Your Source for Business Information that Works

Millions of businesspeople use Hoover's Online every day for research, analysis, and prospecting. Hoover's updates information daily on thousands of companies and hundreds of industries worldwide.

USE HOOVER'S ONLINE FOR:

- **COMPANY RESEARCH**
  Overview
  History
  Competitors
  News
  Products
  Location(s)
  Financials
  Stock data

- **INDUSTRY RESEARCH**
  Quick synopsis
  Leading companies
  Analysis of trends
  Associations
  Glossary of terms
  Research reports

- **PROSPECTING**
  Search by industry,
  location, sales, keyword
  Full officer lists
  Company history
  Financials

You simply can't find more information on corporate America in any other single source." —*Business Week*

For accurate online business information, visit us at www.hoovers.com

Hoover's Handbook of American Business

2003

BUSINESS PRESS

Austin, Texas

BUSINESS PRESS

Copyright © 2002 by Hoover's, Inc. All rights reserved. No part of this book may be reproduced or transmitted in any form or by any means, electronic or mechanical, including by photocopying, facsimile transmission, recording, rekeying, or using any information storage and retrieval system, without permission in writing from Hoover's, except that brief passages may be quoted by a reviewer in a magazine, in a newspaper, online, or in a broadcast review.

10 9 8 7 6 5 4 3 2 1

Publishers Cataloging-in-Publication Data

Hoover's Handbook of American Business 2003, vol. 1.

  Includes indexes.

  1. Business enterprises — Directories. 2. Corporations — Directories.

HF3010 338.7

  Hoover's Company Information is also available on America Online, Bloomberg Financial Network, Factiva, LexisNexis, and on the Internet at Hoover's Online (www.hoovers.com), FORTUNE (www.fortune.com), MSN Money (www.moneycentral.com), NewsEdge (www.newsedge.com), ProQuest (www.proquest.com), The Washington Post (www.washingtonpost.com), Yahoo! (www.yahoo.com), and other Web sites.

  A catalog of Hoover's products is available on the World Wide Web at www.hooversbooks.com.

  ISBN 1-57311-081-7

  ISSN 1055-7202

  The Hoover's Handbook series is edited by George Sutton and produced for Hoover's Business Press by Sycamore Productions, Inc., Austin, Texas, using Quark, Inc.'s QuarkXPress 4.04; EM Software, Inc.'s Xtags 4.1; and fonts from Adobe's Clearface, and Myriad families. Cover design is by Shawn Harrington. Electronic prepress and printing were done by Edwards Brothers Incorporated, Ann Arbor, Michigan. Text paper is 50# Arbor.

US AND WORLD DIRECT SALES
Hoover's, Inc.
5800 Airport Blvd.
Austin, TX 78752
Phone: 512-374-4500
Fax: 512-374-4538
e-mail: orders@hoovers.com

EUROPE
William Snyder Publishing Associates
5 Five Mile Drive
Oxford OX2 8HT
England
Phone & fax: +44-186-551-3186
e-mail: snyderpub@aol.com

HOOVER'S, INC.

Founder: Gary Hoover
Chairman, President and CEO: Jeffrey R. Tarr
EVP, Corporate Strategy and Development: Carl G. Shepherd
EVP, Marketing: Russell Secker
SVP and CFO: Lynn Atchison

EDITORIAL

VP and Managing Editor: Nancy Regent
Assistant Managing Editor: Valerie Pearcy
Senior Editors: Rachel Brush, Margaret Claughton, Paul Geary, Joe Grey, Kathleen Kelly, Tom Ziegler
Senior Editor, Financials: Dennis Sutton
Research Manager: Amy Degner
Editors: Joy Aiken, Sally Alt, Linnea Anderson, Alex Biesada, Larry Bills, Angela Boeckman, Joe Bramhall, Travis Brown, James Bryant, Ryan Caione, Jason Cella, Jason Cother, Danny Cummings, Lesley Dings, Michaela Drapes, Bobby Duncan, Alison Ehlig, Carrie Geis, Todd Gernert, Allan Gill, David Hamerly, Stuart Hampton, Jeanette Herman, Guy Holland, Andreas Knutsen, Jay Koenig, Julie Krippel, Anne Law, Diane Lee, Josh Lower, John MacAyeal, Michael McLellan, Barbara Murray, Nell Newton, Anna Porlas, David Ramirez, Rob Reynolds, Kcevin Rob, Melanie Robertson, Matt Saucedo, Amy Schein, Seth Shafer, Joe Simonetta, Daysha Taylor, Vanita Trippe, Tim Walker, Josh Wardrip, Randy Williams, David Woodruff, Chris Zappone
Financial Editors: Adi Anand, Troy Bryant, John Flynn, Chris Huston, Joel Sensat, Matthew Taylor
Editorial Projects Manager: Audra Martin
QC Editors: Anthony Staats, John Willis
Chief Copyeditor: Emily Domaschk
Research Coordinator: Jim Harris
Library Coordinator: Kris Stephenson
Library Assistant: Makiko Schwartz

HOOVER'S BUSINESS PRESS

Director, Hoover's Business Press: Dana Smith
Distribution Manager: Rhonda Mitchell
Fulfillment and Shipping Manager: Michael Febonio
Order Processing Clerk: James H. Taylor IV

ABOUT HOOVER'S, INC. – THE BUSINESS INFORMATION AUTHORITY™

Hoover's, Inc. (Nasdaq: HOOV) is a leading provider of business information. Hoover's publishes authoritative information on public and private companies worldwide, and provides industry and market intelligence that helps sales, marketing, and business development professionals and senior-level executives get the global intelligence they need to grow their businesses. This information, along with advanced searching tools, is available through Hoover's Online (www.hoovers.com), the company's premier online service. Hoover's business information is also available through corporate intranets and distribution agreements with licensees, as well as via print and CD-ROM products from Hoover's Business Press. Hoover's investors include AOL Time Warner (NYSE: AOL), Media General (NYSE: MEG), and Knowledge Universe. Hoover's is headquartered in Austin, Texas, and has offices in New York City and San Francisco.

Abbreviations

AFL-CIO – American Federation of Labor and Congress of Industrial Organizations
AMA – American Medical Association
AMEX – American Stock Exchange
ARM – adjustable-rate mortgage
ASP – application services provider
ATM – asynchronous transfer mode
ATM – automated teller machine
CAD/CAM – computer-aided design/computer-aided manufacturing
CD-ROM – compact disc – read-only memory
CD-R – CD-recordable
CEO – chief executive officer
CFO – chief financial officer
CMOS – complementary metal-oxide semiconductor
COO – chief operating officer
DAT – digital audiotape
DOD – Department of Defense
DOE – Department of Energy
DOS – disc operating system
DOT – Department of Transportation
DRAM – dynamic random access memory
DVD – digital versatile disk/digital videodisk
DVD-R – DVD-recordable
EPA – Environmental Protection Agency
EPROM – erasable programmable read-only memory
EPS – earnings per share
ESOP – employee stock ownership plan
EU – European Union
EVP – executive vice president
FCC – Federal Communications Commission
FDA – Food and Drug Administration
FDIC – Federal Deposit Insurance Corporation
FTC – Federal Trade Commission
FTP – file transfer protocol
GATT – General Agreement on Tariffs and Trade
GDP – gross domestic product
HMO – health maintenance organization
HR – human resources
HTML – hypertext markup language
ICC – Interstate Commerce Commission
IPO – initial public offering
IRS – Internal Revenue Service
ISP – Internet service provider
kWh – kilowatt-hour
LAN – local-area network
LBO – leveraged buyout

LCD – liquid crystal display
LNG – liquefied natural gas
LP – limited partnership
Ltd. – limited
mips – millions of instructions per second
MW – megawatt
NAFTA – North American Free Trade Agreement
NASA – National Aeronautics and Space Administration
NASDAQ – National Association of Securities Dealers Automated Quotations
NATO – North Atlantic Treaty Organization
NYSE – New York Stock Exchange
OCR – optical character recognition
OECD – Organization for Economic Cooperation and Development
OEM – original equipment manufacturer
OPEC – Organization of Petroleum Exporting Countries
OS – operating system
OSHA – Occupational Safety and Health Administration
OTC – over-the-counter
PBX – private branch exchange
PCMCIA – Personal Computer Memory Card International Association
P/E – price-to-earnings ratio
RAM – random access memory
R&D – research and development
RBOC – regional Bell operating company
RISC – reduced instruction set computer
REIT – real estate investment trust
ROA – return on assets
ROE – return on equity
ROI – return on investment
ROM – read-only memory
S&L – savings and loan
SEC – Securities and Exchange Commission
SEVP – senior executive vice president
SIC – Standard Industrial Classification
SOC – system on a chip
SVP – senior vice president
USB – universal serial bus
VAR – value-added reseller
VAT – value-added tax
VC – venture capitalist
VoIP – Voice over Internet Protocol
VP – vice president
WAN – wide-area network
WWW – World Wide Web

Contents

List of Lists

Companies Profiled

ABOUT *HOOVER'S HANDBOOK* OF AMERICAN BUSINESS 2003

T hings aren't always what they seem, or so the events in the world of business this past year suggest. Fact-finding and digging for information are the order of the day, and when you need information about companies, we believe that Hoover's Business Press is the place to turn.

For our Hoover's Handbooks series of guides to businesses, we've done the sorting and sifting of information, leaving you with the facts you need to make the important decisions you face.

Hoover's Handbook of American Business is the first of our four-title series of handbooks that covers, literally, the world of business. The series is available as an indexed set, and also includes *Hoover's Handbook of World Business, Hoover's Handbook of Private Companies* and *Hoover's Handbook of Emerging Companies*. This series brings you information on the biggest, fastest-growing, and most influential enterprises in the world.

In addition to the 2,550 companies featured in our handbooks, coverage of some 50,000 business enterprises is available in electronic format on our Web site, Hoover's Online. Our goal is to provide one site that addresses all the needs of business professionals. Hoover's has partnered with other prestigious business information and service providers to bring you all the right business information, services, and links in one place. Additionally, Hoover's Company Information is available on more than 25 other sites on the Internet, including The Wall Street Journal, The New York Times, and through online services Reuters, Yahoo!, and America Online.

We welcome the recognition we have received as the premier provider of high-quality company information — online, electronically, and in print — and continue to look for ways to make our products more available and more useful to you.

We believe that anyone who buys from, sells to, invests in, lends to, competes with, interviews with, or works for a company should know all there is to know about that enterprise. Taken together, this book and the other Hoover's products and resources represent the most complete source of basic corporate information readily available to the general public.

This latest version of *Hoover's Handbook of American Business* contains, as always, profiles of the largest and most influential companies in the United States. Each of the companies profiled here was chosen because of its important role in American business. For more details on how these companies were selected, see the section titled "Using the Profiles."

This book has four sections in two volumes:

1. "Using the Profiles" describes the contents of our profiles and explains the ways in which we gather and compile our data.

2. "A List-Lover's Compendium" contains lists of the largest, smallest, best, most, and other superlatives related to companies involved in American business.

3. The Profiles section makes up the largest and most important part of the book — 750 profiles of major US enterprises, arranged alphabetically, with A-K in Volume 1 and L-Z in Volume 2.

4. Three indexes complete the book: In addition to the main index, which contains the names of brands, companies, and people mentioned in the profiles, the companies are also indexed by industry group and headquarters location. The indexes are at the end of Volume 2.

Additionally, a list of all profiled companies is found near the front of each volume.

As always, we hope you find our books useful. We invite your comments via phone (512-374-4500), fax (512-374-4538), mail (5800 Airport Boulevard, Austin, Texas 78752), or e-mail (comments@hoovers.com).

The Editors,
Austin, Texas,
October 2002

USING THE PROFILES

SELECTION OF THE COMPANIES PROFILED

The 750 enterprises profiled in this book include the largest and most influential companies in America. Among them are:

- almost 700 publicly held companies, from 3Com to Zale
- more than 30 large private companies (such as Hallmark Cards and Cargill)
- several mutual and cooperative organizations (such as USAA and Ace Hardware)
- a selection of other enterprises (such as Kaiser Foundation Health Plan, the United States Postal Service, and the Tennessee Valley Authority) that we believe are sufficiently large and influential enough to warrant inclusion.

In selecting these companies, our foremost question was "What companies will our readers be most interested in?" Our goal was to answer as many questions as we could in one book — in effect, trying to anticipate your curiosity. This approach resulted in four general selection criteria for including companies in the book:

1. Size. The 500 or so largest American companies, measured by sales and by number of employees, are included in the book. In general, these companies have sales in excess of $2 billion, and they are the ones you will have heard of and the ones you will want to know about. These are the companies at the top of the *FORTUNE*, *Forbes*, and *Business Week* lists. We have made sure to include the top private companies in this number.

2. Growth. We believe that relatively few readers will be going to work for, or investing in, the savings and loan industry. Therefore, only a few S&Ls are in the book. On the other hand, we have included a number of computer and peripheral makers and numerous other electronics and software firms.

3. Visibility. Most readers will have heard of Hilton Hotels and Wm. Wrigley. Their consumer or service natures make them household names, even though they are not among the corporate giants in terms of sales and employment.

4. Breadth of coverage. To show the diversity of economic activity, we've included, among others, two professional sports teams, one ranch, the Big Four accounting firms, two of the largest law firms in the US, and the principal US stock exchanges. We feel that these businesses are important enough to enjoy at least "token" representation. While we might not emphasize certain industries, the industry leaders are present.

ORGANIZATION

The profiles are presented in alphabetical order. This alphabetization is generally word by word, which means that Advance Publications precedes Advanced Micro Devices. We have shown the full legal name of the enterprise at the top of the page, unless the name is too long, in which case you will find it above the address in the Locations section of the profile. If a company name is also a person's name, like Walt Disney, it will be alphabetized under the first name; if the company name starts with initials, like J. C. Penney or H.J. Heinz, look for it under the combined initials (in the above examples, JC and HJ, respectively). All company names (past and present) used in the profiles are indexed in the last index in the book. Basic financial data is listed under the heading Historical Financials & Employees; where the company's stock is traded if it is public, the ticker symbol used by the stock exchange, and the company's fiscal year-end.

The annual financial information contained in the profiles is current through fiscal year-ends occurring as late as June 2002. We have included certain nonfinancial developments, such as officer changes, through September 2002.

OVERVIEW

In the first section of the profile, we have tried to give a thumbnail description of the company and what it does. The description will usually include information on the company's strategy, reputation, and ownership. We recommend that you read this section first.

HISTORY

This extended section reflects our belief that every enterprise is the sum of its history and that you have to know where you came from in order to know where you are going. While some companies have limited historical awareness and were unable to help us much and other companies are just plain boring, we think the vast majority of the enterprises in this book have colorful backgrounds. We have tried to focus on the people who made the enterprises what they are today. We have found these histories to be full of twists and ironies; they make fascinating reading.

OFFICERS

Here we list the names of the people who run the company, insofar as space allows. In the case of public companies, we have shown the ages and pay of key officers. In some cases the published data is for the previous year although the company has announced promotions or retirements since year-end. The pay represents cash compensation, including bonuses, but excludes stock option programs.

Although companies are free to structure their management titles any way they please, most modern corporations follow standard practices. The ultimate power in any corporation lies with the shareholders, who elect a board of directors, usually including officers or "insiders" as well as individuals from outside the company. The chief officer, the person on whose desk the buck stops, is usually called the chief executive officer (CEO). Often, he or she is also the chairman of the board.

As corporate management has become more complex, it is common for the CEO to have a "right-hand person" who oversees the day-to-day operations of the company, allowing the CEO plenty of time to focus on strategy and long-term issues. This right-hand person is usually designated the chief operating officer (COO) and is often the president of the company. In other cases one person is both chairman and president.

A multitude of other titles exists, including chief financial officer (CFO), chief administrative officer, and vice chairman. We have always tried to include the CFO, the chief legal officer, and the chief human resources or personnel officer. Our best advice is that officers' pay levels are clear indicators of who the board of directors thinks are the most important members of the management team. The Officers section also includes the name of the company's auditing (accounting) firm, where available.

The people named in the profiles and officers section are indexed at the back of the book.

LOCATIONS

Here we include the company's headquarters, street address, telephone and fax numbers, and Web site, as available. The back of the book includes an index of companies by headquarters locations.

In some cases we have also included information on the geographic distribution of the company's business, including sales and profit data. Note that these profit numbers, like those in the Products/Operations section below, are usually operating or pretax profits rather than net profits. Operating profits are generally those before financing costs (interest income and payments) and before taxes, which are considered costs attributable to the whole company rather than to one division or part of the world. For this reason the net income figures (in the Historical Financials & Employees section) are usually much lower, since they are after interest and taxes. Pretax profits are after interest but before taxes.

PRODUCTS/OPERATIONS

This section lists as many of the company's products, services, brand names, divisions, subsidiaries, and joint ventures as we could fit. We have tried to include all its major lines and all familiar brand names. The nature of this section varies by company and the amount of information available. If the company publishes sales and profit information by type of business, we have included it. The brand, division, and subsidiary names are listed in the last index in the book.

COMPETITORS

In this section we have listed companies that compete with the profiled company. This feature is included as a quick way to locate similar companies and compare them. The universe of competitors includes all public companies and all private companies with sales in excess of $500 million. In a few instances we have identified smaller private companies as key competitors.

HISTORICAL FINANCIALS & EMPLOYEES

Here we have tried to present as much data about each enterprise's financial performance as we could compile in the allocated space. While the information varies somewhat from industry to industry and is less complete in the case of private companies that do not release data (although we have always tried to provide annual sales and employment), the following information is generally present.

A 10-year table, with relevant annualized compound growth rates, covers:

- **Sales** — fiscal year sales (year-end assets for most financial companies)
- **Net income** — fiscal year net income (before accounting changes)
- **Income as a percent of sales** — fiscal year net income as a percent of sales (as a percent of assets for most financial firms)
- **Earnings per share** — fiscal year earnings per share (EPS)
- **Stock price** — the fiscal year high, low, and close
- **P/E** — high and low price/earnings ratio
- **Dividends per share** — fiscal year dividends per share
- **Book Value per share** — fiscal year-end book value (common shareholders' equity per share)
- **Employees** — fiscal year-end or average number of employees

The information on the number of employees is intended to aid the reader interested in knowing whether a company has a long-term trend of increasing or decreasing employment. As far as we know, we are the only company that publishes this information in print format.

The numbers at the top of each column in the Historical Financials & Employees section give the month and the year in which the company's fiscal year actually ends. Thus, a company with a February 28, 2002, year-end is shown as 2/02.

In addition, we have provided in graph form a stock price history for each company that was public prior to June 2002. The graphs show the range of trading between the high and the low price as well as the closing price for each quarter from January 1, 1992, through September 30, 2002. Generally, for private companies, we have graphed net income, or, if that is unavailable, sales.

Key year-end statistics in this section generally show the financial strength of the enterprise, including:

- Debt ratio (long-term debt as a percent of long-term debt and shareholders' equity)
- Return on equity (net income divided by the average of beginning and ending common shareholders' equity)
- Cash and cash equivalents
- Current ratio (ratio of current assets to current liabilities)
- Total long-term debt (including capital lease obligations)
- Number of shares of common stock outstanding
- Dividend yield (fiscal year dividends per share divided by the fiscal year-end closing stock price)
- Dividend payout (fiscal year dividends divided by fiscal year EPS)
- Market value at fiscal year-end (fiscal year-end closing stock price multiplied by fiscal year-end number of shares outstanding)

Per share data has been adjusted for stock splits. The data for public companies has been provided to us by Media General Financial Services, Inc. Other public company information was compiled by Hoover's, which takes full responsibility for the content of this section.

In the case of private companies that do not publicly disclose financial information, we usually did not have access to such standardized data. We have gathered estimates of sales and other statistics from numerous sources.

Hoover's Handbook of American Business

A List-Lover's Compendium

The 300 Largest Companies by Sales in
Hoover's Handbook of American Business 2003

Rank	Company	Sales ($ mil.)	Rank	Company	Sales ($ mil.)
1	Wal-Mart Stores, Inc.	217,799	51	Pfizer Inc	32,259
2	Exxon Mobil Corporation	187,510	52	J. C. Penney Corporation, Inc.	32,004
3	General Motors Corporation	177,260	53	Metropolitan Life Insurance	
4	Ford Motor Company	162,412		Company	31,928
5	Blue Cross and Blue Shield		54	Dell Computer Corporation	31,168
	Association	143,200	55	The Goldman Sachs Group, Inc.	31,138
6	General Electric Company	125,679	56	United Parcel Service, Inc.	30,646
7	Citigroup Inc.	112,022	57	Motorola, Inc.	30,004
8	ChevronTexaco Corporation	104,409	58	Nationwide	29,538
9	Philip Morris Companies Inc.	89,924	59	The Allstate Corporation	28,802
10	International Business		60	TXU Corp.	27,927
	Machines Corporation	85,866	61	The Dow Chemical Company	27,805
11	Verizon Communications Inc.	67,190	62	ConAgra Foods, Inc.	27,630
12	United States Postal Service	65,834	63	United Technologies Corporation	27,486
13	American Electric Power		64	Prudential Financial, Inc.	27,177
	Company, Inc.	61,257	65	Shell Oil Company	26,943
14	Duke Energy Corporation	59,503	66	PepsiCo, Inc.	26,935
15	The Boeing Company	58,198	67	Wells Fargo & Company	26,891
16	El Paso Corporation	57,475	68	Intel Corporation	26,539
17	American International Group, Inc.	55,459	69	International Paper Company	26,363
18	The Home Depot, Inc.	53,553	70	Delphi Corporation	26,088
19	Bank of America Corporation	53,116	71	Sprint Corporation	26,071
20	AT&T Corp.	52,550	72	Microsoft Corporation	25,296
21	Fannie Mae	50,803	73	The Walt Disney Company	25,269
22	Cargill, Incorporated	50,800	74	Aetna Inc.	25,191
23	J.P. Morgan Chase & Co.	50,429	75	Ingram Micro Inc.	25,187
24	The Kroger Co.	50,098	76	Georgia-Pacific Corporation	25,016
25	McKesson Corporation	50,006	77	E. I. du Pont de Nemours	
26	Cardinal Health, Inc.	47,948		and Company	24,726
27	State Farm Insurance Companies	47,863	78	Walgreen Co.	24,623
28	Merck & Co., Inc.	47,716	79	BANK ONE CORPORATION	24,527
29	CenterPoint Energy, Inc.	46,226	80	BellSouth Corporation	24,130
30	SBC Communications Inc.	45,908	81	ConocoPhillips	24,050
31	Hewlett-Packard Company	45,226	82	PricewaterhouseCoopers	24,000
32	Morgan Stanley	43,727	83	Lockheed Martin Corporation	23,990
33	Dynegy Inc.	42,242	84	Honeywell International Inc.	23,652
34	Sears, Roebuck and Co.	41,078	85	TIAA-CREF	23,411
35	Aquila, Inc.	40,377	86	Viacom Inc.	23,223
36	The Procter & Gamble Company	40,238	87	UnitedHealth Group Incorporated	23,173
37	Koch Industries, Inc.	40,000	88	PG&E Corporation	22,959
38	Target Corporation	39,888	89	Alcoa Inc.	22,859
39	Merrill Lynch & Co., Inc.	38,757	90	American Express Company	22,582
40	AOL Time Warner Inc.	38,234	91	New York Life Insurance Company	22,514
41	Albertson's, Inc.	37,931	92	Wachovia Corporation	22,396
42	Berkshire Hathaway Inc.	37,668	93	Lehman Brothers Holdings Inc.	22,392
43	Freddie Mac	36,173	94	Cisco Systems, Inc.	22,293
44	Kmart Corporation	36,151	95	CVS Corporation	22,241
45	Costco Wholesale Corporation	34,797	96	Lowe's Companies, Inc.	22,111
46	Safeway Inc.	34,301	97	SYSCO Corporation	21,785
47	Tyco International Ltd.	34,037	98	Electronic Data Systems	
48	Kraft Foods Inc.	33,875		Corporation	21,543
49	Marathon Oil Corporation	33,066	99	Lucent Technologies Inc.	21,294
50	Johnson & Johnson	33,004	100	IGA, INC.	21,000

Source: Hoover's, Inc., Database, September 2002

The 300 Largest Companies by Sales in
Hoover's Handbook of American Business 2003 (continued)

Rank	Company	Sales ($ mil.)	Rank	Company	Sales ($ mil.)
101	SUPERVALU INC.	20,909	151	Tenet Healthcare Corporation	13,913
102	FedEx Corporation	20,607	152	Delta Air Lines, Inc.	13,879
103	Caterpillar Inc.	20,450	153	The Gap, Inc.	13,848
104	The Coca-Cola Company	20,092	154	Eckerd Corporation	13,847
105	Archer Daniels Midland Company	20,051	155	Schlumberger Limited	13,746
106	AutoNation, Inc.	19,989	156	Lear Corporation	13,625
107	Kaiser Foundation Health Plan, Inc.	19,700	157	Northrop Grumman Corporation	13,558
108	Qwest Communications	19,695	158	Amerada Hess Corporation	13,413
109	Best Buy Co., Inc.	19,597	159	Bechtel Group, Inc.	13,400
110	Bristol-Myers Squibb Company	19,423	160	Eastman Kodak Company	13,234
111	Loews Corporation	19,417	161	CNA Financial Corporation	13,203
112	FleetBoston Financial Corporation	19,133	162	Deere & Company	13,108
113	CIGNA Corporation	19,115	163	AdvancePCS, Inc.	13,107
114	AMR Corporation	18,963	164	Halliburton Company	12,939
115	California Public Employees' Retirement System	18,845	165	Cinergy Corp.	12,923
116	Solectron Corporation	18,692	166	Anheuser-Busch Companies, Inc.	12,912
117	Johnson Controls, Inc.	18,427	167	Avnet, Inc.	12,814
118	Sun Microsystems, Inc.	18,250	168	Deloitte Touche Tohmatsu	12,400
119	HCA Inc.	17,953	169	Winn-Dixie Stores, Inc.	12,334
120	Sara Lee Corporation	17,747	170	Sunoco, Inc.	12,322
121	Washington Mutual, Inc.	17,692	171	Textron Inc.	12,321
122	Tech Data Corporation	17,198	172	Travelers Property Casualty Corp.	12,231
123	Xerox Corporation	17,008	173	WellPoint Health Networks Inc.	12,187
124	Raytheon Company	16,867	174	General Dynamics Corporation	12,163
125	Mars, Incorporated	16,500	175	Union Pacific Corporation	11,973
126	U.S. Bancorp	16,443	176	Farmland Industries, Inc.	11,763
127	Abbott Laboratories	16,285	177	KPMG International	11,700
128	AmerisourceBergen Corporation	16,191	178	PacifiCare Health Systems, Inc.	11,560
129	UAL Corporation	16,138	179	Eli Lilly and Company	11,543
130	3M Company	16,079	180	Edison International	11,436
131	Massachusetts Mutual Life	15,980	181	Computer Sciences Corporation	11,426
132	Coca-Cola Enterprises Inc.	15,700	182	Waste Management, Inc.	11,322
133	Federated Department Stores, Inc.	15,651	183	Office Depot, Inc.	11,154
134	Fleming Companies, Inc.	15,628	184	The Williams Companies, Inc.	11,035
135	Emerson Electric Co.	15,480	185	Toys "R" Us, Inc.	11,019
136	Publix Super Markets, Inc.	15,370	186	Carlson Wagonlit Travel	11,000
137	Northwestern Mutual	15,345	187	The Great Atlantic & Pacific Tea Company, Inc.	10,973
138	Rite Aid Corporation	15,171	188	Tyson Foods, Inc.	10,751
139	The Hartford Financial Services	15,147	189	Staples, Inc.	10,744
140	Exelon Corporation	15,140	190	The TJX Companies, Inc.	10,709
141	Valero Energy Corporation	14,988	191	Dominion Resources, Inc.	10,558
142	McDonald's Corporation	14,870	192	Manpower Inc.	10,484
143	Xcel Energy Inc.	14,811	193	Anthem, Inc.	10,445
144	Weyerhaeuser Company	14,545	194	Dana Corporation	10,386
145	Kimberly-Clark Corporation	14,524	195	Allegheny Energy, Inc.	10,379
146	The May Department Stores	14,175	196	Whirlpool Corporation	10,343
147	The Goodyear Tire & Rubber	14,147	197	Southern Company	10,155
148	Wyeth	14,129	198	Marriott International, Inc.	10,152
149	Occidental Petroleum Corporation	13,985	199	MBNA Corporation	10,145
150	Household International, Inc.	13,916	200	Arrow Electronics, Inc.	10,128

The 300 Largest Companies by Sales in
Hoover's Handbook of American Business 2003 (continued)

Rank	Company	Sales ($ mil.)	Rank	Company	Sales ($ mil.)
201	Humana Inc.	10,076	251	Smurfit-Stone Container Corporation	8,377
202	Ernst & Young International	10,000	252	Anadarko Petroleum Corporation	8,369
203	Health Net, Inc.	9,980	253	Masco Corporation	8,358
204	Marsh & McLennan Companies	9,943	254	US Airways Group, Inc.	8,288
205	Northwest Airlines Corporation	9,905	255	Genuine Parts Company	8,221
206	NIKE, Inc.	9,893	256	Texas Instruments Incorporated	8,201
207	Public Service Enterprise Group		257	PPG Industries, Inc.	8,169
	Incorporated	9,815	258	Dillard's, Inc.	8,155
208	Schering-Plough Corporation	9,802	259	CSX Corporation	8,110
209	FMR Corp.	9,800	260	Conseco, Inc.	8,108
210	7-Eleven, Inc.	9,782	261	Sempra Energy	8,029
211	Liberty Mutual Insurance Cos.	9,716	262	FirstEnergy Corp.	7,999
212	Ingersoll-Rand Company Limited	9,682	263	Clear Channel Communications	7,970
213	Comcast Corporation	9,674	264	General Mills, Inc.	7,949
214	Oracle Corporation	9,673	265	DTE Energy Company	7,849
215	Consolidated Edison, Inc.	9,634	266	ARAMARK Corporation	7,789
216	Entergy Corporation	9,621	267	The Chubb Corporation	7,754
217	AFLAC Incorporated	9,598	268	Centex Corporation	7,748
218	CMS Energy Corporation	9,597	269	Ashland Inc.	7,719
219	Circuit City Group	9,590	270	Nextel Communications, Inc.	7,689
220	ABC, Inc.	9,556	271	Aon Corporation	7,676
221	NiSource Inc.	9,459	272	Baxter International Inc.	7,663
222	H.J. Heinz Company	9,431	273	ALLTEL Corporation	7,599
223	Colgate-Palmolive Company	9,428	274	Credit Suisse First Boston	7,548
224	UNUMProvident	9,395	275	Kohl's Corporation	7,489
225	Limited Brands, Inc.	9,363	276	The Progressive Corporation	7,488
226	Express Scripts, Inc.	9,329	277	American Standard Companies Inc.	7,465
227	The AES Corporation	9,327	278	Boise Cascade Corporation	7,422
228	Illinois Tool Works Inc.	9,293	279	CBS Television Network	7,373
229	Burlington Northern Santa Fe	9,208	280	Smithfield Foods, Inc.	7,356
230	John Hancock Financial Services, Inc.	9,109	281	KeyCorp	7,352
231	National City Corporation	9,093	282	Applied Materials, Inc.	7,343
232	Fluor Corporation	8,972	283	Eaton Corporation	7,299
233	USAA	8,970	284	Capital One Financial Corporation	7,254
234	Continental Airlines, Inc.	8,969	285	Crown Cork & Seal Company, Inc.	7,187
235	The Gillette Company	8,961	286	The Bank of New York Company	7,160
236	The St. Paul Companies, Inc.	8,943	287	EMC Corporation	7,091
237	Cendant Corporation	8,882	288	Automatic Data Processing, Inc.	7,018
238	Kellogg Company	8,853	289	Tennessee Valley Authority	6,999
239	Principal Financial Group, Inc.	8,818	290	Yum! Brands, Inc.	6,953
240	The Bear Stearns Companies Inc.	8,701	291	Newell Rubbermaid Inc.	6,909
241	Cox Enterprises, Inc.	8,693	292	Omnicom Group Inc.	6,889
242	EOTT Energy Partners, L.P.	8,609	293	Northeast Utilities	6,874
243	R.J. Reynolds Tobacco Holdings, Inc.	8,585	294	Plains All American Pipeline, L.P.	6,868
244	Fox Entertainment Group, Inc.	8,504	295	SAFECO Corporation	6,863
245	The Trump Organization	8,500	296	ArvinMeritor, Inc.	6,805
246	FPL Group, Inc.	8,475	297	ONEOK Inc.	6,803
247	Progress Energy, Inc.	8,462	298	Highmark Inc.	6,799
248	The Pepsi Bottling Group, Inc.	8,443	299	The Interpublic Group of	
249	SunTrust Banks, Inc.	8,435		Companies, Inc.	6,727
250	Agilent Technologies, Inc.	8,396	300	The PNC Financial Services	6,680

The 300 Most Profitable Companies in
Hoover's Handbook of American Business 2003

Rank	Company	Net Income ($ mil.)	Rank	Company	Net Income ($ mil.)
1	Exxon Mobil Corporation	15,320	51	Abbott Laboratories	1,550
2	Citigroup Inc.	14,284	52	3M Company	1,430
3	General Electric Company	13,684	53	Exelon Corporation	1,428
4	Philip Morris Companies Inc.	8,560	54	National City Corporation	1,388
5	Pfizer Inc	7,788	55	SunTrust Banks, Inc.	1,376
6	International Business Machines	7,723	56	Target Corporation	1,368
7	AT&T Corp.	7,715	57	Electronic Data Systems	1,363
8	Microsoft Corporation	7,346	58	The Bank of New York Company	1,343
9	Merck & Co., Inc.	7,282	59	FMR Corp.	1,320
10	SBC Communications Inc.	7,242	60	Mellon Financial Corporation	1,318
11	Bank of America Corporation	6,792	61	American Express Company	1,311
12	Wal-Mart Stores, Inc.	6,671	62	Intel Corporation	1,291
13	Fannie Mae	5,894	63	Southern Company	1,262
14	Johnson & Johnson	5,668	64	Lehman Brothers Holdings Inc.	1,255
15	American International Group, Inc.	5,363	65	Safeway Inc.	1,254
16	Bristol-Myers Squibb Company	5,245	66	Dell Computer Corporation	1,246
17	The Procter & Gamble Company	4,352	67	The Allstate Corporation	1,158
18	E. I. du Pont de Nemours	4,339	68	Occidental Petroleum Corporation	1,154
19	Freddie Mac	4,147	69	Colgate-Palmolive Company	1,147
20	Tyco International Ltd.	3,971	70	Amgen Inc.	1,120
21	The Coca-Cola Company	3,969	71	PG&E Corporation	1,099
22	Morgan Stanley	3,521	72	Fifth Third Bancorp	1,094
23	Wells Fargo & Company	3,423	73	New York Life Insurance Company	1,086
24	ChevronTexaco Corporation	3,288	74	ALLTEL Corporation	1,067
25	Washington Mutual, Inc.	3,114	75	Travelers Property Casualty Corp.	1,065
26	The Home Depot, Inc.	3,044	76	The Kroger Co.	1,043
27	The Boeing Company	2,827	77	Edison International	1,035
28	Eli Lilly and Company	2,780	78	Emerson Electric Co.	1,032
29	PepsiCo, Inc.	2,662	79	Lowe's Companies, Inc.	1,023
30	BANK ONE CORPORATION	2,638	80	Cablevision Systems Corporation	1,008
31	BellSouth Corporation	2,570	81	CIGNA Corporation	989
32	United Parcel Service, Inc.	2,399	82	Medtronic, Inc.	984
33	The Goldman Sachs Group, Inc.	2,310	83	CenterPoint Energy, Inc.	981
34	Wyeth	2,285	84	Marsh & McLennan Companies, Inc.	974
35	Sara Lee Corporation	2,266	85	BB&T Corporation	974
36	Oracle Corporation	2,224	86	American Electric Power Company	971
37	Shell Oil Company	2,184	87	Union Pacific Corporation	966
38	Schering-Plough Corporation	1,943	88	General Dynamics Corporation	943
39	United Technologies Corporation	1,938	89	FleetBoston Financial Corporation	931
40	Household International, Inc.	1,924	90	Sun Microsystems, Inc.	927
41	Duke Energy Corporation	1,898	91	Carnival Corporation	926
42	Kraft Foods Inc.	1,882	92	Automatic Data Processing, Inc.	925
43	U.S. Bancorp	1,707	93	Amerada Hess Corporation	914
44	Anheuser-Busch Companies, Inc.	1,705	94	UnitedHealth Group Incorporated	913
45	MBNA Corporation	1,694	95	The Gillette Company	910
46	J.P. Morgan Chase & Co.	1,694	96	Alcoa Inc.	908
47	ConocoPhillips	1,661	97	HCA Inc.	886
48	McDonald's Corporation	1,637	98	Walgreen Co.	886
49	Wachovia Corporation	1,619	99	First Data Corporation	872
50	Kimberly-Clark Corporation	1,610	100	Cardinal Health, Inc.	857

Source: Hoover's, Inc., Database, September 2002

The 300 Most Profitable Companies in
Hoover's Handbook of American Business 2003 (continued)

Rank	Company	Net Income ($ mil.)	Rank	Company	Net Income ($ mil.)
101	H.J. Heinz Company	834	151	SouthTrust Corporation	555
102	Gannett Co., Inc.	831	152	Dominion Resources, Inc.	544
103	Cargill, Incorporated	827	153	Progress Energy, Inc.	542
104	Golden West Financial Corporation	813	154	SCANA Corporation	539
105	Halliburton Company	809	155	Jefferson-Pilot Corporation	538
106	Illinois Tool Works Inc.	806	156	AmSouth Bancorporation	536
107	Caterpillar Inc.	805	157	Publix Super Markets, Inc.	530
108	Berkshire Hathaway Inc.	795	158	Schlumberger Limited	522
109	Xcel Energy Inc.	795	159	Limited Brands, Inc.	519
110	Massachusetts Mutual Life	791	160	Sempra Energy	518
111	Tenet Healthcare Corporation	785	161	Southwest Airlines Co.	511
112	ConAgra Foods, Inc.	783	162	Regions Financial Corporation	509
113	FPL Group, Inc.	781	163	The Hartford Financial Services	507
114	CBS Television Network	780	164	Omnicom Group Inc.	503
115	Applied Materials, Inc.	775	165	Waste Management, Inc.	503
116	Public Service Enterprise Group	770	166	Albertson's, Inc.	501
117	Cox Communications, Inc.	755	167	The TJX Companies, Inc.	500
118	Entergy Corporation	751	168	Kohl's Corporation	496
119	Sears, Roebuck and Co.	735	169	Yum! Brands, Inc.	492
120	Burlington Northern Santa Fe	731	170	UST Inc.	492
121	Apache Corporation	723	171	Pitney Bowes Inc.	488
122	FedEx Corporation	710	172	Northern Trust Corporation	488
123	Comerica Incorporated	710	173	Kerr-McGee Corporation	487
124	The May Department Stores	703	174	Countrywide Credit Industries, Inc.	486
125	Consolidated Edison, Inc.	696	175	Franklin Resources, Inc.	485
126	AFLAC Incorporated	687	176	Guidant Corporation	484
127	TXU Corp.	677	177	Johnson Controls, Inc.	478
128	NIKE, Inc.	663	178	Kellogg Company	474
129	Dynegy Inc.	650	179	Metropolitan Life Insurance	473
130	Northwestern Mutual	650	180	Ameren Corporation	469
131	Campbell Soup Company	649	181	General Mills, Inc.	458
132	FirstEnergy Corp.	646	182	The New York Times Company	445
133	Capital One Financial Corporation	642	183	Union Planters Corporation	444
134	State Street Corporation	628	184	Cinergy Corp.	442
135	The Bear Stearns Companies Inc.	619	185	Baker Hughes Incorporated	438
136	John Hancock Financial Services	619	186	Harley-Davidson, Inc.	438
137	Unocal Corporation	615	187	R.J. Reynolds Tobacco Holdings	435
138	Baxter International Inc.	612	188	H&R Block, Inc.	434
139	Comcast Corporation	609	189	Praxair, Inc.	430
140	USAA	604	190	Avon Products, Inc.	430
141	Costco Wholesale Corporation	602	191	Northrop Grumman Corporation	427
142	General Motors Corporation	601	192	McKesson Corporation	419
143	SYSCO Corporation	597	193	Lennar Corporation	418
144	Lincoln National Corporation	590	194	Allegheny Energy, Inc.	418
145	UNUMProvident	579	195	Ashland Inc.	417
146	Merrill Lynch & Co., Inc.	573	196	WellPoint Health Networks Inc.	415
147	Best Buy Co., Inc.	570	197	CVS Corporation	413
148	Valero Energy Corporation	564	198	The Progressive Corporation	411
149	Burlington Resources Inc.	561	199	State Farm Insurance Companies	408
150	Air Products and Chemicals, Inc.	560	200	Hewlett-Packard Company	408

The 300 Most Profitable Companies in
Hoover's Handbook of American Business 2003 (continued)

Rank	Company	Net Income ($ mil.)	Rank	Company	Net Income ($ mil.)
201	Becton, Dickinson and Company	402	251	D.R. Horton, Inc.	257
202	Sunoco, Inc.	398	252	Royal Caribbean Cruises Ltd.	255
203	Rohm and Haas Company	395	253	Transocean Inc.	253
204	Verizon Communications Inc.	389	254	Northeast Utilities	251
205	PPG Industries, Inc.	387	255	Dover Corporation	249
206	Fortune Brands, Inc.	386	256	Ingersoll-Rand Company Limited	246
207	Cendant Corporation	385	257	Avery Dennison Corporation	243
208	SLM Corporation	384	258	Darden Restaurants, Inc.	238
209	USA Interactive, Inc.	384	259	NVR, Inc.	237
210	Archer Daniels Midland Company	383	260	Jones Apparel Group, Inc.	236
211	Centex Corporation	382	261	Marriott International, Inc.	236
212	The McGraw-Hill Companies, Inc.	377	262	Lafarge North America Inc.	234
213	Norfolk Southern Corporation	375	263	AutoNation, Inc.	232
214	The PNC Financial Services Group	372	264	Cooper Industries, Ltd.	231
215	Wm. Wrigley Jr. Company	363	265	PPL Corporation	231
216	Principal Financial Group, Inc.	359	266	The Washington Post Company	230
217	Owens-Illinois, Inc.	357	267	Brown-Forman Corporation	228
218	Analog Devices, Inc.	356	268	Engelhard Corporation	226
219	Weyerhaeuser Company	354	269	Allergan, Inc.	225
220	Torchmark Corporation	351	270	KeySpan Corporation	224
221	Computer Sciences Corporation	344	271	Vulcan Materials Company	223
222	Anthem, Inc.	342	272	Cintas Corporation	223
223	CIT Group Inc.	334	273	Bed Bath & Beyond Inc.	220
224	Scientific-Atlanta, Inc.	334	274	NCR Corporation	217
225	DTE Energy Company	332	275	NiSource Inc.	216
226	The Clorox Company	323	276	Harrah's Entertainment, Inc.	209
227	Oxford Health Plans, Inc.	322	277	Dollar General Corporation	208
228	Pinnacle West Capital Corporation	312	278	Hershey Foods Corporation	207
229	Synovus Financial Corp.	312	279	Adobe Systems Incorporated	206
230	Fidelity National Financial, Inc.	306	280	SUPERVALU INC.	206
231	The Estée Lauder Companies Inc.	305	281	Molex Incorporated	204
232	Rockwell Automation, Inc.	305	282	Aon Corporation	203
233	The Pepsi Bottling Group, Inc.	305	283	HEALTHSOUTH Corporation	202
234	Pulte Homes, Inc.	301	284	Office Depot, Inc.	201
235	Mattel, Inc.	299	285	The Charles Schwab Corporation	199
236	Danaher Corporation	298	286	Masco Corporation	199
237	Genuine Parts Company	297	287	Smithfield Foods, Inc.	197
238	American Standard Companies Inc.	295	288	Wendy's International, Inc.	194
239	Monsanto Company	295	289	Cincinnati Financial Corporation	193
240	CSX Corporation	293	290	Liz Claiborne, Inc.	192
241	Goodrich Corporation	289	291	PeopleSoft, Inc.	192
242	Zions Bancorporation	283	292	Circuit City Group	191
243	Simon Property Group, Inc.	281	293	Caremark Rx, Inc.	191
244	Aquila, Inc.	279	294	Family Dollar Stores, Inc.	190
245	ITT Industries, Inc.	277	295	Mohawk Industries, Inc.	189
246	Lexmark International, Inc.	274	296	Ecolab Inc.	188
247	The AES Corporation	273	297	Leggett & Platt, Incorporated	188
248	Staples, Inc.	265	298	Deluxe Corporation	186
249	Newell Rubbermaid Inc.	265	299	Knight Ridder Inc.	185
250	The Sherwin-Williams Company	263	300	Hormel Foods Corporation	182

The 300 Most Valuable Public Companies in
Hoover's Handbook of American Business 2003

Rank	Company	Market Value* ($mil.)	Rank	Company	Market Value* ($mil.)
1	Berkshire Hathaway Inc.	449,064	51	Oracle Corporation	43,014
2	General Electric Company	397,832	52	Wachovia Corporation	42,727
3	Microsoft Corporation	392,959	53	E. I. du Pont de Nemours	42,593
4	Exxon Mobil Corporation	306,147	54	The Goldman Sachs Group, Inc.	42,384
5	Wal-Mart Stores, Inc.	267,091	55	U.S. Bancorp	40,849
6	Citigroup Inc.	259,906	56	Target Corporation	40,093
7	Pfizer Inc	250,138	57	Anheuser-Busch Companies, Inc.	39,744
8	Intel Corporation	210,401	58	The Walt Disney Company	39,102
9	International Business Machines	208,438	59	FleetBoston Financial	38,099
10	American International Group	207,665	60	QUALCOMM Incorporated	36,287
11	Johnson & Johnson	180,090	61	Liberty Media Corporation	36,262
12	Cisco Systems, Inc.	140,767	62	Lowe's Companies, Inc.	35,737
13	AOL Time Warner Inc.	136,682	63	Fifth Third Bancorp	35,735
14	Merck & Co., Inc.	133,636	64	The Gillette Company	35,270
15	SBC Communications Inc.	131,385	65	Walgreen Co.	35,017
16	Verizon Communications Inc.	128,924	66	Comcast Corporation	34,027
17	Philip Morris Companies Inc.	128,653	67	Kimberly-Clark Corporation	34,002
18	The Home Depot, Inc.	117,506	68	McDonald's Corporation	33,900
19	The Coca-Cola Company	117,226	69	Motorola, Inc.	33,855
20	The Procter & Gamble Company	116,161	70	Electronic Data Systems	32,720
21	Bristol-Myers Squibb Company	98,770	71	Hewlett-Packard Company	32,651
22	Bank of America Corporation	98,158	72	The Boeing Company	32,481
23	ChevronTexaco Corporation	95,634	73	Baxter International Inc.	32,119
24	Eli Lilly and Company	88,228	74	Colgate-Palmolive Company	31,803
25	Tyco International Ltd.	88,064	75	Schlumberger Limited	31,645
26	Abbott Laboratories	86,665	76	Automatic Data Processing, Inc.	31,010
27	PepsiCo, Inc.	85,500	77	Cardinal Health, Inc.	30,960
28	Wyeth	81,030	78	The Dow Chemical Company	30,565
29	Fannie Mae	79,262	79	United Technologies Corporation	30,516
30	Viacom Inc.	77,611	80	Duke Energy Corporation	30,505
31	Wells Fargo & Company	73,703	81	Clear Channel Communications	30,444
32	J.P. Morgan Chase & Co.	71,732	82	Alcoa Inc.	30,132
33	BellSouth Corporation	71,608	83	Ford Motor Company	29,994
34	Dell Computer Corporation	71,529	84	MBNA Corporation	29,985
35	General Motors Corporation	69,816	85	First Data Corporation	29,854
36	AT&T Corp.	64,259	86	EMC Corporation	29,842
37	United Parcel Service, Inc.	60,793	87	The Bank of New York Company	29,797
38	Morgan Stanley	60,662	88	Marsh & McLennan Companies	29,479
39	Amgen Inc.	59,025	89	Genentech, Inc.	28,661
40	Medtronic, Inc.	54,308	90	Washington Mutual, Inc.	28,550
41	Schering-Plough Corporation	52,462	91	Applied Materials, Inc.	27,834
42	Sun Microsystems, Inc.	51,059	92	Honeywell International Inc.	27,562
43	Kraft Foods Inc.	49,514	93	Household International, Inc.	26,486
44	Texas Instruments Incorporated	48,550	94	Cox Communications, Inc.	25,171
45	CBS Television Network	48,033	95	Tenet Healthcare Corporation	24,276
46	American Express Company	47,503	96	The Allstate Corporation	23,994
47	3M Company	46,256	97	El Paso Corporation	23,676
48	BANK ONE CORPORATION	45,570	98	Qwest Communications	23,506
49	Freddie Mac	45,473	99	General Mills, Inc.	22,841
50	Merrill Lynch & Co., Inc.	43,963	100	Metropolitan Life Insurance	22,667

* Market value at most recent fiscal year-end
Source: Hoover's, Inc., Database, September 2002

The 300 Most Valuable Public Companies in
Hoover's Handbook of American Business 2003 (continued)

Rank	Company	Market Value* ($mil.)	Rank	Company	Market Value* ($mil.)
101	Micron Technology, Inc.	22,506	151	Northern Trust Corporation	13,348
102	Kohl's Corporation	22,216	152	ConAgra Foods, Inc.	13,217
103	UnitedHealth Group Incorporated	21,841	153	EchoStar Communications	13,170
104	The Charles Schwab Corporation	21,529	154	The Williams Companies, Inc.	13,156
105	Caterpillar Inc.	20,951	155	CIGNA Corporation	13,108
106	Lockheed Martin Corporation	20,693	156	SLM Corporation	13,065
107	Illinois Tool Works Inc.	20,666	157	Raytheon Company	12,840
108	Safeway Inc.	20,378	158	AFLAC Incorporated	12,811
109	Fox Entertainment Group, Inc.	20,201	159	Computer Associates International, Inc.	12,634
110	USA Interactive, Inc.	20,179	160	TXU Corp.	12,495
111	Waste Management, Inc.	20,040	161	The Gap, Inc.	12,466
112	Emerson Electric Co.	19,748	162	PeopleSoft, Inc.	12,288
113	HCA Inc.	19,628	163	John Hancock Financial	12,278
114	Lucent Technologies Inc.	19,563	164	Baker Hughes Incorporated	12,254
115	International Paper Company	19,433	165	Kellogg Company	12,239
116	Prudential Financial, Inc.	19,369	166	Weyerhaeuser Company	11,890
117	Cendant Corporation	19,173	167	The McGraw-Hill Companies, Inc.	11,782
118	ALLTEL Corporation	19,169	168	The Chubb Corporation	11,735
119	SunTrust Banks, Inc.	18,095	169	Albertson's, Inc.	11,701
120	SYSCO Corporation	18,058	170	Capital One Financial Corporation	11,695
121	Gannett Co., Inc.	17,870	171	CVS Corporation	11,570
122	National City Corporation	17,759	172	Wm. Wrigley Jr. Company	11,556
123	Southern Company	17,720	173	Gemstar-TV Guide International	11,489
124	Omnicom Group Inc.	17,033	174	Masco Corporation	11,247
125	State Street Corporation	16,912	175	The TJX Companies, Inc.	11,225
126	JDS Uniphase Corporation	16,808	176	Campbell Soup Company	11,190
127	Mellon Financial Corporation	16,798	177	The Interpublic Group of Companies, Inc.	11,181
128	Costco Wholesale Corporation	16,733	178	Tribune Company	11,154
129	BB&T Corporation	16,455	179	Burlington Northern Santa Fe	11,006
130	Harley-Davidson, Inc.	16,445	180	Avon Products, Inc.	11,006
131	The Kroger Co.	16,377	181	KLA-Tencor Corporation	10,979
132	FedEx Corporation	16,108	182	The Progressive Corporation	10,959
133	General Dynamics Corporation	15,987	183	Northrop Grumman Corporation	10,944
134	Dominion Resources, Inc.	15,908	184	Transocean Inc.	10,782
135	The PNC Financial Services	15,905	185	McKesson Corporation	10,690
136	Lehman Brothers Holdings Inc.	15,713	186	Loews Corporation	10,605
137	Exelon Corporation	15,370	187	The May Department Stores	10,569
138	The Hartford Financial Services Group, Inc.	15,364	188	KeyCorp	10,320
139	Carnival Corporation	15,305	189	The Estée Lauder Companies Inc.	10,287
140	Sears, Roebuck and Co.	15,266	190	Agilent Technologies, Inc.	10,266
141	Guidant Corporation	15,197	191	Yahoo! Inc.	10,210
142	Sara Lee Corporation	14,810	192	Comerica Incorporated	10,146
143	H.J. Heinz Company	14,734	193	Marriott International, Inc.	9,951
144	Best Buy Co., Inc.	14,348	194	Occidental Petroleum Corporation	9,926
145	NIKE, Inc.	14,303	195	FPL Group, Inc.	9,918
146	Southwest Airlines Co.	14,170	196	Progress Energy, Inc.	9,849
147	Anadarko Petroleum Corporation	14,156	197	Boston Scientific Corporation	9,775
148	American Electric Power Company, Inc.	14,027	198	Bed Bath & Beyond Inc.	9,734
149	Union Pacific Corporation	13,883	199	Xcel Energy Inc.	9,593
150	Analog Devices, Inc.	13,804	200	Becton, Dickinson and Company	9,592

The 300 Most Valuable Public Companies in
Hoover's Handbook of American Business 2003 (continued)

Rank	Company	Market Value* ($mil.)	Rank	Company	Market Value* ($mil.)
201	Aon Corporation	9,563	251	Mattel, Inc.	7,411
202	Allergan, Inc.	9,485	252	Synovus Financial Corp.	7,382
203	Air Products and Chemicals, Inc.	9,299	253	Newell Rubbermaid Inc.	7,355
204	Marathon Oil Corporation	9,282	254	H&R Block, Inc.	7,267
205	Hershey Foods Corporation	9,183	255	Yum! Brands, Inc.	7,183
206	Golden West Financial Corporation	9,153	256	Molex Incorporated	7,135
207	The St. Paul Companies, Inc.	9,145	257	Norfolk Southern Corporation	7,072
208	Pitney Bowes Inc.	9,103	258	Ingersoll-Rand Company Limited	7,024
209	Lincoln National Corporation	9,080	259	Jefferson-Pilot Corporation	6,941
210	Dynegy Inc.	9,058	260	Regions Financial Corporation	6,889
211	Franklin Resources, Inc.	9,042	261	AmSouth Bancorporation	6,861
212	Praxair, Inc.	8,958	262	Apache Corporation	6,839
213	Solectron Corporation	8,952	263	DTE Energy Company	6,758
214	Unocal Corporation	8,801	264	Scientific-Atlanta, Inc.	6,660
215	Deere & Company	8,779	265	The Pepsi Bottling Group, Inc.	6,604
216	Nextel Communications, Inc.	8,757	266	CNA Financial Corporation	6,522
217	PPG Industries, Inc.	8,726	267	The New York Times Company	6,522
218	Monsanto Company	8,724	268	UNUMProvident	6,421
219	The AES Corporation	8,715	269	Genuine Parts Company	6,366
220	Computer Sciences Corporation	8,685	270	Georgia-Pacific Corporation	6,353
221	Public Service Enterprise Group Incorporated	8,684	271	Avery Dennison Corporation	6,212
222	Danaher Corporation	8,643	272	Union Planters Corporation	6,201
223	Principal Financial Group, Inc.	8,642	273	Tellabs, Inc.	6,186
224	Entergy Corporation	8,633	274	Cincinnati Financial Corporation	6,162
225	Eastman Kodak Company	8,562	275	Devon Energy Corporation	5,957
226	Univision Communications Inc.	8,475	276	Starwood Hotels & Resorts Worldwide, Inc.	5,902
227	Staples, Inc.	8,454	277	UST Inc.	5,866
228	Coca-Cola Enterprises Inc.	8,430	278	Fortune Brands, Inc.	5,859
229	Federated Department Stores, Inc.	8,357	279	Ameren Corporation	5,839
230	Cablevision Systems Corporation	8,323	280	LSI Logic Corporation	5,814
231	SouthTrust Corporation	8,250	281	HEALTHSOUTH Corporation	5,805
232	Archer Daniels Midland Company	8,227	282	Johnson Controls, Inc.	5,708
233	Corning Incorporated	8,215	283	Halliburton Company	5,685
234	Textron Inc.	8,101	284	Parker Hannifin Corporation	5,640
235	CenterPoint Energy, Inc.	8,034	285	Starbucks Corporation	5,640
236	The Clorox Company	8,012	286	Sabre Inc.	5,639
237	Limited Brands, Inc.	7,958	287	Office Depot, Inc.	5,619
238	Cintas Corporation	7,899	288	The Bear Stearns Companies Inc.	5,607
239	FirstEnergy Corp.	7,835	289	Telephone and Data Systems, Inc.	5,604
240	Lexmark International, Inc.	7,694	290	Amerada Hess Corporation	5,547
241	Delphi Corporation	7,652	291	National Semiconductor	5,537
242	Rohm and Haas Company	7,633	292	SPX Corporation	5,530
243	Consolidated Edison, Inc.	7,625	293	Kerr-McGee Corporation	5,490
244	Xerox Corporation	7,576	294	Teradyne, Inc.	5,459
245	Adobe Systems Incorporated	7,571	295	Knight Ridder Inc.	5,453
246	Burlington Resources Inc.	7,538	296	Apple Computer, Inc.	5,443
247	Dover Corporation	7,510	297	Advanced Micro Devices, Inc.	5,400
248	CSX Corporation	7,490	298	Brown-Forman Corporation	5,374
249	WellPoint Health Networks Inc.	7,469	299	Cinergy Corp.	5,329
250	PG&E Corporation	7,463	300	RadioShack Corporation	5,322

The 300 Largest Employers in
Hoover's Handbook of American Business 2003

Rank	Company	Employees	Rank	Company	Employees
1	Manpower Inc.	2,042,400	51	AT&T Corp.	117,800
2	Wal-Mart Stores, Inc.	1,383,000	52	Lear Corporation	116,000
3	United States Postal Service	797,795	53	Honeywell International Inc.	115,000
4	Kelly Services, Inc.	698,600	54	Starwood Hotels & Resorts	115,000
5	McDonald's Corporation	395,000	55	Federated Department Stores	115,000
6	United Parcel Service, Inc.	371,000	56	Kraft Foods Inc.	114,000
7	General Motors Corporation	365,000	57	The Walt Disney Company	114,000
8	Ford Motor Company	354,431	58	Toys "R" Us, Inc.	113,000
9	International Business Machines	319,876	59	Winn-Dixie Stores, Inc.	112,500
10	General Electric Company	310,000	60	Johnson Controls, Inc.	112,000
11	Sears, Roebuck and Co.	310,000	61	Motorola, Inc.	111,000
12	The Kroger Co.	288,000	62	Kaiser Foundation Health Plan	111,000
13	Target Corporation	280,000	63	Berkshire Hathaway Inc.	110,000
14	Citigroup Inc.	272,000	64	Lowe's Companies, Inc.	108,317
15	The Home Depot, Inc.	256,000	65	CVS Corporation	107,000
16	Verizon Communications Inc.	247,000	66	KPMG International	103,000
17	Tyco International Ltd.	242,500	67	The Procter & Gamble Company	102,000
18	Kmart Corporation	234,000	68	Johnson & Johnson	101,800
19	J. C. Penney Corporation, Inc.	229,000	69	Limited Brands, Inc.	100,300
20	Robert Half International Inc.	221,300	70	International Paper Company	100,000
21	Albertson's, Inc.	220,000	71	H&R Block, Inc.	99,100
22	Yum! Brands, Inc.	210,000	72	Exxon Mobil Corporation	97,900
23	ARAMARK Corporation	200,000	73	Cargill, Incorporated	97,000
24	Delphi Corporation	195,000	74	Northrop Grumman Corporation	96,800
25	Safeway Inc.	193,000	75	The Goodyear Tire & Rubber	96,430
26	SBC Communications Inc.	192,550	76	J.P. Morgan Chase & Co.	95,812
27	The Boeing Company	188,000	77	Deloitte Touche Tohmatsu	95,000
28	FedEx Corporation	184,953	78	Best Buy Co., Inc.	94,000
29	Philip Morris Companies Inc.	175,000	79	IGA, INC.	92,000
30	HCA Inc.	174,000	80	Pfizer Inc	90,000
31	The Gap, Inc.	165,000	81	AOL Time Warner Inc.	89,300
32	PricewaterhouseCoopers	160,000	82	Blockbuster Inc.	89,100
33	United Technologies Corporation	152,000	83	ConAgra Foods, Inc.	89,000
34	Blue Cross and Blue Shield	150,000	84	The TJX Companies, Inc.	89,000
35	PepsiCo, Inc.	143,000	85	Ernst & Young International	88,000
36	Electronic Data Systems Corporation	143,000	86	BellSouth Corporation	87,875
37	Bank of America Corporation	142,670	87	Raytheon Company	87,200
38	Sara Lee Corporation	141,500	88	Hewlett-Packard Company	86,200
39	Marriott International, Inc.	140,000	89	Costco Wholesale Corporation	86,000
40	Darden Restaurants, Inc.	133,200	90	Halliburton Company	85,000
41	Alcoa Inc.	129,000	91	American Express Company	84,400
42	Walgreen Co.	129,000	92	UAL Corporation	84,000
43	AMR Corporation	128,215	93	Sprint Corporation	83,700
44	The May Department Stores	127,000	94	Intel Corporation	83,400
45	Publix Super Markets, Inc.	126,000	95	Schlumberger Limited	81,000
46	Lockheed Martin Corporation	125,000	96	American International Group	81,000
47	Emerson Electric Co.	124,500	97	Hyatt Corporation	80,000
48	Tyson Foods, Inc.	124,000	98	State Farm Insurance Companies	79,300
49	Viacom Inc.	122,770	99	The Great Atlantic & Pacific Tea Company, Inc.	79,000
50	Wells Fargo & Company	119,714	100	E. I. du Pont de Nemours	79,000

Source: Hoover's, Inc., Database, September 2002

The 300 Largest Employers in
Hoover's Handbook of American Business 2003 (continued)

Rank	Company	Employees	Rank	Company	Employees
101	Xerox Corporation	78,900	151	Aon Corporation	53,000
102	Brinker International, Inc.	78,500	152	Kindred Healthcare, Inc.	52,800
103	Merck & Co., Inc.	78,100	153	The Dow Chemical Company	52,689
104	Lucent Technologies Inc.	77,000	154	Wyeth	52,289
105	Delta Air Lines, Inc.	76,273	155	Illinois Tool Works Inc.	52,000
106	Cox Enterprises, Inc.	76,000	156	General Dynamics Corporation	51,700
107	Eastman Kodak Company	75,100	157	HEALTHSOUTH Corporation	51,537
108	Georgia-Pacific Corporation	75,000	158	Gannett Co., Inc.	51,500
109	Eckerd Corporation	75,000	159	Fluor Corporation	51,313
110	Rite Aid Corporation	75,000	160	Textron Inc.	51,000
111	Hilton Hotels Corporation	74,000	161	U.S. Bancorp	50,461
112	BANK ONE CORPORATION	73,519	162	Bechtel Group, Inc.	50,000
113	Caterpillar Inc.	72,004	163	Nordstrom, Inc.	50,000
114	Coca-Cola Enterprises Inc.	72,000	164	Newell Rubbermaid Inc.	49,425
115	3M Company	71,669	165	Eaton Corporation	49,000
116	DHL Worldwide Express, Inc.	71,480	166	Federal-Mogul Corporation	49,000
117	Abbott Laboratories	71,426	167	Cardinal Health, Inc.	48,900
118	VF Corporation	71,000	168	Sanmina-SCI Corporation	48,774
119	Administaff, Inc.	70,730	169	Parker Hannifin Corporation	48,176
120	Dana Corporation	70,000	170	Union Pacific Corporation	48,000
121	Computer Sciences Corporation	67,000	171	Baxter International Inc.	48,000
122	Kimberly-Clark Corporation	64,200	172	Dollar General Corporation	48,000
123	Morgan Stanley	61,000	173	Microsoft Corporation	47,600
124	Qwest Communications	61,000	174	US Airways Group, Inc.	46,600
125	Prudential Financial, Inc.	60,792	175	H.J. Heinz Company	46,500
126	American Standard Companies Inc.	60,000	176	Big Lots, Inc.	46,246
127	Solectron Corporation	60,000	177	Bristol-Myers Squibb Company	46,000
128	Kohl's Corporation	60,000	178	Metropolitan Life Insurance Company	46,000
129	Dole Food Company, Inc.	59,000	179	Northwest Airlines Corporation	45,700
130	Whirlpool Corporation	59,000	180	Deere & Company	45,100
131	Manor Care, Inc.	59,000	181	Office Depot, Inc.	45,000
132	SUPERVALU INC.	57,800	182	Weyerhaeuser Company	44,800
133	Marsh & McLennan Companies	57,800	183	AutoZone, Inc.	44,600
134	Merrill Lynch & Co., Inc.	57,400	184	Wendy's International, Inc.	44,000
135	Dillard's, Inc.	57,257	185	Avon Products, Inc.	43,800
136	Beverly Enterprises, Inc.	57,000	186	Sun Microsystems, Inc.	43,700
137	Omnicom Group Inc.	57,000	187	Jack in the Box Inc.	43,600
138	Waste Management, Inc.	57,000	188	SYSCO Corporation	43,000
139	FleetBoston Financial Corp.	56,000	189	Continental Airlines, Inc.	42,900
140	Ingersoll-Rand Company Limited	56,000	190	Oracle Corporation	42,006
141	ChevronTexaco Corporation	55,763	191	MGM Mirage	42,000
142	CBRL Group, Inc.	55,715	192	Harrah's Entertainment, Inc.	42,000
143	Masco Corporation	55,400	193	Circuit City Group	41,679
144	Park Place Entertainment	55,000	194	RadioShack Corporation	41,400
145	The Interpublic Group of Companies, Inc.	54,100	195	Eli Lilly and Company	41,100
146	Outback Steakhouse, Inc.	54,000	196	Regis Corporation	41,000
147	Starbucks Corporation	54,000	197	Agilent Technologies, Inc.	41,000
148	Staples, Inc.	53,918	198	Automatic Data Processing, Inc.	41,000
149	Saks Incorporated	53,000	199	The Allstate Corporation	40,830
150	Cendant Corporation	53,000	200	Foot Locker, Inc.	40,104

The 300 Largest Employers in
Hoover's Handbook of American Business 2003 (continued)

Rank	Company	Employees	Rank	Company	Employees
201	Washington Mutual, Inc.	39,465	251	Norfolk Southern Corporation	30,894
202	CSX Corporation	39,011	252	Marathon Oil Corporation	30,671
203	Burlington Northern Santa Fe	39,000	253	Cooper Industries, Ltd.	30,500
204	Unisys Corporation	38,900	254	OfficeMax, Inc.	30,500
205	ConocoPhillips	38,700	255	NCR Corporation	30,445
206	Smurfit-Stone Container	38,500	256	Burger King Corporation	30,166
207	Colgate-Palmolive Company	38,500	257	Chiquita Brands International	30,000
208	Comcast Corporation	38,000	258	AutoNation, Inc.	30,000
209	The AES Corporation	38,000	259	Yellow Corporation	30,000
210	Cisco Systems, Inc.	38,000	260	UnitedHealth Group Incorporated	30,000
211	ITT Industries, Inc.	38,000	261	Mars, Incorporated	30,000
212	The Coca-Cola Company	38,000	262	General Mills, Inc.	29,859
213	Michaels Stores, Inc.	37,700	263	Schering-Plough Corporation	29,800
214	IKON Office Solutions, Inc.	37,600	264	The Hertz Corporation	29,800
215	American Greetings Corporation	37,600	265	Denny's Corporation	29,700
216	The Pittston Company	37,500	266	Owens-Illinois, Inc.	29,700
217	The Pepsi Bottling Group, Inc.	37,000	267	Ryder System, Inc.	29,536
218	Barnes & Noble, Inc.	37,000	268	Exelon Corporation	29,200
219	The ServiceMaster Company	37,000	269	First Data Corporation	29,000
220	Smithfield Foods, Inc.	36,500	270	Allied Waste Industries, Inc.	29,000
221	Sun Healthcare Group, Inc.	36,000	271	Roadway Corporation	29,000
222	Family Dollar Stores, Inc.	36,000	272	CBS Television Network	28,900
223	Clear Channel Communications	35,700	273	Payless ShoeSource, Inc.	28,400
224	Aetna Inc.	35,700	274	SunTrust Banks, Inc.	28,391
225	Liberty Mutual Insurance	35,000	275	MBNA Corporation	28,000
226	Nationwide	35,000	276	Loews Corporation	27,820
227	PPG Industries, Inc.	34,900	277	American Electric Power	27,726
228	Texas Instruments Incorporated	34,724	278	The Hartford Financial Services	27,400
229	Dell Computer Corporation	34,600	279	Williams-Sonoma, Inc.	27,000
230	Interstate Bakeries Corporation	34,000	280	Pathmark Stores, Inc.	27,000
231	Service Corporation International	33,430	281	Mattel, Inc.	27,000
232	7-Eleven, Inc.	33,313	282	Baker Hughes Incorporated	26,800
233	Mandalay Resort Group	33,300	283	Cablevision Systems Corporation	26,780
234	Carnival Corporation	33,200	284	Dover Corporation	26,600
235	Crown Cork & Seal Company	33,046	285	Kellogg Company	26,424
236	R. R. Donnelley & Sons Company	33,000	286	Southern Company	26,122
237	ArvinMeritor, Inc.	33,000	287	CNF Inc.	26,100
238	Pitney Bowes Inc.	32,724	288	Universal Corporation	26,000
239	National City Corporation	32,360	289	Burlington Coat Factory	26,000
240	Household International, Inc.	32,000	290	Collins & Aikman Corporation	25,850
241	Borders Group, Inc.	32,000	291	The Sherwin-Williams Company	25,789
242	Corning Incorporated	31,700	292	Tribune Company	25,600
243	Southwest Airlines Co.	31,580	293	Ashland Inc.	25,100
244	Dean Foods Company	31,503	294	Wyndham International, Inc.	25,000
245	The Gillette Company	31,500	295	Kinko's, Inc.	25,000
246	Mohawk Industries, Inc.	31,350	296	Fortune Brands, Inc.	24,998
247	FMR Corp.	31,033	297	Cummins, Inc.	24,900
248	Leggett & Platt, Incorporated	31,000	298	Becton, Dickinson and Company	24,800
249	Genuine Parts Company	31,000	299	Pilgrim's Pride Corporation	24,500
250	Encompass Services Corporation	31,000	300	Praxair, Inc.	24,271

The 100 Fastest-Growing Companies by Sales Growth in
Hoover's Handbook of American Business 2003

Rank	Company	Annual % Change	Rank	Company	Annual % Change
1	EarthLink, Inc.	284.6	51	The AES Corporation	41.9
2	Caremark Rx, Inc.	186.4	52	Health Net, Inc.	41.6
3	Yahoo! Inc.	182.9	53	Washington Mutual, Inc.	41.5
4	McLeodUSA Incorporated	168.5	54	Anadarko Petroleum Corporation	41.2
5	Palm, Inc.	156.7	55	Plains All American Pipeline, L.P.	40.8
6	Martha Stewart Living Omnimedia Inc.	137.7	56	Citigroup Inc.	40.3
7	E*TRADE Group, Inc.	137.4	57	EMC Corporation	39.7
8	Encompass Services Corporation	130.4	58	Whole Foods Market, Inc.	38.7
9	AdvancePCS, Inc.	117.8	59	The Shaw Group Inc.	38.1
10	AOL Time Warner Inc.	114.4	60	Tech Data Corporation	37.5
11	Qwest Communications	98.3	61	Outback Steakhouse, Inc.	37.1
12	Loral Space & Communications Ltd.	95.2	62	Sun Healthcare Group, Inc.	37.0
13	Waste Management, Inc.	81.8	63	URS Corporation	37.0
14	AutoNation, Inc.	78.3	64	Dynegy Inc.	36.9
15	Budget Group, Inc.	77.1	65	BB&T Corporation	36.4
16	Allied Waste Industries, Inc.	75.6	66	UnitedHealth Group Incorporated	36.1
17	Nextel Communications, Inc.	73.9	67	Abercrombie & Fitch Co.	36.1
18	Dean Foods Company	73.2	68	Dell Computer Corporation	35.6
19	Express Scripts, Inc.	72.0	69	Duke Energy Corporation	35.1
20	JDS Uniphase Corporation	70.6	70	Lennar Corporation	34.1
21	USA Interactive, Inc.	69.1	71	Affiliated Computer Services, Inc.	33.8
22	Charter Communications, Inc.	66.4	72	Bed Bath & Beyond Inc.	33.5
23	Clear Channel Communications	66.2	73	KLA-Tencor Corporation	33.5
24	Rent-A-Center, Inc.	64.7	74	Transocean Inc.	33.5
25	Gemstar-TV Guide International	63.3	75	CellStar Corporation	33.5
26	MGM Mirage	62.8	76	PETsMART, Inc.	33.3
27	El Paso Corporation	60.7	77	ConocoPhillips	33.1
28	Cisco Systems, Inc.	59.2	78	Liberty Media Corporation	33.1
29	PeopleSoft, Inc.	59.2	79	KeySpan Corporation	32.7
30	Tower Automotive, Inc.	58.7	80	Viacom Inc.	32.3
31	Sanmina-SCI Corporation	58.3	81	Berkshire Hathaway Inc.	32.3
32	Saks Incorporated	53.5	82	Staples, Inc.	32.0
33	Solectron Corporation	53.0	83	American Electric Power Company, Inc.	32.0
34	Devon Energy Corporation	52.6	84	Valero Energy Corporation	32.0
35	Wyndham International, Inc.	50.2	85	Best Buy Co., Inc.	31.9
36	Starwood Hotels & Resorts	47.8	86	Cendant Corporation	31.8
37	Aquila, Inc.	46.5	87	Constellation Brands, Inc.	31.6
38	Capital One Financial Corporation	45.9	88	Robert Half International Inc.	30.7
39	Cardinal Health, Inc.	45.4	89	Tyco International Ltd.	30.7
40	CDW Computer Centers, Inc.	45.1	90	Kindred Healthcare, Inc.	30.3
41	Starbucks Corporation	45.1	91	HEALTHSOUTH Corporation	30.2
42	Oxford Health Plans, Inc.	45.0	92	Comcast Corporation	30.2
43	U.S. Bancorp	43.4	93	Administaff, Inc.	30.1
44	Jabil Circuit, Inc.	43.0	94	Providian Financial Corporation	30.0
45	QUALCOMM Incorporated	43.0	95	Fidelity National Financial, Inc.	29.4
46	MPS Group, Inc.	42.9	96	CenterPoint Energy, Inc.	29.2
47	D.R. Horton, Inc.	42.6	97	Southern Union Company	29.2
48	TMP Worldwide Inc.	42.5	98	Performance Food Group Company	29.1
49	EchoStar Communications	42.5	99	The Pittston Company	28.9
50	HCA Inc.	42.1	100	Mohawk Industries, Inc.	28.8

Note: Growth rates (compounded and annualized) are based on the sales histories detailed in each profile's HISTORICAL FINANCIALS & EMPLOYEES section; most, but not all, growth rates are for nine-year periods. These rates reflect acquisitions and divestitures.
Source: Hoover's, Inc., Database, September 2002

The 100 Fastest-Growing Companies by Employment Growth in
Hoover's Handbook of American Business 2003

Rank	Company	Annual % Change	Rank	Company	Annual % Change
1	Amazon.com, Inc.	148.7	51	TMP Worldwide Inc.	32.6
2	Qwest Communications	143.0	52	Valero Energy Corporation	31.7
3	Loral Space & Communications	132.5	53	Tower Automotive, Inc.	31.4
4	E*TRADE Group, Inc.	107.0	54	Capital One Financial Corporation	31.3
5	USA Interactive, Inc.	87.8	55	The Shaw Group Inc.	30.5
6	Encompass Services Corporation	82.4	56	Cendant Corporation	30.0
7	Yahoo! Inc.	80.9	57	Tyco International Ltd.	29.9
8	Waste Management, Inc.	73.5	58	Gateway, Inc.	29.5
9	MGM Mirage	68.2	59	L-3 Communications Holdings	29.2
10	JDS Uniphase Corporation	65.9	60	Berkshire Hathaway Inc.	28.9
11	AdvancePCS, Inc.	64.8	61	Best Buy Co., Inc.	28.9
12	Sanmina-SCI Corporation	64.0	62	Oxford Health Plans, Inc.	28.8
13	McLeodUSA Incorporated	62.5	63	PETsMART, Inc.	28.8
14	EarthLink, Inc.	61.8	64	Transocean Inc.	28.4
15	Allied Waste Industries, Inc.	60.4	65	Dynegy Inc.	28.3
16	The AES Corporation	59.9	66	AGCO Corporation	28.3
17	EchoStar Communications	55.8	67	Abercrombie & Fitch Co.	28.0
18	Budget Group, Inc.	55.2	68	Citigroup Inc.	27.8
19	Hicks, Muse, Tate & Furst	54.6	69	Whole Foods Market, Inc.	27.4
20	Gemstar-TV Guide International	53.0	70	BB&T Corporation	27.0
21	PeopleSoft, Inc.	52.6	71	Performance Food Group	26.7
22	Cisco Systems, Inc.	51.9	72	Tech Data Corporation	26.7
23	Starwood Hotels & Resorts	51.1	73	Lear Corporation	26.0
24	AutoNation, Inc.	50.5	74	Bed Bath & Beyond Inc.	25.8
25	Plains All American Pipeline, L.P.	49.5	75	Cablevision Systems Corporation	25.6
26	Cardinal Health, Inc.	48.4	76	QUALCOMM Incorporated	25.4
27	Clear Channel Communications	46.5	77	Dell Computer Corporation	25.0
28	Nextel Communications, Inc.	46.4	78	Mohawk Industries, Inc.	24.9
29	Rent-A-Center, Inc.	44.4	79	Administaff, Inc.	24.8
30	Dean Foods Company	43.6	80	Sun Healthcare Group, Inc.	24.6
31	Viacom Inc.	42.7	81	Comcast Corporation	24.4
32	Jabil Circuit, Inc.	42.7	82	HEALTHSOUTH Corporation	24.4
33	Devon Energy Corporation	42.6	83	Boston Scientific Corporation	24.2
34	D.R. Horton, Inc.	42.0	84	BMC Software, Inc.	24.1
35	Saks Incorporated	41.7	85	The Home Depot, Inc.	23.3
36	CDW Computer Centers, Inc.	40.1	86	Sealed Air Corporation	23.1
37	Solectron Corporation	39.6	87	KLA-Tencor Corporation	22.9
38	Starbucks Corporation	38.6	88	Palm, Inc.	22.8
39	Royal Caribbean Cruises Ltd.	38.3	89	Williams-Sonoma, Inc.	22.3
40	Express Scripts, Inc.	36.3	90	Charter Communications, Inc.	22.3
41	URS Corporation	36.1	91	AmerisourceBergen Corporation	22.1
42	Jones Apparel Group, Inc.	34.5	92	Jefferson-Pilot Corporation	22.0
43	Liberty Media Corporation	34.3	93	The Vanguard Group, Inc.	21.8
44	Providian Financial Corporation	34.0	94	Credit Suisse First Boston	21.7
45	Outback Steakhouse, Inc.	33.5	95	Lennar Corporation	21.6
46	EMC Corporation	33.4	96	U.S. Bancorp	21.6
47	The Pantry, Inc.	33.2	97	Lennox International Inc.	21.5
48	Washington Mutual, Inc.	33.2	98	Amkor Technology, Inc.	21.4
49	HCA Inc.	33.1	99	El Paso Corporation	21.3
50	Affiliated Computer Services, Inc.	32.6	100	Compuware Corporation	21.1

Note: Growth rates (compounded and annualized) are based on the employment histories detailed in each profile's HISTORICAL FINANCIALS & EMPLOYEES section; most, but not all, growth rates are for nine-year periods. These rates reflect acquisitions and divestitures.
Source: Hoover's, Inc., Database, September 2002

The 70 Shrinking Companies by Sales Growth in
Hoover's Handbook of American Business 2003

Rank	Company	Annual % Change	Rank	Company	Annual % Change
1	Triarc Companies, Inc.	(23.7)	36	Lincoln National Corporation	(2.5)
2	Tenneco Automotive Inc.	(14.0)	37	Ashland Inc.	(2.3)
3	ContiGroup Companies, Inc.	(13.7)	38	Chiquita Brands International, Inc.	(2.3)
4	Denny's Corporation	(13.2)	39	Revlon, Inc.	(2.3)
5	W. R. Grace & Co.	(12.1)	40	AT&T Corp.	(2.3)
6	Fluor Corporation	(10.2)	41	Principal Financial Group, Inc.	(2.2)
7	Rockwell Automation, Inc.	(9.9)	42	Universal Corporation	(2.2)
8	Ingram Industries Inc.	(9.5)	43	NCR Corporation	(2.1)
9	Foot Locker, Inc.	(8.7)	44	Bethlehem Steel Corporation	(2.0)
10	Imation Corp.	(8.1)	45	Deluxe Corporation	(2.0)
11	PerkinElmer, Inc.	(7.9)	46	American Express Company	(2.0)
12	FMC Corporation	(7.6)	47	CBS Television Network	(1.9)
13	Viad Corp	(7.6)	48	The Penn Traffic Company	(1.6)
14	Olin Corporation	(6.7)	49	Trinity Industries, Inc.	(1.5)
15	Hartmarx Corporation	(6.0)	50	Delphi Corporation	(1.5)
16	CONSOL Energy Inc.	(5.7)	51	King Ranch, Inc.	(1.2)
17	TIAA-CREF	(5.5)	52	Baxter International Inc.	(1.1)
18	McDermott International, Inc.	(5.2)	53	Advance Publications, Inc.	(1.1)
19	Ryerson Tull, Inc.	(4.8)	54	The Black & Decker Corporation	(1.1)
20	Fortune Brands, Inc.	(4.8)	55	Pathmark Stores, Inc.	(1.0)
21	Tektronix, Inc.	(4.7)	56	Hercules Incorporated	(1.0)
22	Harris Corporation	(4.7)	57	MAXXAM Inc.	(1.0)
23	Eastman Kodak Company	(4.6)	58	D&B	(0.8)
24	Lyondell Chemical Company	(4.3)	59	CSX Corporation	(0.8)
25	ITT Industries, Inc.	(4.1)	60	Solutia Inc.	(0.8)
26	Cooper Industries, Ltd.	(4.1)	61	Sequa Corporation	(0.7)
27	Unisys Corporation	(3.7)	62	Xerox Corporation	(0.7)
28	National Semiconductor Corporation	(3.3)	63	Yum! Brands, Inc.	(0.6)
29	E. I. du Pont de Nemours	(3.2)	64	Kmart Corporation	(0.5)
30	Unocal Corporation	(3.2)	65	The Reader's Digest Association, Inc.	(0.4)
31	DIMON Incorporated	(3.2)	66	Ryder System, Inc.	(0.4)
32	Apple Computer, Inc.	(3.0)	67	Dow Jones & Company, Inc.	(0.3)
33	Levi Strauss & Co.	(2.9)	68	General Mills, Inc.	(0.3)
34	GenCorp Inc.	(2.9)	69	Brown Shoe Company, Inc.	(0.2)
35	Sears, Roebuck and Co.	(2.7)	70	Reebok International Ltd.	(0.1)

Note: Growth rates (compounded and annualized) are based on the sales histories detailed in each profile's HISTORICAL FINANCIALS & EMPLOYEES section; most, but not all, growth rates are for nine-year periods. These rates reflect acquisitions and divestitures.
Source: Hoover's, Inc., Database, September 2002

The 100 Shrinking Companies by Employment Growth in
Hoover's Handbook of American Business 2003

Rank	Company	Annual % Change	Rank	Company	Annual % Change
1	Host Marriott Corporation	(45.1)	51	Lincoln National Corporation	(6.1)
2	Triarc Companies, Inc.	(36.7)	52	Eastman Kodak Company	(6.1)
3	Premcor Inc.	(24.8)	53	Texas Instruments Incorporated	(6.0)
4	Wyndham International, Inc.	(22.6)	54	Cooper Industries, Ltd.	(5.9)
5	Imation Corp.	(19.0)	55	NCR Corporation	(5.8)
6	Level 3 Communications, Inc.	(17.3)	56	The Black & Decker Corporation	(5.8)
7	CBS Television Network	(17.3)	57	IGA, INC.	(5.6)
8	Viad Corp	(16.7)	58	Sabre Inc.	(5.4)
9	W. R. Grace & Co.	(16.6)	59	Beverly Enterprises, Inc.	(5.3)
10	Carlson Wagonlit Travel	(16.6)	60	Hercules Incorporated	(5.1)
11	Ryerson Tull, Inc.	(15.4)	61	E. I. du Pont de Nemours	(5.0)
12	D&B	(14.6)	62	Chiquita Brands International, Inc.	(4.9)
13	General Mills, Inc.	(14.4)	63	Apple Computer, Inc.	(4.7)
14	Tenneco Automotive Inc.	(14.1)	64	Kmart Corporation	(4.6)
15	Denny's Corporation	(14.0)	65	Phillips-Van Heusen Corporation	(4.6)
16	FMC Corporation	(13.5)	66	American Financial Group, Inc.	(4.5)
17	Foot Locker, Inc.	(13.3)	67	Tennessee Valley Authority	(4.4)
18	Revlon, Inc.	(13.2)	68	FPL Group, Inc.	(4.3)
19	Rockwell Automation, Inc.	(12.7)	69	The Reader's Digest Association	(4.3)
20	Yum! Brands, Inc.	(12.0)	70	OshKosh B'Gosh, Inc.	(4.1)
21	PerkinElmer, Inc.	(12.0)	71	CNF Inc.	(4.1)
22	Occidental Petroleum Corp.	(11.0)	72	The Penn Traffic Company	(4.0)
23	Harris Corporation	(10.8)	73	Domino's, Inc.	(3.9)
24	GATX Corporation	(10.4)	74	S.C. Johnson & Son, Inc.	(3.7)
25	AT&T Corp.	(10.3)	75	Armstrong Holdings, Inc.	(3.7)
26	The Pittston Company	(10.2)	76	Unisys Corporation	(3.6)
27	PepsiCo, Inc.	(10.1)	77	ITT Industries, Inc.	(3.6)
28	Hartmarx Corporation	(10.1)	78	Hasbro, Inc.	(3.5)
29	Deluxe Corporation	(9.9)	79	American Express Company	(3.3)
30	Equifax Inc.	(9.2)	80	Seaboard Corporation	(3.3)
31	Kindred Healthcare, Inc.	(8.9)	81	Torchmark Corporation	(3.3)
32	National Semiconductor Corp.	(8.9)	82	Northeast Utilities	(3.3)
33	Olin Corporation	(8.8)	83	Ashland Inc.	(3.2)
34	Tektronix, Inc.	(8.8)	84	Consolidated Edison, Inc.	(3.2)
35	Millennium Chemicals Inc.	(8.7)	85	Phelps Dodge Corporation	(3.2)
36	Lucent Technologies Inc.	(8.5)	86	Allmerica Financial Corporation	(3.2)
37	Shell Oil Company	(8.3)	87	The Dial Corporation	(3.2)
38	Unocal Corporation	(7.9)	88	CONSOL Energy Inc.	(3.2)
39	Broadwing Inc.	(7.8)	89	Peoples Energy Corporation	(3.0)
40	General Motors Corporation	(7.7)	90	Scholastic Corporation	(2.9)
41	Levi Strauss & Co.	(7.7)	91	Sears, Roebuck and Co.	(2.9)
42	Brown Shoe Company, Inc.	(7.4)	92	MacAndrews & Forbes Holdings	(2.9)
43	Magellan Health Services, Inc.	(7.4)	93	The Stanley Works	(2.8)
44	McDermott International, Inc.	(7.2)	94	Storage Technology Corporation	(2.8)
45	Anheuser-Busch Companies, Inc.	(6.9)	95	Ingram Industries Inc.	(2.8)
46	Bethlehem Steel Corporation	(6.9)	96	Adolph Coors Company	(2.8)
47	Marathon Oil Corporation	(6.7)	97	Sequa Corporation	(2.8)
48	Fortune Brands, Inc.	(6.6)	98	GenCorp Inc.	(2.7)
49	Campbell Soup Company	(6.3)	99	Baxter International Inc.	(2.7)
50	International Multifoods Corp.	(6.3)	100	Ball Corporation	(2.6)

Note: Growth rates (compounded and annualized) are based on the employment histories detailed in each profile's HISTORICAL FINANCIALS & EMPLOYEES section; most, but not all, growth rates are for nine-year periods. These rates reflect acquisitions and divestitures.
Source: Hoover's, Inc., Database, September 2002

The Hoover's 500:
America's Largest Business Enterprises

Rank	Company	Revenue ($ mil.)	Rank	Company	Revenue ($ mil.)
1	Centers for Medicare & Medicaid Services	350,738	51	WorldCom, Inc.	35,179
2	US Department of Defense	305,558	52	International Business Machines Corporation — Services	34,956
3	Wal-Mart Stores, Inc.	217,799	53	Costco Wholesale Corporation	34,797
4	Exxon Mobil Corporation	187,510	54	Safeway Inc.	34,301
5	General Motors Corporation	177,260	55	Tyco International Ltd.	34,037
6	Ford Motor Company	162,412	56	Kraft Foods Inc.	33,875
7	Blue Cross and Blue Shield Association	143,200	57	International Business Machines Corporation — Hardware	33,392
8	General Electric Company	125,679	58	Marathon Oil Corporation	33,066
9	Citigroup Inc.	112,022	59	Johnson & Johnson	33,004
10	ChevronTexaco Corporation	104,409	60	Federal Reserve System	32,803
11	Enron Corp.	100,789	61	Pfizer Inc	32,259
12	Philip Morris Companies Inc.	89,924	62	Metropolitan Life Insurance	31,928
13	International Business Machines	85,866	63	Mirant Corporation	31,502
14	Verizon Communications Inc.	67,190	64	Dell Computer Corporation	31,168
15	United States Postal Service	65,834	65	The Goldman Sachs Group, Inc.	31,138
16	American Electric Power	61,257	66	United Parcel Service, Inc.	30,646
17	Duke Energy Corporation	59,503	67	Motorola, Inc.	30,004
18	The Boeing Company	58,198	68	Nationwide	29,538
19	El Paso Corporation	57,475	69	Sam's Club	29,395
20	American International Group	55,459	70	The Allstate Corporation	28,802
21	The Home Depot, Inc.	53,553	71	Walgreen Co.	28,681
22	Bank of America Corporation	53,116	72	Microsoft Corporation	28,365
23	El Paso Merchant Energy Group	53,071	73	TXU Corp.	27,927
24	AT&T Corp.	52,550	74	The Dow Chemical Company	27,805
25	Cardinal Health, Inc.	51,136	75	ConAgra Foods, Inc.	27,630
26	Fannie Mae	50,803	76	United Technologies Corporation	27,486
27	Cargill, Incorporated	50,800	77	Marathon Ashland Petroleum LLC	27,348
28	J.P. Morgan Chase & Co.	50,429	78	Prudential Financial, Inc.	27,177
29	The Kroger Co.	50,098	79	PepsiCo, Inc.	26,935
30	McKesson Corporation	50,006	80	Wells Fargo & Company	26,891
31	Merck & Co., Inc.	47,716	81	Intel Corporation	26,539
32	State Farm Insurance Companies	46,700	82	International Paper Company	26,363
33	CenterPoint Energy, Inc.	46,226	83	Delphi Corporation	26,088
34	SBC Communications Inc.	45,908	84	Sprint Corporation	26,071
35	Hewlett-Packard Company	45,226	85	The Walt Disney Company	25,269
36	Morgan Stanley	43,727	86	Aetna Inc.	25,191
37	Dynegy Inc.	42,242	87	Ingram Micro Inc.	25,187
38	Sears, Roebuck and Co.	41,078	88	Georgia-Pacific Corporation	25,016
39	Aquila, Inc.	40,377	89	E. I. du Pont de Nemours	24,726
40	The Procter & Gamble Company	40,238	90	BANK ONE CORPORATION	24,527
41	Koch Industries, Inc.	40,000	91	Motorola, Inc. — Telecommunications	24,169
42	Target Corporation	39,888	92	BellSouth Corporation	24,130
43	Merrill Lynch & Co., Inc.	38,757	93	ConocoPhillips	24,050
44	AOL Time Warner Inc.	38,234	94	PricewaterhouseCoopers	24,000
45	Albertson's, Inc.	37,931	95	Lockheed Martin Corporation	23,990
46	Berkshire Hathaway Inc.	37,668	96	Honeywell International Inc.	23,652
47	Hewlett-Packard Company — Hardware	37,218	97	Archer Daniels Midland Company	23,454
48	Reliant Resources, Inc.	36,546	98	TIAA-CREF	23,411
49	Freddie Mac	36,173	99	SYSCO Corporation	23,351
50	Kmart Corporation	36,151	100	Viacom Inc.	23,223

Source: Hoover's, Inc., Database, September 2002

The Hoover's 500:
America's Largest Business Enterprises (continued)

Rank	Company	Revenue ($ mil.)	Rank	Company	Revenue ($ mil.)
101	UnitedHealth Group Incorporated	23,173	151	Fleming Companies, Inc.	15,628
102	PG&E Corporation	22,959	152	Emerson Electric Co.	15,480
103	Alcoa Inc.	22,859	153	Publix Super Markets, Inc.	15,370
104	American Express Company	22,582	154	Northwestern Mutual	15,345
105	New York Life Insurance Company	22,514	155	Time Warner Entertainment	15,302
106	Wachovia Corporation	22,396	156	Rite Aid Corporation	15,171
107	Lehman Brothers Holdings Inc.	22,392	157	The Hartford Financial Services	15,147
108	CVS Corporation	22,241	158	Exelon Corporation	15,140
109	Lowe's Companies, Inc.	22,111	159	Valero Energy Corporation	14,988
110	Electronic Data Systems Corporation	21,543	160	McDonald's Corporation	14,870
111	WorldCom Group	21,348	161	Xcel Energy Inc.	14,811
112	Lucent Technologies Inc.	21,294	162	Weyerhaeuser Company	14,545
113	IGA, INC.	21,000	163	Kimberly-Clark Corporation	14,524
114	SUPERVALU INC.	20,909	164	Cingular Wireless	14,300
115	FedEx Corporation	20,607	165	The May Department Stores	14,175
116	Caterpillar Inc.	20,450	166	The Goodyear Tire & Rubber	14,147
117	GE Power Systems	20,211	167	Wyeth	14,129
118	The Coca-Cola Company	20,092	168	NASA	14,035
119	AutoNation, Inc.	19,989	169	Occidental Petroleum Corporation	13,985
120	Kaiser Foundation Health Plan	19,700	170	Household International, Inc.	13,916
121	Qwest Communications	19,695	171	Tenet Healthcare Corporation	13,913
122	Best Buy Co., Inc.	19,597	172	Delta Air Lines, Inc.	13,879
123	Motiva Enterprises LLC	19,446	173	The Gap, Inc.	13,848
124	Bristol-Myers Squibb Company	19,423	174	Pharmacia Corporation	13,837
125	Loews Corporation	19,417	175	MCI Group	13,831
126	FleetBoston Financial Corporation	19,133	176	Schlumberger Limited	13,746
127	CIGNA Corporation	19,115	177	Lear Corporation	13,625
128	AMR Corporation	18,963	178	AT&T Wireless Services, Inc.	13,610
129	Cisco Systems, Inc.	18,915	179	Northrop Grumman Corporation	13,558
130	Johnson Controls, Inc.	18,427	180	Amerada Hess Corporation	13,413
131	HCA Inc.	17,953	181	Bechtel Group, Inc.	13,400
132	Visteon Corporation	17,843	182	Eastman Kodak Company	13,234
133	Washington Mutual, Inc.	17,692	183	CNA Financial Corporation	13,203
134	Sara Lee Corporation	17,628	184	Deere & Company	13,108
135	Verizon Wireless Inc.	17,393	185	AdvancePCS, Inc.	13,107
136	Tech Data Corporation	17,198	186	United Technologies Corp. — Aerospace	12,971
137	Xerox Corporation	17,008	187	Federal Reserve Bank of New York	12,946
138	Sprint FON Group	16,924	188	Halliburton Company	12,939
139	Raytheon Company	16,867	188	IBM — Software	12,939
140	Mars, Incorporated	16,500	190	Cinergy Corp.	12,923
141	U.S. Bancorp	16,443	191	Anheuser-Busch Companies, Inc.	12,912
142	TRW Inc.	16,383	192	Circuit City Stores, Inc.	12,791
143	Abbott Laboratories	16,285	193	Sun Microsystems, Inc.	12,496
144	AmerisourceBergen Corporation	16,191	194	Boeing Military Aircraft and Missile Systems	12,451
145	UAL Corporation	16,138	195	Deloitte Touche Tohmatsu	12,400
146	3M Company	16,079	196	Winn-Dixie Stores, Inc.	12,334
147	Massachusetts Mutual Life Insurance Company	15,980	197	Sunoco, Inc.	12,322
148	University of California	15,887	198	Textron Inc.	12,321
149	Coca-Cola Enterprises Inc.	15,700	199	Solectron Corporation	12,276
150	Federated Department Stores, Inc.	15,651	200	Travelers Property Casualty Corp.	12,231

The Hoover's 500:
America's Largest Business Enterprises (continued)

Rank	Company	Revenue ($ mil.)	Rank	Company	Revenue ($ mil.)
201	Federal Aviation Administration	12,230	251	Comcast Corporation	9,674
202	WellPoint Health Networks Inc.	12,187	252	Oracle Corporation	9,673
203	General Dynamics Corporation	12,163	253	Honeywell Aerospace	9,653
204	Union Pacific Corporation	11,973	254	Consolidated Edison, Inc.	9,634
205	Blue Cross Blue Shield of Michigan	11,883	255	Entergy Corporation	9,621
206	Farmland Industries, Inc.	11,763	256	AFLAC Incorporated	9,598
207	GE Industrial Products and Systems	11,647	257	Duke Energy Field Services Corporation	9,598
208	PacifiCare Health Systems, Inc.	11,560	258	CMS Energy Corporation	9,597
209	Eli Lilly and Company	11,543	259	Circuit City Group	9,590
210	Bunge Limited	11,484	260	NiSource Inc.	9,459
211	Edison International	11,436	261	H.J. Heinz Company	9,431
212	Computer Sciences Corporation	11,426	262	Colgate-Palmolive Company	9,428
213	GE Aircraft Engines	11,389	263	UNUMProvident	9,395
214	Waste Management, Inc.	11,322	264	Limited Brands, Inc.	9,363
215	Office Depot, Inc.	11,154	265	Andersen	9,340
216	Liberty Mutual Insurance Companies	11,037	266	Express Scripts, Inc.	9,329
217	The Williams Companies, Inc.	11,035	267	The AES Corporation	9,327
218	Toys "R" Us, Inc.	11,019	268	Illinois Tool Works Inc.	9,293
219	Penske Corporation	11,000	269	Burlington Northern Santa Fe	9,208
219	Carlson Wagonlit Travel	11,000	270	The ASCII Group, Inc.	9,200
221	The Great Atlantic & Pacific Tea Company, Inc.	10,973	271	John Hancock Financial Services	9,109
222	Tyson Foods, Inc.	10,751	272	National City Corporation	9,093
223	Staples, Inc.	10,744	273	Fluor Corporation	8,972
224	The TJX Companies, Inc.	10,709	274	USAA	8,970
225	Meijer, Inc.	10,600	275	Continental Airlines, Inc.	8,969
226	Dominion Resources, Inc.	10,558	276	H. E. Butt Grocery Company	8,965
227	Manpower Inc.	10,484	277	The Gillette Company	8,961
228	Anthem, Inc.	10,445	278	The St. Paul Companies, Inc.	8,943
229	Dana Corporation	10,386	279	Avnet, Inc.	8,920
230	Allegheny Energy, Inc.	10,379	280	Cendant Corporation	8,882
231	Boeing Space and Communications	10,364	281	Kellogg Company	8,853
232	Whirlpool Corporation	10,343	282	Principal Financial Group, Inc.	8,818
233	Southern Company	10,155	283	America Online, Inc.	8,718
234	Marriott International, Inc.	10,152	284	The Bear Stearns Companies Inc.	8,701
235	MBNA Corporation	10,145	285	Cox Enterprises, Inc.	8,693
236	Arrow Electronics, Inc.	10,128	286	EOTT Energy Partners, L.P.	8,609
237	Humana Inc.	10,076	287	R.J. Reynolds Tobacco Holdings, Inc.	8,585
238	Ernst & Young International	10,000	288	C&S Wholesale Grocers, Inc.	8,500
239	Health Net, Inc.	9,980	288	Huntsman Corporation	8,500
240	Marsh & McLennan Companies	9,943	288	The Trump Organization	8,500
241	Northwest Airlines Corporation	9,905	291	FPL Group, Inc.	8,475
242	NIKE, Inc.	9,893	292	Progress Energy, Inc.	8,462
243	Public Service Enterprise Group	9,815	293	The Pepsi Bottling Group, Inc.	8,443
244	Schering-Plough Corporation	9,802	294	SunTrust Banks, Inc.	8,435
245	Carlson Companies, Inc.	9,800	295	GE Medical Systems	8,409
245	FMR Corp.	9,800	296	Agilent Technologies, Inc.	8,396
247	7-Eleven, Inc.	9,782	297	Smurfit-Stone Container Corporation	8,377
248	Sprint PCS Group	9,725	298	Anadarko Petroleum Corporation	8,369
248	Fox Entertainment Group, Inc.	9,725	299	Masco Corporation	8,358
250	Ingersoll-Rand Company Limited	9,682	300	US Airways Group, Inc.	8,288

The Hoover's 500:
America's Largest Business Enterprises (continued)

Rank	Company	Revenue ($ mil.)	Rank	Company	Revenue ($ mil.)
301	Hughes Electronics Corporation	8,262	351	Warner Bros.	6,889
302	Genuine Parts Company	8,221	352	Northeast Utilities	6,874
303	Texas Instruments Incorporated	8,201	353	Plains All American Pipeline, L.P.	6,868
304	PPG Industries, Inc.	8,169	354	SAFECO Corporation	6,863
305	Dillard's, Inc.	8,155	355	Ascension Health	6,853
306	CSX Corporation	8,110	356	ArvinMeritor, Inc.	6,805
307	Conseco, Inc.	8,108	357	ONEOK Inc.	6,803
308	Sempra Energy	8,029	358	Highmark Inc.	6,799
309	Tyco Fire and Security Services	8,000	359	Avaya Inc.	6,793
309	Raytheon Electronic Systems	8,000	360	The Interpublic Group of Companies, Inc.	6,727
311	FirstEnergy Corp.	7,999	361	CFM International, Inc.	6,700
312	Clear Channel Communications, Inc.	7,970	362	The PNC Financial Services	6,680
313	General Mills, Inc.	7,949	363	Navistar International Corporation	6,679
314	Dairy Farmers of America	7,902	364	Unocal Corporation	6,664
315	DTE Energy Company	7,849	365	ACE Limited	6,645
316	JM Family Enterprises, Inc.	7,800	366	KeySpan Corporation	6,633
317	ARAMARK Corporation	7,789	367	Fifth Third Bancorp	6,506
318	The Chubb Corporation	7,754	368	The Marmon Group, Inc.	6,500
319	Cenex Harvest States Cooperatives	7,753	369	The University of Texas System	6,461
320	Centex Corporation	7,748	370	Sara Lee Branded Apparel	6,455
321	Ashland Inc.	7,719	371	First Data Corporation	6,451
322	Swift & Company	7,700	372	Premcor Inc.	6,418
323	Nextel Communications, Inc.	7,689	373	Medtronic, Inc.	6,411
324	Pratt & Whitney	7,679	374	Lincoln National Corporation	6,381
325	Aon Corporation	7,676	375	United States Steel Corporation	6,375
326	Baxter International Inc.	7,663	376	Gannett Co., Inc.	6,344
327	Hewlett-Packard Company — Services	7,599	377	Sonic Automotive, Inc.	6,337
328	ALLTEL Corporation	7,599	378	Enterprise Rent-A-Car	6,300
329	Calpine Corporation	7,590	379	Corning Incorporated	6,272
330	Kohl's Corporation	7,489	380	Dean Foods Company	6,230
331	The Progressive Corporation	7,488	381	BB&T Corporation	6,228
332	American Standard Companies Inc.	7,465	382	United Auto Group, Inc.	6,221
333	Boise Cascade Corporation	7,422	383	Health Care Service Corporation	6,198
334	Smithfield Foods, Inc.	7,356	384	Norfolk Southern Corporation	6,170
335	KeyCorp	7,352	385	MicroAge, Inc.	6,150
336	Applied Materials, Inc.	7,343	386	Parker Hannifin Corporation	6,149
337	Eaton Corporation	7,299	387	Campbell Soup Company	6,133
338	Capital One Financial Corporation	7,254	388	Walt Disney Studio Entertainment	6,106
339	Crown Cork & Seal Company, Inc.	7,187	389	Science Applications International	6,095
340	The Bank of New York Company, Inc.	7,160	390	PACCAR Inc	6,089
341	Army and Air Force Exchange Service	7,133	391	Seagate Technology LLC	6,087
342	EMC Corporation	7,091	392	Gateway, Inc.	6,080
343	GE Plastics	7,069	393	Saks Incorporated	6,071
344	Automatic Data Processing, Inc.	7,004	394	Vivendi UNIVERSAL Entertainment	6,032
345	Walt Disney Parks & Resorts	7,004	395	Lennar Corporation	6,029
346	Tennessee Valley Authority	6,999	396	Unisys Corporation	6,018
347	Yum! Brands, Inc.	6,953	397	Chevron Phillips Chemical Company LP	6,010
348	The Guardian Life Insurance Company of America	6,947	398	Avista Corporation	6,010
349	Newell Rubbermaid Inc.	6,909	399	Rosenbluth International	6,000
350	Omnicom Group Inc.	6,889	400	Avon Products, Inc.	5,995

Rank	Company	Revenue ($ mil.)	Rank	Company	Revenue ($ mil.)
401	Land O'Lakes, Inc.	5,973	451	The LTV Corporation	4,934
402	NCR Corporation	5,917	452	Barnes & Noble, Inc.	4,870
403	Equistar Chemicals, LP	5,909	453	CNF Inc.	4,863
404	Wakefern Food Corporation	5,900	454	Graybar Electric Company, Inc.	4,815
405	GE Consumer Products	5,810	455	Mattel, Inc.	4,804
406	DuPont Performance Coatings and Polymers	5,754	456	Catholic Healthcare West	4,800
407	Catholic Health Initiatives	5,742	457	American Express Financial Advisors	4,791
408	PPL Corporation	5,725	458	RadioShack Corporation	4,776
409	Air Products and Chemicals, Inc.	5,717	459	Owens Corning	4,762
410	MacAndrews & Forbes Holdings	5,700	460	W.W. Grainger, Inc.	4,754
411	Cummins, Inc.	5,681	461	The Estee Lauder Companies Inc.	4,744
412	Fortune Brands, Inc.	5,679	462	Adams Resources & Energy, Inc.	4,717
413	Rohm and Haas Company	5,666	463	American Family Insurance Group	4,714
414	IDACORP, Inc.	5,648	464	New United Motor Manufacturing	4,699
415	State Street Corporation	5,637	465	ITT Industries, Inc.	4,676
416	Nordstrom, Inc.	5,634	466	The McGraw-Hill Companies, Inc.	4,646
417	Caremark Rx, Inc.	5,614	467	OfficeMax, Inc.	4,636
418	Allied Waste Industries, Inc.	5,565	468	Empire HealthChoice, Inc.	4,631
419	Southwest Airlines Co.	5,555	469	Park Place Entertainment Corporation	4,631
420	Providian Financial Corporation	5,530	470	Sierra Pacific Resources	4,589
421	VF Corporation	5,519	471	Sony Music Entertainment Inc.	4,568
422	Menard, Inc.	5,500	472	Hershey Foods Corporation	4,557
423	Monsanto Company	5,462	473	Pinnacle West Capital Corporation	4,551
424	Federal-Mogul Corporation	5,457	474	CIT Group Inc.	4,548
425	Owens-Illinois, Inc.	5,403	475	Carnival Corporation	4,536
426	Eastman Chemical Company	5,384	476	Carolina Group	4,530
427	Baker Hughes Incorporated	5,382	477	Catholic Healthcare Network	4,523
428	Pulte Homes, Inc.	5,382	478	Ameren Corporation	4,506
429	Apple Computer, Inc.	5,363	479	KB Home	4,502
430	MidAmerican Energy Holdings	5,337	480	Trinity Health	4,500
431	AutoZone, Inc.	5,326	480	S.C. Johnson & Son, Inc.	4,500
432	Dollar General Corporation	5,323	482	Murphy Oil Corporation	4,467
433	VT Inc.	5,299	483	Dover Corporation	4,460
434	R. R. Donnelley & Sons Company	5,298	484	D.R. Horton, Inc.	4,456
435	USA Interactive, Inc.	5,285	485	Dole Food Company, Inc.	4,449
436	The Charles Schwab Corporation	5,281	486	Golden West Financial Corporation	4,446
437	BJ's Wholesale Club, Inc.	5,280	487	Giant Eagle Inc.	4,435
438	IKON Office Solutions, Inc.	5,274	488	Oxford Health Plans, Inc.	4,421
439	Tribune Company	5,253	489	Cablevision Systems Corporation	4,405
440	Tesoro Petroleum Corporation	5,218	490	HEALTHSOUTH Corporation	4,381
441	State University of New York	5,211	491	Foot Locker, Inc.	4,379
442	Doctor's Associates Inc.	5,170	492	Universal Studios, Inc.	4,374
443	Praxair, Inc.	5,158	493	Administaff, Inc.	4,373
444	Blockbuster Inc.	5,157	494	Darden Restaurants, Inc.	4,369
445	Engelhard Corporation	5,097	495	The Black & Decker Corporation	4,333
446	The Sherwin-Williams Company	5,066	496	Maytag Corporation	4,324
447	Dean Dairy Group	5,052	497	Golden State Bancorp Inc.	4,320
448	Kemper Insurance Companies	5,026	498	Asbury Automotive Group, Inc.	4,318
449	Ryder System, Inc.	5,006	499	DuPont Agriculture & Nutrition	4,316
450	Comcast Cable Communications	5,003	500	Longs Drug Stores Corporation	4,305

The *FORTUNE* 500 Largest US Corporations

Rank	Company	Revenue ($ mil.)	Rank	Company	Revenue ($ mil.)
1	Wal-Mart Stores	219,812	51	MetLife	31,928
2	Exxon Mobil	191,581	52	Mirant	31,502
3	General Motors	177,260	53	Dell Computer	31,168
4	Ford Motor	162,412	54	Goldman Sachs Group	31,138
5	Enron	138,718	55	United Parcel Service	30,646
6	General Electric	125,913	56	Motorola	30,004
7	Citigroup	112,022	57	Allstate	28,865
8	ChevronTexaco	99,699	58	TXU	27,927
9	IBM	85,866	59	United Technologies	27,897
10	Philip Morris	72,944	60	Dow Chemical	27,805
11	Verizon Communications	67,190	61	ConAgra	27,194
12	American International Group	62,402	62	Prudential Financial	27,177
13	American Electric Power	61,257	63	PepsiCo	26,935
14	Duke Energy	59,503	64	Wells Fargo	26,891
15	AT&T	59,142	65	Intel	26,539
16	Boeing	58,198	66	International Paper	26,363
17	El Paso Energy	57,475	67	Delphi	26,088
18	Home Depot	53,553	68	Sprint	26,071
19	Bank of America Corp.	52,641	69	New York Life	25,678
20	Fannie Mae	50,803	70	Du Pont	25,370
21	J.P. Morgan Chase	50,429	71	Georgia-Pacific	25,309
22	Kroger	50,098	72	Microsoft	25,296
23	Cardinal Health	47,948	73	Walt Disney	25,269
24	Merck	47,716	74	Aetna	25,191
25	State Farm Insurance	46,705	75	Ingram Micro	25,187
26	Reliant Energy	46,226	76	Lucent Technologies	25,132
27	SBC Communications	45,908	77	Lockheed Martin	24,793
28	Hewlett-Packard	45,226	78	Walgreen	24,623
29	Morgan Stanley	43,727	79	Bank One Corp.	24,527
30	Dynegy	42,242	80	TIAA-CREF	24,231
31	McKesson	42,010	81	Phillips Petroleum	24,189
32	Sears, Roebuck	41,078	82	BellSouth	24,130
33	Aquila	40,377	83	Honeywell International	23,652
34	Target	39,888	84	UnitedHealth Group	23,454
35	Procter & Gamble	39,244	85	Viacom	23,223
36	Merrill Lynch	38,793	86	Supervalu	23,194
37	AOL Time Warner	38,234	87	PG&E Corp.	22,959
38	Albertson's	37,931	88	Alcoa	22,859
39	Berkshire Hathaway	37,668	89	American Express	22,582
40	Kmart	36,910	90	Wachovia Corp.	22,396
41	Freddie Mac	35,523	91	Lehman Brothers Hldgs.	22,392
42	WorldCom	35,179	92	Cisco Systems	22,293
43	Marathon Oil	35,041	93	CVS	22,241
44	Costco Wholesale	34,797	94	Lowe's	22,111
45	Safeway	34,301	95	Sysco	21,785
46	Compaq Computer	33,554	96	Bristol-Myers Squibb	21,717
47	Johnson & Johnson	33,004	97	Electronic Data Systems	21,543
48	Conoco	32,795	98	Caterpillar	20,450
49	Pfizer	32,259	99	Coca-Cola	20,092
50	J. C. Penney	32,004	100	Archer Daniels Midland	20,051

Source: *FORTUNE;* April 15, 2002

The *FORTUNE* 500 Largest US Corporations (continued)

Rank	Company	Revenue ($ mil.)	Rank	Company	Revenue ($ mil.)
101	AutoNation	19,989	151	Northrop Grumman	13,558
102	Qwest Communications	19,743	152	Amerada Hess	13,413
103	FedEx	19,629	153	Halliburton	13,405
104	Massachusetts Mutual Life	19,340	154	Deere & Company	13,293
105	Pharmacia	19,299	155	Eastman Kodak	13,234
106	FleetBoston	19,190	156	CMS Energy	12,977
107	Cigna	19,115	157	Circuit City Stores	12,959
108	AMR	18,963	158	Cinergy	12,923
109	Loews	18,799	159	Anheuser-Busch	12,912
110	Solectron	18,692	160	Winn-Dixie Stores	12,903
111	Johnson Controls	18,427	161	Avnet	12,814
112	Sun Microsystems	18,250	162	WellPoint Health Networks	12,429
113	HCA	17,953	163	Sunoco	12,402
114	Visteon	17,843	164	Textron	12,321
115	Sara Lee	17,747	165	Edison International	12,184
116	Washington Mutual	17,692	166	General Dynamics	12,163
117	Tech Data	17,198	167	Tenet Healthcare	12,053
118	Federated Department Stores	16,895	168	Union Pacific	11,973
119	Raytheon	16,867	169	PacifiCare Health	11,844
120	Xerox	16,502	170	Farmland Industries	11,763
121	U.S. Bancorp	16,443	171	Eli Lilly	11,543
122	TRW	16,383	172	Waste Management	11,322
123	Abbott Laboratories	16,285	173	Office Depot	11,154
124	Northwestern Mutual	16,212	174	Williams	11,055
125	UAL	16,138	175	Toys "R" Us	11,019
126	3M	16,079	176	Oracle	10,860
127	AmerisourceBergen	15,823	177	Tyson Foods	10,751
128	Coca-Cola Enterprises	15,700	178	Staples	10,744
129	Fleming	15,628	179	TJX	10,709
130	Emerson Electric	15,480	180	Dominion Resources	10,558
131	Best Buy	15,327	181	Computer Sciences	10,524
132	Rite Aid	15,297	182	Manpower	10,484
133	Publix	15,284	183	Dana	10,469
134	Hartford Financial Services	15,147	184	Anthem	10,445
135	Exelon	15,140	185	Allegheny Energy	10,379
136	Nationwide	15,118	186	Whirlpool	10,343
137	Xcel Energy	15,028	187	Humana	10,195
138	Valero Energy	14,988	188	Southern	10,155
139	McDonald's	14,870	189	Marriott International	10,152
140	Weyerhaeuser	14,545	190	MBNA	10,145
141	Kimberly-Clark	14,524	191	Arrow Electronics	10,128
142	Liberty Mutual Group	14,256	192	Health Net	10,065
143	May Department Stores	14,175	193	Marsh & McLennan	9,943
144	Goodyear Tire & Rubber	14,147	194	NWA	9,905
145	Wyeth	14,129	195	Public Service Enterprise Group	9,815
146	Occidental Petroleum	14,126	196	Schering-Plough	9,802
147	Household International	13,916	197	Illinois Tool Works	9,698
148	Delta Air Lines	13,879	198	Comcast	9,674
149	The Gap	13,848	199	Consolidated Edison	9,634
150	Lear	13,625	200	Entergy	9,621

The *FORTUNE* 500 Largest US Corporations (continued)

Rank	Company	Revenue ($ mil.)	Rank	Company	Revenue ($ mil.)
201	AES	9,614	251	Calpine	7,590
202	AFLAC	9,598	252	Nextel Communications	7,574
203	NiSource	9,565	253	Kohl's	7,489
204	Nike	9,489	254	Progressive	7,488
205	UNUMProvident	9,435	255	American Standard	7,465
206	H.J. Heinz	9,430	256	Boise Cascade	7,422
207	Colgate-Palmolive	9,428	257	KeyCorp	7,352
208	Limited	9,363	258	Applied Materials	7,343
209	John Hancock Financial	9,361	259	Eaton	7,299
210	Express Scripts	9,329	260	Capital One Financial	7,254
211	Burlington Northern Santa Fe	9,208	261	Bank of New York	7,192
212	Agilent Technologies	9,161	262	Crown Cork & Seal	7,187
213	National City Corp.	9,093	263	EMC	7,091
214	Fluor	8,972	264	General Mills	7,078
215	USAA	8,971	265	AdvancePCS	7,024
216	Continental Airlines	8,969	266	Automatic Data Processing	7,018
217	Cendant	8,950	267	Safeco	6,953
218	St. Paul Companies	8,943	267	Tricon Global Restaurants	6,953
219	Guardian Life of America	8,907	269	PNC Financial Services	6,921
220	Kellogg	8,853	270	Newell Rubbermaid	6,909
221	Principal Financial	8,818	271	KeySpan	6,900
222	SCI Systems	8,714	272	Omnicom Group	6,889
223	Bear Stearns	8,701	273	Northeast Utilities	6,874
224	R.J. Reynolds Tobacco	8,585	274	Plains All American Pipeline	6,868
225	Ashland	8,547	275	ArvinMeritor	6,805
226	FPL Group	8,475	276	ONEOK	6,803
227	Progress Energy	8,462	277	Avaya	6,793
228	Pepsi Bottling	8,443	278	Unocal	6,752
229	SunTrust Banks	8,435	279	Interpublic Group	6,727
230	Dillard's	8,388	280	Navistar International	6,722
231	Smurfit-Stone Container	8,377	281	Centex	6,711
232	Anadarko Petroleum	8,369	282	Campbell Soup	6,664
233	Masco	8,358	283	Fifth Third Bancorp	6,506
234	US Airways Group	8,288	284	First Data	6,451
235	Genuine Parts	8,221	285	Premcor	6,418
236	Texas Instruments	8,201	286	Lincoln National	6,411
237	PPG Industries	8,169	287	Gannett	6,344
238	CSX	8,110	288	Sonic Automotive	6,337
239	Conseco	8,108	289	Corning	6,272
240	Gillette	8,084	290	Dean Foods	6,230
241	Sempra Energy	8,029	291	BB&T Corp.	6,228
242	FirstEnergy	7,999	292	United Auto Group	6,221
243	Clear Channel	7,970	293	Norfolk Southern	6,170
244	Cenex Harvest States	7,875	294	Science Applications International	6,163
245	DTE Energy	7,849	295	PACCAR	6,089
246	Aramark	7,789	296	Gateway	6,080
247	Aon	7,676	297	Saks	6,071
248	Baxter International	7,663	298	Lennar	6,029
249	Chubb	7,600	299	Avista	6,021
250	ALLTEL	7,599	300	Unisys	6,018

The *FORTUNE* 500 Largest US Corporations (continued)

Rank	Company	Revenue ($ mil.)	Rank	Company	Revenue ($ mil.)
301	Owens-Illinois	6,013	351	Adams Resources & Energy	4,717
302	Avon Products	5,995	352	Pitney Bowes	4,691
303	Parker Hannifin	5,980	353	Dole Food	4,688
304	NCR	5,917	354	ITT Industries	4,676
305	Smithfield Foods	5,900	355	KB Home	4,647
306	Rohm & Haas	5,896	356	McGraw-Hill	4,646
307	Conectiv	5,836	357	OfficeMax	4,636
308	ServiceMaster	5,811	358	Park Place Entertainment	4,631
309	PPL	5,725	359	Sierra Pacific Resources	4,612
310	Air Products & Chemicals	5,723	360	Estée Lauder	4,608
311	Cummins	5,681	361	Maytag	4,564
312	IDACORP	5,648	362	Hershey Foods	4,557
313	State Street Corporation	5,637	363	Pinnacle West Capital	4,551
314	Nordstrom	5,634	364	Dover	4,528
315	Caremark Rx	5,614	365	Micron Technology	4,516
316	Allied Waste Industries	5,565	366	Ameren	4,506
317	Southwest Airlines	5,555	367	Murphy Oil	4,479
318	Medtronic	5,552	368	D.R. Horton	4,456
319	Providian Financial	5,530	369	Willamette Industries	4,454
320	VF	5,519	370	Quantum	4,452
321	Federal-Mogul	5,457	371	Golden West Financial	4,446
322	Eastman Chemical	5,384	372	Oxford Health Plans	4,421
323	Baker Hughes	5,382	373	Cablevision Systems	4,405
324	Pulte Homes	5,382	374	HEALTHSOUTH	4,381
325	Apple Computer	5,363	375	Foot Locker	4,379
326	Dollar General	5,323	376	Administaff	4,373
327	Fortune Brands	5,318	377	Black & Decker	4,333
328	R.R. Donnelley & Sons	5,298	378	Jabil Circuit	4,331
329	USA Networks	5,285	379	Mutual of Omaha Insurance	4,328
330	Charles Schwab	5,281	380	Rockwell Automation	4,323
331	BJ's Wholesale Club	5,280	381	Golden State Bancorp	4,320
332	IKON Office Solutions	5,274	382	Longs Drug Stores	4,305
333	Tribune	5,253	383	Levi Strauss	4,259
334	TransMontaigne	5,223	384	Kelly Services	4,257
335	Tesoro Petroleum	5,218	385	NorthWestern	4,238
336	Praxair	5,158	386	Cooper Industries	4,210
337	American Family Insurance Group	5,109	387	Computer Assoc. Intl.	4,198
338	Engelhard	5,097	388	Comerica	4,197
339	Sherwin-Williams	5,066	389	Temple-Inland	4,172
340	Goodrich	5,013	390	Lexmark International	4,143
341	Ryder System	5,006	391	Nucor	4,139
342	CNF	4,874	392	Hormel Foods	4,124
343	Barnes & Noble	4,870	393	SPX	4,114
344	Graybar Electric	4,829	394	Leggett & Platt	4,114
345	Countrywide Credit	4,819	395	Nash Finch	4,107
346	AutoZone	4,818	396	Jones Apparel Group	4,073
347	Mattel	4,804	397	Cox Communications	4,059
348	RadioShack	4,776	398	Mellon Financial Corporation	4,055
349	Owens Corning	4,762	399	Sanmina-SCI	4,054
350	W.W. Grainger	4,754	400	Regions Financial	4,038

The *FORTUNE* 500 Largest US Corporations (continued)

Rank	Company	Revenue ($ mil.)	Rank	Company	Revenue ($ mil.)
401	Darden Restaurants	4,021	451	Interstate Bakeries	3,497
402	Pathmark Stores	4,017	452	Roundy's	3,452
403	Amgen	4,016	453	SCANA	3,451
404	MGM Mirage	4,010	454	Liz Claiborne	3,449
405	Pittston	4,008	455	Mohawk Industries	3,446
406	Phelps Dodge	4,002	456	Adelphia Communications	3,435
407	Echostar Communications	4,001	457	Big Lots	3,433
408	Group 1 Automotive	3,996	458	Core-Mark International	3,425
409	AK Steel Holding	3,994	459	Emcor Group	3,420
410	Autoliv	3,991	460	Foster Wheeler	3,397
411	MeadWestvaco	3,984	461	Borders Group	3,388
412	Encompass Services	3,981	462	Shopko Stores	3,387
413	Starwood Hotels & Resorts	3,967	463	AmSouth Bancorporation	3,383
414	CDW Computer Centers	3,962	464	Puget Energy	3,374
415	Jacobs Engineering Group	3,957	465	Tenneco Automotive	3,364
416	LTV	3,956	466	Harley-Davidson	3,363
417	Charter Communications	3,953	467	Western Gas Resources	3,355
418	American Financial Group	3,948	468	Bethlehem Steel	3,334
419	York International	3,931	469	Jefferson-Pilot	3,332
420	Wisconsin Energy	3,929	470	Burlington Resources	3,326
421	Constellation Energy	3,928	471	Allmerica Financial	3,312
422	United Stationers	3,926	472	USG	3,296
423	Clorox	3,903	473	Yellow	3,277
424	Advanced Micro Devices	3,892	474	Northern Trust Corp.	3,262
425	Steelcase	3,886	475	Aid Association for Lutherans	3,258
426	Fidelity Natl. Financial	3,874	476	Performance Food Group	3,237
427	Peter Kiewit Sons'	3,871	477	JDS Uniphase	3,233
428	FMC	3,871	478	Lyondell Chemical	3,226
429	Owens & Minor	3,815	479	Airborne	3,211
430	Avery Dennison	3,803	480	Comdisco	3,202
431	Maxtor	3,797	481	NSTAR	3,192
432	Danaher	3,782	482	OGE Energy	3,182
433	Energy East	3,760	483	Staff Leasing	3,180
434	NTL	3,755	484	Enterprise Products	3,180
435	Becton Dickinson	3,754	485	PepsiAmericas	3,171
436	Host Marriott	3,754	486	Cooper Tire & Rubber	3,155
437	First American Corporation	3,751	487	Coventry Health Care	3,147
438	SouthTrust Corp.	3,742	488	Anixter International	3,144
439	Pacific LifeCorp	3,735	489	Union Planters Corp.	3,144
440	Harrah's Entertainment	3,709	490	Armstrong Holdings	3,135
441	Ball	3,686	491	Equity Office Properties	3,130
442	Brunswick	3,684	492	Amazon.com	3,122
443	Family Dollar Stores	3,665	493	Lennox International	3,120
444	Wesco International	3,658	494	American Axle & Manufacturing	3,107
445	Ames Dept. Stores	3,648	495	C.H. Robinson Worldwide	3,090
446	Kerr-McGee	3,638	496	Kindred Healthcare	3,081
447	Quest Diagnostics	3,628	497	Devon Energy	3,075
448	Smith International	3,551	498	Sealed Air	3,068
449	Spartan Stores	3,520	499	Hilton Hotels	3,050
450	USA Education	3,515	500	New York Times	3,043

The *Forbes* 500 Largest Private Companies in the US

Rank	Company	Revenue ($ mil.)	Rank	Company	Revenue ($ mil.)
1	Cargill	49,408	51	International Data Group	3,010
2	Koch Industries	40,700	52	Allegis Group	3,000
3	PricewaterhouseCoopers	23,100	53	Raley's	3,000
4	Mars	15,500	54	Schwan's Sales Enterprises	3,000
5	Publix Super Markets	14,575	55	J.R. Simplot	3,000
6	Bechtel	14,300	56	QuikTrip	2,929
7	Deloitte Touche Tohmatsu	12,200	57	Bloomberg	2,850
8	KPMG International	11,800	58	RaceTrac Petroleum	2,811
9	Fidelity Investments	11,096	59	Wegmans Food Markets	2,800
10	Ernst & Young	10,000	60	Perdue Farms	2,700
11	Meijer	10,000	61	Keystone Foods	2,650
12	Andersen	9,340	62	A-Mark Financial	2,600
13	H. E. Butt Grocery	8,965	63	Clark Retail Enterprises	2,600
14	C&S Wholesale Grocers	8,500	64	Consolidated Electrical Distributors	2,600
15	Huntsman	8,500	65	Gordon Food Service	2,600
16	Aramark	7,745	66	Kohler	2,600
17	Premcor	7,312	67	Sinclair Oil	2,600
18	JM Family Enterprises	7,100	68	Pilot	2,586
19	Marmon Group	6,786	69	Micro Warehouse	2,565
20	Alliant Exchange	6,600	70	Stater Bros. Markets	2,550
21	Seagate Technology	6,387	71	Transammonia	2,447
22	Enterprise Rent-A-Car	6,300	72	Clark Enterprises	2,445
23	Science Applications International	5,896	73	Connell	2,425
24	Graybar Electric	5,214	74	Parsons	2,400
25	Menard	4,850	75	Platinum Equity	2,400
26	Levi Strauss & Co.	4,645	76	Quality King Distributors	2,400
27	S.C. Johnson & Son	4,500	77	Venture Industries	2,400
28	Peter Kiewit Sons'	4,463	78	Gilbane	2,388
29	Giant Eagle	4,435	79	Allied Worldwide	2,372
30	Advance Publications	4,400	80	Black & Veatch	2,358
31	Hallmark Cards	4,233	81	H Group Holding	2,300
32	ContiGroup Companies	4,000	82	H.T. Hackney	2,300
33	InterTech Group	4,000	83	Metaldyne	2,300
34	Cox Enterprises	3,925	84	Advance Stores	2,288
35	Hy-Vee	3,900	85	Springs Industries	2,275
36	Milliken & Company	3,900	86	Belk	2,270
37	Reyes Holding	3,900	87	Edward Jones	2,212
38	MBM	3,823	88	Kinko's	2,184
39	Guardian Industries	3,800	89	Renco Group	2,150
40	Synnex Information Technologies	3,700	90	BDO International	2,135
41	Alticor	3,525	91	Structure Tone	2,100
42	Southern Wine & Spirits	3,500	92	Scoular	2,098
43	Hearst	3,413	93	Carlson Companies	2,083
44	Eby-Brown	3,400	94	Ingram Industries	2,075
45	McKinsey & Company	3,400	95	Haworth	2,060
46	Flying J	3,330	96	TravelCenters of America	2,060
47	Capital Group of Companies	3,300	97	UniGroup	2,009
48	Gulf States Toyota	3,200	98	Apex Oil	2,000
49	Schneider National	3,089	99	Booz, Allen & Hamilton	2,000
50	Core-Mark International	3,035	100	Golub	2,000

Source: *Forbes;* November 26, 2001

The *Forbes* 500 Largest Private Companies in the US (continued)

Rank	Company	Revenue ($ mil.)	Rank	Company	Revenue ($ mil.)
101	Hunt Consolidated/Hunt Oil	2,000	151	Save Mart Supermarkets	1,524
102	JELD-WEN Holding	2,000	152	Cumberland Farms	1,500
103	KB Toys	2,000	153	Delaware North Companies	1,500
104	LifeStyle Furnishings	2,000	154	Grocers Supply	1,500
105	Vertis	1,994	155	Hewitt Associates	1,500
106	Gulf Oil	1,970	156	National Gypsum	1,500
107	Schnuck Markets	1,969	157	Southwire	1,500
108	Crown Central Petroleum	1,961	158	Wawa	1,500
109	DPR Construction	1,958	159	DHL Airways	1,497
110	Sammons Enterprises	1,934	160	DiGiorgio	1,496
111	Ergon	1,905	161	Glazer's Wholesale Drug	1,480
112	Dr Pepper/Seven-Up Bottling	1,900	162	Services Group of America	1,480
113	HR Logic	1,900	163	Asplundh Tree Expert	1,473
114	Sheetz	1,900	164	General Parts	1,459
115	BCom3 Group	1,894	165	Metromedia	1,450
116	Alex Lee	1,890	166	Purity Wholesale Grocers	1,450
117	DreamWorks SKG	1,873	167	Sierra Pacific Industries	1,450
118	J. F. Shea	1,863	168	Towers Perrin	1,448
119	DeMoulas Super Markets	1,850	169	Frank Consolidated Enterprises	1,431
120	Central National-Gottesman	1,825	170	Heico Companies	1,425
121	DynCorp	1,809	171	Breed Technologies	1,422
122	Heafner Tire Group	1,807	172	Hunt Construction Group	1,418
123	Beaulieu of America Group	1,803	173	Flint Ink	1,400
124	Quad/Graphics	1,800	174	W. L. Gore & Associates	1,400
125	84 Lumber	1,775	175	Software House International	1,400
126	Golden State Foods	1,764	176	H. B. Zachry	1,400
127	BE&K	1,756	177	Walsh Group	1,388
128	Leprino Foods	1,714	178	AEI Resources	1,380
129	Builders FirstSource	1,710	179	EBSCO Industries	1,375
130	Kinray	1,710	180	ViewSonic	1,371
131	CH2M Hill Companies	1,707	181	Hensel Phelps Construction	1,368
132	Andersen	1,700	182	Schreiber Foods	1,352
133	Brookshire Grocery	1,694	183	Devcon Construction	1,351
134	Grant Thornton	1,690	184	IMG	1,350
135	Amsted Industries	1,650	185	Epix Holdings	1,331
136	Bruno's Supermarkets	1,650	186	Maritz	1,318
137	Whiting-Turner Contracting	1,646	187	Dunn Industries	1,311
138	Tishman Realty & Construction	1,640	188	Young's Market	1,310
139	National Distributing	1,630	189	Ritz Camera Centers	1,305
140	Rich Products	1,620	190	Cc Industries	1,300
141	E&J Gallo Winery	1,600	191	SC Johnson Commercial Markets	1,300
142	Kingston Technology	1,600	192	Lanoga	1,300
143	AECOM Technology	1,575	193	Taylor	1,300
144	Comark	1,560	194	WinCo Foods	1,300
145	A. G. Spanos Companies	1,560	195	SF Holdings Group	1,282
146	Follett	1,554	196	Tang Industries	1,270
147	Day & Zimmermann Group	1,554	197	Life Care Centers of America	1,265
148	Swinerton	1,550	198	Republic Technologies International	1,265
149	Fry's Electronics	1,530	199	ICC Industries	1,260
150	Borden	1,524	200	Dillingham Construction	1,258

Rank	Company	Revenue ($ mil.)	Rank	Company	Revenue ($ mil.)
201	Bose	1,250	251	Delco Remy International	1,087
202	Meridian Automotive Systems	1,250	252	UIS	1,087
203	ABC Supply	1,239	253	GSC Enterprises	1,082
204	Holiday Companies	1,225	254	Conair	1,082
205	G-I Holdings	1,208	255	Michael Foods	1,081
206	McCarthy Building Companies	1,205	256	M. A. Mortenson	1,080
207	DeBruce Grain	1,201	257	MTS	1,080
208	Austin Industries	1,200	258	Watkins Associated Industries	1,076
209	Barnes & Noble College Bookstores	1,200	259	Parsons & Whittemore	1,075
210	Mary Kay	1,200	260	ClubCorp	1,069
211	Purdue Pharma	1,200	261	Ben E. Keith	1,068
212	Swagelok	1,200	262	Anderson News	1,063
213	Parsons Brinckerhoff	1,193	263	Earle M. Jorgensen	1,060
214	Discount Tire	1,192	264	Ingram Entertainment Holdings	1,057
215	Connell Limited Partnership	1,185	265	Rooney Brothers	1,053
216	Dade Behring	1,184	266	Carpenter	1,050
217	United Defense	1,184	267	Dick Corporation	1,050
218	Bashas'	1,170	268	MediaNews Group	1,042
219	Dart Container	1,170	269	Primus	1,040
220	Noveon	1,168	270	Rooms to Go	1,040
221	Domino's Pizza	1,167	271	Arctic Slope Regional	1,038
222	Knoll	1,163	272	MSX International	1,035
223	Barton Malow	1,160	273	Dunavant Enterprises	1,030
224	Skadden, Arps, Slate, Meagher & Flom	1,154	274	Battelle Memorial Institute	1,029
225	L.L. Bean	1,150	275	Printpack	1,027
226	Big Y Foods	1,150	276	New Age Electronics	1,024
227	NESCO	1,150	277	J. M. Huber	1,022
228	North Pacific Group	1,150	278	Buffets	1,021
229	Petco Animal Supplies	1,150	279	Medline Industries	1,016
230	TTI	1,146	280	Horseshoe Gaming Holding	1,013
231	Regal Cinemas	1,131	281	Parkdale Mills	1,001
232	Wilbur-Ellis	1,131	282	Baker & McKenzie	1,000
233	Riverwood International	1,129	283	Baker & Taylor	1,000
234	Crown Equipment	1,127	284	Bass Pro	1,000
235	Foster Farms	1,127	285	Boscov's	1,000
236	Quality Stores	1,126	286	Cantor Fitzgerald Securities	1,000
237	SAS Institute	1,120	287	Genmar Holdings	1,000
238	Truman Arnold Companies	1,120	288	Longaberger	1,000
239	Modern Continental Companies	1,118	289	TIC-The Industrial Co.	998
240	Goodman Manufacturing	1,115	290	VarTec Telecom	995
241	Menasha	1,112	291	Beck Group	990
242	Shamrock Foods	1,109	292	Big V Supermarkets	990
243	Dot Foods	1,107	293	Stevedoring Services of America	989
244	Sealy	1,102	294	Warren Equities	984
245	American Century Investments	1,100	295	Honickman Affiliates	983
246	Boston Consulting Group	1,100	296	K-VA-T Food Stores	963
247	Swifty Serve	1,100	297	Hoffman	954
248	TAC Worldwide Companies	1,100	298	Ashley Furniture Industries	952
249	Duchossois Industries	1,090	299	O'Neal Steel	941
250	Red Apple Group	1,090	300	M. Fabrikant & Sons	930

Rank	Company	Revenue ($ mil.)	Rank	Company	Revenue ($ mil.)
301	Chemcentral	917	351	ASI Corp.	818
302	Micro Electronics	916	352	Plastipak Packaging	812
303	Sunbelt Beverage	915	353	Bartlett and Company	810
304	Pella	914	354	Gould Paper	810
305	Royster-Clark	913	355	Journal Communications	810
306	24 Hour Fitness Worldwide	911	356	MTD Products	810
307	Hobby Lobby Stores	905	357	U.S. Can	810
308	New Balance Athletic Shoe	901	358	TTC Illinois	809
309	Colfax	900	359	Jordan Industries	807
310	McKee Foods	900	360	Landmark Communications	805
311	Minyard Food Stores	900	361	Linsco/Private Ledger	801
312	Love's Travel Stops & Country Stores	894	362	Bain & Company	800
313	Dick's Sporting Goods	893	363	Columbia Forest Products	800
314	Iasis Healthcare	892	364	MicronPC	800
315	Doane Pet Care	892	365	National Textiles	800
316	R. B. Pamplin	890	366	Rosen's Diversified	800
317	Oxford Automotive	885	367	Crowley Maritime	790
318	Newark Group	883	368	Les Schwab Tire Centers	790
319	Freeman Companies	878	369	Turner Industries Group	788
320	Soave Enterprises	878	370	Cinemark USA	786
321	P.C. Richard & Son	875	371	Charmer Industries	785
322	Topa Equities	865	372	PMC Global	784
323	Wirtz	865	373	Simpson Investment	780
324	Berwind Group	860	374	Deseret Management	778
325	Hale-Halsell	859	375	Ilitch Holdings	777
326	Texas Petrochemicals	859	376	S. Abraham & Sons	776
327	Freedom Communications	855	377	Feld Entertainment	776
328	MA Laboratories	855	378	Findlay Industries	776
329	Fisher Development	854	379	Bellco Health	775
330	Rudolph and Sletten	852	380	Cabela's	775
331	Brasfield & Gorrie	849	381	Formica	774
332	Pliant	844	382	Avondale	773
333	Alberici	837	383	Miller & Hartman	773
334	Inserra Supermarkets	834	384	King Kullen Grocery	770
335	Pepper Construction Group	834	385	S&P Company	770
336	Solo Cup	833	386	Fiesta Mart	769
337	Bozzuto's	830	387	Horsehead Industries	765
338	Goya Foods	830	388	Sigma Plastics Group	765
339	Icon Health & Fitness	830	389	U.S. Oil	760
340	Roll International	830	390	Webcor Builders	760
341	Sutherland Lumber	830	391	Ty Inc.	758
342	Golden Rule Financial	829	392	Concentra	752
343	David Weekley Homes	828	393	Brookshire Brothers	750
344	World Kitchen	828	394	Lifetouch	750
345	Green Bay Packaging	826	395	McWane	750
346	J. Crew Group	826	396	RTM Restaurant Group	750
347	CenTra	825	397	Superior Group	750
348	Graham Packaging Holdings	825	398	Walbridge, Aldinger	750
349	Houchens Industries	820	399	Petro Stopping Centers	749
350	OmniSource	820	400	F. Dohmen	748

The *Forbes* 500 Largest Private Companies in the US (continued)

Rank	Company	Revenue ($ mil.)	Rank	Company	Revenue ($ mil.)
401	Holiday Retirement/Colson & Colson	747	451	Jones, Day, Reavis & Pogue	675
402	Cupertino Electric	746	452	Angelo Iafrate Companies	674
403	R.A.B. Holdings	745	453	Kimball Hill Homes	673
404	Wintec Industries	745	454	Darby Group Companies	670
405	KinderCare Learning Centers	743	455	Sidley Austin Brown & Wood	670
406	W.G. Yates & Sons Construction	743	456	Haggen	666
407	McJunkin	741	457	Schottenstein Stores	665
408	Express Services	741	458	Suffolk Construction	663
409	Colorado Boxed Beef	740	459	National Wine & Spirits	661
410	Marc Glassman	740	460	American Golf	660
411	Pinnacle Foods	740	461	Everett Smith Group	660
412	Inductotherm Industries	735	462	Amerigroup	660
413	Orius	735	463	HBE	658
414	American Commercial Lines	734	464	Northern Tool & Equipment	655
415	Washington Companies	734	465	E-Z Mart Stores	654
416	Cigarettes Cheaper	730	466	Electek Group	651
417	Georgia Crown Distributing	730	467	Dawn Food Products	650
418	Harold Levinson Associates	730	468	Fellowes	650
419	WWF Paper	730	469	National Envelope	650
420	Simmons	727	470	Ukrop's Super Markets	650
421	Pacific Coast Building Products	725	471	Veridian	650
422	Roseburg Forest Products	725	472	Weitz	650
423	Safelite Glass	725	473	Merrill	649
424	Koppers Industries	724	474	AppleOne Employment Services	648
425	MWH	722	475	Stewart's Shops	648
426	Hampton Affiliates	721	476	TNP Enterprises	644
427	Academy Sports & Outdoors	719	477	APi Group	643
428	Great Lakes Cheese	717	478	Latham & Watkins	643
429	Chas. Levy	717	479	Tutor-Saliba	642
430	Steiner	712	480	Grove Worldwide	640
431	Kraus-Anderson	710	481	Kerr Drug	640
432	CIC International	709	482	WorkPlaceUSA	640
433	Interactive Brokers Group	707	483	Grede Foundries	633
434	Wherehouse Entertainment	706	484	KI	631
435	Bradco Supply	700	485	Forsythe Technology	631
436	Fairchild Dornier	700	486	Crescent Electric Supply	630
437	GS Industries	700	487	Fareway Stores	630
438	H.P. Hood	700	488	Cactus Feeders	625
439	Ormet	700	489	Goss Graphic	623
440	Sauder Woodworking	700	490	ACF Industries	623
441	Wells' Dairy	700	491	Koch Enterprises	617
442	Motor Coach Industries International	692	492	Drummond	615
443	Estes Express Lines	691	493	Gate Petroleum	615
444	Variety Wholesalers	691	494	Leiner Health Products Group	612
445	Peerless Importers	690	495	Schonfeld Securities	612
446	Empire Beef	682	496	Hudson Group	610
447	Modus Media International	682	497	telcobuy.com	609
448	Forever Living Products International	680	498	Atlas World Group	607
449	TRT Holdings	680	499	Marathon Cheese	605
450	Henkels & McCoy	675	500	Jockey International	604

Forbes 25 Greatest US Fortunes

Rank	Name	Age	Net Worth ($ bil.)	Source
1	Gates, William H. III	46	43.0	Microsoft
2	Buffett, Warren Edward	72	36.0	Berkshire Hathaway
3	Allen, Paul Gardner	49	21.0	Microsoft
4	Walton, Alice L.	53	18.8	Wal-Mart
4	Walton, Helen R.	83	18.8	Wal-Mart
4	Walton, Jim C.	54	18.8	Wal-Mart
4	Walton, John T.	56	18.8	Wal-Mart
4	Walton, S. Robson	58	18.8	Wal-Mart
9	Ellison, Lawrence Joseph	58	15.2	Oracle
10	Ballmer, Steven Anthony	46	11.9	Microsoft
11	Dell, Michael	37	11.2	Dell Computer
12	Kluge, John Werner	88	10.5	Metromedia
13	Mars, Forrest Edward Jr.	71	10.0	Candy
13	Mars, Jacqueline	63	10.0	Candy
13	Mars, John Franklyn	66	10.0	Candy
16	Anthony, Barbara Cox	79	9.5	Media
16	Chambers, Anne Cox	82	9.5	Media
18	Redstone, Sumner M.	79	9.0	Viacom
19	Johnson, Abigail	40	8.2	Mutual funds
20	Newhouse, Donald Edward	72	7.7	Media
20	Newhouse, Samuel Irving Jr.	74	7.7	Media
22	Pritzker, Robert Alan	76	7.6	Hotels, investments
22	Pritzker, Thomas J.	52	7.6	Hotels, investments
24	Johnson, Samuel Curtis	74	7.0	S.C. Johnson & Son
24	Soros, George	72	7.0	Hedge funds

Source: *Forbes;* September 30, 2002

Top 20 in CEO Compensation

Rank	Name	Company	Total Pay* ($ mil.)
1	Lawrence Ellison	Oracle	706.1
2	Jozef Straus	JDS Uniphase	150.8
3	Howard Solomon	Forest Laboratories	148.5
4	Richard Fairbank	Capital One Financial	142.2
5	Louis Gerstner	IBM	127.4
6	Charles Wang	Computer Associates Intl.	119.1
7	Richard Fuld, Jr.	Lehman Brothers	105.2
8	James McDonald	Scientific-Atlanta	86.8
9	Steve Jobs	Apple Computer	84.0
10	Timothy Koogle	Yahoo!	64.6
11	Tony White	Applied Biosystems Group	61.9
12	David Rickey	Applied Micro Circuits	59.5
13	John Gifford	Maxim Integrated Products	58.0
14	Paul Folino	Emulex	56.2
15	Douglas Daft	Coca-Cola	55.0
16	Geoffrey Bible	Philip Morris	49.9
17	Michael Devlin	Rational Software	47.3
18	Bruce Karatz	KB Home	44.4
19	Sanford Weill	Citigroup	42.6
20	Micky Arison	Carnival	40.5

*Includes salary, bonus, and long-term compensation
Source: *Business Week;* April 15, 2002

Forbes 40 Most Powerful Celebrities

Rank*	Name	Earnings ($ mil.)	Rank	Name	Earnings ($ mil.)
1	Britney Spears	39.2	21	Michael Schumacher	67.0
2	Tiger Woods	69.0	22	Tom Clancy	47.8
3	Steven Spielberg	100.0	23	David Letterman	32.0
4	Madonna	43.0	24	Dave Matthews Band	50.0
5	U2	69.0	25	Elton John	30.0
6	*NSYNC	42.3	26	Adam Sandler	47.0
7	Mariah Carey	58.0	27	Nicole Kidman	15.0
8	Oprah Winfrey	150.0	28	Jennifer Aniston	24.0
9	Michael Jordan	36.0	29	Arnold Schwarzenegger	35.0
10	Tom Hanks	45.0	30	Shaquille O'Neal	24.0
11	George Lucas	200.0	31	Kobe Bryant	22.0
12	Jennifer Lopez	37.0	32	Rosie O'Donnell	25.0
13	Julia Roberts	20.0	33	Harrison Ford	30.0
14	Stephen King	52.4	34	J.K. Rowling	41.8
15	Ben Affleck	40.0	35	Mike Tyson	23.0
16	Mel Gibson	40.0	36	Robert DeNiro	40.0
17	Bruce Willis	46.0	37	Samuel L. Jackson	34.0
18	Bill Clinton	25.0	38	Lennox Lewis	28.0
19	Backstreet Boys	36.8	39	Meg Ryan	25.0
20	Cameron Diaz	40.0	40	Rush Limbaugh	32.0

*Forbes' rankings are based on income and media recognition (Web prominence, magazine covers, radio/TV and newspaper coverage)
Source: *Forbes*; June 20, 2002

The 20 Most Powerful Women in Business

Rank	Name	Title	Company
1	Carly Fiorina	Chairman and CEO	Hewlett-Packard
2	Betsy Holden	Co-CEO	Kraft Foods
3	Meg Whitman	President and CEO	eBay
4	Indra Nooyi	President and CFO	PepsiCo
5	Andrea Jung	Chairman and CEO	Avon Products
6	Anne Mulcahy	Chairman and CEO	Xerox
7	Karen Katen	EVP and President, Pharmaceuticals Group	Pfizer
8	Pat Woertz	EVP, Downstream	ChevronTexaco
9	Abigail Johnson	President	Fidelity Management & Research
10	Oprah Winfrey	Chairman	Harpo Entertainment Group
11	Ann Moore	Chairman and CEO, Time Inc.	AOL Time Warner
12	Judy McGrath	President, MTV Networks Music Group	Viacom
13	Colleen Barrett	President and COO	Southwest Airlines
14	Shelly Lazarus	Chairman and CEO	Ogilvy & Mather Worldwide
15	Pat Russo	President and CEO	Lucent Technologies
16	Betsy Bernard	President and CEO, AT&T Consumer	AT&T
17	Amy Brinkley	Chief Risk Officer	Bank of America
18	Lois Juliber	COO	Colgate-Palmolive
19	Sherry Lansing	Chairman, Motion Picture Group, Paramount	Viacom
20	Stacey Snider	Chairman, Universal Pictures	Vivendi Universal

Source: *FORTUNE;* October 14, 2002

Top 25 US Banks by Total Assets

Rank	Company	Headquarters	2001 Total Assets ($ mil.)
1	JPMorgan Chase Bank	New York	541,342.0
2	Bank of America, National Association	Charlotte, NC	540,610.0
3	Citibank, N.A.	New York	454,867.0
4	First Union National Bank	Charlotte, NC	226,897.0
5	Fleet National Bank	Providence, RI	178,224.0
6	U.S. Bank National Association	Cincinnati	160,955.1
7	BANK ONE, National Association	Chicago	157,768.0
8	Wells Fargo Bank, National Association	San Francisco	141,221.0
9	Suntrust Bank	Atlanta	103,675.1
10	HSBC Bank USA	Buffalo, NY	84,694.1
11	The Bank of New York	New York	73,954.9
12	Wachovia Bank, National Association	Winston-Salem, NC	72,117.5
13	Keybank National Association	Cleveland	71,111.2
14	State Street Bank and Trust Company	Boston	68,571.2
15	Merrill Lynch Bank USA	Salt Lake City	64,410.1
16	PNC Bank, National Association	Pittsburgh	59,298.7
17	Lasalle Bank, National Association	Chicago	56,115.2
18	Branch Banking and Trust Company	Winston-Salem, NC	55,339.5
19	Wells Fargo Bank Minnesota, National Association	Minneapolis	53,167.8
20	Southtrust Bank	Birmingham, AL	48,312.9
21	BANK ONE, National Association	Columbus, OH	45,618.0
22	MBNA America Bank, National Association	Wilmington, DE	43,996.0
23	Regions Bank	Birmingham, AL	41,165.2
24	Bankers Trust Company	New York	40,856.0
25	Standard Federal Bank National Association	Troy, MI	40,370.5

Source: Federal Reserve Board's National Information Center; March 31, 2002

America's Top 20 Money Managers

Rank	Company	Headquarters	2001 Total Assets ($ mil.)
1	Fidelity Investments	Boston	853,542
2	State Street Global Advisors	Boston	785,421
3	Barclays Global Investors	San Francisco	768,700
4	J.P. Morgan Fleming Asset Management	New York	604,660
5	Capital Group Cos.	Los Angeles	589,257
6	Mellon Financial Corp.	Pittsburgh	537,294
7	Merrill Lynch Investment Managers	Plainsboro, NJ	528,701
8	Citigroup	New York	502,641
9	Axa Financial	New York	480,994
10	Morgan Stanley Investment Management	New York	414,995
11	Vanguard Group	Valley Forge, PA	412,593
12	UBS Global Asset Management	Chicago	405,079
13	Allianz Dresdner Asset Management of America	Newport Beach, CA	382,953
14	Amvescap	Atlanta	331,745
15	Putnam Investments	Boston	314,566
16	Bank of America Corp.	Charlotte, NC	314,240
17	Northern Trust Global Investments	Chicago	314,028
18	Wellington Management Co.	Boston	311,372
19	Goldman Sachs Asset Management	New York	306,014
20	BlackRock/PNC	New York	282,550

Source: *Institutional Investor;* July 2002

Top 25 US Law Firms

Rank	Law Firm	Gross Revenue ($ mil.)	Number of Lawyers
1	Skadden, Arps, Slate, Meagher & Flom	1,225.0	1,602
2	Baker & McKenzie	1,000.0	3,031
3	Jones, Day, Reavis & Pogue	790.0	1,481
4	Latham & Watkins	769.5	1,165
5	Sidley Austin Brown & Wood	715,.0	1,276
6	Shearman & Sterling	619.5	1,039
7	White & Case	603.0	1,315
8	Weil, Gotshal & Manges	581.0	845
9	Morgan, Lewis & Bockius	574.5	1,083
10	Mayer, Brown & Platt	573.0	893
11	Davis Polk & Wardwell	570.0	594
12	Sullivan & Cromwell	568.0	596
13	McDermott, Will & Emery	562.5	874
14	Akin, Gump, Strauss, Hauer & Feld	553.0	949
15	Gibson, Dunn & Crutcher	537.0	709
16	Kirkland & Ellis	530.0	725
17	Simpson Thacher & Bartlett	516.0	588
18	Cleary, Gottlieb, Steen & Hamilton	492.0	610
19	Morrison & Foerster	490.0	889
19	O'Melveny & Myers	490.0	738
21	Holland & Knight	466.5	1,094
22	Paul, Hastings, Janofsky & Walker	455.5	722
22	Vinson & Elkins	455.5	777
24	Foley & Lardner	452.5	907
25	Brobeck, Phleger & Harrison	447.0	792

Source: *American Lawyer;* July 2002

America's Top 20 Tax & Accounting Firms Ranked by US Revenue

Rank	Firm	Headquarters	2001 US Revenue ($ mil.)
1	PricewaterhouseCoopers	New York	8,057.0
2	Deloitte & Touche	New York	6,130.0
3	Ernst &Young	New York	4,485.0
4	Andersen	Chicago	4,300.0
5	KPMG	New York	3,400.0
6	H&R Block	Kansas City, MO	3,001.6
7	RSM McGladrey/McGladrey & Pullen	Bloomington, MN	507.4
8	BDO Seidman	Chicago	420.0
9	Century Business Services Inc.	Cleveland	388.6
10	Grant Thornton	Chicago	380.0
11	American Express Tax & Business Services Inc.	New York	350.0
12	Jackson Hewitt Tax Service	Parsippany, NJ	253.1
13	BKD	Springfield, MO	197.6
14	Crowe, Chizek and Co.	Indianapolis	182.6
15	Moss Adams	Seattle	167.0
16	Centerprise Advisors Inc.	Chicago	162.3
17	Plante & Moran	Southfield, MI	153.0
18	Clifton Gunderson	Peoria, IL	123.2
19	Fiducial	New York	118.3
20	Gilman & Ciocia Inc.	White Plains, NY	106.5

Source: *Accounting Today;* March 18–April 7, 2002

Advertising Age's Top 50 Media Companies by Revenue

Rank	Company	Headquarters	Total 2001 Media Revenue ($ mil.)
1	AOL Time Warner	New York	27,205
2	Viacom	New York	15,211
3	AT&T Broadband (AT&T Corp.)	Denver	10,329
4	Walt Disney Co.	New York/Burbank, CA	10,228
5	Cox Enterprises	Atlanta	6,266
6	NBC Television (General Electric Co.)	New York/Fairfield, CT	6,034
7	News Corp.	Sydney	5,915
8	Clear Channel Communications	San Antonio	5,703
9	Gannett Co.	McLean, VA	5,571
10	DirecTV (General Motors Corp.)	El Segundo, CA	5,550
11	Comcast Corp.	Philadelphia	5,131
12	Tribune Co.	Chicago	5,104
13	Advance Publications	Newark, NJ	4,000
14	Hearst Corp.	New York	3,986
15	Charter Communications	St. Louis	3,953
16	EchoStar Communications Corp.	Littleton, CO	3,683
17	Cablevision Systems Corp.	Bethpage, NY	3,064
18	Adelphia Communications Corp.	Coudersport, PA	3,060
19	New York Times Co.	New York	3,027
20	Knight Ridder	San Jose, CA	2,900
21	Bloomberg	New York	2,109
22	Washington Post Co.	Washington	1,923
23	Primedia	New York	1,922
24	Dow Jones & Co.	New York	1,773
25	Belo	Dallas	1,365
26	E.W. Scripps	Cincinnati	1,354
27	ADVO	Windsor, CT	1,137
28	Vivendi Universal	New York/Paris	1,119
29	International Data Group	Boston	1,104
30	McClatchy Co.	Sacramento, CA	1,040
31	Discovery Communications	Bethesda, MD	985
32	MediaNews Group	Denver	979
33	Meredith Corp.	Des Moines, IW	886
34	Univision Communications	Los Angeles	878
35	Reed Elsevier	London	855
36	Valassis Communications	Livonia, MI	850
37	McGraw-Hill Cos.	New York	846
38	MediaCom Communications Corp.	Middletown, NY	839
39	Media General	Richmond, VA	809
40	A&E Television Networks	New York	804
41	Reader's Digest Association	Pleasantville, NY	791
42	Freedom Communications	Irvine, CA	760
43	Gemstar-TV Guide International	Pasadena, CA	741
44	Gruner & Jahr (Bertelsmann)	New York/Hamburg, Germany	735
45	Landmark Communications	Norfolk, VA	732
46	Lamar Advertising Corp.	Baton Rouge, LA	729
47	Lifetime Entertainment Services	New York	727
48	Insight Communications Co.	New York	704
49	Sinclair Broadcast Group	Hunt Valley, MD	646
50	Zuckerman Media Properties	New York	613

Source: *Advertising Age;* August 19, 2002

Chain Store Age's Top 25 US Retailers

Rank	Company	Headquarters	2001 Revenue ($ mil.)
1	Wal-Mart	Bentonville, AR	219,812.0
2	The Home Depot	Atlanta	53,553.0
3	The Kroger Co.	Cincinnati	50,098.0
4	Sears, Roebuck and Co.	Hoffman Estates, IL	41,078.0
5	Target Corp.	Minneapolis	39,888.0
6	Albertson's	Boise, ID	37,931.0
7	Kmart Corp.	Troy, MI	36,151.0
8	Costco	Issaquah, WA	34,797.0
9	Safeway	Pleasanton, CA	34,301.0
10	J. C. Penney	Plano, TX	32,004.0
11	Dell Computer	Round Rock, TX	31,168.0
12	Walgreen	Deerfield, IL	24,623.0
13	Ahold USA	Chantilly, VA	23,212.0
14	CVS Corp.	Woonsocket, RI	22,241.4
15	Lowe's Cos.	Wilkesboro, NC	22,111.1
16	Best Buy	Eden Prairie, MN	19,597.0
17	Federated Department Stores	Cincinnati	15,651.0
18	Publix Super Markets	Lakeland, FL	15,370.0
19	Rite Aid	Camp Hill, PA	15,171.1
20	Delhaize America	Salisbury, NC	14,900.0
21	May Department Stores	St. Louis	14,215.0
22	Gap Inc.	San Francisco	13,847.9
23	Winn-Dixie	Jacksonville, FL	12,903.4
24	Meijer	Grand Rapids, MI	11,923.0
25	Office Depot	Delray Beach, FL	11,200.0

Source: *Chain Store Age;* August 2002

Supermarket News' Top 20 Supermarket Companies

Rank	Company	Headquarters	2001 Revenue ($ bil.)
1	Wal-Mart Supercenters	Bentonville, AR	65.3
2	Kroger Co.	Cincinnati	50.1
3	Albertson's	Boise, ID	37.9
4	Safeway	Pleasanton, CA	34.3
5	Ahold USA Retail	Chantilly, VA	23.2
6	Supervalu	Minneapolis	21.3
7	Costco Wholesale Corp.	Issaquah, WA	20.5
8	Sam's Clubs	Bentonville, AR	18.4
9	Fleming	Dallas	15.6
10	Publix Super Markets	Lakeland, FL	15.1
11	Delhaize America	Salisbury, NC	14.9
12	Loblaw Cos.	Toronto	14.6
13	Winn-Dixie Stores	Jacksonville, FL	13.0
14	A&P	Montvale, NJ	11.0
15	Meijer, Inc.	Grand Rapids, MI	10.6
16	7-Eleven	Dallas	9.8
17	H. E. Butt Grocery Co.	San Antonio	9.0
18	C&S Wholesale Grocers	Brattleboro, VT	8.5
19	Sobeys	Stellarton, Nova Scotia	7.6
20	Wakefern Food Corp.	Elizabeth, NJ	5.9

Source: *Supermarket News;* January 2002

The Top 25 Full-Service Restaurant Chains

Rank	Chain	2001 Sales ($ mil.)
1	Applebee's	2,926.0
2	Denny's	2,290.0
3	Outback Steakhouse	2,287.0
4	Red Lobster	2,200.0
5	Chili's Grill & Bar	2,049.3
6	T.G.I. Friday's	1,967.0
7	Olive Garden	1,700.0
8	International House of Pancakes	1,345.8
9	Cracker Barrel	1,345.8
10	Golden Corral	1,030.0
11	HomeTown/Old Country	979.4
12	Perkins	834.0
13	Bob Evans	806.0
14	Ryan's Grill	787.2
15	Ruby Tuesday	775.9
16	Bennigan's	690.0
17	Waffle House	675.0
18	Boston Market	660.0
19	Ponderosa/Bonanza	650.0
20	Hooters	611.0
21	Friendly's	604.5
22	Big Boy	600.0
23	Shoney's	583.0
24	Romano's Macaroni Grill	550.6
25	Coco's	538.7

Source: *Restaurants and Institutions;* July 15, 2002

The Top 25 Quick-Service Restaurant Chains

Rank	Chain	2001 Sales ($ mil.)
1	McDonald's	39,653.3
2	Burger King	11,200.0
3	KFC	9,700.0
4	Pizza Hut	7,600.0
5	Wendy's	6,837.0
6	Subway	5,170.0
7	Taco Bell	5,000.0
8	Domino's	3,785.0
9	Dairy Queen	2,790.0
10	Arby's	2,623.2
11	Dunkin' Donuts	2,375.0
12	7-Eleven	2,218.2
13	Jack in the Box	2,121.0
14	Starbucks	2,047.0
15	Sonic Drive-Ins	2,016.3
16	Hardee's	2,004.4
17	Little Caesars	1,900.0
18	Papa John's	1,800.0
19	Tim Hortons	1,462.0
20	Popeyes	1,300.0
21	Chick-fil-A	1,241.9
22	Carl's Jr.	1,103.1
23	Church's Chicken	900.0
24	Baskin-Robbins	820.0
25	Long John Silver's	812.0

Source: *Restaurants and Institutions;* July 15, 2002

Top 15 Convenience Store Companies

Rank	Company	Headquarters	No. of Stores
1	7-Eleven Inc.	Dallas	5,829
2	Royal Dutch/Shell Group of Companies	The Hague/London	5,372
3	Phillips Petroleum Co.	Bartlesville, OK	4,990
4	BP plc	London	4,900
5	Exxon Mobil Corp.	Irving, TX	2,799
6	Chevron Texaco Corp.	San Francisco	2,749
7	Speedway SuperAmerica LLC	Enon, OH	2,100
8	Alimentation Couche-Tard Inc.	Laval, Quebec	1,955
9	Valero Energy Corp.	San Antonio	1,942
10	FEMSA Comercio S.A. de C.V.	Monterrey, Mexico	1,779
11	Imperial Oil Co.	Toronto, Ontario	1,664
12	Casey's General Stores Inc.	Ankeny, IA	1,334
13	The Pantry Inc.	Sanford, NC	1,305
14	Clark Retail Enterprises Inc.	Oak Brook, IL	1,136
15	Amerada Hess Corp.	Woodbridge, NJ	1,112

Source: *CSNews Online;* August 22, 2002

Software Magazine's Top 50 Software Companies by Revenue

Rank	Company	2001 Revenue* ($ mil.)	Rank	Company	2001 Revenue* ($ mil.)
1	IBM	47,895.0	26	PeopleSoft	1,970.5
2	Microsoft Corporation	24,666.0	27	SunGard Data Systems Inc.	1,928.7
3	Electronic Data Systems	21,543.0	28	Compuware Corporation	1,835.8
4	Accenture Ltd.	13,348.0	29	Fiserv, Inc.	1,818.2
5	Oracle Corporation	10,859.7	30	DST Systems, Inc.	1,660.0
6	Computer Sciences	10,524.0	31	CSK Corporation	1,655.5
7	Compaq Computer	7,746.7	32	Logica plc	1,602.8
8	PwCC Limited Pvt	7,481.0	33	Amdocs Limited	1,533.9
9	Cap Gemini Ernst & Young	7,454.9	34	VERITAS Software	1,492.3
10	NTT DATA Corporation	6,460.0	35	Cadence Design Systems	1,430.4
11	SAP	6,454.0	36	BMC Software, Inc.	1,375.9
12	Unisys Corporation	6,018.1	37	Hitachi, Ltd.	1,357.6
13	NEC Corporation	5,892.0	38	Intuit Inc.	1,261.5
14	Computer Associates Int'l	4,190.0	39	Adobe Systems	1,229.7
15	Sun Microsystems, Inc.	4,015.0	40	Misys plc	1,224.7
16	Getronics NV	3,675.2	41	Perot Systems Corporation	1,204.7
17	Cisco Systems, Inc.	3,566.9	42	SAS Institute Pvt	1,130.0
18	NCR Corporation	3,197.0	43	Corporate Software Pvt	1,076.6
19	Lockheed Martin	2,878.8	44	Novell, Inc.	1,040.1
20	Atos Origin	2,690.7	45	Samsung SDS	1,031.7
21	EMC Corporation	2,532.0	46	Symantec	1,011.3
22	Apple Computer, Inc.	2,276.0	47	Reynolds and Reynolds	1,004.0
23	Hewlett-Packard Company	2,261.3	48	i2 Technologies, Inc.	985.6
24	Affiliated Computer Services	2,063.6	49	VeriSign, Inc.	983.6
25	Siebel Systems, Inc.	2,048.4	50	BEA Systems, Inc.	975.9

*Worldwide software and services revenue includes license revenue, maintenance and support, training, and software-related services and consulting revenue.

Source: *Software Magazine;* June/July 2002

Top 10 Telecommunications Companies

Rank	Company	Headquarters	2001 Sales ($ bil.)
1	Verizon	New York	67.2
2	SBC	San Antonio	54.3
3	AT&T	Basking Ridge, NJ	52.6
4	BellSouth	Atlanta	29.6
5	Sprint	Overland Park, KS	26.0
6	WorldCom	Jackson, MS	21.3
7	Qwest	Denver	19.7
8	Northern Telecom	Toronto	17.5
9	Alltel	Little Rock, AR	7.6
10	Global Crossing	Beverly Hills, CA	3.2

Source: *Brandweek;* June 17, 2002

FORTUNE's 100 Best Companies to Work for in America

Rank	Company	US Employees	Rank	Company	US Employees
1	Edward Jones	27,092	51	David Weekley Homes	1,037
2	Container Store	1,987	52	Arbitron	1,105
3	SAS Institute	8,309	53	Lands' End	5,131
4	TDIndustries	1,368	54	McCutchen, Doyle,	
5	Synovus Financial Corp.	11,022		Brown & Enersen	702
			55	Continental Airlines	40,115
6	Xilinx	2,649			
7	Plante & Moran	1,240	56	Lenscrafters	16,999
8	QUALCOMM	6,314	57	Pfizer	89,936
9	Alston & Bird	1,338	58	Starbucks	59,541
10	Baptist Health Care	4,068	59	Genentech	4,859
			60	Bright Horizons Family Solutions	12,303
11	Frank Russell	1,397			
12	Hypertherm	604	61	Four Seasons Hotels	25,321
13	CDW Computer Centers	2,781	62	REI	6,195
14	Fenwick & West	626	63	Kingston Technology	1,015
15	Cisco Systems	37,546	64	American Cast Iron Pipe	2,313
			65	Timberland	5,248
16	Granite Rock	792			
17	Beck Group	652	66	First Tennessee National Corp.	6,875
18	East Alabama Medical Center	1,846	67	A.G. Edwards	17,595
19	Goldman Sachs Group	22,585	68	Wegmans Food Markets	29,072
20	JM Family Enterprises	3,227	69	Barton Protective Svcs.	12,189
			70	MFS	2,802
21	International Data				
	Group (IDG)	11,113	71	National Instruments	2,900
22	Stew Leonard's	1,729	72	Acxiom	5,291
23	American Century	2,937	73	Medtronic	25,830
24	J.M. Smucker	2,380	74	Harley-Davidson	7,858
25	Vision Service Plan	2,283	75	Stratus	1,114
26	MBNA	27,907	76	Ukrop's Super Markets	5,943
27	Adobe Systems	3,017	77	ACUITY	646
28	Microsoft	49,675	78	Brobeck, Phleger & Harrison	1,760
29	Valassis Communications	1,546	79	Fannie Mae	4,455
30	Duncan Aviation	1,898	80	Guidant	10,259
31	Agilent Technologies	40,795	81	Carlson Companies	46,596
32	Capital One Financial	19,868	82	Merck	75,399
33	AFLAC	5,744	83	Publix Super Markets	128,742
34	W.L. Gore & Associates	6,099	84	Nordstrom	42,133
35	Deloitte & Touche	29,154	85	FedEx	200,676
36	Third Federal S&L	1,017	86	St. Luke's Episcopal	3,886
37	SRA International	1,746	87	Ernst & Young	83,184
38	VHA	1,417	88	Vanguard Group	10,886
39	Pella	6,884	89	Discovery Communications	2,018
40	MITRE	4,907	90	Marriott International	139,500
41	Patagonia	812	91	American Express	81,489
42	Paychex	7,406	92	Kimberly-Clark	62,501
43	Griffin Hospital	1,111	93	Eli Lilly	39,823
44	SEI Investments	1,963	94	Wal-Mart Stores	1,269,585
45	Intuit	6,587	95	Texas Instruments	34,857
46	Charles Schwab	19,477	96	R.J. Reynolds Tobacco	8,216
47	Alcon Laboratories	11,695	97	Procter & Gamble	106,000
48	Whole Foods Market	21,514	98	Johnson & Johnson	99,863
49	Intel	89,792	99	Worthington Industries	6,826
50	Sun Microsystems	39,020	100	Men's Wearhouse	8,370

Source: *FORTUNE*; February 4, 2002

America's 10 Most Admired Companies

Rank	Company	CEO	2001 Revenue ($ mil.)
1	General Electric	Jeffrey Immelt	125,913.0
2	Southwest Airlines	James Parker	5,555.2
3	Wal-Mart Stores	H. Lee Scott Jr.	219,812.0
4	Microsoft	Steve Ballmer	25,296.0
5	Berkshire Hathaway	Warren Buffett	37,668.0
6	Home Depot	Robert Nardelli	53,553.0
7	Johnson & Johnson	William Weldon	33,004.0
8	FedEx	Frederick W. Smith	19,629.0
9	Citigroup	Sanford Weill	112,022.0
10	Intel	Craig Barrett	26,539.0

Source: *FORTUNE*; March 4, 2002

The Top 20 Black-Owned Businesses

Rank	Company*	2001 Sales ($ mil.)
1	CAMAC Holdings, Inc.	979.5
2	telcobuy.com	604.0
3	Philadelphia Coca-Cola	419.0
4	Johnson Publishing Company Inc.	412.4
5	Sayers Group	330.0
6	Barden Companies Inc.	326.0
7	World Wide Technology Inc.	320.0
8	The Bing Group	287.0
9	Harpo Inc.	285.0
10	Pacific Network Supply	268.5
11	Spiral Inc.	252.0
12	Hawkins Food Group	246.0
13	Total Premier Services Inc.	242.0
14	H. J. Russell & Company	240.3
15	Global Automotive Alliance	235.0
16	Rush Communications of NYC Inc.	192.0
17	Anderson-Dubose Co.	176.7
18	Bridgewater Interiors L.L.C.	174.0
19	Commodities Management Exchange	170.0
20	Exemplar Manufacturing Co.	168.9

*Manufacturing and service companies only
Source: *Black Enterprise*; June 2002

The Top 20 Hispanic-Owned Businesses

Rank	Company	2001 Sales ($ mil.)
1	Burt Automotive Network	1,493.8
2	MasTec Inc.	1,220.0
3	Codina Group Inc.	783.0
4	Goya Foods Inc.	715.0
5	Ancira Enterprises Inc.	655.0
6	Brightstar Corp.	621.0
7	The Related Group of Florida	547.0
8	Elder Automotive Group	538.8
9	Molina Healthcare Inc.	502.0
10	Pharmed Group Corp.	389.1
11	Sedano's Supermarkets	360.2
12	Lloyd A. Wise Cos.	344.0
13	Lopez Foods Inc.	342.0
14	International Bancshares Corp.	312.5
15	The Diez Group	303.0
16	Supreme International Inc.	287.4
17	Physicians Healthcare Plans Inc.	260.0
18	Lou Sobh Automotive	257.0
19	Barrett Holdings Inc.	210.0
20	Mike Shaw Chevrolet-Buick Pontiac-Saab GMC	203.4

Source: *Hispanic Business*; June 2002

The Top 25 Companies for Female Executives

Rank	Company	Total Employees	Women Employees	Women Dept./ Division Heads (%)	Women on Board of Directors (%)
1	Avon	7,188	5,332	47	55
2	Scholastic	7,430	5,120	52	31
3	Liz Claiborne	6,745	4,923	63	30
4	Aetna	36,148	28,469	36	33
5	Washington Mutual Inc.	42,049	29,073	49	24
6	Prudential Financial Group	31,899	17,709	39	14
7	TIAA-CREF	6,044	3,312	35	30
8	Hewlett-Packard	41,000	15,000	23	22
9	The New York Times Company	14,000	5,861	29	21
10	WellPoint Health Networks Inc.	14,020	10,699	46	38
11	Lincoln Financial Group	6,536	4,218	30	27
12	SBC Communications Inc.	199,029	95,534	29	29
13	Advantica Restaurant Group	42,856	22,182	39	20
14	Fannie Mae	4,499	2,396	45	31
15	CIGNA	39,574	30,460	41	18
16	Merck & Co., Inc.	43,896	24,132	33	23
17	Principal Financial Group	13,861	9,846	35	29
18	USA Education, Inc. (Sallie Mae)	5,695	3,909	41	13
19	State Street	15,628	7,468	34	17
20	The Phoenix Companies, Inc.	1,461	823	40	13
21	Sears, Roebuck and Co.	122,332	60,714	26	20
22	Con Edison	12,655	1,937	23	23
23	Federated Department Stores	150,009	113,311	18	18
24	The Allstate Corporation	39,384	23,769	31	17
25	IBM	147,862	46,043	22	13

Source: National Association for Female Executives; February 13, 2002

The 25 Best Companies for Minorities

Rank	Company	2001 Revenue ($mil.)	Minorities as % of Management	Minorities as % of Work Force
1	Fannie Mae	50,803	29.1	42.8
2	Sempra Energy	8,029	29.3	48.0
3	Advantica	1,391	31.1	49.6
4	SBC Communications	45,908	28.7	37.7
5	McDonald's	14,870	37.8	55
6	PNM Resources	2,352	33.2	47.9
7	Southern California Edison	12,184	26.6	43.1
8	U. S. Postal Service	65,834	31.0	36.2
9	Freddie Mac	35,523	27.3	32.0
10	BellSouth	24,130	26.2	30.9
11	UnionBanCal Corporation	2,912	37.8	56.0
12	Lucent Technologies	25,132	23.1	29.6
13	Consolidated Edison	9,634	20.7	36.0
14	Xerox	16,502	23.0	30.2
15	PepsiCo	26,935	16.4	26.6
16	Colgate-Palmolive	9,428	26.6	29.3
17	Wyndham International	2,105	29.0	60.8
18	Silicon Graphics	1,854	24.1	23.1
19	Hyatt	3,950	35.8	59.3
20	Procter & Gamble	39,244	16.7	16.7
21	DTE Energy	7,849	18.4	27.1
22	Hilton Hotels	3,050	28.3	57.6
23	Levi Strauss	4,259	32.7	56.5
24	Marriott International	10,152	23.3	59.3
25	United Parcel Service	30,646	27.9	35.1

Source: FORTUNE; July 8, 2002

Hoover's Handbook of American Business

THE COMPANY PROFILES A-K

3COM CORPORATION

3Com's attacking the networking sector from two sides. The Santa Clara, California-based company addresses the networking needs of businesses, manufacturers, and telecom carriers through two units. 3Com sells infrastructure gear (hubs, switches, and servers), networked telephony systems, and wireless networking equipment for enterprises through its Business Networks Company (BNC). BNC also provides PC makers and other manufacturers with network interface cards (NICs) and PC cards. 3Com's CommWorks subsidiary sells carrier-class IP networking hardware and software to telecommunications providers.

Recent years have seen 3Com shuffle its operations numerous times. Restructuring measures have included chewing up and spitting out U.S. Robotics; the company took its handheld unit (gained from its U.S. Robotics acquisition) public in 2000 as Palm, Inc., and later spun off the remaining U.S. Robotics operations (analog modems). Since forming CommWorks as a separate unit focused on telecommunications customers and realigning its other businesses under BNC, 3Com has decided to discontinue its consumer cable and DSL modem operations and increase its outsourced manufacturing agreements.

Tough times in the networking sector have led to more belt-tightening measures at 3Com, including significant reductions to its workforce.

HISTORY

Engineer Robert Metcalfe led the Xerox research team that invented Ethernet (now a PC networking standard) in 1973. Six years later, Metcalfe and several colleagues founded 3Com, for "computer, communication, and compatibility." The company began as a computer network consulting firm before there were many PCs to network. In 1980 Xerox agreed to share its Ethernet patent to make the technology an industry standard, and $1.1 million in venture capital helped get 3Com rolling. The upstart introduced an Ethernet transceiver and adapter the next year. William Krause was hired away from Hewlett-Packard in 1981 to be 3Com's president. Sales took off in 1982 after IBM introduced its 16-bit PC.

In 1984, 3Com went public. Initially it sold network adapter cards to large computer makers and resellers, but by 1986 its manufacturing customers were integrating their own networking hardware. Krause responded by broadening the company's focus, and 3Com started providing network hardware and software systems.

In 1987 the company gained a direct sales force when it acquired router supplier Bridge

Communications. When Bridge co-founder Eric Benhamou was named to head 3Com in 1990, Metcalfe departed. Benhamou shed noncore businesses and developed the company's prosperous line of network adapters, hubs, and routers. He also started acquiring complementary companies, including British hub specialist BICC Data Networks (1992) and network switch company Synernetics (1993). The company went into the red in 1994 when it bought Centrum Communications (remote-access technology) and NiceCom (a bandwidth data allocation innovator).

To build name recognition, the company paid $3.9 million in 1995 to rename San Francisco's venerable Candlestick Park as 3Com Park through the year 2000. Also in 1995 the company bought high-end competitor Chipcom.

3Com's $7.3 billion purchase of U.S. Robotics in 1997 added remote-access units and the PalmPilot personal digital assistant to the company's lineup. However, problems digesting the modem giant led to layoffs and inventory backups. The first of several shareholder lawsuits alleging securities violations was filed that year. In 1998 the company named former Digital Equipment heir apparent Bruce Claflin president and COO. (Benhamou remained chairman and CEO.) The following year 3Com acquired Smartcode, a French data communications software company, and Interactive Web Concepts, a provider of Web business technology.

In 2000, 3Com sold shares of Palm to the public in an $875 million offering. (3Com distributed its remaining stake in Palm to shareholders later that year.) The company made plans to exit the high-end networking market and implement staff cuts. Also that year 3Com spun off U.S. Robotics as a private company concentrated on analog modems and other digital access products. Shortly thereafter 3Com reached a settlement in the lawsuit attached to its 1997 acquisition of U.S. Robotics: a $259 million cash payment, one of the largest shareholder settlements ever awarded. At the end of 2000, 3Com made its carrier networks unit a subsidiary called CommWorks.

In early 2001 Claflin succeeded Benhamou as CEO, with Benhamou retaining his chairmanship. Amid a slowdown in the telecommunications equipment sector that year, 3Com eliminated 1,200 jobs; only months later it cut another 3,000 (an additional 30% of its workforce). Soon after the company announced it would exit the high-speed consumer modem business.

3Com merged its business connectivity unit (PC cards and NICs) into its business networks division in 2002.

OFFICERS

Chairman: Eric A. Benhamou, age 46, $933,248 pay
CEO and Director: Bruce L. Claflin, age 50, $991,625 pay
SVP, Corporate Services: Gwen McDonald, age 47
SVP, Finance and Planning and CFO: Mark A. Slaven, age 45
SVP, Legal and Government Relations, Secretary, and General Counsel: Mark D. Michael, age 51
President, Business Networks: John F. McClelland, age 57, $631,111 pay
President, CommWorks: Dennis Connors, age 48, $520,917 pay (prior to title change)
VP; General Manager, LAN Infrastructure, Business Networks: Patrick Guay
VP; General Manager, Product Group, Business Networks: Kathy Rocha
VP, Corporate Branding and Communications: Jeanne Cox, age 47
CIO: Ari Bose
Auditors: Deloitte & Touche LLP

LOCATIONS

HQ: 5400 Bayfront Plaza, Santa Clara, CA 95052
Phone: 408-326-5000   **Fax:** 408-326-5001
Web: www.3com.com

3Com has offices in more than 40 countries.

2002 Sales

	$ mil.	% of total
Americas	696	47
Europe	496	34
Asia/Pacific	286	19
Total	**1,478**	**100**

PRODUCTS/OPERATIONS

2002 Sales

	$ mil.	% of total
BNC	774	52
BCC	475	32
CommWorks	219	15
Exited lines	10	1
Total	**1,478**	**100**

Selected Products

Business Networks Company (BNC)

Business connectivity	Firewalls
Bluetooth cards	Hubs and switches
CompactFlash cards	Servers
Modem PC cards	Web cache appliances
Network interface cards	Networked telephony
LAN infrastructure	systems
DSL routers	Wireless access points

CommWorks
CDMA (Code Division Multiple Access) gateways
Multiservice access platforms
Switching software and hardware (Softswitch)

COMPETITORS

Accton Technology	Efficient Networks	IBM
Alcatel	Enterasys	Linksys
Allied Telesyn	Ericsson	Lucent
Avaya	Extreme Networks	Motorola
Cisco Systems		NETGEAR
Comverse	Foundry Networks	Nokia
Dell Computer		Nortel Networks
D-Link	Hewlett-Packard	Siemens
	Intel	Sonus Networks

HISTORICAL FINANCIALS & EMPLOYEES

Nasdaq: COMS FYE: May 31	Annual Growth	5/93	5/94	5/95	5/96	5/97	5/98	5/99	5/00	5/01	5/02
Sales ($ mil.)	10.2%	617	827	1,295	2,327	3,147	5,420	5,772	4,334	2,821	1,478
Net income ($ mil.)	—	39	(29)	126	178	374	30	404	674	(965)	(596)
Income as % of sales	—	6.3%	—	9.7%	7.6%	11.9%	0.6%	7.0%	15.6%	—	—
Earnings per share ($)	—	0.24	(0.24)	0.86	1.00	2.01	0.08	1.09	1.88	(2.80)	(1.71)
Stock price - FY high ($)	—	2.10	3.34	7.27	11.25	17.08	12.52	10.73	25.12	21.17	7.00
Stock price - FY low ($)	—	0.51	1.03	2.11	6.39	5.03	5.30	4.20	4.75	4.44	3.37
Stock price - FY close ($)	16.5%	1.41	2.47	6.71	10.33	10.18	5.32	5.73	8.77	5.56	5.56
P/E - high	—	9	—	8	11	8	139	10	13	—	—
P/E - low	—	2	—	2	6	2	59	4	2	—	—
Dividends per share ($)	—	0.00	0.00	0.00	0.00	0.00	0.00	0.00	0.00	0.00	0.00
Book value per share ($)	11.2%	2.09	2.16	3.35	5.80	8.51	7.82	8.94	11.05	6.85	5.45
Employees	9.9%	1,971	2,306	3,072	5,190	7,109	12,920	13,027	10,957	8,165	4,615

STOCK PRICE HISTORY

2002 FISCAL YEAR-END

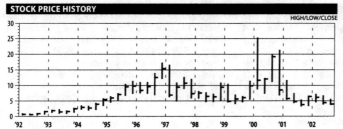

HIGH/LOW/CLOSE

Debt ratio: 3.4%
Return on equity: —
Cash ($ mil.): 679
Current ratio: 3.30
Long-term debt ($ mil.): 68
No. of shares (mil.): 358
Dividends
  Yield: —
  Payout: —
Market value ($ mil.): 1,989

3M COMPANY

It's hard to keep tabs on all of 3M's products, although its Post-it Notes can help. The St. Paul, Minnesota-based manufacturer operates six divisions: transportation, graphics, and safety (reflective materials, respirators, and optical films — accounting for about 20% of sales); industrial (advanced adhesives, tapes, and abrasives — about 20%); health care (drugs, dental, and skin products — 20%); consumer and office (tape — just over 15%); electro and communications (insulating products — a little less than 15%); and specialty material (gases and plastics). 3M's well-known brands include Scotchgard fabric protectors, Post-it Notes, Scotch-Brite scouring products, and Scotch tapes.

Back in 2000, 3M restructured, cut its workforce, and sold its Eastern Heights Bank and several health care businesses (including its cardiovascular systems unit), and was rewarded with its second-best financial performance in 14 years. The company cut thousands of jobs after profits and sales dipped due to the economic slowdown in 2001. CEO James McNerney, a former General Electric executive, has announced more job cuts (bringing the total to 8,500 in all — about 11% of the company's workforce) and is aiming for 10% earnings growth.

HISTORY

Five businessmen in Two Harbors, Minnesota, founded Minnesota Mining and Manufacturing (3M) in 1902 to sell corundum to grinding-wheel manufacturers. The company soon needed to raise working capital. Co-founder John Dwan offered his friend Edgar Ober 60% of 3M's stock. Ober persuaded Lucius Ordway, VP of a plumbing business, to help underwrite 3M. In 1905 the two took over the company and moved it to Duluth.

In 1907 future CEO William McKnight joined 3M as a bookkeeper. Three years later the plant moved to St. Paul. The board of directors declared a dividend to shareholders in the last quarter of 1916, and 3M hasn't missed a dividend since. The next two products 3M developed — Scotch-brand masking tape (1925) and Scotch-brand cellophane tape (1930) — assured its future.

McKnight introduced one of the first employee pension plans in 1931, and in the late 1940s he implemented a vertical management structure. 3M introduced the first commercially viable magnetic recording tape in 1947.

In 1950, after a decade of work and $1 million in development costs, 3M employee Carl Miller completed the Thermo-Fax copying machine, which was the foundation of 3M's duplicating division.

Products in the 1960s included 3M's dry-silver microfilm, photographic products, carbonless papers, overhead projection systems, and medical and dental products. The company moved into pharmaceuticals, radiology, energy control, and office markets in the 1970s and 1980s.

A 3M scientist developed Post-it Notes (1980) because he wanted to attach page markers to his church hymnal. Recalling that a colleague had developed an adhesive that wasn't very sticky, he brushed some on paper and began a product line that now generates hundreds of millions of dollars each year.

In 1990 the company bought sponge maker O-Cel-O. But not all of its inventions have brought 3M good news. In 1995, along with fellow silicone breast-implant makers Baxter International and Bristol-Myers Squibb, it agreed to settle thousands of personal-injury claims related to implants. The companies paid an average $26,000 per claim.

3M spun off its low-profit imaging and data-storage businesses in 1996 as Imation Corp. and closed its audiotape and videotape businesses. The next year 3M sold its National Advertising billboard business to Infinity Outdoor for $1 billion and its Media Network unit (a printer of advertising inserts) to Time Warner.

The company created the 3M Nexcare brand for its line of first-aid and home health products in 1998. To regain earnings growth, 3M closed about 10% of its plants in the US and abroad and cut 6% of its workforce by the end of 1999. The next year 3M sold its heart-surgery-equipment health care unit to Japan's Terumo and its Eastern Heights Bank subsidiary to Norwest Bank of Minnesota.

3M bought Polaroid's Technical Polarizer and Display Films business and a controlling stake in Germany-based Quante AG (telecom systems) in 2000. In addition, the company decided to stop making many of its Scotchgard-brand repellant products due to research revealing that one of the compounds (perfluorooctane sulfonate) used in the manufacturing process is "persistent and pervasive" in the environment and in people's bloodstreams. As 2000 drew to a close, 3M named GE executive James McNerney to succeed L.D. DeSimone as its chairman and CEO.

3M bought Robinson Nugent (electronic connectors) and MicroTouch Systems (touch screens) in 2001. It also announced plans to cut 6,000 jobs. 3M said in 2002 that it would cut another 2,500 jobs — total cuts in 2001 and 2002 equal about 11% of its workforce.

After 100 years of using Minnesota Mining and Manufacturing Company as its legal name, in 2002 the firm shortened it to 3M Company.

OFFICERS

Chairman and CEO: W. James McNerney Jr., age 52, $3,700,000 pay
EVP, Consumer and Office Markets: Moe S. Nozari, age 59
EVP, Electro and Communications Markets and Corporate Services: Charles Reich, age 59
EVP, Health Care Markets: John W. Benson, age 57, $899,952 pay
EVP, Industrial Markets: Harold J. Wiens, age 55, $850,363 pay
EVP, International Operations: Joseph A. Giordano, age 53
EVP, Specialty Material Markets and Corporate Services: Frederick J. Palensky, age 52
SVP and CFO: Patrick D. Campbell, age 49
SVP, Legal Affairs and General Counsel: John J. Ursu, age 62, $786,694 pay
VP, Human Resources: M. Kay Grenz, age 55
Auditors: PricewaterhouseCoopers LLP

LOCATIONS

HQ: 3M Center, St. Paul, MN 55144
Phone: 651-733-1110   **Fax:** 651-736-2133
Web: www.mmm.com

2001 Sales

	$ mil.	% of total
US	7,546	47
Europe & Middle East	3,960	25
Asia/Pacific	3,043	19
Latin America, Africa & Canada	1,496	9
Other regions	34	—
Total	**16,079**	**100**

PRODUCTS/OPERATIONS

2001 Sales & Operating Income

	Sales		Operating Income	
	$ mil.	% of total	$ mil.	% of total
Transportation, graphics & safety	3,526	22	695	25
Health care	3,419	21	760	27
Industrial	3,199	20	518	19
Consumer & office	2,724	17	447	16
Electro & communications	2,171	14	218	8
Specialty material	1,022	6	141	5
Corporate	18	—	(506)	—
Total	**16,079**	**100**	**2,273**	**100**

COMPETITORS

ALZA	Henkel
American Biltrite	Hercules
American Superconductor	Honeywell International
Armstrong Holdings	Illinois Tool Works
Avery Dennison	Imperial Chemical
BASF AG	International Paper
Bayer AG	International Specialty
Beiersdorf	Products
Borden Chemical	Johnson & Johnson
Bostik Findley	Pfizer
Dial	PPG
DuPont	S.C. Johnson
Exxon Mobil	Tyco International
GE	USG
Henkel Consumer Adhesives	

HISTORICAL FINANCIALS & EMPLOYEES

NYSE: MMM FYE: December 31	Annual Growth	12/92	12/93	12/94	12/95	12/96	12/97	12/98	12/99	12/00	12/01
Sales ($ mil.)	1.6%	13,883	14,020	15,079	13,460	14,236	15,070	15,021	15,659	16,724	16,079
Net income ($ mil.)	1.6%	1,236	1,263	1,322	976	1,526	2,121	1,175	1,763	1,782	1,430
Income as % of sales	—	8.9%	9.0%	8.8%	7.3%	10.7%	14.1%	7.8%	11.3%	10.7%	8.9%
Earnings per share ($)	2.7%	2.82	2.59	3.10	2.29	3.57	5.06	2.88	4.34	4.45	3.58
Stock price - FY high ($)	—	53.50	58.50	57.13	69.88	85.88	105.50	97.88	103.38	122.94	127.00
Stock price - FY low ($)	—	42.75	48.63	46.38	50.75	61.25	80.00	65.63	69.31	78.19	85.86
Stock price - FY close ($)	10.0%	50.31	54.38	53.38	66.38	83.00	82.06	71.13	97.88	120.50	118.21
P/E - high	—	19	22	18	30	24	21	33	24	26	35
P/E - low	—	15	19	15	22	17	16	22	16	17	24
Dividends per share ($)	4.6%	1.60	1.66	1.76	1.88	1.92	2.12	2.20	2.24	2.32	2.40
Book value per share ($)	0.4%	15.06	15.16	16.04	16.44	15.08	14.64	14.77	15.77	16.49	15.55
Employees	(2.2%)	87,292	86,168	85,166	70,687	74,289	75,639	73,564	70,549	75,000	71,669

STOCK PRICE HISTORY

HIGH/LOW/CLOSE

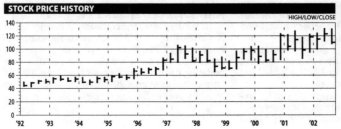

2001 FISCAL YEAR-END

Debt ratio: 20.0%
Return on equity: 22.7%
Cash ($ mil.): 616
Current ratio: 1.40
Long-term debt ($ mil.): 1,520
No. of shares (mil.): 391
Dividends
  Yield: 2.0%
  Payout: 67.0%
Market value ($ mil.): 46,256

7-ELEVEN, INC.

"If convenience stores are open 24 hours, why the locks on their doors?" If anyone knows, it's 7-Eleven. The Dallas-based company (formerly The Southland Corporation) operates about 5,800 7-Eleven convenience stores in more than 30 states and Canada (over half are franchised). Stores range from 2,400-3,000 sq. ft. and sell about 2,800 items. Less than half of its stores offer gasoline (mostly Citgo brand), and its merchandise (including Slurpees, beer, perishables, and tobacco items) accounts for more than 70% of sales.

Worldwide, 7-Eleven operates, franchises, or licenses more than 22,600 stores throughout North America and 16 other countries. Seven-Eleven Japan, which is more than 50%-owned by Ito-Yokado (a retailer that owns about 73% of 7-Eleven), runs more than 9,000 7-Eleven stores in Japan and Hawaii under a license agreement. 7-Eleven has an interest in more than 300 stores in Mexico.

To boost sales 7-Eleven is increasing the percentage of its stores that offer fresh foods to 90% and it has rolled out new products, including the popular Code Red Mountain Dew Slurpee. Additionally, the company plans to add Web-based cash machine/kiosks to about 1,000 stores. 7-Eleven is also setting up high-tech systems that lower the costs of keeping top-selling items in stock. To help compensate for reduced royalty payments from Ito-Yokado, 7-Eleven is expanding in China.

HISTORY

Claude Dawley formed the Southland Ice Company in Dallas in 1927 when ice was a precious necessity during Texas summers for storing and transporting food. Dawley bought four other Texas ice plant operations with backing from Chicago utility magnate Martin Insull. The purchases included Consumers Ice, where Joe Thompson had increased profits by selling chilled watermelons off the truck docks.

After the Dawley enterprise was underway, a dock manager in Dallas began stocking a few food items for customers. (Ice docks were exempt from Texas' blue laws and could operate even on Sundays.) He relayed the idea to Thompson, then running the ice operations, who adopted it at all company locations.

Thompson promoted the grocery operations by calling them Tote'm Stores and erecting totem poles by the docks. In 1928 he added gas stations to some store locations.

Insull bought out Dawley in 1930, and Thompson became president. He expanded Southland's operations even as the company operated briefly under the direction of bankruptcy court (1932-34). Having become the largest dairy retailer in the Dallas/Fort Worth area, in 1936 the company began its own dairy, Oak Farms, to supply some of its milk (sold in 1988). Ten years later the company changed its name to The Southland Corporation and adopted the store name 7-Eleven, a reference to the stores' hours of operation at the time.

After Thompson died in 1961, his eldest son, John, became president. John opened stores in Colorado, New Jersey, and Arizona in 1962 and in Utah, California, and Missouri in 1963. The company introduced the Slurpee, a fizzy slush drink, in 1965. Southland franchised the 7-Eleven format in the UK (1971) and in Japan (1973).

To supply its gas pumps, in 1983 the company purchased Citgo, a gasoline refining and marketing business with about 300 gas stations. It soon sold a 50% interest of the business to the Venezuelan government-owned oil company, Petróleos de Venezuela (PDVSA), in 1986.

In 1988 John and his two brothers borrowed heavily to buy 70% of Southland's stock in an LBO. Stymied by debt, the company sold its remaining 50% stake in Citgo to PDVSA in 1990. However, Southland defaulted on $1.8 billion in publicly traded debt later that year and filed for bankruptcy protection. The company then persuaded bondholders to restructure its debt and take 25% of its stock, clearing the way for the purchase of 70% of Southland in 1991 by its Japanese partner, Ito-Yokado. Company veteran Clark Matthews was named CEO that year.

From 1991 to 1993 sales declined as Southland closed stores, renovated others, and upgraded its merchandise. In 1998 Southland began testing in-store electronic banking kiosks, which allow users to cash checks, pay bills, and transfer funds. New store openings and acquisitions (Christy's in New England, red D marts in Indiana) added 299 more units that year.

Southland changed its name to 7-Eleven in 1999 to better reflect the lone business of the company. In early 2000 Ito-Yokado raised its stake in 7-Eleven to nearly 73%. COO Jim Keyes (a 15-year veteran who began managing 7-Eleven's Citgo gasoline business) replaced Matthews as CEO in April 2000.

In January 2002 the company announced that it was closing up to 120 unprofitable stores. In honor of its 75th anniversary, among other reasons, 7-Eleven launched the most extensive advertising campaign in its history in May 2002. It announced in August 2002 that it would open up to 500 stores in Beijing by 2007.

Chairman: Masatoshi Ito, age 77
Vice Chairman: Toshifumi Suzuki, age 69
Co-Vice Chairman: Clark J. Matthews II, age 65
President, CEO, and Director: James W. Keyes, age 46, $612,214 pay
EVP, General Counsel, and Corporate Secretary: Bryan F. Smith Jr., $361,339 pay
EVP, Operations: Gary R. Rose, $340,166 pay
SVP, Demand Chain Integration: David Podeschi
SVP, Finance and CFO: Edward W. Moneypenny, age 56
SVP, International Liaison, and Director: Masaaki Asakura, age 59
SVP, Merchandising and Marketing: Michael J. Gade, $311,108 pay (partial-year salary)
VP and Treasurer: Stanley W. Reynolds
VP, Business Development/E-Commerce: Rick Updyke
VP, Chesapeake Division: Joseph M. Strong
VP, Field Merchandising: Nancy A. Smith
VP, Florida Division: John W. Harris
VP, Fresh Food: Des Hague
VP, Gasoline Supply: Gary Clifton Lockhart
VP, Great Lakes Division: Jeffrey A. Schenck
VP, Human Resources: Joseph R. Eulberg
VP, Information Systems: Phillip K. Morrow
Auditors: PricewaterhouseCoopers LLP

LOCATIONS

HQ: 2711 N. Haskell Ave., Dallas, TX 75204
Phone: 214-828-7011   **Fax:** 214-828-7848
Web: www.7-eleven.com

PRODUCTS/OPERATIONS

2001 Sales

	$ mil.	% of total
Merchandise	7,020	72
Gasoline	2,762	28
Total	**9,782**	**100**

COMPETITORS

Allsup's	Marathon Oil
Casey's General Stores	Minyard Food Stores
ChevronTexaco	Murphy Oil
Cigarettes Cheaper	The Pantry
Clark Retail Group	Pilot
Cumberland Farms	QuikTrip
Dairy Mart	Racetrac Petroleum
Eckerd	Royal Dutch/Shell Group
Exxon Mobil	Sheetz
Gate Petroleum	Shell
H-E-B	Swifty Serve
Holiday Companies	Uni-Marts
Kiel Brothers	United Petroleum
Krause Gentle	Walgreen
Kroger	Wawa
Loblaw	

HISTORICAL FINANCIALS & EMPLOYEES

NYSE: SE FYE: December 31	Annual Growth	12/92	12/93	12/94	12/95	12/96	12/97	12/98	12/99	12/00	12/01
Sales ($ mil.)	3.1%	7,426	5,851	5,692	5,754	5,907	6,000	6,214	8,252	9,346	9,782
Net income ($ mil.)	—	(131)	71	92	271	90	70	74	83	108	84
Income as % of sales	—	—	1.2%	1.6%	4.7%	1.5%	1.2%	1.2%	1.0%	1.2%	0.9%
Earnings per share ($)	—	(1.60)	0.85	1.10	3.25	1.00	0.80	0.85	0.90	0.98	0.75
Stock price - FY high ($)	—	21.25	38.44	33.75	23.59	24.69	18.44	15.16	13.75	21.25	14.00
Stock price - FY low ($)	—	5.94	14.84	19.06	14.38	12.19	8.59	7.81	7.97	8.00	8.25
Stock price - FY close ($)	(2.8%)	15.16	33.75	22.50	16.56	14.84	10.63	9.53	8.91	8.75	11.71
P/E - high	—	—	—	31	12	25	22	25	14	20	16
P/E - low	—	—	—	17	7	12	10	13	8	8	9
Dividends per share ($)	—	0.00	0.00	0.00	0.00	0.00	0.00	0.00	0.00	0.00	0.00
Book value per share ($)	—	(16.08)	(15.23)	(14.11)	(10.74)	(9.62)	(8.80)	(7.83)	(6.82)	0.78	1.46
Employees	(0.7%)	35,646	32,406	30,417	30,523	29,532	30,323	32,368	33,687	33,400	33,313

STOCK PRICE HISTORY

HIGH/LOW/CLOSE

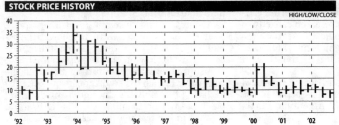

2001 FISCAL YEAR-END

Debt ratio: 91.6%
Return on equity: 71.4%
Cash ($ mil.): 126
Current ratio: 0.78
Long-term debt ($ mil.): 1,664
No. of shares (mil.): 105
Dividends
 Yield: —
 Payout: —
Market value ($ mil.): 1,227

ABBOTT LABORATORIES

Don't expect this Abbott to stay in seclusion. Long known as a staid firm, the Abbott Park, Illinois-based Abbott Laboratories is trying to update its image and expand its pipeline. Abbott's best-known brands are nutritional products — such as Similac, a top infant formula, and Ensure, a leading nutrition supplement — made by its Ross Products division, but far more of Abbott's sales come from pharmaceutical and hospital products. The company sells its products in about 130 countries; nearly one-third of sales are outside the US.

The company's drug treatments focus on metabolic diseases (such as diabetes and obesity), antibiotics, and antiviral treatments for AIDS/HIV. The company is also attempting to find new cardiology and cancer treatments. Abbott purchased BASF's Knoll Pharmaceuticals unit in order to expand its drug sector activities, and maintains a significant stake in Triangle Pharmaceuticals. TAP Pharmaceutical Products, Abbott's joint venture with Takeda Chemical Industries, makes prostate cancer drug Lupron.

Abbott's hospital products unit makes drug-delivery systems and products for anesthesia, critical care, and infection control. Another division makes medical diagnostic systems.

Adversity has been no stranger to Abbott in recent years: the TAP joint venture has plead guilty to conspiring to overbill government insurers for Lupron, and was consequently levied with heavy criminal and civil penalties. This follows on the heels of battles the company has had with the FDA and FTC over manufacturing processes, fair trade practices, and possible mergers. It has also run afoul of the FDA for deficiencies in the firm's reporting of negative drug reactions.

HISTORY

Dr. Wallace Abbott started making his dosimetric granule (a pill that supplied uniform quantities of drugs) at his home outside Chicago in 1888. Aggressive marketing earned Abbott the American Medical Association's criticism, though much of the medical profession supported him.

During WWI, Abbott scientists synthesized anesthetics previously available only from Germany. Abbott improved its research capacity in 1922 by buying Dermatological Research Laboratories; in 1928 it bought John T. Milliken and its well-trained sales force. Abbott went public in 1929.

Salesman DeWitt Clough became president in 1933. International operations began in the mid-1930s with branches in Argentina, Brazil, Cuba, Mexico, and the UK.

Abbott was integral to the WWII effort; the US made only 28 pounds of penicillin in 1943 before the company began to ratchet up production. Consumer, infant, and nutritional products (such as Selsun Blue shampoo, Murine eye drops, and Similac formula) joined the roster in the 1960s. The FDA banned Abbott's artificial sweetener Sucaryl in 1970, saying it might be carcinogenic, and in 1971 millions of intravenous solutions were recalled following contamination deaths.

Robert Schoellhorn became CEO in 1979; profits increased but research and development was cut. In the 1980s Abbott began selling Japanese-developed pharmaceuticals in the US.

Duane Burnham became CEO in 1989; under his conservative management the company received FDA approvals to market insomnia treatment ProSom (1990), hypertension drug for enlarged prostates Hytrin (1994), and ulcer treatment Prevacid and manic depression treatment Depakote (1995).

In 1997 FTC action prompted Abbott to stop claiming that doctors recommended its Ensure nutritional supplement for healthy adults. In 1998 the company pulled blood-clot dissolver Abbokinase off the market to address manufacturing problems.

In 1999 Abbott agreed to buy pharmaceutical research company ALZA, but the deal fell through in part because of FTC antitrust concerns. That year the FDA fined the company $100 million and pulled 125 of its medical diagnostic kits off the market, citing quality assurance problems.

The company sold its agricultural products business to Sumitomo Chemical in 2000. That year the FDA approved Gengraf, a drug that fights organ transplant rejection, and Kaletra, a promising protease inhibitor designed to combat AIDS.

The following year, Abbott bought Knoll Pharmaceuticals, a pharmaceutical unit of German chemicals giant BASF.

Also that year Abbott purchased Visys, thereby acquiring that company's worldwide distribution network and adding its products for the evaluation and management of cancer, prenatal disorders, and other genetic diseases to its portfolio of diagnostics.

Abbott, hoping to avoid government price controls, joined forces with six fellow druggernauts in 2002 to offer Together Rx, a drug discount card for low-income seniors in the US.

Also that year the FDA further thwarted the company's launch of new diagnostic products by declaring that Abbott's Chicago manufacturing plant was not up to snuff. Attempting to move forward in the test market despite the setback, the company licensed a patent to OraSure Technologies and made plans to jointly distribute OraSure's rapid HIV diagnostic test. It also struck an alliance with Celera Diagnostics to develop molecular diagnostic tests.

OFFICERS

Chairman and CEO: Miles D. White, age 46, $3,545,662 pay
Chief Scientific Officer and Director; President and COO, Pharmaceutical Products Group: Jeffrey M. Leiden, age 46, $1,319,569 pay
Director; President and COO, Medical Products Group: Richard A. Gonzalez, age 48, $1,235,754 pay (prior to promotion)
SVP, Finance and CFO: Thomas C. Freyman, age 47
SVP, Secretary, and General Counsel: Jose M. de Lasa, age 60
SVP, Hospital Products: Christopher B. Begley, age 49, $855,384 pay
SVP, Human Resources: Thomas M. Wascoe
SVP, International Operations: William G. Dempsey, age 50, $962,723 pay
SVP, Pharmaceutical Operations: David B. Goffredo
SVP, Ross Products: Gary L. Flynn, age 52
SVP, Specialty Products: Lance B. Wyatt
Auditors: Deloitte & Touche LLP

LOCATIONS

HQ: 100 Abbott Park Rd., Abbott Park, IL 60064
Phone: 847-937-6100   **Fax:** 847-937-1511
Web: www.abbott.com

2001 Sales

	$ mil.	% of total
US	10,249	63
Japan	748	5
Germany	644	4
Italy	496	3
Canada	468	3
The Netherlands	349	2
Other countries	3,331	20
Total	**16,285**	**100**

PRODUCTS/OPERATIONS

2001 Sales

	$ mil.	% of total
International	4,418	27
Pharmaceuticals	3,759	23
Diagnostics	2,929	18
Hospital	2,778	17
Ross	2,088	13
Other	313	2
Total	**16,285**	**100**

COMPETITORS

Amgen	GlaxoSmithKline
AstraZeneca	Johnson & Johnson
Aventis	Mallinckrodt
Bausch & Lomb	Merck
Baxter	Novartis
Bayer AG	Pfizer
Becton Dickinson	Roche
Bristol-Myers Squibb	Schering-Plough
Eli Lilly	Solvay
Genentech	Wyeth

HISTORICAL FINANCIALS & EMPLOYEES

NYSE: ABT FYE: December 31	Annual Growth	12/92	12/93	12/94	12/95	12/96	12/97	12/98	12/99	12/00	12/01
Sales ($ mil.)	8.4%	7,852	8,408	9,156	10,012	11,014	11,884	12,478	13,178	13,746	16,285
Net income ($ mil.)	2.5%	1,239	1,399	1,517	1,689	1,882	2,095	2,333	2,446	2,786	1,550
Income as % of sales	—	15.8%	16.6%	16.6%	16.9%	17.1%	17.6%	18.7%	18.6%	20.3%	9.5%
Earnings per share ($)	3.3%	0.74	0.85	0.94	1.05	1.19	1.34	1.51	1.57	1.78	0.99
Stock price - FY high ($)	—	17.09	15.44	17.00	22.38	28.69	34.88	50.06	53.31	56.25	57.17
Stock price - FY low ($)	—	13.06	11.31	12.69	15.31	19.06	24.88	32.53	33.00	29.38	42.00
Stock price - FY close ($)	15.5%	15.19	14.81	16.31	20.81	25.38	32.75	49.00	36.31	48.44	55.75
P/E - high	—	23	18	18	21	24	26	33	34	31	57
P/E - low	—	18	13	14	14	16	18	21	21	16	42
Dividends per share ($)	12.2%	0.29	0.33	0.37	0.41	0.47	0.53	0.59	0.66	0.74	0.82
Book value per share ($)	12.6%	2.00	2.24	2.52	2.79	3.07	3.27	3.77	4.80	5.54	5.83
Employees	4.5%	48,118	49,659	49,464	50,241	52,817	54,847	56,236	57,100	60,571	71,426

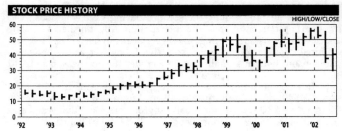

STOCK PRICE HISTORY HIGH/LOW/CLOSE

2001 FISCAL YEAR-END
Debt ratio: 32.4%
Return on equity: 17.6%
Cash ($ mil.): 657
Current ratio: 1.06
Long-term debt ($ mil.): 4,336
No. of shares (mil.): 1,555
Dividends
  Yield: 1.5%
  Payout: 82.8%
Market value ($ mil.): 86,665

ABC, INC.

High TV ratings are not as easy as ABC, the struggling network has learned. The company successfully defended its third place ranking against FOX for the 2001-02 season, but fell far behind front-runners NBC and CBS. The New York City-based ABC Television Network, part of Walt Disney, has failed to find a winning combination of shows and is ready to make some changes. The network's popular *Monday Night Football* is a regular ratings favorite, and the company hopes to duplicate that success with a new contract to broadcast NBA games. The ABC network broadcasts through about 230 affiliate stations around the country.

In addition to TV broadcasting, ABC produces many of its own programs (as well as programs for other networks and syndication) through ABC Entertainment Television and Buena Vista Television. The company also operates the ABC Radio Networks, which broadcasts on more than 4,600 affiliates. ABC owns 10 TV stations and more than 50 radio stations in key markets, as well as several cable channels, including the Disney Channel and ToonDisney. To expand ABC's cable portfolio, Disney in 2001 bought Fox Family Worldwide, which it renamed ABC Family, and the international assets of the Fox Kids Network for $5.2 billion. Through its ABC Cable unit, the company also owns stakes in cable networks ESPN (80%), Lifetime Entertainment Services (50%), and A&E Television Networks (38%).

In 2002 ABC president Steven Bornstein resigned (a successor was not immediately named). ABC is attempting to tap into HBO's recent success (*Sex in the City, Sopranos, Six Feet Under*) with a new two-year development deal with the pay-TV network, in which HBO's production unit will give ABC first dibs on new projects.

HISTORY

ABC was launched in 1927 as the Blue Network by RCA. A sister network to NBC (now owned by General Electric), Blue Network was sold to Life Savers candy magnate Edward J. Noble in 1943 after an FCC ruling that prohibited ownership of more than one network. Renamed the American Broadcasting Company three years later, ABC struggled with just 100 radio stations in its network and no big stars. By 1953 the company had expanded into television with 14 affiliates. That year United Paramount Theatres, led by Leonard Goldenson, bought ABC for $25 million.

To compete with CBS and NBC, Goldenson turned to Hollywood. He signed a $40 million deal with Walt Disney in 1953 that gave ABC access to the Disney film library and an exclusive

programming alliance. The network turned to other studios for programming such as *77 Sunset Strip* and *Maverick*. During the 1960s ABC fended off takeover attempts by ITT and Howard Hughes, and in the 1970s it pioneered the long-form mini-series with *Roots* and *Rich Man, Poor Man*. Hit shows, including *Happy Days* and *Charlie's Angels*, helped put the network on top during the 1976 season. In 1984 the company bought cable sports channel ESPN. (It sold 20% of ESPN to Hearst in 1991.) The next year ABC was sold to Capital Cities Communications for $3.5 billion.

Founded by Frank Smith as Hudson Valley Broadcasting, Capital Cities had started out as a bankrupt TV station in Albany, New York. In 1957 it acquired a second station in Raleigh, North Carolina, changed its name, and went public in 1964. Smith died in 1966, and Thomas Murphy took over as chairman and CEO. The company bought magazine publisher Fairchild Publications in 1968 and newspapers such as the *Fort Worth Star-Telegram* and *Kansas City Star* in the 1970s. By the 1980s Capital Cities had revenues of more than $1 billion.

During the early 1990s Capital Cities/ABC saw ratings soar with hits, including *Roseanne* and *Home Improvement*. Robert Iger was appointed president in 1994. Two years later Disney bought the company for $19 billion, selling off its newspapers for $1.65 billion. In 1998 Patricia Fili-Krushel was named president of ABC Television, making her the first woman to head a major broadcast network. Iger was named chairman of ABC in 1999, and ESPN chief Steven Bornstein took over as president.

In 1999 Disney sold ABC's Fairchild magazine unit to Advance Publications for about $650 million. Bornstein left late that year to head Disney's GO.com (now Walt Disney Internet Group). In early 2000 Iger was named president and COO of Disney, leaving broadcast president Robert Callahan in charge. Fili-Krushel later resigned. Negotiations over rebroadcast rights between Disney and Time Warner Cable went south that year and ABC broadcasts were briefly suspended for about 3.5 million viewers. (Time Warner Cable was later admonished by the FCC for dropping the stations during sweeps periods.) Despite the interruption, ABC finished #1 in the ratings for the first time in five years. That success was short-lived, however, as the network's audience share eroded the next season and ABC fell to #2.

Callahan resigned from ABC in 2001, and Bornstein returned from Disney Internet to become broadcast group president that year. Later Disney bought the Fox Family Channel, renamed

ABC Family, and the international assets of the Fox Kids Network from News Corp. and Haim Saban for $5.2 billion (including debt).

In 2002 ABC announced an agreement to broadcast NBA games in conjunction with ESPN and AOL Time Warner.

Bornstein resigned as president in mid 2002.

OFFICERS

President, ABC Television Network: Alex Wallau
EVP and General Counsel: Alan N. Braverman
EVP, Internet Media: Richard Glover
EVP, Television Distribution and CFO: Laurie Younger
SVP, Corporate Legal Affairs: Griffin W. Foxley
SVP, Counsel: Henry Hoberman
SVP, Counsel: T. Scott Fain
SVP, Human Resources: Jeffrey S. Rosen
SVP, Labor Relations: Jeffrey Ruthizer
SVP, Marketing: Mike Benson
SVP, Planning and Control: Dene Stratton
SVP, Drama Programming: Thom Sherman
SVP, Specials and Alternative Series: Andrea Wong
Chairman, ABC Entertainment Television Group:
  Lloyd Braun
Chairman, ABC News: Roone Arledge
President, ABC Cable Neworks Group and Disney Channel Worldwide: Anne M. Sweeney
President, ABC Family: Angela Shapiro
President, ABC Daytime: Brian S. Frons
President, ABC Entertainment Television Group:
  Susan Lyne
President, ABC News: David Westin, age 48
Auditors: PricewaterhouseCoopers LLP

LOCATIONS

HQ: 77 W. 66th St., New York, NY 10023
Phone: 212-456-7777   **Fax:** 212-456-6850
Web: abc.go.com

PRODUCTS/OPERATIONS

Selected Operations and Operating Units
ABC Radio Networks
ABC Television Network
Buena Vista Productions
Buena Vista Television
Cable networks
  ABC Family
  A&E Television Networks (38%)
    The Biography Channel
    The History Channel
  Disney Channel
  E! Entertainment Television (40%)
  ESPN (80%)
  Lifetime Entertainment Services (50%)
  SoapNet
  Toon Disney
  Touchstone Television
TV stations
Walt Disney Television

Selected Network Shows
According to Jim
Alias
America's Funniest Home Videos
The Drew Carey Show
George Lopez
Monday Night Football
My Wife and Kids
NYPD Blue
The Practice
Whose Line Is It Anyway?

Selected Television Productions
Ebert & Roeper and the Movies (syndicated)
LIVE! With Regis and Kelly (syndicated)
Win Ben Stein's Money (Comedy Central)

COMPETITORS

AOL Time Warner
Cablevision Systems
Clear Channel
Cox Radio
Cumulus Media
Discovery
  Communications

Fox Entertainment
Infinity Broadcasting
Liberty Media
NBC
Rainbow Media
Viacom
Westwood One

HISTORICAL FINANCIALS & EMPLOYEES

Subsidiary FYE: September 30	Annual Growth	9/92	9/93	9/94	9/95	9/96	9/97	9/98	9/99	9/00	9/01
Sales ($ mil.)	6.7%	5,344	5,674	6,379	6,879	6,231	6,522	7,142	7,512	9,615	9,556
Employees	0.5%	19,250	19,250	20,200	20,000	20,000	20,000	20,000	20,000	—	—

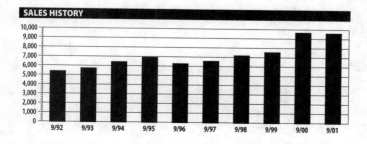

SALES HISTORY

ABERCROMBIE & FITCH CO.

Although it once outfitted Ernest Hemingway, Abercrombie & Fitch (A&F) now outfits kids reading Papa for English 101. Through about 490 stores nationwide (mostly in malls), New Albany, Ohio-based A&F sells upscale, casual apparel for men, women, and kids. Its clothing includes shirts, khakis, jeans, underwear, and outerwear. Most items are emblazoned with the A&F logo. The company also sells merchandise through its subscription catalog, A&F Quarterly, which doubles as a youth-oriented magazine featuring sometimes racy and raucous models. Its products are available on its Web site as well.

Though college students are the company's target market, A&F has an adult and teen following. It has children's stores (simply called abercrombie) and a teen store concept called Hollister Co., which is based on the West Coast lifestyle. The company's carefully selected college-age sales staff and photos of twentysomething models adorning the walls imbue its main stores with an upscale fraternity house feel. A&F's image as the clothier for a preppy social elite has, in some circles, earned its clientele the nickname "Aber-Snobbies."

A&F is no stranger to controversy. In the last four years, various marketing techniques and product choices (including sexually suggestive ads and children's thong underwear) have drawn complaints and criticism from conservative politicians, family advocacy groups, cultural groups, and Mothers Against Drunk Driving and other women's groups.

HISTORY

Scotsman David Abercrombie began selling camping equipment in lower Manhattan in 1892. Joined by lawyer Ezra Fitch, Abercrombie & Fitch (A&F) soon established itself as the purveyor of outdoors equipment for the very rich. A&F supplied Theodore Roosevelt and Ernest Hemingway for safaris and provided gear for Charles Lindbergh and polar explorer Richard Byrd. In 1917 the company moved into a 12-story edifice in Manhattan that included a log cabin (which Fitch lived in) and a casting pool.

A&F thrived through the 1960s. Mounted animal heads adorned its New York store, which offered 15,000 types of lures and 700 different shotguns. However, by the 1970s A&F's core customers were as extinct or endangered as the animals they had hunted, and the company struggled to find new markets.

In 1977 A&F filed for bankruptcy. A year later sports retailer Oshman's bought the company and expanded the number of stores while providing an eclectic assortment of goods. In 1988

clothing retailer The Limited bought A&F, then with about 25 stores, and shifted the company's emphasis to apparel.

Michael Jeffries took over in 1992 and transformed the still money-losing chain into an outfitter for college students. The new *jefe* micromanaged, issuing a 29-page book on everything from how A&F salespeople (who earned around $6 an hour) must look to exactly how many sweaters can be placed in a stack. Draconian perhaps, but the strategy worked, and A&F returned to profitability in fiscal 1995. The company went public in 1996 with more than 110 stores.

In 1998 The Limited spun off its remaining 84% stake. Also that year A&F sued rival American Eagle Outfitters, claiming it illegally copied A&F's clothing and approach (the suit was dismissed in 1999), and it raised the hackles of Mothers Against Drunk Driving with a catalog article entitled "Drinking 101."

The company got attention of a different sort in 1999 when the SEC launched an investigation after A&F leaked sales figures to an analyst before they were made available to the public. In 2000 A&F launched its new teen store concept called Hollister Co.

A&F continued to push the envelope with its A&F Quarterly in summer 2001. Under the theme "Let Summer Begin," the catalog featured naked and half-naked models having "wet 'n' wild summer fun" and T-shirts that read "I Have a Big One" and "Get on the Stick."

The company pushed a little further in Spring 2002 with a line of T-shirts portraying Asian caricatures. Vocal protests from Asian groups forced A&F to pull the T-shirts from its shelves and issue an apology.

Later that spring, A&F may have pushed a little too hard. A line of children's-sized thong underwear bearing sexually suggestive messages caused a furor among family-advocacy groups.

OFFICERS

Chairman and CEO: Michael S. Jeffries, age 57,
$1,851,515 pay
EVP, COO, and Director: Seth R. Johnson, age 48,
$1,021,431 pay
**SVP General Merchandise Manager for Abercrombie &
Fitch Boys':** Raymond C. Attanasio, age 50,
$678,000 pay
SVP Planning and Allocation: Leslee K. O'Neill, age 41,
$670,700 pay
SVP Sourcing: Diane Chang, age 46, $676,558 pay
SVP Stores: David L. Leino
VP and CFO: Wesley S. McDonald, age 39
VP Human Resources: John Fiske
Auditors: PricewaterhouseCoopers LLP

LOCATIONS

HQ: 6301 Fitch Path, New Albany, OH 43054
Phone: 614-283-6500   **Fax:** 614-283-6710
Web: www.abercrombie.com

Abercrombie & Fitch has nearly 500 stores in 48 states
and the District of Columbia.

PRODUCTS/OPERATIONS

2002 Stores

	No.
Abercrombie & Fitch	309
abercrombie	148
Hollister Co.	34
Total	**491**

Selected Products

Backpacks
Belts
Caps
Footwear
Fragrances
Hats
Jackets
Jeans
Outerwear
Pants
Shirts
Shorts
Skirts
Sweaters
Swimwear
Tank tops
Underwear

COMPETITORS

Aeropostale	Lands' End
American Eagle Outfitters	Levi Strauss
American Retail	Limited Brands
Benetton	L.L. Bean
The Bon	May
Buckle	Mossimo
Dillard's	Nordstrom
Eddie Bauer	Pacific Sunwear
Express	Polo
Federated	Quiksilver
Gadzooks	Target
The Gap	Tommy Hilfiger
Guess?	Urban Outfitters
H&M	Wet Seal
J. Crew	

HISTORICAL FINANCIALS & EMPLOYEES

NYSE: ANF FYE: Saturday nearest Jan. 31	Annual Growth	1/93	1/94	1/95	1/96	1/97	1/98	1/99	1/00	1/01	1/02
Sales ($ mil.)	36.1%	85	111	166	236	335	522	816	1,042	1,238	1,365
Net income ($ mil.)	—	(6)	(2)	8	14	25	48	102	150	158	169
Income as % of sales	—	—	—	5.0%	6.1%	7.4%	9.3%	12.5%	14.4%	12.8%	12.4%
Earnings per share ($)	43.6%	—	—	—	—	0.27	0.47	0.96	1.39	1.55	1.65
Stock price - FY high ($)	—	—	—	—	—	13.50	18.06	38.56	50.75	31.31	47.50
Stock price - FY low ($)	—	—	—	—	—	6.31	6.25	14.75	19.56	8.00	16.21
Stock price - FY close ($)	31.0%	—	—	—	—	6.88	15.56	38.38	21.38	29.81	26.55
P/E - high	—	—	—	—	—	50	38	39	35	20	28
P/E - low	—	—	—	—	—	23	13	15	13	5	10
Dividends per share ($)	—	—	—	—	—	0.00	0.00	0.00	0.00	0.00	0.00
Book value per share ($)	122.8%	—	—	—	—	0.11	0.58	1.81	3.05	4.27	6.02
Employees	28.0%	—	—	—	3,800	4,900	6,700	9,500	11,300	13,900	16,700

STOCK PRICE HISTORY

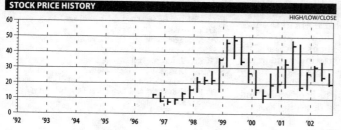

2002 FISCAL YEAR-END

Debt ratio: 0.0%
Return on equity: 33.1%
Cash ($ mil.): 168
Current ratio: 2.48
Long-term debt ($ mil.): 0
No. of shares (mil.): 99
Dividends
  Yield: —
  Payout: —
Market value ($ mil.): 2,625

ACE HARDWARE CORPORATION

Luckily, Ace has John Madden up its sleeve. Despite the growth of warehouse-style competitors, Ace Hardware has remained a household name, thanks to ads featuring Madden, a former Oakland Raiders football coach and TV commentator. The Oak Brook, Illinois-based company is the #2 hardware cooperative in the US, behind TruServ (operator of True Value and several other hardware chains). Ace dealer-owners operate about 5,000 Ace Hardware stores throughout the US and in about 70 other countries.

Ace distributes products such as electrical and plumbing supplies, power tools, hand tools, garden equipment, and housewares to its members through more than 20 warehouses nationwide. It also makes its own brand of paint and offers thousands of other Ace-brand products. Subsidiary Ace Insurance Agency offers dealers insurance for their stores and employees. Ace also provides training programs and advertising campaigns.

Challenged by big-box chains such as The Home Depot and Lowe's, Ace is remodeling stores and polishing its image. Ace dealers own the company and receive dividends from Ace's profits.

HISTORY

A group of Chicago-area hardware dealers — William Stauber, Richard Hesse, Gern Lindquist, and Oscar Fisher — decided in 1924 to pool their hardware buying and promotional costs. In 1928 the group incorporated as Ace Stores, named in honor of the superior WWI fliers dubbed aces. Hesse became president the following year, retaining that position for the next 44 years. The company also opened its first warehouse in 1929, and by 1933 it had 38 dealers.

The organization had 133 dealers in seven states by 1949. In 1953 Ace began to allow dealers to buy stock in the company through the Ace Perpetuation Plan. During the 1960s Ace expanded into the South and West, and by 1969 it had opened distribution centers in Georgia and California — its first such facilities outside Chicago. In 1968 it opened its first international store in Guam.

By the early 1970s the do-it-yourself market began to surge as inflation pushed up plumber and electrician fees. As the market grew, large home center chains gobbled up market share from independent dealers such as those franchised through Ace. In response, Ace and its dealers became a part of a growing trend in the hardware industry — cooperatives.

Hesse sold the company to its dealers in 1973 for $6 million (less than half its book value), and the following year Ace began operating as a cooperative. Hesse stepped down in 1973. In 1976 the dealers took full control when the company's first Board of Dealer-Directors was elected.

After signing up a number of dealers in the eastern US, Ace had dealers in all 50 states by 1979. The co-op opened a plant to make paint in Matteson, Illinois, in 1984. By 1985 Ace had reached $1 billion in sales and had initiated its Store of the Future Program, allowing dealers to borrow up to $200,000 to upgrade their stores and conduct market analyses. Former head coach John Madden of the National Football League's Oakland Raiders signed on as Ace's mouthpiece in 1988.

A year later the co-op began to test ACENET, a computer network that allowed Ace dealers to check inventory, send and receive e-mail, make special purchase requests, and keep up with prices on commodity items such as lumber. In 1990 Ace established an International Division to handle its overseas stores. (It had been exporting products since 1975.) EVP and COO David Hodnik became president in 1995. That year the co-op added a net of 67 stores, including a three-store chain in Russia. Expanding further internationally, Ace signed a five-year joint-supply agreement in 1996 with Canadian lumber and hardware retailer Beaver Lumber. Hodnik added CEO to his title in 1996.

Ace fell further behind its old rival, True Value, in 1997 when ServiStar Coast to Coast and True Value merged to form TruServ, a hardware giant that operated more than 10,000 outlets at the completion of the merger.

Late in 1997 Ace launched an expansion program in Canada. (The co-op already operated distribution centers in Ontario and Calgary.) In 1999 Ace merged its lumber and building materials division with Builder Marts of America to form a dealer-owned buying group to supply about 2,700 retailers. In 2000, Ace gained 208 member outlet stores, but saw 279 member outlets terminated. The next year it gained 220, but lost 255. Also in 2001 more than 160 stores operating under TruServ, which acknowledged financial irregularities in 2000, applied to join Ace.

OFFICERS

Chairman: Howard J. Jung, age 54
President and CEO: David F. Hodnik, age 54, $752,840 pay
EVP, Strategic Planning: Rita D. Kahle, age 45, $434,280 pay
EVP, Retail: Ray A. Griffith, age 48
SVP, International and Technology:
Paul M. Ingevaldson, age 56, $377,800 pay
SVP, Retail Support and Logistics: David F. Myer, age 56, $380,980 pay

VP, Marketing, Advertising, Retail Development, and Company Stores: Michael C. Bodzewski, age 52, $367,380 pay
VP, Merchandising: Lori L. Bossmann, age 41
VP, Retail Operations: Ken L. Nichols, age 53
VP, Human Resources: Jimmy Alexander, age 45
Treasurer: Sandy Brandt
Controller: Ron Knutson
Director, People Development and Learning Systems: Ron Wagner
Director of Retail Operations for the Midwest Division: Bob Guido
Manager, Advertising: Frank Rothing
Manager, Corporate Communications and Public Relations: Paula Erickson
Manager, General Merchandise: Gary Paulson
Manager, Marketing: John Venhvizen
Manager, New Business: Bill Jablonowski
Manager, Retail Program Execution: Art Freedman
Auditors: KPMG LLP

LOCATIONS

HQ: 2200 Kensington Ct., Oak Brook, IL 60523
Phone: 630-990-6600   **Fax:** 630-990-6838
Web: www.acehardware.com

Ace Hardware wholesales products to dealers with retail operations in the US and about 70 other countries.

PRODUCTS/OPERATIONS

2001 Sales

	% of total
Paint, cleaning and related supplies	21
Plumbing and heating supplies	15
Garden, rural equipment and related supplies	14
Hand and power tools	14
Electrical supplies	12
General hardware	11
Sundry	8
Housewares and appliances	5
Total	**100**

Subsidiaries
Ace Corporate Stores, Inc. (operation of company-owned stores)
Ace Hardware Canada, Limited (hardware wholesaler)
Ace Hardware de México, S.A. de C.V. (hardware wholesaler)
Ace Insurance Agency, Inc. (dealer insurance program)
A.H.C. Store Development Corp. (operation of company-owned stores)
Loss Prevention Services, Inc. (security training and loss prevention services for dealers)
National Hardlines Supply, Inc. (sells to retailers outside the Ace dealer network)

COMPETITORS

84 Lumber	Lowe's
Akzo Nobel	McCoy
Benjamin Moore	Menard
Building Materials Holding	Northern Tool
	Réno-Dépôt
Carolina Holdings	Sears
Costco Wholesale	Sherwin-Williams
Do it Best	Sutherland Lumber
Fastenal	TruServ
Grossman's	United Hardware
Home Depot	Distributing Co.
ICI American Holdings	Wal-Mart
Kmart	Wickes
Lanoga	Wolohan Lumber

HISTORICAL FINANCIALS & EMPLOYEES

Cooperative FYE: December 31	Annual Growth	12/92	12/93	12/94	12/95	12/96	12/97	12/98	12/99	12/00	12/01
Sales ($ mil.)	5.0%	1,871	2,018	2,326	2,436	2,742	2,907	3,120	3,182	2,945	2,894
Net income ($ mil.)	2.1%	61	57	65	64	72	76	88	93	80	73
Income as % of sales	—	3.2%	2.8%	2.8%	2.6%	2.6%	2.6%	2.8%	2.9%	2.7%	2.5%
Employees	5.4%	3,256	3,405	3,664	3,917	4,352	4,685	4,672	5,180	5,513	5,229

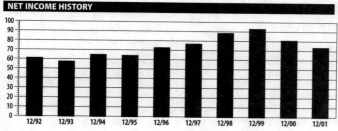

NET INCOME HISTORY

2001 FISCAL YEAR-END
Debt ratio: 37.8%
Return on equity: 25.9%
Cash ($ mil.): 25
Current ratio: 1.37
Long-term debt ($ mil.): 170

ADAMS RESOURCES & ENERGY, INC.

While the name Tennessee is now synonymous with NFL team-owner Bud Adams, his oil and gas business remains deeply rooted in Texas. Houston-based Adams Resources & Energy and its subsidiaries market crude oil and petroleum products, which account for about 99% of the company's sales. The company explores for and produces oil and gas, mainly in Texas, and has proved reserves of about 8.6 billion cu. ft. of natural gas and 626,000 barrels of oil.

Adams Resources Exploration (Exco) explores for and produces oil and gas primarily onshore on third-party properties in Texas. GulfMark Energy purchases crude oil and transports it via company-owned trucks, third-party vehicles, common carrier pipelines, and barges. GulfMark primarily serves oil producers in Texas and off the coast of Louisiana.

Other subsidiaries include Service Transport, which operates tanker trucks that haul petrochemicals and other hazardous liquids throughout the continental US and Canada. Ada Resources purchases, stores, transports, and sells motor fuels and lubrication oils for service stations, including CITGO, Conoco, and Phillips. Bayou City Pipelines operates two crude oil pipelines off the coast of Louisiana. Adams Resources Marketing is a wholesale purchaser, distributor, and marketer of natural gas, serving 100 independent producers primarily offshore in the Gulf of Mexico.

The company has also expanded in the Northeast through the formation of the New England Energy Group. Adams, who owns the NFL's Tennessee Titans, controls about 50% of Adams Resources.

HISTORY

Born in Bartlesville, Oklahoma, in 1923 K. S. "Bud" Adams founded Ada Oil in 1947 to explore for and produce oil and gas. These operations, with some real estate holdings, formed the core of what became Adams Resources when the company went public in 1974. An investment in coal in Illinois and Kentucky led to $65 million in losses in 1981 and the closure of those operations. In 1992 Adams Resources bought GulfMark Energy, a crude oil trading company that specialized in oil transport and the marketing of specialty grades of crude.

When intrastate trucking was deregulated in 1995, Adams Resources faced new competition in Texas, where it made 40% of its trucking sales. The company had to cut prices that year, and transportation earnings fell 30%. Adams Resources enjoyed greater production from a series of successful gas wells in the Austin Chalk region

in 1996, and the company and partner Nuevo Energy added three wells in Austin Chalk the next year.

Adams Resources completed a 7.5-mile offshore Louisiana crude oil pipeline in 1998 that boosted the company's Gulf of Mexico crude oil throughput by more than 15,000 barrels per day.

The company expanded its operations in 1999 by setting up Adams Resources Marketing as a wholesale purchaser, distributor, and marketer of natural gas. In connection with the formation of the new company, Adams Resources Marketing hired almost all of the personnel formerly employed by Houston-based gas marketer H&N Gas Ltd. In addition Adams Resources Marketing signed a service agreement with H&N to administer H&N's existing contracts.

In 2000 Adams Resources ramped up operations in the US Northeast by forming New England Energy Group, a regional retail marketer of natural gas and other energy products. Also in 2000 the company expanded its crude oil operations into Michigan and California. Adams Resources also signed a joint venture deal with Oklahoma-based energy producer The Williams Companies. The deal teamed Adams subsidiary Gulfmark Energy Marketing and Williams Energy Marketing & Trading to form Williams-Gulfmark Energy Co. for purchase, distribution, and marketing of crude oil from the Gulf of Mexico.

In 2000 Adams Resources signed an agreement with British Petroleum (BP) to transport fuels and lubricants to BP outlets in southeastern Texas and Southern Louisiana. Revenues skyrocketed during 1999 and 2000 thanks to rising crude oil prices, but warm winter weather and charges related to its Enron contracts depressed the company's results in 2001.

OFFICERS

Chairman, President, and CEO: K. S. Adams Jr., age 79, $150,406 pay
EVP and General Counsel: Vincent H. Buckley
VP Finance and Director; President, Gulfmark Energy and Adams Resources Marketing GP: Richard B. Abshire, age 49, $206,869 pay
VP Land Transportation and Director: Claude H. Lewis, age 58, $126,191 pay
President, Ada Resources: Lee A. Beauchamp, age 49, $142,171 pay
President, Adams Resources Exploration: James Brock Moore III, $153,454 pay
Secretary: David B. Hurst, age 49
Director Human Resources: Jay Grimes
Auditors: Deloitte & Touche LLP

HQ: 4400 Post Oak Pkwy., Ste. 2700, Houston, TX 77027
Phone: 713-881-3600   **Fax:** 713-881-3491

Adams Resources produces oil and gas in Texas and
Louisiana; markets oil and gas products on the Gulf
Coast and in New England; and provides energy
transportation services throughout the US and Canada.

PRODUCTS/OPERATIONS

2001 Sales

	$ mil.	% of total
Marketing	4,678	99
Transportation	33	1
Oil & gas	6	—
Total	**4,717**	**100**

Selected Subsidiaries
Ada Crude Oil Company
Ada Mining Corporation
Ada Resources, Inc. (petroleum products marketing)
Ada Resources Marketing, Inc. (wholesale natural gas
  marketing)
Adams Resources Exploration Corporation
Adams Resources Marketing, Ltd. (natural gas
  marketing)
Bayou City Pipelines, Inc.
Buckley Mining Corporation
CJC Leasing, Inc.
Classic Coal Corporation
GulfMark Energy, Inc. (crude oil marketing)
New England Energy Group (retail natural gas
  marketing)
Service Transport Company (liquid chemicals and
  petroleum products transport)

COMPETITORS

Abraxas Petroleum
Anadarko Petroleum
Apache
BP
Cabot Oil & Gas
ChevronTexaco
EOG
Exxon Mobil
Howell
Pioneer Natural Resources
Pogo Producing
Royal Dutch/Shell Group

HISTORICAL FINANCIALS & EMPLOYEES

AMEX: AE FYE: December 31	Annual Growth	12/92	12/93	12/94	12/95	12/96	12/97	12/98	12/99	12/00	12/01
Sales ($ mil.)	27.0%	550	695	635	831	1,497	1,963	1,974	3,996	7,022	4,717
Net income ($ mil.)	—	4	2	3	1	6	6	2	6	9	(5)
Income as % of sales	—	0.8%	0.2%	0.5%	0.1%	0.4%	0.3%	0.1%	0.2%	0.1%	—
Earnings per share ($)	—	1.00	0.35	0.72	0.29	1.34	1.36	0.55	1.51	2.10	(1.08)
Stock price - FY high ($)	—	6.50	6.13	10.75	10.00	13.88	18.38	14.75	11.38	21.06	16.75
Stock price - FY low ($)	—	3.00	4.00	4.44	4.88	5.63	11.63	5.25	5.81	8.13	6.10
Stock price - FY close ($)	4.8%	5.13	4.50	9.88	7.13	12.25	14.38	5.75	8.50	14.00	7.80
P/E - high	—	36	18	15	34	10	14	27	8	10	—
P/E - low	—	17	11	6	17	4	9	10	4	4	—
Dividends per share ($)	—	0.00	0.00	0.03	0.05	0.07	0.10	0.10	0.10	0.13	0.13
Book value per share ($)	17.9%	2.11	2.47	3.16	3.74	5.42	6.66	7.14	8.53	10.50	9.29
Employees	8.5%	309	322	377	378	403	512	565	643	685	643

STOCK PRICE HISTORY

HIGH/LOW/CLOSE

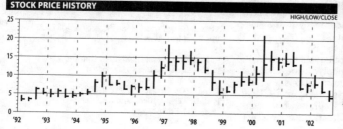

2001 FISCAL YEAR-END

Debt ratio: 22.7%
Return on equity: —
Cash ($ mil.): 14
Current ratio: 1.18
Long-term debt ($ mil.): 12
No. of shares (mil.): 4
Dividends
  Yield: 1.7%
  Payout: —
Market value ($ mil.): 33

ADC TELECOMMUNICATIONS, INC.

ADC's climb up the telecom equipment heap isn't as easy as 1, 2, 3. Minnetonka, Minnesota-based ADC Telecommunications makes systems and software for communications networks. Its products are used in telecom service carrier central offices and in the infrastructure that links network operators and customers; broadband infrastructure and access products account for three-quarters of sales. Products include communications service platforms, integrated access devices, fiber-optic and wireless components, and network management software. ADC also designs and builds networks and offers other professional services. The company targets local telephone (55% of sales), long-distance, cable TV, and ISPs.

CEO Richard Roscitt has his work cut out for him. Former ADC chairman and CEO William Cadogan built up a head of steam for ADC — the company's sales have tripled in the past five years — before his retirement after a decade at the helm. Under his leadership ADC made more than 20 acquisitions since 1996 that have expanded the company's geographic reach and its broadband access product lines. This shopping spree left the company overextended as it attempts to weather bleak market conditions.

ADC began cutting its staff and selling noncore product lines in 2001 to reduce costs. The company has announced that it plans to get out of the optical components business and continue shedding employees and closing facilities through the end of 2002 (ADC has shuttered more than 40 locations worldwide since it began its 2002 fiscal year).

HISTORY

Engineer Ralph Allison founded Audio Development Company (ADC) in 1935 to make devices to test hearing. The company soon diversified into products for the broadcast industry before Allison's departure in 1949, the year ADC sold its audiometer unit.

In 1961 ADC merged with power supply maker Magnetic Controls, becoming ADC Magnetic Controls. In 1970 the Bell family, founders of General Mills and 51% owners of ADC, recruited Honeywell executive Charles Denny as president and CEO. He turned the company into a telephone equipment maker. ADC benefited from the 1983 AT&T breakup, when the Baby Bells began buying equipment from outside sources. ADC sold its struggling power supply business in 1984 and became ADC Telecommunications.

Denny stepped down as president in 1990 and as CEO in 1991 after leading two decades of annual 20% compound earnings. Ex-AT&T

executive William Cadogan took over both positions. ADC's acquisitions let it fill market niches not addressed by larger companies. Profit margins rose as ADC expanded from copper-based telecom gear to fiber-optic, wireless, and digital technologies.

Deregulation positioned the company to benefit from increased industry competition. In the mid-1990s ADC began using acquisitions to fuel global and wireless expansion, including Finland's Solitra Oy (1996), signaling and control expert NewNet (1997), and Israel-based digital loop system maker Teledata Communications (1998). Other 1998 purchases expanded its systems integration business and optical component line.

The company's spree continued in 1999, when it bought Hadax (remote test and access systems), NVision (TV distribution and switching products), Pathway (ATM transmission), Austria-based Phasor Electronics (cable TV transmission products), Spectracom (optical components), and Ireland-based Saville Systems (billing and customer care software).

In 2000 ADC further diversified its product line by acquiring chief rival and digital subscriber line (DSL) specialist PairGain Technologies for $1.6 billion, wireless communications software maker Centigram, and privately held cable and DSL access equipment maker Broadband Access Systems; these purchases totalled over $4 billion.

The company eliminated about 40% of staff in 2001 due to an industrywide downturn in sales. Cadogan retired and Richard Roscitt (another ex-AT&T executive) took the reins. ADC bought privately held CommTech (account and services management software) soon after.

That year the company sold the units responsible for its high-speed WAN access, digital TV broadcasting, and broadband wireless transmission equipment to Platinum Equity. It also sold its radio-frequency filtration equipment business, Solitra, and its enhanced services unit (SS7 signalling gateways and wireless and unified messaging software).

OFFICERS

Chairman, President, and CEO: Richard R. Roscitt, age 50, $2,156,385 pay
EVP and CFO: Robert E. Switz, age 55, $387,423 pay
SVP; President, Wireline: Larry J. Ford, age 60, $335,712 pay
VP; President, Connectivity: Jeff Quiram, age 41
VP; President, Systems Integration: Jo Anne M. Anderson, age 44
VP and CIO: Kamalesh Dwivedi, age 46
VP, Chief Legal Officer, and Secretary: Jeffrey D. Pflaum, age 42

VP, Business Development: Barclay Fitzpatrick, age 41
VP, Human Resources: Laura N. Owen, age 45
VP, Worldwide Operations: Peter W. Hemp,
$251,538 pay
Chief Marketing Officer: William F. O'Brien, age 53
Auditors: Ernst & Young LLP

LOCATIONS

HQ: 13625 Technology Dr., Eden Prairie, MN 55343
Phone: 952-938-8080 **Fax:** 952-917-1717
Web: www.adc.com

ADC Telecommunications has sales, manufacturing, and
development offices in more than 35 countries, and it
has customers in about 100 countries. ADC's main
manufacturing facilities are in China, Mexico, the UK,
and the US.

2001 Sales

	$ mil.	% of total
US	1,711	71
Other countries	692	29
Total	**2,403**	**100**

PRODUCTS/OPERATIONS

2001 Sales

	$ mil.	% of total
Broadband infrastructure & access	1,811	75
Integrated solutions	592	25
Total	**2,403**	**100**

Selected Products and Services

Broadband Infrastructure and Access
Active and passive optical components
Broadband connection and access devices
  Modular fiber-optic cable routing systems
  Network management software
  Radio-frequency signal management
  Routers and switches
Transport systems
  Broadband telephony and DSL platforms
  Carrier access platforms
  Carrier and customer cable broadband and telephony
    systems
  Internet Protocol access switches and routers
Wireless systems and components
  Wideband digital microcells
  Wireless infrastructure equipment and subsystems
  Wireless WAN and LAN equipment

Integrated Solutions
Systems integration services
Operations support systems solutions

COMPETITORS

3Com	CommWorks	Portal Software
ADTRAN	Convergys	Redback
Advanced Fibre	Corning	Networks
Communications	ECI Telecom	Scientific-Atlanta
Agere Systems	Ericsson	Siemens
Alcatel	Fujitsu	Sycamore
Amdocs	JDS Uniphase	Networks
ARRIS	Lucent	Telect
Aurora Networks	Marconi	Tellabs
Avaya	Networks	Westell
CIENA	Motorola	Technologies
Cisco Systems	Nortel Networks	

HISTORICAL FINANCIALS & EMPLOYEES

Nasdaq: ADCT FYE: October 31	Annual Growth	10/92	10/93	10/94	10/95	10/96	10/97	10/98	10/99	10/00	10/01
Sales ($ mil.)	25.3%	317	366	449	586	828	1,165	1,380	1,927	3,288	2,403
Net income ($ mil.)	—	21	32	39	55	88	109	147	88	868	(1,288)
Income as % of sales	—	6.6%	8.6%	8.7%	9.4%	10.6%	9.3%	10.6%	4.5%	26.4%	—
Earnings per share ($)	—	0.05	0.07	0.08	0.12	0.17	0.21	0.27	0.15	1.13	(1.64)
Stock price - FY high ($)	—	1.19	2.75	2.98	6.17	8.78	11.25	10.91	13.41	49.00	27.06
Stock price - FY low ($)	—	0.64	1.13	1.94	2.47	3.56	5.31	3.94	5.81	11.50	2.63
Stock price - FY close ($)	16.7%	1.13	2.28	2.95	5.00	8.55	8.28	5.75	11.92	21.38	4.55
P/E - high	—	24	39	33	51	52	54	39	89	41	—
P/E - low	—	13	16	22	21	21	25	14	39	10	—
Dividends per share ($)	—	0.00	0.00	0.00	0.00	0.00	0.00	0.00	0.00	0.00	0.00
Book value per share ($)	21.4%	0.42	0.50	0.59	1.02	1.18	1.41	1.69	2.08	3.78	2.39
Employees	20.1%	2,303	2,462	2,644	2,984	4,620	5,924	8,000	13,500	22,450	12,000

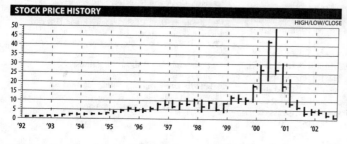

STOCK PRICE HISTORY HIGH/LOW/CLOSE

2001 FISCAL YEAR-END
Debt ratio: 0.2%
Return on equity: —
Cash ($ mil.): 349
Current ratio: 2.18
Long-term debt ($ mil.): 3
No. of shares (mil.): 792
Dividends
  Yield: —
  Payout: —
Market value ($ mil.): 3,604

ADMINISTAFF, INC.

Administaff helps its client companies administer their businesses with fewer staff. One of the leading professional employer organizations (PEOs) in the country, the Kingwood, Texas-based company handles payroll and benefits administration, health and workers' compensation insurance programs, and employee recruiting for small and midsized companies. In a system known as employee leasing, clients' employees are put on Administaff's payroll, and then "leased" back to the client for a fee.

Most of its 4,000 client companies are engaged in the business services, financial services, and health care industries. Administaff has three service centers in Atlanta, Dallas, and Houston, as well as 35 sales offices in 19 major US markets. Its business in Texas accounts for about 50% of sales.

To offer immediate and more personalized services for its clients, the company runs Administaff Assistant, an online service and resource Web site where its client companies and their employees can access and update payroll information, create reports, and receive online training. It also runs the bizzport Internet portal, where clients can purchase goods and services from vendors like BANK ONE, Continental Airlines, Dell, and IBM or from other Administaff clients.

The company continues to expand by adding offices in new territories, with a long-term expansion goal of having 90 offices serving 40 markets. It is also building a fourth service center in Los Angeles. It hopes to handle human resource services for about 10% of the small businesses in the US.

American Express Travel Related Services Company has a 13% stake in the company. Administaff co-founder and CEO Paul Sarvadi owns 12%.

HISTORY

Gerald McIntosh and Paul Sarvadi founded Administaff in 1986. The two entrepreneurs saw growth potential in employee leasing, despite the industry's image problems. (Sarvadi had worked for James Borgelt, who founded several Dallas-area employee leasing firms and was sentenced to three years in prison in 1996 for stealing from clients.)

By 1991 Administaff had become one of the largest employee leasing companies in the US. That year it joined 17 other leasing companies in filing a suit against the Texas State Board of Insurance, which had tried to prohibit leasing companies from buying workers' compensation insurance. Regulators claimed leasing companies

were touting their services as a way to avoid high workers' comp premiums. In 1993 a compromise law allowed employee leasing companies to buy workers' comp insurance based on the clients' on-the-job accident history.

With about 1,500 clients, Administaff went public in 1997. The following year the company formed a marketing agreement with American Express, under which the travel and financial services giant refers smaller business clients to Administaff for a fee.

Administaff entered the world of barter in 1999 when it signed a services agreement with Web developer Luminant Worldwide. Under the agreement, Adminstaff provided human resource services to Luminant in exchange for e-commerce consulting services. Administaff began offering Web-based services in 1999 with Administaff Assistant.

The company launched Internet portal site bizzport in 2000. It also formed several co-marketing deals designed to provide extra perks to its clients' employees. Among the companies it signed agreements with were Web florist FTD.com (for special pricing on flowers and other gifts), Continental Airlines (for travel bonuses), and Spiegel Catalog (for special pricing and reward programs on Spiegel merchandise).

Also in 2000 Administaff opened new offices in New Jersey and Maryland, and added offices in Atlanta, Los Angeles, San Francisco, and Washington, DC.

The company continued to expand in 2001, adding new offices in Boston and San Diego. It also continued to sign co-marketing agreements, including deals with e-Realty.com and Wells Fargo Home Mortgage. By 2001 the company's client roster had grown to more than 4,000 companies.

In 2002 Administaff acquired the assets of Virtual Growth Incorporated, which provided outsourced accounting services. Also that year it launched (with IBM) HR PowerHouse, a human resources Web site targeting small businesses.

OFFICERS

President, CEO, and Director: Paul J. Sarvadi, age 45, $304,672 pay

EVP Administration, CFO, Treasurer, and Director: Richard A. Rawson, age 53, $366,610 pay

EVP Client Services: A. Steve Arizpe, age 44, $266,513 pay

EVP Sales and Marketing: Jay E. Mincks, age 48, $240,631 pay

VP Benefits and Corporate Human Resources: Howard G. Buff, age 41

VP Client Services Coordination: Gwen Fey

VP Enterprise Project Management: Samuel G. Larson, age 40
VP Finance and Controller: Douglas S. Sharp, age 40
VP Legal, General Counsel, and Secretary:
John H. Spurgin II, age 55, $209,252 pay
VP Marketing: Gregory J. Morton
VP Sales: John F. Orth
VP Sales Development: Roger L. Gaskamp
VP Service Center Operations: Gregory R. Clouse
VP Strategic Alliances: Randall H. McCollum, age 57
VP Technology Solutions and CTO: David C. Dickson
VP Web Services: Jeff W. Hutcheon
Director Community Involvement: Corinn Price
Director Corporate Communications: Alan Dodd
Director Sales Automation: Lori Haynes
Application Manager: John Sheridan
Auditors: Ernst & Young LLP

LOCATIONS

HQ: 19001 Crescent Springs Dr., Kingwood, TX 77339
Phone: 281-358-8986   **Fax:** 281-358-3354
Web: www.administaff.com

Administaff has 38 offices in 21 markets around the US.

Selected Markets

Atlanta	Los Angeles
Boston	New York City
Chicago	Orlando, FL
Cleveland	San Diego
Dallas	St. Louis
Houston	

PRODUCTS/OPERATIONS

Selected Services
Benefits and payroll administration
e-business services
Employee recruiting and selection
Employer liability management
Health insurance programs
Performance management
Personnel records management
Training and development
Workers' compensation programs

COMPETITORS

ADP
EPIX
Express Personnel
Gevity HR
Paychex
TEAM America
TeamStaff

HISTORICAL FINANCIALS & EMPLOYEES

NYSE: ASF FYE: December 31	Annual Growth	12/92	12/93	12/94	12/95	12/96	12/97	12/98	12/99	12/00	12/01
Sales ($ mil.)	30.1%	409	496	564	716	900	1,214	1,683	2,261	3,709	4,373
Net income ($ mil.)	89.5%	0	2	4	1	3	7	9	9	17	10
Income as % of sales	—	0.0%	0.4%	0.7%	0.2%	0.3%	0.6%	0.5%	0.4%	0.5%	0.2%
Earnings per share ($)	7.5%	—	—	—	—	—	0.27	0.31	0.34	0.58	0.36
Stock price - FY high ($)	—	—	—	—	—	—	13.25	26.47	17.25	44.56	36.48
Stock price - FY low ($)	—	—	—	—	—	—	6.88	10.81	5.56	10.38	15.40
Stock price - FY close ($)	20.6%	—	—	—	—	—	12.94	12.50	15.13	27.20	27.41
P/E - high	—	—	—	—	—	—	47	83	51	72	96
P/E - low	—	—	—	—	—	—	25	34	16	17	41
Dividends per share ($)	—	—	—	—	—	—	0.00	0.00	0.00	0.00	0.00
Book value per share ($)	17.6%	—	—	—	—	—	2.30	2.99	2.99	3.85	4.40
Employees	24.8%	—	12,000	16,000	16,220	25,000	30,205	34,819	48,800	62,140	70,730

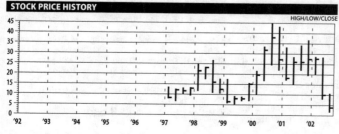

STOCK PRICE HISTORY — HIGH/LOW/CLOSE

2001 FISCAL YEAR-END
Debt ratio: 0.0%
Return on equity: 9.1%
Cash ($ mil.): 53
Current ratio: 1.25
Long-term debt ($ mil.): 0
No. of shares (mil.): 28
Dividends
  Yield: —
  Payout: —
Market value ($ mil.): 766

ADOBE SYSTEMS INCORPORATED

Don't accuse Adobe of having feet of clay. At the forefront of the desktop publishing software industry, San Jose, California-based Adobe Systems offers the ubiquitous Acrobat Reader (distributed free of charge), a tool that displays portable document format (PDF) files on the Internet. Adobe generates nearly 70% of its sales through Web and print products such as Photoshop (photo enhancement), Illustrator (illustration and page design), and PageMaker (page layout). The company's offerings also include print technology geared toward manufacturers, as well as Web design and electronic book publishing software.

Adobe's activities aren't limited to developing its own software. In addition to direct investments in a handful of high-tech companies, it operates four venture partnerships with GraniteVentures. Adobe has investments in more than 30 companies (including AvantGo and Vignette) whose products and services complement its own.

Adobe is emerging from a sales slump — which resulted in a floundering stock price and a takeover bid (unsuccessful) from rival Quark — through a restructuring effort and the debut of its InDesign publishing package, branded a "Quark-killer" by industry experts.

HISTORY

When Charles Geschke hired John Warnock as chief scientist for Xerox's new graphics and imaging lab, he set the stage for one of the world's largest software makers. While at the Xerox lab, the pair developed the PostScript computer language, which tells printers how to reproduce digitized images on paper. When Xerox refused to market it, the duo left that company and started Adobe (named after a creek near their homes in San Jose, California) in 1982.

Their original plan was to produce an electronic document processing system based on PostScript, but the company changed direction when Apple Computer whiz Steve Jobs hired it to co-design the software for his company's LaserWriter printer. A year later Adobe went public. Meanwhile, PostScript was pioneering the desktop publishing industry by enabling users to laser print nearly anything they created on a computer.

In 1987 the company branded into the European market with the establishment of subsidiary Adobe Systems Europe. It also entered the PC market by adapting PostScript for IBM's operating system. Two years later the company began marketing its products in Asia.

Adobe grew throughout the 1990s by acquiring other software firms, including OCR Systems and Nonlinear Technologies (1992), and AH Software and Science & Art (1993). In 1993 the company began licensing its PostScript software to printer manufacturers; it also started marketing its Acrobat software.

Adobe bought Aldus (1994), whose PageMaker software had been instrumental in establishing the desktop publishing market. (PageMaker's success depended on the font software that Adobe made and the two companies had a history of cooperation.) Next the company bought Frame Technology (FrameMaker publishing software, 1995), but that acquisition proved disastrous. Frame sales plummeted, partly the result of Adobe's move to eliminate Frame's technical support operations.

In 1996 Adobe spun off its pre-press applications operations as Luminous. The next year the company issued stock dividends in technology startups in which it held stakes, such as Netscape (now part of AOL Time Warner). That year its licensing sales suffered a blow when one of its largest customers, Hewlett-Packard, introduced a clone version of PostScript.

In 1998 a takeover bid by competitor Quark proved unsuccessful. Drooping sales that year, which Adobe blamed on the Asian crisis (some analysts blamed its product strategy), prompted the company to shed a layer of executives, 10% of its workforce, and its Adobe Enterprise Publishing Services and Image Club Graphics units. Its 1999 acquisition of GoLive Systems expanded its Web publishing product line. That year Adobe released professional page layout application InDesign, which immediately spurred the biggest backlog in the company's history.

In December 2000 chief executive Warnock passed the helm to president Bruce Chizen. Warnock remained co-chairman along with Geschke. The company boosted its electronic book offerings by acquiring software maker Glassbook. In 2002, in a move to expand its ePaper division, Adobe purchased electronic forms provider Accelio for $72 million.

OFFICERS

Co-Chairman: John E. Warnock, age 61, $1,343,240 pay
Co-Chairman: Charles M. Geschke, age 62
President, CEO, and Director: Bruce R. Chizen, age 46, $1,129,497 pay
EVP, Worldwide Product Marketing and Development: Shantanu Narayen, age 38, $582,788 pay
SVP and CFO: Murray Demo, age 40, $499,331 pay
SVP, General Counsel, and Secretary: Karen O. Cottle, age 51
SVP, Corporate Marketing and Communications: Melissa Dyrdahl
SVP, Cross Media: James J. Heeger, age 43

SVP, ePaper Solutions: Ivan Koon, age 43
SVP, Graphics Products: Bryan Lamkin
SVP, Human Resources: Theresa Townsley
**SVP, Worldwide Sales, Customer Care, and Field
  Marketing:** Jim E. Stephens, age 44, $386,758 pay
Senior Corporate Counsel: Ray Campbell
Auditors: KPMG LLP

LOCATIONS

HQ: 345 Park Ave., San Jose, CA 95110
Phone: 408-536-6000   **Fax:** 408-537-6000
Web: www.adobe.com

Adobe Systems has offices in Australia, Denmark,
France, Germany, Ireland, Italy, Japan, the Netherlands,
Norway, Spain, Sweden, the UK, and the US.

2001 Sales

	$ mil.	% of total
Americas	592	48
Europe, Middle East & Africa	326	27
Asia	312	25
Total	**1,230**	**100**

PRODUCTS/OPERATIONS

2001 Sales

	$ mil.	% of total
Web publishing	483	39
Print publishing	350	28
ePaper solutions	292	24
OEM PostScript & other	105	9
Total	**1,230**	**100**

Selected Products and Services

Web Publishing
After Effects (motion graphics and visual effects)
GoLive (Web site creation)
LiveMotion (Web animation creation)
Photoshop (photo enhancement)
Premiere (digital video editing)

Print Publishing
Dimensions (3-D graphics tool)
Font Folio (typefaces)
FrameMaker (technical document publishing)
Illustrator (illustration tool)
InDesign (page layout and publishing program)
PageMaker (page layout for business)
PressReady (printing software)
Streamline (conversion of images to line art)
Type Library (typefaces)

ePaper Solutions
Acrobat (document exchange)
Acrobat Reader (view and print Adobe PDF files)
Document Server (Web-based exchange for workgroups)

COMPETITORS

Apple Computer
Avid Technology
Corel
IBM
Macromedia
Media 100
Microsoft
Quark
Vignette

HISTORICAL FINANCIALS & EMPLOYEES

Nasdaq: ADBE FYE: Friday nearest Nov. 30	Annual Growth	11/92	11/93	11/94	11/95	11/96	11/97	11/98	11/99	11/00	11/01
Sales ($ mil.)	18.5%	266	314	598	762	787	912	895	1,015	1,266	1,230
Net income ($ mil.)	18.8%	44	57	6	94	153	187	105	238	288	206
Income as % of sales	—	16.4%	18.2%	1.1%	12.3%	19.5%	20.5%	11.7%	23.4%	22.7%	16.7%
Earnings per share ($)	14.8%	0.24	0.31	0.06	0.32	0.51	0.63	0.39	0.92	1.13	0.83
Stock price - FY high ($)	—	8.56	9.25	9.63	17.56	18.56	13.28	12.97	39.50	87.31	77.56
Stock price - FY low ($)	—	3.16	3.63	4.94	6.81	7.13	8.13	5.91	9.19	26.72	22.20
Stock price - FY close ($)	25.2%	4.25	5.78	8.25	16.91	9.88	10.50	11.19	34.06	63.38	32.08
P/E - high	—	36	30	161	55	36	21	32	40	72	90
P/E - low	—	13	12	82	21	14	13	15	9	22	26
Dividends per share ($)	2.5%	0.04	0.05	0.05	0.05	0.05	0.05	0.05	0.05	0.05	0.05
Book value per share ($)	8.4%	1.26	1.51	1.87	2.40	2.47	2.60	2.12	2.16	3.12	2.61
Employees	14.6%	887	1,000	1,584	2,319	2,266	2,702	2,680	2,760	3,007	3,029

STOCK PRICE HISTORY

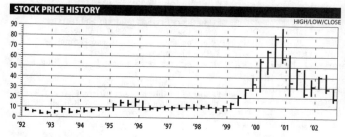

HIGH/LOW/CLOSE

2001 FISCAL YEAR-END

Debt ratio: 0.0%
Return on equity: 30.0%
Cash ($ mil.): 219
Current ratio: 2.45
Long-term debt ($ mil.): 0
No. of shares (mil.): 236
Dividends
  Yield: 0.2%
  Payout: 6.0%
Market value ($ mil.): 7,571

ADOLPH COORS COMPANY

Tapping the Rocky Mountains has been good to Adolph Coors Company's bottom line. Golden, Colorado-based Adolph Coors, the parent of Coors Brewing, rolls out about a dozen beers and malt-based brews, the majority of which are brewed in Colorado. Coors is the #3 US brewer, behind Anheuser-Busch and Philip Morris' Miller Brewing.

Nicknamed "The Silver Bullet," Coors Light is the company's premier product and the #4 US beer. Coors also makes Blue Moon Belgian White Ale, George Killian's Irish Red Lager (licensed), and Zima, a clear, lightly carbonated malt-based beverage. Once known as a single-product, regional beer maker, the brewer has not been afraid to try new varieties, though it has discontinued several that have fallen short (Blue Moon Abbey Ale, Keystone Dry, and Killian's Irish Honey). Coors also owns 49.9% of Molson USA, which sells and distributes Molson products in the US. It also owns the Carling brand under the new name Coors Brewers Limited (CBL). CBL, the #2 brewer in the UK, also brews the Calring, Worthington, and Caffrey's beer brands, as well as Grolsch (under license).

Coors' Colorado plant is the world's largest single-site brewery. The heirs of founder Adolph Coors own all of the company's voting stock.

HISTORY

Adolph Coors landed in Baltimore in 1868, a 21-year-old stowaway fleeing Germany's military draft. He worked his way west to Denver, where he bought a bottling company in 1872 and became partners with Jacob Schueler, a local merchant, in 1873. The partners built a brewery in Golden, Colorado, a small town in the nearby Rocky Mountain foothills. Coors became sole owner of the Adolph Coors Company in 1880.

For most of its history, Coors confined its sales to western states. The cost of nationwide distribution was prohibitive because the company used a single brewery, natural brewing methods, and no preservatives; Coors beer was made, transported, and stored under refrigeration, with a shelf life of only one month.

The brewer survived Prohibition by making near beer and malted milk and by entering cement and porcelain chemical ware production. The Coors family built a vertically integrated company that did everything from growing brewing ingredients to pumping the oil that powered its breweries. By 1929, when Adolph died, son Adolph Jr. was running Coors. After repeal of the 18th Amendment, beer sales grew steadily in the company's 11-state market.

By the 1960s Coors beer had achieved cult status. Another result of the company's national reputation was that the Coors family had become notoriously private. In 1960 Adolph III was kidnapped and murdered, sending the clan into an even deeper state of secrecy.

Adolph Jr. died in 1970; his son Bill was named chairman and started the country's first aluminum-recycling program. Coors beer was the top seller in 10 of its 11 state markets by 1975, when the company went public. However, sales began to decline as Miller Brewing and Anheuser-Busch introduced new light and super-premium beers. Coors responded by introducing its own light and superpremium brands and expanding its market area to 16 states.

In the late 1970s and 1980s, Coors began rapid expansion while enduring boycotts and strikes due to alleged discriminatory labor practices. The brewer eventually developed progressive employment policies.

Coors spun off its packaging and ceramics firm ACX Technologies in 1992. Also that year Coors introduced Zima, a clear, malt-based brew. Leo Kiely became the first president of the company's brewing operations from outside the Coors family in 1993. The company also cut its workforce by nearly 700; the severance program cost $70 million and resulted in Coors' first loss in over 10 years.

Coors' specialty Blue Moon products were piloted at its SandLot microbrewery in 1995. Coors formed a partnership with Molson Breweries and Foster's in 1997 to manage the distribution of its brands in Canada. (Foster's later sold its stake to Molson.)

In 2000 Peter Coors (Adolph's great-grandson) was named president and CEO of Adolph Coors Company and chairman of Coors Brewing Company. In January 2001 the brewer formed a new joint venture with Molson to distribute Molson's beers in the US. In 2002 Belgium's Interbrew sold the Carling division of its Bass Brewers holding to Coors for nearly $1.8 billion.

OFFICERS

Chairman: William K. Coors, age 85, $339,360 pay
President, CEO, and Director; Chairman of Coors Brewing Company: Peter H. Coors, age 55
CEO of Coors Brewing Company and Director: W. Leo Kiely III, age 55, $997,894 pay
SVP of Container, Operations, and Technology: L. Don Brown, age 55, $584,336 pay
SVP of Corporate Development: Robert D. Klugman, age 54
SVP of Sales: Carl L. Barnhill, age 53
SVP and Chief International Officer; CEO of Coors Brewing Limited (UK): Peter M. R. Kendall, age 55
SVP and Chief People Officer: Mara Swan, age 52

VP and CFO; SVP and CFO, Coors Brewing:
Timothy V. Wolf, age 48, $550,025 pay
VP and Controller (ACC and CBC):
Ronald A. Tryggestad, age 45
VP of Finance and Treasurer: David G. Barnes, age 40
VP of Process Development: Olivia M. Thompson,
age 50
VP, International and Control:
Katharine L. MacWilliams, age 46
Chief Marketing Officer, CBC: Ronald G. Askew
Auditors: PricewaterhouseCoopers LLP

LOCATIONS

HQ: 311 10th St., Golden, CO 80401
Phone: 303-279-6565   **Fax:** 303-277-6246
Web: www.coors.com

Adolph Coors Company has production facilities in
Canada, Colorado, Tennessee, Spain, and Virginia. It also
has aluminum can and glass bottling plants in Colorado,
as well as distribution facilities in California, Colorado,
Idaho, and Oklahoma. The company's products are sold
in the US and more than 30 international markets in
Asia, Australia, Europe, and North and South America.

2001 Sales

	% of total
US	97
Rest of world	3
Total	**100**

PRODUCTS/OPERATIONS

Selected Brands and Products
Blue Moon Belgian White Ale
Carling
Coors Dry
Coors Extra Gold
Coors Light
Coors Non-Alcoholic
Coors Original
George Killian's Irish Red Lager (licensed)
Keystone Ice
Keystone Light
Keystone Premium
Winterfest (seasonal)
Zima
Zima Citrus

COMPETITORS

Anheuser-Busch	Genesee
Boston Beer	Guinness/UDV
Brauerei BECK	Heineken
Carlsberg	Interbrew
Constellation Brands	Kirin
Yuengling & Son	Miller Brewing
FEMSA	Grupo Modelo
Foster's	S&P
Gambrinus	Scottish & Newcastle

HISTORICAL FINANCIALS & EMPLOYEES

NYSE: RKY FYE: Last Sunday in December	Annual Growth	12/92	12/93	12/94	12/95	12/96	12/97	12/98	12/99	12/00	12/01
Sales ($ mil.)	5.1%	1,551	1,582	2,040	2,061	2,112	2,208	2,291	2,463	2,842	2,430
Net income ($ mil.)	—	(2)	(42)	58	43	43	82	68	92	110	123
Income as % of sales	—	—	—	2.8%	2.1%	2.1%	3.7%	3.0%	3.7%	3.9%	5.1%
Earnings per share ($)	—	(0.05)	(1.10)	1.51	1.13	1.14	2.16	1.81	2.46	2.93	3.31
Stock price - FY high ($)	—	22.88	22.63	20.88	23.25	24.25	41.25	56.75	65.81	82.31	81.19
Stock price - FY low ($)	—	15.50	15.00	14.75	15.13	16.75	17.50	29.25	45.25	37.38	42.65
Stock price - FY close ($)	13.9%	16.50	16.25	16.75	22.13	19.00	33.25	56.44	52.50	80.31	53.40
P/E - high	—	—	—	14	21	21	19	30	26	28	24
P/E - low	—	—	—	10	13	15	8	16	18	13	13
Dividends per share ($)	5.4%	0.50	0.50	0.50	0.50	0.50	0.50	0.60	0.65	0.72	0.80
Book value per share ($)	4.3%	18.17	16.54	17.59	18.29	18.87	19.98	21.14	22.92	25.11	26.46
Employees	(2.8%)	7,100	6,200	6,300	6,200	5,800	5,800	5,800	5,800	5,850	5,500

STOCK PRICE HISTORY

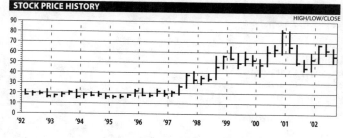

HIGH/LOW/CLOSE

2001 FISCAL YEAR-END

Debt ratio: 2.1%
Return on equity: 13.1%
Cash ($ mil.): 77
Current ratio: 1.17
Long-term debt ($ mil.): 20
No. of shares (mil.): 36
Dividends
  Yield: 1.5%
  Payout: 24.2%
Market value ($ mil.): 1,920

ADVANCE PUBLICATIONS, INC.

This company is propelled forward by magazine and newspaper publishing. Based in Staten Island, New York, Advance Publications is one of the top periodical publishers in the US. Its newspaper operations include 22 titles such as *The Cleveland Plain Dealer, The Star-Ledger* (New Jersey), and its namesake *Staten Island Advance.* Its American City Business Journals unit produces 41 weekly papers and niche publications, including Street & Smith's *SportsBusiness Journal.* Advance is also the #2 magazine publisher in the US (behind Time Inc.), with subsidiaries such as Condé Nast Publications (*Vogue, Glamour, The New Yorker,* and *Vanity Fair*) and trade journal publisher Fairchild Publications (*Women's Wear Daily*). In addition, Advance owns Parade Publications (*Parade Magazine* Sunday insert).

Aside from publishing, Advance is a major online publisher with nearly a dozen regional news Web sites. Its CondéNet unit runs Web versions of Condé Nast's magazines and other Internet properties, including Epicurious (food and dining) and Concierge (travel). The company also has stakes in cable TV systems (33%, with AOL Time Warner), broadband ISP Road Runner (9%), and cable broadcaster Discovery Communications (25%).

Advance took steps to increase its magazine portfolio by acquiring The New York Times Company's Golf Properties unit (*Golf Digest*) for about $430 million and Miami-based Ideas Publishing Group, which produces Spanish language versions of US magazines. Chairman Samuel "Si" Newhouse and his brother Donald (president) control the very closely held company.

HISTORY

Solomon Neuhaus (later Samuel I. Newhouse) got started in the newspaper business after dropping out of school at age 13. He went to work at the *Bayonne Times* in New Jersey and was put in charge of the failing newspaper in 1911; he managed to turn the paper around within a year. In 1922 he bought the *Staten Island Advance* and formed the Staten Island Advance Company in 1924. After buying up more papers, he changed the name of the company to Advance Publications in 1949. By the 1950s the company had local papers in New York, New Jersey, and Alabama.

In 1959 Newhouse bought magazine publisher Condé Nast as an anniversary gift for his wife. (He joked that she had asked for a fashion magazine, so he bought her *Vogue.*) His publishing empire continued to grow with the addition of the *Times-Picayune* (New Orleans) in

1962 and *The Cleveland Plain Dealer* in 1967. In 1976 the company paid more than $300 million for Booth Newspapers, publisher of eight Michigan papers and *Parade Magazine.*

Newhouse died in 1979, leaving his sons Si and Donald to run the company, which encompassed more than 30 newspapers, a half-dozen magazines, and 15 cable systems. The next year Advance bought book publishing giant Random House from RCA. Si resurrected the Roaring Twenties standard *Vanity Fair* in 1983 and added *The New Yorker* under the Condé Nast banner in 1985. The Newhouses scored a victory over the IRS in 1990 after a long-running court battle involving inheritance taxes. Condé Nast bought Knapp Publications (*Architectural Digest*) in 1993 and Advance later acquired American City Business Journals in 1995.

In 1998 the company sold the increasingly unprofitable Random House to Bertelsmann for about $1.2 billion. It later bought hallmark Internet magazine *Wired* (though it passed on Wired Ventures' Internet operations). That year revered *New Yorker* editor Tina Brown, credited with jazzing up the publication's content and increasing its circulation, left the magazine; staff writer and Pulitzer Prize winner David Remnick was named as Brown's replacement.

In 1999 Advance joined Donrey Media Group (now called Stephens Media Group), E.W. Scripps, Hearst Corporation, and MediaNews Group to purchase the online classified advertising network AdOne (later named PowerOne Media). It also bought Walt Disney's trade publishing unit, Fairchild Publications, for $650 million. In 2000 the company shifted *Details* from Condé Nast to Fairchild and relaunched the magazine as a fashion publication. Later that year the company announced it would begin creating Web versions of its popular magazine titles.

In 2001 Condé Nast bought a majority stake in Miami-based Ideas Publishing Group (Spanish language versions of US magazines). Also that year Advance bought four golf magazines, including *Golf Digest,* from the New York Times Company for $430 million. Condé Nast picked up *Modern Bride* magazine from PRIMEDIA in early 2002 for $52 million.

OFFICERS

Chairman and CEO; Chairman, Condé Nast Publications: Samuel I. Newhouse Jr.
President: Donald E. Newhouse
COO, Advance Magazine Publishers; COO, Condé Nast: Charles H. Townsend
VP Finance and Human Resources; Comptroller, Staten Island Advance: Arthur Silverstein
VP Investor Services: George Fries
VP Marketing: Jack Furnari
VP Sales: Gary Cognetta
Chairman, CEO, and Publisher, Parade Publications: Walter Anderson
Chairman and Editorial Director, Golf Digest Companies: Jerry Tarde
Chairman, American City Business Journals: Ray Shaw
President and CEO, Condé Nast Publications: Steven T. Florio
President and CEO, Golf Digest Companies: Mitchell Fox
President and CEO, Fairchild Publications: Mary G. Berner
President and Creative Director, Advance.net: Jeff Jarvis
President, Advance Internet: Peter Wienberger
President, CondéNet: Sarah Chubb
Executive Director of Human Resources Recruiting: Pammy Brooks

LOCATIONS

HQ: 950 Fingerboard Rd., Staten Island, NY 10305
Phone: 718-981-1234   **Fax:** 718-981-1456
Web: www.advance.net

PRODUCTS/OPERATIONS

Selected Operations

Broadcasting and Communications
Cartoonbank.com (database of cartoons from *The New Yorker*)
Discovery Communications (25%, cable TV channel)
Newhouse Broadcasting (33%, cable TV joint venture with AOL Time Warner)
Newhouse News Service
Religion News Service
Road Runner (9%, broadband Internet service)

Magazine Publishing
Condé Nast Publications
  Allure
  Architectural Digest
  Bon Appetit
  Bride's
  Condé Nast Traveler
  Glamour
  Gourmet
  GQ
  House & Garden
  Modern Bride
  The New Yorker
  Self
  Vanity Fair
  Vogue
  Wired
Fairchild Publications
  Details
  Jane
  W
  Women's Wear Daily
The Golf Digest Companies
  Golf Digest
  Golf for Women
  Golf World

Newspaper Publishing
American City Business Journals (41 weekly titles in 22 states)
Newhouse Newspapers (22 papers in more than 20 cities)
Parade Publications

Online Publishing
Advance Internet
CondéNet
  Concierge.com (travel information)
  Epicurious (recipes and fine dining)
  Style.com (fashion and beauty)

Selected Newspapers
The Birmingham News (Alabama)
The Oregonian (Portland)
The Plain Dealer (Cleveland)
The Star-Ledger (Newark, NJ)
Staten Island Advance (New York)
The Times-Picayune (New Orleans)

COMPETITORS

American Express
Crain Communications
Dow Jones
E. W. Scripps
Freedom Communications
Gannett
Gruner + Jahr
Hachette Filipacchi Médias
Hearst
Knight Ridder
MSO
McClatchy Company
Meredith
New York Times
North Jersey Media
PRIMEDIA
Reader's Digest
Reed Elsevier Group
Time
Tribune
Washington Post

HISTORICAL FINANCIALS & EMPLOYEES

Private FYE: December 31	Annual Growth	12/92	12/93	12/94	12/95	12/96	12/97	12/98	12/99	12/00	12/01
Sales ($ mil.)	(1.1%)	4,416	4,690	4,855	5,349	4,250	3,669	3,859	4,228	4,542	4,000
Employees	2.4%	19,000	19,000	19,000	24,000	24,000	24,000	24,000	26,300	23,000	—

SALES HISTORY

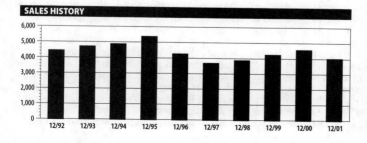

ADVANCED MICRO DEVICES, INC.

In this horse race, AMD is second by somewhat more than a nose. Sunnyvale, California-based Advanced Micro Devices (AMD) ranks #2 in PC microprocessors, far behind industry king-pin Intel. (Intel commands about four-fifths of the world processor market. AMD has eroded that market share only to see Intel strike back with steep price cuts and faster introduction of new models.) AMD is also the world's #2 maker — again behind Intel — of flash memory chips, key components of electronic devices including cellular phones. AMD also makes embedded processors and other chips for communications and networking applications.

AMD has attacked Intel's dominant market share with a lineup of microprocessors that includes the high-performance Athlon and the inexpensive Duron (which is now being phased out). The company's eighth-generation products, speedy 64-bit processors code-named Hammer, are scheduled for release (after some delays) late in 2002. (One of the first releases, called Opteron, is set to compete with Intel's Itanium chip in the server market.) PC bigwig Compaq (now part of Hewlett-Packard) accounts for more than a tenth of AMD's sales.

In its battle with Intel, AMD has sometimes been its own worst enemy. Design flaws and other manufacturing problems, including lack of production capacity, have plagued the company over the years, contributing to losses and testing the market's patience. After a banner year in 2000, the company announced layoffs and plant closures amid a global chip industry slump in 2001. AMD has announced a long-term alliance with chip foundry United Microelectronics aimed at boosting its long-term production capacity — and competitiveness with Intel.

Company founder Jerry Sanders, the colorful (or notorious) leader who ran AMD for over 30 years, has retired as CEO; he is slated to remain chairman through 2003.

HISTORY

Silicon Valley powerhouse Fairchild Camera & Instrument axed marketing whiz Jerry Sanders, reportedly for wearing a pink shirt on a sales call to IBM. In 1969 Sanders started a semiconductor company (just as his former boss, Intel founder Robert Noyce, had done a year earlier) based on chip designs licensed from other companies.

Advanced Micro Devices (AMD) went public in 1972. Siemens, eager to enter the US semiconductor market, paid $30 million for nearly 20% of AMD in 1977 (sold by 1991). In 1982 AMD inked a deal with Intel that let AMD make exact copies of Intel's iAPX86 microprocessors, used in IBM and compatible PCs.

By the mid-1980s the company was developing its own chips. In 1987 AMD sued Intel for breaking the 1982 agreement that allowed AMD to second-source Intel's new 386 chips. Intel countersued for copyright infringement when AMD introduced versions of Intel's 287 math coprocessor (1990), 386 chip (1991), and 486 chip (1993).

In 1993 AMD formed a joint venture with Fujitsu to make flash memory devices. A federal jury decided in AMD's favor in the 287 math coprocessor case in 1994. AMD and Intel settled their legal differences in 1995. Each agreed to pay damages, and AMD won a perpetual license to the microcode of Intel's 386 and 486 chips. AMD's K5 microprocessor (a rival of Intel's Pentium) hit the market in 1996 — more than a year late.

In 1996 AMD bought microprocessor developer NexGen and its technology for use in the K6 chip. That year AMD restructured its programmable logic chip unit as subsidiary Vantis. AMD unveiled its K6 microprocessor the next year, but had trouble increasing production to meet demand. In 1999 AMD sold Vantis to Lattice Semiconductor, raising $500 million. The company debuted its Athlon (K7) chip in 1999 to positive reviews and soon won Compaq and IBM as customers.

In early 2000 AMD named Hector Ruiz (former head of Motorola's semiconductor operations) president and COO — and thus heir apparent — to Sanders. Also in 2000 AMD sold 90% of its communications circuits business (chips for telephony and Internet access) to Francisco Partners for $375 million; the deal calls for AMD to provide manufacturing services to the new company (renamed Legerity).

Improved manufacturing processes, increased sales of high-end Athlons, and a worldwide shortage of flash memory helped AMD turn a profit in 2000, its first since 1995.

In the face of a dismal slump in the global chip business, AMD announced later in 2001 that it would cut costs by closing two chip plants in Texas and by cutting about 2,300 jobs — 15% of its total workforce — there and in Malaysia.

Early in 2002 the company announced a major production alliance with Taiwan-based foundry giant United Microelectronics (UMC). The companies' joint venture, AU Pte Ltd., is slated to begin production at a new cutting-edge fab (wafer factory) in Singapore in 2005; meanwhile, UMC will use its current facilities to boost AMD's microprocessor production capacity.

Also in 2002 AMD acquired Alchemy

Semiconductor, a maker of embedded micro-processors for wireless networking applications, for $50 million in cash.

Sanders handed over the CEO reins to Ruiz in 2002; Sanders is expected to remain chairman through 2003.

OFFICERS

Chairman: W. J. Sanders III, age 65, $2,217,412 pay
President, CEO, and Director: Hector de J. Ruiz, age 56, $795,299 pay
EVP and Chief Sales and Marketing Officer: Robert R. Herb, age 40, $1,404,649 pay
SVP and CFO: Robert J. Rivet Sr., age 47
SVP, General Counsel, and Secretary: Thomas M. McCoy, age 51, $692,900 pay
SVP, Computation Products Group: Dirk Meyer, age 40
SVP, Human Resources: Stanley Winvick, age 62
SVP, Market Development: Stephen J. Zelencik, age 67
SVP, Technology and Manufacturing Operations and Chief Scientist: William T. Siegle, age 63
VP, Information Technology and CIO: Frederick Mapp
Auditors: Ernst & Young LLP

LOCATIONS

HQ: 1 AMD Place, Sunnyvale, CA 94086
Phone: 408-732-2400   **Fax:** 408-894-0547
Web: www.amd.com

2001 Sales

	$ mil.	% of total
Europe	1,493	38
US	1,327	34
Asia/Pacific	1,072	28
Total	**3,892**	**100**

PRODUCTS/OPERATIONS

2001 Sales

	$ mil.	% of total
PC microprocessors	2,419	62
Memory chips	1,133	29
Other integrated circuits	242	6
Foundry services	98	3
Total	**3,892**	**100**

Selected Products
Athlon (K7) high-performance chips
Duron (K7) budget chips
Embedded processors (used in communications products, disk drives, and handheld computers)
Erasable programmable read-only memories (EPROMs)
Flash memory
K6 family (K6, K6 with 3DNow!)
Networking chips
Platform products

COMPETITORS

Atmel
Broadcom
Fairchild Semiconductor
Fujitsu
Hitachi
Infineon Technologies
Integrated Device Technology
Intel
IBM Microelectronics
Macronix International
Micron Technology
Mitsubishi Corporation
Motorola
NEC
Philips Semiconductors
Samsung Electronics
Sharp
STMicroelectronics
Sun Microsystems
Toshiba
Transmeta
VIA Technologies

HISTORICAL FINANCIALS & EMPLOYEES

NYSE: AMD FYE: Last Sunday in December	Annual Growth	12/92	12/93	12/94	12/95	12/96	12/97	12/98	12/99	12/00	12/01
Sales ($ mil.)	11.1%	1,515	1,648	2,135	2,430	1,953	2,356	2,542	2,858	4,644	3,892
Net income ($ mil.)	—	245	229	305	301	(69)	(21)	(104)	(89)	983	(61)
Income as % of sales	—	16.2%	13.9%	14.3%	12.4%	—	—	—	—	21.2%	—
Earnings per share ($)	—	1.25	0.82	1.02	1.40	(0.26)	(0.08)	(0.36)	(0.30)	2.89	(0.18)
Stock price - FY high ($)	—	10.75	16.44	15.88	19.63	14.19	24.25	16.38	16.50	48.50	34.65
Stock price - FY low ($)	—	3.69	8.50	8.38	8.06	5.13	8.56	6.38	7.28	13.56	7.69
Stock price - FY close ($)	6.4%	9.06	8.88	12.44	8.25	12.88	8.88	14.50	14.47	13.81	15.86
P/E - high	—	8	19	14	14	—	—	—	—	15	—
P/E - low	—	3	10	8	6	—	—	—	—	4	—
Dividends per share ($)	—	0.38	0.00	0.00	0.01	0.00	0.00	0.00	0.00	0.00	0.00
Book value per share ($)	6.5%	5.93	7.31	9.09	10.05	7.35	7.14	6.89	6.66	10.10	10.44
Employees	2.5%	11,554	12,065	11,793	12,730	12,200	12,800	13,800	13,387	14,696	14,415

STOCK PRICE HISTORY

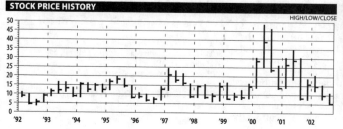

HIGH/LOW/CLOSE

2001 FISCAL YEAR-END
Debt ratio: 15.9%
Return on equity: —
Cash ($ mil.): 427
Current ratio: 1.79
Long-term debt ($ mil.): 673
No. of shares (mil.): 341
Dividends
  Yield: —
  Payout: —
Market value ($ mil.): 5,400

ADVANCEPCS, INC.

Health plans farming out their pharmacy operations turn to AdvancePCS, the largest independent pharmacy benefits provider in the US (Medco, a subsidiary of pharmaceutical company Merck, is larger). The company, based in Irving, Texas, was formed when Advance Paradigm bought PCS Health Systems from Rite Aid.

The firm provides pharmacy and health management services to health plan sponsors covering more than 75 million enrollees. The company's services include mail-order and online pharmacies, disease management programs (for asthma, diabetes, and congestive heart failure), and a broad system of information management capabilities. Subsidiaries Innovative Medical Research and Baumel-Eisner Neuromedical Institute provide a range of clinical trials, outcomes research, and health survey services.

The company has grown quickly — both through acquisitions and the aggressive courting of such groups as the United Mine Workers and the Oklahoma State Education Employees Group Insurance Board. AdvancePCS includes among its clients many Blue Cross and Blue Shield organizations, insurance companies and HMOs, corporate employers, labor unions, and state and local governments.

AdvancePCS is looking for more growth over the next few years as more patients switch to mail-order drug delivery, cutting out local pharmacies and saving on distribution costs. Also, as more high-tech drugs hit the market, the company sees a chance to enhance sales and profits by handling the delivery and administration of these expensive and complex treatments.

HISTORY

David Halbert, a former energy company executive, founded Advance Health Care in 1986 as a mail-order pharmacy. His brother Jon, formerly of Bear Stearns, became COO in 1988. In 1992 the company began building a retail pharmacy network. The next year Advance Health Care bought Paradigm Pharmacy Management, a benefits management subsidiary of Blue Cross and Blue Shield of Maryland. This acquisition enabled the company to strike bargains with drug companies and to attract cost-conscious managed care clients. After the acquisition, the company was renamed Advance Paradigm and moved into integrated health benefits management. The company went public in 1996.

Advance Paradigm had been expanding its customer base through marketing and acquisitions. In keeping with the industry's focus on disease management, it also began acquiring clinical trial and research companies (Innovative Medical Research and Baumel-Eisner Neuromedical Institute, 1998). In 1998 Advance Paradigm launched its online pharmacy operations. In 1999 it bought Foundation Health System's (now Health Net) pharmacy benefit management operations, adding about 27 million members to its system.

In 2000 Advance Paradigm purchased PCS Health Systems from Rite Aid. Rite Aid had acquired PCS from Eli Lilly, but was forced to sell it for a loss to reduce debt. Founded in 1969 as Pharmaceutical Card System, PCS was the first pharmacy benefit management company in the US. PCS entered the mail-order pharmacy business in 1996 when it opened a distribution center in Fort Worth, Texas. After the merger, the two companies became AdvancePCS. In 2000 the company acquired pharmacy benefits manager FFI Health Services, and it invested in Consumer Health Interactive, a Web-based health services marketing company.

In 2001 AdvancePCS launched a specialty pharmacy unit, AdvancePCS SpecialtyRx, by acquiring specialty pharmacy provider TheraCom and forming a joint venture with specialty pharmacy and distribution company Priority Healthcare. The new division offers services to patients who need expensive and technologically advanced drugs to treat complex diseases.

Also in 2001 AdvancePCS teamed with pharmacy benefits companies Express Scripts and Merck-Medco to form RxHub, an electronic exchange that will link patients' doctors with pharmacies, pharmacy benefit managers, and health plans. Later in 2001 the company renewed its contract with the Blue Cross and Blue Shield Association Federal Employee Program, which serves more than 4 million customers.

OFFICERS

Chairman and CEO: David D. Halbert, age 46, $2,264,309 pay
Vice Chairman: Jon S. Halbert, age 42, $934,864 pay
President and Director: David A. George, age 46, $934,864 pay
EVP and CFO: Yon Yoon Jorden, age 47
EVP, Sales and Account Services: John H. Sattler, age 50, $456,923 pay
EVP, Corporate Development: T. Danny Phillips, age 43, $572,192 pay
EVP: Joseph J. Filipek Jr., age 45
SVP, Human Resources: Steven C. Mizell, age 42
SVP and CIO: Mitch Henry
SVP and Chief Marketing Officer: Craig S. Schub, age 47
SVP and Chief Medical Officer: Alan T. Wright
SVP and CTO: Julie Hall

SVP, Chief of Staff — Office of the CEO:
Leslie Simmons, age 31
SVP, Chief Medical Officer: Andrew Garling
SVP, Corporate Affairs and Secretary:
Laura I. Johansen, age 37
SVP and General Counsel: Susan S. de Mars, age 42
SVP, Mail Services: Phil Pearce
SVP, Medical Affairs: Marsha Moore
SVP, Operations: Ernest Buys, age 58
SVP, Trade Relations: Rudy Mladenovac, age 44
Auditors: PricewaterhouseCoopers LLP

LOCATIONS

HQ: 750 W. John Carpenter Frwy., Ste. 1200,
Irving, TX 75039
Phone: 469-524-4700   **Fax:** 469-524-4702
Web: www.advparadigm.com

AdvancePCS operates throughout the US.

PRODUCTS/OPERATIONS

2002 Sales

	$ mil.	% of total
Data services	10,987	84
Mail services	1,555	12
Clinical & other	565	4
Total	**13,107**	**100**

Selected Subsidiaries
AdvancePCS Health, L.P. (dba - IMR)
AdvancePCS Health Systems, L.L.C.
AdvancePCS Holding Corporation
AdvancePCS Mail Services of Birmingham, Inc.
AdvancePCS Puerto Rico, Inc.
AdvancePCS Research, LLC (dba - IMR)
AdvancePCS SpecialtyRx, L.L.C.
AdvancePriority SpecialtyRx, L.L.C.
AdvanceRx.com, L.P.
Advance Funding Corporation
ADVP Consolidation, L.L.C.
ADVP Management, L.P.
AFC Receivables Holding Corporation
Ambulatory Care Review Services, Inc.
Baumel Eisner Neuromedical Institute, Inc.
Consumer Health Interactive, Inc.
Dresing-Lierman, Inc.
FFI Rx Managed Care, Inc.
First Florida International Holdings, Inc.
HMN Health Services, Inc.
TheraCom, Inc.

COMPETITORS

Caremark
Chronimed
Express Scripts
Merck
MIM
National Medical Health Card Systems
Owen Healthcare
Rite Aid
Walgreen

HISTORICAL FINANCIALS & EMPLOYEES

Nasdaq: ADVP FYE: March 31	Annual Growth	3/93	3/94	3/95	3/96	3/97	3/98	3/99	3/00	3/01	3/02
Sales ($ mil.)	117.8%	12	23	66	125	252	477	775	1,968	7,024	13,107
Net income ($ mil.)	—	(0)	(0)	0	1	3	8	13	21	23	116
Income as % of sales	—	—	—	0.0%	0.8%	1.2%	1.7%	1.6%	1.0%	0.3%	0.9%
Earnings per share ($)	71.1%	—	—	—	—	0.09	0.18	0.28	0.43	0.32	1.32
Stock price - FY high ($)	—	—	—	—	—	6.31	10.19	16.94	17.38	29.63	40.15
Stock price - FY low ($)	—	—	—	—	—	1.94	2.72	4.25	5.56	4.75	25.03
Stock price - FY close ($)	55.5%	—	—	—	—	3.31	9.91	15.80	5.94	27.13	30.09
P/E - high	—	—	—	—	—	57	46	55	35	76	28
P/E - low	—	—	—	—	—	18	12	14	11	12	18
Dividends per share ($)	—	—	—	—	—	0.00	0.00	0.00	0.00	0.00	0.00
Book value per share ($)	22.7%	—	—	—	—	3.39	1.42	1.64	2.31	5.56	9.45
Employees	64.8%	—	—	—	282	336	697	891	1,370	4,534	5,655

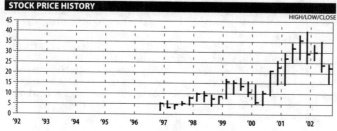

STOCK PRICE HISTORY
HIGH/LOW/CLOSE

2002 FISCAL YEAR-END
Debt ratio: 36.3%
Return on equity: 18.0%
Cash ($ mil.): 139
Current ratio: 0.86
Long-term debt ($ mil.): 499
No. of shares (mil.): 93
Dividends
 Yield: —
 Payout: —
Market value ($ mil.): 2,794

THE AES CORPORATION

AES does not stand for "an excellent start," but it could. By focusing on providing electricity to customers around the world, the relatively young Arlington, Virginia-based company has rapidly become a leading global independent power producer. AES owns and operates its facilities; it has interests in about 180 power plants (some of which are under construction) that give it a net generating capacity of nearly 51,000 MW on six continents. AES sells its power to wholesale and retail customers, including electric utilities, other power traders, commercial and industrial businesses, and residences. AES has interests in distribution utilities that serve 19 million customers, primarily in Latin America; AES also has telecom operations in Latin America.

The company has announced major restructuring initiatives: it is cutting new power plant construction spending and plans to sell noncore assets such as its Illinois utility CILCORP (which fellow utility Ameren will buy), a minority stake in its Indiana utility IPALCO, and some generation facilities. AES also plans to reduce its Latin American operations and its merchant generation operations (either by selling plants or entering into long-term power supply contracts). Chairman Roger Sant and former CEO Dennis Bakke, who founded the company in 1981, own 8% and 7%, respectively, of AES.

HISTORY

Applied Energy Services (AES) was founded in 1981, three years after passage of the Public Utilities Regulation Policies Act, which enabled small power firms to enter electric generation markets formerly dominated by utility monopolies. Co-founders Roger Sant and Dennis Bakke, who had served in President Nixon's Federal Energy Administration, saw that an independent power producer (IPP) could make money by generating cheap power in large volumes to sell to large power consumers and utilities.

AES set about building massive cogeneration plants (producing both steam and electricity) in 1983. The first plant, Deepwater, went into operation near Houston in 1986. By 1989 AES had three plants on line, and it then opened plants in Connecticut and Oklahoma. In 1991 the company, formally renamed AES, went public, but one plant's falsified emissions reports caused AES's stock to plummet in 1992.

Facing environmental groups' opposition to new power plant construction and an overall glut in the US power market, AES bought interests in two Northern Ireland plants in 1992 and began expanding into Latin America in 1993. Also in 1993 AES set up a separately traded subsidiary,

AES China Generating Co., to focus on Chinese development projects. AES won a plant development contract with the Puerto Rico Electric Power Authority (1994) and a bid to privatize an Argentine hydrothermal company (1995).

In 1996 AES began adding stakes in electric utility and distribution companies to its portfolio, including interests in formerly state-owned Brazilian electric utilities Light Serviços de Eletricidade (1996) and CEMIG (1997); two Argentine and one Brazilian distribution companies (1997); and a distribution company in El Salvador (1998).

AES almost doubled its revenues after buying Destec Energy's international operations from NGC (now Dynegy) in 1997. By the next year, prospects in international markets were dimming, so AES turned to the US market again. It bought three California plants from Edison International and arranged for The Williams Companies to supply natural gas to the facilities and market the electricity generated. AES also won a bid to buy six plants from New York State Electric & Gas (now Energy East) affiliate NGE.

Also in 1998, despite black days in many world markets, AES bought 90% of Argentine electric distribution company Edelap and a 45% stake in state-owned Orissa Power Generation in India.

It bought CILCORP, an Illinois utility holding company, in an $886 million deal in 1999. Boosting its presence in the UK, AES bought the Drax power station, a 3,960-MW coal-fired plant, from National Power. It also bought a majority stake in Brazilian data transmission company Eletronet from Brazil's government-owned utility ELETROBRÁS. In 2000 AES increased its interests in Brazilian power distributors. It also gained a 73% stake (later expanded to 87%) in Venezuelan electric utility Grupo EDC in a $1.5 billion hostile takeover.

The next year AES bought IPALCO, the parent of Indianapolis Power & Light, in a $3 billion deal. Also in 2001 AES acquired the outstanding shares of Chilean generation company Gener, in which it previously held a 60% stake.

In 2002 AES sold its 24% interest in Light Serviços de Eletricidade (Light) to Electricité de France (EDF) in exchange for a 20% stake in Brazilian utility Eletropaulo (increasing its stake to 70%). Later that year, in response to credit rating and stock price decreases, AES announced that it would sell noncore assets and restructure its operations. It agreed to sell its CILCORP subsidiary, which holds utility Central Illinois Light, to utility company Ameren in a $1.4 billion deal; it also agreed to sell its retail energy marketing unit to Constellation Energy Group.

Chairman: Roger W. Sant, age 70
President, CEO, and Director: Paul T. Hanrahan,
 age 43, $250,000 pay (prior to title change)
**EVP Competitive Supply and COO; Managing Director,
 AES Pacific:** J. Stuart Ryan, age 43
EVP Contract Generation and COO: John R. Ruggirello,
 age 51, $250,000 pay
EVP Large Utilities, CFO, and COO: Barry J. Sharp,
 age 42, $260,000 pay
EVP; CEO, Eletropaulo: Mark S. Fitzpatrick,
 $260,000 pay (prior to title change)
SVP; President, AES Aurora: Sarah Slusser
SVP; Managing Director, AES Oasis: Shahzad S. Qasim
SVP, Secretary, and General Counsel:
 William R. Luraschi, age 38
SVP; Managing Director; AES Orient:
 William L. Ruccius
SVP Business Development and Investor Relations:
 Kenneth R. Woodcock, age 58
SVP Planning: Roger F. Naill, age 55
Auditors: Deloitte & Touche LLP

LOCATIONS

HQ: 1001 N. 19th St., Arlington, VA 22209
Phone: 703-522-1315 **Fax:** 703-528-4510
Web: www.aesc.com

AES has operations in Argentina, Australia, Bangladesh,
Brazil, Cameroon, Canada, Chile, China, Colombia, the
Czech Republic, the Dominican Republic, El Salvador,
Georgia, Germany, Hungary, India, Italy, Kazakhstan,
Mexico, the Netherlands, Nigeria, Oman, Pakistan,
Panama, Qatar, Sri Lanka, Tanzania, Uganda, the
Ukraine, the UK, the US, and Venezuela.

PRODUCTS/OPERATIONS

2001 Sales

	$ mil.	% of total
Competitive supply	2,729	29
Contract generation	2,466	27
Large utilities	2,444	26
Growth distribution	1,688	18
Total	**9,327**	**100**

Selected Electric Utilities and Distribution Companies
AES Edelap (60%, electric utility, Argentina)
AES Gener (electric generation, Chile)
AES NewEnergy (retail energy marketing)
AES Sul (96%, electric utility, Brazil)
AES Telasi (75%, electric utility, Georgia)
CESCO (48%, electric utility, India)
Grupo La Electricidad de Caracas (EDC, 87%, electric
 distribution, Venezuela)
IPALCO Enterprises, Inc. (holding company)
 Illinois Power & Light Company (IPL, electric utility)
Light Telecom (Brazil)

COMPETITORS

Alliant Energy	Endesa (Spain)	NRG Energy
Calpine	Enersis	PG&E
CMS Energy	Exelon	PowerGen
Duke Energy	FPL	Reliant Energy
Duke/Fluor	Iberdrola	Reliant
Daniel	Indeck Energy	Resources
Dynegy	International	Sempra Energy
Edison	Power	Siemens
International	MidAmerican	Sithe Energies
Electricidade de	Energy	Tractebel
Portugal	Mirant	TXU
El Paso	Nicor	Xcel Energy

HISTORICAL FINANCIALS & EMPLOYEES

NYSE: AES FYE: December 31	Annual Growth	12/92	12/93	12/94	12/95	12/96	12/97	12/98	12/99	12/00	12/01
Sales ($ mil.)	41.9%	401	519	533	685	835	1,411	2,398	3,253	6,691	9,327
Net income ($ mil.)	19.3%	56	71	100	107	125	185	311	228	641	273
Income as % of sales	—	13.9%	13.7%	18.8%	15.6%	15.0%	13.1%	13.0%	7.0%	9.6%	2.9%
Earnings per share ($)	10.4%	0.21	0.25	0.34	0.36	0.41	0.55	0.85	0.58	1.43	0.51
Stock price - FY high ($)	—	6.11	5.67	5.95	6.00	12.53	24.81	29.00	38.19	72.81	60.15
Stock price - FY low ($)	—	2.67	4.21	3.94	4.00	5.25	11.19	11.50	16.41	34.25	11.60
Stock price - FY close ($)	15.4%	4.49	5.67	4.88	5.97	11.63	23.31	23.69	37.38	55.38	16.35
P/E - high	—	29	23	18	17	31	44	33	60	50	116
P/E - low	—	13	17	12	11	13	20	13	26	23	22
Dividends per share ($)	—	0.10	0.15	0.00	0.00	0.00	0.00	0.00	0.00	0.00	0.00
Book value per share ($)	36.1%	0.65	1.07	1.34	1.83	2.33	4.24	4.97	6.38	10.00	10.39
Employees	59.9%	557	570	680	1,258	5,700	10,000	11,700	14,500	26,606	38,000

STOCK PRICE HISTORY

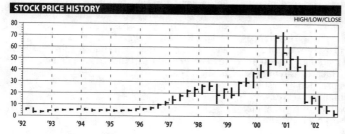

HIGH/LOW/CLOSE

2001 FISCAL YEAR-END

Debt ratio: 78.0%
Return on equity: 5.3%
Cash ($ mil.): 922
Current ratio: 0.92
Long-term debt ($ mil.): 19,586
No. of shares (mil.): 533
Dividends
 Yield: —
 Payout: —
Market value ($ mil.): 8,715

AETNA INC.

It's Splitsville for troubled managed health care provider Aetna.

The Hartford, Connecticut-based managed health care provider offers group and individual indemnity health insurance (including dental, pharmacy, and vision), PPOs, and HMOs. Hammered by government reimbursement cutbacks and rising medical costs, it is also struggling to integrate Prudential's troubled health care operations with U.S. Healthcare. These problems, compounded by a growing managed care backlash, have led the firm to sell its financial services and international divisions to giant ING Groep.

Customers' increased use of pharmacy, outpatient, and specialty services is deteriorating the company's bottom line. Volatile changes within the company, as well as increases in medical spending, have led Aetna to announce that it may take two years to recover. In December of 2001, Aetna announced that it would reduce its workforce by 16% as part of its turnaround plan.

Capital Research and Management Company owns about 11% of the company, and AXA Financial owns about 9% of the company.

HISTORY

Hartford, Connecticut, businessman and judge Eliphalet Bulkeley started Connecticut Mutual Life Insurance in 1846. Agents gained control of the firm the following year. Undeterred, Bulkeley and a group of Hartford businessmen founded Aetna Life Insurance in 1853 as a spinoff of Aetna Fire Insurance. Among its offerings was coverage for slaves, a practice for which the company apologized in 2000.

A nationwide agency network fueled early growth at Aetna, which expanded in the 1860s by offering a participating life policy, returning dividends to policyholders based on investment earnings. (This let Aetna compete with mutual life insurers.) In 1868 Aetna became the first firm to offer renewable term life policies.

Eliphalet's son, Morgan, became president in 1879. Aetna moved into accident (1891), health (1899), workers' compensation (1902), and auto and other property insurance (1907) during his 43-year tenure. He served as Hartford mayor, Connecticut governor, and US senator, all the while leading Aetna.

By 1920 the company sold marine insurance, and by 1922 it was the US's largest multiline insurer. Aetna overexpanded its nonlife lines (particularly autos) during the 1920s, threatening its solvency. It survived the Depression by restricting underwriting and rebuilding reserves.

After WWII the firm expanded into group life, health, and accident insurance. In 1967 it reorganized into holding company Aetna Life and Casualty.

The 1960s, 1970s, and 1980s were go-go years: The company added lines and bought and sold everything from an oil services firm to commercial real estate. The boom period led to a bust and a 1991 reorganization in which Aetna eliminated 8,000 jobs, withdrew from such lines as auto insurance, and sold its profitable American Reinsurance.

To take advantage of the boom in retirement savings, Aetna got permission to set up bank AE Trust in 1995 to act as a pension trustee.

With its health care business accounting for some 60% of sales by 1995, the company restructured in the late 1990s. Aetna sold its property/casualty, behavioral managed care (1997), and individual life insurance (1998) businesses. It then expanded overseas and bought U.S. Healthcare and New York Life's NYLCare managed health business (1998).

Controversy marred 1998. Contract terms — including a "gag" clause against discussing uncovered treatments — prompted 400 Texas doctors to leave its system; defections followed in Kentucky and West Virginia. Consumers balked over Aetna's refusal to cover some treatments, including experimental procedures and advanced fertility treatments. One group sued for false advertising.

The American Medical Association that year decried Aetna's plan to buy Prudential's health care unit as anticompetitive; in 1999 the government required Aetna to sell operations, including NYLCare (completed 2000), to gain approval. Also in 1999 Aetna became the second insurer (after Humana) to be sued for misleading clients about treatment decisions; it reached a settlement the next year with the State of Texas over capitation, physician incentives, and other matters.

In 2000 Aetna restated earnings for seven previous quarters at the behest of the SEC. Flagging earnings prompted CEO Richard Huber to resign; William Donaldson, one of the founders of Donaldson, Lufkin & Jenrette, now Credit Suisse First Boston (USA), took his place. Also in 2000 Aetna went through major restructuring and sold its financial services and international divisions to Netherlands-based ING Groep.

Jack Rowe took over the helm as CEO in 2001 and announced that Aetna may require two years to recover from turbulent changes and rising medical costs.

OFFICERS

Chairman, President, and CEO: John W. Rowe, age 57,
$2,000,000 pay
President: Ronald A. Williams, age 52, $1,221,538 pay
Chief of Staff: Patricia Hassett
EVP, Strategy and Finance: David B. Kelso, age 49,
$588,462 pay
EVP and General Counsel: L. Edward Shaw Jr.,
$945,000 pay
SVP and CFO: Alan M. Bennett, age 51
SVP and CIO: Wei-Tih Cheng
SVP and Chief Medical Officer: William C. Popik, age 56
SVP and Chief Investment Officer: Timothy A. Holt
SVP, Corporate Communications: Roger Bolton
SVP, Federal Government Relations:
Vanda B. McMurtry
SVP, Human Resources: Elease E. Wright
SVP, Strategic Marketing and Consumer Insights:
Arthur Redmond, age 48
VP and Controller: Ronald M. Olejniczak
VP and Corporate Secretary: William J. Casazza
**VP, Sales and Service, Maryland, Virginia and
Washington, D.C. Markets:** Nancy Dudman-Cavalier
VP, Investor Relations: Dennis Oakes, age 50
VP, Public Relations: Roy Clason Jr., age 39
Head of Aetna Group Insurance: Doug Ahn, age 42
Regional Manager, Mid-Atlantic Region:
Felicia Norwood
Auditors: KPMG LLP

LOCATIONS

HQ: 151 Farmington Ave., Hartford, CT 06156
Phone: 860-273-0123   **Fax:** 860-273-3971
Web: www.aetna.com

Aetna operates throughout the US.

PRODUCTS/OPERATIONS

2001 Sales

	$ mil.	% of total
Premiums		
Health care	19,940	80
Other	1,832	7
Administrative services	1,835	7
Investments	1,412	6
Other	76	—
Adjustments	96	—
Total	**25,191**	**100**

COMPETITORS

Blue Cross
CIGNA
Guardian Life
Health Net
Humana
Kaiser Foundation
Mid Atlantic Medical
Oxford Health Plans
PacifiCare
Prudential
UniHealth
UnitedHealth Group
USAA
WellPoint Health Networks

HISTORICAL FINANCIALS & EMPLOYEES

NYSE: AET FYE: December 31	Annual Growth	12/92	12/93	12/94	12/95	12/96	12/97	12/98	12/99	12/00	12/01
Sales ($ mil.)	4.1%	17,497	17,118	17,525	12,978	15,163	18,540	20,604	26,453	26,819	25,191
Net income ($ mil.)	—	230	(366)	468	252	651	901	848	717	127	(280)
Income as % of sales	—	1.3%	—	2.7%	1.9%	4.3%	4.9%	4.1%	2.7%	0.5%	—
Earnings per share ($)	—	0.49	(3.30)	4.13	2.18	4.73	5.59	5.41	4.73	0.90	(1.95)
Stock price - FY high ($)	—	24.84	33.67	33.42	39.01	41.93	60.04	45.43	50.76	42.38	42.69
Stock price - FY low ($)	—	19.31	22.05	21.47	23.76	28.14	33.70	30.59	23.63	19.57	23.01
Stock price - FY close ($)	3.8%	23.63	30.69	23.95	35.20	40.66	35.86	39.96	28.37	41.06	32.99
P/E - high	—	21	—	8	18	9	11	8	11	47	—
P/E - low	—	17	—	5	11	6	6	6	5	22	—
Dividends per share ($)	(37.5%)	2.76	2.76	2.76	2.76	2.46	0.81	0.81	0.81	0.80	0.04
Book value per share ($)	0.5%	65.66	62.79	48.86	63.41	72.58	76.81	80.64	74.94	71.01	68.56
Employees	(2.0%)	43,000	42,600	40,900	40,200	38,600	40,300	33,500	55,900	40,700	35,700

STOCK PRICE HISTORY

HIGH/LOW/CLOSE

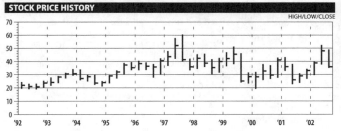

2001 FISCAL YEAR-END

Debt ratio: 13.9%
Return on equity: —
Cash ($ mil.): —
Current ratio: —
Long-term debt ($ mil.): 1,591
No. of shares (mil.): 144
Dividends
 Yield: 0.1%
 Payout: —
Market value ($ mil.): 4,759

AFFILIATED COMPUTER SERVICES

Affiliated Computer Services, Inc. (ACS) makes money out of the mundane. The Dallas-based company generates nearly half of its sales from its business process outsourcing division, which processes, scans, and analyzes company documents such as health care invoices and financial transactions. ACS's services include data processing (loan and mortgage, accounts payable), systems integration, network management, Internet/intranet development, supply chain management, and custom programming. The company also offers program management, processing services, and consulting for state and local governments' health and human services agencies.

Commercial clients, such as Motorola and Blue Cross and Blue Shield, bring in about two-thirds of sales. The rest comes from contracts with various agencies of the US government, including the Senate, the Labor Department, and the National Security Agency.

The company has acquired more than 50 businesses since its founding in 1988, including its $825 million purchase of Lockheed Martin's IMS subsidiary.

Founder and chairman Darwin Deason owns 12% of ACS, and controls about 45% of the voting power.

HISTORY

In 1967 Darwin Deason took over a company called Affiliated Computer Services (ACS). Eight years later he sold that company to Dallas-based MTech, but stayed on as its president. Under Deason, ACS helped MTech become the US's largest provider of financial data processing. When MTech was bought by General Motors subsidiary Electronic Data Systems in 1988, Deason left to start an entirely new ACS.

The new company was created as a financial computer services provider, focused on processing bank transactions. Its 1992 acquisition of Dataplex ushered the company into business process outsourcing, and ACS went public two years later. ACS's 1995 acquisition of The Systems Group extended the company's offerings to include professional services.

The company continued pursuing its rapid rate of growth throughout the late 1990s, building a string of acquisitions that included Intelligent Solutions (1997), Computer Data Systems (1997), Betac International (1998), and Canmax's retail systems subsidiary (1998). In 1998 ACS agreed to buy the Unclaimed Property Services Division of State Street Corporation. Early the following year it acquired information technology (IT) services company BRC Holdings.

Deason also stepped down as CEO (he remains chairman), passing the reigns to president Jeffrey Rich, a former Citibank investment banker. Later in 1999 ACS bought Consultec, a provider of IT services for state health programs, from General American Life in a $105 million deal.

In 2000 the company sold its ATM business for about $180 million. It also boosted its government outsourcing capabilities with the acquisition of Intellisource Group. Additionally, it bought Birch & Davis, a provider of management and consulting services to federal and state government agencies that manage government health care programs, for approximately $75 million.

Also in 2000 ACS's Defense business unit signed a deal with J.S. Wurzler Underwriting Managers to provide a total risk management service, offering online security services and insurance against potential losses from business outages caused by online security breaches.

In 2001 ACS acquired Lockheed Martin's IMS subsidiary, which provides outsourcing services to municipal and state governments, for $825 million. Also that year ACS acquired the business process outsourcing services unit of National Processing Company, which was a subsidiary of National Processing, Inc. for $42 million. The unit provides health care claim, credit card application, and airline lift ticket processing.

Also in 2001 it bought Systems & Computer Technology's Global Government Solutions unit, a provider of outsourcing services to local and state governments, for $85 million. It also acquired Tyler Technologies' subsidiary Business Resources Corporation, a provider of records management, document workflow, and imaging services to state and local governments, for $71 million.

In 2002 the company acquired FleetBoston Financial education services subsidiary AFSA Data for about $410 million, and with it a student loan portfolio worth about $85 billion. Also that year COO Mark King took over the president post from Rich, who remained CEO.

OFFICERS

Chairman: Darwin Deason, age 61, $2,010,045 pay
CEO and Director: Jeffrey A. Rich, age 41,
$1,500,000 pay (prior to title change)
President, COO, and Director: Mark A. King, age 44,
$933,000 pay (prior to promotion)
EVP and CFO: Warren Edwards
EVP; Group President, Government Services:
Harvey Braswell, $582,596 pay
EVP, General Counsel, Secretary, and Director:
William L. Deckelman Jr., age 44

EVP, Global Business Development; Director:
Henry G. Hortenstine, age 57, $750,000 pay
EVP, Mergers and Acquisitions: John Rexford
SVP, Human Resources: Lora Villarreal
Group President, Business Process Solutions:
Lynn Blodgett, $486,000 pay
Group President, State and Local Solutions:
John M. Brophy
Group President, IT Solutions: Donald G. Liedtke
Public Affairs Officer: Audrey Rowe
VP, Real Estate: David Jarrett
Auditors: PricewaterhouseCoopers LLP

LOCATIONS

HQ: 2828 N. Haskell Ave., Dallas, TX 75204
Phone: 214-841-6111   **Fax:** 214-821-8315
Web: www.acs-inc.com

Affiliated Computer Services has more than 200 offices
worldwide.

PRODUCTS/OPERATIONS

2001 Sales

	$ mil.	% of sales
Business process outsourcing	974	47
Systems integration services	649	31
Technology outsourcing	441	22
Total	**2,064**	**100**

Selected Services
Business process outsourcing
  Accounts payable and accounts receivable
    administration
  Benefits and claims administration
  Check processing
  Customer care and support
  Loan processing and administration
  Merchandise fulfillment
  Shareholder support
  Supply chain management
  Trade marketing
Professional support
  Contract programming
  Network design and installation
  Systems conversion
  Systems development
  Telecommunications integration
Technology outsourcing
  Call center support
  Client/server support
  Desktop support
  Hardware and software procurement
  Help desk support
  Network management, support, and maintenance
  Online and batch data processing
  Telemarketing support

COMPETITORS

Accenture	Fiserv
ADP	IBM
BISYS	ManTech
Cap Gemini	Perot Systems
Computer Sciences	SAIC
EDS	Unisys
First Data	

HISTORICAL FINANCIALS & EMPLOYEES

NYSE: ACS FYE: June 30	Annual Growth	6/92	6/93	6/94	6/95	6/96	6/97	6/98	6/99	6/00	6/01
Sales ($ mil.)	33.8%	150	189	271	313	397	625	1,189	1,642	1,963	2,064
Net income ($ mil.)	44.4%	5	10	12	18	24	39	54	86	109	134
Income as % of sales	—	3.3%	5.0%	4.5%	5.6%	6.0%	6.2%	4.6%	5.2%	5.6%	6.5%
Earnings per share ($)	22.7%	—	—	—	0.36	0.43	0.53	0.56	0.83	1.04	1.23
Stock price - FY high ($)	—	—	—	—	7.88	13.44	16.00	19.88	25.88	26.50	38.84
Stock price - FY low ($)	—	—	—	—	4.25	6.94	9.75	10.75	11.19	15.50	16.31
Stock price - FY close ($)	29.5%	—	—	—	7.63	11.75	14.00	19.25	25.31	16.56	35.96
P/E - high	—	—	—	—	21	31	30	35	29	24	29
P/E - low	—	—	—	—	11	16	18	19	13	14	12
Dividends per share ($)	—	—	—	—	0.00	0.00	0.00	0.00	0.00	0.00	0.00
Book value per share ($)	27.6%	—	—	—	2.03	4.30	4.85	5.22	6.17	7.17	8.75
Employees	32.6%	—	2,200	2,200	2,800	5,580	7,030	12,300	15,700	18,500	21,000

STOCK PRICE HISTORY   HIGH/LOW/CLOSE

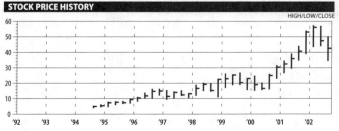

2001 FISCAL YEAR-END
Debt ratio: 42.3%
Return on equity: 16.8%
Cash ($ mil.): 243
Current ratio: 2.88
Long-term debt ($ mil.): 649
No. of shares (mil.): 101
Dividends
  Yield: —
  Payout: —
Market value ($ mil.): 3,638

AFLAC INCORPORATED

AFLAC has taken enough flack for selling "dread disease" and cancer insurance policies. The company sells plenty of accident/disability premiums, too.

Despite its US roots, AFLAC makes most of its insurance sales in Japan. In the US, AFLAC sells insurance that supplements customers' existing medical policies. The Columbus, Georgia-based company sells policies that pay cash benefits for hospital confinement, emergency treatment, and medical appliances. The company also offers on- and off-the-job disability insurance.

AFLAC's reliance on Japan (about 80% of its sales) has a downside: The company is vulnerable to currency fluctuations between the dollar and the yen. It also faces increased competition because of deregulation of Japan's insurance industry.

In Japan, AFLAC primarily sells through an agency system in which a corporation forms a subsidiary to sell AFLAC insurance to its employees. The company also has a marketing alliance with Dai-ichi Mutual Life, Japan's second-largest life insurer. The company's US approach is similar in that AFLAC sells to individuals through their workplaces.

Moving to a tax-friendlier climate, AFLAC plans to relocate its charter from Georgia to Nebraska before the end of 2002.

HISTORY

American Family Life Assurance Co. (AFLAC) was founded in Columbus, Georgia, in 1955 by brothers John, Paul, and William Amos to sell life, health, and accident insurance. Competition was fierce, and the little company did poorly.

With AFLAC nearing bankruptcy, the brothers looked for a niche.

The polio scares of the 1940s and 1950s had spawned insurance coverage written especially against that disease; the Amos brothers (whose father was a cancer victim) took a cue from that concept and decided to sell cancer insurance. In 1958 they introduced the world's first cancer-expense policy. It was a hit, and by 1959 the company had written nearly a million dollars in premiums and expanded across state lines.

The enterprise grew quickly during the 1960s, especially after developing its cluster-selling approach in the workplace, where employers were usually willing to make payroll deductions for premiums. By 1971 the company was operating in 42 states.

While visiting the World's Fair in Osaka in 1970, John Amos decided to market supplemental cancer coverage to the Japanese, whose national health care plan left them exposed to considerable expense from cancer treatment. After four years the company finally won approval to sell in Japan because the policies did not threaten existing markets and because the Amoses found notable backers in the insurance and medical industries. AFLAC became one of the first US insurance companies to enter the Japanese market, and it enjoyed an eight-year monopoly on the cancer market. In 1973 AFLAC organized a holding company and began buying television stations in the South and Midwest.

The 1980s were marked by US and state government inquiries into dread disease insurance. Critics said such policies were a poor value because they were relatively expensive and covered only one disease. However, the inquiries led nowhere and demand for such insurance increased, bringing new competition. In the 1980s, AFLAC's scales tilted: US growth slowed, while business grew in Japan, which soon accounted for most of the company's sales.

In 1990 John Amos died of cancer and was replaced as CEO by his nephew Dan. Two years later the company officially renamed itself AFLAC (partly because Dan planned to increase the company's US profile and so many US companies already used the name "American").

AFLAC has sought to supplement its cancer insurance by introducing new products and improving old ones to encourage policyholders to add on or trade up. Its Japanese "living benefit" product, which includes lump sum payments for heart attacks and strokes, struck a chord with the aging population.

Connecticut repealed its ban on specified-disease insurance in 1997, and New York eventually followed suit. Also in 1997 AFLAC sold its seven TV stations to Raycom Media to concentrate on insurance.

The company boosted its name recognition in the US from 2% in 1990 to more than 56%, primarily through advertising, including slots during the 1998 Olympic Winter Games and NASCAR races. In 1999 the company signed a three-year cross-selling agreement for its supplemental insurance with what is now HR Logic, a human resources outsourcing firm.

Accident/disability premiums surpassed cancer premiums in the US for the first time in the company's history in 2000. Facing up to Japan's deregulated life insurance industry, AFLAC formed a marketing alliance with one of Japan's biggest life insurers, Dai-ichi Mutual Life.

Chairman and CEO, AFLAC Incorporated and AFLAC:
Daniel P. Amos, age 50, $2,476,754 pay
President, CFO, Treasurer, and Director:
Kriss Cloninger III, age 54, $1,300,956 pay
EVP, Corporate Finance, AFLAC Incorporated and AFLAC: Norman P. Foster, age 66
EVP, Deputy Legal Counsel, Assistant Secretary, and Director of Corporate Communications:
Kathelen V. Spencer, age 44
EVP, General Counsel, and Corporate Secretary/ Director of Legal and Governmental Relations, AFLAC: Joey M. Loudermilk, age 48
SVP, Corporate Risk Management: Mark E. Shaw
SVP, Investor Relations: Kenneth S. Janke Jr.
SVP and Chief Investment Officer: Joseph W. Smith Jr.
SVP and Corporate Actuary: Kermitt L. Cox
SVP and Director of Human Resources:
Audrey B. Tillman
Chairman, AFLAC Japan and Director: Yoshiki Otake, age 62, $1,066,319 pay
Chairman, AFLAC International: Minoru Nakai, age 59
President, AFLAC International; Deputy CFO, AFLAC Incorporated; President, aflacdirect.com:
Allan O'Bryant, age 43
President, AFLAC Japan: Hidefumi Matsui, age 57, $793,893 pay
Auditors: KPMG LLP

LOCATIONS

HQ: 1932 Wynnton Rd., Columbus, GA 31999
Phone: 706-323-3431   **Fax:** 706-324-6330
Web: www.aflac.com

AFLAC conducts business throughout the US and several of its territories and in Japan.

PRODUCTS/OPERATIONS

2001 Sales

	$ mil.	% of total
AFLAC Japan		
Cancer life premiums	4,508	47
Other accident & health	1,075	11
Life insurance & annuities	634	7
Investments & other	1,235	13
AFLAC U.S.		
Cancer expense	654	7
Accident/disability	713	7
Other health	416	4
Life insurance	61	1
Investments & other	311	3
Adjustments	(9)	
Total	**9,598**	**100**

COMPETITORS

Allianz	Jefferson-Pilot
AIG	Lincoln National
American National Insurance	MetLife
	Provident Mutual
Aon	Sony
AXA Nichidan Life Insurance	Taiyo Mutual Life
	Torchmark
Conseco	UnitedHealth Group
Daido Life Insurance	UNUMProvident
ING	

HISTORICAL FINANCIALS & EMPLOYEES

NYSE: AFL FYE: December 31	Annual Growth	12/92	12/93	12/94	12/95	12/96	12/97	12/98	12/99	12/00	12/01
Assets ($ mil.)	13.7%	11,901	15,443	20,287	25,338	25,023	29,454	31,183	37,041	37,232	37,860
Net income ($ mil.)	15.8%	183	255	293	349	394	585	487	571	687	687
Income as % of assets	—	1.5%	1.7%	1.4%	1.4%	1.6%	2.0%	1.6%	1.5%	1.8%	1.8%
Earnings per share ($)	17.5%	0.30	0.41	0.48	0.59	0.69	1.04	0.88	1.04	1.26	1.28
Stock price - FY high ($)	—	4.65	5.67	6.02	7.46	11.00	14.47	22.66	28.38	37.47	36.09
Stock price - FY low ($)	—	3.20	4.13	4.21	5.32	7.06	9.38	11.34	19.50	16.78	23.00
Stock price - FY close ($)	20.5%	4.60	4.75	5.34	7.25	10.69	12.78	21.94	23.59	36.09	24.56
P/E - high	—	16	14	12	12	15	13	25	26	29	28
P/E - low	—	11	10	9	9	10	9	12	18	13	18
Dividends per share ($)	13.7%	0.06	0.07	0.08	0.09	0.10	0.12	0.13	0.15	0.17	0.19
Book value per share ($)	21.9%	1.75	2.20	2.93	3.76	3.85	6.44	7.09	7.28	8.87	10.40
Employees	5.3%	3,618	3,902	4,321	4,070	4,421	4,032	4,450	4,673	5,015	5,739

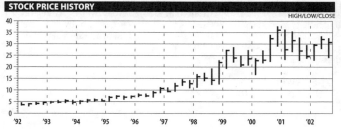

STOCK PRICE HISTORY HIGH/LOW/CLOSE

2001 FISCAL YEAR-END
Equity as % of assets: 14.3%
Return on assets: 1.8%
Return on equity: 13.6%
Long-term debt ($ mil.): 1,207
No. of shares (mil.): 522
Dividends
  Yield: 0.8%
  Payout: 14.8%
Market value ($ mil.): 12,811
Sales ($ mil.): 9,598

A.G. EDWARDS, INC.

With an attitude that's more Main Street than Wall Street, A.G. Edwards brings a midwestern sensibility to the investment business.

The St. Louis-based company owns investment firm A.G. Edwards & Sons, which operates one of the US's largest retail brokerage networks with some 700 offices nationwide. It provides securities and commodities brokerage, asset management, trust services, insurance, mortgage services, and investment banking to individual, corporate, government, and institutional clients. The firm also specializes in underwriting bonds for such public projects as schools and sports facilities.

Unlike most competitors, A.G. Edwards' brokers have no sales quotas. Traditionally a commission-based brokerage, the firm reluctantly added fee-based transactions on some types of accounts in order to keep pace with discount brokers and full-service firms that have discount operations. The company offers no proprietary mutual funds but does offer two fund advisory programs, Fund Navigator and Pathways, for a fee. A.G. Edwards had been family-run for four generations until chairman Robert Bagby took the helm in 2001.

Like most other brokers, A.G. Edwards has been hurt as investors have shied away from the market. To cut costs, the firm cut approximately 400 workers in early 2002, mostly from its nonbranch workforce.

HISTORY

A. G. Edwards was born in 1812, six years before Illinois became a state. His father, Ninian Edwards (later the third governor of Illinois), named the child Albert Gallatin, after the secretary of the treasury during the presidencies of Jefferson and Madison.

When the Civil War broke out in 1861, the Edwardses were fiercely loyal to Lincoln and the Union. Albert was a brigadier general in the Missouri state militia, then was appointed assistant secretary of the US Treasury in 1865, just six days before Abraham Lincoln's assassination. After serving five presidents, he retired in 1887 at age 75. Less than a year later he and his eldest son, Benjamin Franklin Edwards, formed brokerage firm A.G. Edwards & Son to handle trades on the NYSE for St. Louis banks. Albert died in 1892.

The brokerage survived the 1890s recession through conservative fiscal policies and in 1898 bought a seat on the NYSE. Two years later it opened a Wall Street office. After WWI the firm began targeting new middle-class investors. It handled its first IPO in 1925.

Although the firm weathered the Wall Street crash of 1929 better than many, the Depression and skepticism about investments made the 1930s a tough decade. But as a testament to A.G. Edwards' reputation, floor manager William McChesney Martin was elected the NYSE's first paid president in 1938. The company had six offices in 1940; four closed during WWII.

Third-generation president Presley Edwards (1929 to 1965) attended an IBM seminar in 1948 and, impressed by the new technology, had a computer system installed at company headquarters in St. Louis. In the postwar boom A.G. Edwards grew its branch network to 19 offices and 200 brokers by 1960.

Benjamin Edwards III, great-grandson of the founder, took over in 1965 and restructured the company, placing its emphasis squarely on retail business. To this end, the company, which went public in 1971, expanded its retail offices in small communities from 44 in the mid-1960s to 450 in the early 1990s.

In 1990 the firm installed a satellite-based communications system to link its headquarters with its branch offices. In 1994 it introduced a computerized bond-processing system and the Edwards Information Network, a regularly updated electronic information service for brokers. It put up its own Web site in 1996 to give investors access to investment information.

In 1997, in the face of the inevitable, A.G. Edwards began following the lead of the competition and introduced straight execution services as an alternative to its commissioned accounts. However, company brokers weren't happy about it, cautioning that clients rarely become wealthy when they trade on their own account. The company expanded its headquarters and added almost 500 more employees in 1998. It also received a thrift charter that would allow it to conduct its trust business nationwide; in 2000 the firm announced plans to consolidate its trust subsidiaries under this federal charter.

Realizing that resistance was futile, in 1999 A.G. Edwards gave in to the pressure of the competition and announced plans to offer online trading beginning in late 2000. It held the line against discounting, however, offering only its traditional commission services.

Chairman Benjamin Edwards III retired in 2001. His successor, Robert Bagby, became the first person from outside the Edwards family to head the company.

OFFICERS

Chairman and CEO, A.G. Edwards and A.G. Edwards & Sons: Robert L. Bagby, age 58, $1,103,985 pay
Vice Chairman and President: Benjamin F. Edwards IV, age 45, $681,495 pay
Vice Chairman and EVP, Director of Operations: Ronald J. Kessler, age 54, $580,676 pay
VP, CFO, Secretary, and Treasurer; EVP, CFO, Secretary, Director of Law and Compliance, and Treasurer, A.G. Edwards & Sons: Douglas L. Kelly, age 53, $592,391 pay
EVP and Director of Branch Division, A.G. Edwards & Sons: Robert A. Pietroburgo, age 45
EVP and Director of Investment Banking, A.G. Edwards & Sons: Paul F. Pautler, age 57
EVP and Director of Market Analysis, A.G. Edwards & Sons: Alfred E. Goldman, age 68, $597,952 pay
EVP and Director of Staff Division, A.G. Edwards & Sons: Donnis L. Casey, age 54
EVP, A.G. Edwards & Sons; President, A.G. Edwards Technology Group: Mary V. Atkin, age 47
SVP and Regional Manager, A.G. Edwards & Sons: Charles J. Galli, age 61
Chairman and CEO, A.G. Edwards Trust Company: Richard F. Grabish, age 53
Head of Sales and Marketing: Pete M. Miller, age 44
Auditors: Deloitte & Touche LLP

LOCATIONS

HQ: 1 N. Jefferson Ave., St. Louis, MO 63103
Phone: 314-955-3000   **Fax:** 314-955-5402
Web: www.agedwards.com

A.G. Edwards has offices across the US and in London.

PRODUCTS/OPERATIONS

2002 Sales

	$ mil.	% of total
Commissions	950	40
Asset management & service fees	659	28
Principal transactions	320	14
Investment banking	256	11
Interest	172	7
Other	7	—
Total	**2,364**	**100**

Selected Subsidiaries
A.G. Edwards Capital, Inc.
A.G. Edwards Life Insurance Company
A.G. Edwards Trust Company
A.G.E. Properties, Inc.
AGE Capital Holding, Inc.
AGE Commodity Clearing Corp.
AGE International, Inc.
CPI Qualified Plan Consultants, Inc.
Edwards Development Corporation
GULL-AGE Capital Group, Inc.

COMPETITORS

Ameritrade	Morgan Keegan
Charles Schwab	Morgan Stanley
CIBC World Markets	Principal Financial
E*TRADE	Quick & Reilly/Fleet
FMR	Raymond James Financial
Harrisdirect	SEI
Jones Financial Companies	Siebert Financial
J.P. Morgan H&Q	Stephens
Lehman Brothers	TD Waterhouse
Merrill Lynch	UBS PaineWebber
	U. S. Bancorp Piper Jaffray

HISTORICAL FINANCIALS & EMPLOYEES

NYSE: AGE FYE: Last day in February	Annual Growth	2/93	2/94	2/95	2/96	2/97	2/98	2/99	2/00	2/01	2/02
Sales ($ mil.)	9.2%	1,074	1,279	1,178	1,455	1,697	2,004	2,241	2,819	2,839	2,364
Net income ($ mil.)	(5.5%)	119	155	124	171	219	269	292	383	288	72
Income as % of sales	—	11.1%	12.1%	10.5%	11.7%	12.9%	13.4%	13.0%	13.6%	10.1%	3.0%
Earnings per share ($)	(4.7%)	1.37	1.71	1.33	1.77	2.24	2.75	3.00	4.08	3.43	0.89
Stock price - FY high ($)	—	14.81	16.94	15.01	18.01	27.51	43.00	48.81	38.19	57.94	48.29
Stock price - FY low ($)	—	9.20	12.01	11.01	13.59	15.01	20.51	22.63	24.25	31.50	29.76
Stock price - FY close ($)	13.1%	13.47	14.84	15.01	16.17	23.68	42.25	32.56	31.69	38.87	40.85
P/E - high	—	11	10	11	10	12	15	16	9	17	55
P/E - low	—	7	7	8	8	7	7	7	6	9	34
Dividends per share ($)	9.6%	0.28	0.33	0.37	0.39	0.43	0.50	0.55	0.60	0.64	0.64
Book value per share ($)	12.4%	7.11	8.72	9.84	11.70	13.13	15.21	17.16	19.69	20.29	20.42
Employees	6.5%	9,487	10,206	10,471	11,279	12,031	12,967	13,953	15,451	17,000	16,700

STOCK PRICE HISTORY

HIGH/LOW/CLOSE

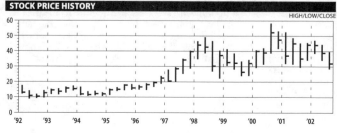

2002 FISCAL YEAR-END

Debt ratio: 0.0%
Return on equity: 4.4%
Cash ($ mil.): —
Current ratio: —
Long-term debt ($ mil.): 0
No. of shares (mil.): 81
Dividends
  Yield: 1.6%
  Payout: 71.9%
Market value ($ mil.): 3,296

AGCO CORPORATION

AGCO has turned its dream of fields into reality. Based in Duluth, Georgia, the company is the third-largest US farm equipment maker, behind leaders #1, Deere and #2, CNH Global. AGCO sells tractors, rotary combines, harvesters, sprayers, related spare parts, and other farm equipment under more than a dozen brand names, including Massey Ferguson, GLEANER, Fendt, and Tye. AGCO offers financing services to customers and some of its 7,350 dealers through a joint venture with Netherlands-based Rabobank. AGCO also distributes tractors made by Italy-based SAME Deutz-Fahr, which has a 10% stake in AGCO. The company sells its products in more than 140 countries.

AGCO has rapidly increased its product line by acquiring makers of other well-known brands of farm equipment, including agricultural equipment maker Ag-Chem Equipment and Caterpillar's high-tech MT tractor line. With its broad brand variety, AGCO tries to keep costs low by maintaining common parts platforms among them. Decreased demand for agricultural equipment worldwide has contributed to sluggish sales for AGCO, which has been trimming its workforce and the number of its manufacturing plants.

AGCO suffered a tragic loss in early 2002 when president and CEO John Shumejda and SVP Ed Swingle were killed in an airplane accident in the UK. Chairman Robert Ratliff was appointed president and CEO in the wake of the accident.

HISTORY

In 1861 American Edward Allis purchased the bankrupt Reliance Works, a leading Milwaukee-based manufacturer of sawmills and flour-milling equipment. Under shrewd management, The Reliance Works of Edward P. Allis & Co. weathered financial troubles — bankruptcy in the Panic of 1873 — but managed to renegotiate its debt and recover. By the time Allis died in 1889, Reliance Works employed some 1,500 workers.

The company branched into different areas of manufacturing in the late 19th century, and by the 20th century the Edward P. Allis Co. (as it was then known) was the world leader in steam engines. In 1901 the company merged with another manufacturing giant, Fraser & Chalmers, to form the Allis-Chalmers Company. In the 1920s and 1930s, Allis-Chalmers entered the farm equipment market.

Although overshadowed by John Deere and International Harvester (IH), Allis-Chalmers made key contributions to the industry — the first rubber-tired tractor (1932) and the All-Crop harvester. Allis-Chalmers spun off its farm equipment business in the 1950s, and phased out

several unrelated products. The company, with its orange-colored tractors, expanded and prospered from the 1940s through the early 1970s. Then the chaffing farm economy of the late 1970s and early 1980s hurt Allis-Chalmers' sales.

After layoffs and a plant shutdown in 1984, the company was purchased in 1985 by German machinery maker Klockner-Humbolt-Deutz (KHD), who moved the company (renamed Deutz-Allis) to Georgia. In the mid-1980s low food prices hurt farmers and low demand hurt the equipment market. KHD was never able to bring profits up to a satisfactory level, and in 1990 the German firm sold the unit to the US management in a buyout led by Robert Ratliff. Ratliff believed the company could succeed by acquiring belly-up equipment makers, turning them around, and competing on price.

Renamed AGCO, the company launched a buying spree in 1991 that included Fiat's Hesston (1991), White Tractor (1991), the North American distribution rights for Massey Ferguson (1993), and White-New Idea (1993). The bumper crop of product growth enabled AGCO to slice into competitors Deere and Case's market share. AGCO went public in 1992. Its 1994 purchase of the remainder of Massey Ferguson (with 20% of the world market) vaulted AGCO among world's leading farm equipment makers.

In 1996 AGCO launched a five-year plan for European growth. In 1997 the company acquired German farm equipment makers Fendt and Dronniberg. It also picked up Deutz Argentina, a supplier of agricultural equipment, engines, and vehicles, as part of an effort to expand into Latin and South America.

AGCO entered the agricultural sprayer market in 1998 by acquiring the Spra-Coupe line from Ingersoll-Rand and the Willmar line from Cargill. A worldwide drop in farm equipment sales caused AGCO to cut about 10% of its workforce.

To further overcome stalled sales and slumping profits, in 1999 the company announced it was permanently closing an Ohio plant and would cease production at a Texas plant. The next year AGCO closed its Missouri plant and trimmed its workforce by about 5%.

In 2001 AGCO acquired fertilizer equipment manufacturer Ag-Chem Equipment, and the next year it completed the purchase of certain assets relating to the design, assembly, and marketing of the MT 700 and MT 800 series of Caterpillar's Challenger rubber-tracked farm tractors.

OFFICERS

Chairman, President, and CEO: Robert J. Ratliff, age 70, $1,000,000 pay
EVP and COO: Donald R. Millard, age 53, $472,516 pay
SVP and Chief Financial Officer: Andrew Beck
SVP, Corporate Development and General Counsel: Stephen D. Lupton, age 57
SVP, Corporate Human Relations: Norman L. Boyd, age 58, $328,881 pay
SVP, Engineering and Product Development: Garry L. Ball, age 54
SVP, Manufacturing Technologies and Quality: Brian C. Truex, age 42
SVP, Sales and Marketing Worldwide: James M. Seaver, age 55
SVP, Special Projects: Adri Verhagen, age 60
SVP, Product Development: Dexter E. Schaible, age 51
CIO: Jose Marrero
Auditors: KPMG LLP

LOCATIONS

HQ: 4205 River Green Pkwy., Duluth, GA 30096
Phone: 770-813-9200   **Fax:** 770-813-6118
Web: www.agcocorp.com

2001 Sales

	$ mil.	% of total
Europe	1,164	45
North America	870	35
South America	249	10
Asia	50	2
Australia	48	2
Africa	29	1
Other regions	132	5
Total	**2,542**	**100**

PRODUCTS/OPERATIONS

2001 Sales

	$ mil.	% of total
Tractors	1,470	58
Replacement parts	472	19
Combines	195	8
Sprayers	154	6
Other machinery	251	9
Total	**2,542**	**100**

Selected Products and Brand Names

Combines	Massey Ferguson
AGCO Allis	White
Deutz	
Fendt	**Other**
GLEANER	Hay and Forage Equipment
Massey Ferguson	AGCO Allis
	Hesston
Tractors	Massey Ferguson
AGCO Allis	White-New Idea
Challenger MT	Implements and Planters
Deutz	AGCO Allis
Fendt	Deutz
Massey Ferguson	Farmhand
White	Glencoe
	Massey Ferguson
Utility Tractors	White-New Idea
AGCO Allis	Willmar
Deutz	
Fendt	

COMPETITORS

Caterpillar	Partek
CNH Global	Steyr-Daimler-Puch
Deere	Aktiengesellschaft
Kubota	Volvo

HISTORICAL FINANCIALS & EMPLOYEES

NYSE: AG FYE: December 31	Annual Growth	12/92	12/93	12/94	12/95	12/96	12/97	12/98	12/99	12/00	12/01
Sales ($ mil.)	26.1%	315	596	1,359	2,125	2,318	3,224	2,941	2,413	2,336	2,542
Net income ($ mil.)	15.9%	6	34	116	129	126	169	61	(12)	4	23
Income as % of sales	—	1.9%	5.7%	8.5%	6.1%	5.4%	5.2%	2.1%	—	0.1%	0.9%
Earnings per share ($)	2.3%	0.27	0.93	2.35	2.30	2.20	2.71	0.99	(0.20)	0.06	0.33
Stock price - FY high ($)	—	5.17	11.42	18.38	27.31	31.63	36.31	30.94	14.13	14.50	16.95
Stock price - FY low ($)	—	1.67	3.34	10.76	12.38	19.25	25.00	5.25	6.00	9.44	7.90
Stock price - FY close ($)	18.2%	3.50	11.38	15.19	25.50	28.63	29.25	7.88	13.44	12.13	15.78
P/E - high	—	19	10	6	10	14	13	31	—	242	50
P/E - low	—	6	3	4	4	8	9	5	—	157	23
Dividends per share ($)	0.0%	0.01	0.02	0.02	0.02	0.04	0.04	0.04	0.04	0.04	0.01
Book value per share ($)	13.6%	3.50	7.87	10.99	11.65	13.53	15.75	16.50	13.92	13.26	11.06
Employees	28.3%	1,201	2,417	5,789	5,548	7,800	11,000	10,500	9,300	9,800	11,300

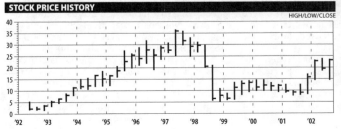

STOCK PRICE HISTORY   HIGH/LOW/CLOSE

2001 FISCAL YEAR-END
Debt ratio: 43.6%
Return on equity: 2.8%
Cash ($ mil.): 29
Current ratio: 1.84
Long-term debt ($ mil.): 618
No. of shares (mil.): 72
Dividends
  Yield: 0.1%
  Payout: 3.0%
Market value ($ mil.): 1,141

AGILENT TECHNOLOGIES, INC.

The quickening pace of advancements in science and technology keeps Agilent Technologies on its toes. The Palo Alto, California-based company, a leading manufacturer of technical analysis equipment and scientific instruments, is the world's top supplier of electrical test and measurement equipment, including multimeters, oscilloscopes, and protocol analyzers used by manufacturers and researchers in the fields of electronics, semiconductors, and telecommunications. Its test and measurement unit, which accounts for two-thirds of Agilent's revenue, also offers a wide range of services, such as consulting on hardware purchases, equipment repair and calibration, and professional engineering services.

In addition to test and measurement equipment, Agilent's semiconductor products division manufactures integrated circuits and fiber-optic devices, primarily for use in communications gear. Its life sciences and chemical analysis unit also makes a wide range of laboratory equipment and scientific instruments. Agilent's customers include global giants such as Bayer, Boeing, Cisco Systems, General Electric, IBM, Merck, Nokia, and Siemens.

That Agilent is a leader in the test and measurement equipment industry should come as no surprise — it is the original business started by technology pioneers William Hewlett and David Packard. Hewlett-Packard spun off the business in 1999 so that it could focus on its computer products operations. Being a leader has not spared the company from tough times in the electronics industry, however. Agilent has made serious job cuts and reduced salaries to control costs, and in 2001 the company sold its health care business (patient monitoring and other clinical measurement and diagnostic equipment) to Philips Electronics. Agilent is depending on its strength in research and development of new products to drive its business and maintain its market leadership.

HISTORY

Agilent Technologies was formed in 1999 when Hewlett-Packard (HP) split off its measurement business. But Agilent's roots run as deep as HP's — Agilent's core products served as the original business of Stanford-trained electrical engineers William Hewlett and David Packard. The friends started HP in 1939 as a test and measurement equipment maker. Their first product, developed in Packard's garage (Hewlett was living in a rented cottage behind Packard's house) was an audio oscillator for testing sound equipment; Walt Disney Studios bought eight to help make the animation classic *Fantasia*.

Demand for electronic test equipment during WWII pushed sales from $34,000 in 1940 (when HP had three employees and eight products) to nearly $1 million three years later. The company entered the microwave field in 1943, creating signal generators for the Naval Research Laboratory. Its postwar line of microwave test products made it a market leader for signal generation equipment.

Expanding beyond the US in the late 1950s, HP established a plant in West Germany. The company went public in 1957. It entered the medical field in 1961 with the purchase of Sanborn, and the analytical instrumentation business in 1965 with the purchase of F&M Scientific. In the 1970s president Hewlett and chairman Packard began shifting HP's focus toward the computer market. Late in that decade they stepped back from day-to-day management (they would retire in 1987 and 1992, respectively).

Sales hit $3 billion in 1980. In 1991 HP broadened its communications component offerings when it bought Avantek. HP moved into the DNA analysis field in 1994 with pharmaceutical research and health care products. David Packard died in 1996. In 1997 HP bought Heartstream, maker of an automatic external defibrillator.

In 1999 HP formed Agilent as a separate company for its test and measurement and other noncomputer operations, which by then accounted for 16% of sales. Edward Barnholt, a 30-year HP veteran, was named CEO of the new company. In a move to energize its computer business, HP spun off 15% of Agilent to the public in November 1999. The remainder was distributed to HP shareholders in mid-2000.

In 2000 Agilent bought Salient 3's subsidiary SAFCO Technologies (engineering services, analysis tools, and wireless network planning software). Later that year Philips Electronics agreed to buy Agilent's Healthcare Solutions unit for $1.7 billion.

In a move to bolster its networking business, Agilent completed its $665 million acquisition of network management software maker Objective Systems Integrators in early 2001. The company also implemented cost-cutting measures such as temporary pay cuts. Later that year, in the face of harsh market conditions, Agilent announced two separate layoffs of 4,000 employees each, representing a total staff reduction of about 18%. William Hewlett died that same year.

In 2002 the company announced plans to consolidate the operations of three older California fabs (wafer fabrication plants) into a new facility in Colorado; the new fab is to specialize in chips made from high-performance indium phosphide (InP) rather than silicon.

OFFICERS

Chairman: Gerald Grinstein, age 69
President, CEO, and Director: Edward W. Barnholt, age 58, $941,666 pay
EVP and COO: William P. Sullivan, age 52, $473,125 pay (prior to promotion)
EVP and CFO: Adrian T. Dillon
SVP and CTO; Director of Agilent Laboratories: Thomas A. Saponas, age 52
SVP, General Counsel, and Secretary: D. Craig Nordlund
SVP and General Manager, Automated Test Group: Jack P. Trautman, age 52
SVP and General Manager, Life Sciences and Chemical Analysis: Chris van Ingen, age 55
SVP and General Manager, Electronics Products and Solutions Group: Byron J. Anderson, age 58, $488,125 pay
SVP Human Resources: Jean M. Halloran, age 49
SVP Sales, Marketing, and Customer Support: Larry Holmberg, age 55
Auditors: PricewaterhouseCoopers LLP

LOCATIONS

HQ: 395 Page Mill Rd. PO Box 10395, Palo Alto, CA 94306
Phone: 650-752-5000   **Fax:** 650-752-5633
Web: www.agilent.com

2001 Sales

	$ mil.	% of total
US	3,373	40
Japan	1,083	13
Other countries	3,940	47
Total	**8,396**	**100**

PRODUCTS/OPERATIONS

2001 Sales

	$ mil.	% of total
Products	7,485	89
Services	911	11
Total	**8,396**	**100**

Product Groups
Chemical Analysis Products
Semiconductor Products
Test and Measurement Products

COMPETITORS

Acterna
Advantest
Affymetrix
Agere Systems
Anritsu
Applied Biosystems
Conexant Systems
Danaher
Emulex
Fisher Scientific
IFR Systems
Inet Technologies
Infineon Technologies
IBM
JDS Uniphase
Keithley Instruments
LeCroy
Lite-On Technology
LSI Logic
Marconi
Networks
Micromuse
Motorola
National Instruments
NEC
Network Associates
NPTest
PerkinElmer
QLogic
RF Micro Devices
Rohde & Schwarz
Shimadzu
Spirent
Tektronix
Teradyne
Texas Instruments
Thermo Electron
Toshiba
Vishay Intertechnology
Vitesse Semiconductor
Waters Corporation

HISTORICAL FINANCIALS & EMPLOYEES

NYSE: A FYE: October 31	Annual Growth	10/92	10/93	10/94	10/95	10/96	10/97	10/98	10/99	10/00	10/01
Sales ($ mil.)	6.1%	—	—	5,546	6,595	7,379	7,785	7,952	8,331	10,773	8,396
Net income ($ mil.)	(7.1%)	—	—	282	499	542	543	257	512	757	168
Income as % of sales	—	—	—	5.1%	7.6%	7.3%	7.0%	3.2%	6.1%	7.0%	2.0%
Earnings per share ($)	(71.1%)	—	—	—	—	—	—	—	—	1.66	0.48
Stock price - FY high ($)	—	—	—	—	—	—	—	—	—	162.00	68.00
Stock price - FY low ($)	—	—	—	—	—	—	—	—	—	38.19	18.00
Stock price - FY close ($)	(52.9%)	—	—	—	—	—	—	—	—	47.25	22.27
P/E - high	—	—	—	—	—	—	—	—	—	96	128
P/E - low	—	—	—	—	—	—	—	—	—	23	34
Dividends per share ($)	—	—	—	—	—	—	—	—	—	0.00	0.00
Book value per share ($)	5.8%	—	—	—	—	—	—	—	—	11.60	12.28
Employees	(1.2%)	—	—	—	—	—	—	—	42,000	47,000	41,000

STOCK PRICE HISTORY

HIGH/LOW/CLOSE

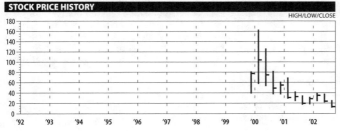

2001 FISCAL YEAR-END

Debt ratio: 0.0%
Return on equity: 3.1%
Cash ($ mil.): 1,170
Current ratio: 2.40
Long-term debt ($ mil.): 0
No. of shares (mil.): 461
Dividends
  Yield: —
  Payout: —
Market value ($ mil.): 10,266

AIR PRODUCTS AND CHEMICALS

Air Products and Chemicals produces the goods that help astronauts breathe easy. A leader in the US industrial and specialty gases markets, the Allentown, Pennsylvania-based company produces argon, helium, hydrogen, nitrogen, oxygen, and other gases which account for almost 70% of sales. Customers include NASA and companies in steel and oil production, chemicals processing, health care, and electronics manufacturing. Air Products distributes industrial gases by building on-site plants (a strategy nearly as old as the company itself) or by truck for companies with less-extensive needs. The company also makes air pollution control systems and gas separation systems.

Air Products' #2 business is chemicals, which accounts for just over a quarter of sales. Its main chemical offerings are chemical intermediates and performance and polymer chemicals, including polyurethanes, amines, epoxy additives and resins, process chemicals, and surfactants.

Air Products and France's L'Air Liquide (the #1 worldwide industrial gas supplier) planned to acquire and break up the #2 player, BOC Group (UK), but the companies stepped back due to regulatory problems. Going forward the company is focused on four growth areas — the electronics industry, the chemical and processing industries, the health care industry, and the Asian region — all of which grew at double-digit rates during 2001 despite the economic woes of the time.

HISTORY

In the early 1900s Leonard Pool, the son of a boilermaker, began selling oxygen to industrial users. By the time he was 30, he was district manager for Compressed Industrial Gases. In the late 1930s Pool hired engineer Frank Pavlis to help him design a cheaper, more-efficient oxygen generator. In 1940 they had the design, and Pool established Air Products in Detroit (initially sharing space with the cadavers collected by his brother, who was starting a mortuary science college). The company was based on a simple, breakthrough concept: the provision of on-site gases. Instead of delivering oxygen in cylinders, Pool proposed to build oxygen-generating facilities near large-volume gas users and then lease them, reducing distribution costs.

Although industrialists encouraged Pool to pursue his ideas, few orders were forthcoming, and the company faced financial crisis. The outbreak of WWII got the company out of difficulty, as the US military became a major customer. During the war the company moved to Chattanooga, Tennessee, for the available labor.

The end of the war brought with it another downturn as demand dried up. By waiting at the Weirton Steel plant until a contract was signed, Pool won a contract for three on-site generators. Weirton was nearly the company's only customer. Pool relocated the company to Allentown, Pennsylvania, to be closer to the Northeast's industrial market, where he could secure more contracts with steel companies.

The Cold War and the launching of the Sputnik satellite in 1957 propelled the company's growth. Convinced that Soviet rockets were powered by liquid hydrogen, the US government asked Air Products to supply it with the volatile fuel. The company entered the overseas market that year through a joint venture with Butterley (UK), to which it licensed its cryogenic processes and equipment. The company went public in 1961 and formed a subsidiary in Belgium in 1964.

Air Products diversified into chemicals when it bought Houdry Process (chemicals and chemical-plant maintenance, 1962) and Airco's plastics and chemicals operations in the 1970s. The company continued to diversify in the mid 1980s as it built large-scale plants for its environmental- and energy-systems business and added Anchor Chemical and the industrial chemicals unit of Abbott Labs.

In 1995 and 1996 Air Products expanded into China and other countries by winning 20 contracts with semiconductor makers. It bought Carburos Metalicos, Spain's #1 industrial gas supplier, in 1996. To focus on its core gas and chemical lines, the company shed most of its environmental- and energy-systems business.

Expanding further in Europe, Air Products bought the methylamines and derivatives unit of UK-based Imperial Chemical Industries (ICI) in 1997. The company sold its remaining interest in American Ref-Fuel (a waste-to-energy US operation).

In 1999 Air Products and France's L'Air Liquide agreed to buy and break up BOC Group. European Union regulators initially approved the deal, but in 2000 the companies shelved the plan when regulatory issues arose. Also in 2000 Air Products sold its polyvinyl alcohol business to Celanese for about $326 million. The company boosted its European presence in 2001 with the acquisition of Messer Griesheim's (Germany) respiratory home-care business and 50% of AGA's Netherlands industrial gases operations.

OFFICERS

Chairman, President, and CEO: John P. Jones III, age 50, $1,665,000 pay
EVP, Gases and Equipment: Robert E. Gadomski, age 53, $1,023,000 pay
Group VP, Chemicals: Andrew E. Cummins, age 56, $651,000 pay
Group VP, Engineered Systems and Development: Arthur T. Katsaros
VP, Business Commercialization Center of Excellence: C.J. Sutton
VP, Energy and Materials: Diane L. Sheridan
VP, Finance and Controller: Leo J. Daley, age 55
VP, General Counsel, and Secretary: W. Douglas Brown, age 55
VP, Human Resources: Leonard V. Brouse Van Groenou
VP and CTO: Miles P. Drake
President, Air Products Europe: Ronaldo Sullam, age 60, $553,750 pay
Auditors: KPMG LLP

LOCATIONS

HQ: Air Products and Chemicals, Inc.
7201 Hamilton Blvd., Allentown, PA 18195
Phone: 610-481-4911   **Fax:** 610-481-5900
Web: www.airproducts.com

2001 Sales

	$ mil.	% of total
US	3,825	67
UK	440	8
Europe		
Spain	295	5
Other Europe	582	10
Canada/Latin America	243	4
Asia/other	332	6
Total	**5,717**	**100**

PRODUCTS/OPERATIONS

2001 Sales

	$ mil.	% of total
Gases	3,944	69
Chemicals	1,523	27
Equipment	250	4
Total	**5,717**	**100**

Selected Products and Services

Industrial Gases
Argon
Carbon dioxide
Carbon monoxide
Helium
Hydrogen
Nitrogen
Oxygen
Synthesis gas

Chemicals
Amines (alkyl and specialty)
Epoxy additives
Polymer emulsions

Polyurethane chemicals and intermediates
Process chemicals
Resins
Specialty additives
Surfactants

Equipment and Services
Air-pollution control systems
Air-separation equipment
Hydrogen-purification equipment
Natural gas-liquefaction equipment

COMPETITORS

Airgas
BASF AG
BOC Group
CHEMCENTRAL
Dow Chemical
Honeywell Specialty Materials
Huntsman
Imperial Chemical
L'Air Liquide
Linde
Praxair

HISTORICAL FINANCIALS & EMPLOYEES

NYSE: APD FYE: September 30	Annual Growth	9/92	9/93	9/94	9/95	9/96	9/97	9/98	9/99	9/00	9/01
Sales ($ mil.)	6.6%	3,217	3,328	3,485	3,865	4,008	4,638	4,919	5,020	5,467	5,717
Net income ($ mil.)	8.4%	271	201	248	368	416	429	547	451	124	560
Income as % of sales	—	8.4%	6.0%	7.1%	9.5%	10.4%	9.3%	11.1%	9.0%	2.3%	9.8%
Earnings per share ($)	6.8%	1.17	0.87	1.07	1.62	1.83	1.91	2.48	2.09	0.57	2.12
Stock price - FY high ($)	—	24.75	24.56	25.19	29.81	30.44	44.81	45.34	49.25	39.13	49.00
Stock price - FY low ($)	—	15.91	18.75	19.06	21.56	24.88	29.00	29.75	27.69	23.00	30.50
Stock price - FY close ($)	6.3%	22.19	19.38	23.38	26.06	29.13	41.47	29.75	29.25	36.00	38.58
P/E - high	—	20	28	24	18	16	23	18	23	67	21
P/E - low	—	13	21	19	13	13	15	12	13	40	13
Dividends per share ($)	7.3%	0.41	0.44	0.47	0.50	0.53	0.57	0.45	0.69	0.73	0.77
Book value per share ($)	3.7%	9.25	9.21	9.78	10.74	11.65	12.05	11.60	12.92	12.30	12.89
Employees	2.3%	14,500	14,100	13,300	14,800	15,200	16,400	16,700	17,400	17,500	17,800

STOCK PRICE HISTORY

HIGH/LOW/CLOSE

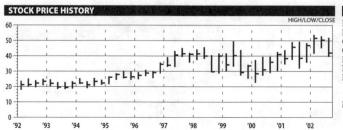

2001 FISCAL YEAR-END

Debt ratio: 39.5%
Return on equity: 18.9%
Cash ($ mil.): 66
Current ratio: 1.25
Long-term debt ($ mil.): 2,028
No. of shares (mil.): 241
Dividends
Yield: 2.0%
Payout: 36.3%
Market value ($ mil.): 9,299

AIRBORNE, INC.

Logistically speaking, lots of shippers are going Airborne. For more than a decade, Seattle-based Airborne (formerly Airborne Freight) has been the third-largest domestic airfreight express carrier by volume in the US, trailing FedEx and UPS.

The holding company's Airborne Express subsidiary specializes in express service for high-volume corporate clients. Overnight delivery accounts for more than half of its domestic shipments, but it also offers next-afternoon and second-day services and ocean shipping. Subsidiary ABX Air flies about 120 airplanes and runs the company's airport in Wilmington, Ohio. ABX Air also owns or contracts approximately 15,000 radio-dispatched delivery trucks and vans.

To better compete domestically with UPS and FedEx, Airborne has added ground delivery services to its portfolio of services, and it reduced the size of its aircraft fleet to trim costs. The company also is extending an agreement with the US Postal Service to go after e-commerce customers. The nation's mail carriers already deliver Airborne's two-day shipments directly to residences. Airborne sells software and hardware for rate and tracking information and provides automated and online shipping services.

HISTORY

Airborne Flower Traffic Association of California was founded in 1946 to ship fresh flowers from Hawaii to the mainland; it became Airborne Freight, an airfreight forwarder, in 1956. In 1968 it merged with Pacific Air Freight, which was founded in Seattle in 1947 by former US Army Air Corps officer Holt Webster to transport perishables to Alaska. Webster became the new company's first CEO.

Airborne introduced FOCUS, its proprietary package tracking system, in 1972 and began buying its own fleet of airplanes and trucks when the airline industry deregulated in 1977. Two years later it expanded into Europe and entered the young overnight delivery business. In 1980 Airborne bought Midwest Air Charter and its Wilmington, Ohio, airport, a former US Air Force base. Later called Airborne Air Park, the property became the company's principal hub and central sorting facility. In the early 1980s the company surpassed Emery Air Freight in shipments to become the third-largest express carrier in the US; it also entered the Australian and New Zealand markets. Webster retired in 1984.

In 1987 Australian transportation conglomerate TNT, which owned 15% of Airborne, tried to buy the rest, but after six months of negotiations, no agreement could be reached. That year,

with a fleet of 37 planes, the company landed two major contracts: one to handle the US express air shipments of Purolator Courier of Canada; another to carry all of IBM's express shipments of 150 pounds or less (Airborne lost IBM's Pacific business in 1989). The company bought same-day shipper Sky Courier in 1989 and also created subsidiary ABX Air as its US airline.

In 1990 Airborne joined Japan's Mitsui and Panther Express International (owned by Mitsui and another Japanese firm, Tonami Transportation) to form Airborne Express Japan (40%-owned by Airborne). When FedEx challenged the company's high-volume corporate business the next year, Airborne cut prices, and in 1994 it began offering ocean shipping services as a less-expensive method of international transportation.

Airborne bought a small service partner in Scotland in 1996 and set up international ventures in Thailand and Malaysia. The next year, as the UPS strike was boosting Airborne's business — though severely taxing its resources — Airborne formed a joint venture in South Africa. It also increased its investment in Amarex International, an airfreight firm with a major presence in the Middle East, to about 9%, and in 1998 Airborne upped its stake in Pioneer Air Cargo of Thailand to 49%.

The next year the company teamed up with the US Postal Service to offer residential delivery services in a service named airborne@home. Airborne diversified as well. It opened a facility, Optical Village (near its Wilmington hub), to provide storage, inventory, logistics, and delivery specifically for the designers, makers, and marketers of eyeglasses.

The company rolled out a new service, QuikMail, in 2000. It offered customers generic bulk shipments of flat mail for 15% to 20% less than the US Postal Service's First Class mail delivery. Also in 2000 Airborne adopted a holding company structure. The holding company took the Airborne name, and its express carrier subsidiary officially became Airborne Express. The following year the company rolled out ground delivery services to better compete with domestic rivals UPS and FedEx Ground.

OFFICERS

Chairmand & CEO: Carlton D. Donaway, age 50, $500,000 pay (prior to title change)
EVP and CFO, Airborne and Airborne Express: Lanny H. Michael, age 50, $275,000 pay
SVP and CIO, Airborne and Airborne Express: David A. Billings, age 56
SVP International, Airborne and Airborne Express: Bruce E. Grout, age 55

SVP Planning, Airborne and Airborne Express:
Darby Langdon, age 56
SVP Sales, Airborne and Airborne Express:
Kenneth J. McCumber, age 56, $275,000 pay
SVP Field Services Area IV, Airborne Express:
John P. Bunyan
SVP Marketing, Airborne Express: Richard F. Corrado
SVP Field Services Area II, Airborne Express:
Thomas E. Nelson Jr.
SVP Customer Service, Airborne Express:
Gary L. Reynolds
SVP Field Services Area III, Airborne Express:
Carl Rodriguez
SVP Revenue Control, Airborne Express:
David H. Scheevel
SVP Field Services, Airborne Express:
William R. Simpson
**VP, General Counsel, and Corporate Secretary, Airborne
and Airborne Express:** David C. Anderson, age 48
Auditors: Deloitte & Touche LLP

LOCATIONS

HQ: 3101 Western Ave., Seattle, WA 98111
Phone: 206-285-4600　　**Fax:** 206-281-1444
Web: www.airborne.com

Airborne provides delivery services from 305 shipping
facilities in more than 200 countries.

2001 Sales

	$ mil.	% of total
US	2,851	89
Other countries	360	11
Total	**3,211**	**100**

PRODUCTS/OPERATIONS

Selected Services
US Services
Customer Software and Technology
　EDI: Electronic Data Interchange
　LIBRA: Shipping and Tracking Software and Hardware
　LIGHTSHIP: Shipment and Tracking Software
　WORLD DIRECTORY: International Service Guide
Delivery Services
　Next Afternoon Service
　Overnight Air Express
　Same-Day/Next-Flight-Out Service
　Second Day Service
Logistics Services
　Airborne stock exchange (warehousing and
　　distribution services)
　Asset Recovery (product retrieval and support services)
　Hub based warehousing (leased distribution facilities)
　Parts on time (time sensitive distribution services)

International Services
Customs Brokerage Services
Delivery Services
International Documentation Requirements
International Logistics Services
International Service Center Locator

COMPETITORS

Arkansas Best	Delta	UPS
BAX Global	DHL Worldwide	UPS Freight
Celadon	Express	Services
CF	FedEx	US Airways
CNF	J. B. Hunt	U.S. Postal
Continental	Roadway	Service
Airlines	UAL	Yellow

HISTORICAL FINANCIALS & EMPLOYEES

NYSE: ABF FYE: December 31	Annual Growth	12/92	12/93	12/94	12/95	12/96	12/97	12/98	12/99	12/00	12/01
Sales ($ mil.)	9.0%	1,484	1,720	1,971	2,239	2,484	2,912	3,075	3,140	3,276	3,211
Net income ($ mil.)	—	5	39	39	24	27	120	137	91	29	(20)
Income as % of sales	—	0.4%	2.3%	2.0%	1.1%	1.1%	4.1%	4.5%	2.9%	0.9%	—
Earnings per share ($)	—	0.06	0.92	0.87	0.56	0.64	2.44	2.72	1.85	0.59	(0.40)
Stock price - FY high ($)	—	14.88	17.63	19.94	14.75	14.19	37.22	42.88	42.56	26.88	15.08
Stock price - FY low ($)	—	6.25	9.00	9.00	9.19	9.75	11.38	14.25	19.50	8.25	7.00
Stock price - FY close ($)	5.3%	9.31	17.56	10.25	13.31	11.69	31.06	36.06	22.00	9.75	14.83
P/E - high	—	248	21	22	26	22	14	15	23	90	—
P/E - low	—	104	11	10	16	15	4	5	10	28	—
Dividends per share ($)	0.7%	0.15	0.15	0.30	0.30	0.30	0.15	0.12	0.20	0.16	0.16
Book value per share ($)	8.3%	8.48	9.26	9.24	9.64	10.13	13.44	15.92	17.63	17.96	17.33
Employees	5.0%	14,500	15,700	17,400	19,500	20,700	22,500	23,000	23,500	24,100	22,500

STOCK PRICE HISTORY

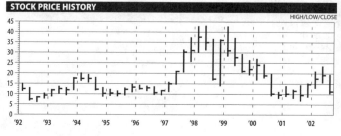

2001 FISCAL YEAR-END

Debt ratio: 20.7%
Return on equity: —
Cash ($ mil.): 202
Current ratio: 0.96
Long-term debt ($ mil.): 218
No. of shares (mil.): 48
Dividends
　Yield: 1.1%
　Payout: —
Market value ($ mil.): 714

AK STEEL HOLDING CORPORATION

Automobile sales have galvanized AK Steel Holding's business. Through subsidiary AK Steel Corporation, the Middletown, Ohio-based holding company produces flat-rolled steel. Its products include coated hot- and cold-rolled carbon steel, cold-rolled and aluminum-coated stainless steel, hot-dipped galvanized steel, and steel pipe and tubing. Carmakers account for over half of sales, with General Motors accounting for 18% of sales. AK Steel's flat-rolled steel is used for appliance manufacturing and construction; its stainless steel is also used to make equipment for food handling, chemical processing, and health care. The company also makes snowplows for light trucks, and it provides electrical steels (iron-silicon alloys with unique magnetic properties) to manufacturers of power transmission and distribution equipment, electrical motors and generators, and lighting ballasts. Other customers include steel distributors and converters.

The company's revenues have been hurt by lower steel prices and a weakened economy, as well as a decision to exit the spot market business. AK Steel believes if it can maintain a mixture of value-added steel products it can prevent future financial losses. In part because of its lowered profits, AK Steel is often mentioned as a possible takeover target.

HISTORY

George Verity, who was in the roofing business in Cincinnati around the turn of the century, often had trouble getting sheet metal, so in 1900 he founded his own steel company, American Rolling Mill. His first plant, in Middletown, Ohio, was followed by a second production facility 11 years later in Ashland, Kentucky. Plant superintendent John Tytus, whose family was in paper milling, applied those rolling techniques to make American Rolling Mill's steel more uniform in thickness.

In 1926 Columbia Steel developed a process to overcome several production problems inherent in the Tytus method, and in 1930 American Rolling Mill bought Columbia Steel. The company changed its name to Armco Steel in 1948.

Armco began diversifying in the 1950s and continued diversifying until the early 1980s. Subsidiaries were involved in coal, oil, and gas-drilling equipment and insurance and financial services, among other things. In 1978 the company changed its name to Armco Inc.

Armco began shedding subsidiaries in the early 1980s. Sales and market share increased as the company approached the billion-dollar mark at the end of the decade. In 1989 Armco formed Armco Steel Company with Japan's Kawasaki Steel Corporation.

Armco's sales reached $1.3 billion in 1991, although high operating expenses in the steel industry of the 1990s kept profits low. Armco began looking outside the company for help, and in 1992 it persuaded retired steel-industry veteran Tom Graham to head the company. Graham brought another steel veteran with him, current AK Steel CEO Richard Wardrop. After evaluating the company's holdings, the two divested more than 10 subsidiaries and divisions. Armco also worked on improving quality and customer service, with special emphasis placed on timely delivery.

In 1994 Armco's limited partnership with Kawasaki was altered and AK Steel Holding Corporation was formed, with AK Steel Corporation as its main subsidiary and the Middletown and Ashland plants as its production base. The holding company went public the same year, raising more than $650 million, enabling the company to pay off its debt.

AK Steel Holding moved its headquarters to Middletown, Ohio, in 1995 as the company racked up $146 million in profits on sales of about $2.3 billion. Despite many nay-sayers, Graham then pushed a plan to build a state-of-the-art $1.1 billion steel production facility. Many doubted the wisdom of going into long-term debt so soon after coming out of the hole — especially when a similar facility had produced lackluster results for Inland Steel. Graham stuck by his plant, and in 1997 ground was broken on the facility in Spencer County near Rockport, Indiana (Rockport Works). Graham retired that year.

In 1998 the company opened its Rockport Works cold-rolling mill and began operating a hot-dip galvanizing and galvannealing line. The next year AK Steel bought former parent Armco for $842 million. AK Steel acquired welded steel tubing maker Alpha Tube Corporation (renamed AK Tube LLC) in 2001. In late 2001 the company took a charge of $194 million for losses in its pension fund, which had been battered by a weak stock market and lowered interest rates.

OFFICERS

Chairman, President, and CEO: Richard M. Wardrop Jr., age 56, $2,000,000 pay
EVP: John G. Hritz, age 47, $539,500 pay
SVP and CFO: James L. Wainscott, age 44, $429,000 pay
VP and General Counsel: David C. Horn, age 50, $439,563 pay
VP and Controller: Donald B. Korade, age 58
VP, Customer Service: J. Theodore Holmes, age 57

VP, Human Resources and Secretary:
Brenda S. Harmon, age 50
VP, Manufacturing Planning and Steel Sourcing:
Ernest E. Rummler, age 51
VP, Operations: James M. Banker, age 45
VP, Public Affairs: Alan H. McCoy, age 50
VP, Purchasing and Transportation: Michael P. Christy, age 45
VP, Research and Design Engineering:
Thomas C. Graham Jr., age 46
VP, Safety and Health: James W. Stanley, age 57
VP, Sales and Marketing: Michael T. Adams, age 44
Auditors: Deloitte & Touche LLP

LOCATIONS

HQ: 703 Curtis St., Middletown, OH 45043
Phone: 513-425-5000   **Fax:** 513-425-2676
Web: www.aksteel.com

AK Steel Holding has operations in Indiana, Kentucky, Maine, Ohio, Pennsylvania, Tennessee, Texas, and Wisconsin.

PRODUCTS/OPERATIONS

2001 Sales by Market

	% of total
Automotive	55
Appliance, industrial machinery & construction	25
Distributors, service centers & convertors	20
Total	**100**

Selected Products

Steel
Aluminum-coated stainless steel
Coil-coated steel
Cold-rolled coated steel
Cold-rolled steel
Electrogalvanized steel
Hot-dipped galvanized steel
Hot-dipped galvannealed steel
Hot-rolled steel
Stainless steel
Steel pipe and tubing
Univit and IF enamel steel

Other
Snowplows and ice-control products

COMPETITORS

Bethlehem Steel
Co-Steel
Dofasco
Geneva Steel
Ispat
LTV
National Steel
Nucor
Ryerson Tull
Steel Authority of India
Steel Technologies
ThyssenKrupp
United States Steel
Worthington Industries

HISTORICAL FINANCIALS & EMPLOYEES

NYSE: AKS FYE: December 31	Annual Growth	12/92	12/93	12/94	12/95	12/96	12/97	12/98	12/99	12/00	12/01
Sales ($ mil.)	12.3%	1,405	1,595	2,017	2,257	2,302	2,441	2,394	4,285	4,612	3,994
Net income ($ mil.)	—	(532)	(43)	258	269	146	151	115	65	132	(275)
Income as % of sales	—	—	—	12.8%	11.9%	6.3%	6.2%	4.8%	1.5%	2.9%	—
Earnings per share ($)	—	—	—	3.94	4.09	2.35	2.43	1.92	0.56	1.20	(0.87)
Stock price – FY high ($)	—	—	—	16.63	17.81	22.06	24.03	23.75	29.63	20.13	15.00
Stock price – FY low ($)	—	—	—	9.63	10.75	16.50	16.13	13.63	13.75	7.50	7.50
Stock price – FY close ($)	(4.2%)	—	—	15.38	17.13	19.81	17.69	23.50	18.88	8.75	11.38
P/E – high	—	—	—	3	4	9	9	12	43	17	—
P/E – low	—	—	—	2	2	6	6	7	20	6	—
Dividends per share ($)	—	—	—	0.00	0.08	0.33	0.43	0.50	0.50	0.50	0.13
Book value per share ($)	1.5%	—	—	8.61	13.05	14.59	14.46	15.75	11.55	12.26	9.59
Employees	8.1%	—	6,069	5,991	5,762	5,800	5,800	5,800	11,500	11,500	11,300

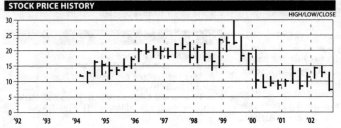

STOCK PRICE HISTORY — HIGH/LOW/CLOSE

2001 FISCAL YEAR-END
Debt ratio: 56.2%
Return on equity: —
Cash ($ mil.): 101
Current ratio: 1.62
Long-term debt ($ mil.): 1,325
No. of shares (mil.): 108
Dividends
  Yield: 1.1%
  Payout: —
Market value ($ mil.): 1,226

ALASKA AIR GROUP, INC.

Whether you want to capture a Kodiak moment or down a daiquiri by the Sea of Cortes, Alaska Air Group can fly you there. The Seattle-based company's Alaska Airlines subsidiary is a top 10 US airline. Alaska Airlines (accounting for about 80% of group sales) serves 40 cities in Alaska and five other western US states, Mexico, and Canada. Alaska Airlines flies out of hubs in Anchorage, Alaska; Portland, Oregon; Los Angeles; and Seattle. The group also owns Horizon Air Industries, a Pacific Northwest regional carrier that serves another 40 airports in five states and Canada.

On the chilling fields of competition the airlines are picking sides. Alaska Air's leadership in West Coast travel has made it an attractive code-sharing partner to American, Continental, KLM Royal Dutch Airlines, and Northwest.

Alaska Air competes in the low-fare market against Southwest Airlines and UAL's United Shuttle. It maintains a young fleet of about 100 jets (737s and MD-80s), keeps costs low, and offers full-service passenger fare such as meals and first-class seating. About 4% of sales come from delivering cargo, including halibut and other Alaskan seafood.

High fuel prices have kept the airline from pursuing an aggressive growth strategy, so it plans to expand its services by building on its existing route structure.

HISTORY

Pilot Mac McGee started McGee Airways in 1932 to fly cargo between Anchorage and Bristol Bay, Alaska. He joined other local operators in 1937 to form Star Air Lines, which began airmail service between Fairbanks and Bethel in 1938. In 1944, a year after buying three small airlines, Star adopted the name Alaska Airlines.

The company expanded to include freight service to Africa and Australia in 1950. This expansion, coupled with the seasonal nature of the airline's business, caused losses in the early 1970s. Developer Bruce Kennedy gained control of the board, turning the firm around by the end of 1973. But the Civil Aeronautics Board forced the carrier to drop service to northwestern Alaska in 1975, and by 1978 it served only 10 Alaskan cities and Seattle.

Kennedy became CEO the next year. The 1978 Airline Deregulation Act allowed Alaska Air to move into new areas as well as regain the routes it had lost. By 1982 it was the largest airline flying between Alaska and the lower 48 states.

In 1985 the airline reorganized, forming Alaska Air Group as its holding company. The next year Alaska Air Group bought Jet America Airlines (expanding its routes eastward to Chicago, St. Louis, and Dallas) and Seattle-based Horizon Air Industries (which served 30 Northwest cities). When competition in the East and Midwest cut profits in 1987, Kennedy shut down Jet America to focus on West Coast operations.

To counterbalance summer traffic to Alaska, the airline began service to two Mexican resorts in 1988. Fuel prices and sluggish traffic hurt 1990 earnings, but Alaska Air Group stayed in the black, unlike many other carriers. Kennedy retired as chairman in 1991.

That year the airline began service to Canada and seasonal flights to two Russian cities. Neil Bergt's MarkAir airline declared war, cutting fares and horning in on Alaska Air Group's territory. Alaska Air Group's profits were slashed, and MarkAir went into bankruptcy.

Alaska Air extended Russian flights to year-round in 1994. In 1995 former Horizon boss John Kelly became CEO of the group, and George Bagley became Horizon's CEO.

The airline began service to Vancouver in 1996. That year it became the first major US carrier to use the GPS satellite navigation system. In 1997 it added service to more than a dozen new cities but in 1998 halted service to Russia because of that country's economic woes.

Alaska Air Group and Dutch airline KLM agreed to a marketing alliance in 1998 that included reciprocal frequent-flier programs and code-sharing, and in 1999 it added code-sharing agreements with several major airlines, including American and Continental. Alaska Airlines developed an online check-in system, a first among US carriers.

In 2000 an Alaska Airlines MD-83 crashed into the Pacific Ocean near Los Angeles, killing all 88 people on board. While a federal investigation of Alaska Airlines' maintenance practices found deficiencies, the FAA eventually accepted the airline's plan to tighten safety standards.

Like most airlines in the latter part of 2001, Alaska Airlines had to reduce its flights as a result of reduced demand after the September 11 attacks on New York and Washington, DC. As capacity slowly grew in 2002, Alaska began to add new destinations and increase the number of flights to some established routes.

OFFICERS

Chairman Emeritus: Bruce R. Kennedy, age 63
Chairman, President, and CEO; Chairman, Alaska Airlines and Horizon Air Industries: John F. Kelly, age 57, $525,000 pay
EVP Finance and CFO, Alaska Air Group and Alaska Airlines: Bradley D. Tilden, age 41, $190,919 pay

VP Legal and Corporate Affairs, General Counsel, and
  Corporate Secretary, Alaska Air Group and Alaska
  Airlines: Keith Loveless, age 45
Director; Chairman Emeritus, Alaska Airlines:
  Ronald F. Cosgrave, age 70
Director; President and COO, Alaska Airlines:
  William S. Ayer, age 47, $340,000 pay
President and CEO, Horizon Air: Jeffrey D. Pinneo
EVP Operations, Alaska Airlines: George D. Bagley,
  $253,133 pay
EVP Marketing and Planning, Alaska Airlines:
  Gregg A. Saretsky, $227,088 pay
SVP Customer Service, Horizon Air: Glenn S. Johnson
SVP Information and Communications Services,
  Alaska Airlines: Robert M. Reeder
SVP Maintenance and Engineering, Alaska Airlines:
  Michael S. Cohen
SVP Operations, Horizon Air: Thomas M. Gerharter
VP Customer Service, Alaska Airlines: Edward W. White
VP Employee Services, Alaska Airlines:
  Dennis J. Hamel
VP Finance and Treasurer, Horizon Air:
  Rudi H. Schmidt
VP Flight Operations, Alaska Airlines: Kevin P. Finan
VP Flight Operations, Horizon Air: Daniel S. Scott
VP Legal and Administration and Corporate Secretary,
  Horizon Air: Arthur E. Thomas
Auditors: Deloitte & Touche LLP

LOCATIONS

HQ: 19300 Pacific Hwy. South, Seattle, WA 98188
Phone: 206-431-7040   **Fax:** 206-431-7038
Web: www.alaskaair.com

Alaska Air Group's major subsidiary, Alaska Airlines,
flies to cities in seven states (Alaska, Arizona, California,
Illinois, Nevada, Oregon, and Washington), Canada, and
Mexico. Horizon Air Industries flies to 35 cities in five
states (California, Idaho, Montana, Oregon, and
Washington) and Canada.

PRODUCTS/OPERATIONS

2001 Sales

	$ mil.	% of total
Passenger service	1,973	92
Freight & mail	86	4
Other	82	4
Total	**2,141**	**100**

COMPETITORS

Air Canada	Lufthansa
America West	SkyWest
AMR	Southwest Airlines
CINTRA	UAL
Continental Airlines	US Airways
Delta	

HISTORICAL FINANCIALS & EMPLOYEES

NYSE: ALK FYE: December 31	Annual Growth	12/92	12/93	12/94	12/95	12/96	12/97	12/98	12/99	12/00	12/01
Sales ($ mil.)	7.5%	1,115	1,128	1,316	1,418	1,592	1,739	1,898	2,082	2,177	2,141
Net income ($ mil.)	—	(85)	(31)	23	17	38	72	124	134	(70)	(40)
Income as % of sales	—	—	—	1.7%	1.2%	2.4%	4.2%	6.6%	6.4%	—	—
Earnings per share ($)	—	(6.87)	(2.51)	1.62	1.26	2.05	3.53	4.81	5.06	(2.66)	(1.49)
Stock price – FY high ($)	—	23.88	18.13	18.88	21.38	30.75	40.13	62.56	54.69	36.88	35.25
Stock price – FY low ($)	—	14.75	12.25	13.13	13.50	15.88	20.75	26.00	33.19	19.50	17.40
Stock price – FY close ($)	6.5%	16.50	14.13	15.00	16.25	21.00	38.75	44.25	35.13	29.75	29.10
P/E – high	—	—	—	11	17	12	8	12	11	—	—
P/E – low	—	—	—	8	11	6	4	5	7	—	—
Dividends per share ($)	—	0.20	0.00	0.00	0.00	0.00	0.00	0.00	0.00	0.00	0.00
Book value per share ($)	5.3%	19.35	12.50	14.30	15.67	18.83	26.00	30.11	35.24	32.59	30.92
Employees	2.7%	8,666	8,458	9,852	10,467	8,406	8,578	9,244	10,040	10,738	11,025

STOCK PRICE HISTORY

HIGH/LOW/CLOSE

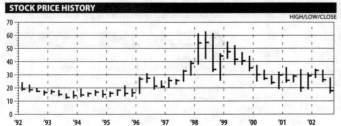

2001 FISCAL YEAR-END

Debt ratio: 51.3%
Return on equity: —
Cash ($ mil.): 490
Current ratio: 1.19
Long-term debt ($ mil.): 863
No. of shares (mil.): 27
Dividends
  Yield: —
  Payout: —
Market value ($ mil.): 772

ALBERTO-CULVER COMPANY

Alberto-Culver puts beauty first. The company, led by Sally Beauty, the world's #1 distributor of professional beauty supplies, also makes Mrs. Dash seasonings, Molly McButter butter alternative, Alberto VO5 and St. Ives Swiss Formula hair and skin care lines, FDS feminine deodorant spray, and Static Guard antistatic spray. These products are sold by wholesale drug sellers and retail outlets.

Sally Beauty accounts for about 60% of Alberto-Culver's sales. It operates more than 2,300 stores in Canada, Germany, Japan, the UK, and the US, selling hair and skin care goods, cosmetics, and styling appliances to beauty professionals and hobbyists alike. Its Beauty Systems Group distributes products directly to beauty salons in the US and Canada.

Although dwarfed by consumer products and beauty care giants such as Unilever, Clairol, and L'Oréal, Alberto-Culver has increased sales by boosting marketing efforts and updating core product lines.

Founder and chairman Leonard Lavin, his wife, daughter, and son-in-law — CEO Howard Bernick — run Alberto-Culver and own about 30% of the company and control about 40% of the voting rights. In June 2002, Alberto-Culver announced that the Lavin family is considering selling approximately $300 million worth of stock, which would reduce the family's ownership of the company to about 27%.

HISTORY

Alberto VO5 Conditioning Hairdressing (featuring five vital oils in a water-free base) was developed in the early 1950s by a chemist named Alberto to rejuvenate the coiffures of Hollywood's movie stars from the damage of harsh studio lights. In 1955, 36-year-old entrepreneur Leonard Lavin and his wife, Bernice, borrowed $400,000, bought the Los Angeles-based firm that made VO5 from Blaine Culver, and relocated it to Chicago. That year Alberto-Culver implemented a key component of its corporate strategy — aggressive marketing — by running the first television commercial for VO5. Within three years Alberto VO5 led its category. In 1959 the company expanded its product line by buying TRESemmé Hair Color.

Lavin built a new plant and headquarters in Melrose Park, Illinois, in 1960, took the company public in 1961, and formed an international marketing division. A series of product innovations included Alberto VO5 Hair Spray (1961), New Dawn Hair Color (the first shampoo-in, permanent hair color; 1963), Consort Hair Spray for Men (1965), and FDS (1966). Acquisitions in 1969 included low-calorie sugar substitute SugarTwin and 10-store beauty supply chain Sally Beauty Supply.

Alberto-Culver restyled TV advertising in 1972 by putting two 30-second ads in a 60-second spot (it later pioneered the "split 30," back-to-back 15-second ads for two different products). It launched TCB (an ethnic hair care line) in 1975 and Static Guard antistatic spray in 1976.

The firm developed a series of food-substitute products in the 1980s, including Mrs. Dash (1983) and Molly McButter (1987). It also expanded the fast-growing Sally chain to the UK (1987). Lavin's son-in-law Howard Bernick succeeded him as president and COO in 1988.

By 1990 the Sally chain had about 800 stores, many added through the purchases of smaller chains. It bought the bankrupt Milo Beauty & Barber Supply chain (about 90 stores) in 1991. That year Alberto-Culver also bought Cederroth International, a Swedish maker of health and hygiene goods. Bernick became CEO in 1994, though Lavin stayed on as chairman.

In 1995 the firm acquired the toiletries division of Swedish beauty and cleaning products maker Molnlycke, combining it with Cederroth to form one of Scandinavia's largest consumer packaged goods marketers. Also that year Lavin's daughter, Carol Bernick, became head of Alberto-Culver USA and led the division to more than $300 million in sales.

The 1,500-store Sally chain opened its first 10 outlets in Japan through a joint venture in 1995 and acquired a small chain in Germany the next year. Also in 1996 Alberto-Culver made its largest acquisition ever, paying $110 million for St. Ives Laboratories, maker of St. Ives Swiss Formula hair and skin care products.

Amid sluggish company-wide sales, in 1999 Alberto-Culver increased marketing spending by 16%. Also in 1999 the company bought Argentina-based La Farmaco, a personal care products company, and professional products distributor Heil Beauty Supply. In 2000 Alberto-Culver bought Pro-Line, a maker of personal care products for African-Americans. Later that year it added beauty products distributors Davidson Supply, with its 32 stores, and B&H Supply Company to its Beauty Systems Group.

OFFICERS

Chairman: Leonard H. Lavin, age 82, $2,816,756 pay
Vice Chairman, Secretary, and Treasurer:
Bernice E. Lavin, age 76, $1,361,755 pay
Vice Chairman and President, Consumer Products
Worldwide: Carol L. Bernick, age 50, $1,771,500 pay
President, CEO, and Director: Howard B. Bernick, age 50, $3,351,000 pay

President, Alberto Personal Care Worldwide:
James Marino, age 52
President, Alberto-Culver International:
Paul H. Stoneham, age 39
President, Culver Business Units Worldwide:
James Chickarello, age 46
President, Sally Beauty Company: Michael H. Renzulli,
age 61, $1,984,500 pay
SVP and CFO: William J. Cernugel, age 59
SVP, Alberto Personal Care Worldwide: Richard Hynes,
age 54
SVP and CFO, Alberto-Culver Consumer Products
Worldwide: Andrew Langert, age 50
VP, General Counsel, and Assistant Secretary:
Gary P. Schmidt, age 50
VP, Worldwide Human Resources: David Bronsweig
Group VP, Worldwide Research and Development:
John R. Berschied Jr., age 58
Auditors: KPMG LLP

LOCATIONS

HQ: 2525 Armitage Ave., Melrose Park, IL 60160
Phone: 708-450-3000 **Fax:** 708-450-3354
Web: www.alberto.com

Alberto-Culver sells its products in more than 120
countries.

2001 Sales & Operating Profit

	Sales		Operating Profit	
	$ mil.	% of total	$ mil.	% of total
US	1,942	77	178	84
Foreign	571	23	35	16
Adjustments	(19)	—	—	—
Total	**2,494**	**100**	**213**	**100**

PRODUCTS/OPERATIONS

2001 Sales

	$ mil.	% of total
Sally Beauty	1,460	58
Alberto-Culver North America	617	25
Alberto-Culver International	446	17
Adjustments	(29)	—
Total	**2,494**	**100**

Selected Brands
Alberto VO5 (hair care products)
Consort (hair care products)
Farmaco (soap, Latin America)
FDS (feminine deodorant spray)
Just For Me (ethnic personal care products)
Molly McButter (butter-flavored sprinkles)
Motions (ethnic hair care products)
Mrs. Dash (salt-free seasoning)
Samarin (antacids, Europe)
Soft & Beautiful (ethnic personal care products)
Static Guard (antistatic spray)
SugarTwin (sugar substitute)

COMPETITORS

Allou	Dial	Nu Skin
Alticor	Estée Lauder	Pharmacia
Avon	Gillette	Procter &
Bristol-Myers	Helen of Troy	Gamble
Squibb	Johnson &	Regis
Burns, Philp	Johnson	Revlon
Colgate-	Johnson	Schwarzkopf &
Palmolive	Publishing	DEP
Cumberland	L'Oréal	Shiseido
Packing	Mary Kay	Unilever
Del Labs	McCormick	Wella

HISTORICAL FINANCIALS & EMPLOYEES

NYSE: ACV FYE: September 30	Annual Growth	9/92	9/93	9/94	9/95	9/96	9/97	9/98	9/99	9/00	9/01
Sales ($ mil.)	9.6%	1,091	1,148	1,216	1,358	1,590	1,775	1,835	1,976	2,247	2,494
Net income ($ mil.)	12.4%	39	41	44	53	63	85	83	86	103	110
Income as % of sales	—	3.5%	3.6%	3.6%	3.9%	3.9%	4.8%	4.5%	4.4%	4.6%	4.4%
Earnings per share ($)	12.2%	0.68	0.72	0.79	0.94	1.06	1.41	1.37	1.51	1.83	1.91
Stock price - FY high ($)	—	16.00	14.13	12.56	16.25	23.75	31.56	32.56	27.88	31.81	46.26
Stock price - FY low ($)	—	10.63	10.13	9.69	10.88	14.94	21.38	19.75	21.56	19.38	28.44
Stock price - FY close ($)	14.0%	11.94	11.31	11.69	15.25	21.69	30.44	23.38	23.13	28.81	38.89
P/E - high	—	24	20	16	17	21	21	22	18	17	24
P/E - low	—	16	14	12	11	13	14	14	14	10	15
Dividends per share ($)	11.5%	0.12	0.14	0.14	0.16	0.18	0.20	0.23	0.26	0.29	0.32
Book value per share ($)	11.1%	5.01	5.23	5.91	6.69	7.64	8.55	9.33	10.21	11.38	12.95
Employees	8.7%	7,600	8,600	9,300	9,900	10,700	11,000	12,700	13,400	15,300	16,100

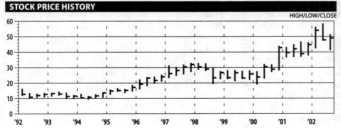

STOCK PRICE HISTORY HIGH/LOW/CLOSE

2001 FISCAL YEAR-END
Debt ratio: 30.4%
Return on equity: 16.1%
Cash ($ mil.): 202
Current ratio: 2.25
Long-term debt ($ mil.): 321
No. of shares (mil.): 57
Dividends
  Yield: 0.8%
  Payout: 16.8%
Market value ($ mil.): 2,210

ALBERTSON'S, INC.

Like a shopper on a budget, Boise, Idaho-based Albertson's is choosy about where it spends money. The #2 supermarket chain in the US (after Kroger) operates more than 2,400 stores under several banners in 33 states. Most of its namesake stores are combination food stores and drugstores, more than 200 with gas stations. The other outlets include smaller conventional grocery stores and no-frills warehouse stores (Max Foods, Super Saver) specializing in discounted meat and produce.

As a result of its 1999 purchase of American Stores, Albertson's added three regional supermarket chains: Acme Markets (in four states anchored by Philadelphia), Jewel (#1 grocer in Chicago), and Lucky (California), which has been converted to the Albertson's banner. The purchase also gave Albertson's the Osco Drug and Sav-on drugstore chains.

Plans to spend $4 billion by the end of 2001 to launch more than 500 new food-and-drug combination stores, stand-alone drugstores, and fuel centers were reversed when new CEO Larry Johnston announced a restructuring plan that would close about 165 underperforming stores and cut 15%-20% of non-store jobs. However, the company is adding stores in key markets in Arizona, Nevada, Oklahoma, and Texas and said it will invest $1 billion to remodel stores and build new ones in California. Albertson's is moving gingerly into online operations — it allows customers in some West Coast markets to order any item available in an Albertson's store and either have their order delivered or picked up at a neighborhood Albertson's.

Theo Albrecht (his family owns supermarket chains ALDI and Trader Joe's) owns about 7% of Albertson's.

HISTORY

J. A. "Joe" Albertson, Leonard Skaggs (whose family ran Safeway), and Tom Cuthbert founded Albertson's Food Center in Boise, Idaho, in 1939. Albertson, who left his position as district manager for Safeway to run the store, thought big from the start. The 10,000-sq.-ft. store was not only eight times the size of the average competitor, it also offered an in-store butcher shop and bakery, one of the country's first magazine racks, and homemade "Big Joe" ice-cream cones. The men ended their partnership in 1945, the year Albertson's was incorporated, and by 1947 it operated six stores in Idaho.

The company opened its first combination food store and drugstore, a 60,000-sq.-ft. superstore, in 1951 and began locating stores in growing suburban areas. Albertson's went public to raise expansion capital in 1959 and by 1960 had 62 stores in Idaho, Oregon, Utah, and Washington. The food retailer acquired Greater All American Markets (1964), a grocery chain based in Downey, California, and Semrau & Sons (1965) of Oakland, which aided the company's thrust into the California market.

Albertson's and the Skaggs chain (by this time run by L. S. Skaggs Jr.) reunited temporarily in 1969, financing six Skaggs-Albertson's food-and-drug-combination stores. (The partnership dissolved in 1977, with each side taking half of the units.) By 1986 the company had reached $5 billion in sales, a fivefold increase over 1975.

The company purchased 74 Jewel Osco combination food stores and drugstores (mostly in Arkansas, Florida, Oklahoma, and Texas) from American Stores in 1992. Co-founder Albertson died in 1993 at age 86.

In 1997 the United Food and Commercial Workers union, which represents supermarket employees, sued Albertson's, alleging the company forced employees to work overtime without pay. (It was settled in 1999, resulting in a $22 million charge.) Also in 1997 Albertson's began selling gasoline at a few stores. Acquisitions the next year (including Buttrey Food and Drug Stores) added stores and states. That year the company began serving online customers in the Dallas-Fort Worth area.

In 1999 the grocer revisited its roots when it acquired American Stores (Skaggs' successor), which operated more than 1,550 stores in 26 states. To obtain regulatory approval for the $12 billion deal, Albertson's sold 145 stores in overlapping markets in three states (most were in California).

In 2001 Larry Johnston, former CEO of GE Appliances, took over as chairman and CEO of Albertson's. Facing increasing competition (especially from Wal-Mart), Johnston announced aggressive restructuring plans that include closing or selling stores and cutting jobs in under-performing markets, specifically Memphis and Nashville, Tennessee, and Houston and San Antonio.

Already allowing customers to order drugs online (from its online drugstore, Savon.com) and groceries in Seattle, Albertson's expanded its online operations to San Diego in 2001 and in early 2002 to Los Angeles, San Francisco, and parts of Oregon and Washington. Albertson's exited the New England drugstore market in 2002 when it sold 80 New England Osco stores to Brooks Pharmacy.

Chairman and CEO: Lawrence R. Johnston, age 53, $3,460,770 pay
President, COO, and Director: Peter L. Lynch, age 50, $1,516,577 pay
EVP and CFO: Felicia D. Thornton, age 38, $658,636 pay
EVP and CTO: Robert J. Dunst Jr., age 41
EVP and General Counsel: John R. Sims, age 52
EVP, Development: Robert K. Banks, age 52
EVP, Distribution: Thomas E. Brother, age 60
EVP, Drug and General Merchandise: Kevin H. Tripp, age 47, $1,048,212 pay
EVP, Human Resources: Kathy J. Herbert, age 48
EVP, Labor Relations and Employment Law: Steven D. Young, age 53
EVP, Marketing and Merchandising: Lawrence A. Stablein, age 44
EVP, Operations: Robert C. Butler, age 53
EVP, Operations: Romeo R. Cefalo, age 52, $1,031,993 pay
SVP and Controller: Richard J. Navarro, age 49
SVP, Corporate Strategy and Business Development: Eric J. Cremers
SVP, Public Affairs: Ertharin Cousin, age 44
VP, Finance and Corporate Planning: Linda Massman
VP and Secretary: Kaye L. O'Riordan
Auditors: Deloitte & Touche LLP

LOCATIONS

HQ: 250 Parkcenter Blvd., Boise, ID 83726
Phone: 208-395-6200 **Fax:** 208-395-6349
Web: www.albertsons.com

Albertson's has more than 2,400 stores in 33 states.

PRODUCTS/OPERATIONS

2002 Stores

	No.
Combination	1,395
Stand-alone drugstore	731
Conventional & warehouse	295
Total	**2,421**

Selected Operations
Acme Markets (supermarkets)
Albertson's (supermarkets)
Jewel Food Stores (supermarkets)
Max Foods (no-frills discount warehouse stores)
Osco Drug (drugstores)
Sav-On Drugs (drugstores)
Seessel's (supermarkets)
Super Saver (no-frills discount warehouse stores)

COMPETITORS

A&P	Meijer
Ahold USA	Minyard Food Stores
Associated Grocers	Pathmark
Bashas'	Publix
Costco Wholesale	Raley's
CVS	Rite Aid
Delhaize America	Safeway
Eckerd	Stater Bros.
H-E-B	Walgreen
IGA	Wal-Mart
Kmart	Whole Foods
Kroger	Winn-Dixie
Longs	

HISTORICAL FINANCIALS & EMPLOYEES

NYSE: ABS FYE: Thursday nearest Jan. 31	Annual Growth	1/93	1/94	1/95	1/96	1/97	1/98	1/99	1/00	1/01	1/02
Sales ($ mil.)	15.7%	10,174	11,284	11,895	12,585	13,777	14,690	16,005	37,478	36,762	37,931
Net income ($ mil.)	7.1%	269	340	400	465	494	517	567	404	765	501
Income as % of sales	—	2.6%	3.0%	3.4%	3.7%	3.6%	3.5%	3.5%	1.1%	2.1%	1.3%
Earnings per share ($)	2.1%	1.02	1.34	1.58	1.84	1.96	2.08	2.30	0.95	1.83	1.23
Stock price - FY high ($)	—	26.69	29.69	30.88	35.25	43.75	48.63	67.13	61.25	39.25	36.99
Stock price - FY low ($)	—	18.50	23.38	25.13	27.25	33.75	30.50	44.00	29.00	20.06	27.00
Stock price - FY close ($)	1.8%	24.44	26.75	29.88	33.88	35.00	47.75	61.00	30.50	28.35	28.75
P/E - high	—	25	22	19	19	22	23	29	61	21	30
P/E - low	—	18	17	15	15	17	15	19	29	11	22
Dividends per share ($)	13.3%	0.31	0.35	0.42	0.50	0.58	0.63	0.67	0.71	0.75	0.95
Book value per share ($)	12.0%	5.25	5.48	6.65	7.75	8.96	9.85	11.44	13.45	14.06	14.53
Employees	13.4%	71,000	75,000	76,000	80,000	88,000	94,000	100,000	235,000	235,000	220,000

STOCK PRICE HISTORY

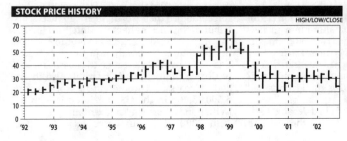

HIGH/LOW/CLOSE

2002 FISCAL YEAR-END

Debt ratio: 47.4%
Return on equity: 8.6%
Cash ($ mil.): 85
Current ratio: 1.29
Long-term debt ($ mil.): 5,336
No. of shares (mil.): 407
Dividends
  Yield: 3.3%
  Payout: 77.2%
Market value ($ mil.): 11,701

ALCOA INC.

Alcoa is a world-class lightweight. The Pittsburgh-based company is the world's #1 producer of alumina (aluminum's principal ingredient — it's refined from bauxite) and aluminum. Alcoa's aluminum products — plate, flat-rolled sheet, extruded rods, tubes, wire, and castings — are used primarily by the construction, consumer packaging, aerospace, automotive, railroad, and shipbuilding industries. Other offerings include alumina chemicals, packaging machinery, plastic bottles, fasteners, and vinyl siding.

Determined to stay on top, Alcoa acquired Reynolds Metals — which had been the world's #3 aluminum producer — after Alcan Aluminium, Algroup, and Pechiney announced they would merge (Pechiney later dropped out). Reynolds has lucrative consumer products (Reynolds Wrap) and packaging businesses, as well as industrial aluminum operations. Alcoa also has diversified its aerospace operations with the purchase of Cordant Technologies, which added Howmet Castings (aerospace castings) and Huck Manufacturing (fasteners).

Alcoa restructured in 2001, selling assets to reduce debt and shutting some aluminum operations because of low demand and energy problems in the western US. It also bought a stake in Aluminium Corporation of China (Chalco). Alcoa expanded its packaging business by purchasing Ivex Packaging (excluding Ivex's interest in Packaging Dynamics Corporation) and raising its stake in Shibazaki Seisakusho (Japanese manufacturer of plastic and aluminum closures and caps).

HISTORY

In 1886 two chemists, one in France and one in the US, simultaneously discovered an inexpensive process for aluminum production. The American, Charles Hall, pursued commercial applications and soon formed the Pittsburgh Reduction Company. Arthur Davis was the company's first salesman and was named to head the company in 1899 (he retired in 1957).

In 1889 the Mellon Bank loaned the company $4,000. In 1891 the firm recapitalized with the Mellon family holding 12% of the stock.

The company introduced aluminum foil (1910) and found applications for aluminum in new products such as airplanes and cars. It became the Aluminum Company of America in 1907.

By the end of WWI, Alcoa had integrated backward into bauxite mining and forward into end-use production. By the 1920s the Mellons had raised their stake to 33%.

The government and Alcoa had debated antitrust issues in court for years since the smelting patent expired in 1912. Finally a 1946 federal ruling forced the company to sell many operations built during WWII, as well as its Canadian subsidiary (Alcan).

In the competitive aluminum industry of the 1960s, Alcoa's lower-cost production helped it seize market share, especially in beverage cans. In the 1970s Alcoa began offering engineered products such as aerospace components, and in the 1980s it invested in research, acquisitions, and plant modernization.

Paul O'Neill (former president of International Paper) arrived as CEO in 1987 and shifted the company's focus back to aluminum. Sales and earnings set records the next two years but plunged afterward, reflecting a weak global economy and record-low aluminum prices. Then the fall of the Soviet Union in the early 1990s led to a worldwide glut as Russian exports soared.

Alcoa formed a joint venture with Shanghai Aluminum Fabrication Plant in China. The company expanded in Europe in 1996, acquiring Italy's state-run aluminum business, followed by the purchase of Inespal, Spain's state-run aluminum operations, in 1998. Alcoa also bought #3 US aluminum producer Alumax for $3.8 billion in 1998, but only after divesting its cast-plate operations.

Known by the nickname "Alcoa" since the late 1920s, the company adopted that as its official name in 1999. O'Neill retired as CEO in 1999; COO Alain Belda succeeded him.

In 2000 Alcoa bought aluminum extrusion maker Excel Extrusions from Noranda and paid $4.5 billion for Reynolds Metals after agreeing to divest some assets — including all of Reynolds' alumina refineries — to satisfy regulators. The same month Alcoa acquired Cordant Technologies. Alcoa also assumed Cordant's 85% ownership of Howmet International (castings) as a result of the transaction — and later acquired the remainder of Howmet. Late in 2000 President-elect George W. Bush named Alcoa's chairman Paul O'Neill to be Treasury Secretary.

Alcoa sold its majority stake in the Worsley alumina refinery (Australia) to BHP Billiton in 2001 for about $1.5 billion as part of its refinery divestments. Also that year Alcoa and BHP Billiton combined their North American metals distribution businesses to create Integris Metals.

Late in 2001 Alcoa agreed to buy an 8% stake in Aluminium Corporation of China (Chalco). The deal gave Alcoa a seat on the board and 27% of Chalco's initial public offering. Also in late 2001 Alcoa said it would cut its workforce by 6,500 (5,400 in the US and 1,100 jobs in the Netherlands, Germany, and Britain).

In 2002 Alcoa purchased Ivex Packaging

(Chicago-based industrial packaging group), which excluded Ivex's 48% stake in Packaging Dynamics for an estimated $790 million in cash and assumed debt. It also raised its stake in Shibazaki Seisakusho (a Japanese manufacturer of plastic and aluminum closures and caps) from 70% to around 95%. The company announced plans to purchase Fairchild Fasteners, an aerospace and industrial fastening maker and unit of The Fairchild Corporation.

OFFICERS

Chairman, President, and CEO: Alain J. P. Belda, age 58, $2,443,477 pay
EVP, CFO, and Chief Compliance Officer: Richard B. Kelson, age 55, $1,085,096 pay
EVP and General Counsel: Lawrence R. Purtell, age 54
EVP, Alcoa Business Center, Customer and Quality: William F. Christopher
EVP, Latin America and Asia: Joseph C. Muscari, age 55
EVP; Group President, Alcoa Industrial Components: L. Patrick Hassey, age 56, $853,200 pay
EVP; Group President, Alcoa Packaging, Consumer, Construction, and Distribution: William E. Leahey Jr., age 52
EVP; Group President, Alcoa Primary Products: G. John Pizzey, age 56, $860,127 pay
Auditors: PricewaterhouseCoopers LLP

LOCATIONS

HQ: 201 Isabella St. at 7th St. Bridge, Pittsburgh, PA 15212
Phone: 412-553-4545 **Fax:** 412-553-4498
Web: www.alcoa.com

2001 Sales

	$ mil.	% of total
US	15,000	66
Australia	1,350	6
Spain	1,011	4
United Kingdom	899	4
Brazil	736	3
Other countries	3,863	17
Total	**22,859**	**100**

PRODUCTS/OPERATIONS

2001 Sales

	$ mil.	% of total
Engineered products	6,098	27
Flat-rolled products	4,999	22
Primary metals	3,432	15
Packaging and consumer	2,720	12
Alumina & chemicals	1,908	8
Other	3,702	16
Total	**22,859**	**100**

COMPETITORS

Alcan	GenCorp	Rio Tinto
Alliant	Hayes Lemmerz	Superior
Techsystems	LTV	Industries
Bethlehem Steel	MAXXAM	Trans-World
BHP Billiton Ltd	Nippon Light	Metals
Boeing	Metal	TUI
Budd Company	Nippon Steel	United States
Commonwealth	Norsk Hydro	Steel
Industries	Nucor	United
Corus Group	Ormet	Technologies
Crown Cork &	Pechiney	
Seal	Quanex	

HISTORICAL FINANCIALS & EMPLOYEES

NYSE: AA FYE: December 31	Annual Growth	12/92	12/93	12/94	12/95	12/96	12/97	12/98	12/99	12/00	12/01
Sales ($ mil.)	10.3%	9,492	9,056	9,904	12,500	13,061	13,319	15,340	16,323	22,936	22,859
Net income ($ mil.)	—	(1,139)	5	375	791	515	805	853	1,054	1,484	908
Income as % of sales	—	—	0.1%	3.8%	6.3%	3.9%	6.0%	5.6%	6.5%	6.5%	4.0%
Earnings per share ($)	—	(1.69)	0.01	0.52	1.11	0.74	1.16	1.21	1.41	1.80	1.05
Stock price – FY high ($)	—	10.08	9.80	11.28	15.06	16.56	22.41	20.31	41.69	43.63	45.71
Stock price – FY low ($)	—	7.63	7.38	8.03	9.22	12.28	16.06	14.50	17.97	23.13	27.36
Stock price – FY close ($)	16.6%	8.95	8.67	10.83	13.22	15.94	17.59	18.64	41.50	33.50	35.55
P/E – high	—	—	980	18	14	22	19	17	29	24	43
P/E – low	—	—	738	13	8	17	14	12	12	13	26
Dividends per share ($)	12.6%	0.20	0.20	0.20	0.23	0.34	0.25	0.38	0.41	0.50	0.58
Book value per share ($)	10.1%	5.26	5.07	5.59	6.30	6.47	6.57	8.25	8.59	13.20	12.52
Employees	8.2%	63,600	63,400	61,700	72,000	76,800	81,600	103,500	127,000	142,000	129,000

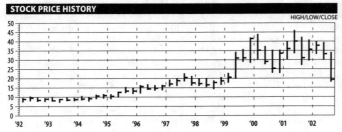

STOCK PRICE HISTORY
HIGH/LOW/CLOSE

2001 FISCAL YEAR-END
Debt ratio: 37.6%
Return on equity: 8.3%
Cash ($ mil.): 512
Current ratio: 1.36
Long-term debt ($ mil.): 6,388
No. of shares (mil.): 848
Dividends
  Yield: 1.6%
  Payout: 55.2%
Market value ($ mil.): 30,132

ALLEGHENY ENERGY, INC.

Even when the Allegheny Moon isn't shining, Hagerstown, Maryland-based Allegheny Energy (AE) can provide plenty of light. Through three regulated utilities, AE's Allegheny Power delivers electricity to 1.5 million customers in Maryland, Ohio, Pennsylvania, Virginia, and West Virginia and natural gas to some 230,000 customers in West Virginia.

AE's nonregulated operations, however, are outshining their utility brethren. To better compete in other energy markets, the company has transferred its generation assets (9,900 MW of capacity) to nonregulated subsidiary Allegheny Energy Supply, which provides power to AE utilities and sells electricity to wholesale and retail customers. The unit has expanded its marketing and generation operations through acquisitions and is building new plants; however, due to investors' lack of confidence in merchant energy companies following Enron's downfall, AE is downsizing its nonregulated expansion plans.

Subsidiary Allegheny Ventures controls Allegheny Energy Solutions, which provides energy consulting services to businesses, and Allegheny Communications Connect, which has a fiber-optic network in the mid-Atlantic region spanning 1,900 route miles, which it is extending. The company also has an interest in AFN, which operates a 7,700-route mile network.

HISTORY

American Water Works & Electric Company was one of many utility holding companies created by financiers as the US power industry consolidated in the 1880s. It bought many electric plants and water facilities in the Northeast and united 53 Pennsylvania power companies to form West Penn Power in 1916. It also formed The Potomac Edison Company in 1923, a similar amalgamation of small utilities that supplied power to western Maryland. The next year American Water Works formed Washington County Light & Power Company (later Monongahela Power) to serve customers in West Virginia and Ohio.

In 1925 West Penn Electric Company was born when American Water Works began integrating the systems' power plants, transformers, and lines under that name. The 1929 stock market crash brought the octopus-like holding companies under scrutiny, and in 1935 the Public Utility Holding Company Act restricted utilities' ownership to contiguous regions. American Water Works was dissolved in 1948, and the newly independent West Penn Electric became the owner of the three geographically linked utilities.

The steel industry — which accounted for the

largest share of the company's sales — began exiting the region in the 1950s. West Penn was saved because its location was in the middle of one of the richest coal regions in the country. The company divested its nonutility interests, and in 1960 it was renamed Allegheny Power System.

In 1981 Allegheny formed Allegheny Generating Company (AGC), which held 40% of a Virginia hydroelectric station it bought that year. Passage of the Clean Air Act of 1990, which set limits on sulfur dioxide emissions, cost coal-dependent Allegheny an estimated $2 billion.

The Energy Policy Act of 1992 opened the door for deregulation of the energy industry, and Allegheny formed a nonutility holding company (AYP Capital) in 1994. Two years later Pennsylvania approved deregulation legislation, and AYP Capital took over two new subsidiaries: AYP Energy (wholesale power) and Allegheny Communications Connect (telecommunications).

In 1997 the company was renamed Allegheny Energy (AE), and it formed Allegheny Energy Solutions to market energy services to Pennsylvania retail customers. It also agreed to buy Pennsylvania utility DQE, but DQE later backed out.

In 1998 AE entered Pennsylvania's deregulation pilot program. Full competition arrived in Pennsylvania's electricity markets in 1999, and AE formed Allegheny Energy Supply to hold its generation assets, including those of AYP Energy. AYP Capital became Allegheny Ventures, which took charge of AE's telecom unit and Allegheny Energy Solutions.

Expanding its West Virginia operations, the company purchased the West Virginia Power unit of UtiliCorp United (now Aquila) for $75 million, and in 2000 bought natural gas distributor Mountaineer Gas (200,000 customers). AE also entered a communications venture with five other companies; the venture, America's Fiber Network (now AFN Communications), operates a 13-state fiber-optic network.

Moving to expand Allegheny Energy Supply's power trading operations, AE in 2001 bought Merrill Lynch's Global Energy Markets unit for $490 million and a 2% stake in Allegheny Energy Supply. It also purchased three gas-fired merchant plants (1,700 MW of capacity) in Illinois, Indiana, and Tennessee from Enron for $1 billion, and announced plans to spin off up to 18% of a holding company that would own Allegheny Energy Supply (it later postponed the plans because of market conditions). It also purchased two energy services firms that year, Fellon-McCord & Associates and Alliance Energy Services Partnership. In 2002 Allegheny Energy Supply sold 150,000 retail accounts in Pennsylvania and Ohio to Dominion's retail marketing unit.

Chairman, President, and CEO, Allegheny Energy; Chairman and CEO, Allegheny Energy Service, Allegheny Generating, Monongahela Power, Potomac Edison, and West Penn Power: Alan J. Noia, age 54, $1,262,500 pay

SVP and CFO; VP and Director, Allegheny Energy, Allegheny Generating, Monongahela Power, Potomac Edison, and West Penn Power; VP, Allegheny Energy Supply: Bruce E. Walenczyk, age 49

SVP Delivery; President and Director, Monongahela Power, Potomac Edison, and West Penn Power; Director, Allegheny Generating: Jay S. Pifer, age 64, $476,300 pay

SVP Supply; President and COO, Allegheny Energy Supply; President and Director, Allegheny Generating, VP and Director, Allegheny Generating, Monongahela Power, Potomac Edison, and West Penn Power: Michael P. Morrell, age 53, $470,700 pay

VP Administration; VP, Allegheny Energy Supply, Allegheny Generating, Monongahela Power, Potomac Edison, and West Penn Power: Richard J. Gagliardi, age 51, $393,400 pay

VP and General Counsel; VP and Director, Allegheny Generating; VP, Allegheny Energy Supply, Monongahela Power, Potomac Edison, and West Penn Power: Thomas K. Henderson, age 61, $368,500 pay

Auditors: PricewaterhouseCoopers LLP

LOCATIONS

HQ: 10435 Downsville Pike, Hagerstown, MD 21740
Phone: 301-790-3400 **Fax:** 301-790-6085
Web: www.alleghenyenergy.com

Allegheny Energy supplies power to parts of Maryland, Ohio, Pennsylvania, Virginia, and West Virginia.

PRODUCTS/OPERATIONS

2001 Sales

	$ mil.	% of total
Unregulated generation & energy marketing	7,486	72
Regulated		
Electric	2,395	23
Gas	235	2
Other	124	1
Allegheny Ventures	139	2
Total	**10,379**	**100**

COMPETITORS

AEP	Duke Energy
Aquila	Exelon
Avista	FirstEnergy
Cinergy	NiSource
Conectiv	Pepco Holdings
Constellation Energy Group	PG&E
	PPL
Dominion	Reliant Energy
DPL	Southern Company
DQE	TVA

HISTORICAL FINANCIALS & EMPLOYEES

NYSE: AYE FYE: December 31	Annual Growth	12/92	12/93	12/94	12/95	12/96	12/97	12/98	12/99	12/00	12/01
Sales ($ mil.)	18.2%	2,307	2,332	2,452	2,648	2,328	2,370	2,576	2,808	4,012	10,379
Net income ($ mil.)	8.3%	204	216	263	240	210	281	(12)	258	237	418
Income as % of sales	—	8.8%	9.3%	10.7%	9.1%	9.0%	11.9%	—	9.2%	5.9%	4.0%
Earnings per share ($)	7.4%	1.83	1.88	2.23	2.00	1.73	2.30	(0.10)	2.22	2.14	3.47
Stock price - FY high ($)	—	24.38	28.44	26.50	29.25	31.13	32.59	34.94	35.19	48.75	55.09
Stock price - FY low ($)	—	20.75	23.44	19.75	21.50	28.00	25.50	26.63	26.19	23.63	32.99
Stock price - FY close ($)	4.7%	23.94	26.50	21.75	28.63	30.38	32.50	34.50	26.94	48.19	36.22
P/E - high	—	13	15	14	15	18	14	—	14	17	15
P/E - low	—	11	12	11	11	16	11	—	11	8	9
Dividends per share ($)	0.7%	1.61	1.63	1.64	1.65	1.69	1.72	1.72	1.72	1.72	1.72
Book value per share ($)	3.7%	16.05	16.62	19.99	19.06	19.24	19.76	18.00	16.02	16.43	22.22
Employees	12.4%	1,957	5,157	6,061	5,750	5,093	4,892	4,817	4,923	5,600	5,600

STOCK PRICE HISTORY

HIGH/LOW/CLOSE

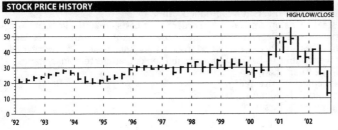

2001 FISCAL YEAR-END

Debt ratio: 53.8%
Return on equity: 18.8%
Cash ($ mil.): 38
Current ratio: 0.43
Long-term debt ($ mil.): 3,236
No. of shares (mil.): 125
Dividends
  Yield: 4.7%
  Payout: 49.6%
Market value ($ mil.): 4,537

ALLEGHENY TECHNOLOGIES

Alloys are allies at Allegheny Technologies. The Pittsburgh-based company, formerly Allegheny Teledyne, formed when diversified Teledyne and stainless-steel manufacturer Allegheny Ludlum merged. It is a top maker of stainless and specialty steels, nickel- and cobalt-based alloys and superalloys, titanium and titanium alloys, tungsten materials, and such exotic alloys as niobium and zirconium. Allegheny Technologies' flat-rolled products (sheet, strip, and plate) account for nearly 60% of sales. Its high-performance metals unit produces metal bar, billet, coil, foil, ingot, plate, rod, and wire. The company's largest markets include aerospace and electrical energy.

To focus on metal products, Allegheny Technologies has spun off its consumer oral hygiene unit and its aerospace, electronics, and high-tech software operations; it also sold some industrial equipment businesses. The company has made several acquisitions, both in the US and Europe. In order to raise funds for continuing acquisitions, Allegheny Technologies has raised prices on several product lines.

Former chairman Richard Simmons owns about 10% of Allegheny Technologies. Caroline Singleton, heir of Teledyne founder Henry Singleton, owns 7%.

HISTORY

Allegheny Ludlum Steel was created in 1938 when Allegheny Steel Company (founded in Pennsylvania in 1898) and Ludlum Steel Company (founded in New Jersey in 1854) merged. Allegheny Steel veteran W. F. Detwiler became the new company's first chairman. During WWII Allegheny Ludlum developed heat-resisting alloys for aircraft turbine engines.

After the war the focus was on stainless steel and flat-rolled silicon electrical steel used to make electrical transformers. In 1956 the company doubled its capacity for making specialty alloys and installed the industry's first semi-automated system for working hot steel. It expanded outside the US by opening a plant in Belgium in the 1960s.

The company adopted the name Allegheny Ludlum Industries in 1970 and, after diversifying, sold its specialty steel division in a management-led buyout that formed Allegheny Ludlum Steel (1980). In 1986 it became Allegheny Ludlum Corp. It went public in 1987.

Henry Singleton and George Kozmetsky, former Litton Industries executives, invested $225,000 each in 1960 to found Teledyne to make electronic aircraft components. First year sales of $4.5 million grew to nearly $90 million by 1964. Kozmetsky left the firm in 1966.

Under Singleton, Teledyne bought more than 100 successful manufacturing and technology firms in defense-related areas such as engines, unmanned aircraft, specialty metals, and computers. Teledyne also moved into offshore oil-drilling equipment, insurance and finance, and the Water Pik line of oral-care products.

Teledyne spun off its Argonaut Insurance unit in 1986 and left the insurance business entirely with its 1990 spinoff of Unitrin. Its defense businesses were caught in a 1989 fraud probe, and the company paid $4.4 million in restitution. In 1991 Teledyne consolidated its 130 operations into 21 companies. It paid a $13 million fine in 1995 on charges of knowingly selling zirconium to a Chilean arms manufacturer for use in cluster bombs sold to Iraq.

Despite Teledyne's rebuff of holding company WHX's 1994 takeover offer, in 1996 WHX came back with a new proposal that led to the $3.2 billion merger of Teledyne and Allegheny Ludlum in 1997. Also in 1997 CEO William Rutledge was succeeded by former Allegheny Ludlum CEO Richard Simmons. Allegheny and Bethlehem Steel entered into a bidding war for steelmaker Lukens. Bethlehem won but in 1998 granted exclusive access to or sold most of Lukens' stainless-steel operations to Allegheny. The company also bought UK-based Sheffield Forgemaster's Group's aerospace division and titanium producer Oregon Metallurgical.

Allegheny restructured to focus on specialty metals in 1999, changing its name to Allegheny Technologies. The company sold Ryan Aeronautical (aerial drones) to Northrop Grumman, its mining equipment business to Astec Industries, and its lift-truck business to Terex. It spun off its consumer oral-hygiene business as Water Pik Technologies and its remaining aerospace businesses as Teledyne Technologies. Lockheed Martin executive Thomas Corcoran became president and CEO in 1999 but abruptly resigned in late 2000. VC Robert Bozzone served as chairman and CEO until insider James Murdy was named CEO in 2001. Also in 2000 the company bought Baker Hughes' tungsten carbide products unit.

In order to cut costs, in 2001 Allegheny Technologies closed a plant in Pennsylvania, made workforce cuts, and sold its North American titanium distribution operations to management.

OFFICERS

Chairman: Robert P. Bozzone, age 68, $650,000 pay
President, CEO, and Director: James L. Murdy, age 63, $880,000 pay
EVP and COO; President, Allegheny Ludlum Corp.: Douglas A. Kittenbrink, age 46, $487,500 pay
EVP, Strategic Initiatives and Technology and CTO: Jack W. Shilling, age 58, $565,000 pay
SVP, Finance and CFO: Richard J. Harshman, age 45, $382,500 pay
SVP and Chief Legal and Administrative Officer: Jon D. Walton, age 59, $495,000 pay
VP, Controller, and Chief Accounting Officer: Dale G. Reid, age 46
VP, Procurement, Information Technology, and CIO: Terry L. Dunlap, age 42
VP and Treasurer: Robert S. Park, age 57
President, Allegheny Rodney: Terrence L. Hartford
President, Allvac: Thomas E. Williams
President, Casting Services: David R. Neil
President, Metalworking Products: David M. Hogan
President, Portland Forge: Patrick W. Bennett
President, Rome Metals: William L. Ringle
President, Wah Chang: Lynn D. Davis
Director Human Resources: Jan Stevens
Auditors: Ernst & Young LLP

LOCATIONS

HQ: Allegheny Technologies Incorporated
1000 6 PPG Place, Pittsburgh, PA 15222
Phone: 412-394-2800 **Fax:** 412-394-3034
Web: www.alleghenytechnologies.com

Allegheny Technologies has operations throughout the US and in China, France, Germany, Spain, Switzerland, and the UK.

PRODUCTS/OPERATIONS

2001 Sales & Operating Profit

	Sales		Operating Profit	
	$ mil.	% of total	$ mil.	% of total
Flat-rolled products	1,088	59	(38)	—
High-performance metals	772	30	82	89
Industrial products	268	11	10	11
Total	**2,128**	**100**	**54**	**100**

Selected Products and Operating Units

Allegheny Ludlum (stainless steel, nickel-based alloys, titanium, silicon electrical steels, tool steels, high-tech alloy and titanium plate)
Allegheny Rodney (stainless steel strip)
Allvac (nickel-based alloys and superalloys, cobalt-based alloys and superalloys, titanium and titanium-based alloys, specialty steel)
Casting Service (large gray iron castings, large ductile iron castings)
Shanghai STAL Precision Stainless Steel Company Ltd. (60%, precision-rolled strip stainless steel, with Baosteel Group)

COMPETITORS

AK Steel Holding Corporation	J & L Specialty Steel	Ryerson Tull
Alcan	Liquidmetal	ThyssenKrupp
A. M. Castle	Metallurg	Timken
Avesta Sheffield	Nippon Steel	United States
Bethlehem Steel	Nucor	Steel
Carpenter Technology	Olympic Steel	WCI Steel
Corus Group	Republic Engineered	WHX
Eramet	Products	

HISTORICAL FINANCIALS & EMPLOYEES

NYSE: ATI FYE: December 31	Annual Growth	12/92	12/93	12/94	12/95	12/96	12/97	12/98	12/99	12/00	12/01
Sales ($ mil.)	8.3%	1,036	1,100	1,077	1,494	3,816	3,745	3,923	2,296	2,460	2,128
Net income ($ mil.)	—	47	71	18	112	213	298	241	300	133	(25)
Income as % of sales	—	4.5%	6.4%	1.7%	7.5%	5.6%	7.9%	6.1%	13.1%	5.4%	—
Earnings per share ($)	—	—	—	—	—	—	—	—	3.13	1.60	(0.31)
Stock price - FY high ($)	—	—	—	—	—	—	—	—	25.94	26.81	21.07
Stock price - FY low ($)	—	—	—	—	—	—	—	—	20.25	12.50	12.50
Stock price - FY close ($)	(13.6%)	—	—	—	—	—	—	—	22.44	15.88	16.75
P/E - high	—	—	—	—	—	—	—	—	14	17	—
P/E - low	—	—	—	—	—	—	—	—	11	8	—
Dividends per share ($)	—	—	—	—	—	—	—	—	0.00	0.80	0.80
Book value per share ($)	(5.9%)	—	—	—	—	—	—	—	13.28	12.94	11.76
Employees	7.9%	5,400	6,100	6,000	6,000	24,000	22,000	21,500	11,500	11,400	10,700

STOCK PRICE HISTORY

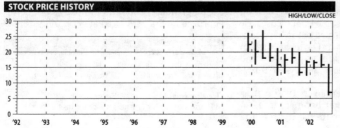

HIGH/LOW/CLOSE

2001 FISCAL YEAR-END

Debt ratio: 37.8%
Return on equity: —
Cash ($ mil.): 34
Current ratio: 2.78
Long-term debt ($ mil.): 573
No. of shares (mil.): 80
Dividends
  Yield: 4.8%
  Payout: —
Market value ($ mil.): 1,345

ALLERGAN, INC.

Which lens is better — one or two? Better with no muscle spasms, or no wrinkles?

Irvine, California-based Allergan's eye care products include eye care medications (glaucoma treatment Alphagan accounts for 15% of sales), contact lens cleaners, and intraocular lenses used in cataract surgery to replace the eye's natural lens. Allergan also makes Azelex acne treatment and Tazorac for acne and psoriasis. Its leading drug Botox — derived from the botulism toxin — treats muscle spasms. Botox has also been found to lessen wrinkles by relaxing facial muscles and has received FDA approval for that indication. The firm is eyeing other Botox uses, including treatments for migraine, lower back pain, and excessive sweating.

Allergan is focusing on new drug discovery to expand its market share and replace older products nearing patent expiration. In addition to expanding existing product lines, the company is also researching vitamin A derivatives (retinoids) for possible diabetes, cancer, and bone disease treatments. To facilitate its focus on pharmaceuticals, Allergan spun off the majority of its optical device unit as Advanced Medical Optics.

HISTORY

In 1950 Gavin Herbert set up a small ophthalmic business above one of his drugstores in Los Angeles. Chemist Stanley Bly invented the company's first product, antihistamine eyedrops called Allergan. The company adopted the name of the eyedrops and expanded the business and the product range. Herbert's son Gavin Jr., then a USC student, helped with the business (he's now chairman emeritus).

By 1960 Allergan was a $1 million company; it moved into the contact lens solution market with its Liquifilm product that year. In 1964 it developed its first foreign distributorship, in Iraq, and the following year it started its first foreign subsidiary, in Canada. International expansion and limited competition for hard contact lens care products sustained sales growth around 20% throughout the 1960s.

Allergan went public in 1971. During the 1970s the company became Bausch & Lomb's contractual supplier of Hydrocare lens solution and enzymatic cleaner for soft contact lenses. By 1975 Allergan had about a third of the hard contact lens care market. When Gavin Sr. died in 1978, Gavin Jr. succeeded him as president and CEO and also became chairman. By 1979 revenues topped $62 million.

SmithKline bought Allergan in 1980 just as the soft contact lens market boomed. In 1984 SmithKline acquired International Hydron, the #2 soft contact lens maker behind Bausch & Lomb; International Hydron became part of Allergan in 1987.

The next year the company acquired the rights to a botulinum toxin product called Oculinum, which would later evolve into Botox. In 1989 SmithKline merged with Beecham and spun off Allergan.

By the early 1990s the contact lens and lens care markets had begun to mature, leading to a company restructuring and a new focus on specialty pharmaceuticals. In 1992 Allergan sold its North and South American contact lens businesses; the rest of its contact lens businesses were sold in 1993.

The company boosted its presence in the intraocular lens market with the 1994 purchase of Ioptex Research. Also in 1994 Allergan and joint venture partner Ligand Pharmaceuticals made their enterprise an independently operating company, Allergan Ligand Retinoid Therapeutics (ALRT). The next year Allergan recalled about 400,000 bottles of contact lens solution because of potential eye irritation.

In 1995 Allergan acquired cataract surgery equipment maker Optical Micro Systems and the contact lens care business of Pilkington Barnes Hind. That year the government probed the company for exporting the botulism toxin in Botox — it feared the product's use in biological weapons — but did not press charges.

The company's 1995 income was hurt by a $50 million contribution to ALRT; its 1996 income was the result of a $70 million write-off for restructuring. In 1996 it was discovered that Allergan's Botox could be used to lessen facial wrinkles.

In 1997 Allergan received approval for a handful of new products, including its multifocus eye lens for cataract patients; acne and psoriasis treatment Tazorac; and glaucoma treatment Alphagan. That year Allergan and Ligand acquired the assets of ALRT and formed subsidiary Allergan Specialty Therapeutics to research and develop new drugs. The unit was spun off in 1998, but Allergan bought it back again in 2001.

In 1998 the firm restructured, cutting some 550 jobs and closing about half of its manufacturing plants. In 2000 the company's Botox was approved by the FDA to treat cervical dystonia.

OFFICERS

Chairman Emeritus: Gavin S. Herbert, age 69
Chairman, President, and CEO: David E. I. Pyott, age 48, $1,540,423 pay
Vice Chairman: Herbert W. Boyer, age 65
SVP and Controller (Principal Accounting Officer): James M. Hindman, age 41

Corporate VP, Corporate Development: Jeffrey Edwards
VP and CFO: Eric K. Brandt, age 39, $572,308 pay
VP and Director; President, Research and Development and Global BOTOX: Lester J. Kaplan, age 51, $595,923 pay
VP, General Counsel, Secretary, and Chief Ethics Officer: Douglas S. Ingram, age 39
VP, Corporate Development: George M. Lasezkay, age 50
VP, Human Resources: Tom Burnham
VP; President, Europe, Africa, and Asia Pacific Region: David A. Fellows, age 45
VP; President, Latin America Region: Nelson R. A. Marques, age 51
VP; President, North America Region and Global Eye Rx Business: F. Michael Ball, age 46, $594,723 pay
VP; President, Surgical and CLCP Businesses: James V. Mazzo, age 44
VP, Worldwide Operations: Jacqueline J. Schiavo, age 53
Corporate Counsel and Assistant Secretary: Aimee S. Weisner, age 33
Associate General Counsel and Assistant Secretary: Martin A. Voet
Director, Investor and Media Relations: Shuki Shattuck
Manager, Treasury and Investor Relations: Vince Scullins
Auditors: KPMG LLP

LOCATIONS

HQ: 2525 Dupont Dr., Irvine, CA 92612
Phone: 714-246-4500   **Fax:** 714-246-4971
Web: www.allergan.com

2001 Sales

	% of total
US	55
Other countries	45
Total	**100**

PRODUCTS/OPERATIONS

2001 Sales

	$ mil.	% of total
Eye care pharmaceuticals	746	43
Botox/neuromuscular	310	17
Contact lens care products	297	17
Ophthalmic surgical devices	254	15
Skin care	79	5
Research	60	3
Total	**1,746**	**100**

Selected Products

Alocril (allergic conjunctivitis treatment)
Alphagan (glaucoma and ocular hypertension treatment)
Array (multifocal silicone intraocular lens)
Azelex (acne treatment)
Betagan (ophthalmic solution)
Blephamide (ophthalmic anti-inflammatory and anti-infective)
Botox (neuromuscular disorder treatment)
Botox Cosmetic (wrinkle reduction)
Ocuflox (conjunctivitis and corneal ulcer solution)
PhacoflexII (intraocular lens)
Propine (ophthalmic solution)
Refresh (artificial tear solution)
Tazorac (treatment for acne and psoriasis)
UltraCare (contact lens neutralizer/disinfectant)

COMPETITORS

Alcon	Hoffmann-La Roche
Bausch & Lomb	Johnson & Johnson
Bristol-Myers Squibb	Merck
Cooper Companies	Novartis
Dermik Laboratories	NutraMax Products
Elan Corporation	Ocular Sciences
GlaxoSmithKline	Schering-Plough

HISTORICAL FINANCIALS & EMPLOYEES

NYSE: AGN FYE: December 31	Annual Growth	12/92	12/93	12/94	12/95	12/96	12/97	12/98	12/99	12/00	12/01
Sales ($ mil.)	7.7%	898	859	947	1,067	1,147	1,149	1,296	1,452	1,626	1,746
Net income ($ mil.)	9.0%	104	109	111	73	77	128	(90)	188	215	225
Income as % of sales	—	11.5%	12.7%	11.7%	6.8%	6.7%	11.2%	—	13.0%	13.2%	12.9%
Earnings per share ($)	9.2%	0.76	0.83	0.87	0.56	0.59	0.98	(0.69)	1.39	1.61	1.68
Stock price - FY high ($)	—	13.12	12.70	14.87	16.25	20.22	17.91	32.02	55.67	97.38	95.70
Stock price - FY low ($)	—	9.81	9.99	9.63	12.40	14.45	12.46	15.29	30.52	42.85	56.82
Stock price - FY close ($)	21.5%	12.52	10.89	13.60	15.65	17.15	16.16	31.18	47.91	93.23	72.27
P/E - high	—	17	15	17	29	34	18	—	39	59	56
P/E - low	—	13	12	11	22	24	13	—	21	26	33
Dividends per share ($)	7.4%	0.19	0.20	0.21	0.24	0.31	0.26	0.26	0.28	0.32	0.36
Book value per share ($)	7.9%	3.74	4.02	4.74	5.18	5.72	6.44	5.26	4.89	6.64	7.45
Employees	2.5%	5,158	4,749	4,903	6,000	6,100	6,100	5,972	5,969	6,181	6,436

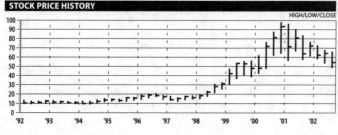

STOCK PRICE HISTORY
HIGH/LOW/CLOSE

2001 FISCAL YEAR-END
Debt ratio: 34.8%
Return on equity: 24.3%
Cash ($ mil.): 782
Current ratio: 2.70
Long-term debt ($ mil.): 521
No. of shares (mil.): 131
Dividends
 Yield: 0.5%
 Payout: 21.4%
Market value ($ mil.): 9,485

ALLIANT TECHSYSTEMS INC.

If Rambo owned stock, he'd want a big chunk of Alliant Techsystems (ATK). The Edina, Minnesota-based company previously had two business segments — aerospace and defense (including the formerly separate conventional munitions unit) — but is now restructuring by adding a third group: Precision Systems, to be accompanied by the Aerospace Group and the newly named Ammunition Group. ATK's Aerospace Group makes reinforced composite structures for aircraft and spacecraft and propulsion systems (ATK Thiokol). The Defense Systems Group turns out conventional munitions ranging from small arms to tank ammunition for the M1A1 Abrams (the US's main battle tank). The Precision Systems Group will be composed of the majority of the tactical munition and propulsion (solid propulsion systems for space vehicles) businesses.

In an attempt to increase its ability to supply munitions to the US government, Alliant has acquired Blount International's ammunition unit and a Boeing ordnance unit. ATK has also bolstered its rocket propulsion operations by purchasing Thiokol Propulsion from Alcoa. The US government and its prime contractors account for about 75% of the company's sales — Boeing and Lockheed Martin each account for about 10% of sales.

HISTORY

Alliant Techsystems (ATK) was formed in 1990 when Honeywell spun off its defense-related businesses to shareholders. Honeywell's roots in the defense business go back to 1941, when it was known as Honeywell-Minnesota. A maker of consumer electronics products such as switches, buttons, and appliances, Honeywell joined the war effort and began producing tank periscopes, turbo engine regulators, automatic ammunition firing control devices, and automatic bomb-release systems.

After WWII Honeywell-Minnesota found that the Cold War provided a reliable and profitable income stream for defense contractors. By 1964 the company had focused on electronics systems. Provisions for the Vietnam War boosted sales, but the fall of Saigon led to downsizing.

When the Iron Curtain fell in the late 1980s, Honeywell's defense operations misfired and ran up huge losses. Honeywell sought to sell its defense businesses as an independent subsidiary, but was unable to obtain an acceptable bid.

Honeywell spun off Alliant Techsystems to shareholders in 1990 under Toby Warson, the CEO of Honeywell's UK subsidiary. A former naval commander, Warson began with about 8,300 employees and lots of bureaucratic layers; he quickly cut about 800 administrative jobs.

Although the Soviet Union and its Eastern Bloc allies had collapsed, a new threat raised its head: Iraq. Cutbacks in the defense budget meant that advanced high-dollar systems were put on the back burner while cheaper alternatives, such as improved ammunition, were moved to the front. During the Gulf War, ATK's ordnance contributions included 120mm uranium-tipped anti-tank shells, 25mm shells for the Bradley Fighting Vehicle, and the 30mm bullets used by Apache helicopters and A-10 Warthog anti-tank planes.

Warson cut another 800 jobs after the Gulf War and reduced the number of management layers from 14 to seven. ATK divested its only non-munitions unit, Metrum Information Storage (data recording and storage devices), in 1992. Metrum had incurred setbacks that caused the company to write off millions of dollars. The next year ATK acquired three companies: Accudyne Corporation (electronic and mechanical assemblies, fuses), Kilgore (sold in 2001), and Ferrulmatic (metal parts). ATK expanded into additional aerospace markets in 1995 with the purchase of the aerospace division of Hercules Incorporated, a maker of space rocket motors, strategic and tactical weapons systems, and ordnance. In 1996 ATK withdrew from demilitarization ventures in the former Soviet republics of Belarus and Ukraine.

ATK refocused on its core operations in 1997 and jettisoned its marine systems group (torpedoes, underwater surveillance systems). The next year the company was awarded a $1 billion contract to make components for Boeing's Delta IV rockets. In 1999 chairman and CEO Dick Schwartz retired from the company and was replaced by retired Navy admiral Paul David Miller.

Miller consolidated plants, improved manufacturing processes, and bought back more than 1.3 million shares of ATK's stock in 2000. While the conventional munitions segment posted slight sales declines that year, primarily due to reduced sales of tactical tank ammunition as the US Army transitions into the next-generation tank round, Miller's efforts led to greater company profitability. In 2001 ATK acquired Thiokol Propulsion Corp. for about $700 million. In September Alliant bought the defense unit of Safety Components International that makes metallic belt links for ammunition. In December the company added another acquisition to the mix with the purchase of the ammunitions unit of Blount International for about $250 million in stock.

In 2002 ATK announced a broad restructuring and bought a small ordnance unit from Boeing.

OFFICERS

Chairman and CEO: Paul David Miller, age 60,
$1,413,333 pay
President: Paul A. Ross, age 64, $669,668 pay
(prior to title change)
SVP and COO: Nicholas G. Vlahakis, age 53,
$517,668 pay (prior to title change)
VP and CFO: Eric S. Rangen, age 45
VP and Chief People Officer: Paula J. Patineau
VP and General Counsel: Ann D. Davidson
VP, Human Resources: Robert E. Gustafson, age 51
VP, Information Technology and CIO:
Geoffrey B. Courtright, age 51
Group VP, Ammunition: Mark W. DeYoung
Group VP, Aerospace: Jeffrey O. Foote
Group VP, Precision Systems: Daniel J. Murphy Jr.
President, ATK Ammunition and Powder:
Patrick S. Nolan
President, ATK Ammunition Systems: Michael McCann
President, ATK Composite Structures:
Travis E. Campbell
President, ATK Integrated Defense: Hubert D. Hopkins
Auditors: Deloitte & Touche LLP

LOCATIONS

HQ: 5050 Lincoln Dr., Edina, MN 55436
Phone: 952-351-3000   **Fax:** 952-351-3025
Web: www.atk.com

2002 Sales

	% of total
US	93
Other countries	7
Total	**100**

PRODUCTS/OPERATIONS

2002 Sales

	$ mil.	% of total
Aerospace	1,031	57
Defense	771	43
Total	**1,802**	**100**

Selected Operations
ATK Aerospace Composite Structures Company
(carbon/carbon graphite, aramid, glass fiber reinforced
composite materials for aircraft, satellites, spacecraft,
and liquid propulsion tank segments)
ATK Aerospace Propulsion Company (solid propulsion
systems; land- and sea-based strategic propulsion
systems)
ATK Ammunition and Powder Company (solid
propellant for ammunition and rockets)
ATK Ammunition Systems Company (medium-caliber
ammunition and tank ammunition)
ATK Integrated Defense Company (infantry weapon
systems, smart artillery systems, barrier systems,
electronic support equipment, electronic warfare
systems, sensors, and missile warning systems)
ATK Lake City Small Caliber Ammunition Company
ATK Tactical Systems Company (missiles)
ATK Thiokol Propulsion Company (propulsion systems
for space launch vehicles)

COMPETITORS

Allied Research	Lockheed Martin
Boeing	Northrop Grumman
Expro Chemical Products	Olin
GenCorp	Raytheon
General Dynamics	United Technologies
ITT Industries	Aerospace

HISTORICAL FINANCIALS & EMPLOYEES

NYSE: ATK FYE: March 31	Annual Growth	3/93	3/94	3/95	3/96	3/97	3/98	3/99	3/00	3/01	3/02
Sales ($ mil.)	6.7%	1,005	775	789	1,194	1,089	1,076	1,090	1,078	1,142	1,802
Net income ($ mil.)	—	(114)	33	(74)	48	59	68	51	74	68	69
Income as % of sales	—	—	4.2%	—	4.0%	5.4%	6.3%	4.7%	6.9%	5.9%	3.8%
Earnings per share ($)	—	(3.51)	0.95	(2.19)	1.06	1.31	1.51	1.24	2.17	2.14	1.96
Stock price - FY high ($)	—	9.20	8.90	12.06	15.73	17.03	20.48	26.11	25.89	39.82	69.13
Stock price - FY low ($)	—	5.68	6.53	6.45	10.57	12.46	12.02	17.17	15.13	17.25	37.32
Stock price - FY close ($)	28.5%	7.12	7.12	11.31	14.35	12.50	18.62	23.05	17.47	39.40	68.03
P/E - high	—	—	9	—	14	13	13	16	12	18	29
P/E - low	—	—	7	—	10	9	8	10	7	8	15
Dividends per share ($)	—	0.00	0.00	0.00	0.00	0.00	0.00	0.00	0.00	0.00	0.00
Book value per share ($)	27.0%	2.00	2.78	3.01	3.60	4.96	5.10	3.42	3.76	6.27	17.19
Employees	11.1%	4,500	4,900	8,200	7,700	6,800	6,550	6,110	6,500	6,022	11,600

STOCK PRICE HISTORY

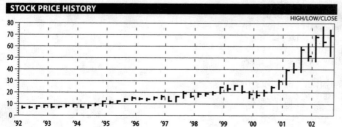

HIGH/LOW/CLOSE

2002 FISCAL YEAR-END

Debt ratio: 60.9%
Return on equity: 18.4%
Cash ($ mil.): 9
Current ratio: 1.80
Long-term debt ($ mil.): 868
No. of shares (mil.): 32
Dividends
Yield: —
Payout: —
Market value ($ mil.): 2,203

ALLIED WASTE INDUSTRIES, INC.

Allied Waste Industries has collected enough garbage and garbage companies to make it the #2 nonhazardous solid waste company in the US, behind Waste Management. The Scottsdale, Arizona-based company serves about 10 million residential, commercial, and industrial customers in 39 states. It operates 355 collection companies, 181 transfer stations, 167 landfills, and 65 recycling facilities.

Allied Waste has worked hard to consolidate the operations of Browning-Ferris Industries, which it acquired in 1999. After major job cuts and shutting down overlapping facilities, the company is focusing on internal growth. Allied Waste is expanding its eight geographic regions to 12 in order to create smaller, more manageable operating areas for the company. It is also working to vertically integrate — controlling the waste stream from collection to transfer station to landfill — all of its markets.

HISTORY

In 1987 entrepreneur Bruce Lessey looked around Houston at all the garbage trucks his Quick Wrench firm was servicing and saw an opportunity. He changed his company's name to Allied Waste, went public, and started buying waste companies. Two years later Allied Waste was in trouble. In stepped Roger Ramsey, co-founder of Browning-Ferris Industries (BFI), who left BFI in 1976. He was a partner in an investment company that owned part of Allied Waste. Ramsey joined the board (becoming CEO in 1989), and Lessey stepped down. Over the next seven years, the company acquired 30 waste haulers in seven states.

One of them (acquired in 1992) was R.18, an Illinois firm owned by Arizona native Thomas Van Weelden. Ramsey, the money man, and Van Weelden, a nonconformist whose entire family was in the garbage business, struck up a close partnership. Van Weelden became Allied Waste's president (and CEO in 1997), and the two moved the company to Scottsdale, Arizona, in 1993 to get away from Houston-based heavyweight (and future partner) BFI.

The two men implemented a rapid growth strategy through the loose consolidation of vertically integrated, locally managed operations. In 1996 Allied Waste bought a rich prize, Laidlaw, for $1.6 billion, which tripled the company's revenues in 1997. It sold Laidlaw's Canadian operation to pay down debt.

Allied Waste acquired 54 other operators in 1998, including Seattle-based Rabanco Cos., which gave it a foothold in the Pacific Northwest. It also paid $1.1 billion for American Disposal

Services. Late that year Van Weelden succeeded Ramsey as chairman, and merger negotiations with big boy BFI got serious.

Between 1992 and the time Allied Waste made its biggest deal, it had collected more than 200 companies. In 1999 it bought its largest company yet, BFI, a $4.7 billion operation. The $9.4 billion acquisition sent Allied Waste's customer base soaring from 2.6 million to 9.9 million. At the time of its acquisition, BFI operated in 46 US states, Canada, and Puerto Rico.

Founded in 1967, BFI had been on the buyout trail for decades. During its first six years it acquired 157 waste-disposal companies and expanded overseas. In the 1980s it bought more than 500 firms and gained another 100 in the early 1990s.

All was not well at BFI, however. The company had slipped in the late 1980s, when price-fixing charges and environmental violations cost it more than $5 million and resulted in a lot of bad press. By 1998 BFI was bloated and revenues were stagnant. It sold all operations outside North America to Suez Lyonnaise, in exchange for $1 billion and a 20% stake in SITA, Europe's #1 waste company. The rest of BFI's holdings went to Allied in 1999 in a deal valued at about $9 billion.

To raise about $1.6 billion and gain regulatory clearance for the BFI acquisition, Allied in 1999 and 2000 sold a number of assets that it gained from BFI. Besides selling selected US solid-waste operations to eliminate overlap, Allied sold all of BFI's operations in Canada, its medical waste business, and its stake in SITA. In integrating BFI's operations with its own, Allied Waste cut 2,900 jobs and closed 51 facilities within a year of the BFI acquisition. Allied continued to trim excess operations in 2001 with the sale of commercial routes in Florida, Georgia, Tennessee, and Virginia.

Chairman, President, and CEO:
Thomas H. Van Weelden, age 47, $1,202,255 pay
EVP and CFO: Thomas W. Ryan, age 55, $461,250 pay
SVP Finance: Peter S. Hathaway, age 46, $425,250 pay
SVP Operations: Donald W. Slager, age 40
VP, Controller, and Chief Accounting Officer:
James E. Gray
VP and Treasurer: Thomas P. Martin
VP Financial Analysis and Planning: John S. Quinn
VP Investor Relations: Michael S. Burnett
VP Legal and Corporate Secretary: Steven M. Helm,
age 54, $399,750 pay
VP Mergers and Aquisitions: Michael G. Hannon
VP Tax: Dale L. Parker
Director, Human Resources: Cheryl Anderson
Auditors: PricewaterhouseCoopers LLP

LOCATIONS

HQ: 15880 N. Greenway-Hayden Loop, Ste. 100,
Scottsdale, AZ 85260
Phone: 480-627-2700   **Fax:** 480-627-2701
Web: www.alliedwaste.com

Allied Waste Industries operates in 39 states in the US.

PRODUCTS/OPERATIONS

2001 Sales

	$ mil.	% of total
Collection	4,204	62
Disposal	2,104	31
Recycling	232	4
Other	197	3
Adjustments	(1,172)	—
Total	**5,565**	**100**

COMPETITORS

Casella Waste Systems
Philip Services
Republic Services
Rumpke
Safety-Kleen
Waste Connections
Waste Industries USA
Waste Management

HISTORICAL FINANCIALS & EMPLOYEES

NYSE: AW FYE: December 31	Annual Growth	12/92	12/93	12/94	12/95	12/96	12/97	12/98	12/99	12/00	12/01
Sales ($ mil.)	75.6%	35	54	97	170	247	875	1,576	3,341	5,708	5,565
Net income ($ mil.)	57.2%	1	1	(8)	9	(79)	0	(223)	(289)	124	59
Income as % of sales	—	2.9%	2.4%	—	5.5%	—	0.0%	—	—	2.2%	1.1%
Earnings per share ($)	—	0.08	0.08	(0.24)	0.35	(0.84)	0.16	(1.22)	(1.69)	0.29	(0.07)
Stock price – FY high ($)	—	12.25	6.88	6.00	10.00	10.38	24.38	31.63	24.06	14.75	19.90
Stock price – FY low ($)	—	4.13	4.00	3.25	3.75	6.44	7.25	16.13	6.50	5.31	8.90
Stock price – FY close ($)	12.8%	4.75	5.25	4.00	7.13	9.25	23.31	23.63	8.81	14.56	14.06
P/E – high	—	153	86	—	26	—	37	—	—	40	—
P/E – low	—	52	50	—	10	—	11	—	—	14	—
Dividends per share ($)	—	0.00	0.00	0.00	0.00	0.00	0.00	0.00	0.00	0.00	0.00
Book value per share ($)	9.3%	4.01	5.98	6.02	2.66	3.64	5.76	5.04	8.67	8.97	8.90
Employees	60.4%	413	639	1,125	1,440	5,000	5,400	9,500	32,500	28,000	29,000

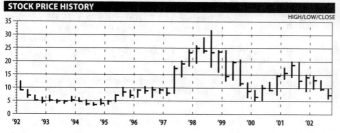

STOCK PRICE HISTORY   HIGH/LOW/CLOSE

2001 FISCAL YEAR-END

Debt ratio: 84.0%
Return on equity: 9.1%
Cash ($ mil.): 159
Current ratio: 0.84
Long-term debt ($ mil.): 9,238
No. of shares (mil.): 197
Dividends
  Yield: —
  Payout: —
Market value ($ mil.): 2,772

ALLMERICA FINANCIAL

All secure? Allmerica Financial wants to help. The Worcester, Massachusetts-based firm sells property/casualty insurance (some 70% of revenues) and asset management services. Citizens Insurance and Hanover Insurance offer homeowners, personal and commercial auto, workers' compensation, and commercial multiperil coverage through independent agents mainly in the Northeast, Midwest, and Southeast. More than 50% of premiums are written in Massachusetts and Michigan.

Allmerica's asset management operations include the sale of life insurance and annuities to affluent individuals and small businesses. Allmerica is seeking partnerships with banks and other financial services firms and advisors through which it can sell its products.

FMR Corp. (better known as Fidelity Investments) owns some 10% of Allmerica.

HISTORY

In 1842 a group of Worcester, Massachusetts, businessmen tried to form a mutual life insurance company. After a failed first attempt, they succeeded with the help of lobbyist Benjamin Balch. In 1844 the State Mutual Life Assurance Co. of Worcester set up business in the back room of secretary Clarendon Harris' bookstore. The first president was John Davis, a US senator. The company issued its first policy in 1845.

In the early years State Mutual reduced risk by issuing policies only for residents of such "civilized" areas as New England, New Jersey, New York, Pennsylvania, and Ohio. It also restricted movement, requiring policyholders to get permission for travel outside these areas. By the 1850s the company had begun issuing policies in the Midwest (with a 25% premium surcharge), the South (for 30% extra), and California (for a pricey extra $25 per $1,000), with a maximum coverage of $5,000.

The Civil War was a problem for many insurers, who had to decide what to do about Southern policyholders and payment on war-related claims. State Mutual chose to pay out its Northern policyholders' benefits, despite the extra cost. In 1896 the firm began offering installment pay-out plans for policyholders afraid that their beneficiaries would fritter away the whole payment.

The first 30 years of the 20th century were, for the company, a time of growth that was stopped short by the Depression. But despite a great increase in the number of policy loans and surrenders for cash value, State Mutual's financial footing remained solid.

After WWII the company entered group insurance and began offering individual sickness and accident coverage. In 1957 it was renamed State Mutual Life Assurance Co. of America. The firm added property/casualty insurance in the late 1950s through alliances with such firms as Worcester Mutual Fire Insurance. During the 1960s State Mutual continued to develop property/casualty, buying interests in Hanover Insurance and Citizens Corp.

The firm followed the industry-wide shift into financial services in the 1970s, adding mutual funds, a real estate investment trust, and an investment management firm. This trend accelerated in the 1980s, and State Mutual began offering financial planning services, as well as administrative and other services for the insurance and mutual fund industries (the mutual fund administration operations were sold in 1995). Managing this growth was another story: Its buys left it bloated and disorganized. Technical systems were in disarray by the early 1990s, and the agency force had grown to more than 1,400. In response, the company began a five-year effort to upgrade systems, cut fat, and reduce sales positions.

In view of its shifting focus, State Mutual became Allmerica Financial in 1992. Three years later it demutualized. In 1997 it bought the 40% of Allmerica Property & Casualty that it didn't already own. The next year heavy spring storms hammered Allmerica's bottom line, and the company incurred $15 million in catastrophe losses. Also in 1998 it bought the portion of Citizens it didn't already own.

In 1999 Allmerica announced plans to sell its group life and health insurance operations to concentrate on its core businesses; Great-West Assurance bought them the next year. Its 1999 purchase of Advantage Insurance Network, a group of affiliated life insurance agencies, grew its distribution channels. In 2000 the firm reduced its workforce by 5% (some 6,000 employees) in an efficiency move. In 2001 Allmerica sold its 401(k) business to Minnesota Life.

OFFICERS

President and CEO, Allmerica Financial and First Allmerica Financial Life Insurance Company, and Director: John F. O'Brien, age 59, $976,923 pay
SVP: Richard M. Reilly, age 63, $450,000 pay
VP and CFO, Allmerica Financial and First Allmerica Financial Life Insurance Company: Edward J. Parry III, age 42
VP and CIO: Gregory D. Tranter, age 45
VP and Chief Investment Officer; VP, Allmerica Financial and First Allmerica Financial Life Insurance Company: John P. Kavanaugh, age 47, $364,231 pay

VP, General Counsel, and Assistant Secretary, Allmerica Financial and First Allmerica Financial Life Insurance Company: J. Kendall Huber, age 47
VP, Human Resources: Renee Mikitarian-Bradley
VP; President and CEO, First Allmerica Financial Life Insurance Company: Mark Hug, age 44
VP, Allmerica Financial and First Allmerica Financial Life Insurance Company; President and CEO, Hanover Insurance: Robert P. Restrepo Jr., age 51, $450,000 pay
Auditors: PricewaterhouseCoopers LLP

LOCATIONS

HQ: Allmerica Financial Corporation
440 Lincoln St., Worcester, MA 01653
Phone: 508-855-1000   **Fax:** 508-853-6332
Web: www.allmerica.com

PRODUCTS/OPERATIONS

2001 Assets

	$ mil.	% of total
Cash & equivalents	350	1
State & municipal bonds	1,830	6
Corporate bonds	6,326	21
Mortgage-backed securities	1,032	4
Stocks	62	—
Mortgage loans	322	1
Policy loans	380	1
Separate account assets	14,838	49
Recoverables & receivables	2,055	7
Other	3,141	10
Total	**30,336**	**100**

Selected Subsidiaries
Allmerica Asset Management, Inc.
  Allmerica Asset Management, Limited (Bermuda)
Allmerica Benefits, Inc.
Allmerica Financial Insurance Brokers, Inc.
Citizens Insurance Company of Illinois
The Hanover Insurance Company
Sterling Risk Management Services, Inc.
Allmerica Funding Corp.
Allmerica, Inc.
Financial Profiles, Inc.
First Allmerica Financial Life Insurance Company
  Advantage Insurance Network, Inc.
  Allmerica Financial Life Insurance and Annuity Company
  Allmerica Trust Company, N.A. (99%)
First Sterling Limited (Bermuda)
VeraVest, Inc.

COMPETITORS

AIG	Lincoln National
Allstate	MassMutual
American Financial	MetLife
AXA Financial	Nationwide
Chubb	New York Life
CIGNA	Northwestern Mutual
CNA Financial	Progressive Corporation
GEICO	Prudential
GenAmerica	St. Paul Companies
Guardian Life	State Farm
The Hartford	TIG Specialty Insurance
John Hancock Financial Services	Travelers
	USAA
Liberty Mutual	

HISTORICAL FINANCIALS & EMPLOYEES

NYSE: AFC FYE: December 31	Annual Growth	12/92	12/93	12/94	12/95	12/96	12/97	12/98	12/99	12/00	12/01
Assets ($ mil.)	13.9%	9,367	10,291	10,503	17,758	18,998	22,549	27,608	30,770	31,588	30,336
Net income ($ mil.)	—	104	115	40	134	182	209	201	296	200	(3)
Income as % of assets	—	1.1%	1.1%	0.4%	0.8%	1.0%	0.9%	0.7%	1.0%	0.6%	—
Earnings per share ($)	—	—	—	—	2.61	3.63	3.82	3.33	5.33	3.75	(0.06)
Stock price - FY high ($)	—	—	—	—	28.63	34.38	51.00	75.25	64.81	74.25	71.75
Stock price - FY low ($)	—	—	—	—	23.38	24.75	32.63	38.38	46.06	35.06	36.70
Stock price - FY close ($)	8.7%	—	—	—	27.00	33.50	49.94	57.88	55.63	72.50	44.55
P/E - high	—	—	—	—	11	9	13	22	11	20	—
P/E - low	—	—	—	—	9	7	9	11	8	9	—
Dividends per share ($)	—	—	—	—	0.00	0.20	0.20	0.20	0.25	0.25	0.25
Book value per share ($)	6.2%	—	—	—	31.42	34.43	39.69	41.96	41.33	45.71	45.20
Employees	(3.2%)	—	—	—	6,800	6,800	6,300	6,300	6,300	5,700	5,600

STOCK PRICE HISTORY

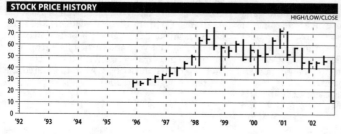

HIGH/LOW/CLOSE

2001 FISCAL YEAR-END

Equity as % of assets: 7.9%
Return on assets: —
Return on equity: —
Long-term debt ($ mil.): 200
No. of shares (mil.): 53
Dividends
  Yield: 0.6%
  Payout: —
Market value ($ mil.): 2,357
Sales ($ mil.): 3,312

THE ALLSTATE CORPORATION

Allstate has all hands on deck to bolster its reputation. Although Allstate is the #2 home and auto insurer in the US (State Farm is #1), it has been fighting an uphill battle to stay competitive, profitable, and well-regarded by its customers.

Auto insurance accounts for some 70% of Allstate's property/casualty premiums, which make up more than three-quarters of sales. The company also offers life and annuity products (through Allstate Life, Northbrook Life, and Glenbrook Life) and specialty lines. To reduce distribution expenses, Allstate has turned its agent-employees into independent contractors and launched an integrated distribution system that allows customers to do business through the Internet, the telephone, or through agents.

For some folks, Allstate's good hands have been clutching a double-edged sword, as the company has been fighting several court battles. These include lawsuits from former employees and the Equal Employment Opportunity Commission over a dispute with about 300 agents who refused to accept the new employment contract.

The company is focusing on expanding its property/casualty business and life insurer Allstate Financial, which targets affluent and middle-income consumers. Adding to its products, Allstate has launched a nationwide bank. The company has been hit by declining equity markets and increased homeowners claims.

HISTORY

Allstate has its origins in a friendly game of bridge played in 1930 on a Chicago-area commuter train by Sears president Robert Wood and a friend, insurance broker Carl Odell. The insurance man suggested Sears sell auto insurance through the mail. Wood liked the idea, financed the company, and in 1931 put Odell in charge (that hand of bridge must have shown Wood that Odell was no dummy). The company was named Allstate, after one of Sears' tire brands. Allstate was born just as Sears was beginning its push into retailing, and Allstate went with it, selling insurance out of all the new Sears stores.

Growth was slow during the Depression and WWII, but the postwar boom was a gold mine for both Sears and Allstate. Suburban development made cars a necessity; 1950s prudence necessitated car insurance; and Sears made it easy to buy the insurance at their stores and, increasingly, at freestanding agencies.

In the late 1950s Allstate added home and other property/casualty insurance lines. It also went into life insurance — in-force policies zoomed from zero to $1 billion in six years, the industry's fastest growth ever.

Sears formed Allstate Enterprises in 1960 as an umbrella for all its noninsurance operations. In 1970 that firm bought its first savings and loan (S&L). The insurer continued to acquire other S&Ls and to add subsidiaries throughout the 1970s and 1980s.

This strategy dovetailed with Sears' strategy, which was to become a diversified financial services company. In 1985 Sears introduced the Discover Card through Allstate's Greenwood Trust Company. However, by the late 1980s it was obvious Sears would never be a financial services giant. Moreover, it was losing so much in retailing that by 1987 Allstate was the major contributor to corporate net income. Sears began to dismantle its financial empire in the 1990s.

Allstate also suffered from a backlash against high insurance rates. When Massachusetts instituted no-fault insurance in 1989, Allstate stopped writing new auto insurance there. Later the company had to refund $110 million to customers to settle a suit with California over rate rollbacks required by 1988's Proposition 103.

Allstate went public in 1993, when Sears sold about 20% of its stake. That year it began reducing its operations in Florida to protect itself against high losses from hurricanes. Two years later the retailer sold its remaining interest to its shareholders. Also in 1995 Allstate sold 70% of PMI, its mortgage insurance unit, to the public.

In 1996 Allstate worked to reduce its exposure to hurricane and earthquake losses. (Together, Hurricane Andrew and the Northridge quake helped account for almost $4 billion in casualty losses.) It created a Florida-only subsidiary that would buy reinsurance to protect against losses that could arise from another major hurricane. That year Allstate sold its Northbrook (property/casualty) and Allstate Reinsurance operations to St. Paul and SCOR, respectively.

In 1998 Allstate sold its real estate portfolio for nearly $1 billion; chairman and CEO Jerry Choate retired and was succeeded by president and COO Edward Liddy; and Allstate opened a savings bank. In 2000 Allstate restructured and added online and telephone distributions to increase its sales and bought Provident National Assurance Co. from UNUMProvident. Reducing expenses, Allstate cut some 10% of its staff (some 4,000 jobs) that year and turned its agents into independent contractors. With its purchase of Sterling Collision Centers, Allstate entered the car repair business in 2001.

OFFICERS

Chairman, President, and CEO: Edward M. Liddy, age 56, $1,093,356 pay
Acting CFO; SVP and CIO, Allstate Insurance: Casey J. Sylla, age 58
SVP and Chief Investment Officer; President, Allstate Investments: Eric A. Simonson
VP and General Counsel; SVP and General Counsel, Allstate Insurance: Michael J. McCabe, age 56
VP and Secretary; EVP and Secretary, Allstate Insurance: Robert W. Pike, age 60
Chairman and President, Allstate Life Insurance: Thomas J. Wilson II, age 44, $914,535 pay
President, Direct Distribution and E-Commerce, Allstate Insurance: Steven L. Groot, age 52
President, Ivantage Group, Allstate Insurance; President, Encompass Insurance: Ernest A. Lausier, age 56
SVP and Chief Marketing Officer, Allstate Insurance: Robert S. Apatoff, age 43
SVP, Allstate Insurance; President, Allstate Property and Casualty: Richard I. Cohen, age 57, $746,464 pay
SVP, Human Resources, Allstate Insurance: Joan M. Crockett, age 51
Auditors: Deloitte & Touche LLP

LOCATIONS

HQ: Allstate Plaza, 2775 Sanders Rd., Northbrook, IL 60062
Phone: 847-402-5000   **Fax:** 847-836-3998
Web: www.allstate.com

Allstate is licensed to sell life and property/casualty insurance in Canada, Germany, Indonesia, Italy, the Philippines, Puerto Rico, and the US.

PRODUCTS/OPERATIONS

2001 Assets

	$ mil.	% of total
Cash & equivalents	263	—
Treasury & agency securities	3,810	3
Foreign governments' securities	911	1
Mortgage-backed securities	10,929	10
Municipal bonds	19,724	18
Corporate bonds	26,117	24
Equity securities	5,245	5
Mortgage loans	5,710	5
Assets in separate account	13,587	12
Recoverables	2,698	3
Receivables	3,976	4
Other	16,205	15
Total	**109,175**	**100**

Selected Subsidiaries
Allstate Bank
Allstate Insurance Company
Allstate International Insurance Holdings, Inc.
American Heritage Life Investment Corporation

COMPETITORS

21st Century	CNA Financial	Ohio Casualty
AIG	GEICO	Old Republic
American	The Hartford	Progressive
General	Kemper	Corporation
American	Insurance	Prudential
National	Liberty Mutual	SAFECO
Insurance	Lincoln National	St. Paul
Chubb	MetLife	Companies
CIGNA	Mutual of	State Farm
Cincinnati	Omaha	Travelers
Financial	Nationwide	USAA

HISTORICAL FINANCIALS & EMPLOYEES

NYSE: ALL FYE: December 31	Annual Growth	12/92	12/93	12/94	12/95	12/96	12/97	12/98	12/99	12/00	12/01
Assets ($ mil.)	8.6%	52,098	59,358	61,369	70,029	74,508	80,918	87,691	98,119	104,808	109,175
Net income ($ mil.)	—	(826)	1,302	484	1,904	2,075	3,105	3,294	2,720	2,211	1,158
Income as % of assets	—	—	2.2%	0.8%	2.7%	2.8%	3.8%	3.8%	2.8%	2.1%	1.1%
Earnings per share ($)	0.7%	—	1.50	0.54	2.12	2.32	3.56	3.94	3.38	2.95	1.59
Stock price - FY high ($)	—	—	17.13	14.94	21.19	30.44	47.19	52.38	41.00	44.75	45.90
Stock price - FY low ($)	—	—	13.56	11.31	11.75	18.69	28.13	36.06	22.88	17.19	30.00
Stock price - FY close ($)	10.9%	—	14.75	11.88	20.56	28.94	45.25	38.50	24.06	43.56	33.70
P/E - high	—	—	11	28	10	13	13	13	12	15	29
P/E - low	—	—	9	21	6	8	8	9	7	6	19
Dividends per share ($)	22.8%	—	0.18	0.36	0.39	0.43	0.36	0.53	0.59	0.66	0.93
Book value per share ($)	9.9%	—	11.44	9.38	14.17	16.07	19.25	21.99	22.32	25.00	24.43
Employees	(2.5%)	51,515	49,000	46,300	44,300	48,200	51,400	53,000	52,000	41,800	40,830

STOCK PRICE HISTORY

HIGH/LOW/CLOSE

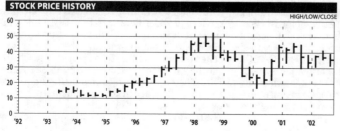

2001 FISCAL YEAR-END

Equity as % of assets: 15.9%
Return on assets: 1.1%
Return on equity: 6.7%
Long-term debt ($ mil.): 3,694
No. of shares (mil.): 712
Dividends
  Yield: 2.8%
  Payout: 58.5%
Market value ($ mil.): 23,994
Sales ($ mil.): 28,802

ALLTEL CORPORATION

ALLTEL wants to be all things to all of its communications customers. The Little Rock, Arkansas-based telecommunications provider offers wireless, local, and long-distance phone service and Internet access to more than 10 million customers in 24 states, primarily in the southeastern and midwestern US.

ALLTEL is the incumbent provider of local phone service for 2.6 million customers in 15 states through mostly rural exchanges. It provides CLEC (competitive local-exchange carrier) service in 12 states, though it is pulling out of seven. ALLTEL provides long-distance service to about 1 million customers in its local service territories, and paging services to about 500,000 subscribers in Arkansas, Florida, Louisiana, and Ohio, on both a facilities-based and resale basis. The company provides wireless phone service to about 6.8 million consumers in 21 states. ALLTEL also has purchased cellular systems and licenses in six states from Louisiana-based CenturyTel in a $1.65 billion cash deal.

ALLTEL's information services units focus primarily on clients in the financial services and telecommunications industries. The company also publishes phone directories and distributes telecom equipment and materials.

HISTORY

ALLTEL traces its roots to the Western Reserve Telephone Company of Hudson, Ohio. In 1960 Weldon Case, grandson of Western Reserve's founder, merged it with four other Ohio phone companies to form the Mid-Continent Telephone Company. In 1983 Mid-Continent merged with Allied Telephone to form ALLTEL Corporation, creating the US's fifth-largest phone service. The merger, inspired by the competitive environment resulting from the AT&T breakup, included Mid-Continent's purchase of satellite-based carrier Argo Communications. Case became ALLTEL's chairman.

In 1984 ALLTEL Mobile launched its first wireless system in Charlotte, North Carolina. To concentrate on fast-growing Sun Belt markets, in 1987 ALLTEL sold cellular interests it had acquired in Ohio, Pennsylvania, and West Virginia.

As the 1990s began, ALLTEL combined its telecom business with information services. It bought Systematics, a provider of processing services and software to the financial industry (1990), C-TEC's cellular phone billing and information systems software (1991), and Computer Power, which did data processing for the mortgage banking industry (1992). These businesses would become part of ALLTEL Information Services.

When Case retired in 1991, Joe Ford became chairman and moved the company's headquarters to Little Rock. Building its southern presence, ALLTEL bought GTE's phone directory publishing business and Georgia phone properties in 1993. It also acquired cellular properties in Arkansas, North Carolina, South Carolina, and Texas. In 1996 the company sold phone and cable TV lines in eight (mainly western) US states to Citizens Utilities and bought a 5% stake in Apex Global Information Services, a global Internet access provider. The next year the company began offering Internet access in several US markets, began long-distance service, and applied for permission to offer competitive local phone service in Arkansas and North Carolina.

ALLTEL won PCS licenses for 73 markets in 12 US states (including seven key southern states) in 1997. In a move to offer more bundled services, the company consolidated its wireline and wireless phone operations that year into one unit, ALLTEL Communications.

In 1998 ALLTEL acquired Chicago-based 360 Communications (which had been struggling since its 1996 spinoff from Sprint) in a $6 billion deal; 360 brought 2.6 million cellular customers in 15 states, mostly in the Southeast and Mid-Atlantic. ALLTEL also bought about 2,400 miles of fiber-optic lines from Qwest, primarily in the South.

In 1999 the company bought Aliant Communications, a provider of both wireless and wireline services in Nebraska, for $1.8 billion. ALLTEL spent another $600 million to acquire Kansas-based Liberty Cellular. In 2000 it swapped wireless properties in 13 states with Bell Atlantic and GTE. The deal, completed in 2000, was tied to Bell Atlantic's purchase of GTE, which formed Verizon Communications. ALLTEL also purchased wireless and paging properties in Louisiana in a $388 million deal with SBC Communications.

ALLTEL cut 1,000 jobs, or about 4% of its workforce, in 2001 to reduce expenses. That year the company dropped out of the US auction for wireless spectrum and later took a majority stake in a UK-based joint venture with IBM to offer Internet banking systems in Europe.

Also in 2001 ALLTEL offered to buy telecom services provider CenturyTel for $6.1 billion in cash and stock and $3.3 billion in assumed debt. ALLTEL released information about the unsolicited bid after CenturyTel had rejected it, which led the Louisiana based company to sue ALLTEL. The two companies mended animosities and in 2002 reached an agreement that sent CenturyTel's cellular operations and licenses to ALLTEL for $1.65 billion in cash. Also that year

ALLTEL completed the purchase of local phone properties in Kentucky from Verizon in a $1.9 billion cash deal. The company also announced plans to discontinue offering competitive local service in seven of the 12 states it operates in.

OFFICERS

Chairman: Joe T. Ford, age 64, $2,250,000 pay
President, CEO, and Director: Scott T. Ford, age 39, $1,870,000 pay
Group President, Communications: Kevin L. Beebe, age 42, $1,017,500 pay
Group President and CIO: Michael T. Flynn, age 53
Group President, Information Services: Jeffrey H. Fox, age 39, $1,017,500 pay
EVP External Affairs, General Counsel, and Secretary: Francis X. Frantz, age 48, $810,000 pay
SVP and CFO: Jeffery R. Gardner, age 42
SVP and CTO: John S. Haley, age 46
SVP Strategic Planning: Keith A. Kostuch, age 39
VP Human Resources: Frank A. O'Mara, age 41
VP Investor Relations: Kerry Brooks
Treasurer: Scott H. Settelmyer
Controller: David A. Gatewood, age 44
Auditors: PricewaterhouseCoopers LLP

LOCATIONS

HQ: 1 Allied Dr., Little Rock, AR 72202
Phone: 501-905-8000   **Fax:** 501-905-5444
Web: www.alltel.com

PRODUCTS/OPERATIONS

2001 Sales & Operating Income

	Sales $ mil.	Sales % of total	Operating Income $ mil.	Operating Income % of total
Communications services				
Wireless	3,832	48	819	46
Wireline	1,813	23	723	40
Emerging businesses	462	6	38	2
Information services	1,323	17	191	11
Other operations	514	6	24	1
Adjustment	(345)	—	(38)	—
Total	**7,599**	**100**	**1,757**	**100**

Selected Operations
Cellular phone operations
Directory publishing
Information processing primarily for financial services and telecom industries
Internet access services
Local phone services (15 states)
Long-distance services
Network management
Paging networks
PCS (personal communications services)

COMPETITORS

Amdocs	Global Crossing	Telephone &
AT&T	Nextel	Data Systems
BellSouth	Price	U.S. Cellular
CenturyTel	Communications	Verizon
Cingular	Qwest	Verizon Wireless
Wireless	R. R. Donnelley	VoiceStream
Convergys	SBC	Wireless
EDS	Communications	WorldCom
Fiserv	Sprint FON	

HISTORICAL FINANCIALS & EMPLOYEES

NYSE: AT FYE: December 31	Annual Growth	12/92	12/93	12/94	12/95	12/96	12/97	12/98	12/99	12/00	12/01
Sales ($ mil.)	15.4%	2,092	2,342	2,962	3,110	3,192	3,264	5,194	6,302	7,067	7,599
Net income ($ mil.)	18.7%	229	262	272	355	292	508	526	784	1,929	1,067
Income as % of sales	—	10.9%	11.2%	9.2%	11.4%	9.1%	15.6%	10.1%	12.4%	27.3%	14.0%
Earnings per share ($)	11.8%	1.25	1.39	1.43	1.85	1.52	2.70	1.89	2.47	6.08	3.40
Stock price - FY high ($)	—	25.00	31.25	31.38	31.13	35.63	41.63	61.38	91.81	82.94	68.69
Stock price - FY low ($)	—	17.38	22.88	24.00	23.25	26.63	29.75	38.25	56.31	47.75	49.43
Stock price - FY close ($)	11.1%	23.88	29.50	30.13	29.50	31.38	41.06	59.81	82.69	62.44	61.73
P/E - high	—	20	22	22	17	23	15	32	37	13	20
P/E - low	—	14	16	17	12	17	11	20	23	8	15
Dividends per share ($)	6.6%	0.74	0.80	0.88	0.96	1.04	1.10	1.16	1.22	1.28	1.32
Book value per share ($)	10.8%	7.12	8.34	8.68	10.26	11.23	12.01	11.63	13.34	16.28	17.92
Employees	7.1%	12,876	14,864	16,333	15,865	16,307	16,393	21,504	24,440	27,257	23,955

STOCK PRICE HISTORY

HIGH/LOW/CLOSE

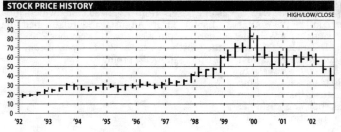

2001 FISCAL YEAR-END

Debt ratio: 41.0%
Return on equity: 20.0%
Cash ($ mil.): 85
Current ratio: 1.38
Long-term debt ($ mil.): 3,862
No. of shares (mil.): 311
Dividends
  Yield: 2.1%
  Payout: 38.8%
Market value ($ mil.): 19,169

AMAZON.COM, INC.

A map of the Amazon River shows its tributaries spreading out like fingers across the land, and a map showing namesake Amazon.com's reach within the online world would look pretty much the same. The Seattle-based company, best known for being the #1 online seller of books (as well as videos and music), is also the Internet's largest retailer, period.

Although it still goes toe-to-toe with Barnes & Noble and others in the book business, Amazon.com now sells a wide variety of products from household goods to tools. It also allows individuals and companies to sell their products through Amazon.com — for a price.

Amazon.com's network of online investments offer a host of other consumer products and services, including prescription drugs, luxury goods, and more. But in the rapidly changing world of e-tailing, not all of its investments have panned out (think of no-longer living.com and expired Pets.com, for example). Amazon.com is linking its virtual stores to the bricks-and-mortar kind; it runs both the Toys "R" Us Web site and the online operations of rival bookseller Borders.

Amazon.com has gone from a venture-capital-funded startup in CEO Jeff Bezos' garage to a bellwether Internet stock. It defined the red-ink-drenched, spend-to-grow style of Internet companies whose jaw-dropping market values outpaced those of much larger enterprises. Founder, chairman, and CEO Bezos owns about one-third of Amazon.com, which reported its first profit ever during the fourth quarter of 2001.

HISTORY

Jeff Bezos was researching the Internet in the early 1990s for hedge fund D.E. Shaw. He realized that book sales would be a perfect fit with e-commerce because book distributors already kept meticulous electronic lists. Bezos, who as a teen had dreamed of entrepreneurship in outer space, took the idea to Shaw. The company passed on the idea, but Bezos ran with it, trekking cross country to Seattle (close to a facility owned by major book distributor Ingram) and typing up a business plan along the way.

Bezos founded Amazon.com in 1994. After months of preparation, he launched a Web site in July 1995 (Douglas Hofstadter's *Fluid Concepts and Creative Analogies* was its first sale); it had sales of $20,000 a week by September. Bezos and his team kept working with the site, pioneering features that now seem mundane, such as one-click shopping, customer reviews, and e-mail order verification.

Amazon.com went public in 1997. Moves to cement the Amazon.com brand included becoming the sole book retailer on America Online's public Web site and Netscape's commercial channel.

In 1998 the company launched its online music and video stores, and it began to sell toys and electronics. Amazon.com also expanded its European reach with the purchases of online booksellers in the UK and Germany, and it acquired the Internet Movie Database. Bezos also expanded the company's base of online services, buying Junglee (comparison shopping) and PlanetAll (address book, calendar, reminders).

By midyear Amazon.com had attracted so much attention that its market capitalization equaled the combined values of profitable bricks-and-mortar rivals Barnes & Noble and Borders Group, even though their combined sales were far greater than the upstart's. Late that year Amazon.com formed a promotional link with Hoover's, publisher of this profile.

After raising $1.25 billion in a bond offering early in 1999, Amazon.com began a spending spree with deals to buy all or part of several dotcoms. However, some have since been sold (HomeGrocer.com) and others have gone out of business or bankrupt — Pets.com, living.com (furniture). It also bought the catalog businesses of Back to Basics and Tool Crib of the North.

Amazon.com began conducting online auctions in early 1999 and partnered with venerable auction house Sotheby's. Also that year Amazon.com added distribution facilities, including one each in England and Germany.

In 2000 Amazon.com inked a 10-year deal with Toysrus.com to set up a co-branded toy and video game store. Also that year Amazon.com added foreign-language sites for France and Japan.

In 2001 Amazon.com cut 15% of its workforce as part of a restructuring plan that also forced a $150 million charge. That year the company also made a deal with Borders to provide inventory, fulfillment, content, and customer service for borders.com. As part of a deal to expand their marketing partnership, America Online invested $100 million in Amazon.com in July 2001. In November Amazon.com purchased some assets from Egghead.com (which filed Chapter 11 in August) and relaunched the Egghead.com Web site in December 2001. For the fourth quarter of 2001, Amazon.com surprisingly showed a profit.

Chairman, President, and CEO: Jeffrey P. Bezos, age 38, $81,840 pay
SVP and CFO: Thomas J. Szkutak, age 41
SVP Human Resources, Secretary, and General Counsel: L. Michelle Wilson, age 38
SVP Worldwide Architecture and Platform Software and CIO: Richard L. Dalzell, age 44
SVP Worldwide Operations and Customer Service: Jeffrey A. Wilke, age 35, $676,463 pay
SVP Worldwide Retail and Marketing: Diego Piacentini, age 41, $1,408,333 pay
VP Electronics: Frank Sadowski, age 48
Auditors: Ernst & Young LLP

LOCATIONS

HQ: 1200 12th Ave. South, Ste. 1200, Seattle, WA 98144
Phone: 206-266-1000 **Fax:** 206-266-1821
Web: www.amazon.com

Amazon.com has customers in all 50 states and more than 150 countries, with distribution facilities in New Castle, Delaware; Coffeyville, Kansas; Campbellsville and Lexington, Kentucky; Fernley, Nevada; Grand Forks, North Dakota; and Seattle in the US and in France, Germany, and the UK. It jointly operates a fulfillment center with Nippon Express in Japan.

2001 Sales

	% of total
US	71
Other regions	29
Total	**100**

PRODUCTS/OPERATIONS

2001 Sales

	% of total
Books, music, DVDs, videos	54
International segment	21
Electronics, tools, kitchen goods	18
Services segment	7
Total	**100**

COMPETITORS

Advanced Marketing	Hastings Entertainment
Autobytel	HMV
AutoNation	Hollywood Entertainment
Barnes & Noble	Home Depot
Bertelsmann	Indigo Books & Music
Best Buy	Lowe's
Blockbuster	Maruzen
Books-A-Million	Microsoft
Borders	MTS
BUY.COM	Musicland
CDnow	mySimon
Cendant	PETsMART
Columbia House	Pinault-Printemps-
CVS	Redoute
Disney Internet	Toys "R" Us
eBay	Wal-Mart
Federated	WHSmith
France Telecom	Yahoo!

HISTORICAL FINANCIALS & EMPLOYEES

Nasdaq: AMZN FYE: December 31	Annual Growth	12/92	12/93	12/94	12/95	12/96	12/97	12/98	12/99	12/00	12/01
Sales ($ mil.)	—	—	—	0	1	16	148	610	1,640	2,762	3,122
Net income ($ mil.)	—	—	—	(0)	(0)	(6)	(28)	(125)	(720)	(1,411)	(567)
Income as % of sales	—	—	—	—	—	—	—	—	—	—	—
Earnings per share ($)	—	—	—	—	—	—	(0.11)	(0.42)	(2.20)	(4.02)	(1.56)
Stock price - FY high ($)	—	—	—	—	—	—	5.49	60.25	113.00	91.50	22.38
Stock price - FY low ($)	—	—	—	—	—	—	1.31	4.14	41.00	14.88	5.51
Stock price - FY close ($)	21.2%	—	—	—	—	—	5.02	53.49	76.13	15.56	10.82
P/E - high	—	—	—	—	—	—	—	—	—	—	—
P/E - low	—	—	—	—	—	—	—	—	—	—	—
Dividends per share ($)	—	—	—	—	—	—	0.00	0.00	0.00	0.00	0.00
Book value per share ($)	—	—	—	—	—	—	0.10	0.44	0.77	(2.71)	(3.86)
Employees	148.7%	—	—	—	33	151	614	2,100	7,600	9,000	7,800

STOCK PRICE HISTORY	2001 FISCAL YEAR-END

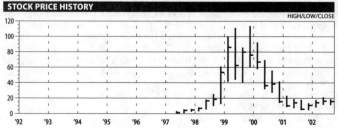

HIGH/LOW/CLOSE

2001 FISCAL YEAR-END
Debt ratio: 100.0%
Return on equity: —
Cash ($ mil.): 540
Current ratio: 1.31
Long-term debt ($ mil.): 2,156
No. of shares (mil.): 373
Dividends
  Yield: —
  Payout: —
Market value ($ mil.): 4,038

AMERADA HESS CORPORATION

Amerada Hess has an armada of black gold assets. Based in New York City, the integrated oil and gas company conducts exploration and production activities mainly in Denmark, Gabon, Norway, the UK, and the US. It also has operations in Azerbaijan, Algeria, Brazil, Indonesia, and Thailand. Amerada Hess has proved reserves of more than 1.4 billion barrels of oil equivalent. Its North Sea properties account for 42% of its proved reserves. The company has gained reserves in West Africa, Latin America, and Southeast Asia by buying exploration and production company Triton Energy.

On the downstream side, Amerada Hess owns a refinery in New Jersey, and it operates the 50%-owned Hovensa refinery in the US Virgin Islands in a venture with Venezuela's state oil company, PDVSA. Amerada Hess markets its petroleum products mainly in the eastern US. It has more than 1,150 HESS gas stations, mostly in Florida, New Jersey, and New York. About 75% of the stations are company-owned, and more than half include Hess Express and Hess Mart convenience stores.

CEO John Hess owns 15% of the company, which he hopes to sail toward a profitable future by exploiting attractive properties in Southeast Asia, Azerbaijan, Latin America, and Algeria.

HISTORY

It was a logical match: Amerada Petroleum, which had been in the exploration and production business since the early 1900s, and Hess Oil and Chemical, involved in refining and marketing since the 1930s.

In 1919 British oil entrepreneur Lord Cowdray formed Amerada Corporation to explore for oil in North America. Cowdray soon hired geophysicist Everette DeGolyer, a pioneer in oil geology research. DeGolyer's systematic methods helped Amerada not only find oil deposits faster but also pick up fields missed by competitors. DeGolyer became president of Amerada in 1929 but left in 1932 to work independently.

After WWII Amerada began exploring overseas and during the 1950s entered pipelining and refining. It continued its overseas exploration through Oasis, a consortium formed in 1964 with Marathon, Shell, and Continental to explore in Libya.

Leon Hess began to buy stock in Amerada in 1966. The son of immigrants, he had entered the oil business during the Depression, selling "resid" — thick refining leftovers that refineries discarded — from a 1929 Dodge truck in New Jersey. He bought the resid cheap and sold it as heating fuel to hotels. Hess also speculated, buying oil at low prices in the summer and selling it for a profit in the winter. He later bought more trucks, a transportation network, refineries, and gas stations and went into oil exploration. Expansion pushed up debt, so in 1962 Leon's company went public as Hess Oil and Chemical after merging with Cletrac Corporation.

Hess acquired Amerada in 1969, after an ownership battle with Phillips Petroleum. During the 1970s Arab oil embargo, Amerada Hess began drilling on Alaska's North Slope. Oilman T. Boone Pickens bought up a chunk of Amerada Hess stock during the 1980s, spurring takeover rumors. They proved premature.

Amerada Hess completed a pipeline in 1993 to carry natural gas from the North Sea to the UK. In 1995 Leon Hess stepped down as CEO (he died in 1999), and his son John took the position. Amerada Hess sold its 81% interest in the Northstar oil field in Alaska to BP, and the next year Petro-Canada bought the company's Canadian operations. In 1996 the company acquired a 25% stake in UK-based Premier Oil.

The company teamed with Dixons Stores Group in 1997 to market gas in the UK. It also purchased 66 Pick Wick convenience store/service stations.

In 1998 Amerada Hess signed production-sharing contracts with a Malaysian oil firm as part of its strategy to move into Southeast Asia and began to sell natural gas to retail customers in the UK.

To offset losses brought on by depressed oil prices, Amerada Hess sold assets worth more than $300 million in 1999, including its southeastern pipeline network, gas stations in Georgia and South Carolina, and Gulf Coast terminals. It also moved into Latin America, acquiring stakes in fields in offshore Brazil.

In 2000 Amerada Hess acquired Statoil Energy Services, which markets natural gas and electricity to industrial and commercial customers in the northeastern US. It also announced its intention to buy LASMO, a UK-based exploration and production company, before Italy's Eni topped the Amerada Hess offer.

Undeterred, in 2001 the company bought Dallas-based exploration and production company Triton Energy for $2.7 billion in cash and $500 million in assumed debt. Amerada Hess also acquired the Gulf of Mexico assets of LLOG Exploration Company for $750 million. That year, however, stiff competition prompted Amerada Hess to put its UK gas and electricity supply business on the auction block. The unit was sold to TXU in 2002.

OFFICERS

Chairman and CEO: John B. Hess, age 47,
$2,500,000 pay
EVP, CFO, and Director: John Y. Schreyer, age 62,
$1,100,000 pay
EVP and President, Refining and Marketing:
F. Borden Walker, age 48, $750,000 pay
**EVP and President Worldwide Exploration and
Production, and Director:** John J. O'Connor, age 56,
$412,500 pay (partial-year salary)
EVP, General Counsel, and Director:
J. Barclay Collins II, age 57, $1,100,000 pay
SVP and Treasurer: Gerald A. Jamin, age 60
SVP Human Resources: Neal Gelfand, age 57
SVP: Alan A. Bernstein, age 57
SVP: F. Lamar Clark, age 68
SVP: John A. Gartman, age 54
SVP: Lawrence H. Ornstein, age 50
SVP: Robert P. Strode, age 45
VP and Controller: J. P. Reily
VP Investor Relations and Secretary: Carl T. Tursi
Auditors: Ernst & Young LLP

LOCATIONS

HQ: 1185 Avenue of the Americas, New York, NY 10036
Phone: 212-997-8500   **Fax:** 212-536-8390
Web: www.hess.com

Amerada Hess conducts exploration and production
activities in Algeria, Azerbaijan, Colombia, Denmark,
Equatorial Guinea, Gabon, Greece, Indonesia, Malaysia,
Thailand, the UK, and the US. It operates refineries in
St. Croix on the US Virgin Islands and in New Jersey.

2001 Sales

	$ mil.	% of total
US	9,824	73
Europe	3,138	24
Other regions	451	3
Total	**13,413**	**100**

PRODUCTS/OPERATIONS

2001 Sales

	$ mil.	% of total
Refining & marketing	9,454	70
Exploration & production	3,957	30
Other	2	—
Total	**13,413**	**100**

COMPETITORS

BP	Norsk Hydro
ChevronTexaco	Occidental Petroleum
ConocoPhillips	PDVSA
Devon Energy	PEMEX
Eni	PETROBRAS
Exxon Mobil	Royal Dutch/Shell Group
Kerr-McGee	Sinclair Oil
Koch	Sunoco
Marathon Ashland	TOTAL FINA ELF
Petroleum	Unocal
Marathon Oil	

HISTORICAL FINANCIALS & EMPLOYEES

NYSE: AHC FYE: December 31	Annual Growth	12/92	12/93	12/94	12/95	12/96	12/97	12/98	12/99	12/00	12/01
Sales ($ mil.)	9.6%	5,875	5,852	6,602	7,302	8,272	8,234	6,590	7,039	11,993	13,413
Net income ($ mil.)	70.5%	8	(268)	74	(394)	660	8	(459)	438	1,023	914
Income as % of sales	—	0.1%	—	1.1%	—	8.0%	0.1%	—	6.2%	8.5%	6.8%
Earnings per share ($)	69.2%	0.09	(2.91)	0.79	(4.26)	7.09	0.08	(5.12)	4.85	11.38	10.25
Stock price - FY high ($)	—	51.25	56.38	52.63	53.63	60.50	64.50	61.06	66.31	76.25	90.40
Stock price - FY low ($)	—	36.63	42.38	43.75	43.25	47.50	47.38	46.00	43.75	47.81	53.75
Stock price - FY close ($)	3.5%	46.00	45.13	45.63	53.00	57.88	54.88	49.75	56.75	73.06	62.50
P/E - high	—	569	—	66	—	8	806	—	14	7	9
P/E - low	—	407	—	55	—	7	592	—	9	4	5
Dividends per share ($)	5.4%	0.75	0.45	0.60	0.60	0.60	0.60	0.60	0.60	0.60	1.20
Book value per share ($)	4.7%	36.59	32.72	33.33	28.60	36.35	35.16	29.26	33.51	43.76	55.29
Employees	0.6%	10,263	10,173	9,858	9,574	9,085	9,216	9,777	8,485	9,891	10,838

STOCK PRICE HISTORY

HIGH/LOW/CLOSE

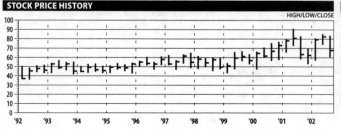

2001 FISCAL YEAR-END

Debt ratio: 51.8%
Return on equity: 20.8%
Cash ($ mil.): 37
Current ratio: 1.06
Long-term debt ($ mil.): 5,283
No. of shares (mil.): 89
Dividends
  Yield: 1.9%
  Payout: 11.7%
Market value ($ mil.): 5,547

AMERCO

AMERCO is in business for the long haul. The Reno, Nevada-based company, best known for operating U-Haul International (based in Phoenix), has moved past the bitter legal battles within its founding Shoen family. With its house in order, AMERCO has refocused its attention on customers who need to get their stuff from here to there.

U-Haul has about 1,350 company-owned locations and about 15,000 independent dealers that rent about 205,000 trucks, trailers, and tow dollies to do-it-yourself movers across the US and Canada. It also sells and rents moving supplies; some sites rent carpet-cleaning equipment and install trailer hitches.

U-Haul is also a top provider of self-storage facilities, with more than 1,000 locations in the US and Canada. In addition, it manages units owned by others and has an interest in Private Mini Storage Realty of Texas.

Subsidiary Republic Western Insurance grew by providing short-term property/casualty insurance to U-Haul customers. AMERCO's other insurance unit, Oxford Life Insurance, offers life, health, and annuity insurance and manages the company's self-insured benefits programs.

The Shoen family, led by chairman and president Edward "Joe" Shoen, controls the company.

Leonard Samuel (L. S.) Shoen earned his nickname, "Slick," as a poor kid trying to make a buck during the Depression. In 1945, as a Navy veteran, he started U-Haul International in Ridgefield, Washington, to serve long-distance do-it-yourself movers who could not return a truck to its origin. Shoen bought used equipment and hit the road, convincing gas station owners to act as agents.

Shoen and his first wife, Anna Mary, who died in 1957, had six children. In 1958 Shoen remarried and with his second wife, Suzanne, had five children. Shoen bestowed stock on all his offspring but neglected to keep a controlling interest. In the 1960s Shoen brought his sons into the company.

U-Haul moved to Phoenix in 1967. Two years later it bought Oxford Life Insurance Co. Shoen formed AMERCO in 1971 as U-Haul's parent. The oil crunch of the 1970s caused U-Haul's network to shrink as gas stations closed, so the company opened its own agencies. New competitors entered the market, and the company's share of business dropped to below 50%. Shoen took AMERCO into debt to diversify into general consumer rentals. The company also established real estate and insurance subsidiaries.

Shoen's second wife divorced him after the out-of-wedlock birth of his 12th child in 1977. His brief marriage to the mother ended in divorce, and he remarried again (and, later, yet again). Meanwhile, Shoen tapped his eldest son Sam for help in pursuing the diversification strategy. In 1979 sons Edward "Joe" and Mark left the company in dispute. Sam became president.

In 1986 Joe and Mark gained the support of enough siblings to constitute a voting majority and ousted their father and brother. L. S. and Sam almost regained control two years later but were outmaneuvered by Joe, who as chairman issued enough stock to a few loyal employees to shift the balance. Then the outside faction sued the people who had been directors in 1988 over issuance of the stock.

Joe refocused on the self-moving business and began upgrading the fleet, reducing the average age of the equipment from 11 to 5 years. In 1993 AMERCO preferred stock began trading on the NYSE, and the next year its common stock was listed on Nasdaq.

Meanwhile, the lawsuit moved glacially through the courts. In 1994 the 1988 directors were found to have wrongfully excluded dissenting family members from the board. An initial award of $1.47 billion was later reduced to $462 million, due from the 1988 directors individually. However, they declared bankruptcy, and AMERCO indemnified them for the award. So in 1996 the company issued new stock and sold (and leased back) tens of thousands of vehicles and trailers to fulfill the judgment. In return, the dissenting family faction (including founder L. S.) gave up their 48% stake in AMERCO.

In 1997 AMERCO held its first stockholders' meeting since 1993. The next year Joe lost an appeal to overturn a ruling that he had acted with malice in dealing with family members in the 1988 stock transaction; he was ordered to pay $7 million in punitive damages to relatives, exclusive of the $462 million previously awarded.

In 1999 founder L. S. died at age 83 in a one-car accident believed to be suicide. In 2001 the company debuted its online storage reservation system. AMERCO denied reports published in August 2002 by the Financial Times that the Securities and Exchange Commission was investigating AMERCO's accounts and probing why it dismissed its auditor of 24 years, PricewaterhouseCoopers.

Chairman and President of AMERCO and U-Haul:
Edward J. Shoen, age 53, $503,708 pay
Secretary and General Counsel of AMERCO and U-Haul: Gary V. Klinefelter, age 54, $289,547 pay
Treasurer of AMERCO and U-Haul: Gary B. Horton, age 58, $289,232 pay
Assistant Treasurer: Rocky D. Wardrip, age 44
President of Amerco Real Estate: Carlos Vizcarra, age 55
President of Oxford Life Insurance:
Mark A. Haydukovich, age 45
President of Republic Western Insurance:
Richard M. Amoroso, age 43, $290,004 pay
President of U-Haul Phoenix Operations:
Mark V. Shoen, age 51, $623,077 pay
EVP and Director of U-Haul: John C. Taylor, age 44
VP Human Resources of U-Haul: Henry P. Kelly
Auditors: BDO Seidman, LLP

LOCATIONS

HQ: 1325 Airmotive Way, Ste. 100, Reno, NV 89502
Phone: 775-688-6300 **Fax:** 775-688-6338
Web: www.uhaul.com

AMERCO's primary subsidiary, U-Haul International, rents consumer moving trucks and trailers throughout the US and Canada.

2002 Sales

	$ mil.	% of total
US	2,016	97
Canada	52	3
Total	**2,068**	**100**

PRODUCTS/OPERATIONS

2002 Sales

	$ mil.	% of total
Moving & Storage	1,585	73
Property/Casualty insurance	302	14
Life insurance	187	9
Real estate	88	4
Adjustments	(94)	—
Total	**2,068**	**100**

Operating Units

Amerco Real Estate Company (owner and manager of the company's real estate assets)
Oxford Life Insurance Company (life, health, and annuity direct writing and reinsurance)
Private Mini Storage (storage, 50%)
Republic Western Insurance Company (property/casualty direct writing and reinsurance for U-Haul employees and customers)
U-Haul International, Inc. (self-moving truck rental and sales of packing supplies)

COMPETITORS

Budget Group
Penske Truck Leasing
Ryder
Shurgard Storage
Sovran
Storage USA

HISTORICAL FINANCIALS & EMPLOYEES

Nasdaq: UHAL FYE: March 31	Annual Growth	3/93	3/94	3/95	3/96	3/97	3/98	3/99	3/00	3/01	3/02
Sales ($ mil.)	7.9%	1,041	1,135	1,241	1,294	1,425	1,425	1,552	1,683	1,814	2,068
Net income ($ mil.)	(24.0%)	32	40	60	60	52	35	63	66	13	3
Income as % of sales	—	3.1%	3.5%	4.8%	4.7%	3.6%	2.5%	4.0%	3.9%	0.7%	0.1%
Earnings per share ($)	—	—	—	1.23	1.33	1.35	0.66	2.07	2.36	0.00	(0.49)
Stock price - FY high ($)	—	—	—	22.50	25.50	49.25	37.00	33.88	30.25	24.38	22.77
Stock price - FY low ($)	—	—	—	15.75	14.75	19.50	22.63	19.63	16.00	16.00	14.27
Stock price - FY close ($)	(2.9%)	—	—	21.38	24.25	25.50	30.75	21.50	18.38	21.25	17.41
P/E - high	—	—	—	18	19	34	29	16	13	—	—
P/E - low	—	—	—	13	11	14	18	9	7	—	—
Dividends per share ($)	—	—	—	0.00	0.00	0.00	0.00	0.00	0.00	0.00	0.00
Book value per share ($)	1.7%	—	—	20.87	24.03	35.74	35.31	36.55	26.12	28.06	23.49
Employees	4.4%	10,900	13,500	12,000	13,000	14,400	14,000	14,400	15,800	16,800	16,100

STOCK PRICE HISTORY

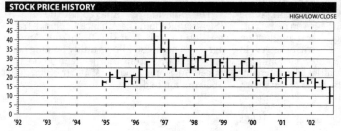

HIGH/LOW/CLOSE

2002 FISCAL YEAR-END

Debt ratio: 67.7%
Return on equity: 0.5%
Cash ($ mil.): 48
Current ratio: —
Long-term debt ($ mil.): 1,046
No. of shares (mil.): 21
Dividends
  Yield: —
  Payout: —
Market value ($ mil.): 370

AMEREN CORPORATION

Ameren knows its current events. The St. Louis-based holding company operates mainly through utility subsidiaries Union Electric and Central Illinois Public Service (known as AmerenUE and AmerenCIPS, respectively). The two serve 1.5 million electricity customers (more than 90% of revenues) and 300,000 natural gas customers in Missouri and Illinois. Ameren has a generating capacity of nearly 13,000 MW (60% coal-fired), most of which is controlled by AmerenUE. Ameren has agreed to purchase CILCORP, the holding company for utility Central Illinois Light, from independent power producer AES.

Since deregulation arrived in Illinois, AmerenCIPS has transferred its power plants to unregulated subsidiary AmerenEnergy Resources, which also procures natural gas for its affiliated companies, builds new power plants, and provides long-term energy supply contracts. Another subsidiary, AmerenEnergy, Inc., markets and trades energy to wholesale and retail customers and provides energy-related services.

Ameren is focusing on its core energy operations and plans to improve its infrastructure assets, including its generating capacity. Other operations include metering system installation and consulting services, and energy and utility construction, financing, and management services.

HISTORY

More than 30 St. Louis companies had built a chaotic grid of generators and power lines throughout the city by 1900. Two years later many of them merged into the Union Company, which attracted national notice when it lit the St. Louis World's Fair in the first broad demonstration of electricity's power. In 1913 the company, by then named Union Electric (UE), began buying electricity from an Iowa dam 150 miles away — the greatest distance power had ever been transmitted in such quantity.

UE pushed into rural Missouri and began buying and building fossil-fuel plants. Despite a slowdown during the Depression, UE built Bagnell Dam on Missouri's Osage River in the early 1930s to gather power for a hydroelectric plant. At the onset of WWII, construction began on new plants with larger generators and lower production costs; however, demand for electricity lagged. In the late 1940s UE compensated by joining a "power pool," a system of utilities with interconnected transmission lines that shared electricity.

Growth in the 1950s came from acquisitions, including Missouri Power & Light (1950) and Missouri Edison (1954). During the 1960s

and 1970s, UE built five new plants, including the Labadie plant (2,300 MW), one of the largest coal-fired plants in the US.

UE began producing nuclear energy in 1984 at its Callaway nuke. High costs and the expenses of a scrapped second plant caused UE to battle the Missouri Public Service Commission throughout the 1980s for rate increases.

Charles Mueller became president in 1993 and CEO one year later. He oversaw continued staff reductions and cost cutting through the 1990s in an increasingly competitive market. In 1997 UE expanded into Illinois through its purchase of CIPSCO, which owned utility Central Illinois Public Service Company (CIPS).

CIPS began as a Mattoon, Illinois, streetcar company in the early 1900s. The firm bought Mattoon's electric power plant in 1904 and began growing its power business, buying small electric companies in the 1920s and 1930s. CIPS built five generating units in the 1940s and 1950s and became part-owner (along with UE) of Electric Energy Inc., which built a power plant on the Ohio River. The company bought Illinois Electric and Gas Company in the 1960s and the state's Gas Utilities in the 1980s. To prepare for competition under deregulation, CIPS created holding company CIPSCO in the 1990s to diversify.

UE's purchase of CIPSCO expanded its geographic scope, and the new company was named Ameren in 1997 to reflect its American energy focus. The next year the company committed to adding generating capacity through several natural gas-fired combustion turbines. It joined nine other utilities to form the Midwest Independent System Operator to manage their transmission needs.

In 1999 Ameren bought a 245-mile railroad line between St. Louis and Kansas City to help the area's economic development. Looking for new opportunities in deregulated energy markets, the company purchased Data & Metering Specialties and rolled it into newly created subsidiary AmerenDMS. In 2000 Ameren created non-regulated subsidiary AmerenEnergy Generating to operate its power plants and affiliate AmerenEnergy Marketing to sell the generating facilities' power.

The following year Ameren left the Midwest ISO group to join the Alliance Regional Transmission Organization (RTO). In 2002 Ameren agreed to purchase Illinois utility holding company CILCORP from independent power producer AES for about $540 million, plus $860 million in debt.

OFFICERS

Chairman and CEO; CEO, AmerenUE and Ameren Services; President, Ameren Development: Charles W. Mueller, age 63, $977,200 pay
President and COO; President and CEO, AmerenCIPS: Gary L. Rainwater, $586,097 pay
SVP Finance: Warner L. Baxter
VP, General Counsel, and Secretary: Steven R. Sullivan
President, AmerenEnergy Resources: Daniel F. Cole
SVP, AmerenEnergy: Clarence J. Hopf Jr.
SVP, AmerenEnergy Resources: R. Alan Kelley
SVP, Ameren Services: David A. Whiteley
SVP, Ameren Services, AmerenUE, and AmerenCIPS: Paul A. Agathen, $354,600 pay
SVP Energy Delivery, Ameren Services: Thomas R. Voss
SVP Generation and Chief Nuclear Officer, AmerenUE and AmerenCIPS: Garry L. Randolph
VP and Tax Counsel, Ameren Services: Gregory L. Nelson
VP AmerenEnergy Marketing, Ameren Energy Resources: Andrew M. Serri
VP Corporate Communications and Public Policy, Ameren Services: J. Kay Smith
VP Corporate Planning, Ameren Services: Craig D. Nelson
VP Customer Service, Ameren Services: Richard J. Mark
Auditors: PricewaterhouseCoopers LLP

LOCATIONS

HQ: 1901 Chouteau Ave., St. Louis, MO 63103
Phone: 314-621-3222 **Fax:** 314-554-3801
Web: www.ameren.com

Ameren distributes electricity and natural gas throughout Missouri and in central and southern Illinois.

PRODUCTS/OPERATIONS

2001 Sales

	$ mil.	% of total
Electric	4,154	92
Natural gas	342	8
Other	10	—
Total	4,506	100

Selected Subsidiaries

AmerenDMS (utility metering and billing services)
AmerenEnergy, Inc. (power marketing and trading, risk management, and energy services)
AmerenEnergy Resources Co. (holding company)
Ameren Development Company (nonregulated holding company)
   AmerenEnergy Generating Company (nonregulated subsidiary operating Ameren's generating facilities)
   AmerenEnergy Fuels and Services Company (natural gas procurement)
   AmerenEnergy Marketing Company (markets Ameren Generating Company's power output)
Central Illinois Public Service Company (AmerenCIPS, Illinois utility)
CIPSCO Investment Company
Electric Energy, Inc. (60%, power generation)
Union Electric Company (AmerenUE, Missouri utility)

COMPETITORS

AES	Enron	MidAmerican
Aquila	Exelon	Energy
CenterPoint	Great Plains	Nicor
Energy	Energy	Peoples Energy
Empire District	Illinois Power	Southern Union
Electric	Laclede Group	

HISTORICAL FINANCIALS & EMPLOYEES

NYSE: AEE FYE: December 31	Annual Growth	12/92	12/93	12/94	12/95	12/96	12/97	12/98	12/99	12/00	12/01
Sales ($ mil.)	5.7%	—	—	—	3,236	3,328	3,327	3,318	3,524	3,856	4,506
Net income ($ mil.)	3.9%	—	—	—	373	372	335	387	385	457	469
Income as % of sales	—	—	—	—	11.5%	11.2%	10.1%	11.6%	10.9%	11.9%	10.4%
Earnings per share ($)	6.4%	—	—	—	—	—	—	2.82	2.81	3.33	3.40
Stock price - FY high ($)	—	—	—	—	—	—	—	44.31	42.94	46.94	46.00
Stock price - FY low ($)	—	—	—	—	—	—	—	35.56	32.00	27.56	36.53
Stock price - FY close ($)	(0.3%)	—	—	—	—	—	—	42.69	32.75	46.31	42.30
P/E - high	—	—	—	—	—	—	—	16	15	14	13
P/E - low	—	—	—	—	—	—	—	13	11	8	11
Dividends per share ($)	10.0%	—	—	—	—	—	—	1.91	2.54	2.54	2.54
Book value per share ($)	2.7%	—	—	—	—	—	—	23.99	24.23	25.01	25.96
Employees	(2.2%)	—	—	—	—	—	8,149	7,450	7,347	7,342	7,447

STOCK PRICE HISTORY

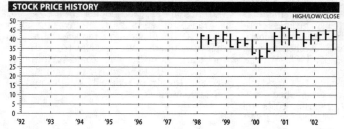

HIGH/LOW/CLOSE

2001 FISCAL YEAR-END

Debt ratio: 44.2%
Return on equity: 14.3%
Cash ($ mil.): 67
Current ratio: 0.55
Long-term debt ($ mil.): 2,835
No. of shares (mil.): 138
Dividends
   Yield: 6.0%
   Payout: 74.7%
Market value ($ mil.): 5,839

AMERICA WEST HOLDINGS

For some, the American West means rattlesnakes, Vegas, and golfing in a desert oasis, and America West Holdings specializes in delivering high-rollers, vacationers, and other travelers there. The Tempe, Arizona-based holding company owns America West Airlines (AWA), a top 10 US carrier. AWA flies to about 90 North American destinations, including seven Mexican cities and two Canadian cities.

AWA, which operates more than 500 flights per day, has more than 145 aircraft (most of them Boeing 737s). Its primary hubs are in Phoenix and Las Vegas, and it has a mini-hub in Columbus, Ohio. It connects to about 115 additional destinations through code-sharing agreements with British Airways, Northwest Airlines, and Taiwan's EVA Airways.

Controlling costs allows AWA to compete with both full-service and low-cost carriers. The airline plans to expand by increasing flights to and from its Phoenix and Las Vegas hubs as well as expanding code-share agreements. To increase its online presence AWA is a partner along with seven other US carriers in Hotwire, an online bargain airfare site competing with priceline.com.

America West also owns a travel services subsidiary, The Leisure Company, which markets tour packages, such as golf vacations, under the America West Vacations brand. A unit of investment firm Texas Pacific Group controls 59% of America West.

As a result of terrorist attacks on New York and Washington, DC, America West cut back on its flight frequency and laid off 2,000 workers (about 15% of its workforce). It was the first major US airline to apply for the federally guaranteed loans that were authorized after the attacks. In its application, America West had to agree to issue warrants that could give the US government a 33% stake in the company.

HISTORY

For years airline consultant Edward Beauvais envisioned a Phoenix airline linking cities in the Southwest to California. He founded America West Airlines (AWA) in 1981 in the wake of airline deregulation. Beauvais' idea was simple: Offer low-fare flights with certain amenities (such as free newspapers) to woo business commuters and create a niche in a region overlooked by the major airlines. In 1983 AWA began flying from Phoenix to four cities. By 1986 AWA was serving 34 cities

AWA added flights to Chicago, New York, and Baltimore in 1987. Beauvais established a second hub in Las Vegas, but expansion costs and competition from Southwest Airlines and USAir

(now US Airways) in Phoenix led to a $46 million loss in 1987. To fuel its rapid expansion and keep its stock in friendly hands, Beauvais and president Michael Conway (formerly of Continental) sold a 20% stake in AWA to its aircraft lessor, Australia's Ansett Airlines. AWA's employees already owned a 30% interest and were guaranteed up to 250% of their annual salaries in the event of a takeover.

Beauvais and Conway cut flights, sold planes, and furloughed 500 employees in 1988. But then AWA tried to expand by buying up bankrupt Eastern Airlines' Washington, DC, route and, in 1991, by initiating service to Nagoya, Japan, via Hawaii. By the end of 1989, AWA had 286 daily flights to 56 cities, including Honolulu, New York, and Seattle.

Burdened with expansion-related debt, AWA succumbed to Chapter 11 in 1991. The airline cut its fleet and sold its Nagoya route to Northwest. But it still opened a third hub, in Columbus, Ohio, and began offering flights to Mexico City in 1992. That year Beauvais resigned as chairman and was replaced by turnaround specialist William Franke.

Conway and Franke never saw eye to eye. Their dispute gained force after an investment bid by the Pritzkers (owners of Hyatt Hotels) favored by Conway was blocked by Franke, who enjoyed support from the board. In 1994 Conway was fired and replaced by Franke.

AWA emerged from bankruptcy in 1994. As part of restructuring, the carrier announced a 10% payroll reduction in 1995. In 1997 Richard Goodmanson became CEO of the airline, replacing Franke, who remained chairman.

In 1998 AWA was hit by the largest penalty yet levied against an airline by the FAA: $2.5 million for lapses in maintenance and structural inspections. Flight attendants threatened the company with a holiday strike and did not reach a contract agreement until 1999. Goodmanson then resigned, and Franke succeeded him as CEO of AWA.

Labor headaches continued for AWA in 2000 when pilots began talks to have their pay and benefits increased shortly before the company agreed to increase pay for baggage and cargo handlers. That year AWA won a coveted slot at Washington's Reagan National Airport.

Franke retired in 2001, and AWA president and COO Douglas Parker replaced him. Also that year, America West was affected by the terrorist attacks on New York and Washington, DC. In response to an anticipated reduction in demand, the airline reduced its flights and laid off 2,000 workers.

Chairman, President, and CEO, America West Holdings and America West Airlines; Chairman, The Leisure Company: W. Douglas Parker, age 40, $354,583 pay

EVP and CFO, America West Holdings and America West Airlines: Bernard L. Han, age 37, $263,401 pay

EVP Corporate, America West Holdings and America West Airlines: Stephen L. Johnson, age 45, $301,212 pay

EVP Sales and Marketing, America West Holdings and America West Airlines: J. Scott Kirby, age 34

SVP Public Affairs, America West Holdings and America West Airlines: C. A. Howlett, age 58, $227,333 pay

President and CEO, The Leisure Company: Jack E. Richards, age 48

EVP Operations, America West Airlines: Jeffrey D. McClelland, age 42, $299,668 pay

SVP Customer Service, America West Airlines: Anthony V. Mulé, age 58

SVP Financial Planning and Analysis, America West Airlines: Derek J. Kerr, age 37

SVP Human Resources, America West Airlines: Lonnie D. Bane, age 43

SVP Marketing and Sales, America West Airlines: Michael A. Smith, age 47

SVP Technical Operations, America West Airlines: Hal M. Heule, age 53

VP Corporate Communications, America West Airlines: James W. Sabourin

VP Employee Relations and Human Resources Legal Compliance, America West Airlines: Shirley Kaufman

Auditors: KPMG LLP

LOCATIONS

HQ: America West Holdings Corporation
111 W. Rio Salado Pkwy., Tempe, AZ 85281
Phone: 480-693-0800 **Fax:** 480-693-5546
Web: www.americawest.com

America West Holdings' America West Airlines serves about 90 destinations in North America, including seven in Mexico and two in Canada. It has hubs in Columbus, Ohio; Las Vegas; and Phoenix.

PRODUCTS/OPERATIONS

2001 Sales

	$ mil.	% of total
Passenger	1,942	94
Cargo	34	2
Other	90	4
Total	**2,066**	**100**

COMPETITORS

AMR	Northwest Airlines
Delta	Southwest Airlines
Frontier Airlines	UAL
Hawaiian Holdings	US Airways

HISTORICAL FINANCIALS & EMPLOYEES

NYSE: AWA FYE: December 31	Annual Growth	12/92	12/93	12/94	12/95	12/96	12/97	12/98	12/99	12/00	12/01
Sales ($ mil.)	5.3%	1,294	1,325	1,409	1,551	1,740	1,875	2,023	2,211	2,344	2,066
Net income ($ mil.)	—	(132)	37	62	54	9	75	109	119	8	(148)
Income as % of sales	—	—	2.8%	4.4%	3.5%	0.5%	4.0%	5.4%	5.4%	0.3%	—
Earnings per share ($)	—	—	—	1.58	1.16	0.18	1.63	2.40	3.03	0.22	(4.39)
Stock price – FY high ($)	—	—	—	16.38	19.00	23.75	18.94	31.31	24.13	20.94	14.19
Stock price – FY low ($)	—	—	—	6.38	6.38	10.88	12.00	9.56	16.00	8.94	1.45
Stock price – FY close ($)	(11.1%)	—	—	8.00	17.00	15.88	18.63	17.00	20.75	12.81	3.50
P/E – high	—	—	—	—	16	113	11	12	8	95	—
P/E – low	—	—	—	—	5	52	7	4	5	41	—
Dividends per share ($)	—	—	—	0.00	0.00	0.00	0.00	0.00	0.00	0.00	0.00
Book value per share ($)	—	—	—	0.00	14.36	14.00	14.87	14.40	14.38	19.85	15.93
Employees	2.1%	10,929	10,544	10,715	8,712	9,652	11,639	12,204	13,336	14,146	13,229

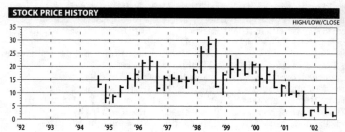

STOCK PRICE HISTORY

HIGH/LOW/CLOSE

2001 FISCAL YEAR-END

Debt ratio: 29.9%
Return on equity: —
Cash ($ mil.): 157
Current ratio: 0.52
Long-term debt ($ mil.): 223
No. of shares (mil.): 33
Dividends
  Yield: —
  Payout: —
Market value ($ mil.): 115

AMERICAN ELECTRIC POWER

American Electric Power (AEP) takes its slice of the US power pie out of Middle America. Besides being one of the top energy marketers in North America, the Columbus, Ohio-based utility holding company is one of the nation's largest electricity distributors: Its utilities serve more than 4.9 million customers in 11 states and generate more than 38,000 MW of primarily coal-fired capacity.

AEP markets and trades electricity, natural gas, and other commodities in North America and Europe and has independent power plant interests (4,000 MW) in the Americas, Europe, and the Asia/Pacific region.

AEP also operates 6,200 miles of natural gas pipeline in Louisiana and Texas, storage facilities, and a fleet of 1,800 barges. Other operations include communication infrastructure services, coal mining, and energy construction and consulting services.

In response to US utility deregulation, AEP is focusing on expanding wholesale marketing activities and is selling noncore retail businesses. It has sold its UK utility interests (Yorkshire Power Group and SEEBOARD) and its Australian electric utility (CitiPower). AEP plans to separate its regulated and nonregulated operations.

HISTORY

In 1906 Richard Breed, Sidney Mitchell, and Henry Doherty set up American Gas & Electric (AG&E) in New York to buy 23 utilities from Philadelphia's Electric Company of America. With properties in seven northeastern US states, AG&E began acquiring and merging small electric properties, creating the predecessors of Ohio Power (1911), Kentucky Power (1919), and Appalachian Power (1926). AG&E also bought the predecessor of Indiana Michigan Power (1925).

By 1926 the company was operating in Indiana, Kentucky, Michigan, Ohio, Virginia, and West Virginia. In 1935 AG&E engineer Philip Sporn, later known as the Henry Ford of power, introduced his high-voltage, high-velocity circuit breaker. Becoming president in 1947, Sporn began an ambitious building program that continued through the 1960s. Plants designed by AG&E (renamed American Electric Power in 1958) were among the world's most efficient, and electric rates stayed 25% to 38% below the national average.

AEP bought Michigan Power in 1967, six years after Donald Cook succeeded Sporn as president. Cook, who refused to attach scrubbers to the smokestacks of coal-fired plants, was criticized in the early 1970s by environmental protesters. AEP's first nuclear plant, named in

Cook's honor, went on line in Michigan in 1975. He retired in 1976.

The firm moved from New York to Columbus, Ohio, in 1980 after buying what is now Columbus Southern Power (formed in 1883). It set up AEP Generating in 1982 to provide power to its electric utilities. AEP began converting its second nuke, Zimmer, to coal in 1984. In 1992 AEP finally began installing scrubbers at its coal-fired Gavin plant in Ohio after being ordered to comply with the Clean Air Act.

In 1997 AEP jumped into the UK's deregulated electric market; AEP and New Century Energies bought Yorkshire Electricity (later Yorkshire Power Group) for $2.8 billion. AEP agreed in 1997 to buy Central and South West (CSW) of Texas in a $6.6 billion deal. AEP's sales would nearly double, and CSW was to bring its own UK utility, SEEBOARD, and other overseas holdings.

In 1998 AEP bought a 20% stake in Pacific Hydro, an Australian power producer, and CitiPower, an Australian electric distribution company. In 1999 China's Pushan Power Plant (70%-owned by AEP) began operations. Environmental concerns resurfaced that year when the EPA sued the utility, alleging its old coal-powered plants, which had been grandfathered from the Clean Air Act, had been quietly upgraded to extend their lives.

In 2000 regulators approved the company's acquisition of CSW, but AEP had to agree to relinquish control of its 22,000 miles of transmission lines to an independent operator. The CSW deal closed later that year. (However, the SEC's approval of the deal was challenged by a federal appeals court in 2002.)

AEP sold its 50% stake in Yorkshire Power Group to Innogy Holdings in 2001; it also purchased Houston Pipe Line Co. (4,200 miles of pipeline in Texas) from Enron for $727 million. AEP became one of the largest US barge operators that year when it bought MEMCO Barge Line from Progress Energy. It also purchased two UK coal-fired power plants (4,000 MW) from Edison Mission Energy, a subsidiary of Edison International, in a $960 million deal.

In 2002 AEP agreed to sell two of its competitive Texas retail electric providers (WTU Retail Energy and CPL Retail Energy, 850,000 customers) to UK utility Centrica; AEP would keep the regulated transmission and distribution networks of West Texas Utilities and Central Power and Light.

Later that year AEP sold its UK utility, SEE-BOARD, to Electricité de France in a $2.2 billion deal; it also sold its Australian utility, CitiPower, to a consortium led by Cheung Kong Infrastructure and Hongkong Electric.

OFFICERS

Chairman, President, and CEO, American Electric Power and AEP Service; Chairman and CEO, Central Power and Light, Southwestern Electric Power, Appalachian Power, Indiana Michigan Power, and Ohio Power: E. Linn Draper Jr., age 60, $1,592,090 pay
Vice Chairman and COO, AEP and AEP Service: Thomas V. Shockley III, age 56, $943,788 pay
EVP Policy, Finance, and Strategic Planning, CFO, and Corporate Secretary: Susan Tomasky, $710,365 pay
EVP; President, Regulated Businesses: Henry W. Fayne, $720,365 pay
EVP Nuclear Generation and Technical Services: Robert P. Powers
VP Human Resources: Mark Welsh
Auditors: Deloitte & Touche LLP

LOCATIONS

HQ: American Electric Power Company, Inc.
1 Riverside Plaza, Columbus, OH 43215
Phone: 614-223-1000 **Fax:** 614-223-1823
Web: www.aep.com

American Electric Power distributes electricity in Arkansas, Indiana, Kentucky, Louisiana, Michigan, Ohio, Oklahoma, Tennessee, Texas, Virginia, and West Virginia. It has natural gas pipeline interests in Louisiana and Texas. Overseas, the company has assets in Australia, Brazil, China, Mexico, the Philippines, and the UK.

PRODUCTS/OPERATIONS

2001 Sales

	$ mil.	% of total
Wholesale	55,929	91
Energy delivery	3,356	6
Other	1,972	3
Total	**61,257**	**100**

Selected Subsidiaries
AEP Coal, Inc. (coal mining)
AEP Communications, LLC (fiber-optic infrastructure, wireless communications towers)
AEP Energy Services, Inc. (energy marketing and trading)
AEP Energy Services, Ltd. (Europe)
AEP Gas Power Systems (50%, gas turbine generators)
AEP Generating Co. (electricity generator, marketer)
AEP Pro Serv, Inc. (engineering, construction, and other services for electric power projects)
AEP Retail Energy (retail energy marketing)
Louisiana Intrastate Gas Company (natural gas pipeline)
MEMCO Barge Line Inc. (barges and towboats)

COMPETITORS

Allegheny Energy	Dominion	PG&E
Aquila	DTE	Southern
CenterPoint	Duke Energy	Company
Energy	Dynegy	TVA
Cinergy	El Paso	TXU
CMS Energy	Entergy	Xcel Energy
Conectiv	FirstEnergy	
Constellation	Mirant	
Energy Group	NiSource	

HISTORICAL FINANCIALS & EMPLOYEES

NYSE: AEP FYE: December 31	Annual Growth	12/92	12/93	12/94	12/95	12/96	12/97	12/98	12/99	12/00	12/01
Sales ($ mil.)	32.0%	5,045	5,269	5,505	5,670	5,849	6,161	6,346	6,916	13,694	61,257
Net income ($ mil.)	8.4%	468	354	500	530	587	511	536	520	267	971
Income as % of sales	—	9.3%	6.7%	9.1%	9.3%	10.0%	8.3%	8.4%	7.5%	1.9%	1.6%
Earnings per share ($)	1.9%	2.54	1.92	2.71	2.85	3.14	2.70	2.81	2.69	0.83	3.01
Stock price - FY high ($)	—	35.25	40.38	37.38	40.63	44.75	52.00	53.31	48.19	48.94	51.20
Stock price - FY low ($)	—	30.38	32.00	27.25	31.25	38.63	39.13	42.06	30.56	25.94	39.25
Stock price - FY close ($)	3.1%	33.13	37.13	32.88	40.50	41.13	51.63	47.06	32.13	46.50	43.53
P/E - high	—	14	21	14	14	14	16	19	18	52	16
P/E - low	—	12	17	10	11	12	12	15	11	28	13
Dividends per share ($)	0.0%	2.40	2.40	2.40	2.40	2.40	2.40	2.40	2.40	2.40	2.40
Book value per share ($)	(0.7%)	27.16	26.67	27.28	26.81	27.34	25.54	26.15	25.79	25.01	25.54
Employees	3.2%	20,841	20,007	19,660	18,502	17,951	17,844	17,943	17,306	26,376	27,726

STOCK PRICE HISTORY

HIGH/LOW/CLOSE

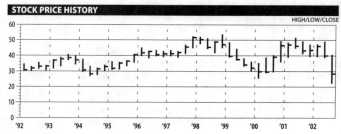

2001 FISCAL YEAR-END

Debt ratio: 54.2%
Return on equity: 11.9%
Cash ($ mil.): 333
Current ratio: 0.69
Long-term debt ($ mil.): 9,753
No. of shares (mil.): 322
Dividends
  Yield: 5.5%
  Payout: 79.7%
Market value ($ mil.): 14,027

AMERICAN EXPRESS COMPANY

"Don't leave home without it" says the famous ad slogan from the 1970s, and the reference is of course to New York City-based American Express' flagship charge card. But today, it could just as easily say "don't invest without it" or "don't retire without it." American Express has become a more diversified financial services firm, all the while keeping its brand cachet intact and remaining synonymous with travel.

The company operates the #1 travel agency in the world, with more than 1,700 locations in more than 200 countries and publishes food- and travel-related magazines. Its Travelers Cheque Group is the world's largest issuer of travelers checks.

The company is probably best known, though, for its charge and credit cards. They account for more than half of American Express' revenue, and their recent evolution, like the company as a whole, has been toward diversification. The company offers four levels of charge cards (the standard green card, Gold, Platinum, and the super-premium Centurion card). The company also offers revolving credit though its Optima and Blue cards.

American Express may boost its share of the credit card market thanks to a Justice Department lawsuit against Visa and MasterCard in 2001 alleging monopolistic practices. The two credit card systems bar member banks from issuing cards of rivals and control 75% of the nation's credit card use. The courts found in favor of American Express (and Morgan Stanley, issuer of the Discover card); Visa and MasterCard are appealing.

American Express also offers corporate financial services; its American Express Financial Corporation and marketing subsidiary American Express Financial Advisors sell life insurance, annuities, investment funds, and financial advisory services.

Warren Buffett's Berkshire Hathaway owns about 11% of American Express.

HISTORY

In 1850 Henry Wells and his two main competitors combined their delivery services to form American Express. When directors refused to expand to California in 1852, Wells and VP William Fargo formed Wells Fargo while remaining at American Express.

American Express merged with Merchants Union Express in 1868 and developed a money order to compete with the government's postal money order. Fargo's difficulty in cashing letters of credit in Europe led to the offering of Travelers Cheques in 1891.

In WWI the US government nationalized and consolidated all express delivery services, compensating the owners. After the war, American Express incorporated as an overseas freight and financial services and exchange provider (the freight operation was sold in 1970). In 1958 the company introduced the American Express charge card. It bought Fireman's Fund American Insurance (sold gradually between 1985 and 1989) and Equitable Securities in 1968.

James Robinson, CEO from 1977 to 1993, hoped to turn American Express into a financial services supermarket. The company bought brokerage Shearson Loeb Rhoades in 1981 and investment banker Lehman Brothers in 1984, among others. In 1987 it introduced Optima, a revolving credit card, to compete with MasterCard and Visa; it had no experience in underwriting credit cards and was badly burned by losses.

Most of the financial units were combined as Shearson Lehman Brothers. But the financial services supermarket never came to fruition, and losses in this area brought a steep drop in earnings in the early 1990s. Harvey Golub was brought in as CEO in 1993 to restore stability.

The company sold its brokerage operations as Shearson (to Travelers, now Citigroup) and spun off investment banking as Lehman Brothers in 1994. In late 1996 the company announced an alliance with Advanta Corp., allowing Advanta Visa and MasterCard holders to earn points in the American Express Membership Rewards program. The move sparked a lawsuit from Visa and MasterCard, which prohibit their member banks from doing business with American Express. Efforts by Visa to set up similar restrictions in the European Union have been rebuffed, Advanta has countersued, and the US Justice Department filed a lawsuit alleging antitrust violations by Visa and MasterCard. In 1997 Kenneth Chenault was named president and COO, a move that put him in line to succeed Golub.

Membership B@nking, an online banking service, was launched in 1999. That year American Express invested in Ticketmaster Online-CitySearch (now Ticketmaster). In 2000 the company established a headquarters in Beijing to develop business in China. Also that year American Express bought more than 4,500 ATMs from Electronic Data Systems, making it a leading US operator of ATMs.

In 2001 Chenault replaced Golub as chairman and CEO. American Express was hit hard that year by bad investments in below-investment grade bonds by its money-management unit, which shaved about $1 billion from earnings. Adding to its woes, the company's employees at its New York City headquarters, which was across the street from the World Trade Center, were displaced by the 2001 terrorist attacks (They moved back into their offices in May 2002). In 2002 the company beefed up its Financial Advisors segment by hiring four managers away from Boston's Fidelity Investments to open a Boston-based asset management office.

OFFICERS

Chairman and CEO: Kenneth I. Chenault, age 50, $3,218,000 pay
Vice Chairman: Jonathan S. Linen, age 58, $1,110,000 pay
EVP and CFO: Gary L. Crittenden, age 48, $1,075,000 pay
EVP and CIO: Glen Salow, age 45
EVP and General Counsel: Louise M. Parent, age 51
EVP American Express Financial Advisors Products and Corporate Marketing: Barbara Fraser
EVP Human Resources and Quality: Ursula F. Fairbairn, age 59
President, Global Financial Services Group: James M. Cracchiolo, age 43, $1,185,000 pay
President, US Consumer and Small Business Services, TRS: Alfred F. Kelly Jr., age 43, $1,170,000 pay
Auditors: Ernst & Young LLP

LOCATIONS

HQ: World Financial Center 200 Vesey Street, New York, NY 10285
Phone: 201-640-2000   **Fax:** 201-209-4261
Web: www.americanexpress.com

2001 Sales

	$ mil.	% of total
US	17,522	77
Europe	2,556	10
Asia/Pacific	1,523	6
Other regions	1,667	7
Adjustments	(686)	—
Total	**22,582**	**100**

PRODUCTS/OPERATIONS

2001 Sales

	$ mil.	% of total
Discount revenue	7,714	34
Management and distribution fees	2,458	11
Net interest and dividends	2,137	9
Net card fees	1,675	7
Travel commissions and fees	1,537	7
Other commissions and fees	2,432	11
Cardmember lending net finance charge revenue	912	4
Life and other insurance revenues	674	3
Other	3,043	14
Total	**22,582**	**100**

COMPETITORS

Advance Publications	FMR	Merrill Lynch
Allstate	John Hancock	MetLife
BANK ONE	Financial	Morgan Stanley
Barclays	Services	Prudential
Carlson Wagonlit	J.P. Morgan	Rosenbluth
Citigroup	Chase	International
Discover	JTB	Visa
First USA Bank	MasterCard	WorldTravel
	MBNA	

HISTORICAL FINANCIALS & EMPLOYEES

NYSE: AXP FYE: December 31	Annual Growth	12/92	12/93	12/94	12/95	12/96	12/97	12/98	12/99	12/00	12/01
Sales ($ mil.)	(2.0%)	26,961	14,173	14,282	15,841	16,237	17,760	19,132	21,278	23,675	22,582
Net income ($ mil.)	12.3%	462	1,478	1,413	1,564	1,901	1,991	2,141	2,475	2,810	1,311
Income as % of sales	—	1.7%	10.4%	9.9%	9.9%	11.7%	11.2%	11.2%	11.6%	11.9%	5.8%
Earnings per share ($)	14.1%	0.30	0.77	0.92	1.03	1.19	1.38	1.54	1.80	2.07	0.98
Stock price - FY high ($)	—	8.45	12.20	11.03	15.03	20.10	30.47	39.50	56.24	63.00	57.06
Stock price - FY low ($)	—	6.66	7.45	8.41	9.66	12.86	17.86	22.31	31.59	39.79	24.20
Stock price - FY close ($)	17.6%	8.28	10.28	9.82	13.78	18.81	29.72	34.13	55.36	54.94	35.69
P/E - high	—	30	16	12	14	16	21	25	31	30	58
P/E - low	—	24	10	9	9	11	12	14	17	19	24
Dividends per share ($)	(0.3%)	0.33	0.33	0.32	0.30	0.30	0.30	0.30	0.30	0.31	0.32
Book value per share ($)	6.3%	5.20	5.94	4.32	5.67	6.01	6.84	7.51	7.52	8.81	9.04
Employees	(3.3%)	114,352	64,654	72,412	70,347	72,300	73,620	85,000	88,378	89,000	84,400

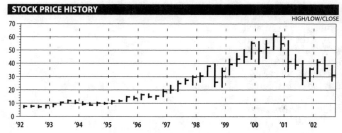

STOCK PRICE HISTORY
HIGH/LOW/CLOSE

2001 FISCAL YEAR-END

Debt ratio: 39.3%
Return on equity: 11.1%
Cash ($ mil.): —
Current ratio: —
Long-term debt ($ mil.): 7,788
No. of shares (mil.): 1,331
Dividends
  Yield: 0.9%
  Payout: 32.7%
Market value ($ mil.): 47,503

AMERICAN FINANCIAL GROUP, INC.

Carl Lindner is bananas for insurance.

Lindner is chairman and CEO of Cincinnati-based American Financial Group (AFG), an insurance holding company that also owns more than 30% of Chiquita Brands International. But it's the specialty lines, such as workers' compensation, professional liability, ocean and inland marine, and multiperil crop insurance, that drive the company's bottom line. AFG is also a major provider of car insurance, especially nonstandard (read: high-risk) insurance.

Additionally, the growing retirement-savings market plays a big role in AFG's product mix — especially flexible and single-premium deferred annuities sold through its Great American Financial Resources subsidiary.

AFG's results in the 1990s have been uneven, and it has typically not made an underwriting profit. The company has shed its commercial lines to concentrate on property/casualty and life and annuities businesses, though it continues to hold investments in noncore companies such as Chiquita and Provident Financial Group (about 15%). Lindner and his family own about 45% of the company.

HISTORY

When his father became ill in the mid-1930s, Carl Lindner dropped out of high school to take over his family's dairy business. He built it into a large ice-cream store chain called United Dairy Farmers (now run by his brother Robert). Lindner branched out in 1955 with Henthy Realty, and in 1959 he bought three savings and loans. The next year Lindner changed the company's name to American Financial Corp. (AFC). He took it public in 1961, using the proceeds to buy United Liberty Life Insurance (1963) and Provident Bank (1966).

Lindner also formed the American Financial Leasing & Services Company in 1968 to lease airplanes, computers, and other equipment. In 1969 the company acquired Phoenix developer Rubenstein Construction and renamed it American Continental. AFC bought several life, casualty, and mortgage insurance firms in the 1970s, including National General, parent of Great American Insurance Group, later the core of AFC's insurance segment. The company also moved into publishing by buying 95% of the Cincinnati Enquirer, paperback publisher Bantam Books, and hardback publisher Grosset & Dunlap.

But the publishing interests soon went back on the block, as Lindner concentrated on insurance, which was then suffering from an industrywide slowdown. In addition to selling the *Enquirer,* AFC spun off American Continental in 1976.

American Continental's president was Charles Keating, who had joined AFC in 1972 and whose brother published the *Enquirer.* Keating (who was later jailed, released, then eventually pleaded guilty in connection with the failure of Lincoln Savings) underwent an SEC investigation during part of his time at AFC for alleged improprieties at Provident Bank. The bank was spun off in 1980.

Lindner took AFC private in 1981. That year, following a strategy of bottom-feeding, the company began building its interest in the nonrailroad assets of Penn Central, the former railroad that had emerged from bankruptcy as an industrial manufacturer. Later that decade AFC increased its ownership in United Brands (later renamed Chiquita Brands International) from 29% to 45%. Lindner installed himself as CEO and reversed that company's losses. In 1987 AFC acquired a TV company, Taft Communications (renamed Great American Communications), entailing a heavy debt load. To reduce its debt, AFC trimmed its holdings, including Circle K, Hunter S&L, and an interest in Scripps Howard Broadcasting.

Great American Communications went bankrupt in 1992 and emerged the next year as Citicasters Inc. (sold 1996). In 1995 Lindner created American Financial Group to effect the merger of AFC and American Premier Underwriters, of which he owned 42%. The result was American Financial Group (AFG).

In 1997 Lindner's bipartisan political donations gained publicity when it became known that his gifts to Republicans had brought support in a dispute with the EU over the banana trade. The next year AFG sold some noncore units, including software consultancy Millennium Dynamics and its commercial insurance operations. In 1999 AFG bought direct-response auto insurer Worldwide Insurance Company as part of its efforts to build depth in the highly commodified auto insurance market.

In 2000 American Financial Group agreed to pay $75 million over the next 30 years to get its name on the Cincinnati Reds' new stadium. It will be known as the Great American Ball Park. Also in 2000, AFG sold its Japanese property and casualty division to Japanese insurer Mitsui Marine & Fire (now Mitsui Sumitomo Insurance).

OFFICERS

Chairman and CEO: Carl H. Lindner, age 82, $1,365,600 pay
Co-President and Director: Keith E. Lindner, age 42, $1,365,600 pay
Co-President and Director: S. Craig Lindner, age 47, $1,365,600 pay
Co-President and Director: Carl H. Lindner III, age 48, $1,365,600 pay
SVP, General Counsel, and Director: James E. Evans, age 56, $1,350,000 pay
SVP: Keith A. Jensen, age 51
SVP, Taxes: Thomas E. Mischell, age 54
SVP and Treasurer: Fred J. Runk, age 59
VP and CIO: Julie J. Murphy
VP, Secretary, and Deputy General Counsel: James C. Kennedy
VP and Controller: Robert H. Ruffing
VP, Human Resources: Lawrence Otto
VP, Investor Relations: Anne N. Watson
VP, Taxes: Kathleen J. Brown
Auditors: Ernst & Young LLP

LOCATIONS

HQ: 1 E. 4th St., Cincinnati, OH 45202
Phone: 513-579-2121   **Fax:** 513-579-2113
Web: www.amfnl.com

American Financial Group operates primarily in the US, but also in Asia, Canada, Europe, Mexico, and Puerto Rico.

PRODUCTS/OPERATIONS

2001 Assets

	$ mil.	% of total
Cash & equivalents	544	3
Treasury & agency securities	1,018	6
Mortgage-backed securities	2,702	16
State & municipal bonds	415	2
Utility bonds	779	4
Corporate bonds	5,674	33
Stocks	314	2
Real estate	267	2
Policy loans	211	1
Recoverables & receivables	3,207	18
Other	2,271	13
Total	**17,402**	**100**

COMPETITORS

21st Century	Kemper Insurance
Allmerica Financial	Liberty Mutual
Allstate	MetLife
AXA Financial	Nationwide
Chubb	New York Life
CIGNA	Northwestern Mutual
Cincinnati Financial	Ohio Casualty
Citigroup	Progressive Corporation
Dole	Prudential
Fresh Del Monte Produce	Reliance Group Holdings
GEICO	St. Paul Companies
The Hartford	State Farm

HISTORICAL FINANCIALS & EMPLOYEES

NYSE: AFG FYE: December 31	Annual Growth	12/92	12/93	12/94	12/95	12/96	12/97	12/98	12/99	12/00	12/01
Assets ($ mil.)	19.4%	3,531	4,050	4,194	14,954	15,051	15,755	15,845	16,054	16,416	17,402
Net income ($ mil.)	—	305	232	0	191	233	192	124	141	(56)	(15)
Income as % of assets	—	8.6%	5.7%	0.0%	1.3%	1.6%	1.2%	0.8%	0.9%	—	—
Earnings per share ($)	—	6.48	6.85	(0.83)	3.85	3.79	0.64	2.00	2.35	(0.95)	(0.22)
Stock price - FY high ($)	—	27.13	39.75	33.25	32.13	38.88	49.25	45.75	43.63	29.00	30.75
Stock price - FY low ($)	—	18.00	23.50	21.63	22.88	28.50	32.38	30.50	24.50	18.38	18.35
Stock price - FY close ($)	(0.1%)	24.88	32.38	25.88	30.63	37.75	40.31	43.88	26.38	26.56	24.55
P/E - high	—	21	6	—	8	9	15	22	18	—	—
P/E - low	—	14	3	—	6	7	10	15	10	—	—
Dividends per share ($)	2.5%	0.80	0.84	0.88	1.00	1.00	1.00	1.00	1.00	1.00	1.00
Book value per share ($)	(4.3%)	32.40	36.30	33.46	23.95	25.45	27.24	28.17	22.94	22.97	21.88
Employees	(4.5%)	11,100	5,400	4,300	9,800	9,500	10,500	10,000	10,400	10,600	7,300

STOCK PRICE HISTORY

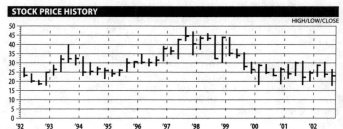

HIGH/LOW/CLOSE

2001 FISCAL YEAR-END

Equity as % of assets: 8.6%
Return on assets: —
Return on equity: —
Long-term debt ($ mil.): 880
No. of shares (mil.): 68
Dividends
  Yield: 4.1%
  Payout: —
Market value ($ mil.): 1,681
Sales ($ mil.): 3,907

AMERICAN GREETINGS

American Greetings has been building its sturdy house of cards for nearly a century. The #2 US maker of greeting cards (behind Hallmark), the Cleveland-based company markets its missives under the American Greetings, Carlton Cards, and Gibson Greetings brand names. American Greetings' cards are available in some 125,000 stores throughout the world. The company's 2000 acquisition of #3 greeting card maker Gibson Greetings (and Gibson's online spinoff, Egreetings Network, acquired the next year) helped it further cut into Hallmark's dominant market share.

While greeting cards generate nearly two-thirds of its sales, American Greetings has branched into other products including DesignWare party goods, GuildHouse candles, Balloon Zone balloons, calendars, and stationery. Subsidiaries include Plus Mark (seasonal gift wrap and accessories), Learning Horizons (supplemental educational products), and Magnivision (nonprescription reading glasses).

American Greetings made the leap into cyberspace in 1995 when it began offering greetings via the Internet. The company shelved plans to spin off a minority interest in its online subsidiary, AmericanGreetings.com, in 2000 and began charging an annual fee in 2001 for access to its e-greeting card services. The company has been hurt by the increasing use of e-mail (AmericanGreetings.com has been a drag on its parent's earnings) and announced in 2001 it would lay off some 1,500 workers (about 13% of its total). It has also shuttered its Forget Me Not line of cards and sold its Mylar balloon subsidiary M&D Industries. Members of the founding Sapirstein family (including CEO Morry Weiss) own about 5% of the company but control about 30% of the voting power.

HISTORY

In 1906 Polish immigrant Jacob Sapirstein founded Sapirstein Greeting Card Company and began selling postcards from a horse-drawn wagon. The outbreak of WWI and the resulting separation of families helped spur demand for the company's products. The impact of the war also helped shape the company's future: After an embargo was imposed on cards produced in Germany, Sapirstein decided to begin manufacturing his own cards.

Sapirstein's sons eventually joined the burgeoning company and, in 1940, after adopting the American Greetings Publishers name, the company's sales topped $1 million. The company incorporated as American Greetings in 1944 and went public in 1952. It introduced Hi

Brows, a line of funny studio cards, in 1956 and broke ground on a 1.5 million-sq.-ft. headquarters building the same year.

In 1960 Sapirstein's son, Irving Stone (all three Sapirstein sons changed their surname to Stone, a derivative of Sapirstein) was appointed president, and Jacob Sapirstein became chairman. The ubiquitous Holly Hobbie made her first appearance on greeting cards in 1967 (within a decade, she had become the world's most popular licensed female character). In 1968 American Greetings' sales exceeded $100 million.

American Greetings introduced the Ziggy character in 1972 and launched Plus Mark, a maker of seasonal wrapping paper, boxed cards, and accessories six years later. Irving Stone succeeded his father as chairman and CEO in 1978, and Morry Weiss, Irving Stone's son-in-law, was appointed president.

The success of Holly Hobbie licensing prompted American Greetings to create its own licensing division in 1980. In 1982 it introduced the Care Bears, licensed characters that appeared in animated films. Following the death of Jacob Sapirstein in 1987 (at age 102), Morry Weiss became chairman and CEO, and Irving Stone became founder-chairman.

The company bought Magnivision (nonprescription reading glasses) in 1993. It ventured onto the Internet two years later, when it began offering online greeting cards. The company branched into supplemental educational products the following year when it unveiled its Learning Horizons product line.

Its acquisitions of greeting card companies Camden Graphics and Hanson White in 1998 helped American Greetings double its presence in the UK. In 1999, in an expansion of its existing agreement with America Online (now part of AOL Time Warner), American Greetings' online unit (AmericanGreetings.com) became AOL's exclusive provider of electronic greetings.

Founder-chairman Irving Stone died in early 2000 at the age of 90. Also that year American Greetings paid $175 million for smaller rival Gibson Greetings, along with Gibson's stake in Egreetings Network. In 2001 the company bought the remaining shares of Egreetings Network and folded the business into its online business, and announced its intent to do the same with Excite@Home's BlueMountain.com. Also that year the company announced a restructuring that includes the elimination of the Forget Me Not card line, the divestiture of Mylar balloon subsidiary M&D Industries (sold to Amscan in early 2002), and the reduction of about 1,500 jobs.

OFFICERS

Chairman and CEO: Morry Weiss, age 62,
$2,524,602 pay
President, COO, and Director: James C. Spira, age 59,
$500,000 pay
EVP North American Greeting Cards: Jeffrey M. Weiss,
age 37, $366,046 pay
SVP and CFO: William S. Meyer, age 54, $737,837 pay
EVP AG Ventures and Enterprise Management:
Zev Weiss, age 34
SVP and President, Carleton Cards Retail:
Patricia A. Papesh, age 53
SVP Business Innovation: Mary Ann Corrigan-Davis,
age 47
SVP Creative: David R. Beittel, age 53
SVP Human Resources: Pamela L. Linton
SVP Information Services: Doug Ronnel
SVP Mass Merchandise Channel: George A. Wenz,
age 56
SVP Program Realization: Erwin Weiss, age 52,
$396,366 pay
SVP Retailer Logistics: Patricia L. Ripple, age 45
SVP Sales: William R. Mason, age 57, $757,112 pay
SVP, Secretary, and General Counsel:
Jon Groetzinger Jr., age 52, $321,268 pay
Auditors: Ernst & Young LLP

LOCATIONS

HQ: American Greetings Corporation
    1 American Rd., Cleveland, OH 44144
Phone: 216-252-7300   **Fax:** 216-252-6777
Web: corporate.americangreetings.com

2002 Sales

	$ mil.	% of total
US	1,961	83
Other countries	395	17
Total	**2,356**	**100**

PRODUCTS/OPERATIONS

2002 Sales

	$ mil.	% of total
Everyday greeting cards	934	40
Seasonal greetings cards	473	20
Gift wrap & wrap accessories	395	17
Other	554	23
Total	**2,356**	**100**

Selected Products
AG Industries (retails display fixtures)
American Greetings (cards)
Balloon Zone (balloons)
Carlton Cards (cards)
Designers' Collection (stationery)
DesignWare (party goods)
Gibson Greetings (cards)
John Sands (cards)
Learning Horizons (supplemental educational products)
Magnivision (nonprescription reading glasses)
Plus Mark (seasonal gift wrap, boxed cards, and
    accessories)

COMPETITORS

Blyth, Inc.	Marchon	Taylor
CSS Industries	Eyewear	Corporation
CTI Industries	SPS Studios	Yankee Candle
Hallmark	Successories	

HISTORICAL FINANCIALS & EMPLOYEES

NYSE: AM FYE: Last day in February	Annual Growth	2/93	2/94	2/95	2/96	2/97	2/98	2/99	2/00	2/01	2/02
Sales ($ mil.)	3.9%	1,672	1,770	1,869	2,003	2,161	2,199	2,206	2,175	2,519	2,356
Net income ($ mil.)	—	112	114	149	115	167	190	180	90	(114)	(122)
Income as % of sales	—	6.7%	6.4%	8.0%	5.7%	7.7%	8.6%	8.2%	4.1%	—	—
Earnings per share ($)	—	1.55	1.54	1.98	1.53	2.22	2.55	2.53	1.37	(1.79)	(1.92)
Stock price - FY high ($)	—	26.19	34.25	31.38	33.00	31.38	45.88	53.75	32.38	24.06	16.00
Stock price - FY low ($)	—	18.88	23.88	25.75	25.50	23.50	29.25	22.00	17.25	8.19	9.75
Stock price - FY close ($)	(6.0%)	24.00	27.88	29.38	27.38	31.00	45.63	23.69	17.25	13.06	13.77
P/E - high	—	17	19	16	21	14	18	21	24	—	—
P/E - low	—	12	13	13	17	11	11	9	13	—	—
Dividends per share ($)	(0.3%)	0.41	0.47	0.53	0.60	0.66	0.70	0.74	0.78	0.82	0.40
Book value per share ($)	0.9%	13.07	14.21	15.61	16.53	17.76	18.90	19.49	16.10	16.49	14.15
Employees	2.0%	31,400	36,600	35,600	36,800	36,300	35,600	35,475	34,200	38,700	37,600

STOCK PRICE HISTORY

HIGH/LOW/CLOSE

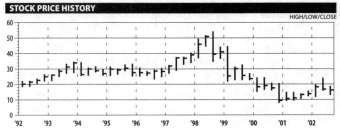

2002 FISCAL YEAR-END

Debt ratio: 48.6%
Return on equity: —
Cash ($ mil.): 101
Current ratio: 1.49
Long-term debt ($ mil.): 853
No. of shares (mil.): 64
Dividends
    Yield: 2.9%
    Payout: —
Market value ($ mil.): 878

AMERICAN INTERNATIONAL GROUP

American International Group (AIG) has the world covered. New York City-based AIG is a global insurance presence, offering life insurance, property/casualty lines, mortgage guaranty, financial services, and jet leasing in the US and internationally (foreign insurance premiums account for more than a third of sales). AIG has been expanding its role in asset management, mostly through acquisitions (including the purchase of retirement specialist SunAmerica) and joint ventures. The company has a long history of insurance operations in the Far East and supported China's accession to the World Trade Organization. Chairman and CEO Maurice Greenberg owns more than 20% of AIG.

AIG is one of the few insurers that makes an underwriting profit instead of depending on investments to stay in the black, largely due to the legendary Greenberg. Greenberg had taken steps to ensure his legacy continues by naming his second son, Evan, as his successor (eldest son Jeff is president at Marsh & McClennan Companies). Evan resigned, and a new heir has not yet become apparent.

AIG wooed insurer American General away from rival suitor Prudential plc to bolster its share of the lucrative US retirement planning market. The combination of the two companies will result in 1,500 jobs being cut in both AIG and American General positions.

The company is paying out about $800 million in claims related to the attacks on the World Trade Center. Taking advantage of rising premiums, AIG has formed Bermuda-based insurer Allied World Assurance together with Goldman Sachs and specialty insurer Chubb.

HISTORY

Former ice cream parlor owner Cornelius Starr founded property/casualty insurer American Asiatic Underwriters in Shanghai in 1919. After underwriting business for other insurers, Starr began selling life insurance policies to the Chinese in 1921 (foreign companies were loath to do so despite the longevity of the Chinese). In 1926 he opened a New York office specializing in foreign risks incurred by American companies. As WWII loomed, Starr moved his base to the US; when the war cut off business in Europe, he focused on Latin America. After a brief postwar return to China, the company was kicked out by the communist government.

In the 1950s the company began providing disability, health, and life insurance and pension plans for employees who moved from country to country. Starr chose his successor, Maurice Greenberg, in 1967 and died the next year.

Greenberg, who had come aboard in 1960 to develop overseas operations, took over the newly formed American International Group, a holding company for Starr's worldwide collection of insurance concerns. Greenberg's policy of achieving underwriting profits forced the company to use tight fiscal discipline. AIG went public in 1969.

By 1975 AIG was the largest foreign life insurer in much of Asia and the only insurer with global sales and support facilities. AIG's underwriting policies saved it when price wars from 1979 to 1984 brought heavy losses to most insurers. In 1987 AIG became the second US-owned insurer (after Chubb) to enter the traditionally closed South Korean market.

The 1980s saw AIG begin investment operations in Asia, increase its presence in health care, and form a financial services group. It bought International Lease Finance Corporation, which leases and remarkets jets to airlines, in 1990. AIG soon moved into parts of Eastern Europe.

The company resumed its Chinese operations in 1993 after triumphing over stiff opposition from state-owned monopolies.

With a strong presence in many developing nations, AIG began cross-selling an array of financial products in those markets. In 1995 the company formed the Asian Infrastructure Fund, a mutual fund for individual investors.

In 1998 AIG bought SunAmerica for $18.3 billion, giving the company access to a sales-driven distribution network and greater flexibility in the consolidating financial services industry.

In 1999, AIG continued to live up to the "international" in its name. The company won licenses for insurance businesses in Azerbaijan, Romania, Bulgaria, and Sri Lanka. As part of a crackdown on foreign insurers, in 1999 the Chinese government stopped AIG from selling what it considered group policies — historically the sole province of Chinese companies — though a US-China pact reached later that year will allow foreign firms gradual entrance to the group-policy market.

Seizing opportunities created by the booming Internet economy, in 2000 AIG launched aigdirect.com, a consumer and small business e-commerce site providing insurance products to users of E*TRADE and worldlyinvestor.com. The company also decided to augment its specialty insurance business with its purchase of HSB Group, the parent company of The Hartford Steam Boiler Inspection and Insurance Company. In 2001 AIG agreed to be the business sponsor for the troubled Chiyoda Mutual Life Insurance Company (now AIG Star Life Insurance) and bought American General.

OFFICERS

Chairman and CEO; Chairman, Transatlantic Holdings:
Maurice R. Greenberg, age 76, $1,000,000 pay
Senior Vice Chairman, General Insurance, and Director: Thomas R. Tizzio, age 64, $1,134,700 pay
Vice Chairman, CFO, and Chief Administrative Officer: Howard I. Smith, age 57, $1,011,924 pay
Vice Chairman and Co-COO: Martin J. Sullivan, age 48
Vice Chairman and Co-COO: Edmund S. W. Tse, age 64, $1,180,742 pay
Vice Chairman, External Affairs, and Director: Frank G. Wisner, age 63
Vice Chairman, Investments and Financial Services, and Director: Edward E. Matthews, age 70, $1,180,000 pay
EVP and Chief Investment Officer: Win J. Neuger, age 52
EVP; CEO, AIG Companies in Japan and Korea: Donald P. Kanak, age 49
EVP, Life Insurance: R. Kendall Nottingham, age 63
EVP, Life Insurance; Vice Chairman and Group Executive, Life Insurance; Chairman, American General Life Insurance: Rodney O. Martin Jr., age 48
EVP, Retirement Savings and Director; President and CEO, SunAmerica: Jay S. Wintrob, age 45
SVP, Human Resources: Axel I. Freudmann, age 55
Auditors: PricewaterhouseCoopers LLP

LOCATIONS

HQ: American International Group, Inc.
70 Pine St., New York, NY 10270
Phone: 212-770-7000　　**Fax:** 212-509-9705
Web: www.aig.com

American International Group's subsidiaries operate throughout the US and in about 130 other countries.

PRODUCTS/OPERATIONS

2001 Assets

	$ mil.	% of total
Cash	698	—
Government securities	3,843	1
State & municipal bonds	34,821	7
Foreign governments' securities	30,145	6
Corporate bonds	130,965	26
Stocks	7,937	2
Mortgage loans	10,744	2
Policy loans	5,786	1
Reinsurance assets	28,758	6
Assets in separate account	51,954	11
Receivables	11,647	2
Other investments & assets	175,684	36
Total	**492,982**	**100**

COMPETITORS

AEGON	The Hartford	MGIC
Allianz	ING	Investment
Allmerica	Jefferson-Pilot	Millea Holdings
Financial	John Hancock	New York Life
Allstate	Financial	Prudential
American Family	Services	Prudential plc
Insurance	Kemper	Reliance Group
Aon	Insurance	Holdings
AXA	Legal & General	SAFECO
Berkshire	Group	St. Paul
Hathaway	Liberty Mutual	Companies
Chubb	Lloyd's of	State Farm
CIGNA	London	Travelers
CNA Financial	MassMutual	Zurich Financial
Fortis (NL)	Meiji Life	Services
GeneralCologne	Insurance	
Re	MetLife	

HISTORICAL FINANCIALS & EMPLOYEES

NYSE: AIG FYE: December 31	Annual Growth	12/92	12/93	12/94	12/95	12/96	12/97	12/98	12/99	12/00	12/01
Assets ($ mil.)	22.4%	79,835	101,015	114,346	134,136	148,431	163,971	194,398	268,238	306,577	492,982
Net income ($ mil.)	13.9%	1,657	1,939	2,176	2,510	2,897	3,332	3,766	5,055	5,636	5,363
Income as % of assets	—	2.1%	1.9%	1.9%	1.9%	2.0%	2.0%	1.9%	1.9%	1.8%	1.1%
Earnings per share ($)	10.4%	0.83	0.97	1.08	1.25	1.45	1.68	1.91	2.15	2.41	2.02
Stock price - FY high ($)	—	12.82	15.87	15.95	22.67	27.63	41.02	54.76	75.29	103.75	98.31
Stock price - FY low ($)	—	8.66	11.63	12.94	15.22	20.92	25.28	34.62	51.03	52.40	66.00
Stock price - FY close ($)	23.1%	12.25	13.89	15.52	21.96	25.70	38.71	51.56	72.12	98.56	79.40
P/E - high	—	16	16	15	18	19	24	29	35	43	47
P/E - low	—	11	12	12	12	14	15	18	23	22	31
Dividends per share ($)	13.8%	0.05	0.06	0.07	0.07	0.09	0.10	0.09	0.13	0.14	0.16
Book value per share ($)	13.5%	6.38	7.59	8.23	9.93	11.15	12.21	13.79	14.34	16.91	19.94
Employees	10.5%	33,000	33,000	32,000	34,500	36,600	40,000	48,000	55,000	61,000	81,000

STOCK PRICE HISTORY

HIGH/LOW/CLOSE

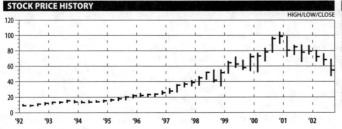

2001 FISCAL YEAR-END

Equity as % of assets: 10.6%
Return on assets: 1.3%
Return on equity: 11.7%
Long-term debt ($ mil.): 53,839
No. of shares (mil.): 2,615
Dividends
　Yield: 0.2%
　Payout: 7.9%
Market value ($ mil.): 207,665
Sales ($ mil.): 55,459

AMERICAN STANDARD COMPANIES

Few businesses have cooler customers than American Standard Companies, a leading maker of air-conditioning equipment. Based in Piscataway, New Jersey, the company makes residential and commercial air-conditioning and indoor environmental control systems sold under both the American Standard and Trane names. Air-conditioning equipment accounts for about 60% of American Standard's sales.

Its other lines of business — also market leaders — include plumbing fixtures and automotive braking systems. The company sells plumbing fixtures (about 25% of sales) mostly to the residential market under the American Standard, Ideal Standard, and Porcher brands. The company's WABCO unit makes braking systems, primarily for trucks and buses; it also makes suspension control systems for SUVs and luxury cars. WABCO's principal customers are OEMs such as DaimlerChrysler and aftermarket resellers.

American Standard has suffered throughout the 1990s from slow sales growth and poor earnings. A sputtering economy has adversely affected 2001 sales, especially for braking systems. CEO Frederic Poses has been dealing with the company's heavy debt and sluggish profit margins by improving employee performance and cutting jobs.

HISTORY

In 1881 American Radiator began making steam and water-heating equipment in Buffalo, New York. J. P. Morgan acquired the company, along with almost every other US heating-equipment firm, and consolidated them as American Radiator in 1899. That year Ahrens & Ott joined with Standard Manufacturing to create Standard Sanitary, which produced enameled cast-iron plumbing fixtures.

Both American Radiator and Standard Sanitary grew through acquisitions early in the 20th century. In 1929 the companies merged to form American Radiator & Standard Sanitary, expanding operations across the Americas and into Europe. By the 1960s the company was the world's #1 manufacturer of plumbing fixtures.

The firm became American Standard in 1967 and began diversifying through acquisitions. In 1968 it bought Westinghouse Air Brake (WABCO), which made railway brakes and, later, automotive products. (WABCO traces its history to Union Switch and Signal, founded in 1882.) During the 1970s and 1980s the firm consolidated operations and sold numerous businesses. It bought Trane (air conditioners) in 1984.

American Standard fought off a hostile takeover by Black & Decker in 1988 and then agreed to be purchased by ASI Holding (formed by LBO firm Kelso & Co.) and taken private. The transaction left the firm deeply in debt. To raise cash, it sold its Manhattan headquarters, its railway signal business, its Steelcraft division, and its pneumatic-controls business in 1988. American Standard sold its railway brake operations in 1990 and Tyler Refrigeration in 1991, losing $22 million in the deal.

In 1994 American Standard acquired 70% of Deutsche Perrot-Bremsen's automotive brake business in a joint venture. American Standard went public again in 1995 and bought the 67% of Etablissements Porcher Paris (bathroom fixtures) that it did not already own. Late in 1996 American Standard fought off a takeover bid by Tyco. Continued poor results in the 1990s prompted the company to streamline operations, shake up management in several areas, and institute a just-in-time manufacturing system to help pare inventory. In late 1997 Horst Hinrichs (SVP at WABCO) was appointed VC of the corporation to provide management succession.

In 1999 the company bought the bathroom-fixtures business of Blue Circle (UK) for $417 million to boost its sales in Europe. American Standard also hired AlliedSignal's president, Frederic Poses, to replace Emanuel Kampouris as chairman and CEO and began seeking a buyer for its medical diagnostics operations that year. (The company's medical systems group, which began operating in 1989, made low-cost analyzers and diagnostic supplies for use in doctors' offices.) American Standard sold its medical unit in 2000. Later that year the company sold its Calorex water heater business.

To reduce costs, American Standard laid off about 8% of its workforce in 2001. Also that same year the company's air conditioning subsidiary, Trane, announced plans for a global alliance with a Japanese air conditioning manufacturer, Daikin, to cross-market and sell each other's products beginning in 2002.

OFFICERS

Chairman and CEO: Frederic M. Poses, age 58, $2,192,000 pay
SVP and CFO: G. Peter D'Aloia, age 57, $700,000 pay
SVP, General Counsel, and Secretary: J. Paul McGrath, age 61, $700,000 pay
SVP, Human Resources: Lawrence B. Costello, age 54, $570,000 pay
SVP, Plumbing Products: Marc R. Olivié, age 48
SVP, Vehicle Control Systems: W. Craig Kissel, age 50
VP and General Manager, Plumbing Products, Americas: Laurie Breininger
VP and General Manager, Plumbing Products, Europe: Wilfried Delker, age 60
VP and General Tax Counsel: Nicholas A. Anthony

VP and Treasurer: R. Scott Massengill, age 39
VP, Communications: Shelly J. London
VP, Marketing: Sally G. Robling
VP, Strategic Planning and Investor Relations:
R. Bruce Fisher
**VP, Supply Chain Management, Air Conditioning
Systems and Services:** Bryan Cook
VP, Trane Residential Systems: David R. Pannier, age 51
Auditors: Ernst & Young LLP

LOCATIONS

HQ: American Standard Companies Inc.
1 Centennial Ave., Piscataway, NJ 08855
Phone: 732-980-6000   **Fax:** 732-980-3340
Web: www.americanstandard.com

American Standard Companies operates nearly 110
manufacturing facilities in about 30 countries.

2001 Sales

	$ mil.	% of total
US	4,265	55
Europe		
Germany	520	7
UK	433	5
France	419	5
Italy	300	4
Other countries	456	6
Other regions	1,413	18
Adjustments	(341)	—
Total	**7,465**	**100**

PRODUCTS/OPERATIONS

2001 Sales & Operating Income

	Sales		Operating Income	
	$ mil.	% of total	$ mil.	% of total
Air conditioning	4,692	63	515	65
Plumbing	1,813	24	148	19
Automotive	960	13	124	16
Total	**7,465**	**100**	**787**	**100**

Selected Products
Applied air conditioning systems (custom-engineered for
commercial use)
ABS braking systems
Bathroom and kitchen fittings and fixtures
Bathtubs
EBS braking systems
Mini-split air conditioning systems (small unitary
systems without ducts, for residential use)
Pneumatic braking control systems
Unitary air conditioning systems (factory-assembled
systems for residential and commercial use)

COMPETITORS

ArvinMeritor,	Goodman	TOTO
Inc.	Manufacturing	United
Black & Decker	Knorr-Bremse	Technologies
BorgWarner	Kohler	U.S. Industries
Carrier	Lennox	Villeroy & Boch
Daikin Industries	Masco	Watsco
Dana	Moen	Whirlpool
Eaton	Mueller	York
Electrolux AB	Industries	International
Grohe	Robert Bosch	
Gerber Plumbing	Tecumseh	
Fixtures	Products	

HISTORICAL FINANCIALS & EMPLOYEES

NYSE: ASD FYE: December 31	Annual Growth	12/92	12/93	12/94	12/95	12/96	12/97	12/98	12/99	12/00	12/01
Sales ($ mil.)	7.8%	3,792	3,831	4,458	5,222	5,805	6,008	6,654	7,190	7,598	7,465
Net income ($ mil.)	—	(57)	(117)	(86)	112	(47)	96	(16)	138	315	295
Income as % of sales	—	—	—	—	2.1%	—	1.6%	—	1.9%	4.1%	4.0%
Earnings per share ($)	18.4%	—	—	—	1.47	(0.60)	1.26	(0.22)	1.90	4.36	4.04
Stock price - FY high ($)	—	—	—	—	32.00	39.75	51.63	49.25	49.44	49.75	70.90
Stock price - FY low ($)	—	—	—	—	19.63	25.50	34.63	21.63	31.13	34.31	46.75
Stock price - FY close ($)	16.0%	—	—	—	28.00	38.25	38.31	36.00	45.88	49.31	68.23
P/E - high	—	—	—	—	17	—	32	—	25	11	17
P/E - low	—	—	—	—	10	—	21	—	16	8	11
Dividends per share ($)	—	—	—	—	0.00	0.00	0.00	0.00	0.00	0.00	0.00
Book value per share ($)	—	—	—	—	(5.08)	(4.84)	(8.47)	(10.03)	(7.02)	(5.65)	(1.25)
Employees	6.7%	33,500	36,000	38,000	43,000	44,000	51,000	57,100	58,000	61,000	60,000

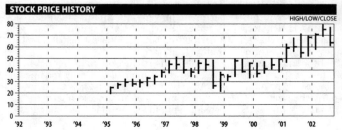

STOCK PRICE HISTORY
HIGH/LOW/CLOSE

2001 FISCAL YEAR-END
Debt ratio: 100.0%
Return on equity: —
Cash ($ mil.): 82
Current ratio: 1.12
Long-term debt ($ mil.): 2,142
No. of shares (mil.): 72
Dividends
  Yield: —
  Payout: —
Market value ($ mil.): 4,917

AMERISOURCEBERGEN

What happens when two major rivals team up to create one company? For AmerisourceBergen, the union created more than just an awkward-sounding name. Based in Chesterbrook, Pennsylvania, the firm was formed when drug distributor AmeriSource bought competitor Bergen Brunswig to become one of the largest distributors of pharmaceuticals and health care products in the US.

AmerisourceBergen's pharmaceutical distribution division supplies hospitals, managed care facilities, drugstores, nursing homes, clinics, supermarkets, and mass merchandisers through more than 40 distribution facilities. The division primarily distributes generic, branded, and OTC pharmaceuticals. The federal government's Veterans Administration accounts for nearly a third of the division's sales.

In addition to its traditional pharmaceutical distribution operations, the company's PharMerica subsidiary distributes pharmaceuticals and provides services through institutional pharmacies. The firm's other services include the iECHO and iBergen Internet ordering systems. AmeriSource Bergen's Family Pharmacy and Good Neighbor Pharmacy programs provide online shopping and help connect independent and small chain drug stores to various merchandising programs and other services.

Its Pharmacy Healthcare Solutions offers consulting services to hospitals. Other divisions supply pharmacies with packaging and distribute cosmetics.

HISTORY

In 1977 Cleveland millionaire and horse racing enthusiast Tinkham Veale went into the drug wholesaling business. His company, Alco Standard (now IKON Office Solutions), already owned chemical, electrical, metallurgical, and mining companies, but by the late 1970s the company was pursuing a strategy of zeroing in on various types of distribution businesses.

Alco's first drug wholesaler purchase was The Drug House (Delaware and Pennsylvania); next was Duff Brothers (Tennessee). The company then bought wholesalers in the South, East, and Midwest. Its modus operandi was to buy small, well-run companies for cash and Alco stock and leave the incumbent management in charge.

By the early 1980s Alco was the US's third-largest wholesale drug distributor and growing quickly (28% between 1983 and 1988) at a time of mass consolidation in the industry (the number of wholesalers dropped by half between 1980 and 1992). In 1985 Alco Standard spun off its

drug distribution operations as Alco Health Services, retaining 60% ownership.

Alco Health boosted its sales above $1 billion mostly via acquisitions and expanded product lines. The company offered marketing and promotional help to its independent pharmacy customers (which were beleaguered by the growth of national discounters) and also targeted hospitals, nursing homes, and clinics.

The US was in the midst of its LBO frenzy in 1988, but an Alco management group failed in its attempt. Rival McKesson then tried to acquire Alco Health, but that deal fell through for antitrust reasons. Later in 1988 management turned for backing to Citicorp Venture Capital in another buyout attempt. This time the move succeeded, and a new holding company, Alco Health Distribution, was formed.

In 1993 Alco Health was named as a defendant in suits by independent pharmacies charging discriminatory pricing policies; a ruling the next year limited its liability. To move away from a reliance on independent drugstores, Alco Health began targeting government entities and others.

Alco Health went public as AmeriSource Health in 1995. Throughout the next year, AmeriSource made a series of acquisitions to move into related areas, including inventory management technology, drugstore pharmaceutical supplies, and disease-management services for pharmacies.

In 1997 AmeriSource made its largest purchase to date when it acquired Alabama-based Walker Drug for $140 million, adding 1,500 independent and chain drugstores in the Southeast to its customer list. Also in 1997 McKesson once again made an offer to buy AmeriSource, this time for $2.4 billion, while two other major wholesale distributors, Cardinal Health and Bergen Brunswig, reached a similar pact. But once again antitrust concerns reared up. The deals were scrapped in 1998 when the Federal Trade Commission voted against both pacts (and was upheld in court).

Later in 1998 AmeriSource signed a five-year deal to become the exclusive pharmaceutical supplier to not-for-profit Sutter Health; in 1999 it renewed similar contracts with the US Department of Veterans Affairs and Pharmacy Provider Services Corporation. That year AmeriSource bought Midwest distributor C.D. Smith Healthcare.

In 2001 AmeriSource bought Bergen Brunswig, and the combined company renamed itself AmerisourceBergen. In 2002 the company bought a maker of automated pharmacy dispensing equipment, AutoMed Technologies.

Chairman: Robert E. Martini, age 67
President, CEO, and Director: R. David Yost
EVP and COO; President, AmerisourceBergen Drug:
Kurt J. Hilzinger
SVP and CFO: Michael D. DiCandilo, age 41
SVP; President, AmerisourceBergen Specialty Group:
Steven H. Collis
SVP; President, PharMerica: Charles J. Carpenter
SVP, Health Systems Sales and Marketing:
Thomas P. Connolly
SVP, Integration: Terrance P. Haas
SVP, Retail Sales and Marketing: David W. Neu
VP and CIO: Linda M. Burkett, age 49
VP, General Counsel, and Secretary: William D. Sprague
VP, Human Resources: Eileen Coyne Clark
Auditors: Ernst & Young LLP

LOCATIONS

HQ: AmerisourceBergen Corporation
1300 Morris Dr., Ste. 100, Chesterbrook, PA 19087
Phone: 610-727-7000   **Fax:** 610-727-3600
Web: www.amerisourcebergen.net

AmerisourceBergen operates nationwide.

PRODUCTS/OPERATIONS

2001 Sales

	$ mil.	% of total
Pharmaceutical distribution	15,770	97
PharMerica	117	1
Bulk deliveries to customer warehouses	368	2
Adjustments	(64)	—
Total	**16,191**	**100**

Selected Services
American Health Packaging (unit dose, punch card, and
unit-of-use packaging)
AmeriSource Select (best-priced generic products)
Diabetes Shoppe & Diabetes Corner (products for
diabetes patients)
ECHO Inventory Module (physical inventory
management)
Family Pharmacy (merchandising and promotional
campaigns)
Health Services Plus (oncology and specialty product
distribution)
iECHO (Internet access for pharmacies)
iECHO Plus (multiple sites Internet access)
Pharmacy Healthcare Solutions (hospital consulting to
improve efficiency)
RECOVERx (indigent patient pharmaceutical
reimbursement recovery)
Rita Ann (fragrance and cosmetic specialty distributor)

COMPETITORS

Cardinal Health	Kinray	PSS World
D & K	McKesson	Medical
Healthcare	Owens & Minor	Quality King
Resources		

HISTORICAL FINANCIALS & EMPLOYEES

NYSE: ABC FYE: September 30	Annual Growth	9/92	9/93	9/94	9/95	9/96	9/97	9/98	9/99	9/00	9/01
Sales ($ mil.)	19.2%	3,330	3,719	4,302	4,669	5,552	7,816	8,669	9,807	11,645	16,191
Net income ($ mil.)	—	(6)	(19)	(208)	10	36	45	51	68	99	125
Income as % of sales	—	—	—	—	0.2%	0.6%	0.6%	0.6%	0.7%	0.9%	0.8%
Earnings per share ($)	39.9%	—	—	—	0.28	0.77	0.95	1.04	1.31	1.90	2.10
Stock price - FY high ($)	—	—	—	—	13.88	22.25	32.63	40.38	41.38	48.00	71.59
Stock price - FY low ($)	—	—	—	—	9.88	12.63	18.81	22.23	22.94	11.00	38.38
Stock price - FY close ($)	31.9%	—	—	—	13.50	22.25	29.22	27.22	23.69	47.00	70.95
P/E - high	—	—	—	—	18	24	33	38	30	25	33
P/E - low	—	—	—	—	13	13	19	21	16	6	18
Dividends per share ($)	—	—	—	—	0.00	0.00	0.00	0.00	0.00	0.00	0.00
Book value per share ($)	—	—	—	—	(2.66)	(0.68)	0.26	1.37	2.88	4.81	27.42
Employees	22.1%	2,269	2,403	2,370	2,600	3,000	3,700	3,298	3,200	3,700	13,700

STOCK PRICE HISTORY

HIGH/LOW/CLOSE

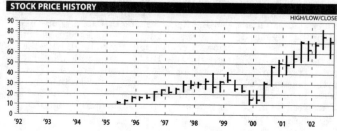

2001 FISCAL YEAR-END

Debt ratio: 36.0%
Return on equity: 8.0%
Cash ($ mil.): 298
Current ratio: 1.36
Long-term debt ($ mil.): 1,597
No. of shares (mil.): 104
Dividends
  Yield: —
  Payout: —
Market value ($ mil.): 7,346

AMGEN INC.

Warriors ate the hearts of their enemies to make themselves stronger. Amgen, the world's largest biotechnology firm, hopes gobbling up near-rival Immunex will give it future fiscal and pharmaceutical fortitude.

The Thousand Oaks, California-based firm develops drugs for nephrology, cancer, inflammatory disorders, neurology, and metabolic diseases. Its top products are anti-anemia drug Epogen (54% of sales), a recombinant version of the hormone EPO, and immune system stimulator Neupogen (about 33%). Amgen also sells hepatitis C treatment Infergen in the US and Canada. Stemgen, which supports stem cell transplantation, is sold in Australia, Canada, and New Zealand.

Its lead products enjoy several more years of patent protection, but Amgen is launching new products that may best its best sellers. One such future blockbuster is ARANESP, a longer-lasting version of Epogen. With Epogen and ARANESP in its arsenal, the company is battling Johnson & Johnson (the maker of Procrit, which it licensed from Amgen some 15 years ago), Baxter (with its Epoetin Omega), and other firms to control the anemia therapy market. Amgen is challenging Transkaryotic Therapies and partner Aventis in US courts: It claims their Dynepo, an EPO genetically engineered drug, infringes Epogen's patents. It lost its patent infringement claims against the duo in the UK in mid-2002.

Amgen is also looking to control the rheumatoid arthritis market. Not only does it have Enbrel, the firm also has Kineret, a proprietary rheumatoid arthritis drug the FDA approved for patients for whom other treatments have failed.

Wyeth, which had owned about 40% of Immunex, now owns about 10% of the combined company.

HISTORY

Amgen was formed as Applied Molecular Genetics in 1980 by a group of scientists and venture capitalists to develop health care products based on molecular biology. George Rathmann, a VP at Abbott Laboratories and researcher at UCLA, became the company's CEO and first employee. Rathmann decided to develop a few potentially profitable products rather than conduct research. The company initially raised $19 million.

Amgen operated close to bankruptcy until 1983, when company scientist Fu-Kuen Lin cloned the human protein erythropoietin (EPO), which stimulates the body's red blood cell production. Amgen went public that year. It formed a joint venture with Kirin Brewery in 1984 to develop and market EPO. The two firms also collaborated on recombinant human granulocyte colony stimulating factor (G-CSF, later called Neupogen), a protein that stimulates the immune system.

Amgen joined Johnson & Johnson subsidiary Ortho Pharmaceutical in a marketing alliance in 1985 and created a tie with Roche in 1988. Fortunes soared in 1989 when the FDA approved Epogen (the brand name of EPO) for anemia. (It is most commonly used to counter side effects of kidney dialysis.) In 1991 Amgen received approval to market Neupogen to chemotherapy patients. A federal court ruling also gave it a US monopoly for EPO. The following year Amgen won another dispute, forcing a competitor to renounce its US patents for G-CSF.

As the company grew, it needed to transform itself from startup to going concern; to do so, Amgen hired MCI veteran Kevin Sharer as president in 1992. Neupogen's usage was expanded in 1993 to include treatment of severe chronic neutropenia (low white blood cell count).

In 1993 Amgen became the first American biotech to gain a foothold in China through an agreement with Kirin Pharmaceuticals to sell Neupogen (under the name Gran) and Epogen there. In 1997 Amgen and partner Regeneron Pharmaceuticals reported the failure of human trials for a drug to treat Lou Gehrig's disease. Still its new drug Stemgen for breast cancer patients undergoing chemotherapy was recommended for approval by an FDA advisory committee in 1998.

In 1998 a dispute with J&J over Amgen's 1985 licensing agreement with Ortho Pharmaceutical ended when an arbiter ordered Amgen to pay about $200 million. Later that year, however, Amgen won a legal battle with J&J over the rights to a promising anemia drug.

In 1999 Amgen ended development of obesity and Parkinson's disease drugs after clinical trials produced discouraging results. Also that year it began human tests with partner Guilford Pharmaceuticals on a drug designed to regenerate damaged nerve cells in the brain in Parkinson's disease patients. (Guilford and Amgen ended the collaboration in 2001.) In 2000 the firm resumed its battle to keep its stranglehold on the Epogen market: It sued Transkaryotic Therapies and Aventis for alleged patent violations over its Epogen product in both the US and the UK. That year it won EU and US approval for ARANESP, an updated version of Epogen; in 2002 Amgen teamed with former J&J partner Fresenius to sell ARANESP in Germany and take some market share away from J&J.

OFFICERS

Chairman, President, and CEO: Kevin W. Sharer, age 54, $2,168,599 pay
EVP, Finance, Strategy, and Communications and CFO: Richard D. Nanula, age 41
EVP, Operations: Dennis M. Fenton, age 50, $1,015,057 pay
EVP, Research and Development: Roger M. Perlmutter, age 49
EVP, Worldwide Sales and Marketing: George Morrow, age 49
SVP, General Counsel, and Secretary: Steven M. Odre, age 52, $847,794 pay
SVP and CIO: Hassan Dayem
SVP, Development and Chief Medical Officer: George Morstyn, $1,009,213 pay
SVP, Human Resources: Brian McNamee, age 45
Auditors: Ernst & Young LLP

LOCATIONS

HQ: One Amgen Center Dr., Thousand Oaks, CA 91320
Phone: 805-447-1000   **Fax:** 805-447-1010
Web: www.amgen.com

Amgen has facilities in Asia and the Pacific Rim, Europe, and North America.

2001 Sales

	$ mil.	% of total
US	3,689	92
Other countries	327	8
Adjustments	(253)	—
Total	**3,763**	**100**

PRODUCTS/OPERATIONS

2001 Sales

	$ mil.	% of total
Products		
Epogen	2,150	57
Neupogen	1,346	36
Other	15	—
Corporate partner revenues	252	7
Total	**3,763**	**100**

COMPETITORS

Abbott Labs	Human Genome	Novartis
ALZA	Sciences	Ortho Biotech
AstraZeneca	IDEC	Pfizer
Atrix Labs	Pharmaceuticals	Pharmacia
Aventis	Immunex	Regeneron
Baxter	Interferon	Pharmaceuticals
Bayer AG	Sciences	Roche
Bone Care	IntraBiotics	Sanofi-
International	Pharmaceuticals	Synthélabo
Bristol-Myers	Johnson &	Schering
Squibb	Johnson	Schering-Plough
Centocor	Kosan	TAP
Cephalon	Biosciences	Pharmaceutical
Chugai	Kyowa Hakko	Products
Degussa	Kogyo	Transkaryotic
Eli Lilly	MedImmune	Therapies
Genentech	Merck	Vertex
GlaxoSmithKline	Millennium	Pharmaceuticals
	Pharmaceuticals	Wyeth

HISTORICAL FINANCIALS & EMPLOYEES

Nasdaq: AMGN FYE: December 31	Annual Growth	12/92	12/93	12/94	12/95	12/96	12/97	12/98	12/99	12/00	12/01
Sales ($ mil.)	14.9%	1,080	1,355	1,620	1,904	2,198	2,346	2,642	3,204	3,448	3,763
Net income ($ mil.)	13.5%	358	383	320	538	680	644	863	1,096	1,139	1,120
Income as % of sales	—	33.1%	28.3%	19.7%	28.2%	30.9%	27.5%	32.7%	34.2%	33.0%	29.8%
Earnings per share ($)	14.3%	0.31	0.35	0.29	0.48	0.61	0.59	0.82	1.02	1.05	1.03
Stock price - FY high ($)	—	9.78	8.97	7.53	14.94	16.63	17.34	27.00	66.44	80.44	75.06
Stock price - FY low ($)	—	6.16	3.88	4.34	7.02	12.84	11.22	11.66	25.69	50.00	45.44
Stock price - FY close ($)	22.9%	8.83	6.19	7.38	14.84	13.59	13.53	26.14	60.06	63.94	56.44
P/E - high	—	32	26	26	29	26	28	32	62	70	70
P/E - low	—	20	11	15	14	20	18	14	24	43	42
Dividends per share ($)	—	0.00	0.00	0.00	0.00	0.00	0.01	0.00	0.00	0.00	0.00
Book value per share ($)	21.6%	0.86	1.09	1.20	1.57	1.80	2.07	2.52	2.97	4.16	4.99
Employees	14.2%	2,335	3,100	3,546	4,046	4,646	5,308	5,500	6,400	7,300	7,700

STOCK PRICE HISTORY

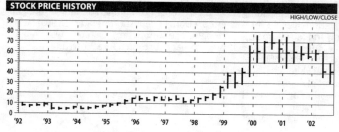

HIGH/LOW/CLOSE

2001 FISCAL YEAR-END

Debt ratio: 4.1%
Return on equity: 23.5%
Cash ($ mil.): 689
Current ratio: 3.85
Long-term debt ($ mil.): 223
No. of shares (mil.): 1,046
Dividends
  Yield: —
  Payout: —
Market value ($ mil.): 59,025

AMKOR TECHNOLOGY, INC.

Wanna test that chip before you send it on its way? Amkor Technology would love to help. The West Chester, Pennsylvania-based company is an independent provider of semiconductor packaging and test services. Packaging includes dicing of a semiconductor wafer into separate chips, die bonding, wire bonding, and encapsulation of the chip in protective plastic. Amkor's testing procedures verify function, current, timing, and voltage. The company also offers wafer fabrication services, through which it makes finished semiconductor wafers for customers. Amkor has more than 300 customers worldwide, including such industry leaders as Toshiba (14% of sales), Texas Instruments (10%), Agilent, Intel, IBM, and STMicroelectronics.

Amkor was originally the US marketing arm of South Korean manufacturer Anam Industrial Co. (now Anam Semiconductor), and the two companies are still very closely linked. After purchasing Anam's four packaging plants, Amkor retains exclusive rights to the output of Anam's remaining wafer foundry. Though it has tried to pare its stake, Amkor remains Anam's controlling shareholder.

Founder, chairman, and CEO James Kim and his family own 45% of Amkor.

HISTORY

Kim Joo-Jin (James Kim), the oldest of seven children, came to the US from South Korea in 1955 to study business. A year later his father started electronics firm Anam Industrial, and in 1968 James Kim (chairman and CEO) founded Amkor (short for "American-Korean") Electronics as its US marketing agent.

To lessen its dependence on the volatile semiconductor market, Anam Industrial began diversifying in 1975, first into watchmaking, and eventually into banking, construction, environmental services, and electronics. (James Kim's wife, Agnes, began selling electronic watches and calculators from a kiosk near the family home in Pennsylvania; the business grew into the Electronics Boutique chain.)

James Kim joined the board of California semiconductor maker VLSI Technology (now part of Philips Semiconductors) in 1982, leading the company into the application-specific integrated circuit market. Anam Industrial, meanwhile, continued to grow along with the semiconductor industry. By 1990 it had 50% of the world's semiconductor package assembly business, and was only one unit of South Korean *chaebol* (family-run, non-legal conglomerate) Anam Group. That year the group took over a plant in Manila from Advanced Micro Devices

and established Amkor/Anam Pilipinas on that site. It also acquired Scotland-based ITEQ Europe Ltd., Europe's leading semiconductor assembly contractor.

During the early 1990s Anam Industrial developed the tape-automated bonding manufacturing process. When the senior Kim retired in 1992, James Kim also became head of the Anam Group.

In 1993 Amkor licensed ball-grid array (BGA) packaging technology from Motorola. At the time BGA — in which tiny balls of solder are used for connections, instead of fragile lead wires — was still an emerging standard. By 1995 Amkor had become a leader in BGA packaging. That year the company announced that it would build the US's first independent BGA facility, in Arizona (it opened in 1999).

Anam Industrial began building its fourth semiconductor assembly plant in 1996, this one in the Philippines, with a production goal of 50 million chips per month. In 1997 Amkor opened its complementary metal oxide semiconductor wafer (CMOS) plant near Seoul, using Texas Instruments' technology, as part of a 10-year cooperative agreement. It also created Amkor Industries to consolidate the various Amkor companies. Also that year Amkor/Anam formed an agreement with Acer and Taiwan Semiconductor Manufacturing to build a semiconductor assembly and test facility in Taiwan.

Amkor went public in 1998. That year Anam Industrial changed its name to Anam Semiconductor and announced plans to divest its noncore businesses to focus on chip packaging. In 1999 Amkor opened a support center in France and bought a packaging plant in South Korea from Anam Semiconductor. In 2000 Amkor bought three more plants from Anam Semiconductor — which was still restructuring as its *chaebol* broke up — and upped its stake in Anam to 42%. In 2001 Amkor announced that, because of erosion in chip demand, it would lay off 2,200 employees — 10% of its workforce.

In 2002 Amkor acquired the Japan-based chip assembly business of Citizen Watch. Also that year the company announced the formation of a chip packaging joint venture with Fujitsu. In mid-2002 Amkor agreed to sell about half of its stake in Anam to Korean conglomerate (and foundry operator) Dongbu, but the deal later fell apart when Dongbu could not come to terms with Anam's predominant customer Texas Instruments.

OFFICERS

Chairman and CEO: James J. Kim, age 66, $869,000 pay
President, COO, and Director: John N. Boruch, age 60, $638,000 pay
EVP and CFO: Kenneth T. Joyce, age 55, $258,500 pay
EVP, Corporate Development and Wafer Fab: Eric R. Larson, age 46, $302,500 pay
EVP, Manufacturing and Product Operations: Bruce Freyman, age 41, $387,692 pay
SVP and CIO: Bill White
SVP and General Counsel: Kevin J. Heron
SVP, Business Development: Gary Waterhouse
SVP, Strategic Business Development: Gene Norrett
VP and Country Manager, Japan: Paul B. Grant, age 55, $328,900 pay
VP, Advanced Leadframe Products: Sean Crowley
VP, Advanced Product Development: Mike Steidl
VP, Corporate Communications: Jeffrey M. Luth
VP, Flip Chip Product Business Unit: Richard Groover
VP, Human Resources: Cathy Loucks
VP, Korean Operations: Chang Nam Kim
VP, Philippine Operations: Tony Ng
VP, Product Management: Scott Voss
VP, QRE and Marketing: John McMillan
VP, Sales: Farshad Haghighi
Auditors: PricewaterhouseCoopers LLP

LOCATIONS

HQ: 1345 Enterprise Dr., West Chester, PA 19380
Phone: 610-431-9600 **Fax:** 610-431-5881
Web: www.amkor.com

Amkor Technology has manufacturing facilities in China, Japan, the Philippines, South Korea, and Taiwan; it has sales and services offices in France, Japan, the Philippines, Singapore, South Korea, Taiwan, and the US.

2001 Sales

	$ mil.	% of total
US	601	40
Japan	297	19
Singapore	151	10
Ireland	77	5
Other countries	392	26
Total	**1,518**	**100**

PRODUCTS/OPERATIONS

2001 Sales

	$ mil.	% of total
Packaging & test	1,337	88
Wafer fabrication	181	12
Total	**1,518**	**100**

Products and Services

Chip packaging
　Advanced leadframe (plastic mold with thermal, electrical characteristics)
　Laminate (plastic or tape rather than leadframe substrate)
　Traditional leadframe (plastic mold with metal leads)
Test services (analog, digital logic, and mixed-signal chips)
Wafer fabrication

COMPETITORS

Alphatec
ASAT Holdings
ASE Test Limited
Chartered Semiconductor Manufacturing
ChipPAC
PSi Technologies
Siliconware Precision Industries
ST Assembly Test Services
Taiwan Semiconductor
United Microelectronics
Winbond Electronics

HISTORICAL FINANCIALS & EMPLOYEES

Nasdaq: AMKR FYE: December 31	Annual Growth	12/92	12/93	12/94	12/95	12/96	12/97	12/98	12/99	12/00	12/01
Sales ($ mil.)	19.6%	304	442	573	932	1,171	1,456	1,568	1,910	2,387	1,518
Net income ($ mil.)	—	(16)	17	12	59	34	43	76	77	154	(451)
Income as % of sales	—	—	3.9%	2.0%	6.3%	2.9%	3.0%	4.8%	4.0%	6.5%	—
Earnings per share ($)	—	—	—	—	—	—	—	0.70	0.63	1.02	(2.87)
Stock price - FY high ($)	—	—	—	—	—	—	—	14.00	29.56	65.31	26.24
Stock price - FY low ($)	—	—	—	—	—	—	—	3.00	7.09	11.75	9.00
Stock price - FY close ($)	14.0%	—	—	—	—	—	—	10.81	28.25	15.52	16.03
P/E - high	—	—	—	—	—	—	—	20	46	62	—
P/E - low	—	—	—	—	—	—	—	4	11	11	—
Dividends per share ($)	—	—	—	—	—	—	—	0.00	0.00	0.00	0.00
Book value per share ($)	14.4%	—	—	—	—	—	—	4.16	5.63	8.64	6.23
Employees	21.4%	—	—	—	—	8,180	9,100	10,000	13,285	22,715	21,600

STOCK PRICE HISTORY

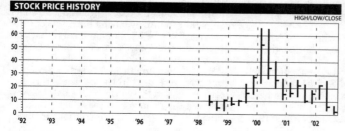

HIGH/LOW/CLOSE

2001 FISCAL YEAR-END

Debt ratio: 63.7%
Return on equity: —
Cash ($ mil.): 200
Current ratio: 1.43
Long-term debt ($ mil.): 1,772
No. of shares (mil.): 162
Dividends
　Yield: —
　Payout: —
Market value ($ mil.): 2,593

AMR CORPORATION

AMR's American Airlines is taking on the world. The #2 airline in the US based on revenue passenger miles (behind UAL's United Airlines), Fort Worth, Texas-based American flies to some 160 destinations (including those served by code-sharing partners) in the Caribbean, the Pacific Rim, Europe, and the Americas. The airline, which has a fleet of more than 800 jets (mostly Boeings), has hubs at Dallas/Fort Worth's DFW, Chicago's O'Hare, and in Miami and San Juan, Puerto Rico. AMR, which expanded in 2001 by buying the assets of bankrupt TWA, also owns commuter carrier American Eagle.

Internationally, American Airlines leads One-world, an extensive marketing alliance that includes British Airways, Cathay Pacific, Qantas, and others. It also has code-sharing agreements with carriers such as China Eastern Airlines and Japan Airlines.

In the airline industry slowdown that has followed the September 11, 2001, terrorist attacks on the US, American Airlines is working to cut costs. In August 2002 the carrier announced plans to reduce its capacity by 9%, lay off about 7,000 employees, and simplify its fleet by retiring its Fokker-100 jets ahead of schedule. American also plans to spread out flight arrivals at its DFW hub, as it has at O'Hare. The move is expected to result in more efficient operations for the airline but longer waits between connections for passengers.

HISTORY

In 1929 Sherman Fairchild created a New York City holding company called the Aviation Corporation (AVCO), combining some 85 small airlines in 1930 to create American Airways. In 1934 the company had its first dose of financial trouble after the government suspended private airmail for months. Corporate raider E. L. Cord took over and named the company American Airlines.

Cord put former AVCO manager C. R. Smith in charge, and American became the leading US airline in the late 1930s. The Douglas DC-3, built to Smith's specifications, was introduced by American in 1936 and became the first commercial airliner to pay its way on passenger revenues alone.

After WWII American bought Amex Airlines, which flew to northern Europe, but another financial crisis prompted Amex's sale in 1950. The airline introduced Sabre, the first automated reservations system, in 1964. Smith left American four years later to serve as secretary of commerce in the Johnson administration.

American moved to Dallas/Fort Worth in 1979,

the year after airline industry deregulation. Former CFO Bob Crandall became president in 1980 (and later, CEO). Using Sabre to track mileage, he introduced the industry's first frequent-flier program (AAdvantage). In 1982 American created AMR as its holding company. After acquiring commuter airline Nashville Eagle in 1987, AMR established American Eagle.

After ducking a 1989 takeover bid by Donald Trump, AMR bought routes to Japan, Latin America, and London from other carriers. American's 1994 attempt to simplify pricing led to a fare war that hurt industry profits. Tragedy struck American Eagle that year — two crashes resulted in 83 deaths. The next year American's 16-year fatality-free flying record ended when an airliner crashed into a mountain near Cali, Colombia, killing 160.

In 1996 AMR spun off nearly 20% of Sabre and announced plans for a code-sharing pact with British Airways (BA) that sparked a wave of alliances, including Oneworld, which took effect in 1999. American's code-sharing deal with BA, however, ran into opposition from regulators, who were concerned about the airlines' dominance of landing slots at London's Heathrow airport.

Crandall retired in 1998 (after a major airline strike was averted only by President Clinton's intervention) and was replaced by Donald Carty. Looking to replace its turboprops, American Eagle rolled out its first regional jets that year. American also bought Reno Air, and concerns about integrating the smaller airline (completed in 1999) culminated in American pilots calling in sick for a week in 1999. The union was later ordered to pay almost $46 million in compensation.

To focus on its airlines, AMR sold its executive aviation services, ground services, and call center units in 1999. That year nine people died when an American jet tried to land in Arkansas during a storm and slid off the runway. The Justice Department dealt another blow in 2000 when it filed a suit accusing American of predatory pricing to fend off low-fare startups. (A federal judge dismissed the case in 2001, however.) Also in 2000 AMR sold its Canadian Airlines stake (bought in 1994) to Air Canada and spun off the rest of Sabre.

In 2001 AMR moved to become a stronger competitor to UAL by buying the assets of troubled rival TWA for $742 million. Later that year American and BA revived plans to seek regulatory clearance for a code-sharing deal.

Also in 2001 American Airlines lost two aircraft that were used in the September 11 terrorist attacks on the World Trade Center in New York and the Pentagon in Washington, DC. In anticipation of reduced demand for air travel,

AMR announced a 20% reduction in flights and layoffs of at least 20,000 employees. Later that year, another American Airlines jet crashed in New York, killing all 260 passengers.

American Airlines' planned partnership with BA, which the airlines had been negotiating since 1996, received conditional approval from the US Department of Transportation (DOT) in 2002, only to be abandoned by the airlines. The DOT wanted the airlines to give up 224 slots at London's Heathrow airport, something they were not willing to do.

OFFICERS

Chairman and CEO, AMR and American Airlines: Donald J. Carty, age 55, $585,813 pay
President and COO, American Airlines: Gerard J. Arpey, age 43, $495,333 pay
EVP Customer Service, AMR and American Airlines: Daniel P. Garton, age 44, $495,333 pay
EVP Marketing and Planning, AMR and American Airlines: Michael W. Gunn, age 56, $495,333 pay
SVP and General Counsel, AMR and American Airlines: Anne H. McNamara, age 54
SVP Finance and CFO: Jeffrey C. Campbell
SVP Government Affairs, American Airlines: William K. Ris Jr.
SVP Human Resources, American Airlines: Susan M. Oliver
SVP Information Technology and CIO, American Airlines: Monte E. Ford
SVP Maintenance and Engineering, American Airlines: Dan P. Huffman
Auditors: Ernst & Young LLP

LOCATIONS

HQ: 4333 Amon Carter Blvd., Fort Worth, TX 76155
Phone: 817-963-1234   **Fax:** 817-967-9641
Web: www.amrcorp.com

American Airlines serves about 160 cities in the Caribbean, Europe, North America, Latin America, and the Pacific Rim. American Eagle serves additional destinations throughout the Caribbean, Canada, and the US.

PRODUCTS/OPERATIONS

2001 Sales

	$ mil.	% of total
Passenger		
American Airlines	14,104	74
TWA	1,676	9
AMR Eagle Holding	1,378	7
Cargo	662	4
Other	1,143	6
Total	**18,963**	**100**

Selected Subsidiaries
American Airlines, Inc.
AMR Eagle Holding Corporation (commuter services)
AMR Investment Services, Inc. (investment management)

COMPETITORS

AirTran Holdings	Mesa Air	UAL
Alaska Air	Mesaba Holdings	UPS
America West	Northwest	US Airways
Continental	Airlines	Virgin Atlantic
Airlines	SkyWest	Airways
Delta	Southwest	
Greyhound	Airlines	

HISTORICAL FINANCIALS & EMPLOYEES

NYSE: AMR FYE: December 31	Annual Growth	12/92	12/93	12/94	12/95	12/96	12/97	12/98	12/99	12/00	12/01
Sales ($ mil.)	3.1%	14,396	15,816	16,137	16,910	17,753	18,570	19,205	17,730	19,703	18,963
Net income ($ mil.)	—	(935)	(110)	228	167	1,016	985	1,314	985	813	(1,762)
Income as % of sales	—	—	—	1.4%	1.0%	5.7%	5.3%	6.8%	5.6%	4.1%	—
Earnings per share ($)	—	(6.27)	(1.12)	1.13	1.05	5.60	5.39	7.52	6.26	5.03	(11.43)
Stock price - FY high ($)		17.93	16.29	16.26	17.93	21.79	29.62	40.20	33.72	39.44	43.94
Stock price - FY low ($)		12.15	12.40	11.93	10.75	15.20	17.49	20.39	23.49	21.93	15.65
Stock price - FY close ($)	4.4%	15.08	14.97	11.90	16.59	19.69	28.72	26.54	29.95	39.19	22.30
P/E - high		—	—	14	14	3	5	5	5	7	—
P/E - low		—	—	10	10	2	3	3	4	4	—
Dividends per share ($)	—	0.00	0.00	0.00	0.00	0.00	0.00	0.00	0.00	0.00	0.00
Book value per share ($)	5.1%	22.21	28.22	22.27	24.35	31.14	35.89	41.51	46.26	47.19	34.78
Employees	0.8%	119,300	118,900	109,800	110,000	88,900	90,600	92,000	124,421	116,054	128,215

STOCK PRICE HISTORY

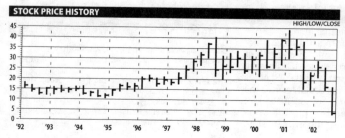

HIGH/LOW/CLOSE

2001 FISCAL YEAR-END

Debt ratio: 64.7%
Return on equity: —
Cash ($ mil.): 120
Current ratio: 0.87
Long-term debt ($ mil.): 9,834
No. of shares (mil.): 154
Dividends
 Yield: —
 Payout: —
Market value ($ mil.): 3,445

AMSOUTH BANCORPORATION

AmSouth makes its sweet home in Alabama, but the bank holding company is growing awfully fond of Florida. The Birmingham-based company is the parent of AmSouth Bank, which has more than 600 branches in Alabama, Florida, Georgia, Louisiana, Mississippi, and Tennessee. It is targeting expansion in the Sunshine State, particularly in major cities, with a focus on its wealth management segment.

The bank offers a full complement of banking services to individuals and small businesses throughout the Southeast (though consumer banking accounts for nearly two-thirds of the company's income).

Its wealth management services (which it is emphasizing outside of Florida as well) include brokerage, trust, custody, estate planning, and philanthropic advice, as well as a family of mutual funds. In addition, AmSouth Bank is one of the nation's leaders in annuity sales. The company also provides capital markets and institutional investment services to large and middle-market corporations.

To woo customers, the bank extended business hours at some locations and is expanding its Web-based services.

HISTORY

AmSouth's roots go back to the First National Bank of Birmingham, formed in 1872. The bank spent the next century serving the residents and businesses of the city, then in 1972 reorganized to become the First Affiliate of Alabama Bank Corp. This reorganization, under the leadership of chairman and CEO John Woods, spurred a buying spree that lasted until 1994.

The bank grew first in its home state. It bought more than 15 banks in the 1970s, including The American National Bank & Trust (1972), The Bank of East Alabama (Opelika) (1979), and Citizens Bank & Trust Co. (Alabaster) (1980). The purchases continued into the 1980s as the company acquired eight more banks around the state. In 1981 the company changed its name to AmSouth and merged all its banks under the AmSouth banner in 1983. Amidst this buying spree, Amsouth branched out into new areas; in 1984 it launched a brokerage subsidiary, and in 1988 it began offering mutual funds.

In the late 1980s AmSouth set its sights beyond the borders of its economically somnolent home state by moving into retiree-rich Florida. Its 1987 purchase of First Mutual Savings Association of Florida (in Pensacola) formed the nucleus of a new subsidiary, AmSouth Bank of Florida, to which it added two more Florida banks in 1988. However, a slump in real estate hammered profits, so AmSouth looked to expand elsewhere.

That opportunity came in 1991, when AmSouth bought the remains of Investors Savings Bank, which had been seized by the government. Two years later it acquired Chattanooga's First Federal Bank, which gave the company entry into not only that city but also Georgia through an office in Summerville. The newly created AmSouth Bank of Georgia grew by acquiring three banks in 1994.

When its buying spree ended in 1994, the bank began to concentrate on internal growth. AmSouth focused on building its brokerage business when mutual funds were in a rut and bank regulators were examining banks' brokerage operations with a fine-tooth comb. During the mid-1990s, clients in Alabama and Florida claimed they'd been misled by advisers (the whistleblower himself was fired), and the federal government investigated possible record keeping violations. Although the lawsuits were dismissed, the company paid substantial fines to securities regulators to settle the record keeping gaffe. In 1996 Woods retired.

During this time AmSouth sought to expand again in Florida, which by then was crawling with carpetbaggers. The bank entered Clearwater, Jacksonville, Orlando, and St. Petersburg (its 1994 wooing of Bank of Tampa was spurned). This growth spurt cost the company as the high costs of buying and integrating the banks along with skyrocketing interest rates eroded its bottom line. AmSouth battled back by restructuring in 1995, selling its mortgage servicing unit.

Following the Riegle-Neal Interstate Banking Act, the company merged its four bank subsidiaries into AmSouth Bank in 1997, allowing it to eliminate redundancies arising from multiple state bank charters. AmSouth failed to buy hometown rival Compass Bancshares, but the proposition marked the bank's emergence as a major regional player. That year it sold its corporate trust unit. In 1999 the bank bought Tennessee bank First American; it completed the integration the next year. Also in 2000 AmSouth exited Arkansas, Kentucky, and Virginia to focus on states where it has a larger presence.

OFFICERS

Chairman, President, and CEO, AmSouth
Bancorporation and AmSouth Bank: C. Dowd Ritter, age 54, $2,759,400 pay
Vice Chairman, CFO, Finance and Credit Group Head, AmSouth and AmSouth Bank: Sloan D. Gibson, age 48, $919,200 pay
SEVP and Consumer Banking Group Head, AmSouth and AmSouth Bank: Candice W. Bagby, age 52

SEVP and Operations and Technology Group Head, AmSouth and AmSouth Bank: Grayson Hall, age 44
SEVP and Alabama/South Louisiana, AmSouth and AmSouth Bank: W. Charles Mayer III, age 47, $678,050 pay
SEVP and Florida and Mississippi Banking Group Head, AmSouth and AmSouth Bank: E. W. Stephenson Jr., age 55, $776,000 pay
SEVP and Tennessee/North Louisiana Banking Group Head, AmSouth and AmSouth Bank: Beth E. Mooney, age 47, $714,150 pay
SEVP and Wealth Management Group Head, AmSouth and AmSouth Bank: Geoffrey A. von Kuhn, age 50
EVP and General Counsel, AmSouth and AmSouth Bank: Stephen A. Yoder, age 48
EVP and Human Resources Director, AmSouth and AmSouth Bank: David B. Edmonds, age 48
COO, Wealth Management: Michael C. Daniel
Head of Private Client Services: Jeffrey P. Botsford
Head of Corporate Banking: Ward Cheatham
Head of Commercial Banking: John M. Gaffney, age 47
Head of Asset Management: Joseph T. Keating, age 47
Auditors: Ernst & Young LLP

LOCATIONS

HQ: AmSouth-Sonat Tower 1900 5th Ave. North, Birmingham, AL 35203
Phone: 205-320-7151   **Fax:** 205-581-7755
Web: www.amsouth.com

AmSouth operates in Alabama, Florida, Georgia, Louisiana, Mississippi, and Tennessee.

PRODUCTS/OPERATIONS

2001 Sales

	$ mil.	% of total
Interest		
Loans	1,976	59
Securities	610	18
Other	49	1
Noninterest		
Service charges on deposit accounts	258	8
Trust income	112	3
Consumer investment services income	95	3
Other	283	8
Total	**3,383**	**100**

Selected Subsidiaries
AmSouth Bank
First American Business Capital, Inc.
First American Enterprises, Inc.

COMPETITORS

BancorpSouth	SouthFirst Bancshares
Bank of America	SouthTrust
BankAtlantic	SunTrust
Compass Bancshares	Union Planters
First Tennessee National	Wachovia
Regions Financial	

HISTORICAL FINANCIALS & EMPLOYEES

NYSE: ASO FYE: December 31	Annual Growth	12/92	12/93	12/94	12/95	12/96	12/97	12/98	12/99	12/00	12/01
Assets ($ mil.)	16.5%	9,751	12,548	16,778	17,739	18,407	18,622	19,902	43,407	38,936	38,600
Net income ($ mil.)	20.3%	102	146	127	175	183	226	263	341	329	536
Income as % of assets	—	1.0%	1.2%	0.8%	1.0%	1.0%	1.2%	1.3%	0.8%	0.8%	1.4%
Earnings per share ($)	7.9%	0.73	0.85	0.66	0.88	0.95	1.23	1.45	0.86	0.86	1.45
Stock price – FY high ($)	—	9.68	10.65	10.35	12.28	15.10	25.39	30.43	34.60	20.06	20.24
Stock price – FY low ($)	—	6.33	8.12	7.53	7.64	10.20	14.02	20.47	18.75	11.69	15.00
Stock price – FY close ($)	7.7%	9.68	9.27	7.64	11.98	14.35	24.16	30.43	19.31	15.25	18.90
P/E – high	—	13	13	15	14	16	21	21	40	23	14
P/E – low	—	9	10	11	9	11	11	14	22	14	10
Dividends per share ($)	11.7%	0.31	0.34	0.41	0.45	0.47	0.50	0.53	0.67	0.80	0.84
Book value per share ($)	3.9%	5.78	6.53	6.70	7.17	6.90	7.65	8.05	7.56	7.53	8.14
Employees	9.8%	5,112	6,032	5,597	5,182	6,461	6,407	6,729	13,882	12,296	11,900

STOCK PRICE HISTORY

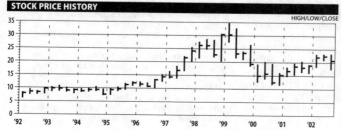
HIGH/LOW/CLOSE

2001 FISCAL YEAR-END

Equity as % of assets: 7.7%
Return on assets: 1.4%
Return on equity: 18.6%
Long-term debt ($ mil.): 6,182
No. of shares (mil.): 363
Dividends
  Yield: 4.4%
  Payout: 57.9%
Market value ($ mil.): 6,861
Sales ($ mil.): 3,383

ANADARKO PETROLEUM

Leaving behind its Anadarko Basin roots, Houston-based Anadarko Petroleum has ventured far afield to become one of the world's largest independent oil and gas exploration and production companies. The company, which has expanded significantly with the acquisition of fellow independent Union Pacific Resources, has proved reserves of 2.3 billion barrels of oil equivalent and daily production of about 570,000 barrels equivalent.

More than half of Anadarko's reserves are located in the US, where it operates in Alaska, Texas, Louisiana, the midcontinent and Rocky Mountain regions, and the Gulf of Mexico. It also operates five gas-gathering systems (more than 2,500 miles of pipeline) in the midcontinent. Internationally, the company has substantial oil and gas interests in Algeria's Sahara Desert, Venezuela, and western Canada. It has gained a stake in the Middle East by purchasing Gulfstream Resources Canada, which has operations in Oman and Qatar.

Since Anadarko became independent in 1986, the company's reserves have shifted from being more than 90% natural gas to being evenly split between gas and crude oil, largely because of oil discoveries in the Gulf of Mexico and Algeria.

HISTORY

In 1959 the Panhandle Eastern Pipe Line Company set up Anadarko (named after the Anadarko Basin) to carry out its gas exploration and production activities. The new company was also formed to take advantage of a ruling by the Federal Power Commission (now the Federal Energy Regulatory Commission) to set lower price ceilings for producing properties owned by pipeline companies.

The company grew rapidly during the early 1960s, largely because of its gas-rich namesake. It bought Ambassador Oil of Fort Worth, Texas, in 1965 — adding interests in 19 states in the US and Canada. The firm also relocated from Kansas to Fort Worth.

Anadarko began offshore exploration in the Gulf of Mexico in 1970 and focused there early in the decade. After moving to Houston in 1974, Anadarko increased its oil exploration activities when the energy crisis led to higher gas prices. A deal with Amoco (now part of BP) led to major finds on Matagorda Island, off the Texas coast, in the early 1980s.

To realize shareholder value, Panhandle spun off Anadarko in 1986 — separating transmission from production. At the time more than 90% of Anadarko's reserves were natural gas.

The next year Anadarko made new discoveries in Canada.

Low domestic natural gas prices led Anadarko overseas. It signed a production-sharing agreement with Algeria's national oil and gas firm, Sonatrach, in 1989. The deal covered 5.1 million acres in the Sahara. Two years later Anadarko began operating in the South China Sea and in Alaska's North Slope.

Back home, the company spent $190 million in 1992 for properties in West Texas, and in 1993 Anadarko began divesting noncore assets. Along with some of its partners, the company also discovered oil in the Mahogany Field offshore Louisiana. Production from Mahogany began in 1996.

In 1997 Anadarko added exploration acreage in the North Atlantic and Tunisia. The next year it made two major oil and gas discoveries in the Gulf of Mexico. Anadarko decided to sell some of its noncore Algerian assets in 1999 and teamed up with Texaco (later acquired by Chevron) in a joint exploration program in the Gulf of Mexico, offshore Louisiana. The next year the company acquired Union Pacific Resources in a $5.7 billion stock swap.

Anadarko expanded its presence in western Canada in 2001 by buying Berkley Petroleum for more than $1 billion in cash and assumed debt; a smaller purchase that year, Gulfstream Resources Canada, landed Anadarko in the Persian Gulf and added 70 million barrels of oil equivalent to its reserves.

OFFICERS

Chairman: Robert J. Allison Jr., age 63, $3,250,000 pay (prior to title change)
President, CEO, and Director: John N. Seitz, age 51, $1,880,000 pay (prior to title change)
EVP Finance and CFO: Michael E. Rose, age 55, $990,000 pay
EVP Administration: Charles G. Manley, age 58, $950,000 pay
EVP Exploration and Production: William D. Sullivan, age 46, $781,167 pay
SVP Algeria: Rex Alman III, age 51
SVP Marketing and Minerals: Richard J. Sharples, age 55
SVP Strategy and Planning: Michael D. Cochran, age 60
SVP Worldwide Business Development: Bruce H. Stover, age 53
VP Information Technology Services and CIO: Morris L. Helbach, age 57
VP and Controller: James R. Larson, age 52
VP and Treasurer: Albert L. Richey, age 53
VP and General Counsel: J. Stephen Martin, age 46
VP Canada: Robert P. Daniels, age 43
VP Corporate Services: Donald R. Willis, age 52
VP Domestic Operations: Mark L. Pease, age 46
VP Exploration: James J. Emme, age 46

VP Government Relations and Public Affairs:
Gregory M. Pensabene, age 52
VP Human Resources: Richard A. Lewis, age 58
VP International and Alaska Operations:
J. Anthony Meyer, age 44
Auditors: KPMG LLP

LOCATIONS

HQ: Anadarko Petroleum Corporation
1201 Lake Robbins Dr., The Woodlands, TX 77380
Phone: 281-636-1000   **Fax:** 281-874-3385
Web: www.anadarko.com

Anadarko Petroleum has US operations in Alaska, the Gulf of Mexico, Louisiana, the Mid-Continent, the Rocky Mountain region, and Texas. Overseas, it operates in Algeria, Australia, Canada, Republic of Congo, Gabon, the North Atlantic, Oman, Qatar, Tunisia, and Venezuela.

2001 Sales

	$ mil.	% of total
US	6,647	80
Canada	1,336	16
Algeria	195	2
Other countries	191	2
Total	**8,369**	**100**

PRODUCTS/OPERATIONS

2001 Sales

	$ mil.	% of total
Marketing	5,256	63
Exploration & production	3,048	36
Minerals & other	65	1
Total	**8,369**	**100**

Selected Subsidiaries
Anadarko Algeria Company, LLC
Anadarko Canada Corporation
Anadarko Canada Energy Ltd.
RME Holding Company
RME Land Corp.
RME Petroleum Company

COMPETITORS

Adams Resources
Apache
BP
Burlington Resources
Cabot Oil & Gas
Chesapeake Energy
ChevronTexaco
Devon Energy
EOG
Exxon Mobil
Hunt Consolidated
Key Energy
Pioneer Natural Resources
Pogo Producing
Royal Dutch/Shell Group

HISTORICAL FINANCIALS & EMPLOYEES

NYSE: APC FYE: December 31	Annual Growth	12/92	12/93	12/94	12/95	12/96	12/97	12/98	12/99	12/00	12/01
Sales ($ mil.)	41.2%	375	476	483	434	569	673	560	701	5,686	8,369
Net income ($ mil.)	—	27	117	41	21	101	107	(42)	43	807	(181)
Income as % of sales	—	7.3%	24.6%	8.5%	4.8%	17.7%	15.9%	—	6.1%	14.2%	—
Earnings per share ($)	—	0.25	1.03	0.35	0.18	0.85	0.89	(0.41)	0.25	4.16	(0.75)
Stock price - FY high ($)	—	16.44	25.88	29.25	27.06	34.44	38.38	44.88	42.75	75.95	73.97
Stock price - FY low ($)	—	9.25	12.81	18.50	17.81	23.38	25.38	24.75	26.25	27.56	43.00
Stock price - FY close ($)	16.2%	14.69	22.69	19.25	27.06	32.38	30.34	30.88	34.13	71.08	56.85
P/E - high	—	66	74	84	150	41	43	—	171	17	—
P/E - low	—	37	37	53	99	28	28	—	105	6	—
Dividends per share ($)	4.9%	0.15	0.15	0.15	0.15	0.15	0.15	0.19	0.20	0.20	0.23
Book value per share ($)	17.6%	5.94	7.37	7.64	7.58	8.38	9.17	10.29	11.84	26.79	25.56
Employees	16.1%	910	970	1,085	1,076	1,229	1,386	1,476	1,431	3,500	3,500

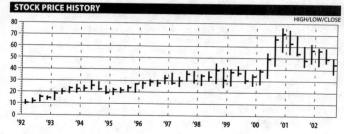

STOCK PRICE HISTORY   HIGH/LOW/CLOSE

2001 FISCAL YEAR-END
Debt ratio: 42.2%
Return on equity: —
Cash ($ mil.): 37
Current ratio: 0.67
Long-term debt ($ mil.): 4,638
No. of shares (mil.): 249
Dividends
Yield: 0.4%
Payout: —
Market value ($ mil.): 14,156

ANALOG DEVICES, INC.

Analog Devices, Inc. (ADI) is fluent in both analog and digital. The Norwood, Massachusetts-based company makes thousands of kinds of integrated circuits (ICs), including analog and mixed-signal chips and digital signal processors (DSPs). The company's analog products process real-world phenomena such as sound, pressure, or temperature in products like video equipment, printers and scanners, industrial robotics, and automobile air bags. ADI's customers include Alcatel, Dell, Ericsson, Philips, Siemens, and Sony. Ford and Volkswagen use the company's products for air bag deployment.

ADI leveraged its early analog know-how to integrate mixed-signal technology on DSPs in time to catch the digital communications and Internet tidal waves. At the same time, the company widened its focus, pioneering tiny silicon devices called micromachines, primarily accelerometers used in airbags.

In the face of a brutal market downturn affecting all parts of the semiconductor industry, ADI has continued to increase R&D spending to promote new product development.

HISTORY

Ray Stata, an MIT graduate and Hewlett-Packard veteran, and Matthew Lorber founded Analog Devices, Inc. (ADI) in 1965 to make amplifiers for strengthening electrical signals. The company soon expanded into converters used to control machinery and take measurements, and went public in 1968. Lorber left the company that year.

In 1969 ADI began manufacturing semiconductors. Stata become chairman and CEO in 1973. In 1977 he launched the influential Massachusetts High Technology Council to fight taxes that he felt were restricting the growth of high-tech firms.

During the early 1980s ADI acquired stakes in several technology firms, including Charles River Data Systems (computer hardware and software), Jupiter Systems (color graphics computers), Photodyne (fiber optics test instruments), and Tau-Tron (high-speed digital instrumentation).

In the mid-1980s ADI's profits declined as Japanese competitors acquired market share. In 1990 the company acquired Precision Monolithics, a maker of passive electronic components. The next year ADI introduced the world's first commercial micromachine, an air bag trigger.

In 1992 the company formed a joint venture with Hewlett-Packard to develop mixed-signal chips. The company extended its global reach in 1996 by acquiring Mosaic Microsystems, a UK radio-frequency design company. It also formed Washington State-based chip producer Wafer-Tech with Taiwan Semiconductor and others. Also in 1996 company veteran Jerald Fishman became ADI's president and CEO; Stata remained chairman.

In 1998 ADI acquired MediaLight, a Toronto-based developer of digital subscriber line software. ADI also sold its disk drive integrated circuit business to Adaptec for about $27 million. The next year the company bought White Mountain DSP (development software for DSPs) and Edinburgh Portable Compilers (software compilers for embedded applications).

In 2000 and early 2001 ADI completed a string of acquisitions, headlined by the purchases of Ireland-based BCO Technologies (wafers for optical components) and Chiplogic (broadband networking chips for voice and video). ADI sold its 4% stake in WaferTech to joint venture partner Taiwan Semiconductor in 2000.

Ray Stata garnered the chip industry's highest honor in 2001 when he received the Semiconductor Industry Association's Robert N. Noyce Award, which is named after the late industry titan who co-founded Intel and co-invented the integrated circuit.

OFFICERS

Chairman: Ray Stata, age 67, $913,077 pay
President, CEO, and Director: Jerald G. Fishman, age 56, $1,177,776 pay
VP, Finance and CFO: Joseph E. McDonough, age 54, $473,199 pay
Group VP, DSP and System Products Group: Brian P. McAloon, age 51, $504,562 pay
VP and Controller: Russ Brennan
VP; General Manager, Analog Semiconductor Components: Robert McAdam
VP; General Manager, Limerick Manufacturing: Dennis Dempsey
VP; General Manager, Wilmington Manufacturing: Mark Norton
VP; General Manager, Santa Clara Manufacturing: Geoffrey R. M. Thomas
VP; General Manager, Micromachined Products: Franklin A. Weigold, age 61
VP, Assembly and Test Operations: John Hassett
VP, Channel and Distribution Marketing: Kevin Styles
VP, Corporate Business Development: Russell K. Johnsen, age 47, $387,311 pay
VP, High Speed Conversion Products: John Hussey
VP, Human Resources: Ross Brown
VP, Linear Products: Lewis W. Counts
VP, North America Sales: Kevin Greene
VP, Planning and Supply: Ger Dundon
VP, Precision Conversion Products: Dick Meaney
VP, Research and Development: Samuel H. Fuller, age 55, $408,662 pay
Auditors: Ernst & Young LLP

LOCATIONS

HQ: 1 Technology Way, Norwood, MA 02062
Phone: 781-329-4700 **Fax:** 781-326-8703
Web: www.analog.com

Analog Devices has manufacturing operations in Ireland, the Philippines, Taiwan, the UK, and the US.

2001 Sales by Product Origin

	$ mil.	% of total
North America	886	39
Europe	554	24
Asia/Pacific		
Japan	341	15
Other countries	496	22
Total	**2,277**	**100**

PRODUCTS/OPERATIONS

2001 Sales by Market

	% of total
Industrial	40
Communications	38
Computers & consumer electronics	22
Total	**100**

Selected Products

Integrated Circuits (ICs)
Analog
  Amplifiers
  Analog signal processing devices
  Comparators
  Data converters
  Interface circuits
  Power management ICs
  Voltage references
Digital signal processing (DSP) devices
Multifunction mixed-signal devices

Assembled Products
Hybrid products (mounted and packaged chips and discrete components)
Multi-chip modules
Printed circuit board modules

Micromachined Products
Accelerometers

COMPETITORS

Agere Systems
Analogic
Broadcom
Cirrus Logic
Conexant Systems
Denso
Fairchild Semiconductor
Infineon Technologies
Intel
Intersil
Linear Technology
Maxim Integrated
  Products

Motorola
National Semiconductor
ON Semiconductor
Philips Semiconductors
PMC-Sierra
Robert Bosch
ROHM
Semtech
Siliconix
STMicroelectronics
Texas Instruments

HISTORICAL FINANCIALS & EMPLOYEES

NYSE: ADI FYE: Saturday nearest Oct. 31	Annual Growth	10/92	10/93	10/94	10/95	10/96	10/97	10/98	10/99	10/00	10/01
Sales ($ mil.)	16.7%	567	666	774	942	1,194	1,244	1,231	1,450	2,578	2,277
Net income ($ mil.)	42.3%	15	45	75	119	172	178	82	197	607	356
Income as % of sales	—	2.6%	6.7%	9.6%	12.7%	14.4%	14.3%	6.7%	13.6%	23.6%	15.7%
Earnings per share ($)	35.6%	0.06	0.15	0.24	0.38	0.52	0.52	0.25	0.55	1.59	0.93
Stock price - FY high ($)	—	2.02	4.67	6.13	9.88	11.30	18.34	19.81	30.22	103.00	67.44
Stock price - FY low ($)	—	1.19	1.94	3.23	5.00	6.38	9.80	6.00	9.66	27.00	29.00
Stock price - FY close ($)	38.7%	2.00	3.71	5.96	9.04	9.75	15.28	9.94	26.59	65.75	38.00
P/E - high	—	34	31	24	25	20	32	54	52	60	67
P/E - low	—	20	13	12	13	11	17	16	17	16	29
Dividends per share ($)	—	0.00	0.00	0.00	0.00	0.00	0.00	0.00	0.00	0.00	0.00
Book value per share ($)	22.1%	1.30	1.46	1.73	2.15	2.72	3.36	3.52	4.62	6.44	7.83
Employees	6.3%	5,200	5,300	5,400	6,000	6,900	7,500	7,200	7,400	9,100	9,000

STOCK PRICE HISTORY

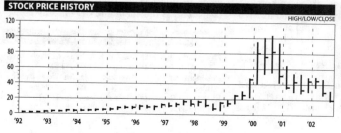

HIGH/LOW/CLOSE

2001 FISCAL YEAR-END

Debt ratio: 29.8%
Return on equity: 13.8%
Cash ($ mil.): 1,365
Current ratio: 6.51
Long-term debt ($ mil.): 1,206
No. of shares (mil.): 363
Dividends
  Yield: —
  Payout: —
Market value ($ mil.): 13,804

ANHEUSER-BUSCH COMPANIES

Anheuser-Busch Companies wants to be the life of the party, whether with its brews or its theme parks. The St. Louis-based company is the world's largest brewer, one of the largest theme park operators and manufacturers of aluminum cans in the US, and the largest recycler of aluminum cans in the world.

Anheuser-Busch leads the US with a market share just shy of 50%, and Budweiser is the nation's top-ranked beer. The company makes more than 30 different beers, including Bud Light, Michelob, and Busch. In an attempt to tap the premium and specialty beer sector, Anheuser-Busch owns several malt and specialty brews, has minority stakes in various small breweries, and has a licensing agreement with Japanese brewer Kirin Brewery to brew its beers in the US. The company has also teamed with drinks giant Bacardi to create Bacardi Silver, a flavored drink in the fast-growing "malternative" segment ruled by Diageo's Smirnoff Ice.

Though Anheuser-Busch is the world's largest brewery, its market share outside the US is rather anemic. It has set its sights on Latin America and Asia to improve international growth. The firm is also seeking to better its sales through investments in top brewers. It owns breweries in the UK and China and about 50% of Mexico's Grupo Modelo (Corona). The company owns about 5% of China's leading brewer, Tsingtao, and may increase its stake in that company to 27%. China is the world's #2 beer market.

The company's theme parks include Busch Gardens and SeaWorld. It also makes labels and cans for itself and soft-drink customers, runs grain elevators and malt plants, grows hops, mills rice, and develops real estate.

Chairman August Busch III represents the fourth generation of the Busch family to lead the company.

HISTORY

George Schneider founded the Bavarian Brewery in St. Louis in 1852. Eight years later he sold the unprofitable brewery to Eberhard Anheuser. Anheuser's son-in-law, Adolphus Busch, joined the company in 1864 and in 1876 assisted restaurateur Carl Conrad in creating Budweiser, a light beer like those brewed in Bohemia. The brewery's rapid growth was based in part on the popularity of Budweiser over heavier, darker beers.

When Adolphus died in 1913, his son August took over the company, which was renamed Anheuser-Busch Companies in 1919. During Prohibition (1920-33), August saved the company by selling yeast, refrigeration units, truck bodies, syrup, and soft drinks. When repeal came in 1933, August quickly resumed brewing; he delivered a case of Budweiser to Franklin Roosevelt in a carriage drawn by Clydesdale horses, which became Anheuser-Busch's symbol. Anheuser-Busch acquired the St. Louis Cardinals baseball team in 1953. Four years later the brewer knocked Schlitz out of first place among US brewers. In 1959 the company established its Busch Entertainment theme park division.

August Busch III was named CEO in 1975, beginning a reign that would last 27 years. The company bought Campbell Taggart (baked goods) and created its Eagle snack foods unit in 1982. Budweiser was introduced in England and Japan in 1984 through licensing. In 1989 Anheuser-Busch acquired SeaWorld from Harcourt Brace Jovanovich.

Anheuser-Busch formed a joint venture with Kirin Brewery in 1993 to distribute Budweiser in Japan. (The arrangement was ended in 1999 and replaced by a licensing agreement.) The company also acquired a minority stake in Redhook Ale Brewery in 1994 and rights to distribute Redhook products.

Anheuser-Busch sold the Cardinals baseball team and stadium for $150 million and spun off its Campbell Taggart baking unit in 1996. The company then closed its Eagle Snacks unit, completing its exit from the food business.

To increase its presence internationally, Anheuser-Busch acquired interests in brewers in China (Budweiser Wuhan International Brewing) in 1995 and Argentina (Compania Cervecarias Unidas) and Brazil (Antarctica Paulista) in 1996. To boost its presence in the specialty beer sector, the company began brewing and selling Kirin beers in the US in 1997.

In 1998 the company increased its holding in Grupo Modelo to over 50% (it bought 18% in 1993). Early in 2001 the company purchased nearly 20% of top Chilean brewer Compania Cervecerias Unidas. It also sold its SeaWorld Cleveland theme park to Six Flags, Inc.

Company veteran Patrick Stokes became the first non-family member to lead Anheuser-Busch when he succeeded Busch III (who remained chairman) as president and CEO in July 2002.

OFFICERS

Chairman; Chairman and CEO, Anheuser-Busch, Inc.: August A. Busch III, age 64, $4,476,000 pay
President, CEO, and Director; CEO, Anheuser-Busch, Inc.: Patrick T. Stokes, age 59, $3,258,000 pay
EVP, Chief Communications Officer and Director: John E. Jacob, age 67, $1,250,000 pay

SVP, World Brewing and Technology:
Gerhardt A. Kraemer
Group VP and General Counsel: Stephen K. Lambright, $945,000 pay
VP and CFO: W. Randolph Baker, $1,050,000 pay
VP and Controller: John F. Kelly
VP and Corporate Representative: James D. Starling
VP and Executive Assistant to the Chairman of the Board: Judith A. Roberts
VP and Group Executive; Chairman and CEO, Busch Agricultural Resources Inc: Donald W. Kloth, age 60
VP and Group Executive; President, Anheuser-Busch Inc.: August A. Busch IV, age 38, $1,075,000 pay (prior to promotion)
VP and Secretary: JoBeth G. Brown
Auditors: PricewaterhouseCoopers LLP

LOCATIONS

HQ: Anheuser-Busch Companies, Inc.
1 Busch Place, St. Louis, MO 63118
Phone: 314-577-2000   **Fax:** 314-577-2900
Web: www.anheuser-busch.com

Anheuser-Busch Companies sells its beer in more than 80 countries.

Selected Beverages
Bud (Dry, Ice, Ice Light, Light)
Budweiser
Busch (regular, Ice, Light)
Doc Otis' Hard Lemon Flavored Malt Beverage
King Cobra
Michelob (regular, Ale, Amber Bock, Classic Dark, Dry, Golden Draft, Hefe-Weizen, Light, Pale Ale)
Natural (Ice, Light)
Red Wolf Lager
Rhumba
Tequiza
ZiegenBock Amber

Theme Parks
Adventure Island (water park, Tampa)
Busch Gardens (theme parks; Tampa and Williamsburg, VA)
Discovery Cove (animal encounters park; Orlando, FL)
Port Adventura, SA (16.1%; Barcelona, Spain)
SeaWorld (marine adventure parks; Orlando, FL; San Antonio; and San Diego)
Sesame Place (family play park; Langhorne, PA)
Water Country USA (water park; Williamsburg, VA)

PRODUCTS/OPERATIONS

2001 Sales

	$ mil.	% of total
Domestic beer	9,988	77
Packaging	1,171	9
Entertainment	848	7
International beer	555	4
Corporate	267	2
Other	83	1
Total	**12,912**	**100**

COMPETITORS

Adolph Coors	Foster's	Scottish &
Asahi Breweries	Gambrinus	Newcastle
Ball Corporation	Guinness/UDV	Six Flags
AmBev	Heineken	Universal
Boston Beer	Interbrew	Studios
Brauerei BECK	Miller Brewing	Recreation
Carlsberg	Molson	Disney Parks &
Cedar Fair	Grolsch	Resorts
Danone	SABMiller	
FEMSA	S&P	

HISTORICAL FINANCIALS & EMPLOYEES

NYSE: BUD FYE: December 31	Annual Growth	12/92	12/93	12/94	12/95	12/96	12/97	12/98	12/99	12/00	12/01
Sales ($ mil.)	1.4%	11,394	11,505	12,054	10,341	10,884	11,066	11,246	11,704	12,262	12,912
Net income ($ mil.)	7.1%	918	595	1,032	642	1,190	1,169	1,233	1,402	1,552	1,705
Income as % of sales	—	8.1%	5.2%	8.6%	6.2%	10.9%	10.6%	11.0%	12.0%	12.7%	13.2%
Earnings per share ($)	10.0%	0.80	0.54	0.97	0.62	1.18	1.17	1.27	1.47	1.69	1.89
Stock price - FY high ($)	—	15.19	15.06	13.84	17.00	22.50	24.13	34.13	42.00	49.88	46.95
Stock price - FY low ($)	—	12.94	10.75	11.78	12.69	16.19	19.25	21.47	32.22	27.31	36.75
Stock price - FY close ($)	13.4%	14.63	12.28	12.72	16.72	20.00	22.00	32.81	35.44	45.50	45.21
P/E - high	—	17	28	14	27	19	20	27	28	29	25
P/E - low	—	15	20	12	20	13	16	17	21	16	19
Dividends per share ($)	9.7%	0.30	0.34	0.38	0.42	0.46	0.50	0.54	0.58	0.63	0.69
Book value per share ($)	1.2%	4.15	3.98	4.29	4.36	4.05	4.15	4.42	4.25	4.57	4.62
Employees	(6.9%)	44,790	43,345	42,622	42,529	25,123	24,326	23,344	23,645	23,725	23,432

STOCK PRICE HISTORY

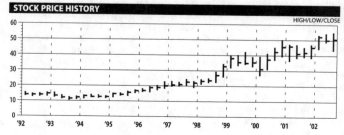

HIGH/LOW/CLOSE

2001 FISCAL YEAR-END
Debt ratio: 59.6%
Return on equity: 41.6%
Cash ($ mil.): 163
Current ratio: 0.89
Long-term debt ($ mil.): 5,984
No. of shares (mil.): 879
Dividends
  Yield: 1.5%
  Payout: 36.5%
Market value ($ mil.): 39,744

ANIXTER INTERNATIONAL INC.

Anixter International's got connections. Based in the Chicago suburb of Skokie, Illinois, the company distributes about 92,000 products that connect PCs, peripheral equipment, mainframe computers, and various networks that carry data, voice, and video.

Anixter sells copper and fiber-optic cable and electrical wiring, as well as active data components for networking applications. Other products include installation-related materials that support central switching offices, Web hosting sites, and remote transmission sites. Anixter also makes electrical wiring products used for the transmission of electricity. With more than 160 sales and distribution centers in 40 countries, Anixter serves 85,000 customers, including Internet service providers, governments, utilities, and manufacturers, as well as resellers such as contractors, architects, engineers, and wholesalers. The US accounts for about 70% of total sales.

The company has shed its network integration operations to focus on distribution. Anixter's chairman, billionaire financier Samuel Zell, owns about 14% of the company.

HISTORY

Two San Francisco businessmen, Gary Friedman and Peter Redfield, founded SSI Computer in 1967 to lease computer systems. The company bought $90 million worth of IBM computers and leased them at rates lower than IBM's.

In 1968 SSI entered the intermodal container and railcar leasing business when it purchased SSI Container Corp. The next year it bought Management Data Processing Corp., and in 1970 the company renamed itself Itel.

During the 1970s the company diversified into aircraft leasing (Itel Air) and capital goods (Itel Capital). By the mid-1970s Itel's computer-leasing business was starting to falter. In 1979 Itel left the computer business, handing most of its sales and service over to National Semiconductor. After both Friedman and Redfield were dismissed, CEO James Maloon focused Itel on transportation services, but by 1981 the company was $1.3 billion in debt and had filed Chapter 11.

When reorganization failed to resurrect the debt-strapped company, Samuel Zell, a Chicago financier, began buying Itel stock. In 1984 he earned a seat on the board and the next year became chairman.

Zell and VC Rod Dammeyer, former Household International CFO, acquired Great Lakes International (marine dredging, 1986), Anixter Bros. (wire and cable, 1986), Pullman (railcars, 1988), and a minority stake in Santa Fe Southern Pacific (railroad, 1988). Other acquisitions included Flexi-Van Leasing (1987), the assets of Evans Asset Holding (railcars, 1987), and B.C. Hydro (rail freight line, 1988). By 1988 Itel was North America's leading railcar leasing company.

In the 1990s Itel repositioned itself, selling its container-leasing business (1990) and its Itel Distribution Systems and Great Lakes Dredge & Deck Co. (1991). When the smoke cleared, Anixter was its core operation. Anixter spun off its cable television products subsidiary ANTEC in 1993. Also that year Dammeyer replaced Zell as Itel's CEO.

Itel's focus became developing new markets in the burgeoning global communications industry. The company sold its remaining rail-leasing interests in 1994. The next year Itel sold its stake in Santa Fe Energy Resources and changed its name to Anixter.

When an ANTEC subsidiary merged with cable TV equipment firm TSX Corp. in 1997, Anixter's ownership in ANTEC was reduced to 19%. That year the company joined with security software maker Check Point Software Technologies to provide network-security products in Europe.

Anixter sold its ANTEC holdings in 1998 to finance the repurchase of its common stock. It also bought Pacer Electronics, an electrical and data cabling distributor. The next year Anixter sold its European network integration business to Persetel Q Data Holdings of South Africa and its data-network design and consulting unit to Ameritech for $200 million in cash. It also sold North America Integration and Asia Pacific Integration, completing the dissolution of its integration segment by the close of 1999.

In 2000 Anixter formed a consortium with Panduit, Rockwell Automation, and Siemens for the production of industrially hardened Ethernet connectors. Anixter signed an agreement to distribute network cabling products for IBM in 2001.

The company recorded a restructuring charge of $31.7 million in 2001 for facility restructuring in North America, staff reductions, and exiting the Korean market.

In 2002 Anixter was named as a *Forbes* "Platinum 400" company, chosen by the magazine's editors as one of America's "best-performing" corporations by industry. The company also purchased the 7% of wiring systems subsidiary Accu-Tech that it did not own.

OFFICERS

Chairman: Samuel Zell, age 60
President, CEO, and Director: Robert W. Grubbs Jr.,
  age 45
SVP, Law and Secretary: James E. Knox, age 64
SVP, Finance and CFO; EVP and CFO, Anixter Inc.:
  Dennis J. Letham, age 50
VP, Controller: Terrance A. Faber, age 50
VP, Taxes: Philip F. Meno, age 43
**VP, Treasurer, Anixter International Inc. and Anixter
  Inc.:** Rodney A. Shoemaker, age 44
VP, Human Resources: Alan Drizd
**General Counsel and Asst. Secretary; General Counsel
  and Secretary, Anixter Inc.:** John A. Dul, age 41
Auditors: Ernst & Young LLP

LOCATIONS

HQ: 4711 Golf Rd., Skokie, IL 60076
Phone: 847-677-2600   **Fax:** 847-677-9480
Web: www.anixter.com

Anixter International operates from a network of 87
locations in the US, 16 in Canada, 24 in continental
Europe, 10 in the UK, 11 in Latin America, nine in Asia,
and four in Australia.

2001 Sales

	$ mil.	% of total
North America		
US	2,179	69
Canada	254	8
Europe	502	16
Asia/Pacific &		
Latin America	209	7
Total	**3,144**	**100**

PRODUCTS/OPERATIONS

Selected Products
Copper and fiber-optic cable
Electrical wiring systems
Mainframe peripheral equipment
PC peripheral equipment

COMPETITORS

Cable Design Technologies
Communications Supply
Graybar Electric
Okonite
Rexel Canada
Scientific-Atlanta
Southwire
Superior TeleCom
WESCO International

HISTORICAL FINANCIALS & EMPLOYEES

NYSE: AXE FYE: Friday nearest Dec. 31	Annual Growth	12/92	12/93	12/94	12/95	12/96	12/97	12/98	12/99	12/00	12/01
Sales ($ mil.)	7.2%	1,682	1,909	1,733	2,195	2,475	2,805	2,349	2,670	3,514	3,144
Net income ($ mil.)	—	(104)	(1)	247	39	36	45	66	124	79	30
Income as % of sales	—	—	—	14.3%	1.8%	1.5%	1.6%	2.8%	4.7%	2.2%	1.0%
Earnings per share ($)	—	(1.90)	(0.07)	3.84	0.70	0.72	0.95	1.45	3.26	2.03	0.80
Stock price - FY high ($)	—	12.19	16.81	18.13	22.06	20.00	19.69	22.75	23.75	37.38	32.00
Stock price - FY low ($)	—	8.00	10.13	11.38	16.63	12.63	12.00	11.88	10.63	17.56	18.81
Stock price - FY close ($)	10.9%	11.44	14.00	17.31	18.63	16.13	16.50	20.31	20.63	21.63	29.01
P/E - high	—	—	—	5	31	27	21	16	7	17	35
P/E - low	—	—	—	3	23	17	13	8	3	8	20
Dividends per share ($)	—	0.00	0.00	0.00	0.00	0.00	0.00	0.00	0.00	0.00	0.00
Book value per share ($)	9.9%	6.54	6.14	9.24	8.55	9.07	10.09	9.83	12.70	14.74	15.25
Employees	0.7%	4,600	4,600	4,200	5,100	5,600	6,300	4,800	5,200	5,900	4,900

STOCK PRICE HISTORY

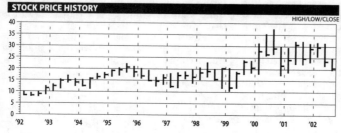

HIGH/LOW/CLOSE

2001 FISCAL YEAR-END

Debt ratio: 30.0%
Return on equity: 5.4%
Cash ($ mil.): 27
Current ratio: 2.35
Long-term debt ($ mil.): 241
No. of shares (mil.): 37
Dividends
  Yield: —
  Payout: —
Market value ($ mil.): 1,071

ANTHEM, INC.

Anthem is finding out what B. B. King already knows: Getting the blues ain't easy. Indianapolis-based Anthem is a health care management company that licenses the Blue Cross and Blue Shield name, providing health insurance to customers in Colorado, Connecticut, Maine, New Hampshire, Nevada, Indiana, Kentucky, Ohio, and Virginia.

Selling noncore health care operations (such as its military health insurance unit, to Humana) has made the company leaner, meaner, and more focused on the Blues, which it is looking to expand left and right. State regulators and public watchdog groups are scrutinizing Anthem's acquisitions of Blue Cross and Blue Shield operations nationwide despite the Blues' eagerness to be acquired. Critics say Anthem's for-profit status would jeopardize health care for the poor, a traditional market for the Blues.

No longer a mutual company, Anthem has gone public and operates through its subsidiary, Anthem Insurance Companies. In order to expand into the Southeastern market, the company acquired Virginia based Trigon Healthcare in 2002.

HISTORY

Anthem's earliest predecessor, prepaid hospital plan Blue Cross of Indiana, was founded in 1944. Unlike other Blues, Blue Cross of Indiana never received tax advantages or mandated discounts, so it competed as a private insurer. Within two years it had 100,000 members; by 1970 there were nearly 2 million.

Blue Shield of Indiana, another Anthem precursor, also grew rapidly after its 1946 formation as a mutual insurance company to cover doctors' services. The two organizations shared expenses and jointly managed the state's Medicare and Medicaid programs.

The 1970s and early 1980s were difficult as Indiana's economy stagnated and health insurance competition increased. In 1982 the joint operation restructured, adding new management and service policies to improve its performance.

Following the 1982 merger of the national Blue Cross and Blue Shield organizations, the Indiana Blues merged in 1985 as Associated Insurance Companies. The next year the company moved outside Indiana, began diversifying to help insulate itself from such industry changes as the shift to managed care, and renamed itself Associated Group to reflect a broader focus.

By 1990 Associated Group had more than 25 operating units with nationwide offerings, including health insurance, HMO services, life insurance, insurance brokerage, financial services, and software and services for the insurance industry.

The group grew throughout the mid-1990s, buying health insurer Southeastern Mutual Insurance (including Kentucky Blue Cross and Blue Shield) in 1992, diversified insurer Federal Kemper (a Kemper Corporation subsidiary) in 1993, and Seattle-based property/casualty brokerage Pettit-Morry in 1994. That year it entered the health care delivery market with the creation of American Health Network.

In 1995 the company merged with Ohio Blues licensee Community Mutual and took the Anthem name. Merger-related charges caused a loss that year.

Anthem bounced back the next year thanks to cost-cutting and customers switching to its more profitable managed care plans. Anthem divested its individual life insurance and annuity business and its Anthem Financial subsidiaries. Its 1996 deal to buy Blue Cross and Blue Shield of New Jersey fell apart in 1997 because of New Jersey Blue's charitable status. Anthem did manage to buy Blue Cross and Blue Shield of Connecticut that year.

Anthem in 1997 sold four property/casualty insurance subsidiaries to Vesta Insurance Group. It bought the remainder of its Acordia property/casualty unit (workers' compensation), then sold Acordia's brokerage operations. That year Anthem was involved in court battles regarding the Blue mergers in Kentucky, as well as in Connecticut, where litigants feared a rise in their premiums. Expenses related to merging Blues organizations contributed to a loss that year.

Anthem shed the rest of its noncore operations in 1998, selling subsidiary Anthem Health and Life Insurance Company to Canadian insurer Great-West Life Assurance. Its proposed purchase of Blue Cross and Blue Shield of Maine (which it acquired in 2000) and merger with the Blues in Rhode Island were met with outcries similar to those that dogged earlier pairings.

In 1999 the company agreed to settle lawsuits related to its 1997 merger with Blue Cross and Blue Shield of Connecticut by financing public health foundations. Anthem also bought the Blues plans in Colorado and New Hampshire that year.

In 2001 Anthem sold its military insurance business to Humana, and became a publicly traded company.

OFFICERS

Chairman: L. Ben Lytle, age 55
President, CEO, and Director: Larry C. Glasscock,
age 53, $3,060,000 pay
EVP and CFO: Michael L. Smith, age 53, $1,066,000 pay
EVP and Chief Legal and Administrative Officer:
David R. Frick, age 57, $1,101,000 pay
EVP and Chief Medical Officer: Samuel R. Nussbaum,
age 53
SVP and CIO: Jane E. Niederberger, age 42
SVP, eBusiness: Mark Boxer
SVP, Human Resources: Randall Brown
VP, Investor Relations: Tami L. Durle
President, Anthem East: Marjorie W. Dorr, age 39,
$1,190,000 pay
President, Anthem Midwest: Keith R. Faller, age 54,
$1,040,000 pay
President, National Accounts: Michael D. Houk, age 57
President, Specialty Business Division of Anthem:
John M. Murphy, age 50
President, Southeast Region; CEO, Trigon:
Thomas G. Snead Jr., age 48
**COO, Anthem Blue Cross and Blue Shield (Colorado
and Nevada):** Caroline S. Matthews, age 42
Auditors: Ernst & Young LLP

LOCATIONS

HQ: 120 Monument Circle, Indianapolis, IN 46204
Phone: 317-488-6000   **Fax:** 317-488-6028
Web: www.anthem-inc.com

Anthem offers Blue Cross and Blue Shield insurance in
Colorado, Connecticut, Indiana, Kentucky, Maine,
Nevada, New Hampshire, Ohio, and Virginia.

PRODUCTS/OPERATIONS

2001 Sales

	$ mil.	% of total
Premiums	9,245	88
Administrative fees	818	8
Investment income	299	3
Other	83	1
Total	**10,445**	**100**

Selected Operations
AdminaStar Federal (Medicare contracting)
Anthem Benefit Administrators, Inc.
Anthem Blue Cross and Blue Shield (Colorado)
Anthem Blue Cross and Blue Shield (Connecticut)
Anthem Blue Cross and Blue Shield (Indiana)
Anthem Blue Cross and Blue Shield (Kentucky)
Anthem Blue Cross and Blue Shield (Maine)
Anthem Blue Cross and Blue Shield (Nevada)
Anthem Blue Cross and Blue Shield (New Hampshire)
Anthem Blue Cross and Blue Shield (Ohio)
Anthem Health of New York
Anthem Insurance Companies, Inc.
Anthem Life
Anthem Prescription Management

COMPETITORS

Aetna	Kaiser Foundation
CIGNA	Maxicare Health Plans
Coventry Health Care	Oxford Health Plans
Empire Blue Cross	UnitedHealth Group
Health Care Service	WellPoint Health
Humana	Networks

HISTORICAL FINANCIALS & EMPLOYEES

NYSE: ATH FYE: December 31	Annual Growth	12/92	12/93	12/94	12/95	12/96	12/97	12/98	12/99	12/00	12/01
Sales ($ mil.)	9.0%	—	—	5,722	6,038	6,270	6,299	5,878	6,270	8,771	10,445
Net income ($ mil.)	21.7%	—	71	72	(98)	64	(159)	172	45	226	342
Income as % of sales	—	—	—	1.3%	—	1.0%	—	2.9%	0.7%	2.6%	3.3%
Earnings per share ($)	—	—	—	—	—	—	—	—	—	—	3.30
Stock price - FY high ($)	—	—	—	—	—	—	—	—	—	—	51.90
Stock price - FY low ($)	—	—	—	—	—	—	—	—	—	—	40.35
Stock price - FY close ($)	—	—	—	—	—	—	—	—	—	—	49.50
P/E - high	—	—	—	—	—	—	—	—	—	—	16
P/E - low	—	—	—	—	—	—	—	—	—	—	12
Dividends per share ($)	—	—	—	—	—	—	—	—	—	—	0.00
Book value per share ($)	—	—	—	—	—	—	—	—	—	—	19.94
Employees	0.0%	—	—	—	—	—	—	—	—	14,800	14,800

STOCK PRICE HISTORY

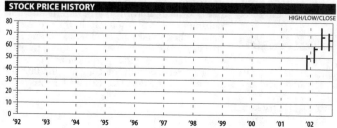

HIGH/LOW/CLOSE

2001 FISCAL YEAR-END
Debt ratio: 28.4%
Return on equity: 17.2%
Cash ($ mil.): —
Current ratio: —
Long-term debt ($ mil.): 818
No. of shares (mil.): 103
Dividends
  Yield: —
  Payout: —
Market value ($ mil.): 5,113

AOL TIME WARNER INC.

Blasting into the 21st century like no other, AOL Time Warner has melded old and new media into a conglomerate that is trying to break new ground in the Internet economy. But, following the bursting of the Internet bubble in mid-2000, the new company has so far failed to live up to expectations. The product of the 2001 acquisition of media titan Time Warner by online king America Online for $106 billion, New York City-based AOL Time Warner is a colossus combination of media and Internet properties contributed by the two companies from which it originated.

It owns AOL (the world's #1 online service) and CompuServe, Netscape Communicator software, and a variety of Internet and portal services. As for the old-school media side of things, AOL Time Warner owns a veritable treasure trove of properties. Its 73% Time Warner Entertainment subsidiary (AT&T owns the other 27%) holds Warner Bros., Time Warner Cable, HBO, and an interest in Road Runner high-speed Internet service. The firm's television assets are held by the Turner Broadcasting System (TBS) and include CNN, TNT, and a majority of the WB Network, as well as sports assets such as the Atlanta Braves, Atlanta Hawks, and Atlanta Thrashers.

Time Inc., is the #1 consumer magazine publisher in the US and the UK and AOL Time Warner Book Group gives the company a host of book publishing operations (it also owns a minority stake in Hoover's, the publisher of this profile). AOL Time Warner also operates the Warner Music Group, which houses several record labels and one of the world's largest music publishers.

Shortly after completing the merger, the new AOL Time Warner announced an aggressive plan to grow revenue to $40 billion a year. The company began streamlining and cut more than 4,000 jobs. By year's end it could not live up to initial expectations and lowered its earnings forecast. New CEO Richard Parsons, who took over in 2002 for the retired Gerald Levin, plans to shift AOL Time Warner's focus away from integration to improving the results of individual subsidiaries.

So far Parsons' biggest success is the unwinding of the Time Warner Entertainment partnership with AT&T. Under the pending deal, AOL Time Warner will buy AT&T's stake with cash and stock. It will then take Time Warner Cable public in 2003.

HISTORY

Though formed in 2001, AOL Time Warner is the result of decades of advancement in the media industry. An elder statesman compared to relative newcomer America Online, Time Warner's roots extend back to 1922 — the year that Henry Luce and Briton Hadden founded publisher Time Inc.,

and brothers Harry, Abe, Jack, and Sam Warner established the origins of Warner Bros., which later became Warner Communications.

America Online's ancestry stretches back to the early 1980s when Stephen Case joined the management of a company called Control Video. Later renamed Quantum Computer Services, the company created the online service that would become America Online in 1985. Quantum Computer Services changed its name to America Online in 1991. It went public the next year.

As America Online was germinating, Time Inc. and Warner Communications were eyeing each other. The two companies merged in 1990 to form Time Warner. Gerald Levin was appointed CEO in 1992. To shave off debt, Time Warner grouped several of its properties into Time Warner Entertainment in 1992, in which U S West (which later became MediaOne Group) bought a 25% interest.

Time Warner's 1996 acquisition of Ted Turner's Turner Broadcasting System further elevated Time Warner's profile on the media stage. For America Online, 1996 marked the first year the company began charging its subscribers a flat rate, vastly increasing the amount of time they spent online.

America Online grew through acquisitions of CompuServe in 1998 and Netscape Communications in 1999. Meanwhile, Time Warner had created Time Warner Telecom and taken it public. After AT&T's announcement that it would acquire MediaOne, MediaOne gave up its 50% management control of Time Warner Entertainment but retained its 25% ownership interest. AT&T's acquisition of MediaOne was completed in 2000, thus giving AT&T 25% of Time Warner Entertainment. (AT&T later boosted its stake to 27%.)

America Online announced that it would acquire Time Warner in early 2000. To please European regulators, Time Warner subsequently abandoned its plans to combine the Warner Music Group with EMI Group's music operations. After a lengthy review by regulatory bodies, America Online acquired Time Warner for $106 billion and formed AOL Time Warner in 2001. Case became chairman, and Levin was appointed CEO. The newly formed company soon began streamlining, cutting more than 2,400 jobs in the process. (It cut another 1,700 jobs at America Online later that year.) Also that year America Online invested about $100 million in Amazon.com.

Levin retired from the company in 2002 and was replaced by Co-COO Richard Parsons.

OFFICERS

Chairman: Stephen M. Case, age 43, $1,000,000 pay
Vice Chairman: Kenneth J. Novack, age 60,
$1,000,000 pay
Vice Chairman and Senior Advisor: R. E. Turner III,
age 63, $1,000,000 pay
CEO and Director: Richard D. Parsons, age 53,
$1,000,000 pay (prior to promotion)
Chairman, Entertainment and Networks Group:
Jeffrey L. Bewkes
Chairman, Media and Communications Group:
Don Logan
EVP and CFO: Wayne H. Pace, age 55
EVP and CTO: William J. Raduchel, age 55
EVP, General Counsel, and Secretary:
Paul T. Cappuccio, age 40
EVP and President, International; President, AOL
International: Michael Lynton, age 42
Auditors: Ernst & Young LLP

LOCATIONS

HQ: 75 Rockefeller Plaza, New York, NY 10019
Phone: 212-484-8000   **Fax:** 212-489-6183
Web: www.aoltimewarner.com

AOL Time Warner has operations worldwide.

2001 Sales

	$ mil.	% of total
US	32,676	85
International	5,558	15
Total	**38,234**	**100**

PRODUCTS/OPERATIONS

2001 Sales

	$ mil.	% of total
Filmed Entertainment	8,759	23
AOL	8,718	22
Networks	7,050	17
Cable	6,992	17
Publishing	4,810	12
Music	3,929	9
Adjustments	(2,024)	—
Total	**38,234**	**100**

Selected Operations
America Online
Time Inc. (magazine publishing)
Time Warner Entertainment (73%)
  Home Box Office (cable network)
  Time Warner Cable (cable system)
Turner Broadcasting System
  The WB Television Network (64%, TV network)
Warner Music Group

COMPETITORS

Advance Publications	Hachette Filipacchi Médias	Reed Elsevier Group
AT&T Broadband	Hearst-Argyle Television	Sony
Bertelsmann	McGraw-Hill	Terra Lycos
Cablevision Systems	Microsoft	Tribune
Comcast	NBC	Viacom
Cox Enterprises	News Corp.	Virgin Group
DIRECTV	Pearson	Vivendi Universal
Dow Jones	PRIMEDIA	Walt Disney
EarthLink	Prodigy	Yahoo!
EMI Group		

HISTORICAL FINANCIALS & EMPLOYEES

NYSE: AOL FYE: December 31	Annual Growth	6/93	6/94	6/95	6/96	6/97	6/98	6/99	6/00	*12/00	12/01
Sales ($ mil.)	114.4%	40	104	394	1,094	1,685	2,600	4,777	6,886	7,703	38,234
Net income ($ mil.)	—	4	6	(34)	30	(499)	92	762	1,232	1,152	(4,921)
Income as % of sales	—	10.5%	5.9%	—	2.7%	—	3.5%	16.0%	17.9%	15.0%	—
Earnings per share ($)	—	0.02	0.01	(0.04)	0.02	(0.33)	0.05	0.30	0.48	0.45	(1.11)
Stock price – FY high ($)	—	0.31	0.72	1.50	4.44	3.88	13.72	87.63	95.81	83.38	58.51
Stock price – FY low ($)	—	0.09	0.29	0.43	1.34	1.40	3.53	8.63	38.47	33.50	27.40
Stock price – FY close ($)	68.7%	0.29	0.45	1.38	2.73	3.48	13.14	55.00	52.63	34.80	32.10
P/E – high	—	31	72	—	148	—	229	237	177	167	—
P/E – low	—	9	29	—	45	—	59	23	71	67	—
Dividends per share ($)	—	0.01	0.00	0.00	0.00	0.00	0.00	0.00	0.00	0.00	0.00
Book value per share ($)	118.4%	0.03	0.11	0.18	0.35	0.08	0.34	1.38	2.66	2.85	35.71
Employees	93.4%	236	527	2,481	5,828	7,371	8,500	12,100	—	88,500	89,300

* Fiscal year change

STOCK PRICE HISTORY

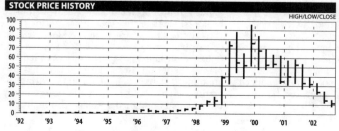

HIGH/LOW/CLOSE

2001 FISCAL YEAR-END
Debt ratio: 13.0%
Return on equity: —
Cash ($ mil.): 719
Current ratio: 0.79
Long-term debt ($ mil.): 22,792
No. of shares (mil.): 4,258
Dividends
  Yield: —
  Payout: —
Market value ($ mil.): 136,682

AON CORPORATION

Aon is the one. The company, whose name is Gaelic for "oneness," is a leader in the insurance brokerage industry. It is also a global purveyor of accident and health insurance, specialty and professional insurance, reinsurance, and risk management consulting services. Aon operates out of about 550 offices in around 130 countries worldwide. Chairman and CEO Patrick Ryan owns about 12% of the company.

Aon operates in three business areas. Aon's youthful commercial insurance brokerage is its largest segment. Anchored by Aon Re, this segment helps groups and businesses choose industry-specific insurance and reinsurance coverage. Its consulting operations include employee benefits, compensation, and other human resources services.

The consumer insurance underwriting segment includes founder W. Clement Stone's original insurance underwriting business, Combined Insurance, which offers supplemental accident, life, and health insurance. The segment's Combined Specialty Group offers extended consumer product warranties. Aon has announced plans to sell this business, scrapping plans to spin it off into a separately quoted company.

In an attempt to reduce costs, Aon has moved administrative functions from local offices to processing centers. Expanding its insurance underwriting operations to include direct property/casualty insurance and reinsurance, Aon launched Endurance Specialty (co-sponsored by Zurich Financial).

Aon's stock took a hit when it was revealed that the SEC is questioning the company's accounting practices.

HISTORY

Aon's story begins with the birth of W. Clement Stone around the turn of the 20th century. At age six he started working as a paperboy in Chicago. The young Stone devoured the optimistic messages of the 19th-century Horatio Alger novels, which detailed the successes of plucky, enterprising heroes.

Stone's mother bought a small Detroit insurance agency and in 1918 brought her son into the business. Young Stone sold low-cost, low-benefit accident insurance, underwriting and issuing policies on-site. The next year he founded his own agency, the Combined Registry Co. While selling up to 122 policies per day, he recruited a nationwide force of agents.

As the Depression took hold, Stone reduced the number of agents and improved training. Forced by his son's respiratory illness to winter in the South, Stone followed the sun to Arkansas

and Texas. In 1939 he bought American Casualty Insurance Co. of Dallas. It was consolidated with other purchases as the Combined Insurance Co. of America in 1947.

The company grew through the 1950s and 1960s, continuing to sell health and accident policies. In the 1970s Combined expanded overseas despite being hit hard by the recession.

In 1982, after 10 years of stagnant growth under Clement Stone Jr., the elder Stone (then 79) resumed control until the completion of a merger with Ryan Insurance Co. allowed him to transfer power to Patrick Ryan.

Ryan, the son of a Wisconsin Ford dealer, had started his company as an auto credit insurer in 1964. In 1976 the company bought the insurance brokerage units of the Esmark conglomerate. Ryan's less-personal management style differed radically from Stone's rah-rah boosterism, but the men's shared interest in philanthropy helped seal the deal.

Ryan focused on insurance brokering and added more upscale insurance products. He also trimmed staff and took other cost-cutting measures, and in 1987 he changed Combined's name to Aon. In 1995 the company sold its remaining direct life insurance holdings to focus on consulting. In 1997 it bought The Minet Group, as well as troubled insurance brokerage Alexander & Alexander Services in a deal that made Aon (temporarily) the largest insurance broker worldwide. In 1998 the firm doubled its employee base with purchases including Spain's largest retail insurance broker, Gil y Carvajal, and the formation of Aon Korea, the first non-Korean firm of its kind to be licensed there.

Responding to industry demands, Aon announced its new fee disclosure policy in 1999, and the company reorganized to focus on buying personal line insurance firms and to integrate its acquisitions. That year it bought Nikols Sedgwick Group, an Italian insurance firm, and formed RiskAttack (with Zurich US), a risk analysis and financial management concern aimed at technology companies. The cost of integrating its numerous purchases, however, hammered profits in 1999.

Despite its troubles, in 2000 Aon bought Reliance Group's accident and health insurance business. Later in that year, however, the company decided to cut 6% of its workforce as part of a restructuring effort. Late in 2001, Aon announced the launch of a new practice called Aon Management Consulting. The company has also announced plans to spin off its underwriting operations to stockholders through a new company to be named Combined Specialty Group, Inc.

Chairman and CEO; Chairman, Aon Group:
Patrick G. Ryan, age 64, $2,587,500 pay
President, COO, and Director; President and COO, Aon Group: Michael D. O'Halleran, age 51, $2,300,000 pay
EVP and CIO: June E. Drewry
EVP and CFO: Harvey N. Medvin, age 64, $1,277,692 pay
EVP: Robert A. Rosholt
EVP, Chief Counsel, and Director: Raymond I. Skilling, age 62, $1,105,930 pay
SVP and Senior Investment Officer: Michael A. Conway, age 54, $690,961 pay
SVP, One Aon: Lawrence I. Geneen
SVP, Aon Group: Dan R. Osterhout
SVP and Controller: Joseph J. Prochaska Jr.
VP, Human Resources: Melody L. Jones
Auditors: Ernst & Young LLP

LOCATIONS

HQ: 200 E. Randolph, Chicago, IL 60601
Phone: 312-381-1000   **Fax:** 312-381-6032
Web: www.aon.com

Aon operates in some 130 countries around the world.

2001 Sales

	$ mil.	% of total
US	4,463	58
Europe		
UK	1,390	18
Other countries	938	12
Other regions	885	12
Total	**7,676**	**100**

PRODUCTS/OPERATIONS

2001 Assets

	$ mil.	% of total
Cash & equivalents	439	2
Corporate bonds	1,203	5
Other bonds	946	4
Stocks	382	2
Other investments	3,615	16
Receivables	7,986	36
Other assets	7,815	35
Total	**22,386**	**100**

Selected Subsidiaries
Aon Consulting Worldwide, Inc.
Aon Group Limited (UK)
Aon Holdings bv (the Netherlands)
Aon Re Worldwide, Inc.
Aon Risk Services Companies, Inc.
Aon Services Group, Inc.
Aon Warranty Group, Inc.
Combined Insurance Company of America
Combined Life Insurance Company of New York
London General Insurance Company Limited (UK)
Virginia Surety Company, Inc.

COMPETITORS

AFLAC	CIGNA	StanCorp
American	Citigroup	Financial Group
General	GeneralCologne	Torchmark
AIG	Re	Trigon
Arthur Gallagher	Health Care	Healthcare
Benfield Greig	Service	UNUMProvident
Heath	Marsh &	Willis
Cerulean	McLennan	
Chubb	MetLife	

HISTORICAL FINANCIALS & EMPLOYEES

NYSE: AOC FYE: December 31	Annual Growth	12/92	12/93	12/94	12/95	12/96	12/97	12/98	12/99	12/00	12/01
Sales ($ mil.)	9.7%	3,337	3,845	4,157	3,466	3,888	5,751	6,493	7,070	7,375	7,676
Net income ($ mil.)	5.4%	127	324	360	403	335	299	541	352	474	203
Income as % of sales	—	3.8%	8.4%	8.7%	11.6%	8.6%	5.2%	8.3%	5.0%	6.4%	2.6%
Earnings per share ($)	3.8%	0.52	1.27	1.39	1.53	1.26	1.12	2.07	1.33	1.79	0.73
Stock price - FY high ($)	—	16.02	17.36	15.90	22.63	28.81	39.27	50.40	46.69	42.75	44.80
Stock price - FY low ($)	—	11.61	13.72	13.01	13.96	21.13	26.80	32.18	26.06	20.69	29.75
Stock price - FY close ($)	9.3%	16.02	14.35	14.24	22.19	27.64	39.10	36.94	40.00	34.25	35.52
P/E - high	—	19	14	11	15	23	34	24	35	23	61
P/E - low	—	14	11	9	9	17	24	15	19	11	41
Dividends per share ($)	7.0%	0.49	0.53	0.56	0.59	0.63	0.68	0.73	0.81	0.87	0.90
Book value per share ($)	3.5%	9.74	10.03	9.79	11.10	11.56	11.24	12.03	12.09	13.16	13.26
Employees	15.1%	15,000	18,000	18,000	27,000	28,000	33,000	44,000	39,000	51,000	53,000

STOCK PRICE HISTORY

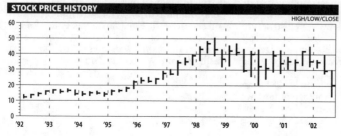

HIGH/LOW/CLOSE

2001 FISCAL YEAR-END

Debt ratio: 32.2%
Return on equity: 5.9%
Cash ($ mil.): —
Current ratio: —
Long-term debt ($ mil.): 1,694
No. of shares (mil.): 269
Dividends
  Yield: 2.5%
  Payout: 123.3%
Market value ($ mil.): 9,563

APACHE CORPORATION

Apache's oil patch is the planet Earth. Houston-based Apache is an independent oil and gas exploration and production company with operations in Argentina, Australia, Canada, China, Egypt, Poland, and the US. The company has proved reserves of 1.3 billion barrels of oil equivalent.

About 75% of Apache's reserves are in North America: the Gulf of Mexico, the Gulf Coast of Texas and Louisiana, the Permian Basin in West Texas, the Anadarko Basin in Oklahoma, and western Canada. The company owns or has interests in more than 6,000 gas wells and more than 6,800 oil wells.

Although Apache has been dumping non-strategic properties, including its Ivory Coast operations, it hasn't stopped buying. It has expanded its Gulf of Mexico operations with the acquisition of Occidental Petroleum's continental shelf properties, and its Canadian operations have been augmented with purchases from Fletcher Challenge Energy and Phillips Petroleum.

HISTORY

Originally, Raymond Plank wanted to start a magazine. Then it was an accounting and tax-assistance service. Plank and his co-founding partner, Truman Anderson, had no experience in any of these occupations, but their accounting business succeeded. In the early 1950s Plank and Anderson branched out again, founding APA, a partnership to invest in new ventures, including oil and gas exploration. The partnership founded Apache Oil in Minnesota in 1954. Investors put up the money, and Apache managed the drilling, spreading the risk over several projects.

As problems with government regulations in the oil industry mounted during the 1960s, Apache diversified into real estate. The real estate operations were pivotal in driving a wedge between Plank and Anderson. In 1963 Anderson called a board meeting to ask the directors to fire Plank. Instead, Anderson resigned, and Plank took over.

Apache's holdings soon encompassed 24 firms, including engineering, electronics, farming, and water-supply subsidiaries. Understanding that its fortunes were tied to varying oil and gas prices, the company reassessed its diversified structure in the 1970s. When the energy crisis rocketed oil prices skyward, Apache sold its non-energy operations, which would have been hurt by the price increases.

Apache formed Apache Petroleum in 1981 as an investment vehicle to take advantage of tax laws favoring limited partnerships. Initially the strategy was a success, but it fell victim in the mid-1980s to a one-two punch: Oil prices sank like a rock, and Congress put an end to the tax advantage. After suffering its first loss in 1986, Apache reorganized into a conventional exploration and production company.

Still under Plank's leadership, the company began steadily buying oil and gas properties and companies in 1991. That year it purchased oil and gas sites with more than 100 million barrels of reserves from Amoco and put the wells back into production. By buying Hadson Energy Resources, which operated fields in western Australia, Apache gained entry into the relatively unexplored region in 1993.

In 1995 Apache merged with Calgary, Canada-based DEKALB Energy (later renamed DEK Energy) and continued picking up properties. It bought $600 million worth of US reserves from Texaco (acquired by Chevron in 2001) that year. In 1996 it expanded its Chinese operations and bought Phoenix Resource Companies, which operated solely in Egypt. A 1998 agreement with Texaco expanded its Chinese acreage thirtyfold. Apache also bought oil and gas properties and production facilities in waters off western Australia from a Mobil unit.

Apache joined with FX Energy and Polish Oil & Gas in 1998 to begin exploratory drilling in Poland. It also worked with XCL and China National Oil & Gas Exploration & Development in Bohai Bay, though the project was slowed by a dispute between Apache and XCL over costs. In 1999 Apache bought Gulf of Mexico assets from a unit of Royal Dutch/Shell and acquired oil and gas properties in western Canada from Shell Canada. That year Apache sold its Ivory Coast oil and gas holdings for $46 million.

Still shopping, however, Apache agreed in 2000 to buy assets in western Canada and Argentina with proved reserves of more than 700 billion cu. ft. of natural gas equivalent from New Zealand's Fletcher Challenge Energy. To help pay for the $600 million acquisition, which closed in 2001, Apache sold $100 million in stock to Shell, which acquired other Fletcher Challenge Energy assets.

Apache bought the Canadian assets of Phillips Petroleum (which merged with Conoco to form ConocoPhillips in 2002) for $490 million in 2000 and acquired the Egyptian assets of Repsol YPF for $410 million in 2001. In 2002 Apache announced three oil discoveries in the Carnarvon Basin offshore Western Australia.

OFFICERS

Chairman and CEO: Raymond Plank, age 79, $1,400,000 pay
President, COO, and Director: G. Steven Farris, age 54, $1,362,500 pay
EVP and CFO: Roger B. Plank, age 45, $537,292 pay
EVP Business Development and Exploration and Production Services: Lisa A. Stewart, age 44, $496,042 pay
EVP Eurasia and New Ventures: John A. Crum, age 49, $439,042 pay
SVP and General Counsel: Zurab S. Kobiashvili, age 59
VP and Treasurer: Matthew W. Dundrea, age 48
VP and Controller: Thomas L. Mitchell, age 41
VP and Associate General Counsel: Eric L. Harry, age 43
VP Corporate Planning: Thomas P. Chambers, age 46
VP Exploration and Production Technology: Michael S. Bahorich, age 45
VP Human Resources: Jeffrey M. Bender, age 50
Auditors: Ernst & Young LLP

LOCATIONS

HQ: 2000 Post Oak Blvd., Ste. 100, Houston, TX 77056
Phone: 713-296-6000   **Fax:** 713-296-6496
Web: www.apachecorp.com

Apache has onshore holdings in Alaska, Arkansas, Colorado, Illinois, Kansas, Louisiana, Michigan, New Mexico, Oklahoma, Pennsylvania, Texas, Utah, and Wyoming and offshore holdings in the Gulf of Mexico. It also owns exploration or production properties in Argentina, Australia, Canada, China, Egypt, and Poland.

2001 Sales

	$ mil.	% of total
US	1,459	52
Canada	613	22
Egypt	461	17
Australia	257	9
Other countries	1	—
Adjustments	(14)	—
Total	**2,777**	**100**

PRODUCTS/OPERATIONS

2001 Sales

	$ mil.	% of total
Natural gas	1,493	53
Oil	1,243	45
Natural gas liquids	55	2
Adjustments	(14)	—
Total	**2,777**	**100**

COMPETITORS

Adams Resources	EEX Corporation	Ocean Energy
Amerada Hess	El Paso	Pioneer Natural
Anadarko	Enron	Resources
Petroleum	EOG	Royal
BP	Exxon Mobil	Dutch/Shell
Burlington	Forest Oil	Group
Resources	Helmerich &	Santos
Chesapeake	Payne	Shell
Energy	KCS Energy	TransTexas Gas
ChevronTexaco	Kerr-McGee	Unocal
Devon Energy	Nuevo Energy	XTO Energy

HISTORICAL FINANCIALS & EMPLOYEES

NYSE: APA FYE: December 31	Annual Growth	12/92	12/93	12/94	12/95	12/96	12/97	12/98	12/99	12/00	12/01
Sales ($ mil.)	23.3%	423	463	538	750	976	1,181	876	1,300	2,284	2,777
Net income ($ mil.)	35.2%	48	37	43	20	121	155	(129)	201	713	723
Income as % of sales	—	11.3%	8.1%	8.0%	2.7%	12.4%	13.1%	—	15.4%	31.2%	26.0%
Earnings per share ($)	19.2%	1.02	0.67	0.65	0.28	1.38	1.65	(1.34)	1.72	5.67	4.97
Stock price - FY high ($)	—	22.13	33.50	29.25	31.00	37.88	45.06	38.75	49.94	74.19	72.88
Stock price - FY low ($)	—	12.00	17.63	22.25	22.25	24.38	30.13	21.06	17.63	32.13	38.25
Stock price - FY close ($)	11.5%	18.75	23.38	25.00	29.50	35.13	35.06	25.31	36.94	70.06	49.88
P/E - high	—	22	50	45	111	27	26	—	29	13	14
P/E - low	—	12	26	34	79	17	18	—	10	5	7
Dividends per share ($)	0.0%	0.28	0.28	0.28	0.28	0.28	0.28	0.28	0.35	0.28	0.28
Book value per share ($)	13.7%	10.12	12.87	13.28	14.11	16.86	18.53	18.43	23.42	29.68	32.23
Employees	9.1%	875	844	1,182	1,285	1,256	1,287	1,281	1,429	1,546	1,915

STOCK PRICE HISTORY

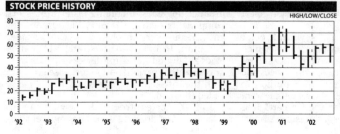

HIGH/LOW/CLOSE

2001 FISCAL YEAR-END

Debt ratio: 33.7%
Return on equity: 19.1%
Cash ($ mil.): 36
Current ratio: 1.34
Long-term debt ($ mil.): 2,244
No. of shares (mil.): 137
Dividends
  Yield: 0.6%
  Payout: 5.6%
Market value ($ mil.): 6,839

APPLE COMPUTER, INC.

The company that has urged customers to "Think Different" now wants them to "Think Digital." Cupertino, California-based Apple Computer aims its colorful iMac (desktop) and iBook (laptop) computers at the consumer and education markets. It targets high-end consumers and professionals involved in design and publishing with its more powerful G4 portable and desktop computers. Apple also makes publishing and multimedia software, and offers Internet services such as Web page hosting. The company's File-Maker subsidiary makes database software.

Once the world's top PC maker, Apple Computer has been relegated to niche status in a market dominated by "Wintel" machines (computers using Microsoft Windows software and Intel processors). Macintosh computers (Macs) forgo the ubiquitous Intel Pentium for processors made by IBM and Motorola. Apple co-founder, CEO, and crusader Steve Jobs has championed unique designs such as the colorful iMac that distinguish Apple computers from their beige brethren. Looking to shepherd consumers into what he has dubbed "the era of the Digital Lifestyle," Jobs has pushed a marketing campaign that casts Macs as the centerpiece for a myriad of digital devices such as cameras, video recorders, and music players.

Apple has traditionally maintained popularity in classrooms, Web design shops, and graphic arts studios. Although more than a quarter of its sales are to schools, Apple has felt increasing pressure in that market, particularly from Dell. In an effort to boost its appeal among consumers, the company has opened more than 30 Apple retail stores across the US.

HISTORY

College dropouts Steve Jobs and Steve Wozniak founded Apple in 1976 in California's Santa Clara Valley. After Jobs' first sales call brought an order for 50 units, the duo built the Apple I in his garage and sold it without a monitor, keyboard, or casing. Demand convinced Jobs there was a distinct market for small computers, and the company's name (a reference to Jobs' stint on an Oregon farm) and the computer's user-friendly look and feel set it apart from others.

By 1977 Wozniak added a keyboard, color monitor, and eight peripheral device slots (which gave the machine considerable versatility and inspired numerous third-party add-on devices and software). Sales jumped from $7.8 million in 1978 to $117 million in 1980, the year Apple went public. In 1983 Wozniak left the firm and Jobs hired PepsiCo's John Sculley as president. Apple

rebounded from failed product introductions that year by unveiling the Macintosh in 1984. After tumultuous struggles with Sculley, Jobs left in 1985 and founded NeXT Software, a designer of applications for developing software. That year Sculley ignored Microsoft founder Bill Gates' appeal for Apple to license its products and make the Microsoft platform an industry standard.

In 1986 Apple blazed the desktop publishing trail with its Mac Plus and LaserWriter printers. The late 1980s brought new competition from Microsoft, whose Windows operating system (OS) featured a graphical interface akin to Apple's. Apple sued but lost its claim to copyright protection in 1992.

In 1993 Apple unveiled the Newton handheld computer, but sales were slow. Earnings fell drastically, so the company trimmed its workforce. (Sculley was among the departed.) In 1994 Apple cried "uncle" and began licensing clones of its OS, hoping a flurry of cheaper Mac-alikes would encourage software developers. By 1996 struggling Apple realized Mac clones were stealing sales. That year it hired Gilbert Amelio, formerly of National Semiconductor, as CEO.

In 1997 Apple bought NeXT, but sales kept dropping and it subsequently cut about 30% of its workforce, canceled projects, and trimmed research costs. Meanwhile Apple's board ousted Amelio and Jobs took the position back on an interim basis. The CEO forged a surprising alliance with Microsoft, which included releasing a Mac version of Microsoft's popular office software. To protect market share, Jobs also stripped the cloning license from chief imitator Power Computing and put it out of business.

In 1998 Apple jumped back into the race with its colorful cocktail of iMacs, and its first server software, Mac OS X. Apple in 1999 opened a new chapter in portable computing with the introduction of its iBook laptop and (taking a cue from Dell) began selling built-to-order systems online. In early 2000, after two-and-a-half years as the semipermanent executive in charge, Jobs took the "interim" out of his title. Jobs unveiled overhauled desktop lines later that year, including an eight-inch cube-shaped G4.

Apple opened 2001 with another round of product upgrades, including faster processors, components such as CD and DVD burners, and an ultraslim version of its Powerbook, called Titanium. In line with its strategy to market Macs as "digital hubs" for devices such as cameras and other peripherals, Apple closed the year with the introduction of a digital music player called the iPod.

In 2002 Apple introduced a new look for its iMac line. And, looking to reclaim market share in the education sector, Apple then introduced the eMac — a computer similar to the iMac to be sold only to students and educators (Apple later introduced a retail version). It continued its new product push that year with the announcement that it would begin offering a rack-mount server called Xserve. Apple also acquired Emagic, a leading maker of music production software, in 2002.

OFFICERS

CEO and Director: Steven P. Jobs, age 47, $1 pay
EVP and CFO: Fred D. Anderson, age 58, $657,039 pay
EVP, Worldwide Sales and Operations:
Timothy D. Cook, age 41, $952,219 pay
SVP, Secretary, and General Counsel: Nancy R. Heinen, age 45
SVP, Applications: Sina Tamaddon, age 44
SVP, Finance: Peter Oppenheimer
SVP, Hardware Engineering: Jonathan Rubinstein, age 45, $469,737 pay
SVP, Retail: Ronald B. Johnson, age 43
SVP, Software Engineering: Avadis Tevanian Jr., age 40, $461,373 pay
SVP, Worldwide Product Marketing: Philip W. Schiller
VP, Human Resources: Dan Walker
Auditors: KPMG LLP

LOCATIONS

HQ: 1 Infinite Loop, Cupertino, CA 95014
Phone: 408-996-1010　　**Fax:** 408-974-2113
Web: www.apple.com

Apple Computer has manufacturing operations in Ireland, Singapore, and the US.

2001 Sales

	$ mil.	% of total
Americas	2,996	56
Europe	1,249	23
Japan	713	13
Other regions	405	8
Total	**5,363**	**100**

PRODUCTS/OPERATIONS

2001 Sales

	$ mil.	% of total
Power Macintosh	1,664	31
iMac	1,117	21
PowerBook	813	15
iBook	809	15
Software, services & other	960	18
Total	**5,363**	**100**

Selected Products

Multimedia software	Rack-mount servers
Networking software	Server software
Operating systems	Wireless networking
Personal and portable computers	systems

COMPETITORS

Acer	IBM	RealNetworks
Casio Computer	Matsushita	Samsung
Dell Computer	Microsoft	SGI
eMachines	NEC	Sony
Fujitsu Siemens	Novell	Sun
Computers	Oracle	Microsystems
Gateway	Philips	Toshiba
Hewlett-Packard	Electronics	

HISTORICAL FINANCIALS & EMPLOYEES

Nasdaq: AAPL FYE: Last Friday in September	Annual Growth	9/92	9/93	9/94	9/95	9/96	9/97	9/98	9/99	9/00	9/01
Sales ($ mil.)	(3.0%)	7,087	7,977	9,189	11,062	9,833	7,081	5,941	6,134	7,983	5,363
Net income ($ mil.)	—	530	87	310	424	(816)	(1,045)	309	601	786	(25)
Income as % of sales	—	7.5%	1.1%	3.4%	3.8%	—	—	5.2%	9.8%	9.8%	—
Earnings per share ($)	—	2.17	0.37	1.31	1.73	(3.30)	(4.15)	1.05	1.81	2.18	(0.07)
Stock price - FY high ($)	—	35.00	32.63	19.25	25.06	21.25	14.88	21.88	40.06	75.19	27.12
Stock price - FY low ($)	—	20.75	11.50	11.00	16.25	8.00	6.38	6.38	14.25	25.38	13.63
Stock price - FY close ($)	(4.1%)	22.56	11.69	16.84	18.63	11.09	10.84	19.06	31.66	25.75	15.51
P/E - high	—	16	88	15	14	—	—	19	19	31	—
P/E - low	—	10	31	8	9	—	—	5	7	10	—
Dividends per share ($)	—	0.24	0.24	0.24	0.24	0.06	0.00	0.00	0.00	0.00	0.00
Book value per share ($)	2.1%	9.23	8.72	9.97	11.80	8.27	4.69	6.07	9.65	12.23	11.17
Employees	(4.7%)	14,798	14,938	14,592	17,615	10,896	10,176	9,663	9,736	8,568	9,603

STOCK PRICE HISTORY

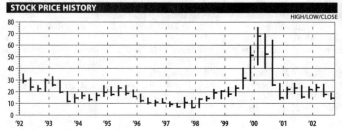

HIGH/LOW/CLOSE

2001 FISCAL YEAR-END

Debt ratio: 7.5%
Return on equity: —
Cash ($ mil.): 2,310
Current ratio: 3.39
Long-term debt ($ mil.): 317
No. of shares (mil.): 351
Dividends
　Yield: —
　Payout: —
Market value ($ mil.): 5,443

APPLIED MATERIALS, INC.

Applied keeps applying itself to dominating its industry. Santa Clara, California-based Applied Materials is — by far — the world's largest maker of semiconductor production equipment. As microchips are incorporated into more and more products, demand for ever-smaller and more complex chips grows. Just as quickly, chip making machinery becomes obsolete — which is good news for Applied's sales. The company's top customer is chip kingpin Intel; other customers include Advanced Micro Devices and Motorola. More than half of Applied's sales come from the Asia/Pacific region, mainly Taiwan and Japan.

Applied's machines dominate many segments of the chip making process, including deposition (layering film on wafers), etching (removing portions of chip material to allow precise construction of circuits), and ion implantation (altering electrical characteristics of certain areas in wafer coatings). The company also makes wafer and photomask inspection tools, and has partnered with specialized construction firms to offer services to speed installation of chip equipment in new plants.

To keep up with the chip industry's constant drive toward smaller circuits, larger wafers, and new technologies such as copper interconnects, Applied relies on heavy R&D efforts. The company has also used a combination of acquisitions and internal development to bolster its moves into the few areas of chip manufacturing — such as atomic layer deposition equipment — where it isn't a major player.

A harsh decline in the worldwide semiconductor industry has led to brutal business conditions for Applied. After pursuing a series of austerity measures intended to forestall layoffs, the company has implemented two rounds of staff cuts, each of which reduced its workforce by about 10%.

HISTORY

Applied Materials was founded in 1967 in Mountain View, California, as a maker of chemical vapor deposition systems for fabricating semiconductors. After years of rapid growth, the company went public in 1972. Two years later it purchased wafer maker Galamar Industries.

In 1975 Applied Materials suffered a 45% drop in sales as the semiconductor industry (and the US economy) contracted. Financial and managerial problems plagued the company following the recession, so in 1976 James Morgan, a former division manager for conglomerate Textron, was chosen to replace founder Michael McNeilly as CEO. Two years later Morgan also became chairman.

After selling Galamar (1977) and other non-core units and extending the company's line of credit, Morgan announced a plan to move into Japan. The company's first joint venture, Applied Materials Japan, was set up in 1979.

Morgan's hunch that Japan would become a semiconductor hub paid off. His early arrival, plus his attention to Japanese ways of doing business, put Applied way ahead of its American competitors. Morgan wrote *Cracking the Japanese Market* about his experiences doing business in Japan.

When another slump hit the chip industry in 1985, Morgan revved up research and development. With two separate manufacturing technologies poised to compete, Morgan essentially bet on the fast but unproven one-at-a-time, multiple-chamber method (as opposed to the existing batch process system). The resulting Precision 5000 series machines revolutionized the industry and catapulted Applied Materials to the top of it. Applied's sales passed the $1 billion mark for the first time in 1993.

Shaking off an industry slump, in 1996 Applied acquired two Israeli companies, Opal (scanning electronic microscopes used in wafer inspection) and Orbot Instruments (wafer and photomask inspection systems), to grab nearly 5% of the crowded chip inspection tools market.

Responding to an industry slowdown, in 1998 Applied began cutting its workforce by 25%. Late that year the company bought Consilium, a maker of factory floor management software. It also bought Obsidian, a maker of chemical mechanical polishing systems.

In early 2000 Applied began its move into photolithography — one of the few industry segments in which it didn't operate — by acquiring Etec Systems, a leading maker of semiconductor mask pattern generation equipment, for nearly $2 billion.

A sharp global downturn in the chip industry led the company in early 2001 to take a variety of cost-cutting measures (including executive pay cuts, a voluntary separation plan, and temporary plant shutdowns) that stopped short of layoffs. Later that year, though, Applied let go about 2,000 employees — about 10% of its workforce — in response to continuing poor conditions in the chip market.

Also in 2001 Applied bought Schlumberger's electron-beam wafer inspection business, as well as privately held Global Knowledge Services, a provider of data-mining services for chip factory yield enhancement.

Late in 2001 the company announced another 10% layoff, this one affecting 1,700 workers.

OFFICERS

Chairman and CEO: James C. Morgan, age 63,
$809,558 pay
President and Director: Dan Maydan, age 66,
$682,212 pay
EVP, Office of the President and CFO:
Joseph R. Bronson, age 53, $454,808 pay
EVP, Office of the President: Sasson Somekh, age 55,
$454,808 pay
EVP, Office of the President: David N. K. Wang, age 55,
$454,808 pay
**SVP; Chairman and CEO, Applied Materials Japan;
Chairman, AKT:** Tetsuo Iwasaki
Group VP, Global Human Resources: Julio A. Aranovich
Auditors: PricewaterhouseCoopers LLP

LOCATIONS

HQ: 3050 Bowers Ave., Santa Clara, CA 95054
Phone: 408-727-5555 **Fax:** 408-748-9943
Web: www.appliedmaterials.com

Applied Materials has operations in China, France,
Germany, Ireland, Israel, Italy, Japan, Malaysia, the
Netherlands, Singapore, South Korea, Taiwan, the UK,
and the US.

2001 Sales

	$ mil.	% of total
Asia/Pacific		
Japan	1,876	26
Taiwan	1,109	15
South Korea	449	6
Other countries	693	9
North America	2,131	29
Europe	1,085	15
Total	**7,343**	**100**

PRODUCTS/OPERATIONS

Selected Products
Chemical mechanical polishing/planarization systems
(wafer polishing)
Deposition systems (deposit layers of conducting and
insulating material on wafers)
 Dielectric deposition (chemical vapor deposition, or
 CVD)
 Metal (CVD, electroplating, or physical vapor
 deposition)
 Silicon and thermal deposition
Etch systems (remove portions of a wafer surface for
circuit construction)
Inspection systems
Ion implant systems (implant ions into wafer surface to
change conductive properties)
Metrology systems
Photolithography mask pattern generation equipment
Rapid thermal processing systems (heat wafers to
change electrical characteristics)

COMPETITORS

ADE	Hitachi	Sumitomo Heavy
ASM	KLA-Tencor	Industries
International	Lam Research	Sumitomo Metal
ASML	Mattson	Industries
Axcelis	Technology	Tokyo Electron
Technologies	Nanometrics	Toshiba
Brooks-PRI	Nikon	Trikon
Automation	Corporation	Varian
Canon	Novellus	Semiconductor
Ebara	Systems	Veeco
Electroglas	NPTest	Instruments
FEI	Semitool	
FSI International	SpeedFam-IPEC	

HISTORICAL FINANCIALS & EMPLOYEES

Nasdaq: AMAT FYE: Last Sunday in October	Annual Growth	10/92	10/93	10/94	10/95	10/96	10/97	10/98	10/99	10/00	10/01
Sales ($ mil.)	28.8%	751	1,080	1,660	3,062	4,145	4,074	4,042	4,859	9,564	7,343
Net income ($ mil.)	39.2%	40	100	221	454	600	499	231	747	2,064	775
Income as % of sales	—	5.3%	9.2%	13.3%	14.8%	14.5%	12.2%	5.7%	15.4%	21.6%	10.6%
Earnings per share ($)	25.1%	0.04	0.08	0.17	0.32	0.41	0.33	0.15	0.48	1.20	0.30
Stock price - FY high ($)	—	0.95	2.50	3.41	7.48	6.94	13.55	10.03	22.55	57.56	29.55
Stock price - FY low ($)	—	0.35	0.91	1.83	2.31	2.72	3.23	5.39	8.05	20.00	13.30
Stock price - FY close ($)	38.3%	0.92	1.97	3.25	6.27	3.30	8.34	8.67	22.45	26.56	17.06
P/E - high	—	24	31	21	23	17	41	63	44	45	62
P/E - low	—	9	11	11	7	7	10	34	16	16	28
Dividends per share ($)	—	0.00	0.00	0.00	0.00	0.00	0.00	0.00	0.00	0.00	0.00
Book value per share ($)	32.2%	0.38	0.47	0.72	1.24	1.64	2.00	2.12	2.83	4.37	4.66
Employees	18.0%	3,909	4,739	6,497	10,537	11,403	13,924	12,060	12,755	19,220	17,365

STOCK PRICE HISTORY

HIGH/LOW/CLOSE

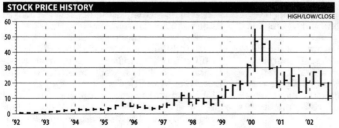

2001 FISCAL YEAR-END

Debt ratio: 6.9%
Return on equity: 10.5%
Cash ($ mil.): 1,356
Current ratio: 5.08
Long-term debt ($ mil.): 565
No. of shares (mil.): 1,632
Dividends
 Yield: —
 Payout: —
Market value ($ mil.): 27,834

AQUILA, INC.

Aquila (formerly UtiliCorp United) isn't just in Kansas City anymore: The company is establishing itself in deregulating energy markets around the world. Close to home, the Kansas City, Missouri-based firm operates regulated utilities that serve some 1.3 million electricity and gas customers in seven states and generate 2,100 MW of capacity. Aquila also serves some 5.1 million energy customers in Canada, Australia, New Zealand, and the UK. Aquila (Italian for eagle, pronounced ah-KWIL-uh) changed its name in 2002 after it had bought back the 20% stake in its Aquila Merchant Services unit (AMS, formerly Aquila, Inc.) that it sold to the public in 2001.

AMS markets and trades wholesale electricity and gas in the US and Canada and holds about 25 independent power projects in the US and the Caribbean (4,700 MW), some of which are under construction or in planning stages. The unit also has a 3,800-mile pipeline system in Texas and Oklahoma, as well as 12 gas processing and treatment plants.

Aquila has been expanding through acquisitions; it gained 2.3 million customers through its 2002 purchase of an 80% stake in UK regional utility Midlands Electricity (operating as Aquila Networks UK), and it is developing global telecom operations.

But as the finances of wholesale energy companies have come under scrutiny, Aquila has announced plans to sell up to $1 billion in assets in an effort to improve its credit rating. The company has laid off about 30% of AMS's employees.

Employees own more than 12% of Aquila.

HISTORY

After coming to Kansas in the 1870s, Lemuel Green worked in a flour mill and then became a farmer. In 1902 he built a steam-powered flour mill (Solomon Valley Milling) and added an electric generator. Green sold the mill in 1908 and bought the struggling H. M. Spalding Electric Light Plant in Concordia, Kansas.

Green turned the business around and built transmission lines to nearby towns. He sold out in 1916 and bought Reeder Light, Ice & Fuel in Pleasant Hill, Missouri (renamed Green Power & Light). In 1922 it went public and was renamed West Missouri Power.

In 1927 Green sold out again and moved to California to grow oranges. West Missouri Power merged with Missouri Public Service (MPS, a subsidiary of Samuel Insull's huge Middle West). Green died in 1930, and his son Ralph pursued the citrus business while watching the utility's decline from afar.

Congress broke up the utility trusts in 1935, ushering in 60 years of regulated regional monopolies. Seeing his chance, Ralph Green bought a controlling interest in the divested MPS (1940) and Missouri Gas & Electric (1943). Ralph's son Richard took over in 1958 and guided the company along a slower growth curve.

Ralph's grandson, Richard Green Jr. became CEO in 1982. He bought a Kansas natural gas utility in 1984, and MPS changed its name to UtiliCorp United in 1985. That year UtiliCorp bought Peoples Natural Gas and its PSI gas marketing unit, and in 1986 it formed UtilCo to develop independent power plants. UtiliCorp reeled in a Minnesota gas distributor in 1986, then a West Virginia electric utility and a British Columbia hydroelectric firm in 1987.

UtiliCorp added an electric utility operating in Colorado and Kansas in 1991; it also changed PSI's name to Aquila Energy (which absorbed UtilCo in 1998). The next year it began marketing gas in the UK, and in 1994 it bought stakes in two New Zealand electric utilities.

In an attempt to offer "branded" electricity nationwide, UtiliCorp introduced its EnergyOne brand name in 1995. That year it began marketing wholesale electricity. In 1996 UtiliCorp tried to buy Kansas City Power & Light, but the firm was bought by rival Western Resources. Undaunted, that year UtiliCorp bought 40% of Oasis Pipe Line and took a stake in United Energy, an Australian electricity distributor.

In 1998 UtiliCorp increased its stake in Power New Zealand to almost 80% and took United Energy public, retaining a 34% share. The following year UtiliCorp and investment partner AMP bought Australian gas utility Multinet Gas/Ikon Energy.

EnergyOne developed into a joint venture in 1997 with PECO Energy (now Exelon), AT&T, and ADT, which offered bundled electricity, phone, and alarm services. The idea seemed to be ahead of its time, and EnergyOne died in 1998.

UtiliCorp also sold its West Virginia Power unit and took a 28% stake in utility and communications construction firm Quanta Services. In 2000 the company filed for an IPO of its Aquila Energy arm as part of the separation of its regulated and nonregulated activities. (Aquila Energy changed its name to Aquila and went public in 2001.)

In 2001 UtiliCorp acquired St. Joseph Light & Power. UtiliCorp also agreed to buy an 80% stake in UK utility Midlands Electricity from First-Energy in a $2 billion deal (completed in 2002). Later that year UtiliCorp formed a new unit, Global Networks Group, to operate its global electric, gas, and telecom networks. It also offered to buy back the 20% stake in Aquila that it had sold to the public; the exchange offer was completed in 2002. Aquila teamed up with NiSource to form an energy marketing joint venture that year.

As a result of the successful exchange offer, UtiliCorp changed its name to Aquila in 2002. Aquila agreed to sell its Texas gas storage assets to PacifiCorp in 2002; it also agreed to sell AMS's gas transmission and processing assets to private firm Energy Transfer Co.

OFFICERS

Chairman: Richard C. Green Jr., age 47, $3,972,116 pay
President, CEO, and Director; Chairman and CEO, Aquila Merchant Services: Robert K. Green, age 40, $3,869,038 pay
CFO; CFO and Treasurer, Aquila Merchant Services: Dan Streek, $1,732,269 pay
SVP; President and COO, Aquila Merchant Services: Edward K. Mills, $4,614,217 pay
SVP; President and COO, Global Networks; Chairman, United Energy, United Networks, and Uecomm: Keith G. Stamm, $4,633,077 pay
SVP and Chief Administrative Officer: Leo E. Morton
SVP, General Counsel, and Corporate Secretary: Leslie J. Parrette Jr., age 39
Director Human Resources: Adrienne Edmondson
Auditors: KPMG LLP

LOCATIONS

HQ: 20 W. Ninth St., Kansas City, MO 64105
Phone: 816-421-6600   **Fax:** 816-467-3591
Web: www.aquila.com

PRODUCTS/OPERATIONS

2001 Sales

	$ mil.	% of total
Energy merchant	37,770	93
Domestic delivery networks	2,292	6
International delivery networks	354	1
Corporate and other	(39)	—
Total	**40,377**	**100**

Selected Subsidiaries and Operations

Energy Merchant Businesses
Aquila Merchant Services (electricity and natural gas marketing and independent power projects)

Energy Delivery Networks
Global Networks Group (network management)
   Aquila Networks (domestic utility operations)
   Aquila Networks UK (80%, formerly Midlands Electricity, utility operations)
   Everest Connections (89%, broadband services)
   United Energy Limited (34%, Australian investments)
   UnitedNetworks Limited (55%, New Zealand, electric distribution utility)

COMPETITORS

AEP	Edison	Mirant
Ameren	International	PG&E
Avista	El Paso	Sempra Energy
CenterPoint	Corporation	Southern
Energy	Entergy	Company
Cinergy	Great Plains	Tractebel
Constellation	Energy	TXU
Energy Group	Koch	Westar Energy
Duke Energy	MidAmerican	Williams
Dynegy	Energy	Companies
		Xcel Energy

HISTORICAL FINANCIALS & EMPLOYEES

NYSE: ILA FYE: December 31	Annual Growth	12/92	12/93	12/94	12/95	12/96	12/97	12/98	12/99	12/00	12/01
Sales ($ mil.)	46.5%	1,299	1,572	1,515	2,799	4,332	8,926	12,563	18,622	28,975	40,377
Net income ($ mil.)	20.3%	53	86	94	80	106	122	132	161	204	279
Income as % of sales	—	4.1%	5.5%	6.2%	2.9%	2.4%	1.4%	1.1%	0.9%	0.7%	0.7%
Earnings per share ($)	12.0%	0.87	1.28	1.37	1.14	1.46	1.51	1.63	1.75	2.21	2.42
Stock price – FY high ($)	—	19.34	22.68	21.26	19.76	20.18	26.05	26.64	26.00	31.31	37.85
Stock price – FY low ($)	—	14.76	18.09	15.84	17.59	17.18	16.76	22.51	18.56	15.19	21.85
Stock price – FY close ($)	3.5%	18.43	21.18	17.68	19.59	18.01	25.89	24.47	19.44	31.00	25.17
P/E – high	—	22	17	15	17	14	17	16	15	14	15
P/E – low	—	17	14	11	15	12	11	14	11	7	9
Dividends per share ($)	1.3%	1.07	1.08	1.13	1.15	1.17	1.17	1.20	1.20	1.20	1.20
Book value per share ($)	5.0%	14.24	14.85	13.95	14.10	14.81	14.44	15.82	16.30	19.30	22.01
Employees	5.4%	4,600	4,700	4,683	4,700	4,700	4,640	5,500	—	8,228	7,377

STOCK PRICE HISTORY

HIGH/LOW/CLOSE

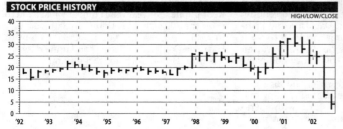

2001 FISCAL YEAR-END

Debt ratio: 40.7%
Return on equity: 98.5%
Cash ($ mil.): 263
Current ratio: 0.85
Long-term debt ($ mil.): 1,748
No. of shares (mil.): 116
Dividends
   Yield: 4.8%
   Payout: 49.6%
Market value ($ mil.): 2,918

ARAMARK CORPORATION

ARAMARK is literally feeding the fan frenzy. Based in Philadelphia, the company is the #3 food service provider in the world (behind Compass and Sodexho Alliance). It serves up refreshments at some 170 sports arenas (Houston's Minute Maid Park, Philadelphia's First Union Center), convention centers, amphitheaters, and other entertainment venues. It also provides food, building maintenance, and housekeeping services for schools, businesses, hospitals, and prisons. In addition to its food business, ARAMARK is the nation's #2 uniform rental company (behind Cintas), providing uniform services to clients in the hospitality, manufacturing, transportation, and utility industries. ARAMARK also provides educational before- and after-school programs and employee on-site child care services.

ARAMARK was propelled to the upper echelon of the concession business in 2000 with its $236 million acquisition of Ogden's sports and entertainment unit (shed as the former conglomerate became electric power marketer Covanta Energy). It plans further expansion through acquisitions and is also focusing on growing organically through new contracts and leveraging existing customers. The company penned a 10-year deal with Boeing in 2000 to supply food services to about 100 locations, one of the biggest food service contracts ever.

ARAMARK continued its expansion with the purchase of ServiceMaster's management services division in 2001 for about $800 million. The company suffered a blow in 2002, however, when it lost a bid to cater the 2002 Olympic Games in Salt Lake City to rival Compass (ARAMARK has catered the Olympics 12 times, including the 2000 games in Sydney). Chairman and CEO Joseph Neubauer controls 17% of the company, which went public at the end of 2001.

HISTORY

Davre Davidson began his career in food service by selling peanuts from the backseat of his car in the 1930s. He landed his first vending contract with Douglas Aircraft (later McDonnell Douglas, now part of Boeing) in 1935. Through that relationship, Davidson met William Fishman of Chicago, who had vending operations in the Midwest. Davidson and Fishman merged their companies in 1959 to form Automatic Retailers of America (ARA). Davidson became chairman and CEO of the new company; Fishman served as president.

Focusing on candy, beverage, and cigarette machines, ARA became the leading vending machine company in the US by 1961, with operations in 38 states. Despite slimmer profit margins, ARA moved into food vending in the early 1960s. It acquired 150 food services businesses between 1959-1963, quickly becoming a leader in the operation of cafeterias at colleges, hospitals, and work sites. The company (which changed its name to ARA Services in 1966) grew so rapidly that the FTC stepped in; ARA agreed to restrict future food vending acquisitions.

ARA provided food services at the 1968 Summer Olympics in Mexico City, beginning a long-term relationship with the amateur sports event. The company also diversified into publication distribution that year, and in 1970 it expanded into janitorial and maintenance services. A foray into residential care for the elderly began in 1973 (and ended in 1993 with the sale of the subsidiary). ARA also entered into emergency room staffing services (sold 1997). The company expanded into child care (National Child Care Centers) in 1980.

CFO Joseph Neubauer became CEO in 1983 and chairman a year later. To avoid a hostile takeover shortly thereafter, he led a $1.2 billion LBO. After the buyout, ARA began refining its core operations. It acquired Szabo (correctional food services) in 1986, Children's World Learning Centers in 1987, and Coordinated Health Services (medical billing services) in 1993.

ARA changed its name to ARAMARK in 1994 as part of an effort to raise its profile with its ultimate customers, the public. The company's concession operations suffered from long work stoppages in baseball (1994) and hockey (1995). ARAMARK acquired Galls (North America's #1 supplier of public safety equipment) in 1996, and in 1997 announced plans to become 100% employee-owned.

The following year ARAMARK entered into a joint venture with privately held Anderson News Company, exchanging its magazine distribution operations for a minority stake in the new business. In 2000 the company was focused on expansion, buying the food and beverage concessions business of conglomerate Ogden Corp. It also bought Wackenhut's Correctional Foodservice Management division. In 2001 ARAMARK acquired ServiceMaster's management services division for about $800 million. It also went public that year. The company lost a bid to cater the 2002 Olympic Games in Salt Lake City to rival Compass. In 2002 it agreed to buy 14 Harrison Conference Centers and university hotels from Hilton Corp. for $55 million.

Chairman and CEO: Joseph Neubauer, age 60,
$2,200,000 pay
President and COO: William Leonard, age 54,
$1,161,500 pay
EVP and CFO: L. Frederick Sutherland, age 50,
$680,500 pay
EVP; President, Food and Support Services:
John J. Zillmer, age 46, $550,500 pay
EVP Human Resources and Public Affairs:
Brian G. Mulvaney, age 45, $615,500 pay
EVP, General Counsel, and Secretary: Bart J. Colli,
age 54
SVP, Controller, and Chief Accounting Officer:
John M. Lafferty, age 57
SVP and Treasurer: Barbara A. Austell, age 48
Auditors: KPMG LLP

LOCATIONS

HQ: ARAMARK Tower, 1101 Market St.,
Philadelphia, PA 19107
Phone: 215-238-3000   **Fax:** 215-238-3333
Web: www.aramark.com

ARAMARK has operations in Belgium, Canada, the
Czech Republic, Germany, Hungary, Mexico, Spain,
the UK, and the US.

PRODUCTS/OPERATIONS

2001 Sales

	$ mil.	% of total
Food & support services, US	4,782	61
Food & support		
services, International	1,109	14
Uniform & apparel rental	995	13
Educational resources	464	6
Uniform & apparel marketing	439	6
Total	**7,789**	**100**

Selected Operations

Educational Resources
ARAMARK Work/Life Partnerships
Children's World Learning Centers
Medallion School Partnerships
Meritor Academy
Warren Walker

Food Services and Facilities Management
Business services (dining, meeting, janitorial, plant
operation services)
Campus services (maintenance and food and catering
services)
Correctional services (commissary management and
facility maintenance)
Facilities Management (general management and
maintenance)
Health care support services (food services,
groundskeeping, patient transportation)
International (food and support services worldwide)
Refreshment services (coffee and vending services)
School support services (facility and food management
services)
Sports and entertainment services (stadiums,
convention centers, and national parks)

Uniform and Career Apparel
Galls
WearGuard-Crest

COMPETITORS

Alex Lee
Cintas
Compass Group
Delaware North
Fine Host
G&K Services
HMSHost
KinderCare
La Petite Academy
ServiceMaster
Sodexho Alliance
UniFirst
Volume Services

HISTORICAL FINANCIALS & EMPLOYEES

NYSE: RMK FYE: Friday nearest Sept. 30	Annual Growth	9/92	9/93	9/94	9/95	9/96	9/97	9/98	9/99	9/00	9/01
Sales ($ mil.)	5.4%	4,865	4,891	5,162	5,601	6,122	6,310	6,377	6,718	7,263	7,789
Net income ($ mil.)	11.3%	67	77	86	94	110	146	129	150	168	177
Income as % of sales	—	1.4%	1.6%	1.7%	1.7%	1.8%	2.3%	2.0%	2.2%	2.3%	2.3%
Employees	5.5%	124,000	131,000	133,000	140,000	150,000	150,000	150,000	152,000	139,000	200,000

STOCK PRICE HISTORY

HIGH/LOW/CLOSE

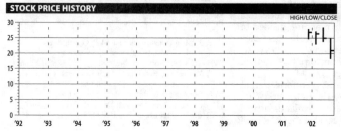

2001 FISCAL YEAR-END

Debt ratio: 86.9%
Return on equity: 98.5%
Cash ($ mil.): 25
Current ratio: 0.94
Long-term debt ($ mil.): 1,636

ARCH COAL, INC.

Your house may be filled with high-tech gadgets, but chances are they're powered by coal. More than half of the electricity generated in the US comes from coal, and St. Louis-based Arch Coal is the country's second-largest coal producer, behind Peabody Energy. The company produces almost 115 million tons of coal a year from 25 mines in the western US and central Appalachian region and has proven and probable reserves of about 3.4 billion tons. Arch ships its coal to 140 power plants in 30 states and exports it to 10 other countries. Wyoming and Central Appalachia hold more than 80% of Arch's recoverable reserves.

Steam coal — low-ash coal used by electric utilities to produce steam in boilers — accounts for 98% of Arch Coal's sales. To store and ship its coal, Arch Coal operates Arch Coal Terminal along the Ohio River, as well as stakes in port facilities at Los Angeles and Newport News, Virginia.

Bush administration energy policies are boosting the outlook for energy coal, but oversupply caused by a mild 2001/2002 winter prompted Arch Coal to cut production and pull back on planned capital expenditures.

HISTORY

Raised in the Oklahoma oil patch, J. Fred Miles founded the Swiss Drilling Company in 1910 and started wildcatting oil wells. Unable to compete against the low prices offered by Standard Oil, Miles moved his company in 1916 to eastern Kentucky and acquired control of 200,000 acres of oil land. With powerful backers such as the Armours of Chicago, Swiss Oil Company soon became one of the leading oil companies in Kentucky.

In the early 1920s the company's oil wells started to play out during a postwar depression. Miles fought back by expanding into refining, buying Tri-State Refining in 1930. The company changed its name in 1936 to Ashland Oil and Refining Company, a business that turned a profit even during the darkest days of the Depression. Miles didn't survive the transition, however. By 1926 Ashland was outperforming its parent, and investors eased Miles out the corporate door.

Pearl Harbor only brought more success to a business the American war machine needed to fuel its ships, planes, and tanks. Although peace brought the inevitable recession, America's postwar love affair with the automobile helped Ashland continue to thrive.

During the 1950s, Ashland's refineries ran at near capacity. In 1969 Merle Kelce and Guy Heckman, along with help from Ashland, formed Arch Mineral. Ashland had decided that it needed

to diversify and lessen its dependence on oil refining. The Hunt family of Dallas, Texas, put their money into the venture in 1971, and in the following years the company bought Southwestern Illinois Coal Corporation, USX's Lynch Properties, Diamond Shamrock Coal, and Lawson-Hamilton Properties. By the end of 1996, the company owned some 1.5 billion tons of recoverable coal reserves.

Ashland struck out on its own in the coal business in 1975, forming Ashland Coal. Ashland Coal then began a series of acquisitions lasting 15 years. The company bought Addington Brothers Mining (1976), Hobet Mining and Construction (1977), Saarbergwerke (1981), Coal-Mac (1989), Mingo Logan (1990), and Dal-Tex Coal (1992). Growing through that binge of acquisitions, the company went public in 1988.

In 1997 Arch Mineral and Ashland Coal merged into Arch Coal, an entity that consolidated Ashland's coal assets. Ashland kept a 58% stake. In 1998 Arch Coal purchased Atlantic Richfield's (ARCO) US coal operations for $1.14 billion, making itself the second-largest coal producer in the US. That year Arch Coal also created Arch Western Resources, a joint venture in which Arch Coal owns 99% and ARCO owns 1%.

Regulatory pressures and low coal prices in 1999 forced the company to close three mines — the Dal-Tex in West Virginia and two surface mines in Kentucky. The company idled its West Elk mine in Colorado when abnormally high levels of carbon monoxide were detected.

Arch Coal recorded a $346 million loss in 1999. To recover from the profit plunge and benefit from increased demand as utilities complied with Clean Air Act mandates, the company boosted production at its low-sulfur coal Black Thunder mine in Wyoming. In 2000 Ashland reduced its stake in Arch Coal to 12%; in 2001 it sold the remainder of its stock. After a mild winter, in early 2002 Arch Coal said it would cut production to offset oversupply. That year Arch Coal and WPP Group formed a partnership, Natural Resource Partners, and filed to take it public.

OFFICERS

Chairman: James R. Boyd, age 55
President, CEO, and Director: Steven F. Leer, age 49, $849,500 pay
EVP, Mining Operations and SVP, Operations: Kenneth G. Woodring, age 52, $499,300 pay
SVP and CFO: Robert J. Messey, age 56, $380,100 pay
SVP, Marketing; President, Arch Coal Sales Co.: John W. Eaves, age 44, $411,800 pay
SVP, Strategic Development: C. Henry Besten, age 53
VP, Business Development: David B. Peugh, age 47
VP, Human Resources: Bradley M. Allbritten, age 44

VP, Federal Government Affairs: Thomas Altmeyer
VP, Law, General Counsel, and Secretary:
Robert G. Jones, age 45
VP, Operations; President, Arch Western Resources:
Robert W. Shanks, age 48, $377,700 pay
Auditors: Ernst & Young LLP

LOCATIONS

HQ: 1 CityPlace Dr., Ste. 300, St. Louis, MO 63141
Phone: 314-994-2700   **Fax:** 314-994-2878
Web: www.archcoal.com

Arch Coal operates 25 mines in Colorado, Kentucky, Utah, Virginia, West Virginia, and Wyoming, and coal terminals in West Virginia and along the Ohio River. It also has stakes in coal terminals in California and Virginia.

PRODUCTS/OPERATIONS

2001 Sales

	% of total
Steam coal	98
Metallurgical coal	2
Total	**100**

Selected Mining Operations

Central Appalachia
Arch of West Virginia (West Virginia)
Campbells Creek (West Virginia)
Coal-Mac (West Virginia)
Dal-Tex (West Virginia)
Hobet 21 (West Virginia)
Lone Mountain (Kentucky)
Mingo Logan (West Virginia)
Pardee (Virginia)
Samples (West Virginia)

Western United States
Arch of Wyoming (Wyoming)
Black Thunder (Wyoming)
Coal Creek (Wyoming)
Dugout Canyon (Utah)
Skyline (Utah)
SUFCO (Utah)
West Elk (Colorado)

Selected Subsidiaries and Affiliates

Arch Coal Terminal
Arch Western Resources, LLC (99%)
 Arch of Wyoming, LLC
 Canyon Fuel Co., LLC (65%, with ITOCHU Corp.)
 Mountain Coal Company, LLC
  West Elk mine (Colorado)
 Thunder Basin Coal Company, LLC
  Black Thunder mine (Wyoming)
Los Angeles Export Terminal (14%)

COMPETITORS

CONSOL Energy	Massey Energy
Drummond	Peabody Energy
Exxon Mobil	Rio Tinto
Lonmin	

HISTORICAL FINANCIALS & EMPLOYEES

NYSE: ACI FYE: December 31	Annual Growth	12/92	12/93	12/94	12/95	12/96	12/97	12/98	12/99	12/00	12/01
Sales ($ mil.)	10.8%	580	498	610	636	577	1,035	1,499	1,556	1,392	1,463
Net income ($ mil.)	(16.3%)	36	27	32	41	17	30	30	(346)	(13)	7
Income as % of sales	—	6.2%	5.3%	5.3%	6.5%	2.9%	2.9%	2.0%	—	—	0.5%
Earnings per share ($)	(24.5%)	1.88	(1.86)	1.68	(0.53)	1.58	1.00	0.76	(9.02)	(0.33)	0.15
Stock price - FY high ($)	—	38.00	31.75	31.25	30.75	28.38	30.50	29.25	16.88	14.94	38.40
Stock price - FY low ($)	—	23.63	22.00	22.50	20.50	20.50	23.75	14.44	8.56	4.75	12.88
Stock price - FY close ($)	(1.2%)	25.38	30.25	28.50	21.25	27.75	27.38	17.13	11.31	14.13	22.70
P/E - high	—	19	—	19	—	18	31	37	—	—	256
P/E - low	—	12	—	13	—	13	24	18	—	—	86
Dividends per share ($)	(6.0%)	0.40	0.40	0.42	0.46	0.46	0.46	0.46	0.46	0.23	0.23
Book value per share ($)	(8.3%)	23.78	25.14	26.88	29.33	29.91	15.42	15.70	6.32	5.76	10.90
Employees	8.1%	1,627	1,687	1,660	1,571	1,528	3,366	4,455	3,764	3,655	3,292

STOCK PRICE HISTORY

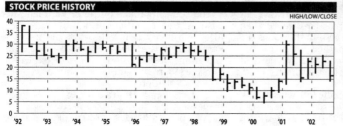

HIGH/LOW/CLOSE

2001 FISCAL YEAR-END

Debt ratio: 57.6%
Return on equity: 1.8%
Cash ($ mil.): 7
Current ratio: 1.21
Long-term debt ($ mil.): 776
No. of shares (mil.): 52
Dividends
 Yield: 1.0%
 Payout: 153.3%
Market value ($ mil.): 1,188

ARCHER DANIELS MIDLAND

Archer Daniels Midland (ADM) knows how to grind and squeeze a fortune out of humble plants. ADM primarily processes the three largest crops in the US: corn, soybeans, and wheat for sale to food, beverage, and chemical industries.

Based in Decatur, Illinois, ADM processes soybeans and other oilseeds into vegetable oils and by-products ranging from salad oils and vitamin E to textured vegetable protein and cotton cellulose pulp. ADM's corn by-products include syrups, sweeteners, citric and lactic acids, and ethanol. ADM also produces wheat and durum flour for bakeries and pasta makers and makes its own pasta products. The company owns or leases about 300 processing plants worldwide.

Thanks to cost cutting and increased prospects for ethanol's use as a fuel, ADM's fortunes have brightened after some tough years. A citric acid and lysine price-fixing scheme cost ADM $100 million. In 1998 a trio of top executives were convicted in the scheme, including Michael Andreas — son of chairman emeritus Dwayne Andreas and cousin of chairman and CEO Allen Andreas. The Andreas family remains significant shareholders in the company.

Effective December 31, 2002, ADM will end its industrial ethanol joint venture with Dow Chemical and will market ethanol on its own. In July 2002 ADM agreed to merge with Minnesota Corn Processors (MCP). MCP is the company's chief competitor in the ethanol market and the merger will increase ADM's ethanol production such that it will control almost half of the US market. The US Department of Justice is reviewing the merger for antitrust violations.

HISTORY

John Daniels began crushing flaxseed to make linseed oil in 1878, and in 1902 he formed Daniels Linseed Company in Minneapolis. George Archer, another flaxseed crusher, joined the company the following year. In 1923 the company bought Midland Linseed Products and became Archer Daniels Midland (ADM). ADM kept buying oil processing companies in the Midwest during the 1920s. It also started to research the chemical composition of linseed oil.

ADM entered the flour milling business in 1930 when it bought Commander-Larabee (then the #3 flour miller in the US). In the 1930s the company discovered a method for extracting lecithin (an emulsifier food additive used in candy and other products) from soybean oil, significantly lowering its price.

The enterprise grew rapidly following WWII. By 1949 it was the leading processor of linseed oil and soybeans in the US and was fourth in

flour milling. During the early 1950s ADM began foreign expansion in earnest.

In 1966 the company's leadership passed to Dwayne Andreas, a former Cargill executive who had purchased a block of Archer family stock. Andreas focused ADM on soybeans, including the production of textured vegetable protein, a cheap soybean by-product used in foodstuffs.

Andreas' restructuring paved the way for productivity and expansion. In 1971 the company acquired Corn Sweeteners (glutens, high-fructose syrups). Other acquisitions included Tabor (grain, 1975) and Colombian Peanut (1981). ADM formed a grain-marketing joint venture with GROWMARK in 1985.

The company continued to expand its global presence in the early 1990s. In 1992 ADM bought Canadian Ogilvie Mills. During the 1992 presidential race, the Andreas family made substantial donations to both parties in hopes that the winner would support the use of ethanol in gasoline. Two years later the EPA required that 10% of all gas sold in the US be blended with ethanol.

In 1995 the FBI — aided by ADM executive-turned-informer Mark Whitacre — joined a federal investigation of lysine and citric acid price-fixing by the company. The next year ADM agreed to plead guilty to two criminal charges of price-fixing and paid $100 million in penalties, a record at that time for a US criminal antitrust case. Whitacre later lost his immunity when convicted of defrauding ADM out of $9 million. He and two other ADM executives, including one-time ADM heir apparent Michael Andreas, were tried and convicted in 1998 and sentenced to prison in 1999.

In 1997 it named Allen Andreas (Dwayne's nephew) as CEO. Also that year it bought a minority stake in pork and beef packer IBP and purchased soybean processor Moorman Manufacturing (renamed Moorman's).

ADM sold its Harvest Burger line of meat-replacement products to Worthington Foods (now owned by Kellogg Company) in 1998. Dwayne turned over the chairman post to Allen in early 1999. In 2000 ADM was again cited for involvement in the price-fixing of lysine and was fined $45 million by the European Commission.

The company took control of Farmland Industries' grain operations in 2001 through a new ADM subsidiary that will share profits with Farmland. In late 2001 the company merged its two animal feed divisions, Consolidated Nutrition and Moorman's, into a new subsidiary, ADM Alliance Nutrition.

In December 2001, in a move to help Mexico's domestic sugar industry, the Mexican government imposed a 20% tax on soft drinks made with corn-syrup sweeteners, of which ADM's plant in Guadalajara is a major producer. However, amid political controversy, Mexican President Vicente Fox suspended the tax until the end of September 2002. In July 2002 the tax was ordered reinstated by the Mexican Supreme Court.

In 2002 the company began a joint venture with Greatocean Oils & Grains Industries, Co. Ltd., to start soy crushing operations in China.

OFFICERS

Chairman Emeritus: Dwayne O. Andreas, age 83
Chairman and CEO: G. Allen Andreas, age 58, $2,398,480 pay
Executive Assistant to the Chairman and Chairman Emeritus: Claudia M. Madding, age 50
President: Paul B. Mulhollem, age 52
SVP and Director of Corporate Marketing: Martin L. Andreas, age 62, $814,539 pay
SVP: Lewis W. Batchelder, age 56
SVP: William H. Camp, age 52
SVP: Larry H. Cunningham, age 57, $709,090 pay
SVP: Richard P. Reising, age 57
SVP: John D. Rice, age 47
President, ADM North American Oilseed Processing: J. Kevin Burgard, age 39
President, ADM Cocoa: Mark A. Bemis, age 40
President, ADM Natural Health and Nutrition: Anthony P. DeLio, age 45
President, ADM Specialty Ingredients: Scott B. Frederickson, age 39
Group VP; Managing Director, ADM International: Brian F. Peterson, age 59
Group VP: Raymond V. Preiksaitis, age 49
VP and CFO: Douglas J. Schmalz, age 55
Auditors: Ernst & Young LLP

LOCATIONS

HQ: Archer Daniels Midland Company
4666 Faries Pkwy., Decatur, IL 62525
Phone: 217-424-5200   **Fax:** 217-424-6196
Web: www.admworld.com

2001 Sales

	$ mil.	% of total
US	13,114	65
Other countries	6,937	35
Total	**20,051**	**100**

PRODUCTS/OPERATIONS

2001 Sales

	$ mil.	% of total
Oilseeds & corn processing	10,464	52
Agricultural services	5,644	28
Other	3,943	20
Total	**20,051**	**100**

COMPETITORS

Ag Processing	Corn Products
Ajinomoto	International
Andersons	Farmland Industries
Bartlett and Company	King Arthur Flour
Buckeye Technologies	Koch
Bunge Limited	Nisshin Oil Mills
Cargill	Riceland Foods
Cenex Harvest States	Scoular
Cereol	Südzucker AG
ConAgra	Tate & Lyle

HISTORICAL FINANCIALS & EMPLOYEES

NYSE: ADM FYE: June 30	Annual Growth	6/92	6/93	6/94	6/95	6/96	6/97	6/98	6/99	6/00	6/01
Sales ($ mil.)	9.0%	9,232	9,811	11,374	12,672	13,314	13,853	16,109	14,283	12,877	20,051
Net income ($ mil.)	(3.0%)	504	568	484	796	696	377	404	266	301	383
Income as % of sales	—	5.5%	5.8%	4.3%	6.3%	5.2%	2.7%	2.5%	1.9%	2.3%	1.9%
Earnings per share ($)	(1.4%)	0.66	0.81	0.66	1.09	0.99	0.54	0.59	0.39	0.45	0.58
Stock price – FY high ($)	—	13.56	12.42	12.37	14.97	15.07	18.76	20.22	16.71	13.26	15.22
Stock price – FY low ($)	—	8.92	9.53	9.42	10.57	10.63	12.19	15.19	11.64	7.98	7.80
Stock price – FY close ($)	2.9%	9.63	10.12	10.51	13.19	14.23	18.37	15.91	13.31	8.89	12.42
P/E – high	—	20	17	18	14	15	35	34	41	29	26
P/E – low	—	13	13	14	10	11	23	26	28	18	13
Dividends per share ($)	13.7%	0.06	0.06	0.06	0.08	0.13	0.16	0.17	0.17	0.18	0.19
Book value per share ($)	4.9%	6.19	6.74	7.29	8.59	9.24	9.82	9.36	8.78	9.20	9.56
Employees	6.0%	13,524	14,168	16,013	14,833	14,811	17,160	23,132	23,603	22,753	22,834

STOCK PRICE HISTORY

HIGH/LOW/CLOSE

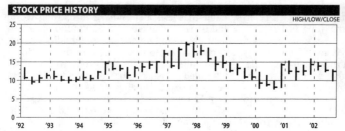

2001 FISCAL YEAR-END

Debt ratio: 34.6%
Return on equity: 6.2%
Cash ($ mil.): 676
Current ratio: 1.59
Long-term debt ($ mil.): 3,351
No. of shares (mil.): 662
Dividends
  Yield: 1.5%
  Payout: 32.8%
Market value ($ mil.): 8,227

ARMSTRONG HOLDINGS, INC.

There is no ceiling too high, no floor too low for Armstrong Holdings, which is the holding company for Armstrong Industries.

Based in Lancaster, Pennsylvania, Armstrong makes a wide variety of floor coverings and ceiling systems for commercial and residential use. Armstrong's flooring products (more than 40% of sales) include wood flooring, linoleum, carpet, and sports surfaces.

Through its Triangle Pacific and DLW Aktiengesellschaft subsidiaries, Armstrong is a leader in the manufacture of hardwood flooring and manufactures kitchen and bathroom cabinets. Its ceiling products include acoustical ceilings and suspended-ceiling systems.

The company markets its products worldwide to dealers, home center chains (The Home Depot accounts for more than 10% of sales), and contractors, with the US accounting for three-fourths of sales.

Armstrong has restructured to focus on its core products — flooring and ceiling products. Armstrong had hoped to sell noncore assets in order to retire debt and fund new acquisitions in its core product segments. This strategy was put on hold when its largest operating subsidiary, Armstrong World Industries, defaulted on a $50 million loan. Armstrong World later filed for bankruptcy protection.

HISTORY

Thomas Armstrong and John Glass started the Armstrong Brothers cork-cutting shop in Pittsburgh in 1860. Armstrong carved the corks by hand, stamped his name on each one, and made his first deliveries in a wheelbarrow.

Concerned with fairness to his customers, Armstrong put a written guarantee in each burlap sack of corks before shipping. By the mid-1890s Armstrong Brothers was the largest cork company in the world. The enterprise changed its name to Armstrong Cork in 1895.

To make up for a dwindling cork market near the turn of the century, Armstrong found new uses for its cork in insulated corkboard and brick. In 1906 the business turned its attention to linoleum (which then was made with cork powder) and started building a new factory in Lancaster, Pennsylvania. Armstrong died in 1908.

The company continued to make flooring and insulating materials through the 1950s while expanding into Canada, Europe, and Australia. During the 1960s Armstrong added home furnishings to its products by purchasing E & B Carpet Mills (1967) and Thomasville Furniture Industries (1968, sold 1995).

The firm changed its name to Armstrong World Industries in 1980. That decade it rapidly expanded through acquisitions, including Applied Color Systems (computerized color systems, 1981; sold 1989), Chemline Industries (chemicals, 1985), and American Olean (ceramic tile, 1988).

Armstrong and Worthington Industries combined their suspended-ceiling businesses in 1992. By the mid-1990s Armstrong began cutbacks and other restructuring moves. Even though the company's building-products division went on a two-year job-slashing spree (cutting its worldwide workforce by 25%), by the end of 1994 Armstrong's North American sheet flooring unit introduced 166 new products, representing nearly 30% of its sheet flooring line. In 1995 Armstrong sold its champagne cork operation to Spanish investors and exchanged its American Tile Olean subsidiary, plus $27 million, for a 37% stake in ceramic-tile maker Dal-Tile.

To expand international operations, Armstrong made a series of strategic moves in 1996, including linking with Shanghai Advanced Building Materials to open a mineral fiber acoustical ceiling plant in China and forming a joint venture to make soft-fiber ceilings in Europe.

In 1998 Armstrong sold its 34% stake in ceramic tile maker Dal-Tile after failing to gain control of the company. Also that year it bought Triangle Pacific, a maker of hardwood flooring and cabinets, for $1.15 billion. It also bought a 93% stake in Germany-based DLW, a flooring and furniture maker. In 1999 Armstrong agreed to form a joint venture by combining its worldwide insulation business with two insulation companies — NMC/Nomaco of Belgium and Thermaflex of the Netherlands. Later that year, Armstrong sold its textile product operations to Day International Group.

In 2000 the company formed Armstrong Holdings as a holding company for Armstrong Industries and bought GEMA Holdings AG, a Swiss-based metal ceiling maker. Continuing the sale of noncore assets, the company sold its insulation business and some of its installation products operations the same year. Also in 2000, former General Signal CEO Michael D. Lockhart was named chairman and CEO of Armstrong. Later that year a subsidiary, Armstrong World Industries, defaulted on a $50 million loan, effectively drying up any excess liquidity by triggering a default clause on an additional $450 million in credit. Armstrong World Industries filed for bankruptcy in late 2000. The next year Armstrong Holdings negotiated for the sale of its European carpet business, Armstrong DLW AG, and its Desso brand, but reconsidered late in the year and decided to keep the unit.

OFFICERS

Chairman and CEO: Michael D. Lockhart, age 52, $1,786,188 pay
SVP and CFO: Leonard A. Campanaro, age 53
SVP and Chief Marketing Officer: April L. Thornton, age 40, $655,985 pay
SVP, Armstrong Strategic Relations: Stephen E. Stockwell, age 56
SVP, Human Resources: Matthew J. Angello, age 42, $632,412 pay
SVP, Secretary, and General Counsel: John N. Rigas, age 52
VP and Controller: William C. Rodruan, age 47
VP and Treasurer: Barry M. Sullivan, age 56
VP, Corporate Communication: Debra L. Miller
VP, Wood Flooring: Michael J. Badar, age 34
President and CEO, Armstrong Building Products Operations: Stephen J. Senkowski, age 50, $763,773 pay
President and CEO, Armstrong Cabinet Pruducts: Charles A. Engle, age 58
President and CEO, Armstrong Floor Products: Chan W. Galbato, age 39, $1,199,375 pay
Auditors: KPMG LLP

LOCATIONS

HQ: 2500 Columbia Ave., Lancaster, PA 17603
Phone: 888-397-0611 **Fax:** 888-446-8061
Web: www.armstrong.com

Armstrong Holdings operates 57 manufacturing plants in 14 countries.

2001 Sales

	$ mil.	% of total
The Americas	2,325	74
Europe	711	23
Asia/Pacific	99	3
Total	**3,135**	**100**

PRODUCTS/OPERATIONS

2001 Sales

	$ mil.	% of total
Flooring		
Resident	1,162	37
Wood	654	21
Building products	831	27
Textiles	263	8
Cabinets	225	7
Total	**3,135**	**100**

Selected Products

Cabinets	Linoleum
Ceiling systems	Wood flooring
Laminate flooring	

COMPETITORS

American Woodmark
Boise Cascade
Mohawk Industries
Nortek
Owens Corning
Pergo
Shaw Industries
Tembec

HISTORICAL FINANCIALS & EMPLOYEES

NYSE: ACK FYE: December 31	Annual Growth	12/92	12/93	12/94	12/95	12/96	12/97	12/98	12/99	12/00	12/01
Sales ($ mil.)	2.3%	2,550	2,525	2,753	2,085	2,156	2,199	2,746	3,444	3,004	3,135
Net income ($ mil.)	—	(234)	64	210	123	156	185	(9)	14	12	93
Income as % of sales	—	—	2.5%	7.6%	5.9%	7.2%	8.4%	—	0.4%	0.4%	3.0%
Earnings per share ($)	—	(6.51)	1.27	4.62	2.54	3.61	4.50	(0.23)	0.36	0.30	2.27
Stock price - FY high ($)	—	37.50	55.25	57.50	64.13	75.25	75.38	90.00	64.31	36.81	5.69
Stock price - FY low ($)	—	24.50	28.75	36.00	38.38	51.88	61.50	46.94	29.00	0.75	2.06
Stock price - FY close ($)	(22.0%)	31.88	53.25	38.50	62.00	69.50	74.75	60.31	33.38	2.06	3.41
P/E - high	—	—	41	11	22	19	17	—	179	123	2
P/E - low	—	—	21	7	13	13	14	—	81	3	1
Dividends per share ($)	—	1.20	1.20	1.26	1.40	1.56	1.72	1.88	1.92	1.44	0.00
Book value per share ($)	2.3%	15.16	15.30	19.72	21.02	19.19	20.20	17.73	16.87	16.28	18.68
Employees	(3.7%)	23,500	21,682	20,583	13,433	10,580	10,600	18,900	18,300	15,400	16,700

STOCK PRICE HISTORY

HIGH/LOW/CLOSE

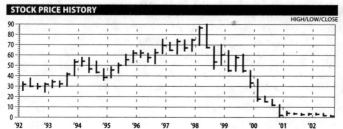

2001 FISCAL YEAR-END

Debt ratio: 6.2%
Return on equity: 13.0%
Cash ($ mil.): 277
Current ratio: 3.06
Long-term debt ($ mil.): 50
No. of shares (mil.): 41
Dividends
  Yield: —
  Payout: —
Market value ($ mil.): 139

ARROW ELECTRONICS, INC.

Arrow Electronics has hit the distribution bull's-eye. The Melville, New York-based company is the world's #1 distributor of electronic components and computer products. Its inventory includes semiconductors, computer peripherals, passive components, and interconnect products. Arrow's customers are primarily manufacturers in industries such as aviation and aerospace, computers and office equipment, industrial equipment, medical and scientific devices, and telecommunications equipment, as well as resellers of computer systems. Arrow has more than 600 suppliers.

Value-added services and the Internet are increasingly important elements of Arrow's business. The company's services have expanded to include product design, inventory management, and manufacturing.

HISTORY

Arrow Radio began in 1935 in New York City as an outlet for used radio equipment. In the mid-1960s the company was selling various home entertainment products and wholesaling electronic parts. In 1968 three Harvard Business School graduates got Arrow in their sights. Duke Glenn, Roger Green, and John Waddell led a group of investors that acquired the company for $1 million in borrowed money. The three also bought a company that reclaimed lead from used car batteries.

With the money they made in the lead reclamation business, the trio expanded Arrow's inventory in its wholesale electronic distribution business. The company expanded rapidly during the 1970s, primarily through internal growth, and by 1977 it had become the US's fourth-largest electronics distributor. In 1979 Arrow bought the #2 US distributor, Cramer Electronics. Although the purchase of West Coast-based Cramer was financed with junk bonds and left Arrow deeply in debt, revenues doubled. Arrow went public in 1979.

One year later a hotel fire killed 13 members of Arrow's senior management, including Glenn and Green. Waddell, who had remained at company headquarters to answer questions about a stock split announced that day, was named acting CEO. Company stock fell 19% the first day it traded after the fire and another 14% before the end of the month. Adding to the company's woes, a slump hit the electronics industry in 1981. That year Arrow's board lured Alfred Stein to leave Motorola and lead the company's new management team as president and CEO; Waddell remained chairman.

Stein did not mesh with Arrow, and in early 1982 the board fired him and put Waddell in charge again. By 1983 the industry slump was over, and Arrow was temporarily back in the black. However, another industry downturn led to significant losses between 1985 and 1987.

In the mid-1980s Arrow began a major global expansion, acquiring in 1985 a 40% interest in Germany's largest electronics distributor, Spoerle Electronic (Arrow owned the company by 2000). President Stephen Kaufman, a former McKinsey & Company consultant, was named CEO in 1986 (Waddell remains VC). Arrow bought Kierulff Electronics, the fourth-largest US distributor, in 1988, and Lex Electronics, the third-largest, three years later.

Arrow expanded into Asia in 1993 with the acquisition of Hong Kong-based Components Agents and Components+Instrumentation of New Zealand in 1995. The next year Italian subsidiary Silverstar acquired Eurelettronica, one of Italy's biggest semiconductor distributors. In 1997 Arrow bought the volume electronic components distribution business of Premier Farnell, a UK-based electronics distributor.

In 1999 Arrow acquired passive components distributor Richey Electronics and the Electronics Distribution Group of Bell Industries. It also joined rival Avnet and others to form online electronics distribution ventures ChipCenter (in 1999) and Viacore (in 2000).

Arrow's purchases in early 2000 included a European distributor (based in France), as well as companies in Israel and Norway. Kaufman stepped down from the CEO post in 2000; company president Francis Scricco was named to the position. Later in 2000 Arrow purchased Wyle Components and Wyle Systems (both North American computer products distributors) from German utility giant E.ON AG.

Also that year the company merged its telephone sales operations with ChipCenter to form a sales and marketing service called eChips. The online service, intended to give contract and electronics equipment makers a place to comparison shop, also counts QuestLink, Avnet, and i2 Technologies as investors.

Facing a broad downturn in the electronics industry, the company in 2001 laid off 1,500 employees. The next year Arrow sold its Gates/Arrow unit (distribution of PC peripherals and software to North American resellers) to SYNNEX Information Technologies. Also in 2002 Scricco resigned as CEO; Kaufman left his post as chairman to take the reins once again as CEO and director David Duval stepped in as chairman.

Chairman: Daniel W. Duval, age 65
Vice Chairman: John C. Waddell, age 63
Interim President, CEO, and Director:
Stephen P. Kaufman, age 60, $1,800,000 pay
EVP, Secretary, and Director: Robert E. Klatell, age 55,
$923,000 pay
SVP and General Counsel: Peter S. Brown
SVP: Betty Jane Scheihing, age 53, $717,000 pay
SVP; President, Arrow Electronics Asia:
Steven W. Menefee, age 55
SVP, Semiconductor Supplier Services Group:
Albert G. Streber
VP and CFO: Paul J. Reilly, age 44
VP; President, Arrow Asia/Pacific: John Tam
VP; President, Arrow Europe: Arthur H. Baer, age 55
VP; President, North American Components Operation:
Jan M. Salsgiver, age 44, $729,000 pay
VP; President, North American Computer Products:
Michael J. Long, age 42
Auditors: Ernst & Young LLP

LOCATIONS

HQ: 25 Hub Dr., Melville, NY 11747
Phone: 516-391-1300   **Fax:** 516-391-1640
Web: www.arrow.com

Arrow Electronics has more than 200 sales facilities and
23 distribution centers in 40 countries.

2001 Sales

	$ mil.	% of total
Americas	6,283	62
Europe	2,975	29
Asia/Pacific	870	9
Total	**10,128**	**100**

PRODUCTS/OPERATIONS

2001 Sales

	$ mil.	% of total
Electric components	7,287	72
Computer products	2,841	28
Total	**10,128**	**100**

Products

Electronic Components	Controllers
Capacitors	Design systems
Connectors	Desktop computers
Potentiometers	Microcomputer boards and
Power supplies	systems
Relays	Printers
Resistors	Servers
Switches	Storage computers
	Terminals
Computer Products	Workstations
Communication control	
equipment	

COMPETITORS

All American	Nu Horizons Electronics
Semiconductor	Pioneer-Standard
Avnet	Electronics
Bell Microproducts	Premier Farnell
Electrocomponents	Rexel, Inc.
Future Electronics	Richardson Electronics
Ingram Micro	SED International
Merisel	Tech Data
New Age Electronics	TTI

HISTORICAL FINANCIALS & EMPLOYEES

NYSE: ARW FYE: December 31	Annual Growth	12/92	12/93	12/94	12/95	12/96	12/97	12/98	12/99	12/00	12/01
Sales ($ mil.)	22.6%	1,622	2,536	4,649	5,919	6,535	7,764	8,345	9,313	12,959	10,128
Net income ($ mil.)	—	45	82	112	203	203	164	146	124	358	(74)
Income as % of sales	—	2.8%	3.2%	2.4%	3.4%	3.1%	2.1%	1.7%	1.3%	2.8%	—
Earnings per share ($)	—	0.77	1.22	1.16	2.03	1.98	1.64	1.50	1.29	3.62	(0.75)
Stock price - FY high ($)	—	15.25	21.56	22.56	29.88	27.69	36.00	36.25	26.56	46.00	33.44
Stock price - FY low ($)	—	7.19	13.25	16.81	17.56	17.63	25.13	11.75	13.19	20.50	18.00
Stock price - FY close ($)	8.5%	14.31	20.88	17.94	21.50	26.75	32.44	26.69	25.38	28.63	29.90
P/E - high	—	17	16	19	14	14	22	24	20	12	—
P/E - low	—	8	10	14	8	9	15	8	10	6	—
Dividends per share ($)	—	0.00	0.00	0.00	0.00	0.00	0.00	0.00	0.00	0.00	0.00
Book value per share ($)	12.8%	6.00	7.30	9.07	11.81	13.27	13.22	15.55	16.16	19.45	17.69
Employees	13.1%	4,100	4,600	6,500	7,000	7,900	9,800	9,700	11,200	12,200	12,400

STOCK PRICE HISTORY

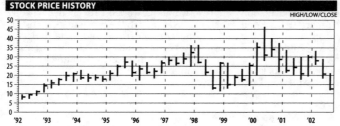

HIGH/LOW/CLOSE

2001 FISCAL YEAR-END

Debt ratio: 58.0%
Return on equity: —
Cash ($ mil.): 557
Current ratio: 3.32
Long-term debt ($ mil.): 2,442
No. of shares (mil.): 100
Dividends
    Yield: —
    Payout: —
Market value ($ mil.): 2,986

ARVINMERITOR, INC.

ArvinMeritor is the name Meritor Automotive adopted after acquiring Arvin Industries. The company's commercial vehicle unit offers axles, brakes, transmissions, and clutches to manufacturers of heavy-duty trucks and off-highway vehicles. The light vehicles unit makes door, roof, exhaust, and suspension systems. Arvin-Meritor also makes automotive aftermarket products such as filters (Purolator) and shocks (Gabriel). The company sells private-label aftermarket parts to retailers such as Pep Boys. DaimlerChrysler and General Motors each account for more than 10% of the company's sales.

ArvinMeritor is anticipating soft sales as the heavy-duty truck and automotive aftermarket sectors suffer from weak demand. To minimize the damage, ArvinMeritor has trimmed its workforce and is consolidating its worldwide manufacturing operations. The company also plans to trim its list of suppliers from 2,700 (at the end of 2001) down to about 1,840 by September 2002. To ensure improved quality and lowest costs, ArvinMeritor plans to buy parts and materials from only 1,000 suppliers by 2006.

HISTORY

ArvinMeritor's earliest progenitor was the Wisconsin Parts Company, a small axle plant Willard Rockwell bought in 1919 to build a truck axle he had designed himself. In 1953 Rockwell merged Wisconsin Parts with Standard Steel and Spring and Timken-Detroit Axle to form Rockwell Spring and Axle Company. Timken-Detroit was a 1909 spinoff of the Timken Roller Bearing Axle Company, whose buggy springs predated the invention of the automobile.

Rockwell Spring and Axle changed its name in 1958 to Rockwell-Standard Corp. In 1967 Rockwell-Standard took over North American Aviation. North American Aviation needed to improve its public image by burrowing into a reputable company after the Apollo space capsule it had built ignited during a ground test, killing all three astronauts aboard. The new company, called North American Rockwell, was headed by Willard.

North American Rockwell made car and truck parts, tools, printing presses, industrial sewing machines, and electronic flight and navigation instruments. In 1973 North American Rockwell bought Rockwell Manufacturing and changed its name once again, to Rockwell International (now Rockwell Automation).

Under Willard Jr.'s leadership, Rockwell bought a number of high-risk businesses. During one period in the early 1970s, the company was losing a million dollars a day. Willard Jr. retired in 1979, and Robert Anderson, who had

come to Rockwell in 1968 from Chrysler Corporation, became chairman. Anderson moved the company away from the high-profile consumer market that Willard Jr. had been so keen on. He also required all company divisions to submit profit goals. Under Anderson's management, Rockwell's debt fell dramatically.

In 1986 Rockwell brought out a new line of single-speed and two-speed drive axles for heavy vehicles, and in 1989 it introduced a family of nine- and 13-speed on-highway transmissions. The next year the company's Meritor WABCO unit (a joint venture with American Standard Companies) began supplying antilock brakes for trailers and tractors.

In the 1990s Rockwell's automotive division began growing through acquisitions and overseas expansion. It bought Czech auto parts maker Skoda Miada Boleslav in 1993 and Dura Automotive Systems' window-regulator business in 1995. The next year the division entered into a joint venture with China's Xuzhou Construction Machinery Axle and Case Co. It also introduced the Engine Synchro Shift transmission system, designed to shift gears easily.

Rockwell spun off Meritor Automotive in 1997 as an independent, publicly traded company. The new company derived its name from the Latin word "meritum," meaning service, worth, and benefit. In 1999 Meritor bought UK-based LucasVarity's heavy vehicle braking system division; Volvo's heavy-duty truck axle unit; and Euclid Industries, which makes replacement parts for medium- and heavy-duty trucks. Meritor further enhanced its aftermarket offerings through an agreement with Pressure Systems International to market automatic tire-inflation systems. Meritor sold its auto seat adjusting system operations for $130 million that year.

Meritor announced in early 2000 that its Meritor Suspension Systems joint venture with Mitsubishi Steel had acquired Tempered Spring Co., a UK-based supplier of automotive suspension components. Also that year Meritor acquired Arvin Industries. Renamed ArvinMeritor, the combined companies formed an automotive systems titan with $7.5 billion in sales. Later that year ArvinMeritor announced that it would reduce its worldwide workforce by about 4% (1,500) because of a slump in the heavy truck industry.

In 2001 ArvinMeritor sold certain electric seat motor assets of its light vehicle systems division to Johnson Electric Holdings Ltd. for $11.7 million.

OFFICERS

Chairman and CEO: Larry D. Yost, age 63, $840,000 pay
President, COO, and Director: Terrence E. O'Rourke, age 54, $370,000 pay (prior to promotion)
SVP and CFO: S. Carl Soderstrom, age 48
SVP and CIO: Perry L. Lipe, age 55
SVP and General Counsel: Vernon G. Baker II, age 48
SVP, Corporate Development and Strategy, Engineering and Procurement: Juan L. De La Riva, age 57
SVP, Human Resources: Ernest T. Whitus, age 46
SVP; President, Commercial Vehicle Systems: Thomas A. Gosnell, age 51, $335,000 pay
SVP; President, Light Vehicle Aftermarket: William K. Daniel, age 36, $300,000 pay
SVP; President, Light Vehicle Systems: Craig Stinson, age 40, $300,000 pay (prior to promotion)
VP, Human Resources: Lisa Corona
Auditors: Deloitte & Touche LLP

LOCATIONS

HQ: 2135 W. Maple Rd., Troy, MI 48084
Phone: 248-435-1000   **Fax:** 248-435-1393
Web: www.arvinmeritor.com

2001 Sales

	$ mil.	% of total
North America		
US	3,476	51
Canada	507	7
Mexico	312	5
Europe		
UK	481	7
France	384	6
Other countries	1,159	17
Other regions	486	7
Total	**6,805**	**100**

PRODUCTS/OPERATIONS

2001 Sales

	$ mil	% of total
Light vehicle systems	3,588	53
Commercial vehicle systems	2,199	32
Light vehicle aftermarket	859	13
Other	159	2
Total	**6,805**	**100**

Selected Products

Access-control systems	Mufflers
Axles	Ride and motion control
Brakes	systems
Catalytic converters	Roof systems
Clutches	Shock absorbers
Door systems	Struts
Drivelines	Suspension systems
Exhaust and tail pipes	Transmissions
Exhaust systems	Wheel products
Filters (Purolator brand)	

COMPETITORS

American Axle & Manufacturing	Federal-Mogul	Tower Automotive
American Standard	Hayes Lemmerz	Transportation
ASC	Magna International	Technologies
Boler	Metaldyne	Valeo
BorgWarner	Oxford	Visteon
Carlisle Companies	Automotive	Williams
Dana	Robert Bosch	Controls
Delphi	Tenneco	ZF
Eaton	Automotive	Friedrichshafen
	Titan	
	International	

HISTORICAL FINANCIALS & EMPLOYEES

NYSE: ARM FYE: September 30	Annual Growth	9/92	9/93	9/94	9/95	9/96	9/97	9/98	9/99	9/00	9/01
Sales ($ mil.)	12.9%	2,279	2,358	2,653	3,125	3,144	3,309	3,836	4,450	5,153	6,805
Net income ($ mil.)	1.7%	30	57	51	123	114	109	147	194	218	35
Income as % of sales	—	1.3%	2.4%	1.9%	3.9%	3.6%	3.3%	3.8%	4.4%	4.2%	0.5%
Earnings per share ($)	(87.1%)	—	—	—	—	—	—	—	—	4.12	0.53
Stock price - FY high ($)	—	—	—	—	—	—	—	—	—	18.63	21.87
Stock price - FY low ($)	—	—	—	—	—	—	—	—	—	13.75	8.88
Stock price - FY close ($)	(2.7%)	—	—	—	—	—	—	—	—	14.69	14.29
P/E - high	—	—	—	—	—	—	—	—	—	5	41
P/E - low	—	—	—	—	—	—	—	—	—	3	17
Dividends per share ($)	245.5%	—	—	—	—	—	—	—	—	0.22	0.76
Book value per share ($)	(12.3%)	—	—	—	—	—	—	—	—	11.17	9.79
Employees	16.6%	—	—	—	—	15,300	16,000	16,900	19,000	36,000	33,000

STOCK PRICE HISTORY

HIGH/LOW/CLOSE

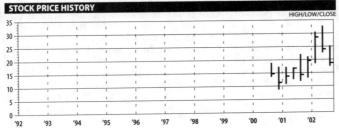

2001 FISCAL YEAR-END

Debt ratio: 66.9%
Return on equity: 4.8%
Cash ($ mil.): 101
Current ratio: 1.05
Long-term debt ($ mil.): 1,313
No. of shares (mil.): 66
Dividends
  Yield: 5.3%
  Payout: 143.4%
Market value ($ mil.): 950

ASHLAND INC.

Ashland, a distributor of chemicals, plastics, and fiber reinforcements, also paves roads and produces Valvoline motor oil. The Covington, Kentucky-based company operates through four subsidiaries. Ashland Distribution (about 35% of sales) buys chemicals and plastics in bulk, then blends and repackages them for distribution. Ashland's APAC subsidiary (about 30% of sales) is a leading US supplier of asphalt and highway materials. It also installs structural foundations and paves streets, primarily in the southern and midwestern US. Ashland Specialty Chemicals supplies chemicals for use in adhesives, composites, plastics, paint, and paper. Ashland's Valvoline unit operates a chain of oil-change centers and markets Valvoline motor oil and Zerex antifreeze.

The company is involved in petroleum refining through a joint venture with Marathon Oil. Marathon Ashland Petroleum (MAP) has a refinery and distribution network and retail gas stations, and it is a leading asphalt producer in the US.

Ashland has been feeding funding from its energy businesses into its other divisions, which have benefited from brand recognition and a focus on lucrative transportation and construction markets. Ashland had a record year in 2001; to stay on track in a slowing economy, the company has closed nine of Ashland Distribution's facilities.

Ashland was recently jolted by the resignation of chairman and CEO Paul Chellgren; Chellgren resigned because he violated a company policy prohiting personal relationships.

HISTORY

After moving to Kentucky in 1917, Fred Miles formed the Swiss Oil Company. In 1924 Swiss Oil bought a refinery in Catlettsburg, a rough town near sedate Ashland, and created a unit called Ashland Refining. Miles battled Swiss Oil directors for control, lost, and resigned in 1927.

Swiss Oil bought Tri-State Refining in 1930 and Cumberland Pipeline's eastern Kentucky pipe network in 1931. Swiss Oil changed its name to Ashland Oil and Refining in 1936. After WWII it bought small independent oil firms, acquiring the Valvoline name in 1950 by buying Freedom-Valvoline.

The firm formed Ashland Chemical in 1967 after buying Anderson-Prichard Oil (1958), United Carbon (1963), and ADM Chemical (1967). Ashland Chemical changed its name to Ashland Oil. It added the SuperAmerica convenience store chain (1970) and started exploring for oil in Nigeria after OPEC nations raised oil prices.

Scandal hit in 1975, the year Ashland Coal was formed. CEO Orin Atkins admitted to ordering Ashland executives to make illegal contributions to the 1972 Nixon presidential campaign. Atkins was deposed in 1981 after the company made questionable payments to highly placed "consultants" with connections to oil-rich Middle Eastern governments. In 1988 Atkins was arrested for trying to fence purloined documents regarding litigation between Ashland and the National Iranian Oil Company (NIOC). Ashland, which launched the federal investigation that led to Atkins' arrest, settled with NIOC in 1989. Atkins pleaded guilty and received probation.

Ashland went on a shopping spree in the 1990s. The company bought Permian (crude oil gathering and marketing) in 1991 and merged it into Scurlock Oil. In 1992 Ashland Chemical bought most of Unocal's chemical distribution business, and two years later it bought two companies that produce chemicals for the semiconductor industry. Also in 1994 Ashland made a promising oil discovery in Nigeria.

The company, by then named Ashland Inc., spent $368 million on 14 acquisitions to expand its energy and chemical divisions in 1995. It received a $75 million settlement with Columbia Gas System (now Columbia Energy Group) for abrogated natural gas contracts resulting from Columbia's bankruptcy.

In 1996 president Paul Chellgren became CEO and, with the company under shareholder fire, began a major reorganization. The next year Arch Mineral and Ashland Coal combined to form Arch Coal, with Ashland owning 58%. Also that year Ashland made more than a dozen acquisitions to bolster its chemical and construction businesses. Its exploration unit, renamed Blazer Energy, was sold to Norway's Statoil for $566 million.

Ashland joined USX-Marathon (now Marathon Oil) in 1998 to create Marathon Ashland Petroleum. It bought 20 companies, including Eagle One Industries, a maker of car-care products, and Masters-Jackson, a group of highway construction companies. In 1999 Ashland bought Denmark-based Superfos, then turned around and sold all but its road-construction operations. The next year Ashland reduced its holdings in Arch Coal from 58% to 12%; it sold the remainder in early 2001. To keep costs in line, the company closed nine Ashland Distribution facilities over the course of 2001.

In 2002 Chellgren announced he would retire after violating a company policy prohibiting romantic office relationships. James O'Brien was named as his successor.

OFFICERS

Chairman and CEO: James J. O'Brien Jr., $615,734 pay (prior to promotion)
SVP and CFO: J. Marvin Quin, age 54, $979,188 pay
SVP and Group Operating Officer, APAC, Inc. and The Valvoline Company: David J. D'Antoni, age 57, $772,545 pay
SVP; President, APAC: Charles F. Potts, age 56
VP; President, Ashland Distribution Company: Frank L. Waters
VP; President, Ashland Specialty Chemical: James A. Duquin, age 54
VP; President, The Valvoline Company: Samuel J. Mitchell Jr., age 40
VP and CIO: Roger B. Craycraft
Auditors: Ernst & Young LLP

LOCATIONS

HQ: 50 E. RiverCenter Blvd., Covington, KY 41012
Phone: 859-815-3333 **Fax:** 859-815-5053
Web: www.ashland.com

PRODUCTS/OPERATIONS

2001 Sales

	$ mil.	% of total
Ashland Distribution	2,849	36
APAC	2,624	34
Ashland Specialty Chemical	1,248	16
Valvoline	1,092	14
Adjustments	(94)	—
Total	**7,719**	**100**

Selected Subsidiaries

APAC, Inc. (construction, including bridges and highways; aggregates, asphalt, and ready-mix concrete)
Ashland Distribution (North American distribution of chemicals, plastics, solvents, fiber reinforcements, and fine ingredients; European distribution of plastics)
Ashland Specialty Chemical (chemicals, petrochemicals, and resins; related services)
Marathon Ashland Petroleum LLC (38%, crude oil refining and marketing, with Marathon Oil)
The Valvoline Co. (motor oil, antifreeze, filters, rust preventatives, automotive coolants, and other automotive products; Valvoline Instant Oil Change car service outlets)

COMPETITORS

BASF AG	Honeywell	PDVSA
Bayer AG	Specialty	Pennzoil-Quaker
ChevronTexaco	Materials	State
DuPont	Hydrite	Peter Kiewit
Exxon Mobil	Ideal Chemical	Sons'
Fluor	Jacobs	Premcor
GE Plastics	Engineering	Royal
Granite	J. F. Shea	Dutch/Shell
Construction	K.A. Steel	Group
Halliburton	Chemicals	Seegott
Hanson Building	Lafarge SA	Shell Chemicals
Materials	Lyondell	Sunoco
America	Chemical	TOTAL FINA
Harcros	Meadow Valley	ELF
Chemicals	Old World	Valero Energy
HELM U.S.	Industries	Vulcan Materials
Holcim	Parsons	Williams
Honeywell	PCL	Companies
International	Construction	

HISTORICAL FINANCIALS & EMPLOYEES

NYSE: ASH FYE: September 30	Annual Growth	9/92	9/93	9/94	9/95	9/96	9/97	9/98	9/99	9/00	9/01
Sales ($ mil.)	(2.3%)	9,552	9,554	9,457	11,179	12,145	13,208	6,534	6,801	7,961	7,719
Net income ($ mil.)	—	(336)	142	197	24	211	279	203	290	70	417
Income as % of sales	—	—	1.5%	2.1%	0.2%	1.7%	2.1%	3.1%	4.3%	0.9%	5.4%
Earnings per share ($)	—	(5.75)	2.20	2.79	0.08	2.96	3.64	2.63	3.89	0.98	5.93
Stock price – FY high ($)	—	34.00	34.38	44.50	39.88	44.13	54.94	57.94	52.50	37.19	44.25
Stock price – FY low ($)	—	22.50	23.63	31.00	31.25	30.38	39.25	44.13	33.63	28.63	30.63
Stock price – FY close ($)	5.0%	24.88	33.88	35.38	33.38	39.75	54.38	46.25	33.63	33.69	38.55
P/E – high	—	—	15	15	499	15	14	22	13	36	7
P/E – low	—	—	10	11	391	10	10	16	9	28	5
Dividends per share ($)	1.1%	1.00	1.00	1.00	1.10	1.10	1.10	1.10	1.10	1.10	1.10
Book value per share ($)	6.6%	18.12	24.24	26.15	25.86	28.34	26.99	28.12	30.56	28.07	32.26
Employees	(3.2%)	33,700	31,800	31,600	32,800	36,100	37,200	21,200	23,000	25,800	25,100

STOCK PRICE HISTORY

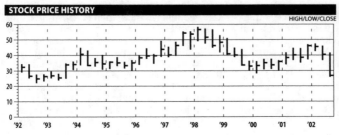

HIGH/LOW/CLOSE

2001 FISCAL YEAR-END

Debt ratio: 44.5%
Return on equity: 19.9%
Cash ($ mil.): 236
Current ratio: 1.48
Long-term debt ($ mil.): 1,786
No. of shares (mil.): 69
Dividends
 Yield: 2.9%
 Payout: 18.5%
Market value ($ mil.): 2,660

AT&T CORP.

Ma Bell is breaking up — again. New York City-based telecom giant AT&T is selling its cable operations and turning its remaining businesses — consumer services and business services — into separately traded units.

AT&T has announced plans to issue a tracking stock for its consumer services unit, still the #1 long-distance provider in the US, although competition has driven down rates. The consumer unit includes AT&T's dial-up Internet access service, WorldNet, and the company plans to introduce consumer DSL service, which it would use to expand its local phone offerings. The company's business services unit, providing a comprehensive array of voice and data services, is AT&T's top revenue generator.

AT&T's cable business — which rival Comcast has agreed to buy — had been a key element of AT&T's growth strategy, and the acquisitions of TCI and MediaOne made the company the #1 US cable operator, ahead of AOL Time Warner. AT&T Broadband is upgrading its cable systems to offer local telephone service, digital video, and high-speed Internet access.

But progress toward offering local phone service over cable has been slower than AT&T had hoped, and the decline in long-distance revenues is slowing the company's overall growth. By splitting itself into separately traded units, AT&T hopes to give investors a chance to value the company's businesses individually. In 2001 AT&T completed its spinoff of AT&T Wireless, the #3 mobile phone operator in the US behind Verizon Wireless and Cingular Wireless. The wireless unit already had its own tracking stock.

HISTORY

Alexander Graham Bell spoke the first words into a telephone in 1876. Bell's backers — fathers of deaf students he was tutoring — founded Bell Telephone (1877) and New England Telephone (1878), combined into National Bell Telephone in 1879.

After much litigation, National Bell barred rival Western Union, which had filed a patent hours after Bell, from the phone business in 1879. National Bell also wrested control of electrical equipment manufacturer Western Electric from Western Union in 1882. Bell was incorporated in 1885 as a subsidiary of American Bell Telephone.

Patents expired in the 1890s, and carriers raced into the market. Bell changed its name to American Telephone and Telegraph (AT&T) and became the parent of the Bell System in 1899.

J. P. Morgan gained control in 1907, and AT&T won Western Union in 1909. Facing antitrust action, AT&T sold it in 1913 and agreed not to buy phone companies without approval, beginning its 70-year run as a monopoly. Bell Labs, the heralded research division, was formed in 1925.

In 1949 the government tried to force AT&T to sell Western Electric. A 1956 settlement allowed AT&T to keep its prize but restricted it to phones. The FCC stripped AT&T of its phone equipment monopoly (1968) and allowed rivals, led by MCI (now WorldCom), to use its network (1969). Finally a 1974 antitrust suit led to AT&T's 1984 breakup. Seven Baby Bells took over local service, and AT&T was left with long distance and telecom equipment businesses.

AT&T made the ill-advised buy of computer maker NCR in 1991. In 1994 the carrier formally became AT&T Corp. and bought McCaw Cellular, then the #1 US cell phone operator. After the Telecommunications Act passed in 1996, AT&T shed noncore businesses NCR and Lucent (telecom equipment and Bell Labs) and began offering PCS and Internet access services.

The first outsider to become AT&T's CEO, Hughes Electronics and IBM veteran Michael Armstrong came on in 1997 and envisioned the firm as a one-stop telecom provider. He began a series of acquisitions, including local carrier Teleport Communications (1998) and portions of IBM's global data network (1999).

But cable TV, which offered a connection to the home to rival that of the Baby Bells, became the centerpiece of Armstrong's strategy. In 1999 AT&T bought cable giant TCI (now AT&T Broadband) and gained Liberty Media (TV programming) and an interest, later expanded, in cable Internet company At Home (which became Excite@Home).

AT&T and BT formed the Concert joint venture to provide telecom services for multinationals in 2000 (the two dismantled the venture in 2002). That year AT&T raised a US-record $10.6 billion in an IPO of a tracking stock tied to its wireless unit and later announced plans to divide itself into four separately traded units — business services, consumer services, cable, and wireless — by 2002. With profits and the company's share price slumping, AT&T in 2000 said it would reduce the dividend paid to shareholders, for the first time in company history. In 2001 AT&T completed the spinoff of its wireless unit.

Also in 2001 Comcast made an unsolicited offer to buy AT&T's cable operations for $44.5 billion in stock and $13.5 billion in assumed debt. AT&T's board rejected the offer, but at the same time delayed plans to issue a tracking stock for the cable unit and suggested it might entertain another bid. In December 2001, after it had heard offers from AOL Time Warner and Cox, AT&T agreed to sell AT&T Broadband to Comcast for $47 billion in stock and $25 billion in assumed debt. Also that year AT&T spun off Liberty Media. AT&T in 2002 launched China's first foreign telecom venture when it teamed up with China Telecom and introduced Shanghai Symphony Telecom.

OFFICERS

Chairman and CEO: C. Michael Armstrong, age 63, $4,014,000 pay
Vice Chairman: Charles H. Noski, age 49, $1,487,500 pay
President and Director: David W. Dorman, age 47, $1,770,000 pay
SEVP and CFO: Thomas W. Horton, age 40
EVP; President, AT&T Network Services: Frank Ianna, age 52, $1,275,000 pay
EVP Corporate Strategy and Business Development: John C. Petrillo, age 53
EVP Human Resources: Mirian M. Graddick-Weir, age 47
EVP Law and Governmental Affairs and General Counsel: James W. Cicconi, age 49
President and CEO, AT&T Broadband: William T. Schleyer
President, Southern Region: Ray M. Robinson, age 54
EVP; President and CEO, AT&T Consumer: Betsy J. Bernard, age 46, $1,028,102 pay
Auditors: PricewaterhouseCoopers LLP

LOCATIONS

HQ: 295 N. Maple Ave., Basking Ridge, NJ 07920
Phone: 908-221-2000   **Fax:** 908-221-2528
Web: www.att.com

2001 Sales

	$ mil.	% of total
Business services	28,024	53
Consumer services	15,079	28
Broadband services	9,799	19
Corporate & other	(352)	—
Total	**52,550**	**100**

Selected Services
Asynchronous transfer mode (ATM) and Internet protocol (IP) technology
Cable Internet access
Dial-up Internet access (AT&T WorldNet)
Digital cable TV
Domestic interstate and intrastate long-distance
Electronic data interchanges
Integrated services digital network (ISDN) technology
International long-distance
Local, long-distance, and toll-free voice transmission
Network management

COMPETITORS

Adelphia Communications	Covad Communications	Level 3 Communications
ALLTEL	Group	McLeodUSA
AOL Time Warner	Cox Communications	Microsoft
BCE	Deutsche Telekom	NTT
BellSouth	DIRECTV	Qwest
Broadwing	EarthLink	SBC Communications
Cable and Wireless	Excel Communications	Sprint
Charter Communications	France Telecom	Teleglobe
Comcast	Global Crossing	Telmex
		TELUS
		Verizon
		WorldCom

HISTORICAL FINANCIALS & EMPLOYEES

NYSE: T FYE: December 31	Annual Growth	12/92	12/93	12/94	12/95	12/96	12/97	12/98	12/99	12/00	12/01
Sales ($ mil.)	(2.3%)	64,904	67,156	75,094	79,609	52,184	51,319	53,223	62,391	65,981	52,550
Net income ($ mil.)	8.2%	3,807	(3,794)	4,710	139	5,908	4,638	6,398	3,428	4,669	7,715
Income as % of sales	—	5.9%	—	6.3%	0.2%	11.3%	9.0%	12.0%	5.5%	7.1%	14.7%
Earnings per share ($)	3.0%	1.91	(1.87)	2.01	0.06	2.40	1.90	2.38	1.74	0.88	2.50
Stock price – FY high ($)	—	25.51	31.22	27.44	32.90	33.08	42.69	52.69	64.12	60.81	25.81
Stock price – FY low ($)	—	17.59	24.13	22.69	22.87	22.18	20.51	32.27	41.50	16.50	14.75
Stock price – FY close ($)	(3.3%)	24.49	25.21	24.13	31.10	28.93	40.90	50.53	50.81	17.25	18.14
P/E – high	—	13	—	14	658	14	23	27	36	68	—
P/E – low	—	9	—	11	457	9	11	16	23	19	—
Dividends per share ($)	(17.8%)	0.88	0.88	0.88	0.88	0.88	0.88	0.88	0.88	0.88	0.15
Book value per share ($)	5.0%	9.42	6.83	7.62	7.22	8.34	9.30	9.71	24.69	27.45	14.59
Employees	(10.3%)	312,700	308,700	304,500	300,000	130,000	128,000	107,800	148,000	166,000	117,800

STOCK PRICE HISTORY
HIGH/LOW/CLOSE

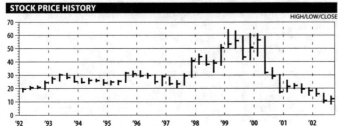

2001 FISCAL YEAR-END
Debt ratio: 44.0%
Return on equity: 10.0%
Cash ($ mil.): 10,592
Current ratio: 0.89
Long-term debt ($ mil.): 40,527
No. of shares (mil.): 3,542
Dividends
 Yield: 0.8%
 Payout: 6.0%
Market value ($ mil.): 64,259

AUTOMATIC DATA PROCESSING, INC.

Every day is payday at Automatic Data Processing (ADP). With more than 500,000 accounts, ADP is the #1 payroll services provider in the world. The Roseland, New Jersey-based company's payroll and tax processing operations generate nearly 60% of sales. Its brokerage services business provides securities transaction processing and support for financial services providers and corporations worldwide, and its dealer services business offers inventory and other computing and data services to more than 16,000 auto and truck dealers. Other offerings include accounting, auto collision estimates for insurers, and employment background checks.

Effective management and a focused strategy have steered ADP to double-digit per-share earnings growth for 40 years running, resulting in strong cash flow. The data processing giant's employer services segment has proven somewhat resilient in economic hard times as clients outsource more human resource functions.

ADP is expanding internationally and extending its services through acquisitions (it has purchased about two dozen established providers around the globe since 1998). The company is also boosting its small business services and its Web-based offerings.

HISTORY

In 1949, 22-year-old Henry Taub started Automatic Payrolls, a manual payroll preparation service in Paterson, New Jersey. Taub's eight accounts created gross revenue of around $2,000 that year. In 1952 his brother Joe joined the company, and a childhood friend, Frank Lautenberg, took a pay cut to become its first salesman.

Automatic Payrolls grew steadily during the 1950s. In 1961 the company went public and changed its name to Automatic Data Processing (ADP). The next year it offered back-office services to brokerage houses and bought its first computer. The company's sales reached $1 million in 1962.

During the 1970s ADP bought more than 30 companies in Brazil, the UK, and the US — all involved in data and payroll processing or financial services. Its stock began trading on the NYSE in 1970. By 1971 revenue had reached $50 million. Lautenberg became CEO in 1975.

ADP bought more than 25 businesses during the 1980s in Canada, Germany, and the US. Its purchases of stock information provider GTE Telenet (1983) and Bunker Ramo's information system business (1986) brought the company 45,000 stock quote terminals in brokerages such as E.F. Hutton, Dean Witter, and Prudential-Bache. When Lautenberg resigned to become one of New Jersey's US senators in 1983, Josh Weston, who had joined the company as a VP in 1970, replaced him.

By 1985 ADP sales had climbed to $1 billion. That year Taub retired. The company installed 15,000 computer workstations at brokerages in 1986; it began installing more than 38,000 new integrated workstations at Merrill Lynch and Shearson Lehman three years later. ADP shed units, including its Canadian stock quote and Brazilian businesses, in 1989 and 1990.

After being deterred from major acquisitions by the inflated prices of the late 1980s, the company bought BankAmerica's 17,000-client Business Services division (1992) and Industry Software's back-office and international equities business (1993).

In 1994 the company purchased Peachtree Software (accounting and payroll software for small companies), National Bio Systems (medical bill auditing), and V-Crest (auto dealership management systems). ADP acquired chief rival AutoInfo and its network of 3,000 salvage yards the next year, and further expanded into Western Europe with its purchase of Paris-based computing services firm GSI.

The buying binge continued in 1996 with acquisitions including Global Proxy Services (proxy processing services), Health Benefits America (benefits management), and Merrin Financial (automated securities trade order management). Former Deloitte & Touche partner Arthur Weinbach, an ADP executive since 1980, was named CEO that year. ADP was ordered in an antitrust settlement in 1997 to help recreate AutoInfo as a viable competitor to its salvage yard business.

Among its dozen acquisitions in 1998 was Swiss Reinsurance's European collision estimates business. Weston retired in 1998; Weinbach was named chairman. The company also filed to spin off Peachtree to the public, but in early 1999 it sold the unit to UK-based software firm The Sage Group. The buying spree continued that year; ADP's largest purchase was The Vincam Group, an employment management contractor, for about $295 million.

In 2000 the company acquired Cunningham Graphics, a provider of printing services to the financial services industry, and Traver Technologies, which offers consulting and training services to automobile dealers in the US. The following year it acquired Avert, a provider of employment screening services, and the output services business of IBM Global Services, specializing in printing and distributing communications for the financial services industry.

OFFICERS

Chairman and CEO: Arthur F. Weinbach, age 58, $1,171,250 pay
President, COO, and Director: Gary C. Butler, age 55, $906,500 pay
SVP: Eugene A. Hall, age 45, $595,021 pay
Group President, Brokerage Service: Richard J. Daly, age 48, $530,969 pay
Group President: Russell P. Fradin, age 46, $698,250 pay
Group President: John P. Hogan, age 53, $531,769 pay
Group President: S. Michael Martone, age 53
President, Employer Services International: John D. Barfitt, age 48
VP Finance: Richard A. Douville, age 46
VP Finance: Karen E. Dykstra, age 42
VP Human Resources: Richard C. Berke, age 56
VP, Secretary, and General Counsel: James B. Benson, age 56
Auditors: Deloitte & Touche LLP

LOCATIONS

HQ: 1 ADP Blvd., Roseland, NJ 07068
Phone: 973-974-5000   **Fax:** 973-974-5495
Web: www.adp.com

Automatic Data Processing has more than 45 processing centers worldwide.

2001 Sales

	$ mil.	% of total
US	5,991	85
Europe	641	9
Canada	279	4
Other regions	107	2
Total	**7,018**	**100**

PRODUCTS/OPERATIONS

2001 Sales

	$ mil.	% of total
Employer services	4,018	57
Brokerage services	1,756	25
Dealer services	691	10
Other	553	8
Total	**7,018**	**100**

Selected Services

Benefits administration and outsourcing
Business management
Collision repair estimating
Employee productivity training
Employment screening and background checks
Hardware maintenance
Human resource record keeping and reporting
Manufacturer and dealer data communications networks
Parts identification, location, and pricing
Payroll processing
Securities transaction processing
Software licensing and support
Tax filing
Unemployment compensation management
Vehicle replacement valuation
Vote tabulation

COMPETITORS

Administaff
Affiliated Computer
BISYS
Century Business Services, Inc.
Ceridian
Concord EFS
DST
EPIX
Fiserv
Gevity HR
Intuit
Kelly Services
Paychex
Payroll 1
ProBusiness Services
Spherion
TEAM America
TriNet

HISTORICAL FINANCIALS & EMPLOYEES

NYSE: ADP FYE: June 30	Annual Growth	6/92	6/93	6/94	6/95	6/96	6/97	6/98	6/99	6/00	6/01
Sales ($ mil.)	15.4%	1,941	2,223	2,469	2,894	3,567	4,112	4,798	5,540	6,288	7,018
Net income ($ mil.)	15.3%	256	294	329	395	455	514	605	697	841	925
Income as % of sales	—	13.2%	13.2%	13.3%	13.6%	12.7%	12.5%	12.6%	12.6%	13.4%	13.2%
Earnings per share ($)	13.5%	0.46	0.52	0.57	0.68	0.77	0.86	0.99	1.10	1.31	1.44
Stock price - FY high ($)	—	12.25	14.03	14.22	16.50	21.69	25.06	36.44	46.88	57.94	69.94
Stock price - FY low ($)	—	7.56	9.69	11.75	12.69	15.47	17.81	22.19	31.75	37.38	48.47
Stock price - FY close ($)	18.6%	10.69	12.00	13.28	15.72	19.31	23.50	36.44	44.00	53.56	49.70
P/E - high	—	27	27	24	24	27	28	36	41	43	48
P/E - low	—	16	19	20	18	20	20	22	28	28	33
Dividends per share ($)	16.0%	0.10	0.12	0.13	0.15	0.19	0.22	0.25	0.29	0.33	0.38
Book value per share ($)	14.0%	2.31	2.65	3.01	3.64	4.02	4.54	5.64	6.43	7.29	7.53
Employees	8.0%	20,500	21,000	22,000	25,000	29,000	30,000	34,000	37,000	40,000	41,000

STOCK PRICE HISTORY

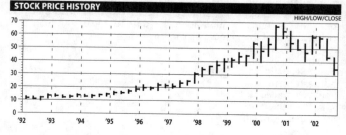

HIGH/LOW/CLOSE

2001 FISCAL YEAR-END

Debt ratio: 2.3%
Return on equity: 19.9%
Cash ($ mil.): 1,275
Current ratio: 2.31
Long-term debt ($ mil.): 110
No. of shares (mil.): 624
Dividends
  Yield: 0.8%
  Payout: 26.4%
Market value ($ mil.): 31,010

AUTONATION, INC.

AutoNation wants to instill patriotic fervor in the fickle car-buying public. The Fort Lauderdale, Florida-based company has used rapid-fire acquisitions to become the nation's #1 car dealer (before Sonic Automotive). It is primarily concerned with new-car sales after abandoning its used-car superstore concept and car-rental and auto-loan businesses.

Formerly known as Republic Industries, the firm, with about 280 new-car dealerships in 17 states, has been a driving force in the consolidation of the US car-sales business. It clusters dealerships within markets so that they can share inventory, cross-sell to customers, and reduce marketing costs — basically cutting and combining costs in an attempt to become the auto industry's Wal-Mart.

AutoNation continues to make acquisitions — with plans to buy seven dealerships in 2002 — while throwing its considerable weight (and national advertising) behind its AutoNation.com Web site, which lists more than 100,000 cars. Regionally, the company will develop brand loyalty by uniting its bricks-and-mortar operations under local brand names as it has done with the John Elway AutoNation group in Denver and the AutoWay dealerships in Tampa Bay.

ESL Investments (chairman Edward Lampert and president William Crowley are AutoNation directors) owns about 24% of the company.

HISTORY

AutoNation started in 1980 as Republic Resources, which brokered petroleum leases, did exploration and production, and blended lubricants. In 1989, after oil prices crashed and a stockholder group tried to force Republic into liquidation, Browning-Ferris Industries (BFI) founder Thomas Fatjo gained control of the company and refocused it on a field he knew well — solid waste. He renamed the firm Republic Waste.

Michael DeGroote, founder of BFI rival Laidlaw, bought into Republic in 1990. (Fatjo left the next year.) DeGroote's investment funded more acquisitions. Republic moved into hazardous waste in 1992, just before the industry nosedived due to stringent new environmental rules. In 1994 Republic spun off its hazardous-waste operations as Republic Environmental Systems, and Republic's stock began rising immediately.

That attracted the attention of Wayne Huizenga, who had founded Waste Management and Blockbuster Video. To him, Republic was not merely a midsized solid-waste firm. No, Huizenga saw Republic as a publicly traded vehicle that could allow him to tap into the stock market to fund his latest project: an integrated, nationwide auto dealer — a first for the highly fragmented and localized industry.

In 1995 Republic bought Hudson Management, a trash business owned by Huizenga's brother-in-law, and Huizenga bought a large interest in Republic. As a result, Huizenga took control of Republic's board. The firm became Republic Industries, and DeGroote stepped back from active management.

Huizenga's investment helped Republic acquire more waste businesses, and his name brought a flood of new investors. The firm diversified with electronic security acquisitions, but growth in this field faltered with a failed bid to buy market leader ADT in 1996. (Republic sold its security division to Ameritech in 1997.)

By 1996 Huizenga's still-separate auto concept, AutoNation, was operational, with 55 automobile franchises and seven used-car stores. Republic bought Alamo Rent A Car and National Car Rental System, and in 1997 AutoNation was bought by Republic. The combined company continued buying dealerships and car rental firms at a sizzling rate.

Republic spun off its solid-waste operations to the public in 1998 as Republic Services. That year Republic bought or agreed to buy 181 new-car franchises, opened nine AutoNation USA dealerships, and opened 62 CarTemps USA insurance-replacement locations.

Republic became AutoNation in 1999 and announced plans to spin off its rental division. In September 1999 Mike Jackson, the former president and CEO of Mercedes-Benz USA, was named CEO of AutoNation. In December the company closed most of its poorly performing used-car superstores and laid off about 1,800 employees.

In May 2000 AutoNation acquired AutoVantage, an online car-buying service linking over 900 dealerships, and inked a deal to be America Online's (now AOL Time Warner) exclusive auto retailer. Later the company completed its spinoff of ANC Rental (Alamo, National, and CarTemps, with more than 3,400 rental car locations worldwide), making AutoNation a pure-play auto retailer. Due to guarantees related to the spinoff, AutoNation took a $20 million charge after ANC Rental filed for Chapter 11 bankruptcy protection in 2001. Also that year AutoNation closed its auto-loan unit to further focus on car sales.

OFFICERS

Chairman: H. Wayne Huizenga, age 64, $500,000 pay
Vice Chairman: Harris W. Hudson, age 59
CEO and Director: Michael J. Jackson, age 53, $1,893,138 pay
President and COO: Michael E. Maroone, age 48, $1,255,262 pay
SVP and CFO: Craig T. Monaghan, age 45, $701,541 pay
SVP, Corporate Development: Thomas S. Butler
SVP, Corporate Real Estate Services: Robert F. Dwors
SVP, Finance: Patricia A. McKay, age 44, $490,189 pay
SVP, Secretary, and General Counsel: Jonathan P. Ferrando, age 36
SVP, Human Resources: Peter C. Smith Jr.
SVP, Information Technology: Keith Holcomb
SVP, Industry Relations and New Vehicle: James D. Evans Jr.
SVP, Brand Development: John R. Drury
SVP, Operations and CIO: Allan Stejskal, age 43
SVP; President, AutoNation Financial Services: Kevin P. Westfall, age 45
VP, Corporate Communications: Marc Cannon
VP, eCommerce: Gary Marcotte
VP, Investor Relations: John M. Zimmerman
VP, IT: Joyce Vonada
VP, Used Vehicles: Adam Simms, age 39
Auditors: Deloitte & Touche LLP

LOCATIONS

HQ: 110 SE 6th St., Fort Lauderdale, FL 33301
Phone: 954-769-6000   **Fax:** 954-769-6537
Web: corp.autonation.com

AutoNation has new-car dealerships in 17 states.

PRODUCTS/OPERATIONS

2001 Sales

	$ mil.	% of total
New vehicles	12,000	60
Used vehicles	3,883	20
Parts and service	2,405	12
Finance and insurance	489	2
Other	1,212	6
Total	**19,989**	**100**

Primary Operations
AutoNation.com (Internet sales)
Franchised vehicle dealerships

COMPETITORS

Asbury Automotive	Hendrick Automotive
Avis Europe	Hertz
Bill Heard	Holman Enterprises
Brown Automotive	JM Family Enterprises
Budget Group	Morse Operations
Burt Automotive	Penske Automotive
CarMax	Planet Automotive Group
Cendant	Sixt
Dollar Thrifty Automotive Group	Sonic Automotive
Enterprise Rent-A-Car	United Auto Group
Group 1 Automotive	VT

HISTORICAL FINANCIALS & EMPLOYEES

NYSE: AN FYE: December 31	Annual Growth	12/92	12/93	12/94	12/95	12/96	12/97	12/98	12/99	12/00	12/01
Sales ($ mil.)	78.3%	110	103	49	260	2,366	10,306	16,118	20,112	20,610	19,989
Net income ($ mil.)	—	(14)	(19)	11	23	(60)	440	500	283	330	232
Income as % of sales	—	—	—	23.4%	8.8%	—	4.3%	3.1%	1.4%	1.6%	1.2%
Earnings per share ($)	—	(0.27)	0.07	0.26	0.07	(0.05)	1.02	1.06	0.66	0.91	0.69
Stock price - FY high ($)	—	6.81	2.75	2.06	18.06	34.63	44.38	30.00	18.38	10.75	13.07
Stock price - FY low ($)	—	2.25	1.38	1.25	1.50	13.19	19.00	10.00	8.50	4.63	4.94
Stock price - FY close ($)	18.7%	2.63	1.69	2.00	18.06	31.19	23.31	14.88	9.25	6.00	12.33
P/E - high	—	—	39	8	226	—	41	27	—	12	19
P/E - low	—	—	20	5	19	—	17	9	—	5	7
Dividends per share ($)	—	0.00	0.00	0.00	0.00	0.00	0.00	0.00	0.00	0.00	0.00
Book value per share ($)	23.5%	1.78	1.42	1.62	2.87	4.93	8.05	11.84	12.26	11.04	11.90
Employees	50.5%	756	683	398	4,090	30,300	56,000	42,000	33,000	31,000	30,000

STOCK PRICE HISTORY

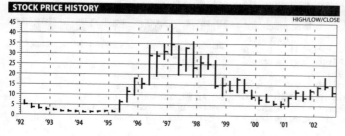

2001 FISCAL YEAR-END

Debt ratio: 14.5%
Return on equity: 6.1%
Cash ($ mil.): 128
Current ratio: 1.22
Long-term debt ($ mil.): 647
No. of shares (mil.): 322
Dividends
 Yield: —
 Payout: —
Market value ($ mil.): 3,967

AUTOZONE, INC.

Imagine that you are in your garage making some weekend car repairs. The wheel cylinders are leaking...the brake shoe adjuster nut is rusted solid . . . you're about to enter . . . the AutoZone. The Memphis-based retailer is the largest auto parts chain in the US. AutoZone operates more than 3,000 stores in 40-plus states and Washington, DC, and more than 20 stores in Mexico. It caters primarily to do-it-yourself consumers, but more than half of its stores also serve professional auto repair shops.

AutoZone stores sell hard parts (alternators, engines, batteries), maintenance items (oil, antifreeze), accessories (car stereos, floor mats), and other merchandise. The stores offer items under brand names as well as under AutoZone private labels such as Duralast and Deutsch. The stores also offer diagnostic testing for starters, alternators, and batteries. They do not sell tires or perform general auto repairs. AutoZone's ALLDATA unit sells automotive diagnostic and repair software and sells related information online. The company has sold its TruckPro subsidiary (heavy-duty truck parts).

AutoZone has grown quickly through a series of acquisitions over the past several years but now is focused on internal growth and development. The company opens around 100 to 200 outlets per year and is adding stores in Mexico, where cars are older — and in need of more repairs — than in the US.

Investor Edward Lampert and his affiliates own 29% of AutoZone.

HISTORY

Joseph "Pitt" Hyde took over the family grocery wholesale business, Malone & Hyde (established 1907) in 1968. He expanded into specialty retailing, opening drugstores, sporting goods stores, and supermarkets, but his fortunes began to race on Independence Day 1979, when he opened his first Auto Shack auto parts store in Forrest City, Arkansas.

Using retailing behemoth Wal-Mart as a model, Hyde concentrated on smaller markets in the South and Southeast, emphasizing everyday low prices and centralized distribution operations. He stressed customer service to provide his do-it-yourself customers with expert advice on choosing parts. While a number of retailers have tried to copy Wal-Mart's successful model, Hyde had an inside track: Before starting Auto Shack he served on Wal-Mart's board for seven years.

Auto Shack had expanded into seven states by 1980, and by 1983 it had 129 stores in 10 states. The next year Malone & Hyde's senior management, with investment firm Kohlberg Kravis

Roberts (KKR), took the company private in an LBO. Auto Shack continued to expand, reaching 192 stores in 1984.

A year later Auto Shack introduced its Express Parts Service, the first service in the industry to offer a toll-free number and overnight delivery of parts. The following year it introduced another first: a limited lifetime warranty on its merchandise. Also in 1986 Auto Shack introduced its own Duralast line of auto products.

The company was spun off to Malone & Hyde's shareholders in 1987, and Malone & Hyde's other operations were sold. Auto Shack brought its electronic parts catalog online that year. The company changed its name to AutoZone in 1987, in part to settle a lawsuit with Radio Shack. By this time it had 390 stores in 15 states.

The company went public in 1991. By the end of that year, it had nearly 600 stores and five distribution centers. The company topped $1 billion in sales in 1992. The next year it opened new distribution centers in Illinois and Tennessee and closed its Memphis operation.

AutoZone began selling to commercial customers such as service stations and repair shops in 1996. It also acquired auto diagnostic software company ALLDATA. Hyde stepped down as CEO that year and as chairman in 1997 and was replaced by COO Johnston (John) Adams.

The company made several key purchases in 1998. It acquired Chief Auto Parts for $280 million, adding 560 stores (most in California) that were converted to AutoZones in 1999. It also purchased Adap and its 112 Auto Palace stores in the Northeast, heavy-duty truck parts distributor TruckPro, and (from Pep Boys) 100 Express stores. Also in 1998 AutoZone opened its first store in Mexico (Nuevo Laredo).

Hyde sold much of his stake by early 1999. Late that year AutoZone expanded its board of directors to 10 members, making room for longtime shareholder Edward Lampert.

In January 2001 Steve Odland, formerly COO at supermarket retailer Ahold USA, succeeded Adams as chairman and CEO. In December 2001 AutoZone sold its TruckPro subsidiary to an investor group led by Paratus Capital Management of Boston and New York.

OFFICERS

Chairman, President, and CEO: Steve Odland, age 43, $895,411 pay
SVP and CFO: Michael G. Archbold, age 41
SVP and CIO: Bruce G. Clark
SVP and President, TruckPro: Michael B. Baird
SVP Advertising: Anthony D. Rose Jr.
SVP Human Resources: Daisy L. Vanderlinde
SVP Marketing: Lisa R. Kranc

SVP Mexico ALLDATA and Store Development:
Robert D. Olsen
SVP, Secretary, and General Counsel:
Harry L. Goldsmith
SVP Store Operations: Michael E. Longo
SVP Supply Chain: William C. Rhodes III
VP and Controller: Tricia K. Greenberger
VP; General Manager, ALLDATA: Jeffery Lagges
VP Investor Relations and External Communications:
Emma J. Kauffman
VP Replenishment: Eric S. Gould
VP Stores: Mike T. Broderick
Auditors: Ernst & Young LLP

PRODUCTS/OPERATIONS

Selected Merchandise

Accessories	Maintenance Items
Car stereos	Antifreeze
Floor mats	Brake fluid
Lights	Engine additives
Mirrors	Oil
	Power steering fluid
Hard Parts	Transmission fluid
Alternators	Waxes
Batteries	Windshield wipers
Brake shoes and pads	
Carburetors	**Other**
Clutches	Air fresheners
Engines	Dent filler
Spark plugs	Hand cleaner
Starters	Paint
Struts	Repair manuals
Water pumps	Tools

Selected Brands

Albany	Duralast
ALLDATA	Ultra Spark
AutoZone	Valucraft
Deutsch	

COMPETITORS

Advance Auto Parts	Kmart
CARQUEST	O'Reilly Automotive
Costco Wholesale	Pep Boys
CSK Auto	Sears
Genuine Parts	Target
Goodyear	Wal-Mart

HISTORICAL FINANCIALS & EMPLOYEES

NYSE: AZO FYE: Last Saturday in August	Annual Growth	8/92	8/93	8/94	8/95	8/96	8/97	8/98	8/99	8/00	8/01
Sales ($ mil.)	19.1%	1,002	1,217	1,508	1,808	2,243	2,691	3,243	4,116	4,483	4,818
Net income ($ mil.)	12.0%	63	87	116	139	167	195	228	245	268	176
Income as % of sales	—	6.3%	7.1%	7.7%	7.7%	7.5%	7.2%	7.0%	5.9%	6.0%	3.6%
Earnings per share ($)	15.2%	0.43	0.59	0.78	0.93	1.11	1.28	1.48	1.63	2.00	1.54
Stock price - FY high ($)	—	21.00	27.56	30.75	27.63	37.63	30.75	38.00	37.31	32.63	49.20
Stock price - FY low ($)	—	9.59	14.13	21.63	21.63	23.38	19.50	23.75	20.50	21.00	21.00
Stock price - FY close ($)	13.7%	14.50	26.88	24.88	26.88	27.25	28.25	25.94	23.81	22.50	46.20
P/E - high	—	49	47	39	30	33	24	25	23	16	32
P/E - low	—	22	24	28	23	21	15	16	13	10	13
Dividends per share ($)	—	0.00	0.00	0.00	0.00	0.00	0.00	0.00	0.00	0.00	0.00
Book value per share ($)	16.4%	2.02	2.75	3.63	4.66	5.77	7.11	8.56	9.17	8.17	7.92
Employees	14.5%	13,200	15,700	17,400	20,200	26,800	28,700	38,500	40,500	43,000	44,600

STOCK PRICE HISTORY   HIGH/LOW/CLOSE

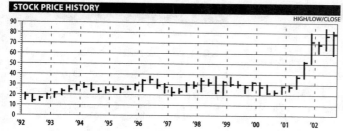

2001 FISCAL YEAR-END

Debt ratio: 58.6%
Return on equity: 18.9%
Cash ($ mil.): 7
Current ratio: 1.05
Long-term debt ($ mil.): 1,225
No. of shares (mil.): 109
Dividends
  Yield: —
  Payout: —
Market value ($ mil.): 5,055

AVERY DENNISON CORPORATION

Some people eschew labels, but Avery Dennison insists on them. The Pasadena, California-based company is, after all, a leading producer of adhesive labels used on everything from wine and shampoo bottles to cassette tapes and overnight mailers.

Under its Avery Dennison and Fasson brands, the company makes papers, films, and foils coated with adhesive and sold in rolls to printers. It also makes school and office products (Avery, Marks-A-Lot, HI-LITER), such as notebooks, three-ring binders, and markers, as well as Duracell battery-testing labels and the USPS's self-adhesive stamps. Pressure-sensitive adhesives and materials account for about 55% of sales.

Avery Dennison operates manufacturing facilities and sales offices around the world; it has been expanding into China.

HISTORY

Avery Dennison was created in 1990 by the merger of Avery International and Dennison Manufacturing. In 1935 Stanton Avery founded Kum-Kleen Products, which would become Avery International. After a fire destroyed the plant's equipment in 1938, Avery, who had renamed the company Avery Adhesives, improved the machinery used in making the labels.

During and after WWII, Avery Adhesives shifted toward the industrial market for self-adhesives. The company incorporated in 1946. At that time Avery Adhesives sold 80% of its production, consisting of industrial labels, to manufacturers that labeled their own products.

The company lost its patent rights for self-adhesive labels in 1952, transforming the firm and the entire industry. As a result, a new division was created — the Avery Paper Company (later renamed Fasson) — to produce and market self-adhesive base materials.

Avery Adhesives went public in 1961. Three years later it had four divisions: label products, base materials, Rotex (hand-operated embossing machines), and Metal-Cal (anodized and etched aluminum foil for nameplates). Renamed Avery International in 1976, the company closed some manufacturing facilities and cut 8% of its workforce in the late 1980s.

In 1990 Avery International merged with Dennison Manufacturing. Dennison was started in 1844 by the father-and-son team of Andrew and Aaron Dennison to produce jewelry boxes. By 1849 Aaron's younger brother, Eliphalet Whorf (E. W.), was running the business and expanding it into tags, labels, and tissue paper. Dennison was incorporated in 1878 with $150,000 in capital.

By 1911 Dennison sold tags, gummed labels, paper boxes, greeting cards, sealing wax, and tissue paper, and it had stores in Boston, Chicago, New York City, Philadelphia, St. Louis, and London. Henry Dennison, E. W.'s grandson, was president from 1917 to 1952.

From the 1960s to the 1980s, Dennison spent heavily on research and development and helped to develop such products as electronic printers and pregnancy test supplies. In the mid-1980s the firm reorganized its operations, selling seven businesses, closing four others, and focusing on stationery, systems, and packaging.

In addition to office products and product identification and control systems, the 1990 merger combined Dennison's office products operations in France (Doret and Cheval Ordex) with Avery International's sizable self-adhesive base materials business.

Avery Dennison sold its 50% interest in a Japanese label converting company, Toppan, in 1996, clearing the way to develop its own businesses in Asia. In 1997 an alliance with Taiwanese rival Four Pillars turned sour when Avery Dennison accused the company of stealing trade secrets. (Two executives at Four Pillars were convicted of espionage in 1999.)

President and COO Philip Neal was promoted to CEO in 1998. (He became chairman in 2000.) In 1999, adhering to its goal of global expansion, Avery Dennison formed office products joint ventures in Germany with Zweckform Buro-Produkte and in Japan with Hitachi Maxell. Record 1998 sales and earnings were dampened by the news of slowing growth, and in 1999 Avery Dennison closed five plants and began laying off workers. Later that year it bought Stimsonite, a maker of reflective highway safety products.

In early 2000 Avery Dennison began a $40 million expansion of its Chinese manufacturing operations while eliminating 1,500 jobs worldwide. The company agreed to jointly package instant imaging and labeling products with Polaroid. Several acquisitions in 2001 included CD Stomper (CD and DVD labels and software). Avery Dennison acquired Jackstadt, a German maker of pressure-sensitive adhesive materials, in 2002.

OFFICERS

Chairman and CEO: Philip M. Neal, age 61, $1,371,667 pay
President, COO, and Director: Dean A. Scarborough, age 46, $726,667 pay
EVP: Kim A. Caldwell, age 53, $676,839 pay
EVP, General Counsel, and Secretary: Robert G. van Schoonenberg, age 55, $602,867 pay
SVP, Corporate Strategy and Technology: Robert M. Malchione, age 44, $494,633 pay

SVP, Finance and CFO: Daniel R. O'Bryant, age 44, $476,833 pay
SVP, Human Resources: J. Terry Schuler
SVP, Worldwide Communications and Advertising: Diane B. Dixon, age 50
Auditors: PricewaterhouseCoopers LLP

LOCATIONS

HQ: 150 N. Orange Grove Blvd., Pasadena, CA 91103
Phone: 626-304-2000   **Fax:** 626-577-5264
Web: www.averydennison.com

Avery Dennison operates more than 200 manufacturing and sales facilities in some 40 countries; it sells its products in 89 countries.

2001 Sales

	$ mil.	% of total
US	2,319	60
Other countries	1,561	40
Adjustments	(77)	—
Total	**3,803**	**100**

PRODUCTS/OPERATIONS

2001 Sales

	$ mil.	% of total
Pressure-sensitive adhesives & materials	2,189	55
Consumer & converted products	1,785	45
Adjustments	(171)	—
Total	**3,803**	**100**

Selected Products

Pressure-Sensitive Adhesives and Materials
Base materials
  Film stock
  Paper
  Pressure-sensitive coated papers, films, and foils
  Proprietary film face stocks
Chemical products
Graphic products
Medical adhesive products
Specialty tape products
Transportation safety products

Consumer and Converted Products
Bar-coded tags
CD and DVD labels, software, and equipment
Computer software
Labels (file folders, data processing, shipping, address)
Markers and highlighters
Notebooks
Paper (laser, ink jet, carbon)
Presentation and organizing systems
Printer labels
Tagging and labeling machinery and data printing systems

COMPETITORS

3M	H.B. Fuller
Bemis	Moore Corporation
Brady	Nashua
Esselte	Newell Rubbermaid
Fleming Packaging	Paxar
Fortune Brands	Standard Register
Four Pillars Enterprise	Wallace Computer

HISTORICAL FINANCIALS & EMPLOYEES

NYSE: AVY FYE: Saturday nearest Dec. 31	Annual Growth	12/92	12/93	12/94	12/95	12/96	12/97	12/98	12/99	12/00	12/01
Sales ($ mil.)	4.2%	2,623	2,609	2,857	3,114	3,223	3,346	3,460	3,768	3,894	3,803
Net income ($ mil.)	13.1%	80	84	109	144	176	205	223	215	284	243
Income as % of sales	—	3.1%	3.2%	3.8%	4.6%	5.5%	6.1%	6.5%	5.7%	7.3%	6.4%
Earnings per share ($)	15.4%	0.68	0.74	1.00	1.32	1.63	1.93	2.15	2.13	2.84	2.47
Stock price - FY high ($)	—	14.56	15.75	18.00	25.06	36.50	45.75	62.06	73.00	78.50	60.50
Stock price - FY low ($)	—	11.63	12.56	12.56	16.56	23.75	33.38	39.44	39.38	41.13	43.25
Stock price - FY close ($)	16.4%	14.38	14.69	17.75	25.06	35.38	44.75	45.06	72.88	54.88	56.53
P/E - high	—	21	22	18	19	22	23	28	34	27	24
P/E - low	—	17	17	13	12	14	17	18	18	14	17
Dividends per share ($)	12.7%	0.42	0.46	0.50	0.56	0.62	0.72	0.87	0.99	1.11	1.23
Book value per share ($)	2.4%	6.82	6.40	6.81	7.69	8.03	8.18	8.33	8.20	8.49	8.46
Employees	0.5%	16,550	15,750	15,400	15,500	15,800	16,200	16,100	17,400	17,900	17,300

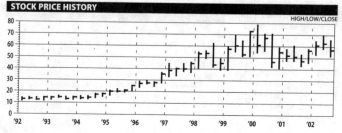

STOCK PRICE HISTORY
HIGH/LOW/CLOSE

2001 FISCAL YEAR-END
Debt ratio: 40.3%
Return on equity: 27.7%
Cash ($ mil.): 19
Current ratio: 1.03
Long-term debt ($ mil.): 627
No. of shares (mil.): 110
Dividends
  Yield: 2.2%
  Payout: 49.8%
Market value ($ mil.): 6,212

AVNET, INC.

Avnet is far above average at its business. Among US-based electronics distributors, Phoenix-based Avnet trails only archrival Arrow Electronics. (The two companies have been known on Wall Street for their ongoing rounds of dueling acquisitions.) Avnet's suppliers include more than 100 makers of electronics components and systems, whose products it distributes to more than 100,000 other manufacturers in more than 60 countries. About two-thirds of Avnet's sales are from its Electronics Marketing unit, which distributes semiconductors and other electronic components to industrial, commercial, and military customers. The company's Computer Marketing Group sells computer products and systems to resellers and end users. Its Avnet Applied Computing unit provides system-level components (such as motherboards) to computer makers.

Avnet has reorganized some of its units and streamlined operations in the face of a global downturn in the electronics industry. Even in the market's worst troughs, though, Avnet has also continued to expand by buying complementary businesses; it has spent more than $2 billion dollars on acquisitions in less than three years.

HISTORY

In 1921, before the advent of commercial battery-operated radios, Charles Avnet started a small ham radio replacement parts distributorship in Manhattan, selling parts to designers, inventors, and ship-to-shore radio users on docked ships. The stock market crash in 1929 left the business strapped; it went bankrupt in 1931. A few years later Avnet founded another company, making car radio kits and antennas. But competition got the best of him, and that company also went bankrupt.

During WWII Charles, joined by his sons Lester and Robert, founded Avnet Electronic Supply to sell parts to government and defense contractors. After the war the company bought and sold surplus electrical and electronic parts. A contract from Bendix Aviation spurred company growth, and Avnet opened a West Coast warehouse. In 1955 the company incorporated as Avnet Electronics Supply, with Robert as chairman and CEO and Lester as president. Sales reached $1 million that year, although the company lost $17,000. It changed its name to Avnet Electronics in 1959.

In 1960 Avnet made its first acquisition, British Industries, and went public. Acquisitions continued throughout the 1960s with Hamilton Electro (1962), Fairmount Motor Products (1963), Carol Wire & Cable (1968), and Time Electronic Sales (1968). To acknowledge its diversification, the company again changed its name, to Avnet, Inc., in 1964. Robert Avnet died the next year and Lester took over as chairman; Lester died in 1970.

In 1973 Intel, which had introduced the microprocessor, signed Avnet as a distributor, and by 1979 Avnet's sales had topped $1 billion. A soft 1982 market caused price declines that led Avnet to sell its wire and cable business. The company consolidated many of its operations to its Arizona headquarters in 1987.

During 1991 and 1992 Avnet spent more than $100 million for acquisitions strategic to the European market. In 1993 the company outbid Wyle Laboratories for Hall-Mark Electronics, the US's third-largest distributor; it also acquired Penstock, the top US distributor of microwave radio-frequency products, in 1994. Thanks to its purchases, Avnet was Europe's #2 electronics distributor by 1994, despite having had almost no European operations prior to 1990.

The company continued to expand globally in 1995, acquiring Hong Kong distributor WKK Semiconductor, among others. In 1998 it reorganized around separate global computer and electronics businesses. Also that year, president and COO Roy Vallee became chairman and CEO. As part of its restructuring, the company sold its Allied Electronics subsidiary to UK-based components distributor Electrocomponents in 1999 for $380 million. That year Avnet acquired rival Marshall Industries in a deal valued at about $760 million.

In 2000 Avnet acquired IBM midrange server distributor Savoir Technology Group in a $140 million deal, making Avnet the leading distributor of IBM midrange products. Later that year the company acquired a part of Germany-based EBV Group (semiconductor distribution) and RKE (computer products and services), both from German utility giant E.ON, in a cash deal worth about $740 million.

In 2001 Avnet acquired smaller rival Kent Electronics for about $600 million. Also that year the company bought Chinese competitor Sunrise Technology.

OFFICERS

Chairman and CEO: Roy A. Vallee, $1,390,000 pay
SVP, CFO, and Assistant Secretary: Raymond Sadowski, age 47
SVP, General Counsel, and Secretary: David R. Birk, age 54
SVP; President, Avnet Applied Computing: Edward B. Kamins, age 52

SVP; President, Avnet Electronics Marketing:
Andrew S. Bryant, age 46, $695,571 pay
(prior to promotion)
SVP; EVP and Director, Finance, Planning &
Operations: Patrick Jewett, age 56
SVP; SVP, Global Materials Management, Avnet
Electronics Marketing: Donald E. Sweet
SVP, Services Business Development:
Steven C. Church, age 52, $895,743 pay
VP and Chief Communications Officer: Allen W. Maag
Auditors: KPMG LLP

LOCATIONS

HQ: 2211 S. 47th St., Phoenix, AZ 85034
Phone: 480-643-2000   **Fax:** 480-643-7240
Web: www.avnet.com

Avnet has operations in more than 50 countries
worldwide.

2001 Sales

	$ mil.	% of total
Americas	8,746	68
Asia/Pacific	556	4
Other regions	3,512	28
Total	**12,814**	**100**

PRODUCTS/OPERATIONS

2001 Sales

	$ mil.	% of total
Electronics Marketing Group	8,287	65
Computer Marketing Group	2,855	22
Avnet Applied Computing	1,672	13
Total	**12,814**	**100**

Selected Operations

Electronics Marketing
Avnet Cilicon (semiconductors)
Avnet Kent (interconnect, passive, and
electromechanical devices)
Design Services (custom-integrated circuit design and
systems-level design services)
Integrated Material Services (electronic components
supply chain management)
MarketSite (online procurement services)
Pivvot (electronic component supply chain services)
Production Supplies & Test (electronics production
supplies and test equipment)
RF & Microwave (radio-frequency and microwave
semiconductors and other components)

Computer Marketing
Avnet Hall-Mark (computers, software, storage, and
services to resellers)
Convergent Technologies (networking, wireless, and
point-of-sale systems)
Enterprise Solutions (systems integration for enterprise
end users)

Avnet Applied Computing (component marketing to
manufacturers)

COMPETITORS

All American Semiconductor	Electro-components	Pioneer-Standard Electronics
Arrow Electronics	Future Electronics	Premier Farnell Reptron
ASCII Group	Ingram Micro	Electronics
ASI Corp.	Merisel	Smith &
Bell Microproducts	Nu Horizons Electronics	Associates Tech Data
CompuCom		TTI

HISTORICAL FINANCIALS & EMPLOYEES

NYSE: AVT FYE: Friday nearest June 30	Annual Growth	6/92	6/93	6/94	6/95	6/96	6/97	6/98	6/99	6/00	6/01
Sales ($ mil.)	24.7%	1,759	2,238	3,548	4,300	5,208	5,391	5,916	6,350	9,172	12,814
Net income ($ mil.)	(12.4%)	51	69	85	140	188	183	151	175	145	15
Income as % of sales	—	2.9%	3.1%	2.4%	3.3%	3.6%	3.4%	2.6%	2.7%	1.6%	0.1%
Earnings per share ($)	(17.2%)	0.71	0.96	1.04	1.66	2.16	2.13	1.90	2.43	1.75	0.13
Stock price – FY high ($)	—	15.00	18.50	22.50	24.88	27.81	32.44	37.25	30.47	40.56	35.41
Stock price – FY low ($)	—	11.63	13.38	15.38	15.75	19.00	19.56	26.84	17.00	18.66	17.19
Stock price – FY close ($)	5.5%	13.81	17.00	15.75	24.13	21.06	28.75	27.34	23.25	29.63	22.42
P/E – high	—	21	19	21	15	13	15	19	12	23	272
P/E – low	—	16	14	14	9	9	9	14	7	11	132
Dividends per share ($)	0.0%	0.30	0.30	0.30	0.30	0.30	0.30	0.30	0.30	0.30	0.30
Book value per share ($)	7.5%	11.78	12.18	13.63	15.19	17.33	18.27	18.04	19.86	21.53	22.59
Employees	8.3%	6,650	6,500	8,000	9,000	9,500	9,400	8,700	8,200	11,500	13,600

STOCK PRICE HISTORY

HIGH/LOW/CLOSE

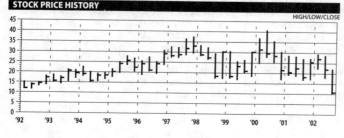

2001 FISCAL YEAR-END

Debt ratio: 27.9%
Return on equity: 0.7%
Cash ($ mil.): 97
Current ratio: 1.46
Long-term debt ($ mil.): 920
No. of shares (mil.): 105
Dividends
 Yield: 1.3%
 Payout: 230.8%
Market value ($ mil.): 2,357

AVON PRODUCTS, INC.

Makeovers are a staple of the cosmetics business, and Avon Products, the world's #1 direct seller of beauty products, is in the midst of its own makeover. Its offerings include cosmetics (Avon Color), fragrances (Perceive, Women of Earth), toiletries (Skin-So-Soft), jewelry, apparel, and home furnishings.

With growth fairly stagnant at home, the New York City-based company has shed many product lines in favor of developing global brands. Printing its brochures in 25 languages, the company has said it wants to become the Coca-Cola of the beauty industry. Avon also is promoting its image as "The Company for Women" by providing business opportunities for women in countries where women have few choices.

To grow in North America, Avon has moved beyond its door-to-door saleslady image by exploring new sales channels for its cosmetics, jewelry, decorative items, and apparel. Although about 90% of revenues still come from its 3.5 million sales representatives, the company believes it can tap new customers and generate brand cachet by expanding its mall kiosk program and its Web site. Avon also intends to sell products in some US department stores.

HISTORY

In the 1880s book salesman David McConnell gave small bottles of perfume to New York housewives who listened to his sales pitch. The perfume was more popular than the books, so in 1886 McConnell created the California Perfume Company and hired women to sell door-to-door. (He renamed the company Avon Products in 1939 after being impressed by the beauty of Stratford-upon-Avon in England.) Through the 1950s these women, mostly housewives seeking extra income, made Avon a major force in the cosmetics industry.

From the 1960s until the mid-1980s, Avon was the world's largest cosmetics company, known for its appeal to middle-class homemakers. But the company hit hard times in 1974 — the recession made many of its products too pricey for blue-collar customers, and women were leaving home for the workforce. Discovering that Avon's traditional products had little appeal for younger women, Avon began an overhaul of its product line, introducing the Colorworks line for teenagers with the slogan, "It's not your mother's makeup."

Avon acquired prestigious jeweler Tiffany & Co. in 1979 (sold 1984) to help improve the company's image. To boost profits, it entered the retail prestige fragrance business by launching a joint venture with Liz Claiborne (1985)

and buying Giorgio Armani (1987, the Giorgio Beverly Hills retail operations were sold in 1994). But Liz Claiborne dissolved the joint venture when Avon bought competitor Parfums Stern in 1987 (sold 1990). It sold 40% of Avon Japan (started 1969) to the Japanese public that year.

Avon Color cosmetics were introduced in 1988, and sleepwear, preschool toys, and videos followed in 1989. The company introduced apparel in 1994 and the next year worked with designer Diane Von Furstenberg to launch a line of clothing.

Mattel and Avon joined forces in 1996 to sell toys — Winter Velvet Barbie became Avon's most successful product introduction ever. In 1997 the company launched a new home furnishings catalog and bought direct seller Discovery Toys (sold in early 1999). Late in 1997 it began a $400 million restructuring program.

Passing over several high-ranking female executives (the company felt they weren't ready), Avon made Charles Perrin its CEO in mid-1998. Andrea Jung, the brain behind the makeover, became president. Avon also began selling makeup in 1998 at mall kiosks and through a catalog.

In 1999 Jung became Avon's first female CEO by replacing the retiring Perrin. Former Goodyear and Rubbermaid CEO Stanley Gault was elected chairman of the board. In March 2000 Avon announced an alliance with Swiss pharmaceutical group Roche to develop a line of women's vitamins and nutritional products (its first). Later that year Avon announced that for the first time in its 115-year history it would begin selling products in US stores — specifically J.C. Penney and Sears, Roebuck & Co. department stores (Sears backed out of the deal in July 2001). In September 2001 Jung was elected chairman of the board.

In 2002 Avon closed its jewelry manufacturing plant in San Sebastian, Puerto Rico, resulting in the loss of 320 jobs. As part of a move to improve operating efficiencies, the closure marked Avon's exit from jewelry manufacturing. It now outsources its full jewelry line by purchasing finished goods from Asia. In another cost-cutting move, Avon laid off 3,500 employees, or 8% of its workforce, in March 2002, saying that the economic recession in Argentina, which accounts for about 5% of Avon's sales, made the layoffs necessary. The next month Avon announced the closing of production operations (with the loss of 465 jobs) in Northampton, UK, and a shift of these operations to its facility in Garwolin, Poland, reflecting what the company called a continuation of its plan to improve efficiency and integration.

Chairman and CEO: Andrea Jung, age 43, $1,829,090 pay
President, COO, and Director: Susan J. Kropf, age 53, $1,219,287 pay
EVP and CFO: Robert J. Corti, age 52, $706,109 pay
SVP and CIO: Harriet Edelman, age 46
SVP and General Counsel: Gilbert L. Klemann II, age 51, $652,950 pay
SVP, Corporate Communications: Brian T. Martin
SVP, Europe, Middle East, and Africa: Robert Toth, age 49
SVP, Global Operations Support: Bennett Gallina
SVP, Human Resources: Jill Kanin-Lovers, age 50
SVP; President, Avon North America: Brian C. Connolly
SVP; President, Global Marketing: William Susetka, age 48
Auditors: PricewaterhouseCoopers LLP

LOCATIONS

HQ: 1345 Avenue of the Americas, New York, NY 10105
Phone: 212-282-5000   **Fax:** 212-282-6049
Web: www.avon.com

Avon Products has operations in the US and 57 other countries. Its products are available in more than 143 countries.

2001 Sales

	% of total
North America	38
Latin America	32
Europe	17
Asia/Pacific	13
Total	**100**

PRODUCTS/OPERATIONS

2001 Sales

	% of total
Cosmetics, fragrances & toiletries	63
Fashion, apparel & jewelry	21
Gift & decorative	16
Total	**100**

Selected Brands

Cosmetics	Hair Care
Beyond Color	Advance Techniques
Color Trend	Avon Kids
	Herbal Care
Fragrances	
Dolce Aura	**Skin Care, Bath, and**
Imari Eau de Cologne	**Body**
Incandessence	Anew
Rare Gold	Clearskin
	Skin-So-Soft

COMPETITORS

Alberto-Culver	Forever Living	New Dana
Alticor	Hanover Direct	Perfumes
Bath & Body	Herbalife	Perrigo
Works	Intimate Brands	Procter & Gamble
BeautiControl	J. C. Penney	Revlon
Cosmetics	Johnson &	Sara Lee
Beiersdorf	Johnson	Shaklee
Body Shop	Johnson	Shiseido
Colgate-	Publishing	Spiegel
Palmolive	L'Oréal	Target
Coty	LVMH	Tupperware
Dillard's	Mary Kay	Unilever
Enesco Group	May	Wal-Mart
Estée Lauder		Wella

HISTORICAL FINANCIALS & EMPLOYEES

NYSE: AVP FYE: December 31	Annual Growth	12/92	12/93	12/94	12/95	12/96	12/97	12/98	12/99	12/00	12/01
Sales ($ mil.)	5.2%	3,810	4,008	4,267	4,492	4,814	5,079	5,213	5,289	5,715	5,995
Net income ($ mil.)	10.5%	175	132	196	257	318	339	270	302	478	430
Income as % of sales	—	4.6%	3.3%	4.6%	5.7%	6.6%	6.7%	5.2%	5.7%	8.4%	7.2%
Earnings per share ($)	12.7%	0.61	0.46	0.69	0.94	1.18	1.27	1.02	1.17	1.99	1.79
Stock price - FY high ($)	—	15.06	16.09	15.91	19.59	29.75	39.00	46.25	59.13	49.75	50.12
Stock price - FY low ($)	—	11.00	11.91	12.09	13.50	18.16	25.31	25.00	23.31	25.25	35.55
Stock price - FY close ($)	14.4%	13.84	12.16	14.94	18.84	28.56	30.69	44.25	33.00	47.88	46.50
P/E - high	—	25	19	19	21	25	30	45	50	24	28
P/E - low	—	18	14	14	14	15	20	24	20	12	20
Dividends per share ($)	8.0%	0.38	0.43	0.48	0.53	0.58	0.63	0.68	0.72	0.74	0.76
Book value per share ($)	—	1.08	1.09	0.67	0.71	0.91	1.08	1.09	(1.71)	(0.91)	(0.32)
Employees	4.4%	29,700	29,800	30,400	31,800	33,700	34,995	33,900	40,500	43,000	43,800

STOCK PRICE HISTORY

HIGH/LOW/CLOSE

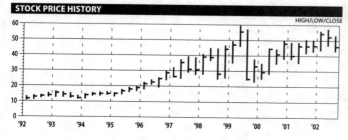

2001 FISCAL YEAR-END

Debt ratio: 100.0%
Return on equity: —
Cash ($ mil.): 509
Current ratio: 1.29
Long-term debt ($ mil.): 1,236
No. of shares (mil.): 237
Dividends
  Yield: 1.6%
  Payout: 42.5%
Market value ($ mil.): 11,006

BAKER & MCKENZIE

How many lawyers does it take to replace a glass ceiling? Whatever the answer, Baker & McKenzie has more than enough. The Chicago-based law firm is one of the world's largest, with more than 3,000 lawyers spread across more than 60 offices in about 35 countries. It also became one of the first major partnerships to elect a woman to manage the firm when Christine Lagarde was chosen in 1999 to replace outgoing chairman John Klotsche. In addition to closing the gender gap, Lagarde is also one of the youngest partners, age 43 when she was elected, to lead the firm.

Baker is a full-service firm offering legal advice in areas such as banking, securities, labor, international trade, and tax. The half-century-old firm has handled the legal affairs of such heavy-duty clients as Chase Manhattan (now J.P. Morgan Chase), Honeywell, and Ingersoll-Rand. Although its size has helped attract clients and employees, Baker has also had to struggle with the image of being more concerned with size than with quality legal work.

The firm is known for the global scale of its practice, with some 80% of Baker attorneys practicing outside the US. However, it is beginning to face new competition on the global scene from firms such as Clifford Chance (which merged with two other practices in 2000 to create a network larger than Baker's).

HISTORY

Russell Baker traveled from his native New Mexico to Chicago on a railroad freight car to attend law school. Upon graduation in 1925 he started practicing law with his classmate Dana Simpson under the name Simpson & Baker. Inspired by Chicago's role as a manufacturing and agricultural center for the world and influenced by the international focus of his alma mater, the University of Chicago, Baker dreamed of creating an international law practice. He began developing an expertise in international law, and in 1934 Abbott Laboratories retained him to handle its worldwide legal affairs. Baker was on his way to fulfilling his dream.

Baker joined forces with Chicago litigator John McKenzie in 1949, forming Baker & McKenzie. In 1955 the firm opened its first foreign office in Caracas, Venezuela, to meet the needs of its expanding US client base. Over the next 10 years it branched out into Asia, Australia, and Europe, with offices in London, Manila, Paris, and Tokyo. Baker's death in 1979 neither slowed the firm's growth nor changed its international character. The next year it expanded into the Middle East and opened its 30th office in 1982 (Melbourne). To manage the sprawling law firm, Baker & McKenzie created the position of chairman of the executive committee in 1984.

In late 1991 the firm dropped the Church of Scientology as a client, losing an estimated $2 million in business. It was speculated that pressure from client Eli Lilly (maker of the drug Prozac, which Scientologists actively oppose) influenced the decision. In 1992 Baker & McKenzie was ordered to pay $1 million for wrongfully firing an employee who later died of AIDS. (The case became the basis for the 1993 film *Philadelphia*.) The firm fought the verdict but eventually settled for an undisclosed amount in 1995.

In 1994 Baker & McKenzie closed its Los Angeles office (the former MacDonald, Halsted & Laybourne; acquired 1988) amid considerable rancor. Also that year a former secretary at the firm received a $7.1 million judgment for sexual harassment by a partner. (A San Francisco Superior Court judge later reduced the award to $3.5 million.)

John Klotsche, a senior partner from the firm's Palo Alto, California, office was appointed chairman in 1995. The following year the firm began a major expansion into California's Silicon Valley as part of an initiative to serve technology companies around the world. It also expanded its Warsaw, Poland, office through a merger with the Warsaw office of Dickinson, Wright, Moon, Van Dusen & Freman.

In 1998 Baker & McKenzie formed a special unit in Singapore to deal with business generated by the financial troubles in Asia. The opening of offices in Taiwan and Azerbaijan in 1998 brought the firm's total number of offices to 59. Klotsche stepped down in 1999 as the firm celebrated its 50th anniversary; Christine Lagarde replaced him. In early 2001 Baker & McKenzie created a joint venture practice with Singapore-based associate firm Wong & Leow. Also that year it merged with Madrid-based Briones Alonso y Martin to create the largest independent law firm in Spain.

OFFICERS

Chairman Executive Committee: Christine Lagarde, age 45
COO: Thomas P. Gaughan, age 36
CFO: Robert S. Spencer
CTO: Craig Courter
General Counsel: Edward J. Zulkey
Director, Special Projects: Suzanne M. Clough
Director, Professional Development: Anne Waldron
Manager, Human Resources: Wilbert Williams

LOCATIONS

HQ: 1 Prudential Plaza, 130 E. Randolph Dr., Ste. 2500, Chicago, IL 60601
Phone: 312-861-8800   **Fax:** 312-861-2899
Web: www.bakerinfo.com

Baker & McKenzie has more than 60 offices throughout Asia, Australia, Europe, Latin America, and North America.

PRODUCTS/OPERATIONS

Selected Practice Areas
Banking and finance
Corporate and securities
E-commerce
International commercial arbitration
International trade
IP, IT, and Communications
Labor and employment
Tax
US Litigation

COMPETITORS

Clifford Chance
Deloitte Touche Tohmatsu
Ernst & Young
Jones, Day
Kirkland & Ellis
KPMG
Mayer, Brown, Rowe & Maw
McDermott, Will
PricewaterhouseCoopers
Sidley Austin Brown & Wood
Skadden, Arps

HISTORICAL FINANCIALS & EMPLOYEES

Partnership FYE: June 30	Annual Growth	6/93	6/94	6/95	6/96	6/97	6/98	6/99	6/00	6/01	6/02
Sales ($ mil.)	7.7%	512	546	594	646	697	785	818	940	1,000	1,000
Employees	5.2%	5,054	5,114	5,248	5,680	6,100	6,700	6,900	8,000	8,000	8,000

SALES HISTORY

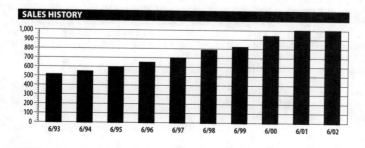

BAKER HUGHES INCORPORATED

Baker Hughes has the drill down pat. The Houston-based company provides products and services to the worldwide oil field and process equipment industries. Through six divisions, the company helps energy companies locate oil and gas reserves and provides drill bits, drilling fluids, and other equipment used in the drilling process. Baker Hughes also makes submersible pumps that deliver oil to the well's surface and provides equipment and services to maintain oil and gas wells. Baker Petrolite makes oil field specialty chemicals, as well as chemicals for the refining and wastewater industries.

Baker Hughes is starting to make a comeback along with the increasing price of oil. With its rig counts at a 10-year high, the company is hoping for a renewed gusher of cash as the increase in per-barrel prices prompts oil companies to reinvest in exploration and production. The company also has been helped by the rising price of natural gas. Unable to sell it in whole, Baker Hughes is planning to sell its Baker Process division (waste-separation equipment) in pieces.

HISTORY

Howard Hughes Sr. developed the first oil well drill bit for rock in 1909. Hughes and partner Walter Sharp opened a plant in Houston, and their company, Sharp & Hughes, soon had a near monopoly on rock bits. When Sharp died in 1912, Hughes bought his partner's half of the company, incorporating as Hughes Tool. Hughes held 73 patents when he died in 1924; the company passed to Howard Hughes Jr.

It is estimated that between 1924 and 1972 Hughes Tool provided Hughes Jr. with $745 million in pretax profits, which he used to diversify into movies (RKO), airlines (TWA), and Las Vegas casinos. In 1972 he sold the company to the public for $150 million. After 1972 the company expanded into tools for aboveground oil production. In 1974, under the new leadership of chairman James Leach, Hughes bought the oil field equipment business of Borg-Warner.

In 1913 drilling contractor Carl Baker organized the Baker Casing Shoe Company in California to collect royalties on his three oil tool inventions. The firm began to make its own products in 1918, and during the 1920s it expanded nationally, opened global trade, and formed Baker Oil Tools (1928). The company grew in the late 1940s and the 1950s as oil drilling boomed.

During the 1960s Baker prospered, despite fewer US well completions. Foreign sales increased. From 1963 to 1975 Baker bought oil-related companies Kobe, Galigher, Ramsey Engineering, and Reed Tool.

US expenditures for oil services fell between 1982 and 1986 from $40 billion to $9 billion. In 1987 both Baker and Hughes faced falling revenues. The two companies merged to form Baker Hughes. By closing plants and combining operations, the venture became profitable by the end of 1988. The company bought Eastman Christensen (the world leader in directional and horizontal drilling equipment) and acquired the instrumentation unit of Tracor Holdings in 1990.

Baker Hughes spun off BJ Services (pumping services) to the public in 1991 and sold the Eastern Hemisphere operations of Baker Hughes Tubular Services (BHTS) to Tuboscope. It sold the Western Hemisphere operations of BHTS to ICO the following year.

Also in 1992 Baker Hughes bought Teleco Oilfield Services, a pioneer in directional drilling techniques, from Sonat. The next year the company consolidated its drilling-technology businesses into a single unit, Baker Hughes INTEQ.

The company continued expanding internationally in 1994, and in 1995 Baker Hughes sold EnviroTech Pumpsystems to the Weir Group of Glasgow, Scotland. In 1996 company veteran Max Lukens became CEO. He replaced James Woods as chairman the next year.

Baker Hughes allied with Schlumberger's oil field service operations in 1996. In a move to boost its oil field chemicals business the company bought Petrolite in 1997 and rival Western Atlas for $3.3 billion in 1998, strengthening its land-based seismic data business (#1 in that market) and testing business. A downturn in the Asian economy, disruptions from tropical storms, and slumping oil prices caused oil companies to reduce demand for Baker Hughes' products. The company suffered a big loss in 1998 and in response trimmed its workforce by about 15% in 1999. It also put its separation-equipment business up for sale.

In 2000 Lukens stepped down after accounting blunders caused the company to restate earnings. Company director and Newfield Exploration Company CEO Joe Foster replaced him as acting CEO until Michael Wiley was named to that office. Baker Hughes combined its seismic oil and gas exploration business with that of Schlumberger Limited to create Western GECO in early 2001.

OFFICERS

Chairman, President, and CEO: Michael E. Wiley, age 51, $2,118,990 pay
SVP, Finance and Administration and CFO:
George S. Finley, age 51, $862,134 pay
SVP and COO: Andrew J. Szescila, age 53, $1,201,692 pay
VP and Controller: Alan J. Keifer, age 47, $191,386 pay
VP and General Counsel: Alan R. Crain Jr., age 50, $734,295 pay
VP and President, Baker Atlas: David H. Barr
VP and President, Baker Hughes INTEQ:
Ray Ballantyne, $808,226 pay
VP and President, Baker Oil Tools: Edwin C. Howell
VP and President, Baker Petrolite: James R. Clark
VP and President, Centrilift: William P. Faubel
VP and President, Hughes Christensen Company:
Douglas J. Wall
VP, Human Resources: Greg Nakanishi, age 50
VP, Marketing and Technology: Trevor Burgess
Director, Investor Relations: Gary R. Flaharty
Auditors: Deloitte & Touche LLP

LOCATIONS

HQ: 3900 Essex Ln., Ste. 1200, Houston, TX 77027
Phone: 713-439-8600   **Fax:** 713-439-8699
Web: www.bakerhughes.com

2001 Sales

	$ mil.	% of total
US	2,082	39
UK	341	6
Norway	312	6
Canada	304	6
Venezuela	233	4
Other countries	2,110	39
Total	**5,382**	**100**

PRODUCTS/OPERATIONS

2001 Sales

	$ mil.	% of total
Oilfield	5,063	94
Process	319	6
Total	**5,382**	**100**

Selected Oilfield Operations

Baker Atlas (downhole data acquisition, processing and analysis; pipe recovery)
Baker Hughes INTEQ (directional drilling, measurement, and drilling fluids)
Baker Oil Tools (completion, workover, and fishing technologies and services)
Baker Petrolite (specialty chemicals for petroleum, transportation, and refining)
Centrilift (electric submersible pumps and downhole oil/water separation)
Hughes Christensen (oil well drill bits)
WesternGeco (30%, seismic exploration services, field development and management)

COMPETITORS

Ahlstrom	Kværner	Smith
BJ Services	Nabors	International
Compagnie	Industries	USFilter
Générale de	Ondeo Nalco	Veritas DGC
Géophysique	Outokumpu	Weatherford
FMC	Petroleum Geo-	International
Halliburton	Services	Wilson
Hercules	Sandvik	Industries
Ingersoll-Rand	Schlumberger	

HISTORICAL FINANCIALS & EMPLOYEES

NYSE: BHI FYE: December 31	Annual Growth	9/92	9/93	9/94	9/95	9/96	9/97	*12/98	12/99	12/00	12/01
Sales ($ mil.)	8.7%	2,539	2,702	2,505	2,638	3,028	3,685	6,312	4,547	5,234	5,382
Net income ($ mil.)	64.4%	5	59	43	105	176	97	(297)	33	102	438
Income as % of sales	—	0.2%	2.2%	1.7%	4.0%	5.8%	2.6%	—	0.7%	2.0%	8.1%
Earnings per share ($)	—	0.00	0.34	0.22	0.57	1.23	0.63	(0.92)	0.10	0.31	1.30
Stock price - FY high ($)		26.00	29.63	24.88	23.75	35.63	47.25	44.13	36.25	43.38	45.29
Stock price - FY low ($)		15.88	17.75	17.00	16.75	18.38	29.50	15.00	15.00	19.63	25.76
Stock price - FY close ($)	5.1%	23.38	23.50	18.63	20.38	30.38	43.81	17.63	21.06	41.56	36.47
P/E - high		—	87	29	35	29	67	—	363	140	35
P/E - low		—	52	20	25	15	42	—	150	63	20
Dividends per share ($)	0.0%	0.46	0.46	0.46	0.46	0.46	0.46	0.58	0.46	0.46	0.46
Book value per share ($)	(2.0%)	11.87	11.47	11.63	10.64	11.69	15.38	9.78	9.31	9.13	9.90
Employees	3.5%	19,600	18,400	14,700	15,200	16,800	21,500	32,300	27,326	24,500	26,800

* Fiscal year change

STOCK PRICE HISTORY

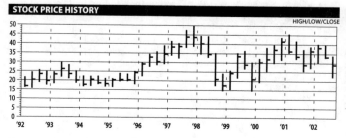

HIGH/LOW/CLOSE

2001 FISCAL YEAR-END

Debt ratio: 33.6%
Return on equity: 13.7%
Cash ($ mil.): 45
Current ratio: 2.22
Long-term debt ($ mil.): 1,682
No. of shares (mil.): 336
Dividends
Yield: 1.3%
Payout: 35.4%
Market value ($ mil.): 12,254

BALL CORPORATION

Ball Corporation is rolling right along as North America's leading maker of beverage cans. The Broomfield, Colorado-based company has two units: packaging (about 90% of sales) and aerospace and technology.

Ball's packaging unit produces metal and polyethylene terephthalate (PET) plastic packaging for food and beverages. Customers include packagers of soft drinks (Pepsi-Cola and Coca-Cola bottlers together account for nearly a third of total sales), beer (Coors, the Miller Brewing Company represents 16% of sales), food, and juices.

The company's Ball Aerospace & Technologies Corporation subsidiary produces aerospace and communications components and systems such as antennas, sensors, satellite ground station-control software, and spacecraft guidance and control instruments. Ball's aerospace and technology unit serves NASA, the US Department of Defense, and foreign governments.

Ball has expanded into key markets through acquisitions. The company has also closed and consolidated some operations in order to reduce excess inventory.

HISTORY

The Ball Corporation began in 1880 when Frank Ball and his four brothers started making wood-jacket tin cans to store and transport kerosene and other materials. In 1884 the company switched to tin-jacketed glass containers for kerosene lamps. The lamps, however, were soon displaced by Thomas Edison's electric light bulb.

The Ball brothers then learned that the patent to the original sealed-glass storage container (the Mason jar) had expired. By 1886 the brothers had entered the sealed-jar business and imprinted their jars with the Ball name. In their first year, they made 12,500 jars and sparked a patent war with the two reigning jar producers, who asserted that they controlled the correct patents and threatened to sue. The Ball lawyers proved that the patents had expired, and the jar remained Ball's mainstay for many years.

The company began diversifying, but a 1947 antitrust ruling prohibited it from buying additional glass subsidiaries. Ball decided to take advantage of the space race by buying Control Cells (aerospace research) in 1957; that operation became Ball Brothers Research Corporation (later Ball Aerospace Systems Division). The Soviets launched Sputnik that year, igniting a massive US response in 1958, and Ball won contracts to make equipment for the US space program.

Ball established its metal beverage-container business in 1969 when it bought Jeffco Manufacturing of Colorado. The operation soon won contracts to supply two-piece cans to Budweiser, Coca-Cola, Dr Pepper, Pepsi, and Stroh's Beer.

John Fisher became president and CEO in 1971. The last company president who was a member of the Ball family, Fisher wanted Ball to diversify. He took the company public in 1972 to fund his efforts. That year he acquired a Singapore-based petroleum equipment company. Next he led Ball into agricultural irrigation systems and prefabricated housing. In 1974 Ball acquired a small California computer firm, which formed the basis of its telecommunications division.

Fisher retired in 1981. Ball's metal-container business suffered in the late 1980s from overcapacity and price wars in its industry. In 1989 Ball's aerospace division was hard hit by $10 million in losses on an Air Force contract and by cuts in defense spending.

Ball spun off its Alltrista canning supplies subsidiary to shareholders in 1993 and purchased Heekin Can, a manufacturer for the food, pet food, and aerosol markets. That year Ball's $50 million mirror system corrected the Hubble Space Telescope's blurred vision. The company entered the polyethylene terephthalate (PET) container business in 1995 and placed its glass-container business into a newly formed company, Ball-Foster Glass Container, and the next year sold its stake to its partner, French materials company Saint-Gobain Group.

Ball sold its aerosol-can business to BWAY Corp in 1996. Ball popped the top on another big deal in 1998 when it bought Reynolds Metals' aluminum-can business (Reynolds is now owned by Alcoa).

In 2001 Ball and ConAgra Grocery Products formed a joint venture, Ball Western Can Company, to make metal food containers. Also that year subsidiary Ball Aerospace & Technologies landed a $260 million contract with the US Air Force, and Ball's president and COO, David Hoover, was named CEO. That November, Ball entered into a joint venture with Coors Brewing Co. called Rocky Mountain Metal Container to operate Coors' can facilities, making 4.5 billion cans per year. The company also acquired Wis-Pak Plastics, Inc., adding to its plastic container operations.

Ball announced in 2002 its plans to acquire German can maker Schmalbach-Lubeca for about $887 million. The deal will make Ball the second-largest can maker in Europe.

OFFICERS

Chairman Emeritus: John W. Fisher
Chairman, President, and CEO: R. David Hoover, age 56, $901,597 pay
EVP and COO, Packaging; Acting President, Metal Food Container Operations: Leon A. Midgett, age 59, $581,650 pay
SVP and CFO: Raymond J. Seabrook, age 51, $404,551 pay
SVP, Administration: David A. Westerlund, age 51, $347,316 pay
VP and Controller: Albert R. Schlesinger, age 60
VP and General Counsel: Donald C. Lewis
VP, Corporate Relations: Harold L. Sohn
Corporate Secretary: Elizabeth A. Overmyer
Auditors: PricewaterhouseCoopers LLP

LOCATIONS

HQ: 10 Longs Peak Dr., Broomfield, CO 80021
Phone: 303-469-3131   **Fax:** 303-460-2127
Web: www.ball.com

Ball Corporation's packaging operations have around 40 manufacturing facilities in the US (including Puerto Rico), Canada, and China. The company's aerospace and technologies group has US offices in California, Colorado, Georgia, New Mexico, Ohio, Texas, and Virginia.

2001 Sales

	$ mil.	% of total
US	3,264	89
Other countries	422	11
Total	**3,686**	**100**

PRODUCTS/OPERATIONS

2001 Sales

	$ mil.	% of total
Packaging	3,267	89
Aerospace & technologies	419	11
Total	**3,686**	**100**

Selected Products and Services

Airborne television
Antennas
Commercial products and technologies manufacturing
Cryogenics
Fuel cell systems
Global communications and video solutions
Laser communications
Lubrication
Mirrors
PET plastic food and beverage containers
Pointing and tracking
Reaction/momentum wheels
Remote sensing
Sensors
Systems engineering
Tactical products
Two- and three-piece metal food containers
Two-piece metal beverage containers
Video products
Wireless communications

COMPETITORS

Alcan
Alcoa
Boeing
BWAY
CLARCOR
Consolidated Container
Constar International
Crown Cork & Seal
Orbital Sciences
Owens-Illinois
PLM AB
Raytheon C3I
Rexam
Rockwell Collins
Schmalbach-Lubeca
Sequa
Silgan
Swales Aerospace Technologies
Tetra Laval

HISTORICAL FINANCIALS & EMPLOYEES

NYSE: BLL FYE: December 31	Annual Growth	12/92	12/93	12/94	12/95	12/96	12/97	12/98	12/99	12/00	12/01
Sales ($ mil.)	6.0%	2,178	2,441	2,595	2,592	2,184	2,389	2,896	3,584	3,665	3,686
Net income ($ mil.)	—	69	(65)	73	(19)	24	58	17	104	68	(99)
Income as % of sales	—	3.2%	—	2.8%	—	1.1%	2.4%	0.6%	2.9%	1.9%	—
Earnings per share ($)	—	1.17	(1.20)	1.18	(0.36)	0.34	0.87	0.22	1.58	1.07	(1.85)
Stock price - FY high ($)	—	19.75	18.63	16.06	19.38	16.13	19.50	23.97	29.56	23.97	36.06
Stock price - FY low ($)	—	14.00	12.56	12.19	12.88	11.56	11.88	14.31	17.69	13.00	19.04
Stock price - FY close ($)	8.0%	17.69	15.13	15.75	13.88	13.13	17.69	22.88	19.69	23.03	35.35
P/E - high	—	16	—	14	—	46	21	50	18	21	—
P/E - low	—	11	—	10	—	33	13	30	11	12	—
Dividends per share ($)	(7.6%)	0.61	0.62	0.30	0.30	0.30	0.30	0.30	0.30	0.30	0.30
Book value per share ($)	(3.0%)	11.43	9.73	10.32	9.67	9.90	10.49	10.22	11.59	12.16	8.72
Employees	(2.6%)	12,589	13,954	12,783	7,500	7,900	10,300	12,100	11,850	11,200	9,950

STOCK PRICE HISTORY

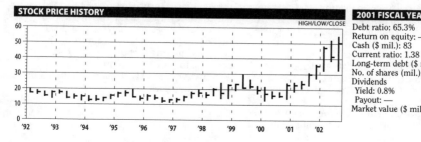

HIGH/LOW/CLOSE

2001 FISCAL YEAR-END

Debt ratio: 65.3%
Return on equity: —
Cash ($ mil.): 83
Current ratio: 1.38
Long-term debt ($ mil.): 949
No. of shares (mil.): 58
Dividends
 Yield: 0.8%
 Payout: —
Market value ($ mil.): 2,044

BANK OF AMERICA CORPORATION

Welcome to the machine. Bank of America is the nation's first coast-to-coast bank.

Based in Charlotte, North Carolina, the US's #3 bank behind Citigroup and J.P. Morgan Chase has more than 4,200 branches in 21 states. It operates through four business segments: Consumer and Commercial Banking is the biggest unit, providing deposit products, credit cards, insurance, loans, treasury services, and financing of car, boat, and RV dealerships. Global Corporate and Investment Banking performs capital markets, mergers and acquisitions advisory, debt and equity underwriting, and other services in more than 30 countries. Asset Management serves institutional investors and high-net-worth individuals, while Equity Investments buys stakes in startups and established firms.

Bank of America is focusing internally, increasing its online presence, pushing its asset management products, and expanding its credit card services (a segment that includes transaction processing subsidiary BA Merchant Services). It is also spending some $100 million on advertising to attract consumer deposits and is building its branch network after years of contraction. Like many of its peers, the company finds itself saddled with bad loans; it formed a subsidiary, Strategic Solutions (about which Bank of America will say little), to sell the liabilities into the secondary market.

HISTORY

Bank of America predecessor NationsBank was formed as the Commercial National Bank in 1874 by citizens of Charlotte, North Carolina. In 1901 George Stephens and Word Wood formed what became American Trust Co. The banks merged in 1957 to become American Commercial Bank, which in 1960 merged with Security National to form North Carolina National Bank.

In 1968 the bank formed holding company NCNB, which by 1980 was the largest bank in North Carolina. Under the leadership of Hugh McColl, who became chairman in 1983, NCNB became the first southern bank to span six states.

NCNB profited from the savings and loan crisis of the late 1980s by managing assets and buying defunct thrifts at fire-sale prices. The company nearly doubled its assets in 1988, when the FDIC chose it to manage the shuttered First Republicbank, then Texas' largest bank. The company renamed itself NationsBank in 1991.

In 1993 the company bought Chicago Research & Trading, a government securities dealer and provider of oil and gas financing. A 1993 joint venture with Dean Witter, Discover to open securities brokerages in banks led to complaints that

customers were not fully informed of the risks of some investments and that brokers were paying rebates to banking personnel for customer referrals. Dean Witter withdrew from the arrangement in 1994, and SEC investigations and a class-action lawsuit ensued. NationsBank settled the lawsuit for about $30 million the next year. (The company agreed to pay nearly $7 million to settle similar charges in 1998.) NationsBank scooped up St. Louis-based Boatmen's Bancshares and Montgomery Securities (now Banc of America Securities) in 1997. The next year it bought Barnett Banks, Florida's #1 bank.

Enter BankAmerica. Founded in 1904 as Bank of Italy, BankAmerica had once been the US's largest bank but had fallen behind as competitors consolidated. As the ink was drying on the Barnett Banks purchase, BankAmerica's board of directors was pondering ways to become more competitive.

BankAmerica decided a merger was the best way; NationsBank obliged. After the merger, the bank announced it would write down a billion-dollar bad loan to D.E. Shaw & Co., which followed the same Russian-investment-paved path of descent as Long-Term Capital Management. David Coulter (head of the old BankAmerica, which made the loan) took the fall for the loss, resigning as president; the balance of power shifted to the NationsBank side when in 1999 Kenneth Lewis took the post.

The Russian debacle and merger hiccups led the firm in early 1999 to reorganize and reduce overseas operations; it sold its private banking operations in Europe and Asia to UBS. Also that year it bought BA Merchant Services. The bank also changed its name to Bank of America and began offering online banking through America Online (now part of AOL Time Warner). To avoid a court battle the bank settled charges that it retained proceeds from unclaimed bonds in California. In 1999 it earned the ire of labor officials for a program in which employees were recruited to maintain ATMs without being paid or provided supplies. EVP Frank Gentry, who crafted the NationsBank/BankAmerica deal, retired in 2000, signalling an end to the company's buying spree. Its focus turned inward as it cleaned up the difficult integration of the two firms.

McColl retired as chairman in 2001. Later that year the company announced it would cease its subprime lending and car leasing operations. In 2002 Bank of America opened an energy trading desk in New York with three former Enron employees.

Chairman Emeritus: Hugh L. McColl Jr., age 66, $500,000 pay

Chairman, President, and CEO: Kenneth D. Lewis, age 55, $6,533,333 pay

Vice Chairman and CFO: James H. Hance Jr., age 57, $4,766,667 pay

President, Global Corporate and Investment Banking: Edward J. Brown III, age 52, $3,450,000 pay

President, Asset Management Group: Richard M. DeMartini, age 49, $3,823,611 pay

President, Bank of America Mid-South: Milton H. Jones Jr.

President, Banc of America Securities: Carter McClelland

President, Bank of America California: Liam E. McGee

President, Consumer and Commercial Banking: R. Eugene Taylor, age 54, $1,950,000 pay

Corporate Personnel Executive: J. Steele Alphin

Chief Marketing Executive; President, Bank of America North Carolina: Catherine P. Bessant

Corporate Risk Management Executive: Amy W. Brinkley, age 46, $2,000,000 pay

Auditors: PricewaterhouseCoopers LLP

LOCATIONS

HQ: Bank of America Corporate Center 100 N. Tryon St., Charlotte, NC 28255
Phone: 704-279-3457   Fax: 704-386-6699
Web: www.bankofamerica.com

Bank of America has branches in Arizona, Arkansas, California, Florida, Georgia, Idaho, Illinois, Iowa, Kansas, Maryland, Missouri, Nevada, New Mexico, North Carolina, Oklahoma, Oregon, South Carolina, Tennessee, Texas, Virginia, Washington, and Washington, DC.

PRODUCTS/OPERATIONS

2001 Sales

	$ mil.	% of total
Interest		
Loans & leases	27,166	51
Securities	3,706	7
Trading account assets	3,623	7
Other	3,798	7
Noninterest		
Consumer service charges	2,866	5
Card income	2,421	5
Investment & brokerage services	2,112	4
Corporate service charges	2,078	4
Trading account profits	1,842	3
Investment banking	1,579	3
Other	1,925	4
Total	**53,116**	**100**

COMPETITORS

American Express	FleetBoston
AmSouth	Golden West Financial
Bank of Montreal	Household International
Bank of New York	J.P. Morgan Chase
BANK ONE	KeyCorp
BB&T	MBNA
Canadian Imperial	Mellon Financial
Citigroup	SunTrust
Countrywide Credit	UnionBanCal
Crédit Lyonnais	U.S. Bancorp
Credit Suisse First Boston	Wachovia
Deutsche Bank	Washington Mutual
First Virginia	Wells Fargo

HISTORICAL FINANCIALS & EMPLOYEES

NYSE: BAC FYE: December 31	Annual Growth	12/92	12/93	12/94	12/95	12/96	12/97	12/98	12/99	12/00	12/01
Assets ($ mil.)	20.3%	118,059	157,686	169,604	187,298	185,794	264,562	617,679	632,574	642,191	621,764
Net income ($ mil.)	21.9%	1,145	1,501	1,690	1,950	2,375	3,077	5,165	7,882	7,517	6,792
Income as % of assets	—	1.0%	1.0%	1.0%	1.0%	1.3%	1.2%	0.8%	1.2%	1.2%	1.1%
Earnings per share ($)	7.1%	2.26	2.86	3.03	3.52	3.92	4.17	2.90	4.48	4.52	4.18
Stock price - FY high ($)	—	26.69	29.00	28.69	37.38	52.63	71.69	88.44	76.38	61.00	65.54
Stock price - FY low ($)	—	19.81	22.25	21.69	22.31	32.19	48.00	44.00	47.63	36.31	45.00
Stock price - FY close ($)	10.5%	25.69	24.50	22.56	34.81	48.88	60.81	60.13	50.19	45.88	62.95
P/E - high	—	12	12	9	11	13	17	30	17	13	15
P/E - low	—	9	9	7	6	8	11	15	10	8	11
Dividends per share ($)	13.0%	0.76	0.82	0.94	1.04	1.20	1.37	1.59	1.85	2.06	2.28
Book value per share ($)	8.1%	15.44	18.42	19.91	23.34	23.90	29.96	26.64	26.49	29.52	31.12
Employees	12.2%	50,828	57,463	61,484	58,322	62,971	80,360	170,975	155,906	142,724	142,670

STOCK PRICE HISTORY

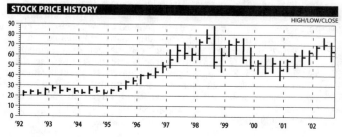

HIGH/LOW/CLOSE

2001 FISCAL YEAR-END

Equity as % of assets: 7.8%
Return on assets: 1.1%
Return on equity: 14.1%
Long-term debt ($ mil.): 62,496
No. of shares (mil.): 1,559
Dividends
  Yield: 3.6%
  Payout: 54.5%
Market value ($ mil.): 98,158
Sales ($ mil.): 53,116

THE BANK OF NEW YORK COMPANY

Big Apple-based Bank of New York is biting deeper into the custody and trust markets.

The company's operations include some 350 retail branches in suburban New York that offer traditional banking services, investment management, and insurance to individuals and small and midsized businesses. However, the fair-haired boy in the corporation is its lucrative (and growing) securities servicing business, which provides mutual fund administration and accounting, collateral management, stock transfer services, foreign exchange, and corporate trust on a global basis. The firm has especially cashed in on services relating to American Depositary Receipts (dollar-denominated foreign securities) and interest rate and currency derivatives. Subsidiary BNY Capital Markets offers investment banking services; BNY Asset Management serves institutions and wealthy individual investors.

As the markets go, so does Bank of New York's securities business, which relies on robust trading volumes. But its retail banking operations still provide a stable base of operations, accounting for about half of the company's income. Bank of New York continues to build its fee-based operations through acquisitions, particularly in securities processing and trust services. Such deals have pushed the firm to the top of the heap of corporate trust providers. Other purchases include equity research firm Jaywalk and hedge fund manager Ivy Asset Management.

HISTORY

In 1784 Alexander Hamilton (at 27, already a Revolutionary War hero and economic theorist) and a group of New York merchants and lawyers founded New York City's first bank, The Bank of New York (BNY). Hamilton saw a need for a credit system to finance the nation's growth and to establish credibility for the new nation's chaotic monetary system.

Hamilton became US secretary of the treasury in 1789 and soon negotiated the new US government's first loan — for $200,000 — from BNY. The bank later helped finance the War of 1812 by offering $16 million in subscription books and the Civil War by loaning the government $150 million. In 1878 BNY became a US Treasury depository for the sale of government bonds.

The bank's conservative fiscal policies and emphasis on commercial banking enabled it to weather economic turbulence in the 19th century. In 1922 it merged with New York Life Insurance and Trust (formed in 1830 by many of BNY's directors) to form Bank of New York and Trust. The bank survived the crash of 1929 and remained profitable, paying dividends throughout the Depression. In 1938 it reclaimed its Bank of New York name.

During the mid-20th century, BNY expanded its operations and its reach through acquisitions, including Fifth Avenue Bank (trust services, 1948) and Empire Trust (serving developing industries, 1966). In 1968 the bank created holding company The Bank of New York Company to expand statewide with purchases such as Empire National Bank (1980).

BNY relaxed its lending policies in the 1980s and began to build its fee-for-service side, boosting its American Depositary Receipts business by directly soliciting European companies and seeking government securities business. The bank bought New York rival Irving Trust in a 1989 hostile takeover and in 1990 began buying other banks' credit card portfolios.

As the economy cooled in the early 1990s, BNY's book of highly leveraged transactions and nonperforming loans suffered, so the company sold many of those loans.

In the mid-1990s BNY bought processing and trust businesses and continued to build its retail business in the suburbs. It pared noncore operations, selling its mortgage banking unit (and in 1998 moved its remaining mortgage operations into a joint venture with Alliance Mortgage); credit card business (1998); and factoring and asset-based lending operations (1999). In late 1997 and again in 1998, the bank tried to woo Mellon Bank (now Mellon Financial) into a merger but was rejected.

The growth of the firm's custody services accelerated in the late 1990s. In 1997 BNY bought operations from Wells Fargo, Signet Bank (now part of First Union), and NationsBank (now Bank of America). It also bought the Bank of Montreal's UK-based fiscal agency business (1998) and Estabrook Capital Management, which manages assets for businesses and wealthy individuals (1999). Scandal rocked the firm in 1999 when the US began investigating the possible flow of money related to Russian organized crime; the following year a former bank executive admitted to having laundered about $7 billion through BNY.

In 2000 BNY bought the corporate trust business of Dai-Ichi Kangyo Bank (now part of Mizuho Holdings) and Harris Trust and Savings Bank. It also purchased a trio of securities clearing and processing firms and opened a direct link with French central depository Sicovam to offer European collateral management services. The next year BNY bought the trust business of New Jersey-based Summit Bancorp (since bought by FleetBoston Financial) and the corporate trust operations of U.S. Trust.

Chairman and CEO, The Bank of New York Company and The Bank of New York: Thomas A. Renyi, age 56, $7,789,800 pay
Vice Chairman, The Bank of New York Company and The Bank of New York: Alan R. Griffith, age 60, $3,691,565 pay
President and Director, The Bank of New York Company and The Bank of New York: Gerald L. Hassell, age 50, $4,476,570 pay
SEVP and CFO; CFO, The Bank of New York: Bruce W. Van Saun, age 44, $3,041,610 pay
SEVP: Robert J. Mueller, age 60, $2,731,600 pay
EVP, General Counsel, and Secretary: J. Michael Shepherd, age 46
Chairman, BNY ESI & Co.: Stephen R. Shloss
CEO, BNY Clearing Services: C. Michael Viviano
President, BNY ESI & Co.: Carey S. Pack, age 45
Director of Personnel: Thomas Angers
Auditors: Ernst & Young LLP

LOCATIONS

HQ: The Bank of New York Company, Inc.
1 Wall St., New York, NY 10286
Phone: 212-495-1784 **Fax:** 212-635-1799
Web: www.bankofny.com

The Bank of New York Company operates bank branches in Connecticut, New Jersey, and New York and also has offices in Argentina, Australia, Belgium, Brazil, the Cayman Islands, China, Egypt, France, Germany, Hong Kong, India, Indonesia, Ireland, Italy, Japan, Lebanon, Luxembourg, Mexico, the Philippines, Russia, Singapore, South Korea, Spain, Thailand, Turkey, United Arab Emirates, and the UK.

PRODUCTS/OPERATIONS

2001 Sales

	$ mil.	% of total
Interest		
Loans	2,271	32
Securities	537	7
Trading assets	401	6
Other	411	6
Noninterest		
Securities servicing fees	1,750	24
Service charges & fees	356	5
Foreign exchange & other trading activities	338	5
Private client services & asset management fees	308	4
Global payment services fees	287	4
Other	501	7
Total	**7,160**	**100**

Selected Subsidiaries
The Bank of New York
  The Bank of New York Europe
BNY Asset Management
BNY Capital Markets, Inc.
BNY ESI & Co., Inc.
BNY International Financing Corp.

COMPETITORS

Bank of America
BANK ONE
Brown Brothers
  Harriman
Canadian
  Imperial
Citigroup
Deutsche Bank
FleetBoston
HSBC Holdings
J.P. Morgan
  Chase
KeyCorp
Mellon Financial
Mizuho Holdings
Northern Trust
State Street
UBS
Wachovia

HISTORICAL FINANCIALS & EMPLOYEES

NYSE: BK FYE: December 31	Annual Growth	12/92	12/93	12/94	12/95	12/96	12/97	12/98	12/99	12/00	12/01
Assets ($ mil.)	7.9%	40,909	45,546	48,879	53,720	55,765	59,961	63,503	74,756	77,114	81,025
Net income ($ mil.)	15.4%	369	559	749	914	1,020	1,104	1,192	1,739	1,429	1,343
Income as % of assets	—	0.9%	1.2%	1.5%	1.7%	1.8%	1.8%	1.9%	2.3%	1.9%	1.7%
Earnings per share ($)	14.6%	0.53	0.68	0.93	1.09	1.20	1.36	1.53	2.27	1.92	1.81
Stock price - FY high ($)	—	6.83	7.81	8.31	12.25	18.06	29.28	40.56	45.19	59.38	58.13
Stock price - FY low ($)	—	3.75	6.33	6.23	7.13	10.88	16.38	24.00	31.81	29.75	29.75
Stock price - FY close ($)	22.2%	6.73	7.13	7.44	12.19	16.88	28.91	40.25	40.00	55.19	40.80
P/E - high	—	12	11	8	10	14	20	26	20	30	32
P/E - low	—	7	9	6	6	8	11	15	14	15	16
Dividends per share ($)	16.0%	0.19	0.22	0.28	0.34	0.42	0.49	0.54	0.58	0.66	0.72
Book value per share ($)	5.3%	5.43	5.44	5.72	6.60	6.63	6.67	7.05	6.95	8.30	8.65
Employees	1.9%	16,167	15,621	15,477	15,810	16,158	16,494	17,157	17,735	18,861	19,181

STOCK PRICE HISTORY

HIGH/LOW/CLOSE

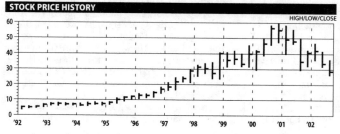

2001 FISCAL YEAR-END

Equity as % of assets: 7.8%
Return on assets: 1.7%
Return on equity: 21.5%
Long-term debt ($ mil.): 4,976
No. of shares (mil.): 730
Dividends
  Yield: 1.8%
  Payout: 39.8%
Market value ($ mil.): 29,797
Sales ($ mil.): 7,160

BANK ONE CORPORATION

BANK ONE used to holler, "Bigger is better!" but now barks, "Get yer banking businesses here!"

The Chicago-based company is the #6 US bank by assets (Citgroup is #1); its First USA unit is a top credit card issuer in the US. BANK ONE has more than 1,800 branches in 14 states and has electronic banking facilities that allow customers to bank anywhere in the US. It has become a "one-stop shop" offering everything to everyone — credit card services, retail and commercial banking, leasing, lease financing, investment management, and consumer finance, including mortgages and other loans. It also owns more than half of Paymentech, a joint venture with First Data that processes merchants' credit card transactions.

BANK ONE has suffered from bottom-line woes (stemming in part from First USA), but the company has been aggressively cutting costs, restructuring, writing off bad loans, and squirreling away credit reserves to square its balance sheet. It pulled the plug on its money-hemorrhaging Internet bank WingspanBank.com and plans to eventually drop the First USA brand in favor of the BANK ONE banner. This belt tightening has fomented speculation that the company may be in line to make an acquisition, possibly of a regional rival or an investment firm. Its existing private capital arm, One Equity Partners, acquired nearly two-thirds of struggling camera maker Polaroid (with Polaroid's creditors assuming ownership of the balance).

HISTORY

It took more than 130 years to get from Columbus, Ohio, to Chicago. The journey started with BANK ONE's predecessor, BANC ONE, the earliest incarnation of which (F. C. Session's bank in Columbus) opened in 1868. By 1929 progenitors Commercial National and City National Bank of Commerce combined to form City National Bank and Trust. John H. McCoy became the bank's president in 1935, spawning a family dynasty.

John G. took his father's place in 1958, and City National began to break with tradition. In the 1960s the bank helped launch comedienne Phyllis Diller by hiring her for radio and TV commercials. Both Diller and City National were on their way.

In 1966 the bank introduced the first Visa (then BankAmericard) card service outside California. McCoy formed a holding company for City National, First Banc Group of Ohio, in 1967 (using a "c" because of legal restrictions on using "bank"). The company grew beyond Columbus, buying Farmers Savings and Trust of Mansfield, Ohio, in 1968. First Banc scored a coup in 1977

when Merrill Lynch hired it to handle the Cash Management Account, the first product to combine a brokerage account with check-writing privileges and a debit card.

First Banc Group became BANC ONE in 1979; all affiliated banks took the name Bank One. Another McCoy, John B., succeeded his father as CEO in 1984 as barriers to interstate banking were loosened. BANC ONE expanded into Indiana, Kentucky, Michigan, and Wisconsin. It broke into the lucrative but troubled Texas market in 1989 by buying 20 failed MCorp bank branches and other failed institutions.

In 1991 the firm entered Illinois, and the next year it moved on to Arizona and Utah (all through stock-swap acquisitions so as not to dilute its investors holdings). It formed a development alliance with Banco Nacional de Mexico in 1992.

The company developed branded services and products, but affiliates could maintain their own offerings and information systems, making it difficult to track regional operations and duplicating many positions. The effect on the bottom line became apparent after 1994's bond market collapse.

In response, BANC ONE began a major consolidation effort. The company continued to make purchases, including Louisiana's #3 bank, Premier Bancorp (1996, built up during the 1980s by C. W. "Chuck" McCoy — John B.'s uncle), and Oklahoma City-based Liberty Bancorp (1997). It became the #3 credit card issuer (behind Citicorp and MBNA) when in 1997 it bought #4 First USA.

Founded in 1863, First Chicago NBD emerged from the Chicago Fire of 1871 and weathered the bank runs of the Great Depression, but it succumbed to the siren call of industry consolidation in early 1998. First Chicago agreed to be acquired by BANC ONE. The combined banks became BANK ONE, based in Chicago and 40%-owned by First Chicago stockholders and 60%-owned by BANC ONE holders.

To reduce bloat, BANK ONE in 1999 cut about 5% of its workforce and sold First Chicago's mortgage servicing portfolio and transaction processing services. John B. retired late in the year and in 2000 James Dimon, former president of Citigroup, stepped in as chairman and CEO.

Under Dimon, who replaced most of the company's executives over the next two years, BANK ONE sold its Canadian card portfolio to Royal Bank of Canada (now known as RBC Financial Group) and its subprime loan portfolio to Household International. It entered the insurance underwriting business with its purchase of Congress Life Insurance.

In 2001 NASD Regulators fined Banc One Capital Markets for bookkeeping inaccuracies.

Also that year BANK ONE converted to a financial holding company, allowing it to expand into such areas as insurance and mutual fund distribution. To bolster its credit card business, the company bought Wachovia's consumer portfolio, which added some 2.8 million customers.

OFFICERS

Chairman and CEO: James Dimon, age 46, $4,000,000 pay
EVP and CTO: Austin A. Adams, age 58
EVP and Chief Risk Management Officer: Linda Bammann, age 45, $2,042,308 pay
EVP; President and CEO, Commercial Banking: James S. Boshart III, age 56, $2,500,000 pay
EVP, Human Resources: David E. Donovan, age 51
EVP, Chief Legal Officer, and Secretary: Christine A. Edwards, age 49
EVP; President and CEO, First USA: Philip G. Heasley, age 52, $1,594,231 pay
EVP; President and CEO, Investment Management: David J. Kundert, age 59
EVP and CFO: Heidi G. Miller, age 49
EVP, Retail Banking: Charles W. Scharf, age 36, $2,500,000 pay (prior to title change)
Auditors: KPMG LLP

LOCATIONS

HQ: 1 Bank One Plaza, Chicago, IL 60670
Phone: 312-732-4000   **Fax:** 312-732-3366
Web: www.bankone.com

PRODUCTS/OPERATIONS

2001 Sales

	$ mil.	% of total
Interest		
Loans	13,213	54
Investment securities	3,219	13
Other	872	4
Noninterest		
Credit card revenue	2,775	11
Banking fees & commissions	1,731	7
Service charges on deposits	1,449	6
Fiduciary & investment management fees	754	3
Other	514	2
Total	**24,527**	**100**

COMPETITORS

ABN AMRO
American Express
Bank of America
Bank of New York
Capital One Financial
Charles Schwab
Citigroup
Comerica
Corus Bankshares

Cullen/Frost Bankers
Fifth Third Bancorp
FleetBoston
Ford
GE
General Motors
Harris Bankcorp
Household International
Huntington Bancshares

J.P. Morgan Chase
KeyCorp
Marshall & Ilsley
MBNA
Mellon Financial
Merrill Lynch
Morgan Stanley
Northern Trust
PNC Financial
U.S. Bancorp
Washington Mutual
Wells Fargo

HISTORICAL FINANCIALS & EMPLOYEES

NYSE: ONE FYE: December 31	Annual Growth	12/92	12/93	12/94	12/95	12/96	12/97	12/98	12/99	12/00	12/01
Assets ($ mil.)	17.8%	61,417	79,919	88,923	90,454	101,848	115,901	261,496	269,425	269,300	268,954
Net income ($ mil.)	14.5%	781	1,140	1,005	1,278	1,427	1,306	3,108	3,479	(511)	2,638
Income as % of assets	—	1.3%	1.4%	1.1%	1.4%	1.4%	1.1%	1.2%	1.3%	—	1.0%
Earnings per share ($)	1.5%	1.96	2.09	1.80	2.20	2.52	1.99	2.61	2.95	(0.45)	2.24
Stock price - FY high ($)	—	32.15	36.95	31.40	33.15	43.52	54.43	65.63	63.56	39.00	41.56
Stock price - FY low ($)	—	25.31	26.66	19.93	20.76	28.41	35.68	36.13	29.75	23.19	27.00
Stock price - FY close ($)	2.3%	31.92	29.39	20.97	31.09	39.09	49.37	51.06	32.00	36.63	39.05
P/E - high	—	16	18	17	15	17	27	25	21	—	18
P/E - low	—	13	13	11	9	11	17	14	10	—	12
Dividends per share ($)	2.0%	0.70	0.85	1.02	1.12	1.24	1.38	1.52	1.64	1.47	0.84
Book value per share ($)	2.8%	13.50	15.27	15.75	17.42	18.40	16.10	17.46	17.51	16.07	17.33
Employees	9.4%	32,700	45,300	48,800	46,900	51,100	56,600	91,310	86,198	80,778	73,519

STOCK PRICE HISTORY

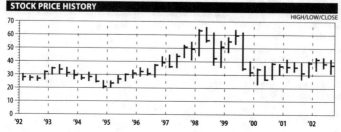

HIGH/LOW/CLOSE

2001 FISCAL YEAR-END

Equity as % of assets: 7.5%
Return on assets: 1.0%
Return on equity: 13.6%
Long-term debt ($ mil.): 43,418
No. of shares (mil.): 1,167
Dividends
  Yield: 2.2%
  Payout: 37.5%
Market value ($ mil.): 45,570
Sales ($ mil.): 24,527

BARNES & NOBLE, INC.

Barnes & Noble books a lot of sales, and it sells a lot of books. The New York City-based retailer is the #1 US bookseller, with nearly 1,000 stores throughout 49 states and the District of Columbia. More than half of its stores are freestanding superstores operating under the Barnes & Noble, Bookstop, and Bookstar banners; the rest are mall-based stores under the names B. Dalton, Doubleday, and Scribner's. Barnes & Noble also owns a direct-mail bookselling business, several publishing companies, 74% of Calendar Club, and 22% of publishing portal iUniverse.com.

The company owns 36% of online book selling unit barnesandnoble.com (a publicly traded joint venture with Bertelsmann, which also owns 36%). Together, Barnes & Noble and barnesandnoble.com own a majority stake in magazine subscription seller enews.com.

Moving beyond books, Barnes & Noble is now the top video game retailer in the US. Built through acquisitions in recent years, the company has a network of more than 1,000 video game and entertainment software stores throughout the US, Puerto Rico, and Guam. The stores operate under the banners Babbages's Etc., Software Etc., GameStop, and FuncoLand.

Chairman Leonard Riggio controls about 20% of the company, including all of the voting power of Barnes & Noble College Bookstores, a private textbook seller.

HISTORY

Barnes & Noble dates back to 1873 when Charles Barnes went into the used-book business in Wheaton, Illinois. By the turn of the century, he was operating a thriving bookselling operation in Chicago. His son William took over as president in 1902. William sold his share in the firm in 1917 (to C. W. Follett, who built Follett Corp. into a major Barnes & Noble competitor) and moved to New York City, where he bought an interest in established textbook wholesalers Noble & Noble. The company was soon renamed Barnes & Noble. It first sold mainly to colleges and libraries, providing textbooks and opening a large Fifth Avenue shop. Over the next three decades, Barnes & Noble became one of the leading booksellers in the New York region.

Enter Leonard Riggio, who worked at a New York University bookstore to help pay for night school. He studied engineering but got the itch for bookselling. In 1965, at age 24, he borrowed $5,000 and opened Student Book Exchange NYC, a college bookstore. Beginning in the late 1960s, he expanded by buying other college bookstores.

In 1971 Riggio paid $1.2 million for the Barnes & Noble store on Fifth Avenue. He soon expanded the store, and in 1974 he began offering jaw-dropping, competitor-maddening discounts of up to 40% for best-sellers. Acquiring Marboro Books five years later, the company entered the mail-order and publishing business.

By 1986 Barnes & Noble had grown to about 180 outlets (including 142 college bookstores). Along with Dutch retailer Vendex, that year it bought Dayton Hudson's B. Dalton mall bookstore chain (about 800 stores), forming BDB Holding Corp. (Vendex had sold its shares by 1997.) In 1989 the company acquired the Scribner's Bookstores trade name and the Bookstop/Bookstar superstore chain. BDB began its shift to superstore format and streamlined its operations to integrate Bookstop and Doubleday (acquired in 1990) into its business.

BDB changed its name to Barnes & Noble in 1991. With superstore sales booming, the retailer went public in 1993 (the college stores remained private). It bought 20% of Canadian bookseller Chapters in 1996 (sold in 1999).

The bookseller went online in 1997 and in 1998 sold a 50% stake in its Web subsidiary to Bertelsmann in an attempt to strengthen both companies in the battle with rival Amazon.com.

Also in 1998 Barnes & Noble agreed to buy #1 US book distributor Ingram Book Group, but the deal was called off in 1999 because of antitrust concerns. Also in 1999 barnesandnoble.com went public and Barnes & Noble bought small book publisher J.B. Fairfax International USA, which included coffee-table book publisher Michael Friedman Publishing Group. Later that year the company bought a 49% stake in book publishing portal iUniverse.com (later reduced to 22%). It also bought Riggio's financially struggling Babbage's Etc., a chain of about 500 Babbage's, Software Etc., and GameStop stores, for $215 million.

Babbage's (renamed GameStop, Inc.) acquired video game retailer Funco for $161.5 million in 2000. In 2001 Barnes & Noble joined barnesandnoble.com in acquiring a majority stake in magazine subscription seller enews.com.

In February 2002 the company completed an initial public offering of its GameStop unit, reducing its ownership interest to about 63%. The same month Leonard handed over the CEO title to his brother, Steve Riggio.

OFFICERS

Chairman: Leonard Riggio, age 61, $725,000 pay
(prior to title change)
Vice Chairman and CEO: Stephen Riggio, age 47
COO: Mitchell S. Klipper, age 44, $725,000 pay
(prior to title change)
CFO: Larry Zilavy
EVP, Distribution and Logistics: William F. Duffy, age 46
EVP, Finance: Maureen O'Connell, age 40, $652,500 pay
SVP, Corporate Communications and Public Affairs:
Mary E. Keating, age 45
VP and CIO: Joseph Giamelli, age 52
VP, Barnes & Noble Development: David S. Deason,
age 43, $630,000 pay
VP, Cafe Operations: Modesto Alcala
VP, Human Resources: Michelle Smith
President, Barnes & Noble Publishing Group:
J. Alan Kahn, age 55, $870,000 pay
Secretary and Director: Michael N. Rosen, age 61
Auditors: BDO Seidman, LLP

LOCATIONS

HQ: 122 Fifth Ave., New York, NY 10011
Phone: 212-633-3300   **Fax:** 212-675-0413
Web: www.barnesandnobleinc.com

Barnes & Noble has book and video game stores in 49
states and Washington, DC, as well as video games stores
in Guam and Puerto Rico.

2002 Stores

	No.
Superstores	591
Mall stores	305
Game & software stores	1,038
Total	**1,934**

PRODUCTS/OPERATIONS

Selected Businesses
Mall stores
  B. Dalton Bookseller
  Doubleday Book Shops
  Scribner's Bookstores
Online sales
  barnesandnoble.com
  (36%)
Publishing
  Barnes & Noble Books
  iUniverse.com
  J.B. Fairfax International
   USA

Michael Friedman
  Publishing
Superstores
  Barnes & Noble
  Bookstar
  Bookstop
Video game and software
  Babbage's Etc.
  FuncoLand
  Gamestop
  Software Etc.

COMPETITORS

Amazon.com
Best Buy
Book-of-the-
  Month Club
Books-A-Million
Borders
BUY.COM
Cendant
Cody's Books
Costco
  Wholesale

Family Christian
  Stores
Follett
Half Price Books
Hastings
  Entertainment
HMV
Hollywood
  Entertainment
Hudson News
Indigo Books &
  Music

KB Toys
MTS
Powell's Books
Rand McNally
Tattered Cover
  Book Store
Toys "R" Us
Viacom
Wal-Mart
WHSmith
Zany Brainy

HISTORICAL FINANCIALS & EMPLOYEES

NYSE: BKS FYE: Saturday nearest Jan. 31	Annual Growth	1/93	1/94	1/95	1/96	1/97	1/98	1/99	1/00	1/01	1/02
Sales ($ mil.)	18.1%	1,087	1,337	1,623	1,977	2,448	2,797	3,006	3,486	4,376	4,870
Net income ($ mil.)	—	(9)	8	26	(53)	51	53	92	125	(52)	64
Income as % of sales	—	—	0.6%	1.6%	—	2.1%	1.9%	3.1%	3.6%	—	1.3%
Earnings per share ($)	25.8%	—	0.15	0.41	(0.85)	0.75	1.10	1.29	1.75	(0.81)	0.94
Stock price - FY high ($)	—	—	17.00	15.69	21.13	18.88	34.25	48.00	40.25	29.94	43.99
Stock price - FY low ($)	—	—	10.31	10.00	10.81	11.88	15.19	22.19	18.50	16.31	23.00
Stock price - FY close ($)	15.8%	—	10.75	14.88	13.44	15.56	31.75	37.44	20.13	25.70	34.81
P/E - high	—	—	113	37	—	25	36	36	22	—	46
P/E - low	—	—	69	24	—	15	16	16	10	—	24
Dividends per share ($)	—	—	0.00	0.00	0.00	0.00	0.00	0.00	0.00	0.00	0.00
Book value per share ($)	11.6%	—	5.50	5.95	6.07	6.87	7.83	9.87	12.92	11.96	13.21
Employees	11.9%	13,500	14,700	20,000	21,400	23,900	29,500	29,000	37,400	39,000	37,000

STOCK PRICE HISTORY

HIGH/LOW/CLOSE

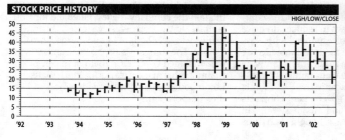

2002 FISCAL YEAR-END

Debt ratio: 33.6%
Return on equity: 7.7%
Cash ($ mil.): 108
Current ratio: 1.40
Long-term debt ($ mil.): 449
No. of shares (mil.): 67
Dividends
  Yield: —
  Payout: —
Market value ($ mil.): 2,340

BAUSCH & LOMB INCORPORATED

Eyes are the windows to profit for Bausch & Lomb. The Rochester, New York-based company is known for its contact lenses and lens care solutions. A pharmaceutical division makes prescription and over-the-counter ophthalmic drugs; its surgical unit makes equipment for cataract and other ophthalmic surgery.

Bausch & Lomb has boosted its surgery business in order to cash in on the boom in cataract and corrective eye surgeries. It also continues to develop new contact lens products, such as "no rub" solutions and lenses that can be worn for longer periods in the eye. The FDA's approval of its 30-day contact lens enters it into a race with such competitors as CIBA Vision (a Novartis unit) and Johnson & Johnson, which have developed or are developing similar products.

Over the past several years, the company has sold off certain operations and cut jobs to remain profitable and keep up with competition, but it is looking now to what it calls a major restructuring to put itself on solid ground. Among the changes will be plant closings as B&L consolidates contact lens and surgical products manufacturing, along with some 450 job cuts around the world. The firm plans to discontinue some older products and focus on newer ones with higher profit margins and potential growth.

HISTORY

In 1853 German immigrant Jacob Bausch opened a small store in Rochester, New York, to sell European optical imports. Henry Lomb soon became a partner by lending Bausch $60.

Bausch & Lomb's first major breakthrough came with Bausch's invention of Vulcanite (a hard rubber) eyeglass frames. The company fitted the frames with European lenses and by 1880 had a New York City sales office. Bausch & Lomb later began making microscopes, binoculars, and telescopes.

The company incorporated in 1908 as Bausch & Lomb Optical Co. In 1912 Jacob's son William became one of the few to make optical-quality glass in the US. During WWI, Bausch & Lomb supplied the military with lenses for binoculars, searchlights, rifle scopes, and telescopes.

The Army Air Corps commissioned the company in 1929 to create lenses to reduce sun glare for pilots. Bausch & Lomb responded with Ray-Ban sunglasses; they were made available to the public in 1936 and went on to become a company mainstay. Bausch & Lomb went public in 1938.

The company won an Oscar in the 1950s for its Cinemascope lens; it won government contracts for lenses used in satellite and missile systems in the 1960s. Bausch & Lomb also bought such firms

as Ferson Optics (1968) and Reese Optical (1969). It began concentrating on contact lenses after the FDA approved its soft lenses in 1971.

In 1981 Daniel Gill, who had helped build the soft contact lens business, became CEO. He sold the company's prescription eyeglass services and industrial instruments units and diversified into medical products and research.

Earnings soared in the 1990s with foreign expansion and acquisitions, including Dahlberg (Miracle-Ear hearing aids); Steri-Oss (dental implants); the Curel and Soft Sense skin care lines from S.C. Johnson & Son; Award, a Scottish manufacturer of disposable contacts (1996); and Arnette Optic Illusions sport sunglasses (1996).

However, Gill's insistence on double-digit growth contributed to a dubious ethical climate in which some executives used questionable tactics to put more sales on the books. This led to an SEC probe (closed in 1997 with no fines or penalties assessed) and a shareholder lawsuit (settled in 1997 for $42 million). That year, the company also paid $1.7 million to settle a class action lawsuit alleging Bausch & Lomb was marketing one type of contact lens under several different product names with varying prices. Gill resigned under fire in 1995 and was replaced by outside director William Waltrip; he turned the reins over to William Carpenter in 1997.

Noncore divisions were sold (oral care and dental implant businesses in 1996; skin care line to Kao subsidiary Andrew Jergens in 1998) in a $100 million restructuring program, and 1,900 jobs were cut. The company entered the cataract and refractive surgery market, buying Chiron's vision unit in 1998 and ophthalmic diagnostic technology company Orbtek in 1999.

To focus on eye care, the company sold its sunglasses unit to Luxottica, Miracle Ear to Italy's Amplifon, and Charles River Laboratories to an affiliate of Donaldson, Lufkin & Jenrette, now Credit Suisse First Boston (USA). Bausch & Lomb then consolidated its manufacturing operations and cut its workforce.

Facing off with rivals Johnson & Johnson and Novartis' CIBA Vision unit over its new PureVision extended-wear lenses, the company withdrew disputed product ads after an FDA warning in 1999. In 2000 the company made a failed bid for tinted contact lensmaker Wesley Jessen VisionCare (which was later bought by and merged into CIBA Vision). The company's successful purchases that year included Groupe Chauvin, a maker of ophthalmic pharmaceuticals. In 2001 Bausch & Lomb bought the ophthalmic business of Pharmos Corporation.

Chairman and CEO: Ronald L. Zarrella, age 52,
$63,462 pay (partial-year salary)
SVP and CFO: Stephen C. McCluski, age 49,
$375,100 pay
SVP and President, Americas Region:
Mark M. Sieczkarek, age 47, $303,846 pay
SVP and President, Asia Region: John M. Loughlin,
age 51
SVP and General Counsel: Robert B. Stiles, age 52
SVP, Global Supply Chain Management: Dwain L. Hahs,
age 49, $376,800 pay
SVP, Research, Development, and Engineering:
Gary M. Aron, age 59, $300,000 pay
VP and CIO: Marie L. Smith, age 44
VP, Corporate Communications and Investor Relations:
Barbara M. Kelley
VP, Human Resources: Ian J. Watkins, age 40
Auditors: PricewaterhouseCoopers LLP

LOCATIONS

HQ: 1 Bausch & Lomb Place, Rochester, NY 14604
Phone: 585-338-6000   **Fax:** 585-338-6007
Web: www.bausch.com

Bausch & Lomb has facilities in Australia, Brazil,
Canada, China, France, Germany, Hong Kong, India,
Italy, Japan, the Netherlands, South Korea, Spain, the
UK, and the US.

2001 Sales

	$ mil.	% of total
Americas	805	47
Europe	584	34
Asia-Pacific	323	19
Total	**1,712**	**100**

PRODUCTS/OPERATIONS

2001 Sales

	$ mil.	% of total
Contact lens	481	28
Lens care	438	26
Pharmaceuticals	350	20
Cataract	305	18
Refractive	138	8
Total	**1,712**	**100**

Selected Products

Vision Care
Boston (contact lenses and lens care products)
PureVision (extended-wear disposable contact lenses)
ReNu (soft contact lens care products)
SoftLens (daily disposable contact lenses)

Pharmaceuticals
Alrex (ophthalmic allergy treatment)
Lotemax (ophthalmic anti-inflammatory)
Ocuvite (OTC vitamin supplement)

Surgical
Hansatome (microkeratome)
Millennium (microsurgical system)
Technolas 217 (excimer laser)
Vitrasert (drug delivery implant devices)

COMPETITORS

Akorn	Essilor	Ocular Sciences
Alcon	International	Paradigm
Allergan	Johnson &	Medical
Cooper	Johnson	STAAR Surgical
Companies	LaserSight	VISX
Escalon Medical	Novartis	

HISTORICAL FINANCIALS & EMPLOYEES

NYSE: BOL FYE: Last Saturday in Dec.	Annual Growth	12/92	12/93	12/94	12/95	12/96	12/97	12/98	12/99	12/00	12/01
Sales ($ mil.)	0.0%	1,709	1,872	1,851	1,933	1,927	1,916	2,363	1,756	1,772	1,712
Net income ($ mil.)	(20.6%)	171	157	14	112	83	49	25	445	83	22
Income as % of sales	—	10.0%	8.4%	0.7%	5.8%	4.3%	2.6%	1.1%	25.3%	4.7%	1.3%
Earnings per share ($)	(13.4%)	2.84	2.31	0.52	1.93	1.47	0.89	0.45	7.59	1.52	0.78
Stock price - FY high ($)	—	60.50	57.50	53.88	44.50	44.50	47.88	60.00	84.75	80.88	54.93
Stock price - FY low ($)	—	44.50	43.00	30.63	30.88	32.50	32.50	37.75	51.38	33.56	27.20
Stock price - FY close ($)	(4.0%)	54.50	51.25	33.88	39.63	35.00	39.63	60.00	68.44	40.44	37.66
P/E - high	—	21	25	102	23	30	54	133	11	54	70
P/E - low	—	15	18	58	16	22	37	84	7	22	35
Dividends per share ($)	3.2%	0.78	0.86	0.93	1.00	1.04	1.04	1.04	1.04	1.04	1.04
Book value per share ($)	2.1%	15.11	15.68	15.50	16.32	15.92	14.82	14.95	21.51	18.12	18.21
Employees	(2.4%)	14,500	15,900	14,400	14,000	13,000	13,000	15,000	11,500	12,400	11,600

STOCK PRICE HISTORY

HIGH/LOW/CLOSE

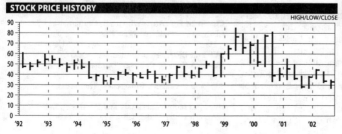

2001 FISCAL YEAR-END

Debt ratio: 41.9%
Return on equity: 2.1%
Cash ($ mil.): 534
Current ratio: 1.99
Long-term debt ($ mil.): 703
No. of shares (mil.): 54
Dividends
  Yield: 2.8%
  Payout: 133.3%
Market value ($ mil.): 2,016

BAXTER INTERNATIONAL INC.

At Baxter International, blood is just the beginning. The Deerfield, Illinois-based medical products maker operates in three segments. Its Medication Delivery unit (nearly 40% of sales) makes intravenous (IV) solutions, bags, tubing, and other supplies to deliver fluids to patients. Its BioScience segment (about 35%) develops therapeutic plasma proteins to treat hemophilia and other blood-related disorders; it also makes blood-collection and separator equipment. Baxter is also a leading maker of such renal dialysis equipment as dialyzers (or dialysis filters), and operates some 200 dialysis clinics outside the US through its Renal division.

With about half of its sales already outside the US, the company continues to build its presence abroad. After encountering problems with some of its dialyzers (involving the deaths of more than 50 patients), Baxter quickly responded by withdrawing equipment, ceasing some product lines, and closing facilities — including the one in Sweden that made the problematic dialyzers. Baxter is now bouncing back and resuming acquisitions; it bought Fusion Medical to expand its BioScience unit.

HISTORY

Idaho surgeon Ralph Falk, his brother Harry, and California physician Donald Baxter formed Don Baxter Intravenous Products in 1931 to distribute the IV solutions Baxter made in Los Angeles. Two years later the company opened its first plant outside Chicago. Ralph Falk bought Baxter's interest in 1935 and began R&D efforts leading to the first sterilized vacuum-type blood collection device (1939), which could store blood for weeks instead of hours. Product demand during WWII spurred sales above $1.5 million by 1945.

In 1949 the company created Travenol Laboratories to make and sell drugs. Baxter went public in 1951 and began an acquisition program the next year. In 1953 failing health caused both Falks to give control to William Graham, a manager since 1945. Under Graham's leadership, Baxter absorbed Wallerstein (1957); Fenwal Labs (1959); Flint, Eaton (1959); and Dayton Flexible Products (1967).

In 1975 Baxter's headquarters moved to Deerfield, Illinois. In 1978 the company debuted the first portable dialysis machine and had $1 billion in sales. Vernon Loucks Jr. became CEO two years later. Baxter claimed the title of the world's leading hospital supplier in 1985 when it bought American Hospital Supply (a Baxter distributor from 1932 to 1962). Offering more than 120,000 products and an electronic system that connected customers with some 1,500 vendors,

Baxter captured nearly 25% of the US hospital supply market in 1988. That year it became Baxter International.

In 1992 Baxter spun off Caremark (home infusion therapy and mail-order drugs) but kept a division that controlled 75% of the world's dialysis machine market.

In 1993 Baxter pleaded guilty (and was temporarily suspended from selling to the Veterans Administration) to bribing Syria to remove Baxter from a blacklist for trading in Israel.

The company entered the US cardiovascular perfusion services market in 1995 with the purchases of PSICOR and SETA. Baxter, along with two other silicone breast-implant makers, agreed to settle thousands of claims (at an average of $26,000 each) from women suffering side-effects from the implants. The next year Baxter spun off its cost management and hospital supply business as Allegiance (sold to Cardinal Health in 1999).

Buys in 1997 boosted Baxter's presence in Europe and its share of the open-heart-surgery devices market. That year it agreed to pay about 20% of a $670 million legal settlement in a suit relating to hemophiliacs infected with HIV from blood products. At the end of 1998, the company chose president Harry Kraemer to succeed Loucks as chairman and CEO.

In response to concerns posed by shareholders, Baxter in 1999 said it would phase out the use of PVC (polyvinyl chloride) in some products by 2010. In 2000 the firm spun off its underperforming cardiovascular unit as Edwards Lifesciences. To strengthen core operations, it lined up a number of purchases, including North American Vaccine.

Purchases in 2001 included the cancer treatment unit of chemicals firm Degussa. Also that year Baxter withdrew dialysis equipment from Spain and Croatia after patients who used its products died. It also ended production of two types of dialyzers that were sold there. As the number of deaths mounted to more than 50 in seven countries, Baxter began facing lawsuits; it later settled with the families of many of the patients.

OFFICERS

Chairman Emeritus: William B. Graham, age 87
Chairman, President, and CEO:
  Harry M. Jansen Kraemer Jr., age 47, $1,408,000 pay
SVP and CFO: Brian P. Anderson, age 51, $718,500 pay
SVP and General Counsel: Thomas J. Sabatino Jr.,
  age 43
SVP and President, Bioscience: Thomas H. Glanzmann,
  age 43, $653,539 pay
**SVP, Intercontinental/Asia and President, Latin
  America:** Carlos del Salto, age 59, $649,000 pay

SVP and President, Medication Delivery:
David F. Drohan, age 62
SVP and President, Renal: Alan L. Heller, age 48,
$840,000 pay
SVP, Corporate Strategy and Development:
Timothy B. Anderson, age 55
SVP, Human Resources, Communications, and Europe:
Michael J. Tucker, age 49
VP and Chief Scientific Officer: Norbert G. Riedel,
age 44
VP and Deputy General Counsel: David C. McKee,
age 54
VP and President, Europe: Eric A. Beard, age 50
VP and President, Fenwal: Gregory P. Young, age 48
VP, Global Manufacturing Operations:
James Michael Gatling, age 52
VP, Human Resources: Karen J. May, age 43
VP, Integration Management: James R. Hurley, age 52
VP, Investor Relations and Financial Planning:
Neville J. Jeharajah, age 48
Auditors: PricewaterhouseCoopers LLP

LOCATIONS

HQ: One Baxter Pkwy., Deerfield, IL 60015
Phone: 847-948-2000   **Fax:** 847-948-3948
Web: www.baxter.com

Baxter International has facilities in Australia, Austria,
Belgium, Brazil, Canada, Chile, China, Colombia, Costa
Rica, the Dominican Republic, France, Germany,
Ireland, Italy, Japan, Malta, Mexico, New Zealand, the
Philippines, Poland, Puerto Rico, Singapore, Spain,
Switzerland, Turkey, the UK, and the US.

2001 Sales

	$ mil.	% of total
US	3,887	51
International	3,776	49
Total	**7,663**	**100**

PRODUCTS/OPERATIONS

2001 Sales

	$ mil.	% of total
Medication Delivery	2,935	38
BioScience	2,786	36
Renal	1,942	26
Total	**7,663**	**100**

COMPETITORS

Abbott Labs	Johnson & Johnson
Amgen	Medtronic
Aventis Behring	Merck
Becton Dickinson	Novartis
Boston Scientific	Novo Nordisk
C. R. Bard	Pfizer
Eli Lilly	Roche
Fresenius Medical Care	Tyco Healthcare
Gambro	United States Surgical
Genentech	Wyeth

HISTORICAL FINANCIALS & EMPLOYEES

NYSE: BAX FYE: December 31	Annual Growth	12/92	12/93	12/94	12/95	12/96	12/97	12/98	12/99	12/00	12/01
Sales ($ mil.)	(1.1%)	8,471	8,879	9,324	5,048	5,438	6,138	6,599	6,380	6,896	7,663
Net income ($ mil.)	3.7%	441	(198)	596	649	669	300	315	797	740	612
Income as % of sales	—	5.2%	—	6.4%	12.9%	12.3%	4.9%	4.8%	12.5%	10.7%	8.0%
Earnings per share ($)	2.9%	0.77	(0.35)	1.07	1.16	1.21	0.53	0.55	1.35	1.25	1.00
Stock price - FY high ($)	—	20.25	16.38	14.44	22.38	24.06	30.13	33.00	38.00	45.13	55.90
Stock price - FY low ($)	—	15.25	10.00	10.81	13.38	19.88	19.94	24.25	28.41	25.88	40.06
Stock price - FY close ($)	14.2%	16.19	12.19	14.13	20.94	20.50	25.22	32.16	31.41	44.16	53.63
P/E - high	—	19	—	13	19	19	56	59	27	36	49
P/E - low	—	14	—	10	11	16	37	43	20	20	35
Dividends per share ($)	—	0.42	0.49	0.51	0.55	0.59	0.57	0.58	0.58	0.73	0.00
Book value per share ($)	(0.9%)	6.79	5.76	6.59	6.81	4.60	4.68	4.96	5.77	4.53	6.27
Employees	(2.7%)	61,300	60,400	53,500	35,500	37,000	41,000	42,000	45,000	43,000	48,000

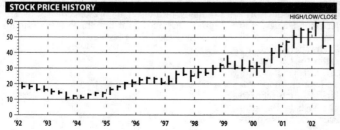

STOCK PRICE HISTORY HIGH/LOW/CLOSE

2001 FISCAL YEAR-END
Debt ratio: 39.8%
Return on equity: 19.1%
Cash ($ mil.): 582
Current ratio: 1.21
Long-term debt ($ mil.): 2,486
No. of shares (mil.): 599
Dividends
  Yield: —
  Payout: —
Market value ($ mil.): 32,119

BB&T CORPORATION

BB&T is banking on the South. Based in Winston-Salem, North Carolina, the wildly acquisitive company serves consumers, small to midsized businesses, and government entities through more than 1,100 banking offices mainly in the Carolinas, Georgia, Kentucky, Maryland, Tennessee, Virginia, West Virginia, and Washington, DC. Its primary subsidiary, Branch Banking and Trust Company, is among the oldest banks in North Carolina.

BB&T's ravenous expansion is all about creating cross-selling opportunities. By snatching up small insurance agencies (it owns about 70) and asset managers throughout the Southeast, the company has the ability to be a one-stop financial products shop. BB&T's bulk allows it to trump smaller competitors, yet the company has a community bank feel. (BB&T maintains decentralized regional management of its banks and most of its senior executives have been with the firm for some 30 years.) In addition to traditional consumer and small business accounts and loans, the company offers life and property/casualty insurance, mutual funds, and financial planning services. Business services include leasing, factoring, and investment banking (through Scott & Stringfellow).

BB&T targets for takeover banks with about $250 million to $10 billion in assets. It bought Washington, DC-area F&M Bank (which retained its name) and added about 100 branches in Kentucky after buying MidAmerica Bancorp and AREA Bancshares. The company also purchased Alabama-based Cooney, Rikard & Curtin, a wholesale insurance broker active in 45 states. After digesting these deals BB&T is on the prowl again: It will enter the coveted Florida market following its purchase of Regional Financial, the privately held parent of First South Bank, a thrift with about 20 bank branches and mortgage offices in the northern part of the state. BB&T is probably not done buying there, either.

HISTORY

The predecessor to Branch Banking and Trust (BB&T) was founded in 1872 by Alpheus Branch, son of a wealthy planter, who founded Branch and Company, a mercantile business, in Wilson, North Carolina. He and Thomas Jefferson Hadley, who was organizing a public school system, created the Branch and Hadley bank. They helped rebuild farms and small businesses after the Civil War.

In 1887 Branch bought out Hadley and changed the bank's name to Branch and Company, Bankers. Two years later Branch secured a state trust charter for the Wilson Banking and Trust Company. He never got the business running, however, and died in 1893. The trust charter was amended to change the name to Branch Banking and Company, and Branch and Company, Bankers, was folded into it in 1900.

In 1907 the bank finally got its trust operations running and began calling itself Branch Banking and Trust Company. In 1922 it opened its first insurance department; the next year it started its mortgage loan activities.

BB&T survived the 1929 stock market crash with the help of the Post Office. Nervous customers withdrew their funds from BB&T and other banks and deposited them in postal savings accounts, unaware that BB&T was the local Post Office's bank and the withdrawn funds went right back to the bank. BB&T opened six more branches between 1929 and 1933.

After WWII consumerism skyrocketed, resulting in more car loans and mortgages. During the 1960s and 1970s the bank embarked on a series of mergers and acquisitions, forming the thin end of a buying wedge that would widen significantly in the coming decades.

By 1994 BB&T was the fourth-largest bank in North Carolina. In 1995 it merged with North Carolina's fifth-largest bank, Southern National Corp., founded in 1897.

With banking regulations loosening to allow different types of operations, BB&T in 1997 made several acquisitions, including banks, thrifts, and securities brokerage Craigie.

BB&T's 1998 activities included three bank acquisitions that pushed it into metro Washington, DC. The company also increased holdings in fields such as insurance sales, venture capital for Southern businesses, and investment banking (through its acquisition of Scott & Stringfellow Financial, the South's oldest NYSE member).

In 1999 Craigie was melded into Scott & Stringfellow. That year BB&T bought several insurance companies and small banks. The company continued its march through the South the following year, buying several Georgia banks and Tennessee's BankFirst. In 2001 BB&T purchased South Carolina's FirstSpartan Financial, multibank holding company Century South Banks, Maryland-based FCNB Corporation, and western Georgia's Community First Banking Company. To bolster its presence in the Washington, DC, market, it bought Virginia Capital Bancshares and F&M National.

Chairman and CEO, BB&T and Branch Banking and Trust Company: John A. Allison IV, age 53, $1,830,104 pay
COO: Henry G. Williamson Jr., age 54, $1,297,120 pay
President: Kelly S. King, age 53, $814,441 pay
SEVP and Manager, Administrative Services; President, Branch Banking and Trust Company:
 Robert E. Greene, age 52, $554,238 pay
SEVP and Chief Credit Officer: W. Kendall Chalk, age 56, $554,238 pay
SEVP and CFO: Scott E. Reed, age 53, $554,238 pay
SEVP and Controller: Sherry A. Kellett, age 57
SEVP and Operations Division Manager:
 C. Leon Wilson III, age 47
SVP, Government Affairs and Public Policy:
 A. Patrick Linton, age 52
VP, Human Resources: Charlie McCurry
East Tennessee Regional President: Lars C. Anderson, age 41
West Virginia Central Regional President:
 Phyllis H. Arnold, age 53
Valley Regional President (Virginia): Wes Beckner, age 43
President, BB&T of South Carolina; Midlands Regional President: Michael R. Brenan, age 49
DC Metro Region President: Ricky K. Brown, age 46
Coastal South Carolina Regional President:
 J. Frank Bullard, age 42
Eastern North Carolina Regional President:
 Danny Daniels, age 53
Southeast North Carolina Regional President:
 Jeff Etheridge, age 53
Mid-South Georgia Regional President: Larry D. Flowers, age 51
Western North Carolina Regional President:
 Fred F. Groce Jr., age 59
Auditors: PricewaterhouseCoopers LLP

HQ: 200 W. 2nd St., Winston-Salem, NC 27101
Phone: 336-733-2000   **Fax:** 336-733-2009
Web: www.bbandt.com

2001 Sales

	$ mil.	% of total
Interest		
Loans	3,808	61
Securities	1,024	16
Short-term investments	17	—
Noninterest		
Service charges on deposits	350	6
Agency insurance commissions	177	3
Investment banking & brokerage fees & commissions	175	3
Mortgage banking	148	2
Securities gains	122	2
Other	407	7
Total	**6,228**	**100**

Allfirst Financial
Bank of America
First Charter
First Virginia
FNB Financial Services
Mercantile Bankshares
Morgan Keegan
National Commerce Financial
RBC Centura Banks
Regions Financial
Southern Financial Bancorp
SunTrust
Synovus
United Bankshares
Wachovia

NYSE: BBT FYE: December 31	Annual Growth	12/92	12/93	12/94	12/95	12/96	12/97	12/98	12/99	12/00	12/01
Assets ($ mil.)	35.5%	4,598	5,898	8,756	20,493	21,247	29,178	34,427	43,481	59,340	70,870
Net income ($ mil.)	39.1%	50	79	111	178	284	360	502	613	626	974
Income as % of assets	—	1.1%	1.3%	1.3%	0.9%	1.3%	1.2%	1.5%	1.4%	1.1%	1.4%
Earnings per share ($)	13.3%	0.69	0.47	0.98	0.80	1.19	1.30	1.71	1.83	1.55	2.12
Stock price - FY high ($)	—	9.88	11.75	11.00	14.00	18.50	32.50	40.75	40.63	38.25	38.84
Stock price - FY low ($)	—	6.50	9.25	8.44	9.38	12.88	17.50	26.25	27.19	21.69	30.24
Stock price - FY close ($)	15.6%	9.81	9.88	9.56	13.13	18.13	32.03	40.31	27.38	37.31	36.11
P/E - high	—	14	20	11	17	15	24	23	22	24	18
P/E - low	—	9	15	8	11	11	13	15	15	14	14
Dividends per share ($)	16.4%	0.25	0.32	0.37	0.43	0.50	0.58	0.66	0.75	0.86	0.98
Book value per share ($)	6.8%	7.48	7.90	7.16	8.10	7.91	8.22	9.51	9.66	11.91	13.50
Employees	27.0%	2,379	2,549	3,609	7,700	7,800	9,800	10,400	13,700	17,500	20,400

HIGH/LOW/CLOSE

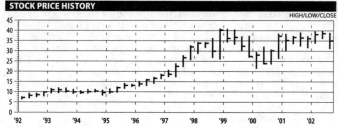

Equity as % of assets: 8.7%
Return on assets: 1.5%
Return on equity: 17.8%
Long-term debt ($ mil.): 11,721
No. of shares (mil.): 456
Dividends
 Yield: 2.7%
 Payout: 46.2%
Market value ($ mil.): 16,455
Sales ($ mil.): 6,228

THE BEAR STEARNS COMPANIES

There are many bears on Wall Street but only one Bear Stearns. One of the US's top securities trading, investment banking, and brokerage firms, New York City-based Bear Stearns Companies serves a worldwide clientele of corporations, governments, and individuals. The company has expertise in equity and bond underwriting, asset management, and market-making activities. In the 1990s it added significant mergers and acquisitions capacities. The firm diversifies its income by performing trade clearing services.

Bear Stearns operates through three divisions: Capital Markets, Global Clearing Services, and Wealth Management. Capital Markets, the largest part of the firm's business, serves institutional clients and offers fixed income, equities, and traditional investment banking services. Global Clearing Services offers prime broker and broker-dealer clearing services, including margin lending and securities borrowing. Wealth Management encompasses Bear Stearns private client and asset management business geared towards wealthy individuals.

Bear Stearns has a large presence in Latin America, where it is a market leader in underwriting equity offerings. It has operated in Europe for 40 years and continues to add offices. The company has also made strides in Asia, especially in China and Japan. The stock market slump, however, prompted Bear Stearns to cut 7% of its staff, with most of the reductions being made in the company's US operations.

HISTORY

Joseph Bear, Robert Stearns, and Harold Mayer formed Bear, Stearns & Co. in 1923 with $500,000 in capital. The firm weathered 1929's crash with no layoffs; during the Depression, Bear Stearns aggressively promoted government bonds.

Its first Chicago branch opened in 1940; it created an international department in 1948 and opened an Amsterdam office in 1955. Branches followed in Geneva (1963), San Francisco (1965), Paris (1967), and Los Angeles (1968).

Formerly a runner at Salomon Brothers, trader Salim "Cy" Lewis guided Bear Stearns in the 1950s and 1960s. He worked his way up to chairman, becoming a Wall Street legend as the driven, Scotch-drinking taskmaster of "The Bear" (and driving out Jerome Kohlberg, Henry Kravis, and George Roberts).

In 1973 Bear Stearns pulled profit out of unused space by giving independent brokers free rent in return for their use of the company for stock trade clearing. The practice became a major contributor to the firm's bottom line.

When Lewis died in 1978, Alan Greenberg became CEO; he surpassed Lewis' reputation for aggressive trading. Kansas-born, Oklahoma-reared Greenberg had worked his way up from clerk to the risk arbitrage desk at age 25.

Under Greenberg's colorful leadership the firm formed departments for government securities (1979) and mortgage-backed securities (1981) and also formed New Jersey bank and trust company Bear Stearns Asset Management and Custodial Trust (1984).

Bear Stearns went public in 1985 as The Bear Stearns Companies Inc. It moved into investment banking in the late 1980s and became the leading underwriter in the Latin American market in 1991. The firm also formed Bear Stearns Securities Corp. to handle clearing.

With success and a high profile came difficulties. The firm's underwriting volume prompted a deluge of lawsuits relating to junk bonds, hot IPOs that fizzled, point-of-sale and in-store advertising, and diet planner Jenny Craig. The 1994 bond market crash mauled Bear Stearns; its non-calendar fiscal year meant that decreased earnings arising from those events were not posted until mid-1995, when most of its competitors had recovered. Lower earnings brought reduced bonuses, which prompted several high-level bond executives to leave.

In 1997 Bear Stearns joined forces with the National Mortgage Bank of Greece to introduce mortgage/asset securitization to that country; it also opened an office in Ireland to provide access to the unifying European market.

Legal woes resurfaced in 1998; the firm suffered adverse judgments over actions in the late 1980s. One jury award ($108 million, reduced to $30 million by 2000) related to now-defunct Daisy Systems' buy of Cadnetix and another to bond underwriting for Weintraub Entertainment Group may eventually cost more than $120 million. In 1999 Bear Stearns agreed to pay $42 million to settle SEC charges relating to the firm's relationship with defunct brokerage A. R. Baron Company, which was accused of defrauding customers; the SEC also charged Richard Harriton, president of Bear Stearns' clearing unit, with fraud in connection with the case.

In 2001, the firm bought NYSE specialist Wagner Stott Mercator and merged it with its market-making joint venture with Hunter Partners; the unit was renamed Wagner Stott Bear Specialists.

In the same year, current CEO James Cayne assumed the mantle of chairman when Greenberg stepped down after more than 50 years with the company.

OFFICERS

Chairman and CEO, Bear Stearns Companies and Bear, Stearns & Co.: James E. Cayne, age 67, $5,172,150 pay
Chairman of the Executive Committee: Alan C. Greenberg, age 74, $3,198,200 pay
President, Co-COO, Bear Stearns Companies and Bear, Stearns & Co.: Alan D. Schwartz, age 51, $4,966,890 pay
President, Co-COO, and Director, Bear Stearns Companies and Bear, Stearns, & Co.: Warren J. Spector, age 44, $4,948,550 pay
EVP and General Counsel, Bear Stearns Companies and Bear, Stearns & Co.: Mark E. Lehman, age 50
EVP and CFO, Bear Stearns Companies and Bear, Stearns & Co.: Samuel L. Molinaro Jr., age 44, $2,744,250 pay
Vice Chairman, Bear, Stearns & Co.: E. John Rosenwald Jr., age 71
Vice Chairman, Bear, Stearns & Co.: Michael L. Tarnopol, age 65
Co-Head of Investment Banking: Jeffrey Urwin
Head of Corporate Marketing: Debra Douglas
Global Head of Mergers and Acquisitions Group: Louis Friedman
Global Head of Equity Capital Markets Group: John Kilgallon
Global Head of Equity Derivative Trading: Steve Meyer
Auditors: Deloitte & Touche LLP

LOCATIONS

HQ: The Bear Stearns Companies, Inc.
383 Madison Ave., New York, NY 10179
Phone: 212-272-2000   **Fax:** 212-272-4785
Web: www.bearstearns.com

PRODUCTS/OPERATIONS

2001 Sales

	$ mil.	% of total
Interest & dividends	4,339	50
Principal transactions	2,283	26
Commissions	1,117	13
Investment banking	772	9
Other income	190	2
Total	**8,701**	**100**

Selected Services

Arbitrage	Mergers, acquisitions, and
Brokerage	restructurings
Equity research	Securities clearance
Fiduciary services	services
Financing customer	Securities lending
activities	Securities trading
Foreign exchange	Trust services
Investment management	Underwriting
and advisory services	Wealth management
Market-making	

COMPETITORS

AIG	Goldman Sachs
Banc of America Securities	Lehman Brothers
Brown Brothers Harriman	Merrill Lynch
Charles Schwab	Morgan Stanley
CIBC World Markets	Salomon Smith Barney
Credit Suisse First Boston	Holdings
Deutsche Banc Alex.	UBS PaineWebber
Brown	UBS Warburg

HISTORICAL FINANCIALS & EMPLOYEES

NYSE: BSC FYE: November 30	Annual Growth	6/92	6/93	6/94	6/95	6/96	6/97	6/98	6/99	*11/00	11/01
Sales ($ mil.)	14.0%	2,677	2,857	3,441	3,754	4,964	6,077	7,980	7,882	10,277	8,701
Net income ($ mil.)	8.6%	295	362	387	241	491	613	660	673	769	619
Income as % of sales	—	11.0%	12.7%	11.2%	6.4%	9.9%	10.1%	8.3%	8.5%	7.5%	7.1%
Earnings per share ($)	9.8%	1.82	2.13	2.27	1.40	2.96	3.81	4.17	4.26	5.35	4.23
Stock price - FY high ($)	—	13.75	16.74	19.36	18.89	21.46	32.51	58.00	55.28	72.50	64.45
Stock price - FY low ($)	—	8.03	9.53	13.20	11.53	15.71	17.80	30.81	23.56	36.50	40.65
Stock price - FY close ($)	20.0%	11.13	16.65	13.29	17.56	20.38	30.98	51.55	44.51	45.94	57.50
P/E - high	—	8	8	9	13	7	9	14	13	14	14
P/E - low	—	4	4	6	8	5	5	7	6	7	9
Dividends per share ($)	4.0%	0.42	0.42	0.44	0.47	0.50	0.53	0.54	0.56	0.84	0.60
Book value per share ($)	23.8%	8.47	11.52	14.93	16.47	20.05	25.25	33.20	39.42	51.88	57.72
Employees	6.7%	5,873	6,036	7,321	7,481	7,749	8,309	9,200	9,500	11,201	10,500

* Fiscal year change

STOCK PRICE HISTORY

HIGH/LOW/CLOSE

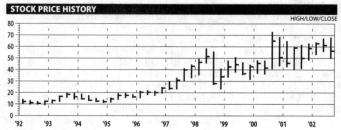

2001 FISCAL YEAR-END

Debt ratio: 80.6%
Return on equity: 12.8%
Cash ($ mil.): —
Current ratio: —
Long-term debt ($ mil.): 23,429
No. of shares (mil.): 98
Dividends
  Yield: 1.0%
  Payout: 14.2%
Market value ($ mil.): 5,607

BECHTEL GROUP, INC.

Whether it's raising an entire city or razing a nuclear power plant, you can bet the Bechtel Group will be there to bid on the business. The engineering, construction, and project management firm, based in San Francisco, is #1 in the US heavy construction industry (ahead of Fluor).

Bechtel builds facilities for diverse industries, ranging from aerospace to civil infrastructure to mining and metals to waste management. The company has made a name for itself by participating in huge projects such as the construction of Hoover Dam and the San Francisco-Oakland Bay Bridge. It completes more than 1,000 projects a year, operating worldwide.

The services Bechtel offers are as broad as the industries it serves. The firm provides such services as project management and design, environmental restoration and remediation, telecommunications (installing cable-optic networks and constructing data centers), and e-business infrastructure (including design, systems integration, and commissioning). Jumping on the international broadband-wagon, Bechtel is expanding its telecommunications services into overseas markets. Through Bechtel Enterprises, the company often invests in infrastructure projects and arranges financing for its clients.

Chairman and CEO Riley Bechtel is the fourth generation of Bechtels to lead the firm. The Bechtel family still controls the private company, which was founded by Warren Bechtel.

HISTORY

In 1898 25-year-old Warren Bechtel left his Kansas farm to grade railroads in the Oklahoma Indian territories, then followed the rails west. Settling in Oakland, California, he founded his own contracting firm. Foreseeing the importance of roads, oil, and power, he won big projects such as the Northern California Highway and the Bowman Dam. By 1925, when he incorporated his company as W.A. Bechtel & Co., it ranked as the West's largest construction company. In 1931 Bechtel helped found the consortium that built Hoover Dam.

Under the leadership of Steve Bechtel (president after his father's death in 1933), the company obtained contracts for large infrastructure projects such as the San Francisco-Oakland Bay Bridge. Noted for his friendships with influential people, including Dwight Eisenhower, Adlai Stevenson, and Saudi Arabia's King Faisal, Steve developed projects that spanned nations and industries, such as pipelines in Saudi Arabia and numerous power projects. By 1960, when Steve Bechtel Jr. took over, the company was operating on six continents.

In the next two decades, Bechtel worked on transportation projects — such as San Francisco's Bay Area Rapid Transit (BART) system and the Washington, DC, subway system — and power projects, including nuclear plants. After the 1979 Three Mile Island accident, Bechtel tried its hand at nuclear cleanup. With nuclear power no longer in vogue, it focused on other markets, such as mining in New Guinea (gold and copper, 1981-84) and China (coal, 1984). Bechtel's Jubail project in Saudi Arabia, begun in 1976, raised an entire industrial port city on the Persian Gulf.

The US recession and rising developing-world debt of the early 1980s sent Bechtel reeling. It cut its workforce by 22,000 and stemmed losses by piling up small projects.

Riley Bechtel, great-grandson of Warren, became CEO in 1990. After the 1991 Gulf War, Bechtel extinguished Kuwait's flaming oil wells and worked on the oil-spill cleanup. During the decade it also worked on such projects as the Channel tunnel (Chunnel) between England and France, a new airport in Hong Kong, and pipelines in the former Soviet Union.

Bechtel was part of the consortium contracted in 1996 to build a high-speed passenger rail line between London and the Chunnel. International Generating (InterGen), Bechtel's joint venture with Pacific Gas and Electric (PG&E), was chosen to help build Mexico's first private power plant. In 1996 Bechtel bought PG&E's share of InterGen, then sold a 50% stake in InterGen to a unit of Royal Dutch/Shell in early 1997.

That year Bechtel began a venture, Netcon (Thailand), with Lucent to build telecom systems abroad. Bechtel also joined with other companies to buy into energy projects in developing regions. In 1998 it won a major contract to construct a gas production plant with Technip in Abu Dhabi. That year it joined Battelle and Electricité de France in project management of a long-term plan to stabilize the damaged reactor of the Chernobyl nuclear plant in Ukraine.

In 1999 Bechtel was hired to decommission the Connecticut Yankee nuclear plant. It also won contracts with Internet companies, including failed online grocer Webvan, to build a series of 26 automated grocery warehouses in the US in a deal worth nearly $1 billion. However, only four were completed before Webvan fizzled in mid-2001. The next year Bechtel teamed up with Shell Oil to build a $400 million power plant in Baja California to meet the high demands of the US-Mexico border region. It also formed Nexant, an energy consulting service for the oil and gas industry and utilities.

Bechtel expanded its telecommunications

operations in 2001 to provide turnkey network implementation services in Europe, the Middle East, and Asia. In 2002 Bechtel was once again called on to work on the UK's rail system, taking over management of the upgrade of the west coast main line from financially troubled Railtrack.

OFFICERS

Chairman Emeritus: Steve Bechtel Jr.
Chairman and CEO: Riley P. Bechtel, age 50
Vice Chairman: Paul Unruh
Vice Chairman, President, and COO: Adrian Zaccaria
SVP, CFO, and Director: Georganne Proctor
EVP and Director; President, Bechtel Enterprises: Tim Statton
EVP and Director; President, Bechtel Systems and Infrastructure: Jude Laspa
EVP and Director; President, Civil Engineering and Construction Business Unit: Lee McIntire
EVP and Director; President, Pipeline Engineering and Construction Business Unit: Mike Thiele
SVP and Director; President, Petroleum and Chemical Engineering and Construction Business Unit: Bill Dudley
SVP and Director; President, Bechtel National: Thomas Hash
SVP and Manager of Procurement and Contracts: Jack Futcher
President, Bechtel Infrastructure: John McDonald
President, Mining and Metals Engineering and Construction Business Unit: Andy Greig
President, Power Engineering and Construction Business Unit: Scott Ogilvie
President, Telecommunications and Industrial Engineering and Construction Business Unit: George Conniff
President, Asia Pacific Region: Bob Baxter
President, Europe, Africa, Middle East, and Southwest Asia Regions: Chuck Redman
President, Latin America Region: Dennis Connell
EVP and Managing Director, Bechtel Enterprises: Daniel K. H. Chao
Auditors: PricewaterhouseCoopers LLP

LOCATIONS

HQ: 50 Beale St., San Francisco, CA 94105
Phone: 415-768-1234   **Fax:** 415-768-9038
Web: www.bechtel.com

Bechtel Group operates worldwide from offices in 10 states in the US, along with international offices in Argentina, Australia, Brazil, Canada, Chile, China, Egypt, France, India, Indonesia, Japan, Korea, Malaysia, Mexico, Oman, Peru, the Philippines, Russia, Saudi Arabia, Singapore, Spain, Taiwan, Thailand, Turkey, United Arab Emirates, the UK, and Venezuela.

PRODUCTS/OPERATIONS

Selected Services
Automation technology
Community relations
Environmental health and safety
Equipment operations
International consulting
Labor relations
Project management, engineering, and financing
Worldwide procurement

COMPETITORS

ABB	HOCHTIEF	Philipp
AMEC	Hyundai	Holzmann
Black & Veatch	Engineering	PowerGen
Bouygues	and	RWE
CH2M HILL	Construction	Safety-Kleen
Chicago Bridge	ITOCHU	Samsung
and Iron	J.A. Jones	Schneider
Chiyoda Corp.	Jacobs	Shaw Group
Duke/Fluor	Engineering	Siemens
Daniel	Kværner	Skanska
Eiffage	Marubeni	Technip-Coflexip
EllisDon	NKK	URS
Construction	Parsons	VINCI
Enron	Perini	Washington
Fluor	Peter Kiewit	Group
Foster Wheeler	Sons'	WESTON
Halliburton		

HISTORICAL FINANCIALS & EMPLOYEES

Private FYE: December 31	Annual Growth	12/92	12/93	12/94	12/95	12/96	12/97	12/98	12/99	12/00	12/01
Sales ($ mil.)	6.2%	7,774	7,337	7,885	8,504	8,157	11,329	12,645	12,600	15,108	13,400
Employees	5.5%	30,900	29,400	29,200	29,400	30,000	30,000	30,000	40,000	40,000	50,000

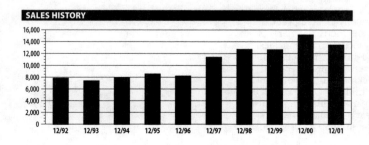

SALES HISTORY

BECKMAN COULTER, INC.

Beckman Coulter is instrumental in keeping people well. Nearly 80% of the Fullerton, California-based company's sales come from clinical diagnostics products and related services. Its cellular analysis, clinical chemistry, immunodiagnostics, sample preparation, and other systems are used mainly by hospital laboratories to test blood and other body fluids. The company also makes laboratory instruments such as centrifuges and DNA sequencers for life sciences and drug research. Beckman Coulter has installed more than 200,000 of its systems in about 130 countries; the US represents some 55% of sales.

Beckman Coulter sees dollar signs in DNA. The company plans to branch out into genetic testing by forming a Molecular Diagnostics unit, which will be part of its newly-created Specialty Testing division. The firm hopes to beef up this segment through alliances and acquisitions.

HISTORY

Arnold Beckman created his first chemistry lab as a child in a shed his blacksmith father had built for him. Beckman studied chemical engineering, worked at Bell Labs (now part of Lucent Technologies), and then earned his doctorate in photochemistry in 1928 from the California Institute of Technology. In 1935, while teaching at CalTech and working as a consultant, Beckman created a special ink for the National Postage Meter Company. He formed the National Inking Appliance Company (later National Technical Laboratories), which was 90% owned by National Postage Meter and 10% owned by Beckman.

In 1935 Beckman also created a device for a Southern California citrus processor that measured lemon juice acidity. Beckman's acidity, or pH, meter soon became a standard tool in chemical laboratories. In 1941 he debuted a wavelength spectrum analysis system, a forerunner of today's analytical precision and chemical analysis instruments. That year the company's sales topped $250,000.

The company became Beckman Instruments in 1950 and went public two years later. During that period the company created products for aerospace, military, and industrial markets. However, it increasingly focused on the medical and research niches, and during the 1960s it introduced glucose analyzers and protein peptide sequencers. By 1975 Beckman Instruments' annual sales neared $230 million.

An 82-year-old Beckman sold his company to SmithKline in 1982, creating SmithKline Beckman. In 1988 Louis Rosso, who as president had guided Beckman's move into life sciences and diagnostics, was named CEO. SmithKline Beckman in 1989 merged with UK pharmaceuticals pioneer Beecham Group, becoming SmithKline Beecham. (That company merged with Glaxo Wellcome to become GlaxoSmithKline plc in 2000.) Beckman, operating as a unit within SmithKline Beecham, suffered financially as a result of cuts in health care spending. SmithKline Beecham spun the company off that year as a medical and research market instrument maker.

New products and cost controls returned Beckman Instruments to health. The company restructured in 1993 (taking writeoffs in 1993 and 1994), then launched a buying spree. It acquired Genomyx, a maker of DNA sequencing products, in 1996, and Sanofi Diagnostics Pasteur's immunoassay product line and related facilities in 1997. Late that year it acquired Coulter, which served the same hospitals and medical offices as Beckman — only with hematology products — for $1.2 billion.

Wallace Coulter in 1948 discovered a new technology for blood cell analysis, dubbed the Coulter Principle. With brother Joe, an electrical engineer, Wallace (who died in 1998) began producing the Coulter Counter cell and particle analyzer. The brothers formed Coulter Electronics in 1958. Over the years the private company made tests to detect everything from colon cancer to strep throat, but it became best known for blood cell analysis diagnostic systems.

Beckman Instruments' purchase of Coulter, which led to job cuts (13% of its workforce), caused losses for 1997. The next year the company changed its name to Beckman Coulter. John Wareham, an executive with Beckman since the early 1980s, replaced Rosso as CEO.

The addition of the Coulter product lines enabled the company to win 1999 contracts from several regional health care networks and large purchasing organizations. In 2000 the company initiated some restructuring by closing plants in Argentina, Brazil, and Hong Kong.

OFFICERS

Chairman, President, and CEO: John P. Wareham, age 60, $1,305,493 pay
VP and CFO: Amin I. Khalifa, age 48, $400,225 pay
VP and Treasurer: James T. Glover, age 52
VP, General Counsel, and Secretary: William H. May, age 59
VP, Human Resources and Corporate Communications: Fidencio M. Mares, age 55
President, Clinical Diagnostics Division: Scott Garrett
President, Life Science Research Division: George E. Bers, age 51, $372,378 pay
President, Specialty Testing Division: Edgar E. Vivanco, age 58, $403,646 pay
Controller: James B. Gray
Auditors: KPMG LLP

LOCATIONS

HQ: 4300 N. Harbor Blvd., Fullerton, CA 92834
Phone: 714-871-4848   **Fax:** 714-773-8283
Web: www.beckmancoulter.com

Beckman Coulter has manufacturing operations in Australia, China, France, Germany, Ireland, Japan, and the US. The company's European administrative center is in Switzerland.

2001 Sales

	$ mil.	% of total
Americas	1,255	63
Europe	485	25
Asia	244	12
Total	**1,984**	**100**

PRODUCTS/OPERATIONS

2001 Sales

	$ mil.	% of total
Clinical diagnostics	1,525	77
Life science research	459	23
Total	**1,984**	**100**

COMPETITORS

Agilent Technologies
Amersham Biosciences
Applera
Bayer AG
Becton Dickinson
Bio-Rad Labs
Dade Behring
Diagnostic Products
Fisher Scientific
Ortho-Clinical Diagnostics
PerkinElmer
Roche
Thermo Electron
Vysis
Waters Corporation

HISTORICAL FINANCIALS & EMPLOYEES

NYSE: BEC FYE: December 31	Annual Growth	12/92	12/93	12/94	12/95	12/96	12/97	12/98	12/99	12/00	12/01
Sales ($ mil.)	9.1%	909	876	889	930	1,028	1,198	1,718	1,809	1,887	1,984
Net income ($ mil.)	13.6%	44	(38)	42	49	75	(264)	34	106	126	138
Income as % of sales	—	4.8%	—	4.7%	5.3%	7.3%	—	1.9%	5.9%	6.7%	7.0%
Earnings per share ($)	12.1%	0.77	(0.68)	0.75	0.85	1.29	(4.79)	0.57	1.79	2.03	2.16
Stock price - FY high ($)	—	12.13	14.13	16.25	17.94	20.56	26.16	32.47	27.88	42.44	47.60
Stock price - FY low ($)	—	8.81	9.81	11.50	13.00	16.00	18.69	20.03	19.75	22.78	32.80
Stock price - FY close ($)	15.7%	11.94	13.69	13.94	17.69	19.19	20.00	27.13	25.44	41.94	44.30
P/E - high	—	16	—	19	21	15	—	54	15	20	20
P/E - low	—	11	—	14	15	12	—	33	11	11	14
Dividends per share ($)	9.5%	0.15	0.18	0.20	0.22	0.26	0.30	0.31	0.32	0.33	0.34
Book value per share ($)	3.6%	6.14	4.95	5.66	6.15	7.12	1.48	2.23	3.93	5.76	8.47
Employees	4.3%	6,900	6,600	6,200	5,700	6,100	11,100	10,000	9,500	9,520	10,094

STOCK PRICE HISTORY

HIGH/LOW/CLOSE

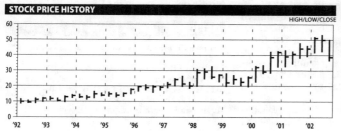

2001 FISCAL YEAR-END

Debt ratio: 59.5%
Return on equity: 32.1%
Cash ($ mil.): 36
Current ratio: 2.03
Long-term debt ($ mil.): 760
No. of shares (mil.): 61
Dividends
  Yield: 0.8%
  Payout: 15.7%
Market value ($ mil.): 2,711

BECTON, DICKINSON

Becton, Dickinson is anything but dull. The Franklin Lakes, New Jersey-based company specializes in "sharps" — it is one of the leading makers of hypodermic needles and syringes in the world. Its Medical Systems division (about half of sales) makes the latter products as well as insulin syringes, anesthesia needles, infusion therapy devices, surgical blades, and scalpels. Other company segments include Clinical Laboratory Solutions (sample collection products, test kits, consulting services) and Biosciences (cell analysis systems, labware, growth media).

Now that is has reorganized into three units under the BD brand, the company can focus on expanding its market overseas, where nearly half of its sales are already generated. BD also continues to cash in on regulations that require safer needle devices — it already had several of such products in the works before the passage of the Needlestick Safety and Prevention Act. BD plans to develop additional versions of its products that are safer and less painful, as well.

HISTORY

Maxwell Becton and Fairleigh Dickinson established a medical supply firm in New York in 1897. In 1907 the company moved to New Jersey and became one of the first US firms to make hypodermic needles.

During WWI, Becton, Dickinson (BD) made all-glass syringes and introduced the cotton elastic bandage. After the war, its researchers designed an improved stethoscope and created specialized hypodermic needles. The company supplied medical equipment to the armed forces during WWII. Becton and Dickinson helped establish Fairleigh Dickinson Junior College (now Fairleigh Dickinson University) in 1942. The company continued to develop products such as the Vacutainer blood-collection apparatus, its first medical laboratory aid.

After the deaths of Dickinson (1948) and Becton (1951), their respective sons, Fairleigh Jr. and Henry, took over. The company introduced disposable hypodermic syringes in 1961. BD went public in 1963 to raise money for new expansion. In the 1960s the company opened plants in Brazil, Canada, France, and Ireland and climbed aboard the conglomeration bandwagon by diversifying into such businesses as industrial gloves (Edmont, 1966) and computer systems (Spear, 1968). BD also went on a major acquisition spree in its core fields during the 1960s and 1970s, buying more than 25 medical supply, testing, and lab companies by 1980.

Wesley Howe, successor to Fairleigh Dickinson Jr., expanded the company's foreign sales in the 1970s. Howe thwarted a takeover by the diversifying oil giant Sun Company (now Sunoco) in 1978 and began to sell BD's nonmedical businesses in 1983, ending with the 1989 sale of Edmont. Acquisitions by the company, including Deseret Medical (IV catheters, surgical gloves and masks; 1986), sharpened BD's focus on medical and surgical supplies.

In the 1990s BD formed a number of alliances and ventures, including a 1991 agreement to make and market Baxter International's Inter-Link needleless injection system, which reduces the risk of accidental needle sticks, and a 1993 joint venture with NeXagen (now part of Gilead Sciences) to make and market in vitro diagnostics. As tuberculosis reemerged in the US as a serious health threat, the firm improved its TB-detection and drug-resistance test systems, which cut testing time from as much as seven weeks to less than two.

In 1996 BD introduced GlucoWatch (a glucose monitoring device developed by Cygnus), and acquired the diagnostic business and brand name of MicroProbe (now Epoch Pharmaceuticals).

Previously known on Wall Street as a homely company that focused on cutting costs, BD changed its image with a string of acquisitions beginning in 1997. The firm acquired PharMingen (biomedical research reagents) and Difco Laboratories (microbiology media), which broadened its product lines. BD also collaborated with Nanogen on diagnosis products for infectious disease.

In 1998 BD bought The BOC Group's medical devices business. The company also settled a lawsuit by a health care worker claiming that BD continued selling conventional syringes that could spread disease through accidental needle sticks instead of promoting safer technology. BD still faced several lawsuits from health workers who had sustained needle sticks. In 1999 the firm joined forces with Millennium Pharmaceuticals to develop cancer tests and treatments; it also bought genetic test maker Clontech Laboratories. In a cost-cutting effort, BD made plans in 2000 to cut its workforce by 1,000 (about 4%).

The following year BD launched the shortest insulin needle ever in the US.

OFFICERS

Chairman, President, and CEO: Edward J. Ludwig, age 50
EVP and CFO: John R. Considine, age 51
SVP, Company Operations: William A. Kozy, age 49
SVP, Technology, Strategy, and Development: Vincent A. Forlenza, age 48
VP, Human Resources: Jean-Marc Dageville, age 42

VP, Secretary, and General Counsel: Bridget M. Healy, age 46
VP and Controller: Richard M. Hyne
President, BD Biosciences: Deborah J. Neff, age 48
VP and Treasurer: Richard K. Berman
President, BD Clinical Laboratory Solutions: Richard O. Brajer
President, Worldwide Medical Systems: Gary M. Cohen, age 42
President, Asia/Pacific: James R. Wessel, age 61
VP, Taxes: Mark H. Borofsky
President, Europe: A. John Hanson, age 57
VP, Quality Management: James R. Brown
President, Japan: Rex C. Valentine, age 50
President, Latin America: Gilberto D. Bulcao, age 54
Auditors: Ernst & Young LLP

LOCATIONS

HQ: Becton, Dickinson and Company
1 Becton Dr., Franklin Lakes, NJ 07417
Phone: 201-847-6800   **Fax:** 201-847-6475
Web: www.bd.com

Becton, Dickinson has offices in some 50 countries in Africa, Asia Pacific, Europe, the Middle East, North America, and South America.

2001 Sales

	$ mil.	% of total
US	2,016	54
International	1,738	46
Total	**3,754**	**100**

PRODUCTS/OPERATIONS

2001 Sales

	$ mil.	% of total
Medical Systems	2,007	53
Clinical Laboratory Solutions	1,155	31
Biosciences	592	16
Total	**3,754**	**100**

Selected Products

Anesthesia needles
Bar-code systems for patient identification and data capture
Cell growth and screening products
Cellular analysis systems
Critical care systems
Diabetes care products
Elastic support products
Hematology instruments
Hypodermic needles and syringes
Immunodiagnostic test kits
Infusion therapy devices
Labware
Microbiology products
Molecular biology reagents (for study of genes)
Monoclonal antibodies (for biomedical research)
Opthalmic surgery devices
Prefillable drug-delivery systems
Sample collection products
Specimen management systems
Surgical blades and scalpels
Thermometers

COMPETITORS

Abbott Labs
Alaris Medical
Apogent Technologies inc.
Baxter
Boston Scientific
Diagnostic Products
Johnson & Johnson
Maxxim Medical
Terumo
Trinity Biotech
United States Surgical

HISTORICAL FINANCIALS & EMPLOYEES

NYSE: BDX FYE: September 30	Annual Growth	9/92	9/93	9/94	9/95	9/96	9/97	9/98	9/99	9/00	9/01
Sales ($ mil.)	5.3%	2,365	2,465	2,560	2,713	2,770	2,811	3,117	3,418	3,618	3,754
Net income ($ mil.)	8.0%	201	72	227	252	284	300	237	276	393	402
Income as % of sales	—	8.5%	2.9%	8.9%	9.3%	10.2%	10.7%	7.6%	8.1%	10.9%	10.7%
Earnings per share ($)	9.7%	0.65	0.22	0.76	0.89	1.05	1.15	0.90	1.04	1.49	1.49
Stock price - FY high ($)	—	9.86	10.52	12.06	15.88	22.44	27.81	43.81	49.63	42.00	39.25
Stock price - FY low ($)	—	7.25	8.16	8.50	11.28	15.53	18.50	20.94	25.13	21.75	25.81
Stock price - FY close ($)	16.5%	9.39	9.41	12.06	15.72	22.13	23.94	41.13	28.06	26.44	37.00
P/E - high	—	15	15	16	18	20	23	46	46	27	25
P/E - low	—	11	12	11	13	14	15	22	23	14	17
Dividends per share ($)	10.9%	0.15	0.17	0.19	0.21	0.23	0.26	0.29	0.34	0.37	0.38
Book value per share ($)	6.2%	5.25	4.87	5.27	5.37	5.36	5.67	6.51	7.05	7.72	8.98
Employees	2.9%	19,100	19,000	18,600	18,100	17,900	18,900	21,700	24,000	25,000	24,800

STOCK PRICE HISTORY

HIGH/LOW/CLOSE

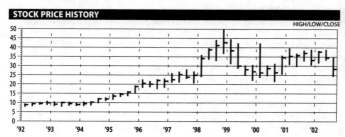

2001 FISCAL YEAR-END

Debt ratio: 25.2%
Return on equity: 19.1%
Cash ($ mil.): 82
Current ratio: 1.39
Long-term debt ($ mil.): 783
No. of shares (mil.): 259
Dividends
  Yield: 1.0%
  Payout: 25.5%
Market value ($ mil.): 9,592

BED BATH & BEYOND INC.

"Beyond" is really not much farther than your kitchen and living room, but it means more alliterative fun for Bed Bath & Beyond. The Union, New Jersey-based company is on top of the towel heap among superstore domestics retailers, a few folds ahead of #2 Linens 'n Things. The company has more than 400 outlets in 44 states (adding more than 50 per year) and Puerto Rico.

Bed Bath & Beyond's stores offer large selections of department-store-quality, brand-name and private-label products. The company has two main categories: domestics (bed linens, bathroom and kitchen items) and home furnishings (a potpourri of goods ranging from cookware and cutlery to ironing boards and coffeemakers to picture frames and soap).

The retailer's decentralized structure allows store managers to have more control than their peers at other retailers (and the company has less manager turnover). The debt-free company cuts costs by locating its stores in strip shopping centers, freestanding buildings, and off-price malls — rather than in pricier regional malls — and by depending on word-of-mouth and inexpensive direct-delivery circulars for advertising. To cut costs further the company's vendors ship merchandise directly to the stores, eliminating the expense of a central distribution center and reducing warehousing costs.

Founders Warren Eisenberg and Leonard Feinstein (who are also co-chairmen and co-CEOs who operate from separate locations) have slowly reduced their holdings in Bed Bath & Beyond.

HISTORY

Warren Eisenberg and Leonard Feinstein, both employed by a discounter called Arlan's, brainstormed an idea in 1971 for a chain of stores offering only home goods. They were betting that customers were, in Feinstein's words, interested in a "designer approach to linens and housewares." The two men started two small linens stores (about 2,000 sq. ft) named bed n bath, one in New York and one in New Jersey.

Expansion came at a fairly slow pace as the company moved only into California and Connecticut by 1985. By then the time was right for such a specialty retailer: Department stores were cutting back on their houseware lines to focus on the more profitable apparel segment, and baby boomers were spending more leisure time at their homes (and more money on spiffing them up). Eisenberg and Feinstein opened a 20,000-sq.-ft. superstore in 1985 that offered a full line of home furnishings. The firm changed its name to Bed Bath & Beyond two years later in order to reflect its new offerings.

With the successful superstore format, the company built all new stores in the larger design. Bed Bath & Beyond grew rapidly; square footage quadrupled between 1992 and 1996. The company went public in 1992. That year it eclipsed the size of its previous stores when it opened a 50,000-sq.-ft. store in Manhattan. (It later enlarged this store to 80,000 sq. ft.; the company's stores now average 42,000 sq. ft.)

Bed Bath & Beyond's management has attributed its success, in part, to the leeway it gives its store managers, who monitor inventory and have the freedom to try new products and layouts. One example often cited by the company is the case of a manager who decided to sell glasses by the piece instead of in sets. Sales increased 30%, and the whole chain incorporated the practice.

The retailer opened 28 new stores in fiscal 1997, 33 in fiscal 1998, and 45 in fiscal 1999, its first-ever billion dollar sales year.

In 1999 the company dipped a toe into the waters of e-commerce by agreeing to buy a stake in Internet Gift Registries, which operates the WeddingNetwork Web site. The company later began offering online sales and bridal registry services. Keeping up its rapid expansion pace, the company opened 70 stores in 2000 and announced plans to open another 80 stores in 2001.

In March 2002 Bed Bath & Beyond acquired Harmon Stores Inc., a health and beauty aid retailer with 27 stores in three states.

OFFICERS

Co-Chairman and Co-CEO: Warren Eisenberg, age 71, $791,667 pay
Co-Chairman and Co-CEO: Leonard Feinstein, age 65, $791,667 pay
President, COO, and Director: Steven H. Temares, age 43, $733,000 pay
CFO and Treasurer: Ronald Curwin, age 72
SVP and Chief Merchandising Officer: Arthur Stark, age 47, $442,000 pay
SVP, Stores: Matthew Fiorilli, age 45, $432,000 pay
VP and CIO: Richard C. McMahon
VP and Controller: Susan E. Lattmann
VP and Corporate Counsel: Michael J. Callahan
VP and General Merchandise Manager, Hardlines: Todd Johnson
VP and General Merchandise Manager, Planning and Allocation: Scott Hames
VP and General Merchandise Manager, Softlines: Nancy J. Katz

VP, Construction and Store Development: Jim Brendle
VP, Corporate Administration and Operations: Michael Honeyman
VP, Corporate Development: G. William Waltzinger Jr.
VP, E-Service Operations: Joseph P. Rowland
VP, Finance: Eugene A. Castagna
VP, Human Resources: Concetta Van Dyke
VP, Information Technology: Stephen J. Murray
VP, Legal and General Counsel: Allan N. Rauch
Auditors: KPMG LLP

LOCATIONS

HQ: 650 Liberty Ave., Union, NJ 07083
Phone: 908-688-0888   **Fax:** 908-688-6483
Web: www.bedbathandbeyond.com

Bed Bath & Beyond has operations in 44 states and in Puerto Rico.

PRODUCTS/OPERATIONS

Selected Merchandise

Domestics
Bath accessories
  Hampers
  Shower curtains
  Towels
Bed linens
  Bedspreads
  Pillows
  Sheets
Kitchen textiles
  Cloth napkins
  Dish towels
  Placemats
  Tablecloths
Window treatments

Home Furnishings
Basic housewares
  Accessories (lamps, chairs, accent rugs)
  General housewares (brooms, ironing boards)
  Small appliances (blenders, coffeemakers, vacuums)
  Storage items (hangers, organizers, shoe racks)
General home furnishings
  Artificial plants and flowers
  Candles
  Gift wrap
  Picture frames
  Seasonal merchandise
  Wall art
Kitchen and tabletop items
  Cookware
  Cutlery
  Flatware
  Gadgets
  Glassware
  Serveware

COMPETITORS

Bombay Company
Burlington Coat Factory
Container Store
Cost Plus
Dillard's
Euromarket Designs
Federated
IKEA
J. C. Penney
Kmart
Lillian Vernon
Linens 'n Things
May
Pier 1 Imports
Ross Stores
Saks Inc.
Sears
Strouds
Target
TJX
Wal-Mart
Williams-Sonoma

HISTORICAL FINANCIALS & EMPLOYEES

Nasdaq: BBBY FYE: Saturday nearest Feb. 28	Annual Growth	2/93	2/94	2/95	2/96	2/97	2/98	2/99	2/00	2/01	2/02
Sales ($ mil.)	33.5%	217	306	440	601	823	1,067	1,397	1,878	2,397	2,928
Net income ($ mil.)	33.8%	16	22	30	40	55	73	97	131	172	220
Income as % of sales	—	7.4%	7.2%	6.8%	6.6%	6.7%	6.9%	7.0%	7.0%	7.2%	7.5%
Earnings per share ($)	32.2%	0.06	0.08	0.11	0.15	0.20	0.26	0.34	0.46	0.59	0.74
Stock price - FY high ($)	—	2.38	4.44	4.13	5.66	7.94	11.22	17.59	19.69	27.81	36.53
Stock price - FY low ($)	—	0.88	1.84	2.84	2.25	4.56	5.72	8.56	11.22	11.00	18.70
Stock price - FY close ($)	37.6%	1.89	3.41	3.03	5.58	6.50	10.80	14.72	14.19	24.63	33.40
P/E - high	—	40	56	38	38	40	42	50	42	46	48
P/E - low	—	15	23	26	15	23	21	24	24	18	25
Dividends per share ($)	—	0.00	0.00	0.00	0.00	0.00	0.00	0.00	0.00	0.00	0.00
Book value per share ($)	38.3%	0.20	0.29	0.40	0.56	0.78	1.07	1.47	1.99	2.84	3.76
Employees	25.8%	2,400	3,200	4,100	5,400	7,000	8,200	9,400	12,000	15,000	19,000

STOCK PRICE HISTORY
HIGH/LOW/CLOSE

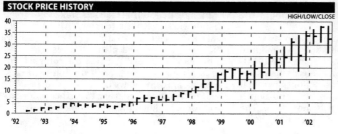

2002 FISCAL YEAR-END
Debt ratio: 0.0%
Return on equity: 23.0%
Cash ($ mil.): 430
Current ratio: 2.40
Long-term debt ($ mil.): 0
No. of shares (mil.): 291
Dividends
  Yield: —
  Payout: —
Market value ($ mil.): 9,734

BELLSOUTH CORPORATION

In the telecommunications world, BellSouth is the belle of the South and beyond, providing services to more than 46 million customers in the US and 15 other countries. As the incumbent local exchange carrier (ILEC) for nine states from Louisiana to Kentucky, the Atlanta-based company is the #3 US local phone company (behind Verizon and SBC Communications). BellSouth has 25 million local phone lines in service.

The company offers consumer and business voice, data, and Internet services, including DSL (digital subscriber line) access and Web hosting. BellSouth also provides both digital wireless and wireline video entertainment systems in its local service area. It has gained permission from regulators to offer long-distance services in Georgia and Louisiana.

BellSouth has expanded beyond its home region by combining its US mobile phone operations with those of SBC to create Cingular Wireless, the #2 US wireless carrier (after Verizon Wireless), with more than 21 million customers in 38 states.

BellSouth is also a hot enchilada south of the border, where it has considered plans to offer a tracking stock for its BellSouth Latin America Group. The company also has stakes in communications providers in Europe and Israel but has announced plans to sell these.

HISTORY

As Boston-based National Bell struggled to market Alexander Graham Bell's telephone, general manager Theodore Vail recruited James Merrill Ormes in 1878 to target the southern US. Ormes created several Bell exchanges, but competitor Western Union hampered growth. The next year the two rivals formed Southern Bell Telephone and Telegraph, and Western Union took the controlling interest. In the 1890s Southern Bell's patents expired, igniting competition, but the Bell responded by upgrading networks, cutting prices, and buying out rivals.

The company relinquished its territory in the Virginias in 1912, and AT&T arranged Southern Bell's merger with Cumberland Telephone and Telegraph (Kentucky, Louisiana, Mississippi, and Tennessee). In the post-WWII boom the company grew rapidly.

Southern Bell was structured into two divisions in 1957, a prelude to its split in 1968 into Birmingham-based South Central Bell (Alabama, Kentucky, Louisiana, Mississippi, and Tennessee) and Atlanta-based Southern Bell (Florida, Georgia, North Carolina, and South Carolina). But the division was short-lived. The 1983 AT&T break up spawned seven Baby Bells,

which were responsible for local phone service. The largest, BellSouth, reunited Southern Bell and South Central Bell.

BellSouth reached beyond local service in the 1980s and 1990s, acquiring a directory publisher (1986), paging and cellular company MCCA (1988), and a cellular license in Argentina (1988). In 1990 it created wireless provider BellSouth New Zealand (sold out to Vodafone in 1998). BellSouth also bought 18 Midwestern cellular systems from McCaw Cellular (1992). Following the 1995 FCC auction, BellSouth teamed up with Northern Telecom (now Nortel Networks) to build one of the first PCS systems in the US. BellSouth sold its paging division to MobileMedia (now a part of Arch Wireless) in 1996.

In 1997 BellSouth made major investments in Latin America, buying 49% of NICACEL, Nicaragua's only wireless company, and majority stakes in telecoms in Ecuador and Peru.

BellSouth tried to enter long-distance markets in South Carolina and Louisiana in 1998, but the FCC turned it down, saying it had not opened its local markets to competition. Undaunted, the company tried again in 1999 when it bought a 10% stake in long-distance provider Qwest. BellSouth also hinted in an SEC filing that it had considered buying control of Qwest. (Qwest began buying back BellSouth's stake in 2001.)

In 1999 BellSouth rolled out its digital subscriber line (DSL) high-speed Internet access and entered the home security market. A year later the company joined Dutch phone company KPN in taking full ownership of German mobile phone operator E-Plus. It also combined its US wireless businesses with those of fellow Baby Bell SBC Communications. BellSouth took a 40% stake in the joint venture, Cingular Wireless, and SBC, which had more wireless customers to contribute, grabbed 60%.

The company announced in 2001 that it was expanding its DSL services and teamed up with Dell Computer to offer DSL-equipped PCs. That year BellSouth announced it would consolidate all of its retail and wholesale domestic operations, effective the first day of 2002, and it said it would reduce its non-management workforce by 1,200 jobs.

In 2002 BellSouth traded its stake in German mobile carrier E-Plus to Royal KPN for a 9% stake in the Dutch operator. It later sold its KPN stake and announced plans to divest its other European holdings. That year the company entered into a four-year, $350 million wholesale services agreement with Qwest. Also in 2002 BellSouth announced plans to further reduce its workforce by 4,000 to 5,000 employees.

OFFICERS

Chairman, President, and CEO: F. Duane Ackerman, age 59, $3,002,000 pay
Vice Chairman, Domestic Operations: Gary D. Forsee, age 52, $1,417,500 pay
CFO: Ronald M. Dykes, age 54, $1,265,500 pay
EVP and General Counsel: Charles R. Morgan, age 55
SVP Corporate Compliance and Corporate Secretary: Rebecca M. Dunn
VP Advertising and Public Relations: William C. Pate
VP Applications, Strategy, and Product Innovation: Jai Menon
VP BellSouth Network Transformation: Ray Smets
VP Consumer Services: Valencia I. Adams
VP Corporate Development: Barry Boniface
VP Corporate Strategy and Planning: Suzanne H. Detlefs
VP Finance and Supply Chain Management: W. Patrick Shannon, age 39
VP Human Resources: Richard D. Sibbernsen
VP Investor Relations: Nancy C. Humphries
Auditors: PricewaterhouseCoopers LLP

LOCATIONS

HQ: 1155 Peachtree St. NE, Atlanta, GA 30309
Phone: 404-249-2000   **Fax:** 404-249-5599
Web: www.bellsouth.com

BellSouth has operations in Alabama, Florida, Georgia, Kentucky, Louisiana, Mississippi, North Carolina, South Carolina, and Tennessee. It has interests in telecommunications operations in Argentina, Brazil, Chile, Colombia, Denmark, Ecuador, Germany, Guatemala, India, Israel, Nicaragua, Panama, Peru, Uruguay, and Venezuela.

PRODUCTS/OPERATIONS

2001 Sales

	$ mil.	% of total
Communications group		
Local service	11,810	49
Network access	4,969	20
Long-distance	747	3
Other communications	1,545	6
BellSouth Latin America		
Services	2,430	10
Equipment sales	170	1
Advertising & publishing	86	—
Other	249	1
Domestic advertising & publishing	2,091	9
Other businesses	140	1
Adjustments	(107)	—
Total	**24,130**	**100**

COMPETITORS

Adelphia Business Solutions	Telecom Italia
Allegiance Telecom	Telecomunicaciones de Chile
ALLTEL	Telefónica
AT&T	Telefónica de Argentina
CenturyTel	Telefónica del Peru
Cox Enterprises	Teleglobe
Focal Communications	Telephone & Data Systems
ITC^DeltaCom	Time Warner Telecom
Millicom	Verizon
Mpower	Vodafone
SBC Communications	WorldCom
Sprint FON	XO Communications
Telecom Argentina	

HISTORICAL FINANCIALS & EMPLOYEES

NYSE: BLS FYE: December 31	Annual Growth	12/92	12/93	12/94	12/95	12/96	12/97	12/98	12/99	12/00	12/01
Sales ($ mil.)	5.3%	15,202	15,880	16,845	17,886	19,040	20,561	23,123	25,224	26,151	24,130
Net income ($ mil.)	5.3%	1,618	880	2,160	(1,232)	2,863	3,261	3,527	3,448	4,220	2,570
Income as % of sales	—	10.6%	5.5%	12.8%	—	15.0%	15.9%	15.3%	13.7%	16.1%	10.7%
Earnings per share ($)	5.6%	0.83	0.43	1.09	(0.62)	1.44	1.64	1.78	1.80	2.23	1.36
Stock price - FY high ($)	—	13.88	15.97	15.88	21.94	22.94	29.06	50.00	51.31	53.50	45.88
Stock price - FY low ($)	—	10.84	12.59	12.63	13.41	17.63	19.06	27.06	39.75	34.94	36.26
Stock price - FY close ($)	12.9%	12.84	14.50	13.53	21.75	20.25	28.16	49.88	46.81	40.94	38.15
P/E - high	—	16	31	15	—	16	18	28	28	24	33
P/E - low	—	13	24	12	—	12	12	15	22	16	26
Dividends per share ($)	1.1%	0.69	0.69	0.69	0.70	0.72	0.72	0.72	0.76	0.76	0.76
Book value per share ($)	3.9%	7.01	6.80	7.24	5.95	6.68	7.64	8.26	7.87	9.03	9.91
Employees	(1.1%)	97,112	95,084	92,100	87,600	81,200	81,000	88,400	96,200	103,900	87,875

STOCK PRICE HISTORY

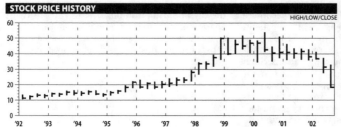

HIGH/LOW/CLOSE

2001 FISCAL YEAR-END

Debt ratio: 44.7%
Return on equity: 14.5%
Cash ($ mil.): 592
Current ratio: 0.68
Long-term debt ($ mil.): 15,014
No. of shares (mil.): 1,877
Dividends
  Yield: 2.0%
  Payout: 55.9%
Market value ($ mil.): 71,608

BEMIS COMPANY, INC.

The folks at Bemis Company can really pack a wallop . . . or a snack . . . or diapers, for that matter. The Minneapolis-based company produces flexible packaging and pressure-sensitive materials (used primarily for labeling). Flexible packaging accounts for nearly 80% of sales and pressure-sensitive materials for the rest. The company's products protect and promote items that range from meat and bread to pet food and diapers. Bemis sells its packaging to the food (its largest market), agribusiness, chemical, graphic arts and printing, medical, and pharmaceutical industries. The company's pressure-sensitive graphics are also used for extra-large "packaging" that includes signage and advertisements on buses and trains.

After an acquisitive period, which included the late 2001 purchase of plastic film maker Duralam, Bemis has been working on integrating its new operations. However, in 2002, the company announced that it is buying plastic films manufacturer Walki Films from UPM-Kymmene for $70 million and simultaneously selling them a self-adhesive materials unit for $420 million.

HISTORY

Judson Moss Bemis founded J. M. Bemis and Company, Bag Manufacturers, in St. Louis in 1858. The 25-year-old received advice and equipment from cousin Simeon Farwell, who owned an established bag-making factory. St. Louis' role as a trading center supported by major railroads and the Mississippi River helped Bemis' business. The company introduced preprinted and machine-sewn flour sacks to the city's millers, and by the end of its first year it was making about 4,000 sacks a day. In its second year Edward Brown, a relative of Farwell's, became Bemis' partner, and the company was renamed Bemis and Brown.

During the Civil War, Brown opened an office in Boston to make the most of fluctuating exchange rates. Bemis also began trading in raw cotton (priced sky-high because of the war), and it started recycling burlap shipping bags into gunnysacks. The company soon began producing its own burlap sacks from imported jute.

Stephen Bemis, Judson's brother, became a partner in the firm in 1870 and took over its St. Louis operations. Judson joined Brown in Boston, where he could be involved in commodity purchases and financial operations. Soon after, he bought out Brown's share of the firm for $300,000, an amount considered extravagant.

By the early 1880s Bemis Bros. and Co. was the US's #2 bag maker. It opened a second factory in 1881 in Minneapolis, which was home to

such companies as General Mills and Pillsbury. During the late 1800s and the early 1900s, Bemis opened plants throughout the US.

Judson retired in 1909, but the company continued to be run by Bemis family members. In 1914 the company entered the emerging industry of paper milling and paper-bag making, but it continued to focus on textile packaging until WWII, when shortages of cotton and jute expanded the role of paper packaging and led to the development of polyethylene packaging.

By the 1950s Bemis' core products were paper and plastic packaging. In 1959 the company opened its own R&D facility. During the late 1950s and 1960s Bemis made several important acquisitions, including Curwood (packaging for medical products) and MACtac (pressure-sensitive materials). The company was renamed Bemis Company in 1965.

Bemis sold more than $100 million of non-core businesses during the 1970s and 1980s. In its effort to become an industry leader, the company began a major capital expansion program. Bemis' sales topped $1 billion in 1988.

The company bought candy-packaging producer Milprint, Inc., in 1990; Princeton Packaging's bakery-packaging business in 1993; and Banner Packaging in 1995. In 1996 Bemis introduced the on-battery tester, developed with Eveready. Bemis' medical packaging segment was rejuvenated that year with the purchase of Malaysia-based Perfecseal. The company sold its packaging-equipment business in 1997 and began closing plants and consolidating operations.

In 1998 Bemis purchased a one-third interest in Brazil-based Dixie Toga's flexible-packaging operations. That year it also acquired Belgium's Techy International, which became Bemis' base for sales and distribution in Europe.

Bemis invested more than $100 million to modernize its packaging manufacturing and printing operations in 1999. The next year it acquired Arrow Industries' flexible packaging operations, Viskase's plastic-films business, and Kanzaki Specialty Papers' pressure sensitive materials business. Bemis acquired plastic film maker Duralam in 2001.

In June 2002 the company agreed to acquire the Clysar shrink film business of DuPont (with operations in both the US and Europe). The purchase gives Bemis a worldwide reach for its shrink bags, film, and heat-set packaging products.

OFFICERS

Chairman: John H. Roe, age 62, $851,332 pay
President, CEO, and Director: Jeffrey H. Curler, age 51,
$1,191,865 pay
SVP, General Counsel, and Secretary: Scott W. Johnson,
age 61, $568,749 pay
VP, Chief Financial Officer, and Treasurer:
Gene C. Wulf, age 51
VP, General Counsel, and Assistant Secretary:
James J. Seifert, age 45
VP, Operations; President, Bemis Flexible Packaging:
Thomas L. Sall, age 57, $774,907 pay
VP and President, Bemis High Barrier Products:
Henry J. Thiesen
VP and Controller: Stanley A. Jaffy, age 53
VP and Asst. Treasurer: Melanie E. R. Miller
VP, Human Resources: Eugene H. Seashore Jr., age 52
Auditors: PricewaterhouseCoopers LLP

LOCATIONS

HQ: 222 S. 9th St., Ste. 2300, Minneapolis, MN 55402
Phone: 612-376-3000   **Fax:** 612-376-3180
Web: www.bemis.com

Bemis Company has operations in Belgium, Brazil,
Canada, France, Germany, Italy, Jamaica, Malaysia,
Mexico, Singapore, Spain, Sweden, Switzerland, the UK,
and the US.

PRODUCTS/OPERATIONS

2001 Sales

	% of total
Flexible packaging	
High-barrier products	49
Polyethylene	21
Paper	9
Pressure-sensitive materials	21
Total	**100**

Selected Products

Flexible Packaging
Coated and laminated film
Industrial and consumer paper-bag packaging
Polyethylene packaging

Pressure-Sensitive Materials
Graphic films
Narrow web roll label products
Printing products
Technical products

COMPETITORS

3M	DuPont	Rexam
AEP Industries	Flexcon	Sealed Air
Alcan	Company	Smurfit-Stone
Amcor	International	Container
Avery Dennison	Paper	Sonoco Products
Constar	Koç	Southern Film
International	Pactiv	Extruders
Crown Cork &	Pechiney	UPM-Kymmene
Seal	Pliant	
Dow Chemical	Printpack	

HISTORICAL FINANCIALS & EMPLOYEES

NYSE: BMS FYE: December 31	Annual Growth	12/92	12/93	12/94	12/95	12/96	12/97	12/98	12/99	12/00	12/01
Sales ($ mil.)	7.6%	1,181	1,204	1,391	1,523	1,655	1,877	1,848	1,918	2,165	2,293
Net income ($ mil.)	10.5%	57	44	73	85	101	108	111	115	131	140
Income as % of sales	—	4.8%	3.7%	5.2%	5.6%	6.1%	5.7%	6.0%	6.0%	6.0%	6.1%
Earnings per share ($)	10.2%	1.10	0.86	1.40	1.63	1.90	2.00	2.09	2.18	2.44	2.64
Stock price - FY high ($)	—	29.63	27.38	25.75	30.00	37.63	47.94	46.94	40.38	39.31	52.47
Stock price - FY low ($)	—	19.75	19.88	20.50	23.00	25.63	33.63	33.50	30.19	22.94	28.69
Stock price - FY close ($)	7.7%	25.13	23.63	24.00	25.63	36.88	44.06	37.94	34.88	33.56	49.18
P/E - high	—	27	31	18	18	20	24	22	18	16	20
P/E - low	—	18	22	15	14	13	17	16	14	9	11
Dividends per share ($)	9.0%	0.46	0.50	0.54	0.64	0.72	0.80	0.88	0.92	0.96	1.00
Book value per share ($)	10.1%	7.06	7.24	8.16	9.76	9.79	12.08	12.83	13.91	15.19	16.76
Employees	4.0%	7,733	7,565	8,120	8,515	8,900	9,300	9,400	9,500	11,000	11,000

STOCK PRICE HISTORY

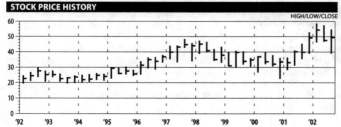

HIGH/LOW/CLOSE

2001 FISCAL YEAR-END

Debt ratio: 40.2%
Return on equity: 16.7%
Cash ($ mil.): 35
Current ratio: 2.46
Long-term debt ($ mil.): 595
No. of shares (mil.): 53
Dividends
  Yield: 2.0%
  Payout: 37.9%
Market value ($ mil.): 2,600

BERKSHIRE HATHAWAY INC.

Berkshire Hathaway, investment firm of the billionaire-populist Warren Buffett, sidestepped the stock market's "Great Bubble" of 2000 along with the "Dot-com Meltdown" only to have its profits hit by losses in the reinsurance industry in the aftermath of the September 11 attacks. Berkshire Hathaway's attachment to safe but boring industries ensures the company maintains a relatively steady course. Under the guidance of the plainspoken Mr. Buffett, who pens his annual shareholder's letter in the first person, the firm proudly eschews get-rich-quick financial swashbuckling in favor of a measured, no-frills approach to growth. Most acquisitions are made with cash, and most firms retain their management after the transaction.

The firm's plain vanilla investments include building products maker Johns Manville , carpet maker Shaw Industries, and sheet rock and other gypsum-based products maker USG. Its extensive insurance holdings have not been immune to a slowing US economy: GEICO Corporation's new premium growth has virtually come to a stop, and GeneralCologne Re has had to endure underwriting losses in recent years. Berkshire Hathaway also holds a sizeable portion of the ubiquitous Coca-Cola, which it plans to hold "forever." Subsidiary MidAmerican Energy Holdings has been picking up bargains in the post-Enron energy industry such as its planned buy of The Northern Natural Gas Co. pipeline from Dynegy. Berkshire Hathaway has even dipped a toe into the telecommunications industry it has traditionally shunned with a planned investment in Level 3 Communications.

While the company's performance (or, rather, its leader's performance) is always a hot topic, investors are becoming increasingly mindful of the health of that leader and the future leadership of Berkshire Hathaway. The septuagenarian Buffett (who owns about 40% of the firm with wife Susan) brushes aside health concerns but has acknowledged his mortality by making plans for succession. Three positions will replace him, including a chairman (his son, Howard Buffett), a director of investments (Louis A. Simpson), and a CEO (a player to be named later).

HISTORY

Warren Buffett bought his first stock — three shares of Cities Service — at age 11. In the 1950s he studied at Columbia University under famed investor Benjamin Graham. Graham's axioms: Use quantitative analysis to discover companies whose intrinsic worth exceeds their stock prices; popularity is irrelevant; the market will vindicate the patient investor.

In 1956 Buffett, then 25, founded Buffett Partnership. Its $105,000 in initial assets multiplied as the company bought Berkshire Hathaway (textiles, 1965) and National Indemnity (insurance, 1967). When Buffett nixed the partnership in 1969 because he believed stocks were overvalued, value per share had risen 30-fold.

Buffett continued investing under the Berkshire Hathaway name, looking for solid businesses, such as See's Candies (1972), advertising agencies (Interpublic, Ogilvy & Mather), newspapers (*Washington Post, Boston Globe*, and *Buffalo News*), and television (Capital Cities/ABC, 1985). Buffett bought Nebraska Furniture Mart (1983) and Scott Fetzer (*World Book* encyclopedias and Kirby vacuum cleaners, 1986). The scale of investments grew as the company bought stakes in Salomon Brothers (investment banking, 1987), Gillette (1989), American Express (1991), Coca-Cola (1988-89), and Wells Fargo (1989-91).

In the 1990s, Buffett sought strong brands and services, including shoes (H. H. Brown, 1991), furniture, jewelry retailing, and pilot-training (FlightSafety International, 1996). Salomon Brothers drew ire when it became known that it had illegally bought up most of two successive issues of US government securities in 1991. Buffett appointed new management. The resulting exodus of talent took Salomon into a tailspin that ended when Travelers bought it to form Salomon Smith Barney. Buffett increased Berkshire Hathaway's insurance holdings, including an 82% stake in Central States Indemnity (credit insurance, 1992) and a buyout of GEICO (1996).

In 1996, as the company's share price soared toward $35,000 and outsiders threatened to start a mutual fund to invest in Berkshire Hathaway stock, Buffett created a cheaper class B stock.

Continuing to invest in what he knew, Buffett bought General Re (1998, now GeneralCologne Re), and time-share private jets through Executive Jet's NetJets (1998).

In 2000 the company's investments included Ben Bridge Jeweler; furniture rental company CORT Business Services; brick and boot maker Justin Industries; paint maker Benjamin Moore and Co.; and more than 80% of Shaw Industries, the world's largest carpet maker.

The next year Buffett did a little housekeeping: He dumped 80% of his Disney stock after Mickey's earnings slipped, and sold most of the firm's holdings in Fannie Mae and Freddie Mac. Berkshire Hathaway also teamed with financial services firm Leucadia National to bail out FINOVA, but later exited that project in response to uncertainty after the terrorist attacks on September 11, 2001.

OFFICERS

Chairman and CEO: Warren E. Buffett, $100,000 pay
Vice Chairman; Chairman and CEO, Wesco Financial: Charles T. Munger, age 78, $100,000 pay
VP, CFO, and Treasurer: Marc D. Hamburg, $412,500 pay
Controller: Daniel J. Jaksich
Secretary: Forrest N. Krutter
Director of Internal Auditing: Rebecca K. Amick
Director of Taxes: Jerry W. Hufton
Director of Financial Assets: Mark D. Millard
Auditors: Deloitte & Touche LLP

LOCATIONS

HQ: 1440 Kiewit Plaza, Omaha, NE 68131
Phone: 402-346-1400   **Fax:** 402-346-3375
Web: www.berkshirehathaway.com

PRODUCTS/OPERATIONS

2001 Assets

	$ mil.	% of total
Cash & equivalents	5,313	3
Securities		
Held for sale	36,509	24
Available for sale	28,675	18
Other	1,974	1
Assets of financial products lines	41,591	26
Goodwill of acquisitions	21,407	13
Recoverables & receivables	4,776	3
Receivables	11,926	7
Other assets	8,755	5
Total	**160,926**	**100**

Selected Holdings

Acme Building Brands (building materials)
Benjamin Moore (architectural and industrial coatings)
Buffalo News (daily and Sunday newspaper)
Dexter Shoe Company (dress, casual, and athletic shoes)
Executive Jet (fractional aircraft ownership programs)
FlightSafety (training for operators of aircraft and ships)
GEICO Corporation (property/casualty insurance)
GeneralCologne Re (property/casualty reinsurance)
H. H. Brown Shoe Co. (work shoes, boots and casual footwear)
Helzberg's Diamond Shops (retailing fine jewelry)
International Dairy Queen (licensing and servicing Dairy Queen Stores)
MidAmerican Energy (production, supply, and distribution of energy)
Star Furniture Company (retailing home furnishings)

Major Equity Investments

American Express (11%)
Coca-Cola (8%)
Gillette (9%)
H&R Block (9%)
Moody's Corp.(15%)
Washington Post Co. (18%)
Wells Fargo & Co. (3%)

COMPETITORS

AEA Investors	Citigroup	Munich Re
AIG	CNA Financial	Onex
Allstate	The Hartford	Progressive
Andersen Group	Hicks, Muse	Corporation
AXA Financial	KKR	Prudential
Blackstone	Lincoln National	State Farm
Group	Loews	Swiss Re
Chubb	MacAndrews &	
CIGNA	Forbes	

HISTORICAL FINANCIALS & EMPLOYEES

NYSE: BRK FYE: December 31	Annual Growth	12/92	12/93	12/94	12/95	12/96	12/97	12/98	12/99	12/00	12/01
Sales ($ mil.)	32.3%	3,029	2,619	3,848	3,713	10,500	10,430	13,832	24,028	33,976	37,668
Net income ($ mil.)	7.7%	407	688	495	725	2,489	1,902	2,830	1,557	3,328	795
Income as % of sales	—	13.4%	26.3%	12.9%	19.5%	23.7%	18.2%	20.5%	6.5%	9.8%	2.1%
Earnings per share ($)	4.3%	355.24	672.00	469.54	669.61	2,065.00	1,542.00	2,262.00	1,025.00	2,185.00	520.55
Stock price - FY high ($)	—	11,750	17,800	20,800	33,400	38,000	48,600	84,000	81,100	71,300	75,600
Stock price - FY low ($)	—	8,575	11,350	15,150	20,250	29,800	33,000	45,800	52,000	40,800	59,000
Stock price - FY close ($)	23.0%	11,750	16,325	20,400	32,100	34,100	46,000	70,000	56,100	71,000	75,600
P/E - high	—	33	25	44	50	18	32	37	79	33	145
P/E - low	—	24	16	32	30	14	21	20	51	19	113
Dividends per share ($)	—	0.00	0.00	0.00	0.00	0.00	0.00	0.00	0.00	0.00	0.00
Book value per share ($)	2.6%	7,743	8,853	10,081	14,420	11,772	13,766	8,941	8,584	9,004	9,756
Employees	28.9%	—	—	—	24,000	34,500	38,000	45,000	45,000	45,000	110,000

STOCK PRICE HISTORY

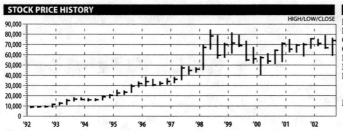
HIGH/LOW/CLOSE

2001 FISCAL YEAR-END

Debt ratio: 5.7%
Return on equity: 1.3%
Cash ($ mil.): —
Current ratio: —
Long-term debt ($ mil.): 3,485
No. of shares (mil.): 6
Dividends
  Yield: —
  Payout: —
Market value ($ mil.): 449,064

BEST BUY CO., INC.

Richard Schulze has been busy building a better Best Buy. The Eden Prairie, Minnesota-based company he founded in 1966 has grown to become the #1 consumer electronics specialty retailer in the US, even though rival Circuit City has more stores. Best Buy's some 490 stores in 44 states offer audio and video equipment (33% of sales), home office equipment (31% of sales), entertainment software (such as CDs, DVDs, videos, and video games), appliances, and other products such as batteries. The company also owns The Musicland Group, which operates the Suncoast, Sam Goody, Media Play, and On Cue retail chains.

Chairman Schulze, who owns about 17% of Best Buy, has been restructuring the chain following a period of ungainly growth. Though the company introduced itself to many consumers by offering a wide selection of cheap CDs, it is now emphasizing higher-margin items such as digital products.

HISTORY

Tired of working for a father who ignored his ideas to improve the business (electronics distribution), Richard Schulze quit. In 1966, with a partner, he founded Sound of Music, a Minnesota home/car stereo store. Schulze bought out his partner in 1971 and began to expand the chain. While chairing a school board, Schulze saw declining enrollment and realized his target customer group, 15- to 18-year-old males, was shrinking. In the early 1980s he broadened his product line and targeted older, more affluent customers by offering appliances and VCRs.

After a 1981 tornado destroyed his best store (but not its inventory), Schulze spent his entire marketing budget to advertise a huge parking-lot sale. The successful sale taught him the benefits of strong advertising and wide selection combined with low prices. In 1983 Schulze changed the company's name to Best Buy and began to open larger superstores. The firm went public two years later.

Buoyed by the format change and the fast-rising popularity of the VCR, Best Buy grew rapidly. Between 1984 and 1987 it expanded from eight stores to 24, and sales jumped from $29 million to $240 million. The next year another 16 stores opened and sales jumped by 84%. But Best Buy began to butt heads with many expanding consumer electronics retailers, and profits took a beating.

To set Best Buy apart from its competitors, in 1989 Schulze introduced the Concept II warehouse-like store format. Thinking that customers could buy products without much help, Schulze cut payroll by taking sales staff off commission and reducing the number of employees per store by about a third. The concept proved to be such a hit in the company's home territory, Minneapolis/St. Paul, that it drove major competitor Highland Appliance to bankruptcy. Customers were happy, but many of Best Buy's suppliers, believing sales help was needed to sell products, pulled their products from Best Buy stores. The losses didn't seem to hurt Best Buy; it took on Sears and Montgomery Ward in the Chicago market in 1989 and continued expanding.

In 1994 the company debuted Concept III, an even larger store format. Best Buy opened 47 new stores in 1995 but found itself swimming in debt. Earnings plummeted in fiscal 1997, partly due to a huge PC inventory made obsolete by Intel's newer product. Best Buy started selling CDs on its Web site in 1997. That year it realized it had overextended itself with its expansion, super-sized stores, and financing promotions. Best Buy underwent a speedy, massive, makeover by scaling back expansion and doing away with its policy of "no money down, no monthly payments, no interest" (and next-to-no profits).

In 1999 Best Buy began to enter new markets (including New England) and introduced its Concept IV stores, which highlight digital products and feature stations for computer software and DVD demonstrations. Also in 1999, Best Buy formed a separate subsidiary for its online operations (BestBuy.com, Inc.) and invested $10 million in consumer electronics information Web site etown.com (etown.com closed down in February 2001).

In 2000 Best Buy agreed to pay $87 million for Seattle-based Magnolia Hi-Fi, a privately held chain of 13 high-end audio and video stores. In early 2001 Best Buy bought The Musicland Group (operator of more than 1,300 Sam Goody, Suncoast, On Cue, and Media Play music stores) for about $377 million. In August 2001 the company announced it would begin its first international expansion of Best Buy stores, opening some 65 stores in Canada over the next three or four years. In November Best Buy acquired Future Shop, Canada's leading consumer electronics retailer. In June 2002 Schulze turned over his responsibilities as CEO to vice chairman Brad Anderson; Schulze remains as chairman.

OFFICERS

Chairman: Richard M. Schulze, age 61, $2,751,875 pay
  (prior to title change)
Vice Chairman and CEO: Bradbury H. Anderson, age 52,
  $1,511,921 pay (prior to title change)

President, COO, and Director: Allen U. Lenzmeier, age 58, $1,096,325 pay
EVP and CIO: Marc D. Gordon, age 41
EVP and General Merchandise Manager: Michael London, age 53
EVP, Business Development: Philip J. Schoonover, age 42
EVP, Consumer and Brand Marketing and Chief Marketing Officer: Michael A. Linton, age 45
EVP, Finance and Treasury and CFO: Darren R. Jackson, age 37
EVP, Human Capital and Leadership: John C. Walden, age 42
EVP, Retail Sales: Brian J. Dunn, age 42
EVP, Strategic Planning: George Z. Lopuch, age 51
SVP and CTO: Clark Becker
SVP, Corporate Communications and Investor Relations: Susan Hoff
SVP, Enterprise Entertainment: Joe Pagano
SVP, Human Resources: Nancy C. Bologna, age 47
SVP, Real Estate and Property Development: Tami Kozikowski
SVP, Retail Operations: Michael W. Marolt, age 44
SVP, Retail Sales: Don Eames
SVP, Retail Sales: Mark Overgard
SVP, Special Projects: Joseph T. Pelano Jr., age 52
Auditors: Ernst & Young LLP

LOCATIONS

HQ: 7075 Flying Cloud Dr., Eden Prairie, MN 55344
Phone: 952-947-2000   **Fax:** 952-947-2694
Web: www.bestbuy.com

Best Buy has more than 480 stores in 44 states.

PRODUCTS/OPERATIONS

2002 Sales

	% of total
Consumer electronics	33
Home office	31
Entertainment software	22
Appliances	6
Other	8
Total	**100**

COMPETITORS

Amazon.com	Fry's Electronics	P.C. Richard &
Blockbuster	Gateway	Son
Borders	Good Guys	RadioShack
BUY.COM	HMV	Sam's Club
Cablevision	Home Depot	Sears
Electronics	J & R	Staples
Investments	Electronics	Target
CDW Computer	J. C. Penney	Toys "R" Us
Centers	Kmart	Tweeter Home
Circuit City	Lowe's	Entertainment
CompUSA	Micro	Group
Costco	Warehouse	Ultimate
Wholesale	MTS	Electronics
Dell Computer	Musicland	Wal-Mart
Dillard's	Office Depot	Wherehouse
Electronics	OfficeMax	Entertainment
Boutique	PC Connection	

HISTORICAL FINANCIALS & EMPLOYEES

NYSE: BBY FYE: Sat. nearest last day in Feb.	Annual Growth	2/93	2/94	2/95	2/96	2/97	2/98	2/99	2/00	2/01	2/02
Sales ($ mil.)	31.9%	1,620	3,007	5,080	7,217	7,771	8,358	10,078	12,494	15,327	19,597
Net income ($ mil.)	45.2%	20	41	58	48	2	95	224	347	396	570
Income as % of sales	—	1.2%	1.4%	1.1%	0.7%	0.0%	1.1%	2.2%	2.8%	2.6%	2.9%
Earnings per share ($)	37.6%	0.10	0.16	0.21	0.19	0.01	0.35	0.71	1.09	1.24	1.77
Stock price - FY high ($)	—	2.62	5.24	7.55	5.04	4.38	10.20	32.68	53.69	59.28	51.49
Stock price - FY low ($)	—	0.79	1.81	3.44	2.00	1.31	1.44	9.83	27.01	14.01	22.43
Stock price - FY close ($)	39.2%	2.29	4.61	3.63	2.79	1.54	9.93	30.93	36.43	27.32	44.96
P/E - high	—	26	31	33	27	438	28	44	48	46	29
P/E - low	—	8	11	15	11	131	4	13	24	11	12
Dividends per share ($)	—	0.00	0.00	0.00	0.00	0.00	0.00	0.00	0.00	0.00	0.00
Book value per share ($)	27.2%	0.90	1.24	1.49	1.68	1.69	2.08	3.49	3.65	5.84	7.90
Employees	28.9%	9,600	15,200	25,300	33,500	36,300	39,000	45,000	55,000	75,000	94,000

STOCK PRICE HISTORY

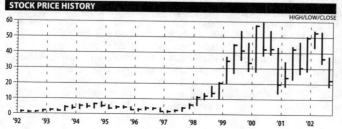

HIGH/LOW/CLOSE

2002 FISCAL YEAR-END

Debt ratio: 24.4%
Return on equity: 26.2%
Cash ($ mil.): 1,855
Current ratio: 1.24
Long-term debt ($ mil.): 813
No. of shares (mil.): 319
Dividends
   Yield: —
   Payout: —
Market value ($ mil.): 14,348

BETHLEHEM STEEL CORPORATION

Bethlehem Steel is tired of getting dumped on and is now seeking cover under Chapter 11 bankruptcy protection. The Bethlehem, Pennsylvania-based company — the #3 US steelmaker (behind United States Steel and Nucor) — makes steel plate, sheet, and specialty steels for the appliance, automotive, construction, and machinery markets. Through its Pennsylvania Steel Technologies division, Bethlehem also makes railroad rails, flat bars, and pipe. The company owns eight short-line railroads to transport its products, and it has stakes in an iron mine in Minnesota.

To cut costs, Bethlehem Steel has cut about 30% of its salaried workforce since 1999; it has also consolidated some operations. However, tough competition from foreign steel companies (that is, "dumping") and giant payouts to retirees led Bethlehem Steel to file for bankruptcy in 2001. Higher-than-expected costs related to modernizing a Maryland facility also have contributed to losses.

The company has amended its shareholder-rights plan to fend off hostile takeover bids. Newly appointed chairman and CEO Steve Miller Jr. has taken the role to stabilize finances and is in discussions with representatives of United States Steel regarding a possible merger. If Bethlehem Steel and United States Steel decide to merge, the two would have to make concessions with the United Steelworkers Union to reduce labor costs. Additionally, the government would have to assist in employee health benefit and pension costs. Arcelor, the world's largest steel producer, has also shown interest in purchasing part of Bethlehem Steel.

HISTORY

Bethlehem Steel began as Saucona Iron in South Bethlehem, Pennsylvania, in 1857, rolling iron railroad rails. It changed its name to Bethlehem Rolling Mills & Iron in 1859 and to Bethlehem Iron in 1861, when it began forging armor plate for US Navy ships. In 1899 it became Bethlehem Steel.

Charles Schwab (president of United States Steel) bought, sold, and again bought Bethlehem Steel in 1901 and 1902. He transferred Bethlehem to United States Shipbuilding, which soon failed. Bethlehem Steel, which then included a steel plant, shipbuilding yards on both US coasts, and Cuban iron-ore mines, was spun off in 1904 with Schwab as president. Schwab saw the potential in Henry Grey's one-piece, wide-flange steel I-beams for large buildings and built a structural mill at Saucon, Pennsylvania. He bought Grey's patents and found a market in the construction industry.

In 1912 Schwab bought the Tofo Iron Mines (Chile) for a cheap source of superior-grade iron ore. Bethlehem acquired Pennsylvania Steel and Maryland Steel in 1916. With its myriad assets, Bethlehem was well prepared for the steel and shipbuilding needs of WWI.

Bethlehem bought Pacific Coast Steel and Southern California Iron & Steel in 1930, and in 1931 it bought the fabricating business of McClintic-Marshall Construction. It made the steelwork for such structures as the Golden Gate Bridge and the US Supreme Court building. During WWII the company built 1,121 ships.

Amid growing US imports in the 1970s and 1980s, Bethlehem reduced production and sold some nonsteel operations. The company undertook a major facilities modernization in 1981 and began building new facilities in 1986.

A slimmer Bethlehem faced an industrywide slump in demand and recession in the early 1990s. The company sold its Freight Car Division in 1991. The next year it sold a coal mine and closed its bar, rod, and wire unit.

In 1993 Bethlehem and Lafayette Steel formed joint venture Precision Blank Welding to produce steel blanks for custom auto parts. Two years later General Motors' Saturn subsidiary agreed to use Bethlehem as its principal steel source. In 1997 Bethlehem agreed to acquire steelmaker Lukens to strengthen its share of the US steel-plate market. After a rival bid by Allegheny Teledyne pushed up the price to $740 million, the two suitors inked a deal in 1998 that gave each company what it wanted: Bethlehem got Lukens but sold most of its stainless-steel operations to Allegheny.

Also in 1998 Bethlehem joined other US steelmakers in filing trade complaints against competitors in Brazil, Japan, and Russia for dumping low-priced steel in the US.

After WHX Corp. amassed about 2 million shares of Bethlehem Steel late in 1999, Bethlehem took defensive "poison-pill" measures to thwart a possible takeover. The company recorded a $183 million loss that year in the face of cheaper foreign imports and from costs related to problems as it relined its blast furnace in Maryland.

Although still one of the largest US steelmakers, the company was dropped from the S&P 500 index late in 2000 (Bethlehem Steel had been listed on the S&P 500 and its forerunner index since 1918), reflecting the company's small market capitalization.

In 2001 the company continued its cost-cutting measures, and it increased the number of planned job cuts. In October 2001, under the new leadership of CEO Steve Miller Jr. (better known for helping in the Chrysler bailout of 1980), the company filed Chapter 11 but quickly secured $450 million in special financing through GE Capital to continue operations.

In 2002 the company began talks with United States Steel about a possible merger. That same year Arcelor, the world's largest steelmaker, began discussions over purchasing a stake in Bethlehem Steel. It also began negotiations with Brazilian steelmaker Companhia Siderúrgica Nacional over a possible joint venture with its Sparrow's Point (Maryland) plant.

OFFICERS

Chairman and CEO: Robert S. Miller Jr., age 60, $242,500 pay (partial-year salary)
SVP, CFO, and Treasurer: Leonard M. Anthony, age 47
SVP, General Counsel, and Secretary:
  William H. Graham, age 56, $365,000 pay
VP Commercial and Chief Commercial Officer:
  Daniel G. Mull, age 50
VP Accounting, Controller, and Chief Accounting Officer: Lonnie A. Arnett, age 55
VP Human Resources: Dorothy L. Stephenson, age 52
President, Burns Harbor Division: Ronald F. Chango, age 54, $339,750 pay
President, Sparrows Point Division: Van R. Reiner, age 53
Auditors: PricewaterhouseCoopers LLP

LOCATIONS

HQ: 1170 8th Ave., Bethlehem, PA 18016
Phone: 610-694-2424   **Fax:** 610-694-6920
Web: www.bethsteel.com

Bethlehem Steel owns mills in Indiana, Maryland, and Pennsylvania; it also operates coke-making facilities in New York, and it has a stake in a Minnesota iron mine.

PRODUCTS/OPERATIONS

2001 Sales

	% of total
Steel mill products	
Coated sheets	29
Plates	22
Cold-rolled sheets	15
Hot-rolled sheets	15
Tin mill products	8
Rail products	4
Other	1
Other products & services	6
Total	**100**

COMPETITORS

AK Steel Holding
  Corporation
Anglo American
BHP Billiton Ltd
Cargill Steel
Chaparral Steel
IPSCO
Ispat

Lone Star
  Technologies
LTV
National Steel
Nippon Steel
Nucor
Roanoke Electric
  Steel

Rowan
Steel Dynamics
ThyssenKrupp
United States
  Steel
Weirton Steel

HISTORICAL FINANCIALS & EMPLOYEES

OTC: BHMS FYE: December 31	Annual Growth	12/92	12/93	12/94	12/95	12/96	12/97	12/98	12/99	12/00	12/01
Sales ($ mil.)	(2.0%)	4,008	4,323	4,819	4,868	4,679	4,631	4,478	3,915	4,197	3,334
Net income ($ mil.)	—	(449)	(266)	81	180	(309)	281	120	(183)	(118)	(1,950)
Income as % of sales	—	—	—	1.7%	3.7%	—	6.1%	2.7%	—	—	—
Employees	(6.9%)	24,900	20,700	19,900	18,300	17,500	15,600	17,000	15,500	14,700	13,100

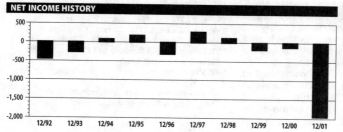

NET INCOME HISTORY

2001 FISCAL YEAR-END

Debt ratio: 100.0%
Return on equity: —
Cash ($ mil.): 104
Current ratio: 4.43
Long-term debt ($ mil.): 628

BEVERLY ENTERPRISES, INC.

The Fort Smith, Arkansas-based company is one of the top nursing home operators in the US. Beverly also runs assisted-living centers and offers outpatient and rehabilitation services; it has more than 500 facilities in 28 states and the District of Columbia.

Like the rest of the nursing home industry, Beverly has grappled with Medicare's payment system (implemented in 1999) that reimburses operators per procedure, not actual costs. Beverly tried to slim down or sell off underperforming operations to deal with the cutbacks and has managed to stay afloat.

HISTORY

In 1963 Utah accountant Roy Christensen founded Beverly as three convalescent hospitals near Beverly Hills, California. The emergence of Medicare and Medicaid in the 1960s fueled the firm's growth. Beverly also dabbled in mirrors, plastics, real estate, and printing before going public in 1966.

Beverly sobered up to losses and industrywide overexpansion by the early 1970s. The company turned to investment firm Stephens to ward off a takeover. Beverly doubled in size in 1977, buying Leisure Lodges nursing homes from Stephens in exchange for 23% of Beverly. Acquisitions pushed Beverly into the #1 nursing home spot by 1983 (by then, Stephens had sold out for a tidy profit). Beverly also diversified, starting its Pharmacy Corporation of America (PCA) institutional pharmacy unit.

Management later wrestled with labor unrest, allegations of patient neglect (including the company's implication in patients' deaths in California and Minnesota), and systemic problems with Medicaid. Beverly again turned to Stephens in the late 1980s to ward off another takeover and to shake up management.

An inventive late 1980s plan to restructure debt by selling nursing homes cast a cloud over some of those involved in it, including lawyers from Little Rock's Rose Law Firm (William Kennedy and Vince Foster, who would later become White House counsels, and Webster Hubbell, who would become an Assistant Attorney General before being convicted of financial irregularities at Rose). A loophole let Beverly sell unprofitable Arkansas and Iowa nursing homes to not-for-profit shell organizations, which bought them with funds raised through tax-free bonds. An $86 million sale was completed in Iowa; after public outcry, the Arkansas deal was killed by then-Governor Bill Clinton.

In 1990 Beverly's headquarters moved to Arkansas, near Stephens' Little Rock home.

Beverly decentralized management of its 883 nursing homes (a move it would later try to use to shield it from liability in labor violations) and began selling some assets. In the mid-1990s Beverly sought relief in higher-margin businesses (post-acute care hospitals, pharmacy services, rehab and respiratory therapy). In 1996 Beverly backed out of managed care; divestitures included PCA. Beverly also exited Texas' punitive regulatory environment, selling 49 nursing homes in the state.

In 1993 the National Labor Relations Board (NLRB) concluded the company had illegally stifled workers' attempts to organize; a similar complaint was filed in 1996. (The company dismisses the NLRB's decisions as "fundamentally flawed.") In 1998 the company filed, then withdrew, a slander suit against a Cornell professor who characterized Beverly as "one of the nation's most notorious labor-law violators." (The company has continued to be a target of union organizers.)

Beverly established records for punitive damages in 1997 and 1998, suffering judgments of $70 million and $95 million (later reduced to $54 million and $3 million, respectively) relating to patient neglect.

Having whittled its nursing homes down to about 560 in 1999 and losing the top spot to Sun Healthcare, Beverly braced itself for a period of austerity as Medicare inaugurated its per-procedure billing method in 1999, the same year the federal government announced it was investigating Beverly's Medicare billings back to 1990; the government charged that Beverly was systematically falsifying records to defraud Medicare. As a result, in 2000 the firm agreed to pay $175 million in restitution (paid over eight years through Medicare reimbursement garnishments) and sell 10 facilities belonging to a California-based subsidiary that were disqualified from federal health insurance programs as part of their punishment for falsifying reimbursement claims.

In 2001 Beverly announced plans to exit its Florida operations.

OFFICERS

Chairman, President, and CEO: William R. Floyd, age 57, $1,264,690 pay
EVP and CFO: Jeffrey P. Freimark, age 46
EVP; President and COO, Nursing Facilities: David R. Devereaux, age 39, $526,597 pay
EVP, Information Technology and CIO: Michael J. Matheny, age 54
EVP, Procurement: Bobby W. Stephens, age 57, $511,136 pay
EVP, Law and Government Relations and Secretary: Douglas J. Babb, age 49, $545,288 pay

SVP, Controller, and Chief Accounting Officer:
Pamela H. Daniels, age 38
SVP and Treasurer: Richard D. Skelly Jr., age 42
SVP, Compliance: Cletus C. Hess, age 37
SVP, Investor Relations and Corporate
Communications: James M. Griffith, age 59
SVP, Marketing and New Business Innovation:
Blaise J. Mercadante, age 48
SVP, Human Resources: Crystal J. Wright, age 53
President, AEGIS Therapies: Cindy H. Susienka, age 42
President, MATRIX Rehabilitation: Chris W. Roussos,
age 37
Auditors: Ernst & Young LLP

LOCATIONS

HQ: 1000 Beverly Way, Fort Smith, AR 72919
Phone: 479-201-2000   **Fax:** 479-201-1101
Web: www.beverlynet.com

Beverly Enterprises has operations in 28 states and
Washington, DC.

2001 Facilities

	Nursing	Assisted Living	Outpatient
California	60	3	39
Pennsylvania	42	3	10
Arkansas	34	3	—
Indiana	30	1	—
Minnesota	30	1	—
Missouri	26	3	—
Wisconsin	25	—	—
Nebraska	24	1	—
Kansas	22	2	—
Other states	173	12	105
Total	**466**	**29**	**154**

PRODUCTS/OPERATIONS

2001 Sales

	% of total
Medicaid	52
Medicare	25
Private & other	23
Total	**100**

Selected Subsidiaries
AGI-Camelot, Inc.
Arborland Management Company, Inc.
Associated Physical Therapy Practitioners, Inc.
Beverly Clinical, Inc.
Beverly Indemnity, Ltd.
Commercial Management, Inc.
Community Care, Inc.
Eastern Home Health Supply & Equipment Co., Inc.
Greenville Rehabilitation Services, Inc.
HomeCare Preferred Choice, Inc.
Las Colinas Physical Therapy Center, Inc.
MATRIX Rehabilitation, Inc.
Peterson Health Care, Inc.
Spectra Healthcare Alliance, Inc.
Theraphysics Corp.
Vantage Healthcare Corporation

COMPETITORS

Centennial HealthCare	Kindred	National HealthCare
Genesis Health Ventures	Life Care Centers	Sun Healthcare
Integrated Health Services	Manor Care	Tenet Healthcare
	Mariner Health Care	

HISTORICAL FINANCIALS & EMPLOYEES

NYSE: BEV FYE: December 31	Annual Growth	12/92	12/93	12/94	12/95	12/96	12/97	12/98	12/99	12/00	12/01
Sales ($ mil.)	0.5%	2,597	2,871	2,969	3,229	3,267	3,230	2,812	2,547	2,626	2,710
Net income ($ mil.)	—	(10)	58	75	(8)	50	59	(31)	(135)	(55)	(301)
Income as % of sales	—	—	2.0%	2.5%	—	1.5%	1.8%	—	—	—	—
Earnings per share ($)	—	(0.14)	0.42	0.76	(0.16)	0.49	0.57	(0.24)	(1.31)	(0.53)	(2.90)
Stock price – FY high ($)	—	8.81	9.90	11.19	11.37	9.69	13.31	16.25	8.19	8.25	12.10
Stock price – FY low ($)	—	4.78	6.21	8.28	6.35	6.52	8.64	5.25	3.50	2.50	5.20
Stock price – FY close ($)	(0.2%)	8.73	8.89	10.13	7.49	8.99	13.00	6.75	4.38	8.19	8.60
P/E – high	—	—	22	14	—	18	23	—	—	—	—
P/E – low	—	—	14	10	—	12	15	—	—	—	—
Dividends per share ($)	—	0.00	0.00	0.00	0.00	0.00	0.00	0.00	0.00	0.00	0.00
Book value per share ($)	(10.4%)	7.60	9.03	9.66	8.32	8.70	8.15	7.58	6.25	5.63	2.84
Employees	(5.3%)	93,000	89,000	82,000	83,000	81,000	74,000	73,000	67,000	64,000	57,000

STOCK PRICE HISTORY

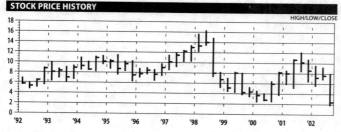

HIGH/LOW/CLOSE

2001 FISCAL YEAR-END

Debt ratio: 69.6%
Return on equity: —
Cash ($ mil.): 89
Current ratio: 1.06
Long-term debt ($ mil.): 677
No. of shares (mil.): 104
Dividends
  Yield: —
  Payout: —
Market value ($ mil.): 897

BIG LOTS, INC.

Big Lots (formerly Consolidated Stores) provides homes for the toys and products that other retailers don't want. The Columbus, Ohio-based holding company is the US's #1 closeout retailer, with more than 1,300 closeout stores.

The company runs four closeout retail chains — Big Lots, Odd Lots, Mac Frugal's, and Pic 'N' Save — in 45 southwestern, midwestern, southern, and mid-Atlantic states, but primarily in California, Florida, Ohio, and Texas. Nearly 90% of the stores operate under the Big Lots name. Its merchandise includes name-brand and private-label housewares, electronics, foods, toiletries, tools, toys, and clothing. To stock the shelves of its stores, Big Lots buys truckloads of orphaned bric-a-brac (discontinued, overproduced, and outdated items) at steep discounts from stores and manufacturers.

It sold its KB Toys unit, one of the largest toy sellers in the US, to a group led by KB management and Bain Capital as part of a restructuring plan to boost its flagging stock price. The deal included online retailer KBkids.com.

Big Lots owns the Big Lots Furniture closeout chain. Big Lots also operates a wholesale business, selling its discounted merchandise to a variety of retailers, manufacturers, distributors, and other wholesalers.

HISTORY

As a kid growing up in Columbus, Ohio, Russian-born Sol Shenk (pronounced "Shank") couldn't stand to pay full price for anything. His frugality blossomed into a knack for buying low and wholesaling. After a failed effort to make auto parts, Shenk began the precursor to Consolidated Stores in 1967, backed by brothers Alvin, Saul, and Jerome Schottenstein.

The company started by wholesaling closeout auto parts and buying retailers' closeout items to sell to other retailers. By 1971 Shenk had branched into retailing, selling closeout auto parts through a chain of Corvair Auto Stores.

One of Shenk's sons suggested they devote space in the Corvair stores to closeout merchandise other than car parts. Sales surged, and Shenk decided to sell the Corvair outlets and focus on closeout stores. The first Odd Lots opened in 1982. Consolidated grew more than 100% annually for the next three years. By 1986, the year after it went public, the company was opening two stores a week in midsized markets around the Midwest.

Shenk found that people would buy anything as long as the price was right. Two years after the mania for Rubik's Cubes ended, Odd Lots bought 6 million of the puzzles (once priced at $8) at

eight cents apiece, marked them up 500%, and sold them all.

By 1987 the company had nearly 300 Odd Lots/Big Lots stores. But runaway growth had created massive inventory shortages and losses as disappointed customers stopped browsing the company's sparsely stocked shelves. The woes coincided with a falling-out with the Schottensteins. Shenk retired in 1989.

Apparel and electronics retail executive William Kelley was named chairman and CEO the next year. Kelley returned Consolidated to its closeout roots and increased sales through acquisitions and creating new discount chains.

Consolidated doubled its size in 1996 with the $315 million purchase of more than 1,000 struggling Kay-Bee Toys (now KB Toys) stores from Melville Corp. The expansion continued with the 1998 purchase of top closeout competitor Mac Frugal's Bargains - Closeouts. (Mac Frugal's had nearly bought Consolidated in 1989 before Consolidated board members vetoed the deal.) The $1 billion acquisition of Mac Frugal's gave Consolidated another 326 western stores under the Pic 'N' Save and Mac Frugal's names.

In 1999 Consolidated combined its online toy sales operations with those of BrainPlay.com to form KBkids.com. In mid-2000 Kelley stepped down as CEO, handing the title over to CFO Michael Potter.

In December 2000 the company sold KB Toys (including KBkids.com) to a group led by KB management and global private equity firm Bain Capital for about $300 million. In mid-2001 the company changed its name to Big Lots and began converting all stores to that name to establish a national brand. Big Lots bought the inventory of bankrupt Internet home furnishings giant Living.com in June.

OFFICERS

Chairman, President, and CEO: Michael J. Potter, age 40, $696,154 pay
Vice Chairman and Chief Administrative Officer: Albert J. Bell, age 42, $671,154 pay
SVP and CFO: Jeffrey G. Naylor, age 43
EVP, Human Resources and Loss Prevention: Brad A. Waite, age 44, $357,692 pay
EVP, Merchandising and Sales Promotion: Kent Larsson, age 58, $339,231 pay
EVP, Store Operations: Donald A. Mierzwa, age 51, $339,231 pay
SVP, CIO: Steven M. Bromet
SVP, Distribution and Transportation Services: Harold A. Wilson
SVP, General Merchandise Manager: John J. Johnson
SVP, General Merchandise Manager: Norman J. Rankin
SVP, Merchandise Planning, Allocation, and Presentation: Lisa M. Bachmann, age 39

SVP, Merchandising: Charles C. Freidenberg
SVP, Wholesale: Armen J. Bahadurian, age 59
VP, General Counsel, and Secretary:
Charles W. Haubiel II, age 36
Auditors: Deloitte & Touche LLP

LOCATIONS

HQ: 300 Phillipi Rd., Columbus, OH 43228
Phone: 614-278-6800 **Fax:** 614-278-6676
Web: www.biglots.com

Big Lots operates stores in 45 states throughout the US.

2002 Stores

	No.
California	183
Ohio	129
Florida	104
Texas	100
Georgia	62
Indiana	52
North Carolina	51
Michigan	47
Pennsylvania	47
Tennessee	46
Kentucky	43
Illinois	39
Virginia	38
New York	36
Alabama	34
Missouri	26
South Carolina	26
West Virginia	25
Other states	247
Total	**1,335**

PRODUCTS/OPERATIONS

Stores
Big Lots
Big Lots Furniture
Mac Frugal's Bargains Close-outs
Odd Lots
Pic 'N' Save

COMPETITORS

99 Cents Only
Amazon.com
Bill's Dollar Stores
BJs Wholesale Club
Costco Wholesale
Dollar General
Dollar Tree
Factory 2-U Stores
Family Dollar Stores
Fred's
Goodwill
J. C. Penney
Kmart
Liquidation World
Odd Job Stores
One Price Clothing Stores
Quality King
Ross Stores
Salvation Army
Sears
Target
TJX
Tuesday Morning
Value City
Variety Wholesalers
Wal-Mart

HISTORICAL FINANCIALS & EMPLOYEES

NYSE: BLI FYE: Saturday nearest Jan. 31	Annual Growth	1/93	1/94	1/95	1/96	1/97	1/98	1/99	1/00	1/01	1/02
Sales ($ mil.)	15.6%	929	1,055	1,279	1,512	2,648	4,055	4,194	4,700	3,277	3,433
Net income ($ mil.)	—	37	43	55	64	84	86	97	96	(381)	(20)
Income as % of sales	—	4.0%	4.1%	4.3%	4.3%	3.2%	2.1%	2.3%	2.0%	—	—
Earnings per share ($)	—	0.50	0.73	0.92	0.78	1.17	0.77	0.86	0.85	(3.39)	(0.18)
Stock price - FY high ($)	—	12.00	14.24	12.80	16.40	28.32	50.00	46.13	38.13	15.88	15.75
Stock price - FY low ($)	—	6.40	9.04	7.36	10.08	12.80	25.80	15.50	13.69	8.25	7.15
Stock price - FY close ($)	(0.2%)	10.96	11.60	11.84	12.80	26.30	41.13	16.69	14.25	13.00	10.72
P/E - high	—	24	19	13	21	23	63	46	44	—	—
P/E - low	—	13	12	8	13	10	32	16	16	—	—
Dividends per share ($)	—	0.00	0.00	0.00	0.00	0.00	0.00	0.00	0.00	0.00	0.01
Book value per share ($)	12.1%	2.90	3.56	4.30	5.22	8.15	9.60	10.79	11.71	8.28	8.11
Employees	12.5%	16,000	16,399	19,699	21,633	38,000	50,324	58,254	65,000	45,676	46,246

STOCK PRICE HISTORY

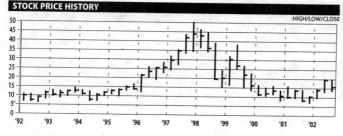

HIGH/LOW/CLOSE

2002 FISCAL YEAR-END

Debt ratio: 18.0%
Return on equity: —
Cash ($ mil.): 29
Current ratio: 3.09
Long-term debt ($ mil.): 204
No. of shares (mil.): 114
Dividends
  Yield: 0.1%
  Payout: —
Market value ($ mil.): 1,226

BJ'S WHOLESALE CLUB, INC.

Long indistinguishable from the nation's leading warehouse retailers (Costco and Sam's Club), BJ's Wholesale Club wants to find its own identity, as well as new space to grow in. The Natick, Massachusetts-based company is the US's #3 discount warehouse chain. It has nearly seven million members and about 130 stores in 15 states, mostly in the Northeast, but also in Florida, North Carolina, Ohio, Virginia, and South Carolina.

Like Costco, BJ's gets about 60% of its sales from typical supermarket items, such as canned goods, dry food items, flowers, fresh produce, frozen food, household products, and meat and dairy products. The rest of its sales come from merchandise common to warehouse stores: apparel, electronics, jewelry, office equipment, tires, among other items. Like both its rivals, BJ's requires membership and offers a limited selection of items in warehouses that span 111,000 sq. ft. (although it does operate some smaller warehouses that cover 69,000 sq. ft. in small cities).

So where does BJ's detect a niche? Unlike Costco, it has liberal membership policies, offers a slightly larger product line — 6,000 items in all — and accepts coupons and most major credit cards. BJ's has added other consumer-minded accoutrements, such as brake and muffler service, food courts with brand-name fast-food restaurants, one-hour photo service, and optical stores.

Opening more than 10 new stores a year, the company plans to expand in Florida and North and South Carolina. At more than 50 of its stores, BJ's sells discounted gas to members. It is also entering the pharmacy business with plans to test pharmacies in five Atlanta clubs scheduled to open in 2002 and in three existing Massachusetts clubs.

HISTORY

In 1984, with Price Club (now part of Costco) thriving and Wal-Mart Stores' Sam's Club beginning to dot the horizon, Zayre Corp. opened BJ's Wholesale Club, New England's first warehouse club. Zayre, a Massachusetts-based chain of discount department stores, placed the first store in Medford, Massachusetts, and named the operation after top executive Mervyn Weich's wife, Barbara Jane. In return for an annual membership fee, customers could buy a mix of goods priced at around 8%-10% above what they cost BJ's.

Zayre's bought the California-based Home-Club chain of home improvement warehouses in 1986 and combined HomeClub with BJ's to form Zayre's warehouse division. Weich was replaced by John Levy the next year.

By mid-1987 BJ's had 15 stores and more than half a billion dollars in annual sales. Over the next few years, the chain expanded into 11 states in the Northeast and Midwest, including stores in the Chicago area. Despite the chain's rapid growth — or because of it — BJ's failed to post profits.

A debt-burdened Zayre began shifting its focus to its moderate-priced chains (including T.J. Maxx and Hit or Miss) during the late 1980s. In 1989 it spun off its warehouse division to shareholders and renamed it Waban (after a nearby Massachusetts town). Zayre was renamed TJX Companies.

Waban cracked the $1 billion sales mark in 1990. During the early 1990s the company moved into the midwestern US, but its stores failed to thrive. In 1991 it closed one of its four Chicago stores and in 1992 turned the other three into HomeBase stores.

Also during those years, BJ's added fresh meats, bakery items, optical departments, and travel agents to its stores. In 1993 Herbert Zarkin, BJ's president, replaced Levy as CEO. That year BJ's had 52 stores and 2.6 million members; its sales reached $2 billion. A new inventory scanning system implemented by the company helped cut costs.

Once again, however, strong sales didn't add up to big profits. In 1993 BJ's per-store profits were far below those of its competitors, primarily due to intense competition and a regional recession. Two years later it became the first warehouse club to accept MasterCard and issued its own store-brand version of that card. BJ's added nine stores in 1995, 10 the next year, and four in 1997.

Meanwhile, Waban was struggling with HomeBase, which was still failing to show a profit due to restructuring charges. In 1997 Waban spun off BJ's Wholesale Club — its star performer — to keep it from being undervalued; Waban then changed its name to HomeBase. Also in 1997 John Nugent was named BJ's CEO.

BJ's began adding gas stations at several of its northeastern stores in 1998. Also that year it introduced its private-label products under the Executive Choice and Berkley & Jensen names. BJ's entered North Carolina in 1999.

OFFICERS

Chairman: Herbert J. Zarkin, age 63, $350,000 pay
President, CEO, and Director: John J. Nugent, age 55, $1,051,152 pay
EVP and CFO: Frank D. Forward, age 47, $361,662 pay
EVP, Merchandising: Laura J. Sen, age 46, $381,500 pay
EVP, Club Operations: Michael T. Wedge, age 48, $381,500 pay
SVP and CIO: Roland A. Laferriere
SVP, Marketing: Edward F. Gillooly

SVP, Sales Operations: Michael R. Brassard
SVP and Controller: Christina M. Neppl
SVP, Field Operations: Edward F. Giles
SVP, Food Merchandise: Paul M. Bass
SVP, General Merchandise: Edward A. Beevers
SVP, Human Resources: Thomas Davis III
SVP, Logistics: Ray R. Sareeram
SVP, Real Estate and Property Development:
George L. Drummey
VP, Financial Reporting: John A. Brent
VP, General Counsel and Secretary: Sarah M. Gallivan, age 59
Auditors: PricewaterhouseCoopers LLP

LOCATIONS

HQ: One Mercer Rd., Natick, MA 01760
Phone: 508-651-7400   **Fax:** 508-651-6114
Web: www.bjswholesale.com

2002 Stores

	No.
New York	28
Florida	19
Massachusetts	14
New Jersey	14
Pennsylvania	11
Ohio	8
Connecticut	7
Maryland	7
Virginia	6
North Carolina	5
New Hampshire	4
Rhode Island	3
Maine	2
Delaware	1
South Carolina	1
Total	**130**

PRODUCTS/OPERATIONS

2002 Sales

	% of total
Merchandise & services	98
Membership fees	2
Total	**100**

Selected Merchandise

Food
Baked goods
Canned goods
Dairy products
Dry grocery items
Fresh produce
Frozen foods
Meat and fish

General Merchandise
Apparel
Auto accessories
Books
Computer software

Consumer electronics
Greeting cards
Hardware
Health and beauty aids
Household paper products
and cleaning supplies
Housewares
Jewelry
Office equipment
Office supplies
Seasonal items
Small appliances
Tires
Toys

COMPETITORS

Ahold USA
Best Buy
Big Lots
Circuit City
Costco
  Wholesale
Family Dollar
  Stores

Hannaford Bros.
IGA
J. C. Penney
Kmart
Office Depot
OfficeMax
Pathmark
Penn Traffic

Sam's Club
Sears
Shaw's
Staples
Stop & Shop
Target
Wal-Mart
Weis Markets

HISTORICAL FINANCIALS & EMPLOYEES

NYSE: BJ FYE: Last Saturday in January	Annual Growth	1/93	1/94	1/95	1/96	1/97	1/98	1/99	1/00	1/01	1/02
Sales ($ mil.)	12.8%	1,787	2,003	2,293	2,530	2,923	3,227	3,552	4,206	4,932	5,280
Net income ($ mil.)	16.3%	21	20	31	42	54	68	63	111	132	82
Income as % of sales	—	1.2%	1.0%	1.3%	1.6%	1.8%	2.1%	1.8%	2.6%	2.7%	1.6%
Earnings per share ($)	5.1%	—	—	—	—	—	0.91	0.82	1.47	1.77	1.11
Stock price - FY high ($)	—	—	—	—	—	—	16.16	23.16	39.00	42.99	57.24
Stock price - FY low ($)	—	—	—	—	—	—	13.00	14.94	20.38	26.75	39.25
Stock price - FY close ($)	33.4%	—	—	—	—	—	15.00	21.88	35.00	42.75	47.55
P/E - high	—	—	—	—	—	—	18	21	26	24	50
P/E - low	—	—	—	—	—	—	14	14	13	15	34
Dividends per share ($)	—	—	—	—	—	—	0.00	0.00	0.00	0.00	0.00
Book value per share ($)	12.7%	—	—	—	—	—	5.95	6.57	7.85	9.18	9.59
Employees	7.5%	—	—	—	—	11,000	11,600	12,500	13,650	14,700	15,800

STOCK PRICE HISTORY

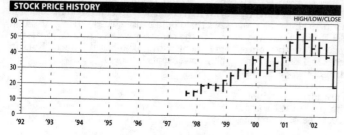

HIGH/LOW/CLOSE

2002 FISCAL YEAR-END

Debt ratio: 8.5%
Return on equity: 12.2%
Cash ($ mil.): 87
Current ratio: 1.20
Long-term debt ($ mil.): 64
No. of shares (mil.): 72
Dividends
  Yield: —
  Payout: —
Market value ($ mil.): 3,404

BLACK & DECKER

Other toolmakers would like to borrow the collection of power tools, hardware, and home improvement products that The Black & Decker Corporation has in its toolshed. The Towson, Maryland-based company is the world's leading maker of power tools and accessories. It also makes electric lawn and garden tools, building products, plumbing products, and industrial fastening systems for do-it-yourselfers and professional tradesmen. Black & Decker's bevy of famous brands includes Black & Decker and DeWALT (power tools and accessories), Kwikset (security hardware), and Price Pfister (faucets). Building products retailer The Home Depot accounts for about 20% of sales.

Despite its brands' high profiles, Black & Decker has done some retooling. The company sold its household appliances operations (toasters, irons, coffeemakers) in North America, Latin America, and Australia — in part because of their low profit margins and in part because the light-duty appliances had hurt its power tools' image. Reacting to a trend of slow sales and high inventories, the company has announced a further restructuring that calls for transferring some operations, especially in the power tools and home improvement businesses, from the US and the UK to China, Mexico, and Central Europe.

HISTORY

When Duncan Black and Alonzo Decker opened The Black & Decker Manufacturing Company in Baltimore in 1910 with a $1,200 investment, they began a partnership that would last over 40 years. Starting with milk-bottle-cap machines and candy dippers, the partners introduced their first major tool in 1916 — a portable half-inch electric drill with patented pistol grip and trigger switch, now on display at the Smithsonian Institute.

In 1917 the company built its first manufacturing plant, which would become its headquarters, in rural Towson, Maryland. Sales passed $1 million in 1919, and the company added a 20,000-sq.-ft. factory. Black & Decker quickly established itself in international markets with sales representatives in Australia, Japan, and Russia that year, and it built a manufacturing plant in England in 1939.

The founders led Black & Decker until they died — Black in 1951 (a year before the company went public) and Decker in 1956 — then family members took control of its operations until the 1970s. Alonzo G. Decker Jr., the co-founder's only son, was president from 1960 to 1972, chief executive from 1964 to 1975, and chairman from 1968 to 1979, remaining on the board of directors until 2001. (It was Decker Jr. who introduced power tools for home use, and he designed the first cordless drill in the 1960s. He died in March 2002.)

The company acquired the General Electric (GE) housewares operations in 1984, replacing the GE trademark with the Black & Decker hexagonal trademark on such items as toaster ovens, can openers, and irons. Nolan Archibald became Black & Decker's CEO in 1986 and began a major restructuring. Renamed The Black & Decker Corporation, it closed five plants, streamlined distribution systems, consolidated overseas facilities, and cut payroll 10%. Earnings doubled in 1987.

Two years later Black & Decker acquired megaconglomerate Emhart (formerly American Hardware), but the purchase caused earnings to fall. To service its debt, the firm sold off pieces of its acquisition, including Emhart's Bostik adhesives, True Temper Hardware, and North American Mallory Controls.

Black & Decker expanded its international presence in 1995, beginning joint operations in India and China and introducing DeWALT power tools to Europe and Latin America.

The company sold its sluggish household products operations in the US and Latin America (except Brazil) to small-appliance maker Windmere-Durable Holdings (now Applica Incorporated) in 1998. (It kept the more profitable lighting and cleaning lines.) Black & Decker also sold True Temper Sports to Cornerstone Equity Investors and sold Emhart Glass to Bucher Holdings of Switzerland. The sales and restructuring eliminated about 5,000 jobs and allowed the company to focus on its DeWALT brand. The company posted a loss in 1998 due to restructuring and $900 million in goodwill charges.

In 1999 heir apparent and EVP Joseph Galli left; GE veteran Paul McBride replaced him. Hurt by slow sales and high inventories in 2001, the company announced in early 2002 that it would undergo restructuring that includes cutting 2,400 jobs, closing several plants, and transferring some operations from the US and the UK to Mexico, China, and Central Europe.

Black & Decker announced in August 2002 that it would recall about 950,000 cordless drills that could overheat and about 6,100 table saws that could cause electric shock. Also that month the company entered into a cooperative agreement with Tokyo-based Hitachi Koki in their power tools business.

Chairman, President, and CEO: Nolan D. Archibald,
age 58, $2,050,000 pay
**EVP; President, Fastening and Assembly Systems
Group:** Paul A. Gustafson, age 59, $573,333 pay
EVP; President, Power Tools and Accessories Group:
Paul F. McBride, age 45, $835,000 pay
SVP and CFO: Michael D. Mangan, age 45, $531,565 pay
SVP and General Counsel: Charles E. Fenton, age 53,
$557,345 pay
SVP, Human Resources: Leonard A. Strom, age 56
**VP; President, Black & Decker Consumer Products,
Power Tools and Accessories Group:** Thomas D. Koos,
age 38
**VP; President, Commercial Operations, North America,
Power Tools and Accessories Group:**
Edward J. Scanlon, age 47
Auditors: Ernst & Young LLP

LOCATIONS

HQ: The Black & Decker Corporation
701 E. Joppa Rd., Towson, MD 21286
Phone: 410-716-3900   **Fax:** 410-716-2933
Web: www.blackanddecker.com

The Black & Decker Corporation's products are
marketed in more than 100 countries.

2001 Sales

	$ mil.	% of total
North America		
US	2,796	65
Canada	140	3
Europe	1,058	24
Other regions	339	8
Total	**4,333**	**100**

PRODUCTS/OPERATIONS

2001 Sales

	$ mil.	% of total
Power tools	2,284	53
Security hardware	547	13
Fastening and assembly systems	477	11
Consumer & professional accessories	315	7
Plumbing products	255	6
Electric lawn and garden products	285	7
Electric cleaning and lighting products	122	2
Household products	48	1
Total	**4,333**	**100**

COMPETITORS

American Standard	Ingersoll-Rand
ASSA ABLOY	Kohler
Atlas Copco	Makita
Cooper Industries	Masco
Danaher	Matsushita
Eaton	Pentair
Electrolux AB	Robert Bosch
Emerson Electric	Royal Appliance
Energizer Holdings	Snap-on
Fortune Brands	Stanley Works
Greenfield Industries	Textron
Hitachi	Toro
Illinois Tool Works	U.S. Industries

HISTORICAL FINANCIALS & EMPLOYEES

NYSE: BDK FYE: December 31	Annual Growth	12/92	12/93	12/94	12/95	12/96	12/97	12/98	12/99	12/00	12/01
Sales ($ mil.)	(1.1%)	4,780	4,882	5,248	4,766	4,914	4,941	4,560	4,521	4,561	4,333
Net income ($ mil.)	—	(334)	66	127	224	230	227	(755)	300	282	108
Income as % of sales	—	—	1.4%	2.4%	4.7%	4.7%	4.6%	—	6.6%	6.2%	2.5%
Earnings per share ($)	—	(4.52)	0.64	1.37	2.37	2.39	2.35	(8.22)	3.40	3.34	1.33
Stock price - FY high ($)	—	26.88	22.25	25.75	38.13	44.25	43.44	65.50	64.63	52.38	46.95
Stock price - FY low ($)	—	14.63	16.63	17.00	22.88	29.00	29.63	37.94	41.00	27.56	28.26
Stock price - FY close ($)	8.5%	18.13	19.75	23.75	35.25	30.13	39.06	56.06	52.25	39.25	37.73
P/E - high	—	—	22	19	13	18	18	—	19	16	35
P/E - low	—	—	17	12	8	12	12	—	12	8	21
Dividends per share ($)	2.0%	0.40	0.40	0.40	0.40	0.48	0.48	0.48	0.48	0.48	0.48
Book value per share ($)	(3.4%)	12.87	12.51	13.81	16.46	17.32	18.89	6.56	9.19	8.62	9.41
Employees	(5.8%)	38,800	37,300	35,800	29,300	29,200	28,600	21,800	22,100	23,600	22,700

STOCK PRICE HISTORY

HIGH/LOW/CLOSE

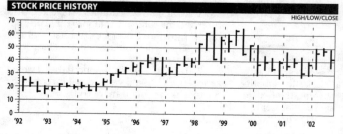

2001 FISCAL YEAR-END

Debt ratio: 61.3%
Return on equity: 15.0%
Cash ($ mil.): 245
Current ratio: 1.77
Long-term debt ($ mil.): 1,191
No. of shares (mil.): 80
Dividends
 Yield: 1.3%
 Payout: 36.1%
Market value ($ mil.): 3,012

BLOCKBUSTER INC.

Anxious parent Viacom has decided to coddle Blockbuster a little longer. The media giant never achieved the synergy it had anticipated with the world's largest home video rental chain and sold 18% of the Dallas-based company to the public in 1999. Viacom planned to shed its remaining 82% stake but decided to keep the company thanks to a turnaround in the retailer's core video rental business. While Blockbuster owns or franchises 8,000 Blockbuster Video outlets in the US and 26 other countries (renting more than 1 billion videos, DVDs, and video games each year) it has had a hard time sustaining growth as more people are building their own video libraries, accessing pay-per-view channels, and buying satellite dishes. As the popularity of DVDs has grown, Blockbuster is scaling back its VHS and video game inventory to make way for more DVDs.

Chairman and CEO John Antioco has helped Blockbuster's bottom line by negotiating revenue-sharing agreements with film studios instead of buying copies from them for around $65 a piece. It allows Blockbuster to stock more copies for less and take in 60%-70% of all rental revenues. The agreements also brought an antitrust lawsuit down on the company from a group of small video store owners in California, New York, and Texas. (The judge eventually dismissed the suit saying the mom-and-pop stores hadn't proved their case.) However, Blockbuster has announced that it will likely start phasing out those revenue-sharing agreements when they expire, an announcement that has been bitterly received in Hollywood. The move is primarily brought on by the growing popularity of DVD rentals, which are not part of the revenue agreements.

A major marketing deal with traditional industry enemy DIRECTV is part of a strategy to explore ways to sell products other than video rentals. Blockbuster in 2001 struck a deal with RadioShack that gave the electronics retailer space in Blockbuster outlets to sell its wares. Both companies pulled out of the agreement the following year when Blockbuster claimed RadioShack sold too many products its customers didn't want. RadioShack said it could never make any money out of the venture. Blockbuster now plans to market its own line of home electronics such as DVD players and VCRs.

HISTORY

After selling his computing services company, David Cook turned to operating flashy, computerized video rental stores, opening his first in 1985 and adopting the moniker Blockbuster Entertainment in 1986. Entrepreneur Wayne Huizenga took over in 1987, injecting $18 million into Blockbuster and buying the company outright by the end of the year. Huizenga's acquisitions rapidly expanded the number of Blockbuster stores to 130. Other acquisitions (including Major Video, a 175-store chain, and Erol's, the US's third-largest video chain) increased the number of stores to 1,500 by 1990.

Blockbuster became the largest video renter in the UK in 1992 through the purchase of 875-unit Cityvision. It also branched into music retailing that year when it bought the Sound Warehouse and Music Plus chains and created Blockbuster Music. The following year it acquired a majority stake in Spelling Entertainment, then was itself acquired in 1994 by Viacom for $8.4 billion. Viacom took Spelling Entertainment under its wing and formed a division for its new chain of video stores called Blockbuster Entertainment Group. Following the deal, Huizenga left the company (he's now chairman of AutoNation).

Over the next few years, Blockbuster experienced a rash of poor business decisions and executive departures starting with Steven Berrard (CEO after Viacom's 1994 takeover), who resigned in 1996 to head Huizenga's used-car operations. Wal-Mart veteran Bill Fields replaced him and started promoting the retailer as a "neighborhood entertainment center," selling videotapes (instead of renting them), books, CDs, gift items, and music. After closing 50 music outlets in 1996, the company moved its headquarters from Florida to Dallas in 1997, a move many employees refused to make.

Fields resigned later that year and current chairman and CEO John Antioco replaced him. Antioco's reign began with Viacom taking a $300 million charge related to the turmoil at Blockbuster. He immediately started unraveling many of Fields' efforts, especially his focus on non-rental operations. Antioco also set the video rental industry on its ear in 1997 by forcing the movie studios into a revenue-sharing agreement that replaced the standard practice of buying rental copies.

The company finished returning to its rental roots by selling Blockbuster Music in 1998. By 1999 Viacom spun off a minority stake in Blockbuster and the company split into three new operating units that oversee its retail outlets, e-commerce operations, and database and brand marketing.

In 2001 Blockbuster announced that it would decrease its VHS and video game inventory by 25% to make room for more DVDs.

OFFICERS

Chairman and CEO: John F. Antioco, age 52, $3,955,000 pay
President and COO: Nigel Travis, age 52, $901,387 pay
EVP, CFO, and Chief Administrative Officer: Larry J. Zine, age 47, $774,144 pay
EVP and Chief Marketing Officer: James Notarnicola, $649,871 pay
EVP, General Counsel, and Secretary: Edward B. Stead, age 55, $695,340 pay
EVP Content Worldwide: Dean M. Wilson, age 44
EVP Merchandising and Chief Concept Officer: Nick Shepherd, age 43
EVP; President, International: Chris Wyatt, age 45
EVP; President, New Media Division: Mark T. Gilman, age 37
EVP; COO, North America Operations: Michael K. Roemer, age 53
SVP Corporate Communications: Karen Raskopf
SVP Human Resources: Dan Satterthawaite
SVP Investor Relations: Mary Bell
SVP and General Manager, Store-in-Store Concepts: Eileen Terry
SVP and General Merchandising Manager: Joyce Woodward
VP Advertising: Marva Cathey
VP Interactive Merchandising: Steven Lundeen
VP Partnership Marketing, Sales, and Promotions: Lisa Zoellner
VP Public Relations: Liz Greene
VP Sales: Laurie Ross
Auditors: PricewaterhouseCoopers LLP

LOCATIONS

HQ: 1201 Elm St., Dallas, TX 75270
Phone: 214-854-3000   **Fax:** 214-854-4848
Web: www.blockbuster.com

Blockbuster operates 8,000 stores in the Americas, Asia, Australia, and Europe.

PRODUCTS/OPERATIONS

2001 Sales

	$ mil.	% of total
Rentals	4,315	84
Merchandise	735	14
Other	107	2
Total	**5,157**	**100**

COMPETITORS

Best Buy
Borders
Circuit City
DIRECTV
Hastings Entertainment
Hollywood Entertainment
Movie Gallery
MTS
Musicland
Trans World Entertainment
Wherehouse Entertainment

HISTORICAL FINANCIALS & EMPLOYEES

NYSE: BBI FYE: December 31	Annual Growth	12/92	12/93	12/94	12/95	12/96	12/97	12/98	12/99	12/00	12/01
Sales ($ mil.)	11.9%	—	—	—	—	2,942	3,314	3,893	4,464	4,960	5,157
Net income ($ mil.)	—	—	—	—	—	78	(318)	(337)	(69)	(76)	(240)
Income as % of sales	—	—	—	—	—	2.6%	—	—	—	—	—
Earnings per share ($)	—	—	—	—	—	—	—	—	(0.44)	(0.43)	(1.37)
Stock price - FY high ($)	—	—	—	—	—	—	—	—	17.13	14.88	28.66
Stock price - FY low ($)	—	—	—	—	—	—	—	—	11.38	6.88	8.19
Stock price - FY close ($)	37.2%	—	—	—	—	—	—	—	13.38	8.38	25.20
P/E – high	—	—	—	—	—	—	—	—	—	—	—
P/E – low	—	—	—	—	—	—	—	—	—	—	—
Dividends per share ($)	100.0%	—	—	—	—	—	—	—	0.02	0.08	0.08
Book value per share ($)	(3.6%)	—	—	—	—	—	—	—	35.00	34.33	32.52
Employees	2.6%	—	—	—	—	—	—	82,400	89,700	95,800	89,100

STOCK PRICE HISTORY

HIGH/LOW/CLOSE

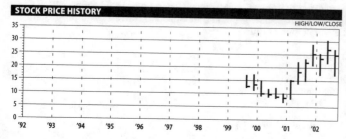

2001 FISCAL YEAR-END

Debt ratio: 8.7%
Return on equity: —
Cash ($ mil.): 200
Current ratio: 0.56
Long-term debt ($ mil.): 546
No. of shares (mil.): 177
Dividends
 Yield: 0.3%
 Payout: —
Market value ($ mil.): 4,455

BLUE CROSS AND BLUE SHIELD

The rise of managed health care has had some of its members singing the blues, but Blue Cross and Blue Shield Association still has major market power. The Chicago-based association governs some 43 chapters that offer health care coverage to more than 80 million Americans via indemnity insurance, HMOs, PPOs, point-of-service (POS) plans, and Medicare plans.

While some Blues always faced competition head-on, most received tax benefits for taking all comers. But as lower-cost plans attracted the hale and hearty, the Blues' customers became older, sicker, and more expensive. With their quasi-charitable status and outdated rate structures, many Blues lost market share.

They have fought back by merging among themselves, creating for-profit subsidiaries, forming alliances with for-profit enterprises, or dropping their not-for-profit status and going public — while still using the Blue Cross Blue Shield name. A history of tax breaks complicates these efforts and usually requires the creation of charitable foundations. As a result, the umbrella association is becoming a licensing and brand-marketing entity. The conversion of the Blues to for-profit status is sparking a backlash by consumer organizations.

HISTORY

Blue Cross was born in 1929, when Baylor University official Justin Kimball offered schoolteachers 21 days of hospital care for $6 a year. A major plan feature was a community rating system that based premiums on the community claims experience rather than members' conditions.

The Blue Cross symbol was devised in 1933 by Minnesota plan executive E. A. van Steenwyck. By 1935 many of the 15 plans in 11 states used the symbol. Many states gave the plans nonprofit status, and in 1936 the American Hospital Association formed the Committee on Hospital Service (renamed the Blue Cross Association in 1948) to coordinate them.

As Blue Cross grew, state medical societies sponsored prepaid plans to cover doctors' fees. In 1946 they united under the aegis of the American Medical Association (AMA) as the Associated Medical Care Plans (later the Association of Blue Shield Plans).

In 1948 the AMA thwarted a Blue Cross attempt to merge with Blue Shield. But the Blues increasingly cooperated on public policy matters while competing for members, and each Blue formed a not-for-profit corporation to coordinate its plan's activities.

By 1960 Blue Cross insured about a third of the US. Over the next decade the Blues started administering Medicare and other government health plans, and by 1970 half of Blue Cross' premiums came from government entities.

In the 1970s the Blues adopted such cost-control measures as review of hospital admissions; many plans even abandoned the community rating system. Most began emphasizing preventive care in HMOs or PPOs. The two Blues finally merged in 1982, but this had little effect on the associations' bottom lines as losses grew.

By the 1990s the Blues were big business. Some of the state associations offered officers high salaries and perks but still insisted on special regulatory treatment.

Blue Cross of California became the first chapter to give up its tax-free status when it was bought by WellPoint Health Networks, a managed care subsidiary it had founded in 1992. In a 1996 deal, WellPoint became the chapter's parent and converted it to for-profit status, assigning all of the stock to a public charitable foundation which received the proceeds of its subsequent IPO. WellPoint also bought the group life and health division of Massachusetts Mutual Life Insurance.

The for-profit switches picked up in 1997. Blue Cross of Connecticut merged with insurance provider Anthem, and other mergers followed. Half the nation's Blues formed an alliance called BluesCONNECT, competing with national health plans by offering employers one nationwide benefits organization. The association also pursued overseas licensing agreements in Europe, South America, and Asia, assembling a network of Blue Cross-friendly caregivers aiming for worldwide coverage.

In 1998 Blues in more than 35 states sued the nation's big cigarette companies to recoup the costs of treating smoking-related illnesses. In a separate lawsuit, Blue Cross and Blue Shield of Minnesota received nearly $300 million from the tobacco industry. In 1999, Anthem moved to acquire or affiliate with Blues in Colorado, Maine, and New Hampshire.

In 2000, after years of discussions, the New York Attorney General permitted Empire Blue Cross and Blue Shield to convert to for-profit status.

Chairman: Michael B. Unhjem
President and CEO: Scott P. Serota
SVP, Corporate Secretary, and General Counsel:
  Roger G. Wilson
SVP, Strategic Services: Maureen Sullivan
SVP and Chief Medical Officer: Allan M. Korn
VP, Finance and Administration: Ralph Rambach
VP, Human Resources: Bill Colbourne
Auditors: PricewaterhouseCoopers LLP

LOCATIONS

HQ: Blue Cross and Blue Shield Association
  225 N. Michigan Ave., Chicago, IL 60601
Phone: 312-297-6000   **Fax:** 312-297-6609
Web: www.bcbs.com

The Blue Cross and Blue Shield Association has offices
in Chicago and Washington, DC, with licensees
operating throughout the US as well as in Africa,
Australia, Asia, Canada, Latin America, the Middle East,
and western Europe.

PRODUCTS/OPERATIONS

2001 Health Care Members

	Members (mil)	% of total
PPO	38	45
Traditional Indemnity	22	26
HMO	17	20
Point-of-service (POS)	7	9
Total	**84**	**100**

Selected Operations
BlueCard Worldwide (care of US members in foreign
  countries)
BluesCONNECT (nationwide alliance)
Federal Employee Health Benefits Program (federal
  employees and retirees)
Health maintenance organizations
Medicare management
Point-of-service programs
Preferred provider organizations

COMPETITORS

Aetna
CIGNA
Health Net
Humana
Kaiser Foundation
Oxford Health Plans
PacifiCare
Prudential
UniHealth
UnitedHealth Group

HISTORICAL FINANCIALS & EMPLOYEES

Association FYE: December 31	Annual Growth	12/92	12/93	12/94	12/95	12/96	12/97	12/98	12/99	12/00	12/01
Sales ($ mil.)	8.1%	70,913	71,161	71,414	74,400	75,200	76,500	94,700	93,700	126,000	143,200
Employees	0.5%	143,000	135,883	146,352	146,000	150,000	150,000	150,000	150,000	150,000	150,000

SALES HISTORY

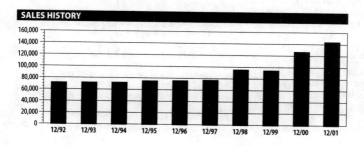

BMC SOFTWARE, INC.

BMC Software simply won't stand to see your enterprise assets mismanaged. The Houston-based company is a leading provider of enterprise management software, offering more than 450 software tools designed to manage enterprise servers, speed up and monitor databases, eliminate unplanned outages, and recover system assets. BMC's software is used to monitor, manage, and maintain a variety of functions, including recovery and storage management, business processes integration, and application and database performance management. The company also offers maintenance, support, and related professional services, which account for about half of sales. BMC's customers include Dow Corning, First Union, and Home Depot.

BMC continues to expand past its core expertise in mainframe management and utility software, investing heavily in research and development and using acquisitions to boost its offerings in fields such as storage management and Web transaction monitoring.

Consistently rated as one of America's best places to work, BMC features whimsical offices with hammocks and cowskin-lined elevators, and a self-contained campus stocked with a dry cleaner, a hairdresser, and other stores catering to workers' needs.

HISTORY

BMC, one of the few profitable software companies not operated by its founders, was launched in 1980 by Scott Boulett, John Moores, and Dan Cloer. Their initials gave the company its name. Its first product — and most that followed — improved communications between IBM databases with connected terminals and PCs.

Through an aggressive telemarketing campaign boasted of internally as "telemuscle," the company's utility software was snapped up by a chunk of the FORTUNE 500, which used it to boost the performance of wall-sized IBM mainframes and database systems. The company started an international expansion in 1984, opening an office in Germany. BMC went public in 1988.

Two years later COO Max Watson replaced Richard Hosley as president and CEO. Hosley stayed on as VC until 1992 when Watson assumed that title as well. Moores, the only founder who held a position with the company, resigned as chairman that year (a 35% stake in BMC that Moores sold that year helped the entrepreneur found rival software company NEON Systems, where he remains chairman, and become majority owner of the San Diego Padres professional baseball team).

In the early 1990s Watson navigated BMC's transition toward networked PC systems as corporate customers began eschewing mainframes. The company continued to take its product development cues from IBM, where Watson had worked for 14 years. As Big Blue developed new technology, BMC would act quickly to release utilities that improved performance for that new technology.

In 1994 BMC bought PATROL Software, adding a network-based performance optimization product that would later become one of the company's flagship lines. The next year the company doubled the size of its marketing. In 1995 BMC launched a lawsuit against Moores for luring away company executives to help run his growing software ventures (the two sides acrimoniously settled in 1999).

Using alliances and acquisitions to expand, the company in 1996 forged an alliance with Sun Microsystems to develop platform management software. The company bought software specialist DataTools in 1997 and system performance analysis software specialist BGS Systems in 1998.

The next year the company doubled its size when it bought rival management software maker Boole & Babbage for about $900 million, and Israeli software developer New Dimension Software for about $675 million. Along with these acquisitions came a corporate reinvention that included a new logo and revamped product divisions. That year the company began tailoring its management software for the e-commerce market.

In 2000 BMC increased its e-commerce offerings by acquiring Evity, a provider of Web transaction monitoring services. Early in 2001, Watson brought Robert Beauchamp on board, passing the president and CEO titles to him. Watson later stepped down as chairman as well, and was replaced by Garland Cupp.

The next year the company restructured, trimming its workforce by about 15%.

OFFICERS

Chairman: B. Garland Cupp, age 60
President, CEO, and Director: Robert E. Beauchamp, age 42, $1,619,836 pay
SVP, Administration: Jerome J. Adams
SVP, General Counsel, and Secretary: Robert H. Whilden Jr., age 67, $725,268 pay
SVP, Operations: Jeffrey S. Hawn, age 38, $1,026,989 pay
SVP, Research and Development: Dan Barnea, age 57, $1,026,985 pay
SVP, Worldwide Field Operations: Darroll Buytenhuys, age 54, $1,079,886 pay
VP, CFO, and Chief Accounting Officer: John W. Cox, age 42
VP and CIO: Jay Gardner
VP and Treasurer: Stephen B. Solcher, age 40

VP and General Manager, Enterprise Data Management: Gene Austin
VP and General Manager, Enterprise Systems Management: Calvin Guidry
VP and General Manager, Subscription Services: Mary Nugent
VP, Common Infrastructure: Carl Coken
VP, Enterprise eBusiness Management: Mary Smars
VP, Human Resources: Johnnie Horn
Director, Customer Relationship Management: Mark Meyer
Director, Engineering: Paul Brownell
Director, Investor Relations: Neil Yekell
Director, Product Marketing, Enterprise Systems Management: Pete DiStefano
Auditors: Ernst & Young LLP

LOCATIONS

HQ: 2101 City West Blvd., Houston, TX 77042
Phone: 713-918-8800   **Fax:** 713-918-8000
Web: www.bmc.com

BMC Software has research and development centers in France, Israel, and the US, and sales offices in more than 30 countries.

2002 Sales

	$ mil.	% of total
North America	752	58
Other regions	537	42
Total	**1,289**	**100**

PRODUCTS/OPERATIONS

2002 Sales

	$ mil.	% of total
License	625	49
Maintenance	576	45
Professional services	88	6
Total	**1,289**	**100**

Selected Software
COMMAND/POST (distributed system centralized application management)
INCONTROL (production, output, and security management)
MAINVIEW (mainframe service, performance, and capacity management)
MAXM (database administration)
PATROL (network, performance, and service management)
RESOLVE (recovery and storage management)

Selected Services
Consulting
Education
Maintenance
Product enhancement and implementation
Technical support

COMPETITORS

Computer Associates	Network Associates
Compuware	Oracle
Hewlett-Packard	SAP
IBM	Sun Microsystems
Microsoft	Sybase

HISTORICAL FINANCIALS & EMPLOYEES

NYSE: BMC FYE: March 31	Annual Growth	3/93	3/94	3/95	3/96	3/97	3/98	3/99	3/00	3/01	3/02
Sales ($ mil.)	20.6%	239	289	345	429	563	731	1,304	1,719	1,504	1,289
Net income ($ mil.)	—	65	57	78	106	164	166	363	243	42	(184)
Income as % of sales	—	27.4%	19.6%	22.5%	24.6%	29.1%	22.7%	27.8%	14.1%	2.8%	—
Earnings per share ($)	—	0.32	0.27	0.38	0.50	0.76	0.77	1.45	0.77	0.17	(0.75)
Stock price - FY high ($)	—	10.52	8.88	8.72	15.34	25.50	42.13	60.25	86.63	51.38	30.50
Stock price - FY low ($)	—	4.66	4.84	5.03	6.91	12.69	19.81	30.13	30.00	13.00	11.50
Stock price - FY close ($)	13.7%	6.11	7.72	7.97	13.69	23.06	41.91	37.06	49.38	21.50	19.45
P/E - high	—	33	33	23	29	31	51	39	—	302	—
P/E - low	—	15	18	13	13	15	24	19	—	76	—
Dividends per share ($)	—	0.00	0.00	0.00	0.00	0.00	0.00	0.00	0.00	0.00	0.00
Book value per share ($)	21.7%	1.06	1.22	1.52	1.92	2.73	3.68	5.92	7.28	7.32	6.25
Employees	24.1%	909	987	1,185	1,444	1,813	2,777	4,914	6,677	7,330	6,335

STOCK PRICE HISTORY

HIGH/LOW/CLOSE

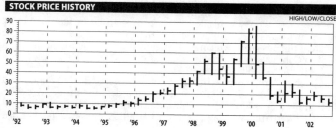

2002 FISCAL YEAR-END

Debt ratio: 0.0%
Return on equity: —
Cash ($ mil.): 330
Current ratio: 1.46
Long-term debt ($ mil.): 0
No. of shares (mil.): 241
Dividends
  Yield: —
  Payout: —
Market value ($ mil.): 4,687

THE BOEING COMPANY

From the Space Shuttle to the Apache helicopter, The Boeing Company is the 800-pound gorilla of US aerospace. The Chicago-based firm is the world's largest aerospace company and the #1 manufacturer of commercial jets, ahead of its only competitor in that business, Airbus. Boeing is also the planet's #2 defense contractor, just behind Lockheed Martin. It has three segments: commercial airplanes, military aircraft and missiles, and space and communications systems. However, the company has embarked on a restructuring, choosing to place more emphasis on its military and space segments while effecting a controlled de-emphasis of its commercial airline business.

Boeing's commercial planes include the Boeing 747, 767, and 777 jets, as well as the 737, the best-selling jetliner in aviation history. Boeing's military aircraft include the F/A-18 Hornet strike fighter, the AH-64D Apache Longbow helicopter, the C-17 Globemaster III transport, and the company's version of an unmanned combat aircraft, the X-45.

Missiles include the Standoff Land Attack Missile (SLAM ER) and the Joint Direct Attack Munition (JDAM). Boeing's space systems include the Space Shuttle (with Lockheed Martin), the Delta family of rockets, global positioning systems (GPS), and communications satellites. It also is the primary contractor for the International Space Station.

Boeing lost out to Lockheed Martin for the Joint Strike Fighter contract, which, at over $200 billion, is the largest defense contract ever. Instead, Boeing is focusing on what it believes is the next big thing in military aircraft: unmanned aerial vehicles (UAVs).

The market for commercial planes has plummeted. To compensate for the downturn in commercial plane orders, Boeing has cut costs, combined operations, and laid off about 30,000 people. It has scrapped plans for the 747X (a competitor of Airbus' A380 superjumbo), instead focusing on the development of the so-called Sonic Cruiser, a faster (flying up to speeds of Mach .95), smaller, and longer-range jetliner with a double delta wing design.

HISTORY

Bill Boeing, who had already made his fortune in Washington real estate, built his first airplane in 1916 with naval officer Conrad Westervelt. His Seattle company, Pacific Aero Products, changed its name to Boeing Airplane Company the next year.

During WWI Boeing built training planes for the US Navy and began the first international airmail service (between Seattle and Victoria, British Columbia). The company added a Chicago-San Francisco route in 1927 and established an airline subsidiary, Boeing Air Transport. The airline's success was aided by Boeing's Model 40A, the first plane to use Frederick Rentschler's new air-cooled engine.

Rentschler and Boeing combined their companies as United Aircraft and Transport in 1929 and introduced the all-metal airliner in 1933. The next year new antitrust rules forced United to sell portions of its operations as United Air Lines and United Aircraft (later United Technologies). This left Boeing Airplane (as it was known until 1961) with the manufacturing concerns.

During WWII Boeing produced such planes as the B-17 "Flying Fortress" and B-29 bombers. At one point the company was producing 362 planes per month for the war effort.

Between 1935 and 1965 Boeing's commercial planes included the Model 314 Clipper, the Model 307 Stratoliner (with the first pressurized cabin), and the 707 (the first successful jetliner) and 727. In the 1960s it built the rockets used in the Apollo space program. The company delivered the first 737 in 1967. The 747 (the first jumbo jet) also went into production in the late 1960s.

Boeing expanded its information services and aerospace capabilities by establishing Boeing Computer Services in 1970. World fuel shortages and concern over aircraft noise prompted Boeing to design the efficient 757 and 767 models in the late 1970s.

The company's wide-body 777 made its maiden flight in 1995. Boeing bought Rockwell's aerospace and defense operations in 1996. The next year it purchased rival and leading military aircraft maker McDonnell Douglas for $16 billion. Boeing's commercial rocket program was thrown into turmoil after its Delta III rocket exploded during its maiden launch. However, the US Air Force awarded the bulk of a satellite-launching contract to Boeing over rival Lockheed Martin.

Boeing acquired Hughes Electronics' satellite-making unit in a $3.85 billion deal in 2000. It also signed an $8.9 billion contract to provide the Navy with 222 of Boeing's new F/A-18E/F Super Hornet fighter aircraft over five years.

In 2001 the company moved its corporate headquarters from Seattle to Chicago. As airlines reduced their flight schedules in the aftermath of September 11, Boeing announced that it would lay off 25,000-30,000 people by the end of 2002.

In a piece of good news, Boeing announced that it had signed a deal for thirty 737s with three Chinese airlines carrying a potential price tag of about $1.6 billion. However, further bad news resulting from the attack was the suspension of production of the 777-200LR.

In 2002 Boeing announced that it had cut a deal with Ryanair for 100 new aircraft, with options on another 50, potentially worth around $9 billion. That same year Boeing announced that it would combine its space and defense units in a bid to boost efficiency. Boeing and the US Air Force signed a $9.7 billion deal for 60 C-17 Globemaster III transport aircraft later that year.

OFFICERS

Chairman and CEO: Philip M. Condit, age 60, $3,337,431 pay
CFO and Office of the Chairman: Michael M. Sears, age 54, $1,307,993 pay (prior to promotion)
Chief People and Administration Officer; Office of the Chairman: Laurette T. Koellner, age 47
CTO and Office of the Chairman: David O. Swain, age 59, $858,112 pay (prior to promotion)
EVP, Airplane Programs: James M. Jamieson, age 52
EVP, Space and Communications; General Manager, Missile Defense Systems: James W. Evatt, age 52
SVP and General Counsel: Doug Bain, age 52
SVP; President and CEO, Boeing Commercial Airplanes Group: Alan R. Mulally, age 56, $1,448,666 pay
Auditors: Deloitte & Touche LLP

LOCATIONS

HQ: 100 N. Riverside Plaza, Chicago, IL 60606
Phone: 312-544-2000   **Fax:** 312-544-2082
Web: www.boeing.com

2001 Sales

	% of total
US	67
Asia	
China	3
Other countries	12
Europe	14
Oceania	1
Africa	1
Other	2
Total	**100**

PRODUCTS/OPERATIONS

2001 Sales & Operating Income

	Sales % of total	Operating Income % of total
Commercial airplanes	59	51
Military aircraft & missiles	21	26
Space & communications	18	12
Financing	1	11
Other	1	—
Total	**100**	**100**

COMPETITORS

Airbus	GE Aircraft	Raytheon
BAE SYSTEMS	Engines	Sextant
Bombardier	Goodrich	Avionique
Cessna	Kaman	Textron
DaimlerChrysler	Lockheed Martin	United
Dassault Aviation	Northrop	Technologies
EADS	Grumman	Vertex Aerospace

HISTORICAL FINANCIALS & EMPLOYEES

NYSE: BA FYE: December 31	Annual Growth	12/92	12/93	12/94	12/95	12/96	12/97	12/98	12/99	12/00	12/01
Sales ($ mil.)	7.6%	30,184	25,438	21,924	19,515	22,681	45,800	56,154	57,993	51,321	58,198
Net income ($ mil.)	19.9%	552	1,244	856	393	1,095	(178)	1,120	2,309	2,128	2,827
Income as % of sales	—	1.8%	4.9%	3.9%	2.0%	4.8%	—	2.0%	4.0%	4.1%	4.9%
Earnings per share ($)	17.3%	0.81	1.64	1.48	0.58	1.60	(0.18)	1.15	2.49	2.44	3.41
Stock price - FY high ($)	—	27.31	22.38	25.06	40.00	53.75	60.50	56.25	48.50	70.94	69.85
Stock price - FY low ($)	—	16.06	16.69	21.06	22.19	37.06	43.00	29.00	32.56	32.00	27.60
Stock price - FY close ($)	7.6%	20.06	21.63	23.50	39.19	53.25	48.94	32.63	41.44	66.00	38.78
P/E - high	—	12	13	17	69	34	—	48	19	29	20
P/E - low	—	7	10	14	38	23	—	25	13	13	8
Dividends per share ($)	3.5%	0.50	0.50	0.50	0.50	0.55	0.56	0.56	0.56	0.56	0.68
Book value per share ($)	1.0%	11.87	13.20	14.23	14.39	15.18	12.95	12.62	12.60	12.59	12.92
Employees	3.2%	142,000	123,000	117,000	105,000	143,000	238,000	231,000	197,000	198,000	188,000

STOCK PRICE HISTORY

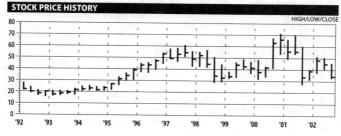

HIGH/LOW/CLOSE

2001 FISCAL YEAR-END

Debt ratio: 50.1%
Return on equity: 25.9%
Cash ($ mil.): 633
Current ratio: 0.79
Long-term debt ($ mil.): 10,866
No. of shares (mil.): 838
Dividends
  Yield: 1.8%
  Payout: 19.9%
Market value ($ mil.): 32,481

BOISE CASCADE CORPORATION

Although Boise Cascade doesn't make paper money, it does make money from paper. The Boise, Idaho-based company manages more than two million acres of forests to support its production of paper and building products. Boise also distributes office supplies such as paper, computer supplies, and furniture through its Boise Office Solutions subsidiary. The company operates about 65 distribution centers in Australia, Canada, New Zealand, and the US. Boise's building products range from laminated veneer lumber to I-joists and plywood. Paper products include newsprint, market pulp, containerboard, and business paper.

Boise Cascade's earnings have been hurt by its building-products unit, which has had to sell product at low prices due to competitive pressure and the economic climate. Although Boise has sold its European office products operations, it has expanded its presence in Australia and New Zealand with the acquisition of the Blue Star Business Supplies Group of US Office Products. In the meantime, Boise Cascade shortened its brand name from Boise Cascade to Boise as part of an effort to revitalize its brand image.

HISTORY

Boise Cascade got its start in 1957 with the merger of two small lumber companies — Boise Payette Lumber Company (based in Boise, Idaho) and Cascade Lumber Company (Yakima, Washington). The business diversified in the 1960s under the leadership of Robert Hansberger, moving into office-products distribution in 1964. A number of acquisitions followed, including Ebasco Industries (1969), a consulting, engineering, and construction firm. By 1970 Boise Cascade had made more than 30 buys to diversify into building materials, paper products, real estate, recreational vehicles (RVs), and publishing.

In the early 1970s the company suffered a timber shortage as its access to public timberlands dwindled. Its plans to develop recreational communities in California, Hawaii, and Washington met opposition from residents, causing Boise Cascade to scrap all but six of the 29 projects.

In 1972 high costs related to the remaining projects left the company in debt. John Fery replaced Hansberger as president that year and sold companies not directly related to the company's core forest-product operations.

In the late 1980s and early 1990s Boise sold more nonstrategic operations, including its Specialty Paperboard Division in 1989. It sold more than half of its corrugated-container plants in 1992 to focus on manufacturing forest products and distributing building materials and office supplies.

Boise Cascade also sold its wholesale office-product business in 1992 to focus on direct sales to big buyers such as IBM and Boeing. The company sold off its Canadian subsidiary, Rainy River Forest Products, during 1994 and 1995. Resurgent paper prices resulted in a profit in 1995, Boise Cascade's first since 1990.

Also in 1995, in a move into the international paper market, Boise Cascade signed a joint venture agreement with Shenzhen Leasing to form Zhuhai Hiwin Boise Cascade, a Chinese manufacturer of carbonless paper. That year it sold a minority stake in Boise Cascade Office Products (BCOP) to the public.

The company sold its coated-papers business to paper and packaging heavyweight Mead in 1996 for $639 million. The following year Boise began harvesting its first quick-growth cottonwood trees (specially grown to cut the cost of harvesting from traditional slow-growth hardwood plantations). Also in 1997 BCOP bought Jean-Paul Guisset, an office-products direct marketer in France. Although this acquisition boosted sales and increased the company's European presence, company profits suffered that year because of weak paper prices.

The low price of paper in 1998 prompted the company to close four sawmills and a research and development center. Restructuring costs associated with the closures and a fire at the company's Medford, Oregon, plywood plant led to a net income loss for the year.

In 1999 Boise bought Wallace Computer Services, a contract stationer business, and broadened its building-supply distribution network nationwide by acquiring Furman Lumber, a building-supplies distributor. In 2000 Boise Cascade completed the purchase of the 19% of Boise Office Solutions that it didn't already own. The company also sold its European office products operations for $335 million and then turned around and purchased the Blue Star Business Supplies Group of US Office Products in Australia and New Zealand for about $115 million.

Because of the decline in federal timber sales, in 2001 the company closed its plywood mill and lumber operations in Emmett, Idaho, and a sawmill in Cascade, Idaho. In 2002 lagging profits prompted Boise to implement cost-cutting procedures.

OFFICERS

Chairman and CEO: George J. Harad, age 57,
   $1,506,313 pay
SVP and CFO: Theodore Crumley, age 57, $581,936 pay
SVP and General Counsel: John W. Holleran, age 47,
   $476,629 pay
SVP, Building Materials, Distribution: Stanley R. Bell,
   age 55
SVP, Building Solutions: John C. Bender, age 62
SVP, Office Solutions: Christopher C. Milliken, age 56,
   $746,409 pay
SVP, Paper Solutions: A. Ben Groce, age 60,
   $504,199 pay
VP and Treasurer: Irving Littman, age 61
VP and Controller: Thomas E. Carlile, age 50
VP, Corporate Communications and Investor Relations:
   Vincent T. Hannity, age 57
VP, Human Resources: John A. Berilla, age 57
VP, Information Technology: Robert Egan, age 42
Auditors: KPMG LLP

LOCATIONS

HQ: 1111 W. Jefferson St., Boise, ID 83728
Phone: 208-384-6161   **Fax:** 208-384-7189
Web: www.bc.com

Boise Cascade has manufacturing and distribution
operations in Australia, Brazil, Canada, New Zealand,
and the US.

2001 Sales

	$ mil.	% of total
US	6,621	92
Other countries	801	8
Total	**7,422**	**100**

PRODUCTS/OPERATIONS

2001 Sales

	$ mil.	% of total
Office solutions	3,534	48
Building solutions	2,361	32
Paper solutions	1,505	20
Other	22	—
Total	**7,422**	**100**

Selected Products

Building Products	Paper Products
I-joists	Business papers
Laminated veneer lumber	Containerboard
Lumber	Corrugated containers
Oriented strand board	Market pulp
Particleboard	Newsprint
Plywood	
Structural panels	

COMPETITORS

Georgia-Pacific Corporation	Office Depot
	OfficeMax
International Paper	Staples
Louisiana-Pacific	Weyerhaeuser

HISTORICAL FINANCIALS & EMPLOYEES

NYSE: BCC FYE: December 31	Annual Growth	12/92	12/93	12/94	12/95	12/96	12/97	12/98	12/99	12/00	12/01
Sales ($ mil.)	8.0%	3,716	3,958	4,140	5,074	5,108	5,494	6,162	6,953	7,807	7,422
Net income ($ mil.)	—	(228)	(77)	(63)	352	9	(30)	(37)	200	179	(43)
Income as % of sales	—	—	—	—	6.9%	0.2%	—	—	2.9%	2.3%	—
Earnings per share ($)	—	(6.73)	(3.17)	(3.08)	5.39	(0.63)	(1.19)	(1.00)	3.06	2.73	(0.96)
Stock price - FY high ($)	—	25.38	27.50	30.50	47.50	47.25	45.56	40.38	47.19	43.94	38.00
Stock price - FY low ($)	—	16.38	19.50	19.00	26.25	27.38	27.75	22.25	28.75	21.75	26.99
Stock price - FY close ($)	5.4%	21.13	23.50	26.75	34.50	31.75	30.25	31.00	40.50	33.63	34.01
P/E - high	—	—	—	—	7	—	—	—	14	15	—
P/E - low	—	—	—	—	4	—	—	—	9	8	—
Dividends per share ($)	0.0%	0.60	0.60	0.60	0.60	0.45	0.60	0.60	0.60	0.60	0.60
Book value per share ($)	(3.0%)	35.78	39.60	35.65	35.48	34.67	28.68	25.35	28.24	30.64	27.18
Employees	3.8%	17,222	17,362	16,618	17,820	19,976	22,514	23,039	23,726	25,257	24,168

STOCK PRICE HISTORY

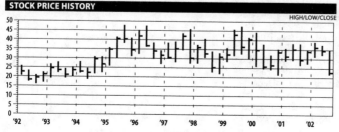

HIGH/LOW/CLOSE

2001 FISCAL YEAR-END

Debt ratio: 42.0%
Return on equity: —
Cash ($ mil.): 57
Current ratio: 0.98
Long-term debt ($ mil.): 1,144
No. of shares (mil.): 58
Dividends
   Yield: 1.8%
   Payout: —
Market value ($ mil.): 1,975

BORDERS GROUP, INC.

Although a great writer's imagination has no borders, inside Borders you can find the works of many great writers. Ann Arbor, Michigan-based Borders Group, the nation's #2 bookstore retailer, operates more than 1,200 US stores (in all 50 states) under two names: Borders (about 375 superstores) and Waldenbooks (about 815 stores, the #1 US mall bookstore chain). Borders also owns more than 30 Books etc. stores in the UK and has opened Borders stores in the UK, Australia, New Zealand, Puerto Rico, and Singapore.

In addition to books, most superstores sell music, videos, and DVDs and have cafes. Borders strives to reflect local tastes and interests in its superstores, even employing community relations representatives. The stores also host literary and community events, including author signings and lectures.

HISTORY

Brothers Louis and Tom Borders founded their first bookstore in 1971 in Ann Arbor, Michigan. The store originally sold used books but soon added new books. As titles were added, Louis developed tracking systems for the growing inventory. It's been said that the former MIT student stumbled upon the system while trying to create a software program to predict horse race winners. In the mid-1970s the brothers formed Book Inventory Systems to market the system to other independent bookstores.

Through the late 1970s and early 1980s, the brothers focused on building the service part of their business, but by the mid-1980s they were having trouble finding enough large, independent bookstore customers. Refocusing on retail, they opened their second store (Birmingham, Michigan) in 1985.

They had five stores by 1988 and hired Robert DiRomualdo (president of cheeselog chain Hickory Farms) to run Borders and mount a national expansion. Discount retailer Kmart bought Book Inventory Systems (including 19 Borders bookstores) in 1992.

Kmart already owned Waldenbooks, which had been founded in 1933 and named for the Massachusetts pond that inspired Thoreau. Started by Larry Hoyt as a book rental library, Waldenbooks had 250 outlets by 1948. In 1968 the bookseller opened its first all-retail bookstore in Pittsburgh.

By placing stores in the growing number of US shopping malls, Waldenbooks expanded rapidly during the 1970s. In 1979 the company hired former Procter & Gamble executive Harry Hoffman to run the company. Hoffman drew the ire of traditionalists in the book retailing industry because he focused on best sellers instead of literary works. Hoffman also added nonbook items such as greeting cards to the stores' merchandise mix.

In 1981 Waldenbooks became the first bookseller to operate in all 50 states. Kmart acquired the chain three years later. As part of a plan to revive its discount business, in 1995 Kmart spun off Borders Group (which by this time included Waldenbooks, Borders, and part of Planet Music, formerly CD Superstore) to the public. Borders consolidated its three divisions under one roof and bought the rest of Planet Music (closed in 1997). With mall traffic slowing nationally, Borders CEO DiRomualdo steered the company away from Waldenbooks and toward superstores.

Moving beyond its existing borders, the company acquired the UK chain Books etc., opened a store in Singapore in 1997, and entered Australia the next year. Borders finally began offering books, music, and videos through its borders.com Web site in 1998, three years after Amazon.com began selling online.

Philip Pfeffer, a former top executive with publisher Random House and book distributor Ingram who succeeded DiRomualdo as CEO in late 1998, was forced out five months later, in part for being slow to address the company's lagging efforts online.

In 1999 Borders acquired 20% of UK stationery retailer Paperchase Products; All Wound Up, a kiosk-based seller of interactive toys and novelties; and 20% of Sprout, which offers on-demand book printing. In November 1999 Greg Josefowicz, the former president of Albertson's Jewel-Osco division, was named CEO.

Slow sales in the 2000 holiday season and disappointing results from the All Wound Up locations triggered Borders to put the toy business up for sale.

In March 2001 Borders turned over its specialty-book operations to distributor Ingram Industries. Also that year Borders laid off its entire borders.com workforce and struck a deal to have the online unit run by rival Amazon.com; the co-branded Web site debuted in August 2001.

In January 2002 DiRomualdo stepped down as chairman, and Josefowicz assumed the role.

OFFICERS

Chairman, President, and CEO: Gregory P. Josefowicz, age 49, $1,148,700 pay
SVP and CFO: Edward W. Wilhelm, age 43, $375,481 pay
VP, General Counsel, and Secretary: Thomas D. Carney, age 55
VP, Cafe Operations: Michael Oprins
VP, Human Resources: Daniel T. Smith, age 37
VP, Information Technology: Mark A. Winterhalter, age 47
President, Borders Stores and Borders Online: Tamara L. Heim, age 44, $397,019 pay
President, International: Vincent E. Altruda, age 52
President, Waldenbooks Stores: Ronald S. Staffieri, age 52, $394,519 pay
Chief Marketing Officer: Michael G. Spinozzi, age 42
Associate Director, Children's Merchandising: Diane Mangan
Managing Director, Borders Pacific Rim: John Campradt
Human Resources Director: Patt Micalef
Director, Consumer Commerce and Human Resource Systems: Greg M. Yarrington
Director, Multimedia and Marketing: Kathryn Popoff
Auditors: Ernst & Young LLP

LOCATIONS

HQ: 100 Phoenix Dr., Ann Arbor, MI 48108
Phone: 734-477-1100   **Fax:** 734-477-1965
Web: www.borders.com

Borders Group has stores in Australia, New Zealand, Puerto Rico, Singapore, the UK, and the US.

PRODUCTS/OPERATIONS

2002 Sales

	% of total
Borders	66
Waldenbooks	27
International stores	7
Total	**100**

COMPETITORS

Amazon.com
Barnes & Noble
Best Buy
Blockbuster
Book-of-the-Month Club
Books-A-Million
CDnow
Cody's Books
Columbia House
Follett
Half Price Books
Harry W. Schwartz Bookshops
Hastings Entertainment
HMV
MTS
Musicland
Powell's Books
Tattered Cover Book Store
Toys "R" Us
Trans World Entertainment
Varsity Group
Wal-Mart
Wherehouse Entertainment
WHSmith

HISTORICAL FINANCIALS & EMPLOYEES

NYSE: BGP FYE: Sun. bef. last Wed. in Jan.	Annual Growth	1/93	1/94	1/95	1/96	1/97	1/98	1/99	1/00	1/01	1/02
Sales ($ mil.)	12.4%	1,183	1,370	1,511	1,749	1,959	2,266	2,595	2,999	3,271	3,388
Net income ($ mil.)	16.0%	23	(38)	21	(211)	58	80	92	90	44	87
Income as % of sales	—	1.9%	—	1.4%	—	3.0%	3.5%	3.5%	3.0%	1.3%	2.6%
Earnings per share ($)	—	—	—	—	(2.94)	0.70	0.98	1.12	1.13	0.54	1.06
Stock price - FY high ($)	—	—	—	—	10.94	22.44	33.44	41.75	17.88	17.81	24.43
Stock price - FY low ($)	—	—	—	—	6.94	9.69	18.50	16.31	11.75	10.88	13.70
Stock price - FY close ($)	14.7%	—	—	—	10.56	22.31	32.25	17.13	13.75	14.10	24.10
P/E - high	—	—	—	—	—	29	32	37	16	32	23
P/E - low	—	—	—	—	—	13	17	15	10	19	13
Dividends per share ($)	—	—	—	—	0.00	0.00	0.00	0.00	0.00	0.00	0.00
Book value per share ($)	11.0%	—	—	—	6.27	6.74	7.93	9.20	10.33	10.76	11.70
Employees	11.2%	—	13,650	16,700	20,000	22,800	24,300	27,200	30,000	30,000	32,000

STOCK PRICE HISTORY

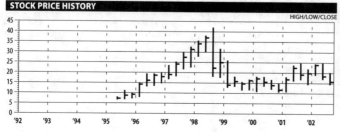

HIGH/LOW/CLOSE

2002 FISCAL YEAR-END

Debt ratio: 5.0%
Return on equity: 9.7%
Cash ($ mil.): 190
Current ratio: 1.30
Long-term debt ($ mil.): 50
No. of shares (mil.): 81
Dividends
  Yield: —
  Payout: —
Market value ($ mil.): 1,957

BORGWARNER INC.

BorgWarner (formerly Borg-Warner Automotive) is happy that millions of American surburbanites are buying four-wheel-drive sport utility vehicles to navigate treacherous cul-de-sacs and mall parking lots. Chicago-based BorgWarner is one of the world's leading makers of four-wheel-drive transfer cases, with more than 40 plants in 14 countries.

In addition to power-train components for cars, light trucks, and RVs, BorgWarner supplies auto parts to every major automaker. Products include automatic transmission components, transfer cases, turbochargers, emission-control systems, clutches, friction plates, and timing-chain systems. Long-term clients Ford (30% of sales), DaimlerChrysler (21%), and General Motors (12%) account for most sales.

As US automakers reduce production to bring inventories in line with reduced demand, companies like BorgWarner are being forced to run leaner as well.

BorgWarner has divested noncore products (fuel systems, HVAC), while stregthening its overseas customer base by forging relationships with the likes of Toyota, Honda, Volkswagen, and Hyundai.

HISTORY

BorgWarner traces its roots to the 1928 merger of major Chicago auto parts companies Borg & Beck (clutches), Warner Gear (transmissions), Mechanics Universal Joint, and Marvel Carburetor. The newly named Borg-Warner Corporation quickly began buying other companies, including Ingersoll Steel & Disc (agricultural blades and discs) and Norge (refrigerators).

The company survived the Depression largely through the contributions of its Norge and Ingersoll units. In the latter 1930s, the company purchased Calumet Steel (1935) and US Pressed Steel (1937), along with several other companies. During the early 1940s Borg-Warner made parts for planes, trucks, and tanks. Between 1942 and 1945 it produced more than 1.6 million automotive transmissions and gained the experience and manufacturing capacity to handle the postwar car boom. Its 1948 contract with Ford to build half of its transmissions resulted in massive growth.

Roy Ingersoll, president of the Ingersoll Steel & Disc division, assumed leadership of Borg-Warner in 1950 and embarked on a major diversification program. Borg-Warner's 1956 purchases included York, Humphreys Manufacturing, Industrial Crane & Hoist, Dittmer Gear, and the Chemical Process Company, among others. James Bert became president in 1968 and continued diversification.

Borg-Warner entered the security business in 1978 by buying Baker Industries (armored transport under the Wells Fargo name). In 1980 Borg-Warner sold its Ingersoll Products division. It acquired Burns International Security Services in 1982 and spun off York to its shareholders in 1986.

In the face of a 1987 takeover attempt, Merrill Lynch Capital Partners organized an LBO and took the company private, assuming $4.5 billion in debt. Borg-Warner then sold everything but its automotive and security units, including its chemical group to General Electric for $2.3 billion (1988) and its credit unit, Chilton, to TRW for $330 million (1989).

The company went public again in 1993 as Borg-Warner Security; it spun off Borg-Warner Automotive to its shareholders. (Borg-Warner Security changed its name to Burns International Services in 1999.) In 1995 Borg-Warner Automotive formed a joint venture in India (Divgi-Warner) to make transmissions and purchased the precision-forged products division of US-based Federal-Mogul.

To expand its air- and fluid-control business, the company acquired Holley Automotive, Coltec Automotive, and Performance Friction Products from component maker Coltec Industries in 1996. The next year it bought a majority stake in Kuhnle, Kopp & Kausch, a Germany-based turbocharger subsidiary of Penske. The same year Borg-Warner Automotive sold its money-losing manual-transmission business to Transmisiones y Equipos Mecanicos of Mexico.

Reduced production of Ford trucks, a weak Asian economy, and a strike at GM hurt 1998 sales. The following year the company bought diesel-engine component maker Kuhlman and then sold Kuhlman's electrical transformer and wire/cable businesses. Borg-Warner Automotive also sold its interests in joint ventures Warner-Ishi and Warner-Ishi Europe to partner Ishikawajima-Harima Heavy Industries.

In 1999 Borg-Warner Automotive bought the Fluid Power Division (automotive cooling systems) of Eaton Corporation for $130 million. The company changed its name to BorgWarner in 2000. Early the next year BorgWarner sold its fuel systems interests to private equity group TMB Industries.

OFFICERS

Chairman and CEO: John F. Fiedler, age 63, $844,401 pay
President, COO, and Director: Timothy M. Manganello, age 52, $399,607 pay
EVP and CFO: George E. Strickler, age 54
EVP; Group President and General Manager, Air/Fluid Systems: Gary P. Fukayama, age 54, $378,990 pay
EVP; Group President and General Manager, Morse TEC and Turbo Systems: Ronald M. Ruzic, age 63, $550,196 pay
EVP; President and General Manager, Transmission Systems: Robert D. Welding, age 53, $554,016 pay
VP, General Counsel, and Secretary: Laurene H. Horiszny, age 46
VP, Human Resources: Kimberly Dickens, age 40
Auditors: Deloitte & Touche LLP

LOCATIONS

HQ: 200 S. Michigan Ave., Chicago, IL 60604
Phone: 312-322-8500   **Fax:** 312-461-0507
Web: www.bwauto.com

Borg-Warner Inc. operates 43 manufacturing facilities in Brazil, Canada, China, France, Germany, Hungary, India, Italy, Japan, Mexico, South Korea, Taiwan, the UK, and the US.

2001 Sales

	$ mil.	% of total
US	1,687	72
Europe		
Germany	348	15
Other countries	162	7
Other regions	155	6
Total	**2,352**	**100**

PRODUCTS/OPERATIONS

2001 Sales

	$ mil.	% of total
Morse TEC	847	36
TorqTransfer systems	499	21
Transmission systems	418	18
Air/fluid systems	350	15
Cooling systems	220	9
Divested operations	18	1
Total	**2,352**	**100**

Selected Products

Air-control valves	Front-wheel and four-wheel-drive chain and timing-chain systems
Chain tensioners and snubbers	
Complete engine induction systems	Four-wheel-drive and all-wheel-drive transfer cases
Complex solenoids and multi-function modules	Friction plates
Crankshaft and camshaft sprockets	Intake manifolds
	On-off fan drives
Electric air pumps	One-way clutches
Engine hydraulic pumps	Torque converter lock-up clutches
Exhaust gas-recirculation valves	Transmission bands
Fan clutches	Single-function solenoids
	Throttle bodies
	Throttle position sensors

COMPETITORS

A. O. Smith	PACCAR	TRW
Dana	Renold	Valeo
Eaton	Siemens	
INTERMET	SPX	

HISTORICAL FINANCIALS & EMPLOYEES

NYSE: BWA FYE: December 31	Annual Growth	12/92	12/93	12/94	12/95	12/96	12/97	12/98	12/99	12/00	12/01
Sales ($ mil.)	10.9%	926	985	1,223	1,329	1,540	1,767	1,837	2,459	2,646	2,352
Net income ($ mil.)	—	(12)	(98)	64	74	42	103	95	132	94	66
Income as % of sales	—	—	—	5.3%	5.6%	2.7%	5.8%	5.2%	5.4%	3.6%	2.8%
Earnings per share ($)	—	—	(4.23)	2.75	3.15	1.75	4.31	4.00	5.07	3.54	2.51
Stock price – FY high ($)	—	—	28.00	34.00	33.88	43.00	61.50	68.38	60.00	45.00	55.19
Stock price – FY low ($)	—	—	20.50	21.63	22.38	28.38	38.38	33.06	36.75	29.75	34.20
Stock price – FY close ($)	8.1%	—	28.00	25.13	32.00	38.50	52.00	55.81	40.50	40.00	52.25
P/E – high	—	—	—	12	11	24	14	17	12	13	22
P/E – low	—	—	—	8	7	16	9	8	7	8	14
Dividends per share ($)	—	—	0.00	0.58	0.60	0.60	0.60	0.60	0.60	0.60	0.60
Book value per share ($)	9.6%	—	20.19	23.13	25.57	26.59	29.46	33.24	39.57	41.45	41.88
Employees	8.8%	—	6,610	7,330	8,600	9,800	10,400	10,100	14,400	14,000	13,000

STOCK PRICE HISTORY

HIGH/LOW/CLOSE

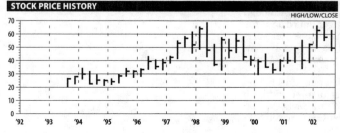

2001 FISCAL YEAR-END

Debt ratio: 38.8%
Return on equity: 6.1%
Cash ($ mil.): 33
Current ratio: 0.97
Long-term debt ($ mil.): 701
No. of shares (mil.): 26
Dividends
  Yield: 1.1%
  Payout: 23.9%
Market value ($ mil.): 1,378

BOSTON CELTICS LIMITED

That lunatic with the shamrock tattooed on his forehead may be more than just an obnoxious Celtics fan — he might own part of the team. A charter member of the Basketball Association of America (which later evolved into the NBA), the Boston Celtics became the first major sports franchise to go public when the partnership that owned the team, Boston Celtics Limited Partnership (BCLP), offered investors a chance to own "units" in the partnership in 1986. BCLP owned all of the team until a 1998 reorganization prompted by changes in the tax code drove it to split into two entities — BCLP, which still owns 48% of the team, and Castle Creek, a private partnership that owns the remaining 52%. The family of BCLP chairman and CEO Paul Gaston controls Castle Creek.

The luck of the Irish hasn't been enough to help the Celtics' fortunes during the past few years. Though the team has a record 16 NBA championships to its credit (including a record eight straight from 1959-66), its last one came in 1986. The Celtics haven't appeared in the NBA playoffs since the 1994-95 season, which also happened to be the team's last in Boston Garden. But the Celtics have rebounded and may find the pot of gold during the 2001-02 season by returning to the postseason. Though it now plays in the 19,600-seat FleetCenter, the team took its famous parquet floor to the new arena.

HISTORY

Walter Brown founded the Boston Celtics basketball team in 1946 and hired Red Auerbach as head coach in 1950. Auerbach turned the Celtics into a competitive organization by acquiring such players as Bob Cousy, Chuck Cooper (the first African-American player in the NBA), Bill Sharman, and Frank Ramsey.

The turning point came in 1956, when Auerbach traded two players to the St. Louis Hawks for Bill Russell. Auerbach crafted a basketball dynasty around Russell's gifted play, winning nine NBA championships from 1957-66 (including a record eight straight). Walter Brown died in 1964, and the team changed hands a number of times over the next two decades. The one constant, however, was Auerbach. Although he quit coaching in 1966, he continued on as the team's general manager. Russell took over Auerbach's coaching duties and, as the first African-American NBA coach, led the team to NBA titles in 1968 and 1969.

During the early 1970s, under coach Tom Heinsohn, the team was restructured and, with the talents of players like John Havlicek, Don Nelson, Jo Jo White, and Dave Cowens, won NBA titles in 1974 and 1976. By the late 1970s, however, it had slipped into last place. The Celtics registered another major turnaround during the 1979-80 season, due largely to the efforts of 1978 draft pick Larry Bird. The Celtics won a 14th title in 1981.

Don Gaston, Paul Dupee, and Alan Cohen bought the team from then-owner Harry Mangurian in 1983 and formed the Boston Celtics Limited Partnership (BCLP). K. C. Jones became head coach that year and led the team to NBA titles in 1984 and 1986. Following its 1986 championship, the Celtics selected University of Maryland forward Len Bias as the second overall draft pick. Bias died two days later from a cocaine overdose.

The three owners also offered "units" in BCLP to investors in 1986. In selling 40% of the team, they made history, becoming the first pro sports franchise to make this type of public offering. Paul Gaston (Don's son) became BCLP chairman in 1993. Future Hall of Famers Larry Bird and Kevin McHale retired before and after the 1992-1993 season, respectively. Tragedy struck again that summer when All Star Reggie Lewis collapsed and died from cardiac arrest.

The Celtics played their final game at historic Boston Garden in 1995, moving to the FleetCenter to start the 1995-96 season. Gaston's stake in the team jumped to more than 44% when he bought out Cohen's and Dupee's stakes in 1995 and 1996, respectively. The Celtics signed University of Kentucky coach Rick Pitino (who led the Wildcats to a national championship in 1995) to a 10-year contract in 1997.

Changes in the tax code prompted a reorganization of BCLP in 1998. BCLP was split into two entities — BCLP, which was left with a 48% stake in the team, and Castle Creek, a private partnership controlled by the family of Paul Gaston, which owned the remainder. An NBA lockout that resulted in the cancellation of nearly three dozen games during the 1998-99 season translated into a loss for BCLP in 1999. After three disappointing seasons, Pitino resigned from the team in early 2001. The Celtics returned to the playoff hunt the next season behind new head coach Jim O'Brien.

Chairman and CEO: Paul E. Gaston, age 44,
$500,000 pay
Vice Chairman and President: Arnold Auerbach
EVP, COO, CFO, Secretary, and Treasurer:
Richard G. Pond, age 41, $660,000 pay
EVP Marketing and Sales: Stuart Layne
General Manager: Chris Wallace
Head Coach: Jim O'Brien, age 50
VP Corporate Relations: Ann Haley
VP Sales: Stephen Riley
Director of Human Resources and Shareholder
Services: Barbara Reed
Director of Marketing: Martin Falkenberg
Director of Sales: Shawn Sullivan
Auditors: Ernst & Young LLP

LOCATIONS

HQ: Boston Celtics Limited Partnership
151 Merrimac St., Boston, MA 02114
Phone: 617-523-6050   **Fax:** 617-523-5949
Web: www.celtics.com

The Boston Celtics play at the FleetCenter in Boston.

PRODUCTS/OPERATIONS

Titles
NBA Champions (1957, 1959-66, 1968-69, 1974, 1976,
1981, 1984, 1986)
Eastern Conference Champions (1957-66, 1968-69,
1974, 1976, 1981, 1984-87)

COMPETITORS

Miami Heat
New Jersey Nets
New York Knicks
Orlando Magic
Philadelphia 76ers
Washington Wizards

HISTORICAL FINANCIALS & EMPLOYEES

NYSE: BOS FYE: June 30	Annual Growth	6/92	6/93	6/94	6/95	6/96	6/97	6/98	6/99	6/00	6/01
Sales ($ mil.)	(49.4%)	46	81	83	52	65	63	76	0	0	0
Net income ($ mil.)	—	8	5	24	16	54	0	12	(10)	(3)	(4)
Income as % of sales	—	16.8%	6.4%	28.7%	30.8%	83.6%	0.6%	16.2%	—	—	—
Earnings per share ($)	—	—	—	—	—	—	—	—	(3.67)	(1.23)	(1.27)
Stock price - FY high ($)	—	—	—	—	—	—	—	—	17.50	12.00	12.11
Stock price - FY low ($)	—	—	—	—	—	—	—	—	7.00	9.13	7.13
Stock price - FY close ($)	(10.8%)	—	—	—	—	—	—	—	11.88	9.81	9.45
P/E - high	—	—	—	—	—	—	—	—	—	—	—
P/E - low	—	—	—	—	—	—	—	—	—	—	—
Dividends per share ($)	—	—	—	—	—	—	—	—	0.00	0.00	0.00
Book value per share ($)	—	—	—	—	—	—	—	—	(15.90)	(17.12)	(18.90)
Employees	1.3%	42	173	125	66	47	43	55	44	47	47

STOCK PRICE HISTORY

HIGH/LOW/CLOSE

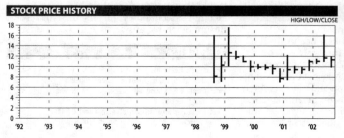

2001 FISCAL YEAR-END

Debt ratio: 100.0%
Return on equity: —
Cash ($ mil.): 3
Current ratio: 20.75
Long-term debt ($ mil.): 44
No. of shares (mil.): 3
Dividends
 Yield: —
 Payout: —
Market value ($ mil.): 26

BOSTON SCIENTIFIC CORPORATION

Boston Scientific hopes it won't need a stent to prop up its own business.

The Natick, Massachusetts-based company makes medical devices for use in minimally invasive surgeries. Boston Scientific's products — steerable catheters, micro-guidewires, and polypectomy snares — are used in a range of medical fields. Cardiovascular products (which focus on the fields of cardiology, radiology, and vascular and neurovascular procedures) account for some 70% of sales. The Endosurgery product line is responsible for the rest, addressing the areas of oncology, vascular surgery, endoscopy, urology, and gynecology. Co-founders John Abele and Peter Nicholas (with their families) together control more than 20% of the company.

In spite of ongoing patent infringement suits (including a particularly ugly one with stent-supplier Medinol), Boston Scientific continues to develop new products and acquire smaller companies. The firm racked up 22 FDA approvals and some half a dozen acquisitions in 2001. It is currently competing in a race with such rivals as Guidant, Johnson & Johnson, and Medtronic to develop a drug-eluting stent — a product that promises to improve the treatment of coronary artery disease.

HISTORY

Many medical companies start near a hospital, but Boston Scientific's roots sprouted at a children's soccer game where two dads found common ground. John Abele and Peter Nicholas had complementary interests: Wharton MBA Nichols wanted to run his own company; philosophy and physics graduate Abele wanted a job that would help people.

In 1979 the two men founded Boston Scientific to buy medical device maker Medi-Tech. Abele and Nichols had to borrow half a million dollars from a bank and raise an additional $300,000. Medi-Tech's primary product was a steerable catheter, a soft-tipped device that could be maneuvered within the body. The catheter revolutionized gallstone operations in the early 1970s, and Boston Scientific expanded on the success of the product. The company adapted it for a slew of new procedures for the heart, lungs, intestines, and other organs.

Boston Scientific's sales were healthy in 1983, but the firm still lacked funds. It eagerly accepted $21 million from Abbott Laboratories in exchange for a 20% stake. New FDA regulations slowed product introduction and put a crimp in the company's growth. Boston Scientific found a legal loophole in the late 1980s to avoid lengthy delays: The company described its products in

the vaguest possible terms so upgraded devices were considered similar enough to predecessors to escape the in-depth scrutiny of the new approval process. Still, Abele and Nicholas had to mortgage their personal properties to stay afloat before this linguistic legerdemain helped to clear government red tape. Boston Scientific returned to profitability in 1991 and went public the next year, buying back Abbott Laboratories' interest in the company as well.

Boston Scientific acquired a bevy of medical device companies in 1995, including SCIMED Life Systems, which specialized in cardiology products; Heart Technology, a maker of systems to treat coronary atherosclerosis; and Meadox Medicals, which made arterial grafts.

The company added EP Technologies and Symbiosis (1996) and Target Therapeutics (1997). Its acquisitions brought operational problems that year, causing inventories to soar while it integrated new operations. Purchases continued in 1998, however, as Boston Scientific bought Pfizer's catheter, stent, and angioplasty equipment business. The Justice Department kicked off an investigation of the Nir-Sox stent, which had been launched and subsequently recalled earlier in the year; the FDA approved a new version of the stent in 2000.

Late in 1998, news came out that Boston Scientific's Japanese subsidiary had inflated sales over several years by as much as $90 million. Restated earnings subsequently revealed a loss, compounding the company's assimilation and recall problems.

Takeover rumors started to fly as well. The 1998 purchase of stent maker Schneider Worldwide fattened Boston Scientific's pipeline and payroll; the company in 1999 cut 14% of workers. That year a federal judge ruled that the company's Bandit PTCA catheter infringed on a Guidant patent. In 2000 the company settled with Guidant and the two companies agreed to license products to each other.

The company began 2001 with a flurry of acquisitions. But its efforts to buy Israel-based Medinol (in which it already had a minority stake) dissolved when Medinol sued the firm, alleging that Boston Scientific had tried to use Medinol's technology for its own purposes. Boston Scientific answered with a countersuit.

OFFICERS

Chairman: Peter M. Nicholas, age 60, $1,191,003 pay
Founder Chairman: John E. Abele, age 64
President, CEO, and Director: James R. Tobin, age 57, $1,373,069 pay
SVP, Finance and Administration and CFO: Lawrence C. Best, age 51, $804,107 pay

SVP and Group President, Cardiovascular:
Paul A. LaViolette, age 44, $790,349 pay
SVP and Group President, Endosurgery:
Stephen F. Moreci, age 50
SVP and Chief Scientific Officer: Arthur L. Rosenthal, age 55
SVP and CTO: Fred A. Colen, age 49
SVP, Secretary, and General Counsel: Paul W. Sandman, age 54, $637,742 pay
SVP, Human Resources: Robert G. MacLean, age 58
VP, Corporate Communications: Paul Donovan, age 46
President, Boston Scientific/Europe: Michael Darnaud
President, Boston Scientific International:
Edward S. Northup
President, EP Technologies: Thomas P. Coen
President, Inter-Continental: Jeffrey H. Goodman
President, Medi-Tech: David N. McClellan
President, Microvasive Endoscopy: Michael P. Phalen
President, Microvasive Urology: John B. Pedersen
President, Target: James R. Feenstra
Auditors: Ernst & Young LLP

LOCATIONS

HQ: 1 Boston Scientific Place, Natick, MA 01760
Phone: 508-650-8000   **Fax:** 508-647-2393
Web: www.bostonscientific.com

Boston Scientific has facilities in France, Ireland, Japan, the Netherlands, Singapore, and the US.

2001 Sales

	% of total
US	58
Japan	21
Europe	14
Other	7
Total	**100**

PRODUCTS/OPERATIONS

2001 Sales

	% of total
Cardiovascular	69
Endosurgery	31
Total	**100**

Selected Subsidiaries
AMS Medinvent S.A. (Switzerland)
Boston Scientific AG (Switzerland)
Boston Scientific Benelux SA (Belgium)
Boston Scientific International B.V. (The Netherlands)
Boston Scientific Japan K.K.
Boston Scientific Korea Co., Ltd.
Boston Scientific Limited (UK)
Boston Scientific Ltd. (Canada)
Boston Scientific Medizintechnik GmbH (Germany)
Boston Scientific Nordic AB (Sweden)
Boston Scientific Pty. Ltd. (Australia)
Boston Scientific, S.A. (France)
Boston Scientific S.p.A. (Italy)
Cardiac Pathways Corporation
Corvita Corporation
EP Technologies, Inc.
SCHNEIDER/NAMIC
SCIMED Life Systems, Inc.
Target Therapeutics, Inc.

COMPETITORS

Arrow International	Cook Group	Maxxim Medical
Ballard Medical	C. R. Bard	Medtronic
Baxter	Datascope	St. Jude Medical
Becton Dickinson	Guidant	Tyco Healthcare
	Johnson & Johnson	United States Surgical

HISTORICAL FINANCIALS & EMPLOYEES

NYSE: BSX FYE: December 31	Annual Growth	12/92	12/93	12/94	12/95	12/96	12/97	12/98	12/99	12/00	12/01
Sales ($ mil.)	26.8%	315	380	449	1,107	1,462	1,872	2,234	2,842	2,664	2,673
Net income ($ mil.)	—	57	70	80	8	167	139	(264)	371	373	(54)
Income as % of sales	—	18.0%	18.3%	17.8%	0.7%	11.4%	7.4%	—	13.1%	14.0%	—
Earnings per share ($)	—	0.29	0.20	0.38	0.03	0.42	0.35	(0.68)	0.90	0.91	(0.13)
Stock price - FY high ($)	—	10.44	11.81	8.94	24.69	30.75	39.22	40.84	47.06	29.19	27.89
Stock price - FY low ($)	—	7.00	4.69	5.94	8.31	18.88	20.50	20.13	17.56	12.19	13.25
Stock price - FY close ($)	9.8%	10.44	6.25	8.69	24.63	30.00	22.94	26.81	21.88	13.69	24.12
P/E - high	—	36	59	24	823	72	96	—	51	32	—
P/E - low	—	24	23	16	277	44	50	—	19	13	—
Dividends per share ($)	—	0.00	0.00	0.00	0.00	0.00	0.00	0.00	0.00	0.00	0.00
Book value per share ($)	16.9%	1.22	1.27	1.75	2.17	2.57	2.54	2.09	4.21	4.84	4.97
Employees	24.2%	2,051	2,051	2,838	8,000	9,580	11,000	14,000	12,615	13,500	14,400

STOCK PRICE HISTORY   HIGH/LOW/CLOSE

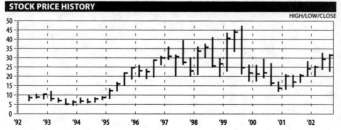

2001 FISCAL YEAR-END
Debt ratio: 32.6%
Return on equity: —
Cash ($ mil.): 180
Current ratio: 1.33
Long-term debt ($ mil.): 973
No. of shares (mil.): 405
Dividends
   Yield: —
   Payout: —
Market value ($ mil.): 9,775

BOWATER INCORPORATED

Extra! Extra! Read all about it! Greenville, South Carolina-based Bowater is the second-largest newsprint producer in North America (behind Canada's Abitibi-Consolidated). The company can churn out more than 3.5 million tons of newsprint (about 60% of sales) annually from its 12 paper mills and 13 sawmills in North America and South Korea. It also produces coated and uncoated groundwood papers, market pulp, lumber, and timber. Company-owned sales offices are located throughout North America and in Brazil, Japan, Singapore, South Korea, and the UK. In addition to the company's 1.5 million acres of owned and leased timber holdings in the US and Canada, Bowater has cutting rights to about 33 million acres in Canada.

With newsprint sales falling, the result of lower newspaper advertising sales, Bowater has moved to broaden its product offerings. Its 2001 acquisition of Canada-based Alliance Forest Products adds higher-margin "fluff pulp" used in consumer and hygiene products. The company converted some US operations to higher grades of paper. It also raised cash by selling more than $130 million worth of timberlands.

HISTORY

The roots of Bowater can be traced to the founders of its British parent, Bowater PLC (renamed Rexam plc in 1995). After several years with a papermaking firm, William Bowater set up his own business in London in 1881. Cashing in on a booming newspaper readership, W. V. Bowater & Sons secured contracts as a paper wholesaler with two leading newspaper publishers: Alfred Harmsworth (of the *Daily Mail* and the *Daily Mirror*) and Edward Lloyd (of the *Daily Chronicle*).

In 1914 Bowater set up a US marketing subsidiary, Hudson Packaging & Paper Co., and in 1919 it opened an office in Sydney, Australia. Eric Bowater, the founder's grandson, took over as chairman at the age of 32 and led the company in a major expansion. By 1936 Bowater accounted for 60% of Britain's newsprint output, up from just 22% only six years before. Bowater began manufacturing in North America in 1938, when it purchased a pulp and newsprint mill in Corner Brook, Newfoundland.

WWII had a devastating impact on the company's UK newsprint business, and output fell by 80%. Bowater PLC diversified into paper packaging in 1944, buying Acme Corrugated Cases. Bowater PLC expanded its presence in the US in 1954 with the opening of Bowater Southern, a newsprint mill in Tennessee. That year Eric

Bowater died. Christopher Chancellor, formerly with Reuters, became CEO.

In 1964 Bowater formed Bowater United States Corp. to manage its US operations. Bowater moved away from paper production in the 1970s, diversifying into such areas as packaging, tissue products, building products, commodity trading, and foodstuffs. In 1984 Bowater exited the paper and pulp business, spinning off its US operations as Bowater Incorporated.

After the spinoff, the new Bowater expanded its range of products. In 1991 the company acquired an 80% interest in Great Northern Paper (GNP); it acquired the remaining 20% in 1992. The next year Bowater started up the GNP recycling facilities, completed the consolidation of its corporate headquarters in Greenville, South Carolina, and sold 70,000 acres of nonstrategic timberlands.

Arnold Nemirow, former CEO of Wausau Paper Mills (Wisconsin), became Bowater's COO in 1994; subsequently, he became CEO and chairman. After three years of losses (largely due to a slump in paper prices), the company turned around in 1995, aided by cost-reduction programs, the sale of timberlands, and higher paper prices. In 1996 Bowater sold its Star Forms subsidiary. The next year Bowater reorganized its US and Canadian forest and wood products operations into a forest products division with plans to spin it off later.

Bowater bought Montreal-based Avenor in 1998 for $2.4 billion, which was 25% more than the hostile takeover bid from rival Abitibi-Consolidated. Although the cost contributed to a loss that year, Bowater became the world's #2 newsprint maker with the acquisition.

A slump in newsprint prices occurred in 1999, and the company sold GNP (exiting the directory paper business) and more than 1.5 million acres of timberlands in Maine and the Carolinas. Also that year Bowater bought a South Korean paper mill.

In 2000 Bowater implemented several price increases as the market for newsprint began to improve. The company bought Canada's Alliance Forest Products in 2001 in a deal worth $770 million. The acquisition added three paper mills and added 10 sawmill facilities. Later Bowater combined its Canadian subsidiaries, Bowater Pulp and Paper Canada and Bowater Canadian Forest Products (formerly Alliance Forest Products), into a new company called Bowater Canadian Forest Products.

OFFICERS

Chairman, President, and CEO: Arnold M. Nemirow, age 57, $1,590,038 pay
EVP and COO: R. Donald Newman, age 55
EVP and CFO: David G. Maffucci, age 51, $606,200 pay
EVP; President, Newsprint Division: Arthur D. Fuller, age 57, $819,721 pay
SVP, Corporate Affairs, General Counsel, and Secretary: Anthony H. Barash, age 58
SVP; President, Coated and Specialty Papers Divisions: E. Patrick Duffy, age 60, $759,902 pay
VP, General Counsel: Harry F. Geair, age 57
VP, Human Resources: James T. Wright, age 55
VP; President, Canadian Forest Products Division: Pierre Monahan, age 55
VP; President, Forest Products Division: Richard K. Hamilton, age 53, $521,763 pay
VP; President, Pulp Division: David J. Steuart, age 55, $571,865 pay
VP, US and Korean Newsprint Operations: Jerry R. Gilmore, age 53
Auditors: KPMG LLP

LOCATIONS

HQ: 55 E. Camperdown Way, Greenville, SC 29602
Phone: 864-271-7733 **Fax:** 864-282-9482
Web: www.bowater.com

Bowater's operations include pulp and paper mills in the US in Michigan, Mississippi, South Carolina, Tennessee, and Washington; in Canada in New Brunswick, Nova Scotia, Ontario, and Quebec; and in South Korea. Bowater also operates sawmills in the US (Alabama) and Canada (Nova Scotia and Quebec). It has newsprint sales offices throughout North America and in Brazil, Japan, Singapore, South Korea, and the UK.

2001 Sales

	$ mil.	% of total
North America	1,961	80
Asia	143	6
Europe	88	3
South America	52	2
Other regions	205	9
Total	**2,449**	**100**

PRODUCTS/OPERATIONS

2001 Sales

	$ mil.	% of total
Newsprint	1,439	59
Coated & specialty papers	479	20
Market pulp	404	16
Lumber & other wood products	127	5
Total	**2,449**	**100**

Selected Products
Bleached kraft pulp
Coated and uncoated groundwood papers
Lumber products (lumber, timber, wood chips)
Newsprints

COMPETITORS

Abitibi-Consolidated
International Paper
Norske Skog
NorskeCanada
Slocan Forest Products
Stora Enso North America
West Fraser Timber
Weyerhaeuser

HISTORICAL FINANCIALS & EMPLOYEES

NYSE: BOW FYE: December 31	Annual Growth	12/92	12/93	12/94	12/95	12/96	12/97	12/98	12/99	12/00	12/01
Sales ($ mil.)	5.6%	1,494	1,354	1,359	2,001	1,718	1,485	1,995	2,135	2,500	2,449
Net income ($ mil.)	—	(82)	(65)	(5)	247	200	54	(19)	79	159	73
Income as % of sales	—	—	—	—	12.3%	11.7%	3.6%	—	3.7%	6.4%	3.0%
Earnings per share ($)	—	(2.34)	(1.84)	(0.59)	5.22	4.55	1.25	(0.44)	1.41	3.02	1.37
Stock price - FY high ($)	—	27.25	24.63	29.63	54.38	41.63	57.00	60.50	60.56	59.56	58.75
Stock price - FY low ($)	—	17.63	18.00	20.38	26.38	31.50	36.88	31.19	36.94	41.88	40.30
Stock price - FY close ($)	7.9%	24.13	23.00	26.63	35.50	37.63	44.44	41.44	54.31	56.38	47.70
P/E - high	—	—	—	—	9	8	45	—	42	20	43
P/E - low	—	—	—	—	4	6	29	—	26	14	29
Dividends per share ($)	(4.4%)	1.20	0.75	0.60	0.60	0.75	0.80	0.80	0.80	0.80	0.80
Book value per share ($)	4.6%	24.59	22.14	26.43	29.28	29.16	28.63	34.22	31.07	35.74	37.01
Employees	3.5%	6,900	6,600	6,000	5,500	5,025	5,000	8,300	6,400	6,400	9,400

STOCK PRICE HISTORY

HIGH/LOW/CLOSE

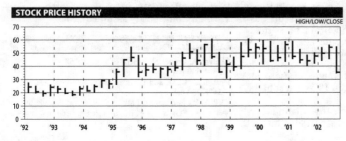

2001 FISCAL YEAR-END

Debt ratio: 47.4%
Return on equity: 3.8%
Cash ($ mil.): 28
Current ratio: 0.80
Long-term debt ($ mil.): 1,828
No. of shares (mil.): 55
Dividends
  Yield: 1.7%
  Payout: 58.4%
Market value ($ mil.): 2,609

BRIGGS & STRATTON CORPORATION

Briggs & Stratton doesn't mind getting yanked around — one good pull can start one of the company's three- to 25-horsepower engines. Briggs & Stratton, based in Wauwatosa, Wisconsin, is the world's #1 maker of air-cooled gasoline engines used in lawn mowers, garden tillers, and other lawn equipment (more than 80% of sales). OEMs AB Electrolux, MTD Products, and Tomkins PLC together account for more than 45% of sales. The company makes its engines in the US, its primary market.

As worldwide emissions standards become more stringent, the company is expanding its product line to serve markets that have been traditionally dominated by two-cycle engine makers. Briggs & Stratton also has acquired generator rival Generac Portable Products.

HISTORY

In 1909 inventor Stephen Foster Briggs and grain merchant Harold Stratton gathered $25,000 and founded Briggs & Stratton to produce a six-cylinder, two-cycle engine that Briggs had developed while in college. However, the engine proved too expensive for mass production. A brief foray into the auto assembly business also failed as the company skirted bankruptcy. But in 1910 Briggs received a patent for a single-spark gas engine igniter. It wasn't a runaway success, but the company had found its niche making automotive electrical components. By 1920 Briggs & Stratton was the largest US producer of specialty lights, ignitions, regulators, and starting switches. These specialties accounted for two-thirds of the firm's total business through the mid 1930s.

The company acquired the A. O. Smith Motor Wheel (a gasoline-driven wheel designed to be attached to bicycles) and the Flyer (a two-passenger vehicle similar to a buckboard) in 1919. Neither product was successful and both were soon sold, but the company gained crucial knowledge and experience. In 1923 Briggs & Stratton introduced a stationary version of the Motor Wheel designed to power washing machines, garden tractors, and lawn mowers. The company continued to diversify, moving into the auto lock business in 1924. Its die-cast cylinder lock outsold competitors' brass models, and by the end of the decade, Briggs & Stratton had the lion's share of the market. The company formed BASCO to make auto body hardware. Briggs & Stratton bought Evinrude Outboard Motor Company in 1928, but sold the business within a year.

As with many other industrial manufacturers, WWII provided a nearly insatiable market for the company. Its wartime contributions included airplane ignition switches, artillery ammunition, and engines for generators, pumps, compressors, fans, repair shops, emergency hospitals, and mobile kitchens.

After the war Briggs & Stratton focused on small engines for lawn and garden equipment, and soon it dominated the market. In 1953 the company introduced an aluminum die-cast engine that was lighter than competing models and could withstand greater operating temperatures and pressures. Baby boomers' parents fueled sales, and the small market attracted little competition; Briggs & Stratton thrived making air-cooled engines and automobile components such as locks and switches.

By the end of the 1970s sales had risen to about $590 million and, as the low-cost producer in the industry, the company was without a rival. During the early 1980s, however, Japanese companies (including Honda, Kawasaki, Mitsubishi, and Suzuki) entered the market after motorcycle sales crested. As a result of the strong dollar, these new competitors were able to provide engines to equipment makers at less expense than could Briggs & Stratton; the company suffered a decline in the late 1980s.

The company experienced a resurgence during the early 1990s. Frederick Stratton Jr., grandson of the co-founder, took over as president in 1992, and Briggs & Stratton benefited from a dollar that was weak relative to the yen. It spun off its car-and-truck lock business as STRATTEC in 1995 and opened three engine plants in Missouri, Alabama, and Georgia in 1996. Over the next few years the company began selling its noncore operations, including foundry businesses in 1997 and 1998 and its long-life engine (for residential heat pumps) and computer software operations, also in 1998.

In 1999 Briggs & Stratton and Eaton Corp. began to jointly develop and market power-generator devices. In mid-2001 CEO Frederick Stratton Jr. stepped down as president (he remains chairman) and COO John Shiely became president and CEO. Also in 2001 Briggs & Stratton acquired rival generator maker Generac Portable Products in a deal worth about $270 million (mostly assumed debt).

OFFICERS

Chairman: Frederick P. Stratton Jr., age 62,
  $604,500 pay
President, CEO, and Director: John S. Shiely, age 49,
  $425,780 pay
EVP, Sales and Service: Michael D. Hamilton, age 59
SVP and CFO: James E. Brenn, age 53, $264,600 pay

SVP, Administration and Secretary: Thomas R. Savage, age 53, $263,400 pay
SVP, Production: Paul M. Neylon, age 54
SVP, Sales and Service: Stephen H. Rugg, age 54
VP and Secretary: Kasandra K. Preston, age 57
VP, Corporate Development: Todd J. Teske, age 36
VP, Distribution Sales and Service: Curtis E. Larson Jr., age 53
VP, Human Resources: Jeffrey Mahlock
VP, Marketing: William H. Reitman, age 45
VP; Director, Briggs & Stratton Europe: Hugo A. Keltz, age 53
Treasurer: Carita R. Twinem, age 46
Auditors: Deloitte & Touche LLP

LOCATIONS

HQ: 12301 W. Wirth St., Wauwatosa, WI 53222
Phone: 414-259-5333   **Fax:** 414-259-5773
Web: www.briggsandstratton.com

Briggs & Stratton has manufacturing facilities in the US in Alabama, Georgia, Kentucky, Missouri, and Wisconsin, and through joint ventures in China, India, and Japan. It conducts sales outside the US through a regional office in Switzerland, a warehouse in the Netherlands, and distributors in Australia, Austria, Canada, Czech Republic, France, Germany, India, Mexico, New Zealand, Russia, South Africa, Sweden, Switzerland, and the UK.

2001 Sales

	$ mil.	% of total
US	1,228	94
Other countries	84	6
Total	**1,312**	**100**

PRODUCTS/OPERATIONS

2001 Sales

	$ mil.	% of total
Engines	1,292	98
Generac Portable Products	30	2
Adjustments	(10)	—
Total	**1,312**	**100**

Selected Applications
Garden tillers
Generators
Lawn mowers (riding and walking)
Pressure washers
Pumps

Selected Brands
Classic
I/C
Industrial Plus
INTEK
Quantum
Quattro
Sprint
Vanguard

COMPETITORS

Coleman
Graco
Honda
Kawasaki Heavy Industries
Suzuki Motor
Tecumseh Products
Toro

HISTORICAL FINANCIALS & EMPLOYEES

NYSE: BGG FYE: Sunday nearest June 30	Annual Growth	6/92	6/93	6/94	6/95	6/96	6/97	6/98	6/99	6/00	6/01
Sales ($ mil.)	2.6%	1,042	1,140	1,286	1,340	1,287	1,316	1,328	1,502	1,591	1,312
Net income ($ mil.)	(0.8%)	52	70	70	105	92	62	71	106	137	48
Income as % of sales	—	4.9%	6.2%	5.4%	7.8%	7.2%	4.7%	5.3%	7.1%	8.6%	3.7%
Earnings per share ($)	2.4%	1.78	2.43	2.40	3.61	3.18	2.15	2.85	4.52	5.97	2.21
Stock price - FY high ($)	—	27.38	34.31	45.13	39.25	46.88	53.63	53.38	71.13	63.63	48.38
Stock price - FY low ($)	—	16.44	21.06	32.44	30.50	32.75	36.50	36.88	33.63	31.00	30.38
Stock price - FY close ($)	7.2%	22.44	33.06	33.44	34.50	41.13	50.00	37.44	57.75	34.25	42.10
P/E - high	—	15	14	13	11	15	25	19	16	11	22
P/E - low	—	9	9	9	8	10	17	13	7	5	14
Dividends per share ($)	5.0%	0.80	0.64	0.90	0.98	1.05	1.09	1.12	1.16	1.19	1.24
Book value per share ($)	6.8%	10.80	12.44	13.96	15.19	17.30	13.82	13.28	15.77	18.83	19.57
Employees	(1.2%)	7,799	7,950	8,628	6,958	7,507	7,661	7,265	7,615	7,233	6,974

STOCK PRICE HISTORY — HIGH/LOW/CLOSE

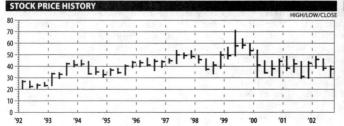

2001 FISCAL YEAR-END
Debt ratio: 54.6%
Return on equity: 11.5%
Cash ($ mil.): 89
Current ratio: 2.53
Long-term debt ($ mil.): 508
No. of shares (mil.): 22
Dividends
 Yield: 2.9%
 Payout: 56.1%
Market value ($ mil.): 909

BRINKER INTERNATIONAL, INC.

Brinker International can't do much for your broken heart, but it can help you get your baby back, baby back (ribs). The Dallas-based restaurateur operates several chains of concept eateries, including the southwestern-themed Chili's Grill & Bar (with its famous Baby Back Ribs), Italian family-style Romano's Macaroni Grill, and casual Mexican diner On The Border Mexican Grill & Cantina. Of its nearly 1,300 units, Brinker's flagship Chili's accounts for more than 800 locations. In addition to its core operations, Brinker is working to build a number of smaller chains, such as its Corner Bakery Cafe (Old World breads and quick foods), Cozymel's Coastal Mexican Grill, and Maggiano's Little Italy.

In the often-fickle world of casual dining, Brinker's Chili's chain has experienced continued popularity, buoyed by an aggressive national marketing campaign. CEO Ronald McDougall has shut down restaurant concepts that weren't working, such as Grady's American Grill and Kona Ranch. (Brinker also sold Wildfire, a 1940s-style steak house.) In their place he developed concepts that didn't face competition from big chains, including Big Bowl Asian cuisine created in partnership with Lettuce Entertain You Enterprises. With Phil Romano, founder of Romano's, Brinker also has developed Eatzi's Market & Bakery, a high-end takeout and grocery business.

HISTORY

Norman Brinker pioneered the so-called "casual-dining" segment in 1966 when he opened his first Steak & Ale in Dallas. In 1971 he took the company public and watched it grow to more than 100 locations by 1976 when Pillsbury (now owned by UK-based Diageo) bought the chain. After serving as president of Pillsbury Restaurant Group (which included Burger King, Poppin' Fresh Restaurants, and Steak & Ale), Brinker left in 1983 to take over Chili's, a chain of southwestern-styled eateries founded by Larry Lavine in 1975. With plans to develop the company into a major chain, Brinker took Chili's public in 1984.

The company began recruiting joint venture and franchise partners. It also expanded the Chili's menu to include items such as fajitas, staking the company's growth on aging baby boomers who were looking for something more than fast food. Stymied in attempts to regain control of his former S&A Restaurant (later bought by Metromedia) and to acquire such fast-food chains as Taco Cabana and Flyer's Island Express, Brinker decided to focus on the casual, low-priced restaurant market. In 1989 Chili's acquired Knoxville,

Tennessee-based Grady's Goodtimes and Romano's Macaroni Grill, a small Italian chain founded by Texas restaurateur Phil Romano in 1988. Reflecting the expansion of its restaurant offerings, the company changed its name to Brinker International in 1990.

Brinker introduced Spageddies (a casual, lower-priced pasta restaurant) in 1992. With two Italian-cuisine chains in his network, the entrepreneur began to take on rival Olive Garden. Brinker suffered a major head injury in 1993 while playing polo, leaving him comatose for two weeks. Despite the traumatic event and poor early prognosis, he made a rapid recovery and returned to running the company. In 1994 Brinker International expanded to cash in on the popularity of Mexican food. It acquired Cozymel's Coastal Mexican Grill that year and bought the $50 million, 21-unit On The Border Mexican-food chain in 1995.

That year Brinker retired as CEO (though he remained chairman) and was replaced by Ronald McDougall. McDougall sold Grady's and Spageddies to Quality Dining, as they no longer fit the company's overall strategy, and acquired two restaurant concepts (Corner Bakery and Maggiano's Little Italy) from Rich Melman's Lettuce Entertain You Enterprises. With Romano in 1996, the company opened a test location (in Dallas) of Eatzi's Market & Bakery, a takeout concept to capitalize on the public's increasing desire not to cook.

The company began a major overhaul of Chili's menu in 1997, led by 34-year-old Brian Kolodziej, a former chef at Dallas' ritzy Mansion on Turtle Creek hotel. In 1998 Brinker announced plans to open as many as 1,500 Corner Bakery shops over a 10-year period. In 1999 Brinker began expanding into Guatemala, Saudi Arabia, and Mexico.

In 2000 the company planned to open up to 140 new restaurants during the next two years, including locations in Puerto Rico and Qatar. The following year it gained complete control of Big Bowl and bought a 40% stake in Rockfish Seafood Grill. With an emphasis on company-owned restaurants, Brinker purchased 47 Chili's and On The Border restaurants from New England Restaurant Co. and 39 Chili's restaurants from Sydran Group in 2001. The company also acquired Sydran's rights to develop locations in all or part of 14 western states.

OFFICERS

Chairman Emeritus: Norman E. Brinker, age 70
Chairman and CEO: Ronald A. McDougall, age 59,
  $2,148,739 pay
President, COO, and Director: Douglas H. Brooks,
  age 49, $1,240,444 pay
**EVP, Chief Administrative Officer, Secretary, and
  General Counsel:** Roger F. Thomson, age 52,
  $650,747 pay
EVP and CFO: Charles M. Sonsteby, age 48
EVP and Chief Strategic Officer, Human Resources:
  Starlette B. Johnson, age 38
SVP IT Concept and Service: Michael B. Webberman
President, Mexican Concepts and On The Border:
  Kenneth D. Dennis, age 48
President, Chili's Grill & Bar Concepts: Todd E. Diener,
  age 44, $679,835 pay
President, Corner Bakery Cafe Concept:
  David Wolfgram, age 43
President, Maggiano's Little Italy Concept:
  Mark F. Tormey
President, Romano's Macaroni Grill: John C. Miller,
  age 46, $651,751 pay
Auditors: KPMG LLP

LOCATIONS

HQ: 6820 LBJ Fwy., Dallas, TX 75240
Phone: 972-980-9917   **Fax:** 972-770-4139
Web: www.brinker.com

Brinker International operates about 1,300 restaurants in
Australia, Austria, Bahrain, Canada, Egypt, Guatemala,
Indonesia, Kuwait, Lebanon, Malaysia, Mexico, Peru, the
Philippines, Saudi Arabia, South Korea, the UK, United
Arab Emirates, the US, and Venezuela.

PRODUCTS/OPERATIONS

Selected Restaurant Concepts
Big Bowl (Asian food)
Chili's Grill & Bar (Southwestern-theme)
Corner Bakery Cafe (retail Old World bakery and quick
  foods)
Cozymel's Coastal Mexican Grill (upscale Mexican
  dining)
Eatzi's Market & Bakery (takeout and catering)
Maggiano's Little Italy (1940s-style Italian diner)
On the Border Mexican Grill & Cantina (casual-style
  Mexican food)
Romano's Macaroni Grill (family-style Italian dining)

COMPETITORS

American Hospitality Concepts	Landry's
American Restaurant Group	Lettuce Entertain You
Applebee's	Lone Star Steakhouse
Avado Brands	Metromedia
Bertucci's	Outback Steakhouse
Carlson Restaurants Worldwide	Panera Bread
Darden Restaurants	Prandium
Denny's	Quality Dining
El Chico Restaurants	RARE Hospitality
	Ruby Tuesday
	Uno Restaurant

HISTORICAL FINANCIALS & EMPLOYEES

NYSE: EAT FYE: Last Wednesday in June	Annual Growth	6/92	6/93	6/94	6/95	6/96	6/97	6/98	6/99	6/00	6/01
Sales ($ mil.)	18.9%	519	653	879	1,042	1,163	1,335	1,574	1,871	2,160	2,474
Net income ($ mil.)	16.9%	36	49	62	73	34	61	69	79	118	145
Income as % of sales	—	6.9%	7.5%	7.0%	7.0%	3.0%	4.5%	4.4%	4.2%	5.5%	5.9%
Earnings per share ($)	17.2%	0.34	0.46	0.55	0.65	0.29	0.54	0.68	0.77	1.17	1.42
Stock price - FY high ($)	—	12.24	16.46	22.47	17.34	12.67	12.67	16.42	20.43	24.01	31.30
Stock price - FY low ($)	—	7.47	9.20	13.34	9.84	7.92	7.09	9.09	10.46	13.26	18.84
Stock price - FY close ($)	11.4%	9.79	15.24	14.01	11.51	10.01	9.50	12.84	18.34	19.76	25.85
P/E - high	—	36	36	38	26	42	23	23	23	20	21
P/E - low	—	22	20	23	15	26	13	13	12	11	13
Dividends per share ($)	—	0.00	0.00	0.00	0.00	0.00	0.00	0.00	0.00	0.00	0.00
Book value per share ($)	14.8%	2.61	3.25	3.92	4.60	5.25	5.35	6.01	6.69	7.72	9.05
Employees	12.1%	28,000	29,000	38,000	37,500	39,900	47,000	53,000	62,300	71,000	78,500

STOCK PRICE HISTORY

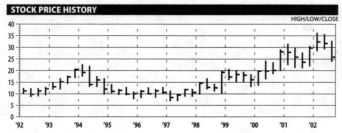

HIGH/LOW/CLOSE

2001 FISCAL YEAR-END

Debt ratio: 20.4%
Return on equity: 17.5%
Cash ($ mil.): 13
Current ratio: 0.57
Long-term debt ($ mil.): 231
No. of shares (mil.): 100
Dividends
  Yield: —
  Payout: —
Market value ($ mil.): 2,572

BRISTOL-MYERS SQUIBB COMPANY

To merge or not to merge — that is the question Bristol-Myers Squibb (BMS) is pondering. With key drugs losing patents and would-be bestsellers on the rocks, the New York City-based company may have to acquire — or be acquired — to survive, and has reportedly brought in Goldman Sachs to help it evaluate options.

Its best-known brands include analgesic Excedrin and nutritional drink Boost, but most of company sales come from prescription pharmaceuticals, particularly anti-cancer, cardiovascular, and anti-infective drugs. Cholesterol-fighting Pravachol (its #1 seller) and diabetes drug Glucophage each account for about 10% of sales. The firm also makes infant formula, nutritional supplements, and wound-cleansing products.

Once among the top five drug firms, BMS has plummeted after several missteps. It had pinned its hopes on hypertension treatment Vanlev (with projected sales of more than $2 billion), but prospects for FDA approval are dim. Meanwhile, the drugmaker bought DuPont's pharmaceutical business, spending $7.8 billion to gain such products as Sustiva, a drug that is part of a "cocktail" AIDS therapy. The company is laying off some 40% of the DuPont unit's workforce and another 2% of its own employees to cut costs.

Another move to boost its pipeline brought problems. It bought a 20% stake in ImClone in hopes of staying on top of the cancer drug market. Instead, BMS finds itself embroiled in the controversy over insider information and stock deals surrounding the biotech.

While the druggernaut frets over its future, its present product line continues to lose clout. Its Glucophage, Taxol, and BuSpar have lost patent protection in the US, and the company's efforts to extend Taxol and BuSpar's patents have increased scrutiny of certain industry tactics used to keep generics off the market. In addition to its product woes, BMS also faces questions from the SEC regarding the possibility that it artificially inflated revenues by offering incentives to wholesalers.

HISTORY

Bristol-Myers Squibb is the product of a merger of rivals.

Squibb was founded by Dr. Edward Squibb in New York City in 1858. He developed techniques for making pure ether and chloroform; he turned the business over to his sons in 1891.

Sales of $414,000 in 1904 grew to $13 million by 1928. The company supplied penicillin and morphine during WWII. In 1952 it was bought by Mathieson Chemical, which in turn was bought by Olin Industries in 1953, forming Olin Mathieson Chemical. Squibb maintained its separate identity.

From 1968 to 1971 Olin Mathieson went through repeated reorganizations and adopted the Squibb name. Capoten and Corgard, two major cardiovascular drugs, were introduced in the late 1970s. Capoten was the first drug engineered to attack a specific disease-causing mechanism. Squibb formed a joint venture with Denmark's Novo (now Novo Nordisk) in 1982 to sell insulin.

William Bristol and John Myers founded Clinton Pharmaceutical in Clinton, New York, in 1887 (renamed Bristol-Myers in 1900) to sell bulk pharmaceuticals. The firm made antibiotics after the 1943 purchase of Cheplin Biological Labs. It began expanding overseas in the 1950s and eventually bought Clairol (1959); Mead Johnson (drugs, infant and nutritional formula; 1967); and Zimmer (orthopedic implants, 1972). Bristol-Myers launched new drugs to treat cancer (Platinol, 1978) and anxiety (BuSpar, 1986).

The firm bought Squibb in 1989. In 1990 the new company bought arthroscopy products and implant business lines and joined Eastman Kodak and Elf Aquitaine to develop new heart drugs in 1993. Despite these initiatives, earnings slipped. In 1994 company veteran Charles Heimbold became CEO and moved to increase profits. In 1995 BMS, along with fellow silicone breast-implant makers 3M and Baxter International, agreed to settle thousands of personal-injury claims at an average of $26,000 per claim.

Facing an antitrust suit filed by independent drugstores, BMS and other major drugmakers agreed in 1996 to charge pharmacies the same prices as managed care groups for medications.

In 1999 the firm pulled its backing for EntreMed after the biotech had problems duplicating results for a cancer drug candidate. It sold its Sea Breeze skin care brand (1999); Matrix Essentials hair care products unit (2000); and Clairol hair and personal care products business (2001). In 2001 it tried to extend BuSpar's protection by filing a secondary patent just as Mylan Labs and Watson Pharmaceuticals were ready to ship their generic versions. Consumer groups and nearly 30 US states sued, alleging BMS illegally blocked generic BuSpar. In early 2002, a judge agreed, opening the floodgates for other lawsuits (BMS faces a similar suit over Taxol).

That year the company joined forces with six fellow pharmas to introduce Together Rx, a drug discount program for low-income senior citizens; critics allege that such programs are merely designed to avoid government price controls.

OFFICERS

Chairman, President, and CEO: Peter R. Dolan, age 46, $2,348,255 pay
EVP and General Counsel: John L. McGoldrick, age 61, $1,233,626 pay
EVP; President, North American Medicines: Donald J. Hayden Jr., age 46, $1,275,949 pay
SVP and CFO: Andrew R. J. Bonfield, age 39
SVP, Corporate and Environmental Affairs: John L. Skule, age 58
SVP, Corporate Development: Tamar D. Howson, age 53
SVP, Corporate Development: George P. Kooluris, age 57
SVP, Human Resources: Stephen E. Bear, age 50
Chief Marketing Officer; President, Global Marketing: Wendy L. Dixon, age 46
Chief Scientific Officer; President, Bristol-Myers Squibb Pharmaceutical Research Institute: Peter S. Ringrose, age 56, $1,122,749 pay
President, Europe: Lamberto Andreotti
Auditors: PricewaterhouseCoopers LLP

LOCATIONS

HQ: 345 Park Ave., New York, NY 10154
Phone: 212-546-4000   **Fax:** 212-546-4020
Web: www.bms.com

2001 Sales

	$ mil.	% of total
Western Hemisphere		
US	13,154	68
Other countries	1,290	7
Europe, Mid-East, & Africa	3,613	18
Pacific	1,366	7
Total	**19,423**	**100**

PRODUCTS/OPERATIONS

2001 Sales

	$ mil.	% of total
Pravachol	2,173	11
Glucophage	2,049	11
Oncology Drugs		
Taxol	1,197	6
Other products	1,433	7
Plavix	1,350	7
Infant formulas	1,255	7
Paraplatin	702	4
Zerit	546	3
Avapro	510	3
Monopril	458	2
Ostomy products	450	2
Serzone	409	2
Cefzil	363	2
BuSpar	338	2
Glucovance	330	2
Tequin	320	2
Glucophage XR	303	1
Capoten/Capozide	285	1
Videx	259	1
Other	4,693	24
Total	**19,423**	**100**

COMPETITORS

Abbott Labs	Dial	Pfizer
Amgen	Eli Lilly	Pharmacia
AstraZeneca	Gillette	Procter &
Aventis	GlaxoSmithKline	Gamble
Bayer AG	Johnson &	Roche
Biomet	Johnson	Schering-Plough
Boehringer	Merck	Solvay
Ingelheim	Novartis	Wyeth

HISTORICAL FINANCIALS & EMPLOYEES

NYSE: BMY FYE: December 31	Annual Growth	12/92	12/93	12/94	12/95	12/96	12/97	12/98	12/99	12/00	12/01
Sales ($ mil.)	6.4%	11,156	11,413	11,984	13,767	15,065	16,701	18,284	20,222	18,216	19,423
Net income ($ mil.)	11.5%	1,962	1,959	1,842	1,812	2,850	3,205	3,141	4,167	4,711	5,245
Income as % of sales	—	17.6%	17.2%	15.4%	13.2%	18.9%	19.2%	17.2%	20.6%	25.9%	27.0%
Earnings per share ($)	12.0%	0.96	0.95	0.91	0.89	1.40	1.57	1.55	2.06	2.36	2.67
Stock price - FY high ($)	—	22.53	16.81	15.25	21.78	29.09	49.09	67.63	79.25	74.88	73.50
Stock price - FY low ($)	—	15.00	12.72	12.50	14.44	19.50	26.63	44.16	57.25	42.44	48.50
Stock price - FY close ($)	13.1%	16.84	14.56	14.47	21.47	27.25	47.31	66.91	64.19	73.94	51.00
P/E - high	—	29	18	17	24	20	30	37	38	31	27
P/E - low	—	19	13	14	16	14	17	24	27	18	18
Dividends per share ($)	2.1%	0.69	0.72	0.73	0.74	0.75	0.76	0.78	0.86	0.98	0.83
Book value per share ($)	7.4%	2.91	2.90	2.81	2.88	3.28	3.63	3.81	4.36	4.70	5.54
Employees	(1.5%)	52,600	49,500	47,700	49,140	51,200	53,600	54,700	54,500	44,000	46,000

STOCK PRICE HISTORY

HIGH/LOW/CLOSE

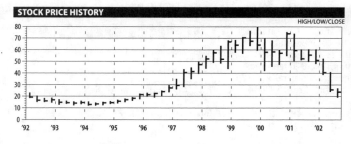

2001 FISCAL YEAR-END

Debt ratio: 36.7%
Return on equity: 52.7%
Cash ($ mil.): 5,500
Current ratio: 1.40
Long-term debt ($ mil.): 6,237
No. of shares (mil.): 1,937
Dividends
 Yield: 1.6%
 Payout: 31.1%
Market value ($ mil.): 98,770

BROADWING INC.

Ohio wasn't big enough for the former Cincinnati Bell. Now Broadwing, the company has spread its wings nationwide by buying fiber-optic network operator IXC Communications (now Broadwing Communications). Though still serving Cincinnati with local phone service, Broadwing hopes to soar with the rise of the Internet as it provides broadband access and long-haul data transport.

The Internet-fueled broadband segment (based on the IXC network) has become the company's focus. Corporations, telecommunications carriers, and ISPs gain access to the network; Broadwing then shuttles traffic across its 18,500-mile, all-optical switched Internet protocol (IP)-based fiber network. The company is consolidating its 11 Web hosting facilities into three main operating locations: Austin, Texas; Cincinnati; and Newark, Delaware.

Broadwing's Cincinnati Bell unit operates in the greater Cincinnati area, providing local phone service (more than 1 million access lines) in parts of Ohio, Kentucky, and Indiana. It also provides dial-up and DSL Internet access and Web hosting. In addition, the company resells long-distance and provides mobile phone service.

HISTORY

Broadwing got its start in the 1870s after Charles Kilgour, injured and homebound, set up a telegraph wire to communicate with his office. Cincinnati manufacturer Andrew Erkenbrecher and other businessmen liked the idea, and the City and Suburban Telegraph Association was incorporated in 1873. For $300 a year, a customer could have a line (up to a mile long), and by 1877 the firm operated 50 lines.

In 1878 the company started selling the telephone under license from Bell Telephone of Boston. The exclusive agent for the Cincinnati area, it added "and Telephonic Exchange" to the end of its name. The next year it published its first phone directory, listing 500 customers. The company began to offer long-distance service through National Bell (which became AT&T) in 1882.

Floods in the 1880s damaged the firm's unwieldy network of overhead wires, and in 1891 it started combining wires into underground cables. In 1903 the company adopted the name Cincinnati and Suburban Bell Telephone.

The firm fell under state regulation in 1911 and soon bought Kentucky's Citizens Telephone, Indiana's Harrison Telephone, and several independent phone companies in Ohio. From 1930 to 1952 it converted its switchboards to dial service.

In 1971 the company became Cincinnati Bell and formed Cincinnati Bell Information Systems (CBIS) in 1983 to develop software. Largely deregulated after the 1984 Bell breakup, the company diversified and spent the late 1980s making acquisitions, including Auxton Computer and Vanguard Technologies. In 1989 Cincinnati Bell formed telemarketing subsidiary MATRIXX.

Technology and telemarketing acquisitions continued into the 1990s. But bad investments hurt profits, and the firm cut 550 jobs in 1991 and sold its equipment-leasing business to AT&T the next year. MATRIXX nearly doubled in size in 1993 with the purchase of telemarketer WATS Marketing. Two years later CBIS bought billing software developers for wireless phones (Europe) and cable TV (US).

Cincinnati Bell began offering Internet access in 1997 and the next year launched its digital mobile phone service in and around Cincinnati through a joint venture with AT&T.

In 1998 CBIS, now a major outsourcing firm for client-data and billing systems, acquired AT&T's Solutions Customer Care segment and became AT&T's preferred supplier of outsourced services. The status irked CBIS clients such as Sprint PCS, an AT&T rival. Cincinnati Bell resolved concerns by spinning off CBIS and MATRIXX into the independent Convergys. It also formed network integration and consulting unit EnterpriseWise IT Consulting.

CEO John LaMacchia retired in 1999 and was succeeded by COO Richard Ellenberger. In a dramatic move, the company that year bought Austin, Texas-based fiber-optic network operator IXC Communications in a $3.2 billion stock-and-debt deal, and Cincinnati Bell changed its name to Broadwing.

Data transport and Internet access (on the network gained from IXC) quickly became the company's top priority. To continue the transformation, Broadwing in 2000 became one of the first to deploy all-optical networking equipment from Corvis on part of its network, which was completed the next year.

Amid the telecom downturn in 2001, Broadwing consolidated its Web hosting centers and closed some sales offices. It also cut about 15% of its workforce. The next year Broadwing sold its Cincinnati Bell Directory Business unit.

OFFICERS

Chairman, President, and CEO: Richard G. Ellenberger, age 49, $1,477,885 pay
COO: Kevin W. Mooney, age 43, $640,385 pay
CFO: Thomas L. Schilling
SVP Corporate Development: Michael W. Callaghan, age 54, $237,728 pay
SVP Internal Controls: Mary E. McCann, age 39

VP Corporate Communications and Chief of Staff:
Thomas G. Osha
VP and Treasurer: Mark W. Peterson
VP and Controller: James H. Reynolds
VP Internal Audit: Robert C. Coogan
VP Investor Relations: Matthew W. Booher
President and COO, Cincinnati Bell: John F. Cassidy,
age 47, $653,077 pay
**President, Broadband Services, Broadwing
Communications:** Mark F. Canha
President, Broadwing Technology Solutions:
Jeffrey A. Lackey
**President, Business Enterprises, Broadwing
Communications:** Jack J. Chidester
**President, Business Markets, Broadwing
Communications:** Richard D. Calder Jr.
**President, National Accounts, Broadwing
Communications:** Richard E. Putt
President, Voice Services: Robert D. Shingler
**Chief Human Resource Officer, Secretary, and General
Counsel:** Jeffrey C. Smith, age 51
CIO: David A. Torline, age 52
CTO, Broadwing and Broadwing Communications:
Michael R. Jones
Auditors: PricewaterhouseCoopers LLP

LOCATIONS

HQ: 201 E. 4th St., Cincinnati, OH 45202
Phone: 513-397-9900 **Fax:** 513-784-1613
Web: www.broadwinginc.com

Broadwing Inc. provides local phone service in the
Cincinnati metropolitan area, which includes a dozen
counties in Indiana, Kentucky, and Ohio. It resells long-
distance service in Indiana, Kentucky, Michigan,
Pennsylvania, and Ohio. The company also operates a
fiber-optic network that extends throughout the US.

PRODUCTS/OPERATIONS

2001 Sales

	$ mil.	% of total
Broadband	1,190	49
Local communications	833	34
Wireless	248	10
Other communications	166	7
Adjustments	(86)	—
Total	**2,351**	**100**

Selected Subsidiaries and Affiliates
AppliedTheory Corporation (23%, ISP)
Broadwing Communications Inc. (formerly IXC
Communications, broadband voice and data services)
Cincinnati Bell Any Distance (long-distance reseller)
Cincinnati Bell Public Communications Inc.
Cincinnati Bell Telephone Company (local phone
services)
Cincinnati Bell Wireless Company (80%, PCS joint
venture with AT&T)

COMPETITORS

Aerie Networks	SBC Communications
AT&T	Sprint
ATX Communications	Teligent
Excel Communications	Time Warner Telecom
Global Crossing	Verizon
Level 3 Communications	Williams Communications
McLeodUSA	Group
Qwest	WorldCom

HISTORICAL FINANCIALS & EMPLOYEES

NYSE: BRW FYE: December 31	Annual Growth	12/92	12/93	12/94	12/95	12/96	12/97	12/98	12/99	12/00	12/01
Sales ($ mil.)	8.4%	1,136	1,090	1,228	1,336	1,574	1,757	885	1,131	2,050	2,351
Net income ($ mil.)	—	35	(57)	73	(32)	185	(16)	150	31	(377)	(286)
Income as % of sales	—	3.1%	—	5.9%	—	11.8%	—	16.9%	2.8%	—	—
Earnings per share ($)	—	0.27	(0.44)	0.56	(0.25)	1.35	0.10	1.08	0.20	(1.82)	(1.36)
Stock price - FY high ($)	—	10.44	12.19	10.06	17.63	30.81	33.75	38.63	37.88	41.06	28.88
Stock price - FY low ($)	—	7.69	8.06	7.69	8.44	15.88	23.06	20.88	16.06	19.06	7.50
Stock price - FY close ($)	1.2%	8.56	9.00	8.50	17.38	30.81	31.00	37.81	36.88	22.81	9.50
P/E - high	—	34	—	17	—	22	24	35	152	—	—
P/E - low	—	25	—	13	—	12	16	19	64	—	—
Dividends per share ($)	—	0.40	0.40	0.40	0.40	0.40	0.40	0.40	0.40	0.30	0.00
Book value per share ($)	4.7%	5.08	3.97	4.19	3.61	4.69	4.25	1.04	11.76	9.38	7.70
Employees	(7.8%)	11,200	14,700	15,600	15,000	19,700	20,800	3,500	6,000	6,400	5,400

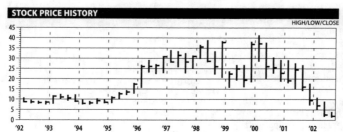

STOCK PRICE HISTORY HIGH/LOW/CLOSE

2001 FISCAL YEAR-END
Debt ratio: 61.7%
Return on equity: —
Cash ($ mil.): 30
Current ratio: 0.51
Long-term debt ($ mil.): 2,702
No. of shares (mil.): 218
Dividends
  Yield: —
  Payout: —
Market value ($ mil.): 2,072

BROWN SHOE COMPANY, INC.

There's no business like shoe business for Brown Shoe Company (formerly Brown Group). A footwear retailer and wholesaler, the St. Louis-based company sells shoes for men, women, and children. Brown Shoe operates three retail chains: Famous Footwear, one of the nation's largest family shoe chains, with more than 900 stores in the US (it accounts for more than half of the company's sales); more than 440 Naturalizer stores in the US and Canada; and 16 F.X. LaSalle stores in malls around Montreal, Canada.

The company's online shops include Shoes.com (purchased in 2000), FamousFootwear.com, and Naturalizer.com. Through its Brown Shoe Wholesale Division, the company sells shoes to 2,200 department stores, mass merchandisers, and independent retailers, primarily in the US and Canada. In addition to its own brands (Buster Brown, Connie, Naturalizer), Brown Shoe sells private-label products and licensed brands such as Barbie, Dr. Scholl's, Hello Kitty, *Star Wars, Bob the Builder*, and Sammy Sosa. More than three-fourths of the company's products are made in China.

Brown Shoe is expanding its Famous Footwear and Naturalizer chains and introducing new styles, including a line designed by rock 'n' roll musician Carlos Santana, to appeal to younger customers. It is opening new larger format stores, but also closing underperforming ones.

HISTORY

Salesman George Brown began mass-producing women's shoes in St. Louis in 1878, unusual at a time when the shoe industry was firmly entrenched in New England. With the financial backing of partners Alvin Bryan and Jerome Desnoyers, Brown hired five shoemakers and opened Bryan, Brown and Company. The firm's fashionable first shoes were a pleasant contrast to the staid, black shoes typical of New England and were an instant success. The enterprise grew rapidly, and in 1893 Brown, by then the sole remaining partner, renamed the operation Brown Shoe Company. By 1900 sales had reached $4 million.

Company executive John Bush introduced cartoonist Richard Outcault's Buster Brown comic strip character in 1902 at the St. Louis World's Fair as a trademark for Brown's children's shoes. Bush failed to purchase the exclusive rights, and Buster Brown became the trademark for scores of products, even cigars and whiskey.

Brown Shoe became a public company in 1913 and introduced its second brand, Naturalizer, in 1927. During the Great Depression, company VP Clark Gamble developed the concept, later commonplace, of having salesmen sell only specific branded shoe lines instead of traveling with samples of all the company's shoes. Brown Shoe modernized its operations and entered the retailing business during the 1950s by purchasing Wohl Shoe, Regal Shoe, and G. R. Kinney (sold in 1963 to Woolworth because of antitrust litigation). The first Naturalizer store opened in Jamaica, New York in 1954.

Diversifying, Brown Shoe bought Cloth World stores (1970), Eagle Rubber (toys and sporting goods, 1971), Hedstrom (bicycles and equipment, 1971), Meis Brothers (department stores, 1972), and Outdoor Sports Industries (1979), among others. It became the Brown Group in 1972.

The company acquired the 32-store Famous Footwear chain in 1981 and expanded it rapidly (especially from 1990 to 1995, when it added more than 500 stores, reaching a total of about 815). In 1985 the company sold its recreational products segment and in 1989 shed all of its specialty retailers except Cloth World.

As the US shoe manufacturing industry fell prey to cheaper foreign imports, Brown Group in 1991 and 1992 closed nine US shoe factories, cutting capacity in half. It discontinued its Wohl Leased Shoe Department business in 1994 and, still facing declining sales and profits, closed five shoe factories and discontinued its Connie and Regal footwear chains. Brown Group also sold its Cloth World chain and discontinued its Maryland Square catalog business.

Brown Group continued its restructuring in 1995, closing its last five plants in the US (it still has two in Canada). Also that year it bought the upscale Larry Stuart Collection and the le coq sportif athletic shoe business. Charges tied to overstocking in its overseas division led to a loss for fiscal 1998.

In 2000 the company opened 92 new Famous Footware stores and added another 26 stores to that chain through its purchase of the Mil-Mar chain and bought a majority interest in e-tailer Shoes.com. The company opened another 100 mostly large-format Famous Footware stores in 2001 and closed 100 smaller stores.

OFFICERS

Chairman, President, and CEO: Ronald A. Fromm, age 51, $775,000 pay
COO; President, Brown Shoe International Division: David H. Schwartz, $495,000 pay (prior to promotion)
CFO and Treasurer: Andrew M. Rosen, $364,115 pay
SVP, Human Resources: Doug Koch
VP and Chief Accounting Officer: Richard C. Schumacher

VP, Legal Department and General Counsel:
Michael I. Oberlander
President, Brown Shoe Wholesale: Gary M. Rich,
$777,069 pay
President, Famous Footwear: Joseph W. Wood
President, Naturalizer: Byron D. Norfleet
Auditors: Ernst & Young LLP

LOCATIONS

HQ: 8300 Maryland Ave., St. Louis, MO 63105
Phone: 314-854-4000 **Fax:** 314-854-4274
Web: www.brownshoecompany.com

Brown Shoe Company has about 1,400 retail stores in
the US and Canada. It also sells shoes wholesale to about
2,200 retailers in Canada and the US.

2002 Country of Origin

	Pairs (mil.)	% of total
China	52	78
Brazil	11	16
Indonesia	3	4
Italy	1	1
Other countries	1	1
Total	**68**	**100**

PRODUCTS/OPERATIONS

2002 Sales

	% of total
Women's	59
Men's	27
Children's	14
Total	**100**

Selected Products

Children's Shoes
Airborne
Barbie (licensed)
Basswood
Bob the Builder (licensed)
Buster Brown
Chill Chasers by Buster
  Brown
Hello Kitty (licensed)
Live Wires
Mary-Kate and Ashley
  (licensed)
Pokémon (licensed)
Sammy Sosa (licensed)
Spider-Man (licensed)
Spy Kids (licensed)
Star Wars (licensed)
Tige
X-Men (licensed)

Men's Shoes
Basswood
Big Country

Brown Shoe
Dr. Scholl's (licensed)
F.X. LaSalle
Francois Xavier Collection
Nature Sole

Women's Shoes
AirStep
Basswood
Bootalinos
Carlos by Carlos Santana
  (licensed)
Connie
Dr. Scholl's (licensed)
Eurosole
Eurostep
F.X. LaSalle
Francois Xavier Collection
Hot Kiss (licensed)
LifeStride
Naturalizer
NaturalSport

COMPETITORS

Berkshire
  Hathaway
Candie's
Dillard's
Federated
Florsheim
Footstar
Genesco
J. C. Penney
Kenneth Cole

Kmart
Maxwell Shoe
May
Nine West
Nordstrom
Payless
  ShoeSource
Phillips-Van
  Heusen
Reebok

Ross Stores
Saks Inc.
Sears
Shoe Carnival
Stride Rite
Target
TJX
Wal-Mart

HISTORICAL FINANCIALS & EMPLOYEES

NYSE: BWS FYE: Saturday nearest Jan. 31	Annual Growth	1/93	1/94	1/95	1/96	1/97	1/98	1/99	1/00	1/01	1/02
Sales ($ mil.)	(0.2%)	1,791	1,598	1,462	1,456	1,525	1,567	1,539	1,593	1,685	1,756
Net income ($ mil.)	—	5	(32)	39	3	20	(21)	24	36	36	(4)
Income as % of sales	—	0.3%	—	2.7%	0.2%	1.3%	—	1.5%	2.2%	2.2%	—
Earnings per share ($)	—	0.27	(1.83)	2.23	0.19	1.15	(1.19)	1.32	1.96	2.04	(0.23)
Stock price - FY high ($)	—	29.88	36.00	38.88	33.38	23.38	20.13	20.00	21.75	18.25	20.50
Stock price - FY low ($)	—	21.00	28.75	29.75	12.50	11.88	12.44	12.50	10.38	8.44	10.25
Stock price - FY close ($)	(6.5%)	29.25	35.13	31.88	13.75	16.50	14.50	16.06	10.38	16.36	15.94
P/E - high	—	111	—	17	176	20	—	15	11	9	—
P/E - low	—	78	—	13	66	10	—	9	5	4	—
Dividends per share ($)	(14.3%)	1.60	1.60	1.60	1.30	0.75	0.85	0.40	0.40	0.40	0.40
Book value per share ($)	(1.4%)	16.69	13.27	13.90	12.92	13.19	11.04	11.96	13.68	15.46	14.68
Employees	(7.4%)	23,000	22,000	14,500	11,000	11,500	11,500	11,000	11,500	11,900	11,500

STOCK PRICE HISTORY

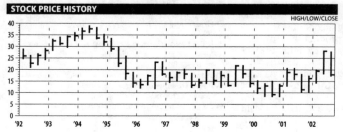

HIGH/LOW/CLOSE

2002 FISCAL YEAR-END

Debt ratio: 32.5%
Return on equity: —
Cash ($ mil.): 23
Current ratio: 1.75
Long-term debt ($ mil.): 124
No. of shares (mil.): 17
Dividends
  Yield: 2.5%
  Payout: —
Market value ($ mil.): 279

BROWN-FORMAN CORPORATION

Straight-up or mixed, whiskey or wine — Brown-Forman's got a drink for you, and a glass to serve it in. The Louisville, Kentucky-based company is best known for producing some of the top-selling wines and spirits in their respective categories, including Jack Daniel's (whiskey), Canadian Mist (Canadian whiskey), Korbel (premium champagne), and Bolla (premium wine). Other drinks include Southern Comfort liqueurs, Old Forester (bourbon), Early Times (whiskey), and Pepe Lopez tequila. The company also licenses its beverage brand names; makes Hartmann luggage and leather goods; and makes tableware, crystal, silver, and collectibles under the Lenox, Dansk, and Gorham names (it is the #1 US maker of fine china). It operates 115 retail stores under the Lenox, Dansk, and Hartmann names.

Brown-Forman has found global success by introducing Jack Daniels into new markets overseas (it has become the leading US whiskey sold worldwide). Its Wines International unit markets Fetzer and 25 other brands in about 75 countries.

Descendants of the co-founding Brown family, including CEO Owsley Brown II, control Brown-Forman.

HISTORY

George Brown and John Forman opened the Brown-Forman Distillery in Louisville, Kentucky, in 1870 to produce Old Forester-brand bourbon. Old Forester sold well through the end of the century, in part because of the company's innovative packaging (safety seals and quality guarantees on the bottles). When Forman died in 1901, Brown bought his interest in the company.

Old Forester continued to be successful under the Brown family. Brown-Forman obtained government approval to produce alcohol for medicinal purposes during Prohibition. In 1923 it made its first acquisition, Early Times, but stored its whiskey in a government warehouse (removed only by permit). The firm went public in 1933 and reestablished the Old Forester image as an alcoholic beverage after the repeal of Prohibition.

During WWII the government greatly curtailed alcoholic beverage production (alcohol was needed for the war effort). The company compensated by providing alcohol for wartime rubber and gunpowder production. In 1941 Brown-Forman correctly predicted that the war would be over by the end of 1945 and started the four-year aging process for its bourbon. As a result, Early Times dominated the whiskey market after the war.

In 1956 Brown-Forman expanded beyond Old Forester by purchasing Jack Daniel's (sour mash whiskey), based in Lynchburg, Tennessee. The company retained the simple, black Jack Daniel's label and promoted the image of a small Tennessee distillery for the brand.

Brown-Forman continued to expand its alcohol line during the 1960s and 1970s, acquiring Korbel (champagne and brandy, 1965), Quality Importers (Ambassador Scotch, Ambassador Gin, and Old Bushmills Irish Whisky; 1967), Bolla and Cella (wines, 1968), and Canadian Mist (blended whiskey, 1971). In 1979 it purchased Southern Comfort (a top-selling liqueur).

Non-beverage acquisitions included Lenox (a leading US maker of fine china, crystal, gifts, and Hartmann luggage; 1983), Kirk Stieff (silver and pewter, 1990), and Dansk International Designs (china, crystal, silver, and the high-quality Gorham line; 1991). Brown-Forman launched Gentleman Jack Rare Tennessee Whiskey in 1988, its first new whiskey from its Jack Daniels distillery in more than 100 years.

The company acquired Jekel Vineyards in 1991 and the next year bought Fetzer Vineyards. In 1993 Owsley Brown II succeeded his brother Lee as CEO. A year later Moore County, Tennessee, voters approved a referendum that allowed whiskey sales in Lynchburg (home of Jack Daniel's) for the first time since Prohibition. Also in 1995 Brown-Forman formed a joint venture with Jagatjit Industries, India's third-largest spirits producer.

A 1997 licensing agreement with Carlson, whose T.G.I. Friday's restaurants came out with a line of Jack Daniel's meat dishes, stealthily slipped the brand into national television advertising. Brown-Forman bought an 80% stake in Sonoma-Cutrer Vineyards in 1999 (and later bought the rest).

In 2000 Brown-Forman bought 45% of Finlandia Vodka Worldwide for $83 million; Altia (owned by the Finnish government) owns 55%. In December 2000 the company (along with its partner Bacardi Limited) lost the bidding battle for the alcoholic drinks business of Seagram (Glenlivet, Sterling Vineyards, Martell Cognac) to rival pair Diageo and Pernod Ricard.

OFFICERS

Chairman and CEO: Owsley Brown II, age 59, $867,973 pay

President and Director; President and CEO, Brown-Forman Beverages Worldwide: William M. Street, age 63, $830,120 pay

EVP and CFO: Phoebe A. Wood, age 48, $586,064 pay

SVP and Director of Corporate Development and Strategy: Donald C. Berg, age 46

SVP Corporate Communications and Corporate Services: Lois A. Mateus, age 54

SVP, Executive Director of Human Resources:
James S. Welch Jr., age 42, $386,932 pay
SVP, General Counsel, and Secretary:
Michael B. Crutcher, age 57, $488,599 pay
President, Brown-Forman Distillery Company:
James D. Hanauer
President, Core Markets Group: J. Andrew Smith
President, Global Spirits Group; EVP, Brown-Forman Beverages Worldwide: Michael V. Cheek
President, Lenox: Stanley E. Krangel, $412,500 pay
President, North American Group: James L. Bareuther
Auditors: PricewaterhouseCoopers LLP

LOCATIONS

HQ: 850 Dixie Hwy., Louisville, KY 40210
Phone: 502-585-1100 **Fax:** 502-774-7876
Web: www.brown-forman.com

2002 Sales

	$ mil.	% of total
US	1,817	82
Other countries	391	18
Total	**2,208**	**100**

PRODUCTS/OPERATIONS

2002 Sales

	$ mil.	% of total
Wine & spirits	1,620	73
Consumer durables	588	27
Total	**2,208**	**100**

Selected Brands

Wines
Bel Arbor
Bolla
Fetzer Vineyards
Korbel champagnes and wines
Michel Picard (marketed in US)
Noilly Prat Vermouths (marketed in US)
Sonoma-Cutrer Vineyards

Spirits
Early Times (whiskey)
Glenmorangie (scotch, marketed in US)
Jack Daniel's (whiskey)
Pepe Lopez (tequila)
Southern Comfort (liqueur)
Usher's (scotch, marketed in US)

Consumer Durables
Dansk (crystal, dinnerware, glassware, flatware, giftware)
Gorham (crystal, flatware, giftware, silver)
Hartmann (luggage, leather goods)
Lenox (china, collectibles, crystal, dinnerware, giftware)

COMPETITORS

Allied Domecq	Gucci	Oneida
Anheuser-Busch	Heaven Hill	Robert Mondavi
ARC	Distilleries	Roll
International	Jim Beam	International
Bacardi USA	Brands	Samsonite
Beringer Blass	Jose Cuervo	Skyy
Constellation	Joseph	Taittinger
Brands	E. Seagram &	V&S
Diageo	Sons	Villeroy & Boch
Gallo	Kendall-Jackson	Waterford
Fortune Brands	Libbey	Wedgwood
Future Brands	LVMH	

HISTORICAL FINANCIALS & EMPLOYEES

NYSE: BFA FYE: April 30	Annual Growth	4/93	4/94	4/95	4/96	4/97	4/98	4/99	4/00	4/01	4/02
Sales ($ mil.)	5.1%	1,415	1,665	1,680	1,807	1,841	1,924	2,030	2,134	2,180	2,208
Net income ($ mil.)	4.3%	156	129	149	160	169	185	202	218	233	228
Income as % of sales	—	11.0%	7.7%	8.8%	8.9%	9.2%	9.6%	10.0%	10.2%	10.7%	10.3%
Earnings per share ($)	6.6%	1.88	1.63	2.15	2.31	2.45	2.67	2.93	3.18	3.40	3.33
Stock price - FY high ($)	—	29.47	30.47	33.88	42.50	51.88	59.00	77.25	75.50	72.00	79.14
Stock price - FY low ($)	—	24.23	24.31	26.13	31.50	35.25	45.00	54.94	41.88	50.00	58.88
Stock price - FY close ($)	12.7%	26.89	29.89	33.00	39.50	50.50	56.63	73.69	54.56	60.80	78.62
P/E - high	—	16	15	16	18	21	22	26	24	21	24
P/E - low	—	13	12	12	14	14	17	19	13	15	18
Dividends per share ($)	5.2%	0.86	0.93	0.97	1.02	1.06	1.10	1.15	1.21	1.28	1.36
Book value per share ($)	7.6%	9.89	6.72	7.91	9.19	10.58	11.89	13.39	15.30	17.34	19.18
Employees	0.5%	6,700	7,100	7,300	7,400	7,500	7,600	7,600	7,400	7,400	7,000

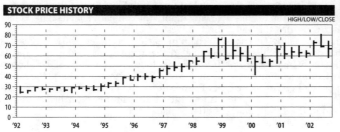

STOCK PRICE HISTORY HIGH/LOW/CLOSE

2002 FISCAL YEAR-END
Debt ratio: 3.0%
Return on equity: 18.3%
Cash ($ mil.): 116
Current ratio: 2.08
Long-term debt ($ mil.): 40
No. of shares (mil.): 68
Dividends
 Yield: 1.7%
 Payout: 40.8%
Market value ($ mil.): 5,374

BRUNSWICK CORPORATION

Brunswick takes the business of leisure quite seriously. The Lake Forest, Illinois-based company once scored most of its sales from making billiards and bowling equipment. Today about 80% of its sales come from making marine equipment, including outboard motors (Mercury, Mariner) and boats designed for sport fishing (Trophy), pleasure (Bayliner), performance (Baja), and yachting (Sea Ray). Brunswick also makes fitness equipment (Life Fitness, ParaBody, and Hammer Strength). The company has unloaded a boatload of outdoor businesses, including its Roadmaster and Mongoose bicycles unit, its Hoppe's gun accessories business, and its camping and fishing goods (Zebco reels and rods).

A longtime kingpin of bowling and billiards equipment, Brunswick has shifted its focus to marine engines and boats. The leisure sector has been hit by slowing sales, however, leading Brunswick to reduce its powerboat workforce. Even so, the company has acquired Princecraft Boats from bankrupt rival Outboard Marine, as well as Hatteras Yachts from Genmar Industries.

HISTORY

Swiss immigrant woodworker John Brunswick built his first billiard table in 1845 in Cincinnati. In 1874 he formed a partnership with Julius Balke, and a decade later they teamed up with H. W. Collender to form Brunswick-Balke-Collender Company.

Following Brunswick's death, son-in-law Moses Bensinger became president. The company diversified into bowling equipment during the 1880s. Bensinger's son, B. E., followed as president (1904) and led the company into wood and rubber products, phonographs, and records. (Al Jolson recorded "Sonny Boy" on the Brunswick label.) Brunswick went public after WWI.

By 1930 Brunswick focused on bowling and billiards, sports that had seedy reputations during the 1920s and 1930s. When B. E. died in 1935, his son Bob became CEO and launched a massive promotional campaign to make his meal tickets respectable.

Bob's brother Ted succeeded him as CEO in 1954. Bowling equipment rival AMF introduced the first automatic pinsetter in 1952, and Brunswick followed four years later, capturing the lead by 1958. Brunswick diversified, adding Owens Yacht, MacGregor (sporting goods, 1958), Aloe (medical supplies, 1959), Mercury (marine products, 1961), and Zebco (fishing equipment, 1961). The company adopted its present name in 1960.

Bowling sales plummeted in the 1960s, and Brunswick cut costs by selling unprofitable units and focusing on new products such as an automatic scorer. Acquisitions in the 1970s brought Brunswick into the medical diagnostics and energy and transportation markets. CEO Jack Reichert, a former pin boy who became chairman in 1983, cut corporate staff in half and promoted the marine business.

Brunswick sparked an industrywide consolidation trend in 1986 by buying Bayliner and Ray Industries (boats), followed by Kiekhaefer Aeromarine (marine propulsion engines, 1990) and Martin Reel Company (fly reels, 1991). In 1992 Brunswick bought the Browning line of rods and reels.

In 1993 Brunswick began selling its businesses in the automotive, electronics, and defense industries. Two years later the company's Brunswick Indoor Recreation division opened family entertainment centers in Brazil, China, Japan, South Korea, and Thailand.

Brunswick expanded its outdoor recreation business in 1996 by purchasing Nelson/Weather Rite (camping equipment) from Roadmaster Industries (later named the RDM Sports Group) along with Roadmaster's bicycle business. Also that year Brunswick acquired the Boston Whaler line of saltwater boats from Meridian Sports. In 1997 the company bought Igloo Holdings (coolers), Bell Sports' Mongoose bicycle unit, Mancuso's Life Fitness (exercise equipment) unit, Hammer Strength (fitness equipment), and DBA products (bowling-lane machines and equipment) The company lost antitrust lawsuits in 1999 that totaled nearly $300 million. However, all but two cases ($65 million) were overturned on appeal.

In early 2001 Brunswick cut some jobs and rolled its bicycle business over to Pacific Cycle. Stung by the US's economic slowdown, the company announced 500 more job cuts in its powerboat division, even as it acquired Princecraft Boats from Outboard Marine. Also in 2001 Brunswick sold Hoppe's (to Michaels of Oregon) and Zebco (to W.C. Bradley) and acquired UK-based luxury boat maker Sealine International. In October the company agreed to buy Hatteras Yachts, a luxury boat maker, from Genmar Holdings for about $80 million. The following month the company sold its Igloo cooler unit to Westar Capital.

Then in early December 2001 Brunswick completed the acquisition of Hatteras Yachts from Genmar Industries for about $80 million in cash. Early in 2002 Brunswick closed the sale of its European fishing business to Zebco Sports Europe Ltd., a company newly formed by the operation's management.

Chairman and CEO: George W. Buckley, age 55,
$1,290,786 pay
**Vice Chairman; President, Brunswick Bowling &
Billiards:** Peter B. Hamilton, age 55, $616,800 pay
SVP and CFO: Victoria J. Reich, age 44, $457,015 pay
VP; President, Brunswick Boat Group:
Dustan E. McCoy, age 52, $512,770 pay
VP; President, Life Fitness Division: Kevin S. Grodzki,
age 46
VP; President, Mercury Marine Group:
Patrick C. Mackey, age 55, $541,322 pay
VP; President, Sea Ray: Cynthia M. Trudell, age 48
VP; President, US Marine Division:
William J. Barrington, age 51, $522,951 pay
VP and Chief Human Resources Officer:
B. Russell Lockridge, age 52
VP, General Counsel, and Secretary: Marschall I. Smith,
age 56
Auditors: Ernst & Young LLP

LOCATIONS

HQ: 1 N. Field Ct., Lake Forest, IL 60045
Phone: 847-735-4700   **Fax:** 847-735-4765
Web: www.brunswickcorp.com

2001 Sales

	$ mil.	% of total
US	2,512	75
Other countries	859	25
Total	**3,371**	**100**

PRODUCTS/OPERATIONS

2001 Sales

	$ mil.	% of total
Marine engines	1,562	44
Boats	1,251	35
Recreation	766	21
Adjustments	(208)	—
Total	**3,371**	**100**

Selected Brands and Products

Marine Engines	Sea Ray
Marine Power	Sealine
Mercury Marine	Trophy
MotoTron	
	Recreation Centers
Boats	Brunswick Zones
Baja	
Bayliner	**Sporting Goods**
Boston Whaler	Billiards
Brunswick	Brunswick
Hatteras Yachts	Bowling
Maxum	Brunswick
Princecraft	

COMPETITORS

AMF Bowling	Giant Manufacturing
Bowl America	Honda
Dave & Buster's	Soloflex
Fountain Powerboat	Yamaha
Genmar Holdings	

HISTORICAL FINANCIALS & EMPLOYEES

NYSE: BC FYE: December 31	Annual Growth	12/92	12/93	12/94	12/95	12/96	12/97	12/98	12/99	12/00	12/01
Sales ($ mil.)	5.6%	2,059	2,207	2,700	3,041	3,160	3,657	3,945	4,284	3,812	3,371
Net income ($ mil.)	—	(26)	23	129	127	186	151	186	38	(96)	82
Income as % of sales	—	—	1.0%	4.8%	4.2%	5.9%	4.1%	4.7%	0.9%	—	2.4%
Earnings per share ($)	—	(0.28)	0.24	1.35	1.32	1.88	1.50	1.88	0.41	(1.08)	0.93
Stock price - FY high ($)	—	17.75	18.50	25.38	24.00	25.88	37.00	35.69	30.00	22.13	25.01
Stock price - FY low ($)	—	12.13	12.50	17.00	16.25	17.25	23.13	12.00	18.06	14.75	14.03
Stock price - FY close ($)	3.3%	16.25	18.00	18.88	24.00	24.00	30.31	24.75	22.25	16.44	21.76
P/E - high	—	—	32	19	17	14	24	15	73	—	26
P/E - low	—	—	22	13	12	9	15	5	44	—	15
Dividends per share ($)	1.4%	0.44	0.44	0.44	0.50	0.50	0.50	0.50	0.50	0.50	0.50
Book value per share ($)	4.3%	8.65	8.44	9.54	10.65	12.16	13.22	14.27	14.16	12.22	12.65
Employees	2.2%	17,000	18,000	20,800	20,900	22,800	25,300	25,500	26,600	23,200	20,700

STOCK PRICE HISTORY

HIGH/LOW/CLOSE

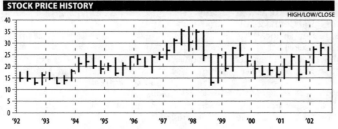

2001 FISCAL YEAR-END

Debt ratio: 35.1%
Return on equity: 7.5%
Cash ($ mil.): 109
Current ratio: 1.55
Long-term debt ($ mil.): 600
No. of shares (mil.): 88
Dividends
  Yield: 2.3%
  Payout: 53.8%
Market value ($ mil.): 1,911

BUDGET GROUP, INC.

Budget Group has gone from franchise player to franchise owner — and then some. The Daytona Beach, Florida-based company used to be Team Rental Group, the largest franchisee of Budget Rent a Car Corporation (BRACC). The renamed company owns BRACC, one of the world's largest car rental firms. It also is the US's #2 renter of moving trucks (behind AMERCO's U-Haul), including Budget trucks as well as yellow Ryder trucks. Worldwide, Budget Group oversees a system of about 6,500 car and truck rental locations, most of them operated by franchisees.

To stem losses caused in part by stiff industry competition, the company has consolidated operations and sold off noncore businesses. All of its domestic rental operations have been consolidated into one organization, North American Vehicle Operations. It has exited the car sales business and has sold its Cruise America RV business and its VPSI vanpool business. To strengthen its brand name, the company will replace its white Budget trucks and yellow Ryder TRS trucks with a fleet of blue trucks.

Chairman and CEO Sandy Miller controls 20% of Budget Group's voting stock; directors Jeffrey Congdon and John Kennedy each control about 10%. Budget Group, which filed for bankruptcy protection, is selling its operations in Australia, Canada, Latin America, New Zealand, and the US to Cendant while searching for a buyer of its other units.

HISTORY

Car-rental industry veteran Sandy Miller had logged miles on his odometer with the Avis, Budget, and Dollar systems by 1987. That year he joined Jeffrey Congdon and John Kennedy in forming Team Rental Group to operate the Budget Rent a Car Corporation (BRACC) franchise in San Diego. In 1991 Team Rental began methodically expanding its BRACC franchise operations with acquisitions in New York and Virginia.

Three years later the company bought franchises in Pennsylvania and Ohio, went public, and began selling used rental cars. Next came acquisitions of franchises in California and Arizona (more than 90 locations combined), as well as in Indiana, North Carolina, and Connecticut.

By 1996 Team Rental's 160 or so locations made it BRACC's largest franchisee. That year it bought Chrysler's Van Pool Services (van rentals for commuter groups), further increasing its vehicle purchasing power.

Amid an industrywide shift in the ownership of major car rental firms, BRACC became available, and in 1997 Team Rental acquired the franchisor — a much larger company — for $350 million.

Morris Mirkin had begun Budget Rent a Car in Los Angeles in 1958 with 10 cars. Distant relative Jules Lederer began leasing cars to Mirkin the next year and in 1960 formed Budget Rent a Car Corp. of America. Lederer's firm grew through franchising and focusing on the leisure travel market. In 1968 Transamerica bought Lederer's company. (Mirkin's company continued to operate in California and Nevada.)

In 1986 BRACC management and LBO firm Gibbons, Green, van Amerongen bought the company for $205 million. It went public in 1987, only to be taken private again two years later in a buyout worth $333 million, with $300 million plunked down by Ford Motor and the rest by BRACC management and Gibbons' general partner.

BRACC began opening corporate-owned units in Europe in 1989 and purchased Diversified Services, its biggest franchisee, in 1990. That buyout gave BRACC direct access to Florida and Los Angeles, the two largest US car rental markets. BRACC lost $125 million in 1995 but broke even the next year after a round of cost-cutting under new management.

Ford owned rental car leader Hertz by 1996 and decided to buy all of BRACC as well. When that deal ran into antitrust concerns the next year, Team Rental bought BRACC and changed its own name to Budget Group. Budget Group agreed to buy about 80,000 vehicles per year from Ford for 10 years. Also in 1997 Budget Group bought Premier Car Rental (insurance replacement rentals).

The company in 1998 acquired Cruise America (RV rentals) and Ryder TRS (consumer rentals of familiar yellow moving trucks). To get more of its cars on the road, in 1999 BRACC launched a Web site allowing customers to bid on cars — an industry first. In 2000 the company sold off finance operations as well as two new-car dealerships, fostering its efforts to exit the car sales business. Budget also sold its Cruise America unit to an investment group led by Cruise America management for $28 million. The company sold its van pooling company (VPSI) to an investment group led by Rockwood Capital.

Several charges related to fleet reduction and refranchising of company-owned locations in Europe accounted for part of the company's huge losses in fiscal 2000. The next year, amid a weak car rental market (reeling further after the terrorist attacks of September 11, 2001), Budget reduced its fleet size by 12,000 cars and cut 12% of its employees.

Budget was delisted from NYSE in March 2002 for failing to meet minimum share prices and began trading in the OTC market. The next month, following the lead of Hertz and Avis, Budget eliminated travel agents' commissions for rentals with corporate or government price plans in North America. The company filed for bankruptcy protection in July 2002. It announced a month later that it was selling its Australian, Canadian, Latin American, New Zealand, and US operations to Cendant.

OFFICERS

Chairman and CEO: Sanford Miller, age 49, $643,502 pay
President, COO, and Director: Mark R. Sotir, age 38, $500,000 pay
EVP and CFO: William S. Johnson, age 44, $371,900 pay
EVP, General Counsel, and Secretary: Robert L. Aprati, age 57
SVP, Human Resources: Vicki R. Pyne
VP and CTO: Tyler Best
VP and Controller: Thomas L. Kram
VP, Shared Services: David Coonfield
Auditors: KPMG LLP

LOCATIONS

HQ: 125 Basin St., Ste. 210, Daytona Beach, FL 32114
Phone: 386-238-7035   **Fax:** 386-238-7461
Web: www.drivebudget.com

Budget Group and its franchisees have operations in more than 120 countries and territories.

PRODUCTS/OPERATIONS

Major Business Units

Car Rental
Budget Rent a Car (car and truck rental system)

Truck Rental
Budget Truck Rental (truck rental system)
Ryder TRS (truck rental system)

COMPETITORS

AMERCO
ANC Rental
AutoNation
Avis Europe
Cendant
Dollar Thrifty Automotive Group
Electricité de France
Enterprise Rent-A-Car
Hertz
Penske
Rent-A-Wreck
Sixt

HISTORICAL FINANCIALS & EMPLOYEES

OTC: BDGPA FYE: December 31	Annual Growth	12/92	12/93	12/94	12/95	12/96	12/97	12/98	12/99	12/00	12/01
Sales ($ mil.)	77.1%	—	22	39	150	357	1,304	2,616	2,350	2,436	2,161
Net income ($ mil.)	—	—	0	0	0	5	37	(49)	(65)	(605)	(139)
Income as % of sales	—	—	1.8%	1.0%	0.2%	1.3%	2.8%	—	—	—	—
Employees	55.2%	—	—	525	1,709	2,000	12,000	14,500	16,400	12,400	11,400

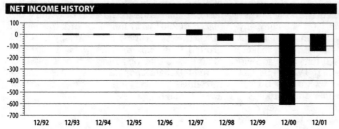

NET INCOME HISTORY

2001 FISCAL YEAR-END
Debt ratio: 98.3%
Return on equity: —
Cash ($ mil.): 43
Current ratio: —
Long-term debt ($ mil.): 3,485

BURGER KING CORPORATION

Burger King is not the burger king, but it's close. The Miami-based company is the world's #2 hamburger chain, ahead of Wendy's but trailing McDonald's. A whopping 1.7 billion Whoppers, Burger King's flame-broiled signature hamburger, are sold each year at its more than 11,400 restaurants worldwide (nearly 75% are in the US). The company's other offerings include the BK Broiler (grilled chicken sandwich), the Croissan'wich, and more pronounceable fast-food fare. Burger King is a subsidiary of British food and spirits giant Diageo, which put the struggling fast-food chain up for sale in 2002. An investor group led by Texas Pacific Group agreed to buy the company that year for about $2.2 billion. Burger King accounts for less than 10% of Diageo's sales.

The company has been looking outside the US for growth in its goal of surpassing McDonald's. However, Europe isn't embracing an encroaching Americanism, and its golden-arched rival may have exhausted Europeans' tastes for fast food. Burger King has pulled out of Poland, as well as Japan, where McDonald's used its market dominance to drive down prices. The threat of mad cow disease in Germany and the UK hasn't helped. One bright spot has been Ireland, where Burger King has 22 locations (and plans to have 50 by 2005; McDonald's has 62 restaurants there). In fiscal 2001 the company added 221 stores overall, compared to 635 the previous year.

Burger King hopes that an increased interest in drive-thru units in Holland, the UK, and other locations will drive sales. It has also upgraded the kitchens at its US locations and added 14 new items to its menu, copy-catting McDonald's successful New Tastes Menu. In 2002 the company introduced the BK Back Porch Griller burger to its permanent menu, expected to be its largest initiative for several years, to bolster its image as the company heads to the auction block. If these measures don't work, new CEO John Dasburg (from Northwest Airlines) may end up right back on the street: Burger King has gone through seven CEOs since 1989.

HISTORY

In 1954 restaurant veterans James McLamore and David Edgerton founded the first Burger King in Miami. Three years later the company added the Whopper sandwich, which then sold for 37 cents, to its menu of hamburgers, shakes, and sodas. Burger King used television to help advertise the Whopper (its first TV commercial appeared in 1958). During its infancy Burger King was the first chain to offer dining rooms.

Looking to expand nationwide, Burger King turned to franchising in 1959. McLamore and Edgerton took a hands-off approach, allowing franchises to buy large territories and operate with autonomy. Although their technique spurred growth, it also created large service inconsistencies among Burger Kings across the US; this bugaboo would haunt the company for years. Having grown to 274 stores in the US and abroad, Burger King was sold to Pillsbury in 1967.

During the early 1970s Burger King continued to add locations. The company did well during this time, launching its successful "Have It Your Way" campaign in 1974 and introducing drive-through service a year later. Yet parent Pillsbury had to fight to rein in large franchisees who argued they could run their Burger Kings better than a packaged-goods company. In 1977 Pillsbury handed control of Burger King to Donald Smith, a McDonald's veteran, who soon silenced the insurrection. Smith tightened franchising regulations, created 10 regional management offices, and instituted annual visits.

Smith left for Pizza Hut in 1980, and by 1982 Burger King had reached the #2 fast-food plateau, trailing McDonald's. The company struggled through the rest of the 1980s, though, hurt by high management turnover and a string of unsuccessful ad campaigns. (Remember "Herb the Nerd"?) Pillsbury became the target of a hostile takeover by UK-based Grand Metropolitan, and in 1988 Grand Met acquired Pillsbury along with its 5,500 Burger King restaurants.

Grand Met bolstered Burger King's foreign operations in 1990 by converting about 200 recently acquired UK-based Wimpey hamburger stores into Burger Kings. International expansion increased, with new restaurants in Mexico (1991), Saudi Arabia (1993), and Paraguay (1995).

In 1997 Grand Met and Guinness combined their operations to form Diageo, making Burger King a subsidiary. That year Dennis Malamatinas left GrandMet's Asian beverage division to become Burger King's CEO. In 1999 the company joined rival TRICON (now called Yum! Brands) in shucking out $150 million to help food distributor AmeriServe stay afloat following AmeriServe's filing for bankruptcy.

Late in 2000 Diageo announced plans to spin off Burger King, but the latter's slow sales delayed action. Malamatinas resigned as CEO and was replaced in 2001 with John Dasburg, former CEO of Northwest Airlines. The company also broke ground that year on its new headquarters in Miami. Late that year Burger King took its cue from McDonald's popular New Tastes Menu and introduced 14 new items to its menu, including a vegetarian burger.

OFFICERS

Chairman, President, and CEO: John H. Dasburg, age 59
EVP and CFO: Bennett Nussbaum
EVP and General Counsel: Richard B. Hirst, age 56
EVP Human Resources: Stephen Cerrone
EVP, Chief Marketing Officer, and President, Burger King Brands: Christopher E. Clouser, age 49
SVP and Chief Development Officer, North America: Paul Novak, age 56
SVP Marketing Programs and Sales: Fredrick Dow
SVP Operations Services and Programs: Jim Hyatt
SVP US Company Operations: Enrique Silva
SVP Worldwide Diversity Resources: Vince Berkeley
VP Business Services: Lisa Vivero
VP Corporate Counsel: Elsie Romero
VP Corporate Communications: Rob Doughty
VP Field Marketing and Sales Manager: Rick N. Brown
VP Global Advertising and Promotions: Craig Braasch
VP Product Marketing: Dana Frydman
VP Strategic Operations Research and Development: John Reckert
VP Supply Chain Management and Quality Assurance: Bruce Burnham
CIO: Rafael Sanchez
Chief Safety Officer: Chet England

LOCATIONS

HQ: 17777 Old Cutler Rd., Miami, FL 33157
Phone: 305-378-7011 **Fax:** 305-378-7262
Web: www.burgerking.com

Burger King has restaurants in all 50 US states and 58 other countries.

**2001 Locations
(includes franchises)**

	No.	% of total
US	8,307	73
Foreign	3,066	27
Total	**11,373**	**100**

PRODUCTS/OPERATIONS

2001 Restaurants

	No.	% of total
Franchised	10,384	91
Company-owned	989	9
Total	**11,373**	**100**

Selected Products
Biscuits
BK Big Fish
BK Broiler
Broiled chicken salad
Cheeseburger
Chicken sandwich
Chicken tenders
Croissan'wich
Double cheeseburger
Double Whopper
Dutch apple pie
French fries
French toast sticks
Hamburger
Hash browns
Onion rings
Salads
Shakes
Soft drinks
Whopper
Whopper, Jr.

COMPETITORS

AFC Enterprises	Long John Silver's
Checkers Drive-In	McDonald's
Chick-fil-A	Pret A Manger
CKE Restaurants	Shoney's
Davco Restaurants	Sonic
Denny's	Taco Cabana
Subway	Wendy's
Domino's Pizza	Whataburger
Dairy Queen	White Castle
Jack in the Box	Yum!
Little Caesar	

HISTORICAL FINANCIALS & EMPLOYEES

Subsidiary FYE: June 30	Annual Growth	6/92	6/93	6/94	6/95	6/96	6/97	6/98	6/99	6/00	6/01
Sales ($ mil.)	1.9%	—	—	—	—	1,342	1,396	1,449	1,379	1,427	1,474
Employees	0.5%	—	—	—	—	—	29,590	27,149	26,000	28,432	30,166

SALES HISTORY

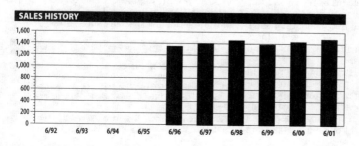

BURLINGTON COAT FACTORY

Cold spells mean hot sales for Burlington Coat Factory Warehouse. The Burlington, New Jersey-based company sells off-price, brand-name men's, women's, and children's clothing and outerwear at its 300-plus stores in more than 40 states. Many of its stores also carry children's apparel and furniture, gifts, housewares, jewelry, linens, and shoes.

The firm, one of the largest coat sellers in the US, is best known for its year-round selection of about 10,000 to 20,000 discounted coats (compared to about 1,500 to 2,000 coats at the typical department store). Burlington Coat Factory also runs stores under the names Baby Depot (infant and toddler clothes and furniture), Cohoes Fashions (upscale apparel and accessories), Decelle (off-priced family apparel), Luxury Linens (bed and bath items), MGM Shoes (designer and fashion shoes), and Totally 4 Kids (children's clothing, books, toys). Some stores, such as Baby Depot and Luxury Linens, are also found as departments within its stores.

Burlington Coat Factory takes less of a markup than its department store competition and has lower profit margins than other clothing retailers, but chairman, president, and CEO Monroe Milstein has kept the company competitive by running a tight ship. It buys the coats early in the season (up to five months before department store rivals) to lock in lower prices. Burlington Coat Factory prefers to lease existing buildings and refurbish rather than build new stores, keeping overhead low. Unlike other off-price retailers, it buys directly from manufacturers and does not rely on leftovers or closeouts.

The Milstein clan owns about 60% of Burlington Coat Factory. Monroe's sons Andrew and Stephen are company executives.

HISTORY

Russian-Jewish immigrant Abe Milstein and a partner started coat wholesaler and manufacturer Milstein and Feigelson in 1924. Abe's son, Monroe, was a quick study. He graduated from New York University with a business degree in 1946 at age 19 and started his own coat and suit wholesaling business called Monroe G. Milstein, Inc. His mother provided free labor at her son's company six days a week to keep the business alive. Abe ended his partnership in 1953 and joined his son's business.

Family relations were strained temporarily in 1972, when Monroe disregarded his father's advice not to buy a faltering coat factory outlet store in Burlington, New Jersey. (Abe believed that his son did not have enough retailing experience.) Monroe, however, thought owning a retail store

would provide a guaranteed sales outlet for their merchandise, and he bought Burlington Coat Factory for $675,000 (using $60,000 of his wife Henrietta's savings). His company also adopted the Burlington Coat Factory Warehouse moniker as its own.

To become less dependent on the season-specific coat business, the company soon expanded its merchandise mix by adding a children's division (started by Henrietta, deceased in 2001) and subleased departments. It opened a second store in Long Island, New York, in 1975.

Settling a trademark dispute with fabric maker Burlington Industries in 1981, Burlington Coat Factory agreed to say in advertising — as it does to this day — that the two companies are not affiliated. The 31-store company went public two years later, using the money it raised to open almost 30 stores that year. As part of its expansion in the 1980s, Burlington Coat Factory opened stores in warmer climates such as Texas and Florida.

The firm tried to grow through acquisitions that decade but failed in its attempts to buy a number of department store retailers. It made a successful bid in 1989 for New York discount retailer Cohoes.

Burlington Coat Factory's bought Boston-based off-price family apparel chain Decelle in 1993. It then opened its first store outside the US (in Mexico) and tried new stand-alone store concepts based on successful in-store departments such as Luxury Linens and Baby Depot. A warm winter in 1994 hurt the company: Profits fell by two-thirds, and it sold off inventory for two years afterward.

The company pulled a line of men's parkas in late 1998 after a Humane Society investigation revealed that the coats were trimmed with hair from dogs killed inhumanely in China. The company launched a baby gift registry in 2000, and later that year opened a silk floral division in selected stores. In 2001 the company acquired 16 stores formerly occupied by bankrupt Montgomery Ward and announced plans to open 20 to 30 stores. Burlington Coat Factory began operating MGM Shoes in fiscal 2002, opening nine of the stand-alone specialty shoe stores.

OFFICERS

Chairman, President, and CEO: Monroe G. Milstein, age 74, $322,400 pay

EVP, Executive Merchandise Manager, Assistant Secretary, and Director: Andrew R. Milstein, age 48, $212,376 pay

EVP, General Merchandise Manager, and Director: Stephen E. Milstein, age 45, $214,698 pay

EVP, COO, and Director: Mark A. Nesci, age 45, $325,405 pay
EVP, General Counsel, and Assistant Secretary: Paul C. Tang, age 47, $222,376 pay
VP and CIO: Michael Prince
VP, Corporate Controller, and Chief Accounting Officer: Robert L. LaPenta Jr.
VP Customer Relations: Carole Abbott
VP Customer Services: David Cestaro
VP Information Services: Brad H. Friedman
VP Logistics: Lorenzo Figueroa
VP Loss Prevention: John Putrino
VP Marketing and Advertising: Mari Ann McCormick
VP Planning and Allocation: Marvin Hearn
VP Real Estate: Robert Grapski
VP Recruiting: Sarah Orleck
VP Store Merchandising: Angel Guzman
VP Store Operations: Albert Cuccorelli
VP Store Planning: Jerry Lupia
VP Store Support and Development: Gloria Johnson
Auditors: Deloitte & Touche LLP

LOCATIONS

HQ: Burlington Coat Factory Warehouse Corporation
1830 Rte. 130, Burlington, NJ 08016
Phone: 609-387-7800 **Fax:** 609-387-7071
Web: www.coat.com

Burlington Coat Factory Warehouse has locations in 42 states across the US.

PRODUCTS/OPERATIONS

2002 Stores

	No.
Burlington Coat Factory	292
MGM Shoes	9
Decelle	7
Cohoes Fashions	5
Luxury Linens	4
Baby Depot (stand-alone)	1
Totally 4 Kids (stand-alone)	1
Total	**319**

Stores

Baby Depot (accessories, clothes, furniture for babies and toddlers)
Burlington Coat Factory (off-price clothing, accessories, linens, bath items, gifts)
Cohoes Fashions (upscale apparel and accessories)
Decelle (off-price family apparel, with an emphasis on youth clothing)
Luxury Linens (linens, bath items, gifts, accessories)
MGM Shoes (designer and fashion shoes)
Totally 4 Kids (children's clothing, furniture, books, toys)

COMPETITORS

Bed Bath & Beyond	Gingiss	Stein Mart
Belk	J. C. Penney	Syms
Dillard's	Limited Brands	Target
Dress Barn	Linens 'n Things	TJX
Federated	May	Toys "R" Us
Filene's Basement	Ross Stores	Value City
	Saks Inc.	Wal-Mart
	Sears	

HISTORICAL FINANCIALS & EMPLOYEES

NYSE: BCF FYE: Saturday nearest May 31	Annual Growth	6/93	6/94	6/95	6/96	6/97	*5/98	5/99	5/00	5/01	5/02
Sales ($ mil.)	8.9%	1,198	1,468	1,585	1,592	1,758	1,796	2,006	2,199	2,400	2,577
Net income ($ mil.)	5.1%	43	45	15	29	57	64	48	61	71	67
Income as % of sales	—	3.6%	3.1%	0.9%	1.8%	3.2%	3.5%	2.4%	2.8%	3.0%	2.6%
Earnings per share ($)	6.2%	0.88	0.93	0.30	0.59	1.17	1.34	1.02	1.34	1.60	1.51
Stock price - FY high ($)	—	15.56	23.64	20.62	11.97	16.66	20.50	28.06	20.75	21.98	23.50
Stock price - FY low ($)	—	6.62	10.97	7.08	7.81	8.33	12.39	10.75	9.69	10.81	12.81
Stock price - FY close ($)	6.5%	12.99	14.37	8.64	8.75	16.24	20.06	16.88	12.50	19.56	22.90
P/E - high	—	18	25	69	20	14	15	28	15	14	16
P/E - low	—	8	12	24	13	7	9	11	7	7	8
Dividends per share ($)	—	0.00	0.00	0.00	0.00	0.00	0.02	0.02	0.02	0.02	0.02
Book value per share ($)	10.5%	6.63	7.49	7.88	8.37	9.29	10.97	11.81	13.16	14.76	16.24
Employees	8.2%	12,800	17,000	15,000	17,000	17,600	20,000	20,000	21,000	22,000	26,000

* Fiscal year change

STOCK PRICE HISTORY

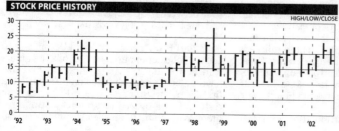

HIGH/LOW/CLOSE

2002 FISCAL YEAR-END

Debt ratio: 3.0%
Return on equity: 9.7%
Cash ($ mil.): 123
Current ratio: 1.46
Long-term debt ($ mil.): 22
No. of shares (mil.): 44
Dividends
  Yield: 0.1%
  Payout: 1.3%
Market value ($ mil.): 1,019

BURLINGTON NORTHERN SANTA FE

It's true that Santa leaves trains as gifts for little boys, but Burlington Northern Santa Fe (BNSF) is a big boy now and has to buy its own rolling stock. Based in Fort Worth, Texas, BNSF is looking to improve its technology services and increase competition with other railroads.

The second-largest US railroad behind Union Pacific, BNSF makes tracks through 28 states in the West, Midwest, and Sunbelt regions of the US and in two Canadian provinces. Trackage rights (which allow BNSF to operate its trains on another railroad's tracks) account for 8,000 miles of BNSF's 33,000-mile system. In addition to its rail system, the company has begun offering an online supplier verification system to aide both minority-owned and women-owned businesses to work with BNSF.

BNSF plans to build a seven-mile rail spur to Dow Chemical's Seadrift, Texas, facility, which will allow it to better compete with Union Pacific, which is the exclusive rail provider in the area for Dow. The company also plans to increase its intermodal operations (shipping by a combination of truck, train, or ship) by forming an alliance with Swift Transportation to haul fresh produce.

HISTORY

Burlington Northern (BN) was largely created by James Hill, who bought the St. Paul & Pacific Railroad in Minnesota in 1878. By 1893 Hill had completed the Great Northern Railway, extending from St. Paul to Seattle. The next year he gained control of Northern Pacific (chartered in 1864), which had been built between Minnesota and Washington.

In 1901, with J.P. Morgan's help, Hill acquired the Chicago, Burlington & Quincy (Burlington), whose routes included Chicago-St. Paul and Billings, Montana-Denver-Fort Worth, Texas-Houston. The Spokane, Portland & Seattle Railway (SP&S), completed in 1908, gave Great Northern an entrance to Oregon.

Hill intended to merge Great Northern, Northern Pacific, SP&S, and Burlington under his Morgan-backed Northern Securities Company, but in 1904 the Supreme Court found that Northern Securities had violated the Sherman Antitrust Act. The holding company was dissolved, but Hill controlled the individual railroads until he died in 1916. Hill's railroads produced well-known passenger trains: Great Northern's Empire Builder (now operated by Amtrak) began service in 1929, and in 1934 Burlington Zephyr was the nation's first streamlined passenger diesel.

After years of deliberation, the Interstate Commerce Commission allowed Great Northern and Northern Pacific to merge in 1970, along with jointly owned subsidiaries Burlington and SP&S. The resulting company, Burlington Northern (BN), acquired the St. Louis-San Francisco Railway in 1980, adding more than 4,650 miles to its rail network.

The company formed Burlington Motor Carriers (BMC) in 1985 to manage five trucking companies it had acquired. It sold BMC in 1988 and spun off Burlington Resources, a holding company for its nonrailroad businesses.

A fiery collision between a BN freight train and a Union Pacific (UP) freight in 1995 propelled the rivals to begin joint testing of global positioning satellites for guiding trains. Besides improving safety, the two hoped to end rail bottlenecks.

That year BN and Santa Fe Pacific (SFP), founded in 1859, formed Burlington Northern Santa Fe in a $4 billion merger. BN's strength lay in transporting manufacturing, agricultural, and natural resource commodities, and SFP specialized in intermodal shipping (combining train, truck, and ship). SFP (originally Atchison, Topeka & Santa Fe) had taken the name Santa Fe Pacific in 1989 after it was forced to sell the Southern Pacific.

The new BNSF acquired Washington Central Railroad in 1996, adding a third connection between central Washington and the Pacific Coast.

In 1997 customers protested when BNSF couldn't come up with enough cars and locomotives for grain shipping. A year later UP was in trouble with clogged rail lines: BNSF opened a joint dispatching center in Houston with UP to help unsnarl traffic. The effort proved successful, and in 1999 BNSF and UP began to combine dispatching in Southern California; the Kansas City, Missouri area; and Wyoming's Powder River Basin.

In 1999 BNSF announced a $2.5 billion capital improvement program, but later decided to trim spending to $2.28 billion and cut 1,400 jobs. Later that year BNSF agreed to merge with Canadian National Railway. The companies terminated the deal in 2000, however, after a US moratorium on rail mergers was upheld on appeal.

BNSF began offering intermodal service in 2000 between the US and Monterrey, Queretaro, and Mexico City, Mexico, its first such US-Mexico service.

In 2001 BNSF became the first US railroad to use the Internet to purchase fuel (via the American Petroleum Exchange). Another first followed, albeit a more dubious one: To settle the first federal lawsuit against workplace genetic testing, BNSF agreed to drop its testing program. Without their knowledge, employees who had been diagnosed with carpal tunnel syndrome were tested for genetic defects.

Also that year BNSF announced plans to join with a group of chemical and plastics companies to build a rail-spur southeast of Houston in order to compete with Union Pacific for petro-chemical shipping business.

OFFICERS

Chairman, President, CEO; Chairman, President, and CEO, BNSF Railway: Matthew K. Rose, age 42, $691,000 pay

EVP and COO: Carl R. Ice, age 45, $574,873 pay

EVP and CFO: Thomas N. Hund, age 48, $282,000 pay

EVP and Chief Marketing Officer: Charles L. Schultz, age 54, $524,570 pay

EVP Law and Government Affairs and Secretary: Jeffrey R. Moreland, age 57, $375,939 pay

VP Technology Services and CIO: Gregory C. Fox

VP and Controller: Dennis R. Johnson, age 50

VP and General Tax Counsel: Shelley J. Venick

VP Corporate Relations: Richard A. Russack

VP Government Affairs: A. R. Endres Jr.

VP Human Resources: Gloria Zamora

VP Investor Relations and Corporate Secretary: Marsha K. Morgan

VP Law and General Counsel: Gary L. Crosby

General Director Public Affairs: Steve Forsberg

Director Corporate Communications: Patrick Hiatte

Director Investor Relations: Jim Ayres

Assistant VP Finance and Treasurer: Linda J. Hurt

Auditors: PricewaterhouseCoopers LLP

LOCATIONS

HQ: Burlington Northern Santa Fe Corporation
2650 Lou Menk Dr., 2nd Fl., Fort Worth, TX 76131
Phone: 817-333-2000 **Fax:** 817-352-7171
Web: www.bnsf.com

Burlington Northern Santa Fe operates in 28 states, primarily in the western US, and in two Canadian provinces.

PRODUCTS/OPERATIONS

2001 Sales

	$ mil.	% of total
Consumer products	3,356	36
Coal	2,123	23
Industrial products	2,080	23
Agricultural commodities	1,531	17
Other	118	1
Total	**9,208**	**100**

Subsidiaries and Affiliates
BNSF Acquisition, Inc.
The Burlington Northern and Santa Fe Railway Company
FreightWise, Inc. (89%)

COMPETITORS

APL	CSX	Schneider
Canadian	J. B. Hunt	National
National	Landstar System	Union Pacific
Railway	Norfolk	U.S. Xpress
CNF	Southern	Werner

HISTORICAL FINANCIALS & EMPLOYEES

NYSE: BNI FYE: December 31	Annual Growth	12/92	12/93	12/94	12/95	12/96	12/97	12/98	12/99	12/00	12/01
Sales ($ mil.)	7.9%	4,630	4,699	4,995	6,183	8,187	8,413	8,941	9,100	9,205	9,208
Net income ($ mil.)	10.4%	299	296	426	92	889	885	1,155	1,137	980	731
Income as % of sales	—	6.5%	6.3%	8.5%	1.5%	10.9%	10.5%	12.9%	12.5%	10.6%	7.9%
Earnings per share ($)	42.9%	—	—	—	0.22	1.90	1.88	2.43	2.44	2.36	1.87
Stock price - FY high ($)	—	—	—	—	28.22	30.01	33.61	35.67	37.94	29.56	34.00
Stock price - FY low ($)	—	—	—	—	23.48	24.48	23.39	26.88	22.88	19.06	22.40
Stock price - FY close ($)	1.6%	—	—	—	25.97	28.76	30.95	34.25	24.25	28.31	28.53
P/E - high	—	—	—	—	50	16	18	15	15	13	18
P/E - low	—	—	—	—	41	13	12	11	9	8	12
Dividends per share ($)	—	—	—	—	0.00	0.40	0.40	0.42	0.48	0.48	0.37
Book value per share ($)	10.4%	—	—	—	11.21	12.93	14.51	16.52	17.98	19.10	20.35
Employees	2.5%	31,204	30,502	30,711	45,500	43,000	44,500	42,900	41,600	39,600	39,000

STOCK PRICE HISTORY

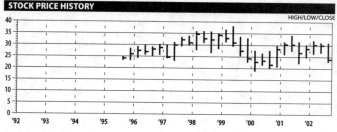

HIGH/LOW/CLOSE

2001 FISCAL YEAR-END

Debt ratio: 44.8%
Return on equity: 9.5%
Cash ($ mil.): 26
Current ratio: 0.33
Long-term debt ($ mil.): 6,363
No. of shares (mil.): 386
Dividends
 Yield: 1.3%
 Payout: 19.8%
Market value ($ mil.): 11,006

BURLINGTON RESOURCES INC.

The bulk of Burlington Resources' resources is in the form of natural gas (67% of its total reserves). Houston-based Burlington Resources is one of the largest independent oil and gas companies in the US, having proved reserves of more than 11.8 trillion cu. ft. of natural gas equivalent. It is also a major natural gas producer in North America. A holding company for a number of operating companies, Burlington Resources is engaged in oil and gas exploration, development, production, and marketing.

North American activities account for most of the company's sales, and its top gas-producing region is the San Juan Basin of New Mexico and Colorado. Burlington Resources also operates in the deepwater provinces of the Gulf of Mexico and the midcontinent region of the US, where it has wells in the Williston Basin in the Dakotas and Montana, Oklahoma's Anadarko Basin, Texas' Permian Basin, and Wyoming's Wind River Basin.

The company has moved into western Canada with the purchases of Poco Petroleums (renamed Burlington Resources Canada) and Canadian Hunter Exploration. Abroad, Burlington Resources has operations in the East Irish Sea and North Sea, Asia, Latin America, and North and West Africa.

HISTORY

Burlington Resources got its start in 1864 when President Abraham Lincoln granted Burlington Northern's predecessor, Northern Pacific Railway, the land and rights-of-way to construct a transcontinental railroad. After the railroad was completed, Northern Pacific retained major land holdings and mineral rights, including the largest private coal reserve in the US, 1.5 million acres of forest, and one of the country's largest reserves of natural gas and oil (discovered in 1951 on Burlington Northern's property in the Williston Basin of North Dakota).

In 1980 the company set up Milestone Petroleum to manage its oil and gas assets. Burlington Northern acquired the El Paso Company and Southland Royalty between 1983 and 1985; it merged these oil and gas firms with Milestone to form Meridian Oil.

During the 1980s, under the leadership of chairman Richard Bressler, Burlington Northern refocused its efforts on its railroad business. However, faced with the possibility of a long strike by railroad workers, Bressler moved to create two companies to protect the group's profits: Burlington Northern would manage the railroad activities, and Burlington Resources (spun off in 1988) would hold all the other interests of the enterprise.

The company spun off El Paso Natural Gas, a gas distribution company, in 1992 to focus exclusively on oil and gas operations. In 1994 Burlington Resources launched an exploration growth strategy that included ramping up its operations in the Gulf of Mexico. To avoid confusion, Meridian Oil's operations were subsumed under the Burlington Resources name in 1996, and the company subsequently divested nonstrategic oil and gas properties.

To position itself as a "super independent" with vast resources and a global reach, Burlington Resources acquired independent oil and gas exploration and production company Louisiana Land and Exploration (LL&E) in 1997. LL&E had been founded in 1926 by speculator Edward Simms to explore for oil on Louisiana coastal property owned by Henry Timken and a group of Midwesterners. During the 1950s and 1960s LL&E acquired other properties across the US, and in the 1980s it bought properties in Australia, Colombia, Indonesia, Mexico, and the UK. By 1997 it had production and exploration operations not only in Louisiana and the Gulf of Mexico but also in Algeria, offshore Indonesia, Venezuela, the North Sea, and the Madden Gas Field in Wyoming. The company also owned 600,000 acres of land in southern Louisiana and about 200 shallow-water and deepwater leases.

In 1998 Burlington Resources, Canada's Talisman Energy, and Sonatrach of Algeria successfully tested a wildcat well in the Berkine Basin of Algeria. Burlington Resources also signed an agreement with Hydrocarbon Resources, a subsidiary of Centrica, to transport and process natural gas from undeveloped gas fields in the UK's East Irish Sea. In 1999 Burlington Resources moved into western Canada by buying Calgary-based Poco Petroleums in a $2.5 billion deal.

In 2000 the company moved into West Africa by acquiring a 25% stake in Agip-operated fields offshore Gabon. The next year Burlington Resources agreed to buy properties in western Canada that had net proved reserves of 297 billion cu. ft. of gas equivalent from Petrobank Energy and ATCO Gas.

It expanded further in 2001, acquiring natural gas exploration and production firm Canadian Hunter Exploration for $2.1 billion.

OFFICERS

Chairman, President, and CEO: Bobby S. Shackouls,
age 51, $2,084,550 pay
SVP and CFO: Steven J. Shapiro, age 49, $855,243 pay
**SVP, Exploration, Burlington Resources, and BROG
GP:** John A. Williams, age 57, $855,243 pay
SVP, Law and Administration: L. David Hanower,
age 42, $780,456 pay
SVP, Production; President and CEO, BROG GP:
Randy L. Limbacher, age 43, $855,243 pay
VP and Chief Engineer: Brent Smolik
VP and Treasurer: Daniel D. Hawk
VP and Controller: Joseph P. McCoy
VP and General Counsel: Frederick J. Plaeger
VP and Managing Director, London: Neil Ritson
VP, Acquisitions: Thomas B. Nusz
VP, Human Resources and Administration:
William Usher
VP, Investor Relations and Corporate Communications:
Ellen R. DeSanctis
VP, Marketing: Clifford Scott Kirk
Auditors: PricewaterhouseCoopers LLP

LOCATIONS

HQ: 5051 Westheimer, Ste. 1400, Houston, TX 77056
Phone: 713-624-9500   **Fax:** 713-624-9645
Web: www.br-inc.com

Burlington Resources operates primarily in the US
(Colorado, Louisiana, Montana, New Mexico, North
Dakota, Oklahoma, Texas, Wyoming, and the Gulf of
Mexico) and Canada. International operations include the
East Irish Sea and the UK and Dutch sectors of the North
Sea (Northwest European Shelf), the Far East (including
offshore China), Latin America (Colombia, Ecuador,
Suriname, and Venezuela), and North and West Africa.

2001 Sales

	$ mil.	% of total
US	2,199	66
Canada	938	28
Other countries	189	6
Total	**3,326**	**100**

PRODUCTS/OPERATIONS

2001 Reserves

	Bill. cu. ft.	% of total
Gas	7,925	67
Oil	3,883	33
Total	**11,808**	**100**

Major Subsidiaries
Burlington Resources Canada Ltd.
Burlington Resources Oil & Gas Company LP
Canadian Hunter Exploration Ltd.
The Louisiana Land and Exploration Company

COMPETITORS

Adams Resources	Kerr-McGee
Anadarko Petroleum	Koch
Apache	Ocean Energy
BP	Pioneer Natural Resources
Calpine	Royal Dutch/Shell Group
Devon Energy	Talisman Energy
EOG	TOTAL FINA ELF
Exxon Mobil	Unocal
Helmerich & Payne	Vintage Petroleum

HISTORICAL FINANCIALS & EMPLOYEES

NYSE: BR FYE: December 31	Annual Growth	12/92	12/93	12/94	12/95	12/96	12/97	12/98	12/99	12/00	12/01
Sales ($ mil.)	12.6%	1,141	1,249	1,055	873	1,293	2,000	1,637	2,065	3,147	3,326
Net income ($ mil.)	9.0%	258	256	154	(280)	255	319	86	1	675	561
Income as % of sales	—	22.6%	20.5%	14.6%	—	19.7%	16.0%	5.3%	0.0%	21.4%	16.9%
Earnings per share ($)	3.7%	1.95	1.53	1.20	(1.47)	1.88	1.79	0.48	0.01	3.12	2.70
Stock price - FY high ($)	—	43.63	53.88	49.63	42.25	53.50	54.50	49.63	47.63	52.88	53.63
Stock price - FY low ($)	—	33.00	36.50	33.13	33.63	35.13	39.75	29.44	29.50	25.75	31.69
Stock price - FY close ($)	(0.7%)	40.00	42.38	35.00	39.25	50.38	44.81	35.81	33.06	50.50	37.54
P/E - high	—	22	35	41	—	28	30	103	4,763	17	20
P/E - low	—	17	24	28	—	19	22	61	2,950	8	12
Dividends per share ($)	(1.8%)	0.65	0.54	0.55	0.55	0.55	0.55	0.55	0.55	0.55	0.55
Book value per share ($)	(0.7%)	18.67	20.11	20.30	17.54	18.68	17.07	17.01	15.03	17.40	17.56
Employees	2.7%	1,705	1,729	1,846	1,796	2,004	1,819	1,678	1,997	1,783	2,167

STOCK PRICE HISTORY

HIGH/LOW/CLOSE

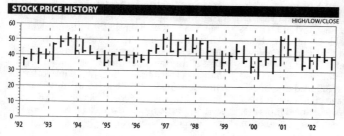

2001 FISCAL YEAR-END

Debt ratio: 55.2%
Return on equity: 15.4%
Cash ($ mil.): 116
Current ratio: 1.01
Long-term debt ($ mil.): 4,337
No. of shares (mil.): 201
Dividends
  Yield: 1.5%
  Payout: 20.4%
Market value ($ mil.): 7,538

In the city that never sleeps, Cablevision Systems never stops. Bethpage, New York-based Cablevision operates one of the nation's largest collections of cable systems and has stakes in a wide array of programming and entertainment assets. The company has sold and swapped cable systems in order to concentrate its operations in a regional cluster around New York City, where Cablevision has more than 3 million subscribers. It is moving to offer telephone service over cable networks, and it also operates competitive local-exchange carrier Lightpath.

Cablevision's majority-owned Rainbow Media Holdings operates five national cable networks, including American Movie Classics, Bravo, and the Independent Film Channel. Other Rainbow properties include regional sports channels and a stake in Fox Sports Net. A tracking stock, Rainbow Media Group, represents Cablevision's stake in Rainbow's assets.

Cablevision also controls Madison Square Garden — not only the famous arena, but also the professional basketball and hockey teams that play there, the New York Knicks and the New York Rangers. The company's Radio City Entertainment unit oversees the Music Hall and Rockettes. Cablevision's Clearview Cinema Group owns 65 theaters, including Manhattan's famous Ziegfeld. In addition, the company owns electronics retailer The Wiz.

Chairman and founder Charles Dolan and his family (including son James Dolan, the CEO) control Cablevision's voting stock.

HISTORY

In 1954 Charles Dolan helped form Sterling Manhattan Cable, which won the cable TV franchise for Lower Manhattan in 1965. It began broadcasting pro basketball and hockey, via Madison Square Garden (MSG), in 1967. In 1970 Dolan started Home Box Office (HBO), the first nationwide pay-TV channel, and hired Gerald Levin (later AOL Time Warner's CEO) to run it.

Dolan took the company public as Sterling Communications; its partner, media giant Time (now part of AOL Time Warner), came to own 80% of Sterling. Costs mounted, however, and in 1973 Time liquidated Sterling (but kept HBO).

Dolan bought back the New York franchises and formed Long Island Cable Communications Development. He changed its name to Cablevision and expanded around New York and Chicago. In 1980 Cablevision formed Rainbow Programming, which soon included the American Movie Classics and Bravo channels; in 1983 it launched the popular SportsChannel (now Fox Sports New York). Cablevision went public in

1986. It bought two Connecticut cable systems that year and one in Massachusetts the next.

In 1989 Cablevision helped NBC launch the CNBC cable network but sold its interest to NBC in 1991. Cablevision began offering cable phone service to businesses on Long Island — two years before the Telecommunications Act of 1996 was passed. Subsidiary Cablevision Lightpath, a competitive local-exchange carrier, signed a groundbreaking co-carrier agreement with Baby Bell NYNEX (now part of Verizon) in 1995.

To get a grip on NYC entertainment, Cablevision partnered with ITT in 1995 to buy the MSG properties. Three years later Starwood acquired ITT. Meanwhile, on-again, off-again merger talks with U S WEST Media stalled over Dolan's high asking price. In late 1996 Charles' son, James, became CEO.

In 1997 Cablevision began dumping cable holdings, which were spread over 19 states, to focus on its New York City area operations and the upgrading of its cable infrastructure. It began a series of swaps with TCI to cluster its cable systems. (As a result, TCI, which had been bought by AT&T, held 33% of Cablevision stock by 1999. AT&T sold the stake in 2001.) Cablevision traded its Boston-area subscribers to MediaOne (also acquired by AT&T) for more NYC customers (2001) and sold its Cleveland cable system to Adelphia and its Kalamazoo, Michigan, cable system to Charter (2000).

Cablevision sold 40% of Rainbow Media's regional sports business to Fox/Liberty (now Fox Sports Networks, owned by News Corp.) to create a rival to Disney's ESPN. Fox/Liberty got 40% of MSG, and Cablevision got Fox Sports Net, a chain of 22 regional sports networks. MSG also bought Radio City Entertainment (and the famed Rockettes) in 1997.

In 1998 Cablevision sold cable systems in 10 states to Mediacom. That year it bought beleaguered electronics retailer Nobody Beats The Wiz, Clearview Cinema, and 16 New York theaters from Loews Cineplex. It also began offering business phone service in Connecticut and residential service on Long Island.

Rainbow Media Group, a tracking stock representing Cablevision's stakes in several of its programming assets, began trading in 2001. That year MGM paid $825 million for a 20% stake in four of Rainbow's national networks. But the recession forced the company to take steps to improve operations, including the elimination of 600 jobs, or about 4% of its workforce. The company in 2002 battled with the Yankees Entertainment & Sports Network (YES Network) over the rights to broadcast New York Yankees games.

Chairman: Charles F. Dolan, age 75, $1,600,000 pay
Vice Chairman, General Counsel, and Secretary; Vice Chairman, Madison Square Garden: Robert S. Lemle, age 49, $2,875,000 pay
Vice Chairman: William J. Bell, age 62, $2,875,000 pay
President, CEO, and Director; Chairman, Madison Square Garden: James L. Dolan, age 46, $1,600,000 pay
EVP Communications, Government, and Public Affairs and Director: Sheila A. Mahony, age 60
EVP Corporate Administration: Joseph J. Lhota, age 47
EVP Engineering and Technology: Wilt Hildenbrand, age 54
EVP Finance and Controller: Andrew B. Rosengard, age 44, $2,150,000 pay
EVP Planning and Operations: Margaret A. Albergo, age 48
EVP, CIO, and Director: Thomas C. Dolan, age 49
SVP Investor Relations: Frank Golden
Director; President, News 12 Networks: Patrick F. Dolan, age 50
President and CEO, Rainbow Media Holdings: Joshua W. Sapan
President, Retail Group: Jeffrey Yapp
President, Madison Square Garden and Radio City Entertainment: Seth Abraham
Auditors: KPMG LLP

LOCATIONS

HQ: Cablevision Systems Corporation
1111 Stewart Ave., Bethpage, NY 11714
Phone: 516-803-2300   **Fax:** 516-803-2273
Web: www.cablevision.com

PRODUCTS/OPERATIONS

2001 Sales

	$ mil.	% of total
Cablevision NY Group		
Telecommunications	2,276	52
Madison Square Garden	842	19
Retail electronics	679	15
Rainbow Media Group	589	13
Other	36	1
Adjustments	(17)	—
Total	**4,405**	**100**

COMPETITORS

AT&T	RCN
Circuit City	SBC Communications
CompUSA	Time Warner Cable
DIRECTV	Time Warner
EchoStar Communications	Entertainment
NBC	Verizon
P.C. Richard & Son	Viacom
RadioShack	Walt Disney

HISTORICAL FINANCIALS & EMPLOYEES

NYSE: CVC FYE: December 31	Annual Growth	12/92	12/93	12/94	12/95	12/96	12/97	12/98	12/99	12/00	12/01
Sales ($ mil.)	25.4%	573	667	837	1,078	1,315	1,949	3,265	3,943	4,411	4,405
Net income ($ mil.)	—	(251)	(247)	(315)	(318)	(332)	137	(449)	(801)	229	1,008
Income as % of sales	—	—	—	—	—	—	7.0%	—	—	5.2%	22.9%
Earnings per share ($)	—	(2.80)	(2.71)	(3.43)	(3.55)	(4.63)	(0.12)	(3.16)	(5.12)	1.29	3.71
Stock price – FY high ($)	—	9.13	18.00	16.97	17.44	15.09	24.56	50.25	91.88	86.88	91.50
Stock price – FY low ($)	—	6.22	7.34	9.75	12.19	6.25	6.78	21.78	49.88	55.00	32.50
Stock price – FY close ($)	20.7%	8.75	16.97	12.63	13.56	7.66	23.94	50.13	75.50	84.94	47.45
P/E – high	—	—	—	—	—	—	—	—	—	66	24
P/E – low	—	—	—	—	—	—	—	—	—	42	9
Dividends per share ($)	—	0.00	0.00	0.00	0.00	0.00	0.00	0.00	0.00	0.00	0.00
Book value per share ($)	—	(13.82)	(16.19)	(19.27)	(16.54)	(13.78)	(12.51)	(6.81)	(9.60)	(5.63)	(9.04)
Employees	25.6%	3,444	3,636	4,698	5,801	7,118	15,020	15,824	23,413	24,463	26,780

STOCK PRICE HISTORY

HIGH/LOW/CLOSE

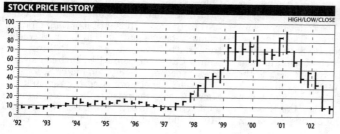

2001 FISCAL YEAR-END

Debt ratio: 100.0%
Return on equity: —
Cash ($ mil.): 108
Current ratio: 0.62
Long-term debt ($ mil.): 6,978
No. of shares (mil.): 175
Dividends
 Yield: —
 Payout: —
Market value ($ mil.): 8,323

CABOT CORPORATION

Even if it lost money, Cabot still would be in the black. The Boston-based company is the world's #1 producer of carbon black, a reinforcing and pigmenting agent used in tires and printing. Cabot also makes fumed silica, which is used as an anticaking, thickening, and reinforcing agent. Other products include tantalum (used in electronics), thermoplastic concentrates, ink-jet colorants, and fluids used in gas and oil drilling. Cabot also owns about 41% of safety products maker Aearo Corporation (formerly Cabot Safety Holding Corporation).

Consolidation of the tire industry and a slowing economy has hurt Cabot's carbon black business. In response, the company has cut capacity and costs — primarily in that segment. The company's fumed silica sales have also suffered, but long-range contracts have boosted its tantalum sales and the company is developing its newer businesses, including inkjet colorants, specialty fluids, and elastomer composites. Cabot has spun off the remainder of its microelectronics materials business and has sold Cabot LNG (liquified natural gas).

HISTORY

A descendant of two old-line Boston merchant families, Godfrey Lowell Cabot graduated from Harvard in 1882. His brother had a paint business in Pennsylvania that used coal tars to make black pigment, and the two decided that carbon black — an abundant waste product of the oil fields — would be their business. The brothers built a carbon black plant in Pennsylvania in 1882; five years later Godfrey bought his brother's share in the company. A carbon black glut and the increasing use of natural gas led Godfrey to drill his first gas well in 1888. He took advantage of the glut by buying distressed carbon black factories.

As the Pennsylvania oil fields dried up near the turn of the century, Godfrey moved operations to West Virginia, where he added to his gas holdings and, in 1914, built a natural gas extraction plant. Meanwhile, products such as high-speed printing presses increased the demand for carbon black. The reinforcing and stabilizing properties of the compound became widely known after its use in tires during WWI. The company was incorporated in 1922 as Godfrey L. Cabot, Inc.

The production of carbon black soon moved west, and by 1930 Cabot had eight plants in Texas and one in Oklahoma. Early that decade the company developed dustless carbon black pellets, which, along with gas profits, got Cabot through the Depression. In 1935 Cabot began drilling for oil and gas and processing natural gas

in Texas. Soon natural gas accounted for more than half of sales.

WWII led to rubber shortages and temporary government control over the industry. It also led to the construction and improvement (with government assistance) of Cabot plants in Louisiana, Oklahoma, and Texas. The company was the #1 producer of carbon black in 1950 and began its fumed silica operations in 1952. The postwar economic boom allowed Cabot to open carbon black plants in Canada, France, Italy, and the UK by the end of the decade.

In 1960 the company's businesses were united under the Cabot Corporation name. During the 1960s expansion continued into Argentina, Colombia, Germany, and Spain. Godfrey Cabot died in 1962. The next year the company started producing titanium, sold a 12% stake in a public offering, and began experimenting with plastic polymers.

CEO Robert Sharpie used the cash derived from Cabot's chemical businesses during the 1970s for acquisitions — including Kawecki Berylco Industries (tantalum, 1978) and TUCO, Inc. (gas processing and pipeline, 1979) — while its chemical plants deteriorated. The oil crisis early in the decade resulted in the rapid growth of Cabot's energy business. However, when gas prices fell in the 1980s, Cabot's revenue base shrank and its liabilities didn't.

The Cabot family, which owned 30% of the company, replaced Sharpie with Samuel Bodman as CEO in 1987. Bodman invested in the plants and divested many of Cabot's noncore assets, including ceramics, metal manufacturing, and semiconductors. He also exited the energy production and exploration businesses.

In 1996 Cabot formed divisions to make pigment-based inks (ink-jet colorants) and drilling fluids (Cabot Specialty Fluids) and sold TUCO. Two years later the company began field testing a drilling fluid (cesium formate) that would half the drilling time in high-temperature, high-pressure wells. Cabot opened a slurry plant (for semiconductor manufacturing) in Japan in 1999 and completed the second phase of its carbon black plant in China, a joint venture with a Chinese firm. It also spun off 15% of its microelectronics materials business and sold Cabot LNG to Tractebel. In 2000 Cabot spun off its remaining stake (about 80%) in Cabot Microelectronics. The next year Kennett F. Burnes was named CEO after Samuel W. Bodman stepped down to become Deputy Commerce Secretary.

In 2002 Cabot purchased the remainder of Showa Cabot Supermetals (tantalum) from its joint venture partner, Showa Denko, for about $100 million and another $100 million in debt.

Chairman, President, and CEO: Kennett F. Burnes, age 58, $1,462,500 pay
EVP and General Manager, Carbon Black: William P. Noglows, age 43, $820,833 pay
EVO and CFO: John A. Shaw, age 53
VP and Director, Corporate Affairs: Karen M. Morrissey
VP; President, Cabot Specialty Fluids: U. Roger Weems
VP and Director, Safety, Health and Environmental Affairs: John E. Anderson, age 61, $352,500 pay
VP and General Counsel: Ho-il Kim, age 43
VP and General Manager, Cabot Performance Materials: Thomas H. Odle, $545,833 pay
VP and General Manager, Fumed Metal Oxides: William J. Brady, age 40, $506,250 pay
VP and General Manager, Inkjet Colorants Business: Peter H. Shepard
VP and General Manager, New Product Development: Daniel Gilliland
Auditors: PricewaterhouseCoopers LLP

LOCATIONS

HQ: Two Seaport Lane, Ste. 1300, Boston, MA 02109
Phone: 617-345-0100   **Fax:** 617-342-6103
Web: www.cabot-corp.com

Cabot operates about 40 manufacturing facilities in 23 countries.

2001 Sales

	% of total
North America	47
Europe	29
Asia/Pacific	15
Latin America	9
Total	**100**

PRODUCTS/OPERATIONS

2001 Sales

	$ mil.	% of total
Chemical businesses	1,335	79
Performance materials	329	19
Specialty fluids	27	2
Adjustments	(21)	—
Total	**1,670**	**100**

Selected Products
Carbon black
  Industrial product blacks
  Special blacks
  Tire blacks
Fumed metal oxides
  Fumed alumina
  Fumed silica
Ink-jet colorants
Performance materials
  Niobium
  Tantalum
Specialty fluids (cesium formate drilling fluids)
Thermoplastic concentrates

COMPETITORS

Akzo Nobel	Eastman Resins	Mitsubishi
Allegheny	Engelhard	Chemical
Technologies	Flint Ink	Phelps Dodge
BASF AG	GE Plastics	Smith
Clariant	Imperial	International
Crompton	Chemical	Tauber Oil
Degussa	J. M. Huber	Tokai Carbon
Desc	Keystone	
Dow Chemical	MacDermid	

HISTORICAL FINANCIALS & EMPLOYEES

NYSE: CBT FYE: September 30	Annual Growth	9/92	9/93	9/94	9/95	9/96	9/97	9/98	9/99	9/00	9/01
Sales ($ mil.)	0.8%	1,557	1,614	1,680	1,830	1,856	1,630	1,648	1,695	1,523	1,670
Net income ($ mil.)	8.0%	62	11	79	172	194	93	122	97	453	124
Income as % of sales	—	4.0%	0.7%	4.7%	9.4%	10.5%	5.7%	7.4%	5.7%	29.7%	7.4%
Earnings per share ($)	9.2%	0.75	0.10	0.92	2.03	2.42	1.19	1.61	1.31	5.22	1.66
Stock price – FY high ($)	—	13.09	14.06	14.62	29.38	31.63	29.38	39.94	31.69	38.44	41.60
Stock price – FY low ($)	—	7.00	9.28	12.19	12.75	22.75	21.50	21.75	19.75	17.94	18.19
Stock price – FY close ($)	14.3%	12.00	13.87	13.63	26.56	27.88	26.94	24.94	23.75	31.69	39.90
P/E – high	—	16	31	14	13	12	22	22	22	17	22
P/E – low	—	9	21	12	6	8	16	12	13	8	10
Dividends per share ($)	6.6%	0.27	0.27	0.26	0.30	0.36	0.40	0.42	0.44	0.44	0.48
Book value per share ($)	9.6%	6.64	6.03	7.51	9.44	10.41	10.47	10.49	10.52	15.47	15.17
Employees	(2.3%)	5,300	5,400	5,400	4,100	4,700	4,800	4,800	4,450	4,500	4,300

STOCK PRICE HISTORY

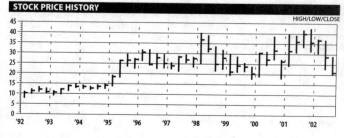

HIGH/LOW/CLOSE

2001 FISCAL YEAR-END

Debt ratio: 30.6%
Return on equity: 13.4%
Cash ($ mil.): 364
Current ratio: 3.33
Long-term debt ($ mil.): 419
No. of shares (mil.): 63
Dividends
  Yield: 1.2%
  Payout: 28.9%
Market value ($ mil.): 2,499

CALPERS

California's public sector retirees already have a place in the sun; CalPERS gives them the money to enjoy it.

The Sacramento-based California Public Employees' Retirement System (CalPERS) is one of the largest public pension systems in the US, with nearly $145 billion in assets. It manages retirement and health plans for nearly 1.3 million beneficiaries from nearly 2,500 government agencies and school districts. CalPERS uses its size to influence such corporate governance issues as company performance, executive compensation, and sometimes social policy. It is also a powerful negotiator for such services as insurance; rates established by the system serve as benchmarks for other employers.

Most of CalPERS revenue comes from its enormous investment program: It has interests in US and foreign securities, real estate development and investment, and even hedge funds and venture capital activities. CalPERS has steadily increased its investments in private equity, looking to take ownership stakes in more firms (it already owns 10% of investment bank Thomas Weisel). The system has invested $485 million in LBO firm Texas Pacific Group and $425 million in investment firm The Carlyle Group (netting a stake of just more than 5%, with an option to double it), and closed a $500 million fund targeting investments in corporate partners. In addition, the system spent about $2 billion to acquire Cabot Industrial Trust and its approximately 350 industrial properties in 20 states. Over the next few years CalPERS may be forced to sell assets, as it is expected to be hit with a wave of early retirements by middle-aged workers.

CalPERS' board consists of six elected, three appointed, and four designated members (the director of the state's Department of Personnel Administration, the state controller, the state treasurer, and a member of the State Personnel Board). The board has seen its share of disputes, on issues ranging from staff salaries to how to invest assets. The sometimes nasty (and public) donnybrooks have led to the exodus of several key personnel, including former CEO James Burton and former chief investment officer Daniel Szente.

HISTORY

The state of California founded CalPERS in 1931 to administer a pension fund for state employees. By the 1940s the system was serving other public agencies and educational institutions on a contract basis.

When the Public Employees' Medical and Hospital Care Act was passed in 1962, CalPERS added health coverage. The fund was conservatively managed in-house, with little exposure to stocks. Despite slow growth, the state used the system's funds to meet its own cash shortfalls.

CalPERS became involved in corporate governance issues in the mid-1980s, when California treasurer Jesse Unruh became outraged by corporate greenmail schemes. In 1987 he hired as CEO Wisconsin pension board veteran Dale Hanson, who led the movement for corporate accountability to institutional investors.

In the late 1980s CalPERS moved into real estate and Japanese stocks. When both crashed around 1990, Hanson came under pressure. CalPERS was twice forced to take major write-downs for its real estate holdings and turned to expensive outside fund managers, but its investment performance deteriorated and member services suffered.

Legislation in 1990 enabled CalPERS to offer long-term health insurance. Governor Pete Wilson's 1991 attempt to use $1.6 billion from CalPERS to help meet a state budget shortfall resulted in legislation banning future raids. CalPERS made its first direct investment in 1993, an energy-related infrastructure partnership with Enron.

CalPERS suffered in the 1994 bond crash. That year Hanson resigned amid criticism that his focus on corporate governance had depressed fund performance. The system moved to an indexing strategy.

CalPERS eased its corporate relations stance, creating a separate office to handle investor issues and launching an International Corporate Governance Program. However, the next year CalPERS was uninvited from a KKR investment pool because of criticism of its fund management and fee structure.

In 1996 the system teamed with the Asian Development Bank to invest in the Asia/Pacific region; it took a major hit in the Asian financial crisis the next year, but used the downturn as an opportunity to expand its position there in undervalued stocks. In 1998 CalPERS pressured foreign firms to adopt more transparent financial reporting methods.

In 2000 the system raised health care premiums almost 10% to keep up with rising care costs. It widened the scope of its direct investments with stakes in investment bank Thomas Weisel Partners (10%) and asset manager Arrowstreet Capital (15%); it also moved into real estate development, buying Genstar Land Co. with Newland Communities, and announcing plans to invest in high-tech firms focused on B2B online real estate services. CalPERS said that year it would sell off more than $500 million in tobacco holdings; it then invested the same amount in five biotech funds (including one from what is now GlaxoSmithKline), its first foray into the sector.

In 2001 California state controller and CalPERS board member Kathleen Connell successfully sued the system for not following state-sanctioned rules regarding pay increases. CalPERS was forced to cut salaries for investment managers, a move that prompted chief investment officer Daniel Szente to resign.

OFFICERS

Interim CEO; Assistant Executive Officer, Governmental Affairs, Planning, and Research: Robert D. Walton
Deputy Executive Officer: James H. Gomez
Assistant Executive Officer, Financial and Administration Services: Vincent P. Brown
Assistant Executive Officer, Investment Operations: Robert Aguallo
Assistant Executive Officer, Health Benefit Services: Allen D. Feezor
Assistant Executive Officer, Member and Benefit Services: Barbara D. Hegdal
Chief, Human Resources: Tom Pettey
Chief, Information Technology Services Division: Jack Corrie
Chief Investment Officer: Mark J.P. Anson
Chief, Office of Public Affairs: Patricia K. Macht
Chief Actuary: Ronald L. Seeling
Auditors: PricewaterhouseCoopers LLP

LOCATIONS

HQ: California Public Employees' Retirement System
Lincoln Plaza, 400 P St., Sacramento, CA 95814
Phone: 916-326-3000   **Fax:** 916-558-4001
Web: www.calpers.ca.gov

PRODUCTS/OPERATIONS

Selected Retirement Plans
Defined Benefit Plans
  Judges' Retirement Fund
  Judges' Retirement Fund II
  Legislators' Retirement System
  Public Employees' Retirement Fund
  Volunteer Firefighters' Length of Service Award System
Defined Contribution Plans
  State Peace Officers' and Firefighters' Defined Contribution Plan Fund
Health Care Plans
  Public Employees' Health Care Fund
  Public Employees' Contingency Reserve Fund
Others
  Replacement Benefit Fund
  Public Employees' Long-Term Care Fund
  Public Employees' Deferred Compensation Fund
  Old Age & Survivors' Insurance Revolving Fund

COMPETITORS

A.G. Edwards	Nationwide Financial
Alliance Capital	Principal Financial
Management	Putnam Investments
AXA Financial	Raymond James Financial
Charles Schwab	Salomon Smith Barney
FMR	Holdings
Franklin Resources	State Street
Janus	SunAmerica Inc.
Legg Mason	T. Rowe Price
MFS	TIAA-CREF
Mellon Financial	UBS PaineWebber
Merrill Lynch	USAA
Morgan Stanley	Vanguard Group

HISTORICAL FINANCIALS & EMPLOYEES

Government-owned FYE: June 30	Annual Growth	6/92	6/93	6/94	6/95	6/96	6/97	6/98	6/99	6/00	6/01
Sales ($ mil.)	(20.4%)	—	13,027	4,986	16,174	17,179	23,918	27,514	20,889	18,845	2,095
Employees	8.7%	—	—	900	1,000	1,037	1,089	1,247	1,500	1,594	1,614

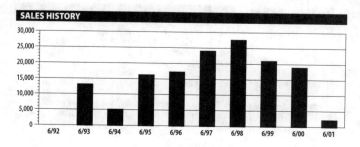

SALES HISTORY

CAMPBELL SOUP COMPANY

Soup means M'm! M'm! Money! for the Campbell Soup Company. The Camden, New Jersey-based company is the world's biggest soup maker; its 70% share in the US is led by chicken noodle, tomato, and cream of mushroom. The company also makes Franco-American sauces and canned pasta, Godiva chocolates, Pace picante sauce, Pepperidge Farm baked goods, and V8 beverages.

Campbell is striving to heat up lukewarm sales as consumers seek more convenience in the kitchen and competitors slurp into its market share. The company has launched meal-kits, ready-to-serve soups in pop-top, resealable, and microwaveable containers; it also has redesigned its distinctive red-and-white label and revived its "M'm! M'm! Good!" advertising jingle.

The company's Away From Home unit is following customers out of the kitchen, selling soup and buns to cafeterias and fast-food restaurants. The company also operates Godiva boutiques around the world. In 2002 Campbell said it would purchase Irish soup maker Erin Foods from Greencore.

Descendants of condensed soup inventor John Dorrance own about 50% of Campbell Soup Company.

HISTORY

Campbell Soup Company began in Camden, New Jersey, in 1869 as a canning and preserving business founded by icebox maker Abram Anderson and fruit merchant Joseph Campbell. Anderson left in 1876 and Arthur Dorrance took his place. The Dorrance family assumed control after Campbell retired in 1894.

Arthur's nephew, John Dorrance, joined Campbell in 1897. The young chemist soon found a way to condense soup by eliminating most of its water. Without the heavy bulk of water-filled cans, distribution was cheaper; Campbell products quickly spread.

In 1904 the firm introduced the Campbell Kids characters. Entering the California market in 1911, Campbell became one of the first US companies to achieve national distribution of a food brand. It bought Franco-American, the first American soup maker, in 1915.

The company's ubiquity in American kitchens made its soup can an American icon (consider Andy Warhol's celebrated 1960 print) and brought great wealth to the Dorrance family.

With a reputation for conservative management, Campbell began to diversify, acquiring V8 juice (1948), Swanson (1955), Pepperidge Farm (1961), Godiva Chocolatier (33% in 1966, full ownership in 1974), Vlasic pickles (1978), and

Mrs. Paul's seafood (1982, sold 1996). It introduced Prego spaghetti sauce and LeMenu frozen dinners in the early 1980s.

Much of Campbell's sales growth in the 1990s came not from unit sales but from increasing its prices. In 1993 it took a $300 million restructuring charge, and over the next two years it sold poor performers at home and abroad. John Sr.'s grandson Bennett Dorrance took up the role of VC in 1993, becoming the first family member to take a senior executive position in 10 years.

Two years later Campbell paid $1.1 billion for Pace Foods (picante sauce) and acquired Fresh Start Bakeries (buns and muffins for McDonald's) and Homepride (#1 cooking sauce in the UK).

As part of its international expansion, in 1996 the firm acquired #1 German soup maker, Erasco, and Cheong Chan, a food manufacturer in Malaysia. However back at home it sold Mrs. Paul's. In 1997 Campbell sold its Marie's salad dressing operations and bought Groupe Danone's Liebig (France's leading wet-soup brand). Also that year Dale Morrison, a relative newcomer to the firm, succeeded David Johnson as president and CEO. To reduce costs and focus on other core segments, in 1998 Campbell spun off Swanson frozen foods and Vlasic pickles into Vlasic Foods International. (Vlasic later filed bankruptcy and was snapped up in a leveraged buyout.) In 1999 Campbell redesigned its soup can labels, altering an American icon.

Morrison resigned abruptly as president and CEO in 2000; Johnson returned to the helm during the search for a permanent chief. In early 2001 Douglas Conant, previously of Nabisco Foods, joined Campbell as president and CEO. A fresh plan was introduced to spend up to $600 million on marketing, product development, and quality upgrades (at the expense of shareholder dividends). In 2001 Campbell also bought the Batchelors, Royco, and Heisse Tasse brands of soup, as well as Oxo brand of bouillon cubes, from Unilever for about $900 million. The deal made Campbell the leading soup maker in Europe. In 2002 Campbell bought Snack Foods Limited, a leading snack food maker in Australia.

OFFICERS

Chairman: George M. Sherman, age 60
President, CEO, and Director: Douglas R. Conant, age 51, $1,585,307 pay
SVP and CFO: Robert A. Schiffner, age 51
SVP and CIO: Doreen A. Wright, age 45
SVP and Chief Strategy Officer: M. Carl Johnson III, age 53
SVP, Chief Customer Officer, and Interim President, North American Soup: Larry S. McWilliams, age 45
SVP, Distributor Sales: Rudolph Juarez, age 43

SVP, Human Resources: D. Eric Pogue, age 52
SVP, Law and Government Affairs: Ellen Oran Kaden, age 49, $785,271 pay
VP, Controller: Gerald S. Lord, age 54
VP, Corporate Development and Strategic Planning: Robert J. Zatta
VP, Global Research and Development: R. David C. Macnair, age 47
VP, Global Supply Chain: Patrick O'Malley, age 52
VP, Governmental Affairs: Kelly Johnston
VP, Human Resources: Ed Walsh
VP; President, North American Beverages and Sauces: James A. Goldman, age 43
President, Campbell Europe: Brian Mirsky, age 48
President, Campbell Sales Company: James M. Kenney, age 54
Auditors: PricewaterhouseCoopers LLP

LOCATIONS

HQ: Campbell Place, Camden, NJ 08103
Phone: 856-342-4800   **Fax:** 856-342-3878
Web: www.campbellsoup.com

Campbell Soup Company has principal manufacturing facilities in Australia, Belgium, Canada, France, Germany, Indonesia, Malaysia, Mexico, Papua New Guinea, Sweden, the UK, and the US.

2001 Sales

	$ mil.	% of total
US	5,021	75
Europe	613	9
Australia & Asia/Pacific	589	9
Other regions	513	7
Adjustments	(72)	—
Total	**6,664**	**100**

PRODUCTS/OPERATIONS

2001 Sales

	$ mil.	% of total
Soup & sauces	4,539	68
Biscuits & confectionery	1,613	24
Away From Home	573	8
Other	4	—
Adjustments	(65)	—
Total	**6,664**	**100**

Selected Brand Names

Domestic	International
Campbell's (soups)	Batchelors (soups, UK)
Godiva (chocolates, ice cream)	Erasco (soups, Germany)
	Godiva (chocolate)
Pace (Mexican sauces)	Heisse Tasse (soups, Germany)
Pepperidge Farm (cookies and crackers)	Kettle Chip (salty snacks, Australia)
Prego (pasta sauces)	Kimball (sauces, Malaysia)
Swanson (broths)	Liebig (soups, France)
V8 and V8 Splash (vegetable and fruit juices)	Oxo (bouillon cubes, UK)
	V8 Splash (beverages)

COMPETITORS

Borden Chemical	Hershey	Nestlé
Bush Brothers	Heinz	Ocean Spray
Cadbury Schweppes	Hormel	PepsiCo
	Keebler	Quaker Foods
Lindt & Sprungli	Kraft Foods	Thorntons
ConAgra	Kraft Foods International	Unilever
Diageo		
General Mills	Mars	

HISTORICAL FINANCIALS & EMPLOYEES

NYSE: CPB FYE: Sunday nearest July 31	Annual Growth	7/92	7/93	7/94	7/95	7/96	7/97	7/98	7/99	7/00	7/01
Sales ($ mil.)	0.7%	6,263	6,586	6,690	7,278	7,678	7,964	6,696	6,424	6,267	6,664
Net income ($ mil.)	3.2%	491	8	630	698	802	713	660	724	714	649
Income as % of sales	—	7.8%	0.1%	9.4%	9.6%	10.4%	9.0%	9.9%	11.3%	11.4%	9.7%
Earnings per share ($)	5.2%	0.98	0.01	1.26	1.40	1.59	1.51	1.44	1.63	1.65	1.55
Stock price - FY high ($)	—	21.94	22.69	21.63	25.63	35.38	52.81	62.88	59.94	47.00	35.44
Stock price - FY low ($)	—	15.75	17.63	17.13	18.50	22.13	32.00	46.00	38.06	25.44	23.75
Stock price - FY close ($)	4.2%	18.94	17.94	18.50	23.38	33.94	51.88	54.00	44.00	26.50	27.36
P/E - high	—	22	44	17	18	22	35	42	37	28	23
P/E - low	—	16	35	14	13	14	21	31	23	15	15
Dividends per share ($)	14.8%	0.26	0.43	0.53	0.75	0.68	0.56	0.81	0.87	1.13	0.90
Book value per share ($)	—	4.04	3.38	4.01	4.95	5.55	3.10	1.95	0.55	0.33	(0.60)
Employees	(6.3%)	43,256	46,920	44,378	43,781	40,650	37,000	24,250	24,500	22,000	24,000

STOCK PRICE HISTORY — HIGH/LOW/CLOSE

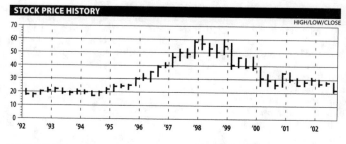

2001 FISCAL YEAR-END

Debt ratio: 100.0%
Return on equity: —
Cash ($ mil.): 24
Current ratio: 0.39
Long-term debt ($ mil.): 2,243
No. of shares (mil.): 409
Dividends
  Yield: 3.3%
  Payout: 58.1%
Market value ($ mil.): 11,190

CAPITAL ONE FINANCIAL

Maybe the company should be called Capital Four-One-One.

Capital One Financial takes information from its over 40 million accounts and uses it to match customers with thousands of Visa and MasterCard credit card products. The Falls Church, Virginia-based company offers the cards through its Capital One Bank and Capital One F.S.B. banking subsidiaries (the company has no retail banking operations). All told, the company manages more than $30 billion in consumer debt.

Capital One works hard to keep the *custom* in customer. Its cards sport themes ranging from kittens to pro wrestlers; card terms run the gamut from a $200-limit secured card with an annual fee (for those with spotty credit) to a 9.9% annual interest rate and no fee (for affluent, "superprime" customers). Capital One has extended its superprime credit offerings to Canada, France, and the UK. The company also markets to college and high school students.

Capital One Financial hopes to pursue mammon through its mammoth database. When customers call Capital One to check balances or make payments, chances are they'll be offered goods or services that match their profiles. Under its information-based strategy, Capital One pitches such customized products as home mortgages, car insurance, and shopping catalogs to incoming callers.

As part of the strategy, Capital One has moved into subprime auto financing (Capital One Auto Finance). Though a latecomer to the Internet, the company now offers Internet shopping (via its CapitalOnePlace.com site).

Financial Services Firm J.P. Morgan Chase owns about 6% of Capital One.

HISTORY

Capital One Financial is a descendant of the Bank of Virginia, which was formed in 1945. The company began issuing products similar to credit cards in 1953 and was MasterCard issuer #001. Acquisitions and mergers brought some 30 banks and several finance and mortgage companies under the bank's umbrella between 1962 and 1986, when Bank of Virginia became Signet Banking.

Signet's credit card operations had reached a million customers in 1988, when the bank hired consultants Richard Fairbank and Nigel Morris (now the top two officers at Capital One) to implement their "Information-Based Strategy." Under the duo's leadership, the bank began using sophisticated data-collection methods to gather massive amounts of information on existing or prospective customers; it then used the information to design and mass-market customized products to the customer.

In 1991 — after creating an enormous database and developing sophisticated screening processes and direct-mail marketing tactics — Signet escalated the credit card wars, luring customers from rivals with its innovative balance-transfer credit card. The card let customers of other companies transfer what they owed on higher-interest cards to a Signet card with a lower introductory rate.

The new card immediately drew imitators (by 1997 balance-transfer cards accounted for 85% of credit card solicitations). After skimming off the least risky customers, Fairbank and Morris began going after less desirable credit customers who could be charged higher rates. The result was what they call second-generation products — secured and unsecured cards with lower credit lines and higher annual percentage rates and fees for higher-risk customers.

The credit card business had grown to five million customers by 1994, but at a high cost to Signet, which had devoted most of its resources to finding and servicing credit card holders. That year Signet spun off its credit card business as Capital One to focus on banking. (Signet was later acquired by First Union.)

The company expanded into Florida and Texas in 1995 and into Canada and the UK in 1996; that year it established its savings bank, mainly to offer products and services to its cardholders. In 1997 the company used this unit to move into deposit accounts, buying a deposit portfolio from J. C. Penney. In 1998 the company began marketing its products to such clients as immigrants and high school students (whose parents must co-sign for the card). The company also expanded in terms of products and geography, acquiring auto lender Summit Acceptance and opening a new office in Nottingham, England.

In 1999 the firm's growth continued. The company stepped up its marketing efforts and was rewarded with significant boosts to its non-interest income and customer base. The next year the company launched The Capital One Place, an Internet shopping site. In 2001 the company acquired AmeriFee, which provides loans for elective medical and dental surgery.

In response to industry-wide concern over subprime lending, Capital One agreed to beef up reserves on its subprime portfolio in 2002.

OFFICERS

Chairman and CEO: Richard D. Fairbank, age 51
President, COO, and Director: Nigel W. Morris, age 43
EVP Operations and Technology and CIO:
Gregor S. Bailar, age 38
EVP Enterprise Services Group: Marjorie M. Connelly, age 40
EVP, Corporate Secretary, and General Counsel:
John G. Finneran Jr., age 51, $1,303,333 pay
EVP Corporate Development: Larry Klane, age 37
EVP Human Resources: Dennis H. Liberson, age 46, $1,123,667 pay
EVP Brand Management: William J. McDonald, age 45, $589,219 pay
EVP: Peter Schnall, age 38
EVP US Consumer Operations: Catherine West, age 42
EVP and CFO: David M. Willey, age 41, $1,228,083 pay
Auditors: Ernst & Young LLP

LOCATIONS

HQ: Capital One Financial Corporation
2980 Fairview Park Dr., Ste. 1300,
Falls Church, VA 22042
Phone: 703-205-1000   **Fax:** 703-205-1755
Web: www.capitalone.com

Capital One Financial has operations centers in Florida, Idaho, Massachusetts, Texas, Virginia, Washington, and internationally in Canada, France, and the UK.

PRODUCTS/OPERATIONS

2001 Sales

	$ mil.	% of total
Interest		
Consumer loans	2,643	36
Securities	138	2
Other	53	1
Noninterest		
Servicing & securitizations	2,441	34
Service charges & fees	1,599	22
Other	380	5
Total	**7,254**	**100**

Subsidiaries

AmeriFee Corporation (loans for medical and dental procedures)
Capital One Auto Finance (automobile loans)
Capital One Bank (credit card products)
Capital One, F.S.B. (consumer lending and deposit services)
Capital One Services, Inc. (operating, administrative, and other services to the corporation and its subsidiaries)

COMPETITORS

American
   Express
AmeriCredit
Bank of America
BANK ONE
CellStar
CIT Group
Citigroup
Credit
   Acceptance
Household
   International
J.P. Morgan
   Chase
MBNA
Morgan Stanley
Providian
   Financial
Toronto-
   Dominion Bank
Wells Fargo

HISTORICAL FINANCIALS & EMPLOYEES

NYSE: COF FYE: December 31	Annual Growth	12/92	12/93	12/94	12/95	12/96	12/97	12/98	12/99	12/00	12/01
Sales ($ mil.)	45.9%	242	455	656	1,010	1,424	1,787	2,600	3,966	5,424	7,254
Net income ($ mil.)	39.4%	32	111	95	127	155	189	275	363	470	642
Income as % of sales	—	13.3%	24.3%	14.5%	12.5%	10.9%	10.6%	10.6%	9.2%	8.7%	8.8%
Earnings per share ($)	29.4%	—	—	0.48	0.64	0.77	0.93	1.32	1.72	2.24	2.91
Stock price – FY high ($)	—	—	—	5.54	9.87	12.28	18.09	43.27	60.19	73.25	72.58
Stock price – FY low ($)	—	—	—	4.62	5.12	7.24	10.16	16.84	35.81	32.06	36.40
Stock price – FY close ($)	39.2%	—	—	5.33	7.95	11.99	18.04	38.30	48.19	65.81	53.95
P/E – high	—	—	—	12	15	16	19	31	33	31	24
P/E – low	—	—	—	10	8	9	11	12	19	13	12
Dividends per share ($)	—	—	—	0.00	0.08	0.11	0.11	0.11	0.11	0.11	0.11
Book value per share ($)	30.4%	—	—	2.39	3.02	3.72	4.55	6.44	7.59	9.94	15.33
Employees	31.3%	—	2,451	2,629	3,500	5,552	5,913	10,432	14,343	19,247	21,648

STOCK PRICE HISTORY

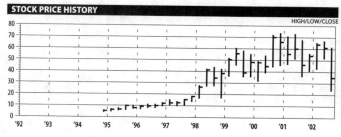

HIGH/LOW/CLOSE

2001 FISCAL YEAR-END

Debt ratio: 61.6%
Return on equity: 24.3%
Cash ($ mil.): —
Current ratio: —
Long-term debt ($ mil.): 5,335
No. of shares (mil.): 217
Dividends
   Yield: 0.2%
   Payout: 3.8%
Market value ($ mil.): 11,695

CARDINAL HEALTH, INC.

Cardinal Health is the big bird of drug distribution. The Dublin, Ohio-based company is #1 in the field, ahead of McKesson. Cardinal distributes pharmaceuticals, surgical and hospital supplies, and provides related services from more than 110 facilities throughout the world.

Always acquisitive, Cardinal Health has absorbed more than a dozen companies since 1984. Its Medicine Shoppe subsidiary is the US's largest franchisor of independent retail pharmacies. Other units include Owen Healthcare (pharmacy management), Pyxis (automated drug-dispensing and medication management systems), Allegiance (medical products distribution), and R.P. Scherer (maker of gelatin capsules).

If Cardinal can't consolidate, it diversifies; federal opposition stymied the company's 1998 bid to buy wholesaler Bergen Brunswig (now part of AmerisourceBergen), but Cardinal bought Allegiance in an even bigger deal the next year. Cardinal Health has bought Bindley Western, an Indianapolis, Indiana-based pharmaceutical distributor, and Boron, LePore & Associates, a pharmaceutical marketing services firm. It also intends to acquire radiopharmaceutical maker Syncor International.

HISTORY

Cardinal Health harks back to Cardinal Foods, a food wholesaler named for Ohio's state bird. In 1971 Robert Walter, then 26 and with the ink still fresh on his Harvard MBA, acquired Cardinal in a leveraged buyout. He hoped to grow Cardinal by acquisitions but was frustrated when he found that the food distribution industry was already highly consolidated.

In 1980 Cardinal moved into pharmaceuticals distribution with the acquisition of Zanesville. It went public in 1983 as Cardinal Distribution and Walter began looking for more acquisitions.

Cardinal soon expanded nationwide by swallowing other distributors. During the 1980s these purchases included two pharmaceuticals distributors headquartered in New York and a Massachusetts-based pharmaceuticals and food distributor. In 1988 Cardinal sold its food group, including Midland Grocery Co. and Mr. Moneysworth Inc., to Roundy's and narrowed its focus to pharmaceuticals.

During the 1990s the drug distributors joined the rest of the pharmaceutical industry in its rush toward consolidation.

Cardinal's acquisitions during those years included Ohio Valley-Clarksburg (1990, the Mid-Atlantic), Chapman Drug Co. (1991, Tennessee), PRN Services (1993, Michigan), Solomons Co.

(1993, Georgia), Behrens (1994, Texas), and Humiston-Keeling (1994, Illinois).

One of Cardinal's most important acquisitions during this period was its cash purchase of Whitmire Distribution in 1994. Formerly Amfac Health Care, Whitmire had been a subsidiary of Amfac, one of Hawaii's "Big Five" landholders. When Amfac Health Care was spun off in 1988, its president, Melburn Whitmire, led a management group that acquired a majority interest. When Cardinal bought it, Whitmire was the US's #6 drug wholesaler; the purchase bumped Cardinal up to #3. At that time the company changed its name to Cardinal Health and Melburn Whitmire became Cardinal's vice chairman.

In 1995 Cardinal made its biggest acquisition yet when it purchased St. Louis-based Medicine Shoppe International, the US's largest franchisor of independent retail pharmacies. Founded by two St. Louis obstetricians in 1970, the Medicine Shoppe had 987 US outlets and 107 abroad at the time of its purchase by Cardinal (for $348 million in stock).

A 1996 stock swap brought the company Pyxis, which provides hospitals with machines that automatically distribute pills to patients; Pyxis also provides pharmacy management services to hospital pharmacies. Later that year Cardinal bought PCI Services, a pharmaceutical packaging company.

In 1997 Cardinal acquired Owen Healthcare, a provider of pharmacy management services. When Cardinal agreed to buy Bergen Brunswig, market leader McKesson countered with a bid to acquire AmeriSource Health. In 1998 the Federal Trade Commission voted to block both deals; a federal judge supported that decision, and the agreements were scrapped.

That year Cardinal further expanded beyond marketing and distribution when it acquired R.P. Scherer, the world's largest maker of softgels. In 1999 Cardinal bought Allegiance, the largest medical products distributor in the US. That year it announced plans to buy Automatic Liquid Packaging, which packages liquid drugs for such companies as Pfizer.

Chairman and CEO: Robert D. Walter, age 56
EVP and CFO: Richard J. Miller, age 44
EVP and Chief Administrative Officer:
Anthony J. Rucci, age 50
EVP and CIO: Kathy Brittain White, age 52
EVP, Chief Legal Officer, and Secretary:
Paul S. Williams, age 41
EVP; Group President, Medical-Surgical Products and Services: Ronald K. Labrum
EVP; Group President, Pharmaceutical Technologies and Services: George L. Fotiades, age 48
EVP; Group President and COO, Pharmaceutical Distribution and Provider Services: James F. Millar, age 54
EVP; Group President, Automation and Information Services: Stephen S. Thomas, age 46
SVP, Controller, and Principal Accounting Officer:
Michael E. Beaulieu, age 42
SVP, Human Resources: Carole S. Watkins, age 40
SVP; President, Cardinal Health Capital:
Stephanie A. Wagoner, age 41
President, R.P. Scherer: John Lowry, age 42
Auditors: Ernst & Young LLP

LOCATIONS

HQ: 7000 Cardinal Place, Dublin, OH 43017
Phone: 614-757-5000 **Fax:** 614-757-8871
Web: www.cardinal-health.com

Cardinal Health operates from more than 50 pharmaceutical distribution facilities throughout the US and Puerto Rico, as well as facilities in Argentina, Australia, Brazil, Canada, the Dominican Republic, France, Germany, Italy, Japan, Malaysia, Malta, Mexico, the Netherlands, Thailand, and the UK.

PRODUCTS/OPERATIONS

2001 Sales

	$ mil.	% of total
Pharmaceutical distribution & provider services	31,186	65
Bulk deliveries to customer warehouses	9,288	19
Medical-surgical products & services	5,902	12
Pharmaceutical technologies & services	1,178	3
Automation & information services	472	1
Other	(78)	—
Total	**47,948**	**100**

Selected Subsidiaries

Allegiance Corporation (manufacturer and distributor of professional-use health care products)
Medicine Shoppe International, Inc. (franchisor of apothecary-style retail pharmacies)
National Specialty Services, Inc. (distributor of therapeutic plasma products, oncology products and other specialty pharmaceuticals)
Owen Healthcare, Inc. (pharmacy-management services)
PCI Services, Inc. (packager of pharmaceuticals for health care industry)
R.P. Scherer Corporation (softgels and other drug-delivery systems)

COMPETITORS

AmerisourceBergen
D & K Healthcare
Resources
McKesson

Moore Medical
Owens & Minor
PSS World Medical
Quality King

HISTORICAL FINANCIALS & EMPLOYEES

NYSE: CAH FYE: June 30	Annual Growth	3/92	3/93	*6/94	6/95	6/96	6/97	6/98	6/99	6/00	6/01
Sales ($ mil.)	45.4%	1,648	1,967	5,790	7,806	8,862	10,968	15,918	25,034	29,871	47,948
Net income ($ mil.)	48.0%	25	34	35	85	112	181	247	456	680	857
Income as % of sales	—	1.5%	1.7%	0.6%	1.1%	1.3%	1.7%	1.6%	1.8%	2.3%	1.8%
Earnings per share ($)	22.6%	0.30	0.39	0.39	0.62	0.53	0.75	0.99	1.09	1.59	1.88
Stock price - FY high ($)	—	9.20	7.77	12.29	15.10	22.70	29.08	43.32	55.53	49.36	77.32
Stock price - FY low ($)	—	5.34	5.64	6.29	10.83	12.91	19.62	24.25	35.84	24.68	44.81
Stock price - FY close ($)	28.3%	7.30	7.06	11.63	14.02	21.40	25.47	41.71	42.77	49.36	69.00
P/E - high	—	30	19	29	23	42	38	43	50	30	40
P/E - low	—	17	13	15	17	24	25	24	32	15	23
Dividends per share ($)	16.7%	0.02	0.02	0.03	0.03	0.03	0.05	0.05	0.07	0.07	0.08
Book value per share ($)	17.8%	2.77	3.18	2.89	3.88	4.32	5.45	6.52	8.43	9.60	12.12
Employees	48.4%	1,400	1,600	3,500	4,000	4,800	11,000	11,200	36,000	42,200	48,900

* Fiscal year change

STOCK PRICE HISTORY

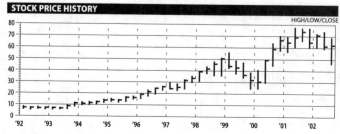

HIGH/LOW/CLOSE

2001 FISCAL YEAR-END

Debt ratio: 25.6%
Return on equity: 18.2%
Cash ($ mil.): 934
Current ratio: 1.63
Long-term debt ($ mil.): 1,871
No. of shares (mil.): 449
Dividends
  Yield: 0.1%
  Payout: 4.3%
Market value ($ mil.): 30,960

CAREMARK RX, INC.

Caremark Rx hits the mark when it comes to managing prescription drug costs. Once known as MedPartners, the US's #1 practice management company, the firm jettisoned its clinics to build its prescription benefits management (PBM) program and is now one of the leading PBMs in the US.

The Birmingham, Alabama-based company buys drugs directly from manufacturers to distribute through some 50,000 pharmacies; it also provides mail-order service. The firm provides these services to some 20 million patients covered by more than 1,200 corporate, insurance, managed-care, government, and union health plans. Caremark also offers disease management programs through 17 specialty pharmacies to members suffering from chronic, genetic, or otherwise high-cost conditions.

With drug prices rising, Caremark is focused on keeping its costs down and making its operations more efficient.

HISTORY

MedPartners was formed in 1993 by Richard Scrushy, the entrepreneurial chairman and president of HEALTHSOUTH, the leading US rehabilitation services company. HEALTHSOUTH grew by consolidating rehabilitation practices, many of which had a financial interest in the rehabilitation facilities to which they referred patients. In the 1990s, as HEALTHSOUTH restructured its agreements after self-referrals were restricted, Scrushy became interested in physician practice management (PPM).

Scrushy formed MedPartners in January 1993 and the next month bought a medical billing service. In June MedPartners landed its first contract, managing one of HEALTHSOUTH's practices. Larry House, HEALTHSOUTH's COO, became the company's chairman, president, and CEO. Funded by venture capitalists, House began acquiring other PPM companies. In 1993 MedPartners managed four practices; by the end of 1994, it managed 25.

MedPartners went public in 1995 and used the proceeds to buy more practices in the Southeast. Later that year it expanded to the West Coast, merging with Mullikin Medical Enterprises, then the US's largest private PPM (with about 3,000 doctors).

The new MedPartners/Mullikin had the size (4,900 doctors in 23 states) to go after market share. It targeted practices in markets where it could represent at least 20% of the physicians and thus have some clout to negotiate with the big HMOs.

In 1996 MedPartners/Mullikin secured its position as the leader in its field by buying Caremark, which managed the practices of about 1,000 doctors, provided pharmacy benefits management services nationwide, and had international operations.

After the Caremark deal, the company (which by then had changed its name back to the simpler MedPartners) had some 7,400 doctors in its network. In 1997 it bought Florida-based In-PhyNet Medical Management and formed a Southern California hospital-doctor network with Tenet Healthcare, the #2 US hospital chain, that increased both companies' negotiating heft with HMOs.

MedPartners moved into several more southwestern markets before agreeing to merge with PhyCor (now known as Aveta Health). However, the company was badly bloated, and the PhyCor deal quickly fell apart when its fiscal shape came to light. To recover, the company cut operations and sold low-performance practices, racking up nearly $700 million in restructuring charges and recording another in a string of annual losses.

In the aftermath, House resigned as chairman and CEO. Mac Crawford, who had earlier turned around managed behavioral care provider Magellan Health Services, replaced him. In 1998 the company announced plans to leave physician management entirely to focus on Caremark.

The next year the company sold its contract emergency physicians management operations and all but four of its PPM clinics (including its troubled California operations that had gone into involuntary Chapter 11 bankruptcy protection that year). The company then changed its name to Caremark Rx. The following year the company was blocked from selling its remaining clinics until arrangements could be made for patients using those clinics to continue receiving care; however, it later completed the sale.

In 2001 Caremark announced an agreement with McKesson that would allow McKesson to be the primary supplier to the pharmacies and warehouses of the company.

Chairman and CEO: Edwin M. Crawford, age 53,
$1,294,231 pay
President and COO: A. D. Frazier Jr.
EVP and CFO: Howard A. McLure, age 45, $520,674 pay
EVP, General Counsel, and Director:
Edward L. Hardin Jr., age 61, $963,885 pay
EVP, Corporate Development: Bradley S. Karro, age 40
EVP, Corporate Strategies: Charles C. Clark, age 52
SVP, Assistant General Counsel, and Secretary:
Sara J. Finley, age 41
SVP, Finance, and Treasurer: Peter J. Clemens IV,
age 37
EVP and Chief Administrative Officer: Kirk McConnell,
age 41
SVP and Controller: Mark S. Weeks, age 39
VP, Human Resources: Migdalia Penaloza
Auditors: KPMG LLP

LOCATIONS

HQ: 3000 Galleria Tower, Ste. 1000,
Birmingham, AL 35244
Phone: 205-733-8996
Web: www.caremark.com

Caremark Rx operates throughout the US.

PRODUCTS/OPERATIONS

Selected Subsidiaries
Caremark International Inc.
Caremark Inc.
MP Receivables Company

COMPETITORS

Accredo Health
AdvancePCS
Chronimed
CVS
Express Scripts
Gentiva
Medco Health Solutions
MIM
Priority Healthcare
Rite Aid

HISTORICAL FINANCIALS & EMPLOYEES

NYSE: CMX FYE: December 31	Annual Growth	12/92	12/93	12/94	12/95	12/96	12/97	12/98	12/99	12/00	12/01
Sales ($ mil.)	186.4%	—	1	75	726	4,814	6,331	2,634	3,308	4,430	5,614
Net income ($ mil.)	—	—	(1)	(2)	(10)	(159)	(821)	(1,260)	(140)	(163)	191
Income as % of sales	—	—	—	—	—	—	—	—	—	—	3.4%
Earnings per share ($)	—	—	—	—	(0.66)	(0.85)	(4.42)	(6.66)	(0.74)	(0.82)	0.73
Stock price - FY high ($)	—	—	—	—	34.50	36.00	28.38	22.38	9.00	13.94	18.50
Stock price - FY low ($)	—	—	—	—	14.75	16.38	17.88	1.63	2.88	3.75	10.75
Stock price - FY close ($)	(11.1%)	—	—	—	33.00	20.75	22.38	5.25	5.06	13.56	16.31
P/E - high	—	—	—	—	—	—	—	—	—	—	23
P/E - low	—	—	—	—	—	—	—	—	—	—	14
Dividends per share ($)	—	—	—	—	0.00	0.00	0.00	0.00	0.72	0.00	0.00
Book value per share ($)	—	—	—	—	3.24	4.47	0.46	(5.75)	(5.66)	(3.33)	(3.32)
Employees	19.3%	—	—	1,175	20,000	20,400	29,256	19,636	4,373	3,474	4,037

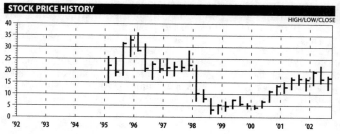

STOCK PRICE HISTORY
HIGH/LOW/CLOSE

2001 FISCAL YEAR-END
Debt ratio: 100.0%
Return on equity: —
Cash ($ mil.): 159
Current ratio: 0.95
Long-term debt ($ mil.): 696
No. of shares (mil.): 233
Dividends
Yield: —
Payout: —
Market value ($ mil.): 3,795

CARGILL, INCORPORATED

Being private doesn't mean Cargill is cut off from the world. The Wayzata, Minnesota-based agribusiness giant — the US's largest private corporation — has operations in 59 countries throughout the world. Cargill is the US's #1 grain producer, the #2 US meatpacker (after Tyson Foods), a commodity trader, and a producer of animal feed and crop fertilizers. A global supplier of oils, syrups, flour, and other products used in food processing, Cargill's own retail brands include Honeysuckle White and Riverside (poultry), Sterling Silver (beef), and Gerkens (cocoa).

Cargill also is involved in petroleum trading, financial trading, futures brokering, shipping, and steelmaking (subsidiary North Star is a major minimill steelmaker in the US). To focus on processing, Cargill sold its seed operations and coffee trading business and is selling part of its steel business.

Descendants of the founding Cargill and MacMillan families own about 85% of Cargill.

HISTORY

William W. Cargill founded Cargill in 1865 when he bought his first grain elevator, in Conover, Iowa. He and his brother Sam bought grain elevators all along the Southern Minnesota Railroad in 1870, just as Minnesota was becoming an important shipping route. Sam and a third brother, James, expanded the elevator operations while William worked with the railroads to monopolize transport of grain to markets and coal to farmers.

Around the turn of the century, William's son William S. invested in a number of ill-fated projects. William W. found that his name had been used to finance the projects; shortly afterward, he died of pneumonia. Cargill's creditors pressed for repayment, which threatened to bankrupt the company. John MacMillan, William W.'s son-in-law, took control and rebuilt Cargill. It had recovered by 1916 but lost its holdings in Mexico and Canada. MacMillan opened offices in New York (1922) and Argentina (1929), expanding grain trading and transport operations.

In 1945 Cargill bought Nutrena Mills (animal feed) and entered soybean processing; corn processing began soon after and grew with the demand for corn sweeteners. In 1954 Cargill benefited when the US began making loans to help developing countries buy American grain. Subsidiary Tradax, established in 1955, became one of the largest grain traders in Europe. A decade later Cargill began trading sugar by purchasing sugar and molasses in the Philippines and selling them abroad.

Cargill made its finances public in 1973 (as a requirement for its unsuccessful takeover bid of Missouri Portland Cement), revealing it to be one of the US's largest companies, with $5.2 billion in sales. In the 1970s it expanded into coal, steel, and waste disposal and became a major force in metals processing, beef, and salt production.

In the early 1990s Cargill began selling branded meats and packaged foods directly to supermarkets. To placate family heirs who wanted to take Cargill public, CEO Whitney MacMillan, grandson of John, created an employee stock plan in 1991 that allowed shareholders to cash in their shares. He also boosted dividends and reorganized the board, reducing the family's control. MacMillan retired in 1995 and nonfamily member Ernest Micek became CEO and chairman.

The firm bought Akzo Nobel's North American salt operations in 1997, becoming the #2 US salt company. Cargill bulked up its grain trading business by acquiring the grain export operations of Continental Grain in 1999. Micek resigned as CEO that year and was replaced by Warren Staley. Also in 1999 Cargill fessed up to misappropriating some genetic seed material from rival Pioneer Hi-Bred, killing the $650 million sale of its North American seed assets to Germany's AgrEvo.

Cargill sold its coffee trading unit in 2000 and sought buyers for its rubber business. Also, Cargill sold its North American hybrid seed business to Dow Chemical (Cargill had sold its foreign seed operations to Monsanto in 1998) and bought Agribrands International (Purina and Checkerboard animal feeds sold outside the US).

In 2001 the company bought family-held turkey and chicken processor Rocco Enterprises. That year the North Star Steel subsidiary agreed to sell off its tubing business and laid off employees in other divisions, citing high energy costs and lower demands for steel.

In 2002, Cargill Health & Food Technologies introduced trehalose, a naturally occuring type of sugar made from cornstarch. Trehalose has a blunted insulin response relative to other sugars and helps preserve food flavor, color and texture. Cargill also launched OliggooFiber, a line of natural soluble fiber ingredients which increases calcium absorption as well as the number of beneficial bacteria in the body. Both are marketed to the food industry for use in nutrition bars, sports drinks, bakery products, ice creams, and confections. That same year, Cargill purchased a 56% stake in Cerestar (starches, syrups, feeds) from Montedison SpA, the Italian agriculture and energy conglomerate. It subsequently purchased the bulk of the company's publicly held stock, increasing its ownership of Cerestar to approximately 97%.

OFFICERS

Chairman and CEO: Warren R. Staley, age 60
Vice Chairman and CFO: Robert L. Lumpkins, age 59
Vice Chairman: F. Guillaume Bastiaens, age 59
Vice Chairman: David W. Raisbeck, age 53
Director, President, and COO: Gregory R. Page
EVP: Fredric W. Corrigan
EVP: David M. Larson
EVP: Hubertus P. Spierings
SVP: David W. Rogers
SVP, Director of Corporate Affairs: Robbin S. Johnson
Corporate VP and Controller: Galen G. Johnson
Corporate VP and CTO: Ronald L. Christenson
Corporate VP and Treasurer: William W. Veazey
Corporate VP, Deputy General Counsel: Steven C. Euller
Corporate VP, Human Resources: Nancy P. Siska
Auditors: KPMG LLP

LOCATIONS

HQ: 15407 McGinty Rd. West, Wayzata, MN 55391
Phone: 952-742-7575   **Fax:** 952-742-7393
Web: www.cargill.com

PRODUCTS/OPERATIONS

Selected Divisions and Products

Agriculture

Animal feed	Champions Choice
Aquaculture feed	(agricultural salt
Biosciences	products)
Caprock Industries	Feed phosphates
(cattle feedlots)	Fertilizer
Cargill AgHorizons	Pet food
Cargill Animal Nutrition	

Financial Markets
Financial Markets Group (financial instrument trading, money markets, value investing and trade, and structured finance)
Cargill Technical Services (agricultural consultancy, management, natural resource management, rural development, and technical assistance)

Food Processing
Apples
Bulk and packaged oils
Citric acid
Corn (including dextrose and starch production)
Eggs
Ethanol
High fructose corn syrups
Lactic acid polymers
Oranges
Palm oil
Peanuts
Poultry (production, processing, marketing)
Protein products
Soybeans
Sunflower seeds

Industrial
Cargill Corn Milling (industrial-grade starches)
Cargill Industrial Oils & Lubricants
Cargill Steel and Wire
North Star Recycling
North Star Steel (steel minimills)
Phosphate mining and fertilizer manufacturing
Salt (process evaporated, rock, and solar)

Trading
Cargill Marine and Terminal
G&M Stevedoring
Greenwich Marine (ocean shipping)
Hohenberg Bros (cotton trading)

COMPETITORS

Ag Processing	Dow Chemical	Nippon Steel
ADM	DuPont	Nucor
BASF AG	Farmland	Perdue
Bethlehem Steel	Industries	Rohm and Haas
Bunge Limited	General Mills	Saskatchewan
Cenex Harvest	Hormel	Wheat Pool
States	IBP	Smithfield Foods
Cereol	King Arthur	Tate & Lyle
COFCO	Flour	Tyson Foods
ConAgra	Koch	United States
ContiGroup	Land O' Lakes	Steel
Corn Products	Farmland Feed	
International	Morton Salt	

HISTORICAL FINANCIALS & EMPLOYEES

Private FYE: May 31	Annual Growth	5/93	5/94	5/95	5/96	5/97	5/98	5/99	5/00	5/01	5/02
Sales ($ mil.)	0.8%	47,100	47,135	51,000	56,000	56,000	51,400	50,000	47,602	49,400	50,800
Net income ($ mil.)	9.7%	358	571	671	902	814	468	597	480	358	827
Income as % of sales	—	0.8%	1.2%	1.3%	1.6%	1.5%	0.9%	1.2%	1.0%	0.7%	1.6%
Employees	3.7%	70,000	70,700	73,300	76,000	79,000	80,600	84,000	84,000	90,000	97,000

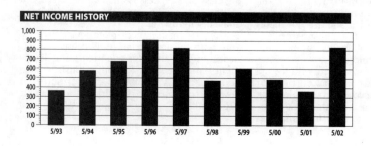

NET INCOME HISTORY

CARLISLE COMPANIES

Manufacturing conglomerate Carlisle Companies could be the poster firm for product diversity. The Syracuse, New York-based enterprise's largest segment, industrial products, includes products such as small bias-ply rubber tires, stamped and roll-formed wheels, rubber belts, tensioners, and pulleys. The construction materials unit produces rubber, plastic, and fleece roof sheeting and roofing accessories such as flashing and sealing tapes. Carlisle's general industry unit makes food service and catering products, specialized cleaning brushes, and cheese-making equipment. The automotive components segment makes rubber and plastic parts for auto makers. Carlisle's transportation unit makes specialty trailers; the specialty products group makes braking systems for heavy-duty trucks and off-highway equipment.

Carlisle grows through acquisitions. The company focuses on niche markets where it can gain a leading market share. However, a slowdown in the manufacturing sector has prompted Carlisle to take cost-cutting measures that included reducing its workforce and closing two plants and several regional offices.

HISTORY

Charles Moomy founded Carlisle Tire and Rubber Company in Carlisle, Pennsylvania, in 1917 to make rubber inner tubes for auto tires. The company debuted its full-molded inner tube in 1926. Success followed until the stock market crash of 1929.

Carlisle limped through the Depression with help from the New Deal's Industrial Loan Act. However, Moomy was forced to turn his stock over to the Federal Reserve Bank of Philadelphia, which became Carlisle's biggest shareholder. Pharis Tire and Rubber Company acquired Carlisle from the Federal Reserve Bank in 1943. Upon Pharis' liquidation in 1949, Carlisle stock was distributed to Pharis stockholders and company officials. Carlisle Corporation was formed, and it bought Dart Truck (mining and construction trucks).

Carlisle continued to diversify. During the 1960s it added jar sealant rings, roofing materials, automotive accessories, and tires for recreational vehicles. It moved to Cincinnati in the 1970s and acquired food service product and computer peripherals companies.

In the 1980s, unable to compete with the big car tire makers, Carlisle focused on tires for smaller vehicles (motorcycles and snowblowers), and it sold car tires to the auto aftermarket. The company restructured as Carlisle Companies

Incorporated in 1986 and moved to Syracuse, New York, the next year.

Carlisle bought Brookpark Plastics (plastic compression molding) and Off-Highway Braking Systems (from B.F. Goodrich Aerospace) in 1990, gaining factories in Europe and South America. After taking a hit in the early 1990's recession, Carlisle consolidated operations and sold its communications and electronics industries. With its 1993 purchase of Goodyear's roofing products business, Carlisle became the US's top maker of nonresidential roofing products.

Since the mid-1990s Carlisle increased its acquisitions, buying Sparta Brush (specialty brushes and cleaning tools), Trail King Industries (specialized low-bed trailers), Ti-Brook (trailers and dump bodies), Walker Stainless (trailers and in-plant processing equipment), Intero (steel and aluminum wheel rims), and Unique Wheel (steel wheels). The company also bought the engineered plastics unit of Johnson Controls and Hartstone (ceramic tableware, cookware, and decorative products).

In 1997 Carlisle acquired several small tire and wheel makers. The next year the company bought Vermont Electromagnetics and Quality Microwave Interconnects, both makers of specialty cable assemblies; Industrial Tire Products, an industrial and recreational vehicle tire distributor; and Hardcast Europe (adhesives and sealants, the Netherlands).

Carlisle stopped making refrigerated marine shipping containers in 1999, and its Carlisle Tire & Wheel Company subsidiary sold its surfacing products division. Carlisle bought privately owned Johnson Truck Bodies that year to boost its production of insulated dairy trucks. It also bought Innovative Engineering (cheese-making system supplier, New Zealand) and Marko International (table coverings and accessories for the food service market).

In 2000 Carlisle bought Damrow Denmark and Damrow USA (cheese-making equipment) as well as Red River Manufacturing (custom trailers and paving equipment). It also bought Titan International's consumer tire and wheel business and Process Controls Engineering, a control systems designer that serves the food and dairy industries.

The deal-making continued apace in early 2001 with the acquisitions of Wincanton Engineering (food- and beverage-processing equipment) and EcoStar (roofing). Carlisle also bought Mark IV Industries' Dayco industrial power transmission business for about $150 million.

Chairman: Stephen P. Munn, age 59, $581,000 pay
Vice Chairman: Dennis J. Hall, age 60, $675,000 pay
President, CEO, and Director: Richmond D. McKinnish, age 52, $525,000 pay
VP and CFO: Kirk F. Vincent, age 53
VP, Corporate Development: Scott C. Selbach, age 46, $284,900 pay
VP, Secretary, and General Counsel: Steven J. Ford, age 42, $247,000 pay
Auditors: KPMG LLP

LOCATIONS

HQ: Carlisle Companies Incorporated
13925 Ballantyne Corporate Place, Ste. 400,
Charlotte, NC 28277
Phone: 704-501-1100   **Fax:** 704-501-1190
Web: www.carlisle.com

Carlisle Companies operates more than 135 office, manufacturing, and warehouse facilities in Canada, China, Denmark, France, Germany, Italy, Japan, Mexico, the Netherlands, New Zealand, Spain, the UK, and the US.

PRODUCTS/OPERATIONS

2001 Sales

	$ mil.	% of total
Industrial components	476	26
Construction materials	465	25
General industry	420	23
Automotive components	252	14
Transportation products	120	6
Specialty products	116	6
Total	**1,849**	**100**

Selected Products

Aerospace wire
Cable assemblies and interconnects
Catering equipment
Ceramic tableware
Cheese and whey processing equipment
Commercial cookware and servingware
Custom-built high payload trailers
Dump bodies
Engineered rubber and plastic components
Fiberglass and composite trays and dishes
Heavy-duty friction and braking systems
Plastic foodservice permanentware
Pulleys
Refrigerated fiberglass truck bodies
Roofing systems
Rubber belts
Small bias-ply tires
Specialty electronic cable
Specialty rubber and plastic cleaning brushes
Specialty trailers
Stainless steel processing and containment equipment
Stamped and roll-formed wheels
Standard and custom-built high payload trailers
Tensioners

COMPETITORS

ArvinMeritor, Inc.	General Cable	Sumitomo Electric
Bridgestone	G-I Holdings	Superior
CertainTeed	Johns Manville	TeleCom
Dana	Michelin	Wabash National
Dover	Owens Corning	
Evergreen	Pirelli S.p.A.	
Marine	Raytech	
	Southwire	

HISTORICAL FINANCIALS & EMPLOYEES

NYSE: CSL FYE: December 31	Annual Growth	12/92	12/93	12/94	12/95	12/96	12/97	12/98	12/99	12/00	12/01
Sales ($ mil.)	14.9%	528	611	693	823	1,018	1,261	1,518	1,611	1,771	1,849
Net income ($ mil.)	0.0%	25	28	36	44	56	71	85	96	96	25
Income as % of sales	—	4.7%	4.6%	5.1%	5.4%	5.5%	5.6%	5.6%	5.9%	5.4%	1.3%
Earnings per share ($)	0.1%	0.81	0.92	1.15	1.41	1.80	2.28	2.77	3.13	3.14	0.82
Stock price - FY high ($)	—	11.88	17.25	18.06	21.81	30.50	47.75	53.06	52.94	51.00	44.00
Stock price - FY low ($)	—	8.81	11.53	15.13	17.25	19.00	27.00	32.56	30.63	30.94	25.50
Stock price - FY close ($)	13.7%	11.63	16.69	18.06	20.19	30.25	42.75	51.63	36.00	42.94	36.98
P/E - high	—	15	19	15	15	17	20	19	17	16	54
P/E - low	—	11	12	13	12	10	12	12	10	10	31
Dividends per share ($)	10.6%	0.33	0.35	0.38	0.42	0.47	0.53	0.60	0.68	0.76	0.82
Book value per share ($)	11.5%	6.68	7.23	8.04	8.92	10.13	11.57	13.48	15.87	18.11	17.85
Employees	10.5%	4,607	4,440	4,440	4,607	6,900	8,500	9,500	10,290	11,710	11,302

STOCK PRICE HISTORY

HIGH/LOW/CLOSE

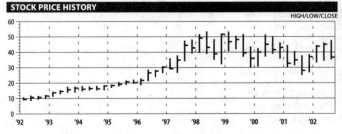

2001 FISCAL YEAR-END

Debt ratio: 46.1%
Return on equity: 4.6%
Cash ($ mil.): 16
Current ratio: 2.02
Long-term debt ($ mil.): 462
No. of shares (mil.): 30
Dividends
  Yield: 2.2%
  Payout: 100.0%
Market value ($ mil.): 1,119

CARLSON WAGONLIT TRAVEL

History was bunk for Henry Ford, but for Carlson Wagonlit Travel it was a bunk bed. Plymouth, Minnesota-based Carlson Wagonlit (pronounced Vah-gon-LEE) Travel descends from Europe's Wagons-Lits (literally, sleeping cars) company, which was founded by the creator of the Orient Express, and from the US's oldest travel agency chain (Ask Mr. Foster). Carlson Wagonlit Travel is the second-largest travel company in the world behind American Express. The company manages business travel from about 3,000 locations in more than 140 countries.

Carlson Wagonlit Travel is co-owned by France's Accor Group (motel and hotel franchises, travel and tourism services) and the US's Carlson Companies. Carlson Companies is a service conglomerate with nonbusiness travel operations such as hospitality (it franchises Radisson Hotels, T.G.I. Friday's and Italianni's restaurants, and luxury cruise lines) and marketing services (motivational and incentive programs for businesses).

The company's two parents have invested €100 million to get Carlson Wagonlit Travel online with business-to-consumer and business-to-business sites. Accor also is reaping the benefits of training the company's travel agents in booking Accor hotel rooms.

HISTORY

Belgian inventor Georges Nagelmackers' first enterprise was adding sleeping compartments to European trains in 1872. Nagelmackers later created the Orient Express. Over the years his Wagons-Lits company expanded its mission to become Wagonlit Travel.

While Nagelmackers was establishing his business in Europe, Ward G. Foster was giving out steamship and train schedules from his gift shop facing the stately Ponce de Leon Hotel in St. Augustine, Florida. As legend has it, hotel patrons with travel questions were directed to Foster's shop with: "Ask Mr. Foster. He'll know." In 1888 he founded Ask Mr. Foster Travel (it became the oldest travel agency in the US). By 1913 the company had offices located in pricey department stores and in the lobbies of upscale hotels and resorts throughout the country. After 50 years at the helm, Foster sold his business in 1937, three years before his death.

After suffering hard times during WWII and into the 1950s, the company changed hands again in 1957 when Donald Fisher and Thomas Orr, two Ask Mr. Foster shareholders, bought controlling interests for $157,000. In 1972 Peter Ueberroth (Major League Baseball commissioner and Los Angeles Olympic Organizing Committee president) bought the company, then sold it in 1979 to Carlson Companies, Inc., Carlson Wagonlit's parent. In 1990 Ask Mr. Foster became Carlson Travel Network. Also that year Carlson Companies acquired the UK's A.T. Mays, the Travel Agents — a leading UK seller of vacation and tour packages. By 1992 Carlson Companies, besides adding a travel agency a day to the 2,000-plus it already owned, was adding a new hotel every 10 days.

Europe's Wagonlit Travel and the US's Carlson Travel Network joined forces in 1994 to pursue expansion efforts. Under a dual-president ownership, the parent companies owned operations in specific world regions. The two companies began developing new business technology and expanded into new global business markets.

In 1994 the venture acquired Germany's Brune Reiseburo travel agency and opened a branch office in Moscow. Through 1995 and 1996 acquisitions targeted the Asia/Pacific region, including Hong Kong's and Japan's Dodwell Travel and the corporate travel business of Singapore's Jetset Travel. The company also formed a partnership with Traveland, an Australian travel agency.

In 1997 Wagonlit Travel and Carlson Travel Network finalized the merger of their business activities operations, renamed Carlson Wagonlit Travel. The following year the new company acquired Florida's Travel Agents International, with more than 300 franchised operations and $600 million in annual sales.

In 1999 three travel agencies in eastern Canada consolidated under the Carlson Wagonlit Travel brand, creating the largest travel network in that region. Also, Carlson Companies founder and Carlson Wagonlit Travel chairman Curtis Carlson died.

In 2000 the company agreed to form a Japan-based joint venture with Japan Travel Bureau (now JTB Corp.). Under the arrangement Carlson Wagonlit will increase its presence in Asia and JTB will increase its number of locations in North America.

In 2001 Carlson Wagonlit cut jobs because of a slowdown in business travel.

CEO and President; President, Europe, Middle East, and Africa: Hervé Gourio
President, Asia Pacific: Geoffrey Marshall
President, North America: Robin Schleien
CFO: Tim Hennessy
EVP Associate Division: Roger E. Block
EVP Business Development and Marketing North America: Bob Briggs
EVP Business Travel: Dan Miles
EVP Europe, Middle East, and Africa: Richard Lovell
EVP Global Sales and Account Management: Liliana Frigerio
EVP Supplier Relations: Robert Deliberto
EVP Vacation and Business Travel: Thomas Baumann
CIO: Loren Brown
CFO, Europe, Middle East, and Africa: Nicholas Francou
VP Account Management Business Travel Services, North America: Michael Woodward
VP Human Resources, North America: Cindy Rodahl
VP Information Technology, Europe, Middle East, and Africa: Len Blackwood
VP Finance Americas: Nick Bluhm
Corporate Communications: Steve Loucks
Public Relations: Mollie Quinn

HQ: 1405 Xenium Ln., Plymouth, MN 55441
Phone: 763-212-4000   **Fax:** 763-212-2219
Web: www.carlsonwagonlit.com

American Express
JTB
Kuoni Travel
Maritz
Rosenbluth International
Thomas Cook AG
TUI
WorldTravel

HISTORICAL FINANCIALS & EMPLOYEES

Joint venture FYE: December 31	Annual Growth	12/92	12/93	12/94	12/95	12/96	12/97	12/98	12/99	12/00	12/01
Sales ($ mil.)	3.0%	—	—	—	—	9,500	10,600	11,000	11,000	12,000	11,000
Employees	(16.6%)	—	—	—	—	20,000	20,000	20,100	7,015	7,702	8,083

SALES HISTORY

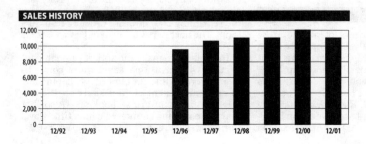

CARNIVAL CORPORATION

The Carnival fleet of ships rules the seven seas. The Miami-based company is the world's #1 cruise operator with six cruise lines and 43 ships catering to more than 2 million passengers each year. (Carnival will sink from the top spot if rival Royal Caribbean completes its merger with P&O Princess Cruises. Carnival has made four separate offers for P&O but has been continually rebuffed by P&O shareholders.) Its Carnival Cruise Lines offers affordable vacation packages primarily to Caribbean locations on its 16 ships, while Holland America offers more luxury-oriented cruises to Europe, South America, and Alaska. Carnival also owns the venerable Cunard Cruise Line and its two ocean liners (*Queen Elizabeth 2* and *Caronia*), the only company offering regularly scheduled passenger service between the UK and America. Carnival's other brands include Windstar, Seabourn, and Italy's Costa Crociere. In addition to cruises, Carnival offers sightseeing tours in Alaska and Canada through Holland America Westours. It sold a 25% stake in UK-based Airtours (now known as MyTravel Group) in 2001.

To maintain its place on the top deck of the cruise industry, Carnival is working to sell its cruises to the 90% of American adults who have never taken one through competitive pricing and by offering more amenities on its ships. It has also launched Web sites for its cruise lines where customers can book their own vacations. But some feel Carnival may be too optimistic about the future: it has committed to building 14 new ships to be launched by 2006, including what will be the world's largest ocean liner, the *Queen Mary 2*. In a move that angered many in the travel agent business, Carnival announced plans to halve agent commissions on the air-travel portion of its cruise bookings in an effort to make its air fare rates more competitive.

Chairman and CEO Micky Arison and his family own 47% of the company. Arison also owns the Miami Heat basketball team. He was identified by *Worth* magazine in 2002 as Miami's wealthiest resident with an estimated worth of $6.2 billion.

HISTORY

Israeli emigrant Ted Arison got into the cruise business in the mid-1960s, forming Norwegian Caribbean Lines with shipping magnate Knut Kloster. After their partnership ended in 1971, Arison persuaded old friend Meshulam Riklis to bankroll his $6.5 million purchase of the *Empress of Canada* in 1972. Riklis owned (among other things) the Boston-based American International Travel Service (AITS). Arison set up

Carnival Cruise Lines as an AITS subsidiary and renamed his ship the *Mardi Gras*. Unfortunately, she ran aground on her maiden voyage, sending Carnival into red ink for three years.

Arison bought out Riklis in 1974 for $1 and assumed Carnival's $5 million debt. He envisioned a cruise line that would offer affordable vacation packages to young, middle-class consumers, and invented a new type of cruise ship featuring live music, gambling, and other entertainment on board. Carnival was profitable within a month, and by the end of the following year, Arison had paid off Carnival's debt and bought its second ship. Arison's son, Micky, became CEO in 1979. Despite the rising costs of shipbuilding and fuel prices, Carnival continued to add to its fleet. It grew to become the world's #1 cruise operator, and the Arisons took Carnival public in 1987.

The company acquired luxury cruise business Holland America Line in 1989 and formed a joint venture with Seabourn Cruise Lines in 1992. Carnival changed its name to Carnival Corporation in 1994 to reflect its diversifying operations, and it took a 50% stake in Seaborn the following year. Carnival stepped up its European expansion in 1996 by buying a stake in UK-based Airtours (now known as MyTravel Group). The next year Carnival and Airtours jointly acquired an interest in European cruise giant Costa Crociere for about $275 million.

Carnival signed a deal with two shipyards in 1998 to build twelve more ships for the company by 2004 (six each for its Carnival and Holland America lines). It also bought a majority-interest in the prestigious Cunard Line (*Queen Elizabeth 2*) that year, merged it with Seabourn, and bought the remainder of the two cruise lines in 1999. An ugly lawsuit reared its head that year after a woman claimed to have been sexually assaulted while on a Carnival ship. Carnival acknowledged that it had received more than 100 other similar complaints against its cruise employees dating back to 1995. (The suit was settled later that year.)

In 2000 the company canceled an agreement to buy time-share company Fairfield Communities (now Fairfield Resorts) due to Carnival's lagging share price. Later in 2000 Carnival acquired the remaining 50% of Costa Crociere from Airtours. The next year, Carnival sold its 25% stake in Airtours.

In an effort to make the air fares sold in connection with cruise packages more competitive, the cruise line announced its plan in 2001 to cut travel agent commissions on the air-travel segment of cruise bookings. Also that year the company countered competitor Royal Caribbean's agreement to merge with P&O

Princess Cruises with its own offer of £2.15 billion. P&O shareholders snubbed the offer but later softened and said it would consider a revised offer, leaving the door open for a bidding war between Carnival and Royal Caribbean. In 2002 Carnival made P&O a series of offers, the latest at £3.8 billion, but it has been continually rejected by P&O shareholders. Also that year the company pleaded guilty to charges of polluting the ocean and falsifying oil-contaminated discharge records. It agreed to pay $18 million in fines and environmental costs, hire overseers to monitor their ships, and hire an environmental standards officer.

OFFICERS

Chairman and CEO: Micky Arison, age 52, $1,951,000 pay
Vice Chairman and COO: Howard S. Frank, age 60, $1,842,000 pay
SVP Audit Services: Richard D. Ames, age 54
SVP Finance and CFO: Gerald R. Cahill, age 50
SVP International: Ian J. Gaunt, age 50
SVP, General Counsel, and Secretary: Arnaldo Perez, age 42
Chairman and CEO, Costa Crociere: Pier Luigi Foschi, age 54
Director; Chairman, President, and CEO, Holland America Line-Westours: A. Kirk Lanterman, age 69
Director; President and COO, Carnival Cruise Lines: Robert H. Dickinson, age 59
President and COO, Cunard Line: Pamela C. Conover, age 46
Director of Human Resources: Susan Herrmann
Auditors: PricewaterhouseCoopers LLP

LOCATIONS

HQ: 3655 NW 87th Ave., Miami, FL 33178
Phone: 305-599-2600 **Fax:** 305-406-4700
Web: www.carnivalcorp.com

2001 Sales

	$ mil.	% of total
US	3,490	77
International	1,046	23
Total	**4,536**	**100**

PRODUCTS/OPERATIONS

2001 Sales

	$ mil.	% of total
Cruises	4,358	96
Tours	230	4
Adjustments	(52)	—
Total	**4,536**	**100**

COMPETITORS

A.B.Sea
Carlson
NCL
Nippon Yusen KK
P&O Princess Cruises
Royal Caribbean Cruises
Royal Olympic Cruise Line
Star Cruises
Walt Disney

HISTORICAL FINANCIALS & EMPLOYEES

NYSE: CCL FYE: November 30	Annual Growth	11/92	11/93	11/94	11/95	11/96	11/97	11/98	11/99	11/00	11/01
Sales ($ mil.)	13.3%	1,474	1,557	1,806	1,998	2,213	2,448	3,009	3,498	3,779	4,536
Net income ($ mil.)	14.4%	277	318	382	451	566	666	836	1,027	966	926
Income as % of sales	—	18.8%	20.4%	21.1%	22.6%	25.6%	27.2%	27.8%	29.4%	25.6%	20.4%
Earnings per share ($)	13.9%	0.49	0.57	0.67	0.79	0.96	1.12	1.40	1.66	1.60	1.58
Stock price - FY high ($)	—	8.50	12.09	13.06	13.56	15.94	27.13	42.63	53.50	51.25	34.94
Stock price - FY low ($)	—	5.63	7.56	10.28	9.56	11.38	14.88	19.00	34.88	18.31	16.95
Stock price - FY close ($)	14.0%	8.06	12.03	10.81	13.00	15.81	27.03	34.50	44.13	22.69	26.11
P/E - high	—	17	21	19	17	16	24	30	32	32	22
P/E - low	—	11	13	15	12	12	13	14	21	11	11
Dividends per share ($)	13.0%	0.14	0.14	0.14	0.15	0.18	0.22	0.30	0.36	0.42	0.42
Book value per share ($)	18.4%	2.45	2.88	3.41	4.12	5.14	6.07	7.20	9.61	10.04	11.24
Employees	9.3%	14,870	15,650	17,250	15,280	18,110	18,100	22,000	25,600	27,000	33,200

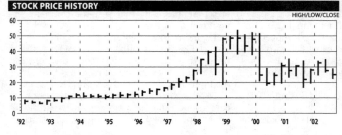

STOCK PRICE HISTORY HIGH/LOW/CLOSE

2001 FISCAL YEAR-END

Debt ratio: 31.0%
Return on equity: 14.9%
Cash ($ mil.): 1,421
Current ratio: 1.32
Long-term debt ($ mil.): 2,955
No. of shares (mil.): 586
Dividends
  Yield: 1.6%
  Payout: 26.6%
Market value ($ mil.): 15,305

CATERPILLAR INC.

Peoria, Illinois-based Caterpillar, like its namesake, is trying to metamorphose and fly away from downturns in the highway construction and agricultural industries. Most people know that Caterpillar (or Cat) is the world's #1 maker of earthmoving machinery and a leading supplier of agricultural equipment, but few realize that engines account for more than one-third of the company's sales. In addition to making engines for its own equipment (and replacement engines), Cat is the largest maker of medium- and heavy-duty truck engines in North America and makes engines for electric power generation systems, locomotives, and for the mining, logging, and oil industries. The company also provides financing and insurance services for Cat customers and dealers.

Although the US accounts for half of Caterpillar's sales, the company operates manufacturing plants on six continents and maintains a global network of some 220 dealers (with 2,700 locations) in about 170 countries. In addition to equipment-related operations, Cat also distributes Cat-branded boots, caps, and jeans, as well as products made by others, such as Daimler-Chrysler auto parts and PUMA sneakers.

Like other manufacturers in the industry, Caterpillar is taking steps to reduce costs. To that end, the company has instituted a 6 Sigma program and set a goal to reduce costs by $1 billion in 2002. The company has seen a downturn in engine sales, but sales of electric power engines and engines designed for the petroleum industry are showing growth.

HISTORY

In 1904 in Stockton, California, combine maker Benjamin Holt modified the farming tractor by substituting a gas engine for steam and replacing iron wheels with crawler tracks. This improved the tractor's mobility over dirt.

The British adapted the "caterpillar" (Holt's nickname for the tractor) design to the armored tank in 1915. Following WWI, the US Army donated tanks to local governments for construction work. The caterpillar's efficiency spurred the development of earthmoving and construction equipment.

Holt merged with Best Tractor in 1925. The company, renamed Caterpillar (Cat), moved to Peoria, Illinois, in 1928. Cat expanded into foreign markets in the 1930s and phased out combine production to focus on construction and road-building equipment.

Sales volume more than tripled during WWII when Cat supplied the military with earthmoving equipment. Returning GIs touted Cat

durability and quality, and high demand continued. Cat held a solid first place in the industry, far ahead of #2 International Harvester.

Moving beyond US borders, Cat established its first overseas plant in the UK (1951). In 1963 it entered a joint venture with Japanese industrial titan Mitsubishi. Cat bought Solar Turbines (gas turbine engines) in 1981. Fifty consecutive years of profits ended, however, when Cat ran up $953 million in losses between 1982 and 1984 as equipment demand fell and foreign competition intensified. Cat doubled its product line between 1984 and 1989 and shifted production toward smaller equipment.

In 1990 CEO Donald Fites reorganized Cat along product lines. The next year the company clashed with the United Auto Workers (UAW) over wage and health benefits. A strike resulted, and Cat reported its first annual loss since 1984. Most of the striking workers returned to work without a contract by mid-1992.

The firm completed a six-year, $1.8 billion modernization program in 1993 that automated many of its plants. That investment benefited the company when almost two-thirds of Cat's UAW employees at eight plants in Colorado, Illinois, and Pennsylvania went on strike in 1994. Company management hired replacement workers and used its foreign factories to help fill orders. In 1995, after two years of record earnings at Cat, the UAW called off the strike. Cat set up a holding company, Caterpillar China Investment Co. Ltd., in 1996 for joint ventures in China.

In 1998 Cat and the UAW (with federal mediation) hammered out their first contract agreement in more than six years. That year Cat paid $1.33 billion for LucasVarity's UK-based Perkins Engines, expanding its capacity to produce small and midsize diesel engines.

Chairman and CEO Fites retired in 1999; vice chairman Glen Barton succeeded him. Cat cut back its workforce and production after slowdowns in the agricultural, mining, and oil exploration industries reduced machinery orders.

In 2000 Cat expanded the range of its marine power systems to include engines below 300 bhp with its purchase of family-owned Sabre Engines Ltd., a UK maker of high-performance marine diesel engines. Late that year the company announced an alliance with DaimlerChrysler to make and market medium-duty engines worldwide. In 2001 Caterpillar announced a restructuring that involved facility consolidation, the retirement of several executives, and the sale of the high-tech MT series tractor line to AGCO.

To secure its equipment financing position on construction and heavy equipment, in early 2002 Cat Financial bought FCC Equipment Financing.

OFFICERS

Chairman and CEO: Glen A. Barton, age 62,
$2,263,006 pay
Group President: Vito H. Baumgartner, age 61,
$1,027,408 pay
Group President: Douglas R. Oberhelman, age 48,
$821,806 pay
Group President: James W. Owens, age 55,
$1,245,933 pay
Group President: Gerald L. Shaheen, age 57,
$1,041,922 pay
Group President: Richard L. Thompson, age 62,
$1,210,933 pay
VP and CFO: F. Lynn McPheeters, age 59
VP; President, Caterpillar Financial Services:
James S. Beard, age 60
VP; President, Caterpillar Industrial:
Richard A. Benson, age 59
VP; President, Perkins Engine Company:
Michael J. Baunton, age 50
VP; President, Solar Turbines: Gary A. Stroup, age 52
VP, General Counsel, and Secretary: James B. Buda,
age 54
VP, Human Services Division: Richard P. Lavin, age 49
Auditors: PricewaterhouseCoopers LLP

LOCATIONS

HQ: 100 NE Adams St., Peoria, IL 61629
Phone: 309-675-1000   **Fax:** 309-675-1182
Web: www.cat.com

2001 Sales

	$ mil.	% of total
United States	10,033	49
Other countries	10,417	51
Total	**20,450**	**100**

PRODUCTS/OPERATIONS

2001 Sales

	$ mil.	% of total
Machinery	12,158	59
Engines	6,869	34
Financial	1,423	7
Total	**20,450**	**100**

Selected Products

Machinery
Backhoe loaders
Log loaders
Log skidders
Mining shovels
Motor graders
Off-highway trucks
Paving products
Pipelayers
Skid steer loaders
Telescopic handlers
Track and wheel excavators, loaders, and tractors
Wheel tractor-scrapers

Engines
Engines for Caterpillar machinery
Engines for electric power generation systems
Engines for marine, petroleum, construction, industrial,
and agricultural applications
Engines for on-highway trucks and locomotives

COMPETITORS

AGCO	Dresser	Komatsu
CNH Global	Ingersoll-Rand	Peugeot Motors
Cummins	Infrastructure	of America, Inc.
Deere	JCB	

HISTORICAL FINANCIALS & EMPLOYEES

NYSE: CAT FYE: December 31	Annual Growth	12/92	12/93	12/94	12/95	12/96	12/97	12/98	12/99	12/00	12/01
Sales ($ mil.)	8.0%	10,194	11,615	14,328	16,072	16,522	18,925	20,977	19,702	20,175	20,450
Net income ($ mil.)	—	(2,435)	652	955	1,136	1,361	1,665	1,513	946	1,053	805
Income as % of sales	—	—	5.6%	6.7%	7.1%	8.2%	8.8%	7.2%	4.8%	5.2%	3.9%
Earnings per share ($)	—	(6.03)	1.52	2.33	2.84	3.50	4.37	4.11	2.63	3.02	2.32
Stock price - FY high ($)	—	15.53	23.28	30.38	37.63	40.50	61.63	60.75	66.44	55.13	56.83
Stock price - FY low ($)	—	10.31	13.47	22.19	24.13	27.00	36.25	39.06	42.00	29.56	39.75
Stock price - FY close ($)	16.3%	13.41	22.25	27.56	29.38	37.63	48.50	46.00	47.06	47.31	52.25
P/E - high	—	—	14	13	13	11	14	15	25	18	24
P/E - low	—	—	8	9	8	8	8	9	16	10	17
Dividends per share ($)	28.0%	0.15	0.15	0.23	0.60	0.75	0.90	1.10	1.25	1.33	1.38
Book value per share ($)	15.3%	3.90	5.40	7.26	8.73	10.81	12.71	14.36	15.45	16.31	13.99
Employees	3.6%	52,340	50,443	53,986	54,352	57,026	59,863	65,824	66,896	68,440	72,004

STOCK PRICE HISTORY

HIGH/LOW/CLOSE

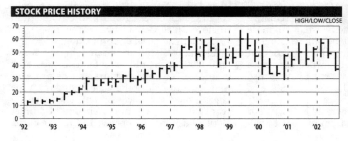

2001 FISCAL YEAR-END

Debt ratio: 66.8%
Return on equity: 14.4%
Cash ($ mil.): 400
Current ratio: 1.30
Long-term debt ($ mil.): 11,291
No. of shares (mil.): 401
Dividends
  Yield: 2.6%
  Payout: 59.5%
Market value ($ mil.): 20,951

CBRL GROUP, INC.

Some say it's not good to live in the past, but for restaurant holding company CBRL Group, it's been fairly profitable. The Lebanon, Tennessee-based company owns the 450-unit Cracker Barrel Old Country Store restaurant chain spanning 40 states. Located primarily on interstate highways, Cracker Barrels are famous for their rustic decor (stone fireplaces, rocking chairs) and country cooking (country ham, turnip greens, grits). The restaurants also feature retail areas where customers can purchase items such as hand-blown glassware, cast iron cookware, and woodcrafts, as well as jellies and old-fashioned candies.

CBRL Group also is home to the Logan's Roadhouse restaurant chain, which includes about 80 company-owned units and 10 franchised locations in 16 states. As the name suggests, Logan's Roadhouse restaurants resemble roadhouses of the 1940s and 1950s with exterior features such as corrugated metal and rough-hewn cedar and interior features such as wooden planked floors and jukeboxes. The restaurants serve steaks, ribs, and fried green tomatoes, among other items.

The company has been the focus of controversy over the years. In 1991 it drew criticism for an openly anti-gay hiring statement that it later rescinded. In 1999 it was the focus of an NAACP racial discrimination suit that alleged discriminatory hiring practices against African Americans. With that case still pending, a group in 2001 filed another racial discrimination suit, this time alleging discriminatory practices toward black customers.

In 2001 CBRL Group sold its gourmet food unit, Carmine Giardini's Gourmet Market, which operated three gourmet markets in Florida. Although CBRL Group intends to keep growing its Cracker Barrel and Logan's Roadhouse chains, the company has scaled back the planned rate of growth to focus on improving its restaurants. Edward Johnson, chairman of FMR Corp., owns about 6% of CBRL Group.

HISTORY

Dan Evins opened the first Cracker Barrel Old Country Store in 1969. As a sales representative for Shell Oil, Evins believed he could sell more gas if he combined gas stations with restaurants. He also envisioned placing his new concept along what was then a relatively new enterprise — the interstate highway system. Evins opened the first Cracker Barrel Old Country Store in Lebanon, Tennessee.

The company was incorporated in 1970. Four years later Evins resigned from his job at Shell Oil to give full attention to his burgeoning restaurant chain, which had grown to a dozen locations. The oil embargo of the mid-1970s prompted the company to back away from the sale of gas, and it completely did away with gas pumps by the mid-1980s. Cracker Barrel went public in 1981.

Company sales slumped in 1985, when a plan to force smaller stores to squeeze out the same amount of revenue as larger stores failed. The company rebounded by remodeling the smaller stores to the dimensions of the larger stores and by creating middle management positions to oversee real estate purchasing, gift shop merchandising, and human resource training. It also introduced an incentive program to reward store managers for curbing costs and increasing sales. Between 1980 and 1990, the company added 84 new restaurants to its rapidly expanding chain.

Controversy struck the company during the 1990s when its old country values clashed with present day reality. In 1991 the company issued a statement declaring that it would no longer employ "individuals whose sexual preferences fail to demonstrate normal heterosexual values." Believing that the sexual orientation of such individuals was not in line with the values of its customer base, the company fired more than a dozen employees. Cracker Barrel rescinded the policy, but the incident deeply scarred the company's image and continued to haunt it throughout the 1990s. The controversy also spurred changes in SEC regulations — a protest by Cracker Barrel stockholders who opposed the policy eventually led to a 1998 SEC decision permitting stockholders to propose resolutions on employment matters.

The company continued opening new restaurants throughout the 1990s. As it expanded beyond the southern states, it also began adapting its menus and decor to the tastes and preferences of each region. With the 1998 purchase of Carmine's Prime Meats, Cracker Barrel expanded the company's interests into gourmet food stores. In keeping with its goal of expanding into other restaurant ventures, the company restructured into the CBRL Group holding company the following year. Also in 1999 the company bought Logan's Roadhouse. A group of African-American employees filed a lawsuit against the company in 1999, claiming racial discrimination.

All Cracker Barrel units were company-owned until 2000, when CBRL executed a sale-leaseback deal for 65 of these restaurants (the proceeds were used to reduce the debt arising from the Logan's Roadhouse acquisition). The following year CBRL sold its Carmine Giardini's Gourmet Market business and opened 15 Cracker Barrel and 13 Logan's restaurants. Even as the 1999 racial discrimination suit was pending, the company in 2001 was hit by a class action discrimination suit by 21 customers claiming that African Americans were seated in segregated areas, denied service, and served food taken from the garbage.

OFFICERS

Chairman: Dan W. Evins, age 66, $1,162,700 pay
President, CEO, and Director: Michael A. Woodhouse, age 56, $927,144 pay
SVP Finance and CFO: Lawrence E. White, age 51, $542,477 pay
SVP, Secretary, and General Counsel: James F. Blackstock, age 54, $379,951 pay
President and COO, Cracker Barrel Old Country Store: Donald M. Turner, age 53, $645,918 pay
President and COO, Logan's Roadhouse: Peter W. Kehayes, age 44
SVP Human Resources: Norman J. Hill
Divisional VP Restaurant Operations, Cracker Barrel Old Country Store: Michael D. Adkins
VP Retail Operations, Cracker Barrel Old Country Store: John W. Boles
VP and Controller, Cracker Barrel Old Country Store: Mattie H. Hankins
VP Government and Community Relations, Cracker Barrel Old Country Store: Bruce C. Cotton
VP Marketing, Cracker Barrel Old Country Store: Paul S. Calkins
SVP Development, Logan's Roadhouse: Ralph W. McCracken
Auditors: Deloitte & Touche LLP

LOCATIONS

HQ: 305 Hartmann Dr., Lebanon, TN 37088
Phone: 615-444-5533   **Fax:** 615-443-9399
Web: www.cbrlgroup.com

CBRL Group has Cracker Barrel Old Country Store restaurants in 40 states. The company's Logan's Roadhouse chain spans 16 states.

PRODUCTS/OPERATIONS

2001 Sales

	$ mil.	% of total
Restaurant	1,544	79
Retail	419	21
Franchise fees & royalties	1	—
Total	**1,964**	**100**

COMPETITORS

Applebee's	Marie Callender
Bob Evans	O'Charley's
Brinker	The Restaurant Company
Buffets	Roadhouse Grill
Carlson Restaurants Worldwide	Ruby Tuesday
	Shoney's
Darden Restaurants	Stuckey's
Denny's	VICORP Restaurants
Furr's	Waffle House
IHOP	Worldwide Restaurant
Investor's Management	Concepts
Luby's	

HISTORICAL FINANCIALS & EMPLOYEES

Nasdaq: CBRL FYE: Friday nearest July 31	Annual Growth	7/92	7/93	7/94	7/95	7/96	7/97	7/98	7/99	7/00	7/01
Sales ($ mil.)	19.3%	401	518	641	783	943	1,124	1,317	1,532	1,773	1,964
Net income ($ mil.)	4.2%	34	46	58	66	64	87	104	70	59	49
Income as % of sales	—	8.5%	8.8%	9.0%	8.4%	6.7%	7.7%	7.9%	4.6%	3.3%	2.5%
Earnings per share ($)	4.0%	0.61	0.78	0.96	1.09	1.04	1.41	1.65	1.16	1.02	0.87
Stock price - FY high ($)	—	24.35	34.25	29.75	27.25	27.38	29.88	43.00	30.50	15.50	24.50
Stock price - FY low ($)	—	13.35	20.84	21.25	17.50	15.75	19.63	26.00	14.81	8.00	11.81
Stock price - FY close ($)	(1.6%)	22.34	26.00	23.25	21.00	21.25	28.63	30.25	15.13	11.88	19.39
P/E - high	—	40	44	31	25	26	21	26	26	15	28
P/E - low	—	22	27	22	16	15	14	15	13	8	13
Dividends per share ($)	8.0%	0.01	0.02	0.02	0.02	0.02	0.02	0.02	0.02	0.01	0.02
Book value per share ($)	16.0%	4.06	6.16	7.18	8.27	9.34	10.81	12.86	13.49	14.63	15.38
Employees	16.1%	14,508	18,035	21,796	26,299	31,683	35,805	38,815	49,314	44,750	55,715

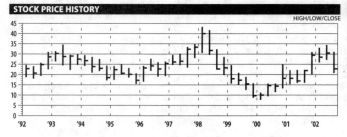

STOCK PRICE HISTORY
HIGH/LOW/CLOSE

2001 FISCAL YEAR-END

Debt ratio: 12.9%
Return on equity: 5.9%
Cash ($ mil.): 12
Current ratio: 0.79
Long-term debt ($ mil.): 125
No. of shares (mil.): 55
Dividends
  Yield: 0.1%
  Payout: 2.3%
Market value ($ mil.): 1,067

CBS TELEVISION NETWORK

The "Tiffany Network" has regained its shine. New York City-based CBS Television Network took second place behind NBC for the 2001-02 ratings season, after winning the #1 spot (ABC ran a very close #2) for the 2000-01 season. The network's usual stable of shows (including *Everybody Loves Raymond, Touched by an Angel,* and *60 Minutes*) appeal to an audience that skews a bit older than those of its rivals, a thorny issue that results in some of its top-rated programs generating lower ad revenue than less popular but "younger" shows from other networks. However the network has gotten a big shot in the arm thanks to its hugely popular *Survivor* franchise. Its new *CSI: Crime Scene Investigation* program is also proving to be a surprise rating hit (placing regularly in the top 10 rated primetime shows).

CBS distributes its programming to more than 200 affiliates including 20 stations owned by parent company Viacom, which bought CBS in 2000 for about $45 billion. CBS, which transferred its cable assets (CMT, TNN) to Viacom's MTV Networks, also owns mega-syndicator King World Productions (*The Oprah Winfrey Show, Wheel of Fortune, Jeopardy!*). The network's investment in Web site MarketWatch.com has been transferred to Viacom. CBS owns 32% of sports Web site SportsLine.com.

CEO Les Moonves, right-hand man of former CBS CEO Mel Karmazin (now Viacom president and COO), orchestrated the network's strategy of appealing to older demographics on the theory that older audiences, as opposed to the 18- to 34-year-olds group more often targeted, actually have money to spend on advertisers' products. CBS has revised that strategy somewhat (in a successful effort to defeat ABC's *Who Wants To Be A Millionaire*) with reality-based shows such as *Survivor* and *Big Brother* that engage younger viewers. *Survivor* set records in its time slot and helped CBS take hold of the #1 spot in the ratings in 2000-01.

CBS and UPN (another Viacom-owned network) have combined operations and are both overseen by Moonves, although he says the two networks will retain separate identities on the air.

HISTORY

Arthur Judson founded radio broadcasting company United Independent Broadcasters (UIB) in 1927. Columbia Phonograph bought UIB's broadcasting rights later that year, and the company was rechristened the Columbia Phonograph Broadcasting System, a moniker later shortened to the Columbia Broadcasting System. When cigar maker Sam Paley took a controlling interest in the company in 1928, he installed his son

William as president, and the younger Paley set about changing the face of broadcasting. He promoted daytime dramas, raided stars from NBC, and built a strong news organization.

CBS branched into TV broadcasting during the 1940s, picking up its Tiffany Network nickname for programming considered classier than the norm. The network found itself red-faced when its *$64,000 Question* was front and center in the 1958 quiz show scandal, but thanks to shows such as *I Love Lucy* and *The Beverly Hillbillies,* CBS was #1 in ratings for much of the 1950s and 1960s.

In spite of a flurry of turnover among top management during the 1970s, programming such as *The Mary Tyler Moore Show* and *All in the Family* helped CBS stay on top in the ratings. Laurence Tisch became CEO in 1987; he led the sale of CBS' publishing and record operations. When William Paley died in 1990, Tisch became chairman.

A stunned CBS lost broadcasting rights to NFL football games and several affiliates to the FOX network in 1994. After a no-confidence vote from one of its top institutional investors the following year, Westinghouse Electric acquired CBS for $5.4 billion.

Committing itself to broadcasting, Westinghouse started selling its non-broadcasting holdings and acquired radio firm Infinity Broadcasting in 1996. It also expanded into cable, buying The Nashville Network and Country Music Television. The company changed its name from Westinghouse to CBS Corporation in 1997.

CBS got back on the gridiron in 1998 when it outbid NBC for an NFL contract ($4 billion over eight years). President and COO Mel Karmazin (former CEO of Infinity Broadcasting) was appointed CEO in 1999 and led CBS to a swarm of Internet acquisitions, including stakes in Hollywood Media Corp., Medscape, Rx.com, and Switchboard. Other deals included the $2.5 billion acquisition of syndication giant King World Productions and an 11-year, $6 billion deal for exclusive rights to the NCAA college basketball championship tournament.

In a mega-deal to keep up with other media giants such as Walt Disney, Time Warner (now part of AOL Time Warner), and News Corp., Viacom bought CBS in 2000 for about $45 billion. Many of CBS' assets, such as its cable networks and radio operations, were reorganized under Viacom. Karmazin became president and COO of Viacom, and Leslie Moonves became CEO of the new CBS Television Network subsidiary. In 2002 the network gained 32% of SportsLine.com, which runs the CBS sports Web site and other sports-related sites. Viacom put fledgling network UPN under the CBS umbrella in 2002, combining management and operations.

OFFICERS

President and CEO; Acting CEO of UPN:
Leslie Moonves, age 52
EVP Communications: Gil Schwartz
EVP Marketing and Communications:
George Schweitzer
EVP: Martin Franks
EVP and General Counsel: Susan J. Holliday
SVP and CFO: Bruce Taub
SVP Diversity: Josie Thomas
SVP Human Resources: Anthony Ambrosio
SVP and Deputy General Counsel: Martin P. Messinger
SVP Drama Series Development: Nina Tassler
SVP Comedy: Wendy Goldstein
SVP Communications, CBS Entertainment:
Chris Ender
VP Broadcast Operations and Engineering: Bob Ross
VP Human Resources: Linda Kalarchian
President, Entertainment: Nancy Tellem
President, News: Andrew Heyward, age 50
President, Sports: Sean McManus
Chairman and CEO, KingWorld Production and CBS
Enterprises: Roger King
President, CBS Broadcasting International:
Armando Nunez Jr.
SVP and General Sales Manager, Domestic Syndication
Sales, KingWorld Entertainment: Joe DiSalvo
Auditors: KPMG LLP

LOCATIONS

HQ: 51 W. 52nd St., New York, NY 10019
Phone: 212-975-4321   **Fax:** 212-975-4516
Web: www.cbs.com

CBS has operations in Los Angeles and New York City.

PRODUCTS/OPERATIONS

Selected Operations
CBS Enterprises
   CBS Broadcast International (foreign distribution)
   King World Productions (domestic syndication)
CBS Entertainment
CBS News
CBS Radio Network
CBS Sports
CBS Television
   CBS.com
   CBSNews.com
Internet properties
   SportsLine.com (32%)
UPN (United Paramount Network)

Selected Programming
48 Hours
The Agency
Becker
CSI:Crime Scene Investigation
CSI:Miami
The District
Everybody Loves Raymond
The Guardian
JAG
Judging Amy
King of Queens
Survivor
Touched By An Angel
Yes, Dear

COMPETITORS

A&E Networks
AOL Time Warner
Discovery Communications
Fox Entertainment
Liberty Media
NBC
Univision
Walt Disney

HISTORICAL FINANCIALS & EMPLOYEES

Subsidiary FYE: December 31	Annual Growth	12/92	12/93	12/94	12/95	12/96	12/97	12/98	12/99	12/00	12/01
Sales ($ mil.)	(1.7%)	8,447	8,875	8,848	6,296	8,449	5,363	6,805	7,373	7,094	7,240
Employees	(17.3%)	109,050	101,654	84,400	77,813	59,275	51,444	46,189	28,900	—	—

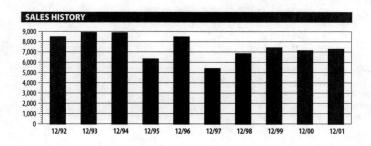

SALES HISTORY

CDW COMPUTER CENTERS, INC.

You can send mail through your computer, so why not get your computer through the mail? Based in Vernon Hills, Illinois, CDW Computer Centers is a leading US direct marketer of computer products, offering more than 80,000 items. The company primarily sells its products through catalogs, over the phone, and online. CDW also has two retail showrooms in Illinois. Business, government, and institutional clients represent about 97% of its sales.

Computers represent nearly 30% of sales. The company offers other hardware (and software) such as printers, accessories, add-on boards, and networking products from companies including 3Com, Hewlett-Packard, Microsoft, Sony, and Toshiba.

CDW is increasing its government and education market share, as well as its breadth of technology lines, focusing on client servers, graphics scanners, and other Internet-related products. Chairman emeritus Michael Krasny owns about 33% of the company.

HISTORY

Michael Krasny started Computer Discount Warehouse at his kitchen table in 1984. Weary of selling used cars at his father's Chicago lot (though he did like using his programming skills to computerize the dealership), Krasny quit and had to sell his own computer to raise cash. A classified ad in the *Chicago Tribune* generated phenomenal response, and Krasny sold his computer almost immediately.

When the calls kept coming in, he bought more computers and sold them to people responding to the original ad, and his mail-order business was under way. Krasny chose new, stripped-down IBM clones, packaged them with monitors and printers, and advertised them as used computer systems. Because PCs were still in their infancy, and customers were lost in the technology, he made a large part of the early business computer setup and repair.

CDW launched its first catalog in 1987. Figuring that some buyers would shy away from purchasing costly PC systems by mail, Krasny in 1990 opened his first retail showroom (one of two) in Chicago.

The company went public in 1993 after changing the name to CDW Computer Centers. By then it had intensified its push into the corporate market, which featured bulk purchases and solid repeat business. Sales that year nearly doubled from 1992. CDW launched an Internet site in 1995. The next year the company expanded its telemarketing-based sales strategy and began taking online orders. Also in 1996 CDW enlarged its Chicago showrooms.

Intense marketing and low prices boosted sales in 1997 with multimedia products, data storage devices, PCs, software, and video products as the fastest sellers. That year the company relocated to a larger facility in Vernon Hills, Illinois. (It moved one of its showrooms there, too.) CDW pushed past the $1 billion mark for the first time in 1997, logging sales of nearly $1.3 billion. The following year the company formed CDW Government, a subsidiary set up to focus on sales to government and education institutions.

In May 2001 Krasny assumed the role of chairman emeritus; president and CEO John Edwardson added chairman to his duties.

OFFICERS

Chairman Emeritus: Michael P. Krasny, age 48
Chairman, President, and CEO: John A. Edwardson, age 52, $1,420,926 pay (partial-year salary)
EVP; President, CDW Government: James R. Shanks, age 37, $788,374 pay
EVP and Director: Daniel B. Kass, age 45, $1,317,359 pay
EVP, Sales: Harry J. Harczak Jr., age 45, $790,189 pay
SVP and CFO: Barbara A. Klein, age 47
SVP, Purchasing and Operations: Douglas E. Eckrote, age 37
VP and CIO: Jonathan J. Stevens, age 32
VP and Controller: Sandra M. Rouhselang
VP, Corporate Secretary, and General Counsel: Christine A. Leahy, age 37
VP, Advertising: Donald M. Gordon
VP, Business Development: Daniel F. Callen
VP, Coworker Services: Arthur S. Friedson, age 47
VP, Marketing: Joseph K. Kremer, age 37
VP, National Sales and Services: Oren J. Hartman, age 31
VP, Sales: James J. Lillis
VP, Training and Sales Recruiting: Maria M. Sullivan
SVP, CDW Government: Larry Kirsch
VP, Program Management, CDW Government: Kevin Adams
Treasurer: Robert Welyki
Auditors: PricewaterhouseCoopers LLP

HQ: 200 N. Milwaukee Ave., Vernon Hills, IL 60061
Phone: 847-465-6000   **Fax:** 847-465-6800
Web: www.cdw.com

CDW Computer Centers has operations in Illinois and
Virginia.

2001 Sales

	% of total
US	
Midwest	
Illinois	12
Other states	15
East	32
West	22
South	18
Other countries	1
Total	**100**

PRODUCTS/OPERATIONS

2001 Sales

	% of total
Software	17
Notebook computers & accessories	15
Data storage devices	15
Desktop computers & servers	13
Printers	13
Networking & communication products	9
Video products	8
Add-on boards & memory	4
Input devices	3
Supplies, accessories, & other	3
Total	**100**

COMPETITORS

Best Buy
Black Box
BUY.COM
Circuit City
Comark
CompuCom
CompUSA
Cyberian Outpost
Dell Computer
Elcom International
En Pointe
Fry's Electronics
Gateway
Insight Enterprises
MCSi
Merisel
Micro Electronics
Micro Warehouse
MoreDirect
Pacific Magtron
PC Connection
PC Mall
PC Warehouse
Pomeroy Computer
RadioShack
Systemax
Zones

HISTORICAL FINANCIALS & EMPLOYEES

Nasdaq: CDWC FYE: December 31	Annual Growth	12/92	12/93	12/94	12/95	12/96	12/97	12/98	12/99	12/00	12/01
Sales ($ mil.)	45.1%	139	271	413	629	928	1,277	1,734	2,561	3,843	3,962
Net income ($ mil.)	71.7%	1	13	12	20	34	51	66	98	162	169
Income as % of sales	—	0.9%	4.7%	2.9%	3.2%	3.7%	4.0%	3.8%	3.8%	4.2%	4.3%
Earnings per share ($)	37.3%	—	0.15	0.16	0.24	0.40	0.59	0.76	1.11	1.79	1.89
Stock price - FY high ($)	—	—	2.38	5.79	10.59	18.50	19.50	25.97	40.00	86.13	56.88
Stock price - FY low ($)	—	—	1.13	2.23	5.09	5.63	9.91	9.00	13.97	22.25	24.88
Stock price - FY close ($)	48.0%	—	2.33	5.69	6.75	14.83	13.03	23.98	39.31	27.88	53.71
P/E - high	—	—	16	36	44	46	33	34	35	46	29
P/E - low	—	—	8	14	21	14	17	12	12	12	13
Dividends per share ($)	—	—	0.00	0.00	0.00	0.00	0.00	0.00	0.00	0.00	0.00
Book value per share ($)	53.4%	—	0.29	0.67	1.23	1.64	2.32	3.15	4.52	7.29	8.80
Employees	40.1%	135	247	390	536	740	986	1,512	1,937	2,700	2,800

STOCK PRICE HISTORY

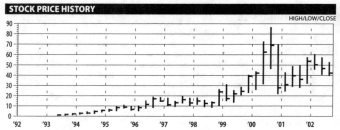

HIGH/LOW/CLOSE

2001 FISCAL YEAR-END

Debt ratio: 0.0%
Return on equity: 23.8%
Cash ($ mil.): 146
Current ratio: 5.39
Long-term debt ($ mil.): 0
No. of shares (mil.): 88
Dividends
  Yield: —
  Payout: —
Market value ($ mil.): 4,752

CELLSTAR CORPORATION

CellStar is good at helping everyday conversations reach new heights. Carrollton, Texas-based CellStar is a leading independent wholesale cellular phone distributor (it competes fiercely with Brightpoint). The company makes three-quarters of its sales to customers outside North America, primarily in countries that lack wireline telecom infrastructure. It distributes products from Nokia, Ericsson, Motorola, and other manufacturers to retailers, carriers, and exporters; the company also operates retail outlets in Asia, Europe, and Latin America. It also provides inventory and logistics management, testing and repair, and wireless activation services.

CellStar has experienced a slight drop in total worldwide sales but the company is making strides in China where cell phone penetration is low but steadily rising. The company has announced plans to exit certain markets — initially Argentina, Peru, and the UK — as it repositions operations in an effort to improve profitability.

Founder Alan Goldfield and his wife own about 35% of the company.

HISTORY

Alan Goldfield started Dallas record store National Tape and Record Center in 1969, later selling car stereos and accessories. In 1981 he formed a relationship with Audiovox that led to a 1984 joint venture to distribute cell phones; in 1988 it began selling phones in Wal-Mart's Sam's Clubs. The company changed its name to CellStar and went public in 1993.

In the early 1990s CellStar opened operations in Mexico, soon branched into other Latin American markets, and became the first company authorized to distribute wireless phones in China (it must buy and sell locally made products and deal in local currency). By 1995 CellStar had 150 retail outlets, and within a year it added 200 more. But rapid expansion depressed earnings.

In 1996 CellStar sold 331 centers located in Sam's Club to MCI and shifted its focus to wholesale. The company started wholesale operations in the UK (1996) and Shanghai and Indonesia (1997), and made acquisitions in Sweden and Poland (1998).

Income fell in fiscal 1998 as CellStar recorded a $29 million investment charge, and shareholder litigation alleging that CellStar had padded sales numbers hit hard when the company settled for $14.5 million. The SEC launched an investigation into the company's finances that year. Also in 1998 CellStar signed an agreement with the Beijing Radio Telecommunications Bureau to be its sole supplier of Motorola cellular phones and accessories and to operate Motorola branded sales outlets for the Bureau. Also in 1998 CellStar introduced an e-commerce site, allowing commercial customers to order mobile phones and accessories via the Internet.

In 1999 CellStar sold all but two of its US retail stores to Baby Bell SBC Communications, cut 10% of its workforce, and consolidated Latin American and North American operations. It bought Dutch distributor Montana Telecommunications that year. Also in 1999 it entered a strategic alliance with Boston Communications Group to market prepaid cellular phones and phone services to international clients.

In 1999 CellStar signed a strategic alliance agreement with Arcoa Communications, Taiwan's largest telecommunications retail store chain, to serve as the primary supplier of Motorola-licensed handsets and accessories to Arcoa's retail stores. CellStar strengthened its ties with Arcoa in early 2000 when it bought a small stake in the Taiwanese retailer.

Despite belt-tightening, CellStar suffered losses for fiscal 2000. Also that year the company signed a joint venture agreement with Asian Internet content provider chinadotcom to provide fulfillment, sales, and distribution for chinadotcom's Wireless Access Protocol (WAP) Internet service. Also in 2000 CellStar signed a deal with Amazon.com to provide logistics, fulfillment support, and service activations for the online retailer's new wireless phones store.

In 2001 Goldfield announced his retirement as chairman and CEO. Board member James L. Johnson was named chairman and Terry S. Parker, former president and COO of CellStar, was named CEO. Goldfield became chairman emeritus. Also in 2001, the SEC dropped its investigation of CellStar.

In 2002 CellStar announced plans to close its Argentina, Peru, and UK operations, in an effort to return to profitability.

OFFICERS

Chairman: James L. Johnson, age 74
President, CEO, and Director: Terry S. Parker, age 56
CFO and Treasurer: Robert A. Kaiser, age 48
SVP, General Counsel, and Secretary:
Elaine Flud Rodriguez, age 44, $265,000 pay
VP, US Sales: Timmy Monico
**Chairman, CEO, and General Manager CellStar (Asia)
Corporation Ltd.:** A. S. Horng, age 43, $800,133 pay
Director, Human Resources: Scott Campbell
Auditors: KPMG LLP

LOCATIONS

HQ: 1730 Briercroft Ct., Carrollton, TX 75006
Phone: 800-466-5000 **Fax:** 800-466-0288
Web: www.cellstar.com

CellStar operates in Chile, China, Colombia, Hong Kong, Mexico, the Netherlands, Singapore, Sweden, Taiwan, and the US.

2001 Sales

	$ mil.	% of total
Asia/Pacific	1,213	50
North America	579	24
Latin America	411	17
Europe	231	9
Total	**2,434**	**100**

PRODUCTS/OPERATIONS

Selected Suppliers
Audiovox
Ericsson
Kenwood
Kyocera
Motorola
NeoPoint
Nokia
Samsung
Sanyo
Qualcomm

Services
Inventory management (order processing, purchasing, returns, and repairs)
Logistics management (tri-party purchasing and custom invoicing)
Multiparty marketing
Package design
Supply chain management
Testing and repair
Web-based procurement (NetXtreme)
Wireless service activation

Subsidiaries
A&S Air Service, Inc.
Audiomex Export Corp.
Celular Express S.A. de C.V. (Mexico)
Florida Properties, Inc.
NAC Holdings, Inc.
National Auto Center, Inc.
Sizemore International B.V. (Netherlands Antilles)
Shanghai CellStar International Trading Co. Ltd. (China)
Shanghai Fengzing CellStar Trading (China)
Shenzhen CellStar Honbo Telecommunication (China)
Sunrise Mobil Sdn Bhd (Malaysia)
Systar Corporation Ltd. (Taiwan)

COMPETITORS

Andrew Corporation
Audiovox
Best Buy
Brightpoint
Casio Computer
Circuit City
Hello Direct
SED International
TESSCO

HISTORICAL FINANCIALS & EMPLOYEES

Nasdaq: CLST FYE: November 30	Annual Growth	11/92	11/93	11/94	11/95	11/96	11/97	11/98	11/99	11/00	11/01
Sales ($ mil.)	33.5%	181	275	518	812	948	1,483	1,996	2,334	2,476	2,434
Net income ($ mil.)	—	0	8	16	23	(6)	54	14	69	(59)	1
Income as % of sales	—	—	2.9%	3.1%	2.8%	—	3.6%	0.7%	3.0%	—	0.0%
Earnings per share ($)	(38.5%)	—	—	1.50	2.05	(0.55)	4.45	1.20	5.60	(4.95)	0.05
Stock price – FY high ($)	—	—	—	34.60	61.91	48.77	124.69	94.06	67.50	65.63	13.50
Stock price – FY low ($)	—	—	—	15.22	26.89	9.59	18.55	15.00	25.00	8.13	3.75
Stock price – FY close ($)	(24.3%)	—	—	30.85	43.77	19.49	64.69	32.19	48.28	8.28	4.40
P/E – high	—	—	—	23	30	—	28	78	12	—	135
P/E – low	—	—	—	10	13	—	4	13	4	—	38
Dividends per share ($)	—	—	—	0.00	0.00	0.00	0.00	0.00	0.00	0.00	0.00
Book value per share ($)	12.1%	—	—	6.88	9.63	9.02	13.75	15.08	20.86	15.72	15.31
Employees	10.6%	524	700	1,250	2,008	1,010	1,100	1,100	1,425	1,300	1,300

STOCK PRICE HISTORY

HIGH/LOW/CLOSE

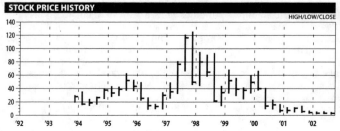

2001 FISCAL YEAR-END

Debt ratio: 0.0%
Return on equity: 0.3%
Cash ($ mil.): 48
Current ratio: 1.25
Long-term debt ($ mil.): 0
No. of shares (mil.): 12
Dividends
  Yield: —
  Payout: —
Market value ($ mil.): 53

CENDANT CORPORATION

Whether you're traveling or ready to settle down, Cendant has a way to serve you. From its headquarters in New York City, Cendant Corporation is the largest hotel franchisor in the world, with such well-known brand names as AmeriHost Inn, Days Inn, Ramada, Super 8, and Howard Johnson. Its mid-market and economy hotels span more than 6,600 locations. Cendant also owns timeshare resort firms Resort Condominiums International and Fairfield Resorts (formerly Fairfield Communities), as well as Avis Group Holdings and its 1,700 worldwide car rental locations.

For those looking for a place to call home, Cendant Real Estate Franchise Group franchises real estate brokerages Century 21, Coldwell Banker, and ERA. It also offers mortgage services and owns NRT, the nation's #1 residential real estate firm and Cendant's top real estate franchisee. Cendant Mobility Services provides corporate relocation services and subsidiary Jackson Hewitt offers tax preparation services.

The company had planned to spin off its direct marketing and membership operations — which offer discount clubs (shopping, dining, and auto) and insurance products — but later decided to license and outsource that business to Trilegiant, a new company formed by the marketing and membership units' management.

Cendant was rocked by a 1998 financial scandal for overstating earnings. The company ended up paying $3.8 billion, the largest securities fraud settlement in history, to resolve ensuing lawsuits. Cendant put itself on the road to recovery by selling off noncore assets, buying back stock, and paying down debt.

The company has been hurt both by post-September 11 jitters in the leisure industry and from indirect fallout related to the Enron scandal. Investors are leery of companies such as Cendant whose off-balance sheet accounting practices and widely dispersed operations mirror those of Enron.

HISTORY

Cendant began life through the 1997 merger of CUC International and HFS. A giant in hospitality, HFS was cobbled together as Hospitality Franchise Systems by LBO specialist Blackstone Group in 1992. With brands including Days Inn, Ramada, and Howard Johnson, HFS went public that year.

In 1995 HFS bought real estate firm Century 21. The next year it added Electronic Realty Associates (ERA) and Coldwell Banker. Also in 1996, HFS acquired the Super 8 Motels brand, as well as car-rental firm Avis. The next year it

sold 75% of Avis' #1 franchisee to the public and later bought relocation service firm PHH.

In an attempt to leverage the power of his brands, HFS CEO Henry Silverman began looking at direct marketing giant CUC International. CUC was founded in 1973 as Comp-U-Card America by Walter Forbes and other investors who envisioned a computer-based home shopping network. During the 1980s CUC developed as a discount direct marketer and catalog-based shopping club. It went public in 1983 with 100,000 members. CUC saw explosive growth as it signed up 7.6 million members between 1989 and 1993. In 1996 CUC acquired Rent Net, an online apartment rental service, and later bought entertainment software publishers Davidson & Associates and Sierra On-Line. In 1997 CUC bought software maker Knowledge Adventure and launched the online shopping site NetMarket.

CUC and HFS completed their $14.1 billion merger in December 1997 with Silverman as CEO and Forbes as chairman. While the name Cendant was derived from "ascendant," the marriage quickly headed in the opposite direction. Accounting irregularities from before the merger that had inflated CUC's revenue and pretax profit by about $500 million were revealed in 1998. Cendant's stock price tumbled, taking a $14 billion hit in one day. Forbes resigned that summer. (Forbes and former vice chairman Kirk Shelton were later indicted on federal fraud charges and sued by the SEC for their part in the scandal.) Silverman quickly took action and began to sell off operations. Cendant Software, National Leisure Group, Match.Com, and National Library of Poetry all were sold that year for a total of about $1.4 billion. The company also acquired Jackson Hewitt, the US's #2 tax-preparation firm, and UK-based National Parking.

Through 1999 the company continued to sell assets. Cendant sold its fleet business — including PHH Vehicle Management Services — to Avis Rent A Car (now Avis Group Holdings) for $5 billion and sold its Entertainment Publications unit, the world's largest coupon book marketer and publisher, to The Carlyle Group.

In 2001 Cendant sought to expand its travel holdings with a slew of acquisitions. Its purchases included the rest of car rental firm Avis Group Holdings it didn't already own, timeshare resort firm Fairfield Communities (renamed Fairfield Resorts), travel services firm Galileo International, online travel reservation service Cheap Tickets, and vacation timeshare marketer Equivest Finance.

In 2002, Cendant agreed to buy Budget Group for about $108 million and assume its $2.7 billion debt to bring it out of bankruptcy. Later that year it agreed to buy Bertelsmann subsidiary TRUST International, a supplier of reservation and distribution databases, to add nonflight revenue to its travel business. It also agreed to buy Novasol AS, which rents out private vacation homes in Northern Europe.

OFFICERS

Chairman, President, and CEO: Henry R. Silverman, age 61, $7,856,760 pay
Vice Chairman and General Counsel:
James E. Buckman, age 57, $2,150,000 pay
Vice Chairman; Chairman and CEO, Hospitality Division: Stephen P. Holmes, age 45, $2,150,000 pay
SEVP and CFO: Kevin M. Sheehan, age 47
SEVP; Chairman and CEO, Financial Services Division and Vehicle Services Division: John W. Chidsey, age 39
SEVP and Chief Strategic Officer; Chairman and CEO, Travel Distribution Division; Chairman, Galileo International: Samuel L. Katz, age 36, $3,538,853 pay
SEVP and Chief Administrative Officer:
Thomas D. Christopoul, age 37
SEVP and Group Managing Director, Cendant Europe, Middle East, and Africa: Scott E. Forbes, age 44
EVP and Deputy General Counsel: Joel R. Buckberg
EVP and CIO: Lawrence E. Kinder
EVP Human Resources: Terence P. Conley
EVP Law and Corporate Secretary: Eric J. Bock
Auditors: Deloitte & Touche LLP

LOCATIONS

HQ: 9 W. 57th St., New York, NY 10019
Phone: 212-413-1800   **Fax:** 212-413-1918
Web: www.cendant.com

2001 Sales

	$ mil.	% of total
US	7,774	88
UK	577	6
Other countries	531	6
Total	**8,882**	**100**

PRODUCTS/OPERATIONS

2001 Sales

	$ mil.	% of total
Vehicle services	3,659	40
Real estate services	1,859	21
Hospitality	1,522	17
Financial services	1,402	16
Travel distribution	437	5
Other	3	1
Total	**8,882**	**100**

COMPETITORS

Accor	Enterprise Rent-	QVC
Amadeus	A-Car	RE/MAX
AutoNation	Experian	Sabre
Bank of America	Fingerhut	Sears
Best Western	GMAC	Six Continents
Budget Group	H&R Block	Hotels
Choice Hotels	Hertz	USAA
Citigroup	Hilton	Worldspan
Concepts Direct	Interval	
Conseco Finance	International	
Direct Marketing	J. C. Penney	
Dollar Thrifty	Marriott	
Automotive	International	
Group	Prudential	

HISTORICAL FINANCIALS & EMPLOYEES

NYSE: CD FYE: December 31	Annual Growth	1/93	1/94	1/95	1/96	1/97	*12/97	12/98	12/99	12/00	12/01
Sales ($ mil.)	31.8%	739	875	1,045	1,415	2,348	5,315	5,284	5,402	3,930	8,882
Net income ($ mil.)	23.2%	59	87	118	163	164	55	540	(55)	602	385
Income as % of sales	—	8.0%	10.0%	11.3%	11.5%	7.0%	1.0%	10.2%	—	15.3%	4.3%
Earnings per share ($)	5.7%	0.25	0.34	0.45	0.56	0.41	0.06	0.61	(0.07)	0.81	0.41
Stock price - FY high ($)	—	8.61	17.68	16.13	26.18	27.50	34.38	41.69	26.94	26.31	21.53
Stock price - FY low ($)	—	5.12	7.38	11.12	15.29	18.34	19.25	6.50	13.63	8.13	9.63
Stock price - FY close ($)	10.3%	8.09	14.24	15.40	24.60	24.88	34.38	19.31	26.56	9.63	19.61
P/E - high	—	34	52	36	47	67	491	65	—	29	46
P/E - low	—	20	22	25	27	45	275	10	—	9	20
Dividends per share ($)	—	0.00	0.00	0.00	0.00	0.00	0.00	0.00	0.00	0.00	0.00
Book value per share ($)	31.4%	0.62	1.13	1.72	2.57	3.12	5.38	5.80	3.12	3.77	7.23
Employees	30.0%	5,000	6,000	6,500	8,000	11,000	34,000	35,000	28,000	28,000	53,000

* Fiscal year change

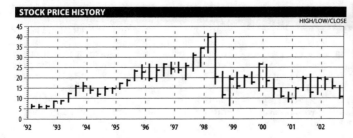

STOCK PRICE HISTORY

HIGH/LOW/CLOSE

2001 FISCAL YEAR-END

Debt ratio: 68.8%
Return on equity: 7.8%
Cash ($ mil.): 1,971
Current ratio: 0.84
Long-term debt ($ mil.): 15,575
No. of shares (mil.): 978
Dividends
 Yield: —
 Payout: —
Market value ($ mil.): 19,173

CENTERPOINT ENERGY, INC.

CenterPoint Energy (formerly Reliant Energy) has become much more than a reliable local utility, but it is taking steps back toward its roots. The Houston-based utility holding company has evolved from a Texas electricity provider into a power broker with expanding energy interests throughout the US and in Western Europe. CenterPoint Energy changed its name in 2002 as part of a restructuring plan; the firm also plans to separate its regulated and nonregulated operations into two companies.

CenterPoint Energy's main stomping ground is Texas, where it generates 14,000 MW of primarily fossil-fueled electricity that it distributes to 1.7 million customers in its hometown and along much of the Texas Gulf Coast. As part of its reorganization and in response to Texas' energy deregulation (which took effect in 2002), CenterPoint Energy has transferred its Texas retail power supply business to nonregulated subsidiary Reliant Resources. The firm has also separated its Texas power generation and distribution operations. The company's natural gas distribution subsidiaries serve about 3 million customers (nearly 1 million are also Texas electricity customers) in the south-central US and Minnesota and operate 8,100 miles of pipeline.

Majority-owned Reliant Resources handles its parent's nonregulated activities. The unit has grown to become one of the leading energy marketers in North America. It operates independent power plants with a capacity of 20,000 MW, and it markets and trades energy in Europe and North America.

As the finances of wholesale energy companies have come under scrutiny, the SEC has issued a formal investigation into "round-trip" energy trades completed by Reliant Resources. These activities artificially inflated the company's trading volumes and led it to restate its 1999, 2000, and 2001 financial results; it has also reduced its energy marketing and trading workforce by about 35%. CenterPoint Energy plans to continue restructuring by spinning off its remaining 83% stake in Reliant Resources to shareholders. The company is also selling its Latin American operations.

HISTORY

CenterPoint Energy's earliest predecessor, Houston Electric Lighting and Power, was formed in 1882 by a group including Emanuel Raphael, cashier at Houston Savings Bank, and Mayor William Baker. In 1901 General Electric's financial arm, United Electric Securities Company, took control of the utility, which became Houston Lighting & Power (HL&P). United

Electric sold HL&P five years later; by 1922 HL&P ended up in the arms of National Power & Light Company (NP&L), a subsidiary of Electric Bond & Share (a public utility holding company that had been spun off by General Electric).

In 1942 NP&L was forced to sell HL&P in order to comply with the 1935 Public Utility Holding Company Act. As the oil industry boomed in Houston after WWII, so did HL&P.

HL&P became the managing partner in a venture to build a nuclear plant on the Texas Gulf Coast in 1973. Construction on the South Texas Project, with partners Central Power and Light and the Cities of Austin and San Antonio, began in 1975. Houston Industries (HI) was formed in 1976 as the holding company for HL&P.

By 1980 the nuke was four years behind schedule and over budget. HL&P and its partners sued construction firm Brown & Root in 1982 and received a $700 million settlement in 1985. (The City of Austin also sued HL&P for damages but lost.) The nuke was finally brought online in 1988, with the final cost estimated at $5.8 billion.

Meanwhile, HI diversified into cable TV in 1986 by creating Enrcom (later Paragon Communications) through a venture with Time Inc. Two years later it bought the US cable interests of Canada's Rogers Communications. HI left the cable business in 1995, selling out to Time Warner.

Developing Latin fever, HI joined a consortium that bought 51% of Argentinean electric company Edelap in 1992. (However, in 1998 HI sold its stake to AES.) On a roll, HI acquired 90% of Argentina's electric utility EDESE (1995); joined a consortium that won a controlling stake in Light, a Brazilian electric utility (1996); and bought interests in three electric utilities in El Salvador (1998).

Back in the US, HI acquired gas dealer NorAm for $2.5 billion in 1997. The next year it bought five generating plants in California from Edison International and laid plans to build merchant plants in Arizona (near Phoenix), Illinois, Nevada (near Las Vegas, in partnership with Sempra Energy), and Rhode Island. Overseas, HI finished a power plant in India in 1998. It also bought a 65% interest in Colombian electric utilities Electricaribe and Electrocosta; Light bought about 75% of Metropolitana (Sao Paulo, Brazil).

In 1999 HI became Reliant Energy and HL&P became Reliant Energy HL&P. That year the company bought a 52% stake in Dutch power generation firm UNA; it bought the remaining 48% the next year. Also in 2000 Reliant Energy paid Sithe Energies $2.1 billion for 21 power plants in the mid-Atlantic states. It sold its operations in Brazil, Colombia, and El Salvador that year, and transferred all of its nonregulated operations to subsidiary Reliant Resources.

Reliant Energy netted about $1.7 billion in 2001 from the sale of nearly 20% of Reliant Resources to the public. Later that year, Reliant Resources announced that it would acquire US independent power producer Orion Power Holdings in a $4.7 billion deal; the deal was completed in 2002. Deregulation took effect in Texas that year, and Reliant Energy transferred its retail power supply business to Reliant Resources.

Reliant Energy announced plans in 2001 to form a new holding company, CenterPoint Energy, for itself and Reliant Resources; it completed the name change in 2002.

LOCATIONS

HQ: 1111 Louisiana St., Houston, TX 77002
Phone: 713-207-3000   **Fax:** 713-207-3169
Web: www.reliantenergy.com

CenterPoint Energy has regulated operations in Arkansas, Louisiana, Minnesota, Mississippi, Oklahoma, and Texas.

OFFICERS

Chairman, President, and CEO; Chairman and CEO, Reliant Resources: R. Steve Letbetter, age 54, $2,723,020 pay
Vice Chairman; President and COO, Reliant Resources: Stephen W. Naeve, age 54, $1,342,250 pay
Vice Chairman; President and COO, Regulated Operations; Manager, CenterPoint Energy Houston Electric: David M. McClanahan, age 52, $1,080,700 pay
Vice Chairman; President, Retail Group; EVP, Reliant Resources: Robert W. Harvey, age 46, $1,342,250 pay
EVP and CFO, CenterPoint Energy and Reliant Resources: Mark M. Jacobs
EVP, General Counsel, and Corporate Secretary; SVP, General Counsel, and Corporate Secretary, Reliant Resources: Hugh Rice Kelly, age 59
SVP Human Resources: Preston R. Johnson Jr.
Auditors: Deloitte & Touche LLP

PRODUCTS/OPERATIONS

2001 Sales

	$ mil.	% of total
Wholesale energy	35,158	74
Electric operations	5,505	12
Gas distribution	4,742	10
European energy	1,192	3
Pipelines & gathering	415	1
Retail energy	211	—
Other	25	—
Adjustments	(1,022)	—
Total	**46,226**	**100**

COMPETITORS

Ameren	Duke Energy	PG&E
AEP	Dynegy	Sempra Energy
Aquila	El Paso	Southern
Avista	Entergy	Company
BP	Exelon	Tractebel
Cinergy	Iberdrola	TXU
Constellation	Koch	Williams
Energy Group	Mirant	Companies
Dominion	Peabody Energy	

HISTORICAL FINANCIALS & EMPLOYEES

NYSE: CNP FYE: December 31	Annual Growth	12/92	12/93	12/94	12/95	12/96	12/97	12/98	12/99	12/00	12/01
Sales ($ mil.)	29.2%	4,596	4,324	4,002	3,730	4,095	6,873	11,489	15,303	29,339	46,226
Net income ($ mil.)	9.5%	435	416	399	1,106	405	421	(141)	1,849	447	981
Income as % of sales	—	9.5%	9.6%	10.0%	29.6%	9.9%	6.1%	—	12.1%	1.5%	2.1%
Earnings per share ($)	7.9%	1.69	1.60	1.62	4.46	1.66	1.66	(0.50)	5.18	1.56	3.35
Stock price - FY high ($)	—	23.44	24.88	23.88	24.50	25.63	27.25	33.38	32.50	49.00	50.45
Stock price - FY low ($)	—	20.06	21.25	15.00	17.69	20.50	18.88	24.44	22.75	19.75	23.27
Stock price - FY close ($)	1.6%	22.94	23.81	17.81	24.25	22.63	26.75	32.06	22.88	43.31	26.52
P/E - high	—	18	16	14	5	15	16	—	6	32	16
P/E - low	—	15	13	9	4	12	11	—	4	13	7
Dividends per share ($)	0.1%	1.49	1.50	1.50	1.50	1.50	1.50	1.50	1.50	1.50	1.50
Book value per share ($)	4.8%	14.84	14.64	15.57	17.23	16.06	16.58	14.59	18.05	18.58	22.64
Employees	4.3%	11,576	11,350	11,498	8,891	8,100	12,711	12,916	14,256	15,633	16,958

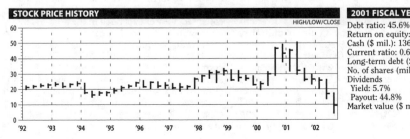

STOCK PRICE HISTORY HIGH/LOW/CLOSE

2001 FISCAL YEAR-END
Debt ratio: 45.6%
Return on equity: 15.9%
Cash ($ mil.): 136
Current ratio: 0.65
Long-term debt ($ mil.): 5,742
No. of shares (mil.): 303
Dividends
  Yield: 5.7%
  Payout: 44.8%
Market value ($ mil.): 8,034

CENTEX CORPORATION

Centex has built its way to the top: The Dallas-based company's Centex Homes unit is one of the largest US home builders, along with Lennar, behind industry leader Pulte Homes. Centex also buys and develops land, provides mortgage loans and insurance to home buyers, and offers commercial contracting and construction services.

Centex Homes, which targets both first-time buyers and move-up buyers, builds houses that range in price from $63,000 to $2.2 million (the average price is about $214,000). The company operates in the US in 23 states, most heavily in the South Central, Southeast, and Mid-Atlantic regions, and in Washington, DC. More than 85% of its homes are single-family detached houses; townhomes and low-rise condominiums make up the balance. Centex also has holdings in Latin America and the UK, including British builder Fairclough Homes, and it owns Cavco Industries, a leading builder of manufactured homes.

The company's commercial building arm, Centex Construction Group, has projects in both the private sector (such as office and apartment buildings) and public sector (such as schools and government buildings). Almost a quarter of the group's sales are derived from the construction of health care facilities.

Centex has cemented its position among the top domestic home builders by offering home-related products and services. Its 65%-owned subsidiary, Centex Construction Products, makes and sells gypsum wallboard, aggregates, and ready-mix concrete. CTX Mortgage makes loans to about 70% of its parent's homebuyers. The firm's Centex HomeTeam Services subsidiary provides pest control and security services; it has sold its chemical lawn care operations to The Scotts Company (Ohio) and will use proceeds of the sale to expand its Centex Pest Management operations.

HISTORY

Tom Lively and Ira Rupley, who built their first large subdivision near Dallas in 1949, founded home builder Centex the next year. Centex's first out-of-Texas project was a development of 7,000 houses near Chicago.

By 1960 it had built 25,000 houses. Branching out from home building, Centex built its first cement plant in 1963 and established four more over the next 25 years. Centex expanded into commercial construction with the 1966 purchase of Dallas contractor J. W. Bateson (founded in 1936). In the 1970s it picked up other general contractors, moving into Florida, California, and Washington, DC. To combine home building with home financing, Centex began mortgage banking in 1973, and when oil prices soared during the 1970s, the enterprising company formed subsidiary Cenergy to go digging for petroleum (spun off in 1984).

Centex increasingly built outside its Southwest territory — from 28% of all new homes in 1979 to 45% in 1984. Larry Hirsch, a New York-reared lawyer who had headed a Houston cement and energy company, became COO in 1984 (and CEO in 1988). The early 1980s was a boom time for Texas real estate as deregulation spurred S&Ls to make loans — any loans. The market became overbuilt, and when oil prices collapsed in 1986 and 1987, credit dried up. With the spectacular failure of several Texas S&Ls, the Texas real estate market crashed. Centex was pinched, but it survived on sales from less-depressed areas of the US.

Centex Development was established in 1987 as a custodian for land the company could not develop during the bust. Centex created Centex Rodgers Construction that year to focus on construction of medical facilities. In 1994 the company took its construction products division public and sold off its S&Ls.

In 1995 Centex entered ventures to build luxury houses in the UK and living centers for sufferers of Alzheimer's disease and memory disorders. The next year Centex purchased parts of security firm Advanced Protection Systems and pest-control company Environmental Safety Systems — both are now part of Centex HomeTeam.

The company was selected by *Builder* and *Home* magazines in 1997 to build the Home of the Future, showcasing cutting-edge products and design. On the other end of the housing spectrum, Centex acquired an 80% stake in manufactured-home maker Cavco Industries (it bought the rest in 2000). The next year Cavco bought AAA Homes, which had about 260 manufactured-home retail outlets in 12 states, Canada, and Japan. Also in 1998 Centex entered Ohio and New Jersey by acquiring Wayne Homes and Calton Homes, respectively. Centex went further abroad in 1999: It bought UK builder Fairclough Homes from AMEC.

In 2000 Centex joined other leading home builders to form HomebuildersXchange, a supply chain services Web site, but the project soon collapsed. Centex expanded in the Midwest by acquiring Detroit home builder Selective Group in 2001. It also acquired City Homes, a Dallas luxury townhome and condo builder. In 2002 the company's Centex HomeTeam Services subsidiary sold its chemical lawn care operations, including 12 branches in Florida, Georgia, and Texas, to The Scotts Company (Ohio); it plans to expand its pest management business with the proceeds of the sale.

OFFICERS

Chairman and CEO: Laurence E. Hirsch, age 56, $4,950,000 pay
President, COO, and Director; Chairman, Centex Homes: Timothy R. Eller, age 53, $5,135,234 pay
EVP and CFO: Leldon E. Echols, age 46, $1,662,500 pay
EVP, Chief Legal Officer, General Counsel, and Secretary: Raymond G. Smerge, age 57, $1,260,000 pay
SVP, Administration: Michael S. Albright
SVP, Finance: Lawrence Angelilli
SVP, Strategic Planning and Marketing: Robert S. Stewart
President and CEO, Mid-Atlantic Division, Centex Construction Company: John P. Tarpey
SVP and Director of Operations, Mid-Atlantic Division, Centex Construction Company: Steven Smithgall
Chairman and CEO, Centex Construction Group; Chairman, Centex Rooney Construction Co., Inc.: Bob L. Moss
Auditors: Ernst & Young LLP

LOCATIONS

HQ: 2728 N. Harwood St., Dallas, TX 75201
Phone: 214-981-5000   **Fax:** 214-981-6859
Web: www.centex.com

Centex builds houses in 79 markets in 23 states in the US (Arizona, California, Colorado, Florida, Georgia, Illinois, Indiana, Maryland, Michigan, Minnesota, Nevada, New Jersey, New Mexico, North Carolina, Ohio, Oregon, Pennsylvania, South Carolina, Tennessee, Texas, Utah, Virginia, and Washington) and the District of Columbia. It also invests in homebuilding activities in Latin America and the UK.

PRODUCTS/OPERATIONS

2002 Sales

	$ mil.	% of total
Homebuilding	4,985	64
Construction services	1,296	17
Financial services	700	9
Construction products	471	6
Investment real estate	72	1
Other	224	3
Total	**7,748**	**100**

COMPETITORS

Barratt Developments
Beazer Homes
C.F. Jordan
Countrywide Credit
David Weekley Homes
Del Webb
D.R. Horton
FleetBoston
Fluor
Foster Wheeler
George Wimpey
Hovnanian Enterprises
KB Home
Kimball Hill Homes
Lennar
M.D.C. Holdings

MGIC Investment
M/I Schottenstein Homes
NVR
Peter Kiewit Sons'
PMI Group
Pulte Homes
Rollins
Ryland
SBC Communications
Taylor Woodrow
Thos. S. Byrne
Toll Brothers
Turner Corporation
Tyco International
Whiting-Turner

HISTORICAL FINANCIALS & EMPLOYEES

NYSE: CTX FYE: March 31	Annual Growth	3/93	3/94	3/95	3/96	3/97	3/98	3/99	3/00	3/01	3/02
Sales ($ mil.)	13.4%	2,503	3,215	3,278	3,103	3,785	3,976	5,155	5,956	6,711	7,748
Net income ($ mil.)	22.6%	61	85	92	53	107	145	232	257	282	382
Income as % of sales	—	2.4%	2.7%	2.8%	1.7%	2.8%	3.6%	4.5%	4.3%	4.2%	4.9%
Earnings per share ($)	22.8%	0.96	1.29	1.51	0.91	1.80	2.36	3.75	4.22	4.65	6.11
Stock price - FY high ($)	—	17.31	22.88	16.19	18.00	21.00	41.63	45.75	42.88	46.20	63.09
Stock price - FY low ($)	—	9.94	13.38	10.06	11.75	12.63	16.75	26.38	17.50	20.63	28.03
Stock price - FY close ($)	14.1%	15.81	15.44	12.13	15.50	17.63	38.13	33.38	23.81	41.65	51.93
P/E - high	—	18	18	11	19	11	17	12	10	10	10
P/E - low	—	10	10	7	13	7	7	7	4	4	4
Dividends per share ($)	5.4%	0.10	0.10	0.10	0.10	0.10	0.12	0.16	0.16	0.16	0.16
Book value per share ($)	15.7%	9.29	10.56	11.90	12.71	14.40	16.65	20.17	24.14	28.60	34.60
Employees	10.7%	6,500	8,430	6,395	6,186	8,926	10,259	13,161	13,368	13,000	16,249

STOCK PRICE HISTORY

HIGH/LOW/CLOSE

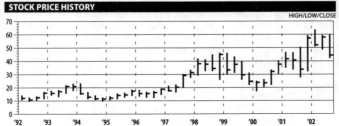

2002 FISCAL YEAR-END

Debt ratio: 71.4%
Return on equity: 20.0%
Cash ($ mil.): 220
Current ratio: 5.18
Long-term debt ($ mil.): 5,277
No. of shares (mil.): 61
Dividends
  Yield: 0.3%
  Payout: 2.6%
Market value ($ mil.): 3,177

CERIDIAN CORPORATION

Ceridian wants to be the king of number crunching. The Minneapolis-based company's Human Resource Services unit (nearly 75% of sales) is a leading provider of human resources information systems, payroll and tax services, employee training, and related services and software. It serves customers in the US, Canada, and the UK. Ceridian's Comdata unit provides services to the transportation industry, including fuel cards, licensing, and fuel tax reporting. In 2001 the company spun off its Arbitron subsidiary, which measures radio and TV audiences to help advertisers decide where to spend their money most effectively.

Having divested its defense electronics business and other remnants of its predecessor, Control Data Corporation, Ceridian is firmly focused on information services. The company is using acquisitions to expand its human resources outsourcing capabilities.

HISTORY

Ceridian has its roots in Control Data Corporation (CDC), which William Norris founded in 1957 to challenge IBM in mainframe computers for scientific applications. A WWII cryptologist, Norris helped found Engineering Research Associates (ERA) after the war. ERA sold to Remington Rand and formed the nucleus of Sperry Rand (now Unisys). Norris managed Sperry Rand's UNIVAC division, where Seymour Cray (who later founded Cray Computers and Cray Research) created a pioneering line of computers.

During the 1960s and 1970s CDC was a powerhouse. It bought more than 80 companies, primarily in peripherals and data services. The company's service segment grew substantially in 1973 when, in the settlement of an antitrust suit, CDC was allowed to buy IBM's service bureau for less than market value. CDC also began providing lease financing services through the 1968 purchase of Commercial Credit Company. During this period Norris directed the company into social remediation projects, building facilities in low-income areas and offering benefits such as day care and counselling.

In the early 1980s CDC plunged into supercomputers and encountered heated competition. It also entered the fiercely competitive semiconductor business. These operations sucked cash out of the organization and never became profitable.

Norris retired following huge losses in 1985. His successor, Robert Price, divested several operations, including Commercial Credit. Sales rose modestly and then fell again. Price resigned and Lawrence Perlman was brought in as CEO in 1990. He turned the company away from proprietary systems and made alliances with other manufacturers, including Silicon Graphics and Volkswagen (to develop computer-assisted engineering and manufacturing software). But new cost controls could not overcome the effects of recession in the early 1990s, and sales remained weak.

As part of a broad restructuring in 1992, Perlman spun off CDC's mainframe, computer leasing, and disk drive units, and changed the company's name to Ceridian (a fictitious word).

The remaining company consisted of the human resources and benefits administration operations, Arbitron media services, and Defense Electronics. Reaching for a common thread, Ceridian redefined itself as a diversified information services company. Bankrolled by higher earnings at last, plus about $1 billion in tax credits from its past losses, the company shopped for acquisitions. In 1995 it bought Comdata, a provider of information services to the trucking industry and of cash advances to casinos. In 1996 the company acquired nine additional human resources and transportation services companies.

In 1997 Ceridian expanded its information business to the UK through the purchase of Continental Research. Later that year it exited the defense electronics business by selling Computing Devices International to General Dynamics for $600 million. In 1998 the company swapped Comdata's casino services unit for First Data's trucking services business and bought the payroll division of Canadian Imperial Bank of Commerce, among others.

Ceridian in 1999 bought competitor ABR Information Services (benefits and payroll services, now part of the Human Resource Solutions unit) for $750 million. It jumped on the Web later that year with the purchase of Powerpay, a maker of online payroll transaction software. In 2000 president and COO Ronald Turner, a former CEO at GEC-Marconi Electronic Systems who joined Ceridian in 1993, replaced Perlman as CEO.

In 2001 the company spun off its Arbitron division in order to focus Ceridian on its human resources and Comdata businesses. The company partnered with ChoicePoint in 2002 to offer the Web-based pre-employment screening service ScreenNow.

OFFICERS

Chairman, President, and CEO: Ronald L. Turner,
age 55, $1,083,750 pay (prior to promotion)
EVP and CFO: John R. Eickhoff, age 61, $617,416 pay
EVP; President, Ceridian Employer/Employee Services:
Tony G. Holcombe, age 46, $603,334 pay
EVP; President, Comdata: Gary A. Krow, age 47,
$574,160 pay
EVP; General Manager, Stored Value Systems:
Mike Berry
EVP, Secretary, and General Counsel: Gary M. Nelson,
age 50, $366,992 pay
SVP Human Resources: Shirley J. Hughes, age 56
SVP LifeWorks: Sharon A. Stein
President, Ceridian Canada: Richard Ball
Managing Director, Ceridian Centrefile: Bruce Thew
VP and Controller: Loren D. Gross, age 56
VP Investor Relations: Craig Manson
VP, Deputy Secretary, and Associate General Counsel:
William E. McDonald
Director Employee Benefits: Peggy Hammond
Director, Executive and Employee Communications:
Linda Falch
Public Relations, Ceridian Centrefile: Ron Wood
Public Relations, Ceridian Canada: Amanda LeRougetel
Marketing, Ceridian HR Solutions: Patrick Smyth
Auditors: KPMG LLP

LOCATIONS

HQ: 3311 E. Old Shakopee Rd., Minneapolis, MN 55425
Phone: 952-853-8100   **Fax:** 952-853-4068
Web: www.ceridian.com

Ceridian has offices in Canada, the UK, and the US.

2001 Sales

	$ mil.	% of total
US	1,008	85
Canada	105	9
UK	69	6
Total	**1,182**	**100**

PRODUCTS/OPERATIONS

2001 Sales

	$ mil.	% of total
Human Resource Services	866	73
Comdata	316	27
Total	**1,182**	**100**

COMPETITORS

Administaff
ADP
Best Software
Century Business Services, Inc.
Gevity HR
Paychex
ProBusiness Services
Spherion
TEAM America
TeamStaff
The Ultimate Software Group

HISTORICAL FINANCIALS & EMPLOYEES

NYSE: CEN FYE: December 31	Annual Growth	12/92	12/93	12/94	12/95	12/96	12/97	12/98	12/99	12/00	12/01
Sales ($ mil.)	4.0%	830	886	916	1,333	1,496	1,075	1,162	1,342	1,176	1,182
Net income ($ mil.)	—	(393)	(30)	79	59	182	472	190	149	100	55
Income as % of sales	—	—	—	8.6%	4.4%	12.2%	44.0%	16.3%	11.1%	8.5%	4.6%
Earnings per share ($)	—	—	—	—	—	—	—	—	—	—	0.41
Stock price - FY high ($)	—	—	—	—	—	—	—	—	—	—	20.55
Stock price - FY low ($)	—	—	—	—	—	—	—	—	—	—	12.50
Stock price - FY close ($)	—	—	—	—	—	—	—	—	—	—	18.75
P/E - high	—	—	—	—	—	—	—	—	—	—	56
P/E - low	—	—	—	—	—	—	—	—	—	—	34
Dividends per share ($)	—	—	—	—	—	—	—	—	—	—	0.00
Book value per share ($)	—	—	—	—	—	—	—	—	—	—	7.24
Employees	0.8%	8,800	7,600	7,500	10,200	10,800	8,000	9,600	10,600	9,600	9,415

STOCK PRICE HISTORY

HIGH/LOW/CLOSE

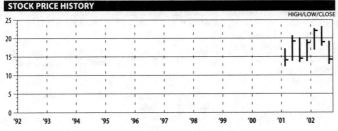

2001 FISCAL YEAR-END

Debt ratio: 18.2%
Return on equity: 0.5%
Cash ($ mil.): 139
Current ratio: 1.48
Long-term debt ($ mil.): 236
No. of shares (mil.): 146
Dividends
  Yield: —
  Payout: —
Market value ($ mil.): 2,747

C.H. ROBINSON WORLDWIDE, INC.

Still trucking along without any trucks, C.H. Robinson Worldwide (CHR) brokers shipping to more than 15,000 customers. Although planeless, rail-less, boatless, and truckless, CHR is never feckless as it transports more than 2.5 million shipments a year through 40 US states, Canada, and Mexico, as well as countries in Europe and South America. The Eden Prairie, Minnesota-based company is one of the largest providers of third-party logistics in North America, with 140 offices and contracts with some 20,000 motor carriers. CHR also procures and distributes fresh produce, provides customs brokerage, and offers T-Chek, a "smart card" fueling service for truckers.

Because almost 90% of its transportation revenue comes from the trucking industry, CHR is expanding its over-the-road business by acquiring logistics providers for less-than-truckload carriers. The company is also in it for the short-haul: It is forming regional transportation networks with its branch offices. CHR employees own a large share of the company, and chairman Sid Verdoorn controls 7% of the firm.

HISTORY

In the early 1900s Charles H. Robinson began a produce brokerage in Grand Forks, North Dakota. Robinson entered a partnership in 1905 with Nash Brothers, the leading wholesaler in North Dakota, and C.H. Robinson (CHR) was born. Robinson became president but soon relinquished control under mysterious circumstances (rumor had it he ran off with Annie Oakley). H. B. Finch took charge, and by 1913 a new company, Nash Finch, became CHR's sole owner. As a subsidiary, CHR primarily procured produce for Nash Finch, which helped it expand into Illinois, Minnesota, Texas, and Wisconsin. To avoid FTC scrutiny over preferential treatment, Nash Finch split CHR into two: C.H. Robinson Co., owned by CHR employees, which sold produce to Nash Finch warehouses; and C.H. Robinson, Inc., owned by Nash Finch.

After WWII the interstate highway system and refrigerated trucks changed the industry. No longer dependent on railroads, CHR began charging for truck brokerage of perishables. The two companies formed by the 1940s split reunited under the C.H. Robinson name in the mid-1960s; Nash Finch kept a 25% stake in the company and sold the rest to employees. Not surprisingly, Nash Finch wanted to divert CHR profits to its other businesses, so in 1976 CHR employees bought out Nash Finch.

The next year D.R. "Sid" Verdoorn was named president and Looe Baker became chairman.

The two focused on increasing CHR's data-processing capability and adding branch offices. In 1980 the Motor Carrier Act deregulated the transportation industry, and CHR entered the freight-contracting business, acting as a middleman for all types of goods. The company grew rapidly, from about 30 offices in 1980 to more than 60 in 1990.

As part of its overall effort to become a full-service provider, CHR formed its Intermodal Division (more than one mode of transport) in 1988. It also established an information services division (1991) and bought fruit juice concentrate distributor Daystar International (1993). By this time the company was working with more than 14,000 shippers and moving more than 500,000 shipments a year.

Meanwhile, CHR had ventured overseas with the launch of its international division in 1989. It entered Mexico in 1990 and added airfreight operations and international freight forwarding through the 1992 purchase of C.S. Green International. In 1993 CHR picked up a 30% stake in French motor carrier Transeco (acquiring the rest later) and opened offices in Mexico City, Chile, and Venezuela.

In 1997 the company went public and became C.H. Robinson Worldwide; the next year Verdoorn, who was CEO, assumed the additional role of chairman. CHR also acquired the Argentinian Comexter transportation group in 1998 as an entry into South America's Mercosur market, which includes Argentina, Brazil, Paraguay, and Uruguay.

CHR expanded its European operation in 1999 through the purchase of Norminter, a French third-party logistics provider. Much closer to home, CHR bought Eden Prairie-based Preferred Translocation Systems, a logistics provider to less-than-truckload carriers, and Chicago-based transportation provider American Backhaulers.

In 2000 the company teamed up with PaperExchange.com, Inc., the global e-business marketplace for the pulp and paper industry, to provide an exclusive logistics service to PaperExchange.com members.

CHR continued to expand in 2002 with the purchase of Miami-based Smith Terminal Transportation Services. Also that year, Verdoorn stepped down as CEO; president Wiehoff assumed the position.

OFFICERS

Chairman: D.R. (Sid) Verdoorn, age 63, $549,017 pay (prior to title change)
President, CEO, and Director: John P. Wiehoff, age 40, $665,609 pay (prior to promotion)
SVP and Director: Barry W. Butzow, age 55, $517,617 pay

SVP and Director: Gregory D. Goven, age 50, $516,400 pay
VP and CFO: Chad M. Lindbloom, age 37
VP and CIO: Paul A. Radunz, age 45
VP, Secretary, and General Counsel: Owen P. Gleason, age 50
VP International: Joseph J. Mulvehill, age 48, $355,913 pay
VP Produce: Michael T. Rempe, age 48
VP Transportation: James V. Larsen, age 48
VP Transportation: Timothy P. Manning, age 37
VP Transportation: Mark A. Walker, age 44
VP: Scott A. Satterlee, age 33
Treasurer: Troy A. Renner, age 37
Corporate Controller: Thomas K. Mahlke, age 30
Director Organizational Resources: Colleen Zwach
Account Manager: Mike Ralston
Branch Manager: Ty Angelus
Corporate Transportation: Molly DuBois
Transportation Sales: Yvonne Belk
Auditors: Deloitte & Touche LLP

LOCATIONS

HQ: 8100 Mitchell Rd., Eden Prairie, MN 55344
Phone: 952-937-8500   **Fax:** 952-937-6714
Web: www.chrobinson.com

C.H. Robinson Worldwide has offices in 40 US states and in Argentina, Belgium, Brazil, Canada, Chile, France, Germany, Italy, Mexico, Poland, Spain, the UK, and Venezuela.

2001 Sales

	$ mil.	% of total
US	2,960	96
Other countries	130	4
Total	**3,090**	**100**

PRODUCTS/OPERATIONS

Services
Transportation (truck, rail, ship, and air transportation through third parties)
Sourcing (fresh produce sourcing and distribution to wholesalers, grocery chains, and food service companies)
Information Services (online Internet-based services including fuel purchase contracts, fuel tax reporting, fleet management and payroll; freight payments through electronic funds transfer)

Selected Subsidiaries
C.H. Robinson Company
C.H. Robinson Company (Canada) Ltd.
C.H. Robinson de Mexico, S.A. de C.V.
C.H. Robinson International, Inc.
C.H. Robinson Poland Sp. Zo.
Comexter Cargo, Inc.
Comexter Robinson S.A. (Argentina)
Comexter Trading Company
Robinson Europe, S.A. (France)
Robinson Logistica Do Brasil Ltda. (Brazil)
T-Chek Systems, Inc.
Wagonmaster Transportation Co.

COMPETITORS

BAX Global
Bilspedition
CNF
CSX
DSC Logistics
EGL
Exel
Expeditors International
FedEx
GeoLogistics
Hub Group
J. B. Hunt
Koninklijke Frans Maas Groep
Ryder
Schneider National
Swift Transportation
UPS Freight Services
USFreightways

HISTORICAL FINANCIALS & EMPLOYEES

Nasdaq: CHRW FYE: December 31	Annual Growth	12/92	12/93	12/94	12/95	12/96	12/97	12/98	12/99	12/00	12/01
Sales ($ mil.)	13.8%	969	1,096	1,258	1,446	1,606	1,791	2,038	2,261	2,882	3,090
Net income ($ mil.)	20.0%	16	20	27	32	35	28	43	53	71	84
Income as % of sales	—	1.7%	1.9%	2.2%	2.2%	2.2%	1.5%	2.1%	2.4%	2.5%	2.7%
Earnings per share ($)	30.3%	—	—	—	—	—	0.34	0.52	0.65	0.83	0.98
Stock price - FY high ($)	—	—	—	—	—	—	13.25	13.50	21.03	32.94	32.25
Stock price - FY low ($)	—	—	—	—	—	—	9.88	7.19	12.00	17.16	22.82
Stock price - FY close ($)	26.8%	—	—	—	—	—	11.19	12.97	19.88	31.44	28.92
P/E - high	—	—	—	—	—	—	39	26	32	39	32
P/E - low	—	—	—	—	—	—	29	14	18	20	23
Dividends per share ($)	—	—	—	—	—	—	0.00	0.13	0.14	0.16	0.20
Book value per share ($)	25.8%	—	—	—	—	—	1.68	2.06	2.92	3.51	4.21
Employees	15.3%	1,050	1,183	1,403	1,436	1,665	1,925	2,205	3,125	3,677	3,770

STOCK PRICE HISTORY

HIGH/LOW/CLOSE

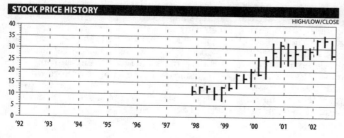

2001 FISCAL YEAR-END

Debt ratio: 0.0%
Return on equity: 25.7%
Cash ($ mil.): 116
Current ratio: 1.56
Long-term debt ($ mil.): 0
No. of shares (mil.): 84
Dividends
  Yield: 0.7%
  Payout: 20.4%
Market value ($ mil.): 2,442

CHAMPION ENTERPRISES, INC.

Its homes may not be so mobile, but Champion Enterprises is still leading the race. Based in Auburn Hills, Michigan, Champion is the #1 maker of manufactured housing in the US. Champion's roughly 40 factories make single-section and multi-section manufactured homes (nearly 80% of sales) that sell for $15,000 to $150,000 and range from 400 sq. ft. to 4,000 sq. ft. The company sells homes in the US and western Canada through independent retailers and about 120 company-owned locations in 27 US states. Other operations include HomePride Finance, which serves retailers and customers by financing Champion purchases, and Champion Development, a developer of manufactured-housing communities. First Pacific Advisors owns 12% of Champion.

In response to increased consumer-finance requirements, high inventory levels, and excess retail locations in the industry, Champion has idled almost 30 manufacturing plants and closed about 175 retail sales facilities since mid-1999. The company has formed HomePride National Mortgage, LP, a real estate financing joint venture with Ohio-based National City Mortgage Co., to provide its Champion Home Center members with real estate mortgages, as well as Veterans Administration and Federal Housing Administration loans.

HISTORY

Champion Home Builders started in 1953, just in time to take advantage of the burgeoning postwar American economy and the passage of a 1956 law allowing mobile homes to be up to 10 feet wide. The increase made mobile homes increasingly popular — by 1960 a majority were "10-wides." The change shifted the main benefit of mobile homes from mobility to affordability. Champion prospered and it went public in 1962. By the mid-1960s the company was one of the leaders in its market.

Part of Champion's success could be attributed to its vertically integrated manufacturing process. Champion made and installed all the components in a home, from plumbing to drapes. This policy increased efficiency, and productivity was twice that of most of its rivals. Despite these advantages, the mid-1970s recession hit the company hard. Industry sales fell about a third from their 1972 peak. Champion felt the recession's brunt in its mobile-home sales, but sales of recreational vehicles (RVs) and low-priced motor homes helped temper the losses. The increase of prices for site-built housing helped Champion and other mobile-home makers out of the slump.

At the start of the 1980s, Champion recovered briefly, but by the mid-1980s the company was again struggling. By 1990 the firm had lost $30 million over the previous five years and was considering bankruptcy proceedings. Walter Young took over that year and quickly revamped the company. To stave off bankruptcy, Young sold some businesses (RV making and component manufacturing) for much-needed cash. Young also gutted the central office and eliminated 248 of 260 jobs.

In 1993 Champion settled on a growth strategy involving both internal sales and acquisitions. The company soon acted on its plan by purchasing Dutch Housing in 1994 and Chandeleur Homes and Crest Ridge Homes a year later.

Champion acquired Redman Industries, the #3 US manufactured-housing builder at the time (Champion was #2). The acquisition pushed Champion to the top spot that year in terms of sales. In addition, Champion opened five new plants that combined with the Redman purchase increased the number of plants Champion operated from 23 to 50. Champion also became vertically integrated from manufacturing to delivery by acquiring a company to provide in-house freight-haul services of its home components to retail and home-building sites.

In 1998 Champion sold its midsize-bus business to narrow its focus on housing. That year the company bought manufactured-housing seller The ICA Group, operator of 23 retail outlets. In 1999 Champion bought Care Free Homes (Utah), Central Mississippi Manufactured Housing, Homes of Merit (Florida), and Heartland Homes (Texas). That year the company created Champion Development Corporation and acquired Phoenix Land Development for developing manufactured-housing communities.

Although sales increased, Champion's profits nearly halved in 1999 because of bad inventory control, excess retail sites, and tighter consumer financing requirements. In response, the company closed or consolidated eight manufacturing plants and streamlined and upgraded inventory-control processes.

Slowing demand and increased competition forced the company to close more than 60 retail outlets and seven of its factories in 2000. The company idled two additional factories and 30 more retail centers in 2001. The next year Champion announced plans to close an additional 64 retails centers and seven manufacturing plants. The company formed a joint venture with loan originator National City Mortgage Co. to provide real estate financing under the name HomePride National Mortgage, LP.

Chairman, President, and CEO: Walter R. Young Jr.,
age 57, $1,193,182 pay
COO: Philip C. Surles, age 60, $719,568 pay
EVP and CFO: Anthony S. Cleburg, age 49,
$803,068 pay
SVP, General Counsel, and Secretary:
John J. Collins Jr., age 50, $471,353 pay
VP and Controller: Richard P. Hevelhorst, age 54
VP, Human Resources: Hugh G. Beswick
VP, Investor Relations: Colleen T. Bauman
VP, Marketing: Grover Tarlton
President, Genesis Homes: Roger D. Lasater
President, Retail Operations: M. Mark Cole, age 40,
$513,832 pay
President, East Manufacturing Region: B. J. Williams
President, West Manufacturing Region:
Richard A. Brugge
President, Central Retail Region: Edward B. Lasater
President, Eastern Retail Region: Gary L. Good
President, Midwestern Retail Region:
Christopher L. Richter
President, Western Retail Region: Robert S. Bagwell
Auditors: PricewaterhouseCoopers LLP

LOCATIONS

HQ: 2701 Cambridge Ct., Ste. 300,
Auburn Hills, MI 48326
Phone: 248-340-9090 **Fax:** 248-340-9345
Web: www.champent.com

Champion Enterprises manufactures its homes at
roughly 40 plants located throughout the US and
western Canada. The company operates a network of 117
company-owned and 618 independent retail Champion
Home Centers in 27 states in the US.

PRODUCTS/OPERATIONS

2001 Sales

	$ mil.	% of total
Manufacturing	1,296	74
Retail	453	26
Adjustments	(201)	—
Total	**1,548**	**100**

Selected Subsidiaries
Champion Development Corp.
Champion Home Builders Co.
Champion Retail, Inc.
Chandeleur Homes, Inc.
Crest Ridge Homes, Inc.
Dutch Housing, Inc.
Grand Manor, Inc.
HomePride Finance Corp.
Homes of Legend, Inc.
Homes of Merit, Inc.
Moduline International, Inc.
Redman Industries, Inc.

COMPETITORS

American Homestar	Horton Industries
Bingham Financial	KIT Manufacturing
Cavalier Homes	Liberty Homes
Cavco	Nobility Homes
Clayton Homes	Oakwood Homes
Coachmen	Palm Harbor Homes
Dynamic Homes	Patriot Homes
Fairmont Homes	Pioneer Housing
Fleetwood Enterprises	Skyline
Four Seasons Housing	Southern Energy Homes
General Housing	Sunshine Homes

HISTORICAL FINANCIALS & EMPLOYEES

NYSE: CHB FYE: Saturday nearest Dec. 31	Annual Growth	12/92	12/93	12/94	12/95	12/96	12/97	12/98	12/99	12/00	12/01
Sales ($ mil.)	23.3%	235	342	616	798	1,644	1,675	2,254	2,489	1,922	1,548
Net income ($ mil.)	—	3	11	27	32	54	75	94	50	(147)	(28)
Income as % of sales	—	1.2%	3.3%	4.4%	4.0%	3.3%	4.5%	4.2%	2.0%	—	—
Earnings per share ($)	—	0.09	0.30	0.96	1.14	1.09	1.54	1.91	1.02	(3.12)	(0.59)
Stock price - FY high ($)	—	2.72	4.94	10.16	15.50	26.13	21.25	30.00	27.38	8.44	13.75
Stock price - FY low ($)	—	0.72	2.28	4.38	6.78	11.88	13.75	17.50	7.88	2.31	2.81
Stock price - FY close ($)	18.7%	2.63	4.41	7.63	15.44	19.50	20.56	27.38	8.50	2.75	12.31
P/E - high	—	30	14	10	13	23	13	15	26	—	—
P/E - low	—	8	7	4	6	11	9	9	8	—	—
Dividends per share ($)	—	0.00	0.00	0.00	0.00	0.00	0.00	0.00	0.00	0.00	0.00
Book value per share ($)	18.6%	1.22	1.59	2.62	3.70	4.75	6.02	8.39	9.39	6.27	5.63
Employees	19.7%	2,100	2,800	4,500	2,300	11,000	11,300	14,000	15,000	12,000	10,600

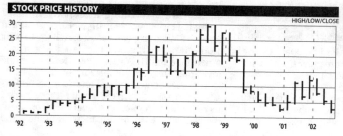

STOCK PRICE HISTORY HIGH/LOW/CLOSE

2001 FISCAL YEAR-END
Debt ratio: 45.3%
Return on equity: —
Cash ($ mil.): 70
Current ratio: 1.18
Long-term debt ($ mil.): 225
No. of shares (mil.): 48
Dividends
  Yield: —
  Payout: —
Market value ($ mil.): 595

CHARLES SCHWAB

My, how times change. Once strictly a discount broker, San Francisco-based Schwab now offers services typical of the traditional brokers it rebelled against some 25 years ago; its purchase of U.S. Trust did nothing to reverse that trend.

Schwab's main business is still as the world's #1 discount brokerage, making trades for investors who make their own decisions. The company's other services include trading by phone, wireless device, or the Internet; futures and commodities trading; access to IPOs; and investment educational material. A top mutual fund distributor, Schwab's Mutual Fund MarketPlace offers retail and institutional clients more than 3,200 funds from 400 fund families, while its One-Source offers investors some 1,300 no-load funds. The firm's online financial services mix also includes mortgages via a partnership with E-Loan. Founder Charles Schwab owns 19% of the company.

Schwab has nearly 400 US offices. Its World Trade Center offices were destroyed by the terrorist attacks, but the company did not lose any of its New York staff. Although the firm has recently cut back on overseas business, Schwab has exported its no-frills concept to the UK, Asia, and the Pacific Rim and has introduced Web sites in Chinese, Korean, and Spanish.

Like its rivals, the firm has been fighting to keep the cooling economy from chilling its revenues. After ramping up its branch and online trading operations, Schwab is now facing a decline in trading activity as investors shy away from stocks. In January 2002 the company reported its first losing quarter in nearly 15 years. In light of the decreased business during the slowdown, the firm has cut about 25% of its workforce since the end of 2000, with the most recent decrease of about 5% coming in summer 2002. The company has refocused its strategy to concentrate primarily on the US market. In keeping with this strategy, Schwab plans to expand into new areas of domestic service and has cut workers at each of its overseas branches, including the complete shutdown of operations in Japan and Australia. In addition, the firm sold its Canadian operations (Charles Schwab Canada) to Bank of Nova Scotia in February 2002.

HISTORY

During the 1960s Stanford graduate Charles Schwab founded First Commander Corp., which managed investments and published a newsletter. But he failed to properly register with the SEC, and after a hiatus, he returned to the business under the name Charles Schwab & Co. in 1971. Initially a full-service broker, Schwab moved into discount brokerage after the SEC outlawed fixed commissions in 1975. While most brokers defiantly raised commissions, Schwab cut its rates steeply.

From 1977 to 1983 Schwab's client list increased thirtyfold, and revenues grew from $4.6 million to $126.5 million, enabling the firm to automate its operations and develop cash-management account systems. To gain capital, Charles sold the company to BankAmerica (now Bank of America) in 1983. Schwab grew, but federal regulations prevented expansion into such services as mutual funds and telephone trading. Charles bought his company back in 1987 and took it public. When the stock market crashed later that year, trading volume fell by nearly half, from 17,900 per day. Stung, Schwab diversified further, offering new fee-based services. Commission revenues fell from 64% of sales in 1987 to 39% in 1990, but by 1995 the long bull market had pushed commissions to more than 50%.

In 1989 Schwab introduced TeleBroker, a 24-hour Touch-Tone telephone trading service available in English, Spanish, Mandarin, or Cantonese.

Schwab continued to diversify, courting independent financial advisors. Other buys included Mayer & Schweitzer (1991, now Schwab Capital Markets), an OTC market maker that accounted for about 7% of all Nasdaq trades. In 1993 the firm opened its first overseas office in London, but traded only in dollar-denominated stocks until it bought Share-Link (now Charles Schwab Europe), the UK's largest discount brokerage, in 1995.

During the next year Schwab made a concerted effort to build its retirement services by creating a 401(k) administration and investment services unit. In 1997 Schwab allied with J.P. Morgan, Hambrecht & Quist (now J.P. Morgan H&Q), and Credit Suisse First Boston (CSFB) to give its customers access to IPOs; the next year the relationship with CSFB deepened to give Schwab access to debt offerings. In late 1997 and early 1998, Schwab reorganized to reflect its new business lines. The firm also began recruiting talent rather than promoting from within.

Expansion was key at the turn of the century. In 1999 Schwab formed Charles Schwab Canada and started a joint venture in Japan with firms led by Tokio Marine & Fire Insurance. It also linked up with FMR and Spear, Leeds, & Kellogg to offer after-hours trading and partnered with rivals Ameritrade and TD Waterhouse to form an online investment bank to compete in the IPO market.

That year Schwab moved toward more broker-advised investing: It inked a deal (geared toward its retirement products customers) with online financial advice firms Financial Engines and mPower.com, and introduced Velocity, a desktop system designed to make trading easier for fiscally endowed investors. In 2000 Schwab bought on-line broker CyBerCorp (now CyberTrader), as well as U.S. Trust, which markets to affluent clients.

Schwab and TD Waterhouse teamed to buy British stock market maker Aitken Campbell in 2001. Also that year, Schwab made plans to expand its products by offering hedge funds to less affluent ($1.5 million net worth) customers.

OFFICERS

Chairman and Co-CEO: Charles R. Schwab, age 64, $650,003 pay
President, Co-CEO, and Director: David S. Pottruck, age 54, $650,003 pay
Vice Chairman and President, Schwab Institutional: John Philip Coghlan, age 50, $499,125 pay
Vice Chairman and President, Schwab Capital Markets: Lon Gorman, age 53, $499,125 pay
Vice Chairman, Technology and Administration: Dawn G. Lepore, age 49, $526,388 pay
EVP and CFO: Christopher V. Dodds, age 42
EVP and Director: Jeffery S. Maurer, age 54, $526,330 pay
EVP and Director: H. Marshall Schwarz, age 65, $673,442 pay
EVP, Global Support Services: Parkash P. Ahuja
EVP, International: William L. Atwell
EVP, Corporate Services: Walter W. Bettinger III
EVP, Technology Services: David E. Dibble
EVP, Corporate Oversight, General Counsel, and Secretary: Carrie E. Dwyer
EVP; CEO, CyberTrader: James M. Hackley
Auditors: Deloitte & Touche LLP

LOCATIONS

HQ: The Charles Schwab Corporation
101 Montgomery St., San Francisco, CA 94104
Phone: 415-627-7000   **Fax:** 415-636-5970
Web: www.schwab.com

Charles Schwab has more than 360 branch offices in Canada, the Cayman Islands, Hong Kong, Puerto Rico, the UK, the US, and the US Virgin Islands.

PRODUCTS/OPERATIONS

2001 Sales

	$ mil.	% of total
Interest	1,857	35
Asset management & administration fees	1,675	32
Commissions	1,355	26
Principal transactions	255	5
Other	139	2
Total	**5,281**	**100**

COMPETITORS

American Express	Jones Financial
Ameritrade	Companies
Citigroup	Merrill Lynch
Datek Online	Morgan Stanley
E*TRADE	Prudential
FMR	Quick & Reilly/Fleet
Harrisdirect	Raymond James Financial
John Hancock Financial	UBS PaineWebber
Services	U. S. Bancorp Piper Jaffray

HISTORICAL FINANCIALS & EMPLOYEES

NYSE: SCH FYE: December 31	Annual Growth	12/92	12/93	12/94	12/95	12/96	12/97	12/98	12/99	12/00	12/01
Sales ($ mil.)	21.6%	909	1,097	1,263	1,777	2,277	2,845	3,388	4,713	7,139	5,281
Net income ($ mil.)	10.5%	81	118	135	173	234	270	349	589	718	199
Income as % of sales	—	8.9%	10.7%	10.7%	9.7%	10.3%	9.5%	10.3%	12.5%	10.1%	3.8%
Earnings per share ($)	8.0%	0.07	0.09	0.11	0.15	0.19	0.22	0.29	0.47	0.51	0.14
Stock price - FY high ($)	—	1.25	1.90	1.83	4.30	4.88	9.84	22.84	51.69	44.77	33.00
Stock price - FY low ($)	—	0.55	0.82	1.18	1.64	2.67	4.51	6.17	16.97	22.47	8.13
Stock price - FY close ($)	37.9%	0.86	1.60	1.73	2.99	4.75	9.33	18.74	25.51	28.38	15.47
P/E - high	—	18	19	15	29	24	43	79	105	88	550
P/E - low	—	8	8	10	11	13	20	21	35	44	136
Dividends per share ($)	16.7%	0.01	0.01	0.02	0.02	0.03	0.03	0.04	0.04	0.04	0.04
Book value per share ($)	33.2%	0.23	0.32	0.41	0.54	0.72	0.96	1.19	1.84	3.05	2.99
Employees	17.8%	4,500	6,500	6,500	9,200	10,400	12,700	13,300	18,853	25,800	19,600

STOCK PRICE HISTORY

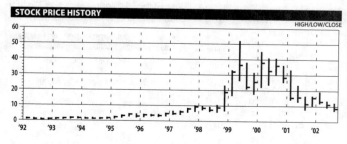

HIGH/LOW/CLOSE

2001 FISCAL YEAR-END

Debt ratio: 14.9%
Return on equity: 4.7%
Cash ($ mil.): —
Current ratio: —
Long-term debt ($ mil.): 730
No. of shares (mil.): 1,392
Dividends
 Yield: 0.3%
 Payout: 28.6%
Market value ($ mil.): 21,529

CHARMING SHOPPES, INC.

At Charming Shoppes, bigger is better. Based in Bensalem, Pennsylvania, Charming Shoppes is the leader among US plus-sized clothing retailers. The company's August 2001 purchase of the Lane Bryant chain from The Limited (which has since changed its name to Limited Brands) added about 650 stores to its already more than 500 plus-sized apparel stores that operate under the Catherine's Plus Sizes, Added Dimensions, The Answer, and Fashion Bug Plus names. The mainly strip mall-based retailer also operates about 1,250 Fashion Bug stores that carry sizes for all ages and shapes (girls, juniors, misses, and plus sizes). The company caters to low- to middle-income women and teens with brand-name and private-label sportswear, dresses, coats, lingerie, shoes, and accessories.

Through a joint venture with upscale UK retailer Monsoon, Charming Shoppes plans to open stores in the US under the Monsoon and Accessorize labels. Charming Shoppes is closing its Added Dimensions and The Answer chains (80 stores) and 130 underperforming Fashion Bug stores, as well as converting about 45 Fashion Bug stores to the Lane Bryant concept.

HISTORY

Morris and Arthur Sidewater opened their first women's apparel store, called Charm Shoppes, in Philadelphia in 1940. Morris, a buyer with apparel company Associated Merchandising, and Arthur, who performed as a dancer on tour with Red Skelton, were challenged from the start: Legal notice came during their first week that the "Charm" name was already taken. The brothers responded by changing the name of the store to Charming Shoppes.

By the end of the 1940s, the brothers began taking on partners to add new stores, with the new partners becoming store managers of the outlets they opened. In 1951 the brothers formed what would become the most significant of their partnerships with a friend of Arthur's, David Wachs, and David's brother Ellis. That year the Sidewater and Wachs brothers opened a store in Norristown, Pennsylvania; later they added another store in Woodbury, New Jersey.

During the 1960s the pairs of brothers moved to follow the steady flight of consumers to malls and large shopping centers, opening new stores in those areas under the Fashion Bug name and renaming old stores. By 1971, the year the company went public, Charming Shoppes operated 21 stores and had a total of 18 partners. As rent at the mall climbed in the mid-1970s, the company began expanding into cheaper strip malls, where rents were less than half those in enclosed malls.

As it entered the 1980s, Charming Shoppes operated nearly 160 stores. That decade marked a period of rapid expansion for the company. Charming Shoppes began opening Fashion Bug Plus stores (and departments within existing stores), featuring sizes for larger women. By 1985 it had more than 500 stores (about 65% of which were located in strip malls). That year the company expanded its product line by adding fashions for preteens.

During the last half of the decade, Charming Shoppes began changing its selection from name brands to private brands. In 1988 David became CEO, replacing Morris, who had served as CEO since the company went public. Although sales had increased unabated for two decades, shrinking profits led the company to curtail expansion, but only slightly. By the end of 1989, it operated more than 900 outlets.

Charming Shoppes continued to grow and increase sales, adding menswear in the early 1990s. With more than 1,400 stores in 1995, the company named Dorrit Bern, a former group VP of apparel and home merchandise at Sears, as CEO. That year Charming Shoppes reported its biggest loss of $139 million. Bern promptly laid off a third of the company's workforce. She closed nearly 300 poorly performing stores and revamped Charming Shoppes' merchandising strategy, stemming losses in 1996 and bringing the company back to profitability the next year.

In 1998 Charming Shoppes closed another 65 poorly performing stores, replacing them with about 65 new sites. Restructuring charges contributed to a loss for fiscal 1999. Charming Shoppes bought plus-sized chain Modern Woman and integrated the stores with its acquisition of 436-store plus-sized retailer Catherines Stores.

Charming Shoppes positioned itself as a leader in plus-size women's apparel in 2001 with the $335 million purchase of plus-size apparel chain Lane Bryant (with more than 650 stores) from retailer The Limited.

In 2002 Charming Shoppes announced the closing of about 200 stores, including its Added Dimensions, The Answer, and 130 Fashion Bug stores. It also planned to move about 45 Fashion Bug stores under the Lane Bryant banner.

OFFICERS

Chairman, President, and CEO: Dorrit J. Bern, age 52, $1,300,000 pay
EVP and CFO: Eric M. Specter, age 44, $455,000 pay
EVP and COO: Joseph M. Baron, age 54
EVP, General Counsel, and Secretary: Colin D. Stern, age 53, $382,000 pay
EVP, Sourcing: Erna Zint, age 58, $400,000 pay

EVP and Corporate Director of Human Resources:
Anthony A. DeSabato, age 53, $355,000 pay
SVP and Chief Administrative Officer, Lane Bryant:
Jeffery Warzel, age 45, $447,376 pay
SVP, Real Estate: Jonathon Graub, age 43
SVP, Supply Chain Managment: James G. Bloise
VP and Corporate Controller: John J. Sullivan, age 55
VP and Director of Stores: Larry Lombardi
VP, Associate General Counsel, and Assistant
Secretary: Kathleen H. Lieberman
VP, Corporate and Store Support: Jon A. Goldberg
VP, Corporate Planning and Customer Database:
Christine Rudy
VP, Credit: Kirk R. Simme
VP, Distribution and Transportation:
William P. Mancuso
VP, Marketing: Carmen Monaco, age 55
VP, Merchandising: Rachel A. Ungaro
President, Catherines Stores: Lorna E. Nagler, age 44
President, Fashion Bug: Elizabeth Williams, age 47,
$525,736 pay
Auditors: Ernst & Young LLP

LOCATIONS

HQ: 450 Winks Ln., Bensalem, PA 19020
Phone: 215-245-9100   **Fax:** 215-633-4640
Web: www.charmingshoppes.com

PRODUCTS/OPERATIONS

Store Names
Accessorize
Catherine's Plus Sizes
Fashion Bug
Fashion Bug Plus
Lane Bryant
Monsoon

COMPETITORS

American Retail
Burlington Coat Factory
Cato
Charlotte Russe Holding
Claire's Stores
Deb Shops
dELiA*s
Dress Barn
Foot Locker
The Gap
Goody's Family Clothing
Hot Topic
J. C. Penney
Kmart

Kohl's
Limited Brands
Ross Stores
Sears
Spiegel
Stage Stores
Stein Mart
Talbots
Target
TJX
Too Inc.
United Retail
Wal-Mart

HISTORICAL FINANCIALS & EMPLOYEES

Nasdaq: CHRS FYE: Saturday nearest Jan. 31	Annual Growth	1/93	1/94	1/95	1/96	1/97	1/98	1/99	1/00	1/01	1/02
Sales ($ mil.)	6.0%	1,179	1,254	1,273	1,102	1,016	1,017	1,035	1,197	1,617	1,994
Net income ($ mil.)	—	81	80	45	(139)	(7)	19	(20)	45	51	(4)
Income as % of sales	—	6.9%	6.4%	3.5%	—	—	1.9%	—	3.8%	3.2%	—
Earnings per share ($)	—	0.75	0.74	0.42	(1.35)	(0.07)	0.18	(0.20)	0.43	0.48	(0.04)
Stock price - FY high ($)	—	19.00	19.50	14.00	6.63	8.38	7.19	5.75	8.25	8.00	7.13
Stock price - FY low ($)	—	12.50	10.63	5.75	2.06	2.69	3.75	3.25	2.81	4.63	4.48
Stock price - FY close ($)	(11.7%)	18.13	11.50	6.38	2.75	4.75	4.06	3.69	6.81	7.00	5.89
P/E - high	—	25	28	33	—	—	40	—	18	16	—
P/E - low	—	17	15	14	—	—	21	—	6	9	—
Dividends per share ($)	—	0.08	0.09	0.09	0.05	0.00	0.00	0.00	0.00	0.00	0.00
Book value per share ($)	1.4%	4.35	5.08	5.43	4.06	3.99	4.14	3.91	4.33	4.85	4.91
Employees	5.2%	15,200	15,200	16,600	14,200	12,100	12,600	12,700	18,000	19,750	24,000

STOCK PRICE HISTORY
HIGH/LOW/CLOSE

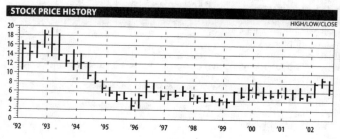

2002 FISCAL YEAR-END
Debt ratio: 27.5%
Return on equity: —
Cash ($ mil.): 37
Current ratio: 1.43
Long-term debt ($ mil.): 209
No. of shares (mil.): 112
Dividends
  Yield: —
  Payout: —
Market value ($ mil.): 659

CHARTER COMMUNICATIONS, INC.

Cable operator Charter Communications is laying the pipeline to billionaire Paul Allen's "wired world." Based in St. Louis, Charter has become one of the US's largest cable TV operators after its acquisition spree (completing 12 in the past year). The company has 6.8 million customers in 40 states; most are clustered in 14 states.

In Allen's vision, conceived when he and Bill Gates were starting Microsoft , a world of information and entertainment arrives through a single connection. Allen has found his conduit in Charter (he controls the firm with a 55% share ownership). The company is spending $3.5 billion to upgrade its cable systems for broadband communications. In selected markets, Charter already offers digital cable (2.3 million customers) and high-speed Internet access (747,000 customers). Charter has also taken on ISP partners, including High Speed Access (in which Allen controls a 49% stake) and EarthLink, to offer Internet access.

Internet over TV is another strand in the "wired world." Agreements with WorldGate allow some Charter cable subscribers to access the Web using TV set-top boxes. With Wink, Charter offers an interactive TV service that allows TV viewers to instantly access Web information related to programming. Charter is also part of Broadband Partners, which is developing a personalized interactive TV service.

What's next in Charter's vision? The company is busy developing cable telephony services.

HISTORY

Crown Media bought St. Louis-based Cencom Cable in 1992. Rather than relocate to Crown's Dallas home, Cencom CEO Howard Wood joined with fellow executives Barry Babcock and Jerry Kent to form Charter Communications as a cable acquisition and management company in St. Louis. With an investment from Crown (owned by Hallmark Cards), the trio partnered with LEB Communications in 1994 to manage Charter's growth. And grow it did.

In 1994 Charter paid about $900 million for a majority stake in Crown. Charter spent $3 billion on 15 cable acquisitions in its first four years. It had more than 1 million subscribers by early 1997 and began offering high-speed cable Internet access and paging services in some of its markets.

Charter went into acquisition overdrive in 1998 when Microsoft co-founder Paul Allen took control with his $4.5 billion investment. The deal closely followed Allen's $2.8 billion takeover of Dallas-based Marcus Cable; Marcus was merged with Charter. The new Charter, based in St. Louis with Kent as CEO, was the #7 US cable

business with 2.5 million subscribers. Also that year the company teamed up with Wink and WorldGate to offer TV Internet services with set-top boxes.

Before the ink was dry on the merger papers, Allen was at it again. The company's 1999 acquisitions included Falcon Communications (1 million cable subscribers) and Fanch Cablevision (more than 500,000); it also bought cable systems from Helicon, InterMedia Partners, Avalon Cable, InterLink Communications, Renaissance Media, and Rifkin. Charter said it would spend $3.5 billion upgrading its systems over three years after raising that amount in a major junk bond sale. Months later the company raised $3.2 billion in its IPO.

In 2000 Charter completed its purchase of Bresnan Communications (700,000 subscribers) and bought a system from Cablevision to form a major cluster in Michigan, Minnesota, and Wisconsin. The next year the company gained 554,000 subscribers by swapping noncore cable systems and $1.8 billion in cash to AT&T Broadband in exchange for systems serving the St. Louis area, parts of Alabama, and the Reno area of Nevada and California. Also in 2001 Kent resigned from the company and its board of directors and was replaced as CEO by former Liberty Media executive Carl Vogel.

OFFICERS

Chairman: Paul G. Allen, age 49
President, CEO, and Director: Carl E. Vogel, age 44, $753,692 pay (partial-year salary)
EVP and COO: David G. Barford, age 43, $826,644 pay
EVP and CFO: Kent D. Kalkwarf, age 42, $826,644 pay
EVP and Assistant to the President: Steven A. Schumm, age 49, $837,000 pay
EVP Corporate Development and CTO: Stephen E. Silva, age 42
SVP, General Counsel, and Secretary: Curtis S. Shaw, age 53
SVP and CIO: Michael E. Riddle, age 43
SVP and Treasurer: Ralph G. Kelly, age 44
SVP Administration: Eric Freesmeier, age 49
SVP Advanced Technology Development: Thomas R. Jokerst, age 52
SVP Communications: David C. Anderson, age 53
SVP Engineering: John C. Pietre, age 52
VP Engineering: Larry Schutz
VP Human Resources: Don Johnson
SVP Operations, Eastern Division: David L. McCall, age 46, $713,150 pay
SVP Operations, Gulf Coast Region: Ron Johnson
SVP Operations, Midwest Division: William J. Shreffler, age 48
SVP Operations, Western Division: J. Christian Fenger, age 46
SVP Operations, Western Region: Tom Schaeffer
Auditors: KPMG LLP

HQ: 12405 Powerscourt Dr., Ste. 100,
St. Louis, MO 63131
Phone: 314-965-0555   **Fax:** 314-965-9745
Web: www.chartercom.com

PRODUCTS/OPERATIONS

2001 Sales

	$ mil.	% of total
Video		
Analog	2,788	71
Digital	307	7
Advertising sales	313	8
Cable modem	154	4
Other	391	10
Total	**3,953**	**100**

Selected Services
Broadband Internet access via cable modems
Cable TV
Digital TV
Interactive video programming
Pay-per-view
Private business networks
Television-based Internet access
Video-on-demand

COMPETITORS

Adelphia Communications
AT&T Broadband
Cablevision Systems
Classic Communications
Comcast
Cox Communications
DIRECTV
EchoStar Communications
Insight Communications
Mediacom Communications
Time Warner Cable

HISTORICAL FINANCIALS & EMPLOYEES

Nasdaq: CHTR FYE: December 31	Annual Growth	12/92	12/93	12/94	12/95	12/96	12/97	12/98	12/99	12/00	12/01
Sales ($ mil.)	66.4%	—	—	—	—	—	—	—	1,428	3,249	3,953
Net income ($ mil.)	—	—	—	—	—	—	—	—	(66)	(829)	(1,178)
Income as % of sales	—	—	—	—	—	—	—	—	—	—	—
Earnings per share ($)	—	—	—	—	—	—	—	—	(2.22)	(3.67)	(4.37)
Stock price – FY high ($)	—	—	—	—	—	—	—	—	27.75	24.19	24.45
Stock price – FY low ($)	—	—	—	—	—	—	—	—	19.50	10.00	10.49
Stock price – FY close ($)	(13.3%)	—	—	—	—	—	—	—	21.88	22.69	16.43
P/E – high	—	—	—	—	—	—	—	—	—	—	—
P/E – low	—	—	—	—	—	—	—	—	—	—	—
Dividends per share ($)	—	—	—	—	—	—	—	—	0.00	0.00	0.00
Book value per share ($)	(16.1%)	—	—	—	—	—	—	—	13.58	13.36	9.56
Employees	22.3%	—	—	—	—	—	—	—	11,970	13,505	17,900

STOCK PRICE HISTORY

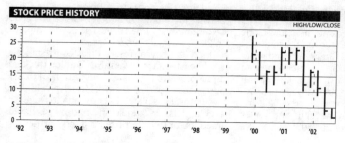

HIGH/LOW/CLOSE

2001 FISCAL YEAR-END

Debt ratio: 85.1%
Return on equity: —
Cash ($ mil.): 2
Current ratio: 0.27
Long-term debt ($ mil.): 16,343
No. of shares (mil.): 300
Dividends
  Yield: —
  Payout: —
Market value ($ mil.): 4,921

CHEVRONTEXACO CORPORATION

Having added a star to its stripes, Chevron-Texaco can pull rank on its rivals. Chevron's acquisition of Texaco in October 2001 created the #2 US integrated oil company (behind Exxon Mobil). San Francisco-based ChevronTexaco has followed the path blazed by the cost-saving mergers of other oil giants (Exxon and Mobil, BP and Amoco).

ChevronTexaco boasts proved reserves of 11.5 billion barrels of oil equivalent and daily production level of 2.7 million barrels of oil equivalent. With a global reach of more than 180 countries, ChevronTexaco also owns stakes in chemicals producer Chevron Phillips Chemical and power producer and marketer Dynegy. The company's brands include Chevron, Texaco, and Caltex. (The Caltex brand comes from a joint venture between the companies that was formed in 1936 to operate in Asia and Africa.)

To obtain US government approval for the deal, ChevronTexaco sold its stakes in its Equilon and Motiva refining and marketing joint ventures. Shell bought ChevronTexaco's 44% interest in Equilon, which operates in the West and Midwest as Shell Oil Products US. Chevron-Texaco's 35% stake in Motiva, which operates along the Gulf Coast and the eastern seaboard, was sold to partners Shell and Saudi Aramco. The company also agreed to sell its interest in the Discovery Pipeline and its stake in the Enterprise Fractionator near Houston.

ChevronTexaco, led by Chevron veteran Dave O'Reilly, has announced plans to lay off some 4,000 workers (from a workforce that numbered 57,000 when the companies were combined) as part of a reorganization intended to save $1.2 billion.

HISTORY

Thirty years after the California gold rush, a small firm began digging for a new product — oil. The crude came from wildcatter Frederick Taylor's well located north of Los Angeles. In 1879 Taylor and other oilmen formed Pacific Coast Oil, attracting the attention of John D. Rockefeller's Standard Oil. The two firms competed fiercely until Standard took over Pacific Coast in 1900.

When Standard Oil was broken up in 1911, its West Coast operations became the stand-alone Standard Oil Company (California), which was nicknamed Socal and sold Chevron-brand products. After winning drilling concessions in Bahrain and Saudi Arabia in the 1930s, Socal summoned Texaco to help, and they formed Caltex (California-Texas Oil Company) as equal partners. In 1948 Socony (later Mobil) and Jersey Standard (later Exxon) bought 40% of Caltex's

Saudi operations, and the Saudi arm became Aramco (Arabian American Oil Company).

Socal exploration pushed into Louisiana and the Gulf of Mexico in the 1940s. In 1961 it bought Standard Oil Company of Kentucky (Kyso). The 1970s brought setbacks: Caltex holdings were nationalized during the OPEC-spawned upheaval, and the Saudi Arabian government claimed Aramco in 1980.

In 1984 Socal was renamed Chevron and doubled its reserves with its $13 billion purchase of Gulf Corp., which had origins in the 1901 Spindletop gusher in Texas. Gulf became an oil power by developing Kuwaiti concessions, but was hobbled when those assets were nationalized in 1975. After Gulf was rocked by disclosures that it had an illegal political slush fund, Socal stepped in. The deal loaded the new company with debt, and it cut 20,000 jobs and sold billions in assets.

Chevron bought Tenneco's Gulf of Mexico properties in 1988, and in 1992 swapped fields valued at $1.1 billion for 15.7 million shares of Chevron stock owned by Pennzoil.

In the 1990s Chevron gave its retailing units a tuneup. It allied with McDonald's (1995) to combine burger stands and gas stations in 12 western states. In addition, the company sold 450 UK gas stations and a refinery to Shell (1997). Meanwhile, Chevron sold its natural gas operation in 1996 for a stake in Houston-based NGC (later Dynegy).

Poor economic conditions in Asia and slumping oil prices in 1998 forced Chevron to shed some US holdings, including California properties. Looking for growth overseas, in 1999 it bought Rutherford-Moran Oil, increasing its interests in Thailand, and Petrolera Argentina San Jorge, Argentina's #3 oil company. As the rest of the industry consolidated, Chevron discussed merging with Texaco, but the talks collapsed in 1999. Later that year CEO Ken Derr retired, and VC Dave O'Reilly replaced him.

In 2000 Chevron formed a joint venture with Phillips Petroleum that combined the companies' chemicals businesses as Chevron Phillips Chemical. That year talks with Texaco were revived and Chevron agreed to acquire its Caltex partner for about $35 billion in stock and about $8 billion in assumed debt. The deal, completed in 2001, formed ChevronTexaco.

In 2002 ChevronTexaco divested its stakes in US downstream joint ventures Equilon (to Shell) and Motiva (to Shell and Saudi Aramco). It also agreed to sell part of a Gulf of Mexico pipeline and two natural gas plants in Louisiana to Duke Energy, and its 12.5% stake in a natural gas liquids fractionator to Enterprise Products Partners.

Chairman and CEO: David J. O'Reilly, age 55,
$5,970,833 pay
Vice Chairman: Peter J. Robertson, age 55,
$1,669,167 pay
EVP Administration and Corporate Services:
Gregory Matiuk
EVP Downstream: Patricia A. Woertz, age 49
EVP Power, Chemicals, and Technology:
Darald W. Callahan, age 59
VP and CFO: John S. Watson, age 45, $2,405,417 pay
VP; President, ChevronTexaco Overseas Petroleum:
George L. Kirkland, age 51
**VP; President, North America Exploration and
Production:** Raymond I. Wilcox, age 56
VP and CTO: Donald Paul
VP and Treasurer: David M. Krattebol
VP and Comptroller: Stephen J. Crowe
VP and General Counsel: Harvey D. Hinman, age 61
VP Health, Environment, and Safety: Warner Williams
VP Human Resources: John E. Bethancourt, age 50
VP Public and Government Affairs: Rosemary Moore
VP Strategic Planning: Patricia E. Yarrington
CEO, Alto Technology Resources: Barbara Dunn
President and CIO, Information Technology:
David Clementz
President and CTO, Alto Technology Resources:
Alfredo Prelat
President, Asia/Middle East/Africa Products:
John McKenzie
Auditors: PricewaterhouseCoopers LLP

LOCATIONS

HQ: 575 Market St., San Francisco, CA 94105
Phone: 415-894-7700   **Fax:** 415-894-0583
Web: www.chevrontexaco.com

ChevronTexaco Corporation has operations in more than
180 countries.

2001 Sales

	$ mil.	% of total
US	50,444	43
Other countries	65,575	57
Adjustments	(11,610)	—
Total	**104,409**	**100**

PRODUCTS/OPERATIONS

2001 Sales

	$ mil.	% of total
Refining, marketing & transportation	81,920	71
Exploration & production	32,393	28
Chemicals	1,171	1
Other	535	—
Adjustments	(11,610)	—
Total	**104,409**	**100**

COMPETITORS

Amerada Hess	Exxon Mobil	Repsol YPF
Anadarko	FFP Marketing	Royal
Petroleum	Imperial Oil	Dutch/Shell
BP	Koch	Group
ConocoPhillips	PETROBRAS	TOTAL FINA
Devon Energy	PDVSA	ELF
Eni	PEMEX	Unocal

HISTORICAL FINANCIALS & EMPLOYEES

NYSE: CVX FYE: December 31	Annual Growth	12/92	12/93	12/94	12/95	12/96	12/97	12/98	12/99	12/00	12/01
Sales ($ mil.)	12.1%	37,464	32,123	30,340	31,322	37,580	35,009	26,187	31,538	46,532	104,409
Net income ($ mil.)	8.6%	1,569	1,265	1,693	930	2,607	3,256	1,339	2,070	5,185	3,288
Income as % of sales	—	4.2%	3.9%	5.6%	3.0%	6.9%	9.3%	5.1%	6.6%	11.1%	3.1%
Earnings per share ($)	—	—	—	—	—	—	—	—	—	—	3.09
Stock price – FY high ($)	—	—	—	—	—	—	—	—	—	—	93.77
Stock price – FY low ($)	—	—	—	—	—	—	—	—	—	—	82.00
Stock price – FY close ($)	—	—	—	—	—	—	—	—	—	—	89.61
P/E – high	—	—	—	—	—	—	—	—	—	—	25
P/E – low	—	—	—	—	—	—	—	—	—	—	22
Dividends per share ($)	—	—	—	—	—	—	—	—	—	—	0.70
Book value per share ($)	—	—	—	—	—	—	—	—	—	—	31.82
Employees	1.4%	49,245	47,576	45,758	43,019	40,820	39,362	39,191	36,490	34,610	55,763

STOCK PRICE HISTORY

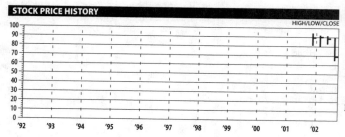

HIGH/LOW/CLOSE

2001 FISCAL YEAR-END

Debt ratio: 20.9%
Return on equity: 9.8%
Cash ($ mil.): 2,117
Current ratio: 0.89
Long-term debt ($ mil.): 8,989
No. of shares (mil.): 1,067
Dividends
 Yield: 0.8%
 Payout: 22.7%
Market value ($ mil.): 95,634

CHIQUITA BRANDS INTERNATIONAL

That's not just a banana in Chiquita's pocket — it's a banana empire. Chiquita Brands International is the world's #1 producer, marketer, and distributor of bananas, which account for more than 50% of the Cincinnati-based company's total sales. Chiquita, which sells its produce in 60 countries, also harvests other fresh fruits and vegetables. Its processed foods unit sells juices and processed bananas and is the largest private-label vegetable canner in the US.

Chiquita has cried foul over European banana trade restrictions, which it says have hurt the company's sales and weakened the banana industry. Frustrated by the long-term failure of the US government to make deals with the European Union to lift the restrictions (finally achieved in an April 2001 agreement), the company is suing the European Commission for damages. As part of an agreement to reduce its debt, Chiquita emerged from a Chapter 11 debt-restructuring plan that gave bondholders a majority interest.

HISTORY

Lorenzo Baker sailed into Jersey City, New Jersey, in 1870 with 160 bunches of Jamaican bananas. Baker arranged to sell bananas through Boston produce agent Andrew Preston and, with the support of Preston's partners, the two formed the Boston Fruit Company in 1885. In 1899 Boston Fruit merged with three other banana importers and incorporated as United Fruit Company. Soon the company was importing bananas from numerous Central American plantations for expanded distribution in the US.

United Fruit entered the Cuban sugar trade with the purchase of Nipe Bay (1907) and Saetia Sugar (1912). It bought Samuel Zemurray's Cuyamel Fruit Company in 1930, leaving Zemurray as the largest shareholder.

Zemurray, who had masterminded the overthrow of the Honduran regime in 1905 to establish one favorable to his business, forcibly established himself as United Fruit's president in 1933. In 1954, when Guatemalan president Jacobo Arbenz threatened to seize United Fruit's holdings, the company claimed he was a communist threat and provided ships to transport CIA-backed troops and ammunition for his ultimate overthrow.

Diversifying in the 1960s, United Fruit purchased A&W (restaurants and root beer, 1966) and Baskin-Robbins (ice cream, 1967). Eli Black, founder of AMK (which included the Morrell meat company), bought United Fruit in 1970 and changed its name to United Brands. Through American Financial Group, Carl Lindner began acquiring large amounts of United Brands' stock in 1973; he became chairman of the company in 1984. During the 1970s and 1980s, United Brands sold many of its holdings, including Baskin-Robbins (1973) and A&W (restaurants, 1982; soft drinks, 1987).

The firm became Chiquita Brands International in 1990. Chiquita acquired Friday Canning two years later. It then began divesting its meat operations, and all were sold by 1995.

In 1993 the European Union (EU) set up trade barriers against banana imports from Latin America, favoring banana-producing former European colonies in the Caribbean. The preference system angered Chiquita, whose bananas come from non-favored countries, although it retained more than 20% of the European market. In 1997 the WTO ruled the EU's trade policy illegal; the battle continued, however, over just how open the market should be.

Chiquita bought vegetable canners Owatonna Canning (1997), American Fine Foods (1997), and Stokely USA (1998) and merged them with Friday Canning in 1998. Also that year Hurricane Mitch destroyed Chiquita plantations in Honduras and Guatemala, costing the company $74 million. Sales were not affected though, as Chiquita was able to turn to growers in Ecuador and Panama. In 2000 the company announced cost-cutting efforts that included job cuts and a reorganization of some divisions.

Beset by a weakened European currency and a banana glut, the company announced in January 2001 that it was unable to pay its public debt. Chiquita also sued the European Commission, demanding $525 million in damages, due to the EU banana trade policy. The EU and the US later reached an agreement modifying quotas and tariffs until 2006, when all such restrictions are set to end. In November 2001 Chiquita filed a debt-restructuring plan under Chapter 11 seeking approval for an agreement the company made with bondholders to change more than $700 million of debt into equity. The plan was approved and the reorganization went into effect in mid-March of 2002, and the company began trading again on the NYSE. That same month, Chiquita announced the resignation of Steve Warshaw as the company president, CEO, and director. Cyrus Friedheim Jr. was named new chairman and CEO.

OFFICERS

Chairman, CEO, and President: Cyrus F. Freidheim Jr., age 67
SVP and CFO: James B. Riley, age 50, $434,423 pay
SVP, General Counsel, and Secretary: Robert W. Olson, age 56, $692,500 pay
SVP, Regulatory Affairs: Dennis M. Doyle
VP and Controller: William A. Tsacalis, age 58
VP, Corporate Communications and Corporate Responsibility Officer: Jeffrey M. Zalla
VP, Human Resources: Barry H. Morris
VP, Information Systems: Jeffrey T. Klare
VP, Strategy and New Business Development: Jill Albrinck, age 38
President and COO, Chiquita Fresh Group and Chiquita Fresh Group-North America: Robert F. Kistinger, age 49, $1,029,500 pay
President and COO, Chiquita Fresh Group-Europe: Peter A. Horekens, $484,848 pay
President and COO, Chiquita Processed Foods: David J. Ockleshaw
President and COO, Far and Middle East/Australia Region: Craig A. Stephen
Auditors: Ernst & Young LLP

LOCATIONS

HQ: Chiquita Brands International, Inc.
250 E. 5th St., Cincinnati, OH 45202
Phone: 513-784-8000   **Fax:** 513-784-8030
Web: www.chiquita.com

Chiquita Brands International leases or owns land for cultivation primarily in Colombia, Costa Rica, Honduras, and Panama. It has 15 vegetable canning facilities in eight states, fruit processing operations in Costa Rica and Ecuador, and edible oils facilities in Honduras.

PRODUCTS/OPERATIONS

2001 Sales

	% of total
Fresh produce	80
Processed foods	20
Total	**100**

Selected Products and Brands

Fresh Produce
Bananas (Amigo, Chiquita, Chiquita Jr., Consul)
Fresh fruit (Chiquita)
Fresh vegetables (Premium)

Processed Foods
Canned vegetables (Read, Stokely's)
Fruit beverages and juices (Chiquita)
Processed banana products (Chiquita)

COMPETITORS

Coca-Cola
Del Monte Foods
Dole
Fresh Del Monte Produce
Fyffes
Goya
Hanover Foods
J. M. Smucker
National Grape Cooperative
Ocean Spray
Pro-Fac
Savia
Seneca Foods
Sunkist
Tropicana Products
United Foods

HISTORICAL FINANCIALS & EMPLOYEES

NYSE: CQB FYE: December 31	Annual Growth	12/91	12/92	12/93	12/94	12/95	12/96	12/97	12/98	12/99	12/00
Sales ($ mil.)	(2.3%)	—	2,723	2,533	3,962	2,566	2,435	2,434	2,720	2,556	2,254
Net income ($ mil.)	—	—	(284)	(51)	(72)	9	(51)	0	(18)	(58)	(95)
Income as % of sales	—	—	—	—	—	0.4%	—	0.0%	—	—	—
Employees	(4.9%)	—	45,000	45,000	40,000	36,000	36,000	40,000	37,000	36,000	30,000

STOCK PRICE HISTORY

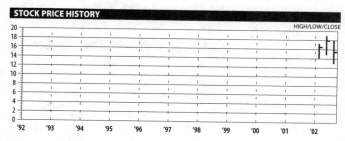

HIGH/LOW/CLOSE

2000 FISCAL YEAR-END

Debt ratio: 64.5%
Return on equity: —
Cash ($ mil.): 97
Current ratio: 1.38
Long-term debt ($ mil.): 1,060
No. of shares (mil.): 67
Dividends
  Yield: —
  Payout: —
Market value ($ mil.): 67

THE CHUBB CORPORATION

Chubb Corporation is trying to stay in shape. Warren, New Jersey-based Chubb offers property/casualty insurance for businesses and personal lines for wealthy individuals. The company's specialty commercial insurance includes the lucrative Executive Risk business that offers professional liability policies to executives. Other specialty commercial insurance includes policies written for marine, surety, and financial institutions. Chubb's Real Estate Group develops commercial and residential properties in Florida and New Jersey. The US accounts for some three-fourths of direct business.

Another element in the company's growth strategy is a focus on developing foreign markets; Chubb does business in some 30 countries in Asia, Australia, Europe, Latin America, and North America.

Severely affected by events of September 11 and the collapse of Enron, Chubb is paying out almost $900 million in claims. The company is taking advantage of soaring insurance rates and has set up insurer Allied World Assurance together with Goldman Sachs.

HISTORY

Thomas C. Chubb and his son Percy formed Chubb & Son in New York in 1882 to underwrite cargo and ship insurance. The company soon became the US manager for Sea Insurance Co. of England and co-founded New York Marine Underwriters (NYMU). In 1901 NYMU became Chubb's chief property/casualty affiliate, Federal Insurance Co.

Chubb expanded in the 1920s, opening a Chicago office (1923) and, just before the 1929 crash, organizing Associated Aviation Underwriters. Growth slowed during the Depression, but Chubb recovered enough by 1939 to buy Vigilant Insurance Co.

The company bought Colonial Life in 1959 and Pacific Indemnity in 1967. That year Chubb Corporation was formed as a holding company, with Chubb & Son designated the manager of the property/casualty insurance businesses. A 1969 takeover attempt by First National City Corp. (predecessor of Citigroup) was foiled by federal regulators.

Chubb acquired Bellemead Development in 1970 to expand its real estate portfolio. Following a strategy of offering specialized insurance, Chubb in the 1970s launched insurance packages for the entertainment industry, including films and Broadway shows. After the Tylenol poisonings of 1982, Chubb developed insurance against product tampering (which it no longer offers). During the 1980s Chubb focused on specialized property/casualty insurance lines; in 1985 it retreated from medical malpractice insurance.

The company combined three subsidiaries into Chubb Life Insurance Co. of America in 1991. The next year Chubb subsidiary Pacific Indemnity settled a suit over Fibreboard Corporation's asbestos liability (Fibreboard was later bought by Owens Corning); the company ultimately paid some $675 million in asbestos-related settlements.

Financial difficulties at Lloyd's of London caused that market to rethink and subsequently relax its rules about doing business with corporate insurance companies. Chubb took advantage of the opportunity and opened an office at Lloyd's in 1993. The next year Chubb's acquisitions included the personal lines business of Alexander & Alexander (now part of Aon Corporation).

Since the 1880s, Chubb had maintained an alliance with UK-based Royal & Sun Alliance Insurance Group and its predecessors. Royal & Sun Alliance owned about 5% of Chubb, and Chubb held about 3% of Royal & Sun Alliance. In 1993 the US insurer formed a new joint venture with the British company, with the purpose of extending to the UK Chubb's insurance products targeting the affluent. But in 1996, a major client of Royal & Sun Alliance Insurance Group defected and Chubb ended the agreement.

To focus on the property/casualty market, Chubb in 1997 sold its life and health insurance operations to Jefferson Pilot and parts of its Bellemead real estate business to Paine Webber and Morgan Stanley Dean Witter. The next year the commercial lines market tanked and with them went Chubb's earnings.

With losses dragging down its otherwise profitable property/casualty segment, Chubb vowed to get tough — raising rates and getting out of unprofitable businesses. It also forged ahead with its overseas plans, buying Venezuelan insurer Italseguros Internacional and creating Chubb Re to offer international reinsurance. In 1999 Chubb bought corporate officer insurer Executive Risk (now with a Chubb prefix) to beef up its executive protection and financial services lines. The next year, UK aviation insurer British Aviation Group bought Chubb's Associated Aviation Underwriters.

OFFICERS

Chairman and CEO: Dean R. O'Hare, age 60, $1,012,501 pay
President: John J. Degnan, age 57, $408,752 pay
EVP and CFO: Weston M. Hicks, age 45, $375,000 pay
EVP: Thomas F. Motamed, age 53, $421,876 pay
EVP; SVP, Chubb Executive Risk: Michael O'Reilly, age 58, $398,893 pay

SVP: Daniel J. Conway
SVP: David S. Fowler, age 56
SVP: Brant W. Free Jr.
SVP: Frederick W. Gaertner
SVP: Ned I. Gerstman
SVP: Mark Greenberg
SVP: Andrew A. McElwee Jr., age 47
SVP: Glenn A. Montgomery, age 49
SVP: Marjorie D. Raines
SVP: Henry B. Schram, age 55
SVP and General Counsel: Joanne L. Bober, age 49
SVP and Counsel: Michael J. O'Neill Jr., age 53
Auditors: Ernst & Young LLP

LOCATIONS

HQ: 15 Mountain View Rd., Warren, NJ 07061
Phone: 908-903-2000 **Fax:** 908-903-3402
Web: www.chubb.com

PRODUCTS/OPERATIONS

2001 Assets

	$ mil.	% of total
Cash	26	—
Treasury & agency securities	1,216	4
Foreign governments' securities	1,626	6
Mortgage-backed securities	2,130	7
State & municipal bonds	9,556	33
Corporate bonds	3,339	11
Stocks	710	2
Real estate	647	2
Goodwill	467	2
Recoverables & receivables	6,198	21
Other	3,534	12
Total	**29,449**	**100**

Selected Subsidiaries
Bellemead Development Corporation
Chubb Atlantic Indemnity Ltd.
  DHC Corporation
    Chubb do Brasil Companhia de Seguros (99%, Brazil)
Chubb Capital Corporation
Chubb Financial Solutions, Inc.
Federal Insurance Company
  CC Canada Holdings Ltd.
    Chubb Insurance Company of Canada
  Chubb Argentina de Seguros, S.A.
  Chubb Custom Insurance Company
  Chubb Indemnity Insurance Company
  Chubb Insurance Company of Australia Limited
  Chubb Insurance Company of Europe, S.A. (Belgium)
  Chubb Insurance Company of New Jersey
  Chubb National Insurance Company
  Executive Risk Indemnity Inc.
    Executive Risk Specialty Insurance Company
    Quadrant Indemnity Company
  Great Northern Insurance Company
  Pacific Indemnity Company
    Northwestern Pacific Indemnity Company
    Texas Pacific Indemnity Company
  Vigilant Insurance Company

COMPETITORS

Allianz	CIGNA	Liberty Mutual
Allstate	Citigroup	Loews
AIG	CNA Financial	Millea Holdings
Aviva	GEICO	St. Paul
AXA	GeneralCologne	Companies
Berkshire	Re	State Farm
Hathaway	The Hartford	Travelers

HISTORICAL FINANCIALS & EMPLOYEES

NYSE: CB FYE: December 31	Annual Growth	12/92	12/93	12/94	12/95	12/96	12/97	12/98	12/99	12/00	12/01
Assets ($ mil.)	7.8%	15,019	19,437	20,723	22,997	19,939	19,616	20,746	23,537	25,027	29,449
Net income ($ mil.)	(17.3%)	617	324	529	697	513	770	707	621	715	112
Income as % of assets	—	4.1%	1.7%	2.6%	3.0%	2.6%	3.9%	3.4%	2.6%	2.9%	0.4%
Earnings per share ($)	(17.3%)	3.48	1.83	2.96	3.90	2.88	4.39	4.19	3.66	4.01	0.63
Stock price - FY high ($)	—	45.50	48.19	41.56	50.31	56.25	78.50	88.81	76.38	90.25	86.63
Stock price - FY low ($)	—	31.19	38.00	34.31	38.06	40.88	51.13	55.38	44.00	43.25	55.54
Stock price - FY close ($)	5.0%	44.44	38.94	38.69	48.38	53.75	75.63	64.75	56.31	86.50	69.00
P/E - high	—	13	25	14	13	20	18	21	21	22	133
P/E - low	—	9	20	12	10	14	11	13	12	11	85
Dividends per share ($)	6.1%	0.79	0.85	0.91	0.97	1.06	1.14	1.53	1.27	1.31	1.35
Book value per share ($)	6.1%	22.59	23.92	24.46	30.14	31.24	33.53	34.78	35.74	39.91	38.37
Employees	2.6%	10,000	10,500	11,200	10,900	11,600	11,000	10,700	11,900	12,400	12,600

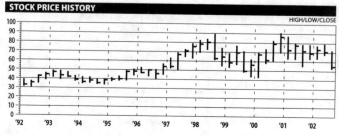

STOCK PRICE HISTORY   HIGH/LOW/CLOSE

2001 FISCAL YEAR-END
Equity as % of assets: 22.2%
Return on assets: 0.4%
Return on equity: 1.7%
Long-term debt ($ mil.): 1,351
No. of shares (mil.): 170
Dividends
  Yield: 2.0%
  Payout: 214.3%
Market value ($ mil.): 11,735
Sales ($ mil.): 7,754

CHURCH & DWIGHT CO., INC.

The same stuff that makes a cake rise also freshens cat boxes and is a soothing bath additive for treating sunburn. Based in Princeton, New Jersey, Church & Dwight Co. is the world's leading maker of baking soda (a.k.a. sodium bicarbonate). The company sells its baking soda to both consumers and industrial customers, who use it in baked goods, pharmaceuticals, and fire extinguishers, as well as for other uses.

Church & Dwight's consumer products (which account for more than 80% of sales) include the long-familiar ARM & HAMMER-brand baking soda in the orange box, along with laundry detergents (its largest business) and baking soda-enriched deodorant, toothpaste, cat litter, and air fresheners. The company combined its laundry detergent business with USA Detergents (Xtra, Nice 'N Fluffy) in order to cut costs and ended up buying the company.

The company's specialty products division makes antacid feed additives for cattle, industrial- and medical-grade sodium bicarbonate (used in kidney dialysis), ammonium bicarbonate, potassium carbonate (used in video monitor glass), and industrial cleaning products.

The siren song of overseas consumer markets has fallen on deaf ears at Church & Dwight, which has stayed focused on building its brands within the US (approximately 90% of sales) and Canada, as well as expanding through domestic acquisitions (Brillo, Clean Shower). A small subsidiary in England produces specialty chemicals for European markets.

The Statue of Liberty's inner walls were cleaned with ARM & HAMMER baking soda in 1986 in preparation for its 100th anniversary. New product introductions intensified in the late 1980s and into the 1990s; offerings included toothpaste (1988), carpet deodorizer (1988), and deodorant and other products (1994). The product introductions were badly handled, and a large earnings drop ensued. Minton resigned in 1995 and was replaced by former marketing VP Robert Davies, the first CEO without ties to the founding family.

Broadening its household cleaning products base, the company bought the Brillo soap pad and five other brands from Dial in 1997 and folded Dial's Toss 'N Soft fabric softener business into its laundry basket in 1998. The following year it bought the Clean Shower brand (from Clean Shower L.P.) and the Scrub Free and Delicare brands (from Benckiser), doubling its household cleaner business.

In 2000 Church & Dwight agreed to combine its laundry detergent business with value-brand cleaning products company USA Detergents. The two companies formed a joint venture, Armus LLC, before Church & Dwight decided to buy all of USA Detergents in 2001.

Also that year the company acquired Carter-Wallace's consumer products business (Arrid, Trojan, and Nair) for about $740 million. It bought the US antiperspirant and pet-care businesses outright, but the larger part of the deal was made in partnership with private equity firm Kelso & Company.

HISTORY

Chemistry enthusiast Dr. Austin Church and John Dwight, his marketing-driven brother-in-law, founded a company to make bicarbonate of soda for baking in 1846. The ARM & HAMMER trademark — representing Vulcan, the Roman god of fire, and originally used by Church's son James, owner of the Vulcan Spice Mills — was adopted in 1867.

After Church's retirement, his sons ran a separate company until 1896, when they formed Church & Dwight. The company became known for direct marketing and distinctive packaging. Church & Dwight began preaching alternative uses for baking soda in the 1920s and accelerated the effort after WWII, when home baking declined.

Dwight Minton, great-great-grandson of Church, was named CEO in 1968. Under his direction the company began appealing to "green" sentiments with new products such as non-phosphate laundry detergent (1970). Church & Dwight went public in 1977.

OFFICERS

Chairman Emeritus: Dwight C. Minton, age 67
Chairman and CEO: Robert A. Davies III, age 66, $1,101,500 pay
President and COO, Specialty Products Division: Joseph A. Sipia Jr., age 53
President Personal Care; President Domestic Operations, Armkel: Bradley A. Casper, age 42
VP, Advertising: Henry Kornhauser, age 69, $324,900 pay
VP, Animal Nutrition, Specialty Products Division: Ronald D. Munson, age 59
VP, Basic Chemicals, Specialty Products Division: W. Patrick Fiedler, age 53
VP, Controller, and CIO: Gary P. Halker, age 51
VP, Corporate Development: James L. Rogula, age 66
VP, Finance and CFO: Zvi Eiref, age 63, $535,000 pay
VP, Financial Analysis and Planning, Arm & Hammer Division: John R. Burke, age 50
VP, General Counsel, and Secretary: Mark A. Bilawsky, age 54
VP, Human Resources: Steven P. Cugine, age 39
VP, International Finance, Specialty Products Division: Jaap Ketting, age 50
VP, Logistics: Kenneth S. Colbert, age 46

VP, Manufacturing: Robert Fingerhut, age 59
VP, Marketing, Arm & Hammer Division:
  Larry B. Koslow, age 50
VP, MIS: Robert J. Carroll, age 43
VP, Operations: Mark G. Conish, age 49, $340,400 pay
VP, Procurement: Alfred H. Falter, age 52
Auditors: Deloitte & Touche LLP

LOCATIONS

HQ: 469 N. Harrison St., Princeton, NJ 08543
Phone: 609-683-5900   **Fax:** 609-497-7269
Web: www.churchdwight.com

Church & Dwight operates facilities in Alabama, Missouri, New Jersey, Ohio, and Wyoming; Ontario, Canada; and Wakefield, UK.

PRODUCTS/OPERATIONS

2001 Sales

	$ mil.	% of total
Consumer products	908	84
Specialty products	173	16
Total	**1,081**	**100**

Selected Products

Consumer	Specialty
ARM & HAMMER baking soda	Armakleen aqueous cleaner
ARM & HAMMER carpet & room deodorizer	Armicarb fungicide
ARM & HAMMER Dental Care toothpaste	ARM & HAMMER ammonium bicarbonate
ARM & HAMMER deodorant/antiperspirant	ARM & HAMMER feed-grade sodium bicarbonate
ARM & HAMMER laundry detergent	ARM & HAMMER sodium bicarbonate
ARM & HAMMER Super Scoop clumping litter	ARM & HAMMER SQ-810 rumen buffer (animal feed supplement)
Arrid antiperspirants	Armand potassium carbonate
Brillo soap pads	Armex blast media
Delicare liquid detergent	Bio-Chlor
First Response pregnancy test kits	Clear Balance swimming pool treatment
Lambert Kay pet care products	Fermenten
Nair depilatories	MEGALAC rumen bypass fat (animal feed supplement)
Nice 'N Fluffy	
Rain Drops water softener	
Sno Bol toilet bowl cleaner	
Trojan condoms	

COMPETITORS

Alticor	Nestlé Purina	Reckitt
Clorox	PetCare	Benckiser
Colgate-	Oil-Dri	Sara Lee
Palmolive	Orange Glo	Household
Dial	Procter &	S.C. Johnson
FMC	Gamble	Unilever
IMC Global		

HISTORICAL FINANCIALS & EMPLOYEES

NYSE: CHD FYE: December 31	Annual Growth	12/92	12/93	12/94	12/95	12/96	12/97	12/98	12/99	12/00	12/01
Sales ($ mil.)	8.6%	516	508	491	486	528	575	684	730	796	1,081
Net income ($ mil.)	5.3%	30	26	6	10	21	25	30	45	34	47
Income as % of sales	—	5.7%	5.2%	1.2%	2.1%	4.0%	4.3%	4.4%	6.2%	4.2%	4.3%
Earnings per share ($)	5.5%	0.71	0.64	0.16	0.26	0.54	0.62	0.76	1.11	0.84	1.15
Stock price - FY high ($)	—	17.88	16.44	14.63	12.44	11.88	16.38	18.00	30.19	27.75	28.44
Stock price - FY low ($)	—	11.00	11.44	8.31	8.50	8.75	10.81	13.28	16.50	14.69	19.56
Stock price - FY close ($)	6.1%	15.63	14.13	9.00	9.25	11.44	14.03	17.97	26.69	22.25	26.63
P/E - high	—	24	25	91	48	22	26	23	26	32	24
P/E - low	—	15	18	52	33	16	17	17	14	17	16
Dividends per share ($)	4.8%	0.19	0.21	0.22	0.22	0.22	0.23	0.24	0.26	0.28	0.29
Book value per share ($)	7.0%	3.91	4.22	3.94	3.94	4.25	4.61	5.04	5.83	6.12	7.21
Employees	7.6%	1,085	1,105	1,028	941	937	1,137	1,127	1,324	1,439	2,099

STOCK PRICE HISTORY

HIGH/LOW/CLOSE

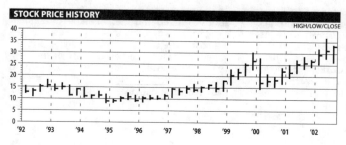

2001 FISCAL YEAR-END

Debt ratio: 59.0%
Return on equity: 18.2%
Cash ($ mil.): 52
Current ratio: 1.50
Long-term debt ($ mil.): 407
No. of shares (mil.): 39
Dividends
 Yield: 1.1%
 Payout: 25.2%
Market value ($ mil.): 1,042

CIGNA CORPORATION

CIGNA wants to signify employers' one-stop benefits shop. The Philadelphia-based company (one of the largest US health insurers along with Aetna and UnitedHealth) offers group life and disability insurance, as well as retirement and investment services and management. Related businesses, such as dental plans, specialty medical management programs, and pharmacy benefits management, cover about 14 million people. Its retirement benefits services include pension, 401(k), and other defined contribution plans; asset management; and other investment and savings packages.

It also operates one of the nation's largest HMOs, with more than 6 million members. The company has pulled its HMO out of all but two Medicare businesses because of reduced payments by the government.

Outside the US, CIGNA offers insurance to individuals (life, accident, and health) and large commercial customers (group insurance and benefits). CIGNA also provides reinsurance (group and individual life, personal accident, and health care coverage). The company operates in Asia, Europe, North and South America, and the Pacific Rim.

Having sold its property/casualty business in 1999, the firm is now concentrated on employee benefits. In addition to expanding its product lines to meet clients' needs, CIGNA plans to expand into serving more small and midsized businesses. The company is cutting some 2,000 jobs as it consolidates service operations in its employee health, life, and disability benefits units.

Financial services conglomerate J.P. Morgan Chase & Co. owns more than 8% of the company.

HISTORY

The Insurance Company of North America (INA) was founded in 1792 by Philadelphia businessmen. INA was the US's first stock insurance company and its first marine insurer. It later issued life insurance, fire insurance, and coverage for the contents of buildings. In 1808 it began using agents outside Pennsylvania. INA grew internationally in the late 1800s, appointing agents in Canada as well as in London and Vienna in Europe. It was the first US company to write insurance in China, beginning in Shanghai in 1897.

In 1942 INA provided both accident and health insurance for men working on the Manhattan Project, which developed the atomic bomb. It introduced the first widely available homeowner coverage in 1950. In 1978 INA bought HMO International, which was then the largest publicly owned health maintenance

organization in the US. INA merged with Connecticut General in 1982 to form CIGNA.

Connecticut General began selling life insurance in 1865 and health insurance in 1912. It wrote its first group insurance (for the *Hartford Courant* newspaper) in 1913 and the first individual accident coverage for airline passengers in 1926. In the late 1930s Connecticut General was a leader in developing group medical coverage. The company offered the first group medical coverage for general use in 1952 and in 1964 added group dental insurance.

After the merger, CIGNA bought Crusader Insurance (UK, 1983; sold 1991) and AFIA (1984). To begin positioning itself as a provider of managed health care, the company sold its individual insurance products division to InterContinental Life in 1988 and its Horace Mann Cos. (individual financial services) to an investor group in 1989. To further its goal, in 1990 CIGNA bought EQUICOR, an HMO started by Hospital Corporation of America (now part of HCA Inc.) and Equitable Life Assurance.

In the early 1990s it began to withdraw from the personal property/casualty business to focus on small and midsized commercial clients in the US, cutting sales overseas and combining them with life and health operations. It also exited such areas as airline insurance and surety bonds.

CIGNA expanded internationally in the mid-1990s, opening a Beijing office in 1993, 43 years after its departure from China. The next year the company bought 60% of an Indonesian insurance company. It also acquired 45% of Mediplan, a managed health care organization in Mexico.

Reeling from unforeseen environmental liabilities (chiefly related to asbestos), CIGNA in 1995 split its remaining property/casualty business between a healthy segment that continued to write new policies and one for run-off business. Four years later it finally sold these operations (including Cigna Insurance Co. of Europe) to ACE Limited in order to fund internal growth and acquisitions.

In the late 1990s, the company continued to cultivate its health care segment, acquiring managed care provider Healthsource in 1997. The company expanded its group benefits operations to India, Brazil, and Poland; at home, it cut its payroll by 1,300 in the US to counter rising costs. The company sold its domestic individual life insurance and annuity business in 1998, but began offering investment and pension products in Japan in 1999. In 2000 CIGNA settled a federal lawsuit over Medicare billing fraud.

OFFICERS

Chairman and CEO: H. Edward Hanway, age 50, $3,611,500 pay
President, CIGNA HealthCare: Patrick E. Welch, age 55
President, CIGNA Health Services: Douglas E. Klinger
President, CIGNA Dental Companies: Sam Westover
President, CIGNA Group Insurance: Michael W. Bell, age 38
President, CIGNA International: Terry L. Kendall, age 55
President, CIGNA Retirement & Investment Services: John Y. Kim, age 41
President, CIGNA Small Case Business Development: Gregory H. Wolf, age 45
EVP and CFO: James G. Stewart, age 59, $1,301,900 pay
EVP Systems and CIO: Andrea Anania, age 49
EVP and Chief Marketing Officer: Robert G. Romasco
EVP and General Counsel: Judith E. Soltz, age 55
EVP, Human Resources and Services: Donald M. Levinson, age 56, $1,061,900 pay
SVP and Treasurer: David B. Gerges
SVP, Public Affairs: Mike Fernandez
SVP, Mergers and Acquisitions: James Hom
VP, Investor Relations: Greg Deavens
Chief Accounting Officer: James A. Sears
Chief Investment Officer; President, TimesSquare Capital Management: Farhan Sharaff, age 51
Auditors: PricewaterhouseCoopers LLP

LOCATIONS

HQ: 1 Liberty Place, Philadelphia, PA 19192
Phone: 215-761-1000   **Fax:** 215-761-5515
Web: www.cigna.com

CIGNA has operations in the Asia/Pacific region, Europe, North America, and South America.

2001 Premiums & Fees

	% of total
US	95
Other countries	5
Total	**100**

PRODUCTS/OPERATIONS

2001 Sales

	$ mil.	% of total
Premiums & fees	15,367	80
Investment income	2,843	15
Realized investment gains	(175)	—
Other	1,080	5
Total	**19,115**	**100**

COMPETITORS

Aetna	ING	Northwestern
AIG	John Hancock	Mutual
Allianz	Financial	Oxford Health
Allstate	Services	Plans
American	Kaiser	Principal
Express	Foundation	Financial
Aon	Kemper	Prudential
AXA	Insurance	State Farm
AXA Financial	Loews	TIAA-CREF
Blue Cross	MassMutual	Travelers
Charles Schwab	Mellon Financial	UnitedHealth
Chubb	Merrill Lynch	Group
CNA Financial	MetLife	WellPoint Health
The Hartford	New York Life	Networks
Highmark		

HISTORICAL FINANCIALS & EMPLOYEES

NYSE: CI FYE: December 31	Annual Growth	12/92	12/93	12/94	12/95	12/96	12/97	12/98	12/99	12/00	12/01
Sales ($ mil.)	0.3%	18,582	18,402	18,392	18,955	18,950	20,038	21,437	18,781	19,994	19,115
Net income ($ mil.)	13.7%	311	234	554	211	1,056	1,086	1,292	1,774	987	989
Income as % of sales	—	1.7%	1.3%	3.0%	1.1%	5.6%	5.4%	6.0%	9.4%	4.9%	5.2%
Earnings per share ($)	18.5%	1.45	1.09	2.50	0.96	4.63	4.88	6.05	8.99	6.08	6.69
Stock price – FY high ($)	—	20.27	22.77	24.64	38.30	47.74	66.85	82.38	98.63	136.75	134.95
Stock price – FY low ($)	—	15.69	18.81	18.98	20.73	33.55	44.66	55.94	63.44	60.75	69.86
Stock price – FY close ($)	18.9%	19.52	20.90	21.19	34.38	45.50	57.40	77.31	80.56	132.30	92.65
P/E – high	—	13	21	10	39	10	14	13	10	22	20
P/E – low	—	10	17	7	21	7	9	9	7	10	10
Dividends per share ($)	2.6%	1.01	1.01	1.01	1.01	1.05	1.10	0.85	1.19	1.23	1.27
Book value per share ($)	3.3%	26.67	30.41	26.87	31.22	32.35	36.56	40.25	36.24	35.61	35.73
Employees	(1.7%)	52,255	50,600	48,300	44,707	42,800	47,700	49,900	41,900	43,200	44,600

STOCK PRICE HISTORY

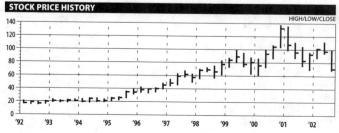

HIGH/LOW/CLOSE

2001 FISCAL YEAR-END

Debt ratio: 24.3%
Return on equity: 18.9%
Cash ($ mil.): —
Current ratio: —
Long-term debt ($ mil.): 1,627
No. of shares (mil.): 141
Dividends
  Yield: 1.4%
  Payout: 19.0%
Market value ($ mil.): 13,108

CINCINNATI FINANCIAL

It's a formula reminiscent of the Hair Club for Men: Not only are they sales agents for Cincinnati Financial Corporation (CFC), they're also owners. The company uses this unusual structure to attract and maintain a qualified, loyal sales force.

The nearly 1,000 independent agents of Fairfield, Ohio-based CFC sell property/casualty and life insurance nationwide, with a focus on the Midwest and Southeast. Serving primarily small to midsized businesses, CFC's Cincinnati Insurance Company offers a full line of commercial and personal insurance products, including workers' compensation, standard and nonstandard auto, and liability policies. The company's Life Horizons line of life insurance is sold through its Cincinnati Life Insurance subsidiary, and its CFC Investment Company offers real estate services and financing and leasing of equipment and vehicles (including to its own agents). CinFin Capital Management offers asset management for internal and external clients. CFC has also made its investment operations a key part of the mix — it owns more than 15% of Fifth Third Bancorp. The founding Schiff family owns nearly 20% of the company.

Cincinnati Financial's operating structure is highly decentralized; its only regional facilities are those maintained by the agents themselves. Although management is selectively adding agencies in targeted states, including Kentucky, Maryland, and North Carolina, the company does not plan to expand its agency force much above its current number.

HISTORY

Jack Schiff spent three years with the Travelers Company before he joined the Navy in WWII. He returned to Cincinnati to start his own independent insurance agency in 1946 and was joined by his younger brother Robert; both were Ohio State graduates whose affection for the Buckeyes led them in later years to close company banquets with the school fight song. The brothers incorporated Cincinnati Insurance with the aid of two elder insurance men and $200,000 from investors.

Cincinnati Insurance was owned by its agents, creating a stable of loyal, long-term employees under the conservative reign of Harry Turner, the company's first president. The company offered property/casualty insurance to small businesses and homeowners through its slow-growing network of agents. By 1956 the company had spread into neighboring Kentucky and Indiana. Over the next decade Cincinnati Insurance expanded its products and network, adding disaster, auto, and burglary lines and enlisting agents throughout the Midwest.

In 1963 Turner took the chairman's seat and Jack Schiff became president, introducing a more aggressive leadership style. That year the company reorganized, forming Cincinnati Financial Corporation as a parent for the insurance operation. This allowed CFC to form two more subsidiaries: CFC Investment Company, in 1970, to deal in commercial real estate and financing, and The Cincinnati Casualty Company, in 1972, to offer preferred-risk personal policies.

Cincinnati Financial went public in 1971, using the money to pay off debts and buy new businesses. By 1973 operations included The Life Insurance Company of Cincinnati, Queen City Indemnity, and fellow Cincinnati giant Inter-Ocean Corporation. That year Jack Schiff added CEO to his title.

With a new emphasis on independent investments, CFC continued to grow throughout the 1970s. In 1982 Cincinnati Financial veteran Robert Morgan became president and CEO. The company's conservative roots and investment base helped it shake off the early-1980s recession and a string of natural disasters that left many other insurers dangling in the wind.

Late in the decade, the company started to shift its focus from personal to commercial lines. In 1988 it reorganized its life insurance subsidiaries under the Cincinnati Life banner and formed The Cincinnati Indemnity Company to offer workers' compensation and nonstandard personal insurance. In 1998 a string of storms (reminiscent of others earlier in the decade) dampened the company's earnings.

Also that year the company — a laggard in the industrywide move into financial services — created CinFin Capital Management. The unit offers the company's in-house asset management skills to corporations, institutions, and wealthy individuals. In 1999 Jack Schiff Jr. succeeded Morgan as president and CEO. The next year, 96-year-old Harry Turner died. After storms hurt the bottom line in 2000, Cincinnati Financial said it would raise renewal rates. Following decisions by the Ohio Supreme Court, CFC set up $110 million in reserves for uninsured motorists claims in 2001.

Chairman, President, and CEO, Cincinnati Financial, Cincinnati Insurance, and Cincinnati Indemnity; Chairman and CEO, Cincinnati Casualty; Chairman, CinFin Capital Management; CEO, Cincinnati Life Insurance: John J. Schiff Jr., age 59, $559,792 pay

SVP, Chief Investment Officer, Assistant Secretary, Assistant Treasurer, and Director; President, CinFin Capital Management; SVP and Chief Investment Officer, Cincinnati Insurance, Cincinnati Indemnity, Cincinnati Casualty, and Cincinnati Life Insurance; SVP and Treasurer, CFC Investment: James G. Miller, age 64, $496,473 pay

SVP, CFO, Secretary, and Treasurer; SVP Accounting, CFO, and Secretary, Cincinnati Insurance, Cincinnati Indemnity, Cincinnati Casualty, Cincinnati Life Insurance, and CFC Investment; Treasurer, Cincinnati Life Insurance and CinFin Capital Management: Kenneth W. Stecher, age 55

Vice Chairman, SVP Claims, and Chief Insurance Officer, Cincinnati Insurance, Cincinnati Indemnity, Cincinnati Casualty; SVP Claims and Chief Insurance Officer, Cincinnati Life Insurance: James E. Benoski, age 63, $440,380 pay

President and COO, Cincinnati Life Insurance: David H. Popplewell

President, Cincinnati Casualty; SVP Personal Lines, Cincinnati Insurance and Cincinnati Indemnity: Larry R. Plum, age 55

SVP Sales and Marketing, Cincinnati Insurance, Cincinnati Indemnity, Cincinnati Casualty, and Cincinnati Life Insurance: Jacob F. Scherer Jr., age 49, $390,153 pay

VP Personnel, Cincinnati Insurance, Cincinnati Indemnity, Cincinnati Casualty, Cincinnati Life Insurance, and CFC Investment: Greg Ziegler

Auditors: Deloitte & Touche LLP

HQ: Cincinnati Financial Corporation
6200 S. Gilmore Rd., Fairfield, OH 45014
Phone: 513-870-2000   **Fax:** 513-870-2911
Web: www.cinfin.com

Cincinnati Financial operates in some 30 states, primarily in the East and Midwest.

2001 Assets

	$ mil.	% of total
Cash	93	1
State & municipal bonds	1,042	7
Stocks	8,495	61
Corporate bonds	1,777	13
Receivables	1,367	10
Separate account assets	390	3
Other	795	5
Total	**13,959**	**100**

Subsidiaries
CFC Investment Company
The Cincinnati Casualty Company
The Cincinnati Indemnity Company
The Cincinnati Insurance Company
The Cincinnati Life Insurance Company
CinFin Capital Management Company

Allstate
American Family Insurance
American Financial
Erie Indemnity
Nationwide
Ohio Casualty
Progressive Corporation
SAFECO
State Farm
Travelers

Nasdaq: CINF FYE: December 31	Annual Growth	12/92	12/93	12/94	12/95	12/96	12/97	12/98	12/99	12/00	12/01
Assets ($ mil.)	14.8%	4,028	4,602	4,734	6,109	7,046	9,493	11,087	11,380	13,287	13,959
Net income ($ mil.)	1.3%	171	216	201	227	224	299	242	255	118	193
Income as % of assets	—	4.3%	4.7%	4.2%	3.7%	3.2%	3.2%	2.2%	2.2%	0.9%	1.4%
Earnings per share ($)	1.6%	1.03	1.33	1.18	1.33	1.31	1.77	1.41	1.52	0.73	1.19
Stock price - FY high ($)	—	19.89	21.16	18.47	21.16	21.81	47.12	46.87	42.50	43.31	42.93
Stock price - FY low ($)	—	11.30	15.85	14.58	16.09	17.73	20.65	30.50	30.13	26.19	34.00
Stock price - FY close ($)	7.8%	19.42	16.96	16.33	20.69	21.60	46.87	36.63	31.19	39.56	38.15
P/E - high	—	19	17	15	16	16	26	32	27	59	36
P/E - low	—	11	13	12	12	13	11	21	19	35	28
Dividends per share ($)	11.0%	0.32	0.35	0.39	0.43	0.48	0.53	0.60	0.66	0.74	0.82
Book value per share ($)	14.6%	10.87	12.27	12.20	16.68	18.93	28.33	33.72	33.46	37.26	37.13
Employees	6.2%	1,925	2,000	2,050	2,289	2,506	2,670	2,770	2,920	3,106	3,299

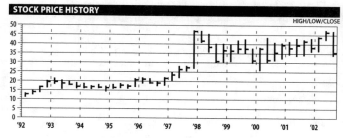

HIGH/LOW/CLOSE

2001 FISCAL YEAR-END
Equity as % of assets: 43.0%
Return on assets: 1.4%
Return on equity: 3.2%
Long-term debt ($ mil.): 426
No. of shares (mil.): 162
Dividends
  Yield: 2.1%
  Payout: 68.9%
Market value ($ mil.): 6,162
Sales ($ mil.): 2,561

CINERGY CORP.

While California has experienced rolling blackouts, Ohio's deregulated energy market is creating smaller waves. Cincinnati-based Cinergy, an electricity and gas distributor at home and abroad, is increasingly focused on the unregulated sectors of wholesale generation, marketing, and infrastructure services, which have grown to account for more than 75% of sales.

Cinergy's energy merchant unit operates the company's regulated and nonregulated generation assets; it owns domestic merchant plants that have a net capacity of 7,000 MW, and it manages Cinergy's regulated utility plants, which generate 6,000 MW of capacity. The unit also markets and trades wholesale energy (primarily in the Midwestern US), offers risk management services, and has international power plant interests (mainly in Europe).

Cinergy's regulated utility businesses transmit and distribute power to about 1.5 million electricity customers and 500,000 gas customers in Ohio, Indiana, and Kentucky. It also includes Cinergy Global Resources' distribution networks in Europe and Africa.

The company's power technology and infrastructure services unit invests in new power technologies (fuel cells, solar energy) and provides consulting and infrastructure services.

Cinergy has announced plans to focus on its merchant and regulated businesses, and is considering the sale of some noncore assets, including international, renewable, and technology investments.

HISTORY

Cinergy is the product of the 1994 merger between Cincinnati Gas & Electric (CG&E) and PSI Resources. CG&E began in 1837 when James Conover was granted a charter for the Cincinnati Gas Light & Coke Company. Conover began supplying manufactured gas to Cincinnati residents in 1843, when the utility industry was still in its early days.

Then the incandescent bulb sprang to light. Hedging its bets, Conover's company began buying the stock of Cincinnati Electric Light in 1887 and renamed itself Cincinnati Gas & Electric Company (CG&E) in 1901. CG&E became a subsidiary of Columbia Gas & Electric in 1911.

After WWII Columbia divested CG&E under the 1935 Public Utility Holding Company Act, which broke up powerful utility trusts and ushered in regulated regional monopolies.

During the 1950s and 1960s CG&E expanded and built new plants fired with cheap, plentiful coal. The lure of cheaper nuclear power led CG&E to begin building Zimmer Station in the early 1970s. However, costs and controversy forced CG&E to convert the nearly completed nuke to coal. Competition was on the horizon in the early 1990s, and CG&E began looking for a merger partner.

Enter PSI. PSI dates back to the early 1900s, when utility magnate Samuel Insull created a huge holding company, Middle West Utilities. In 1902 subsidiary United Gas & Electric Company of New Albany was created to invest in Indiana power plants and electric railways. Renamed Public Service Company of Indiana (PSI) in 1931, the company was divested by Midland United (successor to Middle West) in 1948.

PSI's postwar growth focused on new coal-fired plants, but in 1978 it began building the Marble Hill nuke. Mounting costs nearly bankrupted PSI, but in 1986 it was allowed a rate hike to cover the subsequent $1.34 billion write-off of Marble Hill.

In 1988 PSI hired as its chairman former Federal Energy Regulatory Commission official James Rogers, who realized he needed a partner to help absorb rising industry costs. The company became PSI Resources in 1990, and two years later it agreed to merge with neighboring CG&E.

Cinergy was born in 1994; its name was derived from CG&E's stock symbol (CIN) and the word synergy. Expanding into international markets, Cinergy teamed up with GPU in 1996 to purchase UK regional electric company Midlands Electricity. In 1997 Cinergy and fellow utilities Florida Progress (now Progress Energy) and New Century Energies (now Xcel Energy) teamed up to form Cadence Network to provide energy management services; it also formed a cogeneration partnership with Trigen Energy. Building up its energy trading operations, Cinergy became a member of NYMEX that year.

In 1999 Cinergy sold its 50% interest in Midlands Electricity to GPU (now FirstEnergy). Trading wholesale power in the US proved to be perilous when Cinergy failed to fulfill its power contracts during the Midwest's 1999 heatwave. More trouble surfaced when the EPA included Cinergy in a suit against seven US utilities; the utilities allegedly had increased pollution from old coal-fired generating plants by upgrading them in violation of the Clean Air Act.

Cinergy settled its portion of the EPA lawsuit in 2000 by agreeing to a $1.4 billion settlement. Retail competition took effect in Ohio in 2001.

Chairman, President, and CEO; Chairman and CEO, Cincinnati Gas & Electric and PSI Energy: James E. Rogers, age 54, $2,481,250 pay
EVP and CFO, Cinergy, Cincinnati Gas & Electric, and PSI Energy: R. Foster Duncan, age 47, $1,033,437 pay
EVP and Chief Administrative Officer: Frederick J. Newton III, age 46
EVP, Cinergy and Cincinnati Gas & Electric; Vice Chairman, PSI: Larry E. Thomas, age 56, $1,003,765 pay
EVP, Cinergy, Cincinnati Gas & Electric, and PSI Energy; CEO, Energy Merchant Business Unit: Michael J. Cyrus, age 46, $920,006 pay
EVP, Cinergy, Cincinnati Gas & Electric, and PSI Energy: William J. Grealis, age 56, $941,889 pay
EVP; VP, Cincinnati Gas & Electric, and CEO, Regulated Businesses Business Unit: James L. Turner, age 42
VP, General Counsel, and Assistant Secretary, Cinergy and PSI Energy; VP, General Counsel, and Secretary, Cincinnati Gas & Electric: Jerome A. Vennenmann, age 51
VP, Human Resources and Administration: Timothy J. Verhagen, age 55
VP; President, Cinergy Global Resources and Cinergy Global Power; Managing Director, Cinergy Global Power Services: John Bryant, age 55
VP; COO and CFO, Energy Merchant Business Unit: M. Stephen Harkness, age 53
President, Cincinnati Gas & Electric: Gregory C. Ficke, age 49
President, Power Technology and Infrastructure Services Business Unit: Donald B. Ingle Jr., age 52
VP and CFO, Energy Merchant Business Unit: Douglas F. Esamann, age 44
Auditors: Deloitte & Touche LLP

HQ: 139 E. Fourth Street, Cincinnati, OH 45202
Phone: 513-421-9500   **Fax:** 513-287-3171
Web: www.cinergy.com

Cinergy operates in Africa, Europe, and North America.

2001 Sales

	$ mil.	% of total
Energy merchant	10,024	77
Regulated businesses	2,850	22
Power technology	49	1
Total	**12,923**	**100**

Selected Subsidiaries
The Cincinnati Gas & Electric Company
Cinergy Global Resources, Inc.
Cinergy Investments, Inc.Cinergy Technologies, Inc.
Cinergy Wholesale Energy, Inc.
PSI Energy, Inc.

AEP	DPL	Mirant
Allegheny	Duke Energy	NiSource
Energy	Dynegy	PG&E
Aquila	El Paso	Sempra Energy
Avista	Entergy	TVA
CenterPoint	FirstEnergy	Vectren
Energy	IPALCO	Williams
Delta Natural	Enterprises	Companies
Gas	Koch	
Dominion	LG&E Energy	

NYSE: CIN FYE: December 31	Annual Growth	12/92	12/93	12/94	12/95	12/96	12/97	12/98	12/99	12/00	12/01
Sales ($ mil.)	26.5%	1,553	1,752	2,924	3,032	3,243	4,353	5,876	5,938	8,422	12,923
Net income ($ mil.)	9.1%	202	(9)	191	347	316	253	261	404	400	442
Income as % of sales	—	13.0%	—	6.5%	11.5%	9.8%	5.8%	4.4%	6.8%	4.7%	3.4%
Earnings per share ($)	3.4%	2.04	0.43	1.29	2.20	1.99	1.59	1.65	2.53	2.50	2.75
Stock price - FY high ($)	—	26.60	29.63	27.75	31.13	34.25	39.13	39.88	34.88	35.25	35.60
Stock price - FY low ($)	—	22.26	23.88	20.75	23.38	27.50	32.00	30.81	23.44	20.00	28.00
Stock price - FY close ($)	3.3%	24.88	27.50	23.50	30.63	33.38	38.31	34.38	23.94	35.13	33.43
P/E - high	—	13	69	21	14	16	17	24	14	14	13
P/E - low	—	11	56	16	11	13	14	19	9	8	10
Dividends per share ($)	1.0%	1.65	1.68	1.39	1.72	1.74	1.80	1.80	1.80	1.80	1.80
Book value per share ($)	(0.4%)	19.16	17.25	18.64	18.63	17.62	17.23	16.60	17.28	17.54	18.45
Employees	6.7%	4,900	5,000	8,868	8,602	7,973	7,609	8,794	8,950	8,362	8,769

HIGH/LOW/CLOSE

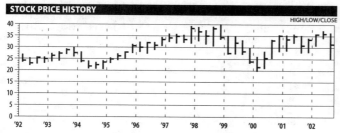

Debt ratio: 55.0%
Return on equity: 15.4%
Cash ($ mil.): 111
Current ratio: 0.66
Long-term debt ($ mil.): 3,597
No. of shares (mil.): 159
Dividends
  Yield: 5.4%
  Payout: 65.5%
Market value ($ mil.): 5,329

CINTAS CORPORATION

If Cintas had its way, you'd never again agonize over what to wear. Based in Cincinnati, the company is the nation's largest supplier of uniforms, with more than 500,000 clients such as Delta Air Lines and DHL. Cintas has about 365 facilities (including 14 manufacturing plants and seven distribution centers) across the US and Canada. More than 5 million people don the company's garb each day.

Uniform rentals generate more than 75% of Cintas' sales. In addition to offering shirts, pants, jackets, belts, and footwear, the company also provides cleanroom apparel and flame resistant clothing. The remainder of Cintas' revenue comes from uniform sales and an array of other products and services offered by the company, including sanitation supplies, first aid and safety products, and cleanroom supplies.

Cintas has been a participant in the industry's consolidation wave and, through acquisitions and internal growth, doubled in size during the late 1990s. It completed the integration of Unitog in 2000 and increased its client base by nearly 100,000 with its acquisition of Omni Services in 2002. Although growth of the company's ancillary services units has been slowed by the downturn in the US economy, Cintas is looking to expand its non-uniform operations. Chairman Richard Farmer owns about 21% of the company; director James Gardner owns about 6%.

HISTORY

In 1929 onetime animal trainer, boxer, and blacksmith Richard "Doc" Farmer started a business of salvaging old rags, cleaning them, and then selling them to factories. Farmer later began renting the rags to his customers. He would pick up the dirty rags, clean them, and return them to the factory. By 1936 the Acme Overall & Rag Laundry had established itself in Cincinnati with plans to convert an old bathhouse into a laundry. Farmer, along with his adopted son Herschell, suffered a setback from flood damage in 1937, but the family rebuilt and continued to grow the business.

In 1952 Doc Farmer died, and Herschell assumed command of the company. Five years later Herschell turned the reins over to his 23-year-old son, Richard. Richard Farmer immediately moved Acme into the uniform rental market, and the company blossomed. Throughout the 1960s the company grew enormously, aided by Richard's innovative leadership. (The company was the first to use a polyester-cotton blend that lasted twice as long as normal cotton work uniforms.) Through a holding company, Richard established a string of uniform plants in the Midwest, starting with a factory in Cleveland in 1968. Four years later the company changed its name to Cintas.

At this time the company began tapping into the new corporate identity market, pushing the idea that uniforms convey a sense of professionalism and present a cleaner, safer image. The company began to custom design the uniforms, adding logos and distinctive colors. This aspect of the business compelled Cintas to expand to help accommodate its national clients; by 1972 the company had offices throughout Ohio and in Chicago, Detroit, and Washington, DC. By 1975 Cintas was operating in 13 states.

The company went public in 1983. For the rest of the 1980s, Cintas rode the wave of consolidation in the uniform rental industry, making a slew of acquisitions. The company also expanded from its blue-collar base into the service industry and began to supply uniforms to hotels, restaurants, and banks. By the early 1990s Cintas was a presence in most major US cities, and its share of the US market had climbed to about 10%. Farmer turned over the title of CEO to president Robert Kohlhepp in 1995. That year the company acquired Cadet Uniform Services, a Toronto uniform rental business, for $41 million.

Scott Farmer, Richard's 38-year-old son, was named president and COO in 1997. That year Cintas made a number of acquisitions, including Micron-Clean Uniform Service and Canadian firms Act One Uniform Rentals and DW King Services. The company also moved into the first aid supplies industry with its purchase of American First Aid, and added clean-room garments to its expanding list of uniform rentals. In 1998 Cintas acquired uniform rental company Apparelmaster, as well as Chicago-based Uniforms To You, a $150 million design and manufacturing company. In an effort to expand its corporate uniform business, the company acquired rival Unitog in 1999 for about $460 million.

As part of the integration of Unitog, in 2000 Cintas closed several of Unitog's uniform rental operations, distribution centers, and manufacturing plants. The company also established first aid supplies and safety equipment unit Xpect. In 2002 Cintas purchased Omni Services, marking its largest acquisition to date.

Founder and Chairman: Richard T. Farmer, age 67, $450,765 pay
CEO and Director: Robert J. Kohlhepp, age 57, $606,200 pay
President, COO, and Director: Scott D. Farmer, age 42, $569,000 pay
SVP; President, Uniform Rental Division: Robert R. Buck, age 54, $570,520 pay
President, National Account Sales Division: William L. Cronin
VP and CFO: William C. Gale
VP and CIO: G. Thomas Thornley
VP and Treasurer: Karen L. Carnahan
VP, Secretary, and General Counsel: Thomas E. Frooman
VP: James J. Krupansky
VP: Robert A. Oswald
VP Central Rental Group: Gregory J. Eling
VP Cleanroom Division: Michael P. Gaburo
VP Distribution: J. Phillip Holloman
VP First Aid & Safety Division: David Pollak Jr.
VP Great Lakes Rental Group: David B. Armbrester
VP Human Resources: Larry Fultz
VP Logistics and Manufacturing: Glenn W. Larsen
VP Marketing and Merchandising: William W. Goetz
VP MidAtlantic Rental Group: John E. Myers
Auditors: Ernst & Young LLP

LOCATIONS

HQ: 6800 Cintas Blvd., Cincinnati, OH 45262
Phone: 513-459-1200   **Fax:** 513-573-4130
Web: www.cintas-corp.com

Cintas has operations in the US and Canada.

PRODUCTS/OPERATIONS

2002 Sales

	$ mil.	% of total
Rentals	1,753	77
Other services	518	23
Total	**2,271**	**100**

Selected Products and Services
Cleanroom supplies
Entrance mats
Fender covers
First aid and safety products and services
Linen products
Mops
Towels
Uniform cleaning
Uniform rental and sales

COMPETITORS

Angelica Corporation
ARAMARK
G&K Services
National Service Industries
NCH
Steiner
Superior Uniform Group
UniFirst

HISTORICAL FINANCIALS & EMPLOYEES

Nasdaq: CTAS FYE: May 31	Annual Growth	5/93	5/94	5/95	5/96	5/97	5/98	5/99	5/00	5/01	5/02
Sales ($ mil.)	19.6%	453	523	615	730	840	1,198	1,752	1,902	2,161	2,271
Net income ($ mil.)	20.1%	45	52	63	75	91	123	139	193	223	234
Income as % of sales	—	9.9%	10.0%	10.2%	10.3%	10.8%	10.3%	7.9%	10.2%	10.3%	10.3%
Earnings per share ($)	17.0%	0.33	0.40	0.50	0.59	0.70	0.79	0.82	1.14	1.30	1.36
Stock price – FY high ($)	—	10.34	11.51	13.42	18.68	21.47	35.27	52.28	47.38	54.50	56.62
Stock price – FY low ($)	—	7.92	8.25	9.92	11.17	16.42	20.51	26.60	23.18	33.75	37.25
Stock price – FY close ($)	21.3%	9.17	10.40	11.51	17.84	20.68	30.47	42.35	44.00	46.64	52.21
P/E – high	—	30	28	26	32	30	44	62	41	41	42
P/E – low	—	23	20	19	19	23	25	32	20	26	27
Dividends per share ($)	19.6%	0.05	0.06	0.07	0.09	0.10	0.12	0.15	0.28	0.22	0.25
Book value per share ($)	17.9%	1.90	2.21	2.58	3.03	3.54	4.17	5.24	6.20	7.27	8.38
Employees	14.8%	7,797	8,581	9,724	10,803	11,996	16,957	22,000	22,500	24,193	27,000

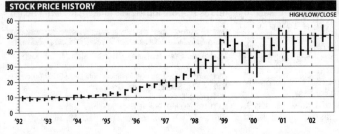

STOCK PRICE HISTORY   HIGH/LOW/CLOSE

2002 FISCAL YEAR-END
Debt ratio: 33.1%
Return on equity: 17.6%
Cash ($ mil.): 41
Current ratio: 2.73
Long-term debt ($ mil.): 703
No. of shares (mil.): 170
Dividends
  Yield: 0.5%
  Payout: 18.4%
Market value ($ mil.): 8,872

CIRCUIT CITY GROUP

Circuit City is plugged into almost every state in the US. Circuit City Stores' Circuit City Group is the #2 US appliance and electronics retailer, even though it has more stores than archrival Best Buy. Most of Richmond, Virginia-based Circuit City Group's more than 620 US locations are Circuit City Superstores, which range from 9,500 to 43,000 sq. ft. and offer a broad selection of merchandise such as computers, software, home stereos, and TVs.

To make up for the shrinking profit levels among PC sales, the company has turned to hot-ticket items such as satellite television systems and cellular phones. The company is also revamping its superstores and has phased out major appliances to make room for more high-profit electronics and home office products. The company also operates about 20 mall-based Circuit City Express stores.

Circuit City Stores is a holding company for Circuit City Group. Circuit City Stores also controlled used-car seller CarMax, which owns about 40 used-car superstores and 20 new-car franchises, but spun it off in October 2002.

HISTORY

While on vacation in Richmond, Virginia, in 1949, Samuel Wurtzel learned from a local barber that the first TV station in the South was about to go on the air. Wurtzel decided to launch a southern TV retailing operation and founded Wards Company (an acronym for family names Wurtzel, Alan, Ruth, David, and Samuel) in Richmond that year, gradually diversifying into small appliances. Wards went public in 1961.

Throughout the 1960s and early 1970s, Wards expanded by acquiring several appliance retailers. Samuel's son Alan joined the business in 1966, when the company was focused on selling stereos. Predicting the end of the stereo boom, Alan converted the stores into full-line electronics specialty retailers.

Wards took a bold step in 1975, when it spent half of its net worth to open an electronics superstore in Richmond. It was an immediate success, and in 1981 it branched into the New York City market with the purchase of Lafayette Radio Electronics. The company found itself unable to compete with exuberant competitors in New York, such as Crazy Eddie (which went out of business), and abandoned the market. From its New York experience, Wards developed a strategy of blitzing single markets in the South and the West with a high number of stores. In 1984 the company changed its name to Circuit City Stores.

Two years later Alan stepped down as CEO, and company leadership passed to Richard Sharp, a former computer consultant who had designed Circuit City's computerized sales system. Sharp made it a priority to maintain an efficient distribution and records system. Earnings slipped in 1990 as consumer spending dropped and the industry was slow to introduce new products. During this time, Circuit City started opening mall stores named Impulse and introduced the Circuit City credit card.

Circuit City began selling recorded music in its superstores in 1992. The next year it entered Chicago with 18 stores and renamed its Impulse stores Circuit City Express. Also in 1993 Circuit City opened its first used-car-retailing venture, a CarMax dealership in Richmond. (The company offered a CarMax tracking stock in 1997.)

Rival Best Buy surpassed Circuit City's sales in fiscal year 1996, partly due to Best Buy's aggressive expansion. That year Circuit City and Mexico City-based electronics retailer Grupo Elektra launched a service whereby products bought at Circuit City stores in the US could be picked up at Elektra stores in Mexico. The next year the firm opened superstores in the New York City metropolitan area, part of its ongoing expansion.

The company formed joint venture Digital Video Express (Divx) in 1998, offering DVD players and movies on limited-use, disposable discs available in Circuit City outlets and other stores. Lack of support from movie studios and other retailers forced an end to Divx in 1999, incurring about a $375 million loss.

In an effort to compete with online computer retailers, in 1999 the company began offering $400 rebates to customers who signed up with Internet service provider CompuServe. In June 2000 president and COO Alan McCollough replaced Sharp as CEO, who remains chairman. The following month Circuit City began a $1 billion remodeling plan for its superstores that would phase out major appliances in favor of high-profit consumer electronics and home office products. It also announced plans to cut about 1,000 employees.

In 2002 Circuit City Stores announced it would spin off its CarMax unit as an independent entity. Chairman Richard Sharp stepped down in June 2002; president and CEO McCollough took on his responsibilities as chairman of the board.

OFFICERS

Chairman, President, and CEO: W. Alan McCollough, age 52, $1,995,000 pay
EVP and COO: John W. Froman, age 48, $985,000 pay
EVP, CFO, Secretary, and Director:
Michael T. Chalifoux, age 55, $988,000 pay
EVP Merchandising: Kim D. Maguire, age 46
SVP and CIO: Dennis J. Bowman, age 48, $655,000 pay

SVP, Treasurer, and Controller: Philip J. Dunn, age 49
SVP and General Counsel: W. Stephen Cannon, age 50
SVP Automotive; President, CarMax: W. Austin Ligon, age 51, $1,166,153 pay
SVP Human Resources and Training: Jeffrey S. Wells, age 56
SVP Marketing: Fiona P. Dias, age 36
Auditors: KPMG LLP

LOCATIONS

HQ: 9950 Mayland Dr., Richmond, VA 23233
Phone: 804-527-4000   **Fax:** 804-527-4194
Web: www.circuitcity.com

2002 Stores

	No.
California	84
Texas	48
Florida	46
Illinois	33
New York	29
Ohio	29
Pennsylvania	27
Virginia	27
Michigan	24
Georgia	23
North Carolina	19
Massachusetts	18
Maryland	16
Indiana	15
New Jersey	13
Tennessee	13
Washington	12
Arizona	11
Colorado	11
Missouri	11
Other states	114
Total	**623**

PRODUCTS/OPERATIONS

2002 Stores

	No.
Circuit City Superstores	603
Circuit City Express (mall stores)	20
Total	**623**

Selected Merchandise

Audio Equipment
CD players
Home stereo systems
Tape recorders

Home Office
Computers
Fax machines
Printers
Software

Mobile Electronics
Car stereo systems
Security systems

Video Equipment
Camcorders
Digital satellite systems
DVD players
TVs
VCRs

Other
Cellular phones
Entertainment Software
Portable audio and video products
Telephones

COMPETITORS

Amazon.com	Electronics	OfficeMax
Best Buy	Boutique	PC Connection
Blockbuster	Fry's Electronics	P.C. Richard
BUY.COM	Gateway	RadioShack
Cablevision	Good Guys	REX Stores
Electronics	HMV	Sears
Investments	J & R Electronics	Staples
CDW	Kmart	Trans World
CompUSA	Micro Warehouse	Entertainment
Costco	MTS	Ultimate
Dell Computer	Musicland	Electronics
	Office Depot	Wal-Mart

HISTORICAL FINANCIALS & EMPLOYEES

NYSE: CC FYE: February 28	Annual Growth	2/93	2/94	2/95	2/96	2/97	2/98	2/99	2/00	2/01	2/02
Sales ($ mil.)	16.4%	3,270	4,130	5,583	7,029	7,664	8,871	10,804	12,614	12,959	12,792
Net income ($ mil.)	8.0%	110	132	168	179	136	104	143	198	161	219
Income as % of sales	—	3.4%	3.2%	3.0%	2.6%	1.8%	1.2%	1.3%	1.6%	1.2%	1.7%
Earnings per share ($)	5.3%	0.58	0.69	0.87	0.92	0.70	0.57	0.75	0.96	0.73	0.92
Stock price - FY high ($)	—	9.40	11.30	9.17	12.67	12.92	15.17	21.39	35.93	43.48	20.68
Stock price - FY low ($)	—	4.61	5.50	5.75	7.17	9.55	10.30	9.61	17.30	5.79	6.37
Stock price - FY close ($)	4.7%	7.92	6.34	7.21	9.88	10.42	12.88	18.09	26.97	10.12	11.93
P/E - high	—	16	16	11	14	18	27	29	37	60	22
P/E - low	—	8	8	7	8	14	18	13	18	8	7
Dividends per share ($)	5.8%	0.03	0.04	0.05	0.06	0.07	0.07	0.07	0.07	0.07	0.05
Book value per share ($)	17.7%	3.01	3.70	4.55	5.46	8.22	8.71	9.45	10.51	11.38	13.09
Employees	10.4%	20,107	23,625	31,413	36,430	40,071	42,246	49,362	53,284	53,445	49,167

NET INCOME HISTORY

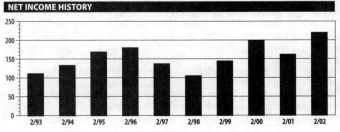

2002 FISCAL YEAR-END

Debt ratio: 0.5%
Return on equity: 8.6%
Cash ($ mil.): 1,252
Current ratio: 2.23
Long-term debt ($ mil.): 14
No. of shares (mil.): 209
Dividends
  Yield: 0.4%
  Payout: 5.4%
Market value ($ mil.): 2,491

CISCO SYSTEMS, INC.

It's lonely at the top? Tell that to Cisco. San Jose, California-based Cisco Systems is the world's leading provider of equipment used to build and connect local and wide area networks; switches and routers account for 40% and 30% of sales, respectively. The company also makes remote access servers, IP telephony equipment used to transmit data and voice communications over the same network, Internet service and security products, optical networking components, and network management software. US customers account for about 60% of sales.

Cisco has used acquisitions — close to 80 since 1993 — to broaden its product lines and secure engineering talent in the highly competitive networking sector. Of course with market breadth comes an abundance of competitors, and Cisco faces fellow giants and swift upstarts across all of its market segments. It shares the Ethernet switch market with companies ranging from the pioneering 3Com to relative newcomer Extreme Networks; hard-charging Juniper Networks has made aggressive moves to wrestle market share in the core router market; and telecommunications powerhouse Nortel Networks is perhaps Cisco's most formidable opponent in virtually every market.

And the once seemingly invincible Cisco has not been immune to market rigors. The company's heavy investment in Internet Protocol-based telecommunications equipment proved costly when an industrywide downturn slowed spending among telecom service providers building next-generation voice networks. Cisco responded with job cuts and other organizational changes, realigning its operations around its core technologies rather than customer segments, and centralizing its engineering and marketing efforts. Cisco's entrenchment has provided it with some buffer against telecom's nose-dive, and the company continues to branch into new markets such as storage networking.

HISTORY

Cisco Systems was founded by Stanford University husband-and-wife team Leonard Bosack and Sandra Lerner and three colleagues in 1984. Bosack developed technology to link his computer lab's network with his wife's network in the graduate business school. Anticipating a market for networking devices, Bosack and Lerner mortgaged their house, bought a used mainframe, put it in their garage, and got friends and relatives to work for deferred pay. They sold their first network router in 1986. Originally targeting universities, the aerospace industry, and the government, the company in 1988 expanded its

marketing to include large corporations. Short of cash, Cisco turned to venture capitalist Donald Valentine of Sequoia Capital, who bought a controlling stake and became chairman. He hired John Morgridge of laptop maker GRiD Systems as president and CEO.

Cisco, whose products had a proven track record, had a head start as the market for network routers opened up. Sales increased from $1.5 million in 1987 to $28 million in 1989.

The company went public in 1990. That year Morgridge fired Lerner, with whom he had clashed, and Bosack quit. The couple sold their stock for about $200 million, giving most to favorite causes, including animal charities and a Harvard professor looking for extraterrestrials.

With competition increasing, Cisco began expanding through acquisitions. Purchases included networking company Crescendo Communications (1993); Ethernet switch maker Kalpana (1994); and asynchronous transfer mode (ATM) switch maker LightStream (1995). In 1995 EVP John Chambers succeeded Morgridge as president and CEO; Morgridge became chairman (and Valentine vice chairman).

Cisco's 1996 acquisition of ATM product maker StrataCom set off a flurry of consolidations within the networking industry. In 1997 Cisco formed an alliance with telecom equipment maker Alcatel to provide networking capabilities to telecommunications and Internet access providers.

Cisco acquired several niche players in 1998, such as Precept Software (video transmission software) and American Internet Corporation (software for set-top boxes and cable modems). That year Cisco's market capitalization passed the $100 billion milestone, a landmark accomplishment for a company its age.

In 1999 Cisco invested $1.5 billion for a 20% stake in KPMG's consulting business. (The stake was reduced to 9% when KPMG Consulting spun off in 2001.) Also in 1999 Cisco teamed with Motorola to acquire the fixed wireless assets of Bosch Telecom, forming joint venture SpectraPoint Wireless to provide high-speed networking services to businesses. In its largest acquisition to date, Cisco bought Cerent (fiber-optic network equipment) for $7 billion.

The company continued its acquisitive ways in 2000, snatching up more than 20 companies, including wireless network equipment maker Aironet. Hard hit by an economic slump that affected companies across the technology sector, mighty Cisco in 2001 responded with the strategy du jour — a 15% workforce reduction. To save a few jobs, Chambers voluntarily cut his salary to $1 for the remainder of the year.

Chairman: John P. Morgridge, age 68
Vice Chairman: Donald T. Valentine, age 69
President, CEO, and Director: John T. Chambers, age 52, $268,131 pay (partial-year salary)
Chief Development Officer: Mario Mazzola, age 55
SVP and CIO: Brad Boston
SVP and Chief Marketing Officer: James Richardson, age 44, $383,108 pay
SVP and General Manager, Technology Development: Charles H. Giancarlo, age 43
SVP, Finance and Administration, CFO, Secretary, and Director: Larry R. Carter, age 59, $424,212 pay
SVP, Human Resources: Kate DCamp
SVP, Internet Business Solutions Group: Susan L. Bostrom, age 41
SVP, Internet Communications Software Group: David Kirk
SVP, Internet Switching and Services: Michelangelo Volpi, age 34, $380,346 pay
Auditors: PricewaterhouseCoopers LLP

LOCATIONS

HQ: 170 W. Tasman Dr., San Jose, CA 95134
Phone: 408-526-4000   **Fax:** 408-526-4100
Web: www.cisco.com

2001 Sales

	$ mil.	% of total
Americas	15,130	60
Europe, Middle East & Africa	6,288	25
Asia/Pacific		
Japan	2,384	9
Other countries	1,540	6
Adjustments	(3,049)	—
Total	**22,293**	**100**

PRODUCTS/OPERATIONS

2001 Sales

	$ mil.	% of total
Switches	10,586	42
Routers	8,655	34
Service	2,734	11
Access	2,333	9
Other	1,034	4
Adjustments	(3,049)	—
Total	**22,293**	**100**

Products

Ethernet concentrators, hubs, and transceivers	Routers
Interfaces and adapters	Switches
Network management software	Telephony access systems
Optical platforms	Video networking
Power supplies	Voice integration applications
	Wireless networking

COMPETITORS

3Com	Foundry	Motorola
ADC Tele-	Networks	MRV
communications	Fujitsu	Communications
Alcatel	Hewlett-Packard	NEC
Avaya	IBM	Network
Avici Systems	Intel	Associates
CIENA	Juniper	Nokia
D-Link	Networks	Nortel Networks
ECI Telecom	Linksys	Novell
Enterasys	Lucent	Redback
Ericsson	Marconi	Networks
Extreme	Networks	Sycamore
Networks	Microsoft	Networks

HISTORICAL FINANCIALS & EMPLOYEES

Nasdaq: CSCO FYE: Last Sunday in July	Annual Growth	7/92	7/93	7/94	7/95	7/96	7/97	7/98	7/99	7/00	7/01
Sales ($ mil.)	59.2%	340	649	1,243	1,979	4,096	6,440	8,459	12,154	18,928	22,293
Net income ($ mil.)	—	84	172	315	421	913	1,049	1,350	2,096	2,668	(1,014)
Income as % of sales	—	24.9%	26.5%	25.3%	21.3%	22.3%	16.3%	16.0%	17.2%	14.1%	—
Earnings per share ($)	—	0.02	0.04	0.06	0.08	0.15	0.17	0.21	0.31	0.36	(0.14)
Stock price - FY high ($)	—	0.75	1.59	2.27	3.27	6.58	9.00	17.43	34.63	82.00	70.00
Stock price - FY low ($)	—	0.26	0.62	1.04	1.13	2.85	5.03	7.58	10.28	28.08	13.19
Stock price - FY close ($)	43.6%	0.74	1.44	1.17	3.10	5.76	8.85	15.97	31.06	65.44	19.22
P/E - high	—	38	40	32	41	44	53	79	105	210	—
P/E - low	—	13	16	15	14	19	30	34	31	72	—
Dividends per share ($)	—	0.00	0.00	0.00	0.00	0.00	0.00	0.00	0.00	0.00	0.00
Book value per share ($)	59.1%	0.06	0.11	0.18	0.28	0.48	0.71	1.14	1.77	3.71	3.70
Employees	51.9%	882	1,451	2,443	4,086	8,782	11,000	15,000	21,000	34,000	38,000

STOCK PRICE HISTORY

HIGH/LOW/CLOSE

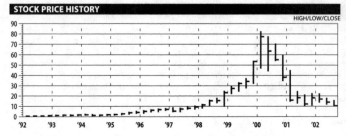

2001 FISCAL YEAR-END

Debt ratio: 0.0%
Return on equity: —
Cash ($ mil.): 4,873
Current ratio: 1.59
Long-term debt ($ mil.): 0
No. of shares (mil.): 7,324
Dividends
  Yield: —
  Payout: —
Market value ($ mil.): 140,767

CIT GROUP INC.

"Credit — the commodity in which we deal — is ever in demand," said Henry Ittleson, founder of what became famous as commercial loan powerhouse CIT Group. The New York-based commercial finance firm, one of the largest commercial lenders on the planet, sates that demand across the spectrum, offering services to clients ranging from consumers borrowing against their houses to captains of industry seeking leasing arrangements for multimillion-dollar manufacturing equipment.

The firm has four divisions: equipment financing, which offers secured financing to a variety of heavy industries and includes a separate unit devoted to aircraft and rail equipment lending; specialty finance, which includes vendor finance programs and home equity loans; commercial finance, which includes factoring, letters of credit, and other traditional commercial financing programs; and structured finance, which offers investment banking services. CIT Group exited the manufactured home and recreational vehicle financing businesses as a means of refocusing on what it considers more robust commercial finance opportunities.

Traditionally known for conservative management, the company passed through several hands in recent decades, including RCA and Dai-Ichi Kangyo Bank, with Tyco International taking control in 2001 and renaming the group Tyco Capital.

But if credit is ever in demand, creditors are ever demanding. In 2002 Tyco International spun off the division as part of a breakup of the parent into four divisions to reduce overall corporate debt. The company has returned to its CIT identity.

HISTORY

Henry Ittleson founded CIT Group as Commercial Credit and Investment Trust in St. Louis in 1908. Initially financing horse-drawn carriages, it moved to New York in 1915 as Commercial Investment Trust (CIT) to participate in one of the milestones of modern consumer debt: Its auto financing program, launched in collaboration with Studebaker, was the first of its kind.

CIT diversified into industrial financing during the 1920s and went public in 1924 on the NYSE. Cars remained a strong focus, though: When Ford Motor Co. ran into difficulties in 1933, it sold financing division Universal Credit Corp. to CIT. The firm continued to expand into industrial financing, incorporating its industrial business as CIT Financial Corp. in 1942.

During the post-WWII boom, CIT began financing manufactured home sales and offering small loans. In 1964 it consolidated factoring operations into Meinhard-Commercial Corp. By the end of the 1960s, the firm started to retreat from auto financing, focusing instead on industrial leasing, factoring, and equipment financing.

In 1980 RCA bought CIT, seeking to buy financing to develop its other businesses. RCA found the debt from the purchase unwieldy, however, and sold CIT to Manufacturers Hanover Bank (Manny Hanny) in 1984. The bank bought CIT to expand outside its home state of New York. Though it could not open banks out of state, Manny Hanny could still offer financial services through CIT, which became The CIT Group in 1986.

Manny Hanny executives tried to bring aggressive management to staid, top-heavy CIT. CIT sold its Inventory Finance division in 1987, divested the consumer loan business in 1988, and consolidated the Meinhard-Commercial and Manufacturers Hanover factoring units in 1989. By then Manny Hanny was cash-strapped over losses incurred from foreign loans, so it sold a 60% stake in CIT to The Dai-Ichi Kangyo Bank of Japan.

CIT gave Dai-Ichi entrée into US financial services, and it began expanding CIT's range of services again, including equity investment (1990), credit finance (from its purchase of Fidelcor Business Credit in 1991), and venture capital (1992). CIT also reentered the consumer loan market (including home equity lending) with a new Consumer Finance group (1992).

In 1995 Chemical Bank (Manny Hanny's successor; now part of J.P. Morgan Chase & Co.) sold an additional 20% share to Dai-Ichi, bumping the Japanese bank's holdings to 80% and arranging to sell its remaining shares to Dai-Ichi. In 1997, instead of Dai-Ichi buying the rest of Chase's shares, CIT bought them and spun them off to the public. In 1998 Dai-Ichi reduced its stake.

The following year CIT bought Newcourt Credit Group, North America's #2 equipment finance and leasing firm; it also bought Heller Financial's commercial services unit. In 2000 the firm worked on integrating Newcourt and sold its Hong Kong consumer finance unit.

Tyco International bought CIT in 2001, renaming the new subsidiary Tyco Capital. Under Tyco's umbrella, it sold its manufactured home loan portfolio to Lehman Brothers and recreational vehicle portfolio to Salomon Smith Barney as a part of its effort to exit noncore businesses. Tyco, however, expanded too far too fast, and the next year announced an about-face on its financial services subsidiary, deciding to spin off the division and return to its CIT identity.

Chairman, President, and CEO: Albert R. Gamper Jr.,
age 60, $3,801,203 pay (partial-year salary)
EVP and Chief Risk Officer: Thomas L. Abate, age 56
EVP and General Counsel: Robert J. Ingato, age 41
EVP and CFO: Joseph M. Leone, age 48, $882,308 pay
(partial-year salary)
EVP, Human Resources: Susan Mitchell
Group CEO, Equipment Financing: John D. Burr,
age 58
Group CEO, Specialty Finance: Thomas B. Hallman,
age 49, $893,846 pay (partial-year salary)
Group CEO, Commercial Finance:
Lawrence A. Marsiello, age 51, $793,846 pay (partial-year salary)
Group CEO, Structured Finance: David D. McKerroll,
age 42
Group CEO, Capital Finance: Nikita Zdanow, age 64,
$869,615 pay (partial-year salary)
Auditors: PricewaterhouseCoopers LLP

LOCATIONS

HQ: 1211 Avenue of the Americas, New York, NY 10036
Phone: 973-536-1390 **Fax:** 973-740-5527
Web: www.citgroup.com

CIT Group has offices in Argentina, Australia, Austria,
Belgium, Brazil, Canada, Chile, China, Colombia,
France, Germany, Hong Kong, Hungary, Ireland, Italy,
Malaysia, Mexico, the Netherlands, New Zealand,
Singapore, South Korea, Spain, Switzerland, Taiwan, the
UK, and the US.

2001 Finance & Leasing Assets

	% of total
United States	
Northeast	24
West	19
Midwest	18
Southeast	14
Southwest	12
Canada	5
Other countries	8
Total	**100**

PRODUCTS/OPERATIONS

2001 Sales

	$ mil.	% of total
Finance income	3,975	86
Factoring commissions	112	3
Gains on securitizations	98	2
Gains on sales of leasing equipment	48	1
Gains on venture capital investments	6	—
Fees & other income	387	8
Special charges	(78)	—
Total	**4,548**	**100**

COMPETITORS

Advanta
AXA Financial
Citigroup
Conseco
Deutsche Bank
FINOVA
GE Commercial Finance
Household International
J.P. Morgan Chase
Lehman Brothers
Merrill Lynch
National City

HISTORICAL FINANCIALS & EMPLOYEES

NYSE: CIT FYE: September 30	Annual Growth	12/92	12/93	12/94	12/95	12/96	12/97	12/98	12/99	12/00	*9/01
Sales ($ mil.)	17.7%	—	1,238	1,429	1,714	1,890	2,131	2,271	2,917	6,160	4,548
Net income ($ mil.)	7.9%	—	182	201	225	260	310	339	389	612	334
Income as % of sales	—	—	14.7%	14.1%	13.1%	13.8%	14.6%	14.9%	13.4%	9.9%	7.3%
Employees	12.5%	—	—	2,700	2,750	2,950	3,025	3,230	8,255	7,355	6,150

* Fiscal year change

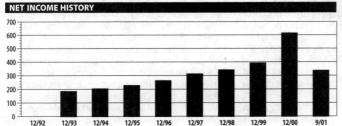

NET INCOME HISTORY

2001 FISCAL YEAR-END

Debt ratio: 67.6%
Return on equity: 3.0%
Cash ($ mil.): 1,541
Current ratio: —
Long-term debt ($ mil.): 35,698

CITIGROUP INC.

Citigroup is more like a Citicrowd. The New York-based company is the world's second-largest financial services firm (behind Japan's Mizuho Holdings), the leading credit card issuer, and the first US bank with more than $1 trillion in assets. But the company may be getting too big for its britches as it finds itself embroiled in a host of controversies regarding conflicts of interests in its investment banking business.

Citigroup serves consumers and businesses through more than 2,600 locations in the US and about 3,000 additional offices in some 100 other countries. Its largest business segment, Global Consumer, offers retail banking (primarily through subsidiary Citibank) and investment and insurance services via Primerica Financial Services and Travelers Life and Annuity. The Global Investment Management and Private Banking division performs asset management services.

Citigroup is parlaying the $4 billion it netted from the spinoff of 20% of Travelers Property Casualty (it distributed most of the remaining stock to Citigroup shareholders) into a planned $5.8 billion purchase of Golden State Bancorp, the parent of the third-largest thrift in the US, Cal Fed.

The company's Corporate and Investment Bank arm provides brokerage, banking, advisory, and financial planning to corporate clients. But subsidiary Salomon Smith Barney, one of the world's largest underwriters of stocks and bonds, is at the center of several brouhahas, including a House of Representatives investigation into Citigroup's connection with bankrupt telecom firm WorldCom, and a Senate investigation exploring Citigroup's role in the Enron collapse.

Legendary chairman Sandy Weill has maintained that Citigroup is not involved in any improprieties, but Weill is being investigated by New York Attorney General Eliot Spitzer over his possible role in Salomon gaining a mandate to underwrite AT&T tracking stock in 2000, which netted Citigroup some $45 million in fees. (Prior to the deal, a Salomon analyst had upgraded his rating of AT&T to a "buy.") Weill is also a member of AT&T's board.

HISTORY

Citigroup travels under an old umbrella. Predecessor Travelers Group (the first US accident insurer) was founded in 1864 by businessmen in Hartford, Connecticut. Travelers soon added life insurance, annuities, and liability insurance; in 1897 it issued the first auto policy. It later added group life, and sold President Woodrow Wilson the first air travel policy.

A decision made on the eve of the 1929 crash to buy federal bonds helped the firm survive the Depression. Travelers thrived after WWII and issued space travel insurance to *Apollo 11* astronauts for the first moon landing.

In the late 1970s and early 1980s Travelers got into financial services. When real estate soured in the late 1980s, it sold its home mortgage units. Enfeebled, Travelers caught the eye of empire builder Sanford "Sandy" Weill.

Weill had built brokerage firm Shearson Loeb Rhoades and sold it to American Express (AmEx) in 1981. Forced out of AmEx in 1985, Weill bounced back in 1986, buying Control Data's Commercial Credit unit.

Primerica caught Weill's eye next. Its predecessor, American Can, was founded in 1901 as a New Jersey canning company; it eventually expanded into the paper and retail industries before turning to financial services in 1986. The firm was renamed Primerica in 1987 and bought brokerage Smith Barney, Harris Upham & Co. Weill's Commercial Credit bought Primerica in 1988. In 1993 Primerica bought Shearson from AmEx, as well as Travelers, taking its name and logo.

Weill set about trimming Travelers. He sold life subsidiaries and bought Aetna's property/casualty business in 1995. In 1996 he consolidated all property/casualty operations to form Travelers Property Casualty and took it public. The next year Travelers bought investment bank Salomon Brothers and formed Salomon Smith Barney Holdings.

Weill sold Citicorp chairman and CEO John Reed on the idea of a merger in 1998, in advance of the Gramm-Leach-Bliley act, which deregulated the financial services industry in the US. By the time the merger went through, a slowed US economy and foreign-market turmoil brought significant losses to both sides. The renamed Citigroup consolidated in 1998 and 1999, laying off more than 10,000 employees.

In 1999 Citigroup moved deeper into subprime lending. It launched Internet banking services on AOL, and emerged as the leading provider of government benefits via ATM cards. Also that year, former Treasury Secretary Robert Rubin joined Citigroup as a co-chairman.

In 2000 John Reed retired and the company bought the investment banking business of British firm Schroders. That same year Citigroup bought subprime lender Associates First Capital (now CitiFinancial) for approximately $27 billion to expand its consumer product lines and its international presence. The deal, however, also brought Citigroup federal scrutiny regarding perceived predatory lending tactics. In 2001 the company bought New York-based European American Bank from ABN AMRO and purchased Grupo Financiero Banamex, one of Mexico's biggest banks.

Chairman and CEO: Sanford I. Weill, age 69,
$17,986,748 pay
Chairman of the Executive Committee and Director:
Robert E. Rubin, age 63, $11,250,000 pay
Senior Vice Chairman: Victor J. Menezes, age 52,
$4,725,000 pay
Senior Vice Chairman and Senior International Officer:
William R. Rhodes, age 66
**Vice Chairman; Chairman and CEO, Citigroup
International:** Sir Deryck C. Maughan, age 54
Vice Chairman; President, Citigroup International:
Stanley Fischer
**President; Chairman and CEO, Global Consumer
Group:** Robert B. Willumstad, age 56, $4,462,500 pay
COO and Corporate Secretary: Charles O. Prince III,
age 52
**SEVP; COO and Chief Administrative Officer,
Consumer Group:** Marjorie Magner, age 52
EVP, Finance and Investments, and CFO:
Todd S. Thomson, age 41
Chairman, Citigroup Europe:
Sir Winfried F. W. Bischoff, age 61
**Chairman and CEO, Global Corporate and Investment
Bank and Salomon Smith Barney:**
Michael A. Carpenter, $9,206,250 pay
**Chairman, President, and CEO, Travelers Life and
Annuity:** George C. Kokulis
Auditors: KPMG LLP

LOCATIONS

HQ: 399 Park Ave., New York, NY 10043
Phone: 212-559-1000   **Fax:** 212-793-3946
Web: www.citigroup.com

PRODUCTS/OPERATIONS

2001 Sales

	$ mil.	% of total
Interest		
Loans	39,616	35
Other	26,949	24
Noninterest		
Commissions & fees	15,944	14
Insurance premiums	13,460	12
Principal transactions	5,544	5
Asset management & administration fees	5,389	5
Other	5,120	5
Total	**112,022**	**100**

COMPETITORS

Allstate	Deutsche Bank	MassMutual
American	FleetBoston	MBNA
Express	FMR	Merrill Lynch
AXA Financial	GE	Mizuho Holdings
Bank of America	Goldman Sachs	Morgan Stanley
Bank of New	The Hartford	New York Life
York	Household	Northwestern
BANK ONE	International	Mutual
Bear Stearns	HSBC Holdings	Prudential
Capital One	ING	State Farm
Financial	John Hancock	UBS
Chubb	Financial	UBS
CIGNA	Services	PaineWebber
CNA Financial	J.P. Morgan	USAA
Credit Lyonnais	Chase	Wachovia
Credit Suisse	Lehman	Wells Fargo
First Boston	Brothers	

HISTORICAL FINANCIALS & EMPLOYEES

NYSE: C FYE: December 31	Annual Growth	12/92	12/93	12/94	12/95	12/96	12/97	12/98	12/99	12/00	12/01
Assets ($ mil.)	52.6%	23,397	101,360	115,297	114,475	151,067	386,555	668,641	716,937	902,210	1,051,450
Net income ($ mil.)	39.2%	728	916	1,326	1,834	2,331	3,104	5,807	9,867	13,519	14,284
Income as % of assets	—	3.1%	0.9%	1.2%	1.6%	1.5%	0.8%	0.9%	1.4%	1.5%	1.4%
Earnings per share ($)	19.7%	0.54	0.91	0.34	0.93	1.20	1.27	1.22	2.13	2.62	2.72
Stock price – FY high ($)	—	4.16	8.26	7.20	10.66	15.85	28.70	36.77	43.69	59.13	57.38
Stock price – FY low ($)	—	2.99	4.02	5.07	5.40	9.43	14.60	14.26	24.51	35.34	34.51
Stock price – FY close ($)	32.4%	4.04	6.49	5.40	10.45	15.14	26.95	24.86	41.77	51.06	50.48
P/E – high	—	7	9	21	11	13	21	29	20	22	20
P/E – low	—	5	4	15	6	7	11	11	11	13	12
Dividends per share ($)	29.2%	0.06	0.08	0.10	0.16	0.15	0.20	0.28	0.41	0.49	0.60
Book value per share ($)	19.5%	3.18	4.81	4.63	6.27	6.85	9.31	9.49	11.07	13.18	15.78
Employees	27.8%	30,000	65,000	52,000	47,600	58,900	68,900	173,700	180,000	230,000	272,000

STOCK PRICE HISTORY

HIGH/LOW/CLOSE

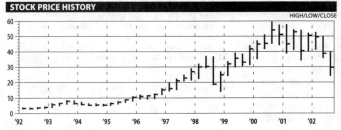

2001 FISCAL YEAR-END

Equity as % of assets: 7.7%
Return on assets: 1.5%
Return on equity: 19.8%
Long-term debt ($ mil.): 136,435
No. of shares (mil.): 5,149
Dividends
  Yield: 1.2%
  Payout: 22.1%
Market value ($ mil.): 259,906
Sales ($ mil.): 112,022

CITIZENS COMMUNICATIONS

The former Citizens Utilities once wanted to be all utilities to all people. But today, Stamford, Connecticut-based Citizens Communications just wants to be the phone company: It is selling its natural gas, electric, and water utility operations.

The company is the incumbent local exchange carrier in parts of 24 states, primarily in rural and suburban markets. It operates about 2.5 million phone lines and provides local, long-distance, and data services, including Internet access. In 2001 Citizens canceled separate plans to buy another 540,000 telephone lines from Qwest and 63,000 lines from Verizon.

Citizens also owns Electric Lightwave, a competitive local exchange carrier (CLEC). ELI offers local and long-distance voice and data services over fiber-optic networks in major markets in the western US, and it provides long-distance and data services nationwide.

HISTORY

Citizens Utilities Company was formed in 1935 to acquire Public Utilities Consolidated Corporation, a Minneapolis-based company with interests in electric, gas, water, and telephone utilities throughout the US. From 1950 to 1970 the company bought utilities in rural and suburban areas of Arizona, California, Hawaii, Illinois, Indiana, Ohio, and Pennsylvania. A major acquisition was Hawaii's Kauai Electric Company, in 1969. By the mid-1970s, electric power brought in 40% of company revenues.

Leonard Tow, head of Century Communications, was brought on board in 1989 and elected chairman the next year. Expanding Citizens through more electric, water, and natural gas acquisitions, he tripled the company's revenues in less than 10 years.

In 1993 Citizens acquired a majority stake in Electric Lightwave, the first CLEC west of the Mississippi River. Citizens started its long-distance telephone service in 1994. It also acquired 500,000 local access lines in nine states from GTE, quadrupling the size of its operations. By 1995 the telecom group was the fastest-growing segment of the company.

After the Telecommunications Act was passed in 1996, Citizens acquired another 110,000 local access lines and cable systems with more than 7,000 customers from ALLTEL and bought three Southern California cable systems with Century Communications. Citizens aggressively marketed local phone service in areas neighboring its service territories, but the company didn't see the return it expected and by 1997 had to cut its workforce and tighten cost controls. In light of the cutbacks, bookkeeping troubles, and 1996 threats from Vermont to revoke Citizens' license in that state for accounting and permit problems, the board voted Tow a pay cut.

The company sold a minority stake in Electric Lightwave to the public in 1997. (Citizens reacquired the stake in 2002 and Electric Lightwave became a wholly owned subsidiary.) Citizens continued its buying spree with telecom and gas firms in New York and Hawaii, and a local phone company in Pennsylvania in 1998.

The next year, Citizens began turning itself into a pure telecom company through a series of transactions. It agreed to pay about $2.8 billion for 900,000 local phone lines owned by U S WEST and GTE, sold its cable TV interests, and agreed to sell its water and wastewater operations (for $835 million). In 2000 the company agreed to sell its electric utility operations and part of its natural gas business (for $375 million — completed in 2001), and it changed its name to Citizens Communications. (The electric properties deal fell through, however.)

In 2001 Citizens bought more than 1 million local phone lines from Global Crossing for about $3.5 billion. Later that year the company canceled its pending acquisition agreements with Qwest, U S WEST's successor, amid a dispute over how much revenue the local lines were producing. The terminated deals, valued at $1.7 billion, would have given Citizens another 540,000 local lines. It later pulled out of a deal to buy an additional 63,000 access lines in Arizona and California from Verizon.

OFFICERS

Chairman and CEO; Chairman, Electric Lightwave: Leonard Tow, age 73, $900,000 pay

Vice Chairman, President, and COO; EVP, Electric Lightwave; Chairman and President, Citizens Capital Ventures: Scott N. Schneider, age 44, $750,000 pay

EVP and Director; President, COO, and Director, ILEC Sector: John H. Casey III, age 45, $468,800 pay

VP and CFO; VP and CFO, Electric Lightwave, Inc.: Jerry Elliott, age 42

VP; President and CEO, Electric Lightwave; EVP, ILEC Sector: Robert Braden, age 56, $496,968 pay

VP, General Counsel, and Secretary: L. Russell Mitten, age 50

VP and Chief Accounting Officer, Citizens Communications and Electric Lightwave: Robert J. Larson, age 42

VP and General Manager, Central Region: John J. Lass

VP and General Manager, Eastern Region: L. Todd Wells

VP and General Manager, Western Region: William C. O'Neill

VP Corporate Development: Michael Zarella, age 41

VP Engineering and New Technology: Michael G. Harris, age 55

VP Finance and Treasurer, Citizens Communications and Electric Lightwave: Donald B. Armour, age 54
VP Government and Regulatory Affairs:
   F. Wayne Lafferty
VP Human Resources: Jeanne M. DiSturco, age 38
VP Information Technology: Stephen D. Ward, age 35
VP Reporting and Audit: Livingston E. Ross, age 53
VP Sales: Vince Bury
VP Strategic Planning and Development:
   Michael Zarrella, age 42
VP Tax: Edward O. Kipperman, age 50
Auditors: KPMG LLP

LOCATIONS

HQ: Citizens Communications Company
   3 High Ridge Park, Stamford, CT 06905
Phone: 203-614-5600   **Fax:** 203-614-4642
Web: www.czn.net

Citizens Communications provides local telephone service in Arizona, California, Illinois, Minnesota, Montana, Nebraska, Nevada, New Mexico, New York, North Dakota, Oregon, Pennsylvania, Tennessee, Utah, West Virginia, and Wisconsin.

PRODUCTS/OPERATIONS

2001 Sales

	$ mil.	% of total
Incumbent telecommunications		
Network access services	655	27
Local network services	583	24
Long-distance and data services	208	8
Directory services	72	3
Other	76	3
Electric Lightwave		
Network services	101	4
Local phone services	73	3
Data services	40	2
Long-distance services	12	—
Public services		
Gas	412	17
Electric	228	9
Adjustments	(3)	—
Total	**2,457**	**100**

COMPETITORS

AT&T
Qwest
SBC Communications
Sprint FON
Time Warner Telecom
Verizon
WorldCom
XO Communications

HISTORICAL FINANCIALS & EMPLOYEES

NYSE: CZN FYE: December 31	Annual Growth	12/92	12/93	12/94	12/95	12/96	12/97	12/98	12/99	12/00	12/01
Sales ($ mil.)	17.2%	589	619	916	1,069	1,307	1,394	1,542	1,087	1,802	2,457
Net income ($ mil.)	—	115	126	144	160	179	10	62	145	(22)	(83)
Income as % of sales	—	19.5%	20.3%	15.7%	14.9%	13.7%	0.7%	4.0%	13.3%	—	—
Earnings per share ($)	—	—	—	0.57	0.54	0.57	0.03	0.22	0.55	(0.11)	(0.38)
Stock price - FY high ($)	—	—	—	12.81	10.25	9.10	8.98	9.00	14.31	19.00	15.88
Stock price - FY low ($)	—	—	—	8.92	7.60	7.42	5.84	5.20	7.25	12.50	8.20
Stock price - FY close ($)	2.6%	—	—	8.92	9.01	7.86	7.17	8.00	14.19	13.13	10.66
P/E - high	—	—	—	22	19	16	299	39	26	—	—
P/E - low	—	—	—	16	14	13	195	23	13	—	—
Dividends per share ($)	—	—	—	0.00	0.00	0.18	0.00	0.00	0.00	0.00	0.00
Book value per share ($)	8.0%	—	—	4.05	5.10	5.21	5.02	5.36	7.30	6.46	6.92
Employees	17.7%	2,335	2,967	4,294	4,760	5,400	6,100	6,700	6,700	7,191	10,121

STOCK PRICE HISTORY
HIGH/LOW/CLOSE

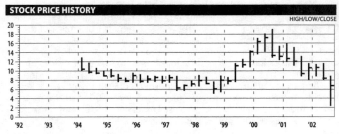

2001 FISCAL YEAR-END
Debt ratio: 74.0%
Return on equity: —
Cash ($ mil.): 58
Current ratio: 1.62
Long-term debt ($ mil.): 5,535
No. of shares (mil.): 281
Dividends
   Yield: —
   Payout: —
Market value ($ mil.): 2,999

CLEAR CHANNEL

In a media landscape dominated by flashy Internet companies, it's tempting to dismiss radio and billboards as yesterday's news. But don't write off these media pioneers just yet — Clear Channel Communications is a reminder that the health of radio and billboards is still vigorous. The San Antonio-based company's 1999 acquisitions of Jacor Communications elevated it to the #2 spot in US radio station ownership. In 2000 the company ascended to the #1 position in radio station ownership with its $23.8 billion acquisition of AMFM. Clear Channel also is one of the world's largest outdoor advertising companies.

Nationwide, the company owns, programs, or sells airtime for more than 1,200 stations (including pending transactions). Clear Channel also has equity stakes in more than 240 radio stations internationally and owns 26% of Hispanic Broadcasting Corporation (one of the largest Spanish-language radio broadcasters in the US). Its acquisition of Jacor brought more than 50 syndicated programs (*Rush Limbaugh, The Dr. Laura Program*) under its umbrella. Clear Channel also operates 19 US TV stations.

The company's outdoor advertising activities encompass more than 730,000 outdoor advertising displays (billboards, transit displays) across the globe.

Not content to dominate just the airwaves, Clear Channel has expanded into live entertainment through its acquisition of events producer and promoter SFX Entertainment (renamed Clear Channel Entertainment). It has also purchased media company The Ackerley Group, which adds another 6,000 outdoor displays, 18 television stations, and four radio stations to its portfolio. The company is also moving in on new turf, announcing in 2001 that it would begin providing online music subscriptions through selected radio stations' Web sites. In 2002, as part of its restructuring plans, Clear Channel discontinued certain operations, closed some of its AMFM and SFX offices, and laid off 630 employees. It expects to cut an additional 170 jobs in connection with the restructuring.

Thomas Hicks of Dallas-based leverage buyout firm Hicks, Muse, Tate & Furst owns about 7% of Clear Channel; CEO L. Lowry Mays, about 5%.

HISTORY

In 1972 investment banker L. Lowry Mays found himself in a predicament. Investors looking to buy a San Antonio radio station had reneged on the financing that he had arranged for them, leaving Mays in a tight spot. He turned to local car dealer B.J. "Red" McCombs, and the two decided to buy the station themselves. They bought three more radio stations in 1973 and another station two years later. In 1975, after leaving investment banking to devote his time to radio stations, Mays changed the company's name from San Antonio Broadcasting to Clear Channel Communications (a moniker borrowed from the term for a high-powered station that has exclusive use of its frequency).

The company went public in 1984, and Clear Channel soon earned a reputation for buying unsuccessful stations and turning them around. By the mid-1980s its collection of radio stations numbered 16. Reluctant to pay the high prices asked for radio stations in the late 1980s, Clear Channel temporarily bowed out of radio acquisitions and tried its luck in the TV market. It created subsidiary Clear Channel Television in 1988; by 1992 it had purchased seven TV stations.

After the Federal Communications Commission loosened restrictions on radio station ownership in 1992, Clear Channel resumed the expansion of its radio empire. By 1994 its portfolio included 35 radio stations and nine TV stations. The company expanded internationally in 1995 with its purchase of a half interest in the Australian Radio Network. It also dipped a toe in the US Spanish-language radio market, buying 20% of Heftel Broadcasting (later renamed Hispanic Broadcasting).

When regulations on nationwide radio station ownership were lifted in 1996, Clear Channel wasted no time extending its reach. By the end of 1997, it owned or programmed 175 radio stations and 18 TV stations. It also crossed the threshold of the outdoor advertising industry with acquisitions of Eller Media in 1997 and Universal Outdoor Holdings and UK-based More Group in 1998. Its $4 billion purchase of Jacor Communications in 1999 marked the company's largest acquisition to date and positioned Clear Channel as the second-largest radio station owner in the country. In 2000 it completed an even larger acquisition: a $23.8 billion buyout of rival AMFM.

Also in 2000 the company bought SFX Entertainment (renamed Clear Channel Entertainment in 2001), the largest events producer and promoter in the US. The following year Clear Channel (and other radio operators) stopped streaming Webcast signals from many of its stations after the American Federation of Television and Radio Artists signed a contract guaranteeing its members 300% of fees for Internet commercials. In 2001 the company agreed to acquire media company The Ackerley Group (completed for $500 million in mid-2002). It closed offices of SFX and AMFM and laid off 630 employees in 2002.

OFFICERS

Chairman and CEO: L. Lowry Mays, age 66, $1,010,626 pay
President, COO, and Director: Mark P. Mays, age 38, $692,915 pay
EVP, CFO, and Director: Randall T. Mays, age 36, $691,649 pay
SVP Finance: Juliana F. Hill, age 32
SVP and Chief Accounting Officer: Herbert W. Hill Jr., age 42
SVP, General Counsel, and Secretary: Kenneth E. Wyker, age 40
Chairman and CEO, Clear Channel Entertainment: Brian Becker, age 45
CEO, Clear Channel New Technologies: Randy Michaels, age 49, $506,471 pay (prior to title change)
CEO, Clear Channel International: Roger G. Parry, age 48, $577,034 pay
CEO, Clear Channel Radio: John E. Hogan
President and CEO, Clear Channel Outdoor: Paul Meyer, age 59
President, International Radio Operations: Bob Cohen
President, Television Division: William Moll, age 64
President, Clear Channel Advantage: Don Howe
VP Human Resources: Bill Hamersly
Auditors: Ernst & Young LLP

LOCATIONS

HQ: Clear Channel Communications, Inc.
200 E. Basse Rd., San Antonio, TX 78209
Phone: 210-822-2828   **Fax:** 210-822-2299
Web: www.clearchannel.com

Clear Channel Communications has operations in Asia, Australia, Europe, North America, and South America.

PRODUCTS/OPERATIONS

2001 Sales

	% of total
Broadcasting	43
Live entertainment	31
Outdoor advertising	22
Other	4
Total	**100**

Selected TV Stations

KCOY (CBS; Santa Maria, CA)
KKFX (FOX; Santa Barbara, CA)
KLRT (FOX; Little Rock, AR)
KOKI (FOX; Tulsa, OK)
KSAS (FOX; Wichita, KS)
WETM (NBC; Elmira, NY)
WFTC (FOX; Minneapolis)
WHP (CBS; Harrisburg, PA)
WIVT (ABC; Binghamton, NY)
WIXT (ABC; Syracuse, NY)
WJTC (UPN; Mobile, AL)
WKRC (CBS; Cincinnati)
WMTU (UPN; Jackson, TN)
WNAC (FOX; Providence, RI)
WOKR (ABC; Rochester, NY)
WPMI (NBC; Mobile, AL)
WPTY (ABC; Memphis, TN)
WTEV (CBS; Jacksonville, FL)

COMPETITORS

ABC
Citadel Broadcasting
Cox Radio
Cumulus Media
Emmis Communications
Entercom
Fisher Communications
Gannett
Hearst-Argyle Television
Infinity Broadcasting
Lamar Advertising
LIN TV
Radio One
Sinclair Broadcast Group
Spanish Broadcasting
Westwood One

HISTORICAL FINANCIALS & EMPLOYEES

NYSE: CCU FYE: December 31	Annual Growth	12/92	12/93	12/94	12/95	12/96	12/97	12/98	12/99	12/00	12/01
Sales ($ mil.)	66.2%	82	118	173	244	352	697	1,351	2,678	5,345	7,970
Net income ($ mil.)	—	4	9	22	32	38	64	54	73	249	(1,144)
Income as % of sales	—	5.2%	7.7%	12.7%	13.1%	10.7%	9.1%	4.0%	2.7%	4.7%	—
Earnings per share ($)	—	0.04	0.08	0.16	0.23	0.26	0.34	0.22	0.22	0.57	(1.93)
Stock price - FY high ($)	—	1.81	4.61	6.50	11.06	22.63	39.94	62.31	91.50	95.50	68.08
Stock price - FY low ($)	—	0.86	1.62	3.93	6.27	10.19	16.81	31.00	52.00	43.88	35.20
Stock price - FY close ($)	46.6%	1.63	4.60	6.34	11.03	18.06	39.72	54.50	89.25	48.44	50.91
P/E - high	—	45	58	41	48	87	111	271	339	162	—
P/E - low	—	22	20	25	27	39	47	135	193	74	—
Dividends per share ($)	—	0.00	0.00	0.00	0.00	0.00	0.00	0.00	0.00	0.00	0.00
Book value per share ($)	79.1%	0.26	0.72	0.95	1.18	3.34	8.89	17.01	29.78	51.82	49.73
Employees	46.5%	1,150	1,354	1,549	1,779	3,219	5,400	7,000	17,650	36,350	35,700

STOCK PRICE HISTORY

HIGH/LOW/CLOSE

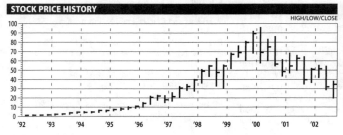

2001 FISCAL YEAR-END

Debt ratio: 21.1%
Return on equity: —
Cash ($ mil.): 155
Current ratio: 0.66
Long-term debt ($ mil.): 7,968
No. of shares (mil.): 598
Dividends
  Yield: —
  Payout: —
Market value ($ mil.): 30,444

THE CLOROX COMPANY

The Clorox Company makes consumer products for cleaning, cooking, and killing. The Oakland, California-based company is best known for its namesake bleach (the top-selling bleach in the world), but its bevy of brand names also includes Armor All and STP auto products; Soft Scrub, Tilex, Formula 409, and S.O.S cleaning products; Brita water filtration systems (in North America); Kingsford charcoal briquettes; Combat and Black Flag insecticides; and cat litters Fresh Step and Jonny Cat.

Clorox sells products in more than 110 countries, and international markets account for about 20% of the firm's total sales; much of Clorox's foreign growth has been from Latin America and Canada. The company has been building on existing lines through acquisitions, such as its 1999 purchase of First Brands, which gave the company its biggest brand — the Glad line of plastic wraps, trash bags, and containers. Ninety percent of sales come from brands ranked #1 or #2 in their respective markets. Clorox has also cleaned up through the introduction of new products (about 115 in 2000, including household items such as Clorox Disinfecting Wipes).

German chemical giant Henkel owns nearly 30% of Clorox.

HISTORY

Known first as the Electro-Alkaline Company, The Clorox Company was founded in 1913 by five Oakland, California, investors to make bleach using water from salt ponds around San Francisco Bay. The next year the company registered the brand name Clorox (the name combines the bleach's two main ingredients, chlorine and sodium hydroxide). At first the company sold only industrial-strength bleach, but in 1916 it formulated a household solution.

With the establishment of a Philadelphia distributor in 1921, Clorox began national expansion. The company went public in 1928, and built plants in Illinois and New Jersey in the 1930s; it opened nine more US plants in the 1940s and 1950s. In 1957 Procter & Gamble (P&G) bought Clorox. The Federal Trade Commission raised antitrust questions, and litigation ensued over the next decade. P&G was ordered to divest Clorox, and in 1969 Clorox again became an independent company.

Following its split with P&G, the firm added household consumer goods and foods, acquiring the brands Liquid-Plumr (drain opener, 1969), Formula 409 (spray cleaner, 1970), Litter Green (cat litter, 1971), and Hidden Valley (salad dressings, 1972). Clorox entered the specialty food products business by purchasing Grocery Store Products (Kitchen Bouquet, 1971) and Kingsford (charcoal briquettes, 1973).

In 1974 Henkel, a large West German maker of cleansers and detergents, purchased 15% of Clorox's stock as part of an agreement to share research. Beginning in 1977, Clorox sold off subsidiaries and brands, such as Country Kitchen Foods (1979), to focus on household goods.

During the 1980s Clorox launched a variety of new products, including Match Light (instant-lighting charcoal, 1980), Tilex (mildew remover, 1981), and Fresh Step (cat litter, 1984). Clorox began marketing Brita water filtration systems in the US in 1988 (adding Canada in 1995). In 1990 it paid $465 million for American Cyanamid's household products group, including Pine-Sol cleaner and Combat insecticide.

In 1991 Clorox left the laundry detergent business (begun in 1988) after it was battered by heavyweights P&G and Unilever. Household products VP Craig Sullivan became CEO the next year. In 1993 Clorox dumped its frozen food and bottled water operations. It began marketing its liquid bleach in Hungary through a Henkel subsidiary in 1994 and also bought S.O.S soap pads from Miles Inc.

A string of acquisitions brought the company into new markets as it built on existing brands. Clorox bought Black Flag and Lestoil in 1996 and car care product manufacturer Armor All in 1997. With its 1999 purchase of First Brands — for about $2 billion in stock and debt — Clorox added four more brands of cat litter and diversified into plastic products (Glad).

Despite adding 115 new products in 2000, the company said it would put more emphasis on core brands going forward; it plans to push its struggling Glad brand with more trade promotion and coupons. In January 2001 Clorox announced a joint venture with Bombril S.A., Brazil's leading name of cleaning utensils, to form Detergentes Bombril S.A.; however, Clorox canceled the agreement in April, claiming that various conditions of the deal had not been met.

OFFICERS

Chairman and CEO: G. Craig Sullivan, age 62, $937,500 pay
President and COO: Gerald E. Johnston, age 54, $537,499 pay
SVP Sales: Frank A. Tataseo, age 47, $445,500 pay
SVP, Secretary, and General Counsel: Peter D. Bewley, age 54
Group VP and CFO: Karen M. Rose, age 52
Group VP: Richard T. Conti, age 45
Group VP: Lawrence S. Peiros, age 45
VP Business Development: Charles F. Schneider
VP Corporate Administration: Robert C. Klaus, age 55

VP Corporate Communications and Public Affairs: Steven S. Silberblatt, age 48
VP Human Resources: Janet M. Brady, age 47
VP Information Services: Keith R. Tandowsky, age 43
VP Marketing: George C. Roeth, age 39
VP Research and Development: Wayne L. Delker, age 46
VP Strategy and Planning: Daniel G. Simpson, age 46
VP Supply Chain: Mark Richenderfer, age 41
VP and Treasurer: Greg S. Frank, age 40
VP and Controller: Dan J. Heinrich, age 45
VP and General Manager, Asia/Pacific: Warwick Every-Burns, age 48
Auditors: Deloitte & Touche LLP

LOCATIONS

HQ: 1221 Broadway, Oakland, CA 94612
Phone: 510-271-7000   **Fax:** 510-832-1463
Web: www.clorox.com

The Clorox Company sells its products in more than 110 countries.

2001 Sales

	$ mil.	% of total
US	3,169	81
Rest of world	734	19
Total	**3,903**	**100**

PRODUCTS/OPERATIONS

2001 Sales

	$ mil.	% of total
US specialty products	1,778	46
North American household products	1,521	39
International	604	15
Total	**3,903**	**100**

Selected Brands

Food-Related Products
Brita
Glad
GladWare
Hidden Valley
KC Masterpiece

Household Cleaning Products
Clorox
Clorox FreshCare
Formula 409
Handi-Wipes
Lestoil
Liquid-Plumr
Pine-Sol
Soft Scrub
S.O.S
Tilex
Wash 'n Dri

International Products
Arela (waxes)
Bluebell (laundry)
Clorisol (bleach)
Gumption (cleaners)

Horizon (trash bags)
Kitty Kit (cat litter)
Mono (aluminum foil)
Roomate (trash cans)
Selton (insecticides)
S.O.S (cleaners)
Super Globo (bleach)
Yuhanrox (bleach)

Specialty Products
Armor All
Black Flag
Combat
EverFresh
Fresh Step
HearthLogg
Jonny Cat
Kingsford
Match Light
Rain Dance
Scoop Away
STP
Tanner's Preserve
Tuff Stuff

COMPETITORS

Alticor
California Cedar Products Company
Church & Dwight
Colgate-Palmolive
Dial
Oil-Dri
Pactiv
Procter & Gamble
Reckitt Benckiser
S.C. Johnson
Turtle Wax
Unilever

HISTORICAL FINANCIALS & EMPLOYEES

NYSE: CLX FYE: June 30	Annual Growth	6/92	6/93	6/94	6/95	6/96	6/97	6/98	6/99	6/00	6/01
Sales ($ mil.)	9.6%	1,717	1,634	1,837	1,984	2,218	2,533	2,741	4,003	4,083	3,903
Net income ($ mil.)	14.1%	99	167	212	201	222	249	298	246	394	323
Income as % of sales	—	5.7%	10.2%	11.5%	10.1%	10.0%	9.8%	10.9%	6.1%	9.6%	8.3%
Earnings per share ($)	12.7%	0.46	0.76	0.99	0.95	1.06	1.19	1.41	1.03	1.64	1.35
Stock price - FY high ($)	—	13.00	13.34	13.94	16.44	22.34	33.55	48.31	66.47	58.25	48.63
Stock price - FY low ($)	—	9.13	10.19	11.75	11.94	15.22	21.72	30.94	39.69	29.06	28.38
Stock price - FY close ($)	12.9%	11.34	13.03	12.22	16.31	22.16	33.05	47.81	53.41	44.81	33.85
P/E - high	—	24	18	14	17	21	28	34	63	35	35
P/E - low	—	17	13	12	13	14	18	21	38	17	21
Dividends per share ($)	8.6%	0.40	0.43	0.45	0.48	0.53	0.58	0.64	0.72	0.80	0.84
Book value per share ($)	8.9%	3.73	4.01	4.26	4.50	4.55	5.02	5.23	6.67	7.62	8.03
Employees	7.4%	5,800	4,700	4,850	4,700	5,300	5,500	6,600	11,000	11,000	11,000

STOCK PRICE HISTORY

HIGH/LOW/CLOSE

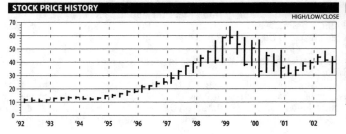

2001 FISCAL YEAR-END

Debt ratio: 26.5%
Return on equity: 17.5%
Cash ($ mil.): 251
Current ratio: 1.03
Long-term debt ($ mil.): 685
No. of shares (mil.): 237
Dividends
  Yield: 2.5%
  Payout: 62.2%
Market value ($ mil.): 8,012

CMS ENERGY CORPORATION

Though a large chunk of its revenue still comes from its utility, CMS Energy is hitching its power lines to a galloping horse that is tromping through energy markets worldwide. The Dearborn, Michigan-based company buys and sells electricity, natural gas, and other commodities in North America through its CMS Marketing, Services and Trading unit. It has also acquired more than 15,000 miles of gas pipeline stretching from Texas to Michigan, and its independent power projects have a generating capacity of more than 9,400 MW (plus 2,000 MW in the works). CMS Energy has international interests in plants, pipelines, and utilities, mostly in Africa, Asia, Latin America, and the Middle East.

Back home in Michigan's lower peninsula, CMS Energy's utility mule, Consumers Energy, still pulls in more than 40% of sales. Consumers provides electricity to 1.7 million customers and has a capacity of about 6,500 MW (primarily coal-fired). It also delivers gas to 1.6 million.

Reigning in on its expansion strategy, CMS Energy is selling nonstrategic international power plants and oil and gas assets, as well as its South American electric utilities. It has also sold Consumers' high-voltage transmission system in preparation for retail competition in Michigan.

The company's CMS Oil and Gas unit, which holds the company's exploration and production operations, has withdrawn its IPO, and CMS Energy has agreed to sell the unit.

HISTORY

In the late 1880s W.A. Foote and Samuel Jarvis formed hydroelectric company Jackson Electrical Light Works in Jackson, Michigan. After building plants in other Michigan towns, Foote formed utility holding company Consumers Power. In 1910 the firm merged with Michigan Light to create Commonwealth Power Railway and Light (CPR&L) and began building a statewide transmission system.

Foote died in 1915, and after nine years of acquisitions, successor Bernard Cobb sold the rail systems and split CPR&L into Commonwealth Power (CP) and Electric Railway Securities. In 1928 Cobb bought Southeastern Power & Light (SP&L) and merged CP with Penn-Ohio Edison to form Allied Power & Light. Commonwealth and Southern (C&S) was then created as the parent of Allied and SP&L.

In 1932 future GOP presidential nominee Wendell Willkie took the helm and became a national political figure by opposing the Public Utility Holding Company Act of 1935, which began 60 years of regulated monopolies. After WWII, Consumers Power was divested from C&S.

Consumers brought a nuclear plant on line in 1962 and the next year began buying Michigan oil and gas fields. In 1967 it formed NOMECO (now CMS Oil and Gas) to guide its oil and gas efforts.

The completion of the Palisades nuke in 1971 began a 13-year run of chronic problems and lengthy shutdowns. Cost overruns and an environmental lawsuit killed the firm's third nuke (Midland) in 1984 — after $4.1 billion was spent.

A rate hike and new CEO William McCormick set the firm on a new path in 1985. He formed a subsidiary to develop and invest in independent power projects in 1986 and created holding company CMS (short for "Consumers") Energy the next year. CMS Gas Transmission was formed in 1989.

Midland Cogeneration Venture (CMS Energy and six partners) completed converting Midland to a natural gas-fueled cogeneration plant in 1990, and CMS Energy wrote off $657 million from its losses at the former nuke. It regained profitability in 1993.

McCormick split the utilities into gas and electric divisions in 1995 and also issued stock for its gas utility and transmission businesses, Consumers Gas Group. The next year CMS Energy formed an energy marketing arm.

In 1996 and 1997 CMS Energy invested in power plants in Morocco and Australia and bought a stake in a Brazilian electric utility.

Michigan's public service commission (PSC) issued utility restructuring orders in 1997 and 1998, but in 1999 the state Supreme Court ruled that the PSC lacked restructuring authority.

CMS Energy bought Panhandle Eastern Pipe Line from Duke Energy for $2.2 billion in 1999. It also grabbed a 77% stake in another Brazilian utility and began building its Powder River Basin gas pipeline. In 2000 the company partnered with Marathon Ashland Petroleum and TEPPCO to operate a pipeline transporting refined petroleum from the US Gulf Coast to Illinois. Later that year CMS Energy announced plans for an IPO for its CMS Oil and Gas unit; however, the IPO was withdrawn in 2001.

CMS Energy agreed in 2001 to sell Consumers' high-voltage electric transmission assets to independent transmission operator Trans-Elect for about $290 million; the deal, which was the first of its kind in the US, was completed in 2002. It also announced plans to sell about $2.4 billion in other noncore assets, including interests in power plants, utilities, and gas assets.

In 2002 the company sold its Equatorial Guinea (West Africa) oil and gas assets to Marathon Oil for about $1 billion. Also that year McCormick stepped down amid controversy over "round trip" power trades that artificially inflated the company's sales and trading volume; CMS Energy later announced that it would restate its 2000 and 2001 financial results to eliminate the effects of the trades.

Later that year, the company agreed to sell its CMS Oil and Gas unit (excluding the unit's Colombian assets) to private French energy firm Perenco.

OFFICERS

Chairman and CEO: Kenneth Whipple, age 67
Vice Chairman and General Counsel:
S. Kinnie Smith Jr.
President, COO, and Director: David W. Joos, age 49, $637,500 pay
EVP and COO, Gas: William J. Haener, age 60, $729,126 pay
EVP and CFO: Thomas J. Webb, age 49
SVP, Chief Accounting Officer, and Controller:
Preston D. Hopper, age 51
SVP Governmental and Public Affairs:
David G. Mengebier, age 44
SVP Human Resources and Business Services, CMS Energy and Consumers Energy: John F. Drake, age 54
VP Investor Relations and Treasurer:
Laura L. Mountcastle
Auditors: Ernst & Young LLP

LOCATIONS

HQ: Fairlane Plaza South, Ste. 1100
330 Town Center Dr., Dearborn, MI 48126
Phone: 313-436-9200   **Fax:** 313-436-9225
Web: www.cmsenergy.com

CMS Energy primarily distributes electricity and natural gas throughout Michigan's lower peninsula. It also has utilities operations in Argentina, Brazil, and Venezuela, and oil and gas exploration and production in Cameroon, Colombia, Republic of the Congo, Eritrea, Tunisia, the US, and Venezuela.

PRODUCTS/OPERATIONS

2001 Sales

	$ mil.	% of total
Utility		
Electric .	2,631	28
Gas	1,338	14
Marketing, services & trading	3,953	41
Natural gas transmission	1,053	11
Independent power production	388	4
Oil & gas exploration & production	212	2
Other	22	—
Total	**9,597**	**100**

COMPETITORS

AEP	Duke Energy	Southern
AES	Dynegy	Company
Allegheny	Edison	Tractebel
Energy	International	Williams
Alliant Energy	Endesa (Spain)	Companies
Aquila	Iberdrola	Wisconsin
CenterPoint	ONEOK	Energy
Energy	SEMCO Energy	WPS Resources
Con Edison	Sempra Energy	Xcel Energy
DTE	Sithe Energies	

HISTORICAL FINANCIALS & EMPLOYEES

NYSE: CMS FYE: December 31	Annual Growth	12/92	12/93	12/94	12/95	12/96	12/97	12/98	12/99	12/00	12/01
Sales ($ mil.)	13.5%	3,073	3,482	3,619	3,890	4,333	4,787	5,141	6,103	8,998	9,597
Net income ($ mil.)	—	(297)	155	179	204	240	268	285	277	36	(545)
Income as % of sales	—	—	4.5%	4.9%	5.2%	5.5%	5.6%	5.5%	4.5%	0.4%	—
Earnings per share ($)	—	(3.72)	1.90	2.08	2.26	2.44	2.61	3.71	2.42	0.32	(4.39)
Stock price - FY high ($)	—	22.75	27.50	25.00	30.00	33.75	44.06	50.13	48.44	32.25	31.80
Stock price - FY low ($)	—	14.88	17.88	19.63	22.50	27.81	31.13	38.75	30.31	14.88	19.49
Stock price - FY close ($)	3.0%	18.38	25.13	22.88	29.88	33.63	44.06	48.44	31.19	31.69	24.03
P/E - high	—	—	14	12	13	14	17	19	20	101	—
P/E - low	—	—	9	9	10	11	12	15	12	47	—
Dividends per share ($)	13.2%	0.48	0.60	0.78	0.90	1.02	1.14	1.56	1.39	1.46	1.46
Book value per share ($)	2.7%	11.13	13.25	12.79	16.04	16.57	18.14	19.01	21.17	19.53	14.16
Employees	1.6%	9,971	10,013	9,972	10,072	9,663	9,659	9,710	11,462	11,652	11,510

STOCK PRICE HISTORY

HIGH/LOW/CLOSE

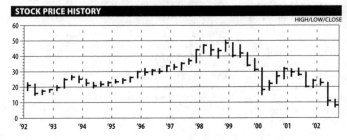

2001 FISCAL YEAR-END

Debt ratio: 78.7%
Return on equity: —
Cash ($ mil.): 189
Current ratio: 0.80
Long-term debt ($ mil.): 6,983
No. of shares (mil.): 133
Dividends
  Yield: 6.1%
  Payout: —
Market value ($ mil.): 3,207

CNA FINANCIAL CORPORATION

It's no accident that CNA Financial writes so many commercial property/casualty insurance policies. The Chicago-based holding company's subsidiaries offer workers' compensation, general liability, multiple peril, reinsurance, marine, and other coverage for businesses, groups, and associations. CNA also provides special liability insurance for such professionals as doctors, lawyers, and architects. Loews, the Tisch family's holding company, owns almost 90% of the firm.

Like so many things in life, CNA is getting commercial. The firm has exited the personal insurance business to focus on the commercial market: It transferred its personal insurance lines, including its auto and homeowners coverage, to Allstate. CNA will continue to write and renew personal policies until Allstate opts to buy out these operations. As part of the restructuring (the company's new organization includes three major segments: property/casualty, life, and group), CNA fired some 10% of its workforce.

CNA paid out more than $450 million in claims related to the attacks on the World Trade Center.

HISTORY

When merchant Henry Bowen could not find the type of fire insurance he wanted, he began Continental Insurance. Bowen assembled a group of investors and started with about $500,000 in capital. In 1882 Continental Insurance added marine and tornado insurance. Seven years later Francis Moore became president; he was developer of the Universal Mercantile Schedule, a system of assessing fire hazards in buildings.

About the time Continental Insurance was writing the book on fire insurance, several midwestern investors were having trouble assessing risk in their own insurance field — disability. In 1897 this group founded Continental Casualty in Hammond, Indiana. In the early years its primary clients were railroads. Continental Casualty eventually merged with other companies in the field and by 1905 had branch offices in nine states and Hawaii, and was writing business in 41 states and territories.

Both Continentals added new insurance lines in 1911: Continental Insurance went into personal auto, and Continental Casualty formed subsidiary Continental Assurance to sell life insurance. By 1915 Continental Insurance had four primary companies; spurred by growing prewar patriotism, they were called the America Fore Group. Both Continentals rose to the challenges presented by the world wars and the Depression; they entered the 1950s ready for new growth.

In the 1960s the companies began to diversify. Continental Insurance added interests in Diners Club and Capital Financial Services; in 1968 it formed holding company Continental Corp. Meanwhile, Continental Assurance (which had formed its own holding company, CNA Financial) went even farther afield, adding mutual fund companies, consumer finance companies, nursing homes, and residential construction.

By the early 1970s CNA was on the ropes because of the recession and setbacks in the housing business. In 1974 Robert and Laurence Tisch bought most of the company and cut costs ruthlessly. Continental had its own problems in the 1970s, including an Iranian joint venture that got caught up in the revolution.

Both companies suffered losses arising from Hurricane Andrew in 1992, but CNA, which did its housecleaning in the 1970s, was better able to deal with the blow than Continental, which entered the 1990s in need of restructuring.

Rising interest rates in 1994 hurt Continental, whose merger with CNA in 1995 made CNA one of the US's top 10 insurance companies. About 5,000 jobs were cut in the consolidation of the two operations.

CNA bought Western National Warranty in 1995, followed by managed care provider Core-Source the next year. In 1997 the company spun off its surety business in a deal with Capsure Holdings and formed CNA Surety. Taking advantage of outsourcing trends, the company created CNA UniSource (payroll and human resources services) and bought its payroll servicer, Interlogic Systems, the next year.

CNA pursued a global strategy, buying majority interests in an Argentine workers' compensation carrier and a British marine insurer, but with 1998 sales flat and earnings down the tube, the company did more slashing than accumulating. It cut 2,400 jobs and exited such lines as agriculture and entertainment insurance.

In 1999 CNA transferred its personal lines to Allstate and in 2000 sold its life reinsurance operations to a subsidiary of Munich Re.

OFFICERS

Chairman: Bernard L. Hengesbaugh, age 55, $1,900,000 pay
CEO and Director; Chairman and CEO, CNA Insurance: Stephen W. Lilienthal, age 52
President and CEO, Property & Casualty Operations: James R. Lewis
EVP and CFO: Robert V. Deutsch, age 42, $1,485,000 pay
EVP, General Counsel, and Secretary: Jonathan D. Kantor
EVP, Global Specialty Lines: Peter W. Wilson, age 42

EVP, Human Resources and Corporate Services:
Thomas Pontarelli
EVP, Worldwide Field Operations: Gary J. Owcar
President and CEO, CNA Life: Robert W. Patin,
$709,615 pay (partial-year salary)
President and CEO, CNA Re: Debra McClenahan
Auditors: Deloitte & Touche LLP

LOCATIONS

HQ: CNA Plaza, Chicago, IL 60685
Phone: 312-822-5000   **Fax:** 312-822-6419
Web: www.cna.com

CNA Financial operates primarily in the US.

PRODUCTS/OPERATIONS

2001 Assets

	$ mil.	% of total
Cash & equivalents	142	—
US treasury & agency securities	5,081	8
Asset-backed securities	7,723	12
State & municipal bonds	2,720	4
Corporate bonds	9,587	14
Stocks	1,338	2
Assets in separate account	3,798	6
Receivables	18,272	28
Other	17,307	26
Total	**65,968**	**100**

Selected Subsidiaries
CNA Casualty of California
CNA Group Life Assurance Company
CNA Lloyd's of Texas
CNA Reinsurance Company, Ltd. (UK)
CNA Surety Corporation
Columbia Casualty Company
Continental Assurance Company
Continental Casualty Company
The Continental Corporation
The Continental Insurance Company
The Continental Insurance Company of New Jersey
Continental Reinsurance Corporation
The Fidelity & Casualty Company of New York
Firemen's Insurance Company of Newark, New Jersey
First Insurance Company of Hawaii, Ltd.
The Mayflower Insurance Company, Ltd.
National Fire Insurance Company of Hartford
National-Ben Franklin Insurance Company of Illinois
Pacific Insurance Company
Transcontinental Insurance Company
Transportation Insurance Company
Valley Forge Insurance Company

COMPETITORS

21st Century	The Hartford	Pacific Mutual
AIG	John Hancock	Prudential
Allstate	Financial	Reliance Group
American	Services	Holdings
Financial	Liberty Mutual	St. Paul
Chubb	MassMutual	Companies
CIGNA	MetLife	State Farm
GEICO	Mutual of	Travelers
GeneralCologne	Omaha	USAA
Re	Nationwide	Zurich Financial
Guardian Life	New York Life	Services

HISTORICAL FINANCIALS & EMPLOYEES

NYSE: CNA FYE: December 31	Annual Growth	12/92	12/93	12/94	12/95	12/96	12/97	12/98	12/99	12/00	12/01
Assets ($ mil.)	6.7%	36,681	41,912	44,320	59,902	60,735	61,269	62,359	61,219	62,068	65,968
Net income ($ mil.)	—	(331)	268	37	757	965	966	282	(130)	1,214	(1,644)
Income as % of assets	—	—	0.6%	0.1%	1.3%	1.6%	1.6%	0.5%	—	2.0%	—
Earnings per share ($)	—	(1.80)	1.42	0.17	4.04	5.16	5.17	1.49	(0.77)	6.61	(8.48)
Stock price - FY high ($)	—	34.80	33.63	27.39	41.04	39.13	44.04	53.26	45.31	41.94	40.24
Stock price - FY low ($)	—	26.14	24.73	19.98	21.56	31.88	32.09	34.50	33.00	24.56	23.00
Stock price - FY close ($)	(1.2%)	32.63	25.81	21.60	37.80	35.63	42.54	40.25	38.94	38.75	29.17
P/E - high	—	—	24	161	10	8	9	36	—	6	—
P/E - low	—	—	17	118	5	6	6	23	—	4	—
Dividends per share ($)	—	0.00	0.00	0.00	0.00	0.00	0.00	0.00	0.00	0.00	0.00
Book value per share ($)	4.2%	25.81	28.98	24.48	36.29	38.04	44.77	49.80	48.47	52.64	37.42
Employees	0.0%	17,200	16,800	15,600	25,000	24,300	24,700	23,600	19,600	19,100	17,274

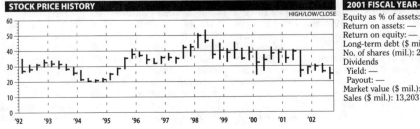

STOCK PRICE HISTORY   HIGH/LOW/CLOSE

2001 FISCAL YEAR-END
Equity as % of assets: 12.7%
Return on assets: —
Return on equity: —
Long-term debt ($ mil.): 2,567
No. of shares (mil.): 224
Dividends
  Yield: —
  Payout: —
Market value ($ mil.): 6,522
Sales ($ mil.): 13,203

CNF INC.

CNF (formerly CNF Transportation) has been traveling long enough to know what works. Based in Palo Alto, California, the global transportation company moves freight on the ground and in the air, and operates through two primary business groups: Con-Way Transportation Services and Menlo Worldwide. Another unit, Road Systems, makes trailers and transportation equipment.

Con-Way, CNF's nonunion carrier, mainly provides regional less-than-truckload services in the US, Puerto Rico, and large cities in Canada and Mexico. It owns some 32,000 trucks, trailers, and tractors. Other Con-Way services include truckload and intermodal shipping.

In December 2001 CNF combined its logistics businesses into Menlo Worldwide, which operates through four divisions. Emery Forwarding, CNF's largest revenue generator, focuses on heavy airfreight in the US. It acts as an airfreight forwarder in more than 200 countries and provides customs brokerage services. Menlo Logistics manages warehouses and distribution networks and provides other supply chain services, and Menlo Worldwide Technologies develops software for logistics and order tracking. Vector SCM, a joint venture with General Motors, provides supply chain management and logistics services strictly for GM.

The company has dropped "transportation" from its name to reflect its growing emphasis on logistics.

Leland James, co-owner of a bus company in Portland, Oregon, founded Consolidated Truck Lines in 1929 to provide transport services in the Pacific Northwest. Operations extended to San Francisco and Idaho by 1934 and to North Dakota by 1936. It adopted the name Consolidated Freightways (CF) in 1939.

James formed Freightways Manufacturing that year, making CF the only trucking company to design and build its own trucks (Freightliners). In the 1940s CF extended service to Chicago, Minneapolis, and Los Angeles.

CF went public in 1951 and moved to Menlo Park, California, in 1956. It continued to buy companies (52 between 1955 and 1960) and extended its reach throughout the US and Canada. When an attempt to coordinate intermodal services with railroads and shipping lines failed in 1960, William White became president and exited intermodal operations to focus on less-than-truckload shipping.

In 1966 CF formed CF AirFreight to offer air cargo services in the US. Three years later it bought Pacific Far East Lines, a San Francisco shipping line (now a part of Con-Way).

In 1981 CF sold Freightways Manufacturing to Daimler-Benz (now DaimlerChrysler). After the US trucking industry was deregulated in 1983, CF started the Con-Way carriers, its regional trucking businesses. In the 1980s Con-Way moved back into intermodal rail, truck, and ocean shipping.

The company bought Emery Air Freight in 1989 and combined it with CF AirFreight to form Emery Worldwide. Founded in 1946, Emery Air Freight had expanded across the US and overseas, first by using extra cargo space on scheduled airline flights, then by chartering aircraft. Later operating its own air fleet, Emery began having troubles in the 1980s, including difficulties in integrating its 1987 acquisition, Purolator Courier. A 1988 takeover attempt by former FedEx president Arthur Bass further plagued Emery; fending off the takeover resulted in losses of about $100 million in 1989. That year Emery brought CF a deal with the U.S. Postal Service (USPS) to handle its next-day express mail.

Amid the beginning of a three-year profit slump, CF formed Menlo Logistics in 1990 to provide its customers with a range of third-party logistics services. A Teamsters' strike in 1994 that halted union carriers nationwide boosted demand for Con-Way's services as customers sought nonunion carriers to move their shipments. That next year Con-Way opened 40 service centers and bought another 3,300 tractors and trailers.

In 1996 CF spun off most of its long-haul transportation businesses (including CF Motor-Freight, Canadian Freightways, and Milne & Craighead) and renamed the resulting entity Consolidated Freightways. CF then changed its own name to CNF Transportation.

CNF Transportation received a five-year, $1.7 billion contract from USPS in 1997 to sort and transport two-day priority mail in the eastern US. Menlo won contracts in 1998 from six companies, including Intel and IBM, expected to generate more than $1 billion by 2003.

In 2000 CNF Transportation shortened its name to CNF and began renegotiating its money-losing second-day priority mail contract with USPS. (FedEx eventually got the job.) That year CNF formed Vector SCM, a supply chain management and logistics joint venture with General Motors. In 2001 CNF's Con-Way Transportation established Con-Way Air Express, an airfreight forwarder that serves the US and Puerto Rico.

Emery grounded its aircraft fleet in 2001 because of maintenance problems discovered by Federal Aviation Administration inspectors. The company hired other carriers in order to continue its airfreight services. In a settlement with the FAA, Emery agreed to pay a $1 million civil fine.

Also that year, to emphasize its focus on logistics, CNF combined the operations of Emery Worldwide, Menlo Logistics, and Vector SCM into a new company, Menlo Worldwide.

OFFICERS

Chairman: Donald E. Moffitt, age 69
President, CEO, and Director: Gregory L. Quesnel, age 53, $712,504 pay
SVP and CFO: Sanchayan Ratnathicam, age 54, $425,048 pay
SVP; President and CEO, Con-Way Transportation Services: Gerald L. Detter, age 57, $673,323 pay
SVP; President and CEO, Menlo Worldwide: John H. Williford, age 45, $525,754 pay
SVP, General Counsel, and Secretary: Eberhard G. H. Schmoller, age 57, $359,008 pay
VP and CIO: Roy L. Swackhamer, age 54
VP Human Resources and Deputy General Counsel: David L. Slate, age 59
President and CEO, Con-Way Central Express: Richard Palazzo
President and CEO, Vector SCM: Gary D. Kowalski, age 47
President, Menlo Worldwide Logistics: Robert L. Bianco
Auditors: KPMG LLP

LOCATIONS

HQ: 3240 Hillview Ave., Palo Alto, CA 94304
Phone: 650-494-2900   **Fax:** 650-813-0160
Web: www.cnf.com

2001 Sales

	$ mil.	% of total
US	3,609	74
Other countries	1,253	26
Total	**4,862**	**100**

PRODUCTS/OPERATIONS

2001 Sales

	$ mil.	% of total
Emery Worldwide	2,044	42
Con-Way Transportation	1,913	39
Menlo Logistics	898	19
Other	7	—
Total	**4,862**	**100**

Selected Subsidiaries and Operations
Con-Way Air Express
Con-Way Canada Express
Con-Way Integrated Services
Emery Forwarding
Menlo Worldwide Logistics

COMPETITORS

Airborne	Expeditors	Schneider
Arkansas Best	International	National
BAX Global	FedEx	TPG
Central Freight	GeoLogistics	UPS
Lines	J. B. Hunt	UPS Freight
CHR	Norfolk	Services
CSX	Southern	USFreightways
Deutsche Post	Overnite	U.S. Postal
DHL Worldwide	Transportation	Service
Express	Roadway	Werner
DSC Logistics	Ryder	Yellow
EGL		

HISTORICAL FINANCIALS & EMPLOYEES

NYSE: CNF FYE: December 31	Annual Growth	12/92	12/93	12/94	12/95	12/96	12/97	12/98	12/99	12/00	12/01
Sales ($ mil.)	2.0%	4,056	4,192	4,681	5,281	3,662	4,267	4,942	5,593	5,572	4,862
Net income ($ mil.)	—	(81)	51	55	57	28	121	139	191	135	(395)
Income as % of sales	—	—	1.2%	1.2%	1.1%	0.8%	2.8%	2.8%	3.4%	2.4%	—
Earnings per share ($)	—	(2.78)	0.46	1.64	1.64	1.48	2.19	2.45	3.35	2.36	(8.26)
Stock price - FY high ($)	—	19.63	24.00	29.25	28.75	29.38	50.88	49.94	45.88	36.88	39.88
Stock price - FY low ($)	—	12.50	13.63	17.88	20.25	16.25	20.25	21.56	28.38	20.19	21.05
Stock price - FY close ($)	7.4%	17.63	23.63	22.38	26.50	22.25	38.75	37.56	34.50	33.81	33.55
P/E - high	—	—	27	27	26	68	21	18	12	14	—
P/E - low	—	—	15	16	18	38	8	8	8	8	—
Dividends per share ($)	—	0.00	0.00	0.00	0.40	0.50	0.40	0.40	0.40	0.40	0.40
Book value per share ($)	(2.5%)	16.39	17.46	18.53	16.45	11.41	13.89	16.22	19.98	21.83	13.05
Employees	(4.1%)	37,900	39,100	40,500	41,600	25,100	26,300	33,700	34,400	28,700	26,100

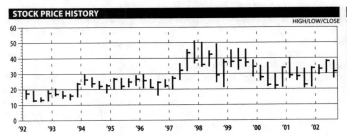

STOCK PRICE HISTORY
HIGH/LOW/CLOSE

2001 FISCAL YEAR-END

Debt ratio: 47.0%
Return on equity: —
Cash ($ mil.): 401
Current ratio: 1.50
Long-term debt ($ mil.): 566
No. of shares (mil.): 49
Dividends
  Yield: 1.2%
  Payout: —
Market value ($ mil.): 1,640

THE COCA-COLA COMPANY

According to The Coca-Cola Company, the two most famous expressions in the world are "OK" and "Coca-Cola." And if Coca-Cola had its way, you'd forget the other one. Atlanta-based Coca-Cola, the #1 soft-drink company (ahead of PepsiCo), sells about 300 beverage brands, including carbonated and sports drinks, juices, teas, and coffees, in almost 200 countries. Outside of Australia, Europe, and North America, Coca-Cola sells the Canada Dry, Dr Pepper, and Schweppes brands.

Worldwide, Coca-Cola has two of the three top-selling soft drinks (#1 Coca-Cola classic and #3 diet Coke) and a 50% market share. More than 60% of Coca-Cola's sales come from outside the US.

The company's rivalry with PepsiCo has moved beyond soda to juice products (Coca-Cola's Minute Maid vs. PepsiCo's Tropicana), bottled water (Dasani vs. Aquafina), and other non-carbonated products. Coca-Cola has increased its presence in the bottled water segment by agreeing to market and distribute Group Danone's Evian, the #1 water brand worldwide, in North America; it also has a deal with Danone to sell its bottled spring water brands in the US. It bought Odwalla, a maker of premium juices, in an effort to strengthen its non-carbonated drink lineup. In May 2002 Coca-Cola agreed to buy the Seagram's Mixers (ginger ale, tonic, seltzer, and club soda) from co-owners Diageo and Pernod Ricard.

Trying to boost consumer interest in its flagship cola, Coca-Cola has announced it will switch the graphics on Coke bottles and cans back to a more traditional look, beginning in 2003.

SunTrust Banks, which helped underwrite Coca-Cola's first public stock sale, owns about 5% of the company, and Warren Buffett's Berkshire Hathaway owns 8%.

HISTORY

Atlanta pharmacist John Pemberton invented Coke in 1886. His bookkeeper, Frank Robinson, named the product after two ingredients, coca leaves (later cleaned of narcotics) and kola nuts. By 1891 druggist Asa Candler had bought The Coca-Cola Company; within four years the soda-fountain drink was available in all states, and it was in Canada and Mexico by 1898.

Candler sold most US bottling rights in 1899 to Benjamin Thomas and John Whitehead of Chattanooga, Tennessee, for $1. The two designed a regional franchise bottling system that created over 1,000 bottlers within 20 years. In 1916 Candler retired to become Atlanta's mayor; his family sold the company to Atlanta banker

Ernest Woodruff for $25 million in 1919. Coca-Cola went public that year.

The firm expanded overseas and introduced the slogans "The Pause that Refreshes" (1929) and "It's the Real Thing" (1941). To keep WWII soldiers in Cokes at a nickel a pop, the government built 64 overseas bottling plants. Coca-Cola bought Minute Maid in 1960 and began launching new drinks — Fanta (1960), Sprite (1961), TAB (1963), and diet Coke (1982).

In 1981 Roberto Goizueta became chairman. In 1985, with Coke slipping in market share, the firm changed its formula and introduced New Coke, which consumers soundly rejected. In 1986 it consolidated the US bottling operations it owned into Coca-Cola Enterprises and sold 51% of the new company to the public. Goizueta also engineered the company's purchase of Columbia Pictures in 1982. (Columbia earned Coke a profit of about $1 billion when it was sold to Sony in 1989.)

In 1995 it bought Barq's root beer. Goizueta died of lung cancer in 1997; while he was at the helm, the firm's value rose from $4 billion to $145 billion. Douglas Ivester, the architect of Coca-Cola's restructured bottling operations, succeeded him. An agreement to buy about 30 Cadbury Schweppes beverage brands — including Canada Dry, Dr Pepper, and Schweppes — outside the US and France was scaled down because of antitrust concerns. Completed in 1999, the deal also excluded Canada, much of Continental Europe, and Mexico.

A battered Ivester resigned in February 2000; president and COO Douglas Daft was named chairman and CEO. Coca-Cola began its largest cutbacks ever, slashing nearly 5,000 jobs, and later agreed to pay nearly $193 million to settle a race-discrimination suit filed by African-American workers.

In order to fortify its portfolio in the fast-growing non-carbonated drinks segment, Coca-Cola acquired Mad River Traders (teas, juices, sodas) and Odwalla (juices and smoothies) in 2001. The company also bought a 35% interest (San Miguel Corporation owns the rest) in bottler Coca-Cola Philippines from Coca-Cola Amatil. The company announced the creation of a huge beverage and snack distribution joint venture with Procter & Gamble, but the multi-billion dollar operation fell apart before it could begin.

In 2002 Coca-Cola introduced Vanilla Coke, its biggest new product launch since the disastrous New Coke debacle. The company also secured distribution rights to Danone's Evian brand in the US; later Coca-Cola paid about $128 million to market and distribute Danone's spring and mineral water brands in the US.

OFFICERS

Chairman and CEO: Douglas N. Daft, age 58,
$5,000,000 pay
Vice Chairman and COO: Brian G. Dyson, age 65,
$1,291,667 pay
**EVP; President and COO, Europe, Eurasia, and Middle
East Group:** Alexander R. C. Allan, age 56
EVP; President and COO, Americas Group:
Jeffrey T. Dunn, age 43
**EVP; President and COO, Coca-Cola Ventures;
President, Latin American Operations:**
Steven J. Heyer, age 49, $2,205,333 pay
EVP; President and COO, Asia Group: Mary E. Minnick,
age 41
EVP; President, Africa Group:
Alexander B. Cummings Jr., age 44
EVP and General Counsel: Deval L. Patrick, age 45
EVP, Global Public Affairs and Administration:
Carl Ware, age 58, $1,266,667 pay
SVP and CFO: Gary P. Fayard, age 49
SVP, Human Resources: Coretha Rushing, age 44
Auditors: Ernst & Young LLP

LOCATIONS

HQ: 1 Coca-Cola Plaza, Atlanta, GA 30313
Phone: 404-676-2121   **Fax:** 404-676-6792
Web: www.cocacola.com

2001 Sales

	% of total
North America	38
Asia	25
Europe/Eurasia/Middle East	23
Latin America	11
Africa	3
Total	**100**

PRODUCTS/OPERATIONS

Selected Brand Names

Carbonated Soft Drinks
Barq's
Canada Dry (outside
Australia, Europe, North
America)
Cherry Coke (regular, diet)
Coca-Cola (regular,
caffeine free)
Coca-Cola classic (regular,
caffeine free)
Crush (outside Australia,
Europe, North America)
diet Coke (regular, caffeine
free)
Dr Pepper (regular, diet;
outside Australia,
Europe, North America)
Fanta
Fresca
Mello Yello

Mr. PiBB
Schweppes (outside
Australia, Europe, North
America)
Smart (soft drink, China)
Sprite (regular, diet)
TAB

Other Beverages
Dasani (bottled water)
Five Alive (fruit beverages)
Fruitopia (fruit juices and
teas)
Hi-C (fruit drinks)
Minute Maid (juices and
juice drinks)
Nestea (tea-based drinks)
Odwalla (non-carbonated
juices)
POWERaDE (sports drink)

COMPETITORS

Cadbury
Schweppes
Chiquita Brands
Clearly Canadian
Cott
Ferolito,
Vultaggio
Florida's Natural
Kirin
Kraft Foods

National
Beverage
National Grape
Cooperative
Nestlé
Northland
Cranberries
Ocean Spray
PepsiCo
Pernod Ricard

Procter &
Gamble
Quaker Foods
Six Continents
Suntory
Triarc
Unilever
Virgin Group
Vitality
Beverages

HISTORICAL FINANCIALS & EMPLOYEES

NYSE: KO FYE: December 31	Annual Growth	12/92	12/93	12/94	12/95	12/96	12/97	12/98	12/99	12/00	12/01
Sales ($ mil.)	4.9%	13,074	13,957	16,172	18,018	18,546	18,868	18,813	19,805	20,458	20,092
Net income ($ mil.)	10.1%	1,664	2,176	2,554	2,986	3,492	4,129	3,533	2,431	2,177	3,969
Income as % of sales	—	12.7%	15.6%	15.8%	16.6%	18.8%	21.9%	18.8%	12.3%	10.6%	19.8%
Earnings per share ($)	11.1%	0.62	0.83	0.98	1.17	1.38	1.64	1.42	0.98	0.88	1.60
Stock price - FY high ($)	—	22.69	22.56	26.75	40.19	54.25	72.63	88.94	70.88	66.88	62.19
Stock price - FY low ($)	—	17.78	18.75	19.44	24.38	36.06	50.00	53.63	47.31	42.88	42.37
Stock price - FY close ($)	9.4%	20.94	22.31	25.75	37.13	52.63	66.69	67.00	58.25	60.94	47.15
P/E - high	—	36	27	27	34	39	43	62	72	76	39
P/E - low	—	28	22	20	21	26	30	38	48	49	26
Dividends per share ($)	11.1%	0.28	0.34	0.39	0.44	0.50	0.56	0.60	0.64	0.68	0.72
Book value per share ($)	13.3%	1.49	1.77	2.05	2.15	2.48	2.96	3.41	3.85	3.75	4.57
Employees	2.2%	31,300	34,000	33,000	32,000	26,000	29,500	28,600	37,400	36,900	38,000

STOCK PRICE HISTORY

HIGH/LOW/CLOSE

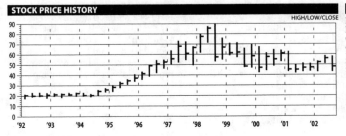

2001 FISCAL YEAR-END

Debt ratio: 9.7%
Return on equity: 38.4%
Cash ($ mil.): 1,866
Current ratio: 0.85
Long-term debt ($ mil.): 1,219
No. of shares (mil.): 2,486
Dividends
  Yield: 1.5%
  Payout: 45.0%
Market value ($ mil.): 117,226

COCA-COLA ENTERPRISES INC.

The scientists and suits at The Coca-Cola Company concoct the secret recipes and market the brands, but Coca-Cola Enterprises (CCE) does much of the bottling and distribution of the soft drinks. Atlanta-based CCE is the world's #1 soft-drink bottler and an "anchor" bottler for The Coca-Cola Company (TCCC). CCE distributes about 80% of TCCC's North American volume and about 24% of TCCC's total volume worldwide. Coca-Cola products, including Coca-Cola classic, Sprite, Minute Maid, Fruitopia, and Barq's, account for 90% of the bottler's sales. CCE also bottles, markets, and/or distributes other beverage brands such as Canada Dry, Dr Pepper, Evian, Nestea, Perrier, and Schweppes.

CCE continues to increase its share of the Coca-Cola market by acquiring other bottlers in the US (where it hopes to become the only Coke bottler), Canada, and Europe. The company is trying to restore consumer confidence and sales volume in Europe after a contamination scare and product recall in 1999. It is also undergoing regulatory scrutiny by the European Commission for anti-competitive practices.

TCCC owns about 38% of CCE's stock, while former CCE chairman Summerfield Johnston Jr. owns about 8%.

HISTORY

Coca-Cola Enterprises (CCE) was formed in 1986 when The Coca-Cola Company bought its two largest bottlers — JTL Corp. and BCI Holdings — and formed a single corporation. The company went public immediately, though Coca-Cola retained a significant interest in it.

CCE set about acquiring smaller bottling concerns across the US, and by 1988 the company had become the #1 bottler in the world. The company centralized operations to boost its slim profit margin.

In 1991 CCE merged with the Johnston Coca-Cola Bottling Group, the #2 US Coca-Cola bottler. The acquisition cost the ailing CCE $125 million, and led a number of disaffected investors to protest. Johnston executives took control when Summerfield Johnston Jr. (whose grandfather had co-founded the first Coke bottling franchisee) assumed the post of CEO, and Henry Schimberg, a former RC Cola route salesman, became president and COO.

In 1992 the bottler was reorganized into 10 US operating regions to allow for better control of individual market dynamics. A $1.5 billion public debt offering occurred that year, and the following year the company began looking outward for growth, acquiring Nederland B.V. (the Coca-Cola bottler of the Netherlands), as well as two Tennessee bottlers. In 1994 CCE recorded its first profitable year since 1990.

The company reorganized again in 1996, forming four operating groups defined by market and geographic lines. Its acquisitions that year included bottlers in Belgium and France.

CCE bought Cadbury Schweppes' 51% stake in the Coca-Cola & Schweppes Beverages UK joint venture for $2 billion in 1997, and it also purchased Coca-Cola's shares in Coca-Cola Beverages Ltd. (Canada's leading bottler) and The Coca-Cola Bottling Company of New York.

A half-dozen deals in 1998 included the $1.1 billion purchase of Coke Southwest and other bottling acquisitions in the US and Luxembourg worth $355 million. Schimberg became CEO that year.

Also in 1998 the bottler expanded its vending-machine business, and many distributors and vending-machine owners (who use CCE as a supplier) complained that the firm was charging lower prices in its own machines than independent owners could for the same products.

Bad news came in 1999 when products bottled by CCE in Antwerp, Belgium, and Dunkirk, France, were contaminated by bad carbon dioxide and paint used on wooden pallets to prevent mold. Coca-Cola products were banned or recalled in Belgium, France, and a handful of other European countries for about two weeks, costing the company more than $100 million. Schimberg retired in 1999 and Summerfield Johnston Jr. became CEO again.

In 1999 CCE acquired seven bottlers in the US for about $628 million and one in Europe. European Commission regulators raided various CCE offices in 1999 and 2000 as part of an investigation into anti-competitive marketing programs.

In 2000 sales of Coca-Cola products in Belgium recovered to pre-contamination scare levels; the rest of CCE's European sales are recovering more slowly. The company spent about $54 million on four acquisitions in the US and Canada that same year.

In April 2001 Summerfield Johnston Jr. stepped down as CEO, but remained chairman. Vice chairman Lowry Kline was named CEO. In July the company bought bottlers Hondo and Herbco Enterprises (collectively known as Herb Coca-Cola, the #3 Coke bottler in the US) for about $1.4 billion. The company then announced it would lay off 2,000 employees as a result of stagnant sales in North America. In 2002 Kline also replaced Johnston as chairman.

OFFICERS

Chairman and CEO: Lowry F. Kline, age 60,
$795,963 pay (prior to promotion)
President and COO: John R. Alm, age 56, $858,375 pay
(prior to title change)
EVP, Marketing: Norman P. Findley III, age 56,
$698,122 pay
EVP; President, North America Group:
G. David Van Houten Jr., age 51, $851,978 pay
EVP, Strategic Planning: Summerfield K. Johnston III,
age 48, $690,888 pay
SVP and CFO: Patrick J. Mannelly, age 46
SVP and Chief Customer Officer: Daniel G. Marr, age 49
SVP and General Counsel: John R. Parker Jr., age 50
SVP, Bottler Relations: Gary P. Schroeder, age 55
SVP, Human Resources: Daniel S. Bowling III
**SVP, North American Marketing and Business
Development:** William A. Holl, age 43
SVP, Operations and Capital Planning: Robert F. Gray,
age 54
SVP, Public Affairs: John H. Downs Jr., age 44
SVP, Treasurer, and Special Assistant to the CEO:
Vicki R. Palmer, age 48
Auditors: Ernst & Young LLP

LOCATIONS

HQ: 2500 Windy Ridge Pkwy., Atlanta, GA 30339
Phone: 770-989-3000 **Fax:** 770-989-3788
Web: www.cokecce.com

Coca-Cola Enterprises bottles and distributes soft drinks
in the US and in Belgium, Canada, France, Great
Britain, Luxembourg, Monaco, and the Netherlands.

2001 Sales

	% mil.	% of total
North America	12,055	77
European	3,645	23
Total	**15,700**	**100**

PRODUCTS/OPERATIONS

2001 Brand Distribution

	% of total
Coca-Cola/Coca-Cola classic	40
diet Coke/Coca-Cola light	21
Sprite	11
Other Coca-Cola products	20
Other franchise products	8
Total	**100**

COMPETITORS

Buffalo Rock
Cadbury
 Schweppes
Coca-Cola
 Bottling
 Consolidated
Cott
Dr Pepper/Seven
 Up Bottling

Georgia Crown
 Distributing
Honickman
Leading Brands
National
 Beverage
Nestlé
Ocean Spray
Pepsi Bottling

Pepsi Bottling
 Ventures
PepsiAmericas
Quaker Foods
Snapple
Suntory
Virgin Group

HISTORICAL FINANCIALS & EMPLOYEES

NYSE: CCE FYE: December 31	Annual Growth	12/92	12/93	12/94	12/95	12/96	12/97	12/98	12/99	12/00	12/01
Sales ($ mil.)	13.2%	5,127	5,465	6,011	6,773	7,921	11,278	13,414	14,406	14,750	15,700
Net income ($ mil.)	—	(186)	(15)	69	82	114	171	142	59	236	(321)
Income as % of sales	—	—	—	1.1%	1.2%	1.4%	1.5%	1.1%	0.4%	1.6%	—
Earnings per share ($)	—	(0.48)	(0.04)	0.18	0.20	0.28	0.43	0.35	0.13	0.54	(0.75)
Stock price - FY high ($)	—	5.41	5.29	6.49	9.95	16.36	36.00	41.56	37.50	30.25	23.90
Stock price - FY low ($)	—	3.75	3.91	4.66	5.91	7.99	15.69	22.88	16.81	14.00	13.46
Stock price - FY close ($)	18.6%	4.08	5.08	5.99	8.95	16.15	35.56	35.75	20.13	19.00	18.94
P/E - high	—	—	—	36	47	58	82	115	288	54	—
P/E - low	—	—	—	26	28	29	36	64	129	25	—
Dividends per share ($)	26.0%	0.02	0.02	0.02	0.02	0.03	0.08	0.15	0.16	0.16	0.16
Book value per share ($)	7.8%	3.23	3.25	3.45	3.72	4.11	4.61	6.07	6.94	6.78	6.34
Employees	12.5%	25,000	26,000	26,500	30,000	43,200	56,000	66,000	69,000	67,000	72,000

STOCK PRICE HISTORY

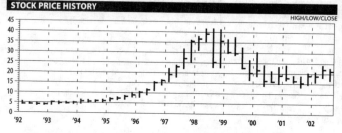

HIGH/LOW/CLOSE

2001 FISCAL YEAR-END

Debt ratio: 78.6%
Return on equity: —
Cash ($ mil.): 284
Current ratio: 0.64
Long-term debt ($ mil.): 10,365
No. of shares (mil.): 445
Dividends
 Yield: 0.8%
 Payout: —
Market value ($ mil.): 8,430

COLGATE-PALMOLIVE COMPANY

Colgate-Palmolive wants you to get up close and personal. Headquartered in New York City, the company is the #1 maker of toothpaste in the US (ahead of Procter & Gamble). It produces mouthwash and dental floss, and leads the world in toothbrush sales by volume. Colgate is also a major supplier of personal care products (baby care, deodorants, shampoos, and soaps), dishwashing soaps (Palmolive is a leading brand worldwide), and household cleaning products (Ajax, Murphy's). Its Hill's Pet Nutrition subsidiary produces Science Diet pet food, a bestseller globally. Colgate has operations in more than 70 countries and markets its products in more than 200.

The company aggressively pursues market share, constantly introducing a bevy of new products and supporting them with a big advertising budget. Colgate relies heavily on foreign sales (about 70% of revenues).

HISTORY

William Colgate founded The Colgate Company in Manhattan in 1806 to produce soap, candles, and starch. Colgate died in 1857, and the company passed to his son Samuel, who renamed it Colgate and Company. In 1873 the company introduced toothpaste in jars, and in 1896 it began selling Colgate Dental Cream in tubes. By 1906 Colgate was making 160 kinds of soap, 625 perfumes, and 2,000 other products. The company went public in 1908.

In 1898 Milwaukee's B. J. Johnson Soap Company (founded 1864) introduced Palmolive, a soap made of palm and olive oils rather than smelly animal fats. It became so popular that the firm changed its name to The Palmolive Company in 1916. Ten years later Palmolive merged with Peet Brothers, a Kansas City-based soap maker founded in 1872. Palmolive-Peet merged with Colgate in 1928, forming Colgate-Palmolive-Peet (shortened to Colgate-Palmolive in 1953). The stock market crash of 1929 prevented a planned merger of the company with Hershey and Kraft.

During the 1930s the firm purchased French and German soap makers and opened branches in Europe. Colgate introduced Fab detergent and Ajax cleanser in 1947, and the brands soon became top sellers in Europe. The company expanded to the Far East in the 1950s, and by 1961 foreign sales were 52% of the total.

Colgate introduced a host of products in the 1960s and 1970s, including Palmolive dishwashing liquid (1966), Ultra Brite toothpaste (1968), and Irish Spring soap (1972). During the same time, the company diversified by buying approximately 70 other businesses, including Kendall hospital and industrial supplies (1972), Helena Rubinstein cosmetics (1973), Ram Golf (1974), and Riviana Foods and Hill's Pet Products (1976). The strategy had mixed results, and most of these acquisitions were sold in the 1980s.

Reuben Mark became CEO of Colgate in 1984. The company bought 50% of Southeast Asia's leading toothpaste, Darkie, in 1985, but changed its name to Darlie in 1989 following protests of its minstrel-in-blackface trademark. Both Palmolive automatic dishwasher detergent and Colgate Tartar Control toothpaste were introduced in 1986. That year Colgate purchased the liquid soap lines of Minnetonka, the most popular of which is Softsoap. In 1992 the company bought Mennen, maker of Speed Stick (the leading US deodorant).

Increasing its share of the oral care market in Latin America to 79% in 1995, Colgate acquired Brazilian company Kolynos (from Wyeth for $1 billion) and 94% of Argentina's Odol Saic. The company also bought Ciba-Geigy's oral hygiene business in India, increasing its share of that toothpaste market. At home, however, sales and earnings in key segments were dismal, so in 1995 Colgate began a restructuring that included cutting more than 8% of its employees and closing or reconfiguring 24 factories over two years.

The company introduced a record 602 products in 1996 and continued to expand its operations in countries with emerging economies. In 1997 Colgate took the lead in the US toothpaste market for the first time in 35 years (displacing Procter & Gamble).

In 1999 the company sold the rights to Baby Magic (shampoos, lotions, and oils) in the US, Canada, and Puerto Rico to Playtex Products, retaining the rights in all other countries. In 2001 the company sold its heavy-duty laundry detergent business in Mexico (primarily the Viva brand) to Henkel, one of Europe's leading detergent producers.

In 2002 Colgate introduced a teeth whitening gel, Simply White, as direct competition with rival Procter & Gamble's Crest Whitestrips.

OFFICERS

Chairman and CEO: Reuben Mark, age 63, $4,937,566 pay
President: William S. Shanahan, $4,162,966 pay
COO: Lois D. Juliber, age 53, $1,720,714 pay
CFO: Stephen C. Patrick, age 52, $1,100,064 pay
EVP; President, Colgate-Latin America: Michael J. Tangney, age 57
EVP; President, Colgate-North America: Ian M. Cook, age 49, $1,401,717 pay

SVP, General Counsel, and Secretary:
Andrew D. Hendry, age 54
CEO, Hill's Pet Nutrition: Robert C. Wheeler, age 60
President, Central Europe and Russia: Tarek S. Hallaba
President, Colgate-Africa/Middle East: Robert R. Martin
President, Colgate-Asia Pacific: S. Peter Dam
President, Colgate-Europe: Franck J. Moison
President, Colgate Oral Pharmaceuticals:
J. Nicholas Vinke
President, Fabric Care: Gregory P. Woodson
President, Global Oral Care: Barrie M. Spelling, age 58
President, Mexico: Guillermo M. Fernandez
VP and Chief Patent Counsel: Paul Shapiro
VP and Treasurer: Susan J. Riley, age 43
VP and Corporate Controller: Dennis J. Hickey, age 53
VP, Advertising: Emilio Alvarez-Recio, age 64
Auditors: PricewaterhouseCoopers LLP

LOCATIONS

HQ: 300 Park Ave., New York, NY 10022
Phone: 212-310-2000   **Fax:** 212-310-3405
Web: www.colgate.com

Colgate-Palmolive has operations in more than 70
countries and sells its products in more than 200.

2001 Sales (Excludes Hill's Pet Nutrition, Inc.)

	% of total
Latin America	39
North America	30
Europe	20
Asia/Africa	11
Total	**100**

PRODUCTS/OPERATIONS

2001 Sales

	% of total
Oral care	34
Personal care	24
Household	16
Fabric care	13
Pet food	13
Total	**100**

Selected Brands

Oral Care	**Household Surface Care**
Actibrush (toothbrush)	Ajax
Colgate	Murphy's oil soap
Navigator (flexible head toothbrush)	Palmolive
Sparkling White	**Fabric Care**
	Dynamo
Personal Care	Fab
Irish Spring	
Mennen	**Pet Nutrition**
Speed Stick	Hill's Prescription Diet
	Science Diet

COMPETITORS

Alberto-Culver	Heinz	Pfizer
Alticor	Henkel	Procter &
Avon	Herbalife	Gamble
Chattem	Iams	Reckitt
Church &	Johnson &	Benckiser
Dwight	Johnson	Sara Lee
Clorox	L'Oréal USA	Household
Dial	Mars	S.C. Johnson
Doane Pet Care	MedPointe	Unilever
Company	Nestlé	
Gillette	Nu Skin	

HISTORICAL FINANCIALS & EMPLOYEES

NYSE: CL FYE: December 31	Annual Growth	12/92	12/93	12/94	12/95	12/96	12/97	12/98	12/99	12/00	12/01
Sales ($ mil.)	3.4%	7,007	7,141	7,588	8,358	8,749	9,057	8,972	9,118	9,358	9,428
Net income ($ mil.)	10.2%	477	190	580	172	635	740	849	937	1,064	1,147
Income as % of sales	—	6.8%	2.7%	7.6%	2.1%	7.3%	8.2%	9.5%	10.3%	11.4%	12.2%
Earnings per share ($)	11.8%	0.69	0.26	0.89	0.26	0.98	1.14	1.31	1.47	1.70	1.89
Stock price - FY high ($)	—	15.16	16.81	17.44	19.34	24.13	39.34	49.44	65.00	66.75	64.75
Stock price - FY low ($)	—	11.28	11.69	12.38	14.50	17.22	22.50	32.53	36.56	40.50	48.50
Stock price - FY close ($)	17.1%	13.94	15.59	15.84	17.56	23.06	36.75	46.44	65.00	64.55	57.75
P/E - high	—	21	20	18	74	23	32	35	41	37	32
P/E - low	—	15	14	13	56	16	18	23	23	22	24
Dividends per share ($)	9.9%	0.29	0.34	0.39	0.44	0.47	0.53	0.55	0.59	0.63	0.68
Book value per share ($)	(10.3%)	4.09	3.14	3.16	2.88	3.46	3.69	3.56	4.32	2.59	1.54
Employees	3.3%	28,800	28,000	32,800	38,400	37,900	37,800	38,300	37,200	38,300	38,500

STOCK PRICE HISTORY

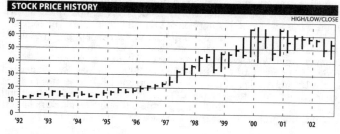

HIGH/LOW/CLOSE

2001 FISCAL YEAR-END
Debt ratio: 76.9%
Return on equity: 141.6%
Cash ($ mil.): 173
Current ratio: 1.04
Long-term debt ($ mil.): 2,812
No. of shares (mil.): 551
Dividends
  Yield: 1.2%
  Payout: 36.0%
Market value ($ mil.): 31,803

COLLINS & AIKMAN CORPORATION

Collins & Aikman loves that new car smell. The Troy, Michigan-based company is a leading maker of automotive interior systems for North America's carmakers. It manufactures floor mats, molded carpeting, plastic trim, acoustic materials, and luggage compartment trim. The company also makes automotive fabric and convertible tops. Major customers include General Motors, Ford, and DaimlerChrysler, which together account for about 70% of sales. The company has more than 80 facilities in 13 countries.

Collins & Aikman sold 25 million of its outstanding shares to Heartland Industrial Partners. Investment firms Blackstone Partners and Wasserstein Pernella Partners have also sold about half of their majority stake in Collins & Aikman to Heartland, so Heartland controls about 60% of Collins & Aikman. The company is using the cash to become a specialized plastics molder. Toward this end, Collins & Aikman has bought injection-molder Becker Group LLC and Textron's TAC-Trim unit (a move that is expected to almost double the company's 2002 sales).

HISTORY

Gibbons Kelty founded G. L. Kelty, a window shade shop, in 1843 in New York City. Following the death of Kelty, investor William Collins and nephew Charles Aikman bought Kelty's holding in a Philadelphia weave plant. They incorporated the company as Collins & Aikman in 1891 and specialized in heavy fabric for upholstery. During the 1920s the company began to make fabrics for auto seats. Collins & Aikman went public in 1926.

When plastics supplanted textiles for many auto interior components after WWII, the company diversified into institutional carpets to boost its upholstery and apparel lines. Retail lumber firm Wickes acquired Collins & Aikman in 1986.

The Wickes Corporation began as a foundry and machine shop in 1854, and developed a steam-powered mill saw that revolutionized the lumber industry. Exploiting the post-WWII building boom, the company's building-supply stores took off; they were renamed Wickes Lumber in 1962. Wickes' continued expansion and acquisitions through the 1970s and early 1980s led the company to bankruptcy, from which it emerged in 1985.

In 1988, two years after Wickes' acquisition of Collins & Aikman, the company sold Wickes Lumber. That year James Birle led a group of investors that took Wickes private, and Wickes Lumber's former parent changed its name to Collins & Aikman.

The company sold its engineering group to Teleflex in 1993 and also closed Builders Emporium. Collins & Aikman reorganized in 1994 and went public. The restructured company placed an emphasis on its automotive division, where contracts with the Big Three automakers helped lift the company to a leading position in the car interior market. The company also expanded globally with plants in Austria and Mexico.

Collins & Aikman got busy in 1996. It acquired Manchester Plastics, which added a variety of plastic-based products such as door panels and headrests, and BTR Fatati Limited, a European maker of floor carpet and trim. Other purchases included JPS Automotive (molded floor carpet and bodycloth) and Perstorp AB's auto supply operations in North America, Spain, and the UK. In 1997 Collins & Aikman sold its floor-coverings operations and its Mastercraft upholstery unit. That year the Manchester Plastics subsidiary entered a joint venture to make instrument panels for GM. The company also sold the airbag-fabric division of JPS to Safety Components International. That next year Collins & Aikman sold its Imperial Wallcoverings unit to a company sponsored by Blackstone Capital Partners.

The company restructured its automotive interior operations into two divisions in 1999. As part of the restructuring, Collins & Aikman put in place a global account manager structure to reduce costs and increase sales to OEMs. That year Thomas Evans, who had been president of Tenneco's automotive parts business, became chairman and CEO.

Moving closer to the car industry, the company transferred its headquarters from Charlotte, North Carolina, to Troy, Michigan, in 2000. In 2001 investment firms Blackstone Partners and Wasserstein Pernella Partners sold about half of their majority stake to Heartland Industrial Partners. Heartland also bought 25 million of Collins & Aikman's outstanding shares. The two deals gave Heartland a controlling 60% stake. That same year Collins & Aikman acquired automotive plastics maker Becker Group LLC in a deal worth about $141 million.

Later in the year Collins & Aikman acquired Textron's automotive trim unit, TAC-Trim, in a deal worth about $1.24 billion (plus the assumption of $100 million in debt). The company also acquired Joan Fabrics' automotive fabrics operations, which it will assimilate into its own North American Automotive Fabric division.

In August of 2002 Thomas Evans stepped down as chairman and CEO. Jerry Mosingo was named CEO, and David Stockman of Heartland Industrial Partners (Collins & Aikman's largest shareholder) was named chairman.

Chairman: David A. Stockman, age 55
Vice Chairman and CFO: J. Michael Stepp, age 57
CEO and Director: Jerry Mosingo, age 51
EVP, Global Manufacturing Operations, Carpet and Acoustic Systems: Millard King, age 57
EVP, Global Manufacturing Operations, Fabrics: Gerald Jones, age 56
EVP, Manufacturing Operations, Interior Trim and Cockpit Systems, Canada: Dana Leavitt
EVP, Manufacturing Operations, Interior Trim and Cockpit Systems, US and Mexico: Eric White
SVP, General Counsel, and Corporate Secretary: Ronald T. Lindsay, age 51, $275,900 pay
SVP, Human Resources: Greg L. Tinnell, age 41
President and Managing Director, European Operations: Bernd Lattemann, age 60
President, Convertible Systems and Mexican Operations: Reed A. White, age 54, $270,000 pay
President, Global Commercial Operations: Michael A. Mitchell, age 58
Auditors: PricewaterhouseCoopers LLP

LOCATIONS

HQ: 250 Stephenson Hwy., Ste. 100, Troy, MI 48083
Phone: 248-824-2500   **Fax:** 248-824-1532
Web: www.collinsaikman.com

Collins & Aikman operates 88 manufacturing plants in Austria, Belgium, Brazil, Canada, France, Germany, Italy, Mexico, the Netherlands, Spain, Sweden, the UK, and the US.

2001 Sales

	$ mil.	% of total
US	1,346	74
Canada	169	9
UK	117	6
Mexico	50	3
Other countries	141	8
Total	**1,823**	**100** *

PRODUCTS/OPERATIONS

2001 Sales

	$ mil.	% of total
Molded floor carpet	477	26
Plastic interior trim	404	24
Automotive fabrics	278	15
Acoustical products	223	12
Floormats	149	8
Convertible top systems	118	6
Luggage compartment trim	61	3
Other	113	6
Total	**1,823**	**100**

COMPETITORS

ASC	Lancaster Colony
Eagle-Picher	Lear
Faurecia	Magna International
Guilford Mills	Milliken
Johnson Controls	Textron
Johnston Industries	Visteon

HISTORICAL FINANCIALS & EMPLOYEES

NYSE: CKC FYE: Last Saturday in Dec.	Annual Growth	1/93	1/94	1/95	1/96	*12/96	12/97	12/98	12/99	12/00	12/01
Sales ($ mil.)	2.5%	—	—	1,536	1,292	1,056	1,629	1,826	1,899	1,902	1,823
Net income ($ mil.)	—	—	—	(31)	206	41	155	(4)	(10)	5	(46)
Income as % of sales	—	—	—	—	16.0%	3.9%	9.5%	—	—	0.2%	—
Earnings per share ($)	—	—	—	(6.01)	7.25	1.46	5.84	(0.15)	(0.40)	0.17	(1.18)
Stock price – FY high ($)	—	—	—	27.50	23.44	20.94	30.94	24.22	19.06	17.66	25.75
Stock price – FY low ($)	—	—	—	19.06	14.38	13.44	15.31	12.19	9.84	7.19	8.75
Stock price – FY close ($)	(0.8%)	—	—	20.31	17.19	15.63	21.56	12.81	14.38	10.47	19.25
P/E – high	—	—	—	—	3	12	5	—	—	88	—
P/E – low	—	—	—	—	2	8	3	—	—	36	—
Dividends per share ($)	—	—	—	0.00	0.00	0.00	0.00	0.00	2.03	0.00	0.00
Book value per share ($)	—	—	—	(14.63)	(8.08)	(7.18)	(2.54)	(3.21)	(6.10)	(6.25)	5.58
Employees	15.1%	—	—	—	—	12,800	15,100	15,900	15,600	15,000	25,850

* Fiscal year change

STOCK PRICE HISTORY

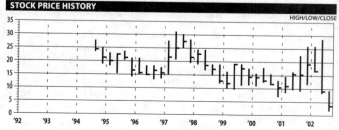

HIGH/LOW/CLOSE

2001 FISCAL YEAR-END

Debt ratio: 77.4%
Return on equity: —
Cash ($ mil.): 74
Current ratio: 0.97
Long-term debt ($ mil.): 1,282
No. of shares (mil.): 67
Dividends
  Yield: —
  Payout: —
Market value ($ mil.): 1,294

COMCAST CORPORATION

Comcast casts its net into the cable and entertainment industries. The Philadelphia-based company is the #3 cable system operator in the US, with 8.5 million subscribers, including 2.7 million digital cable and more than 1 million broadband Internet access customers, and it has agreed to buy market leader AT&T Broadband. The new AT&T Comcast would have 22 million subscribers, dwarfing #2 cable operator Time Warner Cable, a unit of AOL Time Warner. Another deal aimed at separating Time Warner Entertainment's cable and content services will give AT&T Comcast a 21% stake in a restructured Time Warner Cable.

Comcast gets nearly half of its sales from its 57% stake in QVC, the global electronic retailer. Other programming interests include 40% of E! Entertainment Television, a joint venture with Disney. It also has a two-thirds stake in Comcast-Spectacor, a venture that owns Philadelphia's Flyers hockey team and 76ers basketball team, as well as 53% of SportsNet, a regional network that broadcasts home games of the Flyers, 76ers, and Philadelphia Phillies.

President Brian Roberts, son of founder and chairman Ralph Roberts, controls about 87% of the voting rights of the company.

HISTORY

In 1963 Ralph Roberts, Daniel Aaron, and Julian Brodsky bought American Cable Systems in Tupelo, Mississippi. The company soon expanded throughout the state. In 1969 the company got a new name: Comcast, combining "communications" and "broadcast." Two years later it acquired franchises in western Pennsylvania, and when it went public in 1972, it moved to Philadelphia.

Comcast bought up local operations nationwide through the early 1980s and gained its first foreign cable franchise in 1983 in London (it sold its affiliate there to NTL in 1998). It took a 26% stake in the large Group W Cable in 1986. Roberts also lent financial support that year to a fledgling home-shopping channel called QVC — for "quality, value, and convenience."

A big step into telecommunications came in 1988 when Comcast bought American Cellular Network, with Delaware and New Jersey franchises. Two years later Roberts' son Brian — who had trained as a cable installer during a summer away from college — became Comcast's president.

In 1992 Comcast bought Metromedia's Philadelphia-area cellular operations and began investing in fiber-optic and wireless phone companies. By then the company was a major QVC shareholder. With an eye toward Comcast's programming needs, Brian persuaded Fox network head Barry Diller to become QVC's chairman. But when Diller tried to use QVC to take over CBS, Comcast bought control of QVC in 1994 to quash the bid, which went against cross-ownership bans. To pay for QVC, Comcast had to sell its 20% stake in cable firm Heritage Communications in 1995. Diller left the company (he now oversees USA Networks, parent of QVC's archrival Home Shopping Network). Also in 1995 Comcast funded former Disney executive Richard Frank to launch the C3 (Comcast Content and Communication) programming company.

In 1996 the company formed Comcast-Spectacor, a regional sports venture that led to the regional all-sports channel SportsNet. The next year Microsoft invested $1 billion in Comcast, crowning cable as the preferred pathway into the home for information delivery. Comcast's C3 also paired with Disney to buy out Time Warner's majority stake in E! Entertainment Television, but by 1998 C3 had folded and Comcast took control.

Comcast, TCI, and Cox sold Teleport, their local phone venture, to AT&T in 1998, but Comcast turned around and bought long-distance service provider GlobalCom (now Comcast Telecommunications). That year Sprint Spectrum — Comcast's PCS venture with Sprint, Cox, and the former TCI — was rolled into Sprint PCS, under Sprint's management.

Comcast sold its cellular operations to SBC Communications for $1.7 billion in 1999. The company also agreed to acquire rival MediaOne that same year, but soon after the $54 billion deal was struck, AT&T weighed in with a $58 billion offer. Comcast dropped its bid for MediaOne when AT&T offered to sell it 2 million cable subscribers. More than a million of those subscribers came from Pennsylvania cable operator Lenfest Communications, which Comcast bought in 2000 from AT&T and the Lenfest family in a $7 billion deal.

In 2001 Comcast completed a systems swap with Adelphia Communications and completed the $2.75 billion purchase of systems in six states from AT&T. Also that year Comcast offered to buy the rest of AT&T's cable operations for $44.5 million in stock and $13.5 billion in assumed debt. AT&T's board rejected the offer, but left the door open for another bid. After it had heard proposals from AOL Time Warner and Cox, AT&T agreed to sell its cable unit to Comcast for $47 billion in stock and $25 billion in assumed debt.

The next year Comcast reached a deal with United Online to offer broadband Internet access over Comcast's cable network.

OFFICERS

Chairman: Ralph J. Roberts, age 82, $1,756,988 pay
Vice Chairman; Chairman, Comcast Interactive Capital:
Julian A. Brodsky, age 68, $1,196,516 pay
President and Director: Brian L. Roberts, age 42,
$2,756,250 pay
EVP; President, Comcast Cable: Stephen B. Burke,
age 43, $1,389,150 pay
EVP Law and Administration and Secretary:
Stanley L. Wang, age 61
EVP and Treasurer: John R. Alchin, age 53
EVP: David L. Cohen
EVP: Lawrence S. Smith, age 54, $1,237,500 pay
SVP and Chief Accounting Officer: Lawrence J. Salva,
age 45
SVP and General Counsel: Arthur R. Block
SVP Corporate Development: Robert S. Pick
SVP Strategic Planning: Mark A. Coblitz
VP and Corporate Controller: Joseph F. DiTrolio
VP Corporate Human Resources: Sharon D. Ingram
VP Corporate Communications: Karen Buchholz
VP External Affairs and Public Policy Counsel:
Joseph W. Waz Jr.
VP Internal Audit: William J. Montemarano
VP Investor Relations: Marlene S. Dooner
Auditors: Deloitte & Touche LLP

LOCATIONS

HQ: 1500 Market St., Philadelphia, PA 19102
Phone: 215-665-1700   **Fax:** 215-981-7790
Web: www.comcast.com

Comcast Corporation's major cable TV systems are
clustered in the mid-Atlantic region (from northern New
Jersey to the Washington, DC, metro area). QVC is
distributed in Germany, the UK, and the US.

PRODUCTS/OPERATIONS

2001 Sales

	$ mil.	% of total
Cable		
Video	4,278	44
Advertising sales	325	3
Broadband Internet	294	3
Other cable services	153	2
Commerce		
QVC & subsidiaries	3,917	41
Other service revenues	707	7
Total	**9,674**	**100**

Selected Operations and Investments
Comcast Cable (cable TV and broadband Internet access)
Comcast Communications (broadband data, voice, and
  Internet services for business)
E! Entertainment (40%, entertainment-related news and
  original programming)
QVC (57%, electronic retailer)
Philadelphia 76ers (NBA team)
Philadelphia Flyers L.P. (NHL team)

COMPETITORS

Adelphia Communications
AT&T Broadband
Cablevision Systems
Charter Communications
Cox Communications
DIRECTV
EchoStar
 Communications
Insight Communications
Liberty Media

Pegasus Communications
Prodigy
RCN
SBC Communications
Shop At Home
Time Warner Cable
Time Warner
 Entertainment
ValueVision Media
Viacom

HISTORICAL FINANCIALS & EMPLOYEES

Nasdaq: CMCSK FYE: December 31	Annual Growth	12/92	12/93	12/94	12/95	12/96	12/97	12/98	12/99	12/00	12/01
Sales ($ mil.)	30.2%	900	1,338	1,375	3,363	4,038	4,913	5,145	6,209	8,219	9,674
Net income ($ mil.)	—	(270)	(859)	(87)	(44)	(54)	(239)	972	1,066	2,022	609
Income as % of sales	—	—	—	—	—	—	—	18.9%	17.2%	24.6%	6.3%
Earnings per share ($)	—	(0.67)	(2.01)	(0.19)	(0.09)	(0.11)	(0.38)	1.20	1.38	2.13	0.63
Stock price - FY high ($)	—	6.17	13.01	12.01	11.19	10.69	16.53	30.13	57.69	55.69	47.46
Stock price - FY low ($)	—	4.46	5.25	7.00	6.88	6.88	7.31	14.75	28.91	27.88	31.99
Stock price - FY close ($)	21.9%	6.04	12.01	7.84	9.09	8.91	15.78	29.34	50.56	41.75	36.00
P/E - high	—	—	—	—	—	—	—	23	40	25	198
P/E - low	—	—	—	—	—	—	—	11	20	12	133
Dividends per share ($)	—	0.10	0.05	0.05	0.05	0.05	0.05	0.05	0.01	0.00	0.00
Book value per share ($)	—	(0.45)	(1.96)	(1.52)	(1.62)	0.95	2.30	5.16	13.75	14.63	15.31
Employees	24.4%	5,327	5,391	6,700	12,200	16,400	17,600	17,000	25,700	35,000	38,000

STOCK PRICE HISTORY

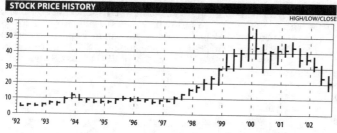

HIGH/LOW/CLOSE

2001 FISCAL YEAR-END

Debt ratio: 44.8%
Return on equity: 4.3%
Cash ($ mil.): 350
Current ratio: 1.45
Long-term debt ($ mil.): 11,742
No. of shares (mil.): 945
Dividends
  Yield: —
  Payout: —
Market value ($ mil.): 34,027

COMERICA INCORPORATED

Comerica's business banks on business banking. The Detroit-based bank holding company has long been strong in commercial lending with an emphasis on small-business loans.

Comerica is organized into three operating units. The Business Bank focuses on business and asset-based lending, global finance, and institutional trusts; it offers lines of credit and international trade finance, among other services. The Individual Bank provides consumer lending and deposits, mortgage loan servicing, small-business banking, private banking, and credit cards. The Investment Bank deals in mutual fund and annuity investment services, as well as life and disability insurance. Comerica operates in California, Florida, Michigan, and Texas, as well as in Canada and Mexico. The company also has offices in several major US cities. To diversify its revenue stream, Comerica owns a majority of publicly traded Official Payments, which allows online remittance of tax bills.

The economic downturn has caused a spike in Comerica's nonperforming loans (it has been particularly burned by the bankruptcy of fellow Michigander Kmart), but the company remains committed to its core small- and middle-market clientele. (With almost 95% of its portfolio wrapped up in commercial loans, the company may have little choice.) To pad its balance sheet, the company could be on the prowl for acquisitions in California and Texas.

HISTORY

Comerica traces its history to 1849, when Michigan governor Epaphroditus Ransom tapped Elon Farnsworth to found the Detroit Savings Fund Institute. At that time Detroit was a major transit point for shipping between Lakes Huron and Erie, as well as between the US and Canada. The bank grew with the town and in 1871 became Detroit Savings Bank.

By 1899 Detroit was one of the top 10 US manufacturing centers and, thanks to a group of local tinkerers and mechanics that included Henry Ford, was on the brink of even greater growth. Detroit Savings also grew, fueled by the deposits of workers whom Ford paid up to $5 a day. Detroit Savings was not, however, the beneficiary of significant business with the auto makers; for corporate banking they turned first to eastern banks and then to large local banks in which they had an interest.

Detroit boomed during the 1920s as America went car-crazy, but after the 1929 crash Detroiters defaulted on mortgages by the thousands. By 1933 Michigan's banks were in such disarray that the governor shut them down three weeks prior to the federal bank holiday. Detroit Savings was one of only four Detroit banks to reopen. None of the major banks associated with auto companies survived.

A few months later Manufacturers National Bank, backed by a group of investors that included Edsel Ford (Henry's son), was founded. Although its start was rocky, Manufacturers National was on firm footing by 1936; around the same time, Detroit Savings Bank renamed itself the Detroit Bank to appeal to a more commercial clientele.

WWII and the postwar boom put Detroit back in gear. In the 1950s and 1960s, both banks thrived. In the 1970s statewide branching was permitted and both banks formed holding companies (DETROITBANK Corp. and Manufacturers National Corp.) and expanded throughout Michigan. As they grew, they added services; when Detroit's economy was hit by the oil shocks of the 1970s, these diversifications helped them through the lean years.

DETROITBANK opened a trust operation in Florida in 1982 to maintain its relationship with retired customers and renamed itself Comerica to be less area-specific. Manufacturers National also began operating in Florida (1983) and made acquisitions in the Chicago area (1987). Comerica went farther afield, buying banks in Texas (1988) and California (1991).

Following the national consolidation trend, in 1992 Comerica and Manufacturers National merged (retaining the Comerica name) but did not fully integrate until 1994, when the new entity began making more acquisitions. To increase sales and develop its consumer business, the company reorganized in 1996. It sold its Illinois bank and its Michigan customs brokerage business and acquired Fairlane Associates to expand its property/casualty insurance line.

As part of its strategy to have operations in all three NAFTA countries, Comerica opened a bank in Mexico in 1997 and one in Canada in 1998. It also added online trading. That year it tapped its Paine Webber (now UBS PaineWebber) connection to expand its trust business, and in 2000 began offering personal trust services to clients of RBC Dain Rauscher (formerly Dain Rauscher). Also that year the firm started a Web-based payment system for its international trade business.

To fortify its business lending operations in California, Comerica acquired Imperial Bancorp in 2001. At the beginning of 2002, chairman Eugene Miller handed the CEO reigns to Ralph Babb.

Chairman, Comerica Incorporated and Comerica Bank:
Eugene A. Miller, age 64, $2,279,500 pay
Vice Chairman, Comerica Incorporated and Comerica Bank: Joseph J. Buttigieg III, age 56, $1,105,800 pay
Vice Chairman, Individual and Investment Banks, Comerica Incorporated and Comerica Bank:
John D. Lewis, age 53, $1,127,800 pay
President, CEO, and Director: Ralph W. Babb Jr., age 53, $1,315,750 pay
EVP and CFO: Elizabeth S. Acton, age 50
EVP and CIO: John R. Beran, age 49, $639,350 pay
EVP, Corporate Staff: Richard A. Collister
EVP, Investment Bank, Comerica Incorporated and Comerica Bank: George C. Eshelman, age 48
EVP; President and CEO, Comerica Bank, California:
J. Michael Fulton
EVP; President and CEO, Comerica Bank, Texas:
Charles L. Gummer
EVP, Small Business Banking and Personal Financial Services: John R. Haggerty, age 58
EVP and Chief Credit Officer: Thomas R. Johnson, age 58
EVP, Corporate Secretary, and General Counsel:
George W. Madison, age 48
EVP, National Business Finance, Comerica Bank:
Ronald P. Marcinelli
SVP, Controller, and Chief Accounting Officer, Comerica Incorporated and Comerica Bank:
Marvin J. Elenbaas, age 50
SVP and General Auditor: Susan R. Joseph
SVP, Human Resources: James R. Tietjen, age 42
EVP, Corporate Banking, Comerica Bank:
Dale E. Greene
EVP, Private Banking, Comerica Bank:
David B. Stephens
Auditors: Ernst & Young LLP

HQ: Comerica Tower at Detroit Center,
500 Woodward Ave., MC 3391, Detroit, MI 48226
Phone: 313-222-4000   **Fax:** 313-965-4648
Web: www.comerica.com

2001 Sales

	$ mil.	% of total
Interest		
Loans	3,121	74
Investment securities	246	6
Short-term investments	27	1
Noninterest		
Service charges on deposit accounts	211	5
Fiduciary income	180	4
Commercial lending fees	67	2
Letter of credit fees	57	1
Brokerage fees	44	1
Other	244	6
Total	**4,197**	**100**

Bank of America	Northern Trust
BANK ONE	Silicon Valley Bancshares
Citigroup	SunTrust
Cullen/Frost Bankers	U.S. Bancorp
Huntington Bancshares	Wells Fargo
National City	

NYSE: CMA FYE: December 31	Annual Growth	12/92	12/93	12/94	12/95	12/96	12/97	12/98	12/99	12/00	12/01
Assets ($ mil.)	7.4%	26,587	30,295	33,430	35,470	34,206	36,292	36,601	38,653	41,985	50,732
Net income ($ mil.)	13.6%	226	341	387	413	417	531	607	673	749	710
Income as % of assets	—	0.9%	1.1%	1.2%	1.2%	1.2%	1.5%	1.7%	1.7%	1.8%	1.4%
Earnings per share ($)	22.2%	0.64	1.90	2.19	2.37	2.38	3.19	3.72	4.14	4.63	3.88
Stock price – FY high ($)	—	21.84	23.51	20.84	28.51	39.60	61.91	73.00	70.00	61.13	65.15
Stock price – FY low ($)	—	17.51	16.76	16.09	16.09	24.18	34.18	46.50	44.00	32.94	44.02
Stock price – FY close ($)	11.6%	21.34	17.76	16.26	26.68	34.93	60.20	68.19	46.69	59.38	57.30
P/E – high	—	34	12	9	12	16	19	19	17	13	17
P/E – low	—	27	9	7	7	10	11	12	10	7	11
Dividends per share ($)	11.8%	0.63	0.70	0.80	0.89	0.99	1.12	1.25	1.40	1.56	1.72
Book value per share ($)	9.7%	11.78	12.67	13.65	15.18	16.33	17.61	19.54	22.20	25.53	27.15
Employees	(1.3%)	13,322	12,670	13,498	13,572	11,969	10,877	10,739	10,842	10,361	11,792

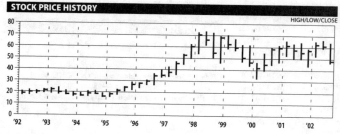

HIGH/LOW/CLOSE

Equity as % of assets: 9.5%
Return on assets: 1.5%
Return on equity: 16.6%
Long-term debt ($ mil.): 5,503
No. of shares (mil.): 177
Dividends
 Yield: 3.0%
 Payout: 44.3%
Market value ($ mil.): 10,146
Sales ($ mil.): 4,197

COMMERCIAL METALS COMPANY

Vertical integration keeps Commercial Metals Company's (CMC) sales from falling flat. The Dallas-based company's manufacturing division operates four steel minimills, 26 steel fabrication plants, and 24 concrete products warehouses. The unit also operates a heat-treating facility and plants that manufacture steel joists, castellated beams, and fence posts. CMC's recycling segment operates 34 secondary metals-processing plants that sort, shred, shear, and pulverize ferrous and nonferrous metals into bales that are sold to steel mills, lead smelters, copper refineries, ingot manufacturers, and others. Subsidiary Howell Metal Company manufactures copper tubing.

CMC's marketing and trading segment operates through 17 international trading offices. It brokers industrial products that include primary and secondary metals, fabricated metals, chemicals, and industrial minerals to customers in the steel, nonferrous metals, metal fabrication, chemical, refractory, and transportation industries.

Despite the gloomy outlook for the steel industry, CMC has managed to make a profit in nearly every quarter for the past 23 years. The company's vertical integration allows for a flagging segment to be compensated for by another's success in tough times. For example, when scrap prices are low, CMC's recycling centers feel the pain, but the company's minimills rake it in. When steel prices are hurt by the dumping of cheap imports, CMC's marketing and trading arm continues to make money.

HISTORY

Russian immigrant Moses Feldman moved to Dallas in 1914 and founded scrap metal company American Iron & Metal the next year. In the 1920s Feldman suffered a heart attack, and his son Jake helped out with the business. Low metal prices hurt the company during the Depression. In 1932 Jake formed a two-man brokerage firm, Commercial Metals Company (CMC), which was combined as a partnership with his father's scrap metal operations. Moses Feldman died in 1937. CMC was incorporated in 1946 and began buying related businesses during the 1950s.

CMC was listed on the American Stock Exchange in 1960. It soon expanded geographically, buying a stake in Texas steelmaker Structural Metals (1963). In 1965 it formed its first overseas subsidiary, Commercial Metals Europa (the Netherlands), and Commonwealth Metal (New York). By 1966 CMC was one of the world's top three scrap metal companies. It bought copper tube manufacturer Howell Metals (Virginia) in 1968, the remainder of Structural Metals, and major stakes in seven affiliated businesses. Over

10 years, CMC opened trading offices around the world. Business continued to grow throughout the 1970s. The company added a small minimill in Arkansas (1971) and certain assets of General Export Iron and Metal in Texas (1976).

CMC began trading on the New York Stock Exchange in 1982. The next year the company bought Connors Steel (Alabama), its third minimill. By the end of 1984 CMC was operating 20 metal recycling plants from Texas to Florida.

The company modernized its minimills in the 1990s. CMC acquired small scrap-metal operations and Shepler's, a concrete-related products business, in 1994. Also that year CEO Stanley Rabin completed the $50 million purchase of Owen Steel (a South Carolina minimill), which expanded CMC's reach into the Mid-Atlantic and Southeast. The company wrapped up a $30 million capital improvement program at its Alabama minimill in 1995 — just in time to ride a strong steel market to record profits.

Although a correction in the steel and metals industry depressed prices in 1996, CMC achieved record sales and profits that fiscal year. However, both dipped the next year, with lower steel and scrap prices widely attributed to an influx of foreign imports. CMC strengthened its vertical integration in 1997 by acquiring Allegheny Heat Treating (heat-treatment services to steel mills) and two auto salvage plants in Florida.

During 1998 CMC moved into the Midwest, buying a metals recycling company in Missouri. It boosted global operations by purchasing a metals trading firm in Australia and also entering a joint venture with Trinec, a Czech Republic steel mill. The next year CMC completed construction of a rolling mill in South Carolina and renovations at an Alabama plant; both were expected to reduce production-related costs and increase efficiency to help counter slumping steel prices.

In 2000 CMC picked up three rebar fabricators — two in California (Fontana Steel and C&M Steel), and one in Florida (Suncoast Steel).

In late 2001 the company announced it would build a facility to develop and manufacture corrosion-resistant stainless steel clad products such as dowels and structural shapes for use in heavy construction industry.

OFFICERS

Chairman, President, and CEO: Stanley A. Rabin, age 63, $770,000 pay
VP and CFO: William B. Larson, age 48
VP and Director; President and COO, CMC Steel Group: Clyde P. Selig, age 69, $561,000 pay
VP; President, Fabrication Plants, CMC Steel Group: Hugh M. Ghormley, age 72, $515,000 pay

VP and Director; President, Howell Metal Company:
A. Leo Howell, age 80, $690,000 pay
VP; President, Marketing and Trading Segment:
Murray R. McClean, age 53
VP; President, Secondary Metals Processing Division:
Harry J. Heinkele, age 69
VP, General Counsel, and Secretary: David M. Sudbury, age 56
Chairman and CEO, CMC Steel Group: Marvin Selig, age 78, $561,000 pay
President, Cometals: Eliezer Skornicki
President, Commonwealth Metal: Eugene L. Vastola
President, Dallas Trading Division: J. Matthew Kramer
President, East Group: Jeff Selig
President, International Division: Kevin S. Aitken
President, West Group: Russ Rinn
EVP, Steel Group: Binh Huynh
EVP Steel Group, West: Phil Seidenberger
Auditors: Deloitte & Touche LLP

LOCATIONS

HQ: 7800 Stemmons Fwy., Dallas, TX 75247
Phone: 214-689-4300   **Fax:** 214-689-5886
Web: www.commercialmetals.com

CMC operates manufacturing and recycling facilities throughout the US; it has 17 trading offices in Australia, Germany, Hong Kong, Singapore, Switzerland, the UK, and the US.

2001 Sales

	$ mil.	% of total
US	1,686	69
Other countries	755	31
Total	**2,441**	**100**

PRODUCTS/OPERATIONS

2001 Sales

	$ mil.	% of total
Manufacturing	1,321	53
Marketing & trading	771	31
Recycling	394	16
Adjustments	(45)	—
Total	**2,441**	**100**

Selected Operations

Manufacturing
Cóncrete-related product warehousing
Copper tube manufacturing
Industrial products supply
Railcar rebuilding
Steel fabrication
Steel joist manufacturing
Steel minimills

Marketing and Trading
Chemicals
Ferroalloys
Nonferrous metals
Ores
Specialty metals
Steel

Recycling
Scrap ferrous and nonferrous metal processing

COMPETITORS

AK Steel Holding Corporation
Bethlehem Steel
BHP Billiton Ltd
Birmingham Steel
Blue Tee
Cargill Steel
Chaparral Steel
Connell Limited Partnership

David J. Joseph
Keywell
LTV
Metal Management
Metals USA
Nucor
OmniSource
Oregon Steel Mills
Quanex

Roanoke Electric Steel
Rouge Industries
Schnitzer Steel
Tang Industries
Tube City
United States Steel
Worthington Industries

HISTORICAL FINANCIALS & EMPLOYEES

NYSE: CMC FYE: August 31	Annual Growth	8/92	8/93	8/94	8/95	8/96	8/97	8/98	8/99	8/00	8/01
Sales ($ mil.)	8.6%	1,166	1,569	1,666	2,117	2,322	2,258	2,368	2,251	2,661	2,441
Net income ($ mil.)	7.7%	13	22	26	38	46	39	43	47	46	24
Income as % of sales	—	1.1%	1.4%	1.6%	1.8%	2.0%	1.7%	1.8%	2.1%	1.7%	1.0%
Earnings per share ($)	8.7%	0.44	0.73	0.88	1.26	1.51	1.27	1.41	1.61	1.63	0.93
Stock price - FY high ($)	—	9.47	14.25	15.00	14.56	16.63	16.75	18.00	17.09	16.97	16.37
Stock price - FY low ($)	—	6.52	8.39	10.50	11.69	11.50	13.56	12.06	9.84	11.06	9.88
Stock price - FY close ($)	6.9%	8.63	14.16	13.38	14.13	15.06	15.38	12.19	15.31	13.97	15.70
P/E - high	—	22	20	17	12	11	13	13	10	10	17
P/E - low	—	15	11	12	9	8	10	8	6	7	11
Dividends per share ($)	3.0%	0.20	0.20	0.23	0.24	0.24	0.26	0.26	0.26	0.26	0.26
Book value per share ($)	9.3%	7.46	7.98	8.50	9.86	11.10	12.02	13.09	14.53	15.97	16.65
Employees	8.5%	3,834	3,904	4,353	6,272	6,700	7,150	7,350	7,581	8,378	7,998

STOCK PRICE HISTORY

HIGH/LOW/CLOSE

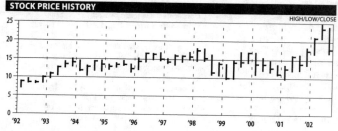

2001 FISCAL YEAR-END

Debt ratio: 36.6%
Return on equity: 5.7%
Cash ($ mil.): 33
Current ratio: 1.84
Long-term debt ($ mil.): 252
No. of shares (mil.): 26
Dividends
  Yield: 1.7%
  Payout: 28.0%
Market value ($ mil.): 411

COMPUCOM SYSTEMS, INC.

CompuCom Systems pieces together the computing puzzle. The Dallas-based company provides desktop, mobile, and wireless computers, networking equipment, peripherals, and software to nearly 6,000 corporations. CompuCom also offers consulting, distribution, help desk support, and other information technology services. Its product vendors include IBM and Hewlett-Packard (65% of product sales).

As manufacturers of technology products turn increasingly to direct sales in an effort to cut costs, CompuCom continues to expand its services business largely through acquisitions.

Investment and management firm Safeguard Scientifics owns 53% of the company.

HISTORY

Stanley Sternberg founded CompuCom Systems in Michigan in 1981 to develop factory automation products. Originally called Cyto-Systems, the company changed its name in 1983 to Machine Vision International (MVI) to reflect its focus on designing artificial vision systems for computers. Its main customers were Detroit automakers, which used MVI's automated guidance systems to control industrial robots. By the mid-1980s MVI was one of the largest machine vision companies in the US.

In 1984 Safeguard Scientifics bought 31.5% of the company; Safeguard was founded in 1953 by Warren Musser and Frank Diamond to raise funds for small, promising businesses. Seeking more capital for MVI, Safeguard and MVI's management took the company public in 1985. However, MVI soon ran into trouble as the machine vision industry slowed down. General Motors, the company's biggest customer, cut its orders, and MVI lost more than $13 million in 1986.

The following year MVI acquired New Jersey-based computer retailer TriStar Data Systems and Office Automation. The company moved its headquarters to New Jersey, renamed itself CompuCom Systems, and shifted its focus to selling and supporting microcomputers.

CompuCom exited the machine vision business in 1988. That year it acquired CompuShop, a Dallas-based computer retailer, from Bell Atlantic. CompuCom then relocated to Dallas.

In 1989 the company named Avery More (EVP of an Apple Computer reseller) president and co-CEO along with CompuShop CEO James Dixon. Safeguard extended its interest in the company that year to 66% (it has since reduced its interest to 53%). In 1991 the company flirted briefly with retailing, but decided to abandon it and focus on direct sales to corporate customers. CompuCom expanded its networking business when it bought network integrator MicroSolutions in 1992 and International Micronet Systems two years later. When More left the company in 1993 to start his own venture capital firm, COO and reseller channel veteran Ed Anderson became CEO.

In 1995 the company bought network integrators in New Jersey and Texas. CompuCom and Unisys joined forces the next year to provide support services for multiple manufacturer desktop and network systems. The company also won a contract in 1996 to establish and operate two computer stores for the State of California (one in Los Angeles, the other in San Francisco). The next year the company added software management to its list of services.

In 1998 CompuCom bought Computer Integration, a computer reseller, and expanded its presence in the Southeast US with its purchase of Florida-based Dataflex. That year, when sales expenses grew faster than revenues, the company laid off close to 10% of its workforce. The reorganization was partly to blame for a drop in profits that year.

Boosting its sales in 1999, CompuCom bought the resale products business of rival ENTEX Information Services (now part of Siemens) for $137 million. That year the company merged its ClientLink applications development subsidiary with Internet security services specialist E-Certify. Anderson left CompuCom to become president and CEO of E-Certify; later in 1999 a veteran of Computer Sciences Corporation, Edward Coleman, took over the CEO position.

Coleman assumed additional duties in 2000 when CompuCom's president and COO Thomas Lynch resigned his position; the following year Coleman also became chairman. In 2001 the company acquired four companies, including MicroAge Technology Services, in an effort to broaden its selection of services.

OFFICERS

Chairman, President, and CEO: J. Edward Coleman, age 50, $1,177,000 pay
SVP and CTO: David W. Hall
SVP, Finance, CFO, Secretary, and Director: M. Lazane Smith, age 47, $700,000 pay
SVP, Corporate Development: Jeffrey H. Sopp
SVP, Human Resources: David A. Loeser, age 47, $410,770 pay
SVP, Information Systems: Suresh V. Mathews
SVP, Sales: Anthony F. Pellegrini, age 59, $410,770 pay
SVP, Outsourcing Services: John F. McKenna, age 38, $453,846 pay
VP, Business Development: Thomas Ducatelli
VP, Enterprise Help Desk: Meg Frantz
VP, Finance, Treasurer, and Controller: Daniel L. Celoni
VP, Financial Operations: Mark J. Loder

VP, Integration and Distribution Services: John DiMuzio
VP, Outsourcing Business Development: Charles Jarrow
VP, Sales Operations: Mark M. Warshauer
VP, Sales Western Region: Rocco Musumeche
VP, Transportation Logistics: Henry Giese
VP, Wireless and Mobile Solutions: Daniel Elliot
President, Clientlink: James H. Hamilton
President, Excell Data Corporation: Richard T. Jorgenson
Auditors: KPMG LLP

LOCATIONS

HQ: 7171 Forest Ln., Dallas, TX 75230
Phone: 972-856-3600 **Fax:** 972-856-5395
Web: www.compucom.com

CompuCom Systems has offices in New Jersey and Texas.

PRODUCTS/OPERATIONS

2001 Sales

	$ mil.	% of total
Product	1,533	84
Services	282	16
Total	**1,815**	**100**

Products

Computers	Networking equipment
Data storage equipment	Peripherals
Mobile and wireless computing products	Software

Selected Services

Asset tracking	Help desk support
Configuration	Network management
Consulting	Networking support
Distribution	Product procurement
Field engineering	Software management

COMPETITORS

Accenture
Avnet
Bell Microproducts
Comark
Computer Sciences
EDS
Hewlett-Packard
IBM
Ingram Micro
Merisel
Siemens
Software House
Software Spectrum
Tech Data
Unisys

HISTORICAL FINANCIALS & EMPLOYEES

Nasdaq: CMPC FYE: December 31	Annual Growth	12/92	12/93	12/94	12/95	12/96	12/97	12/98	12/99	12/00	12/01
Sales ($ mil.)	10.9%	713	1,016	1,256	1,442	1,995	1,950	2,255	2,908	2,711	1,815
Net income ($ mil.)	(0.9%)	7	11	15	21	31	35	0	12	5	7
Income as % of sales	—	1.0%	1.1%	1.2%	1.4%	1.5%	1.8%	0.0%	0.4%	0.2%	0.4%
Earnings per share ($)	(6.5%)	0.22	0.29	0.34	0.45	0.61	0.71	(0.01)	0.22	0.09	0.12
Stock price - FY high ($)	—	2.88	4.63	7.25	10.63	13.88	11.13	9.75	5.63	7.69	4.06
Stock price - FY low ($)	—	1.44	2.19	2.75	3.13	6.25	4.00	2.25	2.75	0.91	1.31
Stock price - FY close ($)	0.4%	2.19	4.06	3.13	9.50	10.75	8.25	3.50	4.13	1.28	2.26
P/E - high	—	13	13	17	20	21	15	—	26	85	34
P/E - low	—	6	6	6	6	9	5	—	13	10	11
Dividends per share ($)	—	0.00	0.00	0.00	0.00	0.00	0.00	0.00	0.00	0.00	0.00
Book value per share ($)	14.9%	1.39	1.78	2.80	3.14	3.61	4.56	4.43	4.64	4.73	4.87
Employees	14.1%	1,156	1,542	1,975	2,615	3,700	4,300	4,800	5,000	4,100	3,800

STOCK PRICE HISTORY

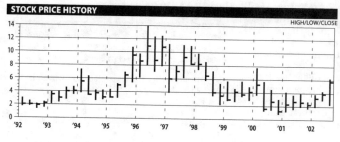

HIGH/LOW/CLOSE

2001 FISCAL YEAR-END

Debt ratio: 0.0%
Return on equity: 3.1%
Cash ($ mil.): 123
Current ratio: 1.42
Long-term debt ($ mil.): 0
No. of shares (mil.): 48
Dividends
  Yield: —
  Payout: —
Market value ($ mil.): 109

COMPUTER ASSOCIATES

Friendly or not, Computer Associates can provide all sorts of software. Islandia, New York-based Computer Associates International (CA) is one of the world's largest software companies, offering more than 800 products that span both mainframe and distributed computing environments. The company's core areas of expertise include products for enterprise management (including its flagship Unicenter software), security, storage, business intelligence, and application development. CA also offers services including consulting, implementation, maintenance, and training. International customers account for about one-third of sales.

While a 20-year practice of acquiring other companies produced an impressive portfolio of software products, it also resulted in CA's reputation for poor customer support and incompatibility among its disparate product lines.

The company has responded to claims of mismanagement (most notably by Sterling Software co-founder Sam Wyly) by restructuring around its core areas of expertise. As part of this effort, CA has spun off certain units as independent subsidiaries and divested other operations.

Swiss billionaire Walter Haefner owns about 20% of the company.

HISTORY

Born in Shanghai, Charles Wang fled Communist China with his family in 1952 and grew up in Queens, New York. After working in sales for software developer Standard Data, Wang started a joint venture in 1976 with Swiss-owned Computer Associates (CA) to sell software in the US. He started with four employees and one product, a file organizer for IBM storage systems. It was a great success, and in 1980 Wang bought out his Swiss partners. CA went public in 1981.

Wang realized that a far-flung distribution and service network (continuously fed by new products) was the key to success. Acquiring existing software (and its customers) reduced risky in-house development and moved products to market sooner.

The company moved beyond mainframe utilities into computer software, buying the popular SuperCalc spreadsheet in 1984. The purchase of chief utilities rival UCCEL in 1987 gave investor Walter Haefner what remains the largest individual stake in CA (21%).

CA's purchases of mostly struggling software firms made it, in 1989, the first independent software company to reach $1 billion in sales. The $300 million acquisition of Cullinet that year added database and banking applications to CA's

product line, but the new software was incompatible with some of CA's other products, causing customer support concerns. This and other problems in assimilating Cullinet prompted CA to develop a way to have its software communicate regardless of hardware platform or operating system.

By the early 1990s, CA's acquisition methods had developed a reputation that were seen by some as ruthless — swoop in, gobble up, cut costs, and get rid of employees. As a new owner, CA strongly defended its licensing contracts — often in court.

In 1994 CA promoted EVP of operations Sanjay Kumar to president. Kumar's shift away from older systems to focus on network software was reflected by the acquisitions of ASK Group (1994), LEGENT (1995), and network management expert Cheyenne Software (1996). CA continued its practice of buying in cash to avoid diluting stock.

Acquisition-related charges caused losses for fiscal 1996. With its lack of a major service operation taking a bite out of potential business, CA made a $9.8 billion hostile takeover offer for consulting firm Computer Sciences Corp. (CSC) in 1998. CA soon dropped its bid in the face of CSC's fierce opposition and later acquired smaller computer service specialist Realogic.

The acquisitions helped cause a drop in profits for fiscal 1999. Later that year CA bought database management software company PLATINUM technology for about $3.5 billion.

In 2000 CA acquired business software specialist Sterling Software in a deal valued at nearly $4 billion. Later that year the company began spinning off some of its promising software businesses; Wang stepped down as CEO to focus on new opportunities for CA as chairman. He handed the CEO reins to Kumar.

Alleging corporate mismanagement, in 2001 Sam Wyly (co-founder of Sterling Software) initiated a proxy fight designed to elect a new board of directors. However, Wyly's bid failed, as it was voted down by shareholders. He initiated a second proxy fight in 2002, but abandoned it after reaching a settlement with the company, which included a $10 million payment.

OFFICERS

Chairman: Charles B. Wang, age 57, $1,000,000 pay
President, CEO, and Director: Sanjay Kumar, age 40, $1,000,000 pay
EVP, Alliances and eTrust Solutions and Director: Russell M. Artzt, age 55, $750,000 pay
EVP, Finance and CFO: Ira H. Zar, age 39, $1,000,000 pay
EVP, Sales: Stephen Richards, age 36, $1,330,600 pay

EVP, Sales and Field Operations: Gary Quinn, age 40, $1,339,209 pay
SVP and General Counsel: Stephen M. Woghin, age 54
SVP and General Manager, CleverPath and AllFusion Solutions: Gary Starkey
SVP and General Manager, Presales Support: Una O'Neill
SVP and General Manager, Unicenter Solutions: Wai Wong
SVP and Secretary: Michael A. McElroy, age 56
SVP, Advantage and Mainframe Solutions: Mark Combs
SVP, BrightStor Solutions: Frank Yang
SVP, Core Values Office: Kevin Long
SVP, Marketing: Nancy Bhagat
SVP, Professional Services and Customer Support: Tommy Bennett, age 46
CTO: Yogesh Gupta
VP and Treasurer: Mary Stravinskas, age 40
VP, Internal Audit: Grace Caden
VP, Investor Relations: Robert Cirabisi
Auditors: KPMG LLP

LOCATIONS

HQ: Computer Associates International, Inc.
1 Computer Associates Plaza, Islandia, NY 11749
Phone: 631-342-5224 **Fax:** 631-342-5329
Web: www.ca.com

Computer Associates International has offices in more than 45 countries.

2002 Sales

	% of total
US	62
Other countries	38
Total	**100**

PRODUCTS/OPERATIONS

2002 Sales

	$ mil.	% of total
Maintenance	958	32
Subscription revenue	827	28
Financing fees	444	15
Professional services	303	10
Software fees & other	432	15
Total	**2,964**	**100**

Selected Software
Application development (Jasmine)
Application lifecycle management (AllFusion)
Business intelligence (CleverPath)
Data access and connectivity
Enterprise management (Unicenter)
Network troubleshooting
Security (eTrust)
Storage management (BrightStor)
Systems management

Selected Services
Consulting	Maintenance
Custom development	Outsourcing
Implementation	Training

COMPETITORS

BMC Software	IBM	SAS Institute
Candle	Microsoft	Software AG
Corporation	Network	Sun
Check Point	Associates	Microsystems
Software	Novell	Sybase
Compuware	Oracle	Symantec
EMC	RSA Security	VERITAS
Hewlett-Packard	SAP	Software

HISTORICAL FINANCIALS & EMPLOYEES

NYSE: CA FYE: March 31	Annual Growth	3/93	3/94	3/95	3/96	3/97	3/98	3/99	3/00	3/01	3/02
Sales ($ mil.)	5.4%	1,841	2,149	2,623	3,505	4,040	4,719	5,253	6,103	4,198	2,964
Net income ($ mil.)	—	246	401	432	(56)	366	1,169	626	696	(591)	(1,102)
Income as % of sales	—	13.3%	18.7%	16.5%	—	9.1%	24.8%	11.9%	11.4%	—	—
Earnings per share ($)	—	0.43	0.69	0.76	(0.10)	0.64	2.06	1.11	1.25	(1.02)	(1.91)
Stock price - FY high ($)	—	8.12	13.32	19.10	34.03	45.27	58.63	61.94	79.44	63.00	38.74
Stock price - FY low ($)	—	3.23	6.49	8.12	16.43	24.85	25.01	26.00	32.88	18.13	14.30
Stock price - FY close ($)	13.4%	7.08	9.16	17.62	31.87	25.93	57.75	35.56	59.25	27.20	21.89
P/E - high	—	19	19	24	—	68	27	54	62	—	—
P/E - low	—	8	9	10	—	37	12	23	25	—	—
Dividends per share ($)	11.5%	0.03	0.04	0.06	0.06	0.07	0.09	0.08	0.08	0.08	0.08
Book value per share ($)	17.6%	1.86	2.26	2.79	2.72	2.77	4.54	5.09	11.94	10.04	8.00
Employees	9.7%	7,200	6,900	7,550	8,800	9,850	11,400	14,650	21,000	18,200	16,600

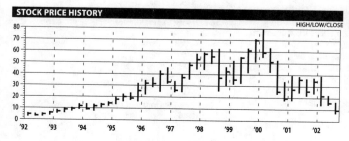

STOCK PRICE HISTORY HIGH/LOW/CLOSE

2002 FISCAL YEAR-END
Debt ratio: 41.9%
Return on equity: —
Cash ($ mil.): 1,093
Current ratio: 1.32
Long-term debt ($ mil.): 3,334
No. of shares (mil.): 577
Dividends
  Yield: 0.4%
  Payout: —
Market value ($ mil.): 12,634

COMPUTER SCIENCES

Wherever there is a cluster of computers, an office of Computer Sciences Corporation (CSC) is probably nearby. With operations in some 70 countries worldwide, El Segundo, California-based CSC is one of the world's largest information technology (IT) services companies. Its offerings include outsourcing (applications development, business process management, and systems analysis), management consulting (including business process and change management), and systems integration. CSC's client list includes corporate giants such as AT&T, D&B, and Raytheon; about 25% of its business comes from the US government.

While IT spending has taken a turn for the worse, CSC has been able to withstand some of the damage due to its long-term outsourcing contracts. However, the company has been forced to make some job cuts, especially in its consulting practice. Realigning its operations, the company sees growing opportunity for its outsourcing business as companies seek to cut costs and squeeze more return from existing technology. CSC has also formed a business unit to focus on security systems such as biometric identification and information security.

HISTORY

Computer Sciences Corporation (CSC) was founded in Los Angeles in 1959 by Fletcher Jones and Roy Nutt to write software for manufacturers such as Honeywell. In 1963 CSC became the first software company to go public. Three years later it signed a $5.5 million contract to support NASA's computation laboratory. Annual sales had climbed to just over $53 million by 1968.

The following year CSC agreed to merge with Western Union, but the deal ultimately fell through. When Jones died in a plane crash in 1972, William Hoover, a former NASA executive who had come aboard eight years earlier, became chairman and CEO. Under Hoover, CSC began transforming itself into a systems integrator. In 1986, when federal contracts still accounted for 70% of sales, the company started diversifying into the commercial sector.

In 1991 CSC signed a 10-year, $3 billion contract with defense supplier General Dynamics. In 1995 Hoover, after more than three decades with CSC, stepped down as CEO (remaining chairman until 1997); he was succeeded by president and COO Van Honeycutt. Also that year CSC bought Germany's largest independent computer services company, Ploenzke. In 1996 CSC acquired insurance services provider Continuum Company for $1.5 billion.

In 1998 CSC found itself on the other side of the bargaining table with a $9.8 billion hostile takeover bid from software giant Computer Associates (CA). After weeks of contentious battle, CA withdrew its bid. The IRS chose CSC to head a team including IBM, Lucent, and Unisys in a multibillion-dollar project to update the agency's computer system.

That year CSC continued its acquisition spree, buying consulting firms in Europe including Informatica Group (Italy), KMPG Peat Marwick (France), Pergamon (Germany), and SYS-AID (the Netherlands). In 1999 CSC inked an 11-year, $1 billion deal to manage the back-office functions of oil and gas giant Enron's energy services unit. (Enron's high-profile bankruptcy leaves the future of this deal uncertain.)

CSC in 2000 boosted its expertise in financial software and services with the cash acquisition of Mynd Corporation (formerly Policy Management Systems) for an estimated $570 million. Also that year CSC signed two large outsourcing contracts — a seven-year, $3 billion deal with telecom equipment maker Nortel Networks that arranged for Nortel to transfer 2,000 employees to CSC, and a $1 billion outsourcing and application development agreement with AT&T.

The company continued to make large deals in 2001, including contracts with the National Security Agency (NSA) and BAE SYSTEMS. The next year saw more of the same: CSC was contracted to operate a central data exchange for the US Environmental Protection Agency, and to collaborate on missile defense systems engineering for the US Army.

OFFICERS

Chairman and CEO: Van B. Honeycutt, age 57, $1,164,123 pay
President and COO: Edward P. Boykin, age 62, $624,591 pay (prior to promotion)
VP; President, European Group: Michael W. Laphen, $641,200 pay
VP; President, Federal Sector: Paul M. Cofoni, $771,000 pay
VP, CFO, and Director: Leon J. Level, age 61, $493,185 pay
VP, Secretary, and General Counsel: Hayward D. Fisk, age 58, $497,077 pay
VP and Controller: Donald G. DeBuck
VP and Deputy General Counsel: Harvey N. Bernstein, age 54
VP and Managing Partner, Global Health Solutions: Daniel Garrett
VP and General Manager, Army Programs: Terry Glasgow
VP and General Manager, Navy/Marine Corps and Missile Defense: Aaron B. Fuller
VP Corporate Development: Paul T. Tucker, age 53
VP Homeland Security: Ben Gianni

VP Human Resources: Frederick E. Vollrath
CEO and Managing Director, Australian Group:
George F. Bell
President, Group President: Mary Jo Morris
President, Application Services Division: Kevin Gaulin
President, Asia Group: Michael W. Brinsford
President, Consulting Group: Rich Wunder
President, Credit Services: Robert M. Denny
Auditors: Deloitte & Touche LLP

LOCATIONS

HQ: Computer Sciences Corporation
2100 E. Grand Ave., El Segundo, CA 90245
Phone: 310-615-0311 **Fax:** 310-322-9768
Web: www.csc.com

Computer Sciences has offices worldwide, plus major
operations in Australia, Denmark, France, Germany,
Hong Kong, and the UK, and throughout the US.

2002 Sales

	$ mil.	% of total
US	7,211	63
Europe		
UK	1,361	26
Other countries	1,585	
Other regions	1,269	11
Total	**11,426**	**100**

PRODUCTS/OPERATIONS

2002 Sales

	$ mil.	% of total
Commercial	8,551	75
US federal	2,875	25
Total	**11,426**	**100**

Selected Services
Management consulting
  Business process reengineering
  Change management
  E-business strategy and implementation
  Information technology strategy
Outsourcing
  Applications development
  Claims processing
  Credit checking
  Customer call centers
  Data center management
  Desktop computing
  Network operations
  Systems analysis
  Web hosting
Systems integration
  Design
  Development
  Implementation
  Integration

COMPETITORS

Accenture	Hewlett-Packard
Affiliated Computer	IBM
American Management	Keane
Atos Origin	Perot Systems
Cap Gemini	PwC Consulting
Deloitte Consulting	SAIC
DynCorp	Siemens
EDS	Titan
GEX	Unisys
Getronics	

HISTORICAL FINANCIALS & EMPLOYEES

NYSE: CSC FYE: Friday nearest March 31	Annual Growth	3/93	3/94	3/95	3/96	3/97	3/98	3/99	3/00	3/01	3/02
Sales ($ mil.)	18.5%	2,480	2,583	3,373	4,242	5,616	6,601	7,660	9,371	10,524	11,426
Net income ($ mil.)	17.9%	78	96	111	142	192	260	341	403	233	344
Income as % of sales	—	3.1%	3.7%	3.3%	3.3%	3.4%	3.9%	4.5%	4.3%	2.2%	3.0%
Earnings per share ($)	11.1%	0.78	0.53	1.00	0.71	1.23	1.64	2.11	2.37	1.37	2.01
Stock price - FY high ($)	—	13.40	20.88	26.31	40.38	43.25	56.75	74.88	94.94	99.88	53.47
Stock price - FY low ($)	—	9.49	11.66	17.63	23.25	30.81	28.94	46.25	52.38	29.50	29.50
Stock price - FY close ($)	16.1%	13.22	18.25	24.69	35.19	31.06	55.00	55.19	79.13	32.35	50.75
P/E - high	—	17	42	26	55	34	34	35	39	72	26
P/E - low	—	12	23	17	31	24	17	21	22	21	14
Dividends per share ($)	—	0.00	0.00	0.00	0.00	0.00	0.00	0.00	0.00	0.00	0.00
Book value per share ($)	13.1%	6.97	7.76	10.41	11.65	10.90	12.75	15.08	18.17	19.06	21.17
Employees	11.1%	26,000	29,000	32,900	33,850	42,200	45,000	50,000	58,000	68,000	67,000

STOCK PRICE HISTORY

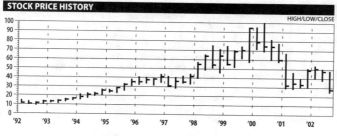

HIGH/LOW/CLOSE

2002 FISCAL YEAR-END

Debt ratio: 34.1%
Return on equity: 10.1%
Cash ($ mil.): 149
Current ratio: 1.22
Long-term debt ($ mil.): 1,873
No. of shares (mil.): 171
Dividends
  Yield: —
  Payout: —
Market value ($ mil.): 8,685

COMPUWARE CORPORATION

Compuware has developed into quite a testy, analytic business. The Farmington Hills, Michigan-based company, a longtime provider of mainframe testing, debugging, and development software, has expanded its operations to include similar software for corporate networks. Its products include debugging, implementation, and support tools for programmers; fault analysis software; and file, data, and systems management tools. Compuware also offers services such as maintenance, implementation, integration, and consulting, which account for more than two-thirds of sales.

Compuware continues to expand its product lines into applications for distributed computing and Web-based systems, including software and services for application development, integration, and performance management.

HISTORY

Peter Karmanos (CEO), Thomas Thewes, and Allen Cutting pooled their tax refunds — a total of $9,000 — in 1973 and founded Compuware in a converted Southfield, Michigan, motel. Starting with a vague sense of purpose ("We will help people do things with computers," read their mission statement), the firm soon was specializing in computer installation, programmer subcontracting, data processing, and mainframe computer troubleshooting.

Compuware entered the software market in 1977 with a fault diagnosis and recommendation tool, Abend-AID, which automated the laborious manual testing and debugging process. The product was named for the programming term "abnormal end," used to designate unexpected computer glitches.

Product expansion kept Compuware busy during the early and mid-1980s. In 1980 it launched tools that helped programmers identify and correct software bugs by evaluating code and logic quality, and in 1983 it introduced file and data management products. In 1985 the company moved into software that let technicians execute transactions and check data.

By the late 1980s Compuware was growing rapidly, with software accounting for 65% of sales. It made inroads in Europe by acquiring a number of its software distributors and reorganizing them as wholly owned subsidiaries. Karmanos, the son of Greek immigrants and chairman since 1978, became CEO in 1987, the year Compuware relocated to larger headquarters in Farmington Hills, Michigan. Cutting died in 1990.

In 1991 it merged with Centura Software, in efforts to strengthen its analysis and debugging line. Sales for the year topped $140 million. Compuware went public in 1992.

As corporations began moving away from the use of established mainframe computers and toward networks of connected desktop PCs in the early 1990s, Compuware responded with acquisitions, building a product base for networked environments, although it kept up sales of diagnostic software and other tools for its established mainframe customer base.

In 1997 Compuware redoubled efforts to strengthen its support to network customers with the purchases of two professional services firms, and it acquired a leading maker of debugging software. In 1998 the company added Underware, a developer of software defect tracking tools, and Vireo Software, a provider of Microsoft Windows device driver software tools.

Compuware in 1999 launched its Rapid Response Survival Kit, a system to correct the year 2000 bug, and continued its acquisitions with the purchase of IT service provider Data Processing Resources, and of Reliant Data Systems, a developer of software for moving data from one computer system to another. It also won a 10-year, $1 billion contract from Detroit Medical Center to manage and maintain the hospital's data center operations, applications, and voice information systems.

In 2000 the company's planned purchase of Viasoft (later acquired by Allen Systems Group) was called off in the wake of Department of Justice antitrust rumblings. The following year the company acquired software providers BlairLake and Nomex.

OFFICERS

Chairman and CEO: Peter Karmanos Jr., age 59, $1,650,000 pay
Vice Chairman: Thomas Thewes, age 69
President and Director: Joseph A. Nathan, age 49, $1,350,000 pay
COO: Tommi A. White, age 51, $750,000 pay
EVP, Human Resources and Administration: Denise A. Knobblock, age 45, $330,000 pay
EVP, Products: Henry A. Jallos, age 53, $1,000,000 pay
SVP and CIO: Christian J. Bockhausen
SVP, CFO, and Treasurer: Laura L. Fournier, age 49
SVP, Professional Services Division: W. Alan Cantrell, age 45, $600,000 pay
SVP, Technology: Kevin Cowsill
VP and CTO: Leslie L. Murphy
VP, General Counsel, and Secretary: Thomas Costello Jr.
VP, Corporate Marketing: Donna Debrodt
Director, Corporate Communications and Investor Relations: Lisa Elkin
Director, Corporate Development: Scott Johnson
Director, Corporate Planning: John Ermanni
Managing Director, Compuware UK: Steve Jobson
Auditors: Deloitte & Touche LLP

HQ: 31440 Northwestern Hwy.,
    Farmington Hills, MI 48334
Phone: 248-737-7300   Fax: 248-737-7108
Web: www.compuware.com

Compuware has offices in more than 45 countries.

2002 Sales

	$ mil.	% of total
US	1,317	76
Europe	308	18
Other regions	104	6
Total	**1,729**	**100**

PRODUCTS/OPERATIONS

2002 Sales

	$ mil.	% of total
Professional services	877	51
Maintenance	434	25
Software licenses	418	24
Total	**1,729**	**100**

Selected Software
Automated testing (QA family)
Error detection and debugging for Windows (NuMega)
Fault management (Abend-AID)
File and data management (File-AID)
Interactive analysis and debugging (XPEDITER)
Network-based application development (UNIFACE)
Network-based systems management (EcoSYSTEMS
    family)
Remote Web site testing (PointForward)

Selected Services
Business systems analysis, design, and programming
Maintenance
Implementation
Integration
Software conversion
Systems consulting
Systems planning
Web site design, integration, and testing

COMPETITORS

BMC Software
Computer Associates
Computer Sciences
EDS
IBM
Keane
Mercury Interactive
Micromuse
Network Associates
Oracle
Rational Software
Sun Microsystems
Sybase

HISTORICAL FINANCIALS & EMPLOYEES

Nasdaq: CPWR FYE: March 31	Annual Growth	3/93	3/94	3/95	3/96	3/97	3/98	3/99	3/00	3/01	3/02
Sales ($ mil.)	24.8%	235	330	534	614	813	1,139	1,638	2,231	2,010	1,729
Net income ($ mil.)	—	35	59	62	44	97	194	350	352	119	(245)
Income as % of sales	—	15.0%	17.9%	11.6%	7.2%	12.0%	17.0%	21.4%	15.8%	5.9%	—
Earnings per share ($)	—	0.13	0.17	0.17	0.13	0.27	0.50	0.87	0.91	0.32	(0.66)
Stock price - FY high ($)	—	4.28	5.91	6.16	4.63	8.66	25.63	39.91	40.00	22.00	14.50
Stock price - FY low ($)	—	3.00	2.41	3.91	1.94	2.84	7.75	17.94	16.38	5.59	7.46
Stock price - FY close ($)	14.8%	3.72	5.27	4.63	2.88	7.84	24.69	23.88	21.06	9.75	12.91
P/E - high	—	33	33	34	36	30	47	42	41	69	—
P/E - low	—	23	13	22	15	10	14	19	17	17	—
Dividends per share ($)	—	0.00	0.00	0.00	0.00	0.00	0.00	0.00	0.00	0.00	0.00
Book value per share ($)	20.3%	0.60	0.80	0.92	0.94	1.30	1.97	2.93	3.33	3.72	3.17
Employees	21.1%	1,808	2,774	4,105	4,844	6,609	8,663	10,908	15,356	13,220	10,164

STOCK PRICE HISTORY

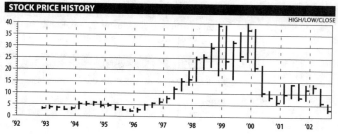

HIGH/LOW/CLOSE

2002 FISCAL YEAR-END
Debt ratio: 0.0%
Return on equity: —
Cash ($ mil.): 233
Current ratio: 1.91
Long-term debt ($ mil.): 0
No. of shares (mil.): 376
Dividends
  Yield: —
  Payout: —
Market value ($ mil.): 4,852

CONAGRA FOODS, INC.

ConAgra Foods dishes it up for those at home or on the road. The Omaha, Nebraska-based firm is the #2 US food company, trailing Kraft Foods. ConAgra Foods' high-profile brands — 33 each rake in more than $100 million a year — are sold through grocery stores and to restaurants and institutions. It also sells agricultural products and services.

As the nation's #2 meat and poultry seller (behind Tyson's IBP Fresh Meats), the company produces beef and pork products, cold cuts, and poultry under such brands as Armour, Butterball, and Eckrich. ConAgra Foods' packaged food segment makes shelf-stable and frozen foods (it's #2 in US frozen foods, after Nestlé USA) under names that include Banquet, Hunt's, Marie Callender's, Orville Redenbacher's, Peter Pan, and Wesson. The company also produces seafood and dairy products such as cheese, dessert toppings, and margarine. The company's agriculture segment is a leading US flour and dry corn miller and also trades and distributes crop protection chemicals, fertilizers, food ingredients, grain-based products, and seeds around the world.

The company has shifted away from its beginnings as a commodity producer and has tried to recast itself as "America's favorite food company." Brisk restructuring and shedding of nonfood related businesses have allowed the company to better pay attention to newly acquired brands, including Chef Boyardee, Louis Kemp, Bumble Bee, and PAM, among others.

HISTORY

Alva Kinney founded Nebraska Consolidated Mills in 1919 by combining the operations of four Nebraska grain mills. It did not expand outside Nebraska until it opened a mill and feed processing plant in Alabama in 1942.

Consolidated Mills developed Duncan Hines cake mix in the 1950s. But Duncan Hines failed to raise a large enough market share, and the company sold it to Procter & Gamble in 1956. Consolidated Mills used the proceeds to expand, opening a flour and feed mill in Puerto Rico the next year. In the 1960s, while competitors were moving into prepared foods, the firm expanded into animal feeds and poultry processing. By 1970 it had poultry processing plants in Alabama, Georgia, and Louisiana. In 1971 the company changed its name to ConAgra (Latin for "in partnership with the land"). During the 1970s it expanded into the fertilizer, catfish, and pet accessory businesses.

Poorly performing subsidiaries and commodity speculation caused ConAgra severe financial problems until 1974, when Mike Harper, a former Pillsbury executive, took over. Harper trimmed properties to reduce debt and had the company back on its feet by 1976. ConAgra stayed focused on the commodities side of the business, but was thus tied to volatile price cycles. In 1978 it bought United Agri Products (agricultural chemicals).

ConAgra moved into consumer food products in the 1980s. It bought Banquet (frozen food, 1980) and within six years had introduced almost 90 new products under that label. Other purchases included Singleton Seafood (1981), Armour Food Company (meats, dairy products, frozen food; 1983), and RJR Nabisco's frozen food business (1986). ConAgra became a major player in the red meat market with the 1987 purchases of E.A. Miller (boxed beef), Monfort (beef and lamb), and Swift Independent Packing.

Confident it had found the right path, ConAgra continued with acquisitions of consumer food makers, including Beatrice Foods (Orville Redenbacher's popcorn, Hunt's tomato products) in 1991. The company agreed to pay $8.3 million in 1997 to settle federal charges of wire fraud and watering down grain. That year ConAgra named VC and president Bruce Rohde as CEO; he became chairman in 1998. Also in 1998 the company bought GoodMark Foods, maker of Slim Jim, and Nabisco's Egg Beaters and tablespreads units (Parkay). ConAgra bought Holly Ridge Foods (pastries) in 1999 and announced a major restructuring.

ConAgra bought Emerge, an agricultural and land-use information software provider, from Litton Industries in 2000. It also acquired Seaboard's poultry division and refrigerated meat alternatives maker Lightlife (Tofu pups, Smart Dogs), before buying major brand holder International Home Foods from Hicks, Muse, Tate & Furst for about $2.9 billion. The company then became ConAgra Foods.

During 2001 the company drew SEC attention and was forced to restate earnings for the previous three years due to accounting no-no's in its United Agri Products division.

In 2002 the USDA forced ConAgra to recall 19 million pounds of ground beef because of possible *E. coli* contamination, making it the second-largest food recall in US history. (The largest recall occurred in 1997 when Hudson Foods, later purchased by Tyson Foods, withdrew 35 million pounds of beef).

OFFICERS

Chairman, President, and CEO: Bruce C. Rohde, age 53, $3,919,267 pay
EVP, CFO, and Corporate Secretary:
James P. O'Donnell, age 54, $1,025,100 pay

EVP, Operations Control and Development:
Dwight J. Goslee, age 51, $1,275,898 pay
EVP, Human Resources and Administration:
Owen C. Johnson, age 55, $1,012,078 pay
SVP and CIO: Kenneth W. Gerhardt, age 51,
$820,080 pay
SVP and Controller: Jay D. Bolding, age 41
SVP, Commodity Procurement and Economic Strategy:
Michael D. Walter, age 52
SVP, Communication and Corporate Marketing:
Timothy P. McMahon, age 47
SVP, Operational Effectiveness: Kevin W. Tourangeau,
age 49
SVP, Supply Chain Management: Stephen J. Tibey,
age 53
VP, Communications: Chris Kircher
Auditors: Deloitte & Touche LLP

LOCATIONS

HQ: 1 ConAgra Dr., Omaha, NE 68102
Phone: 402-595-4000   **Fax:** 402-595-4707
Web: www.conagra.com

·ConAgra Foods' refrigerated goods operations are in
Australia, Panama, Puerto Rico, and the US; its packaged
goods unit has operations in Canada, the Netherlands,
Turkey, the UK, and the US; its agricultural unit has
operations in Argentina, Bolivia, Brazil, Canada, Chile,
China, Ecuador, France, Hong Kong, Italy, Mexico,
Panama, Portugal, Peru, Singapore, South Africa, Spain,
Switzerland, Taiwan, the UK, the US, and Zimbabwe.

PRODUCTS/OPERATIONS

2002 Sales

	$ mil.	% of total
Packaged foods	12,364	45
Meat processing	10,024	36
Agricultural products	3,573	13
Food ingredients	1,669	6
Total	**27,630**	**100**

Selected Brands

Armour	Orville Redenbacher's
Butterball	PAM
Chef Boyardee	Parkay
Chun King	Peter Pan
Healthy Choice	Swift Premium
Hebrew National	Swiss Miss
La Choy	Van Camp's
Manwich	Wesson

COMPETITORS

Agway	Frito-Lay	Mars
ADM	Gardenburger	McCain Foods
Aurora Foods	General Mills	Nestlé
Bunge Limited	Gold Kist	Perdue
Bush Brothers	Hershey	Pharmacia
Campbell Soup	Heinz	Pilgrim's Pride
Cargill	Hormel	Quaker Foods
Carl Buddig	IBP	Sara Lee
Cenex Harvest	J. M. Smucker	Sara Lee Foods
States	JR Simplot	Schwan's
ContiGroup	King Arthur	Smithfield Foods
Dean Foods	Flour	Thai Union
DuPont	Kraft Foods	Tyson Foods
Farmland	Land O'Lakes	
Industries	Luigino's	

HISTORICAL FINANCIALS & EMPLOYEES

NYSE: CAG FYE: Last Sunday in May	Annual Growth	5/93	5/94	5/95	5/96	5/97	5/98	5/99	5/00	5/01	5/02
Sales ($ mil.)	2.8%	21,519	23,512	24,109	24,822	24,002	23,841	24,594	25,535	27,194	27,630
Net income ($ mil.)	12.5%	270	437	496	189	615	613	358	382	639	783
Income as % of sales	—	1.3%	1.9%	2.1%	0.8%	2.6%	2.6%	1.5%	1.5%	2.3%	2.8%
Earnings per share ($)	12.0%	0.53	0.91	1.04	0.40	1.36	1.33	0.75	0.80	1.24	1.47
Stock price - FY high ($)	—	17.13	14.69	17.25	23.56	30.75	38.75	34.38	28.13	26.19	25.71
Stock price - FY low ($)	—	11.38	11.50	14.13	16.31	20.75	27.00	22.56	15.06	17.50	18.80
Stock price - FY close ($)	7.8%	12.56	14.38	16.69	21.31	30.19	29.25	26.06	23.06	20.85	24.61
P/E - high	—	21	16	17	59	23	28	45	35	20	17
P/E - low	—	14	13	14	41	15	19	30	19	13	13
Dividends per share ($)	13.7%	0.29	0.34	0.39	0.45	0.51	0.59	0.67	0.76	0.86	0.92
Book value per share ($)	5.9%	4.79	5.40	5.80	4.64	5.19	5.79	5.96	5.87	7.42	8.02
Employees	0.8%	83,000	87,000	90,871	80,000	80,000	82,169	80,000	85,000	89,000	89,000

STOCK PRICE HISTORY

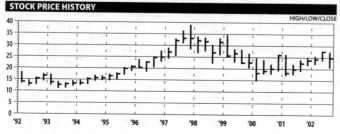

HIGH/LOW/CLOSE

2002 FISCAL YEAR-END

Debt ratio: 57.1%
Return on equity: 18.9%
Cash ($ mil.): 158
Current ratio: 1.49
Long-term debt ($ mil.): 5,744
No. of shares (mil.): 537
Dividends
  Yield: 3.7%
  Payout: 62.6%
Market value ($ mil.): 13,217

CONOCOPHILLIPS

Conoco and Phillips Petroleum brought their operations together in 2002 to form Conoco-Phillips, the #3 oil and gas company in the US, behind Exxon Mobil and ChevronTexaco. The company has net proved reserves of 8.7 billion barrels of oil equivalent and a refining capacity of 2.6 million barrels per day. It sells fuel at more than 17,000 outlets in the US under the 76, Circle K, Conoco, and Phillips 66 brands.

Conoco, formerly a unit of chemical giant DuPont, explored for oil and gas in 20 countries and had proved reserves of about 3.6 billion barrels of oil equivalent in Europe, Southeast Asia, and the Americas. It gained reserves of more than 1 billion barrels of oil equivalent in 2001 by buying Gulf Canada Resources. Conoco also operated about 6,000 miles of US pipeline. It owned or had stakes in nine refineries, and ran a network of gas stations in the US, Europe, and Asia.

Easily recognized by the highway-sign shape of its Phillips 66 logo, Phillips Petroleum had major exploration and production operations in Alaska, and had proved reserves of 5.1 billion barrels of oil equivalent. In 2001 Phillips expanded its refining and marketing business by buying Tosco. Phillips sold fuel under the Phillips 66, Circle K, and 76 brand names.

To gain regulators' blessing for the merger, ConocoPhillips agreed to sell refineries and marketing networks in Colorado and Utah.

HISTORY

The roots of ConocoPhillips go back more than a century and run deep into the history of the US oil industry.

Isaac Elder Blake, an Easterner who had lost everything on a bad investment, came to Ogden, Utah, and founded Continental Oil & Transportation (CO&T) in 1875. In 1885 CO&T merged with Standard Oil's operations in the Rockies and was reincorporated in Colorado as Continental Oil. Continental tightened its grip on the Rocky Mountain area and by 1906 had taken over 98% of the western market. Its monopoly ended in 1911 when the US Supreme Court ordered Standard to divest several holdings: Continental was one of 34 independent oil companies created in 1913.

Seeing opportunity in autos, Continental built a gas station in 1914. Two years later it got into oil production when it bought United Oil, and by 1924 it had become fully integrated by merging with Mutual Oil, which owned production, refining, and distribution assets. Continental's biggest merger came in 1929 when it merged with Marland Oil of Oklahoma.

Continental diversified in the 1960s, acquiring American Agricultural Chemicals in 1963 and Consolidation Coal (Consol) in 1966. Restructuring in the 1970s into Conoco Chemical, Consol, and two petroleum divisions, the company ramped up oil exploration and entered into ventures to develop uranium. In 1979 it changed its name to Conoco.

In the late 1970s, Conoco began joint ventures with chemical titan DuPont. The companies worked together well, and in 1981 Conoco was acquired by DuPont to forestall hostile takeover attempts by Mobil and Seagram. DuPont sold off $1.5 billion of Conoco's assets and absorbed Conoco Chemical. In 1998, however, DuPont spun off Conoco in what was the US's largest-ever IPO at the time (DuPont had completely divested its 70% stake by the next year).

Conoco expanded its natural gas reserves in 2001 by buying Gulf Canada Resources for $4.3 billion in cash and $2 billion in assumed debt. Also that year Conoco agreed to merge with Phillips Petroleum.

The story of Phillips Petroleum begins with Frank Phillips, a prosperous Iowa barber who married a banker's daughter in 1897 and began selling bonds. When a missionary who worked with Native Americans in Oklahoma regaled him with stories about the oil patch, Phillips migrated to Bartlesville, Oklahoma, and established Anchor Oil in 1903.

Anchor's first two wells were dry, but the next one — the Anna Anderson No. 1 — turned into the first of a string of 81 successful wells. Phillips and his brother L.E., doubling as bankers in Bartlesville, transformed Anchor into Phillips Petroleum in 1917.

With continued success on Native American lands in Oklahoma, Phillips moved into refining and marketing. In 1927 the company opened its first gas station in Wichita, Kansas. Frank Phillips retired after WWII and died in 1950.

During the 1980s Phillips became a target of takeover attempts. To fend off bids from corporate raiders T. Boone Pickens (1984) and Carl Icahn (1985), Phillips repurchased stock and ran its debt up to $9 billion. It then cut 8,300 jobs and sold billions of dollars' worth of assets; strong petrochemicals earnings kept it afloat.

As part of an industry trend to share costs of less-profitable operations, Phillips and Conoco flirted with the idea of merging their marketing and refining operations in 1996, but the talks failed. Discussions between Phillips and Ultramar Diamond Shamrock about merging the companies' North American oil refining and marketing operations broke down in 1999.

James Mulva took over as CEO that year, and Phillips decided to shift its focus to its upstream operations. The company combined its natural gas gathering and processing operations with those of Duke Energy in 2000 and received a minority stake in a new company, Duke Energy Field Services. Also that year Phillips acquired ARCO's Alaska assets for $7 billion and merged its chemicals division with that of Chevron (later ChevronTexaco).

In 2001, however, Phillips elected to expand its refining and marketing operations rather than spin them off, and the company bought Tosco for about $7.3 billion in stock and $2 billion in assumed debt. Big as it was, the Tosco deal was eclipsed the next year by the merger of Phillips and Conoco.

VP Upstream Business Development:
Sigmund L. Cornelius
VP Exploration: Dodd W. DeCamp, age 46
VP Upstream Technology: James R. Knudson
President, Alaska: Kevin O. Meyers, age 48
President, Asia Pacific: William B. Berry, age 49
President, Canada: Henry W. Sykes
President, Europe, Russia, and Caspian:
Steven M. Theede

LOCATIONS

HQ: 600 N. Dairy Ashford, Houston, TX 77079
Phone: 281-293-1000   **Fax:** 281-293-1440
Web: www.conocophillips.com

ConocoPhillips has operations in 49 countries.

OFFICERS

Chairman: Archie W. Dunham, age 63
President and CEO: James J. Mulva, age 55
EVP Finance and CFO: John A. Carrig, age 50
EVP Commercial: Philip L. Frederickson, age 45
EVP Exploration and Production: Robert E. McKee III, age 55
EVP Planning and Strategic Transactions:
John E. Lowe, age 43
EVP Refining, Marketing, Supply, and Transportation:
Jim W. Nokes, age 55
EVP: J. Bryan Whitworth, age 64
SVP Services and CIO: Eugene L. Batchelder, age 55
SVP Government Affairs and Communications:
Thomas C. Knudson, age 55
SVP Legal and General Counsel: Rick A. Harrington, age 57
VP Human Resources: Joseph C. High

PRODUCTS/OPERATIONS

2001 Sales (Conoco)

	% of total
Refined products	57
Natural gas	21
Crude oil	15
Other operations	7
Total	**100**

COMPETITORS

Amerada Hess	Occidental Petroleum
BP	Shell Oil Products
ChevronTexaco	Sunoco
Exxon Mobil	TOTAL FINA ELF
Marathon Oil	Valero Energy

HISTORICAL FINANCIALS & EMPLOYEES

NYSE: COP FYE: December 31	Annual Growth	12/92	12/93	12/94	12/95	12/96	12/97	12/98	12/99	12/00	12/01
Sales ($ mil.)	5.1%	12,140	12,545	12,211	13,368	15,731	15,210	11,545	13,571	20,835	24,050
Net income ($ mil.)	24.6%	180	243	484	469	1,303	959	237	609	1,862	1,661
Income as % of sales	—	1.5%	1.9%	4.0%	3.5%	8.3%	6.3%	2.1%	4.5%	8.9%	6.9%
Earnings per share ($)	24.8%	0.69	0.92	1.84	1.78	4.91	3.61	0.91	2.39	7.26	5.63
Stock price - FY high ($)	—	28.88	37.38	37.25	37.13	45.88	52.25	53.25	57.25	70.00	68.00
Stock price - FY low ($)	—	22.00	24.50	25.50	29.88	31.13	37.38	40.19	37.69	35.94	50.00
Stock price - FY close ($)	10.1%	25.13	29.00	32.75	34.13	44.25	48.63	42.63	47.00	56.88	60.26
P/E - high	—	28	40	20	21	9	14	58	24	10	12
P/E - low	—	21	26	14	17	6	10	44	16	5	9
Dividends per share ($)	2.2%	1.12	1.12	1.12	1.20	1.25	1.34	1.36	1.36	1.36	1.40
Book value per share ($)	9.4%	10.37	10.22	11.29	12.16	16.14	18.29	16.74	17.94	23.86	37.52
Employees	(6.5%)	21,400	19,400	18,400	17,400	17,200	17,100	17,300	15,900	12,400	38,700

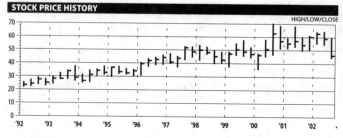

STOCK PRICE HISTORY
HIGH/LOW/CLOSE

2001 FISCAL YEAR-END
Debt ratio: 37.6%
Return on equity: 16.1%
Cash ($ mil.): 142
Current ratio: 0.96
Long-term debt ($ mil.): 8,645
No. of shares (mil.): 382
Dividends
  Yield: 2.3%
  Payout: 25.1%
Market value ($ mil.): 23,029

CONSECO, INC.

Conseco wrote the book on insurance industry consolidation but should have consulted the owner's manual before buying its mobile home loan subsidiary Conseco Finance (formerly Green Tree Financial). The touted cross-selling synergies between the mobile home buyers and Conseco's products didn't materialize, dragging the parent company down.

The Carmel, Indiana-based business pioneered the practice of buying inefficient insurance companies at bargain-basement prices (it gobbled up about 40 firms in a decade and a half). But as copycats adopted the strategy, Conseco continued to buy — at premium prices — piling on the debt. When Conseco Finance fell on hard times, the parent company's house of cards collapsed. GE Capital wizard Gary Wendt was called in to fix the mess — for a hefty upfront signing bonus.

Conseco's insurance companies sell supplemental health, life, annuities; and other insurance products, primarily to lower-middle-income prospects. It also has a family of mutual funds under the aegis of subsidiary Conseco Capital Management. In a continuing effort to cut costs, Conseco has sold or closed five units (including asset-based lending, vendor leasing, and bankcards; the company is also selling its variable annuities unit) of its Conseco Finance subsidiary and combined the company's life insurance, supplemental health insurance, and annuities divisions. Conseco is also getting out of the major medical insurance business.

Due to its financial woes, the NYSE suspended trading in Conseco in August 2002.

HISTORY

Conseco evolved from Security National, an Indiana insurance company formed in 1979 by Stephen Hilbert. The former encyclopedia salesman and Aetna executive believed most insurance companies were bloated and the industry itself overcrowded, as well as ripe for consolidation by a smart, lean organization.

In 1982 the company began its growth-by-acquisition strategy with the purchase of Executive Income Life Insurance (renamed Security National Life Insurance). The next year it bought Consolidated National Life Insurance and renamed the expanded company Conseco.

The firm went public in 1985, using the proceeds to fund an acquisitions spree that included Lincoln American Life Insurance, Lincoln Income Life (sold 1990), Bankers National Life Insurance, Western National Life Insurance (sold 1994), and National Fidelity Life Insurance.

In 1990 the company formed Conseco Capital Partners (with General Electric and Bankers Trust) to finance acquisitions without seeming to burden the parent company with debt. This device financed the purchase of Great American Reserve and the 1991 acquisition of Beneficial Standard Life. Conseco bought Bankers Life Insurance in 1992, then sold 67% of it the next year. Also in 1993 the company formed the Private Capital Group to invest in noninsurance companies.

In 1994 the company tried to acquire the much larger Kemper Corp., but shied away from the debt load that the $2.6 billion deal would have entailed. The aborted deal cost $36 million in bank and accounting fees and spelled the end of the company's relationship with Merrill Lynch, which had underwritten Conseco's IPO, when a Merrill Lynch analyst downgraded Conseco's stock after the fiasco.

Meanwhile, Private Capital's success led Conseco to form Conseco Global Investments. Other investments included stakes in racetrack and riverboat gambling operations in Indiana.

In 1996 and 1997 Conseco absorbed eight life, health, property/casualty, and specialty insurance companies and raised its interest in American Life Holdings to 100%.

Itching to move beyond insurance, in 1998 Conseco bought Green Tree Financial, the US's #1 mobile home financier. Charges of Green Tree's own fuzzy accounting practices helped torpedo Conseco's quest for a federal thrift charter. But the troubles had just begun. The mobile home finance industry took a dive as customers refinanced at lower rates and prepayments slammed Green Tree Financial, reducing Conseco's earnings.

Conseco tried to recoup in 1999 by launching an ad campaign portraying the company as the "Wal-Mart of financial services." It also continued the acquisition spree. But Green Tree Financial (renamed Conseco Finance that year) couldn't stanch the red ink: buyers grew wary of the quality of the finance unit's loan securities and changes in accounting methods cost the parent company a $350 million charge against earnings for 1999.

Conseco in 2000 announced it would unload Conseco Finance, but lowball offers were rebuffed by the company. Nonetheless, amid continuing stockholder and creditor dissatisfaction, chairman and CEO Hilbert and CFO Rollin Dick resigned. Other directors soon followed. Gary Wendt took over as chairman and CEO, and reversed the decision to sell Conseco Finance, launching a corporate restructuring aimed primarily at reducing that unit's operations.

OFFICERS

Chairman and CEO: Gary C. Wendt, age 60
President, COO, and acting CFO: William J. Shea, age 54
EVP, General Counsel, and Secretary: David K. Herzog, age 46, $1,200,000 pay
EVP, Strategic Business Development: David Gubbay, age 49
EVP, External Relations: R. Mark Lubbers
EVP, Operations, Product and Financial Management: Ronald F. Ruhl
EVP and Chief Human Resources Officer: Richard H. Kremer
SVP Investments; President and CEO, Conseco Capital Management: Maxwell E. Bublitz, age 46, $1,075,000 pay
SVP; President, Bankers Life & Casualty: Edward M. Berube, age 52, $1,353,000 pay
SVP, Chief Accounting Officer, and Treasurer: James S. Adams, age 42, $1,000,000 pay
Auditors: PricewaterhouseCoopers LLP

LOCATIONS

HQ: 11825 N. Pennsylvania St., Carmel, IN 46032
Phone: 317-817-6100   **Fax:** 317-817-2847
Web: www.conseco.com

2001 Premiums

	% of total
California	9
Florida	8
Illinois	8
Texas	7
Other states	68
Total	**100**

PRODUCTS/OPERATIONS

2001 Assets

	$ mil.	% of total
Cash & equivalents	3,061	5
US Treasuries	252	—
Foreign securities	107	—
Mortgage-backed securities	7,497	12
State & municipal bonds	229	—
Corporate bonds	12,448	21
Stocks	227	—
Mortgage loans	1,228	2
Policy loans	636	1
Assets in separate account	2,376	4
Recoverables & receivables	18,673	30
Other	14,658	25
Total	**61,392**	**100**

COMPETITORS

Aetna
AFLAC
Allstate
American General
American National Insurance
AXA Financial
Bingham Financial
Fortis
GenAmerica
Guardian Life
Household International
Jefferson-Pilot
John Hancock Financial Services
Lincoln National

MassMutual
MetLife
Minnesota Mutual
Monmouth Capital
MONY
Mutual of Omaha
New York Life
Northwestern Mutual
Pacific Mutual
Phoenix Companies
Principal Financial
Protective Life
Provident Mutual
Prudential
Torchmark

HISTORICAL FINANCIALS & EMPLOYEES

OTC: CNCE FYE: December 31	Annual Growth	12/92	12/93	12/94	12/95	12/96	12/97	12/98	12/99	12/00	12/01
Assets ($ mil.)	20.1%	11,773	13,749	10,812	17,298	25,613	35,915	43,600	52,186	58,589	61,392
Net income ($ mil.)	—	170	297	158	220	252	567	467	595	(1,071)	(406)
Income as % of assets	—	1.4%	2.2%	1.5%	1.3%	1.0%	1.6%	1.1%	1.1%	—	—
Employees	19.6%	2,860	3,290	3,550	3,250	3,700	6,800	14,000	17,000	14,300	14,300

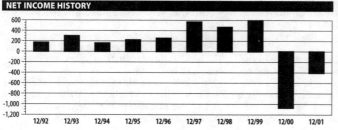

NET INCOME HISTORY

2001 FISCAL YEAR-END

Equity as % of assets: 7.7%
Return on assets: —
Return on equity: —
Long-term debt ($ mil.): 21,100
No. of shares (mil.): 345
Dividends
  Yield: —
  Payout: —
Market value ($ mil.): 1,538
Sales ($ mil.): 8,108

CONSOL ENERGY INC.

Consolation prizes don't interest CONSOL Energy, one of the US's three largest coal companies, along with Peabody and Arch Coal. The Pittsburgh-based company primarily mines bituminous coal, which burns cleaner than lower grades, at its 25 mining complexes located throughout the US and in western Canada.

The holding company's 61 subsidiaries and affiliates produce about 74 million tons of coal annually, which it sells primarily to electricity generators such as Allegheny Energy (14% of sales) and steel companies. CONSOL has around 4.4 billion tons of proven and probable coal reserves. Its Buchanan Production subsidiary and Pocahontas Gas Partnership joint venture (with Conoco) recover coalbed methane gas, an increasingly popular fuel for producing electricity.

A diversified mining company, CONSOL also processes and disposes customers' coal ash, selling the bottom ash for use in road construction. The company's Fairmont Supply subsidiary distributes mining and industrial supplies throughout the US. CONSOL also has extensive shipping operations in the US and Canada: The company delivers coal using its own railroad cars, export terminals, fleet of towboats, and some 300 barges.

While coal remains CONSOL's core business, it has diversified its energy holdings by acquiring additional natural gas reserves (most planned power plants will be gas-fired). The company plans to continue to grow through acquisitions in North America and the Pacific Rim. It is also entering new industries: CONSOL will build an electric generating plant under contract to Allegheny Energy Supply Co.

Germany-based conglomerate RWE owns 74% of CONSOL.

HISTORY

When Consolidation Coal was formed in Maryland in 1864, coal was just beginning to replace wood as the world's top industrial energy source. In the 1880s Consolidation Coal, like other large coal companies, began operations in the Appalachia region of the US. During the 1920s the company built the Kentucky mining city of Van Lear (country music superstar Loretta Lynn's father worked as a Consolidation Coal miner). In 1945 Consolidation Coal merged with Pittsburgh Coal, and the next year it took over Hanna Coal.

In 1966 Continental Oil, founded in 1875 and later renamed Conoco, bought Consolidation Coal. In 1968 78 workers were killed in a Consolidation Coal mine explosion. Also that year a federal jury found the United Mine Workers (UMW) and the company guilty of conspiring to put Kentucky's South East Coal out of business. In 1971 the UMW and Consolidation Coal paid South East almost $9 million in damages, court costs, and interest. Consolidation Coal became part of DuPont when that company bought Conoco in 1981.

Ten years later the mining unit of German conglomerate RWE (Rheinbraun) bought 50% of Consolidation Coal (later increased to 74%) from DuPont. That year Consolidation Coal and Conoco formed the Pocahontas Gas Partnership to recover coalbed methane gas.

A restructuring in 1992 created CONSOL Energy as a holding company for more than 60 subsidiaries, including principal operating subsidiary Consolidation Coal. The next year the UMW initiated a strike against CONSOL, which was using more and more nonunion workers in its mines. CONSOL opened its ash disposal facility the next year and began developing ways to reuse its plant waste and byproducts.

From 1994 to 1997 the firm reduced its workforce by 20% and closed six of its mining complexes. By 1997 about one-third of CONSOL's coal came from nonunion mines. In 1998 CONSOL filed to go public and bought Rochester & Pittsburgh Coal.

CONSOL completed its IPO in 1999. The depressed coal market halved CONSOL's sales that year and the company scaled back production at some of its smaller, high-cost mines in Pennsylvania and West Virginia. During the winter of 2000 and in early 2001, coal prices improved by 36% and natural gas prices skyrocketed as cold temperatures and an energy crisis in California increased demand for energy sources. Despite the improvement in coal prices, the company continued to shut down high-cost mines and restructured its coal operations.

In 2001 CONSOL acquired Conoco's half of the Pocahontas Gas joint venture. It also bought Windsor Coal, Southern Ohio Coal, and Central Ohio Coal from American Electric Power; the deal calls for American Electric Power to purchase 34 million tons of coal from CONSOL through 2008. CONSOL also agreed to buy 50% of the Glennies Creek Mine (in development), its first Australian property.

Also that year CONSOL contracted with Allegheny Energy Supply (an affiliate of largest customer Allegheny Energy) to build an 88-megawatt electric generating plant in Virginia. The facility will be fueled by coalbed methane gas produced by CONSOL.

In 2002 CONSOL said it would expand its McElroy mine to create the largest coal mine east of the Mississippi (CONSOL's Enlow Fork mine is currently the largest eastern mine).

Chairman: John L. Whitmire, age 61
President, CEO, and Director: J. Brett Harvey, age 51, $923,228 pay (partial-year salary)
EVP, Administration and Director: Christoph Koether, age 43, $114,930 pay (partial-year salary)
EVP, Operations: Dan R. Baker, age 52, $448,709 pay
EVP, Engineering Services, Environmental Affairs, and Exploration: Ronald E. Smith, age 53, $467,971 pay (partial-year salary)
SVP, CFO, and Treasurer: William J. Lyons, age 53
VP, General Counsel, and Secretary: Daniel L. Fassio, age 54
Auditors: PricewaterhouseCoopers LLP

HQ: Consol Plaza, 1800 Washington Rd., Pittsburgh, PA 15241
Phone: 412-831-4000 **Fax:** 412-831-4103
Web: www.consolenergy.com

CONSOL Energy has around 25 mining operations in Appalachia, the Illinois Basin, the Ohio Valley, the Western US, and Western Canada, and sales offices in Atlanta; Chicago; Norfolk, Virginia; Philadelphia; Pittsburgh; and Brussels, Belgium.

2001 Sales

	$ mil.	% of total
US	859	82
Europe	98	9
Canada	34	3
South America	36	3
Asia	15	2
Africa	8	1
Total	**1,050**	**100**

2001 Sales

	$ mil.	% of total
Coal	962	88
Gas	49	4
Other	84	8
Adjustments	(45)	—
Total	**1,050**	**100**

Selected Mining Operations

Appalachia	**Ohio Valley**
Amonate Complex	Humphrey Mine
Elk Creek Complex	Loveridge Mine
Enlow Fork Mine	Mahoning Valley Mine
Jones Fork Complex	Robinson Run Mine
Mill Creek Complex	Shoemaker Mine

Australia	**Western US/Canada**
Glennies Creek	Cardinal River Mine
	Emery Mine
Illinois Basin	Line Creek Mine
Ohio No. 11 Mine	
Rend Lake Mine	

Alliance Resource Partners	Penn Virginia
Arch Coal	RAG
Drummond	Rio Tinto
Horizon Natural Resources	Royal Dutch/Shell Group
Massey Energy	TECO Energy
Mitsui Mining Company	United States Steel
NACCO Industries	Walter Industries
Peabody Energy	Westmoreland Coal

NYSE: CNX FYE: December 31	Annual Growth	12/93	12/94	12/95	12/96	12/97	12/98	*6/99	6/00	6/01	*12/01
Sales ($ mil.)	(5.7%)	1,786	2,412	2,314	2,397	2,350	2,350	1,111	2,159	2,298	1,050
Net income ($ mil.)	—	(89)	135	130	153	184	175	40	107	184	1
Income as % of sales	—	—	5.6%	5.6%	6.4%	7.8%	7.4%	3.6%	5.0%	8.0%	0.1%
Earnings per share ($)	(74.7%)	—	—	—	—	—	—	0.62	1.35	2.33	0.01
Stock price - FY high ($)		—	—	—	—	—	—	16.00	17.13	42.48	42.48
Stock price - FY low ($)		—	—	—	—	—	—	10.88	9.63	15.00	18.30
Stock price - FY close ($)	27.4%	—	—	—	—	—	—	12.00	15.13	25.30	24.84
P/E - high		—	—	—	—	—	—	26	13	18	4,248
P/E - low		—	—	—	—	—	—	18	7	6	1,830
Dividends per share ($)		—	—	—	—	—	—	0.00	1.12	1.12	0.56
Book value per share ($)	2.8%	—	—	—	—	—	—	3.17	3.24	4.38	3.45
Employees	(3.2%)	10,036	9,739	8,743	8,206	7,711	8,578	7,658	6,426	7,230	7,523

* Fiscal year change

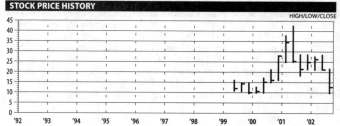

HIGH/LOW/CLOSE

Debt ratio: 63.5%
Return on equity: 0.4%
Cash ($ mil.): 16
Current ratio: 0.89
Long-term debt ($ mil.): 473
No. of shares (mil.): 79
Dividends
 Yield: 2.3%
 Payout: 5,600.0%
Market value ($ mil.): 1,955

CONSOLIDATED EDISON, INC.

Consolidated Edison makes the Big Apple shine. Based in New York City, utility holding company Con Edison supplies electricity through its largest subsidiary — Consolidated Edison Company of New York (better known as Con Ed) — to more than 3.1 million customers in its hometown (except part of Queens) and most of Westchester County. It also distributes gas to nearly 1.1 million customers in Manhattan, The Bronx, and parts of Queens and Westchester County, and it provides steam service in Manhattan. To prepare for deregulation, Con Edison has sold almost all of its New York power plants to focus on distribution and transmission.

The company serves another 280,000 electric customers and more than 120,000 gas customers in southeastern New York and adjacent areas of New Jersey and Pennsylvania through utility Orange and Rockland Utilities. Con Edison's non-utility operations include retail and wholesale energy marketing, energy management services, fiber-optic telecommunications, and merchant power plant development and acquisition.

In the race to competition, Con Edison has faced some tough hurdles, including its failed attempt to expand into New England by buying Northeast Utilities. However, Con Edison is sticking with its growth strategy. It is expanding its competitive operations and improving its regulated infrastructure assets.

HISTORY

Several professionals, led by Timothy Dewey, formed The New York Gas Light Company in 1823 to illuminate part of Manhattan. In 1884 five other gas companies joined New York Gas Light to form the Consolidated Gas Company of New York.

Thomas Edison's incandescent lamp came on the scene in 1879, and The Edison Electric Illuminating Company of New York was formed in 1880 to build the world's first commercial electric power station (Pearl Street), financed by a group led by J.P. Morgan. Edison supervised the project, and in 1882 New York became the first major city with electric lighting.

Realizing electricity would replace gas, Consolidated Gas acquired electric companies, including Anthony Brady's New York Gas and Electric Light, Heat and Power Company (1900), which joined Edison's Illuminating Company in 1901 to form the New York Edison Company. More than 170 purchases followed, including that of the New York Steam Company (1930), a cheap source of steam for electric turbines.

The Public Utility Holding Company Act of 1935 ushered in the era of regulated, regional monopolies. The next year New York Edison combined its holdings to form the Consolidated Edison Company of New York (Con Ed).

Con Ed opened its first nuclear station in 1962. By then Con Ed had a reputation for inefficiency and poor service, and shareholders were angry about its slow growth and low earnings. Environmentalists joined the grousers in 1963 when Con Ed began constructing a pumped-storage plant in Cornwall near the Hudson River. Charles Luce, a former undersecretary with the Department of Interior, was recruited to rescue Con Ed in 1967. He added power plants and beefed up customer service.

In the 1970s inflation and the energy crisis drove up oil prices (Con Ed's main fuel source), and in 1974 Luce withheld dividends for the first time since 1885. He persuaded the New York State Power Authority to buy two unfinished power plants, saving Con Ed $200 million. In 1980 Luce ended the Cornwall controversy and donated the land for park use. He retired in 1982.

The utility started buying power from various suppliers and in 1984 began a two-year price freeze, a boon to rate-hike-weary New Yorkers. The New York State Public Service Commission didn't approve another rate increase until 1992.

In 1997 Con Ed, government officials, consumer groups, and other energy firms outlined the company's deregulation plan, which included the creation of holding company Consolidated Edison, Inc. (known as Con Edison) and a power marketing unit in 1998. The next year Con Edison sold New York City generating facilities to KeySpan, Northern States Power, and Orion Power for a total of $1.65 billion.

Also in 1999 Con Edison bought Orange and Rockland Utilities for $790 million to increase its New York base and expand into New Jersey and Pennsylvania. In an effort to push into New England, the company that year agreed to buy Northeast Utilities (NU) for $3.3 billion in cash and stock and $3.9 billion in assumed debt. But the deal broke down in 2001. NU accused Con Edison of improperly trying to renegotiate terms, while Con Edison accused NU of concealing information about unfavorable power supply contracts.

Con Edison's Indian Point Unit 2 nuclear plant was shut down temporarily in 2000 after a radioactive steam leak; later that year it agreed to sell Indian Point Units 1 and 2 to Entergy for $502 million. The sale was completed in 2001. That year Con Edison also incurred an estimated $400 million in costs related to emergency response and asset damage from the September 11 terrorist attacks on New York City.

Chairman, President, and CEO; Chairman and CEO, Consolidated Edison of New York:
Eugene R. McGrath, age 60, $2,523,333 pay
EVP, CFO, and Director, Consolidated Edison and Consolidated Edison of New York: Joan S. Freilich, age 60, $700,000 pay
SVP and General Counsel, Consolidated Edison and Consolidated Edison of New York: John D. McMahon, age 50, $649,617 pay
VP, Controller, and Chief Accounting Officer:
Edward J. Rasmussen, age 53
President, Consolidated Edison Communications:
Peter A. Rust, age 48
President, Consolidated Edison Development and Consolidated Edison Energy: Charles Weliky, age 55
President, Consolidated Edison of New York:
Kevin Burke, age 51, $660,000 pay
President, Consolidated Edison Solutions: JoAnn Ryan, age 44
President, Orange and Rockland Utilities:
Stephen B. Bram, age 59, $581,067 pay
SVP Electric Operations, Consolidated Edison of New York: Robert W. Donohue Jr., age 59
Auditors: PricewaterhouseCoopers LLP

LOCATIONS

HQ: 4 Irving Place, New York, NY 10003
Phone: 212-460-4600   **Fax:** 212-982-7816
Web: www.conedison.com

Consolidated Edison provides energy in New York, Pennsylvania, and New Jersey, and has interests in independent power projects in Maryland, Massachusetts, New Hampshire, New Jersey, and the Netherlands.

PRODUCTS/OPERATIONS

2001 Sales

	$ mil.	% of total
Electricity	6,889	72
Gas	1,464	15
Steam	501	5
Other	780	8
Total	**9,634**	**100**

Subsidiaries
Consolidated Edison Communications, Inc. (telecommunications services)
Consolidated Edison Company of New York, Inc. (utility)
Consolidated Edison Development, Inc. (investments in power generation projects)
Consolidated Edison Energy, Inc. (wholesale energy marketing and trading)
Consolidated Edison Solutions, Inc. (retail energy marketing and services)
Orange and Rockland Utilities, Inc. (utility)

COMPETITORS

AEP	National Grid USA
CH Energy Group, Inc.	New York Power Authority
Conectiv	NUI
Duke Energy	PPL
Enbridge	PSEG
Energy East	RGS Energy
KeySpan Energy	South Jersey Industries
National Fuel Gas	

HISTORICAL FINANCIALS & EMPLOYEES

NYSE: ED FYE: December 31	Annual Growth	12/92	12/93	12/94	12/95	12/96	12/97	12/98	12/99	12/00	12/01
Sales ($ mil.)	5.5%	5,933	6,265	6,373	6,537	6,960	7,121	7,093	7,491	9,431	9,634
Net income ($ mil.)	1.6%	604	659	734	724	694	713	730	714	596	696
Income as % of sales	—	10.2%	10.5%	11.5%	11.1%	10.0%	10.0%	10.3%	9.5%	6.3%	7.2%
Earnings per share ($)	3.0%	2.46	2.66	2.98	2.93	2.93	2.95	3.04	3.13	2.83	3.21
Stock price – FY high ($)	—	32.88	37.75	32.38	32.25	34.75	41.50	56.13	53.44	39.50	43.37
Stock price – FY low ($)	—	25.00	30.25	23.00	25.50	25.88	27.00	39.06	33.56	26.19	31.44
Stock price – FY close ($)	2.4%	32.63	32.13	25.75	31.75	29.13	41.00	52.88	34.50	38.50	40.36
P/E – high	—	13	14	11	11	12	14	18	17	14	13
P/E – low	—	10	11	8	9	9	9	13	11	9	10
Dividends per share ($)	1.6%	1.90	1.94	2.00	2.04	2.08	2.10	2.12	2.14	2.18	2.20
Book value per share ($)	3.2%	23.63	24.40	25.36	26.23	25.75	26.53	27.26	26.48	26.99	31.31
Employees	(3.2%)	18,718	17,586	17,097	16,582	15,801	15,029	14,322	14,269	13,464	13,953

STOCK PRICE HISTORY

HIGH/LOW/CLOSE

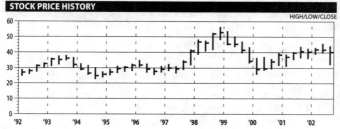

2001 FISCAL YEAR-END

Debt ratio: 48.4%
Return on equity: 12.5%
Cash ($ mil.): 341
Current ratio: 0.65
Long-term debt ($ mil.): 5,542
No. of shares (mil.): 189
Dividends
  Yield: 5.5%
  Payout: 68.5%
Market value ($ mil.): 7,625

CONSTELLATION BRANDS, INC.

Constellation Brands has welcomed some fancier labels to its table, but it still dances with the Wild Irish Rose who brought it to the party. The Fairport, New York-based beverage maker sells 200 or so brands of wine, beer, cider, distilled spirits, and bottled water in the UK and US.

The company, formerly Canandaigua Brands, is the second-largest wine producer in the world, after E. & J. Gallo Winery. Its wines range from the inexpensive Almaden and Inglenook brands up to the classier Franciscan Oakville Estate and Simi labels. Constellation continues to make high-margin, wino-friendly Richards Wild Irish Rose, which brought it early success. It also produces grape juice concentrate, used in making juice-based foods and beverages.

Through its Barton division, Constellation sells a number of imported beers, such as Corona and Tsingtao, as well as several Canadian whiskey labels, including Black Velvet. Its Matthew Clark unit is a leading producer and distributor of wine, cider, and bottled water in the UK.

Constellation has built up a diverse product range in recent years through acquisitions, which, coupled with internal growth, have more than doubled its sales. The founding Sands family controls about 62% of the company's voting power.

HISTORY

Marvin Sands, the son of wine maker Mordecai (Mack) Sands, exited the Navy in 1945 and entered distilling by purchasing an old sauerkraut factory in Canandaigua, New York. His business, Canandaigua Industries, struggled while making fruit wines in bulk for local bottlers in the East. Aiming at regional markets, the company began producing its own brands two years later. Marvin opened the Richards Wine Cellar in Petersburg, Virginia, in 1951 and put his father in charge of the unit. In 1954 Marvin developed his own brand of "fortified" wine — boosted by 190-proof brandy — and named it Richards Wild Irish Rose after his son Richard.

The company slowly expanded, buying a number of small wineries in the 1960s and 1970s. It went public in 1973, changing its name to Canandaigua Wine. A year later the company expanded to the West Coast, thus gaining access to the growing varietal market.

Canandaigua continued to grow though acquisitions and new product introductions in the early 1980s. In 1984, when wine coolers became popular, the company introduced Sun Country Coolers, doubling sales to $173 million by 1986. The short-lived wine cooler fad made Canandaigua realize that its distribution network could handle more volume, so it began looking for additional brands. The company picked up Kosher wine maker Manischewitz and East Coast wine maker Widmer's Wine Cellars, both in 1987. The company made a major purchase in 1991 when it bought Guild Wineries & Distillers (Cook's champagne) for $60 million.

Richard Sands became CEO in 1993. Subsequent acquisitions included Vintners International (Paul Masson and Taylor, 1993), Barton (beer importing, branded spirits; 1993), Heublein's Almaden and Inglenook (1994), and 12 distilled spirits brands from United Distillers Glenmore (1995). The acquisitions doubled Canandaigua's share of the spirits market, making it the #4 US spirits supplier. After the flurry of acquisitions, the company changed its name in 1997 to Canandaigua Brands.

In 1998 it bought Matthew Clark, a UK-based maker of cider, wine, and bottled water, for $359 million. Further stocking its cabinet, in 1999 Canandaigua bought several whiskey brands (including Black Velvet) and two Canadian production facilities from Diageo. Also in 1999 Canandaigua entered the premium wine business with the purchases of vintners Simi Winery and Franciscan Estates.

Founder Marvin died in August 1999. Richard, who had been CEO since 1993, succeeded his father as chairman. In September 2000 the firm changed its name to Constellation Brands.

In March 2001 Constellation Brands acquired Turner Road Vintners, a division of Sebastiani Vineyards, including the Vendange, Talus, Heritage, Nathanson Creek, La Terre, and Farallon brands of wine, as well as two wineries in California. Also that month it acquired the Covey Run, Columbia, Ste. Chapelle, and Alice White wine brands from wine company Corus Brands for about $52 million.

In June 2001 Constellation Brands teamed with Australian vintner BRL Hardy to form a joint venture, Pacific Wine Partners, that targets the mid-price wine market in the US. Ever the acquisitive company, in July Constellation Brands purchased Ravenswood Winery for about $148 million.

OFFICERS

Chairman, President, and CEO: Richard Sands, age 51, $1,449,690 pay
Group President and Director: Robert Sands, age 44, $1,285,930 pay
EVP and CFO: Thomas S. Summer, age 48, $720,720 pay
EVP and Chief Human Resources Officer: George H. Murray, age 55
EVP and General Counsel: Thomas J. Mullin, age 50

President and CEO, Barton: Alexander L. Berk, age 52, $1,037,400 pay
President and CEO, Canandaigua Wine: Jon Moramarco, age 45
President and CEO, Franciscan Vineyards: Agustin Francisco Huneeus, age 36
COO, Constellation International: Tim Kelly, age 44
COO, Matthew Clark: Richard Peters, age 42
Secretary: David S. Sorce
Auditors: KPMG LLP

LOCATIONS

HQ: 300 WillowBrook Office Park, Fairport, NY 14450
Phone: 585-218-2169   **Fax:** 585-218-2155
Web: www.cbrands.com

Canandaigua Brands operates some 29 facilities including wineries, a brewery, cider and water production facilities, distilling plants, a distribution center, and bottling plants in Canada, Chile, the UK, and the US.

PRODUCTS/OPERATIONS

Selected Products and Brands

Canandaigua Wine Company
Brandy (Mt. Boston, Paul Masson Grande Amber)
Dessert wines (Cribari, Wild Irish Rose, Widmer)
Premium table wines (Coastal Vintners, Dunnewood)
Sparkling wines (Cook's, J. Roget, LeDomaine)
Table wines (Almaden, Inglenook, Manischewitz, Nectar Valley, Paul Masson, Taylor, Widmer)

Domestic Beer
Point (Bock, Classic Amber, Maple Wheat, Pale Ale, Special)

Imported
China (Tsingtao)

England (Double Diamond, Tetley's English Pub Ale)
Germany (St. Pauli Girl, St. Pauli Girl Dark)
Italy (Peroni)
Mexico — distribution contract covers Midwest to West Coast (Corona Extra, Corona Light, Modelo especial, Negra Modelo, Pacifico)

Matthew Clark
Bottled water (Strathmore Scottish Spring Water)
Cider (Blackthorn, Gaymers Olde English Cyder)
Wines (Babycham, Stone's Green Ginger Wine, the Stowells of Chelsea — boxed)

Spirits
Bourbon (Colonel Lee Bourbon, Kentucky Gentleman)
Canadian whisky (Black Velvet, Canadian LTD)
Gin (Barton, Fleischmann's)
Prepared drinks (Chi-Chi's)
Schnapps (99)
Scotch (Highland Mist, Inver House, Lauders, Speyburn)
Tequila (Capitan, El Toro, Garduno, Montezuma)
Vodka (Crystal Palace, Glenmore, Fleischmann's, Skol)

COMPETITORS

Allied Domecq	Heineken	S&P
Anheuser-Busch	H P Bulmer	Sebastiani
Bacardi USA	Interbrew	Vineyards
Beringer Blass	Jim Beam	Skyy
Brown-Forman	Brands	Todhunter
Chalone Wine	Kendall-Jackson	Trinchero Family
Diageo	Labatt	Estates
Fortune Brands	Molson	Vincor
Future Brands	National Grape	Wine Group
Gallo	Cooperative	
Heaven Hill	Nestlé	
Distilleries	Robert Mondavi	

HISTORICAL FINANCIALS & EMPLOYEES

NYSE: STZ FYE: Last day in February	Annual Growth	8/93	8/94	8/95	*2/96	2/97	2/98	2/99	2/00	2/01	2/02
Sales ($ mil.)	31.6%	306	630	907	535	1,135	1,213	1,497	2,341	3,154	3,634
Net income ($ mil.)	27.2%	16	12	41	3	28	50	51	77	97	136
Income as % of sales	—	5.1%	1.9%	4.5%	0.6%	2.4%	4.1%	3.4%	3.3%	3.1%	3.8%
Earnings per share ($)	20.0%	0.30	0.19	0.54	0.04	0.36	0.66	0.68	1.05	1.30	1.55
Stock price - FY high ($)	—	5.94	8.00	12.00	13.25	9.88	14.63	15.38	15.30	17.15	27.18
Stock price - FY low ($)	—	2.69	5.06	7.44	7.44	3.94	5.47	8.81	10.72	10.09	15.65
Stock price - FY close ($)	19.3%	5.56	7.63	11.81	9.50	7.69	13.94	13.34	12.25	15.96	27.18
P/E - high	—	18	42	22	331	27	22	18	14	13	17
P/E - low	—	8	27	14	186	11	8	10	10	8	10
Dividends per share ($)	—	0.00	0.00	0.00	0.00	0.00	0.00	0.00	0.00	0.00	0.00
Book value per share ($)	17.8%	2.48	3.20	4.50	4.54	4.83	5.54	6.06	7.16	8.49	10.80
Employees	12.5%	—	—	—	2,500	2,500	2,500	4,230	4,500	4,990	5,080

* Fiscal year change

STOCK PRICE HISTORY

HIGH/LOW/CLOSE

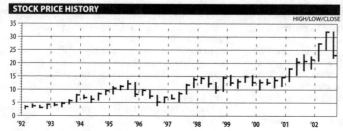

2002 FISCAL YEAR-END
Debt ratio: 57.5%
Return on equity: 17.4%
Cash ($ mil.): 9
Current ratio: 2.07
Long-term debt ($ mil.): 1,293
No. of shares (mil.): 89
Dividends
  Yield: —
  Payout: —
Market value ($ mil.): 2,406

CONSTELLATION ENERGY GROUP

There's a new constellation in the wide-open skies of the US power marketplace. Based in Baltimore, holding company Constellation Energy Group was created in 1999 to separate regulated utility Baltimore Gas and Electric (BGE), which serves nearly 1.2 million electricity customers and more than 600,000 gas customers, from the company's other businesses. In October 2001, however, Constellation canceled plans that would have completed the separation by creating two publicly traded companies: BGE and a merchant energy unit.

Constellation's merchant energy operations consist of the former power plants of BGE (6,200 MW of capacity), which have been separated from its distribution operations; Constellation's interests in independent power projects throughout the US; and Constellation's power marketing and trading subsidiary, which ranks among the top marketers in North America. These assets give Constellation 11,500 MW of owned or operated generating capacity (mostly from coal and nuclear facilities), plus 2,900 MW under construction.

Other nonutility operations include a district cooling operation in Baltimore, heating and air-conditioning and appliance sales, energy consulting services, and retail energy sales.

In the wake of its decision not to split into two companies, Constellation is reorganizing its management and corporate structure. It has announced plans to sell off noncore assets, including its real estate investments and Latin American power projects, and reduce its workforce by 10%.

HISTORY

In 1816, back when gas was made out of tar, Rembrandt Peale (an artist and son of painter Charles Willson Peale), William Lorman, and three others formed the US's first gas utility: Gas Light Company of Baltimore; Lorman was president until 1832. The firm soon ran out of money and issued stock to raise capital.

Baltimore's growth outstripped the firm's gas-main capacity, and by 1860 it had a fierce rival in the People's Gas Light Co. In 1871 the two firms divided the city up and then fought a price war with yet another rival. Finally, the three merged as the Consolidated Gas Company of Baltimore City in 1880.

The next year the Brush Electric Light Company and the United States Electric Light and Power Company were established. In 1906 their descendants merged with Consolidated Gas to form the Consolidated Gas Electric Light and Power Co.

As demand for electricity grew, the company turned from hydroelectric power to steam generators in the 1920s. Its revenues increased despite the Depression, and it later set records producing gas and electricity during WWII. Despite a postwar boom in sales, earnings fell as Consolidated spent money on new plants, shifting to natural gas, and converting downtown Baltimore from DC to AC.

In 1955 Consolidated was renamed Baltimore Gas and Electric Company (BGE). BGE announced plans in 1967 for Maryland's first nuclear power plant; Calvert Cliffs Unit 1 went on line in 1975, and Unit 2 followed two years later.

BGE began adding to the Safe Harbor Hydroelectric Project in 1981. Over the next two years it sought to form a holding company in order to diversify, but state regulators rejected the request in 1983. Undaunted, the firm formed subsidiary Constellation Holdings in 1985 and began investing in nonutility businesses and pursuing independent power projects.

Both Calvert Cliffs nukes were shut down between 1989 and 1990 for repairs, and BGE had to spend $458 million on replacement power.

The Energy Policy Act fundamentally changed the electric utility industry in 1992 by allowing wholesale power competition in monopoly territories. BGE began expanding its gas division that year, and in 1995 it ventured into Latin America and took a stake in a Bolivian power firm.

BGE formed its power marketing arm that year with Goldman Sachs as its advisor. It teamed up with Goldman Sachs again in 1998 when the duo formed joint venture Orion Power Holdings to buy electric plants in the US and Canada. In 1999 Orion bought plants from Niagara Mohawk, Con Ed, and U.S. Generating. The next year Orion snapped up Duquesne Light's generating facilities.

Meanwhile, Maryland passed deregulation legislation in 1999, and Constellation Energy Group was formed in 1999 as the holding company for BGE and its nonregulated subsidiaries. Competition began in BGE's territory in 2000, and Constellation separated BGE's generation assets from its distribution assets in accordance with the state's deregulation laws.

It also announced plans to split into two companies: BGE and a merchant energy business that would retain the Constellation name. But slumping energy prices and a weakened economy caused Constellation to cancel the proposed split in October 2001; it also ended its power advisory relationship with Goldman Sachs, which had planned to invest in the new merchant energy business.

Also in 2001 Constellation purchased the Nine Mile Point Nuclear Station Unit 1 and 82% of

Unit 2 (most of the holdings were bought from Niagara Mohawk), and sold its Guatemalan power plants to Duke Energy.

In 2002 the company sold its 40% stake in Corporate Office Properties Trust, a real estate investment trust (REIT). It also sold its 19% interest in Orion Power Holdings to Reliant Resources, and it agreed to buy the retail marketing unit of power producer AES for $240 million.

OFFICERS

Chairman, President, and CEO: Mayo A. Shattuck III, age 47, $150,000 pay (partial-year salary)
SVP and CFO, Constellation Energy and Baltimore Gas and Electric: E. Follin Smith, age 42
VP, General Counsel, and Corporate Secretary: Kathleen Chagnon
VP and Assistant to the CEO: Judy Pensabene
VP and Chief Risk Officer: John R. Collins, age 44
VP and CIO: Beth S. Perlman
VP Human Resources: Elaine W. Johnson, age 60
President and CEO, Baltimore Gas and Electric: Frank O. Heintz, age 58, $369,500 pay
President and CEO, BGE Home: William H. Munn
President, Constellation Energy Source: Gregory S. Jarosinski
President, Constellation Generation Group: Michael J. Wallace, age 54
President, Constellation Power Source: Thomas V. Brooks, age 39, $1,688,106 pay (partial-year salary)
Auditors: PricewaterhouseCoopers LLP

LOCATIONS

HQ: Constellation Energy Group, Inc.
250 W. Pratt St., Baltimore, MD 21201
Phone: 410-234-5000 **Fax:** 410-234-5220
Web: www.constellationgroup.com

Constellation Energy Group provides electricity and gas in Baltimore and portions of 10 counties in central Maryland. It also owns interests in power projects throughout the US, and it has energy interests in Bolivia and Panama in Latin America.

PRODUCTS/OPERATIONS

2001 Sales

	$ mil.	% of total
Regulated utility		
Electricity	2,040	52
Gas	674	17
Merchant energy	614	16
Other	600	15
Total	**3,928**	**100**

COMPETITORS

AEP	Conectiv	PG&E
Allegheny	Dominion	PPL
Energy	Duke Energy	PSEG
AmerGen Energy	Dynegy	Sempra Energy
Aquila	Edison	Southern
CenterPoint	International	Company
Energy	El Paso Corp.	WGL Holdings
Chesapeake	Entergy	Williams
Utilities	NiSource	Companies
Cinergy	Pepco Holdings	

HISTORICAL FINANCIALS & EMPLOYEES

NYSE: CEG FYE: December 31	Annual Growth	12/92	12/93	12/94	12/95	12/96	12/97	12/98	12/99	12/00	12/01
Sales ($ mil.)	5.2%	2,491	2,669	2,783	2,935	3,153	3,308	3,358	3,786	3,834	3,928
Net income ($ mil.)	(9.8%)	264	310	324	338	311	283	328	274	442	104
Income as % of sales	—	10.6%	11.6%	11.6%	11.5%	9.9%	8.6%	9.8%	7.2%	11.5%	2.7%
Earnings per share ($)	(11.0%)	1.63	1.85	1.93	2.02	1.85	1.72	2.06	1.74	2.21	0.57
Stock price – FY high ($)	—	24.38	27.50	25.50	29.00	29.50	34.31	35.25	31.50	52.06	50.14
Stock price – FY low ($)	—	19.76	22.38	20.50	22.00	25.00	24.75	29.25	24.69	27.06	20.90
Stock price – FY close ($)	1.4%	23.38	25.38	22.13	28.50	26.75	34.13	30.88	29.00	45.06	26.55
P/E – high	—	15	15	13	14	16	20	17	14	24	96
P/E – low	—	12	12	11	11	14	14	14	11	12	40
Dividends per share ($)	(6.4%)	1.42	1.46	1.50	1.54	1.58	1.62	1.66	1.68	1.68	0.78
Book value per share ($)	1.5%	21.56	21.72	21.74	22.53	21.68	21.47	21.25	21.28	22.21	24.64
Employees	(0.1%)	9,265	10,018	9,000	9,379	7,032	9,000	9,400	9,000	7,800	9,200

STOCK PRICE HISTORY

HIGH/LOW/CLOSE

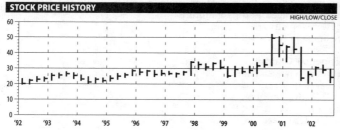

2001 FISCAL YEAR-END

Debt ratio: 40.2%
Return on equity: 3.0%
Cash ($ mil.): 72
Current ratio: 0.52
Long-term debt ($ mil.): 2,713
No. of shares (mil.): 164
Dividends
 Yield: 2.9%
 Payout: 136.8%
Market value ($ mil.): 4,346

CONTIGROUP COMPANIES, INC.

Talk about going against the grain. New York City-based ContiGroup Companies (CGC, formerly Continental Grain) has gotten out of the business in which it literally made its name. CGC was once the US's #2 grain exporter before it sold its commodities marketing business to Cargill to move a bit farther up the food chain.

CGC's largest businesses include ContiBeef LLC, the second-largest cattle feeders (after Cactus Feeders); Premium Standard Farms, the #2 fresh pork producer in the US (after Smithfield Foods); and Wayne Farms, a major poultry producer. In China, the Caribbean, and Latin America, CGC has interests in flour milling, animal feed, and aquaculture. CGC's investment arm, ContiInvestments, maintains interest in real estate and other investments.

Chairman Paul Fribourg (the great-great-great-grandson of ContiGroup's founder) and his family own the company.

Simon Fribourg founded a commodity trading business in Belgium in 1813. It operated domestically until 1848, when a drought in Belgium caused it to buy large stocks in Russian wheat.

As the Industrial Revolution swept across Europe and populations shifted to cities, people consumed more traded grain. In the midst of such rapid changes, the company prospered. After WWI, Russia, which had been Europe's primary grain supplier, ceased to be a major player in the trading game, and Western countries picked up the slack. Sensing the shift, Jules and Rene Fribourg reorganized the business as Continental Grain and opened its first US office in Chicago in 1921.

Throughout the Depression the company bought US grain elevators, often at low prices. Through its purchases, Continental Grain built a North American grain network that included major locations like Kansas City, Missouri; Nashville, Tennessee; and Toledo, Ohio.

In Europe, meanwhile, the Fribourgs were forced to endure constant political and economic upheaval, often profiting from it (they supplied food to Republican forces during the Spanish Civil War). When Nazis invaded Belgium in 1940, the Fribourgs were forced to flee, but they reorganized the business in New York City after the war.

Following the war, Continental Grain pioneered US grain trade with the Soviets. The company went on a buying spree in the 1960s and 1970s, acquiring Allied Mills (feed milling, 1965) and absorbing many agricultural and transport businesses, including Texas feedlots,

a bakery, and the Quaker Oats agricultural products unit.

During the 1980s Continental Grain sold its baking units (Oroweat and Arnold) and its commodities brokerage house. Amid an agricultural bust, it formed ContiFinancial and other financial units.

Michel Fribourg stepped down as CEO in 1988 and was succeeded by Donald Staheli, the first nonfamily-member CEO. The company entered a grain-handling and selling joint venture with Scoular in 1991. Three years later Staheli added the title of chairman, and Michel's son Paul became president. Continental Grain sold a stake in ContiFinancial (home equity loans and investment banking) to the public in 1996. Also in 1996 the firm formed ContiInvestments, an investment arm geared toward the parent company's areas of expertise.

That year Continental Grain and an overseas affiliate (Arab Finagrain) agreed to pay the US government $35 million, which included a $10 million fine against Arab Finagrain, to settle a fraud case involving commodity sales to Iraq.

Paul succeeded Staheli as CEO in 1997. The company bought Campbell Soup's poultry processing units that year, and in 1998 it bought a 51% stake in pork producer/processor Premium Standard Farms. Meanwhile, ContiFinancial diversified into retail home mortgage and home equity lending.

Continental Grain sold its commodities marketing business in July 1999 to #1 grain exporter Cargill. With its grain operations gone, in 1999 the company renamed itself ContiGroup Companies.

During 2000 ContiFinancial declared bankruptcy, and ContiGroup sold its Animal Nutrition Division (Wayne Foods) to feed maker Ridley Inc for $37 million. In mid-2000, Premium Standard Farms doubled its processing capacity with the purchase of Lundy Packing Company.

Chairman emeritus Michel Fribourg, the founder's great-great-grandson, died in 2001. That same year ContiSea, the salmon and seafood processing joint venture between ContiGroup and Seaboard, was sold to Norway's Fjord Seafood, giving ContiGroup a significant share of Fjord.

Chairman, President, and CEO: Paul J. Fribourg
EVP and COO: Vart K. Adjemian
EVP, Investments and Strategy and CFO; President, ContiInvestments: Michael J. Zimmerman, age 51
EVP, Human Resources and Information Systems: Teresa E. McCaslin
CEO, ContiBeef: John Rakestraw
CEO, Premium Standard Farms: John M. Meyer
CEO, Wayne Farms: Elton Maddox
SVP and Managing Director, Asian Industries Division: Michael A. Hoer
VP and General Manager, ContiLatin: Brian Anderson

LOCATIONS

HQ: 277 Park Ave., New York, NY 10172
Phone: 212-207-5100   **Fax:** 212-207-2910
Web: www.contigroup.com

ContiGroup Companies operates in the Caribbean, China, Latin America, and the US.

PRODUCTS/OPERATIONS

Major Business Units

Asian Industries
Feed milling (China)
Pork production (China)
Poultry production (China)

ContiBeef, LLC
Cattle feedlots

ContiInvestments, LLC
Investment management

ContiLatin
Feed and flour milling
Poultry operations
Salmon farming
Seafood processing
Shrimp farming

Premium Standard Farms (51%)
Pork production

Wayne Farms, LLC
Poultry production

COMPETITORS

Bartlett and Company
Cactus Feeders
Cargill
Cenex Harvest States
ConAgra
Farmland Industries
JR Simplot
Salomon Smith Barney Holdings
Smithfield Foods
Tyson Foods

HISTORICAL FINANCIALS & EMPLOYEES

Private FYE: March 31	Annual Growth	3/92	3/93	3/94	3/95	3/96	3/97	3/98	3/99	3/00	3/01
Estimated sales ($ mil.)	(13.7%)	15,000	15,000	15,000	14,000	15,000	16,000	15,000	10,500	10,000	4,000
Employees	(0.2%)	14,750	14,700	15,500	16,000	16,000	16,800	17,500	14,000	13,500	14,500

SALES HISTORY

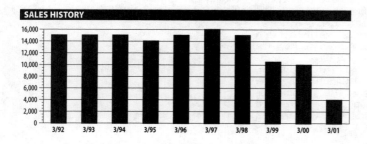

CONTINENTAL AIRLINES, INC.

Based in Houston, Continental Airlines is the fifth-largest US carrier (behind United, American, Delta, and Northwest). The airline offers 2,200 daily flights to more than 120 domestic and more than 90 international destinations, primarily from hubs in Cleveland, Houston, and Newark, New Jersey. Regional feeder Continental Express also operates out of those hubs with more than 1,000 daily departures to more than 115 US cities. Subsidiary Continental Micronesia serves the western Pacific from its hub in Guam.

The carrier is courting business travelers, upgrading and expanding its fleet, adding regional jets to its Continental Express fleet, and expanding international service to Europe and Latin America. Continental code-shares with airlines such as Air France, Alitalia, and Virgin Atlantic to overseas destinations.

Continental has an extensive marketing alliance with Northwest that includes code-sharing and shared frequent-flyer programs. Northwest, which in 2001 sold back shares that gave it a 55% voting stake in Continental, retains a 5% equity interest and the right to block the sale of Continental to a third party.

HISTORY

Varney Speed Lines, the fourth airline begun by Walter Varney, was founded in 1934. It became Continental Airlines three years later when Robert Six, whose own airline had folded during the Depression, bought 40% of the carrier. Six convinced his father-in-law, chairman of drugmaker Charles Pfizer Co., to lend him $90,000 for the stake in Varney.

In 1951 Continental spent $7.6 million to update its fleet, a sum equal to its profit that year. It was a bold move for a small airline in an industry moving toward ever-larger aircraft. Two years later Continental merged with Pioneer Airlines, adding routes to 16 cities in Texas and New Mexico. It also added jets in the late 1950s to compete on cross-country routes. To maintain its small Boeing 707 fleet, Continental developed a maintenance system that enabled it to fly the planes 15 hours a day, seven days a week.

In 1962 the carrier suffered its first crash. The next year it moved its headquarters from Denver to Los Angeles. A transport service contract with the US military during the Vietnam War led to the formation of Air Micronesia in 1968.

Economic downturn, industry deregulation, and rising fuel costs left Continental with a string of losses in the late 1970s (it would lose more than $500 million between 1978 and 1983). Over the objections of Continental's unions, Frank Lorenzo's Texas Air bought the company in 1982.

Texas Air had been founded in 1947 to provide service within Texas, and by 1970 it also flew to the West Coast and Mexico. Bankrupt two years later, the company was acquired by Lorenzo, who returned it to profitability by 1976 — just in time for airline deregulation in 1978.

When Continental's union employees went on strike in 1983, Lorenzo maneuvered the airline into Chapter 11. It emerged from bankruptcy in 1986 as a low-fare carrier with the industry's lowest labor costs. That year Texas Air bought Eastern Air Lines, People Express, and Frontier Airlines.

In 1990 Lorenzo resigned as head of the company, and Texas Air changed its name to Continental Airlines Holdings. With fuel prices soaring because of the Mideast conflict, Continental again filed for bankruptcy. Gordon Bethune became CEO in 1994 and piloted Continental to a comeback with an investment by Air Partners/Air Canada and with a reduction in routes and staff. In 1996 regional subsidiary Continental Express began replacing turboprops with jets from Embraer.

In 1997 Bethune's honeymoon with employees ended as the pilots union negotiated for an accelerated pay-raise schedule; a five-year contract was ratified in 1998. That year Northwest Airlines paid $370 million for 13.5% of Continental, beating a takeover bid from Delta. Meanwhile Continental bought 20 Boeing aircraft and acquired stakes in airlines in Colombia and Panama.

The next year Continental launched its first Mideast route (to Tel Aviv) and sold its stake in the Amadeus computer reservation system. Labor relations remained smooth in 2000 as flight attendants ratified a new contract.

Northwest reduced its voting control of Continental to 5% in 2001, but maintained the right to block the sale of Continental to a third party. Also that year Continental announced plans to sell a minority stake in its ExpressJet unit, the parent of Continental Express, to the public.

Also in 2001 terrorist attacks in New York and Washington, DC, led Continental to reduce its flights and lay off more than 21% of its workforce.

Chairman and CEO; Chairman, Continental Express:
Gordon M. Bethune, age 60, $1,805,470 pay
President and Director: Lawrence W. Kellner, age 43,
$1,231,528 pay
EVP and COO: Clarence McLean, age 60, $1,213,346 pay
EVP Corporate and Secretary: Jeffery A. Smisek, age 47,
$1,163,400 pay
SVP and CFO: Jeffrey J. Misner, age 48
SVP and CIO: Janet P. Wejman, age 44
SVP Airport Services: Mark A. Erwin, age 46
SVP Corporate Development: J. David Grizzle, age 47
SVP Finance and Treasurer: Gerald Laderman, age 44
SVP Flight Operations: Deborah L. McCoy, age 47
SVP Human Resources and Labor Relations:
Michael H. Campbell, age 53, $906,169 pay
SVP International: Barry P. Simon, age 59
SVP Pricing and Revenue Management:
James Compton, age 46
SVP Purchasing and Materials Services:
Kuniaki Tsuruta, age 66
SVP Sales and Distribution: Bonnie S. Reitz, age 49
SVP Scheduling: Glen Hauenstein, age 41
SVP Technical Operations: George L. Mason, age 55
President, Continental Express: James B. Ream, age 46
Auditors: Ernst & Young LLP

LOCATIONS

HQ: 1600 Smith St., Dept. HQSEO, Houston, TX 77002
Phone: 713-324-5000   **Fax:** 713-324-2637
Web: www.continental.com

Continental Airlines has hubs in Cleveland, Guam,
Houston, and Newark, New Jersey, from which the
company serves more than 230 destinations in Asia,
Australia, Europe, and North and South America.

PRODUCTS/OPERATIONS

2001 Sales

	$ mil.	% of total
Passenger	8,457	94
Cargo & mail	512	6
Total	**8,969**	**100**

Major Subsidiaries
Continental Micronesia, Inc. (air service in the Pacific)
ExpressJet Holdings, Inc.
  Continental Express (regional airline)

COMPETITORS

Air Canada
AirTran Holdings
All Nippon Airways
AMR
British Airways
Cathay Pacific
Delta
JAL
Lufthansa
Northwest Airlines
Qantas
SAS
Singapore Airlines
Southwest Airlines
UAL
US Airways

HISTORICAL FINANCIALS & EMPLOYEES

NYSE: CAL FYE: December 31	Annual Growth	12/92	12/93	12/94	12/95	12/96	12/97	12/98	12/99	12/00	12/01
Sales ($ mil.)	5.4%	5,575	3,907	5,670	5,825	6,360	7,213	7,951	8,639	9,899	8,969
Net income ($ mil.)	—	(125)	(39)	(613)	224	319	385	383	485	342	(95)
Income as % of sales	—	—	—	—	3.8%	5.0%	5.3%	4.8%	5.6%	3.5%	—
Earnings per share ($)	—	—	(1.17)	(23.76)	6.29	4.11	4.99	5.02	6.20	5.45	(1.72)
Stock price - FY high ($)	—	—	15.25	13.63	23.75	31.44	50.19	65.13	48.00	54.81	57.88
Stock price - FY low ($)	—	—	6.50	3.75	3.25	19.44	27.00	28.88	30.00	29.00	12.35
Stock price - FY close ($)	12.5%	—	10.25	4.63	21.75	28.25	48.13	33.50	44.38	51.63	26.21
P/E - high	—	—	—	—	3	6	7	10	7	10	—
P/E - low	—	—	—	—	0	4	4	5	4	5	—
Dividends per share ($)	—	—	0.00	0.00	0.00	0.00	0.00	0.00	0.00	0.00	0.00
Book value per share ($)	16.8%	—	5.29	2.93	6.25	10.96	15.55	18.53	24.33	19.85	18.38
Employees	1.3%	38,300	43,100	37,800	32,300	35,400	39,300	43,900	51,275	54,300	42,900

STOCK PRICE HISTORY

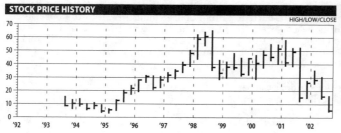

HIGH/LOW/CLOSE

2001 FISCAL YEAR-END

Debt ratio: 78.3%
Return on equity: —
Cash ($ mil.): 1,132
Current ratio: 0.67
Long-term debt ($ mil.): 4,198
No. of shares (mil.): 63
Dividends
  Yield: —
  Payout: —
Market value ($ mil.): 1,656

COOPER INDUSTRIES, LTD.

Cooper Industries can light up your life. The Houston-based company's electrical division (more than 80% of sales) makes electrical and circuit-protection products and lighting for residential and industrial use, as well as electrical power and distribution products for use by utilities. Its tools and hardware division makes and distributes Apex sockets, Crescent wrenches, Plumb hammers, and Weller soldering equipment. It also produces power tools (such as Airetool and Buckeye brands) sold primarily to members of the automotive and aerospace industries. Through its B-Line brand Cooper makes support systems and enclosures that are used in the electrical, mechanical, and telecommunications industries.

The Danaher Corporation, the US-based diversified industrial group, recently withdrew its bid to acquire Cooper, citing concerns over the asbestos liability stemming from the automotive division sold to Federal-Mogul Corporation in 1998. In order to take advantage of tax savings, Cooper has reincorporated in Bermuda.

HISTORY

In 1833 Charles Cooper sold a horse for $50 and borrowed additional money to open a foundry with his brother Elias in Mount Vernon, Ohio. Known as C. & E. Cooper, the company made plows, hog troughs, maple syrup kettles, stoves, and wagon boxes.

C. & E. Cooper began making steam engines in the 1840s for mill and farm use; it later adapted its engines for wood-burning locomotives. In 1868 the company built its first Corliss steam engine, and in 1875 it introduced the first steam-powered farm tractor. By 1900 C. & E. Cooper sold its steam engines in the US and overseas. The company debuted an internal combustion engine-compressor in 1909 for natural gas pipelines.

In the 1920s the company became the #1 seller of compression engines for oil and gas pipelines. A 1929 merger with Bessemer (small engines) created Cooper-Bessemer, which made diesel engines for power boats.

Diversification began in 1959 with the purchase of Rotor Tools. Cooper adopted its current name in 1965 and moved its headquarters to Houston in 1967. It went on to buy other firms, including Lufkin Rule (measuring tapes, 1967), Crescent (wrenches, 1968), and Weller (soldering tools, 1970).

Cooper's 1979 purchase of Gardner-Denver gave it a strong footing in oil-drilling and mining equipment, and the addition of Crouse-Hinds in 1981 was key to its diversification into electrical

materials. The decline in oil prices in the early 1980s caused sales to drop, but Cooper stayed profitable due to its tools and electrical products.

Cooper's electrical segment expanded with the 1985 purchase of McGraw-Edison, maker of consumer products (Buss fuses) and heavy transmission gear for electrical utilities. Growth continued as it added RTE (electrical equipment, 1988), Cameron Iron Works (oil-drilling equipment, 1989), and Ferramentas Belzer do Brasil (hand-tool maker, 1992).

Expanding into auto parts, Cooper bought Champion Spark Plug (1989) and Moog (auto replacement parts, 1992). From 1991 to 1993, the company divested 11 businesses and bought 13. In 1994 it spun off Gardner-Denver Industrial Machinery, sold Cameron Forged Products, and added Abex Friction Products (brake materials) and Zanxx (lighting components) to its auto parts line.

Cooper spun off Cooper Cameron (petroleum equipment) in 1995. The next year Cooper bought electrical fuse supplier Karp Electric, tool manufacturer Master Power, and electrical hub maker Myers Electric Products. Company veteran John Riley took over as chairman that year. Cooper added eight acquisitions in 1997, and some, such as Menvier-Swain Group (emergency lights and alarms, UK), helped to bolster its electrical segment. Despite its growth, the company trimmed its workforce by 30% that year.

Cooper completed 11 acquisitions in 1998 and 10 in 1999; among them were the tool business of Global Industrial Technologies (Quackenbush and Rotor Tool brands), Apparatebau Hundsbach (electronic sensors) and Metronix Elektronik (power tool controls), and several lighting firms. In the meantime, the company sold its automotive operations to Federal-Mogul.

In 2000 Cooper acquired B-Line Systems from Sigma-Aldrich for around $425 million. The next year tool maker Danaher offered to acquire Cooper in a deal worth about $5.5 billion; later it withdrew the bid, due to concerns about asbestos liability stemming from a former division.

In 2002 the company reincorporated in Bermuda for tax reasons and changed its name from Cooper Industries, Inc., to Cooper Industries, Ltd. The company also announced that it would begin expensing the cost of all stock options granted after January 1, 2003.

Chairman, President, and CEO: H. John Riley Jr., age 61
COO: Ralph E. Jackson Jr., age 60
SVP, Strategic Sourcing and Chief Information Technology Officer: Terry A. Klebe, age 47
SVP and CFO: D. Bradley McWilliams, age 61
SVP and General Counsel: Diane K. Schumacher, age 48
SVP, Human Resources: David R. Sheil Jr., age 45
SVP, Strategic Planning and New Venture Development Officer: David A. White Jr., age 60
EVP, Operations: Kirk S. Hachigian
VP, Investor Relations: Richard J. Bajenski, age 49
VP, Public Affairs: Victoria Guennewig, age 51
VP and Treasurer: Alan J. Hill, age 57
VP, Marketing: John J. Peterson
President, Cooper Bussmann: Michael A. Stoessl
Auditors: Ernst & Young LLP

LOCATIONS

HQ: 600 Travis, Ste. 5800, Houston, TX 77002
Phone: 713-209-8400   **Fax:** 713-209-8995
Web: www.cooperindustries.com

Cooper Industries operates manufacturing plants and warehouses in 21 countries around the world.

2001 Sales

	$ mil.	% of total
US	3,241	77
UK	225	5
Germany	219	5
Canada	150	4
Mexico	141	3
Other countries	234	6
Total	**4,210**	**100**

PRODUCTS/OPERATIONS

2001 Sales

	$ mil.	% of total
Electrical products	3,486	83
Tools & hardware	724	17
Total	**4,210**	**100**

Selected Products and Brands

Electrical Products
Architectural recessed lighting (Portfolio)
Aviation lighting products (Crouse-Hinds)
Electrical construction materials (CEAG, Crouse-Hinds)
Emergency lighting and power systems (Blessing, CSA, Pretronica, Univel)
Fire-detection systems (Fulleon, Nugelec, Transmould)
Security equipment (Menvier, Scantronic)
Wiring devices (Arrow Hart)

Tools and Hardware
Chain products (Campbell)
Files and saws (Nicholson)
Industrial power tools (Airetool, Buckeye, Rotor Tool)
Screwdrivers and nutdrivers (Xcelite)
Wrenches and pliers (Crescent)

COMPETITORS

ABB	GE	Siemens Energy
Black & Decker	Illinois Tool	& Automation
Cohesant	Works	SL Industries
Technologies	Ingersoll-Rand	Snap-on
Danaher	Newell	Stanley Works
Eaton	Rubbermaid	Tinnerman
Emerson	Philips	Palnut
Electric	Electronics	Waxman
Fiskars	Siemens	

HISTORICAL FINANCIALS & EMPLOYEES

NYSE: CBE FYE: December 31	Annual Growth	12/92	12/93	12/94	12/95	12/96	12/97	12/98	12/99	12/00	12/01
Sales ($ mil.)	(4.1%)	6,159	6,274	4,588	4,886	5,284	5,289	3,651	3,869	4,460	4,210
Net income ($ mil.)	—	(229)	367	(20)	94	315	395	423	332	357	231
Income as % of sales	—	—	5.9%	—	1.9%	6.0%	7.5%	11.6%	8.6%	8.0%	5.5%
Earnings per share ($)	—	(3.55)	2.15	(0.64)	0.84	2.77	3.26	3.69	3.50	3.80	2.44
Stock price – FY high ($)	—	59.38	54.75	52.25	40.50	44.63	59.69	70.38	56.75	47.00	60.45
Stock price – FY low ($)	—	41.75	45.63	31.63	32.88	34.13	40.00	36.88	39.63	29.38	31.61
Stock price – FY close ($)	(3.3%)	47.38	49.25	34.00	36.75	42.13	49.00	47.69	40.44	45.94	34.92
P/E – high	—	—	20	—	48	15	18	19	16	12	25
P/E – low	—	—	17	—	39	12	12	10	11	8	13
Dividends per share ($)	1.5%	1.22	1.30	1.32	1.65	0.99	1.32	1.32	1.32	1.38	1.40
Book value per share ($)	(1.7%)	25.28	26.13	23.44	15.90	17.50	21.44	16.60	18.50	20.38	21.58
Employees	(5.9%)	52,900	49,500	40,800	40,400	42,000	41,200	28,100	30,100	34,250	30,500

STOCK PRICE HISTORY

HIGH/LOW/CLOSE

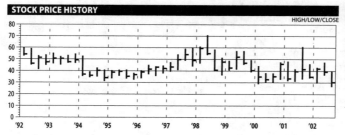

2001 FISCAL YEAR-END

Debt ratio: 35.4%
Return on equity: 11.8%
Cash ($ mil.): 12
Current ratio: 1.49
Long-term debt ($ mil.): 1,107
No. of shares (mil.): 94
Dividends
 Yield: 4.0%
 Payout: 57.4%
Market value ($ mil.): 3,274

COOPER TIRE & RUBBER COMPANY

Cooper Tire & Rubber wants to replace your tired, your poor, your huddled masses of treadbare tires before they threaten the safety on the highways. In addition to tires, the Findlay, Ohio-based company makes inner tubes, hoses, vibration-control products, and automotive sealing systems. Customers include automotive OEMs, wholesalers, retail chains, and independent dealers.

With the purchase of The Standard Products Company (automotive body sealing, exterior plastic trim, and vibration-control products) and Siebe Automotive (automotive fluid-handling systems), Cooper almost doubled in size. The company plans to downsize or close as many as 22 plants, while cutting 1,100 non-tire jobs worldwide. The company has sold its automotive trim and appliance sealing operations, and plans to dispose of the rest of its extruded plastics business.

HISTORY

John Schaefer and Claude Hart (brothers-in-law) bought M and M Manufacturing of Akron, Ohio, in 1914. M and M made tire patches, cement, and repair kits. In 1915 the two bought The Giant Tire & Rubber Company (tire rebuilding). Two years later they moved their business to Findlay, Ohio.

Ira Cooper joined Giant's board in 1917 and soon formed his own company, The Cooper Corporation, which began making tires in 1920. The industry began consolidating in the 1920s, and in 1930 Cooper and Giant merged with Falls Rubber Company (a small tire maker), and Master Tire & Rubber Company was born.

Cooper died in 1941, but the company went on to supply the war effort with tires, pontoons, life jackets, and tank decoys. After WWII the company changed its name to Cooper Tire & Rubber Company.

Cooper earned sales and loyalty from retailers and private-brand customers by promising not to open its own sales outlets — a policy continued to this day. The growth of the interstate system in the postwar years meant more cars, tires, and sales. Cooper went public in 1960. In 1964 it established Cooper Industrial Products to make industrial rubber products.

The 1970s brought the radial tire into widespread use. Radials had been around since the late 1940s, but the manufacturing process hadn't been cheap or easy enough to be practical. After undertaking its own research and development, Cooper rolled out its first radial in 1974. Around the same time it bought a Bowling Green, Ohio, plant that made extruded rubber products and reinforced hose. The plant was quickly adapted to produce rubber parts for cars.

A tire glut in the 1980s (due in part to longer-lasting tires) led to rapid downsizing in the industry. As competitors exited the tire business, Cooper was buying plants and modernizing them for about a third of the cost of building new ones. The company made its first foray outside the US with the acquisition of Rio Grande Servaas (inner tubes, Mexico). Cooper also undertook several projects in the 1980s to upgrade its research capabilities and to improve distribution. By the mid-1980s it could warehouse more than three million tires. By the end of the decade Cooper's stock was 68 times its 1980 level. The success came from growth in the replacement market, which was three times the size of the original equipment market.

The benefits of Cooper's capital investments became clear in the 1990s. As the decade began, the company recorded the best margins in the industry (about 33%), and investment continued. It passed the billion-dollar sales mark in 1991 and spent $110 million in capital investments in 1992.

In 1996 Cooper opened an automotive hose plant in Kentucky. The next year it bought Avon Tyres Limited (UK), its first overseas purchase.

Cooper completed its acquisition of Kentucky-based Dean Tire in 1999, expanding its sales of replacement tires for cars and light trucks to 10 countries. Cooper entered joint ventures with Italy's Pirelli in which Cooper sells and distributes Pirelli passenger car and light truck replacement tires in North America, and Pirelli distributes and markets Cooper tires in South America. The company boosted its automotive sealing system business with its purchase of The Standard Products Company in a deal valued at about $750 million.

In 2000 Cooper bought Siebe Automotive, the automotive fluid-handling division of Invensys, and sold Holm Industries (acquired with Standard Products) to an affiliate of Madison Capital Partners. Cooper also sold its automotive plastic trim plant in Winnsboro, South Carolina. Cooper closed several plants and scaled back operations at other facilities during 2001.

OFFICERS

Chairman, President, and CEO: Thomas A. Dattilo, age 50, $725,000 pay
VP and CFO: Philip G. Weaver, age 49, $335,000 pay
VP; President, Cooper Tire: D. Richard Stevens, age 54
VP; President, Cooper-Standard Automotive: James S. McElya, age 54, $420,000 pay
VP; President, Commercial Products Division: Larry J. Enders

VP; President, North America Tire Division:
Mark F. Armstrong, age 54
VP; EVP, Cooper-Standard Automotive:
Roderick F. Millhof, age 62, $350,000 pay
VP, General Counsel, and Secretary: Richard D. Teeple,
age 59, $302,000 pay
VP, Employee Relations and Development:
James H. Geers
VP: Franklin T. Burnside
VP: Paul C. Gilbert
VP: James P. Keller
VP, Advertising and Communication, Cooper Tire:
Patricia J. Brown
Treasurer: Stephen O. Schroeder
Controller: Eileen B. White, age 51
**Director, Investor Relations and Corporate
Communications:** Roger S. Hendriksen
Asst. General Counsel and Asst. Secretary:
Kathleen L. Diller
Asst. General Counsel and Asst. Secretary:
Richard N. Jacobson
Asst. Treasurer: Charles E. Nagy
Auditors: Ernst & Young LLP

LOCATIONS

HQ: 701 Lima Ave., Findlay, OH 45840
Phone: 419-423-1321 **Fax:** 419-424-4212
Web: www.coopertire.com

Cooper Tire & Rubber Company has manufacturing
facilities throughout the US, as well as in Australia,
Brazil, Canada, the Czech Republic, France, Germany,
India, Mexico, Poland, Spain, and the UK.

2001 Sales

	$ mil.	% of total
North America	2,624	83
Europe	472	15
Other regions	59	2
Total	**3,155**	**100**

PRODUCTS/OPERATIONS

2001 Sales

	$ mil.	% of total
Tire	1,704	54
Automotive	1,477	46
Adjustments	(26)	—
Total	**3,155**	**100**

Selected Products

Tire Group
Inner tubes
Tires (automobile, truck, motorcycle, and racing)
Tread rubber and retreading equipment

Automotive Group
Body sealing systems (rubber seals for trunks, doors,
and windows)
Fluid-handling systems (hose and hose assemblies and
fluid-handling components)
Vibration control systems (body cushions and
suspension components)

COMPETITORS

Bandag	Michelin	Toyo Tire &
Bridgestone	Pneumatiques	Rubber
Continental AG	Kleber	Vredestein
Gates Rubber	Sumitomo	Yokohama
Goodyear	Rubber	Rubber

HISTORICAL FINANCIALS & EMPLOYEES

NYSE: CTB FYE: December 31	Annual Growth	12/92	12/93	12/94	12/95	12/96	12/97	12/98	12/99	12/00	12/01
Sales ($ mil.)	11.6%	1,175	1,194	1,403	1,494	1,619	1,813	1,876	2,196	3,472	3,155
Net income ($ mil.)	(9.2%)	43	102	129	113	108	122	127	136	97	18
Income as % of sales	—	3.7%	8.6%	9.2%	7.6%	6.7%	6.8%	6.8%	6.2%	2.8%	0.6%
Earnings per share ($)	(7.8%)	0.52	1.22	1.53	1.35	1.30	1.55	1.64	1.79	1.31	0.25
Stock price - FY high ($)	—	35.63	39.63	29.50	29.63	27.38	28.44	26.25	25.00	16.00	17.43
Stock price - FY low ($)	—	22.06	20.00	21.63	22.25	17.88	18.00	15.44	13.25	9.19	10.55
Stock price - FY close ($)	(8.1%)	34.00	25.00	23.63	24.63	19.75	24.38	20.44	15.75	10.63	15.96
P/E - high	—	27	32	19	22	21	18	16	14	12	70
P/E - low	—	17	16	14	16	14	12	9	7	7	42
Dividends per share ($)	10.6%	0.17	0.20	0.23	0.27	0.31	0.35	0.39	0.42	0.42	0.42
Book value per share ($)	9.3%	5.65	6.58	7.92	8.95	9.67	10.58	11.45	12.87	13.13	12.54
Employees	13.9%	7,207	7,607	7,872	8,284	8,932	10,456	10,766	21,586	21,185	23,268

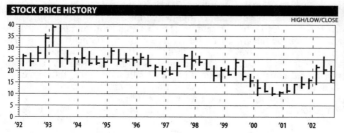

STOCK PRICE HISTORY HIGH/LOW/CLOSE

2001 FISCAL YEAR-END
Debt ratio: 49.2%
Return on equity: 2.0%
Cash ($ mil.): 72
Current ratio: 1.47
Long-term debt ($ mil.): 882
No. of shares (mil.): 73
Dividends
  Yield: 2.6%
  Payout: 168.0%
Market value ($ mil.): 1,159

CORNING INCORPORATED

Corning is the torchbearer for fiber optics. The Corning, New York-based company is the world's top producer of fiber-optic cable, which it invented more than 20 years ago. Corning's telecommunications unit (70% of sales) makes optical fiber and cable and photonic components, which use light to transmit data. The company's advanced materials unit produces industrial and scientific products, including emission controls, semiconductor materials, and optical and lighting products. Its information display segment makes glass products for televisions and VCRs, projection video lenses, and flat-panel displays.

Corning has suffered from slowing sales of its telecom products mainly because telephone service carriers have stopped adding new fiber lines to their networks. The company has shelved plans to buy complementary businesses and expand the capacity of its core fiber-optic cable operations. In 2002 Corning also announced plans for restructuring that will include layoffs, and possibly plant closures and the sale of non-core operations.

Chairman James Houghton returned to the role of chief executive in 2002 after John Loose retired from the company.

HISTORY

Amory Houghton started Houghton Glass in Massachusetts in 1851 and moved it to Corning, New York, in 1868. By 1876 the company, renamed Corning Glass Works, was making several types of technical and pharmaceutical glass. In 1880 it supplied the glass for Thomas Edison's first lightbulb. Other early developments included the red-yellow-green traffic light system and borosilicate glass (which can withstand sudden temperature changes) for Pyrex oven and laboratory ware.

Joint ventures have been crucial to Corning's success. Early ones included Pittsburgh Corning (with Pittsburgh Plate Glass, 1937, glass construction blocks), Owens-Corning (with Owens-Illinois, 1938, fiberglass), and Dow Corning (with Dow Chemical, 1943, silicones).

By 1945 the company's laboratories had made it the undisputed leader in the manufacture of specialty glass. Applications for its glass technology included the first mass-produced television tubes, freezer-to-oven ceramic cookware (Pyroceram, Corning Ware), and car headlights.

After WWII Corning emphasized consumer product sales and expanded globally. In the 1970s the company pioneered the development of optical fiber and auto emission technology (now two of its principal products).

Seeing maturing markets for such established products as lightbulbs and television tubes, Corning began buying higher-growth laboratory services companies — MetPath in 1982, Hazleton in 1987, Enseco in 1989, and G.H. Besse-laar in 1989. Vice chairman James Houghton, who is the great-great-grandson of Corning's founder, was named chairman and CEO in 1988. It also established international joint ventures with Siemens, Mitsubishi, and Samsung. In 1988 Corning bought Revere Ware (cookware). The next year the company dropped Glass Works from its name.

In 1994 Corning joined with Siecor (a joint venture with Siemens) to acquire several fiber and cable businesses from Northern Telecom (now Nortel Networks), expanding Corning's presence in Canada.

Joint venture Dow Corning, under assault from thousands of women seeking damages because of leaking breast implants, entered Chapter 11 bankruptcy protection in 1995. The massive losses incurred by Dow Corning due to litigation and a downturn in Corning's lab products sales prompted the company to recast itself. Corning began selling off its well-known consumer brands and putting greater emphasis on its high-tech optical and display products through acquisitions and R&D.

Company veteran Roger Ackerman was named CEO in 1996. He moved quickly to transform the company from a disjointed conglomerate to a high-tech optics manufacturer. That year the company spun off its laboratory testing division to shareholders, creating Covance and Quest Diagnostics.

After deals to sell a stake in Corning Consumer Products to AEA Investors fell through in 1997, Corning sold a majority stake in the housewares unit to Kohlberg Kravis Roberts the next year. In 1999 Corning bought UK-based BICC Group's telecom cable business.

In 2000 Corning made more than $5 billion worth of acquisitions to expand its optical fiber and hardware business. It bought Siemens' optical cable and hardware operations and the remaining 50% of the companies' Siecor joint venture. Corning acquired Oak Industries (optical components) for $1.8 billion, NetOptix (optical filters) for $2.15 billion, and purchased the 67% of microelectromechanical systems specialist IntelliSense it didn't already own.

Continuing its spending spree, the company bought part of Pirelli's fiber-optic telecom components business for about $3.6 billion; it also acquired Cisco's 10% stake in the business.

In the first half of 2001, Ackerman retired as chairman and CEO of the company. COO John

Loose was named CEO, and Houghton was re-appointed chairman. The company agreed in mid-2001 to acquire Lucent's fiber-optic and cable facilities in China.

Slowing demand prompted Corning to lay off about 25% of its staff, shut down plants, and discontinue its glass tubing operations that year. Houghton became chief executive after Loose retired in 2002.

OFFICERS

Chairman and CEO: James R. Houghton, age 66, $425,000 pay (prior to promotion)
Vice Chairman and CFO: James B. Flaws, age 53, $450,000 pay (prior to title change)
President, COO, and Director: Wendell P. Weeks, age 42, $575,000 pay (prior to promotion)
Director; President, Corning Technologies: Peter F. Volanakis, age 46, $500,000 pay
EVP and CTO: Joseph A. Miller Jr., age 60, $155,000 pay (prior to promotion)
EVP and Chief Administrative Officer: Kirk P. Gregg, age 42
EVP, Environmental Technologies and Strategic Growth: Robert L. Ecklin, age 63
SVP and General Counsel: William D. Eggers, age 57
SVP; Chairman, Steuben: E. Marie McKee
Auditors: PricewaterhouseCoopers LLP

LOCATIONS

HQ: 1 Riverfront Plaza, Corning, NY 14831
Phone: 607-974-9000   **Fax:** 607-974-8091
Web: www.corning.com

Corning and its subsidiaries operate manufacturing facilities at more than 90 plants in 19 countries.

2001 Sales

	$ mil.	% of total
North America	3,183	51
Asia/Pacific	1,461	23
Europe	1,421	22
Latin America	98	2
Other regions	109	2
Total	**6,272**	**100**

PRODUCTS/OPERATIONS

2001 Sales

	$ mil.	% of total
Telecommunications	4,458	71
Advanced materials	993	16
Information display	800	13
Other products	21	—
Total	**6,272**	**100**

COMPETITORS

Agere Systems	Nippon Sheet Glass
Agilent Technologies	Nortel Networks
Alcatel	Pilkington
Alcatel Optronics	Pirelli S.p.A.
Asahi Glass	Saint-Gobain
Cable Design Technologies	Schott Glas
Carl-Zeiss-Stiftung	Showa Electric Wire &
Furukawa Electric	Cable
JDS Uniphase	Sumitomo Electric
Lucent	Tyco International
NGK Insulators	

HISTORICAL FINANCIALS & EMPLOYEES

NYSE: GLW FYE: December 31	Annual Growth	12/92	12/93	12/94	12/95	12/96	12/97	12/98	12/99	12/00	12/01
Sales ($ mil.)	6.0%	3,709	4,005	4,771	5,313	3,652	4,090	3,484	4,297	7,127	6,272
Net income ($ mil.)	—	(13)	(15)	281	(51)	176	440	394	482	423	(5,498)
Income as % of sales	—	—	—	5.9%	—	4.8%	10.8%	11.3%	11.2%	5.9%	—
Earnings per share ($)	—	(0.03)	(0.03)	0.43	(0.08)	0.26	0.61	0.55	0.64	0.49	(5.89)
Stock price - FY high ($)	—	13.42	12.99	11.68	12.45	15.40	21.69	15.21	42.98	113.22	72.19
Stock price - FY low ($)	—	9.57	7.99	9.20	8.03	9.28	11.24	7.62	14.90	34.30	6.92
Stock price - FY close ($)	(3.7%)	12.49	9.32	9.95	10.66	15.40	12.36	14.99	42.94	52.81	8.92
P/E - high	—	—	—	27	—	62	34	27	65	231	—
P/E - low	—	—	—	21	—	37	18	13	23	70	—
Dividends per share ($)	(6.0%)	0.21	0.23	0.23	0.24	0.24	0.24	0.24	0.24	0.24	0.12
Book value per share ($)	7.2%	3.14	2.84	3.87	3.08	1.43	1.82	2.19	3.04	11.47	5.88
Employees	0.2%	31,100	39,200	43,000	41,000	20,000	20,500	15,400	17,000	40,300	31,700

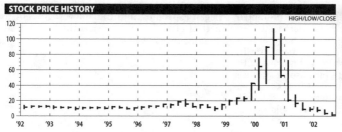

STOCK PRICE HISTORY HIGH/LOW/CLOSE

2001 FISCAL YEAR-END
Debt ratio: 45.2%
Return on equity: —
Cash ($ mil.): 1,037
Current ratio: 2.06
Long-term debt ($ mil.): 4,461
No. of shares (mil.): 921
Dividends
 Yield: 1.3%
 Payout: —
Market value ($ mil.): 8,215

COSTCO WHOLESALE CORPORATION

At Costco Wholesale (formerly Costco Companies), buying paper towels is a privilege, not a right. The Issaquah, Washington-based company is the largest wholesale club operator in the US (ahead of Wal-Mart's Sam's Club). Costco owns or has stakes in some 385 warehouse stores serving more than 36 million members in Canada, Japan, Mexico, South Korea, Taiwan, the UK, and the US. The company's typical warehouse store, averaging 137,000 sq. ft., offers products ranging from alcoholic beverages to pharmaceuticals at sharply discounted prices. (Some are sold in bulk packaging.) Costco carries a tenth of the variety offered by regular discount retailers, instead stocking 3,700 to 4,500 of the fastest-selling, highest-volume products.

In order to shop at Costco stores, customers must be members — a policy the company believes reinforces customer loyalty and provides a steady source of fee revenue. Three types of annual memberships are available: Business ($45 each and $35 for each additional card), Individuals ($45), and Executive ($100; allows members to purchase products and services, including insurance, mortgage services, and long-distance phone service, at reduced rates).

Facing competition from discounters that don't charge a membership fee, as well as from rival Sam's Club, Costco is expanding and retrofitting its warehouses to accommodate fresh food sections and other ancillary units, such as gas stations and optical departments. The company has vowed to open 40 new stores a year, including some in the Midwest. Costco plans to launch a test store — called Costco Home — in Washington state that will offer furniture and appliances.

HISTORY

From 1954 to 1974 retailer Sol Price built his Fed-Mart discount chain into a $300 million behemoth selling general merchandise to government employees. Price sold the company to Hugo Mann in 1975 and the next year, with son Robert, Rick Libenson, and Giles Bateman, opened the first Price Club warehouse, in San Diego, to sell in volume to small businesses at steep discounts.

Posting a large loss its first year prompted Price Club's decision to expand membership to include government, utility, and hospital employees, as well as credit union members. In 1978 it opened a second store, in Phoenix. With the help of his father, Sol's other son Laurence began a chain of tire-mounting stores (located adjacent to Price Club outlets on land leased from the company and using tires sold by the Price Clubs).

The company went public in 1980 with four stores in California and Arizona. Price Club moved into the eastern US with its 1984 opening of a store in Virginia and continued to expand, including a joint venture with Canadian retailer Steinberg in 1986 to operate stores in Canada; the first Canadian warehouse opened that year in Montreal.

Two years later Price Club acquired A. M. Lewis (grocery distributor, Southern California and Arizona), and the next year it opened two Price Club Furnishings, offering discounted home and office furniture.

Price Club bought out Steinberg's interest in the Canadian locations in 1990 and added stores on the East Coast and in California, Colorado, and British Columbia. However, competition in the East from ensconced rivals such as Sam's Club and PACE forced the closure of two stores two years later. A 50-50 joint venture with retailer Controladora Comercial Mexicana led to the opening of two Price Clubs in Mexico City, one each in 1992 and 1993.

Price Club merged with Costco Wholesale in 1993. Founded in 1983 by Jeffrey Brotman and James Sinegal (a former EVP of Price Company), Costco Wholesale went public in 1985 and expanded into Canada.

In 1993 Price/Costco opened its first warehouse outside the Americas in a London suburb. Merger costs led to a loss the following year, and Price/Costco spun off its commercial real estate operations, as well as certain international operations as Price Enterprises (now Price Legacy). In 1997 the company changed its corporate name to Costco Companies.

Costco began online sales and struck a deal to buy two stores in South Korea in 1998 and opened its first store in Japan in 1999. Under industrywide pressure over the way members-only chains record fees, Costco took a $118 million charge for fiscal 1999 to change accounting practices. That year the company made yet another name change to Costco Wholesale (emphasizing its core warehouse operations).

In 2000 the company purchased private retailer Littlewoods' 20% stake in Costco UK, increasing Costco's ownership to 80%. Costco began expanding into the Midwest in 2001 as part of plans to open 40 new clubs a year, including ones in China.

OFFICERS

Chairman: Jeffrey H. Brotman, age 59, $350,000 pay
President, CEO, and Director: James D. Sinegal, age 65, $350,000 pay
SEVP and COO, Merchandising, Distribution, and Construction: Richard D. DiCerchio, age 58, $474,423 pay
EVP and CFO: Richard A. Galanti, age 45, $445,423 pay
EVP and COO, International Operations and Ancillary Businesses: Franz E. Lazarus, age 54
EVP and COO, Northern Division: W. Craig Jelinek, age 49
EVP, Real Estate Development: Paul G. Moulton, age 50
EVP and COO, Eastern US and Canadian Division: Joseph P. Portera, age 48, $438,799 pay
EVP and COO, Southwest Division: Dennis R. Zook, age 52
Auditors: KPMG LLP

LOCATIONS

HQ: 999 Lake Dr., Issaquah, WA 98027
Phone: 425-313-8100   **Fax:** 425-313-8103
Web: www.costco.com

2001 Stores

	No.
US	284
Canada	60
Mexico	20
UK	11
South Korea	5
Taiwan	3
Japan	2
Total	**385**

PRODUCTS/OPERATIONS

2001 Sales

	$ mil.	% of total
Sales	34,137	98
Membership fees	660	2
Total	**34,797**	**100**

Selected Products and Services

Apparel	Health and beauty aids
Appliances	Home insurance
Automobile sales	Housewares
Computer hardware and software	Insurance (automobile, home)
Computer training services	Jewelry
Credit card processing	Mortgage service
Electronics	Payroll processing
Eye exams	Pharmaceuticals
Fresh foods	Real estate services
Furniture	Tools
Glasses and contact lenses	Toys
Hardware	Travel packages and other travel services

COMPETITORS

Albertson's	Circuit City	OfficeMax
ALDI	CompUSA	Petco
Army and Air Force Exchange	Dollar General	PETsMART
AutoZone	Family Dollar Stores	Smart & Final
Barnes & Noble	Home Depot	Staples
Best Buy	Hudson's Bay	Target
Big Lots	Kmart	Toys "R" Us
BJs Wholesale Club	Kroger	Walgreen
Canadian Tire	Loblaw	Wal-Mart
	Office Depot	

HISTORICAL FINANCIALS & EMPLOYEES

Nasdaq: COST FYE: Sunday nearest August 31	Annual Growth	8/92	8/93	8/94	8/95	8/96	8/97	8/98	8/99	8/00	8/01
Sales ($ mil.)	18.9%	7,320	15,155	16,481	17,906	19,567	21,874	24,270	27,456	32,164	34,797
Net income ($ mil.)	18.7%	129	223	(112)	134	249	312	460	397	631	602
Income as % of sales	—	1.8%	1.5%	—	0.7%	1.3%	1.4%	1.9%	1.4%	2.0%	1.7%
Earnings per share ($)	10.4%	0.53	0.50	(0.26)	0.34	0.61	0.73	1.02	0.87	1.35	1.29
Stock price - FY high ($)		15.18	10.55	10.81	9.38	10.94	19.44	32.88	46.88	60.50	46.50
Stock price - FY low ($)		6.92	6.62	6.50	6.00	6.81	8.38	16.94	20.63	25.94	29.31
Stock price - FY close ($)	20.1%	7.21	8.91	7.84	8.44	9.94	18.03	23.53	37.38	34.44	37.41
P/E - high		29	21	—	18	18	26	31	40	43	35
P/E - low		13	13	—	11	11	11	16	17	18	22
Dividends per share ($)	—	0.00	0.00	0.00	0.00	0.00	0.00	0.00	0.00	0.00	0.00
Book value per share ($)	11.6%	4.07	4.14	3.87	3.92	4.53	5.78	6.82	7.98	9.48	10.92
Employees	17.1%	20,777	43,000	47,000	52,000	53,000	57,000	63,000	70,000	78,000	86,000

STOCK PRICE HISTORY

HIGH/LOW/CLOSE

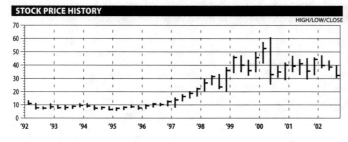

2001 FISCAL YEAR-END

Debt ratio: 15.0%
Return on equity: 13.2%
Cash ($ mil.): 603
Current ratio: 0.94
Long-term debt ($ mil.): 859
No. of shares (mil.): 447
Dividends
 Yield: —
 Payout: —
Market value ($ mil.): 16,733

COUNTRYWIDE CREDIT INDUSTRIES

Countrywide Credit Industries gives credit where credit is due.

The Calabasas, California-based company is the largest independent residential mortgage lending firm in the US. Through Countrywide Home Loans it offers prime first mortgages (about 80% of its business), but the company has been diversifying. Its business is now broken down into five categories: processing and technology (financial transaction processing), consumer businesses (subprime, home equity, and loan closing services), mortgage investments (mortgage servicing rights), capital markets (securities dealing and asset management for institutional clients), and commercial insurance. The company operates more than 550 branch offices located across the US and has a partnership with Sprint to provide home lending services over the Web.

Countrywide Credit's majority-owned Global Home Loans subsidiary services mortgages for Woolwich, one of the leading British mortgage lenders. It has been expanding in the insurance segment with its purchase of the Balboa Life and Casualty Group. With its acquisition of Treasury Bank, a Washington, DC-based commercial bank, Countrywide Credit is transforming itself into a financial services holding company.

HISTORY

Business associates David Loeb and Angelo Mozilo formed Countrywide Credit Industries in 1969. Loeb had already started mortgage banking business United Mortgage Servicing; Mozilo was his best salesman. Loeb was forced to give up his stake in United Mortgage to corporate raiders, and shortly thereafter the pair opened the first Countrywide Credit office in Anaheim, California.

The company went public in the early 1970s, but the partners raised only $800,000 in capital. Business picked up despite inflation and high interest rates. By 1974 Countrywide Credit's eight branches were doing well, but operating costs were eroding the company's bottom line.

Rather than watch Countrywide Credit slowly bleed, Loeb decided to reinvent the company. Mozilo grudgingly agreed; they closed all of the branches and fired all 95 employees except themselves and a secretary. They transformed Countrywide Credit from a sales-driven to a product-driven enterprise, dropping its commissioned sales force in favor of direct solicitation of realtors. Guaranteed low interest rates eventually drummed up enough business to reopen a California branch that was soon seeing more business than it could handle. By 1978 the company was in the black.

By the mid-1980s Countrywide Credit had more than 100 branches in about two dozen states. The company diversified, forming Countrywide Securities (1981) and Countrywide Asset Management (1985). Like other mortgage companies, it benefited from the savings and loan crisis of the late 1980s, filling a void in home loan production.

After the recession that marked the late 1980s and early 1990s, the firm's business picked up again as low interest rates prompted more refinancing. Marginally rising interest rates in 1994 resulted in a flat housing market and a shrinking volume of mortgage refinancing industrywide. In response, Countrywide Credit trimmed staff and took cost-cutting measures. By 1996 the company's profits had rebounded.

But Countrywide Credit still faced the problem of mortgage refinancing, which provides one-time fees but has little effect on loan volume. The company in 1997 responded with a nationwide ad campaign to build brand awareness and target new customer groups, including Hispanics. In an effort to diversify, the firm bought mutual funds broker and administrator Leshner Financial (renamed Countrywide Financial Services, it was sold in 1999).

Another tactic to increase loan volume was more risky. In 1998, as personal bankruptcies continued at record levels, the company moved into the subprime market through its Full Spectrum Lending subsidiary. The next year Countrywide Credit pumped up its insurance business when it bought most of the operations of Balboa Life and Casualty Group.

Also in 1999 the company entered an arrangement to sell most of its loans to Fannie Mae, which began promoting Countrywide Credit's products and accepting loans approved by its new partner's automated underwriting system. The next year the firm teamed with Checkfree to provide online bill payment services to its customers. It also applied to become a financial services holding company and announced plans for a Web site designed to help housing industry professionals get homeowners and home warranty insurance for their customers.

Early in 2000 the long-term partnership driving the firm was broken up when David Loeb left the company. Also that year Countrywide Credit expanded its online operations by forging a deal with Sprint PCS and entered the European market through CCM International Ltd. Countrywide Credit restructured in 2001, in preparation for a more diversified future.

OFFICERS

Chairman, President, and CEO; Chairman, Countrywide Home Loans: Angelo R. Mozilo, age 63, $6,111,934 pay
Executive Managing Director, COO, and Director; President and CEO, Countrywide Home Loans: Stanford L. Kurland, age 49, $3,134,620 pay
Senior Managing Director; COO, Countrywide Home Loans: Thomas H. Boone, age 47, $1,021,203 pay
Senior Managing Director and Chief of Banking and Insurance Operations: Carlos M. Garcia, age 46, $1,065,062 pay
Senior Managing Director and CFO: T. Keith McLaughlin, age 44
Senior Managing Director and Chief of Production: David Sambol, age 42, $2,069,217 pay
Senior Managing Director, Legal, Secretary, and General Counsel: Sandor E. Samuels, age 49
Managing Director, Consumer Markets: Joseph Anderson
Managing Director, Marketing: Andrew S. Bielanski
Managing Director; President, LandSafe: Michael Faine
Managing Director and COO, Banking and Insurance: Marshall M. Gates
Managing Director, Human Resources: Leora I. Goren
Auditors: Grant Thornton LLP

LOCATIONS

HQ: Countrywide Credit Industries, Inc.
4500 Park Granada, Calabasas, CA 91302
Phone: 818-225-3000   **Fax:** 818-225-4051
Web: www.countrywide.com

Countrywide Credit Industries operates in the UK and the US.

2001 Loans

	% of total
California	29
Colorado	5
Florida	5
Michigan	5
Arizona	4
Texas	4
Illinois	3
Massachusetts	3
New Jersey	3
Other states	39
Total	**100**

PRODUCTS/OPERATIONS

2001 Sales

	% of total
Interest income	34
Loan servicing income	24
Gain on sale of loans	17
Loan origination fees	15
Insurance premiums	6
Commissions & other	4
Total	**100**

COMPETITORS

Advanta
Bank of America
Conseco Finance
Fannie Mae
First American Corporation
FleetBoston
Freddie Mac
Golden West Financial
HomeSide International
Impac Mortgage Holdings
Insignia Financial Group
Irwin Financial
J.P. Morgan Chase
NVR
Pelican Financial
Washington Mutual
Wells Fargo

HISTORICAL FINANCIALS & EMPLOYEES

NYSE: CCR FYE: December 31	Annual Growth	2/93	2/94	2/95	2/96	2/97	2/98	2/99	2/00	2/01	*12/01
Assets ($ mil.)	30.9%	3,299	5,586	5,580	8,658	8,089	12,219	15,648	15,822	22,956	37,217
Net income ($ mil.)	14.8%	140	180	88	196	257	345	385	410	374	486
Income as % of assets	—	4.2%	3.2%	1.6%	2.3%	3.2%	2.8%	2.5%	2.6%	1.6%	1.3%
Earnings per share ($)	11.0%	1.52	1.97	0.96	1.95	2.44	3.09	3.29	3.52	3.14	3.89
Stock price - FY high ($)	—	22.07	23.35	18.88	26.75	31.13	48.50	56.25	48.00	52.00	52.00
Stock price - FY low ($)	—	10.85	15.26	12.38	15.50	19.75	24.38	28.63	22.94	22.31	37.39
Stock price - FY close ($)	7.3%	21.75	16.68	16.25	21.00	29.13	44.44	37.88	24.94	44.23	40.97
P/E - high	—	13	12	19	13	12	15	16	13	16	13
P/E - low	—	7	8	13	8	8	8	8	6	7	9
Dividends per share ($)	3.0%	0.23	0.28	0.32	0.32	0.32	0.32	0.32	0.40	0.40	0.30
Book value per share ($)	16.2%	8.61	9.66	10.32	12.91	15.19	19.12	22.37	25.45	30.23	33.31
Employees	21.0%	3,235	4,867	3,613	4,825	6,134	7,983	11,378	10,572	12,090	17,921

* Fiscal year change

STOCK PRICE HISTORY

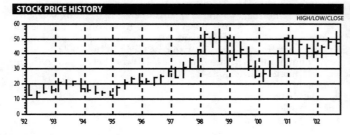

HIGH/LOW/CLOSE

2001 FISCAL YEAR-END

Equity as % of assets: 11.0%
Return on assets: 1.6%
Return on equity: 12.7%
Long-term debt ($ mil.): 16,550
No. of shares (mil.): 123
Dividends
  Yield: 0.7%
  Payout: 7.7%
Market value ($ mil.): 5,027
Sales ($ mil.): 4,110

COX COMMUNICATIONS, INC.

Cox Communications is using its cable cunning to tackle the brave new broadband world. The Atlanta-based MSO (multiple system operator) provides basic cable TV service to more than 6.3 million customers, but it's been expanding its offerings to include digital TV (1.6 million subscribers), telecommunications, and Internet access (1.1 million subscribers). As part of the effort, Cox is deploying fiber-optic cable and upgrading its hybrid fiber-coaxial (HFC) networks.

Using its cable networks, the company offers local phone service and resells long-distance (Cox Digital Telephone). It also provides broadband Internet access via cable modems. Its Cox Business Services (a competitive local-exchange carrier) tackles the business market and provides voice and data services through dedicated fiber-optic and HFC networks.

Cox has investments in several telecom and technology firms, including TiVo (personal video recorders). It also has TV programming interests, which include stakes in Discovery Communications (25%).

Diversified media firm Cox Enterprises holds a majority interest in Cox Communications, controlling 76% of the company's voting stock.

James M. Cox bought the *Dayton Evening News* in 1898 (renamed the *Dayton Daily News*). Soon after he founded the News League of Ohio newspaper chain. Cox was elected to Congress in 1909 and became Ohio's governor in 1913. He was the Democratic Party's presidential nominee in 1920, with Franklin D. Roosevelt as his running mate, but lost to fellow Ohio newspaper publisher Warren G. Harding. Cox returned to Dayton to build a media empire.

In 1934 Cox established Dayton's first radio station (WHIO) in 1934. By the time Cox died in 1957, his media holdings encompassed the new television industry. His son, James Cox Jr., took over, and in 1962 Cox became one of the first broadcasting firms to invest in cable TV (in Pennsylvania). Two years later Cox split the broadcasting (Cox Broadcasting) and newspaper (Cox Enterprises) operations, and Cox Broadcasting acquired cable systems in California, Oregon, and Washington.

The company entered the auto auction business and continued to acquire cable systems in 1968; it also created Cox Cable Communications as a subsidiary. Cox made plans to merge with American Television and Communications in 1972, but the deal was dropped a year later when the Justice Department claimed it would violate antitrust laws. Another proposed merger, with

LVO Cable, was scrapped because of market conditions. Then General Electric began talks to buy Cox Broadcasting in 1979, but they ended with FCC complaints. The government finally caught up with Cox in 1989: The Justice Department brought suit after the company invested in Knight-Ridder in 1986 without SEC approval.

Meanwhile, James Cox Jr. died in 1974, and his brother-in-law Garner Anthony took the helm. In 1977 Cox Cable was merged with Cox Broadcasting, which was renamed Cox Communications in 1982. Three years later the company was purchased by Cox Enterprises.

In 1987 Anthony resigned and James Cox Kennedy, the founder's grandson, was named chairman. Two years later Cox acquired a stake in Blockbuster and became a franchisee, eventually owning 80 video stores, which were put up for sale in 1991.

That year Cox began testing PCS phones and a year later invested in Teleport Communications Group, acquiring 50.1% of the fiber optics company (sold to AT&T in 1998). In 1993 Cox began delivering cable and phone service in the UK through a partnership with SBC Cable-Comms (now Telewest). Two years later Cox teamed with TCI (now AT&T Broadband), Comcast, and Sprint and the alliance won licenses to deliver PCS service in 31 US markets. Also that year Cox acquired Times Mirror Cable Television and created the publicly traded subsidiary Cox Communications.

Cox expanded its cable TV systems in 1996 trades with TCI and U S WEST Media Group, and it began a partnership with Frontier to offer long-distance phone service. A year later the company launched facilities-based digital phone service in one California market and started digital video, Internet access, and local and long-distance switched phone service in another.

In 1999 Cox acquired TCA Cable TV and purchased cable systems from Media General; it also swapped systems with MediaOne and Time Warner Entertainment. It sold its stakes in TeleWest and Flextech in 2000. Also that year Cox acquired systems from Multimedia Cablevision and exchanged its stake in AT&T for cable TV systems.

News reports in 2001 named Cox as a potential bidder for AT&T Broadband, which the telecom giant plans to spin off. That year the company sold its stakes in Outdoor Life, Speedvision, and Cable Network Services to Fox Sports for $439.7 million.

OFFICERS

Chairman; Chairman and CEO, Cox Enterprises:
James Cox Kennedy, age 54
President, CEO, and Director: James O. Robbins,
age 59, $1,528,215 pay
EVP Finance and Administration, CFO, and Director:
Jimmy W. Hayes, age 49, $747,019 pay
EVP Operations: Patrick J. Esser, age 45, $660,339 pay
SVP Engineering and CTO: Christopher J. Bowick,
age 46
SVP Legal and Regulatory Affairs: James A. Hatcher,
age 50
SVP and CIO: Scott A. Hatfield
SVP Operations: John M. Dyer, age 48, $541,194 pay
SVP Operations: Claus F. Kroeger, age 50, $512,234 pay
SVP Strategy and Development: Dallas S. Clement,
age 37
VP Accounting and Financial Planning and Analysis:
William J. Fitzsimmons, age 49
VP Advertising Sales: F. William Farina
VP Business Development: Jayson R. Juraska
VP Communication and Investor Relations:
Ellen M. East
VP Customer Service: Kimberly C. Edmunds
VP Engineering Technology: Hugh A. McCarley
VP Telephony Engineering: Albert W. Young
VP Human Resources and Chief People Officer:
Mae A. Douglas
VP Marketing: Joseph J. Rooney
Auditors: Deloitte & Touche LLP

LOCATIONS

HQ: 1400 Lake Hearn Dr. NE, Atlanta, GA 30319
Phone: 404-843-5000   **Fax:** 404-843-5975
Web: www.cox.com

PRODUCTS/OPERATIONS

2001 Sales

	$ mil.	% of total
Residential		
Video	3,037	75
Data	278	7
Telephony	208	5
Other	62	1
Commercial	144	4
Advertising	338	8
Total	**4,067**	**100**

Selected Investments

Cable TV Programming
Discovery Communications, Inc. (25%, cable TV
networks)
In Demand, L.L.C. (11%, pay-per-view programming)
Product Information Network (45%, infomercial
distribution)

Telecommunications and Technology
Cox Interactive Media Joint Ventures (49%, advertising
supported Internet content)
National Cable Communications (17%, cable TV
advertising sales)
XO Nevada (formerly Nextlink Nevada, 38%,
telecommunications services)

COMPETITORS

Adelphia Communications	DIRECTV
AT&T Broadband	EchoStar
BellSouth	Communications
Cablevision Systems	SBC Communications
Charter Communications	Time Warner Cable
Comcast	Verizon

HISTORICAL FINANCIALS & EMPLOYEES

NYSE: COX FYE: December 31	Annual Growth	12/92	12/93	12/94	12/95	12/96	12/97	12/98	12/99	12/00	12/01
Sales ($ mil.)	22.6%	652	708	736	1,286	1,460	1,610	1,717	2,318	3,507	4,067
Net income ($ mil.)	26.2%	93	98	27	104	(52)	(137)	1,271	882	1,925	755
Income as % of sales	—	14.3%	13.8%	3.6%	8.1%	—	—	74.0%	38.0%	54.9%	18.6%
Earnings per share ($)	34.4%	—	—	—	0.21	(0.10)	(0.25)	2.30	1.51	3.16	1.24
Stock price - FY high ($)	—	—	—	—	10.75	12.06	20.16	35.38	52.00	58.38	50.25
Stock price - FY low ($)	—	—	—	—	7.00	8.31	9.00	17.19	32.00	31.69	36.40
Stock price - FY close ($)	27.5%	—	—	—	9.75	11.56	20.03	34.56	51.50	46.56	41.91
P/E - high	—	—	—	—	51	—	—	15	34	18	838
P/E - low	—	—	—	—	33	—	—	7	21	10	607
Dividends per share ($)	—	—	—	—	0.00	0.00	0.00	0.00	0.00	1.45	0.00
Book value per share ($)	24.5%	—	—	—	4.32	4.18	4.35	9.69	19.11	15.36	16.11
Employees	20.9%	—	4,529	4,375	6,695	7,200	7,700	9,785	12,348	19,000	20,700

STOCK PRICE HISTORY

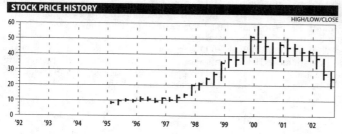

HIGH/LOW/CLOSE

2001 FISCAL YEAR-END

Debt ratio: 46.5%
Return on equity: 8.0%
Cash ($ mil.): 87
Current ratio: 0.75
Long-term debt ($ mil.): 8,418
No. of shares (mil.): 601
Dividends
  Yield: —
  Payout: —
Market value ($ mil.): 25,171

COX ENTERPRISES, INC.

Cox Enterprises is well beyond the printed word. The Atlanta-based company is one of the largest media firms in the US, with interests in newspapers, radio, and broadcast and cable TV. Cox publishes 17 daily newspapers (including its flagship, *The Atlanta Journal-Constitution*) and about 30 weeklies and shoppers in nine states and Washington, DC. It owns 15 TV stations through Cox Television and more than 80 radio stations through its 62% stake in Cox Radio. The company's biggest revenue generator, however, is cable system operator Cox Communications, in which the company controls a 76% voting stake. Cox Communications has more than 6 million subscribers in 23 states.

Cox is online as well, operating the profitable AutoTrader.com, which it operates in conjunction with its Manheim Auctions subsidiary. Manheim is the world's largest used-car auctioneer, with about 115 automobile auctions worldwide. The company's interactive unit operates more than 20 city-sites (such as AccessAtlanta.com). Cox announced in 2002 that it would restructure its interactive unit. Other operations include publishing newsletters and shopping circulars, TV ad sales, and direct mail advertising.

Barbara Cox Anthony (mother of chairman and CEO James Kennedy) and Anne Cox Chambers, daughters of founder James Cox, own the company. The sisters were recently ranked 11th in *Forbes'* list of the richest Americans.

HISTORY

James Middleton Cox, who dropped out of school in 1886 at 16, had worked as a teacher, reporter, and congressional secretary before buying the *Dayton Daily News* in 1898. After acquiring the nearby *Springfield Press-Republican* in 1905, he took up politics, serving two terms in the US Congress (1909-1913) and three terms as Ohio governor (1913-1915; 1917-1921). He even ran for president in 1920 (his running mate was future President Franklin Roosevelt) but lost to rival Ohio publisher Warren G. Harding.

Once out of politics, Cox began building his media empire. He bought the *Miami Daily News* in 1923 and founded WHIO (Dayton, Ohio's first radio station). He bought Atlanta's WSB ("Welcome South, Brother"), the South's first radio station, in 1939 and added WSB-FM and WSB-TV, the South's first FM and TV stations, in 1948. Cox founded Dayton's first FM and TV stations (WHIO-FM and WHIO-TV) the next year, and *The Atlanta Constitution* joined his collection in 1950. He died in 1957.

In the late 1950s and early 1960s the company continued expanding its broadcasting interests. It was one of the first major broadcasting companies to expand into cable TV when it purchased a system in Lewistown, Pennsylvania, in 1962. The Cox family's broadcast properties were placed in publicly held Cox Broadcasting in 1964. Two years later its newspapers were placed into privately held Cox Enterprises, and the cable holdings became publicly held Cox Cable Communications. The broadcasting arm diversified, buying Manheim Services (auto auctions, 1968), Kansas City Automobile Auction (1969), and TeleRep (TV ad sales, 1972).

Cox Cable had 500,000 subscribers in nine states when it rejoined Cox Broadcasting in 1977. Cox Broadcasting was renamed Cox Communications in 1982, and the Cox family took the company private again in 1985, combining it with Cox Enterprises. James Kennedy, grandson of founder James Cox, became chairman and CEO in 1987.

Expansion became the keyword for Cox in the 1990s. The company merged its Manheim unit with the auto auction business of Ford Motor Credit and GE Capital in 1991. It also formed Sprint Spectrum in 1994, a partnership with Sprint, TCI (now part of AT&T), and Comcast to bundle telephone, cable TV, and other communications services (Sprint bought out Cox in 1999). Then, in one of its biggest transactions, Cox bought Times Mirror's cable TV operations for $2.3 billion in 1995 and combined them with its own cable system into a new, publicly traded company called Cox Communications. The following year it spun off its radio holdings into a public company called Cox Radio.

To expand its online presence, the company formed Cox Interactive Media in 1996, establishing a series of city Web sites and making a host of investments in various Internet companies, including CareerPath, Excite@Home, iVillage, MP3.com, and Tickets.com. Cox also applied the online strategy to its automobile auction businesses, establishing AutoTrader.com in 1998 and placing the Internet operations of Manheim Auctions into a new company, Manheim Interactive, in 2000. Manheim spent $1 billion in acquiring ADT Automotive from Tyco International in 2000 and plans on spending another $1 billion over the next five years improving and expanding its operations. Plans for an AutoTrader.com IPO in 2000 were scrapped. In mid-2002 the company cut about 75 jobs from its Cox Interactive unit and dropped a plan to develop a nationwide network of local city Web sites.

OFFICERS

Chairman and CEO: James Cox Kennedy, age 54
President and COO: G. Dennis Berry, age 58
EVP and CFO: Robert C. O'Leary, age 63
SVP Administration: Timothy W. Hughes
SVP Public Policy: Alexander V. Netchvolodoff, age 65
VP and CIO: Gregory B. Morrison, age 43
VP and General Tax Counsel: Preston B. Barnett
VP and Treasurer: Richard J. Jacobson, age 45
VP Business Development: John C. Mellott, age 44
VP Direct Marketing and Database Management:
Tom Whitfield
VP Human Resources: Marybeth H. Leamer, age 45
VP Legal Affairs and Secretary: Andrew A. Merdek
VP Marketing and Communications: John C. Williams
VP Materials Management: Michael J. Mannheimer,
age 54
VP Public Policy: Alexandra M. Wilson
President and CEO, AutoTrader.com: Victor A. Perry III,
age 48
President and CEO, Cox Communications, Inc.:
James O. Robbins, age 59
President, Cox Newspapers, Inc.: Jay R. Smith, age 52
President and CEO, Cox Radio: Robert F. Neil, age 43
President, Cox Television: Andrew S. Fisher, age 54

LOCATIONS

HQ: 6500 Peachtree Dunwoody Rd., Atlanta, GA 30328
Phone: 678-645-0000 **Fax:** 678-645-1079
Web: www.coxenterprises.com

PRODUCTS/OPERATIONS

2001 Sales

	$ mil.	% of total
Cable TV	4,071	47
Auctions	2,260	26
Newspapers	1,350	15
TV stations	617	7
Radio stations	395	5
Total	**8,693**	**100**

Selected Operations

Cox Communications (76%, cable system)
Cox Interactive Media (city sites)
Cox Newspapers
  Daily Newspapers
    The Atlanta Journal-Constitution
    Austin American-Statesman (Texas)
    The Daily Reflector (Greenville, NC)
    Dayton Daily News (Ohio)
    Longview News-Journal (Texas)
    Palm Beach Daily News (Florida)
    The Palm Beach Post (Florida)
    Rocky Mount Telegram (North Carolina)
    Springfield News Sun (Ohio)
  Cox Custom Media
  Valpack (direct mail advertisements)
Cox Radio (62%)
Cox Television
  TV stations
    KFOX (El Paso, TX)
    KICU (San Francisco/San Jose, CA)
    KIRO (Seattle)
    KRXI (Reno, NV)
    KTVU (Oakland/San Francisco, CA)
    WAXN (Charlotte, NC)
    WFTV (Orlando, FL)
    WHIO (Dayton, OH)
    WPXI (Pittsburgh)
    WRDQ (Orlando, FL)
    WSB-TV (Atlanta)
    WSOC (Charlotte, NC)
Manheim Auctions
  Manheim Interactive (online auto auctions)
  AutoTrader.com (majority owned, online auto sales)
Sports teams
  Atlanta Beat (women's professional soccer)
  San Diego Spirit (women's professional soccer)

COMPETITORS

Advance	Gannett	Ticketmaster
Publications	Hearst	Time Warner
AT&T Broadband	Knight Ridder	Cable
Belo	Media General	Tribune
Clear Channel	Morris	Viacom
Comcast	Communications	Walt Disney
Dow Jones	New York Times	Washington Post
E. W. Scripps	News Corp.	

HISTORICAL FINANCIALS & EMPLOYEES

Private FYE: December 31	Annual Growth	12/92	12/93	12/94	12/95	12/96	12/97	12/98	12/99	12/00	12/01
Sales ($ mil.)	14.9%	2,495	2,675	2,939	3,806	4,591	4,936	5,355	6,097	7,824	8,693
Employees	10.5%	30,865	31,000	37,000	38,000	43,000	50,000	55,500	61,000	74,000	76,000

SALES HISTORY

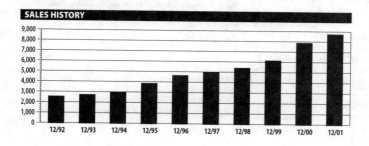

C. R. BARD, INC.

If you laid all of C.R. Bard's catheters end to end — ouch! That would hurt.

The Murray Hill, New Jersey-based company makes diagnostic and treatment devices for oncological, urological, and vascular procedures. These devices include stents; catheters (including its Foley urology catheter); guidewires; implantable fabrics and meshes; and fluid collection systems. Bard also makes special surgical tools, including devices for laparoscopic and orthopedic procedures and for hernia repair.

Having shed its cardiopulmonary operations to focus on products for urology, oncology, and other vascular care, Bard has reorganized around disease-state management lines, delivering products along the continuum of care (prevention, treatment, and cure). The company continues to expand its product lines through development. It has also opted out of its agreement to be bought by Tyco, not long after the conglomerate ran into trouble with its investors regarding its decision to split into four companies.

HISTORY

When visiting Europe at the turn of the century, silk importer Charles Russell Bard discovered that gomenol, a mixture of olive oil with a eucalyptus extract, offered him relief from urinary problems caused by tuberculosis. He brought gomenol to America and began distributing it.

In 1907 C. R. Bard began selling a ureteral catheter developed by French firm J. Eynard. The company incorporated in 1923 with its present name. When Charles Bard's health declined in 1926, he sold the business to John Willits and Edson Outwin (his sales manager and accountant, respectively).

In 1934 Bard became the sole agent for Davol Rubber's new Foley catheter, which helped the company achieve $1 million in sales by 1948. During the 1950s, sales increased more than 400% when the firm introduced its first presterilized packaged product and expanded its product line to include disposable drainage tubes and an intravenous feeding device.

Bard went public in 1963. During the 1960s the firm expanded both vertically, boosting its manufacturing capabilities (it began making its own plastic tubing), and through acquisitions. It also established joint ventures with Davol to manufacture and distribute hospital and surgical supplies internationally.

The company diversified into the cardiovascular, respiratory therapy, home care products, and kidney dialysis fields in the 1970s and introduced the first angioplasty catheter, a nonsurgical device to clear blocked arteries, in 1979.

In 1984 Bard watched its urological business go limp. In response, the company began a buying spree to gain market share in a consolidating hospital products industry. It swallowed up around a dozen companies, including Davol (maker of its best-selling Foley catheter), garnering such products as catheters and other products for angioplasty, diagnostic, and urinary incontinence. In 1988 it faced increasing competition in the coronary catheter market from such giants as Eli Lilly and Pfizer. Bard struck back with innovative products, but it was too little too late — even though the company continued to struggle for 10 more years, it finally pulled out of the cardiovascular market.

Bard agreed in 1993 to pay a then-record $61 million for mislabeling and improperly testing angioplasty catheters blamed for the deaths of two people (and later taken off the market). However, a year later Bard's sales topped $1 billion for the first time, and it purchased catheter-related companies in Canada, France, and Germany.

Purchases in 1995 and 1996 included medical device manufacturers MedChem Products and the Cardiac Assist Division of St. Jude Medical. In 1996 Bard bought a majority stake in Italy-based X-Trode and acquired IMPRA, a leading supplier of vascular grafts (its largest deal ever). That year the ongoing catheter litigation snared three former Bard executives, who received 18-month prison sentences for conspiring to hide potentially fatal flaws in the products.

In 1998 Bard reorganized along disease-state management lines. Over the next two years, it sold its cardiovascular line after deciding it was going to cost too much time and money to re-establish dominance in that field. Bard built its other fields through purchases, including ProSeed (radiation seed therapy, 1998) and Dymax (ultrasound catheter guidance systems, 1999). The next year Bard partnered with medical device distributor Owens & Minor to launch an online purchasing site.

OFFICERS

Chairman and CEO: William H. Longfield, age 63, $2,104,029 pay
Group President: Guy J. Jordan, age 53, $657,894 pay
Group President: Timothy M. Ring, age 44, $766,269 pay
Group President: John H. Weiland, age 46, $779,103 pay
SVP and CFO: Charles P. Slacik, age 47, $694,234 pay
VP, Medical Affairs: James R. Adwers, age 57
VP, Regulatory Sciences: Susan Alpert, age 56
VP, Secretary, and General Counsel: Nadia J. Bernstein, age 57

VP, Operations: Joseph A. Cherry
VP, Quality Assurance: Christopher D. Ganser, age 48
VP, Government and Public Relations: Holly P. Glass
VP and Controller: Charles P. Grom, age 54
VP, Information Technology: Vincent J. Gunari Jr.
VP, Human Resources: Bronwen K. Kelly
VP; President, Corporate Healthcare Services:
James L. Natale
VP, Strategic Planning and Business Development:
Robert L. Mellen
VP and Treasurer: Todd C. Schermerhorn, age 41
Assistant Secretary: Jean F. Miller
Auditors: KPMG LLP

LOCATIONS

HQ: 730 Central Ave., Murray Hill, NJ 07974
Phone: 908-277-8000   **Fax:** 908-277-8240
Web: www.crbard.com

C. R. Bard has plants or offices in Australia, Austria,
Belgium, Canada, China, Denmark, Finland, France,
Germany, Greece, India, Italy, North Korea, Malaysia,
Mexico, the Netherlands, Norway, Portugal, Singapore,
Spain, Sweden, Switzerland, the UK, and the US.

Selected Subsidiaries
American Hydro-Surgical Instruments, Inc.
Angiomed GmbH (Germany)
C.R. Bard GmbH (Germany)
Davol Inc.
Davol International Limited (UK)
Productos Bard de Mexico S.A. de C.V.
ProSeed, Inc.
Vas-Cath, Inc. (Canada)

COMPETITORS

Arrow International
Baxter
Becton Dickinson
Boston Scientific
Guidant
Johnson & Johnson
Maxxim Medical
Medline Industries
St. Jude Medical
United States Surgical

PRODUCTS/OPERATIONS

2001 Sales

	$ mil.	% of total
Urology	390	33
Oncology	275	23
Vascular	251	21
Surgery	205	17
Other	60	6
Total	**1,181**	**100**

HISTORICAL FINANCIALS & EMPLOYEES

NYSE: BCR FYE: December 31	Annual Growth	12/92	12/93	12/94	12/95	12/96	12/97	12/98	12/99	12/00	12/01
Sales ($ mil.)	2.0%	990	971	1,018	1,138	1,194	1,214	1,165	1,037	1,099	1,181
Net income ($ mil.)	7.5%	75	56	75	87	93	72	252	118	107	143
Income as % of sales	—	7.6%	5.8%	7.4%	7.6%	7.7%	6.0%	21.7%	11.4%	9.7%	12.1%
Earnings per share ($)	7.6%	1.42	0.89	1.33	1.52	1.61	1.26	4.51	2.28	2.09	2.75
Stock price - FY high ($)	—	35.88	35.25	30.50	32.25	37.38	39.00	50.25	59.88	54.94	64.95
Stock price - FY low ($)	—	22.50	20.50	22.25	25.50	25.88	26.38	28.50	41.69	35.00	40.86
Stock price - FY close ($)	7.7%	33.13	25.25	27.00	32.25	28.00	31.31	49.50	53.00	46.56	64.50
P/E - high	—	25	35	23	21	23	31	11	26	26	23
P/E - low	—	16	20	17	17	16	21	6	18	17	15
Dividends per share ($)	5.9%	0.50	0.54	0.58	0.62	0.66	0.70	0.74	0.58	0.82	0.84
Book value per share ($)	8.2%	7.43	7.35	8.45	9.89	10.56	10.09	11.02	11.31	12.06	15.06
Employees	(1.5%)	8,850	8,450	8,650	9,400	9,800	9,550	7,700	7,700	8,100	7,700

STOCK PRICE HISTORY HIGH/LOW/CLOSE

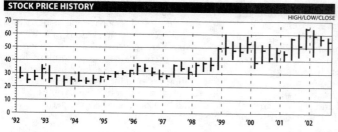

2001 FISCAL YEAR-END
Debt ratio: 16.5%
Return on equity: 20.4%
Cash ($ mil.): 31
Current ratio: 2.76
Long-term debt ($ mil.): 156
No. of shares (mil.): 52
Dividends
  Yield: 1.3%
  Payout: 30.5%
Market value ($ mil.): 3,379

CRANE CO.

When it comes to acquisitions, Crane Co. is accustomed to heavy lifting — it has bought close to 20 companies in the past five years. The Stamford, Connecticut-based company's businesses turn out everything from aircraft components (braking systems, fuel pumps) to vending machines. Its other operations include fluid handling (valves and water-treatment systems), engineered materials (fiberglass panels for trucks), and controls (control valves and regulating switches). Customers include the aerospace, construction, defense, fluid-handling, and food and beverage industries. Crane Co. strives to maintain a competitive advantage by building dominant positions in a number of niche markets through acquisitions.

Crane Co. will attempt to increase its commercial aerospace holdings and microelectronics business. Additionally, the company will boost its inter-company sales of current products into new markets in its control, pump, and valve businesses. The Crane Fund, a charitable trust, owns about 13% of Crane Co.

HISTORY

Crane was founded in 1855 by Richard Teller Crane as a small foundry in a lumberyard owned by his uncle, Martin Ryerson. Crane grew along with Chicago and its railroads. Its first big order was to supply parts to a maker of railroad cars. In 1872 the company began making passenger elevators through the Crane Elevator Company, which was sold in 1895 to a joint venture that became the Otis Elevator Company. Although it had made plumbing materials since 1886, Crane developed a broader line during the 1920s and became a household name. The company remained under the leadership of the Crane family until Thomas Mellon Evans was elected as chief executive in 1959. Evans diversified the company through acquisitions that included Huttig Sash & Door (1968) and CF&I Steel (1969). Crane also added basic materials with its purchase of Medusa (cement and aggregates) in 1979.

Evans' son, Robert, took over as Crane's chairman in 1984 and began restructuring the company. That year Crane sold its U.S. Plumbing division, and the next year it spun off CF&I Steel to its shareholders. The company then began buying manufacturing companies in the defense, aerospace, fluid controls, vending machine, fiberglass panel, and electronic components markets. Crane expanded its Ferguson Machine business with the purchase of PickOmatic Systems of Detroit (mechanical parts-handling equipment), then boosted its wood building distribution

segment with the 1988 acquisitions of Pozzi-Renati Millwork Products and Palmer G. Lewis.

In 1990 Crane acquired Lear Romec (pumps for the aerospace industry) and Crown Pumps' diaphragm pump business. In the early 1990s the company continued its successful strategy of selective buying, adding Jenkins Canada (bronze and iron valves, 1992), Rondel's millwork distributions (1993), Burks Pumps (1993), and Mark Controls (valves, instruments and controls, 1994).

Crane picked up Interpoint (DC-DC power converters) and Grenson Electronics (low-voltage power conversion components, UK) in 1996. The next year Crane bought five businesses, the largest of which was Stockham Valves & Fittings. The company's 1998 acquisitions included Environmental Products USA (water-purification systems), Consolidated Lumber Company (wholesale distributor of lumber and millwork products), Sequentia Holdings (fiberglass-reinforced plastic panels), Liberty Technologies (diagnostic equipment for the power and process industries), and the plastic-lined piping products division of Dow Chemical. Crane also sold two of its foundries in Tennessee and Alabama that year.

In 1999 the company bought Stentorfield (beverage vending machines, UK). Late in the year Crane spun off its distribution subsidiary, Huttig Sash & Door. Huttig sold a 32% stake to UK-based Rugby Group in return for Rugby's US building products business. The combined company was named the Huttig Building Products.

Crane planned to sell two of its telecommunication power supply product lines to Power-One in 2000. That year the company purchased Streamware, a provider of management software for the food service and vending industry, to complement its vending machine business.

In 2001 Crane acquired the industrial flow business of Alfa Laval, Ventech Controls (valve repair), and Laminated Profiles (fiberglass-reinforced panels, UK). In March 2001 the investment firm led by Mario Gabelli increased its stake in Crane to nearly 8%. Crane acquired valve manufacturer Xomox (renamed Crane Process Flow) from Emerson in June and sold its Power Process Controls business (fluid and gas measurement and control) to Watts Industries in October.

Crane continued to add complementary businesses in 2002, purchasing Lasco Composites LP, a Florence, Kentucky manufacturer of fiberglass-reinforced plastic panels, from Tomkins Industries, Inc., a subsidiary of Tomkinsons plc, for $44 million. Later in the year Crane acquired the US-based valve and actuator distributor, Corva Corporation; Corva will become part of Crane's North America valve company.

OFFICERS

Chairman: Robert S. Evans, age 57, $2,518,516 pay
President, CEO, and Director: Eric C. Fast, age 52, $974,578 pay
VP, Finance and CFO: Michael L. Raithel, $572,424 pay
VP, General Counsel, and Secretary: Augustus I. duPont, $457,885 pay
VP and CIO: Bradley L. Ellis, $364,918 pay
VP, Taxes: Thomas N. Noonan, $386,361 pay
VP, Environment, Health, and Safety: Anthony D. Pantaleoni
VP, Human Resources: Elise M. Kopczick
Treasurer: Gil A. Dickoff
Director, Investor Relations and Strategic Planning: Pamela J. S. Styles
Auditors: Deloitte & Touche LLP

LOCATIONS

HQ: 100 First Stamford Place, Stamford, CT 06902
Phone: 203-363-7300   **Fax:** 203-363-7295
Web: www.craneco.com

Crane Co. has more than 30 manufacturing facilities in the US and two in Canada, as well as 24 international sites.

2001 Sales

	$ mil.	% of total
North America		
US	932	59
Canada	184	11
Europe	329	21
Other regions	142	9
Total	**1,587**	**100**

PRODUCTS/OPERATIONS

2001 Sales

	$ mil.	% of total
Fluid handling	585	37
Aerospace	395	25
Engineered materials	291	18
Merchandising systems	216	14
Controls	102	6
Adjustments	(2)	
Total	**1,587**	**100**

Business Segments and Selected Subsidiaries

Azonix Corporation (measurement and control systems)
Barksdale Inc. (pressure switches and transducers)
Crane Ltd. (UK; commercial valves)
Crane Nuclear, Inc. (valve products for the nuclear power industry)
Crane Pumps and Systems (pumps for water, wastewater, chemicals, and power generation)
ELDEC Corporation (sensing and control systems for aircraft)
Ferguson Company (precision motion-control products)
Hydro-Aire, Inc. (anti-skid brake control systems)
Kemlite Company, Inc. (fiberglass-reinforced plastic panels)
National Vendors (vending equipment and systems)
Resistoflex (lined-piping products)

COMPETITORS

AZKOYEN	Kohler
Chori	Kubota
Dover	Legris
Goodrich	Parker Hannifin
IMI	Precision Castparts
K & F Industries	Swagelok

HISTORICAL FINANCIALS & EMPLOYEES

NYSE: CR FYE: December 31	Annual Growth	12/92	12/93	12/94	12/95	12/96	12/97	12/98	12/99	12/00	12/01
Sales ($ mil.)	2.2%	1,307	1,310	1,654	1,782	1,848	2,037	2,269	1,554	1,491	1,587
Net income ($ mil.)	15.5%	24	49	56	76	92	113	138	115	124	89
Income as % of sales	—	1.9%	3.7%	3.4%	4.3%	5.0%	5.5%	6.1%	7.4%	8.3%	5.6%
Earnings per share ($)	17.3%	0.35	0.73	0.83	1.12	1.35	1.63	2.00	1.70	2.02	1.47
Stock price – FY high ($)	—	12.40	13.74	13.12	17.57	21.02	31.52	37.60	32.75	29.50	32.25
Stock price – FY low ($)	—	9.68	10.07	10.73	11.51	16.02	18.34	21.75	16.06	18.63	19.95
Stock price – FY close ($)	10.4%	10.51	11.01	11.96	16.41	19.34	28.93	30.19	19.88	28.44	25.64
P/E – high	—	35	19	16	16	16	19	19	19	15	22
P/E – low	—	28	14	13	10	12	11	11	9	9	14
Dividends per share ($)	2.2%	0.33	0.33	0.33	0.33	0.33	0.33	0.37	0.40	0.40	0.40
Book value per share ($)	11.7%	4.03	4.33	4.86	5.53	6.76	7.80	9.39	9.05	10.04	10.91
Employees	1.4%	8,500	8,700	10,700	8,500	10,700	11,000	12,500	9,000	9,000	9,600

STOCK PRICE HISTORY

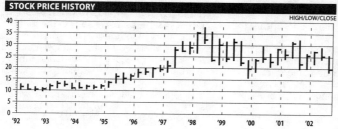

HIGH/LOW/CLOSE

2001 FISCAL YEAR-END

Debt ratio: 31.7%
Return on equity: 14.1%
Cash ($ mil.): 21
Current ratio: 2.10
Long-term debt ($ mil.): 302
No. of shares (mil.): 60
Dividends
 Yield: 1.6%
 Payout: 27.2%
Market value ($ mil.): 1,530

CREDIT SUISSE FIRST BOSTON

The cooling economy hasn't made Swiss cheese out of Credit Suisse First Boston (CSFB) yet. The New York-based firm, a subsidiary of Swiss bank Credit Suisse, is one of the largest international investment banking companies in the world.

The company advises clients on mergers and acquisitions, IPOs (it is one of the world's top IPO underwriters), and privatizations of government companies. It also offers Credit Suisse financial products (the firm accounts for more than half of its parent's revenues) and derivatives-based products. Although its fixed-income business has taken a few hits, CSFB's fee-rich financial services group has helped bolster revenues.

The purchase of Donaldson, Lufkin & Jenrette created a powerhouse for underwriting and mergers and acquisitions, but built on a shaky foundation: A number of top-ranking DLJ officers defected to rivals, and their loss took its toll on CSFB's bottom line. The firm has also been hit hard by the faltering economy and an SEC investigation (regarding IPO distribution) that resulted in a $100 million fine. The NASD recently fined and suspended two top-tier executives for similar violations. To regain its status, CSFB planned an overhaul of its organization and replaced CEO Allen Wheat with former Morgan Stanley Dean Witter head John Mack.

The slow market and irresponsible management hit CSFB hard. Mack responded with a plan to refocus the business through a variety of measures, including cutting approximately 7% of its workforce, slimming down many of its more lucrative employee compensation contracts, and selling CSFBdirect to Bank of Montreal for $520 million. But those measures were not without a cost; the company took a $745 million charge in the fourth quarter of 2001 to cover the layoffs and restructuring. That, coupled with a $213 million loss in Argentina, $126 million loss in Enron, as well as SEC fines of more than $100 million, led to a loss of $1 billion in the quarter. With the investment banking sector still weak, Mack predicts the company's turnaround won't be completed until well into 2003.

HISTORY

Credit Suisse First Boston traces its lineage to an underwriting subsidiary of First National Bank of Boston. Founded as Safety Fund Bank in 1859, the bank entered the national bank system in 1864 and changed its name. First National merged with the venerable Massachusetts National Bank of Boston (founded 1784) but kept the First National name.

In response to the Glass-Steagall Act of 1933, which restricted banks to either commercial or investment banking, First National Bank of Boston and Chase National Bank spun off their securities underwriting affiliates to create First Boston Corp. That year the company opened a London office. The firm suffered during the lean years of the 1930s, but WWII and an increased demand for capital brought it out of its slump. A draining antitrust lawsuit and a disastrous deal to finance a Puerto Rican oil refinery took their toll in the 1940s.

The company — conservative, not aggressive — lost ground against competition in the 1960s. A rising bond market in the 1970s helped, and in 1972 the firm focused on increasing foreign business. It restructured in 1976, creating First Boston, Inc.

In 1978 First Boston and Swiss banking concern Credit Suisse (CS) created Credit Suisse-First Boston (40%-owned by First Boston). CS created 44%-owned holding company Credit Suisse First Boston (CSFB) to own its interests in First Boston, CSFB, and CS First Boston Pacific.

After 1987's stock market crash, First Boston took heavy losses from loans related to mergers and acquisitions. The next year the firm merged with CSFB to form Credit Suisse First Boston (also called CSFB). In 1990 CS injected $300 million into CSFB and shifted $470 million in bad loans from CSFB's books in return for control of the business (becoming the first foreign owner of a major Wall Street investment bank). By 1992 CSFB had repaid its debt to CS, but the organizations did not meld smoothly. Attempts to curb salaries and bonuses at the investment bank led to staff defections in 1993.

From 1992 to 1994, CSFB invested in Russia, setting up a Moscow office and investing in oil and gas stocks. In 1997 the company opened a branch in Seoul and established 75%-owned securities firm Credit Suisse First Boston (India) Securities in Bombay. It got a seat on the Bombay exchange in 1998.

Although the firm in 1998 bought part of Barclays' equity and investment banking businesses in Asia (the price, around $170 million, was considered a steal by many analysts), the late 1990s were not entirely kind to CSFB. In 1998 it agreed to pay $52.5 million to Orange County, California, to settle claims relating to the county's infamous 1994 bankruptcy. The firm also suffered when Russia's economy collapsed and its currency was devalued; CSFB moved to salvage its position by working with Russian companies in default.

In 1999 a CSFB affiliate had its securities license revoked in Japan for obstructing an investigation. The next year, in a preview of things to come, the firm wound up in court with Prudential Securities, which was miffed that Credit Suisse had lured away a number of executives.

In 2000 CSFB bought Donaldson, Lufkin & Jenrette. It announced plans to cut 10% of the combined staff and promptly lost a handful of key DLJ employees to rival firms. The following year CSFB recruited former UK prime minister John Major as a senior adviser. As the hopes of an equities-obsessed culture waned, CSFBdirect, CSFB's online brokerage department, laid off almost a quarter of its employees. CSFB also attracted scrutiny from the SEC and the US Justice Department regarding the way it allocated and promoted scarce IPO shares and the alleged excessive fees it charged to underwrite them. Also in 2001, the company made plans to slash staff at its international private equity division by a third. CSFB also decided to sell DLJdirect, its online European trading division, to TD Waterhouse and made plans to sell CSFBdirect, its US online brokerage, to the Bank of Montreal.

OFFICERS

Chairman: Stephen R. Volk, age 65
Senior Advisor: Joe L. Roby, age 62
Vice Chairman and CEO: John J. Mack, age 57
Vice Chairman and Head of Asset Management: Jeffrey M. Peek, age 55
Vice Chairman, Executive Board, CFO and Head of Support: Richard E. Thornburgh, age 49
Chairman, CSFB Foundation Trust: Joseph T. McLaughlin
Chairman, International: David C. Mulford
Chairman, Pacific: Stephen E. Stonefield
CEO, Europe, Middle East, and Africa: Hector Sants, age 45
COO, Europe: Costas Michaelides, age 52
Global Head of Investment Banking: Adebayo Ogunlesi
Chief Administrative Officer: Thomas R. Nides, age 40
Chairman, Europe: Christopher Carter, age 51

Head of Equity Derivatives and Convertibles: Paul Calello
Head of Equity: Brady W. Dougan
Auditors: KPMG Klynveld Peat Marwick Goerdeler SA

LOCATIONS

HQ: Credit Suisse First Boston Corporation
11 Madison Ave., New York, NY 10010
Phone: 212-325-2000 **Fax:** 212-325-8249
Web: www.csfb.com

Credit Suisse First Boston has about 75 offices in nearly 40 countries.

PRODUCTS/OPERATIONS

Selected Subsidiaries
Credit Suisse First Boston (USA), Inc.
CSFBdirect Inc.
Pershing
Sprout Group (venture capital)

COMPETITORS

Barclays
Bear Stearns
Charles Schwab
Deutsche Banc Alex. Brown
Goldman Sachs
HSBC Holdings
J.P. Morgan H&Q
Merrill Lynch
Morgan Stanley
Salomon Smith Barney Holdings
TD Waterhouse
UBS PaineWebber

HISTORICAL FINANCIALS & EMPLOYEES

Subsidiary FYE: December 31	Annual Growth	12/92	12/93	12/94	12/95	12/96	12/97	12/98	12/99	12/00	12/01
Sales ($ mil.)	20.0%	—	—	—	—	5,493	7,128	6,713	9,133	12,635	13,662
Net income ($ mil.)	12.3%	—	—	—	—	—	826	(154)	1,182	1,461	1,313
Income as % of sales	—	—	—	—	—	—	11.6%	—	12.9%	11.6%	9.6%
Employees	35.7%	—	—	—	—	—	6,183	11,863	14,126	15,185	28,000	28,415

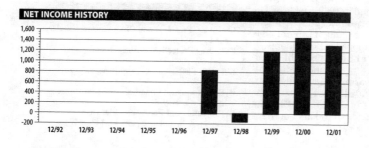

NET INCOME HISTORY

CROMPTON CORPORATION

Crompton always gets mixed results from its chemicals and additives. The company, based in Greenwich, Connecticut, was formed from the merger of Crompton & Knowles and Witco (and was known briefly as CK Witco). The company produces chemicals used in products such as tires, paper, and auto parts. The company's specialty chemicals unit makes rubber chemicals and additives, crop-protection chemicals, and additives for plastics and lubricants. Its Davis-Standard subsidiary makes plastic and rubber extrusion and molding equipment.

Crompton is cutting costs by closing facilities (it's closing six plants) and reducing its workforce. It also is considering selling its industrial surfactants operations to focus on specialty chemicals and polymers.

The company has been hurt by the unfavorable coupling of the sputtering US economy with high energy and raw material costs.

HISTORY

William Crompton started Crompton Loom Works in 1837 in Worcester, Massachusetts, after developing a better version of the textile loom. Twenty-five years later, Lucius Knowles, who became Crompton's nemesis and then his partner, started L.J. Knowles & Bros. in Warren, Massachusetts, featuring his own improved version of the loom. When Knowles moved his company to Worcester in 1879, the two began an intense rivalry that lasted nearly 20 years before the two firms merged in 1897 to form Crompton & Knowles Loom Works.

The new company opened offices in Philadelphia and North Carolina and became known for its machines, which could weave different colors together. By WWII it was one of the world's largest makers of textile machinery.

The company branched into the dye and chemical business in 1954 by purchasing Althouse Chemical Company. In 1956 it changed its name to Crompton & Knowles Corporation and in 1960 began making flavors, food colorings, and fragrances. The next year it bought the Davis-Standard Company, a maker of plastics-processing machinery and in 1969 established its first European subsidiary, in Belgium. A decade later Crompton & Knowles bought DuPont's dye business and in 1981 stopped making looms.

In 1988 Crompton & Knowles bought Ingredient Technology, a leading supplier of ingredients for the food and pharmaceutical industries, and Townley Dyestuffs Auxiliaries Company, one of the largest suppliers of dyes in the UK. The company divested pesticide subsidiary Southern Mill Creek Products.

Crompton & Knowles made two acquisitions in 1990: Atlantic Industries, a US dye manufacturer, and APV Chemical Machinery, maker of the Sterling line of plastic extruders and blow-molding equipment. It made other acquisitions throughout the 1990s in polymers, dyes, and plastics-processing equipment. In 1995 it bought the worldwide crop-protection business of Solvay Duphar and Killion Extruders, maker of small-scale extrusion systems.

In 1996 Crompton & Knowles bought Uniroyal Chemical, a manufacturer of pesticides, rubber, rubber chemicals, and additives. The acquisition helped offset sluggish sales in the company's dyestuffs and food-ingredients units with strong sales from Uniroyal's additives and pesticides products. Also in 1996 the company bought Klöckner ER-WE-PA, a German maker of extrusion coating, cast film, and plastic extrusion equipment. It also bought the Hartig line of plastic blow-molding machines from Battenfeld Gloucester Engineering.

Crompton & Knowles closed its Painesville, Ohio, synthetic rubber plant and moved those operations to its Mexican joint venture with Desc SA in 1999. It also sold its pharmaceutical and food-ingredients division to Denmark's Christian Hansen Holding for $103 million.

Crompton & Knowles in 1999 completed an estimated $2 billion merger with Witco Corporation, another Connecticut-based chemicals company that was founded in 1925. Crompton & Knowles changed its name to CK Witco and later that year announced job cuts and plant consolidations. It also sold its global textile colors and European industrial colors divisions to UK-based dye producer Yorkshire Group.

CK Witco changed its name to Crompton Corporation in 2000, and announced that it was exploring the sale of its industrial surfactants business. The next year Crompton announced that it would close six plants and reduce its workforce by about 8% to cut costs. In October the company announced that it would move its headquarters to Middlebury, Connecticut, by the end of 2002.

OFFICERS

Chairman, President and CEO: Vincent A. Calarco, age 59, $861,667 pay

EVP, Crop Protection: Alfred F. Ingulli, age 60, $541,667 pay

EVP, OSi Specialties and Urethanes: Mary L. Gum, age 54

EVP, Performance Chemicals and Elastomers: James J. Conway, age 58

EVP, Plastics and Petroleum Additives: William A. Stephenson, age 54, $431,667 pay

EVP, Polymer Processing Equipment: Robert W. Ackley, age 60
SVP and CFO: Peter Barna, age 58
SVP and General Counsel: John T. Ferguson II, age 55
SVP, Operations: Walter K. Ruck, age 59
SVP, Organization and Administration: Marvin H. Happel, age 62
SVP, Strategy and Development: Edward L. Hagen, age 60
VP and Treasurer: John R. Jepsen, age 46
VP, Olefins and Styrenics: William H. Murrell
VP, Vinyl Additives: Peter Welch
Regional VP, Asia-Pacific: Mark Harakal
Regional VP, Europe, Africa, and the Middle East: Gerald H. Fickenscher, age 58, $387,500 pay
Regional VP, Latin America: Michel J. Duchesne
Auditors: KPMG LLP

LOCATIONS

HQ: One American Lane, Greenwich, CT 06831
Phone: 203-552-2000 **Fax:** 203-552-2870
Web: www.cromptoncorp.com

Crompton Corporation has more than 50 manufacturing facilities in 20 countries.

2001 Sales

	$ mil.	% of total
North America		
US	1,360	50
Canada	123	5
Europe/Africa	764	28
Asia/Pacific	288	11
Latin America	184	6
Total	**2,719**	**100**

PRODUCTS/OPERATIONS

2001 Sales

	$ mil.	% of total
Polymer Products		
Polymer additives	879	32
Polymers	289	11
Polymer-processing equipment	202	7
Specialty Chemicals		
OrganoSilicones	432	16
Crop-protection products	412	15
Other specialty chemicals	519	19
Adjustments	(14)	—
Total	**2,719**	**100**

Selected Products

Electronic controls	Miticides
EPDM rubber	Plastics additives
Extruders	Rubber chemicals
Fungicides	Seed treatments
Growth regulants	Silanes
Herbicides	Specialty silicones
Insecticides	Surfactants
Integrated extrusion systems	Urethanes

COMPETITORS

American Vanguard	Milliken
BASF Corporation	Mitsubishi Chemical
Bayer AG	Mitsui Chemicals
Ciba Specialty Chemicals	PMC Global
Degussa	Terra Industries
Holliday Chemical	Terra Nitrogen
Jilin Chemical	United-Guardian

HISTORICAL FINANCIALS & EMPLOYEES

NYSE: CK FYE: Saturday nearest Dec. 31	Annual Growth	12/92	12/93	12/94	12/95	12/96	12/97	12/98	12/99	12/00	12/01
Sales ($ mil.)	20.2%	518	558	590	666	1,804	1,851	1,796	2,092	3,038	2,719
Net income ($ mil.)	—	35	52	51	41	(23)	87	162	(175)	89	(124)
Income as % of sales	—	6.7%	9.3%	8.6%	6.1%	—	4.7%	9.0%	—	2.9%	—
Earnings per share ($)	—	0.69	1.00	1.00	1.99	(0.31)	1.15	2.14	(2.10)	0.78	(1.10)
Stock price - FY high ($)	—	23.88	27.25	24.13	20.00	20.13	27.38	32.81	21.38	14.19	12.19
Stock price - FY low ($)	—	16.00	17.63	13.88	12.00	13.00	17.88	12.88	7.25	6.94	6.20
Stock price - FY close ($)	(9.6%)	22.25	22.00	16.25	13.25	19.25	26.50	20.88	13.38	10.50	9.00
P/E - high	—	27	27	24	9	—	22	13	—	18	—
P/E - low	—	18	18	14	6	—	14	5	—	9	—
Dividends per share ($)	(3.3%)	0.27	0.38	0.46	0.53	0.27	0.05	0.05	0.10	0.20	0.20
Book value per share ($)	1.8%	4.14	4.60	4.44	4.53	(1.32)	(0.27)	0.93	9.83	6.69	4.84
Employees	15.3%	2,043	2,309	2,652	2,184	5,665	5,519	5,364	8,600	8,300	7,340

STOCK PRICE HISTORY

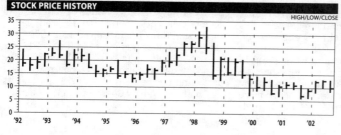

HIGH/LOW/CLOSE

2001 FISCAL YEAR-END

Debt ratio: 71.8%
Return on equity: —
Cash ($ mil.): 22
Current ratio: 1.19
Long-term debt ($ mil.): 1,393
No. of shares (mil.): 113
Dividends
 Yield: 2.2%
 Payout: —
Market value ($ mil.): 1,018

CROWN CORK & SEAL COMPANY

Crown Cork & Seal Company (CC&S) knows how to wrap things up. The Philadelphia-based company is a leading worldwide producer of consumer packaging containers. Its metals packaging unit (which accounts for more than 75% of sales) makes cans, closures, and ends for beverages, pet food, soups, ready-made meals, and other products. CC&S also sells can-making equipment. In addition, the company produces plastic containers for food, lipstick, nasal spray, and other goods, and it designs polyethylene terephthalate (PET) plastic containers to enhance product marketing. CC&S's customers include Coca-Cola, Pepsi-Cola, Nestlé, and Mars.

CC&S has been hit hard by sluggish sales, unfavorable interest rates, and charges related to asbestos litigation, plant closures, and the loss of anticipated tax credits. (The company doesn't expect taxable income until 2004.) As part of its plan to reduce debt by selling $1 billion worth of assets, CC&S has sold several divisions and spun off its PET bottle subsidiary, Constar International.

Rexam PLC is considering a bid to purchase all or part of the debt-ridden company.

HISTORY

Formed as Crown Cork & Seal Co. (CC&S) of Baltimore in 1892, the company was consolidated into its present form in 1927 when it merged with New Process Cork and New York Patents. The next year CC&S expanded overseas and formed Crown Cork International. In 1936 CC&S acquired Acme Can and benefited from the movement at the time from home canning to processed canning. The company was the first to develop the aerosol can (1946).

By 1957 heavy debt had CC&S in trouble. Teetering on the brink of bankruptcy, the company hired John Connelly as president. Connelly immediately stopped can production (sending stockpiled inventory to customers), discontinued unprofitable product lines, and reduced costs (25% of employees were laid off in less than two years). He then directed CC&S to take advantage of new uses for aerosol cans (insecticides, hair spray, and bathroom cleaning supplies) and to expand overseas. CC&S obtained "pioneer rights" between 1955 and 1960 from foreign countries that granted it the first crack at new closure and can businesses.

The introduction of the pull-tab pop-top in 1963 hit the can business like an exploding grenade. Connelly embraced pull tabs, but he rejected getting into the production of two-piece aluminum cans (first introduced in the mid-1970s), focusing instead on existing technology for three-piece cans. He also resisted the diversification trend then popular in the can-making industry, which later led to the declining performances of competitors Continental Can and American Can.

In 1970 CC&S moved into the printing end of the industry. It gained the ability to imprint color lithography on its bottle caps and cans after buying R. Hoe.

Connelly kept CC&S debt-free through most of the 1980s, using cash flow to buy back about half of CC&S's stock. In 1989 he picked Bill Avery to succeed him. With Connelly's blessing, Avery started a buying spree that included the purchase of the plants of Continental Can. Connelly died in 1990. Acquisitions continued throughout the decade of the 1990s. CC&S's purchases included CONSTAR International, the #1 maker of polyethylene terephthalate (PET) plastic containers (1992), can maker Van Dorn (1993), and the can-manufacturing unit of Tri Valley Growers (1994). California's Northridge earthquake in 1994 ruined the company's plant in Van Nuys.

CC&S bought French packaging company CarnaudMetalbox in 1996. The purchase united CC&S's efficient operations and strong presence in North America with the French company's state-of-the-art manufacturing technology and international marketing experience. That year strikes over contract disputes halted production at eight of the company's plants. In addition, CC&S acquired Polish packaging company Fabryka Opakowan Blaszanyck.

In 1997 CC&S bought a 96% stake in Golden Aluminum from ACX Technologies, but returned the aluminum recycler in 1999 at a cost of $10 million. Dropping sales and foreign currency fluctuations in 1998 forced the company to close seven factories and cut 7% of its work force. CC&S closed more factories in 1999 and sold its composite can (paper cans with metal or plastic ends) business. That year the company increased its foreign presence with the purchase of two can manufacturers in Spain and Greece.

CC&S entered into a joint venture with Tempra Technology in 2000 to make and market a self-refrigerating can. The same year Avery announced his retirement; president and COO John Conway succeeded him as CEO in 2001. To reduce debt and move closer to profitability, CC&S sold three product divisions in 2001 and sold its fragrance pump unit to Rexam PLC for about $107 million in 2002. In March 2002 the company sold its Europe-based pharmaceutical packaging business. In May CC&S spun off its PET bottle subsidiary Constar in an IPO offering.

OFFICERS

Chairman, President, and CEO: John W. Conway,
age 56, $1,327,500 pay
Vice Chairman; EVP and CFO: Alan W. Rutherford,
age 58, $728,000 pay
EVP; President, European Division: William R. Apted,
age 54, $455,000 pay
EVP; President, Americas Division: Frank Mechura,
age 59, $447,996 pay
EVP; President, Asia-Pacific Division: William H. Voss,
age 56, $385,000 pay
SVP, Human Resources: Gary L. Burgess
SVP, Finance: Timothy J. Donahue, age 39
VP and President, US Food Can Division:
Raymond L. McGowan
VP, Strategic Marketing and Planning:
William J. Freeman
VP and Corporate Controller: Thomas A. Kelly, age 42
Auditors: PricewaterhouseCoopers LLP

LOCATIONS

HQ: Crown Cork & Seal Company, Inc.
1 Crown Way, Philadelphia, PA 19154
Phone: 215-698-5100   **Fax:** 215-676-7245
Web: www.crowncork.com

Crown Cork & Seal Company operates about 210
manufacturing facilities worldwide, with concentrations
in Europe and the US.

2001 Sales

	$ mil.	% of total
Americas	3,666	51
Europe	3,200	45
Asia/Pacific	321	4
Total	**7,187**	**100**

PRODUCTS/OPERATIONS

2001 Sales

	$ mil.	% of total
Metal Packaging		
Beverage cans & ends	2,349	33
Food cans & ends	2,057	29
Other	1,171	16
Plastic Packaging	1,550	22
Other	60	—
Total	**7,187**	**100**

Selected Products

Metal Packaging
Aerosol cans
Beverage cans
Closures
Crowns
Ends
Food cans
Specialty packaging
(unusual containers)

Plastic Packaging
Bottles
Closures

Personal care product
containers (lipstick,
deodorant, and
cosmetics)
PET (polyethylene
terephthalate)
containers

Other Products
Engineering and spares
(machinery for can
manufacturing)

COMPETITORS

AptarGroup
Ball Corporation
Owens-Illinois
Rexam
Schmalbach-Lubeca
Silgan
U.S. Can

HISTORICAL FINANCIALS & EMPLOYEES

NYSE: CCK FYE: December 31	Annual Growth	12/92	12/93	12/94	12/95	12/96	12/97	12/98	12/99	12/00	12/01
Sales ($ mil.)	7.4%	3,781	4,163	4,452	5,054	8,332	8,495	8,300	7,732	7,289	7,187
Net income ($ mil.)	—	155	99	131	75	284	294	105	181	(174)	(972)
Income as % of sales	—	4.1%	2.4%	2.9%	1.5%	3.4%	3.5%	1.3%	2.3%	—	—
Earnings per share ($)	—	1.79	1.11	1.46	0.83	2.14	2.10	0.71	1.36	(1.40)	(7.74)
Stock price – FY high ($)	—	41.13	41.88	41.88	50.63	55.50	59.75	55.19	37.50	24.19	9.75
Stock price – FY low ($)	—	27.39	33.25	33.50	33.50	40.63	43.56	24.00	19.69	2.94	0.83
Stock price – FY close ($)	(26.4%)	39.88	41.88	37.75	41.75	54.38	50.13	30.81	22.38	7.44	2.54
P/E – high	—	23	20	28	61	26	28	78	28	—	—
P/E – low	—	15	16	23	40	19	20	34	14	—	—
Dividends per share ($)	—	0.00	0.00	0.00	0.00	1.00	1.00	1.00	1.00	1.00	0.00
Book value per share ($)	(7.8%)	13.24	14.09	15.28	16.12	27.75	27.49	24.32	23.88	16.79	6.40
Employees	5.5%	20,378	21,254	22,373	20,409	44,611	40,985	38,459	35,959	34,618	33,046

STOCK PRICE HISTORY

HIGH/LOW/CLOSE

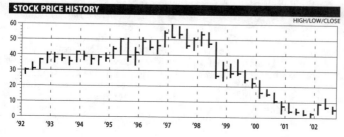

2001 FISCAL YEAR-END

Debt ratio: 84.8%
Return on equity: —
Cash ($ mil.): 456
Current ratio: 0.97
Long-term debt ($ mil.): 4,475
No. of shares (mil.): 126
Dividends
    Yield: —
    Payout: —
Market value ($ mil.): 319

CSX CORPORATION

CSX is banking on the railway and the seaway as the right ways to make money: The Richmond, Virginia-based company delivers freight by rail and ship. CSX Transportation (CSXT), CSX's largest unit, is the #1 railroad company in the eastern US. A major coal carrier, CSXT has some 23,000 route miles in 23 states in the eastern half of the US, the District of Columbia, and two Canadian provinces.

With its 42% ownership of Conrail (Norfolk Southern owns the rest), the firm has taken the fast track in the railroad industry's consolidation. The Conrail operations give CSX major rail links in the Northeast, such as Boston to Cleveland and New York to Chicago, and connect these cities with CSX's southern rail network.

The company's CSX Lines, formerly part of Sea-Land, provides domestic container shipping between the continental US and Alaska, Hawaii, Guam, and Puerto Rico; it operates a fleet of 16 vessels and 27,000 containers. CSX Lines has expanded its Internet-based booking, tracking, and tracing services, and more than half of its bookings are done via the Internet. The company is in talks to sell CSX Lines to boost its profitability.

Another former Sea-Land unit, CSX World Terminals, operates terminal businesses in the Asia/Pacific region, the Caribbean region (Dominican Republic), Latin America, and Europe. The company also offers intermodal services through CSX Intermodal, which operates nearly 50 facilities worldwide. CSX Intermodal is seeking partnerships with intermodal marketing companies to increase business, and in preparation for that increase plans to double its fleet size to more than 9,000 containers.

In addition, CSX owns The Greenbrier, a resort in West Virginia, and develops real estate.

HISTORY

CSX Corporation was formed in 1980, when Chessie System and Seaboard Coast Line (SCL) merged in an effort to improve the efficiency of their railroads.

Chessie's oldest railroad, the Baltimore & Ohio (B&O), was chartered in 1827 to help Baltimore compete against New York and Philadelphia for freight traffic. By the late 1800s the railroad served Chicago, Cincinnati, New York City, St. Louis, and Washington, DC. Chesapeake & Ohio (C&O) acquired it in 1962.

C&O originated in Virginia with the Louisa Railroad in 1836. It gained access to Chicago, Cincinnati, and Washington, DC, and by the mid-1900s was a major coal carrier. After B&O and C&O acquired joint control of Baltimore-based Western Maryland Railway (1967), the

three railroads became subsidiaries of newly formed Chessie System (1973).

One of SCL's two predecessors, Seaboard Air Line Railroad (SAL), grew out of Virginia's Portsmouth & Roanoke Rail Road of 1832. SCL's other predecessor, Atlantic Coast Line Railroad (ACL), took shape between 1869 and 1893 as William Walters acquired several southern railroads. In 1902 ACL bought the Plant System (railroads in Georgia, Florida, and other southern states) and the Louisville & Nashville (a north-south line connecting New Orleans and Chicago), giving ACL the basic form it was to retain until 1967, when it merged with SAL to form SCL.

After CSX inherited the Chessie System and SCL, it bought Texas Gas Resources (gas pipeline, 1983), American Commercial Lines (Texas Gas' river barge subsidiary, 1984), and Sea-Land Corporation (ocean container shipping, 1986). To improve its market value, CSX sold most of its oil and gas properties, its communications holdings (Lightnet, begun in 1983), and most of its resort properties (Rockresorts) in 1988 and 1989. American Commercial Lines acquired Valley Line in 1992.

Sea-Land struck a deal with Danish shipping company Maersk Line in 1996 to share vessels and terminals. That year CSX entered a takeover battle with rival Norfolk Southern for Conrail. Conrail decided to split its assets between the two; CSX paid $4.3 billion for 42%. (The division took place in 1999.)

CSX combined the American Commercial Lines barge business with the barge business of Vectra Group in 1998. In 1999 CSX sold Grand Teton Lodge to Vail Resorts for $50 million. Also that year CSX divided Sea-Land into three businesses: international terminal operations (which became CSX World Terminals), domestic container shipping (CSX Lines), and global container shipping. The international shipping business was sold to Denmark's A.P. Møller (parent of Maersk Line) for $800 million.

Rail service disruptions stemming from the integration of Conrail assets were exacerbated by damage from Hurricane Floyd in 1999. The next year a federal audit found defects in CSX track. Service problems related to the Conrail takeover continued, and the company's rail unit underwent a management shake-up.

Later in 2000 CSX, looking to pay down debt, sold its CTI Logistx unit to TNT Post Group for $650 million. The next year CSX formed a new unit, Transflo Corp., to provide intermodal services. In 2002 CSX established a CSXT office in Europe to focus on international freight and to create partnerships with European freight forwarders and ocean carriers.

OFFICERS

Chairman and CEO: John W. Snow, age 62, $2,200,003 pay (prior to title change)
Vice Chairman and CFO: Paul R. Goodwin, age 59, $802,083 pay
President and Director: Michael J. Ward, age 51
EVP Corporate Services: Andrew B. Fogarty, age 57
SVP Corporate Communications and Investor Relations: Jesse R. Mohorovic, age 59
SVP Government Affairs: Arnold I. Havens
SVP Law: Ellen M. Fitzsimmons, age 41
SVP Mechanical and Engineering: W. Michael Cantrell
SVP Merchandise Service Group: Clarence W. Gooden
SVP Regulatory Affairs and Washington Counsel: Peter J. Shudtz
SVP Strategic Planning: Lester M. Passa, age 47
VP and COO: Glen Soliah
VP, General Counsel, and Corporate Secretary: Stephen R. Larson
VP Administration: James A. Searle Jr.
VP Corporate Human Resources: Jeffrey C. McCutcheon
Auditors: Ernst & Young LLP

LOCATIONS

HQ: 1 James Center, 901 E. Cary St., Richmond, VA 23219
Phone: 804-782-1400   **Fax:** 804-782-6747
Web: www.csx.com

CSX's rail system reaches the District of Columbia and 23 states in the eastern, midwestern, and southern US, as well as the provinces of Ontario and Quebec in Canada. Its domestic container shipping unit links the continental US with Alaska, Hawaii, Guam, and Puerto Rico. CSX also operates terminal businesses in Asia, Australia, China, the Dominican Republic, and Europe.

PRODUCTS/OPERATIONS

2001 Sales

	% of total
CSX Transportation	75
CSX Intermodal	14
CSX Lines	8
CSX World Terminals	3
Total	**100**

Selected Operations
CSX Intermodal Inc. (transcontinental intermodal services)
CSX Lines LLC (domestic container shipping)
CSX Real Property Inc. (property sales, leasing and development)
CSX Transportation Inc. (rail transportation and distribution services)
CSX World Terminals LLC (terminal operations)
The Greenbrier (luxury resort)
Transflo Corp. (intermodal services)
Yukon Pacific Corp. (pipeline development)

COMPETITORS

Alexander & Baldwin
APL
Atlantic Container
Burlington Northern Santa Fe
Canadian National Railway
CHR
CNF
Evergreen Marine
FedEx
Hanjin Shipping
J. B. Hunt
Neptune Orient
Norfolk Southern
P&O
Schneider National
Union Pacific

HISTORICAL FINANCIALS & EMPLOYEES

NYSE: CSX FYE: Last Friday in December	Annual Growth	12/92	12/93	12/94	12/95	12/96	12/97	12/98	12/99	12/00	12/01
Sales ($ mil.)	(0.8%)	8,734	8,940	9,608	10,504	10,536	10,621	9,898	10,811	8,191	8,110
Net income ($ mil.)	34.8%	20	359	652	618	855	799	537	2	565	293
Income as % of sales	—	0.2%	4.0%	6.8%	5.9%	8.1%	7.5%	5.4%	0.0%	6.9%	3.6%
Earnings per share ($)	33.9%	0.10	1.71	3.08	2.91	3.96	3.62	2.51	0.01	2.67	1.38
Stock price - FY high ($)	—	36.81	44.06	46.19	46.13	53.13	62.44	60.75	53.94	33.44	41.30
Stock price - FY low ($)	—	27.25	33.19	31.56	34.69	42.13	41.25	36.50	28.81	19.50	24.81
Stock price - FY close ($)	0.2%	34.38	40.94	34.81	45.63	42.25	54.00	41.50	31.38	25.94	35.05
P/E - high	—	368	25	15	16	13	17	24	225	35	30
P/E - low	—	273	19	10	12	11	11	14	120	21	18
Dividends per share ($)	0.6%	0.76	0.79	0.88	0.92	1.04	1.08	1.20	0.90	1.20	0.80
Book value per share ($)	8.0%	14.38	15.28	17.81	20.15	23.03	26.41	27.08	26.33	28.28	28.64
Employees	(2.2%)	47,597	48,308	47,703	47,965	47,314	46,911	46,147	48,950	45,355	39,011

STOCK PRICE HISTORY

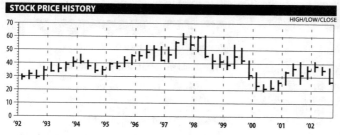

HIGH/LOW/CLOSE

2001 FISCAL YEAR-END

Debt ratio: 48.8%
Return on equity: 4.8%
Cash ($ mil.): 137
Current ratio: 0.63
Long-term debt ($ mil.): 5,839
No. of shares (mil.): 214
Dividends
  Yield: 2.3%
  Payout: 58.0%
Market value ($ mil.): 7,490

CUMMINS, INC.

Instead of taking reds, vitamin C, and cocaine to keep on truckin', many people just fire up a Cummins diesel. Headquartered in Columbus, Indiana, Cummins (formerly Cummins Engine Company) is the world's #1 manufacturer of diesel engines. Cummins' diesel and natural gas engines, which range from 55 hp to 3,500 hp, also power light commercial and midrange trucks, pickups (primarily the Dodge Ram), power generators, buses, construction equipment, farm tractors, and marine vessels.

The company's power generation unit makes Onan generator sets and Newage alternators. Cummins' Fleetguard and Nelson filtration units produce fuel filters, air filters, and exhaust systems for heavy-duty engines.

In response to a slowdown in the North American heavy-duty truck market, Cummins has trimmed its workforce and is focusing on its power generation and filtration segments. Cummins has also created a new international distribution segment with 17 wholly owned and three joint-venture distributors that serve 111 locations in 50 countries.

HISTORY

Chauffeur Clessie Cummins believed that Rudolph Diesel's cumbersome and smoky engine could be improved for use in transportation. Borrowing money and work space from his employer — Columbus, Indiana, banker W. G. Irwin — Cummins founded Cummins Engine in 1919. Irwin invested more than $2.5 million and in the mid-1920s Cummins produced a mobile diesel engine. Truck manufacturers were reluctant to switch from gas to diesel, so Cummins used publicity stunts (such as racing in the Indianapolis 500) to advertise his engine.

The company was profitable by 1937, the year Irwin's grandnephew, J. Irwin Miller, took over. During WWII the Cummins engine was used in cargo trucks. Sales jumped from $20 million in 1946 to more than $100 million by 1956. That year Cummins started its first overseas plant in Scotland, and bought Atlas Crankshafts in 1958. By 1967 it had 50% of the diesel engine market.

Cummins diversified in 1970 by acquiring the K2 Ski Company (fiberglass skis) and Coot Industries (all-terrain vehicles), but sold them by 1976. In the early 1980s Cummins introduced a line of midrange engines developed in a joint venture with J.I. Case (then a subsidiary of Tenneco; now a part of Fiat-controlled CNH Global). To remain competitive, Cummins cut costs by 22%, doubled productivity in its US and UK plants, and spent $1.8 billion to retool its factories.

Having twice repelled unwelcome foreign suitors in 1989, Cummins sold 27% of its stock to Ford, Tenneco, and Japanese tractor maker Kubota for $250 million in 1990. The move raised cash and protected Cummins from future takeover bids.

In 1993 Cummins established engine-making joint ventures with Tata Engineering & Locomotive, India's largest heavy-vehicle maker, and Komatsu, a leading Japanese construction equipment maker. Also in 1993 Cummins introduced a natural-gas engine for school buses and formed a joint venture to produce turbochargers in India. The company began Cummins Wartsila, a joint venture with engineering company Wartsila NSD, to develop high-speed diesel and natural-gas engines in France and the UK in 1995. It also began restructuring that year, selling plants and laying off workers.

Continuing its strategy of teaming with other manufacturers, Cummins agreed in 1996 to make small and midsize diesel engines with Fiat's Iveco and New Holland (now known as CNH Global) subsidiaries.

In 1997 subsidiary Cadec Systems signed a license to develop and sell Montreal-based Canadian Marconi's (now BAE SYSTEMS CANADA) fleet-tracking system, which uses satellites and computers. Cummins bought diesel exhaust and air filtration company Nelson Industries for $490 million in early 1998. The company also agreed, without admission of guilt, to pay a $25 million fine and contribute $35 million to environmental programs after the EPA accused Cummins of cheating on emissions tests.

In 1999 Cummins sold its Atlas Crankshaft subsidiary to ThyssenKrupp's automotive subsidiary. Chairman and CEO James Henderson retired at the end of 1999 and was succeeded by Theodore Solso.

Early in 2001 the company announced that it had signed a long-term deal to supply PACCAR (Peterbilt and Kenworth trucks) with heavy-duty ISX, Signature, N14, ISM and ISL engines. Cummins also formed a joint venture with Westport Innovations (Cummins Westport Inc.) for the building of low-emission, natural gas engines. The company also shortened its name to Cummins, Inc.

OFFICERS

Chairman and CEO: Theodore M. Solso, age 55, $904,575 pay
EVP; Group President, Engine Business: F. Joseph Loughrey, age 52, $562,750 pay
EVP; Group President, Power Generation: John K. Edwards, age 57, $452,000 pay
VP and CFO: Thomas Linebarger, age 38, $341,667 pay
VP and CTO: John C. Wall, age 50

VP and Corporate Controller: Susan Carter
VP and Treasurer: Donald Trapp
VP, General Counsel, and Corporate Secretary:
Marya M. Rose
President and General Manager, Cummins, S de R.L.
de C.V.; VP, Cummins Mexico Operations:
Steve Knaebel
President, Cummins Brasil; General Manager, Latin
America: Ricardo Chuahy
VP; Chairman and Managing Director, Newage
AvK/SEG: Steven Zeller
VP; Managing Director, Holset Engineering Company
Ltd.: David Moorehouse
VP; Managing Director, Newage: Peter McDowell
VP and General Manager, Heavy-Duty Engine Business:
Frank J. McDonald
VP, Automotive Engineering: John H. Stang
Auditors: PricewaterhouseCoopers LLP

LOCATIONS

HQ: 500 Jackson St., Columbus, IN 47201
Phone: 812-377-5000   **Fax:** 812-377-3334
Web: www.cummins.com

Cummins Engine Company has major manufacturing
operations in Australia, Brazil, Canada, France, Mexico,
the UK, and the US.

2001 Sales

	$ mil.	% of total
US	3,045	54
Asia/Australia	901	16
Europe	832	15
Mexico/Latin America	471	8
Canada	303	5
Africa/Middle East	129	2
Total	**5,681**	**100**

PRODUCTS/OPERATIONS

2001 Sales

	$ mil.	% of total
Engine business	3,121	52
Power generation	1,422	24
Filters & other	889	15
International distribution	562	9
Adjustments	(313)	—
Total	**5,681**	**100**

Selected Products

Engines
Bus engines
Heavy- and medium-duty truck engines
    185-315 hp diesel engines for midrange trucks
    280-650 hp diesel engines for heavy-duty trucks
Industrial engines for construction, mining,
    agricultural, rail, and marine equipment
Light, commercial vehicle engines

Power Generation
Alternators (Newage)
Generator sets (Onan)

Filtration
Fleetguard
Nelson

COMPETITORS

Caterpillar	Invensys	Nissan
Detroit Diesel	Isuzu	PACCAR
Emerson	Kohler	Scania
Electric	Mack Trucks	ThyssenKrupp
Hino Motors	Navistar	Volvo

HISTORICAL FINANCIALS & EMPLOYEES

NYSE: CUM FYE: December 31	Annual Growth	12/92	12/93	12/94	12/95	12/96	12/97	12/98	12/99	12/00	12/01
Sales ($ mil.)	4.7%	3,749	4,248	4,737	5,245	5,257	5,625	6,266	6,639	6,597	5,681
Net income ($ mil.)	—	(190)	177	253	224	160	212	(21)	160	8	(102)
Income as % of sales	—	—	4.2%	5.3%	4.3%	3.0%	3.8%	—	2.4%	0.1%	—
Earnings per share ($)	—	(6.01)	4.63	6.11	5.52	4.01	5.48	(0.55)	4.13	0.20	(2.66)
Stock price - FY high ($)	—	40.44	54.38	57.63	48.63	47.75	83.00	62.75	65.69	50.00	45.50
Stock price - FY low ($)	—	26.63	37.38	35.88	34.00	34.50	44.25	28.31	34.56	27.06	28.00
Stock price - FY close ($)	(0.1%)	39.00	53.75	45.25	37.00	46.00	59.06	35.50	48.31	37.94	38.54
P/E - high	—	—	11	9	9	12	15	—	16	250	—
P/E - low	—	—	8	6	6	9	8	—	8	135	—
Dividends per share ($)	31.8%	0.10	0.20	0.63	1.00	1.00	1.08	1.10	1.13	1.20	1.20
Book value per share ($)	6.1%	14.55	21.33	25.78	29.43	33.30	33.78	30.29	34.43	32.27	24.76
Employees	0.7%	23,400	23,600	25,600	24,300	23,500	26,300	28,300	28,500	28,000	24,900

STOCK PRICE HISTORY

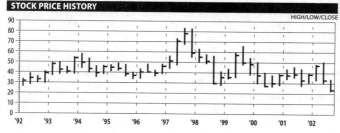

HIGH/LOW/CLOSE

2001 FISCAL YEAR-END

Debt ratio: 47.2%
Return on equity: —
Cash ($ mil.): 92
Current ratio: 1.69
Long-term debt ($ mil.): 915
No. of shares (mil.): 41
Dividends
    Yield: 3.1%
    Payout: —
Market value ($ mil.): 1,596

CVS CORPORATION

Drugs are not merely recreational at CVS, which has more drugstores — more than 4,175, located primarily east of the Mississippi River — and fills more prescriptions than any other drugstore chain. The Woonsocket, Rhode Island-based company makes about 65% of its sales filling prescriptions. Other sales come from over-the-counter medications, cosmetics, food, film processing, and general merchandise. Subsidiary PharmaCare Management Services provides prescription benefit management services and has been key to the company's growth.

Formerly known as Melville, in the mid-1990s the company shucked its apparel, home goods, and shoe-retailing operations to concentrate on its star performer, the CVS chain. CVS then bulked up by acquiring Revco D.S. (nearly 2,600 stores, 1997) and Arbor Drugs (200 stores, 1998).

CVS has since introduced CVS ProCare pharmacies, which cater to customers who require complex drug therapies (HIV, infertility). The company continues to move its stores from strip malls to freestanding locations. In addition, it has tapped into the Internet market with its CVS.com online pharmacy.

HISTORY

Brothers Stanley and Sid Goldstein, who ran health and beauty products distributor Mark Steven, branched out into retail in 1963 when they opened up their first Consumer Value Store in Lowell, Massachusetts, with partner Ralph Hoagland. The chain grew rapidly, amassing 17 stores by the end of 1964 (the year the CVS name was first used) and 40 by 1969. That year the Goldsteins sold the chain to Melville Shoe to finance further expansion.

Melville had been founded in 1892 by shoe supplier Frank Melville. Melville's son, Ward, grew the company, creating the Thom McAn shoe store chain and later buying its supplier. By 1969 Melville had opened shoe shops in Kmart stores (through its Meldisco unit), launched one apparel chain (Chess King, sold in 1993), and purchased another (Foxwood Stores, renamed Foxmoor and sold in 1985).

In 1972 CVS bought the 84-store Clinton Drug and Discount, a Rochester, New York-based chain. Two years later, when sales hit $100 million, CVS had 232 stores — only 45 of which had pharmacies. The company bought New Jersey-based Mack Drug (36 stores) in 1977. By 1981 CVS had more than 400 stores.

CVS's sales hit $1 billion in 1985 as it continued to add pharmacies to many of its older stores. In 1987 Stanley's success was recognized companywide when he was named chairman and CEO of CVS's parent company, which by then had been renamed Melville.

CVS bought the 490-store Peoples Drug Stores chain from Imasco in 1990, giving it locations in Maryland, Pennsylvania, Virginia, West Virginia, and Washington, DC. CVS created PharmaCare Management Services in 1994 to take advantage of the growing market for pharmacy services and managed-care drug programs. Pharmacist Tom Ryan was named CEO that year.

With CVS outperforming Melville's other operations, Melville decided in 1995 to concentrate on the drugstore chain. By that time Melville's holdings had grown to include discount department store chain Marshalls and furniture chain This End Up, both sold in 1995; footwear chain Footaction, spun off as part of Footstar in 1996, along with Meldisco; the Linens 'n Things chain, spun off in 1996; the Kay-Bee Toys chain, sold in 1996; and Bob's Stores (apparel and footwear), sold in 1997.

Melville was renamed CVS in late 1996. Amid major consolidation in the drugstore industry, in 1997 CVS — then with about 1,425 stores — paid $3.7 billion for Revco D.S., which had nearly 2,600 stores in 17 states, mainly in the Midwest and Southeast. The following year the company bought Arbor Drugs (200 stores in Michigan, later converted to the CVS banner) for nearly $1.5 billion. CVS opened about 180 new stores and relocated nearly 200 in 1998 as it shifted from strip malls to freestanding stores. (It also closed nearly 160 stores.) Stanley retired as chairman in 1999 and was succeeded by Ryan.

In 1999 the company bought online drugstore pioneer Soma.com, renamed CVS.com. It also launched the CVS ProCare pharmacy to serve customers in need of complex drug therapies. A year later CVS bought Stadtlander Pharmacy of Pittsburgh from Bergen Brunswig (now AmerisourceBergen) for $124 million.

In early 2001 Wolverine Equities paid $288 million for 96 stores, which CVS said it will continue to operate. In 2001 CVS opened 43 stores in new markets, including Miami and Ft. Lauderdale, Florida; Las Vegas, Nevada; and Dallas, Houston, and Fort Worth, Texas. The company planned to add approximately 150-175 new stores in 2002, including 75 in new markets. However, CVS said in late 2001 that it would close 200 stores, cut staff, and close a distribution plant and one of its mail-order facilities in 2002 in an effort to streamline operations.

In July 2002 CVS was among the winning bidders for the remaining assets of bankrupt rival Phar-Mor. CVS acquired the majority of Phar-Mor's prescription lists.

Chairman, President, and CEO, CVS and CVS Pharmacy: Thomas M. Ryan, age 49, $993,750 pay
EVP, CFO, and Chief Administrative Officer, CVS and CVS Pharmacy: David B. Rickard, age 55, $595,000 pay
EVP Merchandising and Marketing: Chris Bodine, age 46
EVP Stores, CVS and CVS Pharmacy: Larry J. Merlo, age 46, $495,000 pay
EVP Strategy and Business Development: Deborah G. Ellinger, age 43
SVP Advertising and Marketing: Helena B. Foulkes, age 37
SVP Finance and Controller, CVS and CVS Pharmacy: Larry D. Solberg, age 54
SVP, CIO: Howard Edels
SVP, Chief Legal Officer, CVS and CVS Pharmacy; President, CVS Realty: Douglas A. Sgarro, age 43, $390,000 pay
SVP Human Resources and Corporate Communications: V. Michael Ferdinandi
SVP Human Resources, CVS Pharmacy: Rosemary Mede, age 54
Auditors: KPMG LLP

LOCATIONS

HQ: One CVS Dr., Woonsocket, RI 02895
Phone: 401-765-1500   **Fax:** 401-766-2917
Web: www.cvs.com

CVS has stores operating under the CVS and CVS/pharmacy name in 26 states and the District of Columbia; it also has two mail-order facilities and some 45 specialty pharmacies operating under the CVS ProCare name in 20 states and the District of Columbia.

2001 Stores

	No.
New York	414
Ohio	375
Pennsylvania	347
Massachusetts	327
Georgia	281
North Carolina	274
Indiana	268
Michigan	248
Virginia	245
New Jersey	219
South Carolina	175
Maryland	172
Tennessee	140
Alabama	139
Connecticut	129
Illinois	90
Other states	348
Total	**4,191**

PRODUCTS/OPERATIONS

2001 Sales

	% of total
Pharmacy	66
Front of store	34
Total	**100**

COMPETITORS

A&P	Eckerd	Rite Aid
Ahold USA	Kerr Drug	Walgreen
Albertson's	Kmart	Wal-Mart
drugstore.com	Kroger	
Duane Reade	Longs	

HISTORICAL FINANCIALS & EMPLOYEES

NYSE: CVS FYE: December 31	Annual Growth	12/92	12/93	12/94	12/95	12/96	12/97	12/98	12/99	12/00	12/01
Sales ($ mil.)	8.8%	10,433	10,435	11,286	9,689	5,528	12,738	15,274	18,098	20,088	22,241
Net income ($ mil.)	13.4%	133	332	308	(657)	75	38	396	635	746	413
Income as % of sales	—	1.3%	3.2%	2.7%	—	1.4%	0.3%	2.6%	3.5%	3.7%	1.9%
Earnings per share ($)	6.7%	0.56	1.19	2.75	(6.41)	0.49	0.07	0.98	1.55	1.83	1.00
Stock price - FY high ($)	—	27.50	27.38	20.81	19.94	23.00	35.00	56.00	58.38	60.44	63.75
Stock price - FY low ($)	—	21.25	19.44	14.75	14.31	13.63	19.50	30.44	30.00	27.75	22.89
Stock price - FY close ($)	1.2%	26.56	20.31	15.44	15.38	20.69	32.03	55.00	39.88	59.94	29.60
P/E - high	—	41	68	8	—	47	292	57	37	32	63
P/E - low	—	32	49	5	—	28	163	31	19	15	22
Dividends per share ($)	(12.2%)	0.74	0.76	0.76	0.57	0.22	0.22	0.17	0.23	0.23	0.23
Book value per share ($)	1.8%	9.92	10.67	11.28	7.37	5.84	6.85	7.97	9.39	10.97	11.68
Employees	(0.9%)	115,644	111,082	117,000	96,832	44,000	90,000	97,000	100,000	99,000	107,000

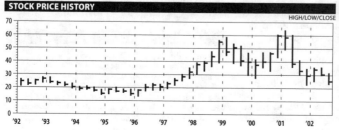

STOCK PRICE HISTORY

HIGH/LOW/CLOSE

2001 FISCAL YEAR-END

Debt ratio: 15.1%
Return on equity: 9.9%
Cash ($ mil.): 236
Current ratio: 1.78
Long-term debt ($ mil.): 810
No. of shares (mil.): 391
Dividends
  Yield: 0.8%
  Payout: 23.0%
Market value ($ mil.): 11,570

DANA CORPORATION

Dana Corporation, based in Toledo, Ohio, manufactures automotive components for carmakers and automotive aftermarket retailers. Its core products include axles, brakes, and driveshafts, along with engine, filtration, fluid-system, sealing, and structural products. Subsidiary Dana Credit Corporation provides leasing and financing services.

The company operates five business groups: automotive systems, automotive aftermarket, engine and fluid mangement, commercial vehicle systems, and off-highway systems. Customers include GM, Ford, DaimlerChrysler, AutoZone, and CARQUEST.

Due to a slowing of North American car production, Dana has closed aging plants and reduced its workforce. The company also continues to sell businesses that no longer fit its core focus. In keeping with this strategy, Dana has divested its Mr. Gasket division and is selling off its global leasing business (Dana Commercial Credit) on a piecemeal basis. Dana also has consolidated its engine and fluid businesses into a single unit.

HISTORY

Clarence Spicer developed a universal joint and a driveshaft for autos while studying at Cornell University. After leaving Cornell in 1904, he patented his designs, founded Spicer Manufacturing in Plainfield, New Jersey, and marketed the product himself.

The company ran into financial trouble in 1913, and the following year New York attorney Charles Dana joined the firm, advancing Spicer money to refinance. Acquisitions after WWI strengthened Spicer's position in the growing truck industry. The business moved to Toledo, Ohio, in 1929 to be nearer the emerging Detroit automotive mecca. In 1946 the company was renamed in honor of Dana, who became chairman two years later.

The company entered the replacement-parts market in 1963, and Charles Dana retired that year. Continuing to expand its offerings, Dana acquired the Weatherhead Company (hoses, fittings, and couplings; 1977) and later branched into financial services. In 1989 Dana introduced a nine-speed, heavy-duty truck transmission (developed jointly with truckmaker Navistar), the first all-new design of its type in over 25 years.

Dana sold its mortgage banking business and some other financial services in 1992. It bought Delta Automotive and Krizman, both leading makers and distributors of automotive aftermarket parts. The following year Dana acquired the Reinz Group, a German gasket maker with worldwide operations. Purchases in 1994 included Sige (axles, Italy), Stieber Heidelberg (industrial components, Germany), Tece (auto parts distribution, the Netherlands), and Tremec (transmissions, Mexico).

Acquisitions in 1995 and 1996 included a number of rubber and plastics makers. The company bought Clark-Hurth Components (drivetrains) and the piston ring and cylinder liner operations of SPX Corporation in 1997; it also increased its shares in Wix Filtron (filtration products, Poland). Dana sold some of its businesses in 1997 as well. These included its sheet-rubber and conveyor-belt business to Coltec Industries, its European warehouse distribution operations to Partco Group, and its Spicer clutch business to Eaton.

In 1998 Dana bought Eaton's heavy-axle and brake business and then paid $3.9 billion for Echlin. Dana then cut 3,500 jobs and closed 15 plants, mostly former Echlin facilities. It paid $430 million in 1998 for the bearings, washers, and camshafts businesses of Federal-Mogul.

In 2000 Dana sold Gresen's hydraulic business to Parker Hannifin and Warner Electric's industrial products business to Colfax. Dana also sold a truck-cab parts unit and its Truckline distribution centers in Australia. Anticipating a slowdown in North American car production, Dana closed five plants, downsized three, and terminated 1,280 employees.

Dana acquired the auto axle manufacturing and stamping operations of Invensys (UK) in 2000. Also that year president and CEO Joseph Magliochetti, a 33-year Dana veteran, became chairman. Late in 2000 the company announced it would cut 3,000 production jobs.

In 2001 Dana sold its Chelsea Products Division (power take-offs) to Parker Hannifin. Later in the year Dana announced 10,000 more job cuts through plant closings and consolidations. Near the end of 2001, Dana announced plans sell its Dana Commercial Credit leasing business and to consolidate its engine and fluid businesses into a single unit; the restructuring of these divisions was complete by early 2002. In June of that year Dana sold the first piece of Dana Commercial Credit for $69 million. The following month the division completed the sale of certain real estate holdings for $150 million.

OFFICERS

Chairman, President, CEO, and COO:
  Joseph M. Magliochetti, age 60, $935,000 pay
VP and CFO; Chairman, Dana Credit Corporation:
  Robert C. Richter, age 50, $451,667 pay
VP and Director e-Business: Kevin P. Moyer, age 44
VP, Chief Accounting Officer, and Assistant Treasurer:
  Charles W. Hinde, age 63

VP, Finance: Rodney R. Filcek, age 49
VP, Human Resources: Caroline Clark
VP, Sales, Dana World Trade (DWT): Rod Nineham
VP, Secretary, and General Counsel:
  Michael L. DeBacker, age 55
President, Automotive Aftermarket Group:
  Terry R. McCormack, age 51
President, Automotive Systems Group:
  William J. Carroll, $520,000 pay
President, Dana International and Global Initiatives:
  Marvin A. Franklin III, age 54, $480,000 pay
President, Engine and Fluid Management Group:
  James M. Laisure, age 50
President, Off-Highway Systems Group:
  Bernard N. Cole, age 49
President, Technology Development and Diversified
  Products: Charles F. Heine, age 49
Auditors: PricewaterhouseCoopers LLP

LOCATIONS

HQ: 4500 Dorr St., PO Box 1000, Toledo, OH 43697
Phone: 419-535-4500   Fax: 419-535-4643
Web: www.dana.com

Dana operates manufacturing and distribution facilities
in more than 30 countries worldwide.

2001 Sales

	$ mil.	% of total
The Americas		
North America	7,684	74
South America	553	5
Europe	1,704	17
Asia/Pacific	330	3
Adjustments	115	1
Total	**10,386**	**100**

PRODUCTS/OPERATIONS

2001 Sales

	$ mil.	% of total
Automotive systems	3,717	36
Automotive aftermarket	2,538	24
Engine and fluid management	2,137	21
Commercial vehicle systems	1,118	11
Off-highway systems	621	6
Other	140	1
Adjustments	115	1
Total	**10,386**	**100**

Selected Products

Air filters	Hard and soft gaskets
Axles	Oil pumps
Brake components and	Power steering pumps
assemblies	Single- and two-speed
Brake hydraulics	drive axles
Camshaft bearings	Stampings
Complete chassis	Tandem drive axles
assemblies	Trailer and auxiliary axles
Cylinder head gaskets	Transaxles
Driveshaft assemblies	Universal joints
Frames	Wet disc brakes
Fuel filters	Wheel-end modules

COMPETITORS

American Axle &	Eaton	Mark IV
Manufacturing	Federal-Mogul	Metaldyne
ArvinMeritor,	Honeywell	Robert Bosch
Inc.	International	SPX
BorgWarner	Ingersoll-Rand	TRW
Budd Company	ITT Industries	Valeo
Champion Parts	Magna	Visteon
Delphi	International	

HISTORICAL FINANCIALS & EMPLOYEES

NYSE: DCN FYE: December 31	Annual Growth	12/92	12/93	12/94	12/95	12/96	12/97	12/98	12/99	12/00	12/01
Sales ($ mil.)	8.8%	4,872	5,460	6,614	7,598	7,686	8,291	12,464	13,270	12,460	10,386
Net income ($ mil.)	—	(382)	80	228	288	306	369	534	513	334	(298)
Income as % of sales	—	—	1.5%	3.5%	3.8%	4.0%	4.5%	4.3%	3.9%	2.7%	—
Earnings per share ($)	—	(4.35)	0.86	2.28	2.80	2.81	3.49	3.20	3.08	2.18	(2.01)
Stock price – FY high ($)	—	24.13	30.13	30.69	32.63	35.50	54.38	61.50	54.06	33.25	26.90
Stock price – FY low ($)	—	13.38	22.00	19.63	21.38	27.25	30.63	31.31	26.00	12.81	10.25
Stock price – FY close ($)	(5.7%)	23.50	29.94	23.50	29.25	32.63	47.50	40.88	29.94	15.31	13.88
P/E – high	—	—	22	13	12	13	15	19	17	15	—
P/E – low	—	—	16	9	8	10	9	10	8	6	—
Dividends per share ($)	1.8%	0.80	0.80	0.83	0.90	0.98	1.04	1.14	1.24	1.24	0.94
Book value per share ($)	6.1%	7.70	8.73	9.51	11.47	13.87	16.19	17.74	18.14	17.76	13.14
Employees	8.0%	35,000	36,000	39,500	42,200	45,500	47,900	86,400	84,200	79,300	70,000

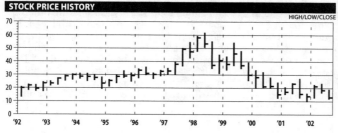

STOCK PRICE HISTORY	HIGH/LOW/CLOSE

2001 FISCAL YEAR-END

Debt ratio: 60.6%
Return on equity: —
Cash ($ mil.): 199
Current ratio: 1.09
Long-term debt ($ mil.): 3,008
No. of shares (mil.): 149
Dividends
  Yield: 6.8%
  Payout: —
Market value ($ mil.): 2,068

DANAHER CORPORATION

Danaher's namesake, a fishing stream off Montana's Flat Head River, took its name from a word meaning "swift flowing." The phrase is also apt for describing the acquisition-fueled growth of Washington, DC-based Danaher's process/environmental controls and tools businesses.

Danaher's controls group (69% of sales) produces a wide range of monitoring, sensing, controlling, and testing products. Notable brands include Veeder-Root (measuring and leak-detection systems for underground fuel-storage tanks), Fluke (devices for measuring electronic voltage, frequency, pressure, and temperature), and Pacific Scientific (electric motors, drives, and safety equipment).

The company also produces mechanics' hand tools, automotive specialty tools, and accessories, which it makes under numerous brand names. For example, Danaher is the sole maker of Sears' line of Craftsman tools. (Sears is the company's largest customer.) Danaher is also the primary tool supplier for auto parts company NAPA.

Together, spotlight-averse brothers Steve Rales (Danaher's chairman) and Mitch Rales (the company's executive committee chairman) own about 30% of the company. The two have proven to be fishers not only of trout but also of companies, buying underperforming companies with strong market shares and recognizable brand names. Noted for cutting costs and improving productivity at purchased companies, Danaher plans further growth through new products, international expansion, and more acquisitions. Citing poor sales, the company announced that it would also restructure its drill chuck, power quality, and industrial controls businesses.

HISTORY

Once dubbed "raiders in short pants" by *Forbes,* Steven and Mitchell Rales began making acquisitions in their 20s. In 1981 they bought their father's 50% stake in Master Shield, a maker of vinyl building products. The brothers bought tire manufacturer Mohawk Rubber the following year. In 1983 they acquired control of publicly traded DMG, a distressed Florida real-estate firm; the next year they sold DMG's real-estate holdings and folded Mohawk and Master Shield into the company, which they renamed Danaher.

Danaher then began taking over low-profile industrial firms that weren't living up to their growth potential. Backed by junk bonds from Michael Milken, within two years it had purchased 12 more companies. Among these early acquisitions were makers of tools (Jacobs, Matco Tools), controls (Partlow, Qualitrol, Veeder-Root), precision components (Allen, maker of the namesake

hexagonal wrench), and plastics (A.L. Hyde). With its purchases, Danaher proceeded to cut costs and pay down debt by unloading underperforming assets.

The Rales brothers' takeover efforts weren't always successful. They lost out to Warren Buffett when they tried to buy Scott & Fetzer (encyclopedias, vacuum cleaners) in 1985 and INTERCO (furniture, shoes, apparel) in 1988. They did, however, make off with $75 million for their troubles, and INTERCO was driven into dismantlement and bankruptcy in the process.

In 1989 Danaher bought Easco Hand Tools, the main maker of tools for Sears, Roebuck and Co.'s Craftsman line. (The Raleses already controlled Easco Hand Tools; a private partnership they controlled had bought the company from its parent in 1985 and taken it public in 1987.) The deal established the tool division as Danaher's largest, and two years later Sears selected Danaher as the sole manufacturer of Craftsman mechanics' hand tools.

The brothers hired Black & Decker power tools executive George Sherman as president and CEO in 1990. Between 1991 and 1995 Danaher grew through purchases such as Delta Consolidated Industries and Armstrong Brothers Tool. The firm improved its international distribution channels by adding West Instruments (UK, 1993) and Hengstler (Germany, 1994).

Focusing on tools and controls, Danaher sold its automotive components business in 1995. After a lengthy battle, the company bought test maker and controls firm Acme-Cleveland in 1996.

Danaher's 1997 purchases included Current Technology and GEMS Sensors. Danaher made its two largest purchases to date in 1998 when it bought Pacific Scientific (motion controls and safety equipment) for $460 million and Fluke (electronic tools) for $625 million.

Boosting its motion-control operations, in 2000 Danaher bought Kollmorgen for about $240 million and American Precision Industries for $185 million. In 2001 Lawrence Culp, formerly the company's COO, was named president and CEO. Later that year Danaher made a $5.5 billion offer for Cooper Industries (electric products and tools). Cooper rejected the offer and announced that it was exploring other options. Further talks with Cooper followed, but Danaher lost interest when Cooper became embroiled in asbestos lawsuits. The following year Danaher completed the divestiture of API Heat Transfer. Also in 2002 Danaher said it would buy motion control products maker Thomson Industries in a deal valued at around $165 million.

Chairman: Steven M. Rales, age 50
Chairman of the Executive Committee:
Mitchell P. Rales, age 45
President, CEO, and Director: H. Lawrence Culp Jr.,
age 38, $1,310,000 pay
EVP, CFO, and Secretary: Patrick W. Allender, age 54,
$895,000 pay
EVP: Philip W. Knisely, age 47
EVP: Steven E. Simms, age 45, $778,000 pay
VP, Finance and Tax: James H. Ditkoff, age 54
VP, Human Resources: Dennis Longo, age 44
VP and Controller: Christopher C. McMahon, age 38
President, Danaher Industrial Controls Group:
Craig B. Purse
**President, General Purpose Systems Division, Danaher
Motion Control Group:** John S. Stroup
**President, Motion Components Division, Danaher
Motion Control Group:** William T. Fejes Jr.
**President, Special Purpose Systems Division, Danaher
Motion Control Group:** Lawrence D. Kingsley
Auditors: Ernst & Young LLP

LOCATIONS

HQ: 1250 24th St. NW, Ste. 800, Washington, DC 20037
Phone: 202-828-0850   **Fax:** 202-828-0860
Web: www.danaher.com

2001 Sales

	$ mil.	% of total
US	2,622	70
Germany	293	8
UK	143	3
Other countries	724	19
Total	**3,782**	**100**

PRODUCTS/OPERATIONS

2001 Sales

	$ mil.	% of total
Environmental controls	2,617	69
Tools & components	1,165	31
Total	**3,782**	**100**

Selected Operations
Acme-Cleveland Corp.
  Communications Technology Corp.
  (telecommunications products)
  Namco Controls Corp. (sensors and proximity
  switches)
The Allen Manufacturing Company (wrenches,
  hexagonal keys)
Armstrong Tools, Inc. (industrial hand tools)
Cyberex, Inc. (solid-state power technology)
Delta Consolidated Industries, Inc. (truck boxes and
  industrial gang boxes)
Dr. Bruno Lange Gmbh (analytical instrumentation and
  reagents, Germany)
Fisher Pierce (outdoor lighting controls)
Fluke Corporation (electronic test tools)
GEMS Sensors, Inc. (level, flow, and pressure sensors)
Hennessy Industries Inc. (wheel-service equipment)
Jacobs Vehicle Systems, Inc. (braking systems for
  commercial vehicles)
Matco Tools Corporation (tools for the automotive
  aftermarket)

COMPETITORS

Black & Decker	Matrix Service
Cooper Industries	Snap-on
Dresser	Stanley Works
Johnson Controls	Tektronix

HISTORICAL FINANCIALS & EMPLOYEES

NYSE: DHR FYE: December 31	Annual Growth	12/92	12/93	12/94	12/95	12/96	12/97	12/98	12/99	12/00	12/01
Sales ($ mil.)	16.6%	949	1,067	1,289	1,487	1,812	2,051	2,910	3,197	3,778	3,782
Net income ($ mil.)	28.3%	32	18	82	108	208	155	183	262	324	298
Income as % of sales	—	3.3%	1.7%	6.3%	7.3%	11.5%	7.5%	6.3%	8.2%	8.6%	7.9%
Earnings per share ($)	24.5%	0.28	0.16	0.70	0.93	2.41	1.29	1.32	1.79	2.23	2.01
Stock price - FY high ($)	—	6.84	9.81	13.28	17.19	23.31	32.00	55.25	69.00	69.81	68.69
Stock price - FY low ($)	—	4.94	6.03	9.00	12.13	14.63	19.50	28.00	42.75	36.44	43.90
Stock price - FY close ($)	28.1%	6.50	9.53	13.06	15.88	23.31	31.56	54.31	48.25	68.38	60.31
P/E - high	—	24	61	19	18	10	24	41	38	31	33
P/E - low	—	18	38	13	13	6	15	21	23	16	21
Dividends per share ($)	—	0.00	0.03	0.03	0.04	0.05	0.05	0.04	0.06	0.07	0.08
Book value per share ($)	19.8%	3.07	3.20	4.08	5.01	6.79	7.84	10.01	12.00	13.68	15.55
Employees	14.0%	7,100	7,300	9,960	10,500	11,600	13,200	18,000	19,000	24,000	23,000

STOCK PRICE HISTORY

HIGH/LOW/CLOSE

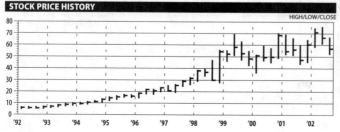

2001 FISCAL YEAR-END

Debt ratio: 33.4%
Return on equity: 14.3%
Cash ($ mil.): 707
Current ratio: 1.84
Long-term debt ($ mil.): 1,119
No. of shares (mil.): 143
Dividends
  Yield: 0.1%
  Payout: 4.0%
Market value ($ mil.): 8,643

D&B

D&B has gone on a diet. Since the mid-1990s, the Murray Hill, New Jersey-based D&B (formerly Dun & Bradstreet Corporation) has spun off several operations, including ACNielsen, Cognizant (later Nielsen Media Research), and R. H. Donnelley. In 2000 the company continued slimming down when it separated from its famous credit rating division, Moody's Investors Service (now part of the publicly traded holding company Moody's Corporation).

Now D&B is focused solely on being one of the world's leading suppliers of business information, services, and research. Its global database contains statistics on some 70 million companies in more than 200 countries. D&B sells that information and integrates it into value-added products built by such software makers as Oracle and SAP. In addition, D&B offers marketing information and purchasing support services. Its Avantrust joint venture with American International Group offers security for e-commerce B2B transactions through a combination of insurance, credit information, and inspections.

The decision to spin off Moody's came at the end of a tumultuous 1999, which saw stock prices plunge because of sagging revenues at D&B. After shareholders (led by Harris Associates, which owns about 7% of the company) demanded that the company put itself up for sale, chairman and CEO Volney Taylor resigned. After the spinoff, Allan Loren took over as chairman and CEO. The company is working to shore up D&B's bottom line with Web-enabled information tools. Warren Buffett's Berkshire Hathaway owns about 7% of D&B.

HISTORY

D&B originated as Lewis Tappan's Mercantile Agency, established in 1841 in New York City. One of the first commercial credit-reporting agencies, the Mercantile supplied wholesalers and importers with reports on their customers' credit histories. The company's credit reporters included four future US presidents (Lincoln, Grant, Cleveland, and McKinley). In the 1840s it opened offices in Boston, Philadelphia, and Baltimore, and in 1857 established operations in Montreal and London.

In 1859 Robert Dun took over the agency and renamed it R.G. Dun & Co. The first edition of the *Dun's Book* (1859) contained information on 20,268 businesses; by 1886 that number had risen to over a million. During this time Dun's was competing fiercely with the John M. Bradstreet Company, founded in 1849 by its namesake in Cincinnati. The rivalry continued until the Depression, when Dun's CEO Arthur Whiteside negotiated a merger of the two firms in 1933; the new company adopted the Dun & Bradstreet name in 1939.

In 1961 Dun & Bradstreet bought Reuben H. Donnelley Corp., a direct-mail advertiser and publisher of the Yellow Pages (first published 1886) and 10 trade magazines. In 1962 Moody's Investors Service (founded 1900) became part of Dun & Bradstreet. The company began computerizing its records in the 1960s and eventually developed the largest private business database in the world. Repackaging that information, the company began creating new products such as Dun's Financial Profiles, first published in 1979.

Dun & Bradstreet continued buying information and publishing companies during the 1970s and 1980s, including Technical Publishing (trade and professional publications, 1978), National CSS (computer services, 1979) and McCormack & Dodge (software, 1983). Later came ACNielsen (1984) and IMS International (pharmaceutical sales data, 1988).

Finding that not all information was equally profitable, Dun & Bradstreet sold its specialty industry and consumer database companies in the early 1990s. Still hoping to cash in on medical and technology information, the company formed D&B HealthCare Information and bought a majority interest in consulting firm Gartner Group. In 1993 the company consolidated its 27 worldwide data centers into four locations. The following year it settled a class-action suit involving overcharging customers for credit reports. After its second earnings decline in three years, management revamped the company in 1996, selling off ACNielsen and Cognizant (consisting of IMS Health and Nielsen Media Research). Volney Taylor was appointed chairman and CEO of Dun & Bradstreet. In 1998 it spun off R. H. Donnelley (formerly Reuben H. Donnelley).

Under pressure from unhappy shareholders, Taylor resigned in late 1999. With director Clifford Alexander Jr. acting as interim CEO, Dun & Bradstreet announced plans to spin off its Moody's unit. After completing the spinoff the following year, Allan Loren took over as chairman and CEO of the new company.

In 2001 the company sold its collections services business. Later that year Dun & Bradstreet changed its name to the already widely used acronym D&B; it also announced in 2002 that it would relocate its headquarters and cut some 1,300 jobs.

OFFICERS

Chairman, President, and CEO: Allan Z. Loren, age 63, $1,975,000 pay
SVP and CFO: Sara Mathew
SVP, Global Marketing, Strategy Implementation, eBusiness Solutions, Asia Pacific/Latin America and Data and Operations: Steve Alesio, age 48, $985,530 pay
SVP and CTO: Cynthia B. Hamburger, age 42, $805,758 pay
SVP, US Sales: Ronald Klausner
SVP, General Counsel, and Corporate Secretary: David J. Lewinter, age 39
SVP and Leader, Data and Operations: Vicki P. Raeburn
SVP, Europe: Bruno de la Rivière
VP, Communications: Joanne Carson
VP and Leader, Human Resources: Patricia A. Clifford
VP and Controller: Chester J. Geveda Jr., age 55, $798,693 pay
VP, eBusiness Solutions: Larry Kutscher, age 38
VP Strategic Development, eBusiness Solutions: Sonny Ajmani, age 38
CFO Europe and VP of Strategy Implementation: Gary S. Michel, age 37
VP, Treasury and Investor Relations: Roxanne E. Parker
Auditors: PricewaterhouseCoopers LLP

LOCATIONS

HQ: 1 Diamond Hill Rd., Murray Hill, NJ 07974
Phone: 908-665-5000   **Fax:** 908-665-5803
Web: www.dnb.com

D&B has offices in 30 countries and correspondents in another 150 countries.

2001 Sales

	% of total
North America	71
Europe	26
Asia Pacific/Latin America	3
Total	**100**

PRODUCTS/OPERATIONS

2001 Sales

	$ mil.	% of total
Risk Management	867	66
Sales and Marketing	333	26
Supply Management	30	2
Divested businesses	79	6
Total	**1,309**	**100**

Selected Products and Services
Credit information
Marketing information
Purchasing information

COMPETITORS

ACNielsen
Acxiom
Experian
Fair, Isaac
Harte-Hanks
Information Resources
infoUSA
Kreller
RoperASW
Thomson Corporation

HISTORICAL FINANCIALS & EMPLOYEES

NYSE: DNB FYE: December 31	Annual Growth	12/92	12/93	12/94	12/95	12/96	12/97	12/98	12/99	12/00	12/01
Sales ($ mil.)	(0.8%)	—	—	—	—	—	1,354	1,421	1,408	1,418	1,309
Net income ($ mil.)	(4.5%)	—	—	—	—	—	184	280	256	207	153
Income as % of sales	—	—	—	—	—	—	13.6%	19.7%	18.2%	14.6%	11.7%
Earnings per share ($)	(25.4%)	—	—	—	—	—	—	—	—	2.52	1.88
Stock price - FY high ($)	—	—	—	—	—	—	—	—	—	27.00	36.90
Stock price - FY low ($)	—	—	—	—	—	—	—	—	—	13.00	20.99
Stock price - FY close ($)	36.4%	—	—	—	—	—	—	—	—	25.88	35.30
P/E - high	—	—	—	—	—	—	—	—	—	11	19
P/E - low	—	—	—	—	—	—	—	—	—	5	11
Dividends per share ($)	—	—	—	—	—	—	—	—	—	0.00	0.00
Book value per share ($)	—	—	—	—	—	—	—	—	(0.64)	(0.27)
Employees	(14.6%)	—	—	—	—	—	—	—	10,700	10,100	7,800

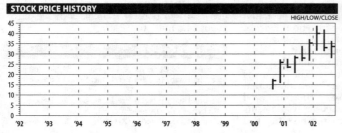

STOCK PRICE HISTORY
HIGH/LOW/CLOSE

2001 FISCAL YEAR-END
Debt ratio: 100.0%
Return on equity: —
Cash ($ mil.): 145
Current ratio: 0.88
Long-term debt ($ mil.): 300
No. of shares (mil.): 77
Dividends
  Yield: —
  Payout: —
Market value ($ mil.): 2,714

DARDEN RESTAURANTS, INC.

Darden Restaurants has clawed its way to the top — with lobster claws. The Orlando, Florida-based company is the #1 casual-dining restaurateur in the world with nearly 1,200 restaurants in the US and Canada. Leading the menu is its chain of Red Lobster seafood restaurants (about 660 in all). Next is the 490-unit Olive Garden Italian restaurant chain, followed by the 24-unit string of Bahama Breeze Caribbean restaurants. With the exception of 34 licensed Red Lobster units in Japan (which it is selling), Darden Restaurants has built its eatery empire without benefit of franchises.

Red Lobster, Darden Restaurants' oldest restaurant chain, serves fish, shrimp, crab, lobster, and other seafood items. Its Olive Garden chain offers Italian appetizers, soups, salads, pastas, seafood, and grilled entrees. Bahama Breeze features Caribbean cuisine spotlighting an array of seafood, beef, pork, and chicken dishes.

Darden Restaurants has started a new chain, Smokey Bones BBQ, a barbecue/sports bar concept with 10 units. The company is taking the concept nationwide.

HISTORY

Nineteen-year-old Bill Darden entered the restaurant business in the late 1930s with a 25-seat luncheonette called the Green Frog in Waycross, Georgia. The restaurant, which featured the slogan "Service with a Hop," was a hit, and his career was born. During the 1950s he owned a variety of restaurants, including several Howard Johnson's, Bonanza, and Kentucky Fried Chicken outlets.

Darden teamed with a group of investors in 1963 to buy an Orlando, Florida, restaurant, Gary's Duck Inn. The restaurant became the prototype for Darden's idea for a moderately priced, sit-down seafood chain. He decided to name the new chain Red Lobster, a takeoff on the old Green Frog.

The first Red Lobster opened in Lakeland, Florida, in 1968 with Joe Lee, who had worked in one of Darden's other restaurants, as its manager. It was such a success that within a month the restaurant had to be expanded. In 1970, when there were three Red Lobsters in operation and two under construction in central Florida, Betty Crocker's boss, General Mills, bought the chain — keeping Darden on to run it.

Red Lobster was not General Mills' first foray into the restaurant business. The company opened the Betty Crocker Tree House Restaurant in 1968, and acquired a fish-and-chips chain and a barbecue chain. But Red Lobster would be its first success. Rather than franchise the Red Lobster name, General Mills chose to develop the chain on its own. Lee was named president of Red Lobster in 1975, and Darden became chairman of General Mills Restaurants.

While General Mills continued to expand Red Lobster, it also sought another restaurant idea to complement the seafood chain. Among concepts tried and discarded were a steak house, as well as Mexican and health-food restaurants. In 1980 the company decided on Italian. After two years of marketing questionnaires and recipe tests, General Mills opened a prototype Olive Garden in Orlando featuring moderately priced Italian food. General Mills began to add outlets in the mid-1980s, and Olive Garden became another success story of the casual-dining industry.

After testing a new Chinese restaurant concept, General Mills opened its first China Coast in Orlando in 1990. The chain grew rapidly, with more than 45 units opening in a single year. The Olive Garden began to cool off in 1993: Same-store sales slid as competitors added Italian items to their menus. That next year Olive Garden increased its advertising budget, introduced new menu items, and began testing new formats, including smaller cafes for malls.

General Mills decided to spin off the restaurant business as a public company in 1995 and focus on consumer foods. The restaurants were renamed Darden Restaurants in honor of Bill Darden (who had died in 1994, the same year that Joe Lee was appointed CEO). That year the company abandoned its China Coast chain.

Darden Restaurants tried again in 1997 with Bahama Breeze, opening a test restaurant in Orlando. Red Lobster's sales flagged in 1997, but the company initiated a turnaround in 1998, in part by revamping Red Lobster's menu. The company dipped into the barbecue sauce in 1999 and opened its inaugural Smokey Bones BBQ in Orlando. The following year Darden Restaurants announced plans to open 36 new restaurants and renovate more than 150 others in 2001. The company announced plans in 2001 to expand its Smokey Bones BBQ concept nationally, beginning with 10 new restaurants in fiscal 2002. In late 2001 Japanese noodle shop operator Reins International agreed to buy Darden's 34 Red Lobster franchises in Japan for about $4.8 million.

OFFICERS

Chairman and CEO: Joe R. Lee, age 61, $1,697,700 pay
Vice Chairman; Interim President, Smokey Bones: Bradley D. Blum, age 48, $1,005,400 pay
Vice Chairman; Interim President, Bahama Breeze: Richard E. Rivera, age 55, $994,500 pay
EVP and CFO: Clarence Otis Jr., age 45, $580,800 pay

EVP, President of New Business Development, and Director: Blaine Sweatt III, age 53, $690,097 pay
EVP Operations: Alan Palmieri
SVP and CIO: Linda J. Dimopoulos, age 50
SVP and Corporate Controller: Stephen E. Helsel, age 56
SVP and General Counsel: Paula J. Shives, age 50
SVP Corporate Affairs: Richard J. Walsh, age 49
SVP Development: Laurie B. Burns, age 39
SVP Human Resources: Daniel M. Lyons, age 48
SVP Purchasing, Distribution, and Food Safety: Barry Moullet, age 43
VP Business Growth and Acquisition: Stoddard Crane
VP Internal Audit: Jim Ingersoll
VP Media and Communications: Jim DeSimone, age 43
VP Taxes: Bob Faisant
VP and Treasurer: Bill White
RVP Operations: Burt Guirado
VP Planning and Analysis: Jill Golder
Auditors: KPMG LLP

LOCATIONS

HQ: 5900 Lake Ellenor Dr., Orlando, FL 32809
Phone: 407-245-4000   **Fax:** 407-245-5114
Web: www.darden.com

Darden Restaurants operates restaurants in the US and Canada. It also licenses restaurants in Japan.

PRODUCTS/OPERATIONS

2002 Sales

	$ mil.	% of total
Red Lobster	2,340	54
Olive Garden	1,860	43
Bahama Breeze	125	3
Smokey Bones	44	—
Total	**4,369**	**100**

Restaurants
Bahama Breeze (Caribbean)
Olive Garden (Italian)
Red Lobster (seafood)
Smokey Bones BBQ (barbecue/sports bar)

COMPETITORS

Angelo & Maxie's
Applebee's
Brinker
Carlson Restaurants Worldwide
Denny's
Il Fornaio
Landry's
Lone Star Steakhouse
Metromedia
Outback Steakhouse
Prandium
Ruby Tuesday
Shoney's

HISTORICAL FINANCIALS & EMPLOYEES

NYSE: DRI FYE: Last Sunday in May	Annual Growth	5/93	5/94	5/95	5/96	5/97	5/98	5/99	5/00	5/01	5/02
Sales ($ mil.)	5.3%	2,737	2,963	3,163	3,192	3,172	3,287	3,458	3,701	4,021	4,369
Net income ($ mil.)	11.1%	92	123	52	74	(91)	102	141	177	197	238
Income as % of sales	—	3.4%	4.2%	1.7%	2.3%	—	3.1%	4.1%	4.8%	4.9%	5.4%
Earnings per share ($)	28.9%	—	—	0.22	0.31	(0.39)	0.45	0.66	0.89	1.06	1.30
Stock price - FY high ($)	—	—	—	7.59	9.34	8.09	12.09	15.59	15.38	19.67	29.78
Stock price - FY low ($)	—	—	—	6.09	6.50	4.50	5.42	9.46	8.30	10.30	15.41
Stock price - FY close ($)	19.2%	—	—	7.34	7.92	5.59	10.30	14.22	11.46	18.61	25.13
P/E - high	—	—	—	35	30	—	26	23	17	18	22
P/E - low	—	—	—	28	21	—	12	14	9	9	11
Dividends per share ($)	—	—	—	0.00	0.03	0.05	0.05	0.05	0.05	0.05	0.05
Book value per share ($)	4.1%	—	—	4.96	5.11	4.71	4.82	4.87	5.24	5.88	6.56
Employees	2.2%	109,875	115,518	124,730	119,123	114,582	114,800	116,700	122,300	128,900	133,200

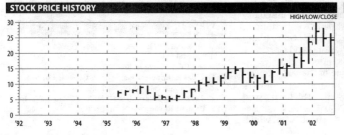

STOCK PRICE HISTORY HIGH/LOW/CLOSE

2002 FISCAL YEAR-END
Debt ratio: 37.0%
Return on equity: 22.0%
Cash ($ mil.): 153
Current ratio: 0.75
Long-term debt ($ mil.): 663
No. of shares (mil.): 172
Dividends
  Yield: 0.2%
  Payout: 3.8%
Market value ($ mil.): 4,326

DEAN FOODS COMPANY

Dean Foods has got milk — and all other things dairy. The Dallas-based company has quickly become the leading producer of fluid milk and other dairy products by herding up regional dairies. Dean Foods was created in 2001 when industry leader Suiza Foods acquired what was then the #2 fluid milk producer, Dean Foods, and took on the Dean Foods name. Since entering the business in 1993, Suiza Foods had acquired more than 80 plants.

Dean Dairy Group's fresh dairy products are sold in the US under a variety of regional and national brand names, including Borden, Pet, Country Fresh, and Meadow Gold. Dean's Morningstar Foods division produces creamers, salad dressings, and specialty dairy products (lactose-free milk, soy milk, flavored milks), while its Specialty Foods division is the leading pickle and pepper packer in the US with regional and private-label brands. In Puerto Rico, Dean has dairy and coffee production facilities.

The company owns 43% of Consolidated Containers (plastic beverage packaging) and holds a majority interest in Leche Celta, Spain's fourth-largest dairy. Dean Foods has purchased soy milk maker White Wave to better tap the growing interest in dairy alternatives, and has formed an alliance with Land O'Lakes to market value-added dairy products under their brand.

HISTORY

Investment banker Gregg Engles formed a holding company in 1988 with other investors, including dairy industry veteran Cletes Beshears, to buy the Reddy Ice unit of Dallas-based Southland (operator of the 7-Eleven chain). The company also bought Circle K's Sparkle Ice and combined it with Reddy Ice. By 1990 it had acquired about 15 ice plants.

The company changed its name to Suiza Foods when it bought Suiza Dairy in 1993 for $99 million. The Puerto Rican dairy was formed in 1942 by Hector Nevares Sr. and named for the Spanish word for "Swiss." By 1993 it was Puerto Rico's largest dairy, controlling about 60% of the island's milk market.

Suiza Foods bought Florida's Velda Farms, manufacturer and distributor of milk and dairy products, in 1994. The company went public in 1996, the same year it bought Swiss Dairy (dairy products, California and Nevada) and Garrido y Compania (coffee products, Puerto Rico).

The company became one of the largest players in the North American dairy industry through its acquisitions in 1997. It paid $960 million for Morningstar (Lactaid lactose-free milk, Second Nature egg substitute), which

— like Suiza Foods itself — was a Dallas-based company formed in 1988 through a Southland divestiture. The company entered the Midwest with its $98 million purchase of Country Fresh and the Northeast with the Bernon family's Massachusetts-based group of dairy and packaging companies, including Garelick Farms and Franklin Plastics (packaging).

Suiza Foods strengthened its presence in the southeastern US in 1998 with its $287 million acquisition of Land-O-Sun Dairies, operator of 13 fluid dairy and ice-cream processing facilities. Also that year Suiza Foods purchased Continental Can (plastic packaging) for about $345 million and sold Reddy Ice to Packaged Ice for $172 million.

After settling an antitrust lawsuit brought by the US Department of Justice, in June 1999 Suiza Foods bought dairy processors in Colorado, Ohio, and Virginia. That same year Suiza Foods combined its US packaging operations with Reid Plastics to form Consolidated Containers, retaining 43% of the new company.

In early 2000 Suiza acquired Southern Foods Group, creating a joint venture with its former 50%-owner, Dairy Farmers of America (DFA), called Suiza Dairy Group. Suiza also bought a majority interest in Spanish dairy processor Leche Celta in 2000.

In April 2001 Suiza Foods announced it had agreed to purchase rival Dean Foods for $1.5 billion and the assumption of $1 billion worth of debt. Dean Foods had begun as Dean Evaporated Milk, founded in 1925 by Sam Dean, a Chicago evaporated-milk broker. By the mid-1930s it had moved into the fresh milk industry. The company went public in 1961 and was renamed Dean Foods in 1963.

Suiza Foods competed the acquisition and took on the Dean Foods name in December 2001. The new Dean Foods bought DFA's interest in Suiza Dairy and merged it with the "old" Dean's fluid dairy operations to create its internal division, Dean Dairy Group.

Along with the purchase of "old" Dean came a 36% ownership of soy milk maker White Wave, and in May 2002 Dean Foods purchased the remaining 64% for approximately $189 million.

OFFICERS

Chairman and CEO: Gregg L. Engles, age 44,
  $1,856,800 pay
EVP and CFO: Barry A. Fromberg, age 46
**EVP, Chief Administrative Officer, General Counsel,
  and Corporate Secretary:** Michelle P. Goolsby, age 44
EVP; President, International: Miguel Calado, age 46
SVP, Human Resources: Robert Dunn

President, Dean Dairy Group, and Director:
Pete Schenkel, age 66, $963,772 pay
President, Morningstar Foods: Herman L. Graffunder,
age 56, $628,873 pay
President, Specialty Foods Group: Jim Greisinger,
age 62
CFO, Morningstar Foods: Craig Miller
COO, Midwest Region, Dean Dairy Group:
Jackie Jackson, age 63
**COO, Northeast Region, Dean Dairy Group, and
Director:** Alan J. Bernon, age 47, $709,803 pay
COO, Southeast Region, Dean Dairy Group: Rick Fehr,
age 50, $785,440 pay
COO, Southwest Region, Dean Dairy Group:
Rick Beaman, age 44, $659,629 pay
Dean Dairy Group: Eric A. Blanchard, age 45
SVP and CFO, Finance, Dean Dairy Group: Pat Ford
SVP, Government and Industry Relations:
Bill Tinklepaugh
SVP, Industry Relations, Dean Dairy Group:
Marty Devine
SVP, Finance, Specialty Foods Group:
Greg Lewandowski
SVP, Marketing, Morningstar Foods: Toby Purdy
SVP, Operations, Dean Dairy Group: Kelly Kading
Auditors: Deloitte & Touche LLP

LOCATIONS

HQ: 2515 McKinney Ave., Ste. 1200, Dallas, TX 75201
Phone: 214-303-3400   **Fax:** 214-303-3499
Web: www.deanfoods.com

Dean Foods operates more than 125 plants in Puerto
Rico, Spain, the UK, and the US.

PRODUCTS/OPERATIONS

2001 Sales

	$ mil.	% total
Dairy Group	5,051	81
Morningstar Foods	767	12
Specialty Foods	19	1
Other	393	6
Total	**6,230**	**100**

Selected Dairy Group Products
Coffee creamers
Cottage cheese
Dairy and nondairy frozen whipped toppings
Half-and-half
Ice cream
Milk
Sour cream
Soymilk
Whipping cream
Yogurt

COMPETITORS

B&G Foods	Land O'Lakes
Blistex	Northwest Dairy
California Dairies Inc.	Parmalat Finanziaria
ConAgra	Pinnacle Foods
Foremost Farms	Corporation
H.P. Hood	Prairie Farms Dairy
Kraft Foods	WestFarm Foods

HISTORICAL FINANCIALS & EMPLOYEES

NYSE: DF FYE: December 31	Annual Growth	12/92	12/93	12/94	12/95	12/96	12/97	12/98	12/99	12/00	12/01
Sales ($ mil.)	73.2%	45	52	341	431	521	1,795	3,321	4,482	5,756	6,230
Net income ($ mil.)	—	(2)	1	4	(10)	26	29	132	110	119	110
Income as % of sales	—	—	2.7%	1.2%	—	4.9%	1.6%	4.0%	2.4%	2.1%	1.8%
Earnings per share ($)	13.4%	—	—	—	—	0.95	0.46	1.79	1.57	1.91	1.78
Stock price - FY high ($)	—	—	—	—	—	10.38	31.25	33.50	25.13	26.22	36.24
Stock price - FY low ($)	—	—	—	—	—	7.00	9.75	12.84	14.81	18.00	21.00
Stock price - FY close ($)	27.5%	—	—	—	—	10.13	29.78	25.47	19.81	24.00	34.10
P/E - high	—	—	—	—	—	10	47	22	15	13	18
P/E - low	—	—	—	—	—	7	15	9	9	9	10
Dividends per share ($)	—	—	—	—	—	0.00	0.00	0.00	0.00	0.00	0.00
Book value per share ($)	31.0%	—	—	—	—	4.35	5.90	9.76	9.97	10.97	16.80
Employees	43.6%	—	1,740	1,800	1,929	2,450	7,050	16,716	18,000	18,000	31,503

STOCK PRICE HISTORY

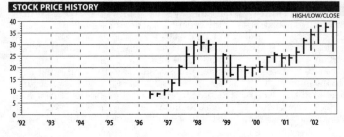

2001 FISCAL YEAR-END

Debt ratio: 66.8%
Return on equity: 10.6%
Cash ($ mil.): 78
Current ratio: 1.26
Long-term debt ($ mil.): 2,972
No. of shares (mil.): 88
Dividends
  Yield: —
  Payout: —
Market value ($ mil.): 2,996

DEERE & COMPANY

Deere hoes rows, tough or not. Based in Moline, Illinois, Deere & Company is one of world's two largest makers of farm equipment (with CNH Global) and a leading producer of construction, forestry, and lawn-care equipment. Farmers use Deere's tractors, harvesters, sprayers, and crop-handling equipment. Homeowners and grounds crews use its signature green chain saws, snow-blowers, and lawn trimmers. Loggers use its forest-harvesting machines, and construction workers use Deere's backhoes and excavators. Deere also offers financing and leasing services for its customers and dealers. The US and Canada account for about three-quarters of sales.

Facing soft demand from a depressed market for agricultural equipment, Deere has implemented production cutbacks. The company has also announced job cuts in its construction-forestry division. Although Deere has become less dependent on the farming industry through its acquisition of forestry equipment maker Timberjack, farming is still its largest business. Deere has expanded its scope by acquiring Richton International Corporation, gaining its landscape irrigation equipment distributor, Century Supply (#1 in the US). However, the company is weeding out non-core assets — it has sold its money-hemorrhaging Homelite home consumer products division and says it will dissolve its farm equipment joint venture with Woods Equipment Company.

Investment firms Capital Research and Management Company and Massachusetts Financial Services Company own 8% and 6% of Deere, respectively.

HISTORY

Vermont-born John Deere moved to Grand Detour, Illinois, in 1836 and set up a blacksmith shop. Deere and other pioneers had trouble with the rich, black soil of the Midwest sticking to iron plows designed for sandy eastern soils, so in 1837 Deere used a circular steel saw blade to create a self-scouring plow that moved so quickly, it was nicknamed the "whistling plow." He sold only three in 1838, but by 1842 he was making 25 a week.

Deere moved his enterprise to Moline in 1847. His son Charles joined the company in 1853, beginning a tradition of family management. (All five Deere presidents before 1982 were related by blood or marriage.) Charles set up an independent dealership distribution system and added wagons, buggies, and corn planters to the product line.

Under Charles' son-in-law, William Butterworth (president, 1907 to 1928), Deere bought agricultural equipment companies and developed harvesters and tractors with internal combustion engines. Butterworth's nephew, Charles Wiman, became president in 1928. He extended credit to farmers during the Depression and won customer loyalty. In 1931 Deere opened its first non-US plant in Canada.

William Hewitt, Wiman's son-in-law, became CEO in 1955. Deere passed International Harvester in 1958 to become the #1 US maker of farm equipment; by 1963 it led the world. Deere expanded into Argentina, France, Mexico, and Spain, and it used research and joint ventures abroad (Yanmar, small tractors, 1977; Hitachi, excavators, 1983) to diversify.

Robert Hanson became the first nonfamily CEO in 1982. He poured $2 billion into research and development during the 1980s. Despite an industrywide sales slump resulting in losses totaling $328 million in 1986 and 1987, Deere was the only major agricultural equipment maker to neither change ownership nor close factories during the 1980s. Instead, Deere cut its workforce 44% and improved efficiency. In 1989 Hans Becherer succeeded Hanson as CEO.

During the 1990s Deere expanded its lawn-care equipment business, mainly in Europe. After spending most of the early 1990s in the doldrums because of recession and weak farm prices, Deere rebounded. By 1994 it had replaced its tractor line with all-new models and bought Homelite (handheld outdoor power equipment) from industrial conglomerate Textron.

Deere signed a deal to sell combines in Ukraine (1996), and it formed a joint venture in 1997 to make combines in China. Fading demand for agricultural equipment at home and jeopardized sales contracts from failing economies in Asia, Brazil, and former Soviet states caused layoffs of about 2,400 workers in 1998 and production cutbacks in 1998 and 1999. Late in 1999 Deere sold its property/casualty insurance operations to Sentry Insurance.

In 2000 Deere purchased regional parts distributor Sunbelt Outdoor Products and Finland-based Metso Corporation's Timberjack forestry-equipment business for about $600 million. President and COO Robert Lane succeeded Becherer as chairman and CEO. Deere bought McGinnis Farms — the US's largest horticultural products distributor — in 2001.

Late in 2001 Deere said it would add to its previously announced job cuts, bringing the total to about 3,000 jobs. It also sold its Homelite consumer products division to Hong Kong-based TechTronics Industries Co., Ltd. Deere acquired Richton International Corporation; that deal included Richton's landscape irrigation equipment distributor, Century Supply (#1 in the US), and

Richton Technology Group (hardware, software, and systems support services).

In 2002 Deere & Company announced plans to pull out of its hay, farm, and forage equipment joint venture, Alloway Industries, with Woods Equipment Company.

OFFICERS

Chairman, President, and CEO: Robert W. Lane, age 52, $1,066,025 pay
Division President (Financial Services Division): Michael P. Orr, age 54, $490,098 pay
Division President (Worldwide Agricultural Operations): David C. Everitt, age 49
Division President (Worldwide Commercial & Consumer Equipment Division): John J. Jenkins, age 56
Division President (Worldwide Construction & Forestry Division & Deere Power Systems Group): Pierre E. Leroy, age 53, $515,801 pay
Division President: James R. Jenkins, age 56
Division President: H.J. Markley, age 51
SVP and CFO: Nathan J. Jones, age 45, $479,270 pay
SVP and CTO: David M. Purvis, age 50
SVP: Samuel R. Allen, age 48
SVP: John K. Lawson, age 61, $495,742 pay
VP, Human Resources: Mertroe B. Hornbuckle
Auditors: Deloitte & Touche LLP

LOCATIONS

HQ: 1 John Deere Place, Moline, IL 61265
Phone: 309-765-8000   **Fax:** 309-765-5671
Web: www.deere.com

Deere & Company operates 30 factories in Canada and the US. The company also operates manufacturing plants in Argentina, Brazil, Finland, France, Germany, Mexico, the Netherlands, New Zealand, South Africa, Spain, and Sweden.

2001 Sales

	% of total
US & Canada	76
Other regions	24
Total	**100**

PRODUCTS/OPERATIONS

2001 Sales

	% of total
Agricultural equipment	47
Commercial & construction equipment	20
Construction & forestry	16
Credit	11
Other	6
Total	**100**

COMPETITORS

AGCO	FMC	Navistar
Black & Decker	Ford	Partek
Blue Cross	GE	Toro
Caterpillar	Honda	Volvo
CIGNA	Ingersoll-Rand	
CNH Global	Kubota	

HISTORICAL FINANCIALS & EMPLOYEES

NYSE: DE FYE: October 31	Annual Growth	10/92	10/93	10/94	10/95	10/96	10/97	10/98	10/99	10/00	10/01
Sales ($ mil.)	7.3%	6,931	7,694	8,967	10,118	11,128	12,617	13,626	11,522	12,964	13,108
Net income ($ mil.)	—	37	(921)	604	706	817	960	1,021	239	486	(64)
Income as % of sales	—	0.5%	—	6.7%	7.0%	7.3%	7.6%	7.5%	2.1%	3.7%	—
Earnings per share ($)	—	0.16	(3.96)	2.32	2.69	3.11	3.74	4.16	1.02	2.06	(0.27)
Stock price - FY high ($)	—	18.94	26.10	30.26	31.72	45.00	60.50	64.13	54.00	49.63	47.13
Stock price - FY low ($)	—	12.28	12.24	21.48	20.40	28.31	39.13	28.38	29.44	30.31	33.55
Stock price - FY close ($)	12.2%	13.15	25.72	23.85	29.76	41.88	52.81	35.63	36.25	36.81	36.99
P/E - high	—	118	—	13	12	14	16	15	52	24	—
P/E - low	—	77	—	9	8	9	10	7	29	15	—
Dividends per share ($)	3.1%	0.67	0.67	0.67	0.73	0.80	0.80	0.86	0.88	0.88	0.88
Book value per share ($)	4.3%	11.56	8.12	9.86	11.78	13.83	16.57	17.56	17.51	18.34	16.82
Employees	6.7%	25,250	33,070	34,300	33,400	33,900	34,400	37,000	38,700	43,700	45,100

STOCK PRICE HISTORY

HIGH/LOW/CLOSE

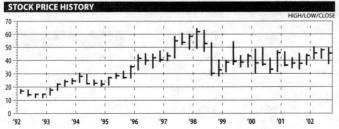

2001 FISCAL YEAR-END

Debt ratio: 62.2%
Return on equity: —
Cash ($ mil.): 1,030
Current ratio: 1.85
Long-term debt ($ mil.): 6,561
No. of shares (mil.): 237
Dividends
  Yield: 2.4%
  Payout: —
Market value ($ mil.): 8,779

DEL MONTE FOODS COMPANY

Del Monte Foods has no problem mixing fruits and vegetables with ketchup on its plate. The San Francisco-based company is the largest produce canner and distributor in the US. It packages vegetables (corn, green beans, peas), fruit (peaches, pineapple, mixed fruit), and tomatoes (ketchup, sauces, diced tomatoes) from produce supplied by mostly US-based growers. Its brands include the Contadina, Del Monte, S&W, and Sunfresh labels, among others.

Del Monte sells 80% of its products through US grocers, warehouse clubs, and other retailers. Wal-Mart rings up approximately 15% of Del Monte's sales. The company has been growing through acquisitions and by rolling out new products with higher profit margins such as Fruit-To-Go single-serve snacks. It is also trying new packaging, including glass and plastic. The Del Monte brand is licensed to other companies internationally and Del Monte hopes to export its other brands, such as S&W, to new markets.

In June 2002 Del Monte said it would buy several North American brands from the H.J. Heinz Company, including Star-Kist, Kibbles 'n Bits, College Inn brand broth, and Nature's Goodness Baby Food. The deal, which is expected to be complete by early 2003, will more than double Del Monte's sales, making it one of the largest branded food providers in the US. The transaction will give Heinz a 75% stake in the company.

HISTORY

Fred Tillman adopted the name Del Monte (originally the name of a coffee blend made for the fancy Hotel Del Monte in Monterey, California) in 1891 for use at his newly formed Oakland Preserving Company. Brand-name labeling was becoming a significant marketing tool, and Del Monte ("of the mountain" in Spanish) became known for high value.

In 1899 Oakland Preserving merged into the California Fruit Canners Association (CFCA) with 17 other canneries (half of California's canning industry). The new company, the largest canner in the world, adopted Del Monte as its main brand name. CFCA merged with other California canneries in 1916 to form Calpak and created national demand for Del Monte products through mass advertising. The company's first ad appeared in the *Saturday Evening Post* in 1917.

Calpak expanded into the Midwest in 1925 by acquiring Rochelle Canneries (Illinois). That year it established British Sales Limited and Philippine Packing Corporation. In later years the company expanded into the Philippines. It weathered slow growth during the Depression, but WWII jump-started Calpak's operations — in 1942 about 40% of the company's products went to feed US troops — and the postwar boom kicked it into high gear.

The company bought control of Canadian Canners Limited, the world's second-largest canner, in 1956, gaining entry into the heavily protected British market. In the 1960s a venture into soft-drink products ended in failure. Calpak changed its name to Del Monte Foods in 1967.

RJR Industries bought Del Monte in 1979 as part of a diversification strategy. In 1989, after its buyout by Kohlberg Kravis Roberts, the newly named, debt-laden RJR Nabisco began selling assets, including Del Monte's Hawaiian Punch line in 1990 and its tropical fruit unit. Merrill Lynch and Del Monte executives bought Del Monte's domestic canning operations in 1990, but the transaction loaded the new company with debt.

To reduce debt, during the 1990s Del Monte sold its dried fruit operations, its pudding division (to Kraft), and its Mexican subsidiary. Texas Pacific Group, an investment partnership known for recruiting specialists to revive companies, acquired a controlling interest in Del Monte in 1997. It installed Richard Wolford, former president of Dole Packaged Foods, as CEO. That year the company bought Contadina's canned tomato products from Nestlé (Nestlé kept the right to use the Contadina brand on refrigerated pasta and sauces).

Interested again in expanding into foreign markets, in 1998 it bought back from Nabisco the rights to the Del Monte brand in South America, and it purchased Nabisco's canned fruits and vegetables business in Venezuela. In 1999 the company completed its IPO. Later that year Del Monte purchased a vegetable processing plant from its competitor Agrilink, and like all food canners, enjoyed robust sales to Y2K-wary shoppers.

In 2000 Del Monte acquired the Sunfresh brand (citrus and tropical fruits) and a distribution center from The UniMark Group for more than $14 million. Del Monte acquired the S&W brand of canned fruits and vegetables, tomatoes, dry beans, and specialty sauces from bankrupted cooperative Tri Valley Growers for about $39 million in March 2001.

OFFICERS

Chairman, President, and CEO: Richard G. Wolford, age 56, $1,223,926 pay
COO and Director: Wesley J. Smith, age 54, $637,175 pay
EVP, Administration, and CFO: David L. Meyers, age 55, $544,000 pay

SVP, Chief Accounting Officer, and Controller:
Richard L. French, age 44
SVP and Chief Corporate Affairs Officer:
William J. Spain, age 59
SVP, Customer Marketing and Sales Development:
Irvin R. Holmes, age 49, $336,121 pay
SVP, Eastern Region: Marvin A. Berg, age 55
SVP, Marketing: Marc D. Haberman, age 38,
$592,933 pay
SVP, Sales: Robert P. Magrann, age 58
SVP and Treasurer: Thomas E. Gibbons, age 53
SVP, Western Region: David L. Withycombe
VP, Corporate Personnel: Mark J. Buxton
VP, General Counsel, and Secretary:
William R. Sawyers, age 38
Auditors: KPMG LLP

LOCATIONS

HQ: One Market St., San Francisco, CA 94105
Phone: 415-247-3000 **Fax:** 415-247-3565
Web: www.delmonte.com

Del Monte Foods owns production facilities in the US
and Venezuela and distributes its products in the US and
South America.

2001 Production Facilities

	No.
California	3
Wisconsin	3
Washington	2
Illinois	1
Indiana	1
Minnesota	1
Texas	1
Venezuela	1
Total	**13**

PRODUCTS/OPERATIONS

2001 Sales

	$ mil.	% of total
Canned fruit (US)	611	40
Canned vegetables (US)	515	34
Tomato products (US)	370	25
South America	16	1
Total	**1,512**	**100**

Selected Brand Names

Contadina	FruitRageous
Del Monte	Orchard Select
FreshCut	S&W
Fruit Cup	Snack Cups
Fruit Naturals	Sunfresh
Fruit Pleasures	

Selected Products
Fruit (apricots, cherries, fruit cocktail, mandarin
oranges, mixed and tropical mixed fruit, peaches,
pears, pineapples)
Sauces (pizza, spaghetti, sloppy joe)
Tomatoes (chunky, crushed, diced, ketchup, stewed,
paste, purée, sauce)
Vegetables (asparagus, carrots, corn, mixed and flavored
vegetables, peas, potatoes, spinach, zucchini, and
green, lima, and wax beans)

COMPETITORS

Campbell Soup	Goya	Nestlé
Chiquita Brands	Hanover Foods	Pro-Fac
ConAgra	Heinz	Seneca Foods
Dole	Maui Land &	Unilever
General Mills	Pineapple	

HISTORICAL FINANCIALS & EMPLOYEES

NYSE: DLM FYE: June 30	Annual Growth	6/92	6/93	6/94	6/95	6/96	6/97	6/98	6/99	6/00	6/01
Sales ($ mil.)	0.6%	1,431	1,555	1,499	1,527	1,305	1,217	1,313	1,505	1,462	1,512
Net income ($ mil.)	—	(58)	(188)	3	5	88	(56)	5	14	129	14
Income as % of sales	—	—	—	0.2%	0.3%	6.7%	—	0.4%	0.9%	8.8%	0.9%
Earnings per share ($)	6.3%	—	—	—	—	—	—	—	0.23	2.42	0.26
Stock price - FY high ($)	—	—	—	—	—	—	—	—	17.00	16.88	11.50
Stock price - FY low ($)	—	—	—	—	—	—	—	—	10.50	6.81	5.63
Stock price - FY close ($)	(29.3%)	—	—	—	—	—	—	—	16.75	6.81	8.38
P/E - high	—	—	—	—	—	—	—	—	25	7	15
P/E - low	—	—	—	—	—	—	—	—	15	3	7
Dividends per share ($)	—	—	—	—	—	—	—	—	0.00	0.00	0.00
Book value per share ($)	—	—	—	—	—	—	—	—	(2.26)	0.20	0.48
Employees	(0.6%)	14,500	14,000	12,500	12,500	12,000	14,100	13,450	14,600	14,000	13,700

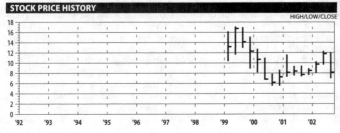

STOCK PRICE HISTORY HIGH/LOW/CLOSE

2001 FISCAL YEAR-END
Debt ratio: 96.6%
Return on equity: 77.7%
Cash ($ mil.): 12
Current ratio: 2.69
Long-term debt ($ mil.): 710
No. of shares (mil.): 52
Dividends
Yield: —
Payout: —
Market value ($ mil.): 438

DELL COMPUTER CORPORATION

Dell Computer may not be known for innovation, but the Round Rock, Texas-based company is thinking outside the box. Dell makes desktop PCs (about half of sales), notebooks, network servers, and storage devices that it sells to customers ranging from home users to large corporations. It also sells refurbished computers, markets third-party peripherals and software, and offers consulting and support services. With the industry-standard Wintel platform (Microsoft Windows operating system and Intel microprocessor) as its foundation, Dell faces intense competition from Hewlett-Packard, whose market share increased dramatically following its acquisition of perennial PC leader Compaq.

Entrepreneurial wunderkind Michael Dell pioneered the direct sales model for computers and took the company from his dorm room to the top of the PC heap by keeping it focused on a simple formula: eliminate the middleman and sell for less. Dell's built-to-order boxes allow for lower inventories, lower costs, and higher profit margins — elements that leave Dell well armed for price wars that characterize the volatile personal computer sector.

Despite its success at grabbing PC market share, Dell continues to attack new markets. It has put increasing emphasis on server computers and storage devices for enterprises. Furthering its push beyond PCs, it has also introduced a line of Ethernet switches. On the services front, Dell has mirrored its straightforward approach to hardware sales, embracing a fixed-price model for offerings such as data migration and storage systems implementation. Dell augmented its storage line when it reached an agreement with market leader EMC to resell that company's enterprise systems. The company is also looking to international revenue to supplant sales in the PC-saturated US market.

Founder and chairman Dell, who is the longest-tenured CEO at any major US computer company, owns 12% of the company.

HISTORY

At age 13 Michael Dell was already a successful businessman. From his parents' home in Houston, Dell ran a mail-order stamp trading business that, within a few months, grossed more than $2,000. At 16 he sold newspaper subscriptions and at 17 Dell bought his first BMW. When he enrolled at the University of Texas in 1983, he was thoroughly bitten by the entrepreneurial bug.

Dell started college as a pre-med student but found time to establish a business selling random-access memory (RAM) chips and disk drives for

IBM PCs. Dell bought products at cost from IBM dealers, who were required at the time to order from IBM large monthly quotas of PCs, which frequently exceeded demand. Dell resold his stock through newspapers and computer magazines at 10%-15% below retail.

By April 1984 Dell's dorm-room computer components business was grossing about $80,000 a month — enough to persuade him to drop out of college. Soon he started making and selling IBM clones under the brand name PC's Limited. Dell sold his machines directly to consumers rather than through retail outlets, as most manufacturers did. By eliminating the retail markup, Dell could sell PCs at about 40% of the price of an IBM.

The company was plagued by management changes during the mid-1980s. Renamed Dell Computer, it added international sales offices in 1987. The company started selling to larger customers in 1988, including government agencies. That year Dell went public.

The company tripped in 1990, reporting a 64% drop in profits. Sales were growing — but so were costs, mostly because of efforts to design a PC using proprietary components and reduced instruction set computer (RISC) chips. Also, the company's warehouses were oversupplied. Within a year Dell turned itself around by cutting inventories and introducing new products.

Dell entered the retail arena by letting Soft Warehouse (now CompUSA) in 1990 and office supply chain Staples in 1991 sell its PCs at mail-order prices. Also that year Dell opened a plant in Ireland.

In 1992 Xerox agreed to sell Dell machines in Latin America. Dell opened subsidiaries in Japan and Australia in 1993. The computer maker abandoned retail stores in 1994 to refocus on its mail-order origins. It also retooled its troubled notebook computer line and introduced servers.

In 1996 the company started selling PCs through its Web site. The next year Dell entered the market for workstations. In 1998 the company stepped up manufacturing in the Americas and Europe and added a production and customer facility in China.

Dell began selling a $999 PC in 1999 despite a history of avoiding low-cost markets. (Dell phased out the WebPC line after just seven months due to slow sales.) That year the company made its first acquisition — storage area network equipment maker ConvergeNet — and opened a plant in Brazil. In 2000 Dell broadened its high-end network servers and Internet-related services offerings, and formed a division for its storage operations.

Faced with slumping PC sales in early 2001,

the company eliminated 1,700 jobs — about 4% of its workforce. Soon after, it announced it would cut as many as 4,000 additional positions. Late that year it expanded its storage offerings when it agreed to resell systems from EMC.

Looking to grow it services unit, Dell acquired Microsoft software support specialist Plural in 2002.

OFFICERS

Chairman and CEO: Michael S. Dell, age 37, $1,273,198 pay
Vice Chairman: James T. Vanderslice, age 61, $960,685 pay
President and COO: Kevin B. Rollins, age 49, $964,543 pay
SVP and CFO: James M. Schneider, age 49
SVP and CIO: Randall D. Mott, age 45
SVP; President, Asia-Pacific/Japan: William J. Amelio, age 44
SVP; President, Europe, Middle East, and Africa: Paul D. Bell, age 41, $633,029 pay
SVP, Americas: Joseph A. Marengi, age 48, $632,579 pay
SVP, Americas: Rosendo G. Parra, age 42
SVP, Human Resources: Paul D. McKinnon, age 51
SVP, Law and Administration and Secretary: Thomas B. Green, age 47
Auditors: PricewaterhouseCoopers LLP

LOCATIONS

HQ: 1 Dell Way, Round Rock, TX 78682
Phone: 512-338-4400   **Fax:** 512-728-3653
Web: www.dell.com

2002 Sales

	$ mil.	% of total
Americas	21,760	70
Europe	6,429	21
Asia/Pacific	2,979	9
Total	**31,168**	**100**

PRODUCTS/OPERATIONS

2002 Sales

	$ mil.	% of total
Desktop computers	16,516	53
Notebooks	8,829	28
Enterprise systems	5,823	19
Total	**31,168**	**100**

Selected Products
Desktop computers (Dell Dimension, OptiPlex)
Notebook computers (Inspiron, Latitude)
Enterprise systems
   Network servers (PowerApp, PowerEdge)
   Storage (PowerVault)
   Workstations (Precision)
Ethernet switches (PowerConnect)
Refurbished systems
Third-party peripherals and software

COMPETITORS

Acer	Hitachi	Sony
Apple Computer	IBM	StorageTek
EMC	Legend Group	Sun
Fujitsu Siemens	Matsushita	Microsystems
Computers	MicronPC	Toshiba
Gateway	NEC	Unisys
Hewlett-Packard	SGI	

HISTORICAL FINANCIALS & EMPLOYEES

Nasdaq: DELL FYE: Sunday nearest Jan. 31	Annual Growth	1/93	1/94	1/95	1/96	1/97	1/98	1/99	1/00	1/01	1/02
Sales ($ mil.)	35.6%	2,014	2,873	3,475	5,296	7,759	12,327	18,243	25,265	31,888	31,168
Net income ($ mil.)	32.1%	102	(36)	149	272	518	944	1,460	1,666	2,177	1,246
Income as % of sales	—	5.0%	—	4.3%	5.1%	6.7%	7.7%	8.0%	6.6%	6.8%	4.0%
Earnings per share ($)	28.0%	0.05	(0.02)	0.05	0.09	0.17	0.32	0.53	0.61	0.79	0.46
Stock price - FY high ($)	—	0.78	0.77	0.75	1.54	4.52	12.98	50.19	55.00	59.69	31.32
Stock price - FY low ($)	—	0.23	0.22	0.30	0.62	0.84	3.74	12.61	31.38	16.25	16.01
Stock price - FY close ($)	49.9%	0.72	0.34	0.67	0.86	4.13	12.43	50.00	38.44	26.13	27.49
P/E - high	—	16	—	13	17	24	36	87	83	69	65
P/E - low	—	5	—	5	7	4	10	22	48	19	33
Dividends per share ($)	—	0.00	0.00	0.00	0.00	0.00	0.00	0.00	0.00	0.00	0.00
Book value per share ($)	31.2%	0.16	0.19	0.26	0.33	0.29	0.50	0.91	2.06	2.16	1.80
Employees	25.0%	4,650	5,980	6,400	8,400	10,350	16,000	24,400	36,500	40,000	34,600

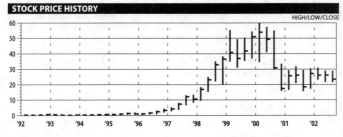

STOCK PRICE HISTORY   HIGH/LOW/CLOSE

2002 FISCAL YEAR-END
Debt ratio: 10.0%
Return on equity: 24.2%
Cash ($ mil.): 3,641
Current ratio: 1.05
Long-term debt ($ mil.): 520
No. of shares (mil.): 2,602
Dividends
   Yield: —
   Payout: —
Market value ($ mil.): 71,529

DELOITTE TOUCHE TOHMATSU

This company isn't "deloitted" by the changes rocking its industry. New York-based Deloitte Touche Tohmatsu (DTT, which operates as Deloitte & Touche in the US) has decided to go with the flow instead of swimming against the tide that was breaking up the combined auditing/consulting operations it built up during the 1980s and 1990s. In the wake of Enron's collapse (which capsized Andersen and put the entire accounting industry under scrutiny), DTT announced in 2002 it would separate its accounting and consulting businesses, shelving the Deloitte Consulting name in favor of new moniker Braxton.

Operating some 700 offices in more than 140 countries, DTT had pursued a strategy of using accountants and consultants in concert to provide seamless service in auditing, accounting, strategic planning, information technology, financial management, and productivity. DTT also provides human resources and tax consulting services, as well as services to governments and international lending agencies working in emerging markets.

HISTORY

In 1845 William Deloitte opened an accounting office in London, at first soliciting business from bankrupts. The growth of joint stock companies and the development of stock markets in the mid-19th century created a need for standardized financial reporting and fueled the rise of auditing, and Deloitte moved into the new field. The Great Western Railway appointed him as its independent auditor (the first anywhere) in 1849.

In 1890 John Griffiths, who had become a partner in 1869, opened the company's first US office in New York City. Four decades later branches had opened throughout the US. In 1952 the firm partnered with Haskins & Sells, which operated 34 US offices.

Deloitte aimed to be "the Cadillac, not the Ford" of accounting. The firm, which became Deloitte Haskins & Sells in 1978, began shedding its conservatism as competition heated up; it was the first of the major accountancy firms to use aggressive ads.

Deloitte Haskins & Sells tried to merge with Price Waterhouse in 1984, but Price Waterhouse's UK partners objected and the deal was dropped.

In 1989 Deloitte Haskins & Sells joined the flamboyant Touche Ross (founded in 1899) to become Deloitte & Touche. Touche Ross's Japanese affiliate, Ross Tohmatsu (founded in 1968) rounded out the current name. The merger was engineered by Deloitte's Michael Cook and Touche's Edward Kangas, in part to unite the former firm's US and European strengths with the latter's Asian presence. Cook continued to oversee US operations, with Kangas presiding over international operations. Many affiliates, particularly in the UK, rejected the merger and defected to competing firms.

As auditors were increasingly held accountable for the financial results of their clients, legal action soared. In the 1990s Deloitte was sued because of its actions relating to Drexel Burnham Lambert junk bond king Michael Milken, the failure of several savings and loans, and clients' bankruptcies.

Nevertheless, in 1995 the SEC chose Michael Sutton, the firm's national director of auditing and accounting practice, as its chief accountant. That year DTT formed Deloitte & Touche Consulting to consolidate its US and UK consulting operations; its Asian consulting operations were later added to the group to facilitate regional expansion.

In 1996 the firm formed a corporate fraud unit (with special emphasis on the Internet) and bought PHH Fantus, the leading corporate relocation consulting company. The next year DTT and Thurston Group (a Chicago-based merchant bank) teamed up to form NetDox, a system for delivering legal, financial, and insurance documents via the Internet. In 1997, amid a new round of industry mergers, rumors swirled that a DTT and Ernst & Young union had been scrapped because the firms could not agree on ownership issues. DTT disavowed plans to merge and launched an ad campaign directly targeted against its rivals.

In 1998 the Asian economic crisis hurt overseas expansion, but provided a boost in restructuring consulting. In 1999 the firm sold its accounting staffing service unit (Resources Connection) to its managers and Evercore Partners, citing possible conflicts of interest with its core audit business. Also that year Kangas (now chairman emeritus) stepped down as CEO to be succeeded by James Copeland, and Deloitte Consulting decided to sell its computer programming subsidiary to CGI Group.

In 2001 the SEC forced Deloitte & Touche to restate the financial results of Pre-Paid Legal Services. In an unusual move, Deloitte & Touche publicly disagreed with the SEC's findings. DTT picked up new business and members in the 2002 collapse of former Big Five rival Andersen.

OFFICERS

Chairman Emeritus: Edward Kangas
Chairman: Piet Hoogendoorn
CEO: James E. Copeland Jr.
COO: J. Thomas Presby
CFO: William A. Fowler
CEO, Deloitte Consulting: Douglas M. McCracken
Chief Executive and Senior Partner, Deloitte & Touche (UK): John P. Connolly
Global Managing Partner, Tax and Legal: Jerry Leamon
National Director, U.S. International Operations: Tom Schiro
Director, Communications: David Read
Director, Human Resources: Martyn Fisher
National Director, Human Capital and Actuary Practice: Ainar D. Aijala Jr.
National Director, Human Resources: James H. Wall
National Director, Operations: William H. Stanton
International Counsel: Joseph J. Lambert
General Counsel: Philip R. Rotner
Director, Finance: Ashish Bali
National Director, Marketing, Communications, and Public Relations: Paul Marinaccio

LOCATIONS

HQ: 1633 Broadway, New York, NY 10019
Phone: 212-492-4000   **Fax:** 212-492-4111
Web: www.deloitte.com

Deloitte Touche Tohmatsu operates through about 700 offices in more than 130 countries.

PRODUCTS/OPERATIONS

Selected Services
Accounting and auditing
Corporate finance
Emerging markets consulting
Human resource, actuarial, insurance, and managed care consulting
Information technology consulting
Management consulting
Mergers and acquisitions consulting
Reorganization services
Tax advice and planning
Transaction services

Industry Specializations
Communications
Consumer business
Financial services
Health care
Manufacturing
Mining
Utilities

COMPETITORS

Accenture
Andersen
BDO International
Booz Allen
Boston Consulting
Cap Gemini
Cap Gemini Ernst & Young U.K.
EDS
Ernst & Young
Grant Thornton International
H&R Block
KPMG
Marsh & McLennan
McKinsey & Company
PricewaterhouseCoopers
Towers Perrin
Watson Wyatt

HISTORICAL FINANCIALS & EMPLOYEES

Partnership FYE: May 31	Annual Growth	8/92	8/93	8/94	8/95	8/96	8/97	8/98	8/99	*5/00	5/01
Sales ($ mil.)	11.1%	4,800	5,000	5,200	5,950	6,500	7,400	9,000	10,600	11,200	12,400
Employees	6.0%	56,000	56,000	56,600	59,000	63,440	65,000	82,000	90,000	90,000	95,000

* Fiscal year change

SALES HISTORY

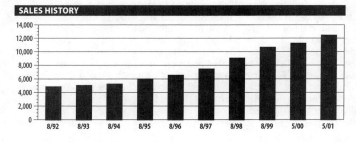

DELPHI CORPORATION

Exactly what goes on beneath the hood of a car might be Greek to most people, but it's no mystery to Delphi Corporation (formerly Delphi Automotive Systems), the world's #1 maker of auto parts. The Troy, Michigan-based company gets its name from ancient Greece, where people sought answers from the oracle at Delphi. Delphi doesn't claim to predict the future, but it can provide answers to almost everything that goes into a car.

Delphi's dynamics and propulsion division accounts for nearly half of sales and produces brake, chassis, ignition, steering, and fuel-management systems. Its safety, thermal, and electrical architecture unit makes powertrain-cooling, climate-control, airbag, and door module systems. Delphi's electronics and mobile communications segment manufactures audio, collision-warning, security, and fiber-optic data-transmission systems. Delphi also plans to offer automotive consumer electronics including satellite digital audio receivers, rear seat entertainment, and MP3 players. The company sells nearly 70% of its products to GM, but also supplies other automakers such as Ford, Toyota, and DaimlerChrysler.

Slower vehicle sales have prompted Delphi to cut jobs (about 8,500 in the first three quarters of 2001), consolidate operations, and focus on its aftermarket business. The company is also considering the sale of up to $5 billion of its underperforming operations. Reflecting its efforts to expand outside the automotive supply business, the company shortened its name to Delphi Corporation early in 2002.

HISTORY

Delphi Corporation traces its roots to the 1908 birth of General Motors (GM), originally formed as a consortium among Buick, Oldsmobile, and Cadillac. During WWI 90% of GM's trucks were targeted for the war effort. Chevrolet joined the group in 1918, and by 1920 GM had bought more than 30 companies.

GM expanded its product line in 1936 to include radios by buying Delco Electronics (transferred to Delphi in 1997). GM spent WWII turning out defense materials, including some 1,300 airplanes and one-fourth of all US aircraft engines. In the 1950s GM introduced the V-8 engine, power steering and brakes, front-seat safety belts, and the first car air-conditioning system.

During the mid-1960s GM diversified into home appliances, insurance, locomotives, electronics, ball bearings, and financing. Delco began to produce AM/FM car stereos. In 1961 J.T. Battenberg III (Delphi's current CEO) joined GM as a GM Institute student.

The 1970s oil crisis contributed to a drop in sales for GM. Additionally, new pollution-control standards forced the company to spend billions on compliance. In the early 1980s GM spent more than $60 billion on new model designs and plant updates. It bought Hughes Electronics and placed Delco under the Hughes umbrella. GM failed to keep up with competing technological developments in the 1980s. Lagging behind, it began venturing out of its own backyard to buy cheaper car components.

Devastating losses in the early 1990s forced GM to restructure. In 1991 it began organizing its parts operations into a separate business group. The next year Battenberg took control of the parts division and began streamlining and exiting noncore operations. GM formed Automotive Components Group (ACG) Worldwide in 1994. That next year GM changed ACG's name to Delphi. In 1997 GM transferred its Delco operations to Delphi.

United Auto Workers (UAW) members at a Delphi plant in Flint, Michigan, joined those from GM's metal-stamping plant across town in a crippling strike in 1998 that lasted almost two months and reduced the company's income by about $726 million. Also that year Delphi recorded a $430 million loss related to the sale of its coil spring, lighting, and seating businesses. In 1999 GM offered 18% of Delphi in an IPO and spun off the rest of Delphi's stock to GM shareholders. Also, Delphi agreed to buy the auto-parts operations of Daewoo Group (South Korea).

Delphi bought Lucas Diesel Systems from TRW in 2000 and renamed it Delphi Diesel Systems. In an effort to expand its non-automotive business by more than $700 million within three to five years, in 2000 Delphi agreed to team up with Ericsson to make in-vehicle communications systems, and acquired an 18% stake in Duraswitch Industries (switches).

In 2001 Delphi bought Eaton Corporation's automotive switch and electronics unit for $300 million. The company also announced that it would cut 5% of its workforce — 11,500 jobs — and close or consolidate nine plants due to slowing vehicle production in Europe and North America. Later in 2001 Delphi acquired Automotive Technical Resources, Inc., for $15 million.

Early in 2002 Delphi shortened its name to Delphi Corporation in hopes of reflecting its efforts to expand outside the automotive industry. Later that year, amid pricing pressures and increasing operating costs, Delphi announced it would lay off an additional 6,100 workers at 25 locations in the US and Europe.

OFFICERS

Chairman, President, and CEO: J. T. Battenberg III, age 59, $1,450,000 pay
EVP; President, Dynamics and Propulsion, and Director: Donald L. Runkle, age 56, $800,000 pay
EVP; President, Electronics and Mobile Communication Sector: David B. Wohleen, age 51, $550,000 pay
EVP; President, Safety, Thermal, and Electrical Architecture Sector: Rodney O'Neal, age 48, $600,000 pay
EVP, CFO, and Director: Alan S. Dawes, age 47, $700,000 pay
EVP, Operations, Human Resource Management and Corporate Affairs: Mark R. Weber, age 53
VP and General Counsel: Logan G. Robinson, age 52
Auditors: Deloitte & Touche LLP

LOCATIONS

HQ: 5725 Delphi Dr., Troy, MI 48098
Phone: 248-813-2000   **Fax:** 248-813-2670
Web: www.delphiauto.com

Delphi Corporation operates 199 wholly owned manufacturing sites, 53 customer centers and sales offices, and 32 technical centers in 43 countries.

2001 Sales

	$ mil.	% of total
North America		
US & Canada	16,393	63
Mexico	3,884	15
Europe	4,801	18
South America	412	2
Other regions	598	2
Total	**26,088**	**100**

PRODUCTS/OPERATIONS

2001 Sales

	$ mil.	% of total
Dynamics & propulsion	12,630	48
Safety, thermal & electrical architecture	9,028	34
Electronics & mobile communication	4,445	17
Mobile multimedia	373	1
Adjustments	(388)	—
Total	**26,088**	**100**

Selected Products

Air and fuel management	Generators
Anti-lock brake systems	Ignition products
Audio systems	Power and signal
Automotive connection	distribution systems
systems	Ride and handling systems
Batteries	Safety/airbag systems
Chassis control systems	Safety systems electronics
Climate-control systems	Security systems
Door modules	Sensors and actuators
Emission control	Thermal-management
Engine-management	systems
systems	Valve train systems

COMPETITORS

ArvinMeritor, Inc.	Federal-Mogul	Motorola
Autoliv	ITT Industries	NSK
Collins &	Johnson	Robert Bosch
Aikman	Controls	Siemens
Dana	Johnson Electric	TRW
Denso	Lear	Valeo
Eaton	Magna	Visteon
	International	Yazaki

HISTORICAL FINANCIALS & EMPLOYEES

NYSE: DPH FYE: December 31	Annual Growth	12/92	12/93	12/94	12/95	12/96	12/97	12/98	12/99	12/00	12/01
Sales ($ mil.)	(1.5%)	—	29,327	31,044	31,661	31,032	31,447	28,479	29,192	29,139	26,088
Net income ($ mil.)	—	—	948	975	1,307	853	215	(93)	1,083	1,062	(370)
Income as % of sales	—	—	3.2%	3.1%	4.1%	2.7%	0.7%	—	3.7%	3.6%	—
Earnings per share ($)	—	—	—	—	—	—	—	—	1.95	1.88	(0.66)
Stock price - FY high ($)	—	—	—	—	—	—	—	—	22.25	20.94	17.50
Stock price - FY low ($)	—	—	—	—	—	—	—	—	14.00	10.50	9.50
Stock price - FY close ($)	(6.9%)	—	—	—	—	—	—	—	15.75	11.25	13.66
P/E - high	—	—	—	—	—	—	—	—	11	11	—
P/E - low	—	—	—	—	—	—	—	—	7	6	—
Dividends per share ($)	41.4%	—	—	—	—	—	—	—	0.14	0.28	0.28
Book value per share ($)	(14.9%)	—	—	—	—	—	—	—	5.69	6.73	4.13
Employees	(0.7%)	—	—	—	—	—	200,463	197,568	203,000	211,000	195,000

STOCK PRICE HISTORY

HIGH/LOW/CLOSE

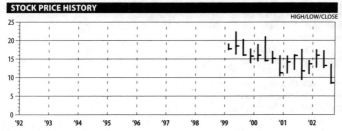

2001 FISCAL YEAR-END

Debt ratio: 47.4%
Return on equity: —
Cash ($ mil.): 757
Current ratio: 1.28
Long-term debt ($ mil.): 2,083
No. of shares (mil.): 560
Dividends
  Yield: 2.0%
  Payout: —
Market value ($ mil.): 7,652

DELTA AIR LINES, INC.

The world's major airlines are picking teams, and Delta Air Lines is playing the game. The Atlanta-based company, a full-service carrier that flies passengers and cargo, ranks #3 in the US behind UAL's United and AMR's American. With a fleet of more than 815 aircraft, Delta operates from hubs in its hometown and in Dallas/Fort Worth, Cincinnati, New York City (Kennedy), and Salt Lake City and serves nearly 210 US cities. It also flies to about 45 international destinations in more than 30 countries. But Delta isn't stopping there: Its code-sharing agreements extend the airline's reach to more than 220 US cities and nearly 120 international destinations.

To better compete with carriers in the Oneworld and Star alliances, Delta formed the Sky-Team global marketing alliance with CINTRA's AeroMéxico, Air France, and Korean Air Lines. In addition, Delta has code-sharing deals with Air Jamaica and China Southern Airlines.

Delta may be thinking globally, but it also acts locally. The company has beefed up regional US offerings with low-fare carrier Delta Express, which offers service between Florida and northeastern and midwestern US cities. Delta also owns regional carriers Atlantic Southeast Airlines and Comair. In addition, the company owns 40% of computer reservation service WORLDSPAN.

HISTORY

Delta Air Lines was founded in Macon, Georgia, in 1924 as the world's first crop-dusting service, Huff-Daland Dusters, to combat boll weevil infestation of cotton fields. It moved to Monroe, Louisiana, in 1925. In 1928 field manager C.E. Woolman and two partners bought the service and renamed it Delta Air Service after the Mississippi Delta region it served.

In 1929 Delta pioneered passenger service from Dallas to Jackson, Mississippi. Flying mail without a government subsidy, Delta finally got a US Postal Service contract in 1934 to fly from Fort Worth to Charleston via Atlanta. Delta relocated to Atlanta in 1941. Woolman became president in 1945 and managed the airline until he died in 1966.

Delta added more flights, including a direct route from Chicago to New Orleans with its 1952 purchase of Chicago and Southern Airlines. The carrier offered its first transcontinental flight in 1961. The airline bought Northeast Airlines in 1972 and added service to New England and Canada; it added service to the UK in 1978, the year that the US airline industry was deregulated.

In 1982 Delta's employees pledged $30 million to buy a Boeing 767 jet, christened *The Spirit of Delta*, as a token of appreciation. In fiscal 1983

the company succumbed to the weak US economy and posted its first loss ever; it quickly became profitable again in 1985. It bought Los Angeles-based Western Air Lines in 1986.

Delta began service to Asia in 1987, the year that longtime employee Ronald Allen became CEO. In 1990 Delta joined TWA and Northwest to form WORLDSPAN, a computer reservation service. Despite a slump in 1990 earnings, in 1991 Delta bought gates, planes, and Canadian routes from Eastern, as well as Pan Am's New York-Boston shuttle, European routes, and Frankfurt hub. The purchases elevated Delta from a domestic player to a top international carrier, but they also contributed to a $2 billion loss between 1991 and 1994.

Allen began a cost-reduction plan in 1994 that cut many routes and 15,000 jobs over the next three years. However, it also drove down employee morale and Delta's customer service reputation. The airline also discontinued unprofitable international routes in 1995 and introduced no-frills Delta Express in 1996.

Allen was let go in 1997 and replaced by Leo Mullin, a former electric utility chief. That year Delta's unprofitable eight-year-old code-sharing agreement with Singapore Airlines was dissolved, and the carrier began a Latin American expansion drive.

Delta held takeover talks with Continental in 1998, but Continental joined with Northwest instead. On the rebound, Delta signed a marketing accord with UAL's United under which the carriers joined their frequent-flier programs.

Spurred by the threat of emerging global alliances Oneworld and Star, Delta announced in 1999 that it would create a competing alliance with Air France and CINTRA's AeroMéxico. SkyTeam, which also includes Korean Air Lines, was launched in 2000. The realignment led Delta to end code-sharing deals with Swissair Group, Sabena, and Austrian Airlines that year. At home, Delta bought regional carriers Atlantic Southeast Airlines and Comair. An 89-day pilots strike led to flight cancellations at Comair in 2001.

Also that year, decreased demand for air travel resulting from terrorist attacks in New York and Washington, DC, prompted Delta to trim its flight schedule and reduce its workforce by about 15% (about 13,000 employees).

Chairman and CEO: Leo F. Mullin, age 59, $596,250 pay
President and COO: Frederick W. Reid, age 51,
  $655,000 pay
EVP and CFO: M. Michele Burns, age 44, $530,000 pay
EVP and Chief Marketing Officer: Vicki B. Escarra,
  age 49, $511,667 pay
EVP Human Resources: Robert L. Colman, age 56,
  $440,000 pay
SVP Airport Customer Service: Richard W. Cordell
SVP and CIO; President and CEO, Delta Technology:
  Curtis W. Robb, age 58
SVP Corporate Communications: Thomas J. Slocum
SVP Delta Air Logistics: Anthony N. Charaf
SVP e-Business: Vincent F. Caminiti
SVP Finance, Treasury, and Business Development:
  James F. Whitehurst, age 34
SVP Finance and Controller: Edward H. Bastian
SVP Flight Operations: David S. Bushy
SVP, General Counsel, and Secretary: Robert S. Harkey
SVP Government Affairs: D. Scott Yohe
SVP International and Alliances: Paul G. Matsen
SVP Sales and Distribution: Lee A. Macenczak
Auditors: Deloitte & Touche LLP

LOCATIONS

HQ: Hartsfield Atlanta International Airport,
  1030 Delta Blvd., Atlanta, GA 30320
Phone: 404-715-2600   **Fax:** 404-715-5042
Web: www.delta.com

Delta Air Lines flies to nearly 210 cities in the US and
more than 45 international destinations in about 30
countries. Through code-sharing, Delta serves more
than 220 cities in the US and about 120 international
destinations in almost 50 countries.

PRODUCTS/OPERATIONS

2001 Sales

	$ mil.	% of total
Passenger	12,964	93
Cargo	506	4
Other	409	3
Total	**13,879**	**100**

Selected Subsidiaries and Affiliates
Atlantic Southeast Airlines, Inc.
Comair, Inc.
WORLDSPAN, L.P. (40%, computer reservation system)

COMPETITORS

Air Canada	Lufthansa
AirTran Holdings	Mesa Air
Alaska Air	Northwest Airlines
Amadeus	Qantas
America West	Sabre
AMR	SAS
British Airways	Singapore Airlines
Cathay Pacific	Southwest Airlines
Continental Airlines	TACA
Galileo International	UAL
Hawaiian Holdings	US Airways
JAL	Virgin Atlantic Airways
KLM	

HISTORICAL FINANCIALS & EMPLOYEES

NYSE: DAL FYE: December 31	Annual Growth	6/93	6/94	6/95	6/96	6/97	6/98	6/99	6/00	*12/00	12/01
Sales ($ mil.)	1.6%	11,997	12,359	12,194	12,455	13,590	14,138	14,711	15,888	16,741	13,879
Net income ($ mil.)	—	(1,002)	(409)	408	156	854	1,001	1,101	1,303	828	(1,216)
Income as % of sales	—	—	—	3.3%	1.3%	6.3%	7.1%	7.5%	8.2%	4.9%	—
Earnings per share ($)	—	(11.16)	(5.16)	2.73	0.72	5.52	6.34	7.20	9.42	6.28	(9.99)
Stock price - FY high ($)	—	30.69	30.56	37.69	43.50	50.56	65.00	72.00	63.56	58.31	52.94
Stock price - FY low ($)	—	22.88	19.75	21.38	31.75	33.38	40.75	40.88	43.56	39.63	20.00
Stock price - FY close ($)	2.1%	24.19	22.63	36.88	41.50	41.31	64.63	57.63	50.56	50.19	29.26
P/E - high	—	—	—	18	60	9	10	9	6	8	—
P/E - low	—	—	—	10	44	6	6	5	4	5	—
Dividends per share ($)	(13.0%)	0.35	0.10	0.10	0.10	0.10	0.10	0.10	0.10	0.05	0.10
Book value per share ($)	5.7%	19.93	15.55	19.16	19.76	21.46	27.90	33.51	41.48	45.34	32.68
Employees	0.4%	73,533	71,412	59,717	60,289	63,441	70,846	74,000	81,000	82,127	76,273

* Fiscal year change

STOCK PRICE HISTORY

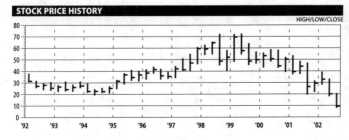

HIGH/LOW/CLOSE

2001 FISCAL YEAR-END

Debt ratio: 67.5%
Return on equity: —
Cash ($ mil.): 2,210
Current ratio: 0.56
Long-term debt ($ mil.): 8,347
No. of shares (mil.): 123
Dividends
  Yield: 0.3%
  Payout: —
Market value ($ mil.): 3,602

DELUXE CORPORATION

When money can move at the speed of a mouse click, Deluxe wants to do more than keep its revenues in check. The Shoreview, Minnesota-based holding company remains the #1 check printer in the US (which, along with printing business forms, accounts for most of its sales). Deluxe believes the check will be in the mail for years to come, especially since it prints checks for some 10,000 of the nation's banks, credit unions, and other financial institutions; 640 million business customers; and 31 million consumers — but it has positioned itself for digital commerce, too.

Accordingly, the company bought eFunds, which provides the retail and financial sectors with electronic transaction and payment protection technology; it spun off the unit in 2000. In addition, Deluxe sells checks and other products to consumers online (its Internet operations account for 15% of sales). Although it sold its greeting card, mail-order stationery, and direct marketing operations, Deluxe offers business cards, personalized business stationery and greeting cards, and promotional specialty products online. It also has developed a number of business and financial services.

ATMs, debit cards, and electronic payments have taken their toll, though — Deluxe has gone from 65 printing plants to nine.

HISTORY

Deluxe Corporation began in 1915 with the determination of William Hotchkiss, a newspaper publisher turned chicken farmer, to produce one product "better, faster, and more economically than anyone else." From his office in St. Paul, Minnesota, Hotchkiss set out to provide banks with business checks within 48 hours of receiving the order. Deluxe Check Printers made just $23 that year. However, when a new Federal Reserve Bank was established in Minneapolis, the region soon became a major national banking center.

During the 1920s Hotchkiss introduced the most successful product in Deluxe's history: the Handy, a pocket-sized check. During the Depression the company cut employee hours and pay, but no jobs.

George McSweeney, a sales manager, created the Personalized Check Program in 1939 and was named president two years later. During WWII he stabilized the company by printing ration forms for banks after persuading Washington to release Deluxe's paper supply. In the 1950s Deluxe was one of the first firms to implement the government's magnetic-ink character-recognition program.

By 1960 the company was selling its printing services to 99% of US commercial banks. Deluxe went public in 1965. The company integrated computers and advanced printing technology into production during the 1970s.

In the following decade Deluxe positioned itself to profit from the increasing automation of transactions, making acquisitions such as Chex-Systems (account verification, 1984), Colwell Systems (medical business forms, 1985), A. O. Smith Data Systems (banking software, 1986), and Current (mail-order greeting cards and checks, 1987). It established a UK base in 1992 with Stockforms Ltd. (computer forms). Deluxe closed about a fourth of its check printing plants in 1993, the first layoffs in its history.

When Gus Blanchard became president and CEO of Deluxe (the first outsider to do so) the following year, he began a major reorganization. In 1996 he began a plan to close more than 20 check printing plants and eliminate 1,200 jobs (completed in 1999). He pursued international business, including a joint venture to provide electronic financial services to India's banking system.

Deluxe bought Fusion Marketing Group (customized database marketing services) in 1997. The next year, through a joint venture with Fair, Isaac & Co. and Acxiom Corp., Deluxe developed FraudFinder, a computerized system to rate a merchant's risk in accepting an individual's check or debit card. Increasing its focus on financial services, the company sold off its greeting card, specialty paper, and marketing database businesses. Also in 1998 it began offering check ordering over the Internet and via voice recognition technology.

In 1999 the company bought eFunds, whose technology converts checks into an electronic transaction at the point of sale. Deluxe also bought the remaining stake of its venture with HCL in 1999, renaming it iDLX. The company merged iDLX into eFunds, which went public in 2000. Also that year Deluxe bought Designer Checks. Deluxe began offering Disney characters on checks in 2001, the first time Disney characters have been licensed to appear on personal checks.

OFFICERS

Chairman and CEO: Lawrence J. Mosner, age 60, $2,188,550 pay
President, COO, and Director: Ronald E. Eilers, age 54, $1,057,500 pay
SVP and CFO: Douglas J. Treff, age 44, $709,375 pay
SVP and CIO: Warner F. Schlais, age 49, $478,125 pay
SVP, General Counsel and Secretary:
  Anthony C. Scarfone, age 40

SVP; President, Deluxe Business Services:
Richard L. Schulte, age 45, $455,550 pay
SVP; President, Direct Checks: Stephen J. Berry, age 39
SVP; President, Deluxe Financial Services:
Guy C. Feltz, age 46
VP, ebusiness and Corporate Development:
Gene H. Peterson, age 57
Executive Director, Human Resources: Mike O'Keefe
Auditors: PricewaterhouseCoopers LLP

LOCATIONS

HQ: 3680 Victoria St. North, Shoreview, MN 55126
Phone: 651-483-7111   **Fax:** 651-481-4163
Web: www.deluxe.com

Deluxe Corporation has production and teleservice centers in Alabama, Arizona, California, Colorado, Illinois, Indiana, Kansas, Minnesota, New Jersey, New York, North Carolina, Ohio, Pennsylvania, Texas, and Utah.

PRODUCTS/OPERATIONS

2001 Sales

	$ mil.	% of total
Financial Services	768	60
Direct Checks	306	24
Business Services	204	16
Total	**1,278**	**100**

Divisions and Selected Products and Services

Financial Services
Account conversion support
Check merchandising
Checks and related products to financial institutions
Customized reporting
Fraud prevention
Program management

Direct Checks
Checks and related products to consumers
   Checks Unlimited
   Designer Checks

Business Services
Checks and related products to small offices and
   home offices
Forms

Other Products and Services
Business cards and stationery
Checkbook covers
Continuous forms
Deposit tickets
Invoices
Personalized office supplies
Promotional specialty products
Statements
Tax forms

COMPETITORS

Adobe	MDC
American Banknote	Moore Corporation
Banta	National Processing
Bowne	New England Business
De La Rue	Service
DST	Northstar Computer
EDS	Forms
Ennis Business Forms	Novar
Equifax	Reynolds and Reynolds
First Data	R. R. Donnelley
ImageX	Standard Register
Intuit	Transaction Systems
iPrint	VeriFone
John Harland	Wallace Computer
Mail-Well	

HISTORICAL FINANCIALS & EMPLOYEES

NYSE: DLX FYE: December 31	Annual Growth	12/92	12/93	12/94	12/95	12/96	12/97	12/98	12/99	12/00	12/01
Sales ($ mil.)	(2.0%)	1,534	1,582	1,748	1,858	1,896	1,919	1,932	1,651	1,263	1,278
Net income ($ mil.)	(1.0%)	203	142	141	87	66	45	145	203	162	186
Income as % of sales	—	13.2%	9.0%	8.1%	4.7%	3.5%	2.3%	7.5%	12.3%	12.8%	14.5%
Earnings per share ($)	1.2%	2.41	1.71	1.71	1.06	0.79	0.55	1.80	2.64	2.24	2.69
Stock price - FY high ($)	—	49.00	47.88	38.00	34.00	39.75	37.00	38.19	40.50	29.00	42.65
Stock price - FY low ($)	—	38.13	31.75	25.63	25.75	27.00	29.75	26.06	24.44	19.63	18.85
Stock price - FY close ($)	(1.3%)	46.75	36.25	26.38	29.00	32.75	34.50	36.56	27.44	25.27	41.58
P/E - high	—	20	28	22	32	50	67	21	15	13	16
P/E - low	—	16	19	15	24	34	54	14	9	9	7
Dividends per share ($)	1.1%	1.34	1.42	1.46	1.48	1.48	1.48	1.48	1.48	1.48	1.48
Book value per share ($)	(20.7%)	9.90	9.71	9.89	9.48	8.69	7.50	7.57	5.79	3.62	1.23
Employees	(9.9%)	17,400	17,748	18,000	19,300	19,600	18,900	15,100	11,900	7,800	6,840

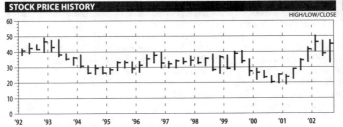

STOCK PRICE HISTORY   HIGH/LOW/CLOSE

2001 FISCAL YEAR-END
Debt ratio: 11.4%
Return on equity: 108.9%
Cash ($ mil.): 10
Current ratio: 0.23
Long-term debt ($ mil.): 10
No. of shares (mil.): 64
Dividends
   Yield: 3.6%
   Payout: 55.0%
Market value ($ mil.): 2,665

DENNY'S CORPORATION

Denny's now has the advantage of being a one-brand company. Spartanburg, South Carolina-based Denny's (formerly Advantica Restaurant Group) is one of the nation's largest restaurant businesses. It owns and franchises more than 1,700 Denny's, making it the US's largest full-service family-style restaurant chain, with breakfast items as the biggest seller. Nearly one-fourth of the company's Denny's are in California; Florida and Texas account for another 20%.

Advantica had emerged from bankruptcy protection in 1998. To cut down on the red meat, it sold the Hardee's, Quincy Family Steakhouse, and El Pollo Loco restaurant chains, but remained burdened by debt. The company decided to focus on Denny's and to rename itself; faced with falling sales, it cut costs by closing some 60 underperforming restaurants and selling another 59 restaurants to franchisees in 2001.

In 2002 it received $32.5 million when subsidiary FRD Acquisition Co. divested itself of the Coco's and Carrows chains as part of FRD's own Chapter 11 reorganization. Director Lloyd Miller owns about 14% of Denny's.

HISTORY

Trans World Airlines began acquiring businesses outside the volatile airline industry in the late 1960s to help stabilize earnings. Starting with Hilton International Hotels in 1967, TWA bought Canteen (food services, 1973), Spartan Food Systems (Hardee's and Quincy's restaurants, 1979), and Century 21 (real estate, 1979). The businesses were consolidated under holding company Trans World Corporation in 1979. However, $128 million in losses at the airline between 1973 and 1980 led Trans World to spin off TWA in 1984. (The airline was later acquired by American Airlines in 2001.) The company sold Century 21 the next year.

After Trans World sold Hilton in 1986, it bought nursing home operator American Medical Services and changed its name to Transworld Services. The company outbid Marriott for Denny's and El Pollo Loco (a Denny's subsidiary) in 1987. TW Services formed a joint venture (EPL Japan) with Japan's Mitsui in 1987 to operate El Pollo Loco restaurants in Japan through 1998 (Japanese operation of Denny's restaurants had begun in 1973).

In 1989 corporate raider Coniston Partners bought TW Services for $1.7 billion; it became a wholly owned subsidiary of TW Holdings, a company formed by Coniston especially for the deal. The buyout left TW Holdings with $1.9 billion in debt. To raise cash, it sold several assets in 1990, including American Medical Services. Kohlberg

Kravis Roberts bought a 47% stake in 1992 (it was sold in a 1997 bankruptcy reorganization).

The company changed its name from TW Holdings to Flagstar Companies in 1993. That year several lawsuits were filed against Denny's by patrons who claimed they were denied service because of race. Most notable was a suit filed by six African-American US Secret Service agents in Maryland. (Denny's settled the suits for $54 million in 1993.) Flagstar sold its Canteen food and vending business the next year.

In 1995 chairman and CEO Jerome Richardson stepped down from his executive position to devote more time to his expansion football franchise, the Carolina Panthers. The company named former Burger King CEO James Adamson as the new CEO. (Adamson also became chairman just four months later; in 1996 the NAACP named him Chief Executive of the Year.) That year Flagstar sold TW Recreational Services (lodging, food, and guest services for national parks and resorts) and Volume Services (stadium concessions). Flagstar bought the Coco's, Jojo's, and Carrows chains from Family Restaurants (now Prandium) in 1996. Many of the 17 Jojo's restaurants were converted to Coco's.

Soft sales and continued losses forced the company to file for Chapter 11 in 1997. It emerged from bankruptcy protection in early 1998 with a new name, Advantica Restaurant Group. That year the company sold its nearly 600 Hardee's fast-food units to CKE Restaurants, the Hardee's franchiser, and its 125-restaurant Quincy's Family Steakhouse chain to Buckley Acquisition. Following successful efforts to make the company more racially sensitive, Advantica ran a series of ads in 1999 to polish its image with the public.

Also in 1999 the company sold its El Pollo Loco chain to American Securities Capital Partners. The following year Advantica announced that it would sell Coco's and Carrows, focus on the Denny's chain, and rename itself (for the fifth time) Denny's. It refranchised nearly 150 restaurants that year, and in early 2001 sold another 28 locations to franchisees and added 40 new Denny's restaurants. Amid falling sales, the company laid off about 90 workers, closed 61 of its underperforming company-owned Denny's, and refranchised 59 others. Late in 2001, chairman James Adamson retired and director Charles Moran was named interim chairman. In 2002 it completed the sale of Coco's and Carrows for about $32.5 million as part of subsidiary and Coco's/Carrows parent FRD Acquisitions Co.'s Chapter 11 reorganization.

OFFICERS

Chairman: Charles F. Moran, age 72
President, CEO, and Director: Nelson L. Marchioli, age 52, $529,664 pay
EVP, Secretary, and General Counsel: Rhonda J. Parish, age 44, $478,436 pay
SVP and CFO: Andrew F. Green, age 46, $374,825 pay
SVP and CIO: Janis S. Emplit, age 46, $376,630 pay
SVP and Chief Marketing Officer: Margaret Jenkins
SVP Human Resources: Linda G. Traylor, age 50, $252,699 pay
VP, Assistant General Counsel, and Assistant Secretary: Timothy E. Fleming
VP and Assistant General Counsel: Robert M. Barrett
VP Communications: Karen F. Randall
VP Business Systems: Karen H. Bird
VP Human Resources and Training: Phyllis J. Calvert
VP Guest Assurance and Employee Relations: Alma F. Jackson
VP Procurement and Distribution: Mark C. Smith, age 41
VP Risk Management: Michael J. Jank
VP and Treasurer: Kenneth E. Jones
VP Tax: Ross B. Nell
VP Training: Kenneth R. Parson
VP Franchise and Development: Mounir N. Sawda, age 44
VP West Coast Operations: Edgardo Hernandez
Auditors: Deloitte & Touche LLP

LOCATIONS

HQ: 203 E. Main St., Spartanburg, SC 29319
Phone: 864-597-8000   **Fax:** 864-597-7532
Web: www.dennys.com

Denny's Corporation has restaurants in Canada, Costa Rica, Guam, Mexico, New Zealand, Puerto Rico, and the US.

PRODUCTS/OPERATIONS

2001 Sales

	% of total
Restaurants	91
Franchise & licensing fees	9
Total	**100**

COMPETITORS

American Hospitality Concepts
Applebee's
Bob Evans
Brinker
Buffets
Carlson Restaurants Worldwide
CBRL Group
Darden Restaurants
Friendly Ice Cream
IHOP
Investor's Management
Lone Star Steakhouse
Luby's
Metromedia
Outback Steakhouse
The Restaurant Company
Ryan's Family Steak Houses
Shoney's
Steak n Shake
VICORP Restaurants
Waffle House
Worldwide Restaurant Concepts

HISTORICAL FINANCIALS & EMPLOYEES

OTC: DNYY FYE: December 31	Annual Growth	12/92	12/93	12/94	12/95	12/96	12/97	12/98	12/99	12/00	12/01
Sales ($ mil.)	(13.2%)	3,720	3,970	2,666	2,572	2,542	2,610	1,721	1,590	1,155	1,040
Net income ($ mil.)	—	(52)	(1,648)	376	(133)	(86)	(135)	(182)	(382)	(82)	(89)
Income as % of sales	—	—	—	14.1%	—	—	—	—	—	—	—
Employees	(14.0%)	116,000	123,000	90,000	88,000	93,000	85,000	54,000	47,700	32,700	29,700

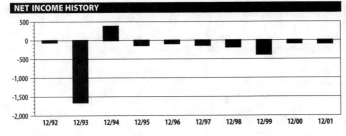

NET INCOME HISTORY

2001 FISCAL YEAR-END

Debt ratio: 100.0%
Return on equity: —
Cash ($ mil.): 7
Current ratio: 0.20
Long-term debt ($ mil.): 645

DEVON ENERGY CORPORATION

Devon Energy explores for and produces oil and gas, but it's developing a reputation as something else: a savvy shopper. By acquiring Northstar Energy, PennzEnergy, and Santa Fe Snyder, Oklahoma City-based Devon has built up its proved reserves to some 2 billion barrels of oil equivalent. The company expanded its reserves further with the acquisitions of Texas-based Mitchell Energy & Development and Canada's Anderson Exploration, deals which made Devon one of the largest independent oil and gas producers in North America.

Devon operates mainly in the US (Colorado, New Mexico, Texas, and Wyoming) and in western Canada. It's also active in the shallow areas of the Gulf of Mexico. Devon is a major producer of coalbed methane gas, and 60% of the company's reserves are natural gas.

Outside North America, the company has operations in the Caspian Sea region (primarily in Azerbaijan), South America, Southeast Asia, and West Africa.

HISTORY

Larry Nichols (a lawyer who clerked for US Supreme Court Chief Justice Earl Warren) and his father, John, founded Devon Energy in 1969. John Nichols was a partner in predecessor company Blackwood and Nichols, an oil partnership formed in 1946.

The company bought a small stake in the Northeast Blanco Unit of New Mexico's San Juan Basin in 1981. To raise capital, Devon formed the limited partnership Devon Resource Investors and took it public in 1985. Devon consolidated all of its units into a single, publicly traded company in 1988.

The firm increased its stake in Northeast Blanco in 1988 and again in 1989, ending up with about 25%. By 1990 Devon had drilled more than 100 wells in the area and had proved reserves of 58 billion cu. ft. of natural gas.

During the 1990s the company launched a major expansion program using a two-pronged strategy: acquiring producing properties and drilling wells in proven fields. In 1990 it bought an 88% interest in six Texas wells; two years later Devon snapped up the US properties of Hondo Oil & Gas. After its 1994 purchase of Alta Energy, which operated in New Mexico, Oklahoma, Texas, and Wyoming, Devon had proved reserves of more than 500 billion cu. ft. of gas.

Between 1992 and 1997 the company also drilled some 840 successful wells. Buoyed by new seismic techniques that raise the odds of finding oil, Devon devoted more resources to pioneering fields in regions where it already had expertise.

Continuing its buying spree, Devon bought Kerr-McGee's onshore assets in 1997. Two years later it bought Alberta, Canada-based Northstar for $775 million, creating a company with holdings divided almost evenly between oil and gas.

Also in 1999 Devon grabbed its biggest prize when it purchased PennzEnergy of Houston in a $2.3 billion stock-and-debt deal that analysts called a bargain. PennzEnergy, spun off from Pennzoil in 1998, dates back to the Texas oil boom after WWII. In addition to new US holdings, the deal gave Devon a number of international oil and gas assets in such places as Azerbaijan, Brazil, Egypt, Qatar, and Venezuela.

On a roll, Devon in 2000 bought Santa Fe Snyder for $2.35 billion in stock and $1 billion in assumed debt. The deal increased Devon's proved reserves by nearly 400 million barrels of oil equivalent.

In 2001 the company agreed to a major deal to supply Indonesian natural gas to Singapore. It also made an unsuccessful bid for rival Barrett Resouces but was trumped by a bid from Williams Companies. Undaunted, that year Devon acquired Anderson Exploration for $3.4 billion in cash and $1.2 billion in assumed debt. It also purchased Mitchell Energy & Development for $3.1 billion in cash and stock and $400 million in assumed debt.

As part of its strategy to refocus on core operations, in 2002 the company agreed to sell its Indonesian assets to PetroChina for $262 million. By mid-2002 the company had raised about $1.2 billion through the disposition of oil properties worldwide.

OFFICERS

Chairman Emeritus: John W. Nichols, age 87
Chairman, President, and CEO: J. Larry Nichols, age 59, $1,650,000 pay
SVP and General Counsel: Duke R. Ligon, age 60, $540,000 pay
SVP Administration: Marian J. Moon, age 51
SVP Canadian Division: John Richels, age 51
SVP Corporate Development: Brian J. Jennings, age 41
SVP Exploration and Production: J. Michael Lacey, age 56, $675,000 pay
SVP Finance: William T. Vaughn, age 55, $565,000 pay
SVP Marketing: Darryl G. Smette, age 54, $675,000 pay
VP; General Manager, Gulf Division: William A. Van Wie, age 56
VP; General Manager, International Division: David J. Sambrooks, age 43
VP; General Manager, Marketing and Midstream Division: Terrence L. Ruder, age 49
VP; General Manager, Permian/Mid-Continent Division: Rick D. Clark, age 54
VP; General Manager, Rocky Mountain Division: Don D. DeCarlo, age 45

VP Accounting: Danny J. Heatley, age 46
VP Communications and Investor Relations:
Vincent W. White, age 44
VP Government Relations: Gary L. McGee, age 52
VP Human Resources: Paul R. Poley, age 48
VP Information Services: Richard E. Manner, age 55
Treasurer: Dale T. Wilson, age 42
Auditors: KPMG LLP

LOCATIONS

HQ: 20 N. Broadway Ave., Ste. 1500,
Oklahoma City, OK 73102
Phone: 405-235-3611   **Fax:** 405-552-4667
Web: www.devonenergy.com

Devon Energy has major operations in Central Asia,
Southeast Asia, North and South America, and West
Africa.

2001 Sales

	$ mil.	% of total
US	2,338	76
Canada	489	16
Other countries	248	8
Total	**3,075**	**100**

PRODUCTS/OPERATIONS

2001 Sales

	$ mil.	% of total
Gas	1,890	62
Oil	958	31
Natural gas liquids	132	4
Other	95	3
Total	**3,075**	**100**

COMPETITORS

Abraxas Petroleum
Amerada Hess
Apache
BP
BHP Billiton Ltd
Burlington Resources
Cabot Oil & Gas
Castle Energy
Chesapeake Energy
ChevronTexaco
ConocoPhillips
EnCana
Exxon Mobil
Forest Oil
Imperial Oil
KCS Energy
Marathon Oil
PDVSA
PETROBRAS
Royal Dutch/Shell Group
Swift Energy
Tom Brown
TOTAL FINA ELF
Unocal
Williams Companies
XTO Energy

HISTORICAL FINANCIALS & EMPLOYEES

AMEX: DVN FYE: December 31	Annual Growth	12/92	12/93	12/94	12/95	12/96	12/97	12/98	12/99	12/00	12/01
Sales ($ mil.)	52.6%	69	99	101	113	163	313	370	716	2,784	3,075
Net income ($ mil.)	24.2%	15	21	14	15	35	75	(60)	95	730	103
Income as % of sales	—	21.3%	20.7%	13.6%	12.8%	21.4%	24.0%	—	13.2%	26.2%	3.3%
Earnings per share ($)	(2.4%)	0.90	1.04	0.63	0.65	1.52	2.17	(1.25)	1.46	5.50	0.72
Stock price – FY high ($)	—	16.00	27.25	26.50	26.00	37.00	49.13	41.13	44.94	64.74	66.75
Stock price – FY low ($)	—	7.63	14.38	16.00	16.75	19.88	27.38	26.13	20.13	31.38	30.55
Stock price – FY close ($)	11.1%	15.00	20.63	18.25	25.50	34.75	38.50	30.69	32.88	60.97	38.65
P/E – high	—	17	28	41	39	24	21	—	30	11	196
P/E – low	—	8	15	25	25	13	12	—	13	6	90
Dividends per share ($)	—	0.00	0.09	0.12	0.12	0.14	0.20	0.20	0.20	0.20	0.20
Book value per share ($)	12.4%	7.39	8.30	9.36	9.90	21.35	16.82	10.80	23.53	25.48	21.15
Employees	42.6%	116	175	192	203	231	383	764	1,549	1,750	2,826

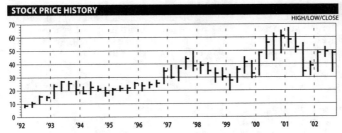

STOCK PRICE HISTORY
HIGH/LOW/CLOSE

2001 FISCAL YEAR-END

Debt ratio: 66.9%
Return on equity: 3.2%
Cash ($ mil.): 193
Current ratio: 1.18
Long-term debt ($ mil.): 6,589
No. of shares (mil.): 154
Dividends
  Yield: 0.5%
  Payout: 27.8%
Market value ($ mil.): 5,957

DHL WORLDWIDE EXPRESS, INC.

By bus, boat, or bicycle, from Albania to Kyrgyzstan, Qatar to Zimbabwe, DHL Worldwide Express delivers. The San Francisco-based company is the world leader in cross-border express deliveries, ahead of FedEx and UPS.

Overall, DHL links 120,000 destinations in about 230 countries and territories. The company has about 4,000 offices worldwide, and it operates a fleet of more than 250 aircraft. It is a licensed customs broker in more than 140 countries. Affiliate DHL Airways provides air cargo services in the US. DHL is expanding its logistics management services, which include Internet tracking and order fulfillment.

Brussels-based DHL International, which is 75%-owned by Deutsche Post, owns 100% of DHL Worldwide Express and 52% of DHL Airways.

HISTORY

In 1969 co-workers Adrian Dalsey (the "D" in DHL Worldwide Express), Larry Lee Hillblom (the "H"), and Robert Lynn (the "L") were looking for a way to improve the turnaround time for ships in ports. Their brainstorm was to fly shipping documents to ports for examination and processing before the ship arrived. This idea rapidly developed into an express delivery service between California and Hawaii, and Bank of America became a major customer.

Service was expanded to the Philippines in 1971. The following year the three original investors asked Hong Kong entrepreneur Po Chung to help them form DHL International, a global delivery network. Chung had no previous experience in the express delivery business, but he pioneered a simplified rate structure and the single network concept, which required that the company take full responsibility for picking up and delivering the package. By the end of 1972, service was extended to Australia, Hong Kong, Japan, and Singapore.

From its Pacific Basin origins, DHL expanded worldwide in the 1970s, moving into Europe in 1974, Latin America in 1977, and the Middle East and Africa in 1978.

An agreement with hotel franchiser Hilton in 1980 to provide daily pickup and international delivery garnered new outlets for DHL.

Having focused on its international network during its early years, DHL invested heavily in developing a delivery network within the US in 1983. It also extended its service to Eastern Europe. In 1985 — the year UPS and FedEx also began providing international express delivery — DHL and Western Union entered a venture to transmit documents by e-mail. That next year DHL established the first air express venture in China. Dalsey ran

the company until his retirement in the mid-1980s (he died in 1994).

In 1990 DHL International sold portions of the company to Japan Airlines, Lufthansa (Germany), and Japanese securities firm Nissho Iwai (which sold back its stake in 1999), giving DHL both customers and expertise in dealing with Japanese and German clients.

Hillblom died in a 1995 plane crash in the Pacific Ocean. The company bought back the 25% stake in DHL International held by his estate. Distribution of his $500 million fortune — much of which was to go for medical research — was delayed by lawsuits, and part of the estate was ordered given to four DNA-linked children born to barmaids in the Pacific Islands where Hillblom retired.

In 1996 DHL opened a gateway in Moscow, and in 1997 the company became one of the first international air carriers to serve North Korea. Deutsche Post acquired a 25% stake in DHL International in 1998. Lynn, DHL's last living co-founder, died that year.

The company in 1999 opened a bigger service center in Silicon Valley (its largest US center); began work on its larger, fully automated North American hub in Cincinnati; and formed an alliance with the US Postal Service guaranteeing a priority mail service across the Atlantic.

That year Japan Airlines reduced its DHL International stake to 6% (from 26%), and DHL announced that it planned an IPO of a 23% stake in DHL International. But the IPO plans were put on hold in 2000: That year Lufthansa and Deutsche Post announced the formation of joint venture Aerologic to oversee their respective 25% stakes in DHL International.

The next year Deutsche Post increased to 51% its stake in DHL International, which owned a majority stake in DHL Airways. Rivals UPS and FedEx complained that the ownership restructuring caused DHL to violate limits on foreign government ownership of US airlines, but the US Department of Transportation ruled in favor of DHL and upheld its air freight forwarding license.

DHL suffered a crash in 2002 when one of its cargo jets collided with a Russian passenger jet, killing 95 people, all but two of whom were on the passenger aircraft. Also that year Deutsche Post increased its stake in DHL International to about 75% by buying out Lufthansa.

Chairman and CEO: John Fellows
SVP and CFO: Ronald F. Dutt
SVP Field and Customer Service: Norm Hurley
SVP Human Resources: Gary Sellers
SVP Sales and Marketing: Randy T. Clark
VP Hub and Gateway Operations: Steve White
**VP Service Management Transit and Operations
  Planning:** Mike Lopez
Acting CEO, DHL Airways: Vicki Bretthauer
SVP and CFO, DHL Airways: Jeffrey J. Simmons
**SVP Corporate Finance and General Counsel, DHL
  Airways:** Steven A. Rossum
VP Marketing and Planning, DHL Airways:
  Joanne Smith
CTO: Oliver Deschryver
Managing Director: Christoph Mueller
Manager Public Relations: Erica Pearson

Airborne
BAX Global
Bilspedition
CD&L
CNF
Expeditors International
FedEx
Ratos
Stinnes
TPG
UPS
UPS Freight Services
USFreightways
U.S. Postal Service

HQ: 50 California St., San Francisco, CA 94111
Phone: 415-677-6100   **Fax:** 415-677-7268
Web: www.dhl-usa.com

Selected Services

International

Import Express (importing of goods or documents into
  the US)
International Document Service
Same Day Service (next-flight-out to more than 125
  international destinations)
ThermoExpress Service (delivery of perishable goods,
  using special packaging)
WorldFreight (worldwide shipment of 220-plus pounds)
Worldwide Priority Express (global door-to-door
  shipment, any size or weight)

Domestic

Same Day Service
ThermoExpress Service
USA Overnight (overnight business delivery)

Subsidiary FYE: December 31	Annual Growth	12/92	12/93	12/94	12/95	12/96	12/97	12/98	12/99	12/00	12/01
Estimated sales ($ mil.)	8.8%	2,800	3,000	3,100	3,800	4,200	4,800	5,000	5,100	5,500	6,000
Employees	11.0%	28,000	34,000	35,000	40,000	50,000	59,200	60,486	63,600	67,000	71,480

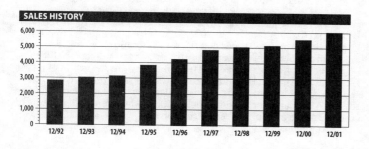

THE DIAL CORPORATION

Sink back in a bath, light an air-freshening candle, pop open a can of Vienna sausages, and you'll be relaxing in Dial style. Scottsdale, Arizona-based The Dial Corporation makes Dial, one of the US's best-selling soaps, and has leading brands in its four core product segments — personal care (Dial, Tone, Breck), laundry (Purex, Borateem, 20 Mule Team), air fresheners (Renuzit), and canned meats (Armour — the top-selling brand of Vienna sausages).

Internationally, the consumer products company has a strong presence in Canada. It has been expanding into Latin America, including Argentina, Mexico, Puerto Rico, and the Caribbean.

In 2001, the company's depressed stock price and flagging earnings stoked rumors that it could be a takeover target. Facing stiff competition and deciding it would fare better as part of a larger company, Dial put itself up for sale in 2002. Due to Argentina's depressed economy, Dial also announced in 2002 that it may exit its business in that country. Altogether, Dial sells its products in more than 50 countries.

HISTORY

In the mid-1940s meatpacker Armour & Company developed a deodorant soap by adding the germicidal agent AT-7 to soap; this limited body odor by reducing bacteria on the skin. The new soap was named Dial because of its 24-hour protection against the odor-causing bacteria. Armour introduced the soap in 1948 in a full-page advertisement (on paper with scented ink) in the *Chicago Tribune*.

By the 1950s Dial was the best-selling deodorant soap in the US. The company adopted the slogan "Aren't you glad you use Dial? Don't you wish everybody did?" in 1953. In the 1960s Armour expanded the Dial line with deodorants and shaving creams.

Canadian bus company Greyhound bought Armour and its Dial brand in 1970. Greyhound kept the company's meatpacking (Armour Foods) and consumer products operations (Armour-Dial), and sold the rest of its assets. Armour-Dial moved its headquarters to Phoenix in 1971.

Greyhound's rapid diversification and frequent unit restructurings led to erratic profitability. In 1981 John Teets was appointed chairman of Greyhound and began selling unprofitable subsidiaries. After meatpackers struck at Armour plants in the mid-1980s, Teets shut 29 plants and sold its meatpacking operation to ConAgra (but kept its canned meat business). A similar labor feud at Greyhound led to the sale of the bus operations in 1987. Armour-Dial acquired laundry soap maker Purex Industries in 1985. Two years later it introduced Liquid Dial soap. In 1990 the company acquired the Breck hair products line.

To reflect its changing focus, the company changed its name to The Dial Corporation in 1991. When it sold Motor Coach Industries to the public in 1993, it exited the US bus industry altogether. Also that year Dial bought Renuzit air fresheners from S.C. Johnson. The company introduced the Nature's Accents line of skin care products in 1995.

Dial chose in 1996 to divide into two companies. Its services units became Viad, while its consumer products businesses continued to operate as Dial. Outsider Malcolm Jozoff — a veteran of Lenox and Procter & Gamble (P&G) — was brought in to head Dial. (Teets was named to head Viad but subsequently announced his retirement.)

The new Dial eliminated about 20% of its management and administrative jobs and trimmed more than half of its 2,300 products. Housecleaning continued when it sold its line of Brillo cleaning products to Church & Dwight in 1997. That same year, to expand its international sales, Dial purchased Argentina's Nuevo Federal (soap, detergent) and then five more Argentine soap brands from P&G.

Dial retired its "Aren't you glad you use Dial . . ." slogan in 1998, hoping to lure younger consumers. To complement its Nature's Accents line, that year the company bought specialty bath care companies Freeman Cosmetic (natural skin care and hair care) and Sarah Michaels (bath and body products). In 1999 Dial formed a joint venture with Germany's Henkel (Dial/Henkel LLC) to develop a new line of Purex detergent products for the North American market. The joint venture later purchased the Custom Cleaner home dry-cleaning business from Creative Products Resource.

In 2000 Herbert Baum (former COO of Hasbro) was named chairman, president, and CEO, replacing Jozoff, who resigned after the company announced it would not meet earnings expectations. In 2001 Dial sold its part of the joint venture it had with Henkel to Henkel. That year Dial also announced it was seeking a buyer. Dial also sold its specialty personal care businesses (the Sarah Michaels and Freeman Cosmetics brands).

In 2002 the company announced that it had decided against putting itself up for sale. However, later that same year, still facing stiff competition from industry giants such as Unilever and Procter & Gamble, Dial reversed this thinking and did, indeed, put itself up for sale, its reasoning being that it would fare better as part of a larger company.

Chairman, President, and CEO: Herbert M. Baum, age 65, $2,585,000 pay
EVP and CFO: Conrad A. Conrad, age 56, $858,596 pay
EVP International and Business Development: Mark R. Shook, age 47, $635,000 pay
EVP Shared Services: Bernhard J. Welle, age 53, $814,384 pay
SVP Investor Relations: Stephen D. Blum, age 58
SVP Research and Development: Mark Cushman, age 44
SVP Sales: Arthur E. Hanke, age 54, $532,577 pay
SVP and CIO: Evon L. Jones, age 37
SVP, General Counsel, and Secretary: Christopher J. Littlefield, age 35
SVP and Treasurer: David M. Riddiford, age 35
SVP and Controller: John F. Tierney, age 49
SVP and General Manager Personal Cleansing: Greg A. Tipsord, age 36
SVP and General Manager Laundry Care: Stephen L. Tooker, age 42
SVP Innovation and Air Fresheners: Mark L. Whitehouse, age 45, $237,629 pay
VP Product Development: Terrell Partee, age 43
VP and General Manager Food Products: Brian T. Shook, age 39
Auditors: Deloitte & Touche LLP

LOCATIONS

HQ: 15501 N. Dial Blvd., Scottsdale, AZ 85260
Phone: 480-754-3425   **Fax:** 480-754-1098
Web: www.dialcorp.com

The Dial Corporation has major manufacturing operations in Argentina, Guatemala, Mexico, and the US.

PRODUCTS/OPERATIONS

Selected Brands

Air Fresheners
Renuzit (adjustables, aerosols, candles)

Body, Hair, and Skin Care Products
Boraxo (hand soap)
Breck
Campos Verdes
Coast (US)
Dial
Liquid Dial
Pure & Natural
Tone

Cleaning and Laundry Products
20 Mule Team
Borateem
Cristal

Enzimax
Fels Naptha
Gran Federal
Gran Llauro
Limzul
Plusbelle
Purex
Sta-Flo
Vano
Zorro
Zout

Food Products
Armour (Vienna sausages, meat spreads, hash, chili)
Armour Star
Cream (corn starch)

COMPETITORS

Alberto-Culver
Alticor
Body Shop
Church & Dwight
Clorox
Colgate-Palmolive
ConAgra
Del Labs

GOJO
Hormel
Huish Detergents
Intimate Brands
Johnson & Johnson
L'Oréal USA
Mary Kay
Nestlé

Procter & Gamble
Reckitt Benckiser
Sara Lee Household
S.C. Johnson
Scott's Liquid Gold
Unilever

HISTORICAL FINANCIALS & EMPLOYEES

NYSE: DL FYE: Saturday nearest Dec. 31	Annual Growth	12/92	12/93	12/94	12/95	12/96	12/97	12/98	12/99	12/00	12/01
Sales ($ mil.)	3.0%	1,275	1,420	1,511	1,365	1,406	1,363	1,525	1,722	1,639	1,663
Net income ($ mil.)	—	31	84	91	(27)	30	84	103	117	(11)	(132)
Income as % of sales	—	2.4%	5.9%	6.0%	—	2.1%	6.1%	6.7%	6.8%	—	—
Earnings per share ($)	—	—	—	—	—	0.33	0.89	1.02	1.17	(0.12)	(1.45)
Stock price - FY high ($)	—	—	—	—	—	15.00	21.81	30.25	38.38	24.06	18.78
Stock price - FY low ($)	—	—	—	—	—	11.13	13.38	19.38	19.50	9.88	11.19
Stock price - FY close ($)	3.2%	—	—	—	—	14.63	20.81	28.88	24.31	11.00	17.15
P/E - high	—	—	—	—	—	45	24	29	32	—	—
P/E - low	—	—	—	—	—	34	15	19	16	—	—
Dividends per share ($)	14.9%	—	—	—	—	0.08	0.32	0.32	0.32	0.32	0.16
Book value per share ($)	(10.1%)	—	—	—	—	1.47	3.12	3.78	4.09	3.10	0.86
Employees	(3.2%)	4,197	4,000	3,995	3,985	2,800	2,533	3,759	3,754	3,351	3,139

STOCK PRICE HISTORY

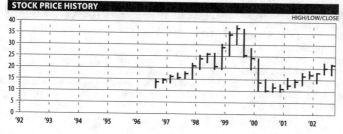

HIGH/LOW/CLOSE

2001 FISCAL YEAR-END

Debt ratio: 84.5%
Return on equity: —
Cash ($ mil.): 29
Current ratio: 1.19
Long-term debt ($ mil.): 445
No. of shares (mil.): 95
Dividends
  Yield: 0.9%
  Payout: —
Market value ($ mil.): 1,627

DIEBOLD, INCORPORATED

Diebold doesn't have to keep bankers' hours. The North Canton, Ohio-based company is a leading provider of automated teller machines (ATMs). In addition to ATMs, Diebold offers automated or staffed banking facilities, such as its MicroBranch prefabricated branch offices, which can be installed in grocery stores and malls. Diebold also develops smart cards, which are used, for example, by students who can carry a single card for cafeteria purchases and campus event access.

Originally a manufacturer of safes, the company is still active in its original market, offering products ranging from vaults to security systems for financial institutions. The company took its ATM technology into the health care market with its MedSelect systems for storing, dispensing, and tracking patient medications, but it has since sold that business.

Diebold is using acquisitions (including purchases of Bull's financial self-service business and Italian ATM machine monitoring service provider Sersi Italia) and alliances to challenge NCR in the developing markets of Europe and Latin America. It also is broadening its services (half of sales) by turning to home Internet transaction processing, Web-enabled ATMs, and other Internet functions.

HISTORY

German immigrant Charles Diebold formed safe and vault maker Diebold Bahmann in Cincinnati in 1859. The Chicago Fire of 1871 gave the company an unexpected boost: All 878 of its safes in the area (and their contents) survived the inferno. The company relocated in 1872 to North Canton, Ohio, where it was incorporated in 1876. During the next two decades, it also made jails, trapdoors for gallows, and padded cells for asylums. In the 1930s Diebold helped develop a bank lobby tear gas system, made in part to deter the notorious John Dillinger.

Compelled to diversify after the Great Depression, Diebold made seven major acquisitions between 1936 and 1947, including bank and office equipment firms and other safe makers. WWII government arms contracts helped boost the company's sales from about $3 million per year to $40 million in 1942. Two years later former Prohibition G-man Eliot Ness (immortalized on television and in films in *The Untouchables*) joined Diebold's board, later becoming chairman and overseeing the 1946 takeover of York Safe, which had been the largest US safe maker before WWII.

The 1947 acquisition of O.B. McClintock Co.'s bank equipment division moved Diebold into the drive-through teller window business. Sales of these windows and other bank equipment were stimulated by suburban growth in the 1950s. By 1957 business equipment represented about half of Diebold's business.

Increased check use in the early 1960s led Diebold to enter check imprinting with the 1963 purchase of Consolidated Business Systems (business forms, magnetic imprinting ink for checks). Diebold went public the next year.

With security equipment sales slowing in the early 1970s, CEO Raymond Koontz gambled on ATMs, investing heavily in R&D. In 1973 Diebold introduced its first ATM. Sales were helped by long-standing relationships with banks, and within five years Diebold had 45% of the US ATM market.

In 1990 Diebold formed InterBold, a joint venture with former rival IBM, to sell ATMs. Diebold acquired Griffin Technology, moving into the market for campus systems, in 1995. The company expanded its Asian presence in 1997 when it acquired Safetell International Security. The next year, after InterBold canceled its agreement with IBM, Diebold bought IBM's 30% interest in the venture, taking direct control over its global distribution. The InterBold purchase and heavy competition in the ATM market caused a decline in sales and earnings for 1998.

Diebold's 1999 acquisitions included Pioneer Systems, a developer of a campus ID card system that provides links to financial institutions as well as off-campus merchants, and Procomp Amazonia Industria Electronica, a Brazil-based information technology company. Later that year Emerson Electric executive Walden O'Dell became CEO. Also in 1999, in a pilot program Bank United (which later became part of Washington Mutual) installed iris-based recognition technology (developed by Diebold) at three ATMs.

In 2000 the company furthered its global push by acquiring the financial self-service businesses of Amsterdam-based Getronics NV and Paris-based Bull for a combined value of about $160 million. Early in 2002 Diebold acquired voting systems maker Global Election Systems, and it renamed the new subsidiary Diebold Election Systems.

OFFICERS

Chairman, President, and CEO: Walden W. O'Dell, age 56, $760,000 pay
COO: Wesley B. Vance, age 44, $518,000 pay
SVP and CFO: Gregory T. Geswein, age 46, $270,000 pay
SVP, Customer Solutions Group: David Bucci, age 50
SVP, Global Manufacturing and Quality: Tom D'Amico
SVP, Global Product Development and Engineering: Danny O'Brien

VP; Managing Director, Asia/Pacific: James L.M. Chen, age 41
VP; Managing Director, Europe, Middle East, and Africa: Reinoud G.J. Drenth, age 38
VP; Managing Director, Latin America: Ernesto R. Unanue, age 60
VP and CIO: John M. Crowther
VP and Secretary: Charee Francis-Vogelsang, age 55
VP and Treasurer: Robert J. Warren, age 55
VP, General Counsel, and Assistant Secretary: Warren W. Dettinger, age 48
VP, Corporate Development: William E. Rosenberg
VP, Customer Satisfaction: Dennis M. Moriarty, age 49
VP, Global Communications and Investor Relations: Donald E. Eagon Jr., age 59
VP, Global Procurement: Larry D. Ingram, age 55
VP, Human Resources: Charles B. Scheurer, age 60
Auditors: KPMG LLP

LOCATIONS

HQ: 5995 Mayfair Rd., North Canton, OH 44720
Phone: 330-490-4000 **Fax:** 330-490-4549
Web: www.diebold.com

Diebold has manufacturing facilities in Argentina, Belgium, Brazil, China, France, India, Mexico, and the US. It has sales and support offices in nearly 30 countries.

2001 Sales

	$ mil.	% of total
The Americas	1,338	76
Europe, Middle East & Africa	312	18
Asia/Pacific	110	6
Total	**1,760**	**100**

PRODUCTS/OPERATIONS

2001 Sales

	$ mil.	% of total
Financial products		
Services	727	41
Hardware	697	40
Security products		
Services	183	10
Hardware	151	9
Other	2	—
Total	**1,760**	**100**

Selected Products

Alarm and monitoring systems
Automated commercial banking systems (Merchant Banking Center)
Automated teller machines (ATMs)
Bill payment terminals (PayStation)
Bullet-resistive barriers
Card-based systems
Cash dispensing systems (Express Delivery XT Systems)
Drive-up banking equipment
Management software
Prefabricated walls (MicroBranch Wall Systems)
Remote bank teller kiosks (RemoteTeller System)
Vaults, safe deposit boxes, locks, and safes

COMPETITORS

Dassault	Hart InterCivic	Shoup Voting
De La Rue	Hypercom	Solutions
Dover	Itautec Philco	Siemens
Election Systems	NCR	Tidel
& Software	Oki Electric	Transaction
Fujitsu	Schlumberger	Systems
Gemplus	Sensormatic	VeriFone

HISTORICAL FINANCIALS & EMPLOYEES

NYSE: DBD FYE: December 31	Annual Growth	12/92	12/93	12/94	12/95	12/96	12/97	12/98	12/99	12/00	12/01
Sales ($ mil.)	13.9%	544	623	760	863	1,030	1,227	1,186	1,259	1,744	1,760
Net income ($ mil.)	12.5%	23	48	64	76	97	123	76	129	137	67
Income as % of sales	—	4.3%	7.8%	8.4%	8.8%	9.5%	10.0%	6.4%	10.2%	7.9%	3.8%
Earnings per share ($)	11.5%	0.35	0.71	0.93	1.10	1.40	1.76	1.10	1.85	1.92	0.93
Stock price - FY high ($)	—	12.27	18.29	20.80	27.64	42.35	50.94	55.31	39.88	34.75	41.50
Stock price - FY low ($)	—	9.25	11.60	15.10	14.68	22.47	28.00	19.13	19.69	21.50	25.75
Stock price - FY close ($)	14.5%	11.97	17.88	18.30	24.64	41.94	50.63	35.69	23.50	33.38	40.44
P/E - high	—	20	26	22	25	30	29	50	21	18	44
P/E - low	—	15	16	16	13	16	16	17	11	11	27
Dividends per share ($)	7.6%	0.33	0.35	0.39	0.43	0.45	0.50	0.56	0.60	0.62	0.64
Book value per share ($)	8.8%	5.91	6.28	6.71	7.37	8.36	9.69	10.15	11.88	13.08	12.66
Employees	13.8%	3,975	4,202	4,731	5,178	5,980	6,714	6,489	9,935	12,544	12,674

STOCK PRICE HISTORY

HIGH/LOW/CLOSE

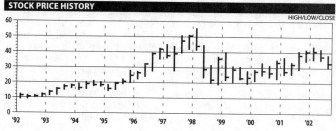

2001 FISCAL YEAR-END

Debt ratio: 2.3%
Return on equity: 7.3%
Cash ($ mil.): 74
Current ratio: 1.45
Long-term debt ($ mil.): 21
No. of shares (mil.): 71
Dividends
  Yield: 1.6%
  Payout: 68.8%
Market value ($ mil.): 2,886

DILLARD'S, INC.

The times they are a-changin' at Dillard's. The #3 upscale department store chain in the US is not only fighting competition from discounters, but it also has to recoup from the loss of its founder and guiding force, William Dillard.

The Little Rock Arkansas-based company operates about 340 stores in 29 states, covering the Sunbelt, the Midwest and the Great Plains. Dillard's caters to middle- and upper-middle-income women, offering name-brand and private-label merchandise, with an emphasis on clothing and home furnishings.

Dillard's prides itself on its attention to quality and a tradition as a grand old department store; but changing consumer buying habits and slumping sales are forcing the company to re-think its strategy. Like its top two competitors, Federated and May, Dillard's has begun to promote its own private-label merchandise. In-house brands now account for 18% of total sales in sections where private brands are sold. The company has long been averse to marking down merchandise, but competition from discount chains is forcing it to put items on sale, often at much lower prices.

One of Dillard's strategies is the double anchor concept: two locations in the same mall. Rather than closing a store when it buys space where it already has a presence, Dillard's uses the additional store, placing women's and children's departments and home furnishings in one location and men's and juniors' departments in the other.

Founder and patriarch William Dillard died in February 2002. His son, William Dillard II, has taken the reins of a company that has been family-controlled for half a century. Dillard family members own 99% of the Class B voting stock and thus elect two-thirds of the company's directors.

HISTORY

At age 12 William Dillard began working in his father's general store in Mineral Springs, Arkansas. After he graduated from Columbia University in 1937, the third-generation retailer spent seven months in the Sears, Roebuck manager training program in Tulsa, Oklahoma.

With $8,000 borrowed from his father, William opened his first department store in Nashville, Arkansas, in 1938. Service was one of the most important things he had to offer, he said, and he insisted on quality — he personally inspected every item and would settle for nothing but the best. William sold the store in 1948 to finance a partnership in Wooten's Department Store in Texarkana, Arkansas; he bought out Wooten and established Dillard's the next year.

Throughout the 1950s and 1960s, the company became a strong regional retailer, developing its strategy of buying well-established downtown stores in small cities; acquisitions in those years included Mayer & Schmidt (Tyler, Texas; 1956) and Joseph Pfeifer (Little Rock, Arkansas; 1963). Dillard's moved its headquarters to Little Rock after buying Pfeifer. When it went public in 1969, it had 15 stores in three states.

During the early 1960s the company began computerizing operations to streamline inventory and information management. In 1970 Dillard's added computerized cash registers, which gave management hourly sales figures.

The chain continued acquiring outlets (more than 130 over the next three decades, including stores owned by Stix, Baer & Fuller, Macy's, Joske's, and Maison Blanche). In a 1988 joint venture with Edward J. DeBartolo, Dillard's bought a 50% interest in the 12 Higbee's stores in Ohio (buying the other 50% in 1992, shortly after Higbee's bought five former Horne's stores in Ohio).

In 1991 Vendamerica (subsidiary of Vendex International and the only major nonfamily holder of the company's stock) sold its 8.9 million shares of Class A stock (25% of the class) in an underwritten public offering.

Dillard's purchase of 12 Diamond stores from Dayton Hudson in 1994 gave it a small-event ticket-sales chain in the Southwest, which it renamed Dillard's Box Office. A lawsuit filed by the FTC against Dillard's that year, claiming the company made it unreasonably difficult for company credit card holders to remove unauthorized charges from their bills, was dismissed the following year.

Dillard's continued to grow; it opened 11 new stores in 1995 and 16 new stores in 1996 (entering Georgia and Colorado). The next year it opened 12 new stores and acquired 20, making its way into Virginia, California, and Wyoming.

William retired in 1998 and William Dillard II took over the CEO position, while brother Alex became president. The company then paid $3.1 billion for Mercantile Stores, which operated 106 apparel and home design stores in the South and Midwest. To avoid redundancy in certain regions, Dillard's sold 26 of those stores and exchanged seven others. The assimilation of Mercantile brought distribution problems that cut into earnings for fiscal 1999. In late 2000, with a slumping stock price and declining sales, Dillard's said it would de-emphasize its concentration on name-brand merchandise and would offer deep discounts on branded items already in stock. Despite these efforts, earnings continued to slide in 2001.

William, founder and chairman of the company, died at age 87 in Little Rock in February 2002. His son was named chairman in May.

Chairman and CEO: William Dillard II, age 57, $710,000 pay
President and Director: Alex Dillard, age 52, $620,000 pay
EVP and Director: Drue Corbusier, age 55, $500,000 pay
EVP and Director: Mike Dillard, age 50, $540,000 pay
SVP, CFO, and Director: James I. Freeman, age 52, $500,000 pay
VP and General Counsel: Paul J. Schroeder Jr., age 53
Personnel: Molly Myers
Auditors: Deloitte & Touche LLP

LOCATIONS

HQ: 1600 Cantrell Rd., Little Rock, AR 72201
Phone: 501-376-5200   **Fax:** 501-399-7831
Web: www.dillards.com

2002 Stores

	No.
Texas	61
Florida	44
Ohio	23
Tennessee	17
Louisiana	15
Missouri	15
North Carolina	15
Arizona	14
Oklahoma	13
Alabama	12
Colorado	11
Kentucky	11
Virginia	11
Georgia	10
Other states	66
Total	**338**

PRODUCTS/OPERATIONS

2002 Sales

	% of total
Women's & juniors' clothing	31
Shoes, accessories & lingerie	20
Men's clothing & accessories	19
Cosmetics	14
Home	9
Children's clothing	7
Leased departments	—
Total	**100**

COMPETITORS

Abercrombie & Fitch	Limited Brands
American Eagle Outfitters	Linens 'n Things
AnnTaylor	May
Bed Bath & Beyond	Men's Wearhouse
Belk	Mervyn's
Best Buy	Neiman Marcus
Brown Shoe	Nordstrom
Burlington Coat Factory	Saks Inc.
Federated	Sears
Foot Locker	Spiegel
The Gap	Stein Mart
J. C. Penney	Talbots
J. Crew	Target
Kohl's	TJX
Lands' End	Tuesday Morning
Levitz	

HISTORICAL FINANCIALS & EMPLOYEES

NYSE: DDS FYE: Saturday nearest Jan. 31	Annual Growth	1/93	1/94	1/95	1/96	1/97	1/98	1/99	1/00	1/01	1/02
Sales ($ mil.)	6.3%	4,714	5,131	5,546	5,918	6,228	6,632	7,797	8,677	8,567	8,155
Net income ($ mil.)	(12.4%)	236	241	252	167	239	258	135	164	(6)	72
Income as % of sales	—	5.0%	4.7%	4.5%	2.8%	3.8%	3.9%	1.7%	1.9%	—	0.9%
Earnings per share ($)	(9.6%)	2.11	2.14	2.23	1.48	2.09	2.31	1.26	1.55	0.15	0.85
Stock price – FY high ($)	—	51.50	52.75	36.63	33.88	41.75	44.75	44.50	37.44	19.94	22.50
Stock price – FY low ($)	—	30.00	33.13	24.63	24.00	28.50	28.00	24.75	17.75	9.44	12.06
Stock price – FY close ($)	(12.7%)	49.00	35.88	26.25	28.75	29.88	35.13	24.81	19.19	15.24	14.38
P/E – high		24	25	16	23	20	19	35	24	19	29
P/E – low		14	15	11	16	14	12	20	11	9	15
Dividends per share ($)	8.0%	0.08	0.08	0.09	0.12	0.13	0.16	0.16	0.16	0.16	0.16
Book value per share ($)	7.7%	16.28	18.43	20.55	18.62	23.92	25.71	26.57	28.68	30.94	31.81
Employees	6.0%	33,883	35,536	37,832	40,312	43,470	44,616	54,921	61,824	58,796	57,257

STOCK PRICE HISTORY

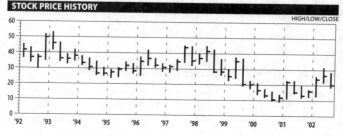

HIGH/LOW/CLOSE

2002 FISCAL YEAR-END

Debt ratio: 44.6%
Return on equity: 2.7%
Cash ($ mil.): 153
Current ratio: 3.03
Long-term debt ($ mil.): 2,145
No. of shares (mil.): 84
Dividends
  Yield: 1.1%
  Payout: 18.8%
Market value ($ mil.): 1,206

DIMON INCORPORATED

DIMON is betting that a lean, mean tobacco-processing machine can still generate a buck. The Danville, Virginia-based company is the world's second-largest leaf tobacco dealer, behind Universal Corporation. DIMON buys tobacco from growers in the US and about 40 other countries.

US cigarette makers Philip Morris (Marlboro) and R.J. Reynolds Tobacco (Camel), together with Japan Tobacco, account for about 45% of DIMON's sales. The company has expanded internationally to provide customers with cheaper leaf tobacco (prices in the US are artificially supported by the government).

DIMON has sold all its non-tobacco operations, cut tobacco facilities and staff, and cleaned up its outstanding accounts to offset falling demand brought on by regional economic crises and litigation-related cigarette price hikes.

HISTORY

DIMON was formed with the 1995 merger of Dibrell Brothers and Monk-Austin, two of the US's leading leaf tobacco dealers. Founded in 1873 by Alphonso and Richard Dibrell, Dibrell Brothers bought and processed tobacco in the South and sold it in North America, expanding overseas during the 1920s. Early sales were for traditional uses such as chewing tobacco and cigars, and it began doing business with large US cigarette makers in the early 1930s.

Publicly traded by the end of WWII, Dibrell Brothers diversified in the 1960s and 1970s, adding makers of ice-cream freezers (Richmond Cedar Works) and wooden lamps (Dunning Industries) and a chain of steakhouses (Kentucky Rib-Eye), but exited those businesses by 1990. Throughout the 1970s Dibrell Brothers established operations in Latin America, the Far East, India, and Italy. It moved into Zimbabwe in 1980 and the next year acquired B.V. Tabak Export & Import Compagnie, a Dutch tobacco firm with holdings in Zimbabwe, West Germany, the Dominican Republic, and Brazil.

In another diversification effort, Dibrell Brothers acquired 54% of Florimex Worldwide in 1987 (buying the rest over the next three years). The flower distributor helped boost sales in 1988. In the 1990s the firm's tobacco fortunes picked up with the growing demand for American-blend tobacco from countries in areas such as Eastern Europe, which previously only had access to high-tar cigarettes.

In 1995 Dibrell Brothers reached an agreement to combine with Monk-Austin, the product of a 1990 merger between tobacco firms A.C. Monk and the Austin Company. Founded by A.C. Monk in 1907, A.C. Monk & Company had interests in North Carolina tobacco plants. Subsequent members of the Monk family expanded its operations. It acquired rival Austin Company in 1990 and went public two years later. In 1993 Monk-Austin acquired tobacco trader T.S. Ragsdale; beefed up its operations in Brazil, Malawi, and Zimbabwe; and began building a tobacco processing plant in China. The company won a contract from R.J. Reynolds Tobacco in 1994 to supply all the domestic leaf tobacco that Reynolds requires.

Upon completion of the 1995 merger, Dibrell Brothers CEO Claude Owen became DIMON's CEO. Also that year the company acquired tobacco operations in Bulgaria, Greece, Italy, and Turkey and reached an agreement to buy and process leaf tobacco for Lorillard Tobacco. DIMON recorded a $30 million loss for the year, largely because of restructuring costs.

The company acquired #4 tobacco merchant Intabex Holdings Worldwide in 1997 for about $246 million. Also in 1997 the firm extended its relationship with R.J. Reynolds, agreeing to process all of its tobacco. In 1998 DIMON sold Florimex to U.S.A. Floral Products for $90 million, in part to finance debt from the purchase of Intabex. Sales were slowed that year and in 1999 by a worldwide glut of leaf tobacco.

In 1999 DIMON settled a lawsuit it had filed against Intabex's owners and management for allegedly misrepresenting its value; the purchase price was reduced by $50 million. In 2000 the company acquired Greece-based facility operator Austro-Hellenique to expand its operations in that country.

In 2001 Dimon's sales decreased somewhat as the company transitioned to direct contract buying (as opposed to buying tobacco at auction).

OFFICERS

Chairman: Joseph L. Lanier Jr., age 70
President, CEO, and Director: Brian J. Harker, age 52, $662,785 pay
SVP and CFO: James A. Cooley, age 51
SVP, Sales and Marketing: H. Peyton Green III, age 52, $281,116 pay
SVP; Regional Director North America/Asia: Larry R. Corbett, age 56, $308,008 pay
SVP; Regional Director Latin America/Africa: Steve B. Daniels, age 44, $318,954 pay
SVP; European Sales Director: E. Shelton Griffin, age 54
SVP; Regional Director Europe: Gustav R. Stangl, age 45, $265,898 pay
SVP, Corporate Affairs and Secretary: Thomas C. Parrish
Director of Human Resources: Don Hare
Auditors: Ernst & Young LLP

LOCATIONS

HQ: 512 Bridge St., Danville, VA 24541
Phone: 804-792-7511 **Fax:** 804-791-0377

DIMON has tobacco operations in more than 30 countries.

PRODUCTS/OPERATIONS

Subsidiaries
Austro-Hellenique S.A. (Greece)
Contentnea, Inc.
DIMON Do Brasil Tabacos Ltda.
DIMON International Tabak AG (S.A. Ltd.) (Switzerland)
DIMON International Tabak B.V. (The Netherlands)
DIMON Tanzania Ltd.
Intabex Netherlands B.V.
Kin-Farm, Inc.
Olima Holdings AG (Switzerland)

COMPETITORS

Altadis
Export Leaf
Standard Commercial
Universal Corporation

HISTORICAL FINANCIALS & EMPLOYEES

NYSE: DMN FYE: June 30	Annual Growth	6/93	6/94	6/95	6/96	6/97	6/98	6/99	6/00	6/01	6/02
Sales ($ mil.)	(3.2%)	1,681	1,449	1,928	2,168	2,513	2,172	1,815	1,474	1,401	1,260
Net income ($ mil.)	(9.2%)	65	(8)	(30)	41	77	44	(5)	18	25	28
Income as % of sales	—	3.9%	—	—	1.9%	3.1%	2.0%	—	1.2%	1.8%	2.2%
Earnings per share ($)	—	—	—	(0.79)	1.01	1.77	0.98	(0.12)	0.40	0.56	0.61
Stock price – FY high ($)	—	—	—	18.63	20.88	26.75	26.50	13.50	6.00	11.61	10.18
Stock price – FY low ($)	—	—	—	14.00	13.75	17.88	10.50	3.25	1.94	2.19	5.35
Stock price – FY close ($)	(12.0%)	—	—	16.88	18.50	26.50	11.25	5.19	2.19	10.00	6.92
P/E – high	—	—	—	—	21	15	27	—	15	21	16
P/E – low	—	—	—	—	14	10	11	—	5	4	9
Dividends per share ($)	5.2%	—	—	0.14	0.54	0.59	0.66	0.40	0.20	0.20	0.20
Book value per share ($)	6.5%	—	—	6.27	7.45	9.21	9.48	8.91	9.06	9.23	9.74
Employees	3.0%	3,000	2,800	3,800	6,900	6,700	8,550	3,200	2,900	3,800	3,900

STOCK PRICE HISTORY

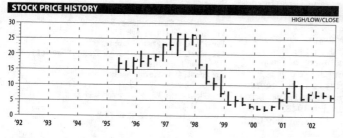

HIGH/LOW/CLOSE

2002 FISCAL YEAR-END

Debt ratio: 48.1%
Return on equity: 6.5%
Cash ($ mil.): 109
Current ratio: 2.18
Long-term debt ($ mil.): 402
No. of shares (mil.): 45
Dividends
  Yield: 2.9%
  Payout: 32.8%
Market value ($ mil.): 309

DOLE FOOD COMPANY, INC.

Bananas might be Dole Food's favorite fruit because they have "a-peel," but as the world's largest producer of fresh fruit and vegetables, it grows and markets much more. The Westlake Village, California-based company also produces canned fruits, pineapple juice, dried fruits, and nuts, almost entirely under the Dole name. Chairman and CEO David Murdock owns 24% of the company.

The company took advantage of its refrigerated distribution network to begin distributing fresh flowers (of which it's now the world's largest producer). During the eight-year-long "banana wars" with the EU, which limited its access to lucrative Western Europe, Dole remained fairly quiet and steadily gained access through acquisitions. Seeking shelter from erratic commodity markets, Dole led the way in introducing value-added produce products, such as precut vegetables and packaged salads.

HISTORY

James Dole embarked on an unlikely career in a faraway land when he graduated from Harvard College in 1899 and sailed to Hawaii. He bought 61 acres of farmland for $4,000 in 1900 and the next year organized the Hawaiian Pineapple Company, announcing that the island's pineapples would eventually be in every US grocery store.

Others had tried and failed to sell fresh fruit to the mainland. Dole decided he would succeed by canning pineapples. He built his first cannery in 1903 and in 1908 introduced a national magazine advertising campaign designed to make consumers associate Hawaii with pineapples (then considered an exotic fruit).

In 1922 Dole expanded his production by buying the island of Lanai, where he set up a pineapple plantation. He financed the purchase by selling a third interest in Hawaiian Pineapple to Waialua Agricultural Company, which was part of Castle & Cooke (C&C). Samuel Castle and Amos Cooke, missionaries to Hawaii, formed C&C in 1851 to manage their church's failing depository, which supplied outlying mission posts with staple goods. In 1858 they entered the sugar business and within 10 years served as agents for several Hawaiian sugar plantations and the ships that carried their cargoes.

C&C gained control of Hawaiian Pineapple in 1932 when it acquired an additional 21% interest in the business. The company began using the Dole name on packaging the next year. Dole became chairman of the board of the reorganized company in 1935 but pursued other business interests until he retired in 1948.

Hawaiian Pineapple was run separately until C&C bought the remainder in 1961. The company started pineapple and banana farms in the Philippines in 1963 to supply markets in East Asia. C&C began importing bananas when it purchased 55% of Standard Fruit of New Orleans in 1964. (It purchased the remainder four years later.)

Heavily in debt and limping from two hostile takeover attempts, C&C agreed in 1985 to merge with Flexi-Van, a container leasing company. The merger brought with it needed capital, Flexi-Van owner David Murdock (who became C&C's CEO), and a fleet of ships to transport produce. Murdock began trimming back, leaving C&C with its fruit and real estate operations. He then decided to end all pineapple operations on Lanai to concentrate on tourist properties. The company took a $168 million writeoff on them in 1995, when it spun off its real estate and resort operations as Castle & Cooke.

C&C became Dole Food in 1991. The company expanded at home and internationally, adding SAMICA (Europe, dried fruits and nuts; 1992), Dromedary (US; dates; 1994), Chiquita's New Zealand produce operations (1995), and SABA Trading (60%, Sweden, produce importing and distribution; 1998).

In 1995 Dole sold its juice business to Seagram's Tropicana Products division, keeping its pineapple juices and licensing the Dole name to Seagram (PepsiCo bought Tropicana in 1998.) Dole entered the fresh flower trade by acquiring four major growers and marketers in 1998.

A worldwide banana glut, Hurricane Mitch, and severe freezes in California hit the company hard in late 1998. The next year Dole launched cost-cutting measures, which by early 2000 had ripened into better earnings. Nonetheless cutbacks and disposals continued throughout 2001.

OFFICERS

Chairman and CEO: David H. Murdock, $1,700,000 pay
President, COO, and Director: Lawrence A. Kern, age 54, $1,168,846 pay
VP and CFO: Richard J. Dahl, age 49
VP, Administration and Support Operations: George R. Horne, age 65
VP, Controller, and Chief Accounting Officer: Gil Borok, age 34
VP, General Counsel, and Corporate Secretary: C. Michael Carter, age 58, $665,000 pay
VP: Roberta Wieman, age 57
President, Dole Fresh Flowers: John T. Schouten
President, Dole North America Tropical Fresh Fruit: Michael J. Cavallero, age 55
President, Dole Worldwide Packaged Foods: Peter M. Nolan, age 59
President, Dole Worldwide Vegetables: Eric M. Schwartz, age 43
Auditors: Deloitte & Touche LLP

LOCATIONS

HQ: One Dole Dr., Westlake Village, CA 91362
Phone: 818-874-4000 **Fax:** 818-879-6615
Web: www.dole.com

Dole Food distributes to more than 90 countries around the world.

2001 Sales

	$ mil.	% of total
US	2,180	49
Japan	516	12
Sweden	353	8
Germany	312	7
France	149	3
Italy	101	2
Other countries	838	19
Total	**4,449**	**100**

PRODUCTS/OPERATIONS

2001 Sales

	$ mil.	% of total
Fresh fruit	2,710	61
Fresh vegetables	874	20
Packaged foods	635	14
Fresh cut Flowers	197	4
Other	33	1
Total	**4,449**	**100**

Divisions and Selected Products

Dried Fruit and Nuts
Almonds
Dates
Pistachios
Prunes
Raisins

Fresh Flowers
Carnations
Chrysanthemums
Roses

Fresh Fruit
Apples
Bananas
Cherries
Cranberries
Grapefruit
Grapes
Kiwi
Lemons
Mangoes
Melons
Oranges
Papayas
Pears
Pineapples

Raspberries
Strawberries
Tangelos

Fresh Vegetables
Artichokes
Asparagus
Broccoli
Carrots
Celery
Lettuce
Onions
Snow peas
Spinach

Fresh-cut Vegetables
Coleslaw
Peeled mini-carrots
Salad mixes
Shredded lettuce

Packaged Foods
Canned mandarin orange
   segments
Canned mixed fruits
Canned pineapple
Pineapple juice

COMPETITORS

Albert Fisher Group	Fresh Del Monte Produce	Maui Land & Pineapple
Blue Diamond Growers	Fyffes	Ocean Spray
Chiquita Brands	Geest	Seneca Foods
Cirio	John Sanfilippo & Son	Sun Growers
Del Monte Foods		Sunkist
		UniMark Group

HISTORICAL FINANCIALS & EMPLOYEES

NYSE: DOL FYE: Saturday nearest Dec. 31	Annual Growth	12/92	12/93	12/94	12/95	12/96	12/97	12/98	12/99	12/00	12/01
Sales ($ mil.)	3.1%	3,376	3,431	3,842	3,804	3,840	4,336	4,424	5,061	4,763	4,449
Net income ($ mil.)	28.5%	16	78	68	23	89	160	12	49	68	150
Income as % of sales	—	0.5%	2.3%	1.8%	0.6%	2.3%	3.7%	0.3%	1.0%	1.4%	3.4%
Earnings per share ($)	29.5%	0.26	1.30	1.14	0.40	1.47	2.65	0.20	0.85	1.21	2.67
Stock price – FY high ($)	—	40.00	37.88	35.50	38.63	43.75	50.06	57.31	34.13	21.50	27.65
Stock price – FY low ($)	—	26.00	25.88	22.50	23.00	30.88	33.75	28.06	13.75	11.75	14.60
Stock price – FY close ($)	(2.0%)	32.13	26.75	23.00	35.00	33.88	45.75	30.00	16.25	16.38	26.83
P/E – high	—	37	29	31	94	30	19	287	40	18	10
P/E – low	—	24	20	20	56	21	13	140	16	10	5
Dividends per share ($)	0.0%	0.40	0.40	0.40	0.40	0.40	0.40	0.40	0.40	0.40	0.40
Book value per share ($)	(2.7%)	16.85	17.70	18.17	8.49	9.10	11.10	10.49	9.53	9.93	13.17
Employees	1.9%	50,000	45,300	46,000	43,000	46,000	44,000	53,500	59,500	61,000	59,000

STOCK PRICE HISTORY

HIGH/LOW/CLOSE

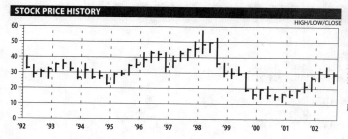

2001 FISCAL YEAR-END

Debt ratio: 52.6%
Return on equity: 23.3%
Cash ($ mil.): 361
Current ratio: 1.63
Long-term debt ($ mil.): 816
No. of shares (mil.): 56
Dividends
   Yield: 1.5%
   Payout: 15.0%
Market value ($ mil.): 1,500

DOLLAR GENERAL CORPORATION

Small town by small town, Dollar General is capturing customers by offering convenience without the high prices associated with convenience stores. The Nashville, Tennessee-based discount retailer operates nearly 5,900 stores in 27 southeastern and midwestern states. The fast-growing company's stores sell a limited selection of best-selling household basics, including cleaning supplies, health and beauty aids, housewares, nonperishable foods, and stationery, as well as basic apparel such as T-shirts. About a third of its items sell for $1 or less; the highest-priced products go for about $35.

Because Dollar General's customers typically live in small towns (less than 20,000 people), the company doesn't advertise. It only sends out direct mailings to announce new stores. It caters to fixed-, lower-, and middle-income customers who find shopping at the small, bare-bones stores (about 6,700 sq. ft.) easier and quicker than at supersized competitors such as Wal-Mart (which are often much farther away). Stores in larger cities (about 30% of its total) are located primarily in low-income neighborhoods.

Chairman and CEO Cal Turner Jr., grandson of the retailer's founder, owns about 15% of Dollar General.

HISTORY

J.L. Turner was 11 when his father was killed during the 1890s in a Saturday night wrestling match. This forced J.L. to drop out of school and work on the family farm, which was weighted by a mortgage. By his 20s J.L., who never learned to read well, was running an area general store. Experiencing some success, he branched out and purchased two stores of his own. They failed. J.L. rebounded, going to work for a wholesaler. With the onset of the Depression, J.L. found he could buy out the inventories of failing merchants for next to nothing, using short-term bank loans that were quickly repaid.

In 1939 J.L. was joined by his son Cal. The two each put up $5,000 to start a new Scottsville, Kentucky-based dry goods wholesaling operation called, not surprisingly, J.L. Turner & Son. It was not until 1945, when the company experienced a glut of women's underwear, that it expanded into retail. J.L. Turner & Son sold off the dainties in their first store, located in Albany, Kentucky. Within a decade the company was operating 35 stores. In 1956 J.L. Turner & Son introduced its first experimental Dollar General Store — all items priced less than a dollar — in Springfield, Kentucky. Like the company's first stores, the dollar store concept would grow: Dollar General Stores numbered 255 a decade later.

Cal Jr., J.L.'s 25-year-old grandson, joined the family business in 1965 and became a director in 1966. The company changed its name to Dollar General and went public two years later. In 1977 Cal Jr. was named president and CEO. That year Dollar General acquired Arkansas-based United Dollar Stores.

The early 1980s saw Dollar General continue its acquisition-powered growth. The company bought INTERCO's 280-store P.N. Hirsch chain and the 203-store Eagle Family Discount chain in 1983 and 1985, respectively. To cope with expanded distribution demands, Dollar General opened an additional distribution center in Homerville, Georgia, the following year to help out the original Scottsville facility. The acquisitions, led by Cal Jr.'s brother Steve, ended up costing the company dearly; Dollar General's 1987 stock price dropped nearly 85%. They also cost Steve his job in 1988: He was forced out by the company's new chairman, Cal Jr. In addition to ousting Steve, Cal Jr. replaced more than half of Dollar General's executives that year. The retailer began moving toward everyday low pricing (à la Wal-Mart) in the late 1980s.

Growth from then on was powered by internal expansion. In 1990 the company operated nearly 1,400 stores; by 1995 it had more than 2,000. To accommodate the growth, Dollar General built a third distribution center in Ardmore, Oklahoma, in 1995 and another in South Boston, Virginia, in 1997. Cal Jr.'s CEO-heir apparent, former Circle K COO Bruce Krysiak, joined the company as president that January, only to resign in December, a casualty of differing corporate visions.

In 1998 Dollar General opted to stop advertising. Cal Turner Sr. died in 2000. The company's stock fell 31% in April 2001 after it announced that earnings over the past 3 years could be cut by 4% because of accounting irregularities. (In January 2002 the company restated net income for the three prior fiscal years by $199.2 million, thereby ending the investigation into accounting problems.)

While continuing to focus on small towns and neighborhoods, Dollar General is expanding beyond the Southeast and Midwest. In 2001 the company opened its first stores in New York and New Jersey.

Chairman and CEO: Cal Turner Jr., age 61,
$1,131,529 pay
President and COO: Donald S. Shaffer, age 58
EVP and CFO: James J. Hagan, age 42
EVP, Merchandising: Tom Hartshorn, age 50,
$286,774 pay
EVP, Operations: Stonie O'Briant, age 46, $349,342 pay
VP, Chief Administrative Officer: Melissa Buffington,
age 43
VP, Controller: Robert A. Lewis, age 40
VP, Distribution: Jeff Sims, age 50
VP, General Counsel, and Corporate Secretary:
Susan S. Lanigan, age 40
VP, General Merchandising Manager: Bob Warner,
age 51
VP, Information and Administrative Services:
Bruce Ash, age 52
VP, Merchandising Support: Bob Layne, age 35
Auditors: Ernst & Young LLP

LOCATIONS

HQ: 100 Mission Ridge, Goodlettsville, TN 37072
Phone: 615-855-4000   **Fax:** 615-855-5252
Web: www.dollargeneral.com

Dollar General operates more than 5,500 neighborhood
stores in 27 states with distribution centers in Florida,
Kentucky, Mississippi, Missouri, Ohio, Oklahoma,
and Virginia.

PRODUCTS/OPERATIONS

Selected Merchandise
Basic apparel
Cleaning supplies
Health and beauty aids
Housewares
Packaged foods
Seasonal goods
Stationery

COMPETITORS

Big Lots
Bill's Dollar Stores
Costco Wholesale
CVS
Dollar Tree
Eckerd
Family Dollar Stores
Fred's
Kmart
One Price Clothing Stores
Rite Aid
Target
TJX
Value City
Variety Wholesalers
Walgreen
Wal-Mart

HISTORICAL FINANCIALS & EMPLOYEES

NYSE: DG FYE: Friday nearest January 31	Annual Growth	1/93	1/94	1/95	1/96	1/97	1/98	1/99	1/00	1/01	1/02
Sales ($ mil.)	21.5%	921	1,133	1,449	1,764	2,134	2,627	3,221	3,888	4,551	5,323
Net income ($ mil.)	21.6%	36	49	74	88	115	145	182	219	71	208
Income as % of sales	—	3.9%	4.3%	5.1%	5.0%	5.4%	5.5%	5.7%	5.6%	1.6%	3.9%
Earnings per share ($)	21.2%	0.11	0.15	0.22	0.26	0.34	0.43	0.54	0.65	0.21	0.62
Stock price – FY high ($)	—	2.66	4.66	5.45	7.13	9.14	16.38	24.19	26.10	23.19	24.05
Stock price – FY low ($)	—	1.48	2.30	3.32	4.04	4.90	7.93	12.80	15.68	13.44	10.50
Stock price – FY close ($)	23.2%	2.41	3.66	5.41	5.22	8.13	14.90	15.96	17.00	19.48	15.80
P/E – high	—	24	31	25	23	22	32	37	37	110	38
P/E – low	—	13	15	15	13	12	16	20	22	64	17
Dividends per share ($)	23.1%	0.02	0.02	0.03	0.04	0.05	0.06	0.08	0.07	0.12	0.13
Book value per share ($)	22.7%	0.50	0.61	1.20	1.53	1.78	2.12	2.62	2.80	2.60	3.13
Employees	18.6%	10,300	10,400	18,000	22,000	25,400	27,400	29,820	34,600	45,000	48,000

STOCK PRICE HISTORY

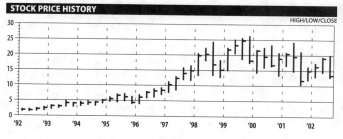

2002 FISCAL YEAR-END

Debt ratio: 24.6%
Return on equity: 21.8%
Cash ($ mil.): 262
Current ratio: 1.37
Long-term debt ($ mil.): 340
No. of shares (mil.): 333
Dividends
  Yield: 0.8%
  Payout: 21.0%
Market value ($ mil.): 5,255

DOMINION RESOURCES, INC.

Dominion Resources wants to dominate the energy market. The Richmond, Virginia-based company generates electricity and transmits it to some 2.1 million customers in Virginia and northeastern North Carolina, and distributes natural gas to about 1.7 million customers in Ohio, Pennsylvania, and West Virginia.

Dominion has prepared for power deregulation, which is being implemented in most of Dominion's service territories, by separating its generation and distribution operations and rebranding several of its units. All of Dominion's generation assets have been transferred to its Dominion Energy unit, which manages 22,000 MW of regulated and nonregulated capacity, markets and trades energy, and operates a 7,600-mile natural gas pipeline. Another unit, Dominion Exploration & Production, owns proved reserves of 4.9 trillion cu. ft. of natural gas equivalent. The company expanded its exploration and production operations in 2001 with the acquisition of Louis Dreyfus Natural Gas.

Dominion is selling all of its overseas operations to focus on its businesses in the northeastern, mid-Atlantic, and Midwest US.

HISTORY

In 1781 the Virginia General Assembly established a group of trustees, including George Washington and James Madison, to promote navigation on the Appomattox River. The trustees (named the Appomattox Trustees) formed the Upper Appomattox Company in 1795 to secure its water rights. The company eventually began operating hydroelectric plants on the river, and by 1888 it had added a steam-powered plant to its portfolio.

The Virginia Railway and Power Company (VR&P), led by Frank Jay Gould, purchased the Upper Appomattox Company (which had changed its name) in 1909. The next year the firm acquired several electric and gas utilities, as well as some electric streetcar lines.

In 1925 New York engineering company Stone & Webster acquired VR&P. The company became known as Virginia Electric and Power Company (Virginia Power), and was placed under Engineers Public Service (EPS), a new holding company. Virginia Power purchased several North Carolina utilities following its acquisition.

During the 1930s the Depression (and the popularity of the automobile) led the company to exit the trolley business. The Public Utility Holding Company Act of 1935 (which ushered in an era of regulated utility monopolies) forced EPS to divest all of its operations except Virginia Power. However, the utility soon merged with the Virginia Public Service Company, thus doubling its service territory.

The company added new power plants to keep up with growing customer demand in the 1950s. Always an innovator, it also built an extra-high-voltage transmission system, the first in the world.

In the 1970s Virginia Power's first nuclear plants became operational. By 1980, however, the firm was near bankruptcy. That year William Berry, who had completed a 23-year rise through the ranks to become president, canceled two other nuclear units. He also became an early supporter of competition in the electric utility industry. In 1983 he formed Dominion Resources as a parent company for Virginia Power, and halted nearly all plant construction. Two additional subsidiaries were soon formed: Dominion Capital in 1985 and Dominion Energy in 1987.

In 1990, the year Thomas Capps took over as CEO, Dominion sold its natural gas distribution business, and Dominion Energy began developing natural gas reserves through joint ventures and by purchasing three natural gas exploration and production companies in 1995.

The company acquired UK utility East Midlands Electricity in 1997. However, after it was hit by a hefty windfall tax by the newly elected Labour Party, and its hopes for mergers with other UK utilities were dashed, it sold East Midlands to PowerGen just 18 months after acquiring it.

In 1999 Dominion prepared for energy deregulation through reorganization. It separated its electricity generation activities from its transmission and distribution operations. In 2000 Dominion bought Consolidated Natural Gas (CNG) for $9 billion, making it one of the largest fully integrated gas and electric power companies in the US; it then sold CNG's Virginia Natural Gas to AGL Resources, and the two firms' combined Latin American assets to Duke Energy.

Virginia Power moved to head off state and federal lawsuits in 2000 by agreeing to spend $1.2 billion over 12 years to reduce pollution from coal-fired plants. It also agreed to pay $1.3 billion for Northeast Utilities' Millstone nuclear power complex that year; the deal closed in 2001. Also in 2000, Dominion changed its brand name from Dominion Resources to simply Dominion.

In 2001 Dominion bought exploration and production company Louis Dreyfus Natural Gas for about $1.8 billion in cash and stock and $500 million in assumed debt; the acquisition added 1.8 trillion cu. ft. of natural gas equivalent to Dominion's proved reserves.

The following year Dominion purchased a 500-MW Chicago power plant from US power producer Mirant for $182 million.

Chairman, President, and CEO: Thomas E. Capps,
age 66, $2,250,000 pay
**EVP and CFO; President and CFO, Consolidated
Natural Gas:** Thomas N. Chewning, age 56,
$707,692 pay
**EVP; President and CEO, Virginia Electric and Power;
EVP, Consolidated Natural Gas:** Edgar M. Roach Jr.,
age 53, $1,028,077 pay
**EVP, Dominion and Consolidated Natural Gas; CEO,
Virginia Electric and Power and Dominion Energy:**
Thomas F. Farrell II, age 47, $1,028,077 pay
**EVP, Dominion and Consolidated Natural Gas;
President and CEO, Dominion Exploration and
Production:** Duane C. Radtke, age 53
**EVP, Dominion and Consolidated Natural Gas;
President and COO, Virginia Electric and Power:**
James P. O'Hanlon, age 58, $700,000 pay
**SVP and Treasurer, Dominion, Virginia Electric and
Power, and Consolidated Natural Gas:**
G. Scott Hetzer, age 45
SVP and Chief Administrative Officer:
Mark F. McGettrick, age 44
SVP Information Technology and CIO:
Margaret E. McDermid
SVP Law, Dominion and Consolidated Natural Gas:
James L. Sanderlin, age 60
VP and General Counsel: James F. Stutts, age 57
Auditors: Deloitte & Touche LLP

LOCATIONS

HQ: 120 Tredegar St., Richmond, VA 23219
Phone: 804-819-2000   **Fax:** 804-819-2233
Web: www.dom.com

PRODUCTS/OPERATIONS

2001 Sales

	$ mil.	% of total
Regulated		
Electric	4,619	44
Gas	1,409	13
Nonregulated		
Gas	1,116	10
Electric	701	7
Gas & oil production	1,118	10
Gas transportation & storage	702	7
Other	893	9
Total	**10,558**	**100**

COMPETITORS

AEP	Exelon
Allegheny Energy	FirstEnergy
Aquila	Koch
BP	LG&E Energy
Cabot Oil & Gas	NiSource
CenterPoint Energy	North Carolina Electric
ChevronTexaco	Membership
Cinergy	North Coast Energy
Devon Energy	Northern Virginia Electric
DPL	Cooperative
DQE	Piedmont Natural Gas
Duke Energy	PPL
Dynegy	Progress Energy
Edison Mission Energy	RGC Resources
El Paso	SCANA
Entergy	UGI
Equitable Resources	Williams Companies

HISTORICAL FINANCIALS & EMPLOYEES

NYSE: D FYE: December 31	Annual Growth	12/92	12/93	12/94	12/95	12/96	12/97	12/98	12/99	12/00	12/01
Sales ($ mil.)	12.1%	3,791	4,434	4,491	4,652	4,842	7,678	6,086	5,520	9,260	10,558
Net income ($ mil.)	2.3%	445	517	478	425	472	399	536	296	436	544
Income as % of sales	—	11.7%	11.7%	10.6%	9.1%	9.7%	5.2%	8.8%	5.4%	4.7%	5.2%
Earnings per share ($)	(2.7%)	2.76	3.12	2.81	2.45	2.65	2.15	2.75	1.48	1.85	2.15
Stock price - FY high ($)	—	41.00	49.50	45.38	41.63	44.38	42.88	48.94	49.38	67.94	69.99
Stock price - FY low ($)	—	34.13	38.25	34.88	34.88	36.88	33.25	37.81	36.56	34.81	55.13
Stock price - FY close ($)	4.8%	39.50	45.38	36.00	41.25	38.50	42.56	46.75	39.25	67.00	60.10
P/E - high	—	15	16	16	17	17	20	18	17	39	32
P/E - low	—	13	12	12	14	14	15	14	13	20	25
Dividends per share ($)	0.8%	2.40	2.48	2.55	2.58	2.58	2.58	2.58	2.58	2.58	2.58
Book value per share ($)	1.0%	30.28	31.25	31.33	30.79	30.98	30.51	30.87	28.24	30.52	33.06
Employees	3.8%	12,217	12,057	10,789	10,592	11,174	15,458	11,033	11,035	15,600	17,100

STOCK PRICE HISTORY

HIGH/LOW/CLOSE

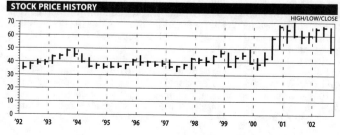

2001 FISCAL YEAR-END

Debt ratio: 58.1%
Return on equity: 7.1%
Cash ($ mil.): 486
Current ratio: 0.72
Long-term debt ($ mil.): 12,119
No. of shares (mil.): 265
Dividends
  Yield: 4.3%
  Payout: 120.0%
Market value ($ mil.): 15,908

DOMINO'S, INC.

Creating its own definition of the domino effect, Domino's Pizza has spread a craving for pizza across the globe. Ann Arbor, Michigan-based Domino's is the world's #1 pizza delivery company and the #2 pizza chain overall (behind Yum! Brands' Pizza Hut).

The company boasts about 7,100 stores (most are franchised; more than two-thirds are in the US) in nearly 65 countries. Toppings vary from place to place — refried beans are popular in Mexico, while pie-lovers elsewhere favor pickled ginger (India), green peas (Brazil), canned tuna and corn (UK), and squid (Japan). The company also owns 18 regional distribution centers in Canada, France, the Netherlands, and the US.

Domino's has built its reputation on speedy delivery, but the company also has begun to emphasize the quality of its fare. In the hard-fought war for market share, the company restructured and closed some underperforming units and has moved aggressively into e-commerce territory by offering online ordering at many locations. It's even testing a $1 delivery charge in certain markets. Domino's founder Thomas Monaghan, a devout Catholic, retired from the company in 1998 to concentrate on his religious activities. He sold 93% of his company to Boston-based investment firm Bain Capital, which has made noises about a possible IPO in late 2002.

Domino's is expanding in Europe through its 2001 majority stake in Dutch Pizza Beheer B.V. The Netherlands franchise operation is Domino's first new office in Europe in almost 20 years.

HISTORY

Thomas Monaghan's early life was one of hardship. After growing up in an orphanage and numerous foster homes, Monaghan spent his young adult life experimenting, trying everything from a Catholic seminary to a stint in the Marine Corps.

In 1960 Monaghan borrowed $500 and bought DomiNick's, a failed pizza parlor in Ypsilanti, Michigan, which he operated with the help of his brother James. In 1961 James traded his share in the restaurant to his brother for a Volkswagen Beetle, but Thomas pressed on, learning the pizza business largely by trial and error. After a brief partnership with an experienced restaurateur with whom he later had a falling out, Monaghan developed a strategy to sell only pizza and to locate stores near colleges and military bases. The company changed its name to Domino's in 1965.

In the 1960s and 1970s Monaghan endured setbacks that brought the company to the brink of bankruptcy. Among these were a 1968 fire that destroyed the Domino's headquarters and a 1975 lawsuit from Domino Sugar maker Amstar (now Tate & Lyle) for trademark infringement. But the company won the ensuing legal battles, and by 1978 it was operating 200 stores.

In the 1980s Domino's grew phenomenally. Between 1981 and 1983 the company doubled its number of US stores to 1,000; it went international in 1983, opening a store in Canada. The company's growth brought Monaghan a personal fortune. In 1983 he bought the Detroit Tigers baseball team and amassed one of the world's largest collections of Frank Lloyd Wright objects.

Domino's expansion continued in the mid-1980s. With sales figures mounting, the company introduced pan pizza (its first new product) in 1989. That year Monaghan put Domino's up for sale, but his practice of linking his personal and professional finances had gotten both the founder and company into such dire fiscal straits that no one wanted to buy the chain. Monaghan removed himself from direct management in 1989 and installed a new management group.

When company performance began to slide, Monaghan returned in 1991, having experienced a religious rebirth. He sold off many of his private holdings (including his resort island and his baseball team, which went to cross-town pizza rival Michael Ilitch of Little Caesar) to reinvigorate the company and reorganize company management.

In 1989 a Domino's driver, trying to fulfill the company's 30-minute delivery guarantee, ran a red light and collided with another car. The $79 million judgment against the company in 1993 prompted Domino's to drop its famous 30-minute policy and replace it with a satisfaction guarantee.

The company revamped its logo and store interiors with a new look in 1997. The following year it introduced a patented delivery bag designed to keep pies hot and crispy. Also in 1998, prompted by his decision to devote more time to religious pursuits, Monaghan retired from the business he had guided for nearly 40 years. He sold 93% of his company to investment firm Bain Capital. David Brandon, former CEO of sales promotion company Valassis Communications, replaced Monaghan as chairman and CEO in 1999.

Monaghan initiated a restructuring in 1999 that involved eliminating 100 managers; he closed or sold 142 stores to franchisees. Also that year the company introduced the first in its line of Italian Originals — specialty pizzas featuring

Italian spices. It also began selling pizza online through a number of franchisees.

In 2001 Domino's bought a majority stake in Dutch Pizza Beheer B.V., an operator of 52 Domino's restaurants in the Netherlands. With the buy, the company is establishing a base to manage future expansion in Europe.

OFFICERS

Chairman and CEO: David A. Brandon, age 49, $1,700,000 pay
EVP, Finance and CFO: Harry J. Silverman, age 43, $860,000 pay
EVP, Build the Brand: Ken C. Calwell
EVP, Distribution: Michael D. Soignet, age 42, $790,000 pay
EVP, Flawless Execution: Patrick W. Knotts, age 47, $768,558 pay
EVP, General Counsel, and Secretary: Elisa D. Garcia, age 44
EVP, International: J. Patrick Doyle, age 38, $715,000 pay
EVP, PeopleFirst: Patricia A. Wilmot, age 53
EVP and Special Assistant to Chairman and CEO: James G. Stansik, age 46
CIO: Timothy Monteith, age 49
VP, Brand Growth: Terri Snyder
VP, Corporate Communications: Tim McIntyre
VP, Purchasing: Jim Caldwell
VP and Corporate Controller: Jeffrey D. Lawrence, age 28
VP and Associate General Counsel: Edwina W. Divins
VP and Treasurer: Joseph Donovan
Manager, Public Relations: Holly Ryan
Auditors: PricewaterhouseCoopers LLP

LOCATIONS

HQ: 30 Frank Lloyd Wright Dr., Ann Arbor, MI 48106
Phone: 734-930-3030   **Fax:** 734-747-6210
Web: www.dominos.com

Domino's Pizza has operations in about 65 countries.

2001 Sales

	$ mil.	% of total
US distribution	692	55
US company-owned restaurants	362	28
US franchised restaurants	134	11
International	70	6
Total	**1,258**	**100**

PRODUCTS/OPERATIONS

2001 Sales

	$ mil.	% of total
Domestic distribution	797	58
Domestic sales	496	36
International sales	70	6
Adjustments	(105)	—
Total	**1,258**	**100**

Menu Items
Pizzas
  Classic Hand Tossed
  Crunchy Thin Crust
  Italian Originals
  Ultimate Deep Dish
Sides
  Breadsticks
  Buffalo wings
  Cheesy bread

COMPETITORS

Bertucci's	Papa John's
Burger King	Pizza Hut
CEC Entertainment	Pizza Inn
CKE Restaurants	Round Table
Godfather's Pizza	Sbarro
KFC	Subway
LDB Corp	Uno Restaurant
Little Caesar	Wendy's
McDonald's	Whataburger

HISTORICAL FINANCIALS & EMPLOYEES

Private FYE: Sunday nearest Dec. 31	Annual Growth	12/92	12/93	12/94	12/95	12/96	12/97	12/98	12/99	12/00	12/01
Sales ($ mil.)	5.3%	—	—	875	905	970	1,045	1,177	1,157	1,166	1,258
Net income ($ mil.)	121.2%	—	—	0	25	20	61	77	2	25	37
Income as % of sales	—	—	—	0.0%	2.8%	2.0%	5.8%	6.5%	0.2%	2.2%	2.9%
Employees	(3.9%)	—	—	—	—	—	—	14,200	14,400	14,600	12,600

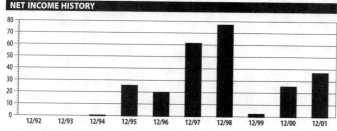

NET INCOME HISTORY

2001 FISCAL YEAR-END

Debt ratio: 100.0%
Return on equity: —
Cash ($ mil.): 35
Current ratio: 0.85
Long-term debt ($ mil.): 612

DOVER CORPORATION

Dover sees diversification as a way to keep its earnings from falling off a cliff (white or otherwise). The New York City-based industrial conglomerate operates more than 50 companies that produce equipment from garbage trucks (Heil Environmental) to ink-jet printers (Imaje).

Dover has four major divisions. Its largest (about 30% of sales), Dover Technologies, produces printed circuit board assembly equipment, electronic components, and ink-jet printing equipment. Dover Industries (26% of sales) makes products for the automotive service, bulk transport, food service, construction, and waste-handling industries. Dover Diversified produces can-making machinery, compressors, food refrigeration and display cases, and heat-transfer equipment. The smallest division, Dover Resources, makes equipment for the automotive, fluid-handling, chemical, and petroleum industries. The Americas account for 70% of sales (62% coming from the US).

Dover maintains a highly decentralized management culture, with a president for each business. The company has maintained a long-term acquisitions strategy (adding anywhere from about 10 to 20 companies a year since 1997). The diversification means that while Dover might benefit from some changing economic tides (such as the increase in oil prices, which boost orders for oil and gas equipment), it can be hurt concurrently by others (such as the sluggish tech sector). This is evidenced by the weak demand for electronics and resulting contraction of the market, which has hurt Dover's technology division.

HISTORY

George Ohrstrom, a New York stockbroker, formed Dover in 1955 and took it public that year. Originally headquartered in Washington, DC, Dover consisted of four companies: C. Lee Cook (compressor seals and piston rings), Peerless (space-venting heaters), Rotary Lift (automotive lifts), and W.C. Norris (components for oil wells). In 1958 Dover made the first of many acquisitions and entered the elevator industry by buying Shepard Warner Elevator.

Dover continued to diversify throughout the 1960s. Acquisitions included OPW (gas pump nozzles) in 1961 and De-Sta-Co (industrial clamps and valves) in 1962. OPW head Thomas Sutton became Dover's president in 1964 and the company moved its headquarters to New York City. Dover acquired Groen Manufacturing (food industry products) in 1967 and Ronningen-Petter (filter-strainer units) in 1968.

During the 1970s Dover expanded beyond its core industries (building materials, industrial components, and equipment). In 1975 it acquired Dieterich Standard, a maker of liquid-measurement instruments. Dieterich Standard's president, Gary Roubos, became Dover's president in 1977 and COO in 1977 and its CEO in 1981. The company sold Peerless in 1977 and acquired electronics assembly equipment manufacturer Universal Instruments in 1979.

Electronics became an increasingly important part of Dover's business during the 1980s. The company bought K&L Microwave, a maker of microwave filters used in satellites and cable TV equipment (1983), Dielectric Laboratories (microwave filter parts, 1985), and NURAD (microwave antennas, 1986). Between 1985 and 1990 Dover bought some 25 companies, including Weldcraft Products (welding equipment, 1985), Wolfe Frostop (salad bars, 1987), Weaver Corp. (automotive lifts, 1987), General Elevator (1988), Texas Hydraulics (1988), Security Elevator (1990), and Marathon Equipment (waste-handling equipment, 1990).

The corporation spun off its DOVatron circuit board assembly subsidiary to shareholders in 1993 after finding that DOVatron was competing with important Dover customers. That same year Dover acquired The Heil Company (garbage trucks).

Dover purchased 10 companies in 1994, including Hill Phoenix (commercial refrigeration cases) and Koolrad Design & Manufacturing (radiators for transformers). In 1995 it bought France-based Imaje (ink-jet printers and specialty inks) for $200 million. It was the largest purchase in the company's history.

The following year Dover bought Everett Charles Technologies, a maker of electronic testing equipment. In 1997 the corporation and its subsidiaries purchased 17 companies, including Vitronics Soltec (soldering equipment for circuit board assembly). The next year the company sold its Dover elevator unit — a popular brand, but a management headache — to German steel giant Thyssen (now ThyssenKrupp) for $1.1 billion.

Dover continued its acquisitive ways in 1999 and 2000, picking up 18 and 23 companies, respectively. Notable were Alphasem, which makes semiconductor-manufacturing equipment, and Graphics Microsystems, which took Dover into the pressroom equipment market. Dover picked up Triton Systems, a maker of ATMs, in 2000. The following year Dover acquired Kurz-Kasch, a US-based, electromagnetic manufacturer with customers in the automotive market.

Chairman, President, and CEO: Thomas L. Reece,
age 59, $1,413,250 pay
VP, Corporate Development: Robert A. Tyre, age 57
VP, Finance and CFO: David S. Smith, age 45,
$713,750 pay
VP, General Counsel, and Secretary:
Robert G. Kuhbach, age 54
VP, Taxation: Charles R. Goulding, age 50
VP and Controller: George F. Messerole, age 55
VP; President and CEO, Dover Industries:
Lewis E. Burns, $970,000 pay
VP; President and CEO, Dover Resources:
Ronald L. Hoffman, age 51
VP; President and CEO, Dover Technologies:
John E. Pomeroy, age 60, $1,100,000 pay
VP; President and CEO, Dover Diversified:
Jerry W. Yochum, age 62, $881,000 pay
President, Dow-Key Microwave: David W. Wightman
President, DT Magnetics: Wm. F. Barry Hegarty
President, Everett Charles Technologies:
David R. Van Loan
President, Imaje: Omar Kerbage
President, K&L Microwave: Louis Abbagnaro
Auditors: PricewaterhouseCoopers LLP

LOCATIONS

HQ: 280 Park Ave., New York, NY 10017
Phone: 212-922-1640   **Fax:** 212-922-1656
Web: www.dovercorporation.com

Dover operates primarily in the US, but the company
has subsidiaries and affiliates in Canada, France,
Germany, the Netherlands, Sweden, and the UK.

2001 Sales

	$ mil.	% of total
The Americas		
US	2,768	62
Other countries	361	8
Europe	847	19
Asia	379	9
Other regions	105	2
Total	**4,460**	**100**

PRODUCTS/OPERATIONS

2001 Sales

	$ mil.	% of total
Dover Technologies	1,258	28
Dover Industries	1,160	26
Dover Diversified	1,105	25
Dover Resources	943	21
Adjustments	(6)	—
Total	**4,460**	**100**

COMPETITORS

Carlisle Companies
Cookson Group
Cooper Industries
Ingersoll-Rand Industrial Solutions
Mark IV
Sequa
York International

HISTORICAL FINANCIALS & EMPLOYEES

NYSE: DOV FYE: December 31	Annual Growth	12/92	12/93	12/94	12/95	12/96	12/97	12/98	12/99	12/00	12/01
Sales ($ mil.)	7.8%	2,272	2,484	3,085	3,746	4,076	4,548	3,978	4,446	5,401	4,460
Net income ($ mil.)	7.5%	130	158	202	278	390	405	379	929	520	249
Income as % of sales	—	5.7%	6.4%	6.6%	7.4%	9.6%	8.9%	9.5%	20.9%	9.6%	5.6%
Earnings per share ($)	9.0%	0.56	0.69	0.88	1.22	1.69	1.79	1.69	4.41	2.54	1.22
Stock price - FY high ($)	—	11.91	15.47	16.72	20.84	27.56	36.69	39.94	47.94	54.38	43.55
Stock price - FY low ($)	—	9.56	11.25	12.44	12.91	18.31	24.13	25.50	29.31	34.13	26.40
Stock price - FY close ($)	13.9%	11.47	15.19	12.91	18.44	25.25	36.13	36.63	45.38	40.56	37.07
P/E - high	—	22	22	19	17	16	20	23	11	21	36
P/E - low	—	18	16	14	10	11	13	15	7	13	22
Dividends per share ($)	6.9%	0.22	0.23	0.25	0.28	0.32	0.36	0.40	0.44	0.48	0.40
Book value per share ($)	15.0%	3.53	3.80	4.39	5.40	6.62	7.65	8.67	10.06	12.02	12.44
Employees	3.9%	18,827	20,445	22,992	25,332	26,234	28,758	23,350	26,600	29,500	26,600

STOCK PRICE HISTORY

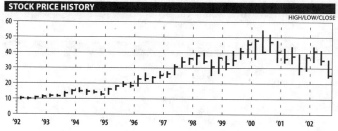

HIGH/LOW/CLOSE

2001 FISCAL YEAR-END

Debt ratio: 29.1%
Return on equity: 10.0%
Cash ($ mil.): 176
Current ratio: 2.02
Long-term debt ($ mil.): 1,033
No. of shares (mil.): 203
Dividends
  Yield: 1.1%
  Payout: 32.8%
Market value ($ mil.): 7,510

THE DOW CHEMICAL COMPANY

Dow Chemical is a maker of Styrofoam brand insulation, Dursban insecticides, and a host of other plastics and chemicals. The Midland, Michigan-based company ranks as the top US chemical firm.

Dow makes performance-plastic products (adhesives, sealants, surfactants, resins, and polymers) used in everything from footwear to automotive interiors. It also produces other plastics (polyethylene resins), performance chemicals (acrylic acid), commodity chemicals (chlorine and caustic soda), fungicides, herbicides (Clincher) and insecticides (Dursban), and crude oil-based materials.

A weakened economy and falling prices have taken a toll on Dow's sales and profits. Reflecting the industry trend toward consolidation, Dow has bolstered its polyethylene business with the acquisition of special and intermediary chemicals company Union Carbide. As a result of costs related to the takeover and the sputtering economy, Dow recorded it first annual loss in nearly ten years.

HISTORY

Herbert Dow founded Dow Chemical in 1897 after developing a process to extract bromides and chlorides from underground brine deposits around Midland, Michigan. Its first product was chlorine bleach. Dow eventually overcame British and German monopolies on bleach, bromides, and other chemicals.

In the mid-1920s Dow rejected a takeover by DuPont. By 1930, the year of Herbert Dow's death, sales had reached $15 million. Dow started building new plants around the country in the late 1930s.

Dow research yielded new plastics in the 1940s, such as Saran Wrap, the company's initial major consumer product. In 1952 Dow built a plant in Japan (Asahi-Dow), its first subsidiary outside North America. Plastics represented 32% of sales by 1957, compared with 2% in 1940. Strong sales of plastics and silicone products propelled the company into the top ranks of US firms. Dow entered the pharmaceutical field with the 1960 purchase of Allied Labs.

Dow suffered earnings drops from 1981 to 1983 from falling chemical prices. To limit the cyclical effect of chemicals on profits, the company expanded its interests in pharmaceuticals and consumer goods. In 1989 it merged its pharmaceutical division with Marion Labs to create Marion Merrell Dow (it sold its 71% stake to Hoechst in 1995). Also in 1989 it formed DowElanco, a joint venture with Eli Lilly to produce agricultural chemicals.

Following allegations that it had put a breast implant on the market without proper testing, Dow Corning (a joint venture with glassmaker Corning), the #1 producer of silicone breast implants, stopped making the devices in 1992. In 1995 a federal judge ordered Dow to pay a Nevada woman $14 million in damages — the first breast-implant verdict against the company as a sole defendant. Facing thousands of pending cases, Dow Corning filed for bankruptcy protection. (In 1998 Dow Corning agreed to pay $3.2 billion to settle most breast-implant claims.)

Dow entered the polypropylene and polyethylene terephthalate markets with the 1996 purchase of INCA International, a subsidiary of Italy's Enichem. It also bought a stake in seed developer Mycogen.

The company sold its 80% of Destec Energy in 1997 and bought Eli Lilly's 40% stake in Dow-Elanco (renamed Dow AgroSciences, 1998). That year Dow bought South Africa's Sentrachem (crop-protection products), but regulators made Dow sell part of it to Akzo Nobel. In 1998 Dow sold its DowBrands unit — maker of bathroom cleaner (Dow), plastic bags (Ziploc), and plastic wrap (Saran Wrap) — to S.C. Johnson & Son. It also paid $322 million for the rest of Mycogen, which became part of Dow AgroSciences.

The company paid $600 million in 1999 to purchase ANGUS Chemical (specialty chemicals) from TransCanada PipeLines. Dow also announced it planned to buy rival Union Carbide for $9.3 billion; it completed the acquisition early in 2002 after agreeing to divest some polyethylene assets to satisfy regulatory concerns.

In 2000 Dow acquired Flexible Products Company (polyurethane foam) and General Latex Chemical Corporation (rigid polyurethane foam). That year Michael Parker succeeded William Stavropoulos as president and CEO (Stavropoulos remains chairman).

Dow acquired Rohm & Haas Co.'s agricultural chemicals (fungicides, insecticides, and herbicides) business for $1 billion in 2001. That year it acquired Celotex Corporation's rigid-foam insulation business and UK fine and specialty chemicals firm Ascot Plc. As the economy slumped late in the year, Dow announced that it would cut about 4,500 jobs (about 8% of its workforce) by 2003.

OFFICERS

Chairman: William S. Stavropoulos, age 62, $2,878,333 pay
Vice Chairman: Anthony J. Carbone, age 61, $1,341,368 pay
President, CEO, and Director: Michael D. Parker, age 55, $1,890,000 pay

EVP, CFO, and Director: J. Pedro Reinhard, age 56, $1,371,970 pay
EVP, Operations and Director: Arnold A. Allemang, age 59, $874,550 pay
VP, Environment, Health and Safety, Human Resources, and Public Affairs: Lawrence J. Washington Jr., age 56, $648,732 pay
VP and Controller: Frank H. Brod, age 47
VP and General Counsel: Richard L. Manetta, age 57, $755,962 pay
VP, Quality and Business Excellence; Business Group President, Styrenics and Engineered Products: Kathleen M. Bader
VP, Research and Development: Richard M. Gross, age 54, $710,341 pay
President and CEO, Dow AgroSciences: A. Charles Fischer
President, Dow Europe; Chairman, Global Geographic Council: Luciano Respini
Auditors: Deloitte & Touche LLP

LOCATIONS

HQ: 2030 Dow Center, Midland, MI 48674
Phone: 989-636-1000   **Fax:** 989-636-1830
Web: www.dow.com

Dow Chemical has about 210 manufacturing facilities in some 40 countries throughout Africa, Asia, Europe, and North and South America. It has customers in about 170 countries.

2001 Sales

	$ mil.	% of total
US	11,725	42
Europe	8,891	32
Other regions	7,189	26
Total	**27,805**	**100**

PRODUCTS/OPERATIONS

2001 Sales

	$ mil.	% of total
Performance plastics	7,321	27
Plastics	6,452	23
Performance chemicals	5,081	18
Chemicals	3,552	13
Agricultural products	2,612	9
Hydrocarbons & energy	2,511	9
Other	276	1
Total	**27,805**	**100**

Selected Products

Benzene	Herbicides
Custom and fine chemicals	Insecticides
Emulsion polymers (latex)	Polyethylene
Engineering plastics	Polyurethanes
Epoxy products	Specialty polymers
Ethylenes	Wire and cable compounds

COMPETITORS

Akzo Nobel	Honeywell	Occidental
BASF AG	International	Petroleum
Bayer AG	Honeywell	Olin
BP	Specialty	OxyChem
BP Chemicals	Materials	Pharmacia
Cargill	Huntsman	PPG
ChevronTexaco	Imperial	RPP
ConAgra	Chemical	Rohm and Haas
Eastman	ITOCHU	Royal
Chemical	Lyondell	Dutch/Shell
DuPont	Chemical	Group
Exxon Mobil	Millennium	
FMC	Chemicals	
Henkel	Novartis	

HISTORICAL FINANCIALS & EMPLOYEES

NYSE: DOW FYE: December 31	Annual Growth	12/92	12/93	12/94	12/95	12/96	12/97	12/98	12/99	12/00	12/01
Sales ($ mil.)	4.3%	18,971	18,060	20,015	20,200	20,053	20,018	18,441	18,929	23,008	27,805
Net income ($ mil.)	—	(489)	644	938	2,071	1,907	1,808	1,310	1,331	1,513	(385)
Income as % of sales	—	—	3.6%	4.7%	10.3%	9.5%	9.0%	7.1%	7.0%	6.6%	—
Earnings per share ($)	—	(0.61)	0.77	1.12	2.54	2.53	2.56	1.92	1.97	2.22	(0.43)
Stock price - FY high ($)	—	22.64	20.65	26.39	25.97	30.80	34.17	33.78	45.95	47.12	39.67
Stock price - FY low ($)	—	16.98	16.32	18.81	20.44	22.73	25.22	24.87	28.47	23.00	25.06
Stock price - FY close ($)	6.6%	19.06	18.90	22.39	23.39	26.10	33.80	30.28	44.50	36.63	33.78
P/E - high	—	—	26	24	10	12	13	17	23	21	—
P/E - low	—	—	21	17	8	9	10	13	14	10	—
Dividends per share ($)	2.9%	0.87	0.87	0.87	0.93	1.00	1.08	1.16	1.16	1.16	1.13
Book value per share ($)	1.3%	9.86	9.77	9.89	10.22	11.03	11.34	11.29	13.23	14.30	11.04
Employees	(1.7%)	61,353	55,436	53,730	39,500	40,289	42,861	39,000	39,239	41,943	52,689

STOCK PRICE HISTORY

HIGH/LOW/CLOSE

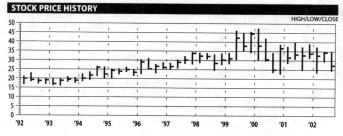

2001 FISCAL YEAR-END

Debt ratio: 48.1%
Return on equity: —
Cash ($ mil.): 220
Current ratio: 1.27
Long-term debt ($ mil.): 9,266
No. of shares (mil.): 905
Dividends
 Yield: 3.3%
 Payout: —
Market value ($ mil.): 30,565

DOW JONES & COMPANY, INC.

Dow Jones & Company has its finger on the pulse of the global economy. The New York City-based company publishes *The Wall Street Journal*, the financial daily whose circulation of about 1.8 million places it just behind Gannett's *USA TODAY* (2.2 million circulation) as the most widely read newspaper in the US. Dow Jones rounds out its print publications with a European version of *The Journal;* financial magazines *Barron's, Far Eastern Economic Review,* and *SmartMoney* (jointly owned with Hearst); and about 50 community newspapers issued by its Ottaway Newspapers group. It also produces pages of *The Wall Street Journal* for distribution in major US newspapers on Sundays.

While its print publications and community newspapers generate some 80% of the company's sales, Dow Jones also distributes information electronically via Dow Jones Newswires, Dow Jones Indexes, Dow Jones Reuters Business Interactive (50%, operates as Factiva), and *The Wall Street Journal Online.* Also, Dow Jones is a partner with NBC in CNBC Europe and CNBC Asia, and it provides content to CNBC in the US.

Dow Jones hit hard times in 2001 as the economy soured; it laid off some 200 workers as a result of declining ad revenue and increased the cover price of its flagship paper. In addition, the company merged the news operations of its *Far Eastern Economic Review* with its Asian version of *The Wall Street Journal* to improve efficiencies. Dow Jones decided to halt publication of its Asian *Wall Street Journal* edition in summer 2002, saying that the WSJ's online operations and expanding global presence made it difficult to sell subscriptions to its Asian version.

Members of the Bancroft family (heirs of early owner Clarence Barron) own 38% of Dow Jones and control 65% of the voting power. The Ottaway family owns about 5% of the company.

HISTORY

Charles Dow, Edward Jones, and Charles Bergstresser founded Dow Jones & Company (1882), which delivered handwritten bulletins of stock and bond trading news to New York subscribers. In 1883 Dow Jones started summarizing the trading day in the *Customers' Afternoon Letter,* which evolved into *The Wall Street Journal* (1889). Jones sold out to his partners in 1899; three years later Dow and Bergstresser sold the company to Clarence Barron. In 1921 the company introduced *Barron's National Business and Financial Weekly.*

Bernard Kilgore, who was appointed managing editor in 1941, shaped the format of *The Journal* that has endured until this day. During the 1960s the company saw the newspaper's circulation exceed 1 million. With its acquisition of the Ottaway group and investments in the *Far Eastern Economic Review* and *The Asian Wall Street Journal* during the 1970s, Dow Jones expanded into community and international publications. It launched *The Wall Street Journal Europe* in 1983, and between 1985 and 1990 acquired Telerate, a real-time financial data network that it renamed Dow Jones Markets.

Peter Kann, who joined *The Journal* as a reporter in 1964, became chairman and CEO of the company in 1991. That next year Dow Jones teamed with Hearst to launch *SmartMoney* magazine. A 1992 alliance with BellSouth to provide telephone access to Dow Jones reports and a 1994 venture with American City Business Journals to publish a monthly magazine fared less well, and both were discontinued in 1995.

In 1997 the company shut down its unprofitable Dow Jones Investor Network (a video news service started in 1993) and tried to revive the ailing Dow Jones Markets service by announcing a $650 million revamping.

Charges associated with Dow Jones Markets led to a sizable loss for 1997, and the company sold the unit to Bridge Information Systems for $510 million the next year. It cut staffing costs in 1998 when more than 500 employees accepted severance packages. That year Dow Jones announced it would expand the number of pages and color capacity of *The Journal,* and inked deals to distribute its newswires through Reuters, Bloomberg, and Bridge.

In 1999 the company joined the *Financial Times* and Independent Media to launch a Russian-language business newspaper, *Vedomosti.* It also formed a joint venture — Factiva — with Reuters that combined their online news databases. In addition, Dow Jones began offering *The Wall Street Journal Sunday,* a weekly package of articles that appears in more than 15 US newspapers.

In 2000 Dow Jones joined with Excite@Home to form online business network Work.com. (Work.com was shut down the next year, and its Internet address was sold to business.com.) Also in 2001 the company increased the price of *The Journal* for the first time in more than a decade.

In 2002 the company was dealt a devastating blow when *Wall Street Journal* reporter Daniel Pearl, who had been kidnapped in Pakistan by suspected Islamic militants, was murdered by his captors. That year the company sold four of its Ottaway daily newspapers (*The Daily Independent* in Ashland, Kentucky; *The Free Press* in Mankato, Minnesota; *The Herald* in Sharton, Pennsylvania; and *The Joplin Globe* in Missouri) to Community Newspaper Holdings for $182 million. Later that year, Ottaway sold three of its Massachusetts-based papers (*The Salem Evening News, The Newburyport Daily News,* and *The Gloucester Daily Times*) to Eagle-Tribune Publishing Company for $70 million.

OFFICERS

Chairman and CEO: Peter R. Kann, age 59, $1,182,000 pay
EVP and COO: Richard F. Zannino, age 43, $1,084,727 pay (prior to promotion)
EVP, General Counsel, and Secretary: Peter G. Skinner, age 57, $716,800 pay
SVP and Publisher of *The Wall Street Journal*: Karen Elliott House, age 43
SVP Electronic Publishing: L. Gordon Crovitz, $607,787 pay
SVP; Chairman and CEO, Ottaway Newspapers; Director: James H. Ottaway Jr., age 64, $549,875 pay
SVP Advertising, The *Wall Street Journal*: Paul Atkinson
VP and CFO: Christopher W. Vieth, age 37
VP and Chief Corporate Marketing Officer: Ann Marks
VP Human Resources: James A. Scaduto
VP Legal: Rosemary C. Spano
Auditors: PricewaterhouseCoopers LLP

LOCATIONS

HQ: 200 Liberty St., New York, NY 10281
Phone: 212-416-2000   **Fax:** 212-416-4348
Web: www.dj.com

Dow Jones & Company has operations in Asia, Europe, Latin America, and North America.

2001 Sales

	$ mil.	% of total
US	1,604	90
International	169	10
Total	**1,773**	**100**

PRODUCTS/OPERATIONS

2001 Sales

	$ mil.	% of total
Advertising	1,052	60
Information services	289	16
Circulation & other	432	24
Total	**1,773**	**100**

Selected Print Publications
Barron's
Far Eastern Economic Review
The Wall Street Journal

Selected Electronic Publications and Services
Barron's Online
dowjones.com (Web portal)
The Wall Street Journal Online

COMPETITORS

Advance Publications	Interactive Data	Pearson
Associated Press	INVESTools	Reed Elsevier Group
Bloomberg	Knight Ridder	Reuters
D&B	LexisNexis	TheStreet.com
EDGAR Online	MarketWatch.com	Thomson
FactSet	McGraw-Hill	Corporation
Forbes	The Motley Fool	Tribune
Gannett	MSCI	Washington Post
Hoover's	New York Times	
	News Corp.	

HISTORICAL FINANCIALS & EMPLOYEES

NYSE: DJ FYE: December 31	Annual Growth	12/92	12/93	12/94	12/95	12/96	12/97	12/98	12/99	12/00	12/01
Sales ($ mil.)	(0.3%)	1,818	1,932	2,091	2,284	2,482	2,573	2,158	2,002	2,203	1,773
Net income ($ mil.)	(1.0%)	108	148	178	190	190	(802)	8	272	(119)	98
Income as % of sales	—	5.9%	7.6%	8.5%	8.3%	7.7%	—	0.4%	13.6%	—	5.5%
Earnings per share ($)	0.8%	1.06	1.47	1.79	1.94	1.95	(8.36)	0.09	2.99	(1.54)	1.14
Stock price - FY high ($)	—	35.38	39.00	41.88	40.13	41.88	55.88	59.00	71.38	77.31	64.30
Stock price - FY low ($)	—	24.50	26.75	28.13	30.63	31.88	33.38	41.56	43.63	51.38	43.05
Stock price - FY close ($)	8.2%	27.00	35.75	31.00	39.88	33.88	53.69	48.13	68.00	56.63	54.73
P/E - high	—	30	26	23	20	21	—	656	24	—	56
P/E - low	—	21	18	15	16	16	—	462	15	—	37
Dividends per share ($)	3.1%	0.76	0.80	0.84	0.92	0.96	0.96	0.96	0.96	1.00	1.00
Book value per share ($)	(31.3%)	14.41	14.96	15.33	16.47	17.22	8.08	5.54	6.16	1.83	0.49
Employees	(2.2%)	9,860	10,006	10,300	11,200	11,800	12,300	8,300	8,175	8,574	8,100

STOCK PRICE HISTORY

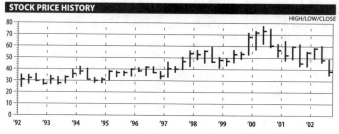

HIGH/LOW/CLOSE

2001 FISCAL YEAR-END

Debt ratio: 80.6%
Return on equity: 97.9%
Cash ($ mil.): 21
Current ratio: 0.41
Long-term debt ($ mil.): 174
No. of shares (mil.): 85
Dividends
  Yield: 1.8%
  Payout: 87.7%
Market value ($ mil.): 4,632

D.R. HORTON, INC.

D.R. Horton rarely hears a "Who?" anymore. The rapidly growing Arlington, Texas-based home builder had been among the largest in the US, and it grew even taller with its February 2002 acquisition of Schuler Homes. Through its 45 or so divisions, the company builds in nearly 40 markets in 20 states. Although D.R. Horton sells mostly entry-level and move-up homes, it also builds luxury models costing up to $900,000. Its homes range in size from 1,000 sq. ft. to 5,000 sq. ft., and the average price is about $200,000. The company also provides mortgage financing and title services, and is building a small number of condominium projects.

Even though the company has been experiencing a major growth spurt (its sales have more than tripled since 1997), D.R. Horton still sticks to its original strategy: letting buyers customize their homes. The company also gives great leeway to its divisional managers, allowing them to run their businesses with minimal interference from the home office and counting on them to understand local tastes and build strong relationships with local contractors.

D.R. Horton is also investing in cyberspace. It has joined with other major homebuilders to create Builder Homesite, an e-commerce site for the industry. It also has invested in other online companies, including Primis, a provider of services to mortgage bankers. Founder Donald Horton owns about 13% of the company; his brother Terrill Horton has a 5% stake.

HISTORY

Donald R. Horton was selling homes in Fort Worth, Texas, when he hit upon a strategy for increasing sales — add options to a basic floor plan. In 1978 he borrowed $33,000 to build his first home, added a bay window for an additional charge, and sold the home for $44,000. Donald soon added floor plans and options that appealed to regional preferences. By the end of 1979 the company had built an additional 19 homes.

The company concentrated on building homes in the Dallas/Fort Worth area in the early and mid-1980s. However, the depressed Texas market drove it to expand beyond DFW in 1987, when it entered the then-hot Phoenix market. It continued to expand into the Southeast, Mid-Atlantic, Midwest, and West in the late 1980s and early 1990s. By 1991 Horton and his family owned more than 25 companies that were combined as D.R. Horton, which went public in 1992.

D.R. Horton acquired six geographically diverse construction firms in 1994 and 1995. In 1996 the company started a mortgage services joint venture, expanded its title operations, and added three more firms.

In 1998 the company bought four builders, including Scottsdale, Arizona-based Continental Homes for $583 million. Continental had been expanding beyond its Arizona and Southern California base and had entered the lucrative retirement community market. After the Continental purchase, Donald Horton stepped down as president, remaining chairman. Richard Beckwitt took over as president, and Donald Tomnitz became CEO. In 1999 the company acquired Century Title and Midwest builder Cambridge Properties, the largest homebuilder in the Chicago area, for $55 million in stock and $103 million in assumed debt.

In 2000 D.R. Horton teamed with several of the nation's largest homebuilders, including Kaufman and Broad, Pulte, and Centex, to create Builder Homesite, a business-to-business Web site serving the homebuilding industry. The site allows users, including contractors, distributors, wholesalers, and manufacturers, to buy and sell building materials, and find subcontractors and other labor.

Also in 2000 D.R. Horton sold its St. Louis assets to McBride & Son Enterprises after spending five years trying to break into the St. Louis home building market. That year Tomnitz took over the duties of president when Beckwitt retired.

The following year the company gained home building operations in Houston and Phoenix when it bought Emerald Builders. Also in 2001 D.R. Horton acquired Fortress-Florida, the leading homebuilder in Jacksonville.

In February 2002 the company acquired Schuler Homes for $1.2 billion, including debt. The deal made D.R. Horton the #2 residential builder in the US, after Pulte Homes.

OFFICERS

Chairman: Donald R. Horton, age 51, $2,400,000 pay
Vice Chairman, President, and CEO: Donald J. Tomnitz, age 53, $2,300,000 pay
EVP, CFO, Treasurer, and Director: Samuel R. Fuller, age 58, $370,000 pay
EVP, Investor Relations: Stacey H. Dwyer, age 35, $164,000 pay
VP and Assistant Controller: Steve Lovett
CIO: Jim Eden
IT Director: Bill Ellis
President, Financial Services: Randy Present
President, Schuler Region and Director: James K. Schuler, age 62
President, Houston Region: Randy Birdwell

President, Northeast Region: George Seagraves
President, South Region: Gordon Jones
President, Southwest Region: Timothy C. Westfall
President, West Region: Thomas F. Noon
Manager Human Resources: Paula Hunter-Perkins
Auditors: Ernst & Young LLP

LOCATIONS

HQ: 1901 Ascension Blvd., Ste. 100, Arlington, TX 76006
Phone: 817-856-8200   Fax: 817-856-8249
Web: www.drhorton.com

D.R. Horton operates in 20 states (Alabama, Arizona, California, Colorado, Delaware, Florida, Georgia, Illinois, Kentucky, Maryland, Minnesota, Nevada, New Jersey, New Mexico, North Carolina, Oregon, South Carolina, Texas, Utah, and Virginia) and in the District of Columbia.

2001 Homebuilding Sales

	$ mil.	% of total
Southwest	1,489	34
West	1,303	30
Mid-Atlantic	616	14
Southeast	518	12
Midwest	458	10
Total	**4,384**	**100**

PRODUCTS/OPERATIONS

2001 Sales

	$ mil.	% of total
Homebuilding	4,384	98
Financial services	72	2
Total	**4,456**	**100**

Selected Operations

Arappco Homes	Milburn Homes
Cambridge Homes	Regency Homes
Continental Homes	Schuler Homes
Dietz-Crane Homes	SGS Communities
Dobson Builders	Stafford Homes
D.R. Horton	Torrey Homes
Emerald Homes	Trimark Communities
Melody Homes	Western Pacific Homes

COMPETITORS

Beazer Homes	Lennar
Centex	M.D.C. Holdings
Century Builders	M/I Schottenstein Homes
Del Webb	NVR
George Wimpey	Pulte Homes
Hovnanian Enterprises	Ryland
J. F. Shea	Standard Pacific
KB Home	Toll Brothers

HISTORICAL FINANCIALS & EMPLOYEES

NYSE: DHI FYE: September 30	Annual Growth	12/92	*9/93	9/94	9/95	9/96	9/97	9/98	9/99	9/00	9/01
Sales ($ mil.)	42.6%	183	190	393	437	547	837	2,177	3,156	3,654	4,456
Net income ($ mil.)	44.8%	9	9	18	21	27	36	93	160	192	257
Income as % of sales	—	5.0%	4.7%	4.5%	4.7%	5.0%	4.3%	4.3%	5.1%	5.2%	5.8%
Earnings per share ($)	28.7%	0.23	0.19	0.38	0.41	0.56	0.69	0.94	1.50	1.69	2.23
Stock price - FY high ($)	—	3.72	5.72	6.85	6.31	7.16	10.37	14.99	13.82	12.62	20.01
Stock price - FY low ($)	—	2.31	2.31	3.50	3.22	4.51	5.18	9.01	6.39	6.01	9.16
Stock price - FY close ($)	17.7%	3.22	5.46	4.65	5.98	5.86	9.47	9.62	7.78	10.33	13.91
P/E - high	—	16	30	18	15	10	13	14	9	7	9
P/E - low	—	10	12	9	8	7	7	9	4	4	4
Dividends per share ($)	—	0.00	0.00	0.00	0.00	0.00	0.02	0.05	0.07	0.09	0.12
Book value per share ($)	26.9%	1.27	1.44	1.88	2.15	3.30	4.23	5.91	7.63	8.32	10.84
Employees	48.0%	—	—	—	—	612	1,160	2,465	3,355	3,631	4,342

* Fiscal year change

STOCK PRICE HISTORY

HIGH/LOW/CLOSE

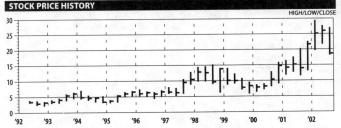

2001 FISCAL YEAR-END

Debt ratio: 60.1%
Return on equity: 23.2%
Cash ($ mil.): 239
Current ratio: 5.98
Long-term debt ($ mil.): 1,884
No. of shares (mil.): 115
Dividends
  Yield: 0.9%
  Payout: 5.4%
Market value ($ mil.): 1,604

DREYER'S GRAND ICE CREAM, INC.

While waiting for Ben & Jerry to come back, Dreyer and Edy curled up in bed with a bowl of Godiva chocolates and Snickers bars. Oakland, California-based Dreyer's Grand Ice Cream is the leading US ice-cream producer. Dreyer's manufactures and distributes premium ice cream and frozen dairy desserts sold under the Dreyer's brand name in 14 western states and parts of Asia and South America. It uses the Edy's brand name elsewhere in the US, and in parts of the Caribbean and Europe. The company also distributes ice cream for ConAgra (Healthy Choice), Nestlé (Häagen-Dazs, Nestlé novelties), and Unilever (Good Humor, Ben & Jerry's).

During a hiatus as the main distributor of Ben & Jerry's superpremium ice creams, Dreyer's began to scoop up sales with its own Dreamery line of superpremium ice creams and Godiva ultrapremium line. The company also teamed up with candy king Mars and the Starbucks coffee company to make ice creams based on their brands. But when Unilever came knocking, Dreyer's agreed to put Ben & Jerry back on its trucks, along with the rest of Unilever's US ice-cream brands.

Dreyer's chairman and CEO, Gary Rogers, owns 10% of the company, and president William Cronk owns 6%; Nestlé owns nearly 30%. Dreyer's has agreed to purchase Nestlé's US ice cream business, in a stock swap that will give Nestlé 67% of the company.

HISTORY

Dreyer's Grand Ice Cream was founded in 1928 by William Dreyer and Joseph Edy as an ice-cream parlor in Oakland, California. Shortly after the stock market crash of 1929, the men created the popular Rocky Road flavor, naming it for the hard times. Edy left in 1947, and Dreyer led the company until his death in 1975.

Fraternity brothers and struggling restaurateurs William Cronk and Gary Rogers bought Dreyer's in 1977 for $1.1 million. The company went public in 1981 and by the mid-1980s had expanded nationally. However, in response to objections from Kraft — then the maker of the Breyer's brand of ice cream — Dreyer's agreed to market its product as Edy's in the eastern US. In 1986 it agreed to distribute Ben & Jerry's superpremium ice cream nationally.

The company was the first premium ice-cream maker to tap the "better-for-you" market, introducing Dreyer's and Edy's Grand Light in 1987 (frozen yogurt and fat-free ice-cream lines followed). In 1994 Nestlé USA acquired about 30% of the company in a deal making Dreyer's

the exclusive distributor of a number of leading Nestlé frozen novelties in selected markets.

Also that year Dreyer's embarked on a five-year marketing plan in an effort to double sales by decade's end. The company formed a joint venture with Starbucks in 1996 to make a line of coffee-flavored ice-cream products. But before Dreyer's grand plan could reach fruition, in late 1997 dairy prices began to skyrocket, doubling costs in 1998. Also, consumers began to tire of healthy stuff, and sales dropped for the reduced-fat, sugar-free ice-cream products.

A rejected bid by Dreyer's to buy Ben & Jerry's in 1998 chilled relations between the two companies: Ben & Jerry's announced that year that it would no longer use Dreyer's as its main US distributor. To counter the resulting loss of income, and newly unfettered from earlier non-compete agreements, Dreyer's introduced its own higher-margin products, starting with the 1999 launch of ultrapremium Godiva Ice Cream (through a licensing agreement with Campbell Soup's Godiva Chocolatier), followed by the introduction of Dreyer's and Edy's Dreamery superpremium ice cream.

In early 2000 the company launched a new line of premium ice-cream products featuring Snickers, M&M's, and other popular Mars candies. Also in 2000 Dreyer's purchased several regional distribution companies, including Cherokee Cream Company, and specialty frozen products. Later that year the company signed a long-term agreement to distribute Unilever's US ice-cream brands nationally, including their newly acquired Ben & Jerry's business.

OFFICERS

Chairman and CEO: T. Gary Rogers, age 59, $777,356 pay
President and Director: William F. Cronk III, $777,356 pay
VP, Sales: Thomas M. Delaplane, age 57, $636,353 pay
VP, Marketing: J. Tyler Johnston, age 48
VP, Finance and Administration, and CFO: Timothy F. Kahn, age 48, $603,205 pay
VP, Operations: William R. Oldenburg, age 55, $636,353 pay
Secretary and Director: Edmund R. Manwell, age 59
Treasurer: William C. Collett
Controller: Jeffrey P. Porter
Manager Corporate Administration (HR): Mary Wold
Auditors: PricewaterhouseCoopers LLP

HQ: 5929 College Ave., Oakland, CA 94618
Phone: 510-652-8187   **Fax:** 510-450-4592
Web: www.dreyersinc.com

Dreyer's Grand Ice Cream has production facilities in California, Indiana, Texas, and Utah.

PRODUCTS/OPERATIONS

2001 Sales

	$ mil.	% total
Dreyer's brand	888	63
Other brands distributed	512	37
Total	**1,400**	**100**

Selected Products
Dreyer's and Edy's products
  Dreamery Ice Cream
  Frozen Yogurt
  Grand Ice Cream
  Grand Soft (soft-serve ice cream and frozen yogurt)
  Homemade Ice Cream
  M&M/Mars Ice Cream
  Sherbet
  Whole Fruit Bars
  Whole Fruit Sorbet
Godiva Ice Cream
Starbucks Ice Cream and Frappuccino Bars

COMPETITORS

Allied Domecq
Blue Bell
CoolBrands
Dean Foods
Friendly Ice Cream
H.P. Hood
Prairie Farms Dairy
Schwan's
TCBY
Unilever
Wells' Dairy
WestFarm Foods
YOCREAM

HISTORICAL FINANCIALS & EMPLOYEES

Nasdaq: DRYR FYE: Last Saturday in Dec.	Annual Growth	12/92	12/93	12/94	12/95	12/96	12/97	12/98	12/99	12/00	12/01
Sales ($ mil.)	14.7%	407	471	564	679	792	970	1,022	1,100	1,194	1,400
Net income ($ mil.)	(6.2%)	16	17	1	(2)	7	8	(47)	11	25	9
Income as % of sales	—	3.9%	3.6%	0.2%	—	0.9%	0.8%	—	1.0%	2.1%	0.6%
Earnings per share ($)	(8.4%)	0.53	0.57	0.03	(0.13)	0.08	0.14	(1.75)	0.33	0.72	0.24
Stock price - FY high ($)	—	18.13	15.75	14.56	20.00	18.88	27.50	26.75	19.94	34.63	40.53
Stock price - FY low ($)	—	7.50	9.88	10.63	12.13	12.00	14.50	9.00	11.31	14.00	23.19
Stock price - FY close ($)	13.6%	12.25	14.75	12.38	16.63	14.50	24.13	15.13	17.00	32.25	38.51
P/E - high	—	39	28	485	—	236	153	—	52	40	156
P/E - low	—	16	17	354	—	150	81	—	30	16	89
Dividends per share ($)	6.4%	0.12	0.12	0.12	0.12	0.12	0.12	0.12	0.12	0.12	0.21
Book value per share ($)	5.6%	3.69	4.19	4.83	7.37	7.60	7.72	5.94	6.24	7.11	6.05
Employees	14.0%	1,447	1,829	2,062	2,500	2,900	3,500	3,450	3,700	4,300	4,700

STOCK PRICE HISTORY

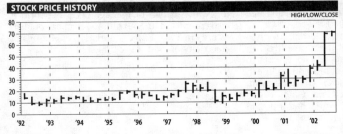

HIGH/LOW/CLOSE

2001 FISCAL YEAR-END
Debt ratio: 41.6%
Return on equity: 5.7%
Cash ($ mil.): 2
Current ratio: 1.72
Long-term debt ($ mil.): 149
No. of shares (mil.): 34
Dividends
  Yield: 0.5%
  Payout: 87.5%
Market value ($ mil.): 1,327

DTE ENERGY COMPANY

Detroit-based DTE Energy keeps the assembly lines rolling in Motor City and the electricity flowing through Michigan power lines. The utility holding company's main subsidiary, Detroit Edison, generates and distributes electricity to some 2.1 million customers in southeastern Michigan. It has a generating capacity of more than 11,000 MW, mainly fossil-fueled. The company expanded into natural gas distribution in 2001 by buying Detroit-based natural gas utility holding company MCN Energy and its MichCon unit, which serves more than 1.2 million customers in Michigan. The enlarged DTE Energy is the state's biggest utility.

DTE Energy is expanding its nonutility businesses such as wholesale power, gas, and coal marketing in the Midwest and northeastern US and eastern Canada (more than 30% of sales); coal transportation and procurement; energy management services for commercial and industrial customers; independent and on-site power generation; and gas exploration, production, and processing. Environmental pursuits by DTE Energy include synthetic fuels production, landfill gas recovery, and fuel cell technology.

Full electric competition in Michigan has taken effect, and DTE Energy prepared by separating its transmission business into a new subsidiary, International Transmission, which it plans to divest.

HISTORY

DTE Energy's predecessor threw its first switch in 1886 when George Peck and local investors incorporated the Edison Illuminating Company of Detroit. Neighboring utility Peninsular Electric Light was formed in 1891, and both companies bought smaller utilities until they merged in 1903 to form Detroit Edison. A subsidiary of holding company North American Co., Detroit Edison was incorporated in New York to secure financing for power plants.

Detroit's growth in the 1920s and 1930s led the utility to build plants and buy others in outlying areas. Detroit Edison acquired Michigan Electric Power, which had been divested from its holding company under the Public Utility Holding Company Act of 1935, and was itself divested from North American in 1940.

The postwar boom prompted Detroit Edison to build more plants, most of them coal-fired. In 1953 it joined a consortium of 34 companies to build Fermi 1, a nuclear plant brought on line in 1963. Still strapped for power, Detroit Edison built the coal-fired Monroe plant, which began service in 1970. In 1972 Fermi 1 had a partial core meltdown and was taken off line.

Detroit Edison began shipping low-sulfur Montana coal through its Wisconsin terminal in 1974, which reduced the cost of obtaining the fuel. That next year it began building another nuke, Fermi 2. The nuke had cost more than $4.8 billion by the time it went on line in 1988. That year the utility began its landfill gas recovery operation (now DTE Biomass Energy).

A recession pounded automakers in the early 1990s, leading to cutbacks in electricity purchases. In 1992 Congress passed the Energy Policy Act, allowing wholesale power competition. In 1993 a fire shut down Fermi 2 for almost two years. Michigan's public service commission (PSC) approved retail customer-choice programs for its utilities in 1994. Detroit Edison and rival Consumers Energy (now CMS Energy) took the PSC to court.

DTE Energy became Detroit Edison's holding company in 1996. The following year it formed DTE Energy Trading to broker power and DTE-CoEnergy to provide energy-management services and sell power to large customers. It also formed Plug Power with Mechanical Technology to develop fuel cells that convert natural gas to power without combustion.

In 1997 and 1998 the PSC, bolstered by state court decisions, issued orders to restructure Michigan's utilities. The transition to retail competition began in 1998. That year DTE Energy and natural gas provider Michigan Consolidated Gas (MichCon) began collaborating on some operations, including billing and meter reading. DTE and GE formed a venture to sell and install Plug Power fuel cell systems.

A higher court shot down the PSC's restructuring orders in 1999, but DTE Energy and CMS Energy decided to implement customer choice using PSC guidelines. That year the US Department of Energy selected DTE Energy to install the world's first super power-cable, which could carry three times as much electricity as conventional copper. Also in 1999, DTE Energy agreed to acquire MCN Energy, MichCon's parent.

In 2000 DTE Energy formed subsidiary International Transmission (ITC) to hold Detroit Edison's transmission assets; the next year ITC joined the Midwest Independent System Operator, which began to manage ITC's network. It also completed its $4.3 billion purchase of MCN Energy in 2001. Full deregulation of Michigan's electricity market was completed in 2002.

Chairman, President, CEO, and COO, DTE Energy and Detroit Edison: Anthony F. Earley Jr., age 52, $1,978,461 pay
SVP and CFO: David E. Meador
SVP and CIO: Lynne Ellyn
SVP and General Counsel: Eric H. Peterson
SVP, Corporate Services: Harold Gardner
SVP, Energy Marketing and Trading: Michael E. Champley
SVP, Human Resources and Corporate Affairs: S. Martin Taylor
SVP, Strategic Planning and Development: Howard L. Dow III
VP and Corporate Secretary, DTE Energy and Detroit Edison: Susan M. Beale
VP, Human Resources: Larry E. Steward
President and COO, DTE Energy Distribution: Robert J. Buckler, age 52, $848,371 pay
President and COO, DTE Energy Resources: Gerard M. Anderson, age 43, $848,371 pay
President and COO, DTE Gas: Stephen E. Ewing, age 57, $636,832 pay
President, DTE Biomass Energy: Curtis T. Ranger
President, DTE Coal Services: Evan O'Neil
Auditors: Deloitte & Touche LLP

PRODUCTS/OPERATIONS

2001 Fuel Mix

	% of total
Fossil	71
Nuclear	15
Purchased power	14
Total	**100**

Selected Subsidiaries and Affiliates
The Detroit Edison Company (electric utility)
DTE Biomass Energy Inc. (landfill gas recovery and methane gas sales)
DTE Coal Services Inc. (coal transportation and sales)
DTE Energy Services Inc. (cogeneration and power generation)
DTE Energy Technologies Inc. (fuel cells and other energy products and services)
DTE Energy Trading Company (energy trading and marketing and risk management)
DTE Rail Services Inc. (rail car repair and maintenance)
DTE Transportation Services Inc. (rail car sourcing and fleet management services)
Edison Development Corporation (28% ownership of Plug Power Inc., a residential fuel cell developer)
International Transmission Company (ITC, transmits electricity)

LOCATIONS

HQ: 2000 2nd Ave., Detroit, MI 48226
Phone: 248-235-4000   **Fax:** 248-223-2150
Web: www.dteenergy.com

DTE Energy provides electricity and natural gas in Michigan and has other operations throughout the US and in Canada.

COMPETITORS

AEP	Nicor	Wisconsin
Aquila	Peabody Energy	Energy
CMS Energy	PG&E	WPS Resources
DPL	SEMCO Energy	Xcel Energy
Duke Energy	Southern	
Dynegy	Company	

HISTORICAL FINANCIALS & EMPLOYEES

NYSE: DTE FYE: December 31	Annual Growth	12/92	12/93	12/94	12/95	12/96	12/97	12/98	12/99	12/00	12/01
Sales ($ mil.)	9.2%	3,558	3,555	3,519	3,636	3,645	3,764	4,221	4,728	5,597	7,849
Net income ($ mil.)	(5.6%)	558	491	390	406	309	417	443	483	468	332
Income as % of sales	—	15.7%	13.8%	11.1%	11.2%	8.5%	11.1%	10.5%	10.2%	8.4%	4.2%
Earnings per share ($)	(6.1%)	3.79	3.34	2.67	2.80	2.13	2.88	3.05	3.33	3.27	2.16
Stock price - FY high ($)	—	35.25	37.13	30.25	34.88	37.25	34.75	49.25	44.69	41.31	47.13
Stock price - FY low ($)	—	30.25	29.88	24.25	25.75	27.63	26.13	33.44	31.06	28.44	33.13
Stock price - FY close ($)	2.8%	32.75	30.00	26.13	34.50	32.38	34.69	43.06	31.63	38.94	41.94
P/E - high	—	9	11	11	12	17	12	16	13	13	22
P/E - low	—	8	9	9	9	13	9	11	9	9	15
Dividends per share ($)	0.6%	1.96	2.04	2.06	2.06	2.06	2.06	2.06	2.06	2.06	2.06
Book value per share ($)	2.2%	23.45	25.01	25.59	25.93	24.73	25.54	25.49	26.95	28.15	28.48
Employees	2.1%	9,183	8,919	8,494	8,340	8,526	8,732	8,482	8,523	9,144	11,030

STOCK PRICE HISTORY
HIGH/LOW/CLOSE

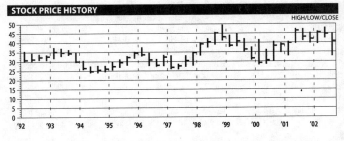

2001 FISCAL YEAR-END

Debt ratio: 62.5%
Return on equity: 7.7%
Cash ($ mil.): 268
Current ratio: 0.89
Long-term debt ($ mil.): 7,654
No. of shares (mil.): 161
Dividends
  Yield: 4.9%
  Payout: 95.4%
Market value ($ mil.): 6,758

DUKE ENERGY CORPORATION

Duke Energy is duking it out with rivals for the title of king of the energy industry. The Charlotte, North Carolina-based company is one of the largest power producers and energy marketers in the US. The company's regulated utilities generate electricity (nearly 18,000 MW capacity, mostly from nuclear and coal-fired plants), which is distributed to 2 million customers in the Carolinas. Duke added more than 1.1 million natural gas customers in Canada with its 2002 acquisition of Westcoast Energy.

Although the Carolinas haven't deregulated their utilities yet, Duke is slugging it out in competitive markets throughout North America. Through its trading and marketing units, which include a venture with Exxon Mobil, Duke buys and sells natural gas, electricity, and other commodities to local utilities, industrial users, and power generators in the US and Canada.

Duke also invests in merchant plants throughout the US (7,400 MW of capacity), and it has power plants, pipelines, and marketing operations in Europe, Latin America, and the Asia-Pacific region. The company provides global engineering and construction services for power projects primarily through its Duke/Fluor Daniel joint venture, which is a top builder of fossil-fuel plants in the US.

Duke also owns and operates a 12,000-mile interstate natural gas pipeline system, which links the Gulf Coast to northeastern US markets. The company is one of the largest US natural gas liquids (NGLs) producers. Duke and Phillips Petroleum have merged their gas gathering and processing and NGL operations into Duke Energy Field Services. Duke is enhancing its generation operations in Latin America and its pipeline operations in Australia, and it has announced plans to buy power generation assets in Europe to supplement its energy trading operations there.

HISTORY

Surgeon W. Gill Wylie founded Catawba Power Company in 1899, which had its first hydroelectric plant in South Carolina on line by 1904. The next year Wylie and James "Buck" Duke (founder of the American Tobacco Company and Duke University's namesake) formed Southern Power Company with Wylie as president.

In 1910 Buck Duke became president of Southern Power and organized Mill-Power Supply to sell electric equipment and appliances. He also began investing in electricity-powered textile mills, which prospered as a result of the electric power, and continued to bring in customers. He formed the Southern Public Utility Company in 1913 to buy other Piedmont-region utilities.

Wylie died in 1924, the same year the company was renamed Duke Power; Buck Duke died the next year.

Growing after WWII, the company went public in 1950 and moved to the NYSE in 1961. It also formed its real estate arm, Crescent Resources, in the 1960s. Insulating itself from the 1970s energy crises, Duke invested in coal mining and three nuclear plants, the first completed in 1974.

In 1988 Duke began to develop power projects outside its home region, and it also bought neighboring utility Nantahala Power and Light. The following year it formed a joint venture with Fluor's Fluor Daniel unit to provide engineering and construction services to power generators. Mill-Power Supply was sold in 1990.

By the 1990s Duke had moved into overseas markets, acquiring an Argentine power station in 1992. It also tried its hand at telecommunications, creating DukeNet Communications in 1994 to build fiber-optic systems, and in 1996 it joined oil giant Mobil to create a power trading and marketing business. As the US power industry traveled toward deregulation, Duke also sought natural gas operations. Duke Power bought PanEnergy in 1997 to form Duke Energy Corporation.

Seeing an opportunity in 1998, Duke formed Duke Communication Services to provide antenna sites to the fast-growing wireless communications industry. It also acquired a 52% stake in Electroquil, an electric power generating company in Guayaquil, Ecuador. That year it purchased a pipeline company in Australia from PG&E; it also bought three PG&E power plants to compete in California's deregulated electric utility marketplace.

Duke merged its pipeline business, Duke Energy Trading and Transport, with TEPPCO Partners and acquired gas processing operations from Union Pacific Resources. To further enhance natural gas operations in other regions, Duke bought El Paso's East Tennessee Natural Gas pipeline unit in 2000 and a 20% stake in Canadian 88 Energy; it also purchased $1.4 billion in South American generation assets, including assets from Dominion Resources, and Mobil's gas trading operations in the Netherlands.

Lawsuits accusing Duke of overcharging California utilities for power during the state's energy crisis were filed in 2000 and 2001; most are still pending. In 2001 Duke announced the $8 billion acquisition of Canadian gas utility Westcoast Energy, which was completed in 2002.

That year Duke announced plans to sell its stake in Canadian 88 Energy. Duke Energy Field Services purchased ChevronTexaco's 33% stake in Discovery Producer Services, which operates a Gulf of Mexico gas pipeline and nearby processing facilities. Also in 2002, after facing scrutiny from the SEC over "round-trip" energy trades, Duke announced that it would combine the energy trading operations of Duke Energy North America, Duke Energy Merchants, and its Canadian marketing business into one unit.

OFFICERS

Chairman, President, and CEO: Richard B. Priory, age 56, $3,265,632 pay
Director; Group President, Duke Power: William A. Coley, age 58
Group President, Energy Services: Harvey J. Padewer, age 55, $1,500,000 pay
Group President, Energy Transmission: Fred J. Fowler, age 56, $1,250,010 pay
EVP and CFO: Robert P. Brace, age 52, $1,265,000 pay
EVP and Chief Risk Officer: Richard J. Osborne, age 51, $1,250,010 pay
EVP and Chief Administrative Officer: Ruth G. Shaw, age 54
EVP, General Counsel, and Secretary: Richard W. Blackburn, age 59
SVP and General Counsel: Brent C. Bailey
SVP Human Resources: Christopher C. Rolfe
Auditors: Deloitte & Touche LLP

LOCATIONS

HQ: 526 S. Church St., Charlotte, NC 28202
Phone: 713-627-5400   **Fax:** 713-989-0363
Web: www.duke-energy.com

2001 Sales

	$ mil.	% of total
US	51,723	87
Canada	5,690	10
Latin America	628	1
Other countries	1,462	2
Total	**59,503**	**100**

PRODUCTS/OPERATIONS

2001 Sales

	$ mil.	% of total
North American wholesale	42,815	72
Field services	7,997	13
Franchised electric	4,737	8
International energy	2,074	3
Natural gas transmission	967	2
Energy services	267	1
Other	646	1
Total	**59,503**	**100**

COMPETITORS

AEP	Dynegy	Piedmont
AES	El Paso	Natural Gas
Aquila	Entergy	Progress Energy
Avista	Exelon	SCANA
BP	Gasunie	Southern
CenterPoint	Iberdrola	Company
Energy	KeySpan Energy	TVA
ChevronTexaco	Koch	Tractebel
Cinergy	Mirant	TXU
Constellation	PG&E	Williams
Energy Group		Companies

HISTORICAL FINANCIALS & EMPLOYEES

NYSE: DUK FYE: December 31	Annual Growth	12/92	12/93	12/94	12/95	12/96	12/97	12/98	12/99	12/00	12/01
Sales ($ mil.)	35.1%	3,962	4,282	4,489	4,677	4,758	16,309	17,610	21,742	49,318	59,503
Net income ($ mil.)	15.8%	508	626	639	715	730	974	1,252	1,507	1,776	1,898
Income as % of sales	—	12.8%	14.6%	14.2%	15.3%	15.3%	6.0%	7.1%	6.9%	3.6%	3.2%
Earnings per share ($)	8.5%	1.11	1.06	1.13	1.34	1.42	1.25	1.70	2.04	2.38	2.32
Stock price – FY high ($)	—	18.75	22.44	21.50	23.94	26.50	28.28	35.50	32.66	45.22	47.74
Stock price – FY low ($)	—	15.69	17.69	16.44	18.69	21.69	20.94	24.47	23.31	22.88	32.22
Stock price – FY close ($)	9.0%	18.06	21.19	19.06	23.69	23.13	27.69	32.03	25.06	42.63	39.26
P/E – high	—	17	21	19	18	18	22	21	29	19	19
P/E – low	—	14	17	15	14	15	17	14	21	10	13
Dividends per share ($)	2.5%	0.88	0.92	0.96	1.00	1.04	1.08	1.10	1.10	1.10	1.10
Book value per share ($)	3.7%	12.03	12.49	12.97	13.35	13.82	11.16	11.66	12.71	13.89	16.63
Employees	2.8%	18,727	18,274	17,052	17,121	17,726	23,000	22,000	21,000	23,000	24,000

STOCK PRICE HISTORY

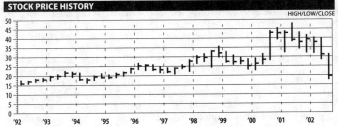

HIGH/LOW/CLOSE

2001 FISCAL YEAR-END

Debt ratio: 48.8%
Return on equity: 16.7%
Cash ($ mil.): 290
Current ratio: 0.92
Long-term debt ($ mil.): 12,321
No. of shares (mil.): 777
Dividends
  Yield: 2.8%
  Payout: 47.4%
Market value ($ mil.): 30,505

DYNEGY INC.

Houston-based Dynegy (short for "dynamic energy" and pronounced DIE-negy) has evolved from a natural gas marketer into a multidimensional energy provider. The company's operations include energy trading, marketing, and generation; natural gas liquids production; electricity and natural gas transmission and distribution; and telecommunications.

Dynegy would have become the world's largest energy trader had it completed its purchase of troubled rival Enron; however, the deal has been canceled, and Enron has since filed for Chapter 11 bankruptcy. Enron's implosion has led to scrutiny of other US energy traders, and Dynegy's accounting practices have attracted regulators' attention. At the urging of board members, longtime Dynegy CEO Chuck Watson resigned in May 2002. Later that year, Dynegy announced that it would take further measures to improve its financial situation, including the sale of some gas transportation and storage assets.

Dynegy's Wholesale Energy Network unit buys and sells electricity, natural gas, and other commodities in the US, Canada, the UK, and continental Europe. The unit has power plant investments that give it a generating capacity of nearly 16,000 MW, primarily located in the US. Dynegy also has alliances with regional utilities to compete in deregulated retail marketplaces.

Dynegy Midstream Services gathers and processes natural gas and produces natural gas liquids, primarily in the US Gulf Coast region. Dynegy has announced plans to spin off part of a new natural gas liquids business, Dynegy Energy Partners, to the public. Regulated utility Illinois Power serves 650,000 natural gas and electricity customers. Dynegy also operates fiber-optic telecommunications networks in the US and Europe.

ChevronTexaco owns nearly 27% of Dynegy.

HISTORY

Dynegy, originally Natural Gas Clearinghouse (NGC), emerged from the deregulation of the natural gas industry. In 1978 the Natural Gas Policy Act reduced interstate pipeline companies' control over the marketplace. Federal Energy Regulatory Commission (FERC) Order 380 (1984) made gas prices on the open market competitive with those of pipeline companies. NGC was founded in late 1984 to match gas buyers and sellers without taking title. Chuck Watson became president and CEO in 1985. The company grew dramatically as deregulation secured larger volumes of gas for independent marketers.

The company developed financial instruments (such as natural gas futures) to provide customers with a hedge against wide fluctuations in natural gas prices. By 1990 NGC was trading natural gas futures on NYMEX. It also branched out by buying gas gathering and processing facilities, and it formed NGC Oil Trading and Transportation to market crude oil.

FERC Order 636 (1992) required most interstate pipeline companies to offer merchant sales, transportation, and storage as separate services, on the same terms that their own affiliates received. With the low-price advantage taken away from pipeline companies, NGC began selling more to local gas utilities.

In 1994 NGC set up partnerships with Canada's NOVA (Novagas Clearinghouse, a natural gas marketer) and British Gas (Accord Energy, an energy marketer), which gave those firms sizable stakes (later reduced) in the company. It also set up an electric power marketing unit, Electric Clearinghouse.

The company changed its name to NGC and went public in 1995 after it bought Trident NGL, an integrated natural gas liquids company. The following year NGC bought Chevron's natural gas business, giving Chevron (which became ChevronTexaco in 2001) a stake in NGC.

In 1997 NGC acquired Destec Energy, a leading independent power producer. It also formed retail energy marketing alliances with regional players in the Midwest (Nicor), the Northeast, and Canada (Enbridge). NGC teamed up with AGL Resources and Piedmont Natural Gas in 1998 to form SouthStar Energy.

Taking the name Dynegy in 1998, the company allied with Florida Power to market wholesale electricity and gas. It also began developing new domestic power plants.

In 2000 Dynegy paid about $4 billion for utility holding company Illinova. The deal gave Dynegy 3,800 MW of generation capacity, which was transferred to its energy marketing unit, and utility operations in the Midwest. However, Dynegy was forced to sell assets to get the merger approved. Later that year it sold its midcontinent natural gas assets to ONEOK, and its Canadian gas assets to Northern Border Partners.

In 2001 the company expanded its power generation operations into the Northeast by buying two New York facilities from CH Energy Group. It also bought BG Group's UK gas storage assets, and agreed to purchase two Arizona plants from Sierra Pacific Resources.

In November 2001 Dynegy announced an agreement to buy energy trading giant Enron for about $9 billion in stock and $13 billion in assumed debt. But after Enron's stock price continued to plunge, Dynegy canceled the deal and announced that it would exercise its option to buy Enron's Northern Natural Gas (NNG) pipeline for $1.5 billion. Enron then filed for Chapter 11 bankruptcy protection, and the two companies filed lawsuits against each other. (Dynegy agreed to pay Enron $25 million to settle the suits in 2002.)

Dynegy announced in 2002 that the SEC would formally investigate how the company accounted for a multi-year natural gas transaction; less than a month later Dynegy restated its 2001 earnings to eliminate a tax benefit related to the gas transaction. Later that year Watson resigned as Dynegy's chairman and CEO.

Dynegy sold the NNG pipeline to MidAmerican Energy Holdings that year for $928 million plus $950 million in assumed debt.

LOCATIONS

HQ: 1000 Louisiana, Ste. 5800, Houston, TX 77002
Phone: 713-507-6400   **Fax:** 713-507-3871
Web: www.dynegy.com

2001 Sales

	$ mil.	% of total
US	32,229	76
Canada	6,085	15
Europe & other	3,928	9
Total	**42,242**	**100**

PRODUCTS/OPERATIONS

2001 Sales

	$ mil.	% of total
Wholesale energy	34,451	81
Transmission & midstream services	6,171	15
Distribution	1,593	4
Communications	27	—
Total	**42,242**	**100**

OFFICERS

Interim CEO and Director: Daniel L. Dienstbier, age 61
President, COO, and Director; CEO, Illinois Power: Stephen W. Bergstrom, age 44, $5,886,493 pay
EVP Finance and Director: Louis J. Dorey
EVP; Chairman and CEO, Dynegy Global Communications: Lawrence A. McLernon, age 63
EVP; President, Global Technology: R. Blake Young, age 43, $756,667 pay
EVP, General Counsel, and Secretary: Kenneth E. Randolph, age 45, $922,000 pay
EVP and Chief Administrative Officer: Milton L. Scott, age 45
EVP and Chief Communications Officer: Deborah A. Fiorito, age 52
EVP Corporate Development: Hugh A. Tarpley, age 45
Auditors: PricewaterhouseCoopers LLP

COMPETITORS

AEP	Duke Energy	PG&E
AES	Edison	Sempra Energy
Alliant Energy	International	TEPPCO
Ameren	El Paso	Partners
Aquila	Entergy-Koch	Tractebel
BP	Enterprise	TXU
CenterPoint	EOTT Energy	Williams
Energy	Partners	Companies
Constellation	Exelon	
Energy Group	Mirant	

HISTORICAL FINANCIALS & EMPLOYEES

NYSE: DYN FYE: December 31	Annual Growth	12/92	12/93	12/94	12/95	12/96	12/97	12/98	12/99	12/00	12/01
Sales ($ mil.)	36.9%	2,493	2,791	3,238	3,666	7,260	13,378	14,258	15,430	29,445	42,242
Net income ($ mil.)	34.9%	44	46	42	45	113	(103)	108	152	501	650
Income as % of sales	—	1.8%	1.6%	1.3%	1.2%	1.6%	—	0.8%	1.0%	1.7%	1.5%
Earnings per share ($)	50.2%	—	—	0.11	0.41	0.42	0.00	0.33	0.46	1.48	1.90
Stock price - FY high ($)	—	—	—	8.87	8.51	17.93	17.48	12.68	17.93	59.88	59.00
Stock price - FY low ($)	—	—	—	5.79	6.07	6.25	10.68	6.79	7.33	17.11	20.00
Stock price - FY close ($)	18.9%	—	—	7.61	6.43	16.84	12.68	7.92	17.61	56.06	25.50
P/E - high	—	—	—	81	21	43	—	35	37	39	30
P/E - low	—	—	—	53	15	15	—	19	15	11	10
Dividends per share ($)	38.9%	—	—	0.03	0.02	0.03	0.03	0.03	0.03	0.25	0.30
Book value per share ($)	54.0%	—	—	0.65	2.50	3.73	3.37	3.71	4.19	11.15	13.28
Employees	28.3%	—	—	1,070	1,055	1,893	2,572	2,434	2,571	5,778	6,139

STOCK PRICE HISTORY

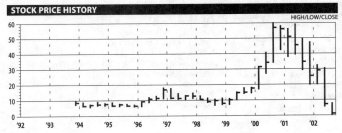

High/Low/Close

2001 FISCAL YEAR-END

Debt ratio: 43.3%
Return on equity: 15.6%
Cash ($ mil.): 218
Current ratio: 1.11
Long-term debt ($ mil.): 3,608
No. of shares (mil.): 355
Dividends
 Yield: 1.2%
 Payout: 15.8%
Market value ($ mil.): 9,058

E. & J. GALLO WINERY

"We don't want most of the business," E. & J. Gallo Winery chairman Ernest Gallo has said. "We want it all." Once known primarily as the maker of cheap jug wine such as Carlo Rossi and Gallo and fortified favorites such as Thunderbird, the world's largest wine maker has siphoned market share from upscale rivals by branching into more profitable middle- and premium-priced wines, including Gallo Sonoma. The Modesto, California-based winery also sells premium wines such as Turning Leaf and Gossamer Bay without the Gallo name on the label.

Already the leader in US table wines, with about 25% of the market, Gallo sells wine worldwide and is the leading US wine exporter. The vintner's strong affiliation with Wal-Mart has boosted wine sales in new Wal-Mart markets such as Germany and the UK. Gallo cultivates 3,000-plus acres in prestigious Sonoma County, California, and buys grapes from other area growers. Gallo sells nearly 35 brands over a wide price range, from alcohol-added wines and wine coolers to upscale varietals that fetch more than $50 a bottle.

The founding Gallo family owns the firm.

HISTORY

Giuseppe Gallo, the father of Ernest and Julio Gallo, was born in 1882 in the wine country of northwest Italy. Around 1900 he and his brother, Michelo (they called themselves Joe and Mike), traveled to America seeking their fame and fortune in the San Francisco area. Both brothers became wealthy by growing grapes and anticipating the growth of the market during Prohibition. (Home winemaking was legal and popular.)

Giuseppe's eldest sons, Ernest and Julio, worked with their father from the beginning. Their relationship was strained, and the father was reluctant to help his sons, particularly Ernest, in business. However, the mysterious murder-suicide that ended the lives of Giuseppe and his wife in 1933 eliminated that problem: The sons inherited the business their father had been unwilling to share.

From then on Ernest ran the business end, assembling a large distribution network and building a national brand, while Julio made the wine and Joe Jr., the third, much younger brother, worked for them. In the early 1940s Gallo opened bottling plants in Los Angeles and New Orleans, using screw-cap bottles, which then seemed more hygienic and modern than corks. Gallo lagged during WWII, when alcohol was diverted for the military. Under Julio's supervision, it upgraded its planting stock and refined its technology.

In an attempt to capitalize on the sweet wines popular in the 1950s, Gallo introduced Thunderbird, a fortified wine (its alcohol content boosted to 20%), in 1957. In the 1960s Gallo spurred its growth by advertising heavily and keeping prices low. It introduced Hearty Burgundy, a jug wine, in 1964, along with Ripple. Gallo introduced the carbonated, fruit-flavored Boone's Farm Apple Wine in 1969, creating an interest in "pop" wines that lasted for a few years.

The company introduced its first varietal wines in 1974. In the 1970s Gallo field workers switched unions, from the United Farm Workers to the Teamsters. Repercussions included protests and boycotts, but sales were largely unaffected. From 1976 to 1982 Gallo operated under an FTC order limiting its control over wholesalers. The order was lifted after the industry's competitive balance changed.

Through the 1970s and 1980s, Gallo expanded its production of varietals; in 1988 it began adding vintage dates to the wines' labels. But it also kept a hand in the lower levels of the market, introducing Bartles & Jaymes wine coolers.

Gallo began a legal battle in 1986 with Joe, who had been eased out of the business, over the use of the Gallo name. In 1992 Joe lost the use of his name for commercial purposes. Julio died the next year when his jeep overturned on a family ranch.

In 1996 rival Kendall-Jackson sued Gallo for trademark infringement over Gallo's new wine brand, Turning Leaf, claiming Gallo copied its Vintner's Reserve bottle and label. A jury ruled in Gallo's favor in 1997; a federal appeals court supported that decision in 1998.

In May 2000 Gallo announced plans to promote wine-cooler market leader Bartles & Jaymes with a new advertising campaign, although the category continues to wane.

In 2001 Gallo's reseach team patented a number of diagnostic tools that can be licensed to winemakers around the world; one tool, for example, can spot an infected vine in a matter of hours, rather than years.

OFFICERS

Chairman: Ernest Gallo
Co-President: James E. Coleman
Co-President: Joseph E. Gallo
Co-President: Robert J. Gallo
EVP and General Counsel: Jack B. Owens
EVP, Marketing: Albion Fenderson
VP, Controller, and Assistant Treasurer: Tony Youga
VP, Human Resources: Mike Chase
VP, Information Systems: Kent Kushar
VP, Media: Sue McClelland
VP, National Sales: Gary Ippolito

LOCATIONS

HQ: 600 Yosemite Blvd., Modesto, CA 95354
Phone: 209-341-3111 **Fax:** 209-341-3569
Web: www.gallo.com

E. & J. Gallo Winery has four wineries in the California counties of Fresno, Livingston, Modesto, and Sonoma, and vineyards throughout the region. Its wine is sold throughout the US and in more than 85 countries.

PRODUCTS/OPERATIONS

Selected Products and Labels

Bargain generic and varietals (Carlo Rossi, Livingston Cellars, Peter Vella, Wild Vines)
Brandy (E&J Brandy, E&J Cask & Cream, E&J VSOP)
Dessert (Fairbanks, Gallo, Sheffield Cellars)
Flagship (Ernest & Julio Gallo Vineyards, Gallo of Sonoma)
Fortified and jug (Gallo, Hearty Burgundy, Night Train, Ripple, Thunderbird)
Hospitality industry (Burlwood, Copperidge by E&J Gallo, William Wycliff Vineyards)
Imported varietals (Ecco Domani)
Mid-priced varietals (Garnet Point, Gossamer Bay, Turning Leaf)
Sparkling (André, Ballatore, Indigo Hills, Tott's)
Ultra-premium (Anapamu, Indigo Hills, Marcelina, Rancho Zabaco)
Wine-based and other beverages (Bartles & Jaymes, Boone's Farm, Hornsby's Pub Draft Cider)

COMPETITORS

Allied Domecq
Asahi Breweries
Bacardi USA
Beringer Blass
Brown-Forman
Chalone Wine
Concha y Toro
Constellation Brands
Foster's
Heaven Hill Distilleries
GIV
Jim Beam Brands
Kendall-Jackson
LVMH
Pernod Ricard
Ravenswood Winery
R.H. Phillips
Robert Mondavi
Sebastiani Vineyards
Taittinger
Terlato Wine
Trinchero Family Estates
UST
Vincor
Wine Group

HISTORICAL FINANCIALS & EMPLOYEES

| Private
FYE: December 31 | Annual
Growth | 12/92 | 12/93 | 12/94 | 12/95 | 12/96 | 12/97 | 12/98 | 12/99 | 12/00 | 12/01 |
|---|---|---|---|---|---|---|---|---|---|---|---|
| Estimated sales ($ mil.) | 6.1% | 1,000 | 1,100 | 980 | 1,100 | 1,200 | 1,300 | 1,500 | 1,520 | 1,610 | 1,700 |
| Employees | 1.7% | 3,000 | 4,000 | 4,000 | 4,000 | 5,000 | 5,000 | 5,000 | 5,250 | 3,600 | 3,500 |

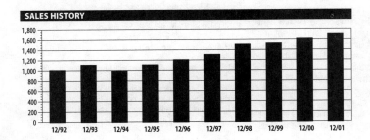

SALES HISTORY

EARTHLINK, INC.

EarthLink is reaching for the stars. The Atlanta-based ISP (formerly EarthLink Network) has 4.6 million consumer and small-business subscribers, making it a leading ISP in the US.

As much of the growth in Internet services is shifting to broadband access, EarthLink is rolling out broadband services, including DSL (digital subscriber line), fixed wireless, and dedicated circuit services. The company, which has about 600,000 broadband subscribers, also offers cable access through an agreement with Time Warner Cable and is in trials to offer service over Comcast Cable's system. EarthLink also provides such services as domain registration, e-commerce, and Web hosting.

The company has been growing through acquisitions, including MindSpring, OneMain.com (which has expanded Earthlink's coverage into more rural markets), e-mail appliance developer Cidco, and the assets of bankrupt wireless services provider OmniSky.

EarthLink and Sprint have ended their exclusive co-branding arrangement and Sprint has reduced its stake in EarthLink to about 17%. EarthLink will continue to provide Internet applications to Sprint and to use Sprint's network services, but the separation of the companies' brands was seen by some analysts as a sign that EarthLink might entertain a takeover offer from another company.

HISTORY

After his first attempt to log onto the Internet took 80 hours in 1993, a frustrated 23-year-old Sky Dayton had an idea for a new business: an ISP focused on customer service. Dayton, who had already co-founded Los Angeles coffeehouse Cafe Mocha and graphics firm Dayton Walker Design, persuaded investors Reed Slatkin and Kevin O'Donnell to contribute $100,000. EarthLink Network was launched in Glendale, California, in 1994.

Dayton, an Ayn Rand fan who graduated from high school at 16 and never attended college, first tried to do everything — from sales to software — himself. He ultimately decided to concentrate on customer service, correctly betting that such elements as browser software and backbone networks would emerge from other providers. Offering phone help and a flat monthly rate of $19.95, EarthLink sold its first account by the end of 1994.

That next year EarthLink released TotalAccess, a package of leading Internet software that included the popular Netscape Navigator browser and QUALCOMM's Eudora, the Internet's most popular e-mail program. Viacom's Macmillan Publishing agreed to sell TotalAccess disks in their Internet books. EarthLink was to gain similar deals with about 90 other partners.

By 1996 EarthLink had won 30,000 subscribers. The company signed a deal with PSINet giving EarthLink customers dial-up access through PSINet's more than 230 locations in the US and Canada. The following year EarthLink went public.

In 1998 EarthLink teamed with Sprint in a 10-year deal that combined the companies' Internet access services and gave Sprint 29.5% of the firm. As EarthLink passed the 1 million-subscriber mark in 1999, it agreed to offer a co-branded version of America Online's instant messaging service.

EarthLink Network agreed to merge with MindSpring in 1999 in a $1.4 billion deal (closed in 2000). The new company, EarthLink, Inc., moved to MindSpring's Atlanta headquarters. MindSpring founder Charles Brewer took over as chairman, and Dayton remained a director. Brewer left EarthLink later in 2000, however, and Dayton stepped back in as chairman.

Investments in EarthLink during 2000 included $200 million from Apple (which made EarthLink the default ISP on Macintoshes) and another $431 million from Sprint (which boosted its stake after heavy dilution from the MindSpring deal). That year, EarthLink gained 700,000 subscribers by buying OneMain.com, an ISP focused on small cities and rural communities, for $262 million.

EarthLink and Sprint stepped back from their co-branding arrangement in 2001, and Sprint sold about 40% of its stake in the company. That year EarthLink agreed to acquire Cidco, a California-based maker of personal e-mail appliances, in a $5 million deal (completed in 2002). Also in 2002 EarthLink acquired the assets of wireless Internet access provider OmniSky, as well as PeoplePC, which sells computers with bundled Internet access.

OFFICERS

Chairman: Sky D. Dayton
CEO and Director: Charles G. Betty, age 45, $683,165 pay
EVP, General Counsel, and Secretary: Samuel R. Desimone Jr., age 42
EVP Acquisitions and Integration: Veronica J. Murdock, age 38
EVP Strategic Brand Marketing: Michael C. Lunsford, age 34
EVP EarthLink Everywhere: Lance Weatherby, age 41
EVP Employee Services: Gregory J. Stromberg, age 49
EVP Finance and Administration and CFO: Lee Adrean, age 50, $392,288 pay

EVP Marketing: Karen L. Gough, age 45
EVP Member Experience: Jon M. Irwin, age 41,
$337,021 pay
EVP Member Support: Carter Calle
EVP Operations: Linda Beck, age 38
EVP Sales: William S. Heys, age 52, $316,972 pay
EVP Strategic Planning: Brinton O. C. Young, age 50
VP Research and Development: Mark S. Petrovi
Chief Privacy Officer: Les Seagraves
Auditors: Ernst & Young LLP

LOCATIONS

HQ: 1375 Peachtree St. 7 North, Atlanta, GA 30309
Phone: 404-815-0770   **Fax:** 404-815-8805
Web: www.earthlink.net

EarthLink provides Internet access primarily in the US
and Canada.

PRODUCTS/OPERATIONS

2001 Sales

	$ mil.	% of total
Narrowband access	999	80
Web hosting	168	14
Broadband access	59	5
Content, commerce & advertising	19	1
Total	**1,245**	**100**

Selected Subsidiaries
Cidco Incorporated (personal Internet communications
    products and services)
EarthLink Communication (Israel) Ltd.
EarthLink/OneMain, Inc.

COMPETITORS

America Online
AT&T
BellSouth
Covad Communications Group
Genuity
Internet America
Microsoft
Prodigy
Qwest
Road Runner
SBC Communications
Verizon

HISTORICAL FINANCIALS & EMPLOYEES

Nasdaq: ELNK FYE: December 31	Annual Growth	12/92	12/93	12/94	12/95	12/96	12/97	12/98	12/99	12/00	12/01
Sales ($ mil.)	284.6%	—	—	0	3	33	79	176	670	987	1,245
Net income ($ mil.)	—	—	—	(0)	(6)	(31)	(30)	(60)	(174)	(346)	(341)
Income as % of sales	—	—	—	—	—	—	—	—	—	—	—
Earnings per share ($)	—	—	—	—	—	—	(0.91)	(1.56)	(1.65)	(2.99)	(2.73)
Stock price - FY high ($)	—	—	—	—	—	—	7.88	47.57	60.22	33.00	18.99
Stock price - FY low ($)	—	—	—	—	—	—	2.61	7.42	21.21	4.75	5.06
Stock price - FY close ($)	11.8%	—	—	—	—	—	7.80	34.54	25.76	5.03	12.17
P/E - high	—	—	—	—	—	—	—	—	—	—	—
P/E - low	—	—	—	—	—	—	—	—	—	—	—
Dividends per share ($)	—	—	—	—	—	—	0.00	0.00	0.00	0.00	0.00
Book value per share ($)	143.2%	—	—	—	—	—	0.16	4.11	6.49	9.09	5.75
Employees	61.8%	—	—	—	376	621	807	1,343	4,828	7,377	6,736

STOCK PRICE HISTORY

HIGH/LOW/CLOSE

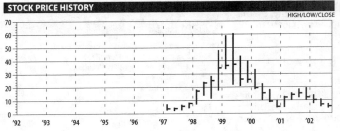

2001 FISCAL YEAR-END

Debt ratio: 0.2%
Return on equity: —
Cash ($ mil.): 424
Current ratio: 1.96
Long-term debt ($ mil.): 2
No. of shares (mil.): 148
Dividends
  Yield: —
  Payout: —
Market value ($ mil.): 1,801

EASTMAN CHEMICAL COMPANY

Eastman Chemical can recall its past through photos — it was once part of film giant Eastman Kodak. The Kingsport, Tennessee-based company has developed into a major producer of chemicals, fibers, and plastics. The company's chemicals — which include raw materials for coatings, adhesives, inks, and performance chemicals — account for more than 50% of sales. Eastman Chemical, through its Voridian unit, also produces polymers used by industrial customers to manufacture such products as food and medical packaging, films, tape, and toothbrushes. Voridian is one of the world's largest makers of polyethylene terephthalate (PET), a plastic used to make packaging for soft drinks, food, and water. Voridian also churns out tons of acetate tow, used in cigarette filters, and yarn used in apparel and fabrics. Eastman Chemical has operations worldwide, with the US and Canada accounting for about 60% of sales.

A sullen stock market nixed Eastman's plans to split into two publicly traded companies, one focused on specialty chemicals and plastics (Eastman Company) and one focused on plastic packaging and acetate fibers (Voridian Company). Eastman Company and Voridian now operate as two separate divisions.

HISTORY

Eastman Chemical went public in 1994, but the company traces its roots to the 19th century. George Eastman, after developing a method for dry-plate photography, established the Eastman Dry Plate and Film Company in 1884 in Rochester, New York (the name was changed to Eastman Kodak in 1892).

In 1886 Eastman hired scientist Henry Reichenbach to help create and manufacture new photographic chemicals. As time passed, Reichenbach and the company's other scientists came up with chemicals that were either not directly related to photography or had uses in addition to photography.

Eastman bought a wood-distillation plant in Kingsport, Tennessee, in 1920 and formed the Tennessee Eastman Corporation to make methanol and acetone for the manufacture of photographic chemicals. The company, by this time called Kodak, introduced acetate yarn and Tenite, a cellulose ester plastic, in the early 1930s. During WWII the company formed Holston Defense to make explosives for the US armed forces.

Kodak began to vertically integrate Tennessee Eastman's operations during the 1950s, acquiring A. M. Tenney Associates, Tennessee Eastman's selling agent for its acetate yarn products, in

1950. It also established Texas Eastman, opening a plant in Longview to produce ethyl alcohol and aldehydes, raw materials used in fiber and film production. At the end of 1952, Kodak created Eastman Chemical Products to sell alcohols, plastics, and fibers made by Tennessee Eastman and Texas Eastman. Also that year Tennessee Eastman developed cellulose acetate filter tow for use in cigarette filters. In the late 1950s the company introduced Kodel polyester fiber.

Kodak created Carolina Eastman Company in 1968, opening a plant in Columbia, South Carolina, to produce Kodel and other polyester products. It also created Eastman Chemicals Division to handle its chemical operations.

In the late 1970s Eastman Chemicals Division introduced polyethylene terephthalate (PET) resin used to make containers. It acquired biological and molecular instrumentation manufacturer International Biotechnologies in 1987.

Eastman Chemicals Division became Eastman Chemical Company in 1990. It exited the polyester fiber business in 1993. When Kodak spun off Eastman Chemical in early 1994, the new company was saddled with $1.8 billion in debt.

Eastman's 1996 earnings were reduced when oversupply lowered prices for PET. Eastman opened plants in Argentina, Malaysia, and the Netherlands in 1998.

Eastman added to its international locations in 1999 by opening a plant in Singapore and an office in Bangkok. It also bought Lawter International (specialty chemicals for ink and coatings) with locations in Belgium, China, and Ireland. In 2000 the company began restructuring into two business segments (chemicals and polymers) and acquired resin and colorant maker McWhorter Technologies.

In 2001 Eastman acquired most of Hercules' resins business. In November the company announced that it had postponed plans to split into two companies (one focusing on specialty chemicals and plastics, the other concentrating on polyethylene, plastics, and acetate fibers) until mid-2002 due to the weak economy. In early 2002 the company announced that it had cancelled those plans and would operate the two as separate divisions.

OFFICERS

Chairman and CEO: J. Brian Ferguson, age 47, $375,268 pay (prior to promotion)
EVP and President, Voridian Company: Allan R. Rothwell, age 54, $404,763 pay (prior to promotion)
SVP, CFO, and COO: James P. Rogers, age 51, $409,981 pay

SVP, General Counsel, and Secretary: Theresa K. Lee, age 49
SVP; Special Growth Initiatives, IT, Marketing/Sales Processes, and Corporate Strategy: Roger K. Mowen Jr., age 56, $376,013 pay
SVP, Human Resources, Communications, and Public Affairs: B. Fielding Rolston, age 60
VP and Controller: Mark W. Joslin, age 42
VP, Communications and Public Affairs: Betty W. DeVinney, age 57
VP and CTO: Gregory O. Nelson, age 50
VP and General Counsel, Voridian: David E. Cotey
VP and CFO, Voridian: Albert J. Wargo
Auditors: PricewaterhouseCoopers LLP

LOCATIONS

HQ: 100 N. Eastman Rd., Kingsport, TN 37660
Phone: 423-229-2000   **Fax:** 423-229-1351
Web: www.eastman.com

Eastman Chemical has about 40 plants scattered throughout Argentina, Belgium, Canada, China, Czech Republic, Finland, France, Germany, Hong Kong, Italy, Ireland, Malaysia, Mexico, the Netherlands, Singapore, Spain, Sweden, the UK, and the US.

2001 Sales

	$ mil.	% of total
US & Canada	3,196	60
Europe, Middle East & Africa	1,148	21
Asia/Pacific	555	10
Latin America	485	9
Total	**5,384**	**100**

PRODUCTS/OPERATIONS

2001 Sales & Operating Income

	Sales		Operating Income	
	$ mil.	% of total	$ mil.	% of total
Chemicals				
Coatings, adhesives, specialty polymers & inks	1,508	28	(35)	—
Performance chemicals & intermediates	1,132	21	(76)	—
Specialty plastics	505	9	40	22
Polymers	1,611	30	(201)	—
Fibers	628	12	146	78
Total	**5,384**	**100**	**(126)**	**100**

COMPETITORS

Acordis	GE
Akzo Nobel	Hercules
BASF AG	Honeywell Specialty
Bayer AG	Materials
BP	Huntsman
Cambrex	Imperial Chemical
Celanese	International Paper
ChevronTexaco	KoSa
Ciba Specialty Chemicals	Lonza Group
Clariant	Lyondell Chemical
Dainippon Ink and	Nan Ya Plastics
Chemicals	Rhodia
Dow Chemical	Rohm and Haas
DSM	Royal Dutch/Shell Group
DuPont	S.C. Johnson
Equistar Chemicals	Teijin
Exxon Mobil	Wellman

HISTORICAL FINANCIALS & EMPLOYEES

NYSE: EMN FYE: December 31	Annual Growth	12/92	12/93	12/94	12/95	12/96	12/97	12/98	12/99	12/00	12/01
Sales ($ mil.)	3.9%	3,811	3,903	4,329	5,040	4,782	4,678	4,481	4,590	5,292	5,384
Net income ($ mil.)	—	292	(209)	336	559	380	286	249	48	303	(179)
Income as % of sales	—	7.7%	—	7.8%	11.1%	7.9%	6.1%	5.6%	1.0%	5.7%	—
Earnings per share ($)	—	—	2.46	4.04	6.78	4.79	3.63	3.13	0.61	3.94	(2.33)
Stock price - FY high ($)	—	—	45.50	56.00	69.50	76.25	65.38	72.94	60.31	54.75	55.65
Stock price - FY low ($)	—	—	42.88	39.50	48.50	50.75	50.75	43.50	36.00	33.63	29.03
Stock price - FY close ($)	(1.8%)	—	45.25	50.50	62.38	55.25	59.56	44.75	47.69	48.75	39.02
P/E - high	—	—	18	14	10	16	18	23	99	14	—
P/E - low	—	—	17	10	7	10	14	14	59	9	—
Dividends per share ($)	—	—	0.00	1.20	1.62	1.70	1.76	1.76	1.76	1.76	1.76
Book value per share ($)	4.2%	—	12.85	15.59	19.11	21.12	22.40	24.45	22.53	23.61	17.90
Employees	(1.7%)	18,457	18,043	17,495	17,709	17,500	16,100	16,000	15,000	14,600	15,800

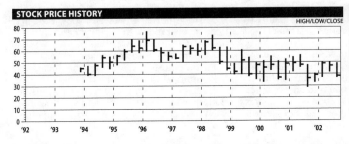

STOCK PRICE HISTORY
HIGH/LOW/CLOSE

2001 FISCAL YEAR-END
Debt ratio: 60.9%
Return on equity: —
Cash ($ mil.): 66
Current ratio: 1.52
Long-term debt ($ mil.): 2,143
No. of shares (mil.): 77
Dividends
  Yield: 4.5%
  Payout: —
Market value ($ mil.): 3,004

EASTMAN KODAK COMPANY

Image-conscious Eastman Kodak has seen the pixels on the wall. The world's largest maker of photographic film, the venerable Rochester, New York-based firm provides amateur and professional photographers with everything they need to create Kodak moments, including digital and traditional cameras, film, photographic paper, and other supplies. It also furnishes photographic products to the health care and entertainment industries.

Kodak has been engaged in fierce price-cutting to compete against global rival Fuji Photo Film to retain its status as the #1 film manufacturer in the US. It is also fighting Fuji for market share on foreign fronts, especially China, where Kodak has invested more than $1 billion. With digital technology transforming photography, the company is aiming for a big share of the digital imaging market, which allows photos to be altered via computer and stored on the Internet; in addition to bundling image manipulation software with its digital cameras, it offers other computerized products such as hot-swappable CD writers. Kodak has also been cropping out thousands of employees.

HISTORY

After developing a method for dry-plate photography, George Eastman established The Eastman Dry Plate and Film Company in 1884. In 1888 it introduced its first camera, a small, easy-to-use device that was loaded with enough film for 100 pictures. Owners mailed the camera back to the company, which returned it with the pictures and more film. The firm settled on the name Eastman Kodak in 1892, after Eastman tried many combinations of letters starting and ending with "k," which he thought was a "strong, incisive sort of letter." The user-friendly Brownie camera followed in 1900. Three years later Kodak introduced a home movie camera, projector, and film.

Ailing and convinced that his work was done, Eastman committed suicide in 1932. Kodak continued to dominate the photography industry with the introduction of color film (Kodachrome, 1935) and a handheld movie camera (1951). The company established US plants to produce the chemicals, plastics, and fibers used in its film production.

The Instamatic, introduced in 1963, became Kodak's biggest success. The camera's foolproof film cartridge eliminated the need for loading in the dark. By 1976 Kodak had sold an estimated 60 million Instamatics, 50 million more cameras than all its competitors combined. Subsequent introductions included the Kodak instant camera (1976) and the unsuccessful disc camera (1982).

In the 1980s Kodak diversified into electronic publishing, batteries, floppy disks (Verbatim, 1985, sold 1990), pharmaceuticals (Sterling Drug, sold 1994), and do-it-yourself and household products (L&F Products, sold 1994).

Kodak entered a joint research and development project with four Japanese photo giants (Canon, Nikon, Minolta, and Fuji Photo Film) in 1992 to develop the Advanced Photography System. Also that year the company introduced the Photo CD, a CD capable of storing photographs.

George Fisher, former chairman of Motorola, became Kodak's chairman and CEO in 1993. Fisher began cutting debt by selling noncore assets. Kodak spun off Eastman Chemical in 1994. Sales in 1996 included its money-losing copier sales and services business.

Kodak wrote off nearly $1.5 billion in 1997, mostly because of costs related to layoffs (cost-cutting measures since 1997 have resulted in more than 13,000 layoffs). That year Kodak bought the document management operations from Wang Laboratories (now part of Getronics), and the following year it formed deals to expand its digital offerings, including a collaboration with Intel and Adobe Systems allowing consumers to manipulate, print, and send personal photos from their PCs. Kodak acquired the medical imaging business of Imation in 1998, but it also unloaded more of its noncore operations, including its 450-store Fox Photo chain.

President and COO Daniel Carp replaced Fisher as CEO in early 2000. Also that year Kodak formed a joint venture with computer giant Hewlett-Packard to develop photofinishing equipment for digital photography; extended its push into the online photo business by buying the remaining shares (it already owned 51%) of PictureVision, a digital image storage service; and acquired Lumisys, a maker of digital imaging systems for the medical industry.

In early 2001 Kodak announced a three-year plan to introduce camera and film vending machines in about 10,000 high-traffic US locations (amusement parks, zoos, airports, ski resorts, and other tourist spots). It also completed its acquisition of Bell & Howell's (now ProQuest) imaging operations. In April former Avaya executive Patricia Russo was named president and COO; Carp remained chairman and CEO.

Further hits to the economy and Kodak's revenue prompted management in 2001 to eliminate regional divisions and realign the business along product lines. In December, Kodak and SANYO Electric Co. announced the formation of a business venture to manufacture OLED displays for cameras, PDAs, and other devices.

In January 2002 Russo left to rejoin Lucent Technologies; Carp assumed her responsibilities. In May, Kodak renewed a multi-year agreement that secured its position as the exclusive imaging supplier of film and related products for The Walt Disney Company.

OFFICERS

Chairman, President, CEO, and COO: Daniel A. Carp, age 53, $1,598,500 pay
EVP and CFO: Robert H. Brust, age 58, $718,484 pay
EVP and Chief Administrative Officer:
Michael P. Morley, age 59, $577,866 pay
EVP; President, Photography Group:
Martin M. Coyne II, age 53, $849,524 pay
SVP and Chief Marketing Officer: Carl E. Gustin Jr., age 49
SVP and Director of Global Manufacturing:
Charles S. Brown Jr., age 50
SVP and General Counsel: Gary P. Van Graafeiland, age 54
SVP; COO, Health Imaging: Candy M. Obourn, age 52
SVP, CTO, and Director of Research and Development:
James C. Stoffel, age 54
SVP; President, Commercial Imaging Group:
Carl A. Marchetto, age 45
SVP; President, Consumer Imaging: Daniel P. Palumbo, age 42
SVP; President, Digital and Applied Imaging:
Willy C. Shih, age 49
SVP; President, Entertainment Imaging: Eric G. Rodli, age 45
VP and CIO: Mark V. Gulling
Auditors: PricewaterhouseCoopers LLP

LOCATIONS

HQ: 343 State St., Rochester, NY 14650
Phone: 585-724-4000   **Fax:** 585-724-1089
Web: www.kodak.com

Eastman Kodak has manufacturing plants in Australia, Brazil, Canada, China, France, Germany, India, Indonesia, Japan, Mexico, Nepal, Russia, the UK, and the US.

PRODUCTS/OPERATIONS

2001 Sales

	$ mil.	% of total
Photography	9,403	71
Health imaging	2,262	17
Commercial imaging	1,459	11
Other imaging	110	1
Total	**13,234**	**100**

COMPETITORS

3M	Minolta
Agfa	Nikon Corporation
Canon	Olympus
Casio Computer	Pentax
China Lucky Film	Philips Electronics
Duracell	PhotoWorks
Fuji Photo	Polaroid
Hewlett-Packard	Ricoh
Konica	Sharp
Leica Camera	Sony
Matsushita	Xerox

HISTORICAL FINANCIALS & EMPLOYEES

NYSE: EK FYE: December 31	Annual Growth	12/92	12/93	12/94	12/95	12/96	12/97	12/98	12/99	12/00	12/01
Sales ($ mil.)	(4.6%)	20,183	16,364	13,557	14,980	15,968	14,538	13,406	14,089	13,994	13,234
Net income ($ mil.)	(26.0%)	1,146	(1,515)	557	1,252	1,288	5	1,390	1,392	1,407	76
Income as % of sales	—	5.7%	—	4.1%	8.4%	8.1%	0.0%	10.4%	9.9%	10.1%	0.6%
Earnings per share ($)	(24.9%)	3.41	(4.64)	1.63	3.67	3.82	0.01	4.24	4.33	4.59	0.26
Stock price – FY high ($)	—	50.75	65.00	56.38	70.38	85.00	94.75	88.94	80.38	67.50	49.95
Stock price – FY low ($)	—	37.75	40.25	40.69	47.13	65.13	53.31	57.94	56.63	35.31	24.40
Stock price – FY close ($)	(3.5%)	40.50	56.25	47.75	67.00	80.25	60.56	72.00	66.25	39.38	29.43
P/E – high	—	17	—	23	19	22	9,475	21	18	15	192
P/E – low	—	12	—	17	13	17	5,331	13	13	8	94
Dividends per share ($)	1.1%	2.00	2.00	1.70	1.60	1.60	1.72	1.76	1.76	1.76	2.21
Book value per share ($)	(7.5%)	20.12	10.15	11.82	14.81	14.27	9.78	12.35	12.60	11.80	9.95
Employees	(6.1%)	132,600	110,400	96,300	96,600	94,800	97,500	86,200	80,650	78,400	75,100

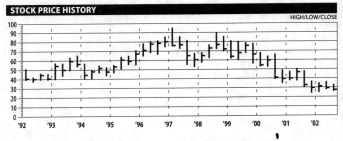

STOCK PRICE HISTORY
HIGH/LOW/CLOSE

2001 FISCAL YEAR-END
Debt ratio: 36.5%
Return on equity: 2.4%
Cash ($ mil.): 448
Current ratio: 0.87
Long-term debt ($ mil.): 1,666
No. of shares (mil.): 291
Dividends
  Yield: 7.5%
  Payout: 850.0%
Market value ($ mil.): 8,562

EATON CORPORATION

Eaton plays for keeps — if it can't win, it doesn't play. The diversified Cleveland-based manufacturing company is nurturing businesses in which it holds a strong market share. Eaton's product line includes electrical power distribution and control equipment, engine components, and hydraulic products for aerospace, automotive, and other industrial uses. The company, which has spun off its semiconductor equipment operations as Axcelis Technologies, operates about 180 manufacturing facilities in 25 countries.

To find the optimum product mix, Eaton has been adjusting its operations. The company is emphasizing its industrial and commercial controls business as demand for cars and heavy trucks has waned. Where deregulation and increasing demand for power has left many in the dark, Eaton sees dollar signs. Similarly, Eaton's line of automotive products are positioned to take advantage of two of the auto industry's greatest challenges — emissions reduction and fuel economy.

HISTORY

In 1911 Joseph Eaton and Viggo Torbensen started the Torbensen Gear and Axle Company to make an internal-gear rear truck axle that Torbensen had patented in 1902. The company moved from Newark, New Jersey, to Cleveland in 1914. After Republic Motor Truck bought Torbensen (1917), Eaton formed the Eaton Axle Company (1919), repurchased Torbensen (1922), and by 1931 had bought 11 more auto parts businesses. In 1932 it became Eaton Manufacturing.

The Depression flattened auto sales, and Eaton's profits fell. WWII sparked demand that helped the company recover. Joseph died in 1949. During the 1950s and 1960s, Eaton diversified and expanded geographically. It bought Fuller Manufacturing (truck transmissions, 1958), Dole Valve (1963), and Yale & Towne Manufacturing (locks and forklifts, 1963). Eaton's international business grew, with foreign sales increasing from almost nil in 1961 to 20% of sales by 1966.

Eaton sold its lock business in 1978 and bought Cutler-Hammer (electronics), Kenway (automated storage and retrieval systems), and Samuel Moore (plastics and fluid power). Downturns in the truck and auto industries forced Eaton to close 30 plants and trim 23,000 jobs between 1979 and 1983. The company reported its first loss in 50 years in 1982 and decided to diversify into high technology and to expand operations overseas.

During the years 1984 to 1993 Eaton spent

almost $4 billion in capital improvements and R&D. In 1986 it bought Consolidated Controls (precision instruments), Pacific-Sierra Research (computer and defense systems), and Singer Controls (valves and switches).

Eaton's acquisitions in the 1990s included Nordhauser Ventil (automotive engine valves, Germany), Control Displays (flight-deck equipment), Heinemann Electric (hydraulic-magnetic circuit breakers), and the automotive switch business of Illinois Tool Works. In 1994 Eaton tripled the size of its electrical power and controls operation with its $1.1 billion purchase of Westinghouse's electrical distribution and control business. The next year it bought Emwest Products (electrical switch gear and controls, Australia) and the IKU Group, a Dutch autocontrols firm. It purchased CAPCO Automotive Products (truck transmissions, Brazil) in 1996, and in 1997 Eaton bought Fusion Systems (semiconductor equipment).

In its repositioning, the company in 1997 sold off its appliance-control business to Siebe PLC and a majority stake in its high-tech defense electronics subsidiary, AIL Systems, to management. That next year Eaton sold its heavy-axle and brake business to Dana and its suspension business to Oxford Automotive. Eaton closed and consolidated plants and laid off more than 1,000 workers in its chip division in 1998.

The company increased its share of the hydraulics market in 1999 by spending $1.7 billion for Aeroquip-Vickers. To help pay for the purchase, Eaton sold its engineered-fasteners business to TransTechnology, its fluid power division (automotive cooling systems) to Borg-Warner (now BorgWarner), and its mobile agricultural hydraulic cylinder business to Hyco International. Eaton also unloaded Vickers' machine-tool controls business later that year.

In 2000 Eaton sold its specialty power resistor business to industrial products maker Halma. That year its Aeroquip unit acquired the fluid connectors business of Honeywell, and Eaton spun off its Axcelis Technologies subsidiary. As part of its bid to reduce debt, the company sold its automotive electronic switch division and its commercial and residential air-conditioning and refrigeration division, in 2001.

Continuing its efforts to divest non-core operations, Eaton agreed in 2002 to sell its naval controls unit (shipboard integrated electrical power distribution and control systems) to DRS Technologies for $92 million.

OFFICERS

Chairman, President, and CEO: Alexander M. Cutler, age 50, $1,596,258 pay
EVP and Chief Financial and Planning Officer: Richard H. Fearon
SVP and Group Executive, Automotive: Stephen M. Buente, age 51, $515,656 pay
SVP and Group Executive, Cutler-Hammer: Randy W. Carson, age 50, $568,526 pay
SVP and Group Executive, Fluid Power: Craig Arnold, age 41, $520,155 pay
SVP and Group Executive, Truck: James E. Sweetnam, age 49
VP and General Counsel: J. Robert Horst, age 58
VP, Human Resources: Susan J. Cook, age 54, $426,019 pay
Auditors: Ernst & Young LLP

LOCATIONS

HQ: Eaton Center, 1111 Superior Ave., Cleveland, OH 44114
Phone: 216-523-5000   **Fax:** 216-523-4787
Web: www.eaton.com

2001 Sales

	$ mil.	% of total
US	5,677	74
Europe	1,108	14
Latin America	406	5
Pacific region	310	4
Canada	177	2
Divested operations	85	1
Adjustments	(464)	—
Total	**7,299**	**100**

PRODUCTS/OPERATIONS

2001 Sales

	$ mil.	% of total
Fluid power	2,507	35
Industrial & commercial controls	2,199	30
Automotive components	1,479	20
Truck components	1,029	14
Divested operations	85	1
Total	**7,299**	**100**

Selected Brand Names

Airflex	Fuller	Starlite
Autoshift	Golf Pride	Supercharger
Cutler-Hammer	Heinemann	Tedeco
Durant	Magnum	Tri-Pac
Eaton	Orbit	Vickers
Eatonite	Panelmate	Vorad
Factorymate	Roadranger	
FMC	Solo	

COMPETITORS

American Standard	Hubbell	Robert Bosch
ArvinMeritor, Inc.	INTERMET	Rockwell Automation
BorgWarner	ITT Industries	Sauer
Cummins	Johnson Controls	Siemens
Dana	Metaldyne	SPX
Detroit Diesel	Navistar	Thomas & Betts
Emerson Electric	PACCAR	TRW
Genus	Parker Hannifin	United Technologies
Honeywell International	Powell Industries	Woodhead
	Precision Castparts	
	Raytheon	

HISTORICAL FINANCIALS & EMPLOYEES

NYSE: ETN FYE: December 31	Annual Growth	12/92	12/93	12/94	12/95	12/96	12/97	12/98	12/99	12/00	12/01
Sales ($ mil.)	7.3%	3,869	4,401	6,052	6,822	6,961	7,563	6,625	8,402	8,309	7,299
Net income ($ mil.)	—	(128)	187	333	399	349	410	349	617	453	169
Income as % of sales	—	—	4.2%	5.5%	5.8%	5.0%	5.4%	5.3%	7.3%	5.5%	2.3%
Earnings per share ($)	—	(1.86)	2.45	4.35	5.08	4.46	5.24	4.80	8.36	6.24	2.39
Stock price - FY high ($)	—	41.63	55.38	62.13	62.50	70.88	103.38	99.63	103.50	86.56	81.43
Stock price - FY low ($)	—	30.88	38.25	43.88	45.25	50.38	67.25	57.50	62.00	57.50	55.12
Stock price - FY close ($)	6.9%	40.81	50.50	49.50	53.63	69.75	89.25	70.69	72.63	75.19	74.41
P/E - high	—	—	22	14	12	16	17	20	12	14	34
P/E - low	—	—	15	10	9	11	11	12	7	9	23
Dividends per share ($)	5.4%	1.10	1.22	1.20	1.50	1.60	1.72	1.76	1.76	1.76	1.76
Book value per share ($)	11.2%	13.67	15.50	21.55	25.45	28.02	27.72	28.69	35.46	35.29	35.61
Employees	2.9%	38,000	38,000	51,000	52,000	54,000	49,000	49,500	63,000	59,000	49,000

STOCK PRICE HISTORY

HIGH/LOW/CLOSE

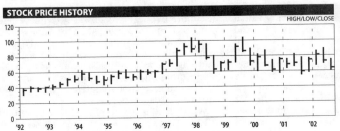

2001 FISCAL YEAR-END

Debt ratio: 47.6%
Return on equity: 6.9%
Cash ($ mil.): 112
Current ratio: 1.43
Long-term debt ($ mil.): 2,252
No. of shares (mil.): 70
Dividends
  Yield: 2.4%
  Payout: 73.6%
Market value ($ mil.): 5,171

ECHOSTAR COMMUNICATIONS

EchoStar Communications serves up a dish that fits almost everyone's entertainment appetite. Based in Littleton, Colorado, EchoStar is the second-largest provider of direct broadcast satellite (DBS) services in the US, behind #1 DIRECTV. The company has agreed to buy Hughes Electronics, DIRECTV's parent, from General Motors. The $25.8 billion deal, which faces regulatory scrutiny, would create one of the largest multichannel TV providers in the US and increase competition with cable systems.

EchoStar's DISH Network provides a wide range of programming (more than 500 digital TV and audio channels) to 7.1 million subscribers. EchoStar has six operational satellites in orbit and maintains sales and service locations throughout the continental US. It operates digital broadcast operations centers in Arizona and Wyoming.

The company's engineering division — EchoStar Technologies — designs the set-top boxes used for the DISH Network's satellite reception (outsourcing the manufacturing activities). The unit also serves other satellite TV operators, supplying similar receiver systems and providing design and construction supervision of uplink centers in Canada and Europe.

EchoStar's Satellite Services unit leases satellite capacity for audio, data, and video services. The company has teamed up with Microsoft and Israel's Gilat Satellite Networks to form StarBand Communications, and it owns a stake in the Colorado-based WildBlue Communications, to develop satellite-delivered two-way broadband Internet service. It also is developing interactive TV services through a partnership with OpenTV.

Co-founder and CEO Charlie Ergen owns about 51% of EchoStar's stock (and controls more than 91% of the vote). Minority shareholders include Rupert Murdoch's News Corp. (11%). To help fund the purchase of DIRECTV, Vivendi Universal has acquired a 10% stake in EchoStar in a $1.5 billion deal that includes a distribution alliance.

HISTORY

Charlie Ergen, a former financial analyst for Frito-Lay, founded a Denver company called Echosphere, a retailer of large-dish, C-band satellite TV equipment, with his wife, Candy, and James DeFranco (currently an EVP) in 1980. Echosphere evolved into a national manufacturer and distributor, which in 1987 began its move toward the new direct broadcast satellite (DBS) delivery system. It filed for a DBS license and set up subsidiary EchoStar Communications Corporation to build, launch, and operate DBS

satellites. In 1992 the FCC granted the company an orbital slot.

By 1994 Echosphere was the US's largest distributor of conventional home satellite equipment, but the future clearly rested with DBS and EchoStar. A 1995 reorganization renamed the company EchoStar Communications; the Echosphere distributor business became a subsidiary. EchoStar also created the DISH (Digital Sky Highway) Network brand, aiming for an easier-to-remember name than its rivals' "DSS" and "USSB."

The company launched the EchoStar I satellite in 1995, followed a year later by EchoStar II. Commencing DISH Network service in 1996, EchoStar competed against other DBS providers, including DIRECTV, to win 350,000 subscribers by year's end.

In 1997 Rupert Murdoch scrubbed a deal that called for News Corp. to buy half of EchoStar for $1 billion; Ergen sued for $5 billion in damages. EchoStar also went public in 1997 and signed up its one-millionth customer.

The next year EchoStar tangled again with Murdoch, winning FCC approval to access programming from FX Networks (owned by News Corp. and the former TCI, now AT&T's cable unit), despite FX Networks' claims that it was locked up in exclusive programming agreements with cable companies. That issue and the 1997 lawsuit were put to rest in 1999 when News Corp. and MCI WorldCom (now WorldCom) traded DBS assets, including an orbital slot, for a combined 15% stake in EchoStar.

That year EchoStar and DIRECTV joined forces to successfully lobby for federal legislation allowing local TV signals to be delivered by satellites nationwide. The company entered the Internet business, providing WebTV Internet access via satellite to customers through an agreement with US software giant Microsoft. EchoStar also bought Media4 (now EchoStar Data Networks), which specializes in providing Internet and data transmission over satellite networks.

In 2000 EchoStar formed a joint venture with OpenTV to offer interactive TV services using digital receivers with built-in hard disk drives. Also that year the company reached an agreement to distribute two-way broadband Internet access using technology developed by the Israel-based Gilat Satellite Networks and Microsoft in a joint venture called StarBand Communications. It also paid $50 million for a 13% stake in startup WildBlue Communications, which has planned to launch two geostationary satellites used to offer the two-way data services.

When Hughes Electronics, the parent of DIRECTV, was put up for sale in 2001, EchoStar expressed interest. After months of negotiations, EchoStar appeared to have given up but instead made an unsolicited offer. Hughes' parent, General Motors, agreed to sell the company to EchoStar for $25.8 billion after News Corp. dropped out of the bidding.

OFFICERS

Chairman and CEO: Charles W. Ergen, age 49, $1,000,006 pay
EVP and Director: James DeFranco, age 49
SVP and CFO: Michael R. McDonnell, age 38, $293,750 pay
SVP, General Counsel, Secretary, and Director: David K. Moskowitz, age 43, $306,730 pay
VP Human Resources: Robert Fuchs
President, COO, and Director: Michael T. Dugan, age 53, $250,000 pay
President, EchoStar International: Steven B. Schaver, age 47
EVP, DISH Network: Soraya Hesabi-Cartwright, age 41, $225,000 pay
SVP, DISH Network Service: Michael Kelly, age 40
SVP, EchoStar Technologies: Mark W. Jackson, age 41
Auditors: PricewaterhouseCoopers LLP

LOCATIONS

HQ: Echostar Communications Corporation
5701 S. Santa Fe Dr., Littleton, CO 80120
Phone: 303-723-1000   **Fax:** 303-723-1399
Web: www.dishnetwork.com

2001 Sales

	$ mil.	% of total
US	3,904	98
Europe	97	2
Total	**4,001**	**100**

PRODUCTS/OPERATIONS

2001 Sales

	$ mil.	% of total
DISH Network		
Subscription TV services	3,588	90
Other revenues	17	—
DTH equipment sales & integration services	271	7
Other services	125	3
Total	**4,001**	**100**

Selected Subsidiaries and Affiliations
EchoStar Broadband Corporation
EchoStar International Corporation
EchoStar Satellite Corporation
EchoStar Technologies Corporation
NagraStar LLC (50%, smart-card encryption service)
VisionStar, Inc. (49.9%, Ka-band satellite operations)
WildBlue Communications Inc. (13%, Ka-band satellite broadband data services)

COMPETITORS

Adelphia Communications	DIRECTV
AT&T Broadband	Pegasus Communications
Cablevision Systems	ReplayTV
Charter Communications	Time Warner Cable
Comcast	TiVo
Cox Communications	

HISTORICAL FINANCIALS & EMPLOYEES

Nasdaq: DISH FYE: December 31	Annual Growth	12/92	12/93	12/94	12/95	12/96	12/97	12/98	12/99	12/00	12/01
Sales ($ mil.)	42.5%	165	221	191	164	211	477	983	1,603	2,715	4,001
Net income ($ mil.)	—	8	12	0	(12)	(101)	(313)	(261)	(793)	(621)	(216)
Income as % of sales	—	4.6%	5.6%	0.1%	—	—	—	—	—	—	—
Earnings per share ($)	—	—	—	—	(0.05)	(0.32)	(0.96)	(0.83)	(1.92)	(1.32)	(0.45)
Stock price - FY high ($)	—	—	—	—	3.22	5.06	3.47	6.13	49.38	81.25	39.03
Stock price - FY low ($)	—	—	—	—	1.50	2.50	1.36	2.02	5.38	21.56	19.49
Stock price - FY close ($)	44.4%	—	—	—	3.03	2.75	2.09	6.05	48.75	22.75	27.47
P/E - high	—	—	—	—	—	—	—	—	—	—	—
P/E - low	—	—	—	—	—	—	—	—	—	—	—
Dividends per share ($)	—	—	—	—	0.00	0.00	0.00	0.00	0.00	0.00	0.00
Book value per share ($)	—	—	—	—	0.49	0.19	(0.25)	(1.03)	(0.11)	(1.33)	(1.62)
Employees	55.8%	—	—	—	—	1,200	1,930	3,815	6,048	11,000	11,000

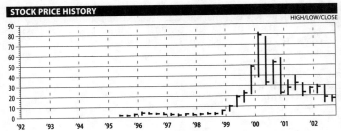

STOCK PRICE HISTORY
HIGH/LOW/CLOSE

2001 FISCAL YEAR-END

Debt ratio: 100.0%
Return on equity: —
Cash ($ mil.): 1,678
Current ratio: 2.36
Long-term debt ($ mil.): 5,707
No. of shares (mil.): 479
Dividends
  Yield: —
  Payout: —
Market value ($ mil.): 13,170

ECKERD CORPORATION

Feed a cold, starve a fever, or close a failing store. Eckerd hopes it knows the right remedy. Based in Largo, Florida, the drugstore chain has struggled along with its parent, J. C. Penney. Eckerd's sales are primarily prescription and over-the-counter drugs (about 64% of sales), although its stores also offer health and beauty aids, convenience foods (including Eckerd-brand soft drinks, bottled water, and cookies), greeting cards, and one-hour Express Photo labs. The company also operates an online and mail-order pharmacy.

Eckerd was forced to close about 300 stores in 2000, leaving about 2,600 stores in the northeastern, southeastern, and Sunbelt regions. Despite its problems, Eckerd still plans to remodel, relocate or open 800 stores annually through the end of 2003. (Penney hasn't ruled out spinning off the drugstore chain either.) Most of the new outlets will be larger, freestanding locations (11,000 to 13,000 sq. ft.), featuring drive-through pharmacies. Eckerd has plans to enter the Phoenix/Tuscon market by late 2002 and open at least 60 stores there by the end of 2004.

CEO J. Wayne Harris (formerly CEO of Grand Union Company) joined the troubled drugstore chain in 2000 and appears to be turning it around. However, Eckerd is facing legal problems. It is being investigated for possible overbilling in its pharmacies and is also the target of a class-action suit contending it routinely charged customers for medications they did not receive.

HISTORY

In 1898 Jack Eckerd's father, Milton, started one of the US's first drugstore chains, in Erie, Pennsylvania. Jack worked for his father during the Great Depression but left to start his own chain of stores in Florida in 1952 by buying three locations in Tampa and Clearwater. He won a case in the Supreme Court of Florida, challenging price restrictions that prevented him from underselling competitors.

Jack took his company public as Eckerd Drugs of Florida in 1961 and began buying other operations, beginning with Old Dominion Candies in 1966 (sold 1972). Two years later the company bought Jackson's/Byrons, renamed J. Byrons, a Miami-based department store chain (sold 1985). Eckerd expanded again in 1969 with its purchases of Gray Security Service and food service supplier Kurman Company, both sold in 1976.

The company continued to expand in the 1970s, buying Brown's Thrift City Wholesale Drugs and Mading-Dugan Drugs (1970), and Ward Cut-Rate Drug and Eckerd Drugs Eastern (1973). Finally, Jack Eckerd Drugs bought Eckerd

Drugs of Charlotte from Edward O'Herron Jr., son-in-law of Milton, bringing all the Eckerd stores under its control in 1977.

Eckerd turned to Merrill Lynch Capital Partners in 1986 to handle a management-led $1.2 billion LBO. That year it closed 45 stores because of poor performance, sold 11 stores in Tulsa, bought 32 Shoppers Drug Mart stores in Florida, and opened 50 new stores.

Between 1987 and 1989 Eckerd expanded its optical services with 23 Visionworks stores (sold 1994) and its photofinishing business with 79 Express Photo locations. In 1990 the company acquired 220 stores from the bankrupt Ohio-based drugstore chain Revco, but it dropped out of a fierce 1991 bidding war for the remaining Revco stores.

During a massive restructuring in 1992 and 1993, the company cut about 600 jobs and consolidated operating divisions. In 1993, seven years after going private, Eckerd once again went public, selling 15% of its stock to relieve debt. The company then changed its name to Eckerd Corporation.

Eckerd acquired Crown Drugs, a 19-unit chain based in North Carolina, in 1994. That year the company sold Insta-Care (prescription drugs and medical consulting) to Beverly Enterprises for about $94 million.

In 1995 Eckerd bought 109 Florida drugstores from Rite Aid for $75 million. Also that year the company teamed with Corning to offer in-store medical testing services. The following year Francis Newman was named CEO.

J. C. Penney bought the chain for $3.3 billion in 1997. Eckerd grew in Virginia that year with the purchase of 114 Revco stores. In 1998 Eckerd was charged with overbilling state and federal health programs by $11.5 million.

In 1999 Eckerd expanded in the Northeast, purchasing 141 Genovese Drug Stores for $418 million. In 2000 Eckerd closed about 300 stores. Also that year CEO Newman resigned to join the dot-com world as CEO of online retailer more.com. J. Wayne Harris took over as Eckerd CEO in October 2000.

At least two states are investigating the drugstore chain for possible overbilling in its pharmacies, and a class action suit alleges that Eckerd routinely charged customers for medications they did not receive.

OFFICERS

Chairman and CEO; EVP, J. C. Penney Company:
J. Wayne Harris, age 62, $1,961,950 pay
EVP and COO: David Aston
SVP and CFO: Dennis Miller
SVP Information Technology: Ken Petersen
SVP Merchandising and Marketing: Enzo Cerra
SVP Pharmacy Services: Jerry Thompson
SVP Real Estate: Thomas M. Nash
SVP Store Operations: Ray Loeffler
SVP Store Operations: Jerry Stettner
VP and Controller: John Carey
VP and General Counsel: Robert E. Lewis
VP Express Photo Operations: Mona Furlott
VP General Merchandise: Kurt Bruder
VP Loss Prevention: Larry Ford
VP Marketing: Jeff Thompson
VP Planning and Analysis: Michael Lisman
Human Resources Manager: Cathy Brown
Auditors: KPMG LLP

LOCATIONS

HQ: 8333 Bryan Dairy Rd., Largo, FL 33777
Phone: 727-395-6000   **Fax:** 727-395-7934
Web: www.eckerd.com

Eckerd has about 2,650 stores in about 20 states,
primarily in the Carolinas, Florida, New York,
Pennsylvania, and Texas.

PRODUCTS/OPERATIONS

Products and Services
Books and magazines
Cosmetics
Food
Fragrances
Greeting cards
Health care products
Household products
Over-the-counter drugs
Photofinishing services
Prescription drugs
Tobacco products
Toys

COMPETITORS

7-Eleven
Albertson's
Bruno's Supermarkets
Chronimed
Costco Wholesale
CVS
Dollar Tree
GNC
H-E-B
Jean Coutu
Kerr Drug
Kmart
Kroger
Longs
Medicine Shoppe
Pathmark
Publix
Rite Aid
Ritz Camera Centers
Safeway
Walgreen
Wal-Mart
Winn-Dixie

HISTORICAL FINANCIALS & EMPLOYEES

Subsidiary FYE: Saturday nearest Jan. 31	Annual Growth	1/93	1/94	1/95	1/96	1/97	1/98	1/99	1/00	1/01	1/02
Sales ($ mil.)	15.2%	3,887	4,191	4,549	4,997	5,376	6,111	10,325	12,427	13,088	13,847
Employees	7.1%	40,300	43,000	42,700	44,600	46,700	53,800	55,000	78,000	78,000	75,000

SALES HISTORY

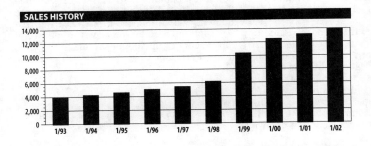

ECOLAB INC.

If cleanliness is next to godliness, Ecolab is rubbing elbows with the Big Guy. The St. Paul, Minnesota-based company provides cleaning and sanitation, pest-control, and maintenance products and services for hospitality, institutional, and industrial customers. Ecolab's cornerstone institutional division offers a variety of cleaning and sanitation products and services (for kitchen equipment, utensils, and laundry) to restaurants, hospitals, hotels, schools, and nursing homes. Other divisions specialize in pest elimination, textile care, water treatment, food processing, and medical and janitorial disinfectants and supplies. Ecolab makes most of its own products and equipment.

Ecolab's hospitality customers have been hurt by the sputtering economy, and the company is undergoing a restructuring that includes job cuts and the closure of some facilities. Since announcing the restructuring, the company has seen several significant changes in its executive offices.

German chemicals firm Henkel KGaA — a maker of cleaning products — owns about 28% of the company.

HISTORY

Salesman Merritt Osborn founded Economics Laboratory in 1924 as a specialty chemical maker; its first product was a rug cleaner for hotels. It added industrial and institutional cleaners and consumer detergents in the 1950s. The company went public in 1957. By 1973 it had been organized into five divisions: industrial (cleaners and specialty chemical formulas), institutional (dishwasher products, sanitation formulas), consumer (dishwasher detergent and laundry aids, coffee filters, floor cleaners), food-processing (detergents), and international (run by future CEO Fred Lanners Jr.).

At the time household dishwasher detergent was Economics Laboratory's top seller, second to Procter & Gamble in the US and #1 overseas. The company began offering services and products as packages in the early 1970s, including on-premise laundry services for hotels and hospitals and sanitation and cleaning services for the food industry.

E. B. Osborn, son of the founder, retired in 1978, and Lanners became the company's first CEO outside the Osborn family. Sales of dishwashing detergent had fallen, while the institutional cleaning business had become its primary segment, quadrupling in sales between 1970 and 1980. International sales were growing rapidly. In 1979 the company bought Apollo Technologies (chemicals and pollution-control equipment) to improve its share of the industrial market.

A depressed industrial sector caused Apollo's sales to drop in early 1980. The man expected to save Apollo, Richard Ashley, succeeded Lanners in 1982 but died in a car crash that year. Pierson "Sandy" Grieve became CEO in 1983 and shut down Apollo. Meanwhile, debt was up, the institutional market had shrunk, and the company was slipping in the dishwashing-detergent market. Grieve sold the firm's coffee-filters unit and several plants, laid off employees, and began new packaging processes. The company changed its name to Ecolab in 1986, and in 1987 it sold its dishwashing-detergent unit and bought lawn-service provider ChemLawn. (ChemLawn was sold in 1992.)

As 1990 neared, Grieve introduced what's now known as "Circle the Customer — Circle the Globe," the aim being to become a worldwide leader in core businesses and broaden product offerings. The company concentrated on building its presence in Africa, the Asia/Pacific region, Latin America, and the Middle East. In 1991 Ecolab also began a highly successful joint venture, Henkel-Ecolab, with German consumer-products company Henkel to better exploit European markets. (It bought Henkel's share in the joint venture in 2001.)

Ecolab acquired Kay Chemical (cleaning and sanitation products for the fast-food industry, 1994), Monarch (cleaning and sanitation products for food processing, 1996), Huntington Laboratories (janitorial products, 1996), and Australia-based Gibson (cleaning and sanitation products, 1997). In 1995 Grieve stepped down, and president Allan Schuman became CEO. Adding a few more degrees to its circle of services, in 1998 Ecolab bought GCS Service (commercial kitchen equipment repair).

The company further secured footholds in Asia and South America in 2000 by acquiring industrial and institutional cleaning firms Dong Woo Deterpan (South Korea), Spartan de Chile, and Spartan de Argentina. At home, it bought kitchen-equipment companies ARR/CRS and Southwest Sanitary Distributing. Late in 2000 Ecolab sold its Johnson dish machines unit to Endonis and announced a restructuring that was soon followed by the departure of several top executives, including president and COO Bruno Deschamps.

OFFICERS

Chairman, President, and CEO: Allan L. Schuman, age 67, $2,075,000 pay
President and COO: Douglas M. Baker Jr., age 43, $402,000 pay
President, International Sector: John P. Spooner, age 55, $697,500 pay
SVP and CFO: Steven L. Fritze, age 47
SVP and Chief Planning Officer: Arthur E. Henningsen Jr., age 54
SVP and CTO: Mary J. Schumacher, age 45
SVP, Global Operations: Maurizio Nisita, age 61
SVP, Human Resources: Diana D. Lewis, age 55
VP and CIO: Alan P. Blumenfeld
VP and Secretary: Kenneth A. Iverson
VP, Law and General Counsel: Lawrence T. Bell, age 54
VP, Tax and Public Affairs: John G. Forsythe
VP and Treasurer: Daniel J. Schemechel
VP and General Manager, Pest Elimination: C. William Snedeker
VP and General Manager, Food & Beverage, North America: Doug Milroy
Auditors: PricewaterhouseCoopers LLP

LOCATIONS

HQ: 370 N. Wabasha St., St. Paul, MN 55102
Phone: 651-293-2233   **Fax:** 651-293-2092
Web: www.ecolab.com

Ecolab has manufacturing facilities in Argentina, Australia, Brazil, Canada, Chile, China, Costa Rica, Fiji, Indonesia, Japan, Kenya, Mexico, New Zealand, the Philippines, Puerto Rico, Singapore, South Africa, South Korea, Tanzania, Thailand, and the US.

2001 Sales

	$ mil.	% of total
US	1,856	79
International	499	21
Total	**2,355**	**100**

PRODUCTS/OPERATIONS

2001 Sales

	$ mil.	% of total
US cleaning & sanitizing	1,583	67
International cleaning & sanitizing	499	21
US other services	273	12
Total	**2,355**	**100**

COMPETITORS

ABM Industries
ARAMARK
Chemed
Colin Service
CPAC
Healthcare Services
ISS
Katy Industries
Reckitt Benckiser
Rollins
ServiceMaster
SYSCO
Tranzonic
UNICCO Service
Unilever
Unisource

HISTORICAL FINANCIALS & EMPLOYEES

NYSE: ECL FYE: December 31	Annual Growth	12/92	12/93	12/94	12/95	12/96	12/97	12/98	12/99	12/00	12/01
Sales ($ mil.)	9.9%	1,005	1,042	1,208	1,341	1,490	1,640	1,888	2,080	2,264	2,355
Net income ($ mil.)	12.7%	64	77	85	99	113	134	193	176	206	188
Income as % of sales	—	6.4%	7.4%	7.0%	7.4%	7.6%	8.2%	10.2%	8.5%	9.1%	8.0%
Earnings per share ($)	12.1%	0.52	0.60	0.63	0.73	0.85	1.00	1.43	1.31	1.56	1.45
Stock price - FY high ($)	—	9.56	11.91	11.75	15.88	19.75	28.00	38.00	44.44	45.69	44.19
Stock price - FY low ($)	—	6.66	9.06	9.63	10.00	14.56	18.13	26.13	31.69	28.00	28.50
Stock price - FY close ($)	17.8%	9.19	11.25	10.44	15.00	18.81	27.72	36.19	39.13	43.19	40.25
P/E - high	—	18	20	19	21	22	27	32	33	28	30
P/E - low	—	13	15	15	13	17	18	22	23	17	19
Dividends per share ($)	12.5%	0.18	0.19	0.22	0.25	0.28	0.32	0.38	0.42	0.48	0.52
Book value per share ($)	10.8%	2.72	2.97	3.31	3.53	4.01	4.27	5.33	5.89	5.95	6.88
Employees	10.9%	7,601	7,822	8,206	9,000	9,500	10,210	12,000	12,900	14,250	19,300

STOCK PRICE HISTORY

HIGH/LOW/CLOSE

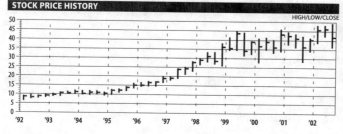

2001 FISCAL YEAR-END

Debt ratio: 36.8%
Return on equity: 23.0%
Cash ($ mil.): 42
Current ratio: 1.12
Long-term debt ($ mil.): 512
No. of shares (mil.): 128
Dividends
 Yield: 1.3%
 Payout: 35.9%
Market value ($ mil.): 5,148

EDISON INTERNATIONAL

Edison International has been around the world, but the Rosemead, California-based company's largest subsidiary is still Southern California Edison (SCE), which distributes electricity to nearly 4.5 million customers in central, coastal, and Southern California.

As part of California's utility industry restructuring, SCE has divested most of its generation assets. But deregulation has been hard on SCE. Prices on the wholesale power market began to soar in 2000, and SCE was unable to pass along the increase to customers because of a rate freeze. The rate freeze has been lifted, but SCE is struggling to pay off debts to wholesalers: the utility has reached a settlement with state regulators that will allow it to keep its current high rates in place until its debts are paid off.

Edison has created a cosmopolitan image through Edison Mission Energy (EME), which has nonregulated power plant interests in Europe, the Asia/Pacific region, and North America (19,000 MW of capacity). To pay down debt, Edison is selling some EME plants and has canceled the unit's growth initiatives. Edison has also sold most of the operations of its Edison Enterprises unit, which engaged in energy management and home security services, and it is cutting back on its venture financing operations.

HISTORY

In 1896 a group including Elmer Peck and George Baker organized West Side Lighting to provide electricity service in Los Angeles. The next year the company merged with Los Angeles Edison Electric, which owned the rights to the Edison name and patents in the region, and Baker became president. Edison Electric installed the first DC-power underground conduits in the Southwest.

John Barnes Miller took over the top spot in 1901. During his 31-year reign the firm bought many neighboring utilities and built several power plants. In 1909 it took the name Southern California Edison (SCE).

SCE doubled its assets by buying Southern California electric interests from rival Pacific Light & Power in 1917. However, in 1912 the City of Los Angeles had decided to develop its own power distribution system, and by 1922 SCE's authority in the city had ended. A 1925 earthquake and the 1928 collapse of the St. Francis Dam severely damaged SCE's facilities.

SCE built 11 fossil-fueled power stations (1948-1973) and moved into nuclear power in 1963, when it broke ground on the San Onofre plant with San Diego Gas & Electric (brought online in 1968). It finished consolidating its

service territory with the 1964 purchase of California Electric Power. In the late 1970s SCE began to build solar, geothermal, and wind power facilities.

Edison Mission Energy (EME) was founded in 1986 to develop, buy, and operate power plants around the world. The next year investment arm Edison Capital was formed, as well as a holding company for the entire group, SCEcorp. EME began to build its portfolio in 1992 when it snagged a 51% stake in an Australian plant (now 100%-owned) and bought hydroelectric facilities in Spain. In 1995 it bought UK hydroelectric company First Hydro; it also began building plants in Italy, Turkey, and Indonesia.

The 1994 Northridge earthquake that cut power to a million SCE customers was nothing compared to the industry's seismic shifts. In 1996 SCEcorp became the more wordly Edison International. California's electricity market opened to competition in 1998, and the utility began divesting SCE's generation assets; it sold 12 gas-fired plants. Overseas EME picked up 25% of a power plant being built in Thailand and a 50% stake in a cogeneration facility in Puerto Rico.

SCE got regulatory approval to offer telecom services in its utility territory in 1999. That year EME snapped up several plants in the Midwest from Unicom for $5 billion. Overseas it purchased two UK coal-fired plants from PowerGen (which it sold to American Electric Power in 2001 for $960 million). The next year EME CEO Edward Muller (who had held the post since 1994) abruptly resigned, and Edison bought Citizens Power from the Peabody Group.

In 2000 SCE got caught in a price squeeze brought on in part by deregulation. Prices on the wholesale power market soared, but the utility was unable to pass along the increase to customers because of a rate freeze. The company gained some prospect of relief in 2001 when California's governor signed legislation to allow a state agency to buy power from wholesalers under long-term contracts. In addition, the California Public Utilities Commission (CPUC) approved a substantial increase in retail electricity rates, and the Federal Energy Regulatory Commission approved a plan to limit wholesale energy prices during periods of severe shortage in 11 western states.

To reduce debt, Edison International agreed to sell its transmission grid to the state for $2.8 billion. While the California legislature debated the agreement, however, the CPUC announced a settlement in which SCE would be allowed to keep its current high rates in place until its debts are paid off. The settlement, which was approved in

2002, was expected to eliminate the need for the sale of the company's transmission grid.

Also in 2001, the company sold most of its Edison Enterprises businesses, including home security services unit Edison Select, which was sold to ADT Security Services.

OFFICERS

Chairman, President, and CEO; Chairman, Edison Mission Energy and Edison Capital: John E. Bryson, age 58, $2,300,000 pay
EVP, CFO, and Treasurer; Chairman, Edison O&M Services: Theodore F. Craver Jr., age 50, $898,600 pay
EVP and General Counsel: Bryant C. Danner, age 64, $894,800 pay
SVP and CIO, Edison International and Southern California Edison: Mahvash Yazdi, age 50
VP and Controller, Edison International and Southern California Edison: Thomas M. Noonan, age 50
VP and General Auditor, Edison International and Southern California Edison: Joseph P. Ruiz
Chairman and CEO, Southern California Edison: Alan J. Fohrer, age 51, $766,800 pay
President and CEO, Edison Capital: Thomas R. McDaniel, age 52
President and CEO, Edison Mission Energy: William J. Heller, age 46
President and COO, Edison O&M Services: Wesley C. Moody
President, Southern California Edison: Robert G. Foster, age 54, $630,000 pay
EVP Generation, Southern California Edison: Harold B. Ray, age 61, $763,100 pay
SVP and General Counsel, Southern California Edison: Stephen E. Pickett, age 51, $476,875 pay
Auditors: PricewaterhouseCoopers LLP

LOCATIONS

HQ: 2244 Walnut Grove Ave., Rosemead, CA 91770
Phone: 626-302-1212   **Fax:** 626-302-2517
Web: www.edison.com

Southern California Edison operates in central, coastal, and Southern California, and other Edison companies have investments in projects in Africa, the Americas, Asia, Australia, and Europe.

PRODUCTS/OPERATIONS

2001 Sales

	$ mil.	% of total
Electric utility	8,126	71
Nonutility power generation	2,968	26
Capital & financial services	202	2
Corporate & other	140	1
Total	**11,436**	**100**

Selected Subsidiaries
Edison Mission Energy (power generation, energy trading and marketing)
Southern California Edison Company (SCE, electric utility)

COMPETITORS

AES	Entergy	Sacramento
Aquila	Iberdrola	Municipal
Avista	Mirant	Sempra Energy
British Energy	NRG Energy	Sierra Pacific
Calpine	PacifiCorp	Resources
Dynegy	PG&E	TVA
El Paso Electric	Portland General	TXU Europe
Endesa (Spain)	Electric	
Enel		

HISTORICAL FINANCIALS & EMPLOYEES

NYSE: EIX FYE: December 31	Annual Growth	12/92	12/93	12/94	12/95	12/96	12/97	12/98	12/99	12/00	12/01
Sales ($ mil.)	4.1%	7,984	7,821	8,345	8,405	8,545	9,235	10,208	9,670	11,717	11,436
Net income ($ mil.)	3.8%	739	639	681	739	717	700	668	623	(1,943)	1,035
Income as % of sales	—	9.3%	8.2%	8.2%	8.8%	8.4%	7.6%	6.5%	6.4%	—	9.1%
Earnings per share ($)	7.5%	1.66	1.42	1.52	1.65	1.63	1.73	1.84	1.79	(5.84)	3.17
Stock price - FY high ($)	—	23.81	25.75	20.50	18.00	20.38	27.81	31.00	29.63	30.00	16.12
Stock price - FY low ($)	—	20.13	19.88	12.38	14.38	15.00	19.38	25.13	21.63	14.13	6.25
Stock price - FY close ($)	(4.1%)	22.00	20.00	14.63	17.63	19.88	27.19	27.88	26.19	15.63	15.10
P/E - high	—	14	18	13	11	12	16	17	17	—	5
P/E - low	—	12	14	8	9	9	11	14	12	—	2
Dividends per share ($)	—	1.38	1.41	1.21	1.00	1.00	1.00	1.03	1.07	1.11	0.00
Book value per share ($)	0.7%	13.30	13.31	15.34	15.94	16.55	16.33	16.07	19.79	12.06	14.13
Employees	(1.6%)	17,259	17,193	17,074	16,434	13,160	12,642	13,177	19,570	18,530	14,964

STOCK PRICE HISTORY

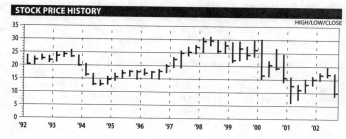

HIGH/LOW/CLOSE

2001 FISCAL YEAR-END
Debt ratio: 73.3%
Return on equity: 36.4%
Cash ($ mil.): 3,991
Current ratio: 0.76
Long-term debt ($ mil.): 12,674
No. of shares (mil.): 326
Dividends
 Yield: —
 Payout: —
Market value ($ mil.): 4,920

E. I. DU PONT DE NEMOURS

E.I. du Pont de Nemours (DuPont) lost its energy but is far from feeling run-down. The #2 US chemical firm (behind Dow Chemical), DuPont exited the energy business to focus on high-performance materials, specialty chemicals, and biotechnology products. The Wilmington, Delaware-based company developed and still produces familiar brand-name materials such as Lycra, Teflon, Corian, Kevlar, and Dacron.

DuPont's chemical and material-science products include performance coatings (engineering polymers, elastomers), nylons (Stainmaster and Antron carpet fibers), and specialty polymers (photopolymer/electronic materials, packaging and industrial polymers). Other products include pigments and chemicals (white pigment, mineral products, specialty chemicals, fluorochemicals), specialty fibers (Lycra, nonwovens, advanced fibers), and polyesters (Dacron, films, resins).

The company's agriculture and nutrition businesses include crop-protection products (herbicides, fungicides, insect control), biotechnology products (animal feed, food ingredients, seed products), and pharmaceuticals.

Seeking refuge from economic cycles, and in order to focus on core chemical operations, DuPont left the energy business by spinning off Conoco. It then sold its pharmaceuticals division (HIV, heart disease, nerve disorder, and cancer drugs) to Bristol-Myers Squibb. (Without the gains from this sale, DuPont would have shown a much weaker net income for 2001; more than 70% of net income came from the capital gains related to the sale.) The company also announced it would spin off its nylon and polyester businesses, two of its weaker segments. DuPont has cut about 5,000 jobs (roughly 6% of its workforce) and has consolidated some of its manufacturing facilities in the face of the sputtering US economy.

HISTORY

Eleuthère Irénée du Pont de Nemours fled to America in 1800 after the French Revolution. Two years later he founded a gunpowder plant in Delaware. Within a decade the DuPont plant was the largest of its kind in the US. After Irénée's death in 1834, his sons Alfred and Henry took over. DuPont added dynamite and nitroglycerine in 1880, guncotton in 1892, and smokeless powder in 1894.

In 1902 three du Pont cousins bought DuPont. By 1906 the company controlled most of the US explosives market, but a 1912 antitrust decision forced it to sell part of the powder business. WWI profits were used to diversify into paints, plastics, and dyes.

DuPont acquired an interest in General Motors in 1917; the stake increased to 37% by 1922 (the company surrendered its stake in 1962 due to antitrust regulations). In the 1920s the firm bought and improved French cellophane technology and began producing rayon. DuPont's inventions include neoprene synthetic rubber (1931), Lucite (1937), nylon (1938), Teflon (1938), and Dacron. The last du Pont to head the company resigned as chairman in 1972. DuPont got into the energy business by acquiring Conoco for $7.6 billion in 1981.

In 1991 DuPont and Merck created DuPont Merck Pharmaceutical to focus on non-US markets. After record earnings in 1994, DuPont spent $8.8 billion the next year to buy back shares of the corporation from Seagram. In 1997 DuPont purchased Protein Technologies International (soy proteins) from Ralston Purina and Imperial Chemical's polyester-resins and intermediates operations (1997) and polyester-film business (1998).

DuPont president Chad Holliday became CEO in early 1998. That year DuPont purchased a 20% stake in Pioneer Hi-Bred International (corn seed) for $1.7 billion and Merck's 50% stake in DuPont Merck Pharmaceutical (now DuPont Pharmaceuticals) for $2.6 billion. DuPont's public offering of Conoco in 1998 raised $4.4 billion, the largest US IPO at the time.

In 1999 DuPont bought the Herberts paints and coatings unit from Hoechst. It also bought the remaining 80% of Pioneer Hi-Bred for $7.7 billion and biotechnology research firm CombiChem for $95 million. Making a clean break with its oil business, DuPont sold its remaining 70% stake in Conoco.

In 2000 DuPont announced plans to close two plants (and reduce production at several others) while restructuring its performance-coatings business. The company announced that it would cut 5,500 jobs and close less-competitive plants in 2001. In October Bristol-Myers Squibb bought DuPont's pharmaceutical operations for $7.8 billion in cash.

In early 2002 DuPont initiated a restructuring that included the possible spinoff of its fibers businesses (now Textiles & Interiors) and the reorganization of its remaining business units into five segments: Electronics & Communication Technologies, Performance Materials, Coatings & Color Technologies, Safety & Protection, and Agriculture & Nutrition. Later that year DuPont acquired ATOFINA's surface protection and fluoroadditives business to become the largest integrated fluorotelomer protectants maker in both Europe and North America.

OFFICERS

Chairman and CEO: Charles O. Holliday Jr., age 54,
$1,085,000 pay
EVP and COO: Richard R. Goodmanson, age 54,
$640,000 pay
EVP: John C. Hodgson, age 57
SVP, Finance and CFO: Gary M. Pfeiffer, age 52,
$438,000 pay
SVP and Chief Science and Technology Officer:
Thomas M. Connelly Jr., age 49, $332,000 pay
**SVP, Chief Administrative Officer, and General
Counsel:** Stacey J. Mobley, age 56, $449,200 pay
SVP, Global Human Resources: Dennis Zeleny, age 46
Auditors: PricewaterhouseCoopers LLP

LOCATIONS

HQ: E. I. du Pont de Nemours and Company
1007 Market St., Wilmington, DE 19898
Phone: 302-774-1000 **Fax:** 302-774-7321
Web: www.dupont.com

2001 Sales

	$ mil.	% of total
North America		
US	12,054	49
Canada	918	4
Other countries	641	3
Europe, Middle East & Africa		
Germany	1,590	6
France	929	4
Italy	854	3
UK	704	3
Other countries	2,354	9
Asia/Pacific	3,657	15
South America	1,025	4
Total	**24,726**	**100**

PRODUCTS/OPERATIONS

2001 Sales & Income

	Sales		Operating Income	
	$ mil.	% of total	$ mil.	% of total
Performance coatings				
& polymers	5,754	21	319	6
Specialty fibers	4,418	16	356	7
Agriculture & nutrition	4,316	15	19	—
Specialty polymers	3,875	14	372	7
Pigments & chemicals	3,554	13	439	8
Nylon	2,696	10	(75)	—
Polyester	1,895	7	(349)	—
Pharmaceuticals	902	3	3,924	72
Other	279	1	(69)	—
Adjustments	(2,963)	—	—	—
Total	**24,726**	**100**	**4,936**	**100**

COMPETITORS

Akzo Nobel	Honeywell	Pharmacia
BASF AG	International	PPG
Bayer AG	Honeywell	Rohm and Haas
BP Chemicals	Specialty	Sherwin-
Cargill	Materials	Williams
Clorox	Huntsman	Siemens
ConAgra	Imperial	Southern Film
Dow Chemical	Chemical	Extruders
Eastman	Koch	Syngenta
Chemical	Lyondell	TOTAL FINA
FMC	Chemical	ELF
Formosa Plastics	Novartis	W. R. Grace
Henkel	Novo Nordisk	
Hercules	OxyChem	

HISTORICAL FINANCIALS & EMPLOYEES

NYSE: DD FYE: December 31	Annual Growth	12/92	12/93	12/94	12/95	12/96	12/97	12/98	12/99	12/00	12/01
Sales ($ mil.)	(3.2%)	33,145	32,621	34,042	36,508	38,349	39,730	24,767	26,918	28,268	24,726
Net income ($ mil.)	—	(3,927)	565	2,727	3,293	3,636	2,405	4,480	7,690	2,314	4,339
Income as % of sales	—	—	1.7%	8.0%	9.0%	9.5%	6.1%	18.1%	28.6%	8.2%	17.5%
Earnings per share ($)	—	(2.92)	0.40	1.98	2.77	3.18	2.08	3.90	6.99	2.19	4.16
Stock price - FY high ($)	—	27.44	26.94	31.19	36.50	49.69	69.75	84.44	77.81	74.00	49.88
Stock price - FY low ($)	—	21.75	22.25	24.13	26.31	34.81	46.38	51.69	50.06	38.19	32.64
Stock price - FY close ($)	6.8%	23.56	24.13	28.06	34.94	47.06	60.06	53.06	65.88	48.31	42.51
P/E - high	—	—	66	16	13	15	33	21	11	33	12
P/E - low	—	—	54	12	9	11	22	13	7	17	8
Dividends per share ($)	5.4%	0.87	0.88	0.91	1.02	1.12	1.23	1.37	1.40	1.40	1.40
Book value per share ($)	5.8%	8.71	8.29	9.41	7.28	9.50	9.78	12.39	12.23	12.75	14.42
Employees	(5.0%)	124,916	114,000	107,000	105,000	97,000	98,000	101,000	94,000	93,000	79,000

STOCK PRICE HISTORY

HIGH/LOW/CLOSE

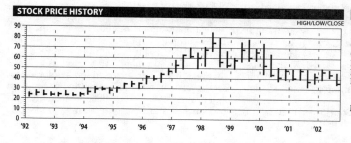

2001 FISCAL YEAR-END

Debt ratio: 27.0%
Return on equity: 31.8%
Cash ($ mil.): 5,763
Current ratio: 1.83
Long-term debt ($ mil.): 5,350
No. of shares (mil.): 1,002
Dividends
  Yield: 3.3%
  Payout: 33.7%
Market value ($ mil.): 42,593

EL PASO CORPORATION

El Paso isn't saying "Pass the picante," but it is spreading its energy throughout del Norte. The Houston-based company, formerly known as El Paso Energy, is a top US energy trader and marketer and owns the largest gas pipeline system in the US. The company also gathers and processes natural gas, generates electricity, and engages in oil and gas exploration and production. El Paso has expanded by buying diversified energy group Coastal. The $24 billion acquisition (completed in 2001) helped boost the company's proved reserves to more than 6 trillion cu. ft. of natural gas equivalent.

El Paso's energy marketing arm, El Paso Merchant Energy, sells and trades gas, electricity, crude oil, and other commodities in North America and operates power plants that generate more than 10,000 MW of capacity. Internationally, this unit has plowed millions of dollars into buying and building power plants in Asia, Europe, and South America. El Paso also has moved into telecommunications bandwidth trading through El Paso Global Networks.

With interests in about 60,000 miles of pipeline throughout the US and in Mexico and Australia, El Paso transports gas from the Gulf Coast to the Midwest and northeastern US; its pipes also reach the West Coast and Southeast. El Paso also explores for and produces oil and gas in the US and Canada. The company's El Paso Field service unit is a leading natural gas gatherer and processor.

El Paso is selling some noncore assets to pay down debt, and it has announced plans to downsize its energy trading operations to focus on core natural gas businesses.

HISTORY

In 1928 Paul Kayser, a Houston attorney, started the El Paso Natural Gas Company and got the rights to sell natural gas to that West Texas town a year later. Despite the 1929 stock market crash, the company built a 200-mile pipeline, first connecting El Paso, Texas, with natural gas wells in Jal, New Mexico. In 1931 it laid pipe again to reach the copper mines of Arizona and Mexico, and three years later expanded to Phoenix and Tucson.

After WWII the company began a 700-mile pipeline to bring natural gas from Texas' Permian Basin to California. As the Golden State's population exploded, sales soared. El Paso also ventured into new business areas, first chemicals and later textiles, mining, land development, and insurance.

In 1974 the Supreme Court ruled that El Paso had to divest its pipeline holdings north of New Mexico and Arizona. Federal regulators had granted the company the right to buy the holdings two decades earlier but later rescinded. Other operations, such as fiber manufacturing, were posting losses, so the company jettisoned some non-gas businesses. El Paso received a boost in 1978 when the Natural Gas Policy Act allowed it more freedom to purchase its own reserves, but later weak demand, coupled with oversupply brought on by the 1970s spike in energy prices, cut into its business by 1982.

Conglomerate Burlington Northern acquired El Paso Natural Gas in 1983. Many of El Paso's operations were spun off when federal regulations required pipeline companies to unbundle their sales and transportation businesses and open up interstate pipelines to third parties. El Paso became mainly a gas transportation company.

The company became independent again when Burlington spun it off in 1992. It entered the big leagues in 1996 by buying Tenneco Energy for $4 billion. With more than 16,000 miles of pipeline, Tenneco more than doubled El Paso's transportation capacity and gave it the only coast-to-coast natural gas pipeline in the US. El Paso Natural Gas began using the name El Paso Energy and moved from its namesake town to Houston, Tenneco's headquarters. In 1997 it sold Tenneco's oil and gas exploration unit to help pay off debt and bought a 29% stake in Capsa, an Argentine energy concern.

Refocusing on Gulf Coast assets, El Paso sold its Anadarko pipeline gas gathering system in Oklahoma and Texas in 1998. In 1999 El Paso bought Sonat, a natural gas transportation and marketing firm that also had an exploration and production unit, in a $6 billion deal. To gain regulators' approval of the Sonat deal, El Paso sold three pipeline systems in 2000, including East Tennessee Natural Gas (to Duke Energy) and Sea Robin Pipeline (to CMS Energy).

El Paso bought PG&E's natural gas and natural gas liquids businesses for about $900 million in 2000. Also that year the company agreed to buy diversified energy company Coastal in a $24 billion deal, which closed early in 2001. The company changed its name from El Paso Energy to El Paso that year.

To raise cash to help offset its heavy debt load, the company agreed in 2002 to sell some of its Texas natural gas pipelines to affiliate El Paso Energy Partners for $750 million. El Paso sold $525 million in oil and gas properties in Texas that year; it also agreed to sell some Colorado assets to Canadian firm Encana for $292 million and properties in Texas, Oklahoma, and Kansas to Pioneer Natural Resources for $113 million.

Chairman, President and CEO; Chairman, El Paso Energy Partners and El Paso Tennessee Pipeline:
William A. Wise, age 56, $4,737,425 pay
EVP and CFO; EVP, El Paso Energy Partners:
H. Brent Austin, age 47, $1,692,091 pay
EVP; President, Merchant Energy Group: Ralph Eads, age 42, $1,980,213 pay
EVP; President, Pipeline Group:
John W. Somerhalder II, age 46, $1,692,091 pay
EVP and General Counsel: Peggy A. Heeg, age 42
EVP Human Resources and Administration, El Paso Corporation: Joel Richards III, age 55
EVP: Greg G. Jenkins, age 44
SVP Communications and Government Affairs:
Norma F. Dunn
VP and Corporate Secretary: David L. Siddall
VP Investor Relations: Bruce Connery
Auditors: PricewaterhouseCoopers LLP

LOCATIONS

HQ: 1001 Louisiana St., Houston, TX 77002
Phone: 713-420-2600 **Fax:** 713-420-6030
Web: www.epenergy.com

El Paso has interests in power plants in Asia, Europe, Latin America, and North America. The company gathers natural gas in major producing areas of the US; it also has exploration and production operations in Canada and has production rights in Australia, Bolivia, Brazil, Hungary, Indonesia, and Turkey. The company also operates gas pipeline systems in Australia, Mexico, and the US.

PRODUCTS/OPERATIONS

2001 Sales

	$ mil.	% of total
Merchant energy	53,071	87
Pipelines	2,748	5
Field services	2,553	4
Production	2,347	4
Other & adjustments	(3,244)	—
Total	**57,475**	**100**

Selected Business Units

El Paso Field Services (natural gas gathering and processing)
El Paso Global LNG (LNG production)
El Paso Global Networks Company (telecommunications bandwidth trading)
El Paso Merchant Energy Group (energy marketing and trading, power generation)
El Paso Pipeline Group
El Paso Production (oil and gas exploration and production)

COMPETITORS

AEP	Entergy	NRG Energy
AES	Enterprise	Peabody Energy
Aquila	Equitable	PG&E
Avista	Resources	Sempra Energy
CenterPoint	Imperial Oil	Southern
Energy	International	Company
Constellation	Power	Tractebel
Energy Group	Kinder Morgan,	TransCanada
Duke Energy	Inc.	PipeLines
Dynegy	MidAmerican	Western Gas
Edison	Energy	Williams
International	Mirant	Companies

HISTORICAL FINANCIALS & EMPLOYEES

NYSE: EP FYE: December 31	Annual Growth	12/92	12/93	12/94	12/95	12/96	12/97	12/98	12/99	12/00	12/01
Sales ($ mil.)	60.7%	803	909	870	1,038	3,010	5,638	5,782	10,581	21,950	57,475
Net income ($ mil.)	2.2%	76	92	90	85	38	186	225	(255)	652	93
Income as % of sales	—	9.5%	10.1%	10.3%	8.2%	1.3%	3.3%	3.9%	—	3.0%	0.2%
Earnings per share ($)	(17.9%)	1.06	1.23	1.23	1.24	0.52	1.59	1.84	(1.12)	2.73	0.18
Stock price - FY high ($)	—	15.75	20.19	20.94	16.25	26.63	33.75	38.94	43.44	74.25	75.30
Stock price - FY low ($)	—	10.13	15.13	14.81	12.38	14.31	24.44	24.69	30.69	30.31	36.39
Stock price - FY close ($)	12.5%	15.50	18.00	15.25	14.38	25.25	33.25	34.81	38.81	71.63	44.61
P/E - high	—	15	16	17	13	50	21	20	—	29	579
P/E - low	—	10	12	12	10	27	15	13	—	12	280
Dividends per share ($)	14.4%	0.25	0.54	0.59	0.65	0.69	0.72	0.76	0.79	0.82	0.84
Book value per share ($)	7.7%	9.01	9.60	9.98	10.40	13.93	16.37	17.53	12.84	15.20	17.63
Employees	21.3%	2,499	2,460	2,403	2,393	4,300	3,500	3,600	4,700	15,000	14,180

STOCK PRICE HISTORY

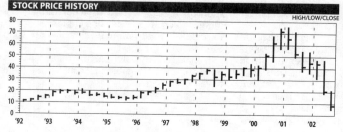

HIGH/LOW/CLOSE

2001 FISCAL YEAR-END
Debt ratio: 58.5%
Return on equity: 1.4%
Cash ($ mil.): 1,139
Current ratio: 0.93
Long-term debt ($ mil.): 13,184
No. of shares (mil.): 531
Dividends
  Yield: 1.9%
  Payout: 466.7%
Market value ($ mil.): 23,676

ELECTRONIC DATA SYSTEMS

EDS thinks big when it comes to information technology services. The Plano, Texas-based company is the largest independent computer management and services company in the US. (IBM is #1 worldwide.) About 75% of sales come from developing and managing complex computer and telecommunications systems for major government and corporate clients, including ChevronTexaco, BellSouth, and the US Navy. EDS also offers management consulting through its A.T. Kearney subsidiary. About 60% of sales come from the US.

For more than a decade, EDS was a General Motors subsidiary (GM still accounts for about 15% of sales). After its 1996 spinoff from GM, profits slumped. CEO Richard Brown restructured, trimming jobs and building a global marketing campaign to revive and recast EDS's image.

Struggling under difficult market conditions — made worse by the bankruptcies of two large clients, WorldCom and US Airways — EDS is relying on its specialty in providing traditional systems integration and computer outsourcing services to large clients. The company has expanded its offerings through consolidations and acquisitions, including the purchase of engineering software firm Structural Dynamics Research Corporation and the airline infrastructure outsourcing business of Sabre.

HISTORY

After 10 years with IBM, disgruntled salesman Ross Perot founded Electronic Data Systems (EDS) in 1962. IBM executives had dismissed Perot's idea of providing electronic data processing management that would relieve clients' data management worries.

Perot took five months to find his first customer, Collins Radio of Cedar Rapids, Iowa. In 1963 EDS pioneered the long-term, fixed-price contract with snack food maker Frito-Lay, writing a five-year contract instead of the 60- to 90-day contracts usually offered by service companies. EDS then got into Medicare and Medicaid claims processing (mid-1960s), data processing for insurance providers (1963), and data management for banks (1968) — moves that would make it the #1 provider of data management services in these markets.

EDS went public in 1968. It established regional data centers and central data processing stations in the early 1970s to pioneer the notion of distributed processing. In 1976 EDS signed one of its first offshore contracts, with Iran. But by 1978 Iran was behind in its payments, and EDS halted operations there. When two EDS employees were later arrested amid the disorder of the Islamic revolution, Perot assembled a rescue team that spirited them out of the country.

On EDS's 22nd anniversary in 1984, General Motors (GM) bought the company for $2.5 billion. GM promised EDS its independence as well as contract work managing its lumbering data processing system. While EDS prospered, Perot and GM chairman Roger Smith had different managerial styles, resulting in an uneasy alliance and, ultimately, divorce. GM bought Perot's EDS shares in 1986 for more than $700 million. Perot formed competitor Perot Systems in 1988.

In 1993 the company launched its management consulting service. Two years later EDS acquired management consulting firm A.T. Kearney and securities industry consultant FCI.

The company won independence from GM in mid-1996 in a spinoff that involved paying $500 million to GM and agreeing to extend the automaker more favorable computer services contracts. In 1998 CEO Lester Alberthal resigned and was replaced by Cable & Wireless executive Richard Brown, who became chairman and CEO in 1999. Brown cut thousands of jobs (including a third of the sales force), and reversed a trend at EDS of spending more money on philanthropy than advertising, launching a $100 million global ad campaign to present a reinvented, more nimble EDS.

In 1999 the company exchanged assets and services from its networking business for communications management services and employees from MCI WorldCom (now WorldCom) in a $17 billion alliance. As one part of that deal, EDS paid $1.65 billion to buy MCI Systemhouse, a move that thrust EDS into the electronic commerce arena. In 2000 EDS scored a record contract with the US Navy worth nearly $7 billion over five years.

In 2001 EDS signed a 10-year, $2.2 billion service contract with Sabre. As part of the deal EDS acquired Sabre's airline infrastructure outsourcing business and its information technology assets for $670 million. EDS continued to expand its territory that year, purchasing Structural Dynamics Research Corporation for $950 million in cash and reacquiring the publicly traded shares of Unigraphics Solutions it spun off in 1998. The two acquisitions were merged to create a design and engineering software division with annual sales of more than $1 billion.

In 2002 EDS consolidated three of its top units into two, and it promoted EVP Paul Chiapparone to vice chairman.

OFFICERS

Chairman and CEO: Richard H. Brown, age 54, $8,500,000 pay
Vice Chairman: Paul J. Chiapparone, age 62, $2,139,720 pay
EVP and CFO: James E. Daley, age 60, $2,124,720 pay
EVP, Leadership and Change Management: Troy W. Todd, age 73, $1,688,880 pay
EVP and Sector Executive, Operations Solutions: Douglas L. Frederick, age 52
President, Application Management Service: Dan Zadorozny
President, Automotive Retail Group: Karen Blunden
President, Business Process Outsourcing: Daniel Henderson
President, Communications, Entertainment, and Media: Reza Jafari
President, Consumer Industries and Retail Global Industry Group: Scott W. Klein
President, Energy Global Industries Group: Tina M. Sivinski
President, Federal Government — Information Solutions: Albert J. Edmonds
President, Global Health Care Industry Group: Charles Saunders
President, Hosting Services: Jeff Kelly
Auditors: KPMG LLP

LOCATIONS

HQ: Electronic Data Systems Corporation
5400 Legacy Dr., Plano, TX 75024
Phone: 972-604-6000 **Fax:** 972-605-2643
Web: www.eds.com

2001 Sales

	$ mil.	% of total
US	12,357	57
UK	3,364	16
Other countries	5,822	27
Total	**21,543**	**100**

PRODUCTS/OPERATIONS

2001 Sales

	$ mil.	% of total
Information solutions	16,182	72
Business process management	3,008	13
Consulting	2,403	11
Product lifecycle management	738	4
Other	(788)	—
Total	**21,543**	**100**

COMPETITORS

Accenture	Fiserv
Affiliated Computer	GEX
American Management	Hewlett-Packard
Atos Origin	IBM
Autodesk	Keane
ADP	KPMG Consulting
Bain & Company	McKinsey & Company
Booz Allen	Parametric Technology
Boston Consulting	Perot Systems
Cap Gemini	PricewaterhouseCoopers
Computer Sciences	SAIC
Dassault	Siemens
Deloitte Touche Tohmatsu	SunGard Data Systems
Ernst & Young	Unisys
First Data	

HISTORICAL FINANCIALS & EMPLOYEES

NYSE: EDS FYE: December 31	Annual Growth	12/92	12/93	12/94	12/95	12/96	12/97	12/98	12/99	12/00	12/01
Sales ($ mil.)	11.4%	8,155	8,507	10,052	12,422	14,441	15,236	16,891	18,534	19,227	21,543
Net income ($ mil.)	8.8%	636	724	822	939	432	731	743	421	1,143	1,363
Income as % of sales	—	7.8%	8.5%	8.2%	7.6%	3.0%	4.8%	4.4%	2.3%	5.9%	6.3%
Earnings per share ($)	8.7%	1.33	1.50	1.69	1.94	0.88	1.48	1.50	0.85	2.40	2.81
Stock price - FY high ($)	—	34.00	35.88	39.50	52.63	63.38	49.63	51.31	70.00	76.69	72.45
Stock price - FY low ($)	—	25.25	26.00	27.50	36.88	40.75	29.56	30.44	44.13	38.38	50.90
Stock price - FY close ($)	8.5%	32.88	29.25	38.38	52.00	43.25	43.94	50.19	66.94	57.75	68.55
P/E - high	—	26	24	23	27	71	33	34	80	31	25
P/E - low	—	19	17	16	19	46	20	20	51	16	17
Dividends per share ($)	5.8%	0.36	0.40	0.48	0.52	0.60	0.60	0.60	0.60	0.60	0.60
Book value per share ($)	8.7%	6.39	7.52	8.79	10.29	9.82	10.80	12.00	9.73	11.04	13.50
Employees	8.2%	70,500	70,000	70,000	96,000	100,000	110,000	120,000	121,000	122,000	143,000

STOCK PRICE HISTORY

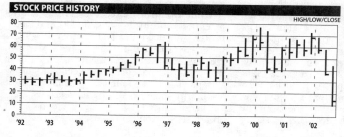

HIGH/LOW/CLOSE

2001 FISCAL YEAR-END

Debt ratio: 42.1%
Return on equity: 23.5%
Cash ($ mil.): 521
Current ratio: 1.69
Long-term debt ($ mil.): 4,692
No. of shares (mil.): 477
Dividends
  Yield: 0.9%
  Payout: 21.4%
Market value ($ mil.): 32,720

ELI LILLY AND COMPANY

Eli Lilly and Company will need to pop more than a Prozac to find escape from its depression.

The Indianapolis-based company makes antidepressant Prozac and pre-menstrual dysphoric disorder treatment Sarafem that, together, contributed almost one-fourth of total company sales in 2000. Since Prozac lost its lucrative patent protection in August 2001, generic versions of the drug have seriously decimated Lilly's hold on the market.

The company's current top five products include Gemzar (pancreatic cancer), Evista (osteoporosis), Humalog (insulin), Actos (Type 2 diabetes), and Zyprexa (schizophrenia and bipolar disorder). In addition to neurological, oncological, and diabetes drugs, Eli Lilly also makes antibiotics, cardiovascular treatments, and animal health products.

The firm's pipeline has become increasingly important since Prozac sales plummeted: Lilly hopes launches of osteoporosis treatment Forteo, antidepressant Duloxetine, and erectile dysfunction treatment Cialis (developed with ICOS) can replace the lost income. The company has some 40 other candidates in development, including treatments for sepsis, cancer, and diabetes. At this crucial time, the company may have more difficulty than expected with rolling new drugs out. The FDA will not approve any of the company's drugs until it addresses manufacturing problems.

Jumping on the bandwagon to avoid government price controls, the company has plans to launch LillyAnswers, a drug discount program for low-income seniors that undercuts other discount programs offered by fellow druggernauts such as GlaxoSmithKline (Orange Card) and Pfizer (Share Card).

The Lilly Endowment, a charitable foundation, owns almost 15% of the company.

HISTORY

Colonel Eli Lilly, pharmacist and Union officer in the Civil War, started Eli Lilly & Company in 1876 with $1,300. His process of gelatin-coating pills led to sales of nearly $82,000 in 1881. Later, the company made gelatin capsules, which it still sells. Lilly died in 1898, and his son and two grandsons ran the business until 1953.

Eli Lilly began extracting insulin from the pancreases of hogs and cattle in 1923; 6,000 cattle or 24,000 hog glands made one ounce of the substance. Other products created in the 1920s and 1930s included antiseptic Merthiolate, sedative Seconal, and treatments for pernicious anemia and heart disease. In 1947 the company began selling diethylstilbestrol (DES), a drug

that prevented miscarriages. Eli Lilly researchers isolated the antibiotic erythromycin from a mold found in the Philippines in 1952. Lilly was also the major supplier of Salk polio vaccine.

The company enjoyed a 70% share of the DES market by 1971, when researchers noticed that a rare form of cervical cancer afflicted many of the daughters of women who had taken the drug. The FDA restricted the drug's use and Lilly found itself on the receiving (and frequently losing) end of a number of trailblazing product-liability suits that stretched into the 1990s.

The firm diversified in the 1970s, buying Elizabeth Arden (cosmetics, 1971; sold 1987) and IVAC (medical instruments, 1977). It launched such products as analgesic Darvon and antibiotic Ceclor.

Lilly's 1982 launch of Humulin, a synthetic insulin developed by Genentech, made it the first company to market a genetically engineered product. In 1986 the company introduced Prozac; that year it also bought biotech firm Hybritech for $300 million (sold in 1995 for less than $10 million). In 1988 Lilly introduced antiulcerative Axid. It founded pesticides and herbicides maker Dow-Elanco with Dow Chemical in 1989.

Eli Lilly bought medical communications network developer Integrated Medical Systems in 1995. That year the firm and developer Centocor introduced ReoPro, a blood-clot inhibitor used in angioplasties. In 1997 the firm sold its Dow-Elanco stake to Dow.

In 1999 a US federal judge found the firm illegally promoted osteoporosis drug Evista as a breast cancer preventative similar to AstraZeneca's Nolvadex. Lilly halted tests on its variation of heart drug Moxonidine after 53 patients died. Also that year, Zyprexa was approved to treat bipolar disorder.

In 2000 the firm began marketing Prozac under the Sarafem name for severe premenstrual syndrome. A federal appeals court knocked more than two years off Prozac's patent, reducing the expected 2003 expiration date to 2001. Lilly suffered another blow when a potential successor to Prozac failed in clinical trials and became embroiled in legal maneuverings with generics maker Barr Laboratories.

While the firm fretted over Prozac and its patents, it continued work to find its next blockbuster. In 2000 Lilly and partner ICOS announced favorable results from a study of erectile dysfunction treatment Cialis; the drug may capture a share of the market dominated by Pfizer's Viagra. The following year Lilly bought a minority stake in Isis Pharmaceuticals, a developer of antisense drugs, and licensed from it an antisense lung cancer drug. Also that year the firm launched Lilly BioVentures, a venture fund aimed at private biotech startup companies. In 2002 the company settled with eight states in an infringement of privacy case involving the company's accidental disclosure of e-mail addresses for more than 600 Prozac patients.

OFFICERS

Chairman, President, and CEO: Sidney Taurel, age 53, $1,865,466 pay
EVP, CFO, and Director: Charles E. Golden, age 55, $973,109 pay
EVP, Pharmaceutical Operations: Gerhard N. Mayr, age 55, $1,010,749 pay
EVP, Pharmaceutical Products and Corporate Development: John C. Lechleiter, age 48, $821,475 pay
EVP, Science and Technology, and Director: August M. Watanabe, age 60, $1,010,749 pay
SVP and General Counsel: Rebecca O. Kendall, age 54
SVP, Human Resources and Manufacturing: Pedro P. Granadillo, age 54
Group VP, Global Marketing and Sales: James A. Harper
Auditors: Ernst & Young LLP

LOCATIONS

HQ: Lilly Corporate Center, Indianapolis, IN 46285
Phone: 317-276-2000 **Fax:** 317-277-6579
Web: www.lilly.com

2001 Sales

	$ mil.	% of total
US	7,364	64
Western Europe	1,953	17
Other regions	2,225	19
Adjustments	1	—
Total	**11,543**	**100**

PRODUCTS/OPERATIONS

2001 Sales

	$ mil.	% of total
Neurosciences	5,328	46
Endocrinology	3,104	27
Anti-infectives	750	7
Oncology	739	6
Animal health	686	6
Cardiovascular	593	5
Other pharmaceutical	343	3
Total	**11,543**	**100**

Selected Products

Actos (type 2 diabetes)
Darvon (line of analgesic products)
Dynabac (antibiotic)
Evista (osteoporosis in post-menopausal women)
Gemzar (pancreatic cancer)
Glucagon (diabetes)
Humalog (insulin)

Keflex (antibiotic)
Kefurox (injectable antibiotic)
Lorabid (antibiotic)
Permax (Parkinson's disease)
Prozac (depression)
Sarafem (premenstrual dysphoric disorder)
Zyprexa (schizophrenia)

COMPETITORS

Abbott Labs
Amgen
AstraZeneca
Aventis
BASF AG
Baxter
Bayer AG

Boehringer Ingelheim
Bristol-Myers Squibb
Genentech
GlaxoSmithKline
Johnson & Johnson

Merck
Novartis
Novo Nordisk
Pfizer
Roche
Schering-Plough
Wyeth

HISTORICAL FINANCIALS & EMPLOYEES

NYSE: LLY FYE: December 31	Annual Growth	12/92	12/93	12/94	12/95	12/96	12/97	12/98	12/99	12/00	12/01
Sales ($ mil.)	7.2%	6,167	6,452	5,712	6,764	7,347	8,518	9,237	10,003	10,862	11,543
Net income ($ mil.)	16.4%	709	480	1,286	2,291	1,524	(385)	2,098	2,721	3,058	2,780
Income as % of sales	—	11.5%	7.4%	22.5%	33.9%	20.7%	—	22.7%	27.2%	28.2%	24.1%
Earnings per share ($)	17.2%	0.61	0.40	1.10	1.99	1.36	(0.35)	1.87	2.46	2.79	2.55
Stock price - FY high ($)	—	21.94	15.50	16.56	28.50	40.19	70.44	91.31	97.75	109.00	95.00
Stock price - FY low ($)	—	14.44	10.91	11.78	15.63	24.69	35.56	57.69	60.56	54.00	70.01
Stock price - FY close ($)	20.0%	15.19	14.84	16.41	28.13	36.50	69.63	88.88	66.50	93.06	78.54
P/E - high	—	31	38	15	14	29	—	48	39	39	36
P/E - low	—	20	27	11	8	18	—	30	24	19	27
Dividends per share ($)	8.2%	0.55	0.61	0.63	0.66	0.69	0.94	0.80	0.92	1.04	1.12
Book value per share ($)	4.7%	4.18	3.90	4.59	4.93	5.52	4.18	4.04	4.60	5.37	6.32
Employees	2.7%	32,200	32,700	24,900	26,800	29,200	31,100	29,800	31,300	35,700	41,100

STOCK PRICE HISTORY

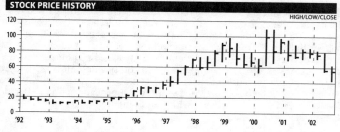

HIGH/LOW/CLOSE

2001 FISCAL YEAR-END

Debt ratio: 30.6%
Return on equity: 42.3%
Cash ($ mil.): 2,702
Current ratio: 1.33
Long-term debt ($ mil.): 3,132
No. of shares (mil.): 1,123
Dividends
  Yield: 1.4%
  Payout: 43.9%
Market value ($ mil.): 88,228

EMC CORPORATION

Don't think EMC is going soft. Despite a shift in focus, the Hopkinton, Massachusetts-based company is still the storage hardware leader. Its refrigerator-sized Symmetrix redundant array of independent disks (RAID) storage systems combine small disk drives into groups to ensure data integrity. EMC's products manage and share data across different types of networked computers. The company targets data-intensive customers, including Internet service providers and many leading airlines and banks. It sells its products directly and through distributors and manufacturers; PC leader Dell Computer is among EMC's reseller partners.

EMC has built a reputation for outstanding service, a feature resulting from a corporate structure that's run with military efficiency. Pressure from relative upstarts such as Network Appliance and stalwarts that include IBM and Hitachi Data Systems has EMC looking to shore up its leading position. The company has used acquisitions to expand its offerings and to gain footholds in emerging storage technologies, with a particular emphasis on growing its software products. However, a slowing economy has forced restructuring measures that have included significant job cuts.

HISTORY

Former Intel executive Dick Egan and his college roommate, Roger Marino, founded EMC in 1979. (Their initials gave the company its name.) Egan, a feisty entrepreneur whose first job was shining shoes, served as a marine in Korea and later worked at MIT on the computer system for NASA's Apollo program. Egan also helped found Cambridge Memory Systems (later Cambex).

EMC was started with no business plan, only the idea that Egan and Marino would be better off working for themselves. At first they sold office furniture, which in short order led to contacts at technology companies and recognition of the niche market for add-on memory boards for minicomputers.

EMC grew steadily throughout the early 1980s and went public in 1986. Two years later Michael Ruettgers, a former COO of high-tech publishing and research company Technical Financial Services, joined the company as EVP of operations. Ruettgers spent his first year and a half at EMC dealing with a crisis that almost ruined the company: Defective disk drives in some of its products were losing customers' files. Ruettgers stepped up quality control and guided EMC through the crisis period. In 1989 he became the company's president and COO.

In the late 1980s EMC expanded into data storage, developing a system that employed small hard disks rather than larger, more expensive disks and tapes used in IBM mainframes. EMC then separated itself from competitors by providing systems with a large cache — a temporary storage area used for quicker data retrieval.

In 1990 EMC pioneered redundant array of independent disks (RAID) storage and eliminated nearly a dozen major product lines, focusing on storage for large IBM computers in a bid to beat Big Blue by undercutting prices. The company introduced its original Symmetrix system, based on the new integrated cached disk array technology that held data from a variety of computer types. Marino left the company in 1990.

Ruettgers became CEO in 1992. The next year the company acquired Epoch Systems, a provider of data management software, and in 1994 it bought storage products company Array Technology and Magna Computer, a leader in tape storage technology for IBM computers. EMC also introduced its first storage product for open systems, the Centriplex series, and its sales passed the $1 billion mark.

EMC increased its presence in this fast-growing data switching and computer connection market with the 1995 acquisition of McDATA. The next year it launched a digital video storage and retrieval system for the TV and film industry and introduced software that let its systems work on networks instead of requiring file servers for data storage management.

In 1997 the company began managing Web sites for customers. Expanding its international service presence, EMC bought French technology services provider Groupe MCI in 1998 and in 1999 opened an Internet services office in Ireland. Also that year the company moved into the market for midrange storage when it acquired data storage and server specialist Data General.

EMC bought data storage software provider SOFTWORKS in early 2000. That year EMC took McDATA public; the following year it distributed its majority stake in that company to EMC shareholders. In early 2001 the company's corporate ladder shifted. Joe Tucci, who had joined EMC in 2000 as president, added CEO to his title. Ruettgers became chairman and Egan was named chairman emeritus. Later that year EMC acquired performance monitoring specialist Luminate Software for approximately $50 million.

Responding to a contracting economy and a subsequent drop in sales, EMC took a restructuring charge in the second half of 2001 that contributed to its first quarterly loss in 12 years. Late that year the company formed a reseller alliance with Dell Computer.

Executive Chairman: Michael C. Ruettgers, age 59,
$1,700,000 pay
President, CEO, and Director: Joseph M. Tucci, age 54,
$1,700,000 pay
EVP and CFO: William J. Teuber Jr., age 50
EVP, Customer Operations: Frank M. Hauck, age 42,
$804,030 pay (prior to title change)
EVP, Global Marketing and Business Development:
David Goulden, age 43
EVP, New Ventures and CTO: Mark S. Lewis
EVP, Open Software Operations: Erez Ofer, age 39,
$1,067,948 pay
EVP, Storage Platforms Operations: David A. Donatelli,
age 36, $796,000 pay
SVP and General Counsel: Paul T. Dacier, age 44
Auditors: PricewaterhouseCoopers LLP

LOCATIONS

HQ: 35 Parkwood Dr., Hopkinton, MA 01748
Phone: 508-435-1000 **Fax:** 508-497-6961
Web: www.emc.com

EMC has more than 100 sales offices worldwide. It has
manufacturing plants in Ireland and the US, and R&D
facilities in France, Israel, and the US.

2001 Sales

	$ mil.	% of total
North America	4,185	59
Europe, Middle East & Africa	1,775	25
Asia/Pacific	894	13
Latin America	237	3
Total	**7,091**	**100**

PRODUCTS/OPERATIONS

2001 Sales

	$ mil.	% of total
Products		
Systems	4,307	61
Software	1,560	22
Services	973	14
Other	251	3
Total	**7,091**	**100**

Selected Products
Systems
   Data storage arrays (CLARiiON)
   Fibre Channel switches and directors (Connectrix)
   Network file and media servers (Celerra)
   Redundant array of independent disks storage systems
      (Symmetrix)
Software (AutoIS)
Services
   Consulting
   Installation
   Support
   Systems upgrades
   Training

COMPETITORS

Brocade Communications Systems	IBM
	Network Appliance
Dell Computer	Quantum
Eurologic	StorageTek
Fujitsu	Sun Microsystems
Hewlett-Packard	VERITAS Software
Hitachi Data Systems	

HISTORICAL FINANCIALS & EMPLOYEES

NYSE: EMC FYE: December 31	Annual Growth	12/92	12/93	12/94	12/95	12/96	12/97	12/98	12/99	12/00	12/01
Sales ($ mil.)	39.7%	349	783	1,378	1,921	2,274	2,938	3,974	6,716	8,873	7,091
Net income ($ mil.)	—	29	127	251	327	386	539	793	1,011	1,782	(508)
Income as % of sales	—	8.2%	16.2%	18.2%	17.0%	17.0%	18.3%	20.0%	15.0%	20.1%	—
Earnings per share ($)	—	0.03	0.08	0.13	0.16	0.19	0.26	0.37	0.46	0.79	(0.23)
Stock price - FY high ($)	—	0.76	2.44	3.00	3.42	4.55	8.14	21.66	55.50	104.94	82.00
Stock price - FY low ($)	—	0.23	0.64	1.56	1.63	1.86	3.97	6.00	21.00	48.50	10.01
Stock price - FY close ($)	38.0%	0.74	2.06	2.75	1.92	4.14	6.86	21.25	54.63	66.50	13.44
P/E - high	—	25	27	21	20	24	30	56	113	128	—
P/E - low	—	8	7	11	10	10	15	15	43	59	—
Dividends per share ($)	—	0.00	0.00	0.00	0.00	0.02	0.00	0.00	0.00	0.00	0.00
Book value per share ($)	44.1%	0.13	0.28	0.46	0.62	0.86	1.20	1.65	2.38	3.72	3.42
Employees	33.4%	1,500	2,452	3,375	4,100	4,800	6,400	9,700	17,700	24,100	20,100

STOCK PRICE HISTORY

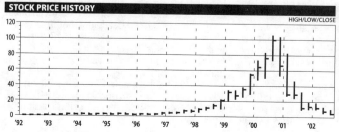

HIGH/LOW/CLOSE

2001 FISCAL YEAR-END

Debt ratio: 0.0%
Return on equity: —
Cash ($ mil.): 2,129
Current ratio: 2.26
Long-term debt ($ mil.): 0
No. of shares (mil.): 2,220
Dividends
   Yield: —
   Payout: —
Market value ($ mil.): 29,842

EMCOR GROUP, INC.

EMCOR's concentration is construction. Norwalk, Connecticut-based EMCOR Group (short for Electrical Mechanical Corp.) is one of the world's largest specialty construction firms. Its metier is the design, installation, and operation of complex mechanical and electrical systems, which provide about 84% of its revenues.

The group operates through more than 50 subsidiaries in the US, Canada, and the UK; it also conducts business internationally through joint ventures in Saudi Arabia, United Arab Emirates, and South Africa. EMCOR units build and maintain electric, lighting, security, and plumbing systems for commercial, industrial, and institutional customers. The group also provides facilities services such as maintenance, management, and support services.

EMCOR has been growing through acquisitions and is focusing on growing its facilities services. The company has expanded its facility services operations in the UK and is establishing additional subsidiaries (mainly through acquisitions) in North America to help aid the increasing demand for such services. One of the largest union employers in the US, EMCOR has a workforce of more than 20,000, and about 75% of its employees belong to unions. The company has acquired 19 subsidiaries from rival Comfort Systems USA, most of that company's union operations.

HISTORY

EMCOR's forerunner, Jamaica Water Supply Co., was incorporated in 1887 to supply water to some residents of Queens and Nassau Counties in New York. In 1902 it bought Jamaica Township Water Co., and by 1906 it was generating revenue — reaching $1.6 million by 1932. Over the next 35 years, the company kept pace with the population of its service area.

In 1966 the enterprise was acquired by Jamaica Water and Utilities, which then bought Sea Cliff Water Co. In 1969 and 1970 it acquired Welsbach (electrical contractors) and A to Z Equipment (construction trailer suppliers); it briefly changed its name in 1974 to Welsbach Corp. before becoming Jamaica Water Properties in 1976.

Diversification proved unprofitable, however, and in 1977, Martin Dwyer and his son Andrew took over the management of the struggling firm. Despite posting million-dollar losses in 1979, it was profitable by 1980.

The Dwyers acquired companies in the electrical and mechanical contracting, security, telecommunications, computer, energy and environmental businesses. In 1985 Andrew Dwyer became president, and the firm changed its name the next year to JWP.

Between 1986 and 1990 JWP acquired more than a dozen companies, including Extel (1986), Gibson Electric (1987), Dynalectric (1988), Drake & Scull (1989), NEECO and Compumat (1990), and Comstock Canada (1990).

In 1991 JWP capped its strategy of buying up US computer systems resellers by acquiring Businessland. It then bought French microelectronics distributor SIVEA. Later that year JWP bought a 34% stake in Resource Recycling Technologies (a solid-waste recycler).

JWP's shopping spree extended the firm's reach, but the company began to struggle when several sectors turned sour. A price war in the information services business and a weak construction market led to a loss of more than $600 million in 1992. That year president David Sokol resigned after questioning JWP's accounting practices. He turned over a report to the SEC that claimed inflated profits.

Cutting itself to about half its former size, the company sold JWP Information Services in 1993. (JWP Information Services later became ENTEX Information Services, which was acquired by Siemens in 2000.) However, JWP continued to struggle, and in early 1994 it filed for bankruptcy. Emerging from Chapter 11 protection in December 1994, the reorganized company took the name EMCOR. That year Frank MacInnis, former CEO of electrical contractor Comstock Group, stepped in to lead EMCOR.

In 1995 the SEC, using Sokol's information, charged several former JWP executives with accounting fraud, claiming they had overstated profits to boost the value of their company stock and their bonuses. EMCOR later reached a nonmonetary settlement with the SEC. The company sold Jamaica Water Supply and Sea Cliff in 1996; it also achieved profitability that year.

Focusing on external growth, EMCOR acquired a number of firms in 1998 and 1999, including Marelich Mechanical Co. and Mesa Energy Systems, BALCO, Inc., and the Poole & Kent group of mechanical contracting companies based in Baltimore and Miami. To meet increased demands for facilities services, in 2000 EMCOR consolidated the operations of three of its mechanical contractors (BALCO, J.C. Higgins, and Tucker Mechanical) into one company, EMCOR Services, which operates in New England.

That year, about six years after emerging from bankruptcy, EMCOR began trading on the New York Stock Exchange. In 2002 EMCOR bought 19 subsidiaries from its financially troubled rival, Comfort Systems USA, including its largest unit, Shambaugh & Son.

Chairman and CEO: Frank T. MacInnis, age 55, $1,767,602 pay
President and COO: Jeffrey M. Levy, age 49, $1,241,699 pay
EVP, General Counsel, and Secretary: Sheldon I. Cammaker, age 62, $777,636 pay
EVP and CFO: Leicle E. Chesser, age 55, $847,069 pay
VP and Controller: Mark A. Pompa, age 37
VP and Treasurer: R. Kevin Matz, age 43, $574,177 pay
VP Corporate Development: Treavor M. Foster
VP Human Resources: J. Edward Buckley
VP Risk Management: Rex C. Thrasher
VP Taxation: Sidney R. Bernstein
Auditors: Ernst & Young LLP

LOCATIONS

HQ: 101 Merritt Seven, 7th Fl., Norwalk, CT 06851
Phone: 203-849-7800   **Fax:** 203-849-7870
Web: www.emcorgroup.com

EMCOR Group operates through offices in 30 states and the District of Columbia in the US, eight provinces in Canada, and 10 locations in the UK. It also operates internationally through joint ventures in Saudi Arabia, South Africa, and the United Arab Emirates.

2001 Sales

	$ mil.	% of total
North America		
US	2,746	80
Canada	198	6
UK	464	14
Other regions	12	—
Total	**3,420**	**100**

PRODUCTS/OPERATIONS

2001 Sales

	$ mil.	% of total
Mechanical & electrical construction	2,873	84
Facility support	547	16
Total	**3,420**	**100**

Selected Mechanical and Electrical Services
Building plant and lighting systems
Data and communications systems
Electrical power distribution systems
Energy recovery
Facilities management
Fire protection systems
Fuel distribution systems
Heating, ventilation, and air-conditioning (HVAC) systems
Piping and plumbing systems
Refrigeration systems
Street lighting and traffic signal systems
Water treatment plants

COMPETITORS

AMPAM	Integrated Electrical
APi Group	Services
Comfort Systems USA	Johnson Controls
Dycom	MasTec
Encompass Services Corp.	MYR Group
Fluor	Quanta Services
Hoffman Corporation	Schneider
Honeywell International	STRATESEC

HISTORICAL FINANCIALS & EMPLOYEES

NYSE: EME FYE: December 31	Annual Growth	12/92	12/93	12/94	12/95	12/96	12/97	12/98	12/99	12/00	12/01
Sales ($ mil.)	4.0%	2,404	2,195	1,764	1,589	1,669	1,951	2,210	2,894	3,460	3,420
Net income ($ mil.)	—	(617)	(114)	303	(11)	9	8	12	28	40	50
Income as % of sales	—	—	—	17.2%	—	0.6%	0.4%	0.6%	1.0%	1.2%	1.5%
Earnings per share ($)	—	—	—	—	(1.13)	0.96	0.74	1.11	2.21	2.95	3.40
Stock price - FY high ($)	—	—	—	—	9.63	17.38	22.25	23.13	26.00	28.13	49.14
Stock price - FY low ($)	—	—	—	—	9.38	9.38	12.75	12.50	16.06	16.81	23.75
Stock price - FY close ($)	29.5%	—	—	—	9.63	13.00	20.50	16.13	18.25	25.50	45.40
P/E - high	—	—	—	—	—	17	25	14	9	7	13
P/E - low	—	—	—	—	—	9	14	7	6	4	6
Dividends per share ($)	—	—	—	—	0.00	0.00	0.00	0.00	0.00	0.00	0.00
Book value per share ($)	24.9%	—	—	—	7.49	8.82	9.94	12.19	16.32	25.00	28.48
Employees	4.0%	14,000	14,000	14,000	12,000	12,000	14,000	15,000	20,000	22,000	20,000

STOCK PRICE HISTORY

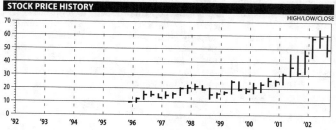

HIGH/LOW/CLOSE

2001 FISCAL YEAR-END
Debt ratio: 0.2%
Return on equity: 15.3%
Cash ($ mil.): 190
Current ratio: 1.42
Long-term debt ($ mil.): 1
No. of shares (mil.): 15
Dividends
  Yield: —
  Payout: —
Market value ($ mil.): 673

EMERSON ELECTRIC CO.

Emerson Electric (more commonly known as simply Emerson) is focused on keeping things under control. The St. Louis-based company divides its products — many of which control the flow of liquids, gases, and electricity — into five segments.

Emerson's electronics and telecommunications unit (23% of sales) makes power distribution and conversion equipment and networking products. The appliance and tools segment (22% of sales) manufactures hand tools, motors for appliances, and appliances such as fans. Its process control unit makes measurement devices and valves used primarily in moving gases and liquids, as well as equipment for power generation. Emerson's industrial automation segment produces motors, drives, and an assortment of equipment used in industrial applications. The HVAC unit makes compressors, thermostats, and other related equipment for heating, ventilating, air-conditioning, and refrigeration systems.

The company has invested heavily in its electronics and telecom segment, with mixed results. Emerson is restructuring that unit and has scaled back about 6% of its salaried workforce since the beginning of 2001.

HISTORY

Emerson Electric was founded in 1890 in St. Louis by brothers Alexander and Charles Meston, inventors who developed uses for the alternating-current electric motor, which was new at the time. The company was named after former Missouri judge and US marshal John Emerson, who financed the enterprise and became its first president. Emerson's best-known product was an electric fan introduced in 1892. Between 1910 and 1920 the company helped develop the first forced-air circulating systems.

The Depression and labor problems in the 1930s brought Emerson close to bankruptcy, but new products, including a hermetic motor for refrigerators, revived it. The company's electric motors were adapted for additional uses during WWII, including powering the gun turrets in B-24 bombers.

Emerson suffered in postwar years, having grown dependent on defense business. Wallace Persons took over as president in 1954 and reorganized the company's commercial product line, seeking to bring in customers from outside the consumer appliance market.

In the early 1960s Persons bought a number of smaller companies to produce thermostats and gas controls, welding and cutting tools, and power transmission products.

Emerson's sales increased from $56 million in 1954 to $800 million in 1973. Persons retired in 1974, and Chuck Knight became CEO. Knight took the company into high-tech fields and expanded its hardware segment with six acquisitions between 1976 and 1986.

In 1989 Emerson expanded its electrical offerings by acquiring a 45% stake in Hong Kong-based Astec (power supplies). The company spun off its defense systems, electronics, and other businesses in 1990 as ESCO Electronics.

Emerson bought Fisher Controls International in 1992 and formed S-B Power Tool with Bosch. It also acquired Buehler International (destructive testing equipment). From 1993 through 1995 Emerson expanded globally by targeting the Asia/Pacific market, setting up operations in China and Eastern Europe, and forming joint ventures in China and India.

Emerson and Caterpillar invested in plants in Northern Ireland in 1996 through their power-generating equipment joint venture, F.G. Wilson. Production began at its Thailand compressor plant in 1997, and Emerson's Appleton Electric division formed EGS Electrical, a joint venture with General Signal (acquired by SPX, 1998), to serve the electrical distribution industry. Also in 1997 Emerson bought Computational Systems, which makes equipment that detects potential problems in machinery at utility and plant facilities.

In 1998 Emerson bought CBS Corporation's Westinghouse Process Control division. Emerson pushed into the telecom market by purchasing Northern Telecom's Advanced Power Systems (power conversion) business.

Emerson sold its F.G. Wilson stake to partner Caterpillar in 1999 in exchange for that company's Kato Engineering electric generator subsidiary. Purchases that year included Daniel Industries (measurement and flow-control equipment) and the rest of Astec.

Early in 2000 Emerson acquired the telecom products division of Jordan Industries for about $980 million and later bought European telecommunications power provider Ericsson Energy Systems from Ericsson for $725 million. Later that year the company dropped "Electric" from its everyday name to reflect its diverse product line. Emerson sold its Chromalox division (electric heating and control products) to JPMorgan Partners in late 2001 for a reported $165 million. The company's Process Management division inked a three-year deal in 2002 with ChevronTexaco to provide control valves and related instrumentation; the deal is estimated to be worth in excess of $20 million a year.

Chairman: Charles F. Knight, age 66, $1,600,000 pay
CEO and Director: David N. Farr, age 47, $1,240,000 pay
President and Director: James G. Berges, age 54,
$1,240,000 pay
COO: Edward Monser, age 51
SEVP, E-Business Leader and Director:
Charles A. Peters, age 46
EVP, CFO, and Director: Walter J. Galvin, age 55,
$855,000 pay
SVP and CTO: Randall D. Ledford, age 52
SVP, Secretary, and General Counsel:
Walter W. Withers, age 61
SVP, Human Resources: P. A. Hutchison
Auditors: KPMG LLP

LOCATIONS

HQ: 8000 W. Florissant Ave., St. Louis, MO 63136
Phone: 314-553-2000   **Fax:** 314-553-3527
Web: www.gotoemerson.com

Emerson operates about 380 manufacturing plants in
Asia, Europe, and North and South America.

2001 Sales

	$ mil.	% of total
US	9,291	60
Europe	3,087	20
Asia	1,412	9
Latin America	670	4
Other regions	1,020	7
Total	**15,480**	**100**

PRODUCTS/OPERATIONS

2001 Sales

	$ mil.	% of total
Electronics & telecommunications	3,600	23
Appliance & tools	3,500	22
Process control	3,300	21
Industrial automation	3,000	19
HVAC	2,400	15
Adjustments	(320)	—
Total	**15,480**	**100**

Selected Products

AC and DC power systems	Mechanical power
Connectivity	transmission
Appliance controls	Motors and drives
Motors	Power distribution
Alternators	Flow controls
Fluid control	Terminal assemblies
Industrial equipment	Thermostats

COMPETITORS

ABB	Ingersoll-Rand	Rockwell
American Power	Climate Control	Automation
Conversion	Ingersoll-Rand	Rolls-Royce
Black & Decker	Industrial	Siemens
Cooper	Solutions	Siemens Energy
Industries	Invensys	& Automation
Dana	Johnson	Snap-on
Dresser	Controls	SPX
Eaton	Magnetek	Stanley Works
GE	Mark IV	Tecumseh
Hitachi	McDermott	Products
Illinois Tool	NEC	Toshiba
Works	Raytheon	United
Ingersoll-Rand		Technologies

HISTORICAL FINANCIALS & EMPLOYEES

NYSE: EMR FYE: September 30	Annual Growth	9/92	9/93	9/94	9/95	9/96	9/97	9/98	9/99	9/00	9/01
Sales ($ mil.)	8.1%	7,706	8,174	8,607	10,013	11,150	12,299	13,447	14,270	15,545	15,480
Net income ($ mil.)	5.0%	663	708	789	908	1,019	1,122	1,229	1,314	1,422	1,032
Income as % of sales	—	8.6%	8.7%	9.2%	9.1%	9.1%	9.1%	9.1%	9.2%	9.2%	6.7%
Earnings per share ($)	5.5%	1.48	1.58	1.76	2.03	2.25	2.50	2.77	3.00	3.30	2.40
Stock price - FY high ($)	—	29.00	31.19	32.94	37.69	45.81	60.38	67.44	71.44	70.38	79.75
Stock price - FY low ($)	—	22.69	25.13	26.94	28.63	34.31	43.75	49.75	51.44	40.50	44.04
Stock price - FY close ($)	6.3%	27.25	29.44	29.81	35.75	45.06	57.63	62.25	63.19	67.00	47.06
P/E - high	—	20	20	16	18	20	24	24	24	21	33
P/E - low	—	15	16	13	14	15	17	18	17	12	18
Dividends per share ($)	9.3%	0.69	0.72	0.78	0.89	0.98	1.08	1.18	1.30	1.43	1.53
Book value per share ($)	6.4%	8.31	8.71	9.71	10.88	11.96	12.30	13.24	14.27	14.98	14.57
Employees	6.7%	69,400	71,600	73,900	78,900	86,400	100,700	111,800	116,900	123,400	124,500

STOCK PRICE HISTORY

HIGH/LOW/CLOSE

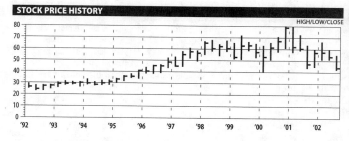

2001 FISCAL YEAR-END

Debt ratio: 26.9%
Return on equity: 16.5%
Cash ($ mil.): 356
Current ratio: 0.99
Long-term debt ($ mil.): 2,256
No. of shares (mil.): 420
Dividends
  Yield: 3.3%
  Payout: 63.8%
Market value ($ mil.): 19,748

ENCOMPASS SERVICES

Here's a company that really tries to cover it all. Formerly Group Maintenance America Corp. (GroupMAC), Houston-based Encompass Services is one of the largest facilities services company in the US, offering a broad range of outsourced electrical, mechanical, janitorial, and maintenance management services through its operations nationwide. The company offers its services in more than 200 locations, including the 100 largest US cities. Corporate clients include General Motors, WorldCom, and Wal-Mart.

Encompass has restructured by combining some of its groups and reorganizing into three main business segments: commercial/industrial services, residential services, and cleaning systems. Nearly 85% of the the company's sales come from its commercial/industrial services group. The group installs and repairs electrical, HVAC (heating, ventilation, and air-conditioning), plumbing, piping, and control systems for commercial and industrial facilities, including manufacturing plants, power generating plants, and office buildings. The company's residential services group provides mechanical, plumbing, and other services for homes, apartments, and condominiums. Encompass' cleaning systems group provides cleaning and maintenance services for a variety of facilities, including retail stores, banks, office buildings, and airport terminals.

Formed in 2000 through the merger of GroupMAC and Building One Services, the company soon eclipsed its rivals in both size and scope. However, the economic slump in the telecommunications and technology sectors has affected the company's sales, and it has discontinued its Maryland-based Global Technologies Group, which provided construction management for colocation facilities and telecom hotels.

Apollo Management controls about 25% of the company.

HISTORY

Houston investor Gordon Cain (founder of the buyout firm Sterling Group) teamed up with Richard Reiling, formerly of Republic Industries (now AutoNation) and Patrick Millinor to form Group Maintenance America Corp. (GroupMAC) in 1996. The group's aim was to consolidate the highly fragmented electrical and mechanical services industry — a sector dominated by more than 100,000 small, owner-operated companies offering limited service in small geographic areas. Its consolidation efforts sought to maximize group buying power, create training programs, and pursue national accounts for its services.

GroupMAC made its first acquisition in early 1997, buying Dayton, Ohio-based Airtron. Airtron was the first of 20 companies with combined sales of about $329 million to be swallowed that year. GroupMAC went public at the end of 1997, using the money for acquisition-related expenses. With most of its revenue coming from low-margin residential contracts, the company began to focus its acquisitions on firms doing more lucrative commercial and industrial work.

In 1998 GroupMAC gobbled up another 39 companies (with combined revenue of more than $700 million), including Texas-based Trinity Contractors. This move put the growing conglomerate past $1 billion in revenue, second only to Washington, DC-based Building One Services. In 1999, 13 more acquisitions (totaling more than $350 million in revenue) followed.

In 2000 GroupMAC merged with Building One to create the country's largest facilities services conglomerate. Founded in 1997, Building One Services Corporation focused on mechanical and electrical systems installation and maintenance services and janitorial and maintenance management services.

Renamed Encompass Services Corporation, the company sold more than $250 million in preferred stock to an affiliate of Apollo Management to help fund the deal, giving the investment firm 23% of Encompass. After the merger the company organized into Mechanical, Electrical/Communications, Industrial, Residential, Janitorial and Maintenance Management, and National Accounts Group business units.

Following the merger, Encompass continued to expand. The company signed a services sharing agreement with Service Resources, a leading provider of facilities management for the retail industry. Encompass also made a minority investment in OAKLEAF Waste Management, a provider of waste management and other services to retail outlets.

In 2001 Encompass launched its Encompass Edge campaign designed to introduce its new, unified brand to residential customers while allowing the local services companies to keep the names that were familiar to their customers. Feeling the effects of an economic downturn in 2001, Encompass decided to cease operations of its Global Technologies Group, which provided construction management services to telecom facilities, such as colocation facilities and Web-hosting centers. That year the group streamlined its operations by reorganizing into three main business segments: commercial/industrial services, residential services, and cleaning systems.

Chairman: J. Patrick Millinor Jr., age 55, $406,831 pay
President, CEO, and Director: Joseph M. Ivey Jr., age 43, $316,961 pay
EVP and COO: Henry P. Holland
SVP and CFO: Darren B. Miller
SVP, CIO, and Administrative Officer: Daniel W. Kipp
SVP, Secretary, and General Counsel: Gray H. Muzzy
SVP Business Solutions Group: James Phillips
SVP Midwest Business Group: James Cocca
SVP Southeast Business Group: Patrick L. McMahon
SVP Southwest Business Group: Ray Naizer
Group President, Cleaning Systems: Bill Hill
Group President, Residential Services: Steven A. Bate
VP Corporate Development: Scott Clingan
VP Marketing & Communications: Larry K. H. Jenkins
VP and Chief Accounting Officer: L. Scott Biar
VP and Treasurer: Todd Matherne
VP Taxes: Layne J. Albert
VP and Associate General Counsel: John A. Hale Jr.
VP and Associate General Counsel: Tony L. Visage
VP Human Resources: Steven C. Ronilo
Auditors: KPMG LLP

LOCATIONS

HQ: Encompass Services Corporation
3 Greenway Plaza, Ste. 2000, Houston, TX 77046
Phone: 713-860-0100   **Fax:** 713-626-4766
Web: www.encompserv.com

Encompass Services Corporation operates through more than 200 locations throughout the US.

PRODUCTS/OPERATIONS

2001 Sales

	$ mil.	% of total
Commercial/industrial services	3,298	84
Residential services	331	8
Cleaning systems	293	8
Adjustments	(17)	—
Total	**3,905**	**100**

COMPETITORS

ABM Industries
Chemed
Comfort Systems USA
EMCOR
Exelon
Integrated Electrical Services
Lennox
Quanta Services
Rentokil Initial
ServiceMaster

HISTORICAL FINANCIALS & EMPLOYEES

NYSE: ESR FYE: December 31	Annual Growth	12/92	12/93	12/94	12/95	12/96	12/97	12/98	12/99	12/00	12/01
Sales ($ mil.)	130.4%	—	—	—	—	—	139	762	1,548	4,099	3,905
Net income ($ mil.)	—	—	—	—	—	—	(4)	26	42	55	(51)
Income as % of sales	—	—	—	—	—	—	—	3.4%	2.7%	1.3%	—
Earnings per share ($)	—	—	—	—	—	—	(0.34)	0.93	1.11	0.63	(1.12)
Stock price - FY high ($)	—	—	—	—	—	—	17.19	20.63	15.44	10.63	9.80
Stock price - FY low ($)	—	—	—	—	—	—	13.00	10.31	7.00	3.25	1.23
Stock price - FY close ($)	(35.0%)	—	—	—	—	—	16.81	12.13	10.69	5.06	3.00
P/E - high	—	—	—	—	—	—	—	22	14	13	—
P/E - low	—	—	—	—	—	—	—	11	6	4	—
Dividends per share ($)	—	—	—	—	—	—	0.00	0.00	0.00	0.00	0.00
Book value per share ($)	12.5%	—	—	—	—	—	6.63	9.53	11.03	16.27	10.60
Employees	82.4%	—	—	—	—	—	2,800	9,000	30,000	34,000	31,000

STOCK PRICE HISTORY

HIGH/LOW/CLOSE

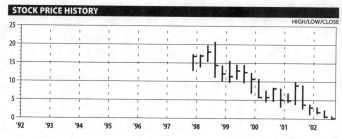

2001 FISCAL YEAR-END

Debt ratio: 54.5%
Return on equity: —
Cash ($ mil.): 21
Current ratio: 1.54
Long-term debt ($ mil.): 810
No. of shares (mil.): 64
Dividends
  Yield: —
  Payout: —
Market value ($ mil.): 191

ENGELHARD CORPORATION

Engelhard Corporation converts base materials into wealth — but no alchemy is involved. Based in Iselin, New Jersey, Engelhard has four major business segments. The largest, materials services, accounts for about 63% of sales and provides manufacturers with base and precious materials (gold, silver, and platinum), as well as related fabricated products. Its environmental technologies segment makes emission-control equipment (such as automotive catalysts). The company's process technologies segment makes catalysts and sorbents used to make a variety of chemicals; its appearance and performance technologies unit provides pigments and additives used in paper (kaolin-based materials), agricultural chemicals, cosmetics, and coatings (such as automobile finishes). Engelhard's biggest customer, the Ford Motor Company, accounts for more than 10% of sales.

Engelhard has been following a productivity and supply-chain initiative to decrease costs. While improving or eliminating peripheral businesses, the acquisitive company is focusing on expanding its bread-and-butter operations in materials services, environmental technologies, and chemical catalysts.

HISTORY

German immigrant Charles Engelhard came to the US in 1891 to work as a representative for a platinum marketer. In a short time he managed to acquire stakes in Baker & Co. (platinum), Irving Smelting (gold and silver), Hanovia, and a number of other precious-metals firms. In 1902 he set up Engelhard Industries as a precious-metals fabricator.

During the early 1900s Engelhard pioneered industrial uses of platinum (such as for lightbulb filaments) while meeting traditional demands in dentistry and ornamentation. But it wasn't until the 1920s that Engelhard secured a regular supply of the previously scarce element. Working with Inco, he became the Canadian mining firm's sole US platinum dealer. In the 1930s Engelhard, working with DuPont, invented a process to mass-produce nitric acid using a platinum and rhodium catalyst. That decade Engelhard benefited from the development of the platinum spinnerette (used in machines that produced synthetic fibers). Engelhard acquired D.E. Makepeace (gold and silver sheet), Amersil (fused quartz), and National Electric Instruments (medical instruments) in the 1940s.

Charles Engelhard Jr. set up his own company, Precious Metals Development, in South Africa in 1949, shortly before his father's death in 1950. He built his business exporting gold in the 1950s. With shipments of bullion banned, gold could be shipped internationally only in the form of art objects. Consequently, Engelhard's company made solid-gold plates, bracelets, and the like for export to markets where the gold was then melted down again. The flamboyant Engelhard, an acquaintance of Ian Fleming, is said to have been the model for the writer's Auric Goldfinger character.

Engelhard expanded its chemicals business in 1963 by buying 20% of Minerals & Chemicals Philipp (MCP), a producer of kaolin and fuller's earth owned by Philipp Brothers. In 1967 Engelhard and MCP merged to become Engelhard Minerals and Chemicals Corp. (EMCC).

The fast-growing Philipp Brothers spun off EMCC as Engelhard Corporation in 1981. During the 1980s much of Engelhard's revenues came from selling fluid catalytic cracking materials to the petroleum industry. Engelhard acquired Harshaw/Filtrol Partnership (pigments and additives) in 1988. The company won a contract in 1992 to produce Russia's first automotive catalytic converters. It opened factories in Germany (1994) and South Africa (1995) and introduced automotive catalysts in Europe and the US.

Engelhard acquired Mearl Corp. (pearlescent pigments and iridescent film) in 1996 for $272 million. That year automaker Ford pulled its support of Engelhard's development of a smog-eating car, claiming that the capacity of the Engelhard radiators to convert ozone into fresh air on contact was much overestimated.

The company formed a joint venture with UCAL Fuel Systems Ltd., called Engelhard Environmental Systems (India) Ltd., in 1997 to make automotive-emission catalysts in India. The next year Engelhard bought Mallinckrodt's catalyst businesses for $210 million. In 1999 Luxembourg-based Minorco sold its 32% stake in Engelhard. The same year Engelhard found itself the target of a Peruvian investigation into tax-fraud charges stemming from its gold operations in that country.

Engelhard sold its electroless gold-plating operations and its metal-joining products business in 2000. In 2001 the company launched a major expansion of its diesel-emission-control technologies in order to take advantage of new legislation passed by the US and Europe reducing emissions for heavy- and medium-duty diesel engines. In early 2002 Engelhard acquired the ceramic coating business of Pittsburgh-based O.Hommel Co.

OFFICERS

Chairman, President, and CEO: Barry W. Perry, age 55, $1,930,000 pay
VP and CFO: Michael A. Sperduto, age 44, $379,429 pay
VP and President, Engelhard Asia Pacific, Inc.:
George C. Hsu
VP, Corporate Communications: Mark Dresner, age 50
VP, General Counsel, and Secretary:
Arthur A. Dornbusch II, age 58, $499,895 pay
VP, Human Resources: John C. Hess, age 49,
$382,838 pay
VP, Investor Relations: Peter B. Martin, age 62,
$321,300 pay
VP, Mergers and Acquisitions: David M. Wexler
VP, Strategic Technologies and CTO: Edward T. Wolynic
Group VP and General Manager, Appearance and Performance Technologies: Stephen D. Lux
Group VP and General Manager, e-Business and Enterprise Processes: James A. Martin
Group VP and General Manager, Environmental Technologies: Edmund A. Stanczak Jr.
Group VP and General Manager, Materials Services:
Eric P. Martens
Group VP and General Manager, Process Technologies:
Victor L. Sprenger
Auditors: Ernst & Young LLP

LOCATIONS

HQ: 101 Wood Ave., Iselin, NJ 08830
Phone: 732-205-5000   **Fax:** 732-906-0337
Web: www.engelhard.com

Engelhard operates manufacturing facilities in Brazil, Canada, China, Finland, France, Germany, India, Italy, Japan, the Netherlands, Peru, Russia, South Africa, South Korea, Switzerland, the UK, and the US.

2001 Sales

	$ mil.	% of total
US	2,984	60
Other countries	2,113	40
Total	**5,097**	**100**

PRODUCTS/OPERATIONS

2001 Sales

	$ mil.	% of total
Materials services	3,208	63
Environmental technologies	647	13
Process technologies	634	12
Appearance & performance technologies	568	11
Other	40	1
Total	**5,097**	**100**

COMPETITORS

Akzo Nobel	Johnson Matthey
Anglo American	MacDermid
BASF AG	Minerals Technologies
Cambrex	NL Industries
Clariant	OM Group
Corning	Ondeo Nalco
Degussa	Penford
Dow Chemical	Siemens Power
Heraeus Holding	Generation
IMERYS	TOR
Imperial Chemical	

HISTORICAL FINANCIALS & EMPLOYEES

NYSE: EC FYE: December 31	Annual Growth	12/92	12/93	12/94	12/95	12/96	12/97	12/98	12/99	12/00	12/01
Sales ($ mil.)	8.7%	2,400	2,151	2,386	2,840	3,184	3,631	4,175	4,405	5,543	5,097
Net income ($ mil.)	40.5%	11	1	118	138	150	48	187	198	168	226
Income as % of sales	—	0.4%	0.0%	4.9%	4.8%	4.7%	1.3%	4.5%	4.5%	3.0%	4.4%
Earnings per share ($)	40.5%	0.08	0.00	0.82	0.94	1.03	0.33	1.29	1.47	1.31	1.71
Stock price - FY high ($)	—	16.24	19.96	21.01	32.50	26.13	23.75	22.81	23.69	21.50	29.20
Stock price - FY low ($)	—	9.27	12.90	13.92	14.92	17.88	17.06	15.75	16.25	12.56	18.25
Stock price - FY close ($)	6.8%	15.29	16.26	14.76	21.75	19.13	17.38	19.50	18.88	20.38	27.68
P/E - high	—	24	—	26	34	25	72	18	16	16	17
P/E - low	—	14	—	17	16	17	52	12	11	9	11
Dividends per share ($)	5.4%	0.25	0.28	0.31	0.35	0.36	0.38	0.40	0.40	0.40	0.40
Book value per share ($)	6.6%	4.38	3.69	4.31	5.13	5.79	5.43	6.29	6.07	6.91	7.77
Employees	0.9%	6,030	5,750	5,830	5,100	6,300	6,400	6,425	6,420	6,420	6,540

STOCK PRICE HISTORY

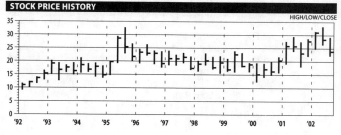

HIGH/LOW/CLOSE

2001 FISCAL YEAR-END

Debt ratio: 19.2%
Return on equity: 24.0%
Cash ($ mil.): 33
Current ratio: 1.00
Long-term debt ($ mil.): 238
No. of shares (mil.): 129
Dividends
  Yield: 1.4%
  Payout: 23.4%
Market value ($ mil.): 3,573

ENTERGY CORPORATION

Entergy is re-energizing its energy operations. The New Orleans-based holding company distributes power to nearly 2.6 million customers in Arkansas, Louisiana, Mississippi, and Texas and natural gas to nearly 240,000 customers in Louisiana. It has interests in regulated and nonregulated power plants in North America and Europe that have a combined generating capacity of more than 27,000 MW; it has sold its Latin American power plant interests.

Entergy is focused on increasing its generating capacity (to support its utilities and its growing marketing and trading operations) through new plant construction, primarily in the US and western Europe, and domestic nuclear plant acquisitions. The company is one of the largest nuclear power generators in the US. Its Entergy Wholesale Operations (EWO) subsidiary oversees plant development, and subsidiary Entergy Nuclear buys nukes and operates those owned by others. Entergy markets and trades energy in North America and Europe through its joint venture with conglomerate Koch Industries; it also has a joint venture with piping systems fabricator The Shaw Group that designs and builds power plants.

HISTORY

Arkansas Power & Light (AP&L, founded in 1913) consolidated operations with three other Arkansas utilities in 1926. Also that year, New Orleans Public Service Inc. (NOPSI, founded in 1922) merged with two other Big Easy electric companies. Louisiana Power & Light (LP&L) and Mississippi Power & Light (MP&L) were both formed in 1927, also through consolidation of regional utilities.

AP&L, LP&L, MP&L, NOPSI, and other utilities were combined into a Maine holding company, Electric Power and Light, which was dissolved in 1949. A new holding company, Middle South Utilities, emerged that year to take over the four utilities' assets.

In 1971 the company bought Arkansas-Missouri Power. In 1974 it brought its first nuclear plant on line and formed Middle South Energy (now System Energy Resources) to develop two more nuclear facilities, Grand Gulf 1 and 2. Unfortunately, Grand Gulf 1 was completed behind schedule and about 400% over budget. When Middle South tried to pass on the costs to customers, controversy ensued. Construction of Grand Gulf 2 was halted, and the CFO, Edwin Lupberger, took charge in 1985. Two years later, nuke-related losses took the company to the brink of bankruptcy.

The company moved to settle the disputes by absorbing a $900 million loss on Grand Gulf 2

in 1989. To distance itself from the controversy, Middle South changed its name to Entergy. In 1991 NOPSI settled with the City of New Orleans over Grand Gulf 1 costs.

That year Entergy, anticipating deregulation, branched out into nonregulated industries and looked abroad for growth opportunities. In 1993 a consortium including Entergy acquired a 51% interest in Edesur, a Buenos Aires electric utility. The next year Entergy signed a deal to build four power plants in China.

Entergy completed its acquisition of CitiPower, an Australian electric distributor, in 1996, and the next year it bought the UK's London Electricity.

But diversification had drained funds. Lupberger resigned in 1998, and a new management team began selling noncore businesses, such as CitiPower and London Electricity. It contracted out construction on two UK power plants, to be owned by Entergy, and moved into eastern Europe through a joint venture with Bulgaria's National Electricity Company. NYMEX began trading electricity futures in 1998, using Entergy and Cinergy as contract-delivery points.

In 1999 Wayne Leonard, Cinergy's former CFO, stepped in as Entergy's CEO. The company bought the Pilgrim nuclear reactor in Massachusetts, its first plant outside its utility territory, from BEC Energy (now NSTAR); it also contracted to operate the Nine Mile Point nuclear plants in New York. Entergy sold its security monitoring business and its interest in a telecom joint venture to partner Adelphia Business Solutions.

Entergy continued its push into the Northeast by buying two nuclear plants — Indian Point 3 and James Fitzpatrick — from the New York Power Authority for $967 million in 2000, and it announced that it would purchase Indian Point 1 and 2 from Consolidated Edison (completed in 2001). In 2001 the company agreed to buy the Vermont Yankee nuclear plant from a group of New England utilities.

Entergy agreed to merge with FPL Group in 2000, but the deal was called off the next year. The company also moved to expand through joint ventures. In 2000 Entergy and The Shaw Group, a piping systems fabricator, formed Entergy-Shaw, which designs and builds power plants. Entergy announced an agreement with Framatome to create a nuclear operations company, and in 2001 Entergy and Koch Industries formed an energy marketing and trading joint venture.

In 2002 Entergy sold its power plant interests in Argentina, Chile, and Peru to Southern Cone Power for $136 million.

OFFICERS

Chairman: Robert Luft, age 66
CEO and Director: J. Wayne Leonard, age 51,
$2,582,300 pay
President: Donald C. Hintz, age 59, $1,378,423 pay
EVP and CFO: C. John Wilder, age 43, $1,093,128 pay
EVP: Jerry D. Jackson, age 57, $1,051,727 pay
EVP, External Affairs: Curtis L. Hébert Jr., age 39
EVP, General Counsel, and Secretary:
Michael G. Thompson, age 61
**SVP, Generation, Transmission, and Energy
Management:** Frank F. Gallaher, age 56, $957,656 pay
SVP, Human Resources and Administration:
William E. Madison
SVP, Merger Integration: Tom Wright
SVP and Chief Accounting Officer: Nathan E. Langston,
age 53
SVP and General Tax Counsel: Joseph T. Henderson,
age 44
Chairman, President, and CEO, Entergy Nuclear:
Jerry W. Yelverton
Group President, Utility Operations: Richard Smith,
age 50
President and CEO, Entergy Arkansas: Hugh McDonald
President and CEO, Entergy Charitable Foundation:
Horace S. Webb
Auditors: Deloitte & Touche LLP

LOCATIONS

HQ: 639 Loyola Ave., New Orleans, LA 70113
Phone: 504-576-4000   **Fax:** 504-576-4428
Web: www.entergy.com

Entergy Corporation provides energy in Arkansas,
Louisiana, Mississippi, and Texas, and owns interests in
energy projects in Europe and North America.

PRODUCTS/OPERATIONS

2001 Sales

	% of total
Domestic utilities	
Electric	75
Natural gas	2
Competitive businesses	23
Total	**100**

Selected Subsidiaries
Energy Commodity Services
Entergy Arkansas, Inc. (electric utility)
Entergy Gulf States, Inc. (electric and gas utility)
Entergy Louisiana, Inc. (electric utility)
Entergy Mississippi, Inc. (electric utility)
Entergy New Orleans, Inc. (electric and gas utility)
Entergy Nuclear, Inc. (nuclear plant operation)
Entergy Operations Services, Inc. (plant management
services)
Entergy-Shaw, LLC (power plant construction joint
venture)
Entergy Solutions Ltd. (retail energy services)
System Fuels, Inc. (fuel storage and delivery to Entergy
utilities)

COMPETITORS

AEP	Constellation	Peabody Energy
AES	Energy Group	PG&E
AmerGen Energy	Dominion	Sempra Energy
Aquila	Duke Energy	Southern
Atmos Energy	El Paso	Company
Avista	El Paso Electric	TVA
CenterPoint	Exelon	TXU
Energy	Mirant	Williams
Cleco	OGE	Companies

HISTORICAL FINANCIALS & EMPLOYEES

NYSE: ETR FYE: December 31	Annual Growth	12/92	12/93	12/94	12/95	12/96	12/97	12/98	12/99	12/00	12/01
Sales ($ mil.)	9.9%	4,117	4,485	5,963	6,274	7,163	9,562	11,495	8,773	10,016	9,621
Net income ($ mil.)	6.2%	438	552	342	485	420	301	786	595	711	751
Income as % of sales	—	10.6%	12.3%	5.7%	7.7%	5.9%	3.1%	6.8%	6.8%	7.1%	7.8%
Earnings per share ($)	3.0%	2.48	3.16	1.49	2.13	1.83	1.03	3.00	2.25	2.97	3.23
Stock price - FY high ($)	—	33.63	39.88	37.38	29.25	30.50	30.25	32.44	33.50	43.88	44.67
Stock price - FY low ($)	—	26.13	32.50	21.25	20.00	24.88	22.38	23.25	23.69	15.94	32.56
Stock price - FY close ($)	1.9%	33.00	36.00	21.88	29.25	27.63	29.94	31.13	25.75	42.31	39.11
P/E - high	—	14	15	25	14	17	29	11	15	15	14
P/E - low	—	11	12	14	9	14	22	8	11	5	10
Dividends per share ($)	(1.4%)	1.45	1.65	1.80	1.80	1.80	1.80	1.50	1.20	1.22	1.28
Book value per share ($)	2.5%	28.46	32.81	32.33	32.60	32.49	32.06	32.35	33.02	33.72	35.41
Employees	2.1%	12,457	16,679	16,037	13,521	13,363	17,288	12,816	12,375	14,100	15,054

STOCK PRICE HISTORY HIGH/LOW/CLOSE

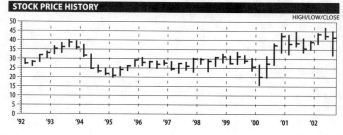

2001 FISCAL YEAR-END
Debt ratio: 49.0%
Return on equity: 10.4%
Cash ($ mil.): 752
Current ratio: 0.84
Long-term debt ($ mil.): 7,502
No. of shares (mil.): 221
Dividends
  Yield: 3.3%
  Payout: 39.6%
Market value ($ mil.): 8,633

EOTT ENERGY PARTNERS, L.P.

Crude oil is dirty stuff, but EOTT Energy Partners is willing to get it together and spread it around. The Houston-based public limited partnership is one of the largest independent gatherers and marketers of crude oil in North America. EOTT purchases about 329,600 barrels per day of crude oil, produced from about 30,000 leases in 19 US states and Canada. It buys mainly from independent producers (91%).

EOTT operates principally in the US's Gulf Coast, Southwest, Rocky Mountains, and mid-continent regions. Acting as an intermediary between supplier and buyer, it transports oil to refineries and other customers via 8,000 miles of pipelines and a fleet of 238 trucks.

The company's former parent, power giant Enron, effectively owns 37% of EOTT, including a 25% stake controlled by Enron's wholly owned subsidiary, EOTT Energy Corp., which is EOTT's general partner.

HISTORY

EOTT Energy Partners was originally a part of Enron, which emerged from the combination of Houston Natural Gas (HNG), formed in 1925, and InterNorth, formed in 1930.

HNG, once a South Texas natural gas distributor, started developing oil and gas fields in 1953. In 1984 Coastal Corp. tried to take over HNG. HNG brought in former Exxon executive Kenneth Lay as CEO to help fend off the bid. Lay shifted HNG's direction to natural gas production and exploration.

Over in Omaha, Nebraska, Northern Natural Gas was a gas pipeline company that started processing and transporting natural gas liquids in 1960. It changed its name to InterNorth in 1980; three years later it bought Belco Petroleum, giving it considerable natural gas and oil reserves.

When InterNorth bought HNG for $2.4 billion in 1985, the US's largest natural gas system (38,000 miles) was created. The next year Lay became CEO of the newly named Enron and moved its headquarters from Omaha to Houston.

Under Lay's direction, Enron bought crude oil terminals and gathering and transportation systems. In 1987 it acquired a terminal and transportation facility from Fairway Crude; a year later Tesoro's gathering and transportation businesses.

But Enron had bigger fish to fry, planning to become the first natural gas giant; it wanted to exit the volatile commodity and trading side of the business. In 1992 it announced the spin-off of Enron Oil Trading & Transportation Company, which brought in high revenues but few profits. In the meantime, Enron acquired Shell's eastern New Mexico oil pipeline system in 1993.

Finally in 1994, Enron combined Enron Oil Trading & Transportation, renamed EOTT Energy, with Enron Products Marketing Company and created EOTT Energy Partners as a public partnership. The IPO raised about $200 million. Philip Hawk took charge of the firm, which was one of the largest independent gatherers and marketers of crude oil in North America.

EOTT had troubles from the start; through the first half of 1995, it suffered through the worst industry refining margins in a decade. To stem the losses from its West Coast operation, EOTT renegotiated its contract with its key processor, Paramount Petroleum, agreeing to sell crude to Paramount and then market the fuel in exchange for a share of the revenues.

EOTT also made several acquisitions, including 600 miles of pipeline in Mississippi and Alabama from oil giant Amerada Hess in 1996 and the 1997 purchase of 400 miles of pipeline in Louisiana and Texas from CITGO.

The company lost money in 1997, and Hawk resigned the next year. He was replaced by venture capital consultant Michael Burke, who guided EOTT toward upgrading its communications and streamlining its business processes. It almost tripled its pipeline mileage with the 1998 acquisition of crude oil marketing and gathering operations from Koch Industries, and in 1999 EOTT bought 2,000 miles of pipeline and other assets from the Texas-New Mexico Pipe Line. The next year the company reported a $6.2 million loss resulting from an internal theft of natural gas liquids.

Chairman Stanley Horton, the CEO of the Enron Gas Pipeline Group, took over as EOTT's CEO in 2000 after Burke stepped down. (Horton was replaced by Thomas Mathews in 2002).

As part of the fall-out from the Enron collapse, Arthur Andersen withdrew as EOTT's auditor in 2002. That year, a financially troubled EOTT sold its West Coast refined products marketing business to Transammonia affiliate, Trammo Petroleum.

OFFICERS

Chairman: Thomas M. Mathews, age 58
President, CEO, COO, and Director: Dana R. Gibbs, age 42, $390,000 pay
SVP and CFO: Lawrence Clayton Jr., age 48, $300,000 pay
VP and Controller: Lori L. Maddox, age 37, $215,000 pay
VP and General Counsel: Molly M. Sample, age 46
VP Human Resources and Administration:
   Mary Ellen Coombe, age 51, $225,000 pay
Auditors: PricewaterhouseCoopers LLP

HQ: 2000 W. Sam Houston Pkwy. S., Ste. 400,
   Houston, TX 77042
Phone: 713-993-5200   **Fax:** 713-993-5821
Web: www.eott.com

EOTT Energy Partners operates in Canada and the US states of Alabama, Arkansas, California, Colorado, Florida, Kansas, Louisiana, Mississippi, Missouri, Montana, Nebraska, New Mexico, North Dakota, Oklahoma, South Dakota, Texas, Utah, and Wyoming.

PRODUCTS/OPERATIONS

2001 Sales

	$ mil.	% of total
North American crude oil (east of the Rockies)	8,112	92
West Coast operations	491	6
Pipeline operations	128	1
Liquids operations	49	1
Adjustments	(171)	—
Total	**8,609**	**100**

Selected Affiliated Limited Partnerships and Subsidiaries
EOTT Energy Canada Limited Partnership
EOTT Energy Financing Corp.
EOTT Energy Operating Limited Partnership
EOTT Energy Pipeline Limited Partnership

COMPETITORS

Amerada Hess
BP
ChevronTexaco
Devon Energy
Exxon Mobil
Genesis Energy
Imperial Oil
Kerr-McGee
Koch
Marathon Oil
Occidental Petroleum
PDVSA
PEMEX
Plains All American Pipeline
Royal Dutch/Shell Group
Sunoco
Sunoco Logistics
TEPPCO Partners
Unocal
Williams Companies

HISTORICAL FINANCIALS & EMPLOYEES

NYSE: EOT FYE: December 31	Annual Growth	12/92	12/93	12/94	12/95	12/96	12/97	12/98	12/99	12/00	12/01
Sales ($ mil.)	1.3%	7,697	6,359	4,557	5,088	7,470	7,646	5,295	8,664	11,614	8,609
Net income ($ mil.)	—	(19)	20	12	(61)	29	(14)	(4)	(1)	14	(15)
Income as % of sales	—	—	0.3%	0.3%	—	0.4%	—	—	—	0.1%	—
Earnings per share ($)	—	—	—	0.71	(3.54)	1.50	(0.75)	(0.21)	(0.02)	0.49	(0.54)
Stock price - FY high ($)	—	—	—	20.13	18.50	22.00	22.38	20.00	19.25	17.00	23.50
Stock price - FY low ($)	—	—	—	14.75	12.75	16.13	14.75	11.25	12.25	11.13	7.40
Stock price - FY close ($)	(0.2%)	—	—	15.25	18.25	21.88	17.13	15.75	13.00	16.38	15.05
P/E - high	—	—	—	28	—	15	—	—	—	35	—
P/E - low	—	—	—	21	—	11	—	—	—	23	—
Dividends per share ($)	11.6%	—	—	0.88	1.80	1.90	1.90	1.90	1.90	1.90	1.90
Book value per share ($)	(23.9%)	—	—	9.33	4.46	5.64	3.30	3.15	5.01	3.51	1.38
Employees	4.4%	—	850	900	800	828	966	1,500	—	1,200	1,200

STOCK PRICE HISTORY

HIGH/LOW/CLOSE

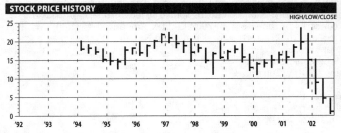

2001 FISCAL YEAR-END

Debt ratio: 86.3%
Return on equity: —
Cash ($ mil.): 3
Current ratio: 0.76
Long-term debt ($ mil.): 240
No. of shares (mil.): 27
Dividends
   Yield: 12.6%
   Payout: —
Market value ($ mil.): 414

EQUIFAX INC.

Equifax knows you. Yes, you.

As one of the US's largest consumer credit reporters (along with Experian and the Marmon Group's Trans Union), the Atlanta-based firm has the goods on some 400 million credit holders around the world. Equifax also provides database marketing consulting, and develops credit scoring software. Customers include retailers, insurance firms, hotels, banks, and other financial institutions.

Equifax has used new technologies to build a database of consumers and their behavior in the US and the developed world. Because its markets (particularly the US) are mature, Equifax is targeting such emerging markets as Latin America, where it is leading the US credit reporter charge. In these areas, the infrastructure for consumer credit reporting is nascent, but fast-growing economies have created a need for Equifax's services. The firm continues to expand its services and its reach through acquisitions.

HISTORY

Brothers Cator and Guy Woolford started Retail Credit Co. in Atlanta in 1899. They compiled credit records of local residents into their Merchants Guide, which they sold to retailers for $25 a year. The brothers extended their services to the insurance industry in 1901, investigating applicants' backgrounds. The company grew steadily and by 1920 had offices across the US and Canada. After several decades, Retail Credit branched into other information sectors, partly through acquisitions of regional credit reporters.

The company came under scrutiny in 1973 when the FTC filed an antimonopoly suit (dropped in 1982) against its consumer credit division and a complaint against its investigative practices (Retail Credit used field investigators to probe people's backgrounds). In 1976 the company became Equifax, short for "equitability in the gathering and presentation of facts."

In the 1980s and 1990s, Equifax continued to buy small businesses in the US and Europe. As the Information Age matured, businesses clamored for its services. By the end of the 1980s, Equifax had passed TRW (now part of Experian) as the largest provider of consumer information.

Receptive to consumer concerns in the late 1980s, the company ended list sales to US direct marketers and scrapped Marketplace, a 1991 joint venture with Lotus Development to compile a database of the shopping habits of 100 million Americans.

During the 1990s Equifax acquired regional credit and collection firms in Florida, Georgia, and Texas. It restructured in 1992, merging its US and Canadian operations, closing field offices, and expanding its international operations.

In 1992 and 1993 the company settled cases with several states over intrusive and inaccurate credit and job reference reports. The California State Lottery ended its scratch ticket terminal contract with an Equifax unit, claiming the subsidiary ran substandard operations. The contract was reinstated in 1995 after Equifax threatened to sue, but the lottery business left a bad impression on Equifax. In 1996 it subcontracted most of its contract obligations to GTECH.

Also in 1996 Equifax exited the health care information business. In 1997 it spun off its insurance services business as Choicepoint. As part of this effort it reassigned CDB Infotek (acquired in 1996) to ChoicePoint. After CDB was alleged to have improperly sold voter registration and social security number lists, shareholders wondered whether Equifax's management had been unaware of the supposed activities, or if it had bought CDB knowing that it could be assuming legal responsibility for them. Equifax spokespeople gave contradictory explanations. At least partially in response to these woes, Equifax helped launch a self-policing initiative for the industry.

Equifax has been building its Latin American business, buying the remaining 50% of South American credit company DICOM in 1997. It also bought 80% of Brazil's largest credit information firm, Seguranca ao Credito e Informacoes (1998), Chilean card processing firm Procard (2000), and one of Uruguay's largest credit information providers, Clearing de Informes (2001).

In 1999 the company entered the UK credit card market with a card processing contract with IKANO Financial Services. The next year it expanded its direct marketing prowess with its acquisition of R.L. Polk's consumer information database. Also in 2000 the company agreed to pay $500,000 to the FTC for blocking or not responding promptly enough to consumers' phone calls.

In 2001 the company spun off credit-card processing and check-management unit Certegy to shareholders, sold its city directory business (acquired in the R.L. Polk acquisition) to infoUSA, and underwent a restructuring that included cutting some 700 jobs, primarily outside the US. In 2002 Equifax announced it would buy direct marketing firm Naviant.

Chairman and CEO: Thomas F. Chapman, age 58,
$1,304,117 pay
President and COO: Mark E. Miller
EVP and Group Executive, Global Operations:
William V. Catucci, age 63, $409,616 pay
EVP and CFO: Philip J. Mazzilli, age 61, $472,135 pay
VP, Financial Administration: John T. Chandler, age 54
**Corporate Vice President and Chief Administration
Officer:** Karen H. Gaston, age 49, $405,600 pay
**Corporate Vice President and General Manager,
Consumer Direct:** Virgil P. Gardaya, age 55
VP, Investor Relations & Public Relations:
Mitchell J. Haws, age 38
VP, General Counsel, and Secretary: Kent E. Mast,
$430,889 pay
VP and Treasurer: Michael G. Schirk, age 52
Auditors: Ernst & Young LLP

LOCATIONS

HQ: 1550 Peachtree St. NW, Atlanta, GA 30309
Phone: 404-885-8000   **Fax:** 404-885-8988
Web: www.equifax.com

Equifax has operations in Argentina, Australia, Brazil,
Canada, Chile, El Salvador, Ireland, Peru, Portugal,
Spain, the UK, the US, and Uruguay.

2001 Sales

	$ mil.	% of total
North America	852	75
Equifax Europe	141	12
Equifax Latin America	107	9
Divested operations	29	3
Other	10	1
Total	**1,139**	**100**

PRODUCTS/OPERATIONS

Selected Subsidiaries
Acrofax Inc. (Canada)
AIF Srl (Italy)
CBI Ventures, Inc.
Compliance Data Center, Inc.
Computer Ventures, Inc.
The Database Company Ltd. (Ireland)
Equifax Canada Inc.
Equifax City Directory, Inc.
Equifax Consumer Services, Inc.
Equifax Decision Solutions, Inc.
Equifax Direct Marketing Solutions, Inc.
Equifax do Brasil Holdings Ltda. (Brazil)
Equifax Europe LLC
Equifax Global Online Inc.
Equifax Healthcare Information Services, Inc.
Equifax Information Technology, Inc.
Equifax Investment (South America) LLC
Equifax Investments (Mexico) Inc.
Equifax Plc (United Kingdom)
Equifax Properties, Inc.
Global Scan Ltd. (United Kingdom)
The Infocheck Group Ltd. (United Kingdom)
Infolink Ltd. (United Kingdom)
Propago S.A. (Chile)
Prospects Unlimited Canada Inc.
SEK S.r.l. (Italy)
UAPT-Infolink Plc (United Kingdom)
Verdad Informatica de Costa Rica, S.A.

COMPETITORS

D&B	First Data	Total System
Experian	Marmon Group	Services
Fair, Isaac	NOVA	

HISTORICAL FINANCIALS & EMPLOYEES

NYSE: EFX FYE: December 31	Annual Growth	12/92	12/93	12/94	12/95	12/96	12/97	12/98	12/99	12/00	12/01
Sales ($ mil.)	0.0%	1,134	1,217	1,422	1,623	1,811	1,366	1,621	1,773	1,966	1,139
Net income ($ mil.)	4.1%	85	64	120	148	178	184	193	216	228	123
Income as % of sales	—	7.5%	5.2%	8.5%	9.1%	9.8%	13.4%	11.9%	12.2%	11.6%	10.8%
Earnings per share ($)	6.0%	0.52	0.42	0.79	0.96	1.19	1.25	1.34	1.55	1.68	0.88
Stock price - FY high ($)	—	5.45	7.24	8.07	11.50	18.25	21.53	26.60	23.57	21.57	27.41
Stock price - FY low ($)	—	3.80	4.60	5.79	6.68	9.39	14.02	17.58	11.89	11.75	16.22
Stock price - FY close ($)	18.0%	5.45	7.24	6.98	11.31	16.20	20.94	20.20	13.93	16.95	24.15
P/E - high	—	10	17	10	12	15	17	19	15	13	31
P/E - low	—	7	11	7	7	8	11	13	8	7	18
Dividends per share ($)	(1.4%)	0.26	0.28	0.31	0.32	0.33	0.35	0.35	0.36	0.37	0.23
Book value per share ($)	(0.1%)	1.70	1.70	2.38	2.40	2.93	2.45	2.62	1.61	2.82	1.68
Employees	(9.2%)	12,400	12,800	14,200	13,400	14,100	10,000	14,000	12,700	12,200	5,200

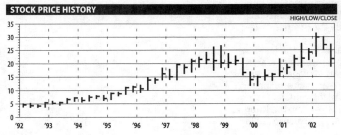

STOCK PRICE HISTORY
HIGH/LOW/CLOSE

2001 FISCAL YEAR-END
Debt ratio: 74.0%
Return on equity: 39.1%
Cash ($ mil.): 33
Current ratio: 1.30
Long-term debt ($ mil.): 694
No. of shares (mil.): 145
Dividends
  Yield: 1.0%
  Payout: 26.1%
Market value ($ mil.): 3,499

EQUITY GROUP INVESTMENTS

Equity Group Investments is the apex of financier Sam Zell's pyramid of business holdings. The Chicago-based private investment group controls a multi-billion-dollar mix of businesses, including real estate investment trusts (REITs), restaurants, and cruise ships. Zell's REITs are #1 in office property (Equity Office Properties Trust), apartments (Equity Residential Properties Trust), and land leased to manufactured home owners (Manufactured Home Communities). Equity Office Properties is one of the largest landlords in San Francisco and Seattle.

A prowess for finding and turning around distressed companies earned Zell the nickname "Grave Dancer." Equity Group Investments has rescued many companies floundering in bankruptcy and often buys during downturns. Many acquisitions are made through the Zell/Chilmark Fund. Zell's Equity Residential Properties continues to build its portfolio through acquisitions.

Zell has made forays into other investments with mixed success. He bought into sugar mills in Mexico that were nationalized by the government. Another holding, American Classic Voyages, suffered a combo of misfortune with the soft Hawaiian cruise industry on one side and the aftermath of September 11 on travel on the other. It has filed for Chapter 11 reorganization.

HISTORY

Sam Zell's first business endeavor was photographing his eighth-grade prom. In 1953 he graduated to reselling 50-cent *Playboy* magazines to schoolmates at a 200% markup.

While at the University of Michigan in the 1960s, Zell teamed with fraternity brother Robert Lurie to manage off-campus student housing. In graduate school, they invested in residential properties and formed Equity Financial and Management Co. after graduation. Their collection of distressed properties grew in the 1970s as Zell made the deals and Lurie made them work. Zell's hands-off management style had its drawbacks, however: In 1976 Zell and three others (including his brother-in-law) were indicted on federal tax-related charges after selling a Reno, Nevada, hotel and apartment complex. The charges were later dropped against Zell and another defendant (only the brother-in-law was convicted).

In the 1980s tax-law changes led the team to begin buying troubled companies. They started in 1983 with Great American Management and Investment, a foundering real estate manager they turned into an investment vehicle. Other targets included Itel (1984, now Anixter International) and oil and gas company Nucorp (1988,

now part of insurer CNA Surety). The true attraction in many of these acquisitions, however, lay in tax-loss carryforwards that could be applied against future earnings.

Lurie died in 1990, after which Zell began to consolidate his power and ease out old friends. (Lurie's estate still owns shares of many Zell enterprises.) That year Zell and David Schulte formed the Zell/Chilmark Fund, which soon owned or controlled such companies as Schwinn (sold 1997), Sealy (sold 1997), and Revco (sold 1997). Among the fund's failures was West Coast retailer Broadway Stores, which Zell bought out of bankruptcy in 1992; when California's slumping economy prevented a rapid turnaround, Zell sold it (once again near bankruptcy) in 1995.

Starting in 1987, Zell formed four real estate funds with Merrill Lynch; six years later, both Equity Residential Properties Trust and Manufactured Home Communities went public. As REITs became popular with investors, more trusts began vying for distressed assets — Zell's traditional lifeblood. In 1997 Zell melded four of his commercial real estate funds into another REIT, Equity Office Properties Trust, and took it public.

In 1998, as investors and financiers looked for fresh opportunities, Zell launched Equity International Properties, a fund targeting acquisitions in Latin America and elsewhere. That year a civil racketeering suit brought against Zell by former executive Richard Perlman shed light on "handshake" loans to top executives and other informal business deals. In 1999 Zell sold Jacor Communications to radio industry consolidator Clear Channel Communications. Equity Group Investments remains diversified, however: That year Equity Office Properties teamed with venture capital firm Kleiner Perkins Caufield & Byers to form Broadband Office to offer Internet and phone services to Zell's tenants and those of other property owners.

Equity Office Properties Trust has continued its buying, claiming New York-based Cornerstone Properties (2000) and California's Spieker Properties (2001).

Chairman: Samuel Zell, age 60
Co-Chairman: Sheli Z. Rosenberg, age 60
President: Donald J. Liebentritt, age 51

LOCATIONS

HQ: Equity Group Investments, L.L.C.
  2 N. Riverside Plaza, Ste. 600, Chicago, IL 60606
Phone: 312-454-1800   **Fax:** 312-454-0610

PRODUCTS/OPERATIONS

Selected Affiliates
American Classic Voyages Co. (36%, cruises)
Angelo & Maxie's, Inc. (38%, restaurants)
Anixter International, Inc. (14%, communications
  network equipment)
Capital Trust, Inc. (commercial real estate finance)
Davel Communications, Inc. (14%, pay-telephone
  operator)
Equity International Properties (overseas buyout fund)
Equity Office Properties Trust (4%, office property REIT)
Equity Residential Properties Trust (3%, apartments
  REIT)
Manufactured Home Communities, Inc. (15%, mobile
  home communities REIT)
Transmedia Network (40%, consumer savings programs)
Zell/Chilmark Fund L.P. (investment vulture fund)

COMPETITORS

Apollo Advisors
Blackstone Group
Carlyle Group
Clayton, Dubilier
Goldman Sachs
JMB Realty
KKR
Thomas Lee
Trump

ERNST & YOUNG INTERNATIONAL

Accounting may actually be the *second*-oldest profession, and Ernst & Young is one of the oldest practitioners. The New York-based concern, one of the world's largest accounting firms, has about 670 offices in about 130 countries.

The company's audit and accounting business provides internal audit, accounting advisory, and risk management services. The firm has one of the world's largest tax practices, serving the needs of multinational clients that have to comply with multiple local tax laws.

After spending most of the 1980s and 1990s building their consulting businesses, the big accountancies have all moved toward spinning off or otherwise shedding these operations, partly from internal pressures and partly because of the perceived conflict of interest in performing audits for clients who may also be large consulting customers. Ernst & Young was the first to split off its consultancy, selling it to France's Cap Gemini (now Cap Gemini Ernst & Young). The SEC since established new rules for disclosure fees paid to auditors, revealing the massive proportion of nonaudit fees and raising further conflict-of-interest concerns.

Ernst & Young is now following the industry trend in adding legal affiliates to provide more comprehensive professional services. The firm has assembled a team of more than 1,850 lawyers in some 60 countries to provide legal services. Ernst & Young also offers a variety of corporate finance, health, and entrepreneurial services.

HISTORY

When Luca Pacioli's *Summa di Arithmetica* was published in Venice in 1494 it was the first text on double-entry bookkeeping, but it was almost 400 years before accounting became a profession. In 1849 Frederick Whinney joined the UK firm of Harding & Pullein. Whinney's ledgers were so clear that he was advised to take up accounting, which was a growth field as stock companies proliferated. Whinney became a name partner in 1859 and his sons followed him into the business. The firm became Whinney, Smith & Whinney (WS&W) in 1894.

After WWII, WS&W formed an alliance with Ernst & Ernst (founded in Cleveland in 1903 by brothers Alwin and Theodore Ernst), with each firm operating on the other's behalf across the Atlantic. Whinney merged with Brown, Fleming & Murray in 1965 to become Whinney Murray. In 1979 Whinney Murray, Turquands Barton Mayhew (also a UK firm), and Ernst & Ernst merged to form Ernst & Whinney.

But Ernst & Whinney wasn't done merging. Ten years later, when it was the fourth-largest accounting firm, it merged with #5 Arthur Young, which had been founded by Scotsman Arthur Young in 1895 in Kansas City. Long known as "old reliable," Arthur Young fell on hard times in the 1980s because its audit relationships with failed S&Ls led to expensive litigation (ultimately settled in 1992 for $400 million).

Thus the new firm of Ernst & Young faced a rocky start. In 1990 it fended off rumors of collapse. The next year it slashed payroll, even thinning its partner roster. Exhausted by the S&L wars, in 1994 the firm replaced its pugnacious general counsel, Carl Riggio, with the more cost-conscious Kathryn Oberly.

In the mid-1990s Ernst & Young concentrated on consulting, particularly in software applications, and grew through acquisitions. It also entered new alliances that year with Washington-based ISD/Shaw, which provided banking industry consulting, and India's Tata Consulting, among others.

In 1997 Ernst & Young was sued for a record $4 billion for its alleged failure to effectively handle the 1993 restructuring of the defunct Merry-Go-Round Enterprises retail chain (it settled the suit for $185 million in 1999). On the heels of a merger deal between Coopers & Lybrand and Price Waterhouse, Ernst & Young agreed in 1997 to merge with KPMG International. But Ernst & Young called off the negotiations in 1998, citing the uncertain regulatory process they faced.

In 1999 Ernst & Young launched a worldwide media blitz aimed at raising awareness of the firm's full range of services, which that year included the company's new technology incubator. That year the firm reached a settlement in lawsuits regarding accounting errors at Informix and Cendant and sold its UK and Southern African trust and fiduciary businesses to Royal Bank of Canada (now RBC Financial Group).

In 2000 the firm became the first of the (then) Big Five firms to sell its consultancy, dealing it to France's Cap Gemini Group for about $11 billion. Later that year the company agreed to buy Washington Counsel, a lobbying firm. The company also started a venture to provide online financial advice with E*TRADE and spun off Intellinex, its online corporate training division.

The following year the UK accountancy watchdog group announced it would investigate Ernst & Young for its handling of the accounts of UK-based The Equitable Life Assurance Society. The insurer was forced to close to new business in 2000 because of massive financial difficulties.

In 2002 Ernst & Young formed an alliance with former New York City mayor Rudy Giuliani to help launch a business consultancy and an investment firm bearing the Giuliani name.

OFFICERS

Global Chairman and Chairman of the Americas Area: James Turley
CEO: William L. Kimsey
Americas CEO: Richard S. Bobrow
Vice Chairman for Law: Patrick Bignon
Vice Chairman Finance, Technology, and Administration: Hilton Dean
Vice Chairman Assurance and Advisory Services: John F. Ferraro
Vice Chairman Consulting Services: Antonio Schneider
Vice Chairman Human Resources: Lewis A. Ting
Vice Chairman Intrastructure: John G. Peetz Jr.
Vice Chairman Regional Integration and Entrepreneurial Growth Companies: Jean-Charles Raufast
Vice Chairman Regional Integration and Planning: Richard N. Findlater
Vice Chairman Tax and Legal Services: Andrew B. Jones
Executive Partner: Paul J. Ostling
General Counsel: Kathryn A. Oberly

LOCATIONS

HQ: 787 7th Ave., New York, NY 10019
Phone: 212-773-3000   **Fax:** 212-773-6350
Web: www.eyi.com

PRODUCTS/OPERATIONS

Selected Services

Assurance and Advisory
Actuarial services
Audits
Employee benefit plan services
Enterprise risk management and risk solutions
Fraud investigation
Internal audit

Corporate Finance
Capital markets advisory
Due diligence
IPO services
Litigation advisory
Mergers and acquisitions advisory
Restructuring advisory
Strategic finance
Valuation advisory

Health
Audit services
Consulting services
Emerging technologies
Tax services

Law
Antitrust, competition, and regulated marks advisory
Banking and securities advisory
Bankruptcy and insolvency assistance and advisory
Commercial and trade advisory and compliance
Corporate mergers and acquisitions advisory and compliance
E-commerce advisory and compliance
Employment advisory and compliance
Environmental advisory and compliance
Intellectual property advisory, protection, and compliance
Real estate/commercial property advisory and compliance

Tax
Consulting on tax consequences of business transactions and decisions
Economics and quantitative analysis
Financial statement effective tax rate management assistance
Global employment solutions
International tax
New tax laws and regulations impact analysis
Online tax advisor
Personal financial counseling
Tax planning
Tax return review and support
Transfer pricing

COMPETITORS

American Management
Bain & Company
BDO International
Deloitte Touche Tohmatsu
Grant Thornton
 International
IBM
KPMG
PricewaterhouseCoopers

HISTORICAL FINANCIALS & EMPLOYEES

Partnership FYE: June 30	Annual Growth	9/92	9/93	9/94	9/95	9/96	9/97	9/98	9/99	*6/00	6/01
Sales ($ mil.)	6.4%	5,701	5,839	6,020	6,867	7,800	9,100	10,900	12,500	9,500	10,000
Employees	4.6%	58,900	58,377	61,287	68,452	72,000	79,750	85,000	97,800	88,625	88,000

* Fiscal year change

SALES HISTORY

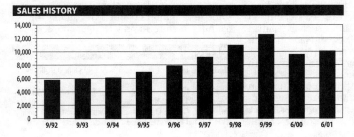

ESTÉE LAUDER COMPANIES

Estée Lauder's products must work: Its customers are getting younger. The New York City-based company, a world leader in upscale makeup, fragrances, and skin care products, captures nearly half of all US prestige cosmetics sales with its Estée Lauder, Clinique, Bobbi Brown *essentials*, and other well-known brands. Estée Lauder has expanded its customer base to include younger, trendier shoppers by acquiring the *jane* and M.A.C cosmetics lines.

Not only has the company expanded its customer base, it has also expanded its distribution channels to include mass merchandisers and salons. The company also has more than 300 free-standing stores, primarily for its M.A.C, Aveda, and Origins lines, and plans to add more. In fact, the company is planning a gradual shift of up to 20% of its business from department stores (which account for 80% of sales) to its own stores and other outlets. Its Origins Internet presence has expanded, too: Clinique, Origins, and Bobbi Brown *essentials* now sell products online, and its long-delayed gloss.com launched in October 2001. Estée Lauder's prestige fragrances (Beautiful), #1 in the US, have been global successes; other fragrances include Tommy Hilfiger and DKNY.

The company's products are available in more than 120 countries. The founding Lauder family owns about 54% of the common stock but controls just over 90% of the voting stock.

HISTORY

Estée Lauder (then Josephine Esther Mentzer) started her beauty career by selling skin care products formulated by her Hungarian uncle, John Schotz, during the 1930s. Eventually she packaged and peddled her variations of his formulas, which included face cream and a cleansing oil.

With the help of her husband, Joseph Lauder, she set up her first office in Queens, New York, in 1944, and added lipstick, eye shadow, and face powder to the line. Joseph oversaw production, and Estée sold her wares to beauty salons and department stores, using samples and gifts to win customers. Throughout the 1950s Estée traveled cross-country, at first to sell her line to high-profile department stores such as Neiman Marcus, I. Magnin, and Saks, and later to train saleswomen in these stores.

Estée Lauder created her first fragrance, Youth Dew perfume and bath oil, in 1953. In the late 1950s US cosmetics firms introduced European skin care lines with scientific names and supposedly advanced skin repair properties. Estée Lauder's contribution was Re-Nutriv cream, which sold for $115 a pound in 1960. The cream's advertising campaign established the sophisticated "Lauder look" — an image that Estée herself cultivated.

In 1964 Estée Lauder introduced Aramis, a fragrance for men, and in 1968, with the help of a *Vogue* editor, it launched Clinique, a hypoallergenic skin care line. In 1972 Estée's son Leonard became president; Estée remained CEO.

Estée Lauder created the Prescriptives skin care and makeup line for young professional women in 1979. Leonard was named CEO in 1983. By 1988 the company had captured a third of the US market in prestige cosmetics.

Estée Lauder unveiled its Origins botanical cosmetics line in 1990. The company launched the All Skins cosmetics line in 1991 and in 1994 bought a controlling stake in hip Make-Up Art Cosmetics (M.A.C).

Leonard became chairman in 1995. The company's IPO that year was structured to allow Estée and her son Ronald (previously an unsuccessful candidate for mayor of New York) to avoid a potential $95 million tax bill (inspiring a 1997 revision of the federal tax law). Filling out a very busy year, Estée Lauder acquired the Bobbi Brown *essentials* line of cosmetics, bought botanical beauty products concern Aveda for $300 million (broadening distribution into hair salons), and entered the mass market with its purchase of Sassaby (*jane* cosmetics) in 1997. In 1998 Estée Lauder, despite potential conflict with the retailers on which it depends, launched a Clinique products Web site.

In 1999 Estée Lauder bought rapidly growing Stila Cosmetics and Jo Malone Limited, a London-based seller of some 200 skin care and fragrance products. Company president Fred Langhammer succeeded Leonard Lauder as CEO in 2000; Leonard Lauder remained chairman.

Also in 2000 Estée Lauder bought a majority interest in Bumble and Bumble, a hair salon and products company. The company delayed the full launch of online beauty site gloss.com until October 2001; the new multi-brand Web site (with Clarins and Chanel) features all of the company's cosmetic brands. In 2002 Estée Lauder restructured by outsourcing gloss.com and closing some distribution channels, including the remaining in-store Tommy Hilfiger shops.

OFFICERS

Chairman: Leonard A. Lauder, age 68, $6,800,000 pay
Vice Chairman: Jeanette S. Wagner, age 71
President, CEO, and Director: Fred H. Langhammer, age 57, $4,300,000 pay
President, Global Operations: Edward M. Straw
EVP, Global Marketing and Finance: Eunice Valdivia

Senior Corporate VP: Evelyn H. Lauder
SVP and CFO: Richard W. Kunes
SVP and General Manager, Clinique North America:
Thia Breen
SVP, General Counsel, and Secretary: Paul E. Konney
SVP, Global Human Resources: Andrew J. Cavanaugh
SVP, Global Marketing, Estée Lauder: Peter Lichtenthal
**Chairman, Clinique Laboratories and Estée Lauder
International and Director:** Ronald S. Lauder, age 57
President, Aramis and Designer Fragrance Brands:
John Bretton Karp
President, Bobbi Brown Worldwide: Rochelle Bloom
President, Clinique Laboratories and Director:
William P. Lauder, age 41, $1,830,000 pay
President, Estée Lauder International:
Patrick Bousquet-Chavanne, $2,558,000 pay
Auditors: KPMG LLP

LOCATIONS

HQ: The Estée Lauder Companies Inc.
767 5th Ave., New York, NY 10153
Phone: 212-572-4200 **Fax:** 212-572-6633
Web: www.elcompanies.com

Estée Lauder sells its products in more than 120
countries and operates plants and research facilities in
Australia, Belgium, Canada, Japan, South Africa,
Switzerland, the UK, and the US.

2002 Sales

	$ mil.	% of total
The Americas	2,878	61
Europe, Middle East, Africa	1,261	26
Asia/Pacific	611	13
Restructuring	(6)	—
Total	**4,744**	**100**

PRODUCTS/OPERATIONS

2002 Sales

	$ mil.	% of total
Skin care	1,791	38
Makeup	1,703	36
Fragrance	1,017	21
Hair care	216	5
Other	23	—
Restructuring	(6)	—
Total	**4,744**	**100**

Selected Brands

Aramis	Kate Spade (licensed)
Aveda	La Mer
Bobbi Brown *essentials*	M.A.C
Bumble and Bumble	Origins
Clinique	Pleasures
Donna Karan (licensed)	Pleasures Intense
Estée Lauder	Prescriptives
jane	Stila
Jo Malone	Tommy Hilfiger (licensed)

COMPETITORS

Alberto-Culver	Chanel	Neiman Marcus
Allou	Clarins	New Dana
Alticor	Coty	Perfumes
Artemis	E Com Ventures	Procter &
Avon	The Gap	Gamble
Bath & Body	Helen of Troy	Revlon
Works	Inter Parfums	Shiseido
BeautiControl	Intimate Brands	Tristar
Cosmetics	Joh. A. Benckiser	Unilever
Body Shop	L'Oréal	Wella
Bristol-Myers	LVMH	
Squibb	Mary Kay	

HISTORICAL FINANCIALS & EMPLOYEES

NYSE: EL FYE: June 30	Annual Growth	6/93	6/94	6/95	6/96	6/97	6/98	6/99	6/00	6/01	6/02
Sales ($ mil.)	7.6%	2,448	2,576	2,899	3,195	3,382	3,618	3,961	4,367	4,608	4,744
Net income ($ mil.)	14.2%	58	70	121	160	198	237	273	314	305	192
Income as % of sales	—	2.4%	2.7%	4.2%	5.0%	5.8%	6.5%	6.9%	7.2%	6.6%	4.0%
Earnings per share ($)	2.9%	—	—	—	0.59	0.73	0.89	1.03	1.20	1.16	0.70
Stock price - FY high ($)	—	—	—	—	22.00	26.75	36.97	51.50	56.50	49.75	43.55
Stock price - FY low ($)	—	—	—	—	15.88	17.38	19.50	23.34	37.25	33.18	29.25
Stock price - FY close ($)	8.9%	—	—	—	21.13	25.13	34.84	50.13	49.44	43.10	35.20
P/E - high	—	—	—	—	37	37	41	49	46	42	56
P/E - low	—	—	—	—	27	24	22	22	31	28	38
Dividends per share ($)	40.8%	—	—	—	0.09	0.17	0.17	0.18	0.20	0.20	0.70
Book value per share ($)	12.2%	—	—	—	3.21	3.84	4.46	5.42	6.39	5.67	6.39
Employees	6.1%	12,000	10,000	9,900	13,500	14,700	15,300	17,700	18,000	19,900	20,400

STOCK PRICE HISTORY

HIGH/LOW/CLOSE

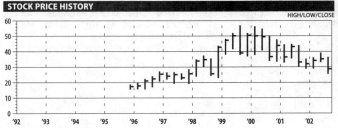

2002 FISCAL YEAR-END

Debt ratio: 21.6%
Return on equity: 15.1%
Cash ($ mil.): 547
Current ratio: 2.01
Long-term debt ($ mil.): 404
No. of shares (mil.): 238
Dividends
  Yield: 0.6%
  Payout: 25.6%
Market value ($ mil.): 8,364

E*TRADE GROUP, INC.

E*TRADE Group wants you to use its services for E*VERYTHING financial. Facing a downturn in online trading volumes, the Menlo Park, California-based company is diversifying its services through a buying spree. It boasts four global divisions (North America, Latin America, Asia-Pacific, and Europe, Africa, and the Middle East) focused on such key operations as retail and institutional brokerage, residential mortgages, banking and asset gathering, and insurance.

One of the top online brokerages (with Charles Schwab and Fidelity), the firm offers trading services via online services, the Internet (the majority of transactions), and the phone to more than 3 million clients. E*TRADE also offers market data, cash and portfolio management, and options and fund trading.

But E*TRADE isn't resting on its online trading laurels. Its E*TRADE Bank offers deposits, loans, credit cards, insurance, and other services online and through more than 10,000 ATMs across the US (although its banking clients are concentrated in major US cities). E*TRADE continues to extend its global network through alliances, such as one to provide ATMs and staffed locations inside Target stores. It has opened its inaugural bricks-and-mortar E*TRADE Center, a financial superstore in New York City. E*TRADE has also entered the stock market-making game with its acquisition of Chicago-based specialist firm Dempsey & Company.

The firm's asset-gathering segment includes mutual fund sales and eAdvisor, the financial advice venture it shares with Ernst & Young. E*TRADE is also targeting affluent individuals, offering premium trading and money management services through such subsidiaries as PrivateAccounts.com. SOFTBANK owns about 20% of the company, but plans to sell its share.

The fallout in Internet stocks packed a one-two punch for the firm: Not only did its stock fall, but online traders cut their use of its service. The company continues to expand its services to make up for shortfalls in its trading income, which accounts for the majority of its revenues.

HISTORY

In 1982 physicist William Porter created Trade Plus, an electronic brokerage service for stockbrokers; clients included Charles Schwab & Co. and Fidelity Brokerage Services. A decade later subsidiary E*TRADE Securities became CompuServe's first online securities trader.

In 1996 E*TRADE moved from the institutional side to retail when it launched its Web site. Christos Cotsakos (a Vietnam and FedEx veteran) became CEO and took the firm public.

But there were problems: E*TRADE covered $1.7 million in customer losses and added backup systems after computer failure stymied user access. In 1997 it formed alliances with America Online and BANK ONE and ended the year with 225,000 accounts.

The firm began to position itself globally in 1997 and 1998, opening sites for Australian, Canadian, German, Israeli, and Japanese customers. It offered its first IPO (Sportline USA) in 1997. Volume grew as Internet trading increased, but technical glitches dogged E*TRADE. In 1999 day trading became fashionable and the company began running ads promoting prudent trading to counter criticism that online trading fosters a get-rich-quick mentality.

The company also continued to add services. In 1999 it teamed with Garage.com to offer affluent clients venture capital investments in young companies and launched online investment bank E*OFFERING with former Robertson Stephens & Co. chairman Sanford Robertson. (E*TRADE sold its stake in the bank to Wit Soundview — now SoundView Technology Group — the next year). It also bought TIR Holdings, which executes and settles multi-currency securities transactions.

Retail banking was a major focus in 2000. The company bought Telebanc Financial (now E*TRADE Financial), owner of Telebank, an online bank with more than 100,000 depositors, and started E*TRADE Bank, which offers retail banking products on the E*TRADE Web site. To provide clients with "real-world" access to their money, it bought Card Capture Services (now E*TRADE Access), an operator of more than 9,000 ATMs across the US.

Continuing to expand its global reach, E*TRADE bought the part of its E*Trade UK joint venture it didn't already own; acquired Canadian firm VERSUS Technologies, a provider of electronic trading services; and teamed with UBS Warburg to allow non-US investors to buy US securities without needing to trade in dollars. Later its E*Trade International Capital announced plans to offer IPOs to European investors.

In 2001 E*TRADE entered consumer lending when it bought online mortgage originator LoansDirect (now E*TRADE Mortgage). That year it moved to the NYSE and announced it may begin bond underwriting. The company's E*TRADE Bank made plans to buy 33,000 accounts from Chase Manhattan Bank USA.

Chairman and CEO: Christos M. Cotsakos, age 53, $4,924,285 pay
President and Chief Customer Operations Officer: Jerry Gramaglia, age 46, $921,302 pay
CFO and Chief Administrative Officer: Leonard C. Purkis, age 53, $745,756 pay
Chief Brokerage Officer and Managing Director, Asia Pacific and Latin America: Robert Jarrett Lilien, age 40, $1,438,859 pay
Chief Financial Products Officer and Managing Director, North America: Mitchell H. Caplan, age 44
Chief Legal Affairs and Human Resources Officer: Russ Elmer
Chief Community Relations Officer and Corporate Secretary: Brigitte VanBaelen, age 33
CTO and Managing Director, Europe, Africa, and the Middle East: Joshua Levine, age 48, $619,726 pay
Chief Communications and Knowledge Officer: Connie M. Dotson, age 52
Chief Strategic Investment Officer: Thomas A. Bevilacqua
Chief Content Development Officer: Pamela S. Kramer, age 41
Chief Government Affairs Officer: Betsy Barclay, age 50
Auditors: Deloitte & Touche LLP

LOCATIONS

HQ: 4500 Bohannon Dr., Menlo Park, CA 94025
Phone: 650-331-6000   **Fax:** 650-331-6804
Web: www.etrade.com

E*Trade has operations in Africa, Asia, Europe, and North America.

PRODUCTS/OPERATIONS

2001 Sales

	$ mil.	% of total
Interest	1,160	57
Transactions	407	20
Sale of investments	171	8
Global & institutional	153	8
Other	144	7
Total	**2,035**	**100**

COMPETITORS

All-Tech Direct
Ameritrade
Charles Schwab
Datek Online
FMR
Harrisdirect
JB Oxford Holdings
Merrill Lynch
Morgan Stanley
NetBank
Quick & Reilly/Fleet
Siebert Financial
TD Waterhouse
UBS PaineWebber

HISTORICAL FINANCIALS & EMPLOYEES

NYSE: ET FYE: December 31	Annual Growth	9/92	9/93	9/94	9/95	9/96	9/97	9/98	9/99	9/00	*12/01
Sales ($ mil.)	137.4%	1	3	11	23	54	158	285	662	2,202	2,035
Net income ($ mil.)	—	(0)	0	1	3	(1)	14	(1)	(54)	19	(242)
Income as % of sales	—	—	3.4%	7.3%	11.1%	—	8.8%	—	—	0.9%	—
Earnings per share ($)	—	—	—	—	—	(0.01)	0.11	(0.01)	(0.23)	0.06	(0.73)
Stock price - FY high ($)	—	—	—	—	—	3.47	11.97	11.94	72.25	40.00	15.38
Stock price - FY low ($)	—	—	—	—	—	2.06	2.19	3.91	2.50	13.13	4.07
Stock price - FY close ($)	25.4%	—	—	—	—	3.30	11.75	4.67	23.50	16.44	10.25
P/E - high	—	—	—	—	—	—	100	—	—	667	—
P/E - low	—	—	—	—	—	—	18	—	—	219	—
Dividends per share ($)	—	—	—	—	—	0.00	0.00	0.00	0.00	0.00	0.00
Book value per share ($)	49.5%	—	—	—	—	0.59	1.82	3.14	3.81	6.10	4.39
Employees	107.0%	5	20	44	115	327	499	833	1,735	3,800	3,495

* Fiscal year change

STOCK PRICE HISTORY

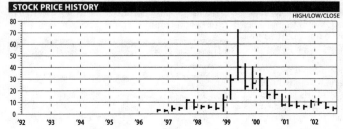

HIGH/LOW/CLOSE

2001 FISCAL YEAR-END

Debt ratio: 76.1%
Return on equity: —
Cash ($ mil.): —
Current ratio: —
Long-term debt ($ mil.): 5,000
No. of shares (mil.): 358
Dividends
  Yield: —
  Payout: —
Market value ($ mil.): 3,672

THE E. W. SCRIPPS COMPANY

One of the oldest newspaper chains in the US, The E. W. Scripps Company has helped shape journalism for more than a century. The Cincinnati-based company's portfolio includes 21 daily newspapers (*Denver Rocky Mountain News, The Commercial Appeal* of Memphis) with a combined circulation of about 1.4 million. Scripps also owns a handful of community newspapers (publishing weekly or semiweekly) and operates the Scripps Howard News Service, a wire service covering US and international news.

While newspapers generate half of the company's revenue, Scripps' 10 TV stations bring in about 20%. Scripps also is active in cable TV through its ownership of Home & Garden Television (HGTV) and the Do It Yourself Network, as well as stakes in the Food Network (68%) and FOX Sports South (12%). It has launched a new channel, Fine Living, which is aimed at affluent households. Through United Media, Scripps' licensing and syndication arm, the company syndicates more than 150 comic strips, including *Dilbert* and the legendary *Peanuts*.

With its foothold in traditional media firmly established, Scripps is looking to broaden its profile in cable TV programming and is stepping up its efforts to boost distribution of HGTV and the Food Network. Along those lines, the company has acquired a 70% stake in cable TV network Shop at Home, the fourth-largest TV home shopping network.

Trusts benefiting members of the Scripps family own about 84% of the company.

HISTORY

Edward Willis "E. W." Scripps launched a newspaper empire in 1878 with his creation of *The Penny Press* in Cleveland. While adding to his string of inexpensive newspapers, Scripps demonstrated his fondness for economy by shunning "extras" such as toilet paper and pencils for his employees.

In 1907 Scripps gave the Associated Press a new rival, combining three wire services to form United Press. E. W. Scripps' health began deteriorating in the 1920s, and Roy Howard was named chairman. Howard's contribution to the burgeoning media enterprise soon was acknowledged when the company's name was changed to the Scripps Howard League. E. W. Scripps died in 1926, leaving a newspaper chain second in size only to Hearst.

In the 1930s Scripps made a foray into radio, buying WCPO (Cincinnati) and KNOX (Knoxville, Tennessee). Roy Howard placed his son Jack in charge of Scripps' radio holdings; under Jack's leadership, Scripps branched into TV. Its first TV station, Cleveland's WEWS, began broadcasting in 1947. Scripps also made Charlie Brown a household name when it launched the *Peanuts* comic strip in 1950. By the time Charles Scripps (E. W. Scripps' grandson) became chairman and Jack Howard was appointed president in 1953, the company had amassed 19 newspapers and a handful of radio and TV stations.

United Press merged with Hearst's International News Service in 1958 to become United Press International (UPI). In 1963 Scripps took its broadcasting holdings public as Scripps Howard Broadcasting Company (Scripps retained controlling interest). Scripps Howard Broadcasting expanded its TV station portfolio in the 1970s and 1980s, buying KJRH (Tulsa, Oklahoma; 1971), KSHB (Kansas City, Missouri; 1977), KNXV (Phoenix; 1985), WFTS (Tampa; 1986), and WXYZ (Detroit; 1986).

With UPI facing mounting losses, Scripps sold the news service in 1982. Under leadership of chief executive Lawrence Leser, Scripps began streamlining, jettisoning extraneous investments and refocusing on its core business lines. In 1988 after decades of family ownership, the company went public as The E. W. Scripps Company (the Scripps family retained a controlling interest).

In 1994 Scripps Howard Broadcasting merged back into E. W. Scripps Company. That year Scripps branched into cable TV when its Home & Garden Television network went on the air. Former newspaper editor William Burleigh became CEO in 1996. Scripps' 1997 purchase of the newspaper and broadcast operations of Harte-Hanks Communications marked the largest acquisition in its history. Scripps promptly traded Harte-Hanks' broadcasting operations for a controlling interest in the Food Network.

Scripps sold television production unit Scripps Howard Productions in 1998. The company sold its Dallas Community Newspaper Group in 1999. In 2000 Scripps' financially struggling *Denver Rocky Mountain News* entered into a joint operating agreement with rival *The Denver Post* (owned by MediaNews). Justice Department approval of the agreement is pending. It launched cable channel Fine Living, aimed at affluent households, in 2002. That year, the company shuttered its Scripps Ventures fund, which invested in Internet and online commerce businesses.

OFFICERS

Chairman: William R. Burleigh, age 66
President, CEO, COO, and Director: Kenneth W. Lowe, age 51, $800,000 pay
EVP: Richard A. Boehne, age 45, $515,000 pay
SVP: Frank Gardner, age 59, $510,000 pay
SVP Newspapers: Alan M. Horton, age 58, $510,000 pay

SVP and CFO: Joseph G. NeCastro, age 45
SVP Television: John F. Lansing, age 44
VP and CTO: B. Jeff Craig, age 43
VP Finance and Treasurer: E. John Wolfzorn, age 56
VP and Controller: Lori Hickok, age 39
VP, Corporate Secretary, and Director of Legal Affairs: M. Denise Kuprionis, age 45
VP Corporate Development: Tim Peterman
VP Engineering: Michael Doback
VP Human Resources: Gregory L. Ebel, age 46
VP Investor Relations and Communications: Timothy E. Stautberg, age 39
VP Newspaper Operations: Stephen W. Sullivan, age 55
President, Do-It-Yourself Network: Jim Zarchin
President, The Food Network: Judy Girard
President, Home and Garden Television: Burton Jablin
President, New Ventures Group: Susan Packard
Auditors: Deloitte & Touche LLP

LOCATIONS

HQ: 312 Walnut St., Cincinnati, OH 45202
Phone: 513-977-3000 **Fax:** 513-977-3721
Web: www.scripps.com

PRODUCTS/OPERATIONS

2001 Sales

	$ mil.	% of total
Newspapers	739	52
Scripps Networks	337	23
Broadcast television	278	19
Licensing & other media	89	6
Adjustment	(6)	—
Total	**1,437**	**100**

Selected Daily Newspapers
Abilene Reporter-News (Texas)
The Albuquerque Tribune (New Mexico)
Birmingham Post-Herald (Alabama)
The Cincinnati Post (includes *The Kentucky Post*)
The Commercial Appeal (Memphis)
Corpus Christi Caller-Times (Texas)
Daily Camera (Boulder, CO)
Denver Rocky Mountain News
The Knoxville News-Sentinel (Tennessee)

Selected TV Stations
KNXV (ABC; Phoenix)
KSHB (NBC; Kansas City, MO)
WCPO (ABC; Cincinnati)
WEWS (ABC; Cleveland)
WFTS (ABC; Tampa)
WMAR (ABC; Baltimore)
WXYZ (ABC; Detroit)

Selected Cable Operations
Food Network (68%)
FOX Sports South (12%)
Home & Garden Television

Other Operations
Scripps Howard News Service (wire news service)
United Media (licensing and syndication)

COMPETITORS

Advance Publications	Dow Jones	MediaNews
Associated Press	Freedom Communications	New York Times
Belo	Gannett	News Corp.
Copley Press	Hearst	Reuters
Cox Enterprises	Knight Ridder	Tribune
Discovery Communications	Liberty Media	Viacom
	Media General	Walt Disney

HISTORICAL FINANCIALS & EMPLOYEES

NYSE: SSP FYE: December 31	Annual Growth	12/92	12/93	12/94	12/95	12/96	12/97	12/98	12/99	12/00	12/01
Sales ($ mil.)	1.4%	1,263	1,206	1,220	1,030	1,122	1,242	1,455	1,571	1,719	1,437
Net income ($ mil.)	2.9%	106	129	123	94	157	158	131	147	164	138
Income as % of sales	—	8.4%	10.7%	10.1%	9.1%	14.0%	12.7%	9.0%	9.3%	9.5%	9.6%
Earnings per share ($)	(2.5%)	—	—	—	—	1.96	1.93	1.62	1.86	2.06	1.73
Stock price - FY high ($)	—	—	—	—	—	35.25	48.94	58.50	53.00	63.25	71.70
Stock price - FY low ($)	—	—	—	—	—	32.75	32.25	38.50	40.50	42.38	54.70
Stock price - FY close ($)	13.5%	—	—	—	—	35.00	48.44	49.75	44.81	62.88	66.00
P/E - high	—	—	—	—	—	18	25	35	28	30	41
P/E - low	—	—	—	—	—	17	16	23	22	20	31
Dividends per share ($)	—	—	—	—	—	0.00	0.39	0.54	0.56	0.56	0.60
Book value per share ($)	7.9%	—	—	—	—	11.70	13.01	13.61	14.90	16.23	17.07
Employees	(1.1%)	8,200	7,600	7,700	6,700	6,800	8,100	7,900	8,000	9,600	7,400

STOCK PRICE HISTORY
HIGH/LOW/CLOSE

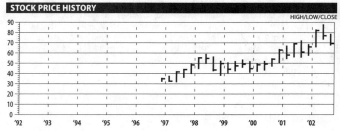

2001 FISCAL YEAR-END
Debt ratio: 7.5%
Return on equity: 10.5%
Cash ($ mil.): 17
Current ratio: 0.50
Long-term debt ($ mil.): 110
No. of shares (mil.): 79
Dividends
  Yield: 0.9%
  Payout: 34.7%
Market value ($ mil.): 5,227

EXELON CORPORATION

The City of Brotherly Love meets the Windy City in utility holding company Exelon, which was formed in 2000 when Philadelphia-based PECO Energy bought Chicago-based Unicom. The company, based in Chicago, distributes electricity to 5 million customers: 3.6 million in Northern Illinois, through Commonwealth Edison (ComEd), and 1.5 million in the five-county Philadelphia region, through PECO. PECO also distributes natural gas to 440,000 customers.

Both PECO and Unicom were leading nuclear plant operators, and about 65% of Exelon's 22,000-MW generating capacity comes from nuclear plants. Most of the power is sold through subsidiary Exelon Power Team, which is a top wholesale electricity marketer in North America. Exelon also has generation operations through a joint venture with British Energy (AmerGen Energy) and a 49.9% interest in Sithe Energies.

Exelon also markets retail energy in the US Midwest and Northeast and offers energy management and infrastructure services. In addition, Exelon is involved in a joint venture in Philadelphia (with Adelphia Business Solutions) that provides voice and data services over its own fiber-optic network; it has agreed to sell its other Philadelphia telecom venture interest to its partner, AT&T Wireless Services.

Exelon is expanding its generation unit through acquisitions and new plant construction; it is also looking to expand its regulated utility operations through the purchase of a smaller utility company.

HISTORY

Thomas Dolan and local investors formed the Brush Electric Light Company of Philadelphia in 1881 to provide street and commercial lighting. Competitors sprang up, and in 1885 Brush merged with the United States Electric Lighting Company of Pennsylvania to form a secret "electric trust," or holding company. Dolan became president in 1886 and bought four other utilities.

In 1895 Martin Maloney formed Pennsylvania Heat Light and Power to consolidate the city's electric companies. By the next year it had acquired, among other businesses, Columbia Electric Light, Philadelphia Edison, and the electric trust. In 1899 a new firm, National Electric, challenged Maloney by acquiring neighboring rival Southern Electric Light. Before retiring, Maloney negotiated the merger of the two firms, forming Philadelphia Electric in 1902.

Demand rose rapidly into the 1920s, fueled in part by the company's promotion of electric appliances. In 1928, the year after it completed the Conowingo Hydroelectric Station, Philadelphia

Electric was absorbed by the much larger United Gas Improvement. United Gas avoided large layoffs during the Depression, but passage of the Public Utility Holding Company Act in 1935 sounded its death knell. In 1943 the SEC forced United Gas to divest Philadelphia Electric.

Philadelphia Electric built several plants in the 1950s and 1960s in response to a postwar electricity boom. A small experimental nuclear reactor was completed at Peach Bottom, Pennsylvania, in 1967, and in 1974 the company placed two nuclear units in service at the plant. The Salem (New Jersey) nuke (Unit 1) followed in 1977. The company relied on these plants during the OPEC oil crisis. Another one, Limerick Unit 1, began operations in 1986, and Unit 2 went on line in 1990, but the Peach Bottom plant was shut down from 1989 to 1991 because of management problems (later resolved).

The company began reorganizing in 1993 and the next year changed its name to PECO Energy Company. It also sold Maryland retail subsidiary Conowingo Power, retaining the hydroelectric plant. In 1995 rival PP&L rejected PECO's acquisition bid, citing PECO's nuclear liabilities.

A year later PECO teamed with AT&T Wireless to offer PCS in Philadelphia (service was launched in 1997). EnergyOne, a national venture formed in 1997 by PECO, UtiliCorp United (now Aquila), and AT&T, offered consumers a package of power, phone, and Internet services on one bill. However, the slow deregulation process caused the venture to fail.

PECO also joined with British Energy in 1997 to form AmerGen, hoping to buy nukes at rock-bottom prices from utilities eager to unload them. AmerGen purchased three nuclear facilities in 1999 and 2000: Unit 1 of the Three Mile Island (Pennsylvania) facility; the Clinton, Illinois, facility; and the Oyster Creek (New Jersey) facility.

In 1999 PECO announced plans to acquire Chicago's Unicom, the parent company of Commonwealth Edison (ComEd). After the deal was completed in 2000, the combined company took the name Exelon and established its headquarters in Chicago.

Pennsylvania's utility markets were fully deregulated in 2000. To expand its power generation business, Exelon bought 49.9% of Sithe Energies that year for $682 million. In 2001 Exelon agreed to buy two gas-fired power plants (2,300 MW) in Texas from TXU for $443 million; the deal was completed in 2002.

OFFICERS

Chairman, President, and CEO; Chairman, Exelon Energy Delivery and Exelon Enterprises:
John W. Rowe, age 56, $2,550,300 pay
EVP; Vice Chairman and CEO, Exelon Energy Delivery; Chairman, ComEd and PECO Energy:
Pamela B. Strobel, age 49, $950,500 pay
EVP; President and CEO, Exelon Generation:
Oliver D. Kingsley Jr., $1,578,000 pay
(prior to promotion)
SVP and CFO: Ruth Ann M. Gillis
SVP; President and CEO, Exelon Business Services:
Honorio J. Padrón
SVP; President, ComEd; SVP, Exelon Energy Delivery:
Frank M. Clark Jr.
SVP; President, Exelon Enterprises:
George H. Gilmore Jr.
SVP; President, Exelon Power Team: Ian P. MacLean
SVP; President, PECO Energy; President and COO, Exelon Energy Delivery: Kenneth G. Lawrence,
$749,277 pay
SVP and Chief Human Resources Officer:
S. Gary Snodgrass
SVP and General Counsel: Randall E. Mehrberg,
$243,979 pay
SVP Communications and Public Affairs, Exelon and Exelon Generation: David W. Woods
Auditors: PricewaterhouseCoopers LLP

LOCATIONS

HQ: 10 S. Dearborn St., 37th Fl., Chicago, IL 60690
Phone: 630-394-7398   **Fax:** 630-663-7599
Web: www.exeloncorp.com

Exelon distributes electricity in Illinois and Pennsylvania.

PRODUCTS/OPERATIONS

2001 Sales

	$ mil.	% of total
Distribution	10,171	51
Generation	7,048	35
Enterprises	2,292	12
Other	341	2
Adjustments	(4,712)	—
Total	**15,140**	**100**

Selected Operating Units and Affiliates
Commonweath Edison Company (ComEd, electric utility)
PECO Energy Company (PECO, electric and gas utility)
AmerGen Energy Company, LLC (joint venture with British Energy, independent power producer)
Exelon Nuclear
Exelon Power
Exelon Power Team (wholesale energy sales)
Exelon Communications
Exelon Energy (nonregulated retail power sales)
Exelon Thermal Technologies (district cooling services, air-conditioning)

COMPETITORS

AES	DQE	Nicor
Allegheny Energy	Duke Energy	NUI
Alliant Energy	Dynegy	Peoples Energy
Ameren	Entergy	PG&E
Aquila	FirstEnergy	PPL
CenterPoint Energy	Green Mountain Energy	PSEG
Conectiv	Indeck Energy	UGI
Dominion	NewPower Holdings	WPS Resources

HISTORICAL FINANCIALS & EMPLOYEES

NYSE: EXC FYE: December 31	Annual Growth	12/92	12/93	12/94	12/95	12/96	12/97	12/98	12/99	12/00	12/01
Sales ($ mil.)	16.1%	3,963	3,988	4,041	4,186	4,284	4,618	5,210	5,437	7,499	15,140
Net income ($ mil.)	12.9%	479	591	427	610	517	(1,497)	513	582	586	1,428
Income as % of sales	—	12.1%	14.8%	10.6%	14.6%	12.1%	—	9.8%	10.7%	7.8%	9.4%
Earnings per share ($)	9.9%	1.90	2.45	1.76	2.64	2.24	(6.80)	2.23	2.89	2.87	4.43
Stock price - FY high ($)	—	26.75	33.50	30.00	30.25	32.50	26.38	42.19	50.50	71.00	70.26
Stock price - FY low ($)	—	22.63	25.50	23.63	24.25	22.50	18.75	18.88	30.75	33.00	38.75
Stock price - FY close ($)	7.0%	26.13	30.25	24.50	30.13	25.25	24.25	41.75	34.75	70.21	47.88
P/E - high	—	14	14	17	11	15	—	18	16	25	16
P/E - low	—	12	10	13	9	10	—	8	10	12	9
Dividends per share ($)	(0.5%)	1.33	1.43	1.55	1.65	1.76	1.80	1.00	1.00	1.00	1.27
Book value per share ($)	2.1%	21.21	22.00	21.09	21.71	22.19	13.29	14.63	10.54	22.62	25.64
Employees	12.9%	9,769	9,391	9,052	7,217	7,186	7,359	6,815	11,737	29,000	29,200

STOCK PRICE HISTORY

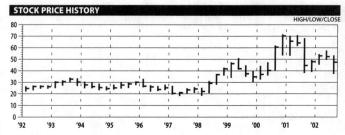

HIGH/LOW/CLOSE

2001 FISCAL YEAR-END

Debt ratio: 61.0%
Return on equity: 18.5%
Cash ($ mil.): 485
Current ratio: 0.86
Long-term debt ($ mil.): 12,876
No. of shares (mil.): 321
Dividends
  Yield: 2.7%
  Payout: 28.7%
Market value ($ mil.): 15,370

EXPRESS SCRIPTS, INC.

Express Scripts knows its clients like their drugs cheap and fast. One of the largest pharmacy benefits management (PBM) companies in the US, Express Scripts has more than 40 million members in the US and Canada. The Maryland Heights, Missouri-based company manages pharmacy benefits plans for HMOs, health insurance plans, self-insured companies, union benefit plans, and other organizations.

Express Scripts offers its enrollees prescription plans through some 55,000 retail drugstores, mail-order pharmacies, and the Internet (the troubled PlanetRx.com became the company's designated online provider when Express Scripts took a stake in the site). Express Scripts processes claims, designs formularies, and offers such services as disease-management programs, infusion therapy, a 24-hour telephone help line, and specialty drug packaging. Unlike most other pharmacy benefit management companies, Express Scripts is not controlled by a large pharmaceutical manufacturer or drug retailer. This independence allows Express Scripts to negotiate deeper discounts, contract with more retailers, and buy direct from manufacturers, not only squeezing a little more profit from the tightly margined business, but avoiding the perceived conflicts of interest that may arise from links to a drug company. New York Life owns more than 20% of the company.

Express Scripts has grown through an aggressive acquisitions program and high-profile marketing efforts to affinity organizations and individuals. The company is teaming with rival PBMs AdvancePCS and Merck-Medco to form RxHub, which will allow electronic prescribing by linking physicians with pharmacies, pharmacy benefit managers, and health plans. In 2001, the company agreed to acquire Phoenix Marketing Group, one of the country's biggest prescription drug sample fulfillment companies. In 2002, the company agreed to acquire National Prescription Administrators, the largest private pharmacy benefits management company in the country.

HISTORY

In 1986 St. Louis-based drugstore chain Medicare-Glaser and HMO Sanus joined forces to create Express Scripts, which would manage the HMO's prescription program. Express Scripts began managing third-party programs in 1988 and later developed other operations: Mail-order prescription, infusion therapy, and vision services. New York Life bought Sanus and picked up the rest of Express Scripts in 1989 when Medicare-Glaser went into bankruptcy.

In 1992 Express Scripts went public. The next year the company formed subsidiary Practice Patterns Science to begin profiling providers and tracking treatment outcomes.

In the late 1990s, the company continued to expand, adding customers in Canada (1996) and building operations — with varying success. A 1996 expansion of its eyecare management services was abandoned in 1998. Although Express Scripts has traditionally grown through big-ticket contracts, such as its 1997 pact with RightCHOICE Managed Care, it has also bought books of business. In 1998 it bought Columbia/HCA's (now HCA) ValueRx unit. The next year Express Scripts bought SmithKline Beecham's Diversified Pharmaceutical Services (DPS). However, it lost DPS's largest customer, when United Healthcare began moving its more than 8 million enrollees to Merck-Medco in 2000.

The company suffered another setback in 2000 when it wrote down its 20% interest in online pharmacy PlanetRx. It had bought into the company in 1999, when dot-coms were soaring, transferring its own Internet pharmacy operations (YourPharmacy.com) into the fledgling company. In 2001 the company joined rivals AdvancePCS and Merck-Medco to form RxHub, which will allow physicians to file prescriptions electronically. The company also agreed to acquire Phoenix Marketing Group, one of the country's biggest prescription drug sample fulfillment companies.

OFFICERS

Chairman and CEO: Barrett A. Toan, age 54, $2,126,152 pay
President and Director: Barbara B. Hill, age 49
COO: David A. Lowenberg, age 52, $770,923 pay
EVP, Health Management Services: Linda L. Logsdon, age 54, $629,323 pay
EVP, Sales and Provider Relations and Director: Stuart L. Bascomb, age 60, $715,520 pay
SVP and CFO: George Paz, age 46, $715,417 pay
SVP and Director of Site Operations: Mabel F. Chen, age 59
SVP and Chief Information Systems Officer: Edward J. Tenholder, age 50
SVP, Integration and Administration: Mark O. Johnson, age 48
SVP, Secretary, and General Counsel: Thomas M. Boudreau, age 50
VP and Chief Accounting Officer: Joseph W. Plum, age 53
VP, eBusiness: Agnes Rey-Giraud
Auditors: PricewaterhouseCoopers LLP

LOCATIONS

HQ: 13900 Riverport Dr., Maryland Heights, MO 63043
Phone: 314-770-1666   **Fax:** 314-702-7037
Web: www.express-scripts.com

Express Scripts has operations in Canada and the US.

PRODUCTS/OPERATIONS

2001 Sales

	$ mil.	% of total
Pharmacy benefits management	9,255	99
Other operations	74	1
Total	**9,329**	**100**

Selected Subsidiaries
Diversified NY IPA, Inc.
Diversified Pharmaceutical Services, Inc.
Diversified Pharmaceutical Services (Puerto Rico), Inc.
ESI Canada Holdings, Inc.
ESI Canada, Inc.
ESI Claims, Inc.
ESI Mail Pharmacy Services, Inc.
Express Scripts Sales Development Co.
Express Scripts Specialty Distribution Services, Inc.
Express Scripts Utilization Management Co.
Express Scripts Vision Corporation
Great Plains Reinsurance Company
IVTx, Inc.
Value Health, Inc.
ValueRx of Michigan, Inc.
YourPharmacy.com, Inc.

COMPETITORS

AARP
AdvancePCS
Caremark
Medco Health Solutions
Merck
MIM
National Medical Health Card Systems

HISTORICAL FINANCIALS & EMPLOYEES

Nasdaq: ESRX FYE: December 31	Annual Growth	12/92	12/93	12/94	12/95	12/96	12/97	12/98	12/99	12/00	12/01
Sales ($ mil.)	72.0%	71	120	385	545	774	1,231	2,825	4,288	6,787	9,329
Net income ($ mil.)	44.3%	5	8	13	18	26	33	43	150	(9)	125
Income as % of sales	—	6.5%	6.7%	3.3%	3.4%	3.4%	2.7%	1.5%	3.5%	—	1.3%
Earnings per share ($)	37.3%	0.09	0.14	0.21	0.30	0.40	0.51	0.64	2.03	(0.13)	1.56
Stock price - FY high ($)	—	4.13	5.88	9.56	13.75	14.50	16.19	34.50	52.75	53.50	61.45
Stock price - FY low ($)	—	1.56	2.34	5.50	6.25	6.63	7.81	13.50	22.19	14.25	34.84
Stock price - FY close ($)	31.1%	4.08	5.88	9.19	12.75	8.97	15.00	33.56	32.00	51.13	46.76
P/E - high	—	46	42	43	44	35	32	53	24	—	38
P/E - low	—	17	17	25	20	16	15	21	10	—	22
Dividends per share ($)	—	0.00	0.00	0.00	0.00	0.00	0.00	0.00	0.00	0.00	0.00
Book value per share ($)	40.1%	0.51	0.65	0.89	1.29	2.52	3.12	3.71	8.97	9.09	10.66
Employees	36.3%	350	710	860	1,217	1,513	1,570	3,354	4,606	5,259	5,671

STOCK PRICE HISTORY

HIGH/LOW/CLOSE

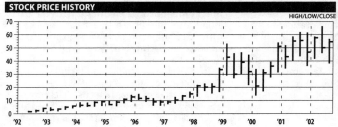

2001 FISCAL YEAR-END

Debt ratio: 29.4%
Return on equity: 16.2%
Cash ($ mil.): 178
Current ratio: 0.97
Long-term debt ($ mil.): 346
No. of shares (mil.): 78
Dividends
  Yield: —
  Payout: —
Market value ($ mil.): 3,649

EXXON MOBIL CORPORATION

Two Big Oil names have become one to make Exxon Mobil the world's #1 oil company, ahead of BP and Royal Dutch/Shell. Irving, Texas-based Exxon Mobil is engaged in oil and gas exploration, production, supply, transportation, and marketing. With major oil and gas holdings in Europe, the US, and eastern Canada, the company has proved reserves of almost 21 billion barrels of oil equivalent. It is looking for new opportunities in West Africa, both onshore and off; in the former Soviet Union; and in South America.

Exxon Mobil's refining capacity exceeds 6 million barrels per day, and the company's refined products are sold at more than 40,000 service stations operating under the Exxon, Esso, and Mobil brands in 118 countries, including 16,000 stations in the US. Exxon Mobil produces and sells petrochemicals (including ethylene, olefin, polyolefin, and paraxylene) and mines coal and other minerals. It also has stakes in electric power plants in China.

Still sorting out the logistical and cost-saving ramifications of the 1999 acquisition of Mobil by Exxon, Exxon Mobil has announced plans to cut 14,000 jobs — about 12% of its workforce — by the end of 2002.

HISTORY

Exxon's 1999 acquisition of Mobil reunited two descendants of John D. Rockefeller's Standard Oil Company. Rockefeller, a commodity trader, started his first oil refinery in 1863 in Cleveland. Realizing that the price of oil at the well would shrink with each new strike, Rockefeller chose to monopolize oil refining and transportation. In 1870 he formed Standard Oil, and in 1882 he created the Standard Oil Trust, which allowed him to set up new, ostensibly independent, companies, including the Standard Oil Company of New Jersey (Jersey Standard); Rochester, New York-based Vacuum Oil; and Standard Oil of New York (nicknamed Socony).

Initially capitalized at $70 million, the Standard Oil Trust controlled 90% of the petroleum industry. In 1911, after two decades of political and legal wrangling, the Supreme Court broke up the trust into 34 companies, the largest of which was Jersey Standard.

Walter Teagle, who became president of Jersey Standard in 1917, secretly bought half of Humble Oil of Texas (1919) and expanded operations into South America. In 1928 Jersey Standard joined in the Red Line Agreement, which reserved most Middle East oil for a few companies. Teagle resigned in 1942 after the company was criticized for a prewar research pact with German chemical giant I.G. Farben.

The 1948 purchase of a 30% stake in Arabian American Oil Company, combined with a 7% share of Iranian production bought in 1954, made Jersey Standard the world's #1 oil company at that time.

Meanwhile, Vacuum Oil and Socony reunited in 1931 as Socony-Vacuum, and the company adopted the Flying Red Horse (Pegasus — representing speed and power) as a trademark. The fast-growing, diversifying company changed its name to Socony Mobil Oil in 1955 and became Mobil in 1976.

Other US companies, still using the Standard Oil name, objected to Jersey Standard's marketing in their territories as Esso (derived from the initials for Standard Oil). To end the confusion, in 1972 Jersey Standard became Exxon, a name change that cost $100 million.

Nationalization of oil assets by producing countries reduced Exxon's access to oil during the 1970s. Though it increased exploration that decade and the next, Exxon's reserves shrank.

Oil tanker *Exxon Valdez* spilled some 11 million gallons of oil into Alaska's Prince William Sound in 1989. Exxon spent billions on the cleanup, and in 1994 a federal jury in Alaska ordered the company to pay $5.3 billion in punitive damages to fishermen and others affected by the spill. (Exxon appealed, and in 2001 the jury award was overturned.)

With the oil industry consolidating, Exxon merged its worldwide oil and fuel additives business with that of Royal Dutch/Shell in 1996.

Still, Exxon was unstoppable. It acquired Mobil for $81 billion in 1999; the new company had Raymond at the helm and Mobil's Lucio Noto as VC. (Noto retired in 2001.) To get the deal done, Exxon Mobil had to divest $4 billion in assets. It agreed to end its European gasoline and lubricants joint venture with BP and to sell more than 2,400 gas stations in the US.

In 2000 Exxon Mobil sold 1,740 East Coast gas stations to Tosco for $860 million. It sold a California refinery and 340 gas stations to Valero Energy for about $1 billion.

In 2001 Exxon Mobil joined the California Fuel Cell Partnership, a group studying possible alternatives to, and supplements for, gasoline in fuel-burning engines. That year Exxon Mobil also announced that it was proceeding with a $12 billion project (with Japanese, Indian and Russian partners) to develop oil fields in the Russian Far East.

In 2002 Exxon Mobil sold its 50% stake in a Colombian coal mine as part of its strategy to divest coal assets in order to focus on its core businesses. That year the company also agreed to sell its Chilean copper mining subsidiary (Disputada de Las Condes) to mineral giant Anglo American for $1.3 billion. Also that year Exxon Mobil and Guangzhou Petrochemical (a subsidiary of China Petroleum & Chemical Corp., or Sinopec Corp., in which Exxon Mobil has a 19% stake), began negotiations on a $3.24 billion deal to jointly expand capacity at Guangzhou's refinery.

2001 Sales

	% of total
US	30
Japan	11
UK	9
Canada	7
Other countries	43
Total	**100**

OFFICERS

Chairman and CEO: Lee R. Raymond, age 63, $5,550,000 pay
EVP and Director: Harry J. Longwell, age 60, $2,113,000 pay
SVP: Edward G. Galante, age 51
SVP: Rex W. Tillerson, age 50
VP and General Counsel: Charles W. Matthews Jr., age 57
VP Human Resources: Lucille J. Cavanaugh
VP; President, ExxonMobil Exploration: Jon L. Thompson, age 62
VP; President, ExxonMobil Fuels Marketing: Hal R. Cramer, age 51
VP; President, ExxonMobil Gas Marketing: Stuart R. McGill, age 59
VP; President, ExxonMobil Production: K. Terry Koonce, age 63, $1,175,000 pay
VP; President, ExxonMobil Refining and Supply: J. Steven Simon, age 58
Auditors: PricewaterhouseCoopers LLP

LOCATIONS

HQ: 5959 Las Colinas Blvd., Irving, TX 75039
Phone: 972-444-1000   **Fax:** 972-444-1350
Web: www.exxon.mobil.com

PRODUCTS/OPERATIONS

2001 Sales

	% of total
Petroleum & natural gas	
Downstream	84
Upstream	9
Chemicals	7
Total	**100**

COMPETITORS

7-Eleven	Eni	PDVSA
Amerada Hess	Enron	PEMEX
Ashland	Huntsman	Racetrac
BHP Billiton Ltd	Imperial	Petroleum
BP	Chemical	Repsol YPF
Celanese	Kerr-McGee	Royal
ChevronTexaco	Koch	Dutch/Shell
ConocoPhillips	Lyondell	Group
Costco	Chemical	Saudi Aramco
Wholesale	Marathon Oil	Sunoco
Dow Chemical	Norsk Hydro	TOTAL FINA
Eastman	Occidental	ELF
Chemical	Petroleum	Unocal
DuPont	PETROBRAS	

HISTORICAL FINANCIALS & EMPLOYEES

NYSE: XOM FYE: December 31	Annual Growth	12/92	12/93	12/94	12/95	12/96	12/97	12/98	12/99	12/00	12/01
Sales ($ mil.)	6.9%	103,160	97,825	99,683	107,893	116,728	120,279	100,697	160,883	206,083	187,510
Net income ($ mil.)	13.8%	4,770	5,280	5,100	6,470	7,510	8,460	6,433	7,910	17,720	15,320
Income as % of sales	—	4.6%	5.4%	5.1%	6.0%	6.4%	7.0%	6.4%	4.9%	8.6%	8.2%
Earnings per share ($)	9.8%	0.95	1.05	1.02	1.29	1.50	1.69	1.29	1.13	2.53	2.21
Stock price - FY high ($)	—	16.38	17.25	16.84	21.50	25.31	33.63	38.66	43.63	47.72	45.84
Stock price - FY low ($)	—	13.44	14.44	14.03	15.03	19.41	24.13	28.31	32.16	34.94	35.01
Stock price - FY close ($)	11.1%	15.28	15.78	15.19	20.28	24.50	30.59	36.56	40.28	43.47	39.30
P/E - high	—	17	16	17	17	17	20	30	38	21	21
P/E - low	—	14	14	14	12	13	14	22	28	15	16
Dividends per share ($)	2.8%	0.71	0.72	0.73	0.75	0.98	0.82	0.82	0.84	0.88	0.91
Book value per share ($)	3.7%	6.80	7.00	7.53	8.14	8.76	8.88	9.01	9.13	8.95	9.39
Employees	0.3%	95,000	91,000	86,000	82,000	79,000	80,000	79,000	123,000	123,000	97,900

STOCK PRICE HISTORY

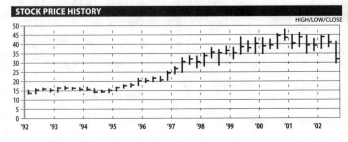

HIGH/LOW/CLOSE

2001 FISCAL YEAR-END

Debt ratio: 8.8%
Return on equity: 21.3%
Cash ($ mil.): 6,547
Current ratio: 1.18
Long-term debt ($ mil.): 7,099
No. of shares (mil.): 7,790
Dividends
  Yield: 2.3%
  Payout: 41.2%
Market value ($ mil.): 306,147

FAMILY DOLLAR STORES, INC.

For families on a budget, the buck stops at Family Dollar Stores. The retail chain, based in Charlotte, North Carolina, operates nearly 4,550 no-frills, low-overhead, small stores (7,000 to 9,000 sq. ft.) in 40 states (from Maine to Florida and as far west as Arizona) and the District of Columbia. Most are located in small communities.

Family Dollar offers discounts on basic merchandise for family and home needs, including apparel, food, health and beauty aids, housewares, and toys. Since price is the most important factor for the company's target customer — a woman shopping for a family making around $25,000 a year — most merchandise sells for less than $10.

In the face of increased competition from mass marketers such as Wal-Mart, Family Dollar has shifted to an everyday-low-pricing strategy (as opposed to short-lived promotional advertising), while increasing the number of brand-name goods it carries. Family Dollar is expanding rapidly, adding freestanding stores and stores in strip malls, without accumulating long-term debt.

Founder and chairman Leon Levine and his family own about 16% of the chain.

HISTORY

Leon Levine came from a retailing family. His father, who founded The Hub, a general store-style department store in Rockingham, North Carolina, in 1908, died when Levine was 13, and the boy and his older brother Al helped his mother run the store. (Al went on to found the Pic 'n Pay self-service shoe stores in 1957.) In 1959, when he was 25, Levine (with his cousin Bernie) opened his own store in Charlotte, with nothing priced over a dollar, targeting low- and middle-income families. The concept of low prices and small neighborhood stores was immediately popular, and Levine began adding stores. By 1970, when he took Family Dollar Stores public, it had 100 stores in five states. That year Levine brought his cousin Lewis into the business.

Family Dollar's profits plummeted in the mid-1970s as the chain's low-income customers, hit by recession, cut back on spending — even though all merchandise was priced at $3 or less. Such pricing made for tight margins, so the company dropped the policy. Family Dollar also improved inventory controls to make operations more efficient and began moving into other states. Sales picked up, topping $100 million in 1977, and the next year the firm bought the 40-store Top Dollar chain from Sav-A-Stop.

As the 1980s began, Family Dollar had nearly 400 stores in eight southern states and was rapidly expanding, it was adding more than 100 stores a year. But in an effort to boost margins, the company had lost its pricing edge to a new threat — Wal-Mart's truckload prices and quick domination of the southern discount retailing market.

After Family Dollar sales were flat in 1986 and dropped 10% in 1987, Levine finally took action. He found his prices were sometimes as much as 10% higher than Wal-Mart's and his stores were often insufficiently stocked with advertised products. He lowered prices, declaring that Family Dollar would not be undersold, and again instituted new inventory controls. But the action had not come quickly enough, argued president and COO Lewis, who left the company in 1987. (He was also upset over a huge salary disparity: Leon — noted for being a hard bargainer with suppliers — was making $1.8 million a year, compared to Lewis' $260,000.) Leon's son Howard, who joined the firm in 1981, also left; he returned to the fold in 1996 and became CEO in 1998.

Family Dollar picked up momentum in the 1990s. It implemented a major renovation of stores and phased out low-margin items such as motor oil and tools in favor of such high-margin items as toys and electronics. The company also accelerated its growth plans, opening stores in a number of new markets and setting up a second distribution center, in Arkansas, in 1994 to support its westward expansion. Also that year Family Dollar began offering everyday low prices and scaled back its sales promotions.

The pace of expansion was steady during the late 1990s, as the company opened hundreds of new stores and more distribution centers and closed underperforming locations. Family Dollar added 165 stores in fiscal 1996, 186 in fiscal 1997, 250 in fiscal 1998, and 366 in fiscal 1999 (its largest single-year increase in stores). It continued adding stores in 2000 and 2001 (although the rate of growth began slowing) and it began emphasizing food, household products, and gift and seasonal items rather than clothing.

OFFICERS

Chairman: Leon Levine, age 64, $1,274,231 pay
Vice Chairman, CFO and Chief Administrative Officer: R. James Kelly, age 54, $573,412 pay
President, CEO, and Director: Howard R. Levine, age 42, $701,095 pay
EVP, COO, and Director: R. David Alexander Jr., age 44, $369,531 pay
EVP, General Counsel, Secretary, and Director: George R. Mahoney Jr., age 59, $353,792 pay
SVP and CIO: Joshua R. Jewett
SVP, Distribution and Logistics: Charles S. Gibson Jr., age 40
SVP, Finance: C. Martin Sowers, age 43

SVP, **Human Resources:** Samuel N. McPherson, age 56
SVP, **Information Technology:** Albert S. Rorie, age 51
SVP, **Merchandising and Advertising:** John J. Scanlon, age 52
SVP, **Real Estate:** Gilbert A. LaFare, age 55
Auditors: PricewaterhouseCoopers LLP

LOCATIONS

HQ: 10401 Old Monroe Rd., Matthews, NC 28105
Phone: 704-847-6961 **Fax:** 704-847-0189
Web: www.familydollar.com.

2001 Stores

	No.
Texas	477
Ohio	262
North Carolina	258
Florida	233
Georgia	232
New York	186
Virginia	182
Pennsylvania	180
Tennessee	176
Michigan	173
Kentucky	156
South Carolina	149
Louisiana	142
Alabama	141
Indiana	132
Illinois	111
Arkansas	97
West Virginia	93
Mississippi	93
Oklahoma	87
Wisconsin	74
Other states	564
Total	**4,198**

PRODUCTS/OPERATIONS

2001 Sales

	% of total
Hardlines	75
Soft goods	25
Total	**100**

Selected Products

Hardlines	Housewares
Automotive supplies	Seasonal goods
Candy, snacks, and other foods	Stationery and school supplies
Electronics	Toys
Gifts	
Hardware	**Soft goods**
Health and beauty aids	Apparel (men's, women's, children's, and infants')
Household chemical products	Domestics (blankets, sheets, and towels)
Household paper products	Shoes

COMPETITORS

Big Lots	Odd Job Stores
Bill's Dollar Stores	Pamida
BJs Wholesale Club	Rite Aid
Costco Wholesale	Sears
CVS	ShopKo Stores
Dollar General	Target
Dollar Tree	Toys "R" Us
Duckwall-ALCO	Value City
J. C. Penney	Variety Wholesalers
Kmart	Walgreen
Meijer	Wal-Mart

HISTORICAL FINANCIALS & EMPLOYEES

NYSE: FDO FYE: August 31	Annual Growth	8/92	8/93	8/94	8/95	8/96	8/97	8/98	8/99	8/00	8/01
Sales ($ mil.)	13.7%	1,159	1,297	1,428	1,547	1,715	1,995	2,362	2,751	3,133	3,665
Net income ($ mil.)	14.6%	56	64	63	58	61	75	103	140	172	190
Income as % of sales	—	4.8%	5.0%	4.4%	3.8%	3.5%	3.7%	4.4%	5.1%	5.5%	5.2%
Earnings per share ($)	13.9%	0.34	0.39	0.38	0.35	0.35	0.44	0.60	0.81	1.00	1.10
Stock price – FY high ($)	—	7.25	8.21	6.59	6.59	6.42	11.75	21.88	26.75	23.44	30.70
Stock price – FY low ($)	—	3.84	5.42	3.67	3.29	3.67	5.34	10.31	11.50	14.00	16.75
Stock price – FY close ($)	20.1%	5.75	6.46	4.21	6.09	5.75	10.63	12.69	19.69	18.00	30.00
P/E – high	—	21	21	18	19	18	27	36	33	23	28
P/E – low	—	11	14	10	9	10	12	17	14	14	15
Dividends per share ($)	12.5%	0.08	0.10	0.11	0.13	0.14	0.16	0.17	0.19	0.21	0.23
Book value per share ($)	14.7%	1.62	1.91	2.18	2.40	2.61	2.91	3.36	4.00	4.66	5.57
Employees	10.5%	14,700	15,900	16,500	18,500	20,700	22,500	26,100	28,300	31,200	36,000

STOCK PRICE HISTORY

HIGH/LOW/CLOSE

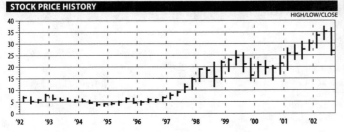

2001 FISCAL YEAR-END

Debt ratio: 0.0%
Return on equity: 21.6%
Cash ($ mil.): 22
Current ratio: 2.07
Long-term debt ($ mil.): 0
No. of shares (mil.): 172
Dividends
 Yield: 0.8%
 Payout: 20.9%
Market value ($ mil.): 5,161

FANNIE MAE

Fannie Mae may be holding your mortgage. Based in Washington, DC, Fannie Mae (formerly known as the Federal National Mortgage Association) is the leading buyer of single-family home mortgages in the US. Fannie Mae buys mortgages from the originating lenders and repackages them as securities for sale, creating liquidity in the mortgage market by transferring risk from lenders, allowing them to offer mortgages to people who might not otherwise qualify.

Fannie Mae is a for-profit, publicly traded government corporation with a federal mandate to make housing more affordable for low- to middle-income families. As such, Fannie Mae enjoys the ability to borrow from the government at advantageous rates and is exempt from certain taxes; it also benefits from an implicit guarantee of federal support that makes its securities desirable.

Criticism has become Fannie Mae's companion. Bureaucrats and mortgage market competitors have called for an end to Fannie Mae's federal charter status because it gives the company an advantage over its competitors in attracting investors and building market share.

HISTORY

In 1938 President Franklin Roosevelt created Fannie Mae as part of the government-owned Reconstruction Finance Corporation; its mandate was to buy FHA (Federal Housing Administration) loans. Fannie Mae began buying VA (Veterans Administration) mortgages in 1948. It was rechartered as a public-private, mixed-ownership corporation in 1954.

The Housing Act of 1968 divided the corporation into the Government National Mortgage Association (Ginnie Mae, which retained explicit government backing) and Fannie Mae, which went public (with only an implicit US guarantee). Fannie Mae retained its treasury backstop authority, whereby the secretary of the treasury can purchase up to $2.24 billion of the company's obligations.

The company introduced uniform conventional loan mortgage documents in 1970, began to buy conventional mortgages in 1972, and started buying condo and planned unit development mortgages in 1974. By 1976 it was buying more conventional loans than FHA and VA loans.

As interest rates rose in the 1970s, Fannie Mae's profits declined and by 1981 it was losing more than $1 million a day. Then it began offering mortgage-backed securities (MBS's) — popular as an investment product because of their implicit guarantee from the government. By 1982 the company funded 14% of US home mortgages.

Fannie Mae began borrowing money overseas and buying conventional multifamily and co-op housing loans in 1984. The next year it tightened credit rules and began issuing securities aimed at foreign investors, such as yen-denominated securities. Fannie Mae issued its first real estate mortgage investment conduit (REMIC) securities (shares in mortgage pools of specific maturities and risk classes) and introduced a program to allow small lenders to pool loans with other lenders to create MBS's in 1987.

After CEO David Maxwell's 1991 retirement with a reported $29 million pension package, Fannie Mae's powerful Washington lobby squelched calls to limit executive salaries. Other attempts to make the company more competitive with private concerns were more successful. In 1992 Fannie Mae's capital requirements were raised; a new mandate also required the organization to lend greater support to inner-city buyers. A new client/server computer system helped the company handle the deluge of new and refinanced loans that came in 1993 (Fannie Mae had struggled to improve its information systems in the 1980s, pouring more than $100 million into a mainframe system that was obsolete before it went online).

In 1997 Fannie Mae officially adopted its long-time nickname. The next year Fannie Mae named White House budget chief Franklin Raines to succeed CEO James Johnson.

In 1999 the Department of Housing and Urban Development began investigating charges that the company's automated underwriting systems were racially biased. The next year the agency released a study that found it to be negligent in promoting homeownership in low-income neighborhoods. In response, Fannie Mae eased credit requirements in an effort to boost minority homeownership (1999) and announced plans to loan some $2 trillion to minority and low-income homebuyers (2000). This move, however, invoked criticism that the company was exposing itself to increased risk from buyers more likely to default.

Following the lead of rival Freddie Mac, in 2000 Fannie Mae offered securities for sale over the Internet.

OFFICERS

Chairman and CEO: Franklin D. Raines, age 53, $2,835,000 pay
Vice Chairman and COO: Daniel H. Mudd, age 43
Vice Chairman: Jamie S. Gorelick, age 51
EVP and CFO: J. Timothy Howard, age 53
EVP, Housing and Community Development: Robert J. Levin, age 46
EVP, Law and Policy: Thomas E. Donilon, age 46

EVP, Single-Family Mortgage Business:
Louis W. Hoyes, age 53
EVP and Chief Credit Officer: Adolfo Marzol, age 41
EVP and CTO: Julie St. John, age 50
SVP, Multifamily Lending and Investment:
Kenneth J. Bacon, age 47
SVP, Regulatory Policy: Arne L. Christenson, age 40
SVP, Human Resources: Kathy G. Gallo, age 42
SVP and Chief Marketing Officer: Vada Hill, age 42
SVP and General Counsel: Ann M. Kappler, age 45
SVP and Treasurer: Linda K. Knight, age 52
SVP, Portfolio Management: Thomas A. Lawler, age 49
SVP, Investor Channel: Thomas Lund, age 43
SVP, Government and Industry Relations:
William R. Maloni, age 57
SVP, Portfolio Strategy: Peter Niculescu, age 42
SVP, Single Family Mortgage Business:
Michael A. Quinn, age 47
Auditors: KPMG LLP

LOCATIONS

HQ: 3900 Wisconsin Ave. NW, Washington, DC 20016
Phone: 202-752-7000   **Fax:** 202-752-3868
Web: www.fanniemae.com

Fannie Mae operates throughout the US, with regional offices in Atlanta; Chicago; Dallas; Pasadena, California; and Philadelphia.

PRODUCTS/OPERATIONS

2001 Assets

	$ mil.	% of total
Cash & equivalents	1,518	—
Mortgage portfolio	705,167	88
Investments	74,554	10
Other assets	18,552	2
Total	**799,791**	**100**

COMPETITORS

Bank of America
BANK ONE
Citigroup
Countrywide Credit
First American Corporation
FleetBoston
Freddie Mac
J.P. Morgan Chase
KeyCorp
Mellon Financial
PNC Financial
Washington Mutual
Wells Fargo

HISTORICAL FINANCIALS & EMPLOYEES

NYSE: FNM FYE: December 31	Annual Growth	12/92	12/93	12/94	12/95	12/96	12/97	12/98	12/99	12/00	12/01
Assets ($ mil.)	18.0%	180,978	216,979	272,508	316,550	351,041	391,673	485,014	575,167	675,072	799,791
Net income ($ mil.)	15.4%	1,623	1,873	2,132	2,144	2,725	3,056	3,418	3,912	4,448	5,894
Income as % of assets	—	0.9%	0.9%	0.8%	0.7%	0.8%	0.8%	0.7%	0.7%	0.7%	0.7%
Earnings per share ($)	16.2%	1.48	1.70	1.93	1.96	2.48	2.83	3.23	3.72	4.29	5.72
Stock price - FY high ($)	—	19.31	21.53	22.59	31.50	41.63	57.31	76.19	75.88	89.38	87.94
Stock price - FY low ($)	—	13.78	18.22	17.03	17.19	27.50	36.13	49.56	58.56	47.88	72.08
Stock price - FY close ($)	17.2%	19.09	19.63	18.22	30.97	37.63	57.06	74.00	62.44	86.75	79.50
P/E - high	—	13	12	12	16	16	20	23	20	21	15
P/E - low	—	9	10	9	9	11	13	15	16	11	12
Dividends per share ($)	14.7%	0.35	0.46	0.60	0.68	0.76	0.84	0.96	1.08	1.12	1.20
Book value per share ($)	12.7%	6.20	7.39	8.74	10.04	12.03	13.30	15.08	17.30	20.86	18.17
Employees	4.6%	3,000	3,200	3,500	3,280	3,400	3,400	3,800	4,000	4,100	4,500

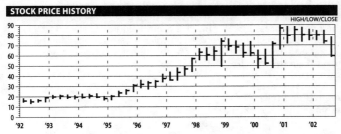

STOCK PRICE HISTORY   HIGH/LOW/CLOSE

2001 FISCAL YEAR-END

Equity as % of assets: 2.3%
Return on assets: 0.8%
Return on equity: 34.3%
Long-term debt ($ mil.): 419,975
No. of shares (mil.): 997
Dividends
  Yield: 1.5%
  Payout: 21.0%
Market value ($ mil.): 79,262
Sales ($ mil.): 50,803

FARMLAND INDUSTRIES, INC.

Farmland Industries helps its members farm land industriously. The Kansas City, Missouri-based enterprise is the #1 agricultural cooperative in the US. Farmland is owned by about 1,700 local co-ops, comprising 600,000 farmers in the US, Canada, and Mexico. To help farmers grow crops and raise livestock, Farmland provides them with fertilizers, feed, herbicides and pesticides. When the harvest is complete, the co-op provides grain storage, delivery, processing, and marketing services — including export to more than 60 countries. Higher up the food chain, the co-op is a major meat company. It makes and markets fresh and processed beef, catfish, and pork through its Farmland National Beef (the #4 US beef slaughterer), Southern Farm Fish Processors, and Farmland Foods subsidiaries.

Farmland also has more than 60 joint ventures and alliances, including WILFARM (with Wilbur-Ellis Company, chemical products).

HISTORY

In 1929 President Herbert Hoover pushed passage of the Agricultural Marketing Act (AMA) to encourage cooperatives as one means to remedy the hard times facing the US agriculture industry in the 1920s. However record grain harvests in 1928 and 1929 foiled its intent; a glut ground down prices, and later the Depression (and drought) dried up markets.

By the time of the AMA, Union Oil Company, Farmland Industries' predecessor, was already in the works. Union Oil was formed in 1929 to provide petroleum supplies to farmers in a period of rapid agricultural mechanization. In the early 1930s, as the government sought to regulate supply by introducing payments for taking land out of production, Union Oil increased the range of its co-op activities. It changed its name to Consumers Cooperative Association in 1935.

Farming did not revive until WWII, though price controls and supports remained an important feature of agricultural policy. Throughout this period the performance of Consumers Cooperative's growing membership of primary producers and local co-ops remained tied to raw commodity prices. In 1959, however, to decrease its reliance on commodity prices, Consumers Cooperative bought a pork processing plant in Denison, Iowa, and began making Farmbest meat products. It was a success, and four years later the co-op opened another plant in Iowa Falls. In 1966 Consumers Cooperative became Farmland Industries, and in the 1970s it expanded into beef production. However, when prices and consumption declined, it exited the field.

Overzealous expansion by American farmers in the 1970s was followed in the 1980s by an industrywide crisis. When the farm economy went down, it hurt the co-op's sales of inputs such as fertilizers. Cheap fertilizer imports, low crude oil prices, and high natural gas prices also took their toll, and the co-op lost more than $210 million in 1985 and 1986. James Rainey took over as CEO in 1986 and turned the operation around. Farmland began placing a greater emphasis on food processing and marketing, otherwise known as outputs.

Harry Cleberg succeeded Rainey in 1991. The co-op had stopped handling grains in 1985, after a period of volatile prices, but it profitably re-entered the market in 1992. The next year it bought the Tradigrain unit of British Petroleum (now BP Amoco). The purchase led Farmland into markets outside the US. Also in 1993 the co-op resumed beef processing and expanded its pork processing facilities.

During the late 1990s, the co-op formed joint ventures and partnerships spanning its range of activities; feeds, grain marketing, energy products and in 1998 absorbed SF Services, an agricultural cooperative.

In 1999 Farmland and Cenex Harvest States voted to merge their entire operations; while Farmland members approved the deal, Cenex members voted it down. Instead Farmland partnered with Land O'Lakes and Cenex to form Agriliance to supply farm products to members. In 2000 Farmland combined its feed business with Land O' Lakes in a joint venture forming North America's top feed company. In the fall of 2000 company veteran Robert Honse was named CEO as Cleberg retired.

Skyrocketing natural gas prices during 2000 hit the co-op's fertilizer business hard, prompting it to shut down one facility. Laden with debt, in mid-2001 the co-op handed the operation of its 24 grain elevators over to Archer Daniels Midland as part of a new grain-marketing venture with the agribusiness giant. In November 2001 the co-op sold its interest in Country Energy to CHS Cooperatives. Farmland lost $90 million in 2001, but the co-op also reduced its debt that year by $268 million and administrative costs by nearly $40 million.

In 2002 Smithfield Foods offered to buy out troubled Farmland; however, Farmland chose to file for Chapter 11 bankruptcy instead.

OFFICERS

Chairman: Albert J. Shivley, age 58
Vice Chairman and VP: Jody Bezner, age 60
President and CEO: Robert B. Terry, age 45
EVP and CFO: Steve Rhodes
EVP; President, Crop Production: Stan A. Riemann, age 50, $298,782 pay
EVP; President, Refrigerated Foods:
William G. Fielding, age 54, $350,000 pay
EVP; President, World Grain: Tim R. Daugherty, age 48
VP, Human Resources: Holly D. McCoy
VP, Strategic Sourcing: Michael T. Sweat, age 56
Auditors: KPMG LLP

LOCATIONS

HQ: 12200 N. Ambassador Dr., Kansas City, MO 64163
Phone: 816-713-7000   **Fax:** 816-713-6323
Web: www.farmland.com

More than 600,000 farmers and their cooperatives, located in the US, Canada, and Mexico, form Farmland Industries, which conducts business in nearly 60 countries.

PRODUCTS/OPERATIONS

Selected Subsidiaries and Joint Ventures
Agriliance, LLC (with Land O'Lakes and Cenex Harvest States to supply fertilizer, pesticides, herbicides, and seed to farmers)
Farmland Foods (99%, 11 food processing plants)
Farmland Hydro, LP (50%, with Norsk Hydro; phosphate fertilizer manufacturing)
Farmland MissChem Limited (50%, anhydrous ammonia manufacturing)
Farmland National Beef Packing Co., LP (71%)
Land O'Lakes Farmland Feed
SF Phosphates, Limited Liability Company (50%, fertilizer manufacturing)
Southern Farm Fish Processors
Tradigrain SA (international grain trading)
WILFARM, LLC (50%, with Wilbur-Ellis Co.; pesticides)

Consumer Product Brands
Black Angus Beef
Carando (bread, specialty meats)
Farmland (processed pork products)
Farmstead
Maple River
OhSe
Regal
Roegelein (processed pork products)
Springwater Farms

COMPETITORS

ADM
Ag Processing
Agway
American Foods
Cargill
Cenex Harvest States
CF Industries
ConAgra
ContiGroup
DeBruce Grain
Exxon Mobil
Gold Kist
GROWMARK
Hormel
IBP
IMC Global
JR Simplot
Rose Packing
Royal Dutch/Shell Group
Scoular
Smithfield Foods
Southern States
Transammonia

HISTORICAL FINANCIALS & EMPLOYEES

Cooperative FYE: August 31	Annual Growth	8/92	8/93	8/94	8/95	8/96	8/97	8/98	8/99	8/00	8/01
Sales ($ mil.)	14.7%	3,429	4,723	6,678	7,257	9,789	9,148	8,775	10,709	12,239	11,763
Net income ($ mil.)	—	62	(30)	74	163	126	135	59	14	(29)	(90)
Income as % of sales	—	1.8%	—	1.1%	2.2%	1.3%	1.5%	0.7%	0.1%	—	—
Employees	7.4%	7,616	8,155	12,000	12,700	14,700	14,600	16,100	17,700	15,000	14,500

NET INCOME HISTORY

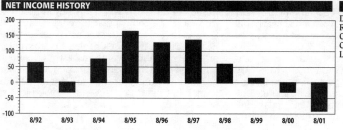

2001 FISCAL YEAR-END

Debt ratio: 47.3%
Return on equity: —
Cash ($ mil.): 0
Current ratio: 1.21
Long-term debt ($ mil.): 711

FEDERAL-MOGUL CORPORATION

Having sent its retail operation to the scrap heap, Federal-Mogul is embracing its core business of making and distributing auto parts. The Southfield, Michigan-based company's product line includes engine components and bearings; sealing products; fuel systems; and ignition, brake, friction, and chassis products for cars, trucks, and construction equipment. Principal customers include automobile and equipment makers such as General Motors, Ford, DaimlerChrysler, BMW, Volkswagen, Caterpillar, and Cummins. Federal-Mogul also provides products to independent warehouse distributors and local parts suppliers and retailers in the global automotive aftermarket.

After more than tripling in size since 1997, Federal-Mogul is feeling the weight of its girth. An ill-advised acquisitions bender, resulting asbestos lawsuits, and falling demand from US automakers have forced the company to purge rather than binge. Federal-Mogul plans to mothball as many as 50 plants, cut its supplier base by 50%, tweak its aftermarket distribution network in North America, and lay off nearly 9% of its salaried work force. Asbestos lawsuits stemming from the company's 1998 acquisition of T&N plc has caused Federal-Mogul to seek Chapter 11 backruptcy protection. A group that includes investor Carl Icahn has cut its stake in the company from just over 6% to just under 4%. State Street Bank and Trust owns nearly 19%.

HISTORY

In 1899 J. Howard Muzzy and Edward Lyon formed the Muzzy-Lyon Company, and later, subsidiary Mogul Metal Company. The two modified a printer's typecasting machine and developed a process for making die-cast engine bearings. Their first big order came in 1910, when Buick ordered 10,000 connecting rod bearings for the Buick 10. In 1924 Mogul Metal merged with Federal Bearing and Bushing to become Federal-Mogul Corporation.

In 1941 Federal-Mogul had about 50 factories dedicated to the war effort, and by 1945 sales had doubled from prewar levels. In 1955 the company acquired Bower Roller Bearing Company and changed its name to Federal-Mogul-Bower Bearings, Inc. By the late 1950s it had nearly 100 distribution centers, and sales had quadrupled in 10 years.

The company began investing in foreign manufacturing plants during the 1960s to safeguard against lower US car exports as more foreign cars entered the global market. It changed its name back to Federal-Mogul in 1965 and the following year moved its headquarters from Detroit to Southfield, Michigan. Following a recession in the mid-1970s, Federal-Mogul realized that it was too dependent on the big automakers and began diversifying. It acquired the Mather Company, a maker of high-performance sealing products, in 1985. The next year it bought Carter Automotive (fuel pumps) and Signal-Stat (lighting and safety components).

In 1989 Dennis Gormley became CEO. He continued the diversification strategy and led the company into the automotive aftermarket. Gormley proposed a push into retail in 1992, and that year Federal-Mogul bought the aftermarket business of TRW Inc. In its effort to become the Pep Boys of the Third World, the company sold parts of its manufacturing business to finance its retail ventures. By 1996 it owned about 130 retail stores, primarily in Latin America. The company lost money, and that year Gormley resigned. His successor, Dick Snell, put an immediate end to the retail fiasco.

By 1998 Federal-Mogul had sold all of its retail holdings and was concentrating on providing parts for entire engine systems. That year it made two major acquisitions: Fel-Pro, a domestic maker of gaskets and other sealing products, for $720 million; and T&N plc, a British maker of bearings, pistons, and brake pads, and Europe's largest asbestos maker during the 1980s. T&N was picked up on the cheap, as its stock was depressed by looming asbestos lawsuits. The decision would prove a grave one for Federal-Mogul.

Driving further into the aftermarket, Federal-Mogul paid $1.9 billion for the automotive business of Cooper Industries (Champion spark plugs, windshield wipers, steering and suspension parts, brake parts). UK-based LucasVarity rejected Federal-Mogul's $6.4 billion buy offer in early 1999 in favor of a $7 billion offer from TRW.

In 2000 Federal-Mogul announced plans to close 22 North American replacement parts warehouses and consolidate 18 manufacturing plants in Europe and Asia. CEO Richard Snell stepped down that year.

Early in 2001 Frank Macher, a former Ford and ITT Automotive executive, was named CEO. Not long after, in the midst of the economic slowdown, Federal-Mogul announced that it would cut its salaried workforce by almost 9%. In August the company acquired 85% of WSK Gorzyce, a Polish piston maker. Later in 2001 Federal-Mogul filed for Chapter 11 bankruptcy protection as a result of the asbestos lawsuits it inherited from the 1998 acquisition of T&N plc.

The following year Federal-Mogul sold its Signal-Stat lighting business to Truck-Lite Co. (a subsidiary of Penske) for $23 million.

Chairman and CEO: Frank E. Macher, $3,200,474 pay
President, COO, and Director: Charles G. McClure, age 48, $2,657,904 pay
EVP and CFO: G. Michael Lynch, age 58, $1,280,379 pay
EVP, Bearings: Wilhelm A. Schmelzer, age 61, $1,280,379 pay
SVP and CIO: Michael P. Gaynor, age 52
SVP and General Counsel: James J. Zamoyski, age 55, $935,363 pay
SVP, Human Resources: Richard P. Randazzo, age 58
SVP, Friction Products: Rene Dalleur, age 48
SVP, Rings and Liners: Kevin Baird, age 40
SVP, Sealing Systems and Systems Protection: Thomas B. Conaghan, age 51
SVP, Worldwide Aftermarket Operations: Joe Felicelli, age 55
Auditors: Ernst & Young LLP

LOCATIONS

HQ: 26555 Northwestern Hwy., Southfield, MI 48034
Phone: 248-354-7700　　**Fax:** 248-354-8950
Web: www.federal-mogul.com

Federal-Mogul operates 180 manufacturing facilities and technical centers worldwide.

2001 Sales

	$ mil.	% of total
United States	3,123	57
Germany	627	12
United Kingdom	426	8
France	345	6
Other	936	17
Total	**5,457**	**100**

PRODUCTS/OPERATIONS

2001 Sales

	$ mil.	% of total
Aftermarket	2,427	44
Powertrain	1,640	30
Sealing systems & systems protection	588	11
Friction	336	6
Other	368	7
Divested operations	98	2
Total	**5,457**	**100**

Selected Products

Bearings and seals	Pads
Brake shoes	Piston pins, rings, and
Camshafts	liners
Connecting rods	Pistons
Discs	Sintered products
Dynamic seals	Spark plugs
Engine bearings	Steering and suspension
Fuel pumps	products
Gaskets	Timing components
Large bearings	Valvetrain components
Lighting products	Wipers
Oil pumps	

COMPETITORS

ArvinMeritor, Inc.	Gates Rubber
Cooper-Standard	Linamar
Automotive	Robert Bosch
Dana	Stant
Delphi	Valeo
Edelbrock	Visteon

HISTORICAL FINANCIALS & EMPLOYEES

OTC Bulletin Board: FDMLQ FYE: December 31	Annual Growth	12/92	12/93	12/94	12/95	12/96	12/97	12/98	12/99	12/00	12/01
Sales ($ mil.)	17.6%	1,264	1,576	1,896	1,996	2,030	1,807	4,469	6,488	6,013	5,457
Net income ($ mil.)	—	(84)	40	63	(10)	(211)	69	54	243	(282)	(1,146)
Income as % of sales	—	—	2.5%	3.3%	—	—	3.8%	1.2%	3.7%	—	—
Employees	14.7%	14,300	14,400	16,200	17,200	15,700	13,300	54,350	50,400	50,000	49,000

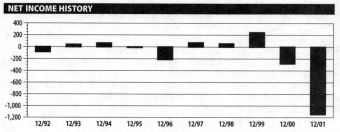

NET INCOME HISTORY

2001 FISCAL YEAR-END

Debt ratio: 38.9%
Return on equity: —
Cash ($ mil.): 347
Current ratio: 2.29
Long-term debt ($ mil.): 267

FEDERATED DEPARTMENT STORES

The nation's #1 upscale department store operator is scaling back on the click-and-order, finding safety in the brick-and-mortar. Including its venerable Bloomingdale's and Macy's chains, Federated Department Stores operates almost 460 stores in 34 states, Puerto Rico, and Guam. Its five regional chains stretch coast to coast and include The Bon Marché (Northwestern US), Burdines (Florida), and Rich's Department Stores, Goldsmith's, and Lazarus (Central and Southeastern US).

Federated stores carry name-brand and private-label merchandise, including apparel, household goods, cosmetics, fragrances, and other accessories for the fashion conscious. The company is trying to sell shoppers on its in-house brands, which account for about 20% of all sales.

Federated has long focused on expanding its catalog and online operations, but losses in that area prompted the company to reorganize those businesses; it has discontinued the Macy's by Mail catalog and turned bloomingdales.com primarily into a marketing tool. (Bloomingdale's by Mail will remain.) Macys.com is getting a makeover to include more housewares, bridal wares, and gifts.

Federated has also unloaded catalog retailer Fingerhut. It has sold most of the assets to a business group led by Fingerhut's former CEO, Theodore Deikel.

HISTORY

In 1929 Fred Lazarus, who controlled Columbus, Ohio's, giant F&R Lazarus department store and the John Shillito Company (the oldest department store west of the Alleghenies; 1830), met with three other great retailers on a yacht in Long Island Sound: Walter Rothschild of Brooklyn-based Abraham & Straus; Louis Kirstein of Boston-based Filene's; and Samuel Bloomingdale, head of Manhattan's Bloomingdale's. Lazarus, Rothschild, and Kirstein agreed to merge their stores into a loose federation. Bloomingdale joined the next year.

Though Federated set up headquarters in Cincinnati in 1945, it continued to be run by powerful merchants in each city where it operated. Under Lazarus' leadership, it was among the first to see the coming growth of the Sunbelt, acquiring Foley's (Houston, 1945), Burdines (Miami, 1956), Sanger's (Dallas, 1958), Bullock's and I. Magnin (California, 1964), and Rich's (Atlanta, 1976).

Federated's growth stalled after Lazarus' son Ralph stepped down in 1981. The company faced stiffer competition from rival department store operators and chains, including May Department Stores, Nordstrom, and Dillard's. By 1989 Federated was no longer a leader, although it was still financially strong.

Years before, when Federated was leader of the department store industry, Allied Stores was #2. Allied was made up mostly of stores that were in small towns or were #2 in their market, with a few leaders (Maas Brothers, The Bon Marché, Jordan Marsh). It had a mediocre track record until Thomas Macioce took the helm in 1971. He closed unprofitable stores, downsized others, and went on an acquisition spree (Brooks Brothers, AnnTaylor).

Campeau Corporation bought Allied and Federated in 1988. Saddled with more than $8 billion in debt from the purchase, both companies declared bankruptcy in 1990. Allen Questrom became Federated's CEO, and in 1992 the companies emerged from bankruptcy as Federated Department Stores. The next year, after being rebuffed in a bid to merge with Macy's, Federated purchased 50% of Macy's unsecured debt, setting the stage for Federated's 1994 acquisition.

Rowland Macy opened a store under his name in Manhattan in 1858. After Macy's death, the Strauses, a New York china merchant family, bought the department store in 1896 and expanded it across the US. In 1986 chairman Edward Finkelstein led a $3.5 billion buyout of Macy's and took it private. Its debt load increased into the early 1990s, and Macy's entered bankruptcy proceedings in 1992.

In 1995 Federated bought the 82-store Broadway Stores and renamed 52 of them Macy's in 1996 (it also renamed 21 Bullock's and 18 Jordan Marsh stores).

Questrom quit (under longstanding tensions with Federated) in 1997, succeeded by president James Zimmerman. The firm paid $10.6 million in 1998 to settle complaints that it illegally collected debts from bankrupt credit card holders.

After relaunching the macys.com Web site, Federated added a number of other hot Web retailing prospects in 1999 by purchasing catalog retailer Fingerhut Companies. It also acquired a 20% stake in WeddingChannel.com.

In 2001 Federated decided to convert 19 of its Stern's locations in New Jersey and New York to its two strongest department store brands, Macy's and Bloomingdale's; it closed the other five Stern's stores.

In July 2002 Federated sold $1.2 billion in Fingerhut credit card receivables to credit card company CompuCredit and other Fingerhut assets to FAC Acquisitions, of which former Fingerhut CEO Thomas Fedders and business partner Theodore Deikel are principals.

OFFICERS

Chairman and CEO: James M. Zimmerman, age 59, $1,250,000 pay
Vice Chairman, Finance and Real Estate: Ronald W. Tysoe, age 49, $825,000 pay
President, COO, Chief Merchandising Officer, and Director: Terry J. Lundgren, age 50, $1,083,333 pay
Group President, Federated Stores: Susan D. Kronick, age 50
EVP, Legal and Human Resources: Thomas G. Cody, age 60, $730,000 pay
EVP, Strategic Initiatives; President, Federated Direct: James J. Amann, age 64
SVP and CFO: Karen M. Hoguet, age 45, $491,667 pay
SVP, Design and Construction: Rudolph V. Javosky
SVP, General Counsel, and Secretary: Dennis J. Broderick, age 53
SVP, Human Resources: David W. Clark, age 50
Chairman and CEO, Bloomingdale's: Michael Gould
Chairman and CEO, Federated Logistics & Operations: Tom Cole, age 52
Chairman and CEO, Federated Merchandising Group: Janet Grove
Chairman and CEO, Macy's West: Robert L. Mettler, age 61
Auditors: KPMG LLP

LOCATIONS

HQ: Federated Department Stores, Inc.
7 W. 7th St., Cincinnati, OH 45202
Phone: 513-579-7000   **Fax:** 513-579-7555
Web: www.federated-fds.com

PRODUCTS/OPERATIONS

Store Chains and Locations
Bloomingdale's
The Bon Marché (northwestern US)
Burdines (Florida)
Goldsmith's (Tennessee)
Lazarus (midwestern US)
Macy's
Rich's (southeastern US)

Other Operations
Bloomingdale's by Mail (catalog business)
bloomingdales.com
macys.com

Private Labels
Alfani
Charter Club
Greendog
I.N.C
Jennifer Moore
Style & Co.
Tools of the Trade

COMPETITORS

American Retail	J. Crew	Nordstrom
AnnTaylor	Jos. A. Bank	Polo
Bed Bath &	Kohl's	Saks Inc.
Beyond	Lands' End	Sears
Belk	Limited Brands	Spiegel
Brown Shoe	Linens 'n Things	Talbots
Dillard's	May	Target
Foot Locker	Men's Wearhouse	TJX
The Gap	Neiman Marcus	Zale
J. C. Penney	Nine West	

HISTORICAL FINANCIALS & EMPLOYEES

NYSE: FD FYE: Saturday nearest Jan. 31	Annual Growth	1/93	1/94	1/95	1/96	1/97	1/98	1/99	1/00	1/01	1/02
Sales ($ mil.)	9.2%	7,080	7,229	8,316	15,049	15,229	15,668	15,833	17,716	18,407	15,651
Net income ($ mil.)	—	113	193	188	75	266	536	662	795	(184)	(276)
Income as % of sales	—	1.6%	2.7%	2.3%	0.5%	1.7%	3.4%	4.2%	4.5%	—	—
Earnings per share ($)	—	1.01	1.50	1.40	0.39	1.24	2.41	2.96	3.62	(0.90)	(1.38)
Stock price - FY high ($)	—	21.50	25.00	25.25	30.13	37.00	48.88	56.19	57.06	46.06	49.90
Stock price - FY low ($)	—	11.25	17.38	17.88	18.75	26.13	31.63	32.81	36.44	21.00	26.05
Stock price - FY close ($)	8.3%	20.38	21.88	18.88	27.00	32.88	42.31	41.81	41.63	44.56	41.62
P/E - high	—	18	16	18	77	29	18	17	15	—	—
P/E - low	—	9	11	13	48	20	12	10	10	—	—
Dividends per share ($)	—	0.00	0.00	0.00	0.00	0.00	0.00	0.00	0.00	0.00	0.00
Book value per share ($)	6.0%	16.46	18.03	19.93	21.09	22.45	25.04	27.38	30.69	29.46	27.71
Employees	5.2%	73,000	67,300	111,700	119,100	117,100	114,700	118,800	133,000	129,000	115,000

STOCK PRICE HISTORY

HIGH/LOW/CLOSE

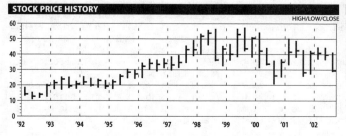

2002 FISCAL YEAR-END

Debt ratio: 41.0%
Return on equity: —
Cash ($ mil.): 636
Current ratio: 1.96
Long-term debt ($ mil.): 3,859
No. of shares (mil.): 201
Dividends
  Yield: —
  Payout: —
Market value ($ mil.): 8,357

FEDEX CORPORATION

Fast delivery made it famous, but FedEx is looking for another burst of speed to win the race in the information economy. The Memphis-based holding company has pulled together its key subsidiaries under the FedEx umbrella to offer customers a single source for a variety of delivery services.

E-mail has stolen thunder from the overnight delivery gig, but FedEx subsidiary Federal Express (doing business as FedEx Express) is still the world's #1 express delivery company, with 55,000 drop-off locations, nearly 650 aircraft, and about 50,000 vehicles. The unit delivers some 3 million packages to more than 210 countries and territories each working day. In a landmark deal with the U.S. Postal Service, FedEx Express is providing air transportation for postal express shipments (but not delivering mail), and FedEx drop boxes are being placed in post offices.

FedEx is also a leading small-package carrier in North America through FedEx Ground (formerly RPS), which ships goods between businesses and offers residential delivery. Surface-expedited carrier FedEx Custom Critical (formerly Roberts Express) specializes in urgent deliveries, and FedEx Trade Networks, created in 2000, provides customs brokerage and trade consulting services through Tower Group International and Caribbean Transportation. Less-than-truckload (LTL) carriers FedEx Freight offers service throughout the US through FedEx Freight East (formerly American Freightways) and FedEx Freight West (formerly Viking Freight).

Founder and CEO Fred Smith owns about 7% of FedEx.

HISTORY

Vietnam vet Fred Smith recognized in the 1960s the need for a reliable, overnight delivery service. He presented the idea in a Yale term paper but only received a C. However, from 1969 to 1971 Smith secured $90 million ($40 million from investors, $8 million from his family, and the balance from bank financing) to make his Federal Express the largest startup funded by venture capital. Overnight and second-day delivery to 22 US cities began in 1973.

Several factors contributed to FedEx's early success: Airlines turned their focus from parcels to passengers; United Parcel Service (UPS) union workers went on strike in 1974; and competitor REA Express went bankrupt. FedEx went public in 1978.

Spotting e-mail's threat to express delivery in the early 1980s, FedEx invested heavily in satellite-based system ZapMail. However, the humble fax machine blindsided FedEx, and it lost over $300 million in 1986 on the short-lived service. The 1987 launch of PowerShip, which processed shipments electronically, was more successful. FedEx expanded internationally in the late 1980s, buying Italy's SAMIMA and three Japanese freight carriers in 1988 and Tiger International (Flying Tigers line) in 1989. That year it doubled overseas sales to become the #1 air cargo company.

In 1991 FedEx introduced EXPRESSfreighter, an international air-express cargo service but suffered a setback when its loss-making European delivery service was scrapped the next year. However, FedEx was back on its feet in 1995 when it created Latin American and Caribbean divisions and became the first US express carrier with direct flights to China.

FedEx jumped back into the Web in 1996 and introduced Internet-based shipping management system interNetShip. It also began selling BusinessLink, a software package that helps businesses use the Internet to sell goods, which are delivered by FedEx.

The 1997 UPS strike put an extra 850,000 packages a day into FedEx's hands. Turning the screws on UPS, FedEx bought ground carrier Caliber System in 1998 and reorganized into holding company FDX. FedEx pilots (unionized in 1993) threatened their own strike during the 1998 holiday season, prompting FedEx to outsource more of its flight operations. Nevertheless, the pilots ratified a five-year contract the following year.

Focusing on the supply chain, in 1999 FedEx restructured Caliber's logistics unit and formed a business-to-business logistics alliance with KPMG. It bought freight forwarder GeoLogistics Air Services (renamed Caribbean Transportation Services), and, internationally, opened its first European hub in Paris and launched a joint venture in China.

In 2000 FDX changed its name to FedEx. In a major rebranding effort, RPS' name was changed to FedEx Ground and Roberts Express became FedEx Custom Critical. Also that year the company formed FedEx Trade Networks to offer customs brokerage and trade consulting services.

The next year FedEx phased out its FedEx Logistics subsidiary, shifting its operations into other subsidiaries. The company acquired less-than-truckload (LTL) carrier American Freightways, and FedEx Freight was created to operate American Freightways and Viking Freight. (By 2002, both carriers were using the FedEx Freight brand name.)

FedEx planes were grounded for a day by the FAA in September 2001 after terrorists used commercial jets to strike the World Trade Center and the Pentagon.

Chairman, President, and CEO: Frederick W. Smith, age 57, $2,467,993 pay
EVP and CFO: Alan B. Graf Jr., age 48, $993,871 pay
EVP, General Counsel, and Secretary: Kenneth R. Masterson, age 58, $1,061,195 pay
EVP, Market Development and Corporate Communications; President and CEO, FedEx Corporate Services: T. Michael Glenn, age 46, $901,999 pay
EVP and CIO: Robert B. Carter, age 43, $787,064 pay
EVP and COO, FedEx Ground: Ivan T. Hofmann
EVP, FedEx Ground: Rodger G. Marticke
EVP, International, FedEx Express: Michael L. Ducker
EVP, Operations and Systems Support, FedEx Express: David F. Rebholz
SVP and Chief Personnel Officer: Larry Brown
Auditors: Ernst & Young LLP

LOCATIONS

HQ: 942 S. Shady Grove Rd., Memphis, TN 38120
Phone: 901-818-7500   **Fax:** 901-395-2000
Web: www.fedex.com

FedEx's subsidiaries operate in the US and provide services to about 210 other countries and territories.

Major Hubs and Sorting Facilities

US
Anchorage, AK
Chicago
Fort Worth, TX
Indianapolis
Los Angeles
Memphis
Newark, NJ

Oakland, CA

International
London
Paris
Subic Bay, Philippines
Tokyo
Toronto

PRODUCTS/OPERATIONS

2002 Sales

	$ mil.	% of total
FedEx Express	15,327	74
FedEx Ground	2,711	13
FedEx Freight	1,960	10
Other	609	3
Total	**20,607**	**100**

Selected Services

FedEx 1Day Freight
FedEx 2Day
FedEx 2Day Freight
FedEx 3Day Freight
FedEx Express Saver
FedEx Extra Hours
FedEx First Overnight
FedEx International Airport-to-Airport
FedEx International Broker Select
FedEx International Economy

FedEx International Express Freight
FedEx International First
FedEx International MailService
FedEx International Priority
FedEx Priority Overnight
FedEx SameDay
FedEx Standard Overnight

COMPETITORS

Airborne
AMR
BAX Global
Burlington Northern Santa Fe
Canada Post
CHR
CNF
CSX

Deutsche Post
DHL Worldwide Express
Landstar System
Nippon Express
Norfolk Southern
Overnite Transportation
Ryder

Stinnes
TPG
UAL
U.S. Postal Service
Union Pacific
UPS
USFreightways
Yellow

HISTORICAL FINANCIALS & EMPLOYEES

NYSE: FDX FYE: May 31	Annual Growth	5/93	5/94	5/95	5/96	5/97	5/98	5/99	5/00	5/01	5/02
Sales ($ mil.)	11.4%	7,808	8,480	9,392	10,274	11,520	15,873	16,774	18,257	19,629	20,607
Net income ($ mil.)	33.2%	54	204	298	308	361	503	631	688	584	710
Income as % of sales	—	0.7%	2.4%	3.2%	3.0%	3.1%	3.2%	3.8%	3.8%	3.0%	3.4%
Earnings per share ($)	28.2%	0.25	0.92	1.32	1.35	1.56	1.69	2.10	2.32	1.99	2.34
Stock price - FY high ($)	—	15.19	19.47	20.19	21.50	28.94	47.13	61.88	57.13	49.97	61.35
Stock price - FY low ($)	—	8.63	11.09	13.38	14.63	18.13	26.25	21.81	30.56	33.38	33.15
Stock price - FY close ($)	17.9%	12.25	19.13	14.97	19.16	26.19	32.06	54.81	35.50	40.00	53.95
P/E - high	—	30	21	15	16	19	25	29	24	25	25
P/E - low	—	17	12	10	11	12	15	10	13	17	14
Dividends per share ($)	—	0.00	0.00	0.00	0.00	0.00	0.00	0.00	0.00	0.00	0.00
Book value per share ($)	12.4%	7.63	8.61	10.09	11.32	15.23	13.44	15.65	16.03	19.76	21.92
Employees	7.7%	95,000	101,000	107,000	114,208	126,000	138,000	141,000	149,000	176,960	184,953

STOCK PRICE HISTORY

HIGH/LOW/CLOSE

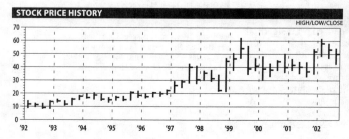

2002 FISCAL YEAR-END

Debt ratio: 21.6%
Return on equity: 11.4%
Cash ($ mil.): 331
Current ratio: 1.25
Long-term debt ($ mil.): 1,800
No. of shares (mil.): 299
Dividends
  Yield: —
  Payout: —
Market value ($ mil.): 16,108

FIDELITY NATIONAL FINANCIAL

Taking a cue from its fast food holdings, title insurer Fidelity National Financial (FNF) has supersized its primary business with its purchase of Chicago Title. The Irvine, California-based firm now claims 30% of the title insurance business in the US, making it #1, bumping First American from the top spot.

FNF's more than 1,100 offices — some 400 from Chicago Title — and more than 8,000 agents across the US primarily serve residential customers, but increasingly target commercial transactions. Subsidiaries also perform such title-related services as escrow, flood certification, credit reporting, and closing; the company offers equipment leases through its FNF Capital unit, while it is active in e-commerce development and services through its majority stake in Micro General.

The firm is expanding its real estate products base; it bought real estate information company Fidelity National Information Solutions and combined the firm with the similar International Data Management, a previous purchase, and its listing service vendor Risco. Fidelity National Information Solutions plans to buy Micro General, FNF will own 72.5% of the combined company.

The firm is expanding the scope of its real estate-related products and is focusing on services online, hoping convenience will attract more clients as rising interest rates deter homeowners from seeking its services.

The company also dabbles in America's favorite pastime: eating. Its fast food holdings include a stake in CKE Restaurants, parent of burgermeisters Hardee's and Carl's Jr.

FNF chairman and CEO William Foley II owns some 5% of the firm.

stake (now about 33%) in Green Burrito restaurants' parent GB Foods (now Santa Barbara Restaurant Group).

In 1998 FNF bought Alamo Title (in #2 title market Texas), equipment leasing firm Granite Financial (now FNF Capital), and a stake in investment bank Cruttenden Roth (sold in 2000). FNF spun off all but 30% of its California operations as American National Financial in 1999. In 2000 FNF bought Chicago Title.

Chicago Title traces its roots back to a Chicago law clerk named Edward Rucker who created a system for tracking real estate transactions. Rucker and his partner James Rees began providing services to real estate businesses in Chicago. In 1871, after the Great Chicago Fire destroyed almost all the official real estate title records in the city, Rucker and Rees, and two other competitors' records became the legal title records for the city, creating the basis for private title insurance. Those three firms merged and in 1891 became Chicago Title and Trust. The company focused solely on Chicago until 1930 when it opened an office in Springfield, Illinois. During the 1950s and 1960s the company began to expand outside Illinois.

Following the acquisition of Chicago Title, Fidelity National cut some 1,500 jobs as it consolidated Chicago Title's operations with its own.

The company spent the first part of the new decade adding real estate information services to its lineup. In 2001 it created Fidelity National Information Solutions to provide real estate-related information and technical information to real estate companies, and in 2002 FNF launched Property Insight to provide real estate property information services to title companies.

HISTORY

Fidelity National Title Insurance was launched in Nebraska in 1961. William Foley (then at Arizona's Security S&L) and colleague Frank Willey bought it in 1984. Foley and Willey already had several small California title firms. Fidelity National Financial (FNF) went public in 1987 and moved to Irvine, California.

FNF was the only title firm with consecutive profits during the real estate crash of the late 1980s and early 1990s (it focused on residential real estate and did in-house research and underwriting). Earnings were flat, but cost controls eased the drop in business.

In the 1990s acquisitions increased geographic reach. FNF bought real estate software and tax information services and sought non-real estate investments to decrease reliance on that volatile market. In 1997 FNF bought a 42%

OFFICERS

Chairman and CEO: William P. Foley II, age 57, $3,810,516 pay
Vice Chairman: Frank P. Willey, age 48, $981,340 pay
President, COO, and Director: Patrick F. Stone, age 54, $3,010,500 pay
EVP and CFO: Alan L. Stinson, age 56, $1,060,516 pay
EVP and General Counsel: Peter T. Sadowski, age 47, $910,500 pay
EVP and Division Manager: Raymond R. Quirk
EVP and Division Manager: Ronald R. Maudsley
EVP and Division Manager: Ernest D. Smith
EVP and Division Manager: Christopher Abbinante
VP, Human Resources: Anne Kulinsky
SVP, Sales and Marketing, Fidelity National Information Solutions: Mark Johnson
Auditors: KPMG LLP

LOCATIONS

HQ: Fidelity National Financial, Inc.,
4050 Talle Real, Santa Barbara, CA 93110
Phone: 949-622-4333
Web: www.fnf.com

Fidelity National Financial operates in Canada, Mexico, Puerto Rico, the US, and the Virgin Islands.

2001 Title Premiums

	% of total
California	25
Texas	13
New York	8
Florida	6
Illinois	5
Arizona	4
Others	39
Total	**100**

PRODUCTS/OPERATIONS

2001 Assets

	$ mil.	% of total
Cash & equivalents	543	12
Treasury & agency securities	461	11
State & municipal bonds	519	12
Corporate bonds	233	6
Stocks	56	1
Other investments	535	12
Receivables	184	4
Cost in excess of net assets acquired	809	18
Other assets	1,076	24
Total	**4,416**	**100**

Selected Subsidiaries

A.S.A.P. Legal Publication Services, Inc.
Alamo Title Company
Alamo Title Insurance
Chicago Title and Trust Company
Chicago Title Company
Chicago Title Insurance Company
Fidelity National Appraisal Services, Inc.
Fidelity National Asset Management Solutions, Inc.
Fidelity National Home Warranty Company
Fidelity National Information Solutions, Inc. (78%)
Fidelity National Insurance Company
Fidelity National Management Services, LLC
Fidelity National Title Company
Fidelity National Title Insurance Company
Fidelity Residential Solutions, Inc.
Fidelity Tax Service, Inc.
FNF Capital, Inc.
FNF Management Corp.
HomeOwnershipTeam.com, Inc.
Inspection One, Inc.
Micro General Corporation (65.7%)
National Title Insurance Services, Inc.
Professional Escrow, Inc.
Real Estate Index, Inc.
Rocky Mountain Aviation, Inc.
Sentry Service Systems, Inc.
The Title Guarantee Company
Title Services, Inc.

COMPETITORS

First American Corporation
Investors Title
LandAmerica Financial Group
National Title Resources
Old Republic
Stewart Information

HISTORICAL FINANCIALS & EMPLOYEES

NYSE: FNF FYE: December 31	Annual Growth	12/92	12/93	12/94	12/95	12/96	12/97	12/98	12/99	12/00	12/01
Assets ($ mil.)	37.6%	249	396	418	405	509	601	970	1,029	3,834	4,416
Net income ($ mil.)	39.7%	15	36	12	7	24	40	106	71	108	306
Income as % of assets	—	6.1%	9.2%	2.9%	1.7%	4.8%	6.6%	10.9%	6.9%	2.8%	6.9%
Earnings per share ($)	19.2%	0.65	1.34	0.45	0.33	1.01	1.50	2.67	1.88	1.47	3.16
Stock price – FY high ($)	—	7.00	15.37	15.16	10.72	11.17	23.61	32.77	25.41	32.53	31.50
Stock price – FY low ($)	—	3.32	6.27	5.50	5.57	7.45	7.85	17.23	11.10	9.61	16.28
Stock price – FY close ($)	14.5%	6.68	15.23	6.13	10.51	10.33	23.38	25.20	11.88	30.52	22.54
P/E – high	—	11	11	40	29	9	12	10	13	21	10
P/E – low	—	5	5	14	15	6	4	6	6	6	5
Dividends per share ($)	14.6%	0.10	0.12	0.16	0.16	0.17	0.21	0.21	0.23	0.33	0.34
Book value per share ($)	23.4%	2.63	4.24	4.61	3.94	5.41	8.18	11.34	13.14	13.16	17.39
Employees	17.9%	4,000	4,700	3,500	4,100	4,500	5,200	7,400	6,000	16,000	17,600

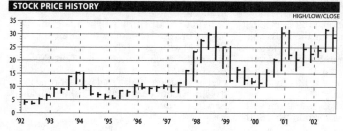

STOCK PRICE HISTORY
HIGH/LOW/CLOSE

2001 FISCAL YEAR-END

Equity as % of assets: 37.1%
Return on assets: 7.4%
Return on equity: 22.3%
Long-term debt ($ mil.): 566
No. of shares (mil.): 94
Dividends
  Yield: 1.5%
  Payout: 10.8%
Market value ($ mil.): 2,125
Sales ($ mil.): 3,874

FIFTH THIRD BANCORP

Fifth Third Bancorp doesn't wait for customers to find it. The Cincinnati-based bank and financial services firm employs an aggressive employee-based sales approach and an ambitious acquisition strategy, putting itself at the beck and telephone call of customers.

Fifth Third's operations consist of consumer and business banking (credit cards, loans, and deposit accounts); investment advisory (proprietary mutual funds, private banking, brokerage, and corporate pension products); and ATM and merchant transaction processing and electronic fund transfers (through subsidiary Midwest Payment Systems). Fifth Third also offers insurance, foreign exchange trading, and import/export services. Its decentralized affiliate banks, located largely in Indiana, Illinois, Kentucky, Ohio, and Michigan (and in Arizona and Florida for snowbirds), emphasize a community-centered approach and operate more than 900 branches, including about 140 Bank Mart seven-days-a-week locations.

Known for its frugality and strong sales culture, Fifth Third offers its employees incentives for bringing in new business. Targeting metropolitan areas within or contiguous to its market area, the company has expanded its geographic reach and product offerings mainly by acquiring relatively small banks, asset managers, and data processing firms. It has arranged to buy Franklin Financial, which will give it a foothold in the growing Nashville, Tennessee area. Fifth Third plans more expansion there and may possibly increase its presence in Pittsburgh. Insurer Cincinnati Financial Corporation owns more than 12% of Fifth Third.

HISTORY

In 1863 a group of Cincinnati businessmen opened the Third National Bank inside a Masonic temple to serve the Ohio River trade. Acquiring the Bank of the Ohio Valley (founded 1858) in 1871, the firm progressed until the panic of 1907. Third National survived and in 1908 consolidated with Fifth National, forming the Fifth Third National Bank of Cincinnati. The newly organized bank acquired two local banks in 1910.

A second bank consolidation, in 1919, resulted in Fifth Third's affiliation with Union Savings Bank and Trust Company, permitting the bank to establish branches, theretofore forbidden by regulators. The company acquired the assets and offices of five more banks and thrifts that year, operating them as branches.

In 1927 the bank merged its operations with the Union Trust Company, forming the Fifth Third Union Trust. With its combined strength, it weathered the Great Depression and acquired three more banks between 1930 and 1933. However, the Depression also brought massive banking regulations to the industry, limiting Fifth Third's acquisitions.

In the postwar years and during the 1950s and 1960s, the bank expanded its consumer banking services, offering traveler's checks. Under CEO Bill Rowe, son of former CEO John Rowe, the firm emphasized the convenience of its locations and increased hours of operations.

In the 1970s Fifth Third shifted its lending program's emphasis from commercial loans to consumer credit and launched its ATM and telephone banking services. Aware that the bank was technologically unprepared for the onslaught of electronic information, Fifth Third expanded its data processing and information services resources, forming the basis for its Midwest Payment Systems division.

The company formed Fifth Third Bancorp, a holding company, and began to branch within Ohio (branching had previously been limited to the home county) in 1975. Ten years later, more deregulation allowed the bank to move into contiguous states. Focused on consumer banking, and with cautious underwriting policies, Fifth Third weathered the leveraged-buyout problems and real estate bust of the 1980s and acquired new outlets cheaply by buying several small banks, as well as branches from larger banks. It acquired the American National Bank in Kentucky and moved further afield with its purchase of the Sovereign Savings Bank in Palm Harbor, Florida, in 1991.

The company continued to expand, buying several banks and thrifts in Ohio in 1997 and 1998. In 1999 Fifth Third moved into Indiana in a big way with its purchase of CNB Bancshares, then solidified its position in the state with the acquisition of Peoples Bank of Indianapolis. Fifth Third also moved into new business areas, buying mortgage banker W. Lyman Case, broker-dealer The Ohio Company (1998), and Cincinnati-based commercial mortgage banker Vanguard Financial (1999). The company began to offer online foreign exchange via its FX Internet Trading Web in 2000.

In 2001 Fifth Third bought money manager Maxus Investments and added some 300 bank branches with its purchase of Capital Holdings (Ohio and Michigan) and Old Kent Financial (Michigan, Indiana, and Illinois), its largest-ever acquisition. It also sold its subprime mortgage servicing portfolio to Wilshire Financial Services Group.

President, CEO, and Director, Fifth Third Bancorp and Fifth Third Bank: George A. Schaefer, age 56, $2,476,170 pay
EVP and CFO, Fifth Third Bancorp and Fifth Third Bank: Neal E. Arnold, age 42, $700,774 pay
EVP, Fifth Third Bancorp and Fifth Third Bank: Michael D. Baker, age 51, $758,480 pay
EVP, Fifth Third Bancorp and Fifth Third Bank: Barry L. Boerstler, age 54
EVP; President and CEO, Fifth Third Bank, Kentucky: James R. Gaunt, age 56
EVP, Fifth Third Bancorp and Fifth Third Bank: James J. Hudepohl, age 49
EVP; President and CEO, Fifth Third Bank, Northeastern Ohio: Robert J. King Jr., age 46, $653,092 pay
EVP, Fifth Third Bancorp and Fifth Third Bank: Robert P. Niehaus, age 55, $712,374 pay
EVP, Secretary, and General Counsel: Paul L. Reynolds, age 40
EVP, Fifth Third Bancorp and Fifth Third Bank: Stephen J. Schrantz, age 52, $922,897 pay
VP, Human Resources, Fifth Third Bancorp and Fifth Third Bank: Mary Sue Findley
Auditors: Deloitte & Touche LLP

LOCATIONS

HQ: Fifth Third Center, 38 Fountain Square Plaza, Cincinnati, OH 45263
Phone: 513-579-5300
Web: www.53.com

Fifth Third Bancorp operates nearly 1,000 branch locations in Arizona, Florida, Indiana, Illinois, Kentucky, Michigan, and Ohio.

PRODUCTS/OPERATIONS

2001 Sales

	$ mil.	% of total
Interest		
Loans & leases	3,420	52
Securities	1,279	20
Other short-term investments	10	—
Noninterest		
Service charges on deposits	367	6
Electronic payment processing	347	5
Investment advisory income	307	5
Other	776	12
Total	**6,506**	**100**

Selected Subsidiaries and Affiliates
Fifth Third Bank
Fifth Third Community Development Corporation
Fifth Third Insurance Services, Inc.
Fifth Third Investment Company
Fountain Square Insurance Company
Heartland Capital Management, Inc.
Old Kent Capital Trust I
USB, Inc.

COMPETITORS

Advest	First Data	National City
BANK ONE	FirstMerit	National
Charter One	Harris Bankcorp	Processing
Comerica	Huntington	Northern Trust
Community First	Bancshares	PNC Financial
Bankshares,	KeyCorp	U.S. Bancorp
Inc.	LaSalle Bank	Wells Fargo
Deluxe	N.A.	
EDS	Marshall & Ilsley	

HISTORICAL FINANCIALS & EMPLOYEES

Nasdaq: FITB FYE: December 31	Annual Growth	12/92	12/93	12/94	12/95	12/96	12/97	12/98	12/99	12/00	12/01
Assets ($ mil.)	24.0%	10,213	11,966	14,957	17,053	20,549	21,375	28,922	41,589	45,857	71,026
Net income ($ mil.)	23.5%	164	196	245	288	335	401	476	668	863	1,094
Income as % of assets	—	1.6%	1.6%	1.6%	1.7%	1.6%	1.9%	1.6%	1.6%	1.9%	1.5%
Earnings per share ($)	14.7%	0.54	0.63	0.73	0.84	0.95	1.15	1.17	1.43	1.83	1.86
Stock price - FY high ($)	—	10.69	11.68	10.89	15.14	22.03	37.15	49.44	50.32	60.88	64.77
Stock price - FY low ($)	—	7.87	9.80	8.91	9.30	12.91	18.03	31.68	38.60	29.35	45.69
Stock price - FY close ($)	21.4%	10.69	10.24	9.50	14.50	18.64	36.37	47.57	48.94	59.75	61.33
P/E - high	—	19	18	15	18	23	32	41	35	33	34
P/E - low	—	14	15	12	11	13	15	26	27	16	24
Dividends per share ($)	20.1%	0.15	0.19	0.23	0.27	0.31	0.37	0.55	0.56	0.68	0.78
Book value per share ($)	16.5%	3.33	3.86	4.28	5.10	6.01	6.53	7.94	8.80	10.50	13.11
Employees	18.5%	4,159	4,987	5,644	6,108	6,549	7,180	8,761	12,240	12,246	19,118

STOCK PRICE HISTORY

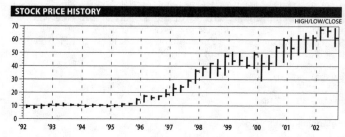

HIGH/LOW/CLOSE

2001 FISCAL YEAR-END
Equity as % of assets: 10.8%
Return on assets: 1.9%
Return on equity: 17.5%
Long-term debt ($ mil.): 7,030
No. of shares (mil.): 583
Dividends
 Yield: 1.3%
 Payout: 41.9%
Market value ($ mil.): 35,735
Sales ($ mil.): 6,506

FIRST AMERICAN CORPORATION

Act locally, think globally.

The First American Corporation (formerly First American Financial), whose First American Title Insurance subsidiary is one of the most prominent title companies in the US, turns the old saw around in its quest for a national database to centralize title records. To help it get there, the company has acquired such firms as Data Tree, owner of an extensive database of imaged property records. Data Trace Information Services, a joint venture with LandAmerica, and First American Real Estate Solutions, a joint venture with Transamerica, will also help First American Financial reach its goal: Eliminating costly local searches by providing a central source for property titles.

Santa Ana, California-based First American also offers real estate tax valuation services, mortgage credit reporting, home warranty, and other services. The company is making use of its extensive databases to offer other services, such as employee screening and credit reporting for landlords. The company operates in Australia, Latin and North America, and the UK. Donald and Parker Kennedy (officers of First American and descendants of its founder) own some 5% of the firm.

HISTORY

In 1889, when Los Angeles was on its way to becoming a real city, the more countrified residents to the south (including the Irvine Company's founding family) formed Orange County, a peaceful realm of citrus groves where land transactions were assisted by title companies Orange County Abstract and Santa Ana Abstract. In 1894 the firms merged under the leadership of local businessman C. E. Parker. For three decades, the resulting Orange County Title limited its business to title searches.

In 1924, as real estate transactions became more complex (in part because of mineral-rights issues related to Southern California's oil boom), Orange County Title began offering title insurance and escrow services. The company remained under Parker family management until 1930, when H. A. Gardner took over and guided it through the Depression. In 1943 the company returned to Parker family control.

In 1957 the company began a major expansion beyond Orange County. The new First American Title Insurance and Trust name acknowledged the firm's expansion into trust and custody operations. Donald Kennedy (C. E. Parker's grandson) took over in 1963 and took the company public the next year.

In 1968 First American Financial was formed as a holding company for subsidiaries First American Title Insurance and First American Trust. This structure facilitated growth as the firm began opening new offices and buying all or parts of other title companies, including Title Guaranty Co. of Wyoming, Security Title & Trust (San Antonio), and Ticore, Inc. (Portland, Oregon), all purchased in 1968.

The 1970s were a quiet time for the company, but it began growing again in the 1980s as savings and loan deregulation jump-started the commercial real estate market in Southern California. First American diversified into home warranty and real estate tax services. In 1988, on the brink of the California meltdown, the company bought an industrial loan corporation to make commercial real estate loans.

Reduced property sales during California's early 1990s real estate crash and recession rocked company results. Fluctuating interest rates didn't help the tremulous bottom lines. In 1994 Donald Kennedy became chairman; his son Parker became president.

As part of its expansion effort, First American bought CREDCO (mortgage credit reporting) and Flood Data Services (flood zone certification) in 1995. A year later it acquired Ward Associates, a property inspection and preservation service provider. In 1997 the company merged its real estate information subsidiaries with those of the Experian Information Solutions, a leading supplier of real estate data; it also bought Strategic Mortgage Services (mortgage information and document preparation), whose software formed the core of software operations for First American's title division.

Earnings jumped in 1998's hot real estate market. That year and the next, First American's acquisitions brought into the company's fold resident screening services and providers of mortgage loan and loan default management software. In 1999 American Financial and Wells Fargo teamed to provide title insurance and appraisal services nationwide.

In 2000 the company bought National Information Group, a provider of tax service, flood certification, and insurance tracking for the mortgage industry. That year the company partnered with Transamerica to create the US's largest property database.

The company purchased Credit Management Solutions in 2001.

Chairman: Donald P. Kennedy, age 83, $801,400 pay
President and Director: Parker S. Kennedy, age 54, $1,350,904 pay
SEVP and General Counsel: Craig I. DeRoy, age 49, $1,090,924 pay
SEVP and CFO: Thomas A. Klemens, age 51, $1,100,224 pay
EVP: Curt A. Caspersen, age 43
EVP: Gary L. Kermott, age 48, $1,091,091 pay
EVP, Technology Initiatives: John M. Hollenbeck, age 40
SVP and CIO: Roger S. Hull
SVP and National Litigation Counsel: Timothy P. Sullivan
VP, Administration: Elizabeth M. Brandon
VP, Affiliated Business Ventures: Linda L. Saunders
VP, Corporate Communications: Jo Etta Bandy
VP, Corporate Services: Karen S. Ebbing
VP, Interactive Division: Thomas E. Huffman
VP and Director, Mergers & Acquisitions: Thomas R. Wawersich
VP, Secretary, and Corporate Counsel: Mark R. Arnesen, age 49
VP and Chief Accounting Officer: Max O. Valdes
Auditors: PricewaterhouseCoopers LLP

LOCATIONS

HQ: The First American Corporation
1 First American Way, Santa Ana, CA 92707
Phone: 714-800-3000   **Fax:** 714-541-6372
Web: www.firstam.com

The First American Corporation operates some 400 offices in the US and Canada, and has other operations in Australia, the Bahamas, Guam, the UK, and the Virgin Islands.

PRODUCTS/OPERATIONS

2001 Assets

	$ mil.	% of total
Cash & equivalents	645	23
US Treasurys	32	1
Mortgage-backed securities	41	2
State & municipal bonds	39	1
Corporate bonds	144	5
Stocks	52	2
Property & equipment	773	27
Goodwill	433	15
Other	678	24
Total	**2,837**	**100**

Selected Subsidiaries

First American Capital Management, Inc. (investment services)
First American Management Company
First American Property Data Services Inc.
First American Real Estate Information Services, Inc.
First American Title Insurance Company, Inc.
First American Trust Co. (trust services)
HireCheck, Inc. (formerly CIC, Inc.; employee screening for employers)
Market Data Center, LLC (automated appraisal systems)
National Information Group (flood certifications and tax services)
Quixsource, Inc.
Strategic Mortgage Services, Inc.

COMPETITORS

Fidelity National
Investors Title
LandAmerica Financial Group
Old Republic
PMI Group
Stewart Information

HISTORICAL FINANCIALS & EMPLOYEES

NYSE: FAF FYE: December 31	Annual Growth	12/92	12/93	12/94	12/95	12/96	12/97	12/98	12/99	12/00	12/01
Assets ($ mil.)	17.0%	691	786	829	874	980	1,168	1,785	2,116	2,200	2,837
Net income ($ mil.)	16.2%	43	66	19	8	54	65	199	33	82	167
Income as % of assets	—	6.3%	8.4%	2.3%	0.9%	5.5%	5.5%	11.1%	1.6%	3.7%	5.9%
Earnings per share ($)	9.4%	1.01	1.29	0.37	0.15	1.03	1.21	3.32	0.50	1.24	2.27
Stock price - FY high ($)	—	5.94	8.72	8.33	6.11	9.13	16.60	43.00	35.19	32.88	35.49
Stock price - FY low ($)	—	2.62	5.00	3.55	3.66	5.50	6.97	15.92	11.50	10.25	16.30
Stock price - FY close ($)	13.9%	5.83	7.77	3.83	5.94	9.13	16.41	32.13	12.44	32.88	18.74
P/E - high	—	6	7	23	41	9	13	12	26	25	14
P/E - low	—	3	4	10	24	5	6	5	8	8	6
Dividends per share ($)	14.0%	0.08	0.11	0.13	0.13	0.15	0.16	0.20	0.24	0.24	0.26
Book value per share ($)	23.5%	2.40	5.54	5.44	5.89	6.78	7.89	12.13	12.54	13.62	16.08
Employees	11.2%	8,694	10,679	9,033	10,149	11,611	12,930	19,669	20,065	20,346	22,597

STOCK PRICE HISTORY

HIGH/LOW/CLOSE

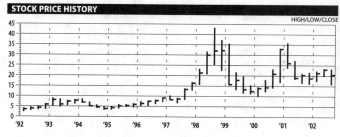

2001 FISCAL YEAR-END

Equity as % of assets: 38.9%
Return on assets: 6.6%
Return on equity: 16.9%
Long-term debt ($ mil.): 415
No. of shares (mil.): 69
Dividends
  Yield: 1.4%
  Payout: 11.5%
Market value ($ mil.): 1,287
Sales ($ mil.): 3,751

FIRST DATA CORPORATION

Paper, plastic, wire, or Internet — First Data has the means to move the money.

The Greenwood Village, Colorado-based company is parent to money transfer powerhouse Western Union; First Data is also the #1 credit card transaction processor in the US. Other subsidiaries handle online transactions and verify paper checks (how quaint!).

The company's payment services segment makes up about 40% of revenues and includes subsidiaries Orlandi Valuta and Western Union, which itself has some 120,000 agent locations worldwide (a number expected to grow thanks to alliances with such entities as 7-Eleven, Rite Aid, Publix, and Banamex).

Its merchant services segment includes subsidiaries focused on credit and debit card transaction processing (First Data Merchant Services), check verification and guarantee (TeleCheck), and ATM network operations (NYCE).

First Data Resources and other subsidiaries make up the card issuing services segment, which provides processing and related products and services (including software) to financial institutions, retailers, and oil companies.

First Data also has operations in electronic tax processing, online payments, telecommunications services, and other areas. It also owns about 45% of card processor Paymentech, a joint venture with BANK ONE.

HISTORY

Both predecessors of today's First Data (First Financial Management and First Data Resources) developed from in-house data processing operations that became independent profit centers for their parent companies and were then spun off.

The older of the two companies, First Financial Management, arose out of the data processing department of the Georgia Railroad Bank & Trust. By the time it went public in 1983, First Financial was the largest banking data processor in the Southeast. It grew rapidly in a consolidating industry and in 1987 entered the credit card transaction processing business with the purchase of NaBANCO.

That year American Express created First Data Resources, a separate unit for its transaction processing functions, under the leadership of Henry Duques. Duques had built up the unit during the 1980s to process a variety of transactions for American Express' charge card processing business and its burgeoning financial services operations, which included the Boston Company (now part of Mellon Financial), Lehman Brothers (spun off in 1994), E. F. Hutton, and IDS. While First Data was growing, First Financial remained active, buying Georgia Federal Bank in 1989 to facilitate the growth of its bank card business.

As the decade of the 1990s dawned, American Express' dreams of a financial services empire were crumbling. The businesses did not fit well with American Express, diverting attention from its core lines. However, First Data had become the largest bank card processing company in the US and a significant power in mutual fund transactions. In 1992 it was spun off.

First Financial began sharpening its focus on merchant (rather than bank) services. It bought TeleCheck (check authorization) in 1992 and began divesting its banking and bank services holdings.

In 1994 First Data and First Financial Management went head-to-head, vying to acquire Western Union (founded 1855) from bankrupt parent New Valley. First Financial was the victor in the bruising bidding war (which also included Forstmann Little).

Although First Data's $6.5 billion merger with First Financial in 1995 raised antitrust concerns, the deal went through with only the stipulation of selling the MoneyGram (money transfer) services business. The new union gave First Data a 30% share of the fragmented credit card processing market and moved it into new service areas, many of which it began divesting in efforts to focus on financial support.

First Data won a 10-year contract in 1996 to process credit and debit transactions for retail giant Wal-Mart Stores — more than 5 billion each year. A 1997 pact with BANK ONE and its First USA subsidiary added another 6 million accounts. First Data also expanded its geographical presence that year, agreeing to provide credit card processing for HSBC Holdings' banks in the UK, the US, and Hong Kong (First Data pulled out of Hong Kong the following year).

In 1999 First Data and BANK ONE strengthened their relationship: First Data took a stake in BANK ONE subsidiary Paymentech and folded it into an existing joint venture with BANK ONE (Banc One Payment Services). To refocus on its electronic payment and commerce services, First Data sold its Investor Services Group.

In 2000 the company slashed some 400 management jobs and made other workforce cuts. First Data continued to grow through acquisitions (including Cardservice International and PaySys) and alliances (with such entities as J.P. Morgan Chase and Deutsche Post) in 2001.

Chairman: Henry C. Duques, age 58, $2,075,577 pay
President, CEO, and Director: Charles T. Fote, age 53, $1,422,693 pay
SEVP: Eula Adams, age 52, $926,293 pay
SEVP; President, Western Union Financial Services: Christina A. Gold
SEVP; President, First Data International: Pamela H. Patsley, age 46
EVP: David P. Bailis, age 45, $750,000 pay
EVP: Guy A. Battista
EVP and CFO: Kimberly S. Patmore, age 45, $838,365 pay
EVP: Alan M. Silberstein, age 53
EVP, Chief Administrative Officer, Secretary, and General Counsel: Michael T. Whealy, age 48, $863,462 pay
SVP, Human Resources: Janet Harris
President, Merchant Services: Scott Betts
President & CEO, TeleCheck Services: Charles D. Drucker
President, Western Union North America: Michael C. Yerington
Auditors: Ernst & Young LLP

LOCATIONS

HQ: 6200 S. Quebec St., Greenwood Village, CO 80111
Phone: 303-967-8000   **Fax:** 303-967-6701
Web: www.firstdatacorp.com

2001 Sales

	$ mil.	% of total
US	6,186	96
Other countries	265	4
Total	**6,451**	**100**

PRODUCTS/OPERATIONS

2001 Sales

	$ mil.	% of total
Payment services	2,706	41
Merchant services	2,256	34
Card issuing services	1,497	22
Emerging payments	91	1
Divested & discontinued businesses	24	—
Other	106	2
Adjustments	(229)	—
Total	**6,451**	**100**

Selected Services

Card Issuer Services	Payment Services
Billing	Bill payment services
Settlement	Nonbank money transfers
Transaction reporting	Pre-paid gift cards
Merchant Processing Services	**Other**
ATM network	Electronic tax processing services
Check verification	Online payment services
Internet-based transaction processing	Voice-center services
Transaction authorization	

COMPETITORS

BA Merchant Services	ECHO	Total System Services
BSI Business Services	EDS	U.S. Postal Service
CheckFree	Fiserv	Vestcom International
Concord EFS	Litle	
Deluxe	MBNA	
	MoneyGram	
	NOVA	

HISTORICAL FINANCIALS & EMPLOYEES

NYSE: FDC FYE: December 31	Annual Growth	12/92	12/93	12/94	12/95	12/96	12/97	12/98	12/99	12/00	12/01
Sales ($ mil.)	20.5%	1,205	1,490	1,652	4,081	4,934	4,979	5,118	5,540	5,705	6,451
Net income ($ mil.)	22.4%	141	173	208	(84)	637	357	466	1,200	930	872
Income as % of sales	—	11.7%	11.6%	12.6%	—	12.9%	7.2%	9.1%	21.7%	16.3%	13.5%
Earnings per share ($)	14.4%	0.33	0.36	0.43	(0.10)	0.69	0.40	0.52	1.38	1.13	1.11
Stock price – FY high ($)	—	8.59	10.56	12.66	17.81	22.00	23.06	18.03	25.75	28.84	40.10
Stock price – FY low ($)	—	5.31	7.81	10.13	11.50	15.19	12.50	9.84	15.66	18.47	24.88
Stock price – FY close ($)	18.4%	8.59	10.19	11.84	16.72	18.25	14.63	15.94	24.66	26.34	39.23
P/E – high	—	26	29	29	—	31	56	34	18	25	36
P/E – low	—	16	22	23	—	21	30	19	11	16	22
Dividends per share ($)	16.7%	0.01	0.03	0.03	0.03	0.03	0.03	0.04	0.04	0.04	0.04
Book value per share ($)	11.0%	1.81	2.16	2.30	3.52	4.14	4.09	4.31	4.68	4.74	4.63
Employees	4.6%	19,400	19,300	22,000	36,000	40,000	36,000	32,000	31,000	27,000	29,000

STOCK PRICE HISTORY

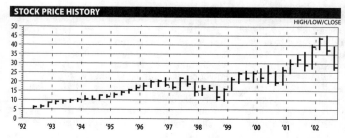

HIGH/LOW/CLOSE

2001 FISCAL YEAR-END

Debt ratio: 46.8%
Return on equity: 24.1%
Cash ($ mil.): 918
Current ratio: 0.99
Long-term debt ($ mil.): 3,102
No. of shares (mil.): 761
Dividends
  Yield: 0.1%
  Payout: 3.6%
Market value ($ mil.): 29,854

FIRSTENERGY CORP.

Competition has FirstEnergy acting like an electrified Tasmanian devil. The Akron, Ohio-based energy holding company is whirling through the northeastern US, picking up companies, putting down others, and creating new subsidiaries in response to retail electricity competition taking effect in its service territories.

FirstEnergy's strategy led to the acquisition of GPU in 2001, making it one of the largest electric utility holding companies in the US. The acquisition nearly doubled FirstEnergy's customer count; the firm's regulated utilities now generate and distribute electricity to some 4.3 million customers in Ohio, Pennsylvania, and New Jersey.

FirstEnergy's domestic power plants have a total generating capacity of more than 13,000 MW; more than half of the company's power is generated by coal-fired plants. Its acquisition of GPU, which sold its US power plants prior to the merger, added 1,500 MW of capacity from international power projects. GPU also contributed overseas utilities; however, FirstEnergy is selling these businesses to focus on its domestic operations. It has divested its Australian utility (GasNet) and 80% of its UK utility (Midlands Electricity); it also plans to sell its Argentine utility and its remaining 20% stake in Midlands Electricity.

Subsidiary FirstEnergy Solutions markets and trades energy commodities in deregulated markets throughout the US. FirstEnergy's other nonregulated businesses include electrical and mechanical contractors (such as GPU's MYR Group), natural gas company MARBEL Energy, and telecommunications subsidiaries.

HISTORY

Ohio Edison came to light in 1893 as the Akron Electric Light and Power Company. After several mergers, the business went bankrupt and was sold in 1899 to Akron Traction and Electric Company, which became Northern Ohio Power and Light (NOP&L).

In 1930 Commonwealth and Southern (C&S) bought NOP&L and merged it with four other Ohio utility holding companies to form Ohio Edison. The new firm increased sales during the Depression by selling electric appliances.

The Public Utility Holding Company Act of 1935 (passed to rein in the uncontrolled utilities) caught up with C&S in 1949, forcing it to divest Ohio Edison. Rival Ohio Public Service was also divested from its holding company, and in 1950 Ohio Edison bought it.

In 1967, after two decades of expansion, Ohio Edison and three other Ohio and Pennsylvania utilities formed the Central Area Power Coordination Group (CAPCO) to share new power plant

costs, including the construction of the Beaver Valley nuclear plant (1970-76). Although the CAPCO partners agreed in 1980 to cancel four planned nukes, in 1985 Ohio Edison took part in building the Perry Unit 1 and Beaver Valley Unit 2 nuclear plants.

The federal Energy Policy Act of 1992 allowed wholesale power competition, and to satisfy new federal requirements, Ohio Edison formed a six-state transmission alliance in 1996 with fellow utilities Centerior Energy, Allegheny Power System, and Dominion Resources' Virginia Power to coordinate their grids.

Ohio Edison paid about $1.5 billion in 1997 for Centerior Energy, formed in 1986 as a holding company for Toledo Edison and Cleveland Electric. Ohio Edison and Centerior, both burdened by high-cost generating plants, merged to cut costs, and the expanded energy concern was renamed FirstEnergy Corp.

The transmission issue arose again in 1997. FirstEnergy left the transmission-coordination alliance Midwest ISO (Independent System Operator) to start a rival, Alliance, with 11 utility members. Looking toward deregulation, FirstEnergy began buying mechanical construction, contracting, and energy management companies in 1997, including Roth Bros. and RPC Mechanical. In 1998 it added nine more. FirstEnergy then ventured into natural gas operations by purchasing MARBEL Energy. The company also created separate subsidiaries for its nuclear and transmission assets.

Power marketers Federal Energy Sales and the Power Co. of America couldn't deliver the juice to FirstEnergy during the summer of 1998's hottest days. FirstEnergy later sued Federal Energy for $25 million in damages. The next year it bought electricity outage insurance.

Pennsylvania began large-scale electric power competition in 1999, when the Ohio legislature passed deregulation legislation. To comply with state laws, FirstEnergy agreed to trade power plants, including Beaver Valley, with DQE. That year brought trouble when the EPA named FirstEnergy and six other utilities in a suit that charged the utility with noncompliance of the Clean Air Act.

In 2000 FirstEnergy agreed to acquire New Jersey-based electric utility GPU in an $11.9 billion deal; it became one of the largest US utilities in 2001 when it completed the acquisition, which added three utilities (Jersey Central Power & Light, Metropolitan Edison, and Pennsylvania Electric) that serve 2.1 million electricity customers.

Following the acquisition, FirstEnergy agreed to sell an 80% stake in GPU's UK utility, Midlands

Electricity, to UtiliCorp (later Aquila) in a $2 billion deal, which was completed in 2002. It also agreed to sell four Ohio coal-fired plants (2,500 MW) to NRG Energy for $1.5 billion; however, the deal was later canceled. The firm also spun off GPU's Australian GasNet subsidiary to the public.

OFFICERS

Chairman and CEO; Chairman, Pennsylvania Power; President, Ohio Edison, The Illuminating Company, Toledo Edison, Metropolitan Edison, and Pennsylvania Electric; CEO, FirstEnergy Services: H. Peter Burg, age 55, $1,452,895 pay
President, COO, and Director; President and COO, First Energy Services: Anthony J. Alexander, age 50, $917,189 pay
SVP and CFO, FirstEnergy, FirstEnergy Service, and FirstEnergy Solutions: Richard H. Marsh, age 51, $491,836 pay
SVP and General Counsel, FirstEnergy, FirstEnergy Service, and FirstEnergy Solutions: Leila L. Vespoli, age 42
SVP, FirstEnergy and FirstEnergy Services: Earl T. Carey, age 59
SVP, FirstEnergy and FirstEnergy Services: Kevin J. Keough
SVP, FirstEnergy and FirstEnergy Services: Carole B. Snyder, age 56
President and CEO, MYR Group: William S. Skibitsky
President, FirstEnergy Solutions: Arthur R. Garfield, age 63, $414,450 pay
SVP Commodity Operations, FirstEnergy Solutions: Guy L. Pipitone
SVP Retail Operations, FirstEnergy Solutions: Douglas S. Elliot
Auditors: PricewaterhouseCoopers LLP

LOCATIONS

HQ: 76 S. Main St., Akron, OH 44308
Phone: 330-633-4766 **Fax:** 330-384-3866
Web: www.firstenergycorp.com

FirstEnergy serves electricity customers in New Jersey, Ohio, and Pennsylvania in the US; it also has energy interests in Argentina, Colombia, Pakistan, Turkey, and the UK.

PRODUCTS/OPERATIONS

2001 Sales

	$ mil.	% of total
Domestic electric	6,379	80
Natural gas	792	10
Facilities services	596	7
MYR	97	1
International	8	—
Other	127	2
Total	**7,999**	**100**

COMPETITORS

AEP	Exelon
Allegheny Energy	NewPower Holdings
Aquila	Peabody Energy
Cinergy	PG&E
Conectiv	PPL
Dominion	PSEG
DPL	Southern Company
DQE	Vectren
Duke Energy	WPS Resources
Dynegy	

HISTORICAL FINANCIALS & EMPLOYEES

NYSE: FE FYE: December 31	Annual Growth	12/92	12/93	12/94	12/95	12/96	12/97	12/98	12/99	12/00	12/01
Sales ($ mil.)	14.7%	2,332	2,370	2,368	2,466	2,470	2,821	5,861	6,320	7,029	7,999
Net income ($ mil.)	9.9%	277	25	304	317	315	306	411	568	599	646
Income as % of sales		11.9%	1.0%	12.8%	12.9%	12.8%	10.8%	7.0%	9.0%	8.5%	8.1%
Earnings per share ($)	9.7%	—	—	—	—	—	1.94	1.82	2.50	2.69	2.81
Stock price - FY high ($)	—	—	—	—	—	—	29.00	34.06	33.19	32.13	36.98
Stock price - FY low ($)	—	—	—	—	—	—	25.13	27.06	22.13	18.00	25.10
Stock price - FY close ($)	4.8%	—	—	—	—	—	29.00	32.56	22.69	31.56	34.98
P/E - high	—	—	—	—	—	—	15	17	13	12	13
P/E - low	—	—	—	—	—	—	13	14	9	7	9
Dividends per share ($)	—	—	—	—	—	—	0.00	1.50	1.50	1.50	1.50
Book value per share ($)	17.5%	—	—	—	—	—	18.59	19.27	20.15	21.26	35.40
Employees	12.9%	6,263	5,978	5,166	4,812	4,273	4,215	1,944	13,461	13,830	18,700

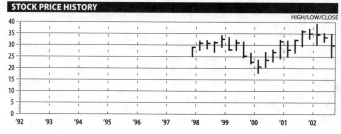

STOCK PRICE HISTORY

HIGH/LOW/CLOSE

2001 FISCAL YEAR-END

Debt ratio: 59.1%
Return on equity: 10.7%
Cash ($ mil.): 220
Current ratio: 0.54
Long-term debt ($ mil.): 11,433
No. of shares (mil.): 224
Dividends
  Yield: 4.3%
  Payout: 53.4%
Market value ($ mil.): 7,835

FISHER SCIENTIFIC INTERNATIONAL

Fisher Scientific International offers scientists an ocean of laboratory products to fish around in. The Hampton, New Hampshire-based company is one of the world's leading wholesale distributors of scientific equipment and instruments — everything from Erlenmeyer flasks to video/microscope systems. Fisher sells more than 600,000 products and services online and through catalogs, distribution centers, and sales offices. The company offers instruments and supplies from independent vendors, and also makes its own products, including chemicals, clinical equipment, diagnostic tools, and laboratory workstations.

Fisher has made a series of acquisitions to expand its offerings into areas such as health care supplies and pharmaceutical packaging services. LBO specialist Thomas H. Lee Company (THL) leads an investor group that controls 48% of Fisher's voting power. As part of that stake, THL itself owns almost 32% of Fisher.

In 1902, 20-year-old Chester Fisher bought the stockroom of Pittsburgh Testing Laboratories (established 1884) and formed Scientific Materials Co. The company's earliest products, supplied from Europe, included simple tools such as microscopes, balances, and calorimeters. It published its first catalog in 1904.

When the outbreak of World War I disrupted supplies from Europe, Scientific Materials established its own R&D and manufacturing facilities. It acquired Montreal-based Scientific Supplies in 1925 and the following year changed its name to Fisher Scientific Company. By 1935 Fisher had doubled its size, adding glass blowing operations and an instrument shop.

In 1940 the company acquired pioneering chemicals supplier Eimer & Amend (founded 1851), whose customers had included Thomas Edison and Henry Ford. Two years later Fisher supplied chemicals used in the Manhattan Project. In 1949 Chester's son Aiken Fisher became president. Jonas Salk relied on Fisher reagents to develop the polio vaccine, introduced in 1955. In 1957 the company bought the laboratory apparatus division of E. Machlett & Son.

Chester Fisher died in 1965 — the same year the company went public — leaving Fisher to sons Aiken, Benjamin, and James. Fisher acquired pipette maker Pfeiffer Glass (1966), scientific teaching equipment maker Stansi Scientific (1967), optical instruments maker Jerrell-Ash Company (1968), and Hi-Pure Chemicals (1974).

Aiken retired as chairman in 1975 and was replaced by Benjamin. That year former Pfeiffer Glass president Edward Perkins was appointed president and CEO — the first nonfamily member to hold this position. In 1977 Fisher bought the diagnostics division of American Cyanamid's Lederle Laboratories.

Fisher acquired laboratory furniture company Conco Industries in 1980. But with earnings flat and the Fisher brothers aging, the company had become vulnerable. It was purchased in 1981 by Allied Corporation (later AlliedSignal, now Honeywell International). Allied wanted Fisher to form the core of its new Health & Science Products unit, but by 1986 Allied was selling off nonstrategic businesses. The Henley Group, an Allied spinoff, bought Fisher, then sold 57% of the renamed Fisher Scientific International to the public in 1991. Its headquarters moved to New Hampshire from Pennsylvania.

In 1992 Fisher bought Hamilton Scientific, the top US maker of laboratory workstations, as well as a majority interest in Kuhn + Bayer, a German supplier of scientific equipment. In 1995 Fisher acquired Curtin Matheson Scientific, a leading US provider of diagnostic instruments. That year the company also boosted its global presence by acquiring Fisons plc, a UK-based laboratory products supplier.

Fisher in 1997 consolidated several international operations. The next year stockholders approved a recapitalization deal giving Thomas H. Lee Company a majority stake in the company (later reduced to about 45%). Fisher also bought Bioblock Scientific, a French distributor of scientific and laboratory instruments. In 1999 the company spun off its ProcureNet (supply chain management software) unit to shareholders and sold UniKix Technology (software).

Early in 2001 Fisher purchased the pharmaceutical packaging services arm of Covance for about $135 million. Late that year Fisher bought Cole-Parmer Instrument Company, a maker and distributor of specialized technical instruments, for about $210 million.

Chairman and CEO: Paul M. Montrone, age 60, $1,851,575 pay
Vice Chairman: Paul M. Meister, age 49
President and COO: David T. Della Penta, age 54, $1,326,915 pay
VP and CFO: Kevin P. Clark, age 39, $535,670 pay
VP, General Counsel, and Secretary: Todd M. DuChene, age 38, $585,050 pay
President, US Distribution Operations: Thomas G. Pitera
Director, Corporate Communications: Gia L. Oei
Investor Relations: Carolyn J. Miller
Auditors: Deloitte & Touche LLP

LOCATIONS

HQ: Fisher Scientific International Inc.,
 1 Liberty Ln., Hampton, NH 03842
Phone: 603-926-5911 **Fax:** 603-926-0222
Web: www.fisherscientific.com

Fisher Scientific International has facilities in Belgium, Canada, France, Germany, Malaysia, Mexico, Singapore, Switzerland, the UK, and the US.

2001 Sales

	% of total
US	83
Other countries	17
Total	**100**

PRODUCTS/OPERATIONS

2001 Sales

	$ mil.	% of total
Distribution	2,865	94
Laboratory equipment	179	6
Adjustments	(164)	—
Total	**2,880**	**100**

Selected Products

Laboratory supplies and consumables
 Chemicals
 Gases
 Gloves
 Lubricants
 Swabs
 Syringes
Laboratory and clinical testing equipment
 Fume hoods
 Incubators
 Laboratory glassware
 Laboratory workstations
 Microscopes
 Mixers
 Safety equipment

Services

Clinical packaging
Facility service management
Laboratory instrument calibration, certification, and
 repair
Pharmaceutical packaging
Safety equipment services
Scientific certification

COMPETITORS

Agilent Technologies
Allegiance
Apogent Technologies inc.
Applera
Beckman Coulter
Carl Zeiss
Corning
Danaher
Honeywell International

Medline Industries
Mettler-Toledo
Owens & Minor
PerkinElmer
Sigma-Aldrich
Thermo Electron
Varian
Waters Corporation

HISTORICAL FINANCIALS & EMPLOYEES

NYSE: FSH FYE: December 31	Annual Growth	12/92	12/93	12/94	12/95	12/96	12/97	12/98	12/99	12/00	12/01
Sales ($ mil.)	15.1%	814	978	1,127	1,436	2,144	2,175	2,252	2,470	2,622	2,880
Net income ($ mil.)	(5.3%)	27	33	36	3	37	(31)	(50)	23	23	16
Income as % of sales	—	3.3%	3.3%	3.2%	0.2%	1.7%	—	—	0.9%	0.9%	0.6%
Earnings per share ($)	(0.7%)	0.33	0.40	0.44	0.04	0.38	(0.30)	(1.24)	0.55	0.51	0.31
Stock price - FY high ($)	—	6.25	7.23	7.75	6.95	9.55	10.25	22.50	44.00	51.00	40.00
Stock price - FY low ($)	—	3.10	5.35	4.58	4.93	6.65	7.03	9.53	16.13	19.88	21.00
Stock price - FY close ($)	18.9%	6.13	7.08	4.95	6.68	9.40	9.55	19.94	36.13	36.88	29.20
P/E - high	—	19	18	17	174	24	—	—	75	89	121
P/E - low	—	9	13	10	123	17	—	—	27	35	64
Dividends per share ($)	—	0.01	0.02	0.02	0.02	0.02	0.02	0.00	0.00	0.00	0.00
Book value per share ($)	(15.2%)	1.89	2.26	2.73	2.78	3.84	8.67	(8.12)	(8.25)	(7.77)	0.43
Employees	12.0%	3,200	4,200	4,800	7,500	6,600	6,800	7,300	7,100	7,400	8,900

STOCK PRICE HISTORY

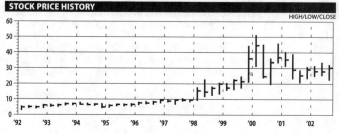

HIGH/LOW/CLOSE

2001 FISCAL YEAR-END

Debt ratio: 97.6%
Return on equity: —
Cash ($ mil.): 75
Current ratio: 1.19
Long-term debt ($ mil.): 956
No. of shares (mil.): 54
Dividends
 Yield: —
 Payout: —
Market value ($ mil.): 1,581

FLEETBOSTON FINANCIAL

This Fleet has seen some choppy waters.

Beantown's FleetBoston Financial has about 1,500 US banking offices and some 250 in two dozen other countries, with a significant presence in Latin America. In addition to offering traditional retail and commercial banking, the company is one of the US's largest loan servicers, especially of credit cards and residential mortgages. The company is placing greater emphasis on its investment management business (operating primarily under the Columbia Management banner), which was bolstered by the purchase of the asset management units of fellow Bostonian Liberty Financial. Other divisions include brokerage Quick & Reilly, which offers online trading and market-making activities, and venture capital investors BancBoston Ventures and BancBoston Capital. FleetBoston sold student loan servicer AFSA Data Corporation to Affiliated Computer Services. Unable to find an outside buyer for investment bank Robertson Stephens, FleetBoston is shuttering its once high-flying unit after plans for a management buyout fell through. The closure will cost Fleet-Boston up to $500 million. The company's bottom line has also suffered from venture capital losses and economic instability in Argentina. Bad loans, including exposure to Enron and battered telecom firms, have led to a bloodletting in Fleet-Boston's risk management department, with top executives of the division losing jobs.

FleetBoston's diverse menu of services (and multiple revenue streams) gives it a competitive edge against smaller regional rivals, but also leaves it vulnerable on many fronts during economic downturns. As FleetBoston regroups and concentrates on internal growth in its core banking business, the traditionally acquisitive firm could find itself the target of a company looking to expand its own range of financial services.

HISTORY

FleetBoston predecessor Fleet National Bank was founded in 1791 in Rhode Island as the Providence Bank. In 1968 it became a subsidiary of Industrial Bancorp, which specialized in loans to Northeastern jewelers. In the 1970s the bank acquired consumer finance and mortgage banking firms.

Terrence Murray was named CEO in 1982, the year the company became Fleet Financial Group; rapid expansion followed. Murray bought consumer lender Credico of New Jersey in 1983. Fleet began expanding its banking operations outside Rhode Island in 1984, buying 46 companies in the 1980s. Even its non-acquisitions were successes: The firm was outbid for bad-loan-heavy Conifer

Group in 1986; the Pyrrhic victor was soon-to-be defunct Bank of New England.

In 1988 Fleet bought New York-based Norstar, taking the name Fleet/Norstar. But its expansion and credit policies left it with bad assets when the economy went into recession. Fleet went into the red for 1990, but soon capitalized on other banks' problems. With the help of Kohlberg Kravis Roberts, Fleet bought the failed Bank of New England (minus its bad loan portfolio) and other banks from the FDIC in 1991. The company's name reverted to Fleet Financial Group, and it made six acquisitions in New England in 1992.

That year a *60 Minutes* report alleged that Fleet charged exorbitant home equity interest rates and fees to low-income minority customers. In 1993 the company agreed to pay $30 million to affected customers in Georgia and to pump $70 million into low-income housing programs. In 1996 Fleet Mortgage took the further step of ceasing to reward employees for making loans exceeding the company's base rates.

In 1995 Fleet merged with Shawmut National Bank, founded in Boston in 1836 as the Warren Bank. The merger doubled Fleet's customer base and strengthened its presence in New Jersey and New York, but organizational problems left many customers upset.

Continuing to diversify, Fleet in 1998 bought Florida-based Quick & Reilly, the US's #3 discount brokerage. To compete with Citicorp's consumer credit cards, Fleet bought three credit card portfolios, including that of Advanta. (It later sued Advanta for misrepresenting the terms of that deal.) Also in 1998, Fleet bought Merrill Lynch Specialists and merged it into its newly named Fleet Specialist.

In 1999 Fleet Financial bought Sanwa Bank's US business credit unit. The plunder most prized by the fleet, though, was venerable rival Bank-Boston, acquired in 1999. BankBoston (founded in 1784) was the Boston area's #1 bank until its capture. Regulators mandated what FleetBoston called the largest bank merger divestiture ever. Also in 1999, the bank began offering online trading to its Internet clients through Quick & Reilly.

In 2000 the company began to sell about 300 branches and announced that merger redundancies would result in about 4,000 layoffs, while fee changes related to the merger sparked activist protests. The company also decided to consolidate its brokerage operations into Quick & Reilly. Later in 2000 the company acquired NYSE specialist firm M.J. Meehan & Co. and combined it with Fleet Specialist to form Fleet Meehan Specialist.

FleetBoston acquired New Jersey's largest bank, Summit Bancorp, in 2001.

OFFICERS

Chairman: Terrence Murray, age 62, $3,492,200 pay
President, CEO, and Director: Charles K. Gifford, age 59, $3,492,200 pay
Vice Chairman and Chief Risk Officer: Paul F. Hogan, age 56
Vice Chairman, New Business Development: Peter J. Manning, age 63
Vice Chairman and CFO: Eugene M. McQuade, age 53
Vice Chairman, Corporate Banking: H. Jay Sarles, age 56, $2,500,000 pay
Vice Chairman; Chairman, Fleet New Jersey: T. Joseph Semrod, age 65
Vice Chairman, Technology and Operations: Joseph A. Smialowski, age 53
Vice Chairman, Consumer Business Group: Bradford H. Warner, age 50
EVP; President, Fleet New Jersey: John G. Collins
EVP and Director, Corporate Marketing and Communications: Anne M. Finucane, age 49
EVP and Treasurer: Douglas L. Jacobs
EVP, General Counsel, and Secretary: Gary A. Spiess, age 61
EVP and Corporate Director, Human Resources and Diversity: M. Anne Szostak, age 51
Auditors: PricewaterhouseCoopers LLP

LOCATIONS

HQ: FleetBoston Financial Corporation, 100 Federal St., Boston, MA 02110
Phone: 617-434-2200   **Fax:** 617-434-6943
Web: www.fleetboston.com

FleetBoston has nearly 1,800 offices primarily in the Northeast, but also throughout the US and in 24 other countries.

PRODUCTS/OPERATIONS

2001 Sales

	$ mil.	% of total
Interest		
Loans & leases	10,921	57
Securities & trading assets	1,900	10
Other	972	5
Noninterest		
Banking fees & commissions	1,603	8
Investment services	1,491	8
Credit cards	757	4
Processing-related revenue	401	2
Capital markets	222	1
Other	866	5
Total	**19,133**	**100**

Selected Subsidiaries and Affiliates
BancBoston Investments Inc.
    BancBoston Capital, Inc. (venture capital)
Fleet National Bank
Quick & Reilly/Fleet Securities, Inc. (discount brokerage)
Robertson Stephens Group, Inc. (investment banking)

COMPETITORS

Bank of America	HSBC USA
Bank of New York	J.P. Morgan Chase
BANK ONE	KeyCorp
Banknorth Group	Merrill Lynch
Charles Schwab	PNC Financial
Citigroup	Sallie Mae
Citizens Financial Group	Sovereign Bancorp
Countrywide Credit	State Street
Deutsche Bank	Wachovia
FMR	

HISTORICAL FINANCIALS & EMPLOYEES

NYSE: FBF FYE: December 31	Annual Growth	12/92	12/93	12/94	12/95	12/96	12/97	12/98	12/99	12/00	12/01
Assets ($ mil.)	17.7%	46,939	47,923	48,757	84,432	85,518	85,535	104,382	190,692	179,519	203,638
Net income ($ mil.)	14.3%	280	488	613	610	1,139	1,303	1,532	2,038	3,420	931
Income as % of assets	—	0.6%	1.0%	1.3%	0.7%	1.3%	1.5%	1.5%	1.1%	1.9%	0.5%
Earnings per share ($)	(0.8%)	0.89	1.51	1.88	0.79	1.99	2.37	2.52	2.10	3.68	0.83
Stock price - FY high ($)	—	16.94	18.94	20.69	21.63	28.13	37.59	45.38	46.81	43.75	44.19
Stock price - FY low ($)	—	12.13	14.13	14.94	14.94	18.81	24.38	30.00	33.25	25.13	31.27
Stock price - FY close ($)	9.3%	16.38	16.69	16.19	20.38	24.94	37.56	44.69	34.81	37.56	36.50
P/E - high	—	19	13	11	25	14	15	17	22	12	53
P/E - low	—	14	9	8	17	9	10	11	15	7	37
Dividends per share ($)	14.2%	0.40	0.48	0.65	0.80	0.86	0.90	0.98	1.08	1.20	1.32
Book value per share ($)	3.7%	12.20	13.24	12.52	12.11	14.15	15.37	16.52	16.72	17.83	16.87
Employees	8.2%	27,500	26,000	21,500	30,800	36,000	34,000	36,000	59,200	53,000	56,000

STOCK PRICE HISTORY
HIGH/LOW/CLOSE

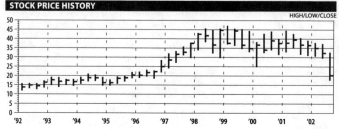

2001 FISCAL YEAR-END
Equity as % of assets: 8.6%
Return on assets: 0.5%
Return on equity: 5.7%
Long-term debt ($ mil.): 25,530
No. of shares (mil.): 1,044
Dividends
  Yield: 3.6%
  Payout: 159.0%
Market value ($ mil.): 38,099
Sales ($ mil.): 19,133

FLEETWOOD ENTERPRISES, INC.

Fleetwood Enterprises makes its customers feel at home, even when they're on the road. The Riverside, California-based company is the #1 US maker of recreational vehicles (RVs), travel trailers, and folding trailers, and it is also the #2 maker of manufactured housing (after Champion Enterprises). Fleetwood makes its homes (features may include vaulted ceilings, walk-in closets, and porches) and its RVs (motor homes, travel trailers, and folding trailers) in 16 states in the US and in Canada. The company retails manufactured homes through about 140 independent dealers and company-owned outlets.

Interest rates for manufactured homes typically are higher than those of site-built homes, and the terms are shorter. These higher interest rates and the fact that many lenders have stopped offering manufactured home loans are causing sales to fall across the industry. An industrywide inventory glut has also negatively impacted revenues. On the upside, Fleetwood's motor-home business is preparing for a baby boom of business, as the boomer generation nears retirement.

HISTORY

In 1950 John Crean started Coach Specialties Company, a California business that made venetian blinds for use by motor-home manufacturers. Headquartered in Riverside, this company was the forerunner of Fleetwood Enterprises, Crean's 1957 entry into the manufactured-housing industry. The company entered the RV market in 1964 by buying a small plant that produced the Terry travel trailer. The firm went public in 1965.

Between 1968 and 1973 sales grew nearly 55% annually. In 1969 the company bought motor-home maker Pace Arrow to expand its offerings in the fast-growing RV market. An industrywide recession caused by the 1973 oil shock and subsequent credit crunch dropped Fleetwood's stock from a 1972 high of $49.50 to $3.50 in 1974. Intensive cost-cutting helped position the company for an eventual upturn, and in 1976 it bought Avion Coach (luxury-class travel trailers and motor homes).

In 1980 Fleetwood closed nine factories in response to a recession, high interest rates, and high gas prices. COO Glenn Kummer became president in 1982. Strong RV sales helped pull the company out of a mild recession in the mid 1980s. Fleetwood opened a credit office in Southern California in 1987 to finance customers' RV purchases; this enabled the company to avoid riskier loans made to mobile-home buyers. Fleetwood added to its existing supply operations (fiberglass and lumber) by buying a maker of cabinet doors in 1988 and a maker of aluminum windows in 1989.

Also in 1989 the company became the first to surpass the $1 billion sales mark in RVs by increasing market share during an industry slump while continuing to avoid long-term debt. Fleetwood also added two new models to its RV line: the lower-priced Flair and the curved-wall Cambria. Another 1989 acquisition included Coleman's folding-trailer business — the largest in the industry, with a 30% market share.

Fleetwood received an order from Saudi Arabia for 2,000 manufactured homes in 1990. Recession and the Persian Gulf War inhibited demand for RVs and manufactured housing, but sales began to rebound by mid 1991.

The company bought 80% of Niesmann & Bischoff (luxury motor homes, Germany) in 1992. The next year Fleetwood finished a plant in Tennessee, followed by a plant near Waco, Texas, in 1994. The travel trailer unit introduced a lightweight line in 1994 for customers with limited towing capacity. Fleetwood began producing manufactured homes in Wichita Falls, Texas, in 1995, and the company broke ground for a housing manufacturing center in Winchester, Kentucky.

Streamlining its operations in 1996, Fleetwood sold its finance subsidiary, Fleetwood Credit, and its money-losing German RV subsidiary. In 1997 Fleetwood became the first US homebuilder to construct a million houses.

Kummer succeeded Crean as chairman and CEO in 1998; Crean became chairman emeritus (he left to start another business in 1999). Also that year the company bought more than half a dozen retailers, including HomeUSA (65 outlets), Better Homes (Kansas), Central Homes (Oregon), and Jasper Homes, Classic City Homes, and America's Best Homes (all in Georgia). Acquisitions continued in 1999 with the purchases of Viking Homes (New Mexico), JR's Mobile Homes (Illinois), and D&D Homes (California).

Because of slowing sales, Fleetwood closed five factories and laid off more than 800 employees in 2000. A 2001 restructuring included several management departures.

In 2002 Kummer retired and Thomas Pitcher became interim chairman. PACCAR VP Edward Caudill was named president designate. The company had 21 idle manufacturing facilities at the end of fiscal 2002. That year the company's manufactured housing group suffered along with the industry in general due to restrictive financing (particularly in Texas) and competition from new home sales.

OFFICERS

Interim Chairman: Thomas B. Pitcher, age 63
President and CEO: Edward B. Caudill
EVP and CFO: Boyd R. Plowman, age 58, $667,217 pay
EVP, Operations: Charles A. Wilkinson, age 61,
  $862,294 pay
SVP, Secretary, and General Counsel:
  Forrest D. Theobald, age 60
VP, Administration and Supply Subsidiaries:
  Larry L. Mace, age 57
VP, Controller, and Chief Accounting Officer:
  James F. Smith, age 54
VP, Folding Trailers: Patrick O. Scanlon
VP, Housing Operations: Ronald L. Brewer, $494,989 pay
VP, Human Resources: John R. Moore
VP, Information Technology and CIO: Todd L. Inlander,
  age 36
VP, Motor Home Division Operations: John M. Green
VP, Retail Housing Division: John H. Darnell Jr., age 50
VP, Travel Trailer Division Operations:
  William F. Bockoven
VP, Sales and Marketing, Housing Group:
  J. Wesley Chancey, age 50, $553,992 pay
VP, Sales and Marketing, RV Group: John C. Draheim,
  age 44
VP, Sales, Housing Group: Kevin Hull
Auditors: Ernst & Young LLP

LOCATIONS

HQ: 3125 Myers St., P.O. Box 7638, Riverside, CA 92513
Phone: 909-351-3500   **Fax:** 909-351-3312

Fleetwood Enterprises operates about 50 RV and
manufactured-housing plants in 16 states in the US and
in Canada.

PRODUCTS/OPERATIONS

2002 Sales

	$ mil.	% of total
Recreational vehicles	1,213	50
Manufactured housing	843	35
Retail	328	14
Supply operations	34	1
Corporate & other	3	—
Adjustments	(141)	—
Total	**2,280**	**100**

Selected Products and Brands
Manufactured housing (up to 2,340 sq. ft.)
Recreational vehicles
  Folding trailers
  Motor homes (American Dream, American Eagle,
    American Heritage, American Tradition, Bounder,
    Discovery, Expedition, Flair, Jamboree, Pace Arrow,
    Southwind, Storm, Tioga)
  Travel trailers (Avion, Mallard, Prowler, Savanna,
    Terry, Westport, Wilderness)

COMPETITORS

Bank of America	HSBC USA
Bank of New York	J.P. Morgan Chase
BANK ONE	KeyCorp
Banknorth Group	Merrill Lynch
Charles Schwab	PNC Financial
Citigroup	Sallie Mae
Citizens Financial Group	Sovereign Bancorp
Countrywide Credit	State Street
Deutsche Bank	Wachovia
FMR	

HISTORICAL FINANCIALS & EMPLOYEES

NYSE: FLE FYE: Last Sunday in April	Annual Growth	4/93	4/94	4/95	4/96	4/97	4/98	4/99	4/00	4/01	4/02
Sales ($ mil.)	1.8%	1,942	2,369	2,856	2,809	2,874	3,051	3,490	3,713	2,532	2,280
Net income ($ mil.)	—	57	66	85	80	125	109	107	84	(284)	(162)
Income as % of sales	—	2.9%	2.8%	3.0%	2.8%	4.3%	3.6%	3.1%	2.2%	—	—
Earnings per share ($)	—	1.23	1.40	1.82	1.71	3.19	3.01	2.94	2.41	(8.67)	(3.90)
Stock price - FY high ($)	—	26.88	26.00	27.25	29.00	37.25	48.00	46.44	27.88	16.00	17.25
Stock price - FY low ($)	—	12.69	16.50	17.75	18.13	24.13	25.88	23.25	14.00	8.10	7.60
Stock price - FY close ($)	(6.4%)	19.38	20.88	23.00	26.25	26.38	46.19	24.69	14.63	12.94	10.67
P/E - high	—	22	18	15	17	11	16	15	11	—	—
P/E - low	—	10	12	10	10	7	8	7	6	—	—
Dividends per share ($)	(13.9%)	0.46	0.50	0.55	0.59	0.63	0.67	0.71	0.75	0.61	0.12
Book value per share ($)	(8.5%)	11.01	11.88	13.20	14.22	12.40	11.96	16.67	17.88	8.74	4.95
Employees	(0.3%)	14,000	16,000	18,000	18,000	18,000	19,000	21,000	20,700	14,000	13,600

STOCK PRICE HISTORY

HIGH/LOW/CLOSE

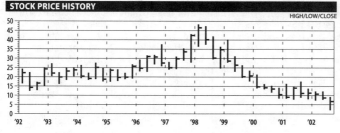

2002 FISCAL YEAR-END

Debt ratio: 4.7%
Return on equity: —
Cash ($ mil.): 26
Current ratio: 1.59
Long-term debt ($ mil.): 9
No. of shares (mil.): 35
Dividends
  Yield: 1.1%
  Payout: —
Market value ($ mil.): 377

FLEMING COMPANIES, INC.

Fleming Companies weighs in as the nation's #1 wholesale food distributor, but it's been trimming some fat. Based in Lewisville, Texas, Fleming supplies brand-name and private-label food and general merchandise to more than 11,500 retailers, including mass merchandisers (Kmart), independent retailers, franchised stores (under its Piggly Wiggly banner), limited assortment stores, and convenience stores. It also owns more than 100 stores that operate under the Food4Less and Rainbow Foods banners.

After losing several of its largest customers (Randall's Food Markets, Furr's Supermarkets), the company initiated a restructuring effort to make itself more efficient. In recent years Fleming has sold or closed 238 of its conventional format supermarkets to focus resources on growing its price impact and limited assortment stores. It also closed or consolidated 12 distribution faciles. But Fleming is making acquisitions, including seven Super1Foods stores from Brookshire Grocery Co., to expand in the Dallas area, and Head Distributing, whose largest customer is Ahold USA convenience stores.

Fleming suffered some ripple effects after its largest customer, Kmart, filed for bankruptcy. However, in July 2002 Fleming inked a $300 million contract with Target to supply candy, cookies, and frozen foods.

HISTORY

Lux Mercantile, a Topeka, Kansas, wholesale grocery founded by O. A. Fleming, Gene Wilson, and Sam Lux, was incorporated in 1915. Three years later the company became Fleming-Wilson Mercantile.

Facing competition from chains, independent wholesalers and grocers banded together to provide competitive mass merchandising, advertising, and efficient store operations. Fleming's son Ned helped establish Fleming-Wilson as the first voluntary wholesaler west of the Mississippi (1927). The enterprise was renamed the Fleming Company (1941), and Ned became president (1945-64) and then chairman and CEO (1964-81). The company went public in 1959 and adopted the name Fleming Companies in 1972.

Fleming has grown by acquisitions since the 1930s, primarily of midwestern wholesale food distributors and supermarkets such as Grainger Brothers (1962, renamed the Fleming Co. of Nebraska); Associated Grocers of Arizona (1985); and Godfrey, with 32 Sentry supermarkets and four Sun warehouse markets (1987). The company also acquired a coffee company, a bakery, a wholesale drug firm, and several distribution centers.

The 1988 purchase of Malone & Hyde, the sixth-largest wholesale food distributor in the US (and owner of the Piggly Wiggly franchise), made Fleming the largest in that field for several years. Later that year the company sold Malone & Hyde's 99-store retail pharmacy subsidiary, M&A Drugs.

Fleming lost important customers when Albertson's began self-distributing in 1990 and when Alpha Beta stores merged with Lucky. As the company saw its supermarkets losing market share to superstores and warehouses in 1993, it began a major restructuring that year (which encountered so much resistance it was delayed until 1998).

In 1994 Fleming added nearly 3,000 stores, including 175 company-owned outlets, with its $1.1 billion purchase of Scrivner, the US's #3 food wholesaler at the time, from German company Franz Haniel & Cie. It acquired ABCO Markets, a nearly bankrupt customer with 71 supermarkets in Arizona, in 1996. That year Fleming sold off underperforming units such as the 28-unit Brooks convenience store chain and cut its workforce again.

With its performance flagging in 1998, Fleming ousted chairman and CEO Robert Stauth and eventually replaced him with Mark Hansen, former CEO of Wal-Mart's Sam's Club. Hansen promptly announced a five-year, $781 million program to improve profit margins by selling or closing seven supply centers and weaker stores.

To that end, in 1999 the company sold its struggling Boogaarts Food Stores, Hyde Park Market, and Consumers Food & Drug chains. Fleming also began converting SuPeRSaVeR stores to its Sentry Foods banner in Wisconsin to streamline marketing efforts in that area.

Fleming signed a three-year deal to supply Kmart stores in 1999. In another move signaling the company might be focusing on mass merchandisers and deepening relationships with other large customers such as Kroger, Fleming announced in 2000 it would sell various chains, including ABCO Desert Markets, Sentry, and Baker's Supermarkets.

In February 2001 Fleming beat out rival SUPERVALU and secured a $4.5 billion contract to be the exclusive food and consumable products distributor to all Kmart and Super Kmart stores. Subsequently Kmart represented 20% of Fleming's sales that year. Nearly a year later, Kmart filed for Chapter 11 bankruptcy protection after suppliers, including Fleming, halted shipments to the troubled discounter.

In August 2001 Fleming bid on the bankrupt Furrs Supermarket chain in New Mexico and Texas and bought 36 of the 71 Furrs stores. Fleming then sold most of the stores to major retail chains and independent grocers, with about half of the new store owners naming Fleming as their supplier. Furrs closed 35 stores for which Fleming was unable to find buyers.

In June 2002 Fleming bought Core-Mark International to strengthen its business in the western US and Canada.

OFFICERS

Chairman and CEO: Mark S. Hansen, age 47, $3,468,179 pay
EVP and CFO: Neal J. Rider, age 40, $1,640,456 pay
EVP and CIO: Ronald B. Griffin, age 48
EVP and President, Convenience Distribution: Robert A. Allen
EVP and President, Wholesale: E. Stephen Davis, age 61, $2,131,562 pay
EVP, Business Development and Chief Knowledge Officer: William H. Marquard, age 42, $1,529,507 pay
EVP, Human Resources: Scott M. Northcutt, age 40
EVP, Merchandising; President, Fleming Retail: J. R. Campbell, age 57
EVP: Thomas G. Dahlen, age 47, $1,586,255 pay
SVP, Finance and Treasurer: Matthew H. Hildreth, age 36
SVP, General Counsel, and Secretary: Carlos M. Hernandez, age 47
Auditors: Deloitte & Touche LLP

LOCATIONS

HQ: 1945 Lakepointe Dr., Box 299013, Lewisville, TX 75029
Phone: 972-906-8000   **Fax:** 972-906-7810
Web: www.fleming.com

PRODUCTS/OPERATIONS

Business Operations

Fleming Brands
BestYet
IGA
Living Well
Marquee
Nature's Finest
Piggly Wiggly
Rainbow
SuperTru

Fleming Retail Group
Food 4 Less
Rainbow Foods (Minnesota and Wisconsin)

Fleming Retail Services
Advertising
Cerespan (electronic communications network)
Finance
Insurance
Marketing
Pricing
Promotions
Store operations
Technology

COMPETITORS

A&P	Homeland	Roundy's
Albertson's	Holding	Royal Ahold
Associated Food	Hy-Vee	Safeway
AWG	Kroger	Spartan Stores
C&S Wholesale	McLane	SUPERVALU
Di Giorgio	Meijer	Wakefern Food
H-E-B	Nash Finch	Wal-Mart
	Publix	Winn-Dixie

HISTORICAL FINANCIALS & EMPLOYEES

NYSE: FLM FYE: Saturday nearest Dec. 31	Annual Growth	12/92	12/93	12/94	12/95	12/96	12/97	12/98	12/99	12/00	12/01
Sales ($ mil.)	2.1%	12,938	13,092	15,754	17,502	16,487	15,373	15,069	14,646	14,444	15,628
Net income ($ mil.)	(16.1%)	113	35	56	42	27	25	(511)	(45)	(122)	23
Income as % of sales	—	0.9%	0.3%	0.4%	0.2%	0.2%	0.2%	—	—	—	0.1%
Earnings per share ($)	(17.9%)	3.06	0.96	1.51	1.12	0.71	0.67	(13.48)	(1.17)	(3.15)	0.52
Stock price - FY high ($)	—	35.13	34.38	30.00	29.88	20.88	20.38	20.75	13.44	17.63	37.89
Stock price - FY low ($)	—	27.25	23.75	22.63	19.13	11.50	13.44	8.63	7.19	8.69	10.75
Stock price - FY close ($)	(5.7%)	31.50	24.75	23.25	20.63	17.25	13.44	10.38	10.25	11.81	18.50
P/E - high	—	11	34	20	27	29	20	—	—	—	60
P/E - low	—	8	23	15	17	16	13	—	—	—	17
Dividends per share ($)	(26.0%)	1.20	1.20	1.20	1.20	0.36	0.08	0.08	0.08	0.08	0.08
Book value per share ($)	(10.0%)	28.90	28.90	28.78	28.72	28.47	28.48	14.79	14.43	10.78	11.21
Employees	0.1%	22,800	23,300	42,400	44,000	41,200	39,700	38,900	36,300	29,567	23,000

STOCK PRICE HISTORY

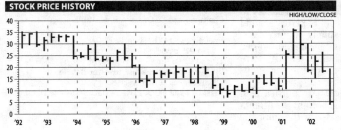

HIGH/LOW/CLOSE

2001 FISCAL YEAR-END

Debt ratio: 77.9%
Return on equity: 5.0%
Cash ($ mil.): 17
Current ratio: 1.38
Long-term debt ($ mil.): 1,760
No. of shares (mil.): 44
Dividends
  Yield: 0.4%
  Payout: 15.4%
Market value ($ mil.): 822

FLOWERS FOODS, INC.

Driven by a knead to succeed, Flowers Foods is using flour power to make — what else? — bread. Thomasville, Georgia-based Flowers Foods consists of the Flowers Bakeries, Flowers Snacks, and Mrs. Smith's Bakeries businesses.

Flowers Bakeries makes fresh breads, rolls, and snack cakes and sells them to retailers in 16 states primarily located in the South and Southeast. Its brands include Nature's Own, Cobblestone Mill, and ButterKrust. Flowers Bakeries also rolls out hamburger buns for Burger King and Whataburger, and private-label breads for retailers such as Kroger and Winn-Dixie. The company's snack unit distributes to vending and wholesale club retailers.

Mrs. Smith's Bakeries produces the #1 frozen-pie brand in the country, along with other fresh and frozen breads, cakes, and desserts for retail and food service customers. Among its national brands are Mrs. Smith's, Pet-Ritz, and Oregon Farms. The division also includes frozen breaded vegetables and cheese sticks under the Stilwell name.

Having long been a regional fresh bread baker, in the late 1990s Flowers bulked up by adding Mrs. Smith's and Keebler (which it sold to Kellogg in 2001). The company is seeking additional growth by building demand for frozen baked goods beyond the holiday season.

HISTORY

Georgia native William Flowers and his brother Joseph opened the Flowers Ice Cream Co. in the winter resort town of Thomasville, Georgia, in 1914 to serve wealthy visitors from the North. Seeing that there was no bakery in the town (the nearest bakery was located more than 200 miles away), the brothers opened Flowers Baking Co. in 1919. During the 1920s William took charge of the bakery, while Joseph continued to run the ice-cream operation. In 1928 Flowers moved into the production of sweet rolls and cakes. As its reputation for high-quality baked goods spread, the firm established a regional network of customers. William died in 1934, and his 20-year-old son, Bill, took over.

Amidst the difficult Depression years, Bill led the company in its first acquisition, a bakery in Florida. Flowers operated its bakeries around the clock during WWII to supply military bases in the Southeast. Bill's brother Langdon joined the firm after the war and helped take the company on a major expansion drive in the 1950s and 1960s.

Flowers acquired additional southeastern bakers in the mid-1960s and bought the Atlanta Baking Co. in 1967. The next year the company changed its name to Flowers Industries and went public.

In 1976 the company diversified, entering the frozen-food business by acquiring Stilwell Foods (frozen fruits, battered vegetables) in Oklahoma and its subsidiary, Rio Grande Foods, in Texas. The firm expanded its fresh bread line, including the Nature's Own brand of variety breads (1978).

During the 1970s and 1980s, the company expanded beyond its southeastern regional base by acquiring bakeries in the Southwest and Midwest. Company veteran Amos McMullian became CEO in 1981 and chairman in 1985, when both Bill and Langdon retired. In 1989 Flowers bought out Winn-Dixie's bakery operations.

The company launched a $377 million, six-year capital investment program in 1991 to upgrade and automate its bakeries. Flowers began a major expansion strategy with the 1996 acquisition of Mrs. Smith's, the US's top frozen-pie brand, from J.M. Smucker. Later that year Flowers and joint venture partners Artal Luxembourg and Benmore acquired cookie maker Keebler Foods. In 1997 the company acquired Allied Bakery Products, a baker of frozen bread and rolls for food service customers in the northeastern US. When Keebler went public in 1998, Flowers increased its controlling stake to 55%.

Further acquisitions included Home Baking Company (food service buns, 1999) and Kroger's bakery operations in Memphis (2000). Weakened by equipment glitches in newly upgraded Mrs. Smith's facilities, earnings suffered at the end of 1999. Flowers snubbed an acquisition inquiry by Sara Lee in early 2000, but as other mega-food company acquisitions dominoed around it, Flowers agreed to sell Keebler to Kellogg in October 2000.

Upon completion of the Keebler/Kellogg deal in March 2001, Flowers Industries recreated itself, spinning off its Flowers Bakeries and Mrs. Smith's Bakeries businesses under the Flowers Foods name; it kept the same FLO stock ticker.

To better control costs, the company cut jobs at Mrs. Smiths in mid-2002, and initiated a restructuring of its operating units.

OFFICERS

Chairman and CEO: Amos R. McMullian, age 64, $1,003,179 pay
President and COO: George E. Deese, age 56, $424,048 pay
VP and CFO: Jimmy M. Woodward, age 41, $348,311 pay
VP, Communications and Investor Relations: Marta Jones Turner, age 48
President and COO, Flowers Bakeries: Gene D. Lord, age 55

President and COO, Flowers Snacks: Allen L. Shiver, age 46
President and COO, Mrs. Smith's Bakeries: William A. Strenglis, age 47
Regional VP, Flowers Bakeries: Robert A. Hocutt, age 48
Regional VP, Flowers Bakeries: David C. Scott, age 45
Regional VP, Flowers Bakeries: Joe G. Tashie, age 47
Secretary and General Counsel: Stephan R. Avera, age 45
Auditors: PricewaterhouseCoopers LLP

LOCATIONS

HQ: 1919 Flowers Circle, Thomasville, GA 31757
Phone: 229-226-9110   **Fax:** 229-225-3823
Web: www.flowersfoods.com

Flowers Foods operates 33 production facilities across 13 states.

PRODUCTS/OPERATIONS

2001 Sales

	$ mil.	% of total
Flowers Bakeries	1,056	65
Mrs. Smith's Bakeries	573	35
Total	**1,629**	**100**

Selected Brands

Fresh Baked Goods
BlueBird
ButterKrust
Cobblestone Mill
Dandee
Evangeline Maid
Flowers
Mary Jane
Nature's Own

Frozen and Vending Baked Goods
Danish Kitchen
European Bakers
Grand Finales (food service desserts)
Mrs. Freshley's (vending products)
Mrs. Smith's
Oregon Farms
Oronoque Orchard
Our Special Touch
Pet-Ritz
Pour-A-Quiche
Stilwell

COMPETITORS

Bimbo	Marie Callender
Campbell Soup	McKee Foods
General Mills	Rich Products
George Weston	Sara Lee Bakery Group
International Multifoods	Tasty Baking
Interstate Bakeries	Weston Foods
Lance	

HISTORICAL FINANCIALS & EMPLOYEES

NYSE: FLO FYE: First Saturday in January	Annual Growth	12/92	12/93	12/94	12/95	12/96	12/97	12/98	12/99	12/00	12/01
Sales ($ mil.)	0.6%	—	—	—	—	—	—	—	—	1,620	1,629
Net income ($ mil.)	—	—	—	—	—	—	—	—	—	5	(14)
Income as % of sales	—	—	—	—	—	—	—	—	—	0.3%	—
Earnings per share ($)	—	—	—	—	—	—	—	—	—	—	(0.48)
Stock price - FY high ($)	—	—	—	—	—	—	—	—	—	—	28.97
Stock price - FY low ($)	—	—	—	—	—	—	—	—	—	—	12.86
Stock price - FY close ($)	—	—	—	—	—	—	—	—	—	—	26.63
P/E - high	—	—	—	—	—	—	—	—	—	—	—
P/E - low	—	—	—	—	—	—	—	—	—	—	—
Dividends per share ($)	—	—	—	—	—	—	—	—	—	—	0.00
Book value per share ($)	—	—	—	—	—	—	—	—	—	—	20.86
Employees	9.6%	—	—	—	—	—	—	—	—	7,300	8,000

STOCK PRICE HISTORY
HIGH/LOW/CLOSE

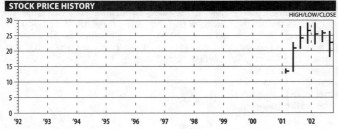

2001 FISCAL YEAR-END
Debt ratio: 28.0%
Return on equity: —
Cash ($ mil.): 12
Current ratio: 1.36
Long-term debt ($ mil.): 242
No. of shares (mil.): 30
Dividends
  Yield: —
  Payout: —
Market value ($ mil.): 794

FLUOR CORPORATION

Towering Fluor is looking for ways to flourish again. The Aliso Viejo, California-based company, one of the world's largest engineering and construction concerns, has decided to get back to the basics of engineering, procurement, construction, and maintenance. The company has undergone a restructuring that involved splitting the old Fluor into two publicly traded companies, one to concentrate on engineering and construction and one on coal mining. Former Fluor subsidiary A. T. Massey Coal has been spun off as Massey Energy, which produces steam and metallurgical-grade bituminous, low-sulfur coal in the Appalachian region of the US.

The new engineering and construction company, which retains the Fluor name, has been restructured into five business segments: energy and chemicals, industrial and infrastructure, power, global services, and government services. A separate unit, Fluor Constructors International, provides unionized management, construction, and management services in the US and Canada to Fluor projects and other companies.

Longtime Fluor veteran Alan Boeckmann has replaced the retired Philip Carroll as chairman and CEO of the company. Carroll, the first outsider to lead Fluor, was instrumental in the company's restructuring.

HISTORY

Fluor's history began in 1890 when three Fluor brothers, immigrants from Switzerland, opened a Wisconsin lumber mill under the name Rudolph Fluor & Brothers. In 1912 John Simon Fluor formed a construction firm in Santa Ana, California, which soon began a relationship with Southern California Gas, leading it to specialize in oil and gas construction. The company, incorporated as Fluor Construction in 1924, later began making engine mufflers. In 1930 it expanded outside of California with a contract to build Texas pipelines.

After WWII, Middle East oil reserves were aggressively developed by Western companies. Fluor cashed in on the stampede, winning major contracts in Saudi Arabia. During the early 1960s it continued to emphasize oil and gas work, establishing a contract drilling unit, and in the 1970s it began work on giant energy projects.

In 1977 Fluor made its biggest purchase: Daniel International, a South Carolina engineering and construction firm with more than $1 billion in annual revenues. The contracting firm, founded by Charles Daniel in 1934, initially did construction work for the textile industry, then later worked for the chemical, pharmaceutical, metal, and power industries.

Flush with cash, Fluor bought St. Joe Minerals in 1981. A drop in oil prices in the 1980s killed demand for the big projects that were its bread and butter. As metal prices fell, St. Joe didn't help the bottom line either. John Robert Fluor, the last of the founding family to head the firm, died in 1984.

When David Tappan stepped in as CEO, he faced a $573 million loss the first year. The white-haired son of missionaries to China, Tappan — known as the Ice Man — dumped subsidiaries and halved the payroll. In 1986 he merged Daniel into Fluor's engineering unit, forming Fluor Daniel.

Leslie McCraw succeeded Tappan as CEO in 1991. McCraw saw Fluor as overly conservative, and three years later he began setting up offices around the world while decentralizing Fluor's structure and adding new business such as temporary staffing and equipment leasing. Fluor also shed some of its commodity companies, including its lead business in 1994. Fluor's environmental services unit merged with Groundwater Technology in 1996 and was spun off as a public company, Fluor Daniel GTI.

Fluor saw mixed results from its expansion. Amid fierce competition and pricing pressure, Fluor Daniel began cutting its overhead in early 1997 by reorganizing and selling noncore businesses. Ill with cancer, McCraw stepped down in 1998, and Philip Carroll, who had overhauled Shell Oil, took over as CEO. Carroll reorganized Fluor into four business units and tagged $90 million to rebuild its internal information management systems. Fluor also unloaded its 52% stake in Fluor Daniel GTI to The IT Group for $36 million.

Fluor in 1999 cut 5,000 jobs, further streamlined operations, and focused on growth industries such as biotechnology and telecommunications. The next year the company split its construction and coal mining operations into two separate publicly traded companies.

Carroll, his restructuring job complete, announced in December 2001 that he would retire the following February. That year the company also made plans to dispose of noncore operations of the company's construction equipment and temporary staffing businesses. Alan Boeckmann, who had been president and COO, succeeded Carroll in 2002.

Chairman and CEO: Alan L. Boeckmann, age 53, $1,365,869 pay
SVP and CFO: D. Michael Steuert, age 53, $504,692 pay
SVP Global Construction: J. Clay Thompson
SVP Human Resources and Administration: H. Steven Gilbert, age 54
SVP Law and Secretary: Lawrence N. Fisher, age 58, $664,800 pay
Group Executive, Energy and Chemicals: Kirk D. Grimes, age 44
Group Executive, Global Services: Mark A. Stevens
Group Executive, Government Services: Ronald G. Peterson
Group Executive, Industrial and Infrastructure: Robert A. McNamara
Group Executive, Investor Relations and Corporate Communications and Director: James O. Rollans, age 59, $899,900 pay
Group Executive, Sales, Marketing, and Strategic Planning: John L. Hopkins, age 48
Group Executive, Strategic Operations: Ronald W. Oakley, age 51
President and CEO, Duke/Fluor Daniel: Jeff L. Faulk
President, AMECO: Gary C. Bernardez
Auditors: Ernst & Young LLP

LOCATIONS

HQ: 1 Enterprise Dr., Aliso Viejo, CA 92656
Phone: 949-349-2000   **Fax:** 949-349-5271
Web: www.fluor.com

Fluor Corporation operates worldwide with offices in Australia, Azerbaijan, Brazil, Canada, Indonesia, Mexico, the Netherlands, Peru, the Philippines, Russia, Saudi Arabia, South Africa, Spain, the UK, and the US.

PRODUCTS/OPERATIONS

Selected Services
Assets performance consulting
Construction management
Design
Engineering, procurement, and construction (EPC)
Equipment rental, sales, and service
Feasibility studies
Maintenance
Procurement
Project management
Technical services
Temporary staffing

Selected Industries Served
Biotechnology
Chemicals
Consumer products
Electronics
Government
Infrastructure
Mining and minerals
Oil and gas
Petrochemicals
Petroleum refining
Pharmaceuticals
Power
Telecommunications

COMPETITORS

ABB	CH2M HILL	McDermott
ARCADIS	Dragados	Parsons
Bechtel	Foster Wheeler	Tetra Tech
Bilfinger Berger	Halliburton	URS
Black & Veatch	Jacobs	Washington
Bouygues	Engineering	Group

HISTORICAL FINANCIALS & EMPLOYEES

NYSE: FLR FYE: December 31	Annual Growth	10/92	10/93	10/94	10/95	10/96	10/97	10/98	10/99	10/00	*12/01
Sales ($ mil.)	(10.2%)	—	—	—	—	—	—	12,377	11,334	9,970	8,972
Net income ($ mil.)	(56.5%)	—	—	—	—	—	—	235	104	124	19
Income as % of sales	—	—	—	—	—	—	—	1.9%	0.9%	1.2%	0.2%
Earnings per share ($)	—	—	—	—	—	—	—	—	—	—	0.25
Stock price - FY high ($)	—	—	—	—	—	—	—	—	—	—	63.20
Stock price - FY low ($)	—	—	—	—	—	—	—	—	—	—	31.20
Stock price - FY close ($)	—	—	—	—	—	—	—	—	—	—	37.40
P/E - high	—	—	—	—	—	—	—	—	—	—	253
P/E - low	—	—	—	—	—	—	—	—	—	—	125
Dividends per share ($)	—	—	—	—	—	—	—	—	—	—	0.48
Book value per share ($)	—	—	—	—	—	—	—	—	—	—	9.85
Employees	8.9%	—	—	—	—	—	—	—	—	47,113	51,313

* Fiscal year change

STOCK PRICE HISTORY

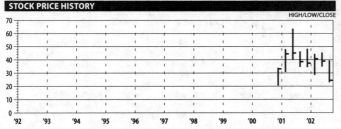

HIGH/LOW/CLOSE

2001 FISCAL YEAR-END

Debt ratio: 2.2%
Return on equity: 1.6%
Cash ($ mil.): 573
Current ratio: 1.02
Long-term debt ($ mil.): 18
No. of shares (mil.): 80
Dividends
  Yield: 1.3%
  Payout: 192.0%
Market value ($ mil.): 2,996

FMC CORPORATION

E may = mc squared, but FMC = chemicals. Philadelphia-based FMC Corporation gets about 40% of its sales from industrial chemicals (including soda ash, hydrogen peroxide, and phosphorus). The company also has a joint venture with Solutia called Astaris that produces phosphorus compounds. The rest of sales come from agricultural products (insecticides and herbicides) and specialty chemicals (food and pharmaceutical additives).

FMC has spun off its energy systems (equipment for the oil and gas industries) and food and transportation systems (food machinery and airport systems) operations as FMC Technologies and moved its headquarters from Chicago to Philadelphia.

As part of the restructuring and spinoff, the company has laid off staff and closed some plants. The company has also sold most of its sodium cyanide business.

HISTORY

After retiring to California, inventor John Bean developed a pump to deliver a continuous spray of insecticide in 1884. This invention led to the Bean Spray Pump Company in 1904. In 1928 Bean Spray Pump went public and bought Anderson-Barngrover (food-growing and food-processing equipment). The company became Food Machinery Corporation the next year. It bought Peerless Pump (agricultural and industrial pumps) in 1933.

During WWII the company began making military equipment. It entered the agricultural chemical field when it bought Niagara Sprayer & Chemical (1943). After the war it added Westvaco Chemical (1948) and changed its name to Food Machinery & Chemical.

The Bean family ran the company until 1956, when John Bean's grandson, John Crummey, retired as chairman. The company extended its product line, buying Oil Center Tool (wellhead equipment, 1957), Sunland Industries (fertilizer and insecticides, 1959), and Barrett Equipment (automotive brake equipment, 1961).

In light of its growing diversification, the company changed its name to FMC Corporation in 1961. Major purchases in the 1960s included American Viscose (rayon and cellophane, 1963) and Link-Belt (equipment for power transmission and for bulk-material handling, 1967).

To be centrally located, FMC moved its headquarters from San Jose to Chicago in 1972. Through the 1970s and early 1980s, the company sold several slow-growing businesses, including its pump and fiber divisions (1976), semiconductor division (1979), industrial packaging division

(1980), Niagara Seed Operation (1980), and Power Transmission Group (1981).

It moved into other markets just as quickly. These included a Nevada gold mine (through a 1979 joint venture with Freeport Minerals), Bradley armored personnel carriers (through an early-1980s contract with the US Army), and lithium (by acquiring Lithium Corp. of America, 1985). In a 1986 antitakeover move, FMC gave employees a larger stake in the company.

FMC bought Ciba-Geigy's flame-retardant and water-treatment businesses in 1992 and combined its defense operations with Harsco as United Defense. FMC's 1994 acquisitions included Abex's Jetway Systems Division (aircraft support systems) and Caterpillar's Automated Vehicle Systems group. FMC formed a joint venture with Nippon Sheet Glass and Sumitomo Corporation in 1995 to mine for soda ash.

FMC made a deal with DuPont in 1996 to commercialize new herbicides. The company debuted its composite (nonmetallic) prototype armored vehicle in 1997. In the long shadow of reduced defense budgets, FMC and Harsco sold their stagnant defense operation for $850 million to The Carlyle Group investment firm.

The sale of its defense division didn't protect FMC from a $310 million damage award in a whistleblower suit against the company in 1998. A federal jury found that FMC had misled the Army about the safety of the Bradley armored infantry vehicle. The court later lowered the penalty to about $90 million.

In 1999 the company agreed to combine its phosphorus operations with Solutia to form a joint venture called Astaris LLC. That year FMC sold its process-additives unit to Great Lakes Chemical. FMC bought Northfield Freezing Systems (food processing) in 2000. The following year the company split into separate chemical and machinery companies by spinning off its machinery business as FMC Technologies.

In early 2002 FMC sold its sodium cyanide business to Cyanco Company, a joint venture between Degussa Corporation and Winnemucca Chemicals (a subsidiary of Nevada Chemicals).

OFFICERS

Chairman, President, and CEO: William G. Walter, age 56, $878,118 pay
SVP and CFO: W. Kim Foster, age 53
SVP and General Manager, Industrial Chemicals Group and Shared Services: Robert I. Harries, age 58, $588,414 pay
CIO: Edward T. Flynn
VP and Controller: Graham R. Wood, age 48
VP and General Manager, Agricultural Products Group: Milton Steele, age 53

VP and Treasurer: Thomas C. Deas Jr., age 51
VP, Communications: Patricia D. Brozowski
VP, General Counsel, and Secretary: Andrea E. Utecht, age 53
VP, Government Affairs: Gerald R. Prout, age 51
VP, Human Resources, Communications, and Public Affairs: Kenneth R. Garrett
Assistant Treasurer and Director Tax: Theodore H. Laws
Investor Relations: Eric Norris
Media: Jeff Jacoby
Auditors: KPMG LLP

LOCATIONS

HQ: 1735 Market St., Philadelphia, PA 19103
Phone: 215-299-6000   **Fax:** 215-299-6618
Web: www.fmc.com

FMC operates about 35 manufacturing facilities in 19 countries.

2001 Sales

	$ mil.	% of total
US	882	45
Other countries	1,061	55
Total	**1,943**	**100**

PRODUCTS/OPERATIONS

2001 Sales

	$ mil.	% of total
Industrial chemicals	822	42
Agricultural chemicals	653	34
Specialty chemicals	472	24
Adjustments	(4)	—
Total	**1,943**	**100**

Selected Products

Agricultural Products
Herbicides
Pesticides

Energy Systems
Drilling, engineering, and metering services
Subsea wellheads

Food and Transportation Systems
Airline cargo loaders
Automated materials-handling systems
Deicers
FMC FoodTech (food equipment)
Jetway passenger-boarding bridges
Push-back tractors

Industrial Chemicals
Hydrogen peroxide
Phosphorus chemicals
Soda ash
Sodium bicarbonate
Sodium sesquicarbonate

Specialty Chemicals
Cellulose (alginate, carrageenan, and microcrystalline)
Lithium

COMPETITORS

Agrium	General	Penwest
Asahi Glass	Chemical	Pharmaceuticals
BASF AG	Hercules	Pharmacia
Cargill	Imperial	Rohm and Haas
Crompton	Chemical	Solvay
Dow Chemical	Novartis	Syngenta
DuPont	Olin	Terra Industries
		Wyeth

HISTORICAL FINANCIALS & EMPLOYEES

NYSE: FMC FYE: December 31	Annual Growth	12/92	12/93	12/94	12/95	12/96	12/97	12/98	12/99	12/00	12/01
Sales ($ mil.)	(7.6%)	3,974	3,754	4,011	4,510	5,081	4,313	4,378	4,111	3,926	1,943
Net income ($ mil.)	—	(76)	36	173	216	211	162	107	213	111	(338)
Income as % of sales	—	—	1.0%	4.3%	4.8%	4.1%	3.8%	2.4%	5.2%	2.8%	—
Earnings per share ($)	—	(2.06)	1.01	4.66	5.72	5.54	4.41	3.05	6.57	3.50	(10.86)
Stock price - FY high ($)	—	27.90	28.30	34.13	41.92	40.87	47.91	43.07	39.43	40.45	44.02
Stock price - FY low ($)	—	22.27	21.75	23.84	29.93	31.90	31.11	25.28	20.57	24.14	23.92
Stock price - FY close ($)	2.1%	25.94	24.69	30.26	35.44	36.75	35.27	29.34	30.03	37.56	31.18
P/E - high	—	—	25	7	7	7	11	10	6	11	—
P/E - low	—	—	19	5	5	6	7	6	3	7	—
Dividends per share ($)	—	0.00	0.00	0.00	0.00	0.00	0.00	0.00	0.00	0.00	0.00
Book value per share ($)	1.5%	6.10	5.99	11.41	17.79	23.02	21.78	22.30	24.49	26.12	6.99
Employees	(13.5%)	22,097	20,696	21,344	22,164	22,048	16,805	16,216	15,609	14,802	6,000

STOCK PRICE HISTORY

HIGH/LOW/CLOSE

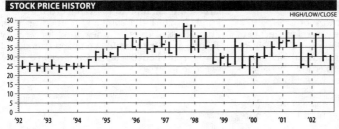

2001 FISCAL YEAR-END

Debt ratio: 74.9%
Return on equity: —
Cash ($ mil.): 23
Current ratio: 0.76
Long-term debt ($ mil.): 652
No. of shares (mil.): 31
Dividends
  Yield: —
  Payout: —
Market value ($ mil.): 976

FMR CORP.

FMR Corp. is *semper fidelis* (ever faithful) to its core business. The Boston-based financial services conglomerate, better known as Fidelity Investments, is the world's #1 mutual fund company.

Serving some 17 million individual and institutional clients, Fidelity manages more than 300 funds and has more than $800 billion of assets under management. Its Magellan fund was for many years the US's largest, but it now jockeys with the Vanguard 500 Index Fund for the top spot. Fidelity's nonfund offerings include life insurance, trust services, securities clearing, retirement services, and a leading online discount brokerage. The firm also has major holdings in telecommunications (COLT Telecom Group) and transportation (BostonCoach). Like many institutional investors, Fidelity uses its clout to sway the boards of companies in which it has significant holdings.

The founding Johnson family controls most of FMR; Abigail Johnson, CEO Ned's daughter and heir apparent, is the largest single shareholder with about 25%.

HISTORY

Boston money management firm Anderson & Cromwell formed Fidelity Fund in 1930. Edward Johnson became president of the fund in 1943, when it had $3 million invested in Treasury bills. Johnson diversified into stocks, and by 1945 the fund had grown to $10 million. In 1946 he established Fidelity Management and Research to act as its investment adviser.

In the early 1950s Johnson hired Gerry Tsai, a young immigrant from Shanghai, to analyze stocks. He put Tsai in charge of Fidelity Capital Fund in 1957. Tsai's brash, go-go investment strategy in such speculative stocks as Xerox and Polaroid paid off; by the time he left to form his own fund in 1965, he was managing more than $1 billion.

The Magellan Fund started in 1962. The company entered the corporate pension plans market (FMR Investment Management) in 1964, and retirement plans for self-employed individuals (Fidelity Keogh Plan) in 1967. It began serving investors outside the US (Fidelity International) in 1968.

Holding company FMR was formed in 1972, and that year Johnson gave control of Fidelity to his son Ned, who vertically integrated FMR by selling directly to customers rather than through brokers. The next year he formed Fidelity Daily Income Trust, the first money market fund to offer check writing.

Peter Lynch was hired as manager of the Magellan Fund in 1977. During his 13-year tenure, Magellan grew from $20 million to $12 billion in assets and outperformed all other mutual funds. Fidelity started Fidelity Brokerage Services in 1978, becoming the first mutual fund company to offer discount brokerage.

In 1980 the company launched a nationwide branch network and in 1986 entered the credit card business. The Wall Street crash of 1987 forced its Magellan Fund to liquidate almost $1 billion in stock in a single day. That year FMR moved into insurance by offering variable life, single premium, and deferred annuity policies. In 1989 the company introduced the low-expense Spartan Fund, targeted toward large, less-active investors.

Magellan's performance faded in the early 1990s, dropping from #1 performer to #3. Most of Fidelity's best performers were from its 36 select funds, which focus on narrow industry segments. FMR founded London-based COLT Telecom in 1993. In 1994 Ned Johnson gave his daughter and heir apparent, Abigail, a 25% stake in FMR.

Jeffrey Vinik resigned as manager of Magellan in 1996, one of more than a dozen fund managers to leave the firm that year and the next. Robert Stansky took the helm of the $56 billion fund, which FMR decided to close to new investors in 1997. Fidelity had a first that year when it went with an outside fund manager, hiring Bankers Trust (now part of Deutsche Bank) to manage its index funds.

FMR did some housecleaning in the late 1990s. It sold its Wentworth art galleries (1997) and *Worth* magazine (1998). Despite continued management turnover, it entered Japan and expanded its presence in Canada.

In 1999 the firm formed a joint venture with Charles Schwab; Donaldson, Lufkin & Jenrette, known now as Credit Suisse First Boston (USA); and Spear, Leeds & Kellogg to form an electronic communications network (ECN) to trade Nasdaq stocks online. That year Fidelity teamed with Internet portal Lycos (now part of Terra Lycos) to develop its online brokerage.

FMR opened savings and loan Fidelity Personal Trust Co. in 2000. That year the Magellan Fund for a time lost its longtime title as the US's largest mutual fund to the Vanguard Index 500 Fund. In 2001 the company teamed up with Frank Russell to offer a new fund for wealthy clients. Also that year the company announced it would cut about 2% of its workforce in the face of economic woes.

Chairman and CEO: Edward C. Johnson III, age 71
Vice Chairman and COO; President, Fidelity Investments Institutional Retirement Group: Robert L. Reynolds
President, Fidelity Management and Research: Abigail P. Johnson, age 40
EVP and CFO: Stephen P. Jonas
SVP and Chief of Administration: David C. Weinstein
VP and General Counsel: Lena G. Goldberg
President, Fidelity Capital: Steven P. Akin
President, Fidelity Corporate Real Estate: Ronald C. Duff
President, Fidelity Corporate Systems and Services: Mark A. Peterson
President, Fidelity International Limited: Barry R.J. Bateman, age 56
President, Fidelity Investments Canada: Jeffrey R. Carney
President, Fidelity Investments European Mutual Funds: Thomas Balk
President, Fidelity Investments Institutional Brokerage Group: David F. Denison
President, Fidelity Investments Institutional Services: Kevin J. Kelly
President, Fidelity Investments Systems: Donald A. Haile
President, Fidelity Security Services: George K. Campbell
President, Fidelity Ventures: Timothy T. Hilton
President, Fidelity-Wide Processing: Chuck Griffith
President, Personal Investments: Gail J. McGovern, age 47
President and Chief Investment Officer, Strategic Advisors: William V. Harlow
Auditors: PricewaterhouseCoopers LLP

LOCATIONS

HQ: 82 Devonshire St., Boston, MA 02109
Phone: 617-563-7000   **Fax:** 617-476-6150
Web: www.fidelity.com

FMR has offices in Australia, Austria, Bermuda, Canada, France, Germany, Hong Kong, India, Ireland, Japan, Luxembourg, the Netherlands, South Korea, Spain, Sweden, Switzerland, Taiwan, the UK, United Arab Emirates, and the US.

PRODUCTS/OPERATIONS

Selected Subsidiaries
Fidelity Capital
Fidelity Financial Intermediary Services
  Fidelity Investments Canada Limited
  Fidelity Investments Institutional Services Company, Inc.
Fidelity International Limited (Bermuda)
Fidelity Investments Institutional Retirement Group
  Fidelity Benefits Center
  Fidelity Group Pensions International
  Fidelity Institutional Retirement Services Company
  Fidelity Investments Public Sector Services Company
  Fidelity Investments Tax-Exempt Services Company
  Fidelity Management Trust Company
Fidelity Investments Life Insurance Company
Fidelity Personal Investments and Brokerage Group
  Fidelity Brokerage Technology Group
  Fidelity Capital Markets
  Fidelity Investment Advisor Group
  National Financial Correspondent Services
Fidelity Technology & Processing Group
Strategic Advisers, Inc.

COMPETITORS

Alliance Capital	MassMutual
American Century	Merrill Lynch
Ameritrade	MetLife
AXA Financial	Morgan Stanley
Barclays	Northwestern Mutual
Charles Schwab	Prudential
Citigroup	Putnam Investments
Datek Online	Quick & Reilly/Fleet
Dow Jones	Raymond James Financial
E*TRADE	T. Rowe Price
Goldman Sachs	TD Waterhouse
John Hancock Financial Services	TIAA-CREF
	UBS PaineWebber
Lehman Brothers	Vanguard Group
Marsh & McLennan	

HISTORICAL FINANCIALS & EMPLOYEES

Private FYE: December 31	Annual Growth	12/92	12/93	12/94	12/95	12/96	12/97	12/98	12/99	12/00	12/01
Sales ($ mil.)	20.5%	1,824	2,570	3,530	4,277	5,080	5,878	6,776	8,845	11,096	9,800
Net income ($ mil.)	29.9%	125	225	315	431	423	536	446	1,008	2,170	1,320
Income as % of sales	—	6.9%	8.8%	8.9%	10.1%	8.3%	9.1%	6.6%	11.4%	19.6%	13.5%
Employees	14.7%	9,000	12,900	14,600	18,000	23,300	25,000	28,000	30,000	33,186	31,033

NET INCOME HISTORY

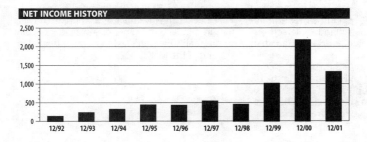

FOOT LOCKER, INC.

The spirit of the venator — which is Latin for "sportsman" or "hunter"— did not help the Venator Group, so it changed its name to Foot Locker. The New York City-based specialty retailer has sold or closed thousands of stores and a number of chains to reverse years of declining sales. The company has more than 3,600 specialty stores in Australia, Europe, and North America, including Foot Locker (the #1 athletic shoe retailer in the US) and Champs Sports.

Hit by the sales slump that has ravaged the entire retail industry, Foot Locker sold its Northern Group stores in Canada and its other noncore units, including gift retailer San Francisco Music Box Co. and some Burger King and Popeyes fastfood franchises. The company changed its name to Foot Locker in November 2001 to underscore its commitment to athletic goods retailing.

Investment group Greenway Partners, which owns about 9% of Foot Locker, launched a failed proxy battle for the company in 1999; FMR Corp owns 8%.

HISTORY

With the idea of selling merchandise priced at no more than five cents, Frank Woolworth opened the Great Five Cent Store in Utica, New York, in 1879; it failed. That year he moved to Lancaster, Pennsylvania, and created the first five-and-dime. Woolworth moved his headquarters to New York City (1886) and spent the rest of the century acquiring other dime-store chains. He later expanded to Canada (1897), England (1909), France (1922), and Germany (1927).

The 120-store chain, with $10 million in sales, incorporated as F.W. Woolworth & Company in 1905, with Woolworth as president. In 1912 the company merged with five rival chains and went public with 596 stores, making $52 million in sales the first year. The next year, paying $13.5 million in cash, Woolworth finished construction of the Woolworth Building, then the world's tallest building (792 feet). When he died in 1919, the chain had 1,081 stores, with sales of $119 million.

Woolworth became more competitive after WWII by advertising, establishing revolving credit and self-service, moving stores to suburbs, and expanding merchandise selections. In 1962 it opened Woolco, a US and Canadian discount chain.

From the 1960s through the 1980s, the company grew by acquiring and expanding in the US and abroad. It picked up Kinney (shoes, 1963), Richman Brothers (men's clothing, 1969), Holtzman's Little Folk Shop (children's clothing,

1983), Champs Sports (sporting goods, 1987), and Mathers (shoes, Australia, 1988).

The company introduced Foot Locker, the athletic shoe chain, in 1974, later developing Lady Foot Locker (1982) and Kids Foot Locker (1987). In 1993 Woolworth launched an ambitious restructuring plan, focusing on specialty stores (mostly apparel and shoes). It also closed 400 US stores and sold 122 Canadian Woolco stores to Wal-Mart that year. Former Macy's president Roger Farah became CEO in 1994. Farah eliminated 16 divisions and dozens of executives.

A year later the firm sold its Kids Mart/Little Folks children's wear chain. In 1996 Woolworth began a major remodeling program that included removing its venerable lunch counters. (Another alleged renovation at the Woolworth chain — the firing of older workers, who were replaced by teenagers — led to an Equal Employment Opportunity Commission lawsuit against the company in 1999.) The changes failed, and the next year the company closed its US Woolworth stores and bought athletic-products catalog company Eastbay.

In 1998 Woolworth changed its name to Venator Group and sold the Woolworth Building, a national landmark (headquarters remained in the building). The company then shed itself of more than 1,400 stores, including Kinney shoes and Footquarters (both closed).

Internet site eVenator was launched in 1999 to sell Eastbay, Champs, and Foot Locker merchandise. Venator came out the champ in a proxy fight against investment group Greenway Partners in July 1999. Shortly thereafter, Farah was replaced as CEO (he remained chairman) by president Dale Hilpert.

In 2000 Venator slashed 7% of its workforce in the US and Canada (a small part of the planned 30% cut) and closed 465 stores. COO Matt Serra became president, and Hilpert became chairman when Farah resigned later that year.

In March 2001 Hilpert resigned, replaced by Carter Bacot as chairman, and Serra added CEO to his title. Venator later sold its Canadian Northern Group unit to investment firm York Management Services and closed its Northern Reflections stores in the US. Venator changed its name to Foot Locker in November. It also finalized deals for gift retailer San Francisco Music Box Co. and its hospitality division's fast-food franchises before the end of the year.

OFFICERS

Chairman: J. Carter Bacot, age 69
President, CEO, and Director: Matthew D. Serra,
age 57, $2,351,367 pay
EVP and CFO: Bruce L. Hartman, age 48, $814,139 pay
SVP and CIO: Terry L. Talley, age 58, $764,875 pay
SVP, General Counsel, and Secretary: Gary M. Bahler,
age 50, $647,136 pay
SVP, Human Resources: Laurie J. Petrucci, age 43
SVP, Real Estate: Jeffrey L. Berk, age 46, $680,537 pay
SVP, Strategic Planning: Lauren B. Peters, age 40
VP and Chief Accounting Officer: Robert W. McHugh,
age 43
VP and Controller: Marc D. Katz, age 37
VP and Deputy General Counsel: Dennis E. Sheehan,
age 49
VP, Corporate Shared Services: Peter M. Cupps
VP, Investor Relations and Treasurer: Peter D. Brown,
age 47
VP, Logistics: Joseph N. Bongiorno, age 54
President and CEO, Foot Locker US and Australia:
Tim Finn, age 51
President and CEO, Foot Locker Europe: Simon Rider,
age 45
President and CEO, Lady Foot Locker: Nick Grayston,
age 39
CEO, Footlocker.com: Thomas J. Slover
President, Foot Locker Canada: Edward Schleicher,
age 55
Auditors: KPMG LLP

LOCATIONS

HQ: 112 W. 34th St., New York, NY 10120
Phone: 212-720-3700   **Fax:** 212-720-4397
Web: www.footlocker-inc.com

2002 Store Locations

	No.
US	2,950
Europe	323
Canada	158
Australia	73
Puerto Rico	73
Virgin Islands	8
Guam	5
Total	**3,590**

PRODUCTS/OPERATIONS

2002 Stores

	No.
Foot Locker	1,993
Lady Foot Locker	632
Champs	574
Kids Foot Locker	391
Total	**3,590**

COMPETITORS

Academy	J. C. Penney
Athlete's Foot	Kmart
Brown Shoe	L.L. Bean
Dillard's	May
Federated	Sears
Finish Line	Shoe Carnival
Footstar	Sports Authority
Forzani Group	Target
The Gap	TJX
Gart Sports	Wal-Mart
Hibbett Sporting Goods	

HISTORICAL FINANCIALS & EMPLOYEES

NYSE: Z FYE: Last Saturday in January	Annual Growth	1/93	1/94	1/95	1/96	1/97	1/98	1/99	1/00	1/01	1/02
Sales ($ mil.)	(8.7%)	9,962	9,626	8,293	8,224	8,092	6,624	4,555	4,647	4,356	4,379
Net income ($ mil.)	(11.6%)	280	(495)	47	(164)	169	(10)	(136)	48	(240)	92
Income as % of sales	—	2.8%	—	0.6%	—	2.1%	—	—	1.0%	—	2.1%
Earnings per share ($)	(12.3%)	2.14	(3.76)	0.36	(1.23)	1.26	(0.07)	(1.00)	0.35	(1.73)	0.66
Stock price - FY high ($)	—	35.00	32.38	25.88	19.38	25.25	28.75	27.25	12.00	16.75	19.10
Stock price - FY low ($)	—	26.00	20.50	12.88	9.38	11.00	18.25	4.25	3.19	5.00	10.20
Stock price - FY close ($)	(6.9%)	29.38	26.00	15.75	11.25	20.38	21.75	5.13	6.00	12.95	15.50
P/E - high	—	16	—	72	—	20	—	—	41	—	29
P/E - low	—	12	—	36	—	9	—	—	11	—	15
Dividends per share ($)	—	1.11	1.15	0.88	0.15	0.00	0.00	0.00	0.00	0.00	0.00
Book value per share ($)	(8.4%)	15.68	10.23	10.25	9.24	9.95	9.42	7.65	8.29	7.31	7.09
Employees	(13.3%)	145,000	111,000	119,000	82,000	82,000	75,000	75,118	47,035	48,815	40,104

STOCK PRICE HISTORY

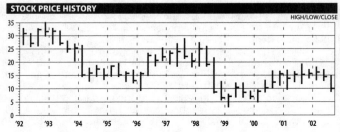

HIGH/LOW/CLOSE

2002 FISCAL YEAR-END

Debt ratio: 26.9%
Return on equity: 9.2%
Cash ($ mil.): 215
Current ratio: 2.07
Long-term debt ($ mil.): 365
No. of shares (mil.): 140
Dividends
  Yield: —
  Payout: —
Market value ($ mil.): 2,169

FORD MOTOR COMPANY

In almost a century of carmaking, Ford Motor has produced enough vehicles — some 270 million — to put every person in the US behind the wheel of a Ford. Parked in Dearborn, Michigan, the company is the world's largest maker of pickup trucks and the #2 overall vehicle manufacturer, behind General Motors. Ford's classic nameplates include Ford, Mercury, Aston Martin, Jaguar, Lincoln, and Volvo (the latter four brands make up Ford's Premier Automotive Group). It also owns a controlling (33%) interest in Mazda Motor.

Among Ford's other holdings, both Ford Motor Credit (auto financing) and Hertz (auto rental) are world leaders, while its Volvo car and Land Rover SUV operations give Ford a larger presence in Europe, where its market share has been slipping. Ford spun off Visteon, its car component subsidiary, as an independent company, and sold Kwik-Fit (European auto maintenance business) to London-based CVC Capital Partners for $505 million in cash and a note to be paid after CVC secures additional financing (although Ford will retain a 19% equity stake).

In what turned out to be the beginning of a major upper management shake-up, Jac Nasser resigned as Ford's CEO. The chairman and great-grandson of the company's founder, William Clay Ford Jr., replaced him. Ford later announced sweeping cost-reduction measures including 35,000 worldwide job cuts (22,000 in North America), the closure of three North American assembly plants, and the discontinuation of four vehicle models — the Mercury Cougar, the Mercury Villager, the Ford Escort, and the Lincoln Continental. The Ford family controls 40% of the company.

HISTORY

Henry Ford started the Ford Motor Company in 1903 in Dearborn, Michigan. In 1908 Ford introduced the Model T, produced on a moving assembly line that revolutionized both carmaking and manufacturing. By 1920 some 60% of all vehicles on the road were Fords.

After Ford omitted its usual dividend in 1916, stockholders sued. Ford responded by buying back all of its outstanding shares in 1919 and didn't allow outside ownership again until 1956.

Ford bought Lincoln in 1922 and discontinued the Model T in 1927. Its replacement, the Model A, came in 1932. With Henry Ford's health failing, his son Edsel became president that year. Despite the debut of the Mercury (1938), market share slipped behind GM and Chrysler. After Edsel's death in 1943, his son, Henry II, took over and decentralized Ford, following the GM model. In 1950 the carmaker recaptured second place. Ford rolled out the infamous Edsel in 1958 and launched the Mustang in 1964.

Hurt by the oil crisis of the 1970s, Ford cut its workforce and closed plants during the 1980s. It also diversified into agricultural equipment by purchasing New Holland (1986) and Versatile (1987). Ford added luxury sports cars in 1987 by buying 75% of Aston Martin (it bought the rest in 1994). The 1988 introduction of the Taurus and Sable spurred Ford to its largest share of the US car market (21.7%) in 10 years. In 1989 it bought the Associates (financial services) and Jaguar (luxury cars).

The company sold Ford Aerospace to Loral in 1990 and merged New Holland (renamed CNH Global, 1999) with a Fiat subsidiary the next year. Ford acquired Hertz in 1994 and two years later bought #3 rental agency Budget Rent a Car (sold 1997). Also in 1996 it sold a 19% stake in finance unit Associates First Capital in an IPO and increased its stake in Mazda to one-third. The next year Ford sold its heavy-duty truck unit to Daimler-Benz's Freightliner and spun off 19% of Hertz in an IPO.

Ford began building a minibus line in China in 1997, beating GM in the race to produce vehicles for the Chinese market. Henry Ford's great-grandson, William Clay Ford Jr., became chairman in 1998. Company veteran Jacques Nasser became president and CEO in early 1999.

Ford bought Volvo's carmaking operations for $6.45 billion in 1999, adding the brand to its new Premier Automotive Group (Aston Martin, Jaguar, and Lincoln), headed by former BMW chairman Wolfgang Reitzle.

In 2000 Ford bought BMW's Land Rover SUV operations for about $2.7 billion in a move to boost its European presence. Also in 2000 the company was embroiled in controversy when Bridgestone/Firestone recalled some 6.5 million tires, many of which were used as original equipment on Ford Explorers.

In 2001 the company also spent about $700 million to buy back the 19% of Hertz. In addition Ford announced that it would take a $2.1 billion charge to cover the replacement of up to 13 million Firestone Wilderness AT tires already on its vehicles. The news led Firestone to announce that it would no longer do business with Ford, thus ending a 95-year relationship. Within days Ford had inked a deal with Goodyear in which Goodyear replaces Ford owners' Firestone Wilderness AT tires with Goodyear tires and then bills Ford.

In August Ford announced that it would use early-retirement incentives to eliminate 4,500-5,000 (about 10%) of its salaried employees. In late 2001 Nasser resigned and was replaced as CEO by chairman Ford.

A week or so into 2002, Ford announced far-reaching cost-cutting measures, including 35,000 worldwide job cuts (22,000 in North America), closure of three North American assembly plants, and the discontinuation of four vehicle models.

OFFICERS

Chairman and CEO: William Clay Ford Jr.
Vice Chairman: Carl E. Reichardt, age 71
Vice Chairman and CFO: Allan D. Gilmour, age 67
President, COO, and Director: Sir Nicholas V. Scheele, age 58, $686,997 pay
Chief of Staff and Secretary: John M. Rintamaki, age 60
Senior Advisor to the Office of the Chairman and the Chief Executive: Carlos E. Mazzorin, age 60
Group VP; Chairman and CEO, Premier Automotive Group: Mark Fields
Group VP Global Product Development and CTO: Richard Parry-Jones, age 50
Group VP North America Marketing Sales and Service: James G. O'Connor
VP and General Counsel: Dennis E. Ross
VP Corporate Human Resources: Joe W. Laymon
Auditors: PricewaterhouseCoopers LLP

LOCATIONS

HQ: 1 American Rd., Dearborn, MI 48126
Phone: 313-322-3000   **Fax:** 313-845-6073
Web: www.ford.com

2001 Sales

	$ mil.	% of total
US	108,296	67
Europe	35,532	22
Other regions	18,584	11
Total	**162,412**	**100**

PRODUCTS/OPERATIONS

2001 Sales

	$ mil.	% of total
Automotive	131,528	81
Financial services		
Ford Credit	24,996	15
Hertz	4,898	3
Other	966	1
Other	24	—
Total	**162,412**	**100**

COMPETITORS

AutoNation	GKN
Bank of America	Honda
BANK ONE	Isuzu
BMW	J.P. Morgan Chase
Boots Company	Navistar
Budget Group	Nissan
Cendant	Peugeot Motors of
Citigroup	America, Inc.
DaimlerChrysler	RAC
Denso	Renault
Dollar Thrifty Automotive	Saab Automobile
Group	Saturn
Enterprise Rent-A-Car	Suzuki Motor
Fiat	Toyota
General Motors	Volkswagen

HISTORICAL FINANCIALS & EMPLOYEES

NYSE: F FYE: December 31	Annual Growth	12/92	12/93	12/94	12/95	12/96	12/97	12/98	12/99	12/00	12/01
Sales ($ mil.)	5.5%	100,132	108,521	128,439	137,137	146,991	153,627	144,416	162,558	170,064	162,412
Net income ($ mil.)	—	(7,385)	2,529	5,308	4,139	4,446	6,920	22,071	7,237	3,467	(5,453)
Income as % of sales	—	—	2.3%	4.1%	3.0%	3.0%	4.5%	15.3%	4.5%	2.0%	—
Earnings per share ($)	—	(7.82)	2.10	4.44	3.33	3.64	5.61	17.74	5.86	2.30	(3.02)
Stock price – FY high ($)	—	9.27	12.54	13.30	12.47	14.13	19.07	35.11	38.79	32.71	31.42
Stock price – FY low ($)	—	5.26	8.16	9.72	9.20	10.34	11.38	16.17	26.43	21.69	14.70
Stock price – FY close ($)	7.6%	8.13	12.24	10.58	10.96	12.24	18.43	33.54	30.46	23.44	15.72
P/E – high	—	—	6	3	3	4	3	7	6	14	—
P/E – low	—	—	4	2	3	3	2	3	4	9	—
Dividends per share ($)	3.1%	0.80	0.80	0.92	1.23	1.47	1.65	1.72	1.87	1.80	1.05
Book value per share ($)	(14.2%)	16.17	17.06	22.97	21.16	22.54	25.54	19.15	22.53	10.13	4.08
Employees	1.0%	325,333	322,213	337,778	346,990	371,702	363,892	345,175	364,550	345,991	354,431

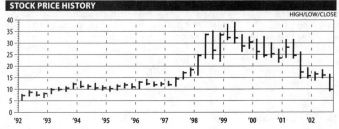

STOCK PRICE HISTORY
HIGH/LOW/CLOSE

2001 FISCAL YEAR-END

Debt ratio: 95.5%
Return on equity: —
Cash ($ mil.): 7,218
Current ratio: 0.81
Long-term debt ($ mil.): 167,035
No. of shares (mil.): 1,908
Dividends
  Yield: 6.7%
  Payout: —
Market value ($ mil.): 29,994

FORTUNE BRANDS, INC.

After kicking butts, Fortune Brands can focus on keeping its brands as strong as a straight shot of bourbon. The Lincolnshire, Illinois-based company spun off UK subsidiary Gallaher in 1997 to become completely tobacco-free. The company boasts leading brands for both the home (Moen faucets, Master Lock padlocks, Aristokraft cabinets) and office (Day-Timers personal planners, Swingline staplers). Fortune is also a leading US golf equipment maker (Titleist balls, Cobra clubs, and FootJoy golf shoes) and a leading producer of distilled spirits, including Jim Beam bourbon and DeKuyper cordials. The company also distributes Absolut vodka in the US through a joint venture (Future Brands) with the Sweden-based Vin & Sprit.

Fortune has added more products to its lines through new product introductions, joint ventures, and acquisitions. The company tried to sell Day-Timers and its parent (ACCO World) but abandoned the idea when it didn't receive an offer it found acceptable. In the meantime, the company is sticking to its strategy of focusing on consumer brands that are #1 or #2 in their markets.

HISTORY

Fortune Brands began in 1864 as W. Duke and Sons, a small tobacco company started by Washington Duke, a North Carolina farmer. James Buchanan Duke joined his father's business at age 14, and by age 25 was its president. James advertised to expanding markets, bought rival tobacco firms, and by 1904 controlled the industry. That year he merged all the competitive groups as American Tobacco Company. In a 1911 antitrust suit, the US Supreme Court dissolved American Tobacco into its original constituents, ordering them to operate independently.

James left American Tobacco the next year. He established a $100 million trust fund composed mainly of holdings in his power company, Duke Power and Light (now Duke Energy Corporation), for Trinity College. The school became Duke University in 1924.

George Washington Hill became president of American Tobacco in 1925. For the next 19 years until his death, George proved himself a consummate adman, pushing Lucky Strike, Pall Mall, and Tareyton cigarettes to top sales.

Smokers began switching to filter-tipped cigarettes in the 1950s because of health concerns. American Tobacco, however, ignored the trend and continued to rely on its popular filterless brands until the mid-1960s. In 1962 the firm sold J. Wix and Sons (Kensitas cigarettes) to UK tobacco firm Gallaher Group for a stake in Gallaher. The company remained solely in the tobacco

business until 1966, when it purchased Sunshine Biscuits (sold 1988) and Jim Beam Distillery. Reflecting its increasing diversity, the firm became American Brands in 1969. The next year it added Swingline (office supplies) and Master Lock. Meanwhile, American Brands increased its stake in Gallaher, controlling 100% by 1975. In 1976 the company bought Acushnet (Titleist and Bulls Eye); it added FootJoy in 1986.

Threatened with a takeover by E-II Holdings (a conglomerate of brands split from Beatrice), American Brands bought E-II in 1988. It kept five of E-II's companies — Day-Timers (time management products), Aristokraft (cabinets), Waterloo (tool boxes), Twentieth Century (plumbing supplies), and Vogel Peterson (office partitions; sold 1995) — and sold the rest (Culligan, Samsonite) to Riklis Family Corporation. Acquisitions in 1990 included Moen (faucets) and Whyte & Mackay (distillers). The company bought seven liquor brands in 1991 from Seagram.

American Brands sold its American Tobacco subsidiary, including the Pall Mall and Lucky Strike brands, to onetime subsidiary B.A.T Industries in 1994. The firm acquired publicly held Cobra Golf in 1996.

The following year American Brands changed its name to Fortune Brands and completed the spinoff of its Gallaher tobacco subsidiary. In 1998 Fortune bought kitchen and bathroom cabinetmaker Schrock from Electrolux, doubling its sales in that category. Also that year it bought Geyser Peak Winery and Apollo Presentation Products (overhead projectors).

Seeking to trim costs, in 1999 Fortune relocated its headquarters to Lincolnshire, Illinois. Norman Wesley was named chairman and CEO in July. In August 1999 Fortune formed Maxxium Worldwide, a non-US wine/spirits sales and distribution joint venture, with Rémy Cointreau and Highland Distillers. Also in 1999 the company bought Boone International (presentation products) and NHB Group, a manufacturer of ready-to-assemble kitchen and bath cabinetry.

In 2001 Fortune and Swedish company Vin & Sprit formed Future Brands, a joint venture to distribute Absolut vodka in the US. In October 2001 the company's Jim Beam Brands Worldwide unit unloaded its UK-based Scotch business for $290 million as part of its strategy to focus on fast-growing, premium brands. Fortune Brands bought The Omega Group, a manufacturer of kitchen and bath cabinetry, for $538 million in April 2002.

OFFICERS

Chairman and CEO: Norman H. Wesley, age 52, $1,622,000 pay
SVP and CFO: Craig P. Omtvedt, age 52, $750,000 pay
SVP, Finance and Treasurer: Mark Hausberg, age 52, $419,500 pay
SVP, General Counsel and Secretary: Mark A. Roche, age 46, $574,100 pay
SVP, Strategy and Corporate Development: Thomas J. Flocco, age 39, $620,000 pay
VP and Chief Internal Auditor: Gary L. Tobison
VP, Associate General Counsel and Assistant Secretary: Kenton R. Rose
VP, Business Development: Allan J. Snape
VP, Corporate Communications: C. Clarkson Hine
VP, Corporate Controller: Nadine A. Heidrich
VP, Human Resources: Anne C. Linsdau, age 47
Auditors: PricewaterhouseCoopers LLP

LOCATIONS

HQ: 300 Tower Parkway, Lincolnshire, IL 60069
Phone: 847-484-4400   **Fax:** 847-478-0073
Web: www.fortunebrands.com

Fortune Brands has facilities in Australia, Canada, Europe, Mexico, South Africa, Taiwan, Thailand, and the US.

2001 Sales

	$ mil.	% of total
US	4,446	78
UK	380	7
Canada	240	4
Australia	142	3
Other countries	471	8
Total	**5,679**	**100**

PRODUCTS/OPERATIONS

2001 Sales

	$ mil.	% of total
Home products	2,107	37
Spirits & wine	1,369	24
Office products	1,256	22
Golf	947	17
Total	**5,679**	**100**

Selected Brands

Absolut (vodka; US distribution joint venture)
ACCO (fastener products)
Cobra (golf clubs)
Day-Timers (organizers)
FootJoy (golf shoes and gloves)
Gilbey's (gin and vodka)
Jim Beam (bourbon)
Master Lock (padlocks)

Moen (faucets)
Old Crow (bourbon)
Old Grand-Dad (bourbon)
Ronrico (rum)
Swingline (staplers)
Titleist (golf balls, clubs, bags, and accessories)
Wilson Jones (binders and labels)

COMPETITORS

Allied Domecq
American Standard
American Woodmark
Armstrong Holdings
Avery Dennison
Bacardi USA
Black & Decker
Brown-Forman

Brunswick
Carbite Golf
Day Runner
Diageo
Eastern Company
Fellowes
Franklin Covey
Grohe
Hunt
Kohler

Logitech
Masco
Microsoft
Newell Rubbermaid
Skyy
Snap-on
Stanley Works
Targus
Waxman
ZAG Industries

HISTORICAL FINANCIALS & EMPLOYEES

NYSE: FO FYE: December 31	Annual Growth	12/92	12/93	12/94	12/95	12/96	12/97	12/98	12/99	12/00	12/01
Sales ($ mil.)	(4.8%)	8,840	8,288	7,490	5,905	5,776	4,845	5,241	5,525	5,845	5,679
Net income ($ mil.)	(8.8%)	884	470	734	540	487	99	263	(891)	(138)	386
Income as % of sales	—	10.0%	5.7%	9.8%	9.2%	8.4%	2.0%	5.0%	—	—	6.8%
Earnings per share ($)	(5.5%)	4.13	2.29	3.77	2.86	2.76	0.56	1.49	(5.35)	(0.88)	2.49
Stock price – FY high ($)	—	31.52	25.68	24.25	29.86	31.68	38.00	42.25	45.88	33.25	40.54
Stock price – FY low ($)	—	24.65	18.01	18.57	23.15	25.20	30.18	25.25	29.38	19.19	28.38
Stock price – FY close ($)	5.0%	25.60	21.01	23.70	28.12	31.36	37.06	31.63	33.06	30.00	39.59
P/E – high	—	7	8	6	10	11	61	25	—	—	16
P/E – low	—	6	5	5	8	9	49	15	—	—	11
Dividends per share ($)	(6.7%)	1.81	1.97	1.99	2.00	2.50	1.41	0.85	0.67	0.93	0.97
Book value per share ($)	(4.4%)	21.23	21.17	23.00	21.50	21.60	23.37	24.40	16.31	13.89	14.21
Employees	(6.6%)	46,220	46,660	34,820	27,050	28,000	24,920	26,040	28,130	27,800	24,998

STOCK PRICE HISTORY

HIGH/LOW/CLOSE

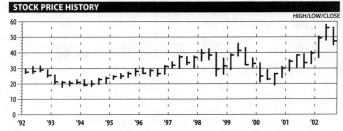

2001 FISCAL YEAR-END

Debt ratio: 31.1%
Return on equity: 18.3%
Cash ($ mil.): 49
Current ratio: 1.57
Long-term debt ($ mil.): 950
No. of shares (mil.): 148
Dividends
  Yield: 2.5%
  Payout: 39.0%
Market value ($ mil.): 5,859

FOSTER WHEELER LTD.

Foster Wheeler has wheeled itself into position as one of the world's leading contractors. This global engineering and construction giant is run from offices in Clinton, New Jersey, but domiciled in Bermuda. It has operations in 30 countries on six continents.

The firm operates through two groups: Engineering and Construction (which accounts for more than 60% of sales) and Energy Equipment. Its Engineering and Construction Group designs and builds chemical, petroleum, and process plants, makes pollution control equipment, and constructs water treatment facilities. It also provides environmental remediation services. The Energy Equipment Group (which incorporated the Power Systems Group) makes steam generating units and auxiliary equipment (such as boilers and condensers) for utilities and industrial customers.

Foster Wheeler is busy with more than 100 projects worldwide. It has built its resume through preferred-contractor arrangements with such big names as Exxon Mobil, Merck, and Electricité de France.

HISTORY

In 1884 Pell and Ernest Foster started Water Works Supply (which became Power Specialty Company in 1900); Ernest hoped to market a European technology that used superheated steam for power. Cousins Frederick and Clifton Wheeler founded Wheeler Condenser & Engineering in New York in 1891 to build condensers and pumps for the marine and power industries.

Power Specialty acquired Wheeler Condenser & Engineering in 1927 and became Foster Wheeler Corporation. That year the company launched a UK subsidiary and in 1928 established a Canadian branch. Foster Wheeler went public in 1929 and bought D. Connelly Boiler in 1931.

US military contracts helped the firm weather the Depression, and the experience won it record business during WWII. After the war Foster Wheeler expanded internationally with subsidiaries in France (1949), Italy (1957), Spain (1965), and Australia (1967).

During the 1960s, shortages in many of Foster Wheeler's core industries (energy, fertilizer, and petrochemicals) boosted sales and prompted diversification. In 1967 the company acquired Glitsch International, which made auto and chemical products and electronics.

The company formed Foster Wheeler Energy and Foster Wheeler International in 1973 and acquired Ullrich Copper, a fabricator of industrial copper products. In 1979 it ducked a takeover attempt by McDonnell Douglas.

In the 1980s Foster Wheeler moved into China and Thailand. In 1987 it set up its headquarters in New Jersey and formed Foster Wheeler Constructors to handle Western Hemisphere projects. In the late 1980s it avoided another takeover attempt by New York investor Asher Edelman.

Foster Wheeler opened a Chile subsidiary in 1991 and two years later organized its business into three groups. In 1994 the company acquired Enserch Environmental and formed Foster Wheeler Environmental. It also bought Optimized Process Designs, a construction firm serving the oil industry. Also in 1994 longtime company executive Richard Swift became CEO.

Foster Wheeler acquired boilermaker Pyropower in 1995 from Finland's Ahlstrom. In 1997 the international builder struggled with the Asian collapse and sold Glitsch to Koch Engineering. It also took a blow on an Illinois waste-to-energy plant (Robbins Resource Recovery) when that state withdrew an interest-free loan and rescinded tax rebates for using that type of energy. The plant cost Foster Wheeler $235 million in charges over the next two years.

Although global sales grew in 1998 (with new contracts in Turkey, Mexico, and China), the oil slump and the Robbins plant hit the company with a $31.5 million loss. That year the company agreed to build a steam generating plant in Ohio and began building Vietnam's first oil refinery.

In 1999 Foster Wheeler formed a recovery plan: It received Chapter 11 bankruptcy protection for the Robbins plant, which it agreed to operate for two years or until sold to a third party, and it filed suit against the state of Illinois. It also cut 1,600 jobs, slashed its quarterly dividend, and closed some facilities. The next year it reorganized its operations, combining the Power Systems Group with the Energy Equipment Group. It also settled a discrimination suit involving about 100 African American and female employees at the Robbins plant.

In 2001 the company reorganized in Bermuda as Foster Wheeler Ltd. That year chairman and CEO Richard Swift retired and was replaced by Raymond Milchovich, a former chairman and CEO of Kaiser Aluminum. To trim down the company, Milchovich launched an aggressive cost-reduction plan in 2002.

OFFICERS

Chairman, President, and CEO: Raymond J. Milchovich, age 52, $695,846 pay (partial-year salary)
SVP and CFO: Joseph T. Doyle, age 55
SVP and General Counsel: Thomas R. O'Brien, age 63, $325,000 pay
VP and Treasurer: Robert D. Iseman, age 53

VP and Secretary: Lisa F. Gardner, age 45
VP and Controller: Thomas J. Mazza, age 48
VP Government Affairs and Corporate Communications: Sherry E. Peske, age 51
VP Project Risk Management: C. James Crumm
VP Sales and Marketing Worldwide, Engineering and Construction Group: Keith E. Batchelor, age 53
Director Corporate Communications: Alastair Davie
Assistant Secretary: John A. Doyle Jr.
Auditors: PricewaterhouseCoopers LLP

LOCATIONS

HQ: Perryville Corporate Park, Clinton, NJ 08809
Phone: 908-730-4000   **Fax:** 908-730-5315
Web: www.fwc.com

Foster Wheeler operates worldwide through locations in Argentina, Brazil, Canada, Chile, China, Colombia, the Czech Republic, Finland, France, Germany, India, Indonesia, Italy, Japan, Malaysia, the Netherlands, Nigeria, the Philippines, Poland, Russia, Saudi Arabia, Singapore, South Africa, Spain, Sweden, Switzerland, Thailand, Turkey, the UK, the US, Venezuela, and Vietnam.

PRODUCTS/OPERATIONS

2001 Sales

	% of total
Engineering & construction	63
Energy equipment	37
Adjustments	—
Total	**100**

Selected Products
Environmental technologies
Fired heaters
Fluidized-bed, pulverized-coal, and package boilers
Gasification of biomass
Heat recovery steam generators
Licensed technologies to the petrochemical markets
Process (oil refining) technologies

Selected Services
After-market service and parts
Construction
Design
Engineering
Environmental remediation
Financing
Plant operation and maintenance
Procurement
Project design, engineering, procurement, fabrication, construction, and financing
Project management
Steam generator design and manufacturing

COMPETITORS

ABB	Day &	ITOCHU
AMEC	Zimmermann	Jacobs
Bechtel	Dresser-Rand	Engineering
Bilfinger Berger	Duke Energy	McDermott
Black & Veatch	Duke/Fluor	Parsons
Bouygues	Daniel	Philipp
Campenon	Fluor	Holzmann
Bernard	GE	Skanska
CH2M HILL	Halliburton	Technip-Coflexip
Chiyoda Corp.	HBG	Washington
Covanta	HOCHTIEF	Group

HISTORICAL FINANCIALS & EMPLOYEES

NYSE: FWC FYE: Last Friday in December	Annual Growth	12/92	12/93	12/94	12/95	12/96	12/97	12/98	12/99	12/00	12/01
Sales ($ mil.)	3.2%	2,495	2,583	2,234	3,042	4,006	4,060	4,537	3,867	3,891	3,315
Net income ($ mil.)	—	(46)	58	65	29	82	(11)	(32)	(175)	40	(309)
Income as % of sales	—	—	2.2%	2.9%	0.9%	2.1%	—	—	—	1.0%	—
Earnings per share ($)	—	(1.29)	1.61	1.82	0.78	2.02	(0.26)	(0.77)	(3.53)	0.97	(7.56)
Stock price – FY high ($)	—	32.88	35.88	45.13	43.50	47.25	48.13	32.25	16.06	9.50	18.74
Stock price – FY low ($)	—	23.00	25.88	26.63	29.38	33.50	26.13	11.75	7.88	3.94	3.93
Stock price – FY close ($)	(17.5%)	28.88	33.50	29.75	42.50	37.13	27.06	13.19	8.88	5.25	5.10
P/E – high	—	—	22	25	55	23	—	—	—	10	—
P/E – low	—	—	16	15	37	17	—	—	—	4	—
Dividends per share ($)	(16.2%)	0.59	0.65	0.72	0.77	0.81	0.84	0.84	0.54	0.24	0.12
Book value per share ($)	(36.4%)	10.87	11.21	12.75	15.46	16.95	15.21	14.05	9.23	8.94	0.18
Employees	0.5%	9,980	9,980	11,685	12,650	12,085	11,090	11,120	10,220	10,170	10,394

STOCK PRICE HISTORY   HIGH/LOW/CLOSE

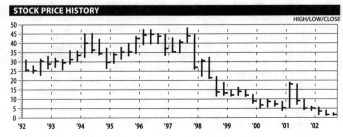

2001 FISCAL YEAR-END
Debt ratio: 94.8%
Return on equity: —
Cash ($ mil.): 224
Current ratio: 0.73
Long-term debt ($ mil.): 138
No. of shares (mil.): 41
Dividends
  Yield: 2.4%
  Payout: —
Market value ($ mil.): 208

FOX ENTERTAINMENT GROUP, INC.

Whether you think this company is smart like one, or crazy like one, the Fox Entertainment Group is one of the world's largest entertainment conglomerates. A vertically integrated company, New York City-based Fox Entertainment develops and produces feature films (*Planet of the Apes, Moulin Rouge*) and TV and cable programming (*Boston Public, Malcolm in the Middle*) that it distributes through its movie and TV studios, as well as its TV network and cable channels. The company also develops programming for third-party clients, such as CBS and NBC. The firm's FOX Broadcasting Company is one of the US's largest television networks with some 200 station affiliates.

Fox Entertainment also owns 34 TV stations, some of which are affiliates of UPN that the company gained through its 2001 acquisition of Chris-Craft. In addition, the company owns Fox Cable Networks, Fox Sports Networks, the Los Angeles Dodgers, and has a 40% stake in Los Angeles' Staples Center.

Rupert Murdoch's News Corporation owns 85% of the company.

HISTORY

Hungarian-born immigrant William Fox (originally Wilhelm Fried) purchased a New York City nickelodeon for $1,600 in 1904. He transformed the failing operation into a success and soon owned (with two partners) 25 theaters across the city. The partners opened a film exchange, The Greater New York Rental Company, and in 1913 began making movies through the Box Office Attraction Company.

Fox became the first to combine film production, leasing, and exhibition when he founded the Fox Film Corporation in 1915. Soon after, he moved the studio to California. One of the first to recognize the value of individual actors, Fox is credited with developing the "star system." Throughout the 1920s, Fox Film continued to grow. The company began experiencing trouble in 1927, and by 1930 William Fox was forced out.

In 1935 the company was merged with Twentieth Century Pictures, a studio started two years earlier by Darryl Zanuck, former head of production at Warner Brothers. Under Zanuck's leadership, the studio flourished in the 1930s and 1940s, producing such films as *The Grapes of Wrath* and *All About Eve*. By the early 1950s, however, TV was dulling some of Hollywood's shine. Zanuck left the studio in 1956 only to return in 1962 to help it recover from the disastrously overbudget *Cleopatra*.

The 1960s brought both good (*The Sound of Music*) and bad (*Tora! Tora! Tora!*). By 1971 infighting between Darryl Zanuck and his son Richard, who had been president of the studio, resulted in the resignation of both men. The studio prospered during the 1970s, culminating in 1977 with the release of *Star Wars,* the biggest box office hit in history at that time.

Oilman Marvin Davis bought Twentieth Century Fox for $722 million in 1981. In 1985 the studio changed hands again when it was purchased by Rupert Murdoch. The next year Murdoch bought six TV stations from Metromedia and launched the FOX Broadcasting Company.

Murdoch became CEO in 1995. In 1996 and 1997, respectively, Murdoch created the Fox News Channel and purchased Pat Robertson's International Family Entertainment. The company also joined Liberty Media in 1996 to create a rival to Disney's ESPN sports network.

Fox Entertainment Group went public in November of 1998, raising $2.8 billion — one of the largest offerings in American history. In 1998 Murdoch bought the Los Angeles Dodgers and acquired 40% of the Staples Center sports arena, acquiring options to buy minority interests in the Los Angeles Kings and the Los Angeles Lakers.

In 1999 News Corp. bought the 50% of the Fox/Liberty Networks business that it didn't already own from Liberty Media and transferred ownership to Fox (the operation was renamed Fox Sports Networks). The deal gave Liberty Media an 8% stake in News Corp. and raised News Corp.'s interest in Fox to 83%. Doug Herzog, Fox's fifth entertainment president in eight years, left in 2000 after only 14 months as programming chief. Gail Berman took over the position in mid-2000. Meanwhile, the company reorganized many of its cable operations into a new division, Fox Cable Networks.

In 2001 Fox and partner Saban sold the Fox Family Channel (jointly owned) to Walt Disney for about $5.2 billion. Fox gained an additional 10 TV stations when News Corp. bought Chris-Craft. The deal boosted News Corp.'s stake in Fox Entertainment to 85%.

In 2002 Fox cancelled *Ally McBeal*, a television dramedy that was once required viewing for water-cooler talk but lost its direction in later seasons. That year the company completed a station swap with the Meredith Corporation, in which it gained two FOX affiliates in Orlando.

OFFICERS

Chairman and CEO: K. Rupert Murdoch, age 71
President, COO, and Director: Peter Chernin, age 50
SEVP, CFO, and Director: David F. DeVoe, age 55
SEVP, General Counsel, and Director:
Arthur M. Siskind, age 62
EVP and Deputy CFO: David DeVoe Jr., age 34

SVP Diversity Development: Mitsy Wilson
VP Investor Relations: Reed Nolte
Co-chairman, Fox Filmed Entertainment:
  James N. Gianopulos, age 49
Co-chairman, Fox Filmed Entertainment:
  Thomas E. Rothman, age 46
Chairman, Fox Sports Networks; Chairman and CEO, Fox Sports Television Group: David Hill, age 55
Chairman and CEO, Fox Television Stations:
  Mitchell Stern, age 47
Chairman and CEO, Los Angeles Dodgers:
  Robert A. Daly
President, Fox Television Entertainment Group:
  Gail Berman
President, Fox Television Studios: David Grant
President, Fox Television Network; CEO, Fox Networks Group: Anthony J. Vinciquerra, age 47
President, Twentieth Century Fox Licensing & Merchandising: Steven M. Ross
President and General Manager, New York Knicks:
  Scott Layden
Auditors: Ernst & Young LLP

LOCATIONS

HQ: 1211 Avenue of the Americas, New York, NY 10036
Phone: 212-852-7111   **Fax:** 212-852-7145
Web: www.newscorp.com/feg

PRODUCTS/OPERATIONS

2002 Sales

	$ mil.	% of total
Filmed entertainment	4,048	42
TV	3,923	40
Cable network programming	1,754	18
Total	**9,725**	**100**

Selected Operations
FOX Broadcasting Company
  FOX (television network)
  Fox Television Stations
Fox Cable Networks
  Canal Fox (entertainment cable channel, Latin America)
  The Fox News Channel
  Fox Sports Networks (interests in regional cable sports networks, Madison Square Garden, Radio City Music Hall, the New York Knicks and New York Rangers)
  FX (general interest cable channel)
  Speedvision Networks (live racing events and related news and documentaries)
  Telecine (12%, pay-television service in Brazil)
Fox Filmed Entertainment
  Fox Searchlight Pictures
  Twentieth Century Fox
Fox Sports Holdings
  Los Angeles Dodgers (professional baseball organization)
  Staples Center (40%, sports complex in Los Angeles; home to the Los Angeles Lakers, Los Angeles Clippers, and Los Angeles Kings)
Fox Television Holdings
  Fox Television Studios
  Twentieth Century Fox Television

COMPETITORS

AOL Time Warner
Carsey-Werner-Mandabach
DreamWorks SKG
Liberty Media
MGM
NBC
Sony Pictures Entertainment
Universal Studios
Viacom
Walt Disney

HISTORICAL FINANCIALS & EMPLOYEES

NYSE: FOX FYE: June 30	Annual Growth	6/93	6/94	6/95	6/96	6/97	6/98	6/99	6/00	6/01	6/02
Sales ($ mil.)	13.3%	—	—	—	4,548	5,847	7,023	8,057	8,589	8,504	9,725
Net income ($ mil.)	—	—	—	—	411	30	176	205	145	(288)	581
Income as % of sales	—	—	—	—	9.0%	0.5%	2.5%	2.5%	1.7%	—	6.0%
Earnings per share ($)	—	—	—	—	—	—	—	0.33	0.20	(0.40)	0.69
Stock price - FY high ($)	—	—	—	—	—	—	—	30.00	33.31	34.75	28.00
Stock price - FY low ($)	—	—	—	—	—	—	—	19.38	19.50	15.44	16.94
Stock price - FY close ($)	1.8%	—	—	—	—	—	—	26.94	30.38	27.90	21.75
P/E - high	—	—	—	—	—	—	—	91	167	—	38
P/E - low	—	—	—	—	—	—	—	59	98	—	23
Dividends per share ($)	—	—	—	—	—	—	—	0.00	0.00	0.00	0.00
Book value per share ($)	(4.9%)	—	—	—	—	—	—	12.18	11.39	11.00	14.23
Employees	5.4%	—	—	—	—	—	10,000	11,000	12,000	11,700	12,800

STOCK PRICE HISTORY

HIGH/LOW/CLOSE

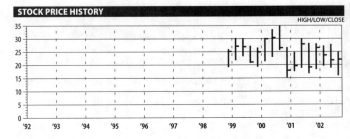

2002 FISCAL YEAR-END

Debt ratio: 7.2%
Return on equity: 6.1%
Cash ($ mil.): 56
Current ratio: 1.43
Long-term debt ($ mil.): 942
No. of shares (mil.): 850
Dividends
  Yield: —
  Payout: —
Market value ($ mil.): 18,486

FPL GROUP, INC.

For a Florida company without any oranges, FPL Group produces a lot of juice. Based in Juno Beach, Florida, the energy holding company generates and distributes electricity to about 3.9 million customers through its main subsidiary, Florida Power & Light (FPL).

FPL's utility service territory includes Florida's southern and eastern coasts. Its power plants, mainly nuclear and fossil-fueled, have a generating capacity of nearly 17,000 MW. Its Energy Marketing and Trading unit buys and sells power, natural gas, and other energy commodities. FPL accounts for nearly 90% of the group's revenues, and its outlook remains sunny because Florida doesn't have set plans for deregulation.

Subsidiary FPL Group Capital owns the firm's nonutility businesses. FPL Energy, an independent power producer and marketer, develops green power; about one-third of its 5,000-MW generating capacity is produced by wind, solar, hydro, and geothermal energy. FPL Energy owns plants in 14 US states; plants that will add another 5,000 MW are under construction or in development phases.

Subsidiary FPL FiberNet leases wholesale fiber-optic capacity to telephone, cable, and Internet providers; the unit operates a 2,500-mile network, which it is expanding.

HISTORY

During Florida's land boom of the early 1920s, new homes and businesses were going up fast. But electric utilities were sparse, and no transmission lines linked systems.

In 1925 American Power & Light Company (AP&L), which operated utilities throughout the Americas, set up Florida Power & Light (FPL) to consolidate the state's electric assets. AP&L built transmission lines linking 58 communities from Miami to Stuart on the Atlantic Coast and Arcadia to Punta Gorda on the Gulf.

FPL accumulated many holdings, including a limestone quarry, streetcars, phone companies, and water utilities, and purchases in 1926 and 1927 nearly doubled its electric properties. In 1927 the company used an electric pump to demonstrate how swamplands could be drained and cultivated.

During the 1940s and 1950s FPL sold its non-electric properties. The Public Utility Holding Company Act of 1935 forced AP&L to spin off FPL in 1950. The company was listed on the NYSE that year.

FPL grew with Florida's booming population. In 1972 its first nuclear plant (Turkey Point, south of Miami) went on line. In the 1980s it began to diversify with the purchase of real estate firm

W. Flagler Investment in 1981, and FPL Group was created in 1984 as a holding company. It subsequently acquired Telesat Cablevision (1985), Colonial Penn Group (1985, insurance), and Turner Foods (1988, citrus groves). FPL Group formed ESI Energy in 1985 to develop nonutility energy projects.

Diversification efforts didn't pan out, and in 1990 the firm wrote off about $750 million. That year, sticking to electricity, the utility snagged its first out-of-state power plant, in Georgia, acquiring a 76% stake (over five years). FPL Group sold its ailing Colonial Penn unit in 1991; two years later it sold its real estate holdings and some of its cable TV businesses.

The utility gave environmentalists cause to complain in 1995. First, the St. Lucie nuclear plant was fined by the NRC for a series of problems. FPL also wanted to burn orimulsion, a cheap, tarlike fuel. (Barred by the governor, the utility gave up the plan in 1998.)

In 1997 FPL Group created FPL Energy, an independent power producer (IPP), out of its ESI Energy and international operations; FPL Energy teamed up with Belgium-based Tractebel the next year to buy two gas-fired plants in Boston and Newark, New Jersey.

FPL Energy built wind-power facilities in Iowa in 1998 and in Wisconsin and Texas in 1999; it also bought 35 generating plants in Maine in 1999. That year FPL Group sold its Turner Foods citrus unit and the rest of its cable TV holdings. By 2000, FPL Energy owned interests in plants in 12 states.

Out of its fiber-optic operations, FPL Group in 2000 created subsidiary FPL FiberNet to market wholesale capacity. That year talks of Spanish utility giant Iberdrola purchasing FPL Group ended when Iberdrola's shareholders objected; in 2001 plans to merge with New Orleans-based Entergy fell through after a series of disagreements. The deal would have created one of the US's largest power companies.

In 2002 FPL Group agreed to purchase an 88% interest in the Seabrook Nuclear Generating Station in New Hampshire for $837 million from a consortium of US utilities, including Northeast Utilities and BayCorp Holdings.

OFFICERS

Chairman, President, and CEO; Chairman and CEO, Florida Power & Light: Lewis Hay III, age 46, $777,070 pay

VP Finance and CFO; SVP Finance and CFO, Florida Power & Light: Moray Dewhurst, age 46

VP Corporate Communications: Mary Lou Kromer

VP Human Resources; SVP Human Resources and
  Corporate Services, Florida Power & Light; Treasurer
  FPL Group and Florida Power & Light:
  Lawrence J. Kelleher, age 54, $924,221 pay
VP Tax: James P. Higgins
President, Florida Power & Light and Director:
  Paul J. Evanson, age 60, $858,207 pay
President, FPL Energy: Ronald F. Green, age 54
President, FPL FiberNet: Neil Flynn
SVP, FPL Energy: Michael O'Sullivan
SVP Nuclear Division, Florida Power & Light:
  John A. Stall, age 47
SVP Power Generation, Florida Power & Light:
  Antonio Rodriguez, age 59
SVP Power Systems, Florida Power & Light:
  Armando J. Olivera, age 52
General Counsel and Secretary, FPL Group and Florida
  Power & Light: Dennis P. Coyle, age 63,
  $1,190,791 pay
Auditors: Deloitte & Touche LLP

LOCATIONS

HQ: 700 Universe Blvd., Juno Beach, FL 33408
Phone: 561-694-4000   Fax: 561-694-4620
Web: www.fplgroup.com

FPL Group provides electric utility services in Florida
through Florida Power & Light (FPL), which owns
generating facilities in Florida and Georgia. It also has
operating US power plants in California, Iowa, Kansas,
Maine, Massachusetts, Minnesota, New Jersey, Oregon,
Pennsylvania, South Carolina, Texas, Virginia,
Washington, and Wisconsin through FPL Energy. FPL
FiberNet markets fiber-optic network capacity in Florida.

PRODUCTS/OPERATIONS

2001 Sales

	$ mil.	% of total
FPL		
Residential	4,187	49
Commercial	2,841	33
Industrial	224	3
Wholesale &		
other customers	225	3
FPL Energy	869	10
Corporate & other	129	2
Total	**8,475**	**100**

COMPETITORS

AES	Florida Public Utilities
AT&T	JEA
BellSouth	MidAmerican Energy
Calpine	Mirant
CenterPoint Energy	PG&E
CMS Energy	Progress Energy
Conectiv	PSEG
Duke Energy	Seminole Electric
Dynegy	Sempra Energy
Edison International	Sithe Energies
Entergy	Southern Company
Exelon	TECO Energy
Florida East Coast	TXU
Industries	Xcel Energy

HISTORICAL FINANCIALS & EMPLOYEES

NYSE: FPL FYE: December 31	Annual Growth	12/92	12/93	12/94	12/95	12/96	12/97	12/98	12/99	12/00	12/01
Sales ($ mil.)	5.6%	5,193	5,316	5,423	5,593	6,037	6,369	6,661	6,438	7,082	8,475
Net income ($ mil.)	5.9%	467	429	519	553	580	618	664	697	704	781
Income as % of sales	—	9.0%	8.1%	9.6%	9.9%	9.6%	9.7%	10.0%	10.8%	9.9%	9.2%
Earnings per share ($)	6.4%	2.65	2.30	2.91	3.16	3.33	3.57	3.85	4.07	4.14	4.62
Stock price - FY high ($)	—	38.38	41.00	39.13	46.50	48.13	60.00	72.56	61.94	73.00	71.63
Stock price - FY low ($)	—	32.00	35.50	26.88	34.00	41.50	42.63	56.06	41.13	36.38	51.21
Stock price - FY close ($)	5.0%	36.25	39.13	35.13	46.38	46.00	59.19	61.63	42.81	71.75	56.40
P/E - high	—	14	18	13	15	14	17	19	15	18	15
P/E - low	—	12	15	9	11	12	12	15	10	9	11
Dividends per share ($)	(0.9%)	2.43	2.47	1.88	1.76	1.84	1.92	2.00	2.08	2.16	2.24
Book value per share ($)	4.4%	24.00	24.46	25.44	25.65	26.99	27.90	29.62	31.24	33.11	35.49
Employees	(4.3%)	14,530	12,400	12,135	11,353	10,011	10,039	10,375	10,717	9,838	9,757

STOCK PRICE HISTORY

HIGH/LOW/CLOSE

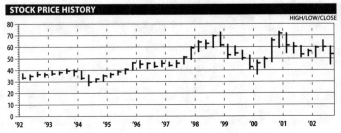

2001 FISCAL YEAR-END

Debt ratio: 43.8%
Return on equity: 13.5%
Cash ($ mil.): 82
Current ratio: 0.44
Long-term debt ($ mil.): 4,858
No. of shares (mil.): 176
Dividends
  Yield: 4.0%
  Payout: 48.5%
Market value ($ mil.): 9,918

FRANKLIN RESOURCES, INC.

To paraphrase this firm's namesake, we must all invest together, or assuredly we shall all invest separately. That philosophy has made San Mateo, California-based Franklin Resources the manager of more than $240 billion in mutual fund assets and some 8.4 million shareholder accounts.

The company is the manager of the Franklin, Templeton, Mutual Series, Bissett, and Fiduciary mutual funds (about 245 in all), suited to investment styles from low to high risk, at home and abroad, taxable and tax-exempt. The firm also provides custody and clearing services. Banking, consumer lending, and trust services are offered through subsidiaries Franklin Templeton Bank & Trust, Franklin Capital, and Fiduciary Trust International. Franklin Resources also owns about half of electronic information display maker Trans-Lux. The Johnson family owns about a third of Franklin.

Franklin Resources continues to expand to its product portfolio and strengthen its geographic reach, while upgrading technology both internally and externally to streamline operations and add online offerings for customers. The company has offices in some 30 countries.

HISTORY

Rupert Johnson Sr. founded Franklin Distributors (capitalizing on Benjamin Franklin's reputation for thrift) in New York in 1947; it launched its first fund, Franklin Custodian, in 1948. Custodian grew into five funds, including conservatively managed equity and bond funds. In 1968 Johnson's son Charles (who had joined the firm in 1957) became president and CEO. The company went public in 1971 as Franklin Resources.

In 1973 Franklin bought San Mateo-based investment firm Winfield & Co. and relocated to the Golden State. The buy provided additional products, including the Franklin Gold Fund (made possible by the end of the prohibition in the US against private interests owning commodity gold). With interest rate spikes in the late 1970s and early 1980s, money drained from savings accounts was poured into more lucrative money market mutual funds.

The Franklin Money Fund, launched in 1975, fueled the firm's tremendous asset growth in the 1980s. In 1981 the Franklin Tax-Free Income Fund (introduced in 1977) began investing solely in California municipal bonds. The fund's success led Franklin to introduce 43 tax-free income funds in later years.

In 1985 Franklin bought Pacific Union Bank and Trust (now Franklin Bank), allowing it to offer consumers such services as credit cards and to compete with financial services supermarkets such as Merrill Lynch. It also bought real estate firm Property Resources (now Franklin Properties).

The 1987 stock crash and the California real estate slump forced Franklin to focus on its funds businesses. In 1992 it bought Bahamas-based Templeton, Galbraith & Hansberger, the manager of Templeton Funds, a major international funds business. The Templeton deal added an aggressive investment management unit to complement the conservatively managed Franklin funds.

In 1940 Sir John Templeton gained control of investment company Templeton, Dobbrow and Vance (TDV). TDV launched Templeton Growth Fund in 1954. In 1969 Templeton sold his interest in TDV but continued to manage the Templeton Growth Fund. John Galbraith became president of Securities Fund Investors (SFI), the distribution company for Templeton Growth Fund, in 1974. In 1977 Galbraith bought SFI from Templeton and began building the Templeton funds broker-dealer network in the US. The Templeton World Fund was formed in 1978. Templeton Investment Counsel was launched to provide investment advice in 1979. In 1986 these companies were combined to form Templeton, Galbraith & Hansberger Ltd.

In 1996 Franklin bought Heine Securities, previous investment adviser to Mutual Series Fund Inc. Max Heine, a leading investor, had established Mutual Shares Corp. in 1949. Heine Securities was formed in 1975. Following the acquisition, Franklin set up a subsidiary, Franklin Mutual Advisers, to serve as the investment adviser for Mutual Series Fund.

In 1997 the weak Asian economy hurt Templeton's international funds, prompting liquidation of a Japanese stocks-based fund. Franklin cut jobs and shuffled management in 1999; the restructuring acknowledged the clash between the firm's value-investing style and investors' bull market optimism.

In 2000 the firm gained a foothold in Canada with its purchase of Bissett & Associates Investment Management. Franklin's purchase of Fiduciary Trust the following year gave the firm greater access to institutional investors and affluent individuals.

OFFICERS

Chairman and CEO: Charles B. Johnson, age 68, $594,330 pay
Vice Chairman: Harmon E. Burns
Vice Chairman: Rupert H. Johnson Jr., age 61
Vice Chairman; Chairman and CEO, Fiduciary Trust Company International: Anne M. Tatlock, age 62
President, Member - Office of the President, COO, and CFO: Martin L. Flanagan, age 41, $823,378 pay

President, Member - Office of the President:
Allen J. Gula Jr., age 47, $855,393 pay
Member - Office of the President and Director:
Charles E. Johnson, age 45, $1,180,128 pay
Member - Office of the President: Gregory E. Johnson, age 40, $1,180,132 pay
EVP and General Counsel: Murray L. Simpson, age 64
SVP and Secretary: Leslie M. Kratter, age 56
SVP: William J. Lippman, age 76
VP: Jennifer J. Bolt, age 37
VP and Deputy General Counsel: Barbara J. Green, age 54
VP - Human Resources: Donna S. Ikeda, age 45
VP - Finance, Chief Accounting Officer, and Treasurer: Charles R. Sims, age 40
Auditors: PricewaterhouseCoopers LLP

LOCATIONS

HQ: 1 Franklin Pkwy., Bldg. 970, 1st Fl.
San Mateo, CA 94404
Phone: 650-312-2000   **Fax:** 650-312-5606
Web: www.franklintempleton.com

Franklin Resources has offices in some 30 countries and sells fund products in more than 125.

2001 Sales

	$ mil.	% of total
US	1,685	67
Bahamas	295	12
Canada	267	10
Europe	129	5
Other regions	144	6
Eliminations	(165)	—
Total	**2,355**	**100**

PRODUCTS/OPERATIONS

2001 Sales

	$ mil.	% of total
Investment management fees	1,407	60
Underwriting & distribution fees	710	30
Shareholder servicing fees & other	238	10
Total	**2,355**	**100**

Selected Subsidiaries
Fiduciary Financial Services Corp.
Fiduciary Investment Corporation
Franklin Advisers, Inc.
Franklin Mutual Advisers, LLC
Franklin Templeton Bank & Trust, F.S.B.
Franklin Templeton Companies, LLC
Franklin Templeton Investor Services, LLC
Franklin/Templeton Travel, Inc.
FTTrust Company
Property Resources, Inc.
Templeton International, Inc.
Templeton Worldwide, Inc.
Templeton/Franklin Investment Services, Inc.

COMPETITORS

AARP	Mellon Financial	Principal
AMVESCAP	Merrill Lynch	Financial
AXA Financial	Morgan Stanley	Putnam
Citigroup	Nationwide	Investments
FleetBoston	Financial	Stilwell
FMR	New York Life	Financial
J.P. Morgan	Old Mutual (US)	T. Rowe Price
Chase	PIMCO	Torchmark
John Hancock	Pioneer	USAA
Financial	Investment	Vanguard Group
Services	Management	

HISTORICAL FINANCIALS & EMPLOYEES

NYSE: BEN FYE: September 30	Annual Growth	9/92	9/93	9/94	9/95	9/96	9/97	9/98	9/99	9/00	9/01
Sales ($ mil.)	22.3%	385	641	827	846	1,523	2,163	2,577	2,263	2,340	2,355
Net income ($ mil.)	16.3%	124	176	251	269	315	434	501	427	562	485
Income as % of sales	—	32.2%	27.4%	30.4%	31.8%	20.7%	20.1%	19.4%	18.9%	24.0%	20.6%
Earnings per share ($)	15.3%	0.53	0.70	1.00	1.07	1.25	1.71	1.98	1.69	2.28	1.91
Stock price - FY high ($)	—	11.13	16.42	17.30	19.34	22.89	47.22	57.88	45.63	45.63	48.30
Stock price - FY low ($)	—	5.98	8.13	11.21	11.01	15.47	21.39	25.75	26.50	24.63	31.65
Stock price - FY close ($)	15.2%	9.67	16.42	12.46	19.22	22.14	46.56	29.88	30.56	44.43	34.67
P/E - high	—	21	23	17	18	18	27	29	27	20	25
P/E - low	—	11	11	11	10	12	12	13	16	11	16
Dividends per share ($)	12.5%	0.09	0.10	0.11	0.13	0.15	0.16	0.20	0.22	0.24	0.26
Book value per share ($)	25.3%	2.00	2.93	3.80	4.78	5.82	7.36	9.06	10.55	12.17	15.25
Employees	12.5%	2,364	3,500	4,100	4,500	4,960	6,400	8,600	6,700	6,500	6,800

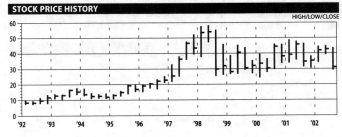

STOCK PRICE HISTORY HIGH/LOW/CLOSE

2001 FISCAL YEAR-END
Debt ratio: 12.5%
Return on equity: 14.0%
Cash ($ mil.): 497
Current ratio: 4.22
Long-term debt ($ mil.): 566
No. of shares (mil.): 261
Dividends
 Yield: 0.7%
 Payout: 13.6%
Market value ($ mil.): 9,042

FREDDIE MAC

McLean, Virginia-based Freddie Mac (formerly the Federal Home Loan Mortgage Corporation) is a shareholder-owned, government-sponsored enterprise established by Congress. Along with sister company Fannie Mae, Freddie Mac provides a continuous flow of funds for residential mortgages, helping Americans achieve the dream of home ownership. Although Freddie Mac is smaller than Fannie Mae (by assets), it indirectly finances one out of every six homes in the US.

Freddie Mac provides liquidity in the housing market by buying mortgage lenders' loans (thus allowing them to make more) and repackaging them into securities. The company is prevented from originating loans, but its work in the secondary market allows home buyers to save up to 0.5% on their mortgage rate. Freddie Mac's automated systems for underwriting, networking, and tracking mortgage payments help reduce origination costs.

Although not part of the US government, Freddie Mac enjoys an implicit guarantee of government support should the company fall on hard times. Because of the perceived backing, investors are willing to lend to Freddie Mac at below-market rates. Consequently, private-sector competitors (and, increasingly, government critics) are growing more vocal with their complaints. Lenders accuse Freddie and Fannie of using their special status to fund expansion into activities outside the scope of their congressional charter.

The two have also been panned by some housing advocates (such as the US Department of Housing and Urban Development), who say the companies have not done enough to remedy discrimination against low-income and minority homebuyers. Freddie has responded in part by toughening its standards for subprime lenders; it also launched an initiative with Jesse Jackson's Rainbow PUSH Coalition to increase minority homeownership.

HISTORY

Ah, the 1960's — free love, great tunes, and a war nobody wanted to pay for with taxes. By the 1970's, inflation was rising and real income was starting to fall. To divert a construction industry recession, Congress created a new entity to buy home mortgages and boost the flow of money into the housing market.

Fannie Mae had been buying mortgages since 1938, but focused on Federal Housing Administration (FHA) and Veterans Administration loans. In 1970 Congress created Freddie Mac and enlarged Fannie Mae's field of action to include conventional mortgages. Still, rising interest rates in the 1970s were brutal to the US real estate market.

In the early 1980s dealers devised a way to securitize the company's loans — seen as somewhat frumpy investments — by packaging them into more alluring, bond-like investments, made even sexier by the implicit government guarantee. When three major government securities dealers collapsed in 1985, ownership of some Freddie Mac securities was in doubt, and the Federal Reserve Bank of New York quickly automated registration of government securities.

In 1984 Freddie Mac issued shares to members of the Federal Home Loan Bank (the overseer of US savings and loans). By 1989 the shares had been converted to common stock and were traded on the NYSE. Freddie Mac's board expanded from three political appointees to 18 members.

Nationwide real estate defaults (rampant in the wake of the late 1980s crash) kindled concern about Freddie Mac's reserve levels and whether it might need to tap its US Treasury line of credit. In response, Congress in 1992 created the Office of Federal Housing Enterprise Oversight to regulate Freddie Mac and Fannie Mae. Initial examinations sounded no alarms. A 1996 Congressional Budget Office report questioned whether the government should continue its implicit guarantees of the pair's debt securities.

In 1997 Freddie Mac officially adopted its longtime nickname. The next year, it launched a system to cut loan approval time from weeks to minutes (it agreed to develop a similar version for the FHA). The streamlining was crucial to pacts in which mortgage lenders (including one of the US's largest, Wells Fargo) promised to sell Freddie Mac their loan originations. In 1999 Freddie Mac hired former House Speaker Newt Gingrich as a consultant.

Freddie Mac made a major Internet push in 2000 with its first online taxable bond offering. A wired venture involving Freddie Mac, Microsoft, and big lenders Chase Manhattan (now J.P. Morgan Chase & Co.), Bank of America, and Wells Fargo drew fire from small banks that said it would push them out of the online lending business. In 2001 Freddie Mac bought Tuttle Decision Systems, a loan-pricing software system provider. Critics responded that Freddie Mac overstepped its government charter with such a move.

OFFICERS

Chairman and CEO: Leland C. Brendsel, $3,255,938 pay
Vice Chairman and President: David W. Glenn, age 58, $2,125,000 pay
EVP, Finance and CFO: Vaughn A. Clarke
EVP, Secretary, and General Counsel: Maud Mater
EVP, Single Family: Paul T. Peterson, $1,145,834 pay

SVP, Single Family Capital Deployment:
David A. Andrukonis
SVP, Credit Risk Management: Donald J. Bisenius
SVP, Single-Family COO: Margaret A. Colon
SVP, Multifamily Housing: Adrian B. Corbiere
SVP, Government Relations: R. Mitchell Delk
SVP, Human Resources: Michael W. Hager
SVP, Information Systems & Services:
William I. Ledman, $908,531 pay
SVP, Investment Funding: Jerome T. Lienhard
SVP, Business Development: Peter F. Maselli
SVP, Customer Services & Control: Michael C. May
SVP and Chief Investment Officer:
Gregory J. Parseghian, $1,750,000 pay
SVP, Corporate Relations: Dwight P. Robinson
SVP and Corporate Controller: Edmond Sannini
SVP and General Manager, National Lending:
Patrick M. Sheehy
SVP and General Manager, Community Lending:
David Stevens
Auditors: PricewaterhouseCoopers LLP

LOCATIONS

HQ: 8200 Jones Branch Dr., McLean, VA 22102
Phone: 703-903-2000   **Fax:** 703-918-8403
Web: www.freddiemac.com

In addition to its home offices in Virginia, Freddie Mac
has regional offices in Atlanta; Carrollton, Texas;
Chicago; New York; and Woodland Hills, California.

PRODUCTS/OPERATIONS

2001 Assets

	$ mil.	% of total
Cash & equivalents	1,508	—
Trading account	33,073	5
Investments	75,894	12
Securities bought under resell agreements	5,531	1
Retained mortgages	62,466	10
Guaranteed mortgage securities	428,927	70
Other assets	9,941	2
Total	**617,340**	**100**

COMPETITORS

Advanta
AIG
Bank of New York
Citigroup
Countrywide Credit
Fannie Mae
FleetBoston
J.P. Morgan Chase
KeyCorp
PNC Financial
TELACU
Washington Mutual

HISTORICAL FINANCIALS & EMPLOYEES

NYSE: FRE FYE: December 31	Annual Growth	12/92	12/93	12/94	12/95	12/96	12/97	12/98	12/99	12/00	12/01
Assets ($ mil.)	29.7%	59,502	83,880	106,199	137,181	173,866	194,597	321,421	386,684	459,297	617,340
Net income ($ mil.)	23.5%	622	786	983	1,091	1,243	1,395	1,700	2,223	2,547	4,147
Income as % of assets	—	1.0%	0.9%	0.9%	0.8%	0.7%	0.7%	0.5%	0.6%	0.6%	0.7%
Earnings per share ($)	23.9%	0.82	1.02	1.26	1.41	1.63	1.88	2.31	2.96	3.40	5.64
Stock price – FY high ($)	—	12.31	14.19	15.72	20.91	29.00	44.56	66.38	65.25	70.13	71.25
Stock price – FY low ($)	—	8.44	11.31	11.75	12.47	19.06	26.69	38.69	45.38	36.88	58.75
Stock price – FY close ($)	20.6%	12.09	12.47	12.63	20.88	27.59	41.94	64.44	47.06	68.88	65.40
P/E – high	—	15	14	12	15	17	23	29	22	21	12
P/E – low	—	10	11	9	9	11	14	17	15	11	10
Dividends per share ($)	17.3%	0.19	0.22	0.26	0.30	0.35	0.40	0.48	0.60	0.68	0.80
Book value per share ($)	18.1%	4.95	6.14	7.14	8.10	9.69	11.08	15.59	16.58	21.42	22.11
Employees	3.0%	—	2,929	3,380	3,320	3,194	3,258	3,503	3,500	3,600	3,700

STOCK PRICE HISTORY	2001 FISCAL YEAR-END

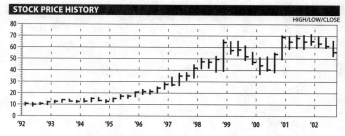

HIGH/LOW/CLOSE

Equity as % of assets: 2.5%
Return on assets: 0.8%
Return on equity: 37.0%
Long-term debt ($ mil.): 314,733
No. of shares (mil.): 695
Dividends
 Yield: 1.2%
 Payout: 14.2%
Market value ($ mil.): 45,473
Sales ($ mil.): 36,173

FREEPORT-MCMORAN

Fending off challenges by Indonesian environmentalists and human rights groups, Freeport-McMoRan Copper & Gold (FCX) keeps digging out profits from its Grasberg Mine — the world's largest and lowest-cost gold and copper mine. New Orleans-based FCX's lifeblood flows from contracts to explore and develop millions of acres in Indonesia's Sudirman Range.

The company's projects contain mineral reserves of more than 88 billion pounds of copper and over 100 million ounces of gold. British mining giant Rio Tinto plc (formerly RTZ) owns about 43% of FCX, and the companies are jointly involved in developing mineral properties in Indonesia's politically and environmentally sensitive Irian Jaya province.

FCX's 86%-owned subsidiary PT Freeport Indonesia (PT-FI; the Indonesian government owns about 10%) operates the vast open-pit Grasberg gold and copper mine (Grasberg also produces silver). One of the world's lowest-cost copper mining operations, PT-FI produces copper for less than 8 cents per pound. FCX also owns a 25% stake in PT Smelting, which operates a copper smelter and refinery in Gresik, Indonesia. Other FCX subsidiaries include P.T. IRJA Eastern Minerals, which explores for minerals in Indonesia, and Atlantic Copper, which operates a copper smelter in Spain.

Political and environmental controversy plagues FCX, now without its major benefactor, Indonesia's former president Suharto, who was forced to resign after more than 30 years in power. Not helping are low copper and gold prices. However, FCX is counting on low-cost operations and strong production to help it weather the rough times.

HISTORY

The Freeport Sulfur Company was formed in Texas in 1912 by Francis Pemberton, banker Eric Swenson, and several investors to develop a sulfur field. The next year Freeport Texas was formed as a holding company for Freeport Sulfur and other enterprises.

During the 1930s the company diversified. In 1936 Freeport pioneered a process to remove hydrocarbons from sulfur. The company joined Consolidated Coal in 1955 to establish the National Potash Company. In 1956 Freeport formed an oil and gas subsidiary, Freeport Oil.

Internationally, Freeport formed an Australian minerals subsidiary in 1964 and a copper-mining subsidiary in Indonesia in 1967. The company changed its name to Freeport Minerals in 1971 and merged with Utah-based McMoRan Oil & Gas (formerly McMoRan Explorations) in 1982.

McMoRan Explorations had been formed in 1969 by William McWilliams, Jim Bob Moffett, and Byron Rankin. In 1973 McMoRan formed an exploration and drilling alliance with Dow Chemical and signed a deal with Indonesia to mine in the remote Irian Jaya region. McMoRan went public in 1978.

In 1984 Moffett became chairman and CEO of Freeport-McMoRan. Freeport-McMoRan Copper was formed in 1987 to manage the company's Indonesian operations. The unit assumed its current name in 1991. Two years later it acquired Rio Tinto Minera, a copper-smelting business with operations in Spain.

To support expansion in Indonesia, FCX spun off its copper and gold division in 1994. In 1995 it formed an alliance with the UK's RTZ Corporation to develop its Indonesian mineral reserves. Local riots that year closed the Grasberg Mine, and Freeport's political risk insurance was canceled. Despite these setbacks, higher metal prices and growing sales in 1995 helped the company double its operating income.

An Indonesian tribal leader filed a $6 billion lawsuit in 1996 charging FCX with environmental, human rights, and social and cultural violations. The company called the suit baseless but offered to set aside 1% of its annual revenues, worth about $15 million, to help local tribes. Tribal leaders rejected the offer, and in 1997 a judge dismissed the lawsuit.

In 1997 FCX pulled out of Bre-X Minerals' Busang gold mine project, which independent tests later proved a fraud of historic proportions. The company made plans to more than double production at the Grasberg Mine. Following a report by an independent consultant on ways to ease tension in Irian Jaya, FCX said it would increase workers' wages by 26% over the next two years.

Amid widespread rioting, Indonesia's embattled president Raden Suharto was forced out of office in 1998. The new government investigated charges of cronyism involving FCX.

FCX received permission from the Indonesian government in 1999 to expand the Grasberg Mine and increase ore output up to 300,000 metric tons per day. However, the next year an overflow accident killed four workers in Grasberg and, as a result of the accident, the Indonesian government ordered FCX to reduce its production at the mine by up to 30%. Normal production at the mine resumed in early 2001. That year FCX established a $2.5 million trust for indigenous workers; the company will add $500,000 annually to the trust.

OFFICERS

Chairman and CEO: James R. Moffett, age 63,
$5,250,000 pay
Vice Chairman: B. M. Rankin Jr., age 72
President and CFO: Richard C. Adkerson, age 55,
$2,281,250 pay
VP, Assistant to the Chairman: Lynne M. Cooney
VP, Communications: William L. Collier III
VP, Environment Affairs: D. James Miller
VP, Investor Relations: Christopher D. Sammons
VP, Security, Safety and Administration:
Josephy I. Molyneux
VP, Social and Development Programs: David B. Lowry
VP and Controller, Financial Reporting:
C. Donald Whitmire Jr.
VP, Tax: Dean T. Falgoust
Treasurer and VP, Finance and Business Development:
Kathleen L. Quirk
**President Director, P.T. Freeport Indonesia and IRJA
Eastern Minerals:** Adrianto Machribie, age 60,
$1,006,250 pay
Managing Director, Atlantic Copper S.A.:
Javier Targhetta
Recruitng Manager: Todd Graver
Auditors: Ernst & Young LLP

LOCATIONS

HQ: Freeport-McMoRan Copper & Gold, Inc.
1615 Poydras St., New Orleans, LA 70112
Phone: 504-582-4000   **Fax:** 504-582-1847
Web: www.fcx.com

Freeport-McMoRan Copper & Gold operates the
Grasberg Mine (gold, silver, and copper) and a copper
smelter and refinery in Indonesia and a copper smelter
and refinery in Spain.

2001 Sales

	$ mil.	% of total
Indonesia	374	20
Spain	359	20
Japan	283	15
Switzerland	222	12
US	146	8
Other countries	455	25
Total	**1,839**	**100**

PRODUCTS/OPERATIONS

2001 Sales

	$ mil.	% of total
Mining & exploration	1,414	65
Smelting & refining	758	35
Adjustments	(333)	—
Total	**1,839**	**100**

Selected Products
Copper concentrates (which include gold)
Copper products (cathodes, wire, and wire rod)
Gold
Silver

COMPETITORS

Anglo American	Mueller	Rio Tinto
Barrick Gold	Industries	Southern Peru
BHP Billiton Ltd	Newmont	Copper
Centromin	Mining	Trelleborg
Codelco	Noranda	Umicore
Grupo Carso	Norddeutsche	Vale do Rio Doce
Grupo México	Affinerie	WMC Limited
Inco Limited	Phelps Dodge	
Lonmin	Placer Dome	

HISTORICAL FINANCIALS & EMPLOYEES

NYSE: FCX FYE: December 31	Annual Growth	12/92	12/93	12/94	12/95	12/96	12/97	12/98	12/99	12/00	12/01
Sales ($ mil.)	11.1%	714	926	1,212	1,834	1,905	2,001	1,757	1,887	1,869	1,839
Net income ($ mil.)	(1.5%)	130	51	130	254	226	245	154	137	77	113
Income as % of sales	—	18.2%	5.5%	10.7%	13.8%	11.9%	12.2%	8.8%	7.2%	4.1%	6.1%
Earnings per share ($)	(9.7%)	—	—	—	0.98	0.89	1.06	0.67	0.61	0.26	0.53
Stock price - FY high ($)	—	—	—	—	30.75	36.13	34.88	21.44	21.38	21.44	17.15
Stock price - FY low ($)	—	—	—	—	22.63	27.38	14.94	9.81	9.13	6.75	8.31
Stock price - FY close ($)	(11.6%)	—	—	—	28.13	29.88	15.75	10.44	21.13	8.56	13.39
P/E - high	—	—	—	—	31	40	33	32	34	82	32
P/E - low	—	—	—	—	23	30	14	15	15	26	16
Dividends per share ($)	—	—	—	—	0.23	0.90	0.90	0.15	0.00	0.00	0.00
Book value per share ($)	(27.8%)	—	—	—	6.06	5.39	3.57	2.76	3.13	4.18	0.86
Employees	8.1%	4,983	6,054	6,074	4,983	8,300	6,300	6,349	7,137	9,777	10,049

STOCK PRICE HISTORY

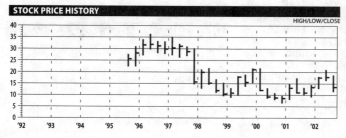
HIGH/LOW/CLOSE

2001 FISCAL YEAR-END

Debt ratio: 95.3%
Return on equity: 36.6%
Cash ($ mil.): 8
Current ratio: 0.87
Long-term debt ($ mil.): 2,133
No. of shares (mil.): 122
Dividends
  Yield: —
  Payout: —
Market value ($ mil.): 1,630

FURNITURE BRANDS

Furniture Brands International is a centerpiece in the furniture industry's showroom. The St. Louis-based company is the #1 maker of residential furniture in the US. Furniture Brands has built its empire on its subsidiaries: Broyhill Furniture Industries, Lane Furniture Industries, and Thomasville Furniture Industries. The company makes bedroom, dining room, and living room furniture, including chairs, home entertainment centers, love seats, recliners, sofas, tables, and accessories. In addition, Lane makes cedar chests and indoor/outdoor wicker and rattan furniture.

Furniture Brands added another notch to its belt in 2001 by purchasing Drexel Heritage, Henredon Furniture Industries, and Maitland-Smith from LifeStyle Furnishings to create its HDM Furniture Industries subsidiary. The company's brands cover different segments of the market — from high-end to ready-to-assemble furniture for mass marketers such as Wal-Mart.

In response to financial troubles at major furniture retailers, Furniture Brands is expanding its network of free-standing independently owned Thomasville Furniture Stores, which exclusively sell Thomasville products. The company is considering similar store networks for its Broyhill and Lane operations.

HISTORY

Although already a diversified firm, INTERCO's purchase of Ethan Allen in 1980 took the company in a direction that would eventually become its only business. INTERCO traces its roots back to the pairing of two shoe manufacturers and made a name for itself by running men's shoemaker and retailer Florsheim, which it acquired in 1953. It added other operations, including department stores and apparel, beginning in the 1960s. The Ethan Allen purchase gave INTERCO 24 furniture factories and 300 retail outlets.

The company grew its furniture business later in 1980 by purchasing Broyhill Furniture Industries, which was founded by J. E. Broyhill as Lenoir Chair Company in 1926. The Broyhill line became popular during the 1930s, and the family had built the company into the largest privately owned maker of furniture, with 20 manufacturing facilities, when INTERCO bought it.

In 1986, after acquiring furniture maker Highland House (Hickory), INTERCO made its largest acquisition in the home furnishings and furniture market the next year when it gained control of the Lane Company for approximately $500 million. Founded in 1912 by Ed Lane to make cedar chests, Virginia-based Lane had

grown into a full-line maker of furniture with 16 plants in operation. The acquisition of Lane lifted furniture and furnishings to 33% of INTERCO's total sales in 1987.

Meanwhile, INTERCO hadn't neglected its shoe business, adding Converse in 1986. Richard Loynd, the Converse CEO, served as INTERCO's CEO from 1989 to 1996. In 1988, under a takeover threat by the Rales brothers of Washington, DC, the company retained the investment banking firm of Wasserstein Perella, which advised payment of a $76 special dividend, for which INTERCO borrowed $1.8 billion via junk bonds. To repay the debt, the firm began selling off assets, including its apparel businesses and Ethan Allen. However, the sales yielded low prices and some businesses failed to attract buyers.

After fighting off the hostile takeover, INTERCO filed bankruptcy in 1991 — one of the largest bankruptcy cases in US history. It also filed a malpractice suit against Wasserstein Perella when it emerged from Chapter 11; the suit was settled the following year, and Apollo Investment Fund acquired a large stake in the firm.

INTERCO sold the last of its 80-year-old shoe-making sole with the spinoff of its Florsheim and Converse units in 1994. The company acquired Thomasville Furniture from Armstrong World Industries for $331 million in 1993, a purchase that made it the leading shaker in residential furniture. Founded in 1904, the Finch brothers ran Thomasville until Armstrong acquired it in 1968.

W. G. "Mickey" Holliman became CEO in 1996, and INTERCO's board decided to change the company's name to Furniture Brands International. In 1997 Apollo Investment Fund, its largest shareholder, sold its 38% stake. The next year Furniture Brands and retailer Haverty Furniture signed a deal whereby Havertys would allocate up to half its retail space for Furniture Brands' items.

In 2000 the company started selling kitchen and bathroom cabinets under the Thomasville brand in Home Depot. In 2001 Furniture Brands bought Drexel Heritage, Henredon, and Maitland-Smith units from LifeStyle Furnishings for $275 million.

OFFICERS

Chairman, President, and CEO: Wilbert G. Holliman, age 64, $1,399,562 pay
SVP, Chief Administrative Officer, Secretary, and General Counsel: Lynn Chipperfield, age 50
VP, CFO, Treasurer, and Controller: David P. Howard, age 51, $411,313 pay
President and CEO, Broyhill Furniture Industries: Dennis R. Burgette, age 54, $481,063 pay

President and CEO, Drexel Heritage Furniture Industries: Jeff Young, age 51
President and CEO, Henredon Furniture Industries: Michael K. Dugan, age 61
President and CEO, Lane Furniture Industries: John T. Foy, age 54, $561,819 pay
President and CEO, Maitland-Smith Furniture Industries: Seamus Bateson, age 50
President and CEO, Thomasville Furniture Industries: Christian J. Pfaff, age 53, $481,906 pay
EVP, Sales and Marketing, Drexel Heritage: Lenwood Rich, age 53
Chief Accounting Officer and Controller: Steven W. Alstadt, age 47
Secretary: Robert L. Kaintz
Human Resources and Employee Benefits Manager: Richard Lockard
Auditors: KPMG LLP

LOCATIONS

HQ: Furniture Brands International, Inc.
101 S. Hanley Rd., St. Louis, MO 63105
Phone: 314-863-1100 **Fax:** 314-863-5306
Web: www.furniturebrands.com

Furniture Brands International's products are sold worldwide, and the company has plants in Mississippi, North Carolina, and Virginia.

PRODUCTS/OPERATIONS

Selected Products
Case Goods Furniture
 Bedroom
 Dining room
 Living room
Occasional Furniture
 Accent items
 Freestanding home entertainment centers
 Home office items
 Wood tables
Stationary Upholstery Products
 Chairs
 Love seats
 Sectionals
 Sofas
Other
 Motion furniture
 Recliners
 Sleep sofas

COMPETITORS

Ashley Furniture	Kimball International
Bassett Furniture	Klaussner Furniture
Bombay Company	La-Z-Boy
Brown Jordan	Masco
International	Meadowcraft
Bush Industries	O'Sullivan Industries
Chromcraft Revington	Pulaski Furniture
Decorize	River Oaks Furniture
DMI Furniture	Rowe Companies
Dorel Industries	Sauder Woodworking
Ethan Allen	Stanley Furniture
Flexsteel	Wellington Hall
Hooker Furniture	

HISTORICAL FINANCIALS & EMPLOYEES

NYSE: FBN FYE: December 31	Annual Growth	12/92	12/93	12/94	12/95	12/96	12/97	12/98	12/99	12/00	12/01
Sales ($ mil.)	12.4%	662	1,657	1,073	1,074	1,697	1,808	1,960	2,088	2,116	1,891
Net income ($ mil.)	11.9%	21	45	38	28	47	67	98	112	106	58
Income as % of sales	—	3.2%	2.7%	3.6%	2.6%	2.8%	3.7%	5.0%	5.4%	5.0%	3.1%
Earnings per share ($)	6.2%	—	—	0.74	0.56	0.76	1.15	1.82	2.14	2.10	1.13
Stock price - FY high ($)	—	—	—	8.38	9.25	15.00	21.50	34.13	28.44	22.44	32.50
Stock price - FY low ($)	—	—	—	6.13	5.50	8.25	13.63	12.94	17.00	13.94	17.65
Stock price - FY close ($)	24.9%	—	—	6.75	9.00	14.00	20.50	27.25	22.00	21.06	32.02
P/E - high	—	—	—	11	14	17	18	18	13	10	28
P/E - low	—	—	—	8	8	9	11	7	8	6	15
Dividends per share ($)	—	—	—	0.00	0.00	0.00	0.00	0.00	0.00	0.00	0.00
Book value per share ($)	14.2%	—	—	5.50	6.01	6.83	6.22	7.99	9.61	11.75	13.91
Employees	2.1%	19,750	20,045	20,400	20,700	20,800	20,700	20,700	21,400	20,700	23,850

STOCK PRICE HISTORY

HIGH/LOW/CLOSE

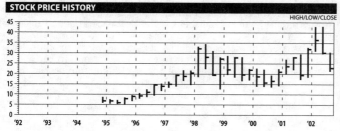

2001 FISCAL YEAR-END

Debt ratio: 37.4%
Return on equity: 8.6%
Cash ($ mil.): 16
Current ratio: 4.44
Long-term debt ($ mil.): 454
No. of shares (mil.): 55
Dividends
 Yield: —
 Payout: —
Market value ($ mil.): 1,749

GANNETT CO., INC.

Gannett satisfies news junkies with a stash of 95 daily US papers. The McLean, Virginia-based company is the nation's largest newspaper publisher; flagship *USA TODAY* (2.2 million circulation) outsells *The Wall Street Journal* (1.8 million circulation, owned by Dow Jones & Company) as the top US newspaper. Gannett's US dailies boast a combined circulation of nearly 8 million and the company also owns some 300 non-daily publications. It has ventured outside the US for the first time through the purchase of UK publisher Newsquest (more than 300 titles, including 15 daily newspapers).

While newspapers generate more than 80% of Gannett's sales, the company also owns 22 TV stations and operates in marketing, commercial printing, and newswire and data services. Gannett has branched into cyberspace with Web sites for most of its newspapers, including its USATODAY.com site. The company went on a buying spree in 2000, acquiring the UK's News Communications & Media, *Arizona Republic* publisher Central Newspapers, and 21 smaller daily papers from Canada's Thomson Corp.

Amid an industry-wide advertising recession, Gannett saw its profits decline in 2001, and *USA TODAY* cut more than 5% of its staff.

HISTORY

In 1906 Frank Gannett started a newspaper empire when he and his associates purchased a stake in New York's *Elmira Gazette*. In 1923 Gannett bought out his associates' interests and formed the Gannett Company. The company's history of technical innovation dates to the 1920s, when Frank Gannett invested in the development of the Teletypesetter; some of his newspapers were printing in color by 1938. The company continued to buy small and medium-sized dailies in the Northeast, and by Gannett's death in 1957, it had accumulated 30 newspapers.

In the 1960s Gannett expanded nationally through acquisitions. It was not until 1966, however, that it started its own paper, *TODAY* (now *FLORIDA TODAY*), in Cocoa Beach, Florida. Gannett went public in 1967.

The company's greatest period of growth came during the 1970s and 1980s under the direction of Allen Neuharth (CEO from 1973 to 1986). Gannett captured national attention in 1979 when it merged with Phoenix-based Combined Communications Corporation (CCC), whose holdings included TV and radio stations, an outdoor advertising business, and pollster Louis Harris & Associates.

In 1982 Gannett started *USA TODAY,* a national newspaper whose splashy format and mini-stories made it an industry novelty. Critics branded it "McPaper," but circulation passed a million copies a day by the end of 1983. (It wasn't profitable until 1993, however.)

In 1990 declines in newspaper advertising, primarily among US retailers, broke the company's string of 89 consecutive quarters of positive earnings. USA TODAY-On-Demand, a fax news service, began in 1992. Gannett bought Multimedia Inc., a newspaper, TV, cable, and program syndication company, for about $2.3 billion in 1995.

Web site *USA TODAY Online* debuted in 1995. The next year Gannett teamed up with newspaper publisher Knight Ridder and privately held media firm Landmark Communications to form Internet service provider InfiNet. In 1996 Gannett sold Louis Harris & Associates and its outdoor advertising operations and traded six radio stations to Jacor Communications for one Tampa TV station.

Gannett exited the radio industry in 1998 by selling its last five stations. It also sold its Multimedia Security Service. That year the company expanded its TV holdings through purchases of three stations in Maine and South Carolina. Gannett's integrity took a blow in 1998 when a reporter for one of its newspapers (*The Cincinnati Enquirer*) illegally obtained information for a report accusing Chiquita Brands International of unscrupulous business practices. Gannett retracted the story and settled with Chiquita to the tune of about $14 million.

The company broke new ground in 1999 when Karen Jurgensen was named editor of *USA TODAY* (she was the first woman to head a national newspaper). Also that year Gannett acquired Newsquest, one of the largest regional newspaper publishers in the UK. In early 2000 Gannett sold its cable operations to Cox Communications for $2.7 billion. The company also formed TV and Web venture USA Today Live to produce news stories for its TV stations. Later that year chairman John Curley passed the title of CEO to president Douglas McCorkindale (McCorkindale would become chair the next year).

Also in 2000 Gannett made a slew of acquisitions, including a purchase of the UK's News Communications & Media, *Arizona Republic* publisher Central Newspapers , and 21 newspapers from Canada's Thomson Corp. The company moved its headquarters in 2001 from Arlington to McLean, Virginia. In early 2002 Gannett sold nearly $2 billion in debt in unsecured global notes; the money will be used to repay short-term loans.

Chairman, President, and CEO:
Douglas H. McCorkindale, age 62, $3,450,000 pay
EVP Operations and CFO: Larry F. Miller, age 63, $1,025,000 pay
SVP Administration; President and Publisher, *USA TODAY*: Thomas Curley, age 53, $940,000 pay
SVP, Secretary, and General Counsel:
Thomas L. Chapple, age 54
SVP Human Resources: Richard L. Clapp, age 61
Chief Executive, Newsquest: Paul Davidson
President and CEO, Gannett Broadcasting Division:
Craig A. Dubow, age 47
President, Gannett Newspaper Division:
Gary L. Watson, age 56, $1,225,000 pay
Auditors: PricewaterhouseCoopers LLP

LOCATIONS

HQ: 7950 Jones Branch Drive, McLean, VA 22107
Phone: 703-854-6000 **Fax:** 703-854-2046
Web: www.gannett.com

Gannett has operations in 43 US states and Washington, DC, as well as in Belgium, Germany, Guam, Hong Kong, Italy, and the UK.

PRODUCTS/OPERATIONS

2001 Sales

	$ mil.	% of total
Newspaper advertising	4,119	65
Newspaper circulation	1,234	20
Broadcasting	662	10
Other	329	5
Total	**6,344**	**100**

Selected Newspapers
The Arizona Republic (Phoenix)
The Cincinnati Enquirer
The Courier-Journal (Louisville, KY)
The Detroit News
The Honolulu Advertiser
The Indianapolis Star (Indiana)
Springfield News-Leader (Missouri)
The Tennessean (Nashville)
Tucson Citizen (Arizona)
USA TODAY

Selected TV Stations
KARE-TV (NBC affiliate, Minneapolis-St. Paul)
KPNX-TV (NBC affiliate, Phoenix)
KUSA-TV (NBC affiliate, Denver)
KXTV-TV (ABC affiliate, Sacramento, CA)
WGRZ-TV (NBC affiliate, Buffalo, NY)
WKYC-TV (NBC affiliate, Cleveland)
WTSP-TV (CBS affiliate, Tampa-St. Petersburg)
WUSA-TV (CBS affiliate; Washington, DC)
WXIA-TV (NBC affiliate, Atlanta)

COMPETITORS

Advance Publications	Hollinger	New York Times
Associated Press	Hubbard Broadcasting	News Corp.
Belo	Journal	Pulitzer
Bloomberg	Communications	Reuters
Clear Channel	Knight Ridder	Sinclair
Copley Press	Landmark	Broadcast
Cox Enterprises	Communications	Group
Dow Jones	Lee Enterprises	Tribune
E. W. Scripps	McClatchy	Viacom
Freedom	Company	Walt Disney
Communications	Media General	Washington Post
Hearst	MediaNews	

HISTORICAL FINANCIALS & EMPLOYEES

NYSE: GCI FYE: Last Sunday in December	Annual Growth	12/92	12/93	12/94	12/95	12/96	12/97	12/98	12/99	12/00	12/01
Sales ($ mil.)	6.9%	3,469	3,642	3,825	4,007	4,421	4,730	5,121	5,260	6,222	6,344
Net income ($ mil.)	17.2%	200	398	465	477	943	713	1,000	958	1,719	831
Income as % of sales	—	5.8%	10.9%	12.2%	11.9%	21.3%	15.1%	19.5%	18.2%	27.6%	13.1%
Earnings per share ($)	18.3%	0.69	1.35	1.60	1.69	3.33	2.50	3.50	3.40	6.41	3.12
Stock price – FY high ($)	—	27.00	29.13	29.50	32.44	39.38	61.81	75.13	83.63	81.56	71.14
Stock price – FY low ($)	—	20.63	23.38	23.06	24.75	29.50	35.69	47.63	60.63	48.38	53.00
Stock price – FY close ($)	11.4%	25.38	28.63	26.63	30.69	37.44	61.81	64.50	81.56	63.06	67.23
P/E – high	—	23	22	19	19	12	25	21	24	22	23
P/E – low	—	17	18	15	15	9	14	13	18	13	17
Dividends per share ($)	3.9%	0.63	0.65	0.67	0.69	0.71	0.73	0.77	0.81	0.85	0.89
Book value per share ($)	16.5%	5.47	6.49	6.52	7.63	10.37	12.26	14.26	16.66	19.31	21.58
Employees	3.8%	36,700	36,500	36,000	39,100	37,200	39,000	39,400	45,800	53,400	51,500

STOCK PRICE HISTORY

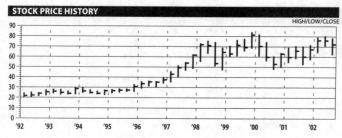

HIGH/LOW/CLOSE

2001 FISCAL YEAR-END

Debt ratio: 47.0%
Return on equity: 15.3%
Cash ($ mil.): 74
Current ratio: 1.04
Long-term debt ($ mil.): 5,080
No. of shares (mil.): 266
Dividends
  Yield: 1.3%
  Payout: 28.5%
Market value ($ mil.): 17,870

THE GAP, INC.

From infancy to affluence, The Gap has got you (or your body) covered. Based in San Francisco, the clothing company operates about 4,170 retail outlets under the names Gap, GapKids, babyGap, GapBody, Banana Republic, and Old Navy. Each chain has its own Web storefront as well. All of Gap's merchandise is private label, including its maternity wear (only available online).

Many retailers have viewed The Gap as a model of successful expansion, in part for its ability to attract shoppers in many price segments. Its fast-growing Old Navy stores target families on a budget, while sophisticated Banana Republic has zeroed in on urban chic. Its flagship Gap stores reach foreign customers mainly in Canada, France, Germany, Japan, and the UK. The Gap plans to deploy Old Navy stores overseas in coming years.

Its expansion zeal came back to bite the Gap, though. Expansion outpaced sales when clothing lines aimed at the Britney Spears and bubblegum set alienated the company's core clientele who count on The Gap for the basics: khaki pants, denim, T-shirts, polos, and other casual fashions, but the company has re-stated its strategy to get back to the basics.

The Fisher family, including founders Donald and Doris Fisher, owns 32% of the company.

HISTORY

Donald Fisher and his wife, Doris, opened a small store in 1969 near what is now San Francisco State University. The couple named their store The Gap (after "the generation gap") and concentrated on selling Levi's jeans. The couple opened a second store in San Jose, California, eight months later, and by the end of 1970 there were six Gap stores. The Gap went public six years later.

In the beginning the Fishers catered almost exclusively to teenagers, but in the 1970s they expanded into activewear that would appeal to a larger spectrum of customers. Nevertheless, by the early 1980s The Gap — which had grown to about 500 stores — was still dependent upon its largely teenage customer base. However, it was less dependent on Levi's (about 35% of sales), thanks to its growing stable of private labels.

In a 1983 effort to revamp the company's image, Donald hired Mickey Drexler, a former president of AnnTaylor with a spotless apparel industry track record, as The Gap's new president. Drexler immediately overhauled the motley clothing lines to concentrate on sturdy, brightly colored cotton clothing. He also consolidated the stores' many private clothing labels into the Gap brand. As a final touch, Drexler replaced circular clothing racks with white shelving so clothes could be neatly stacked and displayed.

Also in 1983 The Gap bought Banana Republic, a unique chain of jungle-themed stores that sold safari clothing. The company expanded the chain, which enjoyed tremendous success in the mid-1980s but slumped after the novelty of the stores wore off late in the decade. In response, Drexler introduced a broader range of clothes (including higher-priced leather items) and dumped the safari lines in 1988. By 1990 Banana Republic was again profitable.

The first GapKids opened in 1985 after Drexler couldn't find clothing that he liked for his son. During the late 1980s and early 1990s, the company grew rapidly, opening its first stores in Canada and the UK. In 1990 it introduced baby-Gap in 25 GapKids stores, featuring miniature versions of its GapKids line. The Gap announced in 1991 it would no longer sell Levi's (which had fallen to less than 2% of total sales) and would sell nothing but private-label items.

Earnings fell in fiscal 1993 because of Gap division losses brought on by low margins and high rents. The company shuffled management positions and titles as part of a streamlining effort. It rebounded in 1994 by concentrating on improving profit margins rather than sales and by launching Old Navy Clothing Co., named after a bar Drexler saw in Paris. Banana Republic opened its first two stores outside the US, both in Canada, in 1995.

Robert Fisher (the founders' son) became the new president of the Gap division (including babyGap and GapKids) in 1997 and was charged with reversing the segment's sales decline. The company refocused its Gap chain on basics (jeans, T-shirts, and khakis) and helped boost its performance with a high-profile advertising campaign focusing on those wares. Later in 1997 the Gap opened an online Gap store. In 1998 it began opening Torpedo Joe submarine-themed shops in select Old Navy flagships.

Also in 1998 the retailer opened its first Gap-Body stores and introduced its only catalog (for Banana Republic). In late 1999, amid sluggish Gap division sales, Robert resigned and CEO Drexler took over his duties. Gap misjudged fashion trends in 2000, which resulted in two years of disappointing earnings. After a 10% reduction in its workforce, the company returned to a more conservative fashion approach.

In January 2002 the company split Gap and Gap International into two separate units to improve performance in the flagship brand. In September Drexler retired and was replaced by Paul Pressler, a veteran of The Walt Disney Company.

OFFICERS

Chairman: Donald G. Fisher, age 73
Vice Chairman: John M. Lillie, age 65, $1,137,091
President and CEO: Paul Pressler, age 46
EVP and CFO: Heidi Kunz, age 47
EVP and Chief Administrative Officer: Anne B. Gust, age 44, $599,572 pay
EVP and Chief Supply Chain Officer: Charles K. Crovitz, age 48
SVP and CIO: Ken Harris, age 52
SVP and General Counsel: Lauri M. Shanahan
SVP, Corporate Administration, Architecture and Construction: Gregory Poole
SVP, Distribution: Joseph D. O'Leary
SVP, Field Real Estate: Alan J. Barocas
SVP, Finance and Business Strategy: George Mazzotta
SVP, Merchandising Systems: Steven R. Luce
SVP, Personal Care: Gary McNatton
SVP, Sourcing: James P. Cunningham
SVP, Sourcing and Logistics: Stanley P. Raggio
President, Banana Republic: Maureen Chiquet, age 39
President, Gap U.S.: Gary P. Muto, age 43
President, Old Navy: Jenny J. Ming, age 46, $848,120 pay
President, Outlet Division: Neal Goldberg, age 42
Auditors: Deloitte & Touche LLP

LOCATIONS

HQ: 2 Folsom St., San Francisco, CA 94105
Phone: 415-952-4400 **Fax:** 415-427-2553
Web: www.gap.com

The Gap sells casual apparel, shoes, and personal care items through about 4,170 Gap, Banana Republic and Old Navy stores in Canada, France, Germany, Japan, the UK, and the US.

PRODUCTS/OPERATIONS

2002 Stores

	No.
Gap	2,298
Old Navy	798
Gap International	634
Banana Republic	441
Total	**4,171**

Stores

babyGap (clothing for infants and toddlers)
Banana Republic (upscale clothing and accessories)
Gap (casual and active clothing and body care products)
GapBody (intimate apparel)
GapKids (clothing for children)
Old Navy (lower-priced family clothing)

COMPETITORS

Abercrombie & Fitch	Guess?	OshKosh B'Gosh
Aeropostale	Gymboree	Phillips-Van Heusen
American Eagle Outfitters	H&M	Polo
Benetton	Inditex	Reebok
Calvin Klein	J. Crew	Retail Brand Alliance
Dillard's	J. C. Penney	Saks Inc.
Eddie Bauer	Lands' End	Sears
Esprit de Corp.	Levi Strauss	Spiegel
Express	Limited Brands	Target
Fast Retailing	L.L. Bean	TJX
Federated	May	Tommy Hilfiger
Foot Locker	Nautica Enterprises	Toys "R" Us
Fruit of the Loom	NIKE	VF
	Nordstrom	

HISTORICAL FINANCIALS & EMPLOYEES

NYSE: GPS FYE: Saturday nearest Jan. 31	Annual Growth	1/93	1/94	1/95	1/96	1/97	1/98	1/99	1/00	1/01	1/02
Sales ($ mil.)	18.7%	2,960	3,296	3,723	4,395	5,284	6,508	9,055	11,635	13,674	13,848
Net income ($ mil.)	—	211	258	320	354	453	534	825	1,127	878	(8)
Income as % of sales	—	7.1%	7.8%	8.6%	8.1%	8.6%	8.2%	9.1%	9.7%	6.4%	—
Earnings per share ($)	—	0.22	0.27	0.33	0.37	0.47	0.58	0.91	1.26	1.00	(0.01)
Stock price - FY high ($)		8.35	6.36	7.33	7.57	10.83	18.35	43.36	52.69	53.75	34.98
Stock price - FY low ($)		4.17	3.78	4.28	4.41	6.88	8.49	17.57	30.81	18.50	11.12
Stock price - FY close ($)	12.2%	5.12	6.27	4.82	6.99	8.53	17.38	42.81	44.69	32.60	14.40
P/E - high	—	36	24	22	20	22	31	46	40	52	—
P/E - low	—	18	14	13	12	14	14	18	23	18	—
Dividends per share ($)	6.7%	0.05	0.06	0.07	0.07	0.09	0.09	0.09	0.09	0.09	0.09
Book value per share ($)	16.0%	0.91	1.15	1.41	1.69	1.79	1.79	1.84	2.63	3.43	3.48
Employees	17.4%	39,000	44,000	55,000	60,000	66,000	81,000	111,000	140,000	166,000	165,000

STOCK PRICE HISTORY

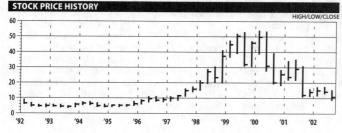

HIGH/LOW/CLOSE

2002 FISCAL YEAR-END

Debt ratio: 39.5%
Return on equity: —
Cash ($ mil.): 1,036
Current ratio: 1.48
Long-term debt ($ mil.): 1,961
No. of shares (mil.): 866
Dividends
  Yield: 0.6%
  Payout: —
Market value ($ mil.): 12,466

GATEWAY, INC.

Gateway's trying to Waitt out the PC slump. The Poway, California-based company is one of the leading computer makers in the US, where it does more than 90% of its business. In addition to desktop, laptop, and server computers, Gateway sells third-party peripherals and offers training, support, and financing services. The company also markets products through its 275-plus Gateway Country stores. Traditionally the stores have not served as retail outlets, rather allowing customers to configure and order systems, but Gateway has begun stocking the outlets with some PC inventory.

Slowing sales across the personal computer sector have hit the PC-centric Gateway hard. Founder and chairman Ted Waitt, who owns 32% of Gateway, has returned as CEO of the troubled company. Under his helm the company has taken aggressive measures to weather the market downturn, including a shakeup among upper management, job cuts, store closings, and a departure from the company-branded Internet service provider, Gateway.net. The company is closing manufacturing facilities in Asia and has pulled out of European markets.

HISTORY

Apparently college and billion-dollar PC retailers don't mix. Like his main competitor, Michael Dell, Ted Waitt dropped out of college to get into the computer business. Waitt had gone to Des Moines, Iowa, to see his roommates' band one weekend. He met a friend who was working for a computer retailer, liked the sound of the job, and left school to go to work. After nine months, he quit to start his own company.

Using his grandmother's certificate of deposit as collateral, Waitt borrowed $10,000 and in 1985 set up shop in the South Dakota barn of his father, a fourth-generation cattleman. There, with his brother Norm and friend Mike Hammond, he founded the TIPC Network, which sold add-on parts by phone for Texas Instruments' PCs.

However, Ted's goal was to sell PCs himself, and in 1987 the three men jumped into the fray. Ted and Hammond put together a fully configured computer system at a price that was near what other companies were charging for a bare-bones system. Sales took off. The next year they changed the enterprise's name to Gateway 2000 to express the belief that their computers were the gateway to the 21st century.

The company's customers were savvy buyers willing to dig through catalogs to find the best price for the exact system they wanted, and much of Gateway's success was rooted in Ted's ability to predict which standard features would sell.

Gateway distinguished itself from competitors with eye-catching ads. Some featured cows and another depicted Ted dressed as Robin Hood. He wanted to convince potential customers that Gateway would be around in the future to service the computers it sold.

In 1990 Gateway moved to North Sioux City, South Dakota. Two years later it introduced a line of notebook computers and created a division to handle component add-ons. Gateway went public in 1993, and opened a manufacturing facility in Ireland. In 1994 it added retail showrooms in Europe.

In 1995 Gateway expanded into Australia when it purchased 80% of the country's largest computer maker. Gateway introduced a cross between a PC and a big-screen TV (called a PCTV) in 1996 and opened two US retail showrooms.

The next year Ted, balking at the thought of his staff becoming subordinate to Compaq's management, rejected a $7 billion takeover bid from the PC giant. Also in 1997 Gateway acquired server maker Advanced Logic Research (ALR) and the patent rights to the venerated Amiga, one of the industry's most resilient, graphics-fueled PCs. (Gateway sold off the Amiga PC assets in 1999.) Inventory excesses and a charge for the ALR buy caused earnings to decline in 1997.

Gateway dropped the "2000" from its name in 1998 to avoid appearing behind the times as the millennium approached, and moved its headquarters to San Diego. In a bolder move that year, Microsoft agreed to let Gateway customize Windows 98 to promote its own Internet service (Gateway.net) over the services of Microsoft-connected providers.

Gateway in 1999 expanded its Web presence by investing in Internet sales specialist NECX to create an online peripheral and software store. Later in 1999 America Online (now AOL Time Warner) made an $800 million investment in Gateway that stipulated a deal for the online services giant to run Gateway.net. As 1999 ended, so did Waitt's reign as CEO — but not as chairman. He turned over the duties to company president and AT&T veteran Jeff Weitzen. In 2000 OfficeMax and Sun Microsystems agreed to sell Gateway products.

At the beginning of 2001 Gateway reduced its workforce by 10% and moved its headquarters to Poway, California, when an industrywide sales slowdown led to heavy losses. Gateway also overhauled its management team, a move that included the departure of Weitzen. Waitt returned to the helm as CEO of a greatly reduced staff. Gateway then began closing many of its Gateway Country stores in North America. It also phased out its Internet service, Gateway.net. The company's next restructuring push included plans to cut its workforce by as much as a quarter worldwide, the closing of manufacturing plants throughout the Pacific Rim, and a withdrawal from European markets. Despite its increased focus on domestic operations, Gateway also announced it would reduce its US call centers and close its Salt Lake City manufacturing plant.

OFFICERS

Chairman and CEO: Theodore W. Waitt, age 39, $20,833 pay
SVP and CFO: Joseph J. Burke, age 44, $384,536 pay
SVP and CIO: Will Headapohl, age 46
SVP and CTO: Robert J. Burnett, age 37
SVP, General Counsel, and Secretary: M. Javade Chaudhri, age 49
SVP, Corporate Communications: Brad Shaw, age 35
SVP, Gateway Solutions Group: Bart R. Brown, age 36, $379,107 pay
SVP, Human Resources: Jack Van Berkel, age 41
SVP, Operations: Michael D. Hammond, age 40, $376,444 pay
SVP, Sales and Marketing: David G. Turner, age 37
SVP, Supply Chain Management: Dave Russell
VP, Gateway Services: Luc Lambert
VP, Mobile Products: Mike Stinson
Auditors: PricewaterhouseCoopers LLP

LOCATIONS

HQ: 14303 Gateway Place, Poway, CA 92064
Phone: 858-848-3401   **Fax:** 858-848-3402
Web: www.gateway.com

2001 Sales

	$ mil.	% of total
US		
Consumer	3,098	51
Business	2,431	40
Asia/Pacific	322	5
Europe, Middle East & Africa	229	4
Total	**6,080**	**100**

PRODUCTS/OPERATIONS

Products
Personal computers
  Desktop
  Portables
Servers
Storage systems
Third-party peripherals and software

Services
Financing
Support
Training

COMPETITORS

Acer	Hewlett-Packard
Apple Computer	IBM
Best Buy	MicronPC
Circuit City Stores	NEC
CompUSA	PC Connection
Dell Computer	Sony
eMachines	Sun Microsystems
Fujitsu	Toshiba

HISTORICAL FINANCIALS & EMPLOYEES

NYSE: GTW FYE: December 31	Annual Growth	12/92	12/93	12/94	12/95	12/96	12/97	12/98	12/99	12/00	12/01
Sales ($ mil.)	20.8%	1,107	1,732	2,701	3,676	5,035	6,294	7,468	8,646	9,601	6,080
Net income ($ mil.)	—	106	151	96	173	251	110	346	428	241	(1,034)
Income as % of sales	—	9.6%	8.7%	3.6%	4.7%	5.0%	1.7%	4.6%	4.9%	2.5%	—
Earnings per share ($)	—	—	0.36	0.31	0.55	0.80	0.35	1.09	1.32	0.73	(3.20)
Stock price - FY high ($)	—	—	5.38	6.19	9.38	16.56	23.13	34.38	84.00	75.13	24.21
Stock price - FY low ($)	—	—	4.19	2.31	4.00	4.50	11.78	15.50	25.59	16.43	4.24
Stock price - FY close ($)	6.4%	—	4.91	5.41	6.13	13.39	16.38	25.59	72.06	17.99	8.04
P/E - high	—	—	15	20	16	20	64	31	62	95	—
P/E - low	—	—	12	7	7	5	33	14	19	21	—
Dividends per share ($)	—	—	0.00	0.00	0.00	0.00	0.00	0.00	0.00	0.00	0.00
Book value per share ($)	22.3%	—	0.97	1.30	1.86	2.66	3.02	4.29	6.32	7.36	4.84
Employees	29.5%	1,369	2,832	5,442	9,300	9,700	13,300	19,300	21,000	24,600	14,000

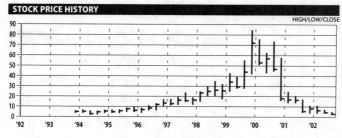

STOCK PRICE HISTORY   HIGH/LOW/CLOSE

2001 FISCAL YEAR-END
Debt ratio: 0.0%
Return on equity: —
Cash ($ mil.): 731
Current ratio: 1.85
Long-term debt ($ mil.): 0
No. of shares (mil.): 323
Dividends
  Yield: —
  Payout: —
Market value ($ mil.): 2,600

GATX CORPORATION

GATX gets around. With operations in North and South America, Europe, and Australia, the Chicago-based holding company offers leasing and finance services through two main groups: GATX Capital and GATX Rail.

GATX Capital leases aircraft and information technology equipment and provides other forms of asset-based financing. With a fleet of more than 300 commercial aircraft, it's one of the largest independent aircraft lessors. The company's Specialty Finance unit offers equipment financing for shipping, construction, and manufacturing companies.

Formerly General American Transportation, GATX Rail is one of the top North American tank car lessors. Its North American fleet includes more than 91,100 railcars. Leasing primarily to shippers of chemicals, petroleum, and food and agricultural products, the unit also maintains and services its railcars. GATX Rail operates in Europe through affiliates; worldwide, the unit owns or manages a fleet of about 150,000 railcars.

GATX has sold its chemical and petroleum logistics operations, along with its pipeline operations (GATX Logistics and GATX Terminals), to focus on finance and leasing operations. It is working to expand its European rail operations.

Investor Warren Buffett owns 15% of GATX. Insurance giant State Farm owns 12%.

HISTORY

Max Epstein, a worker in the Chicago Stockyards, founded the Atlantic Seaboard Dispatch in 1898. He used the $1,000 commission he received for arranging the sale of 20 old railway freight cars as a down payment to purchase 28 cars for himself. In 1902 he incorporated his German-American Car Co., the first to lease specialty railcars on a long-term basis.

By 1907 Epstein had 433 railcars and had begun to specialize in building customized freight cars. In 1916 the firm offered stock under the name General American Tank Car (GATC); its railcars carried the initials GATX (the "X" meant that a car belonged to a private line). In 1925 GATC began a bulk-liquid storage business.

Epstein purchased 13 firms between 1926 and 1931. The Depression was good to GATC: Epstein declared that conditions allowed him to make better deals, and the petroleum and food products hauled in GATC cars were always in demand, despite economic pressures. By the 1940s the company was the US's largest freight-car lessor. It also owned the US's largest public liquid-storage terminal facility and began operating cargo ships on the Great Lakes.

The company was the US's fourth-largest maker of freight cars by 1952. In 1954 GATC acquired Fuller Co., a builder of cement plants, which produced steady profits until its sale in 1986. In 1968 GATC formed GATX Leasing, an airplane lessor (later GATX Capital, a principal subsidiary of GATX Financial Services). That year, as the demand for railcars plummeted, the firm reduced manufacturing and began refocusing. In 1973 GATC acquired American Steamship, which helped expand its role in Great Lakes shipping. The company changed its name to GATX Corporation in 1975.

GATX exited manufacturing and became more service-oriented in the 1980s by expanding its railcar and aircraft fleets and bulk-liquid storage operations. It narrowly escaped several takeover attempts. GATX Terminals expanded rapidly toward the end of the 1980s.

The firm purchased Associated Unit Companies in 1989 (later the Unit Companies and then GATX Logistics) and Sealand Oil Services Ltd. (Scotland) in 1993. It continued to expand overseas by forming a joint venture with EnviroLease in 1994 to provide equipment for moving wastes and recyclables. In 1995 the company leased the 1,200-tank-car fleet of Mexico's state-owned railroad and in 1996 bought a 65% stake in a bulk-liquid storage facility in Altamira, Mexico.

CEO James Glasser, head of GATX since 1978, turned over the reins to Ronald Zech in 1996. The next year mailing-machine maker Pitney Bowes sold part of its lease portfolio to GATX and put other equipment in a joint venture with the company.

Also in 1997, as part of a three-year strategy to sell underperforming units, the company began to sell some of its terminals. By 1999 it had sold six UK terminals. In 2000 GATX changed the name of its main operating unit, General American Transportation Corp., to GATX Rail. It also sold its GATX Logistics subsidiary to two investment groups.

To trim down its operations even further, the firm sold its GATX Terminals subsidiary in 2001 and reorganized its finance and leasing operations under GATX Capital and GATX Rail. Also that year, GATX expanded its European rail operations into Poland with the acquisition of Dyrekcja Eksploatacji Cystern (DEC).

OFFICERS

Chairman, President, and CEO: Ronald H. Zech, age 58, $725,000 pay

SVP and CFO: Brian A. Kenney, age 42, $438,105 pay (prior to promotion)

VP, General Counsel, and Secretary: Ronald J. Ciancio, age 60, $316,763 pay

VP Controller and Chief Accounting Officer: William M. Muckian, age 42
VP Corporate Strategy: Clifford J. Porzenheim, age 38, $226,854 pay
VP Investor Relations: Robert C. Lyons, age 38
VP Human Resources: Gail L. Duddy, age 49, $290,181 pay
President and CEO, GATX Rail: David M. Edwards, $645,379 pay
President, GATX Capital: Jesse V. Crews
SVP and Managing Director, GATX Capital and GATX Technology: Tom McGreal
SVP Customer Support and Solutions, GATX Rail: Tobi D'Andrea
VP and Managing Director Fleet Portfolio Management, GATX Rail Canada: Todd M. Emro
VP and Managing Director Sales and Marketing Administration, GATX Rail Canada: Daniel P. Penovich
VP and Treasurer: William J. Hasek, age 45
VP Customer Service, GATX Rail: Geoff Phillips
VP Engineering, GATX Rail: John Swezey, age 35
VP Fleet Management and Sales Administration, GATX Rail Canada: James V. Pasquini
VP Sales, GATX Rail: Robert Zmudka
VP Sales, GATX Rail Canada: Richard A. Podsiadlo
Midwestern Region Sales Team Member, GATX Rail: John P. Sweeney
Auditors: Ernst & Young LLP

LOCATIONS

HQ: 500 W. Monroe St., Chicago, IL 60661
Phone: 312-621-6200   **Fax:** 312-621-6698
Web: www.gatx.com

PRODUCTS/OPERATIONS

Selected Subsidiaries and Affiliates

Financial Services
American Steamship Company
GATX Financial Services, Inc.
  GATX Capital Corporation

GATX Rail
GATX Rail Corporation
  Ahaus Alstatter Eisenbahn (AAE Cargo, 19%, Switzerland)
  Dyrekcja Eksploatacji Cystern (DEC, Poland)
  GATX de México, S.A. de C.V.
  KVG Kesselwagen Vermietgesellschaft mbH (46%, Germany)

COMPETITORS

ACF
CSX
Electro Rent
Eurofima
Forsythe Technology
GE Equipment Management
General Motors
Greenbrier
International Aircraft Investors
Interpool
Johnstown America
Oglebay Norton
Stolt-Nielsen
Transtar
Trinity Industries
TTX
XTRA

HISTORICAL FINANCIALS & EMPLOYEES

NYSE: GMT FYE: December 31	Annual Growth	12/92	12/93	12/94	12/95	12/96	12/97	12/98	12/99	12/00	12/01
Sales ($ mil.)	4.3%	1,019	1,087	1,155	1,233	1,414	1,702	1,763	1,711	1,312	1,489
Net income ($ mil.)	—	(17)	73	92	101	103	(51)	132	151	67	173
Income as % of sales	—	—	6.7%	7.9%	8.2%	7.3%	—	7.5%	8.8%	5.1%	11.6%
Earnings per share ($)	—	(0.77)	1.52	1.90	2.07	2.10	(1.28)	2.62	3.01	1.37	3.51
Stock price – FY high ($)	—	16.88	21.13	22.31	27.13	25.63	36.69	47.56	40.88	50.50	49.94
Stock price – FY low ($)	—	12.13	15.69	19.13	20.19	21.50	23.75	26.25	28.06	28.38	23.65
Stock price – FY close ($)	7.8%	16.56	20.38	22.00	24.31	24.25	36.28	37.88	33.75	49.88	32.52
P/E – high	—	—	14	11	12	12	—	18	13	36	14
P/E – low	—	—	10	10	9	10	—	10	9	20	7
Dividends per share ($)	7.4%	0.65	0.70	0.77	0.80	0.86	0.92	1.00	1.10	1.20	1.24
Book value per share ($)	2.7%	14.30	14.75	16.64	17.85	19.11	13.39	14.89	17.20	16.54	18.12
Employees	(10.4%)	5,100	5,500	5,800	5,900	6,000	6,000	6,000	6,300	5,500	1,900

STOCK PRICE HISTORY

HIGH/LOW/CLOSE

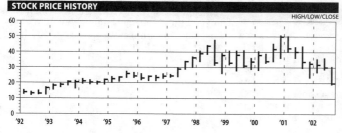

2001 FISCAL YEAR-END

Debt ratio: 81.1%
Return on equity: 20.7%
Cash ($ mil.): 223
Current ratio: 2.77
Long-term debt ($ mil.): 3,789
No. of shares (mil.): 49
Dividends
  Yield: 3.8%
  Payout: 35.3%
Market value ($ mil.): 1,583

GEMSTAR-TV GUIDE

Gemstar-TV Guide International is making sure even TV fans who can't program their VCRs won't miss those late-night *Brady Bunch* reruns. Pasadena, California-based Gemstar-TV Guide International invented VCR Plus+ (the technology that lets users record TV programs using a simple code) as the technological equivalent of Excedrin to relieve VCR programming headaches. The company has licensed its VCR Plus+ technology to essentially every TV and VCR maker across the globe, and its technology also has been installed in other devices such as set-top boxes, PCs, and Internet appliances. The company's programming codes can be found in printed TV listings, including its own popular *TV Guide*.

Gemstar-TV Guide complements VCR Plus+ with its Gemstar Guide Technology and TV Guide Interactive for interactive program guides (IPGs). IPGs allow users to peruse onscreen TV listings and to program their VCRs or TVs from the listings. The company has licensed its IPG technology to some of the most formidable companies on the technology landscape, including AOL Time Warner and Microsoft. The company's pending acquisition of bankrupt DIVA Systems will further expand its interactive TV capabilities. Gemstar also operates the TV Guide Channel, which provides TV listings to some 50 million cable subscribers, and distributes satellite programming through its Superstar/Netlink Group.

But all is far from rosy for the company as it has had to restate $20 million in sales for 2001 and change the way it accounts for revenues. These developments riled News Corporation, which owns 42% of the company through its Sky Global Networks satellite subsidiary. The Australian media giant has had to write down about $6 billion to cover losses brought on by Gemstar's declining stock value. News Corp. is waging a campaign to oust most of Gemstar's top management including founder and CEO Henry Yuen.

Gemstar has expanded its operations through purchases of NuvoMedia and SoftBook Press, two developers of electronic books and related software. The company also has signed an e-book distribution deal with consumer electronics manufacturer THOMSON Multimedia.

HISTORY

Frustrated by a failed attempt to record a Red Sox game, Henry Yuen founded Gemstar Development in 1989 with Daniel Kwoh to simplify VCR programming. Yuen and Kwoh, fellow researchers at TRW, invented a system to translate data about when and where a show aired into a single number. The company introduced the VCR Plus+ system in 1990, selling converter boxes at about $60 and persuading daily newspapers to list coding numbers.

In 1993 the company embarked on a long series of legal battles to protect its patents, exchanging lawsuits with rivals. Its ferocious defense of its technology earned the company the epithet "patent terrorist."

In 1994 Gemstar debuted its VCR Plus+ with CallSet (enabling VCR Plus+ technology via the telephone) and VCR Plus+ Control Tower (a universal remote with built-in VCR Plus+ with CallSet). The company went public in 1995, and changed its name to Gemstar International Group. Through acquisitions of VideoGuide (1996) and StarSight (1997), Gemstar branched into electronic program guides (EPGs). In 1997 THOMSON Multimedia agreed to use the company's EPG technology (called Gemstar Guide Technology) as the industry standard in North and South America.

In 1998 Gemstar fought off a hostile takeover bid by rival United Video Satellite Group. It also inked licensing agreements for its Gemstar Guide Technology with Microsoft and Sony, followed by a licensing agreement with America Online in 1999.

In 2000 Gemstar bought electronic book developers NuvoMedia and SoftBook Press for about $565 million. Later that year it also signed an e-book distribution deal with THOMSON Multimedia. Also that year Gemstar strengthened its grip on the couch potato market when it purchased TV Guide in a stock deal valued at around $14 billion. In acquiring TV Guide, Gemstar gobbled up one of its longtime foes — two years earlier, United Video Satellite Group had purchased TV Guide and adopted the TV Guide name. The deal gave News Corp.'s satellite subsidiary (Sky Global Networks) and Liberty Media each a 21.5% stake in the new company.

In 2001 Liberty swapped the majority of its stake in Gemstar for an interest in Sky Global. Also that year the company entered the retail market through its purchase of SkyMall, which operates an airline catalog distribution business for major retailers such as L.L. Bean. In 2002 Gemstar agreed to purchase interactive TV technology developer DIVA Systems as part of that company's bankruptcy reorganization plan. Also in 2002 the company bought about 17% of online wagering company Youbet.com and has a warrant to purchase up to 51%.

Chairman and CEO: Henry C. Yuen, age 54,
$4,581,198 pay
Co-President, COO, and Director: Jeff Shell, age 36
Co-President, CFO, and Director: Elsie Ma Leung,
age 55, $1,854,215 pay
VP Finance: Lester Sussman
Corporate EVP: Blair Westlake
EVP, General Counsel, and Secretary: Jonathan Orlick,
age 44
Corporate SVP: Michael Benevento
Chairman and CEO, SkyMall: Robert M. Worsley
Director Human Resources: Stacy Wong
Corporate Communications: Lauren Snyder
Auditors: KPMG LLP

LOCATIONS

HQ: Gemstar-TV Guide International, Inc.
135 N. Los Robles Ave., Ste. 800,
Pasadena, CA 91101
Phone: 626-792-5700   **Fax:** 626-792-0257
Web: www.gemstartvguide.com

2001 Sales

	$ mil.	% of total
Media & services	950	69
Technology & licensing	327	24
Interactive platform	101	7
Adjustment	(10)	—
Total	**1,368**	**100**

PRODUCTS/OPERATIONS

Selected Gemstar Guide Technology Licensees
AOL Time Warner
AT&T Broadband
Hitachi
Matsushita Electric Industrial
Microsoft
Motorola
Sony
THOMSON

Media Operations
The Cable Guide (monthly)
TVGuide.com
TV Guide (weekly)
TV Guide Channel

Technology
Gemstar eBook
Interactive programming guides (GUIDE Plus+, TV
Guide Interactive)
Superstar/Netlink Group (80%, marketing and
distribution of programming to C-band satellite dish
owners)
VCR Plus+ system

Other Operations
SkyMall (in-flight retail catalog publishing)

COMPETITORS

ACTV	ReplayTV
AOL Time Warner	Scientific-Atlanta
Charter Communications	TiVo
Cox Communications	TVData
Motorola	Wink Communications
Personalized Media	

HISTORICAL FINANCIALS & EMPLOYEES

Nasdaq: GMSTE FYE: December 31	Annual Growth	3/93	3/94	3/95	3/96	3/97	3/98	3/99	3/00	*12/00	12/01
Sales ($ mil.)	63.3%	—	27	42	53	71	127	167	241	731	1,368
Net income ($ mil.)	—	—	12	14	16	18	39	74	81	(213)	(600)
Income as % of sales	—	—	43.3%	33.6%	30.1%	25.5%	30.6%	44.4%	33.7%	—	—
Earnings per share ($)	—	—	—	—	(0.36)	(0.05)	0.19	0.33	0.33	(0.64)	(1.45)
Stock price - FY high ($)	—	—	—	—	10.44	10.06	9.34	18.97	107.44	107.44	59.56
Stock price - FY low ($)	—	—	—	—	3.28	2.41	2.50	7.19	18.00	33.50	16.05
Stock price - FY close ($)	28.2%	—	—	—	6.25	3.06	7.50	18.81	86.00	46.38	27.70
P/E - high	—	—	—	—	—	—	44	50	269	—	—
P/E - low	—	—	—	—	—	—	12	19	45	—	—
Dividends per share ($)	—	—	—	—	0.00	0.00	0.00	0.00	0.00	0.00	0.00
Book value per share ($)	81.9%	—	—	—	0.50	0.42	0.53	0.93	1.86	19.60	18.21
Employees	53.0%	—	90	100	90	45	178	211	354	3,000	2,700

* Fiscal year change

STOCK PRICE HISTORY

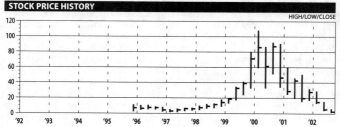
HIGH/LOW/CLOSE

2001 FISCAL YEAR-END

Debt ratio: 3.5%
Return on equity: —
Cash ($ mil.): 349
Current ratio: 1.38
Long-term debt ($ mil.): 271
No. of shares (mil.): 415
Dividends
  Yield: —
  Payout: —
Market value ($ mil.): 11,489

GENCORP INC.

GenCorp can seal you in and fly you to the moon. The Rancho Cordova, California-based company's two biggest subsidiaries make automotive sealing systems and rocket propulsion systems. GenCorp's automotive subsidiary, GDX Automotive, makes molded rubber and plastic sealing systems used to insulate vehicles from air, moisture, and noise. It accounts for nearly 55% of GenCorp sales; Ford and GM account for most of GDX's sales and about 30% of total company sales. GenCorp's Aerojet-General Corporation subsidiary (Aerojet) accounts for almost 45% of sales. Aerojet makes liquid and solid rocket-propulsion systems, smart munitions components, and related defense products. Not surprisingly, the US government and its contractors are responsible for almost all of the division's sales. Bringing up the rear is GenCorp's Aerojet Fine Chemicals subsidiary, which produces chemical intermediates and pharmaceutical ingredients.

GenCorp has narrowed its focus by spinning off its polymer and building products businesses (as OMNOVA Solutions) and selling its electronic and information systems business to Northrop Grumman. Despite the sluggish economy, GDX's sales increased some 67% in 2001, thanks largely to GenCorp's 2000 acquisition of The Laird Group's Draftex business. Aerojet has also agreed to purchase General Dynamics' Space Propulsion and Fire Suppression business for $90 million.

HISTORY

Michael O'Neil and his son, William, a former Firestone dealer, founded General Tire & Rubber in 1915. The elder O'Neil put up most of the $200,000 seed money to start the company and served as president, while his son served as general manager. The two recruited managers from Firestone and began making tires in 1916. Effective advertising and specializing in higher-priced tires helped the company to grow to 14 stores by 1929. During the 1930s the company diversified into radio stations.

WWII proved critical in the company's history. It began producing rockets and motors and acquired missile maker Aerojet. After the war General increased its rubber holdings and entered television broadcasting. It purchased RKO Pictures from Howard Hughes (1955), getting 750 feature films to show on its television stations in New York, Los Angeles, Memphis, and other cities. The company also began an industrial products division to make plastic and metal parts for electric appliances and aircraft. General sold the movie portion of RKO in 1958.

In 1960 William O'Neil died, and his three sons took over. The company had a tumultuous ride under the reins of the O'Neil brothers. The FCC opposed the license renewal of the company's Los Angeles station in 1965 because of poor programming. Later, General was accused of pressuring its suppliers to advertise on its stations and of setting up a slush fund to help overthrow the Allende government in Chile. The oil embargo of 1974 hurt the company. By 1981 General was in trouble and sold several retreading plants, a tire plant, and a cable television operation.

The company created GenCorp as a holding company in 1984, and the next year it hired former TRW executive Bill Reynolds to head the firm. A hostile takeover attempt in 1987 prompted Reynolds to restructure the company. He sold General Tire & Rubber, the rest of the RKO interests, and several radio stations. The leaner company consisted of fast-growing high-tech businesses. Meanwhile Aerojet was cruising along nicely, helped by the 1980s' defense buildup. Analysts and investors applauded the more-focused GenCorp, which made more than $200 million on sales of about $2 billion in 1989.

Defense cutbacks in the 1990s forced GenCorp to seek commercial businesses for growth. In 1991 it bought the assets of Canadian wallcoverings maker General-Tower Ltd. Two years later the company added a latex plant, acquired Reneer Films (vinyl laminates and films), and German automotive supplier HENNIGES. GenCorp sold its reinforced plastics, seat-occupant sensor, and vibration-control businesses in 1996. The next year it acquired Printworld.

In 1998 the company acquired a Sequa unit that makes chemicals for the paper, coatings, and construction industries. GenCorp sold its Penn-brand tennis balls and racquetballs business in 1999 to Austria-based HTM. Also that year it spun off its polymer products and decorative and building products businesses as OMNOVA Solutions.

In 2000 GenCorp's Aerojet Fine Chemicals division took a 35% stake in Pharbil Technologies (contract process and manufacturing, now NextPharma Technologies), which, in turn, acquired a 40% interest in the division. The same year GenCorp bought The Laird Group's car body sealing unit (Draftex) for $208 million.

In 2001 the company's Aerojet unit sold its Electronic and Information Systems business to Northrop Grumman for about $300 million. Late in the year GenCorp regained full ownership of Aerojet Fine Chemicals by reacquiring NextPharma's 40% stake.

The following year GenCorp's Aerojet unit agreed to purchase General Dynamics' Ordnance and Space Propulsion and Fire Suppression business for $90 million.

OFFICERS

Chairman: Robert A. Wolfe, age 63, $540,000 pay
President and CEO: Terry L. Hall, age 48, $400,000 pay
SVP, Law, General Counsel, and Secretary:
William R. Phillips, age 59, $279,000 pay
SVP, Finance and CFO: Yasmin R. Seyal, age 44
VP and Controller: Douglas C. Jeffries
VP, Corporate Communications: Linda B. Cutler, age 48
VP, Deputy General Counsel, and Assistant Secretary:
Robert C. Anderson, age 52
VP, Environment, Health, and Safety: Chris W. Conley,
age 43
VP; President, Aerojet: Michael F. Martin, age 55
President, GDX Automotive: Michael T. Bryant
Human Resources Manager: Brian Ramsey
Auditors: Ernst & Young LLP

LOCATIONS

HQ: Hwy 50 and Aerojet Rd., P.O. Box 537012,
Ranchero Cordova, CA 95853
Phone: 916-355-4000   **Fax:** 916-355-2459
Web: www.gencorp.com

GenCorp has manufacturing facilities in Canada, China,
Czech Republic, France, Germany, Spain, and the US.

2001 Sales By Origin

	$ mil.	% of total
United States	1,037	70
Germany	210	14
Canada	110	7
France	62	4
Spain	57	4
Other countries	10	1
Total	**1,486**	**100**

PRODUCTS/OPERATIONS

2001 Sales

	$ mil.	% of total
GDX Automotive	808	54
Aerospace and Defense	640	43
Fine Chemicals	38	3
Total	**1,486**	**100**

Selected Products

GDX Automotive
Extruded and molded rubber products
Window sealants

Aerospace and Defense
Defense and armaments
Ejection seat propulsion systems
Electron beam welding
Warhead development
Missile and space propulsion
Attitude control systems
Liquid rocket engines
Missile maneuvering engines
Orbital maneuvering engines

Fine Chemicals
Bulk active pharmaceutical ingredients
Fine chemical intermediates

COMPETITORS

Alliant Techsystems	Raytheon
Boeing	Sequa
Cooper Tire & Rubber	Starmet
Harvard Industries	TRW
ITT Industries	United Technologies
Northrop Grumman	

HISTORICAL FINANCIALS & EMPLOYEES

NYSE: GY FYE: November 30	Annual Growth	11/92	11/93	11/94	11/95	11/96	11/97	11/98	11/99	11/00	11/01
Sales ($ mil.)	(2.9%)	1,937	1,905	1,740	1,772	1,515	1,568	1,737	1,071	1,047	1,486
Net income ($ mil.)	21.6%	22	43	(226)	38	42	137	84	72	129	128
Income as % of sales	—	1.1%	2.2%	—	2.1%	2.8%	8.7%	4.8%	6.7%	12.3%	8.6%
Earnings per share ($)	17.6%	0.70	1.24	(7.10)	1.10	1.16	3.40	1.99	1.72	3.07	3.00
Stock price - FY high ($)	—	15.63	17.38	16.38	14.13	18.63	31.00	31.19	27.88	11.06	14.25
Stock price - FY low ($)	—	8.88	10.13	10.00	9.88	11.13	17.50	16.44	9.63	6.63	7.63
Stock price - FY close ($)	2.0%	10.63	13.88	10.38	11.75	18.50	25.06	24.63	10.94	8.00	12.75
P/E - high	—	22	13	—	12	15	8	15	16	8	5
P/E - low	—	13	8	—	8	9	5	8	6	5	3
Dividends per share ($)	(16.4%)	0.60	0.60	0.60	0.60	0.60	0.60	0.60	0.48	0.12	0.12
Book value per share ($)	0.9%	6.72	7.41	(0.22)	1.05	1.67	6.80	8.28	1.91	4.64	7.28
Employees	(2.7%)	13,900	13,300	12,970	11,700	8,950	9,460	10,770	7,480	7,895	10,877

STOCK PRICE HISTORY

HIGH/LOW/CLOSE

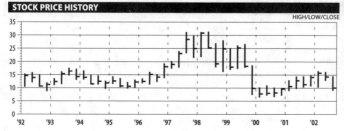

2001 FISCAL YEAR-END

Debt ratio: 38.9%
Return on equity: 50.7%
Cash ($ mil.): 44
Current ratio: 0.90
Long-term debt ($ mil.): 197
No. of shares (mil.): 43
Dividends
 Yield: 0.9%
 Payout: 4.0%
Market value ($ mil.): 543

GENENTECH, INC.

Genentech had better hope 10 isn't its lucky number. Although the South San Francisco, California-based company has several drug-development victories based on its recombinant DNA technology, it has only 10 products on the market.

Rituxan, a treatment for non-Hodgkin's lymphoma, and Herceptin, a breast cancer drug, account for more than half of the biotech's sales. Clot-busting cardiovascular therapies Activase and TNKase together account for about 10% of sales, as do growth hormones Protropin and Nutropin. Pulmozyme, for cystic fibrosis, makes up about 5% of sales.

In addition to product sales, Genentech earns royalties from about 15 approved biotech products it has licensed to such big pharmas as GlaxoSmithKline and Eli Lilly. The firm, however, might have to dole out 30% of its Herceptin sales to Chiron, which claims to hold a key patent for the drug; Genentech licensed its patent from the University of Pennsylvania. One judge ruled in Chiron's favor, but the US Patent Office is investigating the validity of Chiron's patent.

Genentech handles US sales, and international sales are made by drug giant Hoffmann-La Roche, a subsidiary of Swiss druggernaut Roche, which owns about 60% of the company.

The company's pipeline contains almost two dozen drugs: Among them is Raptiva, a psoriasis therapy it developed with XOMA that Serono will co-market outside the US and Asia. Australian approval of Xolair, an asthma therapy developed with Novartis and Tanox, came in mid-2002, but US approval has been delayed by FDA requests for more data. Tracleer, an FDA-approved high blood pressure drug the firm is developing with Actelion for congestive heart failure (CHF), failed to meet expectations in a Phase III trial for CHF, but the partners will try to develop it for other indications. Genentech is hoping to launch at least six new products or expand use of existing ones in 2003, but with the FDA promising to become more cautious about approvals, nearly doubling its product roster might prove difficult for the firm.

HISTORY

Venture capitalist Robert Swanson and molecular biologist Herbert Boyer founded Genentech in 1976 to commercialize Boyer's patented gene-splicing techniques that could mass-produce genetically engineered substances. The company went public in 1980.

Genentech's market debut (the first FDA-approved biotech product) was a bioengineered form of human insulin in 1982. Eli Lilly bought the license and sold it as Humulin. Genentech sold marketing rights for royalties and focused on research; the company next developed the human immune system protein alpha interferon and licensed it to Hoffmann-La Roche, which sold the cancer treatment as Roferon-A. The first product to bear the Genentech name was human growth hormone Protropin, approved by the FDA in 1985.

Genentech released Activase in 1988. Its $180 million in sales was the best first year of any new drug at the time. Roche bought 60% of Genentech for $2.1 billion in 1990, including nearly $500 million to maintain the long-term research pipeline. In 1993 Genentech and Merck developed a compound to prevent activation of the RAS oncogene, a trigger for cancerous cells in the pancreas, colon, and lungs. Merck began human tests of anti-RAS drugs in 1998.

Genentech began shipping human growth hormone Nutropin in early 1994. The next year CEO Kirk Rabb was ousted after trying to secure a $2 million personal loan from Roche. Rabb was replaced by scientist Arthur Levinson. That year the companies signed a pact that gave Roche Genentech's Canadian and European operations, with a provision allowing Roche to buy the rest of the company by mid-1999.

After spending $100 million in 10 years on AIDS-related research, Genentech in 1996 formed a new company to develop its sidetracked HIV vaccine. That year the FDA approved Activase as the first effective treatment for acute stroke. Lymphoma treatment Rituxan (developed with IDEC Pharmaceuticals) became the first monoclonal antibody of its kind approved for cancer in 1998.

The next year saw the demise of Neuleze, once thought to hold promise to treat diabetes-related nerve damage. Meanwhile, charges that Genentech marketed human growth hormone for non-approved uses led to a federal court fine of $50 million. In 1999 co-founder Swanson died of cancer. Also in 1999, Roche bought the shares of Genentech that it didn't own, then spun off 16% of the company in 1999 and 26% more in 2000. Genentech issued a warning to physicians in 2000 after Herceptin was linked to several deaths; together with the FDA, it set about relabeling the drug. That year the FDA approved TNKase to treat heart attacks.

In 2001 the firm won a patent dispute with GlaxoSmithKline over how Genentech makes Herceptin and Rituxan. The next year, though, it lost a royalty dispute with the City of Hope research organization and was hit with $500 million damages from the suit, which the company is appealing.

Chairman, President, and CEO: Arthur D. Levinson, age 52, $1,765,000 pay
EVP and CFO: Louis J. Lavigne Jr., age 53, $689,282 pay
EVP, Development and Product Operations and Chief Medical Officer: Susan D. Desmond-Hellmann, age 44, $925,491 pay
EVP, Commercial Operations and COO: Myrtle S. Potter, age 43, $945,256 pay
SVP, General Counsel, and Secretary: Stephen G. Juelsgaard, age 53, $547,400 pay
SVP, Regulatory, Quality and Compliance: Robert L. Garnick, age 52
SVP, Development Sciences: Paula M. Jardieu, age 51
SVP, Research: Richard H. Scheller, age 48
SVP, Marketing and Sales: Kimberly J. Popovits, age 43
SVP, Product Operations: David A. Ebersman, age 32
VP, Global Manufacturing Operations: W. Robert Arathoon, age 49
VP, Compliance: J. Joseph Barta, age 54
VP, Global Quality: Ronald C. Branning, age 55
VP, Medical Affairs: Hal Barron, age 39
VP, Regulatory Affairs: Genesio Murano, age 60
VP, Product Development: Bernice R. Welles, age 49
VP, Decision Support and Commercial Innovation: Sherine Aly
VP, Intellectual Property and Assistant Secretary: Sean A. Johnston, age 43
Auditors: Ernst & Young LLP

LOCATIONS

HQ: 1 DNA Way, South San Francisco, CA 94080
Phone: 650-225-1000 **Fax:** 650-225-6000
Web: www.gene.com

PRODUCTS/OPERATIONS

2001 Sales

	$ mil.	% of total
Products		
Rituxan	819	39
Herceptin	347	17
Growth hormones	250	12
Activase, TNKase, & Cathflo Activase	197	9
Pulmozyme	130	6
Royalties	265	13
Contracts & other	75	4
Total	**2,082**	**100**

Selected Products
Activase (heart attacks, ischemic stroke)
CathFlo Activase
Herceptin (breast cancer)
Nutropin (human growth hormone)
Nutropin AQ (liquid form of Nutropin)
Nutropin Depot (long-acting human growth hormone)
Protropin (human growth hormone)
Pulmozyme (cystic fibrosis)
Rituxan (non-Hodgkin's lymphoma)
TNKase (heart attack)
Xolair (allergy-induced asthma and rhinitis, with Novartis and Tanox)

COMPETITORS

Bio-Technology General	Genzyme
Bristol-Myers Squibb	IDEC Pharmaceuticals
Centocor	Novo Nordisk
Chiron	Pharmacia
Corixa	Serono
Eli Lilly	

HISTORICAL FINANCIALS & EMPLOYEES

NYSE: DNA FYE: December 31	Annual Growth	12/92	12/93	12/94	12/95	12/96	12/97	12/98	12/99	12/00	12/01
Sales ($ mil.)	16.1%	544	650	753	857	905	948	1,151	1,421	1,646	2,082
Net income ($ mil.)	24.6%	21	59	124	146	118	129	182	(1,145)	(16)	150
Income as % of sales	—	3.8%	9.1%	16.5%	17.1%	13.1%	13.6%	15.8%	—	—	7.2%
Earnings per share ($)	—	—	—	—	—	—	—	—	(2.23)	(0.14)	0.28
Stock price - FY high ($)	—	—	—	—	—	—	—	—	71.50	122.50	84.00
Stock price - FY low ($)	—	—	—	—	—	—	—	—	29.13	42.25	37.99
Stock price - FY close ($)	(10.2%)	—	—	—	—	—	—	—	67.25	81.50	54.25
P/E - high	—	—	—	—	—	—	—	—	—	—	280
P/E - low	—	—	—	—	—	—	—	—	—	—	127
Dividends per share ($)	—	—	—	—	—	—	—	—	0.00	0.00	0.00
Book value per share ($)	4.6%	—	—	—	—	—	—	—	10.23	10.80	11.21
Employees	8.7%	2,331	2,510	2,738	2,842	3,071	3,242	3,389	3,883	4,459	4,950

STOCK PRICE HISTORY

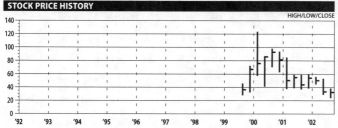

HIGH/LOW/CLOSE

2001 FISCAL YEAR-END

Debt ratio: 0.0%
Return on equity: 2.6%
Cash ($ mil.): 395
Current ratio: 3.39
Long-term debt ($ mil.): 0
No. of shares (mil.): 528
Dividends
  Yield: —
  Payout: —
Market value ($ mil.): 28,661

GENERAL CABLE CORPORATION

General Cable would like to keep you wired. The Highland Heights, Kentucky-based company is a leading maker of copper, aluminum, and fiber-optic wire and cable for the communications and electrical markets. Among its communications products are electronic products, fiber-optic cables, and outside voice, video, and data cables. Its industrial and specialty group's products include automotive parts (jumper cables, ignition wires), custom wire, harnesses, and assemblies. The energy group's products include wire and cable goods that include low-, medium- and high- voltage power distribution and power transmission products for overhead and buried applications.

To combat anticipated weak sales from its industrial and specialty and communication units, the company has reorganized its operating segments and distribution network. General Cable will continue to divest non-core and under performing operations. The company has also introduced lean manufacturing, a system that uses cycle-time and inventory reduction as a means to reduce waste and increase productivity.

HISTORY

General Cable originated from some of the oldest names in the wiring business: Standard Underground Cable (founded by George Westinghouse) and Phillips Wire and Safety Cable Company, both founded in the 1800s. The companies supplied wire for historic events such as Samuel Morse's first telegraph between Baltimore and Washington, DC, in 1844, lighting the Statute of Liberty in 1886, and wiring the first Chicago World's Fair in 1892.

The company's best-known brand of non-metallic sheathed cable, Romex, was invented at the company's Rome, New York, facility in 1922. Five years later, Phillips Wire and Standard Underground Cable joined to form General Cable Corporation. In 1935 the company's cables were used for power lines connecting the Hoover Dam to Los Angeles.

In the early 1980s the company was purchased by Penn Central Corporation (now known as American Premier Underwriters). Later that decade Penn Central added the Carol brand when it purchased the Carol Cable Company (1989) and bought other wiring companies. Construction declined in the early 1990s, leaving wire inventories overstocked. In 1992 Penn Central spun off General Cable to shareholders, but the Lindner family (which owned Penn Central) continued to control most of the stock. The company also made news in 1992 when it moved its corporate headquarters from Cincinnati to northern Kentucky, representing a win in the battle for companies being waged between the bordering states. That year General Cable also sold its equipment-making subsidiary, Marathon LeTourneau, because it was not directly tied to the wire and cable business.

In 1994 Wassall, a British holding company, bought General Cable, which had lost more than $130 million in the previous two years. (Wassall later sold its interest in 1997.) Soon afterward the company hired a new CEO, Stephen Rabinowitz, who had been president of General Electric's electrical distribution and control unit and president of AlliedSignal braking-systems business. He began integrating the company's many units, which previously had been run separately. He also consolidated the company's distribution sites and closed five manufacturing plants.

General Cable went public in 1997. That year it formed a joint venture with glass company Spectran Corporation (since acquired by Lucent) to create fiber-optic cable under the name General Photonics. In 1999 General Cable bought the energy cable businesses of BICC Plc for $440 million. The deal made General Cable one of the largest makers of wire and cable in the world. (The company briefly operated under the BICC-General name.)

When its energy cable businesses in Europe, Africa, and Asia failed to perform up to expectations, General Cable agreed to sell some of those businesses (in the UK, Italy, Africa, and Asia) to Italy-based Pirelli & C. SAPA for $216 million in 2000. Fearing Pirelli's dominant position, the European Commission opened an in-depth investigation of the takeover, but the deal was approved and completed later that year.

In 2001 General Cable sold its Pyrotenax unit to Raychem HTS Canada, Inc. (a division of Tyco International) for $60 million. The company also freed up $175 million in that same year by selling its building wire interests and exiting the cordset (indoor and outdoor extension cords) business. In early 2002 General Cable acquired the New Zealand-based data cable manufacturer Brand-Rex from Novar plc.

OFFICERS

Nonexecutive Chairman: John E. Welsh III, age 50
President, CEO, and Director: Gregory B. Kenny, age 49, $705,577 pay
EVP and CFO: Christopher F. Virgulak, age 46, $415,000 pay
EVP, General Counsel, and Secretary: Robert J. Siverd, age 53, $400,000 pay
SVP and General Manager, Utility Cables: J. Michael Andrews
SVP and General Manager, Communications Cables: James W. Barney

SVP; President and CEO, General Cable Europe: Domingo Goenaga Campmany
SVP, North American Operations: Larry E. Fast
SVP, International Sales: W. Martin Johnsen
SVP, Sales and Business Development: Roderick Macdonald
SVP, Customer Integration and Supply Chain: Elizabeth W. Taliaferro
VP, Communications Sales: Alberto Alsina
VP, Compensation and Benefits: Beth A. Curtis
VP, E-business: Scott D. Freidus
VP, Information Technology: Sharon F. Highlander
VP, Canadian Sales: Robert C. Jamieson
VP, Industrial and Specialty Cables Sales: Gregory J. Lampert
VP, Corporate Communications: Lisa B. Lawson
VP, Retail Sales and General Manager, Automotive Products: Jodi L. Mahon
Auditors: Deloitte & Touche LLP

LOCATIONS

HQ: 4 Tesseneer Dr., Highland Heights, KY 41076
Phone: 859-572-8000   **Fax:** 859-572-8458
Web: www.generalcable.com

General Cable operates 36 facilities in 9 countries worldwide.

2001 Sales

	$ mil.	% of total
US	1,147	69
Europe	321	19
Other regions	183	12
Total	**1,651**	**100**

PRODUCTS/OPERATIONS

2001 Sales

	$ mil.	% of total
Communications	592	36
Industrial & Specialty	537	32
Energy	522	32
Total	**1,651**	**100**

Selected Products

Communications Cables
Electronics cables
Fiber-optic cables
Telecommunications cables

Industrial and Specialty Cables
High temperature cables
Mining cables
Specialty cables and assemblies

Energy Cables
Power cables
Utility cables

COMPETITORS

Alcatel	Furukawa Electric
Balfour Beatty	Pirelli S.p.A.
Belden	Quabbin Wire
Cable Design Technologies	Southwire
Carlisle Companies	Sumitomo Electric
Coleman Cable	Superior TeleCom
CommScope	Tyco International
Corning	Volex
Encore Wire	

HISTORICAL FINANCIALS & EMPLOYEES

NYSE: BGC FYE: December 31	Annual Growth	12/92	12/93	12/94	12/95	12/96	12/97	12/98	12/99	12/00	12/01
Sales ($ mil.)	9.6%	—	794	898	1,061	1,044	1,135	1,151	2,088	2,698	1,651
Net income ($ mil.)	—	—	(58)	(8)	25	39	53	71	34	(26)	(3)
Income as % of sales	—	—	—	—	2.4%	3.8%	4.7%	6.2%	1.6%	—	—
Earnings per share ($)	—	—	—	—	—	—	1.44	1.90	0.95	(0.79)	(0.06)
Stock price - FY high ($)	—	—	—	—	—	—	26.10	32.93	22.88	12.25	19.24
Stock price - FY low ($)	—	—	—	—	—	—	13.59	11.50	6.44	4.19	4.50
Stock price - FY close ($)	(14.2%)	—	—	—	—	—	24.14	20.50	7.56	4.44	13.10
P/E - high	—	—	—	—	—	—	18	17	24	—	—
P/E - low	—	—	—	—	—	—	9	6	7	—	—
Dividends per share ($)	60.7%	—	—	—	—	—	0.03	0.17	0.20	0.20	0.20
Book value per share ($)	(1.1%)	—	—	—	—	—	3.33	4.81	5.21	3.94	3.19
Employees	11.4%	—	—	—	3,900	4,400	4,700	12,300	8,600	6,700	

STOCK PRICE HISTORY

HIGH/LOW/CLOSE

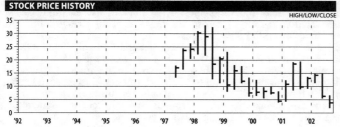

2001 FISCAL YEAR-END

Debt ratio: 80.0%
Return on equity: —
Cash ($ mil.): 17
Current ratio: 1.42
Long-term debt ($ mil.): 421
No. of shares (mil.): 33
Dividends
  Yield: 1.5%
  Payout: —
Market value ($ mil.): 431

GENERAL DYNAMICS CORPORATION

General Dynamics is defending its position in the defense industry and marching on to capitalize on the commercial aircraft market. Through acquisitions, the Falls Church, Virginia-based defense supplier has ventured into systems integration and moved back into aviation. The company operates in four primary areas: marine (warships and nuclear submarines — about 30% of sales), aerospace (business jets — the Gulfstream Aerospace subsidiary accounts for about 25% of sales), information systems and technology (command and control systems — about 25%), and combat systems (tanks and amphibious assault vehicles — about 20%).

General Dynamics derives almost 60% of its revenue from the US government and is the #2 shipbuilder for the US Navy. The company's Bath Iron Works subsidiary builds the Navy's class DDG 51 destroyer and LPD 17 landing craft. Another subsidiary, Electric Boat, builds the Seawolf, Ohio, and Los Angeles class nuclear-attack subs. The Land Systems subsidiary builds the M1 series tank and Abrams armored vehicle.

General Dynamics has been focusing on its commercial aircraft and defense-related electronics operations, but has also expanded into munitions for tanks and other weapons systems. The company's latest bid for rival shipmaker Newport News Shipbuilding (another bid was blocked by the Pentagon in 1999) was thwarted by the Department of Justice, which sued to block General Dynamics' bid on antitrust grounds. General Dynamics then withdrew its bid and Northrop Grumman acquired Newport News. The Crown family controls about 10% of the company, which also lost its bid for the satellite and defense electronics operations of TRW to Northrop Grumman.

In 1899 John Holland founded Electric Boat Company, a New Jersey ship and submarine builder. The company built ships, PT boats, and submarines during WWII, but faced with waning postwar orders, CEO John Jay Hopkins diversified with the 1947 purchase of aircraft builder Canadair. Hopkins formed General Dynamics in 1952, merging Electric Boat and Canadair and buying Consolidated Vultee Aircraft (Convair), a major producer of military and civilian aircraft, in 1954.

Electric Boat launched the first nuclear submarine, the *Nautilus,* in the mid-1950s. In 1955, at the urging of Howard Hughes, Convair began designing its first commercial jetliners. Weakened by the planes' production costs, General Dynamics merged with building-materials supplier Material Service Corporation (1959). Nuclear subs became a mainstay for the company, and it abandoned jetliners in 1961 after losses on the planes reached the staggering sum of $425 million.

During the 1960s General Dynamics developed the controversial F-111 fighter. Despite numerous problems, the aircraft proved financially and militarily successful (F-111s participated in the 1986 US bombing raid on Libya).

In the following years the company won contracts for the US Navy's 688-class attack submarine (1971), liquefied natural gas tankers for the Burmah Oil Company (1972), the Trident ballistic-missile submarine (1974), and the F-16 lightweight fighter aircraft (1975). The company sold Canadair in 1976 and bought Chrysler Defense, which had a contract to build the US Army's new M1 tank, in 1982.

The company bought Cessna Aircraft in 1986. The next year it won a contract to design and build the upper stage of the Titan IV space-launch rocket. Facing defense cuts, General Dynamics sold off pieces of the company: In 1992 it sold Cessna Aircraft to Textron and sold its missile operations to Hughes Aircraft; its electronics business was sold to The Carlyle Group in 1993. The company sold its space-systems business to Martin Marietta in 1994.

The next year General Dynamics began a buying spree with the purchase of shipbuilder Bath Iron Works. In 1996 it added Teledyne's combat vehicle unit, followed in 1997 by Lockheed Martin's Defense Systems and Armament Systems units and defense electronics units from Ceridian and Lucent. Also that year Nicholas Chabraja, director of Ceridian and former general counsel for General Dynamics, became CEO. In 1998 General Dynamics acquired National Steel and Shipbuilding to gain a major naval shipyard on the West Coast. In 1999 it bought business-jet maker Gulfstream Aerospace, which accounts for almost all of the company's commercial-aircraft sales.

In 2000 General Dynamics agreed to acquire Saco Defense Corp., a maker of small- and medium-caliber machine guns and cannon barrels, from New Colt Holding. Early in 2001 the company bought munitions maker Primex Technologies. The company also acquired Galaxy Aerospace, thus adding midsize aircraft to its Gulfstream lineup.

In October General Dynamics' bid for Newport News lost out when the Defense Department approved Northrop Grumman's rival bid and the US Department of Justice sued to stop General Dynamics' acquisition attempt on antitrust grounds. Shortly afterwards General Dynamics withdrew its bid.

OFFICERS

Chairman and CEO: Nicholas D. Chabraja, age 59, $3,050,000 pay
EVP and Group Executive, Aerospace; President and COO, Gulfstream Aerospace: W. William Boisture Jr., age 57, $950,000 pay
EVP and Group Executive, Combat Systems and Resources: Arthur J. Veitch, age 56
EVP and Group Executive, Information Systems and Technology: Kenneth C. Dahlberg, age 56, $950,000 pay
EVP and Group Executive, Marine Systems: John K. Welch, age 51
SVP and CFO: Michael J. Mancuso, age 59, $925,000 pay
SVP, General Counsel, and Secretary: David A. Savner, age 58, $775,000 pay
SVP, Human Resources and Administration: Walter M. Oliver, age 56
Auditors: KPMG LLP

LOCATIONS

HQ: 3190 Fairview Park Dr., Falls Church, VA 22042
Phone: 703-876-3000   **Fax:** 703-876-3125
Web: www.gendyn.com

2001 Sales

	% of total
US	
Government	60
Commercial	30
Other countries	
Commercial	6
Government	4
Total	**100**

PRODUCTS/OPERATIONS

2001 Sales & Operating Income

	Sales $ mil.	Sales % of total	Operating Income $ mil.	Operating Income % of total
Marine Systems	3,612	30	310	21
Aerospace	3,265	27	625	42
Information Systems & Technology	2,800	23	260	18
Combat Systems	2,210	18	238	16
Other	276	2	52	3
Total	**12,163**	**100**	**1,485**	**100**

Selected Operations

Advanced Technology Systems
Armament Systems
Bath Iron Works Corp.
Communications Systems
Defense Systems
Electric Boat Corp.
Electronics Systems
General Dynamics Defense Systems, Inc.
Gulfstream Aerospace
Information Systems
Land Systems
National Steel and Shipbuilding Company
Ordnance and Tactical Systems
Worldwide Telecommunications Systems

COMPETITORS

Airbus
Boeing
Bombardier
Dassault Aviation
EDS
Harris Corp
Harsco
ITT Industries
L-3 Communications
Lockheed Martin
Newport News
Northrop Grumman
Peugeot
Raytheon
Renco
Textron
Titan
United Defense Industries
Westwood

HISTORICAL FINANCIALS & EMPLOYEES

NYSE: GD FYE: December 31	Annual Growth	12/92	12/93	12/94	12/95	12/96	12/97	12/98	12/99	12/00	12/01
Sales ($ mil.)	14.9%	3,472	3,187	3,058	3,067	3,581	4,062	4,970	8,959	10,356	12,163
Net income ($ mil.)	1.6%	815	885	238	321	270	316	364	880	901	943
Income as % of sales	—	23.5%	27.8%	7.8%	10.5%	7.5%	7.8%	7.3%	9.8%	8.7%	7.8%
Earnings per share ($)	(7.0%)	8.93	2.13	1.76	1.95	2.13	2.50	2.86	4.36	4.48	4.65
Stock price - FY high ($)	—	19.21	25.19	23.81	31.50	37.75	45.75	62.00	75.44	79.00	96.00
Stock price - FY low ($)	—	9.50	18.41	19.00	21.19	28.50	31.56	40.25	46.19	36.25	60.50
Stock price - FY close ($)	17.6%	18.45	23.06	21.75	29.56	35.38	43.38	59.00	52.75	78.00	79.64
P/E - high	—	5	12	13	16	18	18	22	17	18	20
P/E - low	—	2	8	11	11	13	13	14	10	8	13
Dividends per share ($)	15.6%	0.37	12.95	0.68	0.74	0.81	0.82	0.65	0.94	1.02	1.36
Book value per share ($)	4.5%	15.15	9.41	10.45	12.39	13.58	15.22	17.51	15.75	19.05	22.56
Employees	(1.0%)	56,800	30,500	24,200	27,700	23,100	29,000	31,000	43,400	43,300	51,700

STOCK PRICE HISTORY

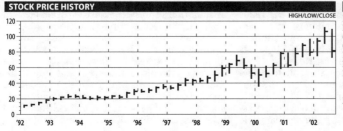

HIGH/LOW/CLOSE

2001 FISCAL YEAR-END

Debt ratio: 13.8%
Return on equity: 22.6%
Cash ($ mil.): 442
Current ratio: 1.07
Long-term debt ($ mil.): 724
No. of shares (mil.): 201
Dividends
  Yield: 1.7%
  Payout: 29.2%
Market value ($ mil.): 15,987

GENERAL ELECTRIC COMPANY

From jet engines to TV broadcasting to power plants, General Electric (GE) is plugged in to several of the businesses that have shaped the modern world. The Fairfield, Connecticut-based conglomerate is one of the largest US companies by sales.

GE's operating segments include aircraft engines (it vies with Rolls-Royce and Pratt & Whitney for industry leadership), consumer products (appliances and lighting), industrial products and systems (electrical distribution and control equipment, diesel-electric locomotives), plastics, power systems (gas turbines, steam turbine-generators, nuclear reactors), and technical products and services (medical imaging systems, data management). Its National Broadcasting Company (NBC) is a major US TV network. GE combined its appliances and lighting units to form GE Consumer Products in 2002.

GE's financial services businesses (formerly GE Capital), which provide consumer and business financing, contributes nearly half of GE's overall sales. In a move intended to provide a clearer picture for investors, GE Capital has been divided into four units — GE Commercial Finance, GE Consumer Finance, GE Equipment Management, and GE Insurance.

Jeff Immelt, formerly president and CEO of GE Medical Systems, has taken over for longtime CEO Jack Welch. For now, at least, Immelt is expected to push forward with Welch's main initiatives: to continue expanding GE outside the US; to build the service businesses tied to many of its products; and to do more business on the Web.

HISTORY

General Electric (GE) was established in 1892 in New York, the result of a merger between Thomson-Houston and Edison General Electric. Charles Coffin was GE's first president, and Thomas Edison, who left the company in 1894, was one of the directors.

GE's financial strength (backed by the Morgan banking house) and its research focus contributed to its initial success. Early products included such Edison legacies as lightbulbs, elevators, motors, toasters, and other appliances under the GE and Hotpoint labels. In the 1920s GE joined AT&T and Westinghouse in a radio broadcasting venture, Radio Corporation of America (RCA), but GE sold off its RCA holdings in 1930 because of an antitrust ruling.

By 1980 GE had reached $25 billion in revenues from plastics, consumer electronics, nuclear reactors, and jet engines. But it had become rigid and bureaucratic. Jack Welch became president in 1981 and shook up the company. He decentralized operations and adopted a strategy of pursuing only high-achieving ventures and dumping those that didn't perform. GE shed air-conditioning (1982), housewares (1984), and semiconductors (1988), and with the proceeds acquired Employers Reinsurance (1984); RCA, including NBC (1986, but sold RCA in 1987); CGR medical equipment (1987); and investment banker Kidder, Peabody (1990).

In the early 1990s GE grew its lighting business. It bought mutual fund wholesaler GNA in 1993, and GE Investment Management (now GE Financial Network) began selling mutual funds to the public.

GE sold scandal-plagued Kidder, Peabody to Paine Webber in 1994. General Electric Capital Services (GECS) expanded its lines, buying Amex Life Insurance (Aon's Union Fidelity unit) and Life Insurance Co. of Virginia in 1995 and First Colony the next year. The company sold its struggling GEnie online service in 1996 and formed an NBC and Microsoft venture, the MSNBC cable news channel.

In 1997 GE acquired Lockheed Martin's medical imaging unit. That next year GECS became the first foreign company to enter Japan's life insurance market when it bought assets from Toho Mutual Life Insurance and set up GE Edison Life.

In 1999 GECS bought the 53% of Montgomery Ward it didn't already own, along with the retailer's direct marketing arm, as Montgomery Ward emerged from bankruptcy. (Ward declared bankruptcy again in 2000.) Later in 2000 the company announced its biggest acquisition of the Welch era. Moving in at the last minute, GE trumped a rival bid from United Technologies and agreed to pay $45 billion in stock for manufacturing giant Honeywell International and to assume $3.4 billion in Honeywell debt.

Welch, by then viewed as one of the best corporate leaders in the US, had agreed to postpone his retirement from April 2001 until the end of that year in order to oversee the completion of the Honeywell acquisition. But European regulators, concerned about the potential strength of the combined GE-Honeywell aircraft-related businesses, blocked the Honeywell deal that summer. Welch then stepped down, and Jeff Immelt, formerly president and CEO of GE Medical Systems, succeeded him in September 2001.

Also in 2001, GE Capital expanded by buying commercial lender Heller Financial for $5.3 billion. That next year GE Industrial Systems acquired electronic security company Interlogix. GE Power Systems purchased Panametrics, a manufacturer of ultrasonic testing equipment for the oil and gas industry, and GE Industrial Systems purchased Kilsen, a fire protection systems manufacturer. Also in 2002 GE Capital was split into four units in order to provide greater transparency to investors. Later that same year, GE Appliances and GE Lighting were combined to form a new business unit, GE Consumer Products.

OFFICERS

Chairman and CEO: Jeffrey R. Immelt, age 46, $6,250,000 pay
Vice Chairman; Chairman, GE Capital Services: Dennis D. Dammerman, age 56, $6,100,000 pay
Vice Chairman; President and CEO, National Broadcasting Company: Robert C. Wright, $5,725,000 pay
Vice Chairman: Gary L. Rogers, age 57, $3,191,304 pay
SVP Finance and CFO: Keith S. Sherin, age 43
SVP, General Counsel, and Secretary: Benjamin W. Heineman Jr., age 58, $3,475,000 pay
SVP Human Resources: William J. Conaty, age 56
Auditors: KPMG LLP

LOCATIONS

HQ: 3135 Easton Tpke., Fairfield, CT 06431
Phone: 203-373-2211   **Fax:** 203-373-3131
Web: www.ge.com

2001 Sales

	$ mil.	% of total
US	89,876	67
Europe	23,878	18
Asia/Pacific	11,447	8
Other regions	8,963	7
Adjustments	(8,485)	—
Total	**125,679**	**100**

PRODUCTS/OPERATIONS

2001 Sales

	$ mil.	% of total
GE Capital Services	58,353	45
Power systems	20,211	16
Industrial products & systems	11,647	9
Aircraft engines	11,389	9
Technical products & services	9,011	7
Materials	7,069	6
Appliances	5,810	4
NBC (broadcasting)	5,769	4
Adjustments	(3,580)	—
Total	**125,679**	**100**

COMPETITORS

Agilent Technologies
AIG
ALSTOM
Bank of America
Caterpillar
CIGNA
CIT Group
Cooper Industries
Electrolux AB
FINOVA
General Motors
GeneralCologne Re
Hitachi
ITT Industries
Johnson Controls
Matsushita
Maytag
News Corp.
Philips Electronics
Polaroid
Raytheon
Rockwell Automation
Rohm and Haas
Rolls-Royce
Siemens
Sony
Textron
ThyssenKrupp
Time Warner Entertainment
Toshiba
United Technologies
U.S. Industries
Viacom
Walt Disney
Washington Group
Whirlpool

HISTORICAL FINANCIALS & EMPLOYEES

NYSE: GE FYE: December 31	Annual Growth	12/92	12/93	12/94	12/95	12/96	12/97	12/98	12/99	12/00	12/01
Sales ($ mil.)	9.3%	56,274	59,827	59,316	69,276	78,541	88,540	99,820	110,832	129,417	125,679
Net income ($ mil.)	12.5%	4,725	4,315	4,726	6,573	7,280	8,203	9,296	10,717	12,735	13,684
Income as % of sales	—	8.4%	7.2%	8.0%	9.5%	9.3%	9.3%	9.3%	9.7%	9.8%	10.9%
Earnings per share ($)	12.9%	0.46	0.41	0.46	0.64	0.72	0.82	0.93	1.07	1.27	1.37
Stock price - FY high ($)	—	7.28	8.91	9.14	12.18	17.67	25.50	34.61	53.11	60.50	53.55
Stock price - FY low ($)	—	6.06	6.73	7.49	8.30	11.57	15.96	22.98	31.32	41.63	28.50
Stock price - FY close ($)	21.2%	7.12	8.73	8.49	11.99	16.46	24.43	33.97	51.53	47.94	40.08
P/E - high	—	16	18	20	19	24	31	36	49	47	38
P/E - low	—	13	13	16	13	16	19	24	29	32	20
Dividends per share ($)	14.4%	0.19	0.21	0.25	0.27	0.31	0.35	0.40	0.47	0.55	0.64
Book value per share ($)	10.3%	2.28	2.51	2.58	2.96	3.15	3.51	3.96	4.31	5.08	5.52
Employees	3.3%	231,000	222,000	221,000	222,000	239,000	276,000	293,000	340,000	313,000	310,000

STOCK PRICE HISTORY

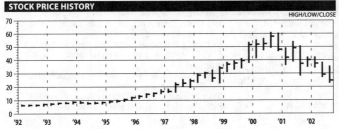

HIGH/LOW/CLOSE

2001 FISCAL YEAR-END

Debt ratio: 59.3%
Return on equity: 26.0%
Cash ($ mil.): 9,082
Current ratio: 1.71
Long-term debt ($ mil.): 79,806
No. of shares (mil.): 9,926
Dividends
  Yield: 1.6%
  Payout: 46.7%
Market value ($ mil.): 397,832

GENERAL MILLS, INC.

In the cereal races, General Mills is stuck behind Kellogg. It had the lead, but fell behind when it stopped to pick up the Pillsbury Doughboy. The Minneapolis-based food producer's Big G Cereals unit includes such brands as Cheerios, Total, and Wheaties. However, the company still has plenty of leaders with Betty Crocker's Gold Medal flour, baking mixes, side dish mixes, and Hamburger Helper. Its snack lineup includes Chex Mix, Pop Secret microwave popcorn, and fruit snacks; it also makes Yoplait and Colombo yogurts. General Mills operates a food service division and holds international joint ventures with PepsiCo and Nestlé.

On a smaller scale, its Small Planet subsidiary markets natural foods brands Muir Glen and Cascadian Farms. General Mills' purchase of Pillsbury doubled the company's size, making it one of the world's largest food companies with expanded frozen and refrigerated foods businesses.

HISTORY

Cadwallader Washburn built his first flour mill in 1866 in Minneapolis, which eventually became the Washburn Crosby Company. After winning a gold medal for flour at an 1880 exposition, the company changed the name of its best flour to Gold Medal Flour.

In 1921 advertising manager Sam Gale created fictional spokeswoman Betty Crocker so that correspondence to housewives could go out with her signature. The firm introduced Wheaties cereal in 1924. James Bell, named president in 1925, consolidated the company with other US mills in 1928 to form General Mills, the world's largest miller. The companies operated independently of one another, with corporate headquarters coordinating advertising and merchandising.

General Mills began introducing convenience foods such as Bisquick (1931) and Cheerios (1941). During WWII it produced war goods such as ordnance equipment and developed chemical and electronics divisions.

When Edwin Rawlings became CEO in 1961, he closed half of the flour mills and divested such unprofitable lines as electronics. This cost $200 million in annual sales but freed resources for such acquisitions as Kenner Products (toys, 1967) and Parker Brothers (board games, 1968), which made General Mills the world's largest toy company.

Through the next 20 years the company made many acquisitions, including Gorton's (frozen seafood, 1968), Monet (jewelry, 1968), Eddie Bauer (outerwear, 1971), and The Talbots (women's clothing, 1973). It bought Red Lobster in 1970 and acquired the US rights to Yoplait

yogurt in 1977. When the toy and fashion divisions' profits fell in 1984, they were spun off as Kenner Parker Toys and Crystal Brands (1985). Reemphasizing food in 1989, the firm sold many businesses, including Eddie Bauer and Talbots.

To expand into Europe, General Mills struck two important joint ventures: Cereal Partners Worldwide (with Nestlé in 1989) and Snack Ventures Europe (with PepsiCo in 1992).

As part of a cereal price war, in 1994 the company cut coupon promotion costs by $175 million and lowered prices on many cereals. But some retailers did not pass on the price cuts to consumers due to shortages that developed after the FDA found an unauthorized pesticide in some cereals. General Mills destroyed 55 million boxes of cereal at a cost of $140 million. Stephen Sanger became CEO in 1995. That year the company sold Gorton's to Unilever and spun off its restaurant businesses as Darden Restaurants.

Focused on a food-only future, in the late 1990s the company picked up several smaller businesses, including Ralcorp Holdings' Chex cereal and snack lines and Gardetto's Bakery snack mixes, as well as the North American rights to Olibra, an appetite suppressant food additive made by Scotia Holdings. Entering the natural foods market in 2000, General Mills launched Sunrise organic cereal and bought organic foods producer Small Planet Foods.

Big changes came in 2001 when General Mills became the #1 cereal maker in the US, overtaking Kellogg for the first time since 1906. The company then completed its $10.5 billion purchase of Pillsbury from Diageo in October 2001. A month later General Mills sold competing product lines to International Multifoods. Also that year the company launched a joint venture with DuPont to develop soy foods marketed under the 8th Continent brand.

While busily integrating Pillsbury, in 2002 General Mills saw its income fall and watched as Kellogg regained the lead in the cereal market.

OFFICERS

Chairman and CEO: Stephen W. Sanger, age 56,
$1,725,506 pay
Vice Chairman: Stephen R. Demeritt, age 58,
$1,008,107 pay
Vice Chairman: Raymond G. Viault, age 58,
$1,104,943 pay
EVP and CFO: James A. Lawrence, age 49, $836,031 pay
SVP; CEO, Cereal Partners Worldwide:
Kendall J. Powell
SVP; President, Bakeries and Foodservice Division:
S. Paul Oliver
SVP; President, Big G Division: Ian R. Friendly
SVP; President, General Mills Foundation:
Christina L. Shea

SVP; President, International: Lucio Rizzi, age 59
SVP; President, Meals Division: Christopher D. O'Leary
SVP; President, Pillsbury USA: Peter B. Robinson
SVP; President, Snacks Unlimited: Peter J. Capell
SVP, Consumer Food Sales and Channel Development:
Jeffrey J. Rotsch, age 52
**SVP, Convenient Food Solutions, Bakeries and
Foodservice:** John T. Machuzick
**SVP, Corporate Affairs, General Counsel, and
Secretary:** Siri S. Marshall, age 54, $601,375 pay
SVP, Corporate Relations: Austin P. Sullivan Jr.
SVP, Financial Operations: Kenneth L. Thome, age 54
SVP, Human Resources and Corporate Services:
Michael A. Peel, age 52
SVP, Innovation, Technology, and Quality:
Danny L. Strickland, age 53
SVP, Strategic Technology Development:
Rory A. Delaney, age 57
Auditors: KPMG LLP

LOCATIONS

HQ: 1 General Mills Blvd., Minneapolis, MN 55426
Phone: 763-764-7600   **Fax:** 763-764-7384
Web: www.generalmills.com/corporate

General Mills has operations throughout the US and
Canada. Its products can be found in more than 100
markets worldwide.

2002 Sales

	$ mil.	% of total
US	7,139	90
Other countries	810	10
Total	**7,949**	**100**

PRODUCTS/OPERATIONS

2002 Sales

	$ mil.	% of total
US Retail		
Big G Cereals	1,866	23
Meals	1,161	15
Yogurt & health	815	10
Pillsbury USA	793	10
Baking products	786	10
Snacks	722	9
Bakeries & food service	1,028	13
International	778	10
Total	**7,949**	**100**

Selected Brand Names

Betty Crocker (baking products)
Bisquick (baking mixes)
Cheerios (cereal)
Chex (cereal)
Chex Mix (snack mix)
Cinnamon Toast Crunch (cereal)
Cocoa Puffs (cereal)
Gold Medal (flour)
Green Giant (canned and frozen vegetables)
Lucky Charms (cereal)
Pop Secret (microwave popcorn)
Progresso (soups)
Total (cereal)
Totino's (frozen pizza)
Wheaties (cereal)
Yoplait (yogurt)

COMPETITORS

Aurora Foods
Campbell Soup
Chelsea Milling
ConAgra
Danone
Del Monte Foods
Frito-Lay
Gilster-Mary Lee
International Multifoods
Kellogg
King Arthur Flour
Kraft Foods
Malt-O-Meal
Mars
McKee Foods
Procter & Gamble
Pro-Fac
Quaker Foods
Ralcorp
Stonyfield Farm

HISTORICAL FINANCIALS & EMPLOYEES

NYSE: GIS FYE: Last Sunday in May	Annual Growth	5/93	5/94	5/95	5/96	5/97	5/98	5/99	5/00	5/01	5/02
Sales ($ mil.)	(0.3%)	8,135	8,517	5,027	5,416	5,609	6,033	6,246	6,700	7,078	7,949
Net income ($ mil.)	(1.1%)	506	470	367	476	445	422	535	614	665	458
Income as % of sales	—	6.2%	5.5%	7.3%	8.8%	7.9%	7.0%	8.6%	9.2%	9.4%	5.8%
Earnings per share ($)	(1.6%)	1.55	1.48	1.17	1.47	1.38	1.30	1.70	2.00	2.28	1.34
Stock price - FY high ($)	—	37.06	34.38	32.31	30.25	34.38	39.13	42.34	43.94	46.35	52.86
Stock price - FY low ($)	—	31.00	24.94	24.69	25.19	26.00	30.00	29.59	29.38	31.38	41.60
Stock price - FY close ($)	3.8%	32.63	27.38	25.94	28.69	31.63	34.13	40.19	39.69	42.36	45.50
P/E - high	—	24	23	28	20	24	29	24	21	20	38
P/E - low	—	20	17	21	17	18	22	17	14	13	30
Dividends per share ($)	3.0%	0.84	0.94	0.94	0.72	1.02	1.06	1.08	1.10	1.10	1.10
Book value per share ($)	7.2%	3.80	3.63	0.45	0.97	1.55	0.61	0.54	(1.01)	0.18	7.12
Employees	(14.4%)	121,290	125,700	9,882	9,800	10,200	10,200	10,660	11,077	11,001	29,859

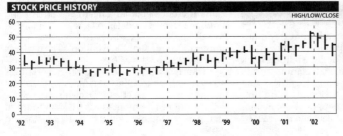

STOCK PRICE HISTORY
HIGH/LOW/CLOSE

2002 FISCAL YEAR-END

Debt ratio: 61.0%
Return on equity: 25.2%
Cash ($ mil.): 975
Current ratio: 0.60
Long-term debt ($ mil.): 5,591
No. of shares (mil.): 502
Dividends
  Yield: 2.4%
  Payout: 82.1%
Market value ($ mil.): 22,841

GENERAL MOTORS CORPORATION

In 1952 former General Motors President Charles E. Wilson stood before the Armed Services Committee and said, "What is good for the country is good for General Motors, and what's good for General Motors is good for the country." Fifty years later, it's still difficult to argue with success. General Motors (GM) remains the world's #1 maker of cars and trucks. Detroit-based GM's North American brands include Buick, Cadillac, Chevrolet, GMC, Oldsmobile, Pontiac, and Saturn. The company also markets vehicles worldwide under the Holden, Opel, Saab, and Vauxhall nameplates. As with rival Ford, GM is trying to better focus its own mega-bureaucratic operations by spinning off noncore units. It has spun off parts maker Delphi Corporation, but its plans to sell Hughes Electronics to EchoStar Communications were blocked by the Federal Communications Commission (FCC).

Even without vehicle sales, GM would boast a formidable array of businesses. Hughes Electronics makes communications equipment such as the digital satellite system for DIRECTV television; GMAC offers financing and insurance; Allison Transmission makes heavy-duty transmissions; and GM Locomotive Group makes train locomotives and components.

After its market share slipped 30% in a decade, GM consolidated its North American car and truck operations to cut costs and is phasing out its weak-selling Oldsmobile nameplate. The company also is pursuing the Asian market, where its goal is to have a 10% share by 2004. To that end, it purchased 20% stakes in Fuji Heavy Industries (Subaru) and Suzuki, and agreed to purchase a 42% stake in South Korea's bankrupt Daewoo Motor for $251 million (with Daewoo's creditors holding much of the rest). GM has entered the Daewoo deal with partner Suzuki (which is taking a 15% stake), and another partner that has yet to be named. Daewoo will help give GM an inroad to the largely closed South Korean car market while creating new opportunities in China.

GM also has a 20% stake in Fiat; in exchange, the Italian company has a 5.6% GM stake, which makes it GM's largest shareholder.

HISTORY

In the early years of the auto industry, hundreds of carmakers each produced a few models. William Durant, who bought a failing Buick Motors in 1904, reasoned that manufacturers could benefit from banding together, and formed the General Motors Company in Flint, Michigan, in 1908. Durant bought 17 companies (including Oldsmobile, Cadillac, and Pontiac) by

1910, the year a bankers' syndicate forced him to step down. In 1915 he regained control when he formed a company with racecar driver Louis Chevrolet. General Motors created the GM Acceptance Corporation (financing) and bought businesses including Frigidaire (sold 1979) and Hyatt Roller Bearing.

With Hyatt came Alfred Sloan (president, 1923-37), who built GM into a corporate colossus via a decentralized management system. GM offered a range of models and colors; by 1927 it was the industry leader. It bought Vauxhall Motors (UK, 1925), merged with Adam Opel (Germany, 1931), added defense products for WWII, and diversified into home appliances and locomotives.

GM spent much of the 1970s making its cars meet federal pollution-control mandates. Under CEO Roger Smith GM laid off thousands of workers. In 1984 GM formed NUMMI with Toyota to see if Toyota's manufacturing techniques would work in the US. GM also bought Electronic Data Systems (1984), Hughes Aircraft (1986), and 50% of Saab Automobile (1989).

GM launched the Saturn car in 1990; that year Robert Stempel became CEO. In 1992 GM made what was the largest stock offering in US history and raised $2.2 billion, and Jack Smith replaced Stempel as CEO.

GM spun off Electronic Data Systems in 1996. That next year it sold the defense electronics business of Hughes Electronics to Raytheon and merged Hughes' auto parts business with Delphi Automotive Systems (now Delphi Corp.).

UAW walkouts at two Michigan GM parts plants in 1998 forced the shutdown of virtually all of the company's North American production lines. In 1999 GM spun off Delphi and boosted its stake in small-truck partner Isuzu to 49%. The following year GM acquired the 50% of Saab Automobile that it didn't already own (from Investor AB) and acquired a 20% stake in Fiat Auto in exchange for a 5.6% Fiat stake in GM.

President Rick Wagoner replaced Smith as CEO in June 2000; Smith remained chairman. In 2001 GM paid about $600 million to double its stake in Suzuki to 20%. That year GM submitted a bid to take over Daewoo Motor. Later in 2001 GM announced that it planned to discontinue the once-popular Chevrolet Camaro and Pontiac Firebird models. In October GM agreed to sell Hughes Electronics to EchoStar Communications for about $26 billion. (The deal was later blocked by the FCC.)

In April 2002 after on-and-off negotiations stretching back to 1998, GM finally inked a deal to buy certain assets of Daewoo Motor for $251 million. Two months later GM announced that partner Suzuki would take a 15% stake in

Daewoo. A third stakeholder in the GM-led Daewoo partnership has yet to be named.

Isuzu and GM decided to revamp their relationship in August 2002. In Isuzu's new business plan GM will write off its entire stake in the company, then inject Isuzu with $84 million in cash. The deal will reduce GM's stake in Isuzu from 49% to 12%. GM will assume a larger share of US-based joint venture DMAX Ltd., and obtain a stake in Isuzu's Polish operations.

OFFICERS

Chairman: John F. Smith Jr., age 64, $1,452,000 pay
Vice Chairman and CFO: John M. Devine, age 58, $2,950,000 pay
Vice Chairman Product Development; Chairman, GM North America: Robert A. Lutz, age 70, $983,333 pay
President, CEO, and Director: G. Richard Wagoner Jr., age 49, $2,784,000 pay
EVP; Chairman and President, General Motors Acceptance Corporation: John D. Finnegan, age 53, $1,000,000 pay
EVP Law and Public Policy: Thomas A. Gottschalk, age 59
Group VP; President, GM Asia Pacific: Frederick A. Henderson, age 43
Group VP; President, GM Europe: Michael J. Burns, age 50
Group VP; President, GM Latin America, Africa, and Middle East: V. Maureen Kempston Darkes, age 53
Group VP; President, GM North America: Gary L. Cowger, age 55
Auditors: Deloitte & Touche LLP

LOCATIONS

HQ: 300 Renaissance Center, Detroit, MI 48265
Phone: 248-556-5000　　**Fax:** 248-874-2760
Web: www.gm.com

2001 Sales

	$ mil.	% of total
North America		
US	132,004	75
Canada & Mexico	11,769	7
Europe	25,897	14
Latin America	5,138	3
Other regions	2,452	1
Total	**177,260**	**100**

PRODUCTS/OPERATIONS

2001 Sales

	$ mil.	% of total
Manufactured products	151,491	85
Financial services	25,769	15
Total	**177,260**	**100**

Selected Brands

Buick	Hummer	Pontiac
Cadillac	Isuzu	Saab
Chevrolet	Opel and	Saturn
GMC	Vauxhall	Subaru

COMPETITORS

BMW	Honda	Renault
DaimlerChrysler	Kia Motors	Suzuki Motor
Fiat	Mazda	Toyota
Ford	Nissan	Volkswagen
Fuji Heavy Ind.	Peugeot	

HISTORICAL FINANCIALS & EMPLOYEES

NYSE: GM FYE: December 31	Annual Growth	12/92	12/93	12/94	12/95	12/96	12/97	12/98	12/99	12/00	12/01
Sales ($ mil.)	3.6%	128,533	133,622	150,592	163,861	158,015	166,445	154,018	167,369	184,632	177,260
Net income ($ mil.)	—	(23,498)	2,466	4,901	6,881	4,963	6,698	2,956	6,002	4,452	601
Income as % of sales	—	—	1.8%	3.3%	4.2%	3.1%	4.0%	1.9%	3.6%	2.4%	0.3%
Earnings per share ($)	—	(31.92)	1.80	5.15	7.21	6.06	8.70	4.18	9.18	6.68	1.77
Stock price - FY high ($)	—	37.01	47.64	54.52	44.31	49.52	60.41	63.96	79.13	94.62	67.80
Stock price - FY low ($)	—	23.87	26.69	30.13	31.07	38.16	43.58	39.25	57.70	48.44	39.17
Stock price - FY close ($)	6.8%	26.90	45.77	35.13	44.10	46.50	50.67	59.68	72.69	50.94	48.60
P/E - high	—	—	26	9	6	8	7	15	8	14	38
P/E - low	—	—	15	5	4	6	5	9	6	7	22
Dividends per share ($)	6.1%	1.17	0.66	0.66	0.93	1.32	1.68	1.26	1.68	2.00	2.00
Book value per share ($)	11.6%	5.09	4.13	11.65	18.06	18.30	25.24	22.88	20.02	21.20	13.72
Employees	(7.7%)	750,000	710,800	728,000	745,000	647,000	608,000	594,000	388,000	386,000	365,000

STOCK PRICE HISTORY

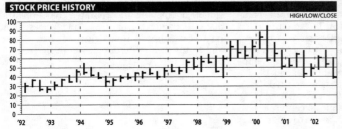

HIGH/LOW/CLOSE

2001 FISCAL YEAR-END

Debt ratio: 89.3%
Return on equity: 2.4%
Cash ($ mil.): 18,555
Current ratio: 3.02
Long-term debt ($ mil.): 163,912
No. of shares (mil.): 1,437
Dividends
　Yield: 4.1%
　Payout: 113.0%
Market value ($ mil.): 69,816

GENUINE PARTS COMPANY

What do spark plugs, hydraulic hoses, note pads, and magnet wire have in common? They're all Genuine Parts. Atlanta-based Genuine Parts Company (GPC) is the largest member of the National Automotive Parts Association (NAPA), a voluntary trade association that distributes auto parts nationwide. Through more than 60 distribution centers, GPC distributes more than 300,000 parts to about 5,000 NAPA Auto Parts stores in the US, including about 850 company-owned outlets. It also serves about 650 corporate and associate resellers in Canada and distributes parts in Mexico through a joint venture with Grupo Auto Todo. GPC's Rayloc division rebuilds automotive parts.

In addition to the automotive market, GPC distributes industrial replacement parts, including bearings, belts, and hoses for transmissions and hydraulic equipment. With nine distribution centers, the division serves more than 500 branches in the US, Mexico, and Canada.

GPC also distributes office products through S. P. Richards, one of the oldest office supply wholesalers in the country. The division has three proprietary brands: Sparco, Nature Saver, and Compucessory. Another subsidiary, EIS, manufactures and distributes electronic and electrical products such as copper foil, magnet wire, and thermal management materials.

HISTORY

Genuine Parts Company (GPC) got its start in Atlanta in 1928 when Carlyle Fraser bought a small auto parts store. That year GPC had the only loss in its history. Three years earlier a group that included Fraser had founded the National Automotive Parts Association (NAPA), an organization of automotive manufacturers, remanufacturers, distributors, and retailers.

The Depression was a boon for GPC because fewer new-car sales meant more sales of replacement parts. During the 1930s GPC's sales rose from less than $350,000 to more than $3 million. One tool it developed to spur sales during the Depression was its monthly magazine, *Parts Pups*, which featured pretty girls and corny jokes (discontinued in the 1990s). GPC acquired auto parts rebuilder Rayloc in 1931 and established parts distributor Balkamp in 1936.

WWII boosted sales at GPC because carmakers were producing for the war effort, but scarce resources limited auto parts companies to producing functional parts. GPC went public in 1948.

The postwar boom in car sales boosted GPC's sales in the 1950s and 1960s. It expanded during this period with new distribution centers across the country. GPC bought Colyear Motor Sales (NAPA's West Coast distributor) in 1965 and introduced a line of filters and batteries in 1966 that were the first parts to carry the NAPA name.

GPC moved into Canada in 1972 when it bought Corbetts, a Calgary-based parts distributor. That acquisition included Oliver Industrial Supply. During the mid-1970s GPC began to broaden its distribution businesses, adding S. P. Richards (office products, 1975) and Motion Industries (industrial replacement parts, 1976). In the late 1970s GPC acquired Bearing Specialty and Michigan Bearing as part of Motion Industries. In 1982 the company introduced its now familiar blue-and-yellow NAPA logo. Canadian parts distributor UAP (formerly United Auto Parts) and GPC formed a joint venture, UAP/NAPA, in 1988, with GPC acquiring a 20% stake in UAP.

During the 1990s GPC diversified its product lines and its geographic reach. Its 1993 acquisition of Berry Bearing made the company a leading distributor of industrial parts. The next year GPC formed a joint venture with Grupo Auto Todo of Mexico.

NAPA formed an agreement in 1995 with Penske Corporation to be the exclusive supplier of auto parts to nearly 900 Penske Auto Centers. GPC purchased Horizon USA Data Supplies that year, adding computer supplies to S. P. Richards' product mix.

A string of acquisitions in the late 1990s increased GPC's industrial distribution business (including Midcap Bearing, Power Drives & Bearings, and Amarillo Bearing).

GPC paid $200 million in 1998 for EIS, a leading wholesale distributor of materials and supplies to the electrical and electronics industries. Late in 1998, after a 10-year joint venture, it bought the remaining 80% of UAP it didn't already own. GPC continued to expand its auto parts distribution network in 1999, acquiring Johnson Industries, an independent distributor of auto supplies for large fleets and car dealers. GPC also acquired Oklahoma City-based Brittain Brothers, a NAPA distributor that serves about 190 auto supply stores in Arkansas, Missouri, Oklahoma, and Texas.

In 2000 the company bought a 15% interest in Mitchell Repair Information (MRIC), a subsidiary of Snap-on Incorporated that provides diagnostic and repair information services. That next year Johnson Industries acquired Coach and Motors, a distribution center in Detroit.

OFFICERS

Chairman and CEO: Larry L. Prince, age 63, $1,057,643 pay
President, COO, and Director: Thomas C. Gallagher, age 54, $750,926 pay
EVP, Finance: Jerry W. Nix, age 56, $234,000 pay
EVP: Robert J. Breci
EVP: George W. Kalafut, age 67, $416,769 pay
SVP, Human Resources: Edward J. Van Stedum, age 52
SVP, Information Technology: G. Thomas Braswell
SVP, Market Development: Robert J. Susor
VP, Corporate Counsel: Scott C. Smith
VP and Corporate Secretary: Carol B. Yancey
VP, Risk Management and Employee Services: R. Bruce Clayton
VP, Planning and Acquisitions: Treg S. Brown
VP and Treasurer: Frank M. Howard
Auditors: Ernst & Young LLP

LOCATIONS

HQ: 2999 Circle 75 Pkwy., Atlanta, GA 30339
Phone: 770-953-1700 **Fax:** 770-956-2211
Web: www.genpt.com

Genuine Parts Company has operations throughout much of the US and in Canada and Mexico.

2001 Sales

	$ mil.	% of total
Automotive	4,253	52
Industrial	2,234	27
Office products	1,380	17
Electrical/electronic materials	387	4
Other	(33)	—
Total	**8,221**	**100**

PRODUCTS/OPERATIONS

2001 Sales

	$ mil.	% of total
United States	7,526	91
Canada	629	8
Mexico	99	1
Other	(33)	—
Total	**8,221**	**100**

Selected Operations

Balkamp, Inc. (majority-owned subsidiary; distributes replacement parts and accessories for cars, heavy-duty vehicles, motorcycles, and farm equipment)
EIS, Inc. (branch locations in 36 US cities and Mexico; products for electrical and electronic equipment, including adhesives, copper foil, and thermal management materials)
Grupo Auto Todo SA de CV (joint venture, distribution and stores, Mexico)
Johnson Industries (auto supply distribution)
Horizon USA Data Supply, Inc. (computer supplies)
Motion Industries, Inc.
S. P. Richards Company (44 distribution centers in 28 states and Canada, office products)
UAP Inc. (auto parts distribution, Canada)

COMPETITORS

Advance Auto Parts
Applied Industrial Technologies
Arrow Electronics
AutoZone
Avnet
Boise Office Solutions
CARQUEST
Ford
General Motors
General Parts
Graybar Electric
Hahn Automotive
Hillman Companies
Ingersoll-Rand
United Stationers

HISTORICAL FINANCIALS & EMPLOYEES

NYSE: GPC FYE: December 31	Annual Growth	12/92	12/93	12/94	12/95	12/96	12/97	12/98	12/99	12/00	12/01
Sales ($ mil.)	9.4%	3,669	4,384	4,858	5,262	5,721	6,005	6,614	7,982	8,370	8,221
Net income ($ mil.)	3.4%	220	258	289	309	330	342	356	378	385	297
Income as % of sales	—	6.0%	5.9%	5.9%	5.9%	5.8%	5.7%	5.4%	4.7%	4.6%	3.6%
Earnings per share ($)	3.3%	1.28	1.38	1.55	1.68	1.81	1.90	1.98	2.11	2.20	1.71
Stock price - FY high ($)	—	23.18	26.01	26.26	28.01	31.68	35.88	38.25	35.75	26.69	37.94
Stock price - FY low ($)	—	19.34	21.93	22.43	23.68	26.68	28.68	28.25	22.25	18.25	23.91
Stock price - FY close ($)	5.5%	22.68	25.10	24.01	27.35	29.68	33.94	33.44	24.81	26.19	36.70
P/E - high	—	18	19	17	17	17	19	19	17	12	22
P/E - low	—	15	16	14	14	15	15	14	11	8	14
Dividends per share ($)	6.2%	0.66	0.70	0.75	0.82	0.88	0.94	0.99	1.03	1.09	1.13
Book value per share ($)	7.3%	7.19	7.76	8.30	9.03	9.62	10.39	11.44	12.28	13.11	13.52
Employees	6.0%	18,400	18,400	21,285	22,500	24,200	24,500	32,000	33,000	33,000	31,000

STOCK PRICE HISTORY

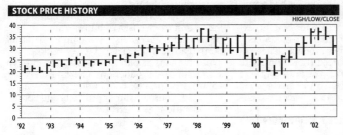

HIGH/LOW/CLOSE

2001 FISCAL YEAR-END

Debt ratio: 26.3%
Return on equity: 12.9%
Cash ($ mil.): 86
Current ratio: 3.42
Long-term debt ($ mil.): 836
No. of shares (mil.): 173
Dividends
  Yield: 3.1%
  Payout: 66.1%
Market value ($ mil.): 6,366

GEORGIA-PACIFIC CORPORATION

As its name implies, Georgia-Pacific (GP) operates from sea to shining sea. The Atlanta-based company is the world's #2 forest products company (behind International Paper). That is changing, however, as GP readies to spin off its consumer products and packaging company as CP&P, Inc.

CP&P's operations will include paper towels (Brawny, Green Forest), toilet paper (Quilted Northern, Angel Soft), plates and cups (Dixie), paper, and packaging businesses. GP retains its plywood, lumber, oriented strand board, gypsum wallboard, particleboard, and wood-bonding adhesives operations. GP is also selling a 60% stake in Unisource Worldwide, a giant distributor of printing and imaging paper. (Investment firm Bain Capital is paying about $850 million for the unit, which GP will use to pay down debt.)

GP's plan to spin off its consumer products operations sprung from its acquisition of Fort James and the company's belief that investors were undervaluing its stock. Fort James (Brawny, Mardi Gras, Quilted Northern, and Dixie brands) gave GP about 40% of the North American tissue market. The decision should shelter its consumer operations from exposure to asbestos litigation related to GP's ongoing building operations. GP's building products and distribution businesses account for just over 50% of sales.

HISTORY

Owen Cheatham founded lumber wholesaler Georgia Hardwood Lumber Company in Augusta, Georgia, in 1927. By 1938 the company was operating five southern sawmills, and during WWII it became the largest lumber supplier to the US armed forces.

Recognizing the potential of plywood, Cheatham bought several plywood mills in the late 1940s, including one in Bellingham, Washington (idled in 2000 because of high energy costs). He began a land-buying spree in 1951 that gave Georgia Hardwood its first timberlands. The company moved its headquarters to Oregon three years later, and in 1957 it adopted the name Georgia-Pacific. By 1960 it had a million acres of timberland.

During the 1960s Georgia-Pacific bought several competitors and diversified into containers, paperboard, tissue, and other products. The Federal Trade Commission forced the company to sell 20% of its assets in 1972. The following year Georgia-Pacific bought Boise Cascade's wood products operations, and in 1975 it acquired Exchange Oil and Gas.

Georgia-Pacific continued to diversify into chemicals in 1976 and introduced cheaper plywood substitutes, such as waferboard. It acquired southern timberland and modernized existing paper mills. In 1979 Georgia-Pacific bought Hudson Pulp and Paper and reached $5 billion in sales. The company returned to Georgia in 1982. Two years later Georgia-Pacific decided to sell most of its chemical operations unrelated to forest products.

In 1988 Georgia-Pacific bought Brunswick Pulp and Paper in Georgia, which increased its southern timber holdings. It purchased Great Northern Nekoosa (pulp and paper) in 1990 (later sold to Bowater).

Georgia-Pacific sold its envelope-making business to the Sterling Group in 1994; it also sold its roofing manufacturing line. In 1995 the pulp and paper industry rebounded from several sluggish years, allowing for price increases and higher profit yields. The trend was short-lived, however.

Georgia-Pacific more than doubled its gypsum production capacity in 1996 by purchasing nine wallboard plants from Domtar (construction materials). The following year Georgia-Pacific Corporation created separate stocks for its timber and building products businesses.

In 1998 Georgia-Pacific purchased CeCorr (corrugated sheets). The company paid $1.2 billion in 1999 for North America's #1 paper distributor, Unisource Worldwide, trumping a previous agreement that Unisource had with propane distributor UGI. Also in 1999, Georgia-Pacific and Chesapeake combined their tissue-making businesses into the Georgia-Pacific Tissue joint venture (95% owned by Georgia-Pacific).

The following year the company announced that it would acquire Fort James Corp. for $7.7 billion. Days later Georgia-Pacific announced that it was selling The Timber Company to Plum Creek Timber in a deal worth around $4 billion. Also in 2000 Georgia-Pacific and other commercial tissue makers, including Kimberly-Clark and Fort James, agreed to pay $56.2 million to settle allegations of price-fixing. The acquisition of Fort James was completed in November after Georgia-Pacific agreed to sell its Georgia-Pacific Tissue commercial tissue unit to satisfy regulators.

In 2001 Georgia-Pacific sold its commercial tissue unit (to Svenska Cellulosa) and four of its US pulp and paper mills (to Domtar for $1.65 billion). It also announced that it would close three gypsum plants as part of a decision to cut gypsum wallboard production in North America by 45%. Early in 2002 GP announced that it was spinning off its consumer products and packaging operations as CP&P, Inc.

Chairman and CEO: Alston D. Correll, age 61
President, Building Products and Distribution:
Lee M. Thomas, age 58
EVP and CFO: James E. Moylan Jr., age 50
EVP, Chief Administrative Officer, and General Counsel: James F. Kelley, age 60
EVP, Human Resources: Patricia A. Barnard, age 53
EVP, Wood Procurement, Gypsum, and Industrial Wood Products: John F. Rasor, age 59
EVP, Wood Products and Distribution: Ronald L. Paul, age 59
EVP, Environmental, Government Affairs, and Communications: James E. Bostic Jr., age 55
President, Unisource: Charles C. Tufano, age 57
VP and Controller, Georgia-Pacific Corporation:
James E. Terrell, age 52
President, Building Products Distribution, Georgia-Pacific Corporation: Charles H. McElrea, age 51
President, Chemical, Georgia-Pacific Corporation:
Mario Concha, age 61
President, Fluff Pulp, Georgia-Pacific Corporation:
W. Wesley Jones, age 47
President, Gypsum, Georgia-Pacific Corporation:
David R. Fleiner, age 55
President, Industrial Wood Products, Georgia-Pacific Corporation: H. Elliott Savage, age 50
Auditors: Ernst & Young LLP

LOCATIONS

HQ: 133 Peachtree St., Atlanta, GA 30303
Phone: 404-652-4000   **Fax:** 404-230-1674
Web: www.gp.com

Georgia-Pacific Group has more than 400 facilities in North America and Europe.

PRODUCTS/OPERATIONS

2001 Sales

	$ mil.	% of total
Bleached pulp & paper	8,713	33
Building products	7,784	30
Consumer products	7,138	27
Packaging	2,610	10
Adjustments	(1,229)	—
Total	**25,016**	**100**

Selected Products

Bath tissue	Fluff pulp
Bleached board	Gypsum products
Bleached paperboard	Kraft paper
Chemicals	Lumber
Communication papers	Market pulp
Containerboard	Napkins
Corrugated containers and packaging	Packaging
	Paper towels
Disposable tableware (plates, cups, cutlery)	Tissue
	Wood panels

COMPETITORS

Boise Cascade
Bowater
Gaylord Container
International Paper
Kimberly-Clark
Smurfit-Stone Container
Weyerhaeuser

HISTORICAL FINANCIALS & EMPLOYEES

NYSE: GP FYE: December 31	Annual Growth	12/92	12/93	12/94	12/95	12/96	12/97	12/98	12/99	12/00	12/01
Sales ($ mil.)	8.7%	11,847	12,330	12,738	14,292	13,024	12,968	13,223	17,796	22,218	25,016
Net income ($ mil.)	—	(124)	(34)	310	1,018	156	(146)	98	716	343	(407)
Income as % of sales	—	—	—	2.4%	7.1%	1.2%	—	0.7%	4.0%	1.5%	—
Earnings per share ($)	—	(0.72)	(0.20)	1.73	5.59	0.86	(0.80)	0.54	4.07	1.94	(2.10)
Stock price - FY high ($)	—	25.63	26.70	28.12	34.09	28.84	38.65	40.50	54.13	51.94	37.65
Stock price - FY low ($)	—	17.18	19.58	20.20	23.41	22.43	25.10	18.69	29.34	19.31	25.39
Stock price - FY close ($)	2.4%	22.21	24.48	25.45	24.43	25.63	30.38	29.28	50.75	31.13	27.61
P/E - high	—	—	—	15	6	32	—	65	13	27	—
P/E - low	—	—	—	11	4	25	—	30	7	10	—
Dividends per share ($)	(5.1%)	0.80	0.80	0.80	0.95	1.00	1.00	0.50	0.38	0.50	0.50
Book value per share ($)	4.6%	14.23	13.30	14.48	19.27	19.26	19.27	18.54	21.78	24.70	21.32
Employees	10.5%	—	—	—	—	45,500	46,500	45,000	59,400	80,000	75,000

STOCK PRICE HISTORY

HIGH/LOW/CLOSE

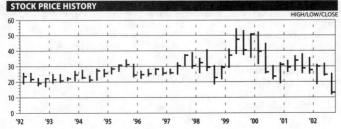

2001 FISCAL YEAR-END

Debt ratio: 67.6%
Return on equity: —
Cash ($ mil.): 31
Current ratio: 0.94
Long-term debt ($ mil.): 10,221
No. of shares (mil.): 230
Dividends
  Yield: 1.8%
  Payout: —
Market value ($ mil.): 6,353

THE GILLETTE COMPANY

Is Warren Buffett a blade man, or does he use a shaver? Either way, The Gillette Company (of which Buffett's Berkshire Hathaway owns around 9%) has what he needs. Boston-based Gillette is the world's #1 maker of shaving supplies for men and women. Buffett's shopping list might also include an Oral-B toothbrush and dental floss, Right Guard deodorant, Duracell batteries, and Braun shavers and small appliances.

Gillette casts a giant shadow worldwide; about 60% of its sales are made outside the US. The firm maintains the top spot in each of its markets with bold advertising campaigns and vigorous research and development operations. Wal-Mart accounts for about 12% of Gillette's sales. The company has sold its stationery and hair care lines of products.

HISTORY

King Gillette, a salesman for the Baltimore Seal Company, originated the idea of a disposable razor blade in 1895 in Brookline, Massachusetts. For the next six years, Gillette developed his idea yet could find no backers. Finally, in 1901 MIT machinist William Nickerson joined Gillette and perfected the safety razor. With the financial support of some wealthy friends, the two men formed The Gillette Safety Razor Company in Boston.

Gillette put his razor on the market in 1903 but sold only 51 sets. The good news spread fast, however, and the next year Gillette Safety Razor sold 90,844 sets. Gillette established his first overseas operation in London in 1905. Five years later Gillette sold most of his interest in the business (he remained president of the company until 1931) to pursue his utopian corporate theories, first described in his 1894 book, *The Human Drift*.

The company introduced self-shaving to a generation of young men by selling shaving kits to the US military during WWI. In the 1920s Gillette Safety Razor distributed free razors through such outlets as banks (via the "Shave and Save" plan) and boxes of Wrigley's gum, winning millions of new customers. Foreign expansion continued, and by 1923 business overseas accounted for 30% of the firm's sales.

In 1939 Gillette Safety Razor paid $100,000 to obtain the radio broadcast rights for the World Series, initiating its practice of advertising during sporting events. The company began diversifying in 1948 by purchasing Toni (home permanent kits), which became the Personal Care Division in 1971. In the 1950s it adopted its present name, The Gillette Company; introduced Foamy (shaving cream, 1953); and bought Paper Mate (pens, 1955).

During the 1960s and 1970s product expansion continued (Right Guard deodorant, Cricket disposable lighters, Eraser Mate pens). It also acquired Braun, maker of electric shavers and appliances, in 1967 and Liquid Paper in 1979. In 1984 Gillette branched into dental care products with the purchase of Oral-B.

In 1989 Warren Buffett's Berkshire Hathaway acquired 11% of the company's stock (later reduced to approximately 9%). In the 1990s Gillette found success in foreign markets; it made acquisitions, but only in sectors where it could operate as the #1 or #2 player. It bought the Parker pen business in 1993 and in 1996 added Duracell, the #1 battery maker.

In 1998 the firm unveiled the triple-bladed Mach3 razor, which quickly became the #1 US razor. Despite that success, tough foreign sales hurt profits in 1998. As a result, the company cut jobs and closed factories. COO Michael Hawley became CEO in 1999 and immediately threatened to dump weak divisions if logistical improvements didn't boost results.

True to Hawley's word, Gillette sold its hair care business (White Rain, Dippity-Do, Toni) in 2000 to health and household products company Diamond Products. The company, frustrated by back-to-back years of earnings disappointments, abruptly fired Hawley in October; president and COO Edward DeGraan was named acting CEO and Richard Pivirotto was named chairman. Before the end of the year, the company announced it would cut 8% of its workforce (2,700 jobs) in a restructuring effort to cut costs and improve cash flow.

In January 2001 Gillette sold its underperforming stationery products business (Paper Mate, Parker, Waterman, and Liquid Paper brands) to Newell Rubbermaid. Former Nabisco president and CEO James Kilts took over as chairman and CEO in February 2001; acting CEO DeGraan (a candidate for the permanent job) stayed on as president and COO. Kilts slashed costs and boosted marketing of major brands.

OFFICERS

Chairman and CEO: James M. Kilts, age 54, $2,197,917 pay
President, COO, and Director: Edward F. DeGraan, age 58, $1,139,375 pay
SVP Corporate Affairs: John F. Manfredi, age 61
SVP Finance and CFO: Charles W. Cramb, age 55, $750,000 pay
SVP Human Resources: Edward E. Guillet, age 50
SVP Strategy and Business Development: Peter Klein, age 56
SVP and CIO: Kathy S. Lane, age 44
SVP and General Counsel: Richard K. Willard, age 53, $660,000 pay

VP Business Development and Strategic Projects:
Patrick F. Graham
VP Corporate Communications: Eric A. Kraus
VP Corporate Investor Relations:
Christopher M. Jakubik
VP, Global Supply Chain and Business Development:
Michael Cowhig
VP New Business Development: Michelle E. Viotty
VP and Controller: Claudio E. Ruben, age 54
VP; President, Blades and Razors - Global Business:
Peter K. Hoffman, age 53, $615,000 pay
VP; President, Commercial Operations, International:
Ernst A. Haberli
VP; President, Commercial Operations, North America:
Joseph F. Dooley, age 48
VP, President, Duracell - Global Business Management:
Mark M. Leckie, age 48
**VP; President, Oral Care - Global Business
Management:** A. Bruce Cleverly, age 56
VP; President, Personal Care Products: Joseph Scalzo,
age 43
Auditors: KPMG LLP

LOCATIONS

HQ: Prudential Tower Bldg., Boston, MA 02199
Phone: 617-421-7000　　**Fax:** 617-421-7123
Web: www.gillette.com

The Gillette Company sells its products in more than
200 countries and territories and manufactures them at
34 locations in 15 countries.

2001 Sales

	$ mil.	% of total
US	3,757	42
Other countries	5,204	58
Total	**8,961**	**100**

PRODUCTS/OPERATIONS

2001 Sales

	$ mil.	% of total
Blades & razors	3,416	39
Duracell products	2,365	26
Braun products	1,033	11
Personal care	877	10
Oral care	1,270	14
Total	**8,961**	**100**

Selected Brand Names
Atra (razors)
Braun Flex (men's electric
　shavers)
Braun Oral-B (electric
　plaque removers)
CrossAction (toothbrush)
Dry Idea (antiperspirant)
Duracell (batteries)
Foamy (shaving cream)
Gillette for Women
　(razors)

Gillette Series (men's
　toiletries)
Good News (razors)
Mach3 (razors)
Oral-B (toothpaste and
　dental products)
Right Guard (deodorant)
Sensor (razors)
Sensor for Women (razors)
Soft & Dri (antiperspirant)
Trac II (razors)

COMPETITORS

American Safety Razor
A. T. Cross
BIC
Bristol-Myers Squibb
Colgate-Palmolive
Dial
Energizer Holdings
Johnson & Johnson
MedPointe
Perrigo
Pfizer

Philips Electronics
Procter & Gamble
Rayovac
Remington Products
SANYO
S.C. Johnson
SEB
Shiseido
Sunbeam
Unilever

HISTORICAL FINANCIALS & EMPLOYEES

NYSE: G FYE: December 31	Annual Growth	12/92	12/93	12/94	12/95	12/96	12/97	12/98	12/99	12/00	12/01
Sales ($ mil.)	6.3%	5,163	5,411	6,070	6,795	9,698	10,062	10,056	9,897	9,295	8,961
Net income ($ mil.)	6.6%	513	288	698	824	949	1,427	1,081	1,260	392	910
Income as % of sales	—	9.9%	5.3%	11.5%	12.1%	9.8%	14.2%	10.7%	12.7%	4.2%	10.2%
Earnings per share ($)	4.5%	0.58	0.25	0.82	0.95	0.83	1.25	0.95	1.14	0.37	0.86
Stock price - FY high ($)	—	15.31	15.94	19.13	27.69	38.88	53.19	62.66	64.38	43.00	36.38
Stock price - FY low ($)	—	10.97	11.84	14.44	17.69	24.13	36.00	32.25	33.06	27.13	24.50
Stock price - FY close ($)	10.0%	14.22	14.91	18.72	26.06	38.88	50.22	47.81	41.19	36.13	33.40
P/E - high	—	26	41	23	29	45	42	65	56	116	42
P/E - low	—	19	30	17	18	28	28	34	29	73	28
Dividends per share ($)	15.3%	0.18	0.21	0.25	0.29	0.35	0.42	0.50	0.57	0.64	0.65
Book value per share ($)	2.0%	1.70	1.67	2.28	2.83	4.04	4.32	4.11	2.87	1.83	2.02
Employees	0.2%	30,900	33,400	32,800	33,500	44,100	44,000	43,100	39,800	35,200	31,500

STOCK PRICE HISTORY

HIGH/LOW/CLOSE

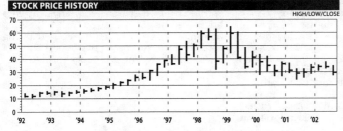

2001 FISCAL YEAR-END

Debt ratio: 43.6%
Return on equity: 44.8%
Cash ($ mil.): 947
Current ratio: 0.92
Long-term debt ($ mil.): 1,654
No. of shares (mil.): 1,056
Dividends
　Yield: 1.9%
　Payout: 75.6%
Market value ($ mil.): 35,270

GOLDEN WEST FINANCIAL

Golden West Financial has got the whole World in its plans. The Oakland, California-based company is the parent of World Savings Bank, the #2 US thrift behind Washington Mutual and just ahead of its rival from across San Francisco Bay, Golden State Bancorp. The company has more than 250 banking branches scattered across nearly 10 states, and some 330 loan production offices nationwide.

Herbert and Marion Sandler, the husband-and-wife team that runs Golden West, have kept it financially healthy by sticking to the unglamorous business of providing deposit accounts and making home loans. Golden West also owns investment management subsidiaries Atlas Advisers and Atlas Securities, which sell insurance and administer and distrubute the company's proprietary Atlas mutual funds.

As many of its savings and loan cousins become more commercial, Golden West remains committed to its bread and butter — earnings from originating and investing in residential loans. The thrift is increasing its short-term adjustable-rate mortgages to take advantage of decreased competition. These loans may also provide some cushion to the company's margins when the Federal Reserve ratchets up interest rates again.

The Sandlers own approximately 10% of Golden West; Marion's brother, Bernard Osher, holds nearly an additional 5%.

HISTORY

World Savings and Loan Association was founded in 1912 as a stock savings and loan (S&L) association. In 1959 Trans-World Financial Co. was incorporated as its parent. The company chugged along until 1963, when Herbert and Marion Sandler bought it. Herbert was a lawyer who had worked with financial institutions and Marion was a securities analyst.

Trans-World went public in 1968. Seven years later it merged with Golden West Financial, parent of Golden West Savings & Loan. The resulting holding company took the Golden West name, but the S&Ls became World Savings and Loan. In 1982 Golden West acquired First S&L Shares and its subsidiary, Majestic Savings & Loan.

During the 1970s and into the 1980s, when many S&Ls were whipsawed by soaring interest rates and a legacy of low fixed-rate mortgages, Golden West concentrated on the pedestrian business of collecting savings deposits and making primarily single-family mortgage loans.

When S&Ls were deregulated in the early 1980s, many institutions ill-advisedly rushed into commercial real estate. Golden West was

there to pick up the pieces when regulators closed the erstwhile high-fliers. In 1985 the company moved into Texas with the acquisition of the failed Bell Savings Banc.

Golden West continued to buy pieces of defunct S&Ls, gaining good loans and deposits while the government retained the bad loans. Such acquisitions included all or part of Blue Valley Federal Savings (Missouri, 1990), American Savings (Colorado, 1990), Security Savings (Arizona, 1991), and Beach Federal Savings (Florida, 1991). These deals helped the company expand nationally at low cost. The Beach Federal Savings deal, for example, involved the acquisition of $1.5 billion in assets for $40 million.

When the recession came to California in the early 1990s, many of Golden West's competitors were devastated by real estate defaults. The company's earnings slipped as well, but because it had little exposure to commercial real estate, it remained strong enough to expand in Arizona (where the thrift and banking industry was wracked by failures). Golden West bought the Arizona operations of PriMerit Bank (seven branches) in 1993 and acquired selected deposits the next year from Polifly Savings & Loan, which extended its operations to New Jersey.

Golden West took advantage of new regulations that favored banks over S&Ls, buying Watchung Hills Bank for Savings (New Jersey), renaming it World Savings Bank, and opening bank branches on some of its S&L premises in California, Colorado, and New Jersey.

Meanwhile, back in California, the economy was looking up. Residential real estate roared back and Golden West rose with its market, more than doubling earnings in 1997 because of improved business, lower reserves for loan losses, and lower deposit insurance premiums. The trend continued through 1998 when the local housing market jump-started the demand for mortgages.

Suffering from stock downturns caused by fear of a Federal Reserve interest rate hike, Golden West repurchased 5% of its stock in 1999. When interest rates did climb, the bank watched its loan originations decline that year and into 2000. Later that year the company merged World Savings and Loan Association into World Savings Bank. The company's fortunes brightened the following year, due to a strong housing market and a mortgage refinancing boom that was spurred by the Fed's slashing of rates an unprecedented 11 times during 2001.

OFFICERS

Co-Chairman and Co-CEO, Golden West Financial and World Savings Bank: Herbert M. Sandler, age 70, $1,245,829 pay
Co-Chairman and Co-CEO, Golden West Financial and World Savings Bank: Marion O. Sandler, age 71, $1,245,829 pay
President, Treasurer, and CFO; SEVP and CFO, World Savings Bank: Russell W. Kettell, age 58, $680,247 pay
SEVP; President and COO, World Savings Bank, FSB and World Savings Bank, FSB (Texas): James T. Judd, age 63, $756,274 pay
EVP, General Counsel, and Secretary: Michael Roster, age 56, $398,596 pay
Group SVP, Golden West Financial, World Savings Bank, FSB, and World Savings Bank, FSB (Texas): Carl Andersen, age 41
Director Human Resources: Susan Lennox
Auditors: Deloitte & Touche LLP

LOCATIONS

HQ: Golden West Financial Corporation
1901 Harrison St., Oakland, CA 94612
Phone: 510-446-4000   **Fax:** 510-446-4259
Web: www.gdw.com

Golden West Financial has banking and lending operations in Arizona, California, Colorado, Florida, Illinois, Kansas, Nevada, New Jersey, and Texas, with additional lending operations in Connecticut, Delaware, Georgia, Idaho, Indiana, Kentucky, Maryland, Massachusetts, Michigan, Minnesota, Missouri, New Mexico, New York, North Carolina, Ohio, Oklahoma, Oregon, Pennsylvania, Rhode Island, South Dakota, Tennessee, Utah, Virginia, Washington, Wisconsin, and Wyoming.

PRODUCTS/OPERATIONS

2001 Sales

	$ mil.	% of total
Interest		
Loans	2,740	62
Mortgage-backed securities	1,276	29
Investments	193	4
Noninterest		
Fees	151	3
Other	86	2
Total	**4,446**	**100**

Selected Subsidiaries
Atlas Advisers, Incorporated
Atlas Agency, Incorporated
Atlas Securities, Incorporated
World Mortgage Investors, Incorporated
World Savings Bank, FSB
World Savings Incorporated

COMPETITORS

Bank of America	J.P. Morgan Chase
Bank of the West	Prudential
BANK ONE	Silicon Valley Bancshares
Citigroup	SunTrust
Countrywide Credit	UnionBanCal
FleetBoston	U.S. Bancorp
FMR	Washington Mutual
Golden State Bancorp	Wells Fargo

HISTORICAL FINANCIALS & EMPLOYEES

NYSE: GDW FYE: December 31	Annual Growth	12/92	12/93	12/94	12/95	12/96	12/97	12/98	12/99	12/00	12/01
Assets ($ mil.)	9.5%	25,891	28,829	31,684	35,118	37,731	39,590	38,469	42,142	55,704	58,586
Net income ($ mil.)	12.4%	284	274	230	235	165	354	435	480	546	813
Income as % of assets	—	1.1%	1.0%	0.7%	0.7%	0.4%	0.9%	1.1%	1.1%	1.0%	1.4%
Earnings per share ($)	14.6%	1.49	1.43	1.24	1.31	0.93	2.04	2.51	2.87	3.41	5.07
Stock price - FY high ($)	—	15.40	16.77	15.32	19.15	22.89	32.61	38.13	38.38	70.50	70.90
Stock price - FY low ($)	—	11.82	12.36	11.41	11.57	16.32	19.61	23.25	28.89	26.88	45.02
Stock price - FY close ($)	16.9%	14.44	12.99	11.74	18.40	21.02	32.57	30.53	33.50	67.50	58.85
P/E - high	—	10	12	12	14	11	16	15	13	20	14
P/E - low	—	8	9	9	9	8	9	9	10	8	9
Dividends per share ($)	14.0%	0.08	0.09	0.10	0.12	0.13	0.15	0.17	0.19	0.22	0.26
Book value per share ($)	13.2%	9.00	10.76	11.37	12.89	13.65	15.74	18.30	19.80	23.28	27.55
Employees	6.6%	4,019	4,376	4,559	4,461	4,028	4,879	5,289	5,650	6,103	7,138

STOCK PRICE HISTORY

HIGH/LOW/CLOSE

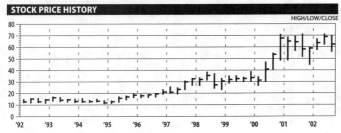

2001 FISCAL YEAR-END

Equity as % of assets: 7.3%
Return on assets: 1.4%
Return on equity: 20.4%
Long-term debt ($ mil.): 798
No. of shares (mil.): 156
Dividends
  Yield: 0.4%
  Payout: 5.1%
Market value ($ mil.): 9,153
Sales ($ mil.): 4,446

THE GOLDMAN SACHS GROUP, INC.

The Goldman Sachs Group may be on top of the financial world now — it is a leader in IPOs in Europe and the US, battling rivals Morgan Stanley Dean Witter and Merrill Lynch — but faced with a cooling economy, how long can the New York City-based investment banker stay there?

The firm's major business lines are Global Capital Markets, which includes trading and principal investments (representing 20% of the firm's sales) and investment banking; and Asset Management and Securities Services, which includes investment management and advice, merchant banking, and institutional brokerage. With its purchase of market makers Spear, Leeds & Kellogg and Benjamin Jacobson & Sons, and more recently TFM Investment Group, the company has become one of the largest specialist firms on the NYSE. Goldman Sachs is also expanding its wealth management operations.

The firm does serve some governments and high net-worth individuals, but unlike rivals that are rushing to diversify operations and income sources, Goldman Sachs has focused almost exclusively on institutional clients. Its reliance on principal transactions could leave it beholden to covering trading losses for those clients should the already cool markets take a more dramatic dip. CEO Hank Paulson is betting that the firm can weather the storm and stay independent despite the wave of consolidation that has swept Wall Street in recent years.

HISTORY

German immigrant-cum-Philadelphia retailer Marcus Goldman moved to New York in 1869 and began buying customers' promissory notes from jewelers to resell to banks. Goldman's son-in-law came aboard in 1882, and the firm became Goldman, Sachs & Co. in 1885.

Two years later Goldman Sachs began offering US-UK foreign exchange and currency services. To serve such clients as Sears, Roebuck, it expanded to Chicago and St. Louis. In 1896 it joined the NYSE.

While the firm increased its European contracts, Goldman's son Henry made it a major source of financing for US industry. In 1906 it co-managed its first public offering, United Cigar Manufacturers (later General Cigar). By 1920 it had underwritten IPOs for Sears, B.F. Goodrich, and Merck.

Sidney Weinberg made partner in 1927 and stayed until his death in 1969. In the 1930s Goldman Sachs entered securities dealing and sales. After WWII it became a leader in investment banking, co-managing Ford's 1956 IPO. In the 1970s it pioneered buying blocks of stock for resale.

Under Weinberg's son John, Goldman Sachs became a leader in mergers and acquisitions. The 1981 purchase of J. Aron gave the firm a significant commodities presence and helped it grow in South America.

Seeking capital after 1987's market crash, Goldman Sachs raised more than $500 million from Sumitomo for a 12% nonvoting interest in the firm (since reduced to 3%). The Kamehameha Schools/Bishop Estate of Hawaii, an educational trust, also invested.

The 1994 bond crash and a decline in new debt issues led Goldman Sachs to cut staffing for the first time since the 1980s. But problems went deeper. Partners began leaving and taking their equity. Cost cuts, a stronger bond market, and the long bull market helped the firm rebound; firm members sought protection through limited liability partnership status. The firm also extended the period during which partners can cash out (slowing the cash drain) and limited the number of people entitled to a share of profits. Overseas growth in 1996 and 1997 focused on the UK and Asia.

After three decades of resistance, the partners in 1998 voted to sell the public a minority stake in the firm, but market volatility led to postponement. Goldman Sachs also suffered from involvement with Long-Term Capital Management, ultimately contributing $300 million to its bailout.

In 1999 Jon Corzine, then co-chairman and co-CEO, announced that he would leave the group after seeing it through its IPO, and Goldman Sachs finally went public that year in an offering valued at close to $4 billion. In 2000 Corzine was elected to a US Senate seat. The New Jersey Democrat spent more than $64 million on his campaign (a record), nearly $61 million of it from his own personal wealth (also a record).

Fortunately, Goldman Sachs did not lose any employees in the September 11 terrorist attacks on the World Trade Center in New York City.

OFFICERS

Chairman and CEO: Henry M. Paulson Jr., age 55, $12,150,500 pay
Vice Chairman: Robert J. Hurst Jr., age 56, $8,528,000 pay
President, Co-COO, and Director: John A. Thain, age 46, $10,544,000 pay
President, Co-COO, and Director: John L. Thornton, age 48, $10,544,000 pay
EVP, General Counsel, and Co-Head of the Legal Department: Gregory K. Palm, age 53

EVP, General Counsel and Co-Head of the Legal Department: Esta E. Stecher, age 44
EVP and CFO: David A. Viniar, age 46, $6,008,000 pay
EVP and CIO: Steve T. Mnuchin, age 39
VP Personnel: Bob Gottlieb
VP and Investment Research Analyst: Brant Thompson
Vice Chairman, Co-Head, Equities, and Co-Head, Fixed Income, Currency, and Commodities: Robert K. Steel
Vice Chairman, Co-Head, Equities, and Co-Head, Fixed Income, Currency, and Commodities: Lloyd C. Blankfein
Vice Chairman and Co-Head, Investment Banking and Investment Management: Robert S. Kaplan, age 44
Vice Chairman, Goldman Sachs International: Mario Draghi
Auditors: PricewaterhouseCoopers LLP

LOCATIONS

HQ: 85 Broad St., New York, NY 10004
Phone: 212-902-1000   **Fax:** 212-902-3000
Web: www.gs.com

2001 Sales

	% of total
North and South America	
US	65
Other countries	1
Europe	
UK	22
Other countries	3
Asia	9
Total	**100**

PRODUCTS/OPERATIONS

2001 Sales

	$ mil.	% of total
Interest	16,620	53
Global Capital Markets		
Trading & principal investments	6,254	20
Investment banking	3,677	12
Asset Management & Securities Services	4,587	15
Total	**31,138**	**100**

Selected Subsidiaries
Goldman, Sachs & Co.
  Goldman Sachs (Asia) Finance Holdings L.L.C.
Goldman Sachs Canada
Goldman Sachs Capital Markets, L.P.
Goldman Sachs Credit Partners, L.P. (Bermuda)
Goldman Sachs Holdings (Netherlands) B.V.
Goldman Sachs (Japan) Ltd. (British Virgin Islands)
Goldman Sachs Mortgage Company
Goldman Sachs (UK) L.L.C.
  Goldman Sachs Holdings (UK)
J. Aron Holdings, L.P.
SLK LLC

COMPETITORS

Bear Stearns	ING
Brown Brothers Harriman	Lehman Brothers
Charles Schwab	Merrill Lynch
CIBC World Markets	Morgan Stanley
Credit Suisse First Boston	Nomura Securities
Credit Suisse First Boston (USA), Inc.	Salomon Smith Barney Holdings
Deutsche Bank	UBS PaineWebber
FMR	

HISTORICAL FINANCIALS & EMPLOYEES

NYSE: GS FYE: Last Friday in November	Annual Growth	11/92	11/93	11/94	11/95	11/96	11/97	11/98	11/99	11/00	11/01
Sales ($ mil.)	9.7%	—	14,848	12,452	14,324	17,289	20,433	22,478	25,363	33,000	31,138
Net income ($ mil.)	20.8%	—	508	1,370	1,348	2,399	2,746	2,428	2,708	3,067	2,310
Income as % of sales	—	—	3.4%	11.0%	9.4%	13.9%	13.4%	10.8%	10.7%	9.3%	7.4%
Earnings per share ($)	(12.5%)	—	—	—	—	—	—	—	5.57	6.00	4.26
Stock price - FY high ($)	—	—	—	—	—	—	—	—	83.00	133.63	120.00
Stock price - FY low ($)	—	—	—	—	—	—	—	—	55.19	65.50	63.27
Stock price - FY close ($)	8.8%	—	—	—	—	—	—	—	75.13	82.13	89.00
P/E - high	—	—	—	—	—	—	—	—	15	21	26
P/E - low	—	—	—	—	—	—	—	—	10	10	14
Dividends per share ($)	41.4%	—	—	—	—	—	—	—	0.24	0.48	0.48
Book value per share ($)	30.1%	—	—	—	—	—	—	—	22.60	36.83	38.28
Employees	13.7%	—	8,103	8,998	8,159	8,977	10,622	14,170	15,361	22,627	22,627

STOCK PRICE HISTORY

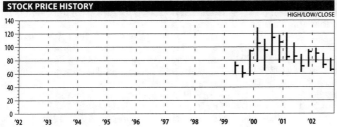

HIGH/LOW/CLOSE

2001 FISCAL YEAR-END
Debt ratio: 63.0%
Return on equity: 13.3%
Cash ($ mil.): —
Current ratio: —
Long-term debt ($ mil.): 31,016
No. of shares (mil.): 476
Dividends
  Yield: 0.5%
  Payout: 11.3%
Market value ($ mil.): 42,384

GOODRICH CORPORATION

Tireless in striving to be good and rich, Goodrich Corporation is a global leader in aerospace systems. The Charlotte, North Carolina-based company, formerly known as BFGoodrich Company, no longer makes tires — it sold its BF-Goodrich tire unit to Michelin a decade ago. The company's aerospace products business, now the focus of the company, comprises four segments: Aerostructures and Aviation Technical Services (about 35% of sales), Landing Systems (almost 30%), Engine and Safety Systems (about 20%), and Electronic Systems. Products include aircraft parts like nacelles and thrust reversers, landing gear, and sensing systems used for navigation and collision avoidance. The company also provides aircraft maintenance and overhaul services. Goodrich's largest customers include Boeing (almost 25% of sales) and Airbus.

Goodrich has sold its performance materials unit, which was struggling against intense competition in the specialty chemical sector. Now, as part of its strategy to focus solely on aerospace operations, the company is spinning off its engineered industrial products unit (air compressors, gas engines, gaskets, spray nozzles, and vacuum pumps) as EnPro Industries and has agreed to acquire TRW Aeronautical Systems from TRW.

HISTORY

Orphan, doctor, Civil War veteran, and entrepreneur Benjamin Franklin Goodrich bought stock in the Hudson River Rubber Co. in 1869 and moved the firm to Akron, Ohio, in 1870. Its rubber products included fire hoses, bottle stoppers, rubber rings for canning jars, and billiard cushions. After the depression of the mid-1870s, the company reorganized as B.F. Goodrich & Co (BFG).

BFG's new uses for rubber galvanized the industry, but it was the advent of rubber tires that secured the company's future. In 1896 bicycle maker Alexander Winton asked BFG to make tires for his "horseless carriage." (A British company named Silvertown had invented the pneumatic tire, and BFG acquired the patent.) As the automobile's popularity grew, BFG continued to improve its tires. It added fabric cords and carbon black to make tires tougher and give them black coloring.

BFG introduced the first rubber sponge in 1902 and began making aircraft tires in 1909 (standard on WWI airplanes). In the 1920s the company added sliding fasteners made by Universal Fastener to its rubber galoshes and began calling the boots "zippers." In 1926 BFG scientists formulated polyvinyl chloride (PVC). The following year the company supplied tires for Charles Lindbergh's *Spirit of St. Louis,* and in the 1930s BFG introduced the first commercial aircraft de-icer.

BFG was at the forefront of the effort to make synthetic rubber, especially after Japan cut the US's supply of natural rubber during WWII. The company's chemicals division was organized in 1943. During the war BFG introduced continuous rubber tracks for tanks, as well as the technology used in pilots' "Mae West" life vests.

The company began selling tubeless tires in 1947, and by the mid-1950s new cars came equipped with the safer tires. In 1956 it formed its aerospace division. A few years later the company provided the space suit worn by Alan Shepard, the first American in space. BFG also made P-F Flyers, sneakers popular with children in the 1960s.

John Ong became chairman in 1979 and reduced the company's dependence on tires. In 1986 BFG and Uniroyal formed the Uniroyal Goodrich Tire Co. When Michelin bought the unit in 1990, BFG was out of the tire business.

BFG sold Geon, its vinyl division, in 1993, and Ong poured the proceeds back into chemical and aerospace businesses. Acquisitions since 1990 include Hercules Aircraft and Electronics Group (1990), Eastern Airlines Avionics (test equipment, 1991), GE Specialty Heating and Avionics Power (heated and electrical components, 1994), Rohr (commercial airline engine nacelles, 1997) and Coltec Industries (aerospace components and engineered industrial products, 1999). David Burner, an executive at BFG since 1983, replaced Ong as chairman in 1997.

In 1999 BFG moved its headquarters from Richfield, Ohio, to Coltec's home — Charlotte, North Carolina. BFG and Boeing agreed in 2000 to cooperate in airplane maintenance and landing-gear overhauling. BFG bought Boeing's airplane ejection-seat maker, IBP Aerospace Group.

Early in 2001 BFGoodrich sold its performance materials operations (industrial plastics and additives) to an investor group for $1.4 billion. In June 2001 the company changed its name to Goodrich Corporation. That same year Goodrich bolstered its aerospace lighting operations with the acquisition of Hella Aerospace GmbH (from privately held Hella KG Hueck & Co.). In late 2001 Goodrich announced that it was closing 16 plants and cutting its workforce by about 10% because of the slowdown in the aircraft manufacturing business.

In 2002 Goodrich paid $1.5 billion in cash for TRW's Aeronautical Systems unit, which manufactures aerospace components and systems.

OFFICERS

Chairman and CEO: David L. Burner, age 62, $2,275,938 pay
President and COO: Marshall O. Larsen, age 53, $1,291,050 pay (prior to promotion)
EVP; President and CEO, BFGoodrich Engineered Industrial Products: Ernest F. Schaub, age 58
EVP; President and COO, BFGoodrich Performance Materials: David B. Price Jr., age 56, $760,250 pay
EVP and CFO: Ulrich Schmidt, age 52
EVP, Human Resources and Administration and General Counsel: Terrence G. Linnert, age 55, $754,737 pay (prior to title change)
SVP, Strategic Resources and Information Technology: Stephen R. Huggins, age 58
SVP, Technology and Innovation: Jerry S. Lee, age 60
VP, Human Resources: Richard C. Driscoll
Auditors: Ernst & Young LLP

LOCATIONS

HQ: 4 Coliseum Centre, 2730 W. Tyvola Rd., Charlotte, NC 28217
Phone: 704-423-7000   **Fax:** 704-423-7100
Web: www.goodrich.com

2001 Sales

	$ mil.	% of total
North America		
US	2,694	65
Canada	177	4
Europe		
France	384	9
Other countries	555	13
Other regions	375	9
Total	**4,185**	**100**

PRODUCTS/OPERATIONS

2001 Sales & Operating Income

	Sales		Operating Income	
	$ mil.	% of total	$ mil.	% of total
Aerostructures & Aviation Technical Services	1,514	36	224	35
Landing Systems	1,149	28	153	24
Engine & Safety Systems	763	18	132	20
Electronic Systems	759	18	135	21
Corporate	—	—	(58)	—
Adjustments	—	—	(94)	—
Merger-related & consolidation costs	—	—	(107)	—
Total	**4,185**	**100**	**385**	**100**

COMPETITORS

Banner Aerospace
Boeing
Crane
General Dynamics
Gulfstream Aerospace
Honeywell International
Lockheed Martin
Meggitt
Northrop Grumman
Raytheon
United Technologies
Vertex Aerospace
Vought Aircraft

HISTORICAL FINANCIALS & EMPLOYEES

NYSE: GR FYE: December 31	Annual Growth	12/92	12/93	12/94	12/95	12/96	12/97	12/98	12/99	12/00	12/01
Sales ($ mil.)	5.8%	2,526	1,818	2,199	2,409	2,239	3,373	3,951	5,538	4,364	4,185
Net income ($ mil.)	—	(296)	128	76	118	152	178	227	170	326	289
Income as % of sales	—	—	7.1%	3.4%	4.9%	6.8%	5.3%	5.7%	3.1%	7.5%	6.9%
Earnings per share ($)	—	(5.96)	(0.37)	0.91	1.34	1.65	2.41	3.02	1.53	3.04	2.76
Stock price - FY high ($)	—	29.06	27.13	24.19	36.31	45.88	48.25	56.00	45.69	43.13	44.50
Stock price - FY low ($)	—	19.44	19.75	19.50	20.81	33.38	35.13	26.50	21.00	21.56	15.93
Stock price - FY close ($)	1.0%	24.44	20.13	21.69	34.00	40.50	41.44	35.88	27.50	36.38	26.62
P/E - high	—	—	—	27	27	28	17	18	30	14	16
P/E - low	—	—	—	21	16	20	13	9	14	7	6
Dividends per share ($)	0.0%	1.10	1.10	1.10	1.35	1.10	1.10	1.10	1.10	1.10	1.10
Book value per share ($)	(2.2%)	16.30	17.53	17.89	16.73	19.53	19.56	21.51	11.73	11.99	13.39
Employees	4.1%	13,375	13,416	13,392	12,287	14,160	16,838	17,175	27,044	22,136	19,200

STOCK PRICE HISTORY

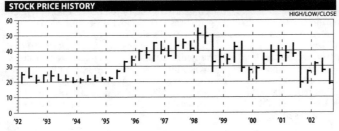

HIGH/LOW/CLOSE

2001 FISCAL YEAR-END

Debt ratio: 49.0%
Return on equity: 22.3%
Cash ($ mil.): 86
Current ratio: 1.66
Long-term debt ($ mil.): 1,307
No. of shares (mil.): 102
Dividends
  Yield: 4.1%
  Payout: 39.9%
Market value ($ mil.): 2,707

GOODYEAR TIRE & RUBBER

Goodyear is #3 in the tire game behind Bridgestone and the Michelin Man. Akron, Ohio-based Goodyear also makes industrial and consumer products from rubber, including belts, hoses, and tire flaps, and it produces organic chemicals and resins. The company operates more than 940 North American retail tire outlets. Goodyear supplies its tire brands (Debica, Dunlop, Fulda, Goodyear, Kelly, and Sava) to automakers and to construction and agricultural equipment makers, as well as to the replacement tire market. Although the company attempted to pass rivals Bridgestone and Michelin to become #1 after acquiring the North American and European Dunlop tire business from Japan's Sumitomo Rubber Industries — the plan has yet to pay off.

Decreasing demand by the US automotive industry has hurt Goodyear's bottom line. In response, the company has cut as many as 10,000 jobs, or 10% of its worldwide workforce. The cuts have decreased Goodyear's annual operating costs by $85 million.

HISTORY

In 1898 Frank and Charles Seiberling founded a tire and rubber company in Akron, Ohio, and named it after Charles Goodyear (inventor of the vulcanization process, 1839). The debut of the Quick Detachable tire and the Universal Rim (1903) made Goodyear the world's largest tire maker by 1916.

Goodyear began manufacturing in Canada in 1910, and over the next two decades it expanded into Argentina, Australia, and the Dutch East Indies. The company established its own rubber plantations in Sumatra (now part of Indonesia) in 1916.

Financial woes led to reorganization in 1921, and investment bankers forced the Seiberlings out. Succeeding caretaker management, Paul Litchfield began three decades as CEO in 1926, a time in which Goodyear had emerged to become the world's largest rubber company.

Goodyear blimps served as floating billboards nationwide by the 1930s. During that decade Goodyear opened company stores, acquired tire maker Kelly-Springfield (1935), and began producing tires made from synthetic rubber (1937). After WWII Goodyear was an innovative leader in technologies such as polyester tire cord (1962) and the bias-belted tire (1967).

By 1980 Goodyear had introduced radial tire brands such as the all-weather Tiempo, the Eagle, and the Arriva, and it led the US market.

Thwarting British financier Sir James Goldsmith's takeover attempt in 1986, CEO Robert Mercer raised $1.7 billion by selling the company's non-tire businesses (Motor Wheel, Goodyear Aerospace) and by borrowing heavily.

Recession, overcapacity, and price-cutting in 1990 led to hard times for tire makers. After suffering through 1990, its first money-losing year since the Depression, Goodyear lured Stanley Gault out of retirement. He ceased marketing tires exclusively through Goodyear's dealer network by selling tires through Wal-Mart, Kmart, and Sears. Gault also cut costs through layoffs, plant closures, and spending reductions and returned Goodyear to profitability in 1991.

The company increased its presence in the US retail market in 1995 when it began selling tires through 860 Penske Auto Centers and 300 Montgomery Ward auto centers. President Samir Gibara succeeded chairman Gault as CEO in 1996. That year Goodyear bought Poland's leading tire maker, T C Debica, and a 60% stake in South African tire maker Contred (acquiring the rest in 1998).

In 1997 Goodyear formed an alliance with Kobe, Japan-based Sumitomo Rubber Industries, under which the companies agreed to make and market tires for one another in Asia and North America. That next year Goodyear sold its Celeron Oil subsidiary, which operated the All American Pipeline, and acquired the remaining 26% stake in tire distributor Brad Ragan.

The company acquired Sumitomo Rubber Industries' North American and European Dunlop tire businesses in 1999. The acquisition returned Goodyear to its #1 position in the tire-making industry. However, the company recorded drastically low profits that year because it had cut tire production and was unable to meet supplier demands.

Goodyear increased tire prices in 2000 and began consolidating its manufacturing operations. Goodyear also announced plans to combine its commercial tire service centers with those of Treadco through a joint venture named Wingfoot Commercial Tire Systems. Despite record sales in 2000, the company's profits hit some hard roads, prompting Goodyear to lay off 10% of its workforce and implement other cost-cutting efforts.

Early in 2001 the company announced that it would close its Mexican tire plant. That same year the company agreed to replace Firestone Wilderness AT tires with Goodyear tires for Ford owners as part of Ford's big Firestone tire recall.

The following year Goodyear announced that it planned to cut 3,000 more jobs to reduce costs. Early in 2002 Goodyear announced that its recent job cuts and manufacturing consolidation resulted in a $85 million decrease in annual operating costs.

OFFICERS

Chairman and CEO: Samir G. Gibara, age 62,
$2,180,675 pay
President, COO, and Director: Robert Keegan, age 54,
$1,392,392 pay
EVP and CFO: Robert W. Tieken, age 62, $743,635 pay
SVP, Business Development and Integration:
Clark E. Sprang, age 59
SVP, Corporate Financial Operations and Treasurer:
Stephanie W. Bergeron, age 48
SVP, General Counsel, and Secretary:
C. Thomas Harvie, age 58, $681,408 pay
SVP, Global Product Supply: Vernon L. Dunkel, age 63
SVP, Human Resources: Kathleen T. Geier, age 45
SVP, Technology and Global Products Planning:
Joseph M. Gingo, age 57
VP and Chief Marketing Officer: Cathryn M. Fischer,
age 40
VP, Finance and Chief Accounting Officer:
Richard J. Kramer, age 38
**VP, Human Resources Planning, Development, and
Change:** Donald D. Harper, age 55
Auditors: PricewaterhouseCoopers LLP

LOCATIONS

HQ: The Goodyear Tire & Rubber Company
1144 E. Market St., Akron, OH 44316
Phone: 330-796-2121 **Fax:** 330-796-2222
Web: www.goodyear.com

2001 Sales

	$ mil.	% of total
US	7,656	54
Other countries	6,491	46
Total	**14,147**	**100**

PRODUCTS/OPERATIONS

2001 Sales

	$ mil.	% of total
Tire Segments		
North American Tire	7,152	49
European Union Tire	3,128	21
Latin American Tire	1,013	7
Eastern Europe, Africa & Middle East Tire	703	5
Asia Tire	494	3
Engineered Products	1,122	8
Chemical Products	1,037	7
Other	19	—
Adjustments	(521)	—
Total	**14,147**	**100**

Selected Products
Aftermarket belts and hoses
Air springs
Chemical products (coating resins, latex polymers, and
rubber chemicals)
Conveyor belts
Industrial hoses
Molded transportation products
Power transmission drive belts
Tires

COMPETITORS

Bandag	Midas
Bridgestone	Pep Boys
Continental AG	Pirelli S.p.A.
Cooper Tire & Rubber	Toyo Tire & Rubber
Michelin	Yokohama Rubber

HISTORICAL FINANCIALS & EMPLOYEES

NYSE: GT FYE: December 31	Annual Growth	12/92	12/93	12/94	12/95	12/96	12/97	12/98	12/99	12/00	12/01
Sales ($ mil.)	2.1%	11,785	11,643	12,288	13,166	13,113	13,155	12,626	12,881	14,417	14,147
Net income ($ mil.)	—	(659)	388	567	611	102	559	682	241	40	(204)
Income as % of sales	—	—	3.3%	4.6%	4.6%	0.8%	4.2%	5.4%	1.9%	0.3%	—
Earnings per share ($)	—	(4.62)	2.64	3.75	3.97	0.65	3.53	4.31	1.52	0.25	(1.27)
Stock price - FY high ($)	—	38.06	47.25	49.25	45.38	53.00	71.25	76.75	66.75	31.63	32.10
Stock price - FY low ($)	—	26.00	32.56	31.63	33.00	41.50	49.25	45.88	25.50	15.60	17.37
Stock price - FY close ($)	(3.9%)	34.19	45.75	33.63	45.38	51.38	63.63	50.44	28.06	22.99	23.81
P/E - high	—	—	14	13	11	80	20	18	43	122	—
P/E - low	—	—	10	8	8	63	14	11	17	60	—
Dividends per share ($)	15.4%	0.28	0.58	0.75	0.95	1.03	1.14	1.20	1.20	1.20	1.02
Book value per share ($)	3.1%	13.36	15.29	18.51	21.38	21.01	21.68	24.02	23.14	22.23	17.55
Employees	0.1%	95,712	91,754	90,712	87,930	88,903	95,472	96,950	100,649	105,128	96,430

STOCK PRICE HISTORY

HIGH/LOW/CLOSE

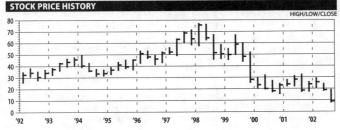

2001 FISCAL YEAR-END

Debt ratio: 52.8%
Return on equity: —
Cash ($ mil.): 959
Current ratio: 1.58
Long-term debt ($ mil.): 3,204
No. of shares (mil.): 163
Dividends
  Yield: 4.3%
  Payout: —
Market value ($ mil.): 3,885

GOODY'S FAMILY CLOTHING, INC.

For shoppers without the money or means to hit Rodeo Drive, Goody's Family Clothing brings moderately priced apparel to small- and medium-sized towns in the Southeast and Midwest. The Knoxville, Tennessee-based retailer sells men's, women's, and children's clothes; accessories; and shoes through more than 330 small department stores in 18 states located mainly in strip centers. Goody's carries brands such as Dockers, Levi's, NIKE, Reebok, Sag Harbor, and Skechers, as well as its own labels (Chandler Hill, GoodKidz, Mountain Lake, and Ivy Crew).

The company had planned an ambitious building schedule, looking to add 10% to its store count per year. However, the weakened economy has led Goody's to cut back on its plan, at least until the economy turns around. Chairman and CEO Robert Goodfriend, the son of the founder, owns about 42% of the company.

HISTORY

M.D. Goodfriend started Athens Outlet Stores in Athens, Tennessee, in 1953 to sell seconds, overstocks, and past-season styles. When his son Robert took over in 1972, the company had 11 stores. Robert overhauled the business, changing its name to Goody's (after his college nickname) Family Clothing and moving the store upmarket by dropping irregulars and spiffing up decor. To differentiate the company from the discount herd, he stocked name-brand items that were frequently hard to get in smaller towns and paid close attention to his clients' lifestyles (such as stocking a wider variety of fancy clothing for a clientele that still dresses up for church).

Goody's Family Clothing went public in 1991. Robert brought in marketing professor Roger Jenkins two years later, and Jenkins hired retail professional George Rubin to take over merchandising; he also assembled a new board of directors. Jenkins and Rubin expanded Goody's casual, trendy choices while narrowing its range of career and formal fashions. But customers didn't want trendy — sales dropped. Robert urged the board to restock its original product mix.

Mired in questionable financial dealings, Robert reduced his power over the board (he owned nearly two-thirds of the stock at the time) and then was fired in 1994. But he returned as CEO in 1995 and removed Jenkins, Rubin, and the rest of the board. He restored the product mix and began aggressive expansion (the company's goal is to increase its store count by about 10% per year), moving the chain west (it entered Texas in 1998) and increasing private-label offerings. In 1999 the chain offered its own credit card to customers through Alliance Data Systems, which handled the network, billing, customer service, and other aspects of the marketing plan. Also that year the company began stocking and operating the shoe departments in its stores after Shoe Corporation of America, which previously had the contract, filed for bankruptcy.

The company looked back on a 16-month sales decline as 2000 started. Robert blamed a failed pricing strategy, murky advertising, and an inability to keep pace with fashion trends — such as missing an opportunity to offer polar fleece and nylon or cotton vests — for the nearly 30% drop in earnings for the previous year. To turn things around, Goody's Family Clothing brought in former Sears SVP Lana Cain Krauter as a president and special assistant to Robert. She was put in charge of Goody's Family Clothing's retail operations, marketing, and advertising. Krauter later replaced president and COO Harry Call, who resigned, and still later was given the title chief merchandising officer.

In 2000 the company announced plans to build a 250,000-sq.-ft. distribution center in Arkansas to cover its expected growth in the southeastern US.

Also that year casual clothes-maker Tommy Hilfiger sued Goody's Family Clothing, alleging the chain sold jeans, shorts, and T-shirts that carried a flag logo similar to Hilfiger's own trademark.

Robert initiated the Goody's Good Friend Bus Tour in 2001, traveling to local stores to listen to improvement suggestions from employees and customers. As a result, the company has added women's and junior's plus sizes and expanded its private labels.

OFFICERS

Chairman and CEO: Robert M. Goodfriend, age 52, $750,000 pay
President and Chief Merchandising Officer: Lana Cain Krauter, age 50, $600,000 pay
EVP, CFO, and Secretary: Edward R. Carlin, age 61, $275,600 pay
EVP, Merchandising: Max W. Jones, age 47, $246,000 pay
EVP, Stores: David R. Mullins, age 50, $275,600 pay
SVP and Chief Accounting Officer: David G. Peek, age 41
SVP and General Merchandise Manager, Men's: John A. Payne, age 5
SVP, Distribution, Transportation and Logistics: Bobby Whaley, age 57
SVP, Management Information Systems: Jay D. Scussel, age 58
SVP, Marketing and Advertising: Thomas Carey
SVP, Planning and Allocation: Bruce E. Halverson, age 47
SVP, Product Development: John J. Okvath III, age 57
VP, Human Resources: Hazel A. Moxim
Auditors: Deloitte & Touche LLP

LOCATIONS

HQ: 400 Goody's Ln., Knoxville, TN 37922
Phone: 865-966-2000   **Fax:** 865-777-4220
Web: www.goodysonline.com

Goody's Family Clothing operates stores in Alabama, Arkansas, Florida, Georgia, Illinois, Indiana, Kentucky, Louisiana, Mississippi, Missouri, North Carolina, Ohio, Oklahoma, South Carolina, Tennessee, Texas, Virginia, and West Virginia.

PRODUCTS/OPERATIONS

2002 Sales

	$ mil.	% of total
Womenswear	511	43
Denim	252	21
Menswear	195	16
Children's wear	86	7
Accessories	76	6
Shoes	64	6
Other	8	1
Total	**1,192**	**100**

COMPETITORS

American Retail
Burlington Coat Factory
Cato
Charming Shoppes
Dress Barn
Dunlap
Elder-Beerman Stores
J. C. Penney
Kmart
Kohl's
One Price Clothing Stores
Payless ShoeSource
Peebles
Stage Stores
Stein Mart
Target
TJX
Value City
Wal-Mart

HISTORICAL FINANCIALS & EMPLOYEES

Nasdaq: GDYS FYE: Saturday nearest Jan. 31	Annual Growth	1/93	1/94	1/95	1/96	1/97	1/98	1/99	1/00	1/01	1/02
Sales ($ mil.)	11.3%	455	505	614	697	819	972	1,091	1,181	1,251	1,192
Net income ($ mil.)	—	16	14	7	11	17	33	28	20	13	(20)
Income as % of sales	—	3.6%	2.7%	1.1%	1.5%	2.1%	3.4%	2.5%	1.7%	1.1%	—
Earnings per share ($)	—	0.50	0.43	0.21	0.32	0.53	0.99	0.81	0.59	0.41	(0.62)
Stock price – FY high ($)	—	12.51	12.51	10.00	7.38	10.41	19.88	29.00	14.63	7.75	6.25
Stock price – FY low ($)	—	7.67	5.50	3.75	3.63	3.38	7.88	7.63	4.50	2.19	2.78
Stock price – FY close ($)	(10.9%)	12.09	6.88	4.25	3.88	10.25	17.13	10.78	4.84	5.19	4.29
P/E – high	—	25	29	45	22	20	19	35	25	19	—
P/E – low	—	15	13	17	11	6	8	9	8	5	—
Dividends per share ($)	—	0.00	0.00	0.00	0.01	0.00	0.00	0.00	0.00	0.00	0.00
Book value per share ($)	11.4%	2.37	2.75	2.96	3.28	3.82	4.90	5.87	6.43	6.85	6.25
Employees	8.4%	4,825	6,000	5,000	4,500	6,100	8,800	8,250	10,100	10,300	10,000

STOCK PRICE HISTORY

HIGH/LOW/CLOSE

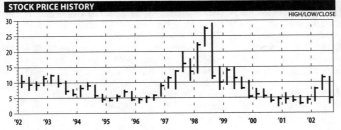

2002 FISCAL YEAR-END

Debt ratio: 0.0%
Return on equity: —
Cash ($ mil.): 54
Current ratio: 1.49
Long-term debt ($ mil.): 0
No. of shares (mil.): 32
Dividends
  Yield: —
  Payout: —
Market value ($ mil.): 139

THE GREAT A&P TEA COMPANY

Once "America's grocery store," blanketing cities from coast to coast, The Great Atlantic & Pacific Tea Company (A&P) now oversees a patchwork of about 700 stores in 17 New England, mid-Atlantic, midwestern, and southern states, and Canada. Although A&P remains its best-known chain, the Montvale, New Jersey-based company also runs Waldbaum's in the New York City area; Food Emporium in New York, Connecticut, and New Jersey; Farmer Jack in Michigan and Ohio; and Super Fresh from New Jersey to Virginia. Other chains include Kohl's in Wisconsin, and Sav-A-Center in Louisiana and Mississippi. In addition, the company is a wholesaler to 67 franchise stores in Canada, which operate under the banners A&P, Dominion, Ultra Food & Drug stores, Food Basics (franchised stores), and The Barn.

Competitors' superstores have eaten into the sales of A&P's aging outlets. As a result, the company is remodeling old stores and aggressively expanding its own superstore prototype. A&P is focusing its growth on existing markets where it can achieve the #1 or #2 position, specifically New York, Michigan, New Orleans, and Ontario. To that end, A&P exited weaker markets, including Richmond, Virginia, and Atlanta.

The company's Compass Foods division makes the Eight O'Clock, Bokar, and Royale brands of coffee (sold not only by A&P but by other food retailers). A&P is also expanding other profitable private-label offerings.

Chairman and CEO Christian Haub and his family own German retailer Tengelmann Group, which owns 57% of A&P.

HISTORY

George Gilman and George Hartford of Augusta, Maine, set up shop in 1859 on New York City's docks to sell tea at a 50% discount by eliminating middlemen. The Great American Tea Company advertised by drawing a red wagon through the city's streets. By 1869 the company, renamed The Great Atlantic & Pacific Tea Company (A&P), had 11 stores offering discounted items.

Gilman retired in 1878, and Hartford brought in his sons George and John. In 1912, when the company had 400 stores, John opened a store on a low-price, cash-and-carry format, without customer credit or premiums, which proved popular. When the company passed to the sons four years later, A&P had more than 1,000 cash-and-carry stores.

The company expanded at a phenomenal pace during the 1920s and 1930s, growing to 15,900 stores by the mid-1930s; however, a movement by small retailers to restrict chain stores tarnished the country's view of A&P in particular. To improve the company's image, John initiated innovative marketing and customer service policies.

A&P grew in the 1940s by converting its stores to supermarkets, but an antitrust suit in 1949 and the company's reluctance to carry more nonfood items pushed it into decline. Management shut stores in California and Washington to shore up its northeastern business.

In 1975, after a long period of poor sales and failed discount format attempts, the board named former Albertson's president Jonathan Scott as CEO. (He eventually left A&P to become CEO of American Stores.) Scott closed stores and reduced the workforce, but the company's sales increases failed to keep ahead of inflation, and A&P lost $52 million in 1978.

A year later the Hartford Foundation sold its A&P holdings to the German Tengelmann Group (owned by the Haub family), which in 1980 appointed English-born James Wood as CEO. A&P made several acquisitions, including Super Fresh (1982), Kohl's (1983), Ontario's Miracle Food Mart (1990), and Atlanta's Big Star (1992).

Rivals' superior supermarkets stripped away market share in New York City, Long Island, and Detroit in the early 1990s. In response, A&P closed hundreds of old stores, remodeled several hundred more, and planned openings of larger stores.

A 14-week strike in 1994 resulted in a complete shutdown of all 63 Miracle stores in Canada. In addition to lost sales, the company paid $17 million in labor settlement costs. In 1995 A&P began converting its Canadian Food Basics stores to franchises.

Christian Haub replaced Wood as CEO in 1998 (and became chairman in mid-2001), and A&P stepped up its modernization efforts.

A&P in 1999 exited the Richmond, Virginia, and Atlanta markets. The grocer boosted its presence in New Orleans with its purchase of six Schwegmann's stores, which were later converted to the Sav-A-Center banner. A&P saw four executive officers leave in six months in 2000, including COO Michael Larkin. Early in 2001 former Nabisco exec Elizabeth Culligan became COO. Also that year A&P shuttered 31 of 39 unprofitable stores slated for closure.

Following the discovery in May 2002 of accounting irregularities related to the timing for recognition of vendor allowances and inventory accounting, in July A&P restated — and improved — its financial results for 1999 and 2000, and adjusted its 2001 results.

OFFICERS

Chairman and CEO: Christian W.E. Haub, age 37, $1,186,851 pay
President, COO and Director: Elizabeth R. Culligan, age 52, $830,000 pay
SVP and CFO: Mitchell P. Goldstein, age 41
SVP, Chief Category Management Officer: Victor T. Alessandro, age 43
SVP, Chief Development Officer: Brian Pall, age 42
SVP and CIO: John E. Metzger, age 47
SVP, General Counsel, and Secretary: William P. Costantini, age 54
SVP, People Resources and Services: Laurane S. Magliari, age 51, $485,000 pay
VP, Corporate Controller: Brenda M. Galgano
VP, Treasurer: William Moss, age 54
Chairman, President, and CEO, The Great Atlantic & Pacific Company of Canada: Brian Piwek, age 55
President, Atlantic Region: David A. Smithies, age 57
President, Midwest Region: Michael Carter
President, Northeast Division: Donald J. Sommerville, age 43
President, Waldbaum's Division: Robert Panasuk
Auditors: Deloitte & Touche LLP

LOCATIONS

HQ: The Great Atlantic & Pacific Tea Company, Inc., 2 Paragon Dr., Montvale, NJ 07645
Phone: 201-573-9700   **Fax:** 201-571-8719
Web: www.aptea.com

The Great Atlantic & Pacific Tea Company operates supermarkets in 17 New England, mid-Atlantic, midwestern, and southern states, the District of Columbia, and Ontario, Canada. It also has franchised stores and wholesale operations in Ontario.

2002 Sales

	$ mil.	% of total
US Retail	8,490	77
Canada Retail	1,807	17
Canada Wholesale	676	6
Total	**10,973**	**100**

PRODUCTS/OPERATIONS

Store Names	Selected Private-Label Brands
A&P	America's Choice
The Barn Markets	The Farm
Dominion	Health Pride
Farmer Jack	Master Choice
Food Basics	Savings Plus
Food Emporium	
Kohl's	
Sav-A-Center	
Super Foodmart	
Super Fresh	
Ultra Food & Drug	
Waldbaum's	

COMPETITORS

Albertson's	Loblaw	Stop & Shop
Delhaize	Meijer	Village Super
America	Pathmark	Market
Foodarama	Penn Traffic	Wakefern Food
Supermarkets	Red Apple Group	Walgreen
Genuardi's	Rite Aid	Wal-Mart
Family Markets	Safeway	Wegmans
Giant Food	Shaw's	Western Beef
King Kullen	ShopRite	Winn-Dixie
Grocery	Sobeys	
Kroger	Stew Leonard's	

HISTORICAL FINANCIALS & EMPLOYEES

NYSE: GAP FYE: Last Saturday in February	Annual Growth	2/93	2/94	2/95	2/96	2/97	2/98	2/99	2/00	2/01	2/02
Sales ($ mil.)	0.5%	10,500	10,384	10,332	10,101	10,089	10,262	10,179	10,151	10,623	10,973
Net income ($ mil.)	—	(190)	4	(172)	57	73	63	(67)	14	(25)	(72)
Income as % of sales	—	—	0.0%	—	0.6%	0.7%	0.6%	—	0.1%	—	—
Earnings per share ($)	—	(4.96)	0.10	(4.49)	1.50	1.91	1.65	(1.75)	0.37	(0.65)	(1.88)
Stock price - FY high ($)	—	35.25	35.00	27.38	29.00	36.75	36.00	35.00	37.69	23.75	28.00
Stock price - FY low ($)	—	21.38	22.75	17.38	19.13	22.13	23.13	21.88	23.06	6.00	8.08
Stock price - FY close ($)	1.7%	23.38	26.38	19.25	22.50	29.75	30.44	31.56	23.44	9.55	27.10
P/E - high	—	—	350	—	19	19	22	—	102	—	—
P/E - low	—	—	228	—	13	12	14	—	62	—	—
Dividends per share ($)	—	0.80	0.80	0.65	0.20	0.20	0.40	0.40	0.40	0.30	0.00
Book value per share ($)	(4.7%)	27.06	26.02	20.27	21.53	23.27	24.22	21.87	22.06	20.79	17.54
Employees	(1.4%)	90,000	94,000	92,000	89,000	84,000	80,000	83,400	80,900	83,000	79,000

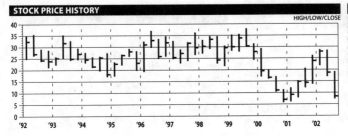

STOCK PRICE HISTORY
HIGH/LOW/CLOSE

2002 FISCAL YEAR-END

Debt ratio: 56.5%
Return on equity: —
Cash ($ mil.): 169
Current ratio: 1.02
Long-term debt ($ mil.): 873
No. of shares (mil.): 38
Dividends
 Yield: —
 Payout: —
Market value ($ mil.): 1,040

GREAT LAKES CHEMICAL

Great Lakes Chemical has tested the waters of change. The Indianapolis, Indiana-based company has restructured to focus on its core specialty chemicals business, which includes polymer additives, water-treatment chemicals, and performance chemicals. From its beginnings in oil and gas exploration, Great Lakes has evolved into a leading global provider of chemicals for uses ranging from fire extinguishers to swimming pools.

The company's polymer additives unit makes flame retardants for a variety of products, including electronics equipment, furniture, and cars. It also makes polymer stabilizers such as antioxidants and ultraviolet absorbers that protect against sun damage. The company's performance chemicals division provides agricultural and pharmaceutical chemicals such as bromine (Great Lakes is the world's #1 producer of the liquid, which mixes easily with organic compounds) and fluorine products (gas used for fire extinguishing, refrigeration, and oil well drilling).

Great Lakes' water-treatment unit makes sanitizers (BioGuard and Aqua Chem), algicides, oxidizers, and pH and mineral balancers for swimming pools, cooling towers, and wastewater plants.

Hurt by weak sales in all product lines except water-treatment chemicals, Great Lakes has been streamlining operations and consolidating facilities. In part to reduce debt, the company has sold its 53% stake in its OSCA subsidiary for about $220 million. Warren Buffett's Berkshire Hathaway owns about 15% of the company.

HISTORY

Entrepreneur "Red" McClanahan started McClanahan Oil Company to explore for oil and gas in Michigan in 1933. By the end of the decade, the company had expanded into Arkansas, Illinois, and Louisiana, but reserves soon dried up and bigger companies started squeezing out McClanahan Oil. In 1946 geologist Charles Hale took hold of the company's reins. Two years later he made the crucial purchase of Great Lakes Chemical Corporation. The two companies merged in 1950 to form Great Lakes Oil and Chemical Company.

Heavy competition during the 1950s caused the company to exit the petroleum business and expand its bromine operations. In 1960 Hale sold enough oil property to fund the purchase of some bromine-rich Arkansas brine wells. That year the company changed its name to Great Lakes Chemical Corporation.

In 1963 the company began to develop its specialty chemicals. From 1969 and throughout the 1970s, Great Lakes expanded internationally through acquisitions and joint ventures.

Longtime employee Emerson Kampen became Great Lakes' president in 1971. (During his tenure the company's yearly revenue grew a hundredfold). Great Lakes doubled its Arkansas brine reserves in 1981 with the purchase of Northwest Industries' Velsicol subsidiary. From 1982 to 1985, Great Lakes moved into developing biotechnology, oil field, and electronic chemicals. The late 1980s brought more acquisitions, and in 1989 Great Lakes bought 51% of Britain's Octel Associates, the world's biggest supplier of motor fuel compounds.

The company continued to grow internationally in the early 1990s. In 1994 Robert McDonald replaced Kampen as president. Strong demand for bromine chemicals proved profitable in 1995. The plastics, auto, and electronics industries were especially good customers because of their need for flame retardants and engineering resins.

In 1996 Great Lakes experienced slower growth, decreased demand, and weaker currencies in Europe. To compensate, it sold two noncore business units. The company continued on this path in 1997 and 1998, selling underperformers and spinning off its Octel subsidiary. In 1998 Great Lakes reorganized into four business units and appointed new management. Also that year the company began a 12% reduction of its workforce.

The following year Great Lakes bought NSC Technologies, a Monsanto division that makes pharmaceutical intermediates, and FMC's process additives unit. In 2000 Great Lakes spun off its OSCA subsidiary (Great Lakes still retained a little more than 50% of its voting rights). That same year it acquired water-treatment company Aqua Clear Industries.

Great Lakes acquired Akzo Nobel's ADC optical monomers business in 2001. The unit, which makes lenses that represent approximately 70% of the world's plastic lens sales, had generated about $25 million in sales in 2000.

In 2002 the company sold its 53% stake in OSCA to BJ Services.

OFFICERS

Chairman, President, and CEO: Mark P. Bulriss, age 50, $810,077 pay

EVP and General Manager, Flame Retardants and Brominated Performance Chemicals: Angelo C. Brisimitzakis, age 42, $230,288 pay

EVP and General Manager, Polymer Stabilizers: Henri Steinmetz, age 45, $246,230 pay

EVP, Performance Chemicals and Business Development: Richard T. Higgons, age 59

EVP; President, Water Treatment: Larry J. Bloom, age 53, $295,000 pay
SVP and CFO: John J. Gallagher III, age 38
SVP and CIO: Zoe Schumaker, age 41
SVP, Environmental, Health, and Safety: John B. Blatz, age 49
SVP, General Counsel and Corporate Secretary: Jeffrey M. Lipshaw, age 47, $259,212 pay
SVP, Global Supply Chain: Bruce G. Davis, age 53
SVP, Human Resources and Communications: Richard J. Kinsley, age 44
VP and Controller: William L. Sherwood
VP and General Manager, Fine Chemicals: Simon Sellers
VP and General Manager, Flourine Chemicals: Jack G. Boss
VP and Treasurer: John E. Kunz
Assistant Secretary: Karen White Duros
Auditors: Ernst & Young LLP

LOCATIONS

HQ: Great Lakes Chemical Corporation
500 E. 96th St., Ste. 500, Indianapolis, IN 46240
Phone: 317-715-3000   **Fax:** 317-715-3050
Web: www.greatlakeschem.com

Great Lakes Chemical has manufacturing facilities around the world.

2001 Sales

	$ mil.	% of total
US	1,058	66
UK	162	10
Switzerland	143	9
Other countries	232	15
Total	**1,595**	**100**

PRODUCTS/OPERATIONS

2001 Sales & Operating Income

	Sales		Operating Income	
	$ mil.	% of total	$ mil.	% of total
Polymer additives	582	36	(71)	—
Water-treatment chemicals	507	32	54	55
Performance chemicals	316	20	26	27
Energy services & products	176	11	18	18
Corporate	14	1	(37)	—
Adjustments	—	—	(267)	—
Total	**1,595**	**100**	**(277)**	**100**

Selected Products

Agricultural products	Flame retardants
Antioxidants	Fluorine chemistry
Bromine intermediates	Optimal monomers
Commercial & specialty chemicals	Polymer stabilizers
	Toxicological services
Fine chemicals	UV absorbers

COMPETITORS

Albemarle	NCH
Arch Chemicals	Occidental Petroleum
Crompton	Ondeo Nalco
Dead Sea Bromine	Orgasynth
Dow Chemical	PPG
DuPont	Praxair
Eastman Chemical	Rohm and Haas
Engelhard	Sigma-Aldrich
Goodrich	TETRA Technologies
Hercules	W. R. Grace

HISTORICAL FINANCIALS & EMPLOYEES

NYSE: GLK FYE: December 31	Annual Growth	12/92	12/93	12/94	12/95	12/96	12/97	12/98	12/99	12/00	12/01
Sales ($ mil.)	0.7%	1,497	1,792	2,065	2,361	2,212	1,311	1,394	1,453	1,671	1,595
Net income ($ mil.)	—	233	273	279	296	250	57	89	140	127	(290)
Income as % of sales	—	15.5%	15.2%	13.5%	12.5%	11.3%	4.3%	6.4%	9.6%	7.6%	—
Earnings per share ($)	—	3.27	3.77	3.96	4.48	3.91	0.94	1.50	2.41	2.42	(5.76)
Stock price - FY high ($)	—	62.67	73.75	72.00	65.52	69.03	48.18	47.58	50.00	40.50	37.63
Stock price - FY low ($)	—	44.12	56.63	42.80	48.95	38.85	36.44	35.12	33.19	26.50	20.00
Stock price - FY close ($)	(9.7%)	60.80	65.52	50.05	63.22	41.05	39.18	40.00	38.19	37.19	24.28
P/E - high	—	19	19	18	14	18	51	32	21	17	—
P/E - low	—	13	15	11	11	10	38	23	14	11	—
Dividends per share ($)	1.9%	0.27	0.34	0.38	0.43	0.54	0.62	0.40	0.32	0.32	0.32
Book value per share ($)	(2.1%)	14.74	17.63	19.48	21.92	24.13	22.18	18.06	18.24	18.88	12.22
Employees	7.2%	2,988	7,000	7,000	8,000	7,000	5,100	5,100	5,800	5,148	5,600

STOCK PRICE HISTORY

HIGH/LOW/CLOSE

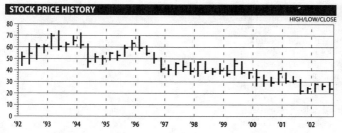

2001 FISCAL YEAR-END

Debt ratio: 46.2%
Return on equity: —
Cash ($ mil.): 72
Current ratio: 1.51
Long-term debt ($ mil.): 528
No. of shares (mil.): 50
Dividends
 Yield: 1.3%
 Payout: —
Market value ($ mil.): 1,219

THE GREEN BAY PACKERS, INC.

Football fans in Green Bay, Wisconsin, bleed green and gold as they chant their mantra, "The Pack is Back." The Green Bay Packers football franchise is among the most storied in the National Football League, winning 12 championship titles, including three Super Bowl victories, since its beginnings in 1919. Icons such as Bart Starr, Ray Nitschke, and legendary coach Vince Lombardi have battled on the frozen tundra at Lambeau Field, where games have been sold out since 1960. (The team's waiting list for season tickets boasts more than 56,000 names.)

In addition to its history, Green Bay is also unique in that it is the only community-owned, not-for-profit franchise in the NFL. It has about 110,000 shareholders who all have voting rights (a stock split in 1997 gave 1,940 holders most of the voting power), though the stock doesn't increase in value nor pay dividends and can only be sold back to the team. No individual is allowed to own more than 200,000 shares.

After a couple of poor seasons, both athletically and financially, the Packers organization has high hopes for the future. Green Bay voters approved public financing for a $295 million renovation of historic Lambeau Field (which the city owns) in 2000. The project (scheduled to be completed by 2003) will add 10,000 seats to the stadium, which is one of the smallest in the NFL, as well as additional luxury seats. The team is also optimistic about its young head coach Mike Sherman (who was named general manager in 2001) and a group of up-and-coming young players.

HISTORY

In 1919 Earl "Curly" Lambeau helped organize a professional football team in Green Bay, Wisconsin, with the help of George Calhoun, the sports editor of the *Green Bay Press-Gazette*. At 20 years old, Lambeau was elected team captain and convinced the Indian Packing Company to back the team, giving the squad its original name, the Indians. The local paper, however, nicknamed the team the Packers and the name stuck. Playing on an open field at Hagemeister Park, the team collected fees by passing the hat among the fans. In 1921 the team was admitted into the American Professional Football Association (later called the National Football League), which had been organized the year before.

The Packers went bankrupt after a poor showing its first season in the league, and Lambeau and Calhoun bought the team for $250. With debts continuing to mount, *Press-Gazette* general manager Andrew Turnbull helped reorganize the team as the not-for-profit Green Bay Football

Corporation and sold stock at $5 a share. Despite winning three straight championships from 1929-31, the team again teetered on the brink of bankruptcy, forcing another stock sale in 1935. With fortunes on and off the field dwindling, Lambeau retired in 1950. A third stock sale was called for that year, raising $118,000. City Stadium (renamed Lambeau Field in 1965) was opened in 1957. In 1959 the team hired New York Giants assistant Vince Lombardi as head coach.

Under Lombardi, the Packers dominated football in the 1960s, winning five NFL titles. With players such as Bart Starr and Ray Nitschke, the team defeated the Kansas City Chiefs in the first Super Bowl after the 1966 season. Lombardi resigned after winning Super Bowl II (he passed away in 1970), and the team again fell into mediocrity. Former MVP Starr was called upon to coach in 1974 but couldn't turn the tide before he was released in 1983.

Bob Harlan, who had joined the Packers as assistant general manager in 1971, became president and CEO in 1989. He hired Ron Wolf as general manager in 1991, who in turn hired Mike Holmgren as head coach early the next year. With a roster including Brett Favre, Reggie White, and Robert Brooks, the Packers posted six straight playoff appearances and won its third Super Bowl in 1997. A fourth stock sale (preceded by a 1,000:1 stock split) netted the team more than $24 million.

After Holmgren resigned in 1999 (he left to coach the Seattle Seahawks), former Philadelphia Eagles coach Ray Rhodes tried to lead the team but lasted only one dismal season. In 2000 Mike Sherman, a former Holmgren assistant, was named the team's 13th head coach. Prompted by falling revenue, the team announced plans to renovate Lambeau Field, and voters in Brown County later approved a sales tax increase to help finance the $295 million project. The following year Wolf retired and coach Sherman was tapped as general manager. That year the team signed quarterback Favre to a 10-year, $100 million contract extension.

OFFICERS

President, CEO, and Director: Robert E. Harlan, age 65
EVP and COO: John M. Jones, age 50
EVP, General Manager, and Head Coach:
Michael F. Sherman, age 47
VP and Director: John J. Fabry
VP Football Operations: Mark Hatley, age 51
VP Player Finance and General Counsel:
Andrew Brandt, age 41
Secretary: Peter M. Platten III
Treasurer and Director: John R. Underwood
Executive Director of Public Relations: Lee Remmel,
age 78
Corporate Counsel: Jason Wied
Director of Accounting: Duke Copp
Director of Administrative Affairs: Mark Schiefelbein
Director of College Scouting: John Dorsey
Director of Corporate Security: Jerry Parins
Director of Corporate Sponsorships: Craig Benzel
Director of Information Technology: Wayne Wichlacz
Director of Facility Operations: Ted Eisenreich
Director of Finance: Vicki Vannieuwenhoven
Director of Player Development: Edgar Bennett
Director of Premium Guest Services: Jennifer Ark
Auditors: Wipfli Ullrich Bertelson LLP

LOCATIONS

HQ: 1265 Lombardi Ave., Green Bay, WI 54304
Phone: 920-496-5700   **Fax:** 920-496-5712
Web: www.packers.com

The Green Bay Packers play at Lambeau Field in Green
Bay, Wisconsin. The team holds its training camp at St.
Norbert College in De Pere, Wisconsin.

PRODUCTS/OPERATIONS

Championship Titles
NFC Championships (1996-97)
NFC Central Division (1972, 1995-97)
NFL Championships (1929-31, 1936, 1939, 1944, 1961-
62, 1965-67)
NFL Western Conference (1936, 1938-39, 1944, 1960-62,
1965-67)
Super Bowl I (1967)
Super Bowl II (1968)
Super Bowl XXXI (1997)

COMPETITORS

Chicago Bears Football Club
Detroit Lions
Minnesota Vikings

HISTORICAL FINANCIALS & EMPLOYEES

Not-for-profit FYE: March 31	Annual Growth	3/93	3/94	3/95	3/96	3/97	3/98	3/99	3/00	3/01	3/02
Sales ($ mil.)	10.4%	54	66	62	70	75	82	103	109	118	132
Employees	8.7%	72	74	80	82	90	92	95	95	140	—

SALES HISTORY

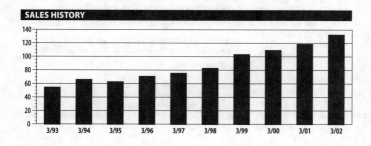

GUIDANT CORPORATION

In matters of the heart, Guidant beats Danielle Steel hands down. The Indianapolis-based company makes cardiovascular therapeutic devices and related products. Its vascular intervention products help open blocked arteries. Guidant's pacemakers and defibrillators detect and correct abnormal heartbeats. The company also develops minimally invasive surgical devices and systems to reduce procedure times and ease patient recovery.

Although there's lots of money to be made in it, the interventional cardiology market is no place for the faint-hearted. Market share can rise and fall precipitously. (Johnson & Johnson, which in 1994 introduced the first stent — a steel mesh used to prop open vessels — saw its share plummet from about 90% in mid-1997 to about one-third the next year.)

Because of this, Guidant has worked hard to diversify into other cardiac and vascular products, particularly cardiac rhythm devices, and through acquisitions and alliances has reduced its reliance on stent-related products to less than half of its business. It is buying Cook Group to get its hands on ACHIEVE, a paclitaxel-coated, restenosis-fighting coronary stent awaiting FDA approval that it hopes will rival J&J's coated stent, available in Europe. Guidant recently gained FDA approval of the ENDOTAK RELIANCE active-fixation defibrillation lead.

HISTORY

Guidant was formed in 1994 when Prozac maker Eli Lilly decided to refocus on its core pharmaceutical business. To this end it merged its medical device units Cardiac Pacemakers (CPI), Advanced Cardiovascular Systems (ACS), Origin Medsystems, Devices for Vascular Intervention, and Heart Rhythm Technologies into the more succinctly named Guidant Corporation. Medical device veterans James Cornelius and Ronald Dollens were named chairman and CEO, respectively. Guidant went public that year. With first-year sales exceeding $800 million, the company made the *FORTUNE* 500 list.

Guidant skipped formative-years angst. In 1995 its ACS subsidiary entered an agreement with Cardiovascular Dynamics, a subsidiary of imaging catheter maker EndoSonics Corporation (now part of Jomed), to develop cardiology device technologies. That year CPI introduced its VENTAK automatic implantable cardioverter defibrillator system to correct abnormally fast heart rhythms, giving Guidant a competitive edge against Medtronic and Ventratech. Also in 1995 Origin Medsystems released the world's first 5mm endoscopic fixation device to treat

hernias and urinary incontinence. Late that year Eli Lilly sold its remaining stake in Guidant.

Guidant's aggressive debut put the screws to established competitors like Johnson & Johnson and St. Jude Medical. But with it came lawsuits: Boston Scientific subsidiary SCIMED Life Systems and Sulzer Medica (now Centerpulse) were among the first to sue Guidant, alleging patent infringement on catheters and stents; Guidant later filed against other competitors. By 1999 the company was involved in more than 20 lawsuits with such rivals as Medtronic, Johnson & Johnson subsidiary Cordis, and Angeion Corporation.

In 1996 the company partnered both with Hewlett-Packard for development of a new catheter and with Physio-Control Corp. to form the Cardiac Rhythm Management Laboratory at the University of Alabama for research on sudden cardiac death. Guidant acquired Endo-Vascular Technologies in 1997 to develop a catheter-based treatment for abdominal aortic aneurysms; the Ancure blood-vessel patch was submitted to the FDA for review two years later.

In 1998 Guidant bought defibrillator specialist InControl and settled two patent infringement suits with C. R. Bard. The company also gained a foothold in Asia in 1998, obtaining permission to distribute its coronary stent products in Japan. The next year the Eastern door opened wider when Chindex International agreed to distribute Guidant's vascular intervention products in China.

Guidant's 1999 purchase of Sulzer Medica's electrophysiology business made it the world's #2 pacemaker manufacturer after Medtronic and defused a lawsuit ongoing since 1995. With coronary stent sales slipping, the company launched its first non-coronary stent, Megalink, to prop open bile ducts. That year Guidant bought CardioThoracic Systems, a maker of less-invasive heart surgery technology. Also that year, the company's TRISTAR stent was cleared for marketing in the US.

In 2000 the company resolved most of its litigation with Johnson & Johnson and as part of the deal will buy some of the drug company's heart-failure technology. Guidant also settled its intellectual property disputes with Boston Scientific and Cordis.

OFFICERS

President, CEO, and Director: Ronald W. Dollens, age 55, $606,600 pay
Group Chairman, Office of the President: A. Jay Graf, age 54, $397,754 pay
Advisor to the President: Ginger L. Graham, age 46
VP, Finance, and CFO: Keith E. Brauer, age 53, $316,650 pay

VP, Human Resources: Roger Marchetti
VP, Corporate Relations and Policy: Dana G. Mead Jr., age 42
VP, General Counsel, and Secretary: Debra F. Minott, age 46
VP, Japan, Asia/Pacific, and Latin America: Rodney R. Nash, age 60
President, US Sales Operations: Mark C. Bartell, age 41
President, Vascular Intervention: John M. Capek, age 40, $261,654 pay
President, Endovascular Solutions: Beverly A. Huss, age 42
President, Cardiac Rhythm Management: R. Frederick McCoy Jr., age 45, $261,654 pay
President, Europe, Middle East, Africa and Canada: Guido J. Neels, age 53
President, Cardiac Surgery: Ronald N. Spaulding, age 38
Corporate Controller and Chief Accounting Officer: Michael A. Sherman, age 35
Auditors: Ernst & Young LLP

LOCATIONS

HQ: 111 Monument Circle, 29th Fl., Indianapolis, IN 46204
Phone: 317-971-2000   **Fax:** 317-971-2040
Web: www.guidant.com

Guidant sells primarily in the US, Europe, and Japan.

2001 Sales

	% of total
US	70
Other regions	30
Total	**100**

PRODUCTS/OPERATIONS

2001 Sales

	% of total
Coronary stents	30
Implantable cardioverter defibrillators	27
Cardiac pacemaker systems	22
Angioplasty systems & accessories	14
Minimally invasive cardiac surgery products	3
ANCURE ENDOGRAFT system	2
Non-coronary products	2
Total	**100**

Selected Products

Abdominal aortic aneurysm repair products (ANCURE ENDOGRAFT system)
Atherectomy catheters
Biliary stent systems
Coronary dilation catheters
Coronary stent systems
Guide wires
Guiding catheters
Implantable cardioverter defibrillators
Lead systems
Minimally invasive cardiac surgery systems
Pacemaker pulse generators

COMPETITORS

Arrow International	Lifecor
Boston Scientific	Medtronic
C. R. Bard	St. Jude Medical
Cordis	United States Surgical
Edwards Lifesciences	ZOLL Medical

HISTORICAL FINANCIALS & EMPLOYEES

NYSE: GDT FYE: December 31	Annual Growth	12/92	12/93	12/94	12/95	12/96	12/97	12/98	12/99	12/00	12/01
Sales ($ mil.)	15.2%	755	795	862	931	1,049	1,328	1,897	2,352	2,549	2,708
Net income ($ mil.)	22.7%	77	52	92	101	66	145	(2)	341	374	484
Income as % of sales	—	10.2%	6.6%	10.7%	10.9%	6.3%	10.9%	—	14.5%	14.7%	17.9%
Earnings per share ($)	30.9%	—	—	0.24	0.32	0.18	0.48	(0.01)	1.10	1.21	1.58
Stock price - FY high ($)	—	—	—	4.03	10.66	15.34	34.75	56.50	69.88	75.38	55.13
Stock price - FY low ($)	—	—	—	3.63	3.88	9.88	13.41	25.50	41.00	44.00	26.90
Stock price - FY close ($)	43.4%	—	—	4.00	10.56	14.25	31.13	55.00	47.00	53.94	49.80
P/E - high	—	—	—	17	33	85	68	—	61	61	34
P/E - low	—	—	—	15	12	55	26	—	36	35	17
Dividends per share ($)	—	—	—	0.00	0.02	0.03	0.03	0.03	0.00	0.00	0.00
Book value per share ($)	27.6%	—	—	0.92	1.33	1.55	1.93	1.84	2.83	3.84	5.07
Employees	9.1%	4,553	4,644	4,507	4,980	4,449	5,100	6,310	8,360	9,252	10,000

STOCK PRICE HISTORY

HIGH/LOW/CLOSE

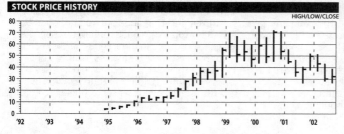

2001 FISCAL YEAR-END

Debt ratio: 22.9%
Return on equity: 35.5%
Cash ($ mil.): 438
Current ratio: 1.96
Long-term debt ($ mil.): 460
No. of shares (mil.): 305
Dividends
  Yield: —
  Payout: —
Market value ($ mil.): 15,197

HALLIBURTON COMPANY

No matter where you are in the oil field of dreams, if you need it built, Halliburton will come. One of the world's largest oil field services providers (along with Schlumberger), the Dallas-based company also makes oil field equipment and offers construction, engineering, and maintenance services, particularly for the petroleum industry, in more than 100 countries.

Halliburton's Energy Services Group accounts for two-thirds of its sales. It includes Halliburton Deepwater, which constructs offshore production facilities. Halliburton Energy Services offers well evaluation, drilling, and maintenance services for oil companies, and Landmark Graphics develops exploration-related software and provides information technology services. The group also manufactures drill bits and field processing equipment.

The company's Engineering and Construction Group, which operates as Halliburton KBR (Kellogg Brown & Root) builds facilities primarily for energy, petrochemical, and refinery clients. Its Brown & Root Services provides engineering, construction, management, and technology services for non-energy businesses and government institutions.

Halliburton is spending big bucks on technology in an effort to develop more efficient oil field products and processes. The company has purchased the assets of Pruett Industries, a fiber optic sensor technology company.

HISTORY

Erle Halliburton began his oil career in 1916 at Perkins Oil Well Cementing. He moved to boomtown Burkburnett, Texas, to start his Better Method Oil Well Cementing Company in 1919. Halliburton used cement to hold a steel pipe in a well, which kept oil out of the water table, strengthened well walls, and reduced the risk of explosions. Though the contribution would later be praised, his technique was considered useless at the time.

In 1920 Halliburton moved to Oklahoma. Incorporating Halliburton Oil Well Cementing Company in 1924, he patented its products and services, forcing oil companies to employ his firm if they wanted to cement wells.

Erle died in 1957, and his company grew through acquisitions between the 1950s and the 1970s. In 1962 it bought Houston construction giant Brown & Root, an expert in offshore platforms. After the 1973 Arab oil embargo Halliburton benefited from the surge in global oil exploration, and later, as drilling costs surged, it became a leader in well stimulation.

When the oil industry slumped in 1982, the firm halved its workforce. Three years later a suffering Brown & Root coughed up $750 million to settle charges of mismanagement at the South Texas Nuclear Project.

In the 1990s Halliburton expanded abroad, entering Russia in 1991 and China in 1993. That next year Brown & Root was named contractor for a pipeline stretching from Qatar to Pakistan. Halliburton drilled the world's deepest horizontal well (18,860 ft.) in Germany in 1995.

Also in 1995 Dick Cheney, a former US defense secretary, became CEO. Brown & Root began providing engineering and logistics services to US Army peacekeeping troops in the Balkans in 1995 and won a major contract to develop an offshore Canadian oil field the next year.

The company nearly doubled in size in 1998 with its $7.7 billion acquisition of oil field equipment manufacturer Dresser Industries. The purchase, coupled with falling oil prices in 1998 and 1999, prompted Halliburton to ax more than 9,000 workers. (Even after oil prices rebounded in 2000, Halliburton had to wait for the effects of the upturn to reach the oil field services sector.)

Brown & Root Energy Services won a contract to provide logistics support for the US Army in Albania in 1999. The company began to sell off portions of its Dresser acquisition that year. Partner Ingersoll-Rand bought Halliburton's stake in Ingersoll-Dresser Pump and bought its stake in Dresser-Rand (industrial compressors) in 2000. Cheney resigned as chairman and CEO that year after he was chosen as George W. Bush's vice presidential running mate. President and COO David Lesar was named to succeed him.

In 2001 a group consisting of investment firms First Reserve and Odyssey Investment Partners and Dresser managers paid $1.55 billion for Dresser Equipment Group. That year a number of multimillion dollar verdicts against Halliburton in asbestos cases sparked rumors that the company was going to file for bankruptcy (flatly denied by Halliburton) and caused the firm's stock price to tumble.

In 2002, in part to protect the company's assets from the unresolved asbestos claims issue, Lesar announced plans to restructure Halliburton into two independent subsidiaries, separating the Energy Services Group from the Halliburton KBR engineering and construction operations. Halliburton took a $483 million (pretax) charge against earnings in the second quarter of 2002 to cover its estimated asbestos liability.

Later that year, in an effort to boost its Energy Services unit, Halliburton purchased Pruett Industries, a fiber optic sensor technology company.

OFFICERS

Chairman, President, and CEO: David J. Lesar, age 48, $3,300,000 pay
EVP and CFO: Douglas L. Foshee, age 42
EVP and General Counsel: Lester L. Coleman, age 59, $950,016 pay
EVP: Gary V. Morris, age 48, $1,100,000 pay
VP, Secretary, and Corporate Counsel: Susan S. Keith
VP and CTO: Robert F. Heinemann, age 48
VP and CIO: Arthur D. Huffman, age 49
VP, Human Resources: Margaret Carriere, age 50
Chairman, Kellogg Brown & Root: A. Jack Stanley
President and CEO, Energy Services Group: Edgar Ortiz, age 59, $1,100,000 pay
President and CEO, Kellogg Brown & Root: R. Randall Harl, age 51, $637,500 pay
President, Halliburton Energy Services: John W. Gibson Jr., age 44
Auditors: KPMG LLP

LOCATIONS

HQ: 3600 Lincoln Plaza 500 N. Akard St., Dallas, TX 75201
Phone: 214-978-2600   **Fax:** 214-978-2611
Web: www.halliburton.com

Halliburton has operations in more than 100 countries.

PRODUCTS/OPERATIONS

2001 Sales

	% of total
Energy Services Group	67
Engineering & Construction Group	33
Total	**100**

Selected Operations, Products, and Services

Halliburton Deepwater (offshore construction and engineering)
Halliburton Energy Services (contract development, drilling, production, and operation of oil fields)
Halliburton KBR, including Brown & Root Services
Contract maintenance operations and services
Economic and technical feasibility studies
Environmental consulting and waste management
Project design, engineering, and construction
Remedial engineering and construction for hazardous waste sites
Site evaluation
Landmark Graphics Corporation (exploration and production software, information systems, and services)

COMPETITORS

ABB	Ishikawajima-Harima
Baker Hughes	McDermott
Bechtel	Nabors Industries
BJ Services	National-Oilwell
Black & Veatch	Noble
Bouygues	Nuovo Pignone Industrie
Caterpillar	Meccaniche
Coflexip	Parsons
Compagnie Générale de	Perini
Géophysique	Peter Kiewit Sons'
Cooper Cameron	Petroleum Geo-Services
Diamond Offshore	Pride International
Duke/Fluor Daniel	Raytheon
ENSCO	Schlumberger
Fluor	Smith International
FMC	Varco International
Foster Wheeler	Weatherford International
GlobalSantaFe	Wilson Industries

HISTORICAL FINANCIALS & EMPLOYEES

NYSE: HAL FYE: December 31	Annual Growth	12/92	12/93	12/94	12/95	12/96	12/97	12/98	12/99	12/00	12/01
Sales ($ mil.)	7.9%	6,525	6,351	5,741	5,699	7,385	8,819	17,353	14,898	11,856	12,939
Net income ($ mil.)	—	(137)	(161)	178	168	300	454	(15)	438	501	809
Income as % of sales	—	—	—	3.1%	3.0%	4.1%	5.2%	—	2.9%	4.2%	6.3%
Earnings per share ($)	—	(0.63)	(0.61)	0.73	0.74	1.19	1.75	(0.03)	0.99	1.13	1.88
Stock price – FY high ($)	—	18.44	22.00	18.63	25.44	31.81	63.25	57.25	51.75	55.19	49.25
Stock price – FY low ($)	—	10.88	12.88	13.94	16.44	22.38	29.69	25.00	28.13	32.25	10.94
Stock price – FY close ($)	(1.0%)	14.38	15.94	16.56	25.31	30.13	51.88	29.63	40.25	36.25	13.10
P/E – high	—	—	—	26	34	27	36	—	76	86	41
P/E – low	—	—	—	20	22	19	17	—	41	50	9
Dividends per share ($)	0.0%	0.50	0.50	0.50	0.50	0.50	0.50	0.50	0.50	0.50	0.50
Book value per share ($)	2.3%	8.90	8.27	8.51	7.64	8.62	9.85	9.23	9.70	9.20	10.95
Employees	2.3%	69,200	64,700	57,200	57,300	60,000	70,750	107,800	103,000	93,000	85,000

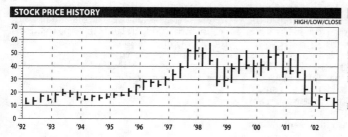

STOCK PRICE HISTORY   HIGH/LOW/CLOSE

2001 FISCAL YEAR-END

Debt ratio: 22.8%
Return on equity: 18.6%
Cash ($ mil.): 290
Current ratio: 1.92
Long-term debt ($ mil.): 1,403
No. of shares (mil.): 434
Dividends
  Yield: 3.8%
  Payout: 26.6%
Market value ($ mil.): 5,685

HALLMARK CARDS, INC.

Hallmark Cards is the #1 producer of warm fuzzies. The Kansas City, Missouri-based company's greeting cards (sold under brand names such as Hallmark, Shoebox, and Ambassador) are sold in more than 47,000 US retail stores. About 7,500 of these stores bear the Hallmark or Hallmark Gold Crown name (the company owns less than 5% of them, and the rest are franchised). Hallmark markets its products in more than 100 countries.

While Hallmark may be best known for its personal expression products, the company has diversified into a host of other areas. Hallmark owns Binney & Smith, maker of Crayola brand crayons and markers, and mall-based portrait studio chain The Picture People (with more than 300 studios nationwide). The company also produces television movies through Hallmark Entertainment's 67%-owned unit, Crown Media, and offers Keepsake brand ornaments. Through its Web site, Hallmark.com, Hallmark offers electronic greeting cards and sells gift items and flowers.

Not resting on well-engraved laurels, Hallmark has announced its intention to triple its revenue by 2010. While it plans to continue expanding its greeting card empire, the company is also intent on stretching its reach in markets such as personal development and family entertainment. The company is bringing a literary slant to its products with a new line of cards and products developed by Pulitzer Prize nominee and poet Maya Angelou.

Members of the Hall family (including chairman Donald Hall, son of founder Joyce Hall) own two-thirds of Hallmark.

HISTORY

Eighteen-year-old Joyce Hall started selling picture postcards from two shoe boxes in his room at the Kansas City, Missouri, YMCA in 1910. His brother Rollie joined him the next year, and the two added greeting cards to their line in 1912. The brothers opened Hall Brothers, a store that sold postcards, gifts, books, and stationery, but it was destroyed in a 1915 fire. The Halls got a loan, bought an engraving company, and produced their first original cards in time for Christmas.

In 1921 a third brother, William, joined the firm, which started stamping the backs of its cards with the phrase "A Hallmark Card." By 1922 Hall Brothers had salespeople in all 48 states. The firm began selling internationally in 1931.

Hall Brothers patented the "Eye-Vision" display case for greeting cards in 1936 and sold it to retailers across the country. The company aired its first radio ad in 1938. That next year it introduced a friendship card, displaying a cart

filled with purple pansies. The card became the company's best-seller. During WWII Joyce Hall persuaded the government not to curtail paper supplies, arguing that his greeting cards were essential to the nation's morale.

The company opened its first retail store in 1950. The following year marked the first production of *Hallmark Hall of Fame,* TV's longest-running dramatic series and winner of more Emmy awards than any other program. Hall Brothers changed its name to Hallmark Cards in 1954 and introduced its Ambassador line of cards five years later.

Hallmark introduced paper party products and started putting *Peanuts* characters on cards in 1960. Donald Hall, Joyce Hall's son, was appointed CEO in 1966. Two years later Hallmark opened Crown Center, which surrounded company headquarters in Kansas City. Disaster struck in 1981 when two walkways collapsed at Crown Center's Hyatt Regency hotel, killing 114 and injuring 225.

Joyce Hall died in 1982, and Donald Hall became both chairman and CEO. Hallmark acquired Crayola crayon maker Binney & Smith in 1984. It introduced Shoebox Greetings, a line of nontraditional cards, in 1986. Irvine Hockaday replaced Donald Hall as CEO the same year (Hall continued as chairman).

The company joined with Information Storage Devices in 1993 to market recordable greeting cards. It unveiled its Web site, Hallmark.com, in 1996 and began offering electronic greeting cards. Hallmark's 1998 acquisition of UK-based Creative Publications boosted the company into the top spot in the British greeting card market. The following year the company acquired portrait studio chain The Picture People and Christian greeting card maker DaySpring Cards. Hallmark also introduced Warm Wishes, a line of 99-cent cards. The company also unveiled the Hallmark Home Collection, a line of home furnishings.

The company began testing overnight flower delivery in the US just in time for Valentine's Day 2000. To further its goal of tripling revenues, it also reorganized its creative and marketing departments. Hallmark Entertainment subsidiary Crown Media went public in 2000. Hockaday retired as president and CEO at the end of 2001; vice chairman Donald Hall Jr. took the additional title of CEO in early 2002.

The company closed its Kansas City-based manufacturing plant in 2002 and transferred some 340 workers to three plants in Kansas.

Chairman: Donald J. Hall
Vice Chairman, President, and CEO: Donald J. Hall Jr.,
  age 45
EVP and CFO: Robert J. Druten, age 53
SVP Corporate Strategy: Anil Jagtiani
SVP Human Resources and Director: David E. Hall
SVP Public Affairs and Communication: Steve Doyal
SVP Sales: Steve Paoletti
VP Marketing: Jan Murley
VP Operations: Wayne Herran
VP Trade Development: Vince G. Burke
Director of Marketing: Jen Weiss
**President and CEO, Hallmark Entertainment;
  Chairman, Crown Media:** Robert Halmi Jr., age 44
President and CEO, Binney & Smith: Mark Schwab
President, Hallmark North America: Donald H. Fletcher

LOCATIONS

HQ: 2501 McGee St., Kansas City, MO 64108
Phone: 816-274-5111   **Fax:** 816-274-5061
Web: www.hallmark.com

Hallmark Cards has operations in Australia, Belgium,
Canada, China, Denmark, France, Japan, Mexico, the
Netherlands, New Zealand, Puerto Rico, Spain, the
UK, and the US. It markets its products in more than
100 countries.

PRODUCTS/OPERATIONS

Selected Product Lines
Ambassador (greeting cards)
Fresh Ink (greeting cards)
Life Mosaic (cards and gifts by poet Maya Angelou)
Hallmark.com (electronic greeting cards, gifts, flowers)
Hallmark en Español (products celebrating Latino
  heritage)
Hallmark Flowers (flower delivery)
Keepsake (holiday ornaments and other collectibles)
Mahogany (products celebrating African-American
  heritage)
Maxine (greeting cards)
Shoebox (greeting cards)
Tree of Life (products celebrating Jewish heritage)

Selected Subsidiaries
Binney & Smith (Crayola brand crayons and markers)
Crown Center Redevelopment (retail complex)
Crown Media Holdings (67%, pay television channels)
DaySpring (Christian greeting cards)
Hallmark Entertainment (television, movies, and home
  video production; majority stake in Crown Media)
Halls Merchandising (department store)
Image Arts (greeting card distributors)
InterArt (Mary Engelbriet and Boyds Bears products)
Irresistible Ink (handwriting service)
Litho-Krome (lithography)
The Picture People (portrait studio chain)
Tapper Candies (maker of candies, party favors)
William Arthur (invitations, stationery)

COMPETITORS

1-800-FLOWERS.COM
American Greetings
Amscan
Andrews McMeel Universal
AOL Time Warner
Blyth, Inc.
CPI Corp.
CSS Industries
Dixon Ticonderoga
Enesco Group
Faber-Castell
Lifetouch
Olan Mills
Party City
PCA International
SPS Studios
Syratech
Thomas Nelson
Viacom
Walt Disney

HISTORICAL FINANCIALS & EMPLOYEES

Private FYE: December 31	Annual Growth	12/92	12/93	12/94	12/95	12/96	12/97	12/98	12/99	12/00	12/01
Sales ($ mil.)	2.9%	3,100	3,400	3,800	3,400	3,600	3,700	3,900	4,200	4,200	4,000
Employees	5.4%	12,487	12,600	12,800	12,100	12,600	12,554	20,945	21,000	24,500	20,000

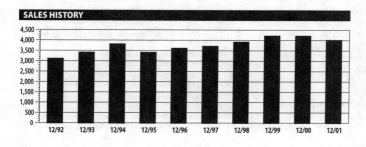

SALES HISTORY

H&R BLOCK, INC.

Only two things are certain in this life, and H&R Block has a stranglehold on one. The Kansas City, Missouri-based company is the US's leading tax preparer. The firm also prepares taxes in Canada, Australia, and the UK, and provides refund-anticipation loans.

H&R Block wants to decrease its dependence on the April 15 deadline. Although tax operations account for almost 60% of sales, the company is rolling out other financial services in hopes of cross-selling them to its more than 19 million tax customers. Its RSM McGladrey unit provides accounting, consulting, tax planning, and other services to midsized companies, while its H&R Block Financial Advisors subsidiary offers brokerage and other investment services to individuals. The firm also sells tax-preparation software and has a division devoted to mortgages.

About 45% of H&R Block's more than 10,000 offices are franchised. Warren Buffett's Berkshire Hathaway owns about 9% of H&R Block.

HISTORY

Brothers Henry and Richard Bloch opened the United Business Co. in Kansas City, Missouri, in 1946 to provide accounting services. As tax preparation monopolized their time, a client suggested they specialize in taxes. The Blochs bought two ads, which brought a stampede of customers.

In 1955 the company became H&R Block (the Blochs didn't want customers to read the name as "blotch"). Basing charges on the number and complexity of tax forms resulted in a low-fee, high-volume business. The first tax season was a success, and the following year the brothers successfully tested their formula in New York City. But neither brother wanted to move to New York, so they worked out a franchise-like agreement with local CPAs. It was the first step toward becoming a nationwide chain.

As the chain grew, H&R Block began training preparers at H&R Block Income Tax Schools. By 1969, when Richard retired, the company had more than 3,000 offices in the US and Canada.

Henry began appearing in company ads in the 1970s; his reassuring manner inspired confidence and aided expansion. Fearing saturation of the tax preparer market, he pushed the company into new areas. H&R Block bought Personnel Pool of America in 1978 (taken public in 1994 as part of Interim Services) and two years later bought 80% of law office chain Hyatt Legal Services (sold in 1987).

In 1980 the firm bought CompuServe, which evolved from a computer time-share firm to a major online service by the 1990s. H&R Block

sought to integrate its two operating areas in hopes that electronic filing and banking would increase its tax business.

In 1992 Henry was succeeded as president by his son, Thomas, who built on the nontax side of the business to try for more even revenue distribution. That next year the company bought MECA Software (personal finance software), mistakenly believing MECA's relationships with banks, based on its refund-anticipation loan program, would help develop online banking services. It sold MECA in 1994, and Thomas stepped down.

That year H&R Block bought Fleet Financial Group's Option One Mortgage, boosting its financial services. In an effort to build a national accounting practice in 1996, it formed HRB Business Services with the purchase of Kansas City accounting firm Donnelly Meiners Jordan Kline and six other regional accounting firms. Frank Salizzoni became CEO in 1996.

After selling 20% of CompuServe in a 1996 IPO, H&R Block in 1998 sold its remaining interest in the company. In 1999 the firm sold its credit card operations and formed RSM McGladrey by purchasing the non-consulting assets of the #7 US accounting firm, McGladrey & Pullen. The McGladrey & Pullen deal didn't please everyone. In May 1999 — even before the McGladrey deal had been reached — a group of franchisees sued H&R Block to ensure that they receive their fair share of royalties from any sales generated in their territories by both the accounting group and H&R Block's tax software. Later in 1999 H&R Block bought discount broker Olde Financial Discount (now H&R Block Financial Advisors).

In 2000 H&R Block's online operations suffered some technology glitches, while its bottom line was blitzed by its string of purchases expanding the firm's financial services offerings. That year co-founder Henry Bloch became honorary chairman, ceding the chairman slot to Salizzoni. In 2001 H&R Block announced a cross-marketing agreement with AOL Time Warner; the pact gives the firms access to each other's customer base. Mark Ernst became CEO in 2001; Salizzoni remained as chairman, but retired in 2002. Ernst became chairman.

OFFICERS

Honorary Chairman: Henry W. Bloch, age 77
Chairman, President, and CEO: Mark A. Ernst, age 43, $1,470,833 pay (prior to promotion)
COO and EVP; President, H&R Block Services: Jeffrey W. Yabuki, age 42, $776,631 pay
SVP and CIO: Jeffery G. Brandmaier
SVP and Chief Marketing Officer: David F. Byers, age 39
SVP and CFO: Frank J. Controneo, age 42, $663,625 pay

SVP, Human Resources: Stephanie R. Otto, age 40
VP, General Counsel, and Secretary: James H. Ingraham, age 47
VP, Communications: Linda M. McDougall, age 48
VP, Corporate Tax: Timothy R. Mertz, age 50
VP and Treasurer: Becky Shulman
VP, Government Relations: Robert A. Weinberger, age 57
VP, Corporate Development and Risk Management: Bret G. Wilson, age 42
President and CEO, Option One Mortgage Corporation: Robert E. Dubrish, age 49, $657,153 pay
President & CEO, H&R Block Financial Advisors: Brian L. Nygaard
President and CEO, RSM McGladrey: Thomas G. Rotherham, age 52, $672,378 pay
Auditors: PricewaterhouseCoopers LLP

LOCATIONS

HQ: 4400 Main St., Kansas City, MO 64111
Phone: 816-753-6900   **Fax:** 816-753-5346
Web: hrblock.com

H&R Block operates in Australia, Canada, the UK, and the US.

2002 Offices

	By location
US	9,015
Canada	955
Australia	362
Other	59
Total	**10,391**

PRODUCTS/OPERATIONS

2002 Sales

	$ mil.	% of total
Services	2,333	80
Gain on sale of mortgage loans	457	16
Product sales	127	4
Total	**2,917**	**100**

Selected Subsidiaries

Block Financial Corporation
Equico, Inc.
H&R Block Canada, Inc.
H&R Block Group, Inc.
McGladrey Contract Business Services, L.L.C
O'Rourke Consulting, LLC
OLDE Financial Corporation
Option One Mortgage Corporation
RSM McGladrey, Inc.
Smart Travel, Inc.
Wallace Sanders Business Consulting, L.P.

COMPETITORS

American Express
Andersen
BDO International
Century Business Services, Inc.
Deloitte Touche Tohmatsu
Ernst & Young
Gilman + Ciocia
Grant Thornton International
Intuit
Jackson Hewitt
KPMG
PricewaterhouseCoopers
Universal Tax

HISTORICAL FINANCIALS & EMPLOYEES

NYSE: HRB FYE: April 30	Annual Growth	4/93	4/94	4/95	4/96	4/97	4/98	4/99	4/00	4/01	4/02
Sales ($ mil.)	8.7%	1,382	1,119	1,234	765	1,806	1,196	1,522	2,452	3,002	2,917
Net income ($ mil.)	10.2%	181	201	107	177	48	392	215	252	281	434
Income as % of sales	—	13.1%	17.9%	8.7%	23.2%	2.6%	32.8%	14.2%	10.3%	9.4%	17.4%
Earnings per share ($)	11.9%	0.84	0.95	0.50	0.84	0.22	1.83	1.07	1.28	1.53	2.31
Stock price - FY high ($)	—	21.38	24.38	23.81	24.44	18.19	24.53	25.88	29.75	27.50	51.46
Stock price - FY low ($)	—	15.19	15.94	16.50	15.75	11.81	15.31	17.66	19.00	13.47	26.24
Stock price - FY close ($)	9.8%	17.31	21.25	21.06	17.63	16.13	22.50	24.06	20.91	27.50	40.12
P/E - high	—	25	26	46	29	79	13	24	23	18	22
P/E - low	—	18	17	32	19	51	8	16	15	9	11
Dividends per share ($)	2.8%	0.49	0.55	0.61	0.64	0.52	0.40	0.48	0.54	0.59	0.63
Book value per share ($)	10.6%	3.06	3.33	3.27	5.03	4.80	6.27	5.44	6.44	6.39	7.56
Employees	2.1%	82,000	82,800	85,000	79,000	78,900	83,500	86,500	103,000	99,400	99,100

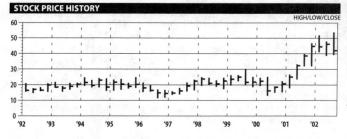

STOCK PRICE HISTORY

HIGH/LOW/CLOSE

2002 FISCAL YEAR-END

Debt ratio: 38.8%
Return on equity: 34.2%
Cash ($ mil.): 436
Current ratio: 1.19
Long-term debt ($ mil.): 868
No. of shares (mil.): 181
Dividends
 Yield: 1.6%
 Payout: 27.3%
Market value ($ mil.): 7,267

HARLEY-DAVIDSON, INC.

"Put your ass on some class," reads one (not necessarily official) Harley-Davidson T-shirt. Offering loads of chrome and the telltale roar of a V-twin engine, the Harley is, to its cult of devotees, the ultimate American machine. Milwaukee-based Harley-Davidson controls about half of the heavyweight motorbike market in the US; its 24 models, which are among the best known in the industry, include the Sportster, Electra Glide, Low Rider, Fat Boy, and Road King. The bikes — built by the company's Harley-Davidson Motor Company unit — are sold through a worldwide network of more than 1,350 dealers. Harley-Davidson also sells an attitude through its line of clothing (MotorClothes) and other goods licensed under the company name.

If Harley-Davidson has a problem, it's with supply, not demand. Devoted customers sometimes wait more than a year for a new bike, depending on the model. To address the lag time, the company increased annual production in 2001 to more than 240,000 bikes (a 15% increase over 2000). Harley ventured into new territory in 2001 with the introduction of the liquid-cooled Harley-Davidson V-Rod. Inspired by Harley's drag racing heritage, the V-Rod combines the attributes of a performance bike with the styling of a custom cycle.

HISTORY

In 1903 William Harley and the Davidson brothers (Walter, William, and Arthur) of Milwaukee sold their first Harley-Davidson motorcycles, which essentially were motor-assisted bicycles that required pedaling uphill. Demand was high, and most sold before leaving the factory. Six years later the company debuted its trademark two-cylinder, V-twin engine. By 1913 it had 150 competitors.

WWI created a demand for US motorcycles overseas that made foreign sales important. During the 1920s Harley-Davidson was a leader in innovative engineering, introducing models with a front brake and the "teardrop" gas tank that became part of the Harley look.

The Depression took a heavy toll on the motorcycle industry. As one of only two remaining companies, Harley-Davidson survived through exports and sales to the police and military. To improve sales, the company added styling features such as art deco decals and three-tone paint. The 1936 EL model, with its "knucklehead" engine (named for the shape of its valve covers), was a forerunner of today's models.

During WWII Harley-Davidson prospered from military orders. It introduced new models after the war to cater to a growing recreational market of consumers with money to spend: the K-model (1952), Sportster "superbike" (1957), and Duo-Glide (1958). Ever since competitor Indian Motorcycle Company gave up the ghost in the 1950s, Harley-Davidson has been the US's only major motorcycle manufacturer. (Indian Motorcycle was revived in 1998, however.)

The company began making golf carts (since discontinued) in the early 1960s. It went public in 1965, and American Machine and Foundry (AMF) bought the company in 1969. But by the late 1970s, sales and quality were slipping. Certain that Harley-Davidson would lose to Japanese bikes flooding the market, AMF put the company up for sale. There was no buyer until 1981, when Vaughn Beals and other AMF executives purchased it. Minutes away from bankruptcy in 1985, then-CFO Richard Teerlink convinced lenders to accept a restructuring plan.

Facing falling demand and increasing imports, Harley-Davidson made one of the greatest comebacks in US automotive history (helped in part by a punitive tariff targeting Japanese imports). Using Japanese management principles, it updated manufacturing methods, improved quality, and expanded the model line. Harley-Davidson again went public in 1986, and by the next year it had control of 25% of the US heavyweight-motorcycle market, up from 16% in 1985.

In 1993 the company acquired a 49% stake in Eagle Credit (financing, insurance, and credit cards for dealers and customers; it bought the rest in 1995) and a 49% share of Wisconsin-based Buell Motorcycle, gaining a niche in the performance-motorcycle market. (Harley-Davidson bought most of Buell's remaining stock in 1998.) The recreational vehicle business, Holiday Rambler, was sold to Monaco Coach Corp. in 1996.

Jeffrey Bleustein, who had headed Harley-Davidson's manufacturing unit, was named the company's chairman and CEO in 1997. Two years later the company began production at its new assembly plant in Brazil, with an eye on increasing sales in Latin America. Harley-Davidson bested Honda in the US in 1999 for the first time in 30 years.

In 2000 Harley-Davidson's production increased by more than 15% over 1999, reaching just over 200,000 bikes. Despite the slowing economy in 2001, demand for Hogs continued to grow. To meet demand, Harley-Davidson again increased production by about 15% — making more than 240,000 bikes in 2001. Also that year Harley introduced the V-Rod. The V-Rod draws design inspiration from Harley's legendary drag racing heritage.

Chairman and CEO; President and COO, Motor Co.:
Jeffrey L. Bleustein, age 62, $2,713,793 pay
VP and CFO: James L. Ziemer, age 50, $886,022 pay
**VP, General Counsel, and Secretary; VP and General
Counsel, Motor Co.:** Gail A. Lione, age 51,
$595,412 pay
VP, Treasurer, and Controller: James M. Brostowitz,
age 49
Chairman and CTO, Buell Motorcycle: Erik F. Buell
President and COO, Buell Motorcycle: John A. Hevey,
age 44
**President and COO, Harley-Davidson Financial
Services:** Donna F. Zarcone, age 43, $853,421 pay
President and COO, Motor Co.: James A. McCaslin,
age 52, $847,805 pay
VP and Managing Director Europe, Motor Co.:
John Russell, age 52
Auditors: Ernst & Young LLP

LOCATIONS

HQ: 3700 W. Juneau Ave., Milwaukee, WI 53208
Phone: 414-343-4680   **Fax:** 414-343-8230
Web: www.harley-davidson.com

Harley-Davidson operates manufacturing facilities in
Missouri, Pennsylvania, and Wisconsin, as well as Brazil.

2001 Sales

	$ mil.	% of total
US	2,766	82
Europe	302	9
Japan	141	4
Canada	97	3
Other regions	57	2
Total	**3,363**	**100**

PRODUCTS/OPERATIONS

2001 Sales

	$ mil.	% of total
Harley-Davidson motorcycles	2,630	78
Parts & accessories	507	15
General merchandise	164	5
Buell motorcycles	62	2
Total	**3,363**	**100**

Selected Motorcycles

Harley-Davidson
Dyna Glide
Softail
Sportster
Touring
VRSC (V-Rod)

Buell
Blast
Cyclone M2
Firebolt XB9R
Lightning X1
Lightning X1W
Thunderbolt S3T

COMPETITORS

BMW
Ducati
Honda
Indian Motorcycle
Kawasaki Heavy Industries
Polaris Industries
Suzuki Motor
Triumph Motorcycles
Yamaha Motor

HISTORICAL FINANCIALS & EMPLOYEES

NYSE: HDI FYE: December 31	Annual Growth	12/92	12/93	12/94	12/95	12/96	12/97	12/98	12/99	12/00	12/01
Sales ($ mil.)	13.2%	1,105	1,217	1,542	1,351	1,531	1,763	2,064	2,453	2,906	3,363
Net income ($ mil.)	26.2%	54	(12)	104	113	166	174	214	267	348	438
Income as % of sales	—	4.9%	—	6.8%	8.3%	10.8%	9.9%	10.3%	10.9%	12.0%	13.0%
Earnings per share ($)	25.9%	0.18	0.25	0.32	0.38	0.47	0.57	0.69	0.87	1.13	1.43
Stock price - FY high ($)	—	4.84	5.94	7.47	7.53	12.38	15.63	23.75	32.03	50.63	55.99
Stock price - FY low ($)	—	2.72	3.94	5.41	5.50	6.59	8.34	11.94	21.25	29.53	32.00
Stock price - FY close ($)	31.2%	4.70	5.52	7.00	7.19	11.75	13.63	23.69	32.03	39.75	54.31
P/E - high	—	25	23	23	20	26	27	34	36	44	39
P/E - low	—	14	15	17	14	14	14	17	24	26	22
Dividends per share ($)	—	0.00	0.02	0.04	0.05	0.06	0.07	0.08	0.09	0.10	0.11
Book value per share ($)	20.2%	1.11	1.07	1.42	1.65	2.19	2.71	3.37	3.84	4.65	5.80
Employees	3.8%	5,800	6,000	6,700	4,800	5,200	6,060	6,200	7,220	7,700	8,100

STOCK PRICE HISTORY

HIGH/LOW/CLOSE

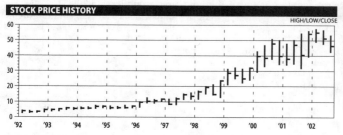

2001 FISCAL YEAR-END

Debt ratio: 17.8%
Return on equity: 27.7%
Cash ($ mil.): 439
Current ratio: 2.33
Long-term debt ($ mil.): 380
No. of shares (mil.): 303
Dividends
 Yield: 0.2%
 Payout: 7.7%
Market value ($ mil.): 16,445

HARMAN INTERNATIONAL

He may be getting up there in years, but hi-fi pioneer Sidney Harman doesn't mind cranking up the volume. Washington, DC-based Harman International Industries makes some of the best-known products in high-end audio under names such as Infinity and JBL (loudspeakers and audio products) and Harman Kardon (audio/video receivers, DVD players, surround-sound systems).

The company gets most of its sales from the consumer market, including sales to car and computer makers who incorporate its audio systems into their products. DaimlerChrysler accounts for more than 20% of Harman's sales. The company also serves the professional market (cinemas, stadiums, concert halls, and broadcasters) with amplifiers, effects devices, microphones, and mixing consoles.

Harman has stood firm in the face of Japan's dominance of the electronics industry and has kept a manufacturing base in the US instead of moving to countries with cheaper labor. Feisty namesake and chairman Sidney Harman, the backbone of the company for nearly half a century, is considered a legend in the audio industry. He owns about 4% of Harman.

HISTORY

Sidney Harman and his partner, Bernard Kardon, left their engineering jobs at a public address system company to found Harman Kardon in 1953. The two marketed their home audio components to the general public instead of to the traditional audio buff. Their novel concept was to package amplifiers and a tuner in a single unit (called a receiver) that appealed to average consumers.

Kardon cashed out in a 1956 IPO that left Harman with about 33% of the firm. Harman Kardon acquired the respected JBL speaker business in 1969.

Harman was also interested in internal growth. He introduced new management techniques emphasizing workers' quality of life, allowing employees to redesign their jobs and leave work after meeting production quotas. His projects, which had varying degrees of success, attracted the attention of President Carter's administration, which brought Harman on board as undersecretary of commerce in 1977. Harman sold the company to Beatrice Foods that year to avoid a conflict of interest. The company did poorly under the conglomerate, and Harman bought much of it back in 1980, taking it private. He then changed the name to Harman International Industries.

Through acquisitions, he quickly expanded the business into the auto OEM market (Essex Loudspeaker from United Technologies, 1981) and professional equipment for recording studios and concert halls (Infinity, 1983). In the mid-1980s Harman signed exclusive deals to supply JBL speakers to Ford (ended in 1995) and Chrysler, and in 1985 it bought back the Harman Kardon trade name (Beatrice Foods had sold it to Japanese company Shin Shirasuna). The company went public again the next year.

In 1991 Harman went into a tailspin (a $20 million loss, 500 layoffs) caused by a worldwide recession, poor auto sales, and four soured acquisitions. Harman, who had been living in Washington, DC, with his politician wife, Jane, moved back to California, site of the company's largest plant. President Donald Esters quit in 1992 and Harman set about reorganizing the firm.

The company bought AKG, a leading Austrian microphone maker, in 1993. Signaling its interest in the new digital age, Harman created a new business unit, Harman Interactive, the following year to focus on PC and home theater systems.

It acquired Becker, supplier of audio systems to Mercedes, and high-end equipment manufacturer Madrigal Audio Laboratories in 1995. Harman expanded its customer base by selling to home electronics superstores such as Circuit City, in addition to specialty stores for audiophiles.

A year later the company began supplying speakers to a Compaq line of computers. In 1997 it boosted its auto audio business with new agreements to supply audio systems to certain models of BMW, Toyota, Hyundai, and Peugeot, and it purchased two car loudspeaker makers (Oxford International and Audio Electronic Systems).

In the late 1990s Harman focused by cutting its consumer product lines from 2,000 to 200. With its sales to Asia down and European sales ailing as well, it closed plants and laid off workers in 1998. That year president Bernard Girod succeeded Harman as CEO. Also in 1998 the company created a remote control with Microsoft and divested several of its international distribution companies to focus on manufacturing and marketing. Harman sold its Orban broadcasting-products business in 1999, and replaced it with Crown International (maker of high-powered amplifiers) in 2000.

In September 2001 Harman sold its Allen & Heath subsidiary, a maker of mixing consoles, to a group consisting of some of the company's top management.

OFFICERS

Executive Chairman: Sidney Harman, age 82, $1,391,667 pay
Vice Chairman and CEO: Bernard A. Girod, age 59, $1,333,333 pay
President, COO, and Director: Gregory P. Stapleton, age 55, $1,229,167 pay
EVP and CFO: Frank Meredith, age 44, $833,333 pay
VP and General Counsel: Edwin C. Summers, age 54
VP, Acoustics: Floyd E. Toole, age 55
VP, Controller: William S. Palin, age 58, $327,308 pay
VP, Financial Operations: Sandra B. Robinson, age 42
Director of Human Resources: Paula Stern
Auditors: KPMG LLP

LOCATIONS

HQ: Harman International Industries, Incorporated
1101 Pennsylvania Ave., NW, Ste. 1010
Washington, DC 20004
Phone: 202-393-1101   **Fax:** 202-393-3064
Web: www.harman.com

Harman International Industries has facilities in Austria, Denmark, France, Germany, Hungary, Mexico, Sweden, Switzerland, the UK, and the US.

PRODUCTS/OPERATIONS

2002 Sales

	$ mil.	% of total
Consumer systems group	1,401	77
Professional group	425	23
Total	**1,826**	**100**

Selected Brand Names

Consumer Systems Group	Professional Group
AudioAccess	AKG
Becker	BSS
Harman Kardon	Crown
Infinity	dbx
JBL	Digitech
Lexicon	DOD
Mark Levinson	JBL Professional
Proceed	Lexicon
Revel	Madrigal
	Soundcraft
	Spirit
	Studer

COMPETITORS

Aiwa	Fender Musical	Philips
Alesis	Instruments	Electronics
Alpine	Kenwood	Pioneer
Electronics	Korg	Polk Audio
AMS Neve	Krell	Recoton
Audio Research	Line 6	Robert Bosch
Bang & Olufsen	Mackie Designs	Roland
Bose	Marshall	Sennheiser
Boston	Amplification	Electronic
Acoustics	Matsushita	Shure
Cambridge	MBT	Siemens
SoundWorks	International	Snell Acoustics
Celestion	Mitek Corp.	Sony
International	Nakamichi	TEAC
Crest Audio	Onkyo	Telex
Delphi	Paradigm	Communications
Denon	Electronics	
Electronics	Peavey	
	Electronics	

HISTORICAL FINANCIALS & EMPLOYEES

NYSE: HAR FYE: June 30	Annual Growth	6/93	6/94	6/95	6/96	6/97	6/98	6/99	6/00	6/01	6/02
Sales ($ mil.)	12.3%	665	862	1,170	1,362	1,474	1,513	1,500	1,678	1,716	1,826
Net income ($ mil.)	28.1%	11	26	41	52	55	50	12	73	32	58
Income as % of sales	—	1.7%	3.0%	3.5%	3.8%	3.7%	3.3%	0.8%	4.3%	1.9%	3.1%
Earnings per share ($)	19.7%	0.50	0.89	1.27	1.55	1.45	1.33	0.33	2.07	0.96	1.70
Stock price - FY high ($)	—	10.17	16.01	19.99	28.25	28.19	28.53	23.75	34.25	50.35	62.15
Stock price - FY low ($)	—	4.28	8.27	12.02	16.00	16.19	17.63	15.75	18.38	23.28	28.94
Stock price - FY close ($)	23.2%	10.00	11.96	19.28	24.63	21.06	19.25	22.00	30.50	38.09	49.25
P/E - high	—	20	17	15	18	19	20	72	16	50	37
P/E - low	—	9	9	9	10	11	12	48	9	23	17
Dividends per share ($)	—	0.00	0.00	0.08	0.10	0.10	0.10	0.10	0.10	0.10	0.10
Book value per share ($)	11.6%	4.87	7.34	9.36	11.72	12.65	13.74	13.18	14.28	13.19	16.21
Employees	9.8%	4,710	6,849	7,929	8,369	8,384	10,010	8,850	9,807	10,676	10,389

STOCK PRICE HISTORY

HIGH/LOW/CLOSE

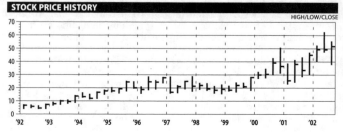

2002 FISCAL YEAR-END

Debt ratio: 47.2%
Return on equity: 12.1%
Cash ($ mil.): 116
Current ratio: 2.02
Long-term debt ($ mil.): 470
No. of shares (mil.): 32
Dividends
  Yield: 0.2%
  Payout: 5.9%
Market value ($ mil.): 1,600

HARRAH'S ENTERTAINMENT, INC.

Harrah's Entertainment likes to spread its bets. The Las Vegas-based company is the third-largest gaming company in the world (behind Park Place Entertainment and MGM Mirage). It's also one of the most geographically diverse US casino operators, owning and/or managing 26 land-based, dockside, riverboat, and Indian gaming casinos in 13 states. Harrah's seeks to trump its competitors with Total Rewards, which is its version of "frequent flier" miles for die-hard gamblers and is maintained by an exclusive database linking the company's locations.

Harrah's derives 75% of its revenues from gambling at its casinos; its locations are in Arizona, California, Colorado, Illinois, Indiana, Iowa, Kansas, Louisiana, Mississippi, Missouri, Nevada, New Jersey, and North Carolina. Operating under the Harrah's, Harveys, Players, Showboat, and Rio names, its facilities boast more than 41,700 slot machines, 14,000 hotel rooms and suites, and about 100 restaurants. Harrah's owned 48% of Las Vegas-based National Airlines until the airline filed for bankruptcy in late 2000.

Revenues at the company's New Orleans casino (it owns 63% of the management firm and has agreed to buy the rest) are slowly picking up. The casino was finally completed in late 1999 after it lay dormant for three years. It emerged from Chapter 11 bankruptcy protection in 2001 after the state of Louisiana agreed to cut its tax payments. Harrah's continues to move forward: It recently opened a new hotel tower at its Atlantic City casino, and plans to complete another by 2003. The company also plans to acquire a 95% stake in Louisiana Downs, a Thoroughbred racetrack in Bossier City, for $157 million.

HISTORY

William Harrah and his father founded their first bingo parlor in Reno, Nevada, in 1937. Using the income from that business, Harrah opened his first casino, Harrah's Club, in downtown Reno in 1946. In 1955 and 1956 he bought several clubs in Stateline, Nevada (near Lake Tahoe). Harrah built the company by using promotions to draw middle-class Californians to his clubs.

During the 1960s the entrepreneur expanded his operations in Lake Tahoe, and in 1968 he built a 400-room hotel tower in Reno. Harrah's went public in 1971. After Harrah's death in 1978, the company expanded outside Nevada by building a hotel and casino in Atlantic City, New Jersey.

Holiday Inns bought Harrah's in 1980 for about $300 million. The hotelier already owned a 40% interest in River Boat Casino, which operated a casino next to a Holiday Inn in Las Vegas. When Holiday Inns acquired the other 60% of the casino/hotel in 1983, Harrah's took over its management. Holiday Inns became Holiday Corporation in 1985. The following year UK brewer Bass PLC (which is now hotel giant Six Continents) put up $100 million for 10% of Holiday Corporation.

In 1990 Bass acquired the Holiday Inn hotel chain for $2.2 billion. The rest of Holiday Corporation, including Harrah's, was renamed Promus under chairman Michael Rose.

In the early 1990s Harrah's built a casino on Ak-Chin Indian land near Phoenix and opened riverboat casinos in Joliet, Illinois; Shreveport, Louisiana; and North Kansas City, Missouri. In 1995 Promus spun off its hotel operations as Promus Hotel Corporation and changed the name of its casino business to Harrah's Entertainment. (Promus was acquired by Hilton Hotels in 1999.)

Also in 1995 Harrah's gambled and lost. Big. Its New Orleans Casino was shelved even before it was finished — a victim of Louisiana's Byzantine politics. Eager for the right to build what would be a $395 million, 200,000-sq.-ft. casino in the heart of the city, Harrah's had made a number of ill-advised concessions to state and municipal officials. It agreed not to offer hotel rooms or food at the casino (forgoing about 20% of anticipated revenues) and promised to make an annual $100 million minimum payment to the state, in addition to 19% of the casino's revenues. In the end the fiasco's price tag reached $900 million (only half of which went to casino construction costs), and Harrah's put the project into bankruptcy to stop the bleeding. (It resumed construction in 1999 and finally opened the casino at the end of the year.)

In 1997 Rose retired as chairman and was replaced by CEO Philip Satre. In 1998 Harrah's bought competitor Showboat, with properties in Las Vegas and Atlantic City and management of a New South Wales, Australia, casino. A Louisiana Supreme Court ruling that year allowed the company to resume work on the New Orleans casino (albeit with a stake of less than 45%, which was later increased to 63%). Harrah's also invested in Las Vegas-based National Airlines that year.

In early 1999 Harrah's bought Rio Hotel & Casino (also a partner in National Airlines), which operates one upscale casino on the Las Vegas Strip, for about $525 million. In 2000 the company bought riverboat casino operator Players International for $425 million. Also that year Harrah's had to write off about $39 million in investments and loans to National Airlines, which filed for bankruptcy. The company had a 48% stake in the airline. In 2001 the company continued its acquisition streak with the purchase of Harveys Casino Resorts, with four locations in Colorado, Iowa, and Nevada, for $675 million. The 452-room Harrah's Atlantic City hotel tower was opened in 2002. Also that year the company began construction of a second, 800-room tower at its Atlantic City Showboat casino.

OFFICERS

Chairman, CEO, and Director: Philip G. Satre, age 52, $2,100,000 pay
President, COO, and Director: Gary W. Loveman, age 41, $1,780,000 pay
SVP and CFO: Charles Atwood, age 53, $492,280 pay
SVP, Operations Products and Services and CIO: John M. Boushy, age 47, $599,154 pay
SVP and General Counsel: Stephen H. Brammell, age 44
SVP Communications and Government Relations: Janis L. Jones, age 52
SVP Marketing: Richard E. Mirman, age 36, $470,645 pay
SVP Human Resources: Marilyn G. Winn, age 49
VP, Corporate Counsel, and Secretary: Brad L. Kerby
General Manager, Lake Tahoe Properties: Joe Hasson
General Manager, Harrah's New Orleans: Bill Noble
President, Central Division: Anthony M. Sanfilippo
President, Western Division: J. Carlos Tolosa
President, Eastern Division: Timothy J. Wilmott, age 43
Director Retail Operations: Katherine Gonzalez
Director Sales: Steve Lowe
Auditors: Deloitte & Touche LLP

LOCATIONS

HQ: One Harrah's Court, Las Vegas, NV 89119
Phone: 702-407-6000 **Fax:** 702-407-6037
Web: www.harrahs.com

PRODUCTS/OPERATIONS

2001 Sales

	$ mil.	% of total
Central Region	1,707	46
(Illinois, Indiana, Iowa, Louisiana, Mississippi, & Missouri)		
Western Region		
Rio Hotel & Casino	391	11
Southern Nevada	422	11
Northern Nevada & Colorado	389	10
Eastern Region		
Harrah's Atlantic City	397	11
Showboat Atlantic City	327	9
Other	76	2
Total	**3,709**	**100**

Selected Casinos
Atlantic City Showboat (NJ)
Harrah's Atlantic City (NJ)
Harrah's Lake Tahoe (NV)
Harrah's Las Vegas
Rio Suite Hotel & Casino (Las Vegas)

COMPETITORS

Ameristar Casinos
Argosy Gaming
Aztar
Boyd Gaming
Hollywood Casino
Isle of Capri Casinos
Kerzner International
Mandalay Resort Group
Mashantucket Pequot Gaming
MGM Mirage
Park Place Entertainment
Pinnacle Entertainment
President Casinos
Station Casinos
Trump Hotels & Casinos

HISTORICAL FINANCIALS & EMPLOYEES

NYSE: HET FYE: December 31	Annual Growth	12/92	12/93	12/94	12/95	12/96	12/97	12/98	12/99	12/00	12/01
Sales ($ mil.)	14.3%	1,113	1,252	1,339	1,550	1,588	1,619	2,004	3,024	3,471	3,709
Net income ($ mil.)	16.6%	53	86	78	79	99	99	102	209	(12)	209
Income as % of sales	—	4.7%	6.9%	5.9%	5.1%	6.2%	6.1%	5.1%	6.9%	—	5.6%
Earnings per share ($)	14.9%	0.52	0.84	0.76	0.76	0.95	0.98	1.00	1.62	(0.10)	1.81
Stock price - FY high ($)	—	13.51	39.62	39.78	33.13	38.88	23.06	26.38	30.75	30.06	38.29
Stock price - FY low ($)	—	5.31	12.58	18.63	21.60	16.38	15.50	11.06	14.19	17.00	22.00
Stock price - FY close ($)	12.1%	13.21	32.94	22.23	24.25	19.88	18.88	15.69	26.44	26.38	37.01
P/E - high	—	26	44	47	43	41	22	22	18	—	21
P/E - low	—	10	14	22	28	17	14	9	8	—	12
Dividends per share ($)	—	0.00	0.00	0.00	0.00	0.00	0.00	0.00	0.00	0.00	0.00
Book value per share ($)	12.6%	4.20	5.24	6.09	5.70	6.99	7.28	8.33	11.95	10.95	12.23
Employees	6.9%	23,000	23,100	28,500	22,000	22,000	23,400	37,400	36,100	40,000	42,000

STOCK PRICE HISTORY
HIGH/LOW/CLOSE

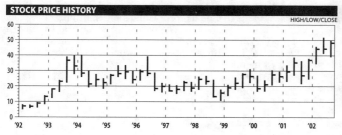

2001 FISCAL YEAR-END

Debt ratio: 73.0%
Return on equity: 15.8%
Cash ($ mil.): 362
Current ratio: 1.09
Long-term debt ($ mil.): 3,719
No. of shares (mil.): 112
Dividends
 Yield: —
 Payout: —
Market value ($ mil.): 4,157

HARRIS CORPORATION

Hail Harris for a high-tech hookup. The Melbourne, Florida-based company makes commercial wireless and broadcast communications products such as microwave radios, satellite systems, high-frequency modems, and television and cable broadcast equipment. Commercial clients include radio and television broadcasters, utilities providers, construction companies, and oil producers. Harris also develops air traffic control systems, space and missile communications equipment, and other military electronics systems for the US government (about 45% of sales).

The company is strengthening its line of communications products with acquisitions and adapting technologies created for its government customers to other markets. Harris has drawn on its expertise in broadcast, high-frequency, and radio-frequency transmission to provide its commercial wireless broadband communications systems. The company has folded or divested most non-communications operations including its semiconductor and prepress publishing systems businesses.

HISTORY

Harris was founded in Niles, Ohio, in 1895 by brothers Alfred and Charles Harris, both jewelers and inventors. Among their inventions was a printing press that became Harris Automatic Press Company's flagship product.

Harris remained a small, family-run company until 1944, when engineer George Dively was hired as general manager. Under Dively the company began manufacturing bindery, typesetting, and paper converting equipment while remaining a leading supplier of printing presses. In 1957 Harris merged with typesetter maker Intertype and became known as Harris-Intertype Corporation.

During the 1960s and 1970s Harris-Intertype grew through acquisitions. In 1967 it bought electronics and data processing equipment maker Radiation, a company heavily dependent on government contracts, and relocated to Radiation's headquarters in Melbourne, Florida. The company also bought RF Communications (two-way radios, 1969), UCC-Communications Systems (data processing equipment, 1972), and General Electric's (GE) broadcast equipment line (1972).

The company changed its name to Harris Corporation in 1974. In 1980 Harris bought Farinon, a manufacturer of microwave radio systems, and Lanier Business Products, the leading maker of dictating equipment. In 1983 it sold its printing equipment business.

Harris formed a joint venture with 3M, called Harris/3M Document Products, in 1986 to market copiers and fax machines, and in 1989 it acquired the entire operation, which became Lanier Worldwide. Other 1980s acquisitions included Scientific Calculations, a CAD software developer (1986), and GE's Solid State group (1988).

Harris won a contract with the FAA in 1992 to modernize voice communications between airports and airplanes. Later that year Harris acquired Westronic, a supplier of automated control systems for electric utilities. Former GE manager and 10-year Harris executive Phillip Farmer was named chairman in 1993. The next year Harris began installing the world's largest private digital telephone network, along Russia's gas pipeline, and it spun off its computer products division as Harris Computer Systems.

In 1996 Harris became the first company to demonstrate a digital TV transmitter. That year it acquired NovAtel, a maker of cellular and wireless local-loop systems for rural areas, and it bought a stake in the Chile-based phone company, Compañía de Telefonos. In 1997 it purchased digital broadcasting specialist Innovation Telecommunications Image and Sound.

The company in 1998 purchased German chemical manufacturer Bayer's Agfa-Gevaert photocopier business, which doubled Lanier's share of the European office equipment market. Hurt by a tough semiconductor market that year, Harris laid off about 8% of its workforce.

Shifting toward a strictly communications-related operation in 1999, Harris sold its semiconductor operation (which now does business as Intersil) in a deal valued at about $600 million and spun off Lanier to shareholders. It also sold its photomask manufacturing unit to Align-Rite.

In 2000 Harris expanded its broadcasting and wireless transmission product lines with the acquisitions of Louth Automation and Wavtrace. That year the company began outsourcing the assembly of its commercial printed circuit boards and folded its telephone switching and alarm management product lines.

The company broadened its communications product portfolio in 2001 with the acquisitions of Exigent, a provider of satellite tracking and control software, and Hirschmann, a maker of digital broadcasting radio transmitters and cable systems. That year Harris also sold its minority stakes in two industrial electronics joint ventures to majority owner General Electric.

Chairman, President, and CEO: Phillip W. Farmer, age 63, $1,570,101 pay
SVP and CFO: Bryan R. Roub, age 60, $590,613 pay
VP and Controller: James L. Christie, age 49
VP and Treasurer: David S. Wasserman, age 58
VP, Secretary, and General Counsel:
Richard L. Ballantyne, age 61, $388,609 pay
VP, Corporate Development: Gary L. McArthur, age 41
VP, Human Resources and Corporate Relations:
Nick E. Heldreth, age 59, $388,609 pay
President, Broadcast Communications Division:
Bruce M. Allen, age 61
**President, Government Communications Systems
Division:** Robert K. Henry, age 54, $454,322 pay
President, Microwave Communications Division:
Allen E. Dukes, age 54, $400,286 pay
President, Network Support Division:
Daniel R. Pearson, age 49
President, RF Communications Division:
Chester A. Massari, age 59
Auditors: Ernst & Young LLP

LOCATIONS

HQ: 1025 W. NASA Blvd., Melbourne, FL 32919
Phone: 321-727-9100   **Fax:** 321-727-9646
Web: www.harris.com

Harris Corporation has about 20 manufacturing plants and 55 offices in the Americas, Europe, and Asia.

2001 Sales

	$ mil.	% of total
US	1,382	71
Other countries	573	29
Total	**1,955**	**100**

PRODUCTS/OPERATIONS

2001 Sales

	$ mil.	% of total
Commercial	1,107	57
Government	848	43
Total	**1,955**	**100**

Selected Products and Services
Advanced avionics systems
Aircraft, shipboard, spacecraft, and missile
  communications
Broadband wireless access systems
Civil and military air traffic control systems
Command, control, communication, and intelligence
  systems, products, and services
Digital and analog AM and FM radio studio and
  transmission systems and products
Electronic warfare simulation
Global Positioning System-based control systems
Law enforcement communication systems
Microwave communications products and systems
Telecommunications tools and test sets
Terrestrial and satellite communication antennas,
  terminals, and networks

COMPETITORS

ADC Telecom	Hitachi	Nokia
Alcatel	L-3	Nortel Networks
Cisco Systems	Communications	Northrop
DMC Stratex	Lucent	Grumman
Ericsson	Marconi	Raytheon
Fujitsu	Motorola	Siemens
General	NEC	Tellabs
Dynamics	Nera	

HISTORICAL FINANCIALS & EMPLOYEES

NYSE: HRS FYE: Friday nearest June 30	Annual Growth	6/92	6/93	6/94	6/95	6/96	6/97	6/98	6/99	6/00	6/01
Sales ($ mil.)	(4.7%)	3,004	3,099	3,336	3,444	3,621	3,797	3,890	1,744	1,807	1,955
Net income ($ mil.)	(13.0%)	75	111	112	155	178	208	133	53	18	21
Income as % of sales	—	2.5%	3.6%	3.4%	4.5%	4.9%	5.5%	3.4%	3.0%	1.0%	1.1%
Earnings per share ($)	(11.5%)	0.96	1.41	1.41	1.98	2.29	2.63	1.66	0.67	0.25	0.32
Stock price – FY high ($)	—	17.00	19.63	26.13	26.81	34.44	46.06	55.31	44.88	39.75	37.88
Stock price – FY low ($)	—	10.63	13.44	18.19	18.88	24.44	25.13	40.19	27.31	18.25	20.75
Stock price – FY close ($)	7.9%	13.75	19.38	22.06	25.81	30.50	42.00	44.69	39.19	32.75	27.21
P/E – high	—	17	14	17	14	15	17	33	57	159	118
P/E – low	—	11	10	12	10	11	9	24	35	73	65
Dividends per share ($)	(10.1%)	0.52	0.52	0.56	0.62	0.68	0.76	0.88	0.96	0.58	0.20
Book value per share ($)	2.4%	13.65	14.41	15.12	16.06	17.66	19.82	20.11	19.96	19.93	16.94
Employees	(10.8%)	28,300	28,300	28,200	26,600	27,600	29,000	28,500	10,500	10,000	10,100

STOCK PRICE HISTORY

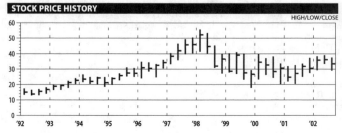

HIGH/LOW/CLOSE

2001 FISCAL YEAR-END

Debt ratio: 25.6%
Return on equity: 1.7%
Cash ($ mil.): 103
Current ratio: 2.65
Long-term debt ($ mil.): 384
No. of shares (mil.): 66
Dividends
  Yield: 0.7%
  Payout: 62.5%
Market value ($ mil.): 1,792

THE HARTFORD FINANCIAL

Like the stag in its logo, The Hartford Financial Services Group takes a heads-up stance. The Hartford, Connecticut-based company provides personal and commercial property/casualty insurance (including homeowners and standard and nonstandard auto coverage) and sells reinsurance. The company owns Hartford Life, a major writer of individual annuities in the US and a provider of disability insurance, investment management services, and both personal and group life insurance.

Hartford Life also offers mutual funds, most of which are managed by Wellington Management Group. The company sells its investment products through a distribution network consisting of about 1,500 broker-dealers and approximately 500 banks.

As the lucrative baby boomer generation ages, Hartford Life is targeting the retirement savings market and seeks marketing alliances, such as its agreement to provide auto and homeowners polices to members of the American Association of Retired Persons (AARP). Focusing on the US market, the company has exited all of its international property/casualty operations.

HISTORY

In 1810 a group of Hartford, Connecticut, businessmen led by Walter Mitchell and Henry Terry founded the Hartford Fire Insurance Co. Frequent fires in America's wooden cities and executive ignorance of risk assessment and premium-setting often left the firm on the edge of insolvency. (In 1835 stockholders staged a coup and threw management out.) Still, each urban conflagration — including the Great Chicago Fire of 1871 — gave the Hartford an opportunity to seek out and pay all its policyholders, thus teaching the company to underwrite under fire, as it were, and to use such disasters to refine its rates.

The company's stag logo was initially a little deer, as shown on a policy sold to Abraham Lincoln in 1861. A few years later, however, Hartford began using the majestic creature (from a Landseer painting) now familiar to customers. By the 1880s Hartford operated nationwide, as well as in Canada and Hawaii.

The company survived both world wars and the Depression but emerged in the 1950s in need of organization. It set up new regional offices and added life insurance, buying Columbian National Life (founded 1902), which became Hartford Life Insurance Co.

In 1969 Hartford was bought by ITT (formerly International Telephone and Telegraph), whose CEO, Harold Geneen, was an avid conglomerateur. Consumer advocate Ralph Nader strongly opposed the acquisition — he fought the merger in court for years and felt vindicated when ITT spun off Hartford in 1995. Others opposed it, too, because ITT had engineered the merger based on an IRS ruling (later revoked) that Hartford stockholders wouldn't have to pay capital gains taxes on the purchase price of their stock.

Insurance operations consolidated under the Hartford Life Insurance banner in 1978. Through the 1980s, Hartford Life remained one of ITT's strongest operations. A conservative investment policy kept Hartford safe from the junk bond and real estate manias of the 1980s.

Hartford reorganized its property/casualty operations along three lines in 1986, and in 1992 it organized its reinsurance business into one unit. The company faced some liability in relation to Dow Corning's breast-implant litigation, but underwriting standards after 1985 reduced long-term risk. In 1994 the company began selling insurance products to AARP members under an exclusive agreement that runs through 2002. In 1996 the company finished its spinoff from ITT, which was acquired by Starwood Hotels & Resorts two years later.

To grow its reinsurance operation, Hartford acquired the reinsurance business of Orion Capital (now Royal & SunAlliance USA) in 1996. It posted a loss of $99 million, due in large part to asbestos and pollution liabilities. Late that year the firm changed its name to The Hartford Financial Services Group.

To shore up reserves and fund growth, in 1997 the company spun off 19% of Hartford Life. The next year The Hartford expanded into nonstandard auto insurance, buying Omni Insurance Group, and sold its London & Edinburgh Insurance Group to Norwich Union (now part of Aviva, formerly CGNU). In 1999 Hartford acquired the reinsurance business of Vesta Fire Insurance, a subsidiary of Vesta Insurance Group.

In 2000 Hartford bought back the part of Hartford Life it had spun off. Hartford also bought the financial products and excess and surplus specialty insurance lines of Reliance Group Holdings. Assurances Générales de France bought Hartford's Dutch subsidiary, Zwolsche Algemeene.

In 2001 the company bought Fortis Financial, a US subsidiary of Belgian insurer Fortis, and sold Hartford Seguros, its Spanish subsidiary, to Liberty Mutual.

Chairman, President, and CEO: Ramani Ayer, age 54, $2,128,917 pay
EVP and Director; President and COO, Hartford Life: Thomas M. Marra, age 43
EVP and Director; President and COO, Hartford Property and Casualty: David K. Zwiener, age 47, $2,107,888 pay
EVP and CFO: David M. Johnson, age 41
EVP and General Counsel: Neal S. Wolin, age 40
SVP and Director, Employer Markets, Group Benefits Division: Richard L. Mucci
SVP and Controller: Robert J. Price, age 51
SVP and Treasurer: John N. Giamalis, age 44
Group SVP and Chief Investment Officer; President, Hartford Investment Management Co.: David M. Znamierowski, $1,056,906 pay
Group SVP, Corporate Relations: Edward L. Morgan Jr., age 58
Group SVP, Human Resources: Randall I. Kiviat, age 51
Group SVP, Information Technology: David H. Annis
SEVP, Business Insurance, Hartford Property and Casualty: Judith A. Blades
Auditors: Deloitte & Touche LLP

LOCATIONS

HQ: The Hartford Financial Services Group, Inc.
Hartford Plaza, 690 Asylum Ave.,
Hartford, CT 06115
Phone: 860-547-5000   **Fax:** 860-547-2680
Web: www.thehartford.com

The Hartford Financial Services Group operates worldwide, primarily in North America.

2001 Sales

	$ mil.	% of total
North America	15,003	99
Other	144	1
Total	**15,147**	**100**

PRODUCTS/OPERATIONS

2001 Assets

	$ mil.	% of total
Cash & equivalents	353	—
Treasury & agency securities	2,543	1
Foreign governments' securities	1,003	1
State & municipal bonds	10,060	6
Corporate bonds	22,008	12
Stocks	1,349	1
Policy loans	3,317	2
Assets in separate account	114,720	63
Recoverables & receivables	7,594	4
Other	18,291	10
Total	**181,238**	**100**

COMPETITORS

Allmerica Financial	Chubb	Mutual of Omaha
Allstate	CIGNA	New York Life
American Financial	Citigroup	Northwestern
American General	CNA Financial	Mutual
AIG	GenAmerica	Prudential
AXA Financial	GeneralCologne Re	SAFECO
Berkshire Hathaway	Liberty Mutual	St. Paul
	Lincoln National	Companies
	MetLife	State Farm
	Millea Holdings	USAA

HISTORICAL FINANCIALS & EMPLOYEES

NYSE: HIG FYE: December 31	Annual Growth	12/92	12/93	12/94	12/95	12/96	12/97	12/98	12/99	12/00	12/01
Assets ($ mil.)	14.4%	54,180	66,179	76,765	93,855	108,840	131,743	150,632	167,051	171,532	181,238
Net income ($ mil.)	—	(274)	537	632	562	(99)	1,332	1,015	862	974	507
Income as % of assets	—	—	0.8%	0.8%	0.6%	—	1.0%	0.7%	0.5%	0.6%	0.3%
Earnings per share ($)	(2.1%)	—	—	—	2.38	(0.42)	5.58	4.30	3.79	4.34	2.10
Stock price - FY high ($)	—	—	—	—	25.06	34.94	47.25	60.00	66.44	80.00	71.15
Stock price - FY low ($)	—	—	—	—	23.69	22.25	32.44	37.63	36.50	29.38	45.50
Stock price - FY close ($)	17.2%	—	—	—	24.19	33.75	46.78	54.88	47.38	70.63	62.83
P/E - high	—	—	—	—	10	—	8	14	17	18	31
P/E - low	—	—	—	—	10	—	6	9	10	7	20
Dividends per share ($)	—	—	—	—	0.00	0.60	0.80	0.83	0.89	0.96	1.00
Book value per share ($)	10.7%	—	—	—	20.07	19.22	25.79	28.25	25.16	32.98	36.86
Employees	3.0%	21,000	21,000	20,000	21,000	22,000	25,000	25,000	26,000	26,600	27,400

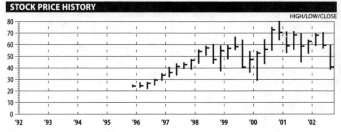

STOCK PRICE HISTORY
HIGH/LOW/CLOSE

2001 FISCAL YEAR-END
Equity as % of assets: 5.0%
Return on assets: 0.3%
Return on equity: 6.2%
Long-term debt ($ mil.): 3,377
No. of shares (mil.): 245
Dividends
   Yield: 1.6%
   Payout: 47.6%
Market value ($ mil.): 15,364
Sales ($ mil.): 15,147

HARTMARX CORPORATION

Hartmarx is the top US maker of men's suits, but as business dress has gone casual, the Chicago-based company has loosened its collar. Hartmarx built a name around its century-old Hart Schaffner & Marx and Hickey-Freeman brands of men's tailored clothing.

Although suits and sports coats are still its biggest business, Hartmarx has ventured into sportswear, including golf wear (Bobby Jones, Jack Nicklaus), slacks (Sansabelt), and accessories, which appeal to younger customers and those not tied to wearing a suit every day.

The company sells its apparel through department and specialty stores, golf shops, resorts, and catalogs in the US and more than a dozen other countries; Dillard's accounts for 20% of its sales. In addition to its own brands, Hartmarx makes clothing under licenses from Tommy Hilfiger, Kenneth Cole, Perry Ellis, and others. Hartmarx also makes women's suits and separates under labels such as Barrie Pace and the licensed Austin Reed name.

Saudi Arabian investor Abdullah Taha Bakhsh owns 17% of the company.

HISTORY

Harry Hart, 21, and his brother Max, 18, of Chicago, opened a men's clothing store, Harry Hart and Brother, in 1872. In 1887, after Marcus Marx and Joseph Schaffner had joined the company, the enterprise was renamed Hart Schaffner & Marx.

The young clothiers contracted with independent tailors to produce suits for their new store. Recognizing the potential of the wholesale garment industry, they began selling to other merchants and in 1897 launched a national ad campaign in leading publications.

A walkout by female workers in 1910 protesting low wages and poor working conditions in one of the company's 48 tailoring shops sparked a citywide garment workers' strike. Schaffner and Harry successfully negotiated a settlement (not honored by other major Chicago companies) in January 1911.

Hart Schaffner & Marx in 1935 began a pattern of purchases over the next three decades that included Wallach Brothers (New York clothing chain), Hastings (a California clothier, 1952), Hanny's (Arizona, 1962), Hickey-Freeman (stores in Chicago, New York, and Detroit; 1964), and Field Brothers (New York, 1968). A 1970 antitrust decree forced it to sell 30 of its 238 men's clothing stores and refrain for 10 years from further purchases without court approval. The company made several approved purchases during the period. In 1981 Hart Schaffner & Marx bought the

Country Miss chain and expanded into women's clothing. A year later it bought Kuppenheimer, a leading maker of lower-priced suits.

The company changed its name to Hartmarx in 1983, creating a holding company to oversee the variety of businesses it had acquired. A costly 1986 reorganization of administrative functions and the retail stores resulted in the loss of 800 jobs; earnings fell 42%. After a brief recovery in 1987 and 1988, earnings declined by more than half to $17 million in 1989, largely because of a dramatic increase in wool prices. Further restructuring, in 1990, Hartmarx reorganized its women's lines into a new unit under the name Barrie Pace and began experimenting with placing Kuppenheimer outlets in Sears stores. It entered the golf wear industry the next year with the introduction of its Bobby Jones line; golf wear grew to $50 million in sales in just five years.

Despite the financial birdie hit by golf wear, CEO Harvey Weinberg was ousted in 1992 due to continued losses (blamed largely on retail operations). COO Elbert Hand took the post and immediately upped the restructuring pace, expanding Hartmarx's core men's apparel business and further divesting retail operations. The company completely exited retailing in 1995, even as some of its retail customers (Barneys, Today's Man) filed for bankruptcy protection. It also closed 10 domestic factories and began moving production to countries such as Costa Rica and Mexico.

Hartmarx in 1996 bought Plaid Clothing Group, a bankrupt supplier of men's tailored clothing. In 1998 it acquired the tropical sportswear wholesale business of Pusser's, as well as Canadian men's apparel maker and Hartmarx licensee Coppley, Noyes and Randall. Hartmarx bought Canada's Royal Shirt in 1999.

Emphasizing the importance of sportswear in a dress-down world, the company brought its various sportswear lines under one roof in early 2000. Late in the year Hartmarx formed a partnership with UK designer Ted Baker to offer the designer's apparel and home furnishings in North and South America. Hartmarx acquired men's sportswear manufacturer Consolidated Apparel Group in August 2001. The Lincoln Company, a group of investors (including suit manufacturer The Tom James Company), made an offer to buy Hartmarx, but the deal fell through.

OFFICERS

Chairman: Elbert O. Hand, age 62, $737,917 pay
(prior to title change)
President, CEO, COO, and Director: Homi B. Patel,
age 52, $578,333 pay (prior to promotion)
EVP, CFO, and Treasurer: Glenn R. Morgan, age 54,
$259,250 pay
SVP, General Counsel, and Secretary: Taras R. Proczko,
$134,125 pay
**SVP, Special Markets for Intercontinental Branded
Apparel:** Joe Diskin
VP, Controller, and Chief Accounting Officer:
Andrew A. Zahr, age 58
VP, Compensation and Benefits: Linda J. Valentine,
$133,950 pay
Chairman and CEO, Hart Schaffner & Marx:
Kenneth Hoffman, age 59
Manager of Human Resources: Susan Klawitter
Auditors: PricewaterhouseCoopers LLP

LOCATIONS

HQ: 101 N. Wacker Dr., Chicago, IL 60606
Phone: 312-372-6300   **Fax:** 312-444-2710
Web: www.hartmarx.com

Hartmarx operates 12 manufacturing plants in the US,
three in Canada, one in Costa Rica, and one in Mexico.

PRODUCTS/OPERATIONS

2001 Sales

	% of total
Men's apparel	91
Women's apparel	9
Total	**100**

Owned Brands

Barrie Pace
Brannoch
Cambridge
Coppley
Desert Classic
Hart Schaffner & Marx
Hawksley & Wight
Hickey-Freeman
Keithmoor
Palm Beach
Pusser's of the West Indies
Racquet Club
Royal Shirt
Sansabelt

Licensed Brands

Alan Flusser
Austin Reed
Bobby Jones
Burberry
Claiborne
Daniel Hechter
Evan-Picone
Gieves & Hawkes
Jack Nicklaus
Kenneth Cole
KM by Krizia
Perry Ellis
Pierre Cardin
Pringle of Scotland
Ted Baker
Tommy Hilfiger

COMPETITORS

Ashworth
Brooks Brothers
Capital Mercury Apparel
Cutter & Buck
Donna Karan
Ellen Tracy
The Gap
Haggar
HdP
Hugo Boss
J. Crew
Jones Apparel

Jos. A. Bank
Lands' End
Levi Strauss
Men's Wearhouse
Nautica Enterprises
Oxford Industries
Perry Ellis International
Phillips-Van Heusen
Polo
S&K Famous Brands
Savane International
Tropical Sportswear

HISTORICAL FINANCIALS & EMPLOYEES

NYSE: HMX FYE: November 30	Annual Growth	11/92	11/93	11/94	11/95	11/96	11/97	11/98	11/99	11/00	11/01
Sales ($ mil.)	(6.0%)	1,054	732	718	595	610	718	725	727	681	602
Net income ($ mil.)	—	(220)	6	16	3	25	25	15	2	9	(14)
Income as % of sales	—	—	0.8%	2.2%	0.5%	4.0%	3.5%	2.0%	0.2%	1.3%	—
Earnings per share ($)	—	(8.59)	0.20	0.50	0.10	0.74	0.74	0.42	0.05	0.31	(0.46)
Stock price - FY high ($)	—	8.63	8.25	7.50	6.88	6.50	10.13	9.00	6.13	4.06	3.90
Stock price - FY low ($)	—	3.00	5.13	5.00	4.25	3.75	4.88	4.38	3.63	2.13	1.35
Stock price - FY close ($)	(11.9%)	5.63	7.00	5.38	4.50	5.25	8.13	5.88	3.81	2.31	1.80
P/E - high	—	—	41	12	69	9	14	21	123	14	—
P/E - low	—	—	26	8	43	5	7	10	73	7	—
Dividends per share ($)	—	0.00	0.00	0.00	0.00	0.00	0.00	0.00	0.00	0.00	0.00
Book value per share ($)	9.5%	2.73	3.41	3.95	4.11	4.86	5.62	6.06	6.43	6.69	6.19
Employees	(10.1%)	13,000	11,200	11,000	8,200	8,600	8,100	9,200	8,000	7,200	5,000

STOCK PRICE HISTORY

HIGH/LOW/CLOSE

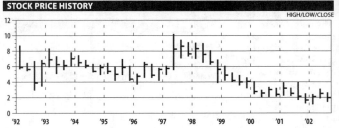

2001 FISCAL YEAR-END

Debt ratio: 43.9%
Return on equity: —
Cash ($ mil.): 2
Current ratio: 2.65
Long-term debt ($ mil.): 147
No. of shares (mil.): 30
Dividends
　Yield: —
　Payout: —
Market value ($ mil.): 54

HASBRO, INC.

The Force may be declining with *Pokémon*, but Hasbro is hoping its other toys, games, and puzzles can stand up to Barbie. Pawtucket, Rhode Island-based Hasbro, the #2 toy company behind Barbie-maker Mattel, has some of the best-known brand names in the industry, including *Star Wars* action figures, *Pokémon* trading cards, G.I. Joe, Playskool, Nerf, and Tonka. The company's games division, which includes Milton Bradley, Parker Brothers, and Wizards of the Coast, accounts for 52% of sales. Some 30% of sales come from Wal-Mart and Toys "R" Us.

Hasbro has tapped into the cross-marketing force of movies, paying at least $600 million for the right to make most of the toys for the *Star Wars* prequels (not to mention giving producer George Lucas warrants to buy stock; he now owns 8% of Hasbro). The initial returns for the first episode were disappointing, but the company is pinning happier endings on the other two episodes.

Hasbro also has licensing deals for *Jurassic Park III* and Disney's *Monsters, Inc.* However, the company is lessening its focus on licensing.

Chairman and CEO Alan Hassenfeld, the third generation of Hassenfelds to control the company, owns about 11% of Hasbro.

HISTORY

Henry and Helal Hassenfeld formed Hassenfeld Brothers in Pawtucket, Rhode Island, in 1923 to distribute fabric remnants. By 1926 the company was manufacturing fabric-covered pencil boxes and shortly thereafter, pencils.

Hassenfeld Brothers branched into the toy industry during the 1940s by introducing toy nurse and doctor kits. The company's toy division was the first to use TV to promote a toy product (Mr. Potato Head in 1952).

Expansion continued in the mid-1960s with the introduction of the G.I. Joe doll, which quickly became its primary toy line. Hassenfeld Brothers went public in 1968 and changed its name to Hasbro Industries. It bought Romper Room (TV productions) the next year.

In the 1970s the toy and pencil divisions, led by different family members, disagreed over the company's finances, future direction, and leadership. The dispute caused the company to split in 1980. The toy division continued to operate under the Hasbro name; the pencil division (Empire Pencil Corporation in Shelbyville, Tennessee, led by Harold Hassenfeld) became a separate corporation.

Hasbro expanded rapidly in the 1980s under new CEO Stephen Hassenfeld. He reduced the number of products by one-third to concentrate on developing a line of toys aimed at specific markets. During that decade the firm released a number of successful toys, including a smaller version of G.I. Joe (1982) and Transformers (small vehicles that transform into robots, 1984). Hasbro acquired Milton Bradley, a major producer of board games (*Chutes and Ladders, Candy Land*), puzzles, and preschool toys (Playskool) in 1984.

The company acquired Cabbage Patch Kids, *Scrabble, Parcheesi,* and other product lines in 1989. Stephen died that year. His brother Alan, who had spearheaded Hasbro's international sales growth in the late 1980s, became CEO.

Hasbro bought Tonka (including the Kenner and Parker Brothers brands) in 1991 and established operations in Greece, Mexico, and Hungary. Hasbro blocked a $5.2 billion hostile takeover attempt by Mattel in 1996, and in 1997 it beat them to an exclusive four-year deal to produce nearly all NFL-related toys and games. It also bought OddzOn Products (sports toys, Koosh balls) and began cutting about 2,500 jobs (20% of Hasbro's employees) that year.

Expanding in the high-tech toys niche, in 1998 Hasbro made several acquisitions, including Tiger Electronics (Giga Pets), the rights to some 75 Atari home console game titles (*Missile Command, Centipede*), MicroProse (3-D video games for PCs), and Galoob Toys, a fellow *Star Wars* prequel licensee and maker of Micro Machines and Pound Puppies. Tiger Electronics had the hit of the 1998 holiday season: a chattering interactive doll called Furby.

In 1999 Hasbro bought game maker and retailer Wizards of the Coast (maker of *Pokémon* trading cards). In late 1999 the company announced it would can another 19% of its workforce (2,200 jobs), close two plants in Mexico and the UK, and launch Games.com with Go2Net (now InfoSpace) to feature online versions of its games.

Another 750 job cuts followed in late 2000. The company sold its Hasbro Interactive and Games.com units in early 2001. Later that year, facing losses caused by the fading *Pokémon* craze, Hasbro said it would focus on favorites such as G.I. Joe and Tonka.

OFFICERS

Chairman and CEO: Alan G. Hassenfeld, age 53, $1,005,900 pay
Vice Chairman: Harold P. Gordon, age 64, $793,016 pay
President, COO, and Director: Alfred J. Verrecchia, age 59, $763,277 pay
EVP and President, International: George B. Volanakis, age 54
SVP and CFO: David D. R. Hargreaves, age 49

SVP and Controller: Richard B. Holt, age 60
SVP Human Resources: Bob Carniaux
SVP, General Counsel, and Secretary: Barry Nagler, age 45
SVP and Treasurer: Martin R. Trueb, age 50
President and CEO, Wizards of the Coast: Vince Caluori
President, Games: E. David Wilson, age 64, $916,828 pay
President, Hasbro U.S. Toys: Brian Goldner, age 38, $932,134 pay
President, Worldwide Marketing and Brand Development: Roger Shiffman
Auditors: KPMG LLP

LOCATIONS

HQ: 1027 Newport Ave., Pawtucket, RI 02862
Phone: 401-431-8697   **Fax:** 401-431-8535
Web: www.hasbro.com

2001 Sales

	$ mil.	% of total
US	1,826	64
Other countries	1,030	36
Total	**2,856**	**100**

PRODUCTS/OPERATIONS

2001 Sales

	$ mil.	% of total
Games & puzzles	1,484	52
Boys' toys	522	18
Preschool toys	222	8
Creative play	191	7
Girls' toys	112	4
Other	325	11
Total	**2,856**	**100**

Selected Brands and Products

Battleship	Play-Doh
Bob the Builder toys	*Pokémon*
Boggle	Raggedy Ann and
Candy Land	Raggedy Andy dolls
Chutes and Ladders	*Risk*
Clue	*Scrabble*
Dungeons and Dragons	Sit 'N Spin
Easy-Bake Oven	*Sorry!*
Furby	Spirograph
The Game of Life	*Star Wars* action figures
G.I. Joe action figures	Super Soaker water
Hungry Hungry Hippos	products
Lite-Brite	Tinkertoys
Magic: The Gathering	Tonka
Monopoly	Transformers
Mr. Potato Head	*Trivial Pursuit*
Nerf	*Twister*
Operation	*Yahtzee*
Ouija	

COMPETITORS

Acclaim	Marvel	SEGA
Entertainment	Enterprises	SMOBY
Applause	Mattel	Sony
Bandai	Nintendo	Toymax
Electronic Arts	Ohio Art	International
Infogrames, Inc.	Play-By-Play	Ty
JAKKS Pacific	Playmates	Vivendi Universal
LEGO	Playmobil	Publishing
Manley Toy	Pleasant	Zindart
Quest	Radio Flyer	

HISTORICAL FINANCIALS & EMPLOYEES

NYSE: HAS FYE: Last Sunday in December	Annual Growth	12/92	12/93	12/94	12/95	12/96	12/97	12/98	12/99	12/00	12/01
Sales ($ mil.)	1.3%	2,541	2,747	2,670	2,858	3,002	3,189	3,305	4,232	3,787	2,856
Net income ($ mil.)	(11.5%)	179	200	175	156	200	135	206	189	(145)	60
Income as % of sales	—	7.1%	7.3%	6.6%	5.4%	6.7%	4.2%	6.2%	4.5%	—	2.1%
Earnings per share ($)	(10.1%)	0.89	0.96	0.85	0.77	0.98	0.68	1.01	0.93	(0.82)	0.34
Stock price – FY high ($)	—	15.96	18.02	16.29	15.68	20.91	24.34	27.30	37.00	18.94	18.44
Stock price – FY low ($)	—	10.29	12.51	12.40	12.62	12.84	15.26	18.67	16.88	8.38	10.31
Stock price – FY close ($)	1.3%	14.51	16.12	12.96	13.79	17.29	21.01	24.09	18.94	10.63	16.23
P/E – high	—	18	18	18	20	20	35	26	38	—	53
P/E – low	—	12	12	14	16	12	22	18	17	—	29
Dividends per share ($)	3.2%	0.09	0.10	0.12	0.14	0.17	0.21	0.21	0.23	0.24	0.12
Book value per share ($)	3.7%	5.64	6.47	7.09	7.77	8.55	9.19	9.91	9.74	7.70	7.82
Employees	(3.5%)	11,000	12,500	12,500	13,000	13,000	12,000	10,000	9,500	8,900	8,000

STOCK PRICE HISTORY HIGH/LOW/CLOSE

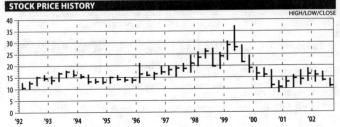

2001 FISCAL YEAR-END

Debt ratio: 46.3%
Return on equity: 4.5%
Cash ($ mil.): 233
Current ratio: 1.80
Long-term debt ($ mil.): 1,166
No. of shares (mil.): 173
Dividends
  Yield: 0.7%
  Payout: 35.3%
Market value ($ mil.): 2,807

HCA INC.

It doesn't take a federal investigation to reveal that HCA is one of the US's top hospital operators. Formerly HCA - The Healthcare Company, the Nashville, Tennessee-based company owns or operates more than 180 acute care, general, and psychiatric hospitals as well as 80 ambulatory surgery centers located primarily in the Sunbelt in the US (plus a few holdings in Switzerland and the UK). The firm draws about 35% of its revenues from Medicare and Medicaid, and its profits have been hit not only by the soaring costs of medical care but also by government cutbacks in reimbursement rates.

After grabbing headlines with its aggressive (some said cutthroat) consumption of hospitals and then with its spectacular downfall in a haze of ongoing federal and state investigations and lawsuits, HCA is becoming a kinder, leaner firm. It jettisoned its former names, has whittled its holdings to the top performers in their markets, and is consolidating administrative and supply operations to cut costs.

HISTORY

In 1987 Dallas lawyer Rick Scott and Fort Worth, Texas, financier Richard Rainwater founded Columbia Hospital Corp. to buy two hospitals in El Paso, Texas. The partners eventually sold 40% of the hospitals to local doctors, hoping that ownership would motivate physicians to increase productivity and efficiency.

The company entered the Miami market the next year and by 1990 had four hospitals. After merging with Smith Laboratories that year, Columbia went public and then acquired Sutter Laboratories (orthopedic products). By the end of 1990 it had 11 hospitals.

Columbia moved into Florida in 1992 with the purchase of several hospitals and facilities. The next year it acquired Galen Health Care, which operated 73 hospitals and had been spun off from health plan operator Humana earlier in the year. The merger thrust the hospital chain into about 15 new markets.

Columbia bought Hospital Corporation of America (HCA) in 1994. Thomas Frist, his son Thomas Frist Jr., and Jack Massey (founder of Kentucky Fried Chicken, now part of TRICON) founded HCA in Nashville, Tennessee, in 1968. By 1973 the company had grown to 50 hospitals. Meanwhile, the medical industry was changing as insurers, Medicare, and Medicaid began scrutinizing payment procedures, while the growth of HMOs (which aimed to restrict hospital admissions) cut hospital occupancy rates. HCA began paring operations in the late 1980s, selling more than 100 hospitals. In 1989 the

younger Frist led a $5.1 billion LBO of the company. He sold more assets and in 1992 took HCA public again, but losses and a tumbling stock price made it a takeover target.

Later in 1994 the newly christened Columbia/HCA acquired the US's largest operator of outpatient surgery centers, Dallas-based Medical Care America. A year later it bought 117-hospital HealthTrust, a 1987 offshoot of HCA.

Columbia/HCA was unstoppable in 1996, with some 150 acquisitions.

In 1997 the government began investigating the company's business practices. After executive indictments, the company fired Scott and several other top officers. Frist Jr. became chairman and CEO, pledging to shrink the company and tone down its aggressive approach. Columbia/HCA sold its home care business, more than 100 of its less-desirable hospitals, and almost all the operations of Value Health, a pharmacy benefits and behavioral health care management firm it had recently bought.

The trimming continued in 1998: The company sold nearly three dozen outpatient surgery centers and more than a dozen hospitals. That year Columbia/HCA sued former financial executive Samuel Greco and several vendors, accusing them of defrauding the company of several million dollars. In 1999 it spun off regional operators LifePoint Hospitals and Triad Hospitals to trim its holdings; the next year it spun off some 120 medical buildings to MedCap Properties, a joint venture formed with First Union Capital Partners.

In 2000 the firm settled with the federal government for about $800 million over charges of fraudulent Medicare billing. It also bought out partner Sun Life and Provincial Holdings' (now AXA UK) interest in several London hospitals and bought three hospitals there from St. Martins Healthcare. That year it became HCA - The Healthcare Company. In 2001 the company continued its strategy of consolidating and streamlining operations, in addition to resolving remaining legal matters. That year it also changed its name again — this time to simply HCA Inc.

HCA seems to be shaking off its shaky past. In 2002, the bottom line has been more kind to HCA, allowing the company to reinvest millions into modernizing facilities and equipment at its hospitals and surgery centers.

OFFICERS

Chairman and CEO: Jack O. Bovender Jr., age 56, $1,027,526 pay
President and COO: Richard M. Bracken, age 49, $587,550 pay
President, Ambulatory Surgery Group: Gregory S. Roth, age 45

President, Eastern Group: Jay F. Grinney, age 50,
$700,313 pay
President, Western Group: Samuel N. Hazen, age 41
SVP, Finance and Treasurer: David G. Anderson, age 54
SVP: Victor L. Campbell, age 55
SVP, Operations Finance: Rosalyn S. Elton, age 40
SVP, Contracts and Operations Support:
James A. Fitzgerald Jr., age 47
SVP, Development: V. Carl George, age 57
SVP, Quality and Medical Director: Frank M. Houser,
age 61, $478,573 pay
SVP and Controller: R. Milton Johnson, age 45
SVP, Government Programs: Patricia T. Lindler, age 54
SVP, Operations Administration: A. Bruce Moore Jr.,
age 42
SVP, Human Resources: Philip R. Patton, age 48
SVP, Internal Audit & Consulting Services:
Joseph N. Steakley, age 47
SVP, Revenue Cycle Operations Management:
Beverly B. Wallace, age 51
SVP and General Counsel: Robert A. Waterman, age 48,
$525,238 pay
SVP and CIO: Noel B. Williams, age 46
SVP, Ethics, Compliance, and Corporate Responsibility:
Alan Yuspeh, age 52
Auditors: Ernst & Young LLP

LOCATIONS

HQ: 1 Park Plaza, Nashville, TN 37203
Phone: 615-344-9551   Fax: 615-344-2266
Web: www.hcahealthcare.com

HCA operates hospitals, outpatient surgery centers,
and home health agencies in 23 states, Switzerland, and
the UK.

2001 Hospital Facilities

	no. facilities
Florida	40
Texas	37
Georgia	17
Louisiana	13
Virginia	12
Tennessee	11
California	7
Colorado	6
Utah	6
Oklahoma	5
West Virginia	4
Other states	19
International	8
Total	**185**

PRODUCTS/OPERATIONS

2001 Sales

	% of total
Managed care	42
Medicare	28
Medicaid	6
Other	24
Total	**100**

COMPETITORS

Allina Health
Ascension
Catholic Health Initiatives
Catholic Healthcare West
HEALTHSOUTH
Integrated Health Services
Kaiser Foundation
New York City Health and
  Hospitals
SSM Health Care
Tenet Healthcare
Trinity Health
Universal Health Services

HISTORICAL FINANCIALS & EMPLOYEES

NYSE: HCA FYE: December 31	Annual Growth	12/92	12/93	12/94	12/95	12/96	12/97	12/98	12/99	12/00	12/01
Sales ($ mil.)	42.1%	762	10,252	11,132	17,695	19,909	18,819	18,681	16,657	16,670	17,953
Net income ($ mil.)	48.3%	26	507	630	961	1,505	(305)	379	657	219	886
Income as % of sales	—	3.3%	4.9%	5.7%	5.4%	7.6%	—	2.0%	3.9%	1.3%	4.9%
Earnings per share ($)	8.7%	0.78	1.03	1.26	1.43	2.22	(0.46)	0.59	1.11	0.39	1.65
Stock price - FY high ($)	—	14.67	22.59	30.18	36.02	41.88	44.88	34.63	29.44	45.25	47.28
Stock price - FY low ($)	—	9.17	10.84	22.18	23.60	31.68	25.75	17.00	17.25	18.75	33.93
Stock price - FY close ($)	11.8%	14.17	22.09	24.35	33.85	40.75	29.63	24.75	29.31	44.01	38.54
P/E - high	—	19	19	21	23	19	—	59	26	116	27
P/E - low	—	12	9	15	15	14	—	29	15	48	20
Dividends per share ($)	—	0.00	0.02	0.08	0.08	0.09	0.08	0.08	0.06	0.08	0.08
Book value per share ($)	3.5%	6.84	6.88	9.63	10.67	12.82	11.30	11.80	9.95	8.11	9.35
Employees	33.1%	13,300	131,600	157,000	240,000	285,000	295,000	260,000	168,000	164,000	174,000

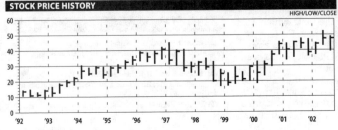

STOCK PRICE HISTORY HIGH/LOW/CLOSE

2001 FISCAL YEAR-END

Debt ratio: 57.9%
Return on equity: 19.3%
Cash ($ mil.): 85
Current ratio: 1.30
Long-term debt ($ mil.): 6,553
No. of shares (mil.): 509
Dividends
  Yield: 0.2%
  Payout: 4.8%
Market value ($ mil.): 19,628

HEALTH NET, INC.

In the basketball game of managed care, Health Net (formerly Foundation Health Systems) is looking to score a slam dunk.

The Woodland Hills, California-based company serves more than 5 million people in 15 states. The firm's Health Plan Services unit offers HMO, PPO, Medicare, and Medicaid plans. The Government Contracts/Specialty Services unit administers government health care contracts, covering almost 1.5 million people in the TRICARE program. This segment also offers behavioral health, vision, and dental care plans, as well as pharmacy benefits management and workers' compensation administrative services.

Health Net continues to pare its operations to deal with the ever-rising costs of health care. The company is exiting certain markets and trimming its Medicare and Medicaid operations.

HISTORY

Foundation Health started as the not-for-profit Foundation Community Health Plan in the 1960s. In 1984 it was bought by AmeriCare Health, which had HMOs in six states. The acquisition was a coup: Foundation Health soon accounted for the bulk of AmeriCare's sales.

AmeriCare went public in 1985. The next year it lost to another firm the rights to that name. Redubbed Foundation Health, the company expanded into new states and unrelated businesses: Commercial real estate, silk flowers, and furniture.

In late 1986 senior management led a $140 million LBO that left Foundation Health hobbled with debt when the industry started to slide. A 1988 Department of Defense (DOD) CHAMPUS contract brightened prospects, but the five-year, $3 billion contract to provide health care to 860,000 military retirees and dependents in California and Hawaii provided little short-term relief against the effects of high debt and rapid growth: The company lost money again.

The CEO slot had been vacant a year when Dan Crowley, a trained accountant with a good turnaround record, came aboard in 1989. He cut staff, slashed budgets, sold unrelated and non-performing units, and kicked off a huge sales effort. To satisfy bankers and the DOD, which was threatening to rescind its contract, Crowley refinanced Foundation's debt. In a little over a year, Foundation Health recorded its best results ever. In 1990 the company went public.

Back on solid ground, the company expanded its services and markets, buying such firms as Western Universal Life Insurance (renamed Foundation Health Benefit Life Insurance,

1991), Occupational Health Services (employee assistance and substance abuse programs, 1992), and California Compensation Insurance (workers' compensation insurance, 1993).

Foundation Health lost the DOD California/Hawaii contract (almost half its revenues) in 1993, but managed to cope until it regained the business — by then worth $2.5 billion — two years later. Also that year Foundation Health won DOD's five-year, $1.8 billion managed-care contract for Oklahoma and parts of Arkansas, Louisiana, and Texas.

Meanwhile, the company had formed Integrated Pharmaceutical Services and bought CareFlorida Health Systems, Intergroup Healthcare, and Thomas-Davis Medical Centers in 1994.

In 1995 the company dropped an offer to buy Health Systems International. The next year it added behavioral health and employee assistance programs with the purchase of Managed Health Network.

Renewed discussions with Health Systems International resulted in the companies merging to become Foundation Health Systems in 1997. Crowley — whose aggressive style garnered profits but was denounced as brutal by some critics — resigned after the merger.

In 1998 the company pushed into the Northeast, buying Connecticut-based HMO Physicians Health Services. It then sold its workers' compensation insurance operations. Chairman Malik Hasan (founder of Health Systems' nucleus, QualMed) resigned that year, partly because president Jay Gellert planned to focus on Arizona and California health plans, CHAMPUS, and behavioral health and pharmacy benefit management.

The financial aftershocks of the companies' merger continued, and FHS pruned its operations in 1999 and 2000, exiting such states as Colorado, New Mexico, and Texas, trimming its Medicare operations, and selling certain noncore administrative business lines. In 2000 the California Medical Association sued the company under RICO statutes, claiming it coerced doctors and interfered in doctor-patient relationships. Later that year, the company changed its name to Health Net in its effort to build a national brand name.

OFFICERS

Chairman: Richard W. Hanselman, age 74
President, CEO, and Director: Jay M. Gellert, age 47, $686,923 pay
EVP, Finance and Operations: Marvin P. Rich, age 56
EVP, Regional Health Plans and Specialty Companies: Jeffrey M. Folick, age 54
SVP, Health Plan Operations: Kate Longworth-Gentry

SVP, Organization Effectiveness: Karin D. Mayhew,
age 51
SVP, General Counsel, and Secretary: B. Curtis Westen,
age 41, $434,769 pay
SVP, Investor Relations: David W. Olson
SVP and Chief Medical Officer: Timothy J. Moore,
age 45
VP, Government Relations: Patricia Clarey
VP, Medical Affairs Operations: Janine Sawaya Eggers
Regional VP, Business Retention and Development and
Acting VP, Sales and Marketing, Health Net of the
Northeast: Susan Ross
President, Health Net of Arizona: Mark S. El-Tawil,
age 37
President, Health Net of California:
Christopher P. Wing, age 44
President, Health Net of Oregon: Stephen Lynch
President, Health Net of the Northeast: Barry Averill
President, Health Net Pharmaceutical Services
(HNPS): John Sivori
CIO: Robert D. Irwin, age 41
Head of National Sales: Dick LaBrecque
Manager of Account Management, Health Net of
Oregon: Susan Burkhart
Auditors: Deloitte & Touche LLP

LOCATIONS

HQ: 21650 Oxnard St., Woodland Hills, CA 91367
Phone: 818-676-6000   Fax: 818-676-8591
Web: www.health.net

Health Net operates both commercial and Government
sponsored health plans in Alaska, Arizona, Arkansas,
California, Connecticut, Hawaii, Idaho, Louisiana, New
Jersey, New York, Oklahoma, Oregon, Pennsylvania,
Texas, and Washington.

PRODUCTS/OPERATIONS

2001 Sales

	$ mil.	% of total
Health plan premiums	8,293	82
Government contracts	1,687	17
Total	**9,980**	**100**

Selected Subsidiaries

Employer & Occupational Services Group, Inc.
FHS Life Holdings
Health Net Federal Services
Health Net of Arizona, Inc.
Health Net of California, Inc.
Health Net of Oregon, Inc.
Health Net of the Northeast, Inc.
HIS Eastern Holdings, Inc.
Managed Health Network, Inc.
QualMed, Inc.

COMPETITORS

Aetna
Blue Cross
CIGNA
Empire Blue Cross
Humana
Kaiser Foundation
Maxicare Health Plans
Oxford Health Plans
PacifiCare
UnitedHealth Group
WellPoint Health Networks

HISTORICAL FINANCIALS & EMPLOYEES

NYSE: HNT FYE: December 31	Annual Growth	12/92	12/93	12/94	12/95	12/96	12/97	12/98	12/99	12/00	12/01
Sales ($ mil.)	41.6%	436	1,957	2,306	2,732	3,204	7,121	8,797	8,706	9,077	9,980
Net income ($ mil.)	18.1%	19	24	88	90	74	(187)	(165)	142	164	87
Income as % of sales	—	4.4%	1.2%	3.8%	3.3%	2.3%	—	—	1.6%	1.8%	0.9%
Earnings per share ($)	(5.2%)	1.12	1.00	0.88	1.55	0.67	(1.52)	(1.35)	1.16	1.33	0.69
Stock price - FY high ($)	—	22.00	20.50	36.75	34.25	37.13	33.94	32.63	20.06	26.94	26.19
Stock price - FY low ($)	—	10.00	10.00	15.88	24.88	19.38	22.06	5.88	6.25	7.63	16.00
Stock price - FY close ($)	1.4%	19.25	16.88	30.38	32.13	24.75	22.25	11.88	9.94	26.19	21.78
P/E - high	—	21	20	41	22	55	—	—	17	20	37
P/E - low	—	9	10	18	16	29	—	—	5	6	23
Dividends per share ($)	—	0.00	0.00	0.00	0.00	0.00	0.00	0.00	0.00	0.00	0.00
Book value per share ($)	4.2%	6.49	3.17	4.61	5.91	7.54	7.18	6.09	7.28	8.64	9.42
Employees	17.1%	2,367	2,455	2,700	2,500	3,825	15,200	14,000	12,000	11,000	9,800

STOCK PRICE HISTORY

HIGH/LOW/CLOSE

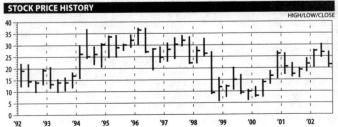

2001 FISCAL YEAR-END

Debt ratio: 33.8%
Return on equity: 7.8%
Cash ($ mil.): 910
Current ratio: 1.33
Long-term debt ($ mil.): 594
No. of shares (mil.): 124
Dividends
  Yield: —
  Payout: —
Market value ($ mil.): 2,694

HEALTHSOUTH CORPORATION

HEALTHSOUTH is the Holiday Inn of standardized health care.

The Birmingham, Alabama-based company owns almost 2,000 inpatient and outpatient rehabilitation facilities, outpatient surgery centers, diagnostic centers, and occupational medicine centers in the US, Australia, Puerto Rico, and the UK. The rehabilitation hospitals provide patients with physical and other therapy for orthopedic injuries, sports and work-related injuries, and neurological/neuromuscular conditions. Patients receive nonemergency surgical procedures at the freestanding surgery centers. The diagnostic centers provide imaging services such as magnetic resonance imaging, X-rays, and mammograms. The occupational medicine centers, which the company is selling, cater exclusively to patients requiring treatment for work-related injuries or illnesses.

HEALTHSOUTH contracts with top insurers, managed care plans, and such major employers as Delta Air Lines, Goodyear Tire & Rubber, and Winn-Dixie Stores.

It also has ongoing relationships with professional sports associations, universities, and high schools to provide sports medicine coverage of events and rehabilitative services for injured athletes. The company hopes to build brand recognition through these partnerships.

Due to lower Medicare reimbursement rates, the company is planning to convert its outpatient surgery center division into a separate publicly traded company.

HISTORY

A one-time service station worker (when he was a 17-year-old married man with a baby on the way), Richard Scrushy got into the health care industry by working in respiratory therapy; he earned a degree in the subject in 1974. Recruited for a job with a Texas health care management firm, Scrushy saw the convergence of several trends: Lowered reimbursements for medical care; a new emphasis on rehabilitation as a way to reduce the need for surgery and get employees back to work faster; and a dearth of brand names in health care. Scrushy decided to establish a national health care brand of rehabilitation hospitals, and in 1984 he and four of his co-workers founded Amcare and built its first outpatient center in Birmingham, Alabama.

From the beginning Scrushy wanted to make his rehabilitation centers less like hospitals and more like upscale health clubs. He sought workers' compensation and rehabilitation contracts from self-insured companies and managed-care operations. The strategies worked. The company had revenues of $5 million in 1985, the year it became HEALTHSOUTH. Other strategies included specializing in specific ailments, such as back problems and sports injuries, and using the same floor plan and furnishings for all HEALTHSOUTH locations to save money. The company went public in 1986.

By 1988 HEALTHSOUTH had nearly 40 facilities in 15 states and kept shopping for more. A merger with its biggest rival, Continental Medical Systems, fell through in 1992, but HEALTHSOUTH became the #1 provider of rehabilitative services the next year with its acquisition of most of the rehabilitation services of National Medical Enterprises (now Tenet Healthcare). (Scrushy and other officers formed MedPartners, a physician management company, in 1993.) Additional acquisitions included the inpatient rehabilitation hospitals of ReLife (1994) and NovaCare (now NAHC) and Caremark's rehabilitation services (1995). HEALTHSOUTH became the #1 operator of outpatient surgery centers with its acquisition of Surgical Care Affiliates in 1995. The $1.1 billion stock swap was the company's largest acquisition ever.

Horizon/CMS Healthcare, the US's largest provider of specialty health care, was acquired in 1997. After completing the Horizon/CMS deal, HEALTHSOUTH sold Horizon's 139 long-term-care facilities, 12 specialty hospitals, and 35 institutional pharmacies to Integrated Health Services; it kept about 30 inpatient and 275 outpatient rehabilitation facilities.

In the late 1990s, HEALTHSOUTH built its outpatient operations through acquisitions, buying nearly three dozen outpatient centers from what is now HCA - The Healthcare Company; it also bought National Surgery Centers, adding another 40 locations in 1998. In 1999 the company bought rival Mariner Post-Acute Network's American Rehability Services outpatient unit. The firm also partnered with Healtheon/WebMD (now known as WebMD Corporation) to form a sports medicine Web site.

In 2001 HEALTHSOUTH decided to sell its occupational medicine division to U.S. Health-Works. In 2002 the company announced that it sold five nursing homes in Massachusetts originally acquired in connection with the 1997 acquisition of Horizon/CMS Healthcare. HEALTHSOUTH no longer holds any remaining ownership interest in any former Horizon/CMS long-term-care facilities, most of which were sold at the end of 1997. The company also announced that it plans to convert its surgical outpatient center division into a new publicly traded company.

OFFICERS

Chairman: Richard M. Scrushy, age 49, $10,461,169 pay
President, CEO, and Director: William T. Owens,
age 43, $2,002,115 pay
President, Inpatient Services: Patrick A. Foster, age 55,
$837,922 pay
President, Ambulatory Services: Larry D. Taylor, age 43,
$952,076 pay
EVP, CFO, and Treasurer: Malcolm E. McVay, age 40
**EVP, Administration, Secretary, and Corporate
Compliance Officer:** Brandon O. Hale, age 52
EVP, Corporate Counsel, and Assistant Secretary:
William W. Horton, age 42
EVP and Chief Development Officer:
Thomas W. Carman, age 50, $436,651 pay
SVP, Reimbursement: Susan M. Jones, age 37
Group VP, Human Resources: Dennis Wade
Auditors: Ernst & Young LLP

LOCATIONS

HQ: 1 HealthSouth Pkwy., Birmingham, AL 35243
Phone: 205-967-7116 **Fax:** 205-969-4719
Web: www.healthsouth.com

HEALTHSOUTH operates approximately 1,900 facilities
in all 50 states and the District of Columbia, as well as
Australia, Puerto Rico, and the UK.

PRODUCTS/OPERATIONS

2001 Sales

	$ mil.	% of total
Outpatient services	2,349	53
Inpatient & other clinical services	2,008	46
Unallocated corporate office	24	1
Total	**4,381**	**100**

Selected Subsidiaries

Advantage Health Corporation
ASC Network Corporation
CMS Capital Ventures, Inc. (15%)
The Company Doctor
Diagnostic Health Corporation
Horizon/CMS Healthcare Corporation
National Imaging Affiliates, Inc.
National Surgery Centers, Inc.
Physical Therapeutix, Inc.
Physician Practice Management Corporation
Professional Sports Care Management, Inc.
ReadiCare, Inc.
Rehabilitation Hospital Corporation of America, Inc.
Surgical Care Affiliates, Inc.
Surgical Health Corporation

COMPETITORS

AmSurg
Beverly Enterprises
BJC Health
Clarent Hospital Corp
Genesis Health Ventures
HCA
Integrated Health Services
Kindred
Manor Care
Occupational Health &
Rehab
RehabCare
Res-Care
Select Medical
Sun Healthcare
Tenet Healthcare

HISTORICAL FINANCIALS & EMPLOYEES

NYSE: HRC FYE: December 31	Annual Growth	12/92	12/93	12/94	12/95	12/96	12/97	12/98	12/99	12/00	12/01
Sales ($ mil.)	30.2%	407	482	1,127	1,557	2,437	3,017	4,006	4,072	4,195	4,381
Net income ($ mil.)	23.8%	30	7	53	79	221	331	47	77	279	202
Income as % of sales	—	7.3%	1.4%	4.7%	5.1%	9.1%	11.0%	1.2%	1.9%	6.6%	4.6%
Earnings per share ($)	8.2%	0.25	0.23	0.30	0.32	0.55	0.91	0.11	0.18	0.71	0.51
Stock price - FY high ($)	—	9.31	6.59	9.84	16.19	19.88	28.94	30.81	17.75	17.50	18.49
Stock price - FY low ($)	—	3.81	3.03	5.84	8.19	13.50	17.75	7.69	4.56	4.75	11.25
Stock price - FY close ($)	9.4%	6.59	6.31	9.11	14.56	19.31	27.75	15.44	5.38	16.31	14.82
P/E - high	—	37	27	31	44	34	30	280	93	24	36
P/E - low	—	15	13	18	22	23	19	70	24	7	22
Dividends per share ($)	—	0.00	0.00	0.00	0.00	0.00	0.00	0.00	0.00	0.00	0.00
Book value per share ($)	16.2%	2.52	2.54	3.12	4.77	4.75	7.99	8.13	8.31	9.11	9.69
Employees	24.4%	7,243	14,562	18,423	26,427	36,410	56,281	51,901	51,260	53,216	51,537

STOCK PRICE HISTORY

HIGH/LOW/CLOSE

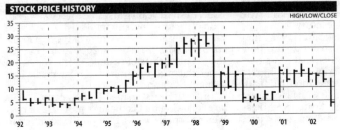

2001 FISCAL YEAR-END

Debt ratio: 44.2%
Return on equity: 5.5%
Cash ($ mil.): 277
Current ratio: 4.84
Long-term debt ($ mil.): 3,005
No. of shares (mil.): 392
Dividends
  Yield: —
  Payout: —
Market value ($ mil.): 5,805

THE HEARST CORPORATION

Like legendary founder William Randolph Hearst's castle, The Hearst Corporation is sprawling. New York City-based Hearst owns 12 daily newspapers (*San Francisco Chronicle, Houston Chronicle*) and 18 weeklies under its Hearst Newspapers unit; 16 US consumer magazines (*Cosmopolitan, Esquire*) under its Hearst Magazine unit; 18 UK magazines; stakes in cable TV networks (A&E, Lifetime, ESPN); TV and radio stations (through Hearst-Argyle Television); King Features, a features and comic syndicate; and business publishers. Hearst sold the *San Francisco Examiner* to the Fang family in conjunction with its 2000 purchase of the larger *San Francisco Chronicle*. Although it no longer owns Hearst Castle (deeded to the State of California in 1951), the company has extensive real estate holdings. Online interests include 30% of iVillage, the top site for women.

Using the selling power of its popular *Cosmopolitan* magazine, the company has capitalized with a TV channel based on the magazine. The company operates a *Cosmopolitan* station in Spain and is adding another one in Latin America and possibly the US. Hearst also plans to turn a TV channel into a magazine; the company will launch *Lifetime* magazine in 2003 in a joint venture with women's cable channel Lifetime.

The company is owned by the Hearst family, but managed by a board of trustees. Upon his death, William Randolph Hearst left 99% of the company's common stock to two charitable trusts controlled by a 13-member board that includes five family and eight non-family members. The will includes a clause that allows the trustees to disinherit any heir who contests the will.

HISTORY

William Randolph Hearst, son of a California mining magnate, started as a reporter — having been expelled from Harvard in 1884 for playing jokes on professors. In 1887 he became editor of the *San Francisco Examiner,* which his father had obtained as payment for a gambling debt. In 1895 he bought the *New York Morning Journal* and competed against Joseph Pulitzer's *New York World*. The "yellow journalism" resulting from that rivalry characterized American-style reporting at the turn of the century.

Hearst branched into magazines (1903), film (1913), and radio (1928). Also during this time it created the Hearst International News Service (it was sold to E.W. Scripps' United Press in 1958 to form United Press International). By 1935 Hearst was at its peak, with newspapers in 19 cities, the largest syndicate (King Features), international news and photo services,

13 magazines, eight radio stations, and two motion picture companies. Two years later Hearst relinquished control of the company to avoid bankruptcy, selling movie companies, radio stations, magazines, and, later, most of his San Simeon estate. (Hearst's rise and fall inspired the 1941 film *Citizen Kane.*)

In 1948 Hearst became the owner of one of the US's first TV stations, WBAL-TV in Baltimore. When Hearst died in 1951, company veteran Richard Berlin became CEO. Berlin sold off failing newspapers, moved into television, and acquired more magazines.

Frank Bennack, CEO since 1979, expanded the company, acquiring newspapers, publishing firms (notably William Morrow, 1981), TV stations, magazines (*Redbook*, 1982; *Esquire*, 1986), and 20% of cable sports network ESPN (1991). Hearst branched into video via a joint venture with Capital Cities/ABC (1981) and helped launch the Lifetime and Arts & Entertainment cable channels (1984).

In 1991 Hearst launched a New England news network with Continental Cablevision. The following year it brought on board former Federal Communications Commission chairman Alfred Sikes, who quickly moved the company onto the Internet. In 1996 Randolph A. Hearst passed the title of chairman to nephew George Hearst (the last surviving son of the founder, Randolph died in 2000). Broadcaster Argyle Television merged with Hearst's TV holdings in 1997 to form publicly traded Hearst-Argyle Television.

In 1999 Hearst combined its HomeArts Web site with Women.com to create one of the largest online networks for women. It also joined with Walt Disney's Miramax Films to publish entertainment magazine *Talk* and Oprah Winfrey's Harpo Entertainment to publish *O, The Oprah Magazine* (launched in 2000). In 1999 the company sold its book publishing operations to News Corp.'s HarperCollins unit. It also agreed to buy the *San Francisco Chronicle* from rival Chronicle Publishing. That deal was called into question over concerns that the *San Francisco Examiner* would not survive and the city would be left with one major paper. To resolve the issue, the next year Hearst sold the *Examiner* to ExIn (a group of investors affiliated with the Ted Fang family and other owners of the *San Francisco Independent*). Also in 2000 Hearst bought the UK magazines of Gruner + Jahr, the newspaper and magazine unit of German media juggernaut Bertelsmann.

In 2001 Hearst gained a 30% stake in iVillage following that company's purchase of rival Women.com Networks. Blaming the downturn in the economy, the company shut down its joint venture with Miramax Films, the magazine *Talk*. In mid-2002 Victor Ganzi took over as CEO and president following Bennack's retirement. Hearst bought shelter magazine *Veranda* from Atlanta-based Veranda Publications in 2002.

OFFICERS

Chairman: George R. Hearst Jr., age 74
President and CEO: Victor F. Ganzi, age 55
EVP, Hearst Newspapers: Steven R. Swartz
SVP; President, Hearst Newspapers: George B. Irish
SVP and President, Hearst Entertainment:
  Raymond E. Joslin
VP and CFO: Ronald J. Doerfler
President, Hearst Magazines: Cathleen P. Black
President, Hearst Business Media: Richard P. Malloch
President, Hearst Interactive Media:
  Kenneth A. Bronfin, age 42
President and CEO, Hearst-Argyle Television:
  David J. Barrett, age 53
SVP, Human Resources, Hearst Magazines: Ruth Diem
SVP, Sales and Marketing, *San Francisco Chronicle*:
  Margaret Krost

LOCATIONS

HQ: 959 8th Ave., New York, NY 10019
Phone: 212-649-2000   **Fax:** 212-765-3528
Web: www.hearstcorp.com

Hearst newspapers are located throughout the US. Hearst Magazines are distributed in more than 110 countries.

PRODUCTS/OPERATIONS

Selected Operations

Broadcasting
Hearst-Argyle Television (60%)

Business Publications
Black Book
Diversion
Electronic Products
First DataBank
Motor Magazine

Entertainment and Syndication
A&E Television Networks (37.5%, with ABC & NBC)
  The History Channel
ESPN (20%)
King Features Syndicate
Lifetime Entertainment Services (50%, with ABC)
Locomotion (with Cisneros Group; all animation TV)
New England Cable News (with AT&T Broadband)

Interactive Media
Circles (invested in online loyalty solutions company)
drugstore.com (invested in online pharmacy site)
Hire.com (invested in career job site)
iVillage (30%, Internet site geared towards women)

Selected Magazines
Cosmopolitan
Country Living
Esquire
Good Housekeeping
Harper's Bazaar
House Beautiful
Marie Claire (with Marie Claire Album)
O, The Oprah Magazine (with Harpo)
Popular Mechanics
Redbook
Town & Country

Major Newspapers
Houston Chronicle
San Antonio Express-News
San Francisco Chronicle
Seattle Post-Intelligencer

COMPETITORS

Advance	E. W. Scripps	New York Times
Publications	Freedom	News Corp.
Andrews McMeel	Communications	PRIMEDIA
Universal	Gannett	Reader's Digest
AOL Time	Hachette	Reed Elsevier
Warner	Filipacchi	Group
Belo	Médias	Rodale
Bertelsmann	IPC Media	Seattle Times
Bloomberg	Knight Ridder	Tribune
Cox Enterprises	Liberty Media	Viacom
Dennis	McGraw-Hill	Walt Disney
Publishing	MediaNews	Washington Post
Emap	Meredith	

HISTORICAL FINANCIALS & EMPLOYEES

Private FYE: December 31	Annual Growth	12/92	12/93	12/94	12/95	12/96	12/97	12/98	12/99	12/00	12/01
Sales ($ mil.)	8.2%	1,973	2,174	2,299	2,513	2,568	2,833	2,200	2,740	3,400	4,000
Employees	4.4%	13,000	13,500	14,000	14,000	14,000	15,000	13,555	14,000	18,300	—

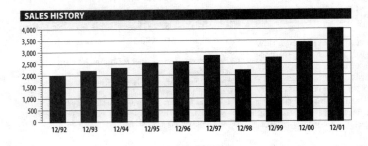

SALES HISTORY

HERCULES INCORPORATED

Hercules puts its muscles to work on water treatments, thickeners, and fibers. Through its pulp and paper division, it produces paper treatment chemicals; through its Aqualon subsidiary, Hercules produces thickeners for water-based products such as latex paints, printing inks, and oral hygiene products. The company also produces fibers used in disposable diapers and automotive textiles.

All bets for the company's future are off after chairman and CEO Vincent Corbo stepped down from the cash-strapped company. Before Corbo's departure, Hercules and Lehman Brothers Holdings formed CP Kelco ApS, a joint venture (Hercules owns 29%), by combining Hercules' food gums business with Pharmacia's Kelco biogums unit. However, that deal has resulted in a $430 million lawsuit against Pharmacia; CP Kelco alleges Pharmacia misrepresented the value of its biogums business.

Heavily in debt since its 1998 purchase of BetzDearborn, Hercules sold the water treatment portion of BetzDearborn (except for the paper process chemicals business) in 2002 to GE Specialty Materials for about $1.8 billion. Hercules also has sold most of its resins business and is looking for a buyer for the remaining resin operations. International Specialty Products, which is leading a proxy fight for control of the board of directors, has a 10% stake in Hercules and has been highly critical of Hercules' board and management, specifically their anti-takeover defenses.

HISTORY

A 1912 federal court decision forced DuPont (which controlled two-thirds of the US's explosives production) to spin off half its business into two companies: Hercules Powder and Atlas Powder. Hercules began operating explosives plants across the US in 1913. During WWI it became the largest US producer of TNT. After the war Hercules diversified into nonexplosive products, which included nitrocellulose for the manufacture of plastics, lacquers, and films.

By the late 1920s Hercules' core business had changed from powders to chemicals. Hercules marketed its rosin products to dozens of industries, including the paper industry, the largest user.

In the early 1950s Hercules developed a new process for making phenol, a substance in plastics, paints, and pharmaceuticals. Its explosives unit made important contributions in rocketry by developing propellants for Nike rockets and by making motors for Minuteman and Polaris missiles. By the late 1950s Hercules was making chemical propellants, petrochemical plastics,

synthetic fibers, agricultural and paper chemicals, and food additives.

During the 1960s and early 1970s, the company, renamed Hercules Incorporated (1966), increased plastic resin and fabricated plastic production. Hercules also developed foreign markets, doubling export sales between 1962 and 1972. Following the 1970s energy crisis, Hercules reduced its dependence on petrochemicals and expanded its specialty chemical and defense-related rocket propulsion businesses. In 1989 Hercules took full ownership of the Aqualon Group, which had been a 50-50 joint venture with Germany's Henkel.

Hercules sold its aerospace business in 1995 to Alliant Techsystems for $440 million. The deal left Hercules with 30% ownership of Alliant. In 1997 Hercules and Mallinckrodt sold their Tastemaker joint venture. Also in 1997 Hercules began selling its stake in Alliant.

The company's acquisitions in 1998 included Houghton International's Citrus Colloids pectin business and, for $2.4 billion and the assumption of $700 million in debt, BetzDearborn, a maker of chemicals for paper production and wastewater treatment. In 1999 president and COO Vincent Corbo replaced R. Keith Elliott as CEO.

In 2000 Hercules combined its food gums business with Pharmacia's Kelco biogums unit into a joint venture, CP Kelco. The company received about $600 million through the sale. The same year Elliott retired and Corbo became chairman; later the same year Corbo resigned and former CEO Thomas Gossage was named interim chairman and CEO. Not long afterwards Hercules let it be known that it was looking for a buyer.

Hercules sold its hydrocarbon resins business — and most of its other resin assets — to Eastman Chemical early in 2001. The same year CP Kelco sued Pharmacia for over $400 million, plus punitive damages, alledging fraud in the joint venture deal. In May former Union Carbide head William Joyce replaced Gossage as CEO.

To reduce its approximately $2.8 billion in debt, Hercules sold its BetzDearborn subsidiary's water-treatment operations to GE Specialty Materials for about $1.8 billion in 2002.

OFFICERS

Chairman and CEO: William H. Joyce, age 66, $1,664,167 pay
EVP, Corporate Development: Dominick W. DiDonna, age 51, $400,008 pay
Corporate Secretary and General Counsel: Israel J. Floyd, age 55, $508,526 pay
Chief Legal Officer: Richard G. Dahlen, age 62
VP and CIO, Information Technology: J. Frank Raboud
VP and Controller: Fred G. Aanonsen, age 54

VP and General Manager, Aqualon Division:
Allen A. Spizzo
VP and General Manager, Pulp and Paper Division:
Brian L. Pahl
VP and President, FiberVisions, Rosin & Terpenes:
Craig A. Rogerson, $457,928 pay
VP and Treasurer: Stuart C. Shears, age 51
VP, Communications and Public Affairs: J. Neil Stalter
VP, Corporate Affairs, Strategic Planning, and Work
Processes: Robert C. Flexon, age 43, $423,000 pay
VP, Hercules International, and President, Hercules
Europe: Hans H. Hjorth
VP, Human Resources and Corporate Resources:
Edward V. Carrington, age 59
VP, Manufacturing and Work Processes:
Matthias Sonneveld, $426,628 pay
Auditors: PricewaterhouseCoopers LLP

LOCATIONS

HQ: Hercules Plaza, 1313 N. Market St.,
Wilmington, DE 19894
Phone: 302-594-5000 **Fax:** 302-594-5400
Web: www.herc.com

Hercules operates about 80 plants in more than 20
countries around the world.

2001 Sales

	$ mil.	% of total
US	1,454	56
Europe	765	29
Asia/Pacific	217	8
The Americas (non-US)	184	7
Total	**2,620**	**100**

PRODUCTS/OPERATIONS

2001 Sales & Operating Income

	Sales		Operating Income	
	$ mil.	% of total	$ mil.	% of total
Process chemical & services	1,654	63	295	65
Functional products	541	21	123	27
Chemical specialties	425	16	38	8
Adjustments	—	—	(169)	—
Total	**2,620**	**100**	**287**	**100**

Business Units

Aqualon (thickeners for water-based products)
FiberVisions (biocomponent fibers, polypropylene
monocomponent fibers)
Pulp and paper (performance additives, process
treatment, water treatment)
Resins (peroxides, rosin resins, terpene resins, terpene
specialties)

COMPETITORS

Akzo Nobel	FMC
Arizona Chemical	Georgia-Pacific
BASF AG	Corporation
Bayer AG	Great Lakes Chemical
BP	Hoffmann-La Roche
Callaway Chemical	Huntsman
Ciba Specialty Chemicals	ICI American Holdings
Cytec	Novo Nordisk
Danisco	Ondeo Nalco
Dow Chemical	Procter & Gamble
DuPont	Rhodia
Eastman Chemical	USFilter
Exxon Mobil	W. R. Grace

HISTORICAL FINANCIALS & EMPLOYEES

NYSE: HPC FYE: December 31	Annual Growth	12/92	12/93	12/94	12/95	12/96	12/97	12/98	12/99	12/00	12/01
Sales ($ mil.)	(1.0%)	2,865	2,773	2,821	2,427	2,060	1,866	2,145	3,248	3,152	2,620
Net income ($ mil.)	—	168	(33)	274	333	325	319	9	168	98	(58)
Income as % of sales	—	5.9%	—	9.7%	13.7%	15.8%	17.1%	0.4%	5.2%	3.1%	—
Earnings per share ($)	—	1.21	(0.28)	2.23	2.87	2.98	3.13	0.10	1.62	0.91	(0.54)
Stock price - FY high ($)	—	21.23	38.25	40.46	62.25	66.25	54.50	51.38	40.69	28.00	20.00
Stock price - FY low ($)	—	14.86	21.06	32.09	38.21	42.75	37.75	24.63	22.38	11.38	6.50
Stock price - FY close ($)	(8.0%)	21.15	37.80	38.42	56.38	43.25	50.06	27.25	27.88	19.06	10.00
P/E - high	—	17	—	17	21	21	17	514	25	31	—
P/E - low	—	12	—	14	13	14	12	246	14	13	—
Dividends per share ($)	—	0.75	0.75	0.75	0.84	0.92	1.00	1.08	1.08	0.62	0.00
Book value per share ($)	(7.6%)	13.36	11.16	11.10	9.97	8.75	7.18	5.54	8.11	7.59	6.54
Employees	(5.1%)	15,419	14,083	11,989	7,892	7,114	6,221	12,357	11,347	9,789	9,665

STOCK PRICE HISTORY

HIGH/LOW/CLOSE

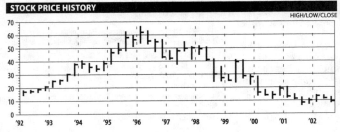

2001 FISCAL YEAR-END

Debt ratio: 73.3%
Return on equity: —
Cash ($ mil.): 76
Current ratio: 0.92
Long-term debt ($ mil.): 1,959
No. of shares (mil.): 109
Dividends
　Yield: —
　Payout: —
Market value ($ mil.): 1,088

HERMAN MILLER, INC.

Desk jockeys can ride Herman Miller's products all the way up the corporate ladder. The Zeeland, Michigan-based company is a top US maker of office furniture. In addition to seating (everything from perch stools to executive chairs), the company makes freestanding furniture, filing and storage systems, wooden casegoods, and ergonomic accessories for corporate, government, and home offices and health care industries.

Most of Herman Miller's worldwide sales come from independent dealers (71%), although the company also uses a direct sales staff and has e-commerce operations. The company's furniture is known for its award-winning contemporary designs and upscale prices; collectors still seek pieces designed and manufactured in the 1940s and 1950s. Previously focused on landing big contracts with major corporations, the Herman Miller has developed new designs to grab medium-size companies and small startups. However, the slowing economy has meant a continuing drop in orders and continuing efforts to cut costs, including extensive layoffs (some 37% of its workforce) and the consolidation of some brands and operations.

HISTORY

In 1923 Herman Miller lent his son-in-law, D. J. De Pree, enough money to buy Star Furniture, started in 1905 in Zeeland, Michigan. (De Pree renamed the furniture maker after Miller.) Designer Gilbert Rohde led Herman Miller's transformation from traditional to more modern styles in the 1930s.

Rohde designed the company's first office component line, the Executive Office Group (introduced in 1942). Rohde died two years later, and in 1946 George Nelson was named Herman Miller's design director. Nelson brought in a number of notable designers, including Charles Eames and Isamu Noguchi.

Throughout its history, the company has maintained a reputation for being open to suggestions and comments from its workers. This policy dates back to De Pree's learning that one of his millwrights who had died had also been a poet; De Pree began to value his employees for their innate talents rather than just for the work they did for him.

Herman Miller grew, largely unimpeded by national competitors, except for neighboring Steelcase. In 1950 the company adopted the Scanlon plan, an employee participation plan that included bonuses based on helpful participation, such as cost-cutting suggestions.

De Pree retired in 1962 and was succeeded by his son, Hugh. Two years later Herman Miller introduced the Action Office, a collection of panels, work surfaces, and storage units that could be moved about to create custom-designed work spaces within an open-plan office; this line has been the company mainstay ever since.

The firm, which went public in 1970, introduced its Ergon ergonomic chair in 1976. Hugh retired in 1980 and was succeeded by his brother Max, who capped executive salaries at 20 times the average wage of factory-line workers. Max became chairman in 1988 and resigned from day-to-day management duties to pursue teaching opportunities.

Max's successor, 33-year company veteran Richard Ruch, began restructuring to sharpen Herman Miller's focus. Then the commercial real estate market collapsed and, with it, the need for new office furnishings. Earnings tumbled in 1991 and 1992. Ruch retired in 1992 to become VC and was succeeded by first-ever company outsider Kermit Campbell.

In 1994 Herman Miller acquired German furniture company Geneal. Earnings plummeted in 1995 and chairman Campbell was forced out. Despite his commitment to its traditionally employee-friendly corporate culture, CEO Michael Volkema led Herman Miller in a shake-up, cutting 180 jobs and closing underperforming plants. The company introduced its cubicle systems office furniture unit Miller SQA ("simple, quick, and affordable") in 1995.

Herman Miller and leading carpet tile maker Interface formed a joint venture in 1997 to provide integrated office furniture and carpeting systems for commercial clients. The next year the company became the first major office furniture maker to target customers over the Internet. Herman Miller acquired wood furniture maker Geiger Brickel in 1999. The company launched a low-cost line of office furniture, dubbed RED, aimed at fledgling Internet-oriented firms in late 2000, shortly before the bubble burst for Web startups.

A slowdown in the US economy prompted cut after cut in 2001; by March 2002 the company had eliminated some 3,900 positions (or 37% of the workforce). The company also phased out its SQA and RED lines that year.

OFFICERS

Chairman, President, and CEO: Michael A. Volkema, age 45, $777,481 pay
CFO: Elizabeth A. Nickels, age 40
EVP, eBusiness: Gary VanSpronsen, age 46
EVP, Sales and Distribution: David M. Knibbe, age 47, $295,568 pay
SVP, Human Resources: Andrew Lock

SVP, Legal Services, and Secretary:
James E. Christenson, age 55
VP, Supply Management: Drew Schramm
President, Herman Miller International: John Portlock
President, Herman Miller North America:
Brian C. Walker, age 40, $530,510 pay
Chief Development Officer: Gary S. Miller, age 52,
$384,073 pay
Auditors: Ernst & Young LLP

LOCATIONS

HQ: 855 E. Main Ave., PO Box 302, Zeeland, MI 49464
Phone: 616-654-3000   **Fax:** 616-654-5234
Web: www.hermanmiller.com

Herman Miller designs and manufactures furniture in
the UK and the US. It has distribution subsidiaries in
Canada, France, Germany, Italy, Japan, Mexico, the
Netherlands, and the UK. Independent dealers sell the
company's products in Asia, the Middle East, and South
America.

2002 Sales

	$ mil.	% of total
US	1,249	85
Other countries	220	15
Total	**1,469**	**100**

PRODUCTS/OPERATIONS

Selected Products and Brands
Accessories (Accents, Aalto, Ibis, Eames)
Freestanding furniture (Passage, Aalto, Burdick, Eames, Arrio, Kiva)
Health care storage and administrative furniture
Modular systems (Action Office, Ethospace, Q System, Resolve)
Screens (Eames)
Seating (Aeron, Ambi, Equa, Ergon, Reaction)
Storage and filing (Meridian)
Textiles (Ituri, Meinecke)
Wooden casegoods (Geiger)

COMPETITORS

Anderson Hickey	Neutral Posture
Falcon Products	Ergonomics
Global Furniture	Open Plan Systems
Haworth	O'Sullivan Industries
HighPoint Furniture	Reconditioned Systems
HON INDUSTRIES	Sauder Woodworking
Inscape	Shelby Williams
Kewaunee Scientific	SMED International
KI	Steelcase
Kimball International	TAB Products
Klaussner Furniture	Teknion
Knoll	Virco Mfg.
MITY	Vitra

HISTORICAL FINANCIALS & EMPLOYEES

Nasdaq: MLHR FYE: Saturday nearest May 31	Annual Growth	5/93	5/94	5/95	5/96	5/97	5/98	5/99	5/00	5/01	5/02
Sales ($ mil.)	6.2%	856	953	1,083	1,284	1,496	1,719	1,766	1,938	2,236	1,469
Net income ($ mil.)	—	22	40	4	46	74	128	142	140	148	(56)
Income as % of sales	—	2.6%	4.2%	0.4%	3.6%	5.0%	7.5%	8.0%	7.2%	6.6%	—
Earnings per share ($)	—	0.22	0.40	0.04	0.46	0.77	1.39	1.67	1.74	1.81	(0.74)
Stock price – FY high ($)	—	6.59	8.75	7.34	8.59	18.81	36.25	30.75	30.00	33.94	27.18
Stock price – FY low ($)	—	3.69	5.94	4.81	5.34	7.31	17.06	15.63	19.13	18.75	18.00
Stock price – FY close ($)	15.5%	6.41	6.13	5.41	7.72	17.88	27.69	20.19	27.00	26.96	23.46
P/E – high	—	30	22	147	19	24	26	18	17	18	—
P/E – low	—	17	15	96	12	9	12	9	11	10	—
Dividends per share ($)	3.7%	0.13	0.13	0.13	0.13	0.13	0.15	0.15	0.15	0.15	0.18
Book value per share ($)	2.2%	2.84	3.01	2.89	3.12	3.12	2.58	2.63	3.76	4.62	3.45
Employees	3.3%	5,446	5,940	7,264	6,964	7,425	7,924	8,555	10,251	9,951	7,291

STOCK PRICE HISTORY

HIGH/LOW/CLOSE

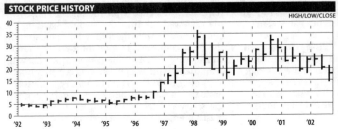

2002 FISCAL YEAR-END

Debt ratio: 45.8%
Return on equity: —
Cash ($ mil.): 124
Current ratio: 1.83
Long-term debt ($ mil.): 222
No. of shares (mil.): 76
Dividends
  Yield: 0.8%
  Payout: —
Market value ($ mil.): 1,787

HERSHEY FOODS CORPORATION

A hard candy coating now surrounds Hershey Foods' rich chocolate center. The Hershey, Pennsylvania-based company is the #1 US candy maker (Mars is #2). In addition to its popular Hershey's bars and Kisses, Reese's candies, Almond Joy, and Milk Duds, the company is a growing presence in the hard- and non-chocolate candy market, with such brands as Good & Plenty and Jolly Rancher. Its grocery offerings include Hershey's chocolate milk mix and Reese's peanut butter. The company is expanding its products with new versions of old favorites, such as Jolly Rancher lollipops and bite-sized bits of its popular chocolate bars.

Hershey's sweets are sold in more than two million retail outlets in North America alone. Still, retail giant Wal-Mart accounts for about 18% of sales. Hershey exports its products to more than 90 countries. The Hershey Trust — which benefits the Milton Hershey School for disadvantaged children — controls about 77% of Hershey's voting power.

HISTORY

Hershey Foods is the legacy of Milton Hershey, of Pennsylvania Dutch origin. Apprenticed in 1872 at age 15 to a candy maker, Hershey started Lancaster Caramel Company at age 30. In 1893, at the Chicago Exposition, he saw a new chocolate-making machine, and in 1900 he sold the caramel operations for $1 million to start a chocolate factory.

The factory was completed in 1905 in Derry Church, Pennsylvania, and renamed Hershey Foods the next year. Chocolate Kisses, individually hand wrapped in silver foil, were introduced in 1907. Two years later the candy man founded the Milton Hershey School, an orphanage; the company was donated to a trust in 1918 and for years existed solely to fund the school. Although Hershey is now publicly traded, the school still controls the majority of shareholder votes.

The candy company pioneered mass-production techniques for chocolates and developed much of the machinery for making and packaging its own products. At one time Hershey supplied its own sugar cane from Cuba and enlarged the world's almond supply sixfold through nut farm ownership. The Hershey bar became so universally familiar that it was used overseas during WWII as currency. Milton refused to advertise, believing that quality would speak for itself. Even after his death in 1945, the company continued his policy. Then, in 1970, facing a sluggish candy market and a diet-conscious public, the company lost share to Mars and management relented.

During the 1960s and 1970s, Hershey diversified in order to stabilize the effects of changing commodity prices. The company got into the pasta business with its 1966 purchase of San Giorgio Macaroni, and it bought the Friendly Ice Cream chain in 1979 (sold 1988). The company expanded candy operations by bringing out large-sized bars (1980) and buying Cadbury's US candy business (Peter Paul, Cadbury, Caramello; 1988).

In 1990 Hershey formed a joint venture with Fujiya to distribute Hershey products in Japan and bought Ronzoni's pasta, cheese, and sauce operations. Kenneth Wolfe was named chairman and CEO in 1994.

Hershey boosted its presence in the non-chocolate candy market with acquisitions of Henry Heide (1995) and the North American operations of Leaf (Good & Plenty, Jolly Rancher) from Finnish candy maker Huhtamäki Oyj (1996). In return, it sold Huhtamäki Oyj its struggling European confectionery interests.

In early 1999 the company sold its pasta business to New World Pasta for $450 million and a 6% interest in that company. Also in 1999 Hershey Trust, wanting to diversify its holdings, sold $100 million of its stock to Hershey.

Business melted during the fall of 1999 when a new company-wide computer system delayed orders during the critical Halloween season. The glitches cost the company more than $100 million in lost sales.

Hershey bought Nabisco Holdings' breath freshener mints and gum businesses (including the Breath Savers, Care*Free, and Fruit Stripe brands) for about $135 million in 2000.

In 2001 Nabisco veteran Rick Lenny replaced Wolfe as CEO. The company announced in October that it was cutting about 400 salaried positions and closing three plants and a distribution facility. In January 2002 Wolfe retired as chairman and Lenny was selected to replace him. Later that year Hershey settled a bitter six-week factory-worker strike. Also in 2002 Hershey sold its non-chocolate Heide brands to Farley's & Sathers Candy Company.

Later in 2002 the Hershey Trust said that to diversify its holdings, it wanted to sell its 77% interest in Hershey Foods. However, the sale was temporarily blocked while the state of Pennsylvania reviewed the impact it would have on the community. Despite the injunction against a sale, the trust continued to look for a buyer and was considering a $12.5 billion offer from chewing gum giant Wm. Wrigley Jr. and a $10.5 billion joint offer from Nestlé and Cadbury Schweppes. Amid the community outcry and legal wrangling, the sale was finally called off after 10 of the 17 trust's members changed their minds.

OFFICERS

Chairman, President, and CEO: Richard H. Lenny, age 50, $1,505,769 pay
SVP and CFO: Frank Cerminara, age 53, $510,546 pay
SVP and Chief Marketing Officer: Wynn A. Willard, age 43, $470,102 pay
SVP Public Affairs, General Counsel, and Secretary: Burton H. Snyder, age 54
VP and Chief Customer Officer: Milton T. Matthews, age 56
VP and CIO: George F. Davis, age 53
VP and Treasurer: R. Montgomery Garrabrant
VP Brand Integration: Dennis N. Eshleman
VP Business Planning and Development: David J. West, age 38
VP Business Process Operations - Analysis & Planning: Richard E. Bentz
VP Consumer and Trade Research: E. Kirk Ward
VP Corporate Communications: John C. Long
VP, Corporate Controller, and Chief Accounting Officer: David W. Tacka, age 48
VP Corporate Development: Bryon Klemens
VP Engineering and Technology: Robert L. Woelfing
VP Human Resources: Marcella K. Arline, age 49
VP Investor Relations: James A. Edris
Auditors: KPMG LLP

LOCATIONS

HQ: 100 Crystal A Dr., Hershey, PA 17033
Phone: 717-534-6799   **Fax:** 717-534-6760
Web: www.hersheys.com

Hershey Foods' main manufacturing facilities are located in Hershey and Lancaster, Pennsylvania; Oakdale, California; Robinson, Illinois; and Stuarts Draft, Virginia.

PRODUCTS/OPERATIONS

Selected Brands

Candy
5th Avenue
Breath Savers
Bubble Yum
Cadbury's Creme Eggs (US only)
Caramello (US only)
Carefree gum
Good & Plenty
Heath
Hershey's Bites
Hershey's Hugs
Hershey's Kisses
Hershey's milk chocolate bars
Hershey's milk chocolate bars with almonds
Jolly Rancher
Kit Kat (US only)
Milk Duds
Mr. Goodbar
Nibs
Oh Henry!
PayDay
Peter Paul Almond Joy

Peter Paul Mounds
Pot of Gold
Reese's peanut butter cups
Reese's Pieces
Rolo (US only)
Skor
Super Bubble
Symphony
Twizzlers
Whatchamacallit
Whoppers
York peppermint patties
Zagnut
Zero

Groceries
Hershey's baking chocolate
Hershey's chocolate milk mix
Hershey's cocoa
Hershey's syrup
Mounds coconut flakes
Reese's peanut butter

COMPETITORS

Brach's
Cadbury Schweppes
Campbell Soup
Chupa Chups
CSM
Ferrara Pan Candy
Ferrero
J. M. Smucker
Mars
Nestlé
Russell Stover
Thorntons
Tootsie Roll
Wrigley
World's Finest Chocolate

HISTORICAL FINANCIALS & EMPLOYEES

NYSE: HSY FYE: December 31	Annual Growth	12/92	12/93	12/94	12/95	12/96	12/97	12/98	12/99	12/00	12/01
Sales ($ mil.)	3.9%	3,220	3,488	3,606	3,691	3,989	4,302	4,436	3,971	4,221	4,557
Net income ($ mil.)	(1.7%)	243	193	184	282	273	336	341	460	335	207
Income as % of sales	—	7.5%	5.5%	5.1%	7.6%	6.8%	7.8%	7.7%	11.6%	7.9%	4.5%
Earnings per share ($)	1.3%	1.34	1.07	1.05	1.69	1.75	2.23	2.34	3.26	2.42	1.50
Stock price - FY high ($)	—	24.19	27.94	26.75	33.94	51.75	63.88	76.38	64.88	66.44	70.15
Stock price - FY low ($)	—	19.13	21.75	20.56	24.00	31.94	42.13	59.69	45.75	37.75	55.13
Stock price - FY close ($)	12.5%	23.50	24.50	24.19	32.50	43.75	61.94	62.19	47.44	64.38	67.70
P/E - high	—	18	17	25	20	29	28	32	20	27	46
P/E - low	—	14	13	19	14	18	19	25	14	15	36
Dividends per share ($)	9.4%	0.52	0.57	0.63	0.69	0.76	0.84	0.92	1.00	1.08	1.17
Book value per share ($)	0.4%	8.12	8.06	8.31	7.25	7.59	5.97	7.28	7.93	8.62	8.46
Employees	1.7%	13,700	14,300	15,600	14,800	15,300	16,200	16,200	15,300	15,700	16,000

STOCK PRICE HISTORY

HIGH/LOW/CLOSE

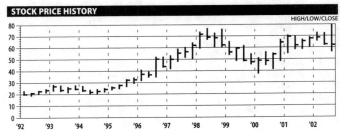

2001 FISCAL YEAR-END

Debt ratio: 43.3%
Return on equity: 17.8%
Cash ($ mil.): 134
Current ratio: 1.93
Long-term debt ($ mil.): 877
No. of shares (mil.): 136
Dividends
  Yield: 1.7%
  Payout: 78.0%
Market value ($ mil.): 9,183

THE HERTZ CORPORATION

If you've ever said, "Don't worry about it, it's a rental," guess who hurts: Hertz, the world's leading car rental company, owned by Ford Motor. Based in Park Ridge, New Jersey, The Hertz Corporation operates a rental fleet of 525,000 vehicles, with about 7,000 locations in more than 140 countries. Its car rental revenues are split almost evenly between business and leisure travelers. Almost 90% of its car rental revenues come from airport pickups. Hertz also has car leasing and used-car sales operations. Ford Motor partially spun off Hertz in a 1997 IPO and bought all its remaining shares in 2001.

Subsidiary Hertz Equipment Rental Corporation (HERC) is a major North American renter of construction and industrial equipment, with about 270 locations in 40 states and Canada (it has some 60 locations in Europe as well). Hertz also administers insurance-related claims for other companies.

Hertz is expanding its presence in the suburban rental market; the company operates about 700 of these locations to capitalize on local use and the insurance replacement business. Its HERC operations are also growing, both organically and through acquisitions.

HISTORY

In 1918, 22-year-old John Jacobs opened a Chicago car rental business with 12 Model T Fords that he had repaired. By 1923, when Yellow Cab entrepreneur John Hertz bought Jacobs' business, it had revenues of about $1 million. Jacobs continued as top executive of the company, renamed Hertz Drive-Ur-Self System. Three years later General Motors (GM) acquired the company when it bought Yellow Truck from John Hertz. Hertz introduced the first car rental charge card in 1926, opened its first airport location at Chicago's Midway Airport in 1932, and initiated the first one-way (rent-it-here/leave-it-there) plan in 1933. The company expanded into Canada in 1938 and Europe in 1950.

Omnibus bought Hertz from GM in 1953, sold its bus interests, and focused on vehicle leasing and renting. The next year Omnibus changed its name to The Hertz Corporation and was listed on the NYSE. Also in 1954 the company purchased Metropolitan Distributors, a New York-based truck leasing firm. In 1961 Hertz began operations in South America.

The company formed its Hertz Equipment Rental subsidiary in 1965. RCA bought Hertz two years later but allowed the company to maintain its board of directors and management. In 1972 it introduced the first frequent traveler's club, the #1 Club, which allowed the rental location to prepare a rental agreement before the customer arrived at the counter. Three years later Hertz began defining the company's image through TV commercials featuring football star/celebrity O. J. Simpson running through airports. (Hertz canceled Simpson's contract in 1994 following his arrest for murder — the TV ads had stopped in 1992.) Frank Olson became CEO in 1977 after serving in the same position at United Airlines.

United Airlines bought Hertz from RCA in 1985, then sold it in 1987 for $1.3 billion to Park Ridge, which had been formed by Hertz management and Ford Motor specifically for the purchase. (Hertz was Ford's largest customer.) In 1988 Ford, which held 80% of Park Ridge, sold 20% to Volvo North America for $100 million. (Ford later reduced its stake to 49% when it sold shares to Volvo.) Also that year Hertz sold its stock in the Hertz Penske truck leasing joint venture for $85.5 million and issued Penske a license to use its name.

Ford bought all the shares of Hertz it didn't already own in 1994. The next year it formed a unit to provide replacement cars for insurance companies. Taking advantage of heightened investor interest in rental car companies (stemming in part from the purchases of some competitors), Ford sold 17% of Hertz to the public in 1997.

Hertz acquired several equipment rental companies in 1998, including the Boireau Group (France) and Matthews Equipment (Canada). In 1999 the company's European acquisitions included French car rental franchise SST and German van rental company Yellow Truck. Also in 1999 Hertz created a referral network with Toyota, Japan's #1 car dealer.

Olson retired as CEO on the last day of 1999, but remained chairman; president Craig Koch was named his successor. In 2000 Hertz continued its acquisitive trend by purchasing Seattle-based AA Rentals equipment leasing company.

In 2001 Ford paid about $722 million for the shares of Hertz it didn't already own. Also that year the company opened about 200 new suburban rental locations. In April 2001 Hertz eliminated commissions for negotiated corporate and government accounts in the US and Canada.

Chairman: Frank A. Olson, age 69
President, CEO, and Director: Craig R. Koch
EVP and CFO: Paul J. Siracusa
EVP, Marketing and Sales: Brian J. Kennedy
EVP; President, Hertz Equipment Rental Corporation: Gerald A. Plescia
EVP; President, Vehicle Rental and Leasing, The Americas and Pacific: Joseph R. Nothwang
SVP, Employee Relations: Donald F. Steele
SVP, General Counsel, and Secretary: Harold E. Rolfe
SVP, Quality Assurance and Administration: Robert J. Bailey
VP; President, Hertz Europe Limited: Charles L. Shafer
VP, Technology and e-Business: Claude B. Burgess
Staff VP and Controller: Richard J. Foti
Treasurer: Robert H. Rillings
Auditors: PricewaterhouseCoopers LLP

LOCATIONS

HQ: 225 Brae Blvd., Park Ridge, NJ 07656
Phone: 201-307-2000   **Fax:** 201-307-2644
Web: www.hertz.com

The Hertz Corporation has about 7,000 locations in more than 140 countries worldwide.

PRODUCTS/OPERATIONS

Selected Services
Car rentals
Claim management services (Hertz Claim Management)
Heavy equipment rental and leasing (Hertz Equipment Rental)
Truck and van rental
Used-car sales

COMPETITORS

AMERCO
Atlas Copco
Budget Group
Cendant
Dollar Thrifty Automotive Group
Enterprise Rent-A-Car
Europcar
National Equipment Services
Neff
Prime Service
Rental Service
Sixt
United Rentals
Western Power

HISTORICAL FINANCIALS & EMPLOYEES

Subsidiary FYE: December 31	Annual Growth	12/92	12/93	12/94	12/95	12/96	12/97	12/98	12/99	12/00	12/01
Sales ($ mil.)	6.4%	2,816	2,855	3,294	3,401	3,589	3,815	4,154	4,611	5,074	4,916
Net income ($ mil.)	(9.1%)	55	53	91	105	159	202	277	336	358	23
Income as % of sales	—	2.0%	1.9%	2.8%	3.1%	4.4%	5.3%	6.7%	7.3%	7.1%	0.5%
Employees	5.8%	18,000	17,950	19,200	19,500	21,000	21,700	24,800	27,700	31,300	29,800

NET INCOME HISTORY

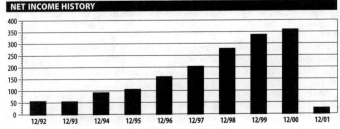

2001 FISCAL YEAR-END

Debt ratio: 76.1%
Return on equity: 1.2%
Cash ($ mil.): 214
Current ratio: —
Long-term debt ($ mil.): 6,314

HEWLETT-PACKARD COMPANY

Bet-the-farm courage or conspicuous consumption? Either way, Palo Alto, California-based Hewlett-Packard (HP) just got a whole lot bigger. Following its monumental acquisition of Compaq Computer, HP rivals in size IBM, which has long been the world's largest computer company by a huge margin. HP's products include PCs, servers, storage products, and printers and other peripherals. The addition of Compaq's sprawling hardware portfolio augments HP's offerings in a number of areas, particularly PCs, storage devices, and servers.

The monster acquisition was championed by CEO Carly Fiorina, whose previous efforts to transform the expansive hardware company included scaling back operations, a push toward services, and a complete overhaul of the company's structure that consolidated more than 80 units into four groups. It was speculated that failure to get the acquisition passed would end Fiorina's career at HP, as the deal met with heated opposition from many of HP's shareholders, including members of both the Hewlett and Packard families.

The embattled CEO is now faced with the staggering task of integrating the two giants while remaining focused on customers. The company's integration plan includes organizing the combined operations into four major business groups: enterprise systems, services, imaging and printing systems, and personal systems. HP is also cutting its workforce by 10%, or some 15,000 employees, as it eliminates redundant product groups.

HISTORY

Encouraged by professor Frederick Terman (considered the founder of Silicon Valley), in 1938 Stanford engineers Bill Hewlett (1913-2001) and David Packard (1912-1996) started Hewlett-Packard (HP) in a garage in Palo Alto, California, with $538. Hewlett was the idea man, while Packard served as manager; the two were so low-key that the company's first official meeting ended with no decision on exactly what to manufacture. Finding good people took priority over finding something to sell. The first product ended up being an audio oscillator. Walt Disney Studios, one of HP's first customers, bought eight to use in the making of *Fantasia*.

Demand for HP's electronic testing equipment during WWII spurred sales growth from $34,000 in 1940 to nearly $1 million just three years later. HP went public in 1957. The company expanded beyond the US during 1959, establishing a marketing organization in Switzerland and a manufacturing plant in West Germany. HP entered the

medical field in 1961 by acquiring Sanborn, and the analytical instrumentation business in 1965 with the purchase of F&M Scientific. Chairman Packard in 1969 began serving two years as deputy defense secretary.

In 1972 the company pioneered personal computing with the world's first handheld scientific calculator. Under the leadership of John Young, the founders' chosen successor (named CEO in 1978), HP introduced its first PCs, the first desktop mainframe, and the LaserJet printer. Its initial PCs were known for their rugged build, tailored for factory operations. They were also more expensive than rival versions and, consequently, didn't enjoy strong sales.

By 1986 a five-year, $250 million R&D project — the company's largest to date — had produced a family of HP computers based on the reduced instruction set computing (RISC) architecture. Hewlett retired in 1987; sons of both Hewlett and Packard were named that year to the company's board of directors. HP became a leader in workstations with the 1989 purchase of market pioneer Apollo Computers, despite technology delays with the merger that resulted in the loss of nearly $750 million in new business.

In 1992 HP acquired Texas Instruments' line of UNIX-based computers and made a new commitment to product cost-cutting. Lewis Platt, an EVP since 1987, was named president and CEO that year. Packard retired in 1993. HP combined its varied computer operations in 1995.

In 1999 HP formed Agilent Technologies for its test and measurement and other noncomputer operations, and spun off 15% of the company to the public. (HP distributed to its shareholders its remaining 85% in mid-2000.) Also in 1999 Platt retired and HP — one of the first major US corporations to be headed by a woman — appointed Lucent executive Carly Fiorina president and CEO. She was named chairman the following year.

In 2001 the company acquired application server specialist Bluestone Software, which helped form HP's Netaction operations. HP agreed to pay $400 million to Pitney Bowes to settle a 1995 patent-infringement case related to printer technology. Also that year HP acquired StorageApps for $350 million in stock and announced that it would cut about 6,000 jobs. Next came the announcement of a blockbuster deal: HP agreed to buy rival Compaq in a stock deal initially valued at about $25 billion. The highly contentious deal eventually met with shareholder approval in early 2002 after months of heated volleys between merger advocates and dissenters. At the time of closing the deal was valued at approximately $19 billion.

Chairman and CEO: Carleton S. Fiorina, age 47,
$1,000,000 pay (prior to merger)
President and Director: Michael D. Capellas, age 47,
$1,600,000 pay (prior to merger)
EVP, Finance and Administration and CFO:
Robert P. Wayman, age 56, $925,000 pay
EVP, HP Enterprise Systems Group: Peter Blackmore,
age 54, $640,385 pay (prior to merger)
EVP, HP Imaging and Printing Group: Vyomesh Joshi,
age 47
EVP, HP Personal Systems Group: Duane E. Zitzner,
age 54, $725,000 pay
EVP, HP Services: Ann M. Livermore, age 43,
$700,000 pay
EVP, HP Worldwide Operations: Michael J. Winkler,
age 56, $620,192 pay (prior to merger)
SVP and CIO, HP Information Technology:
Robert V. Napier, age 55
**SVP and CTO, HP Office of Corporate Strategy and
Technology:** Shane V. Robison, age 48
SVP, HP Human Resources: Susan D. Bowick, age 53
Auditors: Ernst & Young LLP

LOCATIONS

HQ: 3000 Hanover St., Palo Alto, CA 94304
Phone: 650-857-1501   **Fax:** 650-857-5518
Web: www.hp.com

2001 Sales

	$ mil.	% of total
US	18,833	42
Other countries	26,393	58
Total	**45,226**	**100**

PRODUCTS/OPERATIONS

2001 Sales

	$ mil.	% of total
Products	37,498	83
Services	7,325	16
Financing	403	1
Total	**45,226**	**100**

Selected Products and Services

Enterprise Systems	Personal Systems
Management software	Calculators
Networking equipment	Desktop PCs
Servers	Handheld computers
Storage	Notebook computers
	Workstations

Imaging and Printing
Commercial printing
Digital imaging
Personal printing
Shared printing
Supplies

Services
Consulting
Design and installation
Education
Support and maintenance

COMPETITORS

Acer	Lexmark	Sharp
Apple Computer	International	Siemens
Canon	Matsushita	Sony
Dell Computer	Microsoft	Sun
EDS	Minolta	Microsystems
EMC	NEC	Toshiba
Fujitsu	Palm	Unisys
Gateway	Ricoh	Xerox
Hitachi	Seiko Epson	
IBM	SGI	

HISTORICAL FINANCIALS & EMPLOYEES

NYSE: HPQ FYE: October 31	Annual Growth	10/92	10/93	10/94	10/95	10/96	10/97	10/98	10/99	10/00	10/01
Sales ($ mil.)	11.9%	16,410	20,317	24,991	31,519	38,420	42,895	47,061	42,370	48,782	45,226
Net income ($ mil.)	(3.2%)	549	1,177	1,599	2,433	2,586	3,119	2,945	3,491	3,697	408
Income as % of sales	—	3.3%	5.8%	6.4%	7.7%	6.7%	7.3%	6.3%	8.2%	7.6%	0.9%
Earnings per share ($)	(2.8%)	0.27	0.59	0.77	1.16	1.23	1.48	1.39	1.68	1.80	0.21
Stock price - FY high ($)	—	10.63	11.16	12.36	24.16	28.84	36.47	41.19	59.22	77.75	48.00
Stock price - FY low ($)	—	5.58	6.75	8.77	11.48	18.41	21.38	23.53	28.84	35.91	12.50
Stock price - FY close ($)	10.0%	7.11	9.20	12.23	23.16	22.06	30.81	30.13	37.09	46.63	16.83
P/E - high	—	24	19	16	21	23	25	29	34	42	150
P/E - low	—	13	11	11	10	14	14	16	17	19	39
Dividends per share ($)	13.8%	0.10	0.12	0.14	0.18	0.22	0.26	0.30	0.32	0.32	0.32
Book value per share ($)	7.5%	3.74	4.21	4.87	5.80	6.63	7.76	8.33	9.11	7.30	7.19
Employees	(0.8%)	92,600	96,200	98,400	102,300	112,000	121,900	124,600	84,400	88,500	86,200

STOCK PRICE HISTORY

HIGH/LOW/CLOSE

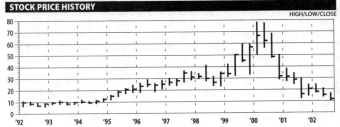

2001 FISCAL YEAR-END

Debt ratio: 21.1%
Return on equity: 2.9%
Cash ($ mil.): 4,197
Current ratio: 1.53
Long-term debt ($ mil.): 3,729
No. of shares (mil.): 1,940
Dividends
  Yield: 1.9%
  Payout: 152.4%
Market value ($ mil.): 32,651

HICKS, MUSE, TATE & FURST

These Texas Hicks know an investment pool ain't no cement pond. Or do they? Dallas-based Hicks, Muse, Tate & Furst creates investment pools in the form of limited partnerships. Investors are mostly pension funds but also include financial institutions and wealthy private investors such as Texas' Hunt family. The firm targets underperforming niche companies and builds them up through add-on investments.

As its target industries consolidated — making US acquisitions scarce — Hicks, Muse had increasingly turned to foreign markets. The firm (which sold its AMFM to Clear Channel Communications to create the US's largest radio, television, and outdoor advertising group) exported its media mogul strategy through investments in Europe and Latin America. Hicks, Muse, along with US-based Liberty Media International, owns CableVision SA, Argentina's largest cable operator. Hicks, Muse's late 1990s hopes for a tidy profit on the more than $1 billion it invested in the South American nation have turned into a 2002 headache as that country wades through an economic depression.

At home, Hicks, Muse has suffered losses in telecommunications and has considered closing funds before they reach their original targets amounts. It abandoned plans to buyout manufacturing firm Johns Manville with Bear Stearns when its stock took a dive.

The firm has closed down offices in Argentina and New York. Hicks, Muse owns the North American assets of bankrupt Vlasic Foods International Inc., including Vlasic pickles, Open Pit barbecue sauces, and Swanson frozen dinners. Hicks, Muse along with UK-based Apax Partners & Co. bought British Telecommunication's yellow pages firm Yell, which in turn is buying US directories publisher McLeodUSA Publishing.

HISTORY

The son of a Texas radio station owner, Thomas Hicks became interested in leveraged buyouts as a member of First National Bank's venture capital group. Hicks and Robert Haas formed Hicks & Haas in 1984; the next year that firm bought Hicks Communications, a radio outfit run by Hicks' brother Steven. (This would be the first of many media companies bought or created by the buyout firm, often with Steven Hicks' involvement.)

Hicks & Haas' biggest coup was its mid-1980s buy of several soft drink makers, including Dr Pepper and Seven-Up. The firm took Dr Pepper/Seven-Up public just 18 months after merging the two companies. In all, Hicks & Haas turned $88 million of investor funding into

$1.3 billion. The pair split up in 1989; Hicks wanted to raise a large pool to invest, but Haas preferred to work deal by deal.

Hicks raised $250 million in 1989 and teamed with former Prudential Securities banker John Muse. Early investments included Life Partners Group (life insurance, 1990; sold 1996). In 1991 Morgan Stanley's Charles Tate and First Boston's Jack Furst became partners.

As part of its buy-and-build strategy, Hicks, Muse bought DuPont's connector systems unit in 1993, renamed it Berg Electronics, added six more companies to it, and doubled its earnings before selling it in 1998. Not every move was a star in the Hicks, Muse crown. Less-than-successful purchases included bankrupt brewer G. Heileman, bought in 1994 and sold two years later for an almost $100 million loss.

The buyout firm's Chancellor Media radio company went public in 1996. That year Hicks, Muse gained entry into Latin America with its purchases of cash-starved Mexican companies, including Seguros Commercial America, one of the country's largest insurers. That year also brought International Home Foods (Jiffy Pop, Chef Boyardee) into the Hicks, Muse fold.

In 1997 Chancellor and Evergreen Media merged to form Chancellor Media (renamed AMFM in 1999). The next year Hicks, Muse continued buying US and Latin American media companies, as well as a few oddities (a UK software maker, a Danish seed company, and US direct-seller Home Interiors & Gifts). Hicks, Muse and Kohlberg Kravis Roberts' merged their cinema operations to form the US's largest theater chain. The company that year also moved into the depressed energy field (Triton Energy) and formed a $1.5 billion European fund.

Buys in 1999 included UK food group Hillsdown Holdings, one-third of Mexican flour maker Grupo Minsa, and (just in time for millennial celebrations) popular champagne brands Mumm and Perrier-Jouet (it quadrupled its investment when it sold the champagne houses in late 2000). Lured by low stock prices on real estate investment trusts (REITs), the company agreed to buy Walden (formerly Walden Residential Properties) that year.

Amid assorted media and other buys in 2000, the firm helped put together several joint deals. With investment bank Bear Stearns, it planned to buy construction-materials manufacturer Johns Manville; the deal soured later that year as the economy cooled. After vying with another buyout group for UK food concern United Biscuits, the two competitors teamed up to complete the deal.

Hicks, Muse sold International Home Foods

to food giant ConAgra in 2000. The next year Hicks, Muse bought bankrupt Vlasic Foods International Inc.'s North American assets, including Vlasic pickles, Open Pit barbecue sauces, and Swanson frozen dinners. Along with UK-based Apax Partners & Co., the firm bought British Telecommunication's yellow pages firm Yell, which is buying US directories publisher McLeodUSA Publishing.

OFFICERS

Chairman and CEO: Thomas O. Hicks, age 56
COO: John R. Muse, age 51
CFO: Darron Ash
General Counsel: Marian Brancaccio
Partner: Lyndon Lea
Partner: Peter Brodsky
Human Resources Manager: Lynita Jessen
Senior Counselor: M. Brian Mulroney, age 63
Senior Counselor, Europe Strategy: Henry A. Kissinger
Latin America Strategy: Richard W. Fisher

LOCATIONS

HQ: Hicks, Muse, Tate & Furst Incorporated
   200 Crescent Ct., Ste. 1600, Dallas, TX 75201
Phone: 214-740-7300   **Fax:** 214-720-7888

Hicks, Muse, Tate & Furst has offices in Dallas and London.

PRODUCTS/OPERATIONS

Selected Holdings
CCI/Triad Systems Corp. (computer systems)
CEI Citicorp Holding (40%, telecommunications and publishing)
Glass Group (automotive information services software)
Grupo Minsa, S.A. de C.V. (32%, corn flour producer, Mexico)
Grupo MVS SA (23%, pay-TV provider and radio station owner, Mexico)
Grupo Vidrio Formas (69%, glass container supplier, Mexico)
Home Interiors & Gifts, Inc. (80%, direct-selling of decorative accessories and gift items)
Ibero-American Media Partners (50%, Latin American media buyout fund)
International Outdoor Advertising (97%; billboards in Argentina, Chile, and Uruguay)
International Wire Holdings Corp. (60%; wire, wire harnesses, and cable)
LIN Holdings (69%, television stations)
Metrocall Inc. (paging systems)
Olympus Real Estate Corp. (real estate equity and mortgage investments)
OmniAmerica Wireless LP (45%, broadcast towers)
Pan-American Sports Network (80%, regional cable sports network)
RCN Corp. (fiber-optic telecommunications networks)
Sunrise Television Corp. (87%, small-market television stations)
Traffic (49%, broadcasting, Brazil)
United Biscuits (Holdings) plc (87%, with Finalrealm; food products; UK)
Viasystems Group (printed circuit boards)
Walden (REIT)

COMPETITORS

Bain Capital	Jordan Company
Berkshire Hathaway	KKR
Boston Ventures	Leonard Green
Clayton, Dubilier	Maseca
CVC Capital Partners	Texas Pacific Group
Equity Group Investments	Thomas Lee
Haas Wheat	Vestar Capital Partners
Heico	Vulcan Northwest
Investcorp	Wingate Partners

HIGHMARK INC.

Highmark is walking the tightrope between high-minded and high income. The Pittsburgh-based company provides insurance coverage to approximately 25 million customers, primarily in Pennsylvania. Highmark offers medical, dental, vision, life, casualty, and other health insurance, as well as such community service programs as the Western Pennsylvania Caring Foundation, which offers free health care coverage to children whose parents earn too much to qualify for public aid but too little to afford private programs.

Highmark continues to operate in western Pennsylvania under the Highmark Blue Cross Blue Shield name and as Pennsylvania Blue Shield statewide. National subsidiaries include United Concordia Companies (dental coverage) and Highmark Life and Casualty Group (disability and life insurance).

HISTORY

Highmark was created from the merger of Blue Cross of Western Pennsylvania (founded in 1937) and Pennsylvania Blue Shield, created in 1964 when the Medical Service Association of Pennsylvania (MSAP) adopted the Blue Shield name.

The Pennsylvania Medical Society, in conjunction with the state of Pennsylvania, had formed MSAP to provide medical insurance to the poor and indigent. MSAP borrowed $25,000 from the Pennsylvania Medical Society to help set up its operations, and Chauncey Palmer (who had originally proposed the organization) was named president. Individuals paid 35 cents per month, and families paid $1.75 each month to join MSAP, which initially covered mainly obstetrical and surgical procedures.

In 1945 Arthur Daugherty replaced Palmer as president (he served until his death in 1968) and helped MSAP recruit major new accounts, including the United Mine Workers and the Congress of Industrial Organizations. MSAP in 1946 became a chapter of the national Blue Shield association, which was started that year by the medical societies of several states to provide prepaid health insurance plans.

In 1951 MSAP signed up the 150,000 employees of United States Steel, bringing its total enrollment to more than 1.6 million. Growth did not lead to prosperity, though, as the organization had trouble keeping up with payments to its doctors. This shortfall in funds led MSAP to raise its premiums in 1961, at which point the state reminded the association of its social mission and suggested it concentrate on controlling costs instead of raising rates.

MSAP changed its name to Pennsylvania Blue Shield in 1964. Two years later the association began managing Pennsylvania's Medicare plan and started the 65-Special plan to supplement Medicare coverage.

In the 1970s Pennsylvania Blue Shield again could not keep up with the cost of paying its doctors, which led to more rate increases and closer scrutiny of its expenses. Competition increased in the 1980s as HMOs cropped up around the state. Pennsylvania Blue Shield fought back by creating its own HMO plans — some of which it owned jointly with Blue Cross of Western Pennsylvania — in the 1980s.

After years of slowly collecting noninsurance businesses, Blue Cross of Western Pennsylvania changed its name to Veritus in 1991 to reflect the growing importance of its for-profit operations.

In 1996 Pennsylvania Blue Shield overcame physicians' protests and state regulators' concerns to merge with Veritus. The company adopted the name Highmark to represent its standards for high quality; it took a loss as it failed to meet cost-cutting goals and suffered early-retirement costs related to the merger consolidation. To gain support for the merger, Highmark sold for-profit subsidiary Keystone Health Plan East to Independence Blue Cross in 1997.

In 1999 Highmark teamed with Mountain State Blue Cross Blue Shield to become West Virginia's primary licensee. Rate hikes and investment returns helped propel the company into the black as the decade closed.

In 2001 Highmark announced that it had uncovered almost $5 million in health care insurance fraud over the course of the previous year.

OFFICERS

Chairman: John N. Shaffer
Vice Chairman: John A. Carpenter
President, CEO, and Director: John S. Brouse
Group EVP, Health Insurance Operations:
James Klingensmith
EVP, Government Business and Corporate Affairs:
George F. Grode
EVP, Strategic Business Development:
Kenneth R. Melani
SVP, CFO, and Treasurer: Robert C. Gray
SVP, Corporate Secretary, and General Counsel:
Gary R. Truitt
SVP and General Auditor: Elizabeth A. Farbacher
SVP, Human Resources and Administrative Services:
S. Tyrone Alexander
Assistant Secretary: Carrie J. Pecht
Assistant Treasurer: Joseph F. Reichard
Corporate Compliance Officer: George A. Welsh
Auditors: PricewaterhouseCoopers LLP

HQ: 5th Ave. Place, 120 5th Ave., Pittsburgh, PA 15222
Phone: 412-544-7000   **Fax:** 412-544-8368
Web: www.highmark.com

PRODUCTS/OPERATIONS

Selected Health Plans and Divisions
Alliances Ventures
Clarity Vision
Davis Vision
HealthGuard (managed care organization)
HGSAdministrators
Highmark Life & Casualty Group
Insurer Physician Services Organization
Keystone Health Plan Central (HMO; central
    Pennsylvania)
Keystone Health Plan West (HMO; western
    Pennsylvania)
United Concordia (dental)
Veritus Medicare Services

COMPETITORS

Aetna
CIGNA
Coventry Health Care
Guardian Life
Humana
New York Life
Prudential
U.S. Healthcare, Inc
UnitedHealth Group

HISTORICAL FINANCIALS & EMPLOYEES

Not-for-profit FYE: December 31	Annual Growth	12/92	12/93	12/94	12/95	12/96	12/97	12/98	12/99	12/00	12/01
Sales ($ mil.)	9.2%	3,083	3,113	3,221	3,367	6,619	7,405	7,544	8,190	9,000	6,799
Net income ($ mil.)	(0.8%)	141	132	128	43	(50)	101	62	69	242	132
Income as % of sales	—	4.6%	4.2%	4.0%	1.3%	—	1.4%	0.8%	0.8%	2.7%	1.9%
Employees	6.2%	—	—	7,200	8,000	10,500	12,000	12,000	11,000	11,000	11,000

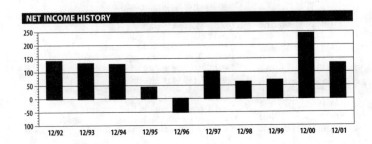

NET INCOME HISTORY

HILLENBRAND INDUSTRIES, INC.

Life. Death. Corpse disposal. Batesville, Indiana-based Hillenbrand Industries serves the verities of existence from cradle to grave.

The holding company operates three major subsidiaries. Hill-Rom makes hospital beds, infant incubators, and related equipment. Hillenbrand's Forethought Financial Services provides burial insurance and trust services, while Forethought Federal Savings Bank enables living customers to save up for their own funerals. And when it's time for the inevitable, another Hillenbrand subsidiary will be there for you: Batesville Casket is one of North America's largest casket makers and a leading provider of cremation products. The Hillenbrand family owns about 25% of the company.

After taking a hit from Medicare reimbursement cutbacks, the company streamlined some operations and appointed its first non-Hillenbrand family CEO.

HISTORY

In 1906 John A. Hillenbrand, a banker, newspaperman, and general store owner in Batesville, Indiana, bought the ailing Batesville Casket Company (founded 1884) to save it from bankruptcy. Under Hillenbrand, and later his four sons (John W., who succeeded his father as president of the company; William; George; and Daniel), the casket company flourished.

In 1929 William Hillenbrand established the Hill-Rom Company in Batesville to make hospital furniture. Hill-Rom made its furniture out of wood instead of tubular steel and quickly became a leader in innovative hospital furnishings.

During the following decades George Hillenbrand created several patented products for both Batesville Casket and Hill-Rom. By the 1940s, for example, the company had developed corrosion-, air-, and water-resistant metal caskets. George constantly sought ways to improve manufacturing techniques and product quality, giving the company a competitive edge in sales and productivity.

Daniel, the youngest son, became president of Batesville Casket in 1964 and consolidated Batesville Casket and Hill-Rom into Hillenbrand Industries five years later. Hoping to make the company more competitive nationally (and eventually globally), Daniel took Hillenbrand public in 1971.

The company acquired Dominion Metalware Industries (1972) and luggage maker American Tourister (1978; sold to Astrum International, maker of Samsonite luggage, in 1993). In 1984 it bought Medeco Security Locks (sold 1998) and a year later purchased Support Systems

International (SSI), provider of specialty rental mattresses for critically ill and immobile patients. (In 1994 SSI was integrated into Hill-Rom.)

Hillenbrand founded the Forethought Group in 1985 to provide special life insurance to cover prearranged funerals and in 1991 entered the European market by acquiring Le Couviour, a French maker of hospital beds. The company also bought Block Medical, a maker of home infusion-therapy products, that year. August Hillenbrand, nephew of Daniel, became CEO in 1989.

In 1992 Batesville Casket set out to consolidate its market, buying casket producer Cormier & Gaudet (Canada). It then bought Bridge Casket (New Jersey), Lincoln Casket (Hamtramck, Michigan); and Industrias Arga (Mexico City), all in 1993. That year Hillenbrand also purchased L & C Arnold, one of the biggest and oldest hospital furniture makers in Germany.

With the casket market flat in the mid-1990s, Hillenbrand grew its business by going after market share in cremation products and diversifying into retail. One venture, which specialized in funeral mementos, expired quietly. A bed store chain, Sleep Options (begun 1995), lived on, opening its seventh store in 1997. In 1996 the company sold its Block Medical subsidiary to infusion systems marketer I-Flow, but it acquired AirShields (UK, infant incubators/warmers) and obtained a federal thrift charter to enter the funeral and cemetery trust market in 1997. In 1998 Hill-Rom entered the medical gas delivery market and expanded its international position by buying UK-based medical gas distributor MEDAES.

As the 20th century drew to a close, Medicare reimbursement cutbacks bit into Hill-Rom's sales. The company cut jobs in both 2000 and 2001. Those years also brought the retirement of both August and Daniel Hillenbrand, though Daniel remains as chairman emeritus. Ray Hillenbrand (nephew of Daniel) was named chairman in 2001.

OFFICERS

Chairman Emeritus: Daniel A. Hillenbrand, age 77
Chairman: Ray J. Hillenbrand, age 66
President, CEO, and Director: Frederick W. Rockwood, age 53, $1,442,025 pay
VP and CFO: Scott K. Sorensen, age 40
VP, General Counsel, and Secretary: Patrick D. de Maynadier, age 41
VP and Chief Accounting Officer: James D. Van De Velde, age 55
VP and CIO: Geoff W. Packwood, age 61
VP and Controller: Gregory N. Miller
VP and Treasurer: Mark R. Lanning, age 47
VP, Corporate Audit: Michael A. Gardner, age 53
VP, Corporate Development: Catherine I. Greany, age 46

VP, Corporate Services: David E. Raver, age 54
VP, Executive Leadership Development:
Stephen W. McMillen, age 48
VP, Taxes: Larry L. Waite
President and CEO, Batesville Casket:
Kenneth A. Camp
President and CEO, Forethought Financial Services:
Stephen R. Lang
President and CEO, Hill-Rom: R. Ernest Waaser, age 46
VP, Marketing, Batesville Casket:
Christopher R. Ruberg, age 42
Director, Human Resources: Tim Dietz
Auditors: PricewaterhouseCoopers LLP

LOCATIONS

HQ: 700 State Rte. 46 East, Batesville, IN 47006
Phone: 812-934-7000 **Fax:** 812-934-7364
Web: www.hillenbrand.com

Hillenbrand Industries operates in Australia, Europe,
Latin America, and North America.

PRODUCTS/OPERATIONS

2001 Sales

	$ mil.	% of total
Health care sales	809	38
Funeral services	613	29
Insurance	346	17
Health care rentals	339	16
Total	**2,107**	**100**

Selected Subsidiaries

Funeral Services
Hillenbrand Funeral Services Group, Inc.
  Batesville Services, Inc.
    Batesville Casket Company, Inc.
    Batesville Casket de Mexico, S.A. de C.V.
    Batesville International Corporation
    Batesville Manufacturing, Inc.
  Hillenbrand Funeral Services International, Inc.
Forethought Financial Services, Inc.
  ForeLife Agency, Inc.
  Forethought Federal Savings Bank
  The Forethought Group, Inc.
  Forethought Investment Management, Inc.
  Forethought Life Assurance Company
  Forethought Life Insurance Company

Health Care
Hill-Rom, Inc.
  Hill-Rom Company, Inc.
  The OR Group, Inc.
  MEDAES Holdings, Inc.

Other
The Acorn Development Group, Inc.
Memory Showcase, Inc.
Sherman House Corporation
Sleep Options, Inc.
Travel Services, Inc.

COMPETITORS

Aurora Casket	Medline Industries
Forever Enterprises	Sunrise Medical
Invacare	Wilbert
Kinetic Concepts	York Group
Matthews International	

HISTORICAL FINANCIALS & EMPLOYEES

NYSE: HB FYE: September 30	Annual Growth	11/92	11/93	11/94	11/95	11/96	11/97	11/98	11/99	11/00	11/01
Sales ($ mil.)	4.4%	1,430	1,448	1,577	1,625	1,684	1,776	2,001	2,047	2,096	2,107
Net income ($ mil.)	4.3%	116	146	90	90	140	157	184	124	154	170
Income as % of sales	—	8.1%	10.1%	5.7%	5.5%	8.3%	8.8%	9.2%	6.1%	7.3%	8.1%
Earnings per share ($)	5.9%	1.62	2.04	1.26	1.27	2.02	2.28	2.73	1.87	2.44	2.71
Stock price – FY high ($)	—	43.63	48.63	43.63	33.13	40.25	48.63	64.69	57.13	51.50	58.51
Stock price – FY low ($)	—	29.31	36.50	26.63	27.00	31.88	33.88	44.38	26.13	28.75	41.56
Stock price – FY close ($)	2.6%	41.63	41.63	29.88	32.75	36.88	44.56	56.81	34.19	51.00	52.64
P/E – high	—	30	26	35	26	20	21	24	31	21	22
P/E – low	—	20	19	21	21	16	15	16	14	12	15
Dividends per share ($)	10.2%	0.35	0.45	0.57	0.60	0.62	0.66	0.72	0.78	0.80	0.84
Book value per share ($)	8.9%	7.65	8.98	9.72	10.63	11.44	12.93	14.26	13.19	13.32	16.42
Employees	(0.5%)	10,700	9,800	10,000	9,800	9,800	10,100	10,400	10,000	10,800	10,200

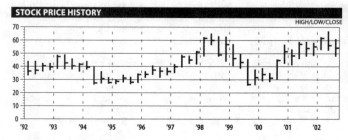

STOCK PRICE HISTORY HIGH/LOW/CLOSE

2001 FISCAL YEAR-END
Debt ratio: 22.9%
Return on equity: 18.3%
Cash ($ mil.): 284
Current ratio: 2.71
Long-term debt ($ mil.): 305
No. of shares (mil.): 62
Dividends
  Yield: 1.6%
  Payout: 31.0%
Market value ($ mil.): 3,288

HILTON HOTELS CORPORATION

With one of the most renowned names in the hotel business, and a little help from the acquisition fairy, Hilton Hotels has become one of the leading hotel enterprises in the country. Headquartered in Beverly Hills, California, the hotelier's lodging empire spans about 2,000 owned, partially owned, managed, or franchised hotels — thanks to the 1999 purchase of Promus Hotel and its 1,450 properties. In addition to its Hilton brands, the company's stable now includes such brands as Hampton Inn (which accounts for about 1,150 hotels) and Embassy Suites. Hilton's hotels are predominantly located in the US, but the company does manage and own hotels and other properties in about 15 other countries, and has plans for a joint venture with Hilton Group to expand the Conrad brand of luxury hotels. It also operates 21 vacation ownership resorts primarily in Florida but also in Nevada and Hawaii.

Hilton spun off its casino business into Park Place Entertainment in 1998 and has continued its withdrawal from gaming by selling the Flamingo Casino-Kansas City. Renewing its focus on lodging, the company planned to open more than 400 new hotels through 2001. (However, it managed to develop only about 170 hotels while it sold off 43 Red Lion hotels and lost another 103 managed properties through a terminated lease agreement with a third party.) It also agreed in 2002 to sell its Harrison Conference Center portfolio, which includes 14 conference centers and university hotels, to ARAMARK for $55 million. Hilton is playing it safe amid a slowed-down economy as occupancy rates dropped across the industry in 2001. It is looking to grow mainly through acquiring new management contracts and by franchising, which require little capital up front.

Chairman Barron Hilton, son of founder Conrad Hilton, owns about 6% of the company and controls an additional 5% through the charitable Conrad N. Hilton Fund.

HISTORY

Conrad Hilton got his start in hotel management by renting out rooms in his family's New Mexico home. He served as a state legislator and started a bank before leaving for Texas in 1919, hoping to make his fortune in banking. Hilton was unable to shoulder the cost of purchasing a bank, however, but recognized a high demand for hotel rooms and made a quick change in strategy, buying his first hotel in Cisco, Texas. Over the next decade he bought seven more Texas hotels.

Hilton lost several hotels during the Depression, but began rebuilding his hotel empire soon

thereafter through the purchase of hotels in California (1938), New Mexico (1939), and Mexico (1942). He even married starlet Zsa Zsa Gabor in 1942 (they later divorced, of course). Hilton Hotels Corporation was formed in 1946 and went public. The company bought New York's Waldorf-Astoria in 1949 (a hotel Hilton called "the greatest of them all") and opened its first European hotel in Madrid in 1953. Hilton paid $111 million for the 10-hotel Statler chain the following year.

Hilton took his company out of the overseas hotel business in 1964 by spinning off Hilton International and began franchising the following year to capitalize on the well-known Hilton name. Barron Hilton, Conrad's son, was appointed president in 1966 (he became chairman upon Conrad Hilton's death in 1979). Hilton bought two Las Vegas hotels (the Las Vegas Hilton and the Flamingo Hilton) in 1970 and launched its gaming division. It returned to the international hotel business with Conrad International Hotels in 1982 and opened its first suite-only Hilton Suites hotel in 1989.

The company expanded its gaming operations in the 1990s, buying Bally's Casino Resort in Reno in 1992 and launching its first riverboat casino, the Hilton Queen of New Orleans, in 1994. Two years later it acquired all of Bally Entertainment, making it the largest gaming company in the world. Also that year, Stephen Bollenbach, the former Walt Disney CFO who negotiated the $19 billion acquisition of Capital Cities/ABC, was named CEO — becoming the first nonfamily member to run the company.

Hilton formed an alliance with Ladbroke Group PLC in 1997 (now Hilton Group, owner of Hilton International and the rights to the Hilton name outside the US) to unify the Hilton brand worldwide. Hilton also put in a bid that year to acquire ITT, owner of Sheraton hotels and Caesars World, but was thwarted when ITT accepted a higher offer from Starwood Hotels & Resorts. Hilton was foiled once again in 1998 when a deal with casino operator Circus Circus (now Mandalay Resort Group) that would have separated Hilton's hotel and casino operations fell through. With a downturn in the gambling industry translating into sluggish results in Hilton's gaming segment, the company spun off its gaming interests as Park Place Entertainment later that year.

In 1999 Hilton made a massive acquisition with the $3.7 billion purchase of Promus Hotel Corp. The following year Hilton sold its Flamingo Casino-Kansas City, a remaining casino property left over from the Park Place spinoff, to Isle of Capri Casinos for $33.5 million. In 2001 it sold

56 of its leases and management contracts to RFS Hotel Investors for about $60 million. In 2002 it unloaded all 41 of its Red Lion hotels (in addition to two Doubltree hotels) on West Coast Hospitality Corporation for about $51 million.

OFFICERS

Chairman: Barron Hilton
President, CEO, and Director: Stephen F. Bollenbach, age 59, $1,900,000 pay
EVP and CFO: Matthew J. Hart, age 49, $941,070 pay
EVP and Director; President, Hotel Operations Owned and Managed: Dieter H. Huckestein, age 58, $724,383 pay
EVP; President, Brand Performance and Franchise Development Group: Thomas L. Keltner, $712,504 pay
EVP, General Counsel, and Corporate Secretary: Madeleine A. Kleiner, $604,872 pay
SVP, Architecture & Construction: Patrick Terwilliger
SVP, Corporate Affairs: Marc A. Grossman
SVP, Franchising and Select Hotels: William B. Fortier
SVP, Human Resources: Molly McKenzie-Swarts
SVP, Sales: Steven Armitage
SVP, and CIO: James T. Harvey
Auditors: Ernst & Young LLP

LOCATIONS

HQ: 9336 Civic Center Dr., Beverly Hills, CA 90210
Phone: 310-278-4321   **Fax:** 310-205-7678
Web: www.hilton.com

Hilton Hotels has operations in Asia, Australia, Canada, Europe (including the UK), Latin America, the Middle East, New Zealand, South Africa, and the US.

PRODUCTS/OPERATIONS

2001 Sales

	$ mil.	% of total
Owned hotels	2,122	81
Management & franchise fees	342	13
Leased hotels	168	6
Total	**2,632**	**100**

Hotel Brands
Conrad Conference Centers
Conrad International Hotels
Doubletree Hotels
Embassy Suites
Hampton Inn
Hampton Inn & Suites
Harrison Conference Centers
Hilton
Hilton Garden Inn
Homewood Suites by Hilton

COMPETITORS

Accor
Best Western
Carlson
Cendant
Choice Hotels
Four Seasons Hotels
Host Marriott
Hyatt
Marriott International
Ritz Carlton
Six Continents Hotels
Starwood Hotels & Resorts
Wyndham International

HISTORICAL FINANCIALS & EMPLOYEES

NYSE: HLT FYE: December 31	Annual Growth	12/92	12/93	12/94	12/95	12/96	12/97	12/98	12/99	12/00	12/01
Sales ($ mil.)	8.8%	1,230	1,394	1,506	1,649	3,940	5,316	1,769	1,959	3,177	2,632
Net income ($ mil.)	5.3%	104	106	122	173	82	250	297	174	272	166
Income as % of sales	—	8.4%	7.6%	8.1%	10.5%	2.1%	4.7%	16.8%	8.9%	8.6%	6.3%
Earnings per share ($)	(2.0%)	0.54	0.56	0.63	0.89	0.41	0.94	1.12	0.65	0.74	0.45
Stock price - FY high ($)	—	13.31	15.25	18.50	19.94	31.75	35.81	35.50	17.13	12.13	13.57
Stock price - FY low ($)	—	9.94	10.38	12.44	15.09	15.28	24.00	12.50	8.38	6.38	6.15
Stock price - FY close ($)	0.1%	10.84	15.19	17.00	15.38	26.25	29.75	19.13	9.56	10.50	10.92
P/E - high	—	25	28	29	22	40	38	31	26	16	30
P/E - low	—	18	19	19	17	19	25	11	13	9	14
Dividends per share ($)	(13.7%)	0.30	0.30	0.30	0.30	0.31	0.32	0.32	0.08	0.08	0.08
Book value per share ($)	(0.9%)	5.25	5.53	5.86	6.49	12.90	13.59	0.72	3.85	4.46	4.83
Employees	6.8%	41,000	43,000	44,000	48,000	65,000	61,000	38,000	78,000	77,000	74,000

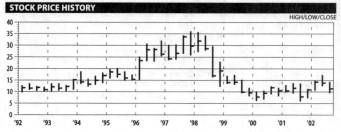

STOCK PRICE HISTORY   HIGH/LOW/CLOSE

2001 FISCAL YEAR-END
Debt ratio: 73.5%
Return on equity: 9.7%
Cash ($ mil.): 35
Current ratio: 1.10
Long-term debt ($ mil.): 4,950
No. of shares (mil.): 369
Dividends
  Yield: 0.7%
  Payout: 17.8%
Market value ($ mil.): 4,029

H.J. HEINZ COMPANY

H.J. Heinz is banging on the bottom of the bottle, trying to get more sales out of ketchup and its other traditional food products. Pittsburgh-based Heinz is a leading global food company with more than 5,700 products, including ketchup, condiments, sauces, frozen foods, tuna, soups, beans, pasta, infant foods, and pet food. Its stable of US retail market leaders includes Heinz ketchup (more than 50% US market share), Ore-Ida potatoes, Star-Kist tuna, 9-Lives cat food, and Weight Watchers food products. Ketchup, condiments, and sauces account for about 28% of its sales.

With brands in mature markets back home, Heinz is expanding overseas through acquisitions and joint ventures.

In an effort to focus on its core food products (sauces, ketchup, frozen foods), Heinz plans to spin off a number of its North American businesses to Del Monte Foods Company. The proposed all-stock transaction includes the company's pet food (Kibbles 'n Bits) and snacks, tuna (Star-Kist), private label soup, and infant feeding (Heinz Nature's Goodness) businesses. The divestitures will total 20% of Heinz's revenues, but the company will gain a 75% stake in Del Monte after the deal is final.

HISTORY

In 1852 eight-year-old Henry J. Heinz started selling produce from the family garden to neighbors in Sharpsburg, Pennsylvania. The young entrepreneur formed a partnership with his friend L. C. Noble in 1869, bottling horseradish sauce in clear glass, but the business went bankrupt in 1875. The following year, with the help of his brother John and his cousin Frederick, Heinz created F. & J. Heinz; the enterprise developed ketchup (1876) and sweet pickles (1880). He gained financial control of the firm in 1888 and changed the name to the H.J. Heinz Company.

Heinz developed a reputation as an advertising and marketing genius. He introduced pickle pins, a popular promotion at the 1893 Chicago World's Fair; coined the catchy "57 Varieties" slogan in 1897 (despite already having 60 products); and in 1900 raised New York City's first large electric advertising sign (a 40-ft. pickle). By 1905 Heinz was manufacturing food products in the UK.

After Heinz's death in 1919 the business, under the direction of his son and later his grandson, continued to rely on its traditional product lines for the next four decades, although some new ones were introduced, such as baby food in 1931. The company went public in 1946. Heinz changed its strategy in 1958 when it made its first acquisition, a Dutch food processor. Major purchases that followed included Star-Kist (tuna and pet food, 1963) and Ore-Ida (potatoes, 1965). In 1966 Burt Gookin became CEO, the first non-family member to hold that position.

The company bought Weight Watchers in 1978. The next year former rugby star Anthony O'Reilly became the company's fifth CEO. He intensified the focus on international expansion and presided over a string of acquisitions throughout the 1980s. O'Reilly became chairman in 1987.

Acquisitions in the 1990s included Wattie's Limited (New Zealand, 1992); Borden's food service business (1994); and pet food divisions from Quaker Oats (1995). However, faced with weak sales growth in its stable markets, in 1997 Heinz began shedding domestic units as it made global acquisitions. It sold its Ore-Ida food service operations (to McCain Foods, 1997) and its bakery products division (to Pillsbury, 1998), but purchased John West Foods (UK, tuna, 1997) and Sonnen Basserman (Germany, convenience meals, 1998).

William Johnson, who had turned around stagnant brands such as 9-Lives, succeeded O'Reilly as CEO in 1998. In 1999 Heinz announced a restructuring intended to eliminate jobs and close or sell about 20 factories over several years. Heinz sold the diet business of Weight Watchers, and, seeking greater access to the US natural foods market, purchased nearly 20% of Hain Food Group (now The Hain Celestial Group).

In 2000 Heinz acquired International Diverse-Foods (food service condiments) and Alden Merrell (frozen desserts). Also in 2000 Dr. O'Reilly retired and Johnson was named chairman.

During 2001 Heinz continued with global acquisitions while being picky with its food back home. It sold its Budget Gourmet frozen entrée business to rival Luigino's and then lapped up pasta sauce and soup businesses from Borden Foods. Overseas, Heinz acquired CSM's food products division, making it the #2 food maker in the Benelux countries, and expanded into Central America by purchasing Productos Columbia and Distribuidora Banquete (makers of the Banquete brand of ketchup, sauces, and condiments). The company also purchased US-based Delimex Holdings (frozen Mexican foods) and the Poppers and T.G.I. Friday's lines of frozen appetizers from Anchor Food Products.

Furthering expansion in China, Heinz purchased Meiweiyuan Food Corp. (flavoring), and Meiweiyuan Food Factory and Fanyu Jinmai Food Factory (food processing) in 2002. Also that year it introduced Heinz organic ketchup.

Chairman, President, and CEO: William R. Johnson,
age 53, $1,691,851 pay
EVP and CFO: Arthur Winkleblack, age 45
EVP; President and CEO, Heinz Europe:
Joseph Jimenez Jr., age 42
EVP; President and CEO, Heinz North America:
Neil Harrison
SVP and Chief Administrative Officer:
William C. Goode III, age 61
SVP and Chief Growth Officer: Michael D. Milone,
age 46
SVP and General Counsel: Laura Stein, age 40,
$486,418 pay
SVP, Corporate and Government Affairs:
D. Edward I. Smyth, age 52
SVP; President, Heinz Asia/Pacific: Michael J. Bertasso,
age 52
Auditors: PricewaterhouseCoopers LLP

LOCATIONS

HQ: 600 Grant Street, Pittsburgh, PA 15219
Phone: 412-456-5700　　**Fax:** 412-456-6128
Web: www.heinz.com

H.J. Heinz operates more than 30 domestic processing
plants and more than 60 foreign plants.

2002 Sales

	$ mil.	% of total
North America	5,205	55
Europe	2,834	30
Asia/Pacific	981	10
Other regions	411	5
Total	**9,431**	**100**

PRODUCTS/OPERATIONS

2002 Sales

	$ mil.	% of total
Ketchup, condiments & sauces	2,670	28
Frozen foods	2,000	21
Soups, beans & pasta meals	1,192	13
Tuna	1,036	11
Pet products	983	11
Infant & nutritional foods	891	9
Other	659	7
Total	**9,431**	**100**

Selected Brand Names

Food
Boston Market (frozen
meals)
Classico (pasta sauce)
Heinz (ketchup, pickles,
relishes, sauces, baby
food)
Ore-Ida (frozen potatoes
and potato products)
Smart Ones (diet frozen
entrees)

Star-Kist (tuna)
Weight Watchers (diet
foods)

Pet Food
9-Lives
Cycle
Gravy Train
Ken-L-Ration
Kibbles 'n Bits
Snausages

COMPETITORS

B&G Foods
Beech-Nut
Campbell Soup
Chicken of the
Sea
International
Cirio
Colgate-
Palmolive

ConAgra
Del Monte Foods
Doane Pet Care
Company
Hibernia Foods
Iams
Jenny Craig
Kraft Foods
North America

La Doria
Luigino's
Mars
Milnot Company
Nestlé
Novartis
Procter &
Gamble
Slim-Fast

HISTORICAL FINANCIALS & EMPLOYEES

NYSE: HNZ FYE: Wednesday nearest Apr. 30	Annual Growth	4/93	4/94	4/95	4/96	4/97	4/98	4/99	4/00	4/01	4/02
Sales ($ mil.)	3.2%	7,103	7,047	8,087	9,112	9,357	9,209	9,300	9,408	9,430	9,431
Net income ($ mil.)	8.6%	396	603	591	659	302	802	474	891	478	834
Income as % of sales	—	5.6%	8.6%	7.3%	7.2%	3.2%	8.7%	5.1%	9.5%	5.1%	8.8%
Earnings per share ($)	10.0%	1.00	1.56	1.58	1.75	0.81	2.15	1.29	2.47	1.36	2.36
Stock price - FY high ($)	—	30.35	26.60	28.68	36.63	44.88	59.94	61.75	54.00	48.00	47.00
Stock price - FY low ($)	—	23.51	20.51	21.09	27.43	29.75	41.13	44.56	30.81	33.13	37.68
Stock price - FY close ($)	6.2%	24.51	21.84	28.01	33.88	41.50	54.50	46.69	34.00	39.15	41.99
P/E - high	—	22	17	18	20	55	27	47	22	34	20
P/E - low	—	17	13	13	15	36	19	34	12	23	16
Dividends per share ($)	8.4%	0.78	0.86	0.94	1.04	1.14	1.24	1.34	1.45	1.55	1.61
Book value per share ($)	(2.4%)	6.09	6.26	6.77	7.34	6.65	6.10	5.02	4.59	3.94	4.90
Employees	2.4%	37,700	35,700	42,200	43,300	44,700	40,500	38,600	49,600	45,800	46,500

STOCK PRICE HISTORY

HIGH/LOW/CLOSE

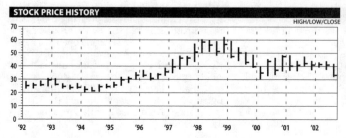

2002 FISCAL YEAR-END

Debt ratio: 73.0%
Return on equity: 53.9%
Cash ($ mil.): 207
Current ratio: 1.34
Long-term debt ($ mil.): 4,643
No. of shares (mil.): 351
Dividends
Yield: 3.8%
Payout: 68.2%
Market value ($ mil.): 14,734

THE HOME DEPOT, INC.

The Home Depot has sketched a simple blueprint for success: Take the service and convenience of a mom-and-pop hardware shop and combine them in a store the size of an airplane hangar. The world's largest home improvement chain and second-largest retailer after Wal-Mart, the Atlanta-based company operates about 1,400 stores in the US, Canada, and Latin America. Included among the company's outlets are more than 40 EXPO Design Center stores (large design showrooms that feature bath and kitchen, flooring, and lighting products).

Home Depot stores, which average about 131,000 sq. ft., primarily cater to do-it-yourselfers. The company has increasingly been selling to professional builders and contractors, courting their business by offering more individualized attention and special services such as same-day delivery. Each Home Depot store stocks more than 40,000 kinds of building materials, home improvement supplies, lawn and garden equipment, and appliances.

Home Depot continually polishes its business plan. The rapidly growing company sells products through the Internet, and it is testing a new smaller-store concept in urban areas and expanding its appliance department. It has also opened a few pilot Home Depot Supply stores for professional builders. Design Place, which focuses on home decor categories and is intended to attract more women customers, has been installed in more than 500 stores and will be part of about another 400 by the end of 2002.

Additionally the company has added a tool rental center to 500 stores, and it is increasing its presence in Mexico.

HISTORY

Bernard Marcus and Arthur Blank founded The Home Depot in 1978 after they were fired (under disputed circumstances) from Handy Dan Home Improvement Centers. They joined Handy Dan co-worker Ronald Brill to launch a "new and improved" home center for the do-it-yourselfer (DIY). (A potential major investment from Ross Perot fell through that year because the wealthy Texan wouldn't allow Home Depot to pick up the payments on Marcus' used Cadillac.) In 1979 they opened three stores in the fast-growing Atlanta area and expanded to four stores in 1980.

Home Depot went public, opened four stores in South Florida, and posted sales of $50 million in 1981. The chain entered Louisiana and Arizona next. By 1983 sales were more than $250 million.

In 1984 Home Depot's stock was listed on the NYSE and the company acquired nine Bowater

Home Centers in the South. Through subsequent stock and debenture offerings, Home Depot continued to grow, entering California (Handy Dan's home turf) with six new stores in 1985.

Back on track in 1986, sales exceeded $1 billion in the firm's 60 stores. Home Depot began the current policy of "low day-in, day-out pricing" the following year, achieving Marcus' dream of eliminating sales events. The company entered the competitive northeastern market with stores in Long Island, New York, in 1988 and opened its first EXPO Design Center in San Diego.

Home Depot's sales continued to rise during the 1990-92 recession and the retailer kept opening stores. It entered Canada in 1994 when it acquired a 75% interest in Aikenhead's, a DIY chain that it converted to the Home Depot name (it bought the remaining 25% in 1998).

A series of gender-bias lawsuits plagued the company in 1994 as female workers claimed they were not treated on an equal basis with male employees. Home Depot reached a $65 million out-of-court settlement in 1997, but not before the company was ordered to pay another female employee $1.7 million in a case in California.

Troubles aside, Home Depot roared past the 500-store mark in 1997. That year Blank succeeded Marcus as the company's CEO; Marcus remained chairman. The company opened stores in Chile in 1998 in a joint venture with Chilean retailer Falabella. In 1999 Home Depot introduced its 40,000-sq.-ft. Villager's Hardware stores, designed to compete with smaller hardware shops, in New Jersey. It also bought Georgia Lighting, an Atlanta lighting designer, distributor, and retailer.

In 2000 Home Depot bought Apex Supply (plumbing distributor). Later that year the company named General Electric executive Robert Nardelli as its president and CEO.

In 2001 the company opened 200 new stores and bought Total HOME, a home improvement chain with four stores in Mexico. Additionally, in 2001 Nardelli became chairman after Marcus stepped down. Also that year the company said it was scrapping its Villager's Hardware experiment to test a small-store concept in urban areas.

In April 2002 Home Depot opened its first small store, a 61,000-sq.-ft. outlet, in New York City. Further increasing its presence in Mexico, the company acquired the four-store Del Norte chain in Juárez in June 2002 and opened a newly constructed store in Mexicali in August 2002. Also that month Home Depot announced that it would begin expensing the cost of stock options granted after February 1, 2003. Additionally in August 2002 Home Depot opened the first of three planned Landscape Supply stores in the Atlanta area.

OFFICERS

Chairman, President, and CEO: Robert L. Nardelli, age 53, $6,528,845 pay
EVP and CFO: Carol B. Tomé, age 45, $925,576 pay
EVP, Corporate Secretary, and General Counsel: Frank L. Fernandez, age 51, $1,219,230 pay
EVP, Human Resources: Dennis M. Donovan, age 53, $1,450,025 pay
EVP, Information Technology, and CIO: Robert P. DeRodes, age 51
EVP, Merchandising: Jerry W. Edwards
EVP, Operations: Larry M. Mercer, age 55, $1,101,922 pay
EVP, Strategy, Business Development, Strategy, and Corporate Operations: Francis S. Blake, age 52
SVP, Customer Service Operations: Ramon K. Gregory
SVP, Executive Services: Lawrence A. Smith
SVP, Global Logistics: Wayne Gibson
SVP, Legal: Laurence B. Appel
SVP, Operations: Troy Rice, age 39
SVP, Real Estate: Michael R. Folio
SVP, Store Merchandising: Millard E. Barron
VP, eBusiness: Chuck Elias
VP, Pro Operations: Ron Bogdanovich
President, EXPO Design Centers: Robert J. Wittman
President, Home Depot Supply: Jim Stoddart
Regional President, Canada: Annette Verschuren
Auditors: KPMG LLP

LOCATIONS

HQ: 2455 Paces Ferry Rd., Atlanta, GA 30339
Phone: 770-433-8211 **Fax:** 770-384-2356
Web: www.homedepot.com

PRODUCTS/OPERATIONS

2002 Sales

	% of total
Plumbing, electrical & kitchen	28
Hardware & seasonal	27
Building materials, lumber & millwork	24
Paint, flooring & wall coverings	21
Total	**100**

Private Labels and Proprietary Brands

Behr Premium Plus (paint)
GE SmartWater (water heaters)
Mill's Pride (cabinets)
RIDGID (power tools)
Thomasville (cabinets)
Vigoro (fertilizer)

COMPETITORS

84 Lumber	Menard
Abbey Carpet	Northern Tool
Ace Hardware	Pacific Coast Building
Amazon.com	Products
Building Materials	Reno-Depot
Holding	Sears
Cameron Ashley	Sherwin-Williams
Carolina Holdings	Sutherland Lumber
Carpet One	Target
Do it Best	TruServ
F.W. Webb	Wal-Mart
Kmart	Wickes
Lanoga	Wolseley
Lowe's	

HISTORICAL FINANCIALS & EMPLOYEES

NYSE: HD FYE: Sunday nearest January 31	Annual Growth	1/93	1/94	1/95	1/96	1/97	1/98	1/99	1/00	1/01	1/02
Sales ($ mil.)	25.1%	7,148	9,239	12,477	15,470	19,536	24,156	30,219	38,434	45,738	53,553
Net income ($ mil.)	26.7%	363	457	605	732	938	1,160	1,614	2,320	2,581	3,044
Income as % of sales	—	5.1%	5.0%	4.8%	4.7%	4.8%	4.8%	5.3%	6.0%	5.6%	5.7%
Earnings per share ($)	23.7%	0.19	0.23	0.29	0.34	0.43	0.52	0.71	1.00	1.10	1.29
Stock price - FY high ($)	—	11.45	11.24	10.79	11.12	13.23	20.55	41.35	69.75	70.00	53.73
Stock price - FY low ($)	—	6.62	7.78	8.26	8.15	9.45	11.01	20.42	35.76	34.69	30.30
Stock price - FY close ($)	18.5%	10.86	8.67	10.40	10.23	11.01	20.17	40.35	56.81	48.20	50.09
P/E - high	—	60	49	37	32	31	39	57	68	63	41
P/E - low	—	35	34	28	23	22	21	28	35	31	23
Dividends per share ($)	26.8%	0.02	0.03	0.03	0.05	0.05	0.07	0.08	0.11	0.16	0.17
Book value per share ($)	23.5%	1.16	1.39	1.69	2.33	2.76	3.23	3.95	5.36	6.46	7.71
Employees	23.3%	38,900	50,600	67,300	80,000	100,000	125,000	157,000	201,000	227,000	256,000

STOCK PRICE HISTORY

HIGH/LOW/CLOSE

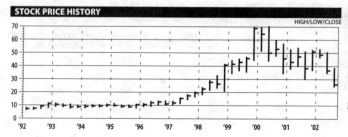

2002 FISCAL YEAR-END

Debt ratio: 6.5%
Return on equity: 18.4%
Cash ($ mil.): 2,477
Current ratio: 1.59
Long-term debt ($ mil.): 1,250
No. of shares (mil.): 2,346
Dividends
  Yield: 0.3%
  Payout: 13.2%
Market value ($ mil.): 117,506

HON INDUSTRIES INC.

Caught in the office during a blizzard? Mad at your office manager? Not to add fuel to the fire, but HON INDUSTRIES makes office furniture and the fireplace to burn it in. Based in Muscatine, Iowa, HON INDUSTRIES is a leading US maker of office furniture (behind #1 Steelcase and racing with Haworth to be #2). Through subsidiaries such as Allsteel, BPI, Gunlocke, and The HON Company, the company makes desks and chairs, filing cabinets, office panel systems, shelving, and related products. Office products make up almost 80% of revenues; one customer, United Stationers, accounts for 14% of HON INDUSTRIES' total sales.

The company's Hearth Technologies subsidiary makes products for the domestic pyrophile. It is the largest US maker of wood- and gas-burning fireplaces, sold under the Heatilator and Heat-N-Glo names; it also makes Aladdin stoves.

HON INDUSTRIES distributes its wares through a system of dealers, wholesalers, and retailers, among others, operating primarily in the US and Canada.

HISTORY

Friends Maxwell Stanley, Clement Hanson, and Wood Miller founded The Home-O-Nize Co. (a name that suggested "modernize" and "economize") in 1944, planning to make home freezers and steel kitchen cabinets. These two products were never made, however, because of a steel shortage.

The first Home-O-Nize product was an aluminum hood used in the installation of natural gas systems. More important than the aluminum hood was the aluminum scrap left behind, which the company made into beverage coasters. These coasters, which could be imprinted with a company's name, were sold to businesses to give out as gifts. Home-O-Nize also transformed the aluminum scraps into boxes for file cards and, due to favorable response, decided to plunge into the office products business.

This move began in earnest in 1951, in an effort dramatically labeled "Operation Independence Home-O-Nize." The program was successful, and in 1952 the company started an unbroken string of profitable years. Helping this streak were such products as Unifile, a file cabinet that featured a single key that would lock all drawers simultaneously (1953). Home-O-Nize added cabinets, coat racks, and desks to its product line during this time and began marking all its products with the "H-O-N" label. Miller retired in 1958.

Home-O-Nize grew during the 1960s under the control of Stanley Howe, a Home-O-Nize employee since 1948. Howe had been appointed president in 1964 and made the company a national manufacturer by purchasing a plant in Georgia in 1967. The firm changed its name to HON INDUSTRIES the next year. Hanson left the company in 1969.

HON INDUSTRIES continued its expansion by purchasing California-based Holga Metal Products in 1971. Acquiring facilities in Pennsylvania and the opening of a plant in Virginia the next year gave HON INDUSTRIES a considerable presence on both US coasts. Howe replaced founder Maxwell Stanley as CEO in 1979.

In 1981 HON INDUSTRIES moved into the fireplace market by acquiring Heatilator, a leading brand of prefabricated fireplaces. By 1987, four decades after shipping its first product, HON INDUSTRIES had become a FORTUNE 500 company that many regarded as the most efficient in the making of office furniture. (It could produce a desk a minute and a chair every 20 seconds.) HON INDUSTRIES acquired Gunlocke, a maker of wooden office furniture, in 1989.

The rise of the office products superstore at the start of the 1990s did not go unnoticed by the company, which quickly positioned itself as a supplier to these businesses. Yet no action could spare HON INDUSTRIES from the office supply bust that occurred soon afterward, as oversupply and a lagging national economy dragged the industry downward.

Jack Michaels became the new CEO in 1991 as the company's sales dropped for the first time in decades. It adapted by investing in new products, and by 1992 sales were climbing again. In 1996 HON INDUSTRIES acquired rival fireplace maker Heat-N-Glo, which it merged with Heatilator to form Hearth Technologies. The next year it acquired three furniture makers, including Allsteel, and further bolstered Hearth by buying stove maker Aladdin Steel Products in 1998.

The company acquired hearth products distributors American Fireplace Company and the Allied Group in 2000. In 2001, for the second year in a row, the company was named one of the "400 Best Big Companies in America" by Forbes magazine. With the office furniture industry in another downturn, HON INDUSTRIES closed three plants that year.

OFFICERS

Chairman, President, and CEO: Jack D. Michaels, $952,150 pay
Vice Chairman: Richard H. Stanley, age 69
EVP; President, Allsteel Inc.: Stanley A. Askren, age 41, $264,805 pay
EVP; President, Hearth Technologies: Daniel C. Shimek

EVP; President, The HON Company:
David C. Burdakin, age 47, $340,417 pay
EVP; President, Wood Furniture Group:
Phillip M. Martineau, age 54, $305,723 pay
VP, Business Analysis and General Auditor:
Robert D. Hayes, age 58
VP and CFO: Jerald K. Dittmer, age 44, $252,117 pay
VP and CTO: Peter R. Atherton, age 49
VP and CIO: Malcolm C. Fields, age 40
VP, Compensation and Benefits: Alysia L. Bensmiller
VP, Financial Reporting: Tamara S. Feldman
VP, General Counsel, and Secretary: James I. Johnson, age 53
VP, Member and Community Relations (HR):
Jeffrey D. Fick, age 40
VP, Treasurer and Investor Relations:
Melinda C. Ellsworth
President, BPI: Jean M. Reynolds
Auditors: PricewaterhouseCoopers LLP

LOCATIONS

HQ: 414 E. 3rd St., Muscatine, IA 52761
Phone: 563-264-7400   **Fax:** 563-264-7217
Web: www.honi.com

HON INDUSTRIES has manufacturing facilities in Alabama, California, Georgia, Iowa, Kentucky, Maryland, Minnesota, New York, North Carolina, Pennsylvania, Tennessee, Virginia, and Washington in the US and in Monterrey, Mexico. The company sells its products primarily in the US and Canada.

2001 Sales

	% of total
US & Canada	99
Other countries	1
Total	**100**

PRODUCTS/OPERATIONS

2001 Sales

	$ mil.	% of total
Office furniture	1,366	76
Hearth products	426	24
Total	**1,792**	**100**

Selected Products

Office Furniture	Hearth Products
Bookcases	Chimney systems
Chairs	Fireplaces
Computer furniture	Fireplace inserts
Credenzas	Gas logs
Desks	Outdoor products (grills,
Filing cabinets	tables)
Seating	Stoves
Storage units	Venting and installation
Tables	products

COMPETITORS

Anderson Hickey	Knoll
Bush Industries	La-Z-Boy
CFM	Lennox
Chromcraft Revington	Martin Industries
Falcon Products	Open Plan Systems
Federal Prison Industries	O'Sullivan Industries
Fireplace Manufacturers	Reconditioned Systems
Global Furniture	Sauder Woodworking
Haworth	SMED International
Herman Miller	Steelcase
HighPoint Furniture	TAB Products
KI	Teknion
Kimball International	Temtex Industries
Klaussner Furniture	Vitra

HISTORICAL FINANCIALS & EMPLOYEES

NYSE: HNI FYE: Saturday nearest Dec. 31	Annual Growth	12/92	12/93	12/94	12/95	12/96	12/97	12/98	12/99	12/00	12/01
Sales ($ mil.)	10.9%	707	780	846	893	998	1,363	1,696	1,789	2,046	1,792
Net income ($ mil.)	7.5%	39	45	54	41	68	87	106	87	106	74
Income as % of sales	—	5.5%	5.8%	6.4%	4.6%	6.8%	6.4%	6.3%	4.9%	5.2%	4.2%
Earnings per share ($)	8.8%	0.59	0.70	0.87	0.67	1.13	1.45	1.72	1.44	1.77	1.26
Stock price – FY high ($)	—	11.75	14.63	17.00	15.63	21.38	32.13	37.19	29.88	27.88	28.85
Stock price – FY low ($)	—	8.25	10.75	12.00	11.50	9.25	16.00	20.00	18.75	15.56	19.96
Stock price – FY close ($)	10.0%	11.75	14.00	13.38	11.63	16.50	29.50	23.94	21.94	25.50	27.65
P/E – high	—	20	21	20	23	19	22	22	21	16	23
P/E – low	—	14	16	14	17	8	11	12	13	9	16
Dividends per share ($)	10.8%	0.19	0.20	0.22	0.24	0.25	0.28	0.32	0.38	0.44	0.48
Book value per share ($)	16.7%	2.52	2.81	3.17	3.56	4.25	6.19	7.48	8.33	9.65	10.10
Employees	4.8%	5,926	6,257	6,131	5,933	6,502	9,400	9,800	10,100	11,500	9,000

STOCK PRICE HISTORY

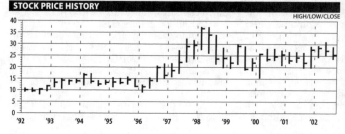

HIGH/LOW/CLOSE

2001 FISCAL YEAR-END

Debt ratio: 12.0%
Return on equity: 12.8%
Cash ($ mil.): 79
Current ratio: 1.39
Long-term debt ($ mil.): 81
No. of shares (mil.): 59
Dividends
  Yield: 1.7%
  Payout: 38.1%
Market value ($ mil.): 1,622

HONEYWELL INTERNATIONAL INC.

Jet engines and thermostats seem worlds apart, but they're Honeywell's bread and butter. The Morristown, New Jersey-based company makes aerospace, automation and control, power and transportation, and specialty materials products. Its biggest division, Honeywell Aerospace (about 40% of sales) makes turbofan and turboprop engines, systems for aircraft landing and flight safety, and communication and navigation gear. The company also provides aircraft maintenance, overhaul, and training services. Honeywell's automation and controls division (some 30% of sales) makes environmental control equipment, access control and security systems, industrial process automation, and industrial measuring equipment.

Other segments include Honeywell's specialty materials division, which makes polymers for electronics, carpet fibers, chemicals used in the manufacture of semiconductors, and nylon and plastic resins; and its transportation and power division, which makes turbochargers and car care products (Prestone, FRAM).

Honeywell agreed to be acquired by General Electric in 2001, but EU regulators vetoed the deal on antitrust concerns and former Allied-Signal CEO Lawrence A. Bossidy (a GE alum) replaced Michael Bonsignore at Honeywell's helm. Bossidy was then replaced by David Cote (another GE alum).

Facing the economic slowdown — and the fallout from the aborted GE deal — Honeywell closed about 50 plants and set about reducing its workforce by about 13%. Speculation about possible mergers or the sale of operations surfaced in the wake of the GE fiasco, but new CEO Cote insists that he wants to run a diverse, independent company.

HISTORY

During WWI Germany controlled much of the world's chemical industry, causing dye and drug shortages. In response, *Washington Post* publisher Eugene Meyer and scientist William Nichols organized the Allied Chemical & Dye Corporation in 1920.

Allied opened a synthetic ammonia plant in 1928 near Hopewell, Virginia, and became the world's leading producer of ammonia. After WWII Allied began making nylon, refrigerants, and other products. The company became Allied Chemical Corporation in 1958.

Seeking a supplier of raw materials for its chemical products, in 1962 Allied bought Union Texas Natural Gas. In the early 1970s CEO John Connor sold many of the firm's unprofitable businesses and invested in oil and gas exploration. By 1979, when Edward Hennessy became CEO, Union Texas produced 80% of Allied's income.

Hennessy led the company into the electronics and technical markets. Under a new name, Allied Corporation (1981), it bought the Bendix Corporation, an aerospace and automotive company, in 1983. In 1985 Allied merged with Signal Companies (founded by Sam Mosher in 1922) to form AlliedSignal.

The company spun off more than 40 unprofitable chemical and engineering businesses over the next two years. Larry Bossidy, hired from GE in 1991 as the new CEO, began to cut waste and buy growth businesses. In 1998 alone the company made 13 acquisitions.

Late in 1999 the company acquired Honeywell in a deal valued at $15 billion and changed its name to Honeywell International. Honeywell, after trying to make a go of it in the computer and telecommunications industries, had refocused on its bread and butter — thermostats, security systems, and other automation equipment. Chairman and CEO of the original Honeywell, Michael Bonsignore, became chairman and CEO of the combined company.

In 2000 Honeywell picked up building-security and fire systems company Pittway for $2 billion. Then, amid lower than expected earnings, the company announced plans to cut an additional 6,000 jobs on top of the 11,000 cuts already planned. Late in the year Honeywell agreed to be acquired by General Electric in a stock deal worth about $45 billion.

In 2001 Honeywell's shareholders approved the deal with GE; the US Justice Department also approved the deal. European Union regulators saw things differently and the deal apparently collapsed in June when GE — which had offered to sell assets that generate about $2.2 billion a year — balked at demands that it sell virtually all of Honeywell's avionics operations. Honeywell then offered itself at a reduced price, but GE declined. The EU formally rejected the acquisition in July, and Honeywell ousted CEO Bonsignore, replacing him with Bossidy — not only the former head of AlliedSignal, but a former GE executive and close friend of Jack Welch.

In September the company said that it would take cost-cutting measures with charges of almost $1 billion and increased the total of previously announced layoffs, cutting about 16,000 jobs by year's end. In December Honeywell agreed to pay Northrop Grumman $440 million to settle an antitrust and patent infringement lawsuit filed against it by Litton (now a part of Northrop) in 1990.

In 2002 the company announced that David Cote (like Bossidy, a former GE executive), the former chairman, president, and CEO of TRW, was named as president and CEO of Honeywell, replacing Bossidy (Cote also replaced Bossidy as chairman in July, 2002). The same year Honeywell agreed to buy Invensys Sensor Systems, which makes vehicle, appliance, and aerospace sensors and controls.

OFFICERS

Chairman, President, and CEO: David M. Cote, age 49
SVP and CFO: Richard F. Wallman, age 50, $785,000 pay
SVP and General Counsel: Peter M. Kreindler, age 56, $805,000 pay
SVP and CTO: Barry C. Johnson, age 57, $770,000 pay
SVP, Information Technology & Administration: Larry E. Kittelberger, age 53
SVP, Human Resources: Tom Weidenkopf
President and CEO, Aerospace: Robert D. Johnson, age 54, $1,000,529 pay
Auditors: PricewaterhouseCoopers LLP

LOCATIONS

HQ: 101 Columbia Rd., PO Box 4000, Morristown, NJ 07962
Phone: 973-455-2000 **Fax:** 973-455-4807
Web: www.honeywell.com

2001 Sales

	$ mil.	% of total
US	17,421	74
Europe	4,264	18
Other regions	1,967	8
Total	**23,652**	**100**

PRODUCTS/OPERATIONS

2001 Sales & Operating Income

	Sales		Operating Income	
	$ mil.	% of total	$ mil.	% of total
Aerospace	9,653	41	1,741	60
Automation & control	7,185	30	819	28
Transportation & power	3,457	15	52	2
Specialty materials	3,313	14	289	10
Corporate	44	—	(153)	—
Total	**23,652**	**100**	**2,748**	**100**

COMPETITORS

Akzo Nobel	Hercules
American Standard	Hexcel
ArvinMeritor, Inc.	ITT Industries
BASF AG	Johnson Controls
Bayer AG	Lockheed Martin
Beaulieu of America	Northrop Grumman
BorgWarner	Parker Hannifin
Carrier	Pratt & Whitney
Dana	Raytheon
Delphi	Robert Bosch
Dow Chemical	Rockwell Automation
DuPont	Rolls-Royce
Eastman Chemical	Sextant Avionique
Eaton	Siemens
Emerson Electric	Tenneco Automotive
Federal-Mogul	TRW
GE	Tyco International
Goodrich	United Technologies
Hamilton Sundstrand	

HISTORICAL FINANCIALS & EMPLOYEES

NYSE: HON FYE: December 31	Annual Growth	12/92	12/93	12/94	12/95	12/96	12/97	12/98	12/99	12/00	12/01
Sales ($ mil.)	7.8%	12,042	11,827	12,817	14,346	13,971	14,472	15,128	23,735	25,023	23,652
Net income ($ mil.)	—	(712)	411	759	875	1,020	1,170	1,331	1,541	1,659	(99)
Income as % of sales	—	—	3.5%	5.9%	6.1%	7.3%	8.1%	8.8%	6.5%	6.6%	—
Earnings per share ($)	—	(1.26)	0.73	1.34	1.52	1.76	2.02	2.32	1.90	2.05	(0.12)
Stock price - FY high ($)	—	15.50	20.03	20.34	24.94	37.19	47.13	47.56	68.63	60.50	53.90
Stock price - FY low ($)	—	10.22	14.38	15.19	16.69	23.56	31.63	32.63	37.81	32.13	22.15
Stock price - FY close ($)	9.3%	15.13	19.75	17.00	23.75	33.50	38.81	44.31	57.69	47.31	33.82
P/E - high	—	—	17	15	16	21	23	20	35	29	—
P/E - low	—	—	12	11	11	13	15	14	19	16	—
Dividends per share ($)	13.0%	0.25	0.29	0.34	0.39	0.45	0.52	0.60	0.68	0.75	0.75
Book value per share ($)	12.3%	3.97	4.21	5.27	6.35	7.39	7.86	9.48	10.81	12.02	11.25
Employees	2.9%	89,300	86,400	87,500	88,500	76,600	70,500	70,400	120,000	125,000	115,000

STOCK PRICE HISTORY

HIGH/LOW/CLOSE

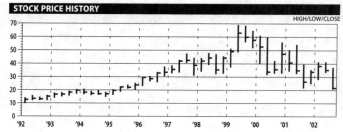

2001 FISCAL YEAR-END

Debt ratio: 34.0%
Return on equity: —
Cash ($ mil.): 1,393
Current ratio: 1.59
Long-term debt ($ mil.): 4,731
No. of shares (mil.): 815
Dividends
 Yield: 2.2%
 Payout: —
Market value ($ mil.): 27,562

HORMEL FOODS CORPORATION

Now that Hormel Foods has launched Turkey SPAM, the world can wonder if it bounces as well as the original. In addition to seeing its SPAM product become an American icon, Hormel Foods is a major US pork processor. Half of its sales come from meat products such as Cure 81 hams and Always Tender fresh pork. It also produces prepared foods such as Mary Kitchen hash, Dinty Moore stews, and Stagg chili. With its Jennie-O turkey and Turkey Shop products, Hormel is the US's #1 turkey processor.

The company has branched into higher-margin convenience, ethnic, low-fat, and frozen foods. Hormel's growing HealthLabs division creates texture-modified foods for hospital and nursing home patients who have difficulty swallowing.

Hormel is expanding globally, forming joint ventures in Australia, China (the world's biggest market for pork), Japan, Mexico, and the Philippines. Back home, the company is forming a joint venture with Cargill to market fresh beef, along with pork under the Always Tender brand. The Hormel Foundation, a charitable trust formed during WWII, owns 46% of the company's stock.

HISTORY

George Hormel opened his Austin, Minnesota, slaughterhouse in an abandoned creamery in 1891. By 1900 Hormel had modernized his facilities to compete with larger meat processors. In 1903 the enterprise introduced its first brand name (Dairy Brand) and a year later began opening distribution centers nationwide. The scandal that ensued after the discovery in 1921 that an assistant controller had embezzled over $1 million almost broke the company, causing Hormel to initiate tighter controls. By 1924 it was processing more than a million hogs annually. Hormel introduced canned ham two years later.

Jay Hormel, George's son, became president in 1929; under his guidance Hormel introduced Dinty Moore beef stew (1936) and SPAM (1937). A Hormel executive won a contest and $100 by submitting the name, a contraction of "spiced ham." During WWII, the US government bought over half of Hormel's output; it supplied SPAM to GIs and Allied forces.

In 1959 Hormel introduced its Little Sizzlers pork sausage and sold its billionth can of SPAM. New products rolled out in the 1960s included Hormel's Cure 81 ham (1963). By the mid-1970s the firm had more than 750 products.

The company survived a violent, nationally publicized strike triggered by a pay cut in 1985. In the end, only 500 of the original 1,500 strikers returned to accept lower pay scales.

Sensing the consumer shift toward poultry, Hormel purchased Jennie-O Foods in 1986. Later acquisitions included the House of Tsang and Oriental Deli (1992), Dubuque (processed pork, 1993) and Herb-Ox (bouillon and dry soup mix, 1993). After more than a century as Geo. A. Hormel & Co., the company began calling itself Hormel Foods in 1993 to reflect its expansion into non-pork foods. Former General Foods executive Joel Johnson was named president and CEO that year (and chairman two years later).

Hormel proved it could take a joke with the 1994 debut of its tongue-in-cheek SPAM catalog, featuring dozens of SPAM-related products. But when a 1996 Muppets movie featured a porcine character named Spa'am, Hormel sued Jim Henson Productions; a federal court gave Spa'am the go-ahead.

Also in 1996 Hormel teamed up with Mexican food processor Grupo Herdez to sell Herdez sauces and other Mexican food products in the US. It then formed a joint venture with Indian food producer Patak Spices (UK) to market its products in the US. Late that year Hormel paid $64 million for a 21% interest in Spanish food maker Campofrio Alimentacion.

Earnings fell in 1996, due in part to soaring hog prices. The company was hit hard again in 1998 when production contracts with hog growers meant it wound up paying premium rates, despite a market glut. In 1998 the Smithsonian Institution accepted two cans of SPAM (one from 1937, the other an updated 1997 version) for its History of Technology collection.

SPAM sales soared in 1999 as nervous consumers stockpiled provisions for the millennium. To build its growing HealthLabs division Hormel acquired Cliffdale Farms (2000), and Diamond Crystal Brands nutritional products (a division of Imperial Sugar) in 2001 — boosting its share of the market for easy-to-swallow foods sold to hospitals and nursing homes.

In early 2001 Hormel acquired family-owned The Turkey Store for approximately $334 million and folded it into its Jennie-O division.

Hormel produced its six billionth can of SPAM in 2002.

OFFICERS

Chairman, President, and CEO: Joel W. Johnson, age 58, $2,121,806 pay
EVP and CFO, Director: Michael J. McCoy, age 54, $487,149 pay
EVP, Refrigerated Foods, Director: Gary J. Ray, age 55, $886,727 pay
SVP, Corporate Staff: James A. Jorgenson, age 57, $482,901 pay

SVP, External Affairs and General Counsel:
Mahlon C. Schneider, age 62
Group VP, Foodservice: Steven G. Binder, age 44
Group VP, Meat Products: Ronald W. Fielding, age 48
Group VP, Prepared Foods, Director: Eric A. Brown,
age 55, $672,537 pay
Group VP; President and COO, Jennie-O Turkey Store:
Jeffrey M. Ettinger, age 43
Group VP; President, Hormel Foods International:
Richard A. Bross, age 50
VP and Controller: James N. Sheehan, age 46
VP and Treasurer: Jody H. Feragen, age 45
VP, Engineering: Larry J. Pfeil, age 52
VP, Foodservice Marketing: Dennis B. Goettsch, age 48
VP, Foodservice Sales: Thomas R. Day, age 43
VP, Fresh Pork Sales and Marketing: Kurt F. Mueller,
age 45
VP, Grocery Products Marketing: Larry L. Vorpahl,
age 38
VP, Grocery Products Sales: Douglas R. Reetz, age 47
VP, Meat Products Marketing: Joe C. Swedberg, age 46
VP, Meat Products Sales: Daniel A. Hartzog, age 50
Auditors: Ernst & Young LLP

LOCATIONS

HQ: 1 Hormel Place, Austin, MN 55912
Phone: 507-437-5611 **Fax:** 507-437-5489
Web: www.hormel.com

Hormel Foods has processing and packaging facilities
in 11 states and China. It sells its products in more
than 40 countries.

PRODUCTS/OPERATIONS

2001 Sales

	$ mil.	% of total
Refrigerated foods	2,210	54
Grocery	889	21
Jennie-O Turkey Store	835	20
Other	190	5
Total	**4,124**	**100**

Selected Brands
Always Tender (fresh pork)
Chi-Chi's (Mexican foods)
Di Lusso (Genoa salami)
Dinty Moore (beef stew)
Herb-Ox (bouillon and stock)
Herdez (Mexican foods)
Hormel (bacon, bacon bits, chili, ham, hot dogs,
   pepperoni)
House of Tsang (Oriental foods)
Jennie-O (turkey products)
Kid's Kitchen (entrees)
Marrakesh Express (couscous)
Mary Kitchen (canned hash)
Mrs. Paterson's Aussie Pies (frozen meat pies)
Patak's (Indian Foods)
SPAM (canned meat)
Stagg (canned chili)
The Turkey Store (fresh and processed turkey products)

COMPETITORS

Bob Evans	Dial	Pilgrim's Pride
Bridgford Foods	Farmland	Sara Lee Foods
Campbell Soup	Industries	Seaboard
Cargill	Foster Farms	Smithfield Foods
ConAgra	Kraft Foods	Tyson Foods

HISTORICAL FINANCIALS & EMPLOYEES

NYSE: HRL FYE: Last Saturday in October	Annual Growth	10/92	10/93	10/94	10/95	10/96	10/97	10/98	10/99	10/00	10/01
Sales ($ mil.)	4.3%	2,814	2,854	3,065	3,046	3,099	3,257	3,261	3,358	3,675	4,124
Net income ($ mil.)	7.5%	95	(27)	118	120	79	110	139	163	170	182
Income as % of sales	—	3.4%	—	3.9%	4.0%	2.6%	3.4%	4.3%	4.9%	4.6%	4.4%
Earnings per share ($)	8.6%	0.62	(0.17)	0.77	0.79	0.52	0.72	0.93	1.11	1.20	1.30
Stock price - FY high ($)	—	11.13	12.75	12.50	14.00	14.00	16.38	19.69	23.09	22.56	26.77
Stock price - FY low ($)	—	8.38	10.13	9.38	11.50	9.69	11.75	12.84	14.69	13.63	16.56
Stock price - FY close ($)	9.5%	10.63	11.31	12.25	11.50	11.81	15.03	16.28	21.56	16.81	24.00
P/E - high	—	18	—	16	18	27	23	21	21	19	20
P/E - low	—	14	—	12	15	19	16	14	13	11	13
Dividends per share ($)	8.3%	0.18	0.21	0.25	0.28	0.30	0.31	0.32	0.33	0.52	0.37
Book value per share ($)	6.1%	4.20	3.71	4.31	4.76	5.07	5.29	5.53	5.89	6.31	7.18
Employees	7.3%	8,300	10,800	9,500	10,600	11,000	11,000	11,200	12,100	12,200	15,600

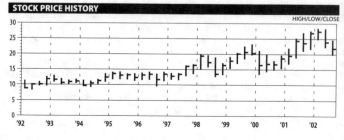

STOCK PRICE HISTORY HIGH/LOW/CLOSE

2001 FISCAL YEAR-END
Debt ratio: 31.7%
Return on equity: 19.5%
Cash ($ mil.): 186
Current ratio: 2.10
Long-term debt ($ mil.): 462
No. of shares (mil.): 139
Dividends
  Yield: 1.5%
  Payout: 28.5%
Market value ($ mil.): 3,328

HOST MARRIOTT CORPORATION

Host Marriott hopes folks heed the President's call to travel, taking up the mantra "refurbish it and they will come." After sprucing itself up as a real estate investment trust (REIT), Host Marriott is joining the ranks of DIYers, albeit to make its chain of upscale hotels just a little bit more posh.

The Bethesda, Maryland-based company is the largest hotel REIT in the US and owns more than 120 luxury and full-service hotels, most of which operate under the Marriott and Ritz-Carlton brands. Other brands include Four Seasons, Swissotel, and Hyatt. The properties are leased to other companies and are managed by sister firm Marriott International.

Host Marriott's New York Marriott World Trade Center hotel, located at Three World Trade Center, was completely devastated on September 11. Two blocks south, the New York Marriott Financial Center hotel sustained heavy damage.

Even before September 11 brought the hotel industry to a screeching halt, the company had curtailed the buying binge that saw it add more than 100 hotels since 1994. It had decided to sell less posh noncore hotels, and focus on renovating remaining holdings. Crashing per-room revenue has the company waiting for the slow return of the health of the industry.

The company, however, may have returned to its purchasing strategy in a buyer's market: It bought the Copley Marriott hotel in Boston, part of the posh Copley Place shopping complex in upscale Back Bay.

The founding Marriott family controls 12% of Host Marriott, while Southeastern Asset Management controls about 17% and Wallace R. Weitz & Company holds about 11%.

HISTORY

That's right — The Four Seasons started as a root beer stand.

Newlyweds John and Alice Marriott left Marriott, Utah (founded by John's grandparents) in 1927 and opened a root beer stand in Washington, DC. As a way to attract customers during the winter, they began selling tamales and tacos — recipes came from a cook at the Mexican Embassy. Dubbed the Hot Shoppe, the Marriotts built the business into a regional chain.

In 1937 the Marriotts began providing boxed lunches for airlines. Hot Shoppes entered the hospital food service business in 1955 and two years later opened its first hotel in Arlington, Virginia. John and Alice's son Bill became president in 1964. The company, which operated four hotels, 45 Hot Shoppes, and the airline catering business, became Marriott-Hot Shoppes.

In the 1960s the company acquired Bob's Big Boy restaurant chain (sold 1987), started Roy Rogers fast-food restaurants (sold 1990), and changed its name to Marriott Corp. Later Marriott bought an Athenian cruise line (Oceanic; sold 1987). Bill Marriott became CEO in 1972.

Marriott diversified its hotel operations in the 1980s, moving into limited-service, middle-priced hotels with the launch of Courtyard by Marriott in 1983. To accelerate growth, the company began building hotels for sale, retaining their control through management contracts. In 1987 it acquired Residence Inn Co., which targeted extended-stay travelers. The company also expanded its airline catering business and moved into retirement facilities. To fund the expansion, Marriott formed limited partnerships and issued corporate bonds; when the late 1980s recession hit, the company was deeply in debt.

In 1993 Marriott Corp. divided into Marriott International (hotel management services) and Host Marriott (real estate and food service), leaving Host Marriott with most of the corporation's debt. Host Marriott began focusing on full-service hotels. It raised money to buy more hotels (many of which belonged to its old limited partnerships) by taking loans from Marriott International and selling assets (including 14 retirement properties and 30 Fairfield Inns). In late 1995 the company further refined its focus by spinning off its food service and concessions business as Host Marriott Services (now Italy-based restaurant operator Autogrill).

Host Marriott acquired three Ritz-Carlton hotels in 1995 through Marriott International, which owns the Ritz-Carlton name, and in 1997 acquired the Forum Group, owner of 29 retirement communities. In 1999 the company expanded its hotel brands, adding controlling stakes in 13 luxury Ritz-Carlton, Four Seasons, Swissotel, and Hyatt properties bought from the Blackstone Group investment firm in exchange for a stake in Host Marriott. It also restructured as a real estate investment trust, or REIT.

Host Marriott and Marriott International were slapped with an investor fraud lawsuit in 2000 relating to its capital-raising efforts in the late 1980s; they reached a tentative settlement under which they would buy back the partnerships. The bulk of the settlements will go to about 2,000 investors in two of the six limited partnerships in question. That year Marriott matriarch Alice died.

The company lost one hotel in the September 11 terrorist attacks on The World Trade Center; The Marriott at Three World Trade Center was a total loss while the nearby Marriott Financial Center hotel was badly damaged.

OFFICERS

Chairman and Director: Richard E. Marriott, age 63, $420,000 pay
President, CEO, and Director: Christopher J. Nassetta, age 39, $1,150,720 pay
EVP and CFO: Robert E. Parsons Jr., age 47, $684,428 pay
EVP Acquisitions and Development: James F. Risoleo, age 47, $509,309 pay
EVP and COO: W. Edward Walter, age 46, $641,276 pay
SVP and Controller: Donald D. Olinger, age 44
SVP, General Counsel and Corporate Secretary: Elizabeth Abdoo, age 43
SVP, Investor Relations: Gregg Larson
SVP Taxes: Richard A. Burton
SVP and Treasurer: John A. Carnella
SVP Acquisitions: Douglas W. Henry
SVP Development: Matthew L. Richardson
SVP Development: Robert H. Shorb Jr.
SVP and CTO: Jules A. Sieburgh
SVP Asset Management: Bruce F. Stemerman
VP Human Resources: Pamela K. Wagoner
Director, Investor Relations: Andrea Morehouse-Jacob
Auditors: KPMG LLP

LOCATIONS

HQ: 10400 Fernwood Rd., Bethesda, MD 20817
Phone: 301-380-9000 **Fax:** 301-380-8413
Web: www.hostmarriott.com

2001 Hotels

	No.
Pacific	23
North Central	15
Atlanta	15
DC Metro	13
South Central	13
Florida	13
Mid-Atlantic	10
Mountain	8
New England	6
International	6
Total	**122**

PRODUCTS/OPERATIONS

2001 Sales

	$ mil.	% of total
Hotel rooms	2,219	59
Food & beverage	1,125	30
Other hotel revenue	282	7
Rental income & other	128	3
Interest	36	1
Gain on property sales	6	—
Affiliate equity	3	—
Total	**3,799**	**100**

COMPETITORS

Accor North America	Hyatt
Boykin Lodging	Lodgian
Carlson	Prime Hospitality
Four Seasons Hotels	Six Continents
Helmsley	Starwood Hotels & Resorts
Hilton	Wyndham International

HISTORICAL FINANCIALS & EMPLOYEES

NYSE: HMT FYE: Friday nearest Dec. 31	Annual Growth	12/92	12/93	12/94	12/95	12/96	12/97	12/98	12/99	12/00	12/01
Sales ($ mil.)	13.7%	1,198	1,354	1,501	484	732	1,147	3,442	1,376	1,473	3,799
Net income ($ mil.)	—	(37)	(60)	(25)	(143)	(13)	50	47	196	156	83
Income as % of sales	—	—	—	—	—	—	4.4%	1.4%	14.2%	10.6%	2.2%
Earnings per share ($)	(16.8%)	—	0.35	(0.26)	(0.90)	(0.07)	0.24	0.27	0.92	0.63	0.08
Stock price - FY high ($)	—	—	10.00	13.75	13.88	16.25	23.75	22.13	14.81	12.94	13.95
Stock price - FY low ($)	—	—	6.25	8.25	9.13	11.25	15.25	9.88	7.38	8.00	6.22
Stock price - FY close ($)	(0.2%)	—	9.13	9.63	13.13	16.00	19.63	13.81	8.25	12.94	9.00
P/E - high	—	—	22	—	—	—	103	24	17	20	155
P/E - low	—	—	14	—	—	—	66	11	8	12	69
Dividends per share ($)	—	—	0.00	0.00	0.00	0.00	0.00	0.00	1.63	0.86	1.04
Book value per share ($)	5.4%	—	4.02	4.62	4.23	8.30	8.59	5.81	6.73	6.43	6.11
Employees	(45.1%)	—	24,000	22,000	800	1,000	525	191	203	215	199

STOCK PRICE HISTORY

HIGH/LOW/CLOSE

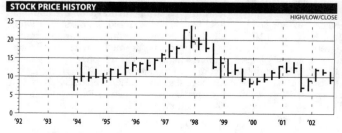

2001 FISCAL YEAR-END

Debt ratio: 77.4%
Return on equity: 6.7%
Cash ($ mil.): —
Current ratio: —
Long-term debt ($ mil.): 5,496
No. of shares (mil.): 263
Dividends
  Yield: 11.6%
  Payout: 1,300.0%
Market value ($ mil.): 2,369

HOUSEHOLD INTERNATIONAL, INC.

Give Household International a little credit — it's made lending to "the little people" profitable.

The Prospect Heights, Illinois-based company is the #2 consumer finance firm in the US (behind Citigroup) and one of the nation's largest home equity lenders. Household Finance, Beneficial, and other subsidiaries serve working-class folks and others with dinged credit who may have trouble borrowing from banks. In addition to its highly profitable unsecured consumer loans and secured home-equity loans, Household provides co-branded and private-label cards for retailers. Household also provides credit cards to members of Microsoft's System Builder Program, allowing developers to buy Microsoft products on credit. The company has more than 1,700 US, Canadian, and UK offices and also offers credit life insurance and finances used cars, mainly through dealers.

Household is looking to expand by combing its client information — it has nearly 50 million customers — to identify cross-selling opportunities. The company continues to try to attract new customers by introducing products (its UK credit card, called marbles, targets online purchases) and upgrading existing ones.

HISTORY

In 1878 Frank Mackey opened a finance company in Minneapolis to lend cash to workers between paychecks. In 1894, when the company had 14 Midwest offices, Mackey moved the headquarters to Chicago (it is now located in a suburb). The firm introduced installment payments on loans in 1905.

More than 30 such Mackey-controlled companies consolidated in 1925 as Household Finance Corporation (HFC), a public company. That year the firm paid its first quarterly dividend.

In 1930 HFC set up the Money Management Institute to teach people how to handle credit. (One pamphlet showed a family of five how to live on $150 a month.) HFC's banks froze the company's credit and stopped lending in 1931, but the freeze was lifted the next year, and the company weathered the Depression. It made its first non-US purchase in 1933, buying Canada's Central Finance.

After WWII the unleashed demand for goods propelled HFC into the suburbs. By 1960 HFC had 1,000 offices and was advertising on TV.

HFC diversified into retailing in the 1960s: hardware stores (Coast to Coast, 1961), variety chains (Ben Franklin and TG&Y, 1965), vacuum jugs (King-Seeley Thermos, 1968), and car rentals (National, 1969). HFC also bought a savings and loan company, four banks, and

Alexander Hamilton Life (1977). This strategy benefited the firm in the 1970s, when rising inflation rates made Household's traditional short-term, fixed-rate loans less profitable.

The company became Household International in 1981. During the mid-1980s chairman Donald Clark refocused Household on financial services, particularly consumer banking, and began divesting noncore operations. Between 1985 and 1988 it bought several finance companies and banks, including BGC Finance in Australia (exiting in 1994). In the late 1980s Household began securitizing some of its receivables (as a bond-like security), freeing it of liability for delinquencies and defaults.

The firm began restructuring in 1994, eventually tossing out brokerage, first-mortgage, banking, and most insurance operations. It was fitting that Clark — who oversaw the expansion of the firm's financial services businesses — gave the reins of power to William Aldinger (who became chairman in 1996) just as Household was getting rid of the last of those businesses.

In 1996 Household increased its credit card reach through an affinity card program for AFL-CIO members and through an agreement to jointly manage Barnett Banks' card business in Florida and Georgia (a deal that came to a close when Barnett was purchased by what is now Bank of America). The following year Household bought the consumer finance operations of Transamerica. The company paid around $8 billion in 1998 for Beneficial Corporation, which in recent years had been struggling with an unfocused business plan. In assimilating Beneficial, Household cut 1,000 jobs and 250 offices.

In the late 1990s Household realigned its credit card operations. The company sold a chunk of its card portfolio to Fleet Financial Group (now FleetBoston Financial) in 1998 and embarked the next year on a program to build its subprime card offerings. In 2000 it bought Renaissance Holdings, an issuer of credit cards to people with bruised credit, as well as a chunk of BANK ONE's real estate lending business worth some $2 billion.

In 2000 and 2001 Household turned much of its focus toward the UK, where banking consolidation created opportunity for the company. Also in 2001 Household announced it would eliminate or modify some of its more controversial products, deemed "predatory" by consumer watchdog organizations.

Under a mandate by the SEC to certify its past financial statements, Household revised its earnings over a nine-year period downward by nearly $400 million in 2002.

OFFICERS

Chairman and CEO: William F. Aldinger, age 54, $5,000,000 pay
President, COO, and Principal Financial Officer: David A. Schoenholz, age 50, $2,500,000 pay
Vice Chairman, Consumer Lending: Gary Gilmer, age 52, $2,500,000 pay
Group Executive, Consumer Lending: Thomas M. Detelich
Group Executive, Retail Services, Refund Lending, Auto Finance, and Insurance Services: Rocco J. Fabiano, age 45, $1,997,115 pay
Group Executive, Credit Card Services and Canada: Siddarth N. Mehta, age 43, $2,009,616 pay
EVP and CIO: Kenneth M. Harvey, age 41
EVP, Administration: Colin P. Kelly, age 59
SVP and Chief Accounting Officer: Steven L. McDonald
SVP, General Counsel, and Corporate Secretary: Kenneth H. Robin, age 55
VP, Investor Relations: Craig A. Streem, age 50
Managing Director, Retail Services: Sandra L. Derickson, age 47
Managing Director, United Kingdom: Adrian R. Hill, age 43
COO, Mortgage Services: Gregory Gibson
Director, Community Relations: Diane Jackson
Hispanic Market Initiatives: Roberto R. Herencia, age 42
Auditors: KPMG LLP

LOCATIONS

HQ: 2700 Sanders Rd., Prospect Heights, IL 60070
Phone: 847-564-5000   **Fax:** 847-205-7401
Web: www.household.com

Household International operates in the US, Canada, Ireland, and the UK.

2001 Sales

	$ mil.	% of total
US	12,662	91
UK	1,014	7
Canada	220	2
Other countries	20	—
Total	**13,916**	**100**

PRODUCTS/OPERATIONS

2001 Sales

	$ mil.	% of total
Finance income	10,021	72
Securitization revenue	1,776	13
Fee income	967	7
Insurance revenue	662	5
Investment income	168	1
Other income	322	2
Total	**13,916**	**100**

Selected Subsidiaries
Beneficial Service Corporation
Household Bank, f.s.b.
Household Capital Corporation
Household Finance Corporation
Household International (U.K.) Limited

COMPETITORS

Advanta	J.P. Morgan Chase
Bank of America	MBNA
BANK ONE	Metris
Capital One Financial	MFN Financial
Citigroup	Providian Financial
Delta Financial	Wells Fargo
ge consumer finance	World Acceptance

HISTORICAL FINANCIALS & EMPLOYEES

NYSE: HI FYE: December 31	Annual Growth	12/92	12/93	12/94	12/95	12/96	12/97	12/98	12/99	12/00	12/01
Sales ($ mil.)	14.3%	4,181	4,455	4,603	5,144	5,059	5,503	8,708	9,499	11,961	13,916
Net income ($ mil.)	29.3%	191	299	368	453	539	687	524	1,486	1,701	1,924
Income as % of sales	—	4.6%	6.7%	8.0%	8.8%	10.6%	12.5%	6.0%	15.6%	14.2%	13.8%
Earnings per share ($)	22.9%	0.64	0.95	1.17	1.43	1.77	2.16	1.03	3.07	3.55	4.08
Stock price - FY high ($)	—	10.07	13.47	13.24	22.77	32.68	43.29	53.69	53.19	57.44	69.98
Stock price - FY low ($)	—	6.91	8.97	9.49	11.95	17.32	26.18	23.00	32.39	29.50	48.00
Stock price - FY close ($)	21.7%	9.87	10.86	12.36	19.81	30.72	42.50	39.63	37.25	55.00	57.94
P/E - high	—	15	14	11	16	18	20	52	17	16	17
P/E - low	—	10	9	8	8	10	12	22	10	8	12
Dividends per share ($)	8.9%	0.38	0.39	0.41	0.43	0.47	0.53	0.44	0.66	0.72	0.82
Book value per share ($)	10.3%	7.81	8.49	8.70	10.18	11.39	15.04	13.22	14.14	17.23	18.94
Employees	10.2%	13,397	16,900	15,500	13,000	14,700	14,900	23,500	23,600	28,000	32,000

Financials are prior to SEC-ordered restatement

STOCK PRICE HISTORY

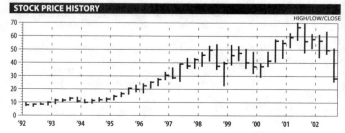

HIGH/LOW/CLOSE

2001 FISCAL YEAR-END

Debt ratio: 86.8%
Return on equity: 23.8%
Cash ($ mil.): —
Current ratio: —
Long-term debt ($ mil.): 56,824
No. of shares (mil.): 457
Dividends
  Yield: 1.4%
  Payout: 20.1%
Market value ($ mil.): 26,486

HUMANA INC.

Although it's one of the US's top health care providers, Humana is finding that maintaining a balance between humane care and healthy earnings might be the trickiest operation of them all.

The Louisville, Kentucky-based firm provides services primarily through HMOs and PPOs; it also serves Medicare and Medicaid patients and, through a contract with the Department of Defense, members of the military. The company also offers group life and dental plans. Humana has more than 6 million members in 18 states and Puerto Rico. Chairman David Jones owns about 5% of Humana.

Pummeled by rising medical costs and lowered reimbursement rates for Medicare (its Medicare HMO accounts for nearly 30% of sales), Humana is raising premiums and has exited certain markets, such as workers' compensation and individual Medicare supplemental insurance.

HISTORY

In 1961 Louisville, Kentucky, lawyers David Jones and Wendell Cherry bought a nursing home as a real estate investment. Within six years their company, Extendicare, was the largest nursing home chain in the US (with only eight homes).

Faced with a glutted nursing home market, the partners noticed that hospitals received more money per patient per day than nursing homes, so they took their company public in 1968 to finance hospital purchases (one per month from 1968 to 1971). The company then sold its 40 nursing homes. Sales rose 13 times over in the next five years, and in 1973 the firm changed its name to Humana.

By 1975 Humana had built 27 hospitals in the South and Southwest. It targeted young, privately insured patients and kept its charity caseload and bad-debt expenses low. Three years later #3 for-profit hospital operator Humana moved up a notch when it bought #2 American Medicorp.

In 1983 the government began reimbursing Medicare payments based on fixed rates. Counting on its high hospital occupancy, the company launched Humana Health Care Plans in 1984, rewarding doctors and patients who used Humana hospitals. However, hospital occupancy dropped, and the company closed several clinics. When its net income fell 75% in 1986, the firm responded by lowering premiums to attract employers.

In 1991 co-founder Cherry died. With hospital profits down, in 1993 Jones spun off Humana's 76 hospitals as Galen Healthcare, which formed the nucleus of what is now HCA - The Healthcare

Company. Humana used the cash to expand its HMO membership, buying Group Health Association (an HMO serving metropolitan Washington, DC) and CareNetwork (a Milwaukee HMO). The next year Humana added 1.3 million members when it bought EMPHESYS, and the company's income, which had stagnated since the salad days of the late 1980s and early 1990s, seemed headed in the right direction.

In the mid-1990s cutthroat premiums failed to cover rising health care costs as members' hospital use soared out of control, particularly in the company's new Washington, DC, market. Profits dropped 94%, and Humana's already tense relationship with doctors and members worsened. President and COO Wayne Smith and CFO Roger Drury resigned as part of a management shake-up, and newly appointed president Gregory Wolf offered to drop the company's gag clause after the Florida Physicians Association threatened to sue.

A reorganized Humana rebounded in 1997. The company pulled out of 13 unprofitable markets, including Alabama (though it did not drop TRICARE, its military health coverage program, in that state) and Washington, DC. Refocusing on core markets in the Midwest and Southeast, Humana bought Physician Corp. of America (PCA) and ChoiceCare, a Cincinnati HMO. Wolf replaced Jones as CEO in 1997.

To cut costs, Humana agreed to be bought by United HealthCare (now UnitedHealth Group) in 1998. The deal was abandoned, however, when United HealthCare took a $900 million charge in advance of the purchase. Humana found savings by pruning its Medicare HMO business.

Humana did everything *but* party in 1999. The company faced RICO charges for allegedly overcharging members for co-insurance; it agreed to repay $15 million in Medicare overpayments to the government; and it became the first health insurance firm to be slapped with a class-action suit over its physician incentives and other coverage policies.

Humana sold PCA in 2000, saying that it had paid too much for the company; subsidiary PCA Property & Casualty was also sold, marking the company's exit from the workers' compensation business. That year Humana also sold its underperforming Florida Medicaid HMO to Well Care HMO, and agreed to pay more than $14 million to the government for submitting false Medicare payment information.

In 2001 Humana bought a unit of Anthem that provides health benefits to the military.

OFFICERS

Chairman: David A. Jones, age 70
Vice Chairman: David A. Jones Jr., age 44
President, CEO, and Director: Michael B. McCallister, age 49, $1,475,753 pay
COO, Service Operations: James E. Murray, age 48, $940,000 pay
COO, Market Operations: Kenneth J. Fasola, age 42, $940,000 pay
SVP and CFO: James H. Bloem, age 51, $581,647 pay
SVP and CIO: Bruce J. Goodman, age 60, $589,945 pay
SVP and Chief Marketing Officer: Steven O. Moya, age 52
SVP and Chief Clinical Strategy and Innovation Officer: Jonathon T. Lord, age 47, $786,250 pay
SVP and Chief Human Resources Officer: Bonnie C. Hathcock, age 53
SVP and General Counsel: Arthur P. Hipwell, age 53
SVP, Government Programs: Gene Shields, age 54
SVP, Corporate Communications: Thomas J. Noland Jr.
SVP, Market Operations: Douglas R. Carlisle
SVP, Strategy and Corporate Development: Thomas J. Liston, age 40
SVP, Government Relations: Heidi Margulis
SVP, National Contracting: Bruce Perkins
VP and Chief Actuary: John M. Bertko, age 52
VP, Service Operations: Kathy Augustian-Hinkfuss
Auditors: PricewaterhouseCoopers LLP

LOCATIONS

HQ: The Humana Bldg., 500 W. Main St., Louisville, KY 40202
Phone: 502-580-1000   **Fax:** 502-580-4188
Web: www.humana.com

Humana operates primarily in 18 states and Puerto Rico.

PRODUCTS/OPERATIONS

2001 Sales

	$ mil.	% of total
Commercial premiums		
Fully insured medical	4,942	49
Specialty	305	3
Government premiums		
Medicare+Choice	2,909	29
TRICARE	1,342	14
Medicaid	441	4
Administrative service fees	137	1
Total	**10,076**	**100**

Selected Subsidiaries

Advanced Care Partners, Inc.
ChoiceCare/Humana
The Dental Concern, Inc.
Humana Medical Plan, Inc.
Humana Military Healthcare Services, Inc.
Managed Care Indemnity, Inc.
Wisconsin Employers Group, Inc.

COMPETITORS

Aetna	New York Life
Blue Cross	Oxford Health Plans
Cerulean	PacifiCare
CIGNA	Prudential
Health Net	UnitedHealth Group
Kaiser Foundation	

HISTORICAL FINANCIALS & EMPLOYEES

NYSE: HUM FYE: December 31	Annual Growth	8/92	*12/93	12/94	12/95	12/96	12/97	12/98	12/99	12/00	12/01
Sales ($ mil.)	10.7%	4,043	3,137	3,654	4,605	6,677	7,880	9,597	9,959	10,395	10,076
Net income ($ mil.)	(0.5%)	123	89	176	190	12	173	129	(382)	90	117
Income as % of sales	—	3.0%	2.8%	4.8%	4.1%	0.2%	2.2%	1.3%	—	0.9%	1.2%
Earnings per share ($)	3.1%	—	0.55	1.07	1.16	0.07	1.05	0.77	(2.28)	0.54	0.70
Stock price – FY high ($)	—	—	19.13	25.38	28.00	28.88	25.31	32.13	20.75	15.81	15.63
Stock price – FY low ($)	—	—	6.13	15.88	17.00	15.00	17.38	12.25	5.88	4.75	8.38
Stock price – FY close ($)	(5.0%)	—	17.75	22.63	27.38	19.00	20.75	17.81	8.19	15.25	11.79
P/E – high	—	—	34	23	24	413	24	42	—	29	22
P/E – low	—	—	11	14	15	214	16	16	—	9	12
Dividends per share ($)	—	—	0.00	0.00	0.00	0.00	0.00	0.00	0.00	0.00	0.00
Book value per share ($)	6.1%	—	5.54	6.56	7.94	7.94	9.15	10.08	7.57	8.04	8.93
Employees	4.6%	—	10,100	12,000	16,800	18,300	19,500	16,300	17,300	15,600	14,500

* Fiscal year change

STOCK PRICE HISTORY

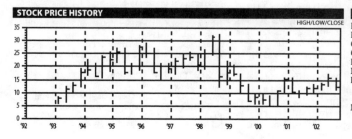

HIGH/LOW/CLOSE

2001 FISCAL YEAR-END

Debt ratio: 17.3%
Return on equity: 8.2%
Cash ($ mil.): 651
Current ratio: 1.14
Long-term debt ($ mil.): 316
No. of shares (mil.): 169
Dividends
 Yield: —
 Payout: —
Market value ($ mil.): 1,990

HYATT CORPORATION

Chicago is Hyatt's kind of town — as well as hundreds of others around the world. Chicago-based Hyatt is one of the largest hotel operators in the nation, with more than 120 full-service luxury hotels and resorts in North America and the Caribbean (Hyatt International, a separate company, operates some 80 hotels and resorts in 37 countries). In addition, Hyatt manages casinos at several of its hotels and runs a luxury retirement community called Classic Residence by Hyatt.

Hyatt caters to business travelers, convention-goers, and upscale vacationers. The company offers specially designed Business Plan rooms with fax machines and 24-hour access to copiers, printers, and other business necessities. Camp Hyatt targets family travelers with educational games, activities, and programs for children. The company is doing much of its growing outside the US. It has some 17 hotels under construction in places such as China, India, Poland, Thailand, and the United Arab Emirates.

Led by chairman, president, and CEO Thomas Pritzker, the company is owned by the Pritzker family, one of the wealthiest in the US.

HISTORY

Nicholas Pritzker left Kiev for Chicago in 1881, where his family's ascent to the ranks of America's wealthiest families began. His son A. N. left the family law practice in the 1930s and began investing in a variety of businesses. He turned a 1942 investment (Cory Corporation) worth $25,000 into $23 million by 1967. A. N.'s son Jay followed in his father's wheeling-and-dealing footsteps. In 1953, with the help of his father's banking connections, Jay purchased Colson Company and recruited his brother Bob, an industrial engineer, to restructure a company that made tricycles and US Navy rockets. By 1990 Jay and Bob had added 60 industrial companies, with annual sales exceeding $3 billion, to the entity they called the Marmon Group.

The family's connection to Hyatt hotels was established in 1957 when Jay Pritzker bought a hotel called Hyatt House, located near the Los Angeles airport, from Hyatt von Dehn. Jay added five locations by 1961 and hired his gregarious youngest brother, Donald, to manage the hotel company. Hyatt went public in 1967, but the move that opened new vistas for the hotel chain was the purchase that year of an 800-room hotel in Atlanta that both Hilton and Marriott had turned down. John Portman's design, incorporating a 21-story atrium, a large fountain, and a revolving rooftop restaurant, became a Hyatt trademark.

The Pritzkers formed Hyatt International in 1969 to operate hotels overseas, and the company grew rapidly in the US and abroad during the 1970s. Donald Pritzker died in 1972, and Jay assumed control of Hyatt. The family decided to take the company private in 1979. Much of Hyatt's growth in the 1970s came from contracts to manage, under the Hyatt banner, hotels built by other investors. When Hyatt's cut on those contracts shrank in the 1980s, the company launched its own hotel and resort developments under Nick Pritzker, a cousin to Jay and Bob. In 1988, with US and Japanese partners, the company built the Hyatt Regency Waikoloa on Hawaii's Big Island for $360 million — a record at the time for a hotel.

The Pritzkers took a side-venture into air travel in 1983 when they bought bedraggled Braniff Airlines through Hyatt subsidiaries as it emerged from bankruptcy. After a failed 1987 attempt to merge the airline with PanAm, the Pritzkers sold Braniff in 1988.

Hyatt opened Classic Residence by Hyatt, a group of upscale retirement communities, in 1989. The company joined Circus Circus (now Mandalay Resort Group) in 1994 to launch the Grand Victoria, the nation's largest cruising gaming vessel, at Elgin, Illinois. The next year, as part of a new strategy to manage both freestanding golf courses and those near Hyatt hotels, the company opened its first freestanding course: an 18-hole par 71 championship course on Aruba.

President Thomas Pritzker, Jay's son, took over as chairman and CEO of Hyatt following his father's death in early 1999. In 2000 Hyatt announced plans to join rival Marriott International in launching an independent company to provide an online procurement network to serve the hospitality industry. The following year the company announced plans to begin building a new headquarters in 2002. The skyscraper, to be called the Hyatt Center, will be located in Chicago's West Loop.

OFFICERS

Chairman, President, and CEO; Chairman Hyatt International Corporation: Thomas J. Pritzker, age 51
Vice Chairman; Chairman and President, Hyatt Development Corporation; President, Hyatt Equities: Nicholas J. Pritzker
SVP Finance and Administration: Frank Borg
Chairman and President, Classic Residence by Hyatt: Penny S. Pritzker
President, Classic Residence by Hyatt: Ronald J. Richardson
President, Hyatt Hotels Corporation: Scott D. Miller
President, Hyatt International Corporation: Bernd Chorengel

EVP and COO, Hyatt Hotels Corporation:
Edward W. Rabin
SVP, Human Resources, Hyatt Hotels Corporation:
Linda Olson
SVP Marketing, Hyatt Hotels Corporation: Tom O'Toole
SVP Operations, Hyatt Hotels Corporation:
Chuck Floyd
Divisional VP (Southern), Hyatt Hotels Corporation:
Tim Lindgren
Divisional VP (Resorts), Hyatt Hotels Corporation:
Victor Lopez, age 51
Divisional VP (Western), Hyatt Hotels Corporation:
John Orr
Divisional VP (Central), Hyatt Hotels Corporation:
Steve Sokal

LOCATIONS

HQ: 200 W. Madison St., Chicago, IL 60606
Phone: 312-750-1234 **Fax:** 312-750-8550
Web: www.hyatt.com

Hyatt Corporation and Hyatt International, a separate entity also controlled by the Pritzer family, own and operate hotels in Argentina, Australia, Azerbaijan, Canada, Chile, China, Egypt, France, Germany, Greece, Guatemala, Hungary, India, Indonesia, Israel, Japan, Jordan, Kazakhstan, Kyrgyzstan, Malaysia, Mexico, Micronesia, Morocco, Nepal, New Zealand, Oman, the Philippines, Puerto Rico, Saudi Arabia, Serbia and Montenegro, Singapore, South Africa, South Korea, Spain, Taiwan, Thailand, Turkey, the UK, the United Arab Emirates, the US, and the West Indies.

PRODUCTS/OPERATIONS

Selected Operations
Camp Hyatt (activities for children)
Classic Residence by Hyatt (upscale retirement communities)
Hyatt Hotels and Resorts
Regency Casinos

COMPETITORS

Accor
Cendant
Four Seasons Hotels
Helmsley
Hilton
Host Marriott
Marriott International
Ritz Carlton
Sandals Resorts
Six Continents Hotels
Starwood Hotels & Resorts
Trump

HISTORICAL FINANCIALS & EMPLOYEES

Private FYE: January 31	Annual Growth	1/91	1/92	1/93	1/94	1/95	1/96	1/97	1/98	1/99	1/00
Estimated sales ($ mil.)	14.4%	—	1,350	1,460	950	1,240	2,500	2,900	1,378	3,400	3,950
Employees	5.7%	—	51,275	52,275	47,000	54,000	65,000	80,000	80,000	80,000	80,000

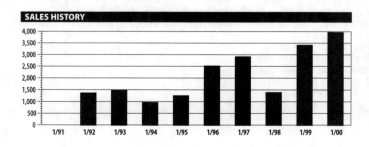

SALES HISTORY

IGA, INC.

Independent grocers have found they can boost their business by being a little less independent. More than 4,400 stores belong to Chicago-based IGA (which stands for both Independent Grocers Alliance and International Grocers Alliance, according to the company). The alliance is the world's largest voluntary supermarket network, owned by 37 marketing and distribution companies worldwide (including the likes of Fleming Companies and SUPER-VALU); it has stores on every inhabited continent — with outlets in nearly all 50 states and about 40 countries. Collectively, its members are one of the largest food operations in terms of sales in North America, and its international operations account for 62% of its total sales.

In addition to flying the IGA Red Oval banner and having access to IGA Brand private-label products, members receive advertising and marketing services, educational programs, and volume discounts through the food distributors that control it. Some stores in the alliance, which primarily caters to smaller towns, also sell gas.

The association continues its expansion overseas. The first US grocer to go into China and Singapore, IGA is now moving into Europe, particularly focusing on Poland.

HISTORY

IGA was founded in Chicago in 1926 by a group led by accountant Frank Grimes. During the 1920s chains began to dominate the grocery store industry. Grimes, an accountant for many grocery wholesalers, saw an opportunity to develop a network of independent grocers that could compete with the burgeoning chains. Grimes and five associates — Gene Flack, Louis Groebe, W. K. Hunter, H. V. Swenson, and William Thompson — created IGA.

Their idea was to "level the playing field" for independent grocers and chain stores by taking advantage of volume buying and mass marketing. IGA originally acted as a purchasing agent for its wholesalers but eventually passed that duty to the wholesalers. The group's first members were Poughkeepsie, New York-based grocery distributor W. T. Reynolds Company and the 69 grocery stores it serviced.

IGA focused on adding distributors and retailers, and it soon added wholesaler Fleming-Wilson (now Fleming Companies) and Winston & Newell (now SUPERVALU). In 1930 it hired Babe Ruth as a spokesman; other celebrity endorsers during the period included Jackie Cooper, Jack Dempsey, and Popeye. IGA also sponsored a radio program called the IGA Home Town Hour.

In 1945 the company introduced the Foodliner format, a design for stores larger than 4,000 sq. ft. The next year IGA introduced the 30-ft.-by-100-ft. Precision Store — designed so customers had to pass all the other merchandise in the store to get to the dairy and bread sections.

Grimes retired as president in 1951. He was succeeded by his son, Don, who continued to expand the company. Don was succeeded in 1968 by Richard Jones, head of IGA member J. M. Jones Co.

Thomas Haggai was named chairman of the company in 1976. A Baptist minister, radio commentator, and former CIA employee, Haggai had come to the attention of Grimes in 1960 when he praised Christian Scientists in one of his radio broadcasts. Grimes, a Christian Scientist, asked Haggai to speak at an IGA convention and eventually asked him to join the IGA board. Haggai, who became CEO in 1986, tightened the restrictions for IGA members, weeding out many of the smaller, low-volume mom-and-pop stores making up much of the group's network.

Haggai also began a push for international expansion. In 1988 the organization signed a deal with Japanese food company C. Itoh (now ITOCHU) to open a distribution outlet in Tokyo.

The 1990s saw expansion into Australia, Papua New Guinea, the Caribbean, China, Singapore, South Africa, and Brazil. IGA also expanded outside the continental US when it entered Hawaii. In 1993 IGA began an international television advertising campaign, a first for the supermarket industry. The next year the company launched its first line of private-label products for an ethnic food market, introducing several Mexican food products. In 1998 the group developed a new format for its stores that included on-site gas pumps.

SUPERVALU signed 54 independent grocery stores (primarily in Mississippi and Arkansas and Trinidad in the Caribbean) to the IGA banner in August 1999.

With more than 60% of sales coming from international operations, IGA realigned its corporate structure in 2001, setting up IGA North America, IGA Southern Hemisphere/Europe/Caribbean, and IGA Asia, each with its own president.

OFFICERS

Chairman and CEO: Thomas S. Haggai
CFO: Robert Grottke
President, IGA Institute: Paulo Goelzer
VP, Events and Communications: Barbara G. Wiest
VP, Information Technology: Nick Liakopulos
VP, Retail Operations: William Benzing
Controller: John Collins
Director, Human Resources: Pat Smiftana
Director, Packaging: Tim Considine

LOCATIONS

HQ: 8725 W. Higgins Rd., Chicago, IL 60631
Phone: 773-693-4520   **Fax:** 773-693-4532
Web: www.igainc.com

IGA has operations in 48 states and about 40 other countries, commonwealths, and territories.

PRODUCTS/OPERATIONS

Distributors/Owners
Bozzuto's Inc.
C.I. Foods Systems Co., Ltd. (Japan)
The Copps Corporation
Davids Limited (Australia)
Fleming Companies, Inc.
Foodland Associated Limited (Australia)
Great North Foods
IGA Brasil (includes 16 individual companies)
Ira Higdon Grocery Company
Laurel Grocery Company
Martahari Putra Prima Tbk (Indonesia)
McLane Polska (Poland)
Merchants Distributors, Inc.
Metro Cash & Carry (Africa)
Nash Finch Company
NTUC Fairprice (Singapore)
Pearl River Distribution Ltd. (China)
SUPERVALU INC.
Tasmania Independent Wholesalers (Tasmania)
Tripifoods, Inc.
Villa Market JP Co., Ltd. (Thailand)
W. Lee Flowers & Co., Inc.
WALTERMART SUPERMARKETS (Philippines)

Affiliates
H.Y. Louie (fraternal relationship, Canada)
Sobey's (fraternal relationship, Canada)

Selected Joint Operations and Services
Advertising
Community service programs
Equipment purchase
IGA Brand (private-label products)
IGA Grocergram (in-house magazine)
Internet services
Marketing
Merchandising
Red Oval Family (manufacturer/IGA collaboration on sales, marketing, and other activities)
Volume buying

COMPETITORS

Albertson's
AWG
BJs Wholesale Club
C&S Wholesale
Carrefour
Casino Guichard
Coles Myer
Daiei
Dairy Farm International Holdings
Delhaize
George Weston
A&P
Hannaford Bros.
H-E-B
Ito-Yokado
Kroger
Meijer
Metro Cash and Carry
Penn Traffic
Publix
Roundy's
Royal Ahold
Safeway
Spartan Stores
Topco Associates
Wakefern Food
Wal-Mart
Winn-Dixie

HISTORICAL FINANCIALS & EMPLOYEES

Holding company FYE: December 31	Annual Growth	12/92	12/93	12/94	12/95	12/96	12/97	12/98	12/99	12/00	12/01
Estimated sales ($ mil.)	3.1%	15,900	16,500	17,000	17,100	16,800	18,000	18,000	19,000	21,000	21,000
Employees	(5.6%)	—	—	—	130,000	128,000	135,000	92,000	92,000	92,000	92,000

SALES HISTORY

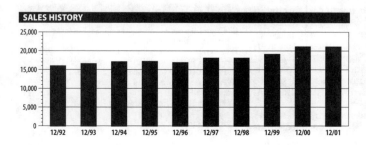

IKON OFFICE SOLUTIONS, INC.

Not satisfied being just another copycat, IKON Office Solutions tries to offer it all. Malvern, Pennsylvania-based business equipment specialist IKON is a leading supplier and servicer of copiers. It sells and leases Canon, Ricoh, Océ, and other name-brand copiers, printers, fax machines, and office equipment; contracts with legal firms and other businesses to help manage huge quantities of documents; and offers information systems design and support. IKON has rapidly shifted away from analog products; digital devices account for almost all of its product sales.

IKON has expanded the number of products and services that it offers, placing an emphasis on high-end products with greater margins. The company continues to push into high-end printers, forging alliances with leading hardware makers such as Hewlett-Packard. IKON has also made a foray into the e-business consulting market with its Sysinct business unit.

HISTORY

Tinkham Veale, a mechanical engineer from Cleveland, married the daughter of A. C. Ernst of the Ernst & Ernst accounting firm in 1941. Ernst helped Veale buy a stake in an engineered goods manufacturer, which prospered during WWII. Veale retired at age 37 to breed and race horses. He invested his earnings, became a millionaire by 1951, and joined the board of Alco Oil and Chemical (formerly Rainbow Production Company). In 1960 Veale and his associates formed a holding company, V & V Associates, and bought a large minority share in Alco.

Alco (renamed Alco Chemical in 1962) acquired four fertilizer companies and in 1965 (renamed Alco Standard) merged with V & V, which had bought stakes in several machinery producers. Veale then implemented the partnership strategy that would serve the company for 25 years: He bought small, privately owned businesses, usually with cash and Alco Standard stock, and let the owners continue to run them. By 1968 Alco Standard had bought 52 companies in this way and had branched into electrical, metallurgical, and distribution businesses.

Alco Standard expanded into coal mining in the 1970s. The company also bought several paper distributors and formed a national paper distributor called Unisource. The division's profitability prompted Alco Standard to enter other distribution businesses, including pharmaceuticals, steel products, auto parts, food service equipment, and liquor. By 1981 distribution provided 75% of sales.

Veale had also acquired several manufacturers (plastics, machinery, rubber, and chemicals), but

they had not grown as rapidly as the distribution units. In 1984 he merged the manufacturers into Alco Industries and sold the new company to its managers; he kept a minority stake. Ray Mundt (who succeeded Veale as chairman) switched Alco Standard's focus in 1986 to office products and paper distribution, cutting seven divisions, including health services and ice cream.

John Stuart succeeded Mundt as CEO in 1993 (and as chairman in 1995) and oversaw a restructuring. Although a 1992 joint venture with Europe-based IMM Office Systems (IMMOS) didn't work out, the dissolution agreement gave Alco two IMMOS subsidiaries: Denmark's Eskofot and France-based STR.

Alco's largest purchase in 1995 was UK-based copier distribution and service company Southern Business Group PLC — renamed A:Copy (UK) PLC. Alco bought 97 businesses in fiscal 1996. The following year it spun off Unisource, which had by then acquired 100 local sales and service operations. After the spinoff Alco Standard changed its name to IKON Office Solutions. It continued a searing rate of acquisitions, including a total of 123 companies for fiscal 1997 and 1998.

Trouble integrating all of its purchases into a united company pushed IKON off its axis, and profits dropped for fiscal 1997. In 1998 EVP James Forese replaced Stuart as president and CEO. Forese, an IBM veteran of 36 years, cut IKON's workforce by 1,500 positions to reduce expenses that year. Charges from this and other restructuring moves caused a loss for 1998. The next year the company's sales force shrank by about 20% thanks to layoffs and attrition. About 1,500 more job cuts — 5% of the workforce — were announced in 2000.

In early 2001 IKON said it would sell and support e-business software from leading vendors through its Sysinct business unit. The next year Forese announced that he would step down as CEO in September 2002 and as chairman in February of the following year; IKON tapped Matthew Espe, former head of GE Lighting, as its new president and CEO.

OFFICERS

Chairman: James J. Forese, age 66, $1,452,000 pay (prior to title change)
President and CEO: Matthew J. Espe, age 43
SVP and CFO: William S. Urkiel, age 56, $539,700 pay
SVP and CIO: David M. Gadra, age 53, $381,700 pay
SVP, General Counsel, and Secretary: Don H. Liu, age 40, $413,600 pay
SVP; SVP, IKON North America: Dennis P. LeStrange, age 47, $495,200 pay
SVP, Human Resources: Beth B. Sexton, age 45

SVP, Marketing: Cathy Lewis, age 49
VP and Controller: Carlyle S. Singer, age 45
VP; President, IKON Europe: David D. Mills
VP, Supply Chain: Stephen R. LaHood
Investor Relations: Veronica L. Rosa
Media Relations: Steven K. Eck
Auditors: PricewaterhouseCoopers LLP

LOCATIONS

HQ: 70 Valley Stream Pkwy., Malvern, PA 19355
Phone: 610-296-8000   **Fax:** 610-408-7025
Web: www.ikon.com

IKON Office Solutions has offices in Canada, Denmark,
France, Germany, Ireland, Mexico, the UK, and the US.

2001 Sales

	$ mil.	% of total
US	4,566	87
UK	324	6
Canada	224	4
Other countries	159	3
Total	**5,273**	**100**

PRODUCTS/OPERATIONS

2001 Sales

	$ mil.	% of total
IKON North America	4,624	88
IKON Europe	454	9
Other	195	3
Total	**5,273**	**100**

Selected Products
Color management software
Copiers (color, monochrome)
Fax machines
Printers (color, large-format, monochrome)
Raster image processors
Workflow management systems

Selected Services
Digital conversion
Facilities management
Financing
Legal document services
Network design and implementation
Outsourcing (document printing, copying, or
  distribution)
Training

Selected Brands
Canon	Lotus
Cisco	Microsoft
Citrix	Novell
Hewlett-Packard	Océ
IBM	Ricoh

COMPETITORS

Buhrmann	Merisel
Canon	Minolta
Danka	Océ
Global Imaging Systems	Office Depot
Hewlett-Packard	Ricoh
Imagistics	Seiko Epson
Ingram Micro	Sharp
Kinko's	Tech Data
Lanier Worldwide	Xerox
Lexmark International	

HISTORICAL FINANCIALS & EMPLOYEES

NYSE: IKN FYE: September 30	Annual Growth	9/92	9/93	9/94	9/95	9/96	9/97	9/98	9/99	9/00	9/01
Sales ($ mil.)	0.9%	4,883	6,387	7,926	9,794	3,942	4,905	5,629	5,522	5,447	5,273
Net income ($ mil.)	(18.5%)	96	0	71	203	211	130	(83)	34	29	15
Income as % of sales	—	2.0%	0.0%	0.9%	2.1%	5.3%	2.7%	—	0.6%	0.5%	0.3%
Earnings per share ($)	(16.0%)	0.53	0.52	(0.09)	0.86	1.12	0.77	(0.76)	0.23	0.20	0.11
Stock price - FY high ($)	—	21.31	25.31	32.75	43.63	66.00	52.25	36.25	16.38	10.88	9.80
Stock price - FY low ($)	—	15.13	16.63	21.75	26.50	37.38	20.63	5.00	6.38	3.88	2.00
Stock price - FY close ($)	(8.9%)	17.94	22.00	31.06	42.38	49.88	25.56	7.19	10.69	3.94	7.72
P/E - high	—	39	48	—	50	58	68	—	71	57	82
P/E - low	—	28	31	—	30	33	27	—	28	20	17
Dividends per share ($)	(11.1%)	0.46	0.48	0.50	0.52	0.56	0.26	0.16	0.16	0.16	0.16
Book value per share ($)	0.6%	9.36	11.13	12.55	17.16	17.14	11.11	10.42	9.79	10.02	9.84
Employees	5.4%	23,500	28,500	30,600	36,500	31,300	41,000	42,600	39,400	31,000	37,600

STOCK PRICE HISTORY
HIGH/LOW/CLOSE

2001 FISCAL YEAR-END
Debt ratio: 58.5%
Return on equity: 1.1%
Cash ($ mil.): 80
Current ratio: 1.11
Long-term debt ($ mil.): 1,966
No. of shares (mil.): 142
Dividends
  Yield: 2.1%
  Payout: 145.5%
Market value ($ mil.): 1,095

ILLINOIS TOOL WORKS INC.

For painting in a pinch, try Illinois Tool Works (ITW). The Chicago-based company makes spray guns, paint-curing systems, and strapping machinery for industrial manufacturers and commercial painters. Other specialty systems (about half of sales) include fluid-mixing and -monitoring equipment. ITW's other business segments include engineered products (adhesives, welding equipment, and metal and plastic fasteners) and leasing and investments. Brands include Paslode (fasteners), Miller (welding products), and Wilsonart (laminates).

With an arsenal of about 600 diversified operating units, ITW's performance is often viewed as a yardstick with which to measure the health of the economy. The prognosis is less than encouraging, but improving. Slowing demand across the industries that ITW serves caused the company to trim jobs at some of its businesses. The company will divest its consumer products holdings (appliances and cookware, exercise equipment, and ceramic tile), many of which it had gained through the acquisition of Premark International, to trim operating costs and relieve debt.

HISTORY

In the early years of the 20th century, Byron Smith, founder of Chicago's Northern Trust Company, recognized that rapid industrialization was outgrowing the capacity of small shops to supply machine tools. Smith encouraged two of his four sons to launch Illinois Tool Works (ITW) in 1912. Harold C. Smith became president of ITW in 1915 and expanded its product line into automotive parts.

ITW developed the Shakeproof fastener, the first twisted-tooth lock washer, in 1923. When Harold C. died in 1936, the torch passed to his son Harold B., who decentralized the company and exhorted salesmen to learn customers' businesses so they could develop solutions even before the customers recognized the problems. Smith plowed profits back into research as WWII spurred demand.

In the 1950s the company began exploring plastics and combination metal and plastic fasteners, as well as electrical controls and instruments, to become a leader in miniaturization. Its major breakthrough came in the early 1960s with the development of flexible plastic collars to hold six-packs of beverage cans. This item, under a new division called Hi-Cone, was ITW's most-profitable offering.

Silas Cathcart became CEO in 1970. Smith's son, another Harold B., was president and COO until 1981 (he remains on the board of directors

and is chairman of the board's executive committee). By the early 1980s ITW had become bureaucratic and susceptible to foreign competition. It was forced to lower prices to hold on to customers. Wary after the 1982 recession, ITW hired John Nichols as CEO.

Nichols broadened the company's product line, introduced more effective production methods, and doubled ITW's size by buying 27 companies, the largest being Signode Industries, bought for $524 million (1986). Nichols broke Signode into smaller units to speed development of 20 new products.

ITW purchased Ransburg Corporation (electrostatic finishing systems, 1989) and the DeVilbiss division of Eagle Industries (1990) and merged the two to form its Finishing Systems and Products division. In 1992 the company introduced the Ring Leader Recycling Program to recycle its plastic six-pack rings.

Through a stock swap, ITW acquired ownership of the Miller Group (arc welding equipment and related systems) in 1993. An 11% increase in car building in Europe in 1994 caused revenues of the company's engineered-components segment to grow dramatically; that year 76% of ITW's international sales came from European operations.

In 1995 ITW named president James Farrell as CEO. He replaced Nichols as chairman in 1996. ITW acquired Hobart Brothers (welding products) and Medalists Industries (industrial fasteners) in 1996 and made 28 acquisitions and joint ventures in 1997. It entered the domestic spray-painting equipment business in 1998 by acquiring Binks Sames (now Sames Corporation) for $106 million.

ITW gained the technology to make bar code printers in 1999 when it acquired industrial ink-jet maker Trident International in a $107 million deal. Other purchases that year included a polyester film-processing plant from South Korea's SKC, Duo-Fast (pneumatic nailing and stapling tools), and for $3.5 billion, Premark International (consumer products, which it began selling off in 2002). ITW sold its Irathane Systems urethane linings and moldings division to Industrial Rubber Products.

The company added to its ink-jet operations in 2000 with the acquisition of Imaging Technologies LLC. ITW also agreed to acquire Trilectron Industries (ground support equipment) from HEICO in a deal worth about $57 million. Early in 2001 the company added to its welding operations by buying four welding component businesses from Dover Corporation. Later in the year it acquired the hot stamp foil company, Foilmark. In early 2002 the company's board of directors gave its stamp of approval for the divestiture of ITW's consumer products segment.

OFFICERS

Chairman and CEO: W. James Farrell, age 59,
$2,040,870 pay
Vice Chairman: Frank S. Ptak, age 59, $953,239 pay
Vice Chairman: James M. Ringler, age 56,
$1,576,897 pay
EVP: Russell M. Flaum, age 51, $561,443 pay
EVP: David T. Flood, age 50
EVP: Philip M. Gresh Jr., age 53
EVP: Thomas J. Hansen, age 53
EVP: David B. Speer, age 51, $657,336 pay
EVP: Hugh J. Zentmyer, age 55
SVP and CFO: Jon C. Kinney, age 59
SVP, General Counsel, and Secretary:
Stewart S. Hudnut, age 62
SVP, Human Resources: John Karpan, age 61
SVP: Allan C. Sutherland, age 38
Auditors: Deloitte & Touche LLP

LOCATIONS

HQ: 3600 W. Lake Avenue, Glenview, IL 60025
Phone: 847-724-7500   **Fax:** 847-657-4261
Web: www.itw.com

Illinois Tool Works has principal plants in Australia,
Belgium, Brazil, Canada, Denmark, France, Germany,
Italy, Mexico, South Korea, Spain, Switzerland, the UK,
and the US. It has operation in nearly 45 countries.

2001 Sales

	$ mil.	% of total
US	5,881	63
Europe	2,350	25
Asia	323	4
Other regions	739	8
Total	**9,293**	**100**

PRODUCTS/OPERATIONS

2001 Sales

	$ mil.	% of total
Specialty systems	5,051	52
Engineered products	4,445	46
Leasing & investments	150	2
Adjustments	(353)	—
Total	**9,293**	**100**

Selected Products

Specialty Systems
Arc welding equipment
Food-preparation equipment
Industrial adhesive-application equipment
Paint application equipment
Recyclable ring packaging
Steel and plastic strapping systems

Engineered Products
Adhesives
Fasteners and assemblies
Fastening tools
Laminates

COMPETITORS

3M	Nordson
Armstrong Holdings	PennEngineering
BASF AG	PPG
Cooper Industries	SPS Technologies
DuPont	Stanley Works
Enodis	Textron
ESAB	TriMas Corporation
GE	Tyco International
Ingersoll-Rand	W. R. Grace
NCH	

HISTORICAL FINANCIALS & EMPLOYEES

NYSE: ITW FYE: December 31	Annual Growth	12/92	12/93	12/94	12/95	12/96	12/97	12/98	12/99	12/00	12/01
Sales ($ mil.)	14.2%	2,812	3,159	3,461	4,152	4,997	5,220	5,648	9,333	9,984	9,293
Net income ($ mil.)	17.3%	192	207	278	388	486	587	673	841	958	806
Income as % of sales	—	6.8%	6.5%	8.0%	9.3%	9.7%	11.2%	11.9%	9.0%	9.6%	8.7%
Earnings per share ($)	13.4%	0.85	0.90	1.22	1.63	1.95	2.33	2.67	2.76	3.15	2.63
Stock price - FY high ($)	—	17.66	20.25	22.75	32.75	43.63	60.13	73.19	82.00	69.00	71.99
Stock price - FY low ($)	—	14.25	16.25	18.50	19.88	25.94	37.38	45.19	58.13	49.50	49.15
Stock price - FY close ($)	17.1%	16.31	19.50	21.88	29.50	39.94	60.13	58.00	67.56	59.56	67.72
P/E - high	—	21	22	19	20	22	26	27	29	22	27
P/E - low	—	17	18	15	12	13	16	17	21	16	19
Dividends per share ($)	15.2%	0.23	0.25	0.27	0.31	0.35	0.43	0.51	0.63	0.74	0.82
Book value per share ($)	14.2%	5.97	5.56	6.76	8.13	9.66	11.24	13.35	16.01	17.86	19.79
Employees	12.7%	17,800	19,000	19,500	21,200	24,400	25,700	29,200	52,800	55,300	52,000

STOCK PRICE HISTORY

HIGH/LOW/CLOSE

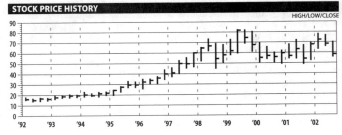

2001 FISCAL YEAR-END

Debt ratio: 17.3%
Return on equity: 14.1%
Cash ($ mil.): 282
Current ratio: 2.08
Long-term debt ($ mil.): 1,267
No. of shares (mil.): 305
Dividends
  Yield: 1.2%
  Payout: 31.2%
Market value ($ mil.): 20,666

IMATION CORP.

Imation wants to start fresh with a blank disk. Based in Oakdale, Minnesota, the company is a leading maker of data storage tapes and diskettes. Imation sells its products directly and through distributors to customers ranging from large corporations to PC owners. It generates 45% of its sales outside the US. Imation was spun off from Post-it Notes and Scotch tape maker 3M in 1996.

Chairman and CEO William Monahan has responded to declining sales across Imation's product lines, overseeing a series of workforce cuts, revamping management, and (tearing a page out of 3M's playbook) divesting Imation of noncore businesses. The company has sold its CD-ROM, photographic film, medical imaging system, and color proofing and color software operations, as well as the North American operations of its Digital Solutions and Services (DSS) business.

HISTORY

Imation's ancestry stretches back to 1902, when five businessmen founded Minnesota Mining and Manufacturing (3M) in Two Harbors, Minnesota, to sell corundum to manufacturers for grinding wheels. Faced with stiff competition and the realization that its mining holdings contained the nearly worthless igneous rock anorthosite instead of corundum, the company shifted gears and began making sandpaper and abrasive wheels.

In a research-fueled corporate culture, 3M's engineers thrived, launching a long line of culturally implanted products including Scotch masking tape, the dry-printing photocopy process, Post-it adhesive notepads, and, in 1947, the first commercially viable magnetic recording tape. This ancestor of the cassette tape would mark 3M's leap into the business that later helped make Imation.

The genesis of Imation's other lines continued in the 1950s and 1960s when 3M ventured into photographic products. It jumped into color proofing systems and X-ray and other medical imaging technologies in the 1970s. When its diskette manufacturing business faced intense global competition in the 1980s, 3M expanded its efforts in the data storage products market.

Imation — a name taken from the words "imaging" and "information" — was born in 1996 when 3M spun off its low-performing data storage, imaging, and printing businesses. 3M's plan was to boost its sagging stock price and let the new company focus on customers, as opposed to the wider corporate goals of 3M, which retained its industrial and consumer and life science units and discontinued its audio- and videotape business. About 75% of 3M's data storage and medical imaging employees made the move; the rest opted for early retirement. That year William Monahan, who began his career in the early 1970s selling 3M data storage products on Wall Street and rose to serve as VP of the company's Electro and Communication Group, was named chairman and CEO.

In 1996 Imation also unveiled the LS-120 diskette for a drive that used both standard floppy disks (1.44 MB) and 120-MB, 3.5-in. disks. Hitachi, Matsushita, and Mitsubishi made products based on the technology. Also that year the company bought Seattle-based pre-press software company Luminous Corp., and was awarded its first non-3M patent for a minicartridge design.

While Imation struggled in an intensely competitive market with plummeting product prices, industry watchers questioned the company's commitment to new technology. Imation intensified restructuring efforts to pare operations and sharpen its focus. In 1997 it stepped up a new technology push by acquiring digital medical imaging specialist Cemax-Icon, as well as Internet service provider Imaginet, resulting in the creation of Imation Internet Studio. (The unit was sold in 1999 to Gage Marketing Group when its strategies conflicted with Imation's.)

More losses piled up in 1997 despite a slew of new products and features. In 1998 Imation tried to turn around its financial results by slashing 3,400 jobs. The company also sold its CD-ROM services unit to optical media company Metatec and its medical imaging systems to Eastman Kodak for about $520 million, partly to settle an intellectual-property lawsuit. In 1999 Imation sold its Photo Color Systems business (photographic film, single-use cameras) to Schroder plc affiliate Schroder Ventures.

In early 2000 Imation introduced Verifi — technology that lets online shoppers verify the accuracy of colors on their monitors. The following year the company agreed to sell its color proofing and color software businesses to Kodak Polychrome Graphics (a joint venture between Kodak and Dainippon Ink and Chemicals subsidiary Sun Chemical); the deal closed in early 2002. Later that year Imation sold its North American Digital Solutions and Services (DSS) operations to DecisionOne, and announced it would close or dispose of DSS operations outside of North America.

OFFICERS

Chairman, President, and CEO: William T. Monahan, age 54, $1,013,742 pay
SVP, CFO, and Chief Administrative Officer: Robert L. Edwards, age 46, $571,820 pay
SVP, Secretary, and General Counsel: John L. Sullivan, age 47, $446,667 pay
President, Data Storage and Information Management: Frank P. Russomanno, age 54
VP and Controller: Paul R. Zeller, age 41
VP, Corporate Communications and Investor Relations: Bradley D. Allen, age 51
VP, Human Resources: Jacqueline A. Chase, age 48
VP, International Operations; President, Imation Digital Solutions and Services: David H. Wenck, age 58, $416,632 pay
VP, Data Storage and Information Management, Manufacturing and Supply Chain: Colleen R. Willhite, age 45
Marketing Manager, Storage Consulting, Imation Storage Professional Services: Bill Peldzus
Auditors: PricewaterhouseCoopers LLP

LOCATIONS

HQ: 1 Imation Place, Oakdale, MN 55128
Phone: 888-704-4000   **Fax:** 888-704-4200
Web: www.imation.com

Imation has offices in Argentina, Australia, Brazil, Canada, Chile, China, Colombia, France, Germany, Guatemala, Hong Kong, India, Italy, Japan, Malaysia, Mexico, the Netherlands, Pakistan, Singapore, South Korea, Spain, Taiwan, Thailand, the United Arab Emirates, the UK, the US, and Venezuela.

2001 Sales

	$ mil.	% of total
US	648	55
Other countries	529	45
Total	**1,177**	**100**

PRODUCTS/OPERATIONS

2001 Sales

	$ mil.	% of total
Data storage & information management	876	75
Color technologies	212	18
Digital solutions & services	87	7
Other	2	—
Total	**1,177**	**100**

Selected Products and Services

Computer diskettes (SuperDisk)
Computer tape cartridges (Travan)
Recordable and rewritable CDs
Storage drives

COMPETITORS

Fuji Photo
Hewlett-Packard
Hitachi
Iomega
Quantum
Seagate
SmartDisk
Sony
TDK
Yamaha

HISTORICAL FINANCIALS & EMPLOYEES

NYSE: IMN FYE: December 31	Annual Growth	12/92	12/93	12/94	12/95	12/96	12/97	12/98	12/99	12/00	12/01
Sales ($ mil.)	(8.1%)	—	2,308	2,281	2,246	2,278	2,202	2,047	1,413	1,235	1,177
Net income ($ mil.)	—	—	75	54	(97)	(21)	(180)	57	44	(4)	(2)
Income as % of sales	—	—	3.2%	2.4%	—	—	—	2.8%	3.1%	—	—
Earnings per share ($)	—	—	—	—	—	(0.49)	(4.54)	1.45	1.17	(0.13)	(0.05)
Stock price - FY high ($)	—	—	—	—	—	33.38	31.88	19.94	34.25	33.88	25.55
Stock price - FY low ($)	—	—	—	—	—	19.25	15.13	13.56	15.00	14.13	14.88
Stock price - FY close ($)	(5.2%)	—	—	—	—	28.13	16.00	17.50	33.56	15.50	21.58
P/E - high	—	—	—	—	—	—	—	14	29	—	—
P/E - low	—	—	—	—	—	—	—	9	13	—	—
Dividends per share ($)	—	—	—	—	—	0.00	0.00	0.00	0.00	0.00	0.00
Book value per share ($)	(3.1%)	—	—	—	—	21.70	16.81	18.56	19.50	18.82	18.58
Employees	(19.0%)	—	—	—	12,000	9,400	9,800	6,400	4,850	4,300	3,400

STOCK PRICE HISTORY

HIGH/LOW/CLOSE

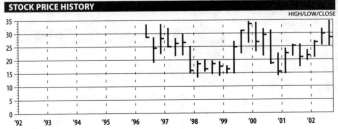

2001 FISCAL YEAR-END

Debt ratio: 0.0%
Return on equity: —
Cash ($ mil.): 390
Current ratio: 2.18
Long-term debt ($ mil.): 0
No. of shares (mil.): 35
Dividends
  Yield: —
  Payout: —
Market value ($ mil.): 762

IMC GLOBAL INC.

The world's leading phosphate producer, IMC Global digs phosphate. The Lake Forest, Illinois-based company produces phosphates and potash, which are used in fertilizers. It also makes additives for livestock and poultry feeds. With production facilities in the US and Canada, the company markets its products mainly in the US, China, Europe, and India. IMC has four phosphate mines in Florida and six potash mines in the US and Canada.

Plowed under by losses caused primarily by weak demand and lower prices, IMC has initiated several plans and programs to reduce costs through plant closures, temporary mine shutdowns, and layoffs. To pay down debt, the company sold several units (including IMC Salt and IMC AgriBusiness) and is selling its IMC Chemicals unit.

HISTORY

In 1897 engineer Thomas Meadows and his brother-in-law Oscar Dortch formed T.C. Meadows & Co. in Tennessee to exploit local phosphorus-rich rock. At that time major sources of potassium (potash) and nitrogen (nitrates) were in Germany and Chile. The company, renamed United States Agricultural Corporation in 1899, began mining in Florida, which soon became the center of the US phosphate industry.

Waldemar Schmidtmann, whose father controlled a major German potash mine, joined Meadows and Dortch in 1909 to form International Agricultural Corp. (IAC), which bought the elder Schmidtmann's mine. Despite an import ban during WWI, IAC's German potash supplies gave it a jump on US firms still searching for domestic potash sources. IAC pioneered a method of separating phosphate rocks from surrounding debris in 1929, doubling the life of rock reserves. By 1939 the company was the world's #1 miner of phosphate rock. US potash was commercially developed by Union Potash in the 1930s, and in 1939 IAC bought Union Potash.

IAC changed its name to International Mineral & Chemical (IMC) in 1941. After WWII, the use of commercial fertilizers by markets in Asia helped sustain 20 years of growth. IMC entered the nitrate market through a 1963 joint venture with Northern Natural Gas of Omaha to build an ammonia plant.

During the 1970s and 1980s IMC suffered financially, in part due to the dominance of Communist Bloc fertilizer firms in markets outside the US, the drop in fertilizer prices, and growing concern about the health risks of inorganic fertilizers. In response, IMC bought Mallinckrodt (pharmaceuticals) and Pitman-Moore (animal

health products) in 1986. IMC reorganized as a holding company with subsidiaries that included Mallinckrodt, IMC Fertilizer, and Pitman-Moore.

IMC Fertilizer went public in 1988 but struggled in the early 1990s due to plant explosions, lawsuits, and depressed prices. In 1992 the company changed its name to IMC Global, and in 1993 it pooled its phosphate assets with those of Freeport-McMoRan Resource Partners (now Phosphate Resource Partners).

To support expansion in China, IMC set up a World Food Production Conference in Beijing and opened a Hong Kong office in 1995. Late that year IMC became the world's #1 miner of phosphate rock and potash by buying Vigoro, a producer and distributor of potash, nitrogen-based fertilizers, and related goods.

In 1996 IMC-Agrico began to explore developing phosphate resources in China's Yunnan province. The next year it bought potash producer Western AG-Minerals and mining company Freeport-McMoRan for $750 million. IMC combined its sulfur business with Freeport-McMoRan's to form Freeport-McMoRan Sulphur in 1997.

IMC bought Harris Chemical for $1.4 billion in 1998. It exited the consumer and professional lawn and garden products market that year by selling IMC Vigoro to privately owned Pursell Industries. IMC hired former Culligan Water CEO Doug Pertz as president that year.

In 1999 IMC sold its IMC AgriBusiness distribution unit to Royster-Clark for about $300 million and its oil and gas operations to McMoRan Exploration for $32 million. The same year IMC sold a majority stake in its chemicals unit and announced that it would lay off at least 10% of its workforce and take an $825 million charge to fund its restructuring. Chairman and CEO Robert Fowler retired late that year, with Pertz succeeding him as CEO.

In 2001 the company sold its salt and Ogden (salt potash) businesses to Compass Minerals Group, an affiliate of investment firm Apollo Management (IMC will keep a minority interest in the business). Meanwhile, IMC's attempt to sell its 30% stake in a joint venture in Huntsman International to Huntsman Chemical has been put on hold.

OFFICERS

Chairman and CEO: Douglas A. Pertz, age 47, $1,171,250 pay (prior to title change)
President and COO: John J. Ferguson
EVP and CFO: Reid Porter, age 53
SVP, General Counsel, and Assistant Secretary: Mary Anne Hynes, age 51, $302,501 pay

SVP, Human Resources: Stephen P. Malia, age 48, $296,252 pay
SVP; President, IMC Sales and Marketing: C. Steven Hoffman, age 53, $357,160 pay
VP and Controller: Robert M. Qualls
VP and Treasurer: E. Paul Dunn Jr.
VP, Environment, Health, and Safety: Marian Whiteman, age 37
VP, Information Technology and Purchasing: Larry Shoemake, age 53
VP, Investor and Corporate Relations: David A. Prichard
VP, Materials: Bruce G. Davis, age 52
Corporate Secretary: Rose Marie Williams
Assistant Treasurer: Joseph A. McGowan, age 35
Auditors: Ernst & Young LLP

LOCATIONS

HQ: 100 S. Saunders Rd., Lake Forest, IL 60045
Phone: 847-739-1200   **Fax:** 847-739-1624
Web: www.imcglobal.com

IMC Global operates production facilities in Canada and the US.

2001 Sales

	$ mil.	% of total
US	950	57
China	164	10
Other countries	548	33
(Adjustments)	297	—
Total	**1,959**	**100**

PRODUCTS/OPERATIONS

2001 Sales

	$ mil.	% of total
PhosFeed	1,171	60
Potash	788	40
Total	**1,959**	**100**

Selected Products

PhosFeed
Diammonium phosphate
Feed Ingredients
Monoammonium phosphate
Triple superphosphate

Potash
Potassium magnesium sulfate
Potassium sulfate
Red muriate of potash
Sulfate
White muriate of potash

COMPETITORS

Agrium
BASF AG
Cargill
CF Industries
Dow Chemical
K + S
MDPA
Mississippi Chemical
Norsk Hydro
Philipp Brothers
Potash Corporation
Terra Industries

HISTORICAL FINANCIALS & EMPLOYEES

NYSE: IGL FYE: December 31	Annual Growth	6/93	6/94	6/95	6/96	6/97	*12/97	12/98	12/99	12/00	12/01
Sales ($ mil.)	9.1%	897	1,442	1,924	2,981	2,982	2,989	2,696	2,369	2,096	1,959
Net income ($ mil.)	—	(167)	(29)	115	144	193	63	(9)	(773)	(345)	(67)
Income as % of sales	—	—	—	6.0%	4.8%	6.5%	2.1%	—	—	—	—
Earnings per share ($)	—	(3.79)	(0.57)	1.94	1.56	2.03	0.67	(0.08)	(6.75)	(3.00)	(0.57)
Stock price – FY high ($)	—	22.94	24.63	27.31	43.25	44.50	42.50	39.50	27.13	19.38	16.69
Stock price – FY low ($)	—	12.19	13.00	17.06	27.00	33.13	29.63	17.81	12.75	11.00	8.00
Stock price – FY close ($)	(1.3%)	14.69	17.31	27.06	37.63	35.00	32.75	21.38	16.38	15.56	13.00
P/E – high	—	—	—	13	28	21	46	—	—	—	—
P/E – low	—	—	—	8	17	15	32	—	—	—	—
Dividends per share ($)	(16.6%)	0.41	0.00	0.15	0.29	0.32	0.16	0.32	0.32	0.32	0.08
Book value per share ($)	(7.8%)	9.76	11.12	12.92	19.42	14.32	16.98	16.27	9.43	5.88	4.70
Employees	(0.4%)	5,400	5,200	6,300	6,800	9,200	9,200	11,244	8,976	7,833	5,194

* Fiscal year change

STOCK PRICE HISTORY

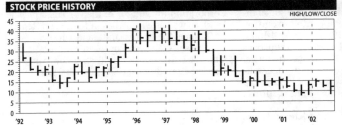

HIGH/LOW/CLOSE

2001 FISCAL YEAR-END

Debt ratio: 80.4%
Return on equity: —
Cash ($ mil.): 249
Current ratio: 1.49
Long-term debt ($ mil.): 2,216
No. of shares (mil.): 115
Dividends
  Yield: 0.6%
  Payout: —
Market value ($ mil.): 1,495

INGERSOLL-RAND COMPANY

Ingersoll-Rand helped shape the face of America (or at least the ones on Mount Rushmore) with its rock drills, but now the company has a more prominent profile in other markets. The Woodcliff Lake, New Jersey-based company (domiciled in Bermuda) makes machinery and equipment for climate control (Thermo King refrigeration units for trucks, Hussmann display cases), security and safety (Schlage locks and Steelcraft doors), construction and mining (Bobcat excavators), and industrial productivity (Torrington bearings and Ingersoll-Rand tools). Ingersoll-Rand's customers include companies involved in infrastructure development, auto manufacturing, food retailing, and construction.

Stung by the general economic downturn, Ingersoll-Rand has been restructuring, closing factories, and laying off workers. The company is emphasizing less-cyclical product lines such as security systems, infrastructure, and refrigeration equipment. It is selling off more-cyclical businesses, including subsidiary Dresser-Rand's compressor business, and plans more divestitures.

HISTORY

Simon Ingersoll invented the steam-driven rock drill in New York City in 1871. In 1874 he sold the patent to Jose Francisco de Navarro, who financed the organization of the Ingersoll Rock Drill Company. Three years later it merged with Sergeant Drill, a company created by Henry Clark Sergeant, Navarro's former foreman.

Meanwhile, the Rand brothers were also establishing a drill company. The companies merged in 1905 to become Ingersoll-Rand.

Ingersoll-Rand initially produced air compressors and a basic line of rock drills. In 1912 the company added centrifugal compressors and turbo blowers. Later, Ingersoll-Rand added portable air tools.

After WWII Ingersoll-Rand, which had mostly served US mining operations, expanded internationally. From the 1960s on, the company diversified into specialized machinery and products. Acquisitions in the 1970s and 1980s made Ingersoll-Rand the largest bearing manufacturer in the US.

The company also developed small air compressors and water-jet systems capable of cutting steel and concrete. In 1986 Ingersoll-Rand formed a joint venture with Dresser Industries called Dresser-Rand to produce gas turbines, compressors, and similar equipment. Ingersoll-Rand and Dresser Industries combined pump operations to form another joint venture, Ingersoll-Dresser Pump, in 1992.

In 1993 16-year Ingersoll-Rand veteran James

Perrella became CEO. That year the company bought the German needle- and cylindrical-bearing business of FAG Kugelfischer Georg Schafer; it also sold its underground coal-mining machinery business (to Long-Airdox), as well as its domestic jet-engine bearing operation. ECOAIR, a unit of MAN GHH, was among several 1994 acquisitions.

Ingersoll-Rand acquired Clark Equipment for $1.5 billion in 1995 in a deal that included the businesses of Bobcat (skid-steer loaders), Clark-Hurth Components (axles and transmissions, sold 1997), Club Car (golf cars), and Blaw-Knox Construction Equipment (asphalt-paving equipment). In 1996 Ingersoll-Rand bought Metaldyne's (formerly Mascotech) Steelcraft Division (steel doors). Ingersoll-Rand bought Newman Tonks Group (UK) and technology from the Master Lock unit of Fortune Brands in 1997, which boosted its architectural hardware line and extended its distribution in Europe and Asia. That year Ingersoll-Rand bought Thermo King from Westinghouse (now CBS) for $2.6 billion.

In 1999 Ingersoll-Rand bought Harrow Industries (access controls, architectural hardware, decorative bath fixtures). The company's industrial production equipment was enhanced when it struck a deal with Cadence Design Systems, a world-leading supplier of electronic design and automation software. James Perrella stepped down as CEO that year; Herbert Henkel, formerly of Textron, succeeded him.

In 2000 Ingersoll-Rand bought Halliburton's stake in its joint ventures with Dresser-Rand and Ingersoll-Dresser Pump. Ingersoll-Rand then sold Ingersoll-Dresser Pump to Flowserve for about $775 million and bought Neal Manufacturing, which makes compact road-paving equipment. That year it also acquired Hussmann International (refrigeration equipment) for about $1.8 billion. Ingersoll-Rand sold its Dresser-Rand compression operations that same year to Hanover Group.

The company closed 20 plants and laid off more than 3,900 employees the next year. But acquisitions continued. Ingersoll-Rand's 2001 purchases included refrigeration company National Refrigeration Services and lock maker Kryptonite Corporation (originator of the U-shaped bicycle lock), as well as companies in the Czech Republic, France, the Netherlands, and Turkey.

Ingersoll-Rand reincorporated in Bermuda in late 2001; the move could save the company nearly $40 million in US taxes every year.

Chairman: George W. Buckley, age 55
President and CEO: Herbert L. Henkel, age 53,
$1,760,000 pay
SVP and CFO: Timothy R. McLevish
SVP, E-business and CTO: Michael D. Radcliff, age 51
SVP, General Counsel, and Director: Patricia Nachtigal,
age 55
SVP, Global Business Services and Human Resources:
Donald H. Rice, age 57
SVP and President, Industrial Productivity Sector:
John E. Turpin, age 55, $638,800 pay
SVP and President, Infrastructure Sector:
Christopher P. Vasiloff, age 50
SVP and President, Security and Safety Sector:
Randy P. Smith, age 52, $764,333 pay
SVP, Climate Control Sector: Gordon A. Mapp, age 55,
$719,883 pay
Auditors: PricewaterhouseCoopers LLP

LOCATIONS

HQ: Ingersoll-Rand Company Limited
200 Chestnut Ridge Rd., Woodcliff Lake, NJ 07675
Phone: 201-573-0123   **Fax:** 201-573-3168
Web: www.ingersoll-rand.com

2001 Sales

	% of total
US	63
Europe	21
Asia/Pacific	8
Canada	4
Latin America	4
Total	**100**

PRODUCTS/OPERATIONS

2001 Sales

	$ mil.	% of total
Industrial Solutions		
Air & productivity solutions	1,308	14
Engineered solutions	1,078	11
Dresser-Rand	881	9
Infrastructure	2,570	27
Climate Control	2,438	25
Security & Safety	1,407	14
Total	**9,682**	**100**

Selected Products

Architectural locks	Pavers
Bearings and components	Personal identification
Case refrigeration	products
equipment	Portable power products
Compactors	Power-operated doors
Compressed air systems	Skid-steer loaders
Drilling equipment	Steel doors
Golf cars and utility	Transport temperature
vehicles	control equipment

COMPETITORS

AMSTED	Emerson	NESCO
Baker Hughes	Electric	Robert Bosch
Black & Decker	Fiat	SPX
Caterpillar	FMC	Stanley Works
Cooper	Fortune Brands	Thermo Electron
Industries	Gardner Denver	ThyssenKrupp
Crown	Graco	Toshiba
Equipment	Hillenbrand	Toyota
Deere	Inductotherm	W.W. Grainger
Dover	ITT Industries	York
Eaton	Joy Global	International

HISTORICAL FINANCIALS & EMPLOYEES

NYSE: IR FYE: December 31	Annual Growth	12/92	12/93	12/94	12/95	12/96	12/97	12/98	12/99	12/00	12/01
Sales ($ mil.)	11.0%	3,784	4,021	4,508	5,729	6,703	7,103	8,292	7,667	8,798	9,682
Net income ($ mil.)	—	(234)	143	211	270	358	381	509	591	669	246
Income as % of sales	—	—	3.5%	4.7%	4.7%	5.3%	5.4%	6.1%	7.7%	7.6%	2.5%
Earnings per share ($)	—	(1.50)	0.90	1.33	1.69	2.21	2.31	3.08	3.57	4.12	1.43
Stock price - FY high ($)	—	22.84	26.60	27.76	28.26	31.77	46.25	54.00	73.81	57.75	50.28
Stock price - FY low ($)	—	16.68	19.18	19.68	18.93	23.43	27.85	34.00	44.63	29.50	30.40
Stock price - FY close ($)	8.9%	19.43	25.51	21.01	23.43	29.68	40.50	47.25	55.06	41.88	41.81
P/E - high	—	—	26	21	17	14	20	17	20	14	34
P/E - low	—	—	18	15	11	11	12	11	12	7	20
Dividends per share ($)	4.4%	0.46	0.47	0.48	0.49	0.52	0.57	0.60	0.64	0.68	0.68
Book value per share ($)	12.2%	8.25	8.55	9.36	11.00	12.74	15.07	16.47	18.23	20.38	23.31
Employees	5.3%	35,308	35,143	35,932	41,133	40,100	46,600	46,500	46,000	51,000	56,000

STOCK PRICE HISTORY

HIGH/LOW/CLOSE

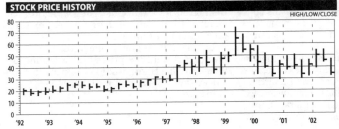

2001 FISCAL YEAR-END

Debt ratio: 42.5%
Return on equity: 6.6%
Cash ($ mil.): 114
Current ratio: 1.12
Long-term debt ($ mil.): 2,901
No. of shares (mil.): 168
Dividends
  Yield: 1.6%
  Payout: 47.6%
Market value ($ mil.): 7,024

INGRAM INDUSTRIES INC.

Book 'em, Martha. Billionaire Martha Ingram heads Nashville-based Ingram Industries, whose Ingram Book Group is one of the US's largest wholesale distributors of trade books and audiobooks to retailers, as well as a leading distributor to libraries. Ingram Book, through its some eight fulfillment centers, distributes about 175 million titles a year. It serves some 32,000 retail outlets and represents over 13,000 publishers. Its Lightning Source subsidiary offers conversion and distribution services for print-on-demand and e-books.

Although Ingram Book accounts for just over half of Ingram Industries' sales, the company also operates Ingram Marine Group, which ships grain, ore, and other products through its some 1,800 barges, and Ingram Insurance Group, which offers high-risk auto insurance in nine states through Permanent General Insurance. Ingram Industries spun off its largest segment, Ingram Micro (the world's largest distributor of microcomputer products), in 1996 and Ingram Entertainment (the US's top distributor of videotapes) in 1997.

Martha Ingram is America's wealthiest active businesswoman, and she and her family own and run Ingram Industries. The Ingram family controls about 75% of Ingram Micro's voting stock.

HISTORY

Orrin Ingram and two partners founded the Dole, Ingram & Kennedy sawmill in 1857 in Eau Claire, Wisconsin, on the Chippewa River, about 50 miles upstream from the Mississippi River. By the 1870s the company, renamed Ingram & Kennedy, was selling lumber as far downstream as Hannibal, Missouri.

Ingram's success was noticed by Frederick Weyerhaeuser, a German immigrant in Rock Island, Illinois, who, like Ingram, had worked in a sawmill before buying one of his own. In 1881 Ingram and Weyerhaeuser negotiated the formation of Chippewa Logging (35%-owned by up-river partners, 65% by down-river interests), which controlled the white pine harvest of the Chippewa Valley. In 1900 Ingram paid $216,000 for 2,160 shares in the newly formed Weyerhaeuser Timber Company. Ingram let his sons and grandsons handle the investment and formed O.H. Ingram Co. to manage the family's interests. He died in 1918.

In 1946 Ingram's descendants founded Ingram Barge, which hauled crude oil to the company's refinery near St. Louis. After buying and then selling other holdings, in 1962 the family formed Ingram Corp., consisting solely of Ingram Barge. Brothers Bronson and Fritz Ingram (Orrin's

great-grandsons) bought the company from their father, Hank, before he died in 1963, and in 1964 they bought half of Tennessee Book, a textbook distributing company founded in 1935. In 1970 they formed Ingram Book Group to sell trade books to bookstores and libraries.

Ingram Barge won a $48 million Chicago sludge-hauling contract in 1971, but later the company was accused of bribing city politicians with $1.2 million in order to land the contract. The brothers stood trial in 1977 for authorizing the bribes; Bronson was acquitted, but the court convicted Fritz on 29 counts. Before Fritz entered prison (he served 16 months of a four-year sentence), he and his brother split their company. Fritz took the energy operations and went bust in the 1980s. Bronson took the barge and book businesses and formed Ingram Industries.

The new company formed computer products distributor Ingram Computer in 1982 and between 1985 and 1989 bought all the stock of Micro D, a computer wholesaler. Ingram Computer and Micro D merged to form Ingram Micro. In 1992 it acquired Commtron, the world's #1 wholesaler of prerecorded videocassettes, and merged it into Ingram Entertainment.

When Bronson died in mid-1995, his wife Martha (the PR director) became chairman and began a restructuring. Ingram Industries closed its non-bookstore rack distributor (Ingram Merchandising) in 1995 and sold its oil-and-gas machinery subsidiary (Cactus Co.) in 1996. It spun off Ingram Micro in 1996, followed in 1997 by Ingram Entertainment. Ingram Industries purchased Christian books distributor Spring Arbor that year and also introduced an on-demand book publishing service (Lightning Print).

The company agreed to sell its book group to Barnes & Noble for $600 million in late 1998, but FTC pressure killed the deal in mid-1999. With customers and competitors increasing distribution capacity in the western US, a resulting drop in business led Ingram Industries to cut more than 100 jobs at an Oregon warehouse in 1999.

In early 2000 Ingram renamed Lightning Print as Lightning Source. Also that year Ingram announced plans to distribute products other than books for e-tailers (starting with gifts). In March 2001 Ingram took over the specialty-book distribution for Borders.

In July 2002 Ingram completed its acquisition of Midland Enterprises LLC, a leading US inland marine transportation company that includes The Ohio River Company LLC and Orgulf Transport LLC.

OFFICERS

Chairman: Martha Ingram
Vice Chairman; Chairman, Ingram Book Group:
John R. Ingram, age 40
**President and CEO; Chairman, Ingram Barge
Company:** Orrin H. Ingram II
VP, Treasurer, and Controller: Mary K. Cavarra
VP, Human Resources: Dennis Delaney
President and CEO, Ingram Book Group:
Michael Lovett
**President, Ingram Book Company and COO, Ingram
Book Group:** Jim Chandler
President, Spring Arbor Distributors: Steve Arthur

LOCATIONS

HQ: 1 Belle Meade Place, 4400 Harding Rd.,
Nashville, TN 37205
Phone: 615-298-8200   **Fax:** 615-298-8242
Web: www.ingram.com

PRODUCTS/OPERATIONS

Selected Operations

Ingram Book Group
Ingram Book Company (wholesaler of trade books and
audiobooks)
Ingram Customer Systems (computerized systems and
services)
Ingram International (international distribution of
books and audiobooks)
Ingram Library Services (distributes books, audiobooks,
and videos to libraries)
Ingram Periodicals (direct distributor of specialty
magazines)
Ingram Publisher Relations (publishing services for
publishers)
Lightning Source (on-demand printing and electronic
publishing)
Specialty Retail (book distributor to nontraditional book
market)
Spring Arbor Distributors (products and services for
Christian retailers)

Ingram Insurance Group
Permanent General Insurance Co. (automobile
insurance in California, Florida, Georgia, Indiana,
Louisiana, Ohio, South Carolina, Tennessee, and
Wisconsin)

Ingram Marine Group
Ingram Barge (ships grain, ore, and other products)
Ingram Materials Co. (produces construction materials
such as sand and gravel)

COMPETITORS

Advanced Marketing
Allstate
American Commercial Lines
American Financial
Baker & Taylor
Chas. Levy
Follett
Hudson News
Kirby
Media Source
Progressive Corporation
SAFECO
State Farm
TECO Energy
Thomas Nelson
Times Publishing

HISTORICAL FINANCIALS & EMPLOYEES

Private FYE: December 31	Annual Growth	12/92	12/93	12/94	12/95	12/96	12/97	12/98	12/99	12/00	12/01
Sales ($ mil.)	(9.5%)	4,657	6,163	8,010	11,000	1,463	1,796	2,000	2,135	2,075	1,900
Employees	(2.8%)	8,407	9,658	10,000	13,000	5,300	6,362	6,500	6,080	6,494	6,500

SALES HISTORY

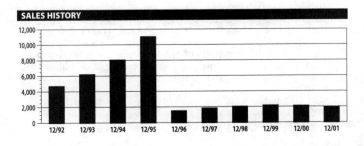

INGRAM MICRO INC.

There's nothing micro about Ingram. Santa Ana, California-based Ingram Micro is the world's largest wholesale distributor of computer products. It offers more than 280,000 items (including PCs, mass storage and networking devices, CD-ROM drives, printers, and software) to 175,000 reseller customers worldwide. Its suppliers include Seagate, Compaq, Corel, and Cisco. The company also provides logistics, financing, marketing, and warehousing services. More than half of its business comes from the US.

Ingram Micro has had a history of summer-movie-plot-thin profit margins, as it has been challenged by the trend toward lower PC prices. Its response has been to streamline operations, offer its order fulfillment and other e-commerce services, look to overseas markets for growth, and most recently expand its array of network and product support services to appease product vendors such as 3Com.

The Ingram family (three members serve as directors) controls more than 70% of the company's voting power.

HISTORY

There is no love lost between the former Micro D and Ingram Industries. Micro D was founded in Fountain Valley, California, in 1979 by husband-and-wife entrepreneurs Geza Csige and Lorraine Mecca. As the company grew, Mecca sought to merge the computer distributor with a partner that could take over daily operations. She relinquished control of Micro D to Linwood "Chip" Lacy in 1986 and sold her 51% share of the company to minority shareholder Ingram Distribution Group.

Sales bottomed out for Micro D that year. Lacy tightened Micro D's belt and took huge charges for outdated inventory it sold at a discount and overdue payments from customers that had gone bankrupt.

At the same time, Ingram Industries was busy merging recently acquired Ingram Software Distribution Services of Buffalo, New York, with Compton, California-based Softeam. The merger made the company one of the nation's largest wholesale distributors of computer software. Lacy saw Ingram's purchase of Micro D shares as a conflict of interest, but he was too busy returning Micro D to profitability: centralizing its marketing and distribution functions, cutting costs, and expanding its market to include more small retailers, which provided higher margins. Micro D went from the fourth-largest distributor of microcomputer products to #1 in just one year.

The surging PC market in the late 1980s fueled Micro D's growth. By 1988 the firm had expanded outside the US for the first time, acquiring Canadian company Frantek Computer Products.

Ingram Industries offered to acquire the 41% of outstanding Micro D stock it did not own in 1988, but Lacy resisted, preferring to let Ingram wait. Though Ingram owned a majority of Micro D stock, it only controlled three of seven seats on the board. Ingram was forced to play Lacy's game and finally acquired the company at a higher cost in 1989. The new company, which controlled 20% of the computer distribution market, was called Ingram Micro D. The merger was anything but smooth, and several Micro D executives jumped ship.

As the PC took hold in the US in the 1990s, Ingram Micro D became the dominant industry player, but relations between Lacy and the Ingram family never improved. The company shortened its name to Ingram Micro in 1991, and two years later, as it was hitting stride, Lacy announced plans to leave. To keep him, Ingram Industries CEO Bronson Ingram (much to his distaste) promised to let Lacy take the company public.

Bronson Ingram died in 1995 and the next year his widow, Martha, forced Lacy's resignation. Lacy was replaced by Jerre Stead, formerly CEO of software maker LEGENT (bought by Computer Associates), who devised a compensation package for himself consisting solely of stock options (no salary) and listed "Head Coach" on his business card. Ingram went public a few months after Stead took over.

In 1998 Ingram Micro forged a distribution alliance with Japanese computer giant SOFTBANK and bought a majority stake in German computer products distributor Macrotron. It also expanded into build-to-order PC manufacturing. Amid softer PC sales industrywide, Ingram Micro in 1999 terminated nearly 600 employees as part of a worldwide realignment, and signed a deal (worth an estimated $10 billion) with CompUSA to be its primary PC manufacturer and distributor.

Later in 1999 Stead — with Ingram Micro's sales slipping and its stock slumping — made plans to step down as CEO. The search for a replacement ended in 2000 when the company named GTE veteran Kent Foster to the post.

The next year Ingram Micro expanded its portfolio of services for enterprises and began offering more extensive network and product support services.

OFFICERS

Chairman and CEO: Kent B. Foster, age 58,
  $1,128,823 pay
President and COO: Michael J. Grainger, age 49,
  $772,305 pay
EVP and CFO: Thomas A. Madden, age 48
EVP and Chief Strategy and Information Officer:
  Guy P. Abramo, age 40, $453,228 pay
EVP; President, Ingram Micro Asia Pacific:
  Hans T. Koppen, age 59
EVP; President, Ingram Micro Europe:
  Gregory M.E. Spierkel, age 45
EVP; President, Ingram Micro North America:
  Kevin M. Murai, age 38, $498,229 pay
SVP, Secretary, and General Counsel:
  James E. Anderson Jr., age 54, $466,469 pay
SVP; General Manager, IM-Logistics: Michael Terrell
SVP; President, Ingram Micro Latin America:
  Asger Falstrup, age 52
SVP, Human Resources: David M. Finley, age 61
VP, Channel and US Marketing: Bob Stegner
Auditors: PricewaterhouseCoopers LLP

LOCATIONS

HQ: 1600 E. St. Andrew Place, Santa Ana, CA 92705
Phone: 714-566-1000   **Fax:** 714-566-7900
Web: www.ingrammicro.com/corp

2001 Sales

	$ mil.	% of total
US	13,507	54
Europe	7,157	28
Other regions	4,523	18
Total	**25,187**	**100**

PRODUCTS/OPERATIONS

Selected Products
CD-ROM, CD-RW, and DVD drives
Computer supplies and accessories
Consumer electronics
Desktop and notebook PCs, servers, and workstations
Mass storage devices
Modems
Monitors
Networking hubs, routers, and switches
Network interface cards
PDAs
Printers
Scanners
Software (business and entertainment)
Wireless devices

Selected Services
Contract manufacturing
Credit and collection management
Customer care
End-to-end order fulfillment
Logistics and transportation management
Marketing services
Product procurement
Warehouse services

COMPETITORS

Arrow Electronics	Deltron International	Otto Versand
ASI Corp.	Intcomex	Pioneer-Standard Electronics
Avnet	MAXDATA	Scribona
Bell Microproducts	Merisel	Software House
Daisytek	New Age Electronics	SYNNEX
		Tech Data

HISTORICAL FINANCIALS & EMPLOYEES

NYSE: IM FYE: Saturday nearest Dec. 31	Annual Growth	12/92	12/93	12/94	12/95	12/96	12/97	12/98	12/99	12/00	12/01
Sales ($ mil.)	28.0%	2,731	4,044	5,830	8,617	12,024	16,582	22,034	28,069	30,715	25,187
Net income ($ mil.)	(15.7%)	31	50	63	84	111	194	245	183	226	7
Income as % of sales	—	1.1%	1.2%	1.1%	1.0%	0.9%	1.2%	1.1%	0.7%	0.7%	0.0%
Earnings per share ($)	(43.6%)	—	—	—	—	0.88	1.32	1.64	1.24	1.52	0.05
Stock price - FY high ($)		—	—	—	—	28.13	34.75	54.63	36.31	21.13	17.48
Stock price - FY low ($)		—	—	—	—	20.00	19.00	26.63	10.00	10.19	10.69
Stock price - FY close ($)	(5.5%)	—	—	—	—	23.00	29.13	35.38	13.13	11.25	17.32
P/E - high		—	—	—	—	28	24	31	29	14	291
P/E - low		—	—	—	—	20	13	15	8	7	178
Dividends per share ($)		—	—	—	—	0.00	0.00	0.00	0.00	0.00	0.00
Book value per share ($)	15.3%	—	—	—	—	6.15	7.69	9.86	13.66	12.82	12.53
Employees	11.4%	—	—	—	7,604	9,008	12,000	14,400	15,363	16,500	14,500

STOCK PRICE HISTORY

HIGH/LOW/CLOSE

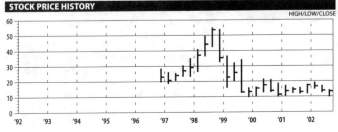

2001 FISCAL YEAR-END

Debt ratio: 9.9%
Return on equity: 0.4%
Cash ($ mil.): 273
Current ratio: 1.42
Long-term debt ($ mil.): 205
No. of shares (mil.): 149
Dividends
  Yield: —
  Payout: —
Market value ($ mil.): 2,581

INTEL CORPORATION

Kingpin. Top dog. Leviathan. Intel. Any way you phrase it, Santa Clara, California-based Intel is by far the world's top semiconductor maker. Though best known for its microprocessors — about four-fifths of all new PCs have them — Intel also makes flash memories (where it's also #1 globally) and embedded semiconductors for the communications and industrial equipment markets. PC giant Dell accounts for 14% of sales. Faced with softening worldwide PC markets, Intel has diversified beyond PC chips, especially with a push into communications chips that has included numerous acquisitions.

Intel's long-running battle with smaller archrival AMD heated up as AMD's successful Athlon processor won market share away from Intel's Pentium. AMD pulled off its coup through timely introductions of high-performance chips during a period when Intel experienced uncharacteristic component shortages and manufacturing glitches. Intel struck back with rounds of price cuts and an unusually aggressive schedule for introducing faster Pentium models.

Intel has also spent billions developing the powerful 64-bit Itanium microprocessor with Hewlett-Packard. After being beset by problems stemming from the complexity of its all-new architecture, Itanium debuted (years behind schedule) in mid-2001. Though sales of the initial generation of Itanium chips were far from impressive, the Itanium project will be worth the effort — and a major headache for competitors such as Sun Microsystems — if its design becomes the de facto standard for servers as the Pentium has been for PCs. (Intel is also pursuing a similar "platform architecture" strategy with its chips for handheld wireless devices and network backbone equipment.)

CEO Craig Barrett, who won a sterling reputation in his days as Intel's manufacturing chief, has launched companywide initiatives to refocus Intel on flawless execution. The company has announced new service offerings directly related to its chip expertise, including design centers to help customers bring to market their own application-specific integrated circuits (ASICs) and telematics devices.

HISTORY

In 1968 three engineers from Fairchild Semiconductor created Intel in Mountain View, California, to develop technology for silicon-based chips. ("Intel" is a contraction of "integrated electronics.") The trio consisted of Robert Noyce (who co-invented the integrated circuit, or IC, in 1958), Gordon Moore, and Andy Grove.

Intel initially provided computer memory

chips such as DRAMs (1970) and EPROMs (1971). These chips' success funded the microprocessor designs that revolutionized the electronics industry. In 1979 Moore became Intel's chairman and Grove its president. (Grove became CEO in 1987.) When Intel's 8088 chip was chosen for IBM's PC in 1981, Intel secured its place as the microcomputer standard-setter.

Cutthroat pricing by Japanese competitors forced Intel out of the DRAM market in 1985; in a breathtaking strategy shift that has become the subject of countless business school case studies, the company refocused on microprocessors. It licensed its 286 chip technology to Advanced Micro Devices (AMD) and others in an effort to create an industry standard. Reacting to AMD's escalating market share (which stood at more than half by 1990), Intel fiercely protected the technology of its 386 (1985) and 486 (1989) chips; AMD sued for breach of contract.

Intel and AMD settled several microcode suits in 1995: AMD got the code license and Intel won $58 million in damages. Rather than fight an accusation from Digital Equipment (later acquired by Compaq) that Intel stole its technology to develop the Pentium processor, Intel bought Digital's semiconductor operations.

Grove handed the CEO reins to president Craig Barrett in 1998; Grove replaced Moore as chairman, while Moore became chairman emeritus. (Thanks to a mandatory retirement age he helped set, Moore retired from Intel's board in 2001.)

Also in 1998 Intel unveiled its low-end Celeron chip. After a wrenching delay, Intel unveiled a chipset to support Rambus' RDRAM memory architecture in 1999. The delay contributed to a big loss of chipset market share, allowing VIA Technologies to pull even with Intel. Late in 1999 the company began shipping prototypes of its Itanium 64-bit processor; Itanium's general release was delayed repeatedly, ultimately into mid-2001.

A string of other problems beset Intel in 2000. The company recalled hundreds of thousands of its motherboards that were distributed with a defective chip, and later cancelled development of a low-cost microprocessor for budget PCs. Also in 2000 Intel began debuting its line of consumer Web appliances and interactive toys. The company later released the long-awaited Pentium 4 processor.

In mid-2001 Intel announced a major deal with Compaq under which Compaq would use the Itanium architecture in all of its high-end servers by 2004; meanwhile Intel gained a license to Compaq's Alpha chip technology. (Intel later absorbed some Compaq chip design teams, as well as Itanium-related engineering groups from Hewlett-Packard, even before those two companies announced their gigantic merger.)

Later in 2001 the company announced that it would phase out its consumer electronics operations (Internet appliances and toys). In a move widely seen as an indication of the company's succession plan for top management, early in 2002 Intel promoted EVP Paul Otellini to president and COO.

OFFICERS

Chairman Emeritus: Gordon E. Moore, age 73
Chairman: Andrew S. Grove, age 65, $1,506,800 pay
CEO and Director: Craig R. Barrett, age 62, $1,650,300 pay
President, COO, and Director: Paul S. Otellini, age 51, $861,000 pay
EVP, CFO, and Chief Enterprise Services Officer: Andy D. Bryant, age 51, $728,000 pay
EVP; President, Intel Capital: Leslie L. Vadasz, age 65, $743,600 pay
EVP; General Manager, Intel Communications Group: Sean M. Maloney, age 45
EVP; Director, Sales and Marketing Group: Michael R. Splinter, age 51
SVP, General Counsel, and Secretary: F. Thomas Dunlap Jr., age 50
Auditors: Ernst & Young LLP

LOCATIONS

HQ: 2200 Mission College Blvd., Santa Clara, CA 95052
Phone: 408-765-8080   **Fax:** 408-765-6284
Web: www.intel.com

2001 Sales

	$ mil.	% of total
Asia/Pacific		
Japan	2,349	9
Other countries	8,308	31
US	9,382	35
Europe	6,500	25
Total	**26,539**	**100**

PRODUCTS/OPERATIONS

2001 Sales

	$ mil.	% of total
Architecture Business Group	21,446	81
Communications Group	2,580	10
Wireless Communications & Computing Group	2,232	8
Other	281	1
Total	**26,539**	**100**

COMPETITORS

3Com	IBM	Philips
AMD	Microelectronics	Semiconductors
Agere Systems	LSI Logic	QUALCOMM
Analog Devices	Micron	Sharp
ATI Technologies	Technology	Sony
Broadcom	Mitsubishi	STMicroelectronics
Cisco Systems	Electric	Sun
Conexant	Motorola	Microsystems
Systems	National	Texas
EDS	Semiconductor	Instruments
Fujitsu	NEC	Toshiba
Hewlett-Packard	NVIDIA	Transmeta
Hitachi		VIA Technologies

HISTORICAL FINANCIALS & EMPLOYEES

Nasdaq: INTC FYE: Last Saturday in Dec.	Annual Growth	12/92	12/93	12/94	12/95	12/96	12/97	12/98	12/99	12/00	12/01
Sales ($ mil.)	18.3%	5,844	8,782	11,521	16,202	20,847	25,070	26,273	29,389	33,726	26,539
Net income ($ mil.)	2.1%	1,067	2,295	2,288	3,566	5,157	6,945	6,068	7,314	10,535	1,291
Income as % of sales	—	18.2%	26.1%	19.9%	22.0%	24.7%	27.7%	23.1%	24.9%	31.2%	4.9%
Earnings per share ($)	1.9%	0.16	0.33	0.33	0.51	0.73	0.97	0.87	1.06	1.51	0.19
Stock price - FY high ($)	—	2.86	4.64	4.59	9.80	17.69	25.50	31.55	44.75	75.81	38.59
Stock price - FY low ($)	—	1.45	2.67	3.17	3.94	6.23	15.72	16.41	25.06	29.81	18.96
Stock price - FY close ($)	31.3%	2.72	3.88	3.99	7.09	16.37	17.56	29.64	41.16	30.06	31.45
P/E - high	—	18	13	13	18	22	24	35	41	48	203
P/E - low	—	9	8	9	7	8	15	18	23	19	100
Dividends per share ($)	26.0%	0.01	0.02	0.02	0.02	0.03	0.03	0.04	0.06	0.07	0.08
Book value per share ($)	23.3%	0.81	1.12	1.40	1.85	2.57	2.96	3.53	4.88	5.55	5.36
Employees	13.9%	25,800	29,500	32,600	41,600	48,500	63,700	64,500	70,200	86,100	83,400

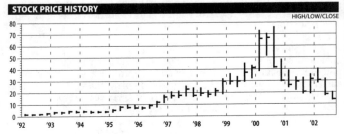

STOCK PRICE HISTORY
HIGH/LOW/CLOSE

2001 FISCAL YEAR-END

Debt ratio: 2.8%
Return on equity: 3.5%
Cash ($ mil.): 7,970
Current ratio: 2.68
Long-term debt ($ mil.): 1,050
No. of shares (mil.): 6,690
Dividends
 Yield: 0.3%
 Payout: 42.1%
Market value ($ mil.): 210,401

IBM

It may be big, but it carries its weight well. Armonk, New York-based International Business Machines (IBM) is the world's largest computer company. Among the leaders in almost every market in which it competes, the company makes desktop and notebook PCs, mainframe and servers, storage systems, microprocessors, and peripherals, among its thousands of products. IBM president Samuel Palmisano, who took over the CEO reins from venerated chairman Louis Gerstner in early 2002, has continued Big Blue's constant efforts to keep up with fast-moving competitors. IBM reorganized its hardware business, merging its desktop and laptop operations and concentrating on its leading enterprise server and storage products.

Though perhaps still best known for its hardware, IBM's growing services business is the largest in the world and accounts for about 40% of its sales. Looking it extend its lead, IBM has announced plans to acquire PricewaterhouseCoopers' consulting and IT services unit, PwC Consulting, for an estimated $3.5 billion in cash and stock.

IBM has largely used acquisitions to become a leader in yet another market — software — where it trails only Microsoft. A pioneer in server operating system software, IBM made an early move into messaging and network management software with its acquisitions of Lotus Development (1995) and Tivoli (1996). Its software operations now focused primarily on e-commerce infrastructure, IBM has continued its push beyond OS software, purchasing the database operations of Informix (2001) and application integration products from CrossWorlds Software (2002).

HISTORY

In 1914 National Cash Register's star salesman, Thomas Watson, left to rescue the flagging Computing-Tabulating-Recording (C-T-R) Company, the pioneer in US punch card processing that had been incorporated in 1911. Watson aggressively marketed C-T-R's tabulators, supplying them to the US government during WWI and tripling company revenues to almost $15 million by 1920. The company became International Business Machines (IBM) in 1924 and soon dominated the global market for tabulators, time clocks, and electric typewriters. It was the US's largest office machine maker by 1940.

IBM perfected electromechanical calculation (the Harvard Mark I, 1944) but initially dismissed the potential of computers. When Remington Rand's UNIVAC computer (1951) began replacing IBM machines, IBM quickly responded.

The company unveiled its first computer in 1952. With its superior research and development and marketing, IBM built a market share near 80% in the 1960s and 1970s. Its innovations included the STRETCH systems, which eliminated vacuum tubes (1960), and the first compatible family of computers, the System/360 (1964). IBM also developed floppy disks (1971) and the first laser printer for computers (1975). The introduction of the IBM PC in 1981 ignited the personal computer industry, sparking a barrage of PC clones. Through it all IBM was the subject of a 12-year government antitrust investigation that ended in 1982.

The shift to smaller, open systems, along with greater competition in all of IBM's segments, caused wrenching change. Instead of responding to the market need for cheap PCs and practical business applications, IBM stubbornly stuck with mainframes, and rivals began capitalizing on Big Blue's technology. After posting profits of $6.6 billion in 1984, the company began a slow slide. It sold many noncomputer businesses, including its copier division to Kodak in 1988 and its Lexmark typewriter business in 1991.

In 1993 CEO John Akers was replaced by Louis Gerstner, the first outsider to run IBM. He began to turn the ailing, artifact-status company around by slashing costs and nonstrategic divisions, cutting the workforce, shaking up entrenched management, and pushing services. In 1994 Big Blue reported its first profit in four years. It also began making computer chips that year.

Beefing up its software offerings, IBM bought spreadsheet pioneer Lotus in 1995 and network management specialist Tivoli in 1996. Expanding its Web focus to include small businesses, IBM bought Internet server maker Sequent in 1999. Hoping to turn around its ailing PC business, IBM axed manufacturing staff and halted sales of its PCs through US retailers that same year.

Looking to bolster its data management division, IBM purchased the database software unit of Informix for $1 billion in 2001. In early 2002, IBM announced it would outsource a significant amount of the manufacturing of its NetVista PC line to Sanmina-SCI; as part of the deal, Sanmina-SCI agreed to purchase IBM's desktop manufacturing operations in the US and Europe.

Later in 2002 COO Samuel Palmisano succeeded Gerstner as CEO; Gerstner remained chairman. IBM then agreed to form a joint venture with Hitachi to combine the companies' disk drive operations, with an initial investment of about $2 billion from Hitachi netting it a 70% stake in the new company, and further payments to IBM over the next three years resulting in full ownership by the Japanese giant.

OFFICERS

Chairman: Louis V. Gerstner Jr., age 60, $10,000,000 pay (prior to title change)
Vice Chairman: John M. Thompson, age 59, $2,125,000 pay
President, CEO, and Director: Samuel J. Palmisano, age 50, $4,100,000 pay (prior to promotion)
SVP and CFO: John R. Joyce, age 48, $1,168,750 pay
SVP and General Counsel: Edward M. Lineen, age 61
SVP; Group Executive, IBM Global Financing: Joseph C. Lane, age 48
SVP; Group Executive, IBM Global Services: Douglas T. Elix, age 53
SVP; Group Executive, Personal Systems and Integrated Supply Chain: Robert W. Moffat Jr., age 45
SVP; Group Executive, Sales and Distribution: J. Michael Lawrie, age 48
SVP; Group Executive, Technology: John E. Kelly III, age 48
SVP; Group Executive, Technology and Manufacturing Group: Nicholas M. Donofrio, age 56, $1,175,000 pay
SVP, Human Resources: J. Randall MacDonald, age 53
Auditors: PricewaterhouseCoopers LLP

LOCATIONS

HQ: International Business Machines Corporation
New Orchard Rd., Armonk, NY 10504
Phone: 914-499-1900 **Fax:** 914-765-7382
Web: www.ibm.com

2001 Sales

	$ mil.	% of total
US	35,215	41
Japan	11,514	13
Other countries	39,137	46
Total	**85,866**	**100**

PRODUCTS/OPERATIONS

2001 Sales

	$ mil.	% of total
Services	37,603	40
Hardware		
Enterprise systems	14,453	15
Personal & printing	12,055	13
Technology	10,295	11
Software	13,920	15
Financing	4,243	5
Enterprise investments & other	1,122	1
Adjustments	(7,825)	—
Total	**85,866**	**100**

COMPETITORS

Accenture	Matsushita
Alcatel	McKinsey & Company
BEA Systems	Microsoft
Canon	Motorola
Cap Gemini	NEC
Computer Associates	Novell
Computer Sciences	NTT DATA
Dell Computer	Oracle
Deloitte Consulting	Ricoh
EDS	SAP
EMC	Seiko Epson
Ericsson	SGI
Fujitsu	Siemens
Gateway	Sony
Hewlett-Packard	Sun Microsystems
Hitachi	Taiwan Semiconductor
Hitachi Data Systems	Texas Instruments
Intel	Toshiba
KPMG Consulting	Unisys
Lexmark International	Xerox

HISTORICAL FINANCIALS & EMPLOYEES

NYSE: IBM FYE: December 31	Annual Growth	12/92	12/93	12/94	12/95	12/96	12/97	12/98	12/99	12/00	12/01
Sales ($ mil.)	3.2%	64,523	62,716	64,052	71,940	75,947	78,508	81,667	87,548	88,396	85,866
Net income ($ mil.)	—	(4,965)	(8,101)	3,021	4,178	5,429	6,093	6,328	7,712	8,093	7,723
Income as % of sales	—	—	—	4.7%	5.8%	7.1%	7.8%	7.7%	8.8%	9.2%	9.0%
Earnings per share ($)	—	(2.17)	(3.56)	1.24	1.77	2.51	3.01	3.29	4.12	4.44	4.35
Stock price – FY high ($)	—	25.09	14.97	19.09	28.66	41.50	56.75	94.97	139.19	134.94	124.70
Stock price – FY low ($)	—	12.19	10.16	12.84	17.56	20.78	31.78	47.81	80.88	80.06	83.75
Stock price – FY close ($)	28.6%	12.59	14.13	18.38	22.84	37.88	52.31	92.19	107.88	85.00	120.96
P/E – high	—	—	—	15	16	16	18	28	33	29	28
P/E – low	—	—	—	10	10	8	10	14	19	17	19
Dividends per share ($)	(8.4%)	1.21	0.40	0.25	0.25	0.33	0.39	0.43	0.41	0.51	0.55
Book value per share ($)	1.4%	12.09	8.49	9.96	10.23	10.64	10.34	10.61	11.50	10.89	13.70
Employees	0.7%	301,542	256,207	219,839	225,347	240,615	269,465	291,067	307,401	316,303	319,876

STOCK PRICE HISTORY

HIGH/LOW/CLOSE

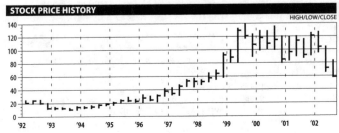

2001 FISCAL YEAR-END

Debt ratio: 40.3%
Return on equity: 35.1%
Cash ($ mil.): 6,330
Current ratio: 1.21
Long-term debt ($ mil.): 15,963
No. of shares (mil.): 1,723
Dividends
  Yield: 0.5%
  Payout: 12.6%
Market value ($ mil.): 208,438

INTERNATIONAL FLAVORS

A rose by any other name would smell sweeter if New York City-based International Flavors & Fragrances (IFF) had anything to do with it. A leading producer of flavors and fragrances, IFF markets primarily to cosmetics manufacturers, household care product makers, and food companies. IFF has manufacturing, sales, and distribution facilities in more than 40 countries. Sales outside North America account for nearly 70% of revenues.

IFF's fragrances, which contribute more than 50% of sales, are sold to producers of perfumes, cosmetics, deodorants, detergents, hair care products, and soaps. IFF's flavors are sold to makers of prepared foods, dairy products, beverages, confectionery products, and pharmaceuticals. The compounds used in the company's products are made both synthetically and from natural ingredients such as flowers and fruits.

IFF's acquisition of rival Bush Boake Allen in 2000 has led to a company-wide reorganization, including the closing of some manufacturing, distribution and sales facilities worldwide. IFF continues to introduce new products and to invest heavily in product development, which accounts for more than 7% of its expenses. The van Ameringen family controls about 20% of the company.

HISTORY

International Flavors & Fragrances (IFF) began in 1929 when Dutch immigrant and perfumer A. L. van Ameringen (who originally came to the US to work for the agent of the Dutch firm Polak & Schwarz, later leaving to form his own business) and William Haebler formed a fragrance company, van Ameringen-Haebler, in New York City.

The company produced the fragrance for Youth Dew, Estée Lauder's first big cosmetics hit, in 1953. One biographer of Estée Lauder linked her romantically with van Ameringen after her 1939 divorce (she later remarried Joseph Lauder). The business association with van Ameringen's company endured, and by the late 1980s it had produced an estimated 90% of Estée Lauder's fragrances.

In 1958 the company changed its name to International Flavors & Fragrances after it bought Polak & Schwarz. The US market for fragrances grew as consumers bought items such as air fresheners and manufacturers began adding fragrances to household cleaning items.

Henry Walter, who became CEO when van Ameringen retired in 1963, expanded IFF's presence overseas. Walter boasted, "Most of the great soap fragrances have been ours." So have many famous French perfumes, but most perfume companies wanted to cultivate product mystique, preventing IFF from taking credit for its scents.

Most of IFF's products were made for manufacturers of consumer goods. But under Walter's direction in the 1970s, IFF's R&D team experimented to find scents for museum exhibits and participated in Masters & Johnson research on the connection between sex and smell. Said Walter, "Our business is sex and hunger."

During the early 1980s IFF conducted fragrance research for relieving stress, lowering blood pressure, and alleviating depression. In 1982 IFF researchers developed a way to bind odors to plastic, a process used by makers of garbage bags and toys.

Walter retired in 1985 and Eugene Grisanti became CEO. After a three-year slump in new creations, IFF developed fragrances for several prestigious perfumes (Eternity and Halston) in 1988. IFF enhanced its position in dairy flavors with its 1991 purchase of Wisconsin-based Auro Tech. In 1993 IFF's Living Flower process successfully synthesized the fragrance of growing flowers for perfumes.

IFF inaugurated its flavor and fragrance facility in China (Guangzhou) and formed a joint venture with China's Hangzhou Xin'anjiang Perfumery Factory. The company reasserted its leadership in the US fragrance market in 1996 with the launch of two IFF-developed fragrances: Elizabeth Taylor's Black Pearls and Escada's Jardin de Soleil.

Sales and profits dipped in 1997, prompting IFF to consolidate production. Asia's economic crisis and turmoil in Russia continued to hurt profits in 1998, and in 1999 IFF was hit by the devaluation of Brazil's currency, weak demand for aroma chemicals, and the US dollar's strength against the euro.

In 2000 Unilever executive Richard Goldstein was appointed chairman and CEO. Boosting its natural ingredients operations, IFF bought Laboratoire Monique Remy (France). The same year IFF acquired rival fragrance and flavor maker Bush Boake Allen in a deal worth about $1 billion.

In 2001 the company sold its US and Brazilian formulated fruit and vegetable preparation businesses and its aroma chemicals business in the UK.

OFFICERS

Chairman and CEO: Richard A. Goldstein, age 60, $1,318,443 pay
EVP, Global Operations: D. Wayne Howard, age 46, $521,850 pay
EVP: Julian W. Boyden, age 57, $653,875 pay
SVP, CFO, and Director: Douglas J. Wetmore, age 44

SVP, General Counsel, and Secretary: Stephen A. Block,
age 57, $3,949,898 pay
VP, Asia-Pacific: Robert Burns
VP, Central Asia and the Middle East: Bruce J. Edwards
VP, Corporate Communications: Gail S. Belmuth,
age 38
VP, Europe: Robert J. Edelman
VP, Fabric, Home and Personal Wash: Robert J. Gordon
VP, Fine Fragrances and Toiletries: Nicolas Mirzayantz
**VP, Flavor and Fragrance Ingredient Sales and
Marketing:** Peter A. Thorburn, age 57
VP, Flavors: Neil Humphreys
VP, Global Human Resources: Steven J. Heaslip, age 44
VP, Latin America: Graciela M. Ferro
VP, North America: James H. Dunsdon
VP, Research and Development: Clint D. Brooks, age 50
VP: Sophia Grojsman
VP: José A. Rodriguez
Treasurer: Charles D. Weller
Auditors: PricewaterhouseCoopers LLP

LOCATIONS

HQ: International Flavors & Fragrances Inc.
521 W. 57th St., New York, NY 10019
Phone: 212-765-5500   **Fax:** 212-708-7132
Web: www.iff.com

2001 Sales

	$ mil.	% of total
Europe	577	31
Central Asia, Middle East	127	7
North America	597	32
Latin America	257	14
Asia/Pacific	286	16
Total	**1,844**	**100**

PRODUCTS/OPERATIONS

2001 Sales

	$ mil.	% of total
Fragrance products	1,008	55
Flavor products	836	45
Total	**1,844**	**100**

Fragrance Uses	Flavor Uses
Aftershave lotions	Alcoholic beverages
Air fresheners	Baked goods
All-purpose cleaners	Candies
Colognes	Dairy products
Cosmetic creams	Desserts
Deodorants	Diet foods
Detergents	Drink powders
Hair care products	Pharmaceuticals
Laundry soap	Prepared foods
Lipsticks	Snacks
Lotions	Soft drinks
Perfumes	
Powders	
Soaps	

COMPETITORS

BASF AG	Imperial Chemical
Bayer	Joh. A. Benckiser
Bayer AG	McCormick
Hauser	Millennium Chemicals
Heller Seasonings	Roche
Henkel	Sensient
Hercules	Unilever
Hoffmann-La Roche	Wrigley
Human Pheromone	
Sciences	

HISTORICAL FINANCIALS & EMPLOYEES

NYSE: IFF FYE: December 31	Annual Growth	12/92	12/93	12/94	12/95	12/96	12/97	12/98	12/99	12/00	12/01
Sales ($ mil.)	5.6%	1,126	1,189	1,315	1,440	1,436	1,427	1,407	1,440	1,463	1,844
Net income ($ mil.)	(4.2%)	171	203	226	249	190	218	204	162	123	116
Income as % of sales	—	15.1%	17.0%	17.2%	17.3%	13.2%	15.3%	14.5%	11.3%	8.4%	6.3%
Earnings per share ($)	(2.3%)	1.48	1.77	2.02	2.22	1.70	1.99	1.90	1.53	1.22	1.20
Stock price - FY high ($)	—	38.71	39.79	47.88	55.88	51.88	53.44	51.88	48.50	37.94	31.69
Stock price - FY low ($)	—	31.47	32.97	35.63	45.13	40.75	39.88	32.06	33.63	14.69	19.75
Stock price - FY close ($)	(2.2%)	36.21	37.88	46.25	48.00	45.00	51.50	44.19	37.63	20.31	29.71
P/E - high	—	25	22	24	25	30	27	27	32	31	26
P/E - low	—	21	19	18	20	24	20	17	22	12	16
Dividends per share ($)	(4.5%)	0.91	1.00	1.08	1.24	1.36	1.44	1.48	1.52	1.52	0.60
Book value per share ($)	(4.6%)	8.47	7.96	9.04	10.06	9.79	9.17	8.91	8.19	5.45	5.53
Employees	3.8%	4,242	4,371	4,570	4,650	4,630	4,640	4,670	4,680	6,610	5,929

STOCK PRICE HISTORY

HIGH/LOW/CLOSE

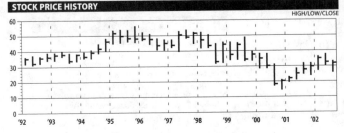

2001 FISCAL YEAR-END

Debt ratio: 64.2%
Return on equity: 20.1%
Cash ($ mil.): 49
Current ratio: 1.60
Long-term debt ($ mil.): 939
No. of shares (mil.): 95
Dividends
  Yield: 2.0%
  Payout: 50.0%
Market value ($ mil.): 2,815

INTERNATIONAL MULTIFOODS

International Multifoods is counting on that spare change in your pocket. The #1 distributor to the vending industry in the US, the Minnetonka, Minnesota-based food processor distributes more than 5,000 products — including candy, snacks, pastries, and beverages — to about 13,000 vending machine operators, coffee service operators, and others. It also distributes food and supplies to independent restaurants, sandwich shops, movie theaters, and other concessionaires. (The company is selling its foodservice distribution business to reduce debt.)

The company's U.S. Foods unit produces commercial baking mixes (including Pillsbury cake mixes), frozen batters, and doughs for in-store and food service baking operations. In Canada its Robin Hood Multifoods unit produces the #1 brand of consumer flours and baking mixes (Robin Hood) and a leading brand of pickles and condiments (Bick's). It also sells hot cereals (Old Mill, Purity).

Once one of the Big Three in the flour business (with General Mills and Pillsbury), International Multifoods changed the ingredients in its business mix a few times before focusing on operations that predominantly serve the foodservice industry. However, it has moved back into consumer foods production with the purchase of the Pillsbury desserts and specialty products businesses from General Mills.

Agricultural processor Archer Daniels Midland owns nearly 9% of International Multifoods.

HISTORY

When Francis Bean's first flour mill went bankrupt, he rented a small mill and started the New Prague Flouring Mill Co. in 1892 in New Prague, Minnesota. Four years later the owner wanted the rented mill back, so Bean had to start over once again. The townspeople put up more than $30,000 to help him build a new mill, which retained the old name. Bean added more mills (including two in Canada in the early 1900s) and changed the company's name to International Milling (IM) in 1910. More than 20 years after his original mill had gone bankrupt, Bean sought out all of its unpaid creditors and paid them a total of more than $200,000.

IM added new mills in the 1920s, including ones in Iowa and New York. During WWII it helped the country meet the increased need for flour and also developed Alcomeal, a wheat product used to make grain alcohol for the production of synthetic rubber.

The company continued to expand, adding more mills (15 during and just after the war), enhancing its product line (acquiring an animal feed maker in 1951), and developing new services (it was the first miller to deliver bulk flour directly to commercial bakeries).

Exporting around the world by the late 1950s, IM decided to concentrate its efforts in Venezuela, where it held more than a third of the market. It went public in 1964 and began diversifying with more than 40 acquisitions ranging from a meat processing plant to Mr. Donut stores, with a particular emphasis on consumer companies. The International Multifoods name was adopted in 1970 to reflect the shift from commodities to consumer items.

In 1984 the company bought Vendors Supply of America, the largest US vending distributor. It then began purchasing food service operations (Fred's Frozen Foods in 1986 and Pueringer Distributing in 1987, among others) while selling off most of its consumer products, flour mills, seafood restaurants, and animal feed businesses. In 1993, two years after deciding to focus on value-added food products in the US, International Multifoods reversed its strategy and began selling its prepared foods operations.

International Multifoods bought Leprino Foods' specialty food distribution business — with an emphasis on supplying pizza restaurants — in 1994. The next year it added Alum Rock Foodservice. In 1997 the company shut down its unprofitable poultry exporting business. To better focus on its North American food service operations, in 1999 International Multifoods sold its Venezuelan operations. It also acquired food service distributor Better Brands for about $28 million.

The company sold its headquarters building in mid-2000 to pay down debt. To meet regulatory concerns, General Mills sold several business lines to International Multifoods in 2001 as part of its purchase of Pillsbury. These lines include the Farmhouse brand of rice and pasta side dishes; La Pina, a tortilla flour sold primarily on the West Coast; the Pet brand of evaporated milk and dry creamer; the Pillsbury line of desserts and specialty products (including Pillsbury cake mixes); Red Band, a biscuit flour sold primarily in the Southeast US; the Robin Hood flour business in the US; and Softasilk, a premium cake flour.

OFFICERS

Chairman and CEO: Gary E. Costley, age 58,
$715,000 pay
President and COO: Dan C. Swander, age 58
SVP, General Counsel, and Secretary:
Frank W. Bonvino, age 60, $297,292 pay
SVP; President, Multifoods Distribution Group:
Robert S. Wright, age 55, $359,300 pay

VP, Communications and Investor Relations:
Jill W. Schmidt, age 43
VP and Controller; CFO and VP, Finance, Multifoods Distribution Group: Dennis R. Johnson, age 50
VP, Finance and CFO: John E. Byom, age 48, $282,292 pay
VP, Human Resources and Administration:
Ralph P. Hargrow, age 50, $255,000 pay
VP, Research and Development: Daryl R. Schaller, age 58
VP, Supply Chain: Randall W. Cochran, age 48
VP and Treasurer: Gregory J. Keup, age 43
Chairman, Robin Hood Multifoods: Donald H. Twiner, age 62
VP; President, Multifoods Foodservice Products Division: Michael J. Wille, age 42
VP; President, Robin Hood Multifoods:
Martin Jamieson, age 42
VP; President, US Consumer Products:
James H. White, age 37
VP, Foodservice Sales and Marketing, Multifoods Distribution Group: Louis E. Kirchem
VP, Human Resources, Multifoods Distribution Group: Jane M. Manion
Auditors: KPMG LLP

LOCATIONS

HQ: International Multifoods Corporation
110 Cheshire Ln., Ste. 300, Minnetonka, MN 55305
Phone: 952-594-3300   **Fax:** 952-594-3304
Web: www.multifoods.com

International Multifoods has processing and distribution centers throughout the US and Canada.

PRODUCTS/OPERATIONS

2002 Sales

	$ mil.	% of total
Multifoods Distribution Group	2,238	78
Canadian Foods	283	10
US Foodservice Products	216	8
US Consumer Products	112	4
Total	**2,849**	**100**

Selected Operations

Food Service Distribution
  Cheeses
  Meats
  Snacks
Vending Distribution
  Candy
  Coffee service supplies
  Refrigerated products
  Snacks
Robin Hood Multifoods (Canada)
  Baking mixes
  Flour

Hot cereals
Pickles
U.S. Foods
Bakery mix products
Desserts
Evaporated milk and dry creamer
Flour
Potato mix and shelf-stable products
Rice and pasta side dishes

COMPETITORS

ARAMARK
ADM
Aurora Foods
BJs Wholesale Club
Chelsea Milling
Costco Wholesale
Country Home Bakers

FlowersFoods
General Mills
George Weston
Heinz
King Arthur Flour
MBM
McLane
Otis Spunkmeyer

Performance Food
Philip Morris
Sam's Club
Smart & Final
Sodexho
SYSCO
U.S. Foodservice

HISTORICAL FINANCIALS & EMPLOYEES

NYSE: IMC FYE: Last day in February	Annual Growth	2/93	2/94	2/95	2/96	2/97	2/98	2/99	2/00	2/01	2/02
Sales ($ mil.)	2.8%	2,224	2,225	2,295	2,523	2,596	2,612	2,297	2,385	2,525	2,849
Net income ($ mil.)	(15.4%)	41	(13)	57	24	3	20	(132)	5	21	9
Income as % of sales	—	1.9%	—	2.5%	1.0%	0.1%	0.8%	—	0.2%	0.8%	0.3%
Earnings per share ($)	(15.1%)	2.10	(0.72)	3.16	1.32	0.15	1.08	(6.98)	0.26	1.12	0.48
Stock price – FY high ($)	—	28.88	26.38	19.63	23.88	22.00	32.44	31.44	24.19	23.31	24.67
Stock price – FY low ($)	—	23.25	16.75	15.13	17.25	15.13	20.00	15.13	10.75	9.81	15.89
Stock price – FY close ($)	(2.2%)	25.75	17.38	18.63	18.63	21.13	27.94	21.69	10.94	18.79	21.05
P/E – high		14	—	6	18	147	30	—	90	21	48
P/E – low		11	—	5	13	101	18	—	40	9	31
Dividends per share ($)	—	0.80	0.80	0.80	0.80	0.80	0.80	0.80	0.80	0.80	0.00
Book value per share ($)	(1.8%)	16.85	13.11	16.36	16.66	16.08	16.51	13.86	13.61	13.66	14.33
Employees	(6.3%)	8,390	8,390	7,495	7,115	7,176	6,807	6,743	4,362	4,654	4,680

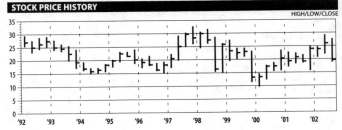

STOCK PRICE HISTORY   HIGH/LOW/CLOSE

2002 FISCAL YEAR-END

Debt ratio: 65.4%
Return on equity: 3.4%
Cash ($ mil.): 27
Current ratio: 1.74
Long-term debt ($ mil.): 515
No. of shares (mil.): 19
Dividends
  Yield: —
  Payout: —
Market value ($ mil.): 400

INTERNATIONAL PAPER COMPANY

More diverse and less international than its name suggests — about 80% of sales are in the US — International Paper is the world's largest forest-products company. Based in Stamford, Connecticut, International Paper's products include paper, pulp, packaging, and plywood. It also processes chemicals such as crude tall oil and crude sulfate turpentine (by-products of the papermaking process) and makes resins and inks through subsidiary Arizona Chemical. International Paper controls about 12 million acres of forest in the US and 1.5 million in Brazil, and it holds interests in 820,000 acres in New Zealand.

International Paper distributes printing, packaging, and graphic-art supplies in North America through subsidiary xpedx and in Europe through subsidiaries Papeteries de France, Scaldia (the Netherlands), and Impap in Poland.

To focus on its core paper, packaging, and forest-product businesses, International Paper has been shedding noncore operations. Total divestitures, including some timberlands, could reach $5 billion. The company has already sold its decorative products, masonite and flexible packaging operations; still on the block are the fine and premium papers, and Arizona Chemical businesses. A zealous consolidator, International Paper's notable purchases have included Union Camp, Shorewood Packaging, and papermaker Champion International. The company — which has announced plans to cut 10% of its US workforce — continues to take production downtimes in order to balance supply with customer demand.

HISTORY

Eighteen northeastern pulp and paper firms consolidated in 1898 to lower costs. The resulting International Paper had 20 mills in Maine, Massachusetts, New Hampshire, New York, and Vermont. The mills relied on forests in New England and Canada for wood pulp. When Canada enacted legislation to stop the export of pulpwood in 1919, International Paper formed Canadian International Paper.

In the 1920s International Paper built a hydroelectric plant on the Hudson River. Between 1928 and 1941 the company called itself International Paper & Power. It entered the market for kraft paper (paper sacks) in 1925 with the purchase of Bastrop Pulp & Paper (Louisiana).

During the 1940s and 1950s, the company bought Agar Manufacturing (shipping containers, 1940), Single Service Containers (Pure-Pak milk containers, 1946), and Lord Baltimore Press (folding cartons, 1958). It diversified in the 1960s and 1970s, buying Davol (hospital products, 1968; sold to C. R. Bard, 1980), American Central

(land development, 1968; sold to developers, 1974), and General Crude Oil (gas and oil, 1975; sold to Mobil Oil, 1979).

In the 1980s International Paper modernized its plants to focus on less-cyclical products. After selling Canadian International Paper in 1981, the company bought Hammermill Paper (office paper, 1986), Arvey (paper manufacturing and distribution, 1987), and Masonite (composite wood products, 1988). International Paper entered the European paper market in 1989 by buying Aussedat Rey (France), Ilford Group (UK), and Zanders (West Germany). In 1990 it bought Dixon Paper (distributor of paper and graphic arts supplies), Nevamar (laminates), and the UK's Cookson Group (printing plates).

International Paper expanded in the early 1990s with acquisitions such as Scaldia Papier (the Netherlands, 1991) and Western Paper (1992) and through investments in Carter Holt Harvey (New Zealand) and Scitex (Israel), a leading maker of electronic prepress systems. In 1994 International Paper formed a Chinese packaging joint venture and bought two Mexican paper-distributing companies. The next year it bought Seaman-Patrick Paper and Carpenter Paper (paper distribution), Micarta (high-pressure laminates), and DSM (inks and adhesives resins). In 1996 it bought Federal Paper Board, a forest- and paper-products firm.

After recording a loss in 1997, International Paper began downsizing: It sold $1 billion in marginal assets and cut its workforce by 10%. Branching its US box-making operations into the South and Midwest, International Paper bought Weston Paper & Manufacturing in 1998; it also bought Mead's distribution business. Then the company announced that it would close 25 plants in the combined enterprise. It also sold xpedx's grocery-supply business to Bunzl in 1998.

To preserve competition, in 1999 federal regulators axed International Paper's deal to sell its laminate business to Formica. However, the company did sell Formica its Fountainhead solid-surfacing business. International Paper paid $7.9 billion in 1999 for rival Union Camp.

International Paper acquired Shorewood Packaging for $850 million in 2000. That year it made an unsolicited $6.2 billion bid for Champion International — which had previously agreed to be acquired by UPM-Kymmene — igniting a bidding war. UPM withdrew its offer, however, and International Paper acquired Champion for about $9.6 billion. Also in 2000, the company sold its 68% stake in Bush Boake Allen for about $640 million.

In 2001 International Paper sold its Masonite Corp. operations to Premdor for $500 million.

The company also began cutting 10% (3,000 jobs) of its US workforce as part of a restructuring program.

International Paper sold its orient strand board facilities to Nexfor in April 2002 and also sold its decorative products division to an affiliate of Kohlberg & Company in July.

OFFICERS

Chairman and CEO: John T. Dillon, age 63, $1,730,625 pay
EVP and CFO: John V. Faraci, age 52, $664,417 pay
EVP, Administration, Information Technology, and Human Resources: Marianne M. Parrs, age 58
EVP, Legal and External Affairs: James P. Melican Jr., age 61, $732,250 pay
EVP, Papers: Robert M. Amen, age 52, $664,417 pay
EVP: David W. Oskin, age 59, $769,825 pay
SVP and CIO: J. Chris Scalet
SVP and General Counsel: William B. Lytton, age 53
SVP, Coated and SC Papers: L. H. Puckett
SVP, Consumer Packaging: Thomas E. Gestrich
SVP, Distribution: Thomas E. Costello
SVP, Human Resources: Jerome N. Carter
SVP, Sales and Marketing: Michael J. Balduino
Auditors: Deloitte & Touche LLP

LOCATIONS

HQ: 400 Atlantic St., Stamford, CT 06921
Phone: 203-541-8000   **Fax:** 203-397-1596
Web: www.ipaper.com

International Paper has manufacturing facilities primarily in the Americas, Asia, and Europe. It sells its products to more than 130 countries.

2001 Sales

	$ mil.	% of total
US	20,563	78
Europe	2,636	10
Pacific Rim	1,846	7
Other regions	1,318	5
Total	**26,363**	**100**

PRODUCTS/OPERATIONS

2001 Sales

	$ mil.	% of total
Forest Products	9,754	37
Paper	7,909	30
Packaging	7,382	28
Other	1,318	5
Total	**26,363**	**100**

Selected Products

Beverage packaging	Kraft paper
Bleached board	Lumber
Commercial printing papers	Molded products
Containerboard	Office and consumer papers
Factory-finished siding	Particleboard
Food service packaging	Plywood
Furniture components	Printing papers
Hardboard	Retail packaging
Industrial papers	Roof decking

COMPETITORS

Boise Cascade	Potlatch
Cascades Inc.	Temple-Inland
Louisiana-Pacific	Weyerhaeuser
Nippon Unipac	

HISTORICAL FINANCIALS & EMPLOYEES

NYSE: IP FYE: December 31	Annual Growth	12/92	12/93	12/94	12/95	12/96	12/97	12/98	12/99	12/00	12/01
Sales ($ mil.)	7.6%	13,598	13,685	14,966	19,797	20,143	20,096	19,541	24,573	28,180	26,363
Net income ($ mil.)	—	86	289	357	1,153	303	(151)	236	183	142	(1,204)
Income as % of sales	—	0.6%	2.1%	2.4%	5.8%	1.5%	—	1.2%	0.7%	0.5%	—
Earnings per share ($)	—	0.35	1.17	1.43	4.41	1.04	(0.50)	0.77	0.44	0.32	(2.50)
Stock price – FY high ($)		39.25	34.94	40.25	45.69	44.63	61.00	55.25	59.50	60.00	43.31
Stock price – FY low ($)		29.25	28.31	30.31	34.13	35.63	38.63	35.50	39.50	26.31	30.70
Stock price – FY close ($)	2.2%	33.31	33.88	37.69	37.88	40.50	43.13	44.81	56.44	40.81	40.35
P/E – high		67	30	23	10	43	—	72	124	73	—
P/E – low		50	24	18	8	34	—	46	82	32	—
Dividends per share ($)	2.0%	0.84	0.84	0.84	0.92	1.00	1.00	1.00	1.00	1.00	1.00
Book value per share ($)	(1.8%)	25.22	25.12	25.87	29.87	31.12	28.82	28.98	24.93	24.99	21.37
Employees	3.6%	73,000	72,500	70,000	81,500	87,000	82,000	80,000	99,000	112,900	100,000

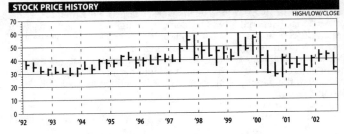

STOCK PRICE HISTORY HIGH/LOW/CLOSE

2001 FISCAL YEAR-END

Debt ratio: 54.8%
Return on equity: —
Cash ($ mil.): 1,224
Current ratio: 1.55
Long-term debt ($ mil.): 12,457
No. of shares (mil.): 482
Dividends
  Yield: 2.5%
  Payout: —
Market value ($ mil.): 19,433

THE INTERPUBLIC GROUP

The ad game has changed to tug-of-war for Interpublic. The New York City-based Interpublic Group of Companies became the world's largest advertising conglomerate after completing its $2.1 billion acquisition of rival True North Communications in 2001. WPP Group took back the #1 spot based on the companies' 2001 billings. It operates through divisions like FCB Group, McCann-Erickson WorldGroup, and The Partnership, each anchored by one of its global advertising agencies: Foote, Cone & Belding Worldwide, McCann-Erickson Worldwide, and Lowe & Partners Worldwide. Each division also includes Interpublic's various independent US agencies such as Bozell, Deutsch, Hill, Holliday, and Temerlin McClain, as well as the firm's various media planning and public relations units. In addition to advertising, Interpublic offers marketing and market research through its Advanced Marketing Services division. The company serves more than 40 global accounts in 20 countries, including General Motors, Nestlé, and Coca-Cola.

Interpublic's rise to the top of the advertising world has come through a number of increasingly larger acquisitions. In 2000 the company bought market researcher NFO Worldwide (now NFO WorldGroup) for $580 million and ad firm Deutsch for about $250 million. Its acquisition of True North was the first orchestrated by chairman and CEO John Dooner, who took charge of the advertising giant at the end of 2000. The company's restructuring efforts relating to acquisitions and the lagging economy resulted in layoffs of 6,800 employees and the closure of 180 offices worldwide through 2002.

HISTORY

Standard Oil advertising executive Harrison McCann opened the H. K. McCann Company in 1911 and signed Standard Oil of New Jersey (later Exxon) as his first client. McCann's ad business boomed as the automobile became an integral part of American life. His firm merged with Alfred Erickson's agency (formed in 1902) in 1930, forming the McCann-Erickson Company. At the end of the decade, the firm hired Marion Harper, a top Yale graduate, as a mailroom clerk. Harper became president in 1948.

Harper began acquiring other ad agencies and by 1961 controlled more than 20 companies. That year he unveiled a plan to create a holding company that would let the ad firms operate separately, allowing them to work on accounts for competing products, but give them the parent firm's financial and informational resources. He named the company Interpublic Inc. after a German research company owned by the former

H. K. McCann Co. The conglomerate continued expanding and was renamed The Interpublic Group of Companies in 1964. Harper's management capabilities weren't up to the task, however, and the company soon faced bankruptcy. In 1967 the board replaced him with Robert Healy, who saved Interpublic and returned it to profitability. The company went public in 1971.

The 1970s were fruitful years for Interpublic; its ad teams created memorable campaigns for Coca-Cola ("It's the Real Thing" and "Have a Coke and a Smile") and Miller Beer ("Miller Time" and Miller Lite ads). After Philip Geier became chairman in 1980, the company gained a stake in Lowe Howard-Spink (1983; it later became The Lowe Group) and bought Lintas International (1987). Interpublic bought the rest of The Lowe Group in 1990.

Interpublic bought Western International Media (now Initiative Media Worldwide), and Ammirati & Puris (merged with Lintas to form Ammirati Puris Lintas) in 1994. As industry consolidation picked up in 1996, Interpublic kept pace with acquisitions of PR company Weber Group and DraftWorldwide. Interpublic bought a majority-stake in artist management and film production company Addis-Wechsler & Associates (now Industry Entertainment) in 1997 and later formed sports marketing and management group Octagon.

Interpublic acquired US agencies Carmichael Lynch and Hill, Holliday, Connors, Cosmopulos in 1998. It also boosted its PR presence with its purchase of International Public Relations (UK), the parent company of public relations networks Shandwick and Golin/Harris. Interpublic strengthened its position in the online world in 1999 when it bought 20% of Stockholm-based Internet services company Icon Medialab International. That year the company merged agencies Ammirati and Lowe & Partners Worldwide to form Lowe Lintas & Partners Worldwide (in 2002 they changed the name to just Lowe & Partners Worldwide).

Interpublic bought market research firm NFO Worldwide for $580 million in 2000 and merged Weber Public Relations with Shandwick International to form Weber Shandwick Worldwide, one of the world's largest PR firms. Later that year, the company bought ad agency Deutsch for about $250 million. John Dooner took the position of chairman and CEO at the end of the year after Geier resigned. Dooner's first move proved a big one: Interpublic acquired True North Communications for $2.1 billion in stock in 2001.

OFFICERS

Chairman, President, and CEO: John J. Dooner Jr.,
age 53, $1,750,000 pay
Vice Chairman: David A. Bell, age 58
EVP, CFO, and Director: Sean F. Orr, age 47,
$1,000,000 pay
EVP and Chief Marketing Officer: Bruce S. Nelson,
age 50, $725,000 pay
EVP Planning and Business Development:
Barry R. Linsky, age 60
SVP, General Counsel, and Secretary:
Nicholas J. Camera, age 55
SVP and Director Corporate Communications:
Philippe Krakowsky
SVP Financial Administration: Thomas J. Dowling,
age 50
SVP Financial Services: Albert Conte, age 51
SVP Human Resources: C. Kent Kroeber, age 63
SVP Investor Relations: Susan V. Watson, age 49
**Chairman, Lowe & Partners Worldwide; Chairman,
Octagon:** Sir Frank B. Lowe, age 59, $1,100,000 pay
Chairman, Magna Global UK: Mick Perry
Chairman, Magna Global USA: Bill Cella
Chairman, MRM Partners Worldwide: Stan Rapp
Chairman, Universal McCann: Ira Carlin, age 53
Auditors: PricewaterhouseCoopers LLP

LOCATIONS

HQ: The Interpublic Group of Companies, Inc.
1271 Avenue of the Americas, New York, NY 10020
Phone: 212-399-8000 **Fax:** 212-399-8130
Web: www.interpublic.com

The Interpublic Group of Companies has offices in
125 countries.

2001 Sales

	$ mil.	% of total
US	3,806	57
International		
Europe (excluding UK)	1,161	17
UK	680	10
Asia Pacific	479	7
Latin America	327	5
Other	274	4
Total	**6,727**	**100**

PRODUCTS/OPERATIONS

2001 Sales

	$ mil.	% of total
Advertising and media management	4,001	60
Marketing communications	1,823	27
Specialized marketing	457	7
Marketing intelligence	446	6
Total	**6,727**	**100**

COMPETITORS

ADVO
Bcom3
Dentsu
Grey Global
Hakuhodo
Havas
Omnicom
Panoramic
Publicis
WPP Group

HISTORICAL FINANCIALS & EMPLOYEES

NYSE: IPG FYE: December 31	Annual Growth	12/92	12/93	12/94	12/95	12/96	12/97	12/98	12/99	12/00	12/01
Sales ($ mil.)	15.7%	1,804	1,794	1,984	2,180	2,538	3,126	3,844	4,427	5,626	6,727
Net income ($ mil.)	—	87	125	93	130	205	239	310	322	359	(505)
Income as % of sales	—	4.8%	7.0%	4.7%	6.0%	8.1%	7.6%	8.1%	7.3%	6.4%	—
Earnings per share ($)	—	0.39	0.56	0.41	0.56	0.85	0.95	1.11	1.11	1.15	(1.37)
Stock price - FY high ($)	—	11.92	11.88	11.96	14.47	16.76	26.50	40.31	58.38	57.69	47.44
Stock price - FY low ($)	—	8.59	7.96	9.17	10.59	13.22	15.67	22.56	34.41	32.69	18.25
Stock price - FY close ($)	10.9%	11.63	10.67	10.71	14.47	15.84	24.91	39.88	57.69	42.56	29.54
P/E - high	—	24	21	23	25	19	27	35	51	49	—
P/E - low	—	17	14	18	19	15	16	20	30	28	—
Dividends per share ($)	10.9%	0.15	0.17	0.19	0.21	0.23	0.25	0.29	0.33	0.37	0.38
Book value per share ($)	9.7%	2.27	2.51	2.79	3.14	3.58	4.23	4.53	5.66	6.50	5.23
Employees	13.9%	16,800	17,600	18,200	19,700	21,700	27,100	34,000	38,600	48,200	54,100

STOCK PRICE HISTORY

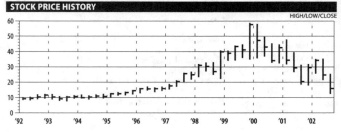

HIGH/LOW/CLOSE

2001 FISCAL YEAR-END

Debt ratio: 55.6%
Return on equity: —
Cash ($ mil.): 935
Current ratio: 1.01
Long-term debt ($ mil.): 2,481
No. of shares (mil.): 379
Dividends
  Yield: 1.3%
  Payout: —
Market value ($ mil.): 11,181

INTERSTATE BAKERIES

It's no Wonder that a Hostess would show her Home Pride by serving breads and sweet treats made by Interstate Bakeries, the largest US wholesale bread and snack cake producer, ahead of Sara Lee Bakery Group. The Kansas City, Missouri-based company operates more than 60 bakeries, making a variety of fresh breads, breakfast pastries, snack cakes, doughnuts, and croutons. The company's national and regional brands include Dolly Madison, Hostess (Twinkies and Ho-Hos), Drake's (Ring Dings, Devil Dogs), Merita, and Mrs. Cubbison's. Its Wonder white bread is the top US bread brand; it also is licensed to sell Sunmaid raisin bread. Unsold products pulled from grocery store shelves are sold through its nearly 1,400 bakery thrift stores.

Interstate Bakeries has held the #1 spot among US bakers since its 1995 purchase of rival Continental Baking (former maker of the popular Wonder and Hostess brands). New baking enzyme technology has made it possible for the company to leave its bread on grocery store shelves longer, cutting down on delivery stops and returns of unsold loaves — all of which caused its bottom line to rise.

HISTORY

Founded in Kansas City, Missouri, in 1930 by Ralph Leroy Nafziger, in 1937 Interstate Bakeries merged with its local rival, Schulze Baking, beginning a strategy of growth through acquisitions and mergers. It acquired Supreme Baking of Los Angeles in 1943 and added O'Rourke Baking, of Buffalo, New York, to its operations in 1950.

The company entered the cake business in 1954 with the purchases of the Ambrosia Cake, Remar Baking, and Butter Cream Baking companies. It added more layers when it acquired Campbell-Sell Baking (1958) and the Kingston Cake Bakery (1959). In 1968 Interstate Bakeries purchased the Millbrook bread division of Nabisco. Interstate Bakeries itself became the object of an acquisition in 1975. DPF, of Hartsdale, New York, an IBM computer-leasing venture that had recorded a $43 million loss over four years, was seeking a low-risk, low-tech acquisition. As the nation's third-largest wholesale baker, Interstate Bakeries fit the bill. The company attempted to block the sale, but DPF prevailed. It spun off its computer business in 1981 and took the Interstate Bakeries name.

Despite efforts to improve plant efficiency, the company recorded declining profits and was saddled with debt. In 1984, in hopes of turning the company around, the firm paid banks $36 million in outstanding loan payments from an overfunded $37 million pension fund.

Interstate Bakeries was taken private in 1987 through an LBO by a group of the company's managers. The company acquired American Bakeries' Merita/Cotton's Bakeries division that year, and Merita president Charles Sullivan was named CEO. The company again went public in 1991. Sullivan decentralized operations, and in 1995 Interstate Bakeries acquired its biggest rival, Ralston Purina's (now Nestlé Purina PetCare) ailing Continental Baking, for $510 million.

Continental was founded as the Ward Baking Co. in New York City in 1849. In 1921 William Ward, grandson of the company's founder, formed United Bakeries, which was renamed Continental Baking in 1924. By 1925, the year Continental bought Taggart Baking (maker of Wonder bread), it had become the US's largest bakery. Continental was sold to hotel and defense conglomerate ITT in 1968. The health-conscious 1970s were hard on Continental, maker of Hostess cupcakes and Twinkies, and in 1984 ITT sold Continental to Ralston Purina, which created a new class of stock in 1993 for separate trading of the company.

To comply with a US Justice Department order related to the Continental acquisition, in 1997 Interstate Bakeries sold its Chicago Butternut Bakery and its Webers brand. That year it bought San Francisco French Bread, a maker of sourdough French bread (Parisian, Colombo, Toscana), from Specialty Foods and the Marie Callender's brand of croutons from International Commissary.

In 1998 Interstate Bakeries bought New England-based John J. Nissen Baking, and Drake's (Ring Dings, Yodels), from Canada's Culinar. In 1999 Interstate Bakeries tried to buy the rest of Culinar, which owns the Canadian trademark for Hostess, but it was outbid by Saputo Group.

In 2000 a San Francisco jury ordered the company to pay $132 million to 19 black employees who charged racial discrimination, but the trial judge reduced the damages to $27 million. In 2000 and 2001, the company shut down several older bakeries and opened new plants in Virginia and Washington.

OFFICERS

Chairman and CEO: Charles A. Sullivan, age 67, $1,920,000 pay
President and COO: Michael D. Kafoure, age 53, $949,385 pay
EVP, Central Division of Brands: Robert P. Morgan, age 46, $410,875 pay
EVP, Eastern Division of Brands:
Thomas S. Bartoszewski, age 59
EVP, Western Division of Brands: Richard D. Willson, age 54

SVP and CFO: Frank W. Coffey, age 59, $454,003 pay
SVP and Counsel, Human Resources: John N. Wiltrakis
SVP, Central Division-North: Timothy W. Cranor
SVP, Central Division-South: Jim Williams
SVP, Director of Corporate Marketing of Brands:
  Mark D. Dirkes, age 55
SVP, Director of Purchasing of Brands:
  Brian E. Stevenson, age 47
SVP, Engineering: Brian A. Poulter
SVP, Southeastern Division: Bob J. McClellan
VP and Corporate Controller: Laura D. Robb, age 44
VP, General Counsel, and Corporate Secretary:
  Kent B. Magill, age 49
VP, National Account Sales: Terry A. Stephens
VP, Research and Development: Theresa S. Cogswell
VP and Treasurer: Paul E. Yarick, age 63
Auditors: Deloitte & Touche LLP

LOCATIONS

HQ: Interstate Bakeries Corporation
  12 E. Armour Blvd., Kansas City, MO 64111
Phone: 816-502-4000   **Fax:** 816-502-4155

Interstate Bakeries operates 62 bakeries in 27 states.

PRODUCTS/OPERATIONS

Selected Brands

Beefsteak	Emperor Norton	Merita
Braun's	Grandma	Millbrook Farms
Bread du Jour	Emilie's	Mrs. Cubbison's
Buttermaid	Holsum	Parisian
Butternut	Home Pride	Roman Meal
Colombo	Hostess	(licensed)
Cotton's Holsum	Ding-Dongs	Sunbeam
DiCarlo	Ho-Hos	Sun-Maid
Dolly Madison	Leopards	(licensed)
Drake's	Sno-Balls	Sweetheart
Devil Dogs	Twinkies	Toscano
Ring Dings	Zingers	Wonder
Yodels	J.J. Nissen	
Eddy's	Marie Callender's	

Selected Products

Bagels	Buns	Snack pies
Bread (white,	Croutons	Stuffing
wheat, crusty,	Cupcakes	Sweet rolls
sourdough,	Doughnuts	Variety cakes
raisin, reduced	English muffins	
calorie)	Rolls	
Breakfast	Shortcakes	
pastries	Snack cakes	

COMPETITORS

Bimbo	Lance
Campbell Soup	McKee Foods
FlowersFoods	Sara Lee Bakery Group
George Weston	Tasty Baking
Kellogg	Weston Foods

HISTORICAL FINANCIALS & EMPLOYEES

NYSE: IBC FYE: Saturday nearest May 31	Annual Growth	5/93	5/94	5/95	5/96	5/97	5/98	5/99	5/00	5/01	5/02
Sales ($ mil.)	13.1%	1,166	1,143	1,223	2,878	3,212	3,266	3,459	3,523	3,497	3,532
Net income ($ mil.)	17.0%	17	16	21	25	97	128	126	89	61	70
Income as % of sales	—	1.4%	1.4%	1.7%	0.9%	3.0%	3.9%	3.6%	2.5%	1.7%	2.0%
Earnings per share ($)	14.9%	0.39	0.39	0.53	0.35	1.28	1.71	1.74	1.31	1.13	1.36
Stock price - FY high ($)	—	10.56	8.75	8.13	13.88	27.94	38.00	35.00	24.94	20.38	28.5
Stock price - FY low ($)	—	7.19	5.81	5.94	7.19	12.63	26.88	20.13	11.31	10.50	14.91
Stock price - FY close ($)	13.7%	8.50	6.00	7.31	13.81	26.88	32.63	21.88	14.50	14.95	27.09
P/E - high	—	14	22	15	40	21	22	20	19	18	21
P/E - low	—	10	15	11	21	10	15	11	9	9	11
Dividends per share ($)	1.7%	0.24	0.25	0.25	0.25	0.27	0.28	0.28	0.28	0.28	0.28
Book value per share ($)	4.0%	4.81	4.77	5.04	6.17	7.17	7.77	8.60	8.98	7.80	6.87
Employees	10.7%	14,000	14,000	35,000	30,000	32,000	34,000	34,000	34,000	34,000	35,000

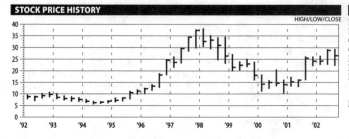

STOCK PRICE HISTORY   HIGH/LOW/CLOSE

2002 FISCAL YEAR-END
Debt ratio: 65.9%
Return on equity: 20.1%
Cash ($ mil.): 0
Current ratio: 0.89
Long-term debt ($ mil.): 581
No. of shares (mil.): 44
Dividends
  Yield: 1.0%
  Payout: 20.6%
Market value ($ mil.): 1,187

ITT INDUSTRIES, INC.

ITT Industries is pumped up to defend its core markets. Based in White Plains, New York, the diversified manufacturer makes the most of its money by controlling liquids and making defense electronics. Its fluid technology unit (about 40% of sales) makes pumps, mixers, valves, and related items for use by the industrial, wastewater, and construction industries; brand names include Flygt, Goulds, and Vogel. ITT's defense electronics segment (nearly 30% of sales) makes tactical communication systems, night-vision devices, and electronic-warfare systems. The company also makes motion and flow control products, such as tubing for brake and fuel lines, boat pumps (Flojet), friction pads, and shock absorbers (KONI). Bringing up the rear is ITT's electronics segment, which produces electronic connectors, switches, control pads, and cable assemblies.

The company has completed a restructuring in which it sold its massive automotive operations to focus on fluid control products, electronics, and defense products. It has also renamed its operating segments to better reflect business operations. ITT's defense electronics and water/wastewater products held their own during 2001, but the electronic components business suffered from a drop in demand.

HISTORY

Colonel Sosthenes Behn founded International Telephone and Telegraph (ITT) in 1920 to build a global telephone company. After three small acquisitions, Behn bought International Western Electric (renamed International Standard Electric, or ISE) from AT&T in 1925, making ITT an international phone equipment maker. In the late 1920s ITT bought Mackay, a US company that made telegraph, cable, radio, and other equipment.

In the 1930s sales outside the US made up two-thirds of revenues. To increase US opportunities during WWII, Behn arranged for a Mackay subsidiary, Federal Telegraph (later Federal Electric), to become part of ITT. Behn took charge of Federal and created Federal Telephone & Radio Laboratories. Meanwhile, ISE scientists who fled war-torn Europe gravitated to ITT's research and development operations and laid the foundation for its high-tech electronics business.

ITT became a diverse and unwieldy collection of companies by the 1950s. In the mid-1950s ISE, its biggest unit, developed advanced telephone-switching equipment. During the 1960s and 1970s, the company added auto-parts makers such as Teves (brakes, West Germany), Ulma (trim, Italy), and Altissimo (lights and accessories, Italy). The firm's electronics acquisitions included Cannon Electric (electrical connectors) and National Computer Products (satellite communications). It also bought Bell & Gossett (the US's #1 maker of commercial and industrial pumps). When ITT bought Sheraton's hotel chain in 1968, it also got auto-parts supplier Thompson Industries. By 1977 its Engineered Products division consisted of nearly 80 automotive and electrical companies. In 1979 ITT began selling all or part of 250 companies, including the last of its telecom operations.

In the 1980s ITT became a major supplier of antilock brakes and, with the 1988 purchase of the Allis-Chalmers pump business, a global force in fluid technology. Its Defense & Electronics unit earned contracts to make equipment used in the Gulf War. In 1994 ITT Automotive purchases solidified its position as the world's top maker of electric motors and wiper systems.

ITT split into three independent companies in 1995: ITT Corporation (hospitality, entertainment, and information services; now part of Starwood Hotels & Resorts), ITT Hartford (insurance; now Hartford Financial Services), and ITT Industries (auto parts, defense and electric systems, and fluid-control products).

In 1997 ITT acquired Goulds Pumps, establishing it as the world's largest pump maker. After the $815 million takeover, ITT reorganized into four segments: Connectors & Switches, Defense Products & Services, Pumps & Complementary Products, and Specialty Products. The company sold its automotive electrical systems unit to Valeo for $1.7 billion and its brake and chassis unit to Germany's Continental for about $1.9 billion.

Beefing up its specialty and defense units, ITT in 1999 bought Hydro Air Industries (spa and swimming pool accessories) and K&M Electronics, and invested $25 million in EarthWatch (imaging satellites). It also spent $110 million for a unit of Singapore-based San Teh (rubber switches used in mobile phones) and $191 million for the space and communications unit of Stanford Telecommunications.

In 2000 ITT bought C&K Components, a privately owned switch maker, for about $117 million and the Man-Machine Interface mobile telephone keypad and switch business of TRW for $60 million. A slowdown in the electronics market in 2001 caused the company to cut its workforce by about 8%. ITT acquired the assets of Waterlink's Pure Water Division in 2002. Later that same year ITT bought submersible pump manufacturer Svedala Robot from the Finland-based Metso Corporation.

Chairman, President, and CEO: Louis J. Giuliano, age 55, $2,199,231 pay
SVP and CFO: David J. Anderson, age 54, $878,215 pay
SVP and Corporate Controller: Edward W. Williams, age 63
SVP and General Counsel: Vincent A. Maffeo, age 51, $615,580 pay
SVP and Director, Human Resources: James D. Fowler Jr., age 58
SVP and Director of Corporate Development: Martin Kamber, age 53
SVP and Director of Corporate Relations: Thomas R. Martin, age 48
SVP; President, Defense: Henry J. Driesse, age 58, $580,246 pay
SVP; President, Fluid Technology: Robert L. Ayers, age 55, $683,809 pay
SVP; President, ITT Cannon Worldwide: Gerard Gendron, age 49
CIO: Steven A. Faas
Auditors: Deloitte & Touche LLP

LOCATIONS

HQ: 4 W. Red Oak Ln., White Plains, NY 10604
Phone: 914-641-2000 **Fax:** 914-696-2950
Web: www.ittind.com

2001 Sales

	$ mil.	% of total
US	2,782	60
Western Europe	1,180	25
Asia/Pacific	295	6
Other regions	419	9
Total	**4,676**	**100**

PRODUCTS/OPERATIONS

2001 Sales

	$ mil.	% of total
Fluid technology	1,830	39
Defense electronics	1,305	28
Motion & flow control	899	19
Electronic components	647	14
Adjustments	(5)	—
Total	**4,676**	**100**

Selected Products

Fluid Technology
Heat exchangers
Mixers
Pumps
Valves

Defense Electronics
Electronic warfare systems
Night-vision devices
Tactical communications
equipment

Motion and Flow Control
Friction pads
Fuel and brake lines

Precision valves
Pumps for boat and spa
baths
Shock absorbers

Electronic Components
Cable assemblies
Connectors
Interconnects
Keypads
LAN components
Network systems
Switches

COMPETITORS

Alliant	Harris Corp	Raytheon
Techsystems	Honeywell	Siemens
BAE SYSTEMS	International	SPX
Dresser	KSB	Swagelok
Ebara	Molex	Texas
FMC	Northrop	Instruments
GenCorp	Grumman	TRW

HISTORICAL FINANCIALS & EMPLOYEES

NYSE: ITT FYE: December 31	Annual Growth	12/92	12/93	12/94	12/95	12/96	12/97	12/98	12/99	12/00	12/01
Sales ($ mil.)	(4.1%)	6,845	6,621	7,758	8,884	8,718	8,777	4,493	4,632	4,829	4,676
Net income ($ mil.)	—	(260)	913	1,033	658	223	108	1,533	233	265	277
Income as % of sales	—	—	13.8%	13.3%	7.4%	2.6%	1.2%	34.1%	5.0%	5.5%	5.9%
Earnings per share ($)	(11.1%)	—	—	—	6.18	1.85	0.89	13.55	2.53	2.94	3.05
Stock price - FY high ($)	—	—	—	—	24.25	28.63	33.69	40.88	41.50	39.63	52.00
Stock price - FY low ($)	—	—	—	—	21.25	21.50	22.13	28.13	30.50	22.38	35.55
Stock price - FY close ($)	13.2%	—	—	—	24.00	24.50	31.38	39.75	33.44	38.75	50.50
P/E - high	—	—	—	—	3	15	35	3	16	13	17
P/E - low	—	—	—	—	2	11	23	2	12	7	11
Dividends per share ($)	—	—	—	—	0.00	0.45	0.60	0.60	0.60	0.60	0.60
Book value per share ($)	19.4%	—	—	—	5.36	6.75	6.94	13.55	12.50	13.78	15.50
Employees	(3.6%)	53,000	50,000	58,400	59,000	59,000	58,500	33,000	38,000	42,000	38,000

STOCK PRICE HISTORY

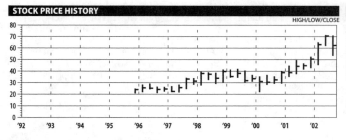

HIGH/LOW/CLOSE

2001 FISCAL YEAR-END

Debt ratio: 24.9%
Return on equity: 21.4%
Cash ($ mil.): 121
Current ratio: 0.77
Long-term debt ($ mil.): 456
No. of shares (mil.): 89
Dividends
  Yield: 1.2%
  Payout: 19.7%
Market value ($ mil.): 4,484

JABIL CIRCUIT, INC.

Let's take a jab at explaining Jabil's operations: St. Petersburg, Florida-based Jabil Circuit is one of the US's leading contract manufacturers of electronics systems and components such as printed circuit boards. Jabil's services range from product design to component procurement, assembly, and order fulfillment. It serves customers in such industries as communications equipment (51% of sales), computer peripherals (19%), PCs (16%), and automobiles. Jabil's top customers include Cisco (23% of sales), Dell (14%), Lucent, and Hewlett-Packard.

Jabil employs innovative business approaches to compete in its rapidly consolidating industry. It provides global parallel production and uses a "workcell" approach, in which semi-autonomous business units are dedicated to individual customers. Despite generally poor market conditions, the company continues to add services and to expand globally through acquisitions, including announced deals to acquire manufacturing operations from Lucent and Philips Electronics.

Chairman William Morean and his family own 19% of Jabil.

HISTORY

Jabil Circuit was named for founders James Golden and Bill Morean. The duo, who originally ran an excavation business, started Jabil in suburban Detroit in 1966 to provide assembly and reworking services to electronics manufacturers. Jabil incorporated in 1969 and began making circuit boards for Control Data Corporation that year.

William D. Morean, the founder's son who had worked summers at Jabil while in high school, joined the company in 1977. The next year he took over Jabil's management. The company entered the automotive electronics business in 1979 through a $12 million contract with General Motors.

During the 1980s Jabil moved into the promising computer field, adding such customers as Dell, NEC, Sun Microsystems, and Toshiba. New production methods and added services spurred the company's growth. Jabil moved its headquarters to St. Petersburg in 1983. William Morean became Jabil's chairman and CEO in 1988.

Production design accounted for most of Jabil's sales for the first time in 1992. The company went public in 1993 and that year opened a factory in Scotland. A major laptop computer manufacturing contract from Epson soured when, in 1995, mysterious cracks appeared in the casings of the laptops and Epson balked at paying its tab. (Jabil eventually won a judgment

against the supplier of the grease used to lubricate the laptops' hinges.)

Jabil opened a factory in Malaysia in 1996. That year disk drive maker Quantum, then Jabil's biggest client, canceled production orders worth about $60 million (expected to total 25% of sales). Jabil quickly filled production gaps by shifting its focus to the booming communications market.

By 1997 Jabil had successfully diversified beyond low-profit margin PC manufacturing, becoming the US's third-largest circuit board manufacturer and adding higher-margin products such as networking hardware. That year Jabil opened a factory in Guadalajara, Mexico, and, in an effort to build its European presence, it more than doubled the size of its manufacturing capacity in Scotland.

The company won a major networking products contract from Northern Telecom (now Nortel Networks) in 1998. It also acquired printed circuit assembly facilities in Idaho and Italy from Hewlett-Packard. Also in 1998 Jabil's sales topped $1 billion for the first time, and it moved from Nasdaq to the New York Stock Exchange.

In 1999 the company expanded into China when it acquired electronics manufacturing services provider GET Manufacturing in a deal valued at about $243 million. It also acquired service and repair provider EFTC Services, Inc. for approximately $30 million. Also in 1999 Thomas Sansone was promoted to vice chairman, and Timothy Main, formerly SVP of business development, succeeded him as president.

Jabil continued its global expansion in 2000, announcing plans to build a manufacturing facility in Tiszaujvaros, Hungary, and acquiring Brazilian electronics manufacturer Bull Information Technology. It also broke ground on two new plants (one for automotive products, the other for consumer products) in Chihuahua, Mexico. Also that year William Morean stepped down as CEO (remaining chairman). He was replaced by Main.

In 2001 the company bought five component factories from UK-based electronics distributor Marconi and created a new technology division to carry out its design, development, and advanced test engineering services. Later that year the company announced it would cut about 300 jobs, or about 10% of its staff.

Also in 2001 Jabil signed an agreement with chip titan Intel under which Jabil will acquire an Intel plant in Malaysia and then supply Intel with parts for three years.

OFFICERS

Chairman: William D. Morean
Vice Chairman: Thomas A. Sansone
President, CEO, and Director: Timothy L. Main,
$726,154 pay
COO: Ronald J. Rapp, $403,077 pay
CFO: Chris A. Lewis, $303,616 pay
General Counsel and Secretary: Robert L. Paver
SVP, Business Development: Mark T. Mondello,
$302,500 pay
SVP, Operations: William E. Peters
SVP, Operational Development: Wesley B. Edwards,
$302,500 pay
SVP, Strategic Planning: Scott D. Brown
VP, Business Development, Asia/Pacific: Rick Evans
VP, Communications: Beth A. Walters
VP, European Business Development:
Roddy A. MacPhee
VP, Global Business Units: Joseph McGee
VP, Global Business Units: John P. Lovato
VP, Jabil Automotive Group: Brian Althaver
VP, Jabil Technology Services: Jeffrey J. Lumetta
VP, Operations, Americas: Bill Muir
VP, Operations, Asia: Teck Ping Yuen
VP, Operations, Europe: Courtney Ryan
Auditors: KPMG LLP

LOCATIONS

HQ: 10560 Ninth St. North, St. Petersburg, FL 33716
Phone: 727-577-9749 **Fax:** 727-579-8529
Web: www.jabil.com

Jabil Circuit has operations in Belgium, Brazil, China,
Hong Kong, Hungary, Ireland, Italy, Japan, Malaysia,
Mexico, the UK, and the US.

2001 Sales by Destination

	$ mil.	% of total
US	2,370	51
Latin America	953	21
Asia	760	16
Europe	537	12
Corporate	5	—
Adjustments	(294)	—
Total	**4,331**	**100**

PRODUCTS/OPERATIONS

2001 Sales by Market

	% of total
Communications	51
Computer peripherals	19
Personal computers	16
Automotive & other	14
Total	**100**

Services
Component selection, sourcing, and procurement
Design and prototyping
Engineering
Printed circuit board assembly
Repair and warranty services
Systems assembly
Test development

COMPETITORS

ACT	Celestica	Plexus
Manufacturing	Flextronics	Sanmina-SCI
APW	Manufacturers'	Solectron
Benchmark	Services	SYNNEX
Electronics	PEMSTAR	Viasystems

HISTORICAL FINANCIALS & EMPLOYEES

NYSE: JBL FYE: August 31	Annual Growth	8/92	8/93	8/94	8/95	8/96	8/97	8/98	8/99	8/00	8/01
Sales ($ mil.)	43.0%	173	335	376	560	863	978	1,277	2,000	3,558	4,331
Net income ($ mil.)	49.4%	3	8	3	7	24	53	57	92	146	119
Income as % of sales	—	1.8%	2.4%	0.7%	1.3%	2.8%	5.4%	4.5%	4.6%	4.1%	2.7%
Earnings per share ($)	28.4%	—	0.08	0.02	0.06	0.17	0.35	0.37	0.56	0.78	0.59
Stock price - FY high ($)	—	—	1.25	1.17	1.83	2.88	15.00	18.00	27.69	64.00	68.00
Stock price - FY low ($)	—	—	0.75	0.56	0.44	0.64	1.44	5.75	5.75	21.81	17.76
Stock price - FY close ($)	47.5%	—	1.03	0.84	1.69	1.53	14.81	5.88	22.41	63.75	23.11
P/E - high	—	—	16	39	26	16	41	46	47	79	110
P/E - low	—	—	9	19	6	4	4	15	10	27	29
Dividends per share ($)	—	—	0.00	0.00	0.00	0.00	0.00	0.00	0.00	0.00	0.00
Book value per share ($)	42.1%	—	0.43	0.45	0.50	0.87	1.23	1.67	3.32	6.68	7.18
Employees	42.7%	—	997	1,516	2,661	2,649	3,661	5,311	6,554	19,115	17,097

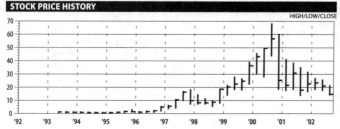

STOCK PRICE HISTORY

HIGH/LOW/CLOSE

2001 FISCAL YEAR-END

Debt ratio: 20.4%
Return on equity: 8.8%
Cash ($ mil.): 431
Current ratio: 2.87
Long-term debt ($ mil.): 362
No. of shares (mil.): 197
Dividends
  Yield: —
  Payout: —
Market value ($ mil.): 4,550

JACK IN THE BOX INC.

Jack in the Box is hoping, when it comes to clown vs. clown, a Ping-Pong-ball-headed mascot proves more popular than its red-haired nemesis. Based in San Diego, Jack in the Box (formerly Foodmaker) is one of the largest fast-food hamburger chains in the US (though badly overshadowed by McDonald's). With more than 1,800 restaurants (some 330 of which are franchised) located in 17 mainly western US states, the company sells burgers, fries, shakes, and other standard fast-food fare. However, it also has developed its own niche by including adult-oriented items, such as the Teriyaki Chicken Bowl, on its menu.

Despite a sluggish economy in 2001 and the restaurant industry's fallout from reduced tourism, Jack in the Box is moving ahead with expansion plans, albeit more conservatively. The company has been making a push into Tennessee, Louisiana, and the Carolinas. About 30 of its 100 planned 2002 openings (down from 126 in 2001) are targeted for the Southeast.

HISTORY

Robert Peterson founded his first restaurant, Topsy's Drive-In, in 1941 in San Diego. He soon renamed it Oscar's (his middle name) and began to expand the restaurant. By 1950 he had four Oscar's drive-in restaurants. That year he changed the name again to Jack in the Box and in 1951 opened one of the country's first drive-through restaurants, which featured a speaker mounted in the chain's signature clown's head.

The drive-through concept took off, and by the late 1960s the company, renamed Foodmaker, operated about 300 Jack in the Box restaurants. In 1968 Peterson sold Foodmaker to Ralston Purina (now named Nestlé Purina Pet-Care). To differentiate itself from competitors, Foodmaker added new food items, including the first breakfast sandwich (1969). The company continued to expand during the 1970s, and by 1979 it had more than 1,000 restaurants. That year it decided to concentrate on the western and southwestern US, selling 232 restaurants in the East and Midwest.

To attract more adult customers, in 1980 Foodmaker began remodeling its stores and adding menu items geared toward adult tastes. The company ran a series of TV ads showing its trademark clown logo being blown up. The ads were meant to show that Jack in the Box was not just for children anymore, but they drew protests from parents worried about the violence in the advertisements.

In 1985 Foodmaker's management acquired the company in a $450 million LBO. The firm went public in 1987, but management took it private again the next year. Led by then-CEO Jack Goodall, Foodmaker expanded its number of franchises. (Unlike most of its competitors, the company had previously owned almost all of its restaurants.) By 1987 about 30% of the company's 900 stores were owned by franchisees.

The next year Foodmaker paid about $230 million for the Chi-Chi's chain of 200 Mexican restaurants. It made its first move outside the US in 1991, opening restaurants in Mexico and Hong Kong. The company went public again the following year.

In 1993 four people died, and more than 700 became ill after eating E. coli-tainted hamburgers from Jack in the Box restaurants in several states, the largest such contamination in US history. Customers, shareholders, and franchisees sued Foodmaker, which in turn sued meat supplier and supermarket chain Vons and Vons' suppliers. Foodmaker's stock and profits plummeted, and the company subsequently enacted a stringent food safety program, which became a model for the fast-food industry and won kudos from the FDA.

Foodmaker sold its Chi-Chi's chain to Family Restaurants (now Prandium) in 1994 for about $200 million and briefly held a stake in that company. In 1996 Goodall retired as CEO, and Robert Nugent succeeded him. The next year Foodmaker announced a major expansion to add 200 Jack in the Box restaurants, primarily in the western US. Foodmaker put the E. coli episode farther behind it in 1998 when it accepted a $58.5 million settlement from Vons and others. In 1999 the company began building units in selected southeastern markets. Also that year Foodmaker dropped its generic moniker and renamed the firm Jack in the Box. The following year it got a nice break from Uncle Sam in the form of a nearly $23 million tax benefit related to the 1995 selling of its stake in Family Restaurants Inc.

In 2001 Goodall stepped down from the board and was replaced by Nugent as chairman. With same store sales down amidst a sagging economy and fewer tourist dollars, the company scaled down its expansion plans. In 2002 it planned to build 100 new locations (down from 126 the previous year), including about 30 in the Southeast.

OFFICERS

Chairman and CEO: Robert J. Nugent, age 60, $851,764 pay
President and COO; Director: Kenneth R. Williams, age 59, $585,558 pay
EVP and CFO: John F. Hoffner, age 54

EVP and Secretary: Lawrence E. Schauf, age 56, $357,831 pay
EVP Marketing: Linda A. Lang, age 44, $319,577 pay
SVP Operations and Franchising: Paul L. Schultz, age 47, $427,232 pay
SVP Quality and Logistics: David M. Theno, age 51
VP and CIO: Stephanie E. Cline, age 56
VP and Treasurer: Harold L. Sachs, age 56
VP Brand Strategy and Product Development: Karen Trissel, age 35
VP Corporate Communications: Karen Bachmann, age 50
VP Financial Planning: Pamela S. Boyd
VP Franchising: Karen G. Gentry, age 41
SVP Human Resources and Strategic Planning: Carlo E. Cetti, age 58
VP Operations, Division I: David Kaufhold, age 44
VP Operations, Division II: Gladys DeClouet, age 44
VP Real Estate and Construction: Charles E. Watson, age 46
VP Restaurant Development: William F. Motts, age 58
Division VP, Advertising: Greg Joumas
Auditors: KPMG LLP

LOCATIONS

HQ: 9330 Balboa Ave., San Diego, CA 92123
Phone: 858-571-2121 **Fax:** 858-571-2101
Web: www.jackinthebox.com

PRODUCTS/OPERATIONS

2001 Sales

	$ mil.	$ of total
Restaurants	1,714	94
Distribution	66	4
Franchise rents & royalties	44	2
Other	10	—
Total	**1,834**	**100**

Selected Menu Items

Breakfast
Breakfast Jack
French Toast Sticks
Sausage Croissants
Ultimate Breakfast Sandwich

Burgers
Bacon Ultimate Cheeseburger
Double Cheeseburger
Jumbo Jack
Sourdough Jack
Ultimate Cheeseburger

Desserts
Cheesecake

Double Fudge Cake
Hot Apple Turnover

Sandwiches
Chicken Fajita Pita
Chicken Supreme
Fish & Chips
Grilled Chicken Fillet
Jack's Spicy Chicken

Sides and Snacks
Chili Cheese Curly Fries
French Fries
Monster Taco
Onion Rings
Stuffed Jalapeños

COMPETITORS

Burger King
Checkers
 Drive-In
CKE Restaurants
Dairy Queen
Domino's Pizza

IHOP
Long John
 Silver's
McDonald's
Sonic
Subway

Taco Cabana
Triarc
Wendy's
Whataburger
Yum!

HISTORICAL FINANCIALS & EMPLOYEES

NYSE: JBX FYE: Sunday nearest Sept. 30	Annual Growth	9/92	9/93	9/94	9/95	9/96	9/97	9/98	9/99	9/00	9/01
Sales ($ mil.)	4.6%	1,219	1,232	1,049	1,019	1,063	1,072	1,224	1,457	1,633	1,834
Net income ($ mil.)	—	(42)	(98)	(40)	(69)	20	34	67	77	100	82
Income as % of sales	—	—	—	—	—	1.9%	3.2%	5.4%	5.3%	6.1%	4.5%
Earnings per share ($)	(2.6%)	2.62	(2.55)	(1.03)	(1.77)	0.51	0.86	1.66	1.95	2.55	2.06
Stock price - FY high ($)	—	18.50	14.00	10.75	7.25	10.25	21.00	21.06	29.44	27.63	34.40
Stock price - FY low ($)	—	9.13	7.50	5.00	3.25	4.75	7.75	12.56	13.00	18.19	19.88
Stock price - FY close ($)	11.7%	10.38	10.00	5.75	5.75	10.00	18.81	15.69	24.94	21.44	28.00
P/E - high	—	28	—	—	—	20	23	12	15	11	16
P/E - low	—	14	—	—	—	9	9	7	7	7	9
Dividends per share ($)	—	0.00	0.00	0.00	0.00	0.00	0.00	0.00	0.00	0.00	0.00
Book value per share ($)	5.6%	6.47	3.64	2.59	0.81	1.32	2.25	3.61	5.69	8.25	10.54
Employees	6.7%	24,350	22,185	26,170	25,785	24,800	29,000	32,600	37,800	40,200	43,600

STOCK PRICE HISTORY
HIGH/LOW/CLOSE

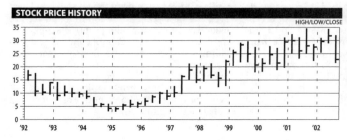

2001 FISCAL YEAR-END
Debt ratio: 40.3%
Return on equity: 22.5%
Cash ($ mil.): 6
Current ratio: 0.55
Long-term debt ($ mil.): 280
No. of shares (mil.): 39
Dividends
 Yield: —
 Payout: —
Market value ($ mil.): 1,099

JACOBS ENGINEERING GROUP INC.

Jacobs Engineering Group continues to climb the ladder. The Pasadena, California-based company provides engineering and design and construction services. Jacobs provides engineering and design services for process plants for companies in the chemical, pharmaceutical, petroleum, pulp and paper, and high-tech industries. It also provides engineering and construction services for commercial, civic, and governmental buildings and transportation infrastructure projects such as highways and bridges.

In addition, Jacobs operates and maintains plants and provides consulting services, such as pricing studies, project feasibility reports, and automation and control system analysis. Consulting customers include US government agencies involved in defense and aerospace programs, which account for 19% of Jacobs' revenues. Jacobs has strengthened its overseas operations by acquiring Dutch engineering firm Stork and the UK's GIBB international engineering and consulting management business.

Founder and chairman Joseph Jacobs owns nearly 13% of his namesake company.

HISTORY

Joseph Jacobs graduated from the Polytechnic Institute of Brooklyn in 1942 with a doctorate in engineering. He went to work for Merck, designing processes for pharmaceutical production. Later he moved to Chemurgic Corp. near San Francisco, where he worked until 1947, when he founded Jacobs Engineering as a consulting firm. Jacobs also sold industrial equipment, avoiding any apparent conflict of interest by simply telling his consulting clients.

When equipment sales outstripped consulting work by 1954, Jacobs hired four salesmen and engineer Stan Krugman, who became his right-hand man. Two years later, the company got its first big chemical design job for Kaiser Aluminum. Jacobs incorporated his sole proprietorship in 1957.

In 1960 the firm won its first construction contract to design and build a potash flotation plant, and Jacobs Engineering became an integrated design and construction firm. In 1967 it opened its first regional office but kept management decentralized to replicate the small size and hard-hitting qualities of its home office. Three years later Jacobs Engineering went public.

The firm merged with Houston-based Pace Companies, which specialized in petrochemical engineering design, in 1974. Also that year the firm became Jacobs Engineering Group and began building its first major overseas chemical plant in Ireland.

By 1977 sales had reached $250 million. A decade of lobbying paid off that year when the firm won a contract for the Arab Potash complex in Jordan. Jacobs began to withdraw from his firm's operations in the early 1980s, but the 1982-1983 recession and poor management decisions pounded earnings. Jacobs returned from retirement in 1985, fired 14 VPs, cut staff in half, and pushed the firm to pursue smaller process plant jobs and specialty construction.

After abandoning a 1986 attempt to take the company private, Jacobs began making acquisitions to improve the firm's construction expertise. In 1992 he relinquished his role as CEO to president Noel Watson. The next year the company expanded its international holdings by acquiring the UK's H&G Process Contracting and H&G Contractors.

The firm's $38 million purchase of CRS Sirrine Engineers and CRSS Constructors in 1994 was the largest at that point in its history and added new markets in the paper and semiconductor industries. By 1995 Jacobs Engineering was working on a record backlog.

Continuing its acquisition drive, the company bought a 49% interest in European engineering specialist Serete Group in 1996 and the rest the next year. Also in 1997 it gained control of Indian engineering affiliate Humphreys & Glasgow (now Jacobs H&G), increasing its 40% stake to 70%, and bought CPR Engineering, a pulp and paper processing specialist. It also formed a joint venture with Krupp UHDE to provide design, engineering, and construction management services in Mexico.

In 1999 the company paid $198 million for St. Louis construction and design firm Sverdrup, which had completed projects in some 65 countries. The next year Jacobs Engineering purchased half of Dutch firm Stork Engineering's business (it acquired the rest in 2001). But the company's bid to buy the assets of bankrupt power plant construction company Stone & Webster in 2000 was topped by Shaw Group.

After being accused of overcharging the US government, Jacobs Engineering settled a whistleblower lawsuit (for $35 million) in 2000 while continuing to deny the allegations. However, the next year Jacobs continued to receive federal contracts, including contracts for boosting security at the US Capitol complex and providing logistics to the US Special Operations Command. In 2001 Jacobs also completed its acquisition of the UK-based Gibb unit of engineering consulting firm LawGibb Group, as well as its purchase of McDermott Engineers and Constructors (Canada).

OFFICERS

Chairman: Joseph J. Jacobs, age 85, $1,130,200 pay
Vice Chairman: Richard E. Beumer, age 63,
$817,350 pay
CEO and Director: Noel G. Watson, age 65,
$1,594,670 pay
President and Director: Craig L. Martin, age 52,
$847,380 pay (prior to promotion)
EVP Operations: Thomas R. Hammond, age 50,
$904,230 pay
EVP Operations: Richard J. Slater, age 55, $904,230 pay
SVP, General Counsel, and Secretary:
William C. Markley III, age 56
SVP Finance and Administration and Treasurer:
John W. Prosser Jr., age 56
SVP and Controller: Nazim G. Thawerbhoy, age 54
SVP Information Technology: Michael P. Miller, age 41
SVP Quality and Safety: Laurence R. Sadoff, age 54
Group VP Asia: Walter C. Barber, age 60
Group VP Central Region: Peter M. Evans, age 56
Group VP Civil: Michael J. Higgins, age 57
Group VP Civil: H. Gerald Schwartz Jr., age 63
Group VP Consulting Operations:
Robert T. McWhinney, age 61
Group VP Facilities: Warren M. Dean, age 57
Group VP Federal Operations: James W. Thiesing,
age 57
Group VP Field Services: Stephen K. Fritschle, age 58
Group VP Field Services: Gregory J. Landry, age 53
Auditors: Ernst & Young LLP

LOCATIONS

HQ: 1111 S. Arroyo Pkwy., Pasadena, CA 91105
Phone: 626-578-3500   **Fax:** 626-578-6916
Web: www.jacobs.com

2001 Sales

	% of total
US	78
Other countries	22
Total	**100**

PRODUCTS/OPERATIONS

2001 Sales

	$ mil.	% of total
Project services	2,340	59
Construction	978	25
Operations & maintenance	505	13
Process, scientific systems consulting	134	3
Total	**3,957**	**100**

Selected Subsidiaries
Jacobs Construction Services, Inc.
Jacobs Engineering, Inc.
Jacobs Facilities, Inc.
Jacobs International Holdings, Inc.
JE Professional Resources Limited (UK)
Sverdrup Technology, Inc.

COMPETITORS

ABB	Hellmuth, Obata	Peter Kiewit
AECOM	+ Kassabaum	Sons'
AMEC	HNTB	Raytheon
BE&K	Honeywell	Turner
Bechtel	International	Corporation
CH2M HILL	Kværner	URS
Day &	Louis Berger	Washington
Zimmermann	Group	Group
Fluor	Parsons	WESTON
Foster Wheeler		

HISTORICAL FINANCIALS & EMPLOYEES

NYSE: JEC FYE: September 30	Annual Growth	9/92	9/93	9/94	9/95	9/96	9/97	9/98	9/99	9/00	9/01
Sales ($ mil.)	15.2%	1,106	1,143	1,166	1,723	1,799	1,781	2,101	2,875	3,419	3,957
Net income ($ mil.)	14.2%	27	29	19	32	40	47	54	65	51	88
Income as % of sales	—	2.4%	2.5%	1.6%	1.9%	2.2%	2.6%	2.6%	2.3%	1.5%	2.2%
Earnings per share ($)	12.5%	0.56	0.58	0.38	0.64	0.78	0.90	1.04	1.24	0.97	1.61
Stock price - FY high ($)	—	18.25	15.50	13.44	12.88	14.69	16.28	17.13	21.38	20.19	37.84
Stock price - FY low ($)	—	10.81	10.00	9.00	8.44	9.81	10.63	12.34	13.47	13.09	18.98
Stock price - FY close ($)	8.8%	14.56	11.63	12.19	12.44	11.25	15.31	15.50	16.25	20.16	31.20
P/E - high	—	33	27	35	20	19	18	16	17	21	23
P/E - low	—	19	17	24	13	12	12	12	11	13	12
Dividends per share ($)	—	0.00	0.00	0.00	0.00	0.00	0.00	0.00	0.00	0.00	0.00
Book value per share ($)	15.7%	2.96	3.51	3.99	4.68	5.51	6.27	7.25	8.58	9.39	11.01
Employees	5.9%	12,300	13,100	13,140	14,500	14,150	15,870	17,240	15,900	18,800	20,600

STOCK PRICE HISTORY

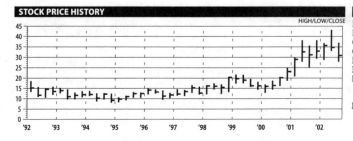

HIGH/LOW/CLOSE

2001 FISCAL YEAR-END

Debt ratio: 21.7%
Return on equity: 16.2%
Cash ($ mil.): 49
Current ratio: 1.35
Long-term debt ($ mil.): 164
No. of shares (mil.): 54
Dividends
  Yield: —
  Payout: —
Market value ($ mil.): 1,677

J.B. HUNT TRANSPORT SERVICES

J.B. Hunt Transport Services keeps its intermodal (train/truck) shipping, logistics, and contract services trucking along. The Lowell, Arkansas-based company is the largest publicly traded truckload carrier in the US (privately held Schneider National is #1 overall). With about 12,300 drivers, 10,770 tractors, 25,500 trailers, and 18,700 containers, J.B. Hunt trucks across the US, Canada, and Mexico. Founder Johnnie Bryan (J.B.) Hunt own and his family own 33% of the firm.

But trucking is just part of the picture. J.B. Hunt's Dedicated Contract Services (DCS) offers dedicated logistics and supply-chain services. DCS puts together customized delivery systems for large clients using the trucking company's equipment and drivers.

The company's intermodal unit, JBI, has agreements with seven railroads in North America (including Burlington Northern Santa Fe, Union Pacific, and Canadian National). Through these agreements, JBI operates throughout North America and Mexico, providing door-to-door intermodal service. J.B. Hunt also has an Internet tracking system that allows trucks to identify the freight waiting to be moved and to post their available equipment and capacity.

HISTORY

Founder Johnnie Bryan Hunt's history is a classic tale of rolling from rags to riches, with a little help from a Rockefeller. Hunt's family members were sharecroppers; he left school at age 12 during the Depression to work for his uncle's Arkansas sawmill. In the late 1950s, after driving trucks for more than nine years, Hunt noticed that the rice mills along his eastern Arkansas route were burning rice hulls. Believing the hulls could be used as poultry litter, Hunt got a contract to haul away the hulls and began selling them to chicken farmers.

In 1961 he began the J.B. Hunt Company with help from future Arkansas governor Winthrop Rockefeller, who owned Winrock grass company, where Hunt bought sod for one of his side businesses. Hunt developed a machine to compress the rice hulls, which made their transportation profitable, and within a few years the company was the world's largest producer of rice hulls for poultry litter.

Still looking for new opportunities, Hunt bought some used trucks and refrigerated trailers in 1969, though the company continued to focus on its original business. In the 1970s it found that the ground rice hulls made a good base for livestock vitamins and medications. Buyers of the ground hulls included Pfizer and Eli

Lilly. J.B. Hunt, with Pfizer's backing, soon began selling a vitamin premix to feed companies.

In the 1980s, J.B. Hunt's trucking division grew dramatically and became lucrative as the trucking industry was being deregulated. In 1981 and 1982 the Hunt trucking business had higher margins than most trucking firms. In 1983, when J.B. Hunt Transport Services went public, Hunt sold the rice hull business to concentrate on trucking.

By 1986 J.B. Hunt was the US's third-largest irregular-route trucking company. The time was ripe to expand, and the company began trucking in Canada (1988) and Mexico (1989). It also formed an alliance in 1989 with Santa Fe Pacific Railroad (now Burlington Northern Santa Fe) to provide intermodal services between the West Coast and the Midwest.

The company began adding computers to its trucks in 1992 to improve data exchange and communication on the road. J.B. Hunt also formed a joint venture with Latin America's largest transportation company, Transportación Marítima Mexicana. Founder Hunt retired in 1995 and became senior chairman.

J.B. Hunt tried hauling automobiles in 1996 but abandoned the idea when it found that cars were easily dented on intermodal trailers. More in line with the trucking company's long-term goals was an effort to stabilize its roster of drivers. It raised wages by one-third in 1997 to counteract driver shortages and high turnover. That year J.B. Hunt sold its underperforming flatbed-trucking unit (renamed Charger Inc.).

In 1998 J.B. Hunt reaped the benefits from its efforts to retain drivers with greater profits. The next year the trucking company began testing a satellite system from ORBCOMM Global to track empty trailers.

In 2000 the company teamed up with five other truckers (including Werner Enterprises and Swift Transportation) to form Transplace.com, an online trucking logistics joint venture. As part of forming the joint venture, J.B. Hunt contributed its J.B. Logistics (JBL) business to Transplace. Also that year the company inked a $100 million deal with Wal-Mart to increase its full truckload services to the retailer by 50%.

OFFICERS

Senior Chairman: J. B. Hunt, age 75, $375,000 pay
Chairman: Wayne Garrison, age 49, $375,000 pay
Vice Chairman: Bryan Hunt, age 43
President, CEO, and Director: Kirk Thompson, age 48, $452,813 pay
EVP Operations and COO: Craig Harper, age 44
EVP Finance and Administration and CFO:
Jerry W. Walton, age 55, $327,031 pay

EVP Enterprise Solutions; President, Dedicated Contract Services: John N. Roberts III, age 37
EVP Equipment and Properties: Bob D. Ralston, age 55
EVP Marketing and Chief Marketing Officer: Paul R. Bergant, age 55, $281,750 pay
VP Strategic Marketing and E-Business: David Roth
CIO: Kay J. Palmer, age 38
Secretary and Director: Johnelle D. Hunt, age 70
Personnel Manager: Jackie Williams
Auditors: KPMG LLP

LOCATIONS

HQ: J.B. Hunt Transport Services, Inc.
615 J.B. Hunt Corporate Dr., Lowell, AR 72745
Phone: 479-820-0000 **Fax:** 479-820-8249
Web: www.jbhunt.com

J.B. Hunt Transport Services provides truckload service to the 48 contiguous US states, Mexico, and the Canadian provinces of British Columbia, Ontario, and Quebec.

PRODUCTS/OPERATIONS

2001 Sales

	$ mil.	% of total
JBT	829	39
JBI	740	35
DCS	549	26
Adjustments	(18)	—
Total	**2,100**	**100**

Operating Groups
Dedicated contract services (DCS)
JBT (dry-van truck)
JBI (intermodal)

Subsidiaries
Comercializadora Internacional de Cargo S.A. de C.V. (Mexico)
FIS, Inc.
Hunt Mexicana, S.A. de C.V. (Mexico)
J.B. Hunt Corp.
J.B. Hunt Transport, Inc.
L.A., Inc.
Servicios de Logistica de Mexico, S.A. de C.V.
Transplace, Inc. (27%)

COMPETITORS

Burlington Northern Santa Fe
Cannon Express
CNF
CSX
EGL
FedEx
Hub Group
Landstar System
Norfolk Southern
Ryder
Schneider National
Swift Transportation
Union Pacific
UPS
UPS Freight Services
U.S. Xpress
Werner

HISTORICAL FINANCIALS & EMPLOYEES

Nasdaq: JBHT FYE: December 31	Annual Growth	12/92	12/93	12/94	12/95	12/96	12/97	12/98	12/99	12/00	12/01
Sales ($ mil.)	9.7%	912	1,021	1,208	1,352	1,487	1,554	1,842	2,045	2,160	2,100
Net income ($ mil.)	(1.8%)	39	38	40	(2)	22	11	47	32	36	33
Income as % of sales	—	4.3%	3.7%	3.3%	—	1.5%	0.7%	2.5%	1.6%	1.7%	1.6%
Earnings per share ($)	(1.9%)	1.08	1.00	1.05	(0.06)	0.58	0.31	1.28	0.89	1.02	0.91
Stock price - FY high ($)	—	26.00	26.75	25.75	20.13	22.13	19.25	38.88	26.25	17.50	25.60
Stock price - FY low ($)	—	16.25	17.25	15.00	12.75	13.75	13.38	12.31	11.88	10.50	12.15
Stock price - FY close ($)	(0.0%)	23.25	23.25	15.25	16.75	14.00	18.75	23.00	13.84	16.81	23.20
P/E - high	—	25	27	25	—	38	62	29	29	17	28
P/E - low	—	16	17	14	—	24	43	9	13	10	13
Dividends per share ($)	—	0.20	0.20	0.20	0.20	0.20	0.20	0.20	0.15	0.05	0.00
Book value per share ($)	5.2%	8.10	8.95	9.81	9.35	9.61	9.48	10.55	11.26	12.15	12.74
Employees	4.3%	11,201	10,476	11,837	12,020	11,575	11,780	14,250	14,700	15,980	16,380

STOCK PRICE HISTORY

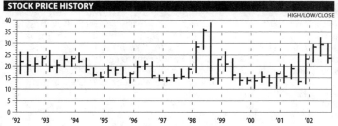

HIGH/LOW/CLOSE

2001 FISCAL YEAR-END

Debt ratio: 43.6%
Return on equity: 7.4%
Cash ($ mil.): 49
Current ratio: 1.45
Long-term debt ($ mil.): 354
No. of shares (mil.): 36
Dividends
  Yield: —
  Payout: —
Market value ($ mil.): 835

J. C. PENNEY CORPORATION, INC.

J. C. Penney Corporation (formerly J. C. Penney Company) is cleaning out its closets. The debt-ridden Plano, Texas-based company is closing some failing JCPenney department stores and some Eckerd drugstores. To boost sales at its nearly 1,100 JCPenney department stores (and lure back customers from discount stores such as Target), J. C. Penney has been expanding its private-label offerings, adding new categories to lines such as the Arizona Jean Co.

Although its department stores have struggled, the company still boasts one of the largest catalog operations in the US and the Eckerd drugstore chain, with 2,600 stores (Eckerd accounts for about 40% of sales). Gearing up for organizational changes, J. C. Penney changed its name in January 2002 (swapping "Company" for "Corporation") and created a holding company that bears its original name. All J. C. Penney stock was converted to that of the publicly traded holding company.

HISTORY

In 1902 James Cash Penney and two former employers opened the Golden Rule, a dry goods store, in Kemmerer, Wyoming. Penney bought out his partners in 1907 and opened stores that sold soft goods in small towns. Basing his customer service policy on his Baptist heritage, he held employees (called "associates") to a high moral code.

The firm incorporated in Utah in 1913 as the J. C. Penney Company, with headquarters in Salt Lake City, but it moved to New York City the next year to improve buying and financial operations. It expanded to nearly 1,400 stores in the 1920s and went public in 1929. The company grew during the Depression with its reputation for high quality and low prices.

J. C. Penney rode the postwar boom, and by 1951 sales had surpassed $1 billion. It introduced credit plans in 1958 and entered catalog retailing in 1962 with its purchase of General Merchandise Co. The next year JCPenney added hard goods, which allowed it to compete with Sears and Montgomery Ward.

The company formed JCPenney Insurance in the mid-1960s and bought Thrift Drug in 1969. The chain continued to grow, and in 1973, two years after Penney's death, there were 2,053 stores. Also in the 1970s J. C. Penney began its ill-fated foray overseas by buying chains in Belgium and Italy in hopes of duplicating its US formula — giant department stores.

The company bought Delaware-based First National Bank in 1983 (renamed JCPenney National Bank in 1984) to issue MasterCard and Visa cards.

JCPenney stores refocused on soft goods during the 1980s and stopped selling automotive services, appliances, paint, hardware, and fabrics in 1983. It discontinued sporting goods, consumer electronics, and photographic equipment in 1987.

The next year JCPenney Telemarketing was formed to take catalog phone orders and provide telemarketing services for other companies. Also in 1988 the company moved its headquarters to Plano, Texas. JCPenney tried to move upmarket in the 1980s, enlisting fashion designer Halston. The line failed, however, so the company developed its own brands.

James Oesterreicher was named CEO in 1995 and J. C. Penney opened its first Mexican department store in Monterrey that year. Facing a slow-growing department store business back home, it then bought 272 drugstores from Fay's Inc. and 200 more from Rite Aid. In 1997 it acquired Eckerd (nearly 1,750 stores) for $3.3 billion, converting its other drugstores to the Eckerd name. Also that year the company sold its $740 million credit card portfolio of JCPenney National Bank to Associates First Capital and dealt its bank branches to First National Bank of Wyoming.

The retailer struggled in 1998, swallowing slumps in sales and a $70 million charge for consolidating its drugstore operations. J. C. Penney also closed 75 underperforming department stores that year. In late 1998 the company bought a controlling stake in Brazilian department store chain Lojas Renner for $33 million.

With its stock value falling, J. C. Penney announced in 1999 it would sell 20% of Eckerd in the form of a tracking stock, but it has postponed the IPO three times since. That year it also sold its private-label credit card operations to GE Capital and sold its store in Chile to department store chain Almacenas Paris.

In 2000 the company closed about 50 department stores and 300 Eckerd drugstores. Also in 2000 CEO Oesterreicher retired and was replaced by Allen Questrom; the company hired Questrom because of the work he did turning around Federated Department Stores and Barneys New York.

In 2001 the company announced plans to shutter about 50 more department stores and drugstores. Also that year Dutch insurer AEGON acquired J. C. Penney's Direct Marketing Services (DMS) unit, including its life insurance subsidiaries, for $1.3 billion.

J. C. Penney changed its name to J. C. Penney Corporation in January 2002 and formed a holding company under its former name.

OFFICERS

Chairman and CEO: Allen I. Questrom, age 62, $3,205,416 pay
EVP and CFO: Robert B. Cavanaugh, age 49
EVP and Chief Human Resources and Administration Officer: Gary L. Davis, age 57, $862,500 pay
EVP and CIO: Stephen F. Raish, age 50
EVP, Chairman and CEO, JCPenney Stores, Catalog and Internet: Vanessa J. Castagna, age 50, $2,033,578 pay
EVP, Secretary, and General Counsel: Charles R. Lotter, age 63, $1,040,201 pay
EVP; Chairman and CEO, Eckerd Drug Stores: J. Wayne Harris, age 62, $1,961,950 pay
SVP; President, Catalog and Internet: John Irvin
SVP and Chief Marketing Officer, JCPenney Stores and Catalog: John Budd
SVP and General Merchandise Manager, Fine Jewelry: Beryl B. Raff, age 51
SVP and General Merchandise Manager, Home: Charles Chinni
SVP and General Merchandise Manager, Men's and Children's: William Cappiello
VP and Director Merchandising, Family Footwear: Edward Mawyer
President and Chief Operating Officer, Stores and Merchandise Operations: Ken C. Hicks, age 49
Auditors: KPMG LLP

LOCATIONS

HQ: 6501 Legacy Dr., Plano, TX 75024
Phone: 972-431-1000   **Fax:** 972-431-1362
Web: www.jcpenney.net

J. C. Penney Corporation operates about 1,100 JCPenney retail stores in Mexico, Puerto Rico, and the US; some 46 Brazilian department stores under the name Renner; and approximately 2,650 Eckerd drugstores in the American northeastern, southeastern, and Sunbelt regions. It has six catalog distribution centers.

PRODUCTS/OPERATIONS

2002 Sales

	% of total
Department store & catalog	57
Eckerd	43
Total	**100**

Major Product Lines
Accessories
Family apparel
Home furnishings
Jewelry
Shoes

Selected Private Labels
Arizona Jean Co.
Crazy Horse by Liz Claiborne (exclusive third-party brand)
Delicates
Hunt Club
Jacqueline Ferrar
JCPenney Home Collection
St. John's Bay
Stafford
USA Olympic
Worthington

COMPETITORS

American Retail	Federated	Otto Versand
Bed Bath &	Foot Locker	Rite Aid
Beyond	The Gap	Ross Stores
Belk	J. Crew	Saks Inc.
BJs Wholesale	J. Jill Group	Sears
Club	Kmart	Signet
Brown Shoe	Kohl's	Spiegel
Comerci	Lands' End	Stage Stores
Costco	Limited Brands	Target
Wholesale	Longs	TJX
CVS	May	Walgreen
Dillard's	Nine West	Wal-Mart
Dress Barn	Nordstrom	Zale

HISTORICAL FINANCIALS & EMPLOYEES

Subsidiary FYE: Last Saturday in January	Annual Growth	1/93	1/94	1/95	1/96	1/97	1/98	1/99	1/00	1/01	1/02
Sales ($ mil.)	6.6%	18,009	18,983	20,380	21,419	23,649	29,618	30,678	32,510	31,846	32,004
Net income ($ mil.)	(20.6%)	777	940	1,057	838	565	566	594	336	(705)	98
Income as % of sales	—	4.3%	5.0%	5.2%	3.9%	2.4%	1.9%	1.9%	1.0%	—	0.3%
Employees	2.0%	192,000	193,000	202,000	205,000	252,000	260,000	262,000	291,000	267,000	229,000

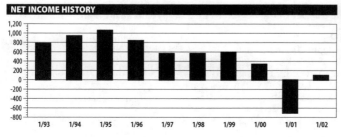

NET INCOME HISTORY

2002 FISCAL YEAR-END
Debt ratio: 45.8%
Return on equity: 1.7%
Cash ($ mil.): 6
Current ratio: 1.93
Long-term debt ($ mil.): 5,179

JDS UNIPHASE CORPORATION

JDS Uniphase grew quickly by eating lightly and got serious indigestion. The San Jose, California-based optoelectronics company makes fiber-optic components and modules used by telecommunications and cable television system manufacturers. These products include source and pump lasers and modulators to send signals across fiber-optic networks, as well as passive components that amplify and guide optical signals on their way. JDS Uniphase also makes cable TV transmission and optical component testing equipment. Nortel Networks, Alcatel, and Lucent account for a combined 36% of sales; other customers include CIENA and Tyco.

JDS Uniphase is in the midst of a monumental restructuring program intended to offset a loss of more than $50 billion (incurred mainly because of write-downs related to companies purchased during the Internet boom) for fiscal 2001. The company faced a sharp drop in sales following the massive spending spree it used to build a presence in the optical equipment market. JDS has since cut its workforce by more than half and is shutting down redundant operations and nonessential facilities worldwide.

JDS plans to sell its MEMS (micro-electro-mechanical) products business, which makes silicon chips with tiny movable mirrors that can be used to direct light as it travels through fiber-optic networks, for about $ 8 million; JDS paid $565 million for the technology in 2000.

·HISTORY

Engineer Dale Crane was already making helium neon lasers in his garage when he left laser developer Spectra-Physics in 1979 to start Uniphase. Initially the company developed and marketed gas laser subsystems to manufacturers of biomedical, industrial process control, and printing equipment. In 1992 Demax Software executive Kevin Kalkhoven became CEO, and Uniphase formed Ultrapointe, introducing the Ultrapointe laser imaging system for semiconductor production the following year. Expenses related to a gas laser subsystem patent-infringement suit filed by Spectra-Physics caused losses in 1993, the year Uniphase went public.

In the mid-1990s Uniphase began to use acquisitions to expand its market share and consolidate product lines. In 1995 the company bought optical components supplier United Technologies Photonics from United Technologies, thereby entering the telecom market. In 1997 it bought IBM's laser business and Australia-based Indx, a maker of reflection filters used to increase the carrying capacity of a fiber-optic strand. Uniphase's 1998 acquisitions included Philips

Optoelectronics (semiconductor laser products) and Broadband Communications Products (fiber-optic transmitters and receivers). The company sold its Ultrapointe unit to chip equipment maker KLA-Tencor late that year. The acquisition spree contributed to losses for fiscal 1997 and 1998.

In 1999 Uniphase merged with JDS FITEL, a Canada-based maker of fiber-optic communications gear, in a $7 billion deal. JDS FITEL, founded in 1981 by four Nortel engineers, focused on making so-called "passive" fiber-optic components that route and manipulate optical signals. It was a complementary fit to Uniphase's "active" gear that generates and transmits signals. The combined company named itself JDS Uniphase. Both JDS FITEL and Uniphase had aggressively pursued acquisitions prior to the merger, and JDS Uniphase continued the buying spree.

In fiscal 2000, following a huge run-up in its share price, JDS Uniphase made 10 acquisitions, including EPITAXX (optical detectors and receivers) and Optical Coating Laboratory. Its largest acquisition was of rival E-Tek Dynamics (for $20.4 billion), which JDS used to further increase its capacity to produce passive components such as amplifiers and better equip itself to offer customers complete optical systems. That year Kalkhoven retired, and co-chairman Jozef Straus (former CEO of JDS FITEL) was named as his replacement.

In 2001 JDS bought rival SDL, a maker of equipment that lets customers send multiple light signals over a single fiber, in a $17 billion stock deal. The company sold a Zurich-based pump laser manufacturing plant to Nortel to gain regulatory approval for the SDL buy. JDS has planned further facility closures and has laid off more than 50% of its staff in response to lagging sales and massive losses incurred from write-downs of its pricey acquisitions.

The company bought IBM's optical transceiver business in early 2002; it also bought optical device startup Scion Photonics.

OFFICERS

Chairman: Martin A. Kaplan, age 64
Co-Chairman and CEO: Jozef Straus, age 56, $521,355 pay
Co-Chairman and Chief Strategy Officer: Don Scifres, age 55, $75,103,649 pay
President and COO: Syrus P. Madavi, age 52
EVP, CFO, and Secretary: Anthony R. Muller, age 59, $306,731 pay (retiring early 2003)
EVP, Strategy and Business Development: M. Zita Cobb, age 42, $275,625 pay
SVP and CTO: Frederick L. Leonberger, age 54
SVP, Business Development and General Counsel: Michael C. Phillips, age 51
SVP, Global Sales: Scott Parker Sr., age 45

SVP, Strategy and Business Development:
Yves Dzialowski
VP and CIO: Joe Riera
VP, Corporate and Marketing Communications:
Jeff Wild
VP, Finance: Steve Moore
President, Transmission Group: Don Bossi
Auditors: Ernst & Young LLP

LOCATIONS

HQ: 210 Baypointe Pkwy., San Jose, CA 95134
Phone: 408-434-1800   **Fax:** 408-954-0540
Web: www.jdsuniphase.com

JDS Uniphase has manufacturing operations in
California, Connecticut, Florida, Massachusetts, New
Jersey, North Carolina, Ohio, Pennsylvania, and Texas,
as well as in Australia, Canada, China, Germany, the
Netherlands, Taiwan, and the UK.

2002 Sales

	$ mil.	% of total
North America	807	74
Europe	197	18
Other regions	94	8
Total	**1,098**	**100**

PRODUCTS/OPERATIONS

Selected Products

Adapters	Isolators, circulators, and
Amplifier modules	hybrids
Array wave guides	Meters
Attenuators	Modulators
Cable assemblies	Optical network monitors
Configurable multiplexers	Optical polarization
Couplers and splitters	components
Dielectric interference	Optical terminators
filters	Optical transport modules
Dispersion compensators	Plug-type attenuators
Emulators	Polarization controllers
Fiber Bragg gratings	Polishing machines and
Filters	accessories
Fixed-fiber optical	Pump lasers
attenuator	Receivers
Fused-fiber couplers and	Switches
wave division	Transmission lasers
multiplexers	Tunable filters
Gain flattening filters	Waveguide
Integrated components	Wavelength lockers

COMPETITORS

Agere Systems	Corning	New Focus
Agilent	Fujitsu	Nortel Networks
Technologies	Furukawa	Oplink
Alcatel Optronics	Electric	Communications
Alcoa Fujikura	Harmonic	PANDATEL
Avanex	Hitachi	Siemens
CIENA	Juniper Networks	Sycamore
Coherent	Lucent	Networks

HISTORICAL FINANCIALS & EMPLOYEES

Nasdaq: JDSU FYE: June 30	Annual Growth	6/93	6/94	6/95	6/96	6/97	6/98	6/99	6/00	6/01	6/02
Sales ($ mil.)	50.9%	27	33	42	69	107	176	283	1,430	3,233	1,098
Net income ($ mil.)	—	(1)	2	1	3	(19)	(81)	(171)	(905)	(56,122)	(8,738)
Income as % of sales	—	—	6.7%	1.7%	4.1%	—	—	—	—	—	—
Earnings per share ($)	—	—	0.02	0.01	0.02	(0.08)	(0.30)	(0.54)	(1.27)	(51.40)	(6.50)
Stock price - FY high ($)	—	—	0.34	0.76	2.25	3.86	8.20	20.90	153.42	140.50	13.2
Stock price - FY low ($)	—	—	0.21	0.24	0.65	1.19	3.28	3.91	19.31	9.55	2.24
Stock price - FY close ($)	34.5%	—	0.25	0.67	2.22	3.64	7.85	20.75	119.88	12.75	2.67
P/E - high	—	—	17	76	113	—	—	—	—	—	—
P/E - low	—	—	11	24	33	—	—	—	—	—	—
Dividends per share ($)	—	—	0.00	0.00	0.00	0.00	0.00	0.00	0.00	0.00	0.00
Book value per share ($)	36.4%	—	0.15	0.16	0.59	0.55	0.71	11.20	26.47	8.12	1.80
Employees	52.8%	203	230	259	409	597	976	6,260	19,000	19,948	9,222

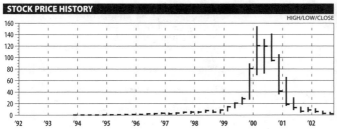

STOCK PRICE HISTORY   HIGH/LOW/CLOSE

2002 FISCAL YEAR-END

Debt ratio: 0.2%
Return on equity: —
Cash ($ mil.): 412
Current ratio: 3.85
Long-term debt ($ mil.): 6
No. of shares (mil.): 1,370
Dividends
  Yield: —
  Payout: —
Market value ($ mil.): 3,659

JEFFERSON-PILOT CORPORATION

The tortoise has become the hare. The subsidiaries (including Jefferson-Pilot Life Insurance, Jefferson Pilot Financial Insurance, and Jefferson Pilot LifeAmerica) of Greensboro, North Carolina-based Jefferson-Pilot (JP) offer such products as annuities and group and individual life insurance. JP also operates three television stations and almost 20 radio stations and produces sports programming. Its insurance operations are responsible for more than 85% of sales.

Historically conservative, JP has greatly increased its activity in recent years; purchases have boosted the company's presence nationally, beyond its previously southern concentration. The company is focusing on its wealth accumulation and business planning segments.

HISTORY

Jefferson Standard Life Insurance was founded in 1907 in Raleigh, North Carolina, by brothers P. D. and Charles Gold and others. Fearing that northern financial institutions were draining the South of capital, they set out to keep the money at home through a regional insurer. A persistent, door-to-door sales force helped the company grow. In 1912 Jefferson acquired two other companies and moved to Greensboro. Increased marketing efforts had the company operating in 14 southern states by the time the last Gold brother retired in 1919. Julian Price, who came to the firm with one of the 1912 acquisitions, was named president. The outspoken and respected Price guided the company through WWII.

In the 1920s Jefferson began investing in newspapers and expanded westward. The company's conservative fiscal strategy helped it weather the Depression and WWII years. In 1945 Jefferson bought a controlling interest in Pilot Life Insurance Company (founded 1903) and merged it with another of its companies, Gate City Life.

Price was killed in a car crash in 1946. He was succeeded briefly by his son, who was replaced in 1950 by Howard Holderness, who had been with the company since the 1920s. By the end of the 1960s, Jefferson was serving more than 1 million policyholders in 32 states. Over the years, Jefferson also invested in several radio stations and TV studios.

After 20 years with the company, W. Roger Soles took the helm in 1967. He reorganized it into a holding company in 1968 to take advantage of changing financial markets and tax laws. The new entity, Jefferson-Pilot Corporation (JP), incorporated the names of both Jefferson Standard and its main subsidiary, Pilot Life.

During the 1970s JP diversified into new markets, including retirement and pension programs, tax-sheltered annuities, and investment and financial planning services. By 1978 the insurance industry was struggling with high interest rates and inflation, but JP's bottom line was aided by its media ventures.

JP grew steadily, if unspectacularly, during the 1980s when many peers grew fat on junk bonds and real estate. Most of JP's sales came from life insurance; its other activities, including casualty and title insurance and communications, accounted for about 20% of income by the end of the decade. Jefferson Standard and Pilot Life were merged to form Jefferson-Pilot Life in 1986. JP sailed merrily along its conservative way in the early 1990s, even as many of its competitors were sent into a tailspin by a junk bond and real estate hangover.

Soles was succeeded in 1993 by David Stonecipher, who began remaking the company. In 1995 JP sold JP Fire & Casualty and JP Data Services to concentrate on core operations, and bought Alexander Hamilton Life Insurance Company (minus its credit insurance business). In 1997 JP bought Chubb Life Insurance Company of America (renamed Jefferson Pilot Financial Insurance Company, 1998).

The next year JP allied with KeyCorp to sell insurance products through the latter's 1,000 banking centers; the firm also began to phase out medical insurance, transferring renewals to United Healthcare.

In 1999 JP and two other insurers invested in Highland Capital Holding, a holding company that aims to expand into a nationwide network of financial services firms. It also began aggressively marketing its LifeLINC annuities program through banks and bought The Guarantee Life Companies to augment its group life and disability insurance operations. In 2000, JP reorganized to better promote the Jefferson-Pilot name, a move that spelled the end of the Guarantee Life and Alexander Hamilton Life brands.

OFFICERS

Chairman and CEO: David A. Stonecipher, age 60, $2,612,410 pay
Vice Chairman and President, Life Companies: Kenneth C. Mlekush, age 63, $1,195,000 pay
President and COO: Dennis R. Glass, $1,035,096 pay
EVP and CFO; President, Jefferson-Pilot Communications: Theresa M. Stone, age 57, $576,377 pay
EVP; President, Benefit Partners: Robert D. Bates, $865,040 pay
EVP and General Counsel: John D. Hopkins, age 63, $625,000 pay
EVP, Marketing and Distribution: Warren H. May

SVP, Finance and Customer Services: Reggie D. Adamson
SVP, IT/New Business: Charles C. Cornelio
SVP and Corporate Actuary: C. Phillip Elam II
SVP and Chief Investment Officer: John C. Ingram
SVP, Product Development: Mark E. Konen
SVP, Human Resources: Hoyt J. Phillips
SVP and Deputy General Counsel: Richard T. Stange
SVP, Corporate Development: John T. Still III
VP and Tax Counsel: Dean F. Chatlain
VP, Corporate Affairs: Paul E. Mason
VP, Internal Auditing: Gary L. McGuirk
VP, Secretary, and Associate General Counsel: Robert A. Reed
Auditors: Ernst & Young LLP

LOCATIONS

HQ: 100 N. Greene St., Greensboro, NC 27401
Phone: 336-691-3000   **Fax:** 336-691-3938
Web: www.jpfinancial.com

Radio Station Locations
Atlanta
Charlotte, NC
Denver
Miami
San Diego

TV Station Locations
Charleston, SC
Charlotte, NC
Richmond, VA

PRODUCTS/OPERATIONS

2001 Assets

	$ mil.	% of total
Cash & equivalents	139	—
Mortgage-backed securities	5,584	19
Corporate bonds	8,344	29
Stocks	511	2
Mortgage loans	3,094	11
Policy loans	911	3
Assets in separate account	2,148	7
Other	8,265	29
Total	**28,996**	**100**

Selected Subsidiaries
The Guarantee Life Companies Inc.
Hampshire Funding Inc.
HARCO Capital Corp.
Jefferson-Pilot Communications Company
Jefferson-Pilot Investments, Inc.
Jefferson-Pilot Life Insurance Company
Jefferson Pilot Securities Corporation

COMPETITORS

Aetna	CNA Financial	New York Life
AFLAC	Conseco	Northwestern
AIG	Guardian Life	Mutual
Allianz	The Hartford	Principal
Allstate	John Hancock	Financial
American	Financial	Prudential
Financial	Services	St. Paul
American	Liberty Mutual	Companies
General	MassMutual	TIAA-CREF
AXA Financial	Merrill Lynch	Torchmark
CIGNA	MetLife	
Citigroup	Nationwide	

HISTORICAL FINANCIALS & EMPLOYEES

NYSE: JP FYE: December 31	Annual Growth	12/92	12/93	12/94	12/95	12/96	12/97	12/98	12/99	12/00	12/01
Assets ($ mil.)	20.9%	5,236	5,641	6,140	16,478	17,562	23,131	24,338	26,446	27,321	28,996
Net income ($ mil.)	11.4%	203	195	239	274	294	396	444	495	537	538
Income as % of assets	—	3.9%	3.5%	3.9%	1.7%	1.7%	1.7%	1.8%	1.9%	2.0%	1.9%
Earnings per share ($)	12.3%	1.18	1.15	1.46	1.68	1.81	2.31	2.61	2.95	3.29	3.35
Stock price - FY high ($)	—	14.69	17.17	16.36	21.48	26.53	38.59	52.28	53.11	50.61	49.69
Stock price - FY low ($)	—	8.98	13.50	12.87	14.99	20.08	22.91	32.48	40.81	33.27	38.00
Stock price - FY close ($)	14.0%	14.28	13.91	15.39	20.69	25.19	34.65	50.03	45.52	49.86	46.27
P/E - high	—	12	13	11	13	15	17	20	18	15	15
P/E - low	—	8	10	9	9	11	10	12	14	10	11
Dividends per share ($)	11.9%	0.39	0.45	0.50	0.55	0.48	0.69	0.57	0.66	0.96	1.07
Book value per share ($)	9.6%	9.92	10.40	10.61	13.78	14.78	17.49	19.24	17.77	20.48	22.61
Employees	22.0%	500	3,850	3,900	2,700	2,700	4,200	2,200	3,200	3,000	3,000

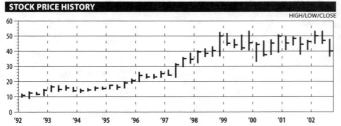

STOCK PRICE HISTORY HIGH/LOW/CLOSE

2001 FISCAL YEAR-END
Equity as % of assets: 11.7%
Return on assets: 1.9%
Return on equity: 16.4%
Long-term debt ($ mil.): 150
No. of shares (mil.): 150
Dividends
　Yield: 2.3%
　Payout: 31.9%
Market value ($ mil.): 6,941
Sales ($ mil.): 3,330

JO-ANN STORES, INC.

Jo-Ann Stores has sewn up the leadership of the fabric store market. The Hudson, Ohio-based company is the #1 fabric retailer in the US, well ahead of Hancock Fabrics. Formerly called Fabri-Centers of America, Jo-Ann sells fabrics and sewing supplies, craft materials, decorating and floral items, and seasonal goods. Most of the company's nearly 850 stores, located mainly in strip shopping centers, operate under the Jo-Ann Fabrics and Crafts name.

Recognizing that sewing these days is more often a hobby than a necessity, the company is luring creative customers with arts and crafts and home-decorating items (including Martha Stewart fabrics). Jo-Ann is pinning its hopes for future growth on its Jo-Ann etc stores, about three times the size of its traditional stores and offering a range of non-sewing items, as well as extras such as educational classes. The superstores account for almost a quarter of Jo-Ann's sales.

The company has been closing underperforming stores, and is scaling down the size of its superstores.

CEO Alan Rosskamm and his mother, Betty (an SVP), own 15% of the firm and SVP Alma Zimmerman and her family control 7%.

HISTORY

Jo-Ann Stores' predecessor began in 1943 when the German immigrant Rohrbach family started Cleveland Fabric with the help of fellow immigrants, the Reichs. Alma, daughter of the Rohrbachs, worked at the store and was joined by Betty Reich in 1947.

Betty's and Alma's respective husbands, Martin Rosskamm and Freddy Zimmerman, also joined the company. At the urging of Martin (who eventually became chairman), Cleveland Fabric opened more stores, mainly in malls. As it moved beyond Cleveland, it adopted a new store name — Jo-Ann — devised from the names of Alma and Freddy's daughter Joan and Betty and Martin's daughter Jackie Ann. It changed its name to Fabri-Centers of America in 1968 and went public the following year.

The very postwar boom that brought Alma and Betty into the workforce worked against the company in the 1970s, as women tucked away their sewing baskets in favor of jobs outside their homes. As department stores responded to the trend and stopped offering sewing supplies, specialty fabric stores found a niche. But they soon faced competition from fabric superstores and heavily discounted ready-made clothing.

Martin and Betty's son Alan took over as president and CEO in 1985 and began to modernize the company and the stores. Trained in real estate

law, he began focusing on opening larger stores in strip shopping centers, which offered cheaper leases than malls. The company had about 625 stores by mid-1989.

As its industry consolidated, Fabri-Centers held on, despite missteps such as its 1984 launch of the Cargo Express housewares chain (the money-losing venture, with about 40 stores at its peak, ended in 1994). The firm became the nation's #1 fabrics and crafts chain in 1994 when it bought 300-plus Cloth World stores. At the close of that deal, Fabri-Centers had nearly 1,000 stores in every state except Hawaii.

In 1995 Fabri-Centers opened a store on its home turf in Hudson, Ohio, that offered not only a range of fabric and craft items, but also home decorating merchandise, furniture, craft classes, and day care. At three times the size of its other stores, the Jo-Ann etc superstore helped the company pull in non-sewers looking for art supplies, picture frames, and decorating ideas. Jo-Ann etc became the focus of the company's growth.

Fabri-Centers paid $3.8 million in 1997 to settle SEC charges that it had overstated its profits during a 1992 debt offering. In 1998 it paid nearly $100 million for ailing Los Angeles-based fabric and craft company House of Fabrics, adding about 260 locations and strengthening its West Coast presence. Fabri-Centers then renamed itself Jo-Ann Stores and began placing all of its stores under the Jo-Ann name.

Jo-Ann continued relocating traditional stores and opening new stores while snipping underperforming locations. In 1999 the company signed a pact with Martha Stewart Living Omnimedia to sell fancy decorating fabrics under the Martha Stewart Home name.

Jo-Ann invested in and partnered with Idea Forest, an Internet-based arts and crafts retailer, in 2000 to run Jo-Ann's e-commerce site. In 2001 the company reported a $13.2 million loss (only the second in its history), in part because of inventory and distribution problems. As a result, Jo-Ann began closing more than 40 underperforming stores, slowing its growth rate, and reducing the number of items carried in its stores.

OFFICERS

Chairman, President, and CEO: Alan Rosskamm, age 52, $465,000 pay
EVP and CFO: Brian P. Carney, age 41, $306,500 pay
EVP, Human Resources: Rosalind Thompson, age 52, $250,000 pay
EVP, Merchandising and Marketing: David E. Bolen, age 50, $342,597 pay
EVP, Operations: Michael J. Edwards, age 41, $338,484 pay
SVP, Secretary, and Director: Betty Rosskamm, age 73

SVP and Director: Alma Zimmerman, age 89
SVP, Supply Chain Management and Logistics:
Anthony Dissinger
SVP, Marketing: William Dandy
SVP, Real Estate: David Stec
VP and Controller: James Kerr
VP, Finance: Donald Tomoff
VP, Merchandise Information Officer: Mark Krebs
VP, Store Operations and Merchandise Support:
Daniel Maguire
VP, System Development: Tim Lemieux
VP, General Merchandise Manager, Fabric: Dotty Grexa
VP, General Merchandise Manager, Home Decor:
Charles S. Domingue
VP, General Merchandise Manager, Seasonal/Floral:
Craig Davis
Regional VP, Central Region: Mary Hultgren
Regional VP, Great Lakes East Region: Dennis Hickey,
age 53
Auditors: Ernst & Young LLP

LOCATIONS

HQ: 5555 Darrow Rd., Hudson, OH 44236
Phone: 330-656-2600   **Fax:** 330-463-6675
Web: www.joann.com

Jo-Ann Stores has about about 890 Jo-Ann Fabrics and
Crafts stores in 49 states and 70 Jo-Ann etc. stores in
16 states.

PRODUCTS/OPERATIONS

2002 Sales

	% of total
Softlines	64
Hardlines	36
Total	**100**

Selected Products

Softlines
Fabrics
Patterns
Sewing machines
Sewing notions

Hardlines
Craft materials (for making stencils, dolls, jewelry, wood
projects, wall décor, rubber stamps, memory books,
plaster)
Fine art materials
Floral products line
Full service framing
Hobby items
Home accessories
Needlecraft items

Seasonal products
Decorations
Gifts
Holiday supplies

COMPETITORS

A.C. Moore	Michaels Stores
Frank's Nursery & Crafts	MJDesigns
Garden Ridge	MSO
Hancock Fabrics	Pier 1 Imports
Hobby Lobby	Rag Shops
Home Interiors & Gifts	Target
Kirkland's	Wal-Mart
Kmart	

HISTORICAL FINANCIALS & EMPLOYEES

NYSE: JAS.A FYE: Saturday nearest Jan. 31	Annual Growth	1/93	1/94	1/95	1/96	1/97	1/98	1/99	1/00	1/01	1/02
Sales ($ mil.)	11.8%	574	582	677	835	929	975	1,243	1,382	1,483	1,570
Net income ($ mil.)	—	4	2	12	18	25	31	14	26	(14)	(15)
Income as % of sales	—	0.7%	0.4%	1.7%	2.1%	2.6%	3.2%	1.1%	1.9%	—	—
Earnings per share ($)	—	0.22	0.11	0.63	0.90	1.26	1.54	0.69	1.38	(0.75)	(0.81)
Stock price - FY high ($)	—	22.50	9.63	9.13	16.13	17.00	27.81	31.88	17.25	10.31	10.70
Stock price - FY low ($)	—	5.00	6.25	5.81	8.19	9.88	15.75	13.00	9.38	5.50	3.10
Stock price - FY close ($)	3.0%	8.19	8.75	8.19	13.63	16.00	24.38	15.25	10.31	5.60	10.70
P/E - high	—	188	96	14	17	12	16	44	12	—	—
P/E - low	—	42	63	9	9	7	9	18	7	—	—
Dividends per share ($)	—	0.00	0.00	0.00	0.00	0.00	0.00	0.00	0.00	0.00	0.00
Book value per share ($)	5.3%	7.84	8.02	8.81	9.80	11.13	14.58	15.47	15.10	13.68	12.49
Employees	7.6%	11,400	11,400	17,600	17,200	17,100	16,400	22,000	22,600	22,300	22,100

STOCK PRICE HISTORY HIGH/LOW/CLOSE

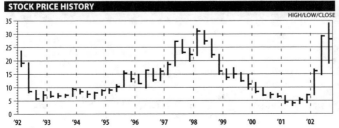

2002 FISCAL YEAR-END
Debt ratio: 49.0%
Return on equity: —
Cash ($ mil.): 21
Current ratio: 2.13
Long-term debt ($ mil.): 224
No. of shares (mil.): 19
Dividends
  Yield: —
  Payout: —
Market value ($ mil.): 199

JOHN HANCOCK

You name it, and John Hancock handles it. John Hancock Financial Services offers insurance, investment products, investment management, and other services. As it has moved from insurance to broader financial services, the company converted to stock ownership in 2000.

Its insurance products, accounting for more than 35% of sales, include variable, universal, and term life. While life insurance is still the Boston-based company's mainstay, the financial planning needs of aging baby boomers has caused John Hancock to put more emphasis on retirement savings products — annuities, mutual funds, and long-term-care insurance. One of the US's largest investors, John Hancock offers institutional asset management services, providing clients with specialty funds in such industries as timber and agriculture. John Hancock operates primarily in the US and Canada but also does business in Asia and the Pacific Rim.

As the competition heats up for financial services, the company is expanding its sales channels. While agents account for about 40% of sales, John Hancock is targeting growth through the Internet and through alliances with other firms, including regional banks.

John Hancock lost more than $300 million relating to Enron's bankruptcy and has eliminated some 1,000 jobs as part of its restructuring program.

HISTORY

In 1862 Albert Murdock and other Boston businessmen founded John Hancock Mutual Life Insurance Company, named after the large-scripted signer of the Declaration of Independence. The firm added agents in Connecticut, Illinois, Missouri, and Pennsylvania in 1865.

The following year the policyholder-owned company began making annual distributions of surplus to paid-up members. It became the first US mutual life insurer to offer industrial insurance (small-face-value weekly premium life insurance) in 1879. Hancock was also a pioneer in granting dividends and cash surrender values (the amount returned to the policyholder when a policy is canceled) with industrial insurance. In 1902 its weekly premium agencies began selling annual premium insurance.

Hancock added annuities in 1922, group insurance in 1924, and individual health insurance in 1957. In 1968 it formed John Hancock Advisers (mutual funds) and John Hancock International Group Program (group health and life insurance overseas). It added property/casualty operations (with Sentry Insurance) in the early 1970s.

Despite forays into new areas, Hancock's mainstay remained whole-life insurance. In the late 1970s, as interest rates soared, members borrowed on their policies at low rates to invest at higher rates, draining company funds. The company saw that it had to diversify. It did so through acquisitions, including brokerages and bond specialists. Other business additions included equipment leasing, universal life, and credit cards. The company also made risky direct investments in the booming real estate market.

Nonetheless, Hancock's position in the industry declined during the 1980s. A 1990s downturn in the real estate industry forced the company to establish hefty reserves against defaults, which contributed to declining earnings. As a result, it sold its banking, credit card, and property/casualty operations.

Hancock expanded overseas, buying interests in insurers in Singapore and Thailand. John Hancock was among many insurers subjected to increased fraud scrutiny in the mid-1990s. In 1994 it agreed to pay more than $1 million in federal and state fines for treating Massachusetts state senators to sports events and dinners over a six-year period, but the problems went deeper. The State of New York fined Hancock $1 million, saying agents persuaded consumers that life insurance policies were retirement savings products (the company responded by fining and laying off agents and altering their compensation plans), and Massachusetts launched an investigation of the company prompted by a 1995 deceptive-sales suit brought by policyholders. (Hancock in 1999 said it would spend more than $700 million to settle the suit.)

John Hancock initiated new sales strategies to bypass agents entirely, including direct mail, telemarketing, and online sales (through a pact with Microsoft). It sold its health care operations in 1997. In 1998 the company also began collaborating with Vietnam Insurance Company to operate in that country, and in 1999 it was among the first insurers approved to sell life insurance in China. The next year the company demutualized and became John Hancock Financial Services.

OFFICERS

Chairman, President, and CEO: David F. D'Alessandro, age 51, $2,600,000 pay
SEVP and CFO: Thomas E. Moloney, age 58, $1,188,346 pay
SEVP, Retail Sector: Michael A. Bell, age 46, $1,537,385 pay (partial-year salary)
EVP; Chairman and CEO, John Hancock Funds, Inc.: Maureen R. Ford, age 46, $1,060,000 pay (partial-year salary)

EVP, General Counsel, and Director: Wayne A. Budd, age 60, $980,000 pay
EVP and Chief Investment Officer: John M. DeCiccio, age 53
EVP and CIO: Robert F. Walters, age 52
EVP, International Operations; Chairman and CEO, John Hancock International, Inc.: Derek Chilvers, age 62
SVP and Chief Compliance Officer: Robert H. Watts
SVP and Chief Investment Strategist: Robert R. Reitano
SVP and Controller: Earl W. Baucom
SVP and Corporate Actuarial: Barry L. Shemin
SVP, Corporate Communications: Stephen P. Burgay
SVP, Human Resources: Page Palmer
SVP, Investor Relations: Jean Peters
Auditors: Ernst & Young LLP

LOCATIONS

HQ: John Hancock Financial Services, Inc.
John Hancock Place, Boston, MA 02117
Phone: 617-572-6000   **Fax:** 617-572-9799
Web: www.johnhancock.com

John Hancock Financial Services has operations in Australia, Belgium, Brazil, Canada, China, Indonesia, Ireland, Malaysia, the Philippines, Singapore, Thailand, the UK, and the US.

2001 Sales

	$ mil.	% of total
US	7,667	84
Canada	1,076	12
Other	366	4
Total	**9,109**	**100**

PRODUCTS/OPERATIONS

2001 Assets

	$ mil.	% of total
Cash and equivalents	1,314	2
Treasury & agency securities	300	—
Foreign governments' securities	1,730	2
Mortgage-backed securities	6,298	7
Corporate bonds	32,625	36
Stocks	1,191	1
Mortgage loans	10,993	12
Real estate	442	—
Policy loans	2,008	2
Assets in separate account	22,719	25
Recoverables	1,909	2
Other	9,615	11
Total	**91,144**	**100**

COMPETITORS

AIG	MassMutual
Allmerica Financial	Merrill Lynch
American General	MetLife
AXA Financial	MONY
Charles Schwab	Morgan Stanley
CIGNA	Mutual of Omaha
Citigroup	National Life Insurance
Conseco	Nationwide
FMR	New York Life
GenAmerica	Northwestern Mutual
Guardian Life	Phoenix Companies
Hartford	Principal Financial
Jefferson-Pilot	Prudential
Kemper Insurance	Prudential plc
Lincoln National	TIAA-CREF

HISTORICAL FINANCIALS & EMPLOYEES

NYSE: JHF FYE: December 31	Annual Growth	12/92	12/93	12/94	12/95	12/96	12/97	12/98	12/99	12/00	12/01
Assets ($ mil.)	7.0%	—	—	56,688	63,321	66,503	71,418	76,967	84,456	87,353	91,144
Net income ($ mil.)	16.9%	—	—	207	350	421	483	449	153	839	619
Income as % of assets	—	—	—	0.4%	0.6%	0.6%	0.7%	0.6%	0.2%	1.0%	0.7%
Earnings per share ($)	(19.9%)	—	—	—	—	—	—	—	—	2.51	2.01
Stock price - FY high ($)	—	—	—	—	—	—	—	—	—	38.25	42.00
Stock price - FY low ($)	—	—	—	—	—	—	—	—	—	5.25	31.50
Stock price - FY close ($)	9.8%	—	—	—	—	—	—	—	—	37.63	41.30
P/E - high	—	—	—	—	—	—	—	—	—	15	21
P/E - low	—	—	—	—	—	—	—	—	—	2	16
Dividends per share ($)	3.3%	—	—	—	—	—	—	—	—	0.30	0.31
Book value per share ($)	6.5%	—	—	—	—	—	—	—	—	18.52	19.73
Employees	(2.1%)	—	—	—	—	—	—	8,900	9,700	8,503	8,355

STOCK PRICE HISTORY

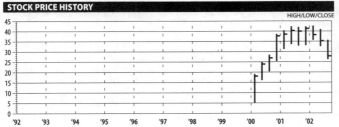

HIGH/LOW/CLOSE

2001 FISCAL YEAR-END

Equity as % of assets: 6.4%
Return on assets: 0.7%
Return on equity: 10.6%
Long-term debt ($ mil.): 1,359
No. of shares (mil.): 297
Dividends
  Yield: 0.8%
  Payout: 15.4%
Market value ($ mil.): 12,278
Sales ($ mil.): 9,109

JOHNSON & JOHNSON

Johnson & Johnson keeps making & making more & more products.

The New Brunswick, New Jersey, company is one of the world's largest manufacturers of health care products and drugs. Its pharmaceutical products (which account for 45% of sales) include Aciphex (gastrointestinal disorders), Duragesic (a skin patch for chronic pain), anemia drug Procrit, Remicade (rheumatoid arthritis and Crohn's disease), and epilepsy medication Topamax. Consumer products include Band-Aids, Neutrogena skin care products, Reach toothbrushes, and Tylenol and Motrin pain relievers. The medical devices and diagnostics segment includes diagnostic equipment, surgical tools, wound management products, and disposable contact lenses (ACUVUE).

Through a broad range of acquisitions and alliances with small companies developing specialized products, Johnson & Johnson continues to expand and strengthen its presence in several medical sectors. The company bought drug and drug-delivery system maker ALZA for more than $12 billion, its largest deal to date. The purchase gave J&J's pipeline a boost in several areas, including the coveted oncology segment, and added several products to its line, including the Nicoderm nicotine patch, incontinence treatment Ditropan XL, and Concerta, a treatment for attention deficit hyperactivity disorder.

Despite its long-standing prominence in the consumer health care market, Johnson & Johnson is focusing more on biotechnology. It bought up-and-coming biotech company Centocor in 1999 and also purchased biotech concern Tibotec-Virtec, which makes antiviral drugs. The firm also sells anemia treatment Procrit (Eprex in Europe) under license from Amgen, one of the largest biotech firms in the world.

HISTORY

Brothers James and Edward Mead Johnson founded their medical products company in 1885 in New Brunswick, New Jersey. In 1886 Robert joined his brothers to make the antiseptic surgical dressings he developed. The company bought gauze maker Chicopee Manufacturing in 1916. In 1921 it introduced two of its classic products, the Band-Aid and Johnson's Baby Cream.

Robert Jr. became chairman in 1932 and served until 1963. A WWII Army general, he believed in decentralization; managers were given substantial freedom, a principle still used today. Product lines in the 1940s included Ortho (birth control products) and Ethicon (sutures). In 1959 Johnson & Johnson bought McNeil Labs, which

launched Tylenol (acetaminophen) as an OTC drug the next year. Foreign acquisitions included Switzerland's Cilag-Chemie (1959) and Belgium's Janssen (1961). The company focused on consumer products in the 1970s, gaining half the feminine protection market and making Tylenol the top-selling painkiller.

J&J bought Iolab, a developer of intraocular lenses used in cataract surgery in 1980. Trouble struck in 1982 when someone laced Tylenol capsules with cyanide, killing eight people. The company's response is now a damage-control classic: It immediately recalled 31 million bottles and totally redesigned its packaging to prevent future tampering. The move cost $240 million but saved the Tylenol brand. The next year prescription painkiller Zomax was linked to five deaths and was pulled.

New products in the 1980s included ACUVUE disposable contact lenses and Retin-A. The company bought LifeScan (blood-monitoring products for diabetics) in 1986. In 1989 Johnson & Johnson began a joint venture with Merck to sell Mylanta and other drugs bought from ICI Americas.

The firm continued its acquisition and diversification strategy in the 1990s. After introducing the first daily-wear, disposable contact lenses in 1993, it bought skin care products maker Neutrogena (1994) to enhance its consumer lines. To diversify its medical products and better compete for hospital business, it bought Mitek Surgical Products (1995) and heart disease product maker Cordis (1996). That year the FDA cleared J&J's Renova wrinkle and fade cream.

In 1997 Johnson & Johnson bought the OTC rights to Motrin from Pharmacia & Upjohn (now Pharmacia). In 1998 the FDA approved the artificial sweetener sucralose and its Indigo LaserOptic system to treat prostate enlargement. That year it bought DePuy and launched Benecol, a margarine said to cut "bad" cholesterol by up to 15%.

In 1999 it purchased S.C. Johnson & Son's skin care business, including the Aveeno line. The next year the firm bought sports medicine device maker Innovasive Devices. After more than 80 deaths were linked to its use, it pulled heartburn drug Propulsid from the US market. Also in 2000 the company started a health care services information technology joint venture with Merrill Lynch and began selling Definity 2 trifocals as its first venture into eyeglass lenses.

In 2001 J&J bought minimally invasive heart surgery equipment maker Heartport. Other acquisitions included BabyCenter, an online parenting resource; drug and drug-delivery system maker ALZA; and the diabetes-care businesses of

Inverness Medical Technology, which it merged into with its LifeScan division. The following year the company joined with six pharmaceuticals companies to offer a discount drug program for the elderly. Also that year the FDA launched a criminal investigation of a company factory in Puerto Rico.

OFFICERS

Chairman and CEO: William C. Weldon, age 53, $1,735,223 pay
Vice Chairman and President; Worldwide Chairman, Medical Devices and Diagnostics Group: James T. Lenehan, age 53, $1,707,273 pay
VP and CIO: JoAnn Heffernan Heisen, age 52
VP and General Counsel: Roger S. Fine, age 59
VP, Finance, CFO, and Director: Robert J. Darretta, age 55, $1,354,679 pay
VP, Human Resources: Michael J. Carey
Worldwide Chairman, Consumer Pharmaceuticals and Nutritionals Group: Brian D. Perkins, age 48
Worldwide Chairman, Consumer and Personal Care Group: Colleen A. Goggins, age 47
Worldwide Chairman, Pharmaceuticals Group: Christine A. Poon, age 49
Company Group Chairman, Pharmaceuticals Group: Joseph C. Scodari
Chairman, Research and Development, Pharmaceuticals Group: Per A. Peterson, age 57
Auditors: PricewaterhouseCoopers LLP

LOCATIONS

HQ: 1 Johnson & Johnson Plaza, New Brunswick, NJ 08933
Phone: 732-524-0400   **Fax:** 732-524-3300
Web: www.jnj.com

2001 Sales

	$ mil.	% of total
US	20,204	61
Europe	6,853	21
Africa & Asia/Pacific	3,805	12
Canada & Latin America	2,142	6
Total	**33,004**	**100**

PRODUCTS/OPERATIONS

2001 Sales

	$ mil.	% of total
Pharmaceuticals	14,851	45
Medical devices and diagnostics	11,191	34
Consumer products	6,962	21
Total	**33,004**	**100**

COMPETITORS

3M	Bristol-Myers	Merck
Abbott Labs	Squibb	Nestlé
Affymetrix	Colgate-	Novartis
Alberto-Culver	Palmolive	Perrigo
Amgen	Dade Behring	Pfizer
Aventis	Dial	Pharmacia
Bausch & Lomb	Eli Lilly	Procter &
Baxter	Genentech	Gamble
Bayer AG	Gillette	Roche
Beckman	GlaxoSmithKline	St. Jude Medical
Coulter	Kimberly-Clark	Unilever
Becton	L'Oréal USA	United States
Dickinson	MedPointe	Surgical
	Medtronic	Wyeth

HISTORICAL FINANCIALS & EMPLOYEES

NYSE: JNJ FYE: Sunday nearest Dec. 31	Annual Growth	12/92	12/93	12/94	12/95	12/96	12/97	12/98	12/99	12/00	12/01
Sales ($ mil.)	10.2%	13,753	14,138	15,734	18,842	21,620	22,629	23,657	27,471	29,139	33,004
Net income ($ mil.)	20.9%	1,030	1,787	2,006	2,403	2,887	3,303	3,059	4,167	4,800	5,668
Income as % of sales	—	7.5%	12.6%	12.7%	12.8%	13.4%	14.6%	12.9%	15.2%	16.5%	17.2%
Earnings per share ($)	31.2%	0.16	0.68	0.77	0.91	1.06	1.21	1.12	1.47	1.70	1.84
Stock price - FY high ($)	—	14.67	12.59	14.13	23.09	27.00	33.66	44.88	53.44	52.97	60.97
Stock price - FY low ($)	—	10.75	8.91	9.00	13.41	20.78	24.31	27.22	38.50	33.06	40.25
Stock price - FY close ($)	18.7%	12.63	11.22	13.69	21.38	24.88	32.94	41.94	46.63	52.53	59.10
P/E - high	—	38	18	18	25	25	27	39	36	31	33
P/E - low	—	28	13	12	14	19	20	24	26	19	22
Dividends per share ($)	13.2%	0.23	0.26	0.29	0.32	0.37	0.43	0.49	0.55	0.62	0.70
Book value per share ($)	16.8%	1.97	2.16	2.77	3.49	4.07	4.59	5.06	5.83	6.76	7.95
Employees	2.0%	84,900	81,600	81,500	82,300	89,300	90,500	93,100	97,800	98,500	101,800

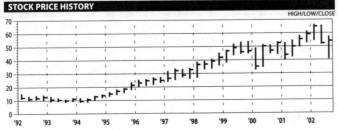

STOCK PRICE HISTORY HIGH/LOW/CLOSE

2001 FISCAL YEAR-END
Debt ratio: 8.4%
Return on equity: 26.3%
Cash ($ mil.): 3,758
Current ratio: 2.30
Long-term debt ($ mil.): 2,217
No. of shares (mil.): 3,047
Dividends
  Yield: 1.2%
  Payout: 38.0%
Market value ($ mil.): 180,090

JOHNSON CONTROLS, INC.

Don't panic, but Johnson Controls has you surrounded. The Milwaukee-based company makes car seats, interior systems, and batteries for automobiles and environmental control systems for commercial buildings. More than 40% of sales are to General Motors, Ford, and DaimlerChrysler. Johnson Controls sells the majority of its batteries through the replacement market via retailers such as AutoZone, Sears, and Wal-Mart. In addition to making systems that regulate temperature and lighting, the company also offers facility management for commercial buildings through its controls division.

Johnson Controls' automotive unit is focused on offering carmakers larger interior modules with the goal of eventually selling complete interiors. The company is also developing interior systems with electronic gadgetry so that its customers can offer more distinctive products. In addition, Johnson Controls is entering the retail store market by way of its controls group's integrated systems, which allow for remote monitoring, diagnostics, and service dispatch via the Internet.

HISTORY

Professor Warren Johnson developed the electric telethermoscope in 1880 so that janitors at Whitewater, Wisconsin's State Normal School could regulate room temperatures without disturbing classrooms. His device, the thermostat, used mercury to move a heat element that opened and shut a circuit. Milwaukee hotelier William Plankinton believed in the invention and invested $150,000 to start production.

The two men formed Johnson Electric Service Company in 1885. They sold the marketing, installation, and service rights to concentrate on manufacturing. Johnson also invented other devices such as tower clocks, and he experimented with the telegraph before becoming interested in the automobile and beginning production of steam-powered cars. He won the US Postal Service's first automotive contract, but never gained support within his own company. Johnson continued to look elsewhere for financing until his death in 1911.

The renamed Johnson Services regained full rights to its thermostats in 1912 and sold its other businesses. During the Depression it produced economy systems, which regulated building temperatures. Johnson Services became a public company in 1940. During WWII it aided the war effort, building weather-data gatherers and test radar sets.

In the 1960s Johnson Services began to develop centralized control systems for temperature, fire alarm, lighting, and security regulation. The company was renamed Johnson Controls in 1974; it acquired automotive battery maker Globe-Union in 1978.

Johnson Controls bought auto seat makers Hoover Universal and Ferro Manufacturing in 1985. It expanded its controls business through the purchases of ITT's European controls group (1982) and Pan Am World Services (1989).

The company sold its car-door components business in 1990 and bought battery maker Varta's Canadian plant. The next year Johnson Controls purchased several car-seat component makers in Europe, and in 1992 it bought a Welsh plastics manufacturer and a Czech seat-cover producer.

The battery unit faced a major setback in 1994 when Sears dropped the company as its battery maker. Two years later, however, the battery business was recharged by an exclusive supply contract with Target stores.

In 1996 Johnson Controls bought most of Roth Frères (auto components) and Prince Automotive (interior systems), becoming a major interior-systems integrator. The company sold its plastic-container operations to the Schmalbach-Lubeca unit of Germany's VIAG in 1997 and regained its Sears business with a three-year deal to make DieHard batteries.

The company bought Becker Group (automotive interior parts), Creative Control Designs (HVAC and lighting-control systems), and Italy-based Commerfin SpA (door systems) in 1998. To slim down after its buying binge, Johnson Controls sold its plastics-machinery division to Cincinnati Milacron and its industrial batteries unit to C&D Technologies.

The company announced in 1999 that it would develop integrated electronics for car interiors through a *keiretsu*-like partnership with Gentex Corporation (mirrors), Jabil Circuit (semiconductors and transistors), and Microchip Technology (microcontrollers). The next year Johnson Controls agreed to buy Nissan's 38% stake in seat maker Ikeda Bussan for about $100 million, as well as Sweden's Gylling Optima Batteries for about $62 million. Late in 2000 the company bought a 15% stake in Donnelly Corporation (automotive components).

The next year it paid $435 million in cash for the automotive electronics business of France's Sagem. Later in 2001 Johnson Controls picked up German automotive battery maker Hoppecke Automotive GmbH & Co. The company finished out the year with the acquisition of SCIENTECH Security Services, a design-build security-system integration services business, specializing in US government projects.

Chairman and CEO: James H. Keyes, age 61,
$2,153,001 pay
President, COO, and Director: John M. Barth, age 56,
$1,354,005 pay
SVP and CFO: Stephen A. Roell, age 51, $830,005 pay
VP and CIO: Subhash Valanju, age 58
VP and Corporate Treasurer: Ben C. M. Bastianen,
age 57
VP and General Manager, Information Technology:
Susan Kampe
VP, Human Resources: Susan F. Davis, age 48
VP; President, Automotive Operations:
Rande S. Somma, age 49
VP; President, Controls Group: Brian J. Stark, age 52,
$749,751 pay
VP; President, Europe, Africa, Latin America, and Asia:
Giovanni Fiori, age 58, $708,504 pay
**VP; President of Battery Operations, Automotive
Systems Group:** Keith E. Wandell, age 51
VP, Secretary, and General Counsel: John P. Kennedy,
age 58
Auditors: PricewaterhouseCoopers LLP

LOCATIONS

HQ: 5757 N. Green Bay Ave., Milwaukee, WI 53209
Phone: 414-524-1200   **Fax:** 414-524-2077
Web: www.johnsoncontrols.com

2001 Sales

	$ mil.	% of total
North America	11,584	63
Europe	4,712	26
Other regions	2,131	11
Total	**18,427**	**100**

PRODUCTS/OPERATIONS

Sales & Operating Income

	$ mil.	% of total	$ mil.	% of total
Automotive systems	13,620	74	720	75
Controls	4,807	26	241	25
Total	**18,427**	**100**	**961**	**100**

Selected Products

Automotive Systems
Batteries
Cockpits
Door systems
Floor consoles
Instrument panels
Overhead systems
Seating systems

Controls
Actuators
Building automation
  systems

Control panels, consoles,
  and instrumentation
Dampers
Digital electronic
  controllers
Electronic sensor controls
Heating products
Pneumatic controls
Refrigeration controls
Valves

COMPETITORS

Alcatel
Ansell
Collins & Aikman
Delphi
Eagle-Picher
Eaton
Exide
Faurecia
General Motors
Hitachi
Honeywell International

Invensys
Johnson Electric
Landis & Gyr
Lear
Magna International
Siemens
SPX
Textron
United Technologies
Varta
Visteon

HISTORICAL FINANCIALS & EMPLOYEES

NYSE: JCI FYE: September 30	Annual Growth	9/92	9/93	9/94	9/95	9/96	9/97	9/98	9/99	9/00	9/01
Sales ($ mil.)	15.2%	5,157	6,182	6,871	8,330	10,009	11,145	12,587	16,139	17,155	18,427
Net income ($ mil.)	16.3%	123	16	165	196	235	289	338	420	472	478
Income as % of sales	—	2.4%	0.3%	2.4%	2.4%	2.3%	2.6%	2.7%	2.6%	2.8%	2.6%
Earnings per share ($)	15.8%	1.37	0.08	1.80	2.14	2.55	3.12	3.63	4.48	5.09	5.11
Stock price - FY high ($)	—	21.88	29.56	30.88	33.00	38.25	49.81	61.88	76.69	70.81	81.70
Stock price - FY low ($)	—	15.19	19.31	22.44	22.88	28.88	35.38	42.19	40.50	45.81	46.44
Stock price - FY close ($)	14.1%	19.94	27.19	24.88	31.63	37.50	49.56	46.50	66.31	53.19	65.24
P/E - high	—	15	19	16	15	14	15	16	16	13	15
P/E - low	—	11	12	12	10	11	11	11	8	8	9
Dividends per share ($)	7.6%	0.64	0.68	0.72	0.78	0.82	0.86	0.92	1.00	1.12	1.24
Book value per share ($)	9.7%	14.78	13.38	14.78	16.30	18.17	20.07	22.92	26.58	29.96	34.12
Employees	10.2%	46,800	50,100	54,800	59,200	65,800	72,300	89,000	95,000	105,000	112,000

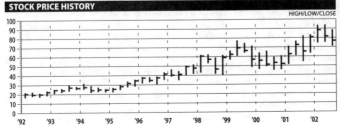

STOCK PRICE HISTORY   HIGH/LOW/CLOSE

2001 FISCAL YEAR-END
Debt ratio: 31.8%
Return on equity: 18.0%
Cash ($ mil.): 375
Current ratio: 0.99
Long-term debt ($ mil.): 1,395
No. of shares (mil.): 87
Dividends
  Yield: 1.9%
  Payout: 24.3%
Market value ($ mil.): 5,708

JONES APPAREL GROUP, INC.

Jones Apparel Group isn't content with keeping up — it wants to set the pace. The Bristol, Pennsylvania-based firm has transformed itself from a supplier of designer-alternative career wear into a provider of a wide range of women's clothing and shoes. Jones also offers men's casual sportswear. It offers more than 20 brands of moderately priced sportswear, business wear, casuals, and shoes, including Jones New York, Nine West, Evan-Picone, Todd Oldham, Rena Rowan, Easy Spirit, and several brands licensed from Polo Ralph Lauren. Its products are manufactured — mainly by third parties — in Asia, Latin America, Mexico, and the US. Footwear is made in China, Brazil, and Italy.

Jones also licenses its Jones New York and Evan-Picone brand names to other makers of women's and men's apparel and accessories. Subsidiary and footwear designer Nine West Group has about 400 stores and more than 340 outlet locations in the US and Australia and operates licensees for stores worldwide. Through Nine West, Jones licenses brands from Esprit for footwear and accessories.

Jones acquired mid-priced clothing retailer McNaughton Apparel Group in June 2001. In August 2002 it bought RSV Sport, maker of l.e.i. jeanswear for girls.

Warren Buffett's Berkshire Hathaway owns about 7% of the company.

HISTORY

When diversifying chemical firm W. R. Grace & Co. began a brief foray into the fashion world in 1970, it hired Sidney Kimmel to run the show. Kimmel had worked in a knitting mill in the 1950s and served as president of women's sportswear maker Villager in the 1960s. He and his companion, designer Rena Rowan, created Grace's fashionable but moderately priced Jones New York line.

Kimmel and Grace accountant Gerard Rubin bought Grace's fashion division in 1975, incorporating it as Jones Apparel Group. Jones expanded quickly by bringing out new labels and licensing others, such as Christian Dior. Talks to sell the company to underwear maker Warnaco fell through in 1981.

Tapping into two trends of the early 1980s, Jones Apparel offered the sweatsuit fashions of Norma Kamali and in 1984 acquired the license for the Gloria Vanderbilt line from Murjani. Swan-adorned Gloria Vanderbilt jeans had been must-haves early in the decade, but the deal turned into an ugly duckling as costs beyond Jones Apparel's' control pushed the company into the red. (Meanwhile, Kimmel produced the films *9 1/2 Weeks* and *Clan of the Cave Bear* and led a group that briefly controlled the Famous Amos Cookie Co.)

Creditors forced Jones Apparel to unload most of its brands — all but Jones New York, Saville, and Christian Dior — and cut jobs, and by 1988 it was profitable again. Kimmel bought Rubin's interest in the company in 1989 and took it public in 1991, retaining about half of the stock.

In the early 1990s, as recession-minded shoppers looked for bargains and the American workplace became more casual, Jones again took off. The company expanded with new lines, such as Rena Rowan (inexpensive suits) and Jones & Co. (career casuals). Jones Apparel moved into women's accessories with the 1993 purchase of the Evan-Picone brand name.

Two years later the company struck its first licensing agreement with Polo Ralph Lauren, for the Lauren by Ralph Lauren line of women's sportswear. Propelled by the new line, Jones reached a billion dollars in sales in 1996. The company ended its long-held licensing agreement with Christian Dior the next year.

Jones Apparel licensed Ralph by Ralph Lauren, a lower-priced juniors' line, in 1998. Also in 1998 it purchased Sun Apparel, picking up the rights to Todd Oldham and Polo jeans, and in 1999 it bought the remaining clothing, footwear, cosmetics, and apparel rights to the youth-oriented Oldham name.

The firm then made its biggest acquisition by far when it paid $1.4 billion for shoe designer and retailer Nine West Group (Easy Spirit, Enzo Angiolini, Bandolino, Amalfi).

With the Nine West purchase, Jones Apparel inherited an FTC investigation into the footwear designer's pricing policies. The company closed several Nine West facilities in 1999, cutting about 1,900 jobs, followed by the sale of its retail operations in Canada (1999), Asia (2000), and the UK (2001). In 2000 Jones Apparel bought costume jewelry designer and marketer Victoria + Co. for $90 million. It purchased mid-market clothing designer McNaughton Apparel Group in June 2001. Continuing its acquisition spree, the company agreed to purchase Gloria Vanderbilt Apparel in March 2002 for about $140 million. The company also said in 2002 that it planned to open 15 to 20 retail stores and close 30 to 40 under-performing locations. In May president Peter Boneparth was named CEO, after Kimmel stepped down (he remains as chairman). Jones Apparel bought RSV Sport, maker of l.e.i. jeanswear for girls, in August 2002.

Chairman: Sidney Kimmel, age 74, $3,700,000 pay
President, CEO, and Director: Peter Boneparth, age 42
COO and CFO: Wesley R. Card, age 54, $1,400,000 pay
EVP, Distribution: John Sammaritano
EVP, Domestic Manufacturing: Ronald Harrison
EVP, Foreign Manufacturing: Martin Marlowe
EVP, Finance and Investor Relations: Anita Britt
SVP and CFO, Moderate Apparel Division:
Amanda J. Bokman
SVP and CTO: Paul Lanham
SVP and Corporate Controller: Patrick M. Farrell, age 52
SVP and Creative Director: Benny Lin
SVP and Treasurer: Efthimios P. Sotos
SVP, Human Resources: Aida Tejero-DeColli
CEO, Gloria Vanderbilt Division: Isaac Dabah
President and CEO, Costume Jewelry Division:
Robert Andreoli
President and CEO, Footwear, Accessories and Retail Group; President and CEO, Nine West Group:
Rhonda J. Brown
President, Gloria Vanderbilt Division: Jack Gross
President, Licensing: Mary Belle
President, Merchandising for Career Collection:
Mark Mendelson
Auditors: BDO Seidman, LLP

LOCATIONS

HQ: 250 Rittenhouse Circle, Bristol, PA 19007
Phone: 215-785-4000   **Fax:** 215-785-1795
Web: www.jny.com

Jones Apparel Group's products are manufactured primarily by contractors in Asia, Latin America, Mexico and the US. They are sold in Australia, Canada, and the US.

PRODUCTS/OPERATIONS

2001 Sales

	$ mil.	% of total
Wholesale apparel	2,369	58
Retail	712	17
Wholesale footwear & accessories	967	24
Other	25	1
Adjustment	(25)	—
Total	**4,048**	**100**

Selected Brands

9 & Co.	Jones New York
Bandolino	Jones Wear
Calico	Lauren by Ralph Lauren
Capezio (licensed)	(licensed)
Easy Spirit	Nine West
Enzo Angiolini	Polo (licensed)
Esprit (licensed)	Ralph by Ralph Lauren
Evan-Picone	(licensed)
Givenchy (jewelry)	Todd Oldham
Gloria Vanderbilt	Tommy Hilfiger
JNY Sport	Westies

COMPETITORS

AnnTaylor	Chico's FAS	Maxwell Shoe
Bally	Coach	Nordstrom
bebe stores	Donna Karan	Payless
Berkshire	Ellen Tracy	ShoeSource
Hathaway	Etienne Aigner	Polo
Bernard Chaus	Gucci	St. John Knits
Brown Shoe	IT Holding	Skechers U.S.A.
Calvin Klein	Kasper	Steven Madden
Candie's	Kenneth Cole	VF
Casual Corner	Liz Claiborne	

HISTORICAL FINANCIALS & EMPLOYEES

NYSE: JNY FYE: December 31	Annual Growth	12/92	12/93	12/94	12/95	12/96	12/97	12/98	12/99	12/00	12/01
Sales ($ mil.)	28.1%	437	541	633	776	1,021	1,373	1,669	3,130	4,121	4,048
Net income ($ mil.)	21.4%	41	50	55	64	81	122	155	188	302	236
Income as % of sales	—	9.5%	9.2%	8.7%	8.2%	7.9%	8.9%	9.3%	6.0%	7.3%	5.8%
Earnings per share ($)	18.3%	0.40	0.49	0.52	0.60	0.76	1.13	1.47	1.60	2.48	1.82
Stock price - FY high ($)	—	10.50	10.25	8.94	9.91	18.69	28.72	37.75	35.88	35.00	47.43
Stock price - FY low ($)	—	5.75	4.66	5.50	5.66	8.91	16.06	15.88	21.50	20.13	23.75
Stock price - FY close ($)	14.9%	9.53	7.47	6.44	9.84	18.69	21.50	22.06	27.13	32.19	33.17
P/E - high	—	26	21	17	16	24	24	25	22	14	26
P/E - low	—	14	10	10	9	11	14	10	13	8	13
Dividends per share ($)	—	0.00	0.00	0.00	0.00	0.00	0.00	0.00	0.00	0.00	0.00
Book value per share ($)	31.0%	1.33	1.87	2.40	3.01	3.62	4.26	5.74	10.12	12.30	15.16
Employees	34.5%	1,160	1,475	2,325	2,560	2,945	3,135	8,685	22,350	13,860	16,690

STOCK PRICE HISTORY

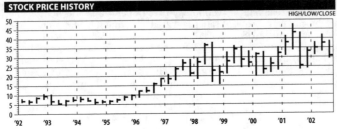

HIGH/LOW/CLOSE

2001 FISCAL YEAR-END

Debt ratio: 33.9%
Return on equity: 14.0%
Cash ($ mil.): 77
Current ratio: 3.02
Long-term debt ($ mil.): 977
No. of shares (mil.): 126
Dividends
  Yield: —
  Payout: —
Market value ($ mil.): 4,169

J.P. MORGAN CHASE & CO.

Could the honeymoon be over for Chase Manhattan and J.P. Morgan & Co.? The 2001 merger of the venerable firms formed J.P. Morgan Chase (the #2 US bank behind Citigroup), intending to take advantage of Chase's lending prowess to lure corporate advisory clients to Morgan.

New York-based J.P. Morgan Chase offers commercial, consumer, and institutional banking in more than 50 nations. Stateside, the bank's retail branches operate mainly in Connecticut, New Jersey, New York, and Texas. It has bragging rights as one of the nation's top mortgage lenders, automobile loan writers, and credit card issuers. The company's asset management business includes institutional investment manager J.P. Morgan Fleming and the prestigious J.P. Morgan Private Bank. J.P. Morgan Chase also claims 45% ownership of mutual fund company American Century.

The company's investment banking operations (including J.P. Morgan H&Q) boast expertise in mergers and acquisitions consulting, risk management, and debt and securities underwriting. J.P. Morgan Chase offers online brokerage services to seasoned investors through Brown & Company and provides equity funding through J.P. Morgan Partners.

J.P. Morgan Chase's commercial lending practices have raised some eyebrows. The company is responsible for nearly half of all corporate enterprise loans (loans secured by debt or market capitalization rather than assets) in the US, leaving it vulnerable to a range of credit risks, such as troubled firms Kmart, Qwest Communications, and Tyco International. J.P. Morgan Chase also has more than $2 billion in exposure to Enron, and is battling with insurers in court in an attempt to recoup some of its losses.

What's more, the marriage of Chase and Morgan has also struggled through steep private equity losses and an industry-wide slowdown in investment banking activity. The firm has cut nearly 9% of its workforce since the merger was announced.

HISTORY

J.P. Morgan Chase & Co.'s roots are in The Manhattan Company, created in 1799 to bring water to New York City. A provision buried in its incorporation documents let the company provide banking services; investor and future US Vice President Aaron Burr brought the company (eventually the Bank of Manhattan) into competition with The Bank of New York, founded by Burr's political rival Alexander Hamilton. J.P. Morgan Chase still owns the pistols from the notorious 1804 duel in which Burr mortally wounded Hamilton.

In 1877 John Thompson formed Chase National, naming it for Salmon Chase, Abraham Lincoln's secretary of the treasury and the architect of the national bank system. Chase National merged with John D. Rockefeller's Equitable Trust in 1930, becoming the world's largest bank and beginning a long relationship with the Rockefellers. Chase National continued growing after WWII, and in 1955 it merged with the Bank of Manhattan. Christened Chase Manhattan, the bank remained the US's largest into the 1960s.

When soaring 1970s oil prices made energy loans attractive, Chase invested in Penn Square, an obscure oil-patch bank in Oklahoma and the first notable bank failure of the 1980s. (The legal aftereffects of Penn Square's 1982 failure dragged on until 1993.) Losses following the 1987 foreign loan crisis hit the company hard, as did the real estate crash. In 1995 the bank went looking for a partner. After talks with Bank of America, it settled on Chemical Bank.

Chemical Bank opened in 1824 and was one of the US's largest banks by 1900. As with Chase, Chemical Bank began as an unrelated business (New York Chemical Manufacturing) in 1823, largely in order to open a bank (it dropped its chemical operations in 1844). Chemical would merge with Manufacturer's Hanover in 1991.

After its 1996 merger with Chase, Chemical Bank was the surviving entity but assumed Chase's more prestigious name. Initial cost savings from the merger were substantial as jobs and branch offices were eliminated. In 1997 Chase acquired the credit business of The Bank of New York and the corporate trustee business of Mellon Financial, but underwent another round of belt-tightening the next year when it took a $320 million charge and cut 4,500 jobs. The bank also suffered losses related to its involvement with the ill-starred Long-Term Capital Management hedge fund.

In 1999 Chase focused on lending, buying two mortgage originators and forming a marketing alliance with subprime auto lender AmeriCredit. Chase also bought Mellon Financial's residential mortgage unit and Huntington Bancshares' credit card portfolio. That year the company created Chase.com to manage Internet and new technology-based operations and bought San Francisco-based investment bank Hambrecht & Quist (since renamed J.P. Morgan H&Q).

In 2000 the bank announced it would offer bond trading via the Web site Market Axess (J.P. Morgan and Bear Stearns were partners in the venture), and it bought UK investment bank Robert Fleming Holdings.

In 2001 it closed its $30 billion buy of J.P. Morgan and renamed itself J.P. Morgan Chase &

Co. The bank eliminated some 3,000 jobs as a result of the merger. Also that year subsidiary Chase Manhattan Mortgage bought the subprime mortgage business of Advanta. Chairman Sandy Warner (who ran J.P. Morgan) retired at year-end and was replaced by former Chase Manhattan leader, CEO William Harrison.

OFFICERS

Chairman and CEO: William B. Harrison Jr., age 58, $6,000,000 pay
Head, Investment Bank, Investment Management, and Private Banking: David A. Coulter, age 54, $5,000,000 pay
Head, Credit Risk Policy: Suzanne Hammett, age 46
Head, Retail Banking: Donald H. Layton, age 51, $8,500,000 pay
Head, Finance, Risk Management, and Administration: Marc J. Shapiro, $4,175,000 pay
Head, J.P. Morgan Partners: Jeffrey C. Walker, age 46
Head, Market Risk Management: Lesley Daniels Webster, age 49
CFO: Dina Dublon, age 48
Director of Human Resources: John J. Farrell Jr., age 49
Chairman, Technology Council: Thomas B. Ketchum, age 51
Chairman, Investment Banking North America: James B. Lee Jr.
Auditing Officer: William J. Moran
Auditors: PricewaterhouseCoopers LLP

LOCATIONS

HQ: 270 Park Ave., New York, NY 10017
Phone: 212-270-6000   **Fax:** 212-270-2613
Web: www.jpmorganchase.com

PRODUCTS/OPERATIONS

2001 Sales

	$ mil.	% of total
Interest		
Loans	15,544	31
Trading assets	7,390	15
Securities	4,990	10
Other	4,257	8
Noninterest		
Fees & commissions	9,208	18
Trading revenue	4,918	10
Investment banking fees	3,612	7
Other	510	1
Total	**50,429**	**100**

COMPETITORS

American Express	Credit Lyonnais	Lehman Brothers
Bank of America	Credit Suisse	MBNA
Bank of New York	First Boston	Merrill Lynch
BANK ONE	Credit Suisse First Boston (USA), Inc.	Mizuho Holdings Morgan Stanley
Bear Stearns	Deutsche Bank	RBC Financial
Canadian Imperial	FleetBoston	Group
Capital One Financial	Goldman Sachs Household International	Salomon Smith Barney Holdings
Citigroup	HSBC Holdings	UBS

HISTORICAL FINANCIALS & EMPLOYEES

NYSE: JPM FYE: December 31	Annual Growth	12/92	12/93	12/94	12/95	12/96	12/97	12/98	12/99	12/00	12/01
Assets ($ mil.)	19.5%	139,655	149,888	171,423	182,926	336,099	365,521	365,875	406,105	715,348	693,575
Net income ($ mil.)	5.1%	1,086	1,604	1,294	1,805	2,461	3,708	3,782	5,446	5,727	1,694
Income as % of assets	—	0.8%	1.1%	0.8%	1.0%	0.7%	1.0%	1.0%	1.3%	0.8%	0.2%
Earnings per share ($)	(5.3%)	1.30	1.60	1.66	2.02	1.65	2.68	2.83	4.18	2.86	0.80
Stock price - FY high ($)	—	13.17	15.47	14.05	21.59	31.97	42.21	51.73	60.78	67.20	57.33
Stock price - FY low ($)	—	7.30	11.67	11.21	11.92	17.38	28.22	23.72	43.90	32.38	29.05
Stock price - FY close ($)	12.2%	12.88	13.38	11.96	19.59	29.81	36.52	47.36	51.82	45.44	36.35
P/E - high	—	10	12	8	10	19	15	18	14	22	69
P/E - low	—	6	9	7	6	10	10	8	10	11	35
Dividends per share ($)	14.4%	0.40	0.43	0.53	0.63	0.73	0.81	0.93	1.06	1.23	1.34
Book value per share ($)	5.3%	13.31	14.72	14.61	15.86	16.68	17.22	18.75	19.04	22.24	21.11
Employees	10.3%	39,687	41,567	42,130	72,696	67,785	69,033	72,683	74,801	99,757	95,812

STOCK PRICE HISTORY

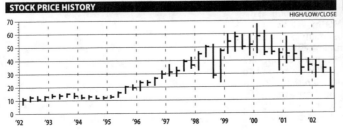

HIGH/LOW/CLOSE

2001 FISCAL YEAR-END

Equity as % of assets: 6.0%
Return on assets: 0.2%
Return on equity: 4.2%
Long-term debt ($ mil.): 39,183
No. of shares (mil.): 1,973
Dividends
  Yield: 3.7%
  Payout: 167.5%
Market value ($ mil.): 71,732
Sales ($ mil.): 50,429

KAISER FOUNDATION

This Kaiser reigns — as a top not-for-profit HMO. Oakland, California-based, Kaiser Foundation Health Plan has an integrated care model, offering both hospital and physician care through a network of hospitals and physician practices operating under the Kaiser Permanente name. Kaiser serves more than 8 million members in 9 states and the District of Columbia; California is its largest market with about 75% of its members.

A string of losses have prompted Kaiser to raise rates and divest underperforming units. Like many competitors, Kaiser also faces the ever-rising costs of health care that threaten the gains it has made to get back in the black.

HISTORY

Henry Kaiser — shipbuilder, war profiteer, builder of the Hoover and Grand Coulee dams, and founder of Kaiser Aluminum — was a bootstrap capitalist who did well by doing good. A high school dropout from upstate New York, Kaiser moved to Spokane, Washington, in 1906 and went into road construction. During the Depression, he headed the consortium that built the great WPA dams.

It was in building the Grand Coulee Dam that, in 1938, Kaiser teamed with Dr. Sidney Garfield, who earlier had devised a prepayment health plan for workers on California public works projects. As Kaiser moved into steelmaking and shipbuilding during WWII (turning out some 1,400 bare-bones Liberty ships — one per day at peak production), Kaiser decided healthy workers produce more than sick ones, and he called on Garfield to set up on-site clinics funded by the US government as part of operating expenses. Garfield was released from military service by President Roosevelt for the purpose.

After the war, the clinics became war surplus. Kaiser and his wife bought them — at a 99% discount — through the new Kaiser Hospital Foundation. His vision was to provide the public with low-cost, prepaid medical care. He created the health plan — the self-supporting entity that would administer the system — and the group medical organization, Permanente (named after Kaiser's first cement plant site). He then endowed the health plan with $200,000. This health plan, the classic HMO model, was criticized by the medical establishment as socialized medicine performed by "employee" doctors.

But the plan flourished, becoming California's #1 medical system. In 1958 Kaiser retired to Hawaii and started his health plan there. Physician resistance limited national growth; HMOs were illegal in some states well into the 1970s. As health care costs rose, Congress legalized

HMOs in all states. Kaiser expanded in the 1980s; as it moved outside its traditional geographic areas, the company contracted for space in hospitals rather than building them. Growth slowed as competition increased.

Some health care costs in California fell in the early 1990s as more medical procedures were performed on an outpatient basis. Specialists flooded the state, and as price competition among doctors and hospitals heated up, many HMOs landed advantageous contracts. Kaiser, with its own highly paid doctors, was unable to realize the same savings and was no longer the best deal in town. Its membership stalled.

To boost membership and control expenses, Kaiser instituted a controversial program in 1996 in which nurses earned bonuses for cost-cutting. Critics said the program could lead to a decrease in care quality; Kaiser later became the focus of investigations into wrongful death suits linked to cost-cutting in California (where it has since beefed up staffing and programs) and Texas (where it has agreed to pay $1 million in fines).

In 1997 Kaiser and Group Health Cooperative of Puget Sound formed Kaiser/Group Health to handle administrative services in the Northwest. Kaiser also tried to boost membership by lowering premiums, but the strategy proved *too* effective: Costs linked to an unwieldy 20% enrollment surge brought a loss in 1997 — Kaiser's first annual loss ever.

A second year in the red in 1998 prompted Kaiser to sell its Texas operations to Sierra Health Services. It also entered the Florida market via an alliance with Miami-based AvMed Health Plan. In 1999 Kaiser announced plans to sell its unprofitable North Carolina operations (it closed the deal the following year).

In 2000 Kaiser announced plans to charge premiums for its Medicare HMO, Medicare+Choice, to offset the shortfall in federal reimbursements. In 2001 the company's hospital division bought the technology and assets of defunct Internet grocer Webvan, in an effort to increase its distribution activity. Also that year, the son of a deceased anthrax victim sued a Kaiser facility for failing to recognize and treat his father's symptoms.

Chairman Emeritus: David M. Lawrence, age 61
Chairman, President and CEO: George C. Halvorson
EVP, Health Plan Operations: Arthur M. Southam
SVP and Chief Administration Officer: Robert M. Crane
SVP and CFO: Robert E. Briggs, age 54
**SVP, National Contracting Purchasing and
  Distribution:** Joseph W. Hummel
SVP, Workforce Development: Leslie A. Margolin
SVP, General Counsel, and Secretary: Kirk E. Miller
SVP and Director for Care and Services Quality:
  Patricia B. Siegel
SVP and CIO: Clifford Dodd
VP, Human Resources, Regions Outside of California:
  Dresdene Flynn-White
**President, Kaiser Permanente Northern California
  Region:** Mary Ann Thode
**President, Kaiser Permanente Southern California
  Region:** Richard Cordova

LOCATIONS

HQ: Kaiser Foundation Health Plan, Inc.
  1 Kaiser Plaza, Oakland, CA 94612
Phone: 510-271-5800   **Fax:** 510-271-6493
Web: www.kaiserpermanente.org

Kaiser Foundation Health Plan operates in California,
Colorado, Georgia, Hawaii, Maryland, Ohio, Oregon,
Virginia, Washington, and the District of Columbia.

PRODUCTS/OPERATIONS

Selected Operations
Kaiser Foundation Health Plans (health coverage)
Kaiser Foundation Hospitals (community hospitals and
  outpatient facilities)
Permanente Medical Groups (physician organizations)

COMPETITORS

Aetna
Blue Cross
Catholic Health East
Catholic Health Initiatives
Catholic Healthcare Network
Catholic Healthcare Partners
Catholic Healthcare West
CIGNA
HCA
Health Net
Humana
Oxford Health Plans
PacifiCare
Sierra Health
UnitedHealth Group
WellPoint Health Networks

HISTORICAL FINANCIALS & EMPLOYEES

Not-for-profit FYE: December 31	Annual Growth	12/92	12/93	12/94	12/95	12/96	12/97	12/98	12/99	12/00	12/01
Sales ($ mil.)	6.7%	11,032	11,930	12,268	12,290	13,241	14,500	15,500	16,841	17,700	19,700
Employees	3.3%	82,858	84,885	84,845	85,000	90,000	100,000	100,000	90,000	90,000	111,000

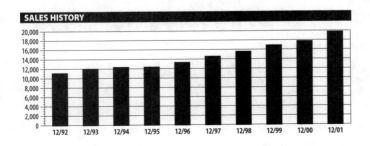

SALES HISTORY

KELLOGG COMPANY

Breakfast is important, but in case you missed it, Kellogg fixed you a snack. The Battle Creek, Michigan-based breakfast giant pioneered ready-to-eat cereal, and among its morning classics are Frosted Flakes, Corn Flakes, Rice Krispies, Special K, and Froot Loops. But these days cereal contributes only slightly more than half of the company's sales. As cereal sales remain soggy and on-the-go consumers grow impatient with the traditional cereal-milk combo, Kellogg is relying increasingly on snacks and convenience foods such as Eggo waffles, Nutri-Grain cereal bars, and Pop-Tarts.

Kellogg briefly snapped under the pressure of ongoing cereal wars, but it has regained US market share and is back to being #1 — just ahead of General Mills. And the company has crackled under fierce store-brand competition. So, Kellogg popped into new markets by acquiring Worthington Foods (Morningstar Farms meat alternatives), and #2 US cookie and cracker maker Keebler Foods (Chips Deluxe, Cheez-it, Famous Amos). Along with big brands, Keebler brought along its direct-to-store distribution system, which Kellogg hopes will improve its product placement on store shelves.

The W. K. Kellogg Foundation, one of the world's largest charities, owns 31% of the company. The Gund family, which sold its coffee business (later Sanka) to Kellogg in 1927, owns about 9%.

HISTORY

Will Keith (W. K.) Kellogg first made wheat flakes in 1894 while working for his brother, Dr. John Kellogg, at Battle Creek, Michigan's, famed homeopathic sanitarium. While doing an experiment with grains (for patients' diets), the two men were interrupted; by the time they returned to the dough, it had absorbed water. They rolled it anyway, toasted the result, and accidentally created the first flaked cereal. John sold the flakes via mail order (1899) in a partnership that W. K. managed. In 1906 W. K. started his own firm to produce corn flakes.

As head of the Battle Creek Toasted Corn Flake Company, W. K. competed against 42 cereal companies in Battle Creek (one run by former patient C. W. Post) and roared to the head of the pack with his innovative marketing ideas. A 1906 *Ladies' Home Journal* ad helped increase demand from 33 cases a day earlier that year to 2,900 a day by year-end. W.K. soon introduced Bran Flakes (1915), All-Bran (1916), and Rice Krispies (1928). International expansion began in Canada (1914) and followed in Australia (1924) and England (1938). Diversifying a little,

the company introduced the Pop-Tart in 1964 and acquired Eggo waffles in the 1970s. By the early 1980s Kellogg's US market share dipped, due to strong competition from General Mills and other rivals. The company pitched new cereals to adults and aggressively pursued the fast-growing European market.

Kellogg spent the mid-1990s reengineering itself, creating the USA Convenience Foods Division and selling such noncore assets as its carton container and Argentine snack-foods makers (1993). It teamed with ConAgra in 1994 to create a cereal line sold under the latter's popular Healthy Choice label.

In 1997 and 1998 the company expanded operations in Australia, the UK, Asia, and Latin America, and it slashed about 25% of its salaried North American workforce and hiked prices on about two-thirds of its cereals. Several top officers left in 1998 and 1999, and Cuban-born president and COO Carlos Gutierrez became CEO.

The company sold the disappointing Lender's division to Aurora Foods in 1999. By the beginning of 2000, cereal competitor General Mills had closed the gap with Kellogg in US market share (in 2001 it passed Kellogg as the #1 cereal maker). In mid-2000 Kellogg added Kashi Company (natural cereals) to its pantry. Later that year Kellogg reorganized its operations into two divisions (USA and International) to reduce costs.

In 2001 Kellogg bulked up its snacks portfolio by acquiring Keebler Foods for $4.5 billion (in cash and assumed debt); in the aftermath of the acquisition, the company trimmed jobs at Keebler and at its own headquarters.

To boost new kid enthusiasm for breakfast, in early 2002 Kellogg launched new cereals featuring Disney characters Buzz Lightyear, Mickey Mouse, and Winnie the Pooh — the first such alliance for The Walt Disney Company. That move, combined with better marketing and General Mills being distracted with its purchase of Pillsbury, helped Kellogg grab back the top spot in the US. Later in the year, to better focus on its branded products, the company sold off Keebler's private-label Bake-Line division to Atlantic Baking Group for $65 million in cash.

OFFICERS

Chairman, President, and CEO: Carlos M. Gutierrez, age 48, $2,165,100 pay
SVP and CFO: John Bryant, age 36
EVP, Corporate Development and Administration, General Counsel, and Secretary: Janet L. Kelly, age 45, $479,600 pay
EVP; President, Kellogg International: Alan F. Harris, age 47, $790,000 pay

EVP; President, Kellogg USA: A. David Mackay, age 46, $1,164,000 pay
SVP; President & CEO, Keebler Snacks: Paul J. Lustig
SVP; President, USA Morning Foods Division: Jeffrey W. Montie, age 41
SVP, Operations: King T. Pouw, age 50, $785,075 pay
SVP, Research, Quality, and Technology: Donna J. Banks, age 45
VP, CIO: H. Ray Shei
VP, Corporate Controller: Jeffrey M. Boromisa, age 46
VP, Deputy General Counsel: Gary H. Pilnick, age 37
VP; EVP, Operations, Kellogg USA: Arthur A. Byrd
VP, External Affairs: George A. Franklin, age 50
VP, Medical Affairs: E. Joseph Alberding, age 59
VP; President, Kellogg Latin America; EVP, Kellogg International: Gustavo Martinez, age 47
VP, Taxes and Treasury: W. Stephen Perry, age 59
VP and Treasurer: Joel R. Wittenberg, age 41
Auditors: PricewaterhouseCoopers LLP

LOCATIONS

HQ: One Kellogg Square, Battle Creek, MI 49016
Phone: 616-961-2000   **Fax:** 616-961-2871
Web: www.kelloggs.com

Kellogg manufactures its products in 19 countries and distributes them in more than 160.

2001 Sales & Operating Income

	Sales		Operating Income	
	$ mil.	% of total	$ mil.	% of total
United States	6,129	70	945	64
Europe	1,363	15	246	17
Latin America	653	7	170	12
Other	708	8	103	7
Corporate	—	—	(173)	—
Total	**8,853**	**100**	**1,291**	**100**

PRODUCTS/OPERATIONS

2001 Sales

	$ mil.	% of total
Cereals	4,914	55
Snacks	2,263	26
Other	1,676	19
Total	**8,853**	**100**

Selected Products

Cereals
Apple Jacks
Froot Loops
Frosted Mini-Wheats
Just Right
Kashi
Kellogg's Corn Flakes
Kellogg's Frosted Flakes
Nutri-Grain
Rice Krispies
Special K

Keebler-Brand Products
Town House crackers
Wheatables crackers
Zesta crackers

Sunshine-Brand Products
Cheez-It crackers
Krispy crackers

Other Products
Eggo (frozen waffles)
Girl Scout cookies
Kellogg's Nutri-Grain (cereal bars, frozen waffles)
Pop-Tarts (toaster pastries)
Pop-Tarts Pastry Swirls (toaster danish)
Rice Krispies Treats (marshmallow snacks)
Worthington (meat alternatives)

COMPETITORS

Aurora Foods
Gardenburger
General Mills
Gilster-Mary Lee
Grist Mill Company

Interstate Bakeries
Kraft Foods
Malt-O-Meal
McKee Foods
Parmalat North America

PowerBar
Quaker Foods
Ralcorp
Weetabix
Wessanen
Weston Foods

HISTORICAL FINANCIALS & EMPLOYEES

NYSE: K FYE: December 31	Annual Growth	12/92	12/93	12/94	12/95	12/96	12/97	12/98	12/99	12/00	12/01
Sales ($ mil.)	4.1%	6,191	6,295	6,562	7,004	6,677	6,830	6,762	6,984	6,955	8,853
Net income ($ mil.)	1.0%	431	681	705	490	531	546	503	338	588	474
Income as % of sales	—	7.0%	10.8%	10.7%	7.0%	8.0%	8.0%	7.4%	4.8%	8.5%	5.3%
Earnings per share ($)	2.9%	0.90	1.47	1.58	1.12	1.25	1.32	1.23	0.83	1.45	1.16
Stock price - FY high ($)	—	37.69	33.94	30.38	39.75	40.31	50.47	50.19	42.25	32.00	34.00
Stock price - FY low ($)	—	27.19	23.63	23.69	26.25	31.00	32.00	28.50	30.00	20.75	24.25
Stock price - FY close ($)	(1.2%)	33.50	28.38	29.06	38.63	32.81	49.63	34.13	30.81	26.25	30.10
P/E - high	—	26	23	19	35	32	37	41	51	22	29
P/E - low	—	19	16	15	23	25	24	23	36	14	20
Dividends per share ($)	6.0%	0.60	0.66	0.70	0.75	0.81	0.87	0.92	0.96	1.00	1.01
Book value per share ($)	(6.9%)	4.10	3.76	4.08	3.67	3.06	2.43	2.20	2.01	2.21	2.14
Employees	5.3%	16,551	16,151	15,657	14,487	14,511	14,339	14,498	15,051	15,200	26,424

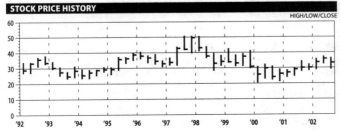

STOCK PRICE HISTORY — HIGH/LOW/CLOSE

2001 FISCAL YEAR-END
Debt ratio: 86.6%
Return on equity: 53.5%
Cash ($ mil.): 232
Current ratio: 0.86
Long-term debt ($ mil.): 5,619
No. of shares (mil.): 407
Dividends
  Yield: 3.4%
  Payout: 87.1%
Market value ($ mil.): 12,239

KELLY SERVICES, INC.

Kelly Services may be a permanent fixture in the personnel services market, but the people it places are free to move around. The Troy, Michigan-based company is one of the largest temporary staffing firms in the US. Kelly Services provides some 700,000 temps to about 150,000 clients in 26 countries in Asia, Australia, Europe, and North America. The company helps reduce its customers' cost of hiring new help during peak business periods by handling the hiring process for them and charging its customers an hourly rate for each assigned temp.

What was once a business that only supplied female clerical help has expanded to include light-industrial, technical, and professional employees of both genders, including information technology specialists, engineers, and accountants. It even has an operation that places lawyers (Kelly Law Registry) and scientists (Kelly Scientific Resources), and its Kelly Home Care Services unit provides personal care and daily living assistance to people who need care at home. The company also places substitute teachers (Kelly Educational Staffing), nurses and other medical staff (Kelly Healthcare Resources), engineers (Kelly Engineering Resources), and teleservices personnel (KellyConnect).

Kelly Services continues to grow by opening new offices in target markets across the US and abroad. Chairman and CEO Terence Adderley controls 92% of the company.

HISTORY

William Russell Kelly, a college dropout and former car salesman, went to Detroit after WWII to seek his fortune. An owner of modern business equipment, he set up Russell Kelly Office Service in 1946 to provide copying, typing, and inventory services for other businesses; first-year sales from 12 customers totaled $848.

Although companies began to acquire their own machines, Kelly knew that they still needed people to work at their offices. He reincorporated his rapidly expanding business as Personnel Service in 1952 and opened the company's first branch office, in Louisville, Kentucky, in 1955; by the end of that year he had 35 offices throughout the US. In 1957 the company was renamed Kelly Girl Service to reflect its all-female workforce.

In the 1960s Kelly ventured beyond office services and began placing convention hostesses, blue-collar workers, data processors, door-to-door marketers, and drafters, among others. Kelly Girl went public in 1962, boasting 148 branches at the time. In 1966 the company adopted its present name, Kelly Services, in

1966. It opened its first non-US office in Toronto in 1968, and one in Paris followed in 1972.

A tough US economy in the 1970s saw a surge in corporate interest in temporary employees. Employers saw the benefits of hiring "Kelly Girls" to meet seasonal needs and special projects. In 1976 Kelly Services acquired a modest health care services company and used it to form Kelly Home Care. In the 1980s this division abandoned the Medicaid and Medicare markets and shifted to private-sector care. Renamed Kelly Assisted Living Services in 1984 (and now known as Kelly Home Care Services), the unit offered aides to perform household duties and nurses to conduct home visits for the elderly and disabled. Also in the 1980s Kelly Services began hiring retired people as part of its ENCORE Program.

The company developed specialty services in the US in the 1990s. It acquired ComTrain (testing and training software products) and Your Staff (an employee-leasing company providing companies with entire human resources departments, including benefits and payroll services) in 1994. The following year it bought the Wallace Law Registry (later renamed Kelly Law Registry), which provides lawyers, paralegals, and clerks. Kelly also established Kelly Scientific Resources to place science professionals. In 1996 that subsidiary acquired Oak Ridge Research Institute, which provided scientists to the defense and energy industries.

Kelly continued its international expansion as well. Since 1988, more than a dozen acquisitions expanded the company in Australasia, Europe, and elsewhere. In response to new legislation allowing companies to hire temporary workers, the company opened five offices in Italy and acquired a personnel placement firm in Russia in 1997.

William Kelly died at the age of 92 in 1998, and the company named president and CEO Terence Adderley, his adopted son, to replace him as chairman (Adderley relinquished the title of president in late 2001). The next year the company made four additions to its staffing services: Kelly Healthcare Resources, Kelly Financial Resources, Kelly Educational Staffing (substitute teachers), and KellyConnect (teleservices).

In 2000 the company made three acquisitions: Extra ETT in Spain (automotive staffing), ProStaff Group in the US (general staffing), and Business Trends Group in Singapore (general staffing). Kelly Services continued with its acquisition strategy the following year, purchasing the engineering services business of Compuware, among others.

Chairman and CEO: Terence E. Adderley, age 68, $817,500 pay
President, COO, and Director: Carl T. Camden, age 47, $655,000 pay
EVP and CFO: William K. Gerber, age 48, $561,667 pay
EVP Human Resources: Michael L. Durik, age 53, $487,500 pay
EVP US Commercial Staffing: Arlene G. Grimsley, age 54, $410,000 pay
SVP, Secretary, and General Counsel: George M. Reardon, age 54
SVP and CIO: Eileen Youds
SVP Administration: James H. Bradley
SVP Global Sales: James A. Tanchon
SVP Marketing: Michael Morrow
SVP Technical Services Group: Larry J. Seyfarth
SVP and General Manager, Strategic Customer Relationships: Joan M. Brancheau
SVP and Division General Manager: George S. Corona
SVP and Division General Manager: Rolf E. Kleiner
SVP and Division General Manager: Andrew R. Watt
SVP and Division General Manager: Michael S. Webster
VP Kelly Automotive Services Group: Jonathan Means
VP Kelly Engineering Resources: Gregory Kruger
VP Kelly Financial Resources: Robert Lyons
VP Kelly HR Solutions: Sue Marks
Auditors: PricewaterhouseCoopers LLP

LOCATIONS

HQ: 999 W. Big Beaver Rd., Troy, MI 48084
Phone: 248-362-4444   **Fax:** 248-244-4360
Web: www.kellyservices.com

Kelly Services has more than 2,300 offices throughout Asia, Australia, Europe, and North America.

PRODUCTS/OPERATIONS

2001 Sales

	$ mil.	% of total
US commercial staffing	2,098	49
International	1,087	26
Professional, technical & staffing alternatives	1,072	25
Total	**4,257**	**100**

Selected Services
Kelly Educational Staffing (substitute teachers)
Kelly Engineering Resources (engineers)
Kelly Financial Resources (accounting, analysts)
Kelly Healthcare Resources (nurses, medical technicians)
Kelly Home Care Services (in-home caregivers)
Kelly Information Technology Resources
Kelly Law Registry
Kelly Light Industrial
Kelly Management Services
Kelly Office Services (clerical staffing)
Kelly Scientific Resources (science staffing)
Kelly Select (temporary to full-time employee service)
Kelly Staff Leasing (human resources management)

COMPETITORS

Adecco	On Assignment
Administaff	Randstad
ATC Healthcare	Robert Half
CDI	Spherion
Gevity HR	TAC Worldwide
Labor Ready	Vedior
Manpower	Volt Information
MPS	

HISTORICAL FINANCIALS & EMPLOYEES

Nasdaq: KELYA FYE: Sunday nearest Dec. 31	Annual Growth	12/92	12/93	12/94	12/95	12/96	12/97	12/98	12/99	12/00	12/01
Sales ($ mil.)	10.6%	1,723	1,955	2,363	2,690	3,302	3,853	4,092	4,269	4,487	4,257
Net income ($ mil.)	(9.2%)	39	45	61	70	73	81	85	85	87	17
Income as % of sales	—	2.3%	2.3%	2.6%	2.6%	2.2%	2.1%	2.1%	2.0%	1.9%	0.4%
Earnings per share ($)	(8.7%)	1.04	1.18	1.61	1.83	1.91	2.12	2.23	2.36	2.43	0.46
Stock price - FY high ($)	—	35.00	36.60	32.00	37.00	32.50	38.75	38.50	32.50	29.00	29.25
Stock price - FY low ($)	—	22.20	22.00	23.00	24.50	25.25	23.25	23.75	22.88	20.25	17.85
Stock price - FY close ($)	(5.1%)	35.00	27.75	27.50	27.75	27.00	30.00	31.75	25.13	23.63	21.89
P/E - high	—	34	31	20	20	17	18	17	14	12	64
P/E - low	—	21	19	14	13	13	11	11	10	8	39
Dividends per share ($)	4.3%	0.58	0.63	0.70	0.78	0.83	0.87	0.91	0.95	0.99	0.85
Book value per share ($)	6.3%	9.74	10.23	11.37	12.52	13.58	14.67	14.72	16.24	17.45	16.93
Employees	2.0%	584,000	634,300	665,000	660,600	692,100	750,000	740,000	757,400	770,000	698,600

STOCK PRICE HISTORY

HIGH/LOW/CLOSE

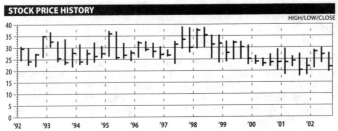

2001 FISCAL YEAR-END

Debt ratio: 0.0%
Return on equity: 2.7%
Cash ($ mil.): 84
Current ratio: 1.92
Long-term debt ($ mil.): 0
No. of shares (mil.): 36
Dividends
 Yield: 3.9%
 Payout: 184.8%
Market value ($ mil.): 785

KERR-MCGEE CORPORATION

Oil and water don't mix, but Kerr-McGee knows oil and chemicals combine quite nicely. The Oklahoma City-based company explores for and produces oil and natural gas and makes inorganic chemicals.

Kerr-McGee has proved reserves of about 1.5 billion barrels of oil equivalent. The company is focusing on deepwater exploration: It has substantial reserves in the Gulf of Mexico and the North Sea, and it also owns deepwater acreage offshore Australia, Brazil, Canada, Gabon, and Thailand. The company nearly doubled its US natural gas reserves by buying HS Resources in 2001.

To offset volatile energy prices, Kerr-McGee is building its chemical business (31% of sales). Its main product is titanium dioxide, a white pigment used in paint, plastics, and paper. After acquiring a major facility in the Netherlands, the company has become the world's third-largest producer of titanium dioxide, with a 16% market share (behind DuPont and Millennium Chemicals). Kerr-McGee has also bought a plant in Georgia and expanded its chemical operation in Mississippi.

In addition to its energy and chemical operations, Kerr-McGee makes timber products, mainly railroad cross ties. It has pursued a decade-long strategy of selling noncore businesses.

HISTORY

In 1929 Robert Kerr (later an Oklahoma governor and US senator) and his brother-in-law James Anderson founded Anderson & Kerr Drilling Company in Ada, Oklahoma. They relocated to Oklahoma City the next year.

Renamed A & K Petroleum in 1932, the company went public in 1935, and Anderson sold his stake the next year. After becoming Kerlyn Oil in 1937, the company recruited Dean McGee, Phillips Petroleum's chief geologist. In 1938 McGee made a major oil find in Arkansas; Kerlyn made another big oil strike in Oklahoma in 1943. Two years later it bought its first refinery and began exploring for oil in the Gulf of Mexico. Kerlyn became Kerr-McGee Oil Industries in 1946.

In the early 1950s Kerr-McGee purchased four natural gas-processing plants in Oklahoma When the production of atomic bombs during the Cold War boosted uranium demand, Kerr-McGee began mining uranium in Arizona (1952). In 1954 McGee became CEO, and the next year Kerr-McGee became a fully integrated oil company with the purchase of Deep Rock Oil, which operated service stations, pipelines, and refineries. In 1957 it bought Triangle Refineries and Cato Oil and Grease Company (sold in 1995).

By the 1960s the company (it was renamed

Kerr-McGee Corporation in 1965) was doing contract drilling in the US and overseas. It also bought two railroad tie plants. Kerr died in 1963.

The company entered the industrial chemicals field through its 1967 acquisition of American Potash & Chemical, including its Hamilton, Mississippi, plant. Two years later Kerr-McGee began mining coal. It opened more uranium plants and bought Southwestern Refining Co. in 1974.

Problems plagued the company's nuclear program in the 1970s and 1980s. Karen Silkwood, a plutonium plant employee who accused the company of safety breaches, was killed in a mysterious car accident (1974), and an explosion at Kerr-McGee's nuclear fuel plant in Gore, Oklahoma, killed a worker and injured dozens (1986).

In 1983 McGee stepped down as CEO (he died in 1989). The company began shedding noncore operations in the late 1980s: It sold its potash and phosphate mines, uranium interests, and contract drilling operations. In 1991 its titanium dioxide plants in Australia and Saudi Arabia began producing.

The company unloaded its downstream operations in 1995. In 1997 Kerr-McGee sold its onshore oil and gas exploration and production businesses to Devon Energy. The deal gave Kerr-McGee a 31% stake in Devon (later reduced to 12%). In 1998 Kerr-McGee acquired 80% of Bayer's European titanium dioxide operations. That year it also sold its coal operations and refocused on the oil business. It bought the North Sea oil and gas reserves of Gulf Canada Resources and formed an exploration alliance with British Petroleum (now BP p.l.c.) in the Gulf of Mexico.

Kerr-McGee began positioning itself as a major US independent oil and gas exploration and production firm in 1999, buying Oryx Energy for about $2.4 billion, as well as the interest in Sun Energy Partners that it didn't already own. In 2000 Kerr-McGee expanded its deepwater operations by buying Repsol-YPF's UK North Sea assets for $555 million and four offshore Canada exploration licenses from Canadian 88 Energy. The company also purchased two titanium dioxide pigment plants from Kemira for $403 million, a move that boosted its world market share to 16%.

In 2000, Kerr-McGee sold its 25% stake in the National Titanium Dioxide Company of Saudi Arabia. The next year the company acquired Bayer's remaining 20% stake in Kerr-McGee's titanium pigment plants in Germany, and Belgium, giving it 100% ownership of the facilities.

To increase its US natural gas reserves, Kerr-McGee in 2001 bought San Francisco-based HS Resources in a $1.7 billion deal.

Chairman and CEO: Luke R. Corbett, age 55,
$1,019,712 pay
SVP and CFO: Robert M. Wohleber, $418,096 pay
SVP, General Counsel, and Corporate Secretary:
Gregory F. Pilcher, $372,673 pay
SVP Chemical: William Peter Woodward, $427,038 pay
SVP Exploration and Production: Kenneth W. Crouch,
$447,885 pay
SVP Corporate Affairs: Carol A. Schumacher, age 45
Corporate VP Human Resources: Theodore Bennett
VP and Controller: John M. Rauh
VP, Deputy Counsel, and Assistant Secretary:
John F. Reichenberger
VP General Administration: Jean B. Wallace
VP Safety and Environmental Affairs:
George D. Christiansen
VP Exploration and Production: Dave Hager
VP Worldwide Exploration: Annell Bay
Auditors: Ernst & Young LLP

LOCATIONS

HQ: Kerr-McGee Center, 123 Robert S. Kerr Ave.,
Oklahoma City, OK 73102
Phone: 405-270-1313   **Fax:** 405-270-3029
Web: www.kerr-mcgee.com

2001 Sales

	$ mil.	% of total
US	2,463	68
Europe		
UK	600	16
Other countries	258	7
Australia	167	5
Other countries	150	4
Total	**3,638**	**100**

PRODUCTS/OPERATIONS

2001 Sales

	$ mil.	% of total
Exploration & production	2,511	69
Chemicals	1,127	31
Total	**3,638**	**100**

Selected Subsidiaries
Kerr-McGee Chemical LLC
Kerr-McGee China Petroleum Ltd.
Kerr-McGee Gryphon Limited
Kerr-McGee (Holland) B.V.
Kerr-McGee North Sea (U.K.) Limited
Kerr-McGee Oil & Gas Corporation
Kerr-McGee Oil and Gas Onshore LP
Kerr-McGee Oil (U.K.) PLC
Kerr-McGee Pigments GmbH & Co. KG
Kerr-McGee Pigments Limited Kerr-McGee Pigments N.V.
Kerr-McGee Pigments (Savannah) Inc.
Kerr-McGee Resources (U.K.) Limited
Kerr-McGee Rocky Mountain Corporation
KMCC Western Australia Pty. Ltd.

COMPETITORS

Amerada Hess	Kemira Oy
Ashland	Marathon Oil
BHP Billiton Ltd	Millennium Chemicals
BP	NL Industries
Burlington Resources	Occidental Petroleum
ChevronTexaco	Royal Dutch/Shell Group
ConocoPhillips	TOTAL FINA ELF
DuPont	Unocal
Exxon Mobil	

HISTORICAL FINANCIALS & EMPLOYEES

NYSE: KMG FYE: December 31	Annual Growth	12/92	12/93	12/94	12/95	12/96	12/97	12/98	12/99	12/00	12/01
Sales ($ mil.)	0.8%	3,382	3,281	3,353	1,801	1,931	1,711	1,396	2,696	4,121	3,638
Net income ($ mil.)	—	(101)	77	90	(31)	220	194	50	142	842	487
Income as % of sales	—	—	2.3%	2.7%	—	11.4%	11.3%	3.6%	5.3%	20.4%	13.4%
Earnings per share ($)	—	(2.08)	1.57	1.74	(0.60)	4.43	4.04	1.06	1.64	8.37	4.93
Stock price - FY high ($)	—	46.38	56.00	51.00	64.00	74.13	75.00	73.19	62.00	71.19	74.10
Stock price - FY low ($)	—	35.63	41.75	40.00	44.00	55.75	55.50	36.19	28.50	39.88	46.94
Stock price - FY close ($)	2.2%	45.00	45.25	46.25	63.50	72.00	63.31	38.25	62.00	66.94	54.80
P/E - high	—	—	36	29	—	17	18	69	37	8	13
P/E - low	—	—	27	23	—	13	14	34	17	4	8
Dividends per share ($)	1.9%	1.52	1.52	1.52	1.52	1.64	1.76	1.80	2.25	1.80	1.80
Book value per share ($)	1.4%	27.96	29.27	28.95	27.73	28.31	30.20	28.26	17.25	27.87	31.68
Employees	(2.6%)	5,866	5,812	5,524	3,976	3,851	3,746	3,367	3,653	4,426	4,638

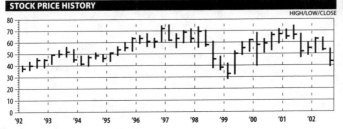

STOCK PRICE HISTORY HIGH/LOW/CLOSE

2001 FISCAL YEAR-END
Debt ratio: 58.9%
Return on equity: 16.8%
Cash ($ mil.): 91
Current ratio: 1.16
Long-term debt ($ mil.): 4,540
No. of shares (mil.): 100
Dividends
  Yield: 3.3%
  Payout: 36.5%
Market value ($ mil.): 5,490

KEYCORP

Cleveland-based KeyCorp is a community banking powerhouse, with more than 900 offices across the northern US. Regulatory changes and strategic acquisitions have increased the bank's presence in such markets as investment banking, financial advice, and stock brokerage. The company's Key Corporate Finance division provides transaction processing (a segment that includes Key Merchant Services, a joint venture with NOVA Information Systems), leases high-tech equipment, and handles small business clients. Key Capital Partners offers investment management, insurance, brokerage services, employee benefits services, and investment banking (through McDonald Investments); it also manages the Victory line of mutual funds.

After a round of belt-tightening, job cuts, and dumping underperforming operations, KeyCorp is looking to beef up its corporate and investment banking business, as well as increase its Internet and telephone banking capabilities.

HISTORY

KeyCorp predecessor Commercial Bank of Albany was chartered in 1825. In 1865 it joined the new national banking system and became National Commercial Bank of Albany. After WWI the company consolidated with Union National Bank & Trust as National Commercial Bank and Trust, which then merged with First Trust and Deposit in 1971.

In 1973 Victor Riley became president and CEO. Under Riley, National Commercial grew during the 1970s and 1980s through acquisitions. Riley sought to make the company a regional powerhouse but was thwarted when several New England states passed legislation barring New York banks from buying banks in the region.

As a result, the company, renamed Key Bank in 1979, turned west, targeting small towns with less competition. Thus situated, it prospered, despite entering Alaska just in time for the 1986 oil price collapse. Its folksy image and small-town success earned it a reputation as the "Wal-Mart of banking."

Meanwhile, in Cleveland, Society for Savings followed a different path. Founded as a mutual savings bank in 1849, the institution succeeded from the start. It survived the Civil War and post-war economic turmoil and built Cleveland's first skyscraper in 1890. It continued to grow even during the Depression and became the largest savings bank outside the Northeast in 1949.

In 1955 the bank formed a holding company, Society National. Society grew through the acquisitions of smaller banks in Ohio until 1979,

when Ohio allowed branch banking in contiguous counties. Thereafter, Society National opened branches as well. In the mid-1980s and the early 1990s, the renamed Society Corporation began consolidating its operations and continued growing.

A 1994 merger of National Commercial with Society more than doubled assets for the surviving KeyCorp; compatibility of the two companies' systems and software simplified consolidation. The company sold its mortgage-servicing unit to NationsBank (now Bank of America) in 1995 and over the next year bought investment management, finance, and investment banking companies.

In 1997 KeyCorp began trimming its branch network, divesting 200 offices, including its 28-branch KeyBank Wyoming subsidiary. It expanded its consumer lending business that year by buying Champion Mortgage. In cooperation with USF&G (now part of The St. Paul Companies) and three HMOs, KeyCorp began offering health insurance to the underserved small-business market.

In 1998 the company bought Leasetec, which leases computer storage systems globally through its StorageTek subsidiary; it also bought McDonald & Company Investments (now McDonald Investments), whose investment banking and brokerage operations could help KeyCorp reach its goal of earning half of revenues from fees. Also in 1998, KeyCorp began offering business lines of credit to customers of Costco Wholesale, the nation's largest wholesale club.

As part of a restructuring effort, KeyCorp sold 28 Long Island, New York, branches to Dime Bancorp in 1999. That next year the company sold its credit card portfolio to Associates First Capital (now part of Citigroup) and bought National Realty Funding, a securitizer of commercial mortgages. In 2001 it acquired Denver-based investment bank The Wallach Company.

OFFICERS

Chairman, President, and CEO: Henry L. Meyer III, age 52, $814,583 pay
Vice Chairman, Chief Administrative Officer, and Secretary: Thomas C. Stevens, age 52, $495,000 pay
SEVP, Key Corporate Finance: Thomas W. Bunn, age 48
SEVP, Consumer Banking: Jack L. Kopnisky, age 45
SEVP and CFO: K. Brent Somers, age 53, $461,250 pay
EVP, Commercial Banking; President, KeyBank National Association: Patrick V. Auletta
EVP and Chief Risk Officer: Kevin M. Blakely
EVP and Director, Civic Affairs and Corporate Diversity: Margot J. Copeland
EVP, Commercial Real Estate: George E. Emmons Jr.
EVP and Chief Marketing Officer: Karen R. Haefling

EVP; Chairman and CEO, KeyBank National Association: Robert B. Heisler Jr., age 53
EVP, Human Resources and Aviation: Thomas E. Helfrich, age 51
EVP and Chief Accounting Officer: Lee G. Irving, age 53
EVP; CEO, McDonald Investments; President, Key Capital Partners: Robert G. Jones
EVP; Senior Managing Director, McDonald Investments: Karen R. Kleinhenz
EVP and General Counsel; Vice Chairman and Secretary, KeyBank National Association: John H. Mancuso
EVP, Public Affairs and Chief Communications Officer: Michael J. Monroe
EVP and CTO: Robert G. Rickert, age 41
EVP; EVP, Credit Administration, KeyBank National Association: David J. Schutter
SVP and Director, Women Business-Owner Initiatives: Maria Coyne
Auditors: Ernst & Young LLP

LOCATIONS

HQ: 127 Public Sq., Cleveland, OH 44114
Phone: 216-689-6300   Fax: 216-689-7009
Web: www.key.com

KeyCorp has more than 900 branches in Alaska, Colorado, Idaho, Indiana, Maine, Michigan, New Hampshire, New York, Ohio, Oregon, Utah, Vermont, and Washington.

PRODUCTS/OPERATIONS

2001 Sales

	$ mil.	% of total
Interest		
Loans	5,067	69
Securities available for sale	451	6
Other investments	109	1
Noninterest		
Trust & investment services	550	7
Service charges on deposits	387	5
Investment banking & capital markets	189	3
Letter of credit & loan fees	124	2
Corporate-owned life insurance	114	2
Other	361	5
Total	**7,352**	**100**

COMPETITORS

Associated Banc-Corp	Huntington Bancshares
Bank of America	J.P. Morgan Chase
Bank of New York	M&T Bank
BANK ONE	Marshall & Ilsley
Charter One	Merrill Lynch
Citigroup	National City
Comerica	Northern Trust
Fifth Third Bancorp	Sovereign Bancorp
FleetBoston	U.S. Bancorp
HSBC USA	Wells Fargo

HISTORICAL FINANCIALS & EMPLOYEES

NYSE: KEY FYE: December 31	Annual Growth	12/92	12/93	12/94	12/95	12/96	12/97	12/98	12/99	12/00	12/01
Assets ($ mil.)	14.0%	24,978	27,007	66,798	66,339	67,621	73,699	80,020	83,395	87,270	80,938
Net income ($ mil.)	(8.8%)	301	347	854	825	783	919	996	1,107	1,002	132
Income as % of assets	—	1.2%	1.3%	1.3%	1.2%	1.2%	1.2%	1.2%	1.3%	1.1%	0.2%
Earnings per share ($)	(14.0%)	1.20	1.43	1.70	1.71	1.67	2.07	2.23	2.45	2.30	0.31
Stock price - FY high ($)	—	16.72	18.63	16.88	18.63	27.13	36.59	44.88	38.13	28.50	29.25
Stock price - FY low ($)	—	12.13	13.63	11.81	12.38	16.69	23.94	23.38	21.00	15.56	20.49
Stock price - FY close ($)	4.7%	16.06	14.88	12.50	18.13	25.25	35.41	32.00	22.13	28.00	24.34
P/E - high	—	14	13	10	11	16	18	20	15	12	79
P/E - low	—	10	9	7	8	10	11	10	9	7	55
Dividends per share ($)	10.3%	0.49	0.56	0.64	0.72	0.76	0.84	0.94	1.04	1.12	1.18
Book value per share ($)	6.8%	8.00	8.68	9.77	11.02	10.92	11.83	13.63	14.41	15.65	14.52
Employees	6.1%	12,451	29,983	29,211	29,563	26,963	24,595	25,862	24,568	22,142	21,230

STOCK PRICE HISTORY
HIGH/LOW/CLOSE

2001 FISCAL YEAR-END
Equity as % of assets: 7.6%
Return on assets: 0.2%
Return on equity: 2.1%
Long-term debt ($ mil.): 15,842
No. of shares (mil.): 424
Dividends
  Yield: 4.8%
  Payout: 380.6%
Market value ($ mil.): 10,320
Sales ($ mil.): 7,352

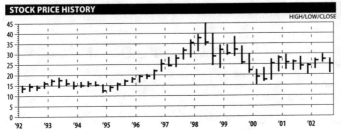

KEYSPAN CORPORATION

KeySpan is trying to fit itself into many areas of the deregulated utility market. The Brooklyn, New York-based energy holding company distributes natural gas to about 2.5 million customers in Brooklyn, Queens, Staten Island, and Long Island and in Massachusetts and New Hampshire through its KeySpan Energy Delivery units. KeySpan also owns some 6,200 MW of electric generating capacity (oil- and gas-fired) in New York City and on Long Island. KeySpan also contracts with the Long Island Power Authority to provide electric transmission and distribution services to 1.1 million customers.

KeySpan's nonregulated activities are helping the firm carve its place in the rapidly-changing utility industry. KeySpan operates in the retail electricity and gas marketplace in the Northeast, and it sells capacity on its fiber-optic network in the New York City area to telecom carriers and ISPs. The company has been building up its HVAC and energy-related engineering operations but has discontinued its general contracting business.

The company also has natural gas exploration, production, and transportation investments, including a 67% stake in Houston Exploration and a 20% interest in the Iroquois Gas Transmission System, which transports gas from Canada to the northeastern US. KeySpan plans to divest some noncore energy assets.

HISTORY

Brooklyn Gas Light Co. was formed in 1825, but a contract dispute with the borough left it defunct until 1847, when it won a contract to light Brooklyn's streets. Two years later it began supplying manufactured gas. By the 1890s 17 gas companies and "gas-house gangs" fought for customers in Brooklyn and Queens. In 1895, though, the company joined six other gas utilities to form the Brooklyn Union Gas Co., which focused on heating buildings.

An emphasis on home heating and cooking helped the company survive the Depression, and by 1952 cheap natural gas allowed the firm to focus on oil-to-gas residential conversions. The company grew through acquisitions during the 1950s, and by 1960 its service area included Brooklyn, Staten Island, and most of Queens. In 1966 Brooklyn Union formed Gas Energy to market gas equipment. The firm diversified in the 1970s and 1980s, forming several nonutility businesses including a gas exploration and production company, Fuel Resources (1974).

In 1985 Fuel Resources formed Brooklyn Union Exploration Company (now the Houston Exploration Company) to explore the Gulf Coast for reserves. In 1986 the company began developing cogeneration plants and brokering gas. The Iroquois Gas Transmission System, a 375-mile pipeline from Canada to the northeastern US, went into service in 1992.

Brooklyn Union formed KeySpan Energy Management in 1996 to serve commercial customers and created KeySpan Energy Services to market gas. The following year Brooklyn Union invested in Phoenix Natural Gas and Premier Transco in Northern Ireland, both units of BG (formerly British Gas).

Also in 1997 Brooklyn Union formed KeySpan Energy as a holding company and sold Gas Energy and Gas Energy Cogeneration to Calpine. KeySpan outsourced Brooklyn Union's gas transportation, supply, and storage operations to Enron in 1998 (taking back control in 2000).

That year KeySpan acquired troubled Long Island Lighting Company (LILCO) and got LILCO's 11 power plants. LILCO's electric power grid was given to the Long Island Power Authority, which contracted KeySpan to keep the power flowing.

At the time of the merger, KeySpan became MarketSpan, but three months later it began doing business as KeySpan again. (It officially became KeySpan Corporation in 1999.) Negative publicity had tainted the MarketSpan name when New York Governor George Pataki made political hay of the $42 million severance package CEO William Catacosinos (former LILCO head) received. Catacosinos was never out of a job but continued working in the same office under the new company's name. He later resigned as CEO; Robert Catell succeeded him.

In 1999 KeySpan bought Ravenswood, a 2,168-MW New York City power plant, from Consolidated Edison and increased its holdings in Ireland's Premier Transco to 50%. The following year it gained 800,000 new customers by acquiring Massachusetts utility Eastern Enterprises (owner of Boston Gas, Colonial Gas, and Essex Gas) and New Hampshire utility EnergyNorth.

In 2001 KeySpan discontinued its general-contract construction business, KeySpan Construction (formerly the Roy Kay Companies). The following year it sold Eastern Enterprises' barge business, Midland Enterprises, to Ingram Industries for about $230 million.

OFFICERS

Chairman and CEO, KeySpan Corporation and KeySpan Energy Delivery; Chairman, President, and CEO, KEDNY and KeySpan Energy; Chairman, Houston Exploration: Robert B. Catell, age 65, $1,761,897 pay
EVP and CFO: Gerald Luterman, age 58, $589,846 pay
EVP and General Counsel: Steven L. Zelkowitz, age 52

EVP; President, KEDNE: Chester R. Messer, age 60
EVP Client Services: Lenore F. Puleo, age 48
EVP Electric Operations: Anthony Nozzolillo, age 53
EVP Strategic Services: John Caroselli, age 47
SVP and CIO: Cheryl T. Smith, age 50
SVP Corporate Affairs: David J. Manning, age 51
SVP Finance Operations and Regulatory Affairs:
Joseph F. Bodanza, age 54
SVP Human Resources: Elaine Weinstein, age 55
SVP Strategic Marketing and E-Business:
Colin P. Watson, age 50
President and CEO, Houston Exploration:
William G. Hargett, age 52
President and CEO, KeySpan Energy Services and
Supply; Vice Chairman and CEO, Keyspan Services:
Robert J. Fani, age 48, $608,870 pay
President, KeySpan Energy Delivery:
Wallace P. Parker Jr., age 52, $604,148 pay
Auditors: Deloitte & Touche LLP

LOCATIONS

HQ: 1 MetroTech Center, Brooklyn, NY 11201
Phone: 718-403-1000   **Fax:** 718-488-1782
Web: www.keyspanenergy.com

KeySpan distributes natural gas in Brooklyn, Long
Island, Queens, and Staten Island in New York; in
eastern, central, and the Cape Cod area of
Massachusetts; and in central New Hampshire.

2001 Natural Gas Customers

	% of total
New York	66
Massachusetts	31
New Hampshire	3
Total	**100**

PRODUCTS/OPERATIONS

2001 Sales

	$ mil.	% of total
Gas distribution	3,614	54
Electric services	1,421	21
Energy-related services	1,100	17
Gas exploration & production	400	6
Other	98	2
Total	**6,633**	**100**

Selected Subsidiaries and Affiliates
The Houston Exploration Company (67%, US oil and gas
exploration)
KeySpan Energy Delivery
Boston Gas (operates as KeySpan Energy Delivery New
England)
The Brooklyn Union Gas Company (operates as
KeySpan Energy Delivery New York)
KeySpan Gas East Corporation (operates as KeySpan
Energy Delivery Long Island)
Premier Transco Limited (50%, pipeline between
Scotland and Northern Ireland)

COMPETITORS

Aquila	Energy East	NiSource
Bay State Gas	Fluor	NSTAR
Bechtel	National Fuel	NUI
CH Energy	Gas	ONEOK
Group, Inc.	National Grid	PG&E
Con Edison	USA	PSEG
Devon Energy	New Jersey	RGS Energy
DualStar	Resources	Star Gas
Technologies	New York Power	Partners
Duke Energy	Authority	Unitil
Dynegy	Nicor	

HISTORICAL FINANCIALS & EMPLOYEES

NYSE: KSE FYE: December 31	Annual Growth	12/92	12/93	12/94	12/95	12/96	12/97	12/98	12/99	12/00	12/01
Sales ($ mil.)	32.7%	—	—	—	1,216	1,432	1,478	1,722	2,955	5,122	6,633
Net income ($ mil.)	16.1%	—	—	—	92	123	115	(167)	259	301	224
Income as % of sales	—	—	—	—	7.5%	8.6%	7.8%	—	8.8%	5.9%	3.4%
Earnings per share ($)	—	—	—	—	—	—	—	(1.34)	1.62	2.10	1.56
Stock price - FY high ($)	—	—	—	—	—	—	—	34.19	31.31	43.63	41.94
Stock price - FY low ($)	—	—	—	—	—	—	—	25.38	22.50	20.19	29.10
Stock price - FY close ($)	3.8%	—	—	—	—	—	—	31.00	23.19	42.38	34.65
P/E - high	—	—	—	—	—	—	—	—	19	21	27
P/E - low	—	—	—	—	—	—	—	—	14	10	18
Dividends per share ($)	—	—	—	—	—	—	—	0.00	1.78	1.78	1.78
Book value per share ($)	(7.1%)	—	—	—	—	—	—	26.61	20.91	21.27	21.33
Employees	14.8%	—	—	—	5,688	5,413	5,187	7,950	7,723	13,000	13,000

STOCK PRICE HISTORY

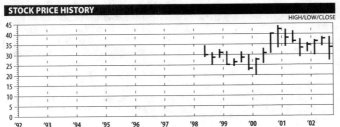

HIGH/LOW/CLOSE

2001 FISCAL YEAR-END
Debt ratio: 61.2%
Return on equity: 7.9%
Cash ($ mil.): 159
Current ratio: 0.84
Long-term debt ($ mil.): 4,698
No. of shares (mil.): 139
Dividends
Yield: 5.1%
Payout: 114.1%
Market value ($ mil.): 4,831

KIMBERLY-CLARK CORPORATION

In good times or bad, Kimberly-Clark is on a roll. The Irving, Texas-based company generates its sales from tissue products (it's the world leader), including Cottonelle toilet paper, Scott toilet paper and paper towels, and Kleenex facial tissues. The company also makes personal care products such as Huggies disposable diapers and baby wipes, Depend undergarments, and Kotex feminine pads. New products, such as Huggies Little Swimmers disposable swimpants and Depend protective underwear, have helped fuel the company's sales growth.

Kimberly-Clark has been adding products for the health care market through acquisitions. The company has become the market leader in sterilization wrap, face masks, surgical drapes and gowns, and closed-suction respiratory products. Kimberly-Clark's purchase of Safeskin made it a leading manufacturer of examination gloves.

Kimberly-Clark also produces Classic Crest business and writing papers, as well as specialty and technical papers and newsprint for many leading US newspapers.

HISTORY

John Kimberly, Charles Clark, Havilah Babcock, and Frank Shattuck founded Kimberly, Clark & Company in Neenah, Wisconsin, in 1872 to manufacture newsprint from rags. The company incorporated as Kimberly & Clark Company in 1880 and built a pulp and paper plant on the Fox River in 1889.

In 1914 the company developed cellu-cotton, a cotton substitute used by the US Army as surgical cotton during WWI. Army nurses used cellu-cotton pads as disposable sanitary napkins, and six years later the company introduced Kotex, the first disposable feminine hygiene product. Kleenex, the first throwaway handkerchief, followed in 1924. Kimberly & Clark joined with The New York Times Company in 1926 to build a newsprint mill (Spruce Falls Power and Paper) in Ontario, Canada. Two years later the company went public.

The firm expanded internationally during the 1950s, opening plants in Mexico, Germany, and the UK. It began operations in 17 more foreign locations in the 1960s. Before retiring in 1971, CEO Guy Minard sold the four mills that handled Kimberly-Clark's unprofitable coated-paper business and entered the paper towel and disposable diaper markets. Minard's successor, Darwin Smith, introduced Kimbies diapers in 1968, but they leaked and were withdrawn from the market. An improved version came out in 1976, followed by Huggies, a premium-priced diaper with elastic leg bands, two years later.

The company formed Midwest Express Airlines from its corporate flight department in 1984 (a business it exited in 1996). Smith moved Kimberly-Clark's headquarters from Neenah to Irving, Texas, the following year.

In 1991 Kimberly-Clark and The New York Times Company sold Spruce Falls Power and Paper. Smith retired as chairman in 1992 and was succeeded by Wayne Sanders, who was largely responsible for designing Huggies Pull-Ups (introduced in 1989). Kimberly-Clark entered a joint venture to make personal care products in Argentina in 1994 and also bought the feminine hygiene units of VP-Schickedanz (Germany) and Handan Comfort and Beauty Group (China).

Kimberly-Clark bought Scott Paper in 1995 for $9.4 billion, which boosted its market share in bathroom tissue from 5% to 31% and its share in paper towels from 6% to 18%, but led to some headaches as the company absorbed Scott's operations.

In 1997 Kimberly-Clark sold its 50% stake in Canada's Scott Paper to forest products company Kruger and bought diaper operations in Spain and Portugal and disposable surgical face masks maker Tecnol Medical Products. A tissue price war in Europe bruised the company's bottom line that year and the company began massive job cuts. (By the end of 1999, nearly 4,000 jobs, mostly in the tissue-based businesses, had been axed.)

In part to focus on its health care business, which it entered in 1997, the company in 1999 sold some of its timber interests and its timber fleet to Cooper/T. Smith Corp. Augmenting its presence in Germany, Switzerland, and Austria, in 1999 the company paid $365 million for the tissue business of Swiss-based Attisholz Holding. Adding to its lineup of medical products, the company bought Ballard Medical Products in 1999 for $744 million and examination glove maker Safeskin in 2000 for about $800 million.

Also in 2000 the company bought virtually all of Taiwan's S-K Corporation; the move made Kimberly-Clark one of the largest manufacturers of consumer packaged goods in Taiwan and set the stage for expanded distribution in the Asia/Pacific region. The company later purchased Taiwan Scott Paper Corporation for about $40 million and merged the two companies together, forming Kimberly-Clark Taiwan. In 2001 Kimberly-Clark bought Italian diaper maker Linostar, and announced it was closing four Latin American manufacturing plants.

In 2002 Kimberly-Clark purchased fellow paper packaging rival Amcor's stake in their Kimberly-Clark Australia joint venture.

Chairman and CEO: Wayne R. Sanders, age 54,
$950,000 pay
President, COO, and Director: Thomas J. Falk, age 43,
$675,000 pay
EVP: Kathi P. Seifert, age 52, $480,000 pay
SVP and CFO: John W. Donehower, age 55,
$440,000 pay
SVP: Tina S. Barry
SVP: Mark R. Hunsader
SVP Law and Government Affairs: O. George Everbach,
age 63, $455,000 pay
Group President, Business-to-Business:
Robert E. Abernathy, age 47
Group President, Consumer Tissue:
Steven R. Kalmanson, age 49
VP, Human Resources: Liz Gottung
Auditors: Deloitte & Touche LLP

LOCATIONS

HQ: 351 Phelps Dr., Irving, TX 75038
Phone: 972-281-1200 **Fax:** 972-281-1490
Web: www.kimberly-clark.com

Kimberly-Clark has operations in the US and 41 other
countries. Its products are sold in 150 countries.

2001 Sales

	$ mil.	% of total
US	9,328	59
Asia, Latin America & Africa	2,864	18
Europe	2,648	17
Canada	938	6
Adjustments	(1,254)	—
Total	**14,524**	**100**

PRODUCTS/OPERATIONS

2001 Sales

	$ mil.	% of total
Personal care products	5,677	39
Consumer tissue	5,383	36
Business-to-business	3,625	25
Adjustments	(161)	—
Total	**14,524**	**100**

Selected Products and Brands

Baby wipes (Huggies)
Bathroom tissue (Cottonelle, Scott)
Business and writing papers (Classic Crest)
Closed-suction respiratory products
Disposable diapers (Huggies, Pull-Ups)
Examination gloves (Safeshield)
Face masks
Facial tissue (Kleenex)

Feminine hygiene products (Kotex, New Freedom, Lightdays)
Infection-control products
Incontinence products (Depend, Poise)
Newsprint
Paper napkins (Scott)
Paper towels (Kleenex, Scott, Viva)
Printing papers
Scrub suits and apparel
Sterile wrap (Kimguard)
Surgical drapes and gowns

COMPETITORS

3M
Akorn
Alba-Waldensian
Allegiance
Becton Dickinson
Bristol-Myers Squibb
CCA Industries
DSG International
Johnson & Johnson

Medline Industries
Molnlycke
Paragon Trade Brands
Playtex
Potlatch
Procter & Gamble
SSI Surgical Services
Unilever

HISTORICAL FINANCIALS & EMPLOYEES

NYSE: KMB FYE: December 31	Annual Growth	12/92	12/93	12/94	12/95	12/96	12/97	12/98	12/99	12/00	12/01
Sales ($ mil.)	8.3%	7,091	6,973	7,364	13,789	13,149	12,547	12,298	13,007	13,982	14,524
Net income ($ mil.)	31.7%	135	511	535	33	1,404	902	1,166	1,668	1,801	1,610
Income as % of sales	—	1.9%	7.3%	7.3%	0.2%	10.7%	7.2%	9.5%	12.8%	12.9%	11.1%
Earnings per share ($)	24.6%	0.42	0.41	1.34	0.06	2.48	1.61	2.11	3.09	3.31	3.05
Stock price - FY high ($)	—	31.63	31.00	30.00	41.50	49.81	56.88	59.44	69.56	73.25	72.19
Stock price - FY low ($)	—	23.13	22.31	23.50	23.63	34.31	43.25	35.88	44.81	42.00	52.06
Stock price - FY close ($)	8.2%	29.50	25.94	25.19	41.38	47.63	49.31	54.50	65.44	70.69	59.80
P/E - high	—	29	60	22	692	20	36	28	22	22	24
P/E - low	—	21	43	17	394	14	27	17	14	13	17
Dividends per share ($)	3.4%	0.82	0.85	0.88	0.90	0.92	0.95	0.99	1.03	1.07	1.11
Book value per share ($)	4.3%	6.81	7.63	8.10	11.39	8.01	7.42	7.22	9.42	10.81	9.93
Employees	4.6%	42,902	42,131	42,707	55,341	54,800	57,000	54,700	54,800	66,300	64,200

STOCK PRICE HISTORY

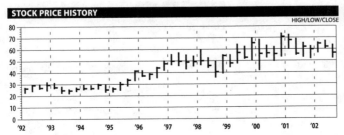

HIGH/LOW/CLOSE

2001 FISCAL YEAR-END

Debt ratio: 30.0%
Return on equity: 28.2%
Cash ($ mil.): 405
Current ratio: 0.94
Long-term debt ($ mil.): 2,424
No. of shares (mil.): 569
Dividends
  Yield: 1.9%
  Payout: 36.4%
Market value ($ mil.): 34,002

KINDRED HEALTHCARE, INC.

Kindred's golden oldies aren't the cash cows they once were. Louisville, Kentucky-based Kindred Healthcare (formerly Vencor) is one of the US's largest long-term health care providers, with about 55 long-term acute care hospitals and more than 300 skilled nursing facilities. Services include long-term intensive care, respiratory services, acute cardiopulmonary care, postoperative care, inpatient and outpatient rehabilitation therapy, and Alzheimer's disease care. Kindred also operates institutional pharmacies. Together, Medicare and Medicaid account for almost 80% of revenues.

The company is the result of its predecessor's split into two: Kindred owns the business operations and non-real estate assets, while real estate investment trust (REIT) Ventas owns most of its properties and leases them to Kindred.

When regulatory changes restricted government health care spending (traditionally more than half of Kindred's revenues), the company tried to shift from Medicaid to wealthier clients, but the move couldn't stave off bankruptcy. With the approval of its reorganization plan, Kindred is hoping that a new name and fresh credit will help it recover.

HISTORY

After a stint as Kentucky's commerce secretary in the 1980s, Bruce Lunsford was approached by respiratory therapist Michael Barr with the idea of establishing long-term hospitals for ventilator-dependent patients. Barr said these hospitals would be cheaper to run than full-service facilities, which require additional equipment. Lunsford (who became chairman, president, and CEO) and Barr (who was COO) founded Vencare in 1983 with backing from Gene Smith (a wealthy political associate of Lunsford). They bought a money-losing, 62-bed Indiana hospital and soon turned the operation around.

Vencare expanded into Florida and Texas and, by the end of the 1980s, operated more than 420 beds in seven facilities. Revenues jumped from less than $1 million in 1985 to $54 million by 1989, the year it changed its name to Vencor.

During the early 1990s, Vencor added facilities in Arizona, California, Colorado, Georgia, and Missouri. Vencor ran 29 facilities by the end of 1993, the same year it launched its Vencare respiratory care program.

Vencor acquisitions in 1995 included hospital respiratory and cardiopulmonary departments in seven states. Later that year it bought the much-larger Hillhaven, the US's #2 nursing home operator at that time. (In 1990 Hillhaven had been spun off from what is now Tenet

Healthcare.) When Vencor bought it, Hillhaven owned 310 nursing homes, 60 pharmacies, and 23 retirement communities. The buy furthered Lunsford's vision of creating a network of long-term-care facilities and services. Vencor also debuted VenTouch, an electronic-pad-based record keeping system for its facilities, in 1995.

The following year Vencor spun off its assisted and independent living properties as Atria Communities; as part of the Hillhaven assimilation, it also consolidated its MediSave pharmacy unit into its hospital operations and sold 34 nursing homes to Lennox Healthcare.

Vencor's 1997 buys included TheraTx (216 rehabilitation centers, 28 nursing centers, and 16 occupational health clinics), and Transitional Hospitals (long-term acute care hospitals). That year Vencor formed an alliance with insurer CNA to develop an insurance product for long-term care.

In 1998 the company split into Ventas (real estate) and Vencor (operations). It also sold most of its remaining interest in an assisted living company (now called Atria Senior Quarters) it had spun off in 1996. To attract wealthier residents, it also launched a program in 1998 to turn away — and turn out — Medicaid patients. Vencor soon abandoned the plan amid heated attacks from advocacy groups. (Welcoming back the evictees didn't stop Florida regulators from fining Vencor.) Several other states and the federal government also began probing Vencor's practices; in 1999 the affair prompted Congressional action designed to protect Medicaid patients. Lunsford and Barr were ousted in the turmoil. The government also demanded that Vencor return $90 million in overpayments over 60 months ($2 million a month) or risk losing Medicare payments.

The company filed for Chapter 11 bankruptcy later that year. Despite bankruptcy protection, the Justice Department in 2000 filed claims for more than $1 billion from Vencor for Medicare fraud since 1992. In 2001, Vencor settled the majority of these claims. That year it also changed its name to Kindred Healthcare.

OFFICERS

Chairman and CEO: Edward L. Kuntz, age 56, $2,188,175 pay
President and COO; Interim President, Health Services Division: Paul J. Diaz, age 40
SVP, CFO, and Treasurer: Richard A. Lechleiter, age 43, $773,164 pay
SVP, CIO, and Chief Administrative Officer: Richard E. Chapman, age 53, $773,164 pay
SVP and General Counsel: M. Suzanne Riedman, age 50

SVP, Planning and Development:
James H. Gillenwater Jr., age 44
VP, Compliance and Government Programs:
William M. Altman, age 42
VP, Human Resources: Keith Sherman
President, Hospital Division: Frank J. Battafarano, age 51, $682,375 pay
Chief Medical Officer, Health Services Division:
James R. Fegan
Chief Medical Officer, Hospital Division:
Sean R. Muldoon
SVP, Pacific Region: Lane Bowen
SVP, Northeast Region: Donna Kelsey
SVP, South Region: David Stordy
SVP, Central Region: Terry Tackett
SVP, Clinical Operations: Richard Gurka
SVP, Operational Reimbursement: Dennis J. Hansen
SVP, Finance: Robert E. Schmidt
SVP, Midwest Region: Steve Monaghan
SVP, East Region: Jim Novak
Auditors: PricewaterhouseCoopers LLP

LOCATIONS

HQ: 1 Vencor Place, 680 S. 4th St., Louisville, KY 40202
Phone: 502-596-7300
Web: www.kindredhealthcare.com

Kindred Healthcare operates in more than 40 states nationwide.

PRODUCTS/OPERATIONS

2001 Sales

	$ mil.	% of total
Medicare	901	38
Medicaid	799	33
Private & other	674	29
Eliminations	(45)	—
Total	**2,329**	**100**

Selected Subsidiaries
Cornerstone Insurance Company (Cayman Islands)
Transitional Hospitals Corporation
Vencor Operating, Inc.
  Horizon Healthcare Services, Inc.
  Medisave Pharmacies, Inc.
  PersonaCare, Inc.
  TheraTx Health Services, Inc.
  Vencare, Inc.
  Vencare Rehab Services, Inc.
  Vencor Home Care Services, Inc.
  Vencor Insurance Holdings, Inc.

COMPETITORS

Ascension	HEALTHSOUTH
Beverly Enterprises	Integrated Health Services
Catholic Healthcare	Life Care Centers
Partners	Manor Care
Centennial HealthCare	Mariner Health Care
Extendicare	Sun Healthcare
Genesis Health Ventures	Tenet Healthcare
HCA	

HISTORICAL FINANCIALS & EMPLOYEES

Nasdaq: KIND FYE: December 31	Annual Growth	12/92	12/93	12/94	12/95	12/96	12/97	12/98	12/99	12/00	12/01
Sales ($ mil.)	30.3%	215	282	400	2,324	2,578	3,116	3,000	2,665	2,889	2,329
Net income ($ mil.)	12.8%	17	23	31	(15)	48	131	(651)	(293)	(65)	52
Income as % of sales	—	8.1%	8.1%	7.9%	—	1.9%	4.2%	—	—	—	2.2%
Earnings per share ($)	—	—	—	—	—	—	—	—	—	—	2.83
Stock price - FY high ($)	—	—	—	—	—	—	—	—	—	—	67.90
Stock price - FY low ($)	—	—	—	—	—	—	—	—	—	—	31.00
Stock price - FY close ($)	—	—	—	—	—	—	—	—	—	—	52.00
P/E - high	—	—	—	—	—	—	—	—	—	—	22
P/E - low	—	—	—	—	—	—	—	—	—	—	10
Dividends per share ($)	—	—	—	—	—	—	—	—	—	—	0.00
Book value per share ($)	—	—	—	—	—	—	—	—	—	—	33.39
Employees	(8.9%)	—	—	—	—	—	76,800	57,900	53,000	51,900	52,800

STOCK PRICE HISTORY

HIGH/LOW/CLOSE

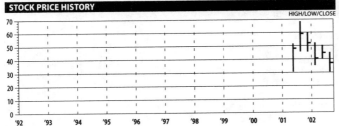

2001 FISCAL YEAR-END

Debt ratio: 26.4%
Return on equity: 86.9%
Cash ($ mil.): 191
Current ratio: 1.62
Long-term debt ($ mil.): 212
No. of shares (mil.): 18
Dividends
  Yield: —
  Payout: —
Market value ($ mil.): 920

KING RANCH, INC.

King Ranch's property is Texas-sized (not really, but it is larger than all of Rhode Island). The company's 825,000-acre namesake ranch still conducts the farming and ranching that made it famous, but the dwindling demand for beef has made it more dependent on oil and gas royalties, fruit and sugar cane farming in Florida, and tourist dollars (from birdwatchers, sightseers, and hunters). The operations are managed from its Houston corporate headquarters.

Considered the birthplace of the American ranching industry, King Ranch also has introduced the new highly fertile breed of beef cattle: the King Ranch Santa Cruz, which is one-fourth Gelbvieh, one-fourth Red Angus, and one-half Santa Gertrudis. About 60,000 cattle still roam the land, but raising animals isn't the only thing King Ranch cottons to — this sprawl of four noncontiguous ranches is also one of the US's largest cotton producers.

Like a good western movie, some things ride into the sunset at King Ranch. The company sold its 670-acre Kentucky Thoroughbred breeding and racing farm, as well as most of its foreign ranches, and its primary oil and gas subsidiary. The descendants of the company's founder, Richard King, own King Ranch.

HISTORY

King Ranch was founded in 1853 by former steamboat captain Richard King and his wife Henrietta, the daughter of a Brownsville, Texas, missionary. On the advice of his friend Robert E. Lee, King used his steamboating profits and occasional strong-arm tactics to buy land — miles of flat, brush-filled, coastal plain and desert south of Corpus Christi, Texas, valued at pennies an acre.

The next year King relocated the residents of an entire drought-ravaged village to the ranch and employed them as ranch hands, known ever after as *kineños* ("King's men"). The Kings built their homestead in 1858 at a site recommended by Lee.

King Ranch endured attacks from Union guerrillas during the Civil War and Mexican bandits after the war. Times were tough, but King was up to the challenge, always traveling armed and with outriders.

In 1867 the ranch used its famed Running W brand for the first time. After King's death in 1885, Robert Kleberg, who married King's daughter Alice, managed the 1.2 million-acre ranch for his mother-in-law. Henrietta died in 1925 and left three-fourths of the ranch to Alice. Before Robert's death in 1932, control of the ranch passed to sons Richard and Bob. In 1933

Bob negotiated an exclusive oil and gas lease with Houston-based Humble Oil, which later became part of Exxon.

While Richard served in Congress, Bob ran the ranch. He developed the Santa Gertrudis, the first breed of cattle ever created in the US, by crossing British shorthorn cattle with Indian Brahmas. The new breed was better suited to the hot, dry South Texas climate.

Bob made King Ranch a leading breeder of quarter horses, which worked cattle, and Thoroughbreds, which he raced. He bought Kentucky Derby winner Bold Venture in 1936 and a Kentucky breeding farm in 1946; that year a King Ranch horse, Assault, won racing's Triple Crown.

When Bob died in 1974, the family asked James Clement, husband of one of the founders' great-granddaughters, to become CEO and bypassed Robert Shelton, a King relative and orphan whom Bob had raised as his own son. Shelton severed ties with the ranch in 1977 over a lawsuit he filed against Exxon, and partially won, alleging underpayment of royalties.

Under Clement, King Ranch became a multinational corporation. In 1980 it formed King Ranch Oil and Gas (also called King Ranch Energy) to explore for and produce oil and gas in five states and the Gulf of Mexico. In 1988 Clement retired, and Kimberly-Clark executive Darwin Smith became the first CEO not related to the founders. Smith left after one year, and the reins passed to petroleum geologist Roger Jarvis and then to Jack Hunt in 1995.

With the help of scientists, in the early 1990s the company developed a leaner, more fertile breed of the Santa Gertrudis called the Santa Cruz. In 1998 Stephen "Tio" Kleberg, the only King descendant still actively working the ranch, was pushed from the saddle of daily operations to a seat on the board. King Ranch sold its Kentucky horse farm in 1998 and teamed up with Collier Enterprises that year to purchase citrus grower Turner Foods from utility holding company FPL Group.

In 2000 King Ranch sold King Ranch Energy to St. Mary Land and Exploration Co. for $60 million.

OFFICERS

Chairman: James H. Clement
President and CEO: Jack Hunt
CFO: Bill Gardiner
VP Livestock: Paul Genho
VP Audit: Richard Nilles
Secretary and General Counsel: Frank Perrone
Director of Human Resources: Martha Breit

LOCATIONS

HQ: 3 River Way, Ste. 1600, Houston, TX 77056
Phone: 832-681-5700   **Fax:** 832-681-5759
Web: www.king-ranch.com

King Ranch operates ranching and farming interests in
South Texas as well as in Florida.

Selected Agricultural Operations
Florida
   3,100 acres (St. Augustine sod)
   12,000 acres (sugar cane)
   40,000 acres (orange and grapefruit groves)
Texas
   60,000 acres (cotton and grain)

PRODUCTS/OPERATIONS

Selected Operations
Consolidated Citrus Limited
   Partnership (southern Florida citrus groves)
King Ranch Museum
King Ranch Nature Tour Program
King Ranch Saddle Shop (leather products)

COMPETITORS

Alico
AZTX Cattle
Bartlett and Company
Cactus Feeders
Calcot
ContiGroup
Devon Energy
Friona Industries
Koch
Lykes Bros.
Southern States

HISTORICAL FINANCIALS & EMPLOYEES

Private FYE: December 31	Annual Growth	12/91	12/92	12/93	12/94	12/95	12/96	12/97	12/98	12/99	12/00
Estimated sales ($ mil.)	(1.2%)	—	330	250	250	250	250	300	300	300	300
Employees	0.0%	—	700	700	700	700	700	700	700	700	700

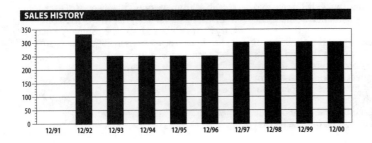

SALES HISTORY

KINKO'S, INC.

Ask someone what they're doing at Kinko's and they might respond, "Makin' copies." But they might also say they're sending documents around the world electronically, shipping packages, getting business cards printed, checking e-mail, or even accessing the Internet. Dallas-based Kinko's began as a one-store, campus-oriented copy shop and has evolved into an entrepreneurial "branch office" for small offices and home businesses. Although the small office/home office market accounts for most of the company's sales, it also provides digital document services to medium and large corporations.

Kinko's operates a global chain of more than 1,100 stores in Australia, Canada, China, Japan, the Netherlands, South Korea, the UK, the United Arab Emirates, and the US. The company's 24-hour-a-day, seven-day-a-week service centers keep up with the latest technologies so that Kinko's customers can focus on their businesses. The firm has also launched Kinkos.com, which allows Web users to design products such as business cards and then forward the order to a nearby Kinko's store for printing.

New CEO Gary Kusin, a longtime Dallas businessman, relocated the company's headquarters to Dallas in early 2002. He cites the area's central location and low tax rate as reasons for uprooting the company. About 350 staffers will be cut as a result of a restructuring of field support positions.

New York buyout firm Clayton, Dubilier & Rice owns 41% of Kinko's.

HISTORY

Kinko's is the creation of Paul Orfalea, who suffers from dyslexia and was inappropriately placed for six weeks in a school for the mentally retarded. The red-haired, Afro-sporting Orfalea (nicknamed Kinko) started selling pencils and spiral notebooks on the campus of UC Santa Barbara in 1970. When he saw a 10-cents-a-page photocopy machine in the library, he decided selling copies would be even better. The self-described hippie borrowed $5,000 that year and opened his first Kinko's shop in a former taco stand near the university. He sold school supplies and made copies on a wheeled copy machine that had to be moved outside because the shop was so small.

Orfalea opened a second California store in San Luis Obispo in 1972, and in the mid-1970s he started providing custom publishing materials for colleges. His innovative approach caught on, and by 1980 he had 80 stores in operation, mostly located near colleges.

In 1983 Kinko's opened its first store outside the US, in Canada, and in 1985 it opened its first 24-hour store, in Chicago. The company moved to Ventura, California, in 1988 and shifted its focus to the growing home office market in 1989 following the loss of a $1.9 million copyright-infringement suit for photocopying texts for professors. By 1990 Kinko's had 420 stores.

Kinko's began positioning itself as "Your Branch Office" in 1992. The following year it teamed up with telecommunications company Sprint and introduced videoconferencing services in 100 stores. Kinko's opened an office in South Korea in 1995 and launched Kinkonet, its electronic communications network. The company teamed up with UUNET in 1996 to make Internet access available at its stores.

Until that year Orfalea was the sole owner of 110 stores and had partnership arrangements with more than 120 other entrepreneurs, a relationship that allowed Orfalea to control the company's rapidly growing network, while giving plenty of incentive for local expansion. This relaxed style of management also led to some unprofitable operations.

To remedy this, Kinko's went corporate in 1996, selling about 30% of the company to buyout firm Clayton, Dubilier & Rice for $219 million; the funds have been used for new technology and expansion. As part of the deal, Kinko's established a single, unified corporation, rolling into it all of the decentralized joint venture, corporate, and partnership companies operating under the Kinko's name.

In 1997 the company opened its first branch in China and made its first acquisition, document management company Electronic Demand Publishing, which became the core of Kinko's corporate document unit. In 1998 Kinko's opened its first stores in the UK (through a joint venture with the Virgin Group) and in the Middle East. The next year it began offering Internet-based custom printing services through an alliance with online print services firm iPrint.com.

In 2000 the company launched a new majority-owned Web firm, Kinkos.com. Orfalea resigned as chairman in 2000. In early 2001 Kinko's bought the rest of Kinkos.com (from Liveprint.com) and absorbed it into the company. Also that year Joseph Hardin Jr. (who had been CEO for more than three years) resigned from the company; Gary Kusin replaced him. The company relocated its headquarters to Dallas in 2002, a move that Orfalea criticized as unnecessary.

Chairman Emeritus: Paul Orfalea
Chairman: George Tamke Jr.
President, CEO, and Director: Gary M. Kusin, age 51
CFO: William P. Benac
EVP Operations: Sue Parks
SVP and CTO: Allen Dickason
SVP General Counsel and Secretary: Leslie Klaassen
SVP Human Resources and Administration:
  Paul Rostron
SVP International: Mark Seals
SVP Operations and Sales: Scott Seay
VP Global Sourcing: Steve Grupe
VP Leasing and Site Selection: Paul Myrick
VP Sales: Jennifer Goodwyn
VP Marketing: Laura Kurzu
Controller: Gary Golden
Marketing Director: Heather Clark
Manager of Environmental Affairs: Larry Rogero
Director of Public Relations: Maggie Thill
Corporate Communications: Chris Barnes

HQ: 13155 Noel Road, Ste. 1600, Dallas, TX 75240
Phone: 214-550-7000   **Fax:** 214-550-7001
Web: www.kinkos.com

Kinko's operates more than 1,100 stores in Australia, Canada, China, Japan, the Netherlands, South Korea, the UK, the United Arab Emirates, and the US.

Selected Products and Services
Binding and finishing services
Business and specialty papers
Computer rentals
Custom printing
Digital printing
E-mail
Fax services
FedEx services
Folding
Instant posters and banners
Internet access
Laminating
Laser printing
Office supplies
Overhead transparencies
Photocopying (black-and-white, color, full-service,
  self-service, oversize)
Pick up and delivery
Presentation materials
Scanning

Black Dot Graphics
Champion Industries
EagleDirect.com
Franchise Services
General Binding
IKON
iPrint
Mail Boxes Etc.
Merrill
Office Depot
OfficeMax
PIP
Pitney Bowes
Staples
TRM
Xerox

Private FYE: June 30	Annual Growth	6/92	6/93	6/94	6/95	6/96	6/97	6/98	6/99	6/00	6/01
Estimated sales ($ mil.)	12.2%	—	—	—	1,100	1,350	1,500	1,600	1,800	2,000	2,200
Employees	4.7%	—	—	—	19,000	23,000	24,000	24,000	25,000	26,000	25,000

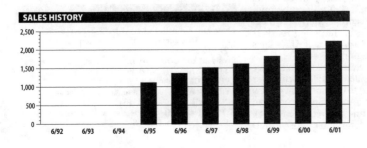

SALES HISTORY

KLA-TENCOR CORPORATION

KLA-Tencor is hard-core when it comes to hunting down flaws in semiconductors. The San Jose, California-based company's equipment and software are used by semiconductor manufacturers to improve factory productivity by detecting defects in the silicon wafers from which chips are made. KLA-Tencor's process control and yield management products inspect circuit patterns (called reticles) and wafers and measure critical production processes. Its software includes products for factorywide yield management and test floor automation and control.

KLA-Tencor's systems are used by most of the world's major semiconductor makers, and by silicon wafer and data storage product manufacturers. KLA-Tencor uses selective acquisitions as well as intensive R&D to keep up with rapid change in chip fabrication, including industry moves to copper interconnects and larger (300mm) wafers.

The company, which is the leader in its niche and one of the top chip equipment firms in the world, tries to position itself as a one-stop shop for its customers' yield management needs, particularly by complementing its technology offerings with consulting services.

HISTORY

In the semiconductor industry's early years (mid-1970s), chip defects rendered about half of some product runs unusable. Silicon Valley entrepreneurs Kenneth Levy — who helped develop image processing equipment pioneer Computervision (merged into Parametric Technology) — and Robert Anderson founded KLA in 1976. Their goal was to develop inspection equipment to improve semiconductor factory yields. In 1978 KLA introduced a first-of-its-kind inspection system that employed advanced optical and image processing technology to test the templates used to etch circuit designs onto silicon wafers. It cut inspection time from eight hours to about 15 minutes.

KLA went public in 1980; within two years it had introduced wafer inspection and wafer metrology systems. As chip yields jumped, so did KLA's sales, shooting past $60 million by mid-decade. When increased competition left US demand faltering, Levy began targeting markets in Europe and Asia. By 1987, 40% of KLA's sales came from those two regions.

Levy named ex-Hewlett-Packard executive Kenneth Schroeder president in 1991 (Schroeder would later become CEO) to take more day-to-day control of the company (Anderson by then had given up his executive duties; he retired in 1994). Restructuring charges, along with extensive R&D

costs, caused the company to lose nearly $14 million in 1992.

KLA returned to profitability in 1993, and the following year it bought Metrologix, a maker of advanced electron beam measurement equipment. In 1995 KLA launched an electron beam-based system that doubled wafer production yields.

Seeking an edge in an increasingly splintered market, the company in 1997 merged with Tencor, at which time it changed its name to KLA-Tencor. The $1.3 billion deal created a company with the broadest line of wafer inspection equipment, film measurement systems, and yield management software.

Czechoslovakian Karel Urbanek had started Tencor in 1976 to make semiconductor measurement and test instruments. Tencor's first product was the Alpha-Step, a film layer profiler, but the company became known for a system that detected and analyzed wafer defects measuring as small as 1/100,000th the width of a human hair. Tencor went public in 1993.

Following the merger, Levy gave up his CEO duties (he remained chairman) to Tencor top executive Jon Tompkins. The two switched titles in 1998 to better reflect their strengths. KLA-Tencor acquired several smaller firms that year in an effort to beef up its technology, including optical defect review firm AMRAY, image archive and retrieval specialist VARS, German wafer inspection equipment maker Nanopro, and software developers DeviceWare and Groff Associates.

Tompkins retired as chairman in 1999. Levy resumed the chairmanship, and Schroeder became CEO. That year KLA-Tencor bought Taiwan-based ACME Systems (engineering analysis software). In 2000 KLA-Tencor bought FINLE Technologies, another maker of yield management software, as well as now-defunct ObjectSpace's Fab Solutions division, which makes process control software.

In 2001 the company acquired QC Optics, a maker of inspection equipment for computer hard disks, flat-panel displays, and semiconductor photomasks, for about $3 million.

OFFICERS

Chairman: Kenneth D. Levy, age 59, $785,115 pay
CEO and Director: Kenneth L. Schroeder, age 55, $1,514,297 pay
President and COO: Gary Dickerson, age 44, $1,075,870 pay (prior to promotion)
EVP and CFO: John H. Kispert, age 37
EVP, E-Beam Inspection and Metrology Group: Neil Richardson, age 46, $632,404 pay
EVP, Optical Surface Inspection & Measurement Group: Dennis J. Fortino, age 55

EVP, Wafer Inspection Group: Richard P. Wallace, age 41
SVP, Data Storage Business: Frank Brienzo
SVP, Strategic Business Development:
  Samuel A. Harrell, age 61
VP and Treasurer: J. Peter Campagna, age 49
VP and General Counsel: Stuart J. Nichols
VP; General Manager, Global Support Services:
  Mike Allison
VP; General Manager, Optical Metrology Division:
  Ami Appelbaum
VP; General Manager, Reticle and Photomask Inspection
  Division: Lance Glasser
VP, Customer Group: Rodney M. Browning, age 39
VP, Finance and Accounting: Maureen L. Lamb, age 40
VP, Human Resources: Tom Coffey
CTO, Software: Robert Rubino
CTO, Systems: Bin-Ming Ben Tsai
Secretary: Larry W. Sonsini, age 61
Auditors: PricewaterhouseCoopers LLP

PRODUCTS/OPERATIONS

Selected Products
Metrology systems
  Critical dimension scanning electron microscopes
    (SEMs)
  Film and film stress measurement
  Optical overlay measurement
  Surface profiling
Reticle (circuit pattern mask) inspection systems
Wafer inspection systems
  Automated defect classification
  Defect analysis software
  In-line monitoring
  Optical and SEM defect review
  Process tool performance monitoring
Yield management software
  Factorywide yield management software
  Test floor automation/control software

LOCATIONS

HQ: 160 Rio Robles, San Jose, CA 95134
Phone: 408-875-6000   Fax: 408-875-3030
Web: www.kla-tencor.com

KLA-Tencor has manufacturing facilities in California
and Massachusetts, and in Israel and the UK

2002 Sales

	$ mil.	% of total
Asia/Pacific		
Japan	351	21
Taiwan	268	16
Other countries	239	15
US	540	33
Western Europe	239	15
Total	**1,637**	**100**

COMPETITORS

ADE
Agilent Technologies
Applied Materials
Carl Zeiss
Electroglas
FEI
Hitachi
Keithley Instruments
Nanometrics
NPTest
Philips Electronics
Rudolph Technologies
Therma-Wave
Veeco Instruments

HISTORICAL FINANCIALS & EMPLOYEES

Nasdaq: KLAC FYE: June 30	Annual Growth	6/93	6/94	6/95	6/96	6/97	6/98	6/99	6/00	6/01	6/02
Sales ($ mil.)	28.9%	167	244	442	695	1,032	1,166	843	1,499	2,104	1,637
Net income ($ mil.)	46.4%	7	30	59	121	105	134	39	254	67	216
Income as % of sales	—	4.2%	12.4%	13.2%	17.4%	10.2%	11.5%	4.6%	16.9%	3.2%	13.2%
Earnings per share ($)	32.1%	0.09	0.30	0.67	1.17	0.62	0.76	0.22	1.32	0.34	1.10
Stock price - FY high ($)	—	4.88	11.25	20.13	24.38	26.56	38.44	32.69	98.50	67.38	70.58
Stock price - FY low ($)	—	1.50	4.13	9.00	10.25	8.75	12.13	10.38	29.91	25.50	28.61
Stock price - FY close ($)	29.4%	4.31	9.38	19.31	11.63	24.38	13.84	32.44	58.56	58.47	43.99
P/E - high	—	54	36	29	20	41	49	142	71	34	64
P/E - low	—	17	13	13	8	13	15	45	22	13	26
Dividends per share ($)	—	0.00	0.00	0.00	0.00	0.00	0.00	0.00	0.00	0.00	0.00
Book value per share ($)	24.1%	1.53	2.49	4.03	5.26	10.11	7.15	6.95	9.11	9.38	10.70
Employees	21.3%	1,000	1,135	1,654	2,500	3,600	4,500	4,200	5,800	6,400	5,700

STOCK PRICE HISTORY

HIGH/LOW/CLOSE

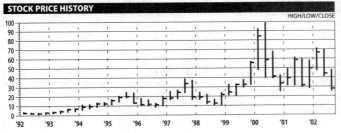

2002 FISCAL YEAR-END

Debt ratio: 0.0%
Return on equity: 11.4%
Cash ($ mil.): 430
Current ratio: 2.36
Long-term debt ($ mil.): 0
No. of shares (mil.): 190
Dividends
  Yield: —
  Payout: —
Market value ($ mil.): 8,374

KMART CORPORATION

Like an overstuffed shopping cart in a narrow aisle, Troy, Michigan-based Kmart has been difficult to turn around. The struggling retail chain was once a major player among US discounters, with more than 1,800 stores. But despite numerous reorganization efforts, including new store concepts, expanded merchandise selections, and adjusted pricing strategies, Kmart has been unable to weather a storm of competition from discount leaders Wal-Mart and Target, as well as the effects of a weak economy.

Kmart sells to low- and middle-income families through its discount stores in all 50 states, Guam, Puerto Rico, and the US Virgin Islands. The company's other retail operations include about 125 Super Kmart Centers (similar to Wal-Mart's Supercenter stores), which offer a full line of groceries and general merchandise. The company also owns e-tailer BlueLight.com, which operates Kmart's online shopping site Kmart.com and offers low-cost Internet access.

A disappointing 2001 holiday season and credit rating downgrades in early 2002 thwarted Kmart's turnaround plans. Finally an erosion of supplier confidence forced Kmart to file for Chapter 11 bankruptcy protection in January 2002, making it the largest retailer ever to seek bankruptcy court protection. As part of its reorganization plan, Kmart closed 283 stores (13%) and cut more than 22,000 jobs. Continued efforts to add exclusive lines and to establish an identity and niche distinct from the competition are part of Kmart's plan for emerging from bankruptcy. Kmart has seen success from its stable of private-label brands, led most notably by the growing Martha Stewart Everyday line.

HISTORY

Sebastian Kresge and John McCrorey opened five-and-dime stores in Memphis and Detroit in 1897. When the partners split two years later, Kresge got Detroit and McCrorey took Memphis. By the time Kresge incorporated as S. S. Kresge Company in 1912, it had become the second-largest dime store chain in the US, with 85 stores. Kresge expanded rapidly in the next several decades, forming S. S. Kresge, Ltd., in 1929 to operate stores in Canada. In the late 1920s and 1930s, the company opened stores in suburban shopping centers. By the 1950s it was one of the largest general merchandise retailers in the US.

A marketing study prompted management to enter discount retailing in 1958, and three unprofitable locations were transformed into Jupiter Discount stores in 1961. The company judged this a success and opened the first Kmart discount store in Detroit in 1962; by 1966 the company had more than 160 Kmart stores. Kresge formed a joint venture with G. J. Coles & Coy (later Coles Myer) to operate Kmart stores in Australia (1968; sold in 1994). The company expanded the Kmart format swiftly in the 1970s, opening more than 270 stores in 1976 alone. With about 95% of its sales coming from Kmart stores, the company changed its name to Kmart in 1977.

Kmart diversified during the 1980s and early 1990s, adding various retailers, including Walden Book Company, then the #1 US bookstore chain, and Builders Square (formerly Home Centers of America) in 1984; PayLess Drug Stores Northwest in 1985; PACE Membership Warehouse in 1989; The Sports Authority in 1990; a 90% stake in OfficeMax by 1991; and the Borders bookstore chain in 1992.

Meanwhile, in 1987 the company sold most of its remaining Kresge and Jupiter locations in the US to McCrory's, the chain started by Kresge's former partner.

In 1994 and 1995, amid falling earnings, the company began shedding operations, spinning off or selling OfficeMax, The Sports Authority; PACE, its US automotive service centers; and Borders. In 1995 CEO Joseph Antonini — architect of the diversification strategy — was replaced by Floyd Hall. More than 200 US stores were closed.

The company then sold Kmart Mexico, a joint venture with El Puerto de Liverpool, and an 87.5% stake in Kmart Canada in 1997 (it sold the rest in 1998). Also in 1997 it unveiled the new Big Kmart format. The company also sold woebegone 162-store Builders Square to Leonard Green & Partners (owners of the Hechinger chain) for a mere $10 million, but retained a $761 million liability for the stores' lease obligations. (Hechinger filed for bankruptcy in 1999, and Kmart assumed the obligations of 115 stores.)

In late 1999 Kmart partnered with Martha Stewart Living Omnimedia, SOFTBANK, and Yahoo! to launch ISP and online retailer BlueLight.com. (Kmart bought the remaining 40% of BlueLight.com it didn't already own in mid-2001.) In May 2000 Hall was replaced by former CVS president and COO Charles Conaway.

In 2001 Kmart said it would close 72 stores in locations that did not fit with expansion plans. Also that year Kmart named distributor Fleming its sole supplier of foods and consumables. The company later said it would offer early retirement to 500 employees.

In a management shakeup that followed downgrades in Kmart's credit rating in January 2002, director James Adamson replaced Conaway as chairman. Soon after, key vendors suspended shipments to the troubled discounter saying

Kmart failed to make regular weekly payments. Kmart filed for Chapter 11 bankruptcy protection that month.

In March 2002 Kmart received bankruptcy court approval to continue its licensing agreements with its five major brands (Martha Stewart; Disney; G.H. Productions, which supplies its Jaclyn Smith line; Joe Boxer Licensing; and Kathy Ireland World Wide). Soon after, Conaway left the company and Adamson was also named CEO. In June the company changed the name of its online shopping site from BlueLight.com to Kmart.com. Since filing for bankruptcy Kmart closed 283 stores, resulting in 22,000 job losses. It announced additional job cuts, including about 400 corporate positions, in August 2002.

OFFICERS

Chairman and CEO: James B. Adamson, age 54
President and COO: Julian C. Day, age 49
EVP and CFO: Albert A. Koch, age 59
EVP, Chief Restructuring Officer: Ronald B. Hutchison, age 52
EVP, Chief Supply Chain Officer: Anthony B. D'Onofrio, age 46
EVP, General Counsel: Janet C. Kelley, age 49
EVP, Human Resources: Michael T. Macik, age 55
EVP, Sourcing and Global Operations: William B. Underwood, age 61
EVP, Store Operations: Gregg Treadway
EVP, Strategic Initiatives and Chief Diversity Officer: Randy L. Allen, age 54, $665,000 pay
Auditors: PricewaterhouseCoopers LLP

LOCATIONS

HQ: 3100 W. Big Beaver Rd., Troy, MI 48084
Phone: 248-463-1000   **Fax:** 248-463-5636
Web: www.bluelight.com

Kmart operates nearly 2,240 retail stores in all 50 states and Guam, Puerto Rico, and the US Virgin Islands.

PRODUCTS/OPERATIONS

2002 Stores

	No.
Big Kmart	2,114
Super Kmart	124
Total	**2,238**

Selected Private Labels
Disney (children's clothing)
Jaclyn Smith (ladies' apparel)
Joe Boxer (apparel)
Kathy Ireland Collection (ladies' apparel)
Martha Stewart Everyday (home fashions, kitchenware)
Sesame Street (kid's clothing and merchandise)

COMPETITORS

Ace Hardware	Costco	Ross Stores
Albertson's	Wholesale	Sears
AutoZone	Dollar General	ShopKo Stores
Bed Bath &	Family Dollar	Staples
Beyond	Stores	Target
Best Buy	J. C. Penney	TJX
Big Lots	Katz Group	Toys "R" Us
BJs Wholesale	Kohl's	TruServ
Club	Kroger	Value City
Circuit City	Linens 'n Things	Walgreen
Stores	Office Depot	Wal-Mart

HISTORICAL FINANCIALS & EMPLOYEES

NYSE: KM FYE: Last Wednesday in Jan.	Annual Growth	1/93	1/94	1/95	1/96	1/97	1/98	1/99	1/00	1/01	1/02
Sales ($ mil.)	(0.5%)	37,724	34,156	34,025	34,389	31,437	32,183	33,674	35,925	37,028	36,151
Net income ($ mil.)	—	941	(974)	296	(571)	(220)	249	518	403	(244)	(2,418)
Income as % of sales	—	2.5%	—	0.9%	—	—	0.8%	1.5%	1.1%	—	—
Earnings per share ($)	—	2.06	(2.40)	0.67	(1.25)	(0.46)	0.51	1.01	0.81	(0.48)	(4.89)
Stock price – FY high ($)	—	28.12	25.75	19.75	16.25	16.00	15.25	20.87	18.63	10.19	13.55
Stock price – FY low ($)	—	20.87	19.25	12.50	5.75	6.00	10.25	10.75	8.28	4.75	0.66
Stock price – FY close ($)	(26.3%)	23.25	19.62	13.62	5.87	11.12	11.00	17.56	8.31	8.75	1.49
P/E – high	—	14	—	29	—	—	30	20	23	—	—
P/E – low	—	10	—	19	—	—	20	10	10	—	—
Dividends per share ($)	—	0.91	0.95	0.96	0.61	0.00	0.00	0.00	0.00	0.00	0.00
Book value per share ($)	(10.4%)	18.52	14.89	13.15	10.85	10.45	11.12	12.12	13.10	12.50	6.87
Employees	(4.6%)	358,000	344,000	348,000	307,000	265,000	261,000	278,525	271,000	252,000	234,000

STOCK PRICE HISTORY

HIGH/LOW/CLOSE

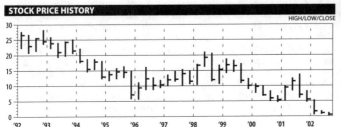

2002 FISCAL YEAR-END

Debt ratio: 25.5%
Return on equity: —
Cash ($ mil.): 1,245
Current ratio: 12.63
Long-term debt ($ mil.): 1,187
No. of shares (mil.): 503
Dividends
  Yield: —
  Payout: —
Market value ($ mil.): 750

KNIGHT RIDDER INC.

The top story for Knight Ridder, the nation's #3 newspaper chain (behind Gannett and Tribune), is the Internet. The fast-growing influence of the World Wide Web convinced the firm to move its headquarters from Miami to San Jose, California, to capitalize on progressive thinking in Silicon Valley. Knight Ridder publishes 32 daily newspapers, including *The Philadelphia Inquirer, The Miami Herald,* the *San Jose Mercury News, The Kansas City Star,* and the *Fort Worth Star-Telegram.* It also owns 25 non-daily papers.

Diversification led the company into cable and specialized information services, but CEO Anthony Ridder (great-grandson of Ridder Publications founder Herman Ridder) has shed the company's non-newspaper operations, taking the firm back to its roots. It has formed a separate unit for its Internet operations called Knight Ridder Digital, with a focus on its employment joint venture, CareerBuilder (with Tribune Company). The firm offers a network of Web sites under its Real Cities umbrella.

HISTORY

Knight Ridder began in 1974 with the merger of Knight Newspapers and Ridder Publications, then the #2 and #3 newspaper groups by circulation in the US.

Knight Newspapers began in 1903 when lawyer-turned-editor Charles Knight purchased the *Akron Beacon Journal.* He died in 1933, leaving the paper to his sons, Jack and Jim. With their guidance the company grew to include 16 metropolitan dailies such as *The Miami Herald* (1937), the *Detroit Free Press* (1940), and *The Philadelphia Inquirer* (1969).

Ridder Publications was founded in 1892 when Herman Ridder bought a German-language newspaper in New York, the *Staats-Zeitung.* He expanded in 1926 with the purchase of the *Journal of Commerce,* a New York shipping daily founded in 1827. Over the next 50 years, the company grew to 19 dailies and eight weeklies, mostly in the West.

After the Knight-Ridder merger, Knight's Lee Hills became chairman and CEO and Ridder's Bernard Ridder became vice chairman. During the 1970s and 1980s the company expanded into TV, radio, and book publishing. It bought HP Books in 1979 (sold 1987) and formed TKR Cable with TCI in 1981. A year later Knight Ridder launched VU/TEXT (online news retrieval), followed in 1983 by Viewtron, America's first consumer videotext system. In 1988 the firm bought DIALOG, the world's largest online full-text

service, from Lockheed. Broadcast properties were sold in 1989.

A newspaper battle between Knight Ridder's *Detroit Free Press* and Gannett's *The Detroit News* in the 1980s ended with the two papers signing a joint operating agreement in 1989 and merging some operations.

Knight Ridder joined the Tribune Company (with whom it operates a news service) in 1992 to deliver business news electronically to PC users. The next year the *San Jose Mercury News,* working with America Online (now AOL Time Warner), became the first newspaper to integrate online services with a daily paper.

The company sold the *Journal of Commerce* in 1995. Also that year Tony Ridder was named chairman and CEO, becoming the first Ridder family member to run the company. He began to sharpen the focus on newspapers. Knight Ridder formed MediaStream, which develops archives for Web sites, in 1996. That year the company sold its financial news unit, Knight-Ridder Financial, to Global Financial Information.

In 1997 the firm bought four newspapers from Walt Disney (including *The Kansas City Star* and the *Fort Worth Star-Telegram*) and swapped its Boulder, Colorado, newspaper for two California newspapers. It also sold several newspapers and sold the Knight Ridder Information unit to M.A.I.D plc. Knight Ridder moved its headquarters to San Jose, California, in 1998. That year it bought Hills Newspapers, a group of weeklies in California, and sold its interest in TKR Cable to partner AT&T Broadband. It joined other powerhouse media companies, including Gannett and Tribune, in 1998 to form Classified Ventures, an online real estate and auto classifieds service.

The following year the company formed KR/NYT Enterprises, a purchasing consortium, with rival New York Times as both firms seek to streamline their purchasing processes. Also that year the company created a new business unit, KnightRidder.com (now Knight Ridder Digital), to house all of its Internet operations. In 2000 KnightRidder.com, with Tribune, formed CareerBuilder, with the acquisitions of online recruiters CareerBuilder and CareerPath.com. Also in 2000 Knight Ridder entered into an agreement with Yahoo! to provide headlines and news briefs on the Web giant's news page.

In 2001 KnightRidder.com changed its name to Knight Ridder Digital. Later that year, CareerBuilder bought job site HeadHunter.NET for about $200 million. That same year the company also started a job reduction program, eliminating some 1,600 positions through early retirements, buyouts, and attrition.

Chairman and CEO: P. Anthony Ridder, age 61, $935,720 pay
SVP Finance and CFO: Gary R. Effren, age 45
SVP Human Resources: Mary Jean Connors, age 49, $518,533 pay
VP and Controller: Margaret Randazzo, age 34
VP and General Counsel: Gordon T. Yamate, age 46, $407,154 pay
VP Human Resources/Compensation and Benefits: Stephen J. Stein, age 48
VP Human Resources Diversity and Development: Jaqui Love Marshall, age 53
VP Marketing: Michael Petrak, age 43
VP News: Jerry Ceppos, age 55
President, Newspaper Division: Steven B. Rossi, age 52, $613,250 pay
Auditors: Ernst & Young LLP

LOCATIONS

HQ: 50 W. San Fernando St., San Jose, CA 95113
Phone: 408-938-7700   **Fax:** 408-938-7766
Web: www.kri.com

Knight Ridder has newspapers in 28 markets in 17 states.

PRODUCTS/OPERATIONS

2001 Sales

	$ mil.	% of total
Advertising	2,254	78
Circulation	512	17
Other	134	5
Total	**2,900**	**100**

Selected Daily Newspapers
Aberdeen American News (SD)
Akron Beacon Journal (OH)
Belleville News-Democrat (IL)
The (Biloxi) Sun Herald (MS)
Bradenton Herald (FL)
The Charlotte Observer (NC)
The (Columbia) State (SC)
Columbus Ledger-Enquirer (GA)
Detroit Free Press
Duluth News-Tribune (MN)
El Nuevo Herald (Miami)
Fort Worth Star-Telegram (TX)
The Kansas City Star (MO)
Lexington Herald-Leader (KY)
The Miami Herald
The (Monterey County) Herald (CA)
The (Myrtle Beach) Sun News (SC)
Philadelphia Daily News
The Philadelphia Inquirer
Saint Paul Pioneer Press (MN)
San Jose Mercury News (CA)
(State College) Centre Daily Times (PA)
Tallahassee Democrat (FL)
The Wichita Eagle (KS)

COMPETITORS

Advance Publications	Media General
Associated Press	Morris Communications
Belo	New York Times
Cox Enterprises	News Corp.
Dow Jones	Pulitzer
E. W. Scripps	Reuters
Gannett	Star Tribune
Hearst	Tribune
McClatchy Company	Washington Post

HISTORICAL FINANCIALS & EMPLOYEES

NYSE: KRI FYE: Last Sunday in December	Annual Growth	12/92	12/93	12/94	12/95	12/96	12/97	12/98	12/99	12/00	12/01
Sales ($ mil.)	2.5%	2,330	2,451	2,649	2,752	2,775	2,877	3,092	3,228	3,212	2,900
Net income ($ mil.)	18.2%	41	148	171	160	268	413	366	340	314	185
Income as % of sales	—	1.8%	6.0%	6.5%	5.8%	9.7%	14.4%	11.8%	10.5%	9.8%	6.4%
Earnings per share ($)	21.7%	0.37	1.34	1.58	1.60	2.75	4.08	3.73	3.49	3.53	2.16
Stock price - FY high ($)	—	32.06	32.50	30.50	33.31	42.00	57.13	59.63	65.00	59.75	65.50
Stock price - FY low ($)	—	25.75	25.31	23.25	25.25	29.88	35.75	40.50	46.00	44.13	50.20
Stock price - FY close ($)	9.4%	29.00	29.88	25.25	31.25	38.25	52.00	51.13	59.56	56.88	64.93
P/E - high	—	24	24	19	20	15	13	13	16	15	28
P/E - low	—	19	19	15	15	11	8	9	11	11	22
Dividends per share ($)	4.0%	0.70	0.70	0.72	0.74	0.77	0.80	0.80	0.89	0.92	1.00
Book value per share ($)	6.3%	10.75	11.33	11.58	11.43	12.12	19.02	21.23	22.37	20.83	18.58
Employees	(0.6%)	20,000	20,000	21,000	22,800	24,000	22,000	22,000	22,000	22,000	19,000

STOCK PRICE HISTORY

HIGH/LOW/CLOSE

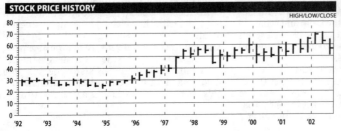

2001 FISCAL YEAR-END

Debt ratio: 50.2%
Return on equity: 11.9%
Cash ($ mil.): 37
Current ratio: 1.12
Long-term debt ($ mil.): 1,573
No. of shares (mil.): 84
Dividends
 Yield: 1.5%
 Payout: 46.3%
Market value ($ mil.): 5,453

KOCH INDUSTRIES, INC.

Among really big privately owned businesses, Koch (pronounced "coke") is the real thing. Wichita, Kansas-based Koch Industries, which has extensive operations in oil and gas, agriculture, and chemicals, is the second-largest private company in the US, after grain merchant Cargill.

Koch's petroleum operations include the purchasing, gathering, and trading of crude oil. Its two refineries in Minnesota and Texas process about 600,000 barrels of crude a day, making it a leading producer of gasoline and petrochemicals. Among its fuels are the low-sulfur Blue Planet brand and soybean diesels. Koch also owns gas gathering systems and about 35,000 miles of pipeline between Texas and Canada, and it purchases, processes, and markets natural gas liquids through a joint venture with Entergy.

Agricultural businesses include cattle ranches (with about 390,000 acres of land and 15,000 cattle), in Kansas, Montana, and Texas. KoSa, Koch's joint venture with Mexico's Saba family, is a leading polyester producer. Koch also produces paraxylene and high-octane missile fuels. Other businesses include asphalt marketing, minerals trading and transport, and making equipment for processing industries.

Brothers Charles and David Koch control the family-run enterprise.

HISTORY

Fred Koch grew up poor in Texas and worked his way through MIT. In 1928 Koch developed a process to refine more gasoline from crude oil, but when he tried to market his invention, the major oil companies sued him for patent infringement. Koch eventually won the lawsuits (after 15 years in court), but the controversy made it tough to attract many US customers. In 1929 Koch took his process to the Soviet Union, but he grew disenchanted with Stalinism and returned home to become a founding member of the anticommunist John Birch Society.

Koch launched Wood River Oil & Refining in Illinois (1940) and bought the Rock Island refinery in Oklahoma (1947). He folded the remaining purchasing and gathering network into Rock Island Oil & Refining (though later sold the refineries). After Koch's death in 1967, his 32-year-old son Charles took the helm and renamed the company Koch Industries. He began a series of acquisitions, adding petrochemical and oil trading service operations.

During the 1980s Koch was thrust into various arenas, legal and political. Charles' brother David, also a Koch Industries executive, ran for US vice president on the Libertarian ticket in 1980. That year the other two Koch brothers, Frederick and

William (David's fraternal twin), launched a takeover attempt, but Charles retained control, and William was fired from his job as VP.

The brothers traded lawsuits, and in a 1983 settlement Charles and David bought out the dissident family members for just over $1 billion. William and Frederick continued to challenge their brothers in court, claiming they had been shortchanged in the deal (the two estranged brothers eventually lost their case in 1998, and their appeals were rejected in 2000). In 1987 they even sued their mother over her distribution of trust fund money.

Despite this legal wrangling, Koch Industries continued to expand, purchasing a Corpus Christi, Texas, refinery in 1981. It expanded its pipeline system, buying Bigheart Pipe Line in Oklahoma (1986) and two systems from Santa Fe Southern Pacific (1988).

In 1991 Koch purchased the Corpus Christi marine terminal, pipelines, and gathering systems of Scurlock Permian (a unit of Ashland Oil). The following year the company bought United Gas Pipe Line (renamed Koch Gateway Pipeline) and its pipeline system extending from Texas to Florida. In 1997 Koch acquired USX-Delhi Group, a natural gas processor and transporter.

In 1998 Koch formed the KoSa joint venture with Mexico's Saba family to buy Hoechst's Trevira polyester unit. Lethargic energy and livestock prices in 1998 and 1999, however, led Koch to lay off several hundred employees, sell its feedlots, and divest portions of its natural gas gathering and pipeline systems.

William Koch sued Koch Industries in 1999, claiming the company had defrauded the US government and Native Americans in oil payments on Indian lands. A jury found for William, but he, Charles, and David agreed to settle the case in 2001 — and sat down to dinner together for the first time in 20 years.

In other legal matters, in 2000 Koch agreed to pay a $30 million civil fine and contribute $5 million toward environmental projects to settle complaints over oil spills from its pipelines in the 1990s. The company agreed to pay $20 million in 2001 to settle a separate environmental case concerning a Texas refinery.

Koch combined its pipeline system and trading units with the power marketing businesses of electric utility Entergy in 2001 to form Entergy-Koch, a joint venture that ranks among the biggest energy commodity traders in the US.

In 2002 Koch acquired Valero Energy's 40% stake in a Mont Belvieu, Texas, natural gas liquids fractionator, boosting its ownership to 80%.

Chairman and CEO: Charles G. Koch, age 66
President, COO, and Director: Joseph W. Moeller
EVP and Director: David H. Koch, age 62
EVP and Director: Richard H. Fink
EVP Operations; Chairman, KoSa: William R. Caffey
SVP and CFO: Steve Feilmeier
SVP Chemicals: Cy S. Nobles
SVP Human Resources: Paul Wheeler
SVP Corporate Strategy: John C. Pittenger
SVP: John M. Van Gelder
SVP; President, Koch Capital Markets: Sam Soliman
VP Business Development: Ron Vaupel
VP, General Counsel, and Secretary: Paul Kaleta
President, Koch Hydrocarbon: Steve Tatum
President, Koch Mineral Services: Jeff Gentry
President, Koch Ventures: Ray Gary
President, Flint Hills Resources: David L. Robertson
President and CEO, Entergy-Koch: Kyle D. Vann
President and CEO, TrueNorth Energy: David G. Park
Managing Director, Environmental and Regulatory Affairs: Don Clay
Auditors: KPMG LLP

LOCATIONS

HQ: 4111 E. 37th St. N, Wichita, KS 67220
Phone: 316-828-5500 **Fax:** 316-828-5739
Web: www.kochind.com

Koch Industries has operations in Argentina, Australia, Belgium, Brazil, Canada, China, the Czech Republic, France, Germany, India, Italy, Japan, Luxembourg, the Netherlands, Poland, Spain, South Africa, Switzerland, the UK, the US, and Venezuela.

PRODUCTS/OPERATIONS

Selected Operations
Flint Hills Resources (formerly Koch Petroleum, crude oil and refined products)
Koch Agriculture Group
  Koch Matador Cattle Company
Koch Chemicals Group
  Koch Chemicals (paraxylene)
  KoSa (polyester, 50%)
  Koch Microelectronic Service Co. (semiconductor chemicals)
  Koch Specialty Chemicals (high-octane missile fuel)
Koch Chemical/Environ Technology Group (specialty equipment and services for refining and chemical industry)
Koch Energy Group
  Entergy-Koch L.P. (50%)
  Koch Exploration
Koch Financial Services, Inc.
  Koch Financial Corp.
Koch Gas Liquids Group
Koch Materials Co. (asphalt)
Koch Mineral Services (bulk ocean transportation and fuel supply)
  Koch Fertilizer Storage & Terminal Co.
  Koch Pipeline Co. LP
Koch Supply & Trading, LLC
Koch Ventures Group (investment in noncore businesses)

COMPETITORS

ADM	Entergy	PEMEX
AEP	EOTT Energy	PG&E
Aquila	Partners	Royal
Ashland	Exxon Mobil	Dutch/Shell
Avista	Imperial Oil	Group
BP	Kerr-McGee	Shell Oil
Cargill	King Ranch	Products
CenterPoint	Lyondell	Southern
Energy	Chemical	Company
ChevronTexaco	Marathon Oil	Sunoco
ConocoPhillips	Motiva	Tractebel
ContiGroup	Enterprises	Williams
Duke Energy	Occidental	Companies
Dynegy	Petroleum	
Enron	Peabody Energy	

HISTORICAL FINANCIALS & EMPLOYEES

Private FYE: December 31	Annual Growth	12/91	12/92	12/93	12/94	12/95	12/96	12/97	12/98	12/99	12/00
Sales ($ mil.)	9.1%	—	19,914	20,000	23,725	25,200	30,000	36,200	35,000	33,050	40,000
Employees	(0.5%)	—	12,000	12,000	12,000	12,500	13,000	15,600	16,000	12,500	11,500

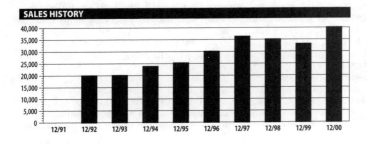

SALES HISTORY

KOHLBERG KRAVIS ROBERTS & CO.

The master of the 1980s buyout universe, Kohlberg Kravis Roberts (KKR) has shed its hostile takeover image for a kinder, gentler, buy-and-build strategy.

New York City-based KKR assembles funds to buy low and sell high. An active investor, it supervises or installs new management and revamps strategy and corporate structure, selling underperforming units or adding new ones. KKR profits not only from its direct interest in these companies but also from fund and company management fees. It has a joint venture with venture capital firm Accel to provide support for companies integrating online and brick-and-mortar businesses. KKR's investment in media company PRIMEDIA makes it the ultimate parent of *Seventeen* and *Fly Fisherman* magazines, among others. Cousins Henry Kravis and George Roberts are the senior partners in KKR. The company, along with Wendel Investissement, is slated to pick up French electrical product maker Legrand from Schneider Electric SA. Other European acquisitions in the works include seven businesses being spun off by German conglomerate Siemens. The businesses are non-core operations such as Mannesmann Plastics Machinery and Demag Cranes & Components. KKR will roll up its acquisitions into a new company called Demag Holding S.a.r.l upon completion of the transactions.

Since 1976 KKR has invested $100 billion in more than 90 companies, with investors receiving returns of around 23%. As the economy cools, though, the firm is weathering its fair share of tumult. KKR is no longer the top fund raiser in the investment industry and has written off investments in such firms as Birch Telecom, which have subsequently slid into bankruptcy.

HISTORY

In 1976 Jerome Kohlberg left investment bank Bear Stearns to form his own leveraged buyout firm; with him he brought protégé Henry Kravis and Kravis' cousin George Roberts. They formed Kohlberg Kravis Roberts & Co. (KKR).

Kohlberg believed LBOs, by giving management ownership stakes in their companies, would yield better results. KKR orchestrated friendly buyouts funded by investor groups and debt. The firm's first buyout was machine-toolmaker Houdaille Industries in 1979.

KKR lost money on its 1981 investment in the American Forest Products division of Bendix. But by 1984 the firm had raised its fourth fund and made its first $1 billion buyout: Wometco Enterprises. That next year KKR turned mean with a hostile takeover of Beatrice. The

deal depended on junk bond financing devised by Drexel Burnham Lambert's Michael Milken and on the sale of pieces of the company. KKR funded the buyouts of Safeway Stores and Owens-Illinois (1986), Jim Walter Homes (1987), and Stop & Shop (1988, sold in 1996).

Unhappy with the firm's hostile image, Kohlberg left in 1987 to form Kohlberg & Co. His suit against KKR over the alleged undervaluing of companies in relation to his departure settlement was resolved for an undisclosed amount. The Beatrice LBO triggered a rash of similar transactions as the financial industry sought fat fees. The frenzy culminated in 1988 with the $31 billion RJR Nabisco buyout, which brought KKR $75 million in fees. As the US slid into recession in 1989, LBOs dwindled and KKR turned to managing its acquisitions.

The firm also did some bottom feeding. In 1991 KKR joined with what is now FleetBoston to buy Bank of New England. The following year it picked up 47% of what was then Advantica Restaurant Group (now just plain Denny's). It sold that holding in 1997.

KKR made its first international foray in 1993 with Russian truck maker Kamaz; it later stalled when Kamaz refused to pay management fees. That next year it freed itself from the RJR morass by swapping its investment in RJR for troubled food company Borden.

In the latter half of the decade, KKR reaped mixed results on its investments, including what is now Spalding Holdings (sporting goods and Evenflo baby products), supermarket chain Bruno's, and KinderCare Learning Centers. The $600 million KKR had sunk into magazine group K-III (now PRIMEDIA) between 1990 and 1994 didn't revive interest in the stock, and it sent Bruno's into bankruptcy in 1998. Disgruntled investors complained about low returns, and in 1996 KKR booted activist megafund CalPERS from its investor ranks.

In 1998 KKR's niche buying continued when it joined with Hicks, Muse, Tate & Furst to buy Regal Cinemas, which it combined with Act III to form the biggest theater chain in the US. The chain's expansion left it on the brink of bankruptcy, and investor Philip Anschutz bought a chunk of its debt and possible control of the company in 2001.

That next year KKR departed from course and unveiled online mortgage lender Nexstar Financial, its first company built from the ground up.

Still focused on Europe, in 2000 the firm claimed the telecommunications business of Robert Bosch (now Tenovis), UK private equity fund Wassall PLC, and Siemens' banking systems unit. That same year it bought the speciality chemicals and pigments operations of Laporte plc to create Rockwood Specialities.

Also in 2000, KKR joined with Internet VC firm Accel Partners to form Accel-KKR, Inc. to invest in companies that combine traditional business and Internet assets. It lost its place as the top fund-raiser to Thomas H. Lee, which closed a record-setting $6.1 billion fund in early 2001.

OFFICERS

Founding Partner: Henry R. Kravis, age 58
Founding Partner, California: George R. Roberts, age 58
General Partner, London: Edward A. Gilhuly, age 42
General Partner: Perry Golkin, age 48
General Partner, California: James H. Greene Jr., age 51
General Partner, California: Robert I. MacDonnell
General Partner: Michael W. Michelson, age 51
General Partner: Paul E. Raether
General Partner: Scott M. Stuart, age 42
Managing Director, London: Johannes Huth
Chairman, Accel-KKR, Inc.: Paul M. Hazen
Office Manager: Sandy Cisneros
Auditors: Deloitte & Touche LLP

LOCATIONS

HQ: 9 W. 57th St., Ste. 4200, New York, NY 10019
Phone: 212-750-8300   **Fax:** 212-750-0003
Web: www.kkr.com

Kohlberg Kravis Roberts & Co. has offices in London; Menlo Park, California; and New York City.

PRODUCTS/OPERATIONS

Selected Investments
Alea Group Holdings AG
Alliance Imaging, Inc.
Amphenol Corporation
Birch Telecom, Inc.
Borden, Inc.
Bristol West Insurance Group
DPL Inc.
Evenflo Company, Inc.
FirstMark Communications Europe SA
IDEX Corporation
Intermedia Communications Inc.
KinderCare Learning Centers, Inc.
KKF.net AG
MedCath Incorporated
NewSouth Communications
Owens-Illinois, Inc.
PRIMEDIA Inc.
Shoppers Drug Mart Inc.
Spalding Holdings Corporation
Tenovis Holding GmbH
Walter Industries, Inc.
Willis Group Limited
Wincor Nixdorf Holding GmbH & Co.
WorldCrest Group
Zhone Technologies, Inc.
Zumtobel AG

COMPETITORS

AEA Investors	Hicks, Muse
American Financial	Interlaken Investment
Apollo Advisors	Investcorp
Bear Stearns	Jordan Company
Berkshire Hathaway	Lehman Brothers
Blackstone Group	Leonard Green
Carlyle Group	MacAndrews & Forbes
Clayton, Dubilier	Merrill Lynch
CVC Capital Partners	Salomon Smith Barney
Dresdner Kleinwort	Holdings
Wasserstein	Texas Pacific Group
Equity Group Investments	Thomas Lee
Forstmann Little	Veronis Suhler Stevenson
Goldman Sachs	Vestar Capital Partners
Haas Wheat	Wingate Partners
Heico	

KOHL'S CORPORATION

The competition is getting hot under the collar over Kohl's. Based in Menomonee Falls, Wisconsin, Kohl's Corporation operates about 420 department stores in about 30 states (primarily in the Midwest). Targeting middle-income customers, Kohl's sells discounted name-brand apparel, shoes, accessories, and housewares for men, women, and children.

Kohl's has become one of the fastest-growing and most successful US department store chains. The company has merchandising relationships that allow it to carry top brands not typically available to other discounters; it sells them at lower prices than department stores by controlling costs. Kohl's one-floor stores (averaging about 85,000 sq. ft.) have fewer areas with a more limited selection than full-line department stores. Centrally located cash registers and wide aisles help get busy shoppers through the store quickly. Stores are generally located in strip malls where rents are cheaper and competition is scarce; customers get easier access to the stores.

Kohl's carries name brands such as Nike, Levi's, Adidas, Danskin, Oshkosh, Healthtex, Nine and Co., and Gloria Vanderbilt. Its private-label lines include the Genuine Sonoma and Croft & Barrow brands. The company tries to simplify and expedite a shopper's trip to the store by limiting the brands it offers in each product category (men's dress pants, for example).

After several years of expanding on its native Midwestern turf and in the mid-Atlantic area, Kohl's is aggressively moving west and south with plans to open 70 stores in 2002 and 80 stores in 2003. AXA Financial owns almost 25% of the company.

HISTORY

Max Kohl (father of Senator Herbert Kohl of Wisconsin) opened his first grocery store in Milwaukee in the late 1920s. Over the years he and his three sons developed it into a chain and in 1938 Kohl's incorporated.

Kohl opened a department store (half apparel, half hard goods) in 1962 next door to a Kohl's grocery. In the mid-1960s he hired William Kellogg, a twentysomething buyer in the basement discount department at Milwaukee's Boston Store, for his expertise in budget retailing. Kellogg came from a retailing family (his father was VP of merchandising at Boston Store; the younger Kellogg had joined that firm out of high school). Kohl and Kellogg began developing the pattern for the store, carving out a niche between upscale department stores and discounters (offering department store quality at discount store prices).

The Kohl family entered real estate development in 1970, building the largest shopping center in the Milwaukee area. By 1972 the family's 65 food stores and five department stores were generating about $90 million in yearly sales. That year the Kohls sold 80% of the two operations to British American Tobacco's Brown & Williamson Industries division (later called BATUS), the first in a string of department store acquisitions that would eventually include Marshall Field's and Saks Fifth Avenue.

BATUS bought the rest of Kohl's in 1978. Herb and Allen Kohl left the business to concentrate on real estate and politics, and Kellogg was named president and CEO. The following year BATUS separated the food and department store operations and eventually sold the food store chain to A&P in 1983.

Kohl's discount image did not fit in with BATUS's other retail operations, so it decided to sell the department store chain. In 1986 Kellogg and two other executives, with the backing of mall developers Herbert and Melvin Simon, led an LBO to acquire the chain's 40 stores and a distribution center; annual sales were about $288 million.

Two years later Kohl's acquired 26 MainStreet department stores from Federated Department Stores, moving the company into new cities such as Chicago and Detroit. When Kohl's went public in 1992, it had 81 stores in six states, and sales topped $1 billion.

In 1996 Kohl's began its mid-Atlantic expansion by opening stores in North Carolina. Sales topped $2 billion in fiscal 1997, and same-store sales were up more than 11%. Early in 1997 the firm acquired a former Bradlees store to enter New Jersey and opened stores in Washington, DC; Philadelphia; New York; and Delaware.

Kohl's continued its expansion in 1998, entering Tennessee and building its mid-Atlantic presence. In early 1999 Kohl's named Larry Montgomery as CEO. The company also bought 30 stores from bankrupt Caldor (mostly in the New York City area) and reopened them as Kohl's in 2000. That next year Kohl's opened a total of 62 new stores with plans to open 150 more over the next two years.

OFFICERS

Chairman: William S. Kellogg, age 58
Vice Chairman and CEO: R. Lawrence Montgomery, age 53, $1,226,067 pay
President and Director: Kevin B. Mansell, age 49, $970,867 pay
COO, Treasurer, and Director: Arlene Meier, age 50, $798,000 pay
EVP and CFO: Patricia K. Johnson, age 44

EVP and General Counsel: Richard D. Schepp, age 41
EVP, Administration: John J. Lesko, age 49
EVP, General Merchandise Manager and Product Development: Richard Leto, age 50, $705,717 pay
EVP, General Merchandise Manager: Jack E. Moore Jr., age 47
EVP, Human Resources: Donald H. Sharpin, age 53
EVP, Marketing: Gary Vasques, age 54, $515,367 pay
Auditors: Ernst & Young LLP

LOCATIONS

HQ: N56 W17000 Ridgewood Dr.,
Menomonee Falls, WI 53051
Phone: 262-703-7000 **Fax:** 262-703-6143
Web: www.kohls.com

2002 Stores

	No.
Illinois	42
Ohio	32
Wisconsin	29
Pennsylvania	26
Michigan	25
Texas	24
Indiana	20
Georgia	18
New Jersey	18
New York	17
Minnesota	17
Virginia	13
North Carolina	12
Maryland	12
Connecticut	12
Missouri	11
Colorado	11
Other states	43
Total	**382**

PRODUCTS/OPERATIONS

Selected Brand Names

adidas	Levi's
Arrow	NIKE
Carter's	OshKosh B'Gosh
Columbia	Pfaltzgraff
Dockers	Reebok
Haggar	Sag Harbor
HealthTex	Unionbay
Jockey	Villager
Lee	Warner

Selected Private-Label Brands
Croft & Barrow
Genuine Sonoma

COMPETITORS

Belk	Ross Stores
BJs Wholesale Club	Saks Inc.
Dillard's	Sears
Dunlap	ShopKo Stores
Federated	Syms
J. C. Penney	Target
Kmart	TJX
Linens 'n Things	Value City
May	Wal-Mart
Men's Wearhouse	

HISTORICAL FINANCIALS & EMPLOYEES

NYSE: KSS FYE: Saturday nearest Jan. 31	Annual Growth	1/93	1/94	1/95	1/96	1/97	1/98	1/99	1/00	1/01	1/02
Sales ($ mil.)	23.8%	1,097	1,306	1,554	1,926	2,388	3,060	3,682	4,557	6,152	7,489
Net income ($ mil.)	38.4%	27	54	69	73	103	141	192	258	372	496
Income as % of sales	—	2.4%	4.1%	4.4%	3.8%	4.3%	4.6%	5.2%	5.7%	6.0%	6.6%
Earnings per share ($)	33.2%	0.11	0.16	0.23	0.25	0.34	0.46	0.59	0.77	1.10	1.45
Stock price - FY high ($)	—	4.36	6.52	6.91	7.09	10.50	18.84	33.88	40.63	72.20	72.24
Stock price - FY low ($)	—	1.66	3.88	4.75	4.98	6.69	9.72	17.03	30.75	34.06	41.95
Stock price - FY close ($)	35.4%	4.34	6.05	5.44	7.05	9.72	17.34	33.88	35.06	71.00	66.29
P/E - high	—	40	34	29	28	30	40	56	51	64	49
P/E - low	—	15	20	20	20	19	21	28	38	30	28
Dividends per share ($)	—	0.00	0.00	0.00	0.00	0.00	0.00	0.00	0.00	0.00	0.00
Book value per share ($)	30.9%	0.74	0.90	1.14	1.39	1.75	3.02	3.67	5.17	6.63	8.33
Employees	17.6%	13,940	14,900	17,600	21,200	25,500	32,200	33,800	43,000	54,000	60,000

STOCK PRICE HISTORY

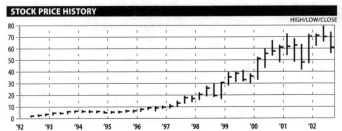

HIGH/LOW/CLOSE

2002 FISCAL YEAR-END

Debt ratio: 28.2%
Return on equity: 19.9%
Cash ($ mil.): 107
Current ratio: 2.80
Long-term debt ($ mil.): 1,095
No. of shares (mil.): 335
Dividends
  Yield: —
  Payout: —
Market value ($ mil.): 22,216

KPMG INTERNATIONAL

KPMG is fighting for dominance in the field of accounting, and is willing to not only tie one hand behind its back, but to cut it off entirely. The Amstelveen, Netherlands-based accounting firm split its consulting operations from its audit offerings and took the former public.

Traditionally a confederation of accounting firms, in recent years KPMG has more closely linked its local operations and has organized them into three regional operating units: the Americas, Europe/Middle East/Africa, and Asia/Pacific. With offices in more than 150 countries, KPMG is the most geographically dispersed of the Big Four (which includes Deloitte Touche Tohmatsu, Ernst & Young, and PricewaterhouseCoopers). In addition to its traditional auditing function, the firm offers tax and financial advisory services; its KLegal International network includes some 1,600 lawyers around the world.

KPMG's consulting operations focus on the Internet. After much regulatory pressure, KPMG Consulting was spun off in an IPO in 2000 that left the firm with a stake of around 20%; Cisco Systems, which had invested $1 billion in the unit, has a 9% stake.

HISTORY

Peat Marwick was founded in 1911, when William Peat, a London accountant, met James Marwick during an Atlantic crossing. University of Glasgow alumni Marwick and Roger Mitchell had formed Marwick, Mitchell & Company in New York in 1897. Peat and Marwick agreed to ally their firms temporarily, and in 1925 they merged as Peat, Marwick, Mitchell, & Copartners.

In 1947 William Black became senior partner, a position he held until 1965. He guided the firm's 1950 merger with Barrow, Wade, Guthrie, one of the US's oldest firms, and built its consulting practice. Peat Marwick restructured its international practice as PMM&Co. (International) in 1972, which was renamed Peat Marwick International in 1978.

That next year several European accounting firms led by Klynveld Kraayenhoff (Netherlands) and Deutsche Treuhand (Germany) began forming an international accounting federation. Needing an American member, the European firms encouraged the merger of two American companies founded around the turn of the century, Main Lafrentz and Hurdman Cranstoun. Main Hurdman & Cranstoun joined the Europeans to form Klynveld Main Goerdeler (KMG), named after two of the member firms and the chairman of Deutsche Treuhand, Reinhard Goerdeler. Other members were C. Jespersen (Denmark), Thorne Riddel

(Canada), Thomson McLintok (UK), and Fides Revision (Switzerland).

Peat Marwick merged with KMG in 1987 to form Klynveld Peat Marwick Goerdeler (KPMG). KPMG lost 10% of its business as competing client companies departed. Professional staff departures followed in 1990 when, as part of a consolidation, the firm trimmed its partnership rolls.

In the 1990s the then-Big Six accounting firms all faced lawsuits arising from an evolving standard holding auditors responsible for the substance, rather than merely the form, of clients' accounts. KPMG was hit by suits stemming from its audits of defunct S&Ls and litigation relating to the bankruptcy of Orange County, California (settled for $75 million in 1998). Nevertheless KPMG kept growing, expanding its consulting division with the acquisition of banking consultancy Barefoot, Marrinan & Associates in 1996.

After Price Waterhouse and Coopers & Lybrand announced their merger in 1997, KPMG and Ernst & Young announced one of their own. But they called it quits the next year, fearing that regulatory approval of the deal would be too onerous.

The creation of PricewaterhouseCoopers (PwC) and increasing competition in the consulting sides of all of the Big Five brought a realignment of loyalties in their national practices. KPMG Consulting's Belgian group moved to PwC and its French group to Computer Sciences Corporation. Andersen nearly wooed away KPMG's Canadian consulting group, but the plan was foiled by the ever-sullen Andersen Consulting group (now Accenture) and by KPMG's promises of more money. Against this background, KPMG sold 20% of its consulting operations to Cisco Systems for $1 billion. In addition to the cash infusion, the deal allowed KPMG to provide installation and system management (neither of which Cisco provides) to Cisco's customers.

In 2000 KPMG announced its IPO plans for the consulting group but continued to rail against the calls by the SEC for the severing of relationships between consulting and auditing organizations. The IPO took place in 2001. The following year the company sold its British and Dutch consultancy units to France's Atos Origin and agreed to sell its German, Swiss, and Austrian units to KPMG Consulting.

OFFICERS

Chairman, KPMG International and KPMG UK:
Mike Rake
CEO: Robert W. Alspaugh
COO: Colin Holland
CFO: Joseph E. Heintz
Chairman and CEO, KPMG LLP: Eugene D. O'Kelly, age 50
Deputy Chairman, KPMG LLP: Jeffrey M. Stein, age 48
Regional Executive Partner, Americas: Lou Miramontes
Regional Executive Partner, Asia-Pacific: John Sim
International Managing Partner, Assurance:
Hans de Munnik
International Managing Partner, Consulting:
Jim McGuire
International Managing Partner, Financial Advisory Services: Gary Colter
International Managing Partner, Markets:
Alistair Johnston
International Managing Partner, Tax and Legal:
Hartwich Lübmann
Chief Marketing Officer, KPMG LLP:
Timothy R. Pearson
General Counsel, KPMG LLP: Claudia L. Taft
National Industry Director, Banking Practice, KPMG LLP: Robert F. Arning
Partner, Human Resources, KPMG LLP:
Timothy P. Flynn

LOCATIONS

HQ: 345 Park Ave., New York, NY 10154
Phone: 212-758-9700   **Fax:** 212-758-9819
Web: www.kpmg.com

2001 Sales

	$ mil.	% of total
Europe/Middle East/Africa	6,300	54
Americas	4,300	37
Asia/Pacific	1,100	9
Total	**11,700**	**100**

PRODUCTS/OPERATIONS

2001 Sales

	$ mil.	% of total
Assurance	5,800	50
Tax & legal	3,100	26
Consulting	1,500	13
Financial advisory	1,200	10
Other	100	1
Total	**11,700**	**100**

Selected Services

Assurance
Advisory services
Financial statement audits
Information Risk Management
Management Assurance Services

Financial Advisory
Corporate finance
Corporate recovery
Forensic & litigation services
Transaction services

Tax and Legal
Business tax services
Global tax services
Indirect tax/customs services
Legal services pertaining to corporate and commercial, banking and financial services, competition, employment/labor, intellectual property, e-commerce, and estates and trusts law
State, local, and property tax services

COMPETITORS

Andersen	H&R Block
Aon	Hewitt Associates
Bain & Company	Marsh & McLennan
BDO International	McKinsey & Company
Booz Allen	PricewaterhouseCoopers
Deloitte Touche Tohmatsu	Towers Perrin
Ernst & Young	Watson Wyatt

HISTORICAL FINANCIALS & EMPLOYEES

Partnership FYE: September 30	Annual Growth	9/92	9/93	9/94	9/95	9/96	9/97	9/98	9/99	9/00	9/01
Sales ($ mil.)	7.4%	6,150	6,000	6,600	7,500	8,100	9,200	10,600	12,200	10,700	11,700
Employees	3.8%	73,488	76,200	76,200	72,000	77,000	83,500	85,300	102,000	108,000	103,000

SALES HISTORY

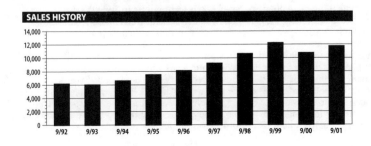

KRAFT FOODS INC.

Kraft Foods has been filling cupboards for about a century. As the #1 food company in the US, Northfield, Illinois-based Kraft Foods holds two operating companies: Kraft Foods North America and Kraft Foods International.

Kraft Foods' major brands include seven — Kraft, Maxwell House, Oscar Mayer, Post, Nabisco, Philadelphia, and Jacobs — that each bring in more than $1 billion in sales annually. Former parent company Philip Morris Companies (the world's top tobacco firm) bought Nabisco (Chips Ahoy!, Oreo, and Ritz crackers) in 2000 and integrated those operations into the Kraft Foods operating companies. Kraft Foods spun off from Philip Morris in 2001 in what was the second-largest IPO in US history; the tobacco giant retained 84% of the company and about 98% of the voting rights.

Kraft Foods also makes Altoids mints, Jell-O, Kool-Aid, Minute rice, Miracle Whip salad dressing, Philadelphia cream cheese, and Velveeta cheese. Kraft Foods North America resulted from the 1995 merger of Kraft and General Foods, both of which were bought by Philip Morris in the 1980s. Philip Morris later combined its Kraft operating companies under the holding company Kraft Foods.

In 2002 Kraft Foods International agreed to sell its Latin American yeast business (Fleischmann) to Australian yeast and spice maker Burns Philp.

HISTORY

The Kraft tale began in 1903 when James L. Kraft began delivering cheese to Chicago grocers. His four brothers joined in, forming the J.L. Kraft & Bros. Company, in 1909. By 1914 the company had opened a cheese factory and was selling cheese across the US. Kraft developed its first blended, pasteurized cheese the following year.

Kraft went public in 1924; four years later it merged with Philadelphia cream-cheese maker Phenix and also created Velveeta cheese spread. In 1930 Kraft was bought by National Dairy, but its operations were kept separate. New and notable products included Miracle Whip salad dressing (1933), macaroni and cheese dinners (1937), and Parkay margarine (1940). In the decades that followed, Kraft expanded into foreign markets.

National Dairy became Kraftco in 1969 and Kraft in 1976, hoping to benefit from its internationally known trademark. To diversify, Kraft merged with Dart Industries in 1980; Dart's subsidiaries (including Duracell batteries) and Kraft kept separate operations. With nonfood sales sagging, Dart & Kraft split up in 1986. Kraft kept its original lines and added Duracell (sold 1988); the rest became Premark International. Tobacco giant Philip Morris Companies bought Kraft in 1988 for $12.9 billion. That next year Philip Morris joined Kraft with another unit, General Foods.

General Foods began when Charles Post, who marketed a wheat/bran health beverage, established the Postum Cereal Co. in 1896; he expanded the firm with such cereals as Grape-Nuts and Post Toasties. The company went public in 1922. Postum bought the makers of Jell-O (1925), Baker's chocolate (1927), Log Cabin syrup (1927), and Maxwell House coffee (1928), and in 1929 it acquired control of General Foods and changed its own name to General Foods.

Its later purchases included Perkins Products (Kool-Aid, 1953) and Kohner Brothers (toys, 1970). Most of its nonfood lines proved unsuccessful and were sold over the years. General Foods also bought Oscar Mayer, the US's #1 hot dog maker, in 1981. Philip Morris bought General Foods for $5.6 billion in 1985.

The 1989 combination of Kraft and General Foods (the units still ran independently) created the largest US food maker, Kraft General Foods. In the early 1990s Kraft General Foods lost market share in areas such as frozen vegetables and processed meat. It introduced "light" meat products and stopped making nearly 300 food items.

To streamline management, Philip Morris integrated Kraft and General Foods in 1995. Kraft bought Del Monte's shelf-stable pudding business (1995) and Taco Bell's grocery line (1996). It also sold its Lender's bagels (1996) and Log Cabin (1997) lines.

In June 2000 parent Philip Morris outbid Danone and Cadbury Schweppes and agreed to buy Nabisco Holdings. It completed the deal that December for $18.9 billion and began integrating those operations into Kraft Foods and Kraft Foods International. Philip Morris created a holding company for the newly combined food operations under the Kraft Foods name in March 2001. The original Kraft Foods was renamed Kraft Foods North America. Kraft Foods International CEO Roger Deromedi was appointed co-CEO of the new holding company, along with Betsy Holden. Kraft Foods went public in June 2001.

In 2002 Kraft acquired the Central and Eastern European confectionery business of Stollwerck AGt. Kraft cut 7,500 jobs in 2002 as a result of the integration of Nabisco operations, paying out $373 million in cash for severance and related costs. The company also announced the phasing out of the Life Savers plant in Holland, Michigan, with the production of the popular candy to be fully moved to Canada by the summer of 2003.

OFFICERS

Chairman: Louis C. Camilleri, age 47
Co-CEO and Director; President and CEO, Kraft Foods International: Roger K. Deromedi, age 49, $1,688,154 pay
Co-CEO and Director; President and CEO, Kraft Foods North America: Betsy D. Holden, age 46, $1,688,154 pay
EVP; General Manager, Pizza Division: Rhonda Jordan, age 44
EVP, Kraft Foods North America and General Manager, Kraft Cheese: Kevin Ponticelli, age 44
EVP, Field Sales and Integrated Logistics Kraft Foods North America: Brian Driscoll
SVP and CFO: James P. Dollive, age 49
SVP, General Counsel, and Corporate Secretary; SVP, General Counsel, and Corporate Affairs, Kraft Foods North America: Calvin J. Collier, age 60, $696,250 pay
Group VP, Kraft Foods International; President, Asia Pacific Region, Kraft Foods International: Hugh H. Roberts, age 49, $787,885 pay
Group VP, Kraft Foods North America; President, Operations, Technology and Informations Systems, Kraft Foods Canada, Mexico and Puerto Rico, and Kraft Foods North America: Irene B. Rosenfeld, $972,500 pay
Group VP, Kraft Foods North America; President, Kraft Cheese, Meals and Enhancers Group, Kraft Foods North America: Mary Kay Haben, age 45, $806,346 pay
Auditors: Deloitte & Touche LLP

LOCATIONS

HQ: Three Lakes Drive, Northfield, IL 60093
Phone: 847-646-2000   **Fax:** 847-646-6005
Web: www.kraft.com

PRODUCTS/OPERATIONS

Selected Brands

A.1. steak sauce	Newtons
Altoids mints	Nilla
Barnum's Animal Crackers	Nutter Butter
Bubble Yum	Oreo
Cheese Nips	Oscar Mayer
Cheez Whiz	Philadelphia (chesse)
Chips Ahoy!	Planters nuts
Claussen pickles	Post (cereal)
Cool Whip	Ritz
Cream of Wheat	Shake 'N Bake coatings
Grey Poupon mustard	Tang
Jell-O	Toblerone chocolates
Jet-Puffed marshmallows	Tombstone pizza
Kool-Aid	Triscuit
Life Savers	Velveeta
Maxwell House	Wheat Thins
Miracle Whip	

COMPETITORS

Bongrain	Hormel	Procter &
Cadbury	Interstate	Gamble
Schweppes	Bakeries	Quaker Foods
Campbell Soup	Keebler	Ralcorp
ConAgra	Kellogg	Rich Products
Danone	Kerry Group	Sara Lee
Dean Foods	Lactalis	Sara Lee Coffee
Diageo	Land O'Lakes	and Tea
Frito-Lay	Lindt & Sprungli	Worldwide
General Mills	Maple Leaf Foods	Sara Lee Foods
George Weston	Mars	Schreiber Foods
Goodman Fielder	McCain Foods	Unilever
Heinz	Nestlé	Uniq plc
Hershey	Northern Foods	United Biscuits

HISTORICAL FINANCIALS & EMPLOYEES

NYSE: KFT FYE: December 31	Annual Growth	12/92	12/93	12/94	12/95	12/96	12/97	12/98	12/99	12/00	12/01
Sales ($ mil.)	3.9%	—	—	—	—	27,950	27,690	27,311	26,797	26,532	33,875
Net income ($ mil.)	5.1%	—	—	—	—	1,467	1,792	1,632	1,753	2,001	1,882
Income as % of sales	—	—	—	—	—	5.2%	6.5%	6.0%	6.5%	7.5%	5.6%
Earnings per share ($)	—	—	—	—	—	—	—	—	—	—	1.17
Stock price - FY high ($)	—	—	—	—	—	—	—	—	—	—	35.57
Stock price - FY low ($)	—	—	—	—	—	—	—	—	—	—	29.50
Stock price - FY close ($)	—	—	—	—	—	—	—	—	—	—	34.03
P/E - high	—	—	—	—	—	—	—	—	—	—	30
P/E - low	—	—	—	—	—	—	—	—	—	—	25
Dividends per share ($)	—	—	—	—	—	—	—	—	—	—	0.13
Book value per share ($)	—	—	—	—	—	—	—	—	—	—	16.14
Employees	(2.6%)	—	—	—	—	—	—	—	—	117,000	114,000

STOCK PRICE HISTORY

HIGH/LOW/CLOSE

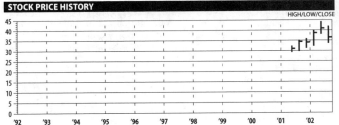

2001 FISCAL YEAR-END

Debt ratio: 35.9%
Return on equity: 10.0%
Cash ($ mil.): 162
Current ratio: 0.79
Long-term debt ($ mil.): 13,134
No. of shares (mil.): 1,455
Dividends
  Yield: 0.4%
  Payout: 11.1%
Market value ($ mil.): 49,514

THE KROGER CO.

Kroger is at the top of the food chain. The Cincinnati-based company is the #1 supermarket chain in the US, with more than 2,400 grocery stores in 32 states from coast to coast — the closest the US has to a national supermarket chain. Kroger also operates nearly 800 convenience stores and about 420 jewelry stores (bringing its store total, under some two dozen names, to about 3,600). It is a major pharmacy operator, with pharmacies in more than half of its food stores.

Its namesake chain has outlets in more than 40 major markets and a sizable share of the market in large cities such as Dallas/Fort Worth and Atlanta. Kroger is buying 17 supermarkets (16 in the Houston area) from Albertson's and another seven stores from Winn-Dixie in the Dallas/Fort Worth area. Kroger's Dillon Companies subsidiary runs more than 200 grocery stores under such names as Dillons Food Stores, City Market, and King Soopers. The subsidiary also runs the company's convenience stores, including Mini-Mart and Kwik Shop, among others.

Kroger's 1999 acquisition of Fred Meyer not only added three supermarket chains (Ralphs, Smith's Food & Drug Centers, and QFC), it gave the company several new retailing formats: multidepartment stores (Fred Meyer), limited selection warehouse outlets (Food 4 Less, PriceRite), and jewelry stores (under the Barclay, Fred Meyer, and Littman names). The purchase gave the company a significant presence in the western US. Kroger also owns about 40 food processing plants that supply its supermarkets with a growing stable of private-label products (accounting for about 25% of its grocery sales).

HISTORY

Bernard Kroger was 22 when he started the Great Western Tea Company in 1883 in Cincinnati. Kroger lowered prices by cutting out middlemen, sometimes by making products such as bread. Growing to 40 stores in Cincinnati and northern Kentucky, the company became Kroger Grocery and Baking Company in 1902. It expanded into St. Louis in 1912 and grew rapidly during the 1910s and 1920s by purchasing smaller, cash-strapped companies. Kroger sold his holdings in the company for $28 million in 1928, the year before the stock market crash, and retired.

The company acquired Piggly Wiggly stores in the late 1920s and bought most of Piggly Wiggly's corporate stock, which it held until the early 1940s. The chain reached its largest number of stores — a whopping 5,575 — in 1929. (The Depression later trimmed that total.) A year later Kroger manager Michael Cullen suggested opening self-service, low-price supermarkets, but company executives demurred. Cullen left Kroger and began King Kullen, the first supermarket. If he was ahead of his time at Kroger, it wasn't by much; within five years, the company had 50 supermarkets.

During the 1950s Kroger acquired companies with stores in Texas, Georgia, and Washington, DC. It added New Jersey-based Sav-on drugstores in 1960 and it opened its first SupeRx drugstore in 1961. The company began opening larger supermarkets in 1971; between 1970 and 1980 Kroger's store count grew just 5%, but its selling space nearly doubled.

In 1983 the grocer bought Kansas-based Dillons Food Stores (supermarkets and convenience stores) and Kwik Shop convenience stores. Kroger sold most of its interests in the Hook and SupeRx drug chains (which later became Hook-SupeRx) in 1987 and focused on its food-and-drugstores. (It sold its remaining stake to Revco in 1994.) That next year it faced two separate takeover bids from the Herbert Haft family and from Kohlberg Kravis Roberts. The company warded off the raiders by borrowing $4.1 billion to pay a special dividend to shareholders and to buy shares for an employee stock plan.

To reduce debt, Kroger sold most of its equity in Price Saver Membership Wholesale Clubs and its Fry's California stores. In 1990 the company made its first big acquisition since the 1988 restructuring by buying 29 Great Scott! supermarkets. Joseph Pichler became CEO that year.

In 1995 Kroger sold its Time Saver Stores unit. In 1999 Kroger acquired Fred Meyer, operator of about 800 stores mainly in the West, in a $13 billion deal. Late that year it announced it was buying nearly 75 stores (mostly in Texas) from Winn-Dixie Stores; the deal was called off in 2000 shortly after the FTC withheld its approval. But the company kept buying — acquisitions included 20 former Hannaford stores in Virginia in 2000, as well as 16 Nebraska food stores bought from food distributor Fleming and seven New Mexico stores bought from Furrs Supermarkets in 2001. That same year it sold five Smith's stores to Fleming. In late 2001 Kroger said it would cut 1,500 jobs. With megadiscounter Wal-Mart breathing down its neck (Wal-Mart Supercenters compete on roughly 55% of Kroger's turf), Kroger cut prices in December 2001.

Chairman and CEO: Joseph A. Pichler, age 62,
$1,705,160 pay
President, COO and Director: David B. Dillon, age 51,
$860,839 pay
EVP and CIO: Michael S. Heschel, age 60, $700,052 pay
EVP, Strategy, Planning, and Finance:
W. Rodney McMullen, age 41, $771,789 pay
EVP: Don W. McGeorge, age 47, $700,052 pay
SVP; President, Manufacturing: Geoffrey J. Covert,
age 50
SVP, Secretary, and General Counsel: Paul W. Heldman,
age 50
Group VP and CFO: J. Michael Schlotman, age 44
Group VP, Drug/GM Merchandising and Procurement:
Michael J. Donnelly, age 43
Group VP, Grocery Merchandising: Bruce A. Macaulay,
age 48
Group VP, Logistics: William T. Boehm, age 55
Group VP, Management Information Systems:
Carver L. Johnson, age 52
**Group VP, Perishables Merchandising and
Procurement:** Derrick A. Penick, age 45
Group VP, Retail Operations: Paul Scutt, age 53
Group VP: Lynn Marmer, age 49
VP, Human Resources: David Avery
Auditors: PricewaterhouseCoopers LLP

LOCATIONS

HQ: 1014 Vine St., Cincinnati, OH 45202
Phone: 513-762-4000   **Fax:** 513-762-1160
Web: www.kroger.com

The Kroger Co. operates supermarkets in more than 30
states and convenience stores in 15 states.

PRODUCTS/OPERATIONS

2002 Sales

	% of total
Kroger stores	14
Other stores	86
Total	**100**

Selected Stores

Barclay Jewelers	Kessel Food Markets
Bell Markets	King Soopers
Cala Foods	Kroger
Dillons Food Stores	Kwik Shop
Food 4 Less	Littman Jewelers
FoodsCo	Loaf 'N Jug
Fox's Jewelers	Mini-Mart
Fred Meyer	Owen's
Fred Meyer Jewelers	Pay Less Super Markets
Fry's Food & Drug Stores	Quik Stop Markets
Fry's Marketplace	Ralphs
Hilander	Smith's Food & Drug
Jay C Food Stores	Centers
Junior Food Stores	Tom Thumb Food Stores

COMPETITORS

7-Eleven	Fleming	Rite Aid
A&P	Companies	Royal Ahold
Albertson's	Hy-Vee	Safeway
Bruno's	IGA	Stater Bros.
Supermarkets	Kmart	SUPERVALU
Costco	Meijer	Walgreen
Wholesale	Publix	Wal-Mart
CVS	Raley's	Winn-Dixie
Delhaize	Randall's	Zale

HISTORICAL FINANCIALS & EMPLOYEES

NYSE: KR FYE: January 31	Annual Growth	12/92	12/93	12/94	12/95	12/96	12/97	12/98	*1/00	1/01	1/02
Sales ($ mil.)	9.5%	22,145	22,384	22,959	23,938	25,171	26,567	28,203	45,352	49,000	50,098
Net income ($ mil.)	—	(6)	(12)	242	303	350	412	411	628	877	1,043
Income as % of sales	—	—	—	1.1%	1.3%	1.4%	1.5%	1.5%	1.4%	1.8%	2.1%
Earnings per share ($)	—	(0.02)	0.01	0.49	0.61	0.67	0.79	0.77	0.73	1.04	1.26
Stock price - FY high ($)	—	5.28	5.44	6.72	9.44	11.88	18.66	30.41	34.91	27.94	27.66
Stock price - FY low ($)	—	2.81	3.50	4.84	5.84	8.38	11.34	17.00	14.88	14.06	19.60
Stock price - FY close ($)	21.2%	3.66	5.03	6.03	9.34	11.63	18.38	30.25	17.38	24.55	20.60
P/E - high	—	—	14	12	14	17	21	35	45	26	22
P/E - low	—	—	9	9	8	12	13	19	19	13	16
Dividends per share ($)	—	0.00	0.00	0.00	0.00	0.00	0.00	0.00	0.00	0.00	0.00
Book value per share ($)	—	(7.38)	(5.71)	(4.85)	(3.23)	(2.33)	(1.54)	(0.75)	3.21	3.79	4.41
Employees	4.7%	190,000	190,000	200,000	205,000	212,000	212,000	213,000	305,000	312,000	288,000

* Fiscal year change

STOCK PRICE HISTORY

HIGH/LOW/CLOSE

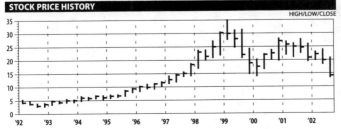

2002 FISCAL YEAR-END

Debt ratio: 70.6%
Return on equity: 31.6%
Cash ($ mil.): 161
Current ratio: 1.00
Long-term debt ($ mil.): 8,412
No. of shares (mil.): 795
Dividends
  Yield: —
  Payout: —
Market value ($ mil.): 16,377